TO:

JANICE

Be Bless with Success

Herbert

MW00454213

It is with great excitement that I recommend to you - The Comprehensive New Testament. I have been able to use it for study and preparation in order to more accurately and clearly present the Word of God to those I teach and preach to weekly. This translation has challenged me to review and compare the text in various versions in order to understand the context and content of the passage. It is an awesome study companion that I strongly recommend for anyone who is serious about accuracy in presentation to acquire and use.

– Dr. Garry Baldwin
Pastor, Midwood Baptist Church
Charlotte, North Carolina

As a Pastor and Preacher, I am finding The Comprehensive New Testament a useful resource for use in ministry. It is both accessible and thorough. I can refer to it with confidence, knowing that it is also an appropriate resource for the church community. I wish I had had access to it during my D.Min. program. As a Ph.D. student, I am finding it to be a wealth of information at my fingertips, a timesaver as well as academically respectable. I anticipate using it regularly in technical studies. As a Daughter of God, I am finding it sensitive and devotional. I can sense that this work was covered in prayer throughout its development, and that the Lord has anointed it. I trust the Spirit to use your work to enrich the lives of many.

– The Reverend Dr. Susan I. Bubbers
Anglican Priest, Province of Uganda
Ph.D. Student, London School of Theology

The editors of The Comprehensive New Testament are talented in their translation skills and thorough in their scholarly translation of the Western texts employed by Protestants and Catholics. The Greek texts translated, while being at places different from those used in our Greek Orthodox Churches, are nevertheless presented with a refreshing forthrightness and honesty regarding available sources, including the Byzantine text, duly referenced in the copious footnotes. The modern English of the Comprehensive New Testament's translation shows good cadence, rhythm and natural good sense, preserving a reverent dignity for the holiness of the text, while at the same time being readable and accessible to the average reader. With great promise, we now look forward to seeing a future companion edition for Orthodox Christian Readers – The Comprehensive *Orthodox* Bible: Old and New Testaments – based in its English translation upon the Greek texts which have been in daily liturgical use in our Greek Orthodox Churches throughout the world for the last two thousand years.

– The Very Reverend Archimandrite Maximos
Abbot of the Monastery of the Holy Cross
Jerusalem Patriarchate
East Setauket, New York

A deft, accurate handling of both Greek and English; and an awesome, easy-to-use research tool for ordinary people interested in the history of the New Testament in its ancient literary context. The Comprehensive New Testament makes available, in English and in a single volume, a great depth of essential cross-references to ancient literature, and quotations from these sources. It is indeed comprehensive. The English syntax and vocabulary are straight-forward, yet shaped carefully by an appreciation of the underlying Greek. So, while this edition of the New Testament is invaluable to scholars, it is also suited to liturgical or devotional use.

– Alastair Haines
Ph.D. Student, Presbyterian Theological Centre
Sydney Australia

I must say that The Comprehensive New Testament is an excellent tool that should not only be on the shelf with other study Bibles but should be with you wherever you go. I have studied and used many different translations of Bibles, and this one is now on my "best five" Bibles list - job well done. I pray that the work on the Old Testament is not far behind. I will recommend the purchase of this book to all of my colleagues, as well as the unsaved.

– The Reverend Tyrone Hayes Sr.
Pastor, The New Mount Zion Baptist Church
Philadelphia, Pennsylvania

As a Certified Chaplain for the State of Florida, I'm doing Bible studies at the Moore Haven GEO Correction Facility. For over 5 years, we've been studying the word of God constantly dealing with people of many faiths and denominations not to mention every type of Bible ever written. During our studies we let the inmates read from their Bibles. The Comprehensive New Testament has allowed me to keep up with all the versions and also gives me an understanding of when, where, and to whom their versions were written. This has been invaluable information because we are studying with 20 Bible versions at one time. The Bible is clear when it reads in Romans 10:17, "So faith comes from hearing; and hearing by the word of Christ." We always have a version that everyone understands.

– C. Manny Padilla
Certified Chaplain
Associate Pastor
Church of God Incorporated

The Comprehensive New Testament is a wonderful modern rendering of the sacred scriptures presented with an accuracy that will be a great help to anyone who desires a better understanding of God's Word.

– Dr. Donald Drawdy
Pastor, Springview Baptist Church
Maryville , Tennessee

I am very impressed with this translation. It has been long needed. I made several checks on needed words and was pleased to find that they had been placed in scripture. Love the word Christ highlighted in the name. I have recommended this Bible to many. Thank you again, excited about this being available. May God add His blessings.

– Deborah Ennis
Beaumont, Texas

I do not have a string of letters behind my name. Some have graciously called me self-educated. I am part of the vast laity, a local church Elder who fills the pulpit at several Indiana churches when asked. I am a retired aircraft maintenance instructor who looks forward to the soon coming of our Lord and Savior, Jesus Christ. Your New Testament is a dream-come-true for me. I have been thrilled and blessed when reading and studying it! My study of Greek ended when I felt confident that our English versions were sufficiently accurate. I became aware of the limitations of any language, and the literary differences in the formal Greek used in the Gospel of John and the somewhat crude Greek of John's Revelation. I have often wished for the time and skill to do exactly what you have done in comparing so many versions. I love them all from the conversational English of the NLT to the "novelty" of Peterson's paraphrase The Message. And also compare them with Nestle's GNT and other manuscripts. Well done! I have been thrilled in learning how to use it with the notes etc. I have shared with several congregations the premise of what will be available. It has become an invaluable aid for developing studies and sermons. Most valuable is having a ready reference to what is and is not in the oldest and most reliable manuscripts. It gives me a way to politely say "that was a later addition" or something to that effect.

– Clyde Best
Mooresville, Indiana

Reading the Comprehensive New Testament for personal study as well as worship and meditation has greatly enriched my spiritual life. I have found the manner of interpretation not only God-honoring, but scripture-centered reflecting the true message of the revelation of God both in words and in the Word who became flesh, Jesus Christ, our Lord and Savior. Thank you for this contribution that not only will make His message clearer, but more consistent with those to whom God entrusted the original task of compiling His record.

– Lawrence Guido, Th.M., Ph.D.
The Guido Evangelistic Association, Inc.
Metter, Georgia

The Comprehensive New Testament

Standardized to the Greek New Testament text of the
Nestle-Aland 27th edition
and the
United Bible Societies 4th edition

with

Complete textual variant mapping and references for the Dead Sea Scrolls, Philo, Josephus,
Nag Hammadi Library, Pseudepigrapha, Apocrypha, Plato, Egyptian Book of the Dead, Talmud,
Old Testament, Patristic Writings, Dhammapada, Tacitus, Epic of Gilgamesh

Edited by T. E. Clontz & J. Clontz

Clewiston, Florida

Cornerstone Publications

The Comprehensive New Testament:
New Testament with complete textual variant mapping and references for the Dead Sea Scrolls, Philo, Josephus, Nag Hammadi Library, Pseudepigrapha, Apocrypha, Plato, Egyptian Book of the Dead, Talmud, Old Testament, Patristic Writings, Dhammapada, Tacitus, Epic of Gilgamesh

Publisher's Cataloging-in-Publication
(Provided by Quality Books, Inc.)

Bible. N.T. English. Clontz. 2008.
    The Comprehensive New Testament : New Testament with complete textual variant mapping and references for the Dead Sea Scrolls, Philo, Josephus, Nag Hammadi Library, Pseudepigrapha, Apocrypha, Plato, Egyptian Book of the Dead, Talmud, Old Testament, Patristic Writings, Dhammapada, Tacitus, Epic of Gilgamesh / edited by T.E. Clontz & J. Clontz.
        p. cm.
    Includes bibliographical references and index.
    LCCN 2007941717
    ISBN-13: 978-0-977873-71-5
    ISBN-10: 0-977873-71-4

    1. Bible--Reference editions.   I. Clontz, T. E.
II. Clontz, J. (Jerry) III. Title.

BS2095.C53 2008   225.5'2
                 QBI07-600339

Solar eclipse photograph credit © **Luc Viatour GFDL/CC**
Used by permission

Printed in Canada

for our Grandparents

You gave us the first Bible we ever read,
and lived by its pages

Contents

Footnote Key

Textual Sources

Alx   Alexandrian Text: The standard text for the Western Church (Roman Catholics, Protestants, and Evangelicals), as represented in the 27th Edition of the Nestle-Aland *Novum Testamentum Graece* 1993 and the 4th Edition of the United Bible Societies *Greek New Testament* 1994. This text is based on the oldest surviving manuscripts. Translations are only indicated in the footnotes when they differ from the NA[27]/UBS[4] text, and will be listed in their matching text-form (Byz, Major, Minor, or Alt) or their nearest approximation if the translation is paraphrased. A translation not listed in the footnote is considered to be in agreement with the NA[27]/UBS[4] text.

Byz   Byzantine Text: The standard text for the Eastern Church (Orthodox), as represented in the *Patriarchal Text* 1904. This text was preserved by the living tradition of Orthodox scholarship from the fifth through the twentieth centuries, and is the authorized text for all Greek speaking congregations.

Major   Majority Text, as represented in the Pierpont-Robinson *The New Testament in the Original Greek* 2005. This scholarly edition reflects the majority of existing manuscripts, and is only noted when it differs from the *Patriarchal Text*.

Minor   Minority reading in Greek.

Alt   Either a reading derived from an ancient translation (e.g. the Peshitta or Vulgate) or an alternate reading in a translation which appears to have no ancient source. The latter instance is marked as *"without textual foundation."*

Peshitta   An Aramaic translation of the New Testament, as represented by the United Bible Societies *The Syriac New Testament and Psalms* 1905.

Vulgate   A Latin translation of the New Testament initiated by Jerome, as represented by the German Bible Society *Biblia Sacra Iuxta Vulgatam* 1969.

Linguistic Notes

Aramaism   Words or phrases in Greek which reflect an Aramaic source.

Hebraism   Words or phrases in Greek which reflect a Hebrew source.

Latinism   Words or phrases in Greek which reflect a Latin source.

Cross Reference Sources

Masoretic   Indicates quotations of the Hebrew Bible which agree with the Masoretic Text as represented in the 5th Edition of the *Biblica Hebraica Stuttgartensia* 1990. The Masoretic text will only be noted when there are differences from either the Dead Sea Scrolls or the Septuagint.

DSS   Dead Sea Scrolls: Indicates quotations of the Hebrew Bible which agree with Hebrew texts found in the Dead Sea Scrolls. DSS will only be noted when there are differences from either the Masoretic Text or the Septuagint.

LXX   Septuagint: Indicates quotations of the Hebrew Bible which agree with the Greek translation found in the Septuagint as represented in the Revised Edition of Rahlfs' *Septuaginta* 1935. LXX will only be noted when there are differences from either the Masoretic Text or the Dead Sea Scrolls.

Conventions

~	A tilde before an abbreviation indicates that it is not an exact match. When used before a translation reference it indicates that the translation does not correspond to a single text-form, and could be a merger of multiple text-forms or a rewording that matches none. When used before a Cross Reference Source it indicates the closest approximation to the New Testament wording.
BOLD	Bold formatting indicates a direct quote. For an Alx note, the **BOLD** text is showing the words that are found in the *Comprehensive New Testament*. For a cross reference the **BOLD** text indicates a cross reference that the original author stated to be from another source (e.g. "as it is written").
ITALICS	*Italic* formatting in the body of the text indicates a quotation or strong allusion to the Old Testament or a secondary source. The cross reference will be listed in the footnotes. *Italic* formatting in a footnote indicates a description provided by the editor (e.g. *Greek*, or *without textual foundation*).

Commentary and Translations

Metzger	Bruce Metzger's *Textual Commentary on the Greek New Testament 2nd Edition*. Unless otherwise noted, the reference can be found in Metzger's commentary with the same or an overlapping verse number. When Metzger is cited before a bracket, he is the primary source for information on the listed variant. When Metzger is cited within parentheses, his commentary reports a minority objection to the textual committee's choice.
ASV	American Standard Version 1901
DRA	Douay-Rheims American Edition 1899 translation of the Vulgate
ESV	English Standard Version 2001, 2007
HCS	Holman Christian Standard Bible 1999
JNT	David Stern's Jewish New Testament 1998
KJV	King James Version 1611, 1769 Blayney revision
MRD	Murdock's translation of the Peshitta 1851
NAB	New American Bible, revised 1991
NAS	New American Standard Bible 1960
NAU	New American Standard Bible, 1995 revision
NET	New English Translation 2004
NIV	New International Version 1984
NJB	New Jerusalem Bible 1985
NKJ	New King James Version 1982
NLT	New Living Translation, 2nd Edition 2004
NRS	New Revised Standard Version 1989
REB	Revised English Bible 1989
RSV	Revised Standard Version, 2nd Edition 1971
TEV	Today's English Version (Good News Bible) 1966
TLB	The Living Bible (paraphrase) 1971

Preface

The Comprehensive New Testament only requires a sixth grade reading level, and it is the most accurate translation of the Nestle-Aland 27th edition Greek New Testament ever produced.

The Greek Text

The Greek text most trusted by Catholic and Protestant pastors, teachers, and churches, is the Nestle-Aland 27th edition. The text represents the oldest surviving Greek manuscripts. Thousands of significant variations in ancient sources are provided in the footnotes. Uncertain readings are clearly marked in brackets. Cross references show parallels not only to the Old Testament, but also to an entire library of ancient religious and philosophical literature.

The English Translation

The Comprehensive New Testament represents the textual choices of the Nestle-Aland in a readable English format. Over 15,000 variations in ancient manuscripts are translated in the footnotes. Uncertain readings are clearly marked in brackets. Cross references show parallels not only to the Old Testament, but also to an entire library of ancient religious and philosophical literature – many of which are identified for the first time in any language.

Although no translation can perfectly reproduce the simplicity and beauty of the original words, it is important to translate the *right* words – and not words created by scribal mistakes or editorial changes.

For those concerned with accuracy in the New Testament text, there are two fundamental factors to keep in mind: 1) the number of textual differences is far larger than is normally admitted, and 2) the seriousness of those differences is far less than is normally feared. In fact, throughout the 15,000 variations translated in this New Testament, we find the same message, and the same gospel. Those who read the old translations can rest assured that the message of the cross has been faithfully preserved even in the few late texts that Erasmus hastily threw together in his Greek edition in 1516. Those who read the modern translations can rest assured that new versions in Chinese, Spanish, Coptic, German, Swahili – and, yes, English – are leading readers to the faith "once delivered to the saints."

The question, then, is not one of fear, but one of faithfulness. The words given through the apostles deserve our best efforts in return. Their own words should be authentically expressed, instead of later redactions, no matter how polished, or how familiar those redactions may be.

Further, our "best efforts" include the best efforts of the entire church, and not the work of a single translation. Though we provide the standard understandings of the text (we make no attempt at novelty), serious Bible readers should use a number of translations and, when possible, learn as much of the original language as they can. As an aid for personal study we provide something that no other translation offers: footnotes for translations beyond our own. Readers can see, at a glance, where other translations agree with the Nestle-Aland, and where they do not. Our notes give more textual information about those translations than they do about themselves – and readers with a favorite translation will find our notes to be an enhancement to their personal Bible, and not a competition to it.

Footnotes

Footnotes are listed by verse number at the bottom of each page, and a footnote key is available at the opening of this book, for ease of reference.

The thousands of Greek manuscripts from the second through the fifteenth centuries fall into two primary groups:

1. The "Alexandrian" group represents the oldest surviving manuscripts.
2. The "Byzantine" group represents the majority of manuscripts from all centuries.

Although the Nestle-Aland 27th edition *Novum Testamentum Graece* 1993 is not entirely an "Alexandrian" text, it is the most respected edition in general agreement with that textual family, and "Alx" is a convenient abbreviation to use for this edition.

The *Patriarchal Text* of 1904, on the other hand, is the most respected edition in the "Byzantine" tradition, and is noted with the abbreviation "Byz."

Neither the Nestle-Aland nor the *Patriarchal Text* can represent the full spectrum of readings available in these two textual families and other minority groups. Majority readings that differ from the *Patriarchal Text* are listed under the abbreviation "Major." Minority readings from all textual groups – Alexandrian, Byzantine, "Western," F1, F13, and more – are listed under the abbreviation "Minor."

Readings *not* originating from Greek sources are listed under the abbreviation "Alt." These readings could come from Latin, Syriac, Coptic, or other ancient sources. When no source can be identified, the reading is listed as "without textual foundation."

Although the Textus Receptus, Latin Vulgate, and Aramaic Peshitta are not explicitly mapped in the notes, readers can trace their textual patterns by observing the notes for the King James Version and New King James Bible (for the Textus Receptus), the Douay-Rheims 1899 American Edition (for the Vulgate), and the Murdock Translation (for the Peshitta). The correspondence is not exact, but will prove accurate to a high degree.

Twenty English translations are included in the footnotes when their textual critical decisions or English stylistic choices agree with a variant reading. In a number of cases these are simple overlaps of meaning. As with all translations, this translation is flexible in the natural range of meaning in the Greek text. An exact word for word equivalence is not only impossible to read in English, it is also unfaithful to the meaning of the Greek text. Greek words have their own meanings and cannot be confined to a single English word. Even in the case of a simple measure of distance, it is sometimes best to translate an equivalent distance (furlongs, miles), while in symbolic passages retaining the word (stadia). Context is the guide, and footnotes are an aid, but there can be no true 100% concordance between any two languages.

Our text and footnotes, then, are not meant to replace the Nestle-Aland. Instead, they are meant to introduce the English reader to textual variations that, before now, have only been available to language experts.

It is impossible for one translator to judge another's labor and decide every case that is a textual critical choice and every case that is a stylistic choice. Instead, our text and notes show all *possible* differences that can be translated into English. When we list a translation, we do so as an aid to the reader to see the differences in ancient texts and their modern translations, and not as criticism of any single work.

That being said, our notes can be helpful in comparing translations with each other. As the charts on the back cover show, the New American Standard Bible agrees with the Nestle-Aland far more than the New King James Bible does. The New American Standard Bible, then, is a more accurate reflection of the Nestle-Aland than the New King James Bible. And in fact, the New King James Bible does not use the Nestle-Aland text, but instead uses the Textus Receptus, which is very similar to the Greek Bible that Erasmus produced

nearly five centuries ago. It is a different text, based on a few late manuscripts, but it stands firmly in church tradition, and many will find a favorite reading which stems from it.

When a translation does *not* completely agree with any of the readings listed in our notes, we mark that translation with a tilde.

Tildes offer an additional measure which has historically been difficult to quantify: paraphrase. Just how literal is one translation in relation to another? By examining each textual variant and measuring translations by the certainty of their textual bases, we have been able to identify the degree of textual ambiguity translators have introduced in order to present a more readable text – as well as the degree in which ambiguity in the original Greek has been resolved in favor of one possible meaning instead of another. With the exception of *The Comprehensive New Testament* (noted below as COM), the Formal Equivalence of each translation is ranked in the same order as the Text-base Equivalence:

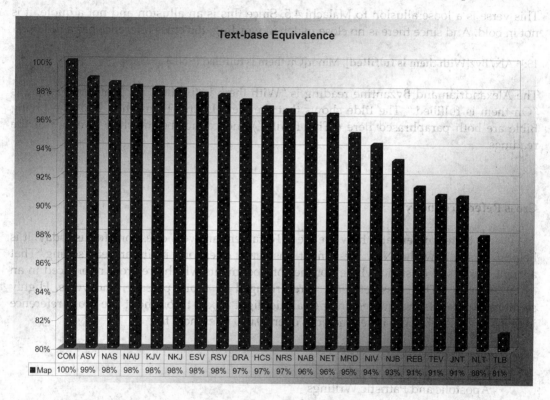

Text-base Equivalence

	COM	ASV	NAS	NAU	KJV	NKJ	ESV	RSV	DRA	HCS	NRS	NAB	NET	MRD	NIV	NJB	REB	TEV	JNT	NLT	TLB
■Map	100%	99%	98%	98%	98%	98%	98%	98%	97%	97%	97%	96%	96%	95%	94%	93%	91%	91%	91%	88%	81%

When there are no textual differences to be noted, *The Comprehensive New Testament* maintains at least a 98% Formal Equivalence rate. When there are differences in the source texts, however, the text approaches as close to a 100% Formal Equivalence as possible between an ancient text and a modern translation. The result is a translation which is textually accurate, easy to understand, and elegant – useful for personal devotions, classroom settings, and worship services.

Footnote Examples (from Matthew)

1:25 Alx[**a son**], Byz[her firstborn son (DRA, KJV, MRD, NKJ)].

The Alexandrian reading is "a son." The Byzantine reading is "her firstborn son." Of the twenty translations in our study, only the Douay-Rheims American, the King James Version, the Murdock translation, and the New King James Bible agree with the Byzantine reading.

2:[18] Alx[**weeping and great mourning**], Byz[lamentation, weeping, and great mourning (KJV, NKJ)];
   Jeremiah 31:15 Alx=Masoretic / Byz=LXX.

The Alexandrian reading is "weeping and great mourning." The Byzantine reading is
"lamentation, weeping, and great mourning." The King James Version and the New King
James Bible agree with the Byzantine reading. Also, since this is a quote from Jeremiah
31:15, the cross reference is in **bold**. The Alexandrian reading quotes the Masoretic Hebrew
version of Jeremiah. The Byzantine reading quotes the Greek Septuagint version of
Jeremiah.

11:[14] ~Malachi 4:5.

This verse is a loose allusion to Malachi 4:5. Since this is an allusion and not a quote, it is
not in bold. And since there is no close match in wording, the cross reference has a tilde (~).

13:[14] Alx/Byz[**With them is fulfilled**], Minor[On them is fulfilled (~NLT, ~TLB)].

The Alexandrian and Byzantine reading is "With them is fulfilled." A Minority reading is
"On them is fulfilled." The tilde shows that the New Living Translation and The Living
Bible are both paraphrased here ("This fulfills") and cannot be matched to either of the
readings.

Cross Reference Index

To better understand how the New Testament answers questions for us today, it is
helpful to see how the New Testament answered questions in its ancient setting. That
ancient world still exists in whole libraries of documents which are cross referenced in an
extensive index. The cross references are arranged by topic, passage, and verse. Highly
significant parallels are quoted in special highlight boxes throughout the cross reference
index. The cross reference index includes over 40,000 references for:

> Old and New Testaments
> Old Testament Apocrypha
> Apostolic and Patristic Writings
> Dead Sea Scrolls
> Dhammapada
> Epic of Gilgamesh
> Golden Verses of Pythagoras
> Greek Literature
> Nag Hammadi Library
> New Testament Apocrypha
> Pseudepigrapha
> Rabbinic Writings
> Tacitus
> The Egyptian Book of the Dead
> Works of Josephus
> Works of Philo
> Works of Plato

The books of the Old Testament were originally composed centuries before the Christian era. The various forms of the Old Testament text are directly quoted more often by the New Testament than any other source. The Septuagint version (LXX) exerts the greatest influence on the New Testament followed by the textual forms exhibited in the Masoretic text, Dead Sea Scrolls, and Aramaic Targums. Some examples are:

Septuagint –"worshipped as he leaned on the top of his staff" (Hebrews 11:21 based on LXX of Genesis 47:31) as compared to "bowed himself upon the head of the bed" (based on the Masoretic text of Genesis 47:31). The dichotomy between the Septuagint and Masoretic versions stems from the Hebrew phrase for "top of the staff" (מטהף) which is written the same as "head of the bed" (מטהף).

Masoretic Text – "Out of Egypt have I called my Son" (Matthew 2:15 based on the Masoretic text of Hosea 11:1) as compared to "out of Egypt have I called his children" (based on LXX of Hosea 11:1).

The Dead Sea Scrolls contain parallels to the Gospels and the book of Revelation – including references to the Messiah and the fishermen, the New Jerusalem, and the Apocalypse. The administrative hierarchy outlined in the Dead Sea Scrolls has parallels to the one outlined in the New Testament including the Messiah, Overseers, and similarities between the office of Maskil and Apostle (compare the use of the word Maskil in Daniel 12:3 to Acts 26:18). The Dead Sea Scrolls comprise over 800 documents, including texts from the Old Testament. The scrolls were discovered between 1947 and 1956 in eleven caves in the Wadi Qumran area on the northwest shore of the Dead Sea. According to carbon dating, the documents were written prior to the 1st century C.E. Dead Sea Scroll 4Q Enoch (4Q204[4QENAR]) COL I 16-18 and Jude 1:14-15 are direct parallels.

Josephus (c. C.E. 37 – C.E. 100) - also known as Flavius Josephus - was a Jewish military leader, historian, and apologist. Josephus was a personal friend of Herod Agrippa and may have been an eye witness to several of the events described in the Book of Acts. His works contain references to the Sadducees, Pharisees, Essenes, the Herodian Temple, Quirinius' census, Pontius Pilate, Herod the Great, Herod Agrippa I, John the Baptist, James, and Jesus.

Philo (c. 20 B.C.E. – C.E. 40) - also known as Philo of Alexandria and as Philo Judeaus – was a Jewish religious instructor and philosopher born in Alexandria, Egypt. Biographical details concerning him are found in his own works and in the works of Josephus (Antiquities xviii. 8). His brother, Alexander, may be mentioned in Acts 4:6. The Works of Philo provide first-hand information of Jewish religious teachings, practices, customs, and beliefs mentioned in the Gospels and the book of Hebrews. His works contain references to the Son of God, the Word, sheep with no shepherd, fishermen letting down their nets, the rich man and his treasure, the woman taken in adultery, rising up in the air to be with the Lord forever, being tested by the fire like gold. Philo provides details of Roman scourgings and crucifixions of Jewish religious leaders in Egypt that contain striking parallels to the details of the crucifixion of Jesus in the New Testament.

Old Testament Apocrypha (c. 500 B.C.E. – C.E. 100) are extra-biblical books that are considered important by various churches, but are not accepted as authoritative. There is no definitive list of apocryphal books, since each church defines its own list. The books that are commonly listed in the Apocrypha contain references to the Holy Spirit and the Apocalypse.

Pseudepigrapha (c. 500 B.C.E. – C.E. 300) are dozens of extra-biblical books with improbable authorship. These texts claim various Old Testament individuals as authors, including Adam, Enoch, Levi, etc. One of the books in this category, 1Enoch, is part of the canon of the Ethiopian Orthodox Church. 1Enoch 1:9 is normally considered the source for

the quote cited in Jude 1:14-15. Two passages in 1Enoch (48:2-7; 69:26-29) describe the son of man in definitive messianic terminology that parallels the New Testament. Portions of 1Enoch were found in the Dead Sea Scrolls.

Plato was a Greek philosopher whose works were originally composed prior to 400 B.C.E. Plato's works were well known throughout Greek speaking areas and provide insight into religious and philosophical concepts prevalent in Greek culture during the apostolic period. Plato's works contain parallels to the Letters of Paul and the Book of Revelation. Plato's description of the judgment of the wicked in Phaedo 113e-114b parallels Revelation 20:10-15.

The books in the Nag Hammadi Library were originally composed prior to C.E. 400. The Nag Hammadi Library is the single largest source of the writings of the Gnostics who are referred to in 1Timothy 6:20-21. The works in the Nag Hammadi Library explore topics such as the Word, the Christ, Jesus, the Incarnation, the Son of God, and the Virgin Birth. The cross reference index facilitates comparisons between passages from the Nag Hammadi Library and commentary concerning these passages from early church fathers such as Irenaeus.

Greek literature (c. 500 B.C.E. – C.E. 100) are texts written primarily by Greek playwrights and philosophers. These writings contain pre-Christian Hellenic concepts that are referred to in the book of Acts and the epistles of Paul. Epimenides, De oraculus and Aratus, Phaenomena 5 are quoted in Acts 17:28.

Rabbinic writings include the Talmud (c. C.E. 200 – C.E. 600) which is a record of rabbinic discussions on Jewish law, Jewish ethics, customs, legends, and stories. Portions of the Talmud parallel the traditions of the elders mentioned in Matthew 15:2-6, Mark 7:3-13, and Galatians 1:14. The Talmud contains references to the Messiah, miraculous healings, the apocalypse, and baptism. Rabbinic writings also include Targums. Targums are Aramaic paraphrases of the Old Testament that contain information not found in the Masoretic Text. The names of Jannes and Jambres mentioned in 2Timothy 3:8 are contained in the Targum Jonathan version of Exodus.

The Egyptian Book of the Dead is a collection of writings from the walls of Egyptian tombs, including the pyramids, which predate Christianity by at least a thousand years. The Egyptian Book of the Dead contains parallels to the Gospel of Matthew and Revelation, including references to the judgment of the dead and the serpent being thrown into the lake of fire.

The Apostolic and Patristic Writings cited in this volume were originally composed in the Ante-Nicene period before C.E. 400. The Apostolic and Patristic Writings provide 1st, 2nd, and 3rd century quotations from the New Testament. The Apostolic and Patristic Writings are crucial for confirming the authentic text of the Gospel of Luke and ten of the Pauline epistles that the heretic Marcion attempted to modify circa C.E. 140.

Tacitus was a Roman senator and historian. His writings were originally composed circa C.E. 130. Tacitus provides insight into Roman religious and philosophical perspectives during the apostolic period. Tacitus is one of the earliest historians to mention Christians.

The Golden Verses of Pythagoras contain philosophical and moral parallels to the New Testament. The Golden Verses of Pythagoras were originally composed centuries before the Christian era.

The Dhammapada is an Indian work that was composed before the Christian era. The Dhammapada contains parallels to the Sermon on the Mount concepts of turning the other cheek, the light of the world, and not looking at a woman with lust.

The Epic of Gilgamesh is an Akkadian text originally composed between 2500 and 1500 B.C.E. and is one of the oldest stories in existence. The Epic of Gilgamesh contains archetypal parallels to the New Testament. There is no known causal connection for parallels between the Epic of Gilgamesh and the New Testament. Any parallels or similarities are believed to have been formed independently, or through secondary means.

The comparison of the Epic of Gilgamesh and the New Testament serves as a demonstration of the formation of textual parallels and allusions due to archetypal similarities.

The books of the New Testament Apocrypha were authored after the beginning of the Christian era and contain a variety of Christian fiction, romances, and letters. The majority of the books are of unknown authorship. One of the books in this category, the Epistula Apostolorum, is part of the canon of the Ethiopian Orthodox Church.

The New Testament contains several Hebrew/Aramaic linguistic structures which are not discernible in either English or Greek. Those portions of the New Testament that preserve oral sayings retain some of their original Hebrew or Aramaic linguistic structures especially puns. Hebrew/Aramaic puns are based on homonyms, letter substitutions, or letter sequence changes in a word to form a new word. For instance in the Old Testament, the word Abram (exalted father) is changed through a pun into Abraham (father of nations) in Genesis 17:5 by adding a single letter. Similarly, in Matthew 3:9 the Hebrew word for "eben" (stones) changes through a pun into the word for "ben" (children) by dropping the first letter, aleph. Hebrew/Aramaic puns underlie the text in Matthew 5:47-48, 7:6, 11:17, 12:39, 16:18, 17:05, 19:12, 19:24, 23:25-29, 26:52.

The Graphs

The back cover and this preface contain three graphs which reflect the goal of our work: to maximize readability and accuracy in a single text.

➤ **Readability** is calculated according to the Coleman-Liau scoring system. For this we reduce the final text to a single file with no titles, verse numbers, or paragraph divisions, and use Readability Studio version 1.2.0.0, Copyright © 2007 to calculate the reading level. We do the same for each of the twenty translations in our comparison study.

➤ **Accuracy** is calculated in several stages:
  - The first stage is to translate textual differences in ancient manuscripts into English.
  - Ignoring brackets, italics, and footnotes, we compare the base text in each translation to the variants and ask a single question: which variation is closer to this translation? If there is no clear answer, we mark the translation with a tilde. A match does not necessarily mean that the translators of that version actually use the variant. It only means that their chosen words are closer to the variant than to the Nestle-Aland. As can be seen by the nature of the variants, many, if not most, are stylistic differences. Ancient copyists faced the same pressures for clarity and style that translators face, and their results will often parallel.
  - Finally, we divide the total number of times each translation is mapped to a variant by the total number of notes, and subtract the result from 100%.

➤ **Formal equivalence** is calculated by dividing the total number of tildes a translation receives by the total number of notes, and subtracting the result from 100%.

For each chart, the first third is generally recognized to be superior to the last third, and our charts offer no surprises. What is new, however, is the completeness of each chart; to our knowledge, no previous study has examined the entire New Testament text in all twenty of these translations for all three categories.

Final Notes

Although this version uses modern language, accuracy has forced the text to return to older conventions in two instances:

1) In Greek, as in English, men do not have the fortune of owning their own gender. Masculine language does not necessarily exclude women in the same way that feminine language excludes men. Both languages offer this advantage to women, and there is no precise way to raise men to an equivalent level.

2) The New Testament was written in a movement that grew out of Judaism, and the general population is often referred to as "the Jews." Those who were born of different nationalities should not feel themselves excluded from the lessons, admonitions, and message of the text.

The editors would like to add that no translation can stand alone. The work of textual accuracy continues with each edition of the Nestle-Aland *Novum Testamentum Graece*, and its sister publication, the United Bible Societies *Greek New Testament*. Knowledge of linguistics, history, and customs continues to shed light on the precise meaning of the text. The English language is itself a moving target, and as human speaking progresses, so too must translation.

Further, no single version, nor any dozen versions, can ever completely capture the style, color, and even puns of the original message. If this version encourages readers to compare and respect the talented and faithful efforts of other versions, it has achieved part of its goal. If this version encourages readers to appreciate the language, history, and customs that were contextually part of the original message then it has achieved more of its goal.

And if this version leads readers to be transformed by the renewing of their minds, that they may prove what is the will of God, what is good and acceptable and perfect (Romans 12:2) – then, indeed, it will have come closer still.

In this past decade of labor, no one has encouraged us more than our grandmother, Mildred Clontz – both by words and by a life lived after this book. She was an inspiration to us and to her church in which she was an active volunteer worker, even at 92. In the final year of her life the production of this text became an urgency, as we wished to give her a bound copy, which finally became possible for her final Christmas.

Our grandparents gave us the first Bible we ever read. Our first effort of translation was the last Bible our grandfather read before his passing in 1996, and the galley proof of *The Comprehensive New Testament* was the last Bible our grandmother read. We miss them both greatly; but we know that the same Spirit which guided them also breathes in the Word that governed their lives, and we are grateful to take this part of them forward in our own lives, and to present it in the hope that it will be of benefit to yours.

The Editors
April 7, 2008

The Comprehensive
New Testament

According to Matthew

1 ¹ The book of the genealogy of Jesus Christ, the son of David, the son of Abraham:

² Abraham was the father of Isaac, Isaac the father of Jacob, and Jacob the father of Judah and his brothers. ³ Judah was the father of Perez and Zerah by Tamar, Perez the father of Hezron, and Hezron the father of Aram. ⁴ Aram was the father of Amminadab, Amminadab the father of Nahshon, and Nahshon the father of Salmon. ⁵ Salmon was the father of Boaz by Rahab, Boaz the father of Obed by Ruth, and Obed the father of Jesse, ⁶ and Jesse the father of David the king.

David was the father of Solomon by the wife of Uriah, ⁷ Solomon the father of Rehoboam, and Rehoboam the father of Abijah. Abijah was the father of Asaph, ⁸ Asaph the father of Jehoshaphat, and Jehoshaphat the father of Joram. Joram was the father of Uzziah, ⁹ Uzziah the father of Jotham, and Jotham the father of Ahaz. Ahaz was the father of Hezekiah, ¹⁰ Hezekiah the father of Manasseh, and Manasseh the father of Amos. Amos was the father of Josiah, ¹¹ and Josiah the father of Jeconiah and his brothers at the time of the exile to Babylon.

¹² And after the exile to Babylon: Jeconiah was the father of Shealtiel, and Shealtiel the father of Zerubbabel. ¹³ Zerubbabel was the father of Abiud, Abiud the father of Eliakim, and Eliakim the father of Azor. ¹⁴ Azor was the father of Zadok, Zadok the father of Achim, and Achim the father of Eliud. ¹⁵ Eliud was the father of Eleazar, Eleazar the father of Matthan, and Matthan the father of Jacob. ¹⁶ And Jacob was the father of Joseph the husband of Mary, of whom Jesus was born, who is called Christ.

¹⁷ So all the generations from Abraham to David were fourteen generations. From David to the exile to Babylon were fourteen generations. And from the exile to Babylon to the Christ were fourteen generations.

¹⁸ Now the birth of Jesus Christ took place in this way: when his mother Mary was betrothed to Joseph, before they came together, she was found to be with child from the Holy Spirit. ¹⁹ Then Joseph her husband, being a just man, and not wanting to disgrace her, was resolved to divorce her quietly. ²⁰ But as he considered this, behold, an angel of the Lord appeared to him in a dream, saying, "Joseph, son of David, do not be afraid to take Mary your wife. For that which is conceived in her is from the Holy Spirit. ²¹ And she

---

Title Alx/Byz[**According to Matthew**], Minor[*variations of* The Gospel According to Saint Matthew].

1:1 **genealogy** *or* birth; **Jesus** *Hebraism* The LORD saves; **Christ** *Anointed One i.e. Messiah.*

1:6 Alx[**David was the father**], Byz[King David was the father (KJV, NKJ)].

1:7-8 Alx[**Asaph**], Byz[Asa (ASV, DRA, HCS, JNT, KJV, MRD, NAS, NAU, NET, NIV, NJB, NKJ, NLT, REB, RSV, TEV, TLB)].

1:8-9 **Joram** *or* Jehoram.

1:10 Alx[**Amos**], Byz[Amon (ASV, DRA, HCS, JNT, KJV, MRD, NAS, NAU, NET, NIV, NJB, NKJ, NLT, REB, TEV)].

1:11 Alx/Byz[**Jeconiah**], Minor[Jehoiakim, Jehoiakim the father of Jeconiah].

1:16 Alx/Byz[*text*], Minor[And Jacob was the father of Joseph, to whom being betrothed the virgin Mary bore Jesus, who is called Christ].

1:17 *The numerical value of* **David** *in Hebrew is fourteen.*

1:18 Alx[**birth** *or* origin], Byz[birth]; Alx/Byz[**Jesus Christ**], Minor[Christ *others* Christ Jesus *others* Jesus]; Alx[**when his mother**], Byz[for when his mother].

1:19 Alx[**disgrace her**], Byz[put her to public shame (ASV, DRA, JNT, KJV, NIV, NKJ, NLT, NRS, ~REB, ~TEV, ~TLB)]; **quietly** *i.e. without legal charges.*

will give birth to a son, and you shall call his name Jesus, for he will save his people from their sins." ²² All this took place to fulfill what the Lord had spoken by the prophet:

²³   *"Behold, the virgin shall be with child and bear a son,*
              and they shall call his name Immanuel,"

which means, *"God with us."* ²⁴ When Joseph woke from sleep, he did as the angel of the Lord commanded him and took his wife. ²⁵ But he did not know her until she had given birth to a son; and he called his name Jesus.

2 ¹ Now after Jesus was born in Bethlehem of Judea in the days of Herod the king, behold, wise men from the East came to Jerusalem, ² saying, "Where is he who has been born king of the Jews? For we have seen his star in the East and have come to worship him." ³ When Herod the king heard this, he was troubled, and all Jerusalem with him. ⁴ And when he had gathered all the chief priests and scribes of the people together, he inquired of them where the Christ was to be born. ⁵ So they said to him, "In Bethlehem of Judea, for thus it is written by the prophet:

⁶   *'But you, Bethlehem, in the land of Judah,*
              are by no means least among the rulers of Judah.
      For out of you shall come a ruler
              who will shepherd my people Israel.'"

⁷ Then Herod called the wise men secretly and determined from them what time the star had appeared. ⁸ And he sent them to Bethlehem and said, "Go and search diligently for the young child, and when you have found him, bring back word to me, so that I too may come and worship him." ⁹ When they had heard the king they went their way. And behold, the star which they had seen in the East went before them, until it came to rest over the place where the child was. ¹⁰ When they saw the star, they were overwhelmed with joy. ¹¹ On coming into the house, they saw the child with his mother Mary, and they fell down and worshipped him. Then they opened their treasures and presented him with gifts of gold, and frankincense, and myrrh. ¹² And being warned in a dream not to return to Herod, they departed to their own country by another way.

¹³ Now when they had departed, behold, an angel of the Lord appeared to Joseph in a dream and said, "Rise, take the child and his mother, and flee to Egypt, and stay there until I tell you; for Herod is about to search for the child, to destroy him." ¹⁴ When he rose, he took the young child and his mother by night and departed for Egypt, ¹⁵ and remained there until the death of Herod. And so was fulfilled what the Lord had spoken by the prophet, *"Out of Egypt have I called my son."*

¹⁶ Then Herod, when he saw that he had been tricked by the wise men, was in a furious rage. And he sent and killed all the male children in Bethlehem and in all its

---

1:22 Alx/Byz[**the prophet**], Minor[*adds* Isaiah].

1:23 Alx/Byz[**they shall call**], Minor[you shall call (MRD, ~REB, ~RSV, ~TEV, ~TLB)]; **Isaiah 7:14, 8:8, 10 LXX/~DSS.**

1:24 Alx[**Joseph woke**], Byz[Joseph was awakened (KJV, NKJ)].

1:25 Alx[**a son**], Byz[her firstborn son (DRA, KJV, MRD, NKJ)].

2:1, 7, 16 **wise men** *or* astrologers *Greek* magi.

2:2, 9 **in the East** *or* when it rose *or* from our country.

2:5 Alx/Byz[**the prophet**], Minor[*adds* Micah (TLB)].

2:6 **shepherd** *or* rule; ~**Micah 5:2**, ~2 Samuel 5:2.

2:9 Alx[**came to rest**], Byz[came and stood (ASV, DRA, ~HCS, ~JNT, KJV, MRD, NAS, NAU, NKJ, ~REB, ~TEV, TLB)].

2:11 Alx/Byz[**they saw**], Minor[they found (DRA)]; **frankincense** *Greek* Lebanon; **myrrh** *Greek* Smyrna.

2:13 Alx/Byz[**appeared** *Greek* appears], Minor[appeared].

2:15 ~**Hosea 11:1 Masoretic.**

region who were two years old or under, according to the time which he had determined from the wise men. **17** Then was fulfilled what was spoken through the prophet Jeremiah:

18 *A voice was heard in Ramah,*
> *weeping and great mourning,*
Rachel weeping for her children,
> *refusing to be comforted, because they are no more."*

19 But when Herod died, behold, an angel of the Lord appeared in a dream to Joseph in Egypt, **20** saying, "Rise, take the young child and his mother, and go to the land of Israel, for those who sought the young child's life are dead." **21** And he rose and took the child and his mother, and went to the land of Israel. **22** But when he heard that Archelaus ruled Judea in place of his father Herod, he was afraid to go there. And being warned in a dream, he withdrew to the district of Galilee. **23** And he went and dwelt in a city called Nazareth, that what was spoken by the Prophets might be fulfilled, *"He shall be called a Nazarene."*

3 **1** In those days John the Baptist came, preaching in the wilderness of Judea, **2** [and] saying, "Repent, for the kingdom of heaven is at hand." **3** For this is he who was declared through the prophet Isaiah when he said,

> *"The voice of one crying in the wilderness:*
> *Prepare the way of the Lord,*
> *make his paths straight."*

4 Now John wore a garment of camel's hair, and a leather belt around his waist; and his food was locusts and wild honey. **5** Then Jerusalem and all Judea and all the region about the Jordan went out to him, **6** and confessing their sins, they were baptized by him in the Jordan River.

7 But when he saw many of the Pharisees and Sadducees coming to his baptism, he said to them, "You brood of vipers! Who warned you to flee from the wrath to come? **8** Bear fruit worthy of repentance. **9** And do not think to say to yourselves, 'We have Abraham as our father.' For I tell you that God is able from these stones to raise children for Abraham. **10** But now the ax is laid at the root of the trees. Every tree therefore that does not bear good fruit is cut down and thrown into the fire. **11** I baptize you with water for repentance. But he who is coming after me is mightier than I, whose sandals I am not worthy to carry. He will baptize you with the Holy Spirit and fire. **12** His winnowing fork is in his hand, and he will clear his threshing floor and gather his wheat into the barn. But the chaff he will burn with unquenchable fire."

2:17 Alx[**through the prophet**], Byz[by the prophet (DRA, ESV, KJV, MRD, NET, NKJ, RSV)].

2:18 Alx[**weeping and great mourning**], Byz[lamentation, weeping, and great mourning (KJV, NKJ)]; **Jeremiah 31:15 Alx=Masoretic / Byz=LXX.**

2:21 Alx[**went to**], Byz[came to (ASV, DRA, ~HCS, KJV, NAS, NAU, NKJ, REB)].

2:22 Alx[**ruled**], Byz[ruled over (ASV, ESV, HCS, NAB, NAS, NAU, NET, NKJ, NRS, RSV)].

2:23 **He shall be called a Nazarene** *unknown reference.*

3:2 Alx/Byz[**and saying**], Minor[saying (ASV, ESV, ~JNT, NAS, NAU, NET, NJB, NLT, NRS, ~REB, RSV, ~TEV, ~TLB)]; **is at hand** *or* has come near.

3:3 Alx[**through the prophet**], Byz[by the prophet (DRA, ESV, ~JNT, KJV, MRD, ~NAB, NAS, NAU, ~NET, NJB, NKJ, ~NLT, ~NRS, ~REB, RSV, TLB)]; **Isaiah 40:3 LXX.**

3:6 Alx[**River**], Byz[*omits* (DRA, KJV, NKJ, TEV)].

3:7 Alx/Byz[**coming to his baptism**], Minor[coming for baptism (ESV 2001 edition, MRD, NAS, NAU, NJB, NRS, REB, RSV, TLB)].

3:8 Alx/Byz[**fruit**], Minor[fruits (KJV, MRD, NKJ, ~TEV, TLB)].

3:10 Alx[**But now**], Byz[But even now (ASV, KJV, NKJ, TLB)].

3:11 Alx/Byz[**and fire**], Major[*omits*]; **with water** *or* in water *or* by water; **with the Holy Spirit** *or* in the Holy Spirit *or* by the Holy Spirit.

3:12 Alx/Byz[**the barn**], Minor[his barn (MRD, NAB, NJB, NLT, REB, TEV)].

[13] Then Jesus came from Galilee to John at the Jordan to be baptized by him. [14] But John tried to prevent him, saying, "I need to be baptized by you, and do you come to me?" [15] But Jesus said to him in reply, "Let it be so now; for thus it is fitting for us to fulfill all righteousness." Then he consented. [16] And when Jesus was baptized, he went up immediately from the water. And behold, the heavens were opened [to him]. And he saw [the] Spirit of God descending like a dove, [and] alighting on him – [17] and behold, a voice from heaven, saying, "This is my beloved Son, with whom I am well pleased."

4 [1] Then Jesus was led by the Spirit into the wilderness to be tempted by the devil. [2] And he fasted forty days and forty nights, and afterward he was hungry. [3] And the tempter came and said to him, "If you are the Son of God, command these stones to become loaves of bread." [4] But he answered, "It is written,

> 'Man shall not live by bread alone,
>> but by every word that proceeds
>>> from the mouth of God.'"

[5] Then the devil took him to the holy city, and stood him on the pinnacle of the temple, [6] and said to him, "If you are the Son of God, throw yourself down. For it is written,

> 'He will give his angels charge of you,'
>> and, 'In their hands they will bear you up,
> lest you strike your foot against a stone.'"

[7] Jesus said to him, "Again it is written, 'You shall not tempt the Lord your God.'" [8] Again, the devil took him to a very high mountain, and showed him all the kingdoms of the world, and their glory. [9] And he said to him, "All these I will give you, if you will fall down and worship me." [10] Then Jesus said to him, "Away, Satan! For it is written,

> 'You shall worship the Lord your God
>> and him only shall you serve.'"

[11] Then the devil left him. And behold, angels came and ministered to him.

[12] Now when he heard that John had been put in prison, he withdrew to Galilee. [13] And leaving Nazareth, he went and dwelt in Capernaum, which is by the sea, in the regions of Zebulun and Naphtali, [14] that what was spoken by the prophet Isaiah might be fulfilled:

[15]
> "The land of Zebulun and land of Naphtali,
>> the way to the sea, beyond the Jordan,
>>> Galilee of the Gentiles –
[16]
> the people who sat in darkness

3:[14] Alx/Byz[**John**], Minor[he].

3:[15-16] Metzger[*Two Latin manuscripts add between verses 15 and 16* And when Jesus was being baptized a great light flashed from the water, so that all who had gathered there were afraid].

3:[16] Alx/Byz[**the heavens were opened to him**], Minor[*omits* to him (JNT, NAS, NAU, NET, NIV, NJB, NLT, REB, RSV); Alx/Byz[**and alighting on him**], Minor[*omits* and (JNT, ~REB, ~TLB)]; **he saw the Spirit** *the pronoun could refer to Jesus or John.*

4:[1] **tempted** *or* tested.

4:[3] Alx[**came and said to him**], Byz[came to him and said (HCS, KJV, NIV, NKJ, REB, TEV, TLB)].

4:[4] Alx/Byz[**by every word**], Minor[in every word (DRA, ~TEV, ~TLB)]; **Deuteronomy 8:3**.

4:[5] Alx[**stood him on the pinnacle**], Byz[stands him on the pinnacle (KJV, ~NLT, ~TLB)].

4:[6] **Psalms 91:11-12**.

4:[7] **Deuteronomy 6:16**.

4:[9] Alx[**he said to him**], Byz[he says to him (KJV)].

4:[10] Alx[**Away**], Byz[Get behind me (~REB, ~TLB)]; **Deuteronomy 6:13 LXX**.

4:[12] Alx[**when he heard**], Byz[when Jesus heard (DRA, JNT, KJV, MRD, NAU, NET, NIV, NKJ, NLT, NRS, TEV, TLB)].

4:[13] Alx[**Capernaum** *Greek* Capharnaum], Byz[Capernaum].

4:[15-16] ~**Isaiah 9:1-2**.

> *have seen a great light,*
> *and on those who sat in the region and shadow of death*
> *light has dawned."*

¹⁷ From that time Jesus began to preach and say, "Repent, for the kingdom of heaven is at hand."

¹⁸ As he was walking by the Sea of Galilee, he saw two brothers, Simon who is called Peter and Andrew his brother, casting a net into the sea; for they were fishermen. ¹⁹ And he said to them, "Follow me, and I will make you fishers of men." ²⁰ Immediately they left their nets and followed him. ²¹ Going on from there, he saw two other brothers, James the son of Zebedee and John his brother, in the boat with Zebedee their father, mending their nets. And he called them, ²² and immediately they left the boat and their father, and followed him.

²³ And he went about all Galilee, teaching in their synagogues, and preaching the gospel of the kingdom, and healing every disease and every sickness among the people. ²⁴ Then his fame spread throughout all Syria. And they brought to him all sick people who were afflicted with various diseases and pains, [and] those who were demon-possessed, those having seizures, and the paralyzed. And he healed them. ²⁵ Great crowds followed him from Galilee, and from the Decapolis, Jerusalem, Judea, and beyond the Jordan.

5 ¹ Seeing the crowds, he went up on a mountain. And when he sat down, his disciples came to him. ² And he opened his mouth and taught them, saying:

³   "Blessed are the poor in spirit,
>   for theirs is the kingdom of heaven.
⁴   Blessed are those who mourn,
>   for they shall be comforted.
⁵   Blessed are the meek,
>   for they shall inherit the earth.
⁶   Blessed are those who hunger and thirst for righteousness,
>   for they shall be filled.
⁷   Blessed are the merciful,
>   for they shall obtain mercy.
⁸   Blessed are the pure in heart,
>   for they shall see God.
⁹   Blessed are the peacemakers,
>   for they shall be called sons of God.
¹⁰ Blessed are those who are persecuted for righteousness' sake,
>   for theirs is the kingdom of heaven.

¹¹ Blessed are you when they revile you and persecute you, and say all kinds of evil against you [falsely] for my sake. ¹² Rejoice and be glad, for great is your reward in heaven, for so they persecuted the prophets who were before you.

4:¹⁷ Alx/Byz[**Repent, for**], Minor/Old Syriac[*omits*]; **is at hand** *or* has come near.

4:¹⁸ Alx/Byz[**As he was walking**], Minor[As Jesus was walking (DRA, JNT, KJV, NAU, NIV, NKJ, NLT, REB, TEV)]; Alx/Byz[**Peter**], Alt/Peshitta[Cephas (JNT, MRD)].

4:²³ Alx[**And he went about all Galilee**], Byz[And Jesus went about all Galilee (ASV, DRA, HCS, JNT, KJV, MRD, NAS, NAU, NET, NIV, NKJ, NLT, NRS, TEV, TLB)]; **gospel** *or* good news.

4:²⁴ Alx/Byz[**and those who were demon-possessed**], Minor[*omits* and (ASV, ESV, HCS, NAB, NAS, NAU, NIV, NJB, ~NLT, NRS, ~REB, RSV, TEV, ~TLB)]; **those having seizures** *Greek* moonstruck.

4:²⁵ **the Decapolis** *or* the Ten Cities.

5:¹ Alx/Byz[**came to him**], Minor[*omits* to him (~TLB)].

5:⁴⁻⁵ Alx/Byz[*text*], Minor[*place verse 4 after verse 5* (DRA)].

5:¹¹ Alx/Byz[**falsely**], Minor[*omits* (REB)].

¹³ "You are the salt of the earth. But if the salt should lose its taste, how shall it be made salty again? It is no longer good for anything, except to be thrown out and trampled under foot by men. ¹⁴ You are the light of the world. A city set on a hill cannot be hidden. ¹⁵ Nor do they light a lamp and put it under a basket, but on a stand. And it gives light to all in the house. ¹⁶ Let your light so shine before men, that they may see your good works and glorify your Father in heaven.

¹⁷ "Do not think that I have come to abolish the Law or the Prophets. I have not come to abolish them but to fulfill them. ¹⁸ For truly, I say to you, till heaven and earth pass away, not an iota, not a dot, will by any means pass from the Law until all is accomplished. ¹⁹ Whoever then breaks one of the least of these commandments and teaches men so, shall be called least in the kingdom of heaven. But he who does them and teaches them shall be called great in the kingdom of heaven. ²⁰ For I tell you, that unless your righteousness exceeds that of the scribes and Pharisees, you will by no means enter the kingdom of heaven.

²¹ "You have heard that it was said to those of old, *'You shall not murder,'* and whoever murders will be liable to judgment. ²² But I say to you that anyone who is angry with his brother shall be subject to judgment. And whoever says to his brother, 'Raca,' shall be in danger of the council. But whoever says, 'You fool!' shall be in danger of the fire of hell. ²³ Therefore, if you are offering your gift at the altar and there remember that your brother has something against you, ²⁴ leave your gift there before the altar, and go. First be reconciled to your brother; and then come and offer your gift. ²⁵ Agree with your adversary quickly, while you are on the way with him, lest your adversary deliver you to the judge, the judge to the officer, and you be thrown into prison. ²⁶ Truly, I say to you, you will never get out till you have paid the last penny.

²⁷ "You have heard that it was said, *'You shall not commit adultery.'* ²⁸ But I say to you that every one who looks at a woman to lust after her has already committed adultery with her in his heart. ²⁹ If your right eye causes you to sin, pluck it out and throw it away. It is better for you to lose one of your members than for your whole body to be thrown into hell. ³⁰ And if your right hand causes you to sin, cut it off and throw it away. It is better for you to lose one of your members than for your whole body to go into hell.

³¹ "It has also been said, *'Whoever divorces his wife, let him give her a certificate of divorce.'* ³² But I say to you that every one who divorces his wife, except for sexual

---

5:¹⁵ **basket** *Greek* modios *a grain-measuring container of about 8 quarts.*

5:¹⁹ **breaks** *or* annuls.

5:²¹ **Exodus 20:13; Deuteronomy 5:17.**

5:²² Alx[**with his brother**], Byz[*adds* without a cause (KJV, MRD, NKJ)]; **Raca** *an Aramaic insult;* **hell** *Greek* Gehenna.

5:²⁵ Alx[**the judge to the officer**], Byz[the judge deliver you to the officer (ASV, DRA, KJV, MRD, NAB, NET, NKJ, NIV, NLT, TEV)].

5:²⁶ Alx/Major[**never get out till**], Byz[never get out; not until].

5:²⁷ Alx/Major[**that it was said**], Byz[*adds* to those of old (DRA, JNT, KJV, NKJ, ~REB)]; **Exodus 20:14; Deuteronomy 5:18.**

5:²⁸ Alx/Byz[**to lust after her**], Minor[lustfully (ESV, MRD, NAB, NIV, NJB, NLT, NRS, REB, RSV, ~TEV, TLB)].

5:²⁹⁻³⁰ **hell** *Greek* Gehenna.

5:³⁰ Alx[**go into hell**], Byz[be cast into hell (JNT, KJV, NKJ, NLT)].

5:³¹ Alx/Byz[**It has also been said**], Major[It has also been said that]; ~**Deuteronomy 24:1.**

5:³² Alx[**every one who**], Byz[whoever (DRA, KJV, MRD, NAB, ~NIV, NKJ, ~NLT, ~NRS, REB, ~TEV)]; Alx[**causes her to become an adulteress** *passive*], Byz[causes her to commit adultery *active* (DRA, ESV, HCS, KJV, MRD, NAB, NAS, NAU, NET, NKJ, NLT, NRS, TEV, TLB)]; Alx/Byz[**And whoever marries a divorced woman commits adultery**], Minor[*omits*].

immorality, causes her to become an adulteress. And whoever marries a divorced woman commits adultery.

33 "Again you have heard that it was said to those of old, *'You shall not swear falsely, but shall perform your oaths to the Lord.'* **34** But I say to you, do not swear at all: either by heaven, for it is God's throne; **35** or by the earth, for it is his footstool; or by Jerusalem, for it is the city of the Great King. **36** And do not swear by your head, for you cannot make even one hair white or black. **37** Simply let your 'Yes' be 'Yes,' and your 'No,' 'No'; anything more than this comes from evil.

38 "You have heard that it was said, *'An eye for an eye and a tooth for a tooth.'* **39** But I tell you, do not resist an evil person. But if someone strikes you on [your] right cheek, turn to him the other also. **40** And if someone wants to sue you and take your tunic, let him have your cloak as well. **41** And if someone forces you to go one mile, go with him two miles. **42** Give to him who asks you, and do not refuse him who wants to borrow from you.

43 "You have heard that it was said, *'You shall love your neighbor'* and hate your enemy. **44** But I say to you, love your enemies and pray for those who persecute you, **45** that you may be sons of your Father in heaven; for he makes his sun rise on the evil and on the good, and sends rain on the just and on the unjust. **46** For if you love those who love you, what reward have you? Do not even the tax collectors do the same? **47** And if you greet only your brothers, what more are you doing than others? Do not even the Gentiles do the same? **48** You, therefore, must be perfect, as your heavenly Father is perfect.

6 **1** "[But] take heed that you do not do your righteousness before men, to be seen by them. If you do, you will have no reward from your Father in heaven.

2 "Thus, when you give alms, do not sound a trumpet before you, as the hypocrites do in the synagogues and in the streets, that they may be praised by men. Truly, I say to you, they have received their reward. **3** But when you give to the needy, do not let your left hand know what your right hand is doing, **4** so that your charitable deed may be in secret. And your Father, who sees in secret, will reward you.

5:33 ~**Leviticus 19:12**; ~**Numbers 30:2**.

5:37 **Simply let your 'Yes' be 'Yes,' and your 'No,' 'No'** *Greek* But let your word be Yes, Yes, No, No; **evil** *or* the evil one.

5:38 **Exodus 21:24; Leviticus 24:20; Deuteronomy 19:21**.

5:39 Alx[**if someone strikes you**], Byz[if someone will strike you (KJV)]; Alx[**on your right cheek**], Byz[on the right cheek (ESV, JNT, NET, NIV, NJB, NLT, NRS, REB, RSV, TEV, ~TLB)].

5:41 **mile** *Greek* milion *(4,854 feet)*.

5:43 ~**Leviticus 19:18**.

5:44 Alx[*text*], Byz[But I say to you, love your enemies, bless those who curse you, do good to those who hate you, and pray for those who spitefully use you and persecute you (~DRA, KJV, MRD, NKJ)].

5:46 Alx/Byz[**do the same**], Minor[do so (DRA, JNT, MRD, NIV, ~NJB, ~NLT, ~REB, TEV, ~TLB)].

5:47 Alx[**brothers**], Byz[friends (JNT, NLT, TEV, TLB)]; Alx[**Gentiles**], Byz[tax collectors (KJV, MRD, ~NJB, NKJ)]; Alx[**do the same**], Byz[do so (DRA, JNT, KJV, MRD, NIV, ~NJB, NKJ, NLT, REB, TEV, TLB)].

5:48 Alx[**as your heavenly Father**], Byz[even as your Father in heaven (JNT, KJV, MRD, NKJ, NLT, TEV, TLB)].

6:1 Alx[**But**], Byz[*omits* (ASV, DRA, ESV, HCS, JNT, KJV, MRD, NAS, NAU, NET, NIV, NJB, NKJ, NLT, NRS, REB, RSV, TEV, TLB)]; Alx[**do your righteousness**], Byz[do your charitable deeds (JNT, KJV, MRD, NKJ, ~NLT, ~TLB)].

6:4 Alx[**will reward you**], Byz[will reward you openly (MRD)], Major[will himself reward you openly (KJV, NKJ)].

⁵ "And when you pray, you shall not be like the hypocrites. For they love to pray standing in the synagogues and on the street corners, that they may be seen by men. Truly, I say to you, they have received their reward. ⁶ But when you pray, go into your room, shut the door and pray to your Father, who is in secret. And your Father, who sees in secret, will reward you. ⁷ And when you pray, do not use empty repetitions as the Gentiles do. For they think that they will be heard for their many words. ⁸ Do not be like them, for your Father knows what you need before you ask him. ⁹ Pray, then, in this way:

> Our Father in heaven,
>> hallowed be your name.
10 >> Your kingdom come.
>> Your will be done
>>> on earth as it is in heaven.
11 >> Give us this day our daily bread.
12 >> And forgive us our debts,
>>> as we also have forgiven our debtors.
13 >> And lead us not into temptation,
>>> but deliver us from the evil one.'

¹⁴ For if you forgive men their trespasses, your heavenly Father will also forgive you. ¹⁵ But if you do not forgive men, neither will your Father forgive your trespasses.

¹⁶ "And when you fast, do not look gloomy, like the hypocrites, for they disfigure their faces that they may be seen by men to be fasting. Truly, I say to you, they have received their reward. ¹⁷ But when you fast, anoint your head and wash your face, ¹⁸ so that you do not appear to be fasting to men, but to your Father who is in secret. And your Father, who sees in secret, will reward you.

¹⁹ "Do not lay up for yourselves treasures on earth, where moth and rust destroy and where thieves break in and steal. ²⁰ But lay up for yourselves treasures in heaven, where neither moth nor rust destroys and where thieves do not break in and steal. ²¹ For where your treasure is, there your heart will be also.

²² "The lamp of the body is the eye. So if your eye is good, your whole body will be full of light. ²³ But if your eye is evil, your whole body will be full of darkness. If then the light in you is darkness, how great is that darkness!

²⁴ "No one can serve two masters. For either he will hate the one and love the other, or he will be devoted to the one and despise the other. You cannot serve God and mammon.

6:5 Alx[**when you** *plural* **pray, you** *plural* **shall not be like**], Byz[when you *singular* pray, you *singular* shall not be just like (KJV, MRD)].

6:6 Alx[**will reward you**], Byz[*adds* openly (KJV, MRD, NKJ)].

6:8 Alx/Byz[**your Father**], Minor[God your Father *others* your heavenly father]; Alx/Byz[**before you ask him**], Minor[before you open your mouth].

6:11 **daily bread** *or* bread for tomorrow.

6:12 Alx[**have forgiven**], Byz[forgive (DRA, KJV, MRD, NAB, NKJ, TEV)].

6:13 Alx[*text*], Minor[*adds* Amen. (DRA)], Byz[*adds* for yours is the kingdom and the power and the glory, forever. Amen. (HCS, KJV, MRD, NAS, NAU, NKJ)]; **the evil one** *or* evil; *compare* 1 Chronicles 29:11-13.

6:15 Alx[**forgive men**], Byz[*adds* their trespasses (ASV, ESV, JNT, KJV, NKJ, RSV)].

6:16 Alx[**like the hypocrites**], Byz[just like the hypocrites]; Alx[**I say to you**], Byz[*adds* that (~NLT)].

6:18 Alx/Major[**reward you**], Byz[*adds* openly (KJV, NKJ)].

6:19-20 **rust** *Greek* eating.

6:21 Alx[**your... your** *singular*], Byz[your... your *plural*]; Alx/Byz[**also**], Minor[*omits* (TEV)].

6:22 Alx/Byz[**So if**], Minor[If (DRA, HCS, NAB, NIV, NLT, REB, TEV, TLB)].

6:24 **mammon** *Aramaic* money *possibly a Syrian deity.*

25 "Therefore I tell you, do not worry about your life, what you will eat [or what you will drink]; nor about your body, what you will put on. Is not life more than food, and the body more than clothing? **26** Look at the birds of the air. They neither sow nor reap nor gather into barns, and yet your heavenly Father feeds them. Are you not of more value than they? **27** Which of you by worrying can add one cubit to his span of life? **28** And why do you worry about clothing? Consider the lilies of the field, how they grow. They neither toil nor spin. **29** Yet I tell you that even Solomon in all his glory was not arrayed like one of these. **30** Now if God so clothes the grass of the field, which today is, and tomorrow is thrown into the oven, will he not much more clothe you, O you of little faith? **31** Therefore do not worry, saying, 'What shall we eat?' or 'What shall we drink?' or 'What shall we wear?' **32** For the Gentiles seek after all these things. And your heavenly Father knows that you need them all. **33** But seek first the kingdom [of God] and his righteousness, and all these things shall be given to you as well. **34** Therefore do not worry about tomorrow, for tomorrow will worry about itself. Sufficient for the day is its own trouble.

7 **1** "Judge not, that you be not judged. **2** For with the same judgment you judge others, you will be judged, and with the measure you use, it will be measured to you. **3** And why do you look at the speck in your brother's eye, but do not consider the log in your own eye? **4** Or how can you say to your brother, 'Let me take the speck out of your eye,' when there is a log in your own eye? **5** You hypocrite! First take the log out of your own eye, and then you will see clearly to remove the speck from your brother's eye. **6** Do not give what is holy to the dogs; do not throw your pearls before swine, lest they trample them under their feet, and turn and tear you in pieces.

7 "Ask, and it will be given to you. Seek, and you will find. Knock, and it will be opened to you. **8** For everyone who asks receives, and he who seeks finds, and to him who knocks it will be opened. **9** Or what man of you, when his son asks him for bread, will give him a stone? **10** Or when he asks for a fish, will give him a serpent? **11** If you then, who are evil, know how to give good gifts to your children, how much more will your Father who is in heaven give good things to those who ask him! **12** So whatever you wish that men would do to you, do also to them, for this is the Law and the Prophets.

13 "Enter by the narrow gate. For the gate is wide, and the way is easy that leads to destruction, and many are those who enter by it. **14** How narrow is the gate and hard the way, that leads to life, and few those who find it!

6:25 Alx[**or what you will drink**], Byz[and what you will drink (MRD, NLT, REB, TEV, ~TLB)], Minor[omits (DRA, NJB)].

6:27 **span of life** or height.

6:28 Alx[**how they grow. They neither toil nor spin**], Byz[how it grows. It neither toils nor spins].

6:32 Alx[**the Gentiles seek** plural], Byz[the Gentiles seek singular (~MRD, ~NET, ~REB)].

6:33 Alx/Byz[**the kingdom of God**], Minor[omits of God (ASV, JNT, NAS, NAU, NET, NIV, NJB, RSV, TLB)], Minor[the kingdom of heaven]; Alx/Byz[**his righteousness**], Minor[omits his (NET, NLT, ~TLB)], Alt[without textual foundation God's righteousness (~NJB)].

6:34 Alx[**worry about itself**], Byz[worry about the things of itself (~JNT, KJV, NKJ, ~NRS, ~TEV)].

7:2 Alx/Byz[**measured to you**], Minor[measured back to you (DRA, KJV, NKJ)].

7:4 Alx[**out of your eye**], Byz[from your eye (MRD, NAB, NET, NKJ, ~NLT)].

7:8 Alx/Byz[**it will be opened**], Minor[it is opened].

7:9 Alx[**when his son**], Byz[if his son (ASV, DRA, ESV, HCS, JNT, KJV, MRD, NET, NIV, NKJ, NLT, NRS, RSV, TLB)].

7:10 Alx[**when he asks**], Byz[if he asks (ASV, DRA, ESV, HCS, JNT, KJV, MRD, NAS, NAU, NET, NIV, NKJ, NLT, NRS, RSV, TLB)].

7:13 Alx/Byz[**For the gate is wide, and the way is easy**], Minor[The way is wide and easy (NJB)].

7:14 Alx/Byz[text], Minor[For the gate is narrow and the way is hard, that leads to life, and few are

¹⁵ "Beware of false prophets, who come to you in sheep's clothing, but inwardly they are ravenous wolves. ¹⁶ You will know them by their fruits. Do men gather grapes from thorn bushes, or figs from thistles? ¹⁷ Even so, every good tree bears good fruit, but a bad tree bears bad fruit. ¹⁸ A good tree cannot bear bad fruit, nor can a bad tree bear good fruit. ¹⁹ Every tree that does not bear good fruit is cut down and thrown into the fire. ²⁰ Thus you will know them by their fruits.

²¹ "Not every one who says to me, 'Lord, Lord,' shall enter the kingdom of heaven, but he who does the will of my Father who is in heaven. ²² On that day many will say to me, 'Lord, Lord, did we not prophesy in your name, and cast out demons in your name, and do many mighty works in your name?' ²³ And then will I declare to them, 'I never knew you. Depart from me, you evildoers!'

²⁴ "Therefore everyone who hears these words of mine and does them will be like a wise man who built his house on the rock. ²⁵ And the rain fell, and the floods came, and the winds blew and beat upon that house, but it did not fall, because it had been founded on the rock. ²⁶ And every one who hears these words of mine and does not do them will be like a foolish man who built his house upon the sand. ²⁷ And the rain descended, the floods came, and the winds blew and beat against that house, and it fell. And great was its fall."

²⁸ And when Jesus had finished these sayings, the crowds were astonished at his teaching, ²⁹ for he taught them as one who had authority, and not as their scribes.

8 ¹ When he came down from the mountain, great crowds followed him. ² And behold, a leper approached and knelt before him, saying, "Lord, if you are willing, you can make me clean." ³ Then he put out his hand and touched him, saying, "I am willing. Be clean." Immediately his leprosy was cleansed. ⁴ And Jesus said to him, "See that you tell no one. But go your way, show yourself to the priest, and offer the gift that Moses commanded, as a testimony to them."

⁵ When he had entered Capernaum, a centurion came to him, asking for help, ⁶ and saying, "Lord, my servant is lying paralyzed at home, in terrible distress." ⁷ And he said to him, "I will come and heal him." ⁸ And the centurion answered him, "Lord, I am not worthy to have you come under my roof. But only say a word, and my servant will be

---

those who find it (ASV, ESV, ~JNT, KJV, NAS, NAU, ~NET, ~NIV, ~NJB, NKJ, ~NLT, NRS, ~REB, RSV, ~TEV, ~TLB) *others* For the way is narrow and hard, that leads to life, and few are those who find it].

7:15 Alx[**Beware of false prophets**], Byz[But beware of false prophets].

7:18 Alx/Byz[**bear bad fruit** *or* produce bad fruit], Minor[carry bad fruit]; Alx/Byz[**bear good fruit** *or* produce good fruit], Minor[carry good fruit].

7:24 Alx/Byz[**these words of mine**], Minor[my words (NLT, TLB)]; Alx[**will be like**], Byz[I will liken him to (KJV, NKJ)].

7:28 Alx[**finished these sayings**], Byz[ended these sayings (DRA, KJV, MRD, NKJ)].

7:29 Alx[**their scribes**], Byz[the scribes (KJV, NKJ, TEV)], Minor/Vulgate[the scribes and Pharisees (DRA, MRD)].

8:2 Alx[**approached**], Byz[came (DRA, JNT, KJV, NIV, NKJ)]; **a leper** *or* a man with a skin disease.

8:3 Alx[**he put out his hand**], Byz[Jesus put out his hand (DRA, ESV, JNT, KJV, MRD, NAU, NIV, NJB, NKJ, NLT, REB, TEV, TLB)].

8:5 Alx/Byz[**When he had entered**]; Minor[When Jesus had entered (JNT, KJV, MRD, NAU, NIV, NKJ, NLT, REB, TEV, TLB)]; Alx[**Capernaum** *Greek* Capharnaum], Byz[Capernaum].

8:7 Alx[**And he said**], Byz[And Jesus said (DRA, JNT, KJV, MRD, NAU, NET, NIV, NJB, NKJ, NLT, REB, TEV, TLB)], Minor[*omits* And (HCS, JNT, MRD, NAB, NAU, NET, NIV, NJB, NLT, REB, TEV, TLB)].

8:8 Alx/Byz[**And the centurion**], Minor[But the centurion (ESV, JNT, NAS, NAU, NET, NLT, REB, RSV)].

healed. **9** For I also am a man under authority, with soldiers under me. And I say to this one, 'Go,' and he goes; and to another, 'Come,' and he comes; and to my servant, 'Do this,' and he does it." **10** When Jesus heard him, he marveled, and said to those who followed him, "Truly, I say to you, I have not found anyone in Israel with such great faith. **11** I say to you that many will come from east and west, and sit down with Abraham, Isaac, and Jacob in the kingdom of heaven. **12** But the sons of the kingdom will be thrown out into the outer darkness – there will be weeping and gnashing of teeth." **13** Then to the centurion Jesus said, "Go. Be it done for you as you have believed." And [his] servant was healed at that very hour.

14 When Jesus came into Peter's house, he saw his mother-in-law lying sick with a fever. **15** He touched her hand, and the fever left her. And she rose and served him. **16** When evening had come, they brought to him many who were demon-possessed. And he cast out the spirits with a word, and healed all who were sick. **17** This was to fulfill what was spoken by the prophet Isaiah:

> *"He took up our infirmities*
> *and bore our diseases."*

18 Now when Jesus saw a crowd around him, he gave orders to go over to the other side. **19** Then a certain scribe came and said to him, "Teacher, I will follow you wherever you go." **20** And Jesus said to him, "Foxes have holes and birds of the air have nests, but the Son of Man has nowhere to lay his head." **21** Another of [his] disciples said to him, "Lord, let me first go and bury my father." **22** But Jesus said to him, "Follow me, and let the dead bury their own dead."

23 And when he got into the boat, his disciples followed him. **24** And behold, a great storm arose on the sea, so that the boat was covered with the waves. But he was asleep. **25** And they went and woke him, saying, "Lord, save! We are perishing!" **26** And he said to them, "Why are you afraid, O you of little faith?" Then he rose and rebuked the winds and the sea, and there was a great calm. **27** And the men marveled, saying, "What sort of man is this, that even the winds and the sea obey him?"

28 When he had come to the other side, to the country of the Gadarenes, two demon-possessed men met him, coming out of the tombs, exceedingly fierce, so that no one could pass that way. **29** And behold, they cried out, "What have you to do with us, O Son of God? Have you come here to torment us before the time?" **30** Now a herd of many

---

8:9 Alx/Byz[**with soldiers under me**], Minor[with soldiers arranged under me (~MRD)].

8:10 Alx[**anyone in Israel with**], Byz[even in Israel (ASV, DRA, KJV, MRD, NKJ, NLT, REB, RSV, TLB)].

8:12 Alx/Byz[**will be thrown out**], Minor[will go out (MRD)].

8:13 Alx[**Go. Be it done**], Byz[Go, and be it done (DRA, KJV, NKJ, TEV)]; Alx/Byz[**And his servant**], Minor[And the servant (ASV, DRA, ESV, NAS, NAU, NET, NJB, NLT, NRS, REB, RSV)].

8:14 Alx/Byz[**Peter's**], Alt/Peshitta[Simon's (MRD)], Alt[*without textual foundation* Cephas' (~JNT)].

8:15 Alx/Byz[**served him**], Minor[served them (DRA, KJV, MRD, NET, NKJ, TLB)].

8:17 ~**Isaiah 53:4**.

8:18 Alx[**a crowd**], Byz[great crowds (ASV, DRA, ~ESV 2001 edition, HCS, KJV, MRD, ~NET, NKJ, NRS, RSV, TLB)].

8:21 Alx/Byz[**his disciples**], Minor[the disciples (ASV, ESV, JNT, NAS, NAU, NET, ~NIV, NJB, TEV)].

8:22 Alx[**But Jesus said** *Greek* But Jesus says], Byz[But Jesus said], Minor[But he says].

8:23 Alx/Byz[**the boat**], Minor[a boat (ASV, KJV, NAB, NKJ, TEV, TLB)].

8:25 Alx[**And they went and**], Byz[And his disciples (KJV, MRD, NKJ)], Major[And the disciples (~HCS, NIV, NLT, TEV, TLB)]; Alx[**Lord, save**], Byz[Lord, save us (DRA, ESV, HCS, KJV, MRD, NAB, NAS, NAU, NET, NIV, NJB, NKJ, NLT, NRS, REB, TEV, TLB)].

8:28 Alx[**Gadarenes**], Byz[Gergesenes (KJV, NKJ)], Minor[Garasenes (DRA)].

8:29 Alx[**O Son of God**], Byz[Jesus, O Son of God (DRA, KJV, NKJ)].

swine was feeding at some distance from them. [31] And the demons begged him, "If you cast us out, send us into the herd of swine." [32] And he said to them, "Go." So they came out and went into the swine. And behold, the whole herd rushed down the steep bank into the sea, and perished in the water. [33] Then those who kept them fled. And they went away into the city and told everything, including what had happened to the demon-possessed men. [34] And behold, the whole city came out to meet Jesus. And when they saw him, they begged him to leave their region.

9 [1] And getting into a boat, he crossed over and came to his own city. [2] And behold, they brought to him a paralytic, lying on a bed. And when Jesus saw their faith he said to the paralytic, "Take heart, my son. Your sins are forgiven." [3] And behold, some of the scribes said to themselves, "This man is blaspheming!" [4] But Jesus, seeing their thoughts, said, "Why do you think evil in your hearts? [5] For which is easier, to say, 'Your sins are forgiven,' or to say, 'Rise and walk'? [6] But that you may know that the Son of Man has authority on earth to forgive sins" – he then said to the paralytic – "Rise, take up your bed and go home." [7] And he rose and went home. [8] When the crowds saw it, they were afraid. And they glorified God, who had given such authority to men.

[9] As Jesus passed on from there, he saw a man named Matthew sitting at the tax office. And he said to him, "Follow me." And he rose and followed him. [10] And as Jesus sat to eat in the house, behold, many tax collectors and sinners came and sat to eat with him and his disciples. [11] And when the Pharisees saw this, they said to his disciples, "Why does your teacher eat with tax collectors and sinners?" [12] But when he heard it, he said, "Those who are well have no need of a physician, but those who are sick. [13] But go and learn what this means: '*I desire mercy, and not sacrifice.*' For I have not come to call the righteous, but sinners."

[14] Then the disciples of John came to him, saying, "Why do we and the Pharisees fast [often], but your disciples do not fast?" [15] And Jesus said to them, "Can the guests of the bridegroom mourn as long as he is with them? The days will come, when the bridegroom will be taken away from them, and then they will fast. [16] No one puts a piece of unshrunk cloth on an old garment, for the patch pulls away from the garment, and the tear is made worse. [17] Neither do they put new wine into old wineskins. If they do, the skins burst, and the wine is spilled, and the skins are ruined. But they put new wine into new wineskins, and so both are preserved."

[18] While he was saying these things to them, behold, a ruler came and knelt before him, saying, "My daughter has just died, but come and lay your hand on her and she will live." [19] So Jesus rose and followed him, and so did his disciples. [20] And behold, a woman

---

8:31 Alx[**send us**], Byz[allow us to go away (KJV, MRD, NKJ)].

8:32 Alx[**the swine**], Byz[the herd of swine (KJV, NKJ)]; Alx[**the whole herd**], Byz[the whole herd of swine (KJV, NKJ)].

9:1 Alx/Byz[**a boat**], Major[the boat (MRD, NJB, REB, TEV)].

9:2 Alx[**Your sins are forgiven**], Byz[Your sins have been forgiven you (~DRA, ~KJV, ~MRD, ~NKJ, ~TLB)].

9:3 **to themselves** *Greek* within themselves.

9:4 Alx/Byz[**seeing their thoughts**], Minor[knowing their thoughts (ASV, ESV, JNT, KJV, MRD, NAB, NAS, NAU, NIV, NJB, NKJ, NLT, REB, RSV, TLB)].

9:5 Alx[**Your sins are forgiven**], Byz[Your sins have been forgiven], Minor[*adds* you (DRA, KJV, MRD, NKJ, ~TLB)].

9:8 Alx[**afraid**], Byz[astonished ~HCS, ~JNT, KJV, ~MRD, NKJ)].

9:12 Alx[**when he heard it, he said**], Byz[when Jesus heard it, he said to them (~DRA, ~JNT, KJV, MRD, ~NAU, ~NET, ~NIV, NKJ, ~NLT, TEV, ~TLB)].

9:13 Alx[**sinners**], Byz[*adds* to repentance (KJV, NKJ, TLB)]; **Hosea 6:6 LXX**.

9:14 Alx/Byz[**often**], Minor[*omits* (ESV, NAS, NAU, NIV, NJB, NLT, REB, RSV, TLB)].

who had suffered from a hemorrhage for twelve years came up behind him and touched the tassel of his garment. 21 For she said to herself, "If I only touch his garment, I shall be made well." 22 Jesus turned, and when he saw her he said, "Take heart, daughter. Your faith has made you well." And the woman was made well from that moment. 23 When Jesus came to the ruler's house, and saw the flute players and the noisy crowd, 24 he said, "Depart; for the girl is not dead but sleeping." And they laughed at him. 25 But when the crowd had been put outside, he went in and took her by the hand, and the girl arose. 26 And the report of this went through all that region.

27 And as Jesus passed on from there, two blind men followed [him], crying out, "Have mercy on us, Son of David." 28 When he had entered the house, the blind men came to him. And Jesus said to them, "Do you believe that I am able to do this?" They said to him, "Yes, Lord." 29 Then he touched their eyes, saying, "According to your faith be it done to you." 30 And their eyes were opened. And Jesus sternly warned them, "See that no one knows it." 31 But they went out and spread the news about him all over that region.

32 As they were going out, behold, a mute and demon-possessed man was brought to him. 33 And when the demon had been cast out, the mute man spoke. And the crowds marveled, saying, "Never was anything like this seen in Israel." 34 But the Pharisees said, "He casts out demons by the prince of demons."

35 And Jesus went about all the cities and villages, teaching in their synagogues and preaching the gospel of the kingdom, and healing every disease and every sickness. 36 When he saw the crowds, he had compassion for them, because they were harassed and helpless, like sheep without a shepherd. 37 Then he said to his disciples, "The harvest is plentiful, but the laborers are few. 38 Therefore pray the Lord of the harvest to send out laborers into his harvest."

10

1 And he summoned his twelve disciples and gave them authority over unclean spirits, to cast them out, and to heal every disease and every sickness. 2 The names of the twelve apostles are these: first, Simon, who is called Peter, and Andrew his brother; and James the son of Zebedee, and John his brother; 3 Philip and Bartholomew; Thomas and Matthew the tax collector; James the son of Alphaeus, and Thaddaeus; 4 Simon the Zealot, and Judas Iscariot, who betrayed him.

9:22 Alx[**Jesus turned**], Byz[Jesus turned back (KJV, ~MRD, NAB, NJB, NKJ, NLT, TEV, TLB)], Minor[He turned].

9:24 Alx[**24 he said**], Byz[he said to them 24], Major[24 he said to them (KJV, MRD, NKJ)], Minor[he said 24 (NJB)].

9:27 Alx/Byz[**followed him**], Minor[omits him (~REB, TLB)].

9:32 Alx/Byz[**mute and demon-possessed man**], Minor[omits man (NAB, NRS, RSV)].

9:33 Alx/Major[**saying**], Byz[saying that].

9:34 Alx/Byz[text], Minor[omits (REB)].

9:35 Alx[**sickness**], Byz[adds among the people (KJV, NKJ, TEV, TLB)].

9:36 Alx/Major[**harassed**], Byz[weary (HCS, KJV, MRD, NKJ)], Alt[confused (NET, NLT, ~TEV, TLB)].

9:38 NJB includes verse 38 in verse 37.

10:2 Alx/Major[apostles **are** Greek apostles is], Byz[apostles are]; Alx/Byz[**Peter**], Alt/Peshitta[Cephas (JNT, MRD)]; Alx[**and James**], Byz[omits and (ASV, ~DRA, ESV, HCS, JNT, KJV, NAB, NET, NIV, NJB, NKJ, NLT, NRS, REB, RSV, TEV, TLB)]; DRA begins verse 3 at James the son of Zebedee.

10:3 Alx[**Thaddaeus**], Byz[Lebbaeus, who was called Thaddaeus (KJV, MRD, NKJ)], Minor[Lebbaeus].

10:4 Alx[**Zealot** Greek Cananean], Byz[Canaanite (KJV, MRD, NKJ)]; Alx/Byz[**Iscariot**], Minor[Scariot], Alt[from Kerioth (~JNT)]; **Iscariot** Hebraism Ish Keriot a man from Kerioth or possibly Sicarios assassin or bandit.

⁵ These twelve Jesus sent out. And he charged them, saying: "Do not go among the Gentiles, or enter any town of the Samaritans. ⁶ But go rather to the lost sheep of the house of Israel. ⁷ And preach as you go, saying, 'The kingdom of heaven is at hand.' ⁸ Heal the sick. Raise the dead. Cleanse the lepers. Cast out demons. Freely you have received, freely give. ⁹ Take no gold, nor silver, nor copper in your belts, ¹⁰ nor bag for your journey, nor two tunics, nor sandals, nor a staff; for the worker deserves his food. ¹¹ Now whatever village or town you enter, inquire who in it is worthy, and stay there until you go out. ¹² As you enter the house, give it your greeting. ¹³ And if the house is worthy, let your peace come upon it. But if it is not worthy, let your peace return to you. ¹⁴ And if any one will not receive you or listen to your words – as you go outside that house or town, shake the dust off your feet. ¹⁵ Truly, I say to you, it will be more tolerable on the day of judgment for the land of Sodom and Gomorrah than for that town.

¹⁶ "Behold, I send you out as sheep in the midst of wolves. Therefore be wise as serpents and innocent as doves. ¹⁷ But beware of men, for they will deliver you up to councils and flog you in their synagogues. ¹⁸ You will be brought before governors and kings for my sake, as a testimony to them and to the Gentiles. ¹⁹ But when they deliver you up, do not worry about how you are to speak or what you are to say. For what you are to say will be given to you in that hour. ²⁰ For it is not you who speak, but the Spirit of your Father speaking through you. ²¹ Now brother will deliver up brother to death, and a father his child. And children will rise up against parents and have them put to death. ²² And you will be hated by all for my name's sake. But he who endures to the end will be saved. ²³ When they persecute you in one city, flee to the next. For truly, I say to you, you will never finish going through the cities of Israel before the Son of Man comes.

²⁴ "A disciple is not above his teacher, nor a servant above his master. ²⁵ It is enough for the disciple to be like his teacher, and the servant like his master. If they have called the master of the house Beelzebul, how much more will they call those of his household!

²⁶ "So do not fear them. For there is nothing covered that will not be revealed, or hidden that will not be known. ²⁷ What I tell you in the dark, speak in the light. And what you hear whispered in your ear, proclaim on the housetops. ²⁸ And do not fear those who kill the body but cannot kill the soul. But rather fear him who can destroy both soul and body in hell. ²⁹ Are not two sparrows sold for a penny? And not one of them will fall to

---

10:⁷ **is at hand** *or* has come near.

10:⁸ Alx[**Raise the dead. Cleanse the lepers**], Byz[Cleanse the lepers. Raise the dead (KJV, MRD, NKJ)], Major[*omits* Raise the dead]; **lepers**, *or* those with skin diseases.

10:¹⁰ Alx/Byz[**a staff**], Major[staffs (KJV, NKJ)]; Alx[**deserves his food**], Byz[is worthy of his food (ASV, DRA, HCS, KJV, MRD, NAS, NAU, NIV, NKJ)].

10:¹² Alx/Major[**greeting**], Byz[*adds* saying, "Peace to this house!" (DRA)], Alt[*without textual foundation adds* saying, "Peace to you." (~JNT, ~TEV)].

10:¹⁴ Alx/Byz[**go outside**], Major[leave (ESV, HCS, JNT, MRD, NET, NIV, NKJ, NLT, NRS, REB, RSV, TEV, TLB)]; Alx/Byz[**off your feet**], Minor[from your feet (DRA, ESV, JNT, MRD, NAB, NJB, NKJ, NLT, NRS, RSV, TLB)].

10:¹⁵ Alx/Major[**of Sodom and Gomorrah** *Greek* of Sodom and of Gomorrah], Byz[of Sodom and Gomorrah].

10:¹⁶ Alx/Byz[**serpents**], Minor[a serpent].

10:²³ Alx[**the next**], Byz[another (DRA, HCS, JNT, KJV, MRD, NAB, NET, NIV, NKJ, REB, TEV)].

10:²⁵ Alx/Byz[**Beelzebul**], Minor/Vulgate/Peshitta[Beelzebub (ASV, DRA, KJV, MRD, NIV, NKJ, ~TLB)].

10:²⁸ Alx[**both soul and body**], Byz[both the soul and the body], Alt[*without textual foundation* both body and soul (NJB, TEV); **hell** *Greek* Gehenna.

10:²⁹ **penny** *Greek* assarion.

the ground apart from your Father's will. ³⁰ But even the hairs of your head are all numbered. ³¹ Fear not, therefore; you are of more value than many sparrows.

³² "Therefore whoever acknowledges me before men, I will also acknowledge before my Father who is in heaven. ³³ But whoever denies me before men, I will also deny before my Father who is in heaven.

³⁴ "Do not think that I have come to bring peace on earth. I did not come to bring peace, but a sword. ³⁵ For I have come to set a man

'against his father,
> and a daughter against her mother,
> and a daughter-in-law against her mother-in-law.

³⁶   And a man's enemies will be those of his own household.'

³⁷ He who loves father or mother more than me is not worthy of me. And he who loves son or daughter more than me is not worthy of me. ³⁸ And he who does not take his cross and follow me is not worthy of me. ³⁹ He who finds his life will lose it, and he who loses his life for my sake will find it.

⁴⁰ "He who receives you receives me, and he who receives me receives him who sent me. ⁴¹ He who receives a prophet because he is a prophet shall receive a prophet's reward, and he who receives a righteous man because he is a righteous man shall receive a righteous man's reward. ⁴² And whoever gives to one of these little ones even a cup of cold water because he is a disciple, truly, I say to you, he shall never lose his reward."

11

¹ And when Jesus had finished instructing his twelve disciples, he went on from there to teach and preach in their cities.

² Now when John heard in prison about the works of Christ, he sent through his disciples ³ to say to him, "Are you the One who is to come, or shall we look for another?" ⁴ And Jesus answered them, "Go and tell John what you hear and see: ⁵ The blind receive their sight and the lame walk. The lepers are cleansed and the deaf hear. And the dead are raised up, and the poor have good news preached to them. ⁶ And blessed is he who is not offended because of me." ⁷ As they went away, Jesus began to speak to the crowds concerning John: "What did you go out into the wilderness to see? A reed shaken by the wind? ⁸ But what did you go out to see? A man in dainty clothes? Indeed, those who wear dainty clothes are in kings' houses. ⁹ Then what did you go out to see? A prophet? Yes, I tell you, and more than a prophet. ¹⁰ This is he of whom it is written:

'Behold, I send my messenger before your face,
> who will prepare your way before you.'

10:³⁵⁻³⁶ ~Micah 7:6.

10:⁴² Alx[**whoever**], Byz[if anyone (JNT, NIV, NJB, ~NLT, ~TLB)].

11:² Alx[**through** *Greek* διά.], Byz[two of *Greek* δύο (DRA, KJV, NKJ)].

11:⁵ Alx/Byz[**and the lame**], Minor[the lame (DRA, HCS, JNT, NAB, NET, NIV, NLT, NRS, REB, TEV)]; Alx[**And the dead**], Byz[the dead (DRA, KCS, JNT, KJV, NAB, NAU, NET, NIV, NJB, NKJ, NLT, NRS, REB, TEV)]; **the lepers** *or* those with skin diseases.

11:⁶ **is not offended** *or* does not fall away.

11:⁸ Alx[**A man in dainty clothes**], Byz[A man dressed in dainty clothes (ASV, DRA, ESV, HCS, KJV, MRD, NAB, NAS, NAU, NET, NIV, NKJ, NLT, ~NRS, REB, RSV, TEV, TLB)]; Alx/Byz[**kings' houses**], Major[royal houses (NAB, ~NJB, ~NLT, NRS, ~REB, ~TEV, ~TLB)]; **what did you go out to see? A man** *or* why did you go out? To see a man; **dainty clothes** *effeminate clothing; NRS words this in neutral gender.*

11:⁹ Alx[*ambiguous* **what did you go out to see? A prophet** *or* why did you go out? To see a prophet], Byz[*can only read* why did you go out? To see a prophet].

11:¹⁰ Alx[**This is he**], Byz[For this is he (DRA, KJV, MRD, NKJ, TEV, TLB)]; ~**Malachi 3:1 Masoretic**.

[11] Truly, I say to you, among those born of women there has not risen one greater than John the Baptist. Yet he who is least in the kingdom of heaven is greater than he. [12] From the days of John the Baptist until now the kingdom of heaven has suffered violence, and men of violence take it by force. [13] For all the Prophets and the Law prophesied until John. [14] And if you are willing to accept it, he is the *Elijah* who is to come. [15] He who has ears, let him hear.

[16] "But to what shall I compare this generation? It is like children sitting in the marketplaces, who call to one another, [17] saying,

'We played the flute for you, and you did not dance.

We sang a dirge, and you did not mourn.'

[18] For John came neither eating nor drinking, and they say, 'He has a demon.' [19] The Son of Man came eating and drinking, and they say, 'Look, a glutton and a drunkard, a friend of tax collectors and sinners!' But wisdom is justified by her deeds."

[20] Then he began to rebuke the cities in which most of his mighty works had been done, because they did not repent. [21] "Woe to you, Chorazin! Woe to you, Bethsaida! For if the mighty works which were done in you had been done in Tyre and Sidon, they would have repented long ago in sackcloth and ashes. [22] But I tell you, it will be more tolerable for Tyre and Sidon on the day of judgment than for you. [23] And you, Capernaum,

will you be exalted to heaven?

No, you shall go down to Hades.

For if the mighty works which were done in you had been done in Sodom, it would have remained until this day. [24] But I tell you that it shall be more tolerable on the day of judgment for the land of Sodom than for you."

[25] At that time Jesus declared, "I thank you, Father, Lord of heaven and earth, that you have hidden these things from the wise and intelligent and have revealed them to babes. [26] Yes, Father, for this was your good pleasure.

[27] "All things have been delivered to me by my Father. No one knows the Son except the Father. And no one knows the Father except the Son and those to whom the Son chooses to reveal him. [28] Come to me, all you who labor and are heavy laden, and I will give you rest. [29] Take my yoke upon you, and learn from me. For I am gentle and lowly in heart, and you will find rest for your souls. [30] For my yoke is easy, and my burden is light."

11:12 **has suffered violence** *or* has been coming violently.

11:14 ~Malachi 4:5.

11:15 Alx[**ears**], Byz[*adds* to hear (ASV, DRA, ESV, KJV, MRD, NAS, NAU, NLT, NKJ, RSV, ~TLB)].

11:16 Alx/Byz[**marketplaces, who call**], Major[marketplaces and calling (ESV, ~JNT, KJV, MRD, NAB, NIV, NKJ, NRS, REB, RSV)]; Alx[**to one another**], Byz[to their companions (ASV, DRA, ESV, KJV, MRD, NKJ, NLT, RSV, TLB)]; *DRA starts verse 17 after* marketplaces.

11:17 Alx[**saying**], Byz[saying 17], Major[and saying (ASV, KJV, MRD, NAS, NAU, NKJ)], Alt[*without textual foundation omits* (~ESV, ~HCS, ~JNT, ~NAB, ~NET, ~NIV, ~NJB, ~NLT, ~NRS, ~REB, ~RSV, ~TEV, ~TLB)]; Alx[**we sang a dirge**], Byz[*adds* for you (KJV, MRD, NKJ)].

11:19 Alx[**deeds**], Byz[children (DRA, KJV, NKJ)].

11:20 Alx/Byz[**he began**], Alt/Peshitta[Jesus began (JNT, MRD, NET, NIV, NLT, ~TEV)].

11:21 Alx/Major[**ashes**], Byz[sitting in ashes (~TLB)].

11:23 Alx[**Capernaum** *Greek* Capharnaum], Byz[Capernaum]; Alx[**will you be exalted to heaven? No, you shall go down**], Byz[who are exalted to heaven, will be thrown down (~ESV, KJV, MRD, ~NET, ~NJB, NKJ, ~NRS, ~RSV, TLB)]; Alx[**it would have remained**], Byz[they would have remained (~REB)].

11:25 **I thank you** *or* I praise you.

11:26 **good pleasure** *or* gracious will.

12

¹ At that time Jesus went through the grainfields on the Sabbath. And his disciples were hungry, and began to pluck heads of grain and to eat. ² But when the Pharisees saw it, they said to him, "Look, your disciples are doing what is not lawful to do on the Sabbath." ³ He said to them, "Have you not read what David did, when he was hungry, and those who were with him: ⁴ how he entered the house of God and ate the consecrated bread which was not lawful for him or his companions to eat, but only for the priests? ⁵ Or have you not read in the Law that on the Sabbath the priests in the temple profane the Sabbath, and are innocent? ⁶ I tell you that something greater than the temple is here. ⁷ And if you had known what this means, '*I desire mercy, and not sacrifice,*' you would not have condemned the guiltless. ⁸ For the Son of Man is Lord of the Sabbath."

⁹ And he went on from there, and went into their synagogue. ¹⁰ And behold, a man with a withered hand… and they asked him, "Is it lawful to heal on the Sabbath?" so that they might accuse him. ¹¹ He said to them, "What man shall there be of you, if he has one sheep and it falls into a pit on the Sabbath, will not lay hold of it and lift it out? ¹² Of how much more value is a man than a sheep! Therefore it is lawful to do good on the Sabbath." ¹³ Then he said to the man, "Stretch out your hand." And he stretched it out, and it was restored as whole as the other. ¹⁴ But the Pharisees went out and plotted against him, how they might destroy him.

¹⁵ Jesus, aware of this, withdrew from there. And many [crowds] followed him. And he healed them all, ¹⁶ and ordered them not to make him known. ¹⁷ This was to fulfill what was spoken by the prophet Isaiah:

¹⁸   *"Behold, my servant whom I have chosen,*
          my beloved in whom my soul is well pleased!
     I will put my Spirit upon him,
          and he will proclaim justice to the Gentiles.
¹⁹   *He will not quarrel or cry out;*
          nor will anyone hear his voice in the streets.
²⁰   *A bruised reed he will not break,*
          and a smoldering wick he will not quench,
     till he sends forth justice to victory.
²¹   *And in his name will the Gentiles hope."*

²² Then a demon-possessed man who was blind and mute was brought to him. And he healed him, so that the mute man spoke and saw. ²³ And all the people were

---

12:3 Alx[**and those who were with him**], Byz[he and those who were with him (NAS, NAU, NKJ)].

12:4 Alx[**to eat** *plural*], Byz[to eat *singular* (ASV, DRA, KJV, MRD, NAS, NKJ, ~NLT, REB, RSV, TLB)].

12:6 Alx/Byz[**something**], Minor[someone (ASV, KJV, NIV, NKJ, NLT, TLB)].

12:7 **Hosea 6:6 LXX**.

12:8 Alx/Major[**Lord of the Sabbath**], Byz[Lord even of the Sabbath (DRA, KJV, NKJ, NLT, TLB)].

12:10 Alx[**behold, a man**], Byz[behold, a man was there (~JNT, ESV, MRD, NAU, NET, NIV, NJB, NRS, REB, ~TLB)], Major[behold, there was a man (DRA, KJV, NAB, NAS, NKJ, ~NLT, NRS, RSV, TEV)].

12:11 Alx/Byz[**shall there be**], Minor[omits (ESV, HCS, JNT, MRD, NAB, NAU, NET, NIV, NJB, NKJ, NLT, NRS, REB, RSV, TEV, TLB)].

12:15 Alx/Byz[**many crowds**], Minor[*omits* crowds (ASV, DRA, ESV, ~JNT, NAS, NAU, NIV, NJB, REB, RSV, TLB)].

12:18-21 **~Isaiah 42:1-4 LXX**.

12:22 Alx/Byz[**was brought to him**], Minor[they brought to him (JNT, MRD, NAB, NET, NIV, NJB, NRS, REB, TEV)]; Alx[**so that the mute man**], Byz[so that the blind and mute man (~HCS, ~JNT, KJV, ~MRD, NKJ, ~REB, ~TEV)]; Alx[**spoke and saw**], Byz[both spoke and saw (HCS, JNT, KJV, MRD, NIV, NKJ, NLT, REB, TLB)].

amazed and said, "Could this be the Son of David?" **24** But when the Pharisees heard this they said, "It is only by Beelzebul, the prince of demons, that this fellow drives out demons." **25** But he knew their thoughts and said to them, "Every kingdom divided against itself is laid waste. And every city or house divided against itself will not stand. **26** If Satan casts out Satan, he is divided against himself. How then will his kingdom stand? **27** And if I cast out demons by Beelzebul, by whom do your sons cast them out? Therefore they shall be your judges. **28** But if it is by the Spirit of God that I cast out demons, then the kingdom of God has come upon you. **29** Or how can one enter a strong man's house and seize his goods, unless he first binds the strong man? And then he will plunder his house. **30** He who is not with me is against me, and he who does not gather with me scatters. **31** Therefore I tell you, every sin and blasphemy will be forgiven men; but the blasphemy against the Spirit will not be forgiven. **32** And if anyone speaks a word against the Son of Man, it will be forgiven him; but whoever speaks against the Holy Spirit will not be forgiven, either in this age or in the age to come.

33 "Either make the tree good, and its fruit good; or make the tree bad, and its fruit bad; for a tree is known by its fruit. **34** You brood of vipers! How can you speak good, when you are evil? For out of the abundance of the heart the mouth speaks. **35** The good man out of his good treasure brings forth good, and the evil man out of his evil treasure brings forth evil. **36** But I tell you that men will have to give account on the day of judgment for every idle word they have spoken. **37** For by your words you will be justified, and by your words you will be condemned."

38 Then some of the scribes and Pharisees said to him, "Teacher, we want to see a sign from you." **39** But he answered them, "An evil and adulterous generation seeks for a sign. But no sign will be given to it except the sign of the prophet Jonah. **40** For as *Jonah was three days and three nights in the belly of the great fish*, so the Son of Man will be three days and three nights in the heart of the earth. **41** The men of Nineveh will rise at the judgment with this generation and condemn it. For they repented at the preaching of Jonah, and now something greater than Jonah is here. **42** The queen of the South will rise at the judgment with this generation and condemn it. For she came from the ends of the earth to hear the wisdom of Solomon, and behold, something greater than Solomon is here.

43 "When an unclean spirit goes out of a man, he goes through dry places, seeking rest, and finds none. **44** Then he says, 'I will return to my house from which I came.' And when he comes he finds it empty, swept, and put in order. **45** Then he goes and takes with

---

12:23 Alx/Major[**the Son of David**], Byz[the Christ, the Son of David (~TLB)].

12:24, 27 Alx/Byz[**Beelzebul**], Alt/Vulgate/Peshitta[Beelzebub (ASV, DRA, KJV, MRD, NIV, NKJ, ~TLB)].

12:25 Alx[**But he knew**], Byz[But Jesus knew (DRA, KJV, MRD, NAU, NET, NIV, NKJ, NLT)].

12:28 Alx/Major[**But if it is by the Sprit of God that I cast out demons**], Byz[But if I by the Spirit of God cast out demons (ASV, DRA, HCS, JNT, KJV, MRD, NAS, NAU, NET, NIV, NKJ, NLT, TLB)].

12:29 Alx/Byz[**seize his goods**], Major[plunder his goods (ASV, DRA, ESV, KJV, MRD, NJB, NKJ, NLT, NRS, RSV, ~TLB)].

12:31 Alx[**will not be forgiven**], Byz[*adds* men (HCS, JNT, KJV, MRD, NKJ, TEV)].

12:32 Alx/Byz[**will not be forgiven**], Minor[will certainly not be forgiven (JNT, NLT, ~REB, TLB)]; Alx[**in this age**], Byz[in the present age (~JNT, ~TEV)].

12:35 Alx/Byz[**his good treasure**], Minor[the good treasure of his heart (KJV, NKJ, NLT)].

12:38 Alx[**said to him**], Byz[*omits* to him (JNT, KJV, NJB, NKJ, REB, TEV)].

12:40 Alx/Major[**as Jonah was**], Byz[as the prophet Jonah came to be (TLB)]; Alx/Major[**the Son of Man will be**], Byz[the Son of Man will also be]; Jonah 1:17.

12:41, 42 **something** *or* someone.

12:44 Alx/Major[**empty, swept**], Byz[empty, and swept (MRD)].

him seven other spirits more wicked than himself, and they enter and dwell there. And the last state of that man is worse than the first. So shall it also be with this wicked generation."

⁴⁶ While he was still talking to the people, behold, his mother and brothers stood outside, seeking to speak to him. ⁴⁷ [Someone told him, "Your mother and brothers are standing outside, wanting to speak to you."] ⁴⁸ But he replied to the man who told him, "Who is my mother, and who are my brothers?" ⁴⁹ And stretching out his hand toward his disciples, he said, "Here are my mother and my brothers! ⁵⁰ For whoever does the will of my Father in heaven is my brother and sister and mother."

13 ¹ That same day Jesus went out of the house and sat by the sea. ² And great crowds gathered around him, so that he got into a boat and sat there. And the whole crowd stood on the shore. ³ Then he told them many things in parables, saying: "A sower went out to sow his seed. ⁴ And as he sowed, some seed fell along the path, and the birds came and devoured them. ⁵ Some fell on rocky places, where they did not have much soil, and they immediately sprang up because they had no depth of soil. ⁶ But when the sun was up they were scorched, and because they had no root they withered away. ⁷ Other seed fell among thorns, and the thorns grew up and choked them. ⁸ But other seed fell on good soil and yielded a crop: some a hundredfold, some sixty, some thirty. ⁹ He who has ears, let him hear."

¹⁰ The disciples came and said to him, "Why do you speak to them in parables?" ¹¹ And he answered them, "To you it has been given to know the secrets of the kingdom of heaven, but to them it has not been given. ¹² For whoever has, to him will more be given, and he will have abundance. But whoever does not have, even what he has will be taken away from him. ¹³ This is why I speak to them in parables, because seeing they do not see, and hearing they do not hear, nor do they understand. ¹⁴ With them is fulfilled the prophecy of Isaiah which says:

'Hearing you will hear and shall never understand.
And seeing you will see and never perceive.
¹⁵   For this people's heart has grown dull,

12:⁴⁶ Alx[**While he was still talking**], Byz[But while he was still talking (MRD)].

12:⁴⁷ Alx/Byz[*verse*], Minor[*omits* (ESV, JNT, RSV, TLB)]; Alx/Major[**wanting to speak to you**], Byz[wanting to see you (~DRA)].

12:⁴⁹ Alx/Byz[**his hand**], Minor[the hand (~JNT, NET, NIV, NLT, NRS, REB, ~TEV, ~TLB)].

12:⁵⁰ Alx/Byz[**is my brother**], Minor[is also my brother].

13:¹ Alx[**That same day**], Byz[But that same day (MRD)]; Alx/Byz[**out of the house**], Major[out from the house].

13:² Alx/Byz[**a boat**], Major[the boat].

13:³ Alx/Major[**saying: "A sower went out to sow his seed. 4**], Byz[saying: 4 "A sower went out to sow his seed].

13:⁴ Alx/Byz[**the birds**], Minor[a bird (MRD)].

13:⁷ Alx[**choked** *or* strangled], Byz[choked *or* drowned].

13:⁹ Alx[**ears**], Byz[*adds* to hear (DRA, KJV, MRD, NKJ, NLT)].

13:¹¹ Alx/Byz[**answered them**], Minor[*omits* them (JNT, NET, NIV, NJB, NLT, NRS, REB, TEV)]; **secrets** *or* mysteries.

13:¹³ Alx/Major[**because seeing they do not see, and hearing they do not hear, nor do they understand**], Byz[so that seeing they do not see, and hearing they do not hear, nor understand (~JNT, ~TLB)].

13:¹⁴ Alx/Major[**understand. 14 With them is fulfilled the prophecy of Isaiah which says**], Byz[understand, 14 lest they turn. And then the prophecy of Isaiah will be fulfilled with them, which says], Minor[On them is fulfilled the prophecy of Isaiah which says (~NLT, ~TLB)].

13:¹⁴⁻¹⁵ **Isaiah 6:9-10 LXX**.

13:¹⁵ Alx/Major[**turn, and I heal**], Byz[turn so that I should heal (ASV, DRA, JNT, KJV, MRD, NAS,

> and their ears are hard of hearing,
> and their eyes they have closed,
> lest they should see with their eyes,
> and hear with their ears,
> and understand with their hearts,
> and turn, and I heal them.'

[16] But blessed are your eyes for they see, and your ears for they hear. [17] For truly, I say to you, many prophets and righteous men longed to see what you see, and did not see it, and to hear what you hear, and did not hear it.

[18] "Hear then the parable of the sower: [19] when anyone hears the word of the kingdom and does not understand it, the evil one comes and snatches away what was sown in his heart. This is the seed sown along the path. [20] But he who received the seed on rocky places, this is he who hears the word and immediately receives it with joy. [21] Yet he has no root in himself, but endures only for a while. And when tribulation or persecution arises because of the word, immediately he falls away. [22] Now he who received seed among the thorns is he who hears the word, but the cares of the world and the deceitfulness of riches choke the word, and he becomes unfruitful. [23] But the one who received seed on the good soil is he who hears the word and understands it, who indeed bears fruit and produces: some a hundredfold, some sixty, some thirty."

[24] Another parable he put forth to them, saying: "The kingdom of heaven is like a man who sowed good seed in his field; [25] but while men were sleeping, his enemy came and sowed weeds also among the wheat, and went away. [26] So when the plants sprouted and bore grain, then the weeds appeared also. [27] And the servants of the householder came and said to him, 'Sir, did you not sow good seed in your field? How then has it weeds?' [28] He said to them, 'An enemy has done this.' The servants said to him, 'Then do you want us to go and gather them up?' [29] But he said, 'No, lest while you gather up the weeds you also root up the wheat with them. [30] Let both grow together until the harvest. And at harvest time I will tell the reapers, "Gather the weeds first and bind them in bundles to be burned, but gather the wheat into my barn."'"

[31] Another parable he put forth to them, saying: "The kingdom of heaven is like a mustard seed, which a man took and sowed in his field. [32] It is the smallest of all seeds, but when it has grown it is the greatest of shrubs and becomes a tree, so that the birds of the air come and make nests in its branches."

NKJ)]; *TLB begins verse 16 after* their eyes they have closed.

13:16 Alx/Byz[**your ears**], Minor[*omits* your].

13:17 Alx/Byz[**For truly**], Minor[*omits* For (ESV 2001 edition, ~JNT, NAB, NJB, NLT, NRS, REB, RSV, TEV, TLB)].

13:18 Alx/Byz[**sower**], Minor[seed (MRD)].

13:19 Alx/Major[**snatches**], Byz[takes (~NJB)].

13:20 Alx/Major[**receives**], Byz[takes and receives].

13:21 **falls away** *Greek* stumbles.

13:22 Alx[**cares of the world**], Byz[cares of this world (DRA, HCS, KJV, MRD, NIV, NKJ, NLT, TEV, TLB)].

13:24 Alx/Byz[**a man who sowed**], Major[a man sowing (TLB)].

13:25 Alx[**sowed weeds also**], Byz[sowed weeds (ESV, HCS, JNT, KJV, MRD, NAU, NET, NIV, NKJ, NLT, NRS, REB, RSV, TEV, TLB)]; **weeds** *darnel, which resembles wheat.*

13:28 Alx/Byz[**The servants said** *Greek* The servants say], Minor[They said (NLT, REB, TEV, TLB)].

13:30 Alx/Byz[**harvest time**], Minor[the time of the harvest (ASV, DRA, KJV, MRD, NAS, NAU, NKJ, ~NLT, ~REB, ~TEV, ~TLB)].

13:32 Alx/Major[**greatest of shrubs**], Byz[greatest of all shrubs (~JNT, DRA, ESV, MRD, ~REB, TEV)].

33 He told them another parable: "The kingdom of heaven is like leaven, which a woman took and hid in three measures of flour till it was all leavened."

34 All these things Jesus spoke to the crowd in parables; and without a parable he did not speak to them. 35 So was fulfilled what was spoken by the prophet:

"*I will open my mouth in parables.*
I will utter things hidden
since the foundation [of the world]."

36 Then he left the crowd and went into the house. And his disciples came to him, saying, "Explain to us the parable of the weeds of the field." 37 He answered, "He who sows the good seed is the Son of Man. 38 The field is the world, and the good seed stands for the sons of the kingdom. The weeds are the sons of the evil one, 39 and the enemy who sowed them is the devil. The harvest is the end of the age, and the reapers are angels. 40 Therefore as the weeds are gathered and burned [up] in the fire, so it will be at the end of the age. 41 The Son of Man will send out his angels, and they will gather out of his kingdom everything that causes sin and all who do evil, 42 and will throw them into the furnace of fire, where there will be weeping and gnashing of teeth. 43 Then the righteous will shine like the sun in the kingdom of their Father. He who has ears, let him hear.

44 "The kingdom of heaven is like treasure hidden in a field, which a man found and hid; and then in his joy over it he goes and sells all that he has and buys that field.

45 "Again, the kingdom of heaven is like a merchantman in search of fine pearls; 46 and, when he had found one pearl of great value, went and sold all that he had and bought it.

47 "Again, the kingdom of heaven is like a net that was thrown into the sea and gathered fish of every kind; 48 which, when it was full, they drew up on the shore. And they sat down and gathered the good into vessels, but threw the bad away. 49 So it will be at the end of the age. The angels will come and separate the wicked from the righteous 50 and throw them into the furnace of fire, where there will be weeping and gnashing of teeth."

51 "Have you understood all these things?" They said to him, "Yes." 52 And he said to them, "Therefore every scribe who has been instructed for the kingdom of heaven is like a householder who brings out of his treasure what is new and what is old."

13:33 Alx/Byz[**He told them**], Minor[*omits*]; Alx/Byz[**hid** *or* mixed], Major[concealed]; **measures** *Greek* sata.

13:34 Alx/Byz[**did not speak**], Major[said nothing (ASV, ESV, JNT, ~NAB, ~NIV, ~NJB, ~NLT, NRS, REB, RSV, TEV, ~TLB)].

13:35 Alx/Byz[**prophet**], Minor[*adds* Isaiah]; Alx/Byz[**foundation of the world**], Minor[*omits* of the world]; ~**Psalms 78:2**.

13:36 Alx/Byz[**he left the crowd** *or* he dismissed the crowd], Major[Jesus left the crowd (KJV, MRD, NKJ, TEV)]; Alx/Major[**the house**], Byz[his house]; Alx[**Explain** *or* Report], Byz[Explain *or* Interpret (TEV)].

13:37 Alx[**He answered** *Greek* He answered and said], Byz[*adds* to them (DRA, KJV, MRD, NKJ)].

13:40 Alx[**the age**], Byz[this age (KJV, NKJ)].

13:43 Alx[**ears**], Byz[*adds* to hear (DRA, KJV, MRD, NKJ, NLT)].

13:44 Alx[**The kingdom of heaven**], Byz[Again, the kingdom of heaven (KJV, MRD, NKJ)]; Alx/Byz[**and sells all that he has**], Minor[and sells what he has].

13:45 Alx/Byz[**merchantman**], Minor[merchant (DRA, ESV, HCS, JNT, NAB, NAS, NAU, NET, NIV, NJB, NKJ, NLT, NRS, REB, RSV, TLB)].

13:46 Alx[**and, when he had found**], Byz[who, when he had found (DRA, ESV, ~HCS, ~JNT, KJV, NKJ, ~REB, RSV, ~TLB)].

13:48 Alx/Major[**they drew up**], Byz[they drew it up (ESV, HCS, MRD, NAB, NAS, NAU, NET, NIV, NJB, NLT, NRS, REB, RSV, TEV, TLB)].

13:51 Alx[*text*], Byz[Jesus asked, "Have you understood all these things?" They said to him, "Yes,

⁵³ When Jesus had finished these parables, he moved on from there. ⁵⁴ And coming to his own country he taught them in their synagogue, so that they were astonished, and said, "Where did this man get this wisdom and these mighty works? ⁵⁵ Is this not the carpenter's son? Is not his mother called Mary; and his brothers James, Joseph, Simon, and Judas? ⁵⁶ And are not all his sisters with us? Where then did this man get all these things?" ⁵⁷ And they took offense at him. But Jesus said to them, "A prophet is not without honor except in his own country and in his own house." ⁵⁸ And he did not do many mighty works there, because of their unbelief.

14 ¹ At that time Herod the tetrarch heard the reports about Jesus. ² And he said to his servants, "This is John the Baptist. He has risen from the dead. That is why these powers are at work in him." ³ For Herod had laid hold of John and bound [him], and put him aside in prison for the sake of Herodias, his brother Philip's wife, ⁴ because John had said to him, "It is not lawful for you to have her." ⁵ And though he wanted to put him to death, he feared the people, because they held him to be a prophet. ⁶ But when Herod's birthday came, the daughter of Herodias danced before them and pleased Herod, ⁷ so that he promised with an oath to give her whatever she might ask. ⁸ Prompted by her mother, she said, "Give me here on a platter the head of John the Baptist," ⁹ and the king was sorry. Because of his oaths and those who sat to eat, he commanded it to be given to her. ¹⁰ So he sent and had John beheaded in prison. ¹¹ And his head was brought on a platter and given to the girl, and she brought it to her mother. ¹² Then his disciples came and took the corpse, and buried him. And they went and told Jesus.

¹³ Now when Jesus heard this, he withdrew from there in a boat to a lonely place by himself. And when the crowds heard it, they followed him on foot from the towns. ¹⁴ When he went ashore he saw a great throng. And he had compassion on them, and healed their sick. ¹⁵ When it was evening, the disciples came to him and said, "This is a remote place, and it is already getting late. Send the crowds away, so they can go to the villages and buy themselves some food." ¹⁶ [Jesus] said, "They do not need to go away. You give them something to eat." ¹⁷ They said to him, "We have only five loaves here and two fish." ¹⁸ He said, "Bring them here to me." ¹⁹ Then he commanded the multitudes to sit down on

---

Lord." (KJV, MRD, ~NIV, NKJ, TEV)].

13:⁵² Alx[**instructed for the kingdom**], Byz[instructed in the kingdom (DRA, HCS, JNT, NAB, NLT, REB, TEV, ~TLB)].

13:⁵⁵ Alx[**Joseph**], Byz[Joses (KJV, MRD, NKJ)].

14:³ Alx/Byz[**and bound him**], Minor[omits him (NLT)]; Alx[**put him aside**], Byz[put him (ASV, DRA, ESV, HCS, JNT, KJV, MRD, NAB, NAS, NAU, NET, NIV, NJB, NKJ, NLT, NRS, REB, RSV, TEV, TLB)]; Alx/Byz[**his brother Philip's**], Minor[his brother's (DRA)].

14:⁶ Alx[**birthday came**], Byz[birthday was celebrated (~HCS, JNT, KJV, ~MRD, ~NAB, NJB, NKJ, ~NLT, ~REB, ~TLB)].

14:⁹ Alx[**Because**], Byz[Nevertheless, because (ASV, DRA, ESV, JNT, KJV, MRD, NAB, NIV, NJB, NKJ, NLT, NRS, REB, RSV, TEV, TLB)].

14:¹² Alx[**corpse**], Byz[body (DRA, ESV, JNT, KJV, NAS, NAU, NET, NIV, NJB, NKJ, NLT, NRS, REB, RSV, TEV, TLB)]; Alx[**buried him**], Byz[buried it (DRA, ESV, HCS, JNT, KJV, MRD, NAS, NAU, NET, NIV, NJB, NKJ, NLT, NRS, REB, RSV, TEV, TLB)].

14:¹³ Alx/Byz[**Now when**], Major[And when (MRD)].

14:¹⁴ Alx[**When he went ashore**], Byz[When Jesus went ashore (KJV, MRD, NIV, NKJ, NLT, TEV, TLB)].

14:¹⁵ Alx[**the disciples**], Byz[his disciples (DRA, KJV, MRD, NET, NKJ, TEV)]; Alx/Byz[**Send the crowds away**], Minor[So send the crowds away (NAS, NAU, NJB)].

14:¹⁶ Alx/Byz[**Jesus said**], Minor[omits Jesus (MRD, NET)].

14:¹⁹ Alx/Byz[**Taking the five loaves**], Minor[And taking the five loaves (ASV, ESV, KJV, MRD, NKJ, REB, RSV, TLB)].

the grass. Taking the five loaves and the two fish, and looking up to heaven, he blessed and broke and gave the loaves to the disciples. And the disciples gave them to the multitudes. ²⁰ And they all ate and were satisfied. And they took up twelve baskets full of the broken pieces that were left over. ²¹ Now those who ate were about five thousand men, besides women and children.

²² Immediately he made the disciples get into the boat and go before him to the other side, while he dismissed the multitudes. ²³ And after he had dismissed the crowds, he went up on the mountain by himself to pray. When evening came, he was there alone. ²⁴ But the boat by this time was many furlongs distant from the land, beaten by the waves; for the wind was against them. ²⁵ And in the fourth watch of the night he came to them, walking on the sea. ²⁶ But when the disciples saw him walking on the sea, they were terrified, saying, "It is a ghost!" And they cried out for fear. ²⁷ But immediately [Jesus] spoke to them, saying, "Take courage! It is I. Do not be afraid." ²⁸ And Peter answered him, "Lord, if it is you, command me to come to you on the water." ²⁹ So he said, "Come." Then Peter got down out of the boat, walked on the water, and came toward Jesus. ³⁰ But when he saw the [strong] wind, he was afraid, and beginning to sink he cried out, "Lord, save me!" ³¹ Jesus immediately reached out his hand and caught him, and said to him, "O you of little faith, why did you doubt?" ³² And when they climbed into the boat, the wind ceased. ³³ Then those who were in the boat worshipped him, saying, "Truly you are God's Son."

³⁴ When they had crossed over, they came to land at Gennesaret. ³⁵ And when the men of that place recognized him, they sent to all that surrounding region and brought to him all who were sick, ³⁶ and begged him that they might only touch the tassel of his garment. And as many as touched it were made well.

15 ¹ Then the Pharisees and scribes from Jerusalem came to Jesus and said, ² "Why do your disciples transgress the tradition of the elders? For they do not wash [their] hands when they eat." ³ He answered them, "And why do you

---

14:²² Alx[**Immediately he**], Byz[Immediately Jesus (DRA, KJV, NET, NIV, NKJ, NLT, TEV, TLB)], Minor[*omits* Immediately (NAB, RSV, TEV)]; Alx/Major[**the disciples**], Byz[his disciples (DRA, KJV, MRD, NKJ, NLT, TLB)]; Alx/Byz[**the boat**], Minor[a boat (KJV, MRD, ~REB)].

14:²⁴ Alx[**many furlongs distant from the land**], Byz[in the middle of the sea (ASV, DRA, KJV, NKJ, ~TEV, ~TLB)]; **furlong** Greek *stadios, about 190 meters.*

14:²⁵ Alx[**he came to them**], Byz[Jesus went to them (KJV, ~MRD, ~NET, NIV, NKJ, ~NLT, ~TEV, ~TLB)].

14:²⁶ Alx/Byz[**the disciples**], Minor[they (DRA, TEV, TLB)].

14:²⁷ Alx/Byz[**Jesus**], Minor[he (RSV)].

14:²⁸ Alx/Byz[**Peter**], Alt/Peshitta[Cephas (JNT, MRD)].

14:²⁹ Alx/Byz[**Peter**], Alt/Peshitta[Cephas (JNT, MRD)]; Alx[**and came toward Jesus**], Byz[to come toward Jesus (ASV, DRA, JNT, KJV, MRD, NAB, NJB, NKJ, NLT, TEV, TLB)].

14:³⁰ Alx/Byz[**strong wind**], Minor[*omits* strong (ASV, ESV, NAS, NAU, NIV, NJB, RSV, ~TLB)].

14:³² Alx[**climbed into the boat**], Byz[got into the boat (ESV, HCS, KJV, MRD, NAB, NAS, NAU, NJB, NKJ, NRS, RSV, TEV)].

14:³³ Alx[**worshipped him**], Byz[came and worshipped him (DRA, KJV, MRD, NKJ)].

14:³⁴ Alx[**to land at Gennesaret**], Byz[into the land of Gennesaret (~DRA, KJV, MRD, NKJ)]; Alx/Byz[**Gennesaret**], Vulgate[Gennesar (DRA, JNT)].

14:³⁶ Alx/Byz[**begged him**], Minor[*omits* him]; Alx/Major[**might only touch**], Byz[might, at least, only touch (~NLT, ~TEV)].

15:¹ Alx[**Pharisees and scribes from Jerusalem**], Byz[scribes and Pharisees who were from Jerusalem (~DRA, KJV, ~MRD, NKJ)].

15:² Alx/Byz[**wash their hands**], Minor[*omits* their (NLT, TLB)].

transgress the commandment of God for the sake of your tradition? ⁴ For God said, *'Honor your father and your mother'*; and, *'He who curses father or mother, let him be put to death.'* ⁵ But you say that if a man says to his father or mother, 'Whatever help you might have received from me is a gift to God,' ⁶ he is not to honor his father with it. Thus you have made the word of God of no effect for the sake of your tradition. ⁷ You hypocrites! Well did Isaiah prophesy about you, when he said:

⁸   *'These people honor me with their lips.*
          But their heart is far from me.
⁹   *In vain do they worship me,*
          teaching as doctrines the precepts of men.'"

¹⁰ And he called the people to him and said to them, "Hear and understand: ¹¹ It is not what goes into the mouth that defiles a man, but what comes out of the mouth; this defiles a man." ¹² Then the disciples came and said to him, "Do you know that the Pharisees were offended when they heard this saying?" ¹³ He answered, "Every plant which my heavenly Father has not planted will be rooted up. ¹⁴ Let them alone. They are blind guides [of the blind]. And if a blind man leads a blind man, both will fall into a pit." ¹⁵ But Peter said to him, "Explain [this] parable to us." ¹⁶ So he said, "Are you also still without understanding? ¹⁷ Do you not see that whatever enters the mouth goes into the stomach and is eliminated? ¹⁸ But those things which proceed out of the mouth come from the heart, and they defile a man. ¹⁹ For out of the heart come evil thoughts, murder, adultery, fornications, theft, false witness, slander. ²⁰ These are what defile a man. But to eat with unwashed hands does not defile a man."

²¹ And Jesus went away from there and withdrew to the region of Tyre and Sidon. ²² And behold, a Canaanite woman from that region came out and cried, "Have mercy on me, O Lord, Son of David! My daughter is severely demon-possessed." ²³ But he did not answer her a word. And his disciples came and urged him, saying, "Send her away, for she is crying out after us." ²⁴ He answered, "I was sent only to the lost sheep of the house of Israel." ²⁵ But she came and knelt before him, saying, "Lord, help me!" ²⁶ And he answered, "It is not good to take the children's bread and throw it to the puppies." ²⁷ But

---

15:4 Alx[**God said**], Byz[God commanded, saying (~ESV, KJV, NKJ, ~RSV, ~TLB)]; **Exodus 20:12, Leviticus 20:9, Deuteronomy 5:16, Exodus 21:17**.

15:5-6 Alx[*text*], Byz[5 But you say that if a man says to his father or mother, 'Whatever help you might have received from me is a gift to God' and he shall not honor his father or his mother. 6 Thus you have made the commandment of God of no effect for the sake of your tradition (~DRA, ~JNT, ~KJV, MRD, ~NAS, ~NAU, ~NJB, ~NKJ, ~NLT, ~NRS, ~RSV, ~TLB)]; **a gift** or an offering.

15:8 Alx[*text*], Byz[These people draw near to me with their mouth, and honor me with their lips. But their heart is far from me (KJV, NKJ)].

15:8-9 **Isaiah 29:13 LXX**.

15:12 Alx[**the disciples**], Byz[his disciples (DRA, KJV, MRD, NAB, NKJ)]; Alx[**and said** Greek and say], Byz[and said].

15:14 Alx/Byz[**of the blind**], Minor[*omits* (ASV, ESV, HCS, NET, NIV, RSV, REB)].

15:15 Alx/Byz[**Peter**], Alt/Peshitta[Simon Cephas (MRD)], Alt[*without textual foundation* Cephas (~JNT)]; Alx/Byz[**this parable**], Minor[the parable (ASV, ESV, JNT, NAS, NAU, NIV, NJB, NLT, RSV, TLB)].

15:16 Alx[**So he said**], Byz[So Jesus said (KJV, NAU, NET, NIV, NJB, NLT, REB, TEV, TLB)].

15:17 Alx[**Do you not see**], Byz[Do you not yet see (KJV, NKJ, ~NLT)].

15:22 Alx[**cried**], Byz[*adds* to him (DRA, ~JNT, KJV, ~NIV, NKJ, ~NLT, REB, ~TEV, ~TLB)]; Alx[**Son of David**], Byz[you Son of David (ASV, DRA, KJV, MRD)].

15:26 Alx/Byz[**It is not good**], Minor[It is not allowed]; **puppies** or little dogs.

15:27 Alx/Byz[**yet even the puppies** Greek for even the puppies], Minor[even the puppies]; **puppies** or little dogs.

she said, "Yes, Lord. Yet even the puppies eat the crumbs that fall from their masters' table." **28** Then Jesus answered her, "O woman, great is your faith! Be it done for you as you desire." And her daughter was healed from that very hour.

29 And Jesus went on from there and passed along the Sea of Galilee. And he went up on the mountain, and sat down there. **30** Then great crowds came to him, bringing with them the lame, the blind, the maimed, the mute, and many others. And they laid them down at his feet, and he healed them. **31** So the multitude marveled when they saw the mute speaking, the maimed made whole, and the lame walking, and the blind seeing. And they glorified the God of Israel.

32 Now Jesus called his disciples to him and said, "I have compassion on the multitude, because they have already been with me three days and have nothing to eat. And I do not want to send them away hungry, lest they faint on the way." **33** Then the disciples said to him, "Where could we get enough bread in the wilderness to feed such a great crowd?" **34** And Jesus said to them, "How many loaves do you have?" They said, "Seven, and a few small fish." **35** He told the crowd to sit down on the ground. **36** He took the seven loaves and the fish, and having given thanks he broke them and gave them to the disciples. And the disciples gave them to the crowds. **37** And they all ate and were satisfied. And they took up seven baskets full of the broken pieces that were left over. **38** Now those who ate were four thousand men, besides women and children. **39** And he sent away the crowds, got into the boat, and went to the region of Magadan.

16 **1** Then the Pharisees and Sadducees came, and to test him they asked him to show them a sign from heaven. **2** He answered them, "[When it is evening, you say, 'It will be fair weather; for the sky is red.' **3** And in the morning, 'It will be stormy today; for the sky is red and threatening.' You know how to interpret the appearance of the sky, but you cannot interpret the signs of the times.] **4** A

15:30 Alx[**the lame, the blind, the maimed, the mute**], Byz[the lame, the blind, the mute, the maimed (ASV, KJV, MRD, NKJ, REB)], Minor[the lame, the maimed, the blind, the mute (NAS, NAU, NJB, NRS, RSV) *others* the mute, the blind, the lame, the maimed (DRA)]; Alx[**at his feet**], Byz[at the feet of Jesus (KJV, MRD, NKJ, NLT, TEV, TLB)].

15:31 Alx[**multitude**], Byz[multitudes (DRA, MRD, NAB, NJB, ~TLB)]; Alx/Major[**the mute speaking**], Byz[the deaf hearing, the mute speaking]; Alx/Byz[**the maimed made whole**], Minor[*omits* (DRA)]; Alx[**and the lame walking**], Byz[*omits* and (DRA, ESV, HCS, JNT, KJV, NAB, NET, NIV, NJB, NKJ, NLT, NRS, REB, RSV, TEV, TLB)].

15:32 Alx/Byz[**already**], Minor[*omits* (~JNT, MRD, NLT, ~TEV)].

15:33 Alx[**the disciples**], Byz[his disciples (KJV, MRD, NIV, NKJ)].

15:35 Alx[**crowd**], Byz[crowds (MRD)].

15:36 Alx[**He took the seven loaves**], Byz[And he took the seven loaves (ASV, DRA, KJV, MRD, NAS, NAU, NIV, NJB, NKJ, NLT, REB, TEV, TLB)]; Alx[**and having given thanks**], Byz[*omits* and (JNT, NAB, NLT, TEV)]; Alx[**to the disciples**], Byz[to his disciples (DRA, KJV, MRD)]; Alx/Byz[**the crowds**], Major[the crowd (DRA, JNT, KJV, NAU, NIV, NKJ, NLT, REB, TEV, TLB)].

15:38 Alx/Byz[**four thousand**], Minor[about four thousand]; Alx/Byz[**women and children**], Minor[children and women (DRA, NET)].

15:39 Alx/Major[**got into the boat**], Byz[went up into the boat], Alt/Vulgate[went up into a boat (DRA)]; Alx[**Magadan**], Byz[Magdala (KJV, MRD, NKJ)], Minor[Magdalan; **Magdala(n)** *Aramaism* Tower *the location is unknown*.

16:1 Alx/Byz[**the Pharisees**], Minor[*omits* the (JNT, MRD, TEV)].

16:2-3 Alx/Byz[*text*], Minor[*omits* all of verses 2 and 3 after **He answered them** (REB)].

16:3 Alx[**You know how**], Byz[Hypocrites! You know how (KJV, MRD, NKJ)]; Alx/Major[**you cannot interpret the signs** *Greek* you cannot the signs], Byz[you cannot know the signs (DRA)].

16:4 Alx[**Jonah**], Byz[the prophet Jonah (DRA, KJV, MRD, NKJ, NLT)].

wicked and adulterous generation seeks for a sign, but no sign shall be given to it except the sign of Jonah." So he left them and departed.

[5] When the disciples reached the other side, they had forgotten to take bread. [6] Then Jesus said to them, "Take heed and beware of the leaven of the Pharisees and the Sadducees." [7] And they discussed among themselves, saying, "It is because we have taken no bread." [8] But Jesus, aware of this, said, "O men of little faith, why do you discuss among yourselves the fact that you have no bread? [9] Do you not yet perceive? Do you not remember the five loaves of the five thousand, and how many baskets you gathered? [10] Or the seven loaves of the four thousand, and how many baskets you gathered? [11] How don't you understand that I did not speak to you about bread? But beware of the leaven of the Pharisees and Sadducees." [12] Then they understood that he did not tell them to beware of the leaven of bread, but of the teaching of the Pharisees and Sadducees.

[13] When Jesus came into the region of Caesarea Philippi, he asked his disciples, "Who do men say that the Son of Man is?" [14] And they said, "Some say John the Baptist, others say Elijah, and others Jeremiah or one of the prophets." [15] He said to them, "But who do you say that I am?" [16] Simon Peter answered, "You are the Christ, the Son of the living God." [17] But Jesus answered him, "Blessed are you, Simon Bar-Jonah! For flesh and blood has not revealed this to you, but my Father who is in heaven. [18] And I tell you, that you are Peter, and on this rock I will build my church, and the gates of Hades shall not prevail against it. [19] I will give you the keys of the kingdom of heaven. And whatever you bind on earth will have been bound in heaven, and whatever you loose on earth will have been loosed in heaven." [20] Then he strictly charged the disciples to tell no one that he was the Christ.

[21] From that time Jesus began to show to his disciples that he must go to Jerusalem, and suffer many things from the elders and chief priests and scribes, and be killed, and be raised on the third day. [22] Peter took him aside and began to rebuke him saying, "God forbid it, Lord! This shall never happen to you!" [23] But he turned and said to Peter, "Get behind me, Satan! You are a stumbling block to me; for you are not mindful of the things of God, but the things of men." [24] Then Jesus said to his disciples, "If anyone

---

16:5 Alx[**the disciples**], Byz[his disciples (DRA, KJV, MRD, NKJ)].

16:8 Alx[**Jesus…said**], Byz[*adds* to them (KJV, MRD, NKJ, TEV, TLB)]; Alx[**have no bread**], Byz[brought no bread (KJV, MRD, NKJ)].

16:11 Alx[**bread** *plural*], Byz[bread *singular*]; Alx[**But beware**], Byz[Beware (DRA, ESV, HCS, JNT, KJV, NAB, NJB, NLT, NRS, REB, RSV, TEV)].

16:12 Alx[**leaven of bread** *plural*], Byz[leaven of bread *singular*], Minor[leaven of the Pharisees and Sadducees *others omit* (~REB, ~TLB)].

16:13 Alx[**say that the Son of Man is**], Byz[say that I, the Son of Man, am (KJV, MRD, NKJ, ~TLB)].

16:16 Alx/Byz[**Peter**], Alt/Peshitta[Cephas (JNT, MRD)].

16:17 Alx[**But Jesus**], Byz[And Jesus (ASV, DRA, ESV, HCS, ~JNT, KJV, ~MRD, ~NAB, NAS, NAU, NET, ~NIV, ~NJB, ~NKJ, ~NLT, NRS, REB, RSV, ~TEV, ~TLB)]; Alx/Byz[**Bar-Jonah** *Aramaism* son of Jonah], Minor[bar Jonah (HCS, MRD, NAB, NET, NIV, NJB, ~NLT, NRS, REB, ~TEV, TLB)].

16:18 **Peter** *Greek* Petros; **rock** *Greek* petra; **prevail against it** *or* be stronger than it.

16:19 Alx[**I will give you**], Byz[And I will give you (DRA, KJV, NKJ, NLT, TLB)].

16:20 Alx/Byz[**strictly charged**], Minor[warned (JNT, NAS, NAU, NIV, NLT, TLB)]; Alx[**the disciples**], Byz[his disciples (DRA, KJV, MRD, NAB, NET, NIV, NKJ, REB, TEV)]; Alx[**the Christ**], Byz[Jesus the Christ (DRA, KJV, NKJ)].

16:21 Alx/Byz[**Jesus**], Minor[Jesus Christ (NAS)].

16:22 Alx/Byz[**Peter**], Alt/Peshitta[Cephas (JNT, MRD)]; Alx/Byz[**began to rebuke**], Minor[began rebuking (JNT)].

16:23 Alx/Byz[**Peter**], Alt/Peshitta[Cephas (JNT, MRD)].

would come after me, let him deny himself and take up his cross and follow me. 25 For whoever desires to save his life will lose it, but whoever loses his life for my sake will find it. 26 What good will it be for a man if he gains the whole world, and forfeits his soul? Or what can a man give in exchange for his soul? 27 For the Son of Man is to come with his angels in the glory of his Father, and then he will reward each man according to what he has done. 28 Truly, I tell you that there are some standing here who will never taste death before they see the Son of Man coming in his kingdom."

17

1 After six days Jesus took with him Peter, James, and John his brother, and led them up a high mountain by themselves. 2 And he was transfigured before them. His face shone like the sun, and his clothes became as white as light. 3 And behold, there appeared to them Moses and Elijah, talking with him. 4 And Peter said to Jesus, "Lord, it is good for us to be here. If you wish, I will make here three tabernacles – one for you, one for Moses, and one for Elijah." 5 While he was still speaking, behold, a bright cloud overshadowed them. And a voice from the cloud said, "This is my beloved Son, with whom I am well pleased. Listen to him!" 6 When the disciples heard this, they fell on their faces, and were filled with awe. 7 But Jesus came, and touching them said, "Rise. Don't be afraid." 8 And when they lifted up their eyes, they saw no one but Jesus himself, alone.

9 And as they were coming down the mountain, Jesus commanded them, "Tell no one the vision, until the Son of Man is risen from the dead." 10 And the disciples asked him, "Why then do the scribes say that Elijah must come first?" 11 He replied, "Elijah is coming and will restore all things. 12 But I tell you that Elijah has come already, and they did not know him but did to him whatever they wished. So also the Son of Man is about to suffer at their hands." 13 Then the disciples understood that he was speaking to them of John the Baptist.

14 And when they came to the crowd, a man came up to him and kneeling before him 15 said, "Lord, have mercy on my son, for he has seizures and he suffers terribly. For often he falls into the fire, and often into the water. 16 And I brought him to your disciples, but they could not heal him." 17 Then Jesus answered, "O faithless and perverse generation! How long shall I be with you? How long shall I bear with you? Bring him here to me." 18 And Jesus rebuked him, and the demon came out of him. And the boy was

---

16:25-26 **life** and **soul** are the same word in Greek.

16:26 Alx[**What good will it be**], Byz[What good is it (DRA, KJV, NET, NKJ, NLT, TLB)].

16:28 Alx[**I tell you that there are**], Byz[I tell you: there are (ASV, DRA, ESV, HCS, KJV, MRD, NAB, NAS, NAU, NET, NIV, NJB, NKJ, NLT, NRS, REB, RSV, ~TLB)].

17:1 Alx/Byz[**Peter**], Alt/Peshitta[Cephas (JNT, MRD)].

17:2 Alx/Byz[**as white as light**], Minor[as white as snow (DRA, ~NRS, ~TEV, ~TLB)].

17:4 Alx/Byz[**Peter**], Alt/Peshitta[Cephas (JNT, MRD)]; Alx[**I will make**], Byz[let us make (DRA, KJV, MRD, NKJ)].

17:7 Alx[**and touching them said**], Byz[and touched them, saying (ASV, DRA, ESV, HCS, JNT, KJV, MRD, NAB, NAS, NAU, NET, NIV, NJB, NKJ, NLT, NRS, REB, RSV, TEV, TLB)].

17:8 Alx[**Jesus himself, alone**], Byz[Jesus alone (ASV, DRA, ESV, KJV, MRD, NAB, NET, NIV, NJB, NKJ, NLT, REB, RSV, TEV, TLB)].

17:9 Alx[**risen from the dead**], Byz[raised from the dead (ESV, HCS, JNT, NAB, NET, NIV, NLT, NRS, REB, RSV, TEV)].

17:10 Alx[**the disciples**], Byz[his disciples (ASV, DRA, KJV, MRD, NAS, NAU, NKJ, NLT, TLB)].

17:11 Alx[**He replied**], Byz[Jesus replied to them (~DRA, KJV, MRD, ~NIV, NKJ, ~TEV, ~TLB)]; Alx[**coming**], Byz[adds first (KJV, MRD, NET, NKJ, NLT, TEV)].

17:15 Alx/Major[**15 said**], Byz[said, 15 (ASV, KJV, NAS, NAU, NKJ, NLT, REB, RSV, TLB)]; Alx/Byz[**suffers terribly**], Minor[has an illness (JNT, NAS, NAU, TEV)]; DRA combines verses 14 and 15 and remains one verse behind to the end of the chapter; **has seizures** Greek moonstruck.

17:18 **rebuked him** or rebuked it.

cured from that moment. [19] Then the disciples came to Jesus privately and said, "Why could we not cast it out?" [20] So he said to them, "Because of your little faith. For truly, I say to you, if you have faith as a grain of mustard seed, you will say to this mountain, 'Move from here to there,' and it will move; and nothing will be impossible to you." [21]

[22] Now while they were gathering in Galilee, Jesus said to them, "The Son of Man is about to be betrayed into the hands of men. [23] And they will kill him, and he will be raised on the third day." And they were greatly distressed.

[24] When they came to Capernaum, the collectors of the half-shekel tax went up to Peter and said, "Does not your teacher pay [the] temple tax?" [25] He said, "Yes." And when he came into the house, Jesus spoke to him first, saying, "What do you think, Simon? From whom do the kings of the earth take customs or taxes, from their sons or from others?" [26] And when he said, "From others," Jesus said to him, "Then the sons are free. [27] Nevertheless, so that we may not offend them, go to the sea, cast in a hook, and take the fish that comes up first. And when you open its mouth, you will find a piece of money. Take that and give it to them for me and you."

18

[1] At that time the disciples came to Jesus, saying, "Who is the greatest in the kingdom of heaven?" [2] He called to him a little child, and put him in the midst of them. [3] And he said, "Truly, I say to you, unless you turn and become like little children, you will never enter the kingdom of heaven. [4] Therefore, whoever will humble himself like this child is the greatest in the kingdom of heaven. [5] Whoever receives one little child like this in my name receives me.

[6] "But whoever causes one of these little ones who believe in me to sin, it would be better for him to have a large millstone hung around his neck and to be drowned in the depth of the sea. [7] Woe to the world because of temptations to sin! For temptations must come, but woe to the man by whom the temptation comes! [8] And if your hand or your foot causes you to sin, cut it off and throw it away. It is better for you to enter life maimed or lame than with two hands or two feet to be thrown into the eternal fire. [9] And if your eye

---

17:20 Alx[he said *Greek* he says], Byz[Jesus said (DRA, KJV, MRD, NKJ, NLT, TEV, TLB)]; Alx[**little faith**], Byz[unbelief (DRA, KJV, MRD, NKJ)].

17:(21) Alx[*omits*], Byz[*adds* But this kind does not go out except by prayer and fasting (ASV, DRA, HCS, KJV, MRD, NAS, NAU, NKJ, TLB)].

17:22 Alx[**gathering**], Byz[staying (ASV, DRA, KJV, MRD, NKJ, ~REB, TLB)].

17:24 Alx[**Capernaum** *Greek* Capharnaum], Byz[Capernaum]; Alx/Byz[**Peter**], Alt/Peshitta[Cephas (JNT, MRD)]; **temple tax** *Greek* didrachma *i.e. two drachmas.*

17:25 **Simon** *Peter.*

17:26 Alx[**And when he said**], Byz[When Peter said to him (KJV, ~MRD, NAU, NIV, NKJ, NLT, NRS, REB, TEV, TLB)]; Alx/Byz[**the sons are free**], Metzger[*Minor adds* give, as being an alien to them].

17:27 **piece of money** *Greek* stater *worth two didrachmas.*

18:1 Alx/Byz[**At that time**], Minor[But at that time].

18:2 Alx[**He called**], Byz[Jesus called (DRA, KJV, MRD, NKJ, NLT, TEV, TLB)].

18:3 Alx/Major[**3 And he said**], Byz[And he said 3].

18:4 Alx/Major[**whoever will humble**], Byz[whoever humbles *or* whoever should humble (ESV, HCS, JNT, NAB, NAS, NAU, NET, NIV, NJB, NKJ, NLT, NRS, REB, RSV, TEV, TLB)].

18:6 Alx[**around his neck**], Byz[on his neck], Major[to his neck (MRD, TLB)].

18:7 Alx[**temptations must come**], Byz[it is necessary that temptations come (ASV, DRA, ESV, KJV, MRD, NAS, NAU, NET, NJB, RSV, ~TEV, TLB)]; Alx[**woe to the man**], Byz[woe to that man (ASV, DRA, HCS, KJV, NAS, NAU, NKJ)].

18:8 Alx[**cut it off**], Byz[cut them off (KJV)]; Alx[**maimed or lame**], Byz[lame or maimed (KJV, MRD, NKJ, ~TLB)].

18:9 **hell** *Greek* Gehenna.

causes you to sin, pluck it out and throw it away. It is better for you to enter life with one eye than to have two eyes and be thrown into the fire of hell.

¹⁰ "See that you do not despise one of these little ones. For I tell you that in heaven their angels always see the face of my Father who is in heaven. (11) ¹² What do you think? If a man has a hundred sheep, and one of them has gone astray, will he not leave the ninety-nine and go to the mountains in search of the one that went astray? ¹³ And if he finds it, truly, I say to you, he rejoices more over that sheep than over the ninety-nine that did not go astray. ¹⁴ So it is not the will of your Father who is in heaven that one of these little ones should perish.

¹⁵ "If your brother sins [against you], go, tell him his fault, between you and him alone. If he listens to you, you have gained your brother. ¹⁶ But if he will not listen, take one or two others along with you, so that 'every matter may be established by the word of two or three witnesses.' ¹⁷ If he refuses to listen to them, tell it to the church. And if he refuses to listen even to the church, let him be to you as a Gentile and a tax collector.

¹⁸ "Truly, I say to you, whatever you bind on earth will have been bound in heaven. And whatever you loose on earth will have been loosed in heaven. ¹⁹ Again [truly] I say to you, that if two of you agree on earth about anything they ask, it will be done for them by my Father in heaven. ²⁰ For where two or three are gathered together in my name, there am I in the midst of them."

²¹ Then Peter came to him and said, "Lord, how often shall my brother sin against me, and I forgive him? Up to seven times?" ²² Jesus said to him, "I do not say to you seven times, but seventy times seven. ²³ Therefore the kingdom of heaven is like a certain king who wanted to settle accounts with his servants. ²⁴ When he began the settlement, one was brought to him who owed him ten thousand talents. ²⁵ And as he was not able to pay, his master ordered that he be sold, with his wife and children and all his possessions, to pay the debt. ²⁶ So the servant fell on his knees before him, saying, 'Have patience with me, and I will pay you everything.' ²⁷ The master of that servant took pity on him, released him, and forgave him the debt. ²⁸ But that servant went out and found one of his fellow

---

18:10 Alx/Byz[**in heaven**], Minor[*omits*].

18:(11) Alx[*omits*], Byz[*adds* For the Son of Man came to save the lost (ASV, DRA, HCS, KJV, MRD, NAS, NAU, NKJ, TLB)].

18:12 Alx[**will he not leave**], Byz[does he not leave (ASV, DRA, ESV, KJV, NAS, NAU, NKJ, NRS, REB, RSV)].

18:14 Alx/Byz[**your Father**], Minor[my Father (ESV, NLT, RSV, TLB)].

18:15 Alx/Byz[**sins against you**], Minor[*omits* against you (NAS, NAU, NET, NJB, REB)]; Alx[**go, tell him**], Byz[go and tell him (DRA, ESV, HCS, JNT, KJV, MRD, NAB, NAS, NAU, NET, NIV, NJB, NKJ, NLT, NRS, REB, RSV, TEV, TLB)].

18:16 Alx/Byz[**along with you**], Minor[along with yourself *others* along with (NIV)]; ~Deuteronomy 19:15.

18:19 Alx/Byz[**Again truly**], Minor[Again (ASV, DRA, ESV, JNT, KJV, MRD, NKJ, NAS, NAU, NIV, REB, RSV) *others* omit (~NLT, ~TEV, ~TLB)]; **truly** *Greek* amen *a Hebraism*.

18:21 Alx/Byz[**Peter**], Alt/Peshitta[Cephas (JNT, MRD)]; Alx/Byz[**came to him**], Minor[*omits* to him].

18:22 **seventy times seven** *or* seventy-seven.

18:24 *a talent is fifteen years' wages for a laborer.*

18:25 Alx[**all his possessions** *Greek* all he has], Byz[had (ASV, DRA, ESV, HCS, KJV, MRD, NAS, NAU, NET, NIV, NKJ, NLT, REB, RSV, TEV, TLB)].

18:26 Alx/Byz[**the servant**], Minor[that servant (DRA, MRD)]; Alx[**Have patience with me**], Byz[*adds* Lord (ASV, KJV, MRD, NKJ, RSV, TLB)].

18:27 Alx/Byz[**that servant**], Minor[the servant (~JNT, NIV, NJB, ~NLT, ~REB, ~TEV, ~TLB)].

18:28 Alx[**Pay, if you owe anything**], Byz[Pay me, if you owe anything], Minor[Pay me what you owe (~ASV, ~DRA, ~ESV, ~HCS, JNT, KJV, MRD, ~NAB, ~NAS, ~NAU, NET, NIV, NJB, NKJ,

servants who owed him a hundred denarii. And he laid hands on him and took him by the throat, saying, 'Pay, if you owe anything.' ²⁹ So his fellow servant fell down and begged him, 'Have patience with me, and I will pay you back.' ³⁰ But he refused, and went and threw him into prison till he should pay the debt. ³¹ So when his fellow servants saw what had taken place, they were greatly distressed, and went and told their master all that had happened. ³² Then his master, after he had called him, said to him, 'You wicked servant! I forgave you all that debt because you begged me. ³³ Should not you have had mercy on your fellow servant, just as I had mercy on you?' ³⁴ And in anger his master delivered him to the jailers to be tortured, until he should pay back all he owed. ³⁵ So also my heavenly Father will do to each of you, if you do not forgive your brother from your heart."

19

¹ Now when Jesus had finished these sayings, he went away from Galilee and entered the region of Judea beyond the Jordan. ² And large crowds followed him. And he healed them there. ³ Some Pharisees came to him to test him. They asked, "Is it lawful for a man to divorce his wife for any reason?" ⁴ And he answered, "Have you not read that he who created them at the beginning 'made them male and female,' ⁵ and said, 'For this reason a man shall leave his father and mother and be joined to his wife, and the two shall become one flesh'? ⁶ So they are no longer two, but one flesh. Therefore what God has joined together, let man not separate." ⁷ They said to him, "Why then did Moses command one to give a certificate of divorce, and to put [her] away?" ⁸ He said to them, "Because of the hardness of your hearts Moses permitted you to divorce your wives. But from the beginning it was not so. ⁹ And I say to you, whoever divorces his wife, except for immorality, and marries another woman commits adultery." ¹⁰ [His] disciples said to him, "If such is the case of a man with his wife, it is better not to marry." ¹¹ But he said to them, "Not all men can accept [this] saying, but only those to whom it has been given. ¹² For there are eunuchs who were born that way from their mother's womb. And there are eunuchs who were made eunuchs by men. And there are eunuchs who have made themselves eunuchs for the sake of the kingdom of heaven. He who is able to accept it, let him accept it."

~NLT, ~NRS, REB, ~RSV, TEV, ~TLB)]; *a denarius was one day's wage for a laborer.*

18:²⁹ Alx[**fell down**], Byz[*adds* at his feet (~JNT, KJV, MRD, NJB, NKJ, ~NLT, REB, ~TLB)]; Alx/Major[**pay you back**], Byz[*adds* all (DRA, KJV, MRD, NKJ)].

18:³⁰ Alx[**the debt**], Byz[what was owed (ASV, HCS, MRD, NAS, NAU)].

18:³¹ Alx[**So when**], Byz[But when (MRD)].

18:³⁴ Alx[**all he owed**], Byz[*adds* to him (KJV, MRD, NAS, NAU, NKJ)].

18:³⁵ Alx[**forgive your brother**], Byz[*adds* their trespasses (KJV, ~MRD, ~NKJ)].

19:³ Alx[**Some Pharisees**], Byz[The Pharisees (DRA, KJV, NKJ)]; Alx[**They asked**], Byz[They asked him (KJV, NKJ)]; Alx/Byz[**lawful for a man to divorce**], Minor[lawful to divorce (ESV, NET, RSV, TLB)].

19:⁴ Alx[**And he answered**], Byz[And he answered them (DRA, KJV, MRD, NKJ)]; Alx[**he who created**], Byz[he who made (ASV, DRA, KJV, MRD, NKJ, NLT, NRS, RSV, ~TLB)]; **Genesis 1:27, 5:2**.

19:⁵ Alx/Major[**5 and said**], Byz[and said 5 (DRA ~TLB)]; Alx/Major[**his father and mother** *Greek* the father and the mother], Byz[his father and the mother]; **Genesis 2:24**.

19:⁷ Alx/Byz[**put her away**], Minor[*omits* her (DRA, NJB)]; ~**Deuteronomy 24:1**.

19:⁹ Alx[*text*], Byz[*adds* And whoever marries a divorced woman commits adultery (ASV, DRA, KJV, MRD, NKJ)].

19:¹⁰ Alx/Byz[**His disciples**], Minor[The disciples (ASV, ESV, JNT, NAS, NAU, NET, NIV, NJB, REB, RSV)].

19:¹¹ Alx/Byz[**this saying**], Minor[the saying (~MRD, NJB)].

[13] Then little children were brought to him that he might put his hands on them and pray. But the disciples rebuked them. [14] But Jesus said, "Let the little children come to me, and do not hinder them; for to such belongs the kingdom of heaven." [15] And he laid his hands on them and went from there.

[16] Now behold, one came up to him and said, "Teacher, what good thing must I do to have eternal life?" [17] And he said to him, "Why do you ask me about what is good? There is only one who is good. If you want to enter life, keep the commandments." [18] He said to him, "Which ones?" And Jesus said, *"You shall not murder. You shall not commit adultery. You shall not steal. You shall not bear false witness.* [19] *Honor father and mother. And, you shall love your neighbor as yourself."'* [20] The young man said to him, "All these I have kept. What do I still lack?" [21] Jesus said to him, "If you want to be perfect, go, sell what you possess and give to [the] poor, and you will have treasure in heaven; and come, follow me." [22] But when the young man heard the saying, he went away sorrowful, for he had great possessions.

[23] Then Jesus said to his disciples, "Truly I say to you, it is hard for a rich man to enter the kingdom of heaven. [24] Again I tell you, it is easier for a camel to go through the eye of a needle than for a rich man to enter the kingdom of God." [25] When the disciples heard this they were greatly astonished, saying, "Who then can be saved?" [26] But Jesus looked at them and said, "With men this is impossible. But with God all things are possible." [27] Then Peter answered him, "Behold, we have left everything and followed you. What then shall we have?" [28] Jesus said to them, "Truly I say to you, at the renewal of all things, when the Son of Man sits on his glorious throne, you who have followed me will also sit on twelve thrones, judging the twelve tribes of Israel. [29] And whoever has left houses or brothers or sisters or father or mother or children or lands, for my name's sake, will receive a hundredfold, and inherit eternal life. [30] But many who are first will be last, and the last first.

19:14 Alx/Byz[**But Jesus said**], Minor[*adds* to them (DRA, MRD)].

19:16 Alx[**came up to him and said**], Byz[came up and said to him (DRA, HCS, KJV, MRD, NKJ, REB)]; Alx[**Teacher**], Byz[Good teacher (DRA, KJV, MRD, NKJ, TLB)].

19:17 Alx[*text*], Byz[And he said to him, "Why do you call me good? No one is good but God alone. If you want to enter life, keep the commandments (KJV, MRD, NKJ, TLB)].

19:18 Alx/Byz[**He said to him**], Minor[*omits* to him (NET, NIV, NJB, NLT, REB, TEV, TLB)].

19:18-19 **Exodus 20:12-16; Deuteronomy 5:16-20**.

19:19 Alx/Byz[**Honor father and mother**], Minor[Honor your father and mother (ASV, DRA, ESV, HCS, KJV, MRD, NAB, NAS, NAU, NET, NIV, NJB, NKJ, NLT, NRS, REB, RSV, TEV, TLB)]; **Leviticus 19:18**.

19:20 Alx[**I have kept**], Byz[*adds* from my youth (DRA, KJV, MRD, NKJ, ~TLB)].

19:21 Alx[**the poor**], Byz[*omits* the].

19:22 Alx/Byz[**the saying**], Minor[*omits* (~ESV, ~JNT, ~NET, ~NIV, ~NLT, ~RSV, ~TEV, ~TLB) *others* this saying (DRA, NAB, NAS, NAU, NJB, NRS, REB)].

19:24 Alx/Byz[**camel**], Minor[cable]; Alx/Byz[**go through...enter**], Minor[enter...into (MRD)]; Alx/Byz[**the kingdom of God**], Minor[the kingdom of heaven (DRA, NJB)].

19:25 Alx[**the disciples**], Byz[his disciples (KJV, NKJ)].

19:26 **looked at them and said** *Greek* looked and said to them.

19:27 Alx/Byz[**Peter**], Alt/Peshitta[Cephas (JNT, MRD)].

19:28 Alx/Byz[**you who have followed**], Minor[yourselves who have followed (NAB, NJB)].

19:29 Alx[**whoever**], Byz[everyone who (ASV, DRA, ESV, HCS, JNT, KJV, MRD, NAB, NAS, NAU, NIV, NKJ, NLT, NRS, REB, RSV, TEV, ~TLB)]; Alx/Byz[**houses or brothers...or lands**], Minor[brothers...or lands or houses]; Alx[**mother**], Byz[*adds* or wife (DRA, KJV, MRD, NKJ, TLB)]; Alx/Byz[**a hundredfold**], Minor[many times as much (NAS, NAU, REB)].

20

¹ "For the kingdom of heaven is like a landowner who went out early in the morning to hire laborers for his vineyard. ² Now when he had agreed with the laborers for a denarius a day, he sent them into his vineyard. ³ And he went out about the third hour and saw others standing idle in the marketplace. ⁴ And to them he said, 'You go into the vineyard too, and whatever is right I will give you.' ⁵ So they went. [And] again he went out about the sixth hour and the ninth hour, and did the same thing. ⁶ And about the eleventh he went out and found others standing, and said to them, 'Why have you been standing here idle all day?' ⁷ They said to him, 'Because no one has hired us.' He said to them, 'You also go into the vineyard.' ⁸ And when evening came, the owner of the vineyard said to his steward, 'Call the laborers and pay them their wages, beginning with the last, up to the first.' ⁹ And when those came who were hired about the eleventh hour, they each received a denarius. ¹⁰ And when the first came, they thought they would receive more. But each of them also received a denarius. ¹¹ And when they had received it, they complained against the landowner, ¹² saying, 'These last men have worked only one hour, and you made them equal to us who have borne the burden and the heat of the day.' ¹³ But he answered one of them, 'Friend, I am doing you no wrong. Did you not agree with me for a denarius? ¹⁴ Take what is yours and go your way. I wish to give to this last man the same as I gave to you. ¹⁵ [Or] is it not lawful for me to do what I want with my own money? Or are you envious because I am generous?' ¹⁶ So the last will be first, and the first will be last."

¹⁷ Now as Jesus was going up to Jerusalem, he took the twelve [disciples] aside. And on the way he said to them, ¹⁸ "Behold, we are going up to Jerusalem, and the Son of Man will be betrayed to the chief priests and to the scribes. And they will condemn him to death, ¹⁹ and deliver him to the Gentiles to be mocked and scourged and crucified. And he will be raised on the third day."

20:² *a* **denarius** *was a day's wage for a laborer.*

20:³ Alx/Major[**about the third hour** *Greek* about third hour], Byz[about the third hour].

20:⁴ Alx/Byz[**the vineyard**], Minor[my vineyard (DRA, HCS, MRD, NAB, NIV, NJB, ~NLT, TLB)].

20:⁵ Alx/Major[**5 So they went**], Byz[So they went 5 (ASV, HCS, JNT, KJV, NAS, NAU, NRS, REB, RSV)]; Alx[**And again**], Byz[*omits* And (ASV, ESV, HCS, JNT, KJV, NAS, NAU, NET, NIV, NJB, NKJ, NLT, NRS, REB, RSV, TEV, TLB)].

20:⁶ Alx[**about the eleventh**], Byz[*adds* hour (ASV, DRA, ESV, JNT, KJV, MRD, NAS, NAU, NIV, NJB, NKJ, REB, RSV)]; Alx[**standing**], Byz[*adds* idle (KJV, MRD, ~NAB, ~NAU, ~NET, ~NIV, ~NJB, NKJ, ~NLT, ~NRS)].

20:⁷ Alx[**vineyard**], Byz[*adds* and whatever is right you will receive (KJV, MRD, NKJ)].

20:⁸ Alx/Byz[**pay them their wages**], Minor[pay them the wages (NET, NLT, TLB)].

20:⁹ Alx/Byz[**And when**], Minor[*omits* And (~DRA, HCS, JNT, NAB, NAU, NET, NIV, NLT, NRS, REB, TEV, TLB) *others* But when].

20:¹⁰ Alx[**And when the first came**], Byz[But when the first came (DRA, KJV, NKJ)].

20:¹⁵ Alx[**Or...Or**], Byz[Or...If (DRA, ~KJV, NAB)]; Minor[...Or (ASV, ESV, ~HCS, JNT, MRD, NAS, NAU, NET, NIV, ~NJB, NKJ, ~NLT, NRS, ~REB, RSV, TEV, ~TLB)]; **are you envious because I am generous** *Greek* is your eye evil because I am good.

20:¹⁶ Alx[**first will be last**], Byz[*adds* for many are called, but few are chosen (DRA, KJV, MRD, NKJ)].

20:¹⁷ Alx/Byz[**as Jesus was going**], Minor[as Jesus was about to go (MRD, NAS, NAU)]; Alx/Byz[**disciples**], Minor[*omits* (NET, NJB, REB)]; Alx[**aside. And on the way he said**], Byz[aside on the way. And he said (KJV, MRD, NJB, NKJ)], Minor[aside. And he said (DRA, NIV, ~NLT, ~TLB)].

20:¹⁸ Alx/Byz[**to death**], Minor[*omits*].

20:¹⁹ Alx[**will be raised**], Byz[will rise (DRA, KJV, MRD, NKJ, TLB)].

20 Then the mother of Zebedee's sons came to him with her sons and, kneeling down, asked something of him. **21** And he said to her, "What do you want?" She said to him, "Grant that these two sons of mine may sit, one at your right hand and one at your left, in your kingdom." **22** But Jesus answered, "You do not know what you are asking for. Are you able to drink the cup that I am about to drink?" They said to him, "We are able." **23** He said to them, "You will indeed drink my cup. But to sit at my right and left, [this] is not mine to grant, but it is for those for whom it has been prepared by my Father." **24** And when the ten heard it, they were indignant with the two brothers. **25** But Jesus called them to him and said, "You know that the rulers of the Gentiles lord it over them, and their great men exercise authority over them. **26** It shall not be so among you. But whoever desires to become great among you shall be your servant. **27** And whoever wants to be first among you shall be your slave – **28** just as the Son of Man did not come to be served, but to serve, and to give his life as a ransom for many."

29 And as they went out of Jericho, a great crowd followed him. **30** And behold, two blind men sitting by the roadside, when they heard that Jesus was passing by, cried out, "Have mercy on us, [Lord,] Son of David!" **31** The crowd rebuked them, telling them to be quiet. But they cried out all the more, "Have mercy on us, Lord, Son of David!" **32** And Jesus stopped and called them, saying, "What do you want me to do for you?" **33** They said to him, "Lord, let our eyes be opened." **34** And Jesus had compassion on them and touched their eyes. Immediately they received their sight and followed him.

20:21 Alx/Major[**your right...your left**], Byz[your right...the left (KJV, NKJ, ~TLB)], Minor[the right...your left].

20:22 Alx[**about to drink**], Byz[*adds* or be baptized with the baptism that I am baptized with (MRD)], Minor[*adds* and be baptized with the baptism that I am baptized with (KJV, NKJ)].

20:23 Alx[**He said**], Byz[And he said (KJV, NKJ)]; Alx[**my cup**], Byz[*adds* and be baptized with the baptism that I am baptized with (KJV, MRD, NKJ)]; Alx[**my right and left**], Byz[my right and my left (ASV, ESV, JNT, KJV, MRD, NAB, NAS, NAU, NET, NJB, NKJ, NRS, RSV, TEV)], Minor[my right or left (DRA, NIV, ~NLT, ~REB, ~TLB)]; Alx[**this is not mine to grant**], Byz[*omits* this (ASV, DRA, ESV, HCS, JNT, KJV, MRD, NET, NIV, NKJ, NLT, REB, RSV, TEV, TLB)].

20:24 Alx/Byz[**And when the ten**], Minor[When the ten (HCS, NAB, NIV, NJB, NLT, NRS, REB, TEV, TLB) *others* But when the ten].

20:26 Alx/Byz[**It shall not be so**], Major[Yet it shall not be so (KJV, NAB, NKJ, NLT, TEV, TLB)], Minor[It is not so (NAS, NAU, NIV, TLB)]; Alx/Byz[**shall be your servant** *or* must be your servant], Minor[must be your servant (DRA, ESV, HCS, JNT, KJV, MRD, NET, NIV, NJB, NKJ, NLT, NRS, REB, RSV, TEV, TLB)].

20:27 Alx[**whoever**], Byz[if anyone (TEV, TLB)]; Alx/Byz[**shall be your slave** *or* must be your slave], Major[must be your slave (ESV, HCS, JNT, KJV, MRD, NET, NIV, NJB, NKJ, NLT, NRS, REB, RSV, TEV, TLB)].

20:28 Alx/Byz[*text*], Metzger[*Minor adds* But seek to increase from that which is small, and from the greater to become less. When you enter into a house and are invited to dine, do not recline in the prominent places, lest perchance one more honorable than you come in, and the host come and say to you, 'Go farther down'; and you will be put to shame. But if you recline in the lower place and one inferior to you comes in, the host will say to you, 'Go farther up'; and this will be advantageous to you *translation is Metzger's*].

20:29 Alx/Byz[**a great crowd**], Minor[a crowd].

20:30 Alx/Byz[**Have mercy on us, Lord**], Minor[*omits* Lord (JNT, REB, RSV, TEV) *others* Lord, have mercy on us (ASV, DRA, ESV, HCS, NAB, NAS, NAU, NIV, NJB, NLT, NRS, TLB)].

20:31 Alx/Byz[**Have mercy on us, Lord**], Minor[Lord, have mercy on us (ASV, DRA, ESV, HCS, JNT, MRD, NAB, NAS, NAU, NET, NIV, NJB, NLT, REB, RSV, ~TEV, ~TLB)].

20:34 Alx[**they received their sight and followed**], Byz[their eyes received sight and they followed (KJV, MRD, NKJ)].

21

¹ Now when they drew near Jerusalem, and came to Bethphage, at the Mount of Olives, Jesus sent two disciples, ² saying to them, "Go into the village opposite you, and immediately you will find a donkey tied, and a colt with her. Untie them and bring them to me. ³ If any one says anything to you, you shall say, 'The Lord has need of them,' and he will send them immediately." ⁴ This took place to fulfill what was spoken by the prophet, saying:

⁵   "Tell the daughter of Zion,
         'Behold, your King is coming to you,
             lowly, and sitting on a donkey,
                 and on a colt, the foal of a donkey.'"

⁶ The disciples went and did as Jesus had instructed them. ⁷ They brought the donkey and the colt, placed cloaks on them, and he sat on them. ⁸ And a very large crowd spread their cloaks on the road, while others cut branches from the trees and spread them on the road. ⁹ The crowds that went before him and those that followed shouted,

        "Hosanna to the Son of David!
            Blessed is he who comes in the name of the Lord!
        Hosanna in the highest!"

¹⁰ And when he entered Jerusalem, all the city was stirred, saying, "Who is this?" ¹¹ So the crowds said, "This is the prophet, Jesus from Nazareth of Galilee."

¹² And Jesus entered the temple and drove out all who sold and bought in the temple. And he overturned the tables of the money-changers and the seats of those who sold doves. ¹³ And he said to them, "It is written,

'My house shall be called a house of prayer.'
But you are making it a den of robbers."

¹⁴ And the blind and lame came to him in the temple, and he healed them. ¹⁵ But when the chief priests and the scribes saw the wonderful things that he did, and the children who were crying out in the temple, "Hosanna to the Son of David!" they were indignant. ¹⁶ And they said to him, "Do you hear what these are saying?" And Jesus said to them, "Yes. Have you never read, 'Out of the mouth of babes and nursing infants you have

---

21:1 Alx/Byz[**Bethphage**], Major[Bethsphage].

21:3 Alx['**The Lord has need of them,' and he will send them immediately** or 'The Lord has need of them, and he will send them back immediately'], Byz['The Lord has need of them' and he sends them immediately].

21:4 Alx[**This took place**], Byz[All this took place (DRA, KJV, MRD, NKJ)]; Alx/Byz[**the prophet**], Minor[adds Zechariah others Isaiah].

21:5 Alx[**on a colt**], Byz[omits on (DRA, KJV, NKJ, ~TLB)]; ~**Isaiah 62:11**, ~**Zechariah 9:9**.

21:6 Alx[**instructed**], Byz[commanded (DRA, KJV, MRD, ~NAB, NKJ, NLT)].

21:7 Alx[**placed cloaks on them**], Byz[placed their cloaks on them (ASV, DRA, ESV, HCS, JNT, KJV, MRD, NAB, NAS, NAU, NET, NIV, NJB, NKJ, NLT, NRS, REB, RSV, TEV, TLB)]; Alx/Major[**and he sat on them**], Byz[and set him on them (DRA, KJV, MRD, NKJ)].

21:8 **A very large crowd** or Most of the crowd.

21:9 Alx[**went before him**], Byz[omits him (DRA, KJV, NKJ, REB, TLB)]; **Hosanna** Hebrew Hoshanah, Please save or Save now; ~Psalms 118:25-26.

21:11 Alx[**the prophet, Jesus**], Byz[Jesus, the prophet (DRA, JNT, KJV, MRD, NAB, NIV, NKJ, NLT, TLB)]; Alx[**Nazareth**], Byz[Nazaret (JNT)].

21:12 Alx[**temple**], Byz[adds of God (ASV, DRA, KJV, MRD, NKJ, RSV)].

21:13 Alx[**you are making it**], Byz[you have made it (DRA, KJV, MRD, NKJ, NLT, TLB)]; **Isaiah 56:7**, ~Jeremiah 7:11.

21:14 Alx[**blind and lame**], Byz[lame and blind].

21:15 Alx[**the children who were crying**], Byz[the children crying (DRA, ESV, HCS, JNT, KJV, MRD, NAB, NET, NIV, NJB, NKJ, NLT, NRS, REB, RSV, TEV, TLB)].

21:16 **Psalms 8:2 LXX**.

perfected praise'?" **17** Then he left them and went out of the city to Bethany, and he lodged there.

18 In the morning, returning to the city, he was hungry. **19** And seeing a fig tree by the road he went to it, and found nothing on it but leaves only. And he said to it, "May no fruit ever come from you again!" And immediately the fig tree withered. **20** And when the disciples saw it, they marveled, saying, "How did the fig tree wither away so soon?" **21** And Jesus answered them, "Truly, I say to you, if you have faith and do not doubt, you will not only do what was done to the fig tree, but even if you say to this mountain, 'Be taken up and cast into the sea,' it will be done. **22** And whatever you ask in prayer, you will receive, if you have faith."

23 And when he entered the temple, the chief priests and the elders of the people came up to him as he was teaching, and said, "By what authority are you doing these things, and who gave you this authority?" **24** And Jesus answered them, "I also will ask you one question; and if you tell me the answer, then I also will tell you by what authority I do these things. **25** The baptism of John – where was it from? From heaven or from men?" And they reasoned among themselves, saying, "If we say, 'From heaven,' he will say to us, 'Why then did you not believe him?' **26** But if we say, 'From men,' we are afraid of the multitude; for all hold that John was a prophet." **27** So they answered Jesus, "We do not know." And he said to them, "Neither will I tell you by what authority I do these things.

28 "What do you think? A man had two sons. And he went to the first and said, 'Son, go and work in the vineyard today.' **29** He answered, 'I will not.' But afterward he regretted it and went. **30** But he went to the other and said the same thing. And he answered, 'I will, sir.' But he did not go. **31** Which of the two did the will of his father?" They said, "The first." Jesus said to them, "Truly, I say to you, the tax collectors and the harlots go into the kingdom of God before you. **32** For John came to you in the way of righteousness, and you did not believe him. But the tax collectors and the harlots believed him. And when you saw it, you did not even repent afterward and believe him.

33 "Hear another parable: there was a landowner who planted a vineyard and set a hedge around it, dug a wine press in it and built a tower. And he leased it to vine dressers and went into a far country. **34** When the harvest time drew near, he sent his servants to the tenants, to get his fruit. **35** And the tenants took his servants, beat one, killed one, and stoned another. **36** Again he sent other servants, more than the first, and they did the same to them. **37** Last of all, he sent his son to them saying, 'They will respect

---

21:18 Alx[**In the morning**], Byz[In the early morning (~HCS, NET, NIV, TEV)]; Alx[**returning**], Byz[as he returned (ASV, ~JNT, KJV, MRD, NAS, NET, NKJ, NRS, ~REB, ~TEV)].

21:24 Alx/Byz[**And Jesus answered**], Minor[*omits* And (DRA, ESV, HCS, JNT, MRD, NAB, NAU, NET, NIV, NJB, NLT, NRS, REB, RSV, TEV, TLB)].

21:25 Alx[**reasoned among themselves**], Byz[reasoned with themselves (ASV, KJV, NRS, RSV)].

21:28 Alx/Major[**A man**], Byz[A certain man (DRA, KJV, MRD)]; Alx/Byz[**and he went**], Minor[*omits* and (HCS, JNT, NAB, NET, NIV, NJB, ~NLT, NRS, REB, TEV, ~TLB)]; Alx[**the vineyard**], Byz[my vineyard (DRA, KJV, NKJ)].

21:29 Alx/Byz[*text*], Minor[He answered, 'I go, sir.' But he did not *others* He answered, 'I will, sir.' But he did not (NAS, REB) *others* He answered, 'I will not.' Afterward he regretted it and went].

21:30 Alx[**But he went to the other**], Byz[And he went to the second (ASV, KJV, NAS, NAU, NJB, NKJ, NRS, REB, RSV)]; Alx/Byz[**'I will, sir.' But he did not go**], Minor['I will not.' But afterward he regretted it and went (NAS, REB)].

21:31 Alx[**They said**], Byz[*adds* to him (DRA, KJV, MRD, NKJ)]; Alx/Byz[**The first**], Minor[The second (NAS, REB) *others* The last].

21:32 Alx[**you did not even repent afterward**], Byz[*omits* even (KJV, NET, NKJ)].

21:33 Alx[**a landowner**], Byz[a certain landowner (KJV, MRD, NKJ, NLT, TLB)].

my son,' 38 But when the tenants saw the son, they said to themselves, 'This is the heir. Come, let us kill him and have his inheritance.' 39 So they took him and cast him out of the vineyard and killed him. 40 Therefore, when the owner of the vineyard comes, what will he do to those tenants?" 41 They said to him, "He will put those wretches to a miserable death, and lease the vineyard to other tenants who will give him the fruits in their seasons." 42 Jesus said to them, "Have you never read in the Scriptures:

> 'The stone which the builders rejected
> > has become the chief cornerstone.
> This was the Lord's doing,
> > and it is marvelous in our eyes'?

43 "Therefore I tell you, the kingdom of God will be taken away from you and given to a nation bearing the fruits of it. 44 [And he who falls on this stone will be broken to pieces. But on whomever it falls, it will crush him.]"

45 When the chief priests and the Pharisees heard his parables, they perceived that he was speaking about them. 46 But when they tried to arrest him, they feared the multitudes, because they held him to be a prophet.

22

1 And again Jesus spoke to them in parables, saying: 2 "The kingdom of heaven is like a king who arranged a marriage for his son, 3 and sent out his servants to call those who were invited to the wedding. But they were not willing to come. 4 Again, he sent out other servants, saying, 'Tell those who are invited, "See, I have prepared my dinner. My oxen and fatted cattle are killed, and everything is ready. Come to the wedding."' 5 But they made light of it and went off, one to his own farm, another to his business. 6 And the rest seized his servants, treated them shamefully, and killed them. 7 But the king was enraged. He sent his army and destroyed those murderers and burned their city. 8 Then he said to his servants, 'The wedding is ready, but those who were invited were not worthy. 9 Go therefore to the highways, and invite to the marriage feast as many as you find.' 10 And those servants went out into the streets and gathered all whom they found, both bad and good. So the wedding hall was filled with guests. 11 But when the king came in to see the guests, he saw a man there who did not have on a wedding garment. 12 And he said to him, 'Friend, how did you get in here without a wedding garment?' And he was speechless. 13 Then the king said to the attendants, 'Bind his feet and hands. Cast him into the outer darkness, where there will be weeping and gnashing of teeth.' 14 For many are called, but few are chosen."

15 Then the Pharisees went and took counsel how to entangle him in his talk. 16 And they sent their disciples to him, along with the Herodians, saying, "Teacher, we know that you are true, and teach the way of God in truth, and you care for no man; for you do not regard the position of men. 17 Tell us, then, what do you think? Is it lawful to pay taxes to Caesar, or not?" 18 But Jesus, aware of their malice, said, "Why are you testing me, you hypocrites? 19 Show me the money for the tax." And they brought him a denarius.

21:38 Alx[**have his inheritance**], Byz[seize his inheritance (ASV, HCS, JNT, KJV, ~MRD, NAS, NAU, NIV, NJB, NKJ)].

21:39 Alx/Byz[**cast him out of the vineyard and killed him**], Minor[killed him and cast him out of the vineyard].

21:42 **chief cornerstone** or capstone or keystone; **Psalms 118:22-23.**

21:44 Alx/Byz[*text*], Minor[*omits* (JNT, NJB, REB, RSV, TEV)].

22:7 Alx[**But the king was enraged**], Byz[But when that king heard it, he was enraged (DRA, KJV, NKJ)], Major[And when that king heard it, he was enraged (MRD)].

22:10 Alx[**all whom they found**], Byz[as many as they found (ASV, KJV)]; Alx/Byz[**the wedding hall**], Minor[the bridal chamber (DRA)].

22:13 Alx[**Cast**], Byz[Take him away, and cast (KJV, NKJ)].

[20] And he said to them, "Whose image and inscription is this?" [21] They said to him, "Caesar's." Then he said to them, "Render therefore to Caesar the things that are Caesar's, and to God the things that are God's." [22] When they heard it, they marveled. And they left him and went away.

[23] That same day the Sadducees, saying there is no resurrection, came to him and asked him a question, [24] saying, "Teacher, Moses said that *if a man dies, having no children, his brother must marry the widow, and raise up children for his brother.* [25] Now there were seven brothers among us. The first one married and died, and having no children, he left his wife to his brother. [26] So the second also, and the third, down to the seventh. [27] After them all, the woman died. [28] Therefore, in the resurrection, whose wife of the seven will she be? For they all had her." [29] But Jesus answered them, "You are wrong, because you do not know the Scriptures or the power of God. [30] For in the resurrection they neither marry nor are given in marriage, but are like angels in heaven. [31] But as for the resurrection of the dead, have you not read what was said to you by God, [32] *'I am the God of Abraham, and the God of Isaac, and the God of Jacob'*? He is not [the] God of the dead, but of the living." [33] And when the multitudes heard this, they were astonished at his teaching.

[34] But when the Pharisees heard that he had silenced the Sadducees, they gathered together. [35] And one of them, [a lawyer,] asked him a question, to test him. [36] "Teacher, which is the great commandment in the Law?" [37] But he said to him, *"'You shall love the Lord your God with all your heart, and with all your soul, and with all your mind.'* [38] This is the great and first commandment. [39] And the second is like it: *'You shall love your neighbor as yourself.'* [40] On these two commandments all the Law hangs, and the Prophets."

[41] While the Pharisees were gathered together, Jesus asked them, [42] "What do you think about the Christ? Whose son is he?" They said to him, "The son of David." [43] He said to them, "How is it then that David, in the Spirit, calls him 'Lord', saying,

[44]   *'The Lord said to my Lord,*
    "Sit at my right hand,
        till I put your enemies under your feet"'?

22:20 Alx/Byz[**And he said to them**], Minor[And Jesus said to them (DRA, ESV, MRD, NET, REB, RSV)].

22:21 Alx/Byz[**They said to him**], Minor[*omits* to him (ESV, JNT, MRD, NAB, NET, NIV, NJB, NLT, NRS, REB, RSV, TEV, TLB)].

22:23 Alx[**saying**], Byz[who say (ASV, DRA, ESV, HCS, JNT, KJV, MRD, NAS, NAU, NET, NIV, NJB, NKJ, NLT, REB, RSV, TLB)].

22:24 ~**Deuteronomy 25:5**.

22:27 Alx[**the woman died**], Byz[*adds* also (DRA, KJV, MRD, NKJ, NLT, TLB)].

22:30 Alx[**angels**], Byz[angels of God (DRA, KJV, MRD, NKJ)].

22:32 Alx[**He is not the God of the dead**], Byz[God is not the God of the dead (ASV, KJV, NKJ, ~REB, TLB)], Minor[He is not God of the dead (ESV, JNT, NJB, NRS, RSV)]; **Exodus 3:6, 15**.

22:35 Alx/Byz[**a lawyer**], Minor[*omits* (NJB, REB)]; Alx[**test him**], Byz[*adds* saying (KJV, NKJ)].

22:37 Alx[**But he said to him**], Byz[But Jesus said to him (DRA, KJV, MRD, NET, NIV, NJB, NKJ, NLT, TEV, TLB)]; ~**Deuteronomy 6:5**.

22:38 Alx[**great and first**], Byz[first and great (KJV, NET, NIV, NKJ, NLT, TLB)].

22:39 Alx/Byz[**And the second**], Minor[*omits* And (HCS, NAB, NAS, NAU, NET, NJB, NLT, REB, TEV, TLB)]; Alx/Byz[**like it**], Minor[like this (ASV, DRA, ~NLT, ~TLB)]; **Leviticus 19:18**.

22:40 Alx[**all the Law hangs, and the Prophets**], Byz[all the Law and the Prophets hang (~DRA, ESV, HCS, JNT, KJV, MRD, NAB, NAS, NAU, NET, NIV, NJB, NLT, NRS, ~REB, RSV, TEV, TLB)].

22:43 Alx/Byz[**He said to them**], Minor[Jesus said to them (NLT, TEV, TLB)]; **in the Spirit** *Greek* in spirit.

22:44 Alx[**till I put your enemies under your feet**], Byz[till I make your enemies your footstool (DRA, KJV, NJB, NKJ)]; **Psalms 110:1**.

⁴⁵ If David then calls him 'Lord,' how is he his son?" ⁴⁶ And no one was able to answer him a word, nor from that day did any one dare to ask him any more questions.

23 ¹ Then Jesus said to the crowds and to his disciples, ² "The scribes and the Pharisees sit in Moses' seat. ³ So you must do and observe whatever they tell you. But do not do what they do; for they preach, but do not practice. ⁴ Rather, they bind heavy burdens, [hard to bear,] and lay them on men's shoulders; but they themselves will not move them with their finger. ⁵ But they do all their works to be seen by men; for they make their *phylacteries* broad and their *tassels* long. ⁶ And they love the place of honor at feasts and the best seats in the synagogues, ⁷ and greetings in the marketplaces, and to be called by men, 'Rabbi.' ⁸ But you are not to be called 'Rabbi,' for you have only one Teacher, and you are all brothers. ⁹ And do not call anyone on earth your 'Father,' for you have one heavenly Father. ¹⁰ Nor are you to be called 'Leader,' since you have one Leader, the Christ. ¹¹ He who is greatest among you shall be your servant. ¹² For whoever exalts himself will be humbled, and whoever humbles himself will be exalted.

¹³ "But woe to you, scribes and Pharisees, hypocrites! Because you shut up the kingdom of heaven against men. For you neither enter yourselves, nor do you allow those who would enter to go in. ⁽¹⁴⁾

¹⁵ "Woe to you, scribes and Pharisees, hypocrites! For you travel land and sea to win a single proselyte, and when he becomes one, you make him twice as much a son of hell as yourselves.

¹⁶ "Woe to you, blind guides, who say, 'If any one swears by the temple, it is nothing; but if any one swears by the gold of the temple, he is bound by his oath.' ¹⁷ You blind fools! For which is greater, the gold or the temple that has made the gold sacred? ¹⁸ And you say, 'If anyone swears by the altar, it means nothing; but if anyone swears by the gift that is on it, he is bound by his oath.' ¹⁹ You blind men! For which is greater, the gift or the altar that makes the gift sacred? ²⁰ Therefore, he who swears by the altar swears by it

---

23:3 Alx[**do and observe whatever they tell you**], Byz[observe and do whatever they tell you to observe (KJV, MRD, NKJ, TEV)].

23:4 Alx[**Rather**], Byz[For (DRA, KJV, NKJ)]; Alx/Byz[**hard to bear**], Minor[*omits* (JNT, MRD, NAS, NAU, NIV, NJB, ~NLT, REB, Metzger)]; Alx[**they themselves**], Byz[*omits* themselves (DRA, JNT, MRD, NAB, NJB, NLT, TEV)].

23:5 Alx/Byz[**for they make**], Major[but they make (~HCS, ~KJV, ~NAB, ~NIV, ~NJB, ~NKJ, ~NLT, ~REB, ~TEV, ~TLB)]; Alx[**their tassels**], Byz[the tassels of their garments (ASV, KJV, MRD, NAS, NAU, NIV, NKJ, NLT, REB, TEV, TLB)]; **phylacteries…tassels** *i.e. tefillin…tzitzit, compare* Exodus 13:9, Numbers 15:38-39, Deuteronomy 6:8, 22:12, Matthew 6:1, 5, 9:20, 14:36.

23:7 Alx[**Rabbi**], Byz[Rabbi, Rabbi (KJV, NKJ, TLB)].

23:8 Alx[**Teacher**], Byz[Teacher, the Christ (NKJ)] , Major[Leader, the Christ (KJV)].

23:9 Alx/Byz[**your 'Father'**], Minor[*omits* your (JNT, ~MRD, NIV, NLT, REB, TEV, TLB)]; Alx[**heavenly Father**], Byz[Father, who is in the heavens (~ASV, ~DRA, ~ESV, ~HCS, ~JNT, ~KJV, ~MRD, ~NAB, ~NAS, ~NAU, ~NET, ~NIV, ~NJB, ~NKJ, ~NLT, ~NRS, REB, ~RSV, ~TEV, ~TLB)].

23:10 Alx[**since**], Byz[for (ASV, DRA, ESV, KJV, MRD, NAS, NAU, NET, NIV, NJB, NKJ, NLT, NRS, ~REB, RSV, TLB)].

23:13 Alx[**But woe to you**], Byz[*omits* But (MRD, NAB, NIV, NJB, NLT, REB, TEV, TLB)].

23:(14) Alx[*omits*], Byz[*adds after verse 12 or 13* Woe to you, scribes and Pharisees, hypocrites! For you devour widows' houses, and for a show make long prayers. Therefore you will receive greater condemnation (ASV, DRA, HCS, KJV, MRD, NAS, NAU, NKJ, TLB)].

23:15 **hell** *Greek* Gehenna.

23:17 Alx[**has made the gold sacred**], Byz[makes the gold sacred (DRA, JNT, KJV, MRD, NET, NIV, NJB, NKJ, NLT, REB, TEV, TLB)].

23:19 Alx[**You blind men**], Byz[You blind fools (KJV, MRD, NKJ)].

and by everything on it. ²¹ And he who swears by the temple, swears by it and by him who dwells in it. ²² And he who swears by heaven, swears by the throne of God and by him who sits on it.

²³ "Woe to you, scribes and Pharisees, hypocrites! For you pay tithe of mint and dill and cummin, and have neglected the weightier matters of the Law, justice and mercy and faith. [But] these you ought to have done, without neglecting the others. ²⁴ You blind guides, who strain out a gnat and swallow a camel!

²⁵ "Woe to you, scribes and Pharisees, hypocrites! For you cleanse the outside of the cup and of the dish, but inside they are full of extortion and self-indulgence. ²⁶ Blind Pharisee! First cleanse the inside of the cup, that the outside of it may be clean also. ²⁷ Woe to you, scribes and Pharisees, hypocrites! For you are like whitewashed tombs which outwardly appear beautiful, but inside they are full of dead men's bones and all uncleanness. ²⁸ Even so you also outwardly appear righteous to men, but inside you are full of hypocrisy and lawlessness.

²⁹ "Woe to you, scribes and Pharisees, hypocrites! For you build the tombs of the prophets and adorn the monuments of the righteous, ³⁰ And you say, 'If we had lived in the days of our forefathers, we would not have taken part with them in shedding the blood of the prophets.' ³¹ Thus you witness against yourselves, that you are sons of those who murdered the prophets. ³² Fill up, then, the measure of your fathers. ³³ You serpents! You brood of vipers, how are you to escape being sentenced to hell? ³⁴ Therefore I send you prophets and wise men and scribes. Some of them you will kill and crucify, and some you will scourge in your synagogues and persecute from town to town, ³⁵ that on you may come all the righteous blood shed on the earth, from the blood of righteous Abel to the blood of Zechariah, son of Berechiah, whom you murdered between the temple and the altar. ³⁶ Truly, I say to you, all this will come upon this generation.

³⁷ "O Jerusalem, Jerusalem, you who kill the prophets and stone those who are sent to you! How often I have longed to gather your children together, as a hen gathers her chicks under her wings, but you were not willing! ³⁸ Behold, your house is left to you desolate. ³⁹ For I tell you, you will never see me again, until you say, *'Blessed is he who comes in the name of the Lord.'"*

24 ¹ Jesus left the temple, and was going away when his disciples came to point out to him the buildings of the temple. ² But he answered them, "You see

---

23:²¹ Alx[**dwells**], Byz[dwelt].

23:²³ Alx/Byz[**But these you ought to have done**], Major[*omits* But (DRA, ESV, HCS, JNT, KJV, MRD, NET, NIV, NJB, NKJ, ~NLT, NRS, REB, RSV, TEV, TLB)].

23:²⁴ Alx/Byz[**who strain**], Minor[straining (ESV, JNT, NJB, RSV)].

23:²⁵ Alx[**self-indulgence**], Byz[unrighteousness (DRA, MRD)].

23:²⁶ Alx[**cup**], Byz[cup and dish (ASV, DRA, ESV, KJV, MRD, NAS, NAU, NIV, NJB, NKJ, NLT, RSV)]; Alx[**outside of it**], Byz[outside of them (~ASV, KJV, MRD, NKJ)], Minor[outside (DRA, ESV, JNT, NAB, NET, NIV, ~NJB, NLT, NRS, REB, RSV, TEV, TLB)].

23:³² Alx/Byz[**Fill up**], Minor[You fill up (TLB)]; **measure** *or* standard.

23:³³ **hell** *Greek* Gehenna.

23:³⁴ Alx[**Some of them**], Byz[And some of them (DRA, KJV, NLT, NRS, RSV, TLB)].

23:³⁶ Alx[**I say to you**], Byz[*adds* that (JNT, MRD)].

23:³⁷ Alx[**her chicks under her wings** *Greek* her chicks under the wings], Byz[her own chicks under the wings], Minor[the chicks under the wings].

23:³⁸ Alx/Byz[**desolate**], Minor[*omits* (~NJB)].

23:³⁹ Psalms 118:26.

24:¹ Alx[**left the temple, and was going away**], Byz[left, and was going away from the temple (HCS, KJV, NKJ, TEV, TLB)].

24:² Alx[**But he answered them**], Byz[But Jesus said to them (KJV, NKJ)].

all these things, do you not? Truly, I say to you, not one stone here can be left upon another, that will not be thrown down."

³ Now as he sat on the Mount of Olives, the disciples came to him privately, saying, "Tell us, when will this be? And what will be the sign of your coming, and of the end of the age?" ⁴ And Jesus answered them: "Take heed that no one deceives you. ⁵ For many will come in my name, saying, 'I am the Christ,' and will deceive many. ⁶ And you will hear of wars and rumors of wars. See that you are not alarmed; for these things must come to pass, but the end is not yet. ⁷ For nation will rise against nation, and kingdom against kingdom, and there will be famines and earthquakes in various places. ⁸ All these are the beginning of birth pains. ⁹ Then they will deliver you up to tribulation, and put you to death; and you will be hated by all nations for my name's sake. ¹⁰ And then many will fall away, and will betray one another, and hate one another. ¹¹ And many false prophets will rise up and deceive many. ¹² And because wickedness will increase, the love of most will grow cold. ¹³ But he who endures to the end will be saved. ¹⁴ And this gospel of the kingdom will be preached in the whole world as a testimony to all nations, and then the end will come.

¹⁵ "So when you see standing in the holy place 'the abomination of desolation,' spoken of by the prophet Daniel (let the reader understand), ¹⁶ then let those who are in Judea flee into the mountains. ¹⁷ Let him who is on the housetop not go down to take things out of his house. ¹⁸ And let him who is in the field not go back to get his coat. ¹⁹ But woe for those who are pregnant and for those who are nursing babies in those days! ²⁰ Pray that your flight may not be in winter or on a Sabbath. ²¹ For then there will be great tribulation, such as has not been from the beginning of the world until now, no, and never will be. ²² And if those days had not been shortened, no flesh would be saved; but for the sake of the elect those days will be shortened. ²³ Then if any one says to you, 'Look, here is the Christ!' or 'There he is!' do not believe it. ²⁴ For false christs and false prophets will arise and show great signs and wonders to deceive, if possible, even the elect. ²⁵ See, I have told you beforehand. ²⁶ So if they say to you, 'There he is, out in the desert,' do not go out; or, 'Here he is, in the inner rooms,' do not believe it. ²⁷ For as the lightning comes from the east and flashes to the west, so will the coming of the Son of Man be. ²⁸ Wherever the carcass is, there the eagles will be gathered together.

²⁹ "Immediately after the tribulation of those days
the sun will be darkened,
and the moon will not give its light.
The stars will fall from heaven,

24:⁶ Alx[**these things**], Byz[all these things (KJV, MRD, NKJ)].

24:⁷ Alx[**famines**], Byz[*adds* and pestilences (DRA, KJV, MRD, NKJ)].

24:¹⁰ **fall away** *or* stumble.

24:¹⁵ ~**Daniel 9:27, 11:31, 12:11**.

24:¹⁶ Alx[**into the mountains**], Byz[over the mountains].

24:¹⁷ Alx/Byz[**to take things out of his house**], Minor[to take anything out of his house (DRA, ESV, KJV, MRD, NET, NIV, NKJ, NRS, RSV, ~TLB)].

24:¹⁸ Alx[**get his coat**], Byz[get his clothes (HCS, KJV, ~MRD, NKJ, TLB)].

24:²⁰ Alx/Major[**on a Sabbath**], Byz[in a Sabbath (~REB)].

24:²⁴ Alx/Byz[**to deceive, if possible, even the elect**], Minor[so that, if possible, even the elect will be deceived (TLB)].

24:²⁶ Alx/Byz[**26 So if they say to you**], Minor[So if they say to you 26].

24:²⁷ Alx[**so will the coming**], Byz[so also will the coming (KJV, NKJ)].

24:²⁸ Alx[**Wherever the carcass is**], Byz[For wherever the carcass is (KJV, ~MRD, NKJ, ~NLT, ~TLB)].

24:²⁹ Isaiah 13:10, 34:4.

and the powers of the heavens will be shaken.

30 Then the sign of the Son of Man will appear in heaven, and then all the tribes of the earth will mourn. And they will see *the Son of Man coming on the clouds of heaven* with power and great glory. **31** And he will send out his angels with a great trumpet, and they will gather together his elect from the four winds, from one end of heaven to [the] other.

32 "Now learn this lesson from the fig tree: as soon as its branch becomes tender and puts forth its leaves, you know that summer is near. **33** So also, when you see all these things, you know that it is near, right at the door. **34** Truly, I tell you that this generation will by no means pass away till all these things take place. **35** Heaven and earth will pass away, but my words will never pass away.

36 "But of that day and hour no one knows, not even the angels of heaven, nor the Son, but the Father only. **37** For as the days of Noah were, so will the coming of the Son of Man be. **38** For as in [those] days before the flood, they were eating and drinking, marrying and giving in marriage, until the day that Noah entered the ark. **39** And they did not know until the flood came and took them all away. So [also] will the coming of the Son of Man be. **40** Then two men will be in the field; one is taken and one left. **41** Two women are grinding at the mill; one is taken and one left. **42** Watch therefore, for you do not know on what day your Lord is coming. **43** But know this, that if the owner of the house had known at what time of the night the thief was coming, he would have watched and would not have let his house be broken into. **44** Therefore you also must be ready, for the Son of Man is coming at an hour you do not expect.

45 "Who then is the faithful and wise servant, whom the master has set over his housekeepers, to give them their food at the proper time? **46** Blessed is that servant whom his master when he comes will find so doing. **47** Truly, I say to you, he will set him over all his possessions. **48** But if that wicked servant says to himself, 'My master is delayed,' **49** and

---

24:30 Alx/Byz[**and then all the tribes**], Minor[*omits* then (JNT, NAB, NET, NIV, NLT, REB, TEV, TLB)]; Daniel 7:13.

24:31 Alx[**a great trumpet**], Byz[a great trumpet sound (ASV, ESV, KJV, ~NAB, NET, NIV, NKJ, NLT, NRS, ~REB, RSV, TEV, TLB)], Minor[a trumpet and a great sound (DRA)].

24:32 Alx/Byz[**and puts forth its leaves**], Minor[and its leaves are put forth (DRA, JNT, MRD, NIV, NJB, NLT, REB, TLB)].

24:33 **it is near** *or* he is near.

24:34 Alx[**I tell you that**], Byz[*omits* that (ASV, DRA, ESV, HCS, KJV, NAB, NAS, NAU, NET, NIV, NJB, NKJ, NLT, NRS, REB, RSV, TEV, TLB)]; **generation** *or* race.

24:36 Alx[**nor the Son**], Byz[*omits* (DRA, KJV, MRD, NET, NKJ)]; Alx[**the Father only**], Byz[my Father only (KJV, NKJ)].

24:37 Alx[**For as the days**], Byz[But as the days (ASV, DRA, ~ESV 2001 edition, ~HCS, KJV, MRD, ~NIV, ~NJB, NKJ, ~NLT, ~REB, ~RSV, ~TEV, ~TLB)]; Alx[**so will**], Byz[so also will (DRA, KJV, NKJ)].

24:38 Alx[**For as in those days**], Byz[For even as in the days (DRA, ~JNT, KJV, MRD, NIV, NKJ, TEV, TLB)]; Alx/Byz[**before the flood**], Minor[of the flood].

24:39 Alx/Byz[**so also will the coming**], Minor[*omits* also (ASV, ESV, HCS, JNT, MRD, NAS, NAU, ~NET, NIV, NJB, NLT, REB, RSV, TEV, TLB)].

24:40 Alx[**one is taken and one left**], Byz[the one is taken and the other left (JNT, KJV, MRD, NIV, NKJ, NLT, ~REB, TEV, TLB)].

24:42 Alx[**day**], Byz[hour (DRA, KJV, MRD, NKJ)].

24:45 Alx[**the master**], Byz[his master (ASV, DRA, ESV, HCS, JNT, KJV, MRD, NAS, NAU, NKJ, NRS, REB, RSV, TEV, ~TLB)]; Alx[**housekeepers**], Byz[caretakers].

24:46 Alx[**so doing**], Byz[doing so (NAB, NIV, NJB, TEV, TLB)].

24:48 Alx/Byz[**that wicked servant**], Minor[the wicked servant (NJB, NLT, ~REB)]; Alx[**delayed**], Byz[delaying his coming (~DRA, KJV, MRD, NAS, NAU, NKJ, REB, TEV, TLB)].

24:49 Alx/Byz[**his fellow servants**], Major[the fellow servants (NLT, REB)]; Alx/Byz[**and shall eat**

he then begins to beat his fellow servants, and shall eat and drink with the drunkards, [50] the master of that servant will come on a day when he does not expect him and at an hour he is not aware of. [51] And he will cut him to pieces and assign him a place with the hypocrites, where there will be weeping and gnashing of teeth.

25

[1] "Then the kingdom of heaven shall be likened to ten virgins who took their lamps and went out to meet the bridegroom. [2] Five of them were foolish, and five were wise. [3] For when the foolish took their lamps, they took no oil with them. [4] But the wise took flasks of oil with their lamps. [5] While the bridegroom was delayed, they all slumbered and slept. [6] But at midnight there was a cry: 'Behold, the bridegroom! Come out to meet [him].' [7] Then all those virgins rose and trimmed their lamps. [8] And the foolish said to the wise, 'Give us some of your oil, for our lamps are going out.' [9] But the wise replied, 'No, there may not be enough for both us and you. Go rather to those who sell oil and buy some for yourselves.' [10] And while they went to buy, the bridegroom came. And those who were ready went in with him to the wedding, and the door was shut. [11] Afterward the other virgins came also, saying, 'Lord, Lord, open to us!' [12] But he replied, 'Truly, I say to you, I do not know you.' [13] Therefore keep watch, for you know neither the day nor the hour.

[14] "For it will be like a man going on a journey, who called his servants and entrusted his property to them. [15] To one he gave five talents, to another two, and to another one, to each according to his ability. Then he went on his journey at once. [16] He who had received the five talents went and traded with them; and he gained five more. [17] Likewise, he who had the two talents gained two more. [18] But he who had received the one talent went and dug in the ground, and hid his master's money. [19] Now after a long time the master of those servants came and settled accounts with them. [20] So he who had received the five talents came and brought five other talents, saying, 'Master, you

---

and drink], Major[and to eat and drink (KJV, NET, NIV, NKJ, REB, TEV)].

24:51 **cut him to pieces** *or* cut him off.

25:1 Alx/Byz[**the bridegroom**], Minor[*adds* and the bride (MRD, DRA)].

25:2 Alx[**foolish...wise**], Byz[wise...foolish (KJV, MRD, NKJ, TLB)].

25:3 Alx[**For when the foolish**], Byz[When those who were foolish (~HCS, ~JNT, KJV, ~MRD, ~NAB, ~NET, ~NIV, ~NJB, NKJ, ~NLT, ~NRS, ~REB, ~TEV, ~TLB)], Minor[But when the foolish (DRA, TLB)]; Alx/Major[**their lamps**], Byz[their own lamps], Minor[the lamps (JNT, ~TLB)].

25:4 Alx[**flasks of oil**], Byz[their flasks of oil (ASV, ~DRA, HCS, KJV, NKJ)].

25:6 Alx[**the bridegroom**], Byz[*adds* is coming (DRA, ~JNT, KJV, MRD, NKJ, NLT, TLB)]; Alx/Byz[**meet him**], Minor[*omits* him].

25:9 Alx[**No, there may not be enough**], Byz[There may not be enough (ASV, DRA, ESV, NJB, NLT, RSV, TLB)]; Alx[**go rather**], Byz[but go rather (KJV, MRD, NKJ)].

25:11 Alx/Byz[**the other virgins came also**], Minor[*omits* also (JNT, NAB, NJB, NLT, REB, TEV, TLB)].

25:13 Alx[**day nor the hour**], Byz[*adds* in which the Son of Man is coming (KJV, NKJ, ~NLT, ~TLB)].

25:15 *a* **talent** *was more than fifteen years' wages for a laborer.*

25:15-16 Alx/Byz[**he went on his journey at once. 16 He who had received the five talents went and traded**], Minor[he went on his journey. 16 He who had received the five talents went at once and traded (ASV, ESV, JNT, NAS, NAU, NET, NIV, NJB, ~NLT, NRS, REB, RSV, TEV, TLB)].

25:16 Alx[**He who had received**], Byz[But he who had received (DRA, KJV, MRD, NKJ)]; Alx[**and he gained five more**], Byz[and he made five talents more (ASV, ESV, KJV, ~NAB, ~NAS, ~NAU, ~NJB, NKJ, ~NRS, ~REB, RSV, ~TEV, ~TLB)].

25:17 Alx[**Likewise**], Byz[And likewise (ASV, DRA, ESV, KJV, MRD, NIV, NKJ, REB, RSV)]; Alx[**gained two more**], Byz[and he gained two more (KJV)].

25:20 Alx[**five more talents**], Byz[*adds* besides them (DRA, KJV, NKJ)].

delivered to me five talents. Look, I have gained five more talents.' 21 His master said to him, 'Well done, good and faithful servant. You have been faithful over a few things. I will make you ruler over many things. Enter into the joy of your master.' 22 [Then] he also who had the two talents came and said, 'Master, you delivered to me two talents. Look, I have gained two more talents.' 23 His master said to him, 'Well done, good and faithful servant. You have been faithful over a few things. I will make you ruler over many things. Enter into the joy of your master.' 24 Then he who had received the one talent came and said, 'Master, I knew you to be a hard man, reaping where you have not sown, and gathering where you have not scattered seed. 25 So I was afraid, and went and hid your talent in the ground. Here you have what is yours.' 26 But his master answered him, 'You wicked and lazy servant! You knew that I reap where I have not sown, and gather where I have not scattered seed? 27 Then you ought to have deposited my money with the bankers, and at my coming I would have received back my own with interest. 28 Therefore take the talent from him, and give it to him who has the ten talents. 29 For to every one who has will more be given, and he will have abundance. But of him who does not have, even what he has will be taken away from him. 30 And cast the worthless servant into the outer darkness, where there will be weeping and gnashing of teeth.'

31 "When the Son of Man comes in his glory, and all the angels with him, then he will sit on his glorious throne. 32 All the nations will be gathered before him, and he will separate them one from another as a shepherd separates the sheep from the goats. 33 And he will put the sheep on his right hand, but the goats on the left. 34 Then the King will say to those on his right hand, 'Come, you blessed of my Father. Inherit the kingdom prepared for you from the foundation of the world. 35 For I was hungry and you gave me food. I was thirsty and you gave me drink. I was a stranger and you took me in. 36 I was naked and you clothed me. I was sick and you visited me. I was in prison and you came to me.' 37 Then the righteous will answer him, 'Lord, when did we see you hungry and feed you, or thirsty and give you drink? 38 When did we see you a stranger and take you in, or naked and clothe you? 39 When did we see you sick or in prison and go to visit you?' 40 And the King will answer them, 'Truly, I say to you, as you did it to one of the least of these my brothers, you did it to me.'

41 "Then he will say to those on his left hand, 'Depart from me, [you who are] cursed, into the eternal fire prepared for the devil and his angels. 42 For I was hungry and you gave me no food. I was thirsty and you gave me no drink. 43 I was a stranger and you did not take me in, naked and you did not clothe me, sick and in prison and you did not visit me.' 44 Then they also will answer, 'Lord, when did we see you hungry or thirsty or a

---

25:21 Alx/Byz[**His master**], Major[And his master].

25:22 Alx[**Then he also**], Byz[He also (JNT, KJV, ~MRD, NAS, NAU, NET, NIV, NJB, NKJ, ~TEV, TLB)]; Alx[**who had the two talents**], Byz[who had received the two talents (ASV, DRA, JNT, KJV, NAB, NAS, NAU, NKJ, TEV, TLB)]; Alx[**two more talents**], Byz[*adds* besides them (KJV, ~MRD, NKJ)].

25:27 Alx[**my money** *plural*], Byz[my money *singular*].

25:29 Alx[**But of him...from him**]; Byz[But from him...from him (~ASV, ~DRA, ~ESV, HCS, ~JNT, ~KJV, ~MRD, ~NAB, ~NAS, ~NAU, ~NKJ, ~NLT, ~NRS, ~REB, ~RSV, TLB)].

25:31 Alx[**angels**], Byz[holy angels (KJV, MRD, NKJ)].

25:39 Alx[**sick**], Byz[weak].

25:40 Alx/Byz[**my brothers**], Minor[*omits*].

25:41 Alx/Byz[**you who are cursed**], Minor[cursed (~NAS, ~NAU)]; Alx/Byz[**fire prepared**], Minor[which was prepared (ASV, DRA, MRD, NAS, NAU, NET, TEV) *others* which my father prepared].

25:42 Alx/Byz[**I was thirsty**], Minor[And I was thirsty (MRD)].

25:44 Alx/Byz[**answer**], Minor[answer him (DRA, KJV, NKJ, TEV)].

stranger or naked or sick or in prison, and did not serve you?' [45] Then he will answer them, 'Truly, I say to you, as you did not do it to one of the least of these, you did not do it to me.' [46] And they will go away into eternal punishment, but the righteous into eternal life."

26

[1] When Jesus had finished all these sayings, he said to his disciples, [2] "You know that after two days is the Passover, and the Son of Man will be delivered up to be crucified." [3] Then the chief priests and the elders of the people assembled in the palace of the high priest, who was called Caiaphas, [4] and they plotted to arrest Jesus by stealth and kill him. [5] But they said, "Not during the feast, lest there be a riot among the people."

[6] Now when Jesus was at Bethany in the house of Simon the leper, [7] a woman came up to him with an alabaster flask of very expensive perfume, and she poured it on his head as he sat at the table. [8] But when the disciples saw it, they were indignant, saying, "Why this waste? [9] For this might have been sold for a high price and given to the poor." [10] But Jesus, aware of this, said to them, "Why do you trouble the woman? For she has done a beautiful thing to me. [11] For you always have the poor with you, but you will not always have me. [12] For in pouring this perfume on my body, she did it to prepare me for burial. [13] Truly, I say to you, wherever this gospel is preached in the whole world, what she has done will also be told in memory of her."

[14] Then one of the twelve, who was called Judas Iscariot, went to the chief priests [15] and said, "What are you willing to give me if I deliver him to you?" And they counted out to him thirty pieces of silver. [16] And from that moment he sought an opportunity to betray him.

[17] Now on the first day of the Feast of Unleavened Bread, the disciples came to Jesus, saying, "Where do you want us to prepare for you to eat the Passover?" [18] He said, "Go into the city to a certain man, and say to him, 'The Teacher says, my time is at hand. I will keep the Passover at your house with my disciples.'" [19] So the disciples did as Jesus had directed them; and they prepared the Passover. [20] When evening had come, he sat at the table with the twelve. [21] And as they were eating, he said, "Truly, I say to you, one of you will betray me." [22] And they were very sorrowful, and each one began to say to him, "Is it I, Lord?" [23] He answered, "He who has dipped his hand in the dish with me will betray me. [24] The Son of Man goes just as it is written of him, but woe to that man by whom the Son of Man is betrayed! It would have been better for that man if he had not been born." [25] Then Judas, who was betraying him, answered, "Rabbi, is it I?" He said to him, "You said it."

26:3 Alx[**chief priests**], Byz[*adds* the scribes (KJV, MRD, NKJ)].

26:6 **leper** *can refer to several skin diseases.*

26:8 Alx[**when the disciples**], Byz[when his disciples (KJV, MRD, NKJ)].

26:9 Alx[**For this might have been sold**], Byz[For this perfume might have been sold (ASV, KJV, MRD, NAS, NAU, NIV, NKJ, NRS, RSV, TEV)].

26:14 Alx/Byz[**Iscariot**], Minor[Scariot], Alt[from Kerioth (~JNT)]; **Iscariot** *Hebraism Ish Keriot* a man from Kerioth *or possibly Sicarios* assassin *or* bandit.

26:17 Alx[**saying**], Byz[*adds* to him (KJV, MRD, NKJ, REB, TEV)].

26:20 Alx/Byz[**twelve**], Minor[*adds* disciples (ASV, DRA, JNT, MRD, NAS, NAU, NLT, REB, RSV, TEV)].

26:22 Alx[**each one**], Byz[each of them (NKJ)], Minor[each one of them (KJV, MRD)]; Alx/Byz[**say to him**], Minor[*omits* to him (DRA, NLT, TLB)].

²⁶ Now as they were eating, Jesus took bread, and blessed, and broke it, and, giving it to the disciples, said, "Take, eat; this is my body." ²⁷ Then he took a cup, and gave thanks, and gave it to them, saying, "Drink from it, all of you. ²⁸ For this is my blood of the covenant, which is poured out for many for the forgiveness of sins. ²⁹ From now on, I tell you, I will never drink of this fruit of the vine until that day when I drink it new with you in my Father's kingdom." ³⁰ And when they had sung a hymn, they went out to the Mount of Olives.

³¹ Then Jesus said to them, "You will all fall away because of me this night; for it is written,

'I will strike the shepherd,
    and the sheep of the flock will be scattered.'

³² But after I have been raised, I will go before you to Galilee." ³³ But Peter declared to him, "If all fall away because of you, I will never fall away." ³⁴ Jesus said to him, "Truly I say to you, this very night, before the rooster crows, you will deny me three times." ³⁵ Peter said to him, "Even if I have to die with you, I will never deny you." And so said all the disciples.

³⁶ Then Jesus went with the disciples to a place called Gethsemane, and he said to them, "Sit here while I go over there and pray." ³⁷ He took Peter and the two sons of Zebedee along with him, and he began to be sorrowful and troubled. ³⁸ Then he said to them, "My soul is exceedingly sorrowful, even to death. Stay here and watch with me." ³⁹ And going a little farther he fell on his face and prayed, "O my Father, if it is possible, let this cup pass from me; nevertheless, not as I will, but as you will." ⁴⁰ Then he came to the disciples and found them sleeping. And he said to Peter, "So, could you not watch with me one hour? ⁴¹ Watch and pray, so that you will not enter into temptation. The spirit indeed is willing, but the flesh is weak." ⁴² Again, a second time, he went away and prayed, saying, "O my Father, if this cannot pass away unless I drink it, your will be

---

26:²⁶ Alx[**Jesus took bread**], Byz[Jesus took the bread]; Alx[**blessed**], Byz[gave thanks (NET, NIV, TEV)]; Alx[**and, giving it to the disciples, said**], Byz[and gave it to the disciples and said (ASV, DRA, ESV, HCS, JNT, KJV, MRD, NAS, NAU, NET, NIV, NJB, NKJ, NLT, NRS, REB, RSV, TEV, TLB)].

26:²⁷ Alx[**took a cup**], Byz[took the cup (DRA, KJV, MRD, NET, NIV, NKJ)].

26:²⁸ Alx[**covenant**], Byz[new covenant (DRA, JNT, KJV, MRD, NKJ, TLB)].

26:²⁹ Alx[**fruit of the vine**], Byz[product of the vine (MRD, ~NJB, ~NLT, ~TEV, ~TLB)].

26:³¹ **Zechariah 13:7.**

26:³³ Alx/Byz[**Peter**], Alt/Peshitta[Cephas (JNT, MRD)]; Alx[**If all fall away because of you, I will never fall away**], Byz[If all fall away because of you, yet I will never fall away (KJV, REB)], Minor[Even if all fall away because of you, I will never fall away (HCS, JNT, NAS, NAU, NIV, NJB, NKJ, NLT, TEV)].

26:³⁵ Alx/Byz[**Peter**], Alt/Peshitta[Cephas (JNT, MRD)]; Alx[**I will never deny you**], Byz[yet I will never deny you (ASV, KJV)], Major[yet I would never deny you].

26:³⁶ Alx/Byz[**the disciples**], Minor[his disciples (ASV, DRA, ESV, JNT, MRD, NAB, NAS, NAU, NIV, NJB, ~NLT, NRS, REB, RSV, TEV, ~TLB)].

26:³⁷ Alx/Byz[**Peter**], Alt/Peshitta[Cephas (JNT, MRD)].

26:³⁸ Alx[**Then he said to them**], Byz[Then Jesus said to them].

26:³⁹ Alx/Byz[**going a little farther**], Major[coming a little (MRD)]; Alx/Byz[**my Father**], Minor[omits my]; Metzger[a few secondary witnesses add Luke 22:43-44 after this verse].

26:⁴⁰ Alx/Byz[**Peter**], Alt/Peshitta[Cephas (JNT, MRD)].

26:⁴¹ **temptation** or the time of trial.

26:⁴² Alx/Byz[**prayed, saying**], Minor[omits saying (ESV, HCS, JNT, NAB, NET, NIV, NJB, NLT, NRS, REB, RSV, TEV, TLB)]; Alx[**if this**], Byz[adds cup (DRA, JNT, KJV, MRD, NAB, NET, NIV, NJB, NKJ, NLT, REB, TEV, TLB)]; Alx[**pass away**], Byz[adds from me (KJV, NKJ, REB)].

done." ⁴³ And again he came and found them sleeping, for their eyes were heavy. ⁴⁴ So he left them again, went away, and prayed the third time, saying the same words again. ⁴⁵ Then he came to the disciples and said to them, "Are you still sleeping and resting? Behold, the hour is at hand, and the Son of Man is being betrayed into the hands of sinners. ⁴⁶ Rise, let us be going; see, my betrayer is at hand."

⁴⁷ While he was still speaking, Judas came, one of the twelve, and with him a great crowd with swords and clubs, from the chief priests and the elders of the people. ⁴⁸ Now the betrayer had given them a sign, saying, "The one I kiss is the man. Seize him." ⁴⁹ And at once he went up to Jesus and said, "Greetings, Rabbi!" and kissed him. ⁵⁰ Jesus said to him, "Friend, why are you here?" Then they came and laid hands on Jesus and arrested him. ⁵¹ And suddenly, one of those who were with Jesus stretched out his hand and drew his sword, struck the servant of the high priest, and cut off his ear. ⁵² But Jesus said to him, "Put your sword back in its place, for all who take the sword will perish by the sword. ⁵³ Do you think that I cannot appeal to my Father, and he will at once send me more than twelve legions of angels? ⁵⁴ But how then could the Scriptures be fulfilled, that it must happen in this way?" ⁵⁵ At that hour Jesus said to the crowds, "Have you come out as against a robber, with swords and clubs to capture me? Every day I sat in the temple teaching, and you did not seize me. ⁵⁶ But all this has taken place, that the Scriptures of the prophets might be fulfilled." Then all the disciples forsook him and fled.

⁵⁷ And those who had seized Jesus led him away to Caiaphas the high priest, where the scribes and the elders had assembled. ⁵⁸ But Peter followed him at a distance, right up to the courtyard of the high priest. He entered and sat down with the guards to see the end. ⁵⁹ Now the chief priests and the whole Sanhedrin sought false testimony against Jesus that they might put him to death, ⁶⁰ but they found none, though many false witnesses came forward. But afterward two came forward ⁶¹ and said, "This fellow said, 'I am able to destroy the temple of God, and to rebuild in three days.'" ⁶² And the high priest stood up and said, "Have you no answer to make? What is it that these men testify against you?" ⁶³ But Jesus remained silent. And the high priest said to him, "I charge you under

---

26:⁴³ Alx[**again he came and found them sleeping**], Byz[he came and found them sleeping again (KJV, NKJ)].

26:⁴⁴ Alx[**he left them again, went away**], Byz[he left them, went away again (DRA, HCS, KJV, MRD, NAB, NIV, NJB, NKJ, ~NLT, REB, ~TLB)]; Alx/Byz[**the third time**], Minor[*omits*]; Alx[**the same words again**], Byz[*omits* again (DRA, JNT, KJV, MRD, NIV, NKJ, NRS, RSV, TEV)].

26:⁴⁵ Alx[**the disciples**], Byz[his disciples (DRA, KJV, MRD, NAB, NKJ)]; Alx/Byz[**Behold**], Minor[For behold (~NLT, ~REB, ~TLB)].

26:⁵⁰ **why are you here?** *or* do what you came to do.

26:⁵² Alx[**perish**], Byz[die (JNT, MRD, NET, NIV, NJB, NLT, REB, TEV, TLB)].

26:⁵³ Alx[**appeal to my Father, and he will at once send**], Byz[appeal to my Father at once, and he will send (KJV, NKJ)].

26:⁵⁵ Alx[**Every day I sat**], Byz[*adds* with you (DRA, KJV, MRD, NKJ, TLB)].

26:⁵⁶ Alx/Byz[**But all this**], Minor[*omits* But]; Alx/Byz[**the disciples**], Minor[his disciples].

26:⁵⁸ Alx/Byz[**Peter**], Alt/Peshitta[Simon Cephas (MRD)], Alt[*without textual foundation* Cephas (~JNT)].

26:⁵⁹ Alx[**chief priests**], Byz[*adds* the elders and (KJV, MRD, NKJ)].

26:⁶⁰ Alx[**though many false witnesses came forward**], Byz[indeed, though many false witnesses came forward, they found none (KJV, NKJ, ~TLB)]; Alx[**But afterward two came forward 61**], Byz[But afterward two false witnesses came forward 61 (DRA, KJV, NKJ)], Major[61 But afterward two false witnesses came forward 61].

26:⁶¹ Alx[**to rebuild**], Byz[to rebuild it (ASV, DRA, ESV, HCS, JNT, KJV, MRD, NAB, NAS, NAU, NET, NIV, NJB, NKJ, NLT, NRS, REB, RSV, TEV, TLB)].

26:⁶³ Alx/Byz[**63 But Jesus remained silent**], Minor[But Jesus remained silent 63]; Alx[**the high priest said**], Byz[the high priest answered and said (KJV, MRD, NKJ)].

oath by the living God: tell us if you are the Christ, the Son of God." ⁶⁴ Jesus said to him, "You said it. But I say to you,

> hereafter you will see *the Son of Man*
> *sitting at the right hand of the Power,*
> *and coming on the clouds of heaven.*"

⁶⁵ Then the high priest tore his clothes and said, "He has spoken blasphemy! Why do we need any more witnesses? Look, now you have heard the blasphemy. ⁶⁶ What do you think?" They answered, "He is worthy of death." ⁶⁷ Then they spat in his face and struck him with their fists. And others slapped him, ⁶⁸ saying, "Prophesy to us, Christ! Who is the one who struck you?"

⁶⁹ Now Peter was sitting outside in the courtyard, and a servant girl came to him and said, "You also were with Jesus of Galilee." ⁷⁰ But he denied in front of everyone, saying, "I do not know what you are talking about." ⁷¹ And when he went out to the gateway, another girl saw him and said to the people there, "This fellow was with Jesus of Nazareth." ⁷² But again he denied it with an oath, "I do not know the man!" ⁷³ After a little while those who stood by came up and said to Peter, "Surely you are also one of them, for your accent betrays you." ⁷⁴ Then he began to invoke a curse on himself and to swear, "I do not know the man." And immediately the rooster crowed. ⁷⁵ And Peter remembered the word Jesus had said, "Before the rooster crows, you will deny me three times." So he went out and wept bitterly.

27

¹ When morning came, all the chief priests and the elders of the people took counsel against Jesus to put him to death. ² And they bound him, and led him away and delivered him to Pilate the governor.

³ When Judas, his betrayer, saw that he was condemned, he repented and brought back the thirty pieces of silver to the chief priests and elders, ⁴ saying, "I have sinned by betraying innocent blood." And they said, "What is that to us? You see to it!" ⁵ Then he threw down the pieces of silver into the temple and departed, and went and hanged himself. ⁶ But the chief priests took the silver pieces and said, "It is not lawful to put them into the treasury, since it is blood money." ⁷ So they took counsel, and bought with them the potter's field, to bury strangers in. ⁸ Therefore that field has been called the Field of Blood to this day. ⁹ Then was fulfilled what was spoken by Jeremiah the prophet, saying,

---

26:⁶⁴ ~Psalms 110:1; ~Daniel 7:13.

26:⁶⁵ Alx[**you have heard the blasphemy**], Byz[you have heard his blasphemy (ESV, JNT, KJV, MRD, NKJ, NLT, NRS, RSV, TEV, TLB)].

26:⁶⁶ Alx/Byz[**66 What do you think?**], Minor[What do you think? 66 (~TLB)].

26:⁶⁹ Alx/Byz[**Peter**], Alt/Peshitta[Cephas (JNT, MRD)]; Alx[**sitting outside**], Byz[outside sitting].

26:⁷⁰ Alx[**in front of everyone** *or* before all], Byz[before them all (ASV, DRA, ESV, KJV, MRD, NAS, NAU, NET, NIV, NJB, NKJ, NRS, REB, RSV, TEV, ~TLB)].

26:⁷¹ Alx[**was with Jesus**], Byz[was also with Jesus (ASV, DRA, KJV, MRD, NKJ)]; **Jesus of Nazareth** *Greek* Jesus the Nazarene.

26:⁷³ Alx/Byz[**Peter**], Alt/Peshitta[Cephas (JNT, MRD)].

26:⁷⁵ Alx/Byz[**Peter**], Alt/Peshitta[Cephas (JNT, MRD)]; Alx[**Jesus had said**], Byz[*adds* to him (KJV, MRD, NKJ, TEV)].

27:² Alx[**Pilate**], Byz[Pontius Pilate (DRA, KJV, NKJ)].

27:³ Alx[**elders**], Byz[the elders (ESV, NET, NIV, NLT, NRS, RSV, TEV)].

27:⁴ Alx/Byz[**innocent blood**], Minor[righteous blood].

27:⁵ Alx[**into the temple**], Byz[in the temple (DRA, KJV, MRD, NJB, NKJ, NLT, NRS, REB, RSV, TEV, ~TLB)].

27:⁹ Alx/Byz[**Jeremiah**], Minor[*omits* (MRD) *others* Zechariah *others* Isaiah]; Alx/Byz[**they took**], Minor[I took (MRD)].

27:⁹⁻¹⁰ ~**Zechariah 11:12-13**, ~Jeremiah 19:1-3, 32:6-9; **price had been set** *Greek* price had been priced.

"And they took the thirty pieces of silver, the price of him on whom a price had been set by some of the sons of Israel. [10] *And they gave them for the potter's field, as the Lord directed me."*

[11] Now Jesus stood before the governor. And the governor asked him, "Are you the king of the Jews?" So Jesus said, "You said it." [12] But when he was accused by the chief priests and elders, he made no answer. [13] Then Pilate said to him, "Do you not hear how many things they testify against you?" [14] But he gave him no answer, not even to a single charge; so that the governor wondered greatly.

[15] Now at the feast the governor was accustomed to release for the crowd any one prisoner whom they wanted. [16] And at that time they had a notorious prisoner, called [Jesus] Barabbas. [17] So when they had gathered, Pilate said to them, "Whom do you want me to release for you, [Jesus] Barabbas or Jesus who is called Christ?" [18] For he knew it was out of envy that they had handed him over. [19] While he was sitting on the judgment seat, his wife sent word to him, "Have nothing to do with that righteous man, for I have suffered greatly today in a dream because of him." [20] But the chief priests and the elders persuaded the crowds to ask for Barabbas and destroy Jesus. [21] The governor answered them, "Which of the two do you want me to release to you?" They said, "Barabbas!" [22] Pilate said to them, "Then what shall I do with Jesus who is called Christ?" They all said, "Let him be crucified!" [23] And he said, "Why, what evil has he done?" But they shouted all the more, "Let him be crucified!" [24] When Pilate saw that he was gaining nothing, but rather that a riot was starting, he took water and washed his hands before the crowd, saying, "I am innocent of this man's blood. See to it yourselves." [25] And all the people answered, "His blood be on us and on our children!" [26] Then he released Barabbas to them. And when he had scourged Jesus, he delivered him to be crucified.

[27] Then the soldiers of the governor took Jesus into the Praetorium and gathered the whole garrison around him. [28] And they stripped him and put a scarlet robe on him. [29] And when they had twisted a crown of thorns, they put it on his head, and a reed in his right hand. And they bowed the knee before him and mocked him, saying, "Hail, King of the Jews!" [30] And they spat on him, and took the reed and struck him on the head. [31] And when they had mocked him, they took the robe off him, and put his own clothes on him, and led him away to crucify him.

[32] Now as they came out, they found a man of Cyrene, Simon by name, and they compelled him to carry his cross. [33] And when they came to a place called Golgotha (which means the place of a skull), [34] they offered him wine to drink, mingled with gall. But when he tasted it, he would not drink it. [35] And when they had crucified him, *they*

27:[10] Alx/Byz[**they gave**], Minor[I gave (MRD)].

27:[11] Alx[**So Jesus said**], Byz[*adds* to him (ASV, DRA, KJV, MRD, NAS, NAU, NKJ)]; **You said it** *Greek* You say it.

27:[12] Alx[**elders**], Byz[the elders (NET, NIV, NJB, NLT)].

27:[16, 17] Alx[**Jesus Barabbas** *i.e. "Jesus, Son of the Father" in Aramaic*], Byz[Barabbas (ASV, DRA, ESV, HCS, ~JNT, KJV, MRD, NAS, NAU, NIV, NJB, NKJ, NLT, RSV, TLB)].

27:[22] Alx[**They all said**], Byz[*adds* to him (KJV, NKJ)].

27:[23] Alx[**And he said**], Byz[And the governor said (DRA, KJV, MRD, ~NIV, NKJ, ~NLT, ~REB, ~TEV, ~TLB)].

27:[24] Alx/Byz[**before the crowd**], Minor[against the crowd]; Alx[**this man's blood**], Byz[this righteous man's blood (ASV, DRA, KJV, MRD, NKJ, TLB)].

27:[28] Alx/Byz[**stripped**], Minor[clothed]; Alx[**put a scarlet robe on him**], Byz[put on him a scarlet robe (ASV, HCS, JNT, KJV, MRD, REB)].

27:[29] Alx[**King of the Jews**], Byz[the King of the Jews (JNT, TEV)].

27:[31] Alx/Byz[**and put his own clothes on him**], Minor[*omits* and (HCS, JNT, NAB, NKJ)].

27:[34] Alx[**wine**], Byz[wine vinegar *or* sour wine (KJV, MRD, NKJ, ~TEV)].

27:[35] Alx/Byz[**casting lots**], Minor[*adds* that it might be fulfilled which was spoken by the prophet:

divided his garments among them by casting lots. ³⁶ And sitting down, they kept watch over him there. ³⁷ And they put above his head the charge written against him:

THIS IS JESUS, THE KING OF THE JEWS.

³⁸ Then two robbers were crucified with him, one on the right and one on the left. ³⁹ And those who passed by hurled insults at him, wagging their heads ⁴⁰ and saying, "You who would destroy the temple and build it in three days, save yourself, if you are the Son of God, [and] come down from the cross." ⁴¹ So also the chief priests, with the scribes and elders, mocked him, saying, ⁴² "He saved others? He cannot save himself! He is the King of Israel? Let him come down now from the cross, and we will believe in him! ⁴³ He trusts in God? Let him deliver now, if he desires him; for he said, 'I am the Son of God!'" ⁴⁴ And the robbers who were crucified with him also reviled him in the same way.

⁴⁵ Now from the sixth hour until the ninth hour there was darkness over all the land. ⁴⁶ And about the ninth hour Jesus cried out with a loud voice, *"Eli, Eli, lema sabachthani?"* that is, *"My God, my God, why have you forsaken me?"* ⁴⁷ When some of those standing there heard this, they said, "This man is calling Elijah." ⁴⁸ Immediately one of them ran and took a sponge, filled it with wine vinegar and put it on a reed, and offered it to him to drink. ⁴⁹ The rest said, "Let him alone. Let us see if Elijah will come to save him." ⁵⁰ And Jesus cried out again with a loud voice, and yielded up his spirit. ⁵¹ And behold, the veil of the temple was torn in two, from top to bottom. And the earth shook. And the rocks were split. ⁵² And the tombs were opened. And many bodies of the saints who had fallen asleep were raised. ⁵³ And coming out of the tombs after his resurrection, they went into the holy city and appeared to many. ⁵⁴ So when the centurion and those with him, who were guarding Jesus, saw the earthquake and the things that were done, they were terrified, and said, "Truly this was God's Son!" ⁵⁵ And many women were there, looking

---

"They divided my garments among them, and for my clothing they cast lots" (DRA, KJV, NKJ)]; Psalms 22:18.

27:38 Alx/Byz[**one on the right and one on the left**], Metzger[*Old Latin* one on the right named Zoatham, and one on the left named Camma].

27:39 **hurled insults at him** *or* blasphemed him.

27:40 Alx[**and come down**], Byz[*omits* and (ASV, DRA, ESV, HCS, KJV, NAS, NAU, NET, NIV, NKJ, NRS, RSV, TEV, TLB)].

27:41 Alx[**So also**], Byz[And so also (~TLB)]; Alx[**scribes and elders**], Byz[*adds* and Pharisees (MRD)].

27:42 Alx[**He is the King**], Byz[If he is the King (DRA, ~JNT, KJV, MRD, NKJ, ~REB, ~TEV, TLB)]; Alx/Byz[**we will believe**], Minor[we would believe *others* we believe]; Alx/Byz[**believe in him**], Minor[believe him (JNT, KJV, NKJ, REB, TLB)]; **he cannot save himself** *or* can he not save himself?

27:43 Alx[**let him deliver now**], Byz[let him deliver him now (ASV, DRA, ESV, HCS, JNT, KJV, MRD, NAB, NAS, NAU, NET, NIV, NJB, NKJ, NLT, NRS, REB, RSV, TEV, TLB)].

27:45 **land** *or* earth.

27:46 Alx/Byz[**Eli** *Hebrew*], Minor[Eloi *Aramaic* (NIV)]; Alx[**lema** *Aramaic*], Byz[lima], Minor[lama *Hebrew* (ASV, DRA, ~JNT, KJV, NAS, NAU, NIV, NJB, NKJ, RSV, TLB)]; Peshitta[*omits as redundant* Eli, Eli, lema sabachthani, that is (MRD)]; **sabachthani** *Aramaic; Codex Bezae reads* zaphthanei *from Hebrew* azavtani; Psalms 22:1 ~Masoretic/~ARAMAIC.

27:49 Alx/Byz[**come to save him**], Minor[*adds* And another took a spear and pierced his side, and water and blood came out].

27:50 **spirit** *or* breath.

27:54 Alx/Byz[**were done**], Minor[were happening (~ESV, HCS, JNT, ~MRD, NAB, NAS, NAU, ~NET, NIV, ~NJB, NKJ, NLT, ~NRS, REB, ~RSV, TEV, TLB)].

27:55 Alx/Major[**many women were there**], Byz[many women were also there (ESV, NRS, REB,

on from afar, who had followed Jesus from Galilee, ministering to him; [56] among whom were Mary Magdalene, Mary the mother of James and Joseph, and the mother of Zebedee's sons.

[57] And when it was evening, there came a rich man from Arimathea, named Joseph, who had himself also become a disciple of Jesus. [58] He went to Pilate and asked for the body of Jesus. Then Pilate ordered it to be given to him. [59] When Joseph took the body, he wrapped it [in] a clean linen cloth, [60] and laid it in his own new tomb, which he had hewn out of the rock. And he rolled a great stone to the door of the tomb, and departed. [61] Mary Magdalene and the other Mary were sitting there opposite the tomb.

[62] The next day, the one after the day of Preparation, the chief priests and the Pharisees gathered to Pilate [63] and said, "Sir, we remember how that deceiver said, while he was still alive, 'After three days I will rise again.' [64] Therefore order that the tomb be made secure until the third day, lest his disciples come and steal him away, and tell the people, 'He has risen from the dead.' So the last deception will be worse than the first." [65] Pilate said to them, "You have a guard; go your way, make it as secure as you know how." [66] So they went and made the tomb secure by sealing the stone and setting a guard.

28

[1] Now after the Sabbath, as the first day of the week began to dawn, Mary Magdalene and the other Mary went to see the tomb. [2] And behold, there was a great earthquake; for an angel of the Lord descended from heaven, and came and rolled back the stone, and sat on it. [3] His appearance was like lightning, and his clothes were white as snow. [4] And the guards shook for fear of him, and became as dead men. [5] But the angel said to the women, "Do not be afraid, for I know that you seek Jesus who was crucified. [6] He is not here; for he has risen, as he said. Come, see the place where he lay. [7] Then go quickly and tell his disciples that he has risen from the dead. And behold, he is going before you to Galilee. There you will see him. Behold, I have told you." [8] So they departed quickly from the tomb with fear and great joy, and ran to tell his disciples. [9] And behold, Jesus met them and said, "Greetings!" And they came to him and took hold of his feet and worshipped him. [10] Then Jesus said to them, "Do not be afraid. Go and tell my brothers to go to Galilee. And there they will see me."

[11] Now while they were going, behold, some of the guard went into the city and reported to the chief priests all the things that had happened. [12] When they had assembled with the elders and consulted together, they gave a large sum of money to the soldiers, [13] and said, "Tell them, 'His disciples came by night and stole him away while we were

---

RSV)].

27:56 Alx[**Joseph**], Byz[Joses (ASV, KJV, MRD, NIV, NKJ)].

27:58 Alx[**Pilate ordered it to be given**], Byz[Pilate ordered the body to be given (DRA, KJV, MRD, NKJ, TEV)].

27:59 Alx[**in a clean linen**], Byz[*omits* in].

27:61 Alx[**Mary** *Miriam* **Magdalene**], Byz[Mary *Maria* Magdalene].

27:64 Alx/Byz[**his disciples**], Minor[the disciples (JNT, NAS)]; Alx[**come**], Byz[*adds* by night (KJV, MRD, NKJ)]; *JNT first edition typographical error omits* 27:62-66.

27:65 Alx[**Pilate said**], Byz[But Pilate said].

28:1 Alx[**Mary** *Miriam* **Magdalene**], Byz[Mary *Maria* Magdalene].

28:2 Alx[**stone**], Byz[*adds* from the door (KJV, MRD, NKJ)].

28:3 Alx[**white as snow**], Byz[white like snow (MRD)].

28:4 Alx[**as dead men**], Byz[like dead men (ESV, HCS, JNT, NAB, NAS, NAU, NET, NIV, NJB, NKJ, ~NLT, NRS, RSV, TEV, ~TLB)].

28:6 Alx[**he lay**], Byz[the Lord lay (ASV, DRA, KJV, MRD, NKJ)].

28:7 Alx/Byz[**risen from the dead**], Minor[risen (DRA)].

28:8 Alx[**departed**], Byz[went out (DRA, ~MRD, NKJ)].

28:9 Alx[**And behold**], Byz[And as they went to tell his disciples, behold (KJV, NKJ, ~TLB)].

28:13 Alx/Major[**13 and said**], Byz[and said 13 (~TLB)].

asleep.' **14** And if this comes to the governor's ears, we will satisfy [him] and keep you out of trouble." **15** So they took the money and did as they were instructed. And this story has been spread among the Jews until today's [day].

16 Then the eleven disciples went to Galilee, to the mountain which Jesus had appointed for them. **17** When they saw him, they worshipped. But some doubted. **18** And Jesus came and said to them, "All authority in heaven and on [the] earth has been given to me. **19** Go therefore and make disciples of all nations, baptizing them in the name of the Father and of the Son and of the Holy Spirit, **20** teaching them to observe all that I have commanded you. And behold, I am with you always, even to the end of the age."

28:14 Alx/Byz[**satisfy him**], Minor[*omits* him (~NLT, ~TLB)].

28:15 Alx/Byz[**the money**], Minor[money]; Alx/Byz[**spread**], Minor[spoken (~KJV, ~MRD, NET, NJB, NRS, ~REB)]; Alx[**today's day**], Byz[today (ASV, DRA, ESV, HCS, KJV, MRD, NAS, NAU, NET, NJB, NKJ, NLT, NRS, REB, RSV)].

28:17 Alx[**they worshipped**], Byz[they worshipped him (ASV, ESV, JNT, KJV, MRD, NAS, NAU, NET, NIV, NJB, NKJ, NLT, NRS, RSV, TEV, TLB)].

28:18 Alx[**the earth**], Byz[*omits* the (ASV, DRA, ESV, HCS, JNT, KJV, MRD, NAB, NAS, NAU, NET, NIV, NJB, NKJ, NLT, NRS, REB, RSV, TEV, TLB)].

28:19 Alx[**Go therefore**], Byz[Go]; Alx/Byz[**baptizing**], Minor[having baptized *others* baptize (MRD, NJB, REB, TEV)].

28:20 Alx[**end of the age**], Byz[*adds* Amen (KJV, MRD, NKJ)].

Subtitle Minor[*adds* According to Matthew].

According to Mark

1

¹ The beginning of the gospel of Jesus Christ, [the Son of God].
² As it is written in Isaiah the prophet:
"Behold, I send my messenger before your face,
who will prepare your way."

³   *"The voice of one crying in the wilderness:*
'Prepare the way of the Lord.
Make his paths straight.'"

⁴ John appeared, who was baptizing in the wilderness and preaching a baptism of repentance for the forgiveness of sins. ⁵ And all the land of Judea, and all the people from Jerusalem, went out to him. And they were baptized by him in the Jordan River, confessing their sins. ⁶ Now John was clothed with camel's hair, and with a leather belt around his waist, and he ate locusts and wild honey. ⁷ And he preached, saying, "After me comes one who is mightier than I, the thong of whose sandals I am not worthy to stoop down and untie. ⁸ I have baptized you with water. But he will baptize you in the Holy Spirit."

⁹ And in those days Jesus came from Nazareth of Galilee and was baptized in the Jordan by John. ¹⁰ And immediately coming up out of the water, he saw the heavens torn open and the Spirit descending into him as a dove. ¹¹ And a voice came from heaven, "You are my beloved Son. With you I am well pleased."

Title Alx/Byz[**According to Mark**], Minor[*variations of* The Gospel According to Saint Mark].

1:1 Alx/Byz[**the Son of God**], Minor[*omits*]; **gospel** *or* good news.

1:2 Alx[**Isaiah the prophet**], Byz[in the Prophets (KJV, NKJ)]; Alx[**prepare your way**], Byz[*adds* before you (DRA, JNT, KJV, NJB, NKJ, ~TEV)]; ~**Malachi 3:1 Masoretic**.

1:3 Alx/Byz[**crying in the wilderness: 'Prepare**], Minor[crying: 'In the wilderness, prepare (JNT)]; **Isaiah 40:3 LXX**.

1:4 Alx[**John appeared, who was baptizing**], Byz[John came baptizing (DRA, ESV, HCS, KJV, MRD, NIV, NKJ, TEV)], Minor[John the Baptist appeared (JNT, NAB, NAS, NAU, NET, NJB, NLT, NRS, REB, RSV, TEV)]; Alx/Byz[**and preaching**], Minor[preaching (JNT, NAB, NAS, NAU, NET, NJB, NRS, REB, RSV)].

1:5 Alx[**all the people from Jerusalem... they were baptized**], Byz[the people from Jerusalem... they were all baptized (KJV, NKJ)].

1:6 Alx/Byz[**camel's hair**], Minor[camel's skin (NJB)].

1:7 Alx/Byz[**After me**], Minor[*omits* me (NLT, TLB)].

1:8 Alx[**I have baptized**], Byz[I indeed have baptized (KJV, NKJ)]; Alx[**with water**], Byz[in water (ASV, JNT)]; Alx/Byz[**in the Holy Spirit**], Minor[with the Holy Spirit (DRA, ESV, HCS, KJT, MRD, NAB, NAS, NAU, NET, NIV, NJB, NKJ, NLT, NRS, REB, RSV, TEV, TLB)].

1:9 Alx/Byz[**And in those days**], Minor[*omits* And (ESV, HCS, JNT, NAB, NAU, NIV, NJB, NKJ, NLT, NRS, REB, RSV, TEV, TLB)]; Alx[**in the Jordan by John**], Byz[by John in the Jordan (ASV, DRA, ESV, KJV, NAS, NAU, NET, NIV, NKJ, NLT, NRS, RSV, TEV, TLB)].

1:10 Alx[**out of**], Byz[from (MRD, NKJ)]; Alx[**into him as a dove**], Byz[upon him as a dove (ASV)], Major[upon him like a dove (ESV, ~HCS, JNT, KJV, MRD, NAB, NAS, NAU, NET, NIV, NJB, NKJ, NLT, NRS, REB, RSV, TEV, ~TLB)], Alt/Vulage[upon him and remaining as a dove (DRA)].

1:11 Alx/Byz[**a voice came from heaven**], Minor[*omits* came (MRD, NLT, TLB)]; Alx/Byz[**You are my beloved Son** *or* You are my Son, the Beloved], Minor[You are my only Son (~NET)], Alx/Byz[**With you**], Major[with whom (KJV, MRD, NKJ)].

¹² The Spirit immediately drove him out into the wilderness. ¹³ And he was in the wilderness forty days, tempted by Satan. And he was with the wild beasts, and the angels ministered to him.

¹⁴ Now after John was put in prison, Jesus came to Galilee, preaching the gospel of God, ¹⁵ and saying, "The time is fulfilled, and the kingdom of God is at hand. Repent, and believe in the gospel."

¹⁶ And as he passed by the Sea of Galilee, he saw Simon, and Andrew the brother of Simon, casting into the sea; for they were fishermen. ¹⁷ And Jesus said to them, "Come follow me, and I will make you become fishers of men." ¹⁸ And immediately they left the nets and followed him. ¹⁹ When he had gone a little farther, he saw James the son of Zebedee, and John his brother, who also were in the boat mending their nets. ²⁰ And immediately he called them. And they left their father Zebedee in the boat with the hired servants, and followed him.

²¹ And they went into Capernaum, and immediately on the Sabbath he entered the synagogue and taught. ²² And they were astonished at his teaching, for he taught them as one who had authority, and not as the scribes. ²³ Now, just then, there was a man in their synagogue with an unclean spirit. And he cried out, ²⁴ saying, "What have we to do with you, Jesus of Nazareth? Have you come to destroy us? I know who you are – the Holy One of God!" ²⁵ But Jesus rebuked him, saying, "Be quiet, and come out of him!" ²⁶ And the unclean spirit, convulsing him and calling with a loud voice, came out of him. ²⁷ And they were all amazed, so that they questioned among themselves, saying, "What is this? A new teaching! With authority he commands even the unclean spirits, and they obey him." ²⁸ And at once his fame spread everywhere throughout all the surrounding region of Galilee.

1:13 Alx[**he was in the wilderness**], Byz[he was there in the wilderness (KJV, MRD, NJB, NKJ, ~NLT, REB, TLB)].

1:14 Alx[**of God**], Byz[of the kingdom of God (DRA, KJV, MRD, NKJ)]; **gospel** *or* good news.

1:15 Alx/Byz[**and saying**], Minor[*omits* and (NET, NIV, NLT, TEV, TLB) *others omit* and saying (HCS, JNT, NAB, NJB, REB)]; **is at hand** *or* has come near; **gospel** *or* good news.

1:16 Alx[**passed by the Sea**], Byz[walked by the Sea (JNT, KJV, MRD, NIV, NJB, NKJ, NLT, REB, TEV, TLB)]; Alx[**Andrew the brother of Simon**], Byz[Andrew his brother (DRA, KJV, MRD, NAB, NIV, NKJ, NLT, NRS, REB, TEV, TLB)]; Alx[**casting**], Byz[casting Simon's net]; Minor[casting a net (ASV, DRA, ESV, HCS, JNT, KJV, MRD, NAB, NAS, NAU, NET, NIV, NJB, NKJ, NLT, NRS, RSV)]; **Simon** *Peter*.

1:18 Alx[**the nets**], Byz[their nets (DRA, ESV, HCS, JNT, KJV, MRD, NAB, NAU, NET, NIV, NJB, NKJ, NLT, NRS, REB, RSV, TEV, TLB)].

1:19 Alx[**a little farther**], Byz[*adds* from there (DRA, KJV, NKJ)].

1:21 Alx[**Capernaum** *Greek* Capharnaum], Byz[Capernaum]; Alx/Byz[**entered the synagogue and taught**], Minor[entered a synagogue and taught *others* taught in the synagogue (MRD)].

1:23 Alx[**just then** *or* immediately], Byz[*omits* (DRA, KJV, MRD, NAB, NKJ, REB, TLB)]; Alx/Byz[**he cried out, 24 saying**], Alt[24 he cried out (NAB)].

1:24 Alx[**What have we to do with you**], Byz[Ha! What have we to do with you (~KJV, ~NET, ~NKJ)]; Alx/Byz[**I know who you are**], Minor[We know who you are]; **Have you come** *or* You have come.

1:25 Alx/Byz[**rebuked him, saying**], Minor[*omits* saying (JNT, NET, NLT, REB, TEV, ~TLB)].

1:26 Alx[**calling with a loud voice**], Byz[crying out with a loud voice (ASV, DRA, ESV, KJV, MRD, NAB, NAS, NAU, NET, NJB, NKJ, NRS, REB, RSV)].

1:27 Alx[**A new teaching! With authority he commands** *or* A new teaching with authority! He commands], Byz[What new teaching is this? With authority he commands (DRA, KJV, MRD, NKJ, TEV, TLB)].

1:28 Alx[**everywhere**], Byz[*omits* (DRA, HCS, JNT, KJV, MRD, NET, NIV, NKJ, NLT, NRS, REB, TLB)].

²⁹ As soon as they left the synagogue, they went with James and John, and entered the house of Simon and Andrew. ³⁰ Now Simon's mother-in-law lay sick with a fever. And immediately they told him about her. ³¹ So he came and took her by the hand and lifted her up, and the fever left her. And she served them. ³² Now at evening, when the sun had set, they brought to him all who were sick and those who were demon-possessed. ³³ And the whole city was gathered together at the door. ³⁴ And he healed many who were sick with various diseases, and cast out many demons. And he would not permit the demons to speak, because they knew him.

³⁵ Now in the morning, a long while before daylight, he rose and went out, and departed to a solitary place, and there he prayed. ³⁶ And Simon searched for him, and those who were with him. ³⁷ And they found him, and said to him, "Everyone is looking for you." ³⁸ And he said to them, "Let us go on to the next towns, so I may preach there also; for that is why I came." ³⁹ And he went into their synagogues throughout all Galilee, preaching and casting out demons.

⁴⁰ Then a leper came to him, imploring him, [kneeling down] and saying to him, "If you are willing, you can make me clean." ⁴¹ And moved with compassion, he put out his hand and touched him, and said to him, "I am willing; be clean." ⁴² And immediately the leprosy left him, and he was made clean. ⁴³ And he strictly warned him and sent him away at once. ⁴⁴ And he said to him, "See that you say nothing to anyone. But go, show yourself to the priest, and offer for your cleansing what Moses commanded, as a testimony to them." ⁴⁵ But he went out and began to talk freely about it, and to spread the news, so that Jesus could no longer openly enter a town, but was outside at the deserted places. And people came to him from every quarter.

1:29 Alx/Byz[**As soon as they**], Minor[As soon as he (~DRA, ESV, MRD, ~NAB, ~NJB, NLT, RSV, ~REB, ~TLB)]; Alx/Byz[**they went**], Minor[he went (~ESV, ~JNT, ~MRD, NAB, NJB, ~RSV, ~TLB)].

1:31 Alx[**took her by the hand**], Byz[took her by her hand (MRD, NAB, NET, NIV, REB)]; Alx[**and the fever left her**], Byz[adds immediately (DRA, KJV, MRD, NKJ, TLB)].

1:34 Alx/Major[**knew him**], Byz[adds to be the Christ].

1:35 Alx/Byz[**and departed**], Minor[omits (MRD, NLT, NRS, RSV, TLB)].

1:36 Alx[text], Byz[And Simon and those who were with him searched for him (ASV, DRA, ESV, HCS, JNT, KJV, MRD, NAB, NAS, NAU, NET, NIV, NJB, NKJ, NLT, NRS, REB, RSV, TEV, TLB)].

1:37 Alx[**And they found him, and said**], Byz[And when they found him, they said (DRA, JNT, KJV, MRD, NET, NIV, NJB, NKJ, NLT, NRS, REB, TEV)].

1:38 Alx[**Let us go on** or Let us go elsewhere], Byz[Let us go (DRA, KJV, MRD, NKJ)]; Alx[**that is why I came**], Byz[that is why I have come (HCS, MRD, NAB, NIV, NKJ)].

1:39 Alx[**he went into**], Byz[he was in (DRA, JNT, KJV, MRD, NIV, NKJ, NLT, TEV, TLB)].

1:40 Alx[**kneeling down**], Byz[adds to him (ASV, KJV, NAS, NAU, NKJ, NLT, REB, TLB)]. Minor[omits; **leper** *can refer to several skin diseases.*

1:41 Alx/Byz[**compassion**], Minor[anger (REB)], Alx[**he put out his hand**], Byz[Jesus put out his hand (DRA, HCS, JNT, KJV, MRD, NAU, NET, NIV, NJB, NKJ, ~NRS, REB, TLB)]; Alx/Byz[**said to him**], Minor[omits to him (MRD, NET, NIV, NLT, REB, TEV, TLB)].

1:42 Alx[**And immediately**], Byz[And when he had spoken, immediately (DRA, KJV, NKJ)].

1:44 Alx/Byz[**say nothing to anyone**], Minor[tell no one (DRA, JNT, MRD, NAB, NJB, NLT, REB)].

1:45 Alx[**at the deserted places**], Byz[in the deserted places (ASV, DRA, ESV, HCS, JNT, KJV, MRD, NAB, NAS, NAU, NET, NIV, NJB, NKJ, NLT, NRS, REB, RSV, TEV, TLB)].

2 ¹ And when he entered Capernaum after some days, it was heard that he was home. ² And many gathered together, so that there was no longer room to receive them, not even near the door. And he preached the word to them. ³ Then they came, bringing to him a paralytic carried by four men. ⁴ And when they could not bring the man to him because of the crowd, they made an opening in the roof above him. And when they had broken through, they let down the pallet where the paralytic was lying. ⁵ When Jesus saw their faith, he said to the paralytic, "Son, your sins are forgiven." ⁶ Now some of the scribes were sitting there, reasoning in their hearts, ⁷ "Why does this man speak like this? He is blaspheming! Who can forgive sins but God alone?" ⁸ And immediately, when Jesus perceived in his spirit that they reasoned thus within themselves, he said to them, "Why do you reason about these things in your hearts? ⁹ Which is easier, to say to the paralytic, 'Your sins are forgiven,' or to say, 'Rise, and take up your pallet and walk'? ¹⁰ But that you may know that the Son of Man has authority to forgive sins on earth" – he said to the paralytic, ¹¹ "I say to you, rise, take up your pallet and go home." ¹² And he rose, and immediately took up the pallet and went out in front of them all; so that they were all amazed and glorified God, saying, "We never saw anything like this!"

¹³ Then he went out again beside the sea. And all the crowd came to him, and he taught them. ¹⁴ As he passed by, he saw Levi the son of Alphaeus sitting at the tax office. And he said to him, "Follow me." So he rose and followed him. ¹⁵ And as he sat to eat in Levi's house, many tax collectors and sinners were sitting to eat with Jesus and his

---

2:1 Alx[**And when he entered…it was heard**], Byz[And he entered…and it was heard (DRA, KJV, MRD, NKJ, REB, TEV, TLB)]; Alx[**Capernaum** *Greek* Capharnaum], Byz[Capernaum].

2:2 Alx[**And many gathered**], Byz[And immediately many gathered (KJV, NKJ, ~TLB)].

2:3 Alx[**they came, bringing to him**], Byz[they came to him, bringing (DRA, HCS, JNT, KJV, MRD, NKJ, ~NLT, ~REB, ~TLB)].

2:4 Alx[**bring the man to him** *Greek* bring to him], Byz[come near him (ASV, ESV, JNT, KJV, MRD, NAB, NAS, NAU, ~NET, NKJ, ~REB, RSV, TLB)]; Alx[**the pallet where**], Byz[the pallet on which (ESV, HCS, JNT, MRD, NAB, NAS, NAU, NET, NIV, NJB, NKJ, NLT, NRS, REB, RSV, TEV, TLB)].

2:5 Alx[**your sins are forgiven**], Byz[your sins have been forgiven you (~DRA, ~KJV, ~MRD, ~NKJ)].

2:7 Alx[**Why does this man speak like this? He is blaspheming!**], Byz[Why does this man speak blasphemies like this? (KJV, NKJ)].

2:8 Alx/Byz[**they reasoned thus**], Minor[*omits* thus (JNT, ~NAB, NIV, NJB, NLT, NRS, ~REB, ~TEV, ~TLB)]; Alx[**he said to them**], Byz[he says to them (ASV, DRA)], Minor[he said (NAB)].

2:9 Alx[**Your sins are forgiven**], Byz[Your sins have been forgiven], Minor[Sins have been forgiven you (~DRA, ~KJV, ~MRD, ~NKJ, ~TLB)]; Alx/Byz[**Rise, and take**], Minor[Rise, take (DRA, ESV, HCS, JNT, MRD, NAB, NET, NIV, NJB, NKJ, NLT, REB, RSV, TEV, ~TLB)]; Alx/Byz[**walk**], Minor[go (TLB)].

2:10 Alx[**to forgive sins on earth**], Byz[on earth to forgive sins (ASV, DRA, ESV, HCS, JNT, KJV, MRD, NAS, NAU, NET, NIV, NKJ, NLT, NRS, REB, RSV, TEV, TLB)]; Alx/Byz[**he said to the paralytic 11**], Minor[11 he said to the paralytic (NAB, NJB, ~TLB)].

2:11 Alx[**rise, take**], Byz[rise, and take (KJV, ~TLB)].

2:12 Alx[**And he rose, and immediately took**], Byz[And he immediately rose, and took (DRA, HCS, KJV, MRD, NET, NKJ, NLT, TLB)]; Alx[**in front of them all**], Byz[in the sight of them all (DRA, NAB, NAS, NAU, NIV, NLT, REB, ~TEV, TLB)]; Alx/Byz[**glorified God, saying**], Minor[*omits* saying (TLB)].

2:13 Alx/Byz[**beside the sea**], Minor[to the sea (DRA, MRD, NJB, NLT, REB, TEV, TLB)].

2:14 Alx/Byz[**Levi**], Minor[James].

2:15 Alx[**as he sat**], Byz[it came to pass as he sat (ASV, DRA, KJV, MRD, NAS, NAU, NKJ, ~NLT, ~TEV, ~TLB)]; Alx/Byz[**there were many who followed him. 16 And the scribes…**], Minor[there were also many scribes…who followed him]; **Levi's** *Greek* his.

disciples; for there were many who followed him. 16 And the scribes of the Pharisees, when they saw that he ate with sinners and tax collectors, said to his disciples, "He eats with tax collectors and sinners!" 17 And when Jesus heard it, he said to them, "Those who are well have no need of a physician, but those who are sick. I did not come to call the righteous, but sinners."

18 Now John's disciples and the Pharisees were fasting. And people came and said to him, "Why do John's disciples and the disciples of the Pharisees fast, but your disciples do not fast?" 19 And Jesus said to them, "Can the guests of the bridegroom fast while he is with them? As long as they have the bridegroom with them, they cannot fast. 20 But the days will come, when the bridegroom will be taken away from them, and then they will fast in that day.

21 "No one sews a patch of unshrunk cloth on an old garment. If he does, the new piece will pull away from the old, and the tear is made worse. 22 And no one puts new wine into old wineskins. If he does, the wine will burst the skins, and the wine and wineskins are ruined. But new wine is for new wineskins."

23 One Sabbath he was going through the grain-fields. And as they made their way his disciples began to pluck heads of grain. 24 And the Pharisees said to him, "Look, why are they doing what is not lawful on the Sabbath?" 25 But he said to them, "Have you never read what David did when he was in need and hungry, he and those who were with him: 26 how he entered the house of God in the days when Abiathar was high priest, and ate the consecrated bread, which is not lawful to eat, except for the priests, and also gave some to those who were with him?" 27 And he said to them, "The Sabbath was made for man, not man for the Sabbath. 28 So the Son of Man is Lord even of the Sabbath."

3 1 He entered the synagogue again, and a man was there who had a withered hand. 2 And they watched him closely, to see whether he would heal him on the Sabbath, so that they might accuse him. 3 And he said to the man who had the

---

2:16 Alx[**scribes of the Pharisees**], Byz[scribes and the Pharisees (DRA, JNT, KJV, MRD, NET, NKJ)]; Alx[**saw that he ate**], Byz[saw him eating (KJV, NIV, NJB, NKJ, NLT, ~REB, TLB)]; Alx[**sinners and tax collectors...tax collectors and sinners**], Byz[tax collectors and sinners...tax collectors and sinners (DRA, KJV, MRD, NKJ, REB)], Minor[sinners and tax collectors...sinners and tax collectors (~NLT, ~TLB]; Alx[**He eats...!**], Byz[Why does he eat and drink...? (ASV, DRA, ~ESV, ~HCS, ~JNT, KJV, MRD, ~NAB, NAS, NAU, ~NET, ~NIV, ~NJB, NKJ, ~NRS, ~REB, ~RSV, ~TEV, ~TLB)].

2:17 Alx[**sinners**], Byz[*adds* to repentance (KJV, NKJ, TLB)].

2:18 Alx[**John's disciples and the Pharisees**], Byz[the disciples of John and of the Pharisees (KJV, MRD, NAB, NKJ, ~TEV)]; Alx[**John's disciples and the disciples of the Pharisees**], Byz[the disciples of John and of the Pharisees (DRA, KJV, MRD, NKJ, ~TLB)]; Alx/Byz[**but your disciples**], Minor[but yours (NIV, REB, TEV)]; **And people came** *Greek* And they came.

2:20 Alx[**in that day**], Byz[in those days (DRA, KJV, ~NET, NKJ, ~NLT, ~REB, ~TEV, ~TLB)].

2:21 Alx/Byz[**No one**], Major[And no one (KJV)]; **If he does** *Greek* Lest.

2:22 Alx[**the wine will burst**], Byz[the new wine bursts (KJV, NKJ)], Alx[**the wine and wineskins are ruined**], Byz[the wine is spilled and the wineskins ruined (DRA, ~HCS, KJV, MRD, NKJ, TLB)], Alx[**But new wine is for new wineskins**], Byz[But new wine must be poured into new wineskins (DRA, KJV, NKJ, TEV)], Minor[omits].

2:23 Alx[**One Sabbath he was going**], Byz[He was going one Sabbath (ASV, DRA, KJV, NAB, NAS, NAU, NET, NKJ, TEV)].

2:26 Alx/Byz[**how he entered**], Minor[omits how (JNT, NIV, NLT, NRS, REB, TEV, TLB)]; Alx/Major[**when Abiathar was high priest**], Byz[of Abiathar the high priest (DRA, ESV, HCS, KJV, NAS, NAU, NIV, NKJ, REB)]; *compare 1 Samuel 21.*

2:27 Alx[**not man for the Sabbath**], Byz[and not man for the Sabbath (ASV, DRA, HCS, KJV, MRD, NAS, NAU, NKJ, NLT, NRS, TLB)].

3:1 Alx/Byz[**the synagogue**], Minor[a synagogue (JNT, MRD, NAS, NAU, REB)].

3:2 Alx/Byz[**would heal**], Minor[heals (~NLT)].

withered hand, "Come here." [4] Then he said to them, "Is it lawful on the Sabbaths to do good or to do evil, to save life or to kill?" But they kept silent. [5] And he looked around at them with anger, grieved at the hardness of their hearts, and said to the man, "Stretch out the hand." He stretched it out, and his hand was restored. [6] Then the Pharisees went out and immediately brought counsel with the Herodians against him, how they might destroy him.

[7] Jesus withdrew with his disciples to the sea, and a great multitude from Galilee [followed]. And from Judea [8] and Jerusalem and Idumea and beyond the Jordan and from around Tyre and Sidon, a great multitude, hearing how many things he was doing, came to him. [9] And he told his disciples to have a small boat ready for him because of the crowd, lest they should crush him. [10] For he had healed many, so that all who had diseases pressed upon him to touch him. [11] And whenever the unclean spirits saw him, they fell down before him and cried out, "You are the Son of God." [12] But he strictly ordered them not to make him known.

[13] And he went up on the mountain, and called to him those he himself wanted. And they came to him. [14] Then he appointed twelve, [whom he also named apostles,] that they might be with him and that he might send them out to preach, [15] and to have authority to cast out the demons. [16] [And he appointed the twelve –] Simon, to whom he gave the name Peter; [17] James the son of Zebedee and John the brother of James, to whom he gave the name Boanerges, that is, "Sons of Thunder"; [18] Andrew, Philip, Bartholomew, Matthew, Thomas, James the son of Alphaeus, Thaddaeus, Simon the Zealot; [19] and Judas Iscariot, who betrayed him.

[20] Then he went into a house; and [the] crowd came together again, so that they could not even eat. [21] When his family heard about this, they went to take charge of him, for they said, "He is out of his mind." [22] And the scribes who came down from Jerusalem said, "He is possessed by Beelzebul, and by the prince of demons he casts out the demons." [23] So he called them to himself and said to them in parables: "How can Satan

---

3:5 Alx[**Stretch out the hand**], Byz[Stretch out your hand (ASV, DRA, ESV, HCS, JNT, KJV, MRD, NAB, NAS, NAU, NET, NIV, NJB, NKJ, NLT, NRS, REB, RSV, TEV, TLB)]; Alx[**restored**], Byz[*adds* as whole as the other (KJV, NKJ)].

3:6 Alx[**brought counsel** *or* gave counsel], Byz[made counsel (DRA, TEV)]; Alx/Byz[**Herodians**], Minor[domestics of Herod (MRD)].

3:7 Alx/Byz[**to the sea**], Minor[into the sea]; Alx[**followed**], Byz[followed him (DRA, JNT, KJV, MRD, NET, NJB, NKJ, NLT, NRS, TEV)], Minor[*omits* (REB)]; Alx/Major[**And from Judea 8**], Byz[8 And from Judea (JNT, NIV, NRS, ~TLB)].

3:8 Alx[**and from around Tyre**], Byz[and those from around Tyre (DRA, KJV, NKJ)]; Alx/Byz[**hearing**], Minor[when they heard (ESV, HCS, JNT, KJV, MRD, NAS, NAU, NET, NIV, NJB, NKJ, ~NLT, REB, TEV, ~TLB)]; Alx/Byz[**he was doing**], Minor[he is doing (~NLT, ~TLB)].

3:14 Alx[**whom he also named apostles**], Byz[*omits* (ASV, DRA, JNT, KJV, MRD, NAS, NAU, NJB, NKJ, REB, RSV, TLB)].

3:15 Alx[**authority**], Byz[*adds* to heal sicknesses and (DRA, JNT, KJV, MRD, NKJ)].

3:16 Alx[**and he appointed the twelve**], Byz[*omits* (ASV, DRA, JNT, KJV, MRD, NKJ, NLT, RSV, TLB)]; Alx/Byz[**Peter**], Alt/Peshitta[Cephas (JNT, MRD)].

3:18 Alx/Byz[**Thaddaeus**], Minor[Lebbaeus]; Alx[**Zealot** *Greek* Cananean], Byz[Cananite (KJV, MRD, NKJ)].

3:19 Alx/Byz[**Iscariot**], Alt/Vulgate/Peshitta[Scariot], Alt[from Kerioth (~JNT)]; **Iscariot** *Hebraism Ish Keriot a man from Kerioth or possibly Sicarios assassin or bandit.*

3:20 Alx/Byx[**20 Then he went into a house**], Major[Then they went into a house 20 (KJV, MRD, NKJ, DRA)].

3:21 Alx/Byz[**his family** *or* his friends], Minor[the scribes and the others].

3:22 Alx/Byz[**Beelzebul**], Alt/Vulgate/Peshitta[Beelzebub (ASV, DRA, KJV, MRD, NKJ, ~NLT, ~TLB)].

cast out Satan? [24] If a kingdom is divided against itself, that kingdom cannot stand. [25] And if a house is divided against itself, that house will not be able to stand. [26] And if Satan has risen up against himself, and is divided, he cannot stand, but is coming to an end. [27] But no one can enter a strong man's house and plunder his goods, unless he first binds the strong man. And then he will plunder his house. [28] Truly, I say to you, all sins will be forgiven the sons of men, and whatever blasphemies they utter; [29] but whoever blasphemes against the Holy Spirit never has forgiveness, but is guilty of eternal sin" – [30] because they said, "He has an unclean spirit."

[31] And then his mother came, and his brothers. And standing outside they sent to him, and called him. [32] And a crowd was sitting around him. And they said to him, "Your mother and your brothers [and your sisters] are outside, asking for you." [33] And answering them, he said, "Who are my mother and [my] brothers?" [34] And he looked at those who sat in a circle around him, and said, "Here are my mother and my brothers! [35] [For] whoever does the will of God is my brother, and sister, and mother."

4 [1] Again he began to teach by the sea. And a very large crowd gathered around him, so that he got into a boat and sat in it on the sea. And the whole crowd was beside the sea on the land. [2] Then he taught them many things by parables, and said to them in his teaching: [3] "Listen! A sower went out to sow. [4] And as he sowed the seed, some fell along the path. And the birds came and devoured it. [5] And some fell on rocky ground, where it did not have much soil. And immediately it sprang up, because it had no depth of soil. [6] And when the sun came up it was scorched, and because it had no root it withered away. [7] Other seed fell among thorns and the thorns grew up and choked it, and it yielded no grain. [8] And other seeds fell on good soil and yielded a crop that

---

3:25 Alx[**will not be able to stand**], Byz[cannot stand (DRA, HCS, JNT, KJV, MRD, NIV, NJB, NKJ, ~NLT, REB, ~TEV, ~TLB)].

3:27 Alx[**But no one**], Byz[No one (DRA, KJV, MRD, NKJ, TEV, TLB)]; Alx/Byz[**will plunder his house**], Major[can plunder his house (ESV, JNT, MRD, NAB, NET, NIV, NJB, NLT, NRS, REB, RSV, TEV, TLB)].

3:28 **whatever blasphemies they utter** *Greek* as many blasphemies they blaspheme.

3:29 Alx[**is guilty of eternal sin**], Byz[is liable to eternal damnation (KJV, MRD, NKJ, ~NLT)], Minor[shall be guilty of eternal sin *others* is liable to eternal torment].

3:31 Alx[**And then his mother came, and his brothers**], Byz[Then his mother came, and his brothers (HCS, JNT, NAB, NAU, NET, NIV, NJB, NKJ, NLT, NRS, REB, TEV, TLB)], Major[Then the brothers and his mother came (KJV, NKJ)].

3:32 Alx[**they said to him** *Greek* they say to him], Byz[they said to him]; Alx/Major[**and your sisters**], Byz[*omits* (ASV, DRA, ESV, JNT, KJV, MRD, NAS, NAU, NET, NIV, NKJ, NLT, REB, RSV, TLB, Metzger)].

3:33 Alx[**And answering them, he said** *Greek* And answering them, he says], Byz[And he answered them, saying (KJV, NKJ)]; Alx[**and my brothers**], Byz[or my brothers (KJV, NKJ, ~NLT, ~TEV, ~TLB)], Minor[and brothers].

3:35 Alx/Byz[**For**], Minor[*omits* (ESV 2001 edition, HCS, JNT, NIV, NJB, NLT, NRS, REB, RSV, TEV, TLB)]; Alx/Byz[**the will of God**], Minor[the things God wills (JNT, TEV)]; Alx[**and sister**], Byz[and my sister (DRA, KJV, MRD, NKJ, TEV, TLB)].

4:1 Alx[**a very large crowd gathered** *Greek* a very large crowd gathers], Byz[a large crowd gathered (DRA, KJV, MRD, NKJ, NLT)].

4:4 Alx/Major[**along the path**], Byz[on the path (NAB, NLT, NRS, TLB)]; Alx/Major[**the birds**], Byz[*adds* of the air (DRA, KJV, NKJ)].

4:5 Alx/Byz[**And some fell**], Major[But some fell]; Alx/Byz[**ground, where**], Minor[ground, and where].

4:6 Alx[**And when the sun came up**], Byz[But at the sun's rising (~JNT, KJV, MRD, ~NIV, NKJ, ~NLT, ~REB, ~TLB)]; Alx/Byz[**it was scorched**], Minor[they were scorched (JNT, NIV, ~TEV)].

4:8 Alx[**And other seeds** *Greek* And others], Byz[And other seed *Greek* And other (JNT, KJV, MRD, NET, NIV, NKJ, NRS)]; Alx[**a thirty, and a sixty, and a hundredfold**], Byz[in thirty, and in sixty,

sprang up, and produced a thirty, and a sixty, and a hundredfold increase." [9] And he said, "He who has ears to hear, let him hear."

[10] And when he was alone, those around him with the twelve asked him about the parables. [11] And he said to them, "To you has been given the secret of the kingdom of God, but to those outside everything is in parables; [12] so that

> 'seeing they may see but not perceive,
>> and hearing may hear but not understand;
> lest they should turn again, and be forgiven.'"

[13] And he said to them, "Do you not understand this parable? How then will you understand all the parables? [14] The sower sows the word. [15] And these are the ones along the path where the word is sown. When they hear, Satan comes immediately and takes away the word that was sown in them. [16] And these are the ones sown on rocky ground who, when they hear the word, immediately receive it with joy. [17] And they have no root in themselves, but endure for only a time. Then, when tribulation or persecution arises on account of the word, immediately they fall away. [18] And others are the ones sown among thorns. They are those who heard the word, [19] but the cares of the world, the deceitfulness of riches, and the desires for other things enter in and choke the word, and it becomes unfruitful. [20] And those are the ones sown on good soil, who hear the word, accept it, and bear a thirty, and a sixty, and a hundredfold crop."

[21] And he said to them, "Is a lamp brought to be put under a basket or under a bed? Is it not to be set on a lampstand? [22] For there is nothing hidden, except to be revealed; nor is anything secret, except to come to light. [23] If anyone has ears to hear, let him hear."

[24] Then he said to them, "Take heed what you hear. With the measure you use, it will be measured to you; and more will be given you. [25] For he who has, to him will more be given. And whoever does not have, from him even what he has will be taken away."

[26] And he said, "The kingdom of God is like a man who should scatter seed on the ground, [27] and should sleep by night and rise by day, and the seed should sprout and

---

and in hundredfold], Minor[into thirty, and into sixty, and into a hundredfold].

4:9 Alx/Major[**he said**], Byz[*adds* to them (KJV, NKJ)].

4:10 Alx[**And when**], Byz[But when (NKJ)]; Alx[**the parables**], Byz[the parable (DRA, KJV, MRD, NKJ, TLB)].

4:11 Alx[**the secret** *or* the mystery], Byz[to know the secrets (~TLB)], Major[to know the secret (DRA, KJV, MRD, NKJ, NLT)].

4:12 Alx[**be forgiven**], Byz[*adds* their sins (DRA, KJV, MRD, ~NJB, NKJ, TLB)]; ~Isaiah 6:9-10 LXX.

4:15 Alx[**sown in them**], Byz[sown in their hearts (DRA, KJV, MRD, NKJ, ~TEV, ~TLB)].

4:16 Alx[**And these are the ones**], Byz[And these likewise are the ones (ASV, DRA, JNT, KJV, NAS, NAU, ~NIV, NJB, NKJ, RSV, ~TEV)].

4:17 **fall away** *or* stumble.

4:18 Alx[**And others are the ones**], Byz[And these are the ones (KJV, ~MRD, ~NAB, NKJ, ~NLT, ~TLB)]; Alx[**They are those**], Byz[*omits* (KJV, ~MRD, ~NAB, ~NLT, ~TLB)]; Alx[**heard the word**], Byz[hear the word (DRA, ESV, HCS, JNT, KJV, MRD, NAB, NET, NIV, NKJ, NLT, NRS, REB, RSV, TEV, TLB)].

4:19 Alx[**cares of the world**], Byz[cares of this world (HCS, KJV, MRD, ~NAB, ~NET, NIV, NKJ, NLT, REB, TEV, TLB)].

4:20 Alx[**And those**], Byz[And these (DRA, KJV, NET, NKJ, NRS)]; Alx[**a thirty, and a sixty, and a hundredfold**], Byz[in thirty, and in sixty, and in a hundredfold (MRD)], Minor[a thirty, and sixty, and hundredfold].

4:21 Alx/Byz[**on a lampstand**], Minor[under a lampstand].

4:22 Alx/Byz[**except to be revealed**], Major[which will not be revealed (DRA, KJV, MRD, ~NIV, NKJ, ~NLT, ~TEV, ~TLB)].

4:24 Alx[**will be given you**], Byz[*adds* who hear (KJV, MRD, NKJ)], Minor[*adds* who believe].

4:25 Alx[**he who has**], Byz[whoever has (JNT, NAS, NAU, NET, NIV, NJB, NKJ)].

grow. He himself does not know how. 28 All by itself the earth produces grain – first the blade, then the head, then the full kernel in the head. 29 But when the grain is ripe, at once he puts in the sickle, because the harvest has come."

30 And he said, "How shall we compare the kingdom of God, or what parable shall we use for it? 31 It is like a mustard seed which, when it is sown on the ground, though the smallest of all seeds in the earth, 32 yet when it is sown it grows up and becomes the greatest of all shrubs, and puts forth large branches, so that the birds of the air can make nests in its shade."

33 With many such parables he spoke the word to them, as they were able to hear it. 34 But without a parable he did not speak to them. And when they were alone, he explained everything to his own disciples.

35 On that day, when evening had come, he said to them, "Let us go over to the other side." 36 And leaving the crowd, they took him along, just as he was, in the boat. There were also other boats with him. 37 And a great storm arose. And the waves beat into the boat, so that the boat was already filling. 38 But he was in the stern, asleep on a cushion. And they woke him and said to him, "Teacher, do you not care if we perish?" 39 Then he rose and rebuked the wind, and said to the sea, "Peace! Be still!" And the wind ceased and there was a great calm. 40 He said to them, "Why are you afraid? Do you still have no faith?" 41 And they were filled with awe, and said to one another, "Who is this? Even the wind and the sea obey him!"

5 1 They came to the other side of the sea, to the country of the Gerasenes. 2 And when he had come out of the boat, immediately there met him out of the tombs a man with an unclean spirit, 3 who lived among the tombs. And no one could bind him any more, not even with a chain, 4 for he had often been bound with shackles and chains. But the chains he wrenched apart. And the shackles he broke in pieces. And no one had the strength to subdue him. 5 Night and day among the tombs and on the mountains he was always crying out, and cutting himself with stones. 6 And when he saw Jesus from a distance, he ran and bowed down to him. 7 And crying out with a loud voice,

---

4:26 Alx/Byz[**like a man who should scatter**], Major[as if a man should scatter (ASV, DRA, ESV, KJV, MRD, NAB, NKJ, NRS, RSV)].

4:28 Alx[**All by itself**], Byz[For all by itself (DRA, KJV, MRD, NKJ, TLB)].

4:30 Alx/Byz[**How shall we compare**], Major[To what shall we compare (DRA, ESV, JNT, KJV, MRD, NAB, NET, NIV, NJB, NKJ, NRS, RSV, TEV)]; Alx[**use for it**], Byz[compare it (DRA, KJV, MRD, NKJ, NLT, TLB)].

4:31 Alx[**though the smallest** *or* being the smallest], Byz[is the smallest (DRA, ESV, HCS, JNT, KJV, MRD, NAB, NIV, NJB, NKJ, NLT, NRS, REB, RSV, TEV)].

4:34 Alx[**his own disciples**], Byz[his disciples (DRA, KJV, MRD, NJB, NKJ, NLT, NRS, REB, TEV, TLB)].

4:36 Alx/Byz[**There were also other boats**], Major[And there were also other little boats (KJV, MRD, NKJ)].

4:37 Alx[**the boat was already filling**], Byz[it was already sinking (~JNT, TLB)], Major[it was already filling (KJV, MRD, NAB, NIV, NJB, NKJ, NLT, REB, TEV)].

4:40 Alx[**Why are you afraid? Do you still have no faith**], Byz[Why are you so afraid? How is it that you have no faith (~ESV, KJV, MRD, NAS, ~NIV, ~NJB, NKJ, ~REB, ~TLB)].

5:1 Alx[**Gerasenes**], Byz[Gergesenes], Major[Gadarenes (KJV, MRD, NKJ, ~TLB)].

5:2 Alx/Byz[**immediately**], Minor[omits (HCS, JNT, MRD, ~NET, NIV, NLT, REB, RSV, ~TEV)].

5:3 Alx[**any more**], Byz[omit (JNT, KJV, MRD, NKJ, TLB)]; Alx[**a chain**], Byz[chains (DRA, HCS, KJV, MRD, NKJ, REB, TEV, TLB)].

5:5 Alx/Byz[**tombs...mountains**], Major[mountains...tombs (KJV, ~MRD, NKJ)].

5:6 Alx[**And when**], Byz[But when (~HCS, ~JNT, KJV, ~NAB, ~NAU, ~NET, ~NIV, ~NJB, ~NKJ, ~NLT, ~NRS, ~REB, ~TEV, ~TLB)]; Alx/Byz[**bowed down to him**], Minor[worshipped him (ASV, DRA, KJV, MRD, NKJ, RSV)].

5:7 Alx/Byz[**he said** *Greek* he says], Major[he said].

he said, "What have you to do with me, Jesus, Son of the Most High God? I implore you by God, do not torment me." [8] For he had said to him, "Come out of the man, you unclean spirit!" [9] Then Jesus asked him, "What is your name?" And he said to him, "My name is Legion, for we are many." [10] And he begged him eagerly not to send them out of the country.

[11] Now a large herd of swine was feeding there on the mountain. [12] So they begged him, "Send us to the swine, that we may enter them." [13] So he gave them permission. And the unclean spirits came out, and entered the swine. And the herd, about two thousand, rushed down the steep bank into the sea, and were drowned in the sea. [14] And those who fed them fled, and told it in the city and in the country. And they went to see what it was that had happened. [15] And they came to Jesus, and saw the man who had been possessed sitting there, clothed and in his right mind, the man who had been possessed by the legion; and they were afraid. [16] And those who had seen it told the people what had happened to the demon-possessed man, and about the swine. [17] Then they began to plead with Jesus to depart from their region. [18] And as he was getting into the boat, the man who had been demon-possessed begged to remain with him. [19] And he did not let him, but said, "Go home to your friends and tell them how much the Lord has done for you, and how he has had mercy on you." [20] And he went away and began to proclaim in the Decapolis how much Jesus had done for him. And all men marveled.

[21] And when Jesus had crossed again [in the boat] to the other side, a great crowd gathered around him; and he was by the sea. [22] Then came one of the rulers of the synagogue, Jairus by name. And seeing him, he fell at his feet, [23] and pleaded earnestly with him, saying, "My little daughter is at the point of death. Come and lay your hands on her, so that she may be healed, and live." [24] So Jesus went with him.

5:9 Alx[he said to him], Byz[he answered, saying (~ESV, ~HCS, ~JNT, KJV, ~MRD, ~NAB, ~NET, ~NIV, ~NJB, NKJ, ~NLT, ~NRS, ~REB, ~RSV, ~TEV, ~TLB)]; Jesus Greek he.
5:10 Alx[them neuter], Byz[them masculine].
5:11 Alx/Byz[mountain], Minor[mountains (KJV, NKJ)].
5:12 Alx[they begged him], Byz[all the demons begged him (KJV, NKJ)], Minor[the demons begged him (DRA, HCS, JNT, MRD, NAS, NAU, NET, NIV, NJB, NLT, NRS, TEV, TLB, REB)].
5:13 Alx[So he gave], Byz[So Jesus immediately gave (DRA, ~JNT, KJV, ~NAU, ~NET, NKJ, ~NLT, ~TLB)]; Alx[about two thousand], Byz[and they were about two thousand (KJV, NKJ, ~TLB)].
5:14 Alx/Byz[And those], Major[Now those (~ESV, ~HCS, ~JNT, ~NAB, ~NAU, NET, ~NIV, ~NJB, NKJ, ~NLT, ~NRS, ~REB, ~RSV, ~TEV, ~TLB)]; Alx[those who fed them], Byz[those who fed the swine (~ESV, ~JNT, KJV, ~NAB, ~NAS, ~NAU, ~NET, NIV, NKJ, ~NLT, ~NRS, ~RSV, TEV, ~TLB)]; Alx[they went to see], Byz[they went out to see (DRA, KJV, MRD, NAB, NET, NIV, NKJ, NLT, REB, TEV, TLB)].
5:15 Alx[clothed], Byz[and clothed (KJV, NKJ)].
5:16 Alx/Byz[And those], Major[Now those (~HCS, ~JNT, ~NAB, ~NAU, ~NET, ~NIV, ~NLT, ~NRS, ~REB, ~TEV, ~TLB)].
5:17 Jesus Greek him.
5:18 Alx/Byz[as he was getting into the boat], Major[as he got into the boat (DRA, ~KJV, MRD, NKJ, TLB)].
5:19 Alx/Byz[And he did not let him], Major[But Jesus did not let him (~HCS, JNT, KJV, ~NAB, NET, ~NIV, ~NJB, NKJ, NLT, NRS, REB, ~RSV, TEV, TLB)].
5:20 Decapolis or Ten Cities.
5:21 Alx/Byz[in the boat], Minor[omits (TEV)].
5:22 Alx/Byz[Then came one of the rulers], Major[Then – behold! – there came one of the rulers (KJV, NKJ)]; Alx/Byz[Jairus by name], Minor[omits].
5:23 Alx[pleaded Greek pleads], Byz[pleaded]; Alx[she may be healed], Byz[she will be healed (JNT, MRD, NAU, NIV, TEV, TLB)].

And a great crowd followed him and thronged around him. ²⁵ And there was a woman who had endured a flow of blood for twelve years. ²⁶ And she had suffered much under many physicians, and had spent all that she owned, and was no better, but instead grew worse. ²⁷ When she heard about Jesus, she came up behind him in the crowd and touched his garment. ²⁸ For she said, "If I touch even his clothes, I shall be made well." ²⁹ And immediately the bleeding stopped. And she felt in her body that she was healed of her disease. ³⁰ And Jesus, immediately knowing in himself that power had gone out from him, turned around in the crowd and said, "Who touched my clothes?" ³¹ And his disciples said to him, "You see the crowd pressing around you, and yet you say, 'Who touched me?'" ³² And he looked around to see who had done it. ³³ But the woman, knowing what had happened to her, came and fell down before him in fear and trembling and told him the whole truth. ³⁴ And he said to her, "Daughter, your faith has made you well. Go in peace, and be healed of your disease."

³⁵ While he was still speaking, some came from the ruler of the synagogue's house who said, "Your daughter is dead. Why trouble the Teacher any further?" ³⁶ But ignoring what they said, Jesus said to the ruler of the synagogue, "Do not be afraid; only believe." ³⁷ And he allowed no one to follow with him except Peter, James, and John the brother of James. ³⁸ When they came to the house of the ruler of the synagogue, he saw a tumult, and people weeping and wailing loudly. ³⁹ And when he came in, he said to them, "Why make this commotion and weep? The child is not dead, but sleeping." ⁴⁰ And they laughed at him. But after he put them all outside, he took the child's father and mother and those who were with him, and went in where the child was. ⁴¹ He took her by the hand and said to her, "Talitha kum!" which means, "Little girl, I say to you, arise." ⁴² Immediately the girl stood up and walked (she was twelve years of age). And they were [immediately] overcome with great amazement. ⁴³ He strictly charged them that no one should know this, and told them to give her something to eat.

6 ¹ He went away from there and came to his hometown. And his disciples followed him. ² And when the Sabbath had come, he began to teach in the synagogue. And many who heard him were astonished, saying, "Where did this

---

5:25 Alx[**there was a woman**], Byz[there was a certain woman (KJV, NKJ)].

5:27 Alx/Byz[**she heard about Jesus**], Minor[she heard the things about Jesus (ASV, ESV, RSV, TLB)].

5:28 Alx/Major[**For she said**], Byz[*adds* in herself (NLT, TEV, TLB)].

5:33 Alx[**happened to her**], Byz[happened in her (DRA, KJV, MRD)].

5:36 Alx[**But ignoring what they said, Jesus** *or* But overhearing what they said, Jesus], Byz[But as soon as Jesus heard what they said, he (KJV, NKJ)].

5:37 Alx[**to follow with him**], Byz[to follow him (DRA, ESV, ~HCS, JNT, KJV, ~NAB, ~NAU, NET, NIV, NKJ, NRS, ~REB, RSV)]; Alx/Byz[**Peter**], Alt/Peshitta[Simon Cephas (~JNT, MRD)].

5:38 Alx[**When they came**], Byz[When he came (KJV, NKJ)]; Alx/Byz[**and people weeping**], Major[*omits* and (ESV, HCS, ~JNT, MRD, NAB, ~NIV, ~NJB, NRS, ~REB, ~TLB)].

5:40 Alx/Major[**40 And they laughed at him**], Byz[And they laughed at him 40]; Alx[**where the child was**], Byz[*adds* lying (DRA, KJV, MRD, NJB, NKJ, NLT, TEV, TLB)].

5:41 Alx[**"Talitha kum!" which means**], Byz["Talitha kumi!" which means (ASV, DRA, ESV, JNT, KJV, NKJ, RSV)], Minor["Tabitha" which means *others omit* (MRD, TLB)]; **Talitha kum** *Aramaic*.

5:42 Alx[**they were immediately overcome**], Byz[*omits* immediately (DRA, HCS, JNT, KJV, MRD, ~NAB, NET, NIV, NKJ, NLT, ~NRS, REB, ~TEV, TLB)].

6:1 Alx[**came** *Greek* comes], Byz[came]; Alx/Major[**his hometown** *Greek* his fatherland], Byz[his own hometown *Greek* his own fatherland (ASV, DRA, KJV, MRD, NKJ, RSV)].

6:2 Alx/Byz[**And many who heard**], Minor[And the many who heard (NAS, NAU, REB, TLB)]; Alx[**given to this one**], Byz[given to him (DRA, ESV, HCS, JNT, KJV, MRD, NAB, NAS, NAU, NET, NIV, NJB, NKJ, NLT, NRS, REB, RSV, TEV, ~TLB)]; Alx/Byz[**and such mighty works performed**], Minor[that such mighty works are performed (KJV, MRD, NIV, NKJ, ~TLB)].

man get these things? And what wisdom is this which is given to this one, and such mighty works performed by his hands! ³ Is not this the carpenter, the son of Mary and brother of James and Joses and Judas and Simon? Are not his sisters here with us?" And they took offense at him. ⁴ And Jesus said to them, "A prophet is not without honor except in his country, among his relatives, and in his house." ⁵ Now he could do no mighty work there, except that he laid his hands on a few sick people and healed them. ⁶ And he marveled because of their unbelief. Then he went around the villages teaching.

⁷ And he called to him the twelve, and began to send them out two by two, and gave them authority over the unclean spirits. ⁸ He commanded them to take nothing for the journey except a staff – no bread, no bag, no money in their belts – ⁹ but to wear sandals and not put on two tunics. ¹⁰ And he said to them, "Where you enter a house, stay there until you leave that place. ¹¹ And if any place will not receive you and they refuse to hear you, when you leave, shake off the dust that is on your feet for a testimony against them." ¹² So they went out and preached that people should repent. ¹³ And they cast out many demons, and anointed with oil many that were sick and healed them.

¹⁴ King Herod heard of it, for Jesus' name had become well known. Some said, "John the Baptist has been raised from the dead, and that is why these powers are at work in him." ¹⁵ But others said, "It is Elijah." And others said, "It is a prophet, like one of the prophets of old." ¹⁶ But when Herod heard, he said, "This is John, whom I beheaded. He has been raised!" ¹⁷ For Herod himself had sent and had John arrested, and bound him in prison for the sake of Herodias, his brother Philip's wife; because he had married her. ¹⁸ For John had said to Herod, "It is not lawful for you to have your brother's wife." ¹⁹ And Herodias had a grudge against him, and wanted to kill him. But she could not, ²⁰ for Herod feared John and protected him, knowing that he was a righteous and holy man. When he heard him, he was greatly perplexed. And yet he heard him gladly. ²¹ But an opportunity came when Herod on his birthday gave a banquet for his high officers and military commanders and the leading men of Galilee. ²² And when his daughter by Herodias came in and danced, she pleased Herod and those who sat to eat. The king said to the girl, "Ask me for whatever you want, and I will give it to you." ²³ And he [eagerly]

6:3 Alx/Byz[**the carpenter, the son of Mary**], Minor[the son of the carpenter and Mary *others* the son of Mary]; Alx[**Joses**], Byz[Joseph (DRA, JNT, NIV, NLT, TEV, TLB)]; **took offense** *or* stumbled.

6:4 Alx[**And Jesus said**], Byz[But Jesus said (~HCS, JNT, KJV, ~NAB, ~NAU, ~NET, ~NIV, NKJ, ~NLT, ~NRS, ~REB, ~TEV, ~TLB)]; Alx/Byz[**in his country**], Minor[in his own country (ASV, DRA, KJV, MRD, NJB, NKJ, NLT, RSV, TEV)]; Alx[**among his relatives**], Byz[among relatives].

6:8 Alx[**bread...bag**], Byz[bag...bread (DRA, KJV, MRD, NKJ)].

6:9 Alx/Major[**not put on two tunics**], Byz[to not put on two tunics (NKJ, NLT, NRS)].

6:11 Alx[**if any place**], Byz[if any one (DRA, JNT, KJV, MRD, NKJ, ~TEV, ~TLB)]; Alx[**testimony against them**], Byz[*adds* Truly I say to you, it will be more tolerable for Sodom and Gomorrah in the day of judgment than for that city (KJV, MRD, NKJ)].

6:14 Alx[**Some said**], Byz[He said (ASV, DRA, KJV, MRD, NKJ)]; **Jesus'** *Greek* his.

6:15 Alx[**But others said**], Byz[*omits* But (JNT, KJV, MRD, NAB, NET, NIV, NJB, NKJ, NLT, REB, TLB)], Alx/Major[**like one**], Byz[or like one (KJV, NKJ)].

6:16 Alx[**He has been raised**], Byz[*adds* from the dead (DRA, KJV, MRD, NIV, NJB, NKJ, NLT, REB, TLB)].

6:17 Alx/Byz[**in prison**], Minor[in the prison].

6:20 Alx[**he was greatly perplexed**], Byz[he did many things (DRA, KJV, ~MRD, NKJ)].

6:22 Alx[**his daughter by Herodias** *Greek* the daughter of him of Herodias], Byz[the daughter of Herodias herself (ASV, DRA, ESV, HCS, JNT, KJV, MRD, NAB, NAS, NAU, NIV, NJB, NKJ, REB, RSV, TEV, TLB)]; Alx[**she pleased**], Byz[and pleased (DRA, KJV, ~MRD, ~NAB, NKJ, ~NLT, REB, TEV, TLB)]; Alx/Byz[**The king said**], Minor[And the king said (ASV, ESV, MRD, NAS, NAU, ~NJB, NRS, RSV, ~TEV)].

6:23 Alx[**eagerly vowed** *or* vowed much], Byz[vowed (ASV, DRA, ESV, JNT, KJV, MRD, NAS, NAU, NET, KJV, NLT, ~REB, RSV, TLB)].

vowed to her, "Whatever you ask me, I will give you, up to half of my kingdom." 24 So she went out and said to her mother, "What should I ask?" And she said, "The head of John the Baptist!" 25 Immediately she came in with haste to the king and asked, saying, "I want you to give me at once the head of John the Baptist on a platter." 26 And the king was exceedingly sorry. But, because of his oaths and the people at the table, he did not want to refuse her. 27 And immediately the king sent an executioner and gave orders to bring his head. He went and beheaded him in the prison, 28 and brought his head on a platter, and gave it to the girl. And the girl gave it to her mother. 29 When his disciples heard of it, they came and took his body, and laid it in a tomb.

30 The apostles gathered to Jesus, and told him all that they had done and that they had taught. 31 And he said to them, "Come away by yourselves to a lonely place and rest a while." For there were many coming and going, and they did not even have time to eat. 32 So they went away in the boat to a lonely place by themselves. 33 But they saw them going, and many knew. And they ran there on foot from all the towns, and got there ahead of them. 34 When he went ashore he saw a great crowd. And he had compassion on them, because they were like sheep without a shepherd. So he began to teach them many things. 35 When it was late in the day, his disciples came to him and said, "This is a deserted place, and already the hour is late. 36 Send them away, so they can go to the surrounding country and villages and buy themselves something to eat." 37 But he answered and said to them, "You give them something to eat." And they said to him, "Should we go and buy two hundred denarii worth of bread, and give it to them to eat?" 38 But he said to them, "How many loaves do you have? Go see." And when they found out they said, "Five, and two fish." 39 Then he commanded them to all sit down in groups

---

6:24 Alx[**What should I ask**], Byz[What shall I ask (ASV, DRA, KJV, MRD, NAB, NAS, NAU, NIV, NJB, NKJ, REB, RSV, TEV, ~TLB)].

6:26 Alx[**at the table**], Byz[*adds* with him (DRA, ~ESV, ~HCS, ~JNT, KJV, ~MRD, ~NAB, ~NAS, ~NAU, ~NET, ~NIV, ~NJB, NKJ, ~NLT, ~NRS, ~REB, ~RSV, ~TEV, ~TLB)].

6:27 Alx[**to bring his head**], Byz[his head to be brought (DRA, KJV, NKJ)]; Alx[**He went and beheaded him in the prison 28**], Byz[28 He went and beheaded him in the prison (DRA, NJB)].

6:29 Alx/Byz[**laid it**], Minor[laid him]; Alx/Byz[**in a tomb**], Minor[in the tomb (~TEV)].

6:30 Alx[**all that they had done and that they had taught**], Byz[all, both that they had done and that they had taught (KJV, NKJ)], Minor[all that they had done and taught (DRA, ESV, HCS, JNT, NAB, NAS, NAU, NET, NIV, NJB, NLT, NRS, REB, RSV, TEV)].

6:31 Alx[**And he said** *Greek* And he says], Byz[And he said].

6:32 Alx[**in the boat to a lonely place**], Byz[to a lonely place in a boat (KJV)], Major[to a lonely place in the boat (NKJ)], Minor[to a lonely place (JNT)].

6:33 Alx/Byz[**they saw them going**], Minor[the crowds saw them going (NKJ)]; Alx[**and many knew**], Byz[and many knew them (ASV, ESV, HCS, JNT, MRD, NAS, NAU, NET, NIV, NJB, NLT, NRS, REB, RSV, TEV, ~TLB)], Major[and many knew him (KJV, NKJ)]; Alx[**got there ahead of him**], Byz[*adds* and gathered to him (KJV, NKJ)].

6:34 Alx[**When he went ashore**], Byz[When Jesus went ashore (DRA, JNT, KJV, MRD, NAU, NET, NIV, NKJ, NLT, TEV)]; Alx[**he had compassion on them**], Byz[he was moved with compassion toward them (JNT, KJV, MRD, NAB, NAS, NAU, NKJ, NRS, REB, TEV)].

6:35 Alx/Byz[**his disciples came to him**], Minor[*omits* to him]; Alx[**and said**], Byz[and saying (DRA, NAS)].

6:36 Alx[**something to eat**], Byz[bread, for they have nothing to eat (KJV, MRD, NKJ)].

6:37 Alx/Byz[**But he answered and said to them**], Minor[*omits* to them (HCS, NIV, NJB, NLT, REB, TEV, TLB)]; **denarii** *a denarius was one day's wages for a laborer.*

6:38 Alx[**Go see**], Byz[Go and see (ASV, DRA, ESV, JNT, KJV, NAB, NET, NIV, NJB, NKJ, NLT, NRS, REB, RSV, TEV, TLB)].

6:39 Alx/Byz[**to all sit down**], Minor[to all be sat down (DRA, HCS, KJV, MRD, NIV, NJB, NKJ, NLT, NRS, REB, TEV)].

on the green grass. ⁴⁰ So they sat down in groups, of hundreds and fifties. ⁴¹ And taking the five loaves and the two fish he looked up to heaven, and blessed, and broke the loaves, and gave them to [his] disciples to set before the people. And he divided the two fish among them all. ⁴² And they all ate and were satisfied. ⁴³ And they took up twelve baskets full of broken pieces and of the fish. ⁴⁴ Now those who had eaten [the loaves] were five thousand men.

⁴⁵ Immediately he made his disciples get into the boat and go before him to the other side, to Bethsaida, while he dismissed the crowd. ⁴⁶ And after he had left them, he went up on the mountain to pray. ⁴⁷ When evening came, the boat was in the middle of the sea, and he was alone on land. ⁴⁸ And seeing them straining at the oars, for the wind was against them, about the fourth watch of the night he came to them, walking on the sea. He was about to pass them by, ⁴⁹ but when they saw him walking on the sea they thought it was a ghost, and cried out. ⁵⁰ For they all saw him, and were terrified. But immediately he spoke to them and said, "Take courage! It is I. Do not be afraid." ⁵¹ Then he climbed into the boat with them, and the wind ceased. And they were [completely] amazed. ⁵² For they had not understood about the loaves, but their heart was hardened.

⁵³ When they had crossed over, they came to land, unto Gennesaret, and anchored there. ⁵⁴ And when they got out of the boat, immediately the people recognized him; ⁵⁵ they ran about that whole country, and began to carry those who were sick around on pallets to wherever they heard he was. ⁵⁶ Wherever he entered, into villages, or into cities, or into the country, they laid the sick in the marketplaces, and begged him that they might touch even the tassel of his garment. And as many as touched him were made well.

7 ¹ Now when the Pharisees and some of the scribes who had come from Jerusalem gathered together to him, ² they saw some of his disciples eating food with hands that were defiled, that is, unwashed. ³ For the Pharisees and all the Jews do

---

6:41 Alx/Major[**his disciples**], Byz[the disciples (ASV, ESV, JNT, NAS, NAU, NLT, REB, RSV, ~TLB)].

6:44 Alx/Byz[**the loaves**], Minor[*omits* (DRA, NIV, TEV, TLB)]; Alx/Byz[**five thousand**], Minor[about five thousand (KJV, NKJ, TLB)].

6:45 Alx/Byz[**to the other side**], Minor[*omits* (~DRA, NIV, ~NLT, ~TLB)]; Alx[**dismissed** *Greek* dismisses], Byz[dismissed].

6:47 Alx/Byz[**in the middle of the sea**], Minor[already in the middle of the sea (REB)].

6:48 Alx/Byz[**seeing them**], Major[he saw them (ESV, HCS, JNT, KJV, MRD, NAB, NET, NIV, NJB, NKJ, NLT, NRS, RSV, TEV, TLB)]; Alx[**about the fourth watch**], Byz[and about the fourth watch (DRA, ESV, KJV, MRD, NJB, NKJ, ~NRS, ~REB, RSV, ~TEV, ~TLB)].

6:51 Alx[**completely amazed**], Byz[completely amazed and wondered (KJV, NKJ)], Minor[amazed].

6:52 Alx/Byz[**but their heart**], Major[for their heart (DRA, KJV, MRD, ~NIV, ~NJB, NKJ, ~NLT, ~REB, ~TEV, TLB)].

6:53 Alx/Major[**they came to land**], Byz[they went to land (~JNT, ~NIV, ~NLT, ~REB, ~TLB)]; Alx[**unto Gennesaret**], Byz[of Gennesaret (DRA, KJV, MRD, NKJ)].

6:55 Alx/Byz[**they ran**], Major[running (DRA, JNT)]; Alx[**country**], Byz[region (ASV, ESV, HCS, JNT, KJV, MRD, NET, NIV, NKJ, NLT, NRS, RSV, TEV, TLB)]; Alx/Byz[**and began to carry**], Major[they began to carry (DRA, NLT, ~TEV)].

6:56 Alx[**or into cities, or into the country**], Byz[or cities, or the country (~DRA, ESV, HCS, JNT, KJV, MRD, NAB, NAS, NAU, NET, NIV, NJB, NKJ, NLT, NRS, REB, RSV, TEV, TLB)].

7:2 Alx[**unwashed**], Byz[*adds* They found fault (DRA, KJV, MRD, NKJ, ~TEV)].

7:3 Alx/Byz[**with the fist**], Minor[often (DRA, KJV)], Alt[*without textual foundation* diligently *or* ritually (~ASV, ~HCS, ~JNT, ~MRD, ~NAB, ~NAS, ~NAU, ~NET, ~NIV, ~NKJ, ~NRS, ~TEV) *others omit without textual foundation* (~ESV, ~REB, ~RSV) *others without textual foundation* over cupped hands (~NLT) *others without textual foundation* to the elbows (~NJB, ~TLB)]; **with the fist** *pouring water on each hand from a (usually double handled) container gripped by the opposing hand (i..e. with the fist). The specific practice requires that the container be actively poured, rather than simply holding the hands under water.*

not eat unless they wash their hands with the fist, holding the tradition of the elders. [4] And, from the marketplace, they do not eat unless they dip themselves. And there are many other traditions which they observe, the washing of cups and pitchers and copper vessels [and beds]. [5] And the Pharisees and the scribes asked him, "Why do your disciples not walk according to the tradition of the elders, but eat with impure hands?" [6] And he said to them, "Well did Isaiah prophesy of you hypocrites; as it is written:

> 'This people honors me with their lips.
>> But their heart is far from me.
> [7] In vain they worship me,
>> teaching as doctrines the precepts of men.'

[8] You let go of the commandment of God, and hold on to the tradition of men." [9] And he said to them, "You have a fine way of rejecting the commandment of God, in order to establish your tradition! [10] For Moses said, 'Honor your father and your mother'; and, 'He who curses father or mother, let him be put to death.' [11] But you say that if a man says to his father or mother, 'Whatever help you might otherwise have received from me is Corban' (that is, an offering devoted to God), [12] you no longer let him do anything for father or mother, [13] thus making void the word of God through your tradition which you have handed down. And many such things you do."

[14] And he called the people to him again, and said to them, "Hear me, everyone, and understand: [15] there is nothing outside a man which by going into him can defile him; but the things which come out of a man are what defile a man." [(16)] [17] When he had left the crowd and entered the house, his disciples asked him this parable. [18] So he said to them, "Are you also without understanding? Do you not see that whatever enters a man from outside cannot defile him, [19] since it does not enter his heart but his stomach, and so

---

7:4 Alx/Byz[**And, from the marketplace**], Minor[And, when they come from the marketplace (ASV, DRA, ESV, HCS, JNT, KJV, ~MRD, ~NAB, NAS, NAU, NET, NIV, ~NJB, NKJ, REB, RSV, TEV)]; Alx/Byz[**dip** *Greek* baptize], Minor[sprinkle (~JNT, ~NAB, ~NAS, ~NAU, NJB, ~RSV, TLB)]; Alx/Byz[**and beds**], Minor[*omits* (ASV, JNT, NAS, NAU, NIV, NJB, NLT, NRS, REB, RSV, TLB)].

7:5 Alx[**And the Pharisees**], Byz[Then the Pharisees (HCS, KJV, ~NAB, ~NIV, ~NJB, NKJ, ~NRS, ~TEV, ~TLB)]; Alx[**impure hands**], Byz[unwashed hands (KJV, MRD, NET, NKJ, NLT, TLB)].

7:6 Alx[**And he said to them**], Byz[And he answered and said to them (DRA, ~HCS, ~JNT, KJV, ~NAB, ~NIV, ~NJB, NKJ, ~NLT, ~REB, ~TEV, ~TLB)].

7:6-7 ~**Isaiah 29:13 LXX**.

7:8 Alx[**You let go of the commandment**], Byz[For you let go of the commandment (DRA, KJV, MRD, NKJ, NLT, TLB)]; Alx[**tradition of men**], Byz[*adds* washings of vessels and cups, and many other such things you do (DRA, KJV, MRD, NKJ)].

7:9 Alx[**establish**], Byz[keep (ASV, DRA, ~HCS, JNT, KJV, NAS, NAU, NIV, ~NJB, NKJ, NLT, NRS, ~REB, RSV, ~TLB)].

7:10 **Exodus 20:12, Deuteronomy 5:16, Exodus 21:17**.

7:11 **Corban** *Hebrew*; **an offering devoted to God** *Greek* an offering.

7:12 Alx[**you no longer**], Byz[and you no longer (DRA, ESV, JNT, KJV, MRD, NET, NIV, NJB, NKJ, ~NLT, NRS, RSV, TLB)]; Alx[**father or mother**], Byz[his father or his mother (ASV, ~DRA, ~ESV, ~HCS, ~JNT, KJV, MRD, ~NAB, NAS, NAU, ~NET, ~NIV, ~NJB, NKJ, ~NLT, ~REB, ~RSV, ~TEV, ~TLB)].

7:14 Alx[**he called the people to him again**], Byz[he called all the people to him (KJV, MRD, NKJ)].

7:15 Alx/Byz[**out of a man are what defile a man**], Major[out of him, those are what defile a man (~ASV, ~DRA, KJV, MRD, ~NAB, NKJ, ~NLT, ~NRS, ~TLB)].

7:(16) Alx/Byz[*omits*], Major[*adds* If anyone has ears to hear, let him hear (ASV, DRA, HCS, KJV, MRD, NAS, NAU, NJB, NKJ)].

7:17 Alx[**asked him this parable**], Byz[asked him concerning this parable (ASV, ESV, HCS, JNT, KJV, MRD, NAB, NAS, NAU, NET, NIV, NJB, NKJ, ~NLT, NRS, REB, RSV, ~TEV, ~TLB)].

7:18 Alx/Major[**Do you not see**], Byz[Do you not yet see].

7:19 Alx/Byz[**and so passes on?" (Thus he declared all foods clean.)**], Minor[and so passes on,

passes on?" (Thus he declared all foods clean.) **20** And he said, "What comes out of a man is what defiles a man. **21** For from within, out of the heart of men, come evil thoughts, fornications, theft, murder, **22** adultery, coveting, wickedness, deceit, lewdness, envy, slander, pride, foolishness. **23** All these evil things come from within, and they defile a man."

24 From there he arose and went away to the region of Tyre. And he entered a house, and did not want anyone to know it; yet he could not be hidden. **25** But immediately a woman whose little daughter was possessed by an unclean spirit heard about him, and she came and fell at his feet. **26** Now the woman was a Greek, a Syrophoenician by birth. And she begged him to cast the demon out of her daughter. **27** And he said to her, "Let the children first be fed, for it is not right to take the children's bread and throw it to the puppies." **28** But she answered him, "Lord, even the puppies under the table eat the children's crumbs." **29** Then he said to her, "For this saying you may go your way; the demon has left your daughter." **30** She went home, and found the child lying on the bed, and the demon gone.

31 Then he departed from the region of Tyre, and went through Sidon to the Sea of Galilee, through the region of the Decapolis. **32** Then they brought to him a man who was deaf and had an impediment in his speech, and they begged him to put his hand on him. **33** And he took him aside from the multitude, and put his fingers into his ears, and he spat and touched his tongue. **34** And looking up to heaven he sighed and said to him, "Ephphatha," that is, "Be opened." **35** And [immediately] his ears were opened, and the impediment of his tongue was loosed, and he spoke plainly. **36** And he commanded them to tell no one. But the more he charged them, the more widely they proclaimed it. **37** And they were astonished beyond measure, saying, "He has done all things well. He even makes the deaf to hear and [the] mute to speak."

8 **1** In those days, when again a great crowd had gathered, and they had nothing to eat, he called the disciples to him, and said to them, **2** "I have compassion on the multitude, because they have now been with me three days and have nothing to eat. **3** And if I send them away hungry to their homes, they will faint on the way; and

---

purifying all the food? (DRA, KJV, MRD, ~NET, NKJ)].

7:21-22 Alx[**fornications, theft, murder, 22 adultery**], Byz[adultery, fornications, murder, 22 theft (DRA, KJV, MRD, NKJ)].

7:24 Alx[**Tyre**], Byz[*adds* and Sidon (ASV, DRA, ESV, HCS, JNT, KJV, MRD, NKJ, RSV, TLB)].

7:25 Alx[**But immediately**], Byz[For (DRA, ~JNT, KJV, ~MRD, NKJ)].

7:27 Alx[**And he said to her**], Byz[But Jesus said to her (KJV, ~MRD, NKJ, ~NLT, TEV, ~TLB)]; **puppies** *or* little dogs.

7:28 Alx[**Lord, even**], Byz[Yes, Lord; even (ASV, ~KJV, ~NJB)], Major[Yes, Lord; for even (~DRA, ~ESV, ~JNT, ~MRD, ~NAS, ~NAU, ~NET, ~NIV, ~NKJ, ~NLT, ~RSV, ~TLB)]; **puppies** *or* little dogs.

7:30 Alx/Byz[**child**], Major[daughter (KJV, MRD, NKJ)].

7:31 Alx/Byz[**he departed**], Alt/Peshitta[Jesus departed (MRD, NET, NIV, NLT, TEV)]; Alx[**Tyre, and went through Sidon to the Sea of Galilee**], Byz[Tyre and Sidon, and went to the Sea of Galilee (KJV, MRD, NKJ, TLB)]; **Decapolis** *or* Ten Cities.

7:34 **Ephphatha** *Aramaic.*

7:35 Alx/Byz[**immediately his ears**], Minor[*omits* immediately (ASV, ESV, JNT, NAS, NAU, NJB, RSV)]; Alx/Byz[**and the impediment**], Minor[and immediately the impediment (NJB)].

7:37 Alx/Byz[**He even makes**], Minor[As he even makes].

8:1 Alx/Byz[**again a great crowd**], Major[a very great crowd (KJV, ~MRD, NKJ)]; Alx[**he called the disciples**], Byz[Jesus called his disciples (~ASV, ~DRA, ~ESV, JNT, KJV, ~MRD, ~NAS, NAU, NET, NIV, ~NJB, NKJ, NLT, ~NRS, REB, ~RSV, ~TEV, TLB)].

8:2 Alx/Byz[**with me**], Minor[*omits* (TLB)].

8:3 Alx[**and some of them have come a from long distance**], Byz[for some of them have come a long distance (DRA, KJV, MRD, ~NIV, NKJ, NLT, TEV, TLB)], Major[for some of them are coming a

some of them have come from a long distance." **4** And his disciples answered him, "How can one feed these men with bread here in the desert?" **5** And he asked them, "How many loaves do you have?" They said, "Seven." **6** So he commanded the crowd to sit down on the ground. And he took the seven loaves, and having given thanks he broke them and gave them to his disciples to set before the people; and they set them before the crowd. **7** They also had a few small fish; and having blessed them, he commanded that these also should be set before them. **8** They ate, and were satisfied. And they took up seven baskets full of the broken pieces left over. **9** And they were about four thousand. And having sent them away, **10** he immediately got into the boat with his disciples, and went to the region of Dalmanutha.

11 The Pharisees came and began to argue with him, seeking from him a sign from heaven, to test him. **12** And he sighed deeply in his spirit, and said, "Why does this generation seek a sign? Truly, I say to you, no sign shall be given to this generation." **13** And he left them. And going aboard again he departed to the other side.

14 Now they had forgotten to bring bread, and they had only one loaf with them in the boat. **15** And he cautioned them, saying, "Watch out! Beware of the leaven of the Pharisees and the leaven of Herod!" **16** And they reasoned with one another, because they had no bread. **17** Being aware of it, he said to them, "Why do you discuss the fact that you have no bread? Do you not yet perceive or understand? Are your hearts hardened? **18** Having eyes do you not see, and having ears do you not hear? And do you not remember? **19** When I broke the five loaves for the five thousand, how many baskets full of broken pieces did you take up?" They said to him, "Twelve." **20** "When I broke the seven

---

long distance], Minor[and some are from a long distance (~ASV, ~REB)].

8:6 Alx[**So he commanded** *Greek* So he commands], Byz[So he commanded].

8:7 Alx/Byz[**blessed**], Minor[given thanks for (NET, NIV, TEV)]; Alx/Byz[**he commanded that these also should be set before them**], Minor[he set these before them].

8:9 Alx/Byz[**And they were about four thousand**], Major[And those who had eaten were about four thousand (DRA, KJV, MRD, NKJ, ~TEV)].

8:10 Alx/Byz[**the boat**], Minor[a boat (DRA, KJV, MRD, NET, NLT, TEV, TLB)]; Alx/Byz[**Dalmanutha**], Minor[Magedan, *others* Magdala].

8:12 Alx[**seek a sign**], Byz[seek for a sign (KJV, MRD, NRS, REB, TEV, ~TLB)]; Alx/Byz[**Truly, I say to you**], Minor[*omits* to you (~TLB)].

8:13 Alx[**And he left them. And going aboard again he departed to the other side**], Byz[And he left them. He departed in the boat again], Major[And he left them. And going aboard into a boat again he departed to the other side], Minor[And he left them. And going aboard into the boat again he departed to the other side (ASV, DRA, ESV, HCS, JNT, KJV, MRD, NAB, NET, NIV, NKJ, NLT, NRS, RSV, TEV, TLB)].

8:14 Alx/Byz[**they had forgotten**], Minor[the disciples had forgotten (JNT, KJV, NIV, NJB, NKJ, NLT, NRS, TEV, TLB)].

8:15 Alx/Byz[**Herod**], Minor[the Herodians].

8:16 Alx[**another, because they had no bread**], Byz[another, saying, "Because we have no bread" (ASV, DRA, KJV, MRD, NIV, NKJ, RSV)], Minor[another, "Because we have no bread" (NJB, NRS)], Alt[...he says this because we have no bread (~TEV, ~TLB)].

8:17 Alx[**he said**], Byz[Jesus said (ASV, DRA, ESV, KJV, MRD, NAS, NAU, NET, NIV, NJB, NKJ, NLT, NRS, RSV, TEV, TLB)]; Alx[**hearts hardened**], Byz[hearts still hardened (DRA, KJV, ~MRD, NKJ)].

8:19 Alx/Major[**how many baskets full of broken pieces**], Byz[how many baskets – even full! – of broken pieces].

8:20 Alx[**When**], Byz[And when (ASV, ESV, JNT, KJV, MRD, NAS, NIV, NJB, NLT, NRS, REB, RSV, TEV, TLB)], Minor[When also (DRA, NKJ)]; Alx[**they said to him** *Greek* they say to him], Byz[they said (HCS, JNT, KJV, NET, NIV, NJB, NKJ, NLT, REB, TEV, TLB)], Minor[they say (MRD)].

for the four thousand, how many large baskets full of pieces did you take up?" And they said [to him], "Seven." ²¹ He said to them, "Do you not yet understand?"

²² And they came to Bethsaida. And some people brought a blind man to him, and begged him to touch him. ²³ So he took the blind man by the hand and brought him out of the village. And when he had spit on his eyes and put his hands on him, he asked him "Do you see anything?" ²⁴ And he looked up and said, "I see men – they look like trees walking." ²⁵ Then he laid his hands on his eyes again and he looked intently. And he was restored, and saw everything clearly. ²⁶ And he sent him away to his home, saying, "Do not even go into the village."

²⁷ And Jesus went on with his disciples, to the villages of Caesarea Philippi. And on the way he asked his disciples, "Who do men say that I am?" ²⁸ They spoke to him, saying, "Some say John the Baptist. Others say Elijah; and still others, one of the prophets." ²⁹ And he asked them, "But who do you say that I am?" Peter answered him, "You are the Christ." ³⁰ And he charged them to tell no one about him.

³¹ And he began to teach them that the Son of Man must suffer many things, and be rejected by the elders and the chief priests and the scribes, and be killed, and after three days rise again. ³² He spoke plainly about this. And Peter took him aside and began to rebuke him. ³³ But when he had turned around and looked at his disciples, he rebuked Peter, and said, "Get behind me, Satan! For you are not mindful of the things of God, but the things of men." ³⁴ And he called the multitude with his disciples, and said to them, "If anyone would follow after me, let him deny himself and take up his cross and follow me. ³⁵ For whoever desires to save his life will lose it. But whoever loses his life for my sake

---

8:21 Alx/Byz[**Do you not yet understand**], Major[How do you not understand (KJV, NKJ, ~TLB)], Minor[How do you not understand (DRA, MRD)].

8:22 Alx[**they came to Bethsaida**], Byz[he came to Bethsaida (KJV, MRD, NKJ)]; **some people** *Greek* they.

8:23 Alx[**brought him out**], Byz[led him out (DRA, ESV, JNT, KJV, MRD, NAB, NIV, NJB, NKJ, NLT, NRS, REB, RSV, TEV, TLB)]; Alx[**asked him, "Do you see anything?"**], Byz[asked him if he saw anything (DRA, KJV, MRD, NKJ, REB)].

8:24 Alx/Major[**I see men – they look like trees walking**], Byz[I see men, as trees walking (DRA, KJV, MRD, NKJ)].

8:25 Alx/Byz[**laid his hands**], Minor[placed his hands (HCS, JNT, KJV, NET, NIV, NKJ, NLT, TEV, TLB)]; Alx[**he looked intently** *or* he saw clearly], Byz[he made him look up (KJV, NKJ)], Minor[*omits* (MRD)]; Alx[**saw everything clearly**], Byz[saw every man clearly (KJV, NKJ)].

8:26 Alx[**Do not even go into the village**], Byz[Do not even go into the village, nor tell anyone in the village (KJV, MRD, NKJ)], Minor[Do not go into the village (JNT, NIV, NLT, TEV) *others* If you go into the village do not tell anyone (DRA)].

8:27 Alx/Byz[**villages of Caesarea Philippi**], Minor[villages – that is, Caesarea Philippi].

8:28 Alx[**They spoke to him, saying**], Byz[They answered (~ESV, ~HCS, ~JNT, KJV, ~MRD, ~NAB, ~NET, NIV, ~NJB, NKJ, NLT, ~NRS, REB, ~RSV, TEV, TLB)].

8:29 Alx[**he asked them**], Byz[he said to them (DRA, KJV, MRD, NKJ)]; Alx[**Peter**], Byz[And Peter (KJV)], Alt/Peshitta[Simon (MRD), Alt[*without textual foundation* Cephas (~JNT)].

8:31 Alx[**by the elders**], Byz[of the elders (KJV)]; Alx/Byz[**the chief priests and the scribes** *or* of the chief priests and of the scribes], Minor[chief priests and scribes (~KJV, NET, NIV, NKJ, REB)].

8:32 Alx/Byz[**Peter**], Alt/Peshitta[Cephas (JNT, MRD)].

8:33 Alx[**Peter, and said** *Greek* Peter, and says], Byz[Peter, saying (DRA, KJV, ~NIV, NKJ, ~NLT, ~REB, ~TEV)], Minor[Peter, and said to him (NJB, ~TLB)], Alt/Peshitta[Simon... (MRD)], Alt[*without textual foundation* Cephas... (~JNT)].

8:34 Alx[**If anyone**], Byz[Whoever (KJV, MRD, NAB, NKJ, ~REB)]; Alx/Byz[**follow after**], Minor[come after (ASV, ESV, JNT, KJV, MRD, NAB, NAS, NAU, NIV, NKJ, RSV, TEV)].

8:35 Alx/Byz[**my sake and the gospel's**], Minor[the sake of the gospel]; Alx[**will save it**], Byz[the same will save it (KJV)].

8:36 Alx[**what does it profit**], Byz[what shall it profit (DRA, JNT, KJV, MRD, NKJ, NRS)]; Alx[to gain

and the gospel's will save it. [36] For what does it profit a man to gain the whole world, and to lose his soul? [37] For what could a man give in exchange for his soul? [38] For whoever is ashamed of me and my words in this adulterous and sinful generation, of him the Son of Man will also be ashamed when he comes in the glory of his Father with the holy angels."

9 [1] And he said to them, "Truly, I say to you that there are some standing here who will never taste death before they see the kingdom of God come with power." [2] After six days Jesus took with him Peter and James and John, and led them up a high mountain apart by themselves. And he was transfigured before them, [3] and his clothes became dazzling, exceedingly white, as no launderer on earth could bleach them. [4] And there appeared to them Elijah with Moses, and they were talking with Jesus. [5] And Peter said to Jesus, "Rabbi, it is good for us to be here. And let us make three tabernacles – one for you, one for Moses, and one for Elijah." [6] For he did not know what to answer, for they became greatly afraid. [7] And a cloud came and overshadowed them. And a voice came out of the cloud, "This is my beloved Son. Listen to him!" [8] Suddenly, when they looked around, they no longer saw anyone but Jesus only with themselves.

[9] And as they were coming down the mountain, he charged them to tell no one what they had seen, until the Son of Man had risen from the dead. [10] So they kept the matter to themselves, questioning what the rising from the dead meant. [11] And they asked him, "Why do the scribes say that Elijah must come first?" [12] Then he said to them, "Elijah does come first and restores all things. And how is it written of the Son of Man, that he must suffer many things and be treated with contempt? [13] But I tell you that Elijah has come, and they did to him whatever they wished, as it is written of him."

[14] And when they came to the disciples, they saw a great crowd around them, and scribes arguing with them. [15] Immediately, when they saw him, all the people were greatly amazed, and ran to him and greeted him. [16] And he asked them, "What are you

---

the whole world], Byz[if he gains the whole world (DRA, JNT, KJV, MRD, NKJ, NLT, TEV, TLB)]; Alx[to lose], Byz[lose (ASV, DRA, ESV, HCS, JNT, KJV, MRD, NAB, NAS, NAU, NET, NIV, NJB, NKJ, NLT, NRS, REB, RSV, TEV, TLB)].

8:35, 36, 37 *The word for* soul *and* life *is the same.*

8:37 Alx[For what could *or* For what should], Byz[Or what can *or* Or what shall (DRA, ~ESV, ~HCS, ~JNT, KJV, MRD, ~NAB, ~NAS, ~NAU, ~NET, ~NIV, ~NJB, NKJ, ~NLT, ~NRS, ~REB, ~RSV, ~TEV, ~TLB)].

8:38 Alx/Byz[my words], Minor[mine]; Alx/Byz[with the holy angels], Minor[and of the holy angels].

9:1 with power *or* in power; *DRA numbers this verse as 8:39.*

9:2 Alx/Byz[Peter], Alt/Peshitta[Cephas (JNT, MRD)].

9:2-50 *DRA begins chapter nine with this verse and numbers 9:2-50 as 9:1-49.*

9:3 Alx[white], Byz[*adds* as snow (DRA, KJV, MRD, NKJ)].

9:5 Alx/Byz[Peter], Alt/Peshitta[Cephas (JNT, MRD)].

9:6 Alx[answer, for they became], Byz[say, for they were (~DRA, ESV, HCS, JNT, KJV, MRD, NAB, NET, NIV, NJB, NKJ, NLT, NRS, REB, RSV, TEV, TLB)].

9:7 Alx/Major[out of the cloud], Byz[*adds* saying (DRA, KJV, MRD, NKJ, NLT, TLB)]; Alx/Byz[This is my beloved Son *or* This is my Son, the Beloved], Minor[This is my only Son (~NET)].

9:8 Alx/Byz[but Jesus only with themselves], Minor[with them but Jesus only (ESV, HCS, JNT, MRD, NAS, NAU, NET, NIV, NJB, NRS, RSV)].

9:11 Alx/Byz[the scribes], Minor[the Pharisees and the scribes (DRA)].

9:12 Alx[he said to them], Byz[he answered and said to them (DRA, ~HCS, ~JNT, KJV, ~NIV, NKJ, ~NLT, ~REB, ~TEV, ~TLB)]; Alx/Byz[Elijah does *or* Elijah indeed], Minor[*omits* does (DRA, ~TLB)].

9:14 Alx[they came...they saw], Byz[he came...he saw (DRA, KJV, MRD, NKJ)].

9:16 Alx[he asked them], Byz[he asked the scribes (KJV, MRD, NKJ, ~TLB)]; Alx/Major[discussing with them], Byz[discussing among yourselves (DRA, ~JNT, ~NLT, ~REB, ~TLB)].

discussing with them?" **17** And one of the crowd answered him, "Teacher, I brought my son to you, who has a mute spirit. **18** And wherever it seizes him, it throws him down; he foams at the mouth, gnashes his teeth and becomes rigid. I asked your disciples to cast out the spirit, but they could not." **19** He answered them, "O faithless generation, how long shall I be with you? How long shall I bear with you? Bring him to me." **20** And they brought the boy to him. And when the spirit saw him, immediately it convulsed the boy, and he fell on the ground and rolled about, foaming at the mouth. **21** And Jesus asked his father, "How long has he been like this?" And he said, "From childhood. **22** And it has often thrown him both into fire and into waters to destroy him. But if you can do anything, have pity on us and help us." **23** Jesus said to him, "If you can, all things are possible to him who believes." **24** Immediately the father of the child cried out and said, "I believe; help my unbelief!" **25** And when Jesus saw that a crowd came running together, he rebuked the unclean spirit, saying to it, "You dumb and deaf spirit, I command you, come out of him, and never enter him again." **26** And the spirit cried out, convulsed terribly, and came out. And the boy was like a corpse; so that most of them said, "He is dead." **27** But Jesus took his hand and lifted him up, and he arose. **28** And when he had come into the house, his disciples asked him privately, "Why could we not cast it out?" **29** And he said to them, "This kind can only come out by prayer."

30 Then they departed from there and passed through Galilee, and he did not want anyone to know it. **31** For he was teaching his disciples and said to them, "The Son of Man is going to be betrayed into the hands of men. They will kill him, and when he is killed, after three days he will rise." **32** But they did not understand the saying, and they were afraid to ask him.

33 And they came to Capernaum. When he was in the house, he asked them, "What were you discussing on the road?" **34** But they kept silent; for on the way they had discussed with one another who was the greatest. **35** And he sat down, called the twelve, and said to them, "If anyone desires to be first, he must be last of all and servant of all." **36** And he took a little child, and put him in the midst of them. And taking him in his arms,

---

9:17 Alx[**answered him**], Byz[answered and said (DRA, KJV, MRD, ~NIV, NKJ, NLT, ~REB, ~TEV, TLB)].

9:19 Alx[**He answered them**], Byz[He answered him (~JNT, KJV, ~NIV, NKJ, ~REB)].

9:20 Alx/Major[**20 And they brought the boy to him.**], Byz[And they brought the boy to him. 20]; Alx[**convulsed the boy**], Byz[tore the boy in a convulsion (ASV, JNT, KJV, NAB, NAS, NAU, NET, NIV, NJB, NLT, REB, TEV, TLB)]; **the boy...the boy** *Greek* him...him.

9:21 Alx[**From childhood**], Byz[Of childhood (~JNT, KJV, ~NAB, ~NLT, ~TEV, ~TLB)]; **Jesus asked** *Greek* he asked.

9:22 Alx/Byz[**fire**], Major[the fire (ASV, DRA, JNT, KJV, MRD, NAS, NAU, NKJ, NLT, NRS, REB, RSV, TEV, TLB)]; *NJB begins verse 23 after* destroy him.

9:23 Alx[**If you can**], Byz[adds believe (DRA, KJV, MRD, NKJ)]; *NJB completes verse 23 as verse 24.*

9:24 Alx[**Immediately**], Byz[And immediately (DRA, KJV, MRD)]; Alx[**cried out**], Byz[adds with tears (DRA, KJV, MRD, NKJ)]; Alx[**I believe**], Byz[adds Lord (DRA, KJV, NKJ)]; *NJB includes verse 23 as the first half of verse 24 and returns to standard numbering.*

9:26 Alx[**convulsed terribly**], Byz[convulsed him terribly (ASV, DRA, ESV, HCS, JNT, KJV, MRD, NAB, NAS, NAU, NET, NIV, NJB, NKJ, NLT, NRS, REB, RSV, TEV, TLB)]; Alx[**most of them**], Byz[many of them (DRA, HCS, KJV, MRD, NAB, NET, NIV, NKJ, ~NLT, REB, ~TEV, ~TLB)].

9:27 Alx[**took his hand**], Byz[took him by the hand (ASV, DRA, ESV, HCS, JNT, KJV, MRD, NAB, NAS, NAU, NIV, NJB, NKJ, NLT, NRS, RSV, TEV, TLB)].

9:29 Alx[**by prayer**], Byz[adds and fasting (DRA, HCS, KJV, MRD, NKJ)].

9:31 Alx/Byz[**said to them**], Minor[said (TEV)], Alx[**after three days**], Byz[on the third day (DRA, KJV, MRD, NKJ)].

9:33 Alx[**they came**], Byz[he came (KJV, NKJ)]; Alx[**Capernaum** *Greek* Capharnaum], Byz[Capernaum]; Alx[**discussing**], Byz[adds among yourselves (KJV, MRD, NKJ)].

he said to them, [37] "Whoever receives one of such little children in my name receives me. And whoever receives me, receives not me but him who sent me."

[38] John said to him, "Teacher, we saw a man casting out demons in your name and we forbade him, because he was not one of us." [39] But Jesus said, "Do not forbid him, for no one who does a miracle in my name can soon afterward speak evil of me. [40] For he who is not against us is for us. [41] For truly, I say to you, whoever gives you a cup of water to drink because you bear the name of Christ, will by no means lose his reward.

[42] "Whoever causes one of these little ones who believe [in me] to sin, it would be better for him if a great millstone were hung around his neck and he were thrown into the sea. [43] If your hand causes you to sin, cut it off. It is better for you to enter life maimed than with two hands to go into hell, to the fire that shall never be quenched. [(44)] [45] And if your foot causes you to sin, cut it off. It is better for you to enter life lame than with two feet to be thrown into hell. [(46)] [47] And if your eye causes you to sin, pluck it out. It is better for you to enter the kingdom of God with one eye than to have two eyes and be thrown into hell, [48] where *their worm does not die, and the fire is not quenched.* [49] For every one will be salted with fire. [50] Salt is good, but if the salt loses its flavor, how will you make it salty again? Have salt in yourselves, and be at peace with one another."

10 [1] Then he left there and went to the region of Judea [and] beyond the Jordan. And crowds gathered to him again; and again, as his custom was, he taught them. [2] And Pharisees came and began to question him, "Is it lawful for a man to divorce his wife?" [3] He answered them, "What did Moses command you?" [4] They said, "Moses permitted a man *'to write a certificate of divorce, and to put her away.'"* [5] But Jesus said to them, "Because of your hardness of heart he wrote you this

---

9:37 Alx/Byz[**such little children**], Minor[these little children (~MRD, NAS, NAU, NET, NIV, NKJ, NLT, REB, TEV, TLB)].

9:38 Alx/Byz[**John**], Major[And John (KJV, NKJ)]; Alx[**said to him**], Byz[answered him, saying (DRA, KJV, NKJ)]; Alx[**a man**], Byz[adds who does not follow us (KJV, ~DRA, NKJ, ~REB)]; Alx/Byz[**in your name**], Major[by your name (NLT, TLB)].

9:39 Alx/Byz[**But Jesus said**], Minor[But he said].

9:40 Alx[**against us is for us**], Byz[against you is for you (DRA, MRD)].

9:41 Alx[**drink because you bear the name of Christ**], Byz[drink in my name, because you belong to Christ (DRA, ~HCS, KJV, NIV, NKJ)].

9:42 Alx/Byz[**these little ones**], Major[the little ones]; Alx/Byz[**who believe in me**], Minor[who believe (NAS, NAU, NJB, REB)]; Alx[**a great millstone** *or* a donkey's millstone], Byz[a millstone (DRA, JNT, KJV, MRD, NKJ, REB)].

9:43, 45, 47 **hell** *Greek* Gehenna.

9:(44) Alx[*omits*], Byz[*adds from verse 48* where 'their worm does not die, and the fire is not quenched' (ASV, DRA, HCS, KJV, MRD, NAS, NAU, NKJ)].

9:45 Alx[**thrown into hell**], Byz[*adds* to the fire that shall never be quenched (DRA, HCS, KJV, NKJ)].

9:(46) Alx[*omits*], Byz[*adds from verse 48* where 'their worm does not die, and the fire is not quenched' (ASV, DRA, HCS, KJV, MRD, NAS, NAU, NKJ)].

9:47 Alx/Major[**two eyes**], Byz[the two eyes (~JNT, ~REB, ~TEV)]; Alx[**be thrown into hell**], Byz[go into the hell of fire (~MRD, ~TLB)], Major[be thrown into the hell of fire (DRA, KJV, NKJ)].

9:48 ~Isaiah 66:24.

9:49 Alx[**salted with fire**], Byz[*adds* and every sacrifice will be salted with salt (DRA, KJV, MRD, NKJ, TEV)]; Leviticus 2:13.

10:1 Alx[**Judea and beyond the Jordan**], Byz[Judea, by the far side of the Jordan (KJV, ~MRD, NKJ)], Minor[Judea, beyond the Jordan (DRA)].

10:2 Alx/Major[**And Pharisees**], Byz[And the Pharisees (DRA, KJV, MRD, NAB, NKJ) *others* And they (~REB, Metzger)]; Alx/Byz[**began to question him**], Major[questioned him (ASV, DRA, ESV, HCS, ~JNT, KJV, MRD, NAB, NET, ~NIV, NJB, NKJ, ~NLT, NRS, ~REB, RSV, TEV, TLB)].

10:4 ~**Deuteronomy 24:1, 3.**

10:5 Alx[**But Jesus said**], Byz[And answering, Jesus said (DRA, KJV, MRD, NKJ)].

commandment. **6** But from the beginning of creation he *'made them male and female.'* **7** *'For this reason a man shall leave his father and mother [and be joined to his wife],* **8** *and the two shall become one flesh.'* So they are no longer two, but one flesh. **9** Therefore what God has joined together, let not man separate." **10** In the house the disciples also asked him again about this matter. **11** So he said to them, "Whoever divorces his wife and marries another commits adultery against her. **12** And if she divorces her husband and marries another man, she commits adultery."

13 And they were bringing children to him, that he might touch them; but the disciples rebuked them. **14** But when Jesus saw it, he was indignant and said to them, "Let the little children come to me. Do not hinder them, for to such belongs the kingdom of God. **15** Truly, I say to you, whoever does not receive the kingdom of God like a little child will never enter it." **16** And he took them in his arms, and blessed them, laying his hands on them.

17 And as he was setting out on his journey, a man ran up and knelt before him, and asked him, "Good Teacher, what must I do to inherit eternal life?" **18** And Jesus said to him, "Why do you call me good? No one is good but God alone. **19** You know the commandments: *'Do not murder. Do not commit adultery. Do not steal. Do not bear false witness. Do not defraud. Honor your father and mother.'"* **20** And he said to him, "Teacher, all these I have observed from my youth." **21** Then Jesus, looking at him, loved him, and said to him, "You lack one thing; go and sell what you have, and give to [the] poor, and you will have treasure in heaven; and come, follow me." **22** But he fell sad at this word, and went away sorrowful, for he had great possessions.

23 Then Jesus looked around and said to his disciples, "How hard it is for those who have riches to enter the kingdom of God!" **24** And the disciples were amazed at his words. But Jesus said to them again, "Children, how hard it is to enter the kingdom of

---

10:6 Alx[**he 'made them**], Byz[God 'made them (DRA, ESV, HCS, JNT, KJV, MRD, NAB, NAS, NAU, NIV, NKJ, NLT, NRS, REB, RSV, TEV, ~TLB) *others omit* them (TLB)]; Genesis 1:27, 5:2.

10:7 Alx/Byz[**his father and mother**], Minor[his father and his mother (MRD)]; Alx/Byz[**and be joined to his wife**], Minor[*omits* (NAS, NAU, NET, NJB, ~TLB)].

10:7-8 Genesis 2:24.

10:10 Alx/Byz[**the disciples**], Major[his disciples (DRA, KJV, NKJ, NLT, TLB)]; Alx/Byz[**this matter**], Major[the same matter (DRA, KJV, NKJ, ~NLT, ~TLB)].

10:12 Alx/Byz[**if she divorces**], Major[if a woman divroces (DRA, JNT, KJV, MRD, NJB, NKJ, TEV, TLB)]; Alx/Byz[**and marries another**], Major[and be married to another (DRA, KJV)].

10:13 Alx[**rebuked them**], Byz[rebuked those that brought them (DRA, ~JNT, KJV, MRD, NET, NKJ, NLT, ~TEV)].

10:14 Alx/Byz[**said to them**], Minor[rebuked them]; Alx[**Do not hinder them**], Byz[And do not hinder them (DRA, KJV, MRD, NET, NIV, NKJ, TEV)].

10:16 Alx/Byz[**and blessed them, laying his hands on them**], Major[laying his hands on them, and blessed them (DRA, HCS, JNT, KJV, MRD, NET, NIV, NJB, NKJ, NLT, NRS, REB, TEV, TLB)].

10:19 Alx[**Do not murder. Do not commit adultery. Do not steal**], Byz[Do not commit adultery. Do not murder. Do not steal (DRA, KJV, NKJ)], Minor[Do not commit adultery. Do not steal. Do not murder (MRD)]; Alx/Byz[**Do not defraud**], Minor[*omits*]; Alx/Byz[**your father and mother**], Minor[your father and your mother (MRD, NAB, NKJ, TEV)]; ~Exodus 20:12-16, ~Deuteronomy 5:16-20.

10:20 Alx[**And he said**], Byz[And answering, he said (DRA, KJV, MRD, NAB, NKJ, ~REB, ~TLB)].

10:21 Alx/Major[**You lack one thing**], Byz[*adds* if you will be perfect]; Alx[**come, follow me**], Byz[come, take up your cross, and follow me (MRD)], Major[come, take up the cross, and follow me (KJV, NKJ)].

10:23 Alx/Byz[*verses 23, 24, 25, 26*], Metzger[*Minor sequence verses 23, 25, 24, 26 others 23, 25, 24, 25, 26*].

10:24 Alx[**how hard it is**], Byz[*adds* for those who trust in riches (ASV, DRA, KJV, MRD, NKJ, TLB)], Metzger[*Minor adds* for a rich man *others add* for those who have possessions].

God! **25** It is easier for a camel to go through [the] eye of [the] needle than for a rich man to enter the kingdom of God." **26** And they were exceedingly astonished, and said to each other, "Then who can be saved?" **27** Jesus looked at them and said, "With men it is impossible, but not with God; for all things are possible with God." **28** Peter began to say to him, "See, we have left everything and followed you." **29** Jesus said, "Truly, I say to you, there is no one who has left house or brothers or sisters or mother or father or children or lands, for my sake and for the sake of the gospel, **30** who will not receive a hundredfold now in this time – house and brothers and sisters and mothers and children and lands, with persecutions, and in the age to come, eternal life. **31** But many who are first will be last, and [the] last first."

32 They were on the road, going up to Jerusalem, and Jesus was walking ahead of them; and they were amazed, but those who followed were afraid. And he took the twelve aside again and began to tell them what was to happen to him. **33** "Behold, we are going up to Jerusalem. And the Son of Man will be betrayed to the chief priests and to the scribes, and they will condemn him to death, and deliver him to the Gentiles. **34** And they will mock him, and spit on him, and scourge him, and kill him. And after three days he will rise."

35 Then James and John, the sons of Zebedee, came to him and said, "Teacher, we want you to do for us whatever we ask of you." **36** And he said to them, "What do you want [me] to do for you?" **37** And they said to him, "Grant us to sit, one at your right hand and the other at the left, in your glory." **38** But Jesus said to them, "You do not know what you are asking. Can you drink the cup that I drink, or be baptized with the baptism I am baptized with?" **39** They said to him, "We are able." So Jesus said to them, "You will drink

---

10:25 Alx/Byz[**camel**], Minor[cable]; Alx[**to go through**], Byz[to go into (MRD)]; Alx/Major[**the eye of the needle**], Byz[an eye of a needle (ASV, ~DRA, ~ESV, ~HCS, JNT, ~KJV, ~MRD, ~NAB, ~NAS, ~NAU, ~NET, ~NIV, ~NJB, ~NKJ, ~NLT, ~NRS, ~REB, ~RSV, ~TEV, ~TLB)].

10:26 Alx/Byz[**said to each other**], Minor[said to him (ASV, ESV, JNT, NAS, NAU, ~NLT, RSV, ~TLB)].

10:27 Alx/Byz[**Jesus looked at them**], Major[And Jesus looked at them (DRA, KJV, MRD, NKJ)].

10:28 Alx/Byz[**Peter began**], Minor[And Peter began (DRA, KJV, NKJ, NLT, TEV, TLB)], Alt/Peshitta[And Cephas began (~JNT, MRD)].

10:29 Alx/Major[**Jesus**], Byz[And Jesus (KJV, NKJ, TLB)]; Alx[**said**], Byz[answered and said (DRA, KJV, MRD, ~NIV, NKJ, ~NLT, ~TLB)]; Alx[**mother or father or children**], Byz[father or mother or wife or children (KJV, MRD, NKJ)], Minor[father or mother or children (DRA)]; Alx/Byz[**the sake of the gospel**], Minor[the gospel (DRA, ESV, HCS, KJV, NIV, NKJ, NLT, REB, RSV, TEV, TLB)]; **gospel** *or* good news.

10:30 Alx/Major[**mothers**], Byz[father and mother].

10:31 Alx/Byz[**the last first**], Major[*omits* the (~JNT, MRD, ~NLT, ~TEV, ~TLB)].

10:32 Alx[**but those who followed**], Byz[and those who followed (ASV, DRA, ESV, JNT, KJV, MRD, NAB, NAS, NAU, ~NIV, NJB, NKJ, NLT, NRS, REB, RSV, ~TEV, ~TLB)].

10:33 Alx[**to the scribes**], Byz[the scribes (ASV, ESV, HCS, JNT, MRD, NAB, NAS, NAU, NET, NIV, NJB, NLT, NRS, REB, RSV, TEV, TLB)].

10:34 Alx[**spit on...scourge**], Byz[scourge...spit on (KJV, MRD, NKJ)]; Alx[**after three days**], Byz[the third day (DRA, KJV, MRD, NKJ)].

10:35 Alx/Major[**the sons of Zebedee**], Byz[sons of Zebedee], Minor[the two sons of Zebedee (NAS, NAU)]; Alx/Byz[**and said**], Minor[*adds* to him (ASV, ESV, MRD, NAB, NAS, NJB, NLT, NRS, RSV)]; Alx[**ask of you**], Byz[ask (DRA, JNT, KJV, MRD, NET, NIV, NJB, NKJ, NLT, REB, TEV, TLB)].

10:37 Alx[**at the left**], Byz[at your left (ASV, DRA, ESV, HCS, JNT, KJV, MRD, NAB, NAS, NAU, NET, NIV, NJB, NKJ, NLT, NRS, REB, RSV, TEV, TLB)].

10:38 Alx[**or be baptized**], Byz[and be baptized (KJV, MRD, NKJ, ~NLT, ~TEV)].

10:39 Alx[**You will drink**], Byz[You will indeed drink (DRA, KJV, NKJ, NLT, TEV, TLB)].

the cup that I drink, and with the baptism I am baptized with you will be baptized. 40 But to sit at my right or left is not mine to grant, but it is for those for whom it has been prepared." 41 And when the ten heard it, they began to be indignant with James and John. 42 And Jesus called them to himself and said to them, "You know that those who are considered rulers over the Gentiles lord it over them, and their great ones exercise authority over them. 43 But it is not so among you. But whoever wants to become great among you shall be your servant, 44 and whoever wants to be first among you must be slave of all. 45 For even the Son of Man did not come to be served, but to serve, and to give his life as a ransom for many."

46 And they came to Jericho. And as he was leaving Jericho with his disciples and a great multitude, Bartimaeus, a blind beggar, the son of Timaeus, was sitting by the roadside. 47 And when he heard that it was Jesus of Nazareth, he began to cry out and say, "Jesus, you Son of David, have mercy on me!" 48 Many rebuked him and told him to be quiet, but he cried out all the more, "Son of David, have mercy on me!" 49 So Jesus stopped and said, "Call him." And they called the blind man, saying to him, "Take heart! Rise, he is calling you." 50 And throwing aside his garment, he sprang up and came to Jesus. 51 And Jesus answered him and said, "What do you want me to do for you?" And the blind man said to him, "Rabboni, let me receive my sight." 52 And Jesus said to him, "Go your way. Your faith has made you well." And immediately he received his sight and followed him on the road.

11 1 And when they drew near Jerusalem, to Bethphage and Bethany, at the Mount of Olives, he sent two of his disciples, 2 and said to them, "Go into the village opposite you. And immediately as you enter it you will find a colt tied, on which no one has ever yet sat. Untie it and bring it. 3 If anyone says to you, 'Why

---

10:40 Alx[**or left**], Byz[and my left (~ASV, ~DRA, ~ESV, JNT, KJV, MRD, ~NAB, ~NAS, ~NAU, ~NET, ~NJB, NKJ, ~NLT, ~NRS, ~REB, ~RSV, ~TEV, ~TLB)]; Alx/Byz[**prepared**], Minor[*adds by my father* (~TEV)]..

10:42 Alx[**And Jesus**], Byz[But Jesus (DRA, ~HCS, JNT, KJV, ~NAB, ~NAU, ~NET, ~NIV, NKJ, ~REB)].

10:43 Alx[**But it is not so**], Byz[But it shall not be so (ESV, ~HCS, ~JNT, KJV, MRD, NAB, ~NJB, NKJ, NLT, REB, RSV)]; Alx/Byz[**shall be your servant**], Minor[must be your servant (ESV, HCS, JNT, MRD, NET, NIV, NJB, NLT, NRS, REB, RSV, TEV, TLB)].

10:44 Alx[**wants to be first among you**], Byz[of you wants to become first (~KJV, ~MRD, ~NIV, ~NKJ, ~REB, ~TEV, ~TLB)].

10:46 Alx[**a blind beggar, the son of Timaeus, was sitting by the roadside**], Byz[a blind man, the son of Timaeus, was sitting by the roadside, begging (KJV, MRD, NAB, NIV, NKJ)], Major[the blind man, a son of Timaeus, was sitting by the roadside, begging (~DRA)].

10:47 Alx/Byz[**you Son of David**], Major[Son of David (DRA, ESV, HCS, JNT, NAB, NAS, NAU, NET, NIV, NJB, NKJ, NLT, NRS, REB, RSV, TEV, TLB)].

10:49 Alx/Byz[**said, Call him."**], Major[commanded him to be called (DRA, KJV, MRD, NKJ)].

10:50 Alx[**sprang up**], Byz[rose (KJV, MRD, NKJ)].

10:51 Alx[**answered him and said**], Byz[answered and says to him (DRA, ~ESV, ~HCS, ~JNT, ~KJV, ~MRD, ~NAB, ~NET, ~NIV, ~NJB, ~NKJ, ~NLT, ~NRS, ~REB, ~RSV, ~TEV, ~TLB)]; **Rabboni** *Aramaic* My teacher.

10:52 Alx/Byz[**And Jesus said**], Major[But Jesus said (~HCS, ~JNT, ~NAB, ~NET, ~NIV, ~NJB, ~NKJ, ~NRS, ~REB, ~TEV)]; Alx[**followed him on the road**], Byz[followed Jesus on the road (KJV, NIV, NKJ, NLT, TEV, TLB)].

11:1 Alx[**to Bethphage and Bethany**], Byz[to Bethsphage and Bethany], Minor[even to Bethany (DRA)].

11:2 Alx[**ever yet**], Byz[ever (ESV, HCS, JNT, KJV, MRD, NAB, NET, NIV, NKJ, NLT, NRS, RSV, TEV, TLB)]; Alx[**Untie it and bring it**]; Byz[Untying it, lead it].

11:3 Alx[**say**], Byz[say that (~NRS)]; Alx/Byz[**'The Lord has need of it and will send it back here immediately.'**], Major['The Lord has need of it,' and he will send it here immediately. (DRA,

are you doing this?' say, 'The Lord has need of it and will send it back here immediately.'" ⁴ They went away and found a colt tied at a door outside in the open street, and they untied it. ⁵ And some of those who stood there said to them, "What are you doing, untying the colt?" ⁶ They answered as Jesus had said, and they let them go. ⁷ Then they brought the colt to Jesus and threw their garments on it, and he sat on it. ⁸ And many spread their garments on the road, and others leafy branches which they had cut from the fields. ⁹ And those who went before and those who followed cried out,

> "Hosanna!
> *Blessed is he who comes in the name of the Lord!*

10　　　Blessed is the kingdom of our father David that is coming!
> *Hosanna* in the highest!"

¹¹ He entered Jerusalem, and went into the temple. And when he had looked round at everything, as it was already evening, he went out to Bethany with the twelve.

¹² On the next day, when they came from Bethany, he was hungry. ¹³ And seeing from a distance a fig tree in leaf, he went to see if he could find anything on it. When he came to it, he found nothing but leaves, for it was not the season for figs. ¹⁴ And answering, he said to it, "May no one ever eat fruit from you again." And his disciples heard it.

¹⁵ And they came to Jerusalem. And he entered the temple and began to drive out those who sold and those who bought in the temple, and overturned the tables of the money changers and the seats of those who sold doves. ¹⁶ And he would not allow anyone to carry merchandise through the temple. ¹⁷ And he taught, and said to them, "Is it not written,

> 'My house shall be called a house of prayer for all the nations'?
> But you have made it a den of robbers."

JNT, KJV, MRD, NKJ)]; **The Lord** *or* Its Lord.

11:4 Alx/Major[**a colt**], Byz[the colt (DRA, KJV, MRD, NKJ, NLT, REB, TLB)]; Alx[**a door**], Byz[the door (ASV, DRA, KJV, MRD, NAS, NAU, NKJ, NLT, RSV, TEV, ~TLB)].

11:6 Alx[**as Jesus had said**], Byz[as Jesus had commanded (DRA, ~JNT, KJV, MRD, ~NAB, ~NAS, ~NAU, ~NET, ~NIV, ~NJB, NKJ, ~NLT, ~REB, ~TEV, ~TLB)].

11:7 Alx[**they brought** *Greek* they are bringing], Byz[they led (~NJB)]; Alx[**threw** *Greek* are throwing], Byz[threw].

11:8 Alx[**fields**], Byz[trees, and spread them in the road (DRA, KJV, MRD, NKJ, ~TLB)].

11:9 Alx[**cried out**], Byz[cried out, saying (DRA, KJV, MRD, NKJ)].

11:9-10 **Hosanna** *Hebrew Hoshanah,* Please save *or* Save now; ~Psalms 118:25-26.

11:10 Alx[**that is coming**], Byz[*adds* in the name of the Lord (KJV, NKJ)].

11:11 Alx[**He entered Jerusalem**], Byz[Jesus entered Jerusalem (JNT, KJV, MRD, NAU, NET, NIV, NKJ, NLT, TEV)]; Alx/Byz[**already evening**], Minor[already late (ESV, HCS, JNT, NAB, NAS, NAU, NET, NIV, NJB, NKJ, NLT, NRS, REB, RSV, TEV, TLB)].

11:13 Alx/Byz[**from a distance**], Major[in the distance (ASV, DRA, ESV, HCS, JNT, KJV, MRD, NAS, NAU, NET, NIV, NJB, NLT, NRS, REB, RSV, TEV, TLB)].

11:14 Alx/Byz[**he said**], Major[Jesus said (KJV, NKJ, NLT, TEV, TLB)].

11:15 Alx[**15 And they came to Jerusalem**], Byz[15 And they went back to Jerusalem (NLT, TLB)], Alt/Peshitta[And they came to Jerusalem (MRD)]; Alx[**he entered the temple**], Byz[Jesus entered the temple (KJV, NET, NIV, NKJ, NLT, TEV)], Alt[Jesus entered the temple of God (MRD)]; Alx/Byz[**and those who bought**], Major[and bought (DRA, HCS, ~JNT, KJV, ~MRD, NAB, ~NAS, ~NAU, NET, ~NIV, NJB, NKJ, NLT, REB, TEV, ~TLB)].

11:17 Alx[**And he taught, and said to them**], Byz[And he taught, saying to them (DRA, ~ESV, ~HCS, ~JNT, KJV, ~MRD, ~NAB, ~NET, ~NIV, ~NJB, ~NLT, ~NRS, ~REB, ~TEV, ~TLB)], Minor[*omits* to them]; **Isaiah 56:7.**

18 And the chief priests and the scribes heard it and sought how they might destroy him. For they feared him, for all the multitude was astonished at his teaching. 19 Whenever evening came, they went out of the city.

20 And as they passed by in the morning, they saw the fig tree withered from the roots. 21 And Peter remembered and said to him, "Rabbi, look! The fig tree which you cursed has withered." 22 And Jesus answered them, "Have faith in God. 23 Truly, I say to you, whoever says to this mountain, 'Be taken up and cast into the sea,' and does not doubt in his heart, but believes that what he says will come to pass, it will be done for him. 24 Therefore I tell you, whatever you pray and ask for, believe that you have received it, and it will be yours. 25 And whenever you stand praying, if you have anything against anyone, forgive him, so that your Father in heaven may also forgive you your trespasses." (26)

27 Then they came again to Jerusalem. And as he was walking in the temple, the chief priests, the scribes, and the elders came to him. 28 And they began to say to him, "By what authority are you doing these things? Or who gave you this authority to do them?" 29 Jesus said to them, "I will ask you one question. Answer me, and I will tell you by what authority I do these things. 30 The baptism of John – was it from heaven or from men? Answer me." 31 And they reasoned among themselves, "If we say, 'From heaven,' He will say, '[Then] why did you not believe him?' 32 But should we say, 'From men'" – they

---

11:18 Alx[**the chief priests and the scribes**], Byz[the scribes and the Pharisees and the chief priests], Major[the scribes and the chief priests (KJV, NKJ)]; Alx/Byz[**how they might destroy him**], Minor[how they would destroy him (ESV, HCS, JNT, NAB, NAS, NAU, NIV, NJB, NLT, NRS, REB, RSV, ~TEV, TLB)]; Alx[**for all the multitude**], Byz[because all the multitude (DRA, ESV, HCS, JNT, KJV, MRD, NAB, NET, NIV, NJB, NKJ, NLT, NRS, REB, RSV, TEV, TLB)]; Alx/Byz[**was astonished**], Minor[were astonished (JNT, ~MRD, NJB, NKJ, NLT, TLB)].

11:19 Alx[**Whenever**], Byz[When (DRA, ESV, JNT, KJV, MRD, NAB, NAU, NET, NIV, NJB, NKJ, NLT, NRS, REB, RSV, TEV, TLB)]; Alx[**they**], Byz[he (ASV, DRA, KJV, ~NET, NJB, NKJ, ~NLT, ~NRS, ~TEV)].

11:20 Alx/Byz[**And as they passed by in the morning**], Major[And in the morning, as they passed by (HCS, JNT, KJV, MRD, NAB, NET, NIV, NJB, NKJ, NLT, NRS, REB, TEV, TLB)].

11:21 Alx/Byz[**Peter**], Alt/Peshitta[Simon (MRD)], Alt[*without textual foundation* Cephas (~JNT)].

11:22 Alx/Byz[**Have faith in God**], Minor[If you have faith in God (TLB)].

11:23 Alx[**Truly, I say**], Byz[For truly I say (KJV, NKJ, ~TLB)]; Alx[**that what he says**], Byz[the things he says (KJV, NKJ, ~NLT, ~TLB)]; Alx[**it will be done for him** *or* he will have it], Byz[he will have whatever he says (KJV, MRD, NKJ, ~TLB)].

11:24 Alx[**pray and ask for**], Byz[ask for in prayer (DRA, ESV, JNT, KJV, NAB, NIV, NJB, NKJ, ~NLT, NRS, REB, RSV, ~TLB)]; Alx[**have received it**], Byz[are receiving it (ASV, JNT, KJV, NKJ, TLB)], Minor[will receive it (DRA, MRD, NAB, NJB)].

11:25 Alx[**whenever you stand**], Byz[whenever you might stand].

11:(26) Alx[*omits*], Byz[*adds* "But if you do not forgive, neither will your Father forgive your trespasses"], Major[*adds* "But if you do not forgive, neither will your Father in heaven forgive your trespasses" (ASV, DRA, HCS, KJV, MRD, NAS, NAU, NKJ)]; *TLB numbers verse 27 as 26.*

11:28 Alx[**And they began to say**], Byz[And they say (~ASV, DRA, ~ESV, ~HCS, ~JNT, KJV, ~MRD, ~NAB, ~NET, ~NIV, ~NJB, ~NKJ, ~NLT, ~NRS, ~REB, ~RSV, ~TEV, ~TLB)]; Alx/Byz[**Or who gave you**], Major[And who gave you (DRA, ~HCS, ~JNT, KJV, MRD, NIV, NKJ, ~NLT, ~NRS, ~REB, ~TEV, ~TLB)].

11:29 Alx[**Jesus said**], Byz[Jesus answering said (DRA, KJV, ~NIV, NKJ, ~NLT, ~TEV, ~TLB)]; Alx[**I will ask**], Byz[I will also ask (DRA, KJV, MRD, NKJ, ~NLT, REB, ~TLB)].

11:31 Alx/Byz[**Then why did you not believe**], Minor[*omits* Then (~NLT, ~TLB)].

11:32 Alx/Byz[**should we say**], Minor[if we say (DRA, HCS, JNT, KJV, MRD, NET, NIV, NKJ, TEV, TLB)]; Alx[**feared the crowd**], Byz[feared the people (ASV, DRA, ESV, JNT, KJV, MRD, NAU, NIV, NJB, NKJ, NLT, REB, RSV, TEV, TLB)]; Alx/Major[**a real prophet**], Byz[a prophet (NLT, TEV, TLB)].

feared the crowd, for all held that John was a real prophet. ³³ So answering Jesus, they said, "We do not know." And Jesus said to them, "Neither will I tell you by what authority I do these things."

12

¹ Then he began to speak to them in parables: "A man planted a vineyard and set a hedge around it, dug a place for the wine vat and built a tower. And he leased it to vine dressers and went into a far country. ² At harvest time he sent a servant to the tenants, to collect from them some of the fruits of the vineyard. ³ And they took him and beat him, and sent him away empty-handed. ⁴ And again, he sent another servant to them. And they wounded him in the head, and treated him shamefully. ⁵ And he sent another. And him they killed; and so with many others, some they beat and some they killed. ⁶ He still had one left to send, a beloved son. He sent him to them last, saying, 'They will respect my son.' ⁷ But those tenants said to one another, 'This is the heir. Come, let us kill him, and the inheritance will be ours.' ⁸ So they took and killed him, and cast him out of the vineyard. ⁹ What [then] will the owner of the vineyard do? He will come and destroy the tenants, and give the vineyard to others. ¹⁰ Have you not read this Scripture:

> 'The stone which the builders rejected
>> has become the chief cornerstone.

¹¹ > This was the Lord's doing,
>> and it is marvelous in our eyes'?"

¹² And they sought to arrest him, but feared the multitude. For they knew he had spoken the parable against them. So they left him and went away.

¹³ Then they sent to him some of the Pharisees and the Herodians, to catch him in his words. ¹⁴ When they came, they said to him, "Teacher, we know that you are true, and care about no man. For you do not regard the person of men, but teach the way of God in truth. Is it lawful to pay taxes to Caesar, or not? Should we pay them, or should we not?" ¹⁵ But knowing their hypocrisy, he said to them, "Why do you put me to the test? Bring

---

11:33 Alx[**Jesus said to them**], Byz[Jesus answering, said to them (DRA, ~JNT, KJV, NKJ, ~NLT, ~TLB)].

12:1 Alx[**speak**], Byz[say (~NLT, ~TLB)].

12:2 Alx[**fruits**], Byz[fruit (DRA, ESV, HCS, ~JNT, KJV, ~NAB, ~NAS, ~NAU, ~NET, NIV, ~NJB, NKJ, ~NLT, ~NRS, ~REB, RSV, ~TEV, ~TLB)].

12:3 Alx/Byz[**And they too him**], Major[But they took him (~DRA, HCS, JNT, NAB, ~NAU, NET, NIV, NJB, NLT, NRS, REB, ~TEV, TLB)].

12:4 Alx[**And they wounded him**], Byz[And they threw stones at him, wounded him (KJV, MRD, NKJ)]; Alx[**treated him shamefully**], Byz[sent him away, treated shamefully (KJV, MRD, NKJ)].

12:5 Alx[**And he sent another**], Byz[And again he sent another (DRA, KJV, MRD, ~NAB, ~NIV, NKJ)].

12:6 Alx[**He still had**], Byz[Therefore still having (DRA, KJV, ~MRD, NKJ)]; Alx[**a beloved son**], Byz[his beloved son (KJV, NET, NJB, NKJ, NLT, REB, ~TEV, TLB)]; Alx[**He sent him**], Byz[He also sent him (DRA, KJV, NKJ)]; Alx/Byz[**to them last**], Minor[omits last (MRD)].

12:7 Alx/Major[**those tenants said**], Byz[those tenants, seeing him coming, said (TLB)].

12:8 Alx/Byz[**cast him out of the vineyard**], Major[omits him (~NET, ~NLT, ~REB, ~TEV, ~TLB)].

12:9 Alx/Byz[**What then**], Minor[omits then (ESV, JNT, NAS, NAU, ~NJB, NLT, REB, RSV, TLB)]; Alx/Major[**the tenants**], Byz[those tenants (DRA, JNT, MRD, NET, NIV, NLT, TEV, ~TLB)].

12:10 **chief cornerstone** or capstone or keystone.

12:10-11 **Psalms 118:22-23**.

12:14 Alx/Byz[**When they came, they said to him**], Minor[When they came, they began to question him deceitfully, and they said to him (~TLB)]; Alx/Major[**Is it lawful**], Byz[So tell us: Is it lawful (NLT, TEV, TLB)]; Alx/Byz[**Should we pay them, or should we not? 15**], Major[15 Should we pay them, or should we not? (ASV, HCS, KJV, NAS, NAU, NIV, NKJ, NLT, NRS, REB, RSV)].

12:15 Alx/Byz[**knowing their hypocrisy**], Minor[seeing their hypocrisy (NET, ~NJB, NLT, REB, TEV, TLB)]; **denarius** a denarius was one day's wages for a laborer.

me a denarius, and let me look at it." **16** And they brought one. And he said to them, "Whose likeness and inscription is this?" They said to him, "Caesar's." **17** Jesus said to them, "Render to Caesar the things that are Caesar's, and to God the things that are God's." And they were utterly amazed at him.

18 Then some Sadducees, who say there is no resurrection, came to him. And they began to question him, saying: **19** "Teacher, Moses wrote for us *'that if a man's brother dies and leaves a wife, but leaves no child, the man must take the wife, and raise up children for his brother.'* **20** There were seven brothers. The first took a wife. And when he died left no children. **21** And the second took her. And he died, leaving behind no children. And the third likewise; **22** so the seven left no children. Last of all the woman died also. **23** In the resurrection, [when they rise,] whose wife will she be? For the seven had her as wife." **24** Jesus said to them, "Is not this why you are wrong, that you do not know the Scriptures nor the power of God? **25** For when they rise from the dead, they neither marry nor are given in marriage, but are like angels in heaven. **26** And as for the dead being raised, have you not read in the book of Moses, in the passage about the bush, how God said to him, *'I am the God of Abraham, and [the] God of Isaac, and [the] God of Jacob'*? **27** He is not God of the dead, but of the living. You are greatly mistaken."

28 And one of the scribes came up and heard them disputing with one another, and seeing that he had answered them well, asked him, "Which commandment is the first

---

12:16 Alx/Major[**They said to him**], Byz[They said (HCS, JNT, NET, NIV, NLT, NRS, REB, TEV, TLB)].

12:17 Alx[**Jesus said**], Byz[And answering, Jesus said (DRA, KJV, NKJ)]; Alx/Byz[**to them**], Minor[*omits* (JNT, NLT, REB, TEV, TLB)]; Alx[**utterly amazed**], Byz[amazed (DRA, ESV, HCS, JNT, KJV, MRD, NAS, NAU, NIV, NJB, NKJ, RSV, TEV, TLB)].

12:18 Alx/Byz[**they began to question him**], Major[they questioned him (ASV, DRA, ESV, HCS, JNT, KJV, MRD, NAB, NET, NIV, NJB, NKJ, NLT, NRS, REB, RSV, TEV, TLB)].

12:19 Alx[**leaves no child**], Byz[leaves no children (DRA, KJV, MRD, NET, NIV, NKJ, NLT, TEV, TLB)]; Alx[**must take the wife**], Byz[must take his wife (ASV, DRA, KJV, MRD, NKJ, TLB)]; **the man must take** *Greek* his brother must take; ~**Deuteronomy 25:5**.

12:20 Alx/Byz[**There were seven brothers**], Major[Now there were seven brothers (DRA, KJV, NAB, NIV, NJB, ~NLT, REB, ~TEV, ~TLB)].

12:21 Alx[**leaving behind no children**], Byz[and neither did he leave behind any children (DRA, KJV, NKJ)], Major[and neither did he leave behind children (~MRD, ~NLT, ~REB, ~TEV, ~TLB)].

12:22 Alx[**the seven left no children**], Byz[the seven had her and left no children (DRA, KJV, MRD, NKJ, ~NLT, TEV)].

12:23 Alx/Major[**In the resurrection**], Byz[In the resurrection, therefore (DRA, KJV, MRD, NKJ, NLT, TEV, TLB)]; Alx/Byz[**when they rise**], Minor[*omits* (ASV, JNT, MRD, NIV, NLT, NRS, RSV, TLB)].

12:24 Alx[**Jesus said to them**], Byz[And answering, Jesus said to them (DRA, KJV, NKJ, ~NLT, ~TEV, ~TLB)].

12:25 Alx[**like angels in heaven**], Byz[like angels which are in heaven (KJV)], Minor[like angels (TLB) *others* like angels of God].

12:26 Alx/Byz[**how God said**], Major[as God said (~NLT, TEV, ~TLB)]; Alx/Byz[**the God of Isaac, and the God of Jacob**], Minor[God of Isaac, God of Jacob]; **Exodus 3:6, 15**.

12:27 Alx[**God of the dead**], Byz[the God of the dead (ASV, DRA, KJV, MRD, NAS, NAU, NET, NIV, NKJ, NLT, ~TEV, ~TLB)]; Alx/Byz[**but of the living**], Major[but God of the living (~KJV, ~NKJ, ~TEV, ~TLB)]; Alx[**You are greatly mistaken**], Byz[Therefore you are greatly mistaken (DRA, KJV, MRD, NKJ)].

12:28 Alx/Byz[**seeing that he had answered**], Major[knowing that he had answered (ASV, ~KJV, NAS, NAU, ~NIV, ~NJB, ~NKJ, NLT, ~REB, TLB)]; Alx[**Which commandment is the first of all** *things*], Byz[Which is the first commandment of all *commandments* (DRA, ~ESV, ~HCS, JNT, KJV, MRD, NAB, ~NAS, ~NAU, ~NET, NIV, NJB, NKJ, NLT, REB, TEV, TLB)].

of all?" **29** Jesus answered, "The first is: *'Hear, O Israel, the Lord our God is one Lord.* **30** *And you shall love the Lord your God with all your heart, and with all your soul,* and with all your mind, *and with all your strength.'* **31** The second is this: *'You shall love your neighbor as yourself.'* There is no other commandment greater than these." **32** And the scribe said to him, "You are right, Teacher. You have well said that *'He is one, and there is no other but he'*; **33** and to *'love him with all the heart, and with all* the understanding, *and with all the strength',* and to *'love one's neighbor as oneself',* is much more than all whole burnt offerings and sacrifices." **34** And when Jesus saw [him,] that he answered wisely, he said to him, "You are not far from the kingdom of God." And after that no one dared to ask him any question.

35 And Jesus said, while he taught in the temple, "How is it that the scribes say that the Christ is the Son of David? **36** David himself, speaking by the Holy Spirit, declared:

> *'The Lord said to my Lord:*
> *"Sit at my right hand*
> *till I put your enemies under your feet."'*

37 David himself calls him 'Lord.' How is he then his son?" And [the] great crowd heard him gladly.

38 And in his teaching he said, "Beware of the scribes, who like to go around in long robes, and to have salutations in the market places **39** and the best seats in the synagogues and the places of honor at feasts, **40** who devour widows' houses, and for a pretense make long prayers. They will receive the greater condemnation."

41 And he sat down opposite the treasury, and watched the multitude putting money into the treasury. Many people who were rich put in large sums. **42** And a poor

---

12:29 Alx[**Jesus answered**], Byz[And Jesus answered him (DRA, KJV, ~MRD, ~NKJ)], Minor[He answered (REB)]; Alx[**The first is**], Byz[The first of all commandments (~DRA, ~NLT)], Major[The first of all the commandments (KJV, MRD, NKJ)]; **the Lord our God is one Lord** *or* the Lord our God, the Lord is one.

12:29-30 ~**Deuteronomy 6:4-5**.

12:30 Alx[**with all your strength**], Byz[*adds* This is the first commandment (DRA, KJV, MRD, NKJ)].

12:31 Alx[**The second is this**], Byz[And the second is like it (DRA, KJV, MRD, NKJ, ~NLT)]; **Leviticus 19:18**.

12:32 Alx/Byz[**And the scribe**], Minor[The scribe (~HCS, JNT, MRD, NAB, NAU, NET, NIV, NJB, NLT, ~NRS, REB, TEV, TLB)]; Alx/Byz[**He is one**], Minor[God is one (DRA, KJV, MRD, NIV, NKJ, NLT, REB, TEV, TLB)]; **Deuteronomy 6:4, 4:35, Isaiah 45:21**.

12:33 Alx[**understanding**], Byz[*adds* with all the soul (DRA, KJV, MRD, NKJ)]; Alx[**much more**], Byz[more (DRA, JNT, KJV, MRD, NAB, NET, NIV, NKJ, NLT, TEV)]; ~**Deuteronomy 6:5, ~Leviticus 19:18**.

12:34 Alx/Major[**Jesus saw him, that he answered wisely**], Byz[Jesus saw that he answered wisely (ASV, DRA, ESV, HCS, JNT, KJV, MRD, NAB, NAS, NAU, NET, NIV, NJB, NKJ, NLT, NRS, REB, RSV, TEV, TLB)].

12:36 Alx[**David himself**], Byz[For David himself (DRA, KJV, MRD, NKJ, NLT, TLB)]; Alx/Byz[**the Holy Spirit, declared**], Minor[the Holy Spirit, declares (DRA, HCS, MRD, ~NIV, ~NLT, ~TEV) *others omit* the]; Alx[**The Lord said to my Lord**], Byz[The Lord says to my Lord]; Alx[**under your feet**], Byz[as a footstool for your feet (ASV, DRA, KJV, MRD, NJB, NKJ, TLB)]; **Psalms 110:1**.

12:37 Alx[**David himself**], Byz[Therefore David himself (DRA, KJV, MRD, NKJ, ~NLT, ~TLB)]; Alx/Byz[**the great crowd**], Minor[a great crowd (DRA, REB, TEV)].

12:38 Alx[**in his teaching he said**], Byz[he said to them in his teaching (DRA, ~JNT, KJV, MRD, NKJ, ~REB, ~TEV, ~TLB)].

12:40 Alx/Byz[**who devour widow's houses**], Minor[who devour widows' property (NET, NJB, NLT, REB)].

12:41 Alx[**he sat down**], Byz[Jesus sat down (DRA, JNT, KJV, MRD, NIV, NKJ, NLT, TEV)].

12:42 Alx/Byz[**poor widow**], Minor[*omits* poor]; **two copper coins, which make a penny** *Greek* two

widow came, and put in two copper coins, which make a penny. 43 And he called his disciples to him, and said to them, "Truly, I say to you, this poor widow put in more than all those who are contributing to the treasury. 44 For they all put in out of their abundance. But she out of her poverty put in everything – all she had to live on."

13

1 And as he came out of the temple, one of his disciples said to him, "Look, Teacher, what wonderful stones and what wonderful buildings!" 2 And Jesus said to him, "Do you see all these great buildings? Not one stone can be left here upon another, that cannot be thrown down."

3 Now as he sat on the Mount of Olives opposite the temple, Peter, James, John, and Andrew asked him privately, 4 "Tell us, when will this be? And what will be the sign when these things are all to be fulfilled?" 5 And Jesus began to say to them: "Take heed that no one deceives you. 6 Many will come in my name, saying, 'I am he,' and will deceive many. 7 When you may hear of wars and rumors of wars, do not be alarmed. Such things must happen, but the end is not yet. 8 For nation will rise against nation, and kingdom against kingdom. There will be earthquakes in various places. There will be famines. These are the beginning of birth pains. 9 But watch out for yourselves. They will deliver you up to councils, and you will be beaten in synagogues. You will be made to stand before governors and kings for my sake, for a testimony to them. 10 And the gospel must first be preached to all nations. 11 And when they bring you to trial and deliver you up, do not worry beforehand what you are to say. But say whatever is given you in that hour. For it is not you who speak, but the Holy Spirit. 12 And brother will betray brother to death, and a father his child. And children will rise up against parents and have them put to death. 13 And you will be hated by all men for my name's sake. But he who endures to the end will be saved.

---

lepta, which make a kodrantes.

12:43 Alx/Byz[**said to them**], Major[says to them (DRA, KJV)]; Alx/Byz[**widow put in more**], Major[widow has put in more (DRA, ESV, HCS, JNT, KJV, MRD, NET, NIV, NJB, NKJ, NLT, NRS, REB, RSV, TLB)].

13:2 Alx[**Jesus said**], Byz[Jesus answering, said (DRA, KJV, NKJ, ~NIV, ~NLT, ~TEV, ~TLB)]; Alx/Byz[**Not one stone can be left here**], Major[omits here (DRA, JNT, KJV, NAB, NAS, NAU, NET, NJB, NKJ, REB, TLB)].

13:3 Alx/Byz[**Peter**], Alt/Peshitta[Cephas (JNT, MRD)].

13:5 Alx[**Jesus began to say to them**], Byz[Jesus answering began to say them (DRA)], Major[Jesus answering them began to say (KJV, NKJ, ~TLB)].

13:6 Alx[**Many will come**], Byz[For many will come (DRA, KJV, MRD, NKJ, NLT, TLB)]; **I am he** Greek I am; Exodus 3:14.

13:7 Alx/Byz[**When you may hear**], Minor[When you hear (ESV, HCS, JNT, NAB, NAS, NAU, NET, NIV, NJB, KJV, NLT, NRS, REB, RSV, TEV, ~TLB) others When you shall hear (ASV, DRA, KJV, MRD)]; Alx[**Such things must happen**], Byz[For such things must happen (DRA, KJV, MRD, NKJ, ~TLB)].

13:8 Alx[**There will be earthquakes**], Byz[And there will be earthquakes (DRA, KJV, MRD, NKJ, TLB)]; Alx[**There will be famines**], Byz[And there will be famines and troubles (KJV, ~MRD, NKJ)]; Alx[**These are the beginning of birth pains 9**], Byz[9 These are the beginnings of birth pangs], Major[These are the beginnings of birth pains 9 (KJV, NAB, NKJ, ~REB, ~TEV, ~TLB)].

13:9 Alx[**They will deliver**], Byz[For they will deliver (ASV, DRA, ESV, KJV, MRD, NAS, NAU, NKJ, NRS, RSV, TLB)]; Alx/Major[**beaten in synagogues**], Byz[beaten in their synagogues]; Alx/Byz[**be made to stand**], Minor[be brought (KJV, ~NAB, NJB, NKJ, REB, TLB)]; **councils** Greek sanhedrins.

13:10 **gospel** or good news.

13:11 Alx[**do not worry beforehand**], Byz[adds or premeditate (KJV, MRD, NKJ)].

13:12 Alx[**And brother will betray brother**], Byz[But brother will betray brother (~HCS, ~JNT, ~KJV, ~NAB, ~NAU, ~NET, ~NIV, ~NJB, ~NKJ, ~NLT, ~NRS, ~REB, ~TEV, ~TLB)].

¹⁴ "When you see 'the abomination of desolation' standing where he ought not to be (let the reader understand), then let those who are in Judea flee to the mountains. ¹⁵ [And] let him who is on the housetop not go down, nor enter to take anything out of his house. ¹⁶ And let the one in the field not go back to get his cloak. ¹⁷ But woe for those who are pregnant and those who are nursing babies in those days! ¹⁸ Pray that it may not happen in winter. ¹⁹ For in those days there will be tribulation, such as has not been from the beginning of the creation which God created until now, and never will be. ²⁰ And if the Lord had not shortened those days, no flesh would be saved. But for the sake of the elect, whom he chose, he shortened the days. ²¹ And then if anyone says to you, 'Look, here is the Christ!' 'Look, he is there!' do not believe it. ²² For false christs and false prophets will rise and give signs and wonders to deceive, if possible, the elect. ²³ But take heed; I have told you all things beforehand.

²⁴   "But in those days, after that tribulation,
            the sun will be darkened.
            And the moon will not give its light.
²⁵   The stars will fall from heaven.
            And the powers in the heavens will be shaken.
²⁶ Then they will see 'the Son of Man coming in the clouds' with great power and glory. ²⁷ And then he will send out the angels, and gather [his] elect from the four winds, from the ends of earth to the ends of heaven.

²⁸ "Now learn this lesson from the fig tree: as soon as its branch becomes tender and puts forth its leaves, you know that summer is near. ²⁹ So also, when you see these things happening, you know that it is near, right at the door. ³⁰ Truly, I say to you, this

---

13:¹⁴ Alx[**the abomination of desolation**], Byz[*adds* spoken of by Daniel the prophet (KJV, MRD, NKJ)]; **Daniel 9:27, 11:31, 12:11**.

13:¹⁵ Alx/Byz[**And let him who is on the housetop**], Minor[*omits* And (ESV, JNT, NAU, NET, NIV, NJB, NKJ, NLT, NRS, REB, RSV, TEV, TLB)]; Alx[**not go down**], Byz[*adds* into the house (DRA, ~ESV, ~JNT, KJV, ~NIV, ~NJB, NKJ, ~NRS, ~REB, ~RSV, ~TEV, ~TLB)].

13:¹⁶ Alx[**the one in the field**], Byz[the one who is in the field (ASV, DRA, ESV, ~JNT, KJV, MRD, NAS, NAU, ~NJB, NKJ, REB, RSV, TEV, ~TLB)].

13:¹⁸ Alx[**Pray that it may not happen**], Byz[Pray that your flight not happen (KJV, MRD, NKJ, TLB)]; Alx/Byz[**in winter**], Minor[*adds* or come on a Sabbath].

13:²⁰ Alx/Byz[**the Lord**], Minor[God (JNT, MRD)].

13:²¹ Alx/Byz[**And then**], Major[Then (HCS, JNT, MRD, NAB, NET, NIV, NKJ, NLT, REB, TEV)]; Alx/Byz[**Christ!' 'Look**], Major[Christ!' or, 'Look (ASV, ESV, JNT, KJV, MRD, NAS, NAU, NET, NIV, NJB, NKJ, NLT, NRS, REB, RSV, TEV, TLB)]; Alx/Byz[**do not believe it**], Minor[you should not believe it].

13:²² Alx/Byz[**For false christs**], Minor[And false christs (~ESV 2001 edition, ~JNT, ~NAB, ~NRS, ~REB, ~RSV)]; Alx/Byz[**false christs**], Minor[*omits*]; Alx/Byz[**give signs**], Minor[make signs (ESV, HCS, JNT, NAB, NET, NIV, NJB, NLT, NRS, REB, TEV, TLB)]; Alx[**the elect**], Byz[even the elect (DRA, KJV, MRD, NKJ, NLT, TEV, TLB)].

13:²³ Alx[**I have told you**], Byz[Behold, I have told you (ASV, DRA, KJV, MRD, NAS, NAU, NKJ)].

13:²⁵ Alx/Byz[**The stars will fall from heaven**], Major[The stars of heaven will fall away (DRA, KJV, NKJ, ~TLB)].

13:²⁶ ~Daniel 7:13.

13:²⁷ Alx[**the angels**], Byz[his angels (DRA, JNT, KJV, MRD, ~NET, NIV, NKJ, NLT)]; Alx/Byz[**his elect**], Minor[the elect]; Alx/Major[**the ends of earth to the ends of heaven**], Byz[the ends of the earth to the ends of (the) heaven (ASV, DRA, ESV, HCS, JNT, KJV, NAB, NAS, NAU, NET, NIV, NJB, NLT, NRS, RSV, TEV, ~TLB)]; **ends** *Greek* boundary *or* limit.

13:²⁸ Alx/Byz[**you know**], Minor[it is known].

13:²⁹ **it is near** *or* he is near.

13:³⁰ **generation** *or* race.

generation will never pass away before all these things take place. [31] Heaven and earth will pass away, but my words will never pass away.

[32] "But of the day or the hour no one knows, not even the angels in heaven, nor the Son, but only the Father. [33] Take heed, watch; for you do not know when the time will come. [34] It is like a man going on a journey, when he leaves his house and puts his servants in charge, each with his work, and commands the doorkeeper to be on the watch. [35] Watch therefore – for you do not know when the master of the house will come, whether in the evening, or at midnight, or when the rooster crows, or in the morning – [36] lest, coming suddenly, he find you sleeping. [37] And what I say to you, I say to all: Watch!"

14

[1] It was now two days before the Passover and the feast of Unleavened Bread. And the chief priests and the scribes were seeking how to arrest him by stealth, and kill him. [2] For they said, "Not during the feast, lest there be a riot among the people."

[3] And while he was at Bethany in the house of Simon the leper, as he sat at table, a woman came with an alabaster flask of ointment of pure nard, very costly. She broke the flask and poured it over his head. [4] But there were some who were indignant among themselves: "Why was the ointment wasted? [5] For the ointment might have been sold for more than three hundred denarii and given to the poor." And they criticized her sharply. [6] But Jesus said, "Let her alone. Why do you trouble her? She has done a beautiful thing to me. [7] For you always have the poor with you, and whenever you will, you can do good to them. But you will not always have me. [8] She has done what she could. She has come beforehand to anoint my body for burial. [9] And truly, I say to you, wherever the gospel is preached in the whole world, what she has done will also be told in memory of her."

[10] Then Judas Iscariot, who was one of the twelve, went to the chief priests to betray him to them. [11] And when they heard it they were glad, and promised to give him money. So he sought an opportunity to betray him.

13:31 Alx/Byz[**will never** *or* will certainly not], Major[should never], Minor[will not (ASV, DRA, ESV, KJV, MRD, NAB, NAS, NAU, NJB, NRS, RSV)].

13:32 Alx/Byz[**or the hour**], Major[or hour (DRA, HCS, NAB, NAS, NAU, NET, NIV, NJB, NLT, NRS, REB, TEV, TLB)], Minor[and that hour (~JNT, KJV, MRD, ~NKJ)]; Alx/Byz[**the angels**], Minor[an angel]; Alx/Byz[**in heaven**], Major[which are in heaven (KJV)].

13:33 Alx[**watch**], Byz[*adds* and pray (ASV, DRA, KJV, MRD, NKJ)]; Alx/Byz[**will come** *Greek* is], Minor[*omits*].

13:34 Alx[**each with his work**], Byz[and each with his work (KJV, MRD, NKJ, ~TLB)].

13:35 Alx[**whether in the evening**], Byz[in the evening (DRA, ESV, KJV, MRD, NJB, NLT, NRS, REB, RSV, ~TEV, TLB)]; *JNT starts verse 35 with* in the evening.

14:2 Alx[**For they said**], Byz[But they said (DRA, ~HCS, KJV, MRD, ~NAB, NIV, NKJ, NLT, ~REB, ~TEV, TLB)].

14:3 Alx[**She broke the flask**], Byz[And she broke the flask (ASV, DRA, ESV, KJV, MRD, NAS, NAU, ~NET, ~NKJ, NRS, RSV, ~TLB)]; Alx[**poured it over**], Byz[poured it down over]; **leper** *can refer to several skin diseases.*

14:4 Alx[**who were indignant among themselves** *Greek* who indignantly among themselves], Byz[*adds* saying (ASV, NAS, NAU, NET, NIV, NJB, NRS, REB, RSV, ~TLB)], Major[*adds* and saying (DRA, KJV, MRD, TEV)].

14:5 Alx/Byz[**the ointment**], Major[it (JNT, KJV, MRD, NAB, NET, NIV, NKJ, NLT, TEV)]; Alx/Byz[**more than**], Minor[*omits* (JNT, NLT, ~TLB)]; **denarii** *a denarius was one day's wages for a laborer.*

14:6 Alx/Byz[**to me** *or* for me], Minor[towards me (MRD)].

14:7 Alx/Byz[**you can do good to them**], Minor[you can always do good to them].

14:9 Alx[**And truly**], Byz[*omits* And (DRA, HCS, JNT, KJV, MRD, NAB, NAU, NET, NIV, NJB, NKJ, NLT, NRS, REB, ~TEV)]; Alx[**the gospel**], Byz[this gospel (DRA, JNT, KJV, MRD, NKJ)].

14:10 Alx/Byz[**Iscariot**], Minor[Scariot], Alt[from Kerioth (~JNT)]; Alx[**who was one** *Greek* the one], Byz[one (DRA, HCS, KJV, MRD, NAB, NET, NIV, NJB, NKJ, NLT, REB, TEV, TLB)]; **Iscariot**

¹² Now on the first day of Unleavened Bread, when they killed the Passover lamb, his disciples said to him, "Where do you want us to go and prepare for you to eat the Passover?" ¹³ And he sent two of his disciples, and said to them, "Go into the city, and a man carrying a jar of water will meet you. Follow him. ¹⁴ And wherever he enters, say to the owner of the house, 'The Teacher says, where is my guest room, where I may eat the Passover with my disciples?' ¹⁵ He will show you a large upper room, furnished and ready; and there make preparations for us." ¹⁶ So the disciples set out and went to the city, and found it just as he had told them; and they prepared the Passover. ¹⁷ And when it was evening he came with the twelve. ¹⁸ And as they were at table eating, Jesus said, "Truly, I say to you, one of you will betray me, one who is eating with me." ¹⁹ They began to be sorrowful, and to say to him one by one, "Is it I?" ²⁰ He said to them, "It is one of the twelve, one who dips bread into the dish with me. ²¹ For the Son of Man goes just as it is written of him. But woe to that man by whom the Son of Man is betrayed! It would have been better for that man if he had not been born."

²² And as they were eating, he took bread, blessed and broke it, and gave it to them and said, "Take; this is my body." ²³ Then he took a cup, and when he had given thanks he gave it to them, and they all drank from it. ²⁴ And he said to them, "This is my blood of the covenant, which is poured out for many. ²⁵ Truly, I say to you, I will never again drink of the fruit of the vine until that day when I drink it new in the kingdom of God." ²⁶ And when they had sung a hymn, they went out to the Mount of Olives.

²⁷ And Jesus said to them, "You will all fall away. For it is written:
'I will strike the shepherd,
        and the sheep will be scattered.'
²⁸ But after I have been raised, I will go before you to Galilee." ²⁹ But Peter said to him, "Even if all fall away, I will not." ³⁰ Jesus said to him, "Truly, I say to you that this night, before the rooster crows twice, you will deny me three times." ³¹ But he insisted, "If I have to die with you, I will never deny you!" And they all said the same.

Hebraism Ish Keriot a man from Kerioth *or possibly Sicarios* assassin *or* bandit.

14:14 Alx/Byz[**my guest room**], Major[the guest room (HCS, KJV, MRD, NJB, NKJ, NLT, REB, TEV, TLB)].

14:15 Alx[**and there**], Byz[*omits* and (ESV, HCS, JNT, KJV, MRD, NAB, NAU, NET, NIV, NJB, NKJ, NLT, NRS, REB, RSV, TEV, TLB)].

14:16 Alx[**the disciples**], Byz[his disciples (DRA, KJV, MRD, NKJ)].

14:19 Alx[**They began to be sorrowful**], Byz[And they began to be sorrowful (DRA, KJV, MRD, NKJ)]; Alx[**Is it I?**], Byz[*adds* And another said, "Is it I?" (KJV, NKJ)].

14:20 Alx[**He said to them**], Byz[He answered and said to them (KJV, ~NIV, NKJ, ~NLT, ~TEV, ~TLB)]; Alx/Byz[**dips bread into the dish** *Greek* dips into the dish], Minor[dips into the same dish (NJB, ~TLB)].

14:21 Alx[**For the Son**], Byz[And indeed the Son (DRA, KJV, ~MRD, ~NIV, ~NJB, ~NKJ, ~REB, ~TEV, ~TLB)].

14:22 Alx[**he took bread**], Byz[Jesus took bread (DRA, JNT, KJV, MRD, NIV, NKJ, NLT, TEV, TLB)]; Alx[**Take; this is my body**], Byz[Take, eat; this is my body (KJV, NKJ, ~TLB)].

14:23 Alx[**a cup**], Byz[the cup (DRA, KJV, MRD, NET, NIV, NKJ)].

14:24 Alx[**the covenant**], Byz[the new covenant (DRA, JNT, KJV, MRD, NKJ, TLB)]; Alx[**for** *on behalf of* **many**], Byz[for *concerning* many].

14:25 Alx/Major[**fruit of the vine**], Byz[offspring of the vine (~NJB, ~NLT, ~TEV, ~TLB)].

14:27 Alx[**fall away**], Byz[*adds* because of me this night (DRA, ~JNT, KJV, MRD, NKJ, ~NLT, ~TLB)]; **Zechariah 13:7**.

14:29 Alx/Byz[**Peter**], Alt/Peshitta[Cephas (JNT, MRD)].

14:30 Alx[**this very night**], Byz[in this night (DRA, KJV, MRD)]; Alx/Byz[**you will deny me**], Minor[*omits* you]; Alx/Byz[**the rooster crows twice**], Minor[*omits* twice].

14:31 Alx/Major[**But he**], Byz[But Peter (NAS, NAU, NET, NLT, REB, TEV, TLB)], Alt[*without textual foundation* But Cephas (~JNT)]; Alx[**insisted** *Greek* spoke insistently], Byz[spoke more insistently

³² They went to a place which was called Gethsemane. And he said to his disciples, "Sit here, while I pray." ³³ And he took Peter, James, and John with him. And he began to be deeply distressed and troubled. ³⁴ And he said to them, "My soul is very sorrowful, even to death. Stay here, and watch." ³⁵ And going a little farther, he fell on the ground and prayed that, if it were possible, the hour might pass from him. ³⁶ And he said, "Abba, Father, all things are possible for you. Take this cup away from me; yet not what I will, but what you will." ³⁷ Then he came and found them sleeping. And he said to Peter, "Simon, are you asleep? Could you not watch one hour? ³⁸ Watch and pray that you may not come into temptation. The spirit indeed is willing, but the flesh is weak." ³⁹ And again he went away and prayed, saying the same words. ⁴⁰ And when he came again, he found them sleeping, for their eyes were heavy. And they did not know what to answer him. ⁴¹ Then he came the third time and said to them, "Are you still sleeping and resting? It is enough! The hour has come. Behold, the Son of Man is being betrayed into the hands of sinners. ⁴² Rise, let us go. See, my betrayer is at hand."

⁴³ And immediately, while he was still speaking, Judas came, one of the twelve, and with him a crowd with swords and clubs, from the chief priests and the scribes and the elders. ⁴⁴ Now the betrayer had given them a signal, saying, "The one I shall kiss is the man. Seize him and lead him away under guard." ⁴⁵ And when he came, he went up to him at once, and said, "Rabbi!" and he kissed him. ⁴⁶ And they laid hands on him and seized him. ⁴⁷ And [a certain] one of those who stood by drew his sword and struck the servant of the high priest, and cut off his ear. ⁴⁸ And Jesus said to them, "Have you come out as against a robber, with swords and clubs to capture me? ⁴⁹ Every day I was with you in the temple teaching, and you did not seize me. But the scriptures must be fulfilled." ⁵⁰ Then they all forsook him and fled.

⁵¹ And a certain young man was following with him, with nothing but a linen cloth around his body. And they seized him, ⁵² and he left the linen cloth and fled naked.

(ASV, DRA, KJV, NJB, NKJ, TEV)]; Alx/Byz[**I will never deny you**], Major[I would never deny you].

14:³³ Alx[**with him**], Byz[with himself]; Alx/Byz[**Peter**], Alt/Peshitta[Cephas (JNT, MRD)].

14:³⁵ Alx/Byz[**going a little farther**], Major[approaching a little].

14:³⁶ Alx/Major[**not what I will, but what you will**], Byz[not what I will, but what you may will (NJB, ~REB)], Alt[not my pleasure, but yours (MRD)]; **Abba** *Aramaic* Father.

14:³⁷ Alx/Byz[**Peter**], Alt/Peshitta[Cephas (JNT, MRD)]; Alx/Major[**Could you** *singular* **not watch**], Byz[Could you *plural* not watch].

14:³⁸ Alx[**come into temptation**], Byz[enter into temptation (ASV, DRA, ESV, HCS, ~JNT, KJV, MRD, ~NAB, ~NET, ~NIV, ~NJB, NKJ, ~NLT, ~REB, RSV, ~TEV, ~TLB)]; **temptation** *or* the time of trial.

14:³⁹ Alx/Byz[**saying the same words**], Minor[*omits* (REB)].

14:⁴⁰ Alx[**when he came again, he found them sleep**], Byz[when he returned, he found them sleeping again (DRA, KJV, NKJ, REB, ~TLB)].

14:⁴¹ Alx/Byz[**It is enough**], Minor[It is all over (MRD, NJB, NLT, TLB)].

14:⁴³ Alx/Major[**Judas**], Byz[*adds* Iscariot (DRA, MRD)]; Alx[**one of the twelve**], Byz[being one of the twelve]; Alx[**a crowd**], Byz[a great crowd (DRA, KJV, ~MRD, ~NJB, NKJ, ~NLT)]; Alx/Major[**from the chief priests**], Byz[sent from the chief priests (~MRD, ~NAB, ~NAU, NET, NIV, NJB, ~NKJ, NLT, REB, TEV, TLB)].

14:⁴⁵ Alx[**said**], Byz[*adds* to him (MRD, NKJ)]; Alx[**Rabbi!**], Byz[Greetings, Rabbi (DRA)], Major[Rabbi! Rabbi! (KJV, MRD, NKJ)].

14:⁴⁶ Alx[**they laid hands on him**], Byz[they laid their hands on him (KJV, NKJ, ~TEV, ~TLB)].

14:⁴⁷ Alx/Byz[**a certain one**], Minor[one (DRA, ESV, HCS, JNT, KJV, MRD, NAB, NAU, NET, NIV, NJB, NKJ, NLT, NRS, REB, RSV, TEV)].

14:⁴⁹ Alx/Byz[**you did not seize me**], Minor[you were not seizing me].

14:⁵¹ Alx[**was following with him**], Byz[followed him (~ASV, DRA, ESV, JNT, KJV, ~MRD, NAB, NJB, NKJ, ~REB, RSV)], Minor[was following him (HCS, NAS, NAU, NET, NIV, ~NLT, NRS,

⁵³ And they led Jesus to the high priest. And all the chief priests and the elders and the scribes were assembled. ⁵⁴ But Peter followed him at a distance, right into the courtyard of the high priest. And he sat with the guards and warmed himself at the fire. ⁵⁵ Now the chief priests and the entire Sanhedrin sought testimony against Jesus to put him to death, but they found none. ⁵⁶ For many bore false witness against him, but their testimonies did not agree. ⁵⁷ Then some stood up and bore false witness against him, saying, ⁵⁸ "We heard him say, 'I will destroy this temple that is made with hands, and in three days I will build another not made with hands.'" ⁵⁹ Yet even then their testimony did not agree. ⁶⁰ And the high priest stood up in the midst, and questioned Jesus, "Have you no answer to make to what these men testify against you?" ⁶¹ But he was silent and made no answer at all. Again the high priest began to question him, "Are you the Christ, the Son of the Blessed?" ⁶² And Jesus said, "I am.

> And *you will see the Son of Man*
>   *sitting at the right hand of the Power,*
>   *and coming with the clouds of heaven.*"

⁶³ The high priest tore his clothes and said, "Why do we need any more witnesses? ⁶⁴ You have heard the blasphemy. What do you think?" And they all condemned him as worthy of death. ⁶⁵ Then some began to spit on him, and to blindfold him, and to beat him, and to say to him, "Prophesy!" And the guards received him with blows.

⁶⁶ Now as Peter was below in the courtyard, one of the servant girls of the high priest came. ⁶⁷ And when she saw Peter warming himself, she looked at him, and said, "You also were with the Nazarene, Jesus." ⁶⁸ But he denied it, saying, "I neither know nor understand what you mean." And he went out into the gateway, [and a rooster crowed]. ⁶⁹ And the servant girl saw him, and began to say again to those who stood by, "This is

---

TEV, ~TLB)]; Alx[**they seized him**], Byz[the young men seized him (KJV, NKJ, ~NLT, ~TLB)].

14:⁵² Alx[**and fled naked**], Byz[and fled from them naked (DRA, KJV, NKJ)].

14:⁵³ Alx[**were assembled**], Byz[*adds* with him (ASV, KJV, MRD, NKJ)].

14:⁵⁴ Alx/Byz[**Peter**], Alt/Peshitta[Simon (MRD)], Alt[*without textual foundation* Cephas (~JNT)].

14:⁶⁰ Alx/Major[**questioned Jesus**], Byz[began to question Jesus]; Alx[**make to what these**], Byz[make? What is it that these (ASV, ESV, KJV, MRD, NAB, NAS, NAU, NET, NIV, NJB, NKJ, NLT, NRS, RSV, TLB)].

14:⁶¹ Alx[**made no answer at all**], Byz[made no answer (ASV, DRA, ESV, JNT, KJV, MRD, NAB, NAS, NAU, NET, NIV, NKJ, NLT, NRS, RSV, TEV, TLB)].

14:⁶² Alx/Major[**with the clouds of heaven**], Byz[on the clouds of heaven (JNT, ~KJV, MRD, NIV, NLT, ~TLB)]; ~Psalms 110:1, ~Daniel 7:13.

14:⁶⁴ Alx/Major[**You have heard**], Byz[You have certainly heard (~NLT)], Alt[Behold, from his own mouth you have heard (MRD)].

14:⁶⁵ Alx/Byz[**spit on him**], Minor[spit in his face (MRD, NJB)]; Alx/Major[**Prophesy!**], Byz[Prophesy for us! Who hit you? (TEV, TLB)], Minor[Christ, prophesy! Who hit you?]; Alx/Byz[**received him with blows**], Major[struck him with blows (DRA, KJV, ~NJB, NKJ)], Minor[struck him in the face (MRD, REB)].

14:⁶⁶ Alx/Byz[**Peter**], Alt/Peshitta[Simon (MRD)], Alt[*without textual foundation* Cephas (~JNT)]; Alx/Byz[**below in the courtyard**], Major[in the courtyard below (DRA, HCS, JNT, NLT)].

14:⁶⁷ Alx/Byz[**Peter**], Alt/Peshitta[him (MRD)], Alt[*without textual foundation* Cephas (~JNT)]; Alx/Major[**with the Nazarene, Jesus**], Byz[with Jesus the Nazarene (DRA, KJV, MRD, NAS, NAU, NJB, NKJ, NLT, NRS, TEV, TLB)].

14:⁶⁸ Alx[**I neither know nor understand**], Byz[I do not know, nor understand (HCS, ~JNT, KJV, ~MRD, ~NET, NIV, NJB, ~NLT, NRS, REB, TEV, ~TLB)]; Alx/Byz[**And a rooster crowed**], Minor[*omits* (NAS, NIV, REB, RSV)].

14:⁶⁹ Alx[**And the servant girl saw him, and began to say again**], Byz[And the servant girl saw him again, and began to say (HCS, MRD, NKJ)], Minor[But the servant girl saw him again, and began to say], Alt[*omits* again (JNT, NLT, TLB) *others* And a servant girl saw him again, and began to say (DRA, KJV)].

one of them." **70** But again he denied it. And after a little while those standing near said to Peter again, "Surely you are one of them; for you are a Galilean." **71** But he began to invoke a curse on himself and to swear, "I do not know this man of whom you speak." **72** And immediately the rooster crowed a second time. Then Peter remembered the word, how Jesus had said to him, "Before the rooster crows twice, you will deny me three times." And he broke down and wept.

15 **1** Very early in the morning, the chief priests held a consultation with the elders and scribes and the entire Sanhedrin. And they bound Jesus, led him away, and delivered him to Pilate. **2** Then Pilate asked him, "Are you the King of the Jews?" And he answered him, "You said it." **3** And the chief priests accused him of many things. **4** And Pilate was again asking him, saying, "Have you no answer to make? See how many things they accuse you of." **5** But Jesus still made no answer, so that Pilate was amazed.

6 Now at the feast he was accustomed to release for them one prisoner whom they excused. **7** And with the rebels in prison, who had committed murder in the insurrection, there was a man called Barabbas. **8** And the crowd came up and began to ask Pilate to do as he had done for them. **9** But Pilate answered them, "Do you want me to release to you the King of the Jews?" **10** For he knew it was out of envy that the chief priests had handed Jesus over to him. **11** But the chief priests stirred up the crowd to have him release for them Barabbas instead. **12** And Pilate again said to them, "Then what [do you want] me to do with [the man you call] the King of the Jews?" **13** And they cried out again, "Crucify him!"

14:70 Alx/Byz[**Peter**], Alt/Peshitta[Cephas (JNT, MRD)]; Alx[**you are a Galilean**], Byz[*adds* and your speech shows it (KJV, MRD, NKJ)].

14:71 Alx/Byz[**to swear**], Minor[*adds* saying (DRA, KJV, ~REB)].

14:72 Alx[**immediately**], Byz[*omits* (KJV, NKJ)]; Alx/Byz[**the rooster crowed a second time**], Minor[the rooster crowed ~DRA)]; Alx/Byz[**Peter**], Alt/Peshitta[Simon (MRD)], Alt[*without textual foundation* Cephas (~JNT)]; Alx[**the word, how**], Byz[the word that (~ASV, DRA, ~HCS, JNT, KJV, ~MRD, NAB, NET, NIV, NJB, NKJ, ~NLT, NRS)]; Alx/Major[**Jesus said to him**], Byz[Jesus said (~NLT, ~TLB)]; Alx/Byz[**the rooster crows twice**], Minor[the rooster crows]; Alx/Byz[**he broke down and wept** *or* he thought on it and wept], Minor[he began to weep (DRA, ~HCS, MRD, NAS, NAU, ~NJB, ~REB, TLB)].

15:1 Alx/Byz[**held a consultation**], Minor[prepared a consultation (NET, NIV, ~NJB, REB)].

15:2 Alx[**he answered him** *Greek* he says to him], Byz[he said to him]; Alx/Byz[**You said it** *Greek* You say it].

15:3 Alx/Major[**many things**], Byz[*adds* But he answered nothing (KJV, NKJ)].

15:4 Alx/Byz[**was again asking him**], Major[again asked him (ASV, DRA, ESV, HCS, JNT, KJV, MRD, NAB, NAU, NET, NIV, NJB, NKJ, NLT, NRS, REB, RSV, TEV, TLB)]; Alx/Byz[**saying**], Minor[*omits* (ESV, HCS, JNT, NAB, NET, NIV, NJB, NLT, NRS, REB, RSV, TEV, TLB)]; Alx[**they accuse you of**], Byz[they testify against you (ESV, JNT, KJV, MRD, NAS, NAU, NET, NJB, NKJ, NLT, NRS, RSV, ~TEV, ~TLB)].

15:6 Alx[**whom they excused**], Byz[whomever they requested (~ASV, DRA, ~ESV, ~HCS, JNT, KJV, ~MRD, ~NAB, ~NAS, ~NAU, NET, ~NIV, NJB, NKJ, NLT, ~NRS, ~REB, ~RSV, TEV, TLB)].

15:7 Alx[**rebels**], Byz[fellow rebels (KJV, NKJ, ~TLB)].

15:8 Alx/Byz[**the crowd**], Minor[the whole crowd]; Alx[**came up**], Byz[cried out (KJV, MRD, NKJ)]; Alx[**as he had done for them**], Byz[as he had always done for them (~ASV, DRA, ~ESV, ~HCS, ~JNT, KJV, ~MRD, ~NAB, ~NAS, ~NAU, ~NET, ~NIV, ~NJB, NKJ, ~NLT, ~NRS, ~REB, ~RSV, ~TEV, ~TLB)].

15:10 Alx/Byz[**the chief priests**], Minor[they (~REB)].

15:12 Alx/Byz[**what do you want me to do**], Minor[what should I do (ASV, ESV, JNT, NAS, NAU, NIV, NJB, NLT, REB, RSV, TLB)], Minor[what do you say I shall do]; Alx/Byz[**the man you call**], Minor[*omits* (DRA) *others omit* the man]; Alx/Byz[**the King of the Jews**], Major[King of the Jews (MRD, NET, NJB, REB, ~TLB)].

14 And Pilate said to them, "Why, what evil has he done?" But they shouted riotously, "Crucify him!" 15 So Pilate, wanting to satisfy the crowd, released Barabbas to them. And he delivered Jesus, after he had scourged him, to be crucified.

16 The soldiers led him away into the palace (that is, the Praetorium) and they called together the whole battalion. 17 And they dressed him in a purple cloak, and they twisted a crown of thorns and put it on him. 18 And they began to salute him, "Hail, King of the Jews!" 19 Then they struck him on the head with a reed and spat on him. And falling on their knees, they paid homage to him. 20 And when they had mocked him, they took the purple robe off him, and put his clothes on him. Then they led him out to crucify him.

21 Then they compelled a certain man, Simon of Cyrene, the father of Alexander and Rufus, as he was coming out of the country and passing by, to carry his cross. 22 And they brought him to the place called Golgotha (which means the place of a skull). 23 Then they offered him wine mingled with myrrh, but he did not take it. 24 And they crucified him, and 'divided his garments, casting lots for them' to determine what each man should take. 25 And it was the third hour, when they crucified him. 26 And the inscription of the charge written against him read:

THE KING OF THE JEWS.

27 And with him they crucified two robbers, one on his right and one on his left. (28) 29 And those who passed by hurled insults at him, wagging their heads, and saying, "Aha! You who would destroy the temple and build it in three days, 30 save yourself by coming down from the cross!" 31 So also the chief priests mocked him among themselves with the scribes, and said, "He saved others? He cannot save himself! 32 Let the Christ, the King of Israel, come down now from the cross, that we may see and believe." Those who were crucified with him also reviled him.

33 And when the sixth hour had come, there was darkness over the whole land until the ninth hour. 34 And at the ninth hour Jesus cried out with a loud voice, *Eloi, Eloi,*

15:14 Alx[**riotously** Greek exceedingly], Byz[more riotously (~DRA, ~ESV, ~HCS, ~JNT, KJV, ~MRD, ~NAS, ~NAU, NET, ~NIV, ~NJB, ~NKJ, NLT, ~NRS, ~REB, ~RSV, ~TEV, ~TLB)].

15:16 **palace** or courtyard.

15:17 Alx[**dressed**], Byz[clothed or put on (ASV, DRA, ESV, KJV, MRD, NAB, NET, NIV, NKJ, NRS, RSV, TEV)].

15:18 Alx[**King of the Jews**], Byz[the King of the Jews (JNT, TEV)].

15:20 Alx[**put his clothes on him**], Byz[put his own clothes on him (DRA, ESV, JNT, KJV, MRD, NAB, NAU, NET, NIV, NJB, NKJ, NLT, NRS, REB, RSV, TEV, TLB)]; Alx/Byz[**to crucify him**], Minor[omits him (JNT, NLT, TLB)].

15:23 Alx[**offered him wine**], Byz[adds to drink (DRA, KJV, MRD, NKJ, ~TEV)].

15:24 Alx[**And they crucified him, and divided**], Byz[And crucifying him, they divided (DRA, ~JNT, KJV, MRD, ~NIV, NKJ, NLT, REB)]; ~Psalms 22:18.

15:25 Alx/Byz[**the third hour**], Minor[the sixth hour].

15:(28) Alx[omits], Byz[adds So the scripture was fulfilled which says, "He was numbered with the transgressors" (ASV, DRA, HCS, KJV, MRD, NAS, NAU, NKJ, TLB)]; Isaiah 53:12.

15:29 **hurled insults at** or blasphemed.

15:30 Alx[**save yourself by coming down** Greek save yourself, coming down], Byz[save yourself, and come down (ASV, ESV, JNT, KJV, MRD, NAS, NAU, NET, NIV, ~NJB, NKJ, NLT, NRS, REB, RSV, TEV, TLB)].

15:31 Alx/Major[**So also** or In the same way also], Byz[And so also (MRD)].

15:32 Alx[**see and believe**], Byz[adds him (JNT, MRD, NLT, TEV, ~TLB)].

15:33 Alx[**And when the sixth hour had come**], Byz[But when the sixth hour had come (~HCS, ~JNT, ~NAB, ~NAU, ~NET, ~NIV, ~NJB, ~NKJ, ~NLT, ~NRS, ~REB, ~TEV, ~TLB)]; **land** or earth.

15:34 Alx[**with a loud voice**], Byz[adds saying (DRA, KJV, MRD, NKJ)]; Alx/Byz[**Eloi, Eloi** Aramaic],

lema sabachthani?" – which means, *"My God, my God, why have you forsaken me?"* 35 When some of those standing near heard this, they said, "Look, he is calling Elijah." 36 But someone ran [and,] filling a sponge full of wine vinegar, put it on a reed, and offered it to him to drink, saying, "Wait, let us see if Elijah will come to take him down." 37 And with a loud cry, Jesus breathed his last. 38 Then the veil of the temple was torn in two from top to bottom. 39 So when the centurion, who stood opposite him, saw how he breathed his last, he said, "Truly this man was God's Son!" 40 There were also women looking on from afar, among whom both Mary Magdalene, and Mary the mother of James the younger and of Joses, and Salome, 41 who followed him and ministered to him when he was in Galilee; and many other women who came up with him to Jerusalem.

42 Now when evening had come, because it was the Preparation Day, that is, the day before the Sabbath, 43 Joseph of Arimathea, a prominent member of the Sanhedrin, who was himself waiting for the kingdom of God, coming and taking courage, went in to Pilate and asked for the body of Jesus. 44 Pilate marveled that he was already dead; and summoning the centurion, he asked him if he had been dead for some time. 45 And when he learned from the centurion that he was dead, he granted the corpse to Joseph. 46 Then he bought fine linen, took him down, and wrapped him in the linen. And he placed him in a tomb which had been hewn out of the rock, and rolled a stone against the door of the tomb. 47 Mary Magdalene and Mary the mother of Joses saw where he was placed.

Minor[Eli, Eli *Hebrew* (~MRD, TLB)]; Alx[**lema** *Aramaic*], Byz[lima], Minor[lama *Hebrew* (ASV, DRA, KJV, NAS, NAU, NIV, NJB, NKJ, RSV, TLB)]; Alx/Byz[**sabachthani** *Aramaic*], Minor[zaphthani *from Hebrew* azavtani]; Alx/Byz[**My God, my God**], Minor[My God]; Alx/Byz[**why have you forsaken me**], Minor[why have you made me a reproach]; Psalms 22:1 *reads in Hebrew* Eli, Eli, lama azavtani.

15:35 Alx/Byz[**Look, he is calling Elijah**], Major[Behold, he is calling Elijah (ASV, DRA, ESV, KJV, NAS, NAU, RSV)], Alt/Peshitta[He is calling Elijah (MRD, ~NLT, ~TLB)], Alt[*without textual foundation* Listen, he is calling Elijah (~NET, ~NIV, ~NJB, ~NRS, ~REB, ~TEV)].

15:36 Alx[**someone**], Byz[one (ASV, DRA, JNT, KJV, MRD, NAB, NIV, NLT, RSV, TEV, TLB)]; Alx/Byz[**and, filling**], Minor[*omits* and (NAB, NET, NIV, NRS, TEV)]; Alx[**put it on a reed**], Byz[and put it on a reed (DRA, KJV, MRD, NJB, ~REB, TEV, TLB)].

15:39 Alx[**how he breathed**], Byz[how he cried out and breathed (DRA, KJV, MRD, NIV, NKJ)].

15:40 Alx[**both Mary** *Maria*], Byz[**were both Mary** *Maria* (ASV)], Minor[both Mary *Miriam* (~JNT)], Alt[*omits* both (~DRA, ~ESV, ~HCS, ~KJV, ~MRD, ~NAB, ~NAS, ~NAU, ~NET, ~NIV, ~NJB, ~NKJ, ~NLT, ~NRS, ~REB, ~RSV, ~TEV, ~TLB)]; Alx[**Joses**], Byz[Jose *or* Jesus (~DRA, JNT, ~NJB, ~NLT, ~TEV)].

15:41 Alx[**who followed him**], Byz[who also followed him (DRA, KJV, NKJ)].

15:42 Alx/Byz[**that is, the day before the Sabbath**], Minor[which is before the Sabbath (MRD)].

15:43 Alx/Byz[**coming and taking courage** *Greek* coming...taking courage], Major[came...taking courage (ASV, DRA, ~ESV, HCS, ~JNT, KJV, MRD, NAB, NAS, NAU, ~NET, ~NIV, NJB, ~NLT, ~NRS, ~REB, ~RSV, TEV, ~TLB)].

15:44 Alx/Byz[**had been dead for some time**], Minor[was already dead (DRA, ESV, HCS, NAB, NAS, NAU, NIV, NLT, REB, RSV, ~TLB)].

15:45 Alx[**corpse**], Byz[body (DRA, KJV, MRD, NAB, NAS, NAU, NET, NIV, NKJ, NLT, NRS, REB, RSV, TEV, TLB)].

15:46 Alx[**took him down** *Greek* taking him down], Byz[and took him down (ASV, DRA, ESV, JNT, KJV, MRD, NET, NRS, RSV, TLB)]; Alx[**placed him**], Byz[laid him (ASV, DRA, ESV, JNT, KJV, MRD, NAB, NAS, NAU, NJB, NKJ, NLT, NRS, REB, RSV, TLB)]; Alx/Byz[**in a tomb**], Minor[in a grave].

15:47 Alx/Byz[**Mary** *Maria*], Minor[**Mary** *Miriam* (~JNT)]; Alx[**Joses**], Byz[Jose *or* Jesus (JNT, ~NJB)], Minor[James *others* James and Joses *others* Joseph (DRA, NLT, TEV)]; **the mother of Joses** *Greek* of Joses.

16

¹ Now when the Sabbath was past, Mary Magdalene, Mary the mother of James, and Salome bought spices, so that they might go and anoint him. ² And very early on the first day of the week, they came to the tomb when the sun had risen. ³ And they asked each other, "Who will roll away the stone from the door of the tomb for us?" ⁴ But when they looked up, they saw that the stone, though it was very large, had been rolled away. ⁵ And entering the tomb, they saw a young man sitting on the right side, dressed in a white robe. And they were alarmed. ⁶ But he said to them, "Do not be alarmed. You seek Jesus of Nazareth, who was crucified. He has risen! He is not here. See the place where they laid him. ⁷ But go, tell his disciples and Peter that he is going before you to Galilee. There you will see him, as he told you." ⁸ So they went out and fled from the tomb, for trembling and astonishment had gripped them. And they said nothing to anyone, for they were afraid.

[[And they briefly reported all they had been commanded to those around Peter. And afterward Jesus himself sent out through them, from east to west, the sacred and imperishable proclamation of eternal salvation. Amen.]]

[[⁹ Now when he rose early on the first day of the week, he appeared first to Mary Magdalene, out of whom he had cast seven demons. ¹⁰ She went and told those who had been with him, as they mourned and wept. ¹¹ And when they heard that he was alive and had been seen by her, they did not believe it.

¹² After this he appeared in another form to two of them, as they were walking into the country. ¹³ And they went and told it to the rest, but they did not believe them either.

¹⁴ [But] later he appeared to the eleven as they sat at the table. And he rebuked them for their unbelief and hardness of heart, because they did not believe those who had

---

16:¹ Alx/Byz[**Mary Magdalene, Mary the mother of James**], Minor[*omits*]; Alx/Byz[**bought**], Minor[went and bought (NLT, TLB)]; Alx/Byz[**anoint him**], Minor[anoint Jesus (DRA, JNT, NIV, NLT, TEV)].

16:² Alx/Byz[**tomb**], Minor[grave]; Alx/Byz[**when the sun had risen**], Minor[at sunrise (HCS, KJV, MRD, NET, NLT, TEV, TLB)].

16:⁴ Alx/Byz[**rolled away**], Minor[rolled back (ASV, DRA, ESV, JNT, NAB, NET, NJB, NRS, RSV, TEV)]; Metzger[*Old Latin Codex Bobiensis adds* "But suddenly at the third hour of the day there was darkness over the whole circle of the earth, and angels descended from the heavens, and as he (the Lord) was rising… in the glory of the living God, at the same time they ascended with him; and immediately it was light. Then the women went to the tomb" *translation is Metzger's*].

16:⁵ Alx/Byz[**entering**], Minor[coming to].

16:⁶ Alx/Byz[**See the place**], Minor[See his place].

16:⁷ Alx/Byz[**Peter**], Alt/Peshitta[Cephas (JNT, MRD)].

16:⁸ Alx/Byz[**they went out**], Minor[*adds* quickly (KJV, NKJ)]; Alx[**for trembling**], Byz[and trembling (~JNT, ~NAB, ~NIV, ~NLT, ~REB, ~TEV, ~TLB)]; Alx[**for they were afraid**], Byz[and they were afraid (~TLB)]; Alx[**And they briefly… Amen**], Byz[*omits* (ASV, DRA, ESV, HCS, JNT, KJV, MRD, NET, NIV, NJB, NKJ, RSV)], Minor[*places this after verse 20* (NAB, NAS, NAU, TEV)].

16:⁹⁻²⁰ Alx/Byz[*text*], Minor[*omits*].

16:¹⁴ Alx[**But later**], Byz[Later (DRA, ESV, HCS, JNT, KJV, NAU, ~NET, NIV, NJB, NKJ, NLT, NRS, REB, RSV, TEV, TLB)]; Alx/Byz[**after he had risen**], Minor[*adds* from the dead (NLT, REB, TLB)], Metzger[*Codex Washingtonianus adds* And they excused themselves, saying, "This age of lawlessness and unbelief is under Satan, who does not allow the truth and power of God to prevail over the unclean things of the spirits. Therefore reveal your righteousness now" – thus they spoke to Christ. And Christ said to them, "The term of years of Satan's power has been fulfilled, but other terrible things draw near. For those who have sinned I was handed over to death, so that they may return to the truth and sin no more, that they may inherit the spiritual and imperishable glory of righteousness that is in heaven" (NRS note, RSV note)].

seen him after he had risen. ¹⁵ And he said to them, "Go into all the world and preach the gospel to all creation. ¹⁶ He who believes and is baptized will be saved; but he who does not believe will be condemned. ¹⁷ And these signs will accompany those who believe: in my name they will cast out demons. They will speak in new tongues. ¹⁸ They will pick up serpents [in their hands]. And if they drink any deadly thing, it cannot hurt them. They will lay their hands on the sick, and they will recover."

¹⁹ So then the Lord Jesus, after he had spoken to them, was taken up into heaven, and sat down at the right hand of God. ²⁰ Then they went out and preached everywhere, and the Lord worked with them and confirmed the word by the signs that accompanied it.]]

16:¹⁵ **gospel** *or* good news.

16:¹⁷ Alx/Byz[**accompany** *or* follow closely], Minor[follow (DRA, KJV, NKJ, ~REB, ~TEV, ~TLB)]; Alx/Byz[**new tongues** *or* strange tongues], Minor[*omits* new (NJB)]; **tongues** *or* languages.

16:¹⁸ Alx[**in their hands**], Byz[*omits* (ASV, DRA, HCS, ~JNT, KJV, MRD, NAS, NAU, NKJ, ~NLT, ~REB, RSV, TEV, ~TLB)]; Alx/Major[**cannot hurt them**], Byz[will not hurt them (~ASV, DRA, ESV, ~HCS, ~JNT, KJV, MRD, NAB, NAS, NAU, NET, NIV, ~NJB, ~NKJ, NLT, NRS, ~REB, RSV, ~TEV, TLB)].

16:¹⁹ Alx[**the Lord Jesus**], Byz[*omits* Jesus (KJV, NKJ)].

16:²⁰ Alx[*text*], Byz[*adds* Amen (ASV, KJV, NKJ, RSV)], Minor[*adds* And they briefly reported all they had been commanded to those around Peter. And afterward Jesus himself sent out through them, from east to west, the sacred and imperishable proclamation of eternal salvation. Amen (NAB, NAS, NAU, TEV)].

According to Luke

1 ¹ Inasmuch as many have undertaken to compile a narrative of the things which have been fulfilled among us, ² just as they were delivered to us by those who from the beginning were eyewitnesses and ministers of the word, ³ it seemed good to me also, having carefully investigated all things from the very first, to write to you an orderly account, most excellent Theophilus, ⁴ so that you may know the certainty of the things which you have been taught.

⁵ In the days of Herod, king of Judea, there was a priest named Zechariah, of the division of Abijah; and he had a wife of the daughters of Aaron, and her name was Elizabeth. ⁶ And they were both righteous in the sight of God, walking in all the commandments and ordinances of the Lord blameless. ⁷ But they had no child, because Elizabeth was barren, and they were both well advanced in years. ⁸ Now while he was serving as priest before God when his division was on duty, ⁹ according to the custom of the priesthood, it fell to him by lot to enter the temple of the Lord and burn incense. ¹⁰ And the whole multitude of the people were praying outside at the hour of incense. ¹¹ Then an angel of the Lord appeared to him, standing on the right side of the altar of incense. ¹² And Zechariah was troubled when he saw him, and fear fell upon him. ¹³ But the angel said to him, "Do not be afraid, Zechariah, for your prayer is heard; and your wife Elizabeth will bear you a son, and you shall call his name John. ¹⁴ And you will have joy and gladness, and many will rejoice at his birth. ¹⁵ For he will be great before [the] Lord, and shall never drink wine or strong drink. He will also be filled with the Holy Spirit, even from his mother's womb. ¹⁶ And he will turn many of the sons of Israel to the Lord their God. ¹⁷ And he will go before him in the spirit and power of *Elijah, 'to turn the hearts of the fathers to the children,'* and the disobedient to the wisdom of the just, to make ready a people prepared for the Lord." ¹⁸ And Zechariah said to the angel, "How shall I know this? For I am an old man, and my wife is well advanced in years." ¹⁹ And the angel answered him, "I am Gabriel, who stands in the presence of God; and I was sent to speak to you, and to bring you this good news. ²⁰ And behold, you will be silent and not able to speak until the day that these things come to pass, because you did not believe my words, which will be fulfilled in their time." ²¹ And the people were waiting for Zechariah and wondering why he stayed so long in the temple. ²² But when he came out, he could not speak to them; and they perceived that he had seen a vision in the temple, for he made signs to them and remained speechless. ²³ And when his time of service was completed, he went to his home. ²⁴ After these days his wife Elizabeth conceived, and for five months she hid herself, saying, ²⁵ "Thus the Lord has done to me, in the days when he looked on me, to take away my reproach among people."

²⁶ In the sixth month the angel Gabriel was sent from God to a city of Galilee named Nazareth, ²⁷ to a virgin betrothed to a man whose name was Joseph, of the house of David.

Title Alx/Byz[**According to Luke**], Minor[*variations of* The Gospel According to Saint Luke].

1:1 **fulfilled** *or* believed.

1:3 Alx/Byz[**it seemed good to me**], Minor[*adds* and to the Holy Spirit]; **from the very first** *or* for a long time.

1:5 Alx[**king of Judea**], Byz[the king of Judea (DRA, KJV, MRD, KJV)]; Alx[**and he had a wife**], Byz[and his wife was (DRA, HCS, JNT, KJV, MRD, NAB, NIV, NKJ, NLT, NRS, REB, TEV, TLB)].

1:6 Alx[**in the sight of**], Byz[before (ASV, DRA, ESV, JNT, KJV, MRD, NKJ, NRS, ~REB, RSV, ~TLB)].

1:15 Alx/Byz[**before the Lord**], Minor[*omits* the (~JNT)].

1:17 ~Malachi 4:5-6.

1:26 Alx[**sent from God**], Byz[sent by God (HCS, JNT, MRD, NET, ~NIV, NJB, NKJ, ~NLT, NRS, REB, ~TEV, ~TLB)]; Alx[**Nazareth**], Byz[Nazaret (JNT)].

The virgin's name was Mary. 28 He went to her and said, "Hail, O highly favored one, the Lord is with you!" 29 But she was greatly troubled at the saying, and considered in her mind what sort of greeting this might be. 30 And the angel said to her, "Do not be afraid, Mary, for you have found favor with God. 31 And behold, you will conceive in your womb and bear a son, and you shall call his name Jesus. 32 He will be great, and will be called the Son of the Most High; and the Lord God will give him the throne of his father David. 33 And he will reign over the house of Jacob forever; and of his kingdom there will be no end." 34 And Mary said to the angel, "How can this be, since I am a virgin?" 35 And the angel answered her, "The Holy Spirit will come upon you, and the power of the Most High will overshadow you; therefore the Holy One to be born will be called the Son of God. 36 And behold, your relative Elizabeth in her old age has also conceived a son, and this is the sixth month with her who was called barren; 37 for no word of God will be impossible." 38 Then Mary said, "Behold, I am the servant of the Lord; let it be to me according to your word." And the angel departed from her.

39 In those days Mary arose and went with haste into the hill country, to a city of Judah, 40 and she entered the house of Zechariah and greeted Elizabeth. 41 And when Elizabeth heard the greeting of Mary, the babe leaped in her womb; and Elizabeth was filled with the Holy Spirit. 42 And she exclaimed with a loud cry, "Blessed are you among women, and blessed is the fruit of your womb! 43 But why is this granted me, that the mother of my Lord should come to me? 44 For behold, as soon as the voice of your greeting came to my ears, the babe in my womb leaped for joy. 45 And blessed is she who believed that there would be a fulfillment of what was spoken to her from the Lord."

46 And Mary said:

47   "My soul magnifies the Lord,
              and my spirit rejoices in God my Savior,
48   for he has regarded the lowly state of his servant;
              for behold, henceforth all generations
                      will call me blessed.
49   For he who is mighty has done great things for me,
              and holy is his name.
50   And his mercy is on those who fear him
              to generations and generations.
51   He has shown strength with his arm;
              he has scattered the proud
                      in the imagination of their hearts.

1:28 Alx[**He went to her**], Byz[the angel went to her (DRA, HCS, JNT, KJV, MRD, NET, NIV, NKJ, ~NLT, REB, TEV, ~TLB)]; Alx[**the Lord is with you**], Byz[*adds* Blessed are you among women (DRA, KJV, MRD, NKJ)].

1:29 Alx[**But she was**], Byz[But when she saw him, she was (KJV, MRD, NKJ)]; Alx[**the saying**], Byz[his saying (DRA, JNT, KJV, MRD, NET, NIV, NKJ, ~NLT, NRS, REB, TEV, TLB)].

1:34 **I am a virgin** *Greek* I do not know a man.

1:35 Alx/Byz[**to be born**], Minor[*adds* of you (DRA, JNT, KJV, MRD, TLB)]; **the Holy One to be born will be called the Son of God** *or* the one to be born will be called holy, Son of God.

1:37 Alx[**no word of God**], Byz[with God no word (DRA, ESV, HCS, JNT, KJV, ~MRD, ~NAB, NAS, NAU, NET, NIV, ~NJB, NKJ, NLT, NRS, ~REB, RSV, ~TEV)].

1:42 Alx[**a loud cry**], Byz[a loud voice (DRA, JNT, KJV, MRD, NAB, NAS, NAU, NET, NIV, NKJ, REB, TEV)].

1:45 **believed that there would be** *or* believed, for there will be.

1:46 Alx/Byz[**Mary**], Minor[Elizabeth].

1:50 Alx[**to generations and generations**], Byz[to generations of generations (~DRA, ~ESV, ~HCS, ~JNT, ~KJV, ~MRD, ~NAB, ~NAS, ~NAU, ~NET, ~NIV, ~NJB, ~NKJ, ~NLT, ~NRS, ~REB, ~RSV, ~TEV, ~TLB)].

52   He has put down the mighty from their thrones,
   and exalted the lowly.
53   He has filled the hungry with good things,
   and the rich he has sent empty away.
54   He has helped his servant Israel,
   in remembrance of his mercy,
55   as he spoke to our fathers,
   to Abraham and to his seed forever."

56 And Mary remained with her about three months, and returned to her home.

57 Now the time came for Elizabeth to be delivered, and she gave birth to a son. 58 Her neighbors and relatives heard that the Lord had shown great mercy to her, and they rejoiced with her. 59 On the eighth day they came to circumcise the child; and they would have named him Zechariah after his father, 60 but his mother said, "No; he shall be called John." 61 They said to her, "There is no one of your family who is called by that name." 62 And they made signs to his father, inquiring what he would have him called. 63 And he asked for a writing tablet, and wrote, "His name is John." And they all marveled. 64 And immediately his mouth was opened and his tongue loosed, and he spoke, praising God. 65 And fear came on all their neighbors. And all these things were discussed throughout all the hill country of Judea; 66 and all who heard them laid them up in their hearts, saying, "What then will this child be?" For indeed the hand of the Lord was with him.

67 Now his father Zechariah was filled with the Holy Spirit, and prophesied, saying:
68   "Blessed be the Lord God of Israel,
   for he has visited and redeemed his people,
69   and has raised up a horn of salvation for us
   in the house of his servant David,
70   as he spoke by the mouth of his holy prophets from ancient times,
71   that we should be saved from our enemies
   and from the hand of all who hate us,
72   to perform the mercy promised to our fathers
   and to remember his holy covenant,
73   the oath which he swore to our father Abraham:
  to grant us 74 that we,
   being delivered from the hand of enemies,
 might serve him without fear,
75   in holiness and righteousness before him
   all our days.
76   And indeed you, child, will be called the prophet of the Most High;

1:55 Alx/Byz[**forever**], Minor[until forever].

1:61 Alx[**of your family**], Byz[in your family (MRD, NAB, NAS, NAU, NIV, NJB, NKJ, NLT, REB, ~TEV, TLB)].

1:66 Alx[**"What then will this child be?" For indeed the hand of the Lord was with him**], Byz["What then will this child be?" Indeed, the hand of the Lord was with him (KJV, MRD, ~NJB, NKJ)], Minor["What then will this child be, for indeed the hand of the Lord is with him?" (TLB)].

1:69 **horn of salvation** or mighty Savior.

1:70 Alx[**ancient times** Greek an age], Byz[the beginning (DRA, JNT, KJV, NKJ)].

1:74 Alx/Byz[**to grant us 74**], Minor[74 to grant us (ASV, JNT, KJV, NAS, NAU, NIV, NJB, NKJ, ~NLT, ~REB, RSV, ~TEV, ~TLB)]; Alx[**of enemies**], Byz[of our enemies (ASV, DRA, ESV, HCS, JNT, KJV, MRD, NAS, NAU, NET, NIV, NJB, NKJ, NLT, NRS, RSV, TEV, TLB)], Minor[of all our enemies].

1:75 Alx[**all our days**], Byz[all the days of our life (KJV, NET, NKJ, NLT, REB, RSV, TEV, ~TLB)].

1:76 Alx[**And indeed you**], Byz[And you (DRA, ESV, HCS, JNT, KJV, MRD, NAB, NAS, NAU, NET, NIV, NJB, NKJ, NLT, NRS, REB, RSV, TEV, TLB)]; Alx[**before the Lord**], Byz[before the face of the Lord (ASV, DRA, KJV, MRD, NKJ)].

for you will go on before the Lord to prepare his ways,

77 to give knowledge of salvation to his people
in the forgiveness of their sins,

78 through the tender mercy of our God,
with which the sunrise from on high will visit us;

79 to give light to those who sit in darkness
and in the shadow of death,
to guide our feet into the way of peace."

80 And the child grew and became strong in spirit, and he was in the wilderness till the day he appeared publicly to Israel.

2 1 In those days a decree went out from Caesar Augustus that a census should be taken of all the world. 2 This was the first census that took place while Quirinius was governor of Syria. 3 And all went to be registered, everyone to his city. 4 And Joseph also went up from Galilee, from the city of Nazareth, to Judea, to the city of David, which is called Bethlehem, because he was of the house and lineage of David, 5 to be registered with Mary, his betrothed, who was with child. 6 And while they were there, the time came for her to be delivered. 7 And she gave birth to her first-born son and wrapped him in swaddling cloths, and laid him in a manger, because there was no room for them in the inn.

8 And in that region there were shepherds living out in the fields, keeping watch over their flock by night. 9 And an angel of the Lord appeared to them, and the glory of the Lord shone around them, and they were filled with fear. 10 Then the angel said to them, "Do not be afraid, for behold, I bring you good news of great joy which will be to all the people. 11 For to you is born this day in the city of David a Savior, who is Christ the Lord. 12 And this will be the sign to you: you will find a babe wrapped in swaddling cloths and lying in a manger." 13 And suddenly there was with the angel a multitude of the heavenly host praising God and saying,

14 "Glory to God in the highest,
and on earth peace among men
with whom he is pleased!"

15 When the angels had gone away from them into heaven, the shepherds spoke to one another, "Let us go over to Bethlehem and see this thing that has happened, which the Lord has made known to us." 16 And they went with haste, and found Mary and Joseph,

---

1:78 Alx[**will visit**], Byz[has visited or visits (DRA, ~JNT, KJV, NJB, NKJ)].

2:2 Alx[**This census first took place**], Byz[This was the first census that took place (ASV, ESV, JNT, NAB, NAS, NAU, NET, NIV, NJB, NLT, NRS, REB, RSV, ~TEV, ~TLB)].

2:3 Alx[**to his city**], Byz[to his own city (ASV, DRA, ESV, HCS, JNT, KJV, MRD, NAB, NAS, NAU, NET, NIV, NJB, NKJ, NLT, NRS, REB, RSV, TEV)].

2:4 Alx[**city of Nazareth**], Byz[city of Nazaret (JNT)], Alt/Peshitta[*omits* city of (MRD)].

2:5 Alx[**betrothed**], Byz[*adds* wife (DRA, KJV, NKJ)].

2:7 Alx[**a manger** *or* a stall], Byz[the manger (MRD)]; **no room for them in the inn** *or* no other space for them in the lodging.

2:9 Alx[**And an angel**], Byz[And behold, an angel (DRA, KJV, NJB, NKJ, ~NLT, ~REB, ~TLB)].

2:12 Alx/Byz[**the sign**], Minor[a sign (DRA, ESV, ~JNT, KJV, NAB, NAS, NAU, NET, NIV, NJB, NRS, REB, RSV, ~TEV, ~TLB)]; Alx[**and lying**], Byz[lying (KJV, NKJ, NLT, TLB)], Minor[*omits*]; Alx/Byz[**a manger**], Minor[the manger].

2:13 Alx/Byz[**heavenly host**], Minor[host of heaven (JNT, MRD, NJB, NLT, ~TEV, TLB)]; **host** *Greek* army.

2:14 Alx[**peace among men with whom he is pleased** *or* peace toward men of (his) good will], Byz[peace, good pleasure toward men (KJV, MRD, NKJ)].

2:15 Alx[**the shepherds spoke**], Byz[and the men keeping sheep said (~ASV, ~DRA, ~ESV, ~HCS, ~JNT, ~KJV, ~MRD, ~NAB, ~NAS, ~NAU, ~NET, ~NIV, ~NJB, ~NKJ, ~NLT, ~NRS, ~REB, ~RSV, ~TEV, ~TLB)].

and the babe lying in a manger. [17] Now when they had seen him, they made known the saying which had been told them concerning this child. [18] And all who heard it were amazed at what the shepherds told them. [19] But Mary kept all these things and pondered them in her heart. [20] Then the shepherds returned, glorifying and praising God for all the things that they had heard and seen, as it had been told them.

[21] And at the end of eight days, when he was circumcised, he was called Jesus, the name given by the angel before he was conceived in the womb.

[22] And when the time of their purification according to the law of Moses was completed, they brought him up to Jerusalem to present him to the Lord [23] (as it is written in the law of the Lord, *"Every male who opens the womb shall be called holy to the Lord"*), [24] and to offer a sacrifice according to what is said in the law of the Lord, *"a pair of turtledoves, or two young pigeons."*

[25] Now there was a man in Jerusalem, whose name was Simeon, and this man was righteous and devout, waiting for the consolation of Israel, and the Holy Spirit was upon him. [26] And it had been revealed to him by the Holy Spirit that he would not see death before he had seen the Lord's Christ. [27] So he came by the Spirit into the temple. And when the parents brought in the Child Jesus, to do for him according to the custom of the law, [28] he took him into his arms and blessed God, and said:

[29]   "Lord, now you are letting your servant depart in peace,
            according to your word;
[30]   for my eyes have seen your salvation
[31]   which you have prepared in the presence of all peoples,
[32]   a light for revelation to the Gentiles,
            and for glory to your people Israel."

[33] And his father and mother marveled at what was said about him. [34] Then Simeon blessed them, and said to Mary his mother, "Behold, this child is destined for the fall and rising of many in Israel, and for a sign that will be spoken against [35] ([and] a sword will pierce through your own soul also), so that the thoughts of many hearts may be revealed."

[36] And there was a prophetess, Anna, the daughter of Phanuel, of the tribe of Asher. She was of a great age, and had lived with her husband seven years from her virginity, [37] and as a widow till she was eighty-four. She did not leave the temple, but worshipped with fasting and prayer night and day. [38] And coming up at that very hour she gave thanks to God, and spoke of him to all who were looking for the redemption of Jerusalem.

2:[17] Alx[**made known**], Byz[reported (HCS, NET, NJB, NLT, TEV, TLB)], Vulgate[understood (DRA)].

2:[19] Alx/Byz[**Mary** *Greek* Miriam], Minor[Mary *Greek* Maria].

2:[20] Alx/Byz[**the shepherds returned**], Minor[the shepherds turned].

2:[21] Alx/Major[**he was circumcised**], Byz[the child was circumcised (DRA, KJV, MRD, NJB, NKJ, NLT, NRS, TEV, TLB)].

2:[22] Alx/Byz[**their purification**], Minor[her purification (DRA, KJV, NKJ, ~REB, TLB)].

2:[23] ~**Exodus 13:2, 12, 15**.

2:[24] Alx[**the law of the Lord**], Byz[a law of the Lord], Alt[*omits* of the Lord (REB, TLB)]; **Leviticus 12:8**.

2:[25, 34] Alx/Byz[**Simeon** *Greek* Symeon], Minor[Simeon].

2:[28] Alx[**he took him into his arms** *Greek* he took him into arms], Byz[he took him into his arms].

2:[29] **now you are letting** *or* now let, **servant** *or* slave.

2:[33] Alx[**his father and mother**], Byz[Joseph and his mother (KJV, MRD, NKJ, ~TLB)], Minor[his father and his mother (ASV, ESV, ~NLT, RSV)].

2:[35] Alx/Byz[**and...also**], Minor[and... (DRA, HCS, ~NAB, ~NLT, TEV, TLB)].

2:[36] **Anna** *Greek* Hanna.

2:[37] Alx[**and as a widow till she was eighty-four**], Byz[and she was a widow of about eighty-four years (JNT, KJV, MRD, NJB, NKJ)]; Alx[**leave the temple**], Byz[depart from the temple (ASV, DRA, ESV, KJV, MRD, NKJ, RSV)].

2:[38] Alx[**she gave thanks**], Byz[she herself gave thanks (~KJV, ~MRD, NLT, TLB)]; Alx[**God**], Byz[the Lord (DRA, KJV, MRD, NKJ)]; Alx[**the redemption of Jerusalem**], Byz[redemption in Jerusalem

³⁹ And when they had performed everything according to the law of the Lord, they turned to Galilee, to their own city, Nazareth. ⁴⁰ And the child grew and became strong; he was filled with wisdom, and the grace of God was upon him.

⁴¹ His parents went to Jerusalem every year at the Feast of the Passover. ⁴² And when he was twelve years old, they went up to the Feast, according to the custom. ⁴³ And when the feast was over, as they were returning, the boy Jesus stayed behind in Jerusalem. His parents did not know it, ⁴⁴ but supposing him to be in the company, they went a day's journey, and they sought him among their relatives and acquaintances. ⁴⁵ And when they did not find him, they returned to Jerusalem, searching for him. ⁴⁶ After three days they found him in the temple, sitting among the teachers, listening to them and asking them questions. ⁴⁷ And all who heard him were amazed at his understanding and his answers. ⁴⁸ And when they saw him they were astonished; and his mother said to him, "Son, why have you treated us so? Behold, your father and I have been looking for you anxiously." ⁴⁹ And he said to them, "Why did you seek me? Did you not know that I must be in my Father's house?" ⁵⁰ But they did not understand the saying which he spoke to them. ⁵¹ Then he went down with them and came to Nazareth, and was obedient to them, but his mother kept all the sayings in her heart. ⁵² And Jesus increased [in] wisdom and stature, and in favor with God and men.

3 ¹ Now in the fifteenth year of the reign of Tiberius Caesar, Pontius Pilate being governor of Judea, Herod being tetrarch of Galilee, his brother Philip tetrarch of Iturea and the region of Trachonitis, and Lysanias tetrarch of Abilene, ² during the high priesthood of Annas and Caiaphas, the word of God came to John son of Zechariah in the wilderness. ³ And he went into all [the] region around the Jordan, preaching a baptism of repentance for the forgiveness of sins. ⁴ As it is written in the book of the words of Isaiah the prophet,

> "The voice of one crying in the wilderness:
> 'Prepare the way of the Lord,
>   make his paths straight.
⁵ Every valley shall be filled
>   and every mountain and hill brought low;

(KJV, NKJ, TLB)], Minor[the redemption in Israel (DRA)].

2:39 Alx[**everything**], Byz[all things (ASV, DRA, KJV, MRD, NAB, NKJ, NLT, TEV, TLB)]; Alx[**turned to Galilee**], Byz[returned to Galilee (ASV, DRA, ESV, HCS, JNT, KJV, MRD, NAB, NAS, NAU, NET, NIV, NJB, NKJ, NLT, NRS, REB, RSV, TEV, TLB)]; Alx/Byz[**their own city**], Minor[their city (DRA, JNT, MRD, ~NLT, ~TEV, ~TLB)]; Alx[**Nazareth**], Byz[Nazaret (JNT)].

2:40 Alx[**became strong**], Byz[*adds* in spirit (KJV, MRD, NKJ)]; Alx[**filled with wisdom**], Byz[full of wisdom (DRA, REB, TEV, ~TLB)].

2:41 Alx/Byz[**His parents**], Minor[Joseph and Mary *others* Joseph and his mother *others* his people (MRD)].

2:42 Alx[**they went up**], Byz[*adds* into Jerusalem (DRA, KJV, NKJ, ~TLB)].

2:43 Alx[**His parents**], Byz[Joseph and his mother (KJV, MRD, NKJ)].

2:45 Alx[**searching for him**], Byz[seeking him (ASV, DRA, KJV, NKJ, RSV)].

2:48 Alx/Byz[**have been looking**], Minor[are looking (~JNT, ~NJB, ~NLT, ~TEV, ~TLB)].

2:49 **house** *or* business *Greek* things.

2:51 Alx[**Nazareth**], Byz[Nazaret (JNT)]; Alx[**the sayings**], Byz[these sayings (ASV, DRA, ESV, HCS, JNT, KJV, MRD, NAB, NAS, NAU, NET, NIV, NJB, NKJ, NLT, NRS, REB, RSV, TEV, TLB)].

2:52 Alx[**in wisdom and stature**], Byz[with wisdom and stature], Minor[in stature and wisdom (MRD, REB, TEV, TLB)].

3:2 Alx/Byz[**during the high priesthood of Annas and Caiaphas**], Minor[while Annas and Caiaphas were high priests (DRA, JNT, KJV, NKJ, NLT, TEV, TLB)].

3:3 Alx/Byz[**all the region**], Minor[*omits* the (JNT, NJB, NLT, REB, TLB)].

3:4 Alx[**Isaiah the prophet**], Byz[*adds* saying (KJV, MRD, NKJ, NLT)].

3:4-6 ~**Isaiah 40:3-5 LXX**.

> *the crooked places shall be made straight*
> *and the rough ways smooth;*
> 6 *and all flesh shall see the salvation of God.'"*

7 Then he said to the multitudes that came out to be baptized by him, "You brood of vipers! Who warned you to flee from the wrath to come? 8 Therefore bear fruits worthy of repentance, and do not begin to say to yourselves, 'We have Abraham as our father.' For I tell you that God is able to raise up children to Abraham from these stones. 9 And even now the ax is laid at the root of the trees; every tree therefore that does not bear good fruit is cut down and thrown into the fire." 10 And the multitudes asked him, "What then should we do?" 11 He answered and said to them, "He who has two tunics, let him share with him who has none; and he who has food, let him do likewise." 12 Tax collectors also came to be baptized, and said to him, "Teacher, what should we do?" 13 And he said to them, "Collect no more than is appointed you." 14 Likewise the soldiers asked him, "And what should we do?" So he said to them, "Rob no one by violence, nor accuse falsely, and be content with your wages."

15 As the people were in expectation, and all men questioned in their hearts concerning John, whether perhaps he were the Christ, 16 John answered them all, "I baptize you with water; but one mightier than I is coming, the thong of whose sandals I am not worthy to untie. He will baptize you with the Holy Spirit and with fire. 17 His winnowing fork is in his hand, to clear his threshing floor, and to gather the wheat into his barn, but the chaff he will burn with unquenchable fire." 18 And with many other exhortations he preached good news to the people. 19 But Herod the tetrarch, being rebuked by him concerning Herodias, his brother's wife, and for all the other evil things Herod had done, 20 added this also to them all, [and] locked John in prison.

21 When all the people were being baptized, Jesus was also baptized. And as he was praying, the heaven was opened 22 and the Holy Spirit descended in bodily form as a dove upon him, and a voice came from heaven, "You are my beloved Son; with you I am well pleased."

3:8 Alx/Byz[**say to yourselves**], Minor[*adds* that (TEV, ~TLB].

3:9 Alx/Byz[**good fruit**], Minor[*omits* good].

3:10 Alx[**should we do**], Byz[shall we do (DRA, ESV, KJV, MRD, NAS, NAU, NKJ, ~REB, RSV, ~TEV, ~TLB)].

3:11 Alx[**said to them**], Byz[says to them (~ESV, ~HCS, ~JNT, KJV, ~NET, ~NIV, ~NJB, ~NLT, ~REB, ~RSV, ~TEV, ~TLB)].

3:12 Alx[**should we do**], Byz[shall we do (DRA, ESV, KJV, MRD, NAS, NAU, NKJ, ~REB, RSV, ~TEV, TLB)].

3:14 Alx[**should we do**], Byz[shall we do (DRA, ESV, KJV, MRD, NAS, NAU, NKJ, ~REB, RSV, ~TEV, ~TLB)]; Alx/Major[**Rob no one by violence, nor accuse falsely**], Byz[Accuse no one falsely, nor rob by violence (~MRD, ~NJB)], Minor[Rob no one by violence, accuse no one falsely (ASV, DRA, JNT, KJV, NAB, NAS, NAU, NIV, ~REB, TEV, ~TLB)].

3:17 Alx[**to clear his threshing floor, and to gather**], Byz[and he will clear his threshing floor, and will gather (DRA, KJV, ~MRD, NKJ, ~NLT, ~REB, TLB)].

3:19 Alx/Byz[**his brother's wife**], Minor[his brother Phillip's wife (KJV, MRD, NKJ)].

3:20 Alx/Byz[**and locked John**], Minor[*omits* and (ASV, ESV, HCS, JNT, KJV, MRD, NAS, NAU, NET, NIV, NJB, NKJ, NLT, NRS, REB, RSV, TEV, TLB)]; Alx[**in prison**], Byz[in the prison].

3:22 Alx[**as a dove**], Byz[like a dove (ESV, HCS, JNT, KJV, MRD, NAB, NAS, NAU, NET, NIV, NJB, NKJ, NLT, NRS, REB, TEV, ~TLB)]; Alx[**a voice came from heaven**], Byz[*adds* saying (KJV, MRD, NKJ, NLT, TLB)]; Alx/Byz[**You are my beloved Son; with you I am well pleased**], Minor[You are my Son, today I have begotten you (NJB)]; **my beloved Son** *or* my Son, the Beloved.

²³ Now Jesus himself, when he began his ministry, was about thirty years of age, being the son (as was supposed) of Joseph, the son of Eli, ²⁴ the son of Matthat, the son of Levi, the son of Melchi, the son of Jannai, the son of Joseph, ²⁵ the son of Mattathias, the son of Amos, the son of Nahum, the son of Hesli, the son of Naggai, ²⁶ the son of Maath, the son of Mattathias, the son of Semein, the son of Josech, the son of Joda, ²⁷ the son of Joanan, the son of Rhesa, the son of Zerubbabel, the son of Shealtiel, the son of Neri, ²⁸ the son of Melchi, the son of Addi, the son of Cosam, the son of Elmadam, the son of Er, ²⁹ the son of Joshua, the son of Eliezer, the son of Jorim, the son of Matthat, the son of Levi, ³⁰ the son of Symeon, the son of Judah, the son of Joseph, the son of Jonam, the son of Eliakim, ³¹ the son of Melea, the son of Menna, the son of Mattatha, the son of Nathan, the son of David, ³² the son of Jesse, the son of Jobed, the son of Boaz, the son of Sala, the son of Nahshon, ³³ the son of Amminadab, the son of Admin, the son of Arni, the son of Hezrom, the son of Perez, the son of Judah, ³⁴ the son of Jacob, the son of Isaac, the son of Abraham, the son of Terah, the son of Nahor, ³⁵ the son of Serug, the son of Reu, the son of Peleg, the son of Eber, the son of Shelah, ³⁶ the son of Cainan, the son of Arphaxad, the son of Shem, the son of Noah, the son of Lamech, ³⁷ the son of Methuselah, the son of Enoch, the son of Jaret, the son of Mahalalel, the son of Cainan, ³⁸ the son of Enos, the son of Seth, the son of Adam, the son of God.

4 ¹ Jesus, full of the Holy Spirit, returned from the Jordan and was led by the Spirit in the wilderness, ² being tempted for forty days by the devil. In those days he ate nothing, and when they had ended, he was hungry. ³ And the devil said to him, "If you are the Son of God, command this stone to become bread." ⁴ But Jesus answered him, "It is written, *'Man shall not live by bread alone.'*" ⁵ And having led him up, he showed him all

---

3:23 Alx[**the son as was supposed**], Byz[as was supposed the son (DRA, HCS, JNT, KJV, MRD, NAS, NAU, NKJ, NLT, TLB)]; Alx[**Eli**], Byz[Heli (ASV, DRA, ESV, HCS, KJV, MRD, NAB, NET, NIV, NJB, NKJ, NRS, REB, RSV, TEV, TLB)].

3:24 Alx/Major[**24 the son of Matthat**], Byz[24 the son of Matthan], Minor[the son of Matthat 24 (DRA)]; Alx[**Jannai**], Byz[Joanna], Major[Janna (DRA, KJV, MRD, NKJ)].

3:25 Alx[**Hesli**], Byz[Eslim], Major[Esli (ASV, ESV, HCS, KJV, MRD, NAB, NET, NIV, NJB, NKJ, NLT, NRS, REB, RSV, TEV, TLB)].

3:26 Alx[**Semein**], Byz[Semeu], Major[Semei (DRA, JNT, KJV, MRD, NKJ)]; Alx[**Josech**], Byz[Joseph (DRA, JNT, KJV, MRD, NKJ)]; Alx/Byz[**Joda**], Major[Judah (DRA, KJV, MRD, NKJ)].

3:27 Alx/Major[**Joanan**], Byz[Joannan (~NKJ)], Minor[Joanna (DRA, KJV, MRD)]; **Shealtiel** *Greek* Salathiel.

3:28 Alx[**Elmadam**], Byz[Elmodam (KJV, MRD, NKJ)], Minor[Helmadan (DRA, ~JNT)].

3:29 Alx[**Joshua**], Byz[Jose (KJV, ~MRD, NKJ)]; Alx[**Jorim**], Byz[Joreim], Minor[Joram (JNT, MRD)].

3:30 Alx/Byz[**Symeon**], Minor[Simeon (DRA, ESV, HCS, JNT, KJV, MRD, NAB, NAS, nAU, NET, NIV, NKJ, NLT, NRS, RSV, TEV, TLB)]; Alx[**Jonam**], Byz[Jonan (~DRA, KJV, NKJ)].

3:31 Alx[**Menna**], Byz[Mainan (~KJV, MRD, ~NKJ)], Minor[Menam]; Alx[**Nathan** *Greek* Natham], Byz[Nathan].

3:32 Alx[**Jobed**], Byz[Obed (ASV, DRA, ESV, HCS, JNT, KJV, MRD, NAB, NAS, NAU, NET, NIV, NJB, NKJ, NLT, NRS, REB, RSV, TEV, TLB)], Minor[Jobel]; Alx[**Sala**], Byz[Salmon (ASV, DRA, HCS, JNT, KJV, MRD, NAS, NAU, NIV, NKJ, NLT, TEV, TLB)], Minor[Salman (~REB)].

3:33 Alx[**Amminadab, the son of Admin, the son of Arni**], Byz[Amminadab, the son of Aram, the son of Joram], Major[Amminadab, the son of Aram (DRA, HCS, KJV, MRD, NIV, NKJ)], Minor[Admin, the son of Arni *others* Amminadab, the son of Arni (ASV, REB) *others* Amminadab, the son of Admin, the son of Ram (NAS, NAU)].

3:35 Alx[**Serug**], Byz[Sarug (DRA, ~JNT, KJV)]; Alx/Byz[**Peleg** *Greek* Pelek], Major[Peleg].

3:36 Alx[**Cainan** *Greek* Cainam], Byz[Cainan].

3:37 Alx[**Jaret**], Byz[Jared (ASV, DRA, ESV, HCS, JNT, KJV, MRD, NAB, NAS, NAU, NET, NIV, NJB, NKJ, NLT, NRS, REB, RSV, TEV, TLB)]; Alx[**Cainan** *Greek* Cainam], Byz[Cainan].

4:1 Alx[**in the wilderness**], Byz[into the wilderness (DRA, KJV, MRD, NAB, NJB, NKJ, TEV, TLB)].

4:2 Alx[**when they had ended**], Byz[after they had ended (~JNT, KJV, MRD, NKJ)].

4:4 Alx[**Jesus answered him**], Byz[*adds* saying (KJV, MRD, NKJ)]; Alx[**by bread alone**], Byz[*adds* but by every word that proceeds from the mouth of God], Major[*adds* but by every word of God (DRA,

the kingdoms of the world in a moment of time. [6] And he said to him, "To you I will give all this authority and their glory; for it has been delivered to me, and I give it to whom I will. [7] If you, then, will worship before me, it shall all be yours." [8] And Jesus answered him, "It is written,

> 'You shall worship the Lord your God,
>> and him only shall you serve.'"

[9] He took him to Jerusalem, set him on the pinnacle of the temple, and said to him, "If you are God's Son, throw yourself down from here; [10] for it is written:

> 'He will give his angels charge of you,
>> to guard you,'

[11] and that,

> 'In their hands they will bear you up,
>> lest you strike your foot against a stone.'"

[12] And Jesus answered him, "It is said, 'You shall not tempt the Lord your God.'" [13] When the devil had ended every temptation, he departed from him until an opportune time.

[14] Then Jesus returned in the power of the Spirit to Galilee, and news of him went out through all the surrounding country. [15] And he taught in their synagogues, being glorified by all.

[16] And he came to Nazara, where he had been brought up. And as his custom was, he went into the synagogue on the Sabbath day, and stood up to read. [17] And the book of the prophet Isaiah was handed to him. And he unrolled the book, and found the place where it was written:

[18]
> "The Spirit of the Lord is upon me,
>> because he has anointed me
>>> to preach the good news to the poor.
> He has sent me to proclaim release to the captives
>> and recovery of sight to the blind,
>>> to set at liberty those who are oppressed,

[19]
> to proclaim the acceptable year of the Lord."

KJV, MRD, NKJ)]; **Deuteronomy 8:3**.

4:5 Alx[**And having led him up, he showed him**], Byz[Then the devil took him up into a high mountain, and showed him (DRA, ~ESV, ~JNT, KJV, MRD, NET, NIV, NJB, NKJ, ~NLT, ~NRS, REB, ~RSV, ~TEV, ~TLB)].

4:5-12 Alx/Byz[*sequence*], Minor[*transpose verses 5-8 after 9-12*].

4:8 Alx[**And Jesus answered him**], Byz[*adds* Get behind me, Satan! For (KJV, NKJ)], Major[*adds* Get behind me, Satan!]; **Deuteronomy 6:13 LXX**.

4:9 Alx/Byz[**said to him**], Minor[*omits* to him (NIV, NLT, REB, TLB)]; Alx[**God's Son**], Byz[the Son of God (ASV, DRA, ESV, HCS, JNT, KJV, MRD, NAB, NAS, NAU, NET, NIV, NKJ, NLT, NRS, REB, RSV, TLB)].

4:10-11 **Psalms 91:11-12**.

4:11 Alx/Byz[**and that**], Major[*omits* that (ASV, ESV, HCS, JNT, KJV, MRD, NAB, NAS, NAU, NET, NIV, NJB, NKJ, NLT, NRS, REB, RSV, TEV, ~TLB)].

4:12 **Deuteronomy 6:16**.

4:16 Alx[**Nazara** *Nazareth*], Byz[Nazaret (JNT)], Minor[Nazareth (ASV, DRA, ESV, HCS, KJV, MRD, NAB, NAS, NAU, NET, NIV, NKJ, NLT, NRS, REB, RSV)]; Alx/Byz[**brought up**], Minor[nurtured (NLT, TLB)].

4:17 Alx[**the prophet Isaiah**], Byz[Isaiah the prophet (DRA, MRD, NLT, TLB)]; Alx/Byz[**unrolled**], Minor[opened (ASV, ~DRA, KJV, MRD, NAS, NAU, NKJ, REB, RSV, TLB)]; Alx/Byz[**the place**], Minor[a place].

4:18 Alx[**He has sent me**], Byz[He has sent me to heal the broken hearted 19 (DRA)], Major[He has sent me to heal the brokenhearted (KJV, MRD, NKJ, TLB)], Minor[He has sent me 19].

4:18-19 **Isaiah 61:1-2 LXX/DSS, Isaiah 58:6 LXX**.

4:19 Alx/Major[**to proclaim the acceptable year of the Lord** *or* to proclaim the year of the Lord's acceptance], Byz[*omits, and instead reads the last half of verse 18 as verse 19* to proclaim release to the

20 Then he closed the book, and gave it back to the attendant, and sat down; and the eyes of all in the synagogue were fixed on him. 21 And he began to say to them, "Today this Scripture is fulfilled in your hearing." 22 And all spoke well of him, and wondered at the gracious words which proceeded out of his mouth; and they said, "Is not this Joseph's son?" 23 He said to them, "Surely you will quote this proverb to me: 'Physician, heal yourself! Do here also in your own country what we have heard that you did in Capernaum.'" 24 Then he said, "Truly, I say to you, no prophet is accepted in his country. 25 But I tell you truly, there were many widows in Israel in the days of Elijah, when the heaven was shut up three years and six months, and there was a great famine throughout all the land; 26 but Elijah was sent to none of them except to Zarephath, in the region of Sidon, to a woman who was a widow. 27 And there were many lepers in Israel in the time of the prophet Elisha; and not one of them was cleansed, but only Naaman the Syrian." 28 When they heard this, all in the synagogue were filled with wrath. 29 And they rose up and cast him out of the city, and led him to an edge of the hill on which their city was built, so that they might throw him down the cliff. 30 But passing through the midst of them, he went his way.

31 Then he went down to Capernaum, a city of Galilee, and he was teaching them on the Sabbath. 32 And they were astonished at his teaching, for his word was with authority. 33 And in the synagogue there was a man who had the spirit of an unclean demon. And he cried out with a loud voice, 34 "Ha! What have you to do with us, Jesus of Nazareth? Have you come to destroy us? I know who you are – the Holy One of God!" 35 But Jesus rebuked him, saying, "Be quiet, and come out from him!" And when the demon had thrown him down in the midst, he came out of him without doing him any harm. 36 And they were all amazed and said to one another, "What is this word? For with authority and power he commands the unclean spirits, and they come out!" 37 And the report about him went out into every place in the surrounding region.

38 And he arose from the synagogue, and entered Simon's house. Now Simon's mother-in-law was ill with a high fever, and they made request of him on her behalf. 39 So he stood over her and rebuked the fever, and it left her. And immediately she rose and served them. 40 When the sun was setting, all those who had any that were sick with various diseases brought them to him; and, laying his hands on every one of them, he

---

captives and recovery of sight to the blind, to set at liberty those who are oppressed], Minor[*adds* and the day of reward (DRA)].

4:23 Alx[**Capernaum** *Greek* Capharnaum], Byz[Capernaum].

4:24 Alx/Byz[**in his country**], Minor[in his own country (ASV, DRA, KJV, MRD, NAB, NJB, NKJ, NLT, REB, RSV, TLB)].

4:25 Alx/Byz[**I tell you truly**], Minor[*adds* that (MRD, NIV, TEV)], Alt[*omits* truly (HCS, TLB)].

4:26 **Zarephath** *Greek* Sarepta.

4:27 **lepers** *can refer to a number of skin diseases.*

4:29 Alx[**an edge of the hill** *Greek* a brow of the hill], Byz[the edge of the hill (ASV, DRA, ESV, HCS, KJV, MRD, NAB, NAS, NAU, NET, NIV, NJB, NKJ, NLT, NRS, REB, RSV, TEV, TLB)]; Alx[**so that they might throw him down**], Byz[in order to throw him down (HCS, JNT, NAB, NAS, NAU, NIV, NJB, NLT, ~REB, TEV, TLB)].

4:31 Alx[**Capernaum** *Greek* Capharnaum], Byz[Capernaum].

4:34 Alx[**"Ha!**], Byz[saying, "Ha! (DRA, KJV, MRD, NKJ)]; **Have you…?** *or* You have…!

4:35 Alx[**come out from him**], Byz[come out of him (ASV, DRA, ESV, HCS, JNT, KJV, MRD, NAB, NAS, NAU, NET, NIV, NJB, NKJ, NLT, NRS, REB, RSV, TEV, ~TLB)].

4:38 Alx/Major[**Simon's mother-in-law**], Byz[the mother-in-law of Simon (MRD)]; Alx[**from the synagogue**], Byz[out of the synagogue (DRA, ~ESV, ~HCS, ~JNT, KJV, MRD, ~NAB, ~NAS, ~NAU, ~NET, ~NIV, ~NJB, ~NLT, ~NRS, ~REB, ~RSV, ~TEV, ~TLB)].

4:40 Alx/Byz[**he began to heal them** *or* he was healing them], Major[he healed them (ASV, DRA, ESV, JNT, KJV, MRD, NAB, NET, NIV, NJB, NKJ, NLT, NRS, REB, RSV, TEV, TLB)].

began to heal them. [41] And demons also came out of many, crying, "You are the Son of God!" But he rebuked them, and would not allow them to speak, because they knew that he was the Christ.

[42] Now when it was day, he departed and went into a deserted place. And the people sought after him and came to him, and tried to keep him from leaving them; [43] but he said to them, "I must preach the good news of the kingdom of God to the other cities also, because I was sent for this purpose." [44] And he was preaching in the synagogues of Judea.

5 [1] Now as the people pressed around him and heard the word of God, he was standing by the Lake of Gennesaret. [2] And he saw two boats by the lake; but the fishermen had gone out of them and were washing their nets. [3] Then he got into one of the boats, which was Simon's, and asked him to put out a little from the land. And he sat down and taught the people out of the boat. [4] When he had finished speaking, he said to Simon, "Put out into the deep, and let down your nets for a catch." [5] And answering, Simon said, "Master, we toiled all night and caught nothing! But at your word I will let down the nets." [6] And when they had done this, they caught a great number of fish, and their nets were breaking. [7] So they signaled to their partners in the other boat to come and help them. And they came and filled both the boats, so that they began to sink. [8] When Simon Peter saw it, he fell down at Jesus' knees, saying, "Depart from me, for I am a sinful man, O Lord!" [9] For he and all who were with him were astonished at the catch of fish which they had taken; [10] and so also were James and John, the sons of Zebedee, who were partners with Simon. And Jesus said to Simon, "Do not be afraid. From now on you will catch men." [11] So when they had brought their boats to land, they left everything and followed him.

[12] While he was in one of the cities, a man who was full of leprosy saw Jesus; and he fell on his face and begged him, saying, "Lord, if you are willing, you can make me clean." [13] And he stretched out his hand, and touched him, saying, "I am willing; be clean." And immediately the leprosy left him. [14] And he charged him to tell no one, "But go and show yourself to the priest, and make an offering for your cleansing as a testimony to them, just as Moses commanded." [15] But the report went around concerning him all the more; and great multitudes came together to hear and to be healed of their infirmities. [16] But he often withdrew to the wilderness and prayed.

4:41 Alx[**You are**], Byz[*adds* the Christ (KJV, MRD, NKJ)].

4:42 Alx/Byz[**sought after him**], Minor[sought him (DRA, ESV, KJV, MRD, NET, NKJ, RSV)].

4:43 Alx[**I was sent for this purpose**], Byz[I have been sent into this purpose (~NAB, ~NET, ~NJB, ~NKJ, ~REB, ~TEV)], Alt[I am sent for this purpose (DRA, KJV)].

4:44 Alx/Byz[**in the synagogues** *Greek* into the synagogues], Major[in the synagogues]; Alx[**Judea**], Byz[Galilee (ASV, DRA, HCS, KJV, MRD, NKJ, ~TEV)].

5:1 Alx[**and heard**], Byz[to hear (DRA, ESV, HCS, JNT, KJV, MRD, NET, NKJ, NLT, NRS, REB, RSV, TEV, TLB)]; **Lake of Gennesaret** *Sea of Galilee*.

5:2 Alx/Byz[**two boats**], Minor[two small boats]; Alx[**washing**], Byz[washing off].

5:3 Alx/Byz[**out of the boat**], Minor[in the boat (REB, TEV, TLB)]; **Simon** *Peter*.

5:5 Alx[**Simon said**], Byz[*adds* to him (DRA, ~ESV, ~HCS, ~JNT, KJV, MRD, ~NET, ~NIV, ~NJB, NKJ, ~NLT, ~NRS, ~REB, ~RSV, ~TEV, ~TLB)]; Alx[**all night** *Greek* through night], Byz[through the night (DRA, KJV, MRD)]; Alx[**the nets**], Byz[the net (DRA, KJV, MRD, NKJ, ~TLB)].

5:6 Alx[**nets**], Byz[net (DRA, KJV, MRD, NKJ)].

5:7 Alx[**their partners**], Byz[*adds* which were (DRA, KJV)].

5:8 Alx/Byz[**Peter**], Alt/Peshitta[Cephas (JNT, MRD)].

5:12 Alx/Byz[**he was in one of the cities**], Alt/Peshitta[Jesus was in one of the cities (JNT, MRD, NET, NIV, NJB, NLT, TEV)]; Alx/Byz[**begged him, saying**], Alt/Peshitta[begged him, and said to him (MRD); **leprosy** *can refer to a number of skin diseases*.

5:15 Alx[**to be healed**], Byz[*adds* by him (DRA, KJV, NKJ)].

¹⁷ One day as he was teaching, there were Pharisees and teachers of the law sitting by, who had come from every village of Galilee and Judea and from Jerusalem. And the power of the Lord was present for him to heal. ¹⁸ Then behold, men brought on a bed a man who was paralyzed, and they sought to bring him in and lay [him] in front of him. ¹⁹ When they could not find a way to bring him in, because of the crowd, they went up on the roof and let him down with his bed through the tiles into the midst before Jesus. ²⁰ When he saw their faith he said, "Man, your sins are forgiven you." ²¹ And the scribes and the Pharisees began to reason, saying, "Who is this who speaks blasphemies? Who can forgive sins but God alone?" ²² But when Jesus perceived their thoughts, he answered them and said, "Why are you reasoning in your hearts? ²³ Which is easier, to say, 'Your sins are forgiven you,' or to say, 'Rise up and walk'? ²⁴ But that you may know that the Son of Man has authority on earth to forgive sins" – he said to the man who was paralyzed – "I say to you, rise, take up your bed, and go home." ²⁵ Immediately he rose up before them, took up what he had been lying on, and went home, glorifying God. ²⁶ And they were all amazed, and they glorified God and were filled with awe, saying, "We have seen strange things today."

²⁷ After this he went out, and saw a tax collector, named Levi, sitting at the tax office; and he said to him, "Follow me." ²⁸ And he left everything, rose up, and began to follow him. ²⁹ Then Levi made him a great feast in his house; and there were a great number of tax collectors and others sitting to eat with them. ³⁰ And the Pharisees and their scribes complained against his disciples, saying, "Why do you eat and drink with the tax collectors and sinners?" ³¹ And Jesus answered them, "Those who are well have no need of a physician, but those who are sick. ³² I have not come to call the righteous, but sinners to repentance."

³³ They said to him, "The disciples of John fast often and offer prayers, and so do the disciples of the Pharisees, but yours eat and drink." ³⁴ And Jesus said to them, "Can you make the guests of the bridegroom fast while he is with them? ³⁵ But the days will come when the bridegroom will be taken away from them; then they will fast in those days." ³⁶ He told them a parable also: "No one tears a piece from a new garment and puts it on an old one; if he does, he will tear the new garment, and the old will not match the piece from

---

5:17 Alx/Byz[**sitting by, who had come**], Minor[sitting by. And there had come (~NLT, REB, ~TLB)]; Alx[**was present for him to heal**], Byz[was present to heal them (DRA, ~JNT, KJV, MRD, ~NIV, NKJ, ~REB, ~TEV)], Minor[was present to heal them all].
5:18 Alx[**lay him**], Byz[*omits* him (~NJB, ~NKJ, ~NLT)].
5:19 Alx/Byz[**find a way**], Minor[find by what way (ASV, DRA, KJV, ~MRD, ~NKJ, ~NLT, ~TLB)].
5:20 Alx[**he said**], Byz[*adds* to him (KJV, ~MRD, NKJ, NLT, REB, TEV, TLB)].
5:22 Alx/Byz[**he answered them and said** *Greek* he, answering, said to them], Minor[he said to them (~ESV, ~HCS, ~JNT, MRD, NET, ~NIV, ~NJB, ~NLT, ~NRS, ~REB, ~RSV, TEV, ~TLB)]; Alx/Byz[**in your hearts**], Minor[in your evil hearts (~NET, ~TLB)].
5:25 Alx/Byz[**what he had been lying on**], Minor[what he had been lying with (~MRD, ~NLT, ~TLB)].
5:28 Alx[**he left everything**], Byz[he left all (ASV, KJV, NKJ)]; Alx[**began to follow him**], Byz[followed him (ASV, DRA, ESV, JNT, KJV, ~MRD, NAB, NET, NIV, NJB, NKJ, NLT, NRS, REB, RSV, TEV, TLB)].
5:29 Alx/Byz[**eat with them**], Minor[eat with him (~TLB)].
5:30 Alx[**the Pharisees and their scribes**], Byz[their scribes and the Pharisees (~DRA, KJV, ~MRD, ~NIV, NKJ)]; Alx/Byz[**the tax collectors**], Minor[*omits* the (DRA, ESV, HCS, JNT, KJV, MRD, NAB, NET, NIV, NJB, NKJ, ~NLT, NRS, REB, RSV, TEV, TLB)]; Alx/Byz[**and sinners**], Minor[*omits* (~NLT, ~TEV)].
5:33 Alx[**The disciples of John**], Byz[Why do the disciples of John (DRA, KJV, MRD, NKJ, NLT, TLB)].
5:34 Alx[**Jesus said**], Byz[he said (DRA, KJV, MRD, NKJ)].
5:36 Alx[**No one tears a piece from a new garment and puts it on an old one**], Byz[No one puts a piece from a new garment on an old one (DRA, KJV, NKJ)]; Alx/Byz[**he will tear the new garment**], Major[he tears the new garment (DRA, KJV, MRD, NKJ, ~NLT, ~TLB)]; Alx/Byz[**the piece from the new**], Major[the new].

the new. [37] And no one puts new wine into old wineskins; if he does, the new wine will burst the skins and it will be spilled, and the skins will be ruined. [38] But new wine must be put into new wineskins. [39] [And] no one after drinking old wine desires the new; for he says, 'The old is good.'"

6 [1] One Sabbath Jesus was going through grain fields, and his disciples plucked and ate some heads of grain, rubbing them in their hands. [2] But some of the Pharisees said, "Why are you doing what is not lawful on the Sabbath?" [3] Jesus answered them, "Have you not read what David did when he was hungry, he and those [who were] with him: [4] [how] he entered the house of God, took and ate the consecrated bread, and gave some to those with him, which is not lawful for any but the priests to eat?" [5] And he said to them, "The Son of Man is Lord of the Sabbath."

[6] On another Sabbath he entered the synagogue and taught, and a man was there whose right hand was withered. [7] The scribes and the Pharisees watched him closely, to see whether he would heal on the Sabbath, so that they might find how to accuse him. [8] But he knew their thoughts, and said to the man who had the withered hand, "Rise and stand here." And he rose and stood there. [9] And Jesus said to them, "I ask you if it is lawful on the Sabbath to do good or to do evil, to save life or to destroy it?" [10] And he looked around at them all, and said to him, "Stretch out your hand." He did, and his hand was restored. [11] But they were filled with fury and discussed with one another what they might do to Jesus.

[12] In those days he went out to the mountain to pray, and all night he continued in prayer to God. [13] And when it was day, he called his disciples to himself; and from them he

---

5:38 Alx[**new wineskins**], Byz[*adds* and both are preserved (DRA, KJV, MRD, NKJ)].

5:39 Alx/Byz[**And no one**], Minor[No one (NET, ~NLT, ~TLB)]; Alx[**desires**], Byz[immediately desires (DRA, KJV, MRD, NKJ)]; Alx[**The old is good**], Byz[The old is better (DRA, KJV, NIV, NKJ, TEV, ~TLB)]; Minor[*omits entire verse*].

6:1 Alx[**One Sabbath**], Byz[On the second Sabbath after the first (DRA, KJV, NKJ)]; Alx[**grain fields**], Byz[the grain fields (ASV, DRA, ESV, HCS, KJV, MRD, NET, NIV, NJB, NKJ, NRS, REB, RSV)]; Alx[**plucked and ate some heads of grain**], Byz[plucked some heads of grain and ate (ASV, DRA, HCS, JNT, KJV, MRD, NAB, NAU, NET, NIV, NJB, NKJ, NLT, NRS, REB, TEV, TLB)].

6:2 Alx[**Pharisees said**], Byz[*adds* to them (DRA, KJV, MRD, NKJ)]; Alx[**lawful**], Byz[*adds* to do (ASV, ESV, KJV, MRD, NKJ, RSV, TEV, ~TLB)].

6:3 Alx/Byz[**those who were with him**], Minor[*omits* who were (~JNT, MRD, ~NET, ~NIV, ~NJB, ~NLT, ~NRS, ~REB, ~TEV, ~TLB)].

6:4 Alx/Byz[**how he entered**], Minor[*omits* how (JNT, NIV, NLT, NRS, REB, TEV, TLB)]; Alx[**and gave some**], Byz[*adds* also (ASV, ESV, KJV, NIV, NKJ, NLT, RSV, TEV)], Alt[*JNT omits without textual foundation* and gave some to those with him]; Metzger[*Codex Bezae transfers verse 5 after verse 10 and in its place adds* On the same day, seeing one working on the Sabbath day, he said to him, "Man, if you know what you are doing, you are blessed; but if you do not know, you are accursed and a transgressor of the law"].

6:5 Alx[**Lord of the Sabbath**], Byz[Lord even of the Sabbath (DRA, KJV, NKJ, NLT, TLB)].

6:6 Alx[**On another Sabbath**], Byz[*adds* also (DRA, KJV, NKJ)].

6:7 Alx[**watched him closely**], Byz[*omits* him (DRA, REB, TLB)]; Alx[**whether he would heal** Greek whether he heals], Byz[whether he would heal]; Alx[**how to accuse him**], Byz[an accusation against him (DRA, HCS, KJV, NKJ, NRS, REB, RSV, TLB)].

6:9 Alx[**And Jesus said**], Byz[Then Jesus said (DRA, HCS, JNT, KJV, NAB, NET, NIV, NJB, NKJ, NLT, NRS, REB, TEV, TLB)]; Alx[**I ask you**], Byz[I will ask you (KJV, NKJ)]; Alx[**if it is lawful**], Byz[is it lawful (ASV, ESV, HCS, JNT, KJV, MRD, NAB, MRD, NAB, NAS, NAU, NET, NIV, NJB, NKJ, NLT, NRS, REB, RSV, TEV, TLB)]; Alx[**on the Sabbath**], Byz[on the Sabbaths]; Alx[**destroy it**], Byz[kill].

6:10 Alx/Byz[**him**], Minor[the man (DRA, KJV, NET, NIV, NJB, NKJ, NLT, REB, TEV, TLB)], Minor[*adds* in anger]; Alx/Byz[**he did**], Minor[*adds* thus (ASV, ESV, HCS, KJV, NAB, NAS, NAU, NET, NIV, NJB, NKJ, ~NLT, NRS, REB, RSV, TEV)]; Alx[**restored**], Byz[restored as the other (MRD)], Major[restored as whole as the other (KJV, NKJ)].

chose twelve, whom he also named apostles: **14** Simon, whom he named Peter, and Andrew his brother, and James and John, and Philip, and Bartholomew, **15** and Matthew, and Thomas, and James the son of Alphaeus, and Simon who was called the Zealot, **16** and Judas the son of James, and Judas Iscariot, who became a traitor.

17 And he came down with them and stood on a level place with a great crowd of his disciples and a great multitude of people from all Judea and Jerusalem, and from the seacoast of Tyre and Sidon, **18** who came to hear him and be healed of their diseases, and those who were troubled with unclean spirits were cured. **19** And all the crowd sought to touch him, for power came from him and healed them all.

20 He lifted up his eyes on his disciples, and said:

"Blessed are you poor,
    for yours is the kingdom of God.
21 Blessed are you who hunger now,
    for you shall be satisfied.
Blessed are you who weep now,
    for you shall laugh.

22 Blessed are you when men hate you, and when they exclude you and revile you, and cast out your name as evil, because of the Son of Man. **23** Rejoice in that day and leap for joy, for behold, your reward is great in heaven; for their fathers did the same to the prophets.

24 But woe to you who are rich,
    for you have received your consolation.
25 Woe to you who are full now,
    for you shall hunger.
Woe to you who laugh now,
    for you shall mourn and weep.

26 Alas! when all men speak well of you, for their fathers did the same to the false prophets.

27 "But I say to you who hear: love your enemies, do good to those who hate you, **28** bless those who curse you, pray for those who mistreat you. **29** To him who strikes you on the cheek, offer the other also. And from him who takes away your cloak, do not withhold your tunic. **30** Give to everyone who asks of you, and from him who takes away your goods

---

6:14   Alx/Byz[**Peter**], Alt/Peshitta[Cephas (JNT, MRD)]; Alx[**and James…and Philip**], Byz[James…Philip (DRA, HCS, JNT, KJV, NAB, ~NET, NIV, NJB, NKJ, NLT, REB, TEV, TLB)].

6:15   Alx[**and Matthew…and James**], Byz[Matthew…James (DRA, HCS, JNT, KJV, NAB, ~NAS, ~NAU, NET, NIV, NJB, NKJ, NLT, REB, TEV, TLB)].

6:16   Alx[**and Judas the son of James**], Byz[*omits* and (HCS, JNT, NAS, NAU, NET, NIV, NJB, NKJ, NLT, REB, TEV, TLB)]; Alx/Byz[**Iscariot**], Alt/Vulgate/Peshitta[Scariot], Alt[from Kerioth (~JNT)]; Alx[**who became a traitor**], Byz[who also became a traitor (KJV, NKJ)]; **Iscariot** *Hebraism Ish Keriot a man from Kerioth or possibly Sicarios* assassin *or* bandit.

6:17   Alx[**a great crowd**], Byz[a crowd (DRA, KJV, NKJ, ~NLT, ~TLB)].

6:18   Alx[**18 who came to hear him and be healed of their diseases**], Byz[who came to hear him and be healed of their diseases 18 (ASV, JNT, KJV, MRD, NET, NKJ, RSV, ~TLB)]; Alx[**and those who were troubled from unclean spirits were cured**], Byz[and those who were troubled from unclean spirits were also cured (NAB, TEV, ~TLB)], Major[and those who were troubled by unclean spirits; and they were cured (KJV, MRD, NKJ)].

6:23   Alx/Byz[**Rejoice…and leap for joy,** *passive*], Minor[Rejoice…and leap for joy! *imperative* (HCS, NAB, NKJ, NLT, TLB)]; Alx/Byz[**the same**], Major[these (DRA, ~HCS, ~NJB, ~TLB)].

6:25   Alx[**who are full now**], Byz[*omits* now (DRA, KJV, MRD, NKJ)].

6:26   Alx[**Alas! when**], Byz[Woe to you when (ASV, DRA, ESV, HCS, JNT, KJV, MRD, NAB, NAS, NAU, NET, NIV, NJB, NKJ, ~NLT, NRS, REB, RSV)]; Alx/Byz[**all men**], Major[men (DRA, MRD, ~NLT, ~TLB)]; Alx/Byz[**the same**], Major[these (DRA, ~TLB)].

6:28   Alx/Byz[**pray**], Minor[and pray (DRA, KJV, MRD, NKJ, TEV, ~TLB)].

6:29   Alx/Byz[**on the cheek**], Minor[in the cheek].

6:30   Alx[**Give to everyone**], Byz[But give to everyone].

do not ask them back. ³¹ And as you wish that men would do to you, do so to them. ³² If you love those who love you, what credit is that to you? For even sinners love those who love them. ³³ [For] if you do good to those who do good to you, what credit is that to you? Even sinners do the same. ³⁴ And if you lend to those from whom you hope to receive back, what credit [is] that to you? Even sinners lend to sinners, to receive as much back. ³⁵ But love your enemies, do good, and lend, expecting nothing in return; and your reward will be great, and you will be sons of the Most High. For he is kind to the ungrateful and evil. ³⁶ Be merciful, [even] as your Father is merciful.

³⁷ "And judge not, and you will never be judged. And condemn not, and you will never be condemned. Forgive, and you will be forgiven. ³⁸ Give, and it will be given to you; good measure, pressed down, shaken together, running over—will be put into your lap. For with what measure you use, it will be measured back to you." ³⁹ He also told them a parable: "Can a blind man lead a blind man? Will they not both fall into a pit? ⁴⁰ No disciple is above the teacher, but everyone who is fully trained will be like his teacher. ⁴¹ And why do you look at the speck in your brother's eye, but do not notice the plank in your own eye? ⁴² How can you say to your brother, 'Brother, let me remove the speck that is in your eye,' when you yourself do not see the plank that is in your own eye? You hypocrite! First take the plank from out of your own eye, and then you will see clearly to take out the speck that is in your brother's eye.

⁴³ "For no good tree bears bad fruit, nor again does a bad tree bear good fruit. ⁴⁴ For each tree is known by its own fruit. For men do not gather figs from thorns, nor do they pick grapes from a bramble bush. ⁴⁵ The good man out of the good treasure of his heart brings forth good, and the evil man out of his evil brings forth evil. For out of the abundance of the heart his mouth speaks.

⁴⁶ "Why do you call me, 'Lord, Lord,' and do not do what I say? ⁴⁷ Every one who comes to me and hears my words and does them, I will show you what he is like: ⁴⁸ he is like a man building a house, who dug deep and laid the foundation on the rock. And when

---

6:³¹ Alx[**do so to them**], Byz[you also do so to them (ASV, DRA, KJV, MRD, NKJ)].

6:³³ Alx[**For if you do good**], Byz[And if you do good (ASV, DRA, ESV, HCS, JNT, KJV, MRD, NAB, NAS, NAU, NET, NIV, NJB, NKJ, NLT, NRS, REB, RSV, TEV, TLB)]; Alx[**Even sinners**], Byz[For even sinners (ASV, ~DRA, ESV, ~KJV, MRD, NAS, NAU, NJB, NKJ, NRS, RSV)].

6:³⁴ Alx[**Even sinners**], Byz[For even sinners (DRA, KJV, MRD, NKJ)], Minor[For even the sinners (~TLB)].

6:³⁵ Alx/Byz[**expecting nothing in return**], Minor[disappointing no one (MRD, ~TLB)].

6:³⁶ Alx[**Be merciful**], Byz[*adds* therefore (DRA, KJV, MRD, NKJ)]; Alx/Byz[**even as**], Minor[as (REB, TLB)].

6:³⁷ Alx/Byz[**And judge not**], Minor[Judge not (DRA, ESV, HCS, JNT, KJV, MRD, NAB, NAU, NET, NIV, NJB, NKJ, NLT, NRS, REB, RSV, TEV, TLB)]; Alx[**And condemn not**], Byz[Condemn not (DRA, ESV, HCS, JNT, KJV, MRD, NAB, NET, NIV, NJB, NKJ, NLT, NRS, REB, RSV, TEV, TLB)].

6:³⁸ Alx[**shaken together, running over**], Byz[and shaken together and running over (DRA, ~HCS, ~JNT, KJV, ~NAB, ~NIV, ~NJB, ~NKJ, ~NLT, REB, ~TLB)], Minor[*omits* shaken together (MRD, TEV)]; Alx[**For with what measure**], Byz[For with the same measure (DRA, KJV, NKJ)]; Alx/Byz[**it will be measured back**], Minor[*omits* back (MRD, ~NET, NIV, ~NJB, TEV)].

6:³⁹ Alx[**He also**], Byz[*omits* also (KJV, MRD, NAB, NKJ, NLT, TEV, TLB)].

6:⁴⁰ Alx[**the teacher**], Byz[his teacher (ASV, DRA, ESV, HCS, JNT, KJV, MRD, NAS, NAU, NET, NIV, NKJ, ~NLT, RSV, TEV, TLB)].

6:⁴² Alx[**How can you say**], Byz[Or how can you say (ASV, DRA, HCS, KJV, MRD, NAS, NAU, NKJ, NRS, RSV)].

6:⁴³ Alx[**nor again**], Byz[*omits* again (DRA, JNT, KJV, MRD, NAB, NIV, NKJ, NLT, ~REB, TEV, TLB)].

6:⁴⁵ Alx[**out of his evil**], Byz[out of the evil treasure of his heart (KJV, MRD, NIV, NKJ, NLT, TEV, TLB)].

6:⁴⁸ Alx/Major[**who dug**], Byz[who also dug (~KJV, MRD, ~TLB)]; Alx[**because it was well built**], Byz[because it was founded on the rock (DRA, KJV, MRD, NKJ)].

a flood arose, the stream broke against that house and could not shake it, because it was well built. **49** But he who hears and does not do them is like a man who built a house on the ground without a foundation; against which the stream broke, and immediately it collapsed. And the ruin of that house was great."

7 **1** When he had finished all his sayings in the hearing of the people, he entered Capernaum. **2** A centurion's servant, who was dear to him, was sick and ready to die. **3** When he heard of Jesus, he sent to him elders of the Jews, asking him to come and heal his servant. **4** And when they came to Jesus, they begged him earnestly, saying, "He is worthy to have you do this for him, **5** for he loves our nation, and has built us our synagogue." **6** And Jesus went with them. When he was not far from the house, the centurion sent friends, saying to him, "Lord, do not trouble yourself, for I am not worthy to have you come under my roof. **7** Therefore I did not even consider myself worthy to come to you. But say the word, and let my servant be healed. **8** For I am a man set under authority, with soldiers under me. And I say to one, 'Go,' and he goes; and to another, 'Come,' and he comes; and to my servant, 'Do this,' and he does it." **9** When Jesus heard this, he marveled at him, and turned and said to the crowd that followed him, "I tell you, I have not found such great faith even in Israel." **10** And when those who had been sent returned to the house, they found the servant well.

11 Soon afterward, he went to a city called Nain, and his disciples and a large crowd went along with him. **12** As he came near the gate of the city, behold, a dead man was being carried out, the only son of his mother; and she was a widow. And a large crowd from the city was with her. **13** When the Lord saw her, he had compassion on her and said to her, "Do not weep." **14** Then he came and touched the open coffin, and those who carried him stood still. And he said, "Young man, I say to you, arise." **15** The dead man sat up, and began to speak. And he gave him to his mother. **16** Fear seized them all; and they glorified God, saying, "A great prophet has arisen among us;" and "God has visited his people." **17** And this report about him spread throughout all Judea and all the surrounding country.

18 Then the disciples of John told him about all these things. And John, calling to him two of his disciples, **19** sent them to the Lord, saying, "Are you the One who is to come, or shall we look for another?" **20** When the men had come to him, they said, "John the

---

6:49 Alx[**it collapsed**], Byz[it fell (DRA, ESV, KJV, MRD, NKJ, NRS, RSV, TEV)].

7:1 Alx[**When he had finished**], Byz[And when he had finished (DRA, KJV, MRD, NKJ)]; Alx[**Capernaum** Greek Capharnaum], Byz[Capernaum].

7:4 Alx/Byz[**begged him**], Minor[asked him (~NRS, ~REB)]; Alx[**have you do this**], Byz[have him do this (KJV, NKJ)].

7:6 Alx[**sent friends**], Byz[*adds* to him (ASV, DRA, KJV, MRD, NJB, NKJ, RSV)]; Alx/Byz[**saying to him**], Minor[*omits* to him (DRA, NLT, REB, TLB)].

7:7 Alx[**and let my servant be healed**], Byz[and my servant will be healed (ASV, DRA, HCS, KJV, MRD, NAS, NAU, NIV, NKJ, NLT, REB, TEV, TLB)].

7:10 Alx[**sent returned to the house**], Byz[sent to the house returned]; Alx[**found the servant well**], Byz[*adds* who had been sick (DRA, KJV, MRD, NKJ)].

7:11 Alx/Byz[**Soon afterward**], Minor[The next day (JNT, KJV, MRD, NKJ)]; Alx/Byz[**Nain**], Minor[Naim (DRA, JNT)]; Alx[**his disciples**], Byz[many of his disciples (KJV, NKJ)].

7:12 Alx/Byz[**and she was a widow**], Major[and she a widow (MRD, ~REB, ~TLB)]; Alx/Byz[**was with her**], Major[with her].

7:17 Alx[**all the surrounding country**], Byz[throughout all the surrounding country *or* in all the surrounding country (DRA, KJV, NAB, NAS, NAU)].

7:18 Alx[**And John, calling to him two of his disciples, 19**], Byz[19 And John, calling to him two of his disciples, (ASV, DRA, ~ESV, KJV, MRD, NAS, NAU, ~NIV, NKJ, REB, RSV, TLB)].

7:19 Alx[**to the Lord**], Byz[to Jesus (DRA, KJV, MRD, NET, NKJ, TLB)]; Alx/Major[**another**], Byz[a different one (HCS, JNT, NAS, NAU, NIV, NJB, NLT, REB, TEV)].

7:20 Alx[**sent us to you**], Byz[has sent us to you (ASV, DRA, ESV, JNT, KJV, MRD, NAB, NAS, NAU, NET, NJB, NKJ, NRS, REB, RSV)]; ~TLB *omits* John the Baptist sent us to you, saying, 'Are you the

Baptist sent us to you, saying, 'Are you the One who is to come, or shall we look for another?'" **21** In that hour he cured many of their diseases and afflictions and evil spirits, and to many that were blind he gave sight. **22** And he answered them, "Go and tell John what you have seen and heard: the blind receive their sight, the lame walk, the lepers are cleansed, and the deaf hear, the dead are raised up, the poor have the good news preached to them. **23** And blessed is he who is not offended because of me." **24** When the messengers of John had departed, he began to speak to the crowds concerning John: "What did you go out into the wilderness to see? A reed shaken by the wind? **25** What then did you go out to see? A man dressed in dainty clothes? Behold, those who are gorgeously appareled and live in luxury are in kings' courts. **26** But what did you go out to see? A prophet? Yes, I tell you, and more than a prophet. **27** This is he of whom it is written:

> *'Behold, I send my messenger before your face,*
> *who will prepare your way before you.'*

28 I tell you, among those born of women there is no one greater than John; yet the one who is least in the kingdom of God is greater than he." **29** (And when they heard him, all the people, even the tax collectors, justified God, having been baptized with the baptism of John. **30** But the Pharisees and the lawyers rejected the purpose of God for themselves, not having been baptized by him.)

31 "To what then shall I compare the men of this generation, and what are they like? **32** They are like children sitting in the marketplace calling to one another who say:

> *'We played the flute for you, and you did not dance;*
> *we sang a dirge, and you did not weep.'*

33 For John the Baptist came neither eating bread nor drinking wine, and you say, 'He has a demon.' **34** The Son of Man has come eating and drinking, and you say, 'Behold, a glutton and a drunkard, a friend of tax collectors and sinners!' **35** But wisdom is justified by all her children."

One who is to come, or shall we look for another.

7:²¹ Alx[**In that hour**], Byz[And in the same hour (~DRA, KJV, ~MRD, ~NAS, ~NAU, ~NET, ~NIV, ~NJB, NKJ, ~NLT, ~NRS, ~REB, ~TEV, ~TLB)].

7:²² Alx[**And he answered**], Byz[And Jesus answered (KJV, MRD, NKJ)]; Alx/Byz[**John** *formal spelling*], Minor[John *informal spelling*]; Alx/Byz[**the blind receive**], Major[that the blind receive (KJV, MRD, NKJ, TLB)]; Alx/Major[**the lame walk**], Byz[and the lame walk (MRD)]; Alx[**and the deaf**], Byz[*omits* and (DRA, HCS, JNT, KJV, NAB, NET, NIV, NKJ, NLT, NRS, REB, TEV, TLB)]; **lepers** *can refer to a number of skin diseases.*

7:²³ **is not offended** *or* does not fall away.

7:²⁴⁻²⁶ Alx[**did you go out**], Byz[have you gone out].

7:²⁴ Alx/Major[**the messengers of John**], Byz[the disciples of John (MRD, NLT, ~TLB)]; **What did you go out into the wilderness to see? A reed** *or* Why did you go out into the wilderness? To see a reed.

7:²⁵ **What then did you go out to see? A man** *or* Why then did you go out? To see a man.

7:²⁶ **But what did you go out to see? A prophet?** *or* But why did you go out? To see a prophet?

7:²⁷ ~**Malachi 3:1 Masoretic**.

7:²⁸ Alx[**I tell you**], Byz[For I tell you (DRA, KJV, NKJ)]; Alx[**no one greater than John**], Byz[no greater prophet than John the Baptist (DRA, KJV, NKJ)], Minor[no greater prophet than John].

7:²⁹ **justified God** *or* praised God.

7:³¹ Alx/Byz[*text*], Minor[*adds to beginning of verse* And the Lord said (DRA, JNT, KJV, NKJ, ~NLT, ~TEV, ~TLB)].

7:³² Alx[**who say**], Byz[and saying (DRA, ~ESV, ~HCS, ~JNT, KJV, MRD, ~NAB, NAS, NAU, ~NET, ~NIV, ~NJB, ~NKJ, ~NLT, ~NRS, ~REB, ~RSV, ~TEV, ~TLB)]; Alx[**sang a dirge**], Byz[*adds* to you (KJV, MRD, NKJ)].

7:³⁵ Alx/Byz[**all her children**], Minor[*omits* all (NLT, TLB)].

³⁶ One of the Pharisees asked him to eat with him, and he went to the Pharisee's house, and sat to eat. ³⁷ And behold, a woman of the city, who was a sinner; and when she learned that Jesus was reclining in the Pharisee's house, brought an alabaster flask of perfume, ³⁸ and as she stood behind him at his feet, weeping, she began to wet his feet with her tears, and wiped them with the hair of her head, and kissed his feet, and anointed them with the perfume. ³⁹ Now when the Pharisee who had invited him saw it, he said to himself, "If this man were a prophet, he would have known who and what sort of woman this is who is touching him, for she is a sinner." ⁴⁰ And Jesus answered him, "Simon, I have something to say to you." And he said, "Teacher, say it." ⁴¹ "A certain creditor had two debtors. One owed five hundred denarii, and the other fifty. ⁴² When they had nothing with which to pay him back, he freely forgave them both. So, which of them will love him more?" ⁴³ Simon, answering, said, "I suppose the one to whom he forgave more." And he said to him, "You have judged rightly." ⁴⁴ Then he turned toward the woman and said to Simon, "Do you see this woman? I entered your house; you gave me no water for my feet, but she has wet my feet with her tears and wiped them with her hair. ⁴⁵ You gave me no kiss, but this woman has not ceased to kiss my feet from the time I came in. ⁴⁶ You did not anoint my head with oil, but she has anointed my feet with perfume. ⁴⁷ Therefore I tell you, her sins, which are many, are forgiven, for she loved much. But he who is forgiven little, loves little." ⁴⁸ And he said to her, "Your sins are forgiven." ⁴⁹ Then those who sat to eat with him began to say among themselves, "Who is this who even forgives sins?" ⁵⁰ He said to the woman, "Your faith has saved you; go in peace."

8 ¹ Soon afterward, he went on through every city and village, preaching and bringing the good news of the kingdom of God. And the twelve were with him, ² and also some women who had been healed of evil spirits and infirmities: Mary, called Magdalene, from whom seven demons had come out, ³ and Joanna the wife of Chuza, Herod's steward, and Susanna, and many others who provided for them out of their means.

⁴ And when a great crowd came together and people from town after town came to him, he said in a parable: ⁵ "A sower went out to sow his seed. And as he sowed, some fell along the path; and it was trampled down, and the birds of the air devoured it. ⁶ Other seed fell down on the rock; and as it grew up, it withered away, because it had no moisture. ⁷ Other seed fell among thorns, and the thorns grew up with it and choked it. ⁸ And other seed fell into good soil, sprang up, and yielded a crop a hundredfold." When he had said this he called out, "He who has ears to hear, let him hear!"

7:37 Alx/Byz[**and when she learned**], Major[*omits* and (DRA, ESV, ~HCS, JNT, KJV, NAB, NET, NIV, NJB, NKJ, NLT, NRS, REB, RSV, TEV, TLB)].

7:39 Alx/Byz[**a prophet**], Minor[the Prophet].

7:41 **denarii** *a denarius was a day's wage for a laborer.*

7:42 Alx[**When they had nothing**], Byz[But when they had nothing (DRA, KJV, MRD, NKJ, NLT, TLB)]; Alx[**So, which of them**], Byz[So, tell me, which of them (KJV, NKJ, NLT, TLB)].

7:43 Alx[**Simon**], Byz[And Simon].

7:44 Alx[**her hair** *Greek* her hairs], Byz[the hairs of her head (KJV, NKJ)].

7:45 Alx/Major[**time I came in**], Byz[time she came in (DRA, MRD)].

7:47 **I tell you, her sins, which are many, are forgiven, for** *or* I can tell you she was forgiven many sins, because.

8:2 Alx/Major[**evil spirits and infirmities**], Byz[illness and scourging and evil spirits and infirmities], Minor[unclean spirits and infirmities (~MRD)].

8:3 Alx/Major[**for them**], Byz[for him (DRA, JNT, KJV, NKJ, ~NLT, ~TEV, ~TLB)].

8:6 Alx[**fell down**], Byz[fell (ASV, DRA, ESV, HCS, JNT, KJV, MRD, NAB, NAS, NAU, NET, NIV, NJB, NKJ, NLT, NRS, REB, RSV, TEV, TLB)].

8:8 Alx/Byz[**into good soil**], Minor[on good soil (DRA, HCS, KJV, MRD, NAB, NET, NIV, NKJ, NLT, TLB)].

⁹ When his disciples asked him what this parable meant, ¹⁰ he said, "To you it has been given to know the secrets of the kingdom of God; but to others it is given in parables, so that

'*Seeing they may not see,*
   and hearing they may not understand.'

¹¹ "Now the parable is this: The seed is the word of God. ¹² The ones along the path are those who heard; then the devil comes and takes away the word from their hearts, that they may not believe and be saved. ¹³ And the ones on the rock are those who, when they hear the word, receive it with joy; but these have no root, they believe for a while and in time of temptation fall away. ¹⁴ And the ones that fell among the thorns, they are those who hear, but as they go on their way they are choked by the cares and riches and pleasures of life, and their fruit does not mature. ¹⁵ But the ones that fell on the good soil are those who, having heard the word with a noble and good heart, keep it and bear fruit with patience.

¹⁶ "No one, when he has lit a lamp, covers it with a vessel or puts it under a bed, but puts it on a lampstand, that those who enter may see the light. ¹⁷ For nothing is secret that will not be revealed, nor anything hidden that cannot be known and come to light. ¹⁸ Therefore take heed how you hear. For whoever has, to him more will be given; and whoever does not have, even what he thinks he has will be taken from him."

¹⁹ Then his mother and brothers came to him, but they could not reach him because of the crowd. ²⁰ And it was told him, "Your mother and your brothers are standing outside, desiring to see you." ²¹ But he said to them, "My mother and my brothers are those who hear and do the word of God."

²² One day he got into a boat with his disciples, and he said to them, "Let us go over to the other side of the lake." So they set out. ²³ As they sailed he fell asleep. And a windstorm came down on the lake, and they were filling with water, and were in danger. ²⁴ And they went and woke him, saying, "Master, Master, we are perishing!" Then he awoke and rebuked the wind and the raging waves; and they ceased, and there was a calm. ²⁵ He said to them, "Where is your faith?" And they were afraid, and they marveled, saying to one another, "Who then is this, that he commands even the winds and water, and they obey him?"

²⁶ Then they sailed to the country of the Gerasenes, which is opposite Galilee. ²⁷ When he stepped out on land, there met him a man from the city who had demons. For a long time he had worn no clothes, and he lived not in a house but in the tombs. ²⁸ When he saw Jesus, he cried out and fell down before him, and said with a loud voice, "What have you to do with me, Jesus, Son of the Most High God? I beg you, do not torment me!" ²⁹ For

---

8:⁹ Alx[**asked him**], Byz[*adds* saying (KJV, NKJ)].

8:¹⁰ **secrets** *or* mysteries; ~Isaiah 6:9 LXX.

8:¹² Alx/Byz[**those who heard**], Major[those who hear (DRA, JNT, KJV, MRD, NIV, NKJ, NLT, REB, TEV, TLB)].

8:¹⁶ Alx[**puts it on a lampstand**], Byz[sets it on a lampstand (DRA, KJV, MRD, NKJ, ~TLB)].

8:¹⁷ Alx[**cannot be known**], Byz[will not be known (ASV, DRA, ESV, HCS, JNT, KJV, MRD, NAB, NAS, NAU, NET, NIV, ~NJB, NKJ, ~NLT, NRS, REB, RSV, ~TEV, ~TLB)].

8:¹⁹ Alx/Byz[**his mother and brothers** *Greek* the mother and his brothers], Minor[his mother and his brothers (ESV, KJV, MRD, NAB, NET, NJB, NRS, REB, RSV)].

8:²⁰ Alx[**it was told him**], Byz[*adds* by some (KJV, ~NIV, NKJ, ~NLT, ~TEV)].

8:²¹ Alx[**hear and do the word of God**], Byz[hear the word of God and do it (ASV, DRA, ESV, JNT, KJV, MRD, NAB, NAS, NAU, NET, NIV, NJB, NKJ, NLT, NRS, REB, RSV, TEV, TLB)].

8:²⁴ Alx[**he awoke**], Byz[he arose (DRA, HCS, KJV, MRD, NAS, NAU, NET, NIV, NKJ, TEV, ~TLB)].

8:²⁶ Alx[**Gerasenes**], Byz[Gadarenes (KJV, MRD, NKJ)], Minor[Gergesenes].

8:²⁷ Alx[**who had demons. For a long time he had worn no clothes**], Byz[who had demons for a long time. He wore no clothes (DRA, KJV, MRD, NKJ, TLB)].

8:²⁸ Alx/Byz[**Son of the Most High God**], Minor[*omits* God].

8:²⁹ Alx/Byz[**he commanded**], Minor[was commanding (ASV, REB, TLB)].

he commanded the unclean spirit to come out of the man. For many times it had seized him, and he was kept under guard, bound with chains and shackles; and he broke the bonds and was driven by the demon into the wilderness. ³⁰ Jesus asked him, "What is your name?" And he said, "Legion"; because many demons had entered him. ³¹ And they begged him repeatedly not to command them to go into the Abyss.

³² Now a large herd of swine was feeding there on the hillside; and they begged him to let them enter them. So he gave them permission. ³³ Then the demons came out of the man and entered the swine, and the herd rushed down the steep bank into the lake and were drowned. ³⁴ When those tending the pigs saw what had happened, they fled, and told it in the city and in the country. ³⁵ Then people went out to see what had happened, and they came to Jesus, and found the man from whom the demons left, sitting at the feet of Jesus, clothed and in his right mind; and they were afraid. ³⁶ Those who had seen it told them how he who had been demon-possessed was healed. ³⁷ Then all the people of the surrounding region of the Gerasenes asked him to depart from them, for they were seized with great fear. So he got into a boat and returned. ³⁸ The man from whom the demons had gone begged that he might be with him; but he sent him away, saying, ³⁹ "Return to your home, and tell how much God has done for you." And he went away, proclaiming throughout the whole city how much Jesus had done for him.

⁴⁰ Now when Jesus was returning, the crowd welcomed him, for they were all waiting for him. ⁴¹ And behold, there came a man named Jairus, who was a ruler of the synagogue; and he fell at Jesus' feet and begged him to come to his house, ⁴² for he had an only daughter, about twelve years of age, and she was dying.

But as he went, the people pressed round him. ⁴³ And a woman who had a flow of blood for twelve years, who [had spent all her living on physicians, and] could not be healed by anyone, ⁴⁴ came up behind him, and touched the tassel of his garment; and immediately her flow of blood stopped. ⁴⁵ And Jesus said, "Who touched me?" When all denied it, Peter said, "Master, the multitudes surround you and press upon you!" ⁴⁶ But Jesus said, "Someone touched me; for I know that power has gone out from me." ⁴⁷ When

---

8:30 Alx[**Jesus asked him**], Byz[*adds* saying (DRA, KJV, NKJ)].

8:31 Alx[**they begged him**], Byz[he begged him].

8:32 Alx[**was feeding**], Byz[were feeding (~NLT)]; Alx[**they begged him**], Byz[they were begging him].

8:33 Alx/Byz[**entered** *plural*], Minor[entered *singular*].

8:34 Alx/Byz[fled, and told], Minor[fled, and went and told (~DRA, ~HCS, KJV, ~NAB, ~NAS, ~NAU, ~NET, ~NIV, ~NJB, ~NLT, ~NRS, ~REB, ~TEV, ~TLB)].

8:35 Alx[**left**], Byz[were left (ASV, DRA, KJV, ~NLT, ~TLB)].

8:36 Alx/Byz[**Those**], Major[*adds* also (DRA, KJV, NKJ)].

8:37 Alx[**Gerasenes**], Byz[Gadarenes (KJV, MRD, NKJ, ~TEV, ~TLB)], Minor[Gergesenes]; Alx[**asked** *singular* him], Byz[asked *plural* him]; Alx[**a boat**], Byz[the boat (DRA, ESV, HCS, JNT, KJV, NET, NIV, NJB, NKJ, NLT, NRS, REB, RSV, TEV, TLB)].

8:38 Alx[**he sent him away**], Byz[Jesus sent him away (DRA, ESV, JNT, KJV, MRD, NET, NIV, NKJ, NLT, NRS, REB, TEV, TLB)].

8:40 Alx[**Now when Jesus**], Byz[Now when it happened that Jesus (DRA, KJV, NKJ, ~NLT, ~TLB)]; Alx[**was returning** *or* as...returned], Byz[returned (~DRA, ESV, HCS, JNT, ~KJV, MRD, NAB, NET, NIV, NKJ, ~NLT, NRS, REB, RSV, TEV, ~TLB)].

8:43 Alx[**had spent all her living on physicians, and**], Byz[had spent all her living in physicians, and], Minor[*omit* (JNT, NAS, NAU, NET, NIV, NJB, NLT, REB, RSV)].

8:44 Alx/Byz[**the tassel of**], Minor[*omits*].

8:45 Alx[**Peter said**], Byz[Peter and those with him said (ASV, DRA, KJV, MRD, NKJ)]; Alx/Byz[**Peter**], Minor[Simon Cephas (~JNT, MRD)]; Alx[**press upon you**], Byz[*adds* and you say, 'Who touched me?' (DRA, KJV, MRD, NKJ)].

8:46 Alx[**has gone out**], Byz[went out (~DRA, JNT, ~KJV, NKJ, NLT, TEV, TLB)].

8:47 Alx[**declared**], Byz[declared to him (KJV, NKJ, TEV)].

the woman saw that she was not hidden, she came trembling, and falling down before him declared in the presence of all the people why she had touched him, and how she had been immediately healed. 48 And he said to her, "Daughter, your faith has made you well; go in peace."

49 While he was still speaking, someone came from the ruler of the synagogue's house and said, "Your daughter is dead; do not trouble the Teacher any more." 50 But Jesus on hearing this answered him, "Do not be afraid; only believe, and she will be well." 51 When he came into the house he did not permit anyone to go in with him except Peter, John, and James, and the father and mother of the girl. 52 Now all were wailing and mourning for her; but he said, "Do not weep; for she is not dead, but sleeping." 53 And they laughed at him, knowing that she was dead. 54 But he took her by the hand and called, saying, "Child, arise." 55 Then her spirit returned, and she got up at once. And he directed that something should be given her to eat. 56 And her parents were astonished, but he charged them to tell no one what had happened.

9 1 Then he called the Twelve together and gave them power and authority over all demons, and to cure diseases. 2 And he sent them out to preach the kingdom of God and to heal [the weak]. 3 And he said to them, "Take nothing for the journey, no staff, nor bag, nor bread, nor money; and do not have two tunics apiece. 4 Whatever house you enter, stay there, and from there depart. 5 And wherever they do not receive you, when you leave that town, shake off the dust from your feet as a testimony against them." 6 So they departed and went through the towns, preaching the gospel and healing everywhere.

7 Now Herod the tetrarch heard of all that was done; and he was perplexed, because it was said by some that John was raised from the dead, 8 by some that Elijah had appeared, and by others that a certain one of the old prophets had risen again. 9 And Herod said, "John I have beheaded, but who is this about whom I hear such things?" So he sought to see him.

10 And when the apostles returned, they told him what they had done. Then he took them with him and withdrew apart to a city called Bethsaida. 11 But when the crowds

---

8:48 Alx[**Daughter, your faith**], Byz[Daughter, take heart, your faith (KJV, MRD, NKJ)].

8:49 Alx[**said**], Byz[*adds* to him (DRA, KJV, MRD, NKJ, NLT, TEV, TLB)]; Alx[**any more**], Byz[*omits* (ASV, DRA, KJV, MRD, NKJ, ~NLT, ~TLB)].

8:50 Alx[**answered him**], Byz[*adds* saying (KJV, ~MRD, ~NIV, ~NJB, NKJ, ~NLT, ~REB, ~TEV, ~TLB)].

8:51 Alx[**did not permit anyone to go in with him**], Byz[permitted no one to go in (KJV, NKJ, TLB)]; Alx/Byz[**Peter**], Minor[Simon (MRD)], Alt[*without textual foundation* Cephas (~JNT)]; Alx/Byz[**John, and James**], Minor[James, and John (DRA, KJV, MRD, NKJ, TLB)].

8:52 Alx[**for she is not dead**], Byz[*omits* for (DRA, JNT, KJV, NET, NIV, NJB, NKJ, NLT, REB, TEV, TLB)].

8:54 Alx[**But he took her by the hand**], Byz[But he put them all outside, and took her by the hand (KJV, MRD, NKJ)].

9:1 Alx/Byz[**the Twelve**], Byz[his twelve disciples (KJV, NKJ, NLT, ~TEV)], Minor[his twelve (MRD) *others* the twelve apostles (DRA, ~TLB)].

9:2 Alx[**the weak**], Byz[the sick (ASV, DRA, HCS, KJV, MRD, NET, NIV, NKJ, NLT, REB, TEV, TLB)], Minor[*omits* (ESV, JNT, NAS, NAU, NJB, NRS, RSV)].

9:3 Alx[**staff**], Byz[staves (KJV, NKJ)]; Alx[**apiece**], Byz[*omits* (ASV, DRA, ESV, HCS, JNT, MRD, NET, NIV, NJB, NLT, ~NRS, REB, RSV, ~TEV, ~TLB)].

9:5 Alx[**the dust**], Byz[even the dust (DRA, KJV, MRD, NKJ)].

9:7 Alx[**that was done**], Byz[*adds* by him (DRA, KJV, MRD, NKJ, ~NLT, ~TLB)]; Alx[**was raised**], Byz[had been raised (ESV, HCS, JNT, NAB, NET, NIV, NLT, NRS, REB, RSV)]; Alx/Byz[**by some that John...from the dead 8**], Minor[8 by some that John...from the dead (DRA)]; Alx/Major[**the dead Greek dead**], Byz[the dead].

9:8 Alx/Byz[**a certain one**], Major[one (ASV, DRA, ESV, HCS, JNT, KJV, ~MRD, NAB, NAS, NAU, NET, NIV, NJB, NKJ, NLT, NRS, REB, RSV, TEV, TLB)].

9:10 Alx[**withdrew**], Byz[*adds* into a desert place (DRA, KJV, NKJ)].

learned it, they followed him; and he welcomed them and began speaking to them about the kingdom of God, and healing those who had need of healing. ¹² Now the day began to wear away; and the twelve came and said to him, "Send the crowd away, to go to the surrounding villages and country, to lodge and get provisions; for we are here in a deserted place." ¹³ But he said to them, "You give them something to eat." And they said, "We have no more than five loaves and two fish – unless we go and buy food for all these people." ¹⁴ For there were about five thousand men. And he said to his disciples, "Make them sit down in groups of [about] fifty each." ¹⁵ And they did so, and made them all sit down. ¹⁶ Taking the five loaves and the two fish and looking up to heaven, he blessed and broke them, and gave them to the disciples to set before the people. ¹⁷ They all ate and were satisfied, and they took up twelve baskets of broken pieces that were left over.

¹⁸ Now it happened that as he was praying alone his disciples were with him; and he asked them, "Who do the crowds say that I am?" ¹⁹ So they answered, "John the Baptist; but others say Elijah; and others say that one of the old prophets has risen again." ²⁰ And he said to them, "But who do you say that I am?" And Peter answered, "The Christ of God."

²¹ But he strictly warned and commanded them to tell this to no one, ²² saying, "The Son of Man must suffer many things, and be rejected by the elders and chief priests and scribes, and be killed, and on the third day be raised." ²³ Then he said to them all, "If anyone would come after me, let him deny himself and take up his cross daily and follow me. ²⁴ For whoever desires to save his life will lose it, but whoever loses his life for my sake will save it. ²⁵ For what profit is it to a man if he gains the whole world, and loses or forfeits his own self? ²⁶ For whoever is ashamed of me and of my words, of him will the Son of Man be ashamed when he comes in his glory and in the glory of the Father and of the holy angels. ²⁷ But I tell you truly, there are some standing here who will never taste death before they see the kingdom of God."

²⁸ Now about eight days after these sayings, he took with him Peter and John and James, and went up on the mountain to pray. ²⁹ And as he was praying, the appearance of his face was altered, and his robe became white and glistening. ³⁰ And behold, two men talked with him, Moses and Elijah, ³¹ who appeared in glory and spoke of his departure, which he was about to accomplish at Jerusalem. ³² But Peter and those with him were heavy with sleep; and when they were fully awake, they saw his glory and the two men who stood with him. ³³ As the men were parting from him, Peter said to Jesus, "Master, it is good

9:11 Alx[**he welcomed them**], Byz[he received them (DRA, KJV, MRD, NAB, NKJ)]; Alx/Major[**and healing**], Byz[and healed (ASV, DRA, ESV, HCS, KJV, MRD, NAB, NET, NIV, NJB, NKJ, NLT, NRS, REB, RSV, TEV)].
9:12 Alx/Byz[**to go to the surrounding villages**], Major[to depart to the surrounding villages (~NLT, ~TLB)].
9:14 Alx/Byz[**For there were**], Minor[And there were (DRA, NAB, NET, NIV, TEV)]; Alx[**about fifty each**], Byz[omits about (DRA, KJV, MRD, NKJ)].
9:15 Alx[**made them all sit down**], Byz[had them all sit down (ESV, HCS, JNT, NAS, NAU, ~NET, ~NIV, ~NLT, ~REB, ~TEV, ~TLB)].
9:18 Alx/Byz[**were with him**], Minor[met with him (NJB, NKJ, TEV)].
9:20 Alx/Byz[**Peter**], Alt/Peshitta[Simon (MRD)], Alt[*without textual foundation* Cephas (~JNT)].
9:22 Alx/Byz[**be raised**], Major[rise (DRA, MRD, TLB)].
9:23 Alx/Byz[**take up his cross daily**], Major[take up his cross].
9:25 Alx/Byz[**what profit is it to a man**], Minor[what does it profit a man (ESV, NET, NLT, NRS, REB, RSV)].
9:26 Alx/Byz[**of me and of my words**], Minor[of me and of mine].
9:28 Alx/Byz[**Peter**], Alt/Peshitta[Simon (MRD)], Alt[*without textual foundation* Cephas (~JNT)].
9:31 **departure** *Greek* exodus.
9:32 Alx/Byz[**Peter**], Alt/Peshitta[Simon (MRD)], Alt[*without textual foundation* Cephas (~JNT)]; **And when they were fully awake** *or* But since they had stayed awake.
9:33 Alx/Byz[**Peter**], Alt/Peshitta[Simon (MRD)], Alt[*without textual foundation* Cephas (~JNT)].

for us to be here; and let us make three tabernacles: one for you, one for Moses, and one for Elijah" – not knowing what he said. ³⁴ While he was saying this, a cloud came and overshadowed them; and they were afraid as they entered the cloud. ³⁵ And a voice came out of the cloud, saying, "This is my Son, my Chosen; listen to him!" ³⁶ When the voice had spoken, Jesus was found alone. But they kept quiet, and told no one in those days any of the things they had seen.

³⁷ The next day, when they had come down from the mountain, a great crowd met him. ³⁸ And behold, a man from the crowd cried aloud, "Teacher, I beg you to look upon my son, for he is my only child. ³⁹ And behold, a spirit seizes him, and he suddenly cries out; it convulses him so that he foams at the mouth, and will hardly leave him, bruising him. ⁴⁰ I begged your disciples to cast it out, but they could not." ⁴¹ Then Jesus answered, "O faithless and perverse generation, how long shall I be with you and bear with you? Bring here your son." ⁴² While he was coming, the demon threw him and convulsed him. But Jesus rebuked the unclean spirit, and healed the boy, and gave him back to his father. ⁴³ And they were all amazed at the majesty of God.

But while everyone was marveling at all that he was doing, he said to his disciples, ⁴⁴ "Let these words sink into your ears, for the Son of Man is about to be betrayed into the hands of men." ⁴⁵ But they did not understand this saying, and it was hidden from them so that they did not perceive it; and they were afraid to ask him about this saying.

⁴⁶ And an argument arose among them as to which of them would be the greatest. ⁴⁷ Jesus, knowing the thought of their heart, took a little child and set him by him, ⁴⁸ and said to them, "Whoever receives this little child in my name receives me, and whoever receives me receives him who sent me. For he who is least among you all is the one who is great."

⁴⁹ Now John answered, "Master, we saw a man casting out demons in your name, and we were forbidding him because he does not follow with us." ⁵⁰ But Jesus said to him, "Do not forbid him, for he that is not against you is for you."

⁵¹ When the time drew near for him to be received up, he set his face to go to Jerusalem. ⁵² And he sent messengers on ahead, who went and entered a village of the

---

9:34 Alx[**as they entered the cloud**], Byz[as they entered that cloud (~TEV, ~TLB)], Alt/Peshitta[as they saw Moses and Elijah go up into the cloud (MRD)].

9:35 Alx[**Chosen**], Byz[Beloved (DRA, KJV, MRD, NKJ)].

9:37 Alx[**The next day**], Byz[In the next day (ASV, ESV, KJV, NAB, NAS, NAU, NET, NJB, NKJ, NRS, RSV)].

9:38 Alx[**cried aloud**], Byz[cried out (~ASV, DRA, ESV, HCS, ~JNT, KJV, MRD, NAB, NAS, ~NAU, NET, NIV, NJB, NKJ, NLT, ~NRS, REB, ~RSV, ~TEV, TLB)]; Alx/Major[**to look**], Byz[look (DRA, JNT, KJV, ~MRD, NAB, NKJ, TEV, ~TLB)].

9:39 Alx/Byz[**hardly leave him**], Minor[only with difficulty leave him (JNT, NAB, NAU, NKJ)]; **he suddenly cries out** *or* it suddenly cries out.

9:41 Alx[**Bring here your son**], Byz[Bring your son here (ESV, HCS, JNT, KJV, NAB, NAS, NAU, NET, NIV, NJB, NKJ, NLT, NRS, REB, RSV, TEV, TLB)].

9:42 Alx/Byz[**But Jesus rebuked...gave him back to his father 43**], Minor[43 But Jesus rebuked him...gave him back to his father (DRA)].

9:43 Alx[**all that he was doing**], Byz[all that Jesus did (~ASV, ~DRA, ~ESV, ~JNT, KJV, MRD, ~NAB, ~NET, NIV, ~NJB, NKJ, ~NLT, ~REB, ~RSV, ~TEV, ~TLB)]; *DRA combines verse 43 into verse 44.*

9:47 Alx[**Jesus, knowing**], Byz[Jesus, seeing (ASV, DRA, KJV, ~NET, NKJ, ~NRS, RSV)].

9:48 Alx/Byz[**one who is great**], Major[one who shall be great (KJV, MRD, NKJ)].

9:49 Alx/Byz[**casting out demons**], Minor[casting out the demons]; Alx[**were forbidding**], Byz[forbade (ASV, DRA, ~ESV, ~HCS, JNT, KJV, MRD, ~NAB, ~NAS, ~NAU, ~NET, ~NIV, ~NJB, NKJ, NLT, ~NRS, ~REB, RSV, ~TEV, TLB)].

9:50 Alx[**But Jesus said**], Byz[And Jesus said (DRA, ~HCS, ~JNT, KJV, ~MRD, ~NAB, ~NIV, ~REB, ~TEV)]; Alx/Major[**Do not forbid him**], Byz[*adds* for he is not against you]; Alx/Byz[**you is for you**], Major[us is for us (KJV, NKJ)].

9:52 Alx/Byz[**village**], Minor[city (DRA)].

Samaritans, to make ready for him; [53] but the people did not receive him, because his face was set for Jerusalem. [54] And when the disciples James and John saw this, they said, "Lord, do you want us to command fire to come down from heaven and consume them?" [55] But he turned and rebuked them, [56] and they went on to another village.

[57] And as they were going along the road, a man said to him, "I will follow you wherever you go." [58] And Jesus said to him, "Foxes have holes and birds of the air have nests, but the Son of Man has nowhere to lay his head." [59] To another he said, "Follow me." But he said, "[Lord,] let me first go and bury my father." [60] He said to him, "Let the dead bury their own dead, but you go and proclaim the kingdom of God." [61] Still another said, "I will follow you, Lord; but first let me go back and say farewell to those at my home." [62] Jesus said [to him], "No one who puts the hand to the plow and looks back is fit for the kingdom of God."

10 [1] After this the Lord appointed seventy-[two] others, and sent them ahead of him, two [by two,] into every town and place where he himself was about to go. [2] And he said to them, "The harvest is plentiful, but the laborers are few; pray therefore the Lord of the harvest to send out laborers into his harvest. [3] Go your way; behold, I send you out as lambs among wolves. [4] Carry no purse, no bag, no sandals; and greet no one on the road. [5] Whatever house you enter, first say, 'Peace to this house.' [6] And if a son of peace is there, your peace will rest on him; if not, it will return to you. [7] And remain in the same house, eating and drinking what they give, for the laborer deserves his wages. Do not go from house to house. [8] Whenever you enter a town and they receive you, eat what is set before you. [9] Heal the sick there and say to them, 'The kingdom of God has come near to you.' [10] But whenever you enter a town and they do not receive you, go into its streets and say, [11] 'Even the dust of your town that clings to the feet, we wipe off against

---

9:54 Alx[**the disciples**], Byz[his disciples (ASV, DRA, ESV, KJV, MRD, NAS, NAU, NET, NKJ, ~NLT, NRS, RSV, ~TLB)]; Alx[**consume them**], Byz[*adds* just as Elijah did (KJV, MRD, NKJ)].

9:55-56 Alx[*text*], Byz[But he turned and rebuked them and said, "You do not know of what kind of spirit you are; 56 the Son of Man came not to destroy men's lives but to save them." And they went on to another village (DRA)], Major[But he turned and rebuked them and said, "You do not know of what sort of spirit you are, 56 for the Son of Man came not to destroy men's lives but to save them." And they went on to another village (KJV, MRD, NAS, NAU, NKJ)].

9:57 Alx[**And as they were going**], Byz[And it happened as they were going (DRA, KJV, NKJ)]; Alx[**I will follow you**], Byz[Lord, I will follow you (KJV, MRD, NKJ)].

9:59 Alx/Byz[**Lord**], Minor[*omits* (NAS, NJB, REB, TLB)].

9:60 Alx[**He said to him**], Byz[Jesus said to him (DRA, ESV, JNT, KJV, MRD, NET, NIV, NKJ, NLT, NRS, REB, TEV, TLB)].

9:62 Alx/Byz[**Jesus said to him**], Minor[*omits* to him (NIV)]; Alx[**the hand to the plow**], Byz[his hand to the plow (ASV, DRA, ESV, HCS, JNT, KJV, MRD, NAS, NAU, NET, NIV, NKJ, REB, RSV, ~TLB)]; Alx[**for the kingdom of God**], Byz[in the kingdom of God (JNT, NIV)].

10:1 Alx/Byz[**After this the Lord appointed**], Minor[After these things, Jesus separated from among his disciples (MRD)]; Alx[**seventy-two**], Byz[seventy (ASV, HCS, JNT, KJV, MRD, NAS, NAU, NKJ, NRS, RSV, TLB)], Metzger[*Kurt Aland holds that* **seventy-two** *should be written without brackets both here and in verse 17*]; Alx[**others**], Byz[*adds* also (DRA, KJV, NKJ)]; Alx[**two by two**], Byz[two (~NAB, ~NAU, ~NJB, ~NLT, ~NRS, ~REB, ~TLB)].

10:2 Alx[**And he said**], Byz[Therefore he said (KJV, NKJ)].

10:4 Alx[**no sandals**], Byz[nor sandals (DRA, ~HCS, KJV, MRD, ~NET, ~NIV, NKJ, NLT, ~REB, ~TEV, ~TLB)], Alt[*omits with no textual foundation* (JNT)]; Alx/Byz[**and greet**], Minor[*omits* and (HCS, NJB; ~REB, TEV)].

10:6 Alx/Byz[**a son of peace**], Minor[the son of peace (DRA, KJV, MRD, ~NLT, ~TLB)].

10:7 Alx[**deserves his wages**], Byz[is worthy of his wages (ASV, DRA, HCS, KJV, MRD, NAS, NAU, NKJ, TLB)].

10:9 **come near to you** *or* come upon you.

10:11 Alx[**the feet**], Byz[our feet (ASV, ESV, HCS, JNT, MRD, NAB, NAS, NAU, NET, NIV, NJB, NLT, NRS, REB, RSV, TEV, TLB)], Major[us (DRA, KJV, NKJ)]; Alx[**has come near** *or* has come],

you. Nevertheless know this, that the kingdom of God has come near.' [12] I tell you, it will be more tolerable on that day for Sodom than for that town.

[13] "Woe to you, Chorazin! Woe to you, Bethsaida! For if the mighty works which were done in you had been done in Tyre and Sidon, they would have repented long ago, sitting in sackcloth and ashes. [14] But it will be more tolerable for Tyre and Sidon in the judgment than for you. [15] And you, Capernaum,

will you be exalted to heaven?
        You shall go down to Hades!

[16] "He who hears you hears me, he who rejects you rejects me, and he who rejects me rejects him who sent me."

[17] The seventy-[two] returned with joy, saying, "Lord, even the demons are subject to us in your name." [18] And he said to them, "I saw Satan fall like lightning from heaven. [19] Behold, I have given you authority to trample on serpents and scorpions, and over all the power of the enemy; and nothing can hurt you. [20] Nevertheless do not rejoice in this, that the spirits are subject to you, but rejoice that your names have been inscribed in heaven."

[21] At that hour he rejoiced [in] the Holy Spirit and said, "I thank you, Father, Lord of heaven and earth, that you have hidden these things from the wise and prudent and revealed them to babes. Yes, Father, for so it was your good pleasure. [22] All things have been delivered to me by my Father, and no one knows who the Son is except the Father, and who the Father is except the Son, and the one to whom the Son chooses to reveal him." [23] Then he turned to his disciples and said privately, "Blessed are the eyes which see what you see. [24] For I tell you that many prophets and kings desired to see what you see, and did not see it, and to hear what you hear, and did not hear it."

[25] And behold, a lawyer stood up to put him to the test, saying, "Teacher, what shall I do to inherit eternal life?" [26] He said to him, "What is written in the law? How do you read?" [27] And he answered, "'You shall love the Lord your God with all your heart, and with all your soul, and with all your strength, and with all your mind'; and 'your neighbor as yourself.'" [28] And he said to him, "You have answered right; do this, and you will live." [29] But he, wanting to justify himself, said to Jesus, "And who is my neighbor?" [30] Jesus said: "A man was going down from Jerusalem to Jericho, and he fell among robbers, who stripped him of his clothing, beat him, and departed, leaving him half dead. [31] Now by chance a priest was going down that road, and when he saw him he passed by on the other side. [32] So likewise,

---

Byz[adds unto you or upon you (KJV, MRD, NKJ, TEV, TLB)].

10:12 Alx/Major[I tell you], Byz[But I tell you (KJV, NKJ)].

10:14 Alx/Byz[in the judgment], Minor[in the day of judgment (MRD, NLT, TEV, TLB)].

10:15 Alx[Capernaum Greek Capharnaum], Byz[Capernaum]; Alx[will you be exalted to heaven? You shall], Byz[who is exalted to heaven, shall (DRA, KJV, MRD, NKJ)]; Alx[go down to Hades], Byz[be brought down to Hades (ASV, DRA, ESV, JNT, KJV, MRD, NAS, NAU, NET, NJB, NKJ, NRS, REB, RSV, TEV, TLB)].

10:17 Alx[seventy-two], Byz[seventy (ASV, HCS, JNT, KJV, MRD, NAS, NAU, NKJ, NRS, RSV, TLB)].

10:19 Alx[I have given], Byz[I give (KJV, MRD, NKJ)]; Alx/Byz[nothing can hurt you], Minor[nothing can hurt us].

10:20 Alx/Byz[but rejoice], Minor[but rather rejoice (KJV, NJB, NKJ, TEV)]; Alx[have been inscribed], Byz[were written (ASV, DRA, ESV, HCS, KJV, MRD, NAB, NAS, NAU, NET, NIV, NJB, NKJ, NLT, NRS, REB, RSV, TEV, TLB)].

10:21 Alx[he rejoiced], Byz[Jesus rejoiced (KJV, MRD, NET, NIV, NKJ, NLT, NRS, REB, TEV)]; Alx[in the Holy Spirit], Byz[in the spirit (KJV, NKJ)]; I thank you or I praise you, good pleasure or gracious will.

10:22 Alx[text], Byz[begins verse And turning to his disciples he said (MRD)].

10:25 Alx[saying], Byz[and saying (DRA, MRD, NAB)].

10:27 Alx/Byz[the Lord your God], Minor[the Lord God]; ~Deuteronomy 6:5, Leviticus 19:18.

10:30 Alx[Jesus said], Byz[But Jesus said (DRA, KJV, NKJ)].

10:32 Alx/Byz[when he came Greek when he became to be coming], Minor[when he was at (DRA)

a Levite, when he came to the place and saw him, passed by on the other side. ³³ But a Samaritan, as he journeyed, came where he was; and seeing, he had compassion. ³⁴ He went to him and bandaged his wounds, pouring on oil and wine; then he set him on his own beast and brought him to an inn, and took care of him. ³⁵ The next day he took out two denarii and gave them to the innkeeper and said, 'Take care of him; and whatever more you spend, I will repay you when I come back.' ³⁶ Which of these three do you think was a neighbor to the man who fell among the robbers?" ³⁷ He said, "The one who showed mercy on him." And Jesus said to him, "Go and do likewise."

³⁸ And as they went on their way, he entered a village; and a woman named Martha welcomed him. ³⁹ And she had a sister called Mary, [who] also sat at the Lord's feet and listened to his word. ⁴⁰ But Martha was distracted with much serving; and she went to him and said, "Lord, do you not care that my sister left me to serve alone? Tell her then to help me." ⁴¹ But the Lord answered her, "Martha, Martha, you are worried and troubled about many things; ⁴² but only one thing is needed for Mary has chosen that good part, which will not be taken away from her."

11

¹ He was praying in a certain place, and when he ceased, one of his disciples said to him, "Lord, teach us to pray, as John taught his disciples." ² He said to them, "When you pray, say:

'Father, hallowed be your name.
        Your kingdom come.
³   Give us each day our daily bread.
⁴   And forgive us our sins,
            for we ourselves also forgive everyone
                who is indebted to us.
        And lead us not into temptation.'"

---

others when he came].

10:33 Alx[**and seeing, he had compassion**], Byz[and seeing him, he had compassion (ASV, DRA, ESV, HCS, JNT, KJV, MRD, NAS, NAU, NET, NIV, NJB, NKJ, NLT, NRS, REB, RSV, TEV, TLB)].

10:35 Alx[**The next day**], Byz[*adds* when he departed (KJV, NKJ)]; Alx[**and said**], Byz[*adds* to him (KJV, NKJ, NLT, TEV, TLB)].

10:36 Alx[**Which of these**], Byz[Now which of these (KJV, MRD, NKJ, NLT, TLB)].

10:37 Alx[**And Jesus said**], Byz[Then Jesus said (HCS, KJV, NAU, NET, NKJ, NLT, TLB)].

10:38 Alx[**And as they went**], Byz[And it happened as they went (DRA, KJV, MRD, NKJ)]; Alx[**he entered a village**], Byz[and he entered a village (DRA, KJV, MRD, NKJ)]; Alx[**Martha welcomed him**], Byz[Martha welcomed him into her house (ASV, DRA, ESV, HCS, JNT, KJV, MRD, NAS, NAU, NIV, NJB, NKJ, NLT, NRS, RSV, TEV, TLB)], Minor[Martha welcomed him into the house (~NET)].

10:39 Alx/Byz[**who also sat**], Minor[*omits* who (MRD, NLT, TLB)]; Alx[**the Lord's feet**], Byz[the feet of Jesus (KJV, NKJ, TLB)].

10:40 Alx/Byz[**my sister left me**], Major[my sister was leaving me (~JNT, ~NJB, ~NLT, ~TLB)].

10:41 Alx[**the Lord**], Byz[Jesus (KJV, MRD, NKJ)].

10:41-42 Alx/Byz[**you are worried and troubled about many things; 42 but only one thing is needed**], Minor[*omits*].

10:42 Alx/Byz[**only one thing is needed**], Minor[only a few things are needed *others* only a few things are needed, or only one (NAS, NJB)]; Alx[**for Mary** *Greek* Miriam], Byz[but Mary *Greek* Maria (DRA, ESV, HCS, JNT, KJV, MRD, NAB, NET, NIV, NJB, NKJ, NLT, NRS, REB, RSV, TEV, TLB)].

11:2 Alx/Byz[**He said**], Jesus said (MRD, NLT, TEV)]; Alx/Byz[**When you pray, say**], Minor[*adds* not vain repetitions, as the Gentiles do: for they think that they shall be heard for their many words, but pray, saying]; Alx[**Father**], Byz[Our Father in heaven (KJV, MRD, NKJ)], Alx[**Your kingdom come**], Byz[*adds* your will be done on earth as it is in heaven (KJV, MRD, NKJ)], Minor[Your kingdom come on us *others* Your Holy Spirit come on us and cleanse us].

11:3 **daily bread** *or* bread for tomorrow.

11:4 Alx/Byz[**4 And forgive us our sins**], Alt[And forgive us our sins 4 (NJB)]; Alx[**lead us not into temptation**], Byz[*adds* but deliver us from evil (KJV, MRD, NKJ)].

⁵ And he said to them, "Which of you who has a friend will go to him at midnight and say to him, 'Friend, lend me three loaves; ⁶ for a friend of mine has come to me on a journey, and I have nothing to set before him'; ⁷ and he will answer from within, 'Do not bother me; the door is now shut, and my children are with me in bed; I cannot get up and give you anything'? ⁸ I tell you, though he will not get up and give to him because he is his friend, yet because of his persistence he will rise and give him as much as he needs. ⁹ So I say to you, ask, and it will be given to you; seek, and you will find; knock, and it will be opened to you. ¹⁰ For everyone who asks receives, and he who seeks finds, and to him who knocks it [will be] opened. ¹¹ And what father from you, if his son asks for a fish, will instead of a fish give him a serpent? ¹² Or if he asks for an egg, will give him a scorpion? ¹³ If you then, who are evil, know how to give good gifts to your children, how much more will your heavenly Father give the Holy Spirit to those who ask him!"

¹⁴ Now he was casting out a demon [that was] mute. So it was, when the demon had gone out, that the mute man spoke; and the multitudes marveled. ¹⁵ But some of them said, "He casts out demons by Beelzebul, the prince of demons." ¹⁶ Others, testing him, sought from him a sign from heaven. ¹⁷ But he, knowing their thoughts, said to them: "Every kingdom divided against itself is laid waste, and a house divided against itself falls. ¹⁸ If Satan also is divided against himself, how will his kingdom stand? For you say that I cast out demons by Beelzebul. ¹⁹ And if I cast out demons by Beelzebul, by whom do your sons cast them out? Therefore they will be your judges. ²⁰ But if [I] cast out demons by the finger of God, then the kingdom of God has come upon you. ²¹ When a strong man, fully armed, guards his own palace, his goods are in peace. ²² But when one stronger than he attacks him and overpowers him, he takes away his armor in which he trusted, and divides his spoils. ²³ He who is not with me is against me, and he who does not gather with me scatters.

²⁴ "When an unclean spirit goes out of a man, he goes through dry places, seeking rest; and finding none, [then] he says, 'I will return to my house from which I came.' ²⁵ And when he comes, he finds it swept and put in order. ²⁶ Then he goes and takes with him

11:5 Alx/Major[**and say to him** or and should say to him], Byz[and say to him or and shall say to him].
11:6 Alx[**a friend of mine**], Byz[*omits* of mine (MRD)].
11:10 Alx/Byz[**will be opened**], Minor[is opened (MRD, TLB)].
11:11 Alx/Byz[**what father from you, if his son asks**], Major[what father of you, if his son asks (ASV, ~ESV, ~HCS, ~JNT, ~KJV, ~MRD, ~NAB, NAS, NAU, ~NET, NIV, ~NJB, ~NKJ, ~NLT, ~NRS, ~REB, ~RSV, TEV, ~TLB)], Alt/Vulgate[which of you, if he asks his father (DRA)]; Alx[**asks for a fish, will instead of a fish give him a serpent?**], Byz[asks for bread, he will not give him a stone will he? Or if he asks for a fish, he will not instead of a fish give him a serpent, will he? (~ASV, ~DRA, ~KJV, ~MRD, ~NKJ, ~TLB)], Minor[asks for a fish, he will not instead of a fish give him a serpent, will he? (NAS, NAU)].
11:12 Alx[**Or if he asks for an egg, will give him a scorpion?**], Byz[Or if he asks for an egg, he will not give him a scorpion, will he? (NAS, NAU)].
11:13 Alx/Byz[**your heavenly Father give the Holy Spirit**], Minor[the Father give the Holy Spirit from heaven (JNT)]; Alx/Major[**the Holy Spirit** Greek Holy Spirit], Byz/Vulgate[the Good Spirit or a good spirit (DRA)].
11:14 Alx/Byz[**a demon that was mute**], Minor[a mute demon]; Alx/Major[**marveled**], Byz[began to marvel].
11:15, 18, 19 Alx/Byz[**Beelzebul**], Vulgate/Peshitta[Beelzebub (ASV, DRA, KJV, MRD, NIV, NKJ, ~NLT, ~TLB)].
11:15 Alx/Byz[**the prince**], Major[prince (REB)].
11:23 Alx/Byz[**scatters**], Minor[*adds* me (NLT, TLB)].
11:24 Alx[**then he says**], Byz[*omits* then (ASV, DRA, ESV, JNT, KJV, MRD, NAB, NAS, NAU, NJB, NKJ, NLT, NRS, REB, RSV, TEV, ~TLB)].
11:25 Alx/Byz[**finds it swept**], Minor[finds it empty, swept].
11:26 Alx/Byz[**they enter**], Major[they come (JNT, ~REB, TEV)].

seven other spirits more wicked than himself, and they enter and dwell there; and the last state of that man is worse than the first."

27 As he said these things, a woman in the crowd raised her voice and said to him, "Blessed is the womb that bore you, and the breasts that nursed you!" 28 But he said, "Blessed rather are those who hear and keep the word of God!"

29 When the crowds were increasing, he began to say, "This generation is an evil generation. It seeks a sign, but no sign will be given to it except the sign of Jonah. 30 For as Jonah became a sign to the Ninevites, so also the Son of Man will be to this generation. 31 The queen of the South will rise at the judgment with the men of this generation and condemn them; for she came from the ends of the earth to hear the wisdom of Solomon, and behold, someone greater than Solomon is here. 32 The Ninevite men will stand up at the judgment with this generation and condemn it; for they repented at the preaching of Jonah, and behold, someone greater than Jonah is here.

33 "No one after lighting a lamp puts it in a cellar [or under a basket], but on a stand, that those who come in may see the light. 34 The lamp of the body is your eye. When your eye is good, your whole body also is full of light. But when it is bad, your body also is full of darkness. 35 Therefore be careful that the light in you is not darkness. 36 If then your whole body is full of light, having no part dark, it will be completely lighted, as when the bright shining of a lamp gives you light."

37 While he was speaking, a Pharisee asked him to dine with him; so he went in and sat at table. 38 The Pharisee was surprised to see that he did not first wash before dinner. 39 But the Lord said to him, "Now you Pharisees clean the outside of the cup and dish, but inside you are full of greed and wickedness. 40 You foolish ones! Did not he who made the outside make the inside also? 41 But give for alms those things which are within; and behold, everything is clean for you. 42 But woe to you Pharisees! For you tithe mint and rue and all manner of herbs, and neglect justice and the love of God. But these you ought to have done, without neglecting the others. 43 Woe to you Pharisees! For you love the best seats in the synagogues and greetings in the marketplaces. 44 Woe to you! For you are like graves which are not seen, and men walk over them without knowing it."

11:28 Alx[**hear and keep the word of God**], Byz[hear the word of God and keep it (ASV, DRA, ESV, HCS, JNT, KJV, MRD, NAB, NAS, NAU, NET, NIV, NJB, NKJ, NLT, NRS, REB, RSV, TEV, TLB)].

11:29 Alx/Byz[**this generation is an evil generation**], Major[this is an evil generation (KJV, MRD, NJB, NKJ, NLT, REB, TEV)]; Alx/Byz[**It seeks a sign**], Major[It seeks for a sign (ASV, ESV, JNT, NAS, NAU, NET, NIV, NJB, NRS, TEV, TLB)]; Alx[**Jonah**], Byz[the prophet Jonah (DRA, KJV, MRD, NKJ)].

11:30 Alx/Major[**the Son of Man will be**], Byz[*adds* a sign (MRD)].

11:31, 32 **someone** *or* something.

11:32 Alx[**The Ninevite men**], Byz[The men of Nineveh (ASV, DRA, ESV, HCS, JNT, KJV, MRD, NAB, NAS, NAU, NET, NIV, NJB, NKJ, NLT, NRS, REB, RSV, TEV, TLB)].

11:33 Alx/Byz[**cellar**], Minor[secret place (DRA, JNT, KJV, MRD, NAB, NET, NIV, NJB, NKJ, NLT, TEV, TLB)]; Alx/Byz[**or under a basket**], Minor[*omit* (NRS, REB, TLB)]; Alx[**see the light**], Byz[see the brightness].

11:34 Alx[**The lamp of the body is your eye. When your eye is good**], Byz[The lamp of the body is the eye. Therefore, when your eye is good (KJV, MRD, NKJ)].

11:37 Alx/Major[**While he was speaking**], Byz[*adds* these things ()]; Alx[**a Pharisee asked** *Greek* A Pharisee asks]; Byz[a certain Pharisee was asking (DRA, KJV, MRD, NKJ, ~NLT, ~TLB)].

11:41 Alx/Major[**everything is clean**], Byz[all things are clean (ASV, DRA, KJV, NAS, NAU, NKJ, ~NLT, ~REB, ~TLB)].

11:42 Alx/Byz[**But these you ought to have done, without neglecting the others**], Major[These you ought to have done, without leaving the others undone (~ASV, ~DRA, ~ESV, ~HCS, ~JNT, KJV, ~MRD, ~NAB, NIV, ~NJB, NKJ, ~NLT, ~NRS, ~REB, ~RSV, ~TEV, ~TLB)], Minor[*omits*].

11:44 Alx[**Woe to you**], Byz[*adds* scribes and Pharisees, hypocrites (KJV, MRD, NKJ)].

⁴⁵ One of the lawyers answered him, "Teacher, by saying these things you reproach us also." ⁴⁶ And he said, "Woe to you also, lawyers! For you load men with burdens hard to bear, and you yourselves do not touch the burdens with one of your fingers. ⁴⁷ Woe to you! For you build the tombs of the prophets, but your fathers killed them. ⁴⁸ So you are witnesses that you approve of the deeds of your fathers; for they killed them, and you build. ⁴⁹ Therefore the wisdom of God also said, 'I will send them prophets and apostles, some of whom they will kill and persecute,' ⁵⁰ that the blood of all the prophets which has been poured out from the foundation of the world may be required of this generation, ⁵¹ from the blood of Abel to the blood of Zechariah, who perished between the altar and the sanctuary. Yes, I tell you, it shall be required of this generation. ⁵² Woe to you lawyers; for you have taken away the key of knowledge! You did not enter in yourselves, and you hindered those who were entering." ⁵³ As he went away from there, the scribes and the Pharisees began to press him hard, and to provoke him to speak of many things, ⁵⁴ lying in wait for him, to catch at something he might say.

12 ¹ In the meantime, when so many thousands of the multitude had gathered together that they trampled one another, he began to say to his disciples first of all, "Beware of the leaven of the Pharisees, which is hypocrisy. ² There is nothing covered up that will not be revealed, or hidden that will not be known. ³ Therefore whatever you have said in the dark will be heard in the light, and what you have whispered in the ear in the inner rooms will be proclaimed from the housetops.

⁴ "I tell you, my friends, do not be afraid of those who kill the body, and after that have no more that they can do. ⁵ But I will show you whom you should fear: fear him who, after he has killed, has power to cast into hell; yes, I tell you, fear him! ⁶ Are not five sparrows sold for two pennies? And not one of them is forgotten before God. ⁷ Indeed, the very hairs of your head are all numbered. Fear not; you are of more value than many sparrows.

⁸ "I tell you, whoever would acknowledge me before men, the Son of Man will also acknowledge him before the angels of God. ⁹ But he who denies me before men will be denied before the angels of God. ¹⁰ And everyone who speaks a word against the Son of Man will be forgiven; but he who blasphemes against the Holy Spirit will not be forgiven. ¹¹

11:47 Alx/Byz[**but your fathers**], Minor[and your fathers (ASV, DRA, ~ESV, HCS, KJV, ~MRD, ~NAB, NAS, NAU, ~NET, NIV, ~NJB, NKJ, ~NLT, ~NRS, ~REB, ~RSV, ~TEV, ~TLB)].

11:48 Alx[**you are witnesses**], Byz[you witness (DRA, JNT, KJV, MRD, NAB, NET, NIV, NJB, NKJ, ~NLT, REB, TEV, TLB)]; Alx[**and you build**], Byz[*adds* their tombs (ASV, DRA, ESV, HCS, KJV, MRD, NAS, NAU, NET, NIV, NKJ, NLT, NRS, REB, RSV, TEV, ~TLB)].

11:49 Alx[**kill and persecute**], Byz[kill and drive out (TLB)].

11:50 Alx[**has been poured out**], Byz[is poured out (~ASV, ~DRA, ~ESV, ~HCS, ~NKJ, ~NAB, ~NAS, ~NAU, ~NKJ, ~NLT, ~NRS, ~REB, ~RSV, ~TEV, ~TLB)].

11:53 Alx[**As he went away from there**], Byz[And as he was saying these things to them (DRA, KJV, MRD, NKJ, ~TLB)].

11:54 Alx[*text*], Byz[lying in wait for him, and seeking to catch at something he might say, that they might accuse him (DRA, KJV, MRD, NKJ, TLB)], Minor[*omits* for him (~JNT, ~NAB, ~NIV, NJB, NLT, REB, ~TLB)].

12:1 Alx/Byz[**disciples first of all, "Beware**], Minor[disciples, "First of all, beware (MRD, TLB)].

12:5 **power** *or* authority, **hell** *Greek* Gehenna.

12:6 **pennies** *Greek* assarion.

12:7 Alx[**Fear not**], Byz[Fear not, therefore (DRA, KJV, MRD, NKJ, TEV)].

12:8 Alx/Byz[**whoever would acknowledge**], Minor[whoever will acknowledge (ASV, DRA, ~ESV, ~HCS, ~JNT, KJV, MRD, ~NAB, ~NAS, ~NAU, ~NET, ~NIV, ~NJB, ~NKJ, ~NLT, ~NRS, ~REB, ~RSV, ~TEV)].

12:11 Alx/Byz[**But when they bring you**], Minor[*omits* But (HCS, JNT, NAB, NAU, NIV, NJB, NRS, REB, TEV)]; Alx/Byz[**how or what**], Minor[*omit* or what (ESV, HCS, JNT, MRD, NET, NIV, NJB, NLT, NRS, REB, TEV, TLB)].

But when they bring you to the synagogues and rulers and authorities, do not worry about how or what you should answer, or what you are to say; [12] for the Holy Spirit will teach you in that very hour what you ought to say."

[13] Someone from the crowd said to him, "Teacher, tell my brother to divide with me the inheritance." [14] But he said to him, "Man, who made me a judge or an arbitrator over you?" [15] And he said to them, "Take heed, and beware of all covetousness; for a man's life does not consist in the abundance of his possessions." [16] And he told them a parable, saying: "The ground of a certain rich man yielded plentifully. [17] And he thought to himself, 'What shall I do, since I have no place to store my crops?' [18] And he said, 'I will do this: I will pull down my barns and build larger ones; and there I will store all the wheat and my goods. [19] And I will say to my soul, "Soul, you have many goods laid up for many years; take your ease; eat, drink, and be merry."' [20] But God said to him, 'Fool! This night your soul will be required of you; then whose will those things be which you have prepared?' [21] So is he who lays up treasure for himself, and is not rich toward God."

[22] Then he said to [his] disciples, "Therefore I tell you, do not worry about life, what you will eat; nor about the body, what you will put on. [23] For life is more than food, and the body more than clothing. [24] Consider the ravens: they neither sow nor reap, they have neither storehouse nor barn, and yet God feeds them. Of how much more value are you than the birds! [25] And which of you by worrying can add a cubit to his span of life? [26] If you then are not able to do this very little thing, why are you anxious about the rest? [27] Consider the lilies, how they grow; they neither toil nor spin; yet I tell you, even Solomon in all his glory was not arrayed like one of these. [28] But if God so clothes the grass in the field, which today is and tomorrow is thrown into the oven, how much more will he clothe you, O you of little faith! [29] And do not seek what you will eat and what you will drink, and do not have an anxious mind. [30] For all the nations of the world seek after these things, and your Father knows that you need them. [31] But seek his kingdom, and these things will be given to

---

12:13 Alx[**Someone from the crowd said to him**], Byz[Someone said to him from the crowd (~NLT, ~TLB)]; Alx/Major[**to divide with me the inheritance**], Byz[to divide the inheritance with me (ASV, DRA, ESV, HCS, KJV, MRD, NAB, NAS, NAU, NET, NIV, NKJ, NLT, NRS, REB, RSV, TLB)].

12:14 Alx/Byz[**or an arbitrator**], Minor[omits (~NLT, ~TLB)].

12:15 Alx/Byz[**all covetousness**], Major[omits all (KJV, NKJ)].

12:18 Alx[**all the wheat**], Byz[all my produce (~ASV, DRA, ~ESV, ~HCS, ~JNT, KJV, ~MRD, ~NAB, ~NAS, ~NAU, ~NET, ~NIV, ~NJB, NKJ, ~NLT, ~NRS, ~REB, ~RSV)], Minor[the produce (~TEV, ~TLB)].

12:19 Alx/Byz[**laid up for many years; take your ease; eat, drink, and be merry**], Minor[omits].

12:21 Alx/Byz[text], Minor[omits, others add Saying these things, he cried out, "He who has ears to hear, let him hear."].

12:22 Alx/Byz[**his disciples**], Minor[the disciples (TEV)]; Alx[**do not worry about life**], Byz[do not worry about your plural life (ASV, DRA, ESV, HCS, JNT, KJV, MRD, NAB, NAS, NAU, NET, NIV, NJB, NKJ, NRS, ~REB, RSV, ~TEV, ~TLB)]; Alx/Byz[**the body**], Minor[your body (ASV, DRA, ESV, JNT, MRD, NAB, NAS, NAU, NET, NIV, NJB, ~NLT, NRS, REB, RSV, TEV, ~TLB)]; Alx/Major[**the body**], Byz[your body (ASV, DRA, ESV, JNT, MRD, NAB, NAS, NAU, NET, NIV, NJB, ~NLT, NRS, REB, RSV, TEV, ~TLB)].

12:23 Alx[**For life**], Byz[Isn't the life…?], Major[The life (DRA, KJV, NIV, NKJ, REB, TEV)].

12:25 Alx[**a cubit**], Byz[one cubit (DRA, ESV, KJV, MRD, NAS, NAU, NIV, NJB, NKJ, NLT, NRS, TLB)]; **span of life** or height.

12:27 Alx/Byz[**Consider the lilies, how they grow; they neither toil nor spin**], Minor[Consider the lilies; how they neither spin nor weave (REB, TLB)].

12:28 Alx/Major[**in the field**], Byz[of the field (~NET, NIV, ~NJB, ~NLT, NRS, ~TEV, ~TLB)].

12:29 Alx/Byz[**and what you will drink**], Major[or what you will drink (DRA, KJV, MRD, NIV, NKJ, REB)].

12:31 Alx[**his kingdom, and these things**], Byz[the kingdom of God, and all these things (DRA, KJV, MRD, NKJ, NLT, TLB)].

you as well. 32 Do not fear, little flock, for it is your Father's good pleasure to give you the kingdom. 33 Sell your possessions, and give alms; provide yourselves purses that do not grow old, a treasure in the heavens that does not fail, where no thief approaches and no moth destroys. 34 For where your treasure is, there your heart will be also.

35 "Let your waist be girded and your lamps burning, 36 and be like men who are waiting for their master, when he should return from the wedding feast, so that they may open to him immediately when he comes and knocks. 37 Blessed are those servants whom the master finds watching when he comes. Truly, I say to you that he will gird himself and have them sit at table, and will come and serve them. 38 If in the second or in the third watch he comes and finds them so, blessed are they. 39 But know this, that if the owner of the house had known at what hour the thief was coming, he would not have allowed his house to be broken into. 40 You also must be ready, for the Son of Man is coming at an hour you do not expect."

41 Peter said, "Lord, are you telling this parable to us, or to all?" 42 And the Lord said, "Who then is the faithful, wise steward, whom his master will set over his household, to give them [their] portion of food at the proper time? 43 Blessed is that servant whom his master will find so doing when he comes. 44 Truly, I say to you, he will set him over all his possessions. 45 But if that servant says to himself, 'My master is delayed in coming,' and begins to beat the menservants and the maidservants, and to eat and drink and get drunk, 46 the master of that servant will come on a day when he does not expect him, and at an hour he is not aware of, and he will cut him to pieces and assign him a place with the unbelievers. 47 And that servant who knew his master's will, and did not ready himself or do according to his will, shall be beaten with many stripes. 48 But he who did not know, and committed things deserving of stripes, shall be beaten with few. From everyone who has been given much, much will be required; and to whom they entrusted much, of him they will ask the more.

49 "I came to cast fire on the earth, and how I wish it were already kindled! 50 But I have a baptism to be baptized with, and how distressed I am until it is accomplished! 51 Do you think that I came to give peace on earth? No, I tell you, but rather division. 52 For from now on there will be five in one house divided: three against two, and two against three.
53   They will be divided, father against son

12:36 Alx/Byz[**when he should return**], Minor[when he shall return (ASV, DRA, ~ESV, ~HCS, ~JNT, KJV, MRD, ~NAB, ~NAS, ~NAU, ~NET, ~NIV, ~NJB, NKJ, ~NLT, ~NRS, ~REB, ~RSV, ~TEV, ~TLB)].

12:38 Alx[**If in the second or in the third watch he comes**], Byz[If he comes in the second watch, or in the third]; Alx[**blessed are they**], Byz[blessed are those servants (ASV, DRA, ESV, HCS, JNT, KJV, MRD, NAB, NAS, NAU, NET, NIV, NJB, NKJ, NLT, NRS, RSV, TLB)], Minor[blessed be].

12:39 Alx[**he would not have allowed**], Byz[he would have watched and not allowed (ASV, DRA, KJV, MRD, NKJ, ~TLB)].

12:40 Alx[**You also must be ready**], Byz[Therefore you also must be ready (DRA, KJV, MRD, NKJ, REB, TLB)].

12:41 Alx[**Peter said**], Byz[*adds* to him (DRA, KJV, NKJ)], Minor[Simon Cephas said to him (~JNT, MRD)].

12:42 Alx[**And the Lord said**], Byz[But the Lord said (~HCS, ~JNT, ~NET, ~NIV, ~NJB, ~REB, ~TEV)]; Minor[And Jesus said (MRD)]; Alx[**the faithful, wise steward**], Byz[the faithful and wise steward (ASV, DRA, ESV, HCS, JNT, KJV, MRD, NAB, NAS, NAU, NET, NIV, NJB, NKJ, NRS, REB, RSV, TEV)]; Alx/Byz[**their portion** *Greek* the portion], Minor[a portion (~NLT, ~TLB)].

12:46 **cut him to pieces** *or* cut him off.

12:47 Alx[**his master's will**], Byz[his own master's will (~TLB)]; Alx[**or do according to his will**], Byz[nor even do according to his will (ASV, DRA, KJV, MRD, NAB, NJB, NLT, TEV, ~TLB)].

12:49 Alx/Byz[**fire on the earth**], Major[fire to the earth (JNT, NJB, NRS, REB, TLB)].

12:53 Alx[**mother against the daughter**], Byz[mother against daughter (ASV, ESV, HCS, JNT, ~MRD, ~NAB, NAS, NAU, NET, NIV, NJB, NKJ, NLT, NRS, REB, RSV, ~TEV, ~TLB)]; Alx[**daughter**

and son against father,
mother against the daughter
and daughter against the mother,
mother-in-law against her daughter-in-law
and daughter-in-law against mother-in-law."

⁵⁴ He also said to the multitudes, "When you see [the] cloud rising over the west, immediately you say that, "A shower is coming'; and so it happens. ⁵⁵ And when you see the south wind blowing, you say that, 'There will be hot weather'; and there is. ⁵⁶ You hypocrites! You know how to interpret the appearance of the earth and the sky; but how is it you do not know how to interpret this present time?

⁵⁷ "And why do you not judge for yourselves what is right? ⁵⁸ As you go with your adversary to the magistrate, make an effort to settle with him on the way, lest he drag you to the judge, and the judge hand you over to the officer, and the officer will throw you into prison. ⁵⁹ I tell you, you will never get out till you have paid the very last copper."

13 ¹ There were some present at that very time who told him about the Galileans whose blood Pilate had mingled with their sacrifices. ² And he answered them, "Do you think that these Galileans were worse sinners than all the other Galileans, because they suffered this way? ³ I tell you, no; but unless you repent you will all likewise perish. ⁴ Or those eighteen on whom the tower in Siloam fell and killed them, do you think that they were worse sinners than all the others who dwelt in Jerusalem? ⁵ I tell you, no; but unless you repent you will all likewise perish."

⁶ He told this parable: "A man had a fig tree planted in his vineyard, and he came seeking fruit on it and found none. ⁷ And he said to the keeper of his vineyard, 'Look, for three years I have come seeking fruit on this fig tree and find none. [So] cut it down; why should it use up the ground?' ⁸ And he answered him, 'Sir, let it alone this year also, until I dig around it and fertilize it. ⁹ And if it bears fruit next year, fine; but if not, you can cut it down.'"

---

against the mother], Byz[daughter against mother (~ASV, ESV, HCS, JNT, ~MRD, ~NAB, NAS, NAU, NET, NIV, NJB, NKJ, NLT, NRS, REB, ~RSV, ~TEV, ~TLB)]; Alx[**mother-in-law against her daughter-in-law and daughter-in-law against mother-in-law**], Byz[mother-in-law against daughter-in-law and daughter-in-law against her mother-in-law (~ASV, ~DRA, ~KJV, ~MRD, ~NAB, ~NAS, ~NAU, ~NIV, ~NJB, ~NKJ, ~REB, ~RSV, ~TEV, ~TLB)].

12:⁵⁴ Alx/Byz[**the cloud**], Minor[a cloud (ASV, DRA, ESV, HCS, JNT, KJV, MRD, NAB, NAS, NAU, NET, NIV, NJB, NKJ, ~NLT, NRS, ~REB, RSV, TEV, ~TLB)]; Alx[**over the west**], Byz[out of the west (DRA, KJV, MRD, NKJ)]; Alx[**say that**], Byz[say (ASV, DRA, ESV, HCS, KJV, MRD, NAS, NAU, NET, NIV, NKJ, NLT, NRS, REB, RSV, TLB)].

12:⁵⁵ Alx/Byz[**you say that**], Minor[you say (ASV, DRA, ESV, HCS, JNT, KJV, MRD, NAS, NAU, NET, NIV, NJB, NKJ, NLT, NRS, REB, RSV, TLB)].

12:⁵⁶ Alx/Major[**the earth and the sky**], Byz[the sky and the earth (DRA, KJV, MRD, NKJ, ~TLB)]; Alx[**do not know how to**], Byz[do not (DRA, KJV, MRD, NAS, NAU, NKJ, ~REB, TLB)].

12:⁵⁸ Alx/Byz[**and the officer will throw**], Major[and the officer should thow (~DRA, ~ESV, ~HCS, ~JNT, ~KJV, ~MRD, ~NAB, ~NAS, ~NAU, ~NET, ~NIV, ~NJB, ~NKJ, ~NRS, ~REB, ~RSV, TLB)].

12:⁵⁹ **copper** *Greek* lepton.

13:² Alx[**he answered them**], Byz[Jesus answered them (KJV, MRD, NAU, NIV, NKJ, NLT, TEV)]; Alx[**suffered this way**], Byz[suffered such a way (DRA, ~JNT, KJV, NKJ, ~NLT, ~TLB)].

13:⁴ Alx[**eighteen**], Byz[ten and eight]; Alx[**they were worse**], Byz[these were worse (~NAS, ~NAU)]; Alx/Byz[**all the others** *Greek* all the men], Major[all others (KJV, NAB, NKJ, ~NLT)].

13:⁷ Alx[**So cut it down**], Byz[Cut it down (ASV, DRA, ESV, HCS, JNT, KJV, MRD, NAS, NAU, NET, NIV, NJB, NKJ, NLT, NRS, REB, RSV, TEV, ~TLB)].

13:⁸ Alx/Major[**answered him** *Greek* answering, says to him], Byz[answering, said to him]; **fertilize it** *Greek* dung it.

13:⁹ Alx[**next year, fine; but if not, you can cut it down**], Byz[fine; but if not, next year you can cut it down (DRA, KJV, ~MRD, NKJ)].

10 Now he was teaching in one of the synagogues on the Sabbath. 11 And there was a woman who had had a spirit of infirmity for eighteen years; she was bent over and could not straighten up at all. 12 When Jesus saw her, he called her forward and said to her, "Woman, you are freed from your infirmity." 13 And he laid his hands on her, and immediately she was made straight, and praised God. 14 But the ruler of the synagogue, indignant because Jesus had healed on the Sabbath, said to the people, "There are six days on which work ought to be done; come on those days and be healed, and not on the Sabbath day." 15 But the Lord answered him, "You hypocrites! Does not each of you on the Sabbath untie his ox or his donkey from the stall, and lead it away to water it? 16 Then ought not this woman, a daughter of Abraham, whom Satan has bound for eighteen years, be loosed on the Sabbath day from this bond?" 17 When he said this, all his adversaries were put to shame; and all the people rejoiced at all the glorious things that were done by him.

18 So he said, "What is the kingdom of God like? And to what shall I compare it? 19 It is like a mustard seed, which a man took and sowed in his garden; and it grew and became a tree, and the birds of the air nested in its branches."

20 And again he said, "To what shall I compare the kingdom of God? 21 It is like leaven, which a woman took and hid in three measures of flour till it was all leavened."

22 He went on his way through towns and villages, teaching, and journeying toward Jerusalem. 23 Then one said to him, "Lord, will those who are saved be few?" And he said to them, 24 "Strive to enter through the narrow door, for many, I tell you, will seek to enter and will not be able. 25 When once the owner of the house has risen up and shut the door, you will begin to stand outside and to knock at the door, saying, 'Lord, open for us.' He will answer you, 'I do not know where you come from.' 26 Then you will begin to say, 'We ate and drank in your presence, and you taught in our streets.' 27 And he will indeed say to you, 'I do not know you or where [you] come from. Depart from me, all you workers of iniquity!'28 There will be weeping and gnashing of teeth, when you see Abraham and Isaac and Jacob and all the prophets in the kingdom of God, and you yourselves thrust out. 29 And men will come from east and west, and from north and south, and sit at table in the kingdom of God. 30 And behold, some are last who will be first, and some are first who will be last."

31 In that very hour some Pharisees came, and said to him, "Get away from here, for Herod wants to kill you." 32 And he said to them, "Go and tell that fox, 'Behold, I cast out demons and perform cures today and tomorrow, and the third day I finish my course.' 33 Nevertheless I must journey today and tomorrow, and the day following; for it cannot be that a prophet should perish outside of Jerusalem. 34 O Jerusalem, Jerusalem, you who kill

---

13:11 Alx[**eighteen years**], Byz[ten and eight years].

13:15 Alx[**But the Lord answered**], Byz[Then the Lord answered (ESV, KJV, NET, NKJ, RSV)]; Alx/Byz[**hypocrites**], Minor[hypocrite (KJV, MRD, NKJ, TLB)].

13:18 Alx[**So he said**], Byz[And he said (MRD, NJB, REB, TEV, ~TLB)].

13:19 Alx[**a tree**], Byz[a large tree (DRA, KJV, MRD, NAB, NKJ, TLB)].

13:20 Alx[**And again**], Byz[Again (HCS, JNT, MRD, NAB, NET, NIV, NJB, ~NLT, REB, TEV, TLB)].

13:21 Alx/Major[**hid**], Byz[concealed (~NLT, ~TLB)]; **measures** Greek sata, about 22 liters..

13:24 Alx[**door**], Byz[gate (DRA, KJV, MRD, NAB, NKJ)].

13:25 Alx[**Lord, open for us**], Byz[Lord, Lord, open for us (KJV, MRD, NKJ)].

13:27 Alx[**And he will indeed say to you** Greek And saying he will say to you], Byz[And he will say, "I tell you (ASV, ESV, HCS, KJV, NAS, NAU, NKJ, NLT, ~REB, RSV, TLB)], Alt[And he will say to you (DRA, JNT, MRD, NAB) others without textual foundation And he will say (~NET, ~NIV, ~NJB, ~NRS) others without textual foundation And he will say again (~TEV); Alx[**I do not know you or where you come from** Greek I do not know you, where you come from], Byz[I do not know where you come from (ASV, ESV, JNT, NAB, NAS, NAU, NET, NIV, NJB, NRS, REB, RSV, TEV, ~TLB)].

13:29 Alx/Byz[**from north and south**], Major[omits from (DRA, JNT, NIV, NLT, ~TLB)].

13:31 Alx[**In that very hour**], Byz[On that very day (DRA, KJV, MRD, NKJ)].

13:34 Alx/Byz[**as a hen gathers her brood**], Minor[as a bird gathers her brood (DRA)].

the prophets and stone those who are sent to you! How often I have longed to gather your children together, as a hen gathers her brood under her wings, but you were not willing! **35** Behold, your house is left to you. [And] I tell you, you will never see me again until [the time comes when] you say, *'Blessed is he who comes in the name of the Lord!'"*

14 **1** One Sabbath, when he went to dine at the house of a ruler who belonged to [the] Pharisees, they watched him. **2** And behold, there was a man before him who had dropsy. **3** And Jesus spoke to the lawyers and Pharisees, saying, "Is it lawful to heal on the Sabbath, or not?" **4** But they kept silent. And he took him and healed him, and let him go. **5** And he said to them, "Which of you, having a son or an ox that has fallen into a well, will not immediately pull him out on the Sabbath day?" **6** And they could not reply to this.

7 So he told a parable to those who were invited, when he noted how they chose the places of honor, saying to them: **8** "When you are invited by anyone to a wedding feast, do not sit down in a place of honor, lest one more distinguished than you be invited by him; **9** and he who invited you both will come and say to you, 'Give place to this man,' and then you will begin with shame to take the lowest place. **10** But when you are invited, go and sit in the lowest place, so that when your host comes he will say to you, 'Friend, go up higher.' Then you will be honored in the presence of all who sit to eat with you. **11** For everyone who exalts himself will be humbled, and he who humbles himself will be exalted." **12** Then he also said to the one who invited him, "When you give a luncheon or a dinner, do not invite your friends or your brothers, your relatives or rich neighbors, lest they also invite you back, and you be repaid. **13** But when you give a feast, invite the poor, the maimed, the lame, the blind, **14** and you will be blessed, because they cannot repay you; for you will be repaid at the resurrection of the just."

15 When one of those who sat to eat with him heard this, he said to him, "Whoever shall eat bread in the kingdom of God is blessed!" **16** Then he said to him, "A certain man was making a great banquet and invited many. **17** And at the time of the banquet he sent his

---

13:35 Alx[**left to you**], Byz[*adds* desolate (ASV, DRA, ~HCS, ~JNT, KJV, MRD, NAS, NAU, NIV, NKJ, ~REB, ~TEV, TLB)]; Alx/Byz[**And I tell you**], Minor[And truly I tell you (KJV, ~NJB, NKJ, ~TEV, ~TLB)], Minor[I tell you (JNT, NIV, ~NLT, REB, ~TLB) *others* For I tell you (MRD)]; Alx/Byz[**the time comes when**], Minor[*omits* (ASV, ESV, JNT, MRD, NET, NIV, NLT, RSV, TLB)]; Psalms 118:26.

14:1 Alx/Byz[**the Pharisees**], Minor[*omits* the].

14:3 Alx[**or not**], Byz[*omits* (DRA, KJV, MRD, NKJ)].

14:4 Alx/Byz[**4 But they kept silent**], Minor[But they kept silent 4].

14:5 Alx[**And he said to them**], Byz[And he answered and said to them (DRA, KJV, NKJ)]; Alx/Byz[**a son**], Minor[a donkey (ASV, DRA, KJV, NKJ, ~TLB)]; Minor[a sheep *others* a sheep or a son].

14:6 Alx[**they could not reply** *or* they could not answer], Byz[they could not answer him (DRA, KJV, MRD, NKJ, TEV)].

14:10 Alx[**he will say to you**], Byz[he may say to you (ASV, DRA, ESV, KJV, MRD, NAB, NAS, NAU, NJB, NKJ, NRS, RSV)]; Alx[**in the presence of all**], Byz[*omits* all (DRA, KJV, NAB, NKJ)].

14:12 Alx/Major[and you *should* be repaid], Byz[and you *will* be repaid].

14:14 Alx/Byz[**for you will be repaid**], Minor[but you will be repaid (~ESV 2001 edition, MRD, ~NIV, ~NJB, ~NLT, ~REB, ~RSV, ~TEV, ~TLB)].

14:15 Alx[**Whoever**], Byz[He who (ASV, DRA, HCS, KJV, MRD, NAB, NIV, NKJ, ~NLT, RSV, ~TLB)]; Alx[**bread**], Byz[dinner (NAB, NET, NIV, NJB, NLT, REB, TEV, ~TLB)].

14:16 Alx[**was making**], Byz[made (ASV, DRA, ESV, JNT, KJV, MRD, NAB, NET, NJB, NKJ, NLT, NRS, RSV, TLB)].

14:17 Alx/Byz[**say to those who had been invited, 'Come, for**], Minor[tell those who had been invited to come, 'For (~DRA, ~TLB)]; Alx[**it is now ready** *or* things are now ready *Greek* things is now ready]; Byz[all is now ready (ASV, DRA, ESV, HCS, JNT, KJV, MRD, NAB, NAS, NAU, NET, NIV, NJB, NKJ, NRS, REB, RSV, TEV, ~TLB)].

servant to say to those who had been invited, 'Come, for it is now ready.' [18] But they all alike began to make excuses. The first said to him, 'I have bought a field, and I must go out to see it. I ask you to have me excused.' [19] And another said, 'I have bought five yoke of oxen, and I am going to test them. I ask you to have me excused.' [20] Still another said, 'I have married a wife, and therefore I cannot come.' [21] So the servant came back and reported this to his master. Then the owner of the house became angry and said to his servant, 'Go out quickly into the streets and lanes of the city and bring in the poor and the maimed, the blind and the lame.' [22] And the servant said, 'Sir, what you commanded has been done, and still there is room.' [23] Then the master said to the servant, 'Go out into the highways and hedges, and compel them to come in, that my house may be filled. [24] For I tell you, none of those men who were invited shall taste my banquet.'"

[25] Now great multitudes went with him; and he turned and said to them, [26] "If any one comes to me and does not hate his own father and mother, wife and children, brothers and sisters, yes, and even his own life, he cannot be my disciple. [27] Whoever does not bear his own cross and come after me cannot be my disciple. [28] For which of you, intending to build a tower, does not sit down first and count the cost, whether he has enough to complete it? [29] Otherwise, when he has laid the foundation, and is not able to finish, all who see it begin to mock him, [30] saying, 'This man began to build, and was not able to finish.' [31] Or what king, going to make war against another king, will not sit down first and consider whether he is able with ten thousand to meet him who comes against him with twenty thousand? [32] And if not, while the other is still a great way off, he sends a delegation and asks terms of peace. [33] So likewise, whoever of you does not give up all that he has cannot be my disciple.

[34] Salt, then, is good; but if even the salt has lost its taste, how shall it be seasoned? [35] It is neither fit for the land nor for the dunghill; men throw it out. He who has ears to hear, let him hear!"

14:18 Alx[**I must go out to see it** *Greek* going out I must see it], Byz[I must go out and see it (ASV, DRA, ESV, HCS, JNT, KJV, MRD, NAS, NAU, NET, NIV, NJB, NKJ, ~NLT, NRS, REB, RSV, TEV, ~TLB)].

14:21 Alx[**the servant**], Byz[that servant (KJV, NKJ)]; Alx[**blind and the lame**], Byz[lame and the blind (KJV, MRD, NKJ, TLB)].

14:22 Alx[**what you commanded has been done**], Byz[it has been done as you commanded (DRA, KJV, MRD, ~NAB, ~NJB, NKJ, ~NLT, ~REB, ~TEV, ~TLB)].

14:23 Alx/Byz[**the servant**], Minor[his servant (MRD, NET, NIV, NJB, ~NLT, ~REB, ~TLB)]; Alx/Byz[**compel them to come**], Minor[make them come (HCS, NAB, NIV, TEV)].

14:24 Alx/Byz[*text*], Major[*adds* For many are called, but few are chosen]; **you** *plural*.

14:25 Alx/Byz[**with him**], Minor[with Jesus (JNT, NET, NIV, NLT, TEV)].

14:26 Alx/Byz[**his own father**], Major[his father (DRA, JNT, KJV, MRD, NAB, NIV, NJB, NKJ, NLT, NRS, REB, TEV)]; Alx/Byz[**his own life** *or* his own soul], Minor[the life of his own soul (~NRS)];

14:27 Alx/Byz[**Whoever does not bear his own cross**], Major[And whoever does not bear his cross (DRA, KJV, MRD, NIV, ~NJB, NKJ, ~NLT, ~NRS, ~REB, ~TLB)]; *Minor omits verse*.

14:28 Alx/Byz[**intending**], Major[who are intending (~JNT, ~NAS, ~NAU, ~NIV, ~TEV, ~TLB)].

14:29 Alx/Major[**is not able**], Byz[will not be able (~HCS, ~JNT, ~NAB, ~NJB, ~NLT, TEV, ~TLB)].

14:31 Alx/Major[**sit down first**], Byz[first sit down (DRA, HCS, JNT, NAB, NAS, NAU, NIV, NJB, NLT, REB, TLB)], Alt/Peshitta[first (MRD)].

14:32 Alx/Byz[**asks terms of peace**], Minor[asks of peace (MRD, NJB)].

14:34 Alx[**then**], Byz[*omits* (DRA, ESV, JNT, KJV, MRD, NAB, NET, NIV, NJB, NKJ, NLT, NRS, REB, RSV, TEV, TLB)]; Alx/Byz[**even**], Major[*omits* (DRA, ESV, HCS, KJV, NET, NIV, NKJ, NLT, NRS, RSV, TEV, TLB)]; **how shall it be seasoned** *or* how shall it season.

14:35 Alx/Byz[**ears to hear**], Minor[*omits* to hear (TEV, ~TLB)].

15

¹ Now the tax collectors and sinners were all drawing near to hear him. ² And both the Pharisees and the scribes murmured, saying, "This man receives sinners and eats with them." ³ So he told them this parable, saying: ⁴ "What man of you, having a hundred sheep, if he loses one of them, does not leave the ninety-nine in the wilderness, and go after the one which is lost until he finds it? ⁵ And when he has found it, he lays it on his shoulders, rejoicing. ⁶ And when he comes home, he calls together his friends and neighbors, saying to them, 'Rejoice with me, for I have found my sheep which was lost.' ⁷ I tell you that in the same way there will be more joy in heaven over one sinner who repents than over ninety-nine righteous persons who need no repentance.

⁸ "Or what woman, having ten silver coins, if she loses one coin, does not light a lamp and sweep the house and search carefully until she finds it? ⁹ And when she has found it, she calls together her friends and neighbors, saying, 'Rejoice with me, for I have found the coin which I had lost.' ¹⁰ In the same way, I tell you, there is joy in the presence of the angels of God over one sinner who repents."

¹¹ Then he said: "There was a man who had two sons. ¹² And the younger of them said to his father, 'Father, give me the share of property that falls to me.' So he divided his living between them. ¹³ Not many days after, the younger son gathered together all he had and took his journey into a far country, and there he squandered his property in loose living. ¹⁴ And when he had spent everything, there arose a severe famine in that country, and he began to be in want. ¹⁵ So he went and joined himself to a citizen of that country, who sent him into his fields to feed swine. ¹⁶ And he would gladly have been filled with the pods that the swine ate, and no one gave him anything. ¹⁷ But when he came to himself, he said, 'How many of my father's hired servants have bread enough and to spare, and here I perish with hunger! ¹⁸ I will arise and go to my father and will say to him, "Father, I have sinned against heaven and before you. ¹⁹ I am no longer worthy to be called your son; make me like one of your hired servants."' ²⁰ And he arose and came to his own father. But while he was still a great way off, his father saw him and had compassion for him, and ran and fell on his neck and kissed him. ²¹ And the son said to him, 'Father, I have sinned against heaven and before you; I am no longer worthy to be called your son.' ²² But the father said to his servants, 'Quick! Bring out the best robe and put it on him, and put a ring on his hand and sandals on his feet. ²³ And bring the fatted calf and kill it, and let us eat and be merry; ²⁴

15:1 Alx/Byz[**all**], Minor[*omits* (DRA, JNT, MRD, NLT, ~TEV, TLB)].

15:2 Alx[**And both**], Byz[*omits* both (DRA, ESV, HCS, JNT, KJV, MRD, NAB, NET, NIV, NJB, NKJ, NLT, NRS, REB, RSV, TEV, TLB)].

15:3 Alx/Byz[**saying**], Minor[*omits* (ESV, HCS, JNT, MRD, NAB, NET, NIV, NJB, NLT, NRS, REB, RSV, TEV, TLB)].

15:4 Alx/Major[**until he finds it**], Byz[not until he finds it].

15:5 Alx/Byz[**his shoulders**], Major[his own shoulders].

15:8 **ten silver coins… coin** *Greek* drachma, *about a day's wage for a laborer.*

15:9 Alx[**her friends and neighbors** *Greek* the friends and neighbors], Byz[the friends and the neighbors (KJV)].

15:16 Alx[**been filled**], Byz[filled his stomach (ASV, DRA, JNT, KJV, MRD, NAS, NAU, NIV, NKJ, REB)].

15:17 Alx[**here I perish**], Byz[*omits* here (KJV, NKJ)].

15:19 Alx/Byz[**I am no longer worthy**], Major[And I am no longer worthy (KJV, MRD, NKJ, NLT, TLB)].

15:20 Alx[**his own father**], Byz[his father (ASV, DRA, ESV, HCS, JNT, KJV, MRD, NAB, NAS, NAU, NET, NIV, NJB, NKJ, NLT, NRS, REB, RSV, TEV, TLB)].

15:21 Alx[**I am no longer worthy**], Byz[and I am no longer worthy (KJV, MRD, NKJ, NLT, TLB)]; Alx/Byz[**called your son**], Minor[*adds* Make me like one of your hired servants].

15:22 Alx[**Quick**], Byz[*omits* (KJV, MRD, NKJ)].

15:23 Alx[**bring the fatted calf and kill it** *Greek* bring the fatted calf, kill it], Byz[bringing the fatted calf, kill it (~NLT, ~TLB)].

for this my son was dead and is alive again; he was lost and is found.' And they began to be merry.

²⁵ "Now his older son was in the field. And as he came and drew near to the house, he heard music and dancing. ²⁶ So he called one of the servants and asked what these things meant. ²⁷ And he said to him, 'Your brother has come, and your father has killed the fatted calf, because he has received him safe and sound.' ²⁸ But he was angry and refused to go in. And his father came out and pleaded with him. ²⁹ But he answered his father, 'Behold, these many years I have been serving you, and I never disobeyed your command; yet you never gave me a young goat, that I might make merry with my friends. ³⁰ But when this son of yours came, who has devoured your living with harlots, you killed for him the fatted calf!' ³¹ And he said to him, 'Son, you are always with me, and all that I have is yours. ³² It was right that we should make merry and be glad, for this your brother was dead, and is alive; he was lost, and is found.'"

16

¹ He also said to the disciples: "There was a certain rich man who had a steward, and an accusation was brought to him that this man was wasting his goods. ² So he called him and said to him, 'What is this I hear about you? Give an account of your stewardship, for you can no longer be steward.' ³ The steward said to himself, 'What shall I do, since my master is taking the stewardship away from me? I am not strong enough to dig, and I am ashamed to beg. ⁴ I have decided what to do, so that people may receive me into their houses when I am put out of the stewardship.' ⁵ So he called in each one of his master's debtors, and he said to the first, 'How much do you owe my master?' ⁶ And he said, 'A hundred measures of oil.' But he said to him, 'Take your bills, and sit down quickly and write fifty.' ⁷ Then he said to another, 'And how much do you owe?' And he said, 'A hundred measures of wheat.' He said to him, 'Take your bills, and write eighty.' ⁸ So the master commended the dishonest steward because he had dealt shrewdly. For the sons of this world are more shrewd in dealing with their own generation than the sons of light. ⁹ And I tell you, make friends for yourselves by means of unrighteous mammon, so that when it fails, they may receive you into the eternal dwellings. ¹⁰ He who is faithful in a very little is faithful also in much; and he who is dishonest in a very little is dishonest also in much. ¹¹ If then you have not been faithful in the unrighteous mammon, who will trust you with the true riches? ¹² And if you have not been faithful in what is another's, who will give you what is your own? ¹³ No servant can serve two masters; for

---

15:24 Alx/Byz[**alive again**], Minor[alive (MRD, TEV)].

15:25 Alx/Byz[**music and dancing**], Alt[*adds* of many (MRD)].

15:26 Alx/Byz[**one of the servants**], Minor[one of his servants].

15:28 Alx[**And his father**], Byz[So his father (HCS, JNT, KJV, NIV, NKJ, TEV)].

15:29 Alx[**his father**], Byz[the father (~JNT, ~NLT, ~REB, ~TLB)].

15:32 Alx[**is alive**], Byz[is alive again (ASV, DRA, HCS, JNT, KJV, NAB, NIV, NKJ, NLT, REB, TLB)].

16:1 Alx[**the disciples**], Byz[his disciples (DRA, KJV, MRD, NAB, NIV, NJB, NKJ, NLT, REB, TEV, TLB)].

16:4 Alx/Major[**their houses**], Byz[their own houses].

16:5 Alx/Major[**his master's**], Byz[the master's].

16:6 Alx[**But he said**], Byz[And he said (ASV, DRA, KJV, MRD, NAS, NAU, RSV)]; Alx[**Take your bills**], Byz[Take your bill (ASV, DRA, ESV, HCS, JNT, KJV, MRD, NAB, NAS, NAU, NET, NIV, NJB, NKJ, NLT, NRS, REB, RSV, TEV, TLB)]; **measures** *or* baths *Greek* batous, *about 3 kiloliters.*

16:7 Alx[**He said to him**], Byz[And he said to him (KJV, MRD, NKJ, REB)]; Alx[**Take your bills**], Byz[Take your bill (ASV, DRA, ESV, HCS, JNT, KJV, MRD, NAB, NAS, NAU, NET, NIV, NJB, NKJ, NLT, NRS, REB, RSV, TEV, TLB)]; **measures** *Greek* korous, *about 35 kiloliters.*

16:8 Alx/Major[**more shrewd in dealing with their own generation than the sons of light**], Byz[shrewd in dealing with their own generation – more than the sons of light].

16:9 Alx[**when it fails**], Byz[when you fail (DRA, KJV, NKJ, ~TLB)].

16:9, 11, 13 **mammon** *Aramaic* money *possibly a Syrian deity.*

16:12 Alx/Byz[**what is your own**], Minor[what is our own].

either he will hate the one and love the other, or else he will be devoted to the one and despise the other. You cannot serve God and mammon."

¹⁴ The Pharisees, who were lovers of money, heard all this, and they scoffed at him. ¹⁵ He said to them, "You are those who justify yourselves before men, but God knows your hearts. For what is highly esteemed among men is an abomination in the sight of God. ¹⁶ The law and the prophets were until John. Since that time the good news of the kingdom of God is preached, and everyone is forcing his way into it. ¹⁷ But it is easier for heaven and earth to pass away, than for one dot of the law to fail. ¹⁸ Everyone who divorces his wife and marries another commits adultery, and he who marries a woman divorced from her husband commits adultery.

¹⁹ "There was a certain rich man who was clothed in purple and fine linen and feasted sumptuously every day. ²⁰ And a certain beggar named Lazarus was laid at his gate, full of sores, ²¹ longing to be fed with what fell from the rich man's table. Moreover the dogs came and licked his sores. ²² So the beggar died, and was carried by the angels to Abraham's bosom. The rich man also died and was buried. ²³ And in Hades, being in torment, he lifted up his eyes, and saw Abraham far off and Lazarus in his bosom. ²⁴ And he called out, 'Father Abraham, have mercy upon me, and send Lazarus to dip the tip of his finger in water and cool my tongue; for I am in agony in this flame.' ²⁵ But Abraham said, 'Son, remember that in your lifetime you received your good things, and Lazarus received evil things; but now he is comforted here and you are in agony. ²⁶ And in all this, between us and you a great chasm has been fixed, so that those who want to pass from here to you cannot, nor can anyone cross over from there to us.' ²⁷ And he said, 'Then I beg you, father, to send him to my father's house, ²⁸ for I have five brothers, so that he may warn them, lest they also come to this place of torment.' ²⁹ But Abraham said, 'They have Moses and the prophets; let them hear them.' ³⁰ And he said, 'No, father Abraham; but if someone goes to them from the dead, they will repent.' ³¹ He said to him, 'If they do not hear Moses and the prophets, neither will they be convinced if some one should rise from the dead.'"

17 ¹ And he said to his disciples, "Things that cause people to sin are bound to come, but woe to him through whom they do come! ² It would be better for him if a millstone were hung round his neck and he were thrown into the sea, than

---

16:¹⁴ Alx[**The Pharisees**], Byz[*adds* also (KJV, NKJ)].

16:¹⁶ **forcing his way into it** *or* urged into it.

16:¹⁷ Alx/Byz[**the law**], Minor[my word].

16:¹⁸ Alx[**he who marries**], Byz[everyone who marries (HCS, KJV, MRD, NKJ, NLT, NRS, REB, TLB)].

16:¹⁹ Alx/Byz[**a certain rich man**], Minor[*adds* named Neues *others* named Nineveh *others* named Phineas *others* named Amenophis].

16:²⁰ Alx[**And a certain beggar named Lazarus was laid**], Byz[And there was a certain beggar named Lazarus who was laid (DRA, KJV, MRD, NKJ, TEV)].

16:²¹ Alx[**what fell**], Byz[the crumbs that fell (ASV, DRA, JNT, KJV, MRD, NAB, NAS, NAU, NKJ, NLT, REB, TEV, TLB)]; Alx/Byz[**from the rich man's table**], Minor[adds and no one was giving anything to him (DRA)].

16:²³ Alx/Byz[**was buried. 23 And in Hades**], Minor[was buried in Hades. 23 (DRA, ~TLB)].

16:²⁵ Alx[**he is comforted here**], Byz[he has this comfort (DRA, KJV, NKJ)].

16:²⁶ Alx[**in all this**], Byz[besides all this (ASV, DRA, ESV, HCS, ~JNT, KJV, NAS, NAU, NET, NIV, NKJ, NLT, NRS, RSV, TEV, TLB)]; Alx/Byz[**pass from here to you**], Minor[pass hence to you (ASV, DRA, KJV)].

16:²⁷ Alx/Byz[**I beg you, father**], Minor[*adds* Abraham (NLT, TEV, TLB)].

16:²⁹ Alx[**But Abraham said**], Byz[Abraham said to him (KJV, MRD, NKJ)], Minor[But Abraham said to him (DRA)].

17:¹ Alx/Major[**he said**], Byz[he began to say]; Alx/Byz[**his disciples**], Major[the disciples (KJV, NKJ)].

17:² Alx/Byz[**millstone**], Major[millstone for a donkey].

that he should cause one of these little ones to sin. ³ Take heed to yourselves; if your brother sins, rebuke him, and if he repents, forgive him. ⁴ And if he sins against you seven times in a day, and turns to you seven times, and says, 'I repent,' you must forgive him."

⁵ The apostles said to the Lord, "Increase our faith!" ⁶ So the Lord said, "If you have faith as a mustard seed, you can say to [this] mulberry tree, 'Be uprooted and be planted in the sea,' and it would obey you.

⁷ "Will any one of you, who has a servant plowing or keeping sheep, say to him when he has come in from the field, 'Come at once and sit down to eat'? ⁸ Will he not rather say to him, 'Prepare my supper, and gird yourself and serve me, till I eat and drink; and afterward you shall eat and drink'? ⁹ Does he thank the servant because he did what was commanded? ¹⁰ So you also, when you have done all that is commanded you, say, 'We are unworthy servants; we have only done what is our duty.'"

¹¹ On the way to Jerusalem he was passing along between Samaria and Galilee. ¹² As he entered a village, ten men who were lepers met [him], who stood at a distance. ¹³ And they lifted up their voices and said, "Jesus, Master, have mercy on us!" ¹⁴ When he saw them, he said to them, "Go, show yourselves to the priests." And as they went, they were cleansed. ¹⁵ Then one of them, when he saw that he was healed, turned back, praising God with a loud voice; ¹⁶ and he fell on his face at Jesus' feet, giving him thanks. And he was a Samaritan. ¹⁷ Then said Jesus, "Were not ten cleansed? But where are the nine? ¹⁸ Was no one found to return and give praise to God except this foreigner?" ¹⁹ And he said to him, "Rise and go your way; your faith has made you well."

²⁰ Now when he was asked by the Pharisees when the kingdom of God would come, he answered them, "The kingdom of God does not come with observation; ²¹ nor will they say, 'Look, here!' or, 'There!' for behold, the kingdom of God is within you." ²² Then he said to the disciples, "The days are coming when you will desire to see one of the days of the Son of Man, and you will not see it. ²³ And they will say to you, 'Look, there!' [or,] 'Look, here!' Do not go after them or follow them. ²⁴ For as the lightning flashes and lights up the sky from one part to the other, so will the Son of Man be [in his day]. ²⁵ But first he must suffer many things and be rejected by this generation. ²⁶ Just as it was in the days of

---

17:3 Alx[**if your brother sins**], Byz[but if your brother sins against you (DRA, KJV, NKJ)].

17:4 Alx[**turns to you seven times**], Byz[turns to you seven times in a day (DRA, KJV, MRD, NKJ)], Major[turns seven times in a day].

17:6 Alx/Byz[**If you have faith**], Minor[If you were having faith (~ASV, ~DRA, ~ESV, ~JNT, ~KJV, ~MRD, ~NAS, ~NAU, ~NET, ~NJB, ~NLT, ~NRS, ~REB, ~RSV, ~TEV, ~TLB)]; Alx/Byz[**this mulberry tree**], Minor[the mulberry tree (~TLB)].

17:7 Alx[**say to him**], Byz[*omits* to him (~NAB, ~NET, NLT, ~NRS, REB, ~TLB)].

17:9 Alx[**the servant**], Byz[that servant (DRA, HCS, KJV, NAB, NKJ, ~TLB)]; Alx[**what was commanded?**], Byz[what was commanded? I think not!], Minor[what he was commanded? I think not! (JNT, KJV, MRD, NKJ, NLT)].

17:12 Alx/Byz[**met him**], Minor[*omits* him (~NLT, ~TLB)]; Alx/Byz[**stood at a distance**], Minor[rose up at a distance (~NRS)]; **lepers** *can refer to a number of skin diseases.*

17:17 Alx/Byz[**But where are the nine**], Minor[*omits* But (ESV, HCS, JNT, MRD, NAB, NET, NIV, NJB, NLT, REB, RSV, TEV, TLB)].

17:21 Alx['**Look, here!' or, 'There!'**], Byz['Look, here!' or, 'Look, there!' (DRA, KJV, MRD, NJB, NKJ, ~TLB)]; **behold** *or* suddenly; **within you** *or* within your grasp *or* among you.

17:22 Alx/Byz[**the days of the Son of Man**], Minor[those days of the Son of Man].

17:23 Alx['**Look, there!' or, 'Look, here!'**], Byz['Look, here!' 'Look, there!' (~DRA)]; Major['Look, here!' or, 'Look, there!' (JNT, KJV, MRD, NKJ)], Minor['Look, there!' 'Look, here!' (ASV, NAS, NAU, ~REB)], Alt[~*NIV and ~TLB omit* Look *both times*, ~*NLT one time*]; Alx/Byz[**Do not go after them or follow them**], Minor[Do not follow (MRD, ~NIV, ~REB, ~TEV)].

17:24 Alx/Byz[**the lightning flashes**], Major[the lightning that flashes (DRA, JNT, KJV, NIV, NKJ, TLB)]; Alx/Major[**so will the Son of Man be**], Byz[so also will the Son of Man be (KJV, NKJ)]; Alx/Byz[**in his day**], Minor[*omits* (~TLB)].

Noah, so also will it be in the days of the Son of Man. 27 They ate, they drank, they married, they were given in marriage, until the day when Noah entered the ark, and the flood came and destroyed them all. 28 Likewise, just as it was in the days of Lot: they ate, they drank, they bought, they sold, they planted, they built; 29 but on the day when Lot went out from Sodom fire and sulfur rained from heaven and destroyed them all. 30 So will it be on the day when the Son of Man is revealed. 31 On that day, let him who is on the housetop, with his goods in the house, not come down to take them away. And likewise let him who is in a field not turn back. 32 Remember Lot's wife. 33 Whoever seeks to keep his life will lose it, and whoever loses his life will preserve it. 34 I tell you, on that night there will be two in one bed; the one will be taken and the other left. 35 Two women will be grinding together; the one will be taken but the other left." (36) 37 And they said to him, "Where, Lord?" He said to them, "Where the body is, there also will the eagles be gathered together."

18 1 And he told them a parable, to show that they ought always to pray and not lose heart. 2 He said: "In a certain city there was a judge who neither feared God nor regarded man. 3 And there was a widow in that city who kept coming to him and saying, 'Grant me justice against my adversary.' 4 For a while he was unwilling; but afterward he said to himself, 'Though I neither fear God nor regard man, 5 yet because this widow bothers me, I will give her justice, or she will wear me out by her continual coming.'" 6 And the Lord said, "Hear what the unjust judge says. 7 And will God never bring about justice for his elect, who cry to him day and night? Will he delay long over them? 8 I tell you that he will bring about justice for them speedily. Nevertheless, when the Son of Man comes, will he find faith on the earth?"

9 Also he told this parable to some who trusted in themselves that they were righteous, and despised others: 10 "Two men went up to the temple to pray, one a Pharisee and the other a tax collector. 11 The Pharisee, standing by himself, prayed these things: 'God, I thank you that I am not like other men – extortioners, unjust, adulterers, or even like

---

17:28 Alx[**Likewise, just as**], Byz[Likewise also, as (KJV, NKJ, ~REB)].

17:31 Alx[**a field**], Byz[the field (ASV, DRA, ESV, HCS, JNT, KJV, MRD, NAB, NAS, NAU, NET, NIV, NJB, NKJ, NLT, NRS, REB, RSV, TEV, TLB)].

17:33 Alx[**keep his life**], Byz[save his life (DRA, KJV, NKJ, TEV)], Minor[preserve his life (MRD) *same word as end of verse*].

17:34 Alx/Byz[**in one bed**], Minor[in a bed (~TEV, ~TLB)]; Alx[**the one will be taken**], Byz[one will be taken (ESV, HCS, JNT, MRD, NAB, NAS, NAU, NET, NIV, NJB, NLT, NRS, REB, RSV, TEV, TLB)].

17:35 Alx[**the one will be taken**], Byz[one will be taken (ESV, HCS, JNT, MRD, NAB, NAS, NAU, NET, NIV, NJB, NLT, NRS, REB, RSV, TEV, TLB)]; Alx[**but the other left**], Byz[and the other left (ASV, DRA, ESV, HCS, JNT, KJV, MRD, NAS, NAU, NET, NIV, NKJ, NRS, RSV)].

17:(36) Alx[*omits*], Byz[*adds* Two men will be in the field; one will be taken and the other left (ASV, DRA, HCS, KJV, MRD, NAS, NAU, NKJ, TLB)]; *DRA places this in the previous verse and remains one verse behind till the end of the chapter.*

17:37 Alx[**there also will the eagles**], Byz[there will the eagles also (ASV, DRA)], Major[*omits* also (ESV, JNT, KJV, MRD, NET, NIV, NKJ, ~NLT, NRS, REB, RSV, TEV, TLB)].

18:1 Alx[**And he told them**], Byz[And he also told them (DRA, MRD)]; Alx/Byz[**they ought always to pray**], Major[*omits* they (DRA, KJV, MRD, NJB, NKJ)].

18:2 Alx/Byz[**He said** *Greek* saying], Minor[*omits* (HCS, JNT, MRD, NAB, REB, TEV)].

18:3 Alx/Byz[**there was a widow**], Minor[there was a certain widow (DRA, MRD)].

18:4 Alx[**he was unwilling**], Byz[he refused (ASV, DRA, ESV, JNT, KJV, MRD, NET, NIV, NJB, NKJ, NLT, NRS, REB, RSV, TEV, TLB)]; Alx[**nor regard man**], Byz[and do not regard man (JNT, MRD, NRS)].

18:5 **wear me out by her continual coming** *or* finally come and strike me in the face.

18:9 Alx/Byz[**Also**], Major[*omits* (DRA, KJV, MRD, NAB, NIV, NJB, NLT, REB, TLB)].

18:11 Alx/Byz[**standing by himself, prayed these things**], Minor[standing, prayed these things by himself (ASV, DRA, ~HCS, JNT, KJV, NAB, NAS, NAU, NET, NIV, NJB, NKJ, RSV) *others* standing, prayed (REB, TLB)].

this tax collector. 12 I fast twice a week; I give tithes of all that I get.' 13 But the tax collector, standing far off, would not even lift up his eyes to heaven, but beat his breast, saying, 'God, be merciful to me a sinner!' 14 I tell you, this man went down to his house justified rather than the other; for everyone who exalts himself will be humbled, and he who humbles himself will be exalted."

15 Now they were also bringing infants to him that he might touch them; but when the disciples saw it, they began to rebuke them. 16 But Jesus invited them, saying, "Let the little children come to me, and do not hinder them; for to such belongs the kingdom of God. 17 Truly, I say to you, whoever does not receive the kingdom of God like a little child will never enter it."

18 Now a certain ruler asked him, "Good Teacher, what shall I do to inherit eternal life?" 19 So Jesus said to him, "Why do you call me good? No one is good but God alone. 20 You know the commandments: 'Do not commit adultery. Do not murder. Do not steal. Do not bear false witness. Honor your father and mother.'" 21 And he said, "All these I have kept from youth." 22 When Jesus heard, he said to him, "One thing you still lack. Sell all that you have and give to the poor, and you will have treasure in the heavens; and come, follow me." 23 But when he heard this, he became very sad, for he was extremely rich.

24 But Jesus saw him [becoming sad] and said, "How hard it is for those who have riches to enter the kingdom of God! 25 For it is easier for a camel to go through the eye of a needle than for a rich man to enter the kingdom of God." 26 Those who heard it said, "Then who can be saved?" 27 But he said, "What is impossible with men is possible with God." 28 Then Peter said, "Behold, we have left our homes to follow you." 29 So he said to them, "Truly, I say to you, there is no one who has left house or wife or brothers or parents or children, for the sake of the kingdom of God, 30 who will not receive many times more in this time, and in the age to come eternal life."

31 Then he took the twelve aside and said to them, "Behold, we are going up to Jerusalem, and everything that is written of the Son of Man by the prophets will be accomplished. 32 For he will be delivered to the Gentiles, and will be mocked and insulted

---

18:13 Alx[**But the tax collector**], Byz[And the tax collector (DRA, KJV, MRD, ~NJB, NKJ)]; Alx[**beat his breast**], Byz[beat upon his breast *Greek* beat into his breast (KJV, MRD, REB, TEV, TLB)].

18:14 Alx/Byz[**rather than the other**], Minor[rather than the Pharisee (MRD, NET, NLT, TEV, TLB)].

18:15 Alx/Major[**but when the disciples**], Byz[and when the disciples (~DRA, ESV, MRD, NAB, ~NIV, NRS, REB, RSV, ~TEV)]; Alx[**they began to rebuke them**], Byz[they rebuked them (ASV, DRA, ESV, HCS, JNT, KJV, MRD, NAB, NIV, NJB, NKJ, NLT, NRS, REB, RSV, TEV, TLB)].

18:16 Alx[**Jesus invited them, saying**], Byz[Jesus, inviting them, said (DRA, ~HCS, ~JNT, ~KJV, ~MRD, ~NAB, ~NIV, ~NJB, ~NKJ, ~NLT, ~NRS, ~REB, ~TEV, ~TLB)], Minor[Jesus invited, saying].

18:20 Alx/Byz[**Do not commit adultery. Do not murder**], Minor[Do not murder. Do not commit adultery (DRA, MRD)]; Alx[**Honor your father and mother**], Byz[Honor your father and your mother (KJV, MRD, NAB, NJB, NKJ, TEV, ~TLB)]; **Exodus 20:12-16, Deuteronomy 5:16-20**.

18:21 Alx[**from youth**], Byz[from my youth (ASV, DRA, ESV, HCS, JNT, KJV, MRD, NAB, NAS, NAU, NET, NIV, NJB, NKJ, NRS, REB, RSV, TEV, TLB)].

18:22 Alx[**When Jesus heard**], Byz[*adds* this *Greek* these (ASV, ESV, HCS, JNT, KJV, MRD, NAB, NAS, NAU, NET, NIV, NJB, NKJ, ~NLT, NRS, REB, RSV, TEV, ~TLB)]; Alx[**in the heavens**], Byz[in heaven (ASV, DRA, ESV, HCS, JNT, KJV, MRD, NAB, NAS, NAU, NET, NIV, NJB, NKJ, NLT, NRS, REB, RSV, TEV, TLB)].

18:24 Alx/Byz[**becoming sad**], Minor[*omits* (JNT, NAS, NAU, NET, NIV, NJB, NLT, NRS, REB, RSV, TLB)].

18:25 Alx/Byz[**camel**], Minor[cable].

18:28 Alx/Byz[**Peter**], Alt/Peshitta[Simon Cephas (~JNT, MRD)]; Alx[**left our homes** *Greek* left our own], Byz[left all (DRA, KJV, MRD, NET, NIV, NJB, NKJ, REB)]; Alx[**to follow you**], Byz[and followed you (ASV, DRA, ESV, HCS, JNT, KJV, MRD, NAB, NAS, NAU, NKJ, NRS, RSV, TLB)].

18:29 Alx[**wife or brothers or parents**], Byz[parents or brothers or wife (DRA, KJV, MRD, NKJ)].

and spit upon. ³³ They will scourge him and kill him, and on the third day he will rise again." ³⁴ But they understood none of these things; this saying was hidden from them, and they did not know what he was talking about.

³⁵ As he drew near to Jericho, a blind man was sitting by the roadside begging. ³⁶ And hearing a multitude going by, he asked what this meant. ³⁷ They told him, "Jesus the Nazarene is passing by." ³⁸ And he cried out, "Jesus, Son of David, have mercy on me!" ³⁹ And those who led the way rebuked him, telling him to be quiet; but he cried out all the more, "Son of David, have mercy on me!" ⁴⁰ So Jesus stopped, and commanded him to be brought to him. And when he came near, he asked him, ⁴¹ "What do you want me to do for you?" He said, "Lord, I want to receive my sight." ⁴² And Jesus said to him, "Receive your sight; your faith has made you well." ⁴³ And immediately he received his sight and followed him, glorifying God. And all the people, when they saw it, gave praise to God.

19 ¹ Jesus entered Jericho and was passing through. ² Now behold, there was a man named Zacchaeus; he was a chief tax collector, and he was rich. ³ And he sought to see who Jesus was, but could not because of the crowd, for he was of short stature. ⁴ So he ran to the front and climbed up into a sycamore tree to see him, because he was to pass that way. ⁵ And when Jesus came to the place, he looked up and said to him, "Zacchaeus, make haste and come down; for I must stay at your house today." ⁶ So he made haste and came down, and received him joyfully. ⁷ And when they saw it they all murmured, "He has gone in to be the guest of a man who is a sinner." ⁸ And Zacchaeus stood and said to the Lord, "Look, Lord, the half of my goods I give to the poor; and if I have defrauded any one of anything, I restore it fourfold." ⁹ And Jesus said to him, "Today salvation has come to this house, because he also is a son of Abraham. ¹⁰ For the Son of Man came to seek and to save what was lost."

¹¹ As they heard these things, he went on to tell a parable, because he was near to Jerusalem, and because they thought that the kingdom of God was to appear immediately. ¹² Therefore he said: "A certain nobleman went into a far country to receive for himself a kingdom and then return. ¹³ So he called ten of his servants, gave them ten minas, and said to them, 'Do business while I am coming.' ¹⁴ But his citizens hated him and sent a delegation after him, saying, 'We do not want this man to reign over us.' ¹⁵ And so it was that when he returned, having received the kingdom, he then commanded these servants, to whom he had given the money, to be called to him, that he might learn what they had gained by trading. ¹⁶ Then came the first, saying, 'Master, your mina has earned ten minas more.' ¹⁷ And he said to him, 'Well done, good servant! Because you have been faithful in a

---

18:³³ Alx/Byz[**They will scourge him and kill him**], Alt[*places this in verse 32* (NIV)].

18:³⁶ Alx/Major[**what this meant**], Byz[what this meant *Greek* what these meant], Minor[whatever this meant (~NAS)].

18:⁴¹ Alx[**"What do you want**], Byz[saying, "What do you want (DRA, KJV, MRD, NKJ, TLB)].

19:² Alx[**and he was rich**], Byz[and this one was rich], Minor[and was rich (ESV, JNT, ~MRD, NAB, NET, NIV, NJB, NLT, NRS, REB, RSV, ~TEV, TLB)].

19:⁴ Alx[**to the front**], Byz[on ahead (ASV, DRA, ESV, HCS, JNT, KJV, NAB, NAS, NAU, NET, NIV, NJB, NKJ, NLT, NRS, REB, RSV, TEV, TLB)], Minor[*adds of Jesus* (MRD)]; Alx/Byz[**pass that way**], Minor[pass through that way (NAS, NAU, ~TLB)].

19:⁵ Alx[**looked up**], Byz[looked up and saw him (DRA, KJV, ~MRD, NKJ)].

19:⁹ Alx/Byz[**he also is a son**], Minor[*omits* is (~NLT, ~TLB)].

19:¹³ Alx/Byz[**Do business**], Minor[to do business (TLB)]; Alx/Byz[**while I am coming**], Major[until I come (ASV, DRA, ESV, HCS, KJV, MRD, NAB, NAS, NAU, NET, NIV, NJB, NKJ, NRS, RSV)]; **ten minas** *a mina was about three months' wages.*

19:¹⁵ Alx[**had given the money**], Byz[gave the money (~TEV)]; Alx/Major[**might learn**], Byz[might know (ASV, DRA, ESV, KJV, MRD, NAS, NAU, NET, NKJ, RSV)]; Alx[**what they had gained**], Byz[how much every man had gained (DRA, JNT, KJV, MRD, NJB, NKJ, REB)].

19:¹⁷ Alx[**Well done**], Byz[Well (KJV, TLB)].

very little, be in authority over ten cities.' ¹⁸ And the second came, saying, 'Master, your mina has earned five minas.' ¹⁹ Likewise he said to him, 'You also be over five cities.' ²⁰ And the other came, saying, 'Master, here is your mina, which I have kept laid away in a handkerchief; ²¹ for I was afraid of you, because you are a hard man. You take up what you did not lay down, and reap what you did not sow.' ²² He said to him, 'I will judge you out of your own mouth, you wicked servant! You knew that I was a hard man, taking up what I did not lay down and reaping what I did not sow? ²³ Why then did you not put my money in a bank, that at my coming I might have collected it with interest?' ²⁴ And he said to those who stood by, 'Take the mina from him, and give it to him who has ten minas.' ²⁵ And they said to him, 'Master, he has ten minas already!' ²⁶ 'I tell you, that to every one who has will more be given; but from him who has not, even what he has will be taken away. ²⁷ But these enemies of mine, who did not want me to reign over them, bring them here and slay them before me.'"

²⁸ When he had said this, he went on ahead, going up to Jerusalem. ²⁹ When he came near to Bethphage and Bethany, at the mount that is called "of Olives," he sent two of the disciples, ³⁰ saying, "Go into the village opposite you, where as you enter you will find a colt tied, on which no one has ever sat. And, untying it, bring it here. ³¹ If any one asks you, 'Why are you untying it?' you shall say, 'The Lord has need of it.'" ³² So those who were sent away and found it just as he had told them. ³³ And as they were untying the colt, its owners said to them, "Why are you untying the colt?" ³⁴ And they said, "Because the Lord has need of it." ³⁵ And they brought it to Jesus, and they threw their garments on the colt and set Jesus on it. ³⁶ And as he went along, many spread their garments on the road.

³⁷ And, as he was now drawing near the descent of the Mount of Olives, the whole multitude of the disciples began to rejoice and praise God with a loud voice for all the mighty works they had seen, ³⁸ saying,

"Blessed is the King
who comes in the name of the Lord!

19:18 **Master, your mina** *word order sequenced by grammar in* Alx[*your mina, Master*], *and by word order in* Byz[*Master, your mina*]; *both translate to the same word order in English.*

19:20 Alx[**the other came**], Byz[another came (ASV, DRA, ESV, HCS, JNT, KJV, MRD, NAS, NAU, NET, NIV, NKJ, ~NLT, ~REB, RSV, TEV, ~TLB)].

19:21 Alx/Major[**reap what you did not sow**], Byz[*adds* and gather where you did not scatter seed].

19:22 Alx/Byz[**He said to him**], Major[But he said to him (KJV, NKJ)]; Alx/Major[**what I did not sow**], Byz[*adds* and gathering where I did not scatter seed].

19:23 Alx[**a bank**], Byz[the bank (ASV, DRA, ESV, HCS, JNT, KJV, MRD, NAS, NAU, NET, NJB, NKJ, NLT, NRS, RSV, TEV, TLB)].

19:25 Alx/Byz[*text*], Minor[*omits verse*].

19:26 Alx[**I tell you**], Byz[For I tell you (~DRA, ~JNT, KJV, NKJ)]; Alx[**will be taken away**], Byz[*adds* from him (ASV, DRA, KJV, ~NJB, NKJ, ~REB, TEV)].

19:27 Alx[**these enemies**], Byz[those enemies (DRA, KJV, MRD, NAB, NIV, ~NJB, NKJ, REB, TEV)]; Alx/Byz[**slay them before me**], Major[*omits* them].

19:29 Alx[**Bethphage**], Byz[Bethsphage]; Alx/Byz[**of Olives**], Minor[Olivet (ASV, DRA, ESV, NAS, NAU, NKJ, REB, RSV)]; Alx[**the disciples**], Byz[his disciples (DRA, KJV, MRD, NAB, NIV, NKJ)].

19:30 Alx[**30 saying**], Byz[30 saying *translated the same as* Alx], Minor[saying 30 (NIV, NJB)]; Alx[**And, untying it**], Byz[*omits* And (~ASV, ~DRA, ~ESV, ~HCS, ~JNT, ~KJV, ~MRD, ~NAB, ~NAS, ~NAU, ~NET, ~NIV, ~NJB, ~NKJ, ~NLT, ~NRS, ~REB, ~RSV, ~TEV, ~TLB)].

19:31 Alx[**you shall say**], Byz[*adds* to him (DRA, JNT, KJV, MRD, NIV, NKJ, TEV)].

19:32 Alx/Major[**found it**], Byz[found the colt standing (DRA, ~NLT, ~TLB)].

19:34 Alx/Byz[**Because the Lord has need of it**], Major[*omits* Because (ASV, ESV, HCS, KJV, NAB, NAS, NAU, NET, NIV, NJB, NKJ, NLT, NRS, REB, RSV, TEV, TLB)].

19:35 Alx[**threw their garments**], Byz[threw their own garments (NKJ)].

19:36 Alx/Byz[**spread their garments**], Minor[spread their own garments].

19:38 Alx[**the King who comes**], Byz[he who comes as king (NJB, REB)], Minor[*omits* who comes (~TLB) *others omit* the King]; Psalms 118:26; 148:1.

Peace in heaven
        and glory in the highest!"

39 And some of the Pharisees in the crowd said to him, "Teacher, rebuke your disciples." **40** And he answered and said, "I tell you, if these will keep silent, the stones will cry out."

41 And when he drew near and saw the city he wept over her, **42** saying, "If you had known, even you, this day, the things that make for peace! But now they are hidden from your eyes. **43** For the days will come upon you when your enemies will build an embankment against you, and surround you and hem you in on every side, **44** and dash you to the ground, you and your children within you, and they will not leave one stone upon another in you; because you did not know the time of your visitation."

45 Then he entered the temple and began to drive out those who were selling, **46** saying to them, "It is written,

'And my house shall be a house of prayer';
        but you have made it a 'den of robbers.'"

47 And he was teaching daily in the temple. But the chief priests, the scribes, and the leaders of the people sought to destroy him, **48** but they could not find anything they could do, for all the people hung upon his words.

20 **1** One day as he was teaching the people in the temple and preaching the gospel, the chief priests and the scribes, together with the elders, came up to him **2** and spoke, saying to him, "Tell us, by what authority are you doing these things? Or who it is that gave you this authority." **3** He answered them, "I also will ask you a question; now tell me, **4** the baptism of John – was it from heaven or from men?" **5** And they reasoned among themselves, saying, "If we say, 'From heaven,' he will say, 'Why did you not believe him?' **6** But if we say, 'From men,' all the people will stone us, for they are persuaded that John was a prophet." **7** So they answered that they did not know where it was from. **8** And Jesus said to them, "Neither will I tell you by what authority I do these things."

19:40 Alx[**answered and said**], Byz[*adds* to them (~DRA, JNT, KJV, MRD, NKJ)]; Alx[**I tell you**], Byz[*adds* that (ASV, DRA, JNT, KJV, MRD, NKJ, TEV)]; Alx[**if these will keep silent**], Byz[if these would keep silent (HCS, KJV, MRD, NKJ)].

19:42 Alx/Major[**42 saying**], Byz[saying 42 (DRA)]; Alx[**this day**], Byz[at least in this your day (DRA, KJV, MRD, NKJ, ~TLB)]; Alx[**peace**], Byz[your peace (DRA, KJV, MRD, NIV, NKJ, ~TLB)].

19:43 Alx[**against you**], Byz[around you (ESV, JNT, ~MRD, NJB, NKJ, NLT, NRS, TEV)].

19:44 Alx[**one stone upon another in you** *Greek* one stone upon stone in you], Byz[in you one stone upon another (ASV, DRA, KJV, MRD, NAS, NAU, NET, ~NIV, NKJ, ~NLT, NRS, REB, ~TEV, ~TLB)].

19:45 Alx[**those who were selling**], Byz[*adds* and those who bought (DRA, ~JNT, KJV, MRD, ~NJB, NKJ, ~REB)].

19:46 Alx/Major[**It is written**], Byz[*adds* that]; Alx[**And my house shall be**], Byz[My house is (DRA, KJV, MRD, NKJ, TLB)]; **Isaiah 56:7**, Jeremiah 7:11.

19:48 Alx/Major[**they could to**], Byz[to do *Greek* they would do (DRA, HCS, JNT, NAB, NET, NIV, NJB, NKJ, ~NLT, ~REB, TEV, ~TLB)].

20:1 Alx[**One day** *Greek* One of the days], Byz[One of those days (KJV, MRD, NKJ, TLB)]; Alx[**chief priests**], Byz[priests].

20:2 Alx[**spoke, saying to him**], Byz[spoke to him, saying (DRA, KJV, NKJ)], Minor[*omits* saying (ESV, HCS, ~JNT, MRD, NAB, NET, ~NIV, ~NJB, ~NLT, ~NRS, ~REB, ~RSV, ~TEV, ~TLB)], Alt[*omits* to him *without textual foundation* (~JNT, ~NIV, ~NJB, ~NLT, ~REB, ~TLB)].

20:3 Alx[**ask you a question** *Greek* ask you a word], Byz[ask you one word (DRA, KJV, NKJ)].

20:5 Alx/Major[**Why did you not believe**], Byz[Why then did you not believe (DRA, JNT, KJV, ~MRD, NKJ, TEV, TLB)].

⁹ Then he began to tell the people this parable: "A [certain] man planted a vineyard, leased it to vine-dressers, and went into another country for a long time. ¹⁰ And at harvest time he sent a servant to the tenants, that they would give him some of the fruit of the vineyard. But the tenants beat him and sent him away empty-handed. ¹¹ And he sent another servant; him also they beat and treated shamefully, and sent him away empty-handed. ¹² He sent a third; and they wounded him and cast him out. ¹³ Then the owner of the vineyard said, 'What shall I do? I will send my beloved son; perhaps they will respect him.' ¹⁴ But when the tenants saw him, they reasoned with one another and said, 'This is the heir. Let us kill him, that the inheritance may be ours.' ¹⁵ So they cast him out of the vineyard and killed him. What then will the owner of the vineyard do to them? ¹⁶ He will come and destroy those tenants, and give the vineyard to others." When they heard this, they said, "May this never be!" ¹⁷ But he looked at them and said, "What then is this that is written:

> 'The stone which the builders rejected
> > has become the chief cornerstone'?

¹⁸ Everyone who falls on that stone will be broken to pieces; but on whomever it falls, it will grind him to powder." ¹⁹ The scribes and the chief priests sought to lay hands on him that very hour, but they feared the people – for they knew that he had spoken this parable against them.

²⁰ So they watched him, and sent spies who pretended to be righteous, that they might catch him on what he said, so as to deliver him up to the power and authority of the governor. ²¹ And they asked him, "Teacher, we know that you speak and teach rightly, and you do not show partiality, but teach the way of God in truth. ²² Is it lawful for us to pay taxes to Caesar or not?" ²³ But he perceived their craftiness, and said to them, ²⁴ "Show me a denarius. Whose likeness and inscription does it have?" And they said, "Caesar's." ²⁵ He said to them, "Then render to Caesar the things that are Caesar's, and to God the things that are God's." ²⁶ And they were not able in the presence of the people to catch him by his word. But marveling at his answer they were silent.

20:9 Alx/Byz[**A certain man**], Major[A man (ASV, ESV, HCS, JNT, NAB, NAS, NAU, NET, NIV, NJB, NLT, NRS, REB, RSV, TEV, TLB)]; *NAB incorrectly brackets* A *instead of* certain.

20:10 Alx[**at harvest time**], Byz[in the harvest time], Major[in harvest time (MRD)]; Alx[**that they would give him**], Byz[that they might give him (ASV, DRA, HCS, KJV, MRD, NAS, NKJ, NRS, RSV)].

20:11 Alx/Major[**he sent another servant**], Byz[*adds* to them].

20:13 Alx[**perhaps they will respect him**], Byz[*adds* when they see him (DRA, KJV, MRD, NKJ)].

20:14 Alx[**with one another**], Byz[among themselves (DRA, ESV, HCS, JNT, KJV, MRD, ~NIV, ~NJB, NKJ, NRS, ~REB, RSV, ~TLB)]; Alx[**Let us kill him**], Byz[Come! Let us kill him (KJV, MRD, NKJ, ~NLT, ~REB, TLB)].

20:17 **cornerstone** *or* capstone *or* keystone; **Psalms 118:22**.

20:19 Alx[**The scribes and the chief priests**], Byz[The chief priests and the scribes (DRA, KJV, MRD, NKJ, TLB)]; Alx/Byz[**they feared the people**], Major[they were afraid (~TLB)]; Alx/Major[**this parable**], Byz[the parables (~NLT)].

20:20 Alx[**so as to deliver him**], Byz[in order to deliver him (~HCS, ~MRD, NAB, NKJ, ~NLT, REB, ~TLB)].

20:23 Alx[**said to them**], Byz[*adds* Why do you test me? (DRA, KJV, MRD, NKJ)].

20:24 Alx[**And they said**], Byz[And answering, they said (DRA, ~JNT, KJV, ~NAB, ~NIV, KJV, ~NLT, ~REB, ~TEV, ~TLB)]; *NIV places the response in verse 25.*

20:26 Alx/Byz[**by his word** *or* by his speech], Minor[by the word (ASV, ~MRD, NAS, NAU, ~REB, ~TEV, ~TLB)].

²⁷ Some of the Sadducees, who [argue] that there is no resurrection, questioned him, ²⁸ saying, "Teacher, Moses wrote for us that *if a man's brother dies, having a wife but no children, his brother must take the wife and raise up children for his brother.* ²⁹ Now there were seven brothers. The first took a wife, and died without children. ³⁰ And the second ³¹ and then the third took her, and in the same way the seven also left no children, and died. ³² And afterward the woman also died. ³³ The woman, then – whose wife is she in the resurrection? For all seven had her as wife." ³⁴ And Jesus said to them, "The sons of this age marry and are given in marriage. ³⁵ But those who are considered worthy to attain that age and the resurrection from the dead neither marry nor are given in marriage, ³⁶ nor can they die any more, for they are equal to the angels and are sons of God, being sons of the resurrection. ³⁷ But that the dead are raised, even Moses showed, in the passage about the bush, where he calls *the Lord 'the God of Abraham and the God of Isaac and the God of Jacob.'* ³⁸ Now he is not the God of the dead but of the living, for all live to him." ³⁹ And some of the scribes answered, "Teacher, you have spoken well." ⁴⁰ For they no longer dared to ask him any question.

⁴¹ And he said to them, "How can they say that the Christ is a Son of David? ⁴² For David himself says in the Book of Psalms,

'The Lord said to my Lord,
"Sit at my right hand,
⁴³   till I make your enemies
                    a stool for your feet."'

⁴⁴ David therefore calls him 'Lord,' and how is he his son?"

⁴⁵ And in the hearing of all the people, he said to [his] disciples, ⁴⁶ "Beware of the scribes, who like to walk in long robes, and love greetings in the marketplaces and the best seats in the synagogues and the places of honor at feasts, ⁴⁷ who devour widows' houses and for a pretense make long prayers. These will receive greater condemnation."

20:²⁷ Alx/Major[**who argue that there is no resurrection** *Greek* who speak against: that there is no resurrection], Byz[who say that there is no resurrection (ASV, HCS, JNT, MRD, NAS, NAU, NIV, NLT, NRS, RSV, TEV, ~TLB)].

20:²⁸ Alx/Byz[**questioned him, 28 saying**], Alt[28 questioned him, saying (ASV, ESV, NAS, NAU, NLT, ~NRS, RSV, TLB) *or* questioned him, saying 28 (HCS, REB, TEV)]; Alx[**having a wife but no children** *Greek* having a wife but being childless], Byz[having a wife but dying childless (~DRA, ~HCS, ~JNT, KJV, ~NJB, NKJ, ~TLB)]; ~**Deuteronomy 25:5-6**.

20:³⁰ Alx[**And the second**], Byz[*adds* took her as wife, and he died childless (DRA, KJV, MRD, NKJ, ~NLT, ~REB, ~TEV, TLB)].

20:³¹ Alx[**took her, and in the same way**], Byz[took her in the same way, and in the same way].

20:³² Alx[**And afterward**], Byz[And last of all (DRA, KJV, NKJ, REB, TEV)].

20:³³ Alx[**The woman, then**], Byz[*omits* The woman (ASV, DRA, JNT, KJV, MRD, NAS, NAU, NIV, NJB, NKJ, NLT, REB, TEV, TLB)]; Alx/Byz[**whose wife is she**], Minor[whose wife will she be (ASV, DRA, ESV, HCS, JNT, MRD, NAB, NAS, NAU, NET, NIV, NJB, NKJ, NLT, NRS, ~REB, RSV, TEV, TLB)].

20:³⁴ Alx[**And Jesus said**], Byz[And Jesus answering, said (KJV, ~NIV, ~NJB, NKJ, ~NLT, ~TEV, ~TLB)]; Alx/Byz[**this age**], Minor[*adds* are begotten and beget].

20:³⁵ A;x/Byz[**who are accounted worthy**], Minor[who shall be accounted worthy (DRA, KJV)].

20:³⁶ Alx/Byz[**nor can they die**], Minor[nor will they die (NLT, ~REB, TLB)].

20:³⁷ **Exodus 3:6**, 15.

20:⁴⁰ Alx[**For they no longer dared**], Byz[But they no longer dared (DRA, HCS, KJV, MRD, NAB, NIV, NJB, NKJ, NLT, REB, TLB)].

20:⁴² Alx[**For David himself says**], Byz[And David himself says (DRA, KJV, MRD, NIV, NJB, NKJ)]; Alx/Major[**Psalms**], Byz[the Psalms]; *JNT places the entire quotation in verse 43*.

20:⁴²⁻⁴³ **Psalms 110:1**.

20:⁴⁵ Alx/Byz[**his disciples**], Minor[the disciples (NAS, NAU, NJB, NRS)], Minor[them].

21

¹ He looked up and saw the rich putting their gifts into the treasury, ² and he saw a poor widow put in two copper coins. ³ So he said, "Truly I tell you, this poor widow has put in more than all of the others; ⁴ for these all put in offerings out of their abundance, but she out of her poverty put in all that she had to live on."

⁵ And as some spoke of the temple, how it was adorned with beautiful stones and offerings, he said, ⁶ "As for these things which you see, the days will come when there shall not be left one stone upon another that will not be thrown down."

⁷ So they asked him, "Teacher, when will these things be? And what will be the sign when they are about to take place?" ⁸ And he said: "Take heed that you are not deceived. For many will come in my name, saying, 'I am he,' and, 'The time is near.' Do not go after them. ⁹ And when you hear of wars and revolutions, do not be terrified; for these things must first take place, but the end will not come immediately." ¹⁰ Then he said to them, "Nation will rise against nation, and kingdom against kingdom. ¹¹ There will be great earthquakes, and in various places famines and pestilences; and there will be fearful sights and great signs from heaven. ¹² But before all this, they will lay their hands on you and persecute you, delivering you up to the synagogues and prisons. And you will be brought before kings and governors for my name's sake. ¹³ This will turn into an opportunity for you to bear testimony. ¹⁴ Therefore settle it in your hearts not to meditate beforehand how you will answer; ¹⁵ for I will give you a mouth and wisdom which none of your adversaries will be able to resist or contradict. ¹⁶ You will be betrayed even by parents and brothers and relatives and friends; and they will put some of you to death. ¹⁷ You will be hated by all for my name's sake. ¹⁸ But not a hair of your head can perish. ¹⁹ By your endurance, gain your lives.

²⁰ "But when you see Jerusalem surrounded by armies, then know that its desolation is near. ²¹ Then let those in Judea flee to the mountains, let those who are in the city depart, and let not those who are out in the country enter it. ²² For these are days of vengeance, to fulfill all that is written. ²³ Woe to those who are pregnant and to those who are nursing babies in those days! For there will be great distress in the land and wrath unto

---

21:2 Alx/Byz[**and he saw**], Major[and he also saw (DRA, ~HCS, ~JNT, KJV, MRD, ~NET, ~NIV, NKJ, ~NLT, ~NRS, TEV, ~TLB)]; **copper coins** *Greek* lepta.

21:3 Alx/Byz[**this poor widow**], Minor[this same poor widow].

21:4 Alx[**offerings**], Byz[*adds* of God (DRA, KJV, MRD, NKJ)].

21:5 Alx/Byz[**offerings** *or* votive offerings], Minor[untouchable things *Greek* anathema *or* banned].

21:6 Alx/Byz[**there shall not be left**], Minor[*adds* here (ASV, ESV, ~JNT, RSV)].

21:8 Alx[**saying, 'I am he'**], Byz[saying that, 'I am he' (~TLB)]; Alx[**Do not go after them**], Byz[Therefore do not go after them (DRA, KJV, NKJ)]; **I am he** *Greek* I am; **near** *or* at hand.

21:11 Alx/Byz[**famines and pestilences**], Minor[pestilences and famines (DRA, JNT, NAS, NAU, NJB)].

21:13 Alx[**This will turn**], Byz[But this will turn (DRA, JNT, KJV, MRD, NJB, NKJ, NLT, TLB)].

21:14 Alx[**settle it in your hearts**], Byz[set it into your hearts (DRA)].

21:15 Alx[**resist or contradict**], Byz[contradict nor resist (KJV, ~NKJ)], Minor[resist (MRD, ~TLB)].

21:16 Alx[**parents and brothers and relatives and friends**], Byz[parents and relatives and friends and brothers].

21:19 Alx/Byz[**gain your lives** *or* win your souls], Minor[you will gain your lives *or* you will win your souls (ASV, DRA, ESV, JNT, MRD, NAB, NAS, NAU, NET, NIV, NJB, NLT, NRS, REB, RSV, TEV, TLB)].

21:20 **near** *or* at hand.

21:23 Alx[**Woe to those**], Byz[But woe to those (DRA, KJV, MRD, NKJ)]; Alx/Major[**For there will be**], Byz[For then there will be (MRD, ~TEV)]; Alx/Byz[**wrath unto this people**], Major[wrath upon this people (DRA, JNT, KJV, MRD, NAB, ~NJB, NKJ, REB, RSV, TEV, TLB)]; *NJB places last sentence in verse 24.*

this people. 24 They will fall by the edge of the sword, and be led captive to all nations. Jerusalem will be trampled by the Gentiles until the times of the Gentiles are fulfilled.

25 "There will be signs in sun and moon and stars, and on the earth distress of nations in perplexity at the roaring of the sea and the waves, 26 men fainting from fear and foreboding of what is coming on the world, for the powers of the heavens will be shaken. 27 Then they will see *the Son of Man coming in a cloud* with power and great glory. 28 Now when these things begin to take place, look up and lift up your heads, because your redemption is drawing near."

29 He told them a parable: "Look at the fig tree, and all the trees. 30 When they are sprouting, you see and know for yourselves that summer is already near. 31 So you also, when you see these things happening, know that the kingdom of God is near. 32 Truly, I say to you, this generation will never pass away till all has taken place. 33 Heaven and earth will pass away, but my words will never pass away.

34 "But take heed to yourselves, lest your hearts be weighed down with dissipation and drunkenness and cares of this life, and that Day come on you unexpectedly 35 like a trap. For it will come upon all those who dwell on the face of the whole earth. 36 But watch at all times, and pray always that you may have strength to escape all these things that will take place, and to stand before the Son of Man."

37 And every day he was teaching in the temple, but at night he went out to spend the night on the mount called "of Olives." 38 And early in the morning all the people came to him in the temple to hear him.

22

1 Now the feast of Unleavened Bread drew near, which is called the Passover. 2 And the chief priests and the scribes were seeking how to kill him, for they feared the people. 3 Then Satan entered Judas, called Iscariot, who was numbered of the twelve. 4 So he went his way and conferred with the chief priests and officers, how he might betray him to them. 5 And they were glad, and agreed to give him money. 6 So he consented, and sought an opportunity to betray him to them in the absence of the multitude.

7 Then came the day of Unleavened Bread, [in] which the Passover lamb had to be sacrificed. 8 So he sent Peter and John, saying, "Go and prepare the Passover for us, that we may eat." 9 They said to him, "Where do you want us to prepare it?" 10 He said to them,

---

21:24 Alx/Byz[**times of the Gentiles are fulfilled**], Minor[*adds* and they shall be].

21:25 Alx/Byz[**in perplexity at the roaring of the sea and the waves**], Minor[in perplexity; the sea and the waves roaring (KJV, NKJ)].

21:27 ~Daniel 7:13.

21:32 **generation** *or* race.

21:33 Alx[**will not pass away**], Byz[should not pass away].

21:34 Alx[**unexpectedly 35 like a trap. For**], Byz[unexpectedly. 35 For like a trap (DRA, KJV, MRD, NKJ)], Alt[unexpectedly like a trap. 35 For (ASV, ESV, JNT, NAS, NAU, NET, NIV, RSV, ~TLB)].

21:36 Alx[**But watch**], Byz[Therefore watch (DRA, KJV, MRD, NKJ)]; Alx[**may have strength**], Byz[may be counted worthy (DRA, KJV, MRD, NKJ, ~TLB)]; Alx[**all these things**], Byz[all things (JNT, MRD, NAB, NIV, NJB, REB)].

21:37 Alx/Byz[**of Olives**], Minor[Olivet (ASV, DRA, ESV, NAS, NAU, NKJ, REB, RSV)].

21:38 Alx/Byz[*verse*], Minor[*adds John 7:53-8:11 here*]; Alx/Major[**temple**], Byz[mountain].

22:3 Alx[**called Iscariot**], Byz[surnamed Iscariot (DRA, KJV, NAB, NJB, NKJ)], Alt/Vulgate/Peshitta[surnamed Scariot], Alt[from Kerioth (~JNT)]; **Iscariot** *Hebraism Ish Keriot* a man from Kerioth *or possibly Sicarios* assassin *or* bandit.

22:4 Alx/Byz[**officers**], Byz[and scribes and the officers (MRD)], Minor[the officers (DRA, JNT, NIV, NJB, ~NLT, ~NRS, TEV)].

22:7 Alx/Byz[**in which**], Minor[*omits* in (HCS, KJV, NAB, NKJ, NLT, TEV, TLB)].

22:8 Alx/Byz[**Peter**], Alt/Peshitta[Cephas (JNT, MRD)].

22:10 Alx[**in which he enters**], Byz[that he enters (ESV, HCS, JNT, ~MRD, NAB, NAS, NAU, NET, NIV, NJB, NKJ, NLT, NRS, REB, RSV, TEV, TLB)].

"Behold, when you have entered the city, a man carrying a jar of water will meet you; follow him into the house in which he enters. ¹¹ And say to the owner of the house, 'The Teacher says to you: Where is the guest room, where I may eat the Passover with my disciples?' ¹² He will show you a large, furnished upper room; there make ready." ¹³ So they went, and found it just as he had told them; and they prepared the Passover.

¹⁴ When the hour came, he sat to eat, and the apostles with him. ¹⁵ And he said to them, "I have earnestly desired to eat this Passover with you before I suffer; ¹⁶ for I tell you, I will never eat it until it is fulfilled in the kingdom of God." ¹⁷ Then he took a cup, and gave thanks, and said, "Take this and divide it among yourselves; ¹⁸ for I tell you [that] from now on I will never drink of the fruit of the vine until the kingdom of God comes." ¹⁹ And he took bread, gave thanks and broke it, and gave it to them, saying, "This is my body which is given for you; do this in remembrance of me." ²⁰ Likewise he took the cup after supper, saying, "This cup is the new covenant in my blood, which is poured out for you. ²¹ But behold the hand of him who betrays me is with me on the table. ²² For the Son of Man goes as it has been determined, but woe to that man by whom he is betrayed!" ²³ Then they began to question among themselves, which of them it was who would do this.

²⁴ A dispute also arose among them, which of them was to be considered the greatest. ²⁵ And he said to them, "The kings of the Gentiles exercise lordship over them; and those who exercise authority over them are called benefactors. ²⁶ But not so among you; on the contrary, he who is greatest among you, let him be as the youngest, and he who leads as one who serves. ²⁷ For who is greater, one who sits at the table, or one who serves? Is it not the one who sits at the table? But I am among you as One who serves. ²⁸ You are those who have continued with me in my trials. ²⁹ And I bestow on you a kingdom, just as my Father bestowed one on me, ³⁰ so that you may eat and drink at my table in my kingdom and will sit on thrones, judging the twelve tribes of Israel.

³¹ "Simon, Simon, behold, Satan has asked to have you, that he might sift you as wheat. ³² But I have prayed for you, that your faith may not fail; and when you have turned again, strengthen your brothers." ³³ But he said to him, "Lord, I am ready to go with you to prison and to death." ³⁴ He said, "I tell you, Peter, the rooster will not crow this day until you deny three times that you know me."

22:14 Alx[**the apostles**], Byz[the twelve apostles (DRA, KJV, MRD, NKJ, ~TLB)].

22:16 Alx[**I will never eat it**], Byz[I will never eat of it again (DRA, HCS, JNT, KJV, MRD, NAB, NAS, NAU, NET, NIV, NKJ, NLT, REB, TLB)].

22:17 Alx/Major[**a cup**], Byz[the cup (DRA, KJV, MRD, NIV, NKJ)]; *some manuscripts omit this verse, or place it after verse 19 or verse 20.*

22:18 Alx/Byz[**I tell you that**], Minor[*omits* that (ASV, HCS, KJV, NAS, NAU, NIV, NJB, NKJ, REB, ~NLT, ~TLB)]; Alx[**from now on I will never drink**], Byz[I will never drink (DRA, KJV, MRD, NKJ, TLB)]; Alx/Byz[**fruit of the vine**], Minor[product of the vine (MRD, ~NJB, ~NLT, ~TEV, ~TLB)]; Alx[**until the kingdom of God comes** *Greek* until when the kingdom of God comes], Byz[until whenever the kingdom of God comes]; *some manuscripts omit this verse, or place it after verse 20.*

22:19-20 Alx/Byz[*text*], Minor[*omits* which is given for you; do this in remembrance of me." 20 Likewise he took the cup after supper, saying, "This cup is the new covenant in my blood, which is poured out for you (REB)]; *some manuscripts place verse 17 within the text of verse 20 before "This cup…".*

22:22 Alx[**For the Son of Man**], Byz[And the Son of Man (DRA, JNT, KJV, MRD, NIV, NKJ, TEV, TLB)].

22:30 Alx/Byz[**in my kingdom**], Major[*omits*]; Alx/Byz[**and will sit**], Minor[and may sit (DRA, ESV, ~JNT, KJV, MRD, NIV, ~NJB, NKJ, ~REB, RSV, ~TEV)].

22:31 Alx[**Simon, Simon**], Byz[And the Lord said, "Simon, Simon (DRA, KJV, NKJ)], Minor[And Jesus said, "Simon, Simon (MRD)]; **you** *plural.*

22:32 Alx/Byz[**may not fail**], Minor[may not be failing].

22:34 Alx/Byz[**Peter**], Alt/Peshitta[Simon (MRD)], Alt[*without textual foundation* Cephas (~JNT)]; Alx/Byz[**will not crow**], Major[will never crow (~NAB, ~NIV, ~NJB, ~NLT, ~TLB)]; Alx[**until you**

³⁵ And he said to them, "When I sent you out with no purse or bag or sandals, did you lack anything?" They said, "Nothing." ³⁶ But he said to them, "But now, let him who has a purse take it, and likewise a bag; and let him who has no sword sell his robe and buy one. ³⁷ For I tell you that this scripture must be fulfilled in me, *'And he was numbered with transgressors'*; for what is written about me has its fulfillment." ³⁸ They said, "Look, Lord, here are two swords." And he said to them, "It is enough."

³⁹ He came out, and went to the Mount of Olives, as was his custom, and the disciples also followed him. ⁴⁰ When he came to the place, he said to them, "Pray that you may not enter into temptation." ⁴¹ And he withdrew from them about a stone's throw, and knelt down and prayed, ⁴² "Father, if you are willing, take this cup from me; nevertheless not my will, but yours, be done." ⁴³ [[An angel appeared to him from heaven, and strengthened him. ⁴⁴ And being in agony, he prayed more earnestly, and his sweat became like drops of blood falling to the ground.]] ⁴⁵ When he rose from prayer, and came to the disciples, he found them sleeping from sorrow. ⁴⁶ He said to them, "Why do you sleep? Rise and pray that you may not enter into temptation."

⁴⁷ While he was still speaking, a crowd came, and the man who was called Judas, one of the twelve, went before them. He drew near to Jesus to kiss him; ⁴⁸ but Jesus said to him, "Judas, are you betraying the Son of Man with a kiss?" ⁴⁹ When those around him saw what was going to happen, they said, "Lord, shall we strike with the sword?" ⁵⁰ And one of them struck the servant of the high priest and cut off his right ear. ⁵¹ But Jesus answered, "No more of this!" And he touched the ear and healed him. ⁵² Then Jesus said to the chief priests, officers of the temple, and the elders who had come to him, "Have you come out as against a robber, with swords and clubs? ⁵³ When I was with you day after day in the temple, you did not lay hands on me. But this is your hour, and the power of darkness."

⁵⁴ Then they seized him and led him away, bringing him into the high priest's house. Peter followed at a distance. ⁵⁵ When they had kindled a fire in the middle of the

---

deny], Byz[before you deny (KJV, NAB, NIV, ~NJB, NKJ, NLT, ~TLB)].

22:³⁶ Alx[**But he said**], Byz[Therefore he said (HCS, KJV, NKJ)]; Alx[**let him who has no sword sell his robe**], Byz[he who has no sword will sell his robe (~NAU)].

22:³⁷ Alx[**this scripture must be fulfilled**], Byz[this scripture must still be fulfilled (DRA, KJV, ~NJB, NKJ)], Minor[*omits rest of the verse after* fulfilled]; Alx/Byz[**for what is written about me**], Minor[*omits* for (~HCS, ~JNT, ~NAB, ~NIV, ~NJB, ~NLT, ~REB, ~TLB)]; **Isaiah 53:12**.

22:³⁹ Alx[**the disciples**], Byz[his disciples (DRA, KJV, MRD, NIV, NKJ)]; Alx/Byz[**also followed him**], Minor[followed him (ESV, HCS, JNT, MRD, NAB, NET, NIV, NJB, NLT, NRS, REB, RSV, TEV, TLB)].

22:⁴² Alx[**take this cup**], Byz[to take this cup].

22:⁴³ Alx/Byz[*text*], Minor[*omits* (RSV)].

22:⁴⁴ Alx/Byz[*text*], Minor[*omits* (RSV)]; Alx/Byz[**44 And being in agony, he prayed more earnestly**], Minor[And being in agony, he prayed more earnestly 44 (DRA)].

22:⁴⁵ Alx/Byz[**the disciples**], Minor[his disciples (DRA, KJV, MRD, NAB, NKJ)].

22:⁴⁷ Alx[**While he was still speaking**], Byz[But while he was still speaking (KJV, MRD, NKJ, NLT, TLB)], Alt[*with no textual foundation* Suddenly while he was still speaking (NJB)]; Alx/Major[**went before them**], Byz[was leading them (ESV, HCS, JNT, NET, NIV, NLT, NRS, RSV, TEV, TLB)]; Alx/Major[**to kiss him**], Byz[*adds* for he gave this sign to them, "Whoever kisses me, is him." (MRD)].

22:⁴⁹ Alx[**they said**], Byz[they said to him (DRA, KJV, MRD, NKJ)].

22:⁵⁰ **servant** *or* slave.

22:⁵¹ Alx[**touched the ear**], Byz[touched his ear (ASV, DRA, ESV, HCS, KJV, NAS, NAU, NKJ, NRS, RSV)], Minor[touched the wounded man's ear (~JNT, MRD, ~NAB, ~NET, ~NIV, ~NJB, ~NLT, ~REB, ~TEV, ~TLB)].

22:⁵⁴ Alx/Byz[**Peter**], Alt/Peshitta[Simon (MRD)], Alt[*without textual foundation* Cephas (~JNT)].

22:⁵⁵ Alx/Major[**kindled a fire**], Byz[kindled a bonfire]; Alx/Byz[**sat down together**], Minor[sat down around it (DRA, MRD, NAB, NLT, REB, TEV, TLB)]; Alx/Byz[**Peter**], Alt/Peshitta[Simon (MRD)], Alt[*without textual foundation* Cephas (~JNT)].

courtyard and sat down together, Peter sat among them. [56] And a servant girl, seeing him as he sat in the firelight, looked at him, and said, "This man also was with him." [57] But he denied it, saying, "Woman, I do not know him." [58] And a little later some one else saw him and said, "You also are of them." But Peter said, "Man, I am not!" [59] Then after about an hour had passed, another insisted, saying, "Certainly this fellow also was with him, for he is a Galilean." [60] But Peter said, "Man, I do not know what you are saying!" Immediately, while he was still speaking, a rooster crowed. [61] And the Lord turned and looked at Peter. And Peter remembered the word of the Lord, how he had said to him, "Before the rooster crows today, you will deny me three times." [62] And he went out and wept bitterly.

[63] Now the men who were holding him mocked him and beat him. [64] They blindfolded him and kept questioning, saying, "Prophesy! Who is the one who struck you?" [65] And they spoke many other blasphemies against him.

[66] As soon as it was day, the council of the elders of the people came together, both chief priests and scribes; and they led him away to their Sanhedrin, [67] saying, "If you are the Christ, tell us." But he said to them, "If I tell you, you will never believe. [68] And if I ask you, you will never answer. [69] But from now on *the Son of Man will be seated at the right hand of the power of God.*" [70] They all said, "Are you the Son of God, then?" He said to them, "You said it – because I am." [71] And they said, "What further testimony do we need? We have heard it ourselves from his own lips."

23 [1] Then the whole body of them arose and led him to Pilate. [2] And they began to accuse him, saying, "We found this man perverting our nation and forbidding the payment of taxes to Caesar, and saying that he himself is Christ, a king." [3] So Pilate asked him, "Are you the King of the Jews?" He answered him, "You said it." [4] Then Pilate said to the chief priests and the crowds, "I find no crime in this man." [5] But

---

22:56 **servant girl** *or* female slave.

22:57 Alx/Byz[**denied it**], Major[denied him (DRA, KJV, NKJ)].

22:58 Alx/Byz[**Peter**], Alt/Peshitta[Cephas (JNT, MRD)].

22:60 Alx/Byz[**Peter**], Alt/Peshitta[Cephas (JNT, MRD)]; Alx/Byz[**a rooster**], Minor[**the rooster** (ASV, DRA, ESV, KJV, MRD, NAB, NIV, NJB, NKJ, NLT, NRS, RSV)].

22:61 Alx/Byz[**Peter…Peter**], Alt/Peshitta[Cephas…Simon (MRD)], Alt[*without textual foundation* Cephas…Cephas (~JNT)]; Alx[**crows today**], Byz[*omits* today (DRA, KJV, MRD, NKJ, ~NLT, ~REB, ~TEV, ~TLB)].

22:62 Alx[**And he went out**], Byz[And Peter went out (DRA, KJV, NKJ, NLT, TEV, TLB)], Minor[And Simon went out (MRD) *others omit entire verse*].

22:63 Alx[**who were holding him**], Byz[who were holding Jesus (ASV, ESV, HCS, JNT, KJV, MRD, NAB, NAS, NAU, NET, NIV, NJB, NKJ, NLT, NRS, REB, RSV, TEV, TLB)].

22:64 Alx[**They blindfolded him and kept questioning, saying**], Byz[They blindfolded him, struck him in the face, and kept questioning him, saying (DRA, KJV, NKJ, TLB)].

22:66 Alx[**both chief priests and scribes**], Byz[and chief priests and scribes (DRA, KJV, MRD, ~NJB, ~NLT, ~REB, ~TEV, ~TLB)]; Alx[**led him away**], Byz[led him (DRA, HCS, KJV, MRD, NAB, NIV, NJB, NKJ, NLT, NRS, REB, TEV, TLB)]; Alx/Byz[**their Sanhedrin**], Minor[their own Sanhedrin.

22:67 Alx[**67 saying**], Byz[saying 67 (ASV, ESV, KJV, NAS, NAU, NKJ, RSV)], Minor[saying, "If you are the Christ, tell us." 67 (DRA)]; Alx/Byz[**If I tell you**], Minor[*omits*].

22:68 Alx[**And if I ask you, you will not answer**], Byz[And if I also ask you, you will not answer me or let me go (DRA, KJV, MRD, NKJ, ~TLB)].

22:69 Alx[**But from now on**], Byz[*omits* But (KJV, MRD, NKJ)]; ~Psalms 110:1.

22:70 Alx/Byz[**He said to them**], Minor[Jesus said to them (MRD)]; **You said it – because I am** *Greek* You say – because I am *or* You say that I am.

23:2 Alx[**our nation**], Byz[the nation (KJV, NKJ)], Metzger[*Marcion adds* and abolishing the law and the prophets]; Alx[**Caesar, and saying**], Byz[Caesar, saying (KJV, NKJ, TEV, TLB)]; **Christ, a king** *or* an anointed king.

23:3 Alx[**Pilate asked** *i.e.* Pilate requested], Byz[Pilate questioned *i.e.* Pilate demanded (MRD, ~NJB)].

23:4 Alx/Major[**said to…the crowds**], Byz[*adds* that].

23:5 Alx[**even to this place**], Byz[*omits* even (DRA, KJV, NKJ, NLT, TLB)]; Alx/Byz[**to this place**],

they were urgent, saying, "He stirs up the people, teaching throughout all Judea, beginning from Galilee even to this place."

⁶ When Pilate heard this, he asked if the man was a Galilean. ⁷ And when he learned that he belonged to Herod's jurisdiction, he sent him to Herod, who also was in Jerusalem at that time. ⁸ Now when Herod saw Jesus, he was very glad, for he had desired to see him for a long time, because he had heard about him, and he hoped to see some miracle done by him. ⁹ Then he questioned him with many words, but he gave him no answer. ¹⁰ The chief priests and the scribes stood by, vehemently accusing him. ¹¹ And [even] Herod with his soldiers treated him with contempt and mocked him. Then, dressing him in a gorgeous robe, he sent him back to Pilate. ¹² That very day Herod and Pilate became friends with each other, for before this they had been enemies.

¹³ Pilate then called together the chief priests, the rulers, and the people, ¹⁴ and said to them, "You have brought this man to me as one who was inciting the people to rebellion. And behold, having examined him in your presence, I have found no guilt in this man concerning those charges which you make against him; ¹⁵ neither did Herod, for he sent him back to us. Behold, nothing deserving death has been done by him; ¹⁶ I will therefore chastise him and release him." ⁽¹⁷⁾ ¹⁸ But they all cried out together, "Away with this man, and release to us Barabbas" – ¹⁹ a man who was thrown into prison for an insurrection in the city, and for murder. ²⁰ But wanting to release Jesus, Pilate addressed them again. ²¹ But they shouted, "Crucify, crucify him!" ²² Then he said to them the third time, "Why, what evil has he done? I have found in him no crime deserving death. I will therefore chastise him and release him." ²³ But they were insistent, demanding with loud voices that he be crucified. And their voices prevailed. ²⁴ So Pilate gave sentence that their demand should be granted. ²⁵ And he released the man who had been thrown into prison for insurrection and murder, the one they asked for; but Jesus he delivered up to their will.

Metzger[*Marcion adds* and he alienates our sons and wives from us, for he is not baptized as we are *others also add* for they are not baptized as also we are, nor do they purify themselves].

23:⁶ Alx[**heard this**], Byz[heard of Galilee (DRA, KJV, MRD, NKJ, ~NLT, ~TLB)].

23:⁸ Alx[**he had desired to see him for a long time**], Byz[he had long desired to see him (ESV, NET, REB, RSV, ~TLB)]; Alx[**he had heard about him**], Byz[he had heard many things about him (DRA, KJV, MRD, NKJ, TLB)].

23:¹⁰ Alx/Major[**chief priests and the scribes**], Byz[scribes and the chief priests].

23:¹¹ Alx[**And even Herod**], Byz[And Herod (ASV, DRA, ESV, HCS, JNT, KJV, MRD, NAS, NAU, NIV, NJB, NKJ, NLT, REB, RSV, TEV, TLB)].

23:¹² Alx/Byz[**Herod and Pilate**], Major[Pilate and Herod (KJV, MRD, NKJ)].

23:¹⁵ Alx[**he sent him back to us**], Byz[I sent you back to him (DRA, KJV, NKJ)], Minor[I sent him back to him (MRD)].

23:⁽¹⁷⁾ Alx[*omits*], Byz[*adds* for he was obligated to release one to them at the festival (ASV, DRA, HCS, KJV, MRD, NAS, NAU, NKJ)], Minor[*adds this verse after verse 19*]; TLB omits this verse, but numbers verse 18 as 17, followed by verse 19.

23:¹⁹ Alx[**a man who was thrown**], Byz[a man having been thrown (ESV, HCS, JNT, MRD, NAB, NAS, NAU, NET, NIV, NJB, NKJ, NRS, REB, RSV, TEV)]; Alx/Major[**prison**], Byz[the prison].

23:²⁰ Alx[**But wanting**], Byz[Therefore wanting (KJV, ~NET, ~NJB, NKJ, ~NLT, TEV, TLB)].

23:²¹ Alx/Byz[**Crucify, crucify him**], Alt[Crucify him, crucify him (DRA, JNT, KJV, MRD, NAB, NIV, NJB, NKJ, NLT, REB, TEV, TLB)].

23:²² Alx/Major[**no crime deserving death** *Greek* no guilt of death], Byz[nothing deserving death (ASV, DRA, ~HCS, JNT, KJV, NIV, NJB, NKJ, NLT, NRS, TEV, TLB)].

23:²³ Alx/Byz[**that he be crucified**], Minor[that he crucify him *others* that they crucify him (MRD)]; Alx[**their voices**], Byz[*adds* and the chief priests' (KJV, NKJ)].

23:²⁵ Alx/Major[**released**], Byz[*adds* to them (DRA, KJV, MRD, NKJ)]; Alx/Major[**the man**], Byz[Barabbas (NLT, TLB)]; Alx[**into prison**], Byz[into the prison].

²⁶ And as they led him away, they seized one Simon, a Cyrenian, who was coming in from the country, and laid on him the cross, to carry it behind Jesus. ²⁷ And a great multitude of the people followed him, and women who mourned and lamented him. ²⁸ But Jesus turning to them said, "Daughters of Jerusalem, do not weep for me, but weep for yourselves and for your children. ²⁹ For behold, the days are coming when they will say, 'Blessed are the barren, and the wombs that never bore, and breasts that never nourished!'

³⁰   Then they will begin *to say to the mountains,*

> *'Fall on us!'*
> *and to the hills,*
> *'Cover us!'*

³¹ For if they do these things when the wood is green, what will happen when it is dry?"

³² Two others, criminals, were also led with him to be put to death. ³³ And when they came to the place called "The Skull," there they crucified him, and the criminals, one from the right and the other from the left. ³⁴ [[Then Jesus said, "Father, forgive them, for they know not what they do."]] And they divided his garments and cast lots. ³⁵ And the people stood watching; but even the rulers sneered at him, saying, "He saved others; let him save himself if he is the Christ of God, the Chosen One." ³⁶ The soldiers also mocked him, coming up, offering him sour wine, ³⁷ and saying, "If you are the King of the Jews, save yourself." ³⁸ There was also an inscription over him:

THIS IS THE KING OF THE JEWS.

³⁹ One of the criminals who were hanged there hurled insults at him, saying, "Are you not the Christ? Save yourself and us!" ⁴⁰ But the other answered, and rebuking him, said, "Do you not fear God, since you are under the same sentence of condemnation? ⁴¹ And we indeed justly, for we are receiving the due reward of our deeds; but this man has done nothing wrong." ⁴² Then he said, "Jesus, remember me when you come into your

---

23:26 Alx[**one Simon**], Byz[Simon (HCS, JNT, MRD, NET, NIV, TLB)]; Alx[**a Cyrenian**], Byz[who was of Cyrene (ASV, DRA, ESV, JNT, NAS, NAU, NET, NIV, NJB, NLT, NRS, REB, RSV, TEV, TLB)].

23:27 Alx[**who mourned**], Byz[who also mourned (KJV, MRD, NJB, NKJ)].

23:29 Alx/Byz[**the days are coming**], Minor[it is coming (~JNT, ~NIV)]; Alx[**the wombs**], Byz[wombs (JNT, NKJ, ~TEV, ~TLB)]; Alx[**nourished**], Byz[nursed (ASV, DRA, ESV, HCS, JNT, KJV, MRD, NAB, NAS, NAU, NET, NIV, NJB, NKJ, NLT, NRS, RSV, TEV, ~TLB)].

23:30 Hosea 10:8.

23:31 Alx/Byz[**the wood is green** *Greek* the green wood], Minor[omits the (KJV, MRD, NJB)].

23:32 Alx/Byz[**with him**], Metzger[*Codex Rehdigeranus adds the names* Joathas and Maggatras *Codex Usserianus reads* ...and Capnatas].

23:33 Alx[**when they came**], Byz[when they departed (~TLB)]; Alx/Byz[**from the right...from the left**], Minor[from the right...on the left (~ASV, ~DRA, ~ESV, ~HCS, ~JNT, ~KJV, ~MRD, ~NAB, ~NAS, ~NAU, ~NET, ~NIV, ~NJB, ~NKJ, ~NLT, ~NRS, ~REB, ~RSV, ~TEV, ~TLB)].

23:34 Alx/Byz[*text*], Minor[*omits verse*]; Alx/Major[**cast lots**], Byz[began to cast lots]; Psalms 22:18.

23:35 Alx[**but even the rulers**], Byz[adds with them (DRA, KJV, NKJ)], Minor[omits even (DRA, ESV, JNT, NAB, NET, NJB, NLT, NRS, REB, RSV, TEV, TLB)]; Alx[**the Christ of God, the Chosen One**], Byz[the Christ, the Chosen One of God (DRA, JNT, KJV, MRD, NKJ, ~TEV, TLB)].

23:36 Alx[**offering him**], Byz[and offering him (DRA, ESV, KJV, MRD, NET, NKJ, NRS, RSV, TEV)].

23:38 Alx[**over him**], Byz[written over him in letters of Greek, Latin, and Hebrew (DRA, KJV, MRD, NKJ)].

23:39 Alx/Byz[**insults at him, saying**], Minor[omits saying (HCS, JNT, NIV, NJB, NLT, REB, TEV, TLB)]; Alx[**Are you not the Christ? Save**], Byz[If you are the Christ, save (DRA, KJV, MRD, NKJ)]; **hurled insults at him** *or* blasphemed him.

23:40 Alx[**rebuking him, said**], Byz[rebuked him, saying (DRA, ESV, ~HCS, JNT, KJV, ~MRD, NET, ~NIV, ~NJB, NKJ, ~NLT, NRS, ~REB, RSV, TEV, ~TLB)].

23:42 Alx[**said, "Jesus, remember me when you come into your kingdom"**], Byz[said to Jesus, "Lord, remember me when you come in your kingdom" (DRA, KJV, MRD, NKJ, ~TEV)], Minor[in the

kingdom." ⁴³ And he said to him, "Truly, I say to you, today you will be with me in Paradise."

⁴⁴ And it was now about the sixth hour, and there was darkness over the whole land until the ninth hour – ⁴⁵ the sun failed; and the veil of the temple was torn in two. ⁴⁶ And Jesus, crying out with a loud voice, said, "Father, *into your hands I commit my spirit.*" And having said this, he breathed his last. ⁴⁷ Now when the centurion saw what had happened, he began to praise God, saying, "Certainly this was a righteous man!" ⁴⁸ When all the multitudes who had gathered to witness this sight saw what had taken place, they beat their breasts, and returned home. ⁴⁹ But all his acquaintances, and the women who had followed him from Galilee, stood at a distance, watching these things.

⁵⁰ Now there was a man named Joseph, a member of the Council, [and] a good and righteous man, ⁵¹ who had not consented to their decision and deed. He came from Arimathea, a city of the Jews, and he was waiting for the kingdom of God. ⁵² This man went to Pilate and asked for the body of Jesus. ⁵³ Then he took it down and wrapped it in linen cloth, and laid it in a tomb that was hewn out of the rock, where no one had ever yet been laid. ⁵⁴ It was the Preparation Day, and the Sabbath was about to begin. ⁵⁵ But the women who had come with him from Galilee followed and saw the tomb, and how his body was laid. ⁵⁶ Then they returned and prepared spices and perfumes.

24 And on the Sabbath they rested according to the commandment. ¹ But on the first day of the week, at early dawn, they came to the tomb, bringing the spices which they had prepared. ² And they found the stone rolled away from the tomb, ³ but when they went in they did not find the body of the Lord Jesus. ⁴ While they were perplexed about this, behold, two men stood by them in dazzling apparel. ⁵ And as the women were terrified and bowed their faces to the ground, the men said to them, "Why do you seek the living among the dead? ⁶ He is not here, but is risen! Remember how he

---

day of your coming].

23:⁴³ Alx[**And he said to him**], Byz[And Jesus said to him (DRA, JNT, KJV, MRD, NET, NIV, NKJ, NLT, REB, TEV, TLB)]; Alx/Byz[**I say to you, today you will be with me**], Minor[I say to you today, you will be with me].

23:⁴⁴ Alx[**it was now**], Byz[*omits* now (DRA, KJV, MRD, NKJ, TEV)]; **land** *or* earth.

23:⁴⁵ Alx[**45 the sun failed** *or* the sun eclipsed *active*], Byz[the sun failed 45 (NJB)], Major[45 and the sun was darkened *passive* (DRA, ~JNT, KJV, MRD, ~NAB, ~NAS, ~NAU, ~NIV, NKJ, NLT)].

23:⁴⁶ Alx[**I commit my spirit**], Byz[I place my spirit (TEV)], Major[I will commit my spirit]; Psalms 31:5.

23:⁴⁷ Alx[**began to praise God**], Byz[praised God (ASV, DRA, ESV, KJV, MRD, NAB, NET, NIV, NJB, NKJ, NLT, NRS, REB, RSV, TEV, ~TLB)]; **a righteous** *or* an innocent.

23:⁴⁸ Alx[**beat their breasts** *Greek* beat the breasts], Byz[beat their own breasts], Alt[*omits without textual foundation* (~NLT, ~TLB)].

23:⁵⁰ Alx/Byz[**and a good**], Major[*omits* and (ASV, DRA, ESV, HCS, JNT, MRD, NAB, NAS, NAU, NET, NIV, NJB, NKJ, NLT, NRS, REB, TEV, TLB)].

23:⁵¹ Alx/Byz[**He came from Arimathea, a city of the Jews**], Minor[*moves to verse 50* (ESV, MRD, RSV, ~TEV, ~TLB)]; Alx[**and he was waiting** *Greek* who was waiting], Byz[and he himself was also waiting *Greek* who himself was also waiting (DRA, KJV, NKJ)], Major[and who himself was also waiting].

23:⁵⁴ Alx[**and the Sabbath**], Byz[*omits* and (TLB)].

23:⁵⁵ Alx[**But the women who had come**], Byz[But women who had come], Minor[But women who had also come (~KJV)].

24:¹ Alx[**prepared**], Byz[*adds* and certain other women with them (KJV, MRD, NKJ)].

24:³ Alx[**but when they went in**], Byz[and when they went in (ASV, ~JNT, DRA, KJV, MRD, ~NKJ, ~NLT, ~TEV, ~TLB)]; Alx/Byz[**of the Lord Jesus**], Minor[*omits* (~MRD, NRS, RSV)].

24:⁴ Alx[**perplexed**], Byz[greatly perplexed (~DRA, KJV, NKJ, REB)].

24:⁵ Alx[**bowed their faces** *Greek* bowed the faces], Byz[bowed the face (DRA, ~HCS, ~REB, ~TEV, ~TLB)].

24:⁶ Alx/Byz[**He is not here, but is risen**], Minor[*omits* (REB, RSV) *others move to verse 5* (NRS)].

told you while he was still in Galilee, [7] 'The Son of Man must be delivered into the hands of sinful men, and be crucified, and on the third day rise again.'" [8] And they remembered his words. [9] Then they returned from the tomb and told all these things to the eleven and to all the rest. [10] It was Mary Magdalene, Joanna, Mary the mother of James, and the other women with them – they told this to the apostles. [11] But these words seemed to them like idle tales, and they did not believe them. [12] But Peter arose and ran to the tomb; and stooping down, he saw the linen wrappings by themselves; and he went away, marveling to himself at what had happened.

[13] Now behold, that same day two of them were going to a village called Emmaus, about seven miles from Jerusalem. [14] And they were talking with each other about all these things that had happened. [15] While they talked and discussed, Jesus himself drew near and went with them. [16] But their eyes were kept from recognizing him. [17] And he said to them, "What is this conversation which you are exchanging with each other as you walk?" And they stood still, looking sad. [18] Then one of them, named Cleopas, answered him, "Are you the only visitor to Jerusalem who does not know the things that have happened there in these days?" [19] And he said to them, "What things?" And they said to him, "The things concerning Jesus the Nazarene, who was a prophet mighty in deed and word before God and all the people, [20] and how the chief priests and our rulers delivered him to be condemned to death, and crucified him. [21] But we had hoped that he was the one who was going to redeem Israel. Indeed, and besides all this, it is the third day since all this happened. [22] In addition, some women of our company amazed us. They were at the tomb early in the morning, [23] and when they did not find his body, they came saying that they had also seen a vision of angels who said he was alive. [24] Some of those who were with us went to the tomb, and found it even so as the women had said; but him they did not see." [25] And he said to them, "O foolish men, and slow of heart to believe all that the prophets have spoken! [26] Did not the Christ have to suffer these things and enter his glory?" [27] And beginning with Moses and all the prophets, he explained to them the things concerning himself in all the scriptures.

24:9 Alx/Byz[**from the tomb**], Minor[*omits* (TLB)].

24:10 Alx/Byz[**It was May Magdalene**], Minor[*omits* It was (HCS)]; Alx[**they told this**], Byz[who told this (DRA, ESV, JNT, KJV, MRD, NET, NIV, KJV, NLT, NRS, RSV, TEV, ~TLB)].

24:11 Alx[**these words**], Byz[their words (~JNT, KJV, NAB, NIV, ~NJB, NKJ, ~NLT)].

24:12 Alx/Byz[**Peter**], Alt/Peshitta[Simon (MRD)], Alt[*without textual foundation* Cephas (~JNT)]; Alx[**wrappings by themselves**], Byz[wrappings lying by themselves (DRA, KJV, NIV, NKJ)], Minor[wrapping lying by itself (MRD) *others* wrappings *others omit entire verse* (REB, RSV)].

24:13 Alx/Byz[**seven miles** *Greek* sixty stadia], Minor[one hundred and sixty stadia].

24:17 Alx[**walk?" And they stood still, looking sad**], Byz[walk, looking sad?" (DRA, KJV, MRD, NKJ)].

24:18 Alx[**named Cleopas**], Byz[whose name was Cleopas (DRA, KJV, MRD, NKJ, NRS)]; Alx/Byz[**visitor to Jerusalem** *Greek* Jerusalem stranger], Minor[visitor in Jerusalem (ASV, HCS, JNT, KJV, MRD, NJB, NKJ, NLT, NRS, REB, TEV, TLB)].

24:19 Alx[**Jesus the Nazarene**], Byz[Jesus of Nazareth (DRA, ESV, KJV, MRD, NIV, NJB, NKJ, NRS, REB, RSV, TEV)].

24:21 Alx[**and besides all this**], Byz[*omits* and (HCS, JNT, ~MRD, NAS, NAU, NET, NKJ, ~NLT, REB, TEV)]; Alx[**it is the third day**], Byz[today is the third day (DRA, JNT, KJV, NKJ)]; **to redeem Israel** *or* to set Israel free.

24:24 Alx/Byz[**found it even so as the women had said**], Minor[*omits* even (DRA, ESV, HCS, ~JNT, MRD, NAB, NET, NIV, ~NJB, NKJ, NLT, NRS, REB, RSV, ~TEV, TLB)].

24:27 Alx[**explained to them**], Byz[began to explain to them]; Alx/Byz[**the things concerning himself**], Minor[the things that were concerning himself (DRA, JNT, NJB)].

²⁸ As they drew near the village to which they were going, he acted as though he would be going further, ²⁹ but they constrained him, saying, "Stay with us, for it is toward evening and the day is now far spent." So he went in to stay with them. ³⁰ When he was at the table with them, he took bread, blessed and broke it, and gave it to them. ³¹ Then their eyes were opened and they recognized him; and he vanished from their sight. ³² And they said to each other, "Did not our hearts burn [within us] while he talked with us on the road, while he opened to us the scriptures?" ³³ So they rose up that very hour and returned to Jerusalem, and they found the eleven and those who were with them assembled, ³⁴ saying, "The Lord has risen indeed, and has appeared to Simon!" ³⁵ Then they told what had happened on the road, and how he was known to them in the breaking of the bread.

³⁶ As they were saying this, he himself stood among them and said to them, "Peace be with you." ³⁷ But they were startled and frightened, and supposed that they saw a spirit. ³⁸ And he said to them, "Why are you troubled, and why do doubts rise in your heart? ³⁹ See my hands and my feet, that it is I myself. Handle me and see, for a spirit does not have flesh and bones as you see I have." ⁴⁰ When he had said this, he showed them his hands and his feet. ⁴¹ And while they still did not believe for joy, and marveled, he said to them, "Have you anything here to eat?" ⁴² They gave him a piece of broiled fish, ⁴³ and he took it and ate in their presence.

⁴⁴ Then he said to them, "These are my words which I spoke to you, while I was still with you, that everything written about me in the law of Moses and the prophets and the psalms must be fulfilled." ⁴⁵ Then he opened their minds, so they could understand the Scriptures. ⁴⁶ And he said to them, "Thus it is written, that the Christ should suffer and rise again from the dead the third day, ⁴⁷ and that repentance for forgiveness of sins should be preached in his name to all nations. Beginning at Jerusalem, ⁴⁸ you are witnesses of these

---

24:²⁸ Alx[**acted as though he would be going further**], Byz[began to act as though he would be going far (~NJB, ~NRS, ~REB, ~TLB)].

24:²⁹ Alx[**the day is now far spent**], Byz[*omits* now (JNT, KJV, MRD, NAB, NET, NIV, NJB, NKJ, NLT, REB, TEV, TLB)].

24:³² Alx/Byz[**Did not our hearts burn**], Metzger[*Minor adds* Were not our hearts veiled *others* Were not our hearts terrified *others* Was not our heart heavy]; Alx/Byz[**within us**], Minor[*omits* (REB, TLB)]; Alx[**while he opened**], Byz[and while he opened (DRA, HCS, KJV, MRD, NAB, NIV, NJB, NKJ, NLT, REB, TEV, TLB)].

24:³³ Alx[**assembled**], Byz[gathered together (ASV, DRA, ESV, HCS, JNT, KJV, NAB, NAS, NAU, NET, NIV, NJB, NKJ, NRS, RSV, TEV, ~TLB)].

24:³⁶ Alx[**he himself**], Byz[Jesus himself (DRA, ESV, KJV, MRD, NET, NIV, NKJ, NLT, NRS, RSV, ~TEV, TLB)]; Alx/Byz[**and said to them, "Peace be with you."**], Minor[*omits* (JNT, NAS, REB, RSV, ~TLB) *others add* It is I; do not be afraid (DRA, MRD)].

24:³⁷ Alx/Byz[**saw a spirit**], Minor[saw a ghost (HCS, JNT, NET, NIV, NJB, NLT, NRS, REB, TEV, TLB)].

24:³⁸ Alx[**your heart**], Byz[your hearts (DRA, ESV, HCS, ~JNT, KJV, MRD, NAB, NAS, NAU, NET, NIV, NJB, NKJ, NLT, NRS, REB, RSV, TEV, ~TLB)].

24:³⁹ Alx/Byz[**my hands and my feet**], Minor[my hands and feet (DRA, REB)]; Alx/Byz[**flesh** *singular*], Minor[flesh *plural*].

24:⁴⁰ Alx/Byz[*text*], Minor[*omits* (REB, RSV)].

24:⁴² Alx[**broiled fish**], Byz[*adds* and some honeycomb (DRA, KJV, MRD, NKJ)].

24:⁴³ Alx/Byz[*text*], Minor[*adds* taking the remains, he gave to them (DRA)].

24:⁴⁴ Alx[**These are my words**], Byz[These are the words (DRA, KJV, MRD, ~NIV, NKJ, ~NLT, ~REB, TEV, ~TLB)].

24:⁴⁶ Alx[**written**], Byz[*adds* and thus it was necessary (DRA, KJV, MRD, NKJ)].

24:⁴⁷ Alx[**repentance for forgiveness** *Greek* repentance into releasing], Byz[repentance and forgiveness (ASV, DRA, ESV, KJV, NIV, NKJ, NRS, RSV, TEV)]; Alx[**to all nations. Beginning at Jerusalem, 48 you are witnesses**], Byz[to all nations, beginning at Jerusalem. 48 And you are witnesses (ASV, DRA, ESV, HCS, JNT, KJV, MRD, NAB, NAS, NAU, NET, NIV, NJB, NKJ, NLT, NRS, REB, RSV, TEV, TLB)].

things. ⁴⁹ And [behold], I send the promise of my Father upon you; but stay in the city, until you are clothed with power from on high."

⁵⁰ Then he led them [out] as far as Bethany, and he lifted up his hands and blessed them. ⁵¹ While he blessed them, he parted from them, and was carried up into heaven. ⁵² Then they worshipped him and returned to Jerusalem with great joy, ⁵³ and were continually in the temple blessing God.

24:⁴⁹ Alx/Byz[**And behold**], Minor[*omits* behold (DRA, ~JNT, MRD, NIV, ~NJB, ~NLT, REB, TEV, ~TLB)]; Alx/Byz[**I send the promise**], Minor[I send forth the promise (ASV, JNT, NAS, NAU)]; Alx[**city**], Byz[*adds* of Jerusalem (KJV, NKJ)], Alt[*omits* city *and reads* Jerusalem (MRD)].

24:⁵⁰ Alx/Byz[**led them out**], Minor[*omits* out (NLT)].

24:⁵¹ Alx/Byz[**and was carried up into heaven**], Minor[*omits* (NAS, REB)].

24:⁵² Alx/Byz[**worshipped him and**], Minor[*omits* (NAS, REB, RSV)].

24:⁵³ Alx[**blessing God**], Byz[praising and blessing God. Amen (DRA, KJV, MRD, NKJ)], Minor[praising God (JNT, NAB, NAS, NAU, NIV, NJB, NLT, REB, ~TEV, TLB)].

According to John

1

¹ In the beginning was the Word,
    and the Word was with God,
    and the Word was God.
² He was with God in the beginning.
³ All things were made through him,
    and without him nothing was made.
    What was made ⁴ in him was life,
  and the life was the light of men.
⁵ The light shines in the darkness,
    and the darkness did not overcome it.

⁶ There was a man sent from God, whose name was John. ⁷ He came for a witness, to bear witness of the light, that all might believe through him. ⁸ He was not the light, but came to bear witness of the light. ⁹ The true light, that gives light to every man, was coming into the world.

¹⁰ He was in the world,
    and the world was made through him,
    and the world did not know him.
¹¹ He came to his own,
    and his own did not receive him.

¹² But to all who received him, to those who believed in his name, he gave the right to become children of God – ¹³ who were born, not of blood, nor of the will of the flesh, nor of the will of man, but of God.

¹⁴ And the Word became flesh
    and dwelt among us,
  and we have seen his glory.
    The glory as of the only begotten from the Father,
    full of grace and truth.

¹⁵ John bore witness of him and cried out, saying, "This was he of whom I spoke, 'He who comes after me ranks before me, for he was before me.'" ¹⁶ For of his fullness have we all received, grace upon grace. ¹⁷ For the law was given through Moses; grace and truth came

---

Title Alx/Byz[**According to John**], Minor[*variations of* The Gospel According to Saint John].

1:¹ *Much of the text of John's gospel hovers at the border of poetry and prose. Translations differ widely in their presentation of its structure;* **God** *or* Deity *Greek* θεός; **the Word was with God, and the Word was God** *literally* the Word was with the Deity, and Deity was the Word *the Greek syntax supports the full quality of the Word as Deity, hence Revised English Bible* …what God was, the Word was, *and New English Translation* …the Word was fully God.

1:³-⁴ Alx[*punctuation*], Byz[*punctuation* 3 All things were made through him, and without him nothing was made that was made. 4 In him was life, and the life was the light of men (Metzger, ASV, DRA, ESV, HCS, JNT, KJV, MRD, NAS, NAU, NET, NIV, NJB, NKJ, NLT, REB, RSV, TEV, TLB)].

1:⁴ Alx/Byz[**4…was life**], Minor[4…is life (TLB)].

1:⁵ **overcome** *or* comprehend *Greek* grasp.

1:⁹ *or* He was the true light, that gives light to every man coming into the world.

1:¹³ Alx/Byz[**who were born**], Minor[who was born]; **blood** *Greek* bloods.

1:¹⁵ Alx/Byz[**This was he of whom I spoke**], Minor[This was he who spoke].

1:¹⁶ Alx[**For of**], Byz[And of (DRA, ESV, HCS, ~JNT, KJV, MRD, ~NAB, ~NIV, NJB, NKJ, ~NRS, ~REB, RSV, TEV, TLB)]; **grace upon grace** *Greek* and grace for grace.

through Jesus Christ. [18] No one has ever seen God; God the only begotten, who is in the bosom of the Father, he has made him known.

[19] Now this is the testimony of John, when the Jews sent [to him] priests and Levites from Jerusalem to ask him, "Who are you?" [20] He confessed, he did not deny, but confessed, "I am not the Christ." [21] And they asked him, "What then? Are you *Elijah*?" And he said, "I am not." "Are you *the prophet*?" And he answered, "No." [22] Then they said to him, "Who are you? Give us an answer for those who sent us. What do you say about yourself?" [23] He said,

"I am the *voice of one crying in the wilderness,*
'*Make straight the way of the Lord,*'

as the prophet Isaiah said." [24] Now they had been sent from the Pharisees. [25] They asked him, "Then why do you baptize, if you are not the Christ, and not Elijah, and not the prophet?" [26] John answered them, "I baptize with water; there has stood One among you whom you do not know, [27] who comes after me; the thong of whose sandal I am not worthy to untie." [28] This took place in Bethany beyond the Jordan, where John was baptizing.

[29] The next day he saw Jesus coming toward him, and said, "Behold, the Lamb of God, who takes away the sin of the world! [30] This is he for whom I said, 'After me comes a man who ranks before me, for he was before me.' [31] I myself did not know him; but for this I came baptizing in water, that he might be revealed to Israel." [32] And John bore witness, "I saw the Spirit descend as a dove from heaven, and it remained on him. [33] I did not know him, but he who sent me to baptize with water said to me, 'He on whom you see the Spirit descend and remain, this is he who baptizes with the Holy Spirit.' [34] And I have seen and testified that this is the Son of God."

[35] Again the next day John was standing with two of his disciples. [36] And he looked at Jesus as he walked, and said, "Behold, the Lamb of God!" [37] And the two disciples heard

---

1:18 Alx[**God the only begotten**], Byz[the only begotten Son (ASV, DRA, HCS, JNT, KJV, ~NAB, NJB, NKJ, ~NRS, ~REB, RSV, ~TEV, TLB, Metzger)], Minor[the only begotten]; **only begotten** *can also mean* only.

1:19 Alx[**to him**], Byz[*omits* (ESV, HCS, JNT, KJV, NET, NIV, NKJ, NLT, NRS, REB, RSV, TLB)].

1:21 Alx/Byz[**And he said**], Minor[*omits* And (ESV, HCS, JNT, NET, NIV, NJB, NKJ, NLT, NRS, REB, RSV, TEV, TLB)]; Malachi 4:5-6, Deuteronomy 18:15, 18.

1:23 ~**Isaiah 40:3 LXX**.

1:24 Alx[**Now they had been sent from the Pharisees**], Byz[Now those who were sent were from the Pharisees (DRA, ~JNT, KJV, MRD, ~NAB, ~NIV, NJB, NKJ, ~REB)].

1:25 Alx[**and not Elijah, and not the prophet**], Byz[nor Elijah, nor the prophet (ASV, DRA, ESV, HCS, JNT, KJV, MRD, NAB, NAS, NAU, NET, NIV, NKJ, NLT, NRS, REB, RSV, TEV, TLB)].

1:26, 31, 33 **with** *or* in.

1:26 Alx[**there has stood**], Byz[but there has stood (DRA, ~ESV, ~HCS, ~JNT, ~KJV, ~MRD, ~NAB, ~NAS, ~NAU, ~NIV, ~NJB, ~NKJ, ~NLT, ~REB, ~RSV, ~TEV, ~TLB)], Minor[there stands (ASV, NET, NRS)].

1:27 Alx[**do not know, 27 who comes after me**], Byz[do not know. 27 It is he who comes after me (DRA, HCS, JNT, KJV, MRD, NAS, NAU, NIV, NKJ, ~NLT, ~TEV)]; Alx[**the thong of whose sandal**], Byz[who is preferred before me, the thong of whose sandal (DRA, KJV, MRD, NKJ)].

1:28 Alx/Byz[**Bethany**], Minor[Bethabara (KJV, NKJ)].

1:29 Alx/Major[**he saw** *Greek* he sees], Byz[John saw *Greek* John sees (DRA, HCS, JNT, KJV, MRD, NET, NIV, NKJ, NLT, TEV, TLB)].

1:30 Alx[**for whom I said** *Greek* on behalf of whom I said], Byz[of whom I said *or* about whom I said (~ASV, ~DRA, ~ESV, HCS, JNT, ~KJV, ~MRD, ~NAB, NET, NIV, ~NJB, ~NKJ, NLT, ~NRS, ~REB, ~RSV, TEV, TLB)].

1:31 Alx[**in water**], Byz[in the water].

1:32 Alx/Byz[**as a dove**], Major[like a dove (ESV, HCS, JNT, KJV, NAB, NET, NJB, NKJ, NLT, NRS, REB, TEV, ~TLB)].

1:34 Alx/Byz[**Son**], Minor[Chosen One (NET, NJB, NLT, REB) *others* Chosen Son].

1:37 Alx/Byz[**And the two disciples**], Minor[*omits* And (ESV, HCS, JNT, NAB, NAU, ~NET, ~NIV, NKJ, ~NLT, NRS, ~REB, RSV, TEV, ~TLB)].

him say this, and they followed Jesus. ³⁸ But Jesus turned, and saw them following, and said to them, "What do you seek?" They said to him, "Rabbi" (which is translated as "Teacher"), "where are you staying?" ³⁹ He said to them, "Come and you will see." So they came and saw where he was staying. And they stayed with him that day. It was about the tenth hour. ⁴⁰ One of the two who heard John speak, and followed him, was Andrew, Simon Peter's brother. ⁴¹ He first found his own brother Simon, and said to him, "We have found the Messiah" (which means the Christ). ⁴² He brought him to Jesus. Jesus looked at him and said, "You are Simon son of John. You shall be called Cephas" (which means Peter).

⁴³ The next day he wanted to go to Galilee, and he found Philip. And Jesus said to him, "Follow me." ⁴⁴ Now Philip was from Bethsaida, the city of Andrew and Peter. ⁴⁵ Philip found Nathanael and said to him, "We have found him of whom Moses in the law, and also the prophets, wrote – Jesus, son of Joseph, from Nazareth." ⁴⁶ And Nathanael said to him, "Can anything good come out of Nazareth?" Philip said to him, "Come and see." ⁴⁷ Jesus saw Nathanael coming toward him, and said of him, "Behold, an Israelite indeed, in whom is no deceit!" ⁴⁸ Nathanael said to him, "How do you know me?" Jesus answered him, "Before Philip called you, when you were under the fig tree, I saw you." ⁴⁹ Nathanael answered him, "Rabbi, you are the Son of God! You are King of Israel!" ⁵⁰ Jesus answered him, "Because I said to you that I saw you under the fig tree, do you believe? You shall see greater things than these." ⁵¹ And he said to him, "Truly, truly, I say to you, you shall see heaven opened, and the angels of God ascending and descending upon the Son of Man."

1:38 Alx/Byz[**But Jesus**], Minor[*omits* But (ESV, ~HCS, JNT, NAB, NET, NIV, NJB, NLT, ~NRS, REB, RSV, TEV, TLB)]; Alx[**which is translated as "Teacher"**], Byz[which means "Teacher" (ASV, DRA, ESV, HCS, JNT, KJV, NIV, NJB, NLT, REB, RSV, TEV)], Alt/Peshitta[*omits as redundant* (MRD, TLB)]; *the Tischendorf and Byzantine texts begin verse 39 after* **and said to them** *and number the verses one number higher through the end of the chapter.*

1:39 Alx[**you will see**], Byz[see (DRA, JNT, KJV, MRD, NJB, NKJ, NLT, NRS, REB, RSV, TEV, TLB)]; Alx/Byz[**So they came**], Major[*omits* So (DRA, KJV, ~MRD, NKJ, ~NLT, NRS, RSV)]; Alx/Byz[**it was about the tenth hour**], Minor[for it was about the tenth hour (DRA, ESV, KJV, MRD, NAS, NAU, NET, NKJ, RSV, ~TLB)].

1:40 Alx/Byz[**Peter**], Alt/Peshitta[*omits* (MRD)], Alt[*without textual foundation* Cephas (~JNT)].

1:41 Alx[**He first found** *the first thing he did was find*], Byz[He was the first to find *the first to get a convert* (~NLT, ~TLB)].

1:42 Alx[**He brought him to Jesus**], Byz[And he brought him to Jesus (DRA, HCS, KJV, MRD, NIV, NJB, NKJ, NLT, TEV, TLB)]; Alx/Byz[**Jesus looked at him**], Minor[And Jesus looked at him (DRA, HCS, KJV, MRD, NKJ)]; Alx[**son of John**], Byz[son of Jonah (DRA, KJV, MRD, NKJ)]; Alx/Byz[**which means Peter** *or* which means a rock], Alt/Peshitta[*omits* (MRD)]; **Cephas** *Aramaic* stone, **Peter** *Greek* rock.

1:43 Alx/Major[**The next day he**], Byz[The next day Jesus (ESV, KJV, MRD, NET, NIV, NJB, NKJ, NLT, NRS, REB, RSV, TEV, TLB)]; Alx/Major[**And Jesus said**], Byz[And he said (ESV, ~HCS, ~JNT, KJV, MRD, NET, NIV, NJB, NKJ, NLT, NRS, REB, RSV, TEV, TLB)].

1:44 Alx/Byz[**Peter**], Alt/Peshitta[Simon (MRD)], Alt[*without textual foundation* Cephas (~JNT)].

1:45 Alx[**son of Joseph**], Byz[the son of Joseph (ASV, DRA, ESV, HCS, KJV, MRD, NAS, NAU, NET, NIV, NKJ, NLT, RSV, TLB)].

1:46 Alx/Byz[**And Nathanael**], Minor[*omits* And (ESV, HCS, JNT, MRD, ~NAB, NAU, NET, NIV, NJB, NLT, NRS, REB, RSV, TEV, TLB)].

1:49 Alx[**Nathanael answered him**], Byz[*adds* and said (KJV, MRD, NKJ, ~REB)]; Alx[**King of Israel**], Byz[the King of Israel (DRA, ESV, HCS, JNT, KJV, MRD, NAB, NAS, NAU, NET, NIV, NKJ, NLT, NRS, RSV, TEV, TLB)].

1:50 Alx[**Because I said to you that**], Byz[*omits* that (ASV, DRA, ESV, HCS, JNT, KJV, NIV, NJB, NKJ, NLT, REB, RSV, TEV, TLB)].

1:51 Alx[**you shall see heaven**], Byz[hereafter you shall see heaven (KJV, MRD, NKJ)]; **you, you** *both are plural*; Genesis 28:10-17.

2 ¹ On the third day there was a wedding at Cana in Galilee, and the mother of Jesus was there. ² And Jesus and his disciples had also been invited to the wedding. ³ When the wine was gone, the mother of Jesus said to him, "They have no wine." ⁴ [And] Jesus said to her, "Woman, what have you to do with me? My hour has not yet come." ⁵ His mother said to the servants, "Do whatever he tells you." ⁶ Now six stone jars were standing there, according to the manner for purification of the Jews, each holding twenty or thirty gallons. ⁷ Jesus said to them, "Fill the jars with water." And they filled them up to the brim. ⁸ He said to them, "Now draw some out, and take it to the master of the feast." So they took it. ⁹ When the master of the feast had tasted the water that was made wine, and did not know where it had come from (though the servants who had drawn the water knew), the master of the feast called the bridegroom. ¹⁰ And he said to him, "Every man sets out the good wine first; and, when the guests have drunk freely, the poor wine. But you have kept the good wine until now." ¹¹ This first of his signs, Jesus did at Cana in Galilee, and revealed his glory; and his disciples believed in him.

¹² After this he went down to Capernaum, with his mother and [his] brothers and his disciples. And there they stayed for a few days.

¹³ The Passover of the Jews was at hand, and Jesus went up to Jerusalem. ¹⁴ In the temple he found those who were selling oxen and sheep and doves, and the money-changers at their business. ¹⁵ And he made a whip of cords, and drove them all, with the sheep and oxen, out of the temple. And he poured out the money of the money-changers and overturned their tables. ¹⁶ And he said to those who sold doves, "Take these things away! You shall not make my Father's house a house of merchandise!" ¹⁷ His disciples remembered that it was written, "*Zeal for your house will consume me.*" ¹⁸ Then the Jews said to him, "What sign do you show to us, since you do this?" ¹⁹ Jesus answered them, "Destroy this temple, and in three days I will raise it up." ²⁰ The Jews then said, "It has taken forty-six years to build this temple, and will you raise it up in three days?" ²¹ But he was speaking of the temple of his body. ²² When therefore he was raised from the dead, his disciples remembered that he had said this; and they believed the scripture and the word which Jesus had spoken.

²³ Now when he was in Jerusalem at the Passover feast, many believed in his name when they saw the signs which he did. ²⁴ But Jesus did not trust himself to them, because he

---

2:1 Alx/Byz[**Cana in Galilee** *Greek* Cana of Galilee], Alt/Peshitta[Cana, a city of Galilee (MRD, NLT, TEV, TLB)].

2:3 Alx/Byz[**When the wine was gone** *Greek* And the wine failing], Minor[And they had no wine, since the wine of the wedding feast had been used up; then (NJB, ~NLT, ~TLB)]; Alx/Byz[**They have no wine**], Minor[There is no wine (~TLB)].

2:4 Alx[**And Jesus said**], Byz[*omits* And (HCS, JNT, KJV, MRD, NET, NIV, NJB, NKJ, NLT, REB, TEV, TLB)].

2:6 **twenty or thirty gallons** *Greek* two or three metretes.

2:10 Alx[**the poor wine**], Byz[then the poor wine (ASV, DRA, ESV, KJV, MRD, NAS, NAU, NET, NIV, NKJ, NLT, NRS, ~REB, RSV, TLB)].

2:11 Alx[**This first of his signs** *Greek* This first of the signs], Byz[This, the first of the signs (ESV, JNT, MRD, NAB, NET, NIV, NJB, NRS, REB, RSV)].

2:12 Alx[**Capernaum** *Greek* Capharnaum], Byz[Capernaum]; Alx/Byz[**his mother and his brothers and his disciples**], Minor[his mother and brothers and his disciples (JNT, NET, NIV) *others* his mother and brothers and disciples (TEV, TLB) *others* his disciples and his mother and his brothers *others* his mother and his brothers].

2:15 Alx/Byz[**he made a whip**], Minor[he made, as it were, a whip (DRA)]; Alx/Byz[**poured out the money** *Greek* poured out the coin], Minor[poured out the coins (ESV, HCS, JNT, NAB, NAS, NAU, NET, NIV, NJB, NLT, NRS, REB, RSV, TEV, TLB)].

2:17 Alx[**His disciples**], Byz[And his disciples (DRA, HCS, KJV, MRD, NJB, NKJ, NLT, TLB)]; Alx/Byz[**will consume**], Minor[consumed (DRA, KJV, MRD, NJB, NKJ, TEV)]; **Psalms 69:9**.

2:22 Alx/Byz[**he had said this**], Minor[*adds* to them (KJV, NKJ)].

knew all men. 25 And he had no need for anyone to bear witness of man, for he knew what was in man.

3   1 Now there was a man of the Pharisees, named Nicodemus, a ruler of the Jews. 2 This man came to him by night and said to him, "Rabbi, we know that you are a teacher come from God. For no one can do these signs that you do unless God is with him." 3 Jesus answered him, "Truly, truly, I say to you, unless one is born again, he cannot see the kingdom of God." 4 Nicodemus said to him, "How can a man be born when he is old? Can he enter a second time into his mother's womb and be born?" 5 Jesus answered, "Truly, truly, I say to you, unless one is born of water and the Spirit, he cannot enter the kingdom of God. 6 That which is born of the flesh is flesh, and that which is born of the Spirit is spirit. 7 Do not marvel that I said to you, 'You must be born again.' 8 The wind blows where it wishes, and you hear the sound of it, but you cannot tell where it comes from or where it goes. So it is with everyone who is born of the Spirit." 9 Nicodemus said to him, "How can this be?" 10 Jesus answered him, "Are you the teacher of Israel, and yet you do not understand these things? 11 Truly, truly, I say to you, we speak of what we know, and testify to what we have seen. But you do not receive our testimony. 12 If I have told you earthly things and you do not believe, how will you believe if I tell you heavenly things? 13 No one has ascended into heaven, but he who descended from heaven – the Son of Man. 14 And as Moses lifted up the serpent in the wilderness, so must the Son of Man be lifted up, 15 that whoever believes may have eternal life in him. 16 For God so loved the world, that he gave the only begotten Son, that whoever believes in him should not perish but have eternal life. 17 For God did not send the Son into the world to condemn the world, but that the world through him might be saved. 18 He who believes in him is not condemned. But he who does not believe is condemned already, because he has not believed in the name of the only begotten Son of God. 19 And this is the judgment, that the light has come into the world, and men loved darkness rather than light, because their deeds were evil. 20 For every one who does evil hates the light, and does not come to the light, lest his deeds should be exposed. 21 But he who does the truth comes to the light, that it may be clearly seen that his deeds have been done in God."

22 After this Jesus and his disciples went into the land of Judea, and there he remained with them and baptized. 23 Now John also was baptizing at Aenon near Salim, because there was much water there; and people came and were baptized. 24 For John had

---

3:2 Alx[**This man came to him**], Byz[This man came to Jesus (DRA, ESV, JNT, KJV, MRD, NAB, NAU, NET, NIV, NJB, NKJ, NRS, REB, RSV, TEV, TLB)].

3:3, 7 **born again** or born from above.

3:5 Alx/Byz[**kingdom of God**], Minor[kingdom of the heavens].

3:5, 6, 8 **spirit…wind** Greek pneuma.

3:7 **you** singular, '**You** plural.

3:8 Alx/Byz[**born of the Spirit**], Minor[born of the water and the Spirit].

3:11 **you do not receive** you is plural.

3:12 **You** plural.

3:13 Alx[**Son of Man**], Byz[adds who is in heaven (ASV, DRA, KJV, MRD, NKJ, REB, ~TEV)].

3:15 Alx[**believes may have eternal life in him** or believes in him may have eternal life], Byz[believes in him may not perish but have eternal life (DRA, KJV, MRD, NKJ)]; the quotation may end here, instead of verse 21.

3:16 Alx[**the only begotten Son**], Byz[his only begotten Son (ASV, DRA, ESV, HCS, JNT, KJV, MRD, NAB, NAS, NAU, NET, NIV, NJB, NKJ, NLT, NRS, REB, RSV, TEV, TLB)].

3:17 Alx[**the Son**], Byz[his Son (DRA, ESV, HCS, KJV, MRD, NAB, NET, NIV, NJB, NKJ, NLT, REB, TEV, TLB)].

3:18 Alx/Byz[**but he who does not**], Minor[omits but (ASV, JNT, NAS, NAU, NET, RSV)].

3:20 Alx/Byz[**his deeds**], Minor[his evil deeds (NLT, REB, TEV, TLB)].

3:23 Alx/Byz[**Salim**], Major[Salem (JNT)].

not yet been put in prison. ²⁵ Now a discussion arose between some of John's disciples and a Jew over purifying. ²⁶ And they came to John and said to him, "Rabbi, he who was with you beyond the Jordan, to whom you have testified – behold, he is baptizing, and all are going to him." ²⁷ John answered, "A man cannot receive even one thing unless it has been given to him from heaven. ²⁸ You yourselves can bear me witness, that I said [that], 'I am not the Christ,' but I have been sent before him. ²⁹ He who has the bride is the bridegroom. But the friend of the bridegroom, who stands and hears him, rejoices greatly because of the bridegroom's voice. Therefore this joy of mine is now full. ³⁰ He must increase, but I must decrease.

³¹ "He who comes from above is above all. He who is of the earth belongs to the earth, and of the earth he speaks. He who comes from heaven [is above all]. ³² He testifies to that which he has seen and heard; yet no one receives his testimony. ³³ He who has received his testimony has certified that God is true. ³⁴ For he whom God has sent speaks the words of God, for he gives the Spirit without measure. ³⁵ The Father loves the Son, and has given all things into his hand. ³⁶ He who believes in the Son has eternal life; but he who does not obey the Son shall not see life, but the wrath of God remains on him."

4 ¹ Now when Jesus knew that the Pharisees had heard that Jesus was making and baptizing more disciples than John ² (although Jesus himself did not baptize, but only his disciples), ³ he left Judea and departed again to Galilee. ⁴ Now he had to go through Samaria. ⁵ So he came to a city of Samaria which is called Sychar, near the plot of ground that Jacob gave to his son Joseph. ⁶ Jacob's well was there, and Jesus, wearied as he was from his journey, sat down by the well. It was about the sixth hour.

⁷ There came a woman of Samaria to draw water. Jesus said to her, "Give me a drink." ⁸ For his disciples had gone away into the city to buy food. ⁹ Then the woman of Samaria said to him, "How is it that you, being a Jew, ask a drink from me, a Samaritan woman?" For Jews have no dealings with Samaritans. ¹⁰ Jesus answered her, "If you knew the gift of God, and who it is that is saying to you, 'Give me a drink,' you would have asked him, and he would have given you living water." ¹¹ [The woman] said to him, "Sir, you

---

3:25 Alx/Byz[**a Jew**], Minor[Jews (DRA, KJV, NKJ, REB, ~TLB) *others* Jesus].

3:27 Alx[**cannot receive even one thing**], Byz[*omits* one (ASV, JNT, KJV, NAB, NAS, NAU, NET, NIV, NJB, NKJ, NLT, NRS, ~REB, RSV, TEV, ~TLB)].

3:28 Alx/Byz[**bear me witness**], Major[*omits* me (HCS, JNT, NAB, NET, NIV, NLT, REB, TLB)]; Alx[**I said that**], Byz[I said (ASV, DRA, ESV, HCS, JNT, KJV, MRD, NAS, NAU, NET, NIV, NJB, NKJ, NLT, NRS, REB, RSV, TEV)]; Alx/Byz[**I am not the Christ**], Minor[I myself am not the Christ].

3:30 **but I must decrease** *the quotation may end here, instead of verse 36.*

3:31-32 Alx[**from heaven is above all. 32 He testifies**], Byz[from heaven is above all. 32 And he testifies (DRA, KJV, MRD, NKJ)], Minor[from heaven 32 testifies (NJB, REB, TLB)].

3:32 Alx/Byz[**testifies to that which he has seen**], Minor[testifies to what he has seen (ESV, HCS, JNT, MRD, NAB, NET, NIV, ~NJB, NLT, NRS, REB, RSV, TEV, TLB)].

3:33 **certified** *or* sealed.

3:34 Alx[**he gives the Spirit**], Byz[God gives the Spirit (DRA, JNT, KJV, MRD, NIV, NKJ, NLT, REB, TEV, TLB)].

3:36 Alx/Byz[**but he who does not obey**], Minor[*omits* but (ESV, NET, NLT, NRS, REB, RSV, TEV, TLB)].

4:1 Alx[**when Jesus knew**], Byz[when the Lord knew (ASV, KJV, NAS, NAU, ~NIV *verse 3*, NKJ, RSV, TLB)]; Alx/Byz[**making and baptizing more disciples than John**], Minor[making more disciples and John baptized].

4:3 Alx[**departed again**], Byz[*omits* again (~NAB, ~NJB, ~NLT, ~NRS, ~TEV, ~TLB)].

4:5 Alx/Byz[**Sychar**], Minor[Shechem (JNT)].

4:9 Alx/Byz[**Then the woman**], Minor[*omits* Then (ESV, HCS, JNT, MRD, NAB, NIV, NJB, NLT, NRS, REB, RSV, TEV, TLB)]; Alx/Byz[**For Jews have no dealings with Samaritans** *or* For Jews do not share things in common with Samaritans], Minor[*omits*].

4:11 Alx/Byz[**The woman said**], Minor[She said (JNT, NAS, NAU, NJB, NLT, TLB)]; Alx/Byz[**So

have nothing to draw with, and the well is deep. So where do you get that living water? [12] Are you greater than our father Jacob, who gave us the well, and drank from it himself, as well as his sons and his cattle?" [13] Jesus answered her, "Everyone who drinks of this water will thirst again, [14] but whoever drinks of the water that I shall give him will never thirst. The water that I shall give him will become in him a spring of water welling up to eternal life." [15] The woman said to him, "Sir, give me this water, that I may not thirst, nor should come all the way here to draw."

[16] He said to her, "Go, call your husband, and come here." [17] The woman answered and said to him, "I have no husband." Jesus said to her, "You are right in saying, 'I have no husband.' [18] For you have had five husbands, and the one whom you now have is not your husband. This you have said truly." [19] The woman said to him, "Sir, I perceive that you are a prophet. [20] Our fathers worshipped on this mountain, and you Jews say that in Jerusalem is the place where men ought to worship." [21] Jesus said to her, "Woman, believe me, the hour is coming when neither on this mountain nor in Jerusalem will you worship the Father. [22] You worship what you do not know; we worship what we know, for salvation is from the Jews. [23] But the hour is coming, and now is, when the true worshippers will worship the Father in spirit and truth, for such the Father seeks to worship him. [24] God is spirit, and those who worship him must worship in spirit and truth." [25] The woman said to him, "I know that Messiah is coming" (who is called Christ). "When he comes, he will tell us all things." [26] "I am he," Jesus said to her, "the one speaking to you."

[27] Just then his disciples came. And they were amazed that he was talking with a woman. But no one said, "What do you wish?" or, "Why are you talking with her?" [28] Then the woman left her water jar, and went away into the city, and said to the people, [29] "Come, see a man who told me all that I ever did. Could this be the Christ?" [30] They went out of the city and came to him.

[31] Meanwhile the disciples urged him, saying, "Rabbi, eat." [32] But he said to them, "I have food to eat of which you do not know." [33] So the disciples said to one another, "Has any one brought him food?" [34] Jesus said to them, "My food is to do the will of him who sent me, and to finish his work. [35] Do you not say, 'There are yet four months and then comes the harvest'? Behold, I tell you, lift up your eyes, and look at the fields! They are white for harvest. Already [36] the reaper is receiving wages, and gathering fruit for eternal

---

where do you get], Minor[Where do you get (ESV, ~MRD, ~NIV, ~NJB, ~NLT, NRS, RSV, ~TEV, ~TLB)].

4:15 Alx[should come], Byz[will come (ASV, DRA, HCS, JNT, KJV, NAS, NAU, NJB, NKJ, RSV)]; Alx[all the way here *Greek* through here], Byz[here (DRA, ESV, HCS, JNT, KJV, ~MRD, NAB, NET, NIV, NJB, NKJ, NLT, NRS, RSV, TEV)].

4:16 Alx[He said to her], Byz[Jesus said to her (ASV, DRA, ESV, KJV, MRD, NAB, NJB, NKJ, NLT, NRS, REB, RSV, TEV, TLB)].

4:17 Alx[said to him], Byz[*omits* to him (DRA, HCS, JNT, KJV, NAS, NAU, NET, NIV, NJB, NKJ, NLT, REB, TEV, TLB)].

4:20, 21, 22 you *plural.*

4:24 Alx/Byz[those who worship him], Minor[*omits* him (NJB, TLB)].

4:27 Alx[they were amazed], Byz[they marveled (ASV, DRA, ESV, KJV, MRD, NAS, NKJ, RSV)].

4:29 Alx/Byz[all that I ever did], Minor[all that I did (NAS, NAU)].

4:30 Alx/Major[They went out], Byz[So they went out (DRA, KJV, NET, NKJ, NLT, TEV, TLB)], Alt/Peshitta[And the people went out (MRD, TLB)].

4:31 Alx[Meanwhile], Byz[But meanwhile]; Alx/Byz[the disciples], Alt[his disciples (KJV, MRD, NIV, NKJ)].

4:33 Alx/Byz[So the disciples], Minor[*omits* So (HCS, ~JNT, MRD, NLT, ~REB, TLB)].

4:35-36 Alx[They are white for harvest. Already 36 the reaper is receiving wages], Byz[They are white for harvest already. 36 And the reaper is receiving wages (ASV, DRA, ~HCS, JNT, KJV, MRD, NET, ~NJB, NKJ, NLT, REB, RSV, ~TEV, ~TLB)]; Alx[so that sower and reaper may rejoice], Byz[so that both sower and reaper may rejoice (DRA, KJV, NKJ, NLT, TLB)].

life, so that sower and reaper may rejoice together. ³⁷ For here the saying is true, 'One sows and another reaps.' ³⁸ I sent you to reap that for which you have not labored. Others have labored, and you have entered into their labor."

³⁹ Many of the Samaritans from that city believed in him because of the woman's testimony, "He told me all that I did." ⁴⁰ So when the Samaritans came to him, they urged him to stay with them; and he stayed there two days. ⁴¹ And many more believed because of his word. ⁴² They said to the woman, "We no longer believe just because of what you said; now we have heard for ourselves, and we know that this man is indeed the Savior of the world."

⁴³ After the two days he left from there to Galilee. ⁴⁴ For Jesus himself testified that a prophet has no honor in his own country. ⁴⁵ So when he came to Galilee, the Galileans welcomed him, having seen everything that he had done in Jerusalem at the feast, for they too had gone to the feast.

⁴⁶ So he came again to Cana in Galilee, where he had made the water wine. And at Capernaum there was a certain official whose son was sick. ⁴⁷ When he heard that Jesus had come from Judea to Galilee, he went to him and begged that he might come down and heal his son, for he was at the point of death. ⁴⁸ Jesus said to him, "Unless you see signs and wonders, you will never believe." ⁴⁹ The official said to him, "Sir, come down before my child dies." ⁵⁰ Jesus said to him, "Go; your son will live." The man believed the word that Jesus spoke to him and went his way. ⁵¹ As he was going down, his servants went to meet him, saying that his child was living. ⁵² Then he inquired of them the hour when his son got better. So they said to him, "Yesterday at the seventh hour the fever left him." ⁵³ So the father knew that it was at the same hour in which Jesus had said to him, "Your son will live." And he himself believed, and all his household. ⁵⁴ [Now,] again, this was the second sign that Jesus did when he had come from Judea to Galilee.

4:38 Alx/Byz[**I sent you to reap**], Minor[I have sent you to reap (DRA, TEV)].

4:39 Alx[**told me all that I did**], Byz[told me all that I ever did (ASV, ESV, HCS, KJV, MRD, NAB, NET, NIV, NKJ, NLT, NRS, REB, RSV, TEV, TLB)].

4:42 Alx[**the Savior**], Byz[the Christ, the Savior (KJV, MRD, NKJ)].

4:43 Alx[**he left from there to Galilee**], Byz[he left from there and departed to Galilee (DRA, KJV, MRD, NKJ, TEV)].

4:45 Alx/Byz[**when he came to Galilee**], Minor[as he came to Galilee (~NJB, ~NLT, ~REB, ~TLB)]; Alx[**everything that he had done**], Byz[all that he had done (ASV, DRA, ESV, JNT, KJV, MRD, NAB, NAS, NAU, NET, NIV, NJB, NKJ, NRS, REB, RSV, ~TEV)].

4:46 Alx[**he came again to Cana**], Byz[Jesus came again to Cana (KJV, MRD, NKJ, TEV)]; Alx[**Capernaum** *Greek* Capharnaum], Byz[Capernaum]; Alx/Byz[**And...there was a certain official**], Minor[But...there was an official (ESV, HCS, JNT, MRD, NAB, NAU, NJB, NLT, NRS, REB, RSV, TEV, TLB)].

4:47 Alx[**begged that he might come down**], Byz[begged him that he might come down (ASV, ~DRA, ~ESV, ~HCS, ~JNT, KJV, MRD, ~NAB, ~NAS, ~NAU, ~NET, ~NIV, ~NJB, ~NKJ, ~NLT, ~NRS, ~REB, ~RSV, ~TEV, ~TLB)].

4:48 **you** *both are plural.*

4:50 Alx[**The man believed**], Byz[And the man believed (KJV, MRD, ~NKJ, NLT, TLB)].

4:51 Alx/Byz[**his servants**], Minor[the servants and a messenger]; Alx[**went to meet him**], Byz[met him (ASV, DRA, ESV, HCS, JNT, KJV, MRD, NAS, NAU, NET, NIV, NJB, NKJ, NLT, NRS, REB, RSV, TEV, TLB)]; Alx[**saying**], Byz[and reported to him, saying (DRA, KJV, MRD, NKJ)], Minor[and reported to him (ESV, JNT, NAB, NET, NIV, NJB, NLT, NRS, REB, RSV, TEV, TLB)]; Alx[**his child**], Byz[your child (KJV, MRD, NKJ, TEV)]; Alx/Byz[**child** *or* boy], Minor[son (ASV, DRA, ESV, JNT, KJV, MRD, NAS, NAU, NET, NKJ, NLT, RSV, TLB)].

4:52 Alx[**So they said to him**], Byz[And they said to him (DRA, ESV, ~HCS, JNT, KJV, MRD, ~NAB, NET, ~NJB, NKJ, NLT, NRS, REB, RSV, TEV, TLB)].

4:54 Alx[**Now, again, this was the second sign** *Greek* But, again, this was the second sign], Byz[*omits* Now (ASV, DRA, ~HCS, JNT, KJV, MRD, NAS, NAU, NET, NIV, NJB, NKJ, NLT, REB, TEV, TLB)].

5 ¹ After this there was a feast of the Jews, and Jesus went up to Jerusalem. ² Now there is in Jerusalem by the Sheep Gate a pool, which is called in Hebrew, Bethzatha, having five porches. ³ In these lay a multitude of disabled people, blind, lame, withered. (⁴) ⁵ One man who was there had been thirty-eight years in his infirmity. ⁶ When Jesus saw him lying there and knew that he had been in this condition for a long time, he said to him, "Do you want to be made well?" ⁷ The sick man answered him, "Sir, I have no man to put me into the pool when the water is stirred up; but while I am coming, another steps down before me." ⁸ Jesus said to him, "Rise, take up your bed, and walk." ⁹ And at once the man was healed, and he took up his bed and walked.

Now that day was the Sabbath. ¹⁰ So the Jews said to the man who was cured, "It is the Sabbath, and it is not lawful for you to carry your bed." ¹¹ But he answered them, "The man who made me well said to me, 'Take up your bed, and walk.'" ¹² They asked him, "Who is the man who said to you, 'Take it up, and walk'?" ¹³ Now the man who had been healed did not know who it was, for Jesus had withdrawn, as there was a crowd in that place. ¹⁴ Afterward, Jesus found him in the temple, and said to him, "See, you are well. Sin no more, so that nothing worse may happen to you." ¹⁵ The man went away and told the Jews that it was Jesus who had made him well. ¹⁶ For this reason the Jews persecuted Jesus, because he was doing these things on the Sabbath. ¹⁷ But [Jesus] answered them, "My Father is working still, and I am working." ¹⁸ For this, therefore, the Jews sought all the more to kill him, because he not only broke the Sabbath, but also said that God was his Father, making himself equal with God.

5:1 Alx[**a feast**], Byz[the feast (~NLT, ~REB, ~TLB)].

5:2 Alx/Byz[**which is called in Hebrew**], Minor[which is spoken in Hebrew], Alt[*without textual foundation omits* (~NLT, ~TLB)]; Alx[**Bethzatha** *Aramaic* Trench *possibly a construction site north of the city*], Byz[Bethesda *Hebrew* House of Mercy (ASV, ESV, HCS, KJV, MRD, NAB, NAS, NAU, NIV, NJB, NKJ, NLT, REB, TLB)], Minor[Bethsaida (DRA) *others* Belzetha]; Alx/Byz[**having five porches**], Alt[*without textual foundation omits* (~JNT)].

5:3 Alx[**a multitude**], Byz[a great multitude (DRA, KJV, MRD, ~NET, ~NIV, NKJ, ~REB, TEV)]; Alx/Byz[**withered**], Minor[paralyzed (ESV, HCS, ~JNT, ~NAB, NET, NIV, NJB, NKJ, NLT, NRS, REB, RSV, TEV, TLB)]; Alx[**withered**], Byz[*adds* waiting for the moving of the water. (⁴) For an angel went down at certain seasons into the pool and stirred up the water; then whoever stepped in first, after the stirring up of the water, was made well from whatever disease he had (~ASV, ~DRA, HCS, KJV, MRD, ~NAS, ~NAU, NKJ, ~TLB)], Minor[*adds* of the Lord *after* angel (ASV, DRA, NAS, NAU, TLB)].

5:5 Alx/Byz[**thirty-eight** *Greek* thirty and eight], Major[thirty-eight]; Alx/Byz[**in his infirmity**], Major[*omits* his (ESV, HCS, JNT, KJV, MRD, NAB, NAU, NET, NIV, NJB, NKJ, NLT, NRS, REB, RSV, TEV, TLB)].

5:9 Alx/Byz[**at once** *or* immediately], Minor[*omits*].

5:10 Alx[**and it is not lawful**], Byz[*omits* and (DRA, HCS, JNT, KJV, MRD, NIV, NJB, NKJ, NLT, NRS, REB, RSV, TLB)]; Alx[**carry your bed**], Byz[carry the bed (NLT, TLB)].

5:11 Alx[**But he answered them**], Byz[*omits* But (DRA, HCS, KJV, NAB, NJB, NKJ, REB, TEV, TLB)], Minor[But who answered them].

5:12 Alx[**They asked him**], Byz[So they asked him (DRA, KJV, NIV, NKJ)]; Alx[**Take it up**], Byz[Take up your bed (ASV, DRA, ESV, HCS, KJV, MRD, NAS, NAU, NET, NJB, NKJ, ~NLT, RSV, ~TEV, ~TLB)].

5:13 Alx/Byz[**who had been healed**], Minor[who had been weak (~NJB, ~NLT, ~TLB)].

5:15 Alx/Byz[**told the Jews**], Minor[said to the Jews].

5:16 Alx[**persecuted Jesus**], Byz[*adds* and sought to kill him (KJV, MRD, NKJ)].

5:17 Alx/Byz[**Jesus answered them**], Minor[he answered them (JNT, NAS, NAU, NET, NJB, REB) *others* the lord answered them].

5:18 Alx/Byz[**For this, therefore**], Minor[For this (ESV, HCS, JNT, ~KJV, MRD, NAB, NET, NIV, NJB, ~NKJ, ~NLT, NRS, REB, RSV, TEV, ~TLB)].

¹⁹ So Jesus said to them, "Truly, truly, I say to you, the Son can do nothing of himself, but only what he sees the Father doing. For whatever he does, the Son also does. ²⁰ For the Father loves the Son, and shows him all things that he himself does. And he will show him greater works than these, that you may marvel. ²¹ For as the Father raises the dead and gives life to them, even so the Son gives life to whom he will. ²² For the Father judges no one, but has given all judgment to the Son, ²³ that all may honor the Son just as they honor the Father. He who does not honor the Son does not honor the Father who sent him. ²⁴ Truly, truly, I say to you, he who hears my word and believes him who sent me, has eternal life; and shall not come into judgment, but has passed from death to life. ²⁵ Truly, truly, I say to you, the hour is coming, and now is, when the dead will hear the voice of the Son of God; and those who hear will live. ²⁶ For as the Father has life in himself, so he has granted the Son also to have life in himself, ²⁷ and has given him authority to execute judgment, because he is the Son of Man. ²⁸ Do not marvel at this; for the hour is coming when all who are in the graves will hear his voice ²⁹ and come forth – those who have done good, to the resurrection of life, but those who have done evil, to the resurrection of judgment.

³⁰ "I can do nothing of myself. As I hear, I judge; and my judgment is just, because I seek not my own will but the will of him who sent me.

³¹ "If I bear witness of myself, my testimony is not true. ³² There is another who bears witness of me, and I know that the testimony which he bears of me is true. ³³ You have sent to John, and he has borne witness to the truth. ³⁴ Not that the testimony which I receive is from man; but I say this that you may be saved. ³⁵ He was a burning and shining lamp, and you were willing to rejoice for a time in his light. ³⁶ But the testimony which I have is greater than that of John; for the works which the Father has given me to finish, these very works which I am doing, bear witness of me, that the Father has sent me. ³⁷ And the Father who sent me; he has testified of me. You have never heard his voice, nor seen his form. ³⁸ And you do not have his word abiding in you, for you do not believe him whom he has sent. ³⁹ You search the Scriptures, because in them you think that you have eternal life; and these are they that testify of me. ⁴⁰ Yet you refuse to come to me that you may have life.

⁴¹ "I do not receive glory from men. ⁴² But I know you, that you do not have the love of God in you. ⁴³ I have come in my Father's name, and you do not receive me. If another comes in his own name, him you will receive. ⁴⁴ How can you believe, who receive glory from one another, and do not seek the glory that comes from the only God? ⁴⁵ Do not think that I shall accuse you to the Father; it is Moses who accuses you, on whom you set your

---

5:19 Alx/Byz[**Jesus said**], Minor[he said]; Alx/Byz[**only what he sees**], Minor[whatever he sees (~NAS, ~NAU)].

5:20 Alx/Byz[**that you may marvel**], Minor[that you will marvel (HCS, JNT, NAU, NET, NIV, NJB, NLT, NRS, REB, TEV, TLB)].

5:27 Alx[**and…to execute judgment**], Byz[*adds* also (KJV, ~MRD, NKJ, ~REB)].

5:29 Alx/Byz[**but those who have done evil**], Minor[*omits* but (NAS, NAU, REB)]; **done evil** *or* done what is worthless.

5:30 Alx[**him who sent me**], Byz[the Father who sent me (KJV, NKJ, ~TLB)].

5:32 Alx/Byz[**I know**], Minor[you know (~NLT, ~TLB) *others* we know].

5:36 Alx/Byz[**But the testimony which I have is greater than that of John**], Minor[But I who am greater than John have the testimony]; Alx[**works which the Father has given me**], Byz[works which the Father gave me (NAB, NLT, TEV)].

5:37 Alx[**he has testified of me** *or* that one has testified of me], Byz[has himself testified of me (DRA, ESV, HCS, JNT, KJV, ~NAB, NET, NIV, NJB, NKJ, NLT, NRS, ~REB, RSV, ~TEV, TLB)].

5:39 Alx[**You search the Scriptures** *indicative or* Search the Scriptures *imperative*], Byz[*only imperative* Search the Scriptures (DRA, KJV, MRD)].

5:42 **in you** *or* among you.

5:44 Alx/Byz[**the only God** *or* God alone], Minor[the only One].

hope. **46** If you believed Moses, you would believe me, for he wrote about me. **47** But if you do not believe his writings, how will you believe my words?"

6 **1** After this Jesus went to the other side of the Galilee-Tiberias Sea. **2** But a great multitude followed him, because they beheld the signs which he performed on those who were diseased. **3** Jesus went up on the mountain, and there sat down with his disciples. **4** Now the Passover, the feast of the Jews, was near. **5** Then Jesus lifted up his eyes, and seeing a great multitude coming toward him, he said to Philip, "Where can we buy bread, that these people may eat?" **6** But this he said to test him, for he himself knew what he would do. **7** Philip answered him, "Two hundred denarii would not buy enough bread for everyone to have a little [something]." **8** One of his disciples, Andrew, Simon Peter's brother, said to him, **9** "There is a boy here who has five barley loaves and two small fish, but what are they among so many?" **10** Jesus said, "Make the people sit down." Now there was much grass in the place; so the men sat down, in number about five thousand. **11** So Jesus took the loaves, and giving thanks, he distributed them to those who were seated; so also the fish, as much as they wanted. **12** And when they had eaten their fill, he said to his disciples, "Gather up the fragments left over, that nothing may be lost." **13** So they gathered them up and filled twelve baskets with the fragments of the five barley loaves, left over by those who had eaten. **14** When the people saw the sign that he did, they said, "Surely this is the *Prophet* who is to come into the world." **15** Perceiving then that they were about to come and take him by force to make him king, Jesus withdrew again to the mountain by himself.

16 When evening came, his disciples went down to the sea, **17** got into a boat, and started across the sea to Capernaum. And it was now dark, and Jesus had not yet come to them. **18** The sea rose because a strong wind was blowing. **19** So when they had rowed about three or four miles, they saw Jesus walking on the sea and drawing near the boat. And they

---

5:47 Alx/Byz[**how will you believe**], Minor[how do you believe (~TEV ~TLB)].

6:1 Alx/Byz[**Galilee-Tiberias Sea** *Greek* Sea of Galilee of Tiberias], Minor[Sea of Galilee and of Tiberias *others* Sea of Galilee, in the regions of Tiberias].

6:2 Alx[**But a great multitude**], Byz[And a great multitude (ASV, DRA, ESV, HCS, JNT, KJV, MRD, NAS, NIV, NJB, ~NKJ, REB, RSV, TLB)]; Alx[**they beheld the signs**], Byz[they saw his signs (KJV, NKJ, NLT, TEV, ~TLB)].

6:5 Alx/Byz[**Where can we buy bread**], Major[Where shall we buy bread (DRA, HCS, KJV, MRD, NIV, NKJ)].

6:7 Alx/Byz[**Philip answered him**], Minor[Philip answers him]; Alx[**everyone**], Byz[everyone of them (ESV, HCS, KJV, NAB, NJB, NKJ, ~NLT, NRS, REB, RSV, ~TLB)]; Alx/Byz[**something**], Minor[omits (ASV, ~JNT, HCS, DRA, ESV, KJV, MRD, NAS, NAU, NET, NKJ, ~NLT, NRS, REB, RSV, TEV, TLB)]; **denarii** *a denarius was a day's wage for a laborer.*

6:8 Alx/Byz[**Peter**], Alt/Peshitta[Cephas (JNT, MRD)].

6:9 Alx[**There is a boy**], Byz[There is one boy].

6:10 Alx[**Jesus said**], Byz[But Jesus said (~DRA, ~HCS, KJV, ~NKJ)], Minor[adds to them (MRD)]; Alx/Byz[**the men sat down**], Minor[men sat down (~HCS, ~JNT, ~NJB, ~NLT, ~NRS, ~TLB)].

6:11 Alx[**So Jesus took the loaves**], Byz[But Jesus took the loaves (DRA, KJV, MRD, NKJ, TEV)]; Alx/Byz[**and giving thanks, he**], Minor[and he gave thanks, and he (MRD, ~NAB, ~NIV, ~NJB, ~NLT, ~REB, ~TEV, TLB)]; Alx[**distributed them to those**], Byz[distributed them to the disciples, and the disciples to those (KJV, NKJ)].

6:14 Alx/Byz[**sign**], Minor[signs]; Alx[**he**], Byz[Jesus (DRA, KJV, MRD, NET, NIV, NKJ, REB, TEV)]; **Prophet** Deuteronomy 18:15, 18.

6:15 Alx/Byz[**Jesus withdrew again**], Major[Jesus withdrew (~JNT, MRD, NLT, TLB)], Minor[Jesus fled again (DRA, NJB)].

6:17 Alx[**Capernaum** *Greek* Capharnaum], Byz[Capernaum]; Alx/Byz[**And it was now dark**], Minor[But darkness had overtaken them (~HCS, ~MRD, ~NLT, ~TEV, ~TLB)]; Alx[**Jesus had not yet come**], Byz[Jesus had not come (DRA, KJV, MRD, NKJ)].

6:19 **three or four miles** *Greek* twenty-five or thirty stadia.

were afraid. 20 But he said to them, "It is I. Do not be afraid." 21 Then they were glad to take him into the boat. And immediately the boat was at the land where they were going.

22 On the next day the people who remained on the other side of the sea saw that there had been only one small boat there, and that Jesus had not entered the boat with his disciples, but that his disciples had gone away alone. 23 But [small] boats from Tiberias came near the place where they ate the bread after the Lord had given thanks. 24 So when the people saw that Jesus was not there, nor his disciples, they got into the small boats and went to Capernaum, seeking Jesus. 25 When they found him on the other side of the sea, they said to him, "Rabbi, when did you come here?" 26 Jesus answered them, "Truly, truly, I say to you, you seek me, not because you saw the signs, but because you ate your fill of the loaves. 27 Do not labor for the food which perishes, but for the food which endures to eternal life, which the Son of Man will give you. For on him has God the Father set his seal." 28 Then they said to him, "What must we do, to be doing the works of God?" 29 Jesus answered them, "This is the work of God, that you should believe in him whom he has sent." 30 So they said to him, "What sign will you perform then, that we may see it and believe you? What work will you do? 31 Our fathers ate the manna in the desert; as it is written, 'He gave them bread from heaven to eat.'" 32 Jesus then said to them, "Truly, truly, I say to you, it was not Moses who has given you the bread from heaven; but my Father gives you the true bread from heaven. 33 For the bread of God is he who comes down from heaven and gives life to the world."

34 Then they said to him, "Lord, give us this bread always." 35 Jesus said to them, "I am the bread of life. He who comes to me shall never hunger, and he who believes in me shall never thirst. 36 But I said to you that you have seen [me] and yet do not believe. 37 All that the Father gives me will come to me, and the one who comes to me I will never cast out. 38 For I have come down from heaven, not to do my own will, but the will of him who sent me. 39 And this is the will of him who sent me, that I should lose nothing of all that he has given me, but raise it up [in] the last day. 40 For this is the will of my Father, that every

---

6:20 **It is I** *Greek* I am.

6:22 Alx[**only one small boat** *Greek* no small boat except one], Byz[*adds* that his disciples had entered (KJV, MRD, NKJ, ~TLB)]; Alx[**Jesus had not entered the boat**], Byz[Jesus had not entered the small boat (~NET, ~NIV, ~NLT, ~REB, ~TEV, ~TLB)].

6:23 Alx[**But small boats from Tiberias**], Byz[However, small boats from Tiberias], Minor[But boats from Tiberias (ASV, DRA, ESV, HCS, JNT, KJV, MRD, NAB, NET, NIV, NJB, NKJ, NLT, NRS, REB, RSV, TEV)]; Alx/Byz[**after the Lord had given thanks**], Minor[*omits* (NJB, TLB)].

6:24 Alx/Byz[**they got into the**], Minor[they also got into the (KJV, NKJ)]; Alx[**small boats**], Byz[boats (DRA, KJV, MRD)]; Alx[**Capernaum** *Greek* Capharnaum], Byz[Capernaum].

6:27 Alx/Byz[**which the Son of Man will give you**], Minor[which the Son of Man gives you (~NLT, ~TLB)].

6:28 Alx/Byz[**what must we do** *or* what should we do], Minor[what shall we do *Greek* what do we do (DRA, KJV, MRD, NAS, NAU, NKJ)].

6:31 ~**Psalms 78:24 LXX**, Exodus 16:4, Nehemiah 9:15.

6:32 Alx/Byz[**it was not Moses who has given**], Minor[it was not Moses who gave (ASV, DRA, ESV, HCS, JNT, KJV, MRD, NAB, NJB, NKJ, NLT, NRS, REB, RSV, TEV, TLB)].

6:33 **he who** *or* that which.

6:35 Alx[**Jesus said**], Byz[But Jesus said (DRA, KJV, NKJ)], Minor[So Jesus said (NIV)].

6:36 Alx/Byz[**me**], Minor[*omits* (JNT, REB)].

6:39 Alx[**him who sent me**], Byz[the Father who sent me (DRA, KJV, NKJ, ~NLT, ~TLB)]; Alx/Byz[**raise it up**], Minor[raise him up (~HCS, ~JNT, ~NET, ~NIV, ~NLT, ~REB, ~TEV, ~TLB)]; Alx/Byz[**in the last day**], Major[at the last day (ASV, KJV, MRD, NET, NIV, NKJ, NLT, RSV, TLB)].

6:40 Alx[**For this is the will**], Byz[But this is the will (DRA, ~JNT, KJV, NJB, NKJ, NRS)]; Alx[**of my Father**], Byz[of the one who sent me (KJV, NKJ)]; Alx[**in the last day**], Byz[*omits* in (ASV, KJV, MRD, NET, NIV, NKJ, NLT, RSV, TLB)].

one who sees the Son and believes in him should have eternal life; and I will raise him up [in] the last day."

⁴¹ The Jews then began to murmur about him, because he said, "I am the bread which came down from heaven." ⁴² And they said, "Is not this Jesus, the son of Joseph, whose father and mother we know? How does he now say, 'I have come down from heaven'?" ⁴³ Jesus answered and said to them, "Do not murmur among yourselves. ⁴⁴ No one can come to me unless the Father who sent me draws him; and I will raise him up in the last day. ⁴⁵ It is written in the prophets, 'And they shall all be taught by God.' Everyone who heard and learned from the Father comes to me. ⁴⁶ Not that any one has seen the Father except the one who is from God; he has seen the Father. ⁴⁷ Truly, truly, I say to you, he who believes has everlasting life. ⁴⁸ I am the bread of life. ⁴⁹ Your fathers ate the manna in the wilderness, and they died. ⁵⁰ This is the bread which comes down from heaven, that a man may eat of it and not die. ⁵¹ I am the living bread which came down from heaven. If anyone eats of this bread, he will live forever. And the bread also which I shall give is my flesh, for the life of the world."

⁵² Then the Jews began to argue among themselves, saying, "How can this man give us [his] flesh to eat?" ⁵³ So Jesus said to them, "Truly, truly, I say to you, unless you eat the flesh of the Son of Man and drink his blood, you have no life in you. ⁵⁴ Whoever eats my flesh and drinks my blood has eternal life, and I will raise him up at the last day. ⁵⁵ For my flesh is true food, and my blood is true drink. ⁵⁶ He who eats my flesh and drinks my blood abides in me, and I in him. ⁵⁷ As the living Father sent me, and I live because of the Father, so he who feeds on me will live because of me. ⁵⁸ This is the bread which came down from heaven, not as the fathers ate, and died. He who eats this bread will live forever." ⁵⁹ This he said in the synagogue as he taught in Capernaum.

⁶⁰ Many of his disciples, when they heard it, said, "This is a hard saying. Who can listen to it?" ⁶¹ When Jesus knew in himself that his disciples complained about this, he said to them, "Does this offend you? ⁶² What then if you should see the Son of Man ascend to where he was before? ⁶³ It is the Spirit who gives life. The flesh profits nothing. The words

---

6:42 Alx[**How does he now say**], Byz[So how does he say (DRA, KJV, ~MRD, NAB, NKJ, ~NLT, ~REB, ~TLB)].

6:43 Alx[**Jesus answered**], Byz[So Jesus answered (DRA, KJV, NKJ, ~NLT, ~TLB)].

6:44 Alx/Major[**in the last day**], Byz[omits in (KJV, MRD, NET, NIV, NKJ, NLT, RSV, TLB)].

6:45 Alx/Byz[**Everyone who heard**], Major[Therefore everyone who hears (~JNT, ~KJV, MRD, ~NAB, ~NET, ~NIV, ~NKJ, ~NLT, ~TEV, ~TLB)]; ~**Isaiah 54:13**.

6:46 Alx/Byz[**he has seen the Father**], Minor[he has seen God (~NLT, ~TLB)].

6:47 Alx[**believes**], Byz[adds in me (DRA, KJV, MRD, NKJ, TLB)].

6:51 Alx/Byz[**If anyone eats of this bread**], Minor[If anyone eats of my bread]; Alx[**the bread also which I shall give is my flesh, for the life of the world**], Byz[the bread also which I shall give is my flesh, which I shall give for the life of the world (JNT, KJV, MRD, NKJ, REB, TEV)]; Minor[the bread also which I shall give for the life of the world is my flesh (ESV, HCS, NAS, NAU, NET, ~NIV, ~NLT, NRS, RSV, TLB)]; DRA moves **If anyone eats of this bread**... to verse 52 and continues one verse higher until the end of the chapter.

6:52 Alx[**his flesh**], Byz[omits his].

6:54 Alx/Byz[**at the last day**], Minor[in the last day (DRA, ~ESV, ~HCS, ~JNT, ~NAB, ~NAS, ~NAU, ~NET, ~NJB, ~NRS, ~REB, ~TEV)].

6:55 Alx[**true food...true drink**], Byz[truly food... truly drink (ASV, DRA, KJV, MRD, NKJ, RSV)].

6:58 Alx[**the fathers ate**], Byz[your fathers ate the manna (~ESV 2007 edition, DRA, HCS, ~JNT, KJV, MRD, ~NAB, NET, NIV, NKJ, NLT, ~NRS, TEV, ~TLB)], Minor[our fathers ate the manna (NJB, REB)].

6:59 Alx[**Capernaum** Greek Capharnaum], Byz[Capernaum].

6:63 Alx[**I have spoken to you are spirit** or I have spoken to you are Spirit], Byz[I speak to you are spirit (KJV, NKJ)].

that I have spoken to you are spirit, and they are life. ⁶⁴ But there are some of you who do not believe." For Jesus knew from the beginning who they were who did not believe, and who would betray him. ⁶⁵ And he said, "This is why I told you that no one can come to me unless it has been granted to him by the Father." ⁶⁶ From this time many [of] his disciples went back and no longer walked with him. ⁶⁷ Then Jesus said to the twelve, "Do you also want to go away?" ⁶⁸ Simon Peter answered him, "Lord, to whom shall we go? You have the words of eternal life. ⁶⁹ And we believe, and have come to know, that you are the Holy One of God." ⁷⁰ Jesus answered them, "Did I not choose you, the twelve, and one of you is a devil?" ⁷¹ He spoke of Judas, the son of Simon Iscariot, for it was he – one of the twelve – who was to betray him.

7 ¹ And after this Jesus went about in Galilee. He would not go about in Judea, because the Jews sought to kill him. ² Now the Jews' feast of Tabernacles was at hand. ³ So his brothers said to him, "Leave here and go to Judea, that your disciples will see the works you are doing. ⁴ For no one works in secret if he seeks to be known openly. If you do these things, show yourself to the world." ⁵ For even his brothers did not believe in him. ⁶ So Jesus said to them, "My time has not yet come, but your time is always ready. ⁷ The world cannot hate you, but it hates me because I testify of it that its works are evil. ⁸ You go up to the feast. I am not going up to this feast, for my time has not yet fully come." ⁹ And having said this, he remained in Galilee.

¹⁰ But after his brothers had gone up to the feast, then he also went up, not publicly, but [as if it were] in secret. ¹¹ The Jews were looking for him at the feast, and saying, "Where is he?" ¹² And there was much grumbling among the crowds about him. Some said,

---

6:⁶⁴ Alx/Byz[**who they were who did not believe, and**], Minor[*omits*].

6:⁶⁵ Alx[**the Father**], Byz[my Father (DRA, KJV, MRD, NAB, NKJ)].

6:⁶⁶ Alx/Byz[**From this time** *or* On account of this *Greek* From this], Minor[*adds* therefore].

6:⁶⁸ Alx[**Simon Peter answered him**], Byz[So Simon Peter answered him (KJV, ~NKJ)], Alt/Peshitta[Simon Cephas answered and said (~JNT, MRD)].

6:⁶⁹ Alx[**the Holy One of God**], Byz[the Christ, the Son of the living God (~DRA, KJV, MRD, NKJ, ~TLB)].

6:⁷⁰ Alx/Byz[**Jesus answered them**], Minor[He answered them].

6:⁷¹ Alx[**Judas, the son of Simon Iscariot**], Byz[Judas Iscariot, the son of Simon (DRA, KJV, MRD, NKJ)]; Alx/Byz[**Iscariot**], Minor[from Karuot (JNT) *others* Scariot]; Alx[**one of the twelve**], Byz[being one of the twelve (ASV, KJV, MRD, NKJ, ~REB)]; **Iscariot** *Hebraism Ish Keriot* a man from Kerioth *or possibly Sicarios* assassin *or* bandit.

7:¹ Alx/Byz[**And after this** *Greek* And after these], Minor[*omits* And (DRA, ESV, HCS, JNT, KJV, MRD, NAB, NAS, NAU, NET, NIV, NJB, NKJ, NLT, NRS, REB, RSV, TEV, TLB)].

7:³ Alx[**will see**], Byz[may see (ASV, DRA, ESV, HCS, JNT, KJV, MRD, NAB, NAS, NAU, NET, NIV, NJB, NKJ, NLT, NRS, REB, RSV, TLB)]; **see the works you are doing** *Greek* see your works which you are doing.

7:⁴ Alx/Byz[**if he seeks to be known** *Greek* and seeks himself to be known], Minor[and seeks it to be known].

7:⁶ Alx/Byz[**So Jesus said**], Minor[Jesus said (ESV, HCS, JNT, MRD, NJB, NLT, NRS, REB, RSV, TEV, TLB)].

7:⁸ Alx[**You go up to the feast**], Byz[You go up to this feast (DRA, KJV, NKJ, ~NLT, ~TLB)]; Alx[**I am not going**], Byz[I am not yet going (HCS, JNT, KJV, MRD, NIV, NKJ, TLB)].

7:⁹ Alx/Byz[**And having said**], Minor[*omits* And (DRA, ESV, HCS, KJV, MRD, NAB, NAU, NET, NIV, NJB, NKJ, NLT, NRS, REB, RSV, TEV, TLB)]; Alx[**said this, he remained** *Greek* said this, he himself remained], Byz[said this to them, he remained (ASV, KJV, NAS, NAU, NKJ, ~TLB)].

7:¹⁰ Alx/Byz[**as if it were**], Minor[*omits* (ESV, HCS, JNT, NET, NIV, NJB, NLT, REB, RSV, TLB)].

7:¹² Alx/Byz[**there was much grumbling among the crowds about him**], Minor[many among the crowds grumbled about him]; Alx/Byz[**the crowds**], Minor[the crowd (DRA, ESV, KJV, MRD, NKJ, RSV, TEV, TLB)]; Alx[**But others said**], Byz[*omits* But (ASV, ESV, HCS, KJV, NAS, NAU, NIV, NJB, NKJ, ~NRS, REB, ~RSV, TEV)].

"He is a good man." [But] others said, "No, on the contrary, he deceives the people." 13 However, no one spoke openly of him for fear of the Jews.

14 Now about the middle of the feast Jesus went up into the temple and taught. 15 So the Jews marveled, saying, "How did this man get such learning, having never studied?" 16 Jesus therefore answered them and said, "My teaching is not mine, but his who sent me. 17 If anyone is willing to do his will, he shall know whether the teaching is from God or whether I speak on my own authority. 18 He who speaks from himself seeks his own glory. But he who seeks the glory of the One who sent him is true, and in him there is no falsehood. 19 Has not Moses given you the law? Yet none of you keeps the law. Why do you seek to kill me?" 20 The people answered, "You have a demon. Who is seeking to kill you?" 21 Jesus answered them, "I did one deed, and you all marvel. 22 For this, Moses gave you circumcision (not that it is from Moses, but from the fathers), and you circumcise a man on the Sabbath. 23 If on the Sabbath a man receives circumcision, so that the law of Moses may not be broken, are you angry with me because on the Sabbath I made a man's whole body well? 24 Do not judge by appearances, but judge with right judgment."

25 Then some of the people of Jerusalem said, "Is not this the man whom they seek to kill? 26 Here he is, speaking publicly, and they say nothing to him! Can it be true that the authorities know that he is the Christ? 27 But we know where this man is from; when the Christ comes, no one will know where he is from." 28 Then Jesus cried out, as he taught in the temple, "You know me, and you know where I am from. And I have not come on my own, but he who sent me is true, and him you do not know. 29 I know him, for I am from him, and he sent me." 30 Then they sought to take him; but no one laid a hand on him, because his hour had not yet come. 31 And many of the people believed in him, and they said, "When the Christ comes, will he do more signs than this man did?"

32 The Pharisees heard the crowd muttering these things about him, and the chief priests and the Pharisees sent officers to arrest him. 33 So Jesus said, "I shall be with you a little while longer, and then I go to him who sent me. 34 You will seek me, and you will not find [me]; where I am you cannot come." 35 The Jews said to one another, "Where does this

---

7:15 Alx[**So the Jews marveled**], Byz[And the Jews marveled (DRA, ~JNT, KJV, MRD, ~NAB, ~NIV, ~NJB, NKJ, ~NLT, ~NRS, ~REB, ~RSV, ~TEV, ~TLB)]; **get such learning** or know his letters.

7:16 Alx/Byz[**Jesus therefore**], Minor[omits therefore (DRA, HCS, KJV, MRD, NAB, NIV, NJB, NKJ, REB, TEV)].

7:19 Alx/Byz[**Has not Moses given**], Minor[Did not Moses give (ASV, DRA, HCS, JNT, KJV, MRD, NAB, NAS, NAU, NJB, NKJ, NLT, NRS, REB, RSV, TEV, ~TLB)]; Alx/Byz[**Why do you seek to kill me? 20**], Minor[20 Why do you seek to kill me? (DRA, MRD)].

7:20 Alx[**The people answered**], Byz[adds and said (DRA, KJV, MRD, NKJ)].

7:21-22 Alx/Major[**you all marvel. 22 For this, Moses gave you**], Byz[you all marvel for this. 22 Moses gave you (JNT, ~NJB, ~RSV, ~TEV, ~TLB)], Minor[you all marvel 22 for this. Moses gave you (~ASV, ~ESV, NAB, ~NLT, ~NRS)].

7:26 Alx[**Can it be true...he is the Christ**], Byz[Can it be true...he is truly the Christ (~JNT, KJV, ~NAB, NKJ, ~REB, ~TLB)].

7:28 **You know me, and you know where I am from** or Do you know me, and do you know where I am from?

7:29 Alx/Byz[**I know him**], Minor[But I know him (KJV, MRD, NET, NIV, NJB, NKJ, NLT, TEV)].

7:31 Alx[**do more signs**], Byz[do more of these signs (ASV, DRA, KJV, MRD, NAS, NAU, NKJ)]; Alx/Byz[**than this man did**], Minor[than this man does (DRA, MRD, ~NIV, ~REB)].

7:32 Alx[**the chief priests and the Pharisees**], Byz[the Pharisees and the chief priests (KJV, NKJ)], Minor[the Pharisees (NJB)]; Alt/Peshitta[they and the chief priests (MRD, NLT, TEV, TLB)]; Alt/Vulgate[rulers and Pharisees (DRA)].

7:33 Alx/Byz[**Jesus said**], Minor[adds to them (DRA, KJV, NKJ, NLT, TLB)].

7:34 Alx[**you will not find me**], Byz[omits me].

7:35 Alx/Byz[**Greeks...Greeks**], Alt/Vulgate[Gentiles...Gentiles (DRA, KJV, MRD, REB, ~TLB)], Alt[without textual foundation Hellenists (~JNT)].

man intend to go that we shall not find him? Does he intend to go to the Dispersion among the Greeks and teach the Greeks? ³⁶ What does he mean when he said, 'You will seek me and you will not find [me],' and, 'Where I am you cannot come'?"

³⁷ On the last day, that great day of the feast, Jesus stood and cried out, "If anyone thirsts, let him come to me and drink. ³⁸ He who believes in me, as the Scripture has said, *'out of his heart will flow rivers of living water.'"* ³⁹ Now this he said about the Spirit, whom those who believed in him were to receive; for the Spirit was not yet, because Jesus was not yet glorified.

⁴⁰ When they heard these words, some of the people said, "Surely this is the *Prophet."* ⁴¹ Others said, "This is the Christ." But some said, "Will the Christ come from Galilee? ⁴² Has not the scripture said that the Christ comes from David's seed, and from *Bethlehem,* the town where David was?" ⁴³ So there was a division among the people because of him. ⁴⁴ Some of them wanted to seize him, but no one laid hands on him.

⁴⁵ The officers then went back to the chief priests and Pharisees, who said to them, "Why did you not bring him?" ⁴⁶ The officers answered, "No man ever spoke like this!" ⁴⁷ So the Pharisees answered them, "Are you deceived, you also? ⁴⁸ Have any of the rulers or Pharisees believed in him? ⁴⁹ But this crowd that does not know the law is accursed." ⁵⁰ Nicodemus, who had gone to him before, and who was one of them, said to them, ⁵¹ "Does our law judge a man without first giving him a hearing and learning what he is doing?" ⁵² They replied, "Are you from Galilee, too? Search and look, and you will find that no prophet rises out of Galilee."

7:36 Alx[**you will not find me**], Byz[*omits* me (~TEV, ~TLB)]; *Minor adds John 7:53-8:11 after this verse.*

7:37 Alx/Byz[**let him come to me**], Minor[*omits* to me].

7:37-38 **let him come to me and drink. He who believes in me** *or* let him come to me. Let him who believes in me drink.

7:38 **heart** *Greek* belly; *possible allusion to Proverbs 18:4 or Apocrypha[Sirach 6:30-34].*

7:39 Alx[**those who believed**], Byz[those who believe (KJV, MRD, ~NAB, NKJ, NLT, NRS, REB, TLB)]; Alx[**for the Spirit was not yet**], Byz[for the Holy Spirit was not yet (KJV, NKJ, ~TLB)], Minor[*adds* given (ASV, DRA, ESV, JNT, KJV, MRD, NAS, NAU, NET, NIV, NKJ, NLT, REB, RSV, TEV, TLB)].

7:40 Alx[**these words**], Byz[the word (~KJV, ~NKJ)], Minor[his words (JNT, MRD, NIV, NLT, REB, TEV, TLB) *others omit* (NJB)]; Alx[**some of the people**], Byz[many of the people (KJV, MRD, NKJ)]; **Prophet** Deuteronomy 18:15, 18.

7:41 Alx[**But some said** *Greek* But they said], Byz[Others said (MRD, NAS, NAU, NIV, NLT, TLB)], Minor[But others said (JNT, NAB, NET, NJB, REB, TEV)].

7:42 ~**Micah 5:2.**

7:46 Alx[**No man ever spoke like this**], Byz[No man ever spoke like this man (DRA, ESV, KJV, ~NAB, NET, NIV, NJB, NKJ, RSV, TEV)], Minor[No man ever spoke like this man speaks (JNT, MRD, NAS, NAU, REB, ~TLB)].

7:47 Alx/Byz[**So the Pharisees answered them**], Minor[*omits* So (ESV, JNT, MRD, NIV, NLT, REB, RSV, TEV, TLB) *others omit* them (JNT, NET, NIV, NJB, NLT, NRS, REB, TLB)].

7:49 Alx[**accursed**], Byz[cursed (~JNT, KJV, ~NIV, NJB, ~NLT, ~REB, ~TEV, ~TLB)].

7:50 Alx[**who had gone to him before**], Byz[who had gone to him by night (DRA)], Minor[*omits*], Minor[who had gone to Jesus by night (KJV, MRD, NKJ)]; Alx/Byz[**and who was one of them**], Minor[*omits* (~NLT, ~TLB)].

7:51 Alx[**without first giving him**], Byz[without earlier giving him (HCS, JNT, KJV, NKJ, NLT, TEV, TLB)].

7:52 Alx[**no prophet rises**], Byz[no prophet has risen (NKJ)].

8   [[53 And each went to his own house. 1 But Jesus went to the Mount of Olives. 2 Early in the morning he came again to the temple. And all the people came to him, and he sat down and taught them. 3 Then the scribes and the Pharisees brought a woman caught in adultery. And when they had set her in the midst, 4 they said to him, "Teacher, this woman has been caught in the act of adultery. 5 Now in the law Moses commanded us to stone such. What, then, do you say?" 6 They said this to test him, that they might have something of which to accuse him. But Jesus bent down and began to trace on the ground with his finger. 7 And when they continued to ask him, he stood up and said to them, "Let him who is without sin among you be the first to throw a stone at her." 8 And again he stooped down and wrote on the ground. 9 Then those who heard it went away one by one, beginning with the oldest, and he was left alone, and the woman in the center. 10 Jesus straightened up and said to her, "Woman, where are they? Has no one condemned you?" 11 She said, "No one, Lord." And Jesus said, "Neither do I condemn you. Go, [and] from now on sin no more."]]

7:53-8:11 Alx/Byz[*adds*], Minor[*omits 7:53-8:11 (RSV 1st edition)* or place it after *7:36, 21:25 (REB),* or *Luke 21:38*], Metzger[*the UBS committee regards this passage as original history, though not originally located within John's gospel*].

7:53 Alx/Major[**And each went to his own house**], Byz[And each departed to his own house (~DRA, JNT, NET)]; *TEV numbers this verse as* 8:1.

8:2 Alx/Byz[**And all the people came to him, and he sat down and taught them**], Major[And all the people came, and he sat down and taught them (NLT, TLB)], Minor[*omits*].

8:3 Alx/Byz[**the scribes and the Pharisees brought**], Major[*adds* to him (DRA, KJV, NKJ)]; Alx/Byz[**caught in adultery**], Minor[caught in sin].

8:4 Alx/Byz[**they said to him**], Major[*adds* to test him]; Alx/Byz[**this woman has been caught**], Major[this woman was caught (DRA, HCS, JNT, KJV, MRD, NAB, NET, NIV, NJB, NKJ, NLT, NRS, TEV, TLB)].

8:5 Alx/Major[**Now in the law Moses commanded us**], Byz[And in our law Moses commanded (JNT, ~MRD, ~NLT, ~REB, TEV, ~TLB)]; Alx[**to stone such**], Byz[that such be stoned (JNT, KJV, NKJ, TEV)]; Alx[**What, then, do you say 6**], Byz[6 What, then, do you say], Minor[*adds* about her (ASV, RSV)].

8:6 Alx/Byz[**They said this to test him, that they might have something of which to accuse him**], Minor[*omits*]; Alx[**trace on the ground**], Byz[write on the ground (ASV, DRA, ESV, HCS, JNT, KJV, MRD, NAB, NAS, NAU, NET, NIV, NJB, NKJ, NLT, NRS, RSV, TEV, TLB)]; Alx/Byz[**with his finger**], Major[*adds* as though he did not hear (KJV, NKJ)].

8:7 Alx/Byz[**they continued to ask him**], Minor[*omits* him (NJB, NLT, TLB)]; Alx/Byz[**he stood up**], Major[standing up], Minor[looking up]; Alx/Byz[**and said to them**], Major[he said to them], Minor[*omits* to them (NET, NJB, NLT, TLB)].

8:8 Alx/Byz[**wrote**], Minor[*adds* with his finger (ASV, RSV)]; Alx/Byz[**on the ground**], Minor[*adds* the sins of each of them].

8:9 Alx/Byz[**went away one by one**], Major[*adds* convicted by their conscience (KJV, NKJ)]; Alx/Byz[**beginning with the oldest**], Minor[*adds* even to the last (ASV, KJV, NJB, NKJ)]; Alx[**and he was left alone**], Byz[and Jesus was left], Major[and Jesus was left alone (ASV, DRA, ESV, KJV, NET, NIV, NJB, NKJ, NLT, NRS, REB, RSV, TEV, TLB)], Minor[and the woman was left alone (MRD)]; Alx/Byz[**the woman in the center**], Minor[the woman standing in the center (DRA, ESV, KJV, MRD, NET, NIV, NKJ, NRS, RSV, TEV)].

8:10 Alx/Byz[**Jesus straightened up**], Major[*adds* and saw her *others* and saw no one but the woman (KJV, NKJ)]; Alx/Byz[**and said to her**], Minor[*omits* to her (NJB) *others* he said to the woman (MRD, NLT)]; Alx/Byz[**Woman**], Major[*omits* (JNT, TEV, TLB)]; Alx/Byz[**where are they**], Major[where are those accusers of yours (DRA, KJV, NKJ)], Minor[where are your accusers (NLT, TLB)]; Alx/Byz[**Has no one condemned you?**], Minor[*omits*].

8:11 Alx/Byz[**Jesus said**], Minor[*adds* to her (KJV, NKJ)]; Alx/Byz[**Neither do I condemn you**], Major[Neither do I judge you (~NLT, ~TLB)]; Alx/Byz[**go, and from now on sin no more**], Major[go, and sin no more (KJV, NKJ, NLT, RSV, ~TEV, TLB)]; Minor[go; from now on sin no more (ASV, NAU)].

¹² Again Jesus spoke to them, saying, "I am the light of the world. He who follows me will never walk in darkness, but shall have the light of life." ¹³ The Pharisees then said to him, "You are bearing witness of yourself; your testimony is not true." ¹⁴ Jesus answered and said to them, "Even if I bear witness of myself, my testimony is true, for I know where I came from and where I am going. But you do not know where I come from or where I am going. ¹⁵ You judge according to the flesh. I judge no one. ¹⁶ And yet if I do judge, my judgment is true, for I am not alone, but I am with the Father who sent me. ¹⁷ In your own law it has been written that *the testimony of two men is true.* ¹⁸ I am one who bears witness of myself, and the Father who sent me bears witness of me." ¹⁹ Then they said to him, "Where is your Father?" Jesus answered, "You know neither me nor my Father. If you knew me, you would know my Father also." ²⁰ These words he spoke in the treasury, as he taught in the temple; but no one arrested him, because his hour had not yet come.

²¹ Then he said to them again, "I am going away, and you will seek me, and will die in your sin. Where I go you cannot come." ²² Then the Jews said, "Will he kill himself, since he says, 'Where I go you cannot come'?" ²³ He said to them, "You are from below; I am from above. You are of this world; I am not of this world. ²⁴ Therefore I told you that you would die in your sins; for if you do not believe that I am he, you will die in your sins." ²⁵ They said to him, "Who are you?" Jesus said to them, "Just what I have been saying to you from the beginning. ²⁶ I have much to say about you and much to judge. But he who sent me is true, and I declare to the world what I have heard from him." ²⁷ They did not understand that he spoke to them of the Father. ²⁸ So Jesus said [to them], "When you have lifted up the Son of Man, then you will know that I am he, and that I do nothing on my own authority but speak just what the Father taught me. ²⁹ And he who sent me is with me. He has not left me alone, for I always do what is pleasing to him." ³⁰ As he spoke these words, many believed in him.

³¹ Jesus then said to the Jews who had believed in him, "If you continue in my word, you are truly my disciples. ³² And you will know the truth, and the truth will make you free." ³³ They answered him, "We are Abraham's descendants, and have never been in bondage to anyone. How can you say, 'You will be made free'?" ³⁴ Jesus answered them, "Truly, truly, I say to you, everyone who commits sin is a slave of sin. ³⁵ And a slave does not continue in the house forever, but a son continues forever. ³⁶ So if the Son makes you free, you will be free indeed. ³⁷ I know that you are Abraham's descendants, yet you seek to

---

8:¹² Alx/Byz[**will never walk in darkness**], Minor[will not walk in darkness (ASV, ESV, KJV, MRD, NAB, NAS, NAU, NJB, NKJ, REB, RSV, TLB) *others* does not walk in darkness (DRA)], Alt[should not walk in darkness (NLT)].

8:¹⁴ Alx/Byz[**but you do not know**], Minor[*omits* but (TEV)]; Alx[**or where I am going**], Byz[and where I am going (KJV, MRD, NKJ, ~NLT, ~TLB)].

8:¹⁶ Alx/Byz[**the Father**], Minor[he (JNT, NAS, NJB, REB, RSV)].

8:¹⁷ ~**Deuteronomy 19:15**.

8:²⁰ Alx[**he spoke**], Byz[Jesus spoke (DRA, KJV, MRD, NET, NKJ, NLT, REB, TEV, TLB)].

8:²¹ Alx[**he said**], Byz[Jesus said (DRA, KJV, MRD, NET, NIV, NKJ, NLT, TEV)].

8:²⁴ **I am he** *Greek* I am.

8:²⁵ Alx[**Jesus said to them**], Byz[And Jesus said to them (KJV, NKJ)]; Alx/Byz[**Just what I have been saying to you from the beginning** *or* Why should I speak to you at all? *or* I am from the beginning what I am telling you], Alt/Vulgate[I am the beginning, who also speaks to you (DRA)], Alt/Peshitta[Although I have begun to speak with you (MRD)].

8:²⁸ Alx/Byz[**Jesus said to them**], Minor[*omits* to them (ASV, JNT, NAS, NAU, NET, NIV, NJB, NLT, NRS, RSV, TLB) *others add* again (MRD)], Alt[*without textual foundation* he said to them (~TEV)]; Alx[**what the Father taught me**], Byz[what my Father taught me (KJV, MRD, NKJ, REB)].

8:²⁹ Alx[**He has not left me alone**], Byz[The Father has not left me alone (KJV, NKJ)], Minor/Peshitta[My Father has not left me alone (MRD)].

8:³³, ³⁷ **descendants** *Greek* seed.

8:³⁴ Alx/Byz[**a slave of sin**], Minor[*omits* of sin (NJB, REB, ~TLB)].

kill me, because my word has no place in you. [38] I speak of what I have seen with the Father, and you, accordingly, do what you have heard from the Father."

[39] They answered him, "Abraham is our father." Jesus said to them, "If you are Abraham's children, you would be doing the works of Abraham, [40] but now you seek to kill me, a man who has told you the truth which I heard from God. This is not what Abraham did. [41] You do the deeds of your father." [So] they said to him, "We have not been born of fornication; we have one Father – God." [42] Jesus said to them, "If God were your Father, you would love me, for I came from God and am now here. I have not come of my own accord, but he sent me. [43] Why do you not understand what I say? It is because you are not able to hear my word. [44] You are of your father the devil, and you want to do your father's desires. He was a murderer from the beginning, and does not stand in the truth, because there is no truth in him. When he lies, he speaks according to his own nature, for he is a liar and the father of lies. [45] But because I tell the truth, you do not believe me. [46] Which of you convicts me of sin? If I tell the truth, why do you not believe me? [47] He who is of God hears the words of God. The reason you do not hear them is that you are not of God."

[48] The Jews answered and said to him, "Are we not right in saying that you are a Samaritan and have a demon?" [49] Jesus answered, "I do not have a demon; but I honor my Father, and you dishonor me. [50] Yet I do not seek my own glory. There is One who seeks it and he will be the judge. [51] Truly, truly, I say to you, if anyone keeps my word he will never see death." [52] [So] the Jews said to him, "Now we know that you have a demon! Abraham died, as did the prophets; and you say, 'If anyone keeps my word, he will never taste death.' [53] Are you greater than our father Abraham? He died, and so did the prophets. Who do you claim to be?" [54] Jesus answered, "If I glorify myself, my glory is nothing. It is my Father who glorifies me, of whom you say that he is our God. [55] But you have not known him. I know him. If I said, I do not know him, I would be a liar like you. But I do know him and keep his word. [56] Your father Abraham rejoiced to see my day; he saw it and was glad." [57] The Jews then said to him, "You are not yet fifty years old, and have you seen Abraham?"

8:38 Alx[**what I have seen with the Father**], Byz[what I have seen with my Father (ASV, DRA, ESV, JNT, KJV, MRD, NAS, NAU, NJB, NKJ, NLT, REB, RSV, TEV, TLB)]; Alx[**what you have heard**], Byz[what you have seen (DRA, KJV, MRD, ~NJB, NKJ, ~REB)]; Alx[**from the Father**], Byz[with your father (ASV, DRA, ESV, HCS, JNT, KJV, MRD, NAS, NAU, NIV, NJB, NKJ, NLT, REB, RSV, TEV, TLB)].

8:39 Alx[**If you are Abraham's children**], Byz[If you were being Abraham's children (ASV, ESV, HCS, KJV, MRD, NAB, NIV, NKJ, NLT, NRS, REB, RSV, TEV, ~TLB)]; Alx/Byz[**you would be doing**], Minor[then do (DRA, NAS, NAU, NJB)].

8:41 Alx/Byz[**So they said to him**], Minor[*omits* So (ASV, ESV, HCS, JNT, MRD, NAS, NAU, NIV, NJB, NLT, NRS, REB, RSV, TEV, TLB)]; Alx/Byz[**we have not been born of fornication**], Minor[we were not born of fornication (ASV, ~DRA, ESV, HCS, ~JNT, ~KJV, ~MRD, ~NAB, NAS, NAU, NET, ~NIV, NJB, NKJ, ~NLT, ~NRS, ~REB, RSV, ~TEV, TLB)].

8:42 Alx[**Jesus said to them**], Byz[So Jesus said to them (DRA)].

8:44 Alx[**does not stand in the truth**], Byz[has not stood in the truth (DRA, HCS, JNT, KJV, MRD, NJB, NLT, TEV, ~TLB)].

8:46 Alx[**If I tell the truth**], Byz[But if I tell the truth (KJV, MRD, NKJ, NLT, TLB)].

8:48 Alx[**The Jews answered**], Byz[So the Jews answered (DRA, KJV, NKJ)].

8:49 Alx/Byz[**my Father**], Alt[*without textual foundation* God (~MRD)].

8:52 Alx/Byz[**So the Jews said**], Minor[*omits* So (ASV, ESV, JNT, MRD, NAS, NAU, ~NIV, NJB, NLT, NRS, REB, RSV, TEV, TLB)].

8:54 Alx/Major[**he is our God**], Byz[he is your God (ASV, DRA, KJV, NIV, NKJ, RSV, TEV, TLB)].

8:56 Alx/Byz[**to see my day**], Minor[to know my day (~NLT)].

8:57 Alx/Byz[**You are not yet fifty**], Minor[You are not yet forty]; Alx/Byz[**have you seen Abraham**], Minor[has Abraham seen you].

[58] Jesus said to them, "Truly, truly, I say to you, before Abraham was, I am." [59] So they took up stones to throw at him; but Jesus hid himself, and went out of the temple.

9 [1] As he passed by, he saw a man blind from birth. [2] And his disciples asked him, "Rabbi, who sinned, this man or his parents, that he was born blind?" [3] Jesus answered, "Neither this man sinned nor his parents sinned. But that the works of God might be revealed in him, [4] we must work the works of him who sent me, while it is day. Night is coming, when no one can work. [5] As long as I am in the world, I am the light of the world." [6] As he said this, he spat on the ground and made clay of the saliva, and anointed the man's eyes with the clay. [7] And he said to him, "Go, wash in the pool of Siloam" (which means, Sent). So he went and washed, and came back seeing. [8] The neighbors and those who had seen him before as a beggar, said, "Is not this the man who used to sit and beg?" [9] Some said, "It is he." Others said, "No, but he is like him." He kept saying, "I am the man." [10] So they said to him, "[Then] how were your eyes opened?" [11] He answered, "The man called Jesus made clay and anointed my eyes and said to me, 'Go to Siloam and wash.' So I went and washed, and I received sight." [12] And they said to him, "Where is he?" He said, "I do not know."

[13] They brought to the Pharisees the man who had formerly been blind. [14] Now it was a Sabbath on the day Jesus made the clay and opened his eyes. [15] Then the Pharisees also asked him again how he had received his sight. He said to them, "He put clay on my eyes, and I washed, and I see." [16] Some of the Pharisees said, "This man is not from God, for he does not keep the Sabbath." [But] others said, "How can a man who is a sinner do such signs?" And there was a division among them. [17] So they again said to the blind man, "What do you say about him, since he has opened your eyes?" He said, "He is a prophet."

[18] The Jews did not believe that he had been blind, and had received his sight, until they called the parents of the man who had received his sight. [19] And they asked them, "Is

---

8:59 Alx[**went out of the temple**], Byz[*adds* going through the midst of them, and so passed by (KJV, MRD, NKJ, TLB)].

9:1 Alx/Byz[**from birth**], Alt/Peshitta[from his mother's womb (MRD)].

9:4 Alx[**we must work**], Byz[I must work (DRA, KJV, MRD, NKJ)]; Alx/Byz[**who sent me**], Minor[who sent us (NLT)]; Alx/Byz[**while it is day**], Minor[as it is day (~NLT, ~TLB)].

9:6 Alx/Byz[**anointed**], Minor[put upon (DRA, HCS, JNT, MRD, NAB, NAS, NAU, NET, NIV, NJB, NLT, NRS, REB, TEV, TLB)]; Alx[**the man's eyes** *Greek* his eyes], Byz[the eyes of the blind (KJV, MRD, NET, NJB, NKJ, NLT, TLB)].

9:7 Alx/Byz[**pool of Siloam**], Minor[baptistery of Siloam (MRD)]; Alx/Byz[**which means, Sent**], Alt/Peshitta[*omits as redundant* (MRD)].

9:8 Alx[**as a beggar**], Byz[as a blind man (KJV, NKJ, ~TLB)].

9:9 Alx/Byz[**9 Some said, "It is he."**], Minor[Some said, "It is he." 9 (DRA)]; Alx[**Others said, "No, but he is like him**], Byz[But others that, "He is like him (~KJV, ~NAB, ~NIV, ~NKJ, ~NLT, ~TEV, ~TLB)], Minor[But others said, "No, but he is like him (DRA)]; Alx/Byz[**He kept saying**], Minor[But he kept saying (DRA, ~JNT, KJV, MRD, NIV, NLT)].

9:10 Alx[**Then how were your eyes opened**], Byz[*omits* Then (DRA, JNT, KJV, MRD, NKJ, NLT, REB, TEV, ~TLB)].

9:11 Alx[**He answered**], Byz[*adds* and said (KJV, NKJ)], Alt/Peshitta[*adds* and said to them (MRD, ~NLT, ~TLB)]; Alx[**The man called Jesus**], Byz[A man called Jesus (KJV, MRD, NKJ, TLB)]; Alx[**Go to Siloam**], Byz[Go to the pool of Siloam (~DRA, KJV, ~MRD, NKJ, NLT, TLB)]; Alx[**So I went and washed**], Byz[And I went and washed (DRA, KJV, MRD, ~TLB)].

9:12 Alx[**And they said**], Byz[So they said (KJV, NKJ)], Minor[They said (ESV, HCS, JNT, MRD, NAU, NET, NIV, NJB, NLT, NRS, REB, RSV, TEV, TLB)].

9:14 Alx[**a Sabbath on the day**], Byz[a Sabbath when (~ASV, DRA, ~ESV, ~KJV, ~NAB, ~NAS, ~NAU, ~NJB, NKJ, ~NRS, ~REB, ~RSV, ~TLB)], Minor[a Sabbath that (~JNT, ~MRD, ~NET, ~NIV, NLT, ~TEV)].

9:15 Alx/Byz[**and I see**], Minor/Peshitta[and my sight was restored (MRD)].

9:16 Alx[**But others said**], Byz[Others said (KJV, NJB, NKJ, NLT, REB, TLB)].

9:17 Alx[**So they again said**], Byz[*omits* So (HCS, KJV, MRD, ~NIV, NKJ)].

this your son, who you say was born blind? How then does he now see?" ²⁰ So his parents answered and said, "We know that this is our son, and that he was born blind. ²¹ But how he now sees we do not know, nor do we know who opened his eyes. Ask him. He is of age. He will speak for himself." ²² His parents said this because they feared the Jews, for the Jews had agreed already that if anyone confessed that he was Christ, he would be put out of the synagogue. ²³ Therefore his parents said, "He is of age. Question him."

²⁴ So for the second time they called the man who had been blind, and said to him, "*Give God the glory*; we know that this man is a sinner." ²⁵ So he answered, "Whether he is a sinner or not, I do not know. One thing I know, that though I was blind, now I see." ²⁶ Then they said to him, "What did he do to you? How did he open your eyes?" ²⁷ He answered them, "I have told you already and you did not listen. Why do you want to hear it again? Do you want to become his disciples, too?" ²⁸ And they reviled him and said, "You are his disciple, but we are disciples of Moses. ²⁹ We know that God spoke to Moses, but as for this fellow, we do not know where he comes from." ³⁰ The man answered, "Why, this is the marvel! You do not know where he comes from, and yet he opened my eyes. ³¹ We know that God does not listen to sinners. But if any one is a worshipper of God and does his will, he listens to him. ³² Never since the world began has it been heard that anyone opened the eyes of a man born blind. ³³ If this man were not from God, he could do nothing." ³⁴ They answered him, "You were born in utter sin, and are you teaching us?" And they cast him out.

³⁵ Jesus heard that they had cast him out, and when he found him, he said, "Do you believe in the Son of Man?" ³⁶ He answered and said, "And who is he, sir, that I may believe in him?" ³⁷ Jesus said to him, "You have seen him, and it is he who speaks with you." ³⁸ Then he said, "Lord, I believe!" And he worshipped him. ³⁹ Jesus said, "For judgment I have come into this world, that those who do not see may see, and that those who see may become blind."

9:20 Alx[**So his parents answered**], Byz[But his parents answered them (~DRA, ~KJV, ~NAS, ~NAU, ~NKJ)], Minor[But his parents answered (~ASV, ~ESV, ~HCS, ~JNT, MRD, ~NAB, ~NIV, ~NJB, ~NLT, ~NRS, ~REB, ~RSV, ~TEV, ~TLB)].

9:23 Alx[**Question him**], Byz[Ask him (ASV, DRA, ESV, HCS, JNT, KJV, MRD, NAS, NAU, NET, NIV, NJB, NKJ, NLT, NRS, REB, RSV, TEV, ~TLB)].

9:24 **Give God the glory** *placing him under oath, compare* Joshua 7:19.

9:25 Alx[**So he answered**], Byz[*adds* and said (~DRA, KJV, MRD, NKJ)], Minor[*adds* to them (DRA, MRD)].

9:26 Alx[**Then they said to him**], Byz[But they said to him again (MRD)], Minor[Then they said to him again (KJV, NKJ)].

9:27 Alx/Byz[**Why do you want to hear**], Minor[Why then do you want to hear].

9:28 Alx[**And they reviled him**], Byz[They reviled him (HCS, NAB, NAU, NET, TEV)], Minor[So they reviled him (DRA, JNT, KJV, NIV, ~NJB, NKJ, NLT, NRS, REB, TLB) *others* But they reviled him (MRD)].

9:30 Alx[**the marvel**], Byz[a marvel (DRA, ESV, HCS, JNT, KJV, ~MRD, NAS, NAU, NET, NKJ, NRS, RSV, TEV)].

9:31 Alx[**We know that God**], Byz[But we know that God (DRA, KJV, MRD, NKJ)].

9:35 Alx[**he said**], Byz[*adds* to him (DRA, KJV, MRD, NET, NJB, NKJ, TEV)]; Alx[**Son of Man**], Byz[Son of God (ASV, DRA, KJV, MRD, NKJ, ~TLB)].

9:36 Alx/Byz[**He answered and said**], Minor[*omits* answered and *others omit* and said (ESV, ~HCS, JNT, NAU, NET, ~NIV, NJB, NLT, NRS, REB, RSV, TEV, TLB)]; Alx/Byz[**And who is he**], Minor[*omits* And (DRA, HCS, JNT, KJV, MRD, NAB, NAU, NIV, NJB, NKJ, NLT, REB, TEV, TLB)]; **sir** *Greek* lord.

9:37 Alx[**Jesus said to him**], Byz[But Jesus said to him (DRA, KJV, NKJ)].

9:38-39 Alx/Byz[**Then he said, "Lord, I believe!" And he worshipped him. 39 Jesus said**], Minor[*omits; others also omit all of verse 39*].

⁴⁰ Some of the Pharisees who were with him heard these things, and said to him, "Are we blind also?" ⁴¹ Jesus said to them, "If you were blind, you would have no guilt. But now that you say, 'We see,' your sin remains.

10

¹ "Truly, truly, I say to you, the man who does not enter the sheepfold by the door, but climbs in by some other way, he is a thief and a robber. ² But he who enters by the door is the shepherd of the sheep. ³ To him the doorkeeper opens, and the sheep hear his voice; and he calls his own sheep by name and leads them out. ⁴ When he has brought out all his own, he goes on before them, and the sheep follow him, for they know his voice. ⁵ A stranger they will not follow, but they will flee from him, for they do not know the voice of strangers." ⁶ This figure Jesus used with them, but they did not understand what he was saying to them.

⁷ Then Jesus said again, "Truly, truly, I say to you, I am the door of the sheep. ⁸ All who ever came [before me] are thieves and robbers, but the sheep did not hear them. ⁹ I am the door. If anyone enters by me, he will be saved, and will go in and out and find pasture. ¹⁰ The thief comes only to steal and kill and destroy. I have come that they may have life, and have it abundantly. ¹¹ I am the good shepherd. The good shepherd lays down his life for the sheep. ¹² He who is a hireling and not the shepherd, who does not own the sheep, sees the wolf coming and leaves the sheep and flees; and the wolf snatches and scatters them. ¹³ This is because he is a hireling and cares nothing for the sheep. ¹⁴ I am the good shepherd; I know my sheep, and my own know me – ¹⁵ just as the Father knows me and I know the Father; and I lay down my life for the sheep. ¹⁶ And I have other sheep that are not of this fold; I must bring them also, and they will heed my voice. And they shall become one flock, one shepherd. ¹⁷ For this reason my Father loves me, because I lay down my life, that I may take it again. ¹⁸ No one takes it from me, but I lay it down of my own accord. I

9:40 Alx[**Some of the Pharisees**], Byz[And some of the Pharisees (DRA, KJV, MRD, ~NKJ)]; Alx/Byz[**heard these things**], Minor[*omits* these things (DRA, NLT, ~REB, ~TLB)].

9:41 Alx[**your sin remains**], Byz[therefore your sin remains (KJV, MRD, NAB, NKJ, ~TLB)].

10:3 Alx[**calls his own sheep**], Byz[invites his own sheep].

10:4 Alx[**When he has brought**], Byz[And when he has brought (DRA, KJV, MRD, NKJ)]; Alx[**all his own**], Byz[his own sheep (DRA, KJV, ~MRD, ~NET, NKJ, ~NLT, ~REB, ~TEV, ~TLB)].

10:5 Alx[**they will not follow**], Byz[they will never follow (HCS, JNT, NET, NIV, NJB, NKJ)].

10:7 Alx[**Jesus said again**], Byz[*adds* to them (ASV, DRA, ESV, JNT, KJV, MRD, NAS, NAU, NET, NJB, NKJ, NLT, NRS, RSV, TLB)], Minor[*omits* again (~NLT, ~TLB)]; Alx/Byz[**door of the sheep**], Minor[shepherd of the sheep].

10:8 Alx/Byz[**All who ever came**], Minor[As many as came (~REB)]; Alx/Byz[**before me**], Major[*omits* (DRA, MRD)].

10:9 **will be saved** *or* will be kept safe.

10:11 Alx/Byz[**the good shepherd. The good shepherd**], Alt/Peshitta[a good shepherd. A good shepherd (MRD, ~NAB, ~TEV)]; Alx/Byz[**lays down his life**], Minor[gives his life (DRA, KJV, ~MRD, NKJ, ~NLT, ~TEV)].

10:12 Alx[**He who is a hireling**], Byz[But he who is a hireling (DRA, KJV, MRD, NKJ)]; Alx[**snatches and scatters them** *Greek* snatches them and scatters], Byz[snatches them and scatters the sheep (~DRA, KJV, ~MRD, ~NIV, ~NJB, ~NKJ, ~NLT, ~REB, ~TEV, ~TLB)].

10:13 Alx[**This is because** *Greek* Because], Byz[But the hireling flees, because (~ASV, DRA, ~ESV, ~JNT, KJV, MRD, ~NAS, ~NAU, ~NET, ~NIV, ~NJB, NKJ, NLT, NRS, ~REB, ~RSV, TEV, TLB)].

10:14 Alx[**my own know me 15**], Byz[I am known by my own 15 (KJV, MRD, NKJ)], Minor[15 I am known by my own].

10:15 Alx/Byz[**I lay down my life**], Minor[I give my life (~MRD, ~NLT, ~TEV)].

10:16 Alx[**they shall become**], Byz[there shall be (DRA, ESV, HCS, JNT, KJV, ~MRD, NAB, NET, NIV, NJB, NKJ, NLT, NLT, NRS, REB, RSV, TLB)]; Alx/Byz[**one flock**], Alt/Vulgate[one fold (DRA, KJV)].

10:18 Alx/Byz[**No one takes**], Minor[No one has taken (NAS, NAU)], Alt[*without textual foundation* No one can take (~NLT, ~TLB)].

have power to lay it down, and I have power to take it again. This command I have received from my Father."

¹⁹ There was again a division among the Jews because of these words. ²⁰ And many of them said, "He has a demon, and is mad. Why listen to him?" ²¹ Others said, "These are not the sayings of one who has a demon. Can a demon open the eyes of the blind?"

²² Then came the Feast of Dedication at Jerusalem. It was winter, ²³ and Jesus was in the temple, walking in Solomon's Porch. ²⁴ So the Jews gathered round him and said to him, "How long will you keep us in suspense? If you are the Christ, tell us plainly." ²⁵ Jesus answered them, "I told you, and you do not believe. The works that I do in my Father's name, they bear witness of me. ²⁶ But you do not believe, because you are not of my sheep. ²⁷ My sheep hear my voice, and I know them, and they follow me. ²⁸ I give them eternal life, and they shall never perish. No one shall snatch them out of my hand. ²⁹ What my Father has given to me is greater than all, and no one is able to snatch it out of the Father's hand. ³⁰ I and the Father are one."

³¹ The Jews took up stones again to stone him. ³² Jesus answered them, "I have shown you many good works from the Father. For which of these do you stone me?" ³³ The Jews answered him, "For a good work we do not stone you, but for blasphemy, and because you, being a man, make yourself God." ³⁴ Jesus answered them, "Is it not written in your law that, 'I said, you are gods'? ³⁵ If he called them gods, to whom the word of God came (and the Scripture cannot be broken), ³⁶ do you say of him whom the Father sanctified and sent into the world, 'You are blaspheming,' because I said, 'I am the Son of God'? ³⁷ If I do not do the works of my father, do not believe me; ³⁸ but if I do them, even though you do not believe me, believe the works, that you may know and understand that the Father is in me, and I am in the Father." ³⁹ [Then] they tried again to seize him, but he escaped from their hands.

10:¹⁹ Alx[**There was again a division**], Byz[So there was again a division (KJV, NKJ)].

10:²⁰ Alx/Byz[**And many of them said**], Minor[So, many of them said].

10:²² Alx[**Then came**], Byz[And it was (ASV, DRA, KJV, MRD, NJB, ~NKJ, ~NLT, REB, RSV, TEV)]; Alx[**It was winter 23**], Byz[And it was winter 23 (DRA, HCS, KJV, MRD, NKJ)], Minor[23 It was winter (ASV, NAS, NAU, NET, RSV)]; **the Feast of Dedication** *Hanukkah*.

10:²⁵ Alx/Byz[**Jesus answered them**], Minor[*omits* them (NET, NIV, NJB, NLT, NRS, REB, TEV, TLB)], Alt/Peshitta[Jesus answered and said to them (MRD)].

10:²⁶ Alx[**because you are**], Byz[for you are (TEV)]; Alx[**not of my sheep**], Byz[*adds* as I said to you (KJV, MRD, NKJ)].

10:²⁹ Alx[*text*], Byz[My Father, who has given them to me, is greater than all; and no one is able to snatch them out of my Father's hand (ASV, ~DRA, ~ESV, ~HCS, ~JNT, KJV, MRD, ~NAB, ~NAS, ~NAU, NET, NIV, ~NJB, NKJ, ~NLT, ~REB, ~RSV, ~TLB)], Minor[What the Father…the Father's hand].

10:³⁰ Alx/Byz[**the Father**], Minor[my Father (KJV, MRD, NKJ)].

10:³¹ Alx[**The Jews took up stones**], Byz[Therefore the Jews took up stones (DRA, KJV, NKJ, TEV, TLB)]; Alx/Byz[**again**], Alt[*omits* (DRA, NJB)].

10:³² Alx[**from the Father**], Byz[from my Father (DRA, KJV, MRD, NAB, NJB, NKJ, NLT, ~TLB)].

10:³³ Alx[**the Jews answered him**], Byz[*adds* saying (KJV, NKJ)], Alt[*without textual foundation omits* him (~HCS, ~JNT, ~NET, ~NIV, ~NLT, ~NRS, ~REB, ~TEV, ~TLB)]; Alx/Byz[**make yourself God** *or* make yourself a god *without definite article*], Minor[make yourself God *with definite article*].

10:³⁴ Alx/Byz[**your law**], Minor[the law *others* the scripture (~NLT)]; Alx[**that**], Byz[*omits* (ASV, DRA, ESV, HCS, JNT, KJV, MRD, NAB, NAS, NAU, NET, NIV, NJB, NKJ, ~NLT, NRS, REB, RSV, ~TEV, ~TLB)]; **Psalms 82:6**.

10:³⁸ Alx[**know and understand**], Byz[know and believe (DRA, KJV, MRD, NKJ, ~TLB)], Minor[know]; Alx[**I am in the Father**], Byz[I am in him (KJV, NKJ)]; Alx/Byz[**the Father…the Father**], Alt/Peshitta[my Father…my Father (MRD)].

10:³⁹ Alx/Byz[**Then they tried**], Minor[They tried (ASV, ESV, JNT, NIV, NLT, RSV, TEV, TLB) *others* But they tried *others* And they tried (MRD)]; Alx/Byz[**again**], Minor[*omits* (DRA)].

40 He went away again across the Jordan to the place where John was baptizing at first, and there he stayed. **41** And many came to him and they said, "John performed no sign, but all that John said about this man was true." **42** And many believed in him there.

11

1 Now a certain man was sick, Lazarus of Bethany, the village of Mary and her sister Martha. **2** It was this Mary who anointed the Lord with fragrant oil and wiped his feet with her hair, whose brother Lazarus was sick. **3** So the sisters sent to him, saying, "Lord, he whom you love is sick." **4** When Jesus heard it, he said, "This sickness is not unto death, but for the glory of God, so that the Son of God may be glorified through it." **5** Now Jesus loved Martha and her sister and Lazarus. **6** So, when he heard that he was sick, he stayed two more days in the place where he was. **7** Then after this he said to the disciples, "Let us go to Judea again." **8** The disciples said to him, "Rabbi, the Jews were just now seeking to stone you, and are you going there again?" **9** Jesus answered, "Are there not twelve hours in the day? If anyone walks in the day, he does not stumble, because he sees the light of this world. **10** But if one walks in the night, he stumbles, because the light is not in him." **11** These things he said, and after that he said to them, "Our friend Lazarus has fallen asleep, but I go to wake him up." **12** So the disciples said to him, "Lord, if he sleeps, he will recover." **13** Now Jesus had spoken of his death, but they thought that he meant taking rest in sleep. **14** So then Jesus told them plainly, "Lazarus is dead. **15** And for your sake I am glad that I was not there, so that you may believe. But let us go to him." **16** Then Thomas, who is called the Twin, said to his fellow disciples, "Let us also go, that we may die with him."

17 So when Jesus came, he found that he had already been in the tomb four days. **18** Bethany was near Jerusalem, about two miles off, **19** and many of the Jews had come to Martha and Mary to comfort them concerning their brother. **20** When Martha heard that Jesus was coming, she went and met him, but Mary sat in the house. **21** Martha said to Jesus, "Lord, if you had been here, my brother would not have died. **22** [But] even now I know that whatever you ask of God, God will give you." **23** Jesus said to her, "Your brother will rise again." **24** Martha said to him, "I know that he will rise again in the resurrection at the last day." **25** Jesus said to her, "I am the resurrection and the life. He who believes in me, though he die, yet shall he live; **26** and whoever lives and believes in me shall never die. Do you believe this?" **27** She said to him, "Yes, Lord, I believe that you are the Christ, the Son of God, who is to come into the world."

10:40 Alx/Byz[**there he stayed**], Minor[there he was staying (NAS, NAU)].

10:41 Alx/Byz[**but all that John said about this man was true." 42**], Alt/Vulgate[42 but all that John said about this man was true." (DRA)].

10:42 Alx/Byz[**many believed in him there**], Minor[*omits* there (DRA, MRD, NJB, TLB)].

11:2 Alx[**Mary** *Greek* Mariam], Byz[Mary *Greek* Maria]; John 12:3.

11:3 Alx/Byz[**So the sisters sent to him**], Minor[So Mary sent to him *others* So the sisters sent to Jesus (JNT, MRD, NET, NIV, NJB, NLT, NRS, TEV, TLB)].

11:12 Alx[**the disciples said to him**], Byz[his disciples said (DRA, KJV, ~MRD, ~NET, NIV, NKJ, ~NLT, ~REB, ~TEV, ~TLB)].

11:16 **the Twin** *Greek* Didymus.

11:17 Alx/Byz[**Jesus came**], Minor[*adds* to Bethany (MRD, NLT, TLB)]; Alx/Byz[**already**], Minor[*omits* (MRD, ~TEV)].

11:18 **two miles** *Greek* fifteen stadia.

11:19 Alx[**had come to Martha and Mary**], Byz[had come to those around Martha and Mary (~NET, NKJ, ~REB)].

11:20 Alx[**Mary** *Greek* Mariam], Byz[Mary *Greek* Maria].

11:21 Alx/Byz[**Lord**], Minor[*omits*].

11:22 Alx/Byz[**But even now**], Minor[*omits* But (~ASV, JNT, NAS, NAU, REB, ~RSV, ~TLB)].

11:25 Alx/Byz[**Jesus said to her**], Minor[But Jesus said to her]; Alx/Byz[**and the life**], Minor[*omits* (NJB)]; Alx/Major[**He who believes in me, though he die, yet shall he live; 26**], Byz[26 He who believes in me, though he die, yet shall he live;].

²⁸ And when she had said this, she went her way and called Mary her sister, saying, "The Teacher is here and is calling for you." ²⁹ And when she heard it, she rose quickly and started to go to him. ³⁰ Now Jesus had not yet come to the village, but was still in the place where Martha had met him. ³¹ The Jews who were with her in the house, and comforting her, when they saw that Mary rose up quickly and went out, followed her, supposing that she was going to the tomb to weep there. ³² Then Mary, when she came where Jesus was and saw him, fell to his feet, saying to him, "Lord, if you had been here, my brother would not have died." ³³ When Jesus saw her weeping, and the Jews who came with her also weeping, he groaned in the spirit and was troubled. ³⁴ And he said, "Where have you laid him?" They said to him, "Lord, come and see."

³⁵ Jesus wept.

³⁶ Then the Jews said, "See how he loved him!" ³⁷ But some of them said, "Could not he who opened the eyes of the blind man have kept this man from dying?"

³⁸ Then Jesus, deeply moved again, came to the tomb. It was a cave, and a stone lay against it. ³⁹ Jesus said, "Take away the stone." Martha, the sister of the dead man, said to him, "Lord, by this time there is a bad odor, for he has been dead four days." ⁴⁰ Jesus said to her, "Did I not tell you that if you would believe you would see the glory of God?" ⁴¹ So they took away the stone. And Jesus lifted up his eyes and said, "Father, I thank you that you have heard me. ⁴² I knew that you always hear me, but I said this for the benefit of the people standing by, that they may believe that you sent me." ⁴³ When he had said this, he cried with a loud voice, "Lazarus, come out!" ⁴⁴ The dead man came out, his hands and feet bound with grave clothes, and his face wrapped with a cloth. Jesus said to them, "Loose him, and let him go."

⁴⁵ Many of the Jews therefore, who had come to Mary and had seen what he did, believed in him. ⁴⁶ But some of them went to the Pharisees and told them what Jesus had done. ⁴⁷ Then the chief priests and the Pharisees gathered the Sanhedrin, and said, "What are we to do? For this man performs many signs. ⁴⁸ If we let him go on like this, everyone will believe in him, and the Romans will come and take away both our place and our nation." ⁴⁹ But one of them, Caiaphas, who was high priest that year, said to them, "You know nothing at all! ⁵⁰ You do not consider that it is expedient for you that one man should

---

11:28 Alx[**when she had said this**], Byz[when she had said these things (DRA, ~KJV, ~MRD, NKJ, ~NLT, ~REB, ~TLB)].

11:29 Alx[**And when she heard it**], Byz[*omits* And (DRA, HCS, JNT, KJV, NAB, ~NET, NIV, NJB, NKJ, ~NLT, REB, TEV, ~TLB)]; Alx[**she rose quickly and started to go to him**], Byz[she rises quickly and goes to him (DRA)].

11:30 Alx[**still**], Byz[*omits* (KJV, MRD, NKJ, ~NLT, ~TLB)].

11:31 Alx[**supposing that she was going to the tomb to weep there**], Byz[saying, "She is going to the tomb to weep there" (DRA, KJV, NKJ)].

11:32 Alx[**Mary** *Greek* Mariam], Byz[Mary *Greek* Maria]; Alx[**fell to his feet**], Byz[fell into his feet].

11:33 Alx/Byz[**he groaned in the spirit** *or* he was angry in spirit], Minor[it was as if he groaned in the spirit].

11:34 Alx/Major[**They said to him, "Lord, come and see." 35**], Byz[35 They said to him, "Lord, come and see."].

11:35 Alx/Byz[**Jesus wept**], Minor/Vulgate[And Jesus wept (DRA, NAB, ~NLT)], Alt/Peshitta[And the tears of Jesus came (MRD, ~TLB)], Alt[*without textual foundation* Jesus began to weep (~NRS)].

11:41 Alx[**took away the stone**], Byz[*adds* from where the dead man was lying (KJV, NKJ)].

11:44 Alx[**The dead man came out**], Byz[And the dead man came out (DRA, KJV, MRD, NKJ, NLT, TLB)]; Alx[**Loose him, and let him go**], Byz[Loose him, and let go (~NIV)].

11:45 Alx[**seen what he did**], Byz[seen what Jesus did (~DRA, JNT, ~KJV, MRD, ~NET, NIV, ~NKJ, ~NLT, NRS, REB, TEV)]; Minor[seen the things he did].

11:48 **place** *or* temple.

11:50 Alx[**You do not consider**], Byz[You do not reason]; Alx[**expedient for you**], Byz[expedient for us (KJV, MRD, NKJ, ~TLB)].

die for the people, and that the whole nation not perish." [51] He did not say this on his own, but being high priest that year he prophesied that Jesus would die for the nation, [52] and not for that nation only, but also that he would gather together into one the children of God who were scattered abroad. [53] So from that day on they plotted to put him to death.

[54] Jesus therefore no longer went about openly among the Jews, but went from there to the country near the wilderness, to a town called Ephraim; and there he stayed with the disciples.

[55] Now the Passover of the Jews was at hand, and many went from the country up to Jerusalem before the Passover, to purify themselves. [56] They were looking for Jesus and saying to one another as they stood in the temple, "What do you think? That he will never come to the feast?" [57] Now the chief priests and the Pharisees had given orders that if anyone knew where he was, he should report it, so that they might arrest him.

12 [1] Then, six days before the Passover, Jesus came to Bethany where Lazarus was, whom Jesus had raised from the dead. [2] There they made him a supper; and Martha served, while Lazarus was one of those who sat to eat with him. [3] Then Mary took a pound of very costly perfume of pure nard, anointed the feet of Jesus, and wiped his feet with her hair. And the house was filled with the fragrance of the perfume. [4] But one [from] his disciples, Judas Iscariot, who was later to betray him, said, [5] "Why was this perfume not sold for three hundred denarii and given to the poor?" [6] This he said, not that he cared for the poor, but because he was a thief; and holding the money box, he was stealing what was put into it. [7] Jesus said, "Let her alone, that she may keep this for the day of my burial. [8] The poor you have with you always, but you do not always have me."

[9] Then [the] great crowd of the Jews learned that he was there, and they came, not only on account of Jesus but also to see Lazarus, whom he had raised from the dead. [10] So the chief priests planned to put Lazarus also to death, [11] because on account of him many of the Jews were going away and believing in Jesus.

11:[51] Alx/Byz[**that year**], Minor[the year *others omit* (~NLT, TLB)].

11:[53] Alx[**plotted**], Byz[plotted together (KJV)].

11:[54] Alx[**stayed with the disciples**], Byz[continued with his disciples (~DRA, KJV, ~MRD, ~NAB, ~NET, ~NIV, ~NJB, ~NKJ, ~NLT, ~REB, ~TLB)].

11:[57] Alx[**the chief priests and the Pharisees**], Byz[both the chief priests and the Pharisees (KJV, NKJ)]; Alx[**given orders**], Byz[given an order (~ASV, DRA, KJV, ~MRD, NKJ, ~NLT, ~TLB)]; *DRA includes this verse in verse 56.*

12:[1] Alx[**where Lazarus was**], Byz[*adds* who had been dead (DRA, KJV, NKJ)]; Alx[**whom Jesus had raised from the dead**], Byz[whom he had raised from the dead (KJV, NET, NJB, NKJ, NLT, NRS, REB, TEV, TLB)].

12:[2] Alx[**of those who sat** *Greek* from those who sat], Byz[of those who sat].

12:[3] Alx[**Mary** *Greek* Mariam], Byz[Mary *Greek* Maria]; **pound** *Greek* litra.

12:[4] Alx[**But one**], Byz[So one (DRA, HCS, KJV, MRD, NAB, NJB, NKJ, ~REB)], Minor[One (TEV)]; Alx/Byz[**from his disciples**], Minor[of his disciples (ASV, DRA, ESV, HCS, KJV, ~NAB, HAS, NAU, NET, NIV, NJB, NKJ, NRS, REB, RSV, ~TEV, TLB)], Alt/Peshitta[one of the disciples (JNT, MRD, ~NLT)]; Alx[**Judas**], Byz[Judas, son of Simon (~KJV, ~NKJ)], Minor[Judas Simon]; Alx/Byz[**Iscariot**], Minor[from Karuot (JNT)], Alt/Vulgate/Peshitta[Scariot; **Iscariot** *Hebraism Ish Keriot* a man from Kerioth *or possibly Sicarios* assassin *or* bandit.

12:[5] *a denarius was a day's wage for a laborer.*

12:[6] Alx[**and holding the money box**], Byz[and he was holding the money box (HCS, JNT, ~KJV, ~MRD, ~NAB, NJB, NKJ, NRS, ~REB, ~TEV, TLB)]; Alx[**he was stealing**], Byz[and he was stealing (HCS, JNT, KJV, MRD, NAB, NJB, NKJ, NRS, REB, TEV, TLB)].

12:[7] Alx[**that she may keep this**], Byz[she has kept this (HCS, JNT, KJV, MRD, NET, NKJ, NLT, TLB)].

12:[8] Alx/Byz[*text*], Minor[*omits*].

12:[9] Alx[**the great crowd** *or* the common people], Byz[a great crowd (DRA, HCS, JNT, KJV, MRD, NET, NIV, NJB, NKJ, ~REB, TEV)].

12 The next day the great crowd that had come to the feast heard that Jesus was coming to Jerusalem. 13 They took branches of palm trees and went out to meet him, crying,

"*Hosanna!*
Blessed is he who comes in the name of the Lord!
[Even] *the King of Israel!*"

14 Jesus found a young donkey and sat upon it, as it is written,

15   "*Fear not, daughter of Zion.*
Behold, your King is coming,
sitting on a donkey's colt."

16 His disciples did not understand this at first; but when Jesus was glorified, then they remembered that these things had been written about him and that they had done these things to him. 17 The crowd that had been with him when he called Lazarus out of the tomb and raised him from the dead bore witness. 18 This was [also] why the people went to meet him, because they heard that he had done this sign. 19 The Pharisees then said to one another, "You see that you are accomplishing nothing. Look, the world has gone after him!"

20 Now there were some Greeks among those who went up to worship at the Feast. 21 Then they came to Philip, who was from Bethsaida in Galilee, and said to him, "Sir, we wish to see Jesus." 22 Philip went and told Andrew; Andrew and Philip went and told Jesus. 23 But Jesus answered them, saying, "The hour has come for the Son of Man to be glorified. 24 Truly, truly, I say to you, unless a grain of wheat falls into the ground and dies, it remains alone; but if it dies, it produces much fruit. 25 He who loves his life destroys it, and he who hates his life in this world will keep it for eternal life. 26 If anyone serves me, he must follow me; and where I am, there my servant will be also. If anyone serves me, him my Father will honor.

27 "Now is my soul troubled, and what shall I say? 'Father, save me from this hour'? No, for this purpose I came to this hour. 28 Father, glorify your name." Then a voice came from heaven, "I have glorified it, and I will glorify it again." 29 So the crowd that stood by

---

12:12 Alx[**the great crowd** *or* the common people], Byz[a great crowd (ASV, DRA, KJV, MRD, NKJ, NLT, RSV, TLB)].

12:13 Alx[**Blessed is he who comes in the name of the Lord! Even the King of Israel**], Byz[Blessed is the King of Israel who comes in the name of the Lord! (DRA, HCS, JNT, KJV, MRD, ~NET, ~NIV, NJB, NKJ, ~NLT, NRS, ~REB, ~TEV, ~TLB)]; **Hosanna** *Hebraism* Please save *or* Save now; Psalms 118:25-26, Zephaniah 3:15.

12:15 ~**Zechariah 9:9**.

12:16 Alx[**His disciples**], Byz[But his disciples].

12:17 Alx/Byz[*text*], Minor[The crowd that had been with him bore witness that he called Lazarus out of the tomb and raised him from the dead (MRD, ~NLT, ~TLB)].

12:18 Alx/Byz[**This was also**], Minor[*omits* also (ESV, ~MRD, NET, NIV, NLT, REB, RSV, TEV, TLB)].

12:20 Alx/Byz[**Greeks**], Alt/Vulgate[Gentiles (DRA, REB)], Alt/Peshitta[people (MRD)].

12:22 Alx[**Andrew and Philip went and told Jesus**], Byz[and again Andrew and Philip told Jesus (DRA, KJV, ~MRD, NIV, NKJ)].

12:23 Alx[**Jesus answered** *Greek* Jesus answers], Byz[Jesus answered].

12:24 Alx/Byz[**it remains alone; but if it dies, it produces much fruit 25**], Alt/Vulgate[25 it remains alone; but if it dies, it produces much fruit (DRA)].

12:25 Alx[**destroys it**], Byz[will destroy it (DRA, HCS, KJV, MRD, NIV, NKJ, NLT, TEV, TLB)]; **destroys** *active, not* loses *passive*.

12:26 Alx[**If anyone serves me, him my Father will honor**], Byz[And if anyone serves me, him my Father will honor (NLT, TEV, TLB)].

12:28 Alx/Byz[**Father, glorify your name**], Minor[Father, glorify my name *others* Father glorify your son *others also add* with the glory I had with you before the foundation of the world].

12:29 Alx/Byz[**So the crowd**], Minor[*omits* So (ESV, HCS, JNT, MRD, NAB, NET, NIV, NJB, NLT, NRS, REB, RSV, TEV, TLB)]; Alx/Byz[**and heard it**], Minor[*omits* and (HCS, MRD, NAB, NJB, NLT, NRS, REB, RSV, TEV, TLB)].

and heard it said that it had thundered. Others said, "An angel has spoken to him." 30 Jesus answered and said, "This voice has come for your sake, not for mine. 31 Now is the judgment of this world; now the ruler of this world will be cast out. 32 And I, when I am lifted up from the earth, will draw all people to myself." 33 He said this to show by what death he was to die. 34 So the crowd answered him, "We have heard from the Law that the Christ remains forever; and how can you say that, 'The Son of Man must be lifted up'? Who is this Son of Man?" 35 Then Jesus said to them, "A little while longer the light is among you. Walk as you have the light, lest the darkness overtake you. He who walks in the darkness does not know where he is going. 36 As you have the light, believe in the light, that you may become sons of light."

When Jesus had said this, he departed and hid himself from them. 37 Though he had done so many signs before them, yet they did not believe in him; 38 that the word of Isaiah the prophet might be fulfilled, which he spoke:

"Lord, who has believed our report?
And to whom has the arm of the Lord been revealed?"

39 Therefore they could not believe, because Isaiah said again:

40   *"He has blinded their eyes*
and hardened their hearts,
lest they should see with their eyes,
and understand with their hearts and turn,
so that I shall heal them."

41 Isaiah said this because he saw his glory and spoke of him. 42 Nevertheless even among the rulers many believed in him, but because of the Pharisees they did not confess him, lest they should be put out of the synagogue; 43 for they loved the praise of men more than the praise of God.

44 Then Jesus cried out and said, "He who believes in me, believes not in me but in him who sent me. 45 And he who sees me sees him who sent me. 46 I have come as a light into the world, that whoever believes in me should not remain in darkness. 47 If anyone hears my words and does not keep them, I do not judge him; for I did not come to judge the world but to save the world. 48 He who rejects me and does not receive my words has a judge; the word that I have spoken will condemn him in the last day. 49 For I have not spoken on my own authority; but the Father who sent me has given me a command, what

---

12:30 Alx/Byz[**Jesus answered and said**], Alt/Peshitta[*adds* to them (MRD, NLT, TEV, TLB)].

12:32 Alx/Byz[**all** *people*], Minor[all *things* (DRA)].

12:34 Alx[**So the crowd answered**], Byz[*omits* So (DRA, JNT, KJV, MRD, NIV, NJB, NKJ, NLT, NRS, REB, RSV, TEV, TLB)]; Alx[**how can you say that**], Byz[*omits* that (ASV, DRA, HCS, JNT, KJV, NAS, NAU, NET, NIV, NJB, NKJ, NLT, ~TLB)].

12:35 Alx[**the light is among you**], Byz[the light is with you (HCS, JNT, KJV, MRD, NET, ~NIV, NJB, NKJ, ~NLT, NRS, RSV, ~TLB)]; Alx[**Walk as you have the light** *i.e. Walk as people who have the light*], Byz[Walk while you have the light (ASV, DRA, ESV, HCS, JNT, KJV, MRD, NAB, NAS, NAU, NET, NIV, NJB, NKJ, NLT, NRS, REB, RSV, TEV, TLB)].

12:36 Alx[**As you have the light** *i.e. As people who have the light*], Byz[While you have the light (ASV, DRA, ESV, HCS, JNT, KJV, MRD, NAB, NAS, NAU, NET, NIV, NJB, NKJ, NLT, NRS, REB, RSV, TEV, TLB)].

12:38 **Isaiah 53:1 LXX**.

12:40 Alx[**and hardened their hearts**], Byz[and has hardened their hearts (NJB)]; Alx[**and turn**], Byz[and return]; Alx[**shall heal them**], Byz[should heal them (ASV, DRA, ESV, HCS, JNT, KJV, MRD, NAB, NET, NIV, ~NJB, NKJ, NRS)]; ~**Isaiah 6:10 LXX**.

12:41 Alx[**because**], Byz[when (DRA, KJV, MRD, NKJ, ~NLT, ~TLB)].

12:47 Alx[**keep them**], Byz[believe (KJV, NKJ, ~REB)].

12:48 Alx/Byz[**in the last day**], Minor[at the last day (MRD, NAS, NAU, NET, NIV, TLB)].

12:49 Alx[**has given me a command**], Byz[gave me a command (DRA, KJV, MRD, NAB, NIV, NJB, NKJ, TLB)].

to say and what to speak. ⁵⁰ And I know that his command is eternal life. Whatever I say, therefore, I say just as the Father has told me."

13 ¹ Now before the feast of the Passover, when Jesus knew that his hour came that he should depart from this world to the Father, having loved his own who were in the world, he loved them to the end. ² And during supper, when the devil had already put into the heart of Judas, son of Simon Iscariot, to betray him – ³ knowing that the Father gave all things into his hands, and that he had come from God and was going to God – he ⁴ rose from supper, laid aside his garments, took a towel and girded himself. ⁵ After that, he poured water into a basin and began to wash the disciples' feet, and to wipe them with the towel with which he was girded. ⁶ Then he came to Simon Peter. He said to him, "Lord, are you going to wash my feet?" ⁷ Jesus answered him, "You do not realize now what I am doing, but later you will understand." ⁸ Peter said to him, "You shall never wash my feet." Jesus answered him, "If I do not wash you, you have no part with me." ⁹ Simon Peter said to him, "Lord, not my feet only, but also my hands and my head!" ¹⁰ Jesus said to him, "He who has bathed does not need to wash, except his feet, but is completely clean; and you are clean, but not every one of you." ¹¹ For he knew who was to betray him; that was why he said that, "You are not all clean."

¹² When he had washed their feet, [and] taken his garments, and sat again, he said to them, "Do you know what I have done to you? ¹³ You call me Teacher and Lord, and you are right, for so I am. ¹⁴ If I then, your Lord and Teacher, have washed your feet, you also ought to wash one another's feet. ¹⁵ For I gave you an example, that you should do as I did to you. ¹⁶ Truly, truly, I say to you, a servant is not greater than his master; nor is he who is sent greater than he who sent him. ¹⁷ If you know these things, blessed are you if you do them. ¹⁸ I am not speaking of you all (I know whom I have chosen); but that the Scripture

13:1 Alx[**that his hour came**], Byz[that his hour had come (ESV, HCS, JNT, MRD, NAB, NAS, NAU, NET, NIV, NJB, NKJ, NLT, NRS, REB, RSV, TEV, ~TLB)]; **to the end** *or* completely.
13:2 Alx[**during supper**], Byz[after supper (DRA, KJV, MRD, NKJ)]; Alx[**put into the heart of Judas...to** *Greek* put into the heart that Judas...should], Byz[put into the heart of Judas...to]; Alx[**Judas, son of Simon Iscariot**], Byz[Judas Iscariot, son of Simon (ASV, DRA, ESV, KJV, MRD, NAS, NAU, NET, NIV, NJB, NKJ, RSV, TLB)], Minor[Judas, son of Simon from Kerioth (JNT)], Alt/Vulgate/Peshitta[Judas, son of Simon Scariot; **Iscariot** *Hebraism Ish Keriot* a man from Kerioth *or possibly Sicarios* assassin *or* bandit.
13:3 Alx[**Knowing...he 4 rose**], Byz[Jesus, knowing... 4 rose (ASV, ESV, HCS, JNT, KJV, MRD, NAS, NAU, NET, NIV, NJB, NKJ, NLT, NRS, REB, RSV, TEV, TLB)]; Alx[**the Father gave all things**], Byz[the Father had given all things (ASV, DRA, ESV, HCS, JNT, KJV, MRD, NAB, NAS, NAU, NET, NIV, NJB, NKJ, NLT, NRS, REB, RSV, TEV, TLB)].
13:6 Alx[**Peter. He**], Byz[Peter. And he], Alt/Vulgate[Peter. And Peter (DRA, KJV, ~NET, NKJ, ~NLT, ~REB, RSV, ~TLB)], Alt/Peshitta[Cephas. Simon (~JNT, MRD)]; Alx[**said to him**], Byz[said to him that].
13:8 Alx/Byz[**Peter**], Alt/Peshitta[Simon Cephas (MRD)], Alt[*without textual foundation* Cephas (~JNT)].
13:9 Alx/Byz[**Peter**], Alt/Peshitta[Cephas (JNT, MRD)]; Alx/Byz[**not my feet only**], Alt/Peshitta[adds shall you wash (MRD)].
13:10 Alx[**does not need to wash, except his feet**], Byz[needs only to wash his feet (NAS, NAU, NET, NIV, NKJ, TLB)], Minor[does not need to wash (NJB, REB)]; **you** *both are plural.*
13:11 Alx[**he said that**], Byz[he said (ASV, DRA, ESV, HCS, JNT, KJV, MRD, NAB, NAS, NAU, NET, ~NIV, NJB, NKJ, ~NLT, NRS, REB, ~RSV, ~TEV, ~TLB)].
13:12 Alx/Byz[**and taken his garments**], Minor[omits and (JNT, MRD, NIV, NKJ, NLT, NRS, REB, TEV, TLB)]; Alx[**and sat again**], Byz[sitting again (DRA, ~HCS, ~NET, ~NJB)].
13:15 Alx/Major[**I gave you an example**], Byz[I have given you an example (ASV, DRA, ESV, HCS, JNT, KJV, MRD, NAB, NET, NIV, NJB, NKJ, NLT, NRS, REB, RSV, TEV, TLB)].
13:16 **servant** *or* slave.
13:18 Alx[**ate my bread**], Byz[ate bread with me (DRA, KJV, MRD, ~NIV, ~NJB, NKJ, REB, ~TEV, TLB)]; ~**Psalms 41:9.**

may be fulfilled, *'He who ate my bread has lifted up his heel against me.'* **19** Now I tell you before it comes, so that when it does take place, you may believe that I am he. **20** Truly, truly, I say to you, he who receives anyone I send receives me; and he who receives me receives him who sent me."

21 When Jesus had said this, he was troubled in spirit, and testified, "Truly, truly, I say to you, one of you will betray me." **22** The disciples looked at one another, uncertain of whom he spoke. **23** One of his disciples, whom Jesus loved, was leaning close to the breast of Jesus. **24** Simon Peter motioned to him to ask who it was of whom he spoke. **25** So, leaning back thus on the breast of Jesus, he said to him, "Lord, who is it?" **26** Jesus answered, "It is he to whom I shall dip this piece of bread and give it to him." And having dipped the bread, he [took it and] gave it to Judas, the son of Simon Iscariot. **27** Then after the bread, Satan entered into him. Jesus said to him, "What you are going to do, do quickly." **28** [But] no one at the table knew why he said this to him. **29** Some thought that, because Judas had the money box, Jesus was telling him, "Buy what we need for the feast"; or, that he should give something to the poor. **30** Having received the piece of bread, he went out immediately. And it was night.

31 So when he had gone out, Jesus said, "Now is the Son of Man glorified, and in him God is glorified. **32** [If God is glorified in him,] God will also glorify him in himself, and glorify him at once. **33** Little children, I shall be with you a little while longer. You will seek me; and as I said to the Jews, 'Where I am going, you cannot come,' so now I say to you. **34** A new commandment I give to you, that you love one another – and that you love one another even as I have loved you. **35** By this all men will know that you are my disciples, if you have love for one another."

36 Simon Peter said to him, "Lord, where are you going?" Jesus answered [him], "Where I am going you cannot follow me now; but you shall follow afterward." **37** Peter

---

13:19 Alx/Byz[**you may believe**], Minor[you may be believing], Alt[*without textual foundation* that you will believe (~HCS, ~NIV, ~NLT, ~TEV, ~TLB)], Alt/Peshitta[that you may know (MRD)]; **I am he** *Greek* I am.

13:22 Alx[**The disciples looked**], Byz[So the disciples looked (DRA, KJV, ~MRD, NKJ)].

13:23 Alx/Byz[**One of his disciples** *Greek* One from his disciples], Major[But one of his disciples (DRA, KJV, MRD, NKJ, ~TLB)].

13:24 Alx/Byz[**Peter**], Alt/Peshitta[Cephas (JNT, MRD)]; Alx/Byz[**motioned to him to ask who it was of whom he spoke** *Greek* motioned to him to ask who is it of whom he speaks], Minor[motioned to him and said to him, "Tell who it is of whom he speaks." (ASV, ~DRA, ~JNT, NAS, NAU, ~NIV, ~NJB, ~NLT, RSV, TEV)].

13:25 Alx[**So, leaning back**], Byz[And, leaning (MRD)], Minor[Leaning back (ASV, JNT, NAB, NAS, NAU, NIV, REB)]; Alx[**thus**], Byz[*omits* (DRA, ESV, HCS, JNT, KJV, MRD, NAB, NET, NIV, NJB, NKJ, NLT, ~NRS, TEV, TLB)].

13:26 Alx/Byz[**Jesus answered**], Minor[So Jesus answered (ASV, NAS, NAU)], Alt/Peshitta[Jesus answered and said (MRD)]; Alx[**to whom I shall dip this piece of bread and give it to him**], Byz[to whom I shall give this piece of bread when I have dipped it (DRA, ESV, HCS, JNT, KJV, MRD, NAB, NET, NIV, NJB, NKJ, NLT, NRS, REB, RSV, TLB)]; Alx[**took it and**], Byz[*omits* (DRA, ESV, HCS, JNT, KJV, MRD, NET, NIV, NJB, NKJ, NLT, NRS, RSV, TLB)]; Alx[**Judas, the son of Simon Iscariot**], Byz[Judas Iscariot, the son of Simon (DRA, KJV, MRD, NET, NIV, NKJ)]; Alx/Byz[**Iscariot**], Minor[from Karuot (JNT)], Alt/Vulgate/Peshitta [Scariot]; **Iscariot** *Hebraism Ish Keriot* a man from Kerioth *or possibly Sicarios* assassin *or* bandit

13:28 Alx/Byz[**But no one at the table**], Minor[*omits* But (HCS, NLT, REB, TEV, TLB)].

13:31 Alx/Byz[**So when he had gone out**], Major[*omits* So (ESV, HCS, JNT, MRD, NAB, NET, NIV, NJB, NLT, NRS, REB, RSV, TEV, TLB)].

13:32 Alx/Byz[**If God is glorified in him**], Minor[*omits* (ASV, NLT, TLB)].

13:36 Alx/Byz[**Peter**], Alt/Peshitta[Cephas (JNT, MRD)]; Alx/Byz[**Jesus answered him**], Minor[*omits* him (ASV, DRA, HCS, JNT, NAS, NAU, NET, NIV, NJB, NLT, NRS, REB, RSV, TEV, TLB)], Alt/Peshitta[Jesus answered and said to him (MRD)]; Alx[**but you shall follow afterward**], Byz[but you shall follow me afterward (KJV, NJB, NKJ, NLT, TEV, TLB)].

said to him, "Lord, why can I not follow you now? I will lay down my life for you." [38] Jesus answered, "Will you lay down your life for me? Truly, truly, I say to you, the rooster will never crow, till you have denied me three times.

14 [1] "Let not your hearts be troubled; believe in God, believe also in me. [2] In my Father's house are many rooms. If it were not so, would I have told you that I go to prepare a place for you? [3] And if I go and prepare a place for you, I will come again and take you to myself, that where I am you may be also. [4] And you know the way where [I] am going." [5] Thomas said to him, "Lord, we do not know where you are going. How can we know the way?" [6] Jesus said to him, "I am the way, and the truth, and the life. No one comes to the Father except through me. [7] If you have known me, you will know my Father also; and from now on you know him and have seen him." [8] Philip said to him, "Lord, show us the Father, and that is enough for us." [9] Jesus said to him, "Have I been with you so long, and yet you do not know me, Philip? He who has seen me has seen the Father. How can you say, 'Show us the Father'? [10] Do you not believe that I am in the Father, and the Father in me? The words that I say to you I do not speak on my own authority; but the Father who dwells in me does his works. [11] Believe me that I am in the Father and the Father in me; or else believe for the sake of the works themselves. [12] Truly, truly, I say to you, he who believes in me will also do the works that I do; and greater works than these will he do, because I go to the Father. [13] And whatever you ask in my name, I

13:37 Alx/Byz[**Peter**], Alt/Peshitta[Simon Cephas (~JNT, MRD)]; Alx/Byz[**Lord**], Minor[omits (DRA, NJB, TLB)].

13:38 Alx[**Jesus answered** Greek Jesus answers], Byz[Jesus answered him (DRA, KJV, MRD, NKJ)]; Alx/Major[**will never crow**], Byz[will not crow (ASV, DRA, ESV, HCS, ~JNT, KJV, MRD, NAB, NAS, NAU, NET, ~NIV, ~NJB, NKJ, ~NLT, ~NRS, ~REB, RSV, ~TEV, ~TLB)].

14:1 **believe in God** or you believe in God.

14:2 Alx[**would I have told you that I go...?** or I would have told you, because I go], Byz[I would have told you. I go (HCS, KJV, NIV, NJB, NKJ, TEV, TLB)].

14:3 Alx/Byz[**go and prepare**], Major[omits and (~NLT, ~TLB)], Alt/Peshitta[go to prepare (MRD)].

14:4 Alx[text], Byz[And where I go you know, and the way you know (DRA, JNT, KJV, MRD, NKJ, ~TLB)].

14:5 Alx[**how can we know the way**], Byz[and how can we know the way (DRA, ~JNT, KJV, MRD, ~NIV, ~NJB, NKJ, ~NLT, ~REB, ~TEV, ~TLB)], Minor[how do we know the way (ASV, NAS, NAU)].

14:7 Alx[**If you have known me**], Byz[If you had known me (ASV, DRA, ESV, KJV, MRD, NAS, NAU, ~NIV, NKJ, NLT, ~REB, RSV, TLB, Metzger)]; Alx[**you will know my Father**], Byz[you would have known my Father (ASV, DRA, ESV, KJV, MRD, NAS, NAU, ~NIV, NKJ, ~NLT, ~REB, RSV, TLB, Metzger)], Minor[you have known my Father]; Alx/Byz[**and from now on**], Minor[from now on (ASV, ESV, HCS, JNT, NAB, NAS, NAU, NIV, NJB, NLT, NRS, REB, RSV, TLB)]; Alx/Byz[**and have seen him**], Minor[and have seen].

14:8 Alx/Byz[**that is enough for us**], Alt[that will be enough for us (JNT, MRD, NAB, ~NET, NIV, ~NJB, ~NLT, ~NRS, ~RSV, ~TLB)].

14:9 Alx[**how can you say** Greek how say you], Byz[and how can you say (~JNT, KJV, MRD, ~NJB, ~NKJ, ~NLT, ~REB, ~TEV, ~TLB)].

14:10 Alx[**say...speak**], Byz[speak...speak (DRA, HCS, ~JNT, KJV, MRD, NAB, ~NIV, NKJ, ~NLT, ~REB, ~TEV, ~TLB)]; Alx[**the Father...does his works**], Byz[the Father...he does the works (DRA, KJV, MRD, ~NKJ)], Minor[the Father...he does his works (TLB)].

14:11 Alx[**or else believe for the sake**], Byz[or else believe me for the sake (ASV, KJV, NKJ, NRS, RSV)], Minor[12 or else believe me for the sake (DRA)]; Alx/Byz[**of the works themselves**], Minor[of his works], Alt[of the works (MRD, ~NJB, ~NLT, ~TEV, ~TLB)].

14:12 Alx[**because I go to the Father 13**], Byz[because I go to my Father 13 (KJV, MRD, NKJ)], Minor[13 Because I go to the Father (DRA)], Alt[without textual foundation because I go with the Father (~TLB)].

14:13 Alx/Byz[**whatever you ask**], Minor[if you ask (~NLT, ~TLB)]; Alx/Byz[**I will do**], Alt[adds for you (MRD)]; Alx/Byz[**the Son**], Alt[his Son (MRD)].

will do, that the Father may be glorified in the Son. [14] If you ask me anything in my name, I will do it.

[15] "If you love me, you will keep my commandments. [16] And I will ask the Father, and he will give you another Counselor, that he may be with you forever – [17] the Spirit of truth, whom the world cannot receive, because it neither sees nor knows him. You know him, for he dwells with you and will be in you. [18] I will not leave you orphans. I will come to you. [19] A little while longer, and the world will see me no more, but you will see me. Because I live, you will live also. [20] In that day you will know that I am in my Father, and you in me, and I in you. [21] He who has my commandments and keeps them, it is he who loves me. And he who loves me will be loved by my Father, and I will love him and reveal myself to him." [22] Judas (not Iscariot) said to him, "Lord, [then] how is it that you will reveal yourself to us, and not to the world?" [23] Jesus answered him, "If anyone loves me, he will keep my word, and my Father will love him, and we will come to him and make our home with him. [24] He who does not love me does not keep my words; and the word which you hear is not mine but the Father's who sent me.

[25] "These things I have spoken to you, while I am still with you. [26] But the Counselor, the Holy Spirit, whom the Father will send in my name, he will teach you all things, and bring to your remembrance all that [I] have said to you. [27] Peace I leave with you; my peace I give to you; not as the world gives do I give to you. Let not your hearts be troubled, neither let them be afraid. [28] You have heard me say to you, 'I am going away and coming back to you.' If you loved me, you would rejoice because I am going to the Father, for the Father is greater than I. [29] And now I have told you before it takes place, so that when it does take place, you may believe. [30] I will no longer talk much with you, for the ruler of the world is coming, and he has nothing in me. [31] But I do as the Father commanded me, so that the world may know that I love the Father. Rise, let us go from here.

14:14 Alx/Major[**If you ask me**], Byz[*omits* me (ASV, KJV, NKJ, REB, RSV, TLB) *others* If you ask the Father]; Alx/Byz[**I will do it**], Minor[I will do this (ASV, DRA)]; Alx/Byz[*verse*], Minor[*omits verse*].

14:15 Alx[**you will keep**], Byz[keep (DRA, KJV, MRD, NKJ, NLT, TLB)], Minor[you should keep].

14:16, 26 **Counselor** *or* Advocate *or* Comforter *or* Encourager *or* Helper *Greek* Paraclete.

14:16 Alx[**that he may be with you**], Byz[that he may abide with you (DRA, KJV, NKJ, ~NLT, TEV, ~TLB)].

14:17 Alx[**it neither sees nor knows him** *Greek* it does not see him nor knows *or* it does not see it nor knows], Byz[it neither sees him nor knows him *or* it neither sees it nor knows it (ASV, DRA, ESV, HCS, KJV, MRD, NAS, NAU, NET, NIV, NKJ, NLT, NRS, RSV, TEV, TLB)]; Alx[**you know him** *or* you know it], Byz[but you know him (HCS, KJV, MRD, NAB, NAS, NAU, NET, NIV, NJB, NKJ, NLT, REB, TEV, TLB)], Alt[but you shall know him (DRA)]; Alx/Byz[**he dwells with you** *or* it dwells with you], Alt[he shall dwell with you (DRA) *others* he is with you (NJB)]; Alx/Byz[**will be in you** *or* will be among you], Minor[is in you (MRD, NJB, TEV)].

14:22 Alx/Byz[**Iscariot**], Minor[from Karuot (JNT)], Alt/Vulgate/Peshitta[Scariot], Alt[*without textual foundation* Judas Iscariot (~NET, ~NIV, ~NJB, ~NLT, ~REB, ~TEV, ~TLB)]; Alx/Byz[**then how is it** *Greek* and how is it], Minor[how is it (ASV, DRA, ESV, HCS, JNT, KJV, MRD, NET, ~NIV, NJB, NKJ, NLT, NRS, REB, RSV, TEV, TLB)]; **Iscariot** *Hebraism Ish Keriot* a man from Kerioth *or possibly Sicarios* assassin *or* bandit.

14:23 Alx/Byz[**he will keep my word**], Alt[*without textual foundation* he will keep my words (~KJV, ~NLT, ~REB, ~TLB)].

14:28 Alx[**because I am going**], Byz[because I said, 'I am going (KJV, NKJ)]; Alx[**for the Father is greater** *Greek* because the Father is greater], Byz[for my Father is greater (KJV, MRD, NKJ, ~NLT, ~TEV, ~TLB)].

14:30 Alx/Byz[**the ruler of the world**], Minor[the ruler of this world (DRA, ESV, JNT, KJV, MRD, NET, NIV, NJB, NKJ, NLT, NRS, REB, RSV, TEV, TLB)].

14:31 Alx/Byz[**as the Father commanded me**], Minor[as the Father gave me a commandment (ASV, DRA, KJV, NAS, NKJ)], Alt/Peshitta[as my Father commanded me (MRD, NIV, ~REB, ~TEV)].

15 ¹ "I am the true vine, and my Father is the vinedresser. ² Every branch in me that bears no fruit he takes away; and every branch that does bear fruit he prunes, so that it may bear more fruit. ³ You are already pruned because of the word which I have spoken to you. ⁴ Abide in me, and I in you. As the branch cannot bear fruit by itself, unless it abides in the vine, neither can you, unless you abide in me. ⁵ I am the vine, you are the branches. He who abides in me, and I in him, he bears much fruit; for apart from me you can do nothing. ⁶ If anyone does not abide in me, he is like a branch that is cast away and withers; and they gather them and throw them into the fire, and it is burned. ⁷ If you abide in me, and my words abide in you, ask whatever you will, and it shall be done for you. ⁸ By this my Father is glorified, that you bear much fruit and be my disciples. ⁹ As the Father has loved me, I also have loved you; abide in my love. ¹⁰ If you keep my commandments, you will abide in my love, just as I have kept my Father's commandments and abide in his love.

¹¹ "These things I have spoken to you, that my joy may be in you, and that your joy may be full. ¹² This is my commandment, that you love one another as I have loved you. ¹³ Greater love has no one than this, that one lay down his life for his friends. ¹⁴ You are my friends if you do the things which I command you. ¹⁵ No longer do I call you servants, for a servant does not know what his master is doing; but I have called you friends, for all that I have heard from my Father I have made known to you. ¹⁶ You did not choose me, but I chose you and appointed you that you should go and bear fruit, and that your fruit should remain, that whatever you ask the Father in my name he may give you. ¹⁷ These things I command you, that you may love one another.

¹⁸ "If the world hates you, know that it hated me – the first of you. ¹⁹ If you were of the world, the world would love its own. But because you are not of the world, but I chose you out of the world, therefore the world hates you. ²⁰ Remember the word that I said to you, 'A servant is not greater than his master.' If they persecuted me, they will also persecute you. If they kept my word, they will keep yours also. ²¹ But all this they will do to you for my name's sake, because they do not know him who sent me. ²² If I had not come and spoken to them, they would not have sin, but now they have no excuse for their sin. ²³ He who hates me hates my Father also. ²⁴ If I had not done among them the works which no

---

15:6 Alx/Byz[**and they gather them and throw them into the fire, and it is burned**], Minor[and they gather it and throw it into the fire, and it is burned (DRA, MRD, ~TLB)].

15:7 Alx/Byz[**ask whatever you will**], Major[you will ask whatever you will (DRA, KJV, MRD, ~NJB, NKJ, ~NLT, TEV, ~TLB)].

15:8 Alx[**and be my disciples**], Byz[and so shall you be my disciples (ASV, DRA, ~ESV, ~HCS, JNT, KJV, MRD, NAB, ~NAS, ~NAU, ~NIV, NKJ, NRS, REB, ~RSV, TEV)].

15:10 Alx/Byz[**just as I**], Minor[just as I also (DRA)], Alt/Peshitta[as I (MRD, REB)]; Alx/Byz[**have kept**], Alt[*without textual foundation* keep (~NLT, ~TLB)]; Alx/Byz[**my Father's commandments**], Minor[the Father's commandments].

15:11 Alx[**my joy may be in you**], Byz[my joy may remain in you (KJV, NKJ)].

15:13 Alx/Byz[**that one lay down**], Minor[that he lay down (NIV, NJB, TEV)].

15:14 Alx[**the things which I command**], Byz[as much as I command (KJV, NKJ)], Minor[the thing which I command (~ESV, ~HCS, ~JNT, ~NAB, ~NAS, ~NAU, ~NET, ~NIV, ~NJB, ~NLT, ~NRS, ~REB, ~RSV, ~TEV, ~TLB)], Alt/Peshitta[all that I command (MRD)].

15:15 **servants** *or* slaves; **servant** *or* slave.

15:17 Alx/Byz[**that you may love one another**], Alt[*without textual foundation* that you will love one another (~ESV) *others without textual foundation* love one another (~HCS, ~JNT, ~NAB, ~NET, ~NIV, ~NJB, ~NLT, ~REB, ~RSV, ~TEV, ~TLB)].

15:18 Alx/Byz[**it hated me – the first of you**], Minor[it hated me first (JNT, NAB, NET, NIV, NLT, REB, TEV)]; **know that it hated** *or* you know that it hated.

15:20 **servant** *or* slave; John 13:16.

15:24 Alx[**which no one else did**], Byz[which no one else has done (DRA, HCS, ~JNT, ~MRD, ~NAB, ~NJB, ~NLT, REB, ~TEV, ~TLB)].

one else did, they would not have sin; but now they have seen and hated both me and my Father. [25] But this is to fulfill the word that is written in their law, *'They hated me without a cause.'*

[26] "When the Counselor comes, whom I shall send to you from the Father, the Spirit of truth who proceeds from the Father, he will testify of me. [27] And you also will bear witness, because you have been with me from the beginning.

16

[1] "I have said all this to you so that you will not go astray. [2] They will put you out of the synagogues; yes, the time is coming when whoever kills you will think he is offering service to God. [3] And they will do these things because they have not known the Father, nor me. [4] But I have told you these things, that when their hour comes, you may remember them, because I told you of them.

"I did not say these things to you at the beginning, because I was with you. [5] But now I am going to him who sent me, yet none of you asks me, 'Where are you going?' [6] But because I have said these things to you, sorrow has filled your heart. [7] Nevertheless I tell you the truth: it is to your advantage that I go away. For if I do not go away, the Counselor will not come to you; but if I go, I will send him to you. [8] And when he comes, he will convict the world of sin, and of righteousness, and of judgment: [9] of sin, because they do not believe in me; [10] of righteousness, because I go to the Father, and you see me no more; [11] of judgment, because the ruler of this world is judged.

[12] "I have many more things to say to you, but you cannot bear them now. [13] But when he, the Spirit of truth, comes, he will guide you in all truth; for he will not speak on his own authority, but whatever he shall hear he will speak; and he will tell you things to come. [14] He will glorify me, for he will take of what is mine and declare it to you. [15] All that the Father has is mine. Therefore I said that he takes of what is mine and will declare it to you.

[16] "A little while, and you will see me no more; again a little while, and you will see me." [17] Then some of his disciples said to one another, "What is this that he says to us, 'A little while, and you will not see me, and again a little while, and you will see me'; and, 'because I go to the Father'?" [18] They said, "What is this that [he says]: 'A little while'? We

---

15:25 ~**Psalms 35:19, 69:4**.

15:26, 16:7 **Counselor** *or* Advocate *or* Comforter *or* Encourager *or* Helper *Greek* Paraclete.

15:26 Alx[**When the Counselor**], Byz[But when the Counselor (ASV, DRA, ESV, KJV, MRD, NKJ, NLT, RSV, TLB)].

16:2 Alx/Byz[**whoever kills you**], Minor[*omits* you].

16:3 Alx/Byz[**they will do these things**], Minor[*adds* to you (DRA, KJV, NKJ, TEV)].

16:4 Alx[**their hour**], Byz[the hour (DRA, JNT, KJV, NIV, ~NJB, NKJ, ~NLT, ~REB, ~TLB)]; Alx/Byz[**I did not say these things**], Alt/Vulgate[5 I did not say these things (DRA)].

16:7 Alx/Byz[**the Counselor will not come**], Minor[the Counselor will by no means come].

16:8 **convict the world of sin** *or* expose the sin of the world.

16:10 Alx[**I go to the Father**], Byz[I go to my Father (KJV, MRD, NKJ)].

16:12 Alx/Byz[**you cannot bear them now**], Alt[you cannot comprehend it now (MRD, TLB)].

16:13 Alx[**in all truth**], Byz[into all truth (ASV, ~DRA, ESV, HCS, JNT, KJV, MRD, NAB, NAS, NAU, NET, NIV, NJB, NKJ, NLT, NRS, REB, RSV, TEV, TLB)]; Alx[**whatever he shall hear** *or* as much as he shall hear], Byz[whatever he may hear], Minor[whatever he hears (ESV, HCS, JNT, MRD, NAB, NAS, NAU, NET, NIV, ~NJB, NKJ, ~NLT, NRS, REB, RSV, TEV, ~TLB)].

16:15 Alx/Major[**takes**], Byz[will take (DRA, ESV, KJV, MRD, NAB, NET, NIV, ~NJB, NKJ, ~NLT, NRS, REB, RSV, TEV, ~TLB)].

16:16 Alx[**you will see me no more**], Byz[you will not see me (DRA, KJV, MRD, NKJ)]; Alx[**you will see me**], Byz[*adds* because I go to the Father (DRA, KJV, MRD, NKJ)].

16:18 Alx/Byz[**What is this that he says**], Minor[What is this (~ESV, JNT, ~NIV, NJB, ~NLT, ~NRS, REB, ~RSV, ~TEV)]; Alx/Byz[**We do not know what he is saying**], Minor[We do not know what (~NAB, ~NJB, NLT, ~REB, ~RSV, ~TLB)].

do not know what he is saying." **19** Jesus knew that they wanted to ask him, and he said to them, "Are you asking yourselves about what I meant when I said, 'A little while, and you will not see me; and again a little while, and you will see me'? **20** Truly, truly, I say to you, you will weep and lament, but the world will rejoice; you will be sorrowful, but your sorrow will turn into joy. **21** When a woman is in labor she has sorrow, because her hour has come; but as soon as she gives birth to the child, she no longer remembers the anguish, for joy that a child has been born into the world. **22** So indeed you have sorrow now, but I will see you again and your heart will rejoice, and no one takes your joy from you. **23** In that day you will ask me nothing. Truly, truly, I say to you, if you ask anything of the Father in my name, he will give it to you. **24** Until now you have asked nothing in my name. Ask, and you will receive, that your joy may be full.

25 "I have said this to you in figurative language; the hour is coming when I will no longer speak to you in figures, but I will tell you plainly about the Father. **26** In that day you will ask in my name. And I do not say to you that I shall pray the Father for you; **27** for the Father himself loves you, because you have loved me and have believed that I came from God. **28** I came from the Father and have come into the world; again, I am leaving the world and going to the Father." **29** His disciples said, "See, now you are speaking plainly, and not using a figure of speech! **30** Now we are sure that you know all things, and have no need for anyone to question you. By this we believe that you came from God." **31** Jesus answered them, "Do you now believe? **32** Behold, the hour is coming, and has come, when you will be scattered, each to his own, and will leave me alone. And yet I am not alone, for the Father is with me. **33** I have said these things to you, that in me you may have peace. In the world you have tribulation. But take courage! I have overcome the world."

17 **1** When Jesus had spoken these words, he lifted up his eyes to heaven, and said: "Father, the hour has come. Glorify your Son, that the Son may glorify you, **2** as you have given him authority over all flesh, that he should give eternal

---

16:19 Alx[**Jesus knew**], Byz[So Jesus knew (~DRA, KJV, ~MRD, NKJ)].

16:20 Alx[**you will be sorrowful**], Byz[and you will be sorrowful (DRA, KJV, ~MRD, NKJ, ~REB, ~TLB)].

16:22 Alx/Byz[**you have sorrow now**], Minor[you will have sorrow now]; Alx/Byz[**no one takes your joy**], Minor[no one will take your joy (DRA, ESV, HCS, JNT, MRD, NAB, NAU, NET, NIV, NJB, NKJ, ~NLT, NRS, REB, RSV, ~TEV, ~TLB)].

16:23 Alx[**if you ask anything of the Father**], Byz[whatever you ask the Father *or* as much as you ask the Father (ESV, JNT, KJV, MRD, NAB, NET, NIV, NKJ, ~NLT)]; Alx/Byz[**in my name, he will give it to you**], Minor[he will give it to you in my name (ASV, JNT, NAS, NIV, NJB, NLT, RSV, TLB)].

16:25 Alx[**the hour is coming**], Byz[but the hour is coming (JNT, KJV, MRD, NKJ, NLT, TEV, TLB)].

16:27 Alx/Byz[**I came from God**], Minor[I came from the Father (ASV, MRD, NAS, NAU, RSV, TLB)].

16:28 Alx/Byz[**I came from the Father**], Minor[I came out from the Father (ASV, DRA, KJV, MRD, NAS, NAU, NKJ)].

16:29 Alx[**His disciples said**], Byz[*adds* to him (DRA, JNT, KJV, MRD, NKJ, TEV)].

16:30 **no need for anyone to question you** *Idiom* no need to ask anyone about their questions.

16:31 Alx/Byz[**Do you now believe**], Alt/Peshitta[*omits* now (MRD)].

16:32 Alx[**and has come**], Byz[and has now come (DRA, JNT, KJV, MRD, NAS, NAU, NJB, NKJ, NLT, REB, TEV)].

16:33 Alx/Major[**you have tribulation**], Byz[you will have tribulation (DRA, ESV, HCS, KJV, MRD, NAB, NIV, NJB, NKJ, NLT, REB, TEV, TLB)].

17:1 Alx[**that the Son**], Byz[that your Son (DRA, KJV, MRD, NAB, NET, NIV, NJB, NKJ, ~NLT, ~TLB)]; Alx[**may glorify you**], Byz[also may glorify you (KJV, NKJ)].

17:2 Alx/Byz[**should give eternal life**], Major[shall give eternal life (~ESV, ~NLT, ~NRS, ~REB, ~RSV, ~TLB)].

life to all those you have given him. ³ And this is eternal life, that they may know you, the only true God, and Jesus Christ whom you have sent. ⁴ I have glorified you on the earth, having finished the work which you have given me to do. ⁵ And now, Father, glorify me in your own presence with the glory which I had with you before the world was made.

⁶ "I have made your name known to the men you gave me out of the world. They were yours; you gave them to me, and they have kept your word. ⁷ Now they have known that everything you have given me comes from you. ⁸ For I have given them the words which you gave me, and they have received them and know in truth that I came from you; and they have believed that you sent me. ⁹ I pray for them. I am not praying for the world, but for those whom you have given me, for they are yours. ¹⁰ And all mine are yours, and yours are mine, and I am glorified in them. ¹¹ And now I am no longer in the world, and they are in the world, and I am coming to you. Holy Father, keep them in your name which you gave me, that they may be one, just as we are. ¹² While I was with them, I kept them in your name which you gave me. I have guarded them, and none of them is lost except the son of perdition, that the Scripture might be fulfilled. ¹³ But now I am coming to you, and these things I speak in the world, that they may have my joy fulfilled in themselves. ¹⁴ I have given them your word. And the world has hated them because they are not of the world, even as I am not of the world. ¹⁵ I do not pray that you should take them out of the world, but that you should keep them from the evil one. ¹⁶ They are not of the world, even as I am not of the world. ¹⁷ Sanctify them in the truth; your word is truth. ¹⁸ As you sent me into the world, I also have sent them into the world. ¹⁹ And for their sakes I sanctify myself, that they also may be sanctified in truth.

²⁰ "I do not pray for these alone, but also for those who believe in me through their word; ²¹ that they all may be one, as you, Father, are in me, and I in you; that they also may be in us, that the world may believe that you sent me. ²² And the glory which you gave me I have given them, that they may be one just as we are one: ²³ I in them, and you in me; that

---

17:3 Alx/Byz[**that they may know**], Minor[that they know (ESV, JNT, NET, NJB, NLT, REB, RSV, TEV, TLB)].

17:4 Alx[**having finished**], Byz[I have finished (DRA, KJV, MRD, NKJ, TEV)].

17:7 Alx/Byz[**Now they have known**], Minor[Now I have known (MRD) *others* Now they know (ASV, ESV, HCS, JNT, NAB, NET, NIV, NLT, NRS, REB, RSV, TEV, TLB)]; Alx/Byz[**everything you have given me**], Minor[everything you gave me (NAB, ~NLT, REB, TEV, ~TLB)].

17:8 Alx[**the words which you gave me**], Byz[the words which you have given me (NET, NKJ)]; Alx/Byz[**received them and know in truth that I came from you**], Minor[truly received them because I came from you].

17:11 Alx[**and they are in the world**], Byz[and these are in the world (ASV, DRA], Alt[but these are in the world (~ESV, ~HCS, KJV, MRD, ~NAB, ~NAS, ~NAU, ~NET, ~NIV, ~NJB, NKJ, ~NRS, ~RSV, ~TEV)]; Alx/Major[**keep them in your name which you gave me**], Byz[keep in your name those whom you have given me (DRA, KJV, NJB, NKJ, TLB)]; Alx/Byz[**just as we are**], Minor[just as also we are (DRA)].

17:12 Alx[**While I was with them**], Byz[*adds* in the world (KJV, MRD, NKJ, ~NLT, ~TLB)]; Alx[**kept them in your name which you gave me**], Byz[kept in your name those you gave me (DRA, KJV, MRD, ~NJB, NKJ, TLB)].

17:13 Alx[**fulfilled in themselves** *or* fulfilled among themselves], Byz[fulfilled in them (HCS, MRD, ~NAB, NIV, NJB, ~NLT, ~REB, ~TLB)], Minor[fulfilled in their own hearts (~TEV)].

17:14 Alx/Byz[**even as I am not of the world**], Minor[*omits* (~REB, ~TLB)].

17:15 **from the evil one** *or* from evil.

17:17 Alx/Byz[**Sanctify**], Alt/Peshitta[Father, sanctify (MRD)]; Alx[**in the truth**], Byz[in your truth (KJV, MRD, NKJ, NLT, TLB)], Alt/Vulgate[in truth (DRA)].

17:20 Alx/Byz[**those who believe**], Minor[those who will believe (DRA, ESV, JNT, KJV, MRD, NAB, NIV, NJB, NKJ, NLT, NRS, TLB)].

17:21 Alx[**be in us**], Byz[be one in us (DRA, HCS, ~JNT, KJV, MRD, NKJ, TEV)].

17:23 Alx[**that the world may know**], Byz[and that the world may know (DRA, JNT, KJV, MRD, NKJ)]; Alx/Byz[**you sent me, and loved them**], Minor[you sent me, and I loved them].

they may become perfectly one, that the world may know that you sent me, and loved them even as you loved me. ²⁴ Father, I desire that they also that you have given me may be with me where I am, that they may behold my glory which you have given me, for you loved me before the foundation of the world. ²⁵ O righteous Father, the world has not known you, but I have known you; and these know that you sent me. ²⁶ I have made known to them your name, and will make it known, that the love with which you loved me may be in them, and I in them."

18

¹ When Jesus had spoken these words, he went out with his disciples over the Kidron valley, where there was a garden, which he and his disciples entered. ² Now Judas (who betrayed him) also knew the place, because Jesus often met there with his disciples. ³ So Judas, having received a detachment of soldiers and some officers from the chief priests and from the Pharisees, came there with lanterns, torches, and weapons. ⁴ Then Jesus, knowing all that was to come upon him, went forward and said to them, "Whom do you seek?" ⁵ They answered him, "Jesus the Nazarene." He said to them, "I am he." And Judas, who betrayed him, was standing with them. ⁶ When he said to them, "I am he," they drew back and fell to the ground. ⁷ Again he asked them, "Whom do you seek?" And they said, "Jesus the Nazarene." ⁸ Jesus answered, "I told you that I am he. So, if you seek me, let these men go." ⁹ This happened so that the words which he had spoken would be fulfilled, that "Of those whom you gave me I have lost none." ¹⁰ Then Simon Peter, having a sword, drew it and struck the high priest's servant, and cut off his right ear. The servant's name was Malchus. ¹¹ Jesus said to Peter, "Put the sword into its sheath. Shall I not drink the cup which the Father has given me?"

¹² Then the detachment of soldiers and their captain and the officers of the Jews arrested Jesus and bound him. ¹³ And they led him to Annas first, for he was the father-in-law of Caiaphas, who was high priest that year. ¹⁴ Now it was Caiaphas who had advised the Jews that it was expedient that one man should die for the people.

¹⁵ Simon Peter followed Jesus, and so did another disciple. As this disciple was known to the high priest, he went with Jesus into the courtyard of the high priest. ¹⁶ But

---

17:24 Alx/Byz[**that you have given me**], Major[whom you have given me (ASV, DRA, ESV, ~HCS, ~JNT, KJV, MRD, NAB, NAS, NAU, ~NET, ~NIV, ~NJB, NKJ, NLT, NRS, REB, RSV, ~TEV, ~TLB)].

17:25 Alx/Byz[**O righteous Father**], Alt/Peshitta[My righteous Father (MRD)].

18:1 Alx/Byz[**the Kidron valley**], Minor[the valley of the cedars *others* the valley of the cedar].

18:2 Alx/Major[**Jesus often met there**], Byz[Jesus also met there often].

18:3 Alx[**and from the Pharisees**], Byz[and Pharisees (~ASV, ~DRA, ~ESV, ~HCS, ~JNT, KJV, MRD, ~NAB, ~NAS, ~NAU, NET, NIV, ~NJB, NKJ, NLT, ~NRS, ~REB, ~RSV, ~TEV, TLB)].

18:4 Alx/Byz[**Then Jesus** *or* So Jesus], Minor[But Jesus (~JNT, MRD, ~NAB, ~NIV, ~NJB, ~NLT, ~REB, ~TEV, ~TLB)]; Alx[**and said** *Greek* and says], Byz[said].

18:5, 6, 8 **I am he** *Greek* I am.

18:5 Alx[**He said to them**], Byz[Jesus said to them (ASV, DRA, ESV, HCS, KJV, MRD, NIV, NKJ, NLT, NRS, REB, RSV, TLB)]; Alx/Byz[**I am he**], Minor[I am Jesus].

18:6 Alx[**When he said to them**], Byz[*adds* that], Alt/Peshitta[And when Jesus said to them (~ESV, MRD, ~NET, ~NIV, ~NJB, ~NLT, ~NRS, ~REB, ~TEV, ~TLB)].

18:7 Alx/Byz[**he asked them**], Alt/Peshitta[Jesus asked them (MRD, NET, TEV)].

18:9 Alx/Byz[**fulfilled, that**], Minor[*omits* that (ASV, DRA, ESV, HCS, JNT, KJV, MRD, NAB, NAS, NAU, NET, NIV, NJB, NKJ, NLT, NRS, REB, RSV, TLB)]; John 6:39, 17:12.

18:10 Alx/Byz[**Peter**], Alt/Peshitta[Cephas (JNT, MRD)].

18:11 Alx/Byz[**Peter**], Alt/Peshitta[Cephas (JNT, MRD)]; Alx/Byz[**the sword**], Major[your sword (DRA, ESV, HCS, JNT, KJV, NAB, NET, NIV, NJB, NKJ, NLT, NRS, REB, RSV, TEV, TLB)].

18:13-27 Alx/Byz[**text**], Minor[*combines verse 24 with, or immediately after, verse 13*], Metzger[*another minority sequence is 13, 24, 14, 15, 16, 17, 18, 19, 20, 21, 22, 23, 25, 26, 27*].

18:15 Alx/Byz[**Peter**], Alt/Peshitta[Cephas (JNT, MRD)]; Alx[**another disciple**], Byz[the other disciple (JNT, ~MRD, ~TLB)]; Alx/Byz[**the courtyard of the high priest**], Alt/Peshitta[the hall (MRD)].

Peter stood at the door outside. Then the other disciple, the one known by the high priest, went out and spoke to the girl who kept the door, and brought Peter in. ¹⁷ Then the girl who kept the door said to Peter, "You are not also one of this man's disciples, are you?" He said, "I am not." ¹⁸ Now the servants and officers had made a charcoal fire, because it was cold, and they were standing and warming themselves. And Peter also was with them, standing and warming himself.

¹⁹ The high priest then questioned Jesus about his disciples and his teaching. ²⁰ Jesus answered him, "I have spoken openly to the world. I always taught in synagogues and in the temple, where all the Jews come together, and I have said nothing in secret. ²¹ Why do you ask me? Ask those who have heard me what I said to them. They know what I said." ²² And when he had said this, one of the officers standing by struck Jesus with his hand, saying, "Is that the way you answer the high priest?" ²³ Jesus answered him, "If I have spoken wrongly, bear witness to the wrong. But if I have spoken rightly, why do you strike me?" ²⁴ So Annas sent him bound to Caiaphas the high priest.

²⁵ Now Simon Peter stood warming himself. Therefore they said to him, "You are not also one of his disciples, are you?" He denied it and said, "I am not." ²⁶ One of the servants of the high priest, a relative of him whose ear Peter had cut off, said, "Did I not see you in the garden with him?" ²⁷ Peter again denied it; and at once a rooster crowed.

²⁸ Then they led Jesus from Caiaphas to the Praetorium, and it was morning. But they did not enter the Praetorium themselves, so that they might not be defiled, but might eat the Passover. ²⁹ So Pilate went out to them and said, "What accusation do you bring [against] this man?" ³⁰ They answered him, "If he were not doing evil, we would not have handed him over to you." ³¹ Pilate said to them, "Take him yourselves and judge him by your own law." The Jews said to him, "It is not lawful for us to put anyone to death." ³² This happened so that the words Jesus had spoken would be fulfilled, showing by what death he was going to die. ³³ Then Pilate entered the Praetorium again, called Jesus, and said to him, "Are you the King of the Jews?" ³⁴ Jesus answered, "Do you say this on your own, or did

18:16 Alx/Byz[**Peter...Peter**], Alt/Peshitta[Simon...Simon (MRD)], Alt[*without textual foundation* Cephas...Cephas (~JNT)]; Alx[**the one known by the high priest** *Greek* the one known of the high priest], Byz[who was known to the high priest (ASV, DRA, ESV, KJV, ~MRD, NAS, NAU, NET, NIV, NKJ, ~NLT, NRS, ~REB, RSV)], Alt[*without textual foundation omits* (~TEV ~TLB)].

18:17 Alx/Byz[**Peter**], Alt/Peshitta[Simon (MRD)], Alt[*without textual foundation* Cephas (~JNT)].

18:18 Alx[**Peter also**], Byz[*omits* also (HCS, KJV, NKJ, NLT, TEV, TLB)], Alt[*without textual foundation* Cephas (~JNT)]; Alx/Byz[**And Peter also was with them, standing and warming himself**], Alt[*without textual foundation omits* (~MRD)].

18:20 Alx[**I have spoken openly**], Byz[I spoke openly (KJV, NKJ, ~NLT, ~TLB)]; Alx/Byz[**where all the Jews come together**], Minor[where the Jews always come together (KJV, NKJ, ~NLT, ~TLB)].

18:21 Alx[**ask...Ask**], Byz[question...Question (HCS, JNT, ~MRD, NAS, NAU, ~NIV, ~NLT, REB, TEV, ~TLB)].

18:24 Alx[**So Annas sent him**], Byz[*omits* So (~DRA)].

18:25 Alx/Byz[**Peter**], Alt/Peshitta[Cephas (JNT, MRD)]; Alx[**He denied it**], Byz[So he denied it (~MRD, ~REB, ~TEV)].

18:26 Alx/Byz[**Peter**], Alt/Peshitta[Simon (MRD)], Alt[*without textual foundation* Cephas (~JNT)].

18:27 Alx/Byz[**Peter**], Alt/Peshitta[Simon (MRD)], Alt[*without textual foundation* Cephas (~JNT)].

18:28 Alx/Byz[**it was morning** *or* it was early], Minor[it was early morning (ESV, HCS, JNT, NET, NIV, NKJ, NLT, NRS, REB, TEV, TLB)].

18:29 Alx[**and said** *Greek* and says], Byz[and said]; Alx/Byz[**against this man**], Minor[of this man (TEV, TLB)].

18:30 Alx[**doing evil**], Byz[an evildoer (ASV, DRA, HCS, KJV, MRD, NAB, NAS, NAU, NET, NIV, NJB, NKJ, NLT, NRS, REB, RSV, TLB)].

18:31 Alx/Byz[**judge him**], Minor[*omits* him]; Alx[**The Jews said**], Byz[So the Jews said (DRA, KJV, NKJ)].

18:32 John 12:32-33.

18:34 Alx[**Jesus answered**], Byz[*adds* him (KJV, NKJ)], Alt/Peshitta[Jesus said to him (MRD)],

others say it to you about me?" ³⁵ Pilate answered, "Am I a Jew? Your own nation and the chief priests have handed you over to me. What have you done?" ³⁶ Jesus answered, "My kingdom is not of this world. If my kingdom were of this world, my servants [would] begin to fight, so that I should not be delivered to the Jews; but now my kingship is not from here." ³⁷ Pilate said to him, "You are a king then?" Jesus answered, "You say that I am a king. For this I was born. And for this I have come into the world, to bear witness to the truth. Everyone who is of the truth hears my voice." ³⁸ Pilate said to him, "What is truth?"

After he had said this, he went out to the Jews again, and told them, "I find no crime in him. ³⁹ But you have a custom that I should release one man for you in the Passover. So do you want me to release to you the King of the Jews?" ⁴⁰ Then they cried again, "Not this man, but Barabbas!" Now Barabbas was a robber.

19

¹ So then Pilate took Jesus and scourged him. ² And the soldiers twisted a crown of thorns and put it on his head, and they clothed him in a purple robe. ³ And they were coming up to him, and saying, "Hail, King of the Jews!" and struck him with their hands. ⁴ And Pilate went out again, and said to them, "See, I am bringing him out to you, that you may know that I find no crime in him." ⁵ So Jesus came out, wearing the crown of thorns and the purple robe. Pilate said to them, "Behold! The man!" ⁶ When the chief priests and officers saw him, they cried out, saying, "Crucify! Crucify!" Pilate said to them, "You take him and crucify him, for I find no fault in him." ⁷ The Jews answered him, "We have a law, and according to that law he ought to die, because he made himself the Son of God."

⁸ When Pilate heard these words, he was the more afraid, ⁹ and he went again into the Praetorium and said to Jesus, "Where are you from?" But Jesus gave him no answer. ¹⁰ So Pilate said to him, "You will not speak to me? Do you not know that I have power to release you, and power to crucify you?" ¹¹ Jesus answered [him], "You would have no power over me unless it had been given you from above. Therefore the one who delivered me to you has the greater sin." ¹² From then on Pilate sought to release him, but the Jews cried out, saying, "If you let this man go, you are not Caesar's friend. Anyone who makes himself a king sets himself against Caesar."

Alt[*without textual foundation* Jesus asked (~NIV, ~TLB)].

18:40 Alx[**they cried again**], Byz[they all cried again (DRA, KJV, MRD, NKJ)].

19:1 Alx/Byz[**So then Pilate took Jesus and scourged him**], Minor[*omits* and (MRD, NLT, TLB)], Alt/Peshitta[Then Pilate scourged Jesus (MRD, ~NLT, ~TLB)], Alt[*without textual foundation omits* So (~ESV, ~HCS, ~JNT, ~NAB, ~NAU, ~NET, ~NIV, ~NJB, ~NLT, ~NRS, ~REB, ~RSV, ~TEV, ~TLB)].

19:3 Alx[**And they were coming up to him, and saying**], Byz[And they were saying (KJV, MRD, NKJ, NLT, TLB)].

19:4 Alx[**And Pilate**], Byz[So Pilate (DRA, KJV, NKJ)]; Alx/Byz[**no crime in him** *Greek* no cause in him], Minor[*omits* in him].

19:5 Alx[**Behold! The man!**], Byz[See the man! (~HCS, ~JNT, ~NIV, ~NJB, ~NRS, REB)].

19:6 Alx/Byz[**cried out, saying**], Minor[*omits* saying (ESV, HCS, JNT, NAB, NET, NIV, NJB, NLT, NRS, REB, RSV, TEV, TLB)]; Alx[**Crucify! Crucify!**], Byz[Crucify! Crucify him! (~ASV, ~DRA, ~ESV, ~JNT, ~KJV, ~MRD, ~NAB, ~NET, ~NJB, ~NKJ, ~NLT, ~NRS, ~RSV, ~TEV)].

19:7 Alx/Byz[**The Jews answered him**], Minor[*omits* him (NAB, NET, NIV, NJB, NLT, REB, TEV, TLB)]; Alx[**according to that law**], Byz[according to our law (KJV, MRD, NET, NKJ, ~NLT, ~TEV, ~TLB)].

19:10 Alx/Byz[**So Pilate**], Minor[*omits* So (MRD, NIV, NLT, REB, TEV, TLB)]; Alx[**release…crucify**], Byz[crucify…release (DRA, KJV, NKJ)].

19:11 Alx[**Jesus answered him**], Byz[*omits* him (DRA, JNT, KJV, NAS, NAU, NET, NIV, NJB, NKJ, ~NLT, REB, TEV, ~TLB)]; Alx/Byz[**You would have no power**], Minor[You have no power (~TEV)]; Alx[**the one who delivered**], Byz[the one who delivers], Alt[*without textual foundation* those who delivered (~TLB)].

19:12 Alx[**the Jews cried out**], Byz[the Jews were crying out (NIV, REB)].

¹³ When Pilate heard these words, he brought Jesus out, and sat down on the judgment seat at a place that is called The Pavement, but in Hebrew, Gabbatha. ¹⁴ Now it was the day of Preparation of the Passover. It was about the sixth hour, and he said to the Jews, "See your King!" ¹⁵ So they cried out, "Away with him! Away with him! Crucify him!" Pilate said to them, "Shall I crucify your King?" The chief priests answered, "We have no King but Caesar." ¹⁶ Then he handed him over to them to be crucified.

So they took Jesus. ¹⁷ And he, bearing his own cross, went out to what is called "Skull Place," which is called in Hebrew, Golgotha. ¹⁸ There they crucified him, and two others with him, one on either side, and Jesus in the center. ¹⁹ Pilate wrote a title and put it on the cross. It read:

JESUS THE NAZARENE, THE KING OF THE JEWS.

²⁰ Many of the Jews read this title, for the place where Jesus was crucified was near the city; and it was written in Hebrew, Latin, and Greek. ²¹ The chief priests of the Jews then said to Pilate, "Do not write, 'The King of the Jews,' but, 'This man said, I am King of the Jews.'" ²² Pilate answered, "What I have written, I have written."

²³ When the soldiers had crucified Jesus, they took his garments, and made four parts, one for each soldier, and also his tunic. Now the tunic was without seam, woven in one piece from top to bottom. ²⁴ So they said to one another, "Let us not tear it, but cast lots for it, whose it shall be." This happened that the Scripture might be fulfilled [which says]:

> *They divided my garments among them,*
> *and for my clothing they cast lots."*

This is what the soldiers did. ²⁵ By the cross of Jesus stood his mother, and his mother's sister, Mary the wife of Clopas, and Mary Magdalene. ²⁶ When Jesus saw the mother, and the disciple whom he loved standing by, he said to the mother, "Woman, see your son." ²⁷

19:13 Alx[**heard these words**], Byz[heard this word (~JNT, KJV, MRD, ~NIV, NKJ, ~NLT, ~REB)]; **sat down** *or* seated him, **Gabbatha** *Aramaic* stone pavement.

19:14 Alx[**it was about the sixth hour**], Byz[and about the sixth hour (HCS, KJV, ~MRD, ~NAB, NKJ, ~NRS)], Minor[it was about the third hour].

19:15 Alx[**So they cried out**], Byz[But they cried out (DRA, ~ESV, HCS, ~JNT, KJV, MRD, ~NAB, NIV, NJB, NKJ, ~NLT, ~NRS, ~REB, ~RSV, ~TEV, ~TLB)].

19:16 Alx[**So they took Jesus 17**], Byz[17 And they took Jesus and led him away], Major[And they took Jesus and led him away 17 (DRA, ~HCS, KJV, MRD, ~NKJ, ~NLT, ~REB)], Minor[17...they took Jesus (ASV, NAS, NAU, RSV, ~TLB)].

19:17 Alx[**bearing his own cross**], Byz[bearing his cross (KJV, MRD, NKJ, TEV, TLB)]; Alx/Byz[**went out to what is called** *Greek* went out to the called], Major[went out to the place called (ASV, ~DRA, ESV, KJV, NAS, NAU, NET, NKJ, NLT, RSV)]; Alx/Byz[**Skull Place**], Alt/Vulgate[Calvary (DRA)]; Alx/Byz[**Hebrew**], Alt[Aramaic-(ESV, JNT, NET, NIV)]; **Golgotha** *Aramaic* place of a skull.

19:20 Alx[**Latin...Greek**], Byz[Greek...Latin (DRA, KJV, MRD, NKJ)].

19:21 Alx/Byz[**the chief priests of the Jews**], Alt/Peshitta[*omits* of the Jews (MRD, NLT, TEV, TLB)].

19:22 Alx/Byz[**Pilate answered**], Alt/Peshitta[Pilate said (MRD)].

19:24 Alx/Byz[**which says**], Minor[*omits* (NAS, NAU, ~REB, RSV, TEV)]; Alx/Byz[**This is what the soldiers did. 25**], Alt[25 This is what the soldiers did. (ASV, NAS, NAU, NRS, RSV, TLB)]; **Psalms 22:18**.

19:25 Alx/Byz[**Mary...Mary** *Greek* Maria...Maria], Minor[Mary...Mary *Greek* Mariam...Mariam (JNT)].

19:26 Alx[**said to the mother**], Byz[said to his mother (ASV, DRA, ESV, HCS, JNT, KJV, MRD, NAB, NAS, NAU, NET, NIV, NJB, NKJ, ~NLT, NRS, ~REB, RSV, TEV, ~TLB)]; Alx/Byz[**see your son**], Major[behold your son (ASV, DRA, ESV, ~HCS, ~JNT, KJV, MRD, NAB, NAS, NAU, ~NET, ~NIV, ~NJB, NKJ, ~NLT, NRS, ~REB, RSV, ~TEV, ~TLB)].

19:27 Alx[**See your mother**], Byz[Behold your mother (ASV, DRA, ESV, ~HCS, ~JNT, KJV, MRD, NAB, NAS, NAU, ~NIV, ~NJB, NKJ, ~NLT, ~NRS, ~REB, RSV, ~TEV, ~TLB)].

Then he said to the disciple, "See your mother." And from that hour the disciple took her to his own home.

²⁸ After this, Jesus, knowing that all was now accomplished, that the Scripture might be fulfilled, said, *"I thirst."* ²⁹ A vessel full of wine vinegar was sitting there. So they put a sponge full of the vinegar on hyssop, and brought it to his mouth. ³⁰ So when he had received the vinegar, Jesus said, "It is finished!" And he bowed his head and gave up his spirit.

³¹ Therefore, because it was the day of Preparation, that the bodies should not remain on the cross on the Sabbath (for that Sabbath was a high day), the Jews asked Pilate that their legs might be broken, and that they might be taken away. ³² Then the soldiers came and broke the legs of the first, and of the other who had been crucified with him. ³³ But when they came to Jesus and saw that he was already dead, they did not break his legs. ³⁴ But one of the soldiers pierced his side with a spear, and immediately blood and water came out. ³⁵ He who saw it has testified, and his testimony is true, and he knows that he tells the truth, that you also may believe. ³⁶ For these things were done that the scripture should be fulfilled, *"Not one of his bones shall be broken."* ³⁷ And again another scripture says, *"They shall look on him whom they have pierced."*

³⁸ But after this Joseph of Arimathea, who was a disciple of Jesus, but secretly, for fear of the Jews, asked Pilate that he might take away the body of Jesus, and Pilate gave him permission. So he came and took away his body. ³⁹ And Nicodemus, who had at first come to him by night, also came, bringing a mixture of myrrh and aloes, about a hundred pounds. ⁴⁰ So they took the body of Jesus, and bound it in strips of linen with the spices, as is the burial custom of the Jews. ⁴¹ Now in the place where he was crucified there was a garden, and in the garden a new tomb in which no one had ever been laid. ⁴² So because of the Jewish day of Preparation, as the tomb was nearby, they laid Jesus there.

20 ¹ On the first day of the week Mary Magdalene went to the tomb early, while it was still dark, and saw that the stone had been taken away from the tomb. ² So she ran, and came to Simon Peter and the other disciple, the one whom Jesus loved, and said to them, "They have taken the Lord out of the tomb, and we do not know where they have laid him." ³ Peter therefore went out with the other disciple, and

---

19:28 Alx/Byz[**knowing**], Major[seeing]; **Psalms 22:15, 69:21**.

19:29 Alx[**A vessel**], Byz[So a vessel (DRA, KJV, NKJ)]; Alx[**so they put a sponge full of the vinegar on hyssop**], Byz[and they filled a sponge with vinegar, and put it on hyssop (~DRA, KJV, MRD, NKJ, ~TEV, ~TLB)]; Alx/Byz[**hyssop**], Minor[a javelin].

19:30 Alx/Byz[**Jesus**], Minor[he (REB)].

19:35 Alx/Byz[**that you also may believe**], Major[that you may believe (KJV, NKJ)]; **he knows that he tells the truth** *or* there is one who knows he tells the truth.

19:36 Alx/Byz[**of his bones**], Major[from his bones]; **Exodus 12:46, Numbers 9:12,** Psalms 34:20.

19:37 ~**Zechariah 12:10 Masoretic**.

19:38 Alx/Byz[**But after this**], Major[After this (ESV, HCS, JNT, MRD, NAB, NAU, NET, NIV, NJB, NKJ, NLT, NRS, REB, RSV, TEV, TLB)]; Alx[**took away his body**], Byz[took away the body of Jesus (DRA, KJV, MRD, NKJ)], Minor[took him away], Alt[took the body away (JNT, NET, NIV, NLT, REB) *others* took it away (NJB, TEV, TLB)].

19:39 Alx[**come to him by night**], Byz[come to Jesus by night (DRA, ESV, JNT, KJV, MRD, NET, NIV, NJB, NKJ, NLT, NRS, REB, TEV, TLB)]; Alx/Byz[**bringing a mixture**], Minor[bringing a roll (~NLT, ~TLB)]; **a hundred pounds** *Greek* a hundred litrai.

19:41 Alx[**no one had ever been laid**], Byz[no one was yet laid (ASV, KJV, ~NLT, ~REB, ~TLB)].

19:42 Alx/Byz[**Jewish day of Preparation**], Alt/Peshitta[sabbath (MRD, ~REB, ~TEV, ~TLB)], Alt/Vulgate[parasceve of the Jews (DRA)].

20:1 Alx/Byz[**Mary** *Greek* Maria], Minor[Mary *Greek* Mariam (JNT)]; Alx/Byz[**from the tomb**], Minor[from the door of the tomb (~NET, ~NIV, ~NLT, ~REB, ~TEV, ~TLB)].

20:2 Alx/Byz[**Peter**], Alt/Peshitta[Cephas (JNT, MRD)].

20:3 Alx/Byz[**Peter**], Alt/Peshitta[Simon (MRD)], Alt[*without textual foundation* Cephas (~JNT)].

they were going toward the tomb. [4] They both ran, but the other disciple outran Peter and reached the tomb first. [5] And stooping to look in, he saw the linen cloths lying there, but he did not go in. [6] Then Simon Peter also came, following him, and went into the tomb; and he saw the linen cloths lying there, [7] and the napkin that had been around his head, not lying with the linen cloths, but folded up in a place by itself. [8] Then the other disciple, who reached the tomb first, also went in; and he saw and believed. [9] For as yet they did not know the Scripture, that he must rise from the dead. [10] Then the disciples went back to their homes.

[11] But Mary stood weeping outside the tomb, and as she wept she stooped into the tomb. [12] And she saw two angels in white, sitting where the body of Jesus had lain, one at the head and the other at the feet. [13] And they said to her, "Woman, why are you weeping?" She said to them, "Because they have taken away my Lord, and I do not know where they have laid him." [14] Saying this, she turned around and saw Jesus standing there, but she did not know that it was Jesus. [15] Jesus said to her, "Woman, why are you weeping? Whom are you seeking?" Supposing him to be the gardener, she said to him, "Sir, if you have carried him away, tell me where you have laid him, and I will take him away." [16] Jesus said to her, "Mary!" She turned and said to him in Hebrew, "Rabboni!" (which means, Teacher). [17] Jesus said to her, "Do not hold me, for I have not yet ascended to the Father. But go to my brothers and say to them, 'I am ascending to my Father and your Father, to my God and your God.'" [18] Mary Magdalene went, announcing to the disciples that, "I have seen the Lord!" And she told them that he had said these things to her.

[19] On the evening of that day, the first day of the week, the doors being shut where the disciples were (for fear of the Jews), Jesus came and stood among them and said to them, "Peace be with you." [20] And saying this, he showed the hands and the side to them. Then the disciples were glad when they saw the Lord. [21] So [Jesus] said to them again, "Peace be with you! As the Father has sent me, I also send you." [22] And when he had said this, he breathed on them, and said to them, "Receive the Holy Spirit. [23] If you forgive the

---

20:4 Alx/Byz[**Peter**], Alt/Peshitta[Simon (MRD)], Alt[*without textual foundation* Cephas (~JNT)].

20:5 Alx/Byz[**he did not go in**], Minor[indeed, he did not go in].

20:6 Alx[**Simon Peter also came**], Byz[Simon Peter came (DRA, ESV, KJV, NAB, NET, NIV, NKJ, NLT, NRS, REB, RSV, TEV, TLB)], Alt/Peshitta[Simon came (MRD)], Alt[*without textual foundation* Simon Cephas came (~JNT)].

20:10 Alx[**their homes**], Byz[their own homes (ASV, ~HCS, ~JNT, KJV, ~NAB, NAS, NAU, ~NJB, NKJ, ~NLT, ~REB, ~TEV, ~TLB)].

20:11 Alx/Byz[**Mary** *Greek* Maria], Minor[Mary *Greek* Mariam (JNT)].

20:13 Alx/Byz[**And they said**], Minor[*omits* And (DRA, ESV, HCS, JNT, NET, NIV, NJB, ~NKJ, NLT, NRS, REB, RSV, TEV, TLB)].

20:14 Alx[**Saying this**], Byz[And saying this (KJV, ~NKJ, ~TEV)].

20:16 Alx[**Mary** *Greek* Mariam], Byz[Mary *Greek* Maria]; Alx[**in Hebrew**], Byz[*omits* (DRA, KJV, NKJ, TLB)], Alt[Aramaic (ESV, NET, NIV)]; **Rabboni** *Aramaic* My teacher.

20:17 Alx[**not yet ascended to the Father**], Byz[not yet ascended to my Father (DRA, KJV, MRD, NET, NKJ)].

20:18 Alx[**Mary** *Greek* Mariam], Byz[Mary *Greek* Maria]; Alx[**announcing to the disciples that, "I have seen the Lord!"**], Byz[reporting to the disciples that she had seen the Lord (JNT, KJV, MRD, NKJ, TEV)].

20:19 Alx[**where the disciples were**], Byz[*adds* assembled (DRA, HCS, JNT, KJV, NET, NIV, NKJ, NLT, NRS, REB, TEV, TLB)].

20:20 Alx[**he showed the hands and the side to them**], Byz[he showed them the hands and his side (ASV, DRA, ESV, HCS, JNT, KJV, MRD, NAB, NET, NIV, NJB, NKJ, NLT, NRS, REB, RSV, TEV, TLB)], Minor[he showed both the hands and the side to them (NAS, NAU)].

20:21 Alx/Byz[**Jesus said**], Minor[he said (NJB, NLT, TLB)]; **Peace be with you** *Hebraic greeting* Shalom aleikhem.

20:23 Alx[**they have been forgiven**], Byz[they are forgiven (ASV, DRA, ESV, HCS, JNT, KJV, NAB, NET, NIV, NJB, NKJ, NLT, NRS, REB, RSV, TEV, TLB)], Minor[they will be forgiven (MRD)].

sins of any, they have been forgiven them. If you retain the sins of any, they have been retained."

²⁴ Now Thomas, one of the twelve, called the Twin, was not with them when Jesus came. ²⁵ So the other disciples told him, "We have seen the Lord." But he said to them, "Unless I see in his hands the mark of the nails, and put my finger in the mark of the nails, and put my hand in his side, I cannot believe." ²⁶ Eight days later, his disciples were again in the house, and Thomas was with them. The doors were shut, but Jesus came and stood among them, and said, "Peace be with you!" ²⁷ Then he said to Thomas, "Put your finger here, and see my hands. Reach out your hand, and put it into my side. Do not be unbelieving, but believing." ²⁸ Thomas answered and said to him, "My Lord and my God!" ²⁹ Jesus said to him, "Have you believed because you have seen me? Blessed are those who have not seen and yet have believed."

³⁰ Jesus did many other signs in the presence of [his] disciples, which are not written in this book. ³¹ But these are written that you may [come to] believe that Jesus is the Christ, the Son of God, and that believing you may have life in his name.

21 ¹ After this Jesus showed himself again to the disciples by the Sea of Tiberias. And in this way he showed himself: ² Simon Peter, Thomas called the Twin, Nathanael of Cana in Galilee, the sons of Zebedee, and two others of his disciples were together. ³ Simon Peter said to them, "I am going fishing." They said to him, "We will go with you." They went out and embarked in the boat; but that night they caught nothing. ⁴ But now when morning came, Jesus stood inshore; yet the disciples did not know that it was Jesus. ⁵ So Jesus said to them, "Children, have you any fish?" They answered him, "No." ⁶ But he said to them, "Cast the net on the right side of the boat, and you will find some." So they cast, and now they were not able to begin hauling it in because of the great number of fish. ⁷ Then that disciple whom Jesus loved said to Peter, "It is the Lord!" Now when Simon Peter heard that it was the Lord, he put on his outer garment (for he had removed it), and threw himself into the sea. ⁸ But the other disciples came in the boat,

---

20:²⁴, 21:² **the Twin** *Greek* Didymus.
20:²⁵ Alx/Byz[**and put my finger in the mark of the nails**], Minor[and put my finger in the place of the nails (DRA, JNT, NAS, NAU, ~NET, ~NIV, REB) *others* and put my finger in the marks of the nails (~MRD, NAB, ~NJB, ~NLT, ~TEV, ~TLB) *others omit* (ASV)].
20:²⁸ Alx[**Thomas answered**], Byz[And Thomas answered (KJV, MRD, NKJ)].
20:²⁹ Alx/Byz[**Have you believed**], Minor[adds Thomas (DRA, KJV, NKJ)].
20:³⁰ Alx/Byz[**his disciples**], Minor[the disciples (ASV, ESV, JNT, NAS, NAU, NET, NJB, NLT, RSV)].
20:³¹ Alx/Byz[**that you may come to believe**], Minor[that you may continue to believe (NLT)].
21:¹ Alx/Byz[**Jesus**], Minor[he]; Alx/Byz[**the disciples**], Minor[his disciples (HCS, MRD, NAB, NIV, REB, TEV) *others add* having come from the dead]; **Sea of Tiberias** *Sea of Galilee*.
21:² Alx/Byz[**Peter**], Alt/Peshitta[Cephas (JNT, MRD)]; **the Twin** *Greek* Didymus.
21:³ Alx/Byz[**Peter**], Alt/Peshitta[Cephas (JNT, MRD)]; Alx[**embarked in the boat**], Byz[adds immediately (KJV, NKJ)], Minor[got into the boat (ASV, DRA, ESV, HCS, JNT, KJV, NAB, NAS, NAU, NET, NIV, NJB, NKJ, ~NLT, NRS, REB, RSV, ~TEV, ~TLB)].
21:⁴ Alx/Byz[**when morning came**], Minor[when morning was coming (ASV, ESV, JNT, NAS, NAU, RSV, TEV)]; Alx/Byz[**Jesus stood inshore**], Minor[Jesus stood on the shore (ASV, DRA, ESV, HCS, JNT, KJV, MRD, NAB, NAS, NAU, NET, NIV, NJB, NKJ, NLT, NRS, REB, RSV, ~TEV, ~TLB)].
21:⁵ Alx/Byz[**Jesus said**], Minor[he said (JNT, NIV, NLT, REB, TEV, TLB)].
21:⁶ Alx/Byz[**But he said**], Minor[He says (DRA, ~ESV, ~HCS, ~JNT, ~MRD, ~NAB, ~NET, ~NIV, ~NJB, ~NLT, ~NRS, ~REB, ~RSV, ~TEV, ~TLB)]; Alx[**not able to begin hauling it in** *Greek* not being able to haul it in], Byz[not able to haul it in (ASV, DRA, ESV, HCS, JNT, KJV, MRD, NAB, NAS, NAU, NET, NIV, NJB, NKJ, NLT, NRS, REB, RSV, TEV, TLB)].
21:⁷ Alx/Byz[**Peter...Simon Peter**], Alt/Peshitta[Cephas...Simon (MRD)], Alt[*without textual foundation* Cephas...Simon Cephas (~JNT)]; Alx/Byz[**It is the Lord**], Minor[It is our Lord (MRD)]; Alx/Byz[**into the sea**], Alt/Peshitta[adds to go to Jesus (MRD)].
21:⁸ **a hundred yards** *Greek* two hundred cubits.

dragging the net full of fish, for they were not far from land, but about a hundred yards off. [9] When they had come to land, they saw a fire of coals there, with fish lying on it, and bread. [10] Jesus said to them, "Bring some of the fish you have just caught." [11] So Simon Peter went aboard and dragged the net to the shore, full of large fish, one hundred and fifty-three; and although there were so many, the net was not torn. [12] Jesus said to them, "Come and have breakfast." But none of the disciples dared ask him, "Who are you?" They knew it was the Lord. [13] Jesus came and took the bread and gave it to them, and did the same with the fish. [14] This was now the third time Jesus appeared to the disciples after he was raised from the dead.

[15] When they had finished breakfast, Jesus said to Simon Peter, "Simon, son of John, do you love me more than these?" He said to him, "Yes, Lord; you know that I like you." He said to him, "Feed my lambs." [16] He said to him again a second time, "Simon, son of John, do you love me?" He said to him, "Yes, Lord; you know that I like you." He said to him, "Tend my sheep." [17] The third time he said to him, "Simon, son of John, do you like me?" Peter was grieved because the third time he said to him, "Do you like me?" And he said to him, "Lord, you know all things; you know that I like you." [Jesus] said to him, "Feed my sheep. [18] Truly, truly, I say to you, when you were younger, you girded yourself and walked where you wished; but when you are old, you will stretch out your hands, and another will gird you and carry you where you do not wish to go." [19] This he said to show by what death he would glorify God. And after this he said to him, "Follow me."

[20] Peter turned and saw following them the disciple whom Jesus loved, who had leaned on his breast at the supper and had said, "Lord, who is the one who is going to betray you?" [21] So when Peter saw him, he said to Jesus, "Lord, what about this man?" [22] Jesus said to him, "If I want him to remain until I come, what is that to you? You follow me." [23] So the saying spread among the brothers that this disciple would not die. Yet Jesus

---

21:11 Alx[**So Simon Peter**], Byz[Simon Peter (DRA, KJV, NAS, NAU, NIV, NJB, NKJ, REB, TEV)], Alt/Peshitta[And Simon Cephas (~JNT, MRD)]; Alx/Byz[**to the shore**], Minor[on the shore (~ESV, ~HCS, ~JNT, ~NAB, ~NIV, ~NJB, ~NRS, ~RSV, ~TEV, ~TLB)].

21:12 Alx/Byz[**But none of the disciples**], Minor[*omits* But (HCS, JNT, NAS, NAU, NIV, NJB, NLT, REB, TEV)].

21:13 Alx[**Jesus came**], Byz[So Jesus came (KJV, NJB, NKJ, NLT, TEV, TLB)], Alt/Vulgate[And Jesus came (DRA, MRD)]; Alx/Byz[**gave it to them**], Minor[gave the Eucharist to them].

21:14 Alx/Byz[**This was now**], Minor[But this was now]; Alx[**the disciples**], Byz[his disciples (DRA, KJV, MRD, NAB, NIV, NKJ, NLT, REB, ~TLB)].

21:15 Alx/Byz[**Simon Peter**], Alt/Peshitta[Simon Cephas (JNT, MRD)]; Alx[**son of John**], Byz[son of Jonah (KJV, MRD, NKJ)]; **love** *Greek* agapao; **like** *or* love *Greek* phileo.

21:16 Alx[**son of John**], Byz[son of Jonah (KJV, MRD, NKJ)]; Alx/Byz[**tend my sheep**], Minor[tend my little sheep (DRA)]; **love** *Greek* agapao; **like** *or* love *Greek* phileo.

21:17 Alx[**son of John**], Byz[son of Jonah (KJV, MRD, NKJ)]; Alx/Byz[**Peter**], Alt/Peshitta[Cephas (MRD)], Alt[*without textual foundation* Simon (~JNT)]; Alx[**And he said to him** *Greek* And he says to him], Byz[And he said to him]; Alx/Byz[**Jesus said to him** *Greek* Jesus says to him], Minor[He says to him (DRA)]; Alx/Byz[**Feed my sheep**], Minor[Feed my little sheep (TLB)], Alt[*omits* (MRD)]; **like** *or* love *Greek* phileo

21:18 Alx/Byz[**another will gird you**], Minor[others will gird you (NET, NLT, TLB)]; Alx/Byz[**carry you**], Minor[carry you away].

21:20 Alx[**Peter turned**], Byz[But Peter turned (~HCS, KJV, NKJ)], Alt/Peshitta[Simon Cephas turned (~JNT, ~MRD)].

21:21 Alx[**So when Peter saw him**], Byz[When Peter saw him (ESV, HCS, KJV, NAB, NIV, NJB, NKJ, ~NLT, NRS, REB, RSV, TEV, ~TLB)], Alt/Peshitta[Cephas saw him (JNT, MRD)].

21:22 Alx/Byz[**If I want him to remain**], Alt/Vulgate[If I want him to remain thus *others* I want him to remain thus (DRA)].

21:23 Alx[**Yet Jesus did not say**], Byz[And Jesus did not say (DRA)]; Alx/Byz[**what is that to you**], Minor[*omits* (NJB)].

did not say to him that he would not die, but, "If I want him to remain until I come, [what is that to you?]"

²⁴ This is the disciple who testifies to these things, and who wrote these things; and we know that his testimony is true.

²⁵ But there are also many other things which Jesus did. If every one of them were to be written, I suppose that even the world itself could not contain the books that would be written.

21:²⁴ Alx/Byz[**the disciple who testifies**], Minor[the disciple who also testifies (~REB)]; Alx[**and who wrote these things** *Greek* and the one writing these things], Byz[and writing these things (ASV, DRA, KJV, MRD, NAB, NAS, NAU, NET, NJB, NKJ, NLT, NRS, TLB)].

21:²⁵ Alx[*text*], Byz[*adds* Amen (KJV, NKJ)], Minor[*omits verse*]; Minor[*inserts John 7:53-8:11 after this verse or after verse 24* (REB)].

The Acts of the Apostles

1 ¹ In the first book, O Theophilus, I wrote about all that Jesus began to do and to teach, ² until the day when he was taken up to heaven, after he had given orders through the Holy Spirit to the apostles whom he had chosen. ³ To these he also presented himself alive after his suffering, by many convincing proofs, appearing to them over a period of forty days and speaking of the things concerning the kingdom of God. ⁴ And while he stayed, he commanded them not to leave Jerusalem, but to wait for what the Father had promised, "Which," he said, "you heard of from me. ⁵ For John baptized with water, but before many days you will be baptized with the Holy Spirit."

⁶ So when they had come together, they asked him, "Lord, are you at this time going to restore the kingdom to Israel?" ⁷ But he said to them, "It is not for you to know times or seasons which the Father has fixed by his own authority. ⁸ But you will receive power when the Holy Spirit has come upon you. And you shall be my witnesses both in Jerusalem, and [in] all Judea and Samaria, and even to the ends of the earth." ⁹ And after he had said this, as they were looking on, he was lifted up, and a cloud took him out of their sight. ¹⁰ And as they were gazing intently into the sky while he was going, behold, two men in white clothing stood beside them. ¹¹ They also said, "Men of Galilee, why do you stand gazing into the sky? This Jesus, who has been taken up from you into heaven, will come in just the same way as you have watched him go into heaven."

¹² Then they returned to Jerusalem from the mount called Olivet, which is near Jerusalem, a Sabbath day's journey away. ¹³ And when they had entered, they went up to the upper room, where they were staying; Peter and John and James and Andrew, Philip and Thomas, Bartholomew and Matthew, James the son of Alphaeus and Simon the Zealot and Judas the son of James. ¹⁴ All these with one mind devoted themselves to prayer, along with the women and Mary the mother of Jesus, and his brothers.

Title Alx/Byz[**The Acts of the Apostles**], Minor[*variations of* The Acts of the Holy Apostles According to the Evangelist Luke *others* Acts].

1:1-22:29 Metzger[*Codex Bezae and other ancient "Western" texts vary significantly from the Alx and Byz readings in Acts. Metzger devotes over 200 pages of commentary to this book alone*].

1:2 Alx/Byz[*text*], Minor[until the day when he chose the apostles through the Holy Spirit and gave them orders].

1:4 Alx/Byz[**stayed** *or* ate], Minor[adds with them (ASV, DRA, ESV, HCS, KJV, MRD, NAB, NAS, NAU, NET, NIV, NJB, NKJ, NLT, NRS, REB, RSV, TEV)]; Alx/Byz[**you heard of from me**], Minor[you heard by my mouth (DRA, ~TLB)].

1:5 Alx/Byz[**before many days**], Minor[adds until Pentecost]; **with** *or* in *or* by.

1:6 Alx[**asked** *requested*], Byz[asked *demanded*].

1:7 Alx/Byz[**But he said**], Minor[omits But (ESV, GCS, JNT, MRD, NAB, NAS, NAU, NET, NIV, NJB, NLT, NRS, REB, RSV, TEV, TLB)]; Alx/Byz[**It is not for you to know**], Alt[No one can know].

1:8 Alx[**my witnesses**], Byz[witnesses to me (DRA, KJV, MRD, NKJ, REB, TEV, TLB)]; Alx/Byz[**in all Judea**], Minor[omits in (NAB, NJB, REB, TLB)].

1:11 Alx/Byz[**gazing**], Minor[looking (ASV, DRA, ESV, HCS, MRD, NAB, NAS, NAU, NET, NIV, NJB, NRS, REB, RSV, TEV)]; Alx/Byz[**taken up from you into heaven**], Minor[omits into heaven].

1:13 Alx/Byz[**Peter**], Alt[*without textual foundation* Cephas (~JNT)]; Alx[**Peter and John and James and Andrew**], Byz[Peter and James and John and Andrew (JNT, KJV, NKJ)], Minor[Peter and Andrew and James and John]; **Judas the son of James** *or* Judas the brother of James *Greek* Judas of James; *TLB places Peter and John and James and Andrew in verse 14.*

1:14 Alx[**to prayer**], Byz[adds and supplication (KJV, NKJ)]; Alx/Byz[**with the women**], Minor[adds and children]; Alx[**and his brothers**], Byz[and with his brothers (ASV, DRA, KJV, MRD, NAS, NAU, NIV, NJB, NKJ, ~NRS, RSV, TEV)].

¹⁵ In those days Peter stood up among the brothers (the company of persons was in all about a hundred and twenty), and said, ¹⁶ "Brothers, the scripture had to be fulfilled, which the Holy Spirit spoke beforehand by the mouth of David, concerning Judas who was guide to those who arrested Jesus. ¹⁷ For he was counted among us and received his share in this ministry." ¹⁸ (Now this man bought a field with the reward of his wickedness. And falling headlong, he burst open in the middle and all his intestines gushed out. ¹⁹ And it became known to all the inhabitants of Jerusalem, so that the field was called in their own language Hakeldamach, that is, Field of Blood.) ²⁰ For it is written in the book of Psalms,

> 'Let his homestead be made desolate,
>> and let there be no one to dwell in it';

and,

> 'let another man take his office.'

²¹ Therefore it is necessary that of the men who have accompanied us all the time that the Lord Jesus went in and out among us, ²² beginning from the baptism of John until the day when he was taken up from us – one of these men must become with us a witness to his resurrection." ²³ So they put forward two men, Joseph called Barsabbas (who was also called Justus), and Matthias. ²⁴ And they prayed and said, "You, Lord, who know the hearts of all men, show which one of these two you have chosen ²⁵ to take the place in this ministry and apostleship from which Judas turned aside, to go to his own place." ²⁶ And they cast lots for them, and the lot fell to Matthias. And he was added to the eleven apostles.

2 ¹ When the day of Pentecost had come, they were all together in one place. ² And suddenly there came from heaven a sound like the rush of a violent wind, and it filled the whole house where they were sitting. ³ And there appeared to them tongues as of fire distributing themselves, and they rested on each one of them. ⁴ And they were all filled with the Holy Spirit and began to speak in other tongues, as the Spirit gave them utterance.

1:15 Alx/Byz[**Peter**], Alt/Peshitta[Simon Cephas (~JNT, MRD)]; Alx[**brothers**], Byz[disciples (~JNT, KJV, MRD, ~NET, ~NIV, NKJ, ~NLT, ~NRS, ~REB, ~TEV, ~TLB)], Minor[apostles].

1:16 Alx[**the scripture**], Byz[this scripture (JNT, KJV, NKJ)].

1:17 Alx[**among us**], Byz[with us (DRA, ~HCS, ~JNT, KJV, MRD, ~NET, ~NIV, ~NJB, NKJ, ~NLT, ~REB, ~TEV, ~TLB)].

1:18 Alx/Byz[**falling headlong** or possibly swelling up], Alt/Vulgate[being hanged (DRA)].

1:19 Alx/Byz[**And it became known**], Minor[which also became known (~HCS, ~JNT, ~NAB, ~NET, ~NIV, ~NJB, ~NLT, ~NRS, ~REB, ~TEV, ~TLB)]; Alx/Byz[**their own language**], Minor[their language (ASV, DRA, JNT, MRD, NAB, NIV, NJB, ~NLT, NRS, RSV, ~TLB)]; Alx[**Hakeldamach** Aramaism of Chakel D'ma], Byz[Akeldama (ASV, ~DRA, ESV, ~HCS, ~JNT, KJV, MRD, NAB, ~NAS, ~NAU, ~NET, NIV, ~NJB, NKJ, NLT, ~NRS, REB, RSV, TEV, ~TLB)]; the final consonant of Hakeldamach in Greek (χ) may be a marker for the final aleph (א) in the Aramaic word, making Hakeldama the intended pronunciation.

1:20 Alx[**let another man take his office**], Byz[may another man take his office (NAB, NIV, TEV)]; **Psalms 69:25, 109:8**.

1:21 Alx/Byz[**Jesus**], Minor[adds Christ].

1:23 Alx/Byz[**they put forward**], Minor[he put forward (~NJB, ~REB)].

1:25 Alx[**take the place**], Byz[take the share (JNT, KJV, MRD, ~NAS, ~NAU, ~NET, NIV, NJB, NKJ, REB)]; Alx[**from which**], Byz[out of which (~HCS, ~JNT, ~NIV, ~NJB, ~NLT, ~REB, ~TEV, ~TLB)].

1:26 Alx[**cast lots for them** or gave lots to them], Byz[cast their lots (JNT, KJV, MRD, NIV, NKJ, NLT, REB, TEV, TLB)]; Alx/Byz[**eleven apostles**], Minor[twelve apostles (NJB) others eleven apostles as the twelfth].

2:1 Alx[**they were all together**], Byz[they were all with one accord (KJV, NKJ)], Minor[while they were all together (MRD, TLB)].

2:4, 11 **tongues** or languages.

⁵ Now there were Jews living in Jerusalem, devout men from every nation under heaven. ⁶ And at this sound the crowd came together, and they were bewildered, because each one heard them speaking in his own language. ⁷ And they were amazed and wondered, saying, "Are not all these who are speaking Galileans? ⁸ And how is it that we hear them, each of us in his own native language? ⁹ Parthians and Medes and Elamites, and residents of Mesopotamia, Judea and Cappadocia, Pontus and Asia, ¹⁰ Phrygia and Pamphylia, Egypt and the parts of Libya around Cyrene, and visitors from Rome, ¹¹ both Jews and proselytes, Cretans and Arabs – we hear them in our own tongues speaking of the mighty deeds of God." ¹² And they were all amazed and perplexed, saying to one another, "What does this mean?" ¹³ But others were jeering and said, "They are full of new wine."

¹⁴ But Peter, taking his stand with the eleven, raised his voice and addressed them: "Men of Judea and all you who live in Jerusalem, let this be known to you and give heed to my words. ¹⁵ For these men are not drunk, as you suppose, since it is only the third hour of the day; ¹⁶ but this is what was spoken by the prophet Joel:

17   'And in the last days it shall be, God says,
           that I will pour out my Spirit upon all flesh,
                 and your sons and your daughters shall prophesy,
           and your young men shall see visions,
                 and your old men shall dream dreams;
18   even on my servants, both men and women,
                 I will pour out my Spirit in those days,
                       and they shall prophesy.
19   And I will show wonders in heaven above
                 and signs on the earth below,
                       blood, and fire, and vapor of smoke.
20   The sun will be turned into darkness
                 and the moon into blood,

2:5 Alx/Byz[**Jews living in Jerusalem, devout men from every nation**], Minor[devout men from every nation living in Jerusalem (NJB) *others* devout Jews from every nation living in Jerusalem (JNT, NET, NIV, NLT, NRS, REB, TLB)].

2:7 Alx[**they were amazed**], Byz[they were all amazed (ASV, DRA, KJV, MRD, NKJ, ~TLB)]; Alx[**saying**], Byz[adds to each other (KJV, MRD, NKJ)].

2:9 Alx/Byz[**Judea**], Metzger[*Minor omits; others substitute one of a number of countries: Armeniam, Syria, India, Idumaea, Ionia, Bithynia, Cilicia, Lydia, Gordyaea, Yaudi, Adiabene, Aramaea*].

2:11 Alx[**11 both Jews and proselytes**], Byz[both Jews and proselytes 11 (ASV, HCS, KJV, MRD, NAS, NAU, NKJ, NLT, NRS, REB, RSV, TLB)].

2:12 Alx/Byz[**to one another**], Minor[adds about what had happened]; Alx[**What does this mean** *Greek* What will is this], Byz[Whatever does this mean *or* What can this mean (HCS, JNT, ~NJB, NKJ, REB, TLB)], Alt[From whom is this thing (MRD)].

2:13 Alx[**jeering**], Byz[mocking (ASV, DRA, ESV, ~HCS, ~JNT, KJV, ~MRD, ~NAB, NAS, NAU, ~NIV, ~NJB, NKJ, ~NLT, ~NRS, ~REB, RSV, ~TEV, TLB)].

2:14 Alx/Byz[**But Peter, taking his stand with the eleven**], Minor[But then Peter, taking his stand first with the ten apostles *others* But then Simon Cephas, taking his stand with the eleven apostles (~JNT, MRD) *others* But then Peter, taking his stand with the eleven apostles (~NLT, ~TEV, ~TLB)].

2:16 Alx/Byz[**Joel**]. Minor[omits (NJB)].

2:17-21 ~**Joel 2:28-32 LXX**.

2:17 Alx/Byz[**And in the last days**], Minor[In the last days (JNT, MRD, NAB, NIV, NJB, NLT, NRS, REB, TEV, TLB) *others* And afterward]; Alx/Byz[**God says**], Minor[the Lord says (DRA, JNT, NJB)]; Alx/Byz[**your sons and your daughters**], Minor[their sons and their daughters].

2:18 Alx/Byz[**in those days**], Minor[omits (NJB, TLB)]; Alx/Byz[**and they shall prophesy**], Minor[omits (NJB)].

2:19 Alx/Byz[**blood, and fire, and vapor of smoke**], Minor[omits (NJB)].

2:20 Alx/Byz[**and glorious**], Minor[omits (~TLB)].

> before the great and glorious day
> of the Lord shall come.

21   And it shall be that everyone
>   who calls on the name of the Lord
>   will be saved.'

²² "Men of Israel, listen to these words: Jesus the Nazarene, a man attested to you by God with miracles and wonders and signs which God did through him in your midst, as you yourselves know – ²³ this man, delivered over by the predetermined plan and foreknowledge of God, you nailed to a cross by the hand of lawless men and put him to death. ²⁴ But God raised him up, having loosed the agony of death, because it was impossible for him to be held in its power. ²⁵ For David says concerning him,

> 'I saw the Lord always before me;
>   for he is at my right hand, so that I will not be shaken.

26   Therefore my heart was glad and my tongue rejoiced.
>   Moreover my flesh also will live in hope,

27   because you will not abandon my soul to hades,
>   nor let your Holy One see decay.

28   You have made known to me the ways of life.
>   You will make me full of gladness with your presence.'

²⁹ "Brothers, I may say to you confidently of the patriarch David that he both died and was buried, and his tomb is with us to this day. ³⁰ And so, because he was a prophet, and knew that God had *sworn with an oath to him that, from the fruit of his loins, he would set one on his throne,* ³¹ he looked ahead and spoke of the resurrection of the Christ,

> *that neither was he abandoned to Hades,*
>   *nor did his flesh see decay.*

³² This Jesus God raised up again, and of that we are all witnesses. ³³ Being therefore exalted at the right hand of God, and having received from the Father the promise of the Holy Spirit, he has poured out this which you [both] see and hear. ³⁴ For David did not ascend into heaven, but he says himself:

> '[The] Lord said to my Lord,
> "Sit at my right hand,

35   until I make your enemies a footstool
>   for your feet."'

³⁶ Therefore let all the house of Israel know for certain that God has made him both Lord and Christ, this Jesus whom you crucified."

2:22 Alx[**as you yourselves know**], Byz[as you yourselves also know (DRA, KJV, NKJ)].

2:23 Alx[**you nailed**], Byz[you have taken, nailed (KJV, ~MRD, NJB, NKJ)]; Alx[**the hand of lawless men**], Byz[lawless hands (~DRA, ~ESV, ~HCS, ~JNT, KJV, ~MRD, ~NAB, ~NAS, ~NAU, ~NET, ~NIV, ~NJB, NKJ, ~NLT, ~NRS, ~REB, ~RSV, ~TEV, ~TLB)].

2:24 Alx/Byz[**death**], Minor[Hades *or* the grave (DRA, MRD, NJB)].

2:25-28 **Psalms 16:8-11 LXX**.

2:25 Alx/Byz[**the Lord**], Minor[my Lord (MRD, ~TLB)].

2:30 Alx[**from the fruit of his loins, he would set one on his throne**], Byz[from the fruit of his loins, according to the flesh, he would raise up Christ to sit on his throne (KJV, NKJ, ~TLB)]; ~**Psalms 132:11**.

2:31 Alx/Byz[**he looked ahead and spoke of the**], Minor[*omits*]; Alx[**neither was he abandoned to Hades**], Byz[his soul was not left in Hades (~ASV, ~DRA, ~ESV, ~HCS, ~JNT, KJV, ~MRD, ~NIV, ~NJB, NKJ, ~NLT, ~NRS, ~REB, ~RSV, ~TEV, TLB)]; ~**Psalms 16:10**.

2:33 Alx[**which you both see and hear**], Byz[which you now see and hear (KJV, NIV, NKJ, ~NLT, TEV, ~TLB)], Minor[which you see and hear (ASV, DRA, ESV, NJB, RSV) *others* gift which you see and hear (JNT, ~MRD, ~NLT, TEV, ~TLB)]; **at the right hand of God** *or* by the right hand of God.

2:34-35 **Psalms 110:1**.

2:36 Alx/Byz[**both Lord and Christ**], Minor[*omits* both (MRD, NJB, TEV, TLB)].

37 Now when they heard this they were stabbed in the heart, and said to Peter and the rest of the apostles, "Brothers, what shall we do?" 38 "Repent!" Peter [said] to them, "and be baptized every one of you on the name of Jesus Christ for the forgiveness of your sins; and you will receive the gift of the Holy Spirit. 39 For the promise is for you and your children and for all who are far off, for all whom the Lord our God will call to himself." 40 And he testified with many other words and exhorted them, saying, "Save yourselves from this perverse generation." 41 So those who received his word were baptized, and there were added in that day about three thousand souls. 42 They devoted themselves to the apostles' teaching and to the fellowship, to the breaking of bread and to prayer.

43 Everyone was filled with awe. And many wonders and signs were done through the apostles. 44 And all who believed were together and had all things in common. 45 And they sold their possessions and goods and distributed them to all, as anyone had need. 46 And day by day, attending the temple together and breaking bread in their homes, they ate together with glad and sincere hearts, 47 praising God and having favor with all the people. And the Lord added to them day by day those who were being saved.

2:37 Alx/Byz[**Peter**], Alt/Peshitta[Simon (MRD)], Alt[*without textual foundation* Cephas (~JNT)]; Alx/Byz[**and said to Peter and the rest of the apostles, "Brothers, what shall we do?"**], Metzger[*Minor* because the entire crowd could not speak to Peter and the apostles, "Brothers, show us what shall we do?"].

2:38 Alx/Byz[**Peter**], Alt/Peshitta[Simon (MRD)], Alt[*without textual foundation* Cephas (~JNT)]; Alx[**"Repent!" Peter said to them, "and be baptized** *Greek* But Peter to them: "Repent!" he said, "and be baptized], Byz[But Peter said to them, "Repent and be baptized (ASV, DRA, ESV, JNT, KJV, MRD, NAB, NAS, NAU, NET, ~NIV, ~NJB, NKJ, ~NLT, NRS, RSV, TEV, ~TLB, ~REB)], Minor[*omits* said (Metzger)]; Alx/Byz[**on the name**], Minor[in the name (ASV, DRA, ESV, HCS, KJV, MRD, NAB, NAS, NAU, NET, NIV, NJB, NKJ, NLT, NRS, REB, RSV, TEV, TLB)]; Alx[**for the forgiveness of your sins** *Greek* into the forgiveness of your sins], Byz[*omits* your (KJV, MRD, NKJ)].

2:39 Alx/Byz[**for you and your children**], Minor[for us and our children].

2:40 Alx[**exhorted them**], Byz[*omits* them (KJV)].

2:41 Alx[**received**], Byz[gladly received (KJV, MRD, NKJ)], Minor[believed (NLT, TEV, TLB)]; Alx[**in that day**], Byz[*omits* in (ESV, HCS, JNT, KJV, ~MRD, NAB, NAS, NAU, NET, NIV, ~NJB, NKJ, NLT, NRS, REB, RSV, TEV, ~TLB)].

2:42 Alx/Byz[**the apostles' teaching**], Minor[*adds* in Jerusalem]; Alx[**to the fellowship, to the breaking of bread**], Byz[to the fellowship, and to the breaking of bread (KJV, MRD, NLT, TEV)], Minor[to the fellowship of the breaking of bread (DRA, MRD, TLB)].

2:43 Alx/Byz[**through the apostles**], Minor[*adds* in Jerusalem (MRD) *others also add here or in verse 44* and there was great fear upon all (DRA)].

2:44 Alx/Byz[**And all who believed**], Minor[And indeed all who believed]; Alx/Byz[**were together and had all things in common**], Minor[together had all things in common (NJB, REB)].

2:45 Alx/Byz[**and they sold their possessions and goods and distributed them to all**], Minor[and as many as had possessions or goods sold them and distributed them to all (MRD)]; Alx/Byz[**as anyone had need. 46 And day by day, attending the temple**], Minor[as anyone had need day by day. 46 And everyone attending the temple].

2:46 Alx/Byz[**attending the temple together and breaking bread in their homes**], Minor[attending the temple and together in their homes (~MRD, ~NJB)]; **in their homes** *or* from house to house; **sincere** *or* generous.

2:47 Alx/Byz[**all the people**], Minor[all the world (~NJB)]; Alx[**to them** *or* to their number *Greek* to it], Byz[to the church (KJV, MRD, ~NJB, NKJ, ~NLT)].

3 ¹ Now Peter and John were going up to the temple at the hour of prayer, the ninth hour. ² And a certain man lame from birth was being carried, whom they set down every day at the gate of the temple which is called Beautiful to beg alms of those who entered the temple. ³ When he saw Peter and John about to go into the temple, he asked to receive alms. ⁴ And Peter, along with John, directed his gaze at him, and said, "Look at us." ⁵ And he gave them his attention, expecting to receive something from them. ⁶ But Peter said, "I do not have silver and gold, but I give you what I have; in the name of Jesus Christ of Nazareth, [rise and] walk." ⁷ And taking him by the right hand, he raised him up. And immediately his feet and ankles were made strong. ⁸ With a leap he stood upright and began to walk. And he entered the temple with them, walking and leaping and praising God. ⁹ And all the people saw him walking and praising God. ¹⁰ But they recognized him as the one who used to sit at the Beautiful Gate of the temple to beg alms. And they were filled with wonder and amazement at what had happened to him.

¹¹ But while he clung to Peter and John, all the people ran together to them in the porch called Solomon's, astounded. ¹² And when Peter saw this he addressed the people, "Men of Israel, why do you wonder at this, or why do you stare at us, as if by our own power or godliness we had made him walk? ¹³ *The God of Abraham, and [the God of] Isaac and [the God of] Jacob, the God of our fathers,* has glorified his servant Jesus, whom you indeed delivered and disowned in the presence of Pilate, when he had decided to release him. ¹⁴ But you disowned the Holy and Righteous One and asked for a murderer to be granted to you, ¹⁵ but killed the Author of Life, whom God raised from the dead. To this we are witnesses. ¹⁶ And his name – by faith in his name – has made this man strong whom you see and know. And the faith which comes through Jesus has given him perfect health in the

---

3:1 Alx/Byz[**Now** *Greek* But], Minor[*adds* in those days (~MRD, ~NIV, ~NJB, ~NRS, ~REB, ~TEV)]; Alx/Byz[**Peter**], Alt/Peshitta[Simon Cephas (~JNT, MRD)]; Alx[**were going up**], Byz[*adds* together (HCS, KJV, MRD, NKJ)]; Alx/Byz[**the temple**], Minor[*adds* toward evening (~HCS, ~JNT, ~NET, ~NIV, ~NLT, ~NRS, ~REB, ~TEV, ~TLB)].

3:2 Alx/Byz[**a certain man**], Minor[behold, a certain man (MRD, ~NJB)].

3:3 Alx/Byz[**Peter**], Alt/Peshitta[Simon (MRD)], Alt[*without textual foundation* Cephas (~JNT)]; Alx[**asked to receive alms**], Byz[asked for alms (HCS, JNT, KJV, MRD, NAB, NET, NIV, NJB, NKJ, NLT, NRS, REB, RSV, TEV, TLB)].

3:4 Alx/Byz[**Peter**], Alt/Peshitta[Simon (MRD)], Alt[*without textual foundation* Cephas (~JNT)].

3:6 Alx/Byz[**Peter**], Alt/Peshitta[Simon (MRD)], Alt[*without textual foundation* Cephas (~JNT)]; Alx/Byz[**rise and walk**], Minor[walk (ASV, JNT, NAS, NAU, NIV, NJB, RSV, TLB)].

3:7 Alx[**raised him up**], Byz[*omits* him]; Alx[**ankles**], Byz[heels (DRA, MRD)].

3:8 Alx/Byz[**began to walk**], Minor[*adds* with joy].

3:10 Alx[**but they recognized him**], Byz[and they recognized this one (~ASV, ~DRA, ~ESV, ~HCS, ~JNT, ~KJV, ~MRD, ~NAB, ~NAS, ~NAU, ~NET, ~NIV, ~NJB, ~NKJ, ~NLT, ~NRS, ~REB, ~RSV, ~TEV, ~TLB)].

3:11 Alx[**while he clung**], Byz[while the lame man who was healed clung (KJV, NKJ)]; Alx/Byz[**Peter**], Alt/Peshitta[Simon (MRD)], Alt[*without textual foundation* Cephas (~JNT)].

3:12 Alx/Byz[**Peter**], Alt/Peshitta[Simon (MRD)], Alt[*without textual foundation* Cephas (~JNT)]; Alx/Byz[**godliness**], Minor[authority (DRA, MRD)].

3:13 Alx[**and the God of Isaac and the God of Jacob**], Byz[and Isaac, and Jacob (ASV, HCS, JNT, KJV, MRD, NAS, NAU, NET, NIV, NJB, NKJ, NLT, REB, RSV, TEV, TLB)]; Alx/Byz[**whom you indeed**], Minor[*omits* indeed (ASV, ESV, HCS, JNT, KJV, MRD, NAB, NAS, NAU, NET, NIV, NJB, NKJ, NLT, NRS, REB, RSV, TEV, TLB)]; Alx[**delivered and disowned**], Byz[delivered, and disowned him (KJV, NIV, TEV)]; **servant** *or* child; Exodus 3:6, 15.

3:14 Alx/Byz[**you disowned**], Minor[you oppressed (~NJB, ~TLB)].

3:15 **Author of Life** *or* Prince of Life.

3:16 Alx/Byz[**And his name – by faith in his name – has made**], Minor[And by faith in his name, he has made (MRD, ~NIV, ~NJB, ~NLT, ~REB, ~TEV, ~TLB)]; Alx/Byz[**whom you see and know; and the faith**], Minor[whom you see; and know that the faith (~NLT, ~TEV, ~TLB)]; **his name** *Hebraism* The Name *i.e. the* LORD; **Jesus** *Greek* him.

presence of you all. [17] And now, brothers, I know that you acted in ignorance, as did also your rulers. [18] But what God foretold by the mouth of all the prophets, that his Christ would suffer, he thus fulfilled. [19] Repent therefore, and turn again, into the blotting out of your sins, [20] that times of refreshing may come from the presence of the Lord, and that he may send the one appointed for you, Christ Jesus, [21] whom heaven must receive until the time for establishing all that God spoke by the mouth of his holy prophets from long ago. [22] Indeed, Moses said, *'The Lord your God will raise up for you a prophet like me from your brothers. You shall listen to everything he tells you. [23] And it shall be that every soul that does not listen to* that prophet *will be destroyed from among the people.'* [24] And likewise, all the prophets who have spoken, from Samuel and those who came afterwards, also announced these days. [25] You are the sons of the prophets and of the covenant which God made with your fathers, saying to Abraham, *'And in your seed all the families of the earth shall be blessed.'* [26] For you first, God raised up his servant and sent him to bless you by turning every one of you from your wicked ways."

4 [1] And as they were speaking to the people, the priests and the captain of the temple guard and the Sadducees came up to them, [2] being greatly disturbed because they were teaching the people and proclaiming in Jesus the resurrection from the dead. [3] And they seized them and put them in jail until the next day, for it was already evening. [4] But many of those who heard the message believed. And [the] number of the men came to [about] five thousand.

3:17 Alx/Byz[**brothers**], Minor[men, brothers]; Alx/Byz[**I know that you**], Minor[*adds* indeed]; Alx/Byz[**acted in ignorance**], Minor[did evil in ignorance].

3:18 Alx[**the prophets...his Christ**], Byz[his prophets...the Christ (KJV, ~MRD, ~NJB, NKJ, ~NLT, ~TLB)].

3:19 Alx[**into the blotting out of your sins**], Byz[for the blotting out of your sins (ASV, DRA, ESV, HCS, JNT, KJV, MRD, NAB, NAS, NAU, NET, NIV, NJB, NKJ, NLT, NRS, REB, RSV, TEV, TLB)].

3:20 Alx/Byz[**20 that times...presence of the Lord**], Major[that times...presence of the Lord 20 (ASV, HCS, KJV, MRD, NAS, NAU, NIV, NKJ, REB, RSV, TLB)]; Alx/Byz[**the one appointed for you, Christ Jesus**], Minor[the one proclaimed to you, Jesus Christ (DRA, KJV, NKJ) *others* the Christ appointed for you, Jesus (ASV, ESV, HCS, JNT, NAB, NAS, NAU, NET, NIV, NJB, NLT, NRS, REB, RSV, TEV, ~TLB)].

3:21 Alx[**his holy prophets**], Byz[all his holy prophets (KJV, NKJ)]; Alx/Byz[**from long ago** *or* from eternity], Minor[*omits* (NJB)].

3:22 Alx[**Moses said**], Byz[For Moses said (DRA, JNT, KJV, MRD, NAB, NIV, NKJ, TEV, ~TLB) *and adds* to the fathers (KJV, NKJ)]; Alx/Byz[**the Lord your God**], Major[the Lord our God], Minor[the Lord God (ASV, ESV, ~JNT, ~MRD, NAS, NAU, NJB, REB, RSV, TLB)]; **like me** *or* as me; **Deuteronomy 18:15-16**.

3:23 ~**Deuteronomy 18:19**, ~**Leviticus 23:29**.

3:24 Alx/Byz[**announced**], Minor[foretold (KJV, NIV, NJB, NKJ, NRS, REB)].

3:25 Alx[**the sons of the prophets**], Byz[sons of the prophets (NKJ, ~TEV)]; Alx[**your fathers**], Byz[our fathers (DRA, JNT, KJV, MRD, NKJ)]; Alx/Byz[**in your seed**], Minor[by your seed (JNT, NIV, NLT, TEV, TLB)]; **Genesis 22:18, 26:4**.

3:26 Alx[**his servant** *or* his child], Byz[*adds* Jesus (KJV, NKJ, NLT)]; Alx/Byz[**you from your wicked ways**], Minor[you from wicked ways *others* you from his wicked ways (KJV, NJB, TEV) *others* him from his wicked ways (DRA)].

4:1 Alx/Byz[**they were speaking**], Minor[*adds* these words (MRD)]; Alx/Byz[**priests**], Minor[chief priests (REB, TLB)]; Alx/Byz[**and the captain**], Minor[*omits*].

4:2 Alx/Byz[**in Jesus the resurrection**], Alt[the resurrection of Jesus (NJB, TEV, TLB)], Alt/Peshitta[a resurrection by the Messiah (MRD)]; Alx[**from the dead**], Byz[of the dead (NAB, NET, NIV, NLT, NRS)].

4:4 Alx/Byz[**the number**], Minor[*omits* the (MRD, ~NRS) *others add* also]; Alx/Byz[**about five thousand**], Minor[*omits* about (DRA)].

⁵ On the next day, their rulers and the elders and the scribes were gathered together in Jerusalem. ⁶ And Annas the high priest was there, and Caiaphas and John and Alexander, and all who were of the high-priestly family. ⁷ And when they had set them in the midst, they began to inquire, "By what power or by what name did you do this?" ⁸ Then Peter, filled with the Holy Spirit, said to them, "Rulers of the people and elders, ⁹ if we are being examined today for a good deed done to a cripple, as to how this man has been healed, ¹⁰ be it known to you all, and to all the people of Israel, that by the name of Jesus Christ of Nazareth, whom you crucified, whom God raised from the dead, by him this man stands before you healed. ¹¹ He is

the stone which was rejected by you, the builders,
but which has become the chief cornerstone.

¹² And there is salvation in no one else, for there is no other name under heaven given among men by which we must be saved." ¹³ Now when they saw the boldness of Peter and John, and perceived that they were uneducated, common men, they were astonished. And they recognized that they had been with Jesus. ¹⁴ And seeing the man who had been healed standing with them, they had nothing to say in reply. ¹⁵ But when they had ordered them to leave the Sanhedrin, they began to confer with one another, ¹⁶ saying, "What should we do with these men? For that a noteworthy miracle has been performed through them is apparent to all the inhabitants of Jerusalem, and we cannot deny it. ¹⁷ But in order that it may spread no further among the people, let us warn them to speak no longer to any one in this name." ¹⁸ And they called them in again and commanded them not to speak or teach at all in the name of Jesus. ¹⁹ But Peter and John answered them, "Whether it is right in the sight of God to listen to you rather than to God, you must judge. ²⁰ For we cannot stop speaking about what we have seen and heard." ²¹ And when they had further threatened them, they let them go, finding no way they could punish them, because of the people. For all the people were praising God for what had happened. ²² For the man on whom this sign of healing was performed was more than forty years old.

4:5 Alx/Byz[**On the next day** *Greek* On the morrow], Minor[On the morrow day]; Alx/Byz[**the elders and the scribes**], Major[elders and scribes (ASV, DRA, ESV, HCS, JNT, KJV, NAB, NAS, NAU, NET, NIV, NJB, NKJ, NLT, NRS, REB, RSV, ~TLB)]; Alx[**in Jerusalem 6**], Byz[into Jerusalem 6], Minor[6 into Jerusalem (~KJV, ~NKJ)], Alt/Peshitta[*omits* (MRD)].

4:6 Alx/Byz[**John**], Minor[Jonathan (NJB)].

4:8 Alx/Byz[**Peter**], Alt/Peshitta[Simon Cephas (~JNT, MRD)]; Alx[**elders**], Byz[*adds* of Israel (KJV, MRD, NKJ, ~TLB)].

4:10 Alx/Byz[**by him**], Minor[*adds* and no other (NJB)].

4:11 **chief cornerstone** *or* capstone *or* keystone; ~Psalms 118:22.

4:12 Alx/Byz[**And there is salvation in no one else**], Minor[*omits* (NJB)]; Alx/Byz[**under heaven**], Major[*omits* (~NJB, ~REB, ~TEV)].

4:13 Alx/Byz[**saw the boldness**], Alt/Peshitta[heard the speech (MRD]; Alx/Byz[**Peter**], Alt/Peshitta[Simon (MRD)], Alt[*without textual foundation* Cephas (~JNT)].

4:14 Alx[**And seeing**], Byz[But seeing (ESV, ~JNT, ~NAB, NIV, NJB, NLT, REB, RSV, TEV)]; Alx/Byz[**nothing to say**], Minor[nothing to do or say].

4:15 Alx/Byz[**to leave the Sanhedrin**], Minor[to be led out of the Sanhedrin (MRD, ~NLT, ~TLB)]; Alx/Byz[**began to confer** *or* were conferring], Minor[conferred (ASV, DRA, ESV, HCS, JNT, KJV, ~MRD, NAB, NIV, ~NJB, NKJ, NLT, NRS, REB, RSV, TLB)].

4:16 Alx[**What should we do**], Byz[What shall we do (ASV, DRA, ESV, KJV, MRD, ~NAB, NAS, NAU, NIV, NJB, NKJ, NRS, ~REB, RSV, TEV, TLB)]; Alx/Byz[**apparent**], Minor[very apparent].

4:17 Alx[**warn them**], Byz[*adds* with a threat (~KJV, ~NAB, ~NKJ, ~TLB)].

4:18 Alx/Byz[**And they called them**], Minor[And having made the decision they called them].

4:19 Alx/Byz[**Peter**], Alt/Peshitta[Simon Cephas (~JNT, MRD)].

4:21 Alx[**they could punish**], Byz[to punish (ESV, HCS, ~MRD, NAB, NAU, NET, NIV, NJB, NKJ, NLT, NRS, ~REB, RSV, TEV, TLB)].

23 When they had been released, they went to their own companions and reported all that the chief priests and the elders had said to them. 24 And when they heard this, they lifted their voices to God together and said, "O Lord, it is you who made the heaven and the earth and the sea, and everything in them, 25 who by the Holy Spirit, through the mouth of our father David your servant, said,

'Why did the Gentiles rage,
        and the peoples plot futile things?
26   The kings of the earth took their stand,
        and the rulers were gathered together
            against the Lord and against his Christ.'

27 For truly in this city there were gathered together against your holy servant Jesus, whom you anointed, both Herod and Pontius Pilate, along with the Gentiles and the peoples of Israel, 28 to do whatever your hand and [your] plan had predestined to take place. 29 And now, Lord, look upon their threats, and grant to your servants to speak your word with all boldness, 30 while you stretch out [your] hand to heal, and signs and wonders take place through the name of your holy servant Jesus." 31 And when they had prayed, the place where they were gathered together was shaken. And they were all filled with the Holy Spirit and spoke the word of God with boldness.

32 Now the company of those who believed were of one heart and soul, and no one claimed that any of the things which he possessed was his own, but they had everything in common. 33 And with great power the apostles gave their testimony to the resurrection of the Lord Jesus, and great grace was upon them all. 34 For there was not a needy person among them, For all who were owners of land or houses sold them and brought the proceeds of the sales 35 and laid it at the apostles' feet, and it was distributed to each as any had need. 36 Thus Joseph who was called by the apostles Barnabas (which means, Son of Encouragement), a Levite, a native of Cyprus, 37 sold a field which he owned, and brought the money and laid it at the apostles' feet.

5 1 But a man named Ananias, with his wife Sapphira, sold a piece of property, 2 and with the wife's full knowledge he kept back some of the money for himself, and brought only a part and laid it at the apostles' feet. 3 But Peter said, "Ananias, why has

---

4:24 Alx/Byz[**when they heard this**], Minor[*adds* they recognized the working of God]; Alx/Byz[**O Lord, it is you who**], Major[O Lord, it is you who are God, who (~ESV, KJV, MRD, ~NAB, ~NIV, NKJ, ~NLT, ~NRS, ~REB, ~RSV)].

4:25 Alx[**by the Holy Spirit, through the mouth of our father David your servant**], Byz[through the mouth of your servant David (KJV, NKJ)]; **servant** *or* child.

4:25-26 **Psalms 2:1-2 LXX**.

4:27 Alx[**in this city**], Byz[*omits* (KJV, MRD, NKJ)]; Alx/Byz[**Pontius Pilate**], Alt/Peshitta[Pilate (MRD)]; Alx/Byz[**peoples of Israel**], Minor[people of Israel (DRA, KJV, NET, NIV, NKJ, NLT, TEV, TLB)], Alt/Peshitta[synagogue of Israel (MRD)]; **servant** *or* child.

4:28 Alx/Byz[**your hand and your plan**], Minor[your hand and plan (JNT, NIV, ~NLT, TEV, ~TLB)].

4:29 **servants** *or* slaves.

4:30 Alx/Byz[**your hand**], Minor[the hand (~TLB)]; **servant** *or* child.

4:31 Alx[**the Holy Spirit**], Byz[Holy Spirit]; Alx/Byz[**with boldness**], Minor[*adds* to all who wished to believe].

4:32 Alx/Byz[**one heart and soul**], Minor[*adds* and there was no division at all in them]; Alx/Byz[**he possessed**], Major[they possessed (KJV, NLT, ~NRS)].

4:33 Alx/Byz[**the Lord Jesus**], Minor[Jesus Christ the Lord (~DRA, ~MRD)].

4:34 Alx[**For there was not**], Byz[For there did not exist (~TLB)].

4:36 Alx[**Joseph**], Byz[Joses (KJV, NKJ)].

4:37 Alx[**at the apostles' feet** *Greek* to the feet], Byz[by the apostles' feet].

5:2 Alx[**the wife's**], Byz[his wife's (ASV, DRA, ESV, HCS, JNT, KJV, MRD, NAB, NAS, NAU, NET, NIV, NJB, NKJ, NLT, NRS, REB, RSV, TEV, TLB)]; Alx[**full knowledge**], Byz[comprehension].

5:3 Alx/Byz[**Peter**], Alt/Peshitta[Simon (MRD)], Alt[*without textual foundation* Cephas (~JNT)];

Satan filled your heart to lie to the Holy Spirit and to keep back some of the price of the land? ⁴ While it remained unsold, did it not remain your own? And after it was sold, was it not at your disposal? How is it that you have conceived this deed in your heart? You have not lied to men but to God." ⁵ When Ananias heard these words, he fell down and died. And great fear came upon all who heard. ⁶ The young men arose and wrapped him up, carried him out, and buried him. ⁷ After an interval of about three hours his wife came in, not knowing what had happened. ⁸ But Peter answered her, "Tell me whether you sold the land for such and such a price." And she said, "Yes, that was the price." ⁹ Then Peter said to her, "How is it that you have agreed together to test the Spirit of the Lord? Look, the feet of those who have buried your husband are at the door, and they will carry you out." ¹⁰ Immediately she fell down to his feet and died. When the young men came in they found her dead, and they carried her out and buried her beside her husband. ¹¹ And great fear came upon the whole church, and upon all who heard of these things.

¹² Now many signs and wonders were being done among the people by the hands of the apostles. And they were all together in Solomon's Porch. ¹³ But none of the rest dared join them, though the people held them in high honor. ¹⁴ And all the more believers in the Lord, multitudes of men and women, were constantly added to their number, ¹⁵ so that they even carried out the sick into the streets, and laid them on beds and pallets, so that as Peter came by at least his shadow might fall on some of them. ¹⁶ The people also gathered from the towns around Jerusalem, bringing the sick and those afflicted with unclean spirits, and they were all healed.

¹⁷ But the high priest rose up and all who were with him, that is, the party of the Sadducees, and they were filled with jealousy ¹⁸ and laid hands on the apostles and put

---

Alx/Byz[**But Peter said, "Ananias, why**], Minor[But Peter said to Ananias, "Why (~JNT)]; Alx/Byz[**Satan filled your heart**], Minor[Satan maimed your heart *others* Satan tempted your heart (DRA, ~NJB, ~REB, ~TEV)].

5:⁴ Alx/Byz[**this deed**], Minor[this evil deed].

5:⁵ Alx[**all who heard**], Byz[*adds* these things (KJV, NKJ)].

5:⁸ Alx/Byz[**Peter**], Alt/Peshitta[Simon (MRD)], Alt[*without textual foundation* Cephas (~JNT)]; Alx[**But Peter answered her** *Greek* But Peter answered to her], Byz[But Peter answered her], Minor[But Peter said to her (DRA, ESV, ~HCS, ~JNT, ~MRD, NAB, NET, ~NIV, ~NJB, ~NLT, NRS, ~REB, RSV, ~TEV, ~TLB)]; Alx/Byz[**Tell me** *Greek* Say to me], Minor[I will ask you (~NLT, ~TLB)].

5:⁹ Alx/Byz[**Peter**], Alt/Peshitta[Simon (MRD)], Alt[*without textual foundation* Cephas (~JNT)]; Alx/Byz[**the Spirit of the Lord**], Minor[the Holy Spirit], Alt[*without textual foundation* the Spirit of God (~TLB)].

5:¹⁰ Alx[**fell down to his feet**], Byz[fell down at his feet (ASV, DRA, ESV, HCS, JNT, KJV, MRD, NAB, NAS, NAU, NET, NIV, NJB, NKJ, ~NLT, NRS, REB, RSV, TEV, ~TLB)]; Alx/Byz[**they carried her out**], Minor[they wrapped her up, carried her out (~MRD)].

5:¹² Alx/Byz[**wonders were being done**], Minor[wonders were done (ASV, DRA, KJV, MRD, NAB, ~NET, NIV, NJB, NKJ, NRS, REB, RSV, TLB)]; Alx/Byz[**they were all together**], Minor[*adds* in the temple (TLB)].

5:¹³ Alx/Byz[**none of the rest dared join them**], Alt[*emendation* none of the Levites dared prevent them *other emendation* none of the elders dared join them *other emendation* none of the leaders dared join them].

5:¹⁵ Alx[**they even carried**], Byz[they carried down (DRA, ~HCS, KJV, MRD, ~NIV, NKJ, NLT, REB, TEV, ~TLB)]; Alx[**beds and pallets**], Byz[couches and pallets (~ESV, ~JNT, ~NAB, ~NAS, ~NAU, ~NET, ~NRS)], Alt/Peshitta[*omits* and pallets (MRD)]; Alx/Byz[**Peter**], Alt/Peshitta[Simon (MRD)], Alt[*without textual foundation* Cephas (~JNT)]; Alx/Byz[**shadow might fall**], Minor[shadow would fall (NET, TLB)]; Alx/Byz[**on some of them**], Minor[*adds* and they might be delivered from their infirmities (DRA)].

5:¹⁶ Alx[**Jerusalem**], Byz[to Jerusalem (DRA, KJV, NKJ)].

5:¹⁷ Alx/Byz[**rose up** *Greek* anastas], Minor[Annas], Alt[*omits* (JNT, MRD, NIV, NLT, ~REB)].

5:¹⁸ Alx[**and laid hands**], Byz[and laid their hands (KJV, NKJ)]; Alx/Byz[**public jail**], Minor[*adds* and

them in the public jail. [19] But during the night an angel of the Lord opened the doors of the prison, and brought them out, and said, [20] "Go, stand and speak to the people in the temple the whole message of this Life." [21] And when they heard this, they entered into the temple about daybreak and began to teach. Now when the high priest and his associates came, they called the Council together, even all the Senate of the sons of Israel, and sent orders to the prison house for them to be brought. [22] But when the officers came, they did not find them in the prison, and they returned and reported back, [23] saying, "We found the prison securely locked, and the guards standing at the doors. But when we opened them, we found no one inside." [24] Now when the captain of the temple guard and the chief priests heard these words, they were much perplexed about them, wondering what would come of this. [25] And someone came and told them, "Look! The men whom you put in prison are standing in the temple and teaching the people." [26] Then the captain went along with the officers and was bringing them back without violence, for they were afraid of the people, lest they should be stoned.

[27] When they had brought them, they set them before the council. The high priest questioned them, [28] saying, "Did we [not] give you strict orders not to teach in this name? And yet you have filled Jerusalem with your teaching and intend to bring this man's blood upon us." [29] But Peter and the apostles answered, "We must obey God rather than men. [30] The God of our fathers raised Jesus – whom you had killed by hanging him on a tree. [31] God exalted him to his own right hand as Prince and Savior, to give repentance and forgiveness of sins to Israel. [32] And we are witnesses of these things, and so is the Holy Spirit, whom God has given to those who obey him."

[33] When they heard this, they were furious and wanted to kill them. [34] But a Pharisee in the council named Gamaliel, a teacher of the law, held in honor by all the people, stood up and ordered the men to be put outside for a while. [35] And he said to them, "Men of Israel, take care what you propose to do with these men. [36] For some time ago Theudas rose up, claiming to be somebody, and a group of about four hundred men joined him. But he was killed, and all who followed him were dispersed and came to nothing. [37]

---

each went to his own home].

5:23 Alx[**We found the prison**], Byz[Indeed, we found the prison (DRA, KJV, NKJ)]; Alx/Byz[**guards standing**], Minor[*adds* outside (KJV, ~NAB, NKJ, ~NLT, ~TLB)]; Alx[**at the doors**], Byz[before the doors (DRA, HCS, KJV, MRD, NKJ)].

5:24 Alx[**the captain**], Byz[the high priest and the captain (KJV, NKJ)].

5:25 Alx/Byz[**told them**], Minor[*adds* saying (KJV, NKJ)].

5:26 Alx[**was bringing them**], Byz[brought them (ASV, DRA, ESV, HCS, JNT, KJV, ~MRD, NAB, NET, NIV, NJB, NKJ, ~NLT, NRS, REB, RSV, TEV, ~TLB)]; Alx[**lest they should be stoned**], Byz[that they should not be stoned (~ESV, ~HCS, ~JNT, ~NAB, ~NUV, ~NET, ~NIV, NJB, ~NLT, ~NRS, ~REB, ~RSV, ~TEV, ~TLB)].

5:28 Alx/Byz[*text*], Minor[We gave you strict orders not to teach in his name. And…upon us (ASV, DRA, ESV, JNT, NAS, NAU, NET, NIV, NJB, NRS, REB, RSV, TEV, Metzger)].

5:29 Alx/Byz[**Peter**], Alt/Peshitta[Simon (MRD)], Alt[*without textual foundation* Cephas (~JNT)].

5:31 Alx/Byz[**to his own right hand** *or* with his own right hand], Minor[for his own glory (~TLB)]; Alx/Byz[**forgiveness of sins**], Minor[*adds* in him].

5:32 Alx[**And we are witnesses**], Byz[And we are his witnesses (KJV, NKJ)], Minor[And, in him, we are witnesses]; Alx[**and so is the Holy Spirit, whom God has given** *Greek* and the Holy Spirit, whom God has given], Byz[and also the Holy Spirit, whom God has given (KJV, MRD, NKJ)], Minor[and God has given the Holy Spirit].

5:33 Alx[**wanted to kill them**], Byz[took counsel to kill them (KJV, NKJ)].

5:34 Alx[**ordered the men**], Byz[ordered the apostles (KJV, MRD, NKJ, TEV, TLB)].

5:35 Alx/Byz[**And he said to them**], Minor[And he said to the rulers and the Sanhedrin (~JNT, ~NET, ~NJB, ~NLT, ~TEV, ~TLB)].

5:36 Alx/Byz[**he was killed**], Minor[he killed himself].

5:37 Alx[**some people**], Byz[many people (KJV, MRD, NJB, NKJ, ~TEV)].

After this man, Judas the Galilean rose up in the days of the census and drew away some people after him. He too perished, and all those who followed him were scattered. **38** And now I say to you, keep away from these men and let them alone, for if this plan or this action is of men, it will fail. **39** But if it is of God, you will not be able to overthrow them – or else you may even be found fighting against God." And they took his advice, **40** and they called the apostles in and had them flogged. Then they ordered them not to speak in the name of Jesus, and let them go. **41** Then they left the presence of the Sanhedrin, rejoicing that they had been counted worthy to suffer dishonor for the Name. **42** And every day, in the temple and from house to house, they never stopped teaching and preaching that the Christ is Jesus.

6 **1** Now in those days when the number of disciples was increasing, the Hellenists among them complained against the Hebrews because their widows were being overlooked in the daily distribution of food. **2** So the twelve summoned the congregation of the disciples and said, "It is not right for us to neglect the word of God in order to serve tables. **3** But, brothers, pick out from among you seven men of good reputation, full of the Spirit and of wisdom, whom we will appoint to this duty. **4** But we will devote ourselves to prayer and to the ministry of the word." **5** And the statement pleased the whole congregation. And they chose Stephen, a man full of faith and of the Holy Spirit, and Philip, Prochorus, Nicanor, Timon, Parmenas and Nicolas, a proselyte from Antioch. **6** These they set before the apostles, and they prayed and laid their hands on them.

7 The word of God increased; and the number of the disciples multiplied greatly in Jerusalem, and a great many of the priests were obedient to the faith.

8 And Stephen, full of grace and power, did great wonders and signs among the people. **9** Then some of those who belonged to the synagogue of the Freedmen (as it was called), and of the Cyrenians, and of the Alexandrians, and of those from Cilicia and Asia, arose and disputed with Stephen. **10** But they could not stand against the wisdom and the Spirit with which he spoke. **11** Then they secretly induced men to say, "We have heard him speak blasphemous words against Moses and against God." **12** They stirred up the people

---

5:38 Alx/Byz[**And now I say to you**], Minor[*adds* brothers]; Alx/Byz[**this plan**], Major[the plan (~NIV, ~NLT, ~REB, ~TEV, ~TLB)].

5:39 Alx[**you will not be able to**], Byz[you cannot (DRA, KJV, MRD, NKJ, ~TEV)]; Alx[**overthrow them**], Byz[overthrow it (DRA, KJV, MRD, NKJ, REB)]; Alx[**And they took his advice 40**], Byz[40 And they took his advice (ASV, KJV, NAS, NAU, NIV, NKJ, NLT, REB, RSV, TLB)].

5:41 Alx[**the Name**], Byz[his name (~JNT, KJV, ~MRD, NAS, NAU, NKJ, TLB)], Major[the name of Jesus (DRA, NLT, ~TEV)], Minor[the name of the Lord Jesus *others* the name of Christ]; **the Name** *Hebraism* the LORD.

5:42 Alx[**that the Christ is Jesus** *Greek* the Christ Jesus], Byz[Jesus as the Christ *Greek* Jesus the Christ (ASV, ESV, JNT, KJV, NAS, NAU, NET, NIB, NKJ, NLT, NRS, REB, RSV, TEV, TLB)], Alt/Peshitta[our Lord Jesus Messiah (MRD)].

6:1 Alx/Byz[**distribution of food**], Minor[*adds* in the distribution of the Hebrews].

6:2 Alx/Byz[**said**], Minor[*adds* to them (~ASV, ~KJV, NJB)]; **tables** *or* accounts.

6:3 Alx[**But, brothers**], Byz[Therefore, brothers (ASV, DRA, ESV, HCS, KJV, MRD, NAU, NKJ, NLT, NRS, REB, RSV, TEV)], Minor[Brothers (JNT, NAB, NIV, NJB)]; Alx[**the Spirit**], Byz[the Holy Spirit (DRA, KJV, NKJ, TEV, TLB)], Alt[the Spirit of the Lord (MRD)]; Alx/Byz[**we will appoint**], Major[we may appoint (ASV, DRA, HCS, KJV, MRD, NAS, NAU, NET, NJB, NKJ, NRS, RSV)].

6:5 Alx/Byz[**Stephen, a man**], Minor[*adds* of the disciples]; Alx/Byz[**Timon**], Alt/Old Latin[Simon].

6:7 Alx/Byz[**word of God**], Minor[word of the Lord (DRA, NJB)]; Alx/Major[**many of the priests**], Byz[many of the Jews (MRD, ~NLT, ~TLB)].

6:8 Alx[**grace**], Byz[faith (KJV, NKJ, TLB)], Alt[*without textual foundation* God's grace (~NIV, ~NLT, ~TEV)]; Alx/Byz[**among the people**], Minor[*adds* through the name of the Lord Jesus Christ].

6:9 Alx/Byz[**Freedmen**], Minor[Libyans]; Alx/Byz[**and Asia**], Minor[*omits*].

6:10 **Spirit** *or* spirit.

and the elders and the scribes, and they came on him and seized him, and brought him before the council. [13] They put forward false witnesses who said, "This man never stops speaking words against [this] holy place, and the law; [14] for we have heard him say that this Jesus the Nazarene will destroy this place, and will change the customs which Moses handed down to us." [15] And fixing their gaze on him, all who were sitting in the Council saw that his face was like the face of an angel.

7 [1] But the high priest said, "Are these things so?" [2] And he said: "Hear me, brothers and fathers! The God of glory appeared to our father Abraham when he was in Mesopotamia, before he lived in Haran, [3] *and said to him, 'Go out from your country and [from] your relatives, and go into the land that I will show you.'* [4] Then he came out of the land of the Chaldeans and settled in Haran. From there, after his father died, God had him move to this country in which you are now living. [5] But He gave him no inheritance in it, not even a foot of ground, and yet, even though he had no child, he promised *that he would give it to him as a possession, and to his descendants after him.* [6] But God spoke to this effect, that *his descendants would be aliens in a foreign land, and that they would be enslaved and mistreated for four hundred years.* [7] *'But I will judge the nation which they serve,'* said God, *'and after that they will come out and worship me in this* place.' [8] And he gave him the covenant of circumcision. And so he became the father of Isaac, and circumcised him on the eighth day. And Isaac became the father of Jacob, and Jacob of the twelve patriarchs.

[9] "And the patriarchs, jealous of Joseph, sold him into Egypt. But God was with him, [10] and rescued him from all his afflictions, and gave him favor and wisdom in the sight of Pharaoh, king of Egypt, and he made him governor over Egypt and [over] all his household. [11] But there came a famine throughout all Egypt and Canaan, and great affliction, and our fathers could find no food. [12] But when Jacob heard that there was grain in Egypt, he sent our fathers there the first time. [13] At the second visit Joseph made himself known again to his brothers, and Joseph's family was made known to Pharaoh. [14] Then Joseph sent and summoned his father Jacob and the whole family, *seventy-five* persons in all. [15] And Jacob went down into Egypt, and there he and our fathers died. [16] They were carried

---

6:13 Alx[**speaking words**], Byz[speaking blasphemous words (HCS, KJV, NKJ)]; Alx[**this holy place**], Byz[the holy place (DRA, NLT, ~TEV, TLB)].

6:15 Alx/Byz[**the face of an angel**], Minor[*adds* standing in their midst].

7:1 Alx/Byz[**the high priest said**], Minor[*adds* to Stephen (NLT, TEV)].

7:2 Alx/Byz[**our father Abraham**], Minor[your father Abraham]; *JNT's* avinu means our father.

7:3 Alx/Byz[**from your relatives**], Minor[*omits* from (JNT, NAS, NAU, NIV, NJB, NLT, NRS, REB, TEV, TLB)]; ~**Genesis 12:1**.

7:4 Alx/Byz[**Then he came out**], Minor[Then Abraham came out (MRD, NLT)].

7:5 Alx/Major[**he had no child**], Byz[there was no child]; ~**Genesis 17:8; 48:4**.

7:6-7 ~**Genesis 15:13-14**.

7:7 ~**Exodus 3:12**.

7:8 Alx/Byz[**he gave him the covenant**], Alt[he gave them the covenant (MRD)].

7:10 Alx/Byz[**in the sight of Pharaoh**], Minor[before Pharaoh (ASV, ESV, JNT, MRD, NAB, ~NIV, ~NJB, NLT, NRS, ~REB, RSV, TEV, ~TLB)]; Alx[**over all his household**], Byz[*omits* over (ASV, KJV, NAS, NAU, NIV, NJB, NKJ, NLT, TEV, ~TLB)].

7:11 Alx[**Egypt**], Byz[the land of Egypt (KJV, NKJ)].

7:12 Alx[**grain** *or* food], Byz[wheat (~DRA, ~KJV)], Alt[*without textual foundation* supplies (~NJB)].

7:13 Alx/Byz[**known again** *or* recognized], Minor[known (ASV, DRA, ESV, HCS, JNT, KJV, MRD, NAB, NAS, NAU, NET, ~NIV, NJB, NKJ, ~NLT, NRS, REB, RSV, TEV, TLB)]; Alx/Byz[**Joseph's family**], Minor[his family (DRA, NJB, ~NLT, REB, ~TLB)].

7:14 Alx/Major[**the whole family**], Byz[his whole family (ASV, DRA, ESV, HCS, JNT, KJV, MRD, NAB, NAS, NAU, NET, NIV, NJB, NKJ, NLT, NRS, RSV, ~TLB)]; **Genesis 46:27 LXX, Exodus 1:5 LXX/DSS, Deuteronomy 10:22 LXX**.

7:15 Alx[**And Jacob went down**], Byz[But Jacob went down (~DRA, ~KJV, ~NET, ~NIV, ~NJB, ~NKJ, ~NLT, ~NRS, ~TEV, ~TLB)]; Alx/Byz[**into Egypt**], Minor[*omits*].

back to Shechem and laid in the tomb that Abraham had bought for a sum of money from the sons of Hamor in Shechem.

¹⁷ "But as the time of the promise drew near, which God had assured to Abraham, the people increased and multiplied in Egypt ¹⁸ until *there arose another king [over Egypt] who knew nothing of Joseph*. ¹⁹ He dealt craftily with our race and forced [our] fathers to expose their infants, so that they would not survive. ²⁰ At this time Moses was born, and was beautiful before God. And he was brought up for three months in his father's house. ²¹ And when he was cast out, Pharaoh's daughter took him and brought him up as her own son. ²² And Moses was educated [in] all the wisdom of the Egyptians, and he was mighty in his words and deeds.

²³ "When he was forty years old, it came to his heart to visit his brothers, the sons of Israel. ²⁴ And when he saw one of them being treated unjustly, he defended him and avenged the oppressed by striking down the Egyptian. ²⁵ And he supposed that [his] brothers understood that God was granting them deliverance through him, but they did not understand. ²⁶ And on the following day he appeared to two of them as they were fighting, and tried to reconcile them into peace, saying, 'Men, you are brothers! Why do you wrong each other?' ²⁷ But the man who was wronging his neighbor pushed him aside, saying, *'Who made you a ruler and a judge over us?* ²⁸ *Do you want to kill me as you killed the Egyptian yesterday?'* ²⁹ But at this remark Moses fled, and became an exile in the land of Midian, where he became the father of two sons.

³⁰ "After forty years had passed, *an angel appeared to him in the wilderness of Mount Sinai, in the flame of a burning bush*. ³¹ When Moses saw it, he began to marvel at the sight. And as he approached to look more closely, there came the voice of the Lord: ³² *'I am the God of your fathers, the God of Abraham and Isaac and Jacob.'* Moses trembled with fear and did not

---

7:16 Alx[**Hamor in Shechem**], Byz[Emor of Shechem (DRA)], Minor[Shechem of Emor (~KJV, ~NJB, ~NKJ, ~TLB)], Alt/Peshitta[Emmor (MRD, TEV)], Alt[*emendation* Hamor at Shechem (NAB, NIV, REB)].

7:17 Alx[**assured to Abraham**], Byz[sworn to Abraham (KJV, MRD, NAB, ~NJB, NKJ)].

7:18 Alx[**over Egypt**], Byz[*omits* (KJV, NKJ, TLB)]; Alx/Byz[**knew nothing of Joseph**], Minor[remembered nothing of Joseph (~NJB, ~TLB)]; **Exodus 1:8**.

7:19 Alx/Byz[**our fathers**], Minor[the fathers (~NLT, ~TLB)].

7:20 Alx/Major[**his father's house** *Greek* the father's house], Byz[his father's house].

7:21 Alx/Byz[**cast out**], Minor[*adds* into the river].

7:22 Alx[**educated in**], Byz[*omits* in (NJB, NLT, TEV, ~TLB)]; Alx[**in his words and deeds**], Byz[in words and in deeds (~DRA, KJV, ~NJB)], Major[in words and deeds (~JNT, NAS, NAU, NIV, NKJ, NLT, REB, TEV, ~TLB)].

7:23 Alx/Major[**to his heart**], Byz[into his heart (ASV, DRA, ESV, ~HCS, KJV, MRD, NAS, NAU, NET, NKJ, NRS, RSV, TLB)].

7:24 Alx/Byz[**one of them**], Minor[one of his race (MRD, ~NLT, ~TLB)]; Alx/Byz[**striking down the Egyptian**], Minor[*adds* and he hid him in the sand].

7:25 Alx/Byz[**his brothers**], Minor[the brothers].

7:26 Alx/Byz[**And on the following day**], Minor[But on the following day (~HCS, ~NAB, ~NAU, ~NET, ~NIV, ~NJB, ~NLT, ~NRS, ~REB, ~TEV, ~TLB) *others* Then on the following day (~JNT)]; Alx[**reconcile them into peace**], Byz[bring them into peace (ASV, HNT, KJV, NET, ~NLT, ~REB, TEV, ~TLB)].

7:27-28 **Exodus 2:14 LXX**.

7:29 Alx/Byz[**But at this remark** *Greek* But in this word], Minor[Thus also in this word].

7:30 Alx[**angel**], Byz[*adds* of the Lord (KJV, MRD, NKJ)]; ~**Exodus 3:2**.

7:31 Alx/Byz[**began to marvel**], Minor[marveled (ASV, DRA, ESV, HCS, JNT, KJV, MRD, NAB, NAU, NET, NIV, NJB, NKJ, NLT, NRS, REB, RSV, TEV, TLB)]; Alx[**voice of the Lord**], Byz[*adds* to him (DRA, KJV, MRD, NKJ, REB, TLB)].

7:32 Alx[**and Isaac and Jacob**], Byz[and the God of Isaac and the God of Jacob (DRA, KJV, NKJ)]; **Exodus 3:6**.

dare to look. ³³ *And the Lord said to him, 'Take off the sandals from your feet, for the place on which you have been standing is holy ground.* ³⁴ *I have certainly seen the oppression of my people in Egypt and have heard their groaning, and I have come down to rescue them. And now come, that I should send you to Egypt.'* ³⁵ This Moses whom they rejected, saying, *'Who made you a ruler and a judge?'* is the one God sent to be [both] a ruler and a deliverer with the hand of the angel who appeared to him in the bush. ³⁶ This man led them out, performing wonders and signs in the land of Egypt and in the Red Sea and in the wilderness for forty years. ³⁷ This is the Moses who said to the Israelites, *'God will raise up for you a prophet like me from your brothers.'* ³⁸ This is he who was in the congregation in the wilderness with the angel who spoke to him at Mount Sinai, and with our fathers; and he received living oracles to pass on to us. ³⁹ Our fathers refused to obey him. But they rejected him and in their hearts turned back to Egypt, ⁴⁰ saying to Aaron, *'Make for us gods who will go before us. As for this Moses who led us out from the land of Egypt – we do not know what happened to him.'* ⁴¹ At that time they made a calf and brought a sacrifice to the idol, and were rejoicing in the works of their hands. ⁴² But God turned away and gave them over to worship the host of heaven, as it is written in the book of the prophets:

> *'Did you offer to me slain beasts and sacrifices,*
>> *forty years in the wilderness, O house of Israel?*

⁴³
> *You took up the tent of Moloch,*
>> *and the star of [your] god Rephan,*
>>> *the figures which you made to worship.*
> *And I will remove you beyond Babylon.'*

7:33 Alx/Byz[**And the Lord said to him**], Minor[And a voice came to him]; Alx[**the place on which**], Byz[the place in which (DRA, ~ESV, ~HCS, ~JNT, ~KJV, ~NAB, ~NET, ~NIV, ~NJB, ~NKJ, ~NRS, ~REB, ~RSV, ~TEV)]; **Exodus 3:5**.

7:34 Alx/Byz[**their groaning**], Minor[his groaning]; Alx[**That I should send** *Greek* I should send], Byz[I shall send (ASV, DRA, ESV, HCS, JNT, KJV, MRD, NAB, NAS, NAU, NET, NIV, ~NJB, NKJ, ~NLT, NRS, REB, RSV, TEV, TLB)]; **~Exodus 3:7-8, 10**.

7:35 Alx/Byz[**a ruler and a judge**], Minor[*adds* over us (MRD, NLT, TEV, TLB)]; Alx[**both a ruler and a deliverer**], Byz[*omits* both (DRA, HCS, KJV, MRD, NIV, NKJ, NLT, REB, TEV, TLB)]; Alx[**with the hand**], Byz[in the hand (~DRA, ~ESV, ~HCS, ~JNT, ~KJV, ~MRD, ~NAB, ~NET, ~NIV, ~NJB, ~NKJ, ~NLT, ~NRS, ~REB, ~RSV, ~TLB)]; **Exodus 2:14**.

7:36 Alx/Byz[**the land of Egypt**], Minor[Egypt (ASV, ESV, JNT, NIV, NJB, NLT, NRS, REB, RSV, TEV, TLB)]; **the Red Sea** *the Sea of Reeds*.

7:37 Alx[**God**], Byz[the Lord your God (KJV, NKJ)], Major[the Lord our God], Minor[the Lord God (MRD)]; Alx/Major[**brothers**], Byz[*adds* him you shall hear (DRA, KJV, MRD, NKJ)]; **a prophet like me** *or* a prophet as me; **Deuteronomy 18:15**.

7:38 Alx/Byz[**living oracles**], Major[a living word (TLB)]; Alx/Byz[**to pass on to us**], Minor[to pass on to you (NAS, NAU, NET, ~TLB)].

7:39 Alx/Byz[**Our fathers**], Minor[Your fathers]; Alx[**their hearts**], Byz[their heart (~NLT, ~REB, ~TEV, ~TLB)].

7:40 Alx[**what happened to him**], Byz[what has happened (~ASV, ~DRA, ESV, ~HCS, JNT, ~KJV, MRD, NAB, NET, NIV, NJB, NKJ, NLT, NRS, REB, RSV, TEV, TLB)]; **we do not know what happened** *Greek* we have not known what happened; **Exodus 32:1, 23**.

7:42 Alx/Byz[**book of the prophets**], Minor[Amos the prophet (~TLB)], Alt/Vulgate[books of the prophets (DRA)].

7:42-43 **~Amos 5:25-27 LXX**.

7:43 Alx/Byz[**your god**], Minor[*omits* your (ASV, MRD, NAS, NAU, NET, NJB, REB, RSV, TEV, ~TLB)]; Alx[**Rephan**], Byz[Remphan (KJV, NKJ)], Minor[Romphan *others* Rompha (NAS, NAU)], Alt/Vulgate[Rempham (DRA)]; Alx/Byz[**beyond Babylon**], Minor[to the parts of Babylon (~NLT)]; **Moloch...Rephan** *from LXX, Hebrew reads* Sikkuth...Kiyyun *TLB paraphrases to the names in Amos*; **beyond Babylon** *Amos 5:27 reads* beyond Damascus.

⁴⁴ "Our fathers had the tabernacle of testimony in the wilderness, just as he who spoke to Moses directed him to make it according to the pattern which he had seen. ⁴⁵ And having received it in their turn, our fathers brought it in with Joshua when they took the land from the nations whom God drove out before our fathers. So it was until the time of David, ⁴⁶ who found favor in God's sight, and asked that he might find a dwelling place for the house of Jacob. ⁴⁷ But it was Solomon who built a house for him. ⁴⁸ However, the Most High does not dwell in what is made by hands; as the prophet says:

⁴⁹   'Heaven is my throne,
                  but the earth is my footstool.
            What kind of house will you build for me? says the Lord,
                  or what is the place of my rest?
⁵⁰   Has not my hand made these all?'

⁵¹ "You stiff-necked people, uncircumcised in hearts and ears, you always resist the Holy Spirit. You are doing just as your fathers did. ⁵² Which of the prophets did your fathers not persecute? And they killed those who announced beforehand the coming of the Righteous One, of whom you are now betrayers and murderers, ⁵³ you who received the law as ordained by angels, and yet did not keep it."

⁵⁴ Now when they heard this they were cut to the heart, and they gnashed their teeth at him. ⁵⁵ But being full of the Holy Spirit, he gazed intently into heaven and saw the glory of God, and Jesus standing at the right hand of God. ⁵⁶ And he said, "Behold, I see the heavens have completely opened, and the Son of Man standing at the right hand of God." ⁵⁷ But they cried out with a loud voice, and covered their ears and rushed together upon him. ⁵⁸ Then they cast him out of the city and began to stone him. And the witnesses laid down their garments at the feet of a young man named Saul. ⁵⁹ And as they were stoning Stephen, he called out, saying, "Lord Jesus, receive my spirit." ⁶⁰ Then he fell on his knees and cried out with a loud voice, "Lord, do not hold this sin against them." When he had said this, he fell asleep. ¹ And Saul was consenting to his death.

7:⁴⁴ Alx/Byz[**Our fathers had the tabernacle of testimony**], Minor[The tabernacle of testimony was among our fathers (~DRA, ~MRD)].

7:⁴⁶ Alx[**house of Jacob**], Byz[God of Jacob (ASV, DRA, ESV, HCS, JNT, KJV, MRD, NAS, NAU, NIV, NKJ, NLT, REB, RSV, TEV, TLB)]; Psalms 132:5.

7:⁴⁸ Alx[**what is made by hands** *Greek* made by hands], Byz[temples made by hands (HCS, KJV, NKJ, NLT, TLB)]; Alx/Byz[**the prophet**], Minor[*adds* Isaiah].

7:⁴⁹ Alx/Byz[**but the earth**], Minor[and the earth (ASV, DRA, ESV, HCS, JNT, KJV, MRD, ~NAB, NAS, NAU, NET, NIV, NJB, NKJ, NLT, NRS, REB, RSV, TEV, TLB)].

7:⁴⁹⁻⁵⁰ **Isaiah 66:1-2**.

7:⁵⁰ Alx/Byz[**these all**], Minor[all these (ASV, DRA, ESV, HCS, JNT, KJV, MRD, NAB, NAS, NAU, NET, NIV, NJB, NKJ, ~NLT, NRS, REB, RSV, TEV, ~TLB)].

7:⁵¹ Alx[**hearts**], Byz[the heart (ASV, DRA, ESV, KJV, MRD, NAB, NAS, NAU, NKJ, NLT, NRS, REB, RSV, ~TLB)].

7:⁵² Alx[**you are now betrayers and murderers**], Byz[you have now become betrayers and murderers (ASV, DRA, ESV, HCS, JNT, KJV, ~MRD, NAB, NAS, NAU, NET, NIV, NJB, NKJ, ~NLT, NRS, REB, RSV, TEV, ~TLB)].

7:⁵⁵ Alx/Byz[**Jesus**], Minor[*adds* the Lord].

7:⁵⁶ Alx[**have completely opened**], Byz[have opened (ASV, DRA, ESV, HCS, JNT, KJV, MRD, NAB, NET, NIV, NKJ, NLT, NRS, REB, RSV, TEV, TLB)]; Alx/Byz[**the Son of Man**], Minor[the Son of God], Alt[*without textual foundation* Jesus the Messiah (~TLB)]; *DRA includes this verse as part of verse 55.*

7:⁵⁸ Alx/Byz[**laid down their garments**], Major[laid down the garments].

8:¹ Alx/Major[**1 And Saul was consenting to his death.**], Byz[And Saul was consenting to his death. 1 (DRA)]; Alx/Byz[**a great persecution**], Minor[*adds* and affliction]; Alx/Byz[**and they were all scattered**], Minor[*omits* and (JNT, TEV)]; Alx/Byz[**except the apostles**], Minor[*adds* who remained in Jerusalem].

8 On that day a great persecution arose against the church in Jerusalem, and they were all scattered throughout the region of Judea and Samaria, except the apostles. ² Devout men buried Stephen, and made great lamentation over him. ³ But Saul began ravaging the church, and, entering house after house, he dragged off men and women and put them in prison.

⁴ Now those who had been scattered went about preaching the word. ⁵ Philip went down to [the] city of Samaria and proclaimed Christ to them. ⁶ And the crowds with one accord were giving attention to what was said by Philip, when they heard and saw the signs which he did. ⁷ For unclean spirits, crying with a loud voice, came out of many who were possessed; and many who were paralyzed and lame were healed. ⁸ And there was much joy in that city.

⁹ Now there was a man named Simon, who had formerly practiced magic in the city and amazed all the people of Samaria. He boasted that he was someone great, ¹⁰ and they all, from the least to the greatest, gave attention to him, saying, "This man is what is called the Great Power of God." ¹¹ And they gave heed to him, because for a long time he had amazed them with his magic. ¹² But when they believed Philip as he preached good news about the kingdom of God and the name of Jesus Christ, they were baptized, both men and women. ¹³ Even Simon himself believed, and after being baptized he continued with Philip. And seeing signs and great miracles performed, he was amazed.

¹⁴ Now when the apostles in Jerusalem heard that Samaria had received the word of God, they sent them Peter and John, ¹⁵ who came down and prayed for them that they might receive the Holy Spirit. ¹⁶ For he had still not fallen upon any of them; they had simply been baptized in the name of the Lord Jesus. ¹⁷ Then they laid their hands on them, and they received the Holy Spirit. ¹⁸ Now when Simon saw that the Spirit was given through the laying on of the apostles' hands, he offered them money, ¹⁹ saying, "Give me also this power, so that everyone on whom I lay my hands may receive the Holy Spirit." ²⁰ But Peter said to him, "May your silver perish with you, because you thought you could obtain the gift of God with money! ²¹ You have no part or share in this matter, for your heart is not right before God. ²² Repent therefore of this wickedness of yours, and pray to

---

8:3 Alx/Byz[**the church**], Alt[*adds* of God (MRD)].

8:4 Alx/Byz[**the word**], Minor[*adds* of God (DRA, MRD)], Alt[*without textual foundation adds* of Jesus (~NLT, ~TLB)].

8:5 Alx[**the city**], Byz[a city (HCS, JNT, MRD, NIV, NJB, REB, RSV)].

8:6 Alx/Byz[**And the crowds** *or* But the crowds], Major[And the crowds], Minor[And when they heard everything, the crowds (~MRD)].

8:7 Alx[**of many** *Greek* many], Byz[of many].

8:8 Alx[**And there was much joy** *or* But there was much joy], Byz[And there was much joy].

8:10 Alx/Byz[**and they all**], Major[*omits* all (~TLB)]; Alx[**what is called**], Byz[*omits* (KJV, MRD, NKJ, ~NLT, ~TLB)].

8:12 Alx[**about the kingdom**], Byz[the things about the kingdom (KJV, NKJ, ~TLB)]; **preached good news** *or* preached.

8:13 Alx[**signs...miracles** *Greek* signs...powers], Byz[miracles...signs (KJV, NKJ)]; Alx[**great miracles**], Byz[*omits* great (KJV, NKJ)], Alt[*puts* great *with* signs (NIV, REB, TEV) *other omits* great *and* signs (TLB)].

8:14 Alx/Byz[**Peter**], Alt/Peshitta[Simon Cephas (~JNT, MRD)].

8:16 Alx[**still not**], Byz[not yet (ASV, DRA, ESV, HCS, KJV, MRD, NAB, NAS, NAU, NET, NIV, NJB, NKJ, NLT, NRS, RSV, TEV, TLB)]; Alx/Byz[**the Lord Jesus**], Major[Christ Jesus].

8:18 Alx/Byz[**Simon saw**], Major[Simon beheld (~REB)]; Alx[**the Spirit**], Byz[the Holy Spirit (ASV, DRA, HCS, KJV, MRD, NKJ, TLB)].

8:19 Alx/Byz[**saying**], Minor[entreating (~NLT, ~TLB)].

8:20 Alx/Byz[**Peter**], Alt/Peshitta[Simon Cephas (~JNT, MRD)]; Alx/Byz[**money**], Alt/Peshitta[a worldly substance (MRD)].

8:22 Alx[**the Lord**], Byz[God (DRA, KJV, MRD, NKJ, TLB)].

the Lord that, if possible, the intent of your heart may be forgiven you. ²³ For I see that you are in the gall of bitterness and in the bond of iniquity." ²⁴ And Simon answered, "Pray for me to the Lord, so that nothing of what you have said may come upon me."

²⁵ Now when they had testified and spoken the word of the Lord, they began to return to Jerusalem, preaching the gospel to many villages of the Samaritans.

²⁶ But an angel of the Lord said to Philip, "Get up and go toward the south to the road that goes down from Jerusalem to Gaza." This is a desert road. ²⁷ So he got up and went. And there was an Ethiopian eunuch, a court official of Kandake (queen) of the Ethiopians, who was in charge of all her treasure, and who had come to Jerusalem to worship. ²⁸ And he was returning and sitting in his chariot, and was reading the prophet Isaiah. ²⁹ And the Spirit said to Philip, "Go up and join this chariot." ³⁰ So Philip ran up to him, and heard him reading Isaiah the prophet, and asked, "Do you understand what you are reading?" ³¹ And he said, "How can I, if someone does not guide me?" And he invited Philip to come up and sit with him. ³² Now the passage of Scripture which he was reading was this:

> "He was led as a sheep to slaughter;
>> and as a lamb, speechless before its shearer,
>>> so he does not open his mouth.

³³
> In [his] humiliation justice was denied him.
>> Who can describe his generation?
>>> For his life is taken up from the earth."

³⁴ And the eunuch said to Philip, "Please tell me, of whom does the prophet say this, about himself or about someone else?" ³⁵ Then Philip opened his mouth, and beginning with this scripture he told him the good news of Jesus. ³⁶ And as they went along the road they came to some water; and the eunuch said, "Look, here is water! What prevents me from being baptized?" ⁽³⁷⁾ ³⁸ And he commanded the chariot to stop, and they both went

---

8:24 Alx/Major[**the Lord**], Byz[God (MRD, ~TLB)]; **you** *plural*.

8:25 Alx/Byz[**the Lord**], Minor[God (MRD)], Alt[*without textual foundation omits* (~TLB)]; Alx[**began to return...preaching**], Byz[returned...preaching (ASV, DRA, ESV, HCS, KJV, MRD, NAB, NIV, NJB, NKJ, NLT, NRS, ~REB, RSV, TEV, TLB)].

8:26 **go toward the south** *or* go at noon.

8:27 Alx/Byz[**Kandake** *Ethiopian title for queen*], Alt[*as a name* Candace (ASV, DRA, ESV, HCS, KJV, MRD, HAS, NAU, NET, NIV, NKJ, TLB) *other omits as redundant for* queen (TEV)]; Alx[**queen**], Byz[the queen (DRA, NAB, NKJ, NLT, TEV, TLB)]; Alx[**and who had come** *Greek* who had come], Minor[*omits* who (DRA, KJV, ~NIV, NJB, NKJ, RSV)].

8:28 Alx/Byz[**and he was returning**], Minor[but he was returning (~KJV, ~NJB)]; Alx/Byz[**and was reading**], Minor[*omits* and (HCS, JNT, KJV, NAB, NET, NIV, NJB, NKJ, NLT, NRS, RSV, TEV, TLB)].

8:29 Alx/Byz[**the Spirit**], Alt[*without textual foundation* the Holy Spirit (~MRD, ~NLT, ~TEV, ~TLB)].

8:30 Alx[**Isaiah the prophet**], Byz[the prophet Isaiah (DRA, HCS, KJV, NKJ, NLT, NRS, REB, TEV)], Alt[*without textual foundation omits* (~TLB)].

8:31 Alx[**if someone does not guide me**], Byz[unless someone guides me (ASV, DRA, ESV, HCS, JNT, KJV, MRD, NAB, NAS, NAU, NET, NIV, NJB, NKJ, NLT, NRS, RSV, TEV)], Alt[when no one guides me (REB, TLB)].

8:32 Alx[**speechless before its shearer**], Byz[before its shearer is silent (ASV, ESV, HCS, MRD, NAB, NAS, NAU, NET, NIV, NKJ, NLT, REB, RSV, TLB)].

8:32-33 **Isaiah 53:7-8 LXX**.

8:33 Alx/Byz[**In his humiliation**], Minor[*omits* his (DRA, ~JNT, ~MRD, NAS, NAU, NET, ~NLT, ~REB, ~TEV)]; Alx[**Who can describe**], Byz[But who can describe (KJV, MRD, NKJ, TLB)].

8:35 Alx/Byz[**Jesus**], Alt[our Lord Jesus (MRD)].

8:⁽³⁷⁾ Alx/Byz[*omits*], Minor[*adds* And Philip said, "If you believe with all your heart, you can." And he answered him, "I believe Jesus Christ is the Son of God" (ASV, DRA, HCS, KJV, MRD, NAS, NAU, NKJ, TLB)].

down into the water, Philip and the eunuch, and he baptized him. ³⁹ And when they came up out of the water, the Spirit of the Lord snatched Philip away. And the eunuch saw him no more, but went on his way rejoicing. ⁴⁰ But Philip found himself at Azotus, and as he passed through he kept preaching the gospel to all the towns until he came to Caesarea.

9 ¹ Now Saul, still breathing threats and murder against the disciples of the Lord, went to the high priest, ² and asked for letters from him to the synagogues at Damascus, so that if he found any belonging to the Way, both men and women, he might bring them bound to Jerusalem. ³ Now as he journeyed he approached Damascus, and suddenly a light out of heaven flashed around him. ⁴ And he fell to the ground and heard a voice saying to him, "Saul, Saul, why do you persecute me?" ⁵ And he said, "Who are you, Lord?" And he said, "I am Jesus whom you are persecuting, ⁶ but get up and enter the city, and it will be told you what you must do." ⁷ The men who were traveling with him stood speechless, hearing the voice but seeing no one. ⁸ Saul got up from the ground. But when his eyes were opened, he could see nothing. So they led him by the hand and brought him into Damascus. ⁹ And for three days he was without sight, and neither ate nor drank.

¹⁰ Now there was a disciple at Damascus named Ananias. And the Lord said to him in a vision, "Ananias." And he said, "Here I am, Lord." ¹¹ And the Lord said to him, "Get up and go to the street called Straight, and inquire at the house of Judas for a man from Tarsus named Saul, for he is praying, ¹² and [in a vision] he has seen a man named Ananias come in and lay [his] hands on him so that he might regain his sight." ¹³ But Ananias answered, "Lord, I heard from many about this man, how much harm he has done to your saints at Jerusalem. ¹⁴ And here he has authority from the chief priests to bind all who call on your name." ¹⁵ But the Lord said to him, "Go, for he is a chosen instrument of mine to carry my name before Gentiles, and also kings and the sons of Israel. ¹⁶ For I will show him how much he must suffer for the sake of my name." ¹⁷ So Ananias departed and entered the house. And after laying his hands on him said, "Brother Saul, the Lord, Jesus, who appeared to you on the road by which you were coming, has sent me so that you may regain your sight and be filled with the Holy Spirit." ¹⁸ And immediately there fell from his

---

8:39 Alx/Byz[**Spirit of the Lord**], Minor[Holy Spirit], Alt[*without textual foundation* Spirit (~REB)].

9:2 Alx/Byz[**the Way**], Minor[this Way (DRA, KJV, MRD, ~TLB)].

9:3 Alx[**out of heaven**], Byz[from heaven (DRA, ESV, HCS, JNT, KJV, MRD, NAB, NAS, NAU, NET, NIV, NJB, NKJ, NLT, NRS, REB, RSV, TEV, TLB)].

9:5 Alx[**he said, "I am Jesus**], Byz[the Lord said, "I am Jesus (KJV, NKJ)], Minor[the Lord said, I am Jesus the Nazarene (MRD)]; Minor[*adds to the end of the verse or to verse 4* It is hard for you to kick against the goads (DRA, KJV, MRD, NKJ)]; *compare* Acts 26:14 *and note.*

9:6 Alx/Byz[**but get up and enter**], Alt/Vulgate[And he, trembling and astonished, said, "Lord, what will you have me do?" And the Lord said to him, "Get up and enter (DRA, KJV, NKJ)]; *DRA begins verse 7 after* have me do.

9:8 Alx[**but when his eyes**], Byz[and when his eyes (ASV, DRA, ~ESV, ~HCS, KJV, ~MRD, ~NAS, ~NAU, NKJ, ~NRS, RSV, ~TEV, ~TLB)]; Alx[**he could see nothing**], Byz[he could see no one (KJV, NKJ)].

9:11 Alx/Byz[**Get up and go** *Greek* Getting up, go], Minor[Get up. Go (~NIV, ~NLT, ~REB, ~TLB)]; Alx/Byz[**Tarsus**], Alt/Peshitta[the city of Tarsus (MRD)].

9:12 Alx/Byz[**in a vision**], Minor[omits (ASV, DRA, NJB, RSV)]; Alx[**his hands** *Greek* the hands], Byz[a hand (KJV, MRD, NKJ)]; Alt[*omits entire verse*].

9:13 Alx[**Lord, I heard**], Byz[Lord, I have heard (ASV, DRA, ESV, HCS, ~JNT, KJV, MRD, NAB, NAS, NAU, NET, NIV, NJB, NKJ, NLT, NRS, REB, RSV, ~TEV, TLB)].

9:15 Alx/Byz[**Gentiles**], Minor[the Gentiles (ASV, DRA, ESV, JNT, KJV, MRD, NAS, NAU, NIV, NLT, REB, RSV, TLB)]; Alx[**and also**], Byz[and (ASV, DRA, ESV, ~HCS, ~JNT, KJV, MRD, ~NAB, NAS, NAU, NET, NIV, NJB, ~NKJ, NLT, NRS, REB, RSV, TEV, TLB)].

9:17 Alx/Byz[**the Lord, Jesus**], Major[*omits* Jesus].

9:18 Alx/Byz[**he regained his sight**], Minor[*adds* immediately (KJV, NKJ, ~TLB)].

eyes something like scales, and he regained his sight. And he got up and was baptized, [19] and he took food and was strengthened.

Now for several days he was with the disciples in Damascus. [20] And immediately he began to proclaim Jesus in the synagogues, saying, "He is the Son of God." [21] All those who heard him were amazed, and said, "Is this not he who made havoc in Jerusalem of those who called on this name, and who had come here for the purpose of bringing them bound before the chief priests?" [22] But Saul increased all the more in strength, and confounded [the] Jews who lived at Damascus by proving that this is the Christ.

[23] When many days had passed, the Jews plotted to kill him, [24] but their plot became known to Saul. But they were also watching the gates day and night, to kill him. [25] But his disciples took him by night and let him down through an opening in the wall, lowering him in a basket.

[26] And when he came to Jerusalem, he tried to join the disciples. But they were all afraid of him, not believing that he was a disciple. [27] But Barnabas took him and brought him to the apostles. And he declared to them how he had seen the Lord on the road, and that he had spoken to him, and how he had preached boldly at Damascus in the name of Jesus. [28] And he was with them moving about freely in Jerusalem, speaking out boldly in the name of the Lord. [29] And he was talking and arguing with the Hellenists. But they were seeking to kill him. [30] But when the brothers learned of it, they brought him down to Caesarea and sent him off to Tarsus.

[31] So the church throughout all Judea and Galilee and Samaria enjoyed peace and was built up. And going on in the fear of the Lord and in the comfort of the Holy Spirit, it continued to increase.

[32] Now as Peter went through all those regions, he came down also to the saints who lived at Lydda. [33] There he found a man named Aeneas, who had been bedridden for eight years and was paralyzed. [34] Peter said to him, "Aeneas, Jesus Christ heals you. Get up and make your bed." Immediately he got up. [35] And all who lived at Lydda and Sharon saw him, and they turned to the Lord.

9:19 Alx/Major[**19 and he took food and was strengthened**], Byz[and he took food and was strengthened 19]; Alx/Byz[**several days** or certain days], Minor[enough days]; Alx[**he was with the disciples**], Byz[Saul was with the disciples (HCS, JNT, KJV, NIV, NKJ, NLT, TEV)]; Alx/Major[**in Damascus**], Byz[who are in Damascus (~ASV, ~DRA, ~KJV, ~NAS, ~NAU)].

9:20 Alx/Byz[**Jesus**], Major[Christ (KJV, NKJ)].

9:22 Alx/Byz[**strength**], Minor[adds in the word (NLT, TEV, TLB)]; Alx/Byz[**the Jews**], Minor[Jews (~MRD)].

9:24 Alx[**But they were also watching**], Byz[And they were watching (ASV, DRA, ESV, HCS, JNT, KJV, MRD, NAB, NIV, NJB, NKJ, NLT, NRS, REB, RSV, TEV, TLB)].

9:25 Alx[**his disciples**], Byz[the disciples (DRA, KJV, MRD, NJB, NKJ, NLT, REB)]; **through an opening in the wall** Greek through the wall.

9:26 Alx[**when he came**], Byz[when Saul came (KJV, NKJ, NLT, TEV)]; Alx[**to Jerusalem**], Byz[in Jerusalem (HCS, ~JNT, NAB, NET, NLT, ~REB, TLB)].

9:28 Alx/Byz[**moving about freely** Greek going in and going out], Major[going in (~TLB)]; Alx/Byz[**Jerusalem, speaking...**], Minor[Jerusalem, 29 speaking... (ASV, KJV, MRD, NKJ, REB, RSV, TLB)]; Alx[**the Lord**], Byz[the Lord Jesus (KJV, NKJ)], Alt[Jesus (MRD)].

9:29 Alx/Byz[**Hellenists** Greek speaking Jews], Minor[Greeks (DRA, ~KJV)].

9:31 Alx[**church... was... it**], Byz[churches... were... they (KJV, NJB, NKJ)].

9:32 Alx/Byz[**Peter**], Alt/Peshitta[Simon (MRD)], Alt[without textual foundation Cephas (~JNT)]; Alx/Byz[**through all those regions** or among all the people], Alt/Peshitta[about the cities (MRD)].

9:34 Alx/Byz[**Peter**], Alt/Peshitta[Simon (MRD)], Alt[without textual foundation Cephas (~JNT)]; Alx[**Jesus Christ**], Byz[Jesus the Christ (JNT, MRD, NET, NKJ)], Alt[the Lord Jesus Christ (DRA)].

9:35 Alx/Byz[**Sharon** or Saron], Major[Assaron].

36 Now there was at Joppa a certain disciple named Tabitha (which is translated Dorcas). She was full of good works and acts of charity. **37** And at that time she fell sick and died. And when they had washed her, they laid [her] in an upper room. **38** Since Lydda was near Joppa, the disciples, having heard that Peter was there, sent two men to him, imploring him, "Please come to us without delay." **39** So Peter rose and went with them. And when he arrived, they took him to the upper room. All the widows stood beside him, weeping and showing the tunics and other garments that Dorcas made while she was with them. **40** But Peter sent them all out and knelt down and prayed. Then turning to the body, he said, "Tabitha, arise." And she opened her eyes, and when she saw Peter, she sat up. **41** And he gave her his hand and raised her up. Then calling the saints and widows he presented her alive. **42** It became known all over Joppa, and many believed in the Lord. **43** And he stayed for many days in Joppa with a tanner named Simon.

10 **1** Now at Caesarea there was a man named Cornelius, a centurion of what was known as the Italian Cohort, **2** a devout man and one who feared God with all his household, and gave alms generously to the people and prayed to God continually. **3** About the ninth hour of the day he clearly saw in a vision an angel of God who had just come in and said to him, "Cornelius!" **4** And he stared at him in terror, and said, "What is it, Lord?" And he said to him, "Your prayers and alms have ascended as a memorial in front of God. **5** Now send men to Joppa, and bring a certain Simon who is called Peter. **6** He is staying with a tanner named Simon, whose house is by the sea." **7** When the angel who spoke to him had left, he called two of the house servants and a devout soldier of those who were his personal attendants, **8** and after he had explained everything to them, he sent them to Joppa.

9 The next day, as they were on their journey and approaching the city, Peter went up on the housetop about the sixth hour to pray. **10** And he became hungry and was

---

9:36 Alx/Byz[**36 Now…Tabitha**], Alt[*without textual foundation* Now…Tabitha 36 (~JNT)]; Alx/Byz[**Joppa**], Alt/Peshitta[the city of Joppa (MRD, TLB)]; **Tabitha** *Aramaic* gazelle; **Dorcas** *Greek* gazelle.

9:37 Alx/Byz[**they laid her**], Minor[*omits* her (NAS, NAU, NET, NIV, NLT, REB, TEV)].

9:38 Alx/Byz[**Lydda**], Alt/Peshitta[the city of Lydda (MRD)]; Alx/Byz[**Peter**], Alt/Peshitta[Simon (MRD)], Alt[*without textual foundation* Cephas (~JNT)]; Alx/Byz[**two men**], Major[*omits*]; Alx[**imploring him, "Please come to us**], Byz[imploring him to come to them (DRA, KJV, MRD, NKJ, TLB)].

9:39 Alx/Byz[**Peter**], Alt/Peshitta[Simon (MRD)], Alt[*without textual foundation* Cephas (~JNT)]; Alx/Byz[**Dorcas**], Alt/Peshitta[Tabitha (JNT, MRD)].

9:40 Alx/Byz[**Peter…Peter**], Alt/Peshitta[Simon…Simon (MRD)], Alt[*without textual foundation* Cephas…Cephas (~JNT)]; Alx[**and knelt**], Byz[*omits* and (DRA, HCS, JNT, NET, ~NIV, ~NLT, ~TLB)]; Alx/Byz[**Tabitha, arise**], Minor[*adds* in the name of our Lord Jesus Christ], Alt[*without textual foundation* Dorcas, arise (~TLB)].

9:42 Alx/Byz[**Joppa**], Alt/Peshitta[the city (MRD, NLT, TLB)].

10:1 Alx/Byz[**there was a man** *Greek* a man], Major[there was a man].

10:3 Alx[**About the ninth hour** *Greek* Around about the ninth hour], Byz[About the ninth hour].

10:4 Alx[**in front of God**], Byz[before God (ASV, ESV, HCS, KJV, MRD, NAB, NAS, NAU, NET, NIV, ~NJB, NKJ, ~NLT, NRS, REB, RSV, ~TEV, ~TLB)].

10:5 Alx/Byz[**Joppa**], Alt/Peshitta[the city of Joppa (MRD)]; Alx[**a certain Simon**], Byz[Simon (HCS, ~JNT, MRD, ~NAS, ~NAU, ~NET, ~NIV, ~NJB, NKJ, ~NLT, ~REB, ~TLB)]; Alx/Byz[**Peter**], Alt/Peshitta[Cephas (JNT, MRD)].

10:6 Alx/Byz[*text*], Minor[*adds* He will tell you what you must do (DRA, KJV, NKJ)].

10:7 Alx[**angel who spoke to him**], Byz[angel who spoke to Cornelius (~JNT, KJV, ~NET, ~NIV, ~NJB, ~NKJ, ~NLT, ~TEV, ~TLB)]; Alx[**the house servants**], Byz[his house servants (ASV, DRA, ESV, HCS, JNT, KJV, MRD, NAB, NAS, NAU, NET, NIV, NKJ, NLT, NRS, REB, RSV, TEV, TLB)].

10:9 Alx/Byz[**Peter**], Alt/Peshitta[Simon (MRD)], Alt[*without textual foundation* Cephas (~JNT)]; Alx/Byz[**sixth hour**], Minor[ninth hour].

10:10 Alx[**he came into a trance**], Byz[he fell into a trance (ASV, ESV, JNT, KJV, MRD, NAB, NAS,

desiring something to eat. But while they were preparing the food, he came into a trance [11] and he saw heaven opened, and something descending, like a great sheet, let down by four corners to the earth. [12] In it were all kinds of four-footed animals and reptiles of the earth and birds of the air. [13] A voice came to him, "Get up, Peter. Kill and eat!" [14] But Peter said, "No, Lord; for I have never eaten anything that is common and unclean." [15] And the voice came to him again a second time, "What God has cleansed, you must not call common." [16] This happened three times, and immediately the thing was taken up to heaven.

[17] Now while Peter was inwardly perplexed as to what the vision which he had seen might mean, behold, the men that were sent by Cornelius, having made inquiry for Simon's house, appeared at the gate. [18] They were calling out, asking whether Simon who was known as Peter was staying there. [19] While Peter was reflecting on the vision, the Spirit said [to him], "Behold, three men are looking for you. [20] But get up, go downstairs and accompany them without hesitation, for I have sent them myself." [21] And Peter went down to the men and said, "Behold, I am the one you are looking for. What is the reason you have come?" [22] And they said, "Cornelius, a centurion, a righteous and God-fearing man, who is well spoken of by the whole Jewish nation, was directed by a holy angel to send for you to come to his house, and to hear what you have to say." [23] So he invited them in to be his guests.

NAU, NIV, NJB, NKJ, NLT, NRS, REB, RSV, TLB)].

10:11 Alx[**something descending**], Byz[something descending on him (KJV)], Minor[something (JNT, MRD, NIV, NJB, NKJ, NLT, TLB)]; Alx[**let down by four corners**], Byz[bound at four corners, and let down (KJV, MRD, NKJ, ~REB)].

10:12 Alx[**four-footed animals and reptiles of the earth**], Byz[four-footed animals of the earth, and wild beasts, and reptiles (KJV, NKJ)].

10:13 Alx/Byz[**Peter**], Alt/Peshitta[Simon (MRD)], Alt[*without textual foundation* Cephas (~JNT)].

10:14 Alx/Byz[**Peter**], Alt/Peshitta[Simon (MRD)], Alt[*without textual foundation* Cephas (~JNT)]; Alx[**common and unclean**], Byz[common or unclean (ESV, JNT, KJV, NIV, NJB, NKJ, NRS, REB, RSV, TEV, ~TLB)].

10:16 Alx[**immediately**], Byz[again (~HCS, KJV, ~MRD, ~NAB, NKJ, ~REB, ~TEV, TLB)]; *Metzger notes that* **immediately** *should be in brackets.*

10:17 Alx/Byz[**Peter**], Alt/Peshitta[Simon (MRD)], Alt[*without textual foundation* Cephas (~JNT)]; Alx[**behold**], Byz[and behold (Metzger)], Minor[*omits* (HCS, JNT, MRD, NAB, NET, NIV, NJB, NLT, ~NRS, REB, TEV, ~TLB)]; Alx[**by Cornelius**], Byz[from Cornelius (DRA, ~JNT, KJV, NKJ, REB)].

10:18 Alx/Byz[**asking**], Minor[asked (ASV, DRA, ~ESV, ~JNT, KJV, MRD, ~NET, ~NJB, NKJ, NLT, ~NRS, REB, ~RSV, TEV)]; Alx/Byz[**Peter**], Alt/Peshitta[Cephas (JNT, MRD)].

10:19 Alx/Byz[**Peter**], Alt/Peshitta[Simon (MRD)], Alt[*without textual foundation* Cephas (~JNT)]; Alx/Byz[**the Spirit said to him**], Minor[*omits* to him (JNT, TEV)]; Alx/Byz[**three men**], Major[men (NJB, REB)], Minor[two men].

10:20 Alx/Byz[**But get up**], Alt[So get up (DRA, KJV, NAB, NIV, NKJ, ~NRS, TEV)], Alt[*without textual foundation* Get up (~ESV, ~HCS, ~JNT, ~MRD, ~NJB, ~NLT, ~REB, ~RSV, ~TLB)].

10:21 Alx/Byz[**Peter**], Alt/Peshitta[Simon (MRD)], Alt[*without textual foundation* Cephas (~JNT)]; Alx/Byz[**And Peter went down**], Minor[Then Peter went down (DRA, HCS, ~JNT, KJV, MRD, NAB, ~NAU, ~NET, ~NIV, ~NJB, NKJ, ~NRS, ~REB, ~TEV, ~TLB)]; Alx/Byz[**the men**], Minor[*adds* who had been sent to him from Cornelius (KJV, NKJ)]; Alx/Byz[**What is the reason**], Minor[What do you want? What is the reason (~TLB)].

10:22 Alx/Byz[**they said**], Minor[*adds* to him (MRD, TLB)]; Alx/Byz[**Cornelius**], Minor[a certain Cornelius (MRD)].

10:23 Alx/Byz[**So he invited them in**], Minor[Then Peter brought them in (~DRA, ~HCS, ~JNT, ~KJV, ~MRD, ~NET, ~NIV, ~NJB, ~NKJ, ~NLT, ~NRS, ~REB, ~TEV, ~TLB)]; Alx/Byz[**he rose and went off** *Greek* rising, he went off], Major[Peter went off (KJV, NIV, ~NJB, NKJ, ~NLT, ~REB, ~TLB)].

And the next day he rose and went off with them, and some of the brothers from Joppa accompanied him. 24 And on the following day he entered Caesarea. Now Cornelius was expecting them and had called together his relatives and close friends. 25 When Peter entered, Cornelius met him and fell down at his feet and worshipped him. 26 But Peter raised him up, saying, "Stand up. I too am just a man." 27 And as he talked with him, he went in and found many people assembled. 28 And he said to them, "You yourselves know how unlawful it is for a Jew to associate with a foreigner or to visit him. But God has shown me that I should not call any man common or unclean. 29 So when I was sent for, I came without raising any objection. I ask then why you sent for me." 30 Cornelius said, "Four days ago to this hour, I was praying in my house during the ninth hour. And behold, a man stood before me in shining garments, 31 and he said, 'Cornelius, your prayer has been heard and your alms have been remembered before God. 32 Send therefore to Joppa and ask for Simon who is called Peter. He is lodging in the house of Simon, a tanner, by the sea.' 33 So I sent for you immediately, and you have been kind enough to come. Now therefore we are all here present in the sight of God, to hear all that you have been commanded by the Lord."

34 And opening his mouth, Peter said: "I most certainly understand now that God is not one to show partiality, 35 but in every nation the man who fears him and does what is right is welcome to him. 36 You know the word [which] he sent to Israel, preaching good news of peace through Jesus Christ – he is Lord of all! 37 You know what has happened throughout all Judea, beginning from Galilee after the baptism which John preached: 38 how God anointed Jesus of Nazareth with the Holy Spirit and with power, and how he went

---

10:24 Alx[**And on the following day** or But on the following day], Byz[And on the following day]; Alx[**he entered Caesarea**], Byz[they entered Caesarea (ASV, ESV, KJV, MRD, NJB, NKJ, NLT, NRS, ~REB, RSV, TLB)].

10:25 Alx/Byz[**Peter**], Alt/Peshitta[Simon (MRD)], Alt[*without textual foundation* Cephas (~JNT)].

10:26 Alx/Byz[**Peter**], Alt/Peshitta[Simon (MRD)], Alt[*without textual foundation* Cephas (~JNT)]; Alx/Byz[**Stand up**], Minor[What are you doing?].

10:27 Alx/Byz[**as he talked with him**], Minor[*omits*].

10:28 Alx/Byz[**You yourselves know**], Minor[*adds* very well (~JNT, ~NIV, ~REB, TEV)]; Alx/Byz[**a foreigner**], Minor[a foreign man (~NJB)].

10:29 Alx/Byz[**I was sent for**], Minor[*adds* by you (~KJV, MRD, NET, REB, TEV)].

10:30 Alx[**Four days ago**], Byz[*adds* I was fasting (KJV, MRD, NKJ)], Minor[Three days ago (JNT, REB, TEV)]; Alx/Byz[**to this hour** or until this hour], Alt[at this hour (ESV, HCS, JNT, ~MRD, NAB, NET, NIV, NJB, NLT, NRS, REB, RSV, TEV, TLB)]; Alx[**during the ninth hour** *Greek* during the ninth], Byz[during the ninth hour].

10:31 Alx/Byz[**and he said** *Greek* and he says], Alt/Peshitta[*adds* to me (MRD)], Alt/Vulgate[*omits* (DRA, NAB)].

10:32 Alx/Byz[**Joppa**], Alt/Peshitta[the city of Joppa (MRD)]; Alx/Byz[**Peter**], Alt/Peshitta[Cephas (JNT, MRD)]; Alx[*text*], Byz[*adds* Who, when he comes, will speak to you (KJV, ~MRD, NKJ)].

10:33 Alx/Byz[**So I sent for you immediately**], Minor[*adds* begging you to come to us]; Alx/Byz[**kind enough to come**], Minor[*adds* quickly (TLB)]; Alx/Byz[**Now therefore we are all here present**], Minor[Now behold we are all here (~JNT, MRD, ~NIV, ~NJB, ~NLT, ~TEV, ~TLB)]; Alx/Byz[**in the sight of God** or before God], Minor[before you (DRA, MRD, NJB)], Alt[*without textual foundation* before the Lord (~TLB)]; Alx/Byz[**to hear**], Minor[wanting to hear from you (~TEV, ~TLB)]; Alx[**by the Lord**], Byz[by God (~KJV, ~MRD, ~NJB, NKJ, ~TLB)], Minor[from… (~ASV, ~JNT, ~KJV, ~MRD, ~NET, ~NIV, ~NJB, ~NLT, ~NRS, ~REB, ~TEV, ~TLB)].

10:34 Alx/Byz[**Peter**], Alt/Peshitta[Simon (MRD)], Alt[*without textual foundation* Cephas (~JNT)].

10:36 Alx/Byz[**You know**], Minor[For you know (MRD)]; Alx/Byz[**You know the word which he sent**], Minor[*omits* which (DRA, HCS, NET, NIV, NJB, ~NLT, NRS, REB, TEV, ~TLB)], Alt[*without textual foundation* the word God sent (~DRA, ~KJV, ~NJB, ~NKJ) *others without textual foundation omit* he sent (~NLT, ~TLB)].

10:37 Alx[**beginning** *masculine*], Byz[beginning *neuter*], Minor[for it began (DRA)], Alt[*because of masculine form, adds* Jesus of Nazareth *from next verse* (NJB)].

about doing good and healing all who were oppressed by the devil, for God was with him. [39] We are witnesses of all that he did both in the country of the Jews and [in] Jerusalem, whom also they put to death by hanging him on a tree. [40] But God raised him up [on] the third day and caused him to be seen, [41] not to all the people but to us who were chosen by God as witnesses, who ate and drank with him after he rose from the dead. [42] And he commanded us to preach to the people, and to testify that this is the one appointed by God to be judge of the living and the dead. [43] Of him all the prophets bear witness that everyone who believes in him receives forgiveness of sins through his name."

[44] While Peter was still speaking these words, the Holy Spirit fell on all who heard the message. [45] All the circumcised believers who came with Peter were amazed, because the gift of the Holy Spirit had been poured out even on the Gentiles. [46] For they heard them speaking in tongues and praising God. Then Peter said, [47] "Can anyone refuse the water for these people to be baptized who have received the Holy Spirit as we have?" [48] And he ordered them to be baptized in the name of Jesus Christ. Then they asked him to stay on for a few days.

11 [1] Now the apostles and the brothers who were throughout Judea heard that the Gentiles also had received the word of God. [2] But when Peter went up to Jerusalem, the circumcised believers criticized him, [3] saying, "You went to uncircumcised men and ate with them." [4] But Peter began and explained to them in order: [5] "I was in the city of Joppa praying. And in a trance I saw a vision, something descending like a great sheet, let down from heaven by four corners. And it came down to me. [6] And when I looked into it I saw four-footed animals of the earth, wild beasts, reptiles, and birds of the air. [7] And I also heard a voice saying to me, 'Get up, Peter. Kill and eat!' [8] But I said,

---

10:39 Alx/Byz[**in Jerusalem**], Minor[omits in]; Alx/Byz[**whom also**], Minor[omits also (DRA, ESV, ~HCS, JNT, KJV, MRD, NAB, NET, NIV, NKJ, NLT, NRS, REB, RSV, ~TEV, ~TLB)].

10:40 Alx[**on the third day** or in the third day], Byz[omits on (ASV, DRA, KJV)], Minor[after three days (TEV, TLB)].

10:41 Alx/Byz[**with him after he rose from the dead**], Minor[with him and accompanied him for forty days after he rose from the dead

10:42 Alx[**this is the one**], Byz[he is the one (ESV, HCS, MRD, NAB, NET, NIV, ~NJB, ~NLT, NRS, REB, RSV, TEV, ~TLB)].

10:44 Alx/Byz[**Peter**], Alt/Peshitta[Simon (MRD)], Alt[without textual foundation Cephas (~JNT)].

10:45 Alx/Byz[**All...who** or As many...who], Minor[omits All (DRA, ESV, HCS, MRD, NAB, NET, NIV, NLT, NRS, REB, RSV, TEV, TLB)]; Alx/Byz[**Peter**], Alt/Peshitta[him (MRD)], Alt[without textual foundation Cephas (~JNT)].

10:46 Alx/Byz[**tongues** or languages], Minor[other tongues (HCS, MRD, NJB, ~REB, TEV)]; Alx/Major[**Then Peter said 47**], Byz[47 Then Peter said (DRA, ~MRD, ~TLB)]; Alx/Byz[**Peter**], Alt/Peshitta[Simon (MRD)], Alt[without textual foundation Cephas (~JNT)].

10:47 Alx[**as we have**], Byz[just as we have (ESV, HCS, JNT, NAB, NAS, NAU, NET, NIV, NJB, NKJ, NLT, NRS, REB, RSV, TEV, TLB)].

10:48 Alx[**Jesus Christ**], Byz[the Lord (KJV, NKJ)], Minor[the Lord Jesus Christ (DRA, MRD)]; Alx/Byz[**Then they asked**], Alt[49 Then they asked (NAB)], Alt[without textual foundation Then Cornelius asked (~NLT, ~TLB)].

11:1 Alx/Byz[**the word of God**], Minor[adds and they glorified God].

11:2 Alx[**But when**], Byz[And when (ASV, DRA, ~ESV, ~HCS, KJV, MRD, ~NAB, NAS, NAU, ~NET, ~NIV, NJB, NKJ, ~NRS, REB, ~RSV, ~TEV)]; Alx/Byz[**Peter**], Alt/Peshitta[Simon (MRD)], Alt[without textual foundation Cephas (~JNT)]; **circumcised believers criticized him** Greek circumcised criticized him.

11:3 Alx/Byz[**You went**], Minor[He went (MRD)]; **saying, "You went to uncircumcised men and ate with them."** could be translated saying, "Why did you go to uncircumcised men and eat with them?"

11:4 Alx/Byz[**Peter**], Alt/Peshitta[Simon (MRD)], Alt[without textual foundation Cephas (~JNT)].

11:6 Alx/Byz[**wild beasts**], Alt[omits (MRD, TLB)].

11:7 Alx[**also**], Byz[omits (ESV, JNT, KJV, MRD, NIV, NJB, NKJ, NLT, REB, RSV, TEV, TLB)];

'No, Lord; for common or unclean things have never entered my mouth.' ⁹ But a voice answered a second time from heaven, 'What God has cleansed you must not call common.' ¹⁰ This happened three times, and all was drawn up again into heaven. ¹¹ And behold, at that moment three men appeared at the house in which we were staying, having been sent to me from Caesarea. ¹² The Spirit told me to go with them, making no distinction. These six brothers also went with me, and we entered the man's house. ¹³ And he told us how he had seen [the] angel standing in his house and saying, 'Send to Joppa and bring Simon, who is also called Peter. ¹⁴ He will declare to you a message by which you will be saved, you and all your household.' ¹⁵ As I began to speak, the Holy Spirit fell on them just as on us at the beginning. ¹⁶ And I remembered the word of the Lord, how he said, 'John baptized with water, but you will be baptized with the Holy Spirit.' ¹⁷ So if God gave them the same gift as he gave us, who believed in the Lord Jesus Christ, who was I that I could oppose God?" ¹⁸ When they heard this, they quieted down and glorified God, saying, "Then God has also granted to the Gentiles the repentance unto life."

¹⁹ Now those who were scattered because of the persecution that arose in connection with Stephen traveled as far as Phoenicia and Cyprus and Antioch, speaking the word to no one except Jews. ²⁰ But there were some of them, men of Cyprus and Cyrene, who came into Antioch and began speaking to the Hellenists also, preaching the Lord Jesus. ²¹ The hand of the Lord was with them, and a great number believed and turned to the Lord. ²² News of this reached the ears of the church at Jerusalem, and they sent Barnabas [to go] as far as Antioch. ²³ When he arrived and saw the grace [which was] of God, he was glad and encouraged them all to remain true to the Lord with all their hearts. ²⁴ For he was a good man, full of the Holy Spirit and of faith. And a great number of people were brought to the Lord. ²⁵ And he went to Tarsus to look for Saul. ²⁶ And when he had found him, he

---

Alx/Byz[**Peter**], Alt/Peshitta[Simon (MRD)], Alt[*without textual foundation* Cephas (~JNT)].

11:8 Alx[**common or unclean**], Byz[any common or unclean (~ASV, ~DRA, ~ESV, ~HCS, ~JNT, ~KJV, MRD, ~NAB, ~NAS, ~NAU, ~NET, ~NIV, ~NJB, ~NKJ, NLT, ~NRS, ~REB, ~RSV, ~TEV, TLB)].

11:9 Alx[**a voice answered**], Byz[*adds* me (KJV, MRD, NKJ)].

11:11 Alx[**we were**], Byz[I was (DRA, JNT, KJV, MRD, NIV, NKJ, REB, TEV, TLB)].

11:12 Alx[**making no distinction**], Byz[with no doubting (DRA, HCS, ~JNT, KJV, ~MRD, ~NAS, ~NAU, ~NET, ~NIV, ~NJB, NKJ, ~NLT, ~TEV, ~TLB)], Minor[*omits* (REB)].

11:13 Alx[**And he told us** *or* But he told us], Byz[And he told us]; Alx/Byz[**the angel**], Minor[an angel (DRA, KJV, MRD, NET, NIV, NJB, NKJ, NLT, REB, TEV, TLB)]; Alx[**and saying**], Byz[*adds* to him (DRA, KJV, MRD, NKJ, NLT, TEV, TLB)]; Alx[**Send to Joppa**], Byz[Send men to Joppa (KJV, ~NAB, NKJ, NLT, ~TEV, TLB)], Alt/Peshitta[Send to the city of Joppa (MRD)]; Alx/Byz[**Peter**], Alt/Peshitta[Cephas (JNT, MRD)].

11:16 **with** *or* in; **the word of the Lord** Acts 1:5.

11:17 Alx/Byz[**if God gave**], Minor[if he gave]; Alx[**who was I**], Byz[but who was I]; Alx/Byz[**oppose God**], Minor[*adds* lest he should give to them the Holy Spirit after they believed in him].

11:18 Alx[**Then God has also granted**], Byz[Then, indeed, God has also granted (~NJB, ~TLB)]; **also granted to the Gentiles** *or* granted even to the Gentiles.

11:20 Alx[**came into Antioch**], Byz[entered into Antioch (DRA)]; Alx/Byz[**Hellenists** *or* Grecians], Minor[Greeks (ASV, DRA, JNT, MRD, NAB, NAS, NAU, NET, NIV, NJB, ~NLT, ~REB, RSV, ~TEV, TLB)]; Alx[**also**], Byz[*omits* (HCS, KJV, MRD, NKJ, NLT)].

11:22 Alx/Byz[**to go**], Minor[*omits* (ASV, DRA, ~ESV, ~JNT, ~MRD, ~NAS, ~NAU, ~NET, ~NIV, ~NJB, ~NKJ, ~NLT, ~NRS, ~REB, ~RSV, ~TEV, ~TLB)].

11:23 Alx[**grace which was of God**], Byz[grace of God (ASV, DRA, ESV, HCS, JNT, KJV, MRD, NAB, NAS, NAU, NET, NIV, NKJ, ~NLT, NRS, ~REB, RSV, ~TLB)]; Alx/Byz[**true to the Lord**], Minor[true in the Lord (DRA)].

11:25 Alx[**he went to Tarsus**], Byz[Barnabas went to Tarsus (DRA, ESV, JNT, KJV, NET, NIV, NJB, NKJ, NLT, NRS, RSV, TEV, TLB)]; Alx/Byz[**Saul**], Alt[*without textual foundation* Paul (~TLB)].

11:26 Alx/Major[**26 and when he had found him, he brought him to Antioch** *Greek* 26 and finding, he brough him to Antioch], Minor[and when he had found him, he brought him to Antioch 26 *Greek* and finding him, he brough him to Antioch 26 (DRA)]; Alx[**even for a whole year**], Byz[*omits*

brought him to Antioch. And even for a whole year they gathered in the assembly and taught great numbers of people. And the disciples were called Christians for the first time in Antioch.

27 Now at this time some prophets came down from Jerusalem to Antioch. 28 One of them named Agabus stood up and foretold by the Spirit that there would be a great famine all over the world. This took place in the reign of Claudius. 29 And the disciples determined, each according to his ability, to send relief for the brothers living in Judea. 30 And this they did, sending it to the elders by Barnabas and Saul.

12 1 Now about that time Herod the king laid hands on some who belonged to the church in order to persecute them. 2 He had James the brother of John put to death with the sword. 3 And when he saw that it pleased the Jews, he proceeded to arrest Peter also. This was during [the] days of Unleavened Bread. 4 When he had seized him, he put him in prison, and delivered him to four squads of soldiers to guard him, intending after the Passover to bring him out to the people. 5 So Peter was kept in prison, but earnest prayer for him was made to God by the church.

6 The very night when Herod was about to bring him out, Peter was sleeping between two soldiers, bound with two chains, and sentries before the door were guarding the prison. 7 And behold, an angel of the Lord suddenly appeared, and a light shone in the cell. And he struck Peter's side and woke him up, saying, "Get up quickly." And the chains fell off his hands. 8 And the angel said to him, "Dress yourself and put on your sandals." And he did so. And he said to him, "Wrap your cloak around you and follow me." 9 So he went out and followed. And he did not know that what was done by the angel was real, but thought he was seeing a vision. 10 When they had passed the first and the second guard, they came to the iron gate leading into the city. It opened for them by itself, and they went out and passed on through one street. And immediately the angel left him. 11 When Peter came to himself, he said, "Now I know for sure that [the] Lord has sent his angel and rescued me from the hand of Herod and from all that the Jewish people were expecting." 12 When he realized this, he went to the house of Mary, the mother of John who was also

---

even (DRA, ESV, HCS, JNT, KJV, MRD, NAB, NAS, NAU, NET, NIV, NJB, NKJ, NLT, NRS, REB, RSV, TEV, TLB)]; Alx/Byz[**in the assembly**], Major[with the assembly (ASV, ESV, HCS, JNT, KJV, NAB, NAS, NAU, NET, NIV, NKJ, NLT, NRS, RSV, TEV, ~TLB)]; Alx[**for the first time**], Byz[first (ASV, DRA, ESV, HCS, KJV, MRD, NAB, NAS, NAU, NET, NIV, NJB, NKJ, NLT, NRS, REB, TEV, TLB)]; **congregation** or church.

11:28 Alx/Byz[**foretold** or signified], Minor[was foretelling (NAS, NAU)]; Alx[**This took place**], Byz[And this took place (MRD, NAB, NAS, NAU, ~NJB, NKJ, NRS, ~REB, RSV)]; Alx[**Claudius**], Byz[adds Caesar (~JNT, KJV, MRD, ~NJB, NKJ, ~TEV)].

12:1 Alx/Byz[**the church**], Minor[adds in Judea].

12:3 Alx[**And when he saw** or But when he saw], Byz[And when he saw]; Alx/Byz[**Peter**], Alt/Peshitta[Simon Cephas (~JNT, MRD)]; Alx/Byz[**This was during the days of Unleavened Bread 4**], Minor[omits the], Alt[4 This was during the days of Unleavened Bread (NJB)].

12:4 Alx/Byz[**Passover**], Alt[without textual foundation Easter (~KJV)]; Alx/Byz[**the people**], Alt/Peshitta[adds of the Jews (MRD, ~TLB)].

12:5 Alx/Byz[**Peter**], Alt/Peshitta[Simon (MRD)], Alt[without textual foundation Cephas (~JNT)]; Alx[**earnest**], Byz[constant (DRA, KJV, MRD, NJB, NKJ)]; Alx[**for him** Greek concerning him], Byz[for him Greek on his behalf (JNT, MRD, NAB, ~TLB)].

12:6 Alx/Byz[**Peter**], Alt/Peshitta[Simon (MRD)], Alt[without textual foundation Cephas (~JNT)].

12:7 Alx/Byz[**struck Peter's side**], Minor[nudged Peter's side (~JNT, ~MRD, ~NAB, ~NJB, ~NRS, ~REB, ~TEV, ~TLB)]; Alx/Byz[**Peter's**], Alt/Peshitta[his (MRD)], Alt[without textual foundation Cephas' (~JNT)].

12:9 Alx[**he went out and followed**], Byz[adds him (DRA, ESV, JNT, KJV, MRD, NAB, NET, ~NIV, NJB, NKJ, ~NLT, NRS, ~REB, RSV, TEV, ~TLB)].

12:11 Alx/Byz[**Peter**], Alt/Peshitta[Simon (MRD)], Alt[without textual foundation Cephas (~JNT)]; Alx/Byz[**the Lord**], Minor[God (MRD)].

called Mark, where many were gathered together and were praying. ¹³ And when he knocked at the door of the gate, a servant-girl named Rhoda came to answer. ¹⁴ When she recognized Peter's voice, in her joy she did not open the gate, but ran in and announced that Peter was standing in front of the gate. ¹⁵ They said to her, "You are out of your mind!" But she kept insisting that it was so. They said, "It is his angel." ¹⁶ But Peter continued knocking. And when they opened the door, they saw him and were amazed. ¹⁷ But motioning to them with his hand to be silent, he described [to them] how the Lord had brought him out of the prison. And he said, "Tell this to James and to the brothers." Then he left and went to another place.

¹⁸ Now when day came, there was no small disturbance among the soldiers as to what had become of Peter. ¹⁹ When Herod had searched for him and could not find him, he examined the guards and ordered that they be put to death. Then he went down from Judea to Caesarea and stayed there a while.

²⁰ Now he was angry with the people of Tyre and Sidon. But they came to him in a body. And having persuaded Blastus, the king's chamberlain, they asked for peace, because their country depended on the king's country for food. ²¹ On an appointed day Herod put on his royal robes, [and] took his seat upon the throne, and made an address to them. ²² And the people shouted, "The voice of a god and not of a man!" ²³ Immediately an angel of the Lord struck him because he did not give God the glory, and he was eaten by worms and died.

²⁴ But the word of God continued to grow and to be multiplied. ²⁵ And Barnabas and Saul returned to Jerusalem when they had fulfilled their mission, taking along with them John, who was also called Mark.

13 ¹ Now in the church that was at Antioch there were prophets and teachers: Barnabas, Simeon who was called Niger, Lucius of Cyrene, Manaen who had been brought up with Herod the tetrarch, and Saul. ² While they were

---

12:13 Alx/Byz[**he knocked**], Major[Peter knocked (KJV, NIV, NKJ, TEV)].

12:14 Alx/Byz[**Peter's...Peter**], Alt/Peshitta[Simon's...Simon (MRD)], Alt[*without textual foundation* Cephas'...Cephas (~JNT)].

12:15 Alx/Byz[**It is his angel**], Minor[Perhaps it is his angel (MRD, ~NIV, ~NJB, ~NLT, ~REB, ~TLB)].

12:16 Alx/Byz[**Peter**], Alt/Peshitta[Simon (MRD)], Alt[*without textual foundation* Cephas (~JNT)].

12:17 Alx/Byz[**he described to them**], Minor[*omits* to them (DRA, NET, NIV) *others* he went in and he described to them (MRD)]; Alx[**And he said**], Byz[But he said].

12:18 Alx/Byz[**Peter**], Alt/Peshitta[Simon (MRD)], Alt[*without textual foundation* Cephas (~JNT)].

12:20 Alx[**he was angry**], Byz[Herod was angry (ESV, JNT, KJV, NET, NJB, NKJ, NLT, NRS, RSV, TEV)]; Alx/Major[**But they came**], Byz[And they came (ASV, ESV, ~HCS, JNT, ~MRD, ~NAB, NAS, NAU, NET, ~NIV, NLT, NRS, ~REB, RSV, TEV)]; Alx/Byz[**the king's country**], Alt[*Peshitta* Herod's country (MRD, NLT, TLB) *others* him (DRA)].

12:21 Alx/Byz[**and took his seat**], Minor[*omits* and (DRA, ESV, JNT, KJV, NAS, NAU, NET, NIV, NKJ, NLT, NRS, RSV, TEV, TLB)]; Alx/Byz[**address to them**], Alt/Peshitta[address to the people of the assembly (~MRD, ~NIV, ~REB, ~TEV)].

12:23 Alx/Byz[**the glory**], Major[glory (NIV, NKJ, NLT, TEV)]; Alx/Byz[**and he was eaten by worms and died**], Minor[and he came down from the platform; while he was still alive he was eaten by worms and thus died (~TLB)].

12:24 Alx/Byz[**word of God**], Minor[word of the Lord (DRA, JNT, NAS, NAU)].

12:25 Alx/Byz[**Saul**], Minor[*adds* who was called Paul *others* Paul (TLB)]; Alx/Byz[**to Jerusalem**], Minor[from Jerusalem (ASV, DRA, ESV, JNT, KJV, MRD, NAS, NAU, NIV, ~NJB, NKJ, REB, RSV, TEV, ~TLB)].

13:1 Alx[**prophets**], Byz[certain prophets (KJV, ~MRD, NKJ, REB, ~TEV)]; Alx/Byz[**Barnabas**], Minor[among whom was Barnabas (DRA)]; Alx/Major[**who was called Niger**], Byz[who was surnamed Niger (~JNT)]; Alx/Byz[**Cyrene**], Alt/Peshitta[the city of Cyrene (MRD)]; **Niger** *from* Latin Dark Skinned.

13:2 Alx/Byz[**Barnabas and Saul**], Minor[both Barnabas and Saul], Alt/Peshitta[Saul and Barnabas (DRA, MRD)], Alt[*without textual foundation* Barnabas and Paul (~TLB)].

worshipping the Lord and fasting, the Holy Spirit said, "Set apart for me Barnabas and Saul for the work to which I have called them." ³ Then after they had fasted and prayed, they laid their hands on them and sent them off.

⁴ So, being sent out by the Holy Spirit, they went down to Seleucia and from there they sailed to Cyprus. ⁵ When they arrived at Salamis, they proclaimed the word of God in the synagogues of the Jews. And they had John as their helper. ⁶ When they had gone through the whole island as far as Paphos, they came upon a certain man – a magician, a Jewish false prophet, named Bar-Jesus, ⁷ who was with the proconsul, Sergius Paulus, a man of intelligence. This man summoned Barnabas and Saul and sought to hear the word of God. ⁸ But Elymas the magician (for that is the meaning of his name) was opposing them, seeking to turn the proconsul away from the faith. ⁹ But Saul, who was also called Paul, filled with the Holy Spirit, gazed into him ¹⁰ and said, "You who are full of all deceit and fraud, you son of the devil, you enemy of all righteousness, will you not stop making crooked the straight ways of [the] Lord? ¹¹ Now, behold, the hand of the Lord is upon you, and you will be blind and unable to see the sun for a time." And immediately a mist and a darkness fell upon him, and he went about seeking someone to lead him by the hand. ¹² Then the proconsul believed, when he saw what had happened, for he was amazed at the teaching of the Lord.

¹³ Now Paul and his companions put out to sea from Paphos and came to Perga in Pamphylia. But John left them and returned to Jerusalem. ¹⁴ But they passed on from Perga and came to Antioch in Pisidia. And on the Sabbath day they [en]tered into the synagogue and sat down. ¹⁵ After the reading of the law and the prophets, the rulers of the synagogue sent to them, saying, "Brothers, if you have any word of exhortation for the people, say it." ¹⁶ Paul stood up, and motioning with his hand said,

"Men of Israel, and you who fear God, listen: ¹⁷ the God of this people Israel chose our fathers and made the people great during their stay in the land of Egypt, and with

---

13:4 Alx[**they went down**], Byz[these went down (JNT, ~NIV, NJB, REB, ~TEV)]; Alx/Byz[**and from there**], Major[but from there].

13:5 Alx/Byz[**Salamis**], Alt/Peshitta[the city of Salamis (MRD)]; Alx/Byz[**the word of God**], Minor[the word of the Lord (MRD, ~TLB)].

13:6 Alx/Byz[**gone through**], Minor[gone around]; Alx[**whole**], Byz[*omits* (KJV, NKJ, TEV)]; Alx/Byz[**Paphos**], Alt/Peshitta[the city of Paphos (MRD)]; Alx[**a certain man – a magician**], Byz[a certain magician (ASV, ESV, HCS, JNT, KJV, NAB, NAS, NAU, NET, NIV, NJB, NKJ, NLT, NRS, REB, RSV, TEV, TLB)].

13:8 Alx/Byz[**Elymas**], Minor[Etoimas]; Alx/Byz[**the magician**], Alt/Peshitta[*adds* Bar Suma (MRD)]; **Elymas** *cf Arabic* Alim *sage.*

13:9 Alx[**gazed**], Byz[and gazed (MRD)]; Alx/Major[**into him**], Byz[toward him (ASV, DRA, ESV, HCS, JNT, KJV, MRD, NAB, NAS, NAU, NET, NIV, NJB, NKJ, NRS, ~REB, RSV, TEV, TLB)]; **Saul** *from Hebrew* asked for; **Paul** *from Latin* small, humble.

13:12 Alx/Byz[**Then the proconsul**], Minor[And the proconsul (MRD, ~NAB, ~NIV, ~NJB, ~NLT, ~NRS, ~REB, ~TEV, ~TLB)].

13:13 Alx/Byz[**Paul**], Alt[*without textual foundation* Saul (~JNT)]; Alx/Byz[**Paphos**], Alt/Peshitta[the city of Paphos (MRD)]; Alx/Byz[**Perga in Pamphylia**], Alt/Peshitta[Perga, a city of Pamphylia (MRD, NLT, TEV, TLB)].

13:14 Alx/Byz[**Antioch in Pisidia**], Alt/Peshitta[Antioch, a city of Pisidia (MRD, TLB)]; Alx/Byz[**entered into the synagogue**], Minor[went into the synagogue (ASV, ESV, HCS, JNT, KJV, ~MRD, NAS, NAU, NET, ~NIV, NJB, NKJ, NLT, NRS, REB, RSV, TEV, TLB)].

13:15 Alx[**if you have any word** *or* if any of you have a word], Byz[if you have a word (MRD, NIV, ~NJB, TEV)].

13:16 Alx/Byz[**Paul**], Alt[*without textual foundation* Saul (~JNT)]; Alx/Byz[**Men of Israel**], Alt/Peshitta[Men, sons of Israel (MRD)].

13:17 Alx/Byz[**Israel**], Major[*omits* (MRD)].

uplifted arm he led them out of it. [18] For about forty years he *put up with them in the wilderness*. [19] And when he had destroyed seven nations in the land of Canaan, he gave their land as an inheritance, [20] for about four hundred and fifty years. And after these things he gave them judges until Samuel [the] prophet. [21] Then they asked for a king, and God gave them Saul the son of Kish, a man of the tribe of Benjamin, for forty years. [22] And after he had removed him, he raised up David to be their king; concerning whom he testified and said, 'I have *found in David the son of Jesse a man after my heart*, who will do all my will.' [23] From this man's descendants God has brought to Israel a Savior, Jesus, as he promised. [24] Before his coming John had preached a baptism of repentance to all the people of Israel. [25] And as John was completing his course, he said, 'What do you suppose that I am? I am not he. No, but after me one is coming, the sandals of whose feet I am not worthy to untie.'

[26] "Brothers, sons of the family of Abraham, and those among you that fear God, to us the message of this salvation was sent forth. [27] For those who live in Jerusalem and their rulers, because they did not recognize him nor the utterances of the prophets which are read every Sabbath, fulfilled these by condemning him. [28] Though they found no ground for a death sentence, they asked Pilate to have him executed. [29] When they had carried out all that was written about him, they took him down from the tree and laid him in a tomb. [30] But God raised him from the dead. [31] And for many days he appeared to those who came up with him from Galilee to Jerusalem, who are [now] his witnesses to the people. [32] And we preach to you the good news that what God promised to the fathers, [33] he has fulfilled for us, [their] children, by raising up Jesus. As it is also written in the second Psalm:

'You are my Son.
Today I have begotten you.'

13:18 Alx/Byz[**put up with them**], Minor[cared for them (ASV, JNT, MRD, NJB, TLB)]; Deuteronomy 1:31 Masoretic *Minor reading is LXX*.

13:19 Alx/Byz[**And when**], Minor[When (~HCS, NAB, NAU, NET, NIV, NJB, NLT, REB, TEV, TLB)]; Alx[**gave their land**], Byz[gave them their land (ASV, DRA, ESV, HCS, JNT, KJV, MRD, NAB, NET, NIV, NJB, NKJ, NLT, NRS, REB, RSV, ~TEV, TLB)]; Alx/Byz[**as an inheritance**], Minor[by lot (DRA, KJV, ~NJB, NKJ, ~TEV)].

13:20 Alx[**20 for about four hundred and fifty years. And after these things**], Byz[20 And after these things, for about four hundred and fifty years (KJV, ~MRD, NKJ, ~REB, ~TLB)], Minor[for about four hundred and fifty years 20 And after these things (ASV, NAS, NAU, RSV, ~TLB)]; Alx/Byz[**the prophet**], Minor[a prophet].

13:22 Alx/Byz[**a man**], Minor[*omits*]; Psalms 89:20, 1 Samuel 13:14.

13:23 Alx/Byz[**brought to Israel**], Minor[raised unto Israel (DRA, KJV, MRD, NJB, NKJ, ~NLT, ~TEV, ~TLB)]; Alx[**a Savior, Jesus**], Byz[salvation].

13:24 Alx[**to all the people of Israel**], Byz[to Israel].

13:25 Alx[**What do you suppose that I am? I am not he** *or* I am not what you suppose I am], Byz[Who do you suppose that I am? I am not he *or* I am not who you suppose that I am (DRA, HCS, JNT, KJV, MRD, NIV, ~NJB, NKJ, ~NLT, REB, TEV, ~TLB)].

13:26 Alx[**to us**], Byz[to you (DRA, KJV, MRD, NJB, NKJ)]; Alx[**sent forth**], Byz[sent (DRA, ESV, HCS, JNT, KJV, MRD, NAB, NAU, NET, NIV, ~NJB, NKJ, NLT, NRS, REB, RSV, TEV, ~TLB)].

13:30 Alx/Byz[**from the dead**], Alt/Vulgate[*adds* the third day (DRA)].

13:31 Alx[**who are now his witnesses**], Byz[*omits* now (KJV, NKJ, ~TLB)].

13:32 Alx/Byz[**And we preach**], Minor[And now we preach (NLT, TLB)]; Alx/Byz[**the fathers**], Minor[our fathers (DRA, HCS, MRD, NAB, NET, NIV, NJB, NLT, NRS, TEV, TLB)].

13:33 Alx/Byz[**33 he has fulfilled...raising up Jesus**], Minor[he has fulfilled...raising up Jesus 33 (~TEV, ~TLB)]; Alx/Byz[**for us, their children**], Minor[for our children (ASV, DRA, NAS, NAU) *others* for us the children (JNT)], Alt[for their children (NJB)], Alt[for the children (REB)], Alt[*paraphrase* in our own time (~TLB)]; Alx/Byz[**Jesus**], Minor[the Lord Jesus Christ *others* our Lord Jesus Christ]; Alx/Byz[**second Psalm**], Minor[first Psalm *others* the Psalms (NJB)]; **Psalms 2:7**; *Minor continues the verse by quoting Psalms 2:8*.

34 As for the fact that he raised him from the dead, no more to return to decay, he spoke in this way:

'I will give *you the holy and sure blessings of David,'*
35 because he also says in another Psalm,

'You will not let your Holy One see decay.'

36 For David, after he had served the purpose of God in his own generation, fell asleep, and was laid with his fathers and saw decay. **37** But he whom God raised did not see decay. **38** Therefore let it be known to you, brothers, that through this man forgiveness of sins is proclaimed to you. [And] from everything in Moses' law which could not make you just – **39** through him everyone who believes is justified. **40** Therefore take care, so that what is said in the prophets may not come:

41   *'Behold, you scoffers,*
           and wonder, and perish.
      For I am going to do a deed in your days,
           a deed which you will never believe,
               if someone declares it to you.'"

42 As Paul and Barnabas were going out, the people begged that these words might be spoken to them the next Sabbath. **43** When the meeting of the synagogue broke up, many Jews and devout converts to Judaism followed Paul and Barnabas, who spoke to them and urged them to remain in the grace of God.

44 The next Sabbath almost the whole city gathered to hear the word of the Lord. **45** But when the Jews saw the crowds, they were filled with jealousy, and contradicted what was spoken by Paul, and blasphemed. **46** And Paul and Barnabas spoke out boldly and said,

---

13:34 ~**Isaiah 55:3 LXX**.

13:35 Alx[**because he also says**], Byz[Therefore he also says (DRA, ESV, HCS, ~JNT, KJV, ~MRD, ~NAB, NAS, NAU, NET, ~NIV, ~NJB, NKJ, ~NLT, NRS, ~REB, RSV, ~TEV, ~TLB)]; **Psalms 16:10 LXX**.

13:38 Alx/Byz[**through this man**], Minor[for this reason *others* through him (DRA, NAB, NAS, NAU, ~NIV, NJB, REB, ~TEV, ~TLB)]; Alx/Byz[**And from everything...**], Minor[And repentance from everything... *others* omit And (ASV, ESV, HCS, JNT, KJV, MRD, NAS, NAU, NET, NIV, NJB, NKJ, NLT, NRS, REB, RSV, TEV, TLB) *others* 39 and from everything... (ASV, ESV 2007 edition, HCS, JNT, KJV, MRD, NAS, NAU, NET, NIV, NKJ, NLT, NRS, REB, RSV, ~TEV, TLB)]; Alx[**Moses' law**], Byz[the law of Moses (ASV, DRA, ESV, HCS, JNT, KJV, MRD, NAB, NAS, NAU, NET, NIV, NJB, NKJ, NLT, NRS, REB, RSV, TEV, ~TLB)].

13:39 Alx/Byz[**through him** *Greek* through this], Minor[*adds* therefore]; Alx/Byz[**is freed**], Minor[*adds* before God (NLT)].

13:40 Alx/Byz[**in the prophets**], Alt[in Habakkuk the prophet]; Alx[**may not come**], Byz[*adds* upon you (ASV, DRA, HCS, JNT, KJV, MRD, NAS, NAU, NET, NIV, NJB, NKJ, NLT, NRS, REB, RSV, TEV, TLB)].

13:41 Alx/Byz[**a deed which**], Major[which (JNT, MRD, NIV, NJB, ~NLT, TEV, ~TLB)]; ~**Habakkuk 1:5 LXX**.

13:42 Alx[**As Paul and Barnabas were going out, the people begged** *Greek* As they were going out, they begged], Byz[As the Jews were going out of the synagogue, the Gentiles begged (KJV, NKJ, ~NIV, ~NLT, ~REB, ~TEV, ~TLB)]; Alx/Byz[**these words**], Major[the words (~MRD, ~TLB)].

13:43 Alx/Byz[**Paul**], Alt/Peshitta[them (MRD)], Alt[*without textual foundation* Saul (~JNT)]; Alx/Byz[**spoke to them**], Major[*omits* to them (~NLT, ~TLB)]; Alx/Byz[**remain in the grace**], Major[continue in the grace (ASV, DRA, ESV, HCS, ~JNT, KJV, ~MRD, NAS, NAU, NET, NIV, NKJ, NLT, NRS, ~REB, RSV, ~TEV, ~TLB)].

13:44 Alx[**the Lord**], Byz[God (ASV, DRA, KJV, MRD, NAS, NJB, NKJ, REB, RSV, TLB)].

13:45 Alx/Byz[**Paul**], Alt[*without textual foundation* Saul (~JNT)]; Alx[**contradicted...and blasphemed**], Byz[contradicted...and contradicted and blasphemed (KJV, NKJ)].

13:46 Alx/Byz[**Paul**], Alt[*without textual foundation* Saul (~JNT)]; Alx[**And Paul and Barnabas**], Byz[But Paul and Barnabas (~DRA, ~HCS, JNT, ~KJV, ~NIV, ~NJB, ~NKJ, ~NLT, ~NRS, REB, TEV, ~TLB)]; Alx[**Since you reject**], Byz[But since you reject (DRA, HCS, JNT, KJV, MRD, NAB, NJB,

"It was necessary that the word of God be spoken to you first. Since you reject it and judge yourselves unworthy of eternal life, behold, we turn to the Gentiles. ⁴⁷ For so the Lord has commanded us:

> 'I have made you a light for the Gentiles,
> that you may bring salvation to the ends of the earth.'"

⁴⁸ When the Gentiles heard this, they began to rejoice and to glorify the word of the Lord. And as many as were appointed to eternal life believed. ⁴⁹ And the word of the Lord spread through the whole region. ⁵⁰ But the Jews incited the devout women of high standing and the leading men of the city, and stirred up persecution against Paul and Barnabas, and drove them out of their district. ⁵¹ But they shook off the dust of the feet against them and went to Iconium. ⁵² And the disciples were filled with joy and with the Holy Spirit.

14 ¹ Now at Iconium they entered together into the Jewish synagogue, and so spoke that a great number believed, both of Jews and of Greeks. ² But the Jews who refused to believe stirred up the Gentiles and poisoned their minds against the brothers. ³ So they spent a long time there, speaking boldly for the Lord, who bore witness [based on] the word of his grace, granting signs and wonders to be done by their hands. ⁴ But the people of the city were divided. Some sided with the Jews, and some with the apostles. ⁵ When an attempt was made by both the Gentiles and the Jews with their rulers, to mistreat them and to stone them, ⁶ they became aware of it and fled to the cities of Lycaonia, Lystra and Derbe, and to the surrounding country. ⁷ And there they continued to preach the gospel.

⁸ At Lystra there was a man sitting who had no strength in his feet, lame from birth, who had never walked. ⁹ He listened to Paul speaking. And Paul, looking intently at him and seeing that he had faith to be made well, ¹⁰ said with a loud voice, "Stand upright on your feet." And he leaped up and began to walk. ¹¹ And when the crowds saw what Paul

---

NKJ, NLT, REB, TEV, TLB)].

13:⁴⁷ **Isaiah 49:6**.

13:⁴⁸ Alx/Byz[**they began to rejoice and to glorify**], Major[he began to rejoice and they began to glorify]; Alx/Byz[**word of the Lord**], Minor[God (MRD) *others* word of God (ASV, RSV)], Alt[*without textual foundation* Paul's message (~TLB)].

13:⁵⁰ Alx[**devout women of high standing**], Byz[devout and honorable women (DRA, KJV, ~MRD, NKJ, ~TLB)]; Alx/Byz[**Paul**], Alt[*without textual foundation* Saul (~JNT)].

13:⁵¹ Alx/Byz[**But they shook off**], Alt[And when they went out, they shook off (MRD)]; Alx[**dust of the feet**], Byz[dust of their feet (ASV, DRA, ESV, HCS, JNT, KJV, MRD, NAB, NAS, NAU, NET, NIV, NJB, NKJ, NRS, REB, RSV, TEV, TLB)]; Alx/Byz[**Iconium**], Alt/Peshitta[the city of Iconium (MRD, NLT, TLB)].

13:⁵² *NJB includes this verse in verse 51.*

14:² Alx[**Jews who refused to believe** *or* Jews who refused to obey], Byz[*present* unbelieving Jews *or* disobedient Jews (DRA, ESV, KJV, ~MRD, NAB, NAS, NAU, NKJ, ~NLT, NRS, ~REB, RSV, ~TLB)].

14:³ Alx[**based on the word**], Byz[to the word (ASV, DRA, ESV, HCS, JNT, KJV, MRD, ~NAB, NAS, NAU, NET, ~NIV, ~NJB, NKJ, ~NLT, NRS, ~REB, RSV, ~TEV, ~TLB)]; Alx/Byz[**granting signs**], Minor[and granting signs (KJV)].

14:⁷ *DRA includes this in verse 6 and remains one verse lower through the end of the chapter.*

14:⁸ Alx/Byz[**At Lystra**], Minor[*omits* (NJB)], Alt/Peshitta[at the city Lystra (MRD)]; Alx[**lame from birth**], Byz[being lame from birth (KJV)].

14:⁹ Alx/Byz[**He listened**], Minor[He was listening (NAS, NAU, NET, NJB, ~NLT, TLB)]; Alx/Byz[**Paul...and Paul** *Greek* Paul...who], Alt[*without textual foundation* Saul...Saul (~JNT)].

14:¹⁰ Alx[**a loud voice**], Byz[the loud voice], Minor[*adds* I say to you in the name of the Lord Jesus Christ (MRD)]; Alx/Byz[**Stand upright**], Major[Stand correctly]; Alx/Byz[**on your feet**], Minor[*adds* and walk], Alt[*without textual foundation* omits (~TLB)]; Alx/Byz[**he leaped up**], Major[he was leaping up], Minor[he immediately leaped up (~NIV) *others* immediately that same hour he leaped up].

14:¹¹ Alx[**And when the crowds saw**], Byz[But when the crowds saw (~NET, ~NKJ)]; Alx/Byz[**Paul**],

had done, they lifted up their voices, saying in the Lycaonian language, "The gods have come down to us in the likeness of men!" **12** And they called Barnabas "Zeus." And Paul, because he was the chief speaker, they called "Hermes." **13** And the priest of Zeus, whose temple was just outside the city, brought oxen and garlands to the gates, and wanted to offer sacrifice with the crowds. **14** But when the apostles Barnabas and Paul heard of it, they tore their robes and rushed out into the crowd, crying out, **15** "Men, why are you doing this? We also are men, of like nature with you, and bring you good news, that you should turn from these vain things to a living God who made the heaven and the earth and the sea and all that is in them. **16** In past generations he allowed all the nations to go their own ways. **17** Yet he did not leave himself without witness, in that he did good and gave you rains from heaven and fruitful seasons, satisfying your hearts with food and gladness." **18** Even with these words, they had difficulty keeping the crowds from offering sacrifice to them.

19 But Jews came there from Antioch and Iconium; and having won over the crowds, they stoned Paul and began to drag him out of the city, supposing him to have died. **20** But after the disciples had gathered around him, he got up and entered the city. And the next day he went with Barnabas to Derbe.

21 After they had preached the gospel to that city and had made many disciples, they returned to Lystra and to Iconium and to Antioch, **22** strengthening the souls of the disciples, encouraging them to continue in the faith, and saying, "Through many tribulations we must enter the kingdom of God." **23** And when they had appointed elders for them in every church, with prayer and fasting they committed them to the Lord in whom they believed. **24** They passed through Pisidia, and came into Pamphylia. **25** And

---

Alt[*without textual foundation* Saul (~JNT)]; Alx/Byz[**the Lycaonian language**], Alt[the language of the country (MRD, NLT, TLB)].

14:12 Alx[**And they called Barnabas**], Byz[And indeed, they called Barnabas]; Alx/Byz[**Zeus** *Greek* Dia], Alt/Vulgate[Jupiter (ASV, DRA, KJV, TLB)], Alt/Peshitta[Lord of the gods (MRD)]; Alx/Byz[**Paul**], Alt[*without textual foundation* Saul (~JNT)]; Alx/Byz[**Hermes**], Alt/Vulgate[Mercury (ASV, DRA, KJV, TLB)].

14:13 Alx[**And the priest**], Byz[But the priest (~HCS, ~KJV, ~NKJ, ~NLT)], Minor[But the priests (NJB)]; Alx/Byz[**Zeus**], Alt/Peshitta[the lord of the gods (MRD)], Alt/Vulgate[Jupiter (ASV, DRA, KJV, TLB)]; Alx[**the city**], Byz[their city (KJV, NKJ)].

14:14 Alx/Byz[**the apostles**], Minor[*omits* (MRD, NLT, TEV, TLB)]; Alx/Byz[**Paul**], Alt[*without textual foundation* Saul (~JNT)]; Alx/Byz[**their robes**], Minor[their own robes]; Alx[**rushed out into the crowd**], Byz[rushed in into the crowd *or* leapt in into the crowd (HCS, JNT, KJV, ~MRD, NJB, NKJ, REB, TEV)].

14:15 Alx[**a living God**], Byz[the living God (DRA, HCS, JNT, KJV, MRD, NAB, NET, NIV, NJB, NKJ, NLT, NRS, REB, TEV, TLB)].

14:17 Alx[**Yet**], Byz[And yet (ASV, NAS, NAU, REB)]; Alx/Byz[**gave you**], Minor[gave us (KJV, NKJ) *others* gave (DRA, MRD)]; Alx/Byz[**your hearts**], Major[our hearts (DRA, KJV, NKJ)], Alt[their hearts (MRD)].

14:19 Alx/Byz[**Paul**], Alt[*without textual foundation* Saul (~JNT)]; Alx/Major[**began to drag**], Byz[dragged (ASV, DRA, ESV, HCS, JNT, KJV, MRD, NAB, NAS, NAU, NET, NIV, NJB, NKJ, NLT, NRS, REB, RSV, TEV, TLB)].

14:20 Alx/Byz[**Derbe**], Alt/Peshitta[the city of Derbe (MRD)].

14:21 Alx/Byz[**After they had preached**], Minor[While they were preaching (MRD)]; Alx/Byz[**Lystra**], Alt/Peshitta[the city of Lystra (MRD)]; Alx[**to Iconium**], Byz[*omits* to (JNT, NIV, NJB, NKJ, NLT, TLB)]; Alx[**to Antioch**], Byz[*omits* to (JNT, KJV, NIV, NJB, NKJ, NLT, NRS, TLB)], Alt[*without textual foundation adds* of Pisidia (~NLT, ~TEV)].

14:23 Alx/Major[**with prayer and fasting** *Greek* praying with fasting], Byz[with prayer and fasting *Greek* and praying with fasting]; Alx/Major[**in whom they believed** *Greek* in whom they had been believing], Byz[in whom they believed]; **appointed** *or* elected.

14:25 Alx/Byz[**the word**], Minor[*adds* of the Lord (DRA, MRD) *others add* of God]; Alx/Byz[**in Perga**], Minor[to Perga (~NAB, ~NJB, ~REB)], Alt/Peshitta[in the city of Perga (MRD)].

when they had spoken the word in Perga, they went down to Attalia. 26 From there they sailed to Antioch, where they had been commended to the grace of God for the work which they had completed. 27 When they arrived, they gathered the church together and declared all that God had done with them, and how he had opened a door of faith to the Gentiles. 28 And they spent a long time with the disciples.

15

1 But some men came down from Judea and were teaching the brothers, "Unless you are circumcised according to the custom of Moses, you cannot be saved." 2 And when Paul and Barnabas had no small dissension and debate with them, Paul and Barnabas and some of the others were appointed to go up to Jerusalem to the apostles and elders about this question. 3 So, being sent on their way by the church, they passed through both Phoenicia and Samaria, reporting the conversion of the Gentiles, and they gave great joy to all the brothers. 4 When they came to Jerusalem, they received welcome from the church and the apostles and the elders, and they reported all that God had done with them. 5 But some believers who belonged to the party of the Pharisees stood up, and said, "It is necessary to circumcise them, and to charge them to keep the Law of Moses."

6 And the apostles and the elders came together to consider this matter. 7 After there had been much debate, Peter stood up and said to them, "Men, brothers, you know that in the early days God made a choice among you, that by my mouth the Gentiles would hear the word of the gospel and believe. 8 And God, who knows the heart, bore witness to them, giving the Holy Spirit, just as he also did to us. 9 And he made no distinction between us and them, but cleansed their hearts by faith. 10 Now therefore why do you test God by putting upon the neck of the disciples a yoke which neither our fathers nor we have been able to bear? 11 But we believe that we are saved through the grace of the Lord Jesus, just as they are."

14:26 Alx/Byz[**grace of God**], Alt[grace of the Lord (MRD)]; Alx/Byz[**26 From there they sailed to Antioch**], Alt[From there they sailed to Antioch 26 (JNT)].

14:28 Alx[**they spent a long time**], Byz[*adds* there (JNT, KJV, NIV, NJB, NKJ, NLT, NRS, REB, TEV, TLB)].

15:1 Alx/Byz[**some men**], Minor[*adds* who had believed from the party of the Pharisees]; Alx[**Unless you are circumcised** *or* Unless you were circumcised], Byz[Unless you are circumcised *present tense*], Minor[*adds* and walk]; Alx/Byz[**Moses**], Alt/Peshitta[the law (MRD, ~NLT, ~TEV, ~TLB)].

15:2 Alx/Byz[**Paul…Paul**], Alt[*without textual foundation* Saul…Saul (~JNT)]; Alx[**And when Paul** *or* But when Paul], Byz[Therefore when Paul (~JNT, KJV, ~NAB, ~NIV, ~NJB, NKJ, ~REB)]; Alx/Byz[**dissension and debate**], Minor[dissension and dispute (JNT, KJV, MRD, NKJ)], Alt[*without textual foundation* contest (~DRA, ~NJB, ~NLT, ~TEV)]; Alx/Byz[**apostles and elders**], Alt[*without textual foundation* apostles and priests (~DRA)].

15:3 Alx[**both Phoenicia and Samaria**], Byz[*omits* both (DRA, JNT, KJV, ~MRD, NAB, NIV, NJB, NKJ, NLT, REB, TEV, TLB)].

15:4 Alx[**they received welcome from** *Greek* they were received from], Byz[they were gladly received by (~DRA, ~ESV, ~HCS, ~JNT, ~MRD, ~NAB, ~NAS, ~NAU, ~NET, ~NIV, ~NJB, ~NKJ, ~NLT, ~NRS, ~REB, ~RSV, ~TEV, ~TLB)]; Alx/Major[**all that God had done with them**], Byz[*adds* and how he had opened a door of faith to the Gentiles].

15:6 Alx[**And the apostles**], Byz[But the apostles (~HCS, ~NKJ, ~NLT, ~TLB)]; Alx/Byz[**came together**], Minor[*adds* with the multitude].

15:7 Alx[**debate**], Byz[dispute (DRA, KJV, NKJ)]; Alx/Byz[**Peter stood up**], Minor[*adds* in the Spirit]; Alx/Byz[**Peter**], Alt/Peshitta[Simon (MRD)], Alt[*without textual foundation* Cephas (~JNT)]; Alx/Byz[**Men, brothers**], Alt[*without textual foundation* Brothers (~ASV, ~ESV, ~HCS, ~JNT, ~NAB, ~NAS, ~NAU, ~NET, ~NIV, ~NJB, ~NLT, ~NRS, ~REB, ~RSV, ~TEV, ~TLB)]; Alx[**made a choice among you**], Byz[made a choice among us (DRA, KJV, NKJ)], Alt[chose (MRD, NET)].

15:8 Alx[**giving the Holy Spirit**], Byz[giving to them the Holy Spirit (ASV, DRA, ESV, JNT, KJV, MRD, ~NAB, NAS, NAU, NET, NJB, NKJ, ~NLT, NRS, ~REB, RSV, ~TEV, ~TLB)].

15:11 Alx/Byz[**the Lord Jesus**], Minor[*adds* Christ (DRA, KJV, MRD, NKJ)].

¹² All the assembly kept silent. And they listened to Barnabas and Paul as they related what signs and wonders God had done through them among the Gentiles. ¹³ After they finished speaking, James replied, "Men, brothers, listen to me. ¹⁴ Simeon has related how God first showed his concern by taking from the Gentiles a people for his name. ¹⁵ With this the words of the Prophets agree, just as it is written,

¹⁶   'After this I will return,
            and I will rebuild the tabernacle of David, which has fallen.
                I will rebuild its ruins,
                    and I will restore it,
¹⁷   so that the rest of mankind may seek the Lord,
            and all the Gentiles who are called by my name,'

says the Lord, who makes these things ¹⁸ known from long ago. ¹⁹ Therefore it is my judgment that we should not trouble those who are turning to God from among the Gentiles, ²⁰ but that we should write to them to abstain from the pollutions of idols and from fornication and from what is strangled and from blood. ²¹ For Moses from ancient generations has in every city those who preach him, since he is read in the synagogues every Sabbath."

²² Then it seemed good to the apostles and the elders, with the whole church, to choose men from among them and send them to Antioch with Paul and Barnabas. They sent Judas called Barsabbas, and Silas, leading men among the brothers, ²³ writing through their hand: "The apostles and the elder brothers, to the brothers in Antioch and Syria and Cilicia who are from the Gentiles, greetings. ²⁴ Since we have heard that some persons [who departed] from us have disturbed you with words, unsettling your minds, although we gave them no instructions, ²⁵ it has seemed good to us, having come to one accord, to choose men and send them to you with our beloved Barnabas and Paul, ²⁶ men who have risked their lives for the name of our Lord Jesus Christ. ²⁷ We have therefore sent Judas and Silas, who themselves will tell you the same things by word of mouth. ²⁸ For it seemed good

---

15:¹² Alx/Byz[**Paul**], Alt[*without textual foundation* Saul (~JNT)].

15:¹⁶ Alx/Byz[**which has fallen**], Minor[which has been overturned (~TEV, ~TLB)].

15:¹⁶⁻¹⁷ ~**Amos 9:11-12 LXX**.

15:¹⁷ Alx/Byz[**says the Lord...these things 18**], Minor[18 says the Lord...these things (ASV, JNT, NAS, NAU, ~NLT, RSV, TEV, TLB)]; Alx[**makes these things**], Byz[makes all these things (KJV, MRD, NKJ)].

15:¹⁸ Alx[**known from long ago**], Byz[Known to God from of old are all his works (KJV, MRD, NKJ)], Minor[Known to the Lord from of old is his work (DRA)].

15:²⁰ Alx/Byz[**from fornication**], Minor[*omits*]; Alx/Byz[**and from what is strangled**], Minor[*omits*]; Alx/Byz[**and from blood**], Minor[*adds* and to refrain from doing to others what they would not like done to themselves].

15:²² Alx/Byz[**Paul**], Alt[*without textual foundation* Saul (~JNT)]; Alx[**Judas called Barsabbas**], Byz[Judas surnamed Barsabbas (DRA, KJV, NKJ, ~REB)]; Alx/Byz[**Barsabbas**], Minor[Barabbas *others* Barnabas].

15:²³ Alx[**writing through their hand**], Byz[writing these through their hand (ASV, ~ESV, ~HCS, ~JNT, KJV, MRD, ~NAB, ~NAS, ~NAU, ~NET, ~NIV, ~NJB, ~NKJ, ~NLT, ~NRS, ~REB, ~RSV, ~TEV, ~TLB)]; Alx[**the elder brothers** *or* the elders, brothers], Byz[the elders and the brothers (KJV, MRD, NKJ, TLB)], Alt[*without textual foundation omits* brothers (~REB)].

15:²⁴ Alx/Byz[**who departed**], Minor[*omits* (NAS, NAU, NLT, REB, RSV, TLB)]; Alx[**unsettling your minds**], Byz[*adds* saying, 'You must be circumcised and keep the law,' (KJV, MRD, NKJ)].

15:²⁵ Alx[**to choose men and send them to you**], Byz[to send chosen men to you (KJV, NKJ, NLT, REB, TLB)]; Alx/Byz[**Paul**], Alt[*without textual foundation* Saul (~JNT)].

15:²⁶ Alx/Byz[**for the name of our Lord Jesus Christ**], Minor[*adds* in every trial].

15:²⁷ Alx/Byz[**will tell you**], Minor[may tell you (MRD, ~NIV, ~NLT)]; *TLB places this verse in verse 26.*

15:²⁸ Alx/Byz[**these essentials**], Minor[*omits* these (~JNT, ~NIV, ~TLB)].

to the Holy Spirit and to us to lay upon you no greater burden than these essentials: ²⁹ that you abstain from things sacrificed to idols and from blood and from things strangled and from fornication. If you keep yourselves free from these, you will do well. Farewell."

³⁰ So when they were sent off, they went down to Antioch. And having gathered the congregation together, they delivered the letter. ³¹ And when they read it, they rejoiced at its encouragement. ³² And Judas and Silas, who were themselves prophets, encouraged the brothers with many words and strengthened them. ³³ And after they had spent some time there, they were sent off in peace by the brothers to those who had sent them. ⁽³⁴⁾ ³⁵ But Paul and Barnabas remained in Antioch, teaching and preaching the word of the Lord, with many others also.

³⁶ After some days Paul said to Barnabas, "Let us return and visit the brothers in every city where we proclaimed the word of the Lord, and see how they are." ³⁷ Barnabas wanted to take John (the one called Mark) with them also. ³⁸ But Paul kept insisting that they should not take along one who had deserted them in Pamphylia, and had not gone with them to the work. ³⁹ And there arose such a sharp disagreement that they separated from one another. And Barnabas took Mark with him and sailed away to Cyprus. ⁴⁰ But Paul chose Silas and left, being commended by the brothers to the grace of the Lord. ⁴¹ And he went through Syria and Cilicia, strengthening the churches.

16 ¹ And he came [also] to Derbe and to Lystra. And behold, a certain disciple was there, named Timothy, the son of a Jewish woman who was a believer; but his father was a Greek. ² And he was well spoken of by the brothers

---

15:²⁹ Alx[**and from things strangled**], Byz[and from a strangled thing (~ESV, ~HCS, ~MRD, ~NET, ~NRS, ~REB, ~RSV, TEV)], Minor[*omits*]; Alx/Byz[**and from fornication**], Minor[*omits*]; Alx/Byz[**you will do well. Farewell**], Minor[you do well. Farewell (~TLB) *others add* and refrain from doing to others what you would not like done to yourselves].

15:³⁰ Alx[**they went down to Antioch**], Byz[they went to Antioch (KJV, MRD, ~NAB, NKJ, ~NLT, TEV, ~TLB)], Minor[*adds* in a few days (~NLT, ~TLB)].

15:³² Alx/Byz[**And Judas**], Minor[But Judas (DRA, ~NKJ, ~NLT, ~TLB)], Alt[And the associates of Judas (MRD)]; Alx/Byz[**prophets**], Minor[*adds* filled with the Holy Spirit], Alt[*without textual foundation* gifted speakers (~TLB)].

15:³³ Alx[**those who had sent them**], Byz[the apostles (KJV, MRD, NKJ, ~TEV)].

15:⁽³⁴⁾ Alx/Byz[*omits*], Minor[*adds* But it seemed good to Silas to remain there (ASV, DRA, KJV, MRD, NAS, NAU, NKJ) *others* But it seemed good to Silas that they remain there *others also add* and Judas journeyed alone (~DRA)]; *TLB numbers verse 35 as 34, 35 without the text of this verse.*

15:³⁵ Alx/Byz[**Paul**], Alt[*without textual foundation* Saul (~JNT)]; Alx/Byz[**the Lord**], Alt/Peshitta[God (MRD)], Alt[*without textual foundation* omits (~TLB)].

15:³⁶ Alx/Byz[**Paul**], Alt[*without textual foundation* Saul (~JNT)]; Alx[**the brothers**], Byz[our brothers (DRA, KJV, NKJ, REB, TEV)]; Alx/Byz[**the Lord**], Alt/Peshitta[God (MRD)], Alt[*without textual foundation* omits (~TLB)].

15:³⁷ Alx[**wanted to take John**], Byz[determined to take John (KJV, NKJ)]; Alx/Major[**called Mark**], Byz[surnamed Mark (DRA, KJV, MRD)]; Alx[**with them also**], Byz[*omits* also (ESV, HCS, JNT, KJV, MRD, ~NIV, NJB, NKJ, NLT, NRS, REB, RSV, TEV, TLB)].

15:³⁸ Alx/Byz[**Paul**], Alt[*without textual foundation* Saul (~JNT)].

15:³⁹ Alx[**And there arose** *or* But there arose], Byz[So there arose (NKJ)].

15:⁴⁰ Alx/Byz[**Paul**], Alt[*without textual foundation* Saul (~JNT)]; Alx[**the Lord**], Byz[God (DRA, KJV, MRD, NJB, NKJ)], Alt[*without textual foundation* omits (~TLB)].

15:⁴¹ Alx/Byz[**the churches**], Minor[*adds* delivering to them the commands of the elders *others add* delivering to them the commands of the apostles and elders (DRA)]; *TLB numbers this with verse 40.*

16:¹ Alx[**also to Derbe**], Byz[*omits* also (DRA, HCS, JNT, KJV, MRD, NIV, NJB, NKJ, NLT, REB, TEV, TLB)], Alt/Peshitta[to the city of Derbe (MRD)]; Alx[**to Lystra**], Byz[*omits* to (DRA, HCS, KJV, NAB, NKJ, TEV)]; Alx[**a Jewish woman**], Byz[a certain Jewish woman (KJV, NKJ)]; Alx/Byz[**Greek**], Alt[Gentile (DRA, MRD, REB)].

who were in Lystra and Iconium. ³ Paul wanted this man to accompany him. And he took him and circumcised him because of the Jews who were in those places, for they all knew that his father was a Greek. ⁴ As they went on their way through the cities, they delivered to them for observance the decisions which had been reached by the apostles and elders who were in Jerusalem. ⁵ So the churches were strengthened in the faith, and increased in numbers daily.

⁶ And they went through the region of Phrygia and Galatia, having been forbidden by the Holy Spirit to speak the word in Asia. ⁷ And when they came to Mysia, they tried to go into Bithynia, but the Spirit of Jesus did not allow them. ⁸ So, passing by Mysia, they went down to Troas. ⁹ A vision appeared to Paul in [the] night: a man of Macedonia was standing and begging him, and saying, "Come over to Macedonia and help us." ¹⁰ When he had seen the vision, immediately we sought to go on into Macedonia, concluding that God had called us to preach the gospel to them.

¹¹ And putting out to sea from Troas, we ran a straight course to Samothrace, and on the day following to Neapolis; ¹² and from there to Philippi, which is a city of the first district of Macedonia, and a Roman colony. We stayed in this city some days. ¹³ And on the Sabbath day we went outside the gate to the riverside, where we supposed there was a place of prayer. And we sat down and began speaking to the women who had come together. ¹⁴ A woman named Lydia, from the city of Thyatira, a seller of purple fabrics, who was a worshipper of God, was listening. The Lord opened her heart to respond to the things spoken by Paul. ¹⁵ When she and her household had been baptized, she urged us, saying, "If you have judged me to be faithful to the Lord, come into my house and stay." And she prevailed upon us.

16:3 Alx/Byz[**Paul**], Alt[*without textual foundation* Saul (~JNT)]; Alx/Byz[**Greek**], Alt[Gentile (DRA, MRD, REB)].

16:4 Alx[**elders**], Byz[the elders (JNT)].

16:6 Alx[**they went through**], Byz[when they had gone through (DRA, KJV, NKJ)]; Alx[**the region of Phrygia and Galatia**], Byz[Phrygia and the region of Galatia (DRA, KJV, NJB, NKJ, ~TLB)]; Alx/Byz[**the word**], Minor[*adds* of God (MRD)].

16:7 Alx[**And when they came**], Byz[*omits* And (HCS, JNT, KJV, NAB, NET, NIV, NJB, NKJ, ~NLT, NRS, REB, TEV, ~TLB)]; Alx[**into Bithynia**], Byz[through Bithynia (~NLT, ~TLB)]; Alx[**the Spirit of Jesus**], Byz[the Spirit (KJV, NKJ)], Minor[the Spirit of the Lord *another* the Spirit of Christ *others* the Holy Spirit].

16:8 Alx/Byz[**passing by Mysia**], Minor[passing through Mysia (~DRA, ~MRD, ~NAB, NET, NJB, NLT, REB, TEV, TLB)].

16:9 Alx/Byz[**Paul**], Alt[*without textual foundation* Saul (~JNT)]; Alx/Byz[**A vision appeared...a man**], Minor[In a vision...a man appeared (MRD, ~TEV, ~TLB)]; Alx/Byz[**standing**], Minor[*adds* before his face (NAB)].

16:10 Alx[**God**], Byz[the Lord (KJV, NKJ)], Alt[our Lord (MRD)].

16:11 Alx[**And putting out to sea**], Byz[So putting out to sea (ASV, ESV, HCS, KJV, NAS, NAU, NKJ, RSV)]; Alx[**Neapolis** *Greek* Neas Polis], Byz[Neapolis *Greek* Neapolis], Alt/Peshitta[the city of Neapolis (MRD)].

16:12 Alx[**and from there to Philippi**], Byz[and so from there to Philippi]; Alx/Byz[**city of the first district**], Minor[leading city of the district (ASV, DRA, ESV, HCS, JNT, KJV, MRD, NAB, NAS, NAU, NET, NIV, NJB, NKJ, NLT, NRS, REB, RSV, ~TLB, Metzger)]; Alx[**stayed in this city**], Byz[stayed in the same city (~NIV, ~NLT, ~REB, ~TEV, ~TLB)]; Alx/Byz[**We stayed...some days 13**], Alt[13 We stayed...some days (NJB)].

16:13 Alx[**outside the gate**], Byz[outside the city (~HCS, KJV, ~MRD, ~NAB, ~NET, ~NIV, NKJ, NLT, ~REB, TEV, TLB)], Alt[*without textual foundation* outside the gates (~NJB)]; Alx[**where we supposed there was a place of prayer**], Byz[where prayer was customarily made (KJV, ~MRD, NJB, NKJ)].

16:14 Alx/Byz[**The Lord**], Alt/Peshitta[Our Lord (MRD)]; Alx/Byz[**Paul**], Alt[*without textual foundation* Saul (~JNT)].

16:15 Alx/Byz[**her household**], Minor[her whole household (TLB)].

¹⁶ It happened that as we were going to the place of prayer, we were met by a slave-girl who had a spirit of divination. She brought her owners much profit by fortune-telling. ¹⁷ Following after Paul and the rest of us, she kept crying out, saying, "These men are servants of the Most High God, who are telling you the way of salvation." ¹⁸ She continued doing this for many days. But Paul was greatly annoyed, and turned and said to the spirit, "I command you in the name of Jesus Christ to come out of her!" And it came out at that very moment. ¹⁹ But when her owners saw that their hope of profit was gone, they seized Paul and Silas and dragged them into the marketplace before the authorities, ²⁰ and when they had brought them to the magistrates they said, "These men are Jews and they are throwing our city into an uproar. ²¹ They advocate customs which it is not lawful for us Romans to accept or practice." ²² The crowd joined against them, and the magistrates tore the garments off them and ordered them to be beaten with rods. ²³ And when they had inflicted many blows upon them, they threw them into prison, charging the jailer to guard them securely. ²⁴ Receiving such a charge, he put them into the inner prison and fastened their feet in the stocks.

²⁵ But about midnight Paul and Silas were praying and singing hymns to God, and the prisoners were listening to them, ²⁶ and suddenly there came a great earthquake, so that the foundations of the prison were shaken. And immediately all the doors were opened and everyone's chains were unfastened. ²⁷ When the jailer woke and saw that the prison doors were open, he drew [the] sword and was about to kill himself, supposing that the prisoners had escaped. ²⁸ But Paul cried with a loud voice, "Do not harm yourself, for we are all here!" ²⁹ And he called for lights and rushed in, and trembling with fear he fell down before Paul and Silas. ³⁰ And he brought them out and said, "Sirs, what must I do to be saved?" ³¹ And they said, "Believe on the Lord Jesus, and you will be saved, you and your household." ³² They spoke the word of the Lord to him, with all who were in his house. ³³ He took them that very hour of the night and washed their wounds, and immediately he was baptized, he and all his family. ³⁴ Then he brought them up into the house, and set food before them. And he rejoiced with his whole household that he had believed in God.

16:16 Alx[**the place of prayer** Greek the prayer], Byz[to prayer (DRA, HCS, KJV, NJB, NKJ)].

16:17 Alx/Byz[**Paul**], Alt[without textual foundation Saul (~JNT)]; Alx/Major[**the rest of us** Greek us], Byz[Silas]; Alx[**telling you the way**], Byz[telling us the way (KJV, NKJ)].

16:18 Alx/Byz[**Paul**], Alt[without textual foundation Saul (~JNT)].

16:19 Alx/Byz[**Paul**], Alt[without textual foundation Saul (~JNT)].

16:20 Alx/Byz[**magistrates** or chief magistrates], Alt[magistrates and chiefs (MRD)], Alt[without textual foundation omits (~TLB)].

16:23 Alx/Byz[**And when they had**], Minor[But when they had].

16:24 Alx[**Receiving such a charge**], Byz[Having received such a charge (ASV, DRA, ESV, KJV, MRD, NAS, NAU, NKJ, RSV)], Alt[without textual foundation omits (~NLT, ~TLB)].

16:25 Alx/Byz[**Paul**], Alt[without textual foundation Saul (~JNT)].

16:26 Alx[**And immediately** or But immediately], Byz[And immediately], Minor[omits immediately (~JNT, ~NAB, ~NJB, ~REB, ~TLB)].

16:27 Alx/Byz[**the jailer**], Minor[adds the faithful Stephanus]; Alx[**the sword**], Byz[a sword (MRD)].

16:28 Alx/Byz[**Paul**], Alt[without textual foundation Saul (~JNT)].

16:29 Alx/Byz[**before**], Minor[to the feet of (DRA, MRD, NET, NJB, TEV)]; Alx/Byz[**Paul**], Alt[without textual foundation Saul (~JNT)].

16:30 Alx/Byz[**he brought them out**], Minor[adds secured the rest].

16:31 Alx/Byz[**And they said** or But they said], Alt[adds to him (MRD, NJB)]; Alx/Byz[**Believe on**], Alt[Believe in (DRA, ESV, JNT, NAB, NAS, NAU, NET, NIV, NJB, NLT, REB, RSV, TEV)]; Alx[**the Lord Jesus**], Byz[adds Christ (KJV, NKJ)], Alt[our Lord Jesus Christ (MRD)].

16:32 Alx/Byz[**word of the Lord**], Minor[word of God]; Alx[**with all**], Byz[and to all (DRA, ESV, JNT, KJV, MRD, NAB, NIV, NJB, NKJ, NRS, REB, RSV, TEV, TLB)].

16:34 Alx[**into the house**], Byz[into his house (ASV, ~DRA, ESV, HCS, JNT, KJV, MRD, NAB, NAS, NAU, NET, NIV, NJB, NKJ, NLT, REB, RSV, TEV, TLB)]; Alx/Byz[**he rejoiced**], Major[he was

³⁵ But when it was day, the magistrates sent their police, saying, "Release those men." ³⁶ And the jailer reported the[se] words to Paul, saying, "The chief magistrates have sent to release you. Therefore come out now and go in peace." ³⁷ But Paul said to them, "They have beaten us publicly, without trial, men who are Roman citizens, and have thrown us into prison. And do they now cast us out secretly? No! Let them come themselves and take us out." ³⁸ The police reported these words to the magistrates, and they were afraid when they heard that they were Roman citizens. ³⁹ And they came and apologized to them, and they took them out and asked them to go away from the city. ⁴⁰ And they went from the prison and came into the house of Lydia, and when they saw the brothers, they encouraged them and departed.

17

¹ Now when they had passed through Amphipolis and Apollonia, they came to Thessalonica, where there was a synagogue of the Jews. ² And Paul went in, as was his custom. And for three weeks he reasoned with them from the scriptures, ³ explaining and proving that the Christ had to suffer and rise again from the dead, and saying, "This Jesus whom I am proclaiming to you is the Christ." ⁴ And some of them were persuaded, and joined Paul and Silas; as did a large number of the God-fearing Greeks and not a few of the leading women. ⁵ But the Jews were jealous. And taking some wicked men from the market place, they formed a mob and set the city in an uproar. They attacked the house of Jason, seeking to bring them out to the people. ⁶ When they did not find them, they dragged Jason and some of the brothers before the city authorities, shouting, "These men who have turned the world upside down have come here also, ⁷ and Jason has welcomed them. And they are all acting against the decrees of Caesar, saying that

---

rejoicing].

16:35 Alx/Byz[**saying**], Alt/Peshitta[*adds to the master of the prison* (MRD, ~NIV, ~NLT, ~TLB)].

16:36 Alx/Byz[**And the jailer** *or* But the jailer], Alt[*without textual foundation* So the jailer (~NKJ, ~NLT, ~TEV, ~TLB)]; Alx/Byz[**the jailer reported these words**], Minor[the jailer reported the words (ASV, ~JNT, ~NIV, NJB, ~NLT, NRS, RSV, ~TEV, ~TLB)], Alt/Peshitta[when the master of the prison heard, he went and said the same thing (MRD)]; Alx/Byz[**Paul**], Alt[*without textual foundation* Saul (~JNT)].

16:37 Alx/Byz[**Paul**], Alt[*without textual foundation* Saul (~JNT)]; Alx/Byz[**without trial**], Minor[innocent (MRD)]; Alx/Byz[**themselves and take us out 38**], Major[*omits* us], Alt[38 themselves and take us out (DRA)].

16:38 Alx/Byz[**these words**], Minor[the words that were told to them (MRD)].

16:39 Alx[**go away from the city**], Byz[leave the city (DRA, ESV, HCS, JNT, KJV, MRD, NAB, NAS, NAU, NET, NIV, ~NJB, NLT, NRS, RSV, TEV, TLB)].

16:40 Alx[**from the prison**], Byz[out of the prison (ASV, DRA, ESV, ~HCS, KJV, NAB, NAS, NAU, NET, NIV, NKJ, ~NLT, ~NRS, ~REB, RSV, ~TEV, ~TLB)]; Alx[**came into**], Byz[entered into (ASV, DRA, ~ESV, KJV, ~RSV)]; Alx[**encouraged them** *Greek* encouraged], Byz[encouraged them].

17:1 Alx/Byz[**Amphipolis...Apollonia**], Alt/Peshitta[the cities of Amphipolis and Apollonia (MRD, NLT, TLB)]; Alx/Byz[**and Apollonia**], Minor[they went down to Apollonia]; Alx/Byz[**they came to Thessalonica**], Minor[and from there to Thessalonica (~NJB)]; Alx[**a synagogue**], Byz[the synagogue].

17:2 Alx/Byz[**Paul**], Alt[*without textual foundation* Saul (~JNT)]; Alx/Major[**he reasoned**], Byz[he was reasoning (~NAB, ~NJB, ~NLT, ~TEV)].

17:3 Alx/Byz[**is the Christ**], Minor[is Christ (~DRA, KJV)].

17:4 Alx/Byz[**Paul**], Alt[*without textual foundation* Saul (~JNT)]; Alx/Byz[**the God-fearing Greeks**], Minor[the God-fearing and Greeks (NJB)], Alt[the God-fearing and the Gentiles (DRA)], Alt[*without textual foundation* the God-fearing Gentiles (~REB)].

17:5 Alx[**But the Jews**], Byz[But Jews who were not persuaded], Major[But the Jews who were not persuaded (JNT, KJV, NKJ)]; Alx[**were jealous**], Byz[*omits* (~MRD, ~NJB)]; Alx[**out to the people** *or* forth to the people], Byz[to the people (~MRD, ~NAB, ~NJB, ~REB, TLB)].

17:6 **authorities** *Greek* politarchs.

there is another king, Jesus." [8] The crowd and the city authorities were disturbed when they heard this. [9] And when they had taken a pledge from Jason and the others, they let them go.

[10] The brothers immediately sent Paul and Silas away by night to Berea. And when they arrived, they went into the Jewish synagogue. [11] Now these were more noble-minded than those in Thessalonica, for they received the word with great eagerness, examining the Scriptures daily to see if these things were so. [12] Therefore many of them believed, along with prominent Greek women and a number of men. [13] But when the Jews of Thessalonica learned that the word of God was proclaimed by Paul in Berea also, they came there too, agitating and stirring up the crowds. [14] And then the brothers immediately sent Paul out to go as far as the sea, and Silas and Timothy remained there. [15] Now those who escorted Paul led as far as Athens. And receiving a command for Silas and Timothy to come to him as soon as possible, they left.

[16] Now while Paul was waiting for them at Athens, his spirit was provoked within him as he saw that the city was full of idols. [17] So he was reasoning in the synagogue with the Jews and the God-fearing Greeks, and in the marketplace every day with those who happened to be there. [18] And also some of the Epicurean and Stoic philosophers were conversing with him. Some said, "What would this word sower wish to say?" Others, "He seems to be a proclaimer of foreign deities," – because he was preaching Jesus and the resurrection. [19] And they took hold of him and brought him to the Areopagus, saying, "May

17:9 Alx/Byz[**And when they**], Minor[And when the authorities (NET, NLT, TEV, ~TLB)]; Alx/Byz[**and the others**], Alt/Peshitta[and the brothers (MRD)].

17:10 Alx/Byz[**Paul**], Alt[*without textual foundation* Saul (~JNT)]; Alx[**night**], Byz[the night (~MRD, NAB, NET, ~NLT, ~NRS, ~TLB)]; Alx/Byz[**Berea**], Alt/Peshitta[the city of Berea (MRD)].

17:11 Alx/Byz[**these were more noble-minded**], Alt/Peshitta[the Jews there were more noble-minded (ESV, MRD, NAB, NET, NJB, NRS, REB, RSV)], Alt[*without textual foundation* the Bereans were more noble-minded (~NIV, ~NLT, ~TLB)]; Alx/Byz[**those in Thessalonica**], Alt/Peshitta[the Jews in Thessalonica (MRD)]; Alx/Byz[**they received the word**], Minor[*adds* of God]; Alx/Byz[**if these things were so**], Minor[*adds* as Paul was reporting (~JNT, NIV, ~NLT, TEV, ~TLB)].

17:12 Alx/Byz[**along with prominent Greek women and a number of men**], Minor[of Greeks, a number of men, and prominent women (MRD)]; Alx/Byz[**Greek**], Alt/Vulgate[Gentile (DRA, REB)]; **a number of men** *Greek* of men not a few.

17:13 Alx/Byz[**Paul**], Alt[*without textual foundation* Saul (~JNT)]; Alx/Byz[**Berea**], Alt/Peshitta[the city of Berea (MRD)]; Alx[**agitating and stirring up**], Byz[agitating (~KJV, ~NKJ, ~TLB)].

17:14 Alx/Byz[**And then the brothers**], Minor[Therefore the brothers (NAB, NJB)], Alt/Peshitta[The brothers (JNT, MRD, NIV, NLT, REB, TEV, TLB)]; Alx/Byz[**immediately**], Alt/Peshitta[*omits* (MRD)]; Alx/Byz[**Paul**], Alt[*without textual foundation* Saul (~JNT)]; Alx[**as far as the sea** *Greek* as far as on the sea], Byz[as if on the sea (KJV)], Minor[on the sea (DRA, ESV, HCS, JNT, MRD, NAB, NET, NIV, NKJ, NLT, NRS, REB, RSV, TEV, TLB)]; Alx[**and Silas and Timothy**], Byz[but Silas and Timothy *or* but both Silas and Timothy (DRA, ESV, HCS, ~JNT, KJV, MRD, ~NAB, NET, NIV, ~NJB, NKJ, ~NLT, NRS, ~REB, RSV, TEV, ~TLB)]; Alx[**remained**], Byz[were remaining (ASV, KJV, ~NJB)].

17:15 Alx/Byz[**Paul**], Alt[*without textual foundation* Saul (~JNT)]; Alx[**led**], Byz[led him (ASV, DRA, ESV, HCS, JNT, KJV, MRD, NAB, NAS, NAU, NET, NIV, NJB, NKJ, NLT, NRS, REB, RSV, TEV, TLB)]; Alx/Byz[**Athens**], Alt/Peshitta[the city of Athens (MRD)].

17:16 Alx/Byz[**Paul**], Alt[*without textual foundation* Saul (~JNT)].

17:17 Alx/Byz[**who happened to be there**], Alt[*without textual foundation* who met him (~ASV, ~KJV, ~NJB)]; **marketplace** *Greek* agora.

17:18 Alx/Major[**also**], Byz[*omits* (DRA, KJV, NIV, NKJ, ~REB)]; Alx[**Stoic**], Byz[of the Stoic (DRA, KJV, ~MRD)]; Alx/Major[**because he was preaching Jesus and the resurrection**], Byz[*adds* to them (DRA, KJV, NKJ)], Minor[*omits entire clause*], Alt/Peshitta[because he was preaching Jesus and his resurrection to them (MRD, NLT, TLB)]; **word sower** *or* idle babbler; **resurrection** *Greek* anastasis *could have been misunderstood by the pagans to be a goddess i.e.* foreign deities...Jesus and Anastasis *compare* NAB, NJB, ~REB.

17:19, 22 **Areopagus** *or* Mar's Hill *both a place and a council.*

we know what this new teaching is which you present? [20] For you are bringing some strange things to our ears. So we want to know what these things mean." [21] (Now all the Athenians and the foreigners who lived there spent their time in nothing other than telling something or hearing something new.)

[22] So Paul stood up in the meeting of the Areopagus and said: "Men of Athens, I see that in every way you are very religious. [23] For as I passed along, and observed the objects of your worship, I found also an altar with this inscription,

'TO AN UNKNOWN GOD.'

What therefore you worship as unknown, this I proclaim to you. [24] The God who made the world and everything in it, since he is Lord of heaven and earth, does not live in temples made by hands. [25] Nor is he served by human hands, as though he needed anything, since he himself gives to all men life and breath and everything. [26] And he made, from one, every nation of men to live on all the face of the earth, having determined their appointed times and the boundaries of their habitation, [27] that they would seek God, if perhaps they might grope for him and find him, though he is not far from each one of us.

[28]   *'For in him we live and move and have our being,'*
as even some of your own poets have said,
        'We are his offspring.'

[29] Being then God's offspring, we ought not to think that the Divine Nature is like gold or silver or stone, an image formed by the art and imagination of man. [30] The times of

---

17:19 Alx/Byz[**And they took hold of him**], Minor[But they took hold of him *others* And after some days they took hold of him], Alt[*without textual foundation* So they took him (~ESV 2007 edition, ~NET, ~NIV, ~NLT, ~NRS, ~TEV, ~TLB)]; Alx/Byz[**the Areopagus**], Alt/Peshitta[the House of Judgments called Areopagus (MRD, ~NIV, ~REB, ~TLB)], Alt[the City Council (~JNT, ~NLT, ~TEV)].

17:20 Alx[**what these things mean**], Byz[whatever these things mean (~TLB)].

17:21 Alx/Byz[**spent their time in**], Alt/Peshitta[cared for (MRD)]; Alx[**telling something or hearing something new**], Byz[telling and hearing something new (NIV, NJB, ~NLT, TEV, ~TLB)].

17:22 Alx/Byz[**Paul**], Alt[*without textual foundation* Saul (~JNT)]; Alx/Byz[**Areopagus**], Alt[Council (~JNT, ~NJB, ~NLT, ~REB, ~TEV, ~TLB)]; Alx/Byz[**very religious**], Alt/Vulgate[too superstitious (DRA, KJV)], Alt/Peshitta[excessive in the worship of demons (MRD)].

17:25 Alx[**human hands**], Byz[men's hands (ASV, DRA, KJV, NKJ, ~REB, ~TEV)]; Alx/Byz[**all men**], Major[all (ASV, DRA, HCS, JNT, KJV, NAB, NAS, NAU, NET, NJB, NKJ, NLT, NRS, REB, TEV, TLB)]; Alx/Byz[**and everything**], Major[through everything (~JNT, ~MRD, ~NJB, ~REB)].

17:26 Alx[**from one**], Byz[from one blood (KJV, MRD, NKJ)]; Alx/Byz[**appointed times**], Minor[pre-appointed times (KJV, NKJ, ~TEV, ~TLB)].

17:27 Alx[**seek God**], Byz[seek the Lord (KJV, NKJ)], Alt[seek the Deity (NJB)]; Alx/Byz[**if perhaps they might grope for him and find him**], Alt/Peshitta[and, by means of his creations, might find him (MRD)]; Alx/Byz[**though he is not far**], Minor[and yet he is not far (ESV, ~NJB, RSV, TEV)], Alt[because he is not far (MRD)].

17:28 Alx/Byz[**some of your own poets**], Alt/Peshitta/Armenian/Ethiopic[one of your own sages *or* one of your own wise men (MRD)], Minor[some of our own poets], Alt[*without textual foundation* some of your own writers (~NJB)], *other without textual foundation* one of your own poets (~TLB)]; Classical[**Epimenides, De oraculus** "They fashioned you a tomb, O holy and high one. The Cretans, always liars, evil beasts, lazy gluttons! But you are not dead. You live and abide forever. For in you we live and move and have our being"; **Aratus, Phaenomena 5** "Let us begin with [god]. Never, O men, let us leave him unmentioned. All the ways are full of [god], and all the market-places of human beings. The sea is full of him; so are the harbors. In every way we have all to do with [god], for we are truly his offspring"]; *compare Titus 1:12.*

17:30 Alx/Byz[**ignorance**], Minor[this ignorance (DRA, ~JNT, KJV, MRD, ~NET, ~NIV, NKJ, ~NLT, ~TLB)]; Alx/Byz[**commands**], Minor[announces to (DRA, NAS, NAU, ~NJB)].

ignorance God overlooked, but now he commands all people everywhere to repent, [31] because he has fixed a day on which he will judge the world in righteousness by a man whom he has appointed. And of this he has given proof to all men by raising him from the dead."

[32] Now when they heard about the resurrection of the dead, some of them sneered. But others said, "We want to hear you on this subject again." [33] Thus, Paul went out from among them. [34] But some men joined him and believed, among whom also were Dionysius the Areopagite and a woman named Damaris and others with them.

18

[1] After this he left Athens and went to Corinth. [2] And he found a Jew named Aquila, a native of Pontus, having recently come from Italy with his wife Priscilla, because Claudius had commanded all the Jews to leave from Rome. He went to see them, [3] and because he was of the same trade he stayed with them and worked, for by trade they were tentmakers. [4] And every Sabbath he was reasoning in the synagogue, and trying to persuade Jews and Greeks.

[5] When Silas and Timothy came from Macedonia, Paul devoted himself exclusively to the word, testifying to the Jews that the Christ was Jesus. [6] But when they opposed him and blasphemed, he shook out his garments and said to them, "Your blood be on your own heads! I am clean. From now on I will go to the Gentiles." [7] Then he left there and entered into the house of a man named Titius Justus, a worshipper of God, whose house was next door to the synagogue. [8] Crispus, the ruler of the synagogue, believed in the Lord, together

---

17:31 Alx/Byz[**by a man**], Minor[*adds* Jesus].

17:33 Alx[**Thus**], Byz[And thus (MRD, NAB, TEV)]; Alx/Byz[**Paul**], Alt[*without textual foundation* Saul (~JNT)].

17:34 Alx/Byz[**the Areopagite**], Alt[from the judges of the Areopagus (~JNT, MRD, ~NAB, ~NLT, REB, ~TEV, ~TLB)]; Alx/Byz[**and a woman named Damaris**], Minor[*omits*].

18:1 Alx[**After this**], Byz[And after this (MRD, ~NLT, ~TLB)]; Alx[**he left Athens**], Byz[Paul left Athens (ESV, ~JNT, KJV, MRD, NET, NIV, NJB, NKJ, NLT, NRS, TEV, TLB)].

18:2 Alx/Byz[**Claudius**], Minor[*adds* Caesar (MRD, NLT, ~TEV, TLB)]; Alx/Byz[**commanded**], Major[ordered (HCS, ~JNT, NAB, NET, NIV, ~NJB, ~NLT, NRS, ~REB, TEV, TLB)]; Alx/Byz[**leave from Rome**], Major[leave out of Rome (~ESV, ~HCS, ~NAB, ~NAS, ~NAU, ~NIV, ~NRS, ~REB, ~TEV)]; Alx/Byz[**He went to see them**], Minor[Paul went to see them (HCS, ~JNT, NET, NIV, NJB, NRS, REB, TEV)], Alt[*without textual foundation* omits (~NLT, ~TLB)].

18:3 Alx/Byz[**the same trade**], Minor[the same tribe and the same trade], Alt[*without textual foundation adds* as they were *or* as he was (~NIV, ~NLT, ~TEV, ~TLB)]; Alx[**he stayed with them and worked**], Byz[he stayed with them, and they worked (ASV, JNT, ~MRD, NAS, NAU, ~NET, ~NIV, ~NJB, ~NLT, ~NRS, RSV, ~TEV, ~TLB, REB)]; Alx/Byz[**he**], Alt[*without textual foundation* Paul (~NLT, ~REB, ~TLB)].

18:4 Alx/Byz[**text**], Alt/Vulgate[*omits verse*]; Alx/Byz[**every Sabbath he was reasoning in the synagogue**], Minor[entering into the synagogue every Sabbath, he was reasoning (~NAB)]; Alx/Byz[**he**], Alt[*without textual foundation* Paul (~JNT, ~NLT, ~TLB)]; Alx/Byz[**and trying to persuade**], Minor[bringing in the name of the Lord Jesus, and trying to persuade (DRA)]; Alx/Byz[**Jews and Greeks**], Minor[not only Jews, but also Greeks (~DRA, ~JNT, ~NAB, ~NET, ~NJB, ~NKJ, ~NLT, ~REB, ~TEV, ~TLB)]; Alx/Byz[**Greeks**], Alt[*without textual foundation* Gentiles (~MRD, ~REB)].

18:5 Alx/Byz[**Paul**], Alt[*without textual foundation* Saul (~JNT)]; Alx[**to the word**], Byz[in the Spirit (KJV, NKJ)]; Alx[**that the Christ was Jesus**], Byz[the Christ Jesus], Alt[that Jesus was the Christ (ASV, DRA, JNT, KJV, MRD, NAS, NAU, NET, NIV, NJB, NKJ, NLT, TEV, TLB)].

18:6 Alx/Byz[**But when they opposed him and blasphemed**], Alt/Peshitta[*places in verse 5* (MRD)].

18:7 Alx[**entered into the house**], Byz[went into the house (ASV, ESV, HCS, JNT, NAB, NAS, NAU, NET, NIV, NJB, NLT, NRS, REB, RSV, TEV, ~TLB)]; Alx[**Titius**], Byz[*omits* (KJV, NJB, NKJ)], Minor[Titus (ASV, DRA, MRD, NAB, TLB)]; Alx/Byz[**Justus**], Alt/Peshitta[*omits* (MRD)].

18:8 Alx/Byz[**who heard him believed**], Alt/Peshitta[*adds* in God (MRD, ~TLB)]; Alx/Byz[**him**], Alt[*without textual foundation* Paul (~ESV, ~NLT, ~NRS, ~RSV)]; Alx/Byz[**baptized**], Minor[*adds*

with all his household. And many of the Corinthians who heard him believed and were baptized. [9] And the Lord said to Paul in the night through a vision, "Do not be afraid, but go on speaking and do not be silent. [10] For I am with you, and no man will attack you to harm you, for I have many people in this city." [11] And he stayed a year and six months, teaching the word of God among them.

[12] But while Gallio was proconsul of Achaia, the Jews made a united attack upon Paul and brought him before the judgment seat, [13] saying, "This man is persuading men to worship God contrary to the law." [14] But when Paul was about to open his mouth, Gallio said to the Jews, "If it were a matter of wrong or of vicious crime, O Jews, it would be reasonable for me to put up with you. [15] But since it is a matter of questions about words and names and your own law, see to it yourselves. I refuse to be a judge of these things." [16] And he drove them from the judgment seat. [17] And they all seized Sosthenes, the ruler of the synagogue, and beat him in front of the judgment seat. And Gallio paid no attention to this.

[18] After this Paul stayed many days longer, and then took leave of the brothers and sailed for Syria, and with him were Priscilla and Aquila. In Cenchrea he had his hair cut, for he had taken a vow. [19] And they came to Ephesus, and he left them there. But he himself went into the synagogue and reasoned with the Jews. [20] When they asked him to stay for a longer time, he declined. [21] But taking leave and saying, "I will return to you if God wills," he set sail from Ephesus. [22] When he had landed at Caesarea, he went up and greeted the church, and then went down to Antioch. [23] After spending some time there, he departed and went from place to place through the region of Galatia and Phrygia, strengthening all the disciples.

---

in the name of the Lord Jesus Christ].

18:9 Alx/Byz[**Paul**], Alt[*without textual foundation* Saul (~JNT)]; Alx/Byz[**in the night**], Alt/Peshitta[*omits* (MRD)].

18:11 Alx/Byz[**he stayed**], Alt[*without textual foundation* Paul stayed (~NIV, ~NJB, ~NLT, ~TEV, ~TLB) *others without textual foundation* Saul stayed (JNT)], Alt/Peshitta[*adds* in Corinth (MRD)].

18:12 Alx/Byz[**Paul**], Alt[*without textual foundation* Saul (~JNT)].

18:14 Alx/Byz[**Paul**], Alt[*without textual foundation* Saul (~JNT)]; Alx[**If it were a matter of wrong**], Byz[If it were therefore a matter of wrong].

18:15 Alx[**a matter of questions**], Byz[a matter of a question (KJV, NAB, NKJ, NLT, ~REB, TEV)]; Alx[**I refuse to be a judge**], Byz[for I refuse to be a judge (KJV, MRD, NKJ)].

18:17 Alx[**they all**], Byz[all the Greeks (KJV, NKJ)], Minor[all the Jews], Alt/Peshitta[all the Gentiles (MRD)]; Alx/Byz[**And Gallio paid no attention to this**], Minor[Then Gallio pretended not to see (~JNT, ~NIV, ~NJB)].

18:18 Alx/Byz[**Paul**], Alt[*without textual foundation* Saul (~JNT)]; Alx/Byz[**he had his hair cut**], Minor[Aquilla had his hair cut *others* Priscilla and Aquila had their hair cut], Alt[Paul had his hair cut (~TLB)]; **hair cut...vow** *Numbers 6.*

18:19 Alx[**they came to Ephesus**], Byz[he came to Ephesus (DRA, KJV, NKJ, ~TLB)]; Alx/Byz[**and he left them there**], Alt/Peshitta[*omits* (MRD)]; Alx/Byz[**he**], Alt/Peshitta[Paul (MRD, NLT, TEV)].

18:20 Alx[**stay for a longer time**], Byz[*adds* with them (KJV, NIV, NKJ)], Alt/Peshitta[stay with them (MRD)].

18:21 Alx[**but taking leave and saying**], Byz[but taking leave of them, saying (ASV, ESV, KJV, NAS, NAU, NET, NKJ, NRS, REB, RSV, ~TEV)], Alt/Peshitta[For he said (MRD, ~TLB)]; Alx[**I will return**], Byz[I must at all costs keep this coming feast in Jerusalem; but I will return (KJV, MRD, NKJ, TLB)]; Alx/Byz[**he set sail from Ephesus**], Minor[and he set sail from Ephesus (ESV, ~HCS, ~JNT, KJV, ~NAB, ~NET, ~NIV, ~NJB, NKJ, ~NLT, ~NRS, ~REB, RSV, ~TEV, ~TLB)], Alt/Peshitta[And he left Aquila and Priscilla at Ephesus *cf. verse 19* (MRD *places in verse 22*)].

18:22 Alx/Byz[**the church**], Alt/Peshitta[the sons of the church (~JNT, MRD)].

18:23 Alx/Byz[**strengthening**], Minor[establishing (ASV, MRD)], Alt/Vulgate[confirming (DRA, ~NJB, ~TLB)].

²⁴ Now a Jew named Apollos, a native of Alexandria, came to Ephesus. He was an eloquent man, well versed in the scriptures. ²⁵ He had been instructed in the way of the Lord; and being fervent in spirit, he spoke and taught accurately the things concerning Jesus, though he knew only the baptism of John. ²⁶ And he began to speak out boldly in the synagogue. But when Priscilla and Aquila heard him, they took him aside and explained to him the way [of God] more accurately. ²⁷ And when he wanted to go across to Achaia, the brothers encouraged him and wrote to the disciples to welcome him. When he had arrived, he greatly helped those who had believed through grace, ²⁸ for he powerfully refuted the Jews in public, proving by the Scriptures that the Christ is Jesus.

19

¹ And it happened that while Apollos was at Corinth, Paul passed through the upper country, came [down] to Ephesus, and found some disciples. ² And he said to them, "Did you receive the Holy Spirit when you believed?" And they said, "No, we have not even heard that there is a Holy Spirit." ³ And he said, "Into what then were you baptized?" They said, "Into John's baptism." ⁴ But Paul said, "John baptized with the baptism of repentance, telling the people to believe in the one who was coming after him, that is, in Jesus." ⁵ On hearing this, they were baptized in the name of the Lord Jesus. ⁶ And when Paul had laid [his] hands upon them, the Holy Spirit came on them, and they were speaking with tongues and prophesying. ⁷ There were about twelve men in all.

⁸ And he entered the synagogue and for three months spoke boldly, arguing and persuading about [the things of] the kingdom of God. ⁹ But when some were stubborn and disbelieved, speaking evil of the Way before the congregation, he withdrew from them, and

---

18:24 **an eloquent** *or* a learned.

18:25 Alx/Byz[**instructed**], Minor[*adds* in his own country (~TLB)]; Alx/Byz[**the way of the Lord**], Minor[the word of the Lord (~TLB)], Alt[ways of the Lord (MRD)]; Alx[**concerning Jesus**], Byz[concerning the Lord (KJV, NKJ, ~TLB)]; **fervent in spirit** *or* fervent in the Spirit.

18:26 Alx[**Priscilla and Aquila**], Byz[Aquila and Priscilla (KJV, MRD, NKJ)]; Alx/Byz[**the way**], Minor[the word], Alt[*too paraphrased to determine* (~TLB)]; Alx/Byz[**of God**], Minor[omits (NJB, REB, ~TLB) *others* of the Lord (DRA, MRD)].

18:28 Alx/Byz[**in public**], Alt/Peshitta[before the congregation (MRD)], Alt[openly (DRA)]; Alx/Byz[**the Christ is Jesus** *present tense*], Alt[*without textual foundation* Jesus was the Christ *past tense* (~ASV, ~ESV, ~KJV, ~NAS, ~NAU, ~NET, ~NIV, ~NJB, ~NLT, ~RSV)].

19:1 Alx/Byz[**Paul**], Alt[*without textual foundation* Saul (~JNT)]; Alx[**came down to Ephesus**], Byz[omits down (ASV, DRA, ESV, HCS, JNT, KJV, ~MRD, NAS, NAU, NET, ~NIV, ~NJB, NKJ, ~NLT, NRS, RSV, ~TEV, ~TLB)]; Alx[**found**], Byz[finding (KJV, NKJ)].

19:2 Alx[**And he said**], Byz[omits And (JNT, KJV, ~MRD, NAB, NAU, NJB, NKJ, NLT, NRS, REB, TLB)], Alt[*without textual foundation* …asked them (~HCS, ~JNT, ~MRD *in verse 1*, ~NIV, ~NJB, ~NLT, ~REB, ~TEV, ~TLB)]; **when you believed** *or* after you believed.

19:3 Alx[**And he said**], Byz[adds to them (HCS, KJV, NKJ)], Minor[But he said (~NRS)], Alt/Peshitta[He said to them (MRD)], Alt[*without textual foundation* …he asked… (~HCS, ~NET, ~NJB, ~NLT)].

19:4 Alx/Byz[**Paul**], Alt[*without textual foundation* Saul (~JNT)]; Alx/Byz[**Paul said**], Alt/Peshitta[adds to them (MRD)]; Alx[**John baptized**], Byz[John indeed baptized (KJV, NKJ)]; Alx[**Jesus**], Byz[Christ Jesus (KJV, MRD, NKJ)].

19:5 Alx/Byz[**the Lord Jesus**], Minor[adds Christ into the remission of sins], Alt/Peshitta[our Lord Jesus Messiah (MRD)].

19:6 Alx/Byz[**Paul**], Alt[*without textual foundation* Saul (~JNT)]; Alx/Byz[**his hands** *Greek* the hands], Minor[hands (NJB, NKJ)]; Alx/Byz[**tongues** *or* languages], Minor[various tongues (~HCS, MRD, ~NLT, ~REB, ~TEV, ~TLB)].

19:8 Alx/Byz[**spoke boldly**], Minor[adds with great power]; Alx/Byz[**the things of** *Greek* the]; Minor[omits (DRA, ESV, JNT, MRD, NAB, NAS, NAU, NET, NIV, NJB, NLT, NRS, REB, RSV, TEV, ~TLB)].

19:9 Alx[**Tyrannus**], Byz[one Tyrannus (DRA, KJV, ~MRD)], Minor[adds from the fifth hour to the tenth *others* from the fifth hour to the ninth].

took the disciples with him, reasoning daily in the hall of Tyrannus. ¹⁰ This took place for two years, so that all who lived in the province of Asia heard the word of the Lord, both Jews and Greeks.

¹¹ And God did extraordinary miracles by the hands of Paul, ¹² so that handkerchiefs or aprons were even carried from his skin to the sick, and diseases left them and the evil spirits went out. ¹³ But also some of the itinerant Jewish exorcists attempted to name over those who had the evil spirits the name of the Lord Jesus, saying, "I adjure you by Jesus whom Paul preaches." ¹⁴ And seven sons of a certain Sceva, a Jewish chief priest, were doing this. ¹⁵ But in answer the evil spirit said to them, "Jesus I [indeed] know, and I know about Paul, but who are you?" ¹⁶ And the man in whom the evil spirit was leaped on them, overpowered both, and prevailed against them, so that they fled out of that house naked and wounded. ¹⁷ And this became known to all, both Jews and Greeks, who lived in Ephesus. And fear fell upon them all and the name of the Lord Jesus was being magnified. ¹⁸ Many also of those who believed now came, confessing and disclosing their practices. ¹⁹ And a number of those who practiced magic arts brought their books together and burned them in the sight of all. And they counted the value of them and found it came to fifty thousand pieces of silver. ²⁰ So the word of the Lord grew mightily and prevailed.

²¹ Now after these things were finished, Paul purposed in the spirit to go to Jerusalem after he had passed through Macedonia and Achaia, saying, "After I have been there, I must also see Rome." ²² And having sent into Macedonia two of his helpers, Timothy and Erastus, he himself stayed in Asia for a while.

²³ About that time there arose no small disturbance concerning the Way. ²⁴ For a man named Demetrius, a silversmith, who made silver shrines of Artemis, brought no little

---

19:10 Alx[**the Lord**], Byz[*adds* Jesus (KJV, NKJ)]; Alx/Byz[**Greeks**], Alt[Gentiles (MRD, REB, TEV)].

19:11 Alx/Byz[**Paul**], Alt[*without textual foundation* Saul (~JNT)]; Alx/Byz[**hands of Paul**], Alt[hand of Paul (DRA, MRD)], Alt[*without textual foundation omits* hands of (~JNT, ~NIV, ~NLT, ~NRS, ~REB, ~TEV, ~TLB)].

19:12 Alx[**carried from his skin**], Byz[brought from his skin *or* applied from his skin (DRA, HCS, JNT, KJV, NAB, NET, NIV, NJB, NKJ, NLT, NRS, TEV, TLB)]; Alx[**evil spirits went out**], Byz[evil spirits came out from them (DRA, ESV, HCS, JNT, KJV, NAB, NET, NIV, NJB, NKJ, NRS, REB, RSV, TEV)].

19:13 Alx[**But also**], Byz[*omits* also (ESV, HCS, JNT, KJV, MRD, NAB, NET, NIV, NKJ, NLT, NRS, RSV, TLB)]; Alx[**I adjure** *or* I implore], Byz[We adjure *or* We implore (KJV, MRD, ~NKJ)], Alt[*without textual foundation* ...exorcise (~DRA, ~JNT, ~NKJ, ~TLB)], Alt[*without textual foundation* I sternly warn (~NET)]; Alx/Byz[**Paul**], Alt[*without textual foundation* Saul (~JNT)].

19:14 Alx/Byz[**seven sons**], Minor[*omits* seven *others* two sons]; Alx/Byz[**chief priest**], Minor[*omits* chief (TLB)].

19:15 Alx[**the evil spirit said to them**], Byz[*omits* to them (KJV, NJB, NKJ, NLT, REB, TLB)]; Alx[**Jesus I indeed know**], Byz[*omits* indeed (ASV, DRA, ESV, HCS, JNT, KJV, NAB, NAS, NAU, NET, NIV, NJB, NKJ, NLT, NRS, RSV, TEV, TLB)]; Alx/Byz[**Paul**], Alt[*without textual foundation* Saul (~JNT)]; **in answer** *Greek* answering.

19:16 Alx[**overpowered both** *or* overpowered all], Byz[overpowered them (JNT, KJV, MRD, NKJ, NLT, ~TLB)].

19:17 Alx/Byz[**Greeks**], Alt[Gentiles (DRA, MRD, REB, TEV)]; Alx/Byz[**the Lord Jesus**], Alt/Peshitta[our Lord Jesus Messiah (MRD)].

19:20 Alx/Byz[**the word**], Minor[the faith (MRD)]; Alx/Byz[**of the Lord**], Minor[of God (DRA, KJV, MRD, TLB)].

19:21 Alx/Byz[**Paul**], Alt[*without textual foundation* Saul (~JNT)].

19:22 Alx/Byz[**in Asia for a while**], Minor[in Asia for a little while (NIV)].

19:23 Alx/Byz[**the Way**], Alt[*without textual foundation* the way of the Lord (~DRA, ~TEV)], Alt/Peshitta[the way of God (MRD)], Alt[*without textual foundation* the Christians (~REB, ~TLB)].

19:24 Alx/Byz[**silver shrines**], Minor[*omits* silver]; Alx/Byz/Peshitta[**Artemis**], Alt/Vulgate[Diana (ASV, DRA, KJV, MRD, NJB, NKJ, TLB)].

business to the craftsmen. ²⁵ These he gathered together, with the workmen of similar trades, and said, "Men, you know that from this business we have our wealth. ²⁶ And you see and hear that not only in Ephesus, but in almost all of Asia, this Paul has persuaded and turned away a considerable number of people, saying that gods made with hands are no gods at all. ²⁷ Not only is there danger that this trade of ours come into disrepute, but also that the temple of the great goddess Artemis be regarded as worthless and that she whom all of Asia and the world worship will even be dethroned from her magnificence."

²⁸ When they heard this, they were enraged and began crying out, "Great is Artemis of the Ephesians!" ²⁹ The city was filled with confusion, and they rushed with one accord into the theater, dragging along Gaius and Aristarchus, Paul's traveling companions from Macedonia. ³⁰ Paul wanted to go in among the crowd, but the disciples would not let him. ³¹ Some of the Asiarchs also, who were friends of his, sent to him and begged him not to venture into the theater. ³² Now some were shouting one thing, some another; for the assembly was in confusion, and most of the people did not know why they had come together. ³³ Some of the crowd prompted Alexander, since the Jews had put him forward. And Alexander motioned with his hand, wishing to make a defense to the people. ³⁴ But when they recognized that he was a Jew, for about two hours they all with one voice shouted, "Great is Artemis of the Ephesians!" ³⁵ And when the town clerk had quieted the crowd, he said, "Men of Ephesus, who of men is there after all who does not know that the city of the Ephesians is guardian of the temple of the great Artemis and of the image which fell down from heaven? ³⁶ Therefore, since these facts are undeniable, you ought to be quiet and do nothing rash. ³⁷ For you have brought these men here who are neither robbers of temples nor blasphemers of our goddess. ³⁸ If then Demetrius and the craftsmen with him have a complaint against anyone, the courts are open, and there are proconsuls. Let them bring charges against one another. ³⁹ But if you seek anything further, it shall be settled in the lawful assembly. ⁴⁰ As it is, we are in danger of being charged with rioting because of

---

19:25 Alx/Byz[**Men**], Minor[*adds* fellow-crasftmen], Alt[*without textual foundation* Sirs (~ASV, ~DRA, ~KJV)], Alt[*without textual foundation omits* (~NJB)].

19:26 Alx/Byz[**this Paul**], Minor[*adds* a somebody (~HCS, ~NIV, ~NJB, ~NLT, ~REB, ~TEV, ~TLB)], Alt[*without textual foundation* this Saul (~JNT)].

19:27 Alx/Byz[**Artemis**], Alt/Vulgate[Diana (ASV, DRA, KJV, MRD, NJB, NKJ, TLB)]; Alx[**be dethroned from her magnificence**], Byz[have her magnificence destroyed (DRA, ~HCS, KJV, NKJ, TEV)].

19:28 Alx/Byz[**and began crying out**], Minor[and running into the street they began crying out]; Alx/Byz[**Artemis**], Alt/Vulgate[Diana (ASV, DRA, KJV, MRD, NJB, NKJ, TLB)].

19:29 Alx/Byz[**The city**], Major[The whole city (DRA, JNT, KJV, MRD, NIV, NJB, NKJ, NLT, REB, TEV)]; Alx/Byz[**Paul**], Alt[*without textual foundation* Saul (~JNT)].

19:30 Alx/Byz[**Paul's**], Alt[*without textual foundation* Saul's (~JNT)]; Alx/Byz[**in among the crowd**], Alt/Peshitta[into the theater (MRD)], Alt[*without textual foundation* in (~NLT, ~TLB)].

19:31 **Asiarchs** *people from Asia.*

19:32 Alx/Byz[**the assembly**], Alt/Peshitta[*adds* in the theater (MRD)].

19:33 Alx[**prompted Alexander**], Byz[drew Alexander (~ASV, DRA, KJV, ~MRD, ~NAS, ~NAU, ~NET, NIV, ~NJB, NKJ, ~NLT, ~TEV, TLB)].

19:34 Alx/Byz[**Great is Artemis of the Ephesians**], Minor[*repeats* (NLT, TLB)]; Alx/Byz[**Artemis**], Alt/Vulgate[Diana (ASV, DRA, KJV, MRD, NJB, NKJ, TLB)].

19:35 Alx[**who of men**], Byz[what man (ASV, DRA, ~ESV, HCS, ~JNT, KJV, MRD, NAB, NAS, NAU, NET, ~NIV, ~NJB, NKJ, ~NLT, ~NRS, ~REB, RSV, ~TEV, ~TLB)]; Alx[**temple of the great**], Byz[*adds* goddess (KJV, NKJ)]; Alx/Byz[**Artemis**], Alt/Vulgate[Diana (ASV, DRA, KJV, MRD, NJB, NKJ, TLB)].

19:37 Alx[**our goddess**], Byz[your goddess (DRA, JNT, KJV, NKJ, ~TLB)].

19:39 Alx[**anything further**], Byz[about other matters (ASV, DRA, ~HCS, KJV, MRD, ~NET, ~NJB, NKJ, NLT, TLB)].

19:40 Alx/Major[**not be able**], Byz[*omits* not (DRA, ESV, HCS, KJV, NET, NKJ, NRS, RSV)]; Alx/Byz[**render an account** *or* give back an account], Major[give an account (ASV, DRA, ESV,

today's events. In that case we would [not] be able to render an account concerning this commotion, since there is no reason for it." After he had said this, he dismissed the assembly.

20

¹ After the uproar had ceased, Paul sent for the disciples, and when he had exhorted them and taken his leave of them, he set out for Macedonia. ² When he had gone through those parts and had given them much encouragement, he came to Greece. ³ There he spent three months. And when a plot was made against him by the Jews as he was about to set sail for Syria, he decided to return through Macedonia. ⁴ He was accompanied by Sopater of Berea, the son of Pyrrhus, and by Aristarchus and Secundus of the Thessalonians, and Gaius of Derbe, and Timothy, and Tychicus and Trophimus of Asia. ⁵ But these went on ahead and were waiting for us at Troas. ⁶ And we sailed away from Philippi after the Days of Unleavened Bread, and in five days came to them at Troas, where we stayed seven days.

⁷ On the first day of the week, when we were gathered together to break bread, Paul began talking to them, intending to leave the next day, and he prolonged his message until midnight. ⁸ There were many lamps in the upper room where we were gathered. ⁹ And there was a young man named Eutychus sitting in the window sill, sinking into a deep sleep. And as Paul talked on and on, he was overcome by sleep and fell down from the

---

HCS, JNT, KJV, MRD, NAB, ~NAS, ~NAU, NET, ~NIV, NJB, NKJ, ~NLT, NRS, REB, RSV, TEV, ~TLB)]; Alx[**concerning this commotion**], Byz[of this commotion (ASV, DRA, KJV, REB)]; Alx[**After he had said this, he dismissed the assembly**], Byz[41 After he had said this, he dismissed the assembly (ASV, ESV, HCS, KJV, MRD, NAS, NAU, NET, NKJ, NLT, NRS, REB, RSV, TEV, TLB)].

20:1 Alx/Byz[**Paul**], Alt[*without textual foundation* Saul (~JNT)]; Alx[**sent for the disciples**], Byz[called to the disciples (DRA, KJV, MRD, ~NAB, NKJ, TEV)]; Alx[**exhorted them and**], Byz[omits (KJV, NKJ)].

20:2 Alx/Byz[**Greece** *Greek* Ellas], Byz[the country of Greece (MRD)], Alt[*without textual foundation* Achaia (~TEV)], Alt[*moves to verse 3* (TLB)].

20:3 Alx/Byz[**decided to return**], Minor[the Spirit said to him to return].

20:4 Alx[**He was accompanied**], Byz[adds as far as Asia (ASV, KJV, MRD, NKJ)], Alt[*without textual foundation adds* as far as Turkey (~TLB)]; Alx[**Sopater of Berea, the son of Pyrrhus**], Byz[omits the son of Pyrrhus (KJV, MRD, NKJ)], Alt[*without textual foundation* Sopater of Berea, the son of Pyrrhus from Berea (~ESV 2001 edition)]; Alx/Byz[**Berea...Derbe**], Minor[Berea...Douberios], Alt/Peshitta[the city of Berea...the city of Derbe (MRD)]; Alx/Byz[**Timothy**], Alt/Peshitta[adds of Lystra (MRD)]; Alx/Byz[**and Tychicus and Trophimus of Asia**], Minor[and the Ephesians Eutychus and Trophimus], Alt[*without textual foundation* and Tychicus and Trophimus, who were returning to their homes in Turkey (~TLB)].

20:5 Alx[**But**], Byz[omits (DRA, ESV, HCS, JNT, KJV, MRD, NAB, NET, NIV, NJB, NKJ, NLT, NRS, REB, RSV, TEV)]; Alx[**went on ahead**], Byz[went on (JNT, NJB, RSV)].

20:6 Alx/Byz[**Philippi**], Alt/Peshitta[Philippi, a city of the Macedonians (MRD, ~NLT, ~TLB)]; Alx/Byz[**came to them**], Alt/Peshitta[proceeded by water and came to them (MRD)]; Alx/Byz[**Unleavened Bread** *Greek* Azymos], Alt/Vulgate[Azymes (DRA)], Alt[*without textual foundation* Passover (~NLT, ~REB, ~TLB)]; JNT Matzah *means* Unleavened Bread.

20:7 Alx[**we were gathered together**], Byz[the disciples were gathered together (KJV, NKJ)]; Alx/Byz[**to break bread**], Alt/Peshitta[to break the Eucharist (MRD)], Alt[to share in the Lord's Supper (~NLT) *or* for the fellowship meal (~TEV) *or* for a Communion Service (~TLB)]; Alx/Byz[**Paul**], Alt[*without textual foundation* Saul (~JNT)].

20:8 Alx/Byz[**many lamps**], Minor[many windows]; Alx/Byz[**we were gathered**], Minor[they were gathered (KJV, NKJ)].

20:9 Alx/Byz[**Paul**], Alt[*without textual foundation* Saul (~JNT)]; Alx/Byz[**sinking into a deep sleep. And as Paul talked on and on, he was overcome by sleep, and fell down**], Alt/Peshitta[and listening. And as Paul talked on and on, he sunk into a deep sleep; and in his sleep he fell down (MRD)].

third story and was picked up dead. [10] But Paul went down and fell on him. And after embracing him, he said, "Do not be alarmed, for his life is in him." [11] When he had gone back up and had broken the bread and eaten, he talked with them a long while until daybreak, and then left. [12] They took away the boy alive, and were greatly comforted.

[13] But going ahead to the ship, we set sail for Assos, intending to take Paul aboard there; for so he had arranged, intending himself to go by land. [14] And when he met us at Assos, we took him on board and came to Mitylene. [15] Sailing from there, we arrived the following day opposite Chios. And the next day we crossed over to Samos. And the day after that we came to Miletus. [16] For Paul had decided to sail past Ephesus, so that he would not have to spend time in Asia. For he was hurrying to be in Jerusalem, if possible, on the day of Pentecost.

[17] From Miletus he sent to Ephesus and called to him the elders of the church. [18] And when they came to him, he said to them: "You yourselves know how I lived the whole time I was with you, from the first day that I set foot in Asia, [19] serving the Lord with all humility and with tears and with trials which came upon me through the plots of the Jews; [20] how I did not shrink from declaring to you anything that was profitable, and teaching you publicly and from house to house, [21] testifying both to Jews and to Greeks of repentance toward God and faith in our Lord Jesus. [22] And now, behold, bound in the Spirit, I am going to Jerusalem, not knowing what will happen to me there, [23] except that the Holy Spirit solemnly testifies to me in every city, saying that bonds and afflictions await me. [24] But I do not consider my life of any account nor as precious to myself, if only I may finish my course and the ministry which I received from the Lord Jesus, to testify to the gospel of the grace of God.

[25] And now, behold, I know that all of you among whom I have gone about preaching the kingdom will see my face no more. [26] Therefore, I testify to you this day that I

20:10 Alx/Byz[**Paul**], Alt[*without textual foundation* Saul (~JNT)].

20:11 Alx[**broken the bread**], Byz[broken bread (DRA, ESV, KJV, NET, NIV, NKJ, NRS, REB, RSV, TEV)], Alt[*without textual foundation* shared in the Lord's Supper (~NLT, ~TLB)]; Alx/Byz[**and then left**], Alt/Peshitta[*adds* to go by land (MRD)].

20:13 Alx/Byz[**going ahead to the ship**], Major[going to the ship (DRA, MRD, ~NLT)]; Alx/Byz[**Assos**], Minor[Thasos (MRD)]; Alx/Byz[**Paul**], Alt[*without textual foundation* Saul (~JNT)].

20:14 Alx/Byz[**Assos**], Minor[Thasos (MRD)], Alt[*without textual foundation omits* (~NLT, ~TLB)].

20:15 Alx/Byz[**the following day**], Minor[in the evening]; Alx/Byz[**Chios**], Alt/Peshitta[the island Chios (MRD, NLT)]; Alx[**Samos. And**], Byz[*adds* after remaining at Trogyllium (KJV, MRD, NJB, NKJ)].

20:16 Alx/Byz[**Paul**], Alt[*without textual foundation* Saul (~JNT)].

20:17 Alx/Byz[**he sent to Ephesus and called to him the elders of the church**], Alt/Peshitta[he sent and called to him the elders of the church at Ephesus (MRD, TLB)].

20:18 Alx/Byz[**when they came to him**], Minor[*adds* and were together (DRA)].

20:19 Alx/Byz[**the Lord**], Alt/Peshitta[God (MRD)]; Alx[**tears**], Byz[many tears (KJV, NKJ, NLT, TEV)].

20:20 Alx/Byz[**publicly**], Alt/Peshitta[in the streets (MRD)].

20:21 Alx/Major[**our Lord Jesus**], Byz[*adds* Christ (ASV, DRA, ESV, JNT, KJV, MRD, NAS, NAU, NKJ, RSV, TLB)].

20:22 Alx/Byz[**behold**], Alt/Peshitta[*omits* (HCS, JNT, MRD, NAB, NET, NIV, NJB, NLT, NRS, TEV, TLB)].

20:23 Alx[**testifies to me**], Byz[*omits* to me (KJV, NKJ)].

20:24 Alx[**But I do not consider my life of any account nor as precious to myself**], Byz[But none of these things move me, nor do I count my life precious to myself (DRA, KJV, NKJ)]; Alx[**finish my course**], Byz[*adds* with joy (KJV, NKJ)]; Alx/Byz[**the ministry**], Alt/Vulgate[*adds* of the word (DRA)]; Alx/Byz[**to testify to the gospel**], Minor[to testify the gospel to Jews and Greeks].

20:25 Alx[**the kingdom**], Byz[*adds* of God (DRA, KJV, MRD, NKJ, TEV)], Minor[*adds* of Jesus *others add* of the Lord Jesus].

am innocent of the blood of all men. [27] For I did not shrink from declaring to you the whole counsel of God. [28] Be on guard for yourselves and for all the flock, among which the Holy Spirit has made you overseers, to shepherd the church of God which he purchased with the blood of his Own. [29] I know that after my departure savage wolves will come in among you, not sparing the flock. [30] And from among your own selves will arise men speaking perverse things, to draw away the disciples after them. [31] Therefore be alert, remembering that for three years I did not cease night and day to admonish each one with tears. [32] And now I commend you to God and to the word of his grace, which is able to build you up and to give the inheritance among all those who are sanctified. [33] I have coveted no one's silver or gold or clothes. [34] You yourselves know that these hands ministered to my own needs and to the men who were with me. [35] In everything I did, I showed you that by this kind of hard work we must help the weak, remembering the words the Lord Jesus himself said: *'It is more blessed to give than to receive.'"*

[36] When he had said this, he knelt down and prayed with them all. [37] And they all wept and embraced Paul and kissed him, [38] grieving most of all over the word which he had spoken, that they would not see his face again. And they accompanied him to the ship.

21 [1] When we had parted from them and set sail, we came by a straight course to Cos, and the next day to Rhodes, and from there to Patara. [2] And having found a ship crossing over to Phoenicia, we went aboard and set sail. [3] When we had come in sight of Cyprus, leaving it on the left we sailed to Syria, and landed at Tyre; for there the ship was to unload its cargo. [4] And having sought out the disciples, we stayed there for seven days. Through the Spirit they told Paul not to set foot in Jerusalem. [5] And when our days there were ended, we left and started on our journey, while they all, with wives and children, brought us on our way until we were out of the city. After kneeling down on the beach and praying, [6] we said farewell to one another. Then we went up into the ship, and they returned home.

20:28 Alx[**Be on guard**], Byz[Therefore be on guard (KJV, MRD, NKJ, NLT, TEV)]; Alx[**church of God**], Byz[church of the Lord and God], Minor[church of the Lord (ASV, REB)]; Alx[**the blood of his Own**], Byz[his own blood (ASV, DRA, ESV, HCS, KJV, MRD, NAB, NAS, NAU, NIV, NKJ, NLT, REB, TLB)]; **overseers**: *or* bishops.

20:29 Alx[**I know**], Byz[For I know this (KJV, ~MRD, NKJ)].

20:31 Alx/Byz[**night and day**], Alt[*without textual foundation* day and night (~MRD, ~TEV)].

20:32 Alx[**I commend you**], Byz[*adds* brothers (KJV, NKJ)]; Alx/Byz[**to God**], Minor[to the Lord (JNT)]; Alx[**give the inheritance**], Byz[give you the inheritance (ASV, ESV, HCS, JNT, KJV, MRD, NAB, NAS, NAU, NET, NIV, NJB, NKJ, NLT, NRS, REB, RSV, TEV, TLB)].

20:33 Alx/Byz[**no one's silver**], Minor[no silver (MRD, TLB)].

20:34 Alx/Byz[**You yourselves know**], Minor[But you yourselves know (KJV, MRD, NKJ)].

20:35 **It is more blessed to give than to receive** *no parallel reference in the gospels*.

20:37 Alx/Byz[**Paul**], Alt/Peshitta[him (JNT, MRD, NIV, NLT, TEV, TLB)].

21:1 Alx/Byz[**Cos**], Alt/Peshitta[the island of Cos (MRD, NLT)]; Alx/Byz[**Patara**], Minor[*adds* and Myra].

21:3 Alx/Byz[**Cyprus**], Alt/Peshitta[the island of Cyprus (MRD, NLT, TLB)].

21:4 Alx/Byz[**the disciples**], Major[disciples (DRA, HCS, KJV, MRD, NKJ, TEV)]; Alx/Byz[**Paul**], Alt[*without textual foundation* Saul (~JNT)]; Alx[**set foot in Jerusalem** *or* go to Jerusalem], Byz[go up to Jerusalem (DRA, JNT, KJV, NKJ)].

21:5-6 Alx[**After kneeling down on the beach and praying, 6 we said farewell to one another. Then**], Byz[And we kneeled down on the beach and prayed. 6 And when we said farewell to one another, (ASV, DRA, ESV, HCS, KJV, MRD, ~NAB, ~NIV, NJB, NKJ, NLT, NRS, REB, RSV, TEV, TLB)], Alt[*places first clause of verse 6 in verse 5* (ASV, NAS, NAU, RSV, TLB)].

21:6 Alx/Byz[**said farewell**], Alt/Peshitta[kissed (MRD)]; Alx[**we went up into the ship**], Byz[we went on board the ship (ASV, ~DRA, ESV, HCS, JNT, ~KJV, ~MRD, NAB, NAS, NAU, NET, NIV, NJB, NKJ, NLT, NRS, REB, RSV, TEV, TLB)].

⁷ When we had finished the voyage from Tyre, we arrived at Ptolemais. And we greeted the brothers and stayed with them for a day. ⁸ On the next day we left and came to Caesarea, and entering the house of Philip the evangelist, who was one of the seven, we stayed with him. ⁹ He had four daughters, virgins, who prophesied. ¹⁰ As we were staying there for some days, a prophet named Agabus came down from Judea. ¹¹ And coming to us, he took Paul's belt, bound his own feet and hands, and said, "This is what the Holy Spirit says, 'In this way the Jews at Jerusalem will bind the man who owns this belt and deliver him into the hands of the Gentiles.'" ¹² When we heard this, we and the people there begged him not to go up to Jerusalem. ¹³ Then Paul answered, "What are you doing, weeping and breaking my heart? For I am ready not only to be bound but even to die at Jerusalem for the name of the Lord Jesus." ¹⁴ And when he would not be persuaded, we ceased and said, "The will of the Lord be done."

¹⁵ And after these days we got ready and went up to Jerusalem. ¹⁶ And some of the disciples from Caesarea went with us, bringing us to the house of Mnason of Cyprus, an early disciple, with whom we were to lodge.

¹⁷ When we arrived at Jerusalem, the brothers welcomed us gladly. ¹⁸ And the following day Paul went in with us to James, and all the elders were present. ¹⁹ After he had greeted them, he related one by one the things that God had done among the Gentiles through his ministry. ²⁰ And when they heard it, they glorified God. And they said to him, "You see, brother, how many tens of thousands there are among the Jews of those who have believed. They are all zealous for the law, ²¹ and they have been told about you that you teach all the Jews who are among the Gentiles to forsake Moses, telling them not to circumcise their children or to walk according to the customs. ²² What then is to be done?

21:7 Alx/Byz[**Ptolemais**], Alt/Peshitta[the city Acco (MRD)]; **finished** *or* continued.

21:8 Alx/Byz[**the next day we**], Major[*adds* who were Paul's companions (KJV, NKJ)]; Alx[**we came to Caesarea**], Byz[*they* came to Caesarea].

21:11 Alx/Byz[**Paul's**], Alt[*without textual foundation* Saul's (~JNT)]; Alx[**belt, bound his own**], Byz[belt, and bound his (~DRA, ~ESV, ~KJV, ~MRD, ~NAS, ~NAU, ~NJB, ~NLT, ~RSV)]; Alx/Byz[**feet and hands**], Minor[hands and feet (JNT, KJV, NET, NIB, NKJ)].

21:12 Alx/Byz[**begged him**], Minor[begged Paul (NIV, NJB, NLT, REB, TEV, TLB)].

21:13 Alx[**Then Paul answered**], Byz[And Paul answered (~JNT, ~NLT, ~TEV, ~TLB)], Alt[*without textual foundation* …he answered (~NJB, ~NLT, ~TEV, ~TLB) *another without textual foundation* …Saul answered (~JNT)], Minor[*adds* us], Alt[*adds* and said (DRA, MRD)]; Alx/Byz[**but even to die**], Minor[but even willing to die]; Alx/Byz[**the Lord Jesus**], Minor[*adds* Christ (MRD)].

21:14 Alx/Byz[**and said**], Minor[*adds* to one another].

21:15 Alx/Byz[**after these days**], Minor[after some days (~JNT, ~NIV, ~NJB, ~NLT, ~REB, TEV, ~TLB)]; Alx[**we got ready**], Byz[we packed up (ASV, JNT, KJV, NKJ, NLT, REB, TLB)], Minor[we told them farewell].

21:16 Alx/Byz[**an early disciple** *or* an old disciple], Alt/Peshitta[a brother from among the earlier disciples (MRD)].

21:17 Alx[**the brothers welcomed us**], Byz[the brothers received us (ASV, DRA, ESV, JNT, KJV, MRD, NAS, NAU, NIV, NKJ, RSV)].

21:18 Alx/Byz[**Paul**], Alt[*without textual foundation* Saul (~JNT)].

21:19 Alx/Byz[**he**], Alt/Peshitta[Paul (MRD, ~NET, ~NIV, NLT, ~TEV, TLB)], Alt[*without textual foundation* Saul (~JNT)].

21:20 Alx[**glorified God**], Byz[glorified the Lord (KJV, NKJ)]; Alx/Byz[**And they said to him**], Major[saying to him], Minor[*omits* to him (HCS, NJB, NLT, TEV, TLB)], Alt[…said to Paul (~NIV, ~REB, ~TEV)]; Alx[**how many tens of thousands there are among the Jews**], Byz[how many tens of thousands of Jews (HCS, KJV, NET, NIV, NJB, NKJ, NLT, TEV, TLB)], Minor[how many tens of thousands], Alt/Peshitta[how many tens of thousands there are in Judea (MRD)].

21:21 Alx/Byz[**all the Jews**], Minor[*omits* all (DRA, TLB)].

21:22 Alx[**What then is to be done?**], Byz[*adds* The multitude must certainly gather, for (DRA, KJV, NJB, NKJ)].

They will certainly hear that you have come. ²³ Therefore do what we tell you. We have four men who are under a vow. ²⁴ Take these men and purify yourself along with them and pay their expenses, so that they may shave their heads. And all will know that there is nothing in what they have been told about you, but that you yourself live in observance of the law. ²⁵ But as for the Gentiles who have believed, we wrote to them our decision that they should abstain from meat sacrificed to idols and from blood and from what is strangled and from fornication." ²⁶ The next day Paul took the men and purified himself along with them. Then he went to the temple to give notice of the date when the days of purification would end and the offering would be made for each one of them.

    ²⁷ When the seven days were almost over, the Jews from Asia, upon seeing him in the temple, stirred up all the crowd and laid hands on him, ²⁸ crying out, "Men of Israel, help! This is the man who is teaching all men everywhere against our people and our law and this place. And besides he also brought Greeks into the temple, and he has defiled this holy place." ²⁹ For they had previously seen Trophimus the Ephesian in the city with him, and they supposed that Paul had brought him into the temple. ³⁰ Then all the city was aroused, and the people rushed together, and taking hold of Paul they dragged him out of the temple. And immediately the gates were shut. ³¹ And while they were trying to kill him, a report came up to the commander of the Roman cohort that all Jerusalem was in confusion. ³² At once he took along some soldiers and centurions and ran down to them. And when they saw the commander and the soldiers, they stopped beating Paul. ³³ Then the commander came up and arrested him, and ordered him to be bound with two chains. He inquired who he was and what he had done. ³⁴ Some in the crowd shouted one thing, and some another. And as he could not learn the facts because of the uproar, he ordered him to be brought into the barracks. ³⁵ When he came to the steps, he was actually carried by the soldiers because of the violence of the mob; ³⁶ for the mob of the people followed, crying out, "Away with him!"

21:23 Alx/Byz[**a vow**], Alt[*adds* to purify themselves (MRD) *another adds* and to shave their heads (TLB)].

21:24 Alx[**all will know**], Byz[all may know (KJV, MRD, ~NLT, NKJ)]; **shave their heads** *cf Numbers 6.*

21:25 Alx/Byz[**we wrote**], Minor[we sent (~ESV, NAB, ~NLT, NRS, REB, RSV, TEV)]; Alx[**should abstain**], Byz[should observe no such thing, but abstain (KJV, NKJ, TLB)]; Alx/Byz[**from what is strangled**], Minor[*omits*]; Alx/Byz[**blood... strangled... fornication**], Alt/Peshitta[fornication... strangled... blood (MRD)].

21:26 Alx/Byz[**Paul**], Alt[*without textual foundation* Saul (~JNT)].

21:28 Alx/Byz[**28 crying out**], Alt/Vulgate[crying out 28 (DRA)]; Alx/Byz[**Greeks**], Alt[Gentiles (DRA, JNT, MRD, NLT, REB, TEV, TLB)].

21:29 Alx[**previously**], Byz[*omits* (DRA, TEV)]; Alx/Byz[**Paul**], Alt[*without textual foundation* Saul (~JNT)].

21:30 Alx/Byz[**Paul**], Alt[*without textual foundation* Saul (~JNT)].

21:31 Alx[**And while they were trying to kill him**], By[But while they were trying to kill him (JNT, NKJ)]; Alx/Byz[**all Jerusalem**], Alt/Peshitta[the whole city (MRD)]; Alx[**was in confusion**], Byz[had been in confusion].

21:32 Alx/Byz[**Paul**], Alt[*without textual foundation* Saul (~JNT)].

21:33 Alx[**Then the commander**], Byz[But the commander (MRD, ~NAB, ~NIV, ~NJB, ~REB, ~TEV, ~TLB)].

21:34 Alx[**shouted**], Byz[cried out (DRA, KJV, ~MRD, NJB, NKJ)].

21:35 Alx/Byz[**he**], Alt/Peshitta[Paul (HCS, MRD, NET, NIV, NJB, NLT, NRS, REB, TLB)], Alt[*without textual foundation* Saul (~JNT)].

21:36 Alx/Byz[**crying out**], Alt/Peshitta[*adds* and saying (MRD)].

37 As Paul was about to be brought into the barracks, he said to the commander, "May I say something to you?" And he said, "Do you know Greek? **38** Then you are not the Egyptian who some time ago stirred up a revolt and led the four thousand men of the Assassins out into the wilderness?" **39** Paul replied, "I am a Jew, from Tarsus in Cilicia, a citizen of no insignificant city. I beg you, let me speak to the people." **40** When he had given him permission, Paul, standing on the steps, motioned to the people with his hand. And when there was a great hush, he addressed them in the Hebrew language, saying,

22 **1** "Men, brothers and fathers, hear my defense which I now offer to you." **2** And when they heard that he addressed them in the Hebrew language, they became more quiet. And he said: **3** "I am a Jewish man, born in Tarsus of Cilicia, but brought up in this city, educated under Gamaliel, strictly according to the law of our fathers, being zealous for God just as you all are today. **4** I persecuted this Way to the death, binding and delivering into prison both men and women, **5** as also the high priest and all the Council of the Elders can testify. From them I also received letters to the brothers, and started off for Damascus in order to bring even those who were there to Jerusalem as prisoners to be punished.

6 "As I made my journey and drew near to Damascus, about noon a bright light from heaven suddenly flashed around me. **7** And I fell to the ground and heard a voice saying to me, 'Saul, Saul, why do you persecute me?' **8** And I answered, 'Who are you, Lord?' And he said to me, 'I am Jesus the Nazarene, whom you are persecuting.' **9** And those who were with me saw the light, but did not hear the voice of the one who was speaking to me. **10** And I said, 'What shall I do, Lord?' And the Lord said to me, 'Get up and go on into Damascus, and there you will be told of all that has been appointed for you to do.' **11** But since I could not see because of the brightness of that light, I was led by the hand by those who were with me and came into Damascus.

12 "A certain Ananias, a devout man according to the Law, and well spoken of by all the Jews who lived there, **13** came to me, and standing near said to me, 'Brother Saul,

21:37 Alx/Byz[**Paul**], Alt[*without textual foundation* Saul (~JNT)]; Alx/Byz[**May I say something**], Major[May I speak (KJV, MRD, ~NJB, NKJ, ~NLT, ~REB, ~TLB)]; Alx/Byz[**Do you know Greek**], Alt[*without textual foundation* Can you speak Greek (~DRA, ~KJV, ~NAB, ~NIV, ~NJB, ~NKJ, ~REB, ~TEV)].

21:38 Alx/Byz[**Assassins** *or* Terrorists *Latinism* sicarius], Alt/Peshitta[doers of evil (MRD)].

21:39 Alx/Byz[**Paul**], Alt[*without textual foundation* Saul (~JNT)]; Alx/Byz[**a citizen of**], Alt/Peshitta[born in (MRD)], Alt[*without textual foundation* omits (~TLB)].

21:40 Alx/Byz[**Paul**], Alt[*without textual foundation* Saul (~JNT)]; Alx/Byz[**he addressed them**], Major[he began to address them (NJB)]; Alx/Byz[**Hebrew**], Alt[*without textual foundation* Aramaic (~NET, ~NIV, ~NLT) *another without textual foundation* Jewish (~REB)].

22:1 Alx/Byz[**Men, brothers and fathers**], Alt/Peshitta[*omits* Men (ASV, ESV, HCS, JNT, MRD, NAB, NAS, NAU, NET, NIV, NJB, NKJ, NLT, NRS, REB, RSV, ~TEV, TLB)].

22:2 Alx/Byz[**Hebrew**], Alt[*without textual foundation* Aramaic (~NET, ~NIV, ~NLT, ~REB)]; Alx/Major[**And he said 3**], Byz[3 And he said (DRA, HCS, NJB, NLT, REB, TLB)].

22:3 Alx[**I am a Jewish man**], Byz[I am indeed a Jewish man (KJV, NKJ, ~REB)]; Alx/Byz[**zealous for God**], Minor[*omits* for God], Alt/Vulgate[zealous for the law (DRA)].

22:5 Alx/Byz[**the high priest**], Minor[*adds* Ananias].

22:6 Alx/Byz[**suddenly**], Alt/Peshitta[from amidst tranquility (MRD)].

22:7 Alx/Byz[**saying to me**], Minor[*adds* in the Hebrew language].

22:8 Alx/Byz[**And I answered**], Alt/Peshitta[*adds* and said (MRD)].

22:9 Alx/Byz[**those who were with me**], Alt/Peshitta[the men who were with me (MRD, TEV, TLB)]; Alx[**saw the light**], Byz[*adds* and were afraid (KJV, NKJ)]; Alx/Byz[**voice of the one who was speaking**], Alt/Peshitta[voice that was speaking (MRD, NJB, NLT, REB, ~TLB)].

22:11 Alx/Byz[**I could not see**], Minor[when I rose up, I could not see *others* I saw nothing (MRD, NAB)].

22:12 Alx/Major[**Jews who lived there**], Byz[*adds* in Damascus (NLT, TLB)].

22:13 Alx/Byz[**13 came to me**], Alt[came to me 13 (~MRD)].

receive your sight!' And at that very time I looked up at him. ¹⁴ Then he said, 'The God of our fathers has appointed you to know his will and to see the Righteous One and to hear words from his mouth. ¹⁵ For you will be a witness for him to all men of what you have seen and heard. ¹⁶ Now why do you delay? Get up and be baptized, and wash away your sins, calling on his name.'

¹⁷ "And it happened that, when I had returned to Jerusalem and was praying in the temple, I fell into a trance ¹⁸ and I saw him saying to me, 'Make haste, and get out of Jerusalem quickly, because they will not accept your testimony about me.' ¹⁹ And I said, 'Lord, they themselves know that in one synagogue after another I used to imprison and beat those who believed in you. ²⁰ When the blood of Stephen your witness was shed, I also was standing by and approving, keeping the garments of those who were killing him.' ²¹ And he said to me, 'Go; for I will send you far away to the Gentiles.'"

²² Up to this word they listened to him, and then they raised their voices and said, "Away with such a fellow from the earth! For he ought not to live." ²³ And as they were crying out and throwing off their cloaks and tossing dust into the air, ²⁴ the commander ordered him to be brought into the barracks, and commanded him to be examined by scourging so that he might find out the reason why they were shouting against him that way. ²⁵ But when they stretched him out with thongs, Paul said to the centurion who was standing by, "Is it lawful for you to scourge a man who is a Roman citizen and uncondemned?" ²⁶ When the centurion heard this, he went to the commander and told him, saying, "What are you about to do? For this man is a Roman." ²⁷ So the commander came and said to him, "Tell me, are you a Roman citizen?" And he said, "Yes." ²⁸ But the

---

22:14 Alx/Byz[**appointed you**], Alt/Vulgate[preordained you (DRA, JNT, ~NET)].

22:15 Alx/Byz[**what you have seen**], Alt/Peshitta[all that you have seen (MRD)].

22:16 Alx/Byz[**wash away your sins**], Minor[release your sins (~MRD, ~TLB)]; Alx[**calling on his name**], Byz[calling on the name of the Lord (KJV, NKJ, NLT, TLB)].

22:17-18 Alx/Major[**I fell into a trance 18 and I saw him saying to me**], Byz[I fell into a trance and I saw him saying to me 18], Alt/Peshitta[18 And I saw him in a vision when he said to me (MRD, ~TLB)].

22:18 Alx/Byz[**I saw him saying to me**], Alt[*without textual foundation* I saw the Lord saying to me (~JNT, ~NAB, ~NET, ~NIV, ~NLT, ~NRS, ~TEV, ~TLB)].

22:20 Alx[**approving**], Byz[*adds* of his death (KJV, ~MRD, ~NJB, NKJ, ~NLT, TEV)]; Alx/Major[**keeping the garments**], Byz[and keeping the garments (ASV, DRA, ESV, HCS, KJV, MRD, NAB, NAS, NAU, NET, NIV, NJB, NKJ, NLT, NRS, REB, RSV, TEV)]; **witness** *Greek* martyr.

22:21 Alx/Byz[**he said to me**], Alt[*without textual foundation* the Lord said to me (~NIV, ~NLT, ~TEV, ~TLB)]; Alx/Byz[**to the Gentiles**], Alt/Peshitta[to preach to the Gentiles (MRD)].

22:22 Alx/Byz[**listened to him**], Alt/Peshitta[listened to Paul (MRD, NIV, NLT, TEV, TLB)]; Alx/Byz[**voices and said**], Alt/Peshitta[voices and cried out (HCS, JNT, MRD, NAB, NET, NIV, NJB, NLT, NRS, ~REB, TEV, TLB)].

22:23 Alx[**And as they were crying out**], Byz[But as they were crying out]; Major[But as they were screaming ~JNT, ~NET, ~TEV].

22:24 Alx/Byz[**examined by scourging**], Alt/Vulgate[scourged and twisted (~DRA)], Alt[*without textual foundation* scourged to confess (~NLT, ~TLB)].

22:25 Alx[**they stretched him out**], Byz[he stretched him out]; Alx/Byz[**Paul**], Alt[*without textual foundation* Saul (~JNT)]; **with thongs** *or* for the lashes.

22:26 Alx/Byz[**When the centurion heard this**], Minor[When the centurion heard that he called himself a Roman], Alt[*without textual foundation* omits (~TLB)]; Alx[**What are you about to do?**], Byz[Take heed what you are about to do (~JNT, KJV, ~NJB, NKJ)]; Alx/Byz[**this man is a Roman**], Alt/Vulgate[*adds* citizen (DRA, ESV, HCS, JNT, NAB, NET, NIV, NJB, NLT, NRS, REB, RSV, TEV, TLB)].

22:28 Alx[**But the commander**], Byz[And the commander (ASV, DRA, KJV, NAS)], Minor[The commander (ESV, HCS, JNT, MRD, NAB, NAU, NET, NKJ, NLT, NRS, REB, RSV, TEV, TLB)], Alt[*without textual foundation* Then the commander (~NIV, ~NJB)]; Alx/Byz[**citizenship**],

commander answered, "I bought this citizenship for a large sum." Paul said, "But I was even born to it." ²⁹ So those who were about to examine him withdrew from him immediately. And the commander also was afraid when he realized that Paul was a Roman and that he had put him in chains.

³⁰ But on the next day, wishing to know for certain why he had been accused by the Jews, he released him and ordered the chief priests and all the Council to assemble, and brought Paul down and set him before them.

23 ¹ And Paul, looking intently at the council, said, "Men, brothers, I have lived my life before God in all good conscience up to this day." ² The high priest Ananias commanded those standing beside him to strike him on the mouth. ³ Then Paul said to him, "God shall strike you, you whitewashed wall! Do you sit to judge me according to the law, and yet contrary to the law you order me to be struck?" ⁴ Those who stood by said, "Would you revile God's high priest?" ⁵ And Paul said, "I did not know, brothers, that he was the high priest; for it is written that, *'You shall not speak evil of a ruler of your people.'"*

⁶ But when Paul perceived that one part were Sadducees and the other Pharisees, he began to cry out in the council, "Brothers, I am a Pharisee, a son of Pharisees; with respect to the hope and the resurrection of the dead [I] am on trial." ⁷ When he said this, a dissension broke out between the Pharisees and Sadducees, and the assembly was divided. ⁸ For the Sadducees say that there is no resurrection, nor an angel, nor a spirit, but the Pharisees acknowledge them all. ⁹ There occurred a great uproar. And some of the scribes of the Pharisees' party stood up and began to argue heatedly, saying, "We find nothing wrong with this man. What if a spirit or an angel has spoken to him?" ¹⁰ And the dispute became so violent that the commander was afraid Paul would be torn to pieces by them and

---

Alt/Peshitta[Roman citizenship (MRD)]; Alx/Byz[**Paul**], Alt[*without textual foundation* Saul (~JNT)].

22:²⁹ Alx/Byz[**examine him**], Alt/Vulgate[torture him (DRA, ~MRD, ~TLB)]; Alx/Byz[**Paul was a Roman**], Alt/Vulgate[*adds* citizen (DRA, ESV, HCS, JNT, NAB, NET, NIV, NJB, NLT, NRS, REB, RSV, TEV, TLB)]; Alx/Byz[**in chains**], Minor[*adds* and at once he released him]; *Codex Bezae ends here; Codex Bezae is the principal Greek record of the "Western Text."*

22:³⁰ Alx[**by the Jews**], Byz[from the Jews (~ASV, ~JNT, ~KJV, ~MRD, ~NJB, ~NLT, ~REB, ~RSV, ~TEV, ~TLB)]; Alx[**he released him**], Byz[*adds* from his bonds (~ESV, KJV, ~MRD, NKJ, ~RSV, TEV, TLB)]; Alx[**the Council**], Byz[their Council (KJV, MRD, NKJ)]; Alx[**to assemble**], Byz[to come (KJV, NKJ)]; Alx/Byz[**Paul**], Alt[*without textual foundation* Saul (~JNT)].

23:¹ Alx/Byz[**Paul**], Alt[*without textual foundation* Saul (~JNT)].

23:³ Alx/Byz[**Paul**], Alt[*without textual foundation* Saul (~JNT)].

23:⁵ Alx/Byz[**Paul**], Alt[*without textual foundation* Saul (~JNT)]; Alx[**it is written that**], Byz[*omits* that (ASV, DRA, ESV, HCS, JNT, KJV, MRD, NAB, NAS, NAU, NET, NIV, NJB, NKJ, NLT, NRS, REB, RSV, TEV, TLB)]; **Exodus 22:28**.

23:⁶ Alx/Byz[**Paul**], Alt[*without textual foundation* Saul (~JNT)]; Alx[**began to cry out**], Byz[cried out (ASV, DRA, ESV, HCS, JNT, KJV, MRD, NAB, NET, NIV, NJB, NKJ, NLT, NRS, REB, RSV, TEV, TLB)]; Alx[**a son of Pharisees**], Byz[a son of a Pharisee (KJV, MRD, NIV, NKJ, ~REB)].

23:⁷ Alx[**When he said this**], Byz[When he spoke this (~NLT, ~REB, ~TLB)]; Alx[**the Pharisees and Sadducees**], Byz[the Pharisees and the Sadducees (DRA, ESV, HCS, JNT, KJV, NET, NIV, NKJ, NLT, NRS, RSV, TLB)], Major[*omits* and the Sadducees].

23:⁹ Alx[**some of the scribes of the Pharisees' party**], Byz[the scribes of the Pharisees' party (KJV, NKJ)], Alt/Vulgate[some of the Pharisees (DRA, ~TLB)]; Alx[**What if a spirit or an angel has spoken to him?**], Byz[But if a spirit or an angel has spoken to him, let us not fight against God (KJV, NKJ)].

23:¹⁰ Alx[**the commander was afraid**], Byz[the commander was concerned]; Alx/Byz[**Paul**], Alt[*without textual foundation* Saul (~JNT)]; Alx[**to go down to take him**], Byz[to go down and take him (ASV, DRA, ESV, KJV, MRD, NAB, NAS, NAU, NIV, NJB, NKJ, NLT, RSV, ~TLB)]; Alx/Byz[**and bring him into the barracks**], Minor[to bring him into the barracks].

ordered the troops to go down to take him away from them by force, and bring him into the barracks.

11 The following night the Lord stood by him and said, "Take courage, for as you have testified about me at Jerusalem, so you must bear witness also at Rome."

12 When it was day, the Jews formed a conspiracy and bound themselves by an oath neither to eat nor drink until they had killed Paul. 13 There were more than forty who formed this plot. 14 They went to the chief priests and the elders and said, "We have bound ourselves under a solemn oath to taste nothing until we have killed Paul. 15 You therefore, along with the council, give notice now to the commander to bring him down to you, as though you were going to determine his case more exactly. And we are ready to kill him before he comes near." 16 But the son of Paul's sister heard of their ambush, and he went and entered the barracks and told Paul. 17 Paul called one of the centurions and said, "Take this young man to the commander; for he has something to tell him." 18 So he took him and brought him to the commander and said, "Paul the prisoner called me and asked me to bring this young man to you, since he has something to tell you." 19 The commander took him by the hand, and going aside asked him privately, "What is it that you have to tell me?" 20 And he said, "The Jews have agreed to ask you to bring Paul down tomorrow to the Council, as though you were going to inquire somewhat more thoroughly about him. 21 But do not yield to them; for more than forty of them are waiting in ambush for him, having bound themselves by an oath neither to eat nor drink until they have killed him. And now they are ready, waiting for the promise from you." 22 So the commander dismissed the young man, instructing him, "Tell no one that you have informed me of this."

23 Then he called [a certain] two centurions and said, "At the third hour of the night get ready two hundred soldiers with seventy horsemen and two hundred spearmen to go as far as Caesarea. 24 Also provide mounts for Paul to ride, and bring him safely to Felix the governor." 25 And he wrote a letter having this form: 26 "Claudius Lysias, to His Excellency, Governor Felix, greetings. 27 This man was seized by the Jews, and was about to be killed by them, when I came upon them with the troops and rescued him, having learned that he was a Roman. 28 And desiring to know the charge for which they were accusing him, I brought him down to their council. 29 I found that he was accused over questions about their Law,

---

23:11 Alx[**Take courage**], Byz[*adds* Paul (KJV, NKJ, NLT, ~TEV, ~TLB)].

23:12 Alx[**the Jews**], Byz[some of the Jews (DRA, JNT, KJV, MRD, NKJ, NLT, TEV, TLB)]; Alx/Byz[**Paul**], Alt[*without textual foundation* Saul (~JNT)].

23:13 Alx[**formed this plot**], Byz[had formed this plot (DRA, HCS, KJV, MRD, NKJ)].

23:14 Alx/Byz[**Paul**], Alt[*without textual foundation* Saul (~JNT)].

23:15 Alx[**bring him down to you**], Byz[*adds* tomorrow (KJV, NKJ)].

23:16 Alx/Byz[**Paul's...Paul**], Alt[*without textual foundation* Saul's...Saul (~JNT)].

23:17 Alx/Byz[**Paul**], Alt[*without textual foundation* Saul (~JNT)].

23:18 Alx/Byz[**Paul**], Alt[*without textual foundation* Saul (~JNT)].

23:20 Alx/Byz[**Paul**], Alt[*without textual foundation* Saul (~JNT)]; Alx[**you were going to inquire**], Byz[they were going to inquire (DRA, ESV, HCS, JNT, KJV, ~MRD, NAB, NAS, NAU, NET, ~NIV, NJB, NKJ, NLT, NRS, ~REB, RSV, TEV, TLB)].

23:23 Alx/Byz[**a certain two centurions**], Minor[*omits* a certain (DRA, KJV, MRD, NKJ)]; Alx/Byz[**seventy horsemen**], Alt[a hundred horsemen]; **spearmen:** *or* bowmen.

23:24 Alx/Byz[**Paul**], Alt[*without textual foundation* Saul (~JNT)].

22:25 Alx/Byz[*text*], Alt[For he feared lest perhaps the Jews might take him away by force and kill him, and he should afterwards be slandered, as if he was to take money. And he wrote a letter having this form (DRA)]; *Metzger notes Alt reading in verse 24.*

23:28 Alx[**And desiring**], Byz[But desiring (~NET, ~NLT, ~NRS, ~REB, ~TLB)]; Alx/Byz[**I brought him down to their council**], Minor[*omits*].

23:29 Alx/Byz[**their Law**], Minor[*adds* of Moses and a certain Jesus]; Alx/Byz[**but there was no accusation**], Major[*omits* but (~HCS, ~MRD, ~NAB, NLT, TEV, TLB)].

but there was no accusation against him deserving death or imprisonment. [30] And when I was informed that there would be a plot against the man, I sent him to you at once, also instructing his accusers to bring [charges] against him before you."

[31] So the soldiers, in accordance with their orders, took Paul and brought him by night to Antipatris. [32] But the next day, leaving the horsemen to go away with him, they returned to the barracks. [33] When these had come to Caesarea and delivered the letter to the governor, they also presented Paul to him. [34] But when he had read it, he asked from what province he was, and when he learned that he was from Cilicia, [35] he said, "I will hear you when your accusers arrive also." And he commanded him to be kept in Herod's Praetorium.

24

[1] After five days the high priest Ananias came down with some elders, with an attorney named Tertullus, and they brought their charges against Paul before the governor. [2] And when he was called, Tertullus began to accuse him, saying: "Since through you we have enjoyed much peace, and since by your provision, reforms are introduced on behalf of this nation, [3] we acknowledge this in every way and everywhere, most excellent Felix, with all gratitude. [4] But, that I may not weary you further, I beg you in your kindness to hear us briefly. [5] For we have found this man a pestilent fellow who stirs up dissensions among all the Jews throughout the world, and a ringleader of the sect of the Nazarenes. [6] He even tried to desecrate the temple; so we seized him. (7) [8] By examining him yourself you will be able to learn the truth about all these charges of which we accuse him." [9] The Jews also joined in the attack, asserting that these things were so.

[10] And when the governor had motioned for him to speak, Paul replied: "Realizing that for many years you have been a judge over this nation, I cheerfully make my defense. [11] Since you can easily verify that no more than twelve days ago I went up to Jerusalem to

---

23:30 Alx[**there would be a plot against the man**], Byz[the Jews lay in wait for the man (KJV, MRD, NKJ)]; Alx/Byz[**I sent him to you at once**], Minor[by them, I sent him to you (DRA)]; Alx[**against him before you**], Byz[*adds* Farewell (DRA, KJV, MRD, NKJ)], Minor[for themselves before you (~DRA, ~NLT, ~TLB)].

23:31 Alx/Byz[**soldiers**], Alt/Peshitta[Romans (MRD)]; Alx/Byz[**Paul**], Alt[*without textual foundation* Saul (~JNT)]; Alx[**night**], Byz[the night (HCS, JNT, NET, NIV, ~NLT, NRS, ~TEV, ~TLB)]; Alx/Byz[**Antipatris**], Alt/Peshitta[the city of Antipatris (MRD)].

23:32 Alx[**go away with him**], Byz[go with him (ASV, DRA, KJV, ~MRD, ~NAB, ~REB)].

23:33 Alx/Byz[**Paul**], Alt[*without textual foundation* Saul (~JNT)].

23:34 Alx[**he had read it**], Byz[the governor had read it (JNT, KJV, NET, NIV, NKJ, TEV)], Minor[he had read the letter (ESV, ~JNT, ~KJV, MRD, ~NET, ~NIV, NRS, REB, RSV, ~TEV)].

24:1 Alx[**some elders**], Byz[the elders (~DRA, KJV, MRD, ~NIV, ~NJB, NKJ, ~NLT, ~REB, ~TLB)]; Alx/Byz[**Paul**], Alt[*without textual foundation* Saul (~JNT)].

24:2 Alx/Byz[**Since through…**], Minor[3 Since through…]; Alx[**reforms**], Byz[very worthy deeds (~JNT, KJV, NKJ, TLB)].

24:5 Alx[**dissensions**], Byz[dissension (~HCS, ~JNT, KJV, MRD, NAB, NAS, NAU, NJB, NKJ, ~NRS, REB, ~RSV)].

24:6-(7)-8 Alx/Major[*text*], Byz[*adds* (6b) And we wanted to judge him according to our law; (7) but Lysias the chief captain came and with great violence took him out of our hands, (8a) commanding his accusers to come before you (ASV, DRA, HCS, KJV, MRD, NAS, NAU, NKJ, TLB)], Alt[*from verse 10* I know that you have administered justice over this nation for many years, and I can therefore speak with confidence in my own defense (~NJB)].

24:9 Alz/Byz[**joined in the attack**], Minor[assented (~DRA, KJV, ~MRD, NJB, NKJ, ~NLT, ~REB, ~TLB)].

24:10 Alx/Byz[**Paul**], Alt[*without textual foundation* Saul (~JNT)]; Alx[**And…Paul replied**], Byz[But…Paul replied (~DRA, ~KJV, ~MRD, ~NAB, ~NKJ, ~NLT, ~REB, ~TEV, ~TLB)], Alt[*adds* having assumed a godlike bearing].

24:11 Alx/Byz[**to Jerusalem** *or* into Jerusalem], Major[in Jerusalem *or* at Jerusalem (ASV, DRA, ESV, HCS, JNT, ~NLT, NRS, RSV, ~TLB)].

worship. ¹² They did not find me disputing with anyone or stirring up a crowd, either in the temple or in the synagogues, or in the city. ¹³ Neither can they prove to you the charges they are now making against me. ¹⁴ But this I admit to you, that according to the Way which they call a sect I do worship the God of our fathers, believing everything that is in accordance with the Law and that is written in the Prophets, ¹⁵ having a hope in God, which these men cherish themselves, that there will certainly be a resurrection of both the righteous and the wicked. ¹⁶ And so I do my best always to have a clear conscience before God and men. ¹⁷ Now after several years I came to bring alms to my nation and to present offerings. ¹⁸ As I was doing this, they found me purified in the temple, without any crowd or uproar. ¹⁹ But there were some Jews from Asia – who ought to be here before you and to make accusation, if they should have anything against me. ²⁰ Or else let these men themselves tell what wrongdoing they found when I stood before the Council, ²¹ except this one thing which I shouted out while standing among them, 'With respect to the resurrection of the dead I am on trial before you today.'"

²² But Felix, having a more exact knowledge about the Way, put them off, saying, "When Lysias the commander comes down, I will decide your case." ²³ He gave orders to the centurion for him to be kept in custody but have some freedom, and not to prevent any of his friends from ministering to him.

²⁴ But some days later Felix came with his own wife Drusilla, who was Jewish, and sent for Paul and heard him speak about faith in Christ Jesus. ²⁵ But as he was discussing righteousness, self-control and the judgment to come, Felix became frightened and said, "Go away for the present, and when I find time I will summon you." ²⁶ And at the same time, he was hoping that money would be given him by Paul. So he sent for him often and conversed with him.

²⁷ But when two years had passed, Felix was succeeded by Porcius Festus, and desiring to do the Jews a favor, Felix left Paul in prison.

24:12 Alx[**stirring up a crowd**], Byz[inciting a crowd (DRA, HCS, NAB, NAS, NAU, ~NJB, NKJ, NLT, TLB)].

24:13 Alx[**prove to you**], Byz[prove (JNT, KJV, NKJ, NLT, REB, TLB)], Major[prove against me].

24:15 Alx/Byz[**hope in God**], Minor[hope with God (ASV, KJV, ~TLB)]; Alx[**resurrection of both**], Byz[resurrection of the dead, both of (KJV, MRD, NKJ, TEV)].

24:16 Alx[**And so I do my best...to have a clear conscience**], Byz[But I also do my best...to have a clear conscience (~ASV)], Major[But I do my best...having a clear conscience (~JNT)].

24:18-19 Alx[*text*], Byz[As I was doing this, some Jews from Asia found me purified in the temple, without any crowd or uproar – 19 who ought to be here before you and to make accusation, if they should have anything against me (HCS, KJV, NKJ)], Minor[*begins Byz reading with* But].

24:20 Alx[**what wrongdoing they found**], Byz[*adds* in me (HCS, JNT, NET, NIV, NJB, NLT, TEV, TLB)], Minor[if they found any wrongdoing in me (DRA, KJV, MRD, NKJ)].

24:21 Alx[**on trial before you**], Byz[on trial by you (DRA, KJV, NKJ, TEV)].

24:22 Alx[**But Felix**], Byz[But when Felix heard these things (KJV, NKJ)]; Alx/Byz[**Lysias**], Alt/Peshitta[*omits* (MRD)].

24:23 Alx[**He gave orders**], Byz[And he gave orders (ASV, DRA, ~ESV, KJV, MRD, NAS, ~NAU, ~NKJ, ~NRS, ~RSV)]; Alx[**for him to be kept**], Byz[for Paul to be kept (HCS, ~JNT, KJV, MRD, NET, NIV, NJB, NKJ, NLT, REB, TEV, TLB)]; Alx[**ministering**], Byz[*adds* or coming (KJV, NKJ, ~TLB)].

24:24 Alx[**his own wife**], Byz[his wife (ASV, DRA, ESV, HCS, JNT, KJV, MRD, NAB, NAS, NAU, NET, NIV, NJB, NKJ, NLT, NRS, RSV, TEV, ~JNT)], Major[the wife]; Alx/Byz[**Paul**], Alt[*without textual foundation* Saul (~JNT)]; Alx[**Christ Jesus**], Byz[Christ (KJV, MRD, NKJ)].

24:26 Alx/Major[**And at the same time**], Byz[But also at the same time (~DRA, ~KJV, ~MRD, ~NKJ, ~NLT, ~REB, ~TLB)]; Alx/Byz[**Paul**], Alt[*without textual foundation* Saul (~JNT)]; Alx[**given him by Paul**], Byz[*adds* so that he might release him (KJV, NKJ)], Minor[given by Paul (~NJB, ~REB)].

24:27 Alx/Major[**and desiring**], Byz[but desiring (JNT, NIV)]; Alx/Byz[**a favor**], Major[favors (~ASV, ~NAB, ~NJB, ~NLT, ~REB, ~TEV, ~TLB)]; Alx/Byz[**Paul**], Alt[*without textual foundation* Saul (~JNT)].

25 ¹ Festus then, three days after arriving in the province, went up to Jerusalem from Caesarea. ² And the chief priests and the principal men of the Jews brought charges against Paul. And they urged him, ³ as a favor to them, to have him transferred to Jerusalem, for they were preparing an ambush to kill him along the way. ⁴ Festus answered that Paul was being kept in Caesarea, and that he himself intended to go there shortly. ⁵ "Therefore," he said, "let the men of authority among you go there with me. And if there is anything wrong about the man, let them prosecute him."

⁶ After he had spent not more than eight or ten days among them, he went down to Caesarea. And on the next day he took his seat on the tribunal and ordered Paul to be brought. ⁷ And when he arrived, the Jews who had come down from Jerusalem stood around him, bringing down many serious charges, which they could not prove. ⁸ Paul said in his defense, "Neither against the law of the Jews, nor against the temple, nor against Caesar have I offended at all." ⁹ But Festus, wishing to do the Jews a favor, said to Paul, "Are you willing to go up to Jerusalem and stand trial before me there on these charges?" ¹⁰ But Paul said, "I am standing before Caesar's tribunal, where I ought to be tried. I have done no wrong to the Jews, as you also very well know. ¹¹ If, then, I am a wrongdoer and have committed anything worthy of death, I do not refuse to die. But if none of the charges brought against me is true, no one can hand me over to them. I appeal to Caesar." ¹² Then when Festus had conferred with his council, he answered, "You have appealed to Caesar, to Caesar you shall go."

¹³ Now when a few days had passed, King Agrippa and Bernice arrived at Caesarea and paid their respects to Festus. ¹⁴ While they were spending many days there, Festus laid Paul's case before the king, saying, "There is a man who was left as a prisoner by Felix. ¹⁵ And when I was at Jerusalem, the chief priests and the elders of the Jews brought charges against him, asking for sentence against him. ¹⁶ I answered them that it is not the custom of the Romans to hand over any man before the accused meets his accusers face to face and has an opportunity to make his defense against the charges. ¹⁷ So when [they] came together here, I did not delay, but on the next day took my seat on the tribunal and ordered the man

---

25:2 Alx[**And the chief priests**], Byz[But the high priest (KJV, NKJ)]; Alx/Byz[**Paul**], Alt[*without textual foundation* Saul (~JNT)].

25:3 **him** *Paul*.

25:4 Alx/Byz[**Paul**], Alt[*without textual foundation* Saul (~JNT)]; Alx[**in Caesarea**], Byz[at Caesarea (ASV, ESV, HCS, KJV, MRD, NAS, NAU, NET, NIV, NKJ, NLT, NRS, REB, RSV, TLB)].

25:5 Alx[**anything wrong**], Byz[*omits* wrong (~TLB)]; Alx[**the man**], Byz[this man (HCS, KJV, NAB, NET, NKJ, ~NLT, ~TLB)].

25:6 Alx[**not more than eight or ten**], Byz[more than ten (KJV, NKJ)], Alt/Peshitta[eight or ten (MRD, NIV, NLT, TEV, TLB)]; Alx/Byz[**Paul**], Alt[*without textual foundation* Saul (~JNT)].

25:7 Alx[**stood around him**], Byz[*omits* him (KJV, NKJ, NLT, REB, TLB)]; Alx[**bringing down many serious charges**], Byz[bringing many serious charges against Paul (~ASV, ~ESV, ~JNT, KJV, ~MRD, ~NAB, ~NAS, ~NAU, ~NIV, NKJ, ~NRS, ~RSV, ~TEV)].

25:8 Alx[**Paul said**], Byz[He said (KJV, NKJ)], Alt[*without textual foundation* Saul said (~JNT)]; .

25:9 Alx/Byz[**Paul**], Alt[*without textual foundation* Saul (~JNT)].

25:10 Alx/Byz[**Paul**], Alt[*without textual foundation* Saul (~JNT)].

25:11 Alx[**If, then**], Byz[For if (DRA, ~JNT, KJV, ~MRD, ~NAB, ~NIV, ~NJB, NKJ, ~NLT, ~NRS, ~REB, ~TEV, ~TLB)].

25:13 Alx/Major[**and paid their respects**], Byz[to pay their respects (DRA, JNT, KJV, MRD, ~NAB, NET, NIV, NKJ, NLT, NRS, ~REB, RSV, TEV, TLB)].

25:14 Alx[**they were spending many days**], Byz[he was spending many days there]; Alx/Byz[**Paul's**], Alt[*without textual foundation* Saul's (~JNT)].

25:15 Alx[**sentence**], Byz[punishment (~TLB)].

25:16 Alx[**hand over any man**], Byz[*adds* to destruction (KJV, MRD, NKJ, ~NLT, ~TLB)].

25:17 Alx/Byz[**they** *expressed*], Minor[they *implied* (Metzger)].

to be brought in. [18] When the accusers stood up, they did not charge him of such crimes as I had expected. [19] But they simply had some points of dispute with him about their own religion and about a dead man, Jesus, whom Paul asserted to be alive. [20] But being at a loss how to investigate such matters, I asked whether he was willing to go to Jerusalem and there stand trial on these matters. [21] But when Paul appealed to be held in custody for the Emperor's decision, I ordered him to be kept in custody until I could send him up to Caesar. [22] But Agrippa said to Festus, "I also would like to hear the man myself." "Tomorrow," he said, "you shall hear him."

[23] So on the next day Agrippa and Bernice came with great pomp and entered the audience room with high ranking officers and the prominent men of the city. At the command of Festus, Paul was brought in. [24] Festus said, "King Agrippa and all who are present with us, you see this man about whom the whole Jewish people petitioned me, both at Jerusalem and here, crying out that he ought not to live any longer. [25] But I found that he had done nothing deserving of death. And as he himself appealed to the emperor, I decided to send him. [26] But I have nothing definite about him to write to my lord. Therefore I have brought him before you all and especially before you, King Agrippa, so that after the investigation has taken place, I may have something to write. [27] For it seems to me unreasonable, in sending a prisoner, not to indicate the charges against him."

26 [1] Agrippa said to Paul, "You have permission to speak about yourself." Then Paul stretched out his hand and began his defense: [2] "I consider myself fortunate that it is before you, King Agrippa, I am to make my defense today against all the accusations of the Jews, [3] because you are especially familiar with all customs and controversies of the Jews. Therefore I beg you to listen to me patiently. [4] So then, all [the] Jews know my manner of life from my youth up, which from the beginning was spent among my own nation and at Jerusalem. [5] They have known about me for a long time, if they are willing to testify, that I lived as a Pharisee according to the strictest sect of our religion. [6] And now I am standing trial for the hope of the promise made by God to our fathers – [7] the promise to which our twelve tribes hope to attain, as they earnestly serve God

---

25:18 Alx[**crimes**], Byz[*omits* (DRA, HCS, KJV, NKJ, REB, TLB)].

25:19 Alx/Byz[**Paul**], Alt[*without textual foundation* Saul (~JNT)].

25:20 Alx/Byz[**investigate such matters**], Minor[investigate into such matters]; **on these matters** *Greek* on these.

25:21 Alx/Byz[**Paul**], Alt/Peshitta[he (MRD)], Alt[*without textual foundation* Saul (~JNT)]; Alx[**send him up to Caesar**], Byz[send him to Caesar (ASV, DRA, ESV, HCS, JNT, KJV, MRD, NAB, NAS, NAU, NET, NIV, NJB, NKJ, NLT, NRS, REB, RSV, TEV, TLB)].

25:22 Alx/Byz[**said to Festus**], Minor[*omits* said]; Alx[**"Tomorrow," he said**], Byz[But he said, "Tomorrow (~MRD, ~NLT, ~TLB)].

25:23 Alx[**high ranking officers**], Byz[the high ranking officers (ASV, DRA, ESV, HCS, KJV, MRD, NAS, NAU, NET, NIV, NJB, NKJ, NRS, RSV, TEV)]; Alx/Byz[**Paul**], Alt[*without textual foundation* Saul (~JNT)].

25:24 Alx[**crying out**], Byz[crying out loudly (NAS, NAU, NET, NJB, ~NLT, REB, ~TLB)].

25:25 Alx[**But I found**], Byz[But when I found (KJV, ~MRD, NKJ)]; Alx[**as he himself**], Byz[*adds* also]; Alx[**to send him** *Greek* to send], Byz[to send him].

26:1 Alx/Byz[**Paul...Paul**], Alt[*without textual foundation* Saul...Saul (~JNT)]; Alx[**to speak about yourself**], Byz[to speak for yourself (ASV, DRA, ESV, HCS, JNT, KJV, MRD, NAB, NAS, NAU, NET, NIV, NJB, NKJ, ~NLT, NRS, RSV, TEV, ~TLB)].

26:3 Alx/Byz[**you are especially familiar**], Minor[I know you are especially familiar (KJV, MRD, NLT, TLB)]; Alx/Byz[**customs**], Major[morals], Alt[laws (MRD, ~TLB)].

26:4 Alx/Byz[**all the Jews**], Minor[all Jews (JNT, NAS, NAU, REB, Metzger)]; Alx[**and at Jerusalem**], Byz[at Jerusalem (DRA, KJV, NKJ)].

26:6 Alx[**our fathers**], Byz[the fathers (DRA)].

26:7 Alx[**O King**], Byz[King Agrippa (KJV, MRD, NKJ)]; Alx/Major[**Jews**], Byz[the Jews (ASV, DRA, HCS, KJV, MRD, NET, NIV, NKJ, ~NLT, TEV, ~TLB)].

night and day. And for this hope, O King, I am being accused by Jews. [8] Why is it thought incredible by any of you that God raises the dead? [9] I myself was convinced that I ought to do many things to oppose the name of Jesus of Nazareth. [10] And that is just what I did in Jerusalem; I not only shut up many of the saints in prison, by authority from the chief priests, but when they were put to death I cast my vote against them. [11] And as I punished them often in all the synagogues, I tried to force them to blaspheme. And being furiously enraged against them, I persecuted them even to foreign cities.

[12] "On one of these journeys I was going to Damascus with the authority and commission of the chief priests. [13] At midday, O King, I saw on the way a light from heaven, brighter than the sun, shining around me and those who journeyed with me. [14] And when we had all fallen to the ground, I heard a voice saying to me in the Hebrew language, 'Saul, Saul, why do you persecute me? It is hard for you to kick against the goads.' [15] And I said, 'Who are you, Lord?' And the Lord said, 'I am Jesus whom you are persecuting. [16] But get up and stand on your feet. For this purpose I have appeared to you: to appoint you a minister and a witness to the things which you have seen [of me], and also to the things in which I will appear to you; [17] rescuing you from the people and from the nations to whom I am sending you, [18] to open their eyes, to turn them from darkness to light and from the power of Satan to God, that they may receive forgiveness of sins and a place among those who are sanctified by faith in me.'

[19] "So, King Agrippa, I was not disobedient to the heavenly vision, [20] but declared first to those at Damascus, and also at Jerusalem and all the country of Judea, and also to the Gentiles, that they should repent and turn to God and perform deeds worthy of their repentance. [21] For this reason Jews seized me [when I was] in the temple and tried to kill me. [22] To this day I have had the help that comes from God. And so I stand here testifying both to small and great, saying nothing but what the prophets and Moses said would happen: [23] that the Christ must suffer, and that, by being the first to rise from the dead, he would proclaim light both to the people and to the nations."

[24] And as he was saying this in his defense, Festus said in a loud voice, "Paul, you are out of your mind! Your great learning is driving you mad." [25] But Paul said, "I am not

---

26:12 Alx[**On one of these journeys**], Byz[And on one of these journeys (MRD)]; Alx[**of the chief priests**], Byz[from the chief priests (HCS, KJV, NET, NJB, NKJ, REB, TEV)].

26:14 Alx[**And when we had all fallen**], Byz[But when we had all fallen]; Alx/Byz[**to the ground**], Minor[*adds* on account of fear, only]; Alx[**saying to me in the Hebrew language**], Byz[speaking to me, and saying in the Hebrew language (KJV, NKJ)]; **the Hebrew language** *or* Aramaic; **kick against the goads** *is sometimes linked to* Classical[**Euripedes, Bacchae 794s**], *but is possibly a cultural idiom.*

26:15 Alx[**the Lord said**], Byz[he said (KJV, NKJ)]; Alx/Byz[**Jesus**], Minor[*adds* the Nazarene (MRD)].

26:16 Alx[**of me**], Byz[*omits* (DRA, HCS, KJV, NAS, NAU, NET, NKJ, NLT, REB, TLB)].

26:17 Alx[**from the people and from the nations**], Byz[from the people and the nations (NLT, TLB)]; Alx/Byz[**to whom I am sending you**], Minor[*adds* now (DRA, HCS, KJV, NKJ)].

26:18 Alx/Byz[**to turn them**], Major[to return them (~TLB)]; Minor[and to turn them (KJV, NIV, NKJ, REB, TEV)].

26:20 Alx[**declared**], Byz[declaring (~NAS, ~NAU, ~NJB)]; Alx[**and also at Jerusalem**], Byz[*omits* also (DRA, ESV, HCS, JNT, KJV, MRD, NAB, NET, NIV, NJB, NKJ, NLT, NRS, REB, RSV, TEV, TLB)]; Alx[**all the country of Judea**], Byz[throughout all the country of Judea (ASV, DRA, ESV, HCS, JNT, KJV, MRD, NAB, NAS, NAU, NET, NIV, NKJ, NLT, NRS, RSV, ~TEV, TLB)].

26:21 Alx[**Jews**], Byz[the Jews (ASV, DRA, ESV, HCS, KJV, MRD, NAB, NET, NIV, NJB, NKJ, NRD, REB, RSV, TEV, TLB)]; Alx[**when I was**], Byz[*omits* (ASV, ESV, HCS, JNT, KJV, MRD, NAS, NAU, NET, NIV, NJB, NKJ, NLT, NRS, REB, RSV, ~TLB)].

26:23 Alx[**both to the people**], Byz[*omits* both (DRA, HCS, KJV, MRD, NIV, NJB, NKJ, NLT, TEV, ~TLB)].

26:24 Alx[**Festus said** *Greek* Festus says], Byz[Festus began to say]; Alx/Byz[**Paul**], Alt[*without textual foundation* Saul (~JNT)].

mad, most excellent Festus, but I am speaking the sober truth. ²⁶ For the king knows about these things, and to him I speak freely. For I am persuaded that [none] of these things has escaped his notice, for this was not done in a corner. ²⁷ King Agrippa, do you believe the prophets? I know that you do." ²⁸ And Agrippa said to Paul, "With a little persuasion you think to make me a Christian!" ²⁹ And Paul said, "Whether with a little or much, I would to God that not only you but also all who hear me this day might become such as I am – except for these chains."

³⁰ And the king rose and the governor and Bernice, and those who were sitting with them. ³¹ And when they had gone aside, they began talking to one another, saying, "This man is not doing [anything] worthy of death or imprisonment." ³² And Agrippa said to Festus, "This man could have been set free if he had not appealed to Caesar."

27 ¹ When it was decided that we would sail for Italy, they delivered Paul and some other prisoners to a centurion of the Augustan cohort named Julius. ² And embarking in a ship from Adramyttium, which was about to sail to the ports along the coast of Asia, we put out to sea, accompanied by Aristarchus, a Macedonian from Thessalonica. ³ The next day we put in at Sidon. And Julius treated Paul kindly, and allowed him to go to his friends and be cared for. ⁴ We put out to sea from there and sailed under the lee of Cyprus, because the winds were against us. ⁵ When we had sailed across the open sea off the coast of Cilicia and Pamphylia, we landed at Myra in Lycia. ⁶ There the centurion found an Alexandrian ship sailing for Italy, and he put us aboard it. ⁷ When we had sailed slowly for a good many days, and with difficulty had arrived off Cnidus, since the wind did not allow us to go farther, we sailed under the lee of Crete, off Salmone. ⁸ We sailed along it with difficulty and came to a place called Fair Havens, near which was the city of Lasea.

26:25 Alx[**But Paul said**], Byz[But he said (KJV, NKJ)], Alt[*without textual foundation* But Saul said (~JNT)]; Alx/Byz[**but I am speaking the sober truth**], Minor[*omits* but (NAB, NIV, NJB, NLT, REB, TEV, TLB)].

26:26 Alx/Byz[**and to him I speak freely**], Minor[*omits* and (HCS, JNT, MRD, NLT, TEV, TLB)].

26:28 Alx/Byz[**Paul**], Alt/Peshitta[him (MRD)], Alt[*without textual foundation* Saul (~JNT)]; Alx[**With a little persuasion you think to make me a Christian** *or* In a little time you think to make me a Christian], Byz[In a short time you think to persuade me to become a Christian (DRA, ESV, HCS, JNT, KJV, MRD, ~NAB, NAS, NAU, NET, NIV, NKJ, NLT, NRS, TLB)].

26:29 Alx/Byz[**Paul**], Alt[*without textual foundation* Saul (~JNT)]; Alx[**Whether with a little or much**], Byz[Whether in a short or a long time (ASV, DRA, ~KJV, ~MRD, NJB, ~NKJ, REB, ~TLB)].

26:30 Alx[**And the king rose**], Byz[And when he had thus spoken, the king rose (KJV, NKJ, ~REB)].

26:31 Alx[**not doing anything**], Byz[doing nothing (ASV, DRA, ESV, HCS, JNT, KJV, MRD, NJB, NKJ, NRS, REB, RSV)].

27:1 Alx/Byz[**sail for Italy**], Alt/Peshitta[*adds* to Caesar (MRD)]; Alx/Byz[**Paul**], Alt[*without textual foundation* Saul (~JNT)].

27:2 Alx[**a ship from Adramyttium, which was about to sail to the ports along the coast of Asia, we put out to sea**]; Byz[a ship from Adramyttium, we put out to sea, meaning to sail by the coasts of Asia (DRA, HCS, KJV, NKJ)]; Alx/Byz[**Adramyttium**], Alt/Peshitta[the city of Adramyttium (MRD)], Alt[*without textual foundation* the Turkish coast (~TLB)]; Alx/Byz[**Macedonian**], Alt[*without textual foundation* Greek (~TLB)]; Alx/Byz[**Thessalonica**], Alt/Peshitta[the city of Thessalonica (MRD)].

27:3 Alx/Byz[**Paul**], Alt[*without textual foundation* Saul (~JNT)]; Alx/Byz[**his friends** *Greek* the friends], Minor[*omits* the (NLT, TLB)].

27:5 Alx/Byz[**in Lycia**], Alt/Peshitta[a city of Lycia (ASV, KJV, MRD, NKJ, ~NLT, ~TLB)], Minor[*adds* for fifteen days].

27:7 Alx/Byz[**Salmone**], Alt/Peshitta[the city of Salmone (MRD)], Alt[*without textual foundation* the port of Salmone (~TLB)].

27:8 Alx/Byz[**Lasea**], Alt/Vulgate[Thalassa (DRA)].

⁹ As much time had been lost, and the voyage was now dangerous because the fast had already gone by, Paul advised them, ¹⁰ and said to them, "Men, I perceive that the voyage will be with injury and great loss, not only of the cargo and the ship, but also of our lives." ¹¹ But the centurion was more persuaded by the pilot and the owner of the ship than by what was being said by Paul. ¹² Because the harbor was not suitable to winter in, the majority reached a decision to put out to sea from there, on the chance that somehow they could reach Phoenix, a harbor of Crete, facing southwest and northwest, and spend the winter there.

¹³ When a gentle south wind came up, supposing that they had obtained their purpose, they weighed anchor and began sailing along Crete, close inshore. ¹⁴ But before very long there rushed down from the land a violent wind, called the northeaster. ¹⁵ And when the ship was caught in it and could not face the wind, we gave way to it and were driven along. ¹⁶ And running under the lee of a small island called Cauda, we were scarcely able to secure the boat. ¹⁷ After they had hoisted it up, they used supports to undergird the ship. And fearing that they might run aground on the shallows of Syrtis, they lowered the sea anchor and in this way let themselves be driven along. ¹⁸ The next day as we were being violently storm-tossed, they began to throw the cargo overboard. ¹⁹ And on the third day they threw the ship's gear overboard with their own hands. ²⁰ When neither sun nor stars appeared for many days, and no small storm was raging on us, all hope of our being saved was finally abandoned.

²¹ When they had gone a long time without food, then Paul stood up among them and said, "Men, you should have followed my advice and not to have set sail from Crete and incurred this damage and loss. ²² Yet now I urge you to keep up your courage; for there will be no loss of life among you, but only of the ship. ²³ For this very night an angel of the God to whom [I] belong and whom I serve stood before me, ²⁴ and he said, 'Do not be afraid, Paul. You must stand before Caesar. And behold, God has granted you all those who sail with you.' ²⁵ So keep up your courage, men. For I have faith in God that it will happen exactly as I have been told. ²⁶ But we must run aground on some island."

²⁷ But when the fourteenth night came, as we were being driven across the Adriatic Sea, about midnight the sailors began to sense that they were approaching land. ²⁸ They took soundings and found it to be twenty fathoms. And a little farther on they took soundings again and found it to be fifteen fathoms. ²⁹ Fearing that we might run aground somewhere on the rocks, they cast four anchors from the stern and prayed for daybreak. ³⁰ But as the sailors were trying to escape from the ship and had let down the lifeboat into the sea, on the pretense of laying out anchors from the bow, ³¹ Paul said to the centurion and

---

27:9 Alx/Byz[**Paul**], Alt[*without textual foundation* Saul (~JNT)].

27:11 Alx/Byz[**Paul**], Alt[*without textual foundation* Saul (~JNT)].

27:12 Alx[**put out to sea from there**], Byz[*adds* also (KJV, ~NIV, NKJ, ~NLT, ~REB, ~TEV, ~TLB)].

27:14 Alx[**northeaster** *Greek* Euraquilo], Byz[southeaster *Greek* Euroclydon (KJV, ~MRD, NKJ)].

27:16 Alx[**Cauda**], Byz[Clauda (KJV, NAS, NAU, NKJ, TLB)], Minor[Cyra (MRD)].

27:17 Alx/Major[**supports** *or* cables], Byz[support *or* a cable (~MRD, ~NJB, ~REB)]; **sea anchor** *or* mainsail *Greek* thing.

27:19 Alx[**they threw...their own hands**], Byz[we threw...our own hands (KJV, MRD, NKJ)], Minor[*adds* into the sea].

27:21 Alx[**When** *or* And when], Byz[But when (KJV, NKJ)]; Alx/Byz[**Paul**], Alt[*without textual foundation* Saul (~JNT)].

27:24 Alx/Byz[**Paul**], Alt[*without textual foundation* Saul (~JNT)].

27:28 **fathoms** *Greek* orguias.

27:29 Alx/Byz[**Fearing that we might**], Minor[Fearing that they might (~TEV, TLB)]; Alx[**run aground**], Byz[run into ground (~HCS, ~MRD)].

27:31 Alx/Byz[**Paul**], Alt[*without textual foundation* Saul (~JNT)].

the soldiers, "Unless these men stay in the ship, you cannot be saved." [32] Then the soldiers cut the ropes of the lifeboat and let it fall away.

[33] As day was about to dawn, Paul urged them all to take some food, saying, "Today is the fourteenth day that you have been in suspense and without food, having taken nothing. [34] Therefore I urge you to take some food. It will give you strength, since not a hair is to perish from the head of any of you." [35] Having said this, he took bread and gave thanks to God in the presence of all, and he broke it and began to eat. [36] Then they all were encouraged and ate some food themselves. [37] All of us in the ship were two hundred and seventy-six persons. [38] When they had eaten enough, they lightened the ship by throwing out the wheat into the sea.

[39] When day came, they could not recognize the land. But they did observe a bay with a beach, and they resolved to drive the ship onto it if they could. [40] So they cast off the anchors and left them in the sea, at the same time loosening the ropes that tied the rudders. Then, hoisting the foresail to the wind, they made for the beach. [41] But striking a place of two seas they ran the vessel aground. The bow stuck fast and remained immovable, and the stern was broken up by the pounding [of the surf]. [42] The soldiers' plan was to kill the prisoners, so that none of them could swim away and escape. [43] But the centurion, wanting to bring Paul safely through, kept them from carrying out their plan. He ordered those who could swim to jump overboard first and get to land, [44] and the rest on planks or on various pieces of the ship. And so it happened that they were all brought safely to land.

28

[1] When we had been brought safely through, then we found out that the island was called Malta. [2] And the natives showed us unusual kindness, for they lit a fire and welcomed us all, because it had begun to rain and was cold. [3] But when Paul had gathered a bundle of sticks and put them on the fire, a viper came out because of the heat and fastened itself on his hand. [4] When the natives saw the creature hanging from his hand, they said to one another, "No doubt this man is a murderer. Though he has escaped from the sea, justice has not allowed him to live." [5] However he shook the creature off into the fire and suffered no harm. [6] They waited, expecting him to swell up or suddenly fall down dead. But after they had waited a long time and saw nothing unusual happen to him, they changed their minds and said that he was a god. [7] Now in the neighborhood of that place were lands belonging to the chief man of the island, named Publius, who welcomed us and entertained us hospitably for three days. [8] It happened that the father of Publius was lying in bed sick with recurrent fever and dysentery. And Paul went in to see him. And after he had prayed, he laid his hands on him

---

27:33 Alx/Byz[**Paul**], Alt[*without textual foundation* Saul (~JNT)].

27:34 Alx/Byz[**take some food**], Major[accept some food (~NJB, ~NLT, ~TEV, ~TLB)]; Alx[**perish**], Byz[fall KJV, NKJ)].

27:37 Alx/Byz[**two hundred and seventy-six**], Minor[about seventy-six *others vary in number*].

27:39 Alx/Byz[**drive the ship onto it**], Minor[bring the ship onto it (RSV)].

27:41 Alx/Byz[**of the surf**], Minor[*omits*]; **place of two seas** *or* reef.

27:43 Alx/Byz[**Paul**], Alt[*without textual foundation* Saul (~JNT)].

28:1 Alx[**we found out**], Byz[they found out (KJV, NKJ)]; Alx/Byz[**Malta** *Greek* Melita], Minor[Malta *Greek* Meliten].

28:2 Alx[**2 And the natives...kindness**], Byz[2 But the natives...kindness], Alt/Vulgate[But the natives...kindness 2 (DRA, ~TLB)]; Alx[**they lit a fire**], Byz[they kindled a fire (ASV, DRA, ESV, KJV, MRD, NAS, NAU, ~NET, ~NIV, NKJ, ~NLT, NRS, RSV, ~TEV, ~TLB)].

28:3 Alx/Byz[**Paul**], Alt[*without textual foundation* Saul (~JNT)]; Alx/Byz[**came out because of the heat**], Major[came out of the heat (DRA, KJV)].

28:6 Alx[**swell up**], Byz[burn up].

28:8 Alx/Byz[**Paul**], Alt[*without textual foundation* Saul (~JNT)]; Alx/Major[**after he had prayed, he laid his hands on him and healed him**], Byz[after he had prayed and laid his hands on him, he healed him (ASV, DRA, ESV, HCS, KJV, MRD, NKJ, NLT, NRS, RSV, TLB)].

and healed him. [9] And when this had happened, the rest of the people on the island who had diseases also came and were cured. [10] They honored us in many ways. And when we were ready to sail, they furnished us with the supplies we needed.

[11] After three months we set sail in a ship which had wintered in the island, an Alexandrian ship, with the Twin Brothers as figurehead. [12] After we put in at Syracuse, we stayed there for three days. [13] From there we sailed off and arrived at Rhegium. And a day later a south wind sprang up. And on the second day we came to Puteoli. [14] There we found some brothers, and were invited to stay with them for seven days. And so we came to Rome. [15] And the brothers, when they heard of us, came as far as the Forum of Appius and Three Taverns to meet us. When Paul saw them, he thanked God and took courage.

[16] And when we entered into Rome, Paul was allowed to stay by himself, with the soldier that guarded him.

[17] After three days he called together the local leaders of the Jews. And when they had gathered, he said to them, "Brothers, though I had done nothing against our people or the customs of our fathers, yet I was delivered prisoner from Jerusalem into the hands of the Romans. [18] And when they had examined me, they were willing to release me because there was no ground for putting me to death. [19] But when the Jews objected, I was compelled to appeal to Caesar – not that I have any charge to bring against my own nation. [20] For this reason therefore I have asked to see you, and speak, since it is because of the hope of Israel that I am bound with this chain." [21] They said to him, "We have not received letters from Judea concerning you, and none of the brothers who have come here has reported or spoken anything bad about you. [22] But we desire to hear from you what your views are. For concerning this sect, we know that everywhere it is spoken against."

[23] When they had appointed a day for him, they came to him at his lodging in great numbers. And he explained the matter to them from morning till evening, testifying to the kingdom of God and trying to convince them about Jesus both from the law of Moses and from the prophets. [24] Some were convinced by what he said, but others would not believe. [25] When they disagreed among themselves, they began to leave, after Paul had made one final

---

28:9 Alx[**And when this had happened**], Byz[So when this had happened (KJV, NKJ, ~NLT, ~REB, ~TLB)]; Alx/Byz[**also came and were cured**], Minor[*omits* also (DRA, JNT, NAB, NAS, NAU, NIV, NLT, REB, TEV, TLB)].

28:11 Alx/Byz[**set sail**], Major[left (KJV, MRD)].

28:12 Alx/Byz[**Syracuse**], Alt/Peshitta[the city of Syracuse (MRD, TEV)].

28:13 Alx[**sailed off**], Byz[sailed around (ASV, DRA, ESV, HCS, KJV, MRD, NAB, NAS, NAU, ~NJB, NKJ, RSV, TLB)]; Alx/Byz[**Rhegium**], Alt/Peshitta[the city Rhegium (MRD)]; Alx/Byz[**Puteoli**], Alt/Peshitta[Puteoli, a city of Italy (MRD)], Alt[*without textual foundation* the town of Puteoli (~TEV)].

28:15 Alx[**came as far as**], Byz[came from there as far as (MRD, NAS, NAU, REB)]; Alx/Byz[**Paul**], Alt[*without textual foundation* Saul (~JNT)].

28:16 Alx[**entered into Rome**], Byz[came into Rome (DRA, ESV, JNT, KJV, MRD, NIV, NJB, NKJ, NLT, NRS, RSV, TEV, TLB)]; Alx/Byz[**Paul**], Alt[*without textual foundation* Saul (~JNT)]; Alx[**Paul was allowed**], Byz[the centurion delivered the prisoners to the captain of the guard, but Paul was allowed (KJV, NKJ)], Alt[the centurion allowed Paul (JNT, MRD)].

28:17 Alx[**he called together**], Byz[Paul called together (~JNT, KJV, MRD, NAU, NET, NKJ, NLT, TEV)].

28:18 Alx/Byz[**examined me**], Minor[much examined me (~TLB)].

28:19 Alx[**not that I have any charge**], Byz[not that I had any charge (ASV, DRA, ESV, HCS, JNT, KJV, MRD, NAB, NAS, NAU, NET, NIV, NJB, NKJ, NLT, NRS, REB, RSV, TEV, ~TLB)].

28:23 Alx[**they came to him**], Byz[they were coming to him].

28:25 Alx/Byz[**Paul**], Alt[*without textual foundation* Saul (~JNT)]; Alx[**your fathers**], Byz[our fathers (DRA, KJV, NKJ, ~TLB)].

statement: "The Holy Spirit spoke the truth to your fathers through Isaiah the prophet, ²⁶ saying,

> 'Go to this people and say,
> > "You will be ever hearing, but will never understand.
> > > And you will be ever seeing, but will never perceive.

²⁷
> > For this people's heart has become dull.
> > > And with their ears they scarcely hear.
> > > > And their eyes they have closed.
> > > > Otherwise they might see with their eyes,
> > > and hear with their ears,
> > and understand with their heart and turn,
> > > and I would heal them."'

²⁸ Therefore let it be known to you that this salvation of God has been sent to the Gentiles. They will listen." ⁽²⁹⁾

²⁰ And he persevered there two whole years in his own rented quarters and welcomed all who came to him, ³¹ preaching the kingdom of God and teaching about the Lord Jesus Christ quite openly and unhindered.

28:²⁶⁻²⁷ **Isaiah 6:9-10 LXX**.

28:²⁷ Alx/Byz[**I would heal them**], Minor[I should heal them (ASV, DRA, JNT, KJV, ~NAB, NAS, ~NJB, NKJ, ~NLT, ~RSV, ~TLB)], Alt/Peshitta[I should forgive them (MRD)].

28:²⁸ Alx/Byz[**this salvation**], Major[the salvation (KJV, ~NIV, NKJ, ~TEV)].

28:⁽²⁹⁾ Alx[*omits*], Byz[*adds* And when he had said these things, the Jews went away, arguing greatly among themselves (ASV, DRA, ESV, HCS, KJV, MRD, NAS, NAU, NKJ)].

28:³⁰ Alx[**he persevered**], Byz[Paul stayed (~JNT, KJV, MRD, NET, NIV, NKJ, NLT, TEV, TLB)].

28:³¹ Alx/Byz[**Jesus Christ**], Minor[Jesus]; Alx/Byz[**unhindered**], Minor[*adds* Amen].

To the Romans

1 ¹ Paul, a servant of Christ Jesus, called to be an apostle, set apart for the gospel of God ² which he promised beforehand through his prophets in the Holy Scriptures, ³ concerning his Son, who was born of the seed of David according to the flesh, ⁴ and declared to be the Son of God with power according to the Spirit of holiness by his resurrection from the dead, Jesus Christ our Lord. ⁵ Through him we have received grace and apostleship to bring about the obedience of faith for the sake of his name among all the nations, ⁶ among whom you also are called to belong to Jesus Christ.

⁷ To all in Rome who are beloved of God, called to be saints:

Grace to you and peace from God our Father and the Lord Jesus Christ.

⁸ First, I thank my God through Jesus Christ for all of you, because your faith is proclaimed in all the world. ⁹ For God is my witness, whom I serve with my spirit in the gospel of his Son, that without ceasing I mention you always in my prayers, ¹⁰ asking that somehow by God's will I may now at last find the way to come to you. ¹¹ For I long to see you, so that I may impart to you some spiritual gift to strengthen you – ¹² that is, that we may be mutually encouraged by each other's faith, both yours and mine. ¹³ I do not want you to be unaware, brothers, that I often planned to come to you (but have been prevented from doing so until now) in order that I might have some harvest among you, just as I have had among the other Gentiles. ¹⁴ I am under obligation both to Greeks and to Barbarians, both to the wise and to the foolish: ¹⁵ so I am eager to preach the gospel to you also who are in Rome.

¹⁶ For I am not ashamed of the gospel: for it is the power of God for the salvation of everyone who believes, to the Jew first and also to the Greek. ¹⁷ For in it the righteousness of God is revealed from faith to faith; as it is written, *"The just shall live by faith."*

¹⁸ For the wrath of God is revealed from heaven against all ungodliness and wickedness of men, who by their wickedness suppress the truth. ¹⁹ For what may be known about God is plain to them, because God has shown it to them. ²⁰ For since the creation of the world his invisible nature, even his eternal power and deity, has been clearly seen, being understood by the things that have been made. So they are without excuse; ²¹ for although they knew God they did not honor him as God or give thanks to him, but they became futile in their thinking, and their foolish hearts were darkened. ²² Claiming to be wise, they became fools, ²³ and exchanged the glory of the immortal God for images made like mortal man and birds and animals and reptiles.

Title Alx/Byz[**To the Romans**], Minor[*variations of* The Letter of Paul the Apostle to the Romans].

1:1 Alx/Byz[**Paul**], Alt[*without textual foundation* Saul (~JNT)]; Alx[**Christ Jesus**], Byz[Jesus Christ (ASV, DRA, KJV, MRD, NKJ, NRS, RSV, TLB)].

1:4 **declared to be the Son of God with power** *or* declared with power to be the Son of God.

1:7 Alx/Byz[**in Rome**], Minor[*omits*]; Alx/Byz[**beloved of God**], Minor[in God's love].

1:8 Alx[**for** *or* on account of], Byz[for *or* for the sake of].

1:13 Alx/Byz[**I do not want you to be unaware**], Minor[I do not suppose you to be unaware], Alt[*without textual foundation* You must remember (~TEV)].

1:15 Alx/Byz[**who are in Rome**], Minor[*omits*].

1:16 Alx[**gospel**], Byz[gospel of Christ (KJV, NKJ, TLB)]; Alx/Byz[**the Jew first**], Minor[*omits* first].

1:17 **The just shall live by faith** *or* The man who through faith is righteous shall live; **Habakkuk 2:4**.

1:19 **because** *or* for.

²⁴ Therefore God gave them up in the lusts of their hearts to impurity, to the dishonoring of their bodies among themselves, ²⁵ because they exchanged the truth of God for a lie and worshipped and served the creature rather than the Creator, who is blessed forever. Amen. ²⁶ For this reason God gave them up to dishonorable passions. Even their women exchanged natural relations for unnatural. ²⁷ And the men likewise gave up natural relations with women and were consumed with passion for one another, men committing shameless acts in men and receiving in their own persons the due penalty for their error. ²⁸ And since they did not see fit to retain the knowledge of God, God gave them over to a base mind, to do what should not be done. ²⁹ They were filled with all manner of unrighteousness, wickedness, covetousness, evil. Full of envy, murder, strife, deceit, malice; they are gossips, ³⁰ slanderers, haters of God, insolent, arrogant, boastful, inventors of evil, disobedient to parents, ³¹ foolish, faithless, heartless, ruthless. ³² Though they know God's righteous decree that those who do such things deserve death, they not only continue to do these very things, but also approve of those who practice them.

2 ¹ Therefore you have no excuse, O man, any one of you who passes judgment; for in whatever point you judge another you condemn yourself, because you, the judge, are doing the very same things. ² But we know that the judgment of God is according to truth against those who do such things. ³ Do you think, O man, that when you judge those who do such things and yet do the same yourself, you will escape the judgment of God? ⁴ Or do you presume upon the riches of his kindness and forbearance and patience? Do you not know that God's kindness is meant to lead you to repentance? ⁵ But by your hardness and your impenitent heart you are storing up wrath for yourself on the day of wrath when God's righteous judgment will be revealed, ⁶ who *"will render to each one according to his works."* ⁷ To those who by patience in doing good seek for glory, honor, and immortality, he will give eternal life. ⁸ But for those who are self-seeking and do not obey the truth, but obey wickedness, there will be wrath and fury. ⁹ There will be tribulation and distress for every human being who does evil, the Jew first and also the Greek, ¹⁰ but glory, honor, and peace for everyone who does good, the Jew first and also the Greek. ¹¹ For God shows no partiality. ¹² All who have sinned without the law will also perish without the law. And all who have sinned under the law will be judged by the law. ¹³ For it is not the hearers of law who are righteous in the sight of God, but the doers of law who will be justified. ¹⁴ When Gentiles, who do not have the law, do by nature things required by the law, they are a law to themselves, even though they do not have the law. ¹⁵ They show that the requirements of the law are written on their hearts, their conscience also bearing witness, and their thoughts accusing or else excusing them ¹⁶ on that day when, according to my gospel, God judges the secrets of men by Christ Jesus.

1:24 Alx[**Therefore**], Byz[*adds* also (KJV, NKJ, TLB)]; Alx/Byz[**among themselves**], Major[among their own selves (~JNT, NJB, ~NLT, ~TEV, ~TLB)].

1:26 Alx/Byz[**Even their women...27**], Alt[27 Even their women... (NJB)].

1:27 Alx/Major[**And the men**], Byz[But the men (~TEV)].

1:29 Alx[**unrighteousness, wickedness, covetousness, evil**], Byz[unrighteousness, immorality, wickedness, covetousness, evil (~DRA, KJV, MRD, NKJ)], Minor[unrighteousness, wickedness, evil, covetousness]; Alx/Major[**they are gossips 30**], Byz[30 they are gossips (MRD, NJB)].

1:30 **haters** *or* hated.

1:31 Alx[**heartless, ruthless**], Byz[heartless, unforgiving, ruthless (KJV, MRD, NKJ)].

2:2 Alx/Byz[**But we know**], Minor[For we know (DRA)].

2:6 Psalms 62:12, Proverbs 24:12.

2:8 Alx[**wrath and fury**], Byz[fury and wrath (KJV, ~NJB, NKJ, NLT, ~REB, ~TLB)].

2:13 Alx[**law...law**], Byz[the law...the law (ASV, DRA, ESV, HCS, KJV, MRD, NAB, NAS, NAU, NET, NIV, NJB, NKJ, NLT, NRS, ~REB, RSV, TEV, ~TLB)].

2:16 Alx/Byz[**on that day when**], Minor[on that day in which (MRD)]; Alx[**God judges**], Byz[God will judge (ASV, DRA, KJV, MRD, NAB, NAS, NAU, NET, NIV, NKJ, NLT, NRS, REB, TEV, TLB)];

[17] But if you call yourself a Jew, and rely on law and boast of your relation to God [18] and know his will and approve of what is excellent, because you are instructed in the law, [19] and if you are sure that you are a guide to the blind, a light to those who are in darkness, [20] an instructor of the foolish, a teacher of infants, having in the law the embodiment of knowledge and truth – [21] you, then, who teach others, do you not teach yourself? You who preach against stealing, do you steal? [22] You who say that one must not commit adultery, do you commit adultery? You who abhor idols, do you rob temples? [23] You who boast in the law, do you dishonor God by breaking the law? [24] For, as it is written, "The *name of God is blasphemed* among the Gentiles because of you." [25] Circumcision indeed is of value if you obey the law. But if you break the law, your circumcision has become uncircumcision. [26] So, if a man who is uncircumcised keeps the requirements of the law, will not his uncircumcision be regarded as circumcision? [27] The one who is not circumcised physically and yet obeys the law will condemn you who, even though you have the written code and circumcision, are a breaker of the law. [28] For he is not a real Jew who is one outwardly, nor is true circumcision something outward and in the flesh. [29] He is a Jew who is one inwardly; and real circumcision is a matter of the heart, by the Spirit, and not by the written code. His praise is not from men but from God.

3 [1] Then what advantage has the Jew, or what is the value of circumcision? [2] Much in every way – [for], first of all, they are entrusted with the oracles of God. [3] What if some did not have faith? Will their faithlessness nullify the faithfulness of God? [4] Certainly not! Let God be true, though every man a liar. As it is written:

> *"That you may be justified in your words*
> *and prevail when you are judged."*

[5] But if our unrighteousness serves to show the righteousness of God, what shall we say? That God is unjust to inflict wrath on us? (I speak in a human way.) [6] Certainly not! For then how could God judge the world? [7] But if through my falsehood God's truthfulness abounds to his glory, why am I still being condemned as a sinner? [8] Why not say – as we are being slanderously reported to say (by some people's claim) – "Let us do evil that good may come"? Their condemnation is just.

[9] What then? Are we Jews any better off? Certainly not! For we have already charged that all men, both Jews and Greeks, are under the power of sin. [10] As it is written:

> *"There is none righteous, no, not one.*
[11]
> *There is no one who understands,*
> *no one who seeks for God.*
[12]
> *All have turned aside. Together they have become worthless.*
> *There is no one who does good,*
> *[no,] not one."*

Alx[**Christ Jesus**], Byz[Jesus Christ (ASV, DRA, KJV, MRD, NIV, NJB, NKJ, NRS, TEV, TLB)].

2:17 Alx[**But if you**], Byz[Behold! You (KJV, NKJ, ~NLT, ~TEV, ~TLB)]; Alx[**law**], Byz[the law (ASV, DRA, ESV, HCS, KJV, MRD, NAB, NAS, NAU, NET, NIV, NJB, NKJ, ~NLT, NRS, REB, RSV, TEV)].

2:24 **Isaiah 52:5 LXX**, Ezekiel 36:22.

2:27 **even though you have the written code and circumcision, are a breaker of the law** *or* by means of the written code and circumcision, you are a breaker of the law.

3:2 Alx/Byz[**for**], Minor[omit (ASV, ESV, HCS, JNT, NAS, NAU, NET, NIV, NJB, NLT, REB, RSV, TEV, TLB)].

3:4 **when you are judged** *or* when you judge; **Psalms 51:4 LXX**.

3:7 Alx[**But if**], Byz[For if (DRA, KJV, NET, ~NIV, ~NJB, NKJ, ~REB, TLB)].

3:9 **better** *or* worse; **Certainly not** *or* Not entirely.

3:10-12 ~**Psalms 14:1-3, 53:1-3 LXX**, Ecclesiastes 7:20.

3:12 Alx/Byz[**no, not one**], Minor[omits no (DRA, ESV, HCS, JNT, NET, NIV, NJB, NLT, RSV, TEV, TLB)].

13   *"Their throat is an open grave.*
                They use their tongues to practice deceit."
        "The poison of asps is under their lips."
14   *"Their mouth is full of cursing and bitterness."*
15   *"Their feet are swift to shed blood.*
16   *In their ways are ruin and misery,*
17   *and the way of peace they do not know."*
18   *"There is no fear of God before their eyes."*

19 Now we know that whatever the law says, it says to those who are under the law, so that every mouth may be stopped and the whole world may be held accountable to God. **20** Therefore no flesh will be justified in his sight by works of the law, for through the law comes knowledge of sin.

21 But now the righteousness of God has been revealed apart from law, although the law and the prophets bear witness to it; **22** the righteousness of God through faith in Jesus Christ to all who believe. For there is no difference, **23** for all have sinned and fall short of the glory of God, **24** and are justified freely by his grace through the redemption that is in Christ Jesus, **25** whom God put forward as an atoning sacrifice by his blood, to be received through faith. This was to demonstrate his righteousness, because in his divine forbearance he had passed over sins committed beforehand. **26** It was to demonstrate his righteousness at the present time, that he might be just and the justifier of the one who has faith in Jesus.

27 Where then is our boasting? It is excluded. On what law? On the law of works? No, but on the law of faith. **28** For we hold that a man is justified by faith apart from works of law. **29** Or is he the God of Jews only? Not of Gentiles also? Yes! – of Gentiles also, **30** since there is one God, who will justify the circumcised by faith and the uncircumcised through their faith. **31** Do we then nullify the law by this faith? Certainly not! On the contrary, we uphold the law.

4 **1** What then shall we say that Abraham, our forefather according to the flesh, has found? **2** For if Abraham was justified by works, he has something to boast about, but not before God. **3** For what does the scripture say? *"Abraham believed God, and it was reckoned to him as righteousness."* **4** Now to him who works, his wages are not reckoned as a gift but as his due. **5** And to one who does not work but trusts him who justifies the ungodly, his faith is reckoned as righteousness. **6** So also David describes the blessedness of the man to whom God reckons righteousness apart from works:

3:13 **Psalms 5:9 LXX, Psalms 140:3 LXX**.

3:14 **Psalms 10:7 LXX**.

3:15-17 **~Isaiah 59:7-8**.

3:18 **Psalms 36:1**.

3:22 Alx/Byz[**Jesus Christ**], Minor[*omits* Jesus (REB)]; Alx[**to all who believe**], Byz[to all and on all who believe (DRA, KJV, MRD, NKJ)]; **faith in Jesus** *or* the faith of Jesus.

3:25 **put forward** *or* designed to be; **an atoning sacrifice** *or* the mercy seat, *compare Hebrews 9:5, Exodus 25:17 LXX*; **in his divine forbearance he had passed over sins committed beforehand. 26 It...** *Greek* he had passed over sins committed beforehand 26 in the forbearance of God. It...

3:26 Alx/Byz[**Jesus**], Minor[Jesus Christ (DRA) *others* our Lord Jesus Christ (MRD)]; **faith in Jesus** *or* the faith of Jesus.

3:27 **law** *or* principle.

3:28 Alx[**For**], Byz[Therefore (ASV, JNT, KJV, MRD, NJB, NKJ, NLT, TLB)].

3:29 Alx[**Not of Gentiles**], Byz[But not of Gentiles (NJB, ~TLB)]; Alx/Byz[**Yes**], Minor[No (MRD, TLB)].

4:1 Alx[**forefather**], Byz[father (DRA, KJV, NKJ)]; Alx/Byz[**say that Abraham...according to the flesh, has found**], Minor[say about Abraham...according to the flesh (~JNT, NJB, REB, RSV)].

4:3 **Genesis 15:6**.

7   *"Blessed are those whose iniquities are forgiven,*
                  and whose sins are covered.
8   *Blessed is the man against whom the Lord*
                  will never count his sin."

9 Is this blessedness only upon the circumcised, or also upon the uncircumcised? For we say *faith was reckoned to Abraham as righteousness.* 10 How then was it reckoned to him? Was it after he had been circumcised, or before? It was not after, but before he was circumcised. 11 And he received the sign of circumcision, a seal of the righteousness which he had by faith while he was still uncircumcised, that he might be the father of all who believe but have not been circumcised, in order that righteousness might be reckoned to them [as well]. 12 And he is also the father of the circumcised who are not only circumcised but who also walk in the footsteps of faith which our father Abraham had before he was circumcised.

        13 The promise to Abraham and his descendants, that he would be heir of the world, was not through the law but through the righteousness of faith. 14 For if those who are of law are to be the heirs, faith has no value and the promise is void, 15 for law brings wrath. But where there is no law there is no transgression. 16 Therefore, the promise comes by faith, so that it may be by grace and may be guaranteed to all his descendants – not only to those who are of the law but also to those who are of the faith of Abraham. For, he is the father of us all 17 (as it is written, *"I have made you the father of many nations"*) in the presence of the God in whom he believed, who gives life to the dead and calls things that do not exist as though they did. 18 In hope, he believed against hope, so that he became the *father of many nations,* as he had been told, *"So shall your descendants be."* 19 And he did not weaken in faith when he considered his own body, which was [already] as good as dead since he was about a hundred years old, or when he considered the barrenness of Sarah's womb. 20 He did not waver at the promise of God through unbelief, but was strengthened in his faith and gave glory to God, 21 being fully convinced that God was able to do what he had promised. 22 [And] that is why it was *"reckoned to him as righteousness."* 23 But the words, "it was reckoned to him," were written not for his sake alone, 24 but for us also. It will be reckoned to us who believe in him who raised from the dead Jesus our Lord, 25 who was delivered to death for our sins and was raised for our justification.

5   1 Therefore, since we have been justified by faith, we have peace with God through our Lord Jesus Christ, 2 through whom we have obtained access [by faith] into this grace in which we stand, and we rejoice in our hope of the glory of God. 3 And not only that, but we rejoice in our sufferings, knowing that suffering produces perseverance; 4

4:7-8 **Psalms 32:1-2**.

4:8 Alx/Byz[**will never count**], Minor[will not count (ASV, DRA, ESV, JNT, KJV, MRD, NAB, NAS, NAU, NJB, NKJ, ~NLT, NRS, REB, RSV, TEV, ~TLB)].

4:9 Alx[**For we say**], Byz[For we say that (DRA, ESV, JNT, KJV, MRD, NAB, NIV, NJB, NKJ, NLT, RSV, TLB)]; ~Genesis 15:6.

4:11 Alx/Byz[**as well** *or* also], Minor[omits (ASV, JNT, NAS, NAU, NIV, NJB, NLT, NRS, REB, RSV, TEV, TLB)].

4:12 Alx/Byz[**faith**], Major[the faith (~ASV, ~DRA, ESV, HCS, JNT, ~KJV, MRD, NAS, NAU, NET, NIV, NKJ, NRS, RSV, ~TLB)].

4:15 Alx[**But where**], Byz[For where (DRA, KJV, MRD, NET, NKJ, TLB)].

4:17 **Genesis 17:5**.

4:18 **Genesis 17:5, 15:5**.

4:19 Alx[**or when he considered**], Byz[He did not consider (DRA, KJV, NKJ, ~TLB)]; Alx/Byz[**already**], Minor[omits (ESV, JNT, MRD, NET, NIV, NJB, NLT, REB, RSV, TLB)].

4:22 Alx/Byz[**And**], Minor[omit (ESV, HCS, JNT, NAB, NET, NIV, NJB, NRS, RSV, TEV)]; Genesis 15:6.

5:1 Alx/Byz[**we have peace**], Minor[we may have peace (TLB) *others* let us have peace (DRA)].

5:2 Alx/Byz[**by faith**], Minor[omits (NRS, REB, RSV)].

5:3 Alx/Byz[**we rejoice**], Minor[rejoicing].

and perseverance, character; and character, hope. [5] And hope does not disappoint us, because God has poured out his love into our hearts by the Holy Spirit who has been given to us. [6] For when we were still weak, at the right time Christ died for the ungodly. [7] Why, one will hardly die for a righteous man – though perhaps for a good man one will dare even to die. [8] But God demonstrates his own love for us, in that while we were still sinners Christ died for us. [9] Since, therefore, we have now been justified by his blood, much more shall we be saved through him from the Wrath. [10] For if, when we were enemies, we were reconciled to God through the death of his Son, much more, having been reconciled, shall we be saved by his life. [11] Not only so, but we also rejoice in God through our Lord Jesus Christ, through whom we have now received our reconciliation.

[12] Therefore, just as sin entered the world through one man, and death through sin, so death spread to all men, because all men sinned. [13] (For sin was in the world before the law was given, but sin is not counted when there is no law. [14] Nevertheless death reigned from Adam to Moses, even over those whose sins were not like the transgression of Adam, who was a type of the one who was to come. [15] But the free gift is not like the trespass. For if by the one man's trespass many died, much more the grace of God and the gift by the grace of the one man, Jesus Christ, abounded to many. [16] And the free gift is not like the effect of that one man's sin. For the judgment following one trespass brought condemnation, but the gift following many trespasses brings justification. [17] For if, by the one man's trespass, death reigned through that one man, much more will those who receive the abundance of grace and of the gift of righteousness reign in life through the one man Jesus Christ.) [18] So then, as one man's trespass led to condemnation for all men, so one man's act of righteousness leads to justification and life for all men. [19] For just as through the disobedience of the one man the many were made sinners, so also through the obedience of the one man the many will be made righteous. [20] Law came in, that the trespass might increase. But where sin increased, grace abounded all the more, [21] so that, as sin reigned in death, grace also might reign through righteousness to eternal life through Jesus Christ our Lord.

6 [1] What shall we say then? Should we continue in sin that grace may abound? [2] Certainly not! How can we who died to sin live any longer in it? [3] Or do you not know that all of us who were baptized into Christ Jesus were baptized into his death? [4] We were buried therefore with him through baptism into death, so that just as Christ was raised from the dead by the glory of the Father, we too might walk in newness of life. [5] For if we have been united with him in a death like his, we shall certainly also be united with him in a resurrection like his. [6] We know that our old self was crucified with him so that the body of sin might be done away with, that we should no longer be slaves to sin. [7] For he who has died has been freed from sin. [8] Now if we died with Christ, we believe that we shall also live with him. [9] For we know that Christ, being raised from the dead, will never

---

5:6 Alx/Byz[**For when**], Minor[For if (~DRA, MRD)]; Alx[**still**], Byz[*omits* (~MRD, NLT, TLB)].

5:8 Alx/Byz[**God**], Minor[*omits*].

5:11 Alx/Byz[**Christ**], Minor[*omits* (REB)].

5:12 Alx/Byz[**because all men sinned** *or* because of which *death* all men sinned], Alt/Vulgate[in whom *Adam* all men sinned (DRA)].

5:17 Alx/Byz[**by one man's trespass**], Minor[by one trespass (MRD)]; Alx/Byz[**of the gift**], Minor[*omits* (~TEV)]; Alx/Byz[**Jesus Christ**], Minor[Christ Jesus].

6:1 Alx[**Should we continue**], Byz[Shall we continue (ASV, DRA, ~JNT, KJV, MRD, NAB, NIV, NKJ, REB, TLB)], Major[Are we continuing].

6:3 Alx/Byz[**Christ Jesus**], Minor[Jesus Christ (KJV, MRD, TLB) *others omit* Jesus].

6:4 Alx/Byz[**We are buried therefore**], Minor[We are buried (JNT, REB, TLB) *others* For we are buried (DRA, MRD, NLT)].

6:6 **done away with** *or* made ineffective.

6:8 Alx/Byz[**Now if we died** *or* But if we died], Minor[For if we died (~MRD, ~NAB, ~NLT, ~TEV, ~TLB)].

die again; death no longer has dominion over him. [10] The death he died, he died to sin once for all; but the life he lives, he lives to God. [11] So you also, consider yourselves [to be] dead to sin but alive to God in Christ Jesus.

[12] Therefore do not let sin reign in your mortal body, that you obey its passions. [13] Do not yield your members to sin as instruments of wickedness, but yield yourselves to God as men who have been brought from death to life, and your members to God as instruments of righteousness. [14] For sin shall not have dominion over you, since you are not under law but under grace.

[15] What then? Should we sin because we are not under law but under grace? Certainly not! [16] Do you not know that if you yield yourselves to anyone to obey as slaves, you are slaves of the one whom you obey, whether of sin, which leads to death, or of obedience, which leads to righteousness? [17] But thanks be to God, that you who were once slaves of sin have become obedient from the heart to the standard of teaching to which you were committed, [18] and, having been set free from sin, you have become slaves of righteousness. [19] I am speaking in human terms, because of the weakness of your flesh. For just as you once yielded your members to impurity and to greater and greater iniquity, so now yield your members to righteousness for holiness. [20] When you were slaves of sin, you were free in regard to righteousness. [21] But then what return did you get from the things of which you are now ashamed? For the end of those things is death. [22] But now that you have been set free from sin and have become slaves of God, the return you get is holiness and its end, eternal life. [23] For the wages of sin is death, but the free gift of God is eternal life in Christ Jesus our Lord.

7 [1] Do you not know, brothers – for I am speaking to those who know the law – that the law has authority over a man only as long as he lives? [2] For a married woman is bound by law to her husband as long as he lives, but if her husband dies she is released from the law of her husband. [3] So then, she will be called an adulteress if she lives with another man while her husband is alive. But if her husband dies, she is free from that law, and though she marries another man, she is not an adulteress. [4] Likewise, my brothers, you have died to the law through the body of Christ, so that you may belong to another, to him who was raised from the dead, in order that we may bear fruit to God. [5] While we were living in the flesh, our sinful passions, aroused by the law, were at work in our members to bear fruit for death. [6] But now, by dying to what once held us, we have been released from the law so that we serve in the new way of the Spirit, and not in the old way of the written code.

6:11 Alx/Byz[to be], Minor[omits (ESV, HCS, NET, NIV, NRS, REB, RSV, TEV, TLB)]; Alx/Byz[**Christ Jesus**], Minor[Jesus Christ (~KJV, ~MRD, ~TLB) others Christ Jesus our Lord (DRA, ~KJV, ~MRD, NKJ, ~TLB)].

6:12 Alx[**obey its passions**], Byz[obey it in its passions (KJV, NKJ, ~TLB)].

6:13 **instruments** or weapons.

6:15 Alx[**Should we sin**], Byz[Shall we sin (ASV, DRA, KJV, MRD, NAB, NAS, NAU, NET, NIV, ~NJB, NKJ, ~NLT, TEV, ~TLB)].

6:16 Alx/Byz[**which leads to death** Greek to death], Minor[omits (MRD)].

6:17 **to which you were committed** or which was committed to you.

6:19 Alx/Byz[**to greater and greater iniquity** Greek iniquity into iniquity], Minor[iniquity (MRD, ~NLT, TLB)].

6:21 Alx/Byz[**For the end**], Minor[For indeed the end (~TLB)].

6:23 Alx/Byz[**Christ Jesus**], Minor[Jesus Christ (KJV, MRD, TLB)].

7:2 Alx/Byz[**from the law of her husband**], Minor[from her husband].

7:6 Alx/Byz[**dying**], Minor[being dead (~DRA, HCS, JNT, KJV, MRD, NAB, NET, NLT, NRS, RSV, TEV, TLB)].

7 What shall we say, then? Is the law sin? Certainly not! Indeed, I would not have known what sin was except through the law. For I would not have known what coveting really was if the law had not said, *"You shall not covet."* 8 But sin, finding opportunity by the commandment, produced in me all kinds of covetous desire. For apart from the law sin lies dead. 9 I was once alive apart from the law, but when the commandment came, sin sprang to life 10 and I died. The very commandment which was to bring life I found to be death to me. 11 For sin, finding opportunity in the commandment, deceived me, and by it killed me. 12 So the law is holy, and the commandment is holy and just and good.

13 Did that which is good, then, become death to me? Certainly not! But it was sin, working death in me through what is good, in order that sin might be recognized as sin, so that through the commandment sin might become sinful beyond measure. 14 For we know that the law is spiritual; but I am flesh, sold under sin. 15 I do not understand what I do. For I do not do what I want to do, but I do what I hate. 16 Now if I do what I do not want to do, I agree that the law is good. 17 So then, it is no longer I who do it, but sin that dwells within me. 18 For I know that nothing good dwells within me, that is, in my flesh. I can will to do what is good, but I cannot do it. 19 For I do not do the good I want to do; but the evil I do not want to do is what I do. 20 Now if [I] do what I do not want to do, it is no longer I who do it, but sin that dwells within me. 21 So I find it to be a law that when I want to do good, evil is present with me. 22 For I delight in the law of God, in my inner being. 23 But I see in my members another law, at war against the law of my mind and making me captive in the law of sin which dwells in my members. 24 Wretched man that I am! Who will deliver me from this body of death? 25 But thanks be to God – through Jesus Christ our Lord! So then, I of myself indeed serve the law of God with my mind, but with my flesh I serve the law of sin.

8 1 There is therefore now no condemnation for those who are in Christ Jesus. 2 For the law of the Spirit of life in Christ Jesus has set you free from the law of sin and death. 3 For what the law could not do, in that it was weakened through the flesh, God did by sending his own Son in the likeness of sinful flesh, and for sin: he condemned sin in the flesh, 4 in order that the righteous requirement of the law might be fulfilled in us, who do not walk according to the flesh but according to the Spirit. 5 For those who live according to the flesh set their minds on the things of the flesh, but those who live according to the Spirit set their minds on the things of the Spirit. 6 To set the mind on the flesh is death, but

---

7:7 **Exodus 20:17, Deuteronomy 5:21**.

7:10 Alx[**10 and I died**], Byz[and I died 10 (ASV, ESV, KJV, MRD, NAS, NAU, NIV, NKJ, REB, RSV, TLB)].

7:14 Alx/Byz[**we know**], Minor[I know indeed (~NLT, ~TLB)]; Alx[**I am flesh** *or* I am of the flesh], Byz[I am carnal (ASV, DRA, ~JNT, KJV, MRD, NAB, ~NET, ~NIV, NKJ, ~NLT, ~REB, RSV, ~TLB)].

7:17 Alx/Byz[**dwells within**], Minor[indwells within (~NAS, ~TLB)].

7:18 Alx[**I cannot do it**], Byz[I cannot find how to do it (DRA, KJV, NKJ)].

7:20 Alx/Byz[**I** *expressed*], Minor[I *implied*].

7:22 Alx/Byz[**law of God**], Minor[law of the mind].

7:23 Alx/Byz[**captive in the law of sin**], Major[captive to the law of sin (~ASV, ESV, HCS, ~JNT, KJV, MRD, NAB, ~NAS, ~NAU, NET, ~NIV, ~NJB, NKJ, NLT, NRS, RSV, TEV, TLB)].

7:25 Alx[**But thanks be to God** *or* But grace to God], Byz[I thank God (ASV, HCS, KJV, MRD, NKJ, ~NLT, ~TLB)], Minor[The grace of God (DRA)]; Alx/Byz[**I of myself indeed**], Minor[*omits* indeed (DRA, ESV, HCS, JNT, KJV, MRD, NAB, NET, NIV, NJB, NKJ, NLT, NRS, REB, RSV, TEV, ~TLB)].

8:1 Alx[**in Christ Jesus**], Byz[*adds* who do not walk according to the flesh but according to the Spirit (KJV, NKJ)], Minor[*adds* who do not walk according to the flesh (DRA, MRD)].

8:2 Alx[**set you free**], Byz[set me free (ASV, DRA, JNT, KJV, NIV, NKJ, RSV, TEV, TLB)], Minor[set us free].

8:3 **for sin** *or* as a sin offering *or* to deal with sin.

to set the mind on the Spirit is life and peace. 7 For the mind that is set on the flesh is hostile to God. It does not submit to God's law, nor can it do so. 8 And those who are in the flesh cannot please God. 9 But you are not in the flesh, you are in the Spirit, if in fact the Spirit of God dwells in you. And if anyone does not have the Spirit of Christ, he does not belong to him. 10 But if Christ is in you, although your body is dead because of sin, your spirit is alive because of righteousness. 11 If the Spirit of him who raised Jesus from the dead dwells in you, he who raised Christ from the dead will give life to your mortal bodies also through his Spirit who dwells in you.

12 Therefore, brothers, we are debtors – not to the flesh, to live according to the flesh. 13 For if you live according to the flesh you will die; but if by the Spirit you put to death the deeds of the body, you will live. 14 For all who are led by the Spirit of God are sons of God. 15 For you did not receive the spirit of bondage again to fear, but you received the Spirit of sonship by whom we cry out, "Abba, Father." 16 The Spirit himself bears witness with our spirit that we are children of God, 17 and if children, then heirs – heirs of God and fellow heirs with Christ, if indeed we suffer with him, in order that we may also be glorified with him.

18 I consider that the sufferings of this present time are not worth comparing with the glory that is to be revealed in us. 19 For the creation waits with eager expectation for the revealing of the sons of God. 20 For the creation was subjected to futility, not of its own will, but by the will of him who subjected it in hope 21 that the creation itself will be set free from its bondage to decay and obtain the glorious liberty of the children of God. 22 We know that the whole creation has been groaning in birth pangs together until now. 23 And not only the creation, but we ourselves, who have the firstfruits of the Spirit, groan inwardly as we wait eagerly for adoption as sons, the redemption of our bodies. 24 For in this hope we were saved. But hope that is seen is not hope. For who hopes for what he sees? 25 But if we hope for what we do not see, we wait for it with patience.

26 Likewise the Spirit helps us in our weakness; for we do not know what to pray for as we ought, but the Spirit himself intercedes with groans that words cannot express. 27 And he who searches the hearts of men knows what is the mind of the Spirit, because he intercedes for the saints according to the will of God. 28 And we know that all things work together for the good of those who love God, who are called according to his purpose. 29 For those whom he foreknew he also predestined to be conformed to the image of his Son, that he might be the firstborn among many brothers. 30 And those whom he predestined, he also

---

8:7 Alx/Major[**7 For the mind that is set on the flesh is hostile to God**], Byz[For the mind that is set on the flesh is hostile to God 7].

8:11 Alx[**raised Christ**], Byz[raised the Christ], Minor[raised Christ Jesus (ASV, DRA, JNT, NAS, NAU, NJB, NLT, REB, RSV, ~TLB) *others* raised our Lord Jesus Christ (MRD)]; Alx/Byz[**also**], Minor[omits (NJB)]; Alx/Byz[**through his Spirit**], Minor[because of his Spirit (DRA, ~KJV, MRD)].

8:15 **sonship** or adoption; **Abba** *Aramaism* Father.

8:20-21 Alx[**subjected it in hope** 21 **that the creation**]; Byz[subjected it in hope; 21 because the creation (DRA, KJV, NKJ, NLT, RSV, ~TLB)].

8:23 Alx/Byz[**we ourselves**], Minor[*omits* we (~NLT, ~REB, ~TLB)]; Alx/Byz[**adoption as sons**], Minor[omits (NJB)].

8:24 Alx[**who hopes for what he sees**], Byz[what a man sees, why does he hope (DRA, KJV, ~MRD, ~NAS, ~NKJ, ~NLT, ~REB, ~TLB)], Minor[who waits for what he sees]; **in this hope** or by this hope.

8:26 Alx[**our weakness**], Byz[our weaknesses (KJV, NKJ, TLB)]; Alx[**intercedes**], Byz[*adds* for us (ASV, DRA, ESV, HCS, JNT, KJV, MRD, NAS, NAU, NET, NIV, NJB, NKJ, NLT, REB, RSV, TEV, TLB)].

8:27 **according to the will of God** *Greek* according to God.

8:28 Alx/Byz[**all things work together**], Minor[God works all things together (JNT, ~MRD, NAS, NAU, ~NIV, ~NJB, NLT, ~REB, ~RSV, ~TEV)].

called; those whom he called, he also justified; and those whom he justified, he also glorified.

   31 What then shall we say to this? If God is for us, who can be against us? **32** He who did not spare his own Son, but gave him up for us all, how will he not also give us all things with him? **33** Who shall bring any charge against God's elect? It is God who justifies. **34** Who is he who condemns? It is Christ [Jesus], who died, yes, who was raised, who is at the right hand of God, who is also interceding for us. **35** Who shall separate us from the love of Christ? Shall tribulation, or distress, or persecution, or famine, or nakedness, or peril, or sword? **36** As it is written:

> "For your sake we are being killed all the day long;
>   we are regarded as sheep to be slaughtered."

37 No, in all these things we are more than conquerors through him who loved us. **38** For I am persuaded that neither death nor life, nor angels nor principalities, nor things present nor things to come, nor powers, **39** nor height nor depth, nor anything else in all creation, will be able to separate us from the love of God which is in Christ Jesus our Lord.

9 **1** I am speaking the truth in Christ, I am not lying; my conscience bears me witness in the Holy Spirit, **2** that I have great sorrow and unceasing anguish in my heart. **3** For I could wish that I myself were accursed and cut off from Christ for the sake of my brothers, my kinsmen according to the flesh. **4** They are Israelites, and to them belong the adoption, the glory, the covenants, the giving of the law, the worship, and the promises. **5** Of them are the patriarchs, and from them, according to the flesh, is the Christ, who is God over all, blessed forever. Amen.

   6 But it is not as though the word of God had failed. For not all who are descended from Israel are Israel, **7** nor are they all children of Abraham because they are his descendants; but, *"Through Isaac shall your descendants be named."* **8** In other words, it is not the children of the flesh who are the children of God, but the children of the promise are reckoned as descendants. **9** For this is what the promise said: *"About this time I will return and Sarah shall have a son."* **10** And not only so, but also when Rebecca had conceived children by one man, our father Isaac, **11** though the twins were not yet born and had done nothing either good or bad, in order that God's purpose of election might stand, **12** not because of works but because of his call, she was told, *"The older will serve the younger."* **13** As it is written,

---

8:34 Alx[**Christ Jesus**], Byz[*omits* Jesus (KJV, MRD, NET, NKJ, REB, TLB)]; Alx/Byz[**who was raised**], Minor[*adds* from the dead (ASV, NJB, RSV)]; Alx/Byz[**who is also interceding**], Minor[*omits* also (HCS, MRD, NLT, REB, TEV, TLB)]; **It is Christ** *or* Is it Christ…?

8:35 Alx/Byz[**the love of Christ**], Minor[the love of God *others* the love of God in Christ Jesus].

8:36 **Psalms 44:22**.

8:38 Alx[**nor things present nor things to come, nor powers**], Byz[nor powers, nor things present, nor things to come (JNT, KJV, MRD, NKJ, ~NLT, TEV, TLB)].

9:4 Alx/Byz[**the covenants**], Minor[the covenant (DRA, ~TLB)].

9:5 Alx/Byz[**Christ, who is God over all, blessed forever**], Alt[Christ. God who is over all be blessed forever (NAB, REB, RSV, TEV) *others* Christ, who is over all, God blessed forever (ASV, DRA, KJV, NAS, NAU, NRS) *others* Christ, who is over all. God be blessed forever (JNT, TLB)]; *the variations are nearly equal in possibility*.

9:7 **children of Abraham because they are his descendants** *or* children of God because they are Abraham's descendants; Genesis 21:12.

9:9 ~Genesis 18:10, 14.

9:11 Alx[**bad** *or* worthless], Byz[bad *or* evil (DRA, KJV, MRD, NKJ, ~REB)].

9:12 Alx[**12 not because of works but because of his call**], Byz[not because of works but because of his call 12 (ASV, ESV, JNT, KJV, MRD, NAS, NAU, NET, NKJ, REB, RSV, ~TEV, ~TLB)]; Genesis 25:23.

9:13 **Malachi 1:2-3**.

> "Jacob I loved,
>   but Esau I hated."

14 What shall we say then? Is there injustice with God? Certainly not! **15** For he says to Moses,

> "I will have mercy on whom I have mercy,
>   and I will have compassion
>   on whom I have compassion."

16 So it depends not upon man's will or exertion, but upon God's mercy. **17** For the scripture says to Pharaoh, "I have raised you up for this very purpose, that I may show my power in you, and that my name may be proclaimed in all the earth." **18** Therefore he has mercy on whom he wills, and he hardens the heart of whom he wills.

19 So you will say to me, "Then why does he still find fault? For who can resist his will?" **20** But who are you, O man, to answer back to God? Will what is formed say to him who formed it, "Why have you made me like this?" **21** Does not the potter have right over the clay, to make out of the same lump one vessel for honor and another for dishonor? **22** What if God, choosing to show his wrath and to make his power known, endured with much patience the vessels of wrath prepared for destruction, **23** in order to make known the riches of his glory for the vessels of mercy, which he has prepared beforehand for glory, **24** even us whom he has called, not from the Jews only, but also from the Gentiles? **25** As indeed he says in Hosea:

> "I will call them who were not my people 'my people,'
>   and her who was not beloved I will call 'my beloved.'"

26
> "And it will happen that in the very place
>   where it was said to them, 'You are not my people,'
>   they will be called 'sons of the living God.'"

27 And Isaiah cries out concerning Israel: "Though the number of the sons of Israel be as the sand of the sea, only the remnant will be saved. **28** For the Lord will carry out his sentence on the earth with speed and finality." **29** And as Isaiah said:

> "Unless the Lord of hosts had left us children,
>   we would have become like Sodom,
>   and we would have been made like Gomorrah."

30 What shall we say, then? That Gentiles who did not pursue righteousness have attained it, that is, righteousness through faith; **31** but Israel, who pursued the law of righteousness, has not attained that law. **32** Why? Because they did not pursue it by faith, but as if it were by works. They have stumbled over the stumbling stone, **33** as it is written:

9:15 **Exodus 33:19.**
9:17 **Exodus 9:16 LXX.**
9:19 Alx[**Then**], Byz[omit (ASV, ~DRA, ESV, KJV, NAS, NAU, NET, NKJ, NLT, RSV, ~TEV, ~TLB)]; Alx/Byz[**For who can resist**], Minor[omits For (~NLT, REB, TEV, ~TLB)].
9:20 Isaiah 29:16, 45:9.
9:23 Alx/Byz[**in order to** Greek and in order that], Minor[omits and].
9:25 ~**Hosea 2:23 LXX.**
9:26 Alx/Byz[**it was said to them**], Minor[omits to them others of them (MRD, TLB)]; **Hosea 1:10.**
9:27-28 ~**Isaiah 10:22-23 LXX.**
9:28 Alx[text], Byz[For he will carry out his work and cut it short in righteousness, because the Lord will make the sentence shortened on the earth (DRA, KJV, NKJ, TLB)].
9:29 **children** Greek seed; **Isaiah 1:9 LXX.**
9:31 Alx[**that law**], Byz[the law of righteousness (DRA, ~JNT, KJV, MRD, NKJ)].
9:32 Alx[**by works**], Byz[adds of the law (JNT, KJV, MRD, NKJ, NLT, TLB)]; Alx[**They have stumbled**], Byz[For they have stumbled (DRA, KJV, MRD, ~NJB, NKJ, ~TEV)].
9:33 Alx[**he who believes**], Byz[whoever believes (DRA, ESV, KJV, NAB, NKJ, NLT, NRS, TEV, TLB)]; **believes in him** or trusts in it; ~**Isaiah 8:14 Masoretic, 28:16 LXX.**

"Behold, I lay in Zion a stone that will make men stumble,
and a rock that will make them fall;
and he who believes in him will not be put to shame."

10 ¹ Brothers, my heart's desire and prayer to God for them is that they may be saved. ² For I bear them witness that they have a zeal for God, but it is not according to knowledge. ³ For, being ignorant of the righteousness that comes from God, and seeking to establish their own [righteousness], they did not submit to God's righteousness. ⁴ For Christ is the end of the law, that there may be righteousness for everyone who believes.

⁵ For Moses writes about the righteousness which is of [the] law, that, *"The man who does those things shall live by them."* ⁶ But the righteousness based on faith says, *"Do not say in your heart, 'Who will ascend into heaven?'"* (that is, to bring Christ down) ⁷ or *"Who will descend into the abyss?"* (that is, to bring Christ up from the dead). ⁸ But what does it say?

"The word is near you,
in your mouth and in your heart"

(that is, the word of faith which we preach); ⁹ because, if you confess with your mouth Jesus as Lord and believe in your heart that God raised him from the dead, you will be saved. ¹⁰ For man believes with his heart and so is justified, and he confesses with his mouth and so is saved. ¹¹ The scripture says, "No one *who believes in him will be put to shame."* ¹² For there is no distinction between Jew and Greek; the same Lord is Lord of all and bestows his riches on all who call upon him. ¹³ For, *"everyone who calls on the name of the Lord will be saved."*

¹⁴ How then can they call on him in whom they have not believed? And how can they believe in him of whom they have not heard? And how can they hear without a preacher? ¹⁵ And how can they preach unless they are sent? As it is written, *"How beautiful are the feet of those who preach [the] good news!"* ¹⁶ But they have not all obeyed the gospel. For Isaiah says, *"Lord, who has believed our message?"* ¹⁷ So faith comes from hearing, and hearing by the word of Christ. ¹⁸ But I ask, have they not heard? Indeed they have; for

"Their voice has gone out to all the earth,
and their words to the ends of the world."

10:1 Alx[**prayer to God for them**], Byz[prayer to God for Israel (JNT, KJV, NIV, NKJ, NLT, TLB)].

10:3 Alx/Byz[**their own righteousness**], Minor[*omits* righteousness (ASV, DRA, ESV, JNT, NAS, NAU, NIV, NJB, NRS, REB, RSV, ~TLB)].

10:4 **end of the law** *or* goal of the law.

10:5 Alx/Byz[**writes about** Greek writes], Minor[that (~ASV, DRA, NAS, NAU, NLT, RSV, TLB)]; Alx/Byz[**the law**], Minor[*omits* the (NAS, NAU, ~TLB)]; Alx/Byz[**that, "The man**], Minor[*omits* that (~ASV, ~DRA, ~HCS, ~MRD, NAB, ~NAS, ~NAU, ~NET, ~NIV, ~NKJ, ~REB, ~RSV, TEV, ~TLB)]; Alx/Byz[**who does those things**], Minor[*omits* those things (ASV, DRA, ~NAS, ~NAU, NJB, REB, RSV, ~TLB)], Alx/Byz[**shall live by them**], Minor[shall live by it (~ASV, DRA, ~NAS, ~NAU, NJB, ~NLT, REB, RSV, ~TEV, ~TLB)]; **Leviticus 18:5**.

10:6 **Deuteronomy 9:4**.

10:6-8 ~**Deuteronomy 30:12-14**.

10:9 Alx/Byz[**Jesus as Lord**], Minor[the word that Jesus is Lord]; **because, if** *or* namely, that if.

10:11 **Isaiah 28:16 LXX**.

10:13 Joel 2:32.

10:14 Alx[**can...can...can** *or* could...could...could], Byz[shall...shall...shall (ASV, DRA, ~ESV, KJV, MRD, NAS, NAU, ~NET, ~NJB, NKJ, ~NRS, ~RSV, TLB)].

10:15 Alx[**can** *or* could], Byz[shall (ASV, DRA, ~ESV, KJV, MRD, NAS, NAU, ~NET, NJB, NKJ, NLT, ~NRS, TLB)]; Alx[**the good news**], Byz[the gospel of peace, and bring the good news (DRA, KJV, MRD, NKJ, TLB)], Minor[good news]; ~**Isaiah 52:7**; Nahum 1:15.

10:16 **Isaiah 53:1 LXX**.

10:17 Alx[**word of Christ**], Byz[word of God (KJV, MRD, NKJ)], Minor[word].

10:18 Psalms 19:4 LXX.

[19] Again I ask, did Israel not understand? First Moses says,

> *"I will make you jealous by those who are not a nation;*
> *by a foolish nation I will make you angry."*

[20] But Isaiah is very bold and says,

> *"I was found [among] those who did not seek me.*
> *I have shown myself to those who did not ask for me."*

[21] But of Israel he says,

> *"All day long I have held out my hands*
> *to a disobedient and contrary people."*

11

[1] I ask, then, has God rejected his people? Certainly not! I myself am an Israelite, a descendant of Abraham, a member of the tribe of Benjamin. [2] God has not rejected his people whom he foreknew. Do you not know what the scripture says of Elijah, how he pleads with God against Israel? – [3] *"Lord, they have killed your prophets, they have torn down your altars, and I alone am left, and they seek my life."* [4] But what is God's reply to him? *"I have reserved for myself seven thousand men who have not bowed the knee to Baal."* [5] So too at the present time there is a remnant, chosen by grace. [6] And if it is by grace, then it is no longer on the basis of works; otherwise, grace would no longer be grace. [7] What then? Israel did not obtain what it sought. The elect obtained it, but the rest were hardened, [8] as it is written:

> *"God gave them a spirit of stupor,*
> *eyes that they should not see*
> *and ears that they should not hear,*
> *down to this very day."*

[9] And David says:

> *"Let their table become a snare and a trap,*
> *a stumbling block and a retribution for them.*

[10]
> *Let their eyes be darkened so that they cannot see,*
> *and bend their backs forever."*

[11] So I ask, have they stumbled so as to fall? Certainly not! But through their trespass salvation has come to the Gentiles, to make them jealous. [12] Now if their trespass means riches for the world, and if their failure means riches for the Gentiles, how much more will their fullness mean!

[13] Now I am speaking to you Gentiles. Inasmuch then as I am an apostle to the Gentiles, I magnify my ministry [14] in the hope that I may somehow arouse to jealousy the kinsmen of my flesh and save some of them. [15] For if their rejection is the reconciliation of

---

10:[19] **Deuteronomy 32:21**.

10:[20] **Isaiah 65:1 LXX/DSS**.

10:[21] **Isaiah 65:2 LXX**.

11:[1] Alx/Byz[**his people**], Minor[his inheritance].

11:[2] Alx[**against Israel**], Byz[*adds* saying (KJV, MRD, NKJ, NLT, ~TLB)].

11:[3] Alx[**they have torn down your altars**], Byz[and torn down your altars (JNT, KJV, MRD, NIV, NKJ, NLT, TEV, TLB)]; **1 Kings 19:10, 14**.

11:[4] **~1 Kings 19:18**.

11:[6] Alx[*text*], Byz[*adds* But if by works, it is no longer grace, or work would no longer be work (KJV, MRD, NKJ)].

11:[8] Alx/Byz[**as it is written**], Minor[just as it is written (JNT, NAS, NAU, NJB, NKJ)]; **Isaiah 29:10, ~Deuteronomy 29:4**.

11:[9-10] **~Psalms 69:22-23 LXX**.

11:[13] Alx[**Now I am speaking**], Byz[For I am speaking (DRA, KJV, NKJ)]; Alx[**Inasmuch then**], Byz[*omits* then (HCS, ~JNT, KJV, MRD, NET, NIV, NJB, NKJ, NLT, REB, TEV, TLB)].

11:[14] **the kinsmen of my flesh** *Greek* my flesh.

the world, what will their acceptance be but life from the dead? [16] If the dough offered as firstfruits is holy, then the whole lump is holy; and if the root is holy, so are the branches.

[17] And if some of the branches were broken off, and you, a wild olive shoot, were grafted in among the rest to share the rich root of the olive tree, [18] do not boast over the branches. If you do boast, remember that you do not support the root, but the root supports you. [19] You will say then, "Branches were broken off so that I might be grafted in." [20] That is true. They were broken off because of their unbelief, but you stand fast only by faith. So do not be proud, but stand in awe. [21] For if God did not spare the natural branches, [perhaps] he will not spare you either. [22] Therefore consider the kindness and the severity of God: severity toward those who fell, but God's kindness to you, provided you continue in his kindness; otherwise you also will be cut off. [23] And they also, if they do not persist in unbelief, will be grafted in, for God is able to graft them in again. [24] For if you were cut out of an olive tree that is wild by nature, and were grafted, contrary to nature, into a cultivated olive tree, how much more will these natural branches be grafted back into their own olive tree!

[25] I do not want you to be ignorant of this mystery, brothers, lest you be wise [in] your own sight: Israel has experienced a hardening in part until the full number of the Gentiles has come in. [26] And so all Israel will be saved, as it is written:

"The Deliverer will come from Zion,
he will turn away ungodliness from Jacob;
[27]   and *this is my covenant with them*
when I take away their sins."

[28] As regards the gospel they are enemies, for your sake; but as regards election they are beloved for the sake of their forefathers. [29] For the gifts and the call of God are irrevocable. [30] Just as you were once disobedient to God but now have received mercy because of their disobedience, [31] so they have now been disobedient in order that by the mercy shown to you they also may [now] receive mercy. [32] For God has bound all men over to disobedience, that he may have mercy upon all.

[33] Oh, the depth of the riches and of the wisdom and knowledge of God! How unsearchable are his judgments and his ways past finding out!
[34]   *"For who has known the mind of the Lord?*
Or who has been his counselor?"
[35]   *"Or who has given a gift to him*
that he might be repaid?"
[36] For from him and through him and to him are all things. To him be glory forever. Amen.

11:[17] Alx[**rich root**], Byz[root and richness (DRA, KJV, MRD, NKJ, REB)].

11:[19] Alx/Major[**Branches**], Byz[The branches (DRA, KJV, MRD, NET, NLT, TEV, TLB)].

11:[21] Alx/Byz[**perhaps**], Minor[*omits* (ASV, ESV, HCS, JNT, NAS, NAU, NIV, NLT, REB, RSV, TEV, TLB)].

11:[22] Alx[**but God's kindness**], Byz[but kindness (KJV, MRD, NIV, NJB, NKJ, NLT, REB, TEV, TLB)].

11:[25] Alx/Byz[**in your own** *or* with your own], Minor[in your own].

11:[26-27] Alx[**he will turn**], Byz[and he will turn (KJV, MRD, NKJ, NLT, TEV, TLB)]; ~**Isaiah 59:20-21 LXX**, ~**27:9 LXX**, ~Jeremiah 31:33-34.

11:[30] Alx[**you were once disobedient**], Byz[you were also once disobedient (DRA)].

11:[31] Alx[**may now receive mercy**], Byz[*omits* now (DRA, KJV, MRD, NJB, NKJ, NLT, REB, RSV, TLB)].

11:[34] Isaiah 40:13 LXX; Jeremiah 23:18.

11:[35] ~Job 41:11 Masoretic.

12 ¹ I appeal to you therefore, brothers, by the mercies of God, to present your bodies as a living sacrifice, holy and acceptable to God, which is your spiritual worship. ² Do not be conformed to this world, but be transformed by the renewing of your mind, that you may prove what is the will of God, what is good and acceptable and perfect.

³ For by the grace given to me I say to every one among you not to think of himself more highly than he ought to think, but to think with sober judgment, each according to the measure of faith which God has assigned him. ⁴ For as in one body we have many members, and all the members do not have the same function, ⁵ so we, though many, are one body in Christ, and individually members one of another. ⁶ Having gifts that differ according to the grace given to us, let us use them: if prophecy, in proportion to faith; ⁷ if service, let us use it in our serving; he who teaches, in his teaching; ⁸ he who exhorts, in exhortation; he who gives, with liberality; he who leads, with diligence; he who does acts of mercy, with cheerfulness.

⁹ Let love be genuine. Hate what is evil; cling to what is good. ¹⁰ Be devoted to one another in brotherly love; outdo one another in showing honor. ¹¹ Never be lacking in zeal, be fervent in spirit, serving the Lord. ¹² Rejoice in your hope, be patient in tribulation, be faithful in prayer. ¹³ Contribute to the needs of the saints, practice hospitality. ¹⁴ Bless those who persecute [you]; bless and do not curse. ¹⁵ Rejoice with those who rejoice, weep with those who weep. ¹⁶ Live in harmony with one another. Do not be proud, but associate with the lowly. Do not be wise in your own sight. ¹⁷ Repay no one evil for evil, but have regard for what is noble in the sight of all men. ¹⁸ If it is possible, as far as it depends on you, live peaceably with all. ¹⁹ Beloved, do not avenge yourselves, but leave it to the Wrath; for it is written, *"Vengeance is mine, I will repay,"* says the Lord. ²⁰ But, *"if your enemy is hungry, feed him; if he is thirsty, give him drink; for in so doing you will heap burning coals on his head."* ²¹ Do not be overcome by evil, but overcome evil with good.

13 ¹ Let every person be subject to the governing authorities. For there is no authority except from God, and those that exist have been instituted by God. ² Therefore he who resists the authority resists what God has appointed, and those who resist will bring judgment on themselves. ³ For rulers are not a terror to good work, but to evil. Do you want to have no fear of him who is in authority? Then do what is good, and you will have praise from him. ⁴ For he is God's servant to you for good. But if you do wrong, be afraid, for he does not bear the sword in vain; he is God's servant, an avenger to execute wrath on the wrongdoer. ⁵ Therefore one must be subject, not only because of wrath but also for the sake of conscience. ⁶ For the same reason you also pay taxes, for the

---

12:¹ **spiritual worship** *or* reasonable service.

12:² Alx[**Do not be conformed...be transformed**], Byz[Not to be conformed...to be transformed]; **world** *or* age; **what is the will of God, what is good and acceptable and perfect** *or* what is the good and acceptable and perfect will of God.

12:⁵ Alx[**individually**], Byz[every one (DRA, JNT, KJV, NIV, ~NLT, TEV, TLB)].

12:⁶ **in proportion to faith** *or* in agreement with faith.

12:¹¹ Alx/Byz[**the Lord**], Minor[the time].

12:¹⁴ Alx/Byz[**persecute you**], Minor[*omits* you].

12:¹⁵ Alx[**rejoice, weep**], Byz[rejoice, and weep (JNT, KJV, MRD, NAS, NAU, NJB, NKJ, NLT)].

12:¹⁶ **associate with the lowly** *or* give yourselves to humble work.

12:¹⁷ Alx/Byz[**of all men**], Minor[of God and of all men (DRA) *others* of men], Alt[*omits* men (ESV, HCS, JNT, NAB, NIV, NJB, NLT, NRS, REB, RSV, TEV, TLB)].

12:¹⁹ ~**Deuteronomy 32:35**.

12:²⁰ Alx[**But**], Byz[Therefore (KJV, NKJ)]; Proverbs 25:21, 22 LXX.

13:¹ Alx[**those that exist**], Byz[the authorities that exist (ASV, JNT, KJV, MRD, NET, NIV, NJB, NKJ, ~NLT, ~NRS, REB, TEV, ~TLB)].

13:³ Alx[**good work**], Byz[good works (KJV, MRD, NKJ, ~REB)].

authorities are God's ministers, attending to this very thing. 7 Pay all of them their dues: taxes to whom taxes are due, revenue to whom revenue is due, respect to whom respect is due, honor to whom honor is due.

8 Owe no one anything, except to love one another; for he who loves his neighbor has fulfilled the law. 9 The commandments, *"You shall not commit adultery," "You shall not murder," "You shall not steal," "You shall not covet,"* and any other commandment there may be, are summed up in this sentence [namely], *"You shall love your neighbor as yourself."* 10 Love does no harm to a neighbor; therefore love is the fulfillment of the law.

11 And do this, knowing the hour, that now it is full time for you to wake from sleep. For now our salvation is nearer than when we first believed. 12 The night is far gone, the day is at hand. Let us then lay aside the works of darkness [and] put on the armor of light. 13 Let us walk properly, as in the day, not in reveling and drunkenness, not in lewdness and lust, not in strife and jealousy. 14 But put on the Lord Jesus Christ, and make no provision for the flesh, to gratify its desires.

14 1 As for the man who is weak in faith, accept him, but not for disputes over opinions. 2 One believes he may eat anything, but the man whose faith is weak eats only vegetables. 3 Let not him who eats despise him who does not, and let not him who does not eat pass judgment on him who eats; for God has accepted him. 4 Who are you to judge the servant of another? To his own master he stands or falls. And he will be made to stand, for the Master is able to make him stand. 5 [For] one man esteems one day as better than another; another man esteems every day alike. Let each one be fully convinced in his own mind. 6 He who observes the day, observes it to the Lord. And he who eats, eats to the Lord, for he gives thanks to God; and he who abstains, does so to the Lord and gives thanks to God. 7 For none of us lives to himself, and none of us dies to himself. 8 If we live, we live to the Lord; and if we die, we die to the Lord. So then, whether we live or whether we die, we are the Lord's. 9 For to this end Christ died and lived again, that he might be Lord both of the dead and of the living. 10 Why do you judge your brother? Or you, why do you despise your brother? For we shall all stand before the judgment seat of God. 11 For it is written:

> *"As I live, says the Lord, every knee shall bow to me,*

13:7 Alx[**Pay**], Byz[Therefore pay (DRA, KJV, MRD, NKJ, TEV)].

13:9 Alx/Byz[**namely**], Minor[*omits* (DRA, ESV, HCS, JNT, MRD, NAS, NAU, NET, NIV, NJB, NLT, NRS, REB, RSV, TEV, TLB)]; Alx/Byz[**You shall not steal**], Minor[*adds* You shall not bear false witness (KJV, NKJ)]; Alx/Byz[**neighbor as yourself**], Minor[neighbor as himself]; **Exodus 20:13-15, 17, Deuteronomy 5:17-19, 21, Leviticus 19:18**.

13:10 **fulfillment** *or* fullness.

13:11 Alx[**for you to wake**], Byz[for us to wake (DRA, ~KJV, MRD, NET, ~NKJ, ~NLT, ~TLB)].

13:12 Alx/Byz[**lay aside** *or* cast off], Minor[throw off (NAB, NJB, REB, ~TEV, ~TLB)]; Alx/Byz[**and put on**], Minor[*omits* and].

13:13 Alx/Byz[**strife and jealousy**], Minor[strifes and jealousies (REB)].

13:14 Alx/Byz[**the Lord Jesus Christ**], Minor[our Lord Jesus Christ (MRD) *others* Christ Jesus (REB)].

14:2 Alx/Byz[**One believes**], Alt[For one believes (DRA, KJV, MRD, NKJ, NLT, ~REB, ~TLB)]; **faith** *or* conviction.

14:4 Alx[**the Master** *or* the Lord], Byz[God (DRA, KJV, NKJ, TLB)].

14:5 Alx[**For**], Byz[*omits* (ASV, ESV, KJV, MRD, NAS, NAU, NET, NIV, NJB, NKJ, ~NLT, NRS, RSV)].

14:6 Alx[**He who observes the day, observes it to the Lord**], Byz[*adds* and he who does not observe the day, to the Lord he does not observe it (KJV, MRD, NKJ)]; Alx/Byz[**And he who eats**], Minor[*omits* And (ESV, HCS, KJV, NET, NIV, NJB, NKJ, NLT, TEV, TLB)].

14:9 Alx[**died and lived again**], Byz[both died and rose and lived again (~DRA, KJV, ~MRD, NKJ, ~NLT)].

14:10 Alx[**seat of God**], Byz[seat of Christ (DRA, KJV, MRD, NKJ)].

14:11 **confess** *or* give praise; **Isaiah 49:18, 45:23 LXX**.

and every tongue shall confess to God."

[12] So [then] each of us shall give account of himself [to God].

[13] Therefore let us not pass judgment on one another anymore, but rather decide never to put a stumbling block or hindrance in our brother's way. [14] I know and am convinced in the Lord Jesus that nothing is unclean in itself; but if anyone regards something as unclean, then for him it is unclean. [15] For if your brother is distressed because of what you eat, you are no longer walking in love. Do not by your eating destroy the one for whom Christ died. [16] So do not let your good be spoken of as evil. [17] For the kingdom of God is not eating and drinking, but righteousness and peace and joy in the Holy Spirit; [18] he who serves Christ in this way is acceptable to God and approved by men. [19] Let us therefore pursue what makes for peace and for mutual edification. [20] Do not, for the sake of food, destroy the work of God. Everything is indeed clean, but it is wrong for a man to eat anything that causes someone else to stumble. [21] It is right not to eat meat or drink wine or do anything that makes your brother stumble. [22] The faith [that] you have, keep between yourself and God. Happy is he who does not condemn himself for what he approves. [23] But he who has doubts is condemned if he eats, because he does not act from faith; for whatever is not from faith is sin.

15

[1] We who are strong ought to bear with the failings of the weak, and not to please ourselves. [2] Let each of us please his neighbor for his good, to build him up. [3] For even Christ did not please himself; but, as it is written, *"The reproaches of those who reproached you fell on me."* [4] For whatever was written in former days was written for our instruction, that through perseverance and through the encouragement of the scriptures we might have hope. [5] May the God of patience and encouragement grant you to live in harmony with one another, according to Christ Jesus, [6] that you may with one mind and one mouth glorify the God and Father of our Lord Jesus Christ.

[7] Therefore, welcome one another, just as Christ also welcomed you, to the glory of God. [8] For I tell you that Christ has become a servant of the circumcised to show God's truth, to confirm the promises made to the patriarchs, [9] and in order that the Gentiles might glorify God for his mercy. As it is written:

"Therefore I will praise you among the Gentiles,

14:12 Alx/Byz[**then**], Minor[*omits* (DRA, NET, NLT, RSV, ~TEV, ~TLB)]; Alx/Byz[**to God**], Minor[*omits*].

14:13 Alx/Byz[**or hindrance**], Minor[*omits* (MRD, TLB)].

14:15 Alx[**For**], Byz[But (JNT, KJV, MRD, ~NAB, ~NIV, ~NJB, NLT, ~NRS, ~REB, ~RSV, ~TEV, TLB)].

14:18 Alx[**in this way**], Byz[in these things (KJV, MRD, NJB, NKJ, TLB)].

14:19 Alx/Byz[**Let us therefore**], Minor[We therefore (NAU, ~TLB)].

14:21 Alx[**stumble**], Byz[*adds* or be offended or made weak (DRA, KJV, NJB, NKJ, TLB)].

14:22 Alx[**The faith that you have, keep between yourself and God**], Byz[Do you have faith? Keep it between yourself and God (DRA, HCS, KJV, NKJ)].

14:23 Alx/Byz[*text*], Minor[*adds* Romans 16:25-27 here]; **faith** or conviction.

15:2 Alx/Byz[**Let each of us**], Minor[For let each of us (~MRD, ~TEV, TLB)].

15:3 Psalms 69:9.

15:4 Alx/Byz[**whatever was written**], Minor[everything that was written (JNT, MRD, NET, NIV, NJB, TEV)]; Alx[**was written for our instruction**], Byz[was written before for our instruction (~NLT)]; Alx/Major[**through the encouragement**], Byz[*omits* through (DRA, JNT, KJV, NAS, NAU, NIV, NJB, NKJ, NLT, ~REB, TEV, TLB)]; Alx/Byz[**we might have hope**], Minor[*adds* of the encouragement].

15:5 Alx/Byz[**Christ Jesus**], Minor[Jesus Christ (DRA, MRD, ~TLB)].

15:7 Alx/Byz[**welcomed you**], Minor[welcomed us (KJV, NAS, NAU, NKJ, REB)].

15:8 Alx[**For**], Byz[Now *or* But (HCS, KJV, MRD, ~NJB, NKJ, ~NLT, ~REB, ~TLB)]; Alx[**Christ**], Byz[Christ Jesus (DRA)], Minor[Jesus Christ (KJV, MRD, NKJ, TLB)]; **circumcised** or circumcision.

15:9 Alx/Major[**Gentiles, and sing**], Byz[Gentiles, Lord, and sing (DRA)]; **praise** or confess; **2 Samuel 22:50, Psalms 18:49.**

and sing to your name."

10 And again it says:

"Rejoice, O Gentiles, with his people!"

11 And again,

"Praise the Lord, all you Gentiles,
and let all peoples praise him."

12 And again, Isaiah says:

"There shall be a root of Jesse;
and he who shall rise to rule over the Gentiles,
in him shall the Gentiles hope."

13 May the God of hope fill you with all joy and peace in believing, so that by the power of the Holy Spirit you may abound in hope.

14 I myself am satisfied about you, my brothers, that you yourselves are full of goodness, filled with all knowledge, and able to instruct one another. 15 But I have written very boldly to you on some points, so as to remind you again, because of the grace that was given me by God, 16 to be a minister of Christ Jesus to the Gentiles in the priestly service of the gospel of God, so that the offering of the Gentiles might be acceptable, sanctified by the Holy Spirit. 17 Therefore I have reason to glory in Christ Jesus in my service to God. 18 For I will not venture to speak of anything except what Christ has accomplished through me to win obedience from the Gentiles, by word and deed – 19 by the power of signs and wonders, by the power of the Spirit [of God], so that from Jerusalem and as far round as Illyricum I have fully preached the gospel of Christ. 20 And so I have made it my ambition to preach the gospel, not where Christ has already been named, lest I build on another man's foundation, 21 but as it is written:

"Those who have not been told of him shall see,
and those who have not heard shall understand."

22 This is the reason why I have often been hindered from coming to you. 23 But now, since I no longer have any place for work in these regions, and since I have longed for many years to come to you, 24 whenever I go to Spain, I hope to see you while passing through, and to be helped by you on my journey there, after I have enjoyed your company for a while. 25 Now, however, I am going to Jerusalem with aid for the saints. 26 For Macedonia and Achaia have been pleased to make a contribution for the poor among the saints in Jerusalem. 27 They were pleased to do it, and indeed they are in debt to them. For if the Gentiles have come to share in their spiritual blessings, they ought also to be of service

---

15:10 **Deuteronomy 32:43**.

15:11 Alx/Byz[**And again**], Minor[*adds* he says (MRD)]; Alx[**and let all peoples praise him**], Byz[and praise him, all you peoples (DRA, KJV, MRD, NIV, NKJ)]; **Psalms 117:1**.

15:12 ~**Isaiah 11:10 LXX**.

15:14 Alx/Byz[**one another**], Major[others (MRD, TLB)].

15:15 Alx[**to you**], Byz[*adds* brothers (DRA, KJV, MRD, NKJ)]; Alx/Byz[**by God**], Minor[from God (~ASV, DRA, ~JNT, ~KJV, NAS, NAU, ~NIV, REB, ~TEV)].

15:16 Alx[**Christ Jesus**], Byz[Jesus Christ (KJV, MRD, NKJ, TLB)].

15:18 Alx/Byz[**will not venture**], Minor[do not venture (DRA, MRD, NJB, NLT, TLB)]; **except what Christ has accomplished** *Greek* that Christ has not accomplished.

15:19 Alx/Byz[**Spirit of God**], Minor[Spirit (NAS, NAU, NIV) *others* Holy Spirit (ASV, DRA, MRD, REB, RSV, TLB)].

15:21 Alx/Byz[**Those who have not been told of him shall see**], Minor[They shall see, who have not been told of him (ASV, RSV)]; **Isaiah 52:15 LXX**.

15:23 Alx/Byz[**many years**], Minor[enough years *or* considerable years (~NLT, ~TLB)].

15:24 Alx[**whenever I go to Spain**], Byz[If I go to Spain, I will come to you (DRA, KJV, ~MRD, NKJ, ~TLB)].

to them in material blessings. [28] When therefore I have completed this, and have delivered to them this fruit, I shall go on by way of you to Spain. [29] And I know that when I come to you, I shall come in the fullness of the blessing of Christ.

[30] Now I urge you, [brothers,] by our Lord Jesus Christ and by the love of the Spirit, to strive together with me in your prayers to God for me, [31] that I may be delivered from the unbelievers in Judea, and my service for Jerusalem may be acceptable to the saints, [32] so that by God's will I may come to you with joy, and together with you be refreshed. [33] The God of peace be with you all. Amen.

16 [1] I commend to you Phoebe our sister, who is [also] a deacon of the church in Cenchrea, [2] that you may receive her in the Lord in a manner worthy of the saints, and help her in whatever she has need from you, for she has been a helper of many and of myself also.

[3] Greet Prisca and Aquila, my fellow workers in Christ Jesus, [4] who risked their necks for my life, to whom not only I but also all the churches of the Gentiles give thanks; [5] greet also the church that meets in their house. Greet my beloved Epaenetus, who was the first fruits of Asia for Christ. [6] Greet Mary, who has worked hard for you. [7] Greet Andronicus and Junias, my kinsmen and my fellow prisoners. They are of note among the apostles, and they were in Christ before me. [8] Greet Ampliatus, my beloved in the Lord. [9] Greet Urbanus, our fellow worker in Christ, and Stachys my beloved. [10] Greet Apelles, who is approved in Christ. Greet those who belong to the household of Aristobulus. [11] Greet Herodion, my kinsman. Greet those in the household of Narcissus who are in the Lord. [12] Greet Tryphena and Tryphosa, those workers in the Lord. Greet the beloved Persis, who has worked hard in the Lord. [13] Greet Rufus, chosen in the Lord, and his mother and mine. [14] Greet Asyncritus, Phlegon, Hermes, Patrobas, Hermas, and the brothers who are with them. [15] Greet Philologus and Julia, Nereus and his sister, and Olympas, and all the saints who are with them. [16] Greet one another with a holy kiss. All the churches of Christ greet you.

[17] I urge you, brothers, to take note of those who cause divisions and difficulties, contrary to the doctrine which you have learned; avoid them. [18] For such persons do not serve our Lord Christ, but their own belly, and by smooth and flattering words they deceive the hearts of the simple. [19] For your obedience has become known to all, so I am full of joy

---

15:28 **delivered** *Greek* sealed.

15:29 Alx[**of Christ**], Byz[of the gospel of Christ (DRA, KJV, MRD, NKJ)].

15:30 Alx/Byz[**brothers**], Minor[*omits* (REB, TLB)].

15:31 Alx[**my service**], Byz[that my service (ASV, ESV, HCS, JNT, KJV, MRD, NAB, NAS, NAU, NET, NIV, NKJ, NRS, RSV, TEV)], Minor[that my bringing a gift (~DRA, NJB, NLT, ~REB, TLB)].

15:32 Alx/Byz[**by God's will**], Minor[by the will of Jesus Christ *others* by the will of Christ Jesus *others* by the will of the Lord Jesus], Alt[*without textual foundation* by his will (~REB)]; Alx/Byz[**and together with you be refreshed**], Minor[*omits*].

15:33 Alx/Byz[**Amen**], Minor[*omits* Amen *others* add Romans 16:25-27 here]; *Metzger brackets* **Amen**.

16:1 Alx[**also**], Byz[*omits* (ASV, DRA, ESV, HCS, JNT, KJV, MRD, NAS, NAU, NET, NIV, NJB, NKJ, NLT, NRS, REB, RSV, TEV, TLB)]; **deacon** *or* servant.

16:3 Alx/Major[**Prisca**], Byz[Priscilla (JNT, KJV, MRD, NIV, NKJ, NLT, TEV, TLB)].

16:5 Alx[**Asia**], Byz[Achaia (KJV, MRD, NKJ)].

16:6 Alx[**worked hard for you**], Byz[worked hard for us (KJV, NKJ, TLB)].

16:7 Alx[**Junias**], Byz[Junia (ESV, HCS, JNT, KJV, MRD, NAB, NET, NKJ, NLT, NRS, REB)], Minor[Julia].

16:8 Alx[**Ampliatus**], Byz[Amplias (KJV, MRD, NKJ)].

16:14 Alx[**Hermes...Hermas**], Byz[Hermas...Hermes (DRA, KJV, MRD, NKJ)].

16:15 Alx/Byz[**Julia**], Minor[Junia *or* Junias].

16:16 Alx[**All the churches**], Byz[The churches (KJV, NKJ)].

16:18 Alx[**Lord Christ**], Byz[Lord Jesus Christ (KJV, MRD, NKJ, ~TLB)].

over you. But I want you to be wise about what is good, and innocent about what is evil. [20] And the God of peace will soon crush Satan under your feet. The grace of our Lord Jesus be with you.

[21] Timothy, my fellow worker, greets you; and Lucius, and Jason, and Sosipater, my kinsmen. [22] I, Tertius, who wrote this letter, greet you in the Lord. [23] Gaius, who is my host and the host of the whole church, greets you. Erastus, the treasurer of the city, greets you, and Quartus, our brother. (24)

[25] [Now to him who is able to establish you according to my gospel and the preaching of Jesus Christ, according to the revelation of the mystery which was kept secret for long ages [26] but is now revealed and made known to all nations through the prophetic writings, according to the command of the eternal God, to bring about the obedience of faith – [27] to the only wise God, through Jesus Christ, to whom be glory forever! Amen.]

16:20 Alx[**The grace of our Lord Jesus be with you**], Byz[The grace of our Lord Jesus Christ be with you (ASV, DRA, ESV, KJV, MRD, NJB, NKJ, NRS, RSV)], Minor[*adds* Amen (KJV, NKJ) *others omit, others place this as verse 24, others after verse 27*].

16:21 Alx/Byz[**my fellow worker**], Minor[*omits* my]; Alx[**greets you** *singular*], Byz[greet you *plural* (HCS, KJV, MRD, NKJ, ~REB, TLB)].

16:(24) Alx[*omits*], Byz[*adds* The grace of our Lord Jesus Christ be with you all, Amen (ASV, DRA, KJV, MRD, NAS, NAU, NKJ)], Minor[*omits* Amen *from Byz reading* (HCS, TLB)].

16:25-27 Alx[*as verses 16:25-27*], Byz[*as verses 14:24-26*], Minor[*as verses 15:34-36*].

16:27 Alx/Byz[**to whom**], Minor[*omits* (ESV, JNT, KJV, NAB, NAS, NAU, NET, NIV, NJB, NKJ, NLT, REB, RSV, TEV, TLB)]; Alx/Byz[**forever**], Minor[for ever and ever (~ESV, DRA, JNT, NAB, NJB, ~REB, ~RSV)]; Alx/Byz[**Amen**], Minor[*adds* to the Romans from Corinthus, and sent by Phoebe deacon of the church at Cenchrea (KJV)].

First Corinthians

1

¹ Paul, called to be an apostle of Christ Jesus by the will of God, and our brother Sosthenes, ² to the church of God which is at Corinth, to those sanctified in Christ Jesus, called to be saints together with all those who in every place call on the name of our Lord Jesus Christ, their Lord and ours: ³ grace to you and peace from God our Father and the Lord Jesus Christ.

⁴ I thank my God always for you because of the grace of God which was given you in Christ Jesus, ⁵ that in every way you were enriched in him in all speech and all knowledge – ⁶ even as the testimony of Christ was confirmed in you, ⁷ so that you are not lacking in any spiritual gift, as you eagerly wait for the revealing of our Lord Jesus Christ; ⁸ who will also confirm you to the end, blameless in the day of our Lord Jesus [Christ]. ⁹ God is faithful, by whom you were called into fellowship with his Son, Jesus Christ our Lord.

¹⁰ I appeal to you, brothers, by the name of our Lord Jesus Christ, that all of you agree and that there be no divisions among you, but that you be united in the same mind and in the same judgment. ¹¹ For I have been informed by Chloe's people that there are quarrels among you, my brothers. ¹² What I mean is this, that each one of you says, "I am of Paul," and "I of Apollos," and "I of Cephas," and "I of Christ." ¹³ Is Christ divided? Was Paul crucified for you? Or were you baptized in the name of Paul? ¹⁴ I give [God] thanks that I baptized none of you except Crispus and Gaius, ¹⁵ so that no one would say you were baptized in my name. ¹⁶ (Now I did baptize also the household of Stephanas; beyond that, I do not know whether I baptized any one else.) ¹⁷ For Christ did not send me to baptize, but to preach the gospel – not with words of human wisdom, lest the cross of Christ be emptied of its power.

¹⁸ For the word of the cross is foolishness to those who are perishing, but to us who are being saved it is the power of God. ¹⁹ For it is written,

> *"I will destroy the wisdom of the wise,*
> *and the cleverness of the clever I will frustrate."*

²⁰ Where is the wise man? Where is the scribe? Where is the debater of this age? Has not God made foolish the wisdom of the world? ²¹ For since in the wisdom of God the world

---

Title Alx/Byz[**First Corinthians** *Greek* To the Corinthians A], Minor[*variations of* The First Letter of Paul the Apostle to the Corinthians].

1:1 Alx/Byz[**Paul**], Alt[*without textual foundation* Saul (~JNT)]; Alx/Byz[**called to be**], Minor[*omits*]; Alx[**Christ Jesus**], Byz[Jesus Christ (ASV, DRA, KJV, MRD, NAS, NAU, NKJ, TLB)].

1:2 Alx/Byz[**which is at Corinth, to those sanctified in Christ Jesus**], Minor[to those sanctified in Christ Jesus, which is at Corinth]; Alx[**their Lord and ours** *Greek* theirs and ours]; Byz[both theirs and ours (ESV, KJV, NKJ, NRS, RSV)].

1:4 Alx/Byx[**my God**], Minor[*omits* my (NIV, NJB, REB, RSV, TLB) *others* our God]; Alx/Byz[**Christ Jesus**], Minor[Jesus Christ (KJV, MRD, ~TLB)].

1:6 **of Christ** *or* to Christ.

1:8 Alx/Byz[**Christ**], Minor[*omits* (REB)].

1:12 Alx/Byz[**Paul**], Alt[*without textual foundation* Saul (~JNT)]; **Cephas** *Peter*.

1:13 Alx/Byz[**Paul...Paul**], Alt[*without textual foundation* Saul...Saul (~JNT)]; **Is Christ divided?** *or* Christ is divided!

1:14 Alx/Byz[**God**], Minor[*omits* (NIV, NJB, RSV, TLB) *others* my God (MRD)].

1:15 Alx[**you were baptized**], Byz[I had baptized (KJV, MRD, NKJ, TLB)].

1:19 **~Isaiah 29:14 LXX**.

1:20 Alx[**wisdom of the world**], Byz[wisdom of this world (DRA, JNT, KJV, MRD, NKJ, NLT, REB, TEV, ~TLB)].

through its wisdom did not know God, God was pleased through the foolishness of what was preached to save those who believe. 22 Jews demand signs and Greeks look for wisdom, 23 but we preach Christ crucified, to Jews a stumbling block and to Gentiles foolishness, 24 but to those who are the called, both Jews and Greeks, Christ the power of God and the wisdom of God. 25 For the foolishness of God is wiser than men, and the weakness of God is stronger than men.

26 For consider your call, brothers; not many of you were wise according to the flesh, not many were powerful, not many were of noble birth. 27 But God chose the foolish things of the world to shame the wise, God chose the weak things of the world to shame the strong, 28 God chose the lowly things of this world and the despised things – the things that are not – to nullify the things that are, 29 so that no flesh may boast before God. 30 It is because of him that you are in Christ Jesus, who became to us wisdom from God, and righteousness and sanctification, and redemption, 31 therefore, as it is written, *"Let him who boasts, boast in the Lord."*

2 1 When I came to you, brothers, I did not come with superiority of speech or of wisdom, proclaiming to you the mystery of God. 2 For I resolved to know nothing among you except Jesus Christ, and him crucified. 3 I was with you in weakness and in fear and in much trembling, 4 and my message and my preaching were not in persuasive [words of] wisdom, but in demonstration of the Spirit and of power, 5 so that your faith might not rest on the wisdom of men, but on the power of God.

6 Yet we do speak a wisdom among the mature; a wisdom, however, not of this age nor of the rulers of this age, who are passing away. 7 But we speak of God's secret wisdom, a wisdom that has been hidden and which God destined for our glory before the ages. 8 None of the rulers of this age understood it; for if they had, they would not have crucified the Lord of glory. 9 But, as it is written,

"*No eye has seen, nor ear heard,*
     nor the heart of man conceived,
   what God has prepared for those who love him,"

10 But God has revealed them to us through the Spirit. For the Spirit searches all things, even the depths of God. 11 For who among men knows the thoughts of a man except the man's spirit which is in him? Even so no one knows the thoughts of God except the Spirit of God. 12 Now we have received not the spirit of the world, but the Spirit who is from God, that we may understand the things freely given to us by God. 13 This is what we speak, not in words taught us by human wisdom but in words taught by the Spirit, expressing spiritual truths in spiritual words. 14 But the natural man does not accept the

---

1:22 Alx[**signs**], Byz[a sign (KJV, NKJ, TLB)].

1:23 Alx[**Gentiles**], Byz[Greeks (JNT, KJV, NKJ)].

1:28 Alx[**the things that are not**], Byz[and the things that are not (ASV, DRA, KJV, MRD, NIV, NKJ, TEV)].

1:29 Alx/Byz[**before God**], Minor[before him (DRA, HCS, KJV, MRD, NET, NIV, NKJ)].

1:31 **in the Lord** *or* of the Lord; ~**Jeremiah 9:24**.

2:1 Alx[**mystery**], Byz[testimony (ASV, DRA, ESV, HCS, KJV, NAS, NAU, NET, NIV, NKJ, REB, RSV, TLB)]; Alx/Byz[**of God**], Minor[of Christ (DRA)].

2:4 Alx[**words of wisdom**], Byz[words of human wisdom (DRA, KJV, NKJ, TEV, TLB)], Minor[persuasion of wisdom (~MRD, ~NJB, ~REB)].

2:9 Alx/Byz[**what God has prepared**], Minor[whatever God has prepared (ASV)]; ~**Isaiah 64:4**.

2:10 Alx/Byz[**But God**], Minor[For God (NAS, NAU) *others* God (ESV, NAB, NET, NRS, RSV)]; Alx[**through the Spirit**], Byz[through his Spirit (KJV, MRD, NIV, NKJ, NLT, TEV, TLB)].

2:11 Alx[**knows the thoughts of God**], Byz[sees the thoughts of God].

2:12 Alx/Byz[**the world**], Minor[this world (DRA, TEV)].

2:13 Alx[**the Spirit**], Byz[the Holy Spirit (KJV, NKJ, TLB)]; **in spiritual words** *or* to spiritual men.

things of the Spirit of God, for they are foolishness to him; and he cannot understand them, because they are spiritually discerned. ¹⁵ But the spiritual man judges all things, yet he himself is rightly judged by no one.

¹⁶   For *"who has known the mind of the Lord*
                    that he may instruct him?"
But we have the mind of Christ.

3 ¹ But I, brothers, could not address you as spiritual men, but as men of flesh, as infants in Christ. ² I gave you milk, not solid food; for you were not yet ready for it. Indeed, even now you are not yet ready, ³ for you are still carnal. For since there is jealousy and strife among you, are you not carnal, and are you not walking like mere men? ⁴ For when one says, "I am of Paul," and another, "I am of Apollos," are you not mere men? ⁵ What then is Apollos? And what is Paul? Servants through whom you believed, even as the Lord assigned to each one. ⁶ I planted, Apollos watered, but God was causing the growth. ⁷ So neither he who plants nor he who waters is anything, but only God who gives the growth. ⁸ Now he who plants and he who waters are one, and each will receive his own reward according to his own labor. ⁹ For we are God's fellow workers; you are God's field, God's building.

¹⁰ According to the grace of God which was given to me, like a wise master builder I laid a foundation, and another is building on it. But each man must be careful how he builds on it. ¹¹ For no other foundation can any one lay than the one which is laid, which is Jesus Christ. ¹² Now if any man builds on the foundation with gold, silver, precious stones, wood, hay, straw, ¹³ each man's work will become evident; for the day will show it, because it is to be revealed with fire, and the fire [itself] will test the quality of each man's work. ¹⁴ If the work that any man has built on the foundation shall survive, he will receive a reward. ¹⁵ If any man's work is burned up, he will suffer loss; but he himself will be saved, but only as through fire. ¹⁶ Do you not know that you are God's temple and that God's Spirit dwells in you? ¹⁷ If any one destroys God's temple, God will destroy him. For God's temple is holy, and that temple you are.

¹⁸ Let no one deceive himself. If any one among you thinks that he is wise in this age, he must become a fool so that he may become wise. ¹⁹ For the wisdom of this world is foolishness with God. For it is written,

---

2:16 Alx/Byz[**the mind of Christ**], Minor[the mind of the Lord]; Isaiah 40:13 LXX.

3:1 Alx[**men of flesh**], Byz[carnal men (ASV, DRA, JNT, KJV, MRD, NAB, NIV, NJB, NKJ, TLB)].

3:2 Alx[**not solid food**], Byz[and not solid food (KJV, MRD, NJB, NKJ, TLB)]; Alx/Byz[**you are not yet ready**], Minor[*omits* yet (ASV, DRA, JNT, MRD, TEV)].

3:3 Alx/Byz[**3 for you are still carnal**], Minor[for you are still carnal 3 (DRA)]; Alx[**strife**], Byz[*adds* and dissensions (KJV, MRD, ~NET, NKJ, TLB)]; Alx/Byz[**among you**], Minor[among us].

3:4 Alx/Byz[**Paul**], Alt[*without textual foundation* Saul (~JNT)]; Alx[**mere men**], Byz[carnal (KJV, MRD, NKJ, ~NLT, ~TEV, ~TLB)].

3:5 Alx[**5 What then is Apollos? And what is Paul?**], Byz[5 Who then is Paul? And who is Apollos, but...? (KJV, MRD, NKJ, ~TLB)], Minor[What then is Apollos? And what is Paul? 5 (DRA)]; Alx/Byz[**Paul**], Alt[*without textual foundation* Saul (~JNT)].

3:10 Alx[**I laid a foundation**], Byz[I have laid a foundation (DRA, HCS, KJV, NKJ, NLT, TLB)].

3:12 Alx[**the foundation**], Byz[this foundation (DRA, JNT, KJV, MRD, NAB, NIV, NJB, NKJ, NLT, REB, TLB)]; Alx/Byz[**gold, silver**], Minor[gold, and silver (TLB)].

3:13 Alx[**itself**], Byz[*omits* (DRA, ESV, HCS, JNT, KJV, MRD, NET, NIV, NKJ, NLT, NRS, REB, RSV, TEV, TLB)].

3:14 Alx[**shall survive**], Byz[survives (DRA, ESV, HCS, JNT, KJV, NAB, NAS, NAU, NET, NIV, NJB, NKJ, NLT, NRS, REB, RSV, TEV, ~TLB)].

3:16 Alx/Byz[**dwells in you** *plural*], Minor[*omits* in you (REB)].

3:17 Alx/Byz[**God will destroy him**], Minor[God destroys him]; **you** *plural*.

3:19 ~**Job 5:13 Masoretic**.

"He catches the wise in their own craftiness."
[20] And again,

"The Lord knows the thoughts of the wise,
that they are futile."

[21] So then let no one boast of men. For all things are yours, [22] whether Paul or Apollos or Cephas or the world or life or death or the present or the future. All belong to you. [23] And you belong to Christ. And Christ belongs to God.

4 [1] This is how one should regard us, as servants of Christ and stewards of the mysteries of God. [2] Moreover, it is required of stewards that they be found trustworthy. [3] But with me it is a very small thing that I should be judged by you, or by any human court; I do not even judge myself. [4] I am not aware of anything against myself, but I am not acquitted by this. It is the Lord who judges me. [5] Therefore do not go on passing judgment before the time, but wait until the Lord comes who will both bring to light the things hidden in the darkness and disclose the motives of men's hearts. Then every man will receive his praise from God.

[6] Now these things, brothers, I have figuratively applied to myself and Apollos for your benefit, so that in us you may learn not to go beyond what is written, so that no one of you will become arrogant in favor of one against the other. [7] For who regards you as different? What do you have that you did not receive? And if you did receive it, why do you boast as if you had not received it? [8] You are already filled! You have already become rich! You have become kings without us! And indeed, I wish that you had become kings so that we also might reign with you. [9] For, I think, God has exhibited us apostles last of all, like men condemned to death; because we have become a spectacle to the world, both to angels and to men. [10] We are fools for Christ's sake, but you are wise in Christ; we are weak, but you are strong; you are distinguished, but we are without honor. [11] To this present hour we are both hungry and thirsty, and we are poorly clothed, and roughly treated, and homeless; [12] and we toil, working with our own hands. When we are reviled, we bless; when we are persecuted, we endure; [13] when we are slandered, we speak kindly; we have become, and are now, as the scum of the world, the refuse of all things.

[14] I do not write this to shame you, but [to] admonish you as my beloved children. [15] For though you have countless guides in Christ, you do not have many fathers, for in Christ Jesus I became your father through the gospel. [16] Therefore I urge you, be imitators of me. [17] For this reason I have sent to you Timothy, who is my beloved and faithful child in the Lord, and he will remind you of my ways which are in Christ [Jesus], just as I teach everywhere in every church. [18] Now some have become arrogant, as though I were not coming to you. [19] But I will come to you soon, if the Lord wills, and I will find out, not the words of these arrogant people, but their power. [20] For the kingdom of God does not consist in talk but in power. [21] What do you desire? Shall I come to you with a rod, or with love and a spirit of gentleness?

3:20 ~**Psalms 94:11**.
3:22 Alx/Byz[**Paul**], Alt[*without textual foundation* Saul (~JNT)]; **Cephas** *Peter*.
4:3 **court** *or* legal day.
4:6 Alx[**learn not to go beyond**], Byz[learn not to esteem beyond (KJV, MRD, NKJ, ~NLT, TLB)].
4:7 **regards you as different** *or* makes you to be different.
4:9 Alx[**For, I think, God**], Byz[For I think that God (DRA, ESV, KJV, MRD, NIV, NJB, NKJ, NRS, RSV, TEV)].
4:13 Alx[**slandered**], Byz[blasphemed (DRA)].
4:14 Alx[**to admonish**], Byz[I admonish (DRA, KJV, MRD, NKJ)].
4:17 Alx/Byz[**For this reason**], Minor[For this very reason (TLB)]; Alx[**Christ Jesus**], Byz[Christ (ASV, ESV, KJV, MRD, NAS, NAU, NET, NJB, NKJ, REB, RSV, TLB)], Minor[the Lord Jesus]; **have sent** *or* am sending.

5 ¹ It is actually reported that there is immorality among you, and of a kind that does not occur even among pagans: a man has his father's wife. ² And you are arrogant! Ought you not rather to have mourned? Let the one who has done this be removed from your midst. ³ For though I am absent in body, I am present in spirit, and have already passed judgment on the one who has committed this, as if I were present. ⁴ In the name of [our] Lord Jesus, when you are assembled, and I with you in spirit, and the power of our Lord Jesus is present, ⁵ you are to deliver this man to Satan for the destruction of the flesh, so that his spirit may be saved in the day of the Lord. ⁶ Your boasting is not good. Do you not know that a little leaven leavens the whole lump of dough? ⁷ Cleanse out the old leaven that you may be a new lump, as you really are unleavened. For Christ, our Passover lamb, has been sacrificed. ⁸ Let us, therefore, celebrate the festival, not with the old leaven, nor the leaven of malice and wickedness, but with the unleavened bread of sincerity and truth.

⁹ I wrote you in my letter not to associate with immoral people; ¹⁰ not at all meaning the immoral people of this world, or with the greedy and swindlers, or with idolaters, for then you would have to go out of the world. ¹¹ But actually, I wrote to you not to associate with any one who bears the name of brother if he is an immoral person, or greedy, or an idolater, or a reviler, or a drunkard, or a swindler – not even to eat with such a one. ¹² For what have I to do with judging outsiders? Is it not those inside the church whom you are to judge? ¹³ God will judge those outside. *"Expel the wicked man from among you."*

6 ¹ When any one of you has a grievance against a brother, does he dare go to law before the unrighteous instead of before the saints? ² Or do you not know that the saints will judge the world? And if the world is to be judged by you, are you not competent to try trivial cases? ³ Do you not know that we will judge angels, not to mention matters of this life? ⁴ So if you have disputes about such matters, do you appoint

---

5:1 Alx[**does not occur**], Byz[is not even named (KJV, MRD, NKJ)].

5:3 Alx[*or* For though I am absent in body, I am present in spirit, and have already passed judgment, as if I were present, on the one who has committed this 4 in the name of our Lord Jesus. When…], Byz[For as though I am absent… (KJV, NKJ, TEV, TLB)].

5:4 Alx[**the name of our Lord Jesus**], Byz[*adds* Christ (DRA, KJV, MRD, NKJ, ~TLB)], Minor[the name of the Lord Jesus (ESV, JNT, NLT, NRS, RSV, ~TLB)]; Alx[**power of our Lord Jesus**], Byz[*adds* Christ (KJV, MRD, NKJ)], Minor[power of the Lord Jesus (NAB)].

5:5 Alx[**the Lord**], Byz[the Lord Jesus (ASV, KJV, NAS, NAU, NKJ, RSV)], Minor[our Lord Jesus Christ (DRA, MRD, TLB)].

5:6 Alx/Byz[**a little leaven**], Minor[a little deceit].

5:7 Alx/Major[**Cleanse out**], Byz[*adds* therefore (KJV, NKJ)]; Alx[**sacrificed**], Byz[*adds* for us (KJV, MRD, NKJ, NLT, TLB)].

5:8 Alx/Byz[**nor the leaven of malice**], Minor[not the leaven of malice (~ESV, ~JNT, ~NAB, ~NET, ~NIV, ~NJB, ~NLT, ~NRS, ~REB, ~RSV, ~TEV, ~TLB)].

5:10 Alx[**not at all meaning**], Byz[yet not at all meaning (KJV, MRD, NKJ, NLT, TLB)]; Alx[**and swindlers**], Byz[or swindlers (DRA, JNT, KJV, MRD, NJB, NKJ, NLT, REB, TEV)].

5:12 Alx[**judging outsiders**], Byz[*adds* also (KJV, NKJ)].

5:13 Alx/Byz[**God will judge**], Minor[God judges (ASV, ESV, HCS, KJV, MRD, NAS, NAU, ~NJB, NKJ, ~REB, RSV, ~TLB)]; Alx[**Expel**], Byz[Therefore expel (KJV, MRD, NKJ, NLT, TLB)]; Deuteronomy 17:7 LXX, 19:19, 21:21, 24, 24:7.

6:2 Alx[**Or do you not know**], Byz[*omits* Or (DRA, JNT, KJV, NAB, NIV, NJB, NKJ, NLT, NRS, REB, RSV, TEV, TLB)].

6:3 Alx[**angels, not to mention matters of this life?**], Byz[angels? How much more matters of this life! (ASV, DRA, ESV, KJV, MRD, ~NAB, NAS, NAU, NET, NIV, NJB, NKJ, NLT, RSV, TEV, TLB)].

6:4 **do you appoint…?** *or* appoint *as a command.*

them as judges who are of no account in the church? [5] I say this to your shame. Can it be that there is no one among you wise enough to decide between his brothers, [6] but brother goes to law against brother, and that before unbelievers? [7] Actually, [then,] it is already a defeat for you, that you have lawsuits with one another. Why not rather be wronged? Why not rather be defrauded? [8] Instead, you yourselves defraud and do wrong, and you even do this to your brothers. [9] Or do you not know that the unrighteous will not inherit the kingdom of God? Do not be deceived; neither the immoral, nor idolaters, nor adulterers, nor dainty nor dominant sodomites, [10] nor thieves, nor the greedy – no drunkards, no revilers, no swindlers will inherit the kingdom of God. [11] And such were some of you. But you were washed, you were sanctified, you were justified in the name of the Lord Jesus Christ and in the Spirit of our God.

[12] "All things are lawful for me," but not all things are helpful. "All things are lawful for me," but I will not be mastered by anything. [13] "Food is for the stomach and the stomach for food" – but God will destroy them both. The body is not meant for immorality, but for the Lord, and the Lord for the body. [14] By his power God raised the Lord, and he will also raise us up. [15] Do you not know that your bodies are members of Christ? Shall I then take the members of Christ and make them members of a prostitute? Never! [16] [Or] do you not know that he who joins himself to a prostitute becomes one body with her? For, as it is written, *The two shall become one flesh.* [17] But he who unites himself with the Lord is one spirit with him. [18] Flee immorality. Every other sin that a man commits is outside the body, but the immoral man sins against his own body. [19] Do you not know that your body is a temple of the Holy Spirit, who is in you, whom you have received from God? You are not your own; [20] you were bought with a price. Therefore glorify God in your body.

7 [1] Now concerning the matters about which you wrote, it is good for a man not to touch a woman. [2] But because of immorality, each man should have his own wife, and each woman her own husband. [3] The husband should fulfill his marital duty to his wife, and likewise the wife to her husband. [4] The wife does not have authority over her own body, but the husband does; and likewise also the husband does not have

---

6:5 Alx/Byz[**Can it be**], Minor[Is it so (DRA, KJV, MRD, NAS, NAU, NET, NIV, NKJ, NLT, ~TEV, TLB)]; Alx[**there is no one**], Byz[there is not one (ASV, DRA, HCS, JNT, KJV, MRD, NAB, NAS, NAU, NKJ, NLT, REB, ~TEV, TLB)].

6:7 Alx/Byz[**then**], Minor[*omits* (ASV, ESV, JNT, NET, NIV, NJB, NLT, NRS, REB, RSV, TEV, TLB)]; Alx/Byz[**a defeat for you**], Minor[a defeat among you (ASV, DRA, KJV, ~MRD, NET, ~NIV, NJB, TEV)].

6:8 Alx[**you even do this**], Byz[you even do these (~ESV, ~MRD, ~NJB, NKJ, ~NLT, ~TEV, ~TLB)].

6:9 Alx/Byz[**nor dainty nor dominant sodomites 10**], Minor[10 nor dainty nor dominant sodomites (DRA, ~TLB)].

6:10 Alx[**nor thieves, nor the greedy – no drunkards, no revilers, no swindlers will inherit the kingdom of God**], Byz[nor the greedy, nor thieves, nor drunkards – no revilers, no swindlers – will not inherit the kingdom of God (MRD)].

6:11 Alx/Byz[**the Lord**], Minor[our Lord (DRA, MRD)]; Alx[**Jesus Christ**], Byz[*omits* Christ (KJV, NKJ, REB, Metzger)].

6:13 *the quotation may extend to the entire sentence.*

6:14 Alx/Byz[**he will also raise us**], Minor[he also raises us *others* he also raised us *others* he will also raise you]; *ASV printed version* will raise up us *electronic versions typo* will raise up as.

6:16 Alx/Byz[**Or**], Major[*omits* (HCS, JNT, ~KJV, NIV, ~NLT, NRS, REB, RSV, ~TLB)]; **Genesis 2:24**.

6:20 Alx/Byz[**Therefore glorify**], Minor[Glorify and bear (DRA)]; Alx[*text*], Byz[*adds* and in your spirit, which are God's (KJV, MRD, NKJ, ~TLB)].

7:1 Alx[**you wrote**], Byz[*adds* to me (DRA, KJV, MRD, NKJ, ~TLB)].

7:3 Alx[**marital duty**], Byz[due affection (KJV, MRD, NKJ)].

authority over his own body, but the wife does. ⁵ Do not deprive one another, except by agreement for a time, so that you may devote yourselves to prayer, and then be together again so that Satan will not tempt you because of your lack of self-control. ⁶ I say this by way of concession, not of command. ⁷ Yet I wish that all men were as I myself am. But each man has his own gift from God, one in this manner and another in that.

⁸ But I say to the unmarried and to the widows that it is good for them if they remain even as I. ⁹ But if they cannot exercise self-control, they should marry; for it is better to marry than to burn with passion. ¹⁰ To the married I give charge, not I but the Lord, that *the wife should not separate from her husband* ¹¹ *(but if she does leave, she must remain unmarried, or else be reconciled to her husband), and that the husband should not divorce his wife.* ¹² But to the rest I say, not the Lord, that if any brother has a wife who is an unbeliever, and she consents to live with him, he must not divorce her. ¹³ If any woman has a husband who is an unbeliever, and he consents to live with her, she must not divorce her husband. ¹⁴ For the unbelieving husband is sanctified through his wife, and the unbelieving wife is sanctified through the brother. Otherwise, your children would be unclean, but as it is they are holy. ¹⁵ But if the unbelieving partner leaves, let him do so; in such a case the brother or sister is not bound. For God has called you to peace. ¹⁶ For how do you know, O wife, whether you will save your husband? Or how do you know, O husband, whether you will save your wife?

¹⁷ Only, let each one lead the life which the Lord assigned to him, and in which God has called him. This is the rule I lay down in all the churches. ¹⁸ Was any man called when he was already circumcised? He is not to become uncircumcised. Has any man been called in uncircumcision? He is not to be circumcised. ¹⁹ Circumcision is nothing and uncircumcision is nothing, but keeping the commandments of God is what counts. ²⁰ Each one should remain in the state in which he was called. ²¹ Were you a slave when you were called? Do not let it trouble you – but if indeed you can gain your freedom, make the most of it. ²² For he who was called in the Lord as a slave is the Lord's freedman; likewise he who was free when called is Christ's slave. ²³ You were bought with a price; do not become slaves of men. ²⁴ Brothers, let each one remain with God in that condition in which he was called.

²⁵ Now concerning virgins, I have no command of the Lord, but I give my opinion as one who by the Lord's mercy is trustworthy. ²⁶ I think that in view of the present

---

7:5 Alx[**prayer**], Byz[fasting and prayer (KJV, MRD, NKJ)]; Alx[**be together**], Byz[come together (DRA, ESV, HCS, JNT, KJV, MRD, NAB, NAS, NAU, ~NET, NIV, NJB, NKJ, NLT, NRS, REB, RSV, ~TEV, TLB)]; Alx/Byz[**your lack of self-control**], Minor[omits your (NJB, REB, RSV, ~TLB)].

7:7 Alx[**Yet I wish**], Byz[For I wish (DRA, KJV, MRD, NKJ)].

7:9 Alx/Byz[**it is better to marry**], Minor[it is better to get married (JNT, MRD, NJB, REB)].

7:10-11 *compare* Matthew 5:32, 19:3-9, Mark 10:2-12, Luke 16:18.

7:13 Alx/Byz[**If any woman**], Major[A woman who (ASV, KJV, MRD, NAS, NAU, NKJ)]; Alx[**divorce her husband**], Byz[divorce him (ESV, JNT, KJV, NET, NIV, NKJ, NLT, NRS, REB, RSV, TEV, TLB)].

7:14 Alx[**sanctified through the brother**], Byz[sanctified through the husband (~DRA, ESV, ~HCS, KJV, ~MRD, ~NAS, ~NAU, NET, ~NIV, NKJ, ~NLT, NRS, ~REB, RSV, ~TEV, ~TLB)].

7:15 Alx[**you**], Byz[us (ASV, DRA, KJV, MRD, NAS, NAU, NIV, NKJ, RSV)].

7:17 Alx/Byz[**assigned to him**], Minor[has assigned to him (ASV, DRA, ESV, JNT, KJV, MRD, NAB, NAS, NAU, NET, NJB, NKJ, NLT, NRS, REB, RSV, TLB)]; Alx[**the Lord...God**], Byz[God...the Lord (KJV, NKJ, ~TLB)].

7:18 Alx[**Has any man been called**], Byz[Was any man called (DRA, ESV, HCS, JNT, KJV, NAB, NET, NIV, ~NJB, NKJ, ~NLT, NRS, REB, RSV, TEV)].

7:21 **make the most of it** *(freedom) or* rather make use of it *(ambiguous, freedom or slavery)*.

7:22 Alx[**likewise**], Byz[adds also (KJV, NJB, NLT, REB, TLB)].

distress it is good for a person to remain as he is. [27] Are you bound to a wife? Do not seek to be free. Are you free from a wife? Do not seek marriage. [28] But if you marry, you have not sinned; and if the virgin marries, she has not sinned. Yet those who marry will have troubles in this flesh, and I am trying to spare you. [29] I mean, brothers, the appointed time has grown very short; so that from now on, those who have wives should live as though they had none, [30] and those who mourn, as though they were not mourning; and those who rejoice, as though they were not rejoicing; and those who buy, as though they did not possess; [31] and those who use the world, as though they did not make full use of it. For the form of this world is passing away. [32] But I want you to be free from concern. One who is unmarried is concerned about the affairs of the Lord, how to please the Lord; [33] but a married man is concerned about the affairs of the world, how to please his wife, [34] and his interests are divided. Also, the unmarried woman, and the virgin, is concerned about the affairs of the Lord, that she may be holy both in body and spirit; but the married woman is concerned about the affairs of the world, how to please her husband. [35] This I say for your own benefit, not to put a restraint upon you, but to promote what is good and to secure undivided devotion to the Lord.

[36] But if any man thinks that he is not acting properly toward his daughter, if she is past her youth, and if it must be so, let him do what he wishes, he does not sin; let them marry. [37] But he who stands firm in his own heart, being under no constraint, but has control over his own will, and has decided this in his own heart, to keep her as his daughter, he will do well. [38] So then he who gives his daughter for marriage does well, and he who does not give her in marriage will do better.

[39] A wife is bound to her husband as long as he lives. But if the husband dies, she is free to be married to whom she wishes, only in the Lord. [40] But in my judgment she is happier if she remains as she is; and I think that I also have the Spirit of God.

7:28 Alx/Byz[**the virgin**], Minor[a virgin (ASV, DRA, ESV, HCS, JNT, KJV, MRD, NAB, NAS, NAU, NET, NIV, NJB, NKJ, NLT, NRS, REB, RSV, TEV, TLB)].

7:29 Alx/Byz[**the appointed time**], Minor[that the appointed time (JNT, MRD, NIV, NJB, TLB)].

7:31 Alx[**the world**], Byz[this world (DRA, KJV, MRD, NKJ)].

7:32 Alx[**how to please the Lord**], Byz[how he may please the Lord (ASV, DRA, HCS, KJV, MRD, NAB, NAS, NAU, NIV, NJB, NKJ)].

7:33 Alx[**how to please his wife**], Byz[how he may please his wife (ASV, DRA, HCS, KJV, MRD, NAB, NAS, NAU, NIV, NJB, NKJ)].

7:34 Alx[*text*], Byz[There is also a difference between the wife and the virgin. The unmarried woman is concerned about the affairs of the Lord, that she may be holy both in body and spirit; but the married woman is concerned about the affairs of the world, how she may please her husband (MRD, KJV)], Minor[*omits* also *from Byz reading* (NKJ)]; Alx/Byz[**holy both in body and spirit**], Minor[*omits* both (ESV, MRD, NJB, NLT, NRS, REB, RSV, TLB)].

7:35 Alx[**your own benefit**], Byz[your own profit (ASV, DRA, KJV, MRD, NKJ)]; Alx/Byz[**devotion**], Major[attention *or* constancy (ASV, DRA, KJV, ~MRD, NAB, NET, NJB, ~NKJ, ~NLT, ~TEV, TLB)].

7:36-38 Alx[**daughter** *Greek* virgin], Byz[*possibly* betrothed *Greek* virgin (ESV, JNT, NIV, NJB, NLT, NRS, REB, RSV, TEV, ~TLB)]; *these verses could refer to a man considering marriage, or a father considering whether to allow such a marriage to take place (see verse 38).*

7:37 Alx[**his own heart**], Byz[his heart (ASV, DRA, ESV, HCS, JNT, KJV, NAB, NAS, NAU, NET, NJB, NKJ, NLT, NRS, REB, RSV, TEV, TLB)]; Alx[**he will do well**], Byz[he does well (DRA, KJV, MRD, NET, NIV, NJB, NKJ, NLT, TEV, TLB)].

7:38 Alx[*text*], Byz[*ambiguous, could be* So then he who marries does well, but he who does not marry does better (ESV, HCS, JNT, NAB, NET, NIV, NJB, NLT, NRS, REB, RSV, TEV, TLB)]; *Alx reading makes the woman his daughter (i.e.. gives in marriage). Byz reading is ambiguous (i.e. marries or gives in marriage) -- the woman could be a daughter or fiancée.*

7:39 Alx[**A wife is bound**], Byz[*adds* by law (DRA, KJV, MRD, NKJ)]; Alx[**if the husband dies**],

8 [1] Now concerning food sacrificed to idols: we know that we all possess knowledge. Knowledge puffs up, but love builds up. [2] If anyone imagines that he knows something, he does not yet know as he ought to know. [3] But if anyone loves God, he is known by him. [4] Therefore concerning the eating of food sacrificed to idols, we know that an idol is nothing in the world, and that there is no God but one. [5] For even if there are so-called gods, whether in heaven or on earth (as indeed there are many "gods" and many "lords"), [6] yet for us there is but one God, the Father, from whom are all things and for whom we exist; and one Lord, Jesus Christ, through whom are all things, and through whom we exist.

[7] However, not all possess this knowledge. But some, being accustomed to the idol, eat food as really sacrificed to an idol; and their conscience, being weak, is defiled. [8] But food will not commend us to God; we are no worse if we do not eat, and no better if we do. [9] But take care that this liberty of yours does not somehow become a stumbling block to the weak. [10] For if a man sees you, who have knowledge, at table in an idol's temple, will not his conscience, if he is weak, be encouraged to eat food sacrificed to idols? [11] For by your knowledge this weak man is destroyed, the brother for whom Christ died. [12] Thus, sinning against your brothers and wounding their conscience when it is weak, you sin against Christ. [13] Therefore, if food causes my brother to fall, I will never eat meat again, so that I will not cause my brother to fall.

9 [1] Am I not free? Am I not an apostle? Have I not seen Jesus our Lord? Are you not my work in the Lord? [2] If to others I am not an apostle, at least I am to you; for you are the seal of my apostleship in the Lord.

[3] This is my defense to those who would examine me. [4] Do we not have the right to food and drink? [5] Do we not have the right to take along a believing wife, even as the other apostles and the brothers of the Lord and Cephas? [6] Or is it only Barnabas and I who have no right to refrain from working for a living? [7] Who at any time serves as a soldier at

---

Major[if the husband also dies], Byz[if her husband dies (DRA, ESV, HCS, KJV, MRD, NAB, NAS, NAU, NET, NIV, NKJ, NLT, TEV, TLB)]; **dies** *Greek* falls asleep.

7:40 Alx/Byz[**and I think**], Minor[for I think]; Alx/Byz[**Spirit of God**], Minor[Spirit of Christ].

8:2 Alx[**If anyone**], Byz[And if anyone (DRA, KJV, MRD, NKJ)]; Alx[**he does not yet know**], Byz[he knows nothing yet (KJV, MRD, NKJ)].

8:3 Alx/Byz[**loves God**], Minor[*omits* God]; Alx/Byz[**he is known by him**], Minor[*omits* by him].

8:4 Alx[**no God but one**], Byz[no other God but one (KJV, MRD, NJB, NKJ, TLB)].

8:5 Alx/Major[**on earth**], Byz[on the earth].

8:6 Alx/Byz[**yet for us**], Minor[*omits* yet]; Alx/Byz[**Christ, through whom**], Minor[Christ, because of whom]; Alx/Byz[**and through whom we exist**], Minor[*adds* and one Holy Spirit, in whom are all things, and in whom we exist].

8:7 Alx[**being accustomed to the idol**], Byz[with conscience of the idol (DRA, KJV, MRD, NJB, NKJ, ~TLB)].

8:8 Alx[**we are no worse if we do not eat, and no better if we do**], Byz[for we are no better if we eat, and no worse if we do not (DRA, KJV, MRD, NKJ)].

8:10 Alx/Byz[**if a man sees you**], Minor[if a man sees him (DRA)].

8:11 Alx[**For by your knowledge**], Byz[And so by your knowledge (DRA, ESV, ~HCS, ~JNT, KJV, MRD, ~NAB, ~NET, ~NIV, NJB, NKJ, ~NLT, ~NRS, ~REB, ~RSV, ~TEV, ~TLB)]; Alx[**this weak man is destroyed, the brother**], Byz[this weak brother is destroyed (DRA, KJV, ~MRD, NET, NIV, NKJ, NLT, NRS)].

8:12 Alx/Byz[**when it is weak**], Minor[*omits* (NLT)].

9:1 Alx[**free...an apostle**], Byz[an apostle...free (KJV, NKJ, TLB)]; Alx[**Jesus**], Byz[Jesus Christ (KJV, MRD, NKJ)], Minor[Christ Jesus (DRA, JNT)].

9:5 **a believing wife** *Greek* a sister as wife; **Cephas** *Peter*.

9:7 Alx[**eat its fruit**], Byz[eat of its fruit (DRA, ESV, KJV, MRD, NAS, NAU, NIV, NKJ, NLT, NRS, RSV, ~TLB)]; Alx/Byz[**Or, who tends**], Minor[*omits* Or (DRA, JNT, NET, NIV, NLT, RSV, TEV,

his own expense? Who plants a vineyard and does not eat its fruit? Or, who tends a flock and does not drink of the milk? **8** Do I say this merely from a human point of view? Does not the Law say the same thing? **9** For it is written in the Law of Moses, *"You shall not muzzle an ox while it is treading out the grain."* Is it for oxen that God is concerned? **10** Or is he speaking altogether for our sake? Yes, for our sake it was written, because the plowman ought to plow in hope, and the thresher to thresh in hope of sharing the crops. **11** If we have sown spiritual seed among you, is it too much if we reap a material harvest from you? **12** If others share this right of support from you, do not we even more?

Nevertheless, we did not make use of this right, but we endure anything rather than put an obstacle in the way of the gospel of Christ. **13** Do you not know that those who work in the temple eat [things] from the temple, and those who serve at the altar share in what is offered on the altar? **14** In the same way, the Lord commanded that those who proclaim the gospel should get their living from the gospel. **15** But I have not used any of these rights. And I am not writing this in the hope that you will do such things for me. I would rather die than have anyone deprive me of my ground for boasting. **16** For if I preach the gospel, I have nothing to boast of, for I am under compulsion. For woe is me if I do not preach the gospel! **17** For if I do this voluntarily, I have a reward; but if it is not of my will, I have a stewardship entrusted to me. **18** What then is my reward? Just this: that in my preaching I may offer the gospel free of charge, and so not make full use of my right in the gospel.

19 For though I am free from all men, I have made myself a slave to all, that I might win the more. **20** To the Jews I became as a Jew, in order to win Jews; to those under the law I became as one under the law – though not being myself under the law – so that I might win those under the law. **21** To those who are without law, I became as one without law, though not being without the law of God but under the law of Christ, so that I might win those who are without the law. **22** To the weak I became weak, that I might win the weak. I have become all things to all men, so that I might by all means save some. **23** I do it all for the sake of the gospel, that I may share in its blessings.

24 Do you not know that in a race all the runners run, but only one receives the prize? Run in such a way that you may win. **25** Everyone who competes in the games exercises self-control in all things. They do it to receive a perishable wreath, but we an imperishable. **26** Therefore I do not run aimlessly. I do not box as a man beating the air. **27**

TLB)].

9:9 **Deuteronomy 25:4.**

9:10 Alx[**the thresher to thresh in hope of sharing the crops**], Byz[he who threshes in hope should be partaker of his hope (KJV, NKJ)].

9:13 Alx[**eat things from the temple**], Byz[eat from the temple (ESV, JNT, MRD, NJB, NRS, RSV, TEV)].

9:16 Alx[**For woe**], Byz[And woe (ESV, HCS, JNT, KJV, MRD, NAB, NET, NIV, NJB, NKJ, NLT, NRS, REB, RSV, TEV, TLB)].

9:18 Alx[**offer the gospel**], Byz[*adds* of Christ (KJV, MRD, NKJ)].

9:20 Alx[**though not being myself under the law**], Byz[*omits* (KJV, MRD, NKJ, ~TLB)], Minor[*breaks verse after* in order to win Jews (DRA)].

9:21 Alx[**of God...of Christ**], Byz[to God...to Christ (ASV, KJV, ~MRD, ~NJB, NKJ, ~RSV, ~TLB)]; Alx[**those who are without the law**], Byz[those who are without law (ASV, KJV, NAS, NAU, NKJ, ~TLB)].

9:22 Alx[**I became weak**], Byz[I became as weak (KJV, MRD, NKJ, ~TLB)]; Alx/Byz[**save some**], Minor[*omits* some (~DRA, ~MRD, ~TLB)].

9:23 Alx[**I do it all**], Byz[I do this (~HCS, KJV, MRD, ~NAB, ~NET, ~NIV, ~NJB, NKJ, ~REB, ~TEV, TLB)].

But I discipline my body and make it my slave, so that, after I have preached to others, I myself will not be disqualified.

10

¹ For I do not want you to be unaware, brothers, that our fathers were all under the cloud and all passed through the sea, ² and all were baptized into Moses in the cloud and in the sea, ³ and all ate the same spiritual food, ⁴ and all drank the same spiritual drink, for they drank from a spiritual rock which followed them, and the rock was Christ. ⁵ Nevertheless, with most of them God was not pleased; for they were overthrown in the wilderness. ⁶ Now these things are examples for us, not to desire evil things as they did. ⁷ Do not be idolaters, as some of them were; just as it is written, *"The people sat down to eat and drink, and rose up to play."* ⁸ We must not indulge in immorality as some of them did, and twenty-three thousand fell in one day. ⁹ We must not put Christ to the test, as some of them did and were destroyed by serpents. ¹⁰ Nor grumble, as some of them did, and were destroyed by the destroyer. ¹¹ Now these things happened to them as an example, and they were written down for our instruction, upon whom the ends of the ages have come. ¹² Therefore let anyone who thinks that he stands take heed lest he fall. ¹³ No temptation has overtaken you but such as is common to man. And God is faithful, who will not let you be tempted beyond what you are able, but with the temptation will provide the way of escape also, so that you will be able to endure it.

¹⁴ Therefore, my beloved, flee from idolatry. ¹⁵ I speak as to sensible men; judge for yourselves what I say. ¹⁶ The cup of blessing which we bless, is it not a participation in the blood of Christ? The bread which we break, is it not a participation in the body of Christ? ¹⁷ Because there is one bread, we who are many are one body, for we all partake of the one bread. ¹⁸ Consider Israel after the flesh; are not those who eat the sacrifices partners in the altar? ¹⁹ What do I mean then? That a thing offered to idols is anything, or that an idol is anything? ²⁰ No, but I say that the things they sacrifice, [they sacrifice] to demons and not to God. I do not want you to be partners with demons. ²¹ You cannot drink the cup of the Lord and the cup of demons. You cannot partake of the table of the Lord and the table of demons. ²² Are we trying to provoke the Lord to jealousy? Are we stronger than he?

²³ "All things are lawful," but not all things are helpful. "All things are lawful," but not all things build up. ²⁴ Let no one seek his own good, but the good of his neighbor.

10:1 Alx[**For**], Byz[But (~ESV 2001 edition, HCS, KJV, MRD, NAB, NJB, NKJ, NLT, NRS, REB, RSV, TEV)].

10:2 Alx[**all were baptized**], Byz[all baptized themselves (JNT, ~REB, ~TLB, Metzger)].

10:3 Alx/Byz[**the same**], Minor[*omits* (~TLB)].

10:6, 11 **examples…an example** *or* types…a type.

10:7 Alx/Major[**just as**], Byz[as (ASV, DRA, ESV, HCS, JNT, KJV, MRD, NAB, NAS, NAU, NET, NIV, NJB, NKJ, NLT, NRS, REB, RSV, TEV, ~TLB)]; **Exodus 32:6**.

10:9 Alx/Byz[**Christ**], Minor[the Lord (ASV, NAS, NAU, NIV, NJB, REB, RSV, TEV, TLB) *others* God]; Alx[**as some of them did**], Byz[as some of them also did (KJV, NKJ)].

10:10 Alx[**as some of them did**], Byz[as some of them also did (KJV, NKJ)].

10:11 Alx[**Now these things**], Byz[Now all these things (DRA, KJV, MRD, NJB, NKJ, TEV, TLB)]; Alx[**as an example**], Byz[as examples (HCS, JNT, KJV, NET, NIV, NKJ, NLT, TEV, TLB)].

10:17 *or* For we who are many are one bread, one body, because we all partake of the one bread.

10:19 Alx[**a thing offered to idols…an idol**], Byz[an idol…a thing offered to idols (KJV, MRD, NET, NKJ, TEV, TLB)].

10:20 Alx[**the things they sacrifice**], Byz[the things the Gentiles sacrifice (ASV, DRA, ESV, JNT, KJV, MRD, NAS, NAU, NET, NIV, NJB, NKJ, NRS, REB, RSV, TEV)]; Alx/Byz[**they sacrifice, they sacrifice to demons**], Minor[they sacrifice to demons (NET)].

10:21 Alx/Byz[**You cannot partake**], Minor[How can you partake…?].

10:23 Alx[**All things are lawful**], Byz[*adds* for me *in both places* (DRA, KJV, MRD, NKJ, NLT, ~REB, ~TEV, ~TLB)]; *DRA places first clause in verse 22.*

25 Eat anything that is sold in the meat market without raising questions of conscience; 26 for, *"The earth is the Lord's, and everything in it."* 27 If one of the unbelievers invites you to dinner and you want to go, eat whatever is set before you without raising questions of conscience. 28 But if anyone says to you, "This has been offered in sacrifice," then do not eat it, both for the sake of the man who informed you and for conscience' sake – 29 the other man's conscience, I mean, not yours. For why should my freedom be judged by another's conscience? 30 If I partake with thankfulness, why am I denounced because of that for which I give thanks? 31 So, whether you eat or drink, or whatever you do, do all to the glory of God. 32 Give no offense either to Jews or to Greeks or to the church of God, 33 just as I try to please all men in everything I do, not seeking my own advantage, but that of many, that they may be saved.

11 1 Be imitators of me, as I am of Christ.
2 I praise you because you remember me in everything and hold firmly to the traditions, just as I delivered them to you. 3 But I want you to understand that Christ is the head of every man, and the man is the head of a woman, and God is the head of Christ. 4 Every man who prays or prophesies with his head covered dishonors his head. 5 But every woman who prays or prophesies with her head uncovered dishonors her head – it is the same as if her head were shaved. 6 For if a woman does not cover her head, she should have her hair cut off; but if it is disgraceful for a woman to have her hair cut or shaved off, let her cover her head. 7 For a man ought not to cover his head, since he is the image and glory of God; but the woman is the glory of man. 8 For man does not originate from woman, but woman from man; 9 neither was man created for woman, but woman for man. 10 Therefore the woman ought to have authority over her head, because of the angels. 11 In the Lord, however, woman is not independent of man, nor is man independent of woman. 12 For as woman was made from man, so also man is born of woman. And all things are from God. 13 Judge for yourselves: is it proper for a woman to pray to God with her head uncovered? 14 Does not even nature itself teach you that if a man has long hair, it is a dishonor to him, 15 but if a woman has long hair, it is her glory? For her hair is given [to her] for a covering. 16 If anyone wants to be contentious, we have no other practice, nor do the churches of God.

17 But in the following instructions, I do not praise you, because you come together not for the better but for the worse. 18 For, in the first place, when you come together as a church, I hear that there are divisions among you; and I partly believe it. 19

10:24 Alx[**but the good of his neighbor**], Byz[but each the good of his neighbor (ASV, KJV, NJB, NKJ)].

10:26 Psalms 24:1.

10:27 Alx[**If one of the unbelievers**], Byz[But if one of the unbelievers (MRD)].

10:28 Alx[*text*], Byz[*adds* for "the earth is the Lord's, and all its fullness (KJV, NKJ)]; Psalms 24:1.

10:30 Alx[**If I partake**], Byz[But if I partake (KJV, NKJ)].

11:2 Alx[**I praise you**], Byz[*adds* brothers (DRA, KJV, MRD, NKJ, TLB)].

11:5 Alx[**dishonors her head**], Byz[dishonors her own head].

11:7 Alx[**the woman**], Byz[woman (ESV, HCS, NAB, NJB, NKJ, NLT, NRS, REB, RSV, TEV)]; **glory** *or* reflection.

11:10 Alx/Byz[**authority**], Minor[a veil of authority (JNT, ~NLT, ~RSV, ~TEV, ~TLB)].

11:11 Alx[**woman...man...man...woman**], Byz[man... woman... woman... man (DRA, KJV, MRD, NKJ, ~TLB)].

11:15 Alx/Byz[**to her**], Major[*omits* (REB, ~TLB)].

11:18 Alx/Byz[**as a church** *or* in church], Minor[in the church (ASV, DRA, KJV, MRD)].

11:19 Alx[**also**], Byz[*omits* (ASV, ESV, HCS, JNT, KJV, MRD, NAS, NAU, NET, NIV, NJB, NKJ, NLT, NRS, REB, RSV, TEV, TLB)].

11:24-25 Matthew 26:26-28, Mark 14:22-24, Luke 22:17-19.

For there must be factions among you in order that [also] those who are approved among you may be recognized. ²⁰ Therefore when you meet together, it is not the Lord's supper that you eat, ²¹ for in eating, each one goes ahead with his own meal, and one is hungry and another is drunk. ²² What! Do you not have houses to eat and drink in? Or do you despise the church of God and humiliate those who have nothing? What shall I say to you? Shall I praise you in this? No, I will not.

²³ For I received from the Lord what I also delivered to you, that the Lord Jesus on the night when he was betrayed took bread, ²⁴ and when he had given thanks, he broke it and said, "*This is my body, which is for you; do this in remembrance of me.*" ²⁵ In the same way he took the cup also after supper, saying, "*This cup is the new covenant in my blood; do this, as often as you drink it, in remembrance of me.*" ²⁶ For as often as you eat this bread and drink the cup, you proclaim the Lord's death until he comes.

²⁷ Whoever, therefore, eats the bread or drinks the cup of the Lord in an unworthy manner will be guilty of profaning the body and the blood of the Lord. ²⁸ Let a man examine himself, and so eat of the bread and drink of the cup. ²⁹ For anyone who eats and drinks, without recognizing the body, eats and drinks judgment on himself. ³⁰ That is why many among you are weak and sick, and a number of you have fallen asleep. ³¹ But if we judged ourselves rightly, we would not be judged. ³² But when we are judged, we are disciplined by [the] Lord so that we will not be condemned along with the world. ³³ So then, my brothers, when you come together to eat, wait for one another. ³⁴ If anyone is hungry, let him eat at home, so that you will not come together for judgment. About the other things I will give directions when I come.

12 ¹ Now concerning spiritual gifts, brothers, I do not want you to be uninformed. ² You know that when you were pagans, you were led astray to mute idols, however you may have been moved. ³ Therefore I tell you that no one who is speaking by the Spirit of God says, "Jesus is cursed," and no one can say, "Jesus is Lord," except by the Holy Spirit.

⁴ Now there are varieties of gifts, but the same Spirit. ⁵ And there are varieties of service, but the same Lord. ⁶ There are varieties of working, but the same God who works all of them in all men. ⁷ But to each one is given the demonstration of the Spirit for the

---

11:²⁴ Alx/Major[**24 and when he had given thanks, he broke it and said**], Byz[and when he had given thanks, he broke it and said 24]; Alx[**This is my body which is for you**], Byz[Take, eat; this is my body, which was broken for you (~DRA, KJV, MRD, NKJ, ~NLT, ~TLB)].

11:²⁶ Alx[**the cup**], Byz[this cup (KJV, MRD, NIV, NJB, NKJ, NLT, TEV, TLB)].

11:²⁷ Alx[**eats the bread**], Byz[eats this bread (DRA, ~JNT, KJV, NKJ, NLT, ~TEV, TLB)]; Alx/Byz[**in an unworthy manner**], Major[in a manner unworthy of the Lord (~TEV)]; Alx/Major[**the body and the blood**], Byz[the body and blood (ESV, HCS, JNT, KJV, NAB, NET, NIV, NKJ, NLT, NRS, REB, RSV, TEV)].

11:²⁹ Alx[**eats and drinks, without recognizing the body**], Byz[eats and drinks in an unworthy manner, without recognizing the body of the Lord (DRA, KJV, MRD, ~NIV, NKJ, ~NLT, ~TEV, TLB)].

11:³⁰ **fallen asleep** *died*.

11:³¹ Alx[**But if we judged**], Byz[For if we judged (KJV, MRD, NKJ)].

11:³² Alx/Byz[**the Lord**], Major[*omits* the], Alt[our Lord (MRD)]; **judged, we are disciplined by the Lord** *or* judged by the Lord, we are disciplined.

11:³⁴ Alx[**If anyone is hungry**], Byz[But if anyone is hungry (KJV, MRD, NKJ, TEV)].

12:² Alx/Byz[**when you were pagans, you were led astray**], Minor[you were pagans, led astray (KJV, MRD, NKJ, ~TLB)]; **pagans** *or* Gentiles.

12:³ Alx[**says, "Jesus is cursed"**], Byz[calls Jesus "cursed" (~DRA, KJV, MRD, NKJ, ~NLT, ~TLB)]; Alx[**say, "Jesus is Lord"**], Byz[call Jesus "Lord" (~DRA, KJV, MRD, NKJ, ~NLT, ~TLB)].

12:⁶ Alx/Byz[**working, but**], Minor[working, and]; Alx[**the same God**], Byz[it is the same God (ESV, JNT, KJV, NJB, NKJ, NLT, NRS, RSV, TLB)].

common good. [8] To one is given through the Spirit the word of wisdom, and to another the word of knowledge according to the same Spirit, [9] to another faith by the same Spirit, to another gifts of healing by the one Spirit, [10] and to another the working of miracles, [and] to another prophecy, [and] to another distinguishing between spirits, to another various kinds of tongues, and to another the interpretation of tongues. [11] But one and the same Spirit works all these things, distributing to each one individually just as he wills.

[12] For just as the body is one and has many members, and all the members of the body, though they are many, are one body, so it is with Christ. [13] For by one Spirit we were all baptized into one body – whether Jews or Greeks, slaves or free – and we were all made to drink of one Spirit. [14] For the body is not made up of one member but of many. [15] If the foot should say, "Because I am not a hand, I do not belong to the body," it would not for that reason be any less a part of the body. [16] And if the ear should say, "Because I am not an eye, I do not belong to the body," it would not for that reason be any less a part of the body. [17] If the whole body were an eye, where would be the hearing? If the whole body were an ear, where would be the sense of smell? [18] But now God has arranged the members in the body, each one of them, just as he desired. [19] If they were all one member, where would the body be? [20] As it is, there are many parts indeed, but one body. [21] And the eye cannot say to the hand, "I have no need of you," nor again the head to the feet, "I have no need of you." [22] On the contrary, the parts of the body that seem to be weaker are indispensable, [23] and those parts of the body which we think less honorable we treat with the greater honor, and our unpresentable parts are treated with greater modesty, [24] while our more presentable members have no need of it. But God has so composed the body, giving the greater honor to the parts that lacked it, [25] so that there may be no division in the body, but that the members may have the same care for one another. [26] And if one member suffers, all the members suffer with it; if [one] member is honored, all the members rejoice with it.

[27] Now you are the body of Christ, and individually members of it. [28] And God has appointed in the church first apostles, second prophets, third teachers, then workers of miracles, then those having gifts of healings, helps, administrations, and those speaking in various kinds of tongues. [29] Are all apostles? Are all prophets? Are all teachers? Do all work miracles? [30] Do all have gifts of healing? Do all speak with tongues? Do all interpret? [31] But earnestly desire the greater gifts.

12:9 Alx[**to another faith**], Byz[and to another faith]; Alx[**the one Spirit**], Byz[the same Spirit (KJV, MRD, NKJ, REB, TEV)], Minor[the Spirit (~TLB)].

12:10-14:39 **tongues** or languages.

12:10 Alx/Byz[**miracles, and...prophecy, and**], Minor[miracles...prophecy (DRA, ESV, HCS, JNT, KJV, NAB, ~NET, NIV, NJB, NKJ, ~NLT, NRS, ~REB, RSV, ~TEV, ~TLB)]; Alx[**spirits, to another**], Byz[spirits, and to another (MRD)].

12:12 Alx[**and all the members of the body**], Byz[and all the members of the one body (KJV, ~NIV, NKJ, ~NLT, ~REB, ~TEV, ~TLB)].

12:13 Alx[**drink of one Spirit**], Byz[drink into one Spirit (DRA, KJV, MRD, NKJ, ~NLT, ~TLB)]; **by** or with or in.

12:20 Alx/Byz[**indeed**], Minor[omits (ASV, ESV, HCS, KJV, MRD, NAB, NAS, NAU, NET, NIV, NJB, NLT, NRS, ~REB, RSV, TEV, TLB)].

12:21 Alx/Major[**And the eye**], Byz[And an eye], Minor[omits And (ESV, MRD, NAB, NET, NIV, NJB, NLT, NRS, REB, RSV, TLB)].

12:25 Alx/Byz[**division**], Major[divisions (JNT, NJB, ~NLT, ~TLB)].

12:26 Alx/Byz[**if one member is honored**], Minor[if a member is honored (NET)]; **honored** or glorified.

12:31 Alx[**greater**], Byz[better (DRA, JNT, KJV, NKJ, ~NLT)]; or But you are earnestly desiring the greater gifts, and yet I will show you a still more excellent way.

13

And I will show you a still more excellent way. [1] If I speak in the tongues of men and of angels, but have not love, I am a noisy gong or a clanging cymbal. [2] If I have the gift of prophecy, and understand all mysteries and all knowledge; and if I have all faith, so as to remove mountains, but have not love, I am nothing. [3] If I give all I have to the poor, and if I surrender my body so I may boast, but have not love, I gain nothing.

[4] Love is patient, love is kind. It is not jealous, [love] is not boastful, it is not arrogant [5] or rude, it does not seek its own, it is not provoked, it keeps no record of wrongs, [6] it does not rejoice in evil, but rejoices with the truth. [7] Love bears all things, believes all things, hopes all things, endures all things.

[8] Love never fails; but where there are prophecies, they will cease; where there are tongues, they will be stilled; where there is knowledge, it will pass away. [9] For we know in part and we prophesy in part; [10] but when the perfect comes, the partial will pass away. [11] When I was a child, I spoke like a child, I thought like a child, I reasoned like a child; when I became a man, I put childish ways behind me. [12] For now we see a riddle in a mirror, but then face to face. Now I know in part, but then I shall know fully – even as I have been fully known. [13] So now faith, hope, love abide – these three; but the greatest of these is love.

14

[1] Pursue love, and earnestly desire the spiritual gifts, especially that you may prophesy. [2] For one who speaks in a tongue does not speak to men but to God; for no one understands him, but in spirit he speaks mysteries. [3] But everyone who prophesies speaks to men for their edification and encouragement and comfort. [4] He who speaks in a tongue edifies himself, but he who prophesies edifies the church. [5] Now, I want you all to speak in tongues, but even more to prophesy. He who prophesies is greater than he who speaks in tongues, unless someone interprets, so that the church may be edified. [6] But now, brothers, if I come to you speaking in tongues, what will I profit you unless I bring you some revelation or knowledge or prophecy or teaching? [7] If even lifeless things, such as the flute or the harp, do not give a distinction in the notes, how will any one know what is played? [8] And if the bugle gives an indistinct sound, who will get ready for battle? [9] So it is with you, unless you utter by the tongue speech that is intelligible, how will anyone know what is spoken? For you will be speaking into the air. [10] Undoubtedly there are many languages in the world, and none is without meaning. [11] If then I do not know the meaning of the language, I will be a

---

13:3 Alx[**so I may boast**], Byz[to be burned (ASV, DRA, ESV, HCS, JNT, KJV, MRD, NAS, NAU, NIV, NJB, NKJ, REB, RSV, TEV, TLB)].

13:4 Alx/Byz[**love is not boastful**], Minor[it is not boastful (DRA, ~ESV, ~HCS, JNT, NIV, ~NLT, ~NRS, ~REB, ~RSV, TEV, TLB)]; Alx/Byz[**it is not arrogant 5**], Minor[5 it is not arrogant (RSV, TLB)].

13:5 Alx/Byz[**rude**], Minor[polite *others* ambitious (DRA)].

13:8 Alx[**Love never fails**], Byz[Love never falls away (DRA)]; Alx/Byz[*are* **prophecies**], Minor[is prophecy (NLT, TLB)].

13:9 Alx[**For we know in part**], Byz[But we know in part (NLT, TLB)].

13:10 Alx[**the partial will pass away**], Byz[then the partial will pass away (KJV, MRD, NKJ, TEV, TLB)].

13:11 Alx[**when I became a man**], Byz[but when I became a man (DRA, KJV, MRD, NET, NJB, NKJ, NLT, TLB)].

13:13 Alx/Byz[**faith, hope, love abide – these three**], Minor[these three abide – faith, hope, love (HCS, JNT, MRD, NET, NIV, NLT, REB, TEV, TLB)].

14:2 **in spirit** *or* in Spirit.

14:5 Alx[**He who prophesies**], Byz[For he who prophesies (DRA, KJV, MRD, NKJ, NLT, TEV, TLB)].

14:10 Alx[**none is without meaning**], Byz[none of them is without meaning (KJV, MRD, NIV, NJB, NKJ, TEV, ~TLB)].

foreigner to the one who is speaking, and the speaker will be a foreigner to me. [12] So it is with you; since you are eager for spiritual gifts, strive to excel in building up the church. [13] Therefore, he who speaks in a tongue should pray that he may interpret. [14] [For] if I pray in a tongue, my spirit prays, but my mind is unfruitful. [15] What am I to do? I will pray with the spirit and I will pray with the mind also; I will sing with the spirit and I will sing with the mind also. [16] Otherwise, if you bless [in] the spirit, how can any one in the position of an outsider say the "Amen" to your thanksgiving, since he does not know what you are saying? [17] For you may be giving thanks well enough, but the other man is not edified. [18] I thank God that I speak in tongues more than you all; [19] but in the church I would rather speak five words with my mind, to instruct others, than ten thousand words in a tongue.

[20] Brothers, do not be children in your thinking; be infants in evil, but in thinking be mature. [21] In the law it is written,

> "By men of strange tongues
>> and by the lips of foreigners
> will I speak to this people,
>> and even then they will not listen to me,"

says the Lord. [22] Tongues, then, are a sign, not for believers but for unbelievers; but prophecy is for believers, not for unbelievers. [23] Therefore if the whole church assembles together and all speak in tongues, and outsiders or unbelievers enter, will they not say that you are mad? [24] But if all prophesy, and an unbeliever or an outsider enters, he is convicted by all, he is called to account by all; [25] the secrets of his heart are disclosed; and so, he will fall on his face, and worship God, declaring that God is really among you.

[26] What is the outcome then, brothers? When you come together, each one has a hymn, or a teaching, or a revelation, or a tongue, or an interpretation. Let all things be done for edification. [27] If anyone speaks in a tongue, it should be by two or at the most three, and each in turn; and one must interpret. [28] But if there is no interpreter, he must keep silent in the church; and let him speak to himself and to God. [29] Let two or three prophets speak, and let the others weigh what is said. [30] But if a revelation is made to another who is sitting, the first one must keep silent. [31] For you can all prophesy one by one, so that all may learn and all be encouraged. [32] Indeed, the spirits of prophets are subject to prophets; [33] for God is not a God of confusion, but of peace.

As in all the churches of the saints, [34] the women should keep silent in the churches. For they are not permitted to speak, but should be submissive, as even the law

---

14:[14] Alx/Byz[**For**], Minor[*omits* (NET, REB)].

14:[15] Alx/Byz[**and I will sing with the mind also**], Minor[and I will sing with the mind *or* I will sing with the mind also (DRA, MRD)].

14:[16] Alx[**in the spirit**], Byz[with the spirit (ASV, DRA, ESV, HCS, JNT, KJV, NAB, NET, NIV, NJB, NKJ, NRS, REB, RSV, TLB)]; **an outsider** *or* the unlearned.

14:[18] Alx[**I thank God**], Byz[I thank my God (DRA, KJV, NKJ)]; Alx/Byz[**in tongues**], Minor[in a tongue].

14:[19] Alx[**with my mind**], Byz[through my mind (~NIV, ~NLT, ~REB, ~TEV, ~TLB)].

14:[21] Alx[**lips of foreigners** *Greek* lips of others], Byz[foreign lips (DRA, KJV, MRD, NAB, NAU, NJB, NKJ, TEV, TLB)]; ~**Isaiah 28:11-12**.

14:[23, 24] **outsiders...an outsider** *or* the unlearned...the unlearned.

14:[25] Alx[**the secrets of his heart**], Byz[and thus the secrets of his heart (KJV, NKJ)].

14:[26] Alx[**each one has a hymn**], Byz[each one of you has a hymn (DRA, KJV, MRD, NJB, NKJ, REB)]; Alx[**revelation...tongue**], Byz[tongue...revelation (KJV, NKJ)].

14:[33] Alx/Major[**As in all the churches of the saints 34**], Byz[34 As in all the churches of the saints].

14:[34] Alx[**the women**], Byz[your women (KJV, MRD, NKJ)], Minor[*omits verses 34-35, others place after verse 40*].

says. 35 If they desire to learn anything, let them ask their own husbands at home; for it is shameful for a woman to speak in church. 36 Did the word of God originate with you? Or are you the only people it has reached?

37 If anyone thinks he is a prophet or spiritual, let him acknowledge that what I am writing to you is the Lord's command. 38 But if anyone does not recognize this, he is not recognized. 39 Therefore, [my] brothers, desire earnestly to prophesy, and do not forbid speaking in tongues. 40 But all things should be done decently and in an orderly way.

15 1 Now I would remind you, brothers, of the gospel I preached to you, which you received, in which you stand, 2 by which also you are saved, if you hold fast the word which I preached to you, unless you believed in vain. 3 For I delivered to you as of first importance what I also received, that Christ died for our sins according to the Scriptures, 4 that he was buried, that he was raised on the third day according to the Scriptures, 5 and that he appeared to Cephas, then to the twelve. 6 After that he appeared to more than five hundred brothers at one time, most of whom are still alive, though some have fallen asleep. 7 Then he appeared to James, then to all the apostles. 8 And last of all, as to one untimely born, he appeared to me also. 9 For I am the least of the apostles, and not fit to be called an apostle, because I persecuted the church of God. 10 But by the grace of God I am what I am, and his grace toward me was not in vain. No, I worked harder than them all – yet not I, but the grace of God [that was] with me. 11 Whether then it was I or they, so we preach and so you believed.

12 Now if Christ is preached that he has been raised from the dead, how can some of you say that there is no resurrection of the dead? 13 But if there is no resurrection of the dead, then not even Christ has been raised. 14 If Christ has not been raised, then our preaching is [also] in vain, and your faith is in vain. 15 More than that, we are even found to be false witnesses of God, because we testified against God that he raised Christ, whom he did not raise, if in fact the dead are not raised. 16 For if the dead are not raised, then Christ has not been raised. 17 And if Christ has not been raised, your faith is futile; you are still in your sins. 18 Then those who have fallen asleep in Christ have also perished. 19 If for this life only we have hoped in Christ, we are of all men most to be pitied.

20 But Christ has indeed been raised from the dead, the first fruits of those who have fallen asleep. 21 For since by a man came death, by a man came also the resurrection of the dead. 22 For as in Adam all die, so also in Christ all will be made alive. 23 But each in

14:35 Alx[**a woman**], Byz[women (KJV, MRD, NKJ, NLT, TLB)].
14:37 Alx[**command**], Byz[commands (DRA, KJV, MRD, NKJ)], Minor[*omits*].
14:38 Alx[**he is not recognized** *or* he is ignorant], Byz[let him not be recognized *or* let him be ignorant (ASV, JNT, KJV, MRD, NKJ, ~REB, TEV, ~TLB)], Minor[he will not be recognized *or* he will be ignorant (DRA, HCS, NIV, ~NLT, ~NRS)].
14:39 Alx[**my**], Byz[*omits* (DRA, KJV, NET, NKJ)].
14:40 Alx[**But all things**], Byz[*omits* But (KJV, NKJ, TEV)].
15:1 **gospel** *or* good news.
15:3 **as of first importance** *or* first.
15:5 Alx/Byz[**twelve**], Minor[eleven (DRA)]; **Cephas** *Peter.*
15:6 Alx[**some have fallen asleep**], Byz[some have also fallen asleep]; **fallen asleep** *died.*
15:10 Alx/Byz[**that was**], Minor[*omits* (DRA, JNT, NAS, NAU, NET, REB, TEV, TLB)].
15:14 Alx[**also**], Byz[*omits* (ASV, DRA, ESV, HCS, JNT, KJV, MRD, NAS, NAU, NET, NIV, NJB, NKJ, NLT, NRS, REB, RSV, TEV, TLB)]; Alx[**and your faith is in vain**], Byz[and your faith is also in vain (DRA, HCS, KJV, MRD, NIV, NJB, NKJ, REB)]; Minor[and our faith is in vain].
15:18 **fallen asleep** *died.*
15:20 Alx[**the first fruits**], Byz[and become the first fruits (KJV, MRD, NKJ, TLB)].
15:23 Alx/Major[**those who belong to Christ** *Greek* those who belong to the Christ], Byz[those who belong to Christ].

his own order: Christ, the first fruits; then, at his coming, those who belong to Christ. 24 Then comes the end, when he hands over the kingdom to God the Father after he has destroyed all rule and all authority and power. 25 For he must reign until he has put all enemies under his feet. 26 The last enemy to be destroyed is death. 27 For he *"has put all things in subjection under his feet."* But when it says, "All things are put in subjection under him," it is plain that he is excepted who put all things under him. 28 When all things are subjected to him, then the Son himself will [also] be subjected to the one who put all things under him, that God may be all in all.

29 Otherwise, what will those do who are baptized for the dead? If the dead are not raised at all, why then are people baptized for them? 30 Why are we also in danger every hour? 31 I protest, [brothers], by my pride in you which I have in Christ Jesus our Lord, I die every day.

32 If I fought wild beasts in Ephesus for merely human reasons, what have I gained? If the dead are not raised,

> *"Let us eat and drink,*
> *for tomorrow we die."*

33 Do not be deceived:

> *"Bad company corrupts good morals."*

34 Come back to your senses as you ought, and stop sinning; for some have no knowledge of God. I say this to your shame.

35 But someone will ask, "How are the dead raised? With what kind of body do they come?" 36 You foolish man! What you sow does not come to life unless it dies. 37 And that which you sow, you do not sow the body which is to be, but a bare grain, perhaps of wheat or of something else. 38 But God gives it a body as he has determined, and to each kind of seed he gives its own body. 39 For not all flesh is the same flesh, but of men there is one kind, another flesh of animals, another of birds, and another of fish. 40 There are also heavenly bodies and there are earthly bodies; but the glory of the heavenly is one, and the glory of the earthly is another. 41 There is one glory of the sun, and another glory of the moon, and another glory of the stars; for star differs from star in glory.

42 So is it with the resurrection of the dead. It is sown a perishable body, it is raised imperishable; 43 it is sown in dishonor, it is raised in glory; it is sown in weakness, it is raised in power; 44 it is sown a natural body, it is raised a spiritual body. If there is a natural body, there is also a spiritual one. 45 So it is written, *"The first man Adam became a living being"*; the last Adam became a life-giving spirit. 46 However, the spiritual is not

---

15:24 **the end** *or* the rest.

15:27 Psalms 8:6.

15:28 Alx[**also**], Minor[*omits* (JNT, MRD, NET, NIV, NJB, NLT, TEV)].

15:29 Alx[**baptized for them**], Byz[baptized for the dead (KJV, MRD, NKJ, NLT, TEV, ~TLB)].

15:30 Alx/Byz[**Why are we**], Alt[*without textual foundation* Why am I (~ESV 2001 edition, ~RSV)].

15:31 Alx/Byz[**my pride in you**], Minor[our pride]; Alx[**brothers**], Byz[*omits* (ASV, DRA, HCS, KJV, NET, NJB, NKJ, TLB)].

15:32 Alx[**gained? If the dead are not raised,**], Byz[gained, if the dead are not raised? (DRA, KJV, MRD, NLT)]; *NJB starts verse 33 with If the dead are not raised*; Isaiah 22:13.

15:33 Classical[**Menander, Thais Fragment 218**].

15:39 Alx/Byz[**but of men there is one kind**], Minor[*adds* of flesh (ASV, DRA, HCS, KJV, MRD, NAS, NAU, NET, NIV, NJB, NKJ, NRS, REB, TEV, ~TLB)]; Alx[**birds...fish**], Byz[fish...birds (KJV, NKJ, TLB)].

15:44 Alx[**If there is a natural body, there is also a spiritual one**], Byz[There is a natural body, and there is a spiritual body (KJV, MRD, NKJ, NLT, TEV, TLB)].

15:45 ~**Genesis 2:7**.

first, but the natural; and then the spiritual. [47] The first man was from the earth, of dust; the second man is from heaven. [48] As was the man of dust, so are those who are of the dust; and as is the man of heaven, so also are those who are of heaven. [49] Just as we have borne the image of the man of dust, we shall also bear the image of the man of heaven.

[50] Now I tell you this, brothers, that flesh and blood cannot inherit the kingdom of God; nor does the perishable inherit the imperishable. [51] Behold, I tell you a mystery; we will not all sleep, but we will all be changed, [52] in a moment, in the twinkling of an eye, at the last trumpet. For the trumpet will sound, and the dead will be raised imperishable, and we shall be changed. [53] For this perishable must put on the imperishable, and this mortal must put on immortality. [54] When the perishable puts on the imperishable, and the mortal puts on immortality, then will come to pass the saying that is written:

    "Death is swallowed up in victory."
[55]   "O death, where is your victory?
        O death, where is your sting?"

[56] The sting of death is sin, and the power of sin is the law. [57] But thanks be to God, who gives us the victory through our Lord Jesus Christ. [58] Therefore, my beloved brothers, be steadfast, immovable, always abounding in the work of the Lord, knowing that in the Lord your labor is not in vain.

16 [1] Now concerning the collection for the saints: as I directed the churches of Galatia, so you must also do. [2] On the first day of every week, each one of you is to put something aside and store it up, as he may prosper, so that no collections be made when I come. [3] And when I arrive, I will send those whom you approve with letters to carry your gift to Jerusalem. [4] If it seems advisable for me to go also, they will accompany me.

[5] But I will come to you after I go through Macedonia, for I am going through Macedonia; [6] and perhaps I will stay with you or even spend the winter, so that you may help me on my journey, wherever I go. [7] For I do not want to see you now just in passing; I hope to spend some time with you, if the Lord permits. [8] But I will stay in Ephesus until Pentecost, [9] for a wide door for effective work has opened to me, and there are many adversaries.

[10] Now if Timothy comes, see that he can be with you without fear, for he is doing the work of the Lord, just as I am also. [11] So let no one despise him. Send him on his way in peace, that he may return to me; for I am expecting him with the brothers.

[12] As for our brother Apollos, I strongly urged him to come to you with the other brothers, but it was not at all his will to come now. He will come when he has opportunity.

15:47 Alx[**from heaven**], Byz[the Lord from heaven (KJV, MRD, NKJ, ~NLT, ~TLB)].

15:49 Alx/Byz[**we shall also bear**], Major[let us also bear (DRA, NET)].

15:51 Alx[**we will not all sleep, but we will all be changed**], Byz[indeed we will not all sleep, but we will all be changed (~DRA)], Minor[we will all sleep, but we will not all be changed]; **sleep** *die*.

15:54 Alx/Byz[**When the perishable puts on the imperishable, and the mortal puts on immortality**], Minor[Now when this mortal body has been clothed with immortality (DRA, ~NLT, ~TEV, ~TLB)]; **~Isaiah 25:8**.

15:55 Alx[*text*], Byz[O death, where is your sting? O Hades, where is your victory? (KJV, MRD, NKJ)]; **Hosea 13:14 LXX**.

16:6 Alx/Byz[**or even spend the winter**], Minor[*omits* even (~KJV, MRD, ~NJB, ~NLT)].

16:7 Alx[**if the Lord permit**], Byz[if the Lord permits (ESV, HCS, JNT, NAB, NAS, NAU, NET, NIV, NKJ, NRS, REB, RSV, TEV, ~TLB)].

16:10 Alx/Byz[**also**], Minor[*omits* (ESV, HCS, JNT, MRD, NAB, NIV, NJB, NLT, NRS, REB, RSV, TEV, TLB)].

16:11 Alx/Major[**11 So let no one despise him**], Byz[So let no one despise him 11].

¹³ Be on your guard. Stand firm in the faith. Act like men. Be strong. ¹⁴ Let all that you do be done in love.

¹⁵ You know that the household of Stephanas were the first converts in Achaia, and they have devoted themselves to the service of the saints. Now I urge you, brothers, ¹⁶ to be subject to such men and to everyone who helps in the work and labors. ¹⁷ I rejoice at the coming of Stephanas and Fortunatus and Achaicus, because they have supplied what was lacking on your part. ¹⁸ For they refreshed my spirit and yours also. Give recognition to such men.

¹⁹ The churches of Asia send you greetings. Aquila and Prisca greet you warmly in the Lord, with the church that is in their house. ²⁰ All the brothers send you greetings. Greet one another with a holy kiss.

²¹ I, Paul, write this greeting in my own hand. ²² If anyone does not love the Lord – let him be anathema. Marana-tha! ²³ The grace of the Lord Jesus be with you. ²⁴ My love be with you all in Christ Jesus.

16:¹² **not at all his will** *could refer to Apollos or to God.*

16:¹⁹ Alx[**Prisca**], Byz[Priscilla (DRA, HCS, JNT, KJV, MRD, NIV, NKJ, NLT, TEV, TLB)]; Alx/Byz[**their house**], Minor[*adds* with whom also I lodge (DRA)].

16:²¹ Alx/Byz[**Paul**], Alt[*without textual foundation* Saul (~JNT)].

16:²² Alx[**the Lord**], Byz[*adds* Jesus Christ (DRA, KJV, MRD, NKJ)]; Alx[**Marana-tha** *Aramaism* Come, O Lord], Byz[Maran-atha *Aramaism* Our Lord has come]; **anathema** *or* accursed.

16:²³ Alx[**the Lord Jesus**], Byz[the Lord Jesus Christ (ASV, NJB)], Minor[our Lord Jesus Christ (DRA, KJV, MRD, NKJ)].

16:²⁴ Alx[*text*], Byz[*adds* Amen (ASV, DRA, ESV, KJV, MRD, NAS, NAU, NIV, NKJ, RSV)], Minor[*adds* To the Corinthians, written from Philippi by Stephanas, Fortunatus, Achaicus, and Timothy (KJV)].

Second Corinthians

1 ¹ Paul, an apostle of Christ Jesus by the will of God, and Timothy our brother, to the church of God which is at Corinth, with all the saints who are throughout Achaia: ² grace and peace to you from God our Father and the Lord Jesus Christ.

³ Blessed be the God and Father of our Lord Jesus Christ, the Father of mercies and the God of all comfort, ⁴ who comforts us in all our affliction, so that we may be able to comfort those who are in any affliction, with the comfort with which we ourselves are comforted by God. ⁵ For just as the sufferings of Christ flow over into our lives, so also through Christ our comfort overflows. ⁶ If we are afflicted, it is for your comfort and salvation. And if we are comforted, it is for your comfort, which is effective in the patient enduring of the same sufferings that we suffer. ⁷ And our hope for you is firm, because we know that just as you share in our sufferings, so also you share in our comfort.

⁸ For we do not want you to be ignorant, brothers, of our affliction which came in Asia: that we were burdened beyond measure, above strength, so that we despaired even of life. ⁹ Indeed, we felt that we had received the sentence of death. But this happened that we might not rely on ourselves but on God, who raises the dead. ¹⁰ He delivered us from so deadly a peril, and he will deliver us; on him we have set our hope [that] he will deliver us again. ¹¹ You also must help us by your prayers, so that many will give thanks on our behalf for the blessing granted us in answer to the prayers of many.

¹² For our boast is this: the testimony of our conscience, that with simplicity and godly sincerity, [and] not in worldly wisdom but in the grace of God, we have conducted ourselves in the world, and still more toward you. ¹³ For we write you nothing but what you can read and understand. And I hope you will understand fully, ¹⁴ as you have understood us in part, that you can be proud of us just as we can be of you, in the day of [our] Lord Jesus.

Title Alx/Byz[**Second Corinthians** *Greek* To the Corinthians B], Minor[*variations of* The Second Letter of the Apostle Paul to the Corinthians]; *commentators sometimes divide 2 Corinthians into two letters: 2 Corinthians A (the severe letter) chapters 10-13, and 2 Corinthians B (the reconciliation letter) chapters 1-9.*

1:1 Alx/Byz[**Paul**], Alt[*without textual foundation* Saul (~JNT)]; Alx[**Christ Jesus**], Byz[Jesus Christ (DRA, KJV, MRD, NKJ, TLB)].

1:6-7 Alx[*text*], Byz[If we are afflicted, it is for your comfort and salvation, which is effective in the patient enduring of the same sufferings that we suffer, and our hope for you is firm. And if we are comforted, it is for your comfort and salvation, 7 because we know that just as you share in our sufferings, so also you share in our comfort], Minor[If we are afflicted, it is for your comfort and salvation, which is effective in the patient enduring of the same sufferings that we suffer. And if we are comforted, it is for your comfort and salvation, and our hope for you is firm, 7 because we know that just as you share in our sufferings, so also you share in our comfort (~DRA, ~KJV, ~NKJ, ~TLB)].

1:8 Alx[**which came in Asia**], Byz[which came to us in Asia (ASV, DRA, KJV, NAS, NAU, NKJ)].

1:10 Alx[**and he will deliver us**], Byz[and he does deliver us (DRA, KJV, NKJ)], Minor[omits (MRD, ~NJB)]; Alx/Byz[**so deadly a peril** *or* the peril of death], Minor[the peril of deaths (~TEV)]; Alx/Byz[**that he will deliver us again**], Minor[and he will yet deliver us (JNT, NAS, NAU, NJB, NLT, REB, TLB)].

1:11 Alx/Byz[**our behalf**], Major[your behalf (~TLB)].

1:12 Alx/Byz[**simplicity**], Minor[holiness (ASV, NAS, NAU, ~NET, NIV, NJB, NLT, REB, RSV, TLB)]; Alx[**and not in worldly**], Byz[omits and (ASV, HCS, JNT, KJV, NAS, NAU, NET, NIV, NJB, NKJ, NLT, NRS, RSV)].

1:13 Alx[**fully** *or* to the end], Byz[even to the end (KJV, NKJ)].

1:14 Alx[**our**], Byz[omits (KJV, NET, NIV, NKJ, NLT, NRS, RSV)].

¹⁵ Because I was sure of this, I wanted to come to you first, so that you might have a double benefit. ¹⁶ I planned to visit you on my way to Macedonia and to come back to you from Macedonia, and then to have you send me on my way to Judea. ¹⁷ When I was planning this, did I do it lightly? Or do I make my plans in a fleshly manner so that in the same breath I say, "Yes, Yes" and "No, No"? ¹⁸ But as surely as God is faithful, our word to you is not, "Yes and No." ¹⁹ For the Son of God, Jesus Christ, who was preached among you by us – by me and Silvanus and Timothy – was not, "Yes and No," but in him it has always been, "Yes." ²⁰ For as many as are the promises of God, in him they are, "Yes." And so through him we speak our Amen to the glory of God. ²¹ Now it is God who establishes us with you in Christ, and has anointed us; ²² he has also put his seal on us and given us his Spirit in our hearts as a guarantee.

2 ²³ But I call God as my witness that it was in order to spare you that I did not return to Corinth. ²⁴ Not that we lord it over your faith; but we work with you for your joy, for you stand firm in your faith. ¹ So I made up my mind that I would not make another painful visit to you. ² For if I cause you pain, who is there to make me glad but the one whom I have pained? ³ And I wrote as I did, so that when I came I might not suffer pain from those who should have made me rejoice, for I had confidence in all of you, that my joy would be the joy of you all. ⁴ For I wrote you out of much affliction and anguish of heart and with many tears, not to cause you pain but to let you know the abundant love that I have for you.

⁵ But if any one has caused pain, he has caused it not to me, but in some measure – not to put it too severely – to all of you. ⁶ Sufficient for such a one is this punishment which was inflicted by the majority, ⁷ so you should rather turn to forgive and comfort him, so that he will not be overwhelmed by excessive sorrow. ⁸ I urge you, therefore, to reaffirm your love for him. ⁹ For this is why I wrote, that I might test you and know whether you are obedient in everything. ¹⁰ Any one whom you forgive, I also forgive. What I have forgiven, if I have forgiven anything, has been for your sake in the presence of Christ, ¹¹ in order that Satan might gain no advantage over us; for we are not ignorant of his schemes.

¹² Now when I came to Troas to preach the gospel of Christ and when a door was opened for me in the Lord, ¹³ I still had no rest in my mind, because I did not find my brother Titus there. So I took my leave of them and went on to Macedonia.

¹⁴ But thanks be to God, who in Christ always leads us in triumph, and through us spreads the fragrance of the knowledge of him everywhere. ¹⁵ For we are the aroma of Christ to God among those who are being saved and among those who are perishing, ¹⁶ to the one a fragrance from death to death, to the other a fragrance from life to life. And who is

---

1:¹⁵ Alx/Byz[**benefit** or grace], Minor[pleasure (RSV)].

1:¹⁶ **I planned** Greek And.

1:¹⁷ Alx/Byz[**planning** or wishing], Major[considering]; **did I do it lightly** or was I fickle.

1:¹⁸ Alx[**our word to you is not**], Byz[our word to you was not (DRA, ESV, KJV, MRD, NKJ, NRS, RSV, TEV)].

1:¹⁹ Alx/Byz[**Jesus Christ**], Minor[Christ Jesus (JNT, NAS, NAU, REB)]; **Silvanus** or Silas.

1:²⁰ Alx[**And so through him**], Byz[omits so (KJV, NKJ, NLT, TLB)].

1:²² Alx/Byz[**he has also**], Minor[omits he (JNT, MRD, NIV, NJB, NRS)].

2:¹ Alx[**So** or For], Byz[But (ASV, DRA, KJV, MRD, NAS, NAU, NKJ, ~TLB)].

2:³ Alx[**I wrote**], Byz[adds to you (DRA, KJV, MRD, NAS, NAU, NET, NKJ, TEV)].

2:⁷ Alx/Byz[**you should rather**], Minor[omits rather (NIV, ~REB, ~TEV, TLB)].

2:⁹ Alx/Byz[**whether**], Minor[whereby (TLB)].

2:¹⁰ **in the presence** or as a representative.

2:¹⁶ Alx[**from death... from life**], Byz[of death... of life (DRA, HCS, JNT, KJV, MRD, NAB, NIV, NJB, NKJ, ~NLT, REB, TEV, TLB)].

sufficient for these things? [17] For we are not, like so many, peddling the word of God; but as men of sincerity, as from God, in the sight of God we speak in Christ.

3 [1] Are we beginning to commend ourselves again? Or do we need, as some do, letters of recommendation to you, or from you? [2] You yourselves are our letter, written in our hearts, known and read by all men. [3] You show that you are a letter from Christ, delivered by us, written not with ink but with the Spirit of the living God, not on tablets of stone but on tablets of fleshly hearts.

[4] Such is the confidence that we have through Christ toward God. [5] Not that we are competent of ourselves to claim anything as coming from ourselves; but our competence is from God, [6] who has made us competent as ministers of a new covenant, not of the letter but of the Spirit; for the letter kills, but the Spirit gives life.

[7] Now if the ministry that brought death, which was engraved in letters on stone, came with glory, so that the Israelites could not look steadily at the face of Moses because of its glory, fading though it was, [8] will not the ministry of the Spirit be even more glorious? [9] For if the ministry of condemnation has glory, much more does the ministry of righteousness exceed it in glory. [10] For even what had glory, in this case has no glory, because of the glory that surpasses it. [11] For if what was fading away came with glory, much more is the glory of that which lasts.

[12] Therefore, since we have such a hope, we are very bold. [13] We are not like Moses, who would put a veil over his face to keep the Israelites from gazing at the end of the radiance of what was fading away. [14] But their minds were hardened; for to this very day, when they read the old covenant, the same veil remains unlifted, because only in Christ is it removed. [15] Even to this day whenever Moses is read, a veil lies over their hearts. [16] But whenever a person turns to the Lord, the veil is taken away. [17] Now the Lord is the Spirit, and where the Spirit of the Lord is, is freedom. [18] And we all, with unveiled face, beholding the reflection of the Lord's glory, are being transformed into his likeness from one degree of glory to another, for this comes from the Lord who is the Spirit.

4 [1] Therefore, since we have this ministry, as we have received mercy, we do not lose heart. [2] But we have renounced secret and shameful ways; we do not use deception, nor do we distort the word of God. On the contrary, by setting forth the truth plainly we commend ourselves to every man's conscience in the sight of God. [3] And even if our gospel is veiled, it is veiled to those who are perishing. [4] In their case the god of this world has blinded the minds of the unbelievers, so that they might not see the light of

---

2:17 Alx[**like so many**], Byz[like the others (MRD, ~NET, ~TEV, ~TLB)].

3:1 Alx[**Or do we need**], Byz[If we need (~TLB)]; Alx[**letters of recommendation to you, or from you**], Byz[letters of recommendation to you, or recommendation from you (KJV, MRD, NKJ, ~NLT, TLB)].

3:2 Alx/Byz[**our hearts**], Minor[your hearts (RSV, TLB)].

3:3 Alx/Byz[**written**], Minor[and written (DRA)]; Alx/Byz[**fleshly hearts**], Minor[a fleshly heart (DRA, KJV, MRD, NKJ, REB)].

3:7 Alx/Byz[**letters**], Minor[a letter *or* writing (~ASV, JNT, ~KJV, MRD, ~NKJ, ~NLT, ~REB, ~TLB)].

3:9 Alx[**has glory**], Byz[is glory (DRA, KJV, ~NIV)].

3:14 Alx[**to this very day** *or* today, to this day], Byz[to this day (ESV, HCS, JNT, KJV, MRD, NIV, NKJ, NLT, RSV, ~TLB)]; Alx/Byz[**because only in Christ is it removed**], Major[which is only removed in Christ (KJV, ~NLT, ~TEV)].

3:15 Alx[**whenever Moses is read**], Byz[when Moses is read (DRA, KJV, MRD, NIV, NKJ, NLT, TLB)].

3:17 Alx[**is freedom**], Byz[there is freedom (ASV, DRA, ESV, HCS, JNT, KJV, MRD, NAB, NAS, NAU, NET, NIV, NJB, NKJ, NLT, NRS, REB, RSV, TEV, TLB)].

3:18 **beholding the reflection** *or* being the reflection *Greek* seeing reflected in a mirror.

4:4 Alx[**they might not see the light of the gospel** *or* the light of the gospel may not shine], Byz[the light of the gospel may not shine to them (ASV, DRA, KJV, MRD, NKJ, REB)].

the gospel of the glory of Christ, who is the image of God. ⁵ For we do not preach ourselves, but Jesus Christ as Lord, and ourselves as your servants for Jesus' sake. ⁶ For it is the God who said, "*Let light shine out of darkness*," who has shone in our hearts to give the light of the knowledge of the glory of God in the face of [Jesus] Christ.

⁷ But we have this treasure in earthen vessels, to show that this all-surpassing power is from God and not from us. ⁸ We are hard pressed on every side, but not crushed; perplexed, but not in despair; ⁹ persecuted, but not forsaken; struck down, but not destroyed; ¹⁰ always carrying about in the body the death of Jesus, so that the life of Jesus may also be revealed in our body. ¹¹ For we who live are always being given up to death for Jesus' sake, so that the life of Jesus may be revealed in our mortal flesh. ¹² So then death is at work in us, but life in you. ¹³ Since we have the same spirit of faith, according to what is written, "*I believed, therefore I spoke*," we also believe and therefore speak, ¹⁴ knowing that he who raised the Lord Jesus will raise us also with Jesus and bring us with you into his presence. ¹⁵ For all this is for your benefit, so that the grace that is reaching more and more people may cause thanksgiving to overflow to the glory of God.

¹⁶ Therefore we do not lose heart. Though our outer nature is wasting away, yet our inner nature is being renewed day by day. ¹⁷ For our light and momentary affliction is producing for us an eternal weight of glory far beyond all comparison, ¹⁸ while we look not at the things which are seen, but at the things which are unseen; for the things which are seen are temporary, but the things which are unseen are eternal.

5 ¹ For we know that if the earthly tent we live in is destroyed, we have a building from God, a house not made with hands, eternal in the heavens. ² Here indeed we groan, longing to be clothed with our heavenly dwelling, ³ so that when we have taken it off, we will not be found naked. ⁴ For while we are in this tent, we groan and are burdened – not that we wish to be unclothed, but to be further clothed, so that what is mortal may be swallowed up by life. ⁵ Now he who has prepared us for this very thing is God, who has given us the Spirit as a guarantee.

⁶ Therefore we are always of good courage. And we know that while we are at home in the body we are away from the Lord, ⁷ for we walk by faith, not by sight. ⁸ We are confident, I say, and would rather be away from the body and at home with the Lord. ⁹ So whether we are at home or away, we make it our aim to please him. ¹⁰ For we must all

---

4:5 Alx[**Jesus Christ**], Byz[Christ Jesus (ASV, JNT, KJV, MRD, NAS, NAU, NJB, NKJ, REB, TLB)]; Alx/Byz[**for Jesus' sake**], Minor[through Jesus (DRA)].

4:6 Alx/Byz[**Jesus Christ**], Minor[*omits* Jesus (NAS, NAU, NET, NIV, NJB, RSV, TEV) *others* Christ Jesus (DRA, JNT)]; **Let light shine out of darkness** *uncertain reference* Genesis 1:3, Psalms 112:4.

4:10 Alx[**the death of Jesus**], Byz[the death of the Lord Jesus (KJV, NKJ)]; Alx/Byz[**our body**], Minor[our bodies (DRA, JNT, NLT, NRS, RSV, TEV, TLB)].

4:13 Alx/Byz[**therefore I spoke**], Minor[and therefore I spoke (ASV, ESV, JNT, KJV, NJB, NKJ, NRS, REB, RSV, TLB)]; **Psalms 116:10 LXX**.

4:14 Alx/Byz[**the Lord Jesus**], Minor[*omits* the Lord (DRA, NET)]; Alx[**raise us also with Jesus**], Byz[raise us also through Jesus (KJV, MRD)].

4:16 Alx[**our inner nature**], Byz[the inner nature (DRA, KJV, MRD, NKJ, ~REB)].

4:17 Alx/Byz[**our light and momentary affliction**], Minor[the light and momentary affliction (ESV, MRD, NAB, NAS, NAU, NRS, RSV, TEV, ~TLB)].

5:3 Alx[**taken it off**], Byz[put it on (ASV, DRA, ESV, HCS, JNT, KJV, MRD, NAS, NAU, NET, NIV, NJB, NKJ, NLT, REB, RSV, TEV, ~TLB)].

5:4 Alx/Byz[**not that we wish**], Minor[because we do not wish (DRA, HCS, NAB, NAS, NAU, NET, NIV, NKJ, NRS, REB, TLB)].

5:5 Alx[**who has given us**], Byz[who has also given us (KJV, NKJ, REB, TEV, TLB)].

5:10 Alx[**good or bad** *or* beneficial or worthless], Byz[good or evil (DRA, ESV, MRD, NAB, NET, NLT, NRS, RSV)].

appear before the judgment seat of Christ, that each one may receive the things done in the body, according to what he has done, whether good or bad.

¹¹ Therefore, knowing the fear of the Lord, we persuade men. But what we are is known to God, and I hope it is known also to your conscience. ¹² We are not again commending ourselves to you, but are giving you an occasion to be proud of us, so that you may have an answer for those who take pride in appearance and not in heart. ¹³ For if we are beside ourselves, it is for God; if we are in our right mind, it is for you. ¹⁴ For the love of Christ controls us, because we are convinced that one has died for all; therefore all have died. ¹⁵ And he died for all, that those who live should no longer live for themselves but for him who died for them and was raised again.

¹⁶ From now on, therefore, we regard no one from a fleshly point of view. Even though we once regarded Christ from a fleshly point of view, we regard him thus no longer. ¹⁷ Therefore, if any one is in Christ, he is a new creation. The old has passed away, behold, the new has come. ¹⁸ All this is from God, who through Christ reconciled us to himself and gave us the ministry of reconciliation. ¹⁹ That is, God was in Christ reconciling the world to himself, not counting their trespasses against them. And he has committed to us the message of reconciliation. ²⁰ We are therefore ambassadors for Christ, as though God were making his appeal through us. We beg you on behalf of Christ, be reconciled to God. ²¹ For our sake he made him to be sin who knew no sin, so that in him we might become the righteousness of God. ¹ Working together with him, then, we urge you not to receive the grace of God in vain. ² For he says,

6   *"At the acceptable time I have listened to you,*
          and helped you on the day of salvation."

Behold, now is the acceptable time; behold, now is the day of salvation. ³ We put no stumbling block in anyone's path, so that our ministry will not be discredited. ⁴ But as servants of God we commend ourselves in every way: through great endurance, in afflictions, hardships, distresses, ⁵ in beatings, imprisonments, tumults, labors, sleeplessness, hunger, ⁶ in purity, knowledge, patience, kindness, in the Holy Spirit, in genuine love, ⁷ in truthful speech, and in the power of God; with the weapons of righteousness for the right hand and for the left; ⁸ through glory and dishonor, evil report and good report; true, yet regarded as impostors; ⁹ as unknown, and yet well known; as dying, and behold we live; as punished, and yet not killed; ¹⁰ as sorrowful, yet always rejoicing; as poor, yet making many rich; as having nothing, and yet possessing everything.

¹¹ Our mouth has spoken freely to you, O Corinthians. Our heart is opened wide. ¹² You are not restricted by us, but you are restricted in your own affections. ¹³ Now in a fair exchange – I speak as to my children – open wide your hearts also.

¹⁴ Do not be unevenly yoked with unbelievers. For what partnership have righteousness and lawlessness? Or what fellowship has light with darkness? ¹⁵ What

---

5:12 Alx[**We are not again commending**], Byz[For we are not again commending (KJV, NKJ)].

5:14 Alx/Major[**14 For the love of Christ controls us**], Byz[For the love of Christ controls us 15]; Alx[**one has died for all**], Byz[if one has died for all (DRA, HCS, KJV, NJB, NKJ)].

5:16 Alx[**even though**], Byz[but even though (~KJV)].

5:17 Alx[**behold, the new has come**], Byz[behold, all things have become new (DRA, KJV, ~MRD, NKJ, NRS)]; **he is a new creation** *or* there is a new creation.

5:18 Alx[**through Christ**], Byz[through Jesus Christ (KJV, NKJ, ~TLB)].

5:19 **God was in Christ** *or* in Christ God was.

5:21 Alx[**For our sake he made him to be sin**], Byz[For he made him to be sin for our sake (KJV, MRD, NKJ, TLB)]; **to be sin** *or* to be a sin offering *or* to share our sin.

6:1 **with him** *Greek lacks.*

6:2 **Isaiah 49:8 LXX.**

6:14 Alx[**Or what fellowship has light**], Byz[And what fellowship has light (~JNT, KJV, NKJ, ~NLT, ~REB, ~TEV, ~TLB)]; **unevenly yoked** *or* mismatched.

harmony has Christ with Beliar? Or what has a believer in common with an unbeliever? **16** What agreement has the temple of God with idols? For we are the temple of the living God; as God said,

> *"I will live in them and walk among them,*
>   *and I will be their God,*
>   *and they shall be my people.*

17   Therefore *come out from them*
          and be separate, says the Lord.
     Touch no unclean thing,
          and I will receive you.

18   And *I will be a father* to you,
          and you shall be my sons and daughters,"

says the Lord Almighty.

7 **1** Since we have these promises, beloved, let us cleanse ourselves from every defilement of flesh and spirit, perfecting holiness in the fear of God.

2 Make room for us in your hearts. We have wronged no one, we have corrupted no one, we have taken advantage of no one. **3** I do not say this to condemn you, for I have said before that you are in our hearts, to die together and to live together. **4** I have great confidence in you. I have great pride in you. I am filled with comfort. With all our affliction, I am overflowing with joy.

5 For even when we came into Macedonia, our flesh had no rest, but we were afflicted at every turn – conflicts on the outside and fears within. **6** But God, who comforts the downcast, comforted us by the coming of Titus, **7** and not only by his coming but also by the comfort with which he was comforted in you, as he told us of your longing, your mourning, your zeal for me, so that I rejoiced still more. **8** For even if I made you sorry with my letter, I do not regret it. Though I did regret it – [for] I see that my letter hurt you, though only for a little while – **9** now I rejoice, not because you were made sorry, but because your sorrow led you to repentance. For you became sorrowful as God intended, so that you suffered no loss through us. **10** For godly sorrow exercises a repentance that leads to salvation and brings no regret, but worldly sorrow produces death. **11** For behold what this very thing, godly sorrow, has produced in you: what earnestness, what eagerness to clear yourselves, what indignation, what alarm, what longing, what zeal, what readiness to see justice done! In every point you have proved yourselves to be innocent in this matter. **12** So although I wrote to you, it was not on account of the one who did the wrong, nor on account of the one who suffered the wrong, but in order that your zeal for us might be revealed to you in the sight of God. **13** Therefore we are comforted.

6:15 Alx/Major[**Beliar**], Byz[Belial (ASV, DRA, ESV, HCS, JNT, KJV, ~MRD, NAS, NAU, NIV, NKJ, ~NLT, REB, RSV, ~TEV, ~TLB)].

6:16 Alx[**we are the temple**], Byz[you are the temple (DRA, KJV, MRD, NKJ, TLB)]; Alx/Byz[**temple**], Minor[temples]; ~**Leviticus 26:12**, ~Jeremiah 32:38, ~**Ezekiel 37:27**.

6:17 **Isaiah 52:11**, ~Ezekiel 20:34, 41.

6:18 ~**2 Samuel 7:8, 14**.

7:2 **in your hearts** *Greek lacks.*

7:8 Alx/Byz[**for I see**], Minor[*omits* for (DRA, NIV, NJB, REB, TEV, TLB)]; **my letter** *see Title note.*

7:10 Alx[**exercises... produces**], Byz[produces... produces (ASV, DRA, ESV, HCS, JNT, KJV, MRD, NAB, NAS, NAU, NIV, NKJ, NRS, REB, RSV)].

7:11 Alx/Byz[**In every point**], Minor[At every point (ESV, NIV, ~NLT, NRS, REB, RSV, ~TEV, ~TLB)].

7:12 Alx[**it was not on account**], Byz[I did not do it on account (ASV, KJV, ~MRD, NKJ, NLT, TLB)]; Alx/Byz[**nor on account of the one who suffered**], Minor[but not on account of the one who suffered]; Alx/Byz[**your zeal for us**], Minor[our zeal for you (DRA, KJV, NKJ)].

7:13 Alx[**besides our own comfort**], Byz[besides your own comfort (KJV, NKJ)].

And besides our own comfort, we rejoiced still more at the joy of Titus, because his spirit has been refreshed by you all. ¹⁴ For if I have boasted to him about you, I was not put to shame. But just as everything we said to you was true, so our boasting which I made before Titus has proved true. ¹⁵ And his affection goes out all the more to you, as he remembers the obedience of you all, how you received him with fear and trembling. ¹⁶ I rejoice, because I have perfect confidence in you.

8 ¹ Now, brothers, we want you to know about the grace of God which has been given in the churches of Macedonia, ² for in a severe test of affliction, their abundance of joy and their extreme poverty have overflowed in the wealth of their liberality. ³ For I testify that according to their ability, and even beyond their ability, they gave of their own free will, ⁴ urgently pleading with us for the grace of sharing in the relief of the saints. ⁵ And they did not do as we expected, but they first gave themselves to the Lord and to us by the will of God. ⁶ So we urged Titus that as he had previously made a beginning, he would also complete in you this work of grace. ⁷ But as you excel in everything – in faith, in utterance, in knowledge, in all earnestness, and in our love for you – see that you excel in this work of grace also.

⁸ I am not speaking this as a command, but I want to test the sincerity of your love by comparing it with the earnestness of others. ⁹ For you know the grace of our Lord Jesus Christ, that though he was rich, yet for your sakes he became poor, so that through his poverty you might become rich. ¹⁰ And in this matter I give my advice: it is best for you now to complete what a year ago you began not only to do but to desire. ¹¹ Now finish the work, so that your readiness to do it may be matched by your completion of it, according to your means. ¹² For if the readiness is there, it is acceptable according to what he has, not according to what he does not have. ¹³ For I do not mean that relief for others should burden you, but that there may be equality – ¹⁴ at the present time your abundance should supply their need, so that their abundance may supply your need, that there may be equality. ¹⁵ As it is written,

> "He who gathered much had nothing left over,
> and he who gathered little had no lack."

¹⁶ But thanks be to God who put the same earnest care for you into the heart of Titus. ¹⁷ For he not only accepted our appeal, but being himself very earnest he is going to

---

7:¹⁴ Alx/Byz[**our boasting which I made**], Minor[your boasting which I made *others omit* which I made (DRA, ESV, HCS, JNT, MRD, NAB, NAS, NAU, NET, NIV, NJB, NKJ, ~NLT, NRS, REB, RSV, TEV, ~TLB)].

7:¹⁶ Alx/Byz[**I rejoice**], Minor[I therefore rejoice (KJV, NKJ)].

8:¹ Alx/Major[**we want you to know** *Greek* we make known], Byz[I want you to know *Greek* I make known (NLT, TLB)].

8:⁴ Alx/Byz[**for the grace**], Minor[that we would receive the grace (KJV, NKJ, TLB)].

8:⁷ Alx[**our love for you**], Byz[your love for us (ASV, DRA, HCS, JNT, KJV, ~NET, NIV, NJB, NKJ, REB, RSV, TEV, TLB)].

8:⁸ Alx/Byz[**sincerity of your love**], Minor[sincerity of our love].

8:⁹ Alx/Byz[**Jesus Christ**], Minor[*omits* Christ (TLB)]; Alx/Byz[**for your sakes he became poor**], Minor[for our sakes he became poor].

8:¹² Alx[**according to what he has**], Byz[according to what a man has (ASV, DRA, ESV, KJV, NAS, NAU, NJB, ~NLT, ~REB, RSV, ~TEV, ~TLB)].

8:¹³ Alx[**relief for others should burden you**], Byz[others should be relieved and you burdened (ASV, DRA, ESV, HCS, KJV, MRD, NAS, NAU, NET, NJB, NKJ, NLT, NRS, RSV, TLB)]; Alx[**but that there may be equality 14**], Byz[14 but that there may be equality (ASV, KJV, MRD, NKJ, REB, RSV, ~TEV, TLB)].

8:¹⁵ **Exodus 16:18**.

8:¹⁶ Alx[**put**], Byz[puts (ASV, NAS, NAU, NKJ, RSV, ~TEV)].

you of his own accord. ¹⁸ And we are sending along with him the brother who is praised by all the churches for his preaching of the gospel. ¹⁹ And not only that, but he has been appointed by the churches to accompany us with this gracious work which we are carrying on, for the glory of the Lord [himself] and to show our good will. ²⁰ We intend that no one should blame us about this liberal gift which we are administering, ²¹ for we have regard for what is honorable, not only in the sight of the Lord, but also in the sight of men. ²² And with them we are sending our brother whom we have often proved diligent in many matters, but who is now more diligent than ever because of his great confidence in you. ²³ As for Titus, he is my partner and fellow worker among you. And as for our brothers, they are apostles of the churches, a glory to Christ. ²⁴ Therefore openly before the churches, show these men the proof of your love and the reason for our boasting about you.

9   ¹ Now it is superfluous for me to write to you about the offering for the saints, ² for I know your readiness, about which I boast of you to the Macedonians, saying that Achaia has been ready since last year. And your zeal has stirred up most of them. ³ But I am sending the brothers so that our boasting about you may not prove vain in this case, so that you may be ready, as I said you would be; ⁴ lest if any Macedonians come with me and find you unprepared, we – not to say anything about you – would be ashamed of our confidence. ⁵ So I thought it necessary to urge the brothers to go on to you before me, and arrange in advance for this gift you have promised, so that it may be ready as a willing gift, and not as an exaction.

      ⁶ The point is this: he who sows sparingly will also reap sparingly, and he who sows bountifully will also reap bountifully. ⁷ Each one must give just as he has chosen in his heart, not reluctantly or under compulsion, for God loves a cheerful giver. ⁸ And God is able to make all grace abound toward you, so that you, always having all sufficiency in everything, may have an abundance for every good work. ⁹ As it is written,

> *"He has scattered abroad. He gives to the poor.*
> *His righteousness endures forever."*

¹⁰ Now he who supplies seed to the sower and bread for food will also supply and increase your store of seed and will multiply the harvest of your righteousness. ¹¹ You will be enriched in every way for all your generosity, which through us will produce thanksgiving to God. ¹² For the ministry of this service is not only fully supplying the needs of the saints, but is also overflowing through many thanksgivings to God. ¹³ Because of the test of this

---

8:18 **gospel** *or* good news.

8:19 Alx/Byz[**accompany us with this gracious work**], Minor[accompany us in this gracious work (ASV, NAB, NAS, NAU, ~NET, ~NIV, NJB, ~NLT, ~NRS, REB, RSV, ~TLB)]; Alx/Byz[**himself**], Minor[*omits* (ASV, DRA, ~MRD, NJB, NLT, RSV, TEV, TLB)]; Alx[**show our good will**], Byz[show your good will (KJV, NKJ)].

8:21 Alx[**for we have regard**], Byz[*omits* for (KJV, NJB, NKJ, NLT, TEV, TLB)].

8:23 **apostles** *or* messengers.

8:24 Alx/Byz[**openly before the churches**], Minor[openly, and before the churches (KJV, NKJ, ~NLT, ~REB, ~TLB)].

9:2 Alx[**your zeal**], Byz[the zeal from you (~TLB)].

9:4 Alx[**not to say anything about you**], Byz[not that we say anything about you (ASV, KJV, ~TLB)]; Alx[**confidence**], Byz[confident boasting (KJV, MRD, NKJ, NLT, TLB)].

9:5 Alx[**promised**], Byz[told beforehand (KJV, MRD)]; Alx/Byz[**gift, and**], Minor[*omits* and (DRA, ESV, JNT, NIV, NLT, ~RSV, TEV)]; Alx/Byz[**as an exaction**], Minor[as of an exaction (KJV, TLB)].

9:7 Alx[**has chosen**], Byz[chooses (KJV, MRD, NKJ, NLT, TLB)].

9:9 **righteousness** *or* benevolence; **Psalms 112:9**.

9:10 Alx[**he who supplies**], Byz[may he who supplies (~KJV, NKJ)]; Alx[**will...will**], Byz[*omits both* (KJV, NKJ)]; Alx/Byz[**harvest**], Minor[children].

9:11 Alx/Byz[**thanksgiving to God**], Minor[thanksgiving of God (~NJB, ~NLT, ~TEV)]; **for all your generosity** *Greek* for all generosity.

service, you will glorify God by your obedience in your confession of the gospel of Christ, and by the generosity of your contribution for them and for all others; [14] while they long for you and pray for you, because of the surpassing grace of God in you. [15] Thanks be to God for his indescribable gift!

10

[1] I, Paul, myself urge you, by the meekness and gentleness of Christ – I who am humble when face to face with you, but bold to you when I am away! – [2] I beg you that when I am present I may not have to be bold with that confidence by which I intend to be bold against some, who think of us as if we walked according to the flesh. [3] For though we live in the flesh, we do not wage war as the flesh does. [4] For the weapons of our warfare are not the weapons of flesh, but they have divine power to destroy strongholds. We demolish arguments [5] and every pretension that sets itself up against the knowledge of God, and we take captive every thought to make it obedient to Christ, [6] and we are ready to punish every disobedience, whenever your obedience is complete.

[7] You look at things as they are outwardly. If anyone is confident in himself that he is Christ's, let him consider this again with himself, that just as he is Christ's, so also are we. [8] For even if I boast somewhat further about our authority, which the Lord gave for building you up and not for destroying you, I shall not be put to shame. [9] I do not wish to seem as if I would terrify you by my letters. [10] For they say, "His letters are weighty and strong, but his personal presence is weak, and his speech of no account." [11] Let such people realize that what we are in our letters when we are absent, we will be in our actions when we are present.

[12] For we do not dare to class or compare ourselves with some of those who commend themselves. But when they measure themselves by themselves, and compare themselves with themselves, they are without understanding. [13] But we will not boast beyond proper limits, but will confine our boasting to the measure God has apportioned to us, a measure that reaches even to you. [14] For we are not overextending ourselves, as if we did not reach you. We were the first to come even as far as you with the gospel of Christ. [15] We do not go beyond limits by boasting in other men's labors, but our hope is that as your faith grows, our sphere among you may be greatly enlarged, [16] so that we can preach the gospel in the regions beyond you. For we do not want to boast of work already done in another man's territory. [17] But, *"Let him who boasts boast in the Lord."* [18] For it is not he who commends himself that is approved, but he whom the Lord commends.

9:15 Alx[**Thanks**], Byz[And thanks].

10:1 Alx/Byz[**Paul**], Alt[*without textual foundation* Saul (~JNT)].

10:4 Alx/Byz[**weapons of our warfare**], Minor[weapons of our army (REB, TLB)]; Alx[**We demolish arguments 5**], Byz[5 We demolish arguments (ASV, ESV, KJV, MRD, NAS, NAU, NIV, NKJ, REB, RSV, TLB)].

10:7 Alx[**with himself**], Byz[from himself (~ESV, ~HCS, ~JNT, KJV, MRD, ~NAB, ~NET, ~NIV, ~NJB, ~NLT, ~NRS, ~REB, ~RSV, ~TLB)]; Alx[**so also are we**], Byz[*adds* Christ's (KJV, NKJ)]; **You look at things as they are outwardly** *or* Look at what is obvious.

10:8 Alx[**which the Lord gave**], Byz[*adds* us (DRA, JNT, KJV, ~MRD, NET, NIV, NJB, NKJ, NLT, TEV, ~TLB)].

10:10 Alx/Byz[**For they say**], Minor[For he says (~HCS, JNT, NAB, NJB, ~REB, TEV)].

10:12 Alx/Byz[**they are without understanding**], Minor[*omits* (DRA)].

10:13 Alx/Byz[**But we**], Minor[*omits*]; **beyond proper limits** *or* beyond what can be measured *Greek* beyond measure; **measure** *or* field.

10:14 Alx/Byz[**we are not overextending**], Minor[we are overextending]; **gospel** *or* good news.

10:15 **beyond limits** *or* beyond what can be measured *Greek* beyond measure.

10:17 ~Jeremiah 9:24.

11

¹ I wish that you would bear with me in some little foolishness; but indeed you are bearing with me. ² I am jealous for you with a godly jealousy; for I betrothed you to one husband, so that to Christ I might present you as a pure virgin. ³ But I am afraid that just as the serpent deceived Eve by his cunning, your minds may somehow be led astray from your sincere [and pure] devotion to Christ. ⁴ For if someone comes to you and preaches a Jesus other than the one we preached, or if you receive a different spirit from the one you received, or a different gospel from the one you accepted, you put up with it easily enough. ⁵ I think that I am not in the least inferior to these "super-apostles." ⁶ But even if I am unskilled in speech, I am not in knowledge; in every way we have made this plain to you in all things.

⁷ Or did I commit a sin in humbling myself that you might be exalted, because I preached the gospel of God to you without charge? ⁸ I robbed other churches by accepting support from them in order to serve you. ⁹ And when I was with you and needed something, I was not a burden to anyone, for the brothers who came from Macedonia supplied what I needed. I have kept myself from being a burden to you in any way, and will continue to do so. ¹⁰ As the truth of Christ is in me, this boasting of mine will not be stopped in the regions of Achaia. ¹¹ Why? Because I do not love you? God knows I do!

¹² And what I am doing, I will also continue to do, in order to cut the ground from under those who want an opportunity to be considered equal with us in the things of which they boast. ¹³ For such men are false apostles, deceitful workmen, disguising themselves as apostles of Christ. ¹⁴ And no wonder, for even Satan disguises himself as an angel of light. ¹⁵ Therefore it is not surprising if his servants also disguise themselves as servants of righteousness. Their end will be according to their deeds.

¹⁶ I repeat, let no one think me foolish; but even if you do, receive me as a fool, so that I too may boast a little. ¹⁷ What I am saying I am not saying as the Lord would, but as a fool, in this confidence of boasting. ¹⁸ Since many boast according to flesh, I too will boast. ¹⁹ For you put up with fools gladly, being so wise yourselves! ²⁰ For you put up with anyone if he makes slaves of you, or preys upon you, or takes advantage of you, or exalts himself, or strikes you in the face. ²¹ To my shame, I must say that we have been too weak for that! But whatever anyone else dares to boast about – I am speaking as a fool – I also dare to boast about. ²² Are they Hebrews? So am I. Are they Israelites? So am I. Are they descendants of

---

11:1 Alx/Byz[**some little foolishness**], Minor[the little foolishness (KJV, MRD, NLT, TEV, TLB)].

11:3 Alx[**cunning, your minds**], Byz[cunning, thus your minds (DRA, ~JNT, KJV, MRD, NKJ, ~NLT, ~TEV, ~TLB)]; Alx[**and pure**], Byz[*omits* (DRA, KJV, MRD, NJB, NKJ, REB)].

11:4 Alx/Byz[**you put up with it**], Major[you might put up with it (DRA, KJV, MRD, NKJ)].

11:5 Alx/Byz[**"super-apostles"**], Major[most eminent apostles (ASV, KJV, MRD, NAS, NAU, NKJ, TEV)].

11:6 Alx[**we have made this plain**], Byz[we have been made plain (DRA, KJV, MRD, NKJ)].

11:7 **gospel** *or* good news.

11:9 Alx[**9 And when I was with you and needed something, I was not a burden to anyone**], Byz[And when I was with you and needed something, I was not a burden to anyone 9 (TLB)], Major[9 And when I was with you and needed something, I was a burden to no one (DRA, KJV, MRD, NKJ, TEV, TLB)].

11:10 Alx/Byz[**this boasting of mine will not be stopped**], Minor[no one will stop this boasting of mine (ASV, KJV, NIV, NKJ, NLT, ~TLB)].

11:14 Alx[**And no wonder**], Byz[And this is nothing wonderful (JNT, MRD, NJB, ~NLT, TLB)].

11:17 Alx/Byz[**the Lord**], Minor[God (DRA) *others* a man (REB)].

11:18 Alx[**according to flesh**], Byz[according to the flesh (ASV, DRA, ESV, KJV, MRD, NAB, NAS, NAU, NIV, NKJ)].

11:21 Alx[**we have been too weak**], Byz[we were too weak (ESV, MRD, NAB, NET, NIV, NKJ, NRS, REB, RSV, TEV, ~TLB)], Minor[*adds* in this matter (DRA, ~NAS, ~NAU)].

Abraham? So am I. ²³ Are they servants of Christ? I am a better one – I am talking like a madman – in more labors, in more imprisonments, with far more beatings, and often in danger of death. ²⁴ Five times I received from the Jews the forty lashes minus one. ²⁵ Three times I was beaten with rods, once I was stoned, three times I was shipwrecked, a night and a day I have spent in the open sea. ²⁶ I have been on frequent journeys, in danger from rivers, in danger from robbers, in danger from my own countrymen, in danger from Gentiles, in danger in the city, in danger in the wilderness, in danger at sea, and in danger from false brothers; ²⁷ with labor and hardship, through many sleepless nights, in hunger and thirst, often without food, in cold and exposure. ²⁸ Besides such external things, there is the daily pressure on me of concern for all the churches. ²⁹ Who is weak, and I am not weak? Who is made to fall, and I do not inwardly burn?

³⁰ If I must boast, I will boast of the things that show my weakness. ³¹ The God and Father of the Lord Jesus, he who is blessed forever, knows that I am not lying. ³² In Damascus the governor under King Aretas had the city of the Damascenes guarded in order to arrest me, ³³ but I was let down in a basket through a window in the wall, and escaped his hands.

12 ¹ I must go on boasting, though there is nothing to be gained by it; but I will go on to visions and revelations of the Lord. ² I know a man in Christ who fourteen years ago was caught up to the third heaven. Whether it was in the body or out of the body I do not know – God knows. ³ And I know that this man – whether in the body or apart from the body I do not know, but God knows – ⁴ was caught up to paradise and heard inexpressible things, which a man is not permitted to tell. ⁵ On behalf of such a man I will boast, but on my own behalf I will not boast, except in weaknesses. ⁶ Though if I should boast, I will not be a fool, for I will be speaking the truth. But I refrain from it, so that no one may think more of me than [something] which he sees in me or hears from me, ⁷ even considering the abundance of revelations. Therefore, to keep me from being too elated, there was given to me a thorn in the flesh, an angel of Satan, to harass me, to keep me from

---

11:²³ Alx[**more imprisonments, with far more beatings**], Byz[far more beatings, with more imprisonments (KJV, ~MRD, NKJ)], Minor[more beatings, with far more imprisonments].

11:²⁴ Alx[**the forty lashes minus one** *Greek* forty lashes minus one *with* forty *as a pronoun*], Byz[forty lashes minus one (ASV, DRA, KJV, MRD, NAB, NAS, NAU, NET, NJB, NKJ, NLT, REB, TEV, TLB)].

11:²⁷ Alx[**with labor and hardship**], Byz[in labor and hardship (ASV, DRA, ESV, KJV, MRD, NAB, NAS, NAU, NET, NKJ, NRS, RSV)].

11:²⁸ Alx[**the daily pressure on me**], Byz[my daily disturbance (DRA, ~JNT, ~NIV, ~NLT, ~NRS, ~TEV)].

11:³⁰ Alx/Byz[**my weakness**], Minor[*omits* my].

11:³¹ Alx[**the Lord Jesus**], Byz[the Lord Jesus Christ], Minor[our Lord Jesus Christ (DRA, KJV, MRD, NKJ, TLB)].

11:³² Alx[**in order to**], Byz[and wanted to (KJV, NKJ)]; **governor** *Greek* ethnarch.

11:³³ **through a window in the wall** *Greek* through the wall.

12:¹ Alx[**I must go on boasting, though there is nothing to be gained by it; but**], Byz[There is doubtless nothing for me to gain by boasting, for (~DRA, KJV, NKJ, ~REB, ~TLB)].

12:³ Alx[**apart from the body**], Byz[outside of the body (DRA, ESV, HCS, KJV, MRD, NAB, NJB, NKJ, NLT, NRS, RSV, ~TEV)]; Alx/Byz[**I do not know**], Minor[*omits* (NLT)].

12:⁵ Alx[**in weaknesses**], Byz[in my weaknesses (ASV, DRA, ESV, HCS, JNT, KJV, MRD, NAB, NAS, NAU, NET, NIV, NJB, NKJ, NLT, NRS, REB, RSV, TEV, TLB)].

12:⁶ Alx/Byz[**something**], Minor[*omits* (ESV, HCS, JNT, MRD, NAB, NAS, NAU, NET, NIV, NJB, NKJ, NLT, NRS, REB, RSV, TEV, TLB)].

12:⁷ Alx[*text*], Byz[...hears from me. 7 And to keep me from being too elated because of the abundance of revelations, there was given to me a thorn in the flesh (ASV, DRA, ESV, KJV, MRD, NAS, NAU, NIV, NJB, NKJ, REB, RSV, TEV)]; Alx/Byz[**to keep me from being too elated...to keep me from being too elated**], Minor[*omits the second* to keep me from being too elated (DRA, NIV)].

being too elated. [8] Three times I pleaded with the Lord about this, that it should depart from me. [9] But he said to me, "My grace is sufficient for you, for power is made perfect in weakness." Therefore I will boast all the more gladly about my weaknesses, so that the power of Christ may rest on me. [10] That is why, for Christ's sake, I am content in weaknesses, in insults, in hardships, in persecutions and difficulties; for when I am weak, then I am strong.

[11] I have been a fool! You forced me to it, for I ought to have been commended by you. For I was not in the least inferior to these "super-apostles," even though I am nothing. [12] The signs of a true apostle were performed among you in all perseverance, signs, and even wonders and mighty works. [13] For in what respect were you inferior to the rest of the churches, except that I myself did not become a burden to you? Forgive me this wrong! [14] Look! For this third time I am ready to come to you. And I will not be a burden, for I seek not what is yours but you; for children ought not to lay up for their parents, but parents for their children. [15] I will most gladly spend and be spent for your souls. If I love you the more, am I to be loved the less? [16] But be that as it may, I did not burden you myself. Yet, crafty fellow that I am, I caught you by trickery! [17] Did I take advantage of you through any of those whom I sent to you? [18] I urged Titus to go, and I sent the brother with him. Titus did not take advantage of you, did he? Did we not act in the same spirit and walk in the same steps?

[19] Have you been thinking all along that we have been defending ourselves before you? It is in the sight of God that we have been speaking in Christ, and all for your upbuilding, beloved. [20] For I am afraid that when I come I may not find you what I wish you to be, and you may not find me what you wish me to be. I fear that there may be quarreling, jealousy, outbursts of anger, factions, slander, gossip, arrogance and disorder. [21] I am afraid that when I come again my God may humble me before you, and I may have to mourn over many of those who sinned before and have not repented of the impurity, immorality, and lewdness which they have practiced.

13 [1] This is the third time I am coming to you. *Every charge must be established by the evidence of two or three witnesses.* [2] I warned those who sinned in the past and all the others, and now while absent, as I did when present the second time, that

---

12:[9] Alx[**power**], Byz[my power (ASV, ESV, JNT, KJV, MRD, NET, NIV, NKJ, NLT, RSV, TEV, TLB)]; Alx/Byz[**about my weaknesses**], Minor[*omits* my].

12:[10] Alx[**in persecutions and difficulties**], Byz[in persecutions, in difficulties (ASV, DRA, ~HCS, KJV, MRD, NAS, NAU, NIV, NKJ)].

12:[11] Alx[**I have been a fool**], Byz[*adds* in boasting (KJV, MRD, NKJ, TEV)]; Alx/Byz["**super-apostles**"], Major[most eminent apostles (ASV, DRA, KJV, MRD, NAS, NAU, NKJ, TEV, ~TLB)].

12:[12] Alx[**signs, and even**], Byz[in signs, and (~ASV, DRA, ESV, KJV, MRD, ~NAS, ~NAU, ~NET, NKJ, REB, ~RSV, ~TEV)].

12:[13] Alx[**inferior to the rest**], Byz[overcome by the rest (ASV, ~DRA, HCS, ~NLT, NRS, ~TLB)].

12:[14] Alx[**For this third time**], Byz[For the third time (DRA, ~ESV, KJV, NET, NIV, NJB, NKJ, NLT, ~REB, RSV, TLB)]; Alx[**And I will not be a burden**], Byz[*adds* to you (ASV, DRA, HCS, JNT, KJV, MRD, NAS, NAU, NET, NIV, NJB, NKJ, NLT, REB, TEV, TLB)].

12:[15] Alx[**If I love you the more**], Byz[Though I love you the more (DRA, KJV, MRD, NKJ, NLT, TLB)].

12:[19] Alx[**Have you been thinking all along**], Byz[Again, do you think (KJV, MRD, NKJ, NLT, ~TLB)].

12:[20] Alx[**quarreling, jealousy**], Byz[quarrelings, jealousies (DRA, KJV, NKJ)].

12:[21] Alx/Byz[**my God**], Minor[God (DRA, NLT, TLB)]; Alx/Byz[**may humble**], Major[will humble (HCS, KJV, NIV, NKJ, NLT, TEV, TLB)].

13:[1] ~Deuteronomy 19:15.

13:[2] Alx[**and now while absent**], Byz[and I write them now while absent (KJV, MRD, NKJ)].

if I come again I will not spare them – ³ since you desire proof that Christ is speaking in me. He is not weak in dealing with you, but is powerful in you. ⁴ For he was crucified in weakness, yet he lives by the power of God. For we also are weak in him, but we shall live with him by the power of God toward you.

⁵ Examine yourselves to see whether you are in the faith. Test yourselves. Do you not realize that Jesus Christ is in you – unless, indeed, you fail the test? ⁶ I trust that you will realize that we have not failed the test. ⁷ Now we pray to God that you may not do wrong – not that we may appear to have met the test, but that you may do what is right, even though we may seem to have failed. ⁸ For we cannot do anything against the truth, but only for the truth. ⁹ For we are glad when we are weak and you are strong. This we also pray for, your perfection. ¹⁰ I write these things while I am absent, in order that when I come I may not have to be severe in my use of the authority which the Lord gave me for building you up, and not for tearing you down.

¹¹ Finally, brothers, farewell. Aim for perfection. Listen to my appeal. Be of one mind. Live in peace. And the God of love and peace will be with you. ¹² Greet one another with a holy kiss.

All the saints greet you. ¹³ The grace of the Lord Jesus Christ, and the love of God, and the fellowship of the Holy Spirit be with you all.

13:⁴ Alx[**For he was crucified**], Byz[For though he was crucified (DRA, JNT, KJV, MRD, NJB, NKJ, NLT, TEV)]; Alx/Byz[**in him**], Minor[with him (MRD, ~NLT)]; Alx/Byz[**the power of God toward you**], Minor[*omits* toward you (ESV, HCS, JNT, NAB, NIV, NJB, ~NLT, REB, TEV)].

13:⁵ Alx/Byz[**Jesus Christ**], Minor[Christ Jesus (DRA, NIV, TEV, ~TLB)].

13:⁷ Alx[**Now we pray**], Byz[Now I pray (KJV, MRD, NKJ, TLB)].

13:⁹ Alx[**This we also pray for**], Byz[And this we also pray for (KJV, MRD, NKJ, TEV)].

13:¹¹ **farewell** *or* rejoice; **Listen to my appeal** *or* Encourage one another.

13:¹³ Alx[**All the saints greet you 13**], Byz[13 All the saints greet you 14 (ASV, ESV, JNT, KJV, MRD, NAS, NAU, NIV, NKJ, NLT, REB, RSV, TLB)], Minor[*omits verse 13* (MRD)]; Alx/Byz[**Jesus Christ**], Minor[*omits* Christ]; Alx[**be with you all**], Byz[*adds* Amen (DRA, NKJ)], Minor[*adds* Amen. The second letter to the Corinthians was written from Philippi, a city of Macedonia, by Titus and Lucas (KJV)]; **fellowship** *or* sharing.

To the Galatians

1 ¹ Paul, an apostle – sent not from men nor through man, but through Jesus Christ and God the Father, who raised him from the dead – ² and all the brothers who are with me, to the churches of Galatia: ³ grace to you and peace from God our Father and the Lord Jesus Christ, ⁴ who gave himself for our sins to rescue us from the present evil age, according to the will of our God and Father, ⁵ to whom be the glory for ever and ever. Amen.

⁶ I am astonished that you are so quickly deserting him who called you by [the] grace [of Christ] and turning to a different gospel – ⁷ which is really not another gospel; but there are some who are disturbing you, and want to pervert the gospel of Christ. ⁸ But even if we, or an angel from heaven, should preach [to you] a gospel contrary to what we preached to you, let him be accursed! ⁹ As we have said before, so I say again now, if any one is preaching to you a gospel contrary to what you received, let him be accursed!

¹⁰ Am I now seeking the favor of men, or of God? Or am I trying to please men? If I were still trying to please men, I would not be a servant of Christ.

¹¹ For I would have you know, brothers, that the gospel which was preached by me is not according to man. ¹² For I did not receive it from man, nor was I taught it, but I received it through a revelation of Jesus Christ.

¹³ For you have heard of my former way of life in Judaism, how intensely I persecuted the church of God and tried to destroy it. ¹⁴ And I was advancing in Judaism beyond many of my own age among my people, so extremely zealous was I for the traditions of my fathers. ¹⁵ But when [God], who had set me apart even from my mother's womb and called me through his grace, was pleased ¹⁶ to reveal his Son in me so that I might preach him among the Gentiles, I did not immediately consult with flesh and blood, ¹⁷ nor did I go up to Jerusalem to those who were apostles before me, but I went away into Arabia; and again I returned to Damascus.

¹⁸ Then after three years, I went up to Jerusalem to become acquainted with Cephas and stayed with him fifteen days. ¹⁹ But I saw none of the other apostles except James, the Lord's brother. ²⁰ (Now in what I am writing to you, I assure you before God that I do not lie.) ²¹ Then I went into the regions of Syria and Cilicia. ²² I was still unknown by sight to the churches of Judea which were in Christ. ²³ They only heard it said, "He who once persecuted us is now preaching the faith he once tried to destroy." ²⁴ And they glorified God because of me.

Title Alx/Byz[**To the Galatians**], Minor[*variations of* The Letter of Paul the Apostle to the Galatians].

1:1 Alx/Byz[**Paul**], Alt[*without textual foundation* Saul (~JNT)].

1:3 Alx[**God our Father and the Lord Jesus Christ**], Byz[God the Father and our Lord Jesus Christ (ASV, DRA, HCS, KJV, MRD, NET, NJB, NKJ, REB, RSV, TLB)].

1:4 Alx/Byz[**for our sins** *or* for the sake of our sins], Major[for our sins *or* on account of our sins].

1:6 Alx/Byz[**the grace of Christ**], Minor[grace (~MRD, REB) *others* the grace of Jesus Christ *others* the grace of Christ Jesus *others* the grace of God].

1:8 Alx/Byz[**to you**], Minor[*omits* (NET, NIV, NLT, TLB)]; **angel** *or* messenger.

1:10 Alx[**If I were still trying**], Byz[For if I were still trying (KJV, MRD, NKJ)]; **servant** *Greek* slave.

1:11 Alx[**For I would have you know**], Byz[But I would have you know (~HCS, ~JNT, KJV, MRD, NAB, NET, ~NIV, NJB, NKJ, ~NLT, ~REB, ~TEV, ~TLB)].

1:15 Alx/Byz[**God**], Minor[*omits* (DRA, ESV, MRD, NAS, NET, RSV, Metzger)].

1:17 Alx/Byz[**up to Jerusalem**], Minor[away to Jerusalem (~DRA, ~MRD)].

1:18 Alx[**Cephas**], Byz[Peter (DRA, KJV, NIV, NKJ, NLT, TEV, TLB)].

2 ¹ Then after fourteen years I went up again to Jerusalem with Barnabas, taking Titus along also. ² I went up because of a revelation. And I set before them the gospel that I preach among the Gentiles. But I did this privately to those who were of repute, for fear that I was running or had run my race in vain. ³ Moreover, even Titus, who was with me, was not compelled to be circumcised, though he was a Greek ⁴ (and that because of the false brothers secretly brought in, who had slipped in to spy out our freedom which we have in Christ Jesus, in order to enslave us). ⁵ We did not yield to them even for a moment, so that the truth of the gospel might remain with you. ⁶ And from those who were reputed to be something (what they were makes no difference to me; God shows no partiality) – those, I say, who were of repute added nothing to me. ⁷ But on the contrary, when they saw that I had been entrusted with the gospel to the uncircumcised, just as Peter had been entrusted with the gospel to the circumcised ⁸ (for he who effectually worked for Peter in his apostleship to the circumcised effectually worked for me also to the Gentiles), ⁹ and when they perceived the grace that was given to me, James and Cephas and John, who were reputed to be pillars, gave to me and Barnabas the right hand of fellowship, that we should go to the Gentiles and they to the circumcised. ¹⁰ All they asked was that we should continue to remember the poor, the very thing I was eager to do.

¹¹ But when Cephas came to Antioch, I opposed him to his face, because he stood condemned. ¹² For before certain men came from James, he used to eat with the Gentiles; but when they came, he began to draw back and separate himself, fearing the party of the circumcision. ¹³ The rest of the Jews [also] joined him in hypocrisy, with the result that even Barnabas was carried away by their hypocrisy. ¹⁴ But when I saw that they were not straightforward about the truth of the gospel, I said to Cephas in the presence of them all, "If you, being a Jew, live like a Gentile and not like a Jew, how is it that you compel the Gentiles to live like Jews?"

¹⁵ We ourselves, who are Jews by birth and not Gentile sinners, ¹⁶ [yet] who know that a man is not justified by works of the law but through faith in Jesus Christ, even we have believed in Christ Jesus, so that we may be justified by faith in Christ, and not by works of the law, because by works of the law will no flesh be justified. ¹⁷ But if, while seeking to be justified in Christ, we ourselves have also been found sinners, is Christ then an agent of sin? Certainly not! ¹⁸ For if I rebuild what I destroyed, I prove myself a

---

2:1 Alx/Byz[**again**], Minor[*omits*].

2:4 Alx[**in order to enslave us**], Byz[that they might enslave us (ASV, DRA, ESV, JNT, KJV, NAB, NKJ, NRS, RSV)], Minor[in order to enslave me (MRD)].

2:5 Alx/Byz[*text*], Minor[I yielded to them only for a moment, so that the truth of the gospel would not be kept from you (~REB)].

2:7 Alx/Byz[**Peter**], Alt/Peshitta[Cephas (JNT, MRD)].

2:8 Alx/Byz[**Peter**], Alt/Peshitta[Cephas (JNT, MRD)].

2:9 Alx/Byz[**Cephas**], Minor[Peter (NIV, NLT, TEV, TLB)]; Alx/Byz[**that we should go to the Gentiles**], Major[that, on the one hand, we should go to the Gentiles].

2:10 **was eager** *or* had been eager.

2:11 Alx[**Cephas**], Byz[Peter (KJV, NKJ, NIV, NLT, TEV, TLB)].

2:12 Alx/Byz[**certain men**], Minor[a certain man (~ASV, ~KJV)].

2:13 Alx/Byz[**also**], Minor[*omits* (DRA, ESV, HCS, JNT, NAS, NAU, NIV, NJB, NLT, NRS, REB, RSV)].

2:14 Alx[**Cephas**], Byz[Peter (KJV, NKJ, NIV, NLT, TEV, TLB)]; Alx[**how is it that you**], Byz[why do you (JNT, KJV, MRD, NKJ, NLT, TEV)]; *the quotation may extend to the end of the chapter.*

2:16 Alx/Byz[**yet**], Major[*omits* (KJV, MRD, NIV, NKJ)]; Alx/Byz[**Jesus Christ…Christ Jesus**], Minor[Christ Jesus…Christ Jesus (JNT, NAS, NAU)], Alt[Jesus Christ…Jesus Christ (KJV, MRD, TLB) *others* Christ Jesus…Jesus Christ (REB)]; **faith in Jesus** *or* the faith of Jesus; **justified** *or* reckoned righteous; **faith in Christ** *or* the faith of Christ.

transgressor. [19] For through the law I died to the law, so that I might live to God. I have been crucified with Christ. [20] It is no longer I who live, but Christ who lives in me. And the life I now live in the flesh I live by faith in the Son of God, who loved me and gave himself for me. [21] I do not nullify the grace of God, for if righteousness comes through the Law, then Christ died for nothing.

3 [1] You foolish Galatians! Who has bewitched you, before whose eyes Jesus Christ was publicly portrayed as crucified? [2] This is the only thing I want to find out from you: did you receive the Spirit by the works of the Law, or by hearing with faith? [3] Are you so foolish? Having begun with the Spirit, are you now being perfected by the flesh? [4] Did you suffer so many things in vain – if it really was in vain? [5] Does he who supplies the Spirit to you and works miracles among you do so by works of the law, or by hearing with faith? [6] Even so Abraham *"believed God, and it was reckoned to him as righteousness."*

[7] Therefore, be sure that it is those who are of faith who are sons of Abraham. [8] And the Scripture, foreseeing that God would justify the Gentiles by faith, preached the gospel beforehand to Abraham, saying, *"In you will all the nations be blessed."* [9] So then those who are of faith are blessed with Abraham, the man of faith. [10] For all who rely on works of the law are under a curse; for it is written that: *"Cursed is everyone who does not obey all things written in the book of the law, to do them."* [11] Now that no one is justified by the Law before God is evident; for, *"The just shall live by faith."* [12] But the Law is not of faith; on the contrary, *"He who does them shall live by them."* [13] Christ redeemed us from the curse of the Law, having become a curse for us – because it is written, *"Cursed is everyone who hangs on a tree"* – [14] in order that in Christ Jesus the blessing of Abraham might come to the Gentiles, so that we might receive the promise of the Spirit through faith.

[15] To give a human example, brothers: even though it is only a man's covenant, yet when it has been ratified, no one sets it aside or adds conditions to it. [16] Now the promises were spoken to Abraham and to his seed. He does not say, "And to seeds," as referring to many, but rather to one, *"And to your seed,"* that is, Christ. [17] What I mean is this: the Law, which came four hundred and thirty years later, does not invalidate a covenant previously ratified by God, so as to nullify the promise. [18] For if the inheritance is based on the law, it is no longer based on a promise. But God gave it to Abraham by a

---

2:19 Alx[**I have been crucified with Christ 20**], Byz[20 I have been crucified with Christ (ASV, JNT, KJV, NAS, NAU, NET, NIV, NKJ, NLT, REB, RSV, TLB)].

2:20 Alx/Byz[**the Son of God**], Minor[God and Christ *others* God]; **by faith in the Son** *or* by the faith of the Son.

2:21 **righteousness** *or* justification.

3:1 Alx[**Who has bewitched you**], Byz[*adds* that you should not obey the truth (DRA, KJV, NKJ)]; Alx[**publicly portrayed as crucified**], Byz[*adds* among you (DRA, KJV, MRD, NKJ, NJB, NLT)].

3:6 Genesis 15:6.

3:8 **Genesis 12:3, 18:18**.

3:10 Alx[**it is written that**], Byz[*omits* that (ASV, DRA, ESV, HCS, JNT, KJV, MRD, NAB, NAS, NAU, NET, NIV, NJB, NKJ, NLT, NRS, REB, RSV, TEV, TLB)]; Alx[**obey all things**], Byz[obey in all things (ASV, DRA, ESV, KJV, NAB, NAS, NAU, NKJ, REB, RSV)]; **Deuteronomy 27:26 LXX**.

3:11 **The just shall live by faith** *or* The one who is righteous through faith shall live; Habakkuk 2:4.

3:12 Alx[**He who does them**], Byz[The man who does them (KJV, NIV, NKJ, TLB)]; **Leviticus 18:5**.

3:13 Alx[**because it is written**], Byz[for it is written (ASV, DRA, ESV, JNT, KJV, MRD, NAB, NAS, NAU, NIV, NKJ, NLT, NRS, REB, RSV, TEV, TLB)]; ~**Deuteronomy 21:23 LXX**.

3:14 Alx/Byz[**Christ Jesus**], Minor[Jesus Christ (JNT, KJV, MRD, REB, ~TLB)].

3:15 **covenant** *or* will.

3:16 Genesis 12:7.

3:17 Alx[**ratified by God**], Byz[*adds* in Christ (KJV, MRD, NKJ)]; **covenant** *or* will.

promise. ¹⁹ Why the Law then? It was added because of transgressions, having been ordained through angels by the agency of a mediator, until the seed would come to whom the promise had been made. ²⁰ Now a mediator does not represent just one party; but God is one.

²¹ Is the law then opposed to the promises [of God]? Certainly not! For if a law had been given which could impart life, then righteousness would indeed have come from the law. ²² But the Scripture has bound everyone under sin, so that what was promised by faith in Jesus Christ might be given to those who believe.

²³ Now before faith came, we were bound under the law, kept under restraint until faith should be revealed. ²⁴ So the law was our tutor to lead us to Christ, that we might be justified by faith. ²⁵ But now that faith has come, we are no longer under a tutor.

²⁶ For you are all sons of God, through faith in Christ Jesus. ²⁷ For all of you who were baptized into Christ have clothed yourselves with Christ. ²⁸ There is neither Jew nor Greek, there is neither slave nor free, there is neither male nor female; for you are all one in Christ Jesus. ²⁹ And if you belong to Christ, then you are Abraham's seed, heirs according to promise.

4 ¹ I mean that the heir, as long as he is a child, is no different from a slave, although he is the owner of all the estate; ² but he is under guardians and trustees until the date set by the father. ³ So also, when we were children, we were in slavery under the elements of the world. ⁴ But when the time had fully come, God sent forth his Son, born of a woman, born under the law, ⁵ to redeem those who were under the law, so that we might receive adoption as sons. ⁶ Because you are sons, God has sent the Spirit of his Son into our hearts, crying, "Abba! Father!" ⁷ So you are no longer a slave, but a son; and if a son, then an heir through God.

⁸ Formerly, when you did not know God, you were slaves to those which by nature are no gods. ⁹ But now that you have come to know God, or rather to be known by God, how is it that you turn back again to the weak and worthless elements? Do you desire to be enslaved all over again? ¹⁰ You observe days and months and seasons and years! ¹¹ I fear for you, that perhaps I have labored over you in vain.

¹² Brothers, I beg you, become as I am, for I also have become as you are. You have done me no wrong. ¹³ You know it was because of an illness in the flesh that I preached the gospel to you at first. ¹⁴ And though my fleshly condition was a trial to you, you did not despise or scorn me, but you received me as an angel of God, as Christ Jesus himself. ¹⁵ Where is the satisfaction you felt? For I bear you witness that, if possible, you would have plucked out your eyes and given them to me. ¹⁶ Have I now become your enemy by telling you the truth? ¹⁷ They seek you, but for no good purpose. They want to shut you out, so that you may seek them. ¹⁸ But it is always good to seek a good purpose, and not only when I am present with you. ¹⁹ My children, with whom I am again in labor until

---

3:19 Alx/Byz[**transgressions**], Minor[traditions].

3:21 Alx/Byz[**of God**], Minor[*omits* (REB)]; Alx/Byz[**from the law**], Minor[in the law].

3:22 **faith in Jesus** *or* the faith of Jesus.

3:24 **tutor to lead us to Christ** *or* guardian until the coming of Christ.

3:28 Alx/Byz[**for you are all one in Christ Jesus**], Minor[for you all belong to Christ Jesus].

3:29 Alx/Byz[**according to promise**], Minor[also according to promise (~TLB)].

4:6 Alx[**our hearts**], Byz[your hearts (DRA, KJV, MRD, NKJ)]; **Abba** *Aramaic* Father.

4:7 Alx[**heir through God**], Byz[heir of God through Christ (KJV, ~MRD, NKJ)].

4:14 Alx[**trial to you**], Byz[trial to me (KJV, ~MRD, NKJ)].

4:15 Alx[**Where is the satisfaction**], Byz[What has become of the satisfaction (HCS, JNT, NIV, NJB, NKJ, NRS, REB, RSV, TEV)].

4:17 Alx/Byz[**shut you out**], Minor[shut us out (~JNT, ~NIV, ~NJB, ~NLT, ~TEV, ~TLB)].

4:19 Alx[**My children**], Byz[My little children (ASV, DRA, ESV, KJV, NKJ, NRS, RSV)].

Christ is formed in you – [20] I could wish to be present with you now and to change my tone, for I am perplexed about you.

[21] Tell me, you who want to be under law, do you not listen to the law? [22] For it is written that Abraham had two sons, one by the slave-girl and one by the free. [23] But the son of the slave-girl was born from flesh, and the son of the free through promise. [24] This is allegorically speaking, for these women are two covenants. One is from Mount Sinai bearing children who are to be slaves; she is Hagar. [25] Now this Hagar is Mount Sinai in Arabia and corresponds to the present Jerusalem, for she is in slavery with her children. [26] But the Jerusalem above is free, and she is our mother. [27] For it is written,

> "Rejoice, O barren woman who does not bear.
> Break forth and shout, you who are not in labor.
> For the children of the desolate are more numerous
> than the children of her who has a husband."

[28] Now you, brothers, like Isaac, are children of promise. [29] But as at that time he who was born according to the flesh persecuted him who was born according to the Spirit, so it is now. [30] But what does the scripture say? "Cast out the slave and her son, for the son of the slave shall not inherit with the son of the free woman." [31] Therefore, brothers, we are not children of the slave, but of the free woman. [1] It was for freedom that Christ has set us free. Therefore keep standing firm and do not be subject again to a yoke of slavery.

[5] [2] Behold I, Paul, say to you that if you receive circumcision, Christ will be of no benefit to you. [3] I testify again to every man who receives circumcision, that he is under obligation to keep the whole Law. [4] You have been severed from Christ, you who are seeking to be justified by law; you have fallen away from grace. [5] For through the Spirit, by faith, we wait for the hope of righteousness. [6] For in Christ Jesus neither circumcision nor uncircumcision is of any avail, but faith working through love.

[7] You were running well; who hindered you from obeying [the] truth? [8] This persuasion did not come from him who calls you. [9] A little leaven leavens the whole lump of dough. [10] I have confidence in the Lord that you will take no other view than mine; and the one who is troubling you will bear his judgment, whoever he is. [11] But if I, brothers, still preach circumcision, why am I still persecuted? In that case the stumbling block of the cross has been abolished. [12] I wish that those who are troubling you would castrate themselves!

4:23 Alx[**through promise**], Byz[through the promise (~JNT, MRD, NAS, NAU, NET, NRS, ~REB, ~TEV, ~TLB)].

4:24 Alx/Byz[**two covenants**], Minor[the two covenants (DRA, HCS, KJV, MRD, NJB, NKJ, ~NLT, ~TLB)].

4:25 Alx[**Now this Hagar is Mount Sinai**], Byz[For this Hagar is Mount Sinai (KJV, MRD, ~NAB, NKJ)], Minor[For Sinai is a Mountain (DRA, ~NJB, ~NLT, ~REB)]; Alx[**for she is in slavery**], Byz[and she is in slavery (DRA, KJV, MRD, ~NIV, NKJ, ~NLT, TEV, ~TLB)].

4:26 Alx[**our mother**], Byz[the mother of us all (KJV, NKJ)].

4:27 **Isaiah 54:1 LXX**.

4:28 Alx[**you**], Byz[we (ASV, DRA, KJV, MRD, NKJ, RSV, TLB)].

4:30 Alx/Byz[**shall not inherit**], Major[cannot inherit *or* shall never inherit (HCS, NIV, TLB)]; ~**Genesis 21:10**.

4:31 Alx[**Therefore**], Byz[So then (DRA, ESV, JNT, KJV, MRD, NAS, NAU, NJB, NKJ, NLT, NRS, REB, RSV, TEV, ~TLB)].

5:1 Alx[**It was for freedom that Christ has set us free. Therefore keep standing firm**], Byz[Stand fast therefore in the freedom by which Christ has set us free (KJV, MRD, NKJ, ~TLB)].

5:2 Alx/Byz[**Paul**], Alt[*without textual foundation* Saul (~JNT)].

5:6 Alx/Byz[**Christ Jesus**], Minor[omits Jesus (TLB)], Alt[Jesus Christ (KJV)]; **working** *or* made effective.

5:7 Alx/Byz[**the truth**], Minor[omits the].

[13] For you were called to freedom, brothers; only do not use your freedom as an opportunity for the flesh, but through love serve one another. [14] For the whole law has been fulfilled in one word, *"You shall love your neighbor as yourself."* [15] But if you bite and devour one another, take care that you are not consumed by one another.

[16] But I say, walk by the Spirit, and you will never gratify the desires of the flesh. [17] For the desires of the flesh are against the Spirit, and the desires of the Spirit are against the flesh; for these are opposed to each other, so that you may not do what you would. [18] But if you are led by the Spirit, you are not under the Law. [19] Now the deeds of the flesh are obvious: immorality, impurity, lewdness, [20] idolatry, sorcery, hatred, rivalry, jealousy, outbursts of anger, disputes, dissensions, factions, [21] envies, bouts of drunkenness, carousings, and the like. I warn you, as I warned you before, that those who do such things will not inherit the kingdom of God.

[22] But the fruit of the Spirit is love, joy, peace, patience, kindness, goodness, faithfulness, [23] gentleness, self-control; against such things there is no law. [24] Those who belong to Christ [Jesus] have crucified the flesh with its passions and desires. [25] If we live by the Spirit, let us also walk by the Spirit. [26] Let us not become conceited, provoking one another, envying one another.

6 [1] Brothers, even if anyone is caught in a trespass, you who are spiritual, restore such a one in a spirit of gentleness; each one looking to yourself, so that you too will not be tempted. [2] Bear one another's burdens, and so you will fulfill the law of Christ. [3] For if anyone thinks he is something when he is nothing, he deceives himself. [4] But let each one test his own work, and then he will have reason to boast in himself alone, and not in his neighbor. [5] For each one will bear his own load. [6] Let the one who is taught the word share in all good things with him who teaches. [7] Do not be deceived; God is not mocked, for whatever a man sows, that he will also reap. [8] For the one who sows to his own flesh will from the flesh reap corruption. But the one who sows to the Spirit will from the Spirit reap eternal life. [9] Let us not lose heart in doing good, for in due time we will reap if we do not grow weary. [10] So then, as we have opportunity, let us do good to all people, and especially to those who are of the household of faith.

[11] See with what large letters I am writing to you with my own hand. [12] Those who want to make a good showing in the flesh try to compel you to be circumcised, and only in order that they may not be persecuted for the cross of Christ. [13] For those who are being circumcised do not even keep the Law themselves, but they desire to have you

---

5:14 Alx[**has been fulfilled**], Byz[is fulfilled (ASV, DRA, ESV, HCS, JNT, KJV, MRD, NAB, NAS, NAU, NET, NJB, NKJ, NLT, NRS, REB, RSV, TEV, TLB)]; Alx/Byz[**neighbor as yourself**], Major[neighbor as himself]; **Leviticus 19:18**.

5:17 Alx[**for these are opposed**], Byz[and these are opposed (HCS, JNT, KJV, MRD, ~NAB, ~NIV, ~NJB, NKJ, ~NLT, REB, TEV, TLB)].

5:19 Alx[**immorality**], Byz[adultery, immorality (KJV, NKJ)].

5:20 Alx[**rivalry, jealousy**], Byz[rivalries, jealousies (~ASV, DRA, ~JNT, ~KJV, NKJ, ~TEV)].

5:21 Alx[**envies**], Byz[*adds* murders (DRA, KJV, MRD, NET, NKJ, TLB)]; Alx[**as I warned you**], Byz[even as I warned you (ASV, KJV, NAS, NAU, NKJ)].

5:23 Alx/Byz[**self-control**], Minor[*adds* patience *others* chastity *others* faith, modesty, chastity (DRA)].

5:24 Alx[**Jesus**], Byz[*omits* (DRA, KJV, MRD, NET, NKJ, TLB)].

6:2 Alx[**and so you will fulfill**], Byz[and so fulfill (ASV, ESV, KJV, NAS, NAU, NKJ, NLT, RSV, TLB)].

6:4 Alx/Byz[**let each one** *or* let each man], Minor[*omits* each (MRD, ~NLT)], *NRS neutral plural.*

6:8 Alx/Byz[**eternal life**], Minor[*omits* eternal].

6:10 Alx/Byz[**as we have opportunity** *or* while we have opportunity], Minor[as we may have opportunity]; Alx/Byz[**let us do good**], Minor[we will do good].

6:12 Alx/Byz[**Christ**], Minor[*adds* Jesus].

6:13 Alx[**those who are being circumcised**], Byz[those who have been circumcised].

circumcised so that they may boast in your flesh. **14** But may it never be that I would boast, except in the cross of our Lord Jesus Christ, through which the world has been crucified to me, and I to the world. **15** For neither is circumcision anything, nor uncircumcision, but what counts is a new creation. **16** Peace and mercy be upon all who walk by this rule, upon the Israel of God.

17 From now on let no one cause me trouble, for I bear on my body the marks of Jesus.

18 The grace of our Lord Jesus Christ be with your spirit, brothers. Amen.

6:14 **which** *or* whom.

6:15 Alx[**For neither is circumcision anything, nor uncircumcision**], Byz[For in Christ Jesus neither circumcision nor uncircumcision avails anything (DRA, KJV, NKJ)].

6:17 Alx[**Jesus**], Byz[the Lord Jesus (DRA, KJV, MRD, NKJ)].

6:18 Alx/Byz[**grace of our Lord Jesus**], Minor[grace of the Lord Jesus]; Alx/Byz[**Amen**], Minor[*adds* To the Galatians, written from Rome (KJV)].

To the Ephesians

1 ¹ Paul, an apostle of Christ Jesus by the will of God, to the saints who are [in Ephesus] and faithful in Christ Jesus: ² grace and peace to you from God our Father and the Lord Jesus Christ.

³ Blessed be the God and Father of our Lord Jesus Christ, who has blessed us with every spiritual blessing in the heavenly places in Christ, ⁴ just as he chose us in him before the foundation of the world, that we would be holy and blameless before him. In love ⁵ he predestined us to be adopted as his sons through Jesus Christ, according to the good pleasure of his will, ⁶ to the praise of his glorious grace, which he freely bestowed on us in the Beloved. ⁷ In him we have redemption through his blood, the forgiveness of our trespasses, according to the riches of his grace ⁸ which he lavished on us. In all wisdom and insight ⁹ he made known to us the mystery of his will according to his good pleasure, which he purposed in Christ, ¹⁰ as a plan for the fullness of the times, to unite all things in Christ – things in heaven and things on earth – in him. ¹¹ And we have obtained an inheritance, having been predestined according to the purpose of him who works all things after the counsel of his will, ¹² in order that we, who were the first to hope in Christ, would be for the praise of his glory. ¹³ In him, you also have heard the word of truth, the gospel of your salvation. Having also believed, you were sealed in him with the promised Holy Spirit, ¹⁴ which is a deposit guaranteeing our inheritance, until the redemption of those who are God's possession – to the praise of his glory.

¹⁵ For this reason, ever since I heard of your faith in the Lord Jesus and your love for all the saints, ¹⁶ I do not cease giving thanks for you, remembering you in my prayers, ¹⁷ that the God of our Lord Jesus Christ, the Father of glory, may give to you a spirit of wisdom and of revelation in the knowledge of him. ¹⁸ I pray also that the eyes of [your] heart may be enlightened, so that you may know what is the hope to which he has called you, what are the riches of his glorious inheritance in the saints, ¹⁹ and what is the

---

Title Alx/Byz[**To the Ephesians**], Minor[*variations of* The Letter of Paul the Apostle to the Ephesians], Alt/Marcion[To the Laodiceans].

1:¹ Alx/Byz[**Paul**], Alt[*without textual foundation* Saul (~JNT)]; Alx[**Christ Jesus**], Byz[Jesus Christ (DRA, KJV, MRD, NKJ, TLB)]; Alx/Byz[**in Ephesus**], Minor[*omits* (NJB, RSV)], Alt/Marcion[in Laodicea]; **faithful** *or* believers.

1:³ Alx/Byz[**in Christ**], Minor[with Christ (MRD, NLT, TEV, TLB)]; **heavenly places** *or* heavenly things.

1:⁴ Alx/Major[**just as he chose**], Byz[just as he also chose].

1:⁴⁻⁵ **blameless before him. In love he predestined** *or* blameless before him in love. He predestined.

1:⁶ Alx[**which**], Byz[in which (DRA, ~ESV, KJV, NKJ, ~TLB)]; Alx/Byz[**in the Beloved**], Minor[in his beloved son (DRA, NET, NLT, ~REB, TEV, TLB)].

1:⁸⁻⁹ **on us. In all wisdom and insight 9 he made** *or* on us in all wisdom and insight. 9 He made

1:¹⁰ Alx/Byz[**in Christ**], Minor[in him (ESV, NRS, RSV)]; Alx/Byz[**things in heaven and things on earth**], Minor[both things in heaven and things on earth (HCS, KJV, NKJ)]; Alx/Byz[**earth – in him. 11 And we**], Major[earth. 11 In him we also (~ASV, ESV, JNT, MRD, NAB, ~NAS, ~NAU, NET, NIV, NJB, ~NLT, ~NRS, RSV, ~TEV, ~REB)].

1:¹¹ **we have obtained an inheritance** *or* we were made a heritage.

1:¹² **who were the first to hope in Christ** *or* who already had hope in Christ.

1:¹⁴ Alx[**which**], Byz[who (DRA, ESV, HCS, JNT, MRD, NAS, NAU, NET, NIV, NJB, NKJ, ~NLT, ~REB, ~TEV, ~TLB)].

1:¹⁵ Alx/Byz[**and your love**], Minor[*omits*].

1:¹⁷ **a spirit of wisdom** *or* the Spirit of wisdom.

1:¹⁸ Alx/Byz[**your**], Minor[*omits*]; Alx/Byz[**heart**], Minor[understanding (KJV, NJB, NKJ, REB, TEV)]; Alx[**what are the riches**], Byz[and what are the riches (DRA, KJV, MRD)].

immeasurable greatness of his power in us who believe. These are in accordance with the working of the strength of his might [20] which he worked in Christ when he raised him from the dead and seated him at his right hand in the heavenly places, [21] far above all rule and authority and power and dominion, and above every name that is named, not only in this age but also in the one to come. [22] And he put all things under his feet and appointed him to be the head over all things for the church, [23] which is his body – the fullness of him who fills all in all.

2 [1] And you were dead in your trespasses and sins, [2] in which you formerly walked according to the course of this world, according to the prince of the power of the air, the spirit that is now at work in the sons of disobedience. [3] Among them we all once lived in the lusts of our flesh, following the desires of flesh and mind, and so we were by nature children of wrath, like the rest of mankind. [4] But God, who is rich in mercy, because of his great love with which he loved us, [5] even when we were dead in our transgressions, made us alive together with Christ (by grace you have been saved), [6] and raised us up with him, and seated us with him in the heavenly places in Christ Jesus, [7] so that in the coming ages he might show the surpassing riches of his grace in kindness toward us in Christ Jesus. [8] For by grace you have been saved through faith; and this is not of yourselves, it is the gift of God – [9] not as a result of works, so that no one may boast. [10] For we are his workmanship, created in Christ Jesus for good works, which God prepared beforehand, that we would walk in them.

[11] Therefore remember that formerly you, the Gentiles in the flesh, who are called "Uncircumcision" by the so-called "Circumcision," which is performed in the flesh by human hands – [12] remember that you were at that time separated from Christ, excluded from the commonwealth of Israel, and strangers to the covenants of promise, having no hope and without God in the world. [13] But now in Christ Jesus you who once were far off have been brought near in the blood of Christ.

[14] For he himself is our peace, who has made both one and has broken down the dividing wall of hostility in his flesh, [15] by abolishing the Law of commandments and ordinances, so that he might create in himself one new man out of the two, thus making peace, [16] and might reconcile them both to God in one body through the cross, by which he put to death the hostility. [17] And he came and preached peace to you who were far away, and peace to those who were near; [18] for through him we both have our access in one Spirit to the Father. [19] So then you are no longer strangers and aliens, but you are fellow citizens with the saints, and are members of God's household, [20] having been built on the foundation of the apostles and prophets, Christ Jesus himself being the cornerstone, [21] in whom the whole building is joined together and rises to become a holy temple in the Lord; [22] in whom you also are being built together into a dwelling of God in the Spirit.

1:20 Alx/Byz[**which he worked**], Minor[which he had worked]; Alx/Byz[**the dead** Greek dead], Major[the dead].

1:23 **all in all** or everything in every way.

2:1 Alx[**your trespasses**], Byz[omits your (ESV, KJV, NJB, NKJ, NRS, RSV)].

2:5 Alx/Byz[**with Christ**], Minor[in Christ (DRA)]; Alx/Byz[**by grace**], Minor[by whose grace (DRA, ~MRD, ~NLT, ~TEV, ~TLB)].

2:11 Alx[**formerly you, the Gentiles**], Byz[you, formerly the Gentiles (DRA, JNT, KJV, MRD, NKJ, ~NLT, ~TEV, ~TLB)].

2:14-15 Alx[**broken down the dividing wall of hostility in his flesh 15**], Byz[broken down the dividing wall 15 of hostility in his flesh (ASV, JNT, KJV, NAS, NAU, ~NET, ~NIV, NKJ, ~RSV, TLB)].

2:16 **by which** or by whom.

2:17 Alx[**and peace to those who were near**], Byz[omits peace (KJV, MRD, NKJ, TEV, TLB)].

2:19 Alx[**but you are fellow citizens**], Byz[omits you are (HCS, KJV, NIV, NKJ, REB)].

2:20 Alx[**Christ Jesus**], Byz[Jesus Christ (DRA, JNT, KJV, MRD, NKJ, TLB)]; **cornerstone** or keystone.

2:21 Alx/Byz[**the whole building** or every building Greek omits the], Major[the whole building].

3 ¹ For this reason I, Paul, am the prisoner of Christ [Jesus] for the sake of you Gentiles – ² assuming that you have heard of the stewardship of God's grace that was given to me for you, ³ [that is], the mystery made known to me by revelation, as I have already written briefly. ⁴ When you read this, you can understand my insight into the mystery of Christ, ⁵ which was not made known to the sons of men in other generations as it has now been revealed to his holy apostles and prophets by the Spirit; ⁶ that is, how the Gentiles are fellow heirs and members of the same body, and partakers of the promise in Christ Jesus through the gospel. ⁷ Of this gospel I was made a minister according to the gift of God's grace which was given me by the working of his power. ⁸ To me, though I am the very least of all saints, this grace was given, to preach to the Gentiles the unsearchable riches of Christ, ⁹ and to reveal [to everyone] the administration of the mystery which for ages has been hidden in God who created all things; ¹⁰ so that the manifold wisdom of God might now be made known through the church to the principalities and powers in the heavenly places. ¹¹ This was according to the eternal purpose which he carried out in Christ Jesus our Lord, ¹² in whom we have boldness and confidence of access through our faith in him. ¹³ Therefore I ask you not to lose heart at my tribulations for you, which are your glory.

¹⁴ For this reason I bow my knees before the Father, ¹⁵ from whom every family in heaven and on earth derives its name, ¹⁶ that according to the riches of his glory he may grant you to be strengthened with power through his Spirit in the inner man, ¹⁷ so that Christ may dwell in your hearts through faith; and that you, being rooted and grounded in love, ¹⁸ may have power to comprehend with all the saints what is the breadth and length and height and depth, ¹⁹ and to know the love of Christ which surpasses knowledge, that you may be filled with all the fullness of God.

²⁰ Now to him who is able to do far more abundantly than all that we ask or think, according to the power that works within us, ²¹ to him be glory in the church and in Christ Jesus to all generations, for ever and ever. Amen.

3:1 Alx/Byz[**Paul**], Alt[*without textual foundation* Saul (~JNT)]; Alx/Byz[**Christ Jesus**], Minor[*omits* Jesus (TLB) *others read* the Lord Jesus (NJB)].

3:3 Alx/Byz[**that is**], Minor[*omits* (HCS, NJB, NLT, TEV, TLB)]; Alx[**made known**], Byz[he made known (KJV, NKJ, NLT, TEV, TLB)].

3:6 Alx[**the promise in Christ Jesus**], Byz[his promise in Christ (JNT, KJV, NKJ)], Minor[the promise in him (MRD)].

3:8 Alx/Major[**all saints**], Byz[all the saints (DRA, ESV, HCS, ~JNT, MRD, NAB, NET, ~NIV, ~NJB, NKJ, ~NLT, NRS, ~REB, RSV, ~TEV, ~TLB)]; Alx[**to the Gentiles**], Byz[among the Gentiles (DRA, KJV, MRD, NKJ)].

3:9 Alx/Byz[**to everyone**], Minor[*omits* (NAS, NAU, NJB, REB)]; Alx/Byz[**administration**], Minor[fellowship (KJV, NKJ)]; Alx[**created all things**], Byz[*adds* through Jesus Christ (KJV, NKJ)]; **reveal** *or* bring to light; **in God** *or* by God.

3:12 **our faith in him** *or* the faith of him.

3:13 Alx/Byz[**tribulations for you**], Minor[*omits* for you].

3:14 Alx[**the Father**], Byz[*adds* of our Lord Jesus Christ (DRA, KJV, MRD, NKJ)].

3:15 **every family** *or* all fatherhood *or* his whole family.

3:17-18 Alx[**and that you, being rooted and grounded in love 18**], Byz[18 and that you, being rooted and grounded in love].

3:18 Alx[**breadth and length and height and depth**], Byz[breadth and length and depth and height (KJV, NKJ, ~TLB)], Minor[height and depth and length and breadth (MRD)].

3:19 Alx/Byz[**that you may be filled with all the fullness of God**], Minor[that all the fullness of God may be complete].

3:20 Alx/Byz[**far more abundantly**], Major[for us more abundantly (MRD)], Minor/Vulgate[all things more abundantly (DRA)].

3:21 Alx[**and in Christ**], Byz[in Christ (KJV, MRD, NKJ, TLB)].

4

¹ I therefore, a prisoner for the Lord, beg you to lead a life worthy of the calling to which you have been called, ² with all humility and gentleness, with patience, showing tolerance for one another in love, ³ being diligent to preserve the unity of the Spirit in the bond of peace. ⁴ There is one body and one Spirit, just as you were called to the one hope that belongs to your call, ⁵ one Lord, one faith, one baptism, ⁶ one God and Father of all, who is over all and through all and in all.

⁷ But to each one of us grace was given according to the measure of Christ's gift. ⁸ Therefore it says,

> "When he ascended on high, he led a host of captives;
> he gave gifts to men."

⁹ (In saying, "He ascended," what does it mean except that he had also descended into the lower [parts] of the earth? ¹⁰ He who descended is also he who ascended far above all the heavens, so that he might fill all things.) ¹¹ And he gave some to be apostles, some prophets, some evangelists, some pastors and teachers, ¹² to equip the saints for the work of service, for the building up of the body of Christ; ¹³ until we all attain to the unity of the faith and of the knowledge of the Son of God, to become mature, to the measure of the stature of the fullness of Christ. ¹⁴ As a result, we are no longer to be children, tossed here and there by waves and carried about by every wind of doctrine, by the cunning of men, by their craftiness in deceitful scheming. ¹⁵ But speaking the truth in love, we are to grow up in all aspects into him, who is the head, into Christ, ¹⁶ from whom the whole body, being joined and held together by what every joint supplies, according to the proper working of each part, causes the growth of the body and builds itself up in love.

¹⁷ Now this I affirm and testify in the Lord, that you must no longer live as the Gentiles do, in the futility of their minds. ¹⁸ They are darkened in their understanding, alienated from the life of God because of the ignorance that is in them, due to the hardness of their heart. ¹⁹ And they, having become callous, have given themselves over to sensuality, greedy for the practice of every kind of impurity. ²⁰ But you did not learn Christ in this way, ²¹ assuming that you have heard about him and were taught in him, as the truth is in Jesus. ²² You were taught, with regard to your former manner of life, to put off your old self, which is being corrupted by its deceitful lusts; ²³ and be renewed in the spirit of your minds, ²⁴ and put on the new nature, created after the likeness of God in true righteousness and holiness.

²⁵ Therefore, laying aside falsehood, *each one of you must speak truth with his neighbor,* for we are members of one another. ²⁶ *Be angry, and yet do not sin;* do not let the sun go down on your anger, ²⁷ and do not give the devil an opportunity. ²⁸ He who has been stealing must steal no longer, but rather must labor, doing useful work with his [own] hands, so that he may have something to share with those in need. ²⁹ Let no unwholesome talk come out of your mouths, but only such as is good for building others up according to the need of the

---

4:6 Alx[**in all**], Byz[in us all (DRA, MRD, TLB)], Minor[in you all (KJV, NKJ)].

4:8 Alx[**he gave gifts**], Byz[and he gave gifts (ASV, ESV, JNT, KJV, MRD, NAS, NAU, NIV, NKJ, NLT, RSV)]; **it says** *or* he says; ~**Psalms 68:18**.

4:9 Alx[**descended**], Byz[*adds* first (DRA, JNT, KJV, MRD, NKJ, TEV, TLB)]; Alx/Byz[**parts**], Minor[*omits* (~NLT, REB)].

4:16 Alx/Byz[**part**], Minor[member (MRD)].

4:17 Alx[**the Gentiles**], Byz[the rest of the Gentiles (KJV, MRD, NKJ)].

4:19 Alx/Byz[**callous**], Minor[despairing (DRA, MRD)].

4:25 Zechariah 8:16.

4:26 Psalms 4:4 LXX.

4:27 Alx/Byz[**and do not give the devil**], Minor[neither give the devil (ASV, ~JNT, KJV, NKJ, ~TLB)].

4:28 Alx[**own**], Byz[*omits* (ASV, DRA, KJV, MRD, NKJ, ~NLT, REB, RSV, TEV)].

4:29 Alx/Byz[**need**], Minor[faith (DRA)].

moment, that it may impart grace to those who hear. [30] And do not grieve the Holy Spirit of God, in whom you were sealed for the day of redemption. [31] Let all bitterness and wrath and anger and clamor and slander be put away from you, along with all malice. [32] [And] be kind and tenderhearted to one another, forgiving each other, just as God in Christ forgave you.

5 [1] Therefore be imitators of God, as beloved children. [2] And walk in love, just as Christ loved us and gave himself up for us as a fragrant offering and sacrifice to God. [3] But immorality or any impurity or greed must not even be named among you, as is proper among saints. [4] And there must be no filthiness and silly talk, or coarse jesting, which are not fitting, but rather let there be thanksgiving. [5] For of this you can be sure, that no immoral, impure, or covetous person – such a man is an idolater – has any inheritance in the kingdom of Christ and of God.

[6] Let no one deceive you with empty words, for because of these things the wrath of God comes upon the sons of disobedience. [7] Therefore do not be partners with them; [8] for once you were darkness, but now you are light in the Lord. Walk as children of light [9] (for the fruit of the light consists in all goodness and righteousness and truth), [10] and try to learn what is pleasing to the Lord. [11] Do not participate in the unfruitful deeds of darkness, but instead expose them. [12] For it is a shame even to speak of the things that they do in secret. [13] But all things become visible when they are exposed by the light, [14] for everything that becomes visible is light. For this reason it is said,

> "Awake, O sleeper,
>   and arise from the dead,
> and Christ will shine upon you."

[15] Be careful, then, how you walk, not as unwise men, but as wise, [16] making the most of your time, because the days are evil. [17] Therefore do not be foolish, but understand what the will of the Lord is. [18] And do not get drunk with wine, for that is recklessness; but be filled with the Spirit, [19] speaking to one another [in] psalms and hymns and spiritual songs, singing and making melody with your heart to the Lord, [20] always giving thanks to God the Father for everything, in the name of our Lord Jesus Christ.

[21] Be subject to one another out of reverence for Christ. [22] Wives: to your husbands, as to the Lord. [23] For a husband is the head of his wife, as Christ is the head of the church.

4:32 Alx/Byz[**And be kind**], Minor[omits And (ESV, NAU, NIV, NJB, REB)]; Alx[**forgave you**], Byz[forgave us (MRD)].

5:2 Alx/Byz[**loved us**], Minor[loved you (ASV, NAS, NAU, NJB, REB, TLB)]; Alx/Byz[**gave himself up for us**], Minor[gave himself up for you (REB, TLB)].

5:4 Alx/Byz[**and silly talk**], Minor[or silly talk (ASV, DRA, ESV, KJV, MRD, NAB, ~NET, ~NIV, NJB, NKJ, ~NLT, ~NRS, REB, RSV, TEV)].

5:5 Alx[**of this you can be sure**], Byz[this you know (HCS, KJV, MRD, NKJ)]; Alx/Byz[**of the Christ and of God** or of the Christ and God], Minor[omits of the Christ (NJB)].

5:9 Alx[**light**], Byz[Spirit (KJV, NKJ)].

5:13-14 Alx[**14 for everything that becomes visible is light**], Byz[for everything that becomes visible is light 14 (ASV, DRA, KJV, MRD, NAS, NAU, NKJ, REB, RSV, TLB)].

5:14 Alx/Byz[**Christ will shine upon you**], Minor[Christ will touch you]; *possible allusion to Isaiah 60:1.*

5:15 Alx/Byz[**Be careful, then**], Minor[adds brothers (DRA)]; Alx/Byz[**how you walk**], Minor[omits how (KJV, MRD, ~NJB, NKJ)].

5:17 Alx[**understand**], Byz[understanding (DRA, KJV, ~NET)].

5:19 Alx[**in psalms**], Byz[omits in (JNT, NJB, NLT, NRS, TLB)]; Alx/Byz[**spiritual**], Minor[omits (MRD, REB)].

5:21 Alx/Byz[**Christ**], Minor[God (KJV, NKJ)].

5:22 Alx[**Wives: to your husbands**], Byz[Wives, be subject to your husbands (ASV, ESV, HCS, JNT, KJV, MRD, NAB, NAS, NAU, NET, NIV, NJB, NKJ, NLT, NRS, REB, RSV, TEV, TLB)], Minor[Let wives be subject to their own husbands (DRA)].

He himself is the Savior of The Body. ²⁴ As the church is subject to Christ, so let wives also be subject to their husbands in everything. ²⁵ Husbands, love your wives, just as Christ loved the church and gave himself up for her, ²⁶ that he might sanctify her, having cleansed her by the washing of water with the word, ²⁷ that he might present the church to himself in all its glory, without spot or wrinkle or any such thing, that she might be holy and blameless. ²⁸ So husbands ought [also] to love their wives as their own bodies. He who loves his wife loves himself. ²⁹ For no one ever hated his own flesh, but nourishes and cherishes it, just as Christ also does the church, ³⁰ because we are members of his body. ³¹ *"For this reason a man shall leave father and mother and be joined to his wife, and the two shall become one flesh."* ³² This is a profound mystery; but I am saying that it refers to Christ and the church. ³³ However, each one of you must also love his wife as himself, and the wife must see that she respects her husband.

6 ¹ Children, obey your parents [in the Lord], for this is right. ² *"Honor your father and mother"* (which is the first commandment with a promise), ³ *"that it may be well with you and that you may live long on the earth."* ⁴ Fathers, do not provoke your children to anger, but bring them up in the discipline and instruction of the Lord.

⁵ Slaves, be obedient to those who are your masters according to the flesh, with fear and trembling, in sincerity of heart, as to Christ; ⁶ not in the way of eye-service, as men-pleasers, but as slaves of Christ, doing the will of God from the heart. ⁷ Render service with good will, as to the Lord, and not to men, ⁸ knowing that whatever good thing each one does, this he will receive back from the Lord, whether he is a slave or free. ⁹ Masters, do the same to them, and give up threatening, knowing that he who is both their Master and yours is in heaven, and that there is no partiality with him.

¹⁰ Finally, be strong in the Lord and in the strength of his might. ¹¹ Put on the full armor of God, so that you may be able to stand against the schemes of the devil. ¹² For our struggle is not against flesh and blood, but against the rulers, against the powers, against the world forces of this darkness, against the spiritual forces of wickedness in the heavenly places. ¹³ Therefore take up the full armor of God, that you may be able to resist in the evil day and, having done everything, to stand firm. ¹⁴ Stand firm therefore, having girded your loins with truth, and having put on the breastplate of righteousness, ¹⁵ and having shod your feet with the preparation of the gospel of peace; ¹⁶ in all this, taking up the shield of

---

5:23 Alx/Major[**a husband**], Byz[the husband (ASV, DRA, ESV, HCS, JNT, KJV, MRD, NAB, NAS, NAU, NET, NIV, NKJ, NRS, REB, RSV)]; Alx[**he himself is the Savior**], Byz[and he himself is the Savior (ESV, HCS, KJV, MRD, NJB, NKJ, REB, RSV, TEV, ~TLB)].

5:24 Alx[**their husbands**], Byz[their own husbands (KJV, NKJ)].

5:26 **having cleansed her** *or* cleansing her.

5:27 Alx[**all its glory**], Byz[all her glory (NAS, NAU, NJB, NLT)].

5:28 Alx[**also**], Byz[*omits* (JNT, KJV, MRD, NAS, NAU, NKJ, TLB)].

5:29 Alx[**Christ**], Byz[the Lord (KJV, NKJ)].

5:30 Alx[**of his body**], Byz[*adds* of his flesh and of his bones (DRA, KJV, MRD, NKJ)].

5:31 Alx[**father**], Byz[his father (ASV, DRA, ESV, HCS, JNT, KJV, MRD, NAB, NAS, NAU, NET, NIV, NJB, NKJ, NLT, NRS, REB, RSV, TEV, TLB)]; Alx/Byz[**his wife**], Minor[the wife]; Genesis 2:24.

6:1 Alx/Byz[**in the Lord**], Minor[*omits* (REB, TLB)].

6:2-3 **Exodus 20:12, Deuteronomy 5:16.**

6:7 Alx/Byz[**as to the Lord**], Minor[to the Lord (NAB, NJB)].

6:9 Alx[**he who is both their Master and yours**], Byz[your own Master (KJV, MRD, NKJ, ~REB, ~TLB)].

6:10 Alx[**Finally**], Byz[*adds* my brothers (~DRA, KJV, MRD, NKJ)].

6:12 Alx/Byz[**our struggle**], Minor[your struggle]; Alx[**this darkness**], Byz[the darkness of this world *or* the darkness of this age (ESV, KJV, MRD, NAB, NIV, NJB, NKJ, NLT, NRS, REB, RSV, TEV, TLB)], Minor[the darkness].

6:16 Alx[**in all this**], Byz[above all this (~JNT, KJV, NKJ, TEV)]; Alx/Byz[**the flaming**], Minor[*omits*

faith, with which you can extinguish all [the] flaming arrows of the evil one. [17] And take the helmet of salvation, and the sword of the spirit, which is the word of God. [18] Pray at all times in the Spirit, with all prayer and petition. And with this in view, keep alert with all perseverance and petition for all the saints, [19] and also pray for me, that in the opening of my mouth, utterance may be given me so that I will fearlessly make known the mystery of the gospel, [20] for which I am an ambassador in chains; that in it I may speak boldly, as I ought to speak.

[21] Tychicus, the beloved brother and faithful minister in the Lord, will tell you everything, so that you also may know how I am and what I am doing. [22] I have sent him to you for this very purpose, that you may know how we are, and that he may encourage your hearts.

[23] Peace be to the brothers, and love with faith, from God the Father and the Lord Jesus Christ. [24] Grace be with all who love our Lord Jesus Christ with an undying love.

---

the].

6:17 Alx/Byz[**And take**], Major[And to take].

6:19 Alx/Byz[**of the gospel**], Minor[*omits* (~TLB)].

6:20 Alx/Byz[**that in it I may speak**], Minor[that I may speak it (ESV, ~JNT, MRD, ~NAB, ~NAS, ~NAU, ~NET, NIV, ~NJB, ~NLT, NRS, REB, RSV, ~TEV, ~TLB)].

6:24 Alx[*or* Grace and immortality be with all who love our Lord Jesus Christ], Byz[*adds* Amen (DRA, MRD, NKJ, ~TLB)], Minor[*adds* To the Ephesians written from Rome, by Tychicus (KJV)].

To the Philippians

1 [1] Paul and Timothy, servants of Christ Jesus, to all the saints in Christ Jesus who are at Philippi, with the overseers and deacons: [2] grace and peace to you from God our Father and the Lord Jesus Christ.

[3] I thank my God in all my remembrance of you, [4] always, in every prayer of mine, making my prayer with joy for you all, [5] because of your partnership in the gospel from the first day until now. [6] I am confident of this, that he who began a good work in you will carry it on to completion until the day of Christ Jesus. [7] For it is only right for me to feel this way about you all, because I have you in my heart, since both in my imprisonment and in the defense and confirmation of the gospel you all are partakers of grace with me. [8] For God is my witness, how I long for you all with the affection of Christ Jesus. [9] And this is my prayer, that your love may abound still more and more in real knowledge and all discernment, [10] so that you may approve what is excellent, and may be pure and blameless until the day of Christ; [11] having been filled with the fruit of righteousness which comes through Jesus Christ, to the glory and praise of God.

[12] Now I want you to know, brothers, that what has happened to me has really served to advance the gospel, [13] so that my imprisonment for Christ has become well known throughout the whole praetorium and to everyone else, [14] and that most of the brothers, trusting in the Lord because of my imprisonment, have been encouraged to speak the word without fear.

[15] Some indeed preach Christ from envy and rivalry, but others from good will. [16] The latter do it out of love, knowing that I am put here for the defense of the gospel. [17] The former proclaim Christ out of selfish ambition, not sincerely, but thinking to raise trouble in my imprisonment. [18] What then? Only that in every way, whether in pretense or in truth, Christ is proclaimed; and in this I rejoice. Yes, and I will rejoice, [19] for I know that through your prayers and the help of the Spirit of Jesus Christ this will turn out for my deliverance, [20] as it is my eager expectation and hope that I will not be ashamed in anything, but that with full courage now as always Christ will be exalted in my body, whether by life or by death. [21] For to me, to live is Christ and to die is gain. [22] But if I am to live on in the flesh, this will mean fruitful labor for me. Yet which I shall choose I do not know. [23] But I am hard pressed between the two. My desire is to depart and be with Christ, [for] that is far better. [24]

Title Alx/Byz[**To the Philippians**], Minor[*variations of* The Letter of Paul the Apostle to the Philippians].

1:1 Alx/Byz[**Paul**], Alt[*without textual foundation* Saul (~JNT)]; Alx[**Christ Jesus**], Byz[Jesus Christ (DRA, KJV, MRD, NKJ, TLB)]; **servants** *or* slaves; **overseers** *or* bishops; **deacons** *or* assistants.

1:6 Alx/Major[**Christ Jesus**], Byz[Jesus Christ (ASV, ESV, KJV, MRD, NJB, NKJ, NRS, RSV, TLB)].

1:7 Alx/Byz[**in the defense**], Minor[to the defense *or* with the defense (~JNT, NIV, NJB, REB, TEV, TLB)]; **For it is only right** *Greek* Even as it is only right.

1:8 Alx[**Christ Jesus**], Byz[Jesus Christ (DRA, KJV, MRD, NKJ, TLB)].

1:11 Alx[**fruit**], Byz[fruits (ASV, KJV, MRD, NJB, NKJ, ~REB, RSV, TEV, TLB)].

1:14 Alx/Byz[**word**], Minor[*adds* of God (ASV, DRA, JNT, MRD, NAS, NAU, NIV, NLT, REB, RSV)].

1:16-17 Alx[*text*], Byz[*places verse 17 before verse 16* (KJV, NKJ)].

1:17 Alx[**raise trouble** *Greek* raise tribulation], Byz[cause trouble (~ESV, HCS, KJV, MRD, NAB, NAS, NAU, NET, NJB, NKJ, ~NLT, NRS, REB, RSV, ~TEV, ~TLB)].

1:18 Alx[**Only that**], Byz[*omits* that (KJV, NAB, REB, TEV)].

1:19 Alx/Byz[**for I know**], Minor[but I know]; **deliverance** *or* salvation.

1:23 Alx/Byz[**But**], Minor[For (~ESV, ~NAB, ~HCS, ~JNT, KJV, MRD, ~NET, ~NIV, ~NJB, NKJ, ~NLT, ~NRS, ~REB, ~RSV, ~TEV, ~TLB)]; Alx/Byz[**for that**], Major[which (DRA, HCS, ~JNT, KJV, NET, NIV, NJB, NKJ, NLT, ~REB, TEV, ~TLB)].

1:24 Alx/Byz[**in**], Minor[to *or* with *or* in (NLT, TEV, TLB)].

But to remain [in] the flesh is more necessary for your sake. [25] Convinced of this, I know that I will remain and continue with you all, for your progress and joy in the faith, [26] so that your proud confidence in me may abound in Christ Jesus through my coming to you again.

[27] Only conduct yourselves in a manner worthy of the gospel of Christ, so that whether I come and see you or remain absent, I will hear of you that you stand firm in one spirit, with one mind striving together for the faith of the gospel, [28] in no way frightened by your opponents. This is a sign of destruction to them, but of your salvation – and this is from God. [29] For to you it has been granted for the sake of Christ, not only to believe in him, but also to suffer for his sake, [30] having the same conflict which you saw in me, and now hear to be in me.

2 [1] Therefore if there is any encouragement in Christ, if there is any consolation of love, if there is any fellowship of the Spirit, if any affection and compassion, [2] make my joy complete by being of the same mind, having the same love, being one in spirit and purpose. [3] Do nothing from selfishness nor from empty conceit, but in humility consider others better than yourselves, [4] each of you looking not only to your own interests, but [also] to the interests of others. [5] Have this attitude in yourselves which was also in Christ Jesus, [6] who, though he was in the form of God, did not consider equality with God a thing to be seized, [7] but emptied himself, taking the form of a servant, being made in the likeness of men. [8] And being found in appearance as a man, he humbled himself and became obedient to death – even death on a cross. [9] Therefore God also highly exalted him, and bestowed on him the name which is above every name, [10] that at the name of Jesus every knee should bow, in heaven and on earth and under the earth, [11] and every tongue confess that Jesus Christ is Lord, to the glory of God the Father.

[12] Therefore, my beloved, as you have always obeyed, so now, not only as in my presence but much more in my absence, work out your own salvation with fear and trembling; [13] for God is the one who works in you, both to will and to work for his good pleasure. [14] Do all things without grumbling or arguing, [15] so that you may be blameless and innocent, children of God without blemish in the midst of a crooked and perverse generation, among whom you shine as lights in the world, [16] holding fast the word of life, so that in the day of Christ I may be proud that I did not run in vain or labor in vain. [17] But even if I am being poured out as a drink offering upon the sacrifice and service of your faith, I am glad and rejoice with you all. [18] So you too should be glad and rejoice with me.

[19] I hope in the Lord Jesus to send Timothy to you soon, that I also may be cheered when I receive news of you. [20] I have no one else like him, who will be genuinely concerned for your welfare. [21] For they all seek after their own interests, not those of Jesus Christ. [22] But you know that he has proved his worth, because as a son with his father he has served with

---

1:28 Alx[**but of your salvation**], Byz[but to you of salvation (DRA, ~JNT, KJV, ~NIV, ~NJB, NKJ, ~NLT, TLB)].

2:2 Alx/Byz[**being one**], Minor[being the same (HCS)].

2:3 Alx[**nor from empty conceit**], Byz[or empty conceit (ESV, HCS, JNT, KJV, NAS, NAU, NET, NIV, NJB, NKJ, ~NLT, NRS, REB, RSV, ~TLB)].

2:4 Alx[**each of you looking**], Byz[Each of you should look (ESV, HCS, JNT, KJV, MRD, NAS, NAU, NET, NIV, NKJ, NLT, NRS, REB, RSV, TEV, TLB)]; Alx/Byz[**also**], Minor[omits (DRA, JNT, NJB, NRS, REB)]; **not only to your own** Greek not to your own.

2:5 Alx[**Have this attitude**], Byz[For let this attitude be (DRA)].

2:9 Alx[**the name**], Byz[a name (DRA, KJV, MRD, TLB)].

2:12 Alx/Byz[**as in my presence**], Minor[omits as (HCS, JNT, MRD, NAB, NET, NIV, NJB, NLT, NRS, ~REB, TEV, TLB)].

2:15 Alx[**without blemish**], Byz[without blame (DRA, KJV, ~NAS, ~NAU, NKJ, ~NLT)].

2:16 **holding fast** or holding out.

2:20 or No one here thinks like I do; he will be genuinely concerned for your welfare.

2:21 Alx[**Jesus Christ**], Byz[the Christ, Jesus (JNT)], Major[Christ Jesus (NAS, NAU, NKJ, REB)].

me in the work of the gospel. [23] Therefore I hope to send him immediately, as soon as I see how things go with me. [24] And I trust in the Lord that shortly I myself will come also.

[25] But I thought it necessary to send to you Epaphroditus, my brother and fellow worker and fellow soldier, who is also your messenger and minister to my need. [26] For he was longing for you all and was distressed because you had heard that he was ill. [27] Indeed he was ill, near to death. But God had mercy on him, and not only on him but on me also, lest I should have sorrow upon sorrow. [28] Therefore I am all the more eager to send him, so that when you see him again you may rejoice and I may have less anxiety. [29] So receive him in the Lord with all joy. And honor men like him, [30] because he almost died for the work of Christ, risking his life to complete what was deficient in your service to me.

3 [1] Finally, my brothers, rejoice in the Lord. To write the same things to you again is no trouble to me, and it is a safeguard for you.

[2] Watch out for the dogs. Watch out for the evil workers. Watch out for those mutilators of the body. [3] For we are the true circumcision, who worship in the Spirit of God, and glory in Christ Jesus, and put no confidence in the flesh, [4] though I myself have reasons for confidence in the flesh. If anyone else thinks he has reasons to put confidence in the flesh, I have more: [5] circumcised on the eighth day, of the people of Israel, of the tribe of Benjamin, a Hebrew of Hebrews; as to the law, a Pharisee; [6] as to zeal, a persecutor of the church; as to righteousness under the law, blameless. [7] [But] whatever was gain to me, I counted as loss for the sake of Christ. [8] More than that, I count everything to be loss because of the surpassing worth of knowing Christ Jesus my Lord. For his sake I have suffered the loss of all things, and count them as rubbish, in order that I may gain Christ [9] and be found in him, not having a righteousness of my own that comes from the law, but that which is through faith in Christ – the righteousness that comes from God and is by faith, [10] that I may know him, and the power of his resurrection, and the fellowship of his sufferings, becoming like him in his death – [11] in order that I may attain to the resurrection from the dead.

[12] Not that I have already obtained this, or have already been made perfect, but I press on to take hold of that for which Christ [Jesus] took hold of me. [13] Brothers, I do not consider myself to have taken hold of it; but one thing I do: forgetting what lies behind and straining forward to what lies ahead, [14] I press on toward the goal for the prize of the upward call of God in Christ Jesus. [15] Let those of us who are mature have this attitude; and

---

2:24 Alx/Byz[**come**], Minor[*adds* to you (DRA, MRD, NET, NLT, TEV, TLB)].

2:25 **messenger** *or* apostle.

2:26 Alx/Byz[**longing for you all**], Minor[longing to see you all (MRD, NLT, TEV)].

2:27 Alx/Major[**ill, near to death**], Byz[near illness of death (~REB)].

2:30 Alx/Byz[**work of Christ**], Minor[work of the Lord *others* work *others* work of God]; Alx[**risking his life**], Byz[not regarding his life (KJV, MRD, NKJ, ~NLT)].

3:1 **rejoice** *or* farewell *the Greek expression is a greeting.*

3:3 Alx/Byz[**worship in the Spirit of God**], Minor[worship God in spirit (DRA, KJV, MRD, NKJ, RSV, TLB)].

3:7 Alx/Byz[**But**], Minor[*omits*].

3:8 Alx/Byz[**More than that, I count**], Major[But indeed, I also count (ASV, ~HCS, KJV, MRD, ~NJB, NKJ, ~NLT)].

3:9 **through faith in Christ** *or* through the faith of Christ.

3:10 Alx/Byz[**the fellowship**], Minor[*omits* the (ESV, MRD, NET, NJB, NLT, REB, RSV, TEV, TLB)].

3:11 Alx[**from the dead**], Byz[of the dead (KJV)].

3:12 Alx/Byz[**Jesus**], Minor[*omits* (REB, TLB)]; **been made perfect** *or* reached the goal.

3:13 Alx/Major[**consider myself**], Byz[*adds* yet (ASV JNT, NAS, NAU, NIV, REB, TEV, TLB)]; Alx/Major[**but one thing...14**], Byz[14 but one thing...].

3:14 Alx[**toward the goal**], Byz[because of the goal (~MRD, ~NET, ~NLT)].

if in anything you have a different attitude, God will reveal that also to you. [16] Only let us live up to what we have already attained.

[17] Brothers, join in following my example, and observe those who live according to the pattern you have in us. [18] For many, of whom I have often told you and now tell you even with tears, live as enemies of the cross of Christ. [19] Their end is destruction, their god is the belly, and they glory in their shame, with minds set on earthly things. [20] For our citizenship is in heaven, from which also we eagerly wait for a Savior, the Lord Jesus Christ; [21] who will transform our lowly body – conformed to his glorious body, by the power that enables him even to subject all things to himself. [1] Therefore, my brothers, whom I love and long for, my joy and crown, stand firm – as beloved – in the Lord.

4 [2] I plead with Euodia and I plead with Syntyche to agree with each other in the Lord. [3] Yes, and I ask you also, true yoke-fellow, to help these women who have struggled at my side in the cause of the gospel, together with Clement also and the rest of my fellow workers, whose names are in the book of life. [4] Rejoice in the Lord always. Again I will say, Rejoice! [5] Let your gentle spirit be known to all men. The Lord is near. [6] Do not be anxious about anything. But in everything, by prayer and supplication, with thanksgiving, let your requests be made known to God. [7] And the peace of God, which passes all understanding, will guard your hearts and your minds in Christ Jesus.

[8] Finally, brothers, whatever is true, whatever is honorable, whatever is right, whatever is pure, whatever is lovely, whatever is gracious, if there is any excellence, if there is anything worthy of praise, think about these things. [9] Practice what you have learned and received and heard and seen in me, and the God of peace will be with you.

[10] I rejoice in the Lord greatly, that now at last you have revived your concern for me. Indeed, you were concerned before, but you had no opportunity. [11] Not that I speak from want, for I have learned to be content in whatever circumstances I am. [12] I know how to be in need, and I also know how to have plenty. In any and every circumstance I have learned the secret of being filled and going hungry, both of having abundance and want. [13] I can do all things through him who strengthens me. [14] Yet it was good of you to share in my troubles.

[15] You yourselves also know, Philippians, that in the first preaching of the gospel, when I left Macedonia, no church shared with me in the matter of giving and receiving except you only. [16] For even in Thessalonica you sent once and again to my need. [17] Not that I seek the gift itself, but I seek for the profit which increases to your account. [18] I have

---

3:16 Alx[**what**], Byz[the rule (ASV, DRA, ~HCS, KJV, MRD, NAS, NAU, NET, NKJ, TEV, ~TLB)]; Alx[**attained**], Byz[*adds* let us be of the same mind (DRA, KJV, MRD, NKJ)].

3:20 Alx/Byz[**For our citizenship**], Minor[But our citizenship (DRA, ESV, HCS, JNT, MRD, NAB, NET, NIV, NJB, NLT, NRS, ~REB, RSV, ~TEV, TLB)]; **citizenship** *or* commonwealth.

3:21 Alx[**conformed**], Byz[that it might be conformed (ASV, ~DRA, ESV, ~HCS, ~JNT, KJV, MRD, NIV, NKJ, NRS, RSV, ~TEV)].

4:1 Alx/Byz[**as beloved**], Minor[as my beloved (ASV, DRA, ESV, JNT, KJV, MRD, NAS, NAU, NET, NRS, REB, RSV, TLB)].

4:2 Alx/Byz[**Euodia** *feminine*], Alt[*without textual foundation* Euodias *masculine* (KJV, MRD, TLB)].

4:3 Alx/Byz[**Yes**], Minor[And (DRA, JNT, KJV, MRD, NJB, NKJ, NLT, RSV, TEV, TLB)]; **yoke-fellow** *or a name* Syzygus.

4:4 **Rejoice** *or* Farewell *the Greek expression is a greeting.*

4:7 Alx/Byz[**your hearts and your minds**], Minor[*adds* and your bodies *others* your hearts and your bodies].

4:8 Alx/Byz[**anything worthy of praise**], Minor[any understanding worthy of praise *others* any discipline worthy of praise (DRA, MRD)]; **think about** *Greek* take account of.

4:10 **rejoice** *or* rejoiced.

4:12 Alx/Byz[**I know how to be in need, and I also know** *or* I know both how to be in need, and I know], Minor[But I know how to be in need, and I know].

4:13 Alx[**through him**], Byz[through Christ (KJV, MRD, NKJ, NLT, TEV, TLB)].

received full payment and even more. I am amply supplied, having received from Epaphroditus the gifts you sent, a fragrant offering, an acceptable sacrifice, pleasing to God. ¹⁹ And my God will supply all your needs according to his riches in glory in Christ Jesus. ²⁰ To our God and Father be glory for ever and ever. Amen.

²¹ Greet every saint in Christ Jesus. The brothers who are with me greet you. ²² All the saints greet you, especially those of Caesar's household. ²³ The grace of the Lord Jesus Christ be with your spirit.

To the Colossians

1 ¹ Paul, an apostle of Christ Jesus by the will of God, and Timothy our brother, ² to the saints and faithful brothers in Christ who are at Colossae: grace to you and peace from God our Father.

³ We always thank God, the Father of our Lord Jesus Christ, when we pray for you, ⁴ because we have heard of your faith in Christ Jesus and of the love which you have for all the saints, ⁵ because of the hope laid up for you in heaven. Of this you have heard before in the word of the truth, the gospel ⁶ which has come to you, just as in all the world it is bearing fruit and growing, even as it has been doing among you since the day you heard it and understood the grace of God in truth; ⁷ as you learned it from Epaphras, our beloved fellow servant, who is a faithful minister of Christ on your behalf, ⁸ and who also told us of your love in the Spirit.

⁹ For this reason also, since the day we heard it, we have not ceased to pray for you, asking that you may be filled with the knowledge of his will in all spiritual wisdom and understanding, ¹⁰ to live a life worthy of the Lord, pleasing him in all respects, bearing fruit in every good work and increasing in the knowledge of God. ¹¹ May you be strengthened with all power, according to his glorious might, for all endurance and patience with joy, ¹² giving thanks to the Father, who has qualified you to share in the inheritance of the saints in light. ¹³ For he has rescued us from the dominion of darkness and transferred us into the kingdom of his beloved Son, ¹⁴ in whom we have redemption, the forgiveness of sins. ¹⁵ He is the image of the invisible God, the firstborn of all creation. ¹⁶ For by him all things were created, in heaven and on earth, visible and invisible, whether thrones or dominions or rulers or authorities – all things were created through him and for him. ¹⁷ He is before all things, and in him all things hold together. ¹⁸ And he is the head of the body, the church. He is the beginning, the firstborn from the dead, so that he might have the first place in everything. ¹⁹ For all fullness was pleased to dwell in him ²⁰ and through him, to reconcile

---

Title Alx/Byz[**To the Colossians**], Minor[*variations of* The Letter of Paul the Apostle to the Colossians].

1:¹ Alx/Byz[**Paul**], Alt[*without textual foundation* Saul (~JNT)]; Alx[**Christ Jesus**], Byz[Jesus Christ (DRA, KJV, MRD, NAS, NAU, NKJ, TLB)].

1:² Alx/Byz[**in Christ**], Minor[*adds* Jesus (DRA, MRD)]; Alx[**God our Father**], Byz[*adds* and the Lord Jesus Christ (DRA, KJV, NKJ)]; **faithful** *or* believing

1:³ Alx[**God, the Father**], Byz[the God and Father (KJV, NKJ)]; Alx/Byz[**our Lord Jesus Christ**], Minor[*omits* Christ].

1:⁴ Alx[**the love which you have**], Byz[your love (MRD, NKJ, NLT, TEV, ~TLB)].

1:⁶ Alx[**it is bearing fruit**], Byz[and it is bearing fruit (DRA, KJV, MRD, NKJ)]; Alx/Byz[**and growing**], Minor[*omits* (KJV, NKJ, NLT, ~TLB)].

1:⁷ Alx[**as you learned**], Byz[as you also learned (KJV, NKJ)]; Alx/Byz[**on your behalf**], Minor[on our behalf (ASV, NAS, NAU, NET, NIV, NJB, REB, RSV, TEV, TLB)]; **servant** *Greek* slave.

1:¹⁰ Alx[**to live a life**], Byz[so that you may live a life (DRA, HCS, JNT, KJV, MRD, NAS, NAU, NET, NIV, NKJ, NLT, NRS, REB, TEV, TLB)].

1:¹¹⁻¹² **for all endurance and patience with joy, giving thanks** *or* patience, with an all enduring joy, giving thanks.

1:¹² Alx/Major[**the Father**], Byz[God the Father *Greek* the God and Father (DRA, MRD)], Minor[the Father of Christ]; Alx[**qualified you**], Byz[qualified us (ASV, DRA, KJV, MRD, NAS, NAU, NKJ, RSV, TLB)].

1:¹⁴ Alx/Byz[**have redemption**], Minor[had redemption (NLT, TLB)]; Alx/Byz[**redemption**], Minor[*adds* through his blood (DRA, KJV, NKJ, TLB)]; *compare Ephesians 1:7.*

1:¹⁶ Alx[**in heaven and on earth**], Byz[that are in heaven and that are on earth (KJV, ~MRD, ~NIV, NKJ)]; **by him** *or* in him.

1:²⁰ Alx/Byz[**in heaven** *Greek* in the heavens], Major[at the heavens (~TEV)]; Alx/Byz[**through him –**],

to himself all things, whether things on earth or things in heaven, by making peace [through him –] through the blood of his cross.

²¹ And although you were once alienated and hostile in mind, doing evil deeds, ²² yet he has now reconciled you in the body of his flesh through death, in order to present you before himself holy and blameless and beyond reproach – ²³ if indeed you continue in the faith, firmly established and steadfast, and are not moved away from the hope of the gospel that you have heard, which has been proclaimed to every creature under heaven, and of which I, Paul, have become a minister.

²⁴ Now I rejoice in suffering for you, and I do my share for the sake of his body, which is the church, in filling up what afflictions of Christ my flesh still lacks. ²⁵ Of this I became a minister according to the stewardship from God which was given to me for you, to make the word of God fully known, ²⁶ the mystery that has been kept hidden for ages and generations, but is now disclosed to the saints. ²⁷ To them God willed to make known what is the riches of the glory of this mystery among the Gentiles, which is Christ in you, the hope of glory. ²⁸ We proclaim him, admonishing every man and teaching every man with all wisdom, so that we may present every man complete in Christ. ²⁹ For this end I labor, striving with all his energy, which so mightily works within me.

2 ¹ For I want you to know how greatly I strive for you, and for those at Laodicea, and for all who have not seen my face in the flesh, ² that their hearts may be encouraged as they are knit together in love, to have all the riches of assured understanding and the knowledge of God's mystery, that is, Christ himself, ³ in whom are hidden all the treasures of wisdom and knowledge. ⁴ I say this so that no one may delude you with fine-sounding arguments. ⁵ For even though I am absent in flesh, nevertheless I am with you in spirit, rejoicing to see your good order and the firmness of your faith in Christ.

⁶ Therefore as you have received Christ Jesus the Lord, so live in him, ⁷ rooted and built up in him and established in the faith, just as you were taught, overflowing with thanksgiving. ⁸ See to it that no one takes you captive through philosophy and empty deception, according to human tradition, according to the elements of the world, rather than according to Christ. ⁹ For in him all the fullness of Deity dwells in bodily form, ¹⁰ and you have been made complete in him, who is the head over all rule and authority. ¹¹ In him you were also circumcised with a circumcision made without hands, by putting off the body of the flesh by the circumcision of Christ; ¹² having been buried with him in baptism, in which you were also raised up with him through faith in the working of God, who raised

---

Minor[*omits* (DRA, ESV, HCS, ~NIV, NJB, ~NLT, NRS, RSV, TEV, TLB)].

1:²² Alx[**22 yet he has now reconciled you**], Byz[yet he has now reconciled you 22 (KJV, NKJ, ~REB, TLB)].

1:²³ Alx[**to every creature** *or* in all creation], Byz[in all the creation (DRA, MRD, REB, TEV, TLB)]; Alx/Byz[**Paul**], Alt[*without textual foundation* Saul (~JNT)].

1:²⁴ Alx/Major[**Now I rejoice in suffering**], Byz[Who now rejoice in my sufferings (~ASV, DRA, ~ESV, ~HCS, ~JNT, KJV, ~NAB, ~NAS, ~NAU, ~NET, ~NKJ, ~NLT, ~NRS, ~REB, ~RSV, ~TEV, ~TLB)]; **what afflictions of Christ my flesh still lacks** *Greek* that which is lacking of the afflictions of Christ in my flesh.

1:²⁸ Alx[**Christ**], Byz[*adds* Jesus (DRA, KJV, ~MRD, NKJ)].

2:¹ Alx[**strive for you** *or* strive on behalf of you], Byz[strive for you *or* strive concerning you].

2:² Alx[**of God's mystery, that is, Christ himself**], Byz[the mystery of God, both of the Father and of Christ (DRA, KJV, MRD, NKJ)], Minor[the mystery of God *others* the mystery of Christ].

2:⁴ Alx[**I say this so that no one**], Byz[But I say this, lest anyone (KJV, MRD, NKJ)].

2:⁶ **live in him** *Greek* walk in him.

2:⁷ Alx[**in the faith** *or* by the faith], Byz[in the faith]; Alx[**overflowing**], Byz[*adds* in it (DRA, KJV, MRD, NKJ, ~TLB)].

2:¹¹ Alx[**body of the flesh**], Byz[body of the sins of the flesh (~JNT, KJV, ~MRD, ~NIV, NKJ, ~NLT, ~REB, TEV, TLB)].

him from the dead. [13] When you were dead [in] your sins and the uncircumcision of your flesh, God made you alive together with him, having forgiven us all sins, [14] having canceled the certificate of debt, which stood against us with its decrees. He has taken what was hostile away from us, nailing it to the cross. [15] And having disarmed the powers and authorities, he made a public spectacle of them, triumphing over them in it.

[16] Therefore let no one judge you in questions of food and drink, or with regard to a festival or a new moon or a Sabbath day. [17] These things are only a shadow of what is to come; but the substance belongs to Christ. [18] Let no one disqualify you for the prize by delighting in self-abasement and the worship of the angels, taking his stand on visions he has seen, puffed up without cause by his fleshly mind, [19] and not holding fast to the head, from whom the whole body, nourished and held together by its joints and ligaments, grows with a growth that is from God.

[20] If with Christ you died to the elements of the world, why, as if you still belonged to it, do you submit to regulations such as, [21] "Do not handle! Do not taste! Do not touch!" [22] (referring to things which are all destined to perish with use), according to human commandments and teachings? [23] These indeed have an appearance of wisdom in promoting self-made religion and self-abasement [and] severe treatment of the body, but they are of no value against fleshly indulgence.

3 [1] If then you have been raised with Christ, seek the things that are above, where Christ is, seated at the right hand of God. [2] Set your minds on the things above, not on things that are on earth. [3] For you have died, and your life is hidden with Christ in God. [4] When Christ, who is your life, appears, then you also will appear with him in glory.

[5] Put to death, therefore, whatever belongs to earthly nature: sexual immorality, impurity, passion, evil desire and greed, which is idolatry. [6] Because of these, the wrath of God is coming [on the sons of disobedience], [7] in which you also once walked, when you lived in these things. [8] But now you must put them all away: anger, wrath, malice, slander, and filthy language from your mouth. [9] Do not lie to one another, since you have put off the old self with its practices, [10] and have put on the new self, which is being renewed in knowledge in the image of its Creator. [11] Here there is no Greek and Jew, circumcised and uncircumcised, barbarian, Scythian, slave, free, but Christ is all, and in all.

2:13 Alx/Byz[**in**], Minor[*omits* (~JNT, NJB, NLT, ~REB, ~TEV)]; Alx/Byz[**made you alive**], Minor[*omits* you (DRA, ESV, KJV, MRD, NKJ, RSV) *others* made us alive]; Alx/Byz[**forgiven us**], Minor[forgiven you (DRA, JNT, KJV, NET, NKJ, TLB)]; **God** *Greek* he.

2:14 Alx/Major[**has taken what was hostile**], Byz[took what was hostile (ESV, JNT, KJV, MRD, NAB, NIV, ~NJB, NLT, NRS, RSV, TEV, TLB)].

2:15 **disarmed the powers** *or* put off his powers; **over them in it** *or* over them in him.

2:16 Alx[**food and drink**], Byz[food or drink (ASV, DRA, KJV, NAS, NAU, NET, NIV, NJB, NKJ, NLT, REB, TEV, TLB)].

2:18 Alx[**visions he has seen**], Byz[visions which he has not seen (DRA, ~ESV, KJV, MRD, ~NET, NKJ, ~NRS)].

2:20 Alx/Major[**If with Christ**], Byz[Therefore if with Christ (DRA, KJV, ~NIV, NKJ, REB, TLB)].

2:23 Alx/Byz[**and severe treatment**], Minor[*omits* and (NET, NJB)]; **against fleshly indulgence** *or* indulging only the flesh.

3:4 Alx[**your life**], Byz[our life (ASV, JNT, KJV, MRD, NAS, NAU, NKJ, REB, RSV, TLB)].

3:5 Alx[**earthly nature**], Byz[your earthly nature (ASV, DRA, ESV, HCS, JNT, KJV, MRD, NAB, NAS, NAU, NET, NIV, NJB, NKJ, NLT, NRS, REB, RSV, TEV, TLB)].

3:6 Alx/Byz[**on the sons of disobedience**], Minor[*omits* (ESV, NAS, NIV, NLT, REB, RSV)].

3:7 Alx[**these things**], Byz[them (DRA, ESV, HCS, KJV, MRD, NAS, NAU, NET, ~NJB, NKJ, ~REB, RSV, TEV, TLB)].

¹² So, as God's chosen ones, holy and beloved, put on a heart of compassion, kindness, humility, gentleness and patience; ¹³ bearing with one another and, if one has a complaint against another, forgiving each other. As the Lord forgave you, so you also must forgive. ¹⁴ And over all these virtues put on love, which binds them all together in perfect unity. ¹⁵ Let the peace of Christ rule in your hearts, to which indeed you were called in one body. And be thankful. ¹⁶ Let the word of Christ dwell in you richly. Teach and admonish one another with all wisdom, and sing psalms, hymns and spiritual songs with thankfulness in your hearts to God. ¹⁷ And whatever you do, in word or deed, do all in the name of the Lord Jesus, giving thanks to God the Father through him.

¹⁸ Wives, be subject to your husbands, as is fitting in the Lord. ¹⁹ Husbands, love your wives, and do not be harsh with them.

²⁰ Children, obey your parents in all things, for this is pleasing in the Lord. ²¹ Fathers, do not exasperate your children, or they will become discouraged.

²² Slaves, in all things obey those who are your masters according to the flesh, not with eye-service, as men-pleasers, but in sincerity of heart, fearing the Lord. ²³ Whatever you do, do your work heartily, as for the Lord and not for men, ²⁴ knowing that you will receive an inheritance from the Lord as a reward. It is the Lord Christ you are serving. ²⁵ For he who does wrong will be paid back for the wrong he has done, and there is no partiality. ¹ Masters, provide your slaves with what is right and fair, knowing that you also have a Master in heaven.

4 ² Devote yourselves to prayer, being watchful in it with thanksgiving. ³ And pray for us as well, that God may open a door to us for the word, so that we may proclaim the mystery of Christ, for which I am in chains, ⁴ so that I may make it clear, as I ought to speak. ⁵ Walk with wisdom toward outsiders, making the most of the opportunity. ⁶ Let your speech always be full of grace, seasoned with salt, so that you may know how you ought to answer everyone.

⁷ Tychicus will tell you all about my affairs. He is a beloved brother, a faithful minister and fellow servant in the Lord. ⁸ I have sent him to you for this very purpose, that

---

3:12 Alx/Byz[**holy and beloved**], Minor[holy, beloved (NJB, NLT, TLB)]; Alx/Byz[**compassion**], Minor[compassions (ESV 2007 edition, ~JNT, KJV, MRD, NKJ)].

3:13 Alx[**the Lord**], Byz[Christ (KJV, MRD, NKJ)].

3:15 Alx[**peace of Christ**], Byz[peace of God (KJV, NKJ)]; Alx/Byz[**one body**], Minor[*omits* one (TLB)].

3:16 Alx/Byz[**the word of Christ**], Minor[the word of God *others* the word of the Lord *others* his word (MRD)]; Alx[**psalms, hymns**], Byz[psalms and hymns (ASV, ESV, KJV, MRD, NAS, NAU, NJB, NKJ, NLT, REB, RSV, TLB)]; Alx[**your hearts**], Byz[your heart (~REB)]; Alx[**to God**], Byz[to the Lord (KJV, NKJ, TLB)].

3:17 Alx/Byz[**the Lord Jesus**], Minor[the Lord Jesus Christ (DRA, MRD) *others* Jesus Christ *others* Christ]; Alx[**God the Father**], Byz[God and the Father (DRA, KJV)].

3:18 Alx/Byz[**your husbands**], Major[your own husbands (KJV, NKJ)].

3:20 Alx/Major[**pleasing in the Lord**], Byz[pleasing to the Lord (DRA, ESV, JNT, KJV, MRD, NAB, NAS, NAU, NIV, NJB, NKJ, NLT, ~REB, RSV, ~TEV, TLB)].

3:21 Alx/Byz[**exasperate**], Minor[provoke (ASV, DRA, ESV, KJV, NAB, NET, NKJ, NRS, RSV)].

3:22 Alx[**eye-service**], Byz[eye-services]; Alx[**fearing the Lord**], Byz[fearing God (DRA, KJV, NKJ)]; **masters** *Greek* lords.

3:23 Alx[**Whatever**], Byz[And whatever (KJV, MRD, NKJ)].

3:24 Alx/Byz[**you will receive**], Major[you will take]; Alx[**It is the Lord Christ**], Byz[For it is the Lord Christ (KJV, MRD, NKJ, TEV)]; **you are serving** *or* you are slaves to.

3:25 Alx[**For he who does wrong**], Byz[But he who does wrong (~JNT, KJV, MRD, ~NIV, ~NJB, NKJ, NLT, ~REB, TEV, TLB)].

4:1 Alx[**in heaven**], Byz[in heavens].

4:3 Alx/Byz[**mystery of Christ**], Minor[mystery of God].

4:5 **opportunity** *or* time.

4:7 **servant** *Greek* slave.

you may know about our circumstances and that he may encourage your hearts; [9] and with him Onesimus, the faithful and beloved brother, who is one of yourselves. They will tell you everything that has taken place here.

[10] My fellow prisoner Aristarchus sends you his greetings, and also Mark, the cousin of Barnabas (about whom you have received instructions; if he comes to you, welcome him) [11] and also Jesus who is called Justus. These are the only men of the circumcision among my fellow workers for the kingdom of God, and they have proved to be a comfort to me. [12] Epaphras, who is one of your number, a servant of Christ [Jesus], sends you his greetings, always laboring earnestly for you in his prayers, that you may stand mature and fully assured in all the will of God. [13] I testify for him that he has worked hard for you and for those who are in Laodicea and Hierapolis. [14] Luke, the beloved physician, and Demas send you greetings. [15] Give my greetings to the brothers at Laodicea, and to Nympha and the church in her house. [16] When this letter has been read among you, have it also read in the church of the Laodiceans; and see that you read the letter from Laodicea. [17] Say to Archippus, "See to the ministry which you have received in the Lord, that you may fulfill it."

[18] I, Paul, write this greeting with my own hand. Remember my chains. Grace be with you.

4:8 Alx[**that you may know about our circumstances**], Byz[that he may know about your circumstances (DRA, KJV, MRD, NKJ, TLB)].

4:12 Alx[**Jesus**], Byz[*omits* (KJV, MRD, NET, NKJ, REB)]; Alx[**fully assured**], Byz[complete (DRA, KJV, MRD, NKJ, TLB)]; **servant** *Greek* slave.

4:13 Alx[**worked hard**], Byz[a great zeal (KJV, MRD, NAS, NAU, NKJ, ~NLT, ~REB)].

4:15 Alx[**Nympha and the church in her house**], Byz[Nymphas and the church in his house (KJV, MRD, NKJ, TLB)], Minor[Nymphas and the church in their house (ASV)].

4:16 **Laodicea** *compare Ephesians 1:1 note.*

4:18 Alx/Byz[**Paul**], Alt[*without textual foundation* Saul (~JNT)]; Alx[*text*], Byz[*adds* Amen (DRA, MRD, NKJ, ~TLB)], Minor[*adds* Written from Rome to the Colossians by Tychicus and Onesimus (KJV)].

First Thessalonians

1 ¹ Paul, Silvanus and Timothy, to the church of the Thessalonians in God the Father and the Lord Jesus Christ: grace and peace to you. ² We give thanks to God always for all of you, mentioning you in our prayers; ³ remembering before our God and Father your work of faith and labor of love and steadfastness of hope in our Lord Jesus Christ. ⁴ For we know, brothers beloved by God, that he has chosen you; ⁵ for our gospel came to you not only in word, but also in power and in the Holy Spirit and [with] full conviction. You know what kind of men we proved to be [among] you for your sake. ⁶ You became imitators of us and of the Lord, for you received the word in much affliction, with the joy of the Holy Spirit; ⁷ so that you became an example to all the believers in Macedonia and in Achaia. ⁸ For not only has the word of the Lord sounded forth from you in Macedonia and [in] Achaia, but your faith in God has gone forth everywhere, so that we have no need to say anything. ⁹ For they themselves report about us what kind of a reception we had with you, and how you turned to God from idols to serve a living and true God, ¹⁰ and to wait for his Son from heaven, whom he raised from [the] dead – Jesus, who rescues us from the wrath to come.

2 ¹ For you yourselves know, brothers, that our visit to you was not in vain. ² But after we had already suffered and been shamefully treated in Philippi, as you know, we had the boldness in our God to speak to you the gospel of God in the face of great opposition. ³ For our appeal does not spring from error or impurity, nor is it made with deceit. ⁴ But just as we have been approved by God to be entrusted with the gospel, so we speak, not to please men, but to please God who tests our hearts. ⁵ For, as you know, we never used flattery nor a pretext for greed – God is witness – ⁶ nor did we seek glory from men, either from you or from others, ⁷ though we might have made demands as apostles of Christ. But we were infants among you, like a mother nursing

---

Title Alx/Byz[**First Thessalonians** *Greek* To the Thessalonians A], Minor[*variations of* The First Letter of Paul the Apostle to the Thessalonians].

1:1 Alx/Byz[**Paul**], Alt[*without textual foundation* Saul (~JNT)]; Alx[**grace and peace to you**], Byz[*adds* from God our Father and the Lord Jesus Christ (KJV, NKJ, TLB)]; **Silvanus** *or* Silas.

1:2 Alx[**mentioning you** *Greek omits* you], Byz[mentioning you].

1:5 Alx/Byz[**our gospel**], Minor[the gospel of God *others* the gospel of our God]; Alx/Byz[**with full conviction**], Minor[*omits* with (JNT, NLT, TLB)]; Alx/Byz[**among**], Minor[*omits* (~ASV, TLB)].

1:7 Alx[**an example**], Byz[examples (KJV, NKJ)]; Alx[**in Achaia**], Byz[*omits* in (HCS, JNT, KJV, NIV, NJB, NKJ, NLT, TEV, ~TLB)].

1:8 Alx/Byz[**in Achaia**], Minor[*omits* in (ASV, ESV, HCS, JNT, KJV, MRD, NAS, NAU, NET, NIV, NJB, NKJ, NLT, NRS, REB, RSV, TEV, ~TLB)]; Alx[**has gone forth**], Byz[has also gone forth (DRA, KJV, NAS, NAU, NKJ)].

1:9 Alx/Byz[**report about us**], Minor[report about you (~MRD, ~NET, ~NIV, ~NJB, ~NLT, ~REB, ~TEV, ~TLB]; Alx/Byz[**reception we had**], Minor[reception we have (~NJB, ~REB)].

1:10 Alx/Byz[**the dead**], Minor[*omits* the (TEV, ~TLB)].

2:2 Alx/Byz[**but after**], Minor[but even after (~ESV, JNT, KJV, ~NET, NKJ, ~NRS, ~RSV, ~TEV)].

2:4 Alx/Byz[**tests our hearts**], Minor[tests your hearts].

2:7 Byz[*divides verse 6 and 7 after* apostles of Christ (ASV, ESV, KJV, MRD, NAS, NAU, NIV, NKJ, RSV, TLB)]; Alx[**infants**], Byz[gentle (ASV, ESV, HCS, JNT, KJV, MRD, NAB, NAS, NAU, NIV, NJB, NKJ, NRS, REB, RSV, TEV, TLB, Metzger)].

her little children. [8] Having so fond an affection for you, we were ready to share with you not only the gospel of God but also our own lives, because you had become very dear to us. [9] For you remember our labor and toil, brothers. We worked night and day, that we might not be a burden to any of you, while we preached to you the gospel of God. [10] You are witnesses, and God also, how holy and righteous and blameless we behaved toward you believers. [11] For you know how, as a father with his own children, [12] we exhorted each one of you and encouraged you and implored you to live a life worthy of God, who calls you into his own kingdom and glory.

[13] And we also thank God constantly for this, that when you received the word of God which you heard from us, you accepted it not as the word of men but as what it really is, the word of God, which is at work in you who believe. [14] For you, brothers, became imitators of the churches of God in Christ Jesus which are in Judea, for you suffered the same things from your own countrymen as they did from the Jews, [15] who both killed the Lord Jesus and the prophets, and also drove us out. They displease God and are hostile to all men, [16] hindering us from speaking to the Gentiles so that they may be saved; with the result that they always fill up the measure of their sins. But wrath has come upon them at last.

[17] But since we were taken away from you, brothers, for a short time, in person not in heart, we endeavored the more eagerly and with great desire to see you face to face. [18] For we wanted to come to you – I, Paul, again and again – but Satan hindered us. [19] For who is our hope or joy or crown of exultation? Is it not even you, in the presence of our Lord Jesus at his coming? [20] For you are our glory and joy.

3 [1] Therefore when we could endure it no longer, we thought it best to be left behind at Athens alone, [2] and we sent Timothy, our brother and God's fellow worker in the gospel of Christ, to strengthen and encourage you for your faith, [3] so that no one would be unsettled by these afflictions. You yourselves know that we have been destined for this. [4] For indeed when we were with you, we kept telling you in advance that we were going to suffer affliction; and so it came to pass, as you know. [5] For this reason, when I could endure it no longer, I also sent to find out about your faith, for fear that the tempter might have tempted you, and our labor would be in vain.

[6] But now that Timothy has come to us from you, and has brought us the good news of your faith and love and reported that you always remember us kindly and long

---

2:9 Alx[**We worked night and day**], Byz[For we worked night and day (KJV, NKJ)].

2:11-12 Alx[*text*]; Byz[*divides verse 11 and 12 after* encouraged you (JNT, MRD)], Minor[*divides verse 11 and 12 after* implored you (ASV, DRA, HCS, KJV, NAS, NAU, NKJ, RSV, TLB)].

2:12 Alx/Byz[**who calls you**], Minor[who has called you (DRA, KJV, MRD, NLT, TLB)].

2:13 Alx[**And we also**], Byz[We also (HCS, JNT, KJV, MRD, NAU, NJB, NKJ, NLT, NRS)]; *DRA omits verse 13.*

2:15 Alx[**the prophets**], Byz[their own prophets (KJV, MRD, NKJ, TLB)]; Alx/Byz[**drove us out**], Minor[drove you out].

2:16 Alx/Byz[**wrath has come**], Minor[God's wrath has come (DRA, ESV, JNT, NAB, NIV, NLT, NRS, RSV, TEV, TLB)]; **at last** *or* completely.

2:18 Alx[**For** *or* Because], Byz[Therefore (HCS, ~JNT, KJV, NKJ, REB, ~TEV, ~TLB)]; Alx/Byz[**Paul**], Alt[*without textual foundation* Saul (~JNT)].

2:19 Alx/Major[**Lord Jesus**], Byz[*adds* Christ (DRA, KJV, NKJ, TLB)].

3:2 Alx[**our brother and God's fellow worker**], Byz[our brother and servant of God and our fellow worker (KJV, MRD, NKJ, ~TEV, TLB)], Minor[our brother and fellow worker]; Alx[**strengthen and encourage you for your faith** *Greek* strengthen you and encourage for your faith], Byz[strengthen you and encourage you about your faith (ASV, DRA, JNT, KJV, MRD, NET, NJB, NKJ, NLT, RSV, TLB)].

to see us, just as we long to see you – [7] for this reason, brothers, in all our distress and affliction we were comforted about you through your faith; [8] for now we really live, if you stand firm in the Lord. [9] For what thanksgiving can we render to God for you in return for all the joy which we feel for your sake before our God, [10] as we night and day keep praying most earnestly that we may see you face to face and supply what is lacking in your faith?

[11] Now may our God and Father himself, and our Lord Jesus, direct our way to you. [12] And may the Lord make you increase and abound in love for one another and for all, just as we do for you, [13] so that he may establish your hearts without blame in holiness before our God and Father, at the coming of our Lord Jesus with all his saints, [Amen].

4 [1] Finally then, brothers, we request and exhort you in the Lord Jesus, that as you learned from us how you ought to live and to please God, just as you are doing, you do so more and more. [2] For you know what instructions we gave you by the authority of the Lord Jesus. [3] For this is the will of God, your sanctification: that is, that you should abstain from sexual immorality; [4] that each one of you know how to control his own body in holiness and honor, [5] not in the passion of lust like the heathen, who do not know God; [6] and that no man transgress and wrong his brother in this matter because the Lord is the avenger in all these things, just as we also told you before and solemnly warned you. [7] For God has not called us to impurity, but to holiness. [8] Therefore, he who rejects this instruction does not reject man but God, who [also] gives you his Holy Spirit.

[9] Now concerning love of the brothers you have no need to have any one write to you, for you yourselves have been taught by God to love one another; [10] and indeed you do love all the brothers [that are] throughout Macedonia. But we urge you, brothers, to do so more and more. [11] Make it your ambition to lead a quiet life, to mind your own business and to work with your [own] hands, just as we told you, [12] so that your daily life may win the respect of outsiders and so that you will not be dependent on anyone.

3:7 Alx[**distress and affliction**], Byz[affliction and distress (JNT, KJV, NKJ)].

3:11 Alx[**our Lord Jesus**], Byz[*adds* Christ (DRA, KJV, MRD, NKJ)].

3:13 Alx/Byz[**without blame**], Minor[blamelessly]; Alx[**our Lord Jesus**], Byz[*adds* Christ (DRA, KJV, MRD, NKJ, TLB)]; Alx[**Amen**], Byz[*omits* (ASV, ESV, JNT, KJV, MRD, NAS, NAU, NET, NIV, NJB, NKJ, NRS, REB, RSV, TEV, TLB)].

4:1 Alx/Major[**Finally then**], Byz[The rest, then (DRA, ~JNT, ~MRD)], Minor[*omits* then (NAB, NIV, NJB, NLT, NRS, REB, RSV, TEV, TLB)]; Alx[**that as you learned**], Byz[as you learned (JNT, NIV, NJB, NLT, REB, TEV, TLB)]; Alx[**just as you are doing**], Byz[*omits* (~DRA, KJV, MRD, NKJ)].

4:4 **control his own body** *or* take his own spouse for himself *Greek* possess his own vessel.

4:8 Alx[**who also gives**]; Byz[who has also given (DRA, KJV, NKJ)], Minor[*omits* also (ASV, ESV, JNT, MRD, NAS, NAU, NET, NIV, NJB, NLT, REB, RSV, TEV, TLB)]; Alx/Byz[**you his Holy Spirit**], Minor[us his Holy Spirit (DRA, KJV, NKJ)].

4:9 Alx/Byz[**you have no need to have any one write to you**], Minor[we have no need to write to you (DRA, JNT, NIV, NJB, NLT, TEV, TLB)].

4:10 Alx/Byz[**brothers that are throughout**], Minor[*omits* that are (DRA, ESV, HCS, JNT, NAB, NET, NIV, NJB, NLT, NRS, REB, RSV, TEV, TLB)].

4:11 Alx/Byz[**your own hands**], Minor[your hands (ASV, ESV, NAS, NAU, NET, NIV, NJB, NLT, NRS, REB, RSV)].

4:12 *DRA combines verse 11 and 12 as a single verse, and remains one verse lower in number to the end of the chapter.*

¹³ But we do not want you to be ignorant, brothers, about those who are asleep, so that you will not grieve as do the rest, who have no hope. ¹⁴ For if we believe that Jesus died and rose again, even so God will bring with him those who have fallen asleep in Jesus.

¹⁵ For this we declare to you by the word of the Lord, *that we who are alive, who are left until the coming of the Lord, cannot precede those who have fallen asleep.* ¹⁶ *For the Lord himself will descend from heaven, with a loud command, with the voice of the archangel and with the trumpet call of God, and the dead in Christ will rise first.* ¹⁷ *Then we who are alive, who are left, will be caught up together with them in the clouds to meet the Lord in the air, and so we shall always be with the Lord.* ¹⁸ Therefore comfort one another with these words.

5 ¹ Now as to the times and the seasons, brothers, you have no need to have anything written to you. ² For you yourselves know well that the day of the Lord will come like a thief in the night. ³ While people are saying, "Peace and safety," then sudden destruction will come upon them, as labor pains upon a woman with child, and they cannot escape. ⁴ But you, brothers, are not in darkness so that this day should surprise you like a thief. ⁵ For you are all sons of light and sons of the day. We are not of the night or of darkness. ⁶ So then let us not sleep, as others do, but let us be alert and sober. ⁷ For those who sleep, sleep at night. And those who get drunk, get drunk at night. ⁸ But, since we belong to the day, let us be sober, and put on the breastplate of faith and love, and as a helmet the hope of salvation. ⁹ For God has not destined us to wrath, but to obtain salvation through our Lord Jesus Christ, ¹⁰ who died for us, so that whether we are awake or asleep, we will live together with him. ¹¹ Therefore encourage one another and build up one another, just as you also are doing.

¹² But we ask you, brothers, to respect those who labor among you and are over you in the Lord and admonish you, ¹³ and that you esteem them very highly in love because of their work. Live in peace with one another. ¹⁴ And we urge you, brothers, admonish the idlers, encourage the fainthearted, help the weak, be patient with everyone. ¹⁵ See that none of you repays evil for evil, but always seek to do good [both] for one another and for all.

¹⁶ Rejoice always. ¹⁷ Pray without ceasing. ¹⁸ Give thanks in all circumstances, for this is God's will for you in Christ Jesus. ¹⁹ Do not quench the Spirit. ²⁰ Do not despise prophecies. ²¹ But test everything. Hold fast to what is good. ²² Abstain from every form of evil.

4:13 Alx[**But we do not want**], Byz[But I do not want (KJV, MRD, NKJ, TLB)]; Alx[**who are asleep**], Byz[who have fallen asleep (JNT, MRD, NAB, NJB, NKJ, NLT, NRS, TEV, ~TLB)].

4:15-17 **Matthew 24:30-31, Mark 13:26-27, Luke 21:27-28**.

4:17 Alx/Byz[**who are alive, who are left**], Minor[*omits* who are left (~HCS, ~REB, ~TEV)].

5:3 Alx[**While people are saying**], Byz[For while people are saying (DRA, KJV, NKJ)], Minor[But while people are saying].

5:4 Alx/Byz[**like a thief**], Minor[like thieves].

5:5 Alx[**For you are all sons**], Byz[You are all sons (KJV, ~NJB, NKJ, REB, TEV)].

5:9 Alx/Byz[**Lord Jesus Christ**], Minor[*omits* Christ].

5:15 Alx/Byz[**both**], Minor[*omits* (ASV, DRA, ESV, HCS, JNT, MRD, NAS, NAU, NET, NIV, NJB, NLT, NRS, REB, RSV, TEV, TLB)].

5:21 Alx/Major[**But test everything**], Byz[Test everything (ASV, KJV, MRD, NAB, NIV, NJB, NKJ, TEV)].

²³ Now may the God of peace himself sanctify you entirely; and may your whole spirit and soul and body be kept blameless at the coming of our Lord Jesus Christ. ²⁴ He who calls you is faithful, and he will do it.

²⁵ Brothers, pray for us [too].

²⁶ Greet all the brothers with a holy kiss. ²⁷ I charge you by the Lord to have this letter read to all the brothers.

²⁸ The grace of our Lord Jesus Christ be with you.

5:23 **blameless** *or* whole.

5:25 Alx[**too**], Byz[*omits* (ASV, DRA, ESV, JNT, KJV, MRD, NAS, NAU, NIV, NJB, NKJ, NLT, NRS, RSV, TLB)].

5:27 Alx[**brothers**], Byz[holy brothers (DRA, KJV, MRD, NKJ)].

5:28 Alx[*text*], Byz[*adds* Amen (DRA, MRD, NKJ, ~TLB)], Minor[*adds* The first letter to the Thessalonians was written from Athens (KJV) *others add* To the Thessalonians A].

Second Thessalonians

1 ¹ Paul, Silvanus and Timothy, to the church of the Thessalonians in God our Father and the Lord Jesus Christ: ² grace and peace to you from God [our] Father and the Lord Jesus Christ.

³ We ought to give thanks to God always for you, brothers, as is fitting, because your faith is growing abundantly, and the love of every one of you for one another is increasing. ⁴ Therefore we ourselves boast of you among the churches of God for your perseverance and faith in all your persecutions and in the afflictions which you are enduring. ⁵ This is evidence of God's righteous judgment, so that you will be considered worthy of the kingdom of God, for which indeed you are suffering. ⁶ For after all it is only just for God to repay with affliction those who afflict you, ⁷ and to give relief to you who are afflicted and to us as well when the Lord Jesus will be revealed from heaven with his mighty angels ⁸ in flaming fire, inflicting vengeance on those who do not know God and on those who do not obey the gospel of our Lord Jesus. ⁹ They will suffer the punishment of eternal destruction and exclusion from the presence of the Lord and from the glory of his power, ¹⁰ when he comes to be glorified in his saints on that day, and to be marveled at among all who have believed – because our testimony to you was believed. ¹¹ To this end we always pray for you, that our God may count you worthy of his calling, and may fulfill every good resolve and work of faith by his power, ¹² so that the name of our Lord Jesus may be glorified in you, and you in him, according to the grace of our God and the Lord Jesus Christ.

2 ¹ Now concerning the coming of our Lord Jesus Christ and our gathering together to him, we beg you, brothers, ² not to be quickly shaken in mind or excited, either by spirit or by word, or by letter as if from us, to the effect that the day of the Lord has come. ³ Let no one deceive you in any way; for that day will not come, unless the rebellion comes first, and the man of lawlessness is revealed, the son of destruction, ⁴ who opposes and exalts himself above every so-called god or object of worship, so that he takes his seat in the temple of God, proclaiming himself to be God. ⁵ Do you not remember that when I was still with you I told you these things? ⁶ And you know what restrains him now, so that in his own time he may be revealed. ⁷ For the mystery of lawlessness is already at work; only he who now restrains will do so until he is taken out of the way. ⁸ And then the lawless one will be revealed, whom the Lord [Jesus] will slay with the breath of his mouth

---

Title Alx/Byz[**Second Thessalonians** *Greek* To the Thessalonians B], Minor[*variations of* The Second Letter of Paul the Apostle to the Thessalonians].

1:¹ Alx/Byz[**Paul**], Alt[*without textual foundation* Saul (~JNT)]; **Silvanus** *or* Silas.

1:² Alx/Byz[**our**], Minor[the (ASV, JNT, NAS, NAU, NET, NIV, NJB, REB, RSV)].

1:⁴ Alx/Byz[**which you are enduring**], Minor[in which you are held].

1:⁸ Alx/Byz[**in flaming fire**], Minor[in a flame of fire (DRA) *others place in verse 7* (ASV, NAS, NAU, NIV, RSV, TLB)]; Alx/Major[**Lord Jesus**], Byz[*adds* Christ (DRA, KJV, MRD, NKJ, TLB)].

1:¹⁰ Alx/Byz[**all who have believed**], Minor[all who believe (KJV, MRD, NJB, NKJ, NLT, REB, ~TEV)].

1:¹² Alx/Major[**the name of our Lord Jesus**], Byz[*adds* Christ (KJV, MRD, NJB, NKJ, TEV, TLB)]; **our God and the Lord Jesus Christ** *or* our God and Lord, Jesus Christ.

2:¹ Alx/Byz[**our Lord**], Minor[the Lord].

2:² Alx[**the Lord**], Byz[Christ (KJV, NKJ, TLB)].

2:³ Alx[**the man of lawlessness**], Byz[the man of sin (ASV, DRA, KJV, MRD, ~NJB, NKJ, ~REB, ~TEV)].

2:⁴ Alx[**temple of God**], Byz[*adds* as God (KJV, MRD, NKJ, TLB)]; **temple** *or* sanctuary.

2:⁸ Alx[**the Lord Jesus will slay**], Byz[the Lord will consume (KJV, ~MRD, ~NAS, ~NAU, ~NET, ~NJB, NKJ, ~TLB)].

and destroy by the splendor of his coming. [9] The coming of the lawless one is by the working of Satan, with all power and with pretended signs and wonders, [10] and with all the deception of wickedness for those who are to perish, because they refused to love the truth and so be saved. [11] For this reason God is sending them a strong delusion so that they will believe what is false, [12] so that all may be condemned who did not believe the truth but had pleasure in wickedness.

[13] But we are bound to give thanks to God always for you, brothers beloved by the Lord, because God chose you as firstfruits to be saved, through sanctification by the Spirit and belief in the truth. [14] [And] he called you to this through our gospel, that you may share in the glory of our Lord Jesus Christ. [15] So then, brothers, stand firm and hold to the traditions which you were taught, whether by word of mouth or by letter from us. [16] Now may our Lord Jesus Christ himself and God our Father, who loved us and gave us eternal comfort and good hope by grace, [17] comfort and strengthen your hearts in every good work and word.

3 [1] Finally, brothers, pray for us that the word of the Lord may spread rapidly and be honored, just as it did also with you, [2] and that we may be delivered from wicked and evil men; for not all have faith. [3] But the Lord is faithful, and he will strengthen and protect you from the evil one. [4] And we have confidence in the Lord about you, that you are [both] doing and will continue to do the things which we command. [5] May the Lord direct your hearts into the love of God and into the steadfastness of Christ.

[6] Now we command you, brothers, in the name of [our] Lord Jesus Christ, that you keep away from every brother who is living in idleness and not according to the tradition which they received from us. [7] For you yourselves know how you ought to follow our example. We were not idle when we were with you, [8] nor did we eat anyone's bread without paying for it, but with labor and hardship we worked night and day so that we would not be a burden to any of you. [9] We did this, not because we do not have the right to such help, but in order to make ourselves an example for you to follow. [10] For even when we were with you, we gave you this rule: "If anyone will not work, he shall not eat." [11] For we hear that some among you are leading an undisciplined life, not doing any work at all, but acting like busybodies. [12] Now such persons we command and exhort in the Lord Jesus Christ to work in quiet fashion and earn their own bread to eat. [13] But as for you, brothers,

---

2:10 Alx[**for those who are to perish**], Byz[in those who are to perish (HCS, ~JNT, KJV, MRD, NKJ)].

2:11 Alx[**is sending**], Byz[will send (DRA, KJV, MRD, NAS, NAU, NKJ, NLT, TLB)]; *DRA is one verse lower from verse 11 to the end of the chapter.*

2:13 Alx[**as firstfruits**], Byz[from the beginning (ASV, HCS, KJV, MRD, NAS, NAU, NET, NIV, NJB, NKJ, REB, RSV, TLB)].

2:14 Alx[**And**], Byz[*omits* (ASV, DRA, ESV, JNT, HCS, KJV, MRD, NAU, NET, NIV, NJB, NKJ, NLT, NRS, REB, RSV, TEV, TLB)].

2:15 **traditions** *or* teachings.

2:16 Alx[**and God our Father**], Byz[and our God and Father (KJV, NKJ)].

2:17 Alx[**comfort and strengthen your hearts**], Byz[comfort your hearts and strengthen you (DRA, HCS, JNT, KJV, MRD, NET, NIV, NJB, NKJ, NLT, ~REB, TEV, ~TLB)]; Alx[**work and word**], Byz[word and work (JNT, KJV, MRD, NJB, NKJ, TLB)].

3:3 **from the evil one** *or* from evil.

3:4 Alx/Byz[**both**], Minor[*omits* (ESV, HCS, JNT, NAS, NAU, NIV, NJB, NLT, NRS, REB, RSV, TEV, TLB)]; Alx[**which we command**], Byz[*adds* you (JNT, KJV, MRD, NAB, NJB, NKJ, NLT, REB, TEV, TLB)].

3:5 Alx/Byz[**the steadfastness of Christ**], Minor[*omits* the (HCS, MRD, NIV)].

3:6 Alx/Byz[**our**], Minor[the (JNT, NIV, NJB)]; Alx/Byz[**they received**], Minor[he received (~HCS, KJV, NKJ) *others* you received (ESV, JNT, MRD, NAS, NAU, NET, NIV, NJB, REB, RSV, TLB)]; **tradition** *or* teaching.

3:8 Alx[**night and day**], Byz[throughout night and day].

3:12 Alx[**in the Lord**], Byz[by our Lord (~DRA, ~HCS, KJV, MRD, NKJ)].

do not grow weary of doing good. [14] If anyone does not obey our instruction in this letter, take special note of that person, to not associate with him, so that he may be ashamed. [15] Yet do not regard him as an enemy, but warn him as a brother.

[16] Now may the Lord of peace himself give you peace at all times in every way. The Lord be with you all.

[17] I, Paul, write this greeting with my own hand. This is a distinguishing mark in every letter; this is the way I write. [18] The grace of our Lord Jesus Christ be with you all.

3:14 Alx[**to not associate**], Byz[and do not associate (DRA, ESV, JNT, KJV, NAS, NAU, NET, NJB, NKJ, REB, RSV, TEV, TLB)].

3:16 Alx/Byz[**in every way**], Minor[in every place (DRA)].

3:17 Alx/Byz[**Paul**], Alt[*without textual foundation* Saul (~JNT)].

3:18 Alx[*text*], Byz[*adds* Amen (DRA, MRD, NKJ)], Minor[*adds* The second letter to the Thessalonians was written from Athens (KJV)].

First Timothy

1 ¹ Paul, an apostle of Christ Jesus by the command of God our Savior and of Christ Jesus our hope, ² to Timothy, my true child in the faith: grace, mercy and peace from God the Father and Christ Jesus our Lord.

³ As I urged you when I went into Macedonia, remain on at Ephesus so that you may instruct certain men not to teach strange doctrines, ⁴ nor to devote themselves to myths and endless genealogies. These promote useless speculations rather than the divine plan – which is by faith. ⁵ But the goal of our instruction is love from a pure heart and a good conscience and a sincere faith. ⁶ For some men have wandered away from these things and turned aside to fruitless discussion, ⁷ wanting to be teachers of the Law, even though they do not understand either what they are saying or the matters about which they make confident assertions.

⁸ But we know that the Law is good, if one uses it lawfully, ⁹ realizing the fact that law is not made for a righteous person, but for those who are lawless and rebellious, for the ungodly and sinners, for the unholy and profane, for those who kill their fathers or mothers, for murderers ¹⁰ and immoral men and homosexuals and kidnappers and liars and perjurers, and whatever else is contrary to sound doctrine, ¹¹ according to the glorious gospel of the blessed God, with which I have been entrusted.

¹² I thank Christ Jesus our Lord, who has given me strength, because he considered me faithful, appointing me to his service. ¹³ Even though I was formerly a blasphemer and a persecutor and a violent aggressor, I was shown mercy because I acted ignorantly in unbelief. ¹⁴ And the grace of our Lord was overflowing for me, with the faith and love that are found in Christ Jesus. ¹⁵ It is a trustworthy saying that deserves full acceptance, that Christ Jesus came into the world to save sinners – of whom I am the foremost. ¹⁶ But I received mercy for this reason, so that in me, as the foremost, Christ Jesus might display his perfect patience for an example to those who would believe in him for eternal life. ¹⁷ Now to the King eternal, immortal, invisible, the only God, be honor and glory for ever and ever. Amen.

¹⁸ I give you this command, Timothy, my son, in accordance with the prophecies once made about you, that by them you may fight the good fight, ¹⁹ holding faith and a good conscience, which some have rejected and made shipwreck of their faith. ²⁰ Among

them are Hymenaeus and Alexander, whom I have handed over to Satan so that they will be taught not to blaspheme.

2 ¹ First of all, then, I urge that requests, prayers, intercessions, and thanksgivings be made for all men, ² for kings and all who are in authority, so that we may lead a quiet and peaceable life in all godliness and dignity. ³ This is good and acceptable in the sight of God our Savior, ⁴ who desires all men to be saved and to come to the knowledge of the truth. ⁵ For there is one God, and one mediator also between God and men, the man Christ Jesus, ⁶ who gave himself as a ransom for all – the testimony given at the proper time. ⁷ For this I was appointed a preacher and an apostle (I am telling the truth, I am not lying), as a teacher of the Gentiles in faith and truth.

⁸ Therefore I want the men in every place to pray, lifting up holy hands, without anger or quarreling. ⁹ Likewise, I [also] want women to adorn themselves with proper clothing, modestly and sensibly, not with braided hair and gold or pearls or costly garments, ¹⁰ but with good deeds, as is proper for women who profess godliness. ¹¹ Let a woman learn in silence with all submissiveness. ¹² But I do not permit a woman to teach or to have authority over a man. She must be silent. ¹³ For Adam was formed first, then Eve. ¹⁴ And it was not Adam who was deceived, but the woman was seduced and became a transgressor. ¹⁵ But she will be saved through child-bearing, if they continue in faith and love and holiness with self-restraint. ¹ It is a trustworthy saying.

3 If any one aspires to the office of overseer, he desires a noble task. ² Now the overseer must be above reproach, the husband of one wife, temperate, self-controlled, respectable, hospitable, able to teach, ³ not given to drunkenness, not violent but gentle, not quarrelsome, not a lover of money. ⁴ He must manage his own household well, keeping his children under control with all dignity. ⁵ If a man does not know how to manage his own household, how can he take care of God's church? ⁶ He must not be a recent convert, or he may become conceited and fall into the same condemnation as the devil. ⁷ He must also have a good reputation with outsiders, so that he will not fall into reproach and the snare of the devil.

⁸ Deacons likewise must be men of dignity, not double-tongued, not addicted to much wine, and not fond of sordid gain. ⁹ They must hold the mystery of the faith with a clear conscience. ¹⁰ They must also first be tested. And then if they are beyond reproach,

---

2:1 Alx/Byz[**I urge**], Minor[I urge you (MRD, NLT, ~TLB)].

2:3 Alx[**This is good**], Byz[For this is good (DRA, KJV, MRD, NKJ)].

2:6 **testimony** *or* proof *Greek* martyrion.

2:7 Alx[**telling the truth**], Byz[*adds* in Christ (KJV, NKJ)].

2:8 Alx/Byz[**quarreling**], Minor[quarrelings (JNT, MRD)].

2:9 Alx/Byz[**also**], Minor[*omits* (ASV, DRA, ~HCS, JNT, ~MRD, NAS, NAU, NET, ~NIV, NJB, ~NLT, ~NRS, REB, ~RSV, ~TEV, TLB)]; Alx[**women**], Byz[the women (JNT, NET, NKJ, NRS, TEV, TLB)]; Alx[**and gold**], Byz[or gold (DRA, ~HCS, KJV, MRD, NIV, NJB, NKJ, NLT, NRS, ~REB, RSV, TEV, TLB)].

2:11 **woman** *or* wife.

2:12 **woman** *or* wife; **a man** *or* her husband.

2:14 Alx[**deceived...seduced**], Byz[deceived...deceived (ASV, ~DRA, ESV, HCS, JNT, KJV, ~MRD, NAB, NAU, NIV, NJB, NKJ, NLT, NRS, REB, RSV, TEV, TLB)].

2:15 **will be saved** *or* will be restored.

3:1-2 **overseer** *or* bishop.

3:1 Alx/Byz[**a trustworthy saying**], Minor[a human saying]; **It is a trustworthy saying** *could be the beginning of the next paragraph.*

3:3 Alx[**not violent**], Byz[*adds* not greedy for money (KJV, NKJ)].

3:7 Alx[**He must also**], Byz[He himself must also].

let them serve as deacons. [11] The women must likewise be dignified, not malicious gossips, but temperate, faithful in all things. [12] Deacons must be the husband of one wife, and must manage their children and their households well. [13] For those who have served well as deacons gain for themselves a high standing and great confidence in the faith that is in Christ Jesus.

[14] Although I hope to come to you soon, I am writing you these instructions so that, [15] if I am delayed, you will know how one ought to conduct himself in the household of God, which is the church of the living God, the pillar and support of the truth. [16] By common confession, great is the mystery of godliness:

> Who was revealed in the flesh,
>> vindicated in the Spirit,
>>> seen by angels,
>> preached among the nations,
>>> believed on in the world,
>>>> taken up in glory.

4 [1] Now the Spirit expressly says that in later times some will fall away from the faith by giving heed to deceitful spirits and doctrines of demons, [2] through the pretensions of liars, whose consciences have been seared as with a hot iron. [3] They forbid marriage and advocate abstaining from foods, which God created to be received with thanksgiving by those who believe and know the truth. [4] For everything created by God is good, and nothing is to be rejected if it is received with thanksgiving; [5] for it is consecrated by the word of God and prayer.

[6] If you point out these things to the brothers, you will be a good servant of Christ Jesus, constantly nourished on the words of the faith and of the good doctrine which you have followed. [7] Have nothing to do with godless myths and old wives' tales. Rather, train yourself in godliness. [8] For bodily training is of some value, but godliness is of value in all things, as it holds promise for the present life and also for the life to come. [9] It is a trustworthy saying and worthy of full acceptance. [10] For to this end we labor and strive, because we have our hope set on the living God, who is the Savior of all men, especially of those who believe.

[11] Command and teach these things. [12] Let no one look down on your youth, but set the believers an example in speech and conduct, in love, in faith, in purity. [13] Until I come, devote yourself to the public reading of Scripture, to preaching and to teaching. [14] Do not neglect the gift that is in you, which was given you through prophetic utterance

---

3:11 Alx/Byz[**temperate** *feminine*], Major[temperate *masculine*]; **women** or deaconesses or wives.

3:14 Alx/Byz[**come to you**], Minor[*omits* to you (~REB)]; Alx[**soon**], Byz[shortly (ASV, DRA, KJV, NKJ)].

3:16 Alx[**Who**], Byz[God (KJV, NKJ, ~NLT, ~TLB)]; **vindicated** or justified.

4:1 **later** or the last.

4:2 **seared** or branded.

4:6 Alx[**Christ Jesus**], Byz[Jesus Christ (KJV, MRD, NKJ, ~TLB)]; Alx/Byz[**which you have followed**], Minor[which you followed]; **servant** Greek deacon.

4:9 *this verse could refer to either the sentence before or after.*

4:10 Alx[**we labor**], Byz[we both labor (KJV, NKJ)]; Alx[**strive**], Byz[suffer reproach (DRA, KJV, MRD, NKJ, TLB)].

4:12 Alx[**in love**], Byz[*adds* in spirit (KJV, NKJ)].

4:13 **the public reading of Scripture** Greek the Reading.

4:14 **gift** Greek charismatos; **the council of elders laid their hands on you** or you were ordained to the council of elders.

when the council of elders laid their hands on you. ¹⁵ Be diligent in these matters. Give yourself wholly to them, so that all may see your progress. ¹⁶ Take heed to yourself and to your teaching. Persevere in them, for if you do, you will save both yourself and your hearers.

5 ¹ Do not rebuke an elder, but exhort him as a father, younger men as brothers, ² older women as mothers, and younger women as sisters, in all purity.

³ Honor widows who are real widows. ⁴ But if a widow has children or grandchildren, they must first learn to practice their religion in regard to their own family and to make some return to their parents; for this is acceptable in the sight of God. ⁵ Now she who is a real widow, and who has been left all alone, has set her hope on God and continues in supplications and prayers night and day. ⁶ But she who lives for pleasure is dead even while she lives. ⁷ Command these things as well, so that they may be above reproach. ⁸ If any one does not provide for his relatives, and especially for his own family, he has denied the faith and is worse than an unbeliever. ⁹ A widow is to be put on the list only if she is not less than sixty years old, having been the wife of one husband. ¹⁰ And she must be well known for her good deeds, as one who has brought up children, shown hospitality, washed the feet of the saints, relieved those in distress, and devoted herself to doing good in every way. ¹¹ But refuse to put younger widows on the list, for when their passions draw them away from Christ, they want to marry, ¹² thus bringing condemnation, because they have set aside their first pledge. ¹³ Besides, they learn to be idle, going about from house to house. And not only do they become idlers, but also gossips and busybodies, saying things they ought not to. ¹⁴ So I would have younger widows marry, bear children, manage their homes, and give the enemy no occasion for reproach. ¹⁵ For some have already turned aside to follow Satan. ¹⁶ If any woman who is a believer has dependent widows, she must assist them, and let not the church be burdened, so that it may assist those who are real widows.

¹⁷ The elders who rule well are to be considered worthy of double honor, especially those who work hard at preaching and teaching. ¹⁸ For the scripture says, *"You shall not muzzle an ox while it is treading out the grain,"* and, *"The laborer deserves his wages."* ¹⁹ Do not receive an accusation against an elder except on the basis of two or three witnesses. ²⁰ Those who continue in sin, rebuke in the presence of all, so that the rest also may be fearful of sinning. ²¹ I charge you, in the presence of God and of Christ Jesus and of the elect angels, to keep these instructions without partiality, doing nothing out of favoritism. ²² Do not be hasty in the laying on of hands, and do not share in the sins of others; keep yourself pure. ²³ No longer drink only water, but use a little wine for the sake of the stomach and your frequent ailments.

4:15 Alx[**so that all may see your progress**], Byz[so that your progress may be evident to all (ASV, DRA, HCS, JNT, KJV, MRD, NAB, NAS, NAU, NKJ, REB, TEV) *or* so that your progress may be evident in all things].

5:4 Alx/Major[**this is acceptable**], Byz[this is good and acceptable (KJV, NKJ)].

5:5 Alx/Byz[**God**], Minor[the Lord].

5:16 Alx[**woman**], Byz[man or woman (~DRA, KJV, MRD, NKJ)], Vulgate[man (DRA)].

5:17 **honor** *or* compensation.

5:18 Alx/Byz[**wages**], Minor[food]; **Deuteronomy 25:4, Luke 10:7.**

5:19 Alx/Byz[**except on the basis of two or three witnesses**], Metzger[*some ancient Latin texts may have omitted this*].

5:20 Alx/Byz[**Those who continue in sin**], Minor[But those who continue in sin].

5:21 Alx[**Christ Jesus**], Byz[the Lord Jesus Christ (KJV, MRD, ~NJB, NKJ, TLB)].

5:23 Alx[**the stomach**], Byz[your stomach (ASV, DRA, ESV, HCS, JNT, KJV, MRD, NAB, NAS, NAU,

24 The sins of some men are obvious, going before them to judgment. For others, their sins appear later. 25 In the same way, good deeds are obvious, and even those that are not cannot be hidden.

6 1 Let all who are under the yoke of slavery regard their masters as worthy of all honor, so that the name of God and the teaching may not be spoken against. 2 Those who have believing masters must not be disrespectful to them because they are brothers, but they must serve them all the better, because those who benefit by their service are believers and beloved.

Teach and urge these duties. 3 If anyone teaches otherwise and does not agree with the sound words of our Lord Jesus Christ and the teaching which accords with godliness, 4 he is conceited and understands nothing; but he has a morbid interest in controversial questions and disputes about words, which produce envy, strife, malicious talk, evil suspicions, 5 and constant friction between men of depraved mind and deprived of the truth, who imagine that godliness is a means of gain. 6 But godliness with contentment is itself great gain. 7 For we brought nothing into the world, and we cannot take anything out of it. 8 But if we have food and clothing, with these we shall be content. 9 But those who want to get rich fall into temptation and a snare and into many foolish and harmful desires that plunge men into ruin and destruction. 10 For the love of money is a root of all sorts of evil, and some by longing for it have wandered away from the faith and pierced themselves with many griefs.

11 But you, man of God, flee from all this, and pursue righteousness, godliness, faith, love, endurance and gentleness. 12 Fight the good fight of the faith. Take hold of the eternal life to which you were called when you confessed the good confession in the presence of many witnesses. 13 I charge [you] in the presence of God, who gives life to all things, and of Christ Jesus, who made the good confession before Pontius Pilate, 14 to keep the commandment without stain or reproach until the appearing of our Lord Jesus Christ, 15 which he will bring about at the proper time – he who is the blessed and only Sovereign, the King of kings and Lord of lords, 16 who alone has immortality and dwells in unapproachable light, whom no man has ever seen or can see. To him be honor and eternal dominion. Amen.

17 Instruct those who are rich in this present world not to be conceited or to fix their hope on the uncertainty of riches, but on God, who richly supplies us with everything to enjoy. 18 Instruct them to do good, to be rich in good deeds, to be generous and ready to share, 19 storing up for themselves the treasure of a good foundation for the future, so that they may take hold of that which is truly life.

NET, NIV, NJB, NKJ, NLT, NRS, REB, RSV, TEV, TLB)].

5:25 Alx/Byz[**In the same way**], Minor[But in the same way]; Alx[**good deeds are obvious**], Byz[there are good deeds that are obvious (ASV, NAS, NAU)].

6:2 Alx/Major[**Teach and urge these duties 3**], Byz[3 Teach and urge these duties].

6:3 Alx/Byz[**agree with**], Minor[keep (NJB, REB)].

6:5 Alx[**means of gain**], Byz[*adds* Withdraw from such people (KJV, MRD, NKJ, TLB)].

6:7 Alx[**and we cannot**], Byz[and it is certain that we cannot (DRA, KJV, MRD, NKJ)].

6:9 Alx/Byz[**snare**], Minor[*adds* of the devil (DRA)].

6:12 Alx/Major[**you were called**], Byz[you were also called (KJV, NKJ)].

6:13 Alx/Byz[**you**], Minor[*omits*]; Alx[**gives life** *or* preserves life], Byz[quickens *or* brings life (DRA, KJV, MRD, ~NJB)]; Alx/Byz[**Christ Jesus**], Minor[Jesus Christ (MRD, REB)]; *RSV places* **I charge you** *in verse 14.*

6:17 Alx[**God**], Byz[the living God (DRA, KJV, MRD, NKJ, TLB)].

6:19 Alx[**truly**], Byz[eternal (KJV, NKJ, ~TLB)].

[20] O Timothy, guard what has been entrusted to you. Avoid the godless chatter and contradictions of what is falsely called knowledge, [21] which some have professed and in so doing have wandered from the faith.

Grace be with you.

6:20 Alx/Major[**entrusted to you**], Byz[deposited with you ()].

6:21 Alx[**Grace be with you** *plural*], Byz[Grace be with you *singular*], Byz[*adds* Amen (DRA, MRD, NKJ)], Minor[*adds* The first to Timothy was written from Laodicea, which is the chief city of Phrygia Pacatiana (KJV)].

Second Timothy

1 ¹ Paul, an apostle of Christ Jesus by the will of God, according to the promise of life that is in Christ Jesus, ² to Timothy, my beloved son: grace, mercy and peace from God the Father and Christ Jesus our Lord.

³ I thank God, whom I serve with a clear conscience the way my forefathers did, as I constantly remember you in my prayers night and day. ⁴ As I recall your tears, I long to see you, so that I may be filled with joy. ⁵ For I am reminded of your sincere faith, which first dwelt in your grandmother Lois, and your mother Eunice, and I am sure is in you as well. ⁶ For this reason I remind you to fan into flame the gift of God which is in you through the laying on of my hands. ⁷ For God did not give us a spirit of timidity, but a spirit of power and love and self-discipline. ⁸ So do not be ashamed to testify of our Lord or of me his prisoner, but join in suffering for the gospel according to the power of God, ⁹ who has saved us and called us with a holy calling, not according to our works, but according to his own purpose and the grace which was granted us in Christ Jesus from all eternity, ¹⁰ but has now been revealed through the appearing of our Savior Christ Jesus, who has abolished death and brought life and immortality to light through the gospel. ¹¹ For this gospel I was appointed a preacher and an apostle and a teacher. ¹² For this reason I also suffer as I do. But I am not ashamed, for I know whom I have believed and I am convinced that he is able to guard my trust until that day. ¹³ Follow the pattern of sound words which you have heard from me, in the faith and love which are in Christ Jesus. ¹⁴ Guard, through the Holy Spirit who dwells in us, the treasure that has been entrusted to you.

¹⁵ You are aware of the fact that all who are in Asia turned away from me, among whom are Phygelus and Hermogenes. ¹⁶ May the Lord grant mercy to the household of Onesiphorus, for he often refreshed me and was not ashamed of my chains. ¹⁷ But when he was in Rome, he diligently searched for me and found me. ¹⁸ (May the Lord grant him to find mercy from the Lord on that Day!) And you know very well all the service he rendered at Ephesus.

2 ¹ You then, my son, be strong in the grace that is in Christ Jesus. ² And the things you have heard from me in the presence of many witnesses, entrust to faithful men who will be able to teach others also. ³ Share in hardship as a good soldier of Christ Jesus. ⁴ No soldier in active service gets entangled in civilian affairs, since his aim is to please the one who enlisted him as a soldier. ⁵ Also, if anyone competes as an athlete, he does not win the prize unless he competes according to the rules. ⁶ The hard-working farmer ought to be the first to receive his share of the crops. ⁷ Consider what I say, for the Lord will give you understanding in everything.

Title Alx/Byz[**Second Timothy** *Greek* To Timothy B], Minor[*variations of* The Second Letter of Paul the Apostle to Timothy].

1:¹ Alx/Byz[**Paul**], Alt[*without textual foundation* Saul (~JNT)]; Alx[**Christ Jesus**], Byz[Jesus Christ (DRA, KJV, MRD, NKJ, TLB)].

1:² Alx/Byz[**Christ Jesus our Lord**], Minor[the Lord Jesus Christ our Lord].

1:¹⁰ Alx[**Christ Jesus**], Byz[Jesus Christ (DRA, KJV, MRD, NKJ, REB, TLB)].

1:¹¹ Alx[**teacher**], Byz[*adds* of the Gentiles (DRA, JNT, KJV, MRD, NKJ, TLB)].

1:¹⁵ Alx/Major[**Phygelus**], Byz[Phygellus (DRA, KJV, MRD, NKJ, TLB)].

1:¹⁷ Alx[**diligently**], Byz[very diligently (KJV, NKJ)].

1:¹⁸ Alx/Byz[**service he rendered**], Minor[*adds* to me (DRA, JNT, KJV, MRD, NET, NIV, NJB, NKJ, TEV, TLB)].

2:³ Alx[**Share in hardship**], Byz[You therefore must endure hardship (KJV, NKJ)]; Alx[**Christ Jesus**], Byz[Jesus Christ (KJV, MRD, NKJ, TLB)].

2:⁷ Alx[**the Lord will give you**], Byz[may the Lord give you (KJV, MRD, NKJ, TLB)].

⁸ Remember Jesus Christ, risen from the dead, descended from David according to my gospel, ⁹ for which I am suffering even to the point of wearing chains like a criminal. But the word of God is not chained. ¹⁰ Therefore I endure everything for the sake of the elect, that they too may obtain the salvation that is in Christ Jesus, with eternal glory. ¹¹ Here is a trustworthy saying:

> If we died with him, we will also live with him.
> ¹² If we endure, we will also reign with him.
> If we shall deny him, he also will deny us.
> ¹³ If we are faithless, he remains faithful,
>   for he cannot deny himself.

¹⁴ Remind them of these things, and charge them in the presence of God to avoid disputing about words, which does no good, but only ruins the hearers. ¹⁵ Do your best to present yourself to God as one approved, a workman who does not need to be ashamed, rightly handling the word of truth. ¹⁶ Avoid godless chatter, for it will lead people into more and more ungodliness, ¹⁷ and their talk will spread like gangrene. Among them are Hymenaeus and Philetus, ¹⁸ who have gone astray from the truth. They say that [the] resurrection has already taken place, and upset the faith of some. ¹⁹ Nevertheless, God's firm foundation stands, having this seal: *"The Lord knows those who are his,"* and, "Everyone who names the name of the Lord must turn away from wickedness." ²⁰ In a large house there are not only vessels of gold and silver but also of wood and earthenware. Some are for noble use. Some are for ignoble – ²¹ if anyone cleanses himself from these, he will be a vessel for noble purposes, made holy, useful to the Master and prepared to do any good work. ²² Now flee from youthful lusts, and pursue righteousness, faith, love and peace, along with those who call on the Lord from a pure heart. ²³ Don't have anything to do with foolish and stupid arguments, because you know that they produce quarrels. ²⁴ And the Lord's servant must not be quarrelsome, but he must be kind to everyone: able to teach, patient when wronged, ²⁵ with gentleness correcting those who are in opposition. It may be that God will grant them repentance leading to the knowledge of the truth, ²⁶ and they may come to their senses and escape from the snare of the devil, having been captured by him to do his will.

3 ¹ But understand this, that in the last days there will come times of stress. ² For men will be lovers of self, lovers of money, boastful, arrogant, abusive, disobedient to their parents, ungrateful, unholy, ³ unloving, unforgiving, slanderous, without self-control, brutal, haters of good, ⁴ treacherous, reckless, conceited, lovers of pleasure rather than lovers of God, ⁵ holding a form of godliness but denying its power. Avoid such people. ⁶ For among them are those who make their way into households and capture weak women, weighed down with sins and swayed by various impulses, ⁷ always learning and never able to come to the knowledge of the truth. ⁸ Just as Jannes and Jambres opposed Moses, so these men also oppose the truth, men of depraved mind, rejected in regard to the faith. ⁹ But they will not get very far, for their folly will be plain to all, as theirs also was.

2:12 Alx[**if we shall deny him**], Byz[if we deny him (DRA, ESV, HCS, JNT, KJV, NAB, NAS, NAU, NET, NIV, NJB, NKJ, NLT, NRS, REB, RSV, TEV, TLB)].

2:13 Alx[**for**], Byz[*omits* (DRA, KJV, NKJ)].

2:14 Alx[**God**], Byz[the Lord (ASV, DRA, JNT, KJV, MRD, NET, NKJ, RSV, TLB)].

2:18 Alx/Byz[**the resurrection**], Minor[*omits* the (~JNT, REB, TEV)].

2:19 Alx/Byz[**the name of the Lord**], Minor[the name of Christ (KJV, NKJ, TLB)]; ~Numbers 16:5 LXX; ~Numbers 16:26, ~Isaiah 52:11 LXX.

2:21 Alx[**holy, useful**], Byz[holy and useful (DRA, JNT, KJV, NKJ, NLT, NRS, RSV)].

2:22 Alx/Byz[**along with those**], Minor[along with all those (NJB, REB)].

2:24 **servant** *Greek* slave.

2:26 **him… his** *the pronouns could refer to God or the devil.*

3:8 Alx/Byz[**Jannes and Jambres**], Minor[Joannes and Mambres (DRA)].

[10] You, however, know all about my teaching, my conduct, my purpose, faith, patience, love, endurance, [11] persecutions, and sufferings, such as happened to me at Antioch, at Iconium and at Lystra; what persecutions I endured, yet the Lord rescued me from them all. [12] Indeed all who desire to live a godly life in Christ Jesus will be persecuted, [13] while evil men and impostors will go from bad to worse, deceiving and being deceived. [14] But as for you, continue in what you have learned and have become convinced of, knowing from whom you learned it, [15] and how from childhood you have known [the] sacred writings which are able to make you wise for salvation through faith in Christ Jesus. [16] Every scripture inspired by God is also profitable for teaching, for reproof, for correction, and for training in righteousness; [17] so that the man of God may be complete, equipped for every good work.

4 [1] I solemnly charge you in the presence of God and of Christ Jesus, who is to judge the living and the dead, and by his appearing and his kingdom: [2] preach the word; be ready in season and out of season; correct, rebuke, exhort, with great patience and instruction. [3] For the time will come when they will not endure sound doctrine. But having itching ears, they will accumulate for themselves teachers to suit their own desires, [4] and will turn their ears away from the truth and turn aside to myths. [5] But you, be sober in all things, endure hardship, do the work of an evangelist, fulfill your ministry.

[6] For I am already being poured out as a drink offering, and the time of my departure has come. [7] I have fought the good fight. I have finished the race. I have kept the faith. [8] In the future there is laid up for me the crown of righteousness, which the Lord, the righteous Judge, will award to me on that day; and not only to me, but also to all who have loved his appearing.

[9] Do your best to come to me soon; [10] for Demas, having loved this present world, has deserted me and gone to Thessalonica. Crescens has gone to Galatia, and Titus to Dalmatia. [11] Only Luke is with me. Get Mark and bring him with you, for he is useful to me in my ministry. [12] But Tychicus I have sent to Ephesus. [13] When you come, bring the cloak that I left with Carpus at Troas, and the books, especially the parchments. [14] Alexander the coppersmith did me great harm. The Lord will repay him for his deeds. [15] Be on guard against him yourself, for he strongly opposed our message.

[16] At my first defense no one stood by me, but all deserted me; may it not be counted against them. [17] But the Lord stood at my side and gave me strength, so that through me the message might be fully proclaimed and all the Gentiles might hear it. And I was rescued from the lion's mouth. [18] The Lord will rescue me from every evil attack and will bring me safely to his heavenly kingdom. To him be the glory for ever and ever. Amen.

3:14 Alx[**from whom** *plural*], Byz[from whom *singular*].

3:15 Alx/Byz[**the sacred writings**], Minor[*omits* the].

3:16 Alx/Byz[**and profitable**], Minor[*omits* and (DRA, MRD, REB)]; Alx[**reproof**], Byz[proof]; **Every scripture inspired by God is also** *or* All scripture is inspired by God and.

4:1 Alx[**I solemnly charge you**], Byz[I therefore solemnly charge you (KJV, NKJ, TLB)]; Alx[**Christ Jesus**], Byz[the Lord Jesus Christ (KJV, MRD, NKJ)]; Alx[**and by his appearing**], Byz[at his appearing (JNT, KJV, MRD, NKJ, NLT, TLB)].

4:2 Alx/Byz[**rebuke, exhort**], Minor[exhort, rebuke (DRA, ~MRD)].

4:8 Alx/Byz[**also to all who have loved**], Minor[also to those who have loved (DRA, MRD)].

4:10 Alx/Byz[**Galatia**], Minor[Gaul].

4:13 Alx/Byz[**cloak**], Minor[bookcase (MRD)].

4:14 Alx[**the Lord will repay**], Byz[the Lord repay (KJV, NKJ)].

4:15 Alx[**he strongly opposed**], Byz[he has strongly opposed (DRA, KJV, NAB, NJB, NKJ)].

4:16 Alx[**stood by me**], Byz[stood with me (DRA, KJV, MRD, NKJ, NLT)].

4:18 Alx[**The Lord will rescue**], Byz[And the Lord will rescue (KJV, MRD, NKJ, NLT, TEV, TLB)].

¹⁹ Greet Prisca and Aquila, and the household of Onesiphorus. ²⁰ Erastus remained at Corinth, but Trophimus I left sick at Miletus. ²¹ Do your best to come before winter. Eubulus greets you, and so do Pudens and Linus and Claudia and all the brothers. ²² The Lord be with your spirit. Grace be with you.

4:¹⁹ **Prisca** *or* Priscilla.
4:²⁰ Alx/Byz[**Miletus**], Alt/Peshitta[the city of Miletus (MRD)].
4:²¹ Alx/Byz[**all the brothers**], Minor[*omits* all].
4:²² Alx[**The Lord**], Byz[*adds* Jesus Christ (DRA, KJV, MRD, NKJ, TLB)]; Alx[**Grace be with you**], Byz[*adds* Amen (DRA, MRD, KJV, NKJ)], Minor[Grace be with us *others add* The second letter to Timothy, ordained the first bishop of the Ephesian church, was written from Rome when Paul was brought before Nero the second time (KJV)].

To Titus

1 ¹ Paul, a servant of God and an apostle of Jesus Christ, for the faith of God's elect and the knowledge of the truth which leads to godliness, ² in the hope of eternal life, which God, who cannot lie, promised long ages ago, ³ and at the proper time revealed in his word through the preaching with which I have been entrusted by the command of God our Savior, ⁴ to Titus, my true child in a common faith: grace and peace from God the Father and Christ Jesus our Savior.

⁵ For this reason I left you in Crete, that you might straighten out what was left unfinished, and appoint elders in every town as I directed you, ⁶ namely, if any man is blameless, the husband of one wife, and his children believe and are not open to the charge of being wild or rebellious. ⁷ For the overseer must be blameless as God's steward, not self-willed, not quick-tempered, not addicted to wine, not violent, not fond of sordid gain, ⁸ but hospitable, a lover of what is good, master of himself, upright, holy, and self-controlled. ⁹ He must hold firm to the sure word as taught, so that he may be able to give instruction in sound doctrine and also to refute those who contradict it.

¹⁰ For there are [also] many rebellious men, empty talkers and deceivers, especially those of the circumcision. ¹¹ They must be silenced, because they are upsetting whole families by teaching things they ought not to teach for the sake of sordid gain. ¹² One of themselves, a prophet of their own, said,

> "Cretans are always liars, evil beasts, lazy gluttons."

¹³ This testimony is true. Therefore, rebuke them sharply, so that they may be sound in the faith ¹⁴ and will pay no attention to Jewish myths or to the commands of men who reject the truth. ¹⁵ To the pure, all things are pure; but to those who are corrupted and unbelieving, nothing is pure, but both their minds and consciences are corrupted. ¹⁶ They profess to know God, but they deny him by their deeds. They are detestable and disobedient, unfit for any good deed.

2 ¹ But as for you, teach what befits sound doctrine. ² The older men are to be temperate, serious, sensible, sound in faith, in love, and in endurance. ³ The older women likewise are to be reverent in behavior, not to be slanderers or slaves to much

---

Title Alx/Byz[**To Titus**], Minor[*variations of* The Letter of Paul the Apostle to Titus].

1:1 Alx/Byz[**Paul**], Alt[*without textual foundation* Saul (~JNT)]; Alx/Byz[**Jesus Christ**], Minor[Christ Jesus *others* Christ]; **servant** *Greek* slave; **for the faith** *or* according to the faith.

1:4 Alx[**grace and peace**], Byz[grace, mercy, peace (KJV, NKJ)]; Alx[**Christ Jesus**], Byz[the Lord Jesus Christ (KJV, ~MRD, NKJ, ~REB)].

1:5 **appoint** *or* ordain.

1:7 **overseer** *or* bishop.

1:9 Alx/Byz[*text*], Metzger[*Minor adds* "Do not appoint those who have married twice or make them deacons, and do not take wives in a second marriage; let them not come to serve the Deity at the altar. As God's servant reprove the rulers who are unjust judges and robbers and liars and unmerciful" *translation is Metzger's*].

1:10 Alx/Byz[**also**], Minor[*omits* (ASV, DRA, ESV, JNT, NAS, NAU, NET, NIV, NJB, NLT, NRS, REB, RSV, TEV, TLB)].

1:11 Alx/Byz[*text*], Metzger[*Minor adds* "The children who abuse or strike their parents you must check and reprove and admonish as a father his children" *translation is Metzger's*].

1:12 Classical[**Epimenides, De oraculus**: "They fashioned you a tomb, O holy and high one. The Cretans, always liars, evil beasts, lazy gluttons! But you are not dead. You live and abide forever. For in you we live and move and have our being."]; *compare Acts 17:28*.

wine. But they are to teach what is good, [4] so they can train the young women to love their husbands and children, [5] to be sensible, pure, workers at home, kind, being subject to their own husbands, so that the word of God will not be dishonored. [6] Likewise urge the young men to be sensible. [7] Show yourself in all respects an example of good deeds, and in your teaching show integrity, seriousness, [8] and sound speech that cannot be condemned, so that an opponent may be put to shame, having nothing bad to say about us. [9] Teach slaves to be subject to their masters in everything, to be well-pleasing, not to talk back to them, [10] and not to steal, but to show all good faith, so that in everything they will adorn the doctrine of God our Savior.

[11] For the grace of God has appeared, bringing salvation to all men, [12] training us to renounce ungodliness and worldly passions, and to live sober, upright, and godly lives in this present age, [13] looking for the blessed hope and the appearing of the glory of our great God and Savior, Jesus Christ, [14] who gave himself for us to redeem us from all wickedness and to purify for himself a people that are his very own, zealous for good deeds. [15] Speak these things. Exhort and reprove with all authority. Let no one disregard you.

3 [1] Remind them to be subject to rulers, authorities, to be obedient, to be ready for every good deed, [2] to speak evil of no one, to be peaceable and gentle, and to show true humility toward all men. [3] For we ourselves were once foolish, disobedient, deceived, enslaved to various passions and pleasures, passing our days in malice and envy, hated by men and hating one another. [4] But when the kindness and love of God our Savior appeared, [5] he saved us, not on the basis of deeds which we have done in righteousness, but because of his own mercy, by the washing of regeneration and renewal in the Holy Spirit, [6] whom he poured out upon us richly through Jesus Christ our Savior, [7] so that we might be justified by his grace and become heirs according to the hope of eternal life.

[8] This is a trustworthy saying. And concerning these things I want you to speak confidently, so that those who have believed God may be careful to devote themselves to good deeds. These things are excellent and profitable for men. [9] But avoid foolish controversies and genealogies and rivalries and quarrels about the Law, for they are unprofitable and useless. [10] Warn a man who is factious once, and then warn him a second time. After that, have nothing to do with him, [11] knowing that such a man is perverted and sinful. He is self-condemned.

[12] When I send Artemas or Tychicus to you, do your best to come to me at Nicopolis, for I have decided to spend the winter there. [13] Do your best to help Zenas the lawyer and Apollos on their way. See that they lack nothing. [14] Our people must also learn

---

2:5 Alx[**workers at home**], Byz[keepers at home (DRA, HCS, JNT, KJV, MRD, NAB, NKJ, NRS, ~RSV, TEV, TLB)].

2:7 Alx[**integrity, seriousness**], Byz[*adds* incorruptibility (KJV, ~NJB, NKJ)].

2:8 Alx/Byz[**say about us**], Minor[say about you (KJV, NKJ, TLB)].

2:10 Alx/Byz[**all good faith**], Minor[*omits* faith]; Alx/Byz[**God our Savior**], Minor[God your Savior].

2:11 Alx[*text*], Byz[For the grace of God that brings salvation has appeared to all men (~DRA, JNT, KJV, ~MRD, NIV, NKJ, TLB)].

2:13 Alx/Byz[**Jesus Christ**], Minor[Christ Jesus (NAS, NAU, NJB, REB)]; **our great God and Savior** *or* the great God and our Savior.

2:15 **authority** *Greek* commandment.

3:1 Alx[**rulers, authorities**], Byz[rulers and authorities (DRA, ESV, HCS, JNT, KJV, MRD, NAB, NET, NIV, NKJ, NLT, NRS, REB, RSV, TEV, TLB)].

3:8 **This is a trustworthy saying** *could be placed with the previous paragraph.*

3:9 Alx/Byz[**rivalries**], Minor[rivalry (NAS, NAU)].

to devote themselves to good deeds, so that they may help cases of urgent need, and not be unfruitful.

15 All who are with me send you greetings. Greet those who love us in the faith. Grace be with you all.

3:15 Alx/Byz[**Grace**], Minor[The grace of the Lord *others* The grace of God]; Alx[*text*], Byz[*adds* Amen (DRA, KJV, MRD, NKJ)], Minor[*adds variations of* To Titus, the first bishop of the Cretan church, from Nicopolis of Macedonia (KJV)].

3:16 Minor[*places* Grace be with you all *as verse 16*].

To Philemon

1

¹ Paul, a prisoner of Christ Jesus, and Timothy our brother, to Philemon our beloved brother and fellow worker, ² and to Apphia our sister, and to Archippus our fellow soldier, and to the church in your house: ³ grace to you and peace from God our Father and the Lord Jesus Christ.

⁴ I thank my God always when I remember you in my prayers, ⁵ because I hear of your love and of the faith which you have for the Lord Jesus and all the saints, ⁶ and I pray that the sharing of your faith may become effective through the knowledge of every good thing that is ours in Christ. ⁷ For I have derived much joy and comfort from your love, my brother, because the hearts of the saints have been refreshed through you.

⁸ Therefore, though I am bold enough in Christ to order you to do what is proper, ⁹ yet for love's sake I rather appeal to you – since I am such a person as Paul, the aged, and now also a prisoner of Christ Jesus – ¹⁰ I appeal to you for my child, Onesimus, whose father I have become in these chains. ¹¹ Formerly he was useless to you, but now he is useful to [both] you and me. ¹² I am sending him back to you, sending my very heart. ¹³ I would have been glad to keep him with me, so that he might serve me on your behalf during my imprisonment for the gospel. ¹⁴ But without your consent I did not want to do anything, so that your goodness would not be, in effect, by compulsion but of your own free will. ¹⁵ Perhaps this is the reason he was separated from you for a while, that you might have him back forever, ¹⁶ no longer as a slave, but more than a slave, as a beloved brother, especially to me, but how much more to you, both in the flesh and in the Lord.

¹⁷ So if you consider me a partner, welcome him as you would welcome me. ¹⁸ If he has wronged you in any way, or owes you anything, charge that to my account. ¹⁹ I, Paul, am writing this with my own hand, I will pay it back – not to mention that you owe me even your own self. ²⁰ Yes, brother, let me have some benefit from you in the Lord. Refresh my heart in Christ.

Title Alx/Byz[**To Philemon**], Minor[*variations of* The Letter of Paul the Apostle to Philemon].

1:1 Alx/Byz[**Paul**], Alt[*without textual foundation* Saul (~JNT)]; Alx/Byz[**Christ Jesus**], Minor[Jesus Christ (KJV, MRD, TLB)]; **our brother** *Greek* the brother.

1:2 Alx[**our sister** *Greek* the sister], Byz[our beloved (~DRA, KJV, MRD, NKJ)].

1:5 Alx/Byz[**for the Lord** *or* toward the Lord], Minor[in the Lord (DRA, NAB, NET, NIV, NLT, ~TEV, TLB)].

1:6 Alx/Byz[**every good thing that is**], Minor[*omits* that is (MRD, NIV, NJB, NLT)]; Alx/Byz[**ours**], Minor[yours (ASV, DRA, KJV, MRD, NAS, NAU, NET, NKJ, TLB)]; Alx[**Christ**], Byz[*adds* Jesus (DRA, KJV, MRD, NKJ, TLB)].

1:7 Alx[**I have derived**], Byz[we have (KJV, MRD, NKJ)]; Alx[**joy**], Byz[grace].

1:9 Alx/Byz[**Paul**], Alt[*without textual foundation* Saul (~JNT)]; Alx/Byz[**the aged**], Alt[*emendation* the ambassador (RSV); Alx[**Christ Jesus**], Byz[Jesus Christ (DRA, KJV, MRD, NKJ, TLB)].

1:10 Alx[**these chains**], Byz[my chains (ASV, DRA, ESV, KJV, MRD, NAB, NAS, NAU, NET, ~NIV, NKJ, NRS, RSV, TLB)].

1:10-11 **Onesimus** *means* useful *or* beneficial (*compare verse 20*).

1:11 Alx[**both**], Byz[*omits* (ASV, ESV, JNT, KJV, NET, NKJ, RSV)].

1:11-12 Alx[*text*], Byz[*ends verse 11 after* sending him back to you (MRD)]; Alx/Byz[**I am sending him back to you**], Minor[him].

1:12 Alx[**sending my very heart**], Byz[Receive my very heart (DRA, KJV, MRD, NKJ)].

1:19 Alx/Byz[**Paul**], Alt[*without textual foundation* Saul (~JNT)].

1:20 Alx[**Christ**], Byz[the Lord (DRA, KJV, NKJ, ~REB, TLB)]; **have some benefit** *Greek* onaimen; *compare verse 10.*

21 Confident of your obedience, I write to you, knowing that you will do even more than I say. **22** At the same time, prepare a guest room for me, for I hope through your prayers to be granted to you.

23 Epaphras, my fellow prisoner in Christ Jesus, sends you greetings, **24** and so do Mark, Aristarchus, Demas, and Luke, my fellow workers. **25** The grace of the Lord Jesus Christ be with your spirit.

To the Hebrews

1 ¹ In the past God spoke to the fathers by the prophets at many times and in various ways. ² But in these last days he has spoken to us by his Son, whom he appointed heir of all things, and through whom also he made the world. ³ He is the radiance of his glory and the exact representation of his being, and upholds all things by the word of his power. When he had made purification for sins, he sat down at the right hand of the Majesty on high, ⁴ having become as much superior to angels as the name he has inherited is more excellent than theirs.

⁵ For to which of the angels did God ever say,

> "You are my son,
>> today I have begotten you"?

And again,

> "I will be a father to him
>> and he shall be a son to me"?

⁶ And again, when God brings the first-born into the world, he says,

> "Let all God's angels worship him."

⁷ Of the angels he says,

> "Who makes his angels winds,
>> and his servants flames of fire."

⁸ But of the Son he says,

> "Your throne, O God, is for ever and ever,
>> and the righteous scepter
>>> is the scepter of your kingdom.

⁹ You have loved righteousness and hated lawlessness;
> therefore God, your God
>> has anointed you with the oil of gladness
>>> above your companions."

¹⁰ And,

> "You, Lord, in the beginning laid the foundation of the earth,
>> and the heavens are the work of your hands.

¹¹ They will perish, but you remain.

Title Alx/Byz[**To the Hebrews**], Minor[*variations of* The Letter of Paul the Apostle to the Hebrews].

1:¹ Alx/Byz[**the fathers**], Minor[our fathers (ESV, MRD, NAB, NET, NIV, NJB, NLT, NRS, REB, RSV, TEV, TLB)].

1:² Alx[**2 but in these last days he has spoken to us by his Son**], Byz[but in these last days he has spoken to us by his Son 2 (~DRA)]; Alx/Byz[**these last days** *Greek* the last of these days], Minor[these last days], Alt[last of all, in these days (DRA)], Alt[*without textual foundation* in this the final age (~REB)].

1:³ Alx[**When he had made purification for sins**], Byz[When he had by himself made purification for our sins (JNT, KJV, ~MRD, NKJ, ~NLT)].

1:⁵ **Psalms 2:7, 2 Samuel 7:14**, 1 Chronicles 17:13.

1:⁶ **Deuteronomy 32:43 LXX/DSS**, Psalms 97:7.

1:⁷ **Psalms 104:4 LXX**.

1:⁸ Alx/Byz[**for ever and ever**], Minor[forever]; Alx[**and the righteous scepter**], Byz[a righteous scepter (JNT, KJV, MRD, NAB, NET, ~NIV, NKJ, ~NLT, ~TEV, ~TLB)]; Alx/Byz[**your kingdom**], Minor[his kingdom (NAS, NAU, NJB, REB)].

1:⁸⁻⁹ **Psalms 45:6-7 LXX**.

1:⁹ Alx/Byz[**hated lawlessness**], Minor[hated unrighteousness (~REB, ~TEV, ~TLB)]; Alx/Byz[**your God has anointed you**], Minor[your God, has anointed you (ASV, DRA, ESV, HCS, KJV, MRD, NAB, NAS, NAU, NET, NIV, NKJ, NRS, RSV, TEV, TLB)].

1:¹⁰⁻¹² ~**Psalms 102:25-27 LXX/DSS**

> They will all grow old like a garment.
12   You will roll them up like a mantle.
> And like a garment they will be changed.
> But you remain the same,
> and your years will never end."

13 But to which of the angels has he ever said,

> "Sit at my right hand,
> until I make your enemies a stool for your feet"?

14 Are they not all ministering spirits, sent forth to serve for the sake of those who will inherit salvation?

2 ¹ Therefore we must pay more careful attention to what we have heard, lest we drift away from it. ² For if the message spoken by angels was valid, and every transgression and disobedience received a just punishment, ³ how shall we escape if we neglect so great a salvation? It was declared at first by the Lord, and it was confirmed to us by those who heard him, ⁴ while God also bore witness, by signs and wonders and various miracles, and by gifts of the Holy Spirit distributed according to his own will.

⁵ For it is not to angels that he subjected the world to come – of which we are speaking. ⁶ But there is a place where someone has testified,

> "What is man that you are mindful of him,
> or the son of man that you care for him?
7   You made him a little lower than the angels;
> you crowned him with glory and honor,
8   and put everything in subjection under his feet."

Now in putting everything in subjection [to him], he left nothing that is not subject to him. As it is, we do not yet see everything subject to him. ⁹ But we see Jesus, who for a little while was made lower than the angels, crowned with glory and honor because of the suffering of death, so that by the grace of God he might taste death for everyone.

¹⁰ For it was fitting that he, for whom and through whom all things exist, in bringing many sons to glory, should make the author of their salvation perfect through suffering. ¹¹ For both he who sanctifies and those who are being sanctified are all of one. That is why he is not ashamed to call them brothers, ¹² saying,

> "I will declare your name to my brothers.
> In the midst of the congregation I will sing your praise."

13 And again,

> "I will put my trust in him."

And again,

> "Here am I, and the children God has given me."

14 Since therefore the children share in blood and flesh, he himself likewise partook of the same nature, that through death he might destroy him who has the power of death, that is,

---

1:12 Alx/Byz[**You will roll them up**], Minor[You will change them (DRA)]; Alx[**like a garment**], Byz[*omits* (DRA, KJV, MRD, NKJ, RSV, TLB)].

1:13 **Psalms 110:1**.

2:6-8 **Psalms 8:4-6 LXX**.

2:7 Alx/Byz[*text*], Minor[*adds* and set him over the works of your hands (ASV, DRA, KJV, MRD, NAS, NAU, NKJ)]; **a little lower** *or* for a little while lower; *compare Psalms 8:7*.

2:8 Alx/Byz[**subjection to him**], Minor[*omits* to him (NLT, TLB)]; NRS *makes* **to him** *into a neutral plural* to them.

2:9 Alx/Byz[**by the grace of God**], Minor[apart from God]; **for a little while** *or* only a little.

2:12 **Psalms 22:22 LXX**.

2:13 2 Samuel 22:3; **Isaiah 8:17 LXX, 8:18**.

2:14 Alx[**blood and flesh**], Byz[flesh and blood (ASV, DRA, ESV, HCS, ~JNT, KJV, MRD, NAS, NAU, NET, NIV, ~NJB, NKJ, NLT, NRS, REB, RSV, TEV, TLB)].

the devil, [15] and might free those who through fear of death were subject to slavery all their lives. [16] For surely it is not with angels that he is concerned, but with the descendants of Abraham. [17] Therefore he had to be made like his brothers in every respect, so that he might become a merciful and faithful high priest in the service of God, to make atonement for the sins of the people. [18] For because he himself has suffered, being tempted, he is able to help those who are tempted.

3 [1] Therefore, holy brothers, who share in a heavenly calling, consider Jesus, the apostle and high priest of our confession. [2] He was faithful to him who appointed him, just as Moses also was faithful in [all] God's house. [3] Yet Jesus has been counted worthy of as much more glory than Moses as the builder of a house has more honor than the house. [4] For every house is built by someone, but the builder of all things is God. [5] Now Moses was faithful in all God's house as a servant, to testify to the things that were to be spoken later, [6] but Christ is faithful as a son over God's house. And we are his house, if [only] we hold fast to our confidence and the hope of which we boast.

[7] Therefore, as the Holy Spirit says:

"Today, if you will hear his voice,
[8]   do not harden your hearts as in the rebellion,
            on the day of testing in the wilderness,
[9]   where your fathers tried, tested,
            and saw my works for [10] forty years.
    Therefore I was angry with this generation,
    and said, 'They always go astray in their hearts;
            and they have not known my ways.'
[11]   As I swore in my wrath,
            'They shall never enter my rest.'"

[12] Take care, brothers, lest there be in any one of you an evil, unbelieving heart, leading you to fall away from the living God. [13] But exhort one another every day, as long as it is called "Today," so that none of you may be hardened by the deceitfulness of sin. [14] For we have come to share in Christ if we hold our first confidence firm to the end, [15] while it is said,

"Today, if you will hear his voice,
    do not harden your hearts as in the rebellion."

[16] For who were they who heard and rebelled? Were they not all those Moses led out of Egypt? [17] And with whom was he angry for forty years? Was it not with those who sinned, whose bodies fell in the wilderness? [18] And to whom did he swear that they would never

---

2:17 **make atonement** *or* bring mercy.

3:1 Alx[**consider Jesus**], Byz[consider Jesus Christ (MRD)], Minor[consider Christ Jesus (KJV, NKJ)].

3:2 Alx/Byz[**all**], Minor[*omits* (NET, REB, RSV, TEV, TLB)]; **God's** *Greek* his; *compare Numbers 12:7 LXX.*

3:3 **Jesus** *Greek* this one.

3:5 **God's** *Greek* his.

3:6 Alx[**only**], Byz[*omits* (ASV, DRA, ~ESV, HCS, JNT, KJV, MRD, NAS, NAU, ~NET, NIV, NJB, NKJ, NLT, NRS, RSV, TEV, TLB)]; Alx[**hold fast to**], Byz[*adds* the end (ASV, DRA, KJV, MRD, NAS, NAU, NKJ, TLB)]; **God's** *Greek* his.

3:7-11 **Psalms 95:7-11 LXX**.

3:9 Alx[**tried, tested**], Byz[tried me, tested me (ASV, ~DRA, ~ESV, HCS, ~JNT, KJV, ~MRD, ~NAB, NAS, NAU, NET, ~NIV, NJB, NKJ, ~NLT, ~NRS, REB, ~RSV, TEV, ~TLB)].

3:10 Alx[**10 forty years**], Byz[forty years 10 (ASV, ESV 2007 edition, JNT, KJV, MRD, NAS, NAU, NET, NIV, NKJ, NLT, REB, RSV, TEV, TLB)]; Alx[**this generation**], Byz[that generation (ESV, JNT, KJV, MRD, NAB, NET, NIV, NJB, NKJ, ~NLT, NRS, REB, RSV, ~TEV, ~TLB)].

3:15 **Psalms 95:7-8 LXX**.

3:16 Alx[**For who were they...?**], Byz[For there were some ... (DRA, KJV)].

3:18 **were disobedient** *or* disbelieved.

enter his rest, but to those who were disobedient? [19] So we see that they were not able to enter because of unbelief.

4 [1] Therefore, while the promise of entering his rest remains, let us fear lest any one of you be judged to have come short of it. [2] For we also have had the good news preached to us, just as they did. But the message they heard was of no value to them, because they were not united in faith with those who listened. [3] For we who have believed enter [that] rest, as he has said,

> "As I swore in my wrath,
> 'They shall never enter my rest,'"

although his works were finished from the foundation of the world. [4] For he has somewhere spoken of the seventh day in this way: "And God rested on the seventh day from all his works." [5] And again in this place he said, "They shall never enter my rest." [6] Since therefore it remains for some to enter it, and those who formerly had the good news preached to them failed to enter because of disobedience, [7] God again set a certain day, "Today," saying through David after so long a time just as has been said before,

> "Today, if you hear his voice,
> do not harden your hearts."

[8] For if Joshua had given them rest, God would not have spoken later of another day. [9] So then, there remains a Sabbath rest for the people of God; [10] for anyone who enters God's rest also rests from his own work, just as God did from his. [11] Therefore let us be diligent to enter that rest, so that no one will fall by following the same example of disobedience.

[12] For the word of God is living and active, sharper than any two-edged sword, piercing even to the division of soul and spirit, and of joints and marrow, and discerning the thoughts and intentions of the heart. [13] And there is no creature hidden from his sight, but all things are open and laid bare to the eyes of him with whom we have to do.

[14] Since then we have a great high priest who has passed through the heavens, Jesus, the Son of God, let us hold fast our confession. [15] For we do not have a high priest who is unable to sympathize with our weaknesses, but one who in every respect has been tempted as we are, yet without sin. [16] Let us then with confidence draw near to the throne of grace, that we may receive mercy and find grace to help in time of need.

5 [1] For every high priest chosen from among men is appointed to act on behalf of men in relation to God, to offer both gifts and sacrifices for sins. [2] He can deal gently with those who are ignorant and going astray, since he himself is beset with weakness. [3] Because of it he has to offer sacrifices for his own sins, as well as for the sins of the people. [4] And no one takes the honor upon himself, but he is called by God, even as Aaron was.

4:2 Alx[**they were not united in faith with those who listened**], Byz[it did not meet with faith in those who listened (ASV, DRA, JNT, KJV, MRD, NAS, NAU, NKJ, REB, RSV, ~TEV, ~TLB)].

4:3 Alx/Byz[**For**], Minor[Then (MRD, NIV, REB, TEV) *others* But (NJB)]; Alx/Byz[**enter that rest** *or* enter the rest], Minor[enter rest (DRA, KJV, MRD, ~NJB, ~NLT, ~TLB)].

4:3, 5 **Psalms 95:11**.

4:4 **Genesis 2:2**.

4:7 Alx[**as has been said before** *or* as quoted above], Byz[*omits* before (KJV, NKJ)], Minor[as he has said before (TEV)]; **Psalms 95:7-8 LXX**.

4:8 **God** *Greek* he.

4:12 Alx[**soul and spirit**], Byz[both soul and spirit].

4:14 **through the heavens** *or* into heaven.

4:15 Alx[**tempted** *or* tested], Byz[tried].

5:1 Alx/Byz[**both gifts**], Minor[*omits* both (DRA, ESV, JNT, MRD, NAB, NIV, NJB, NLT, NRS, REB, RSV, TEV, TLB)].

5:3 Alx[**Because of it**], Byz[Because of this (~ASV, ~DRA, ESV, HCS, JNT, ~KJV, ~MRD, NAB, NET, NIV, NKJ, NRS, REB, RSV, ~TEV, ~TLB)]; Alx[**for his own sins** *Greek* for his], Byz[for himself (ASV, DRA, HCS, KJV, MRD, NAB, NAS, NAU, NET, NJB, NKJ, REB)]; Alx[**for the sins of the people** *or* concerning the sins of the people], Byz[for the sins of the people *or* on behalf of the sins

[5] So also Christ did not exalt himself to become a high priest, but it was he who said to him,

> "You are my son,
>> today I have begotten you";

[6] as he says also in another place,

> "You are a priest forever,
>> after the order of Melchizedek."

[7] In the days of his flesh, Jesus offered up prayers and supplications, with loud cries and tears, to the one who was able to save him from death, and he was heard because of his godly fear. [8] Although he was a Son, he learned obedience from what he suffered; [9] and, once made perfect, he became the source of eternal salvation for all who obey him, [10] being designated by God as a high priest according to the order of Melchizedek.

[11] About this we have much to say which is hard to explain, since you have become dull of hearing. [12] For though by this time you ought to be teachers, you need someone to teach you again the first elements of God's word. You need milk, [and] not solid food; [13] for every one who lives on milk is unskilled in the word of righteousness, for he is a babe. [14] But solid food is for the mature – those who have their sense trained by practice to distinguish good from evil.

6 [1] Therefore let us leave the first teachings about Christ and go on to maturity, not laying again a foundation of repentance from dead works, and of faith toward God, [2] of instruction of baptisms, the laying on of hands, and the resurrection of the dead, and eternal judgment. [3] And this we will do, if God permits. [4] For it is impossible for those who have once been enlightened, who have tasted the heavenly gift, and have become partakers of the Holy Spirit, [5] and have tasted the goodness of the word of God and the powers of the age to come, [6] and then have fallen away, to renew them again to repentance, since they crucify again to themselves the Son of God, and put him to an open shame. [7] For land which drinks the rain that often falls upon it, and brings forth vegetation useful to those for whose sake it is cultivated, receives a blessing from God. [8] But if it bears thorns and thistles, it is worthless and near to being cursed. Its end is to be burned.

[9] Even though we speak like this, beloved, we are confident of better things in your case, things that accompany salvation. [10] For God is not so unjust as to forget your work and the love which you have shown for his sake in serving the saints, as you still do. [11] And we desire each one of you to show the same diligence in realizing the full assurance of hope until the end, [12] so that you may not be sluggish, but imitators of those who through faith and patience inherit the promises.

---

of the people].

5:4 Alx[**even as Aaron was**], Byz[just as Aaron was (DRA, ESV, HCS, JNT, KJV, MRD, NAB, NIV, NJB, NKJ, NLT, NRS, REB, RSV, TEV)].

5:5 **Psalms 2:7**.

5:6 **Psalms 110:4**.

5:7 **Jesus** *Greek* he.

5:11 **About this** *or* About him.

5:12 Alx[**you need someone to teach you again the first elements**], Byz[you need to be taught again what are the first elements (DRA, KJV, MRD)]; Alx/Byz[**and not solid food**], Minor[*omits* and (ESV, HCS, JNT, NET, NIV, NRS, REB, RSV, TEV, TLB)].

6:1 **maturity** *or* perfection; **dead works** *or* works that lead to death.

6:2 Alx/Byz[**of instruction**], Minor[*omits* of (HCS, JNT, MRD, NAB, NET, NIV, NJB, NLT, NRS, ~REB, RSV, TLB)]; Alx/Byz[**and the resurrection**], Minor[*omits* and (ESV, HCS, JNT, NAB, NET, NIV, NJB, NKJ, NLT, NRS, REB, RSV, TEV)].

6:3 Alx/Byz[**And this we will do**], Major[Let us do this (~TEV)].

6:6 **and then have fallen** *or* if they then fall; **since they crucify** *or* while they are crucifying.

6:10 Alx[**your work and the love**], Byz[your work and labor of love (KJV, NKJ)]; Alx/Byz[**which you have shown**], Minor[which you must show].

¹³ For when God made a promise to Abraham, since he had no one greater by whom to swear, *"he swore by himself,"* ¹⁴ saying, *"I will surely bless you and multiply you."* ¹⁵ And so Abraham, having patiently endured, obtained the promise. ¹⁶ For men swear by one greater than themselves. And in all their disputes the oath is final for confirmation. ¹⁷ So when God desired to show more convincingly to the heirs of the promise the unchangeable character of his purpose, he interposed with an oath, ¹⁸ so that, by two unchangeable things in which it is impossible for God to lie, we who have taken refuge might have strong encouragement to take hold of the hope set before us. ¹⁹ We have this as a sure and steadfast anchor of the soul, a hope that enters into the inner sanctuary behind the veil, ²⁰ where Jesus has entered as a forerunner on our behalf, having become a high priest forever according to the order of Melchizedek.

7 ¹ For this *Melchizedek, king of Salem, priest of the Most High God, met Abraham returning from the slaughter of the kings and blessed him.* ² And to him *Abraham gave a tenth part of everything.* He is first, by translation of his name, king of righteousness. And then he is also *king of Salem,* that is, king of peace. ³ Without father, without mother, without genealogy, having neither beginning of days nor end of life, but made like the Son of God, he remains a priest continually.

⁴ See how great he was! [Even] the patriarch Abraham gave him a tenth of the spoils. ⁵ And those descendants of Levi who receive the priestly office have a commandment in the law to take a tenth from the people, that is, from their brothers, though these also are descended from Abraham. ⁶ But this man whose genealogy is not derived from them received a tenth from Abraham and blessed him who had the promises. ⁷ And without dispute the lesser person is blessed by the greater. ⁸ In this case tithes are received by mortal men, but in that case by one of whom it is witnessed that he lives on. ⁹ One might even say that Levi himself, who receives tithes, paid tithes through Abraham, ¹⁰ for he was still in the loins of his ancestor when Melchizedek met him.

¹¹ Now if perfection could have been through the Levitical priesthood (for on the basis of it the people received the Law), what further need was there for another priest to arise according to the order of Melchizedek, and not one designated according to the order of Aaron? ¹² For when there is a change of the priesthood, there must also be a change of the law. ¹³ For the one of whom these things are spoken belonged to another tribe, from which no one has ever served at the altar. ¹⁴ For it is evident that our Lord was descended from Judah, and in regard to that tribe Moses said nothing about priests. ¹⁵ This becomes even more evident if another priest arises in the likeness of Melchizedek, ¹⁶ who has become a priest not on the basis of a law of carnal requirement, but according to the power of an indestructible life. ¹⁷ For it is declared,

> *"You are a priest forever,*
>   *after the order of Melchizedek."*

¹⁸ On the one hand, a former commandment is set aside because of its weakness and uselessness ¹⁹ (for the law made nothing perfect); but on the other hand, a better hope is introduced, through which we draw near to God. ²⁰ And it was not without an oath. For

---

6:13-14 **Genesis 22:16-17**.

6:14 Alx[**surely**], Byz[surely], Minor[unless (DRA)].

6:15 **Abraham** *Greek* he.

6:16 Alx[**For men swear**], Byz[For, to be sure, men swear (KJV, NJB, NKJ, NRS, RSV)].

6:18 Alx/Byz[**might**], Minor[would (NAU)].

7:1-2 ~**Genesis 14:17-20**.

7:4 Alx/Byz[**Even**], Minor[*omits* (ASV, ESV, MRD, NAS, NAU, NET, NJB, REB, RSV, TEV)].

7:14 Alx[**priests**], Byz[priesthood (KJV, MRD, NKJ, TLB)].

7:17 Alx[**it is declared**], Byz[he declares (DRA, KJV, MRD, NKJ, NLT, TLB)].

7:17, 21 **Psalms 110:4**.

7:20 Alx[**For those who formerly became priests took their office without an oath 21**], Byz[21 For

those who formerly became priests took their office without an oath, [21] but he became a priest with an oath through the One who said to him,

> "The Lord has sworn
> and will not change his mind,
> 'You are a priest forever.'"

[22] Because of this oath, Jesus has become the guarantee of [an even] better covenant. [23] The former priests were many in number, because they were prevented by death from continuing in office. [24] But he holds his priesthood forever, because he continues forever. [25] Therefore he is able also to save forever those who draw near to God through him, since he always lives to make intercession for them.

[26] For it was indeed fitting that we should have such a high priest, holy, blameless, unstained, separated from sinners, exalted above the heavens. [27] He does not need, like those high priests, to offer up daily sacrifices, first for his own sins and then for the sins of the people, because he did this once for all when he offered up himself. [28] For the Law appoints men as high priests who are weak. But the word of the oath, which came after the Law, appoints a Son who has been made perfect forever.

8 [1] Now the point in what we are saying is this: we have such a high priest, one who is seated at the right hand of the throne of the Majesty in heaven, [2] a minister in the sanctuary, the true tabernacle which is set up by the Lord, not by man. [3] For every high priest is appointed to offer both gifts and sacrifices; and so it is necessary for this priest also to have something to offer. [4] Now if he were on earth, he would not be a priest at all, since there are those who offer the gifts according to the law. [5] They serve a copy and shadow of the heavenly sanctuary; for when Moses was about to erect the tabernacle, he was instructed by God, saying, *"See that you make everything according to the pattern which was shown you on the mountain."* [6] But as it is, he has obtained a ministry which is as much more excellent than the old as the covenant he mediates is better, since it is enacted on better promises.

[7] For if that first covenant had been faultless, no opportunity would have been sought for a second one. [8] For he finds fault with them when he says:

> "The days are coming, says the Lord,
> when I will make a new covenant
> with the house of Israel and with the house of Judah;
>
> [9] not like the covenant that I made with their fathers
> on the day when I took them by the hand

---

those who formerly became priests took their office without an oath (ASV, KJV, MRD, NAS, NAU, NKJ, ~REB, RSV, TLB)].

7:21 Alx[**a priest forever**], Byz[*adds* after the order of Melchizedek (KJV, MRD, NKJ, TLB)].

7:22 Alx[**an even**], Byz[a (DRA, ESV, KJV, MRD, NET, NIV, NJB, ~NKJ, NLT, RSV, TLB)].

7:25 **forever** *or* completely

7:26 Alx[**For it was indeed fitting**], Byz[For it was fitting (ASV, DRA, HCS, JNT, KJV, NAB, NAS, NAU, NIV, NJB, NKJ, NLT, NRS, RSV, ~TEV, ~TLB)].

7:27 Alx/Byz[**offered up himself**], Minor[offered himself (DRA, HCS, NAB, NET, NIV, NJB, NLT, NRS, TEV, TLB)].

8:2 Alx[**not by man**], Byz[and not by man (DRA, HCS, ~JNT, KJV, MRD, NJB, NKJ, NLT, NRS, ~RSV, TLB)].

8:4 Alx[**Now if he were on earth**], Byz[For if he were on earth (KJV, NKJ)]; Alx[**there are those who offer**], Byz[there are priests who offer (ESV, JNT, KJV, MRD, NET, NKJ, NLT, NRS, REB, RSV, TEV, TLB)].

8:5 **Exodus 25:40**.

8:8 **For he finds fault with them when he says** *or* For he finds fault when he says to them.

8:7 Alx/Byz[**For if that first covenant**], Minor[For if indeed that first covenant (~JNT)].

8:8-12 **Jeremiah 31:31-34 LXX**.

8:9 **and so I paid no heed to them** *from LXX, Hebrew reads* though I was their husband.

> to lead them out of the land of Egypt;
> for they did not continue in my covenant,
> and so I paid no heed to them, says the Lord.

10   This is the covenant that I will make with the house of Israel
> after those days, says the Lord:
> I will put my laws into their mind,
> and I will write them on their hearts,
> and I will be their God,
> and they shall be my people.

11   And they will never teach every one his fellow-citizen
> or every one his brother, saying, 'Know the Lord,'
> for all shall know me,
> from the least to the greatest of them.

12   For I will be merciful to their iniquities,
> and I will remember their sins nevermore."

13 When he said, "A new covenant," he has made the first obsolete. And what is becoming obsolete and growing old is ready to vanish away.

9 ¹ Now [even] the first covenant had regulations for worship and an earthly sanctuary. ² For there was a tabernacle prepared, the first one, in which were the lampstand and the table and the sacred bread. This is called the holy place. ³ Behind the second veil was a tabernacle called the Holy of Holies, ⁴ having the golden altar of incense and the ark of the covenant covered on all sides with gold, which contained a golden jar holding the manna, and Aaron's rod that budded, and the tables of the covenant; ⁵ and above it were the cherubim of glory overshadowing the mercy seat. But of these things we cannot now speak in detail.

⁶ These preparations having thus been made, the priests go continually into the outer tabernacle, performing their ritual duties. ⁷ But into the second only the high priest goes, and he but once a year, and not without taking blood, which he offers for himself and for the unintentional sins of the people. ⁸ The Holy Spirit was showing by this that the way into the holy place had not yet been disclosed as long as the outer tabernacle was still standing. ⁹ This is a parable for the present time. According to this parable, gifts and sacrifices are offered which cannot perfect the conscience of the worshipper, ¹⁰ since they relate only to food and drink and various washings – regulations for the flesh imposed until the time of reformation.

8:10 Alx/Byz[**hearts**], Minor[heart (ESV, HCS, JNT, KJV, MRD, NAB, NAS, NAU, NET, NJB, NKJ, NLT, NRS, REB, RSV, TEV, TLB)].

8:11 Alx/Major[**never teach**], Byz[not teach (ASV, DRA, ESV, HCS, ~JNT, KJV, MRD, NAB, NAS, NAU, ~NET, ~NIV, ~NJB, ~NKJ, ~NLT, NRS, REB, RSV, ~TEV, ~TLB)]; Alx/Byz[**fellow-citizen**], Minor[neighbor (DRA, ESV, KJV, NIV, NJB, NKJ, NLT, ~NRS, TLB)]; Alx[**from the least to the greatest of them**], Byz[from the least of them to the greatest of them (~ESV, ~JNT, ~KJV, ~MRD, ~NAB, ~NET, ~NIV, ~NJB, NKJ, ~NLT, ~NRS, ~REB, ~RSV, ~TEV, ~TLB)].

8:12 Alx[**their sins**], Byz[*adds* and their lawless deeds (KJV, NKJ)].

9:1 Alx/Byz[**even**], Minor[*omits* (MRD, NIV, NLT)]; Alx/Major[**the first covenant had regulations** *Greek* the first had regulations], Byz[the first tabernacle had regulations].

9:2 Alx/Byz[**the sacred bread**], Minor[*adds* and the golden altar]; Alx/Byz[**the holy place**], Minor[*omits* place (DRA)]; **sacred bread** *or* bread of the Presence.

9:4 Alx/Byz[**the golden altar**], Minor[*omits*].

9:5 **mercy seat** *see Romans 3:25n.*

9:7 **unintentional sins of the people** *Leviticus 4:1-31.*

9:9 Alx[**According to this parable**], Byz[According to this time (HCS, KJV, MRD, ~NAB, NET, ~NJB, NKJ, ~NLT, NRS, ~TLB)].

9:10 Alx[**-- regulations for the flesh**], Byz[and regulations for the flesh (DRA, JNT, KJV, MRD, NKJ, TLB)].

¹¹ But when Christ appeared as a high priest of the good things that have come, he entered through the greater and more perfect tabernacle, not made with hands, that is to say, not of this creation. ¹² He did not enter by means of the blood of goats and calves, but he entered the holy place once for all by his own blood, having obtained eternal redemption. ¹³ For if the blood of goats and bulls, and the ashes of a heifer sprinkling those who have been defiled, sanctify for the cleansing of the flesh, ¹⁴ how much more will the blood of Christ, who through the eternal Spirit offered himself without blemish to God, cleanse our conscience from dead works to serve the living God?

¹⁵ For this reason he is the mediator of a new covenant, that those who are called may receive the promised eternal inheritance, now that he has died as a ransom to set them free from the transgressions committed under the first covenant. ¹⁶ For where a will is, there must of necessity be the death of the one who made it. ¹⁷ For a will is in force only when somebody has died, since it never takes effect while the one who made it is living. ¹⁸ This is why even the first covenant was not ratified without blood. ¹⁹ For when every commandment of the law had been declared by Moses to all the people, he took the blood of calves [and goats], with water and scarlet wool and hyssop, and sprinkled both the book itself and all the people, ²⁰ saying, *"This is the blood of the covenant which God has commanded you."* ²¹ And in the same way he sprinkled with the blood both the tabernacle and all the vessels used in worship. ²² Indeed, under the law almost everything is cleansed with blood, and without the shedding of blood there is no forgiveness of sins.

²³ It was necessary, then, for the copies of the heavenly things to be purified with these sacrifices, but the heavenly things themselves with better sacrifices than these. ²⁴ For Christ did not enter a holy place made with hands, a copy of the true one, but into heaven itself, now to appear in the presence of God for us. ²⁵ Nor was it that he should offer himself again and again, as the high priest enters the holy place year by year with blood not his own. ²⁶ For then he would have had to suffer repeatedly since the foundation of the world. But now, he has appeared once for all at the end of the ages to put away sin by the sacrifice of himself. ²⁷ And just as it is appointed for men to die once, and after that comes judgment, ²⁸ so also Christ, having been offered once to bear the sins of many, will appear a second time, not to bear sin but to bring salvation to those who are eagerly waiting for him.

10 ¹ For since the law has only a shadow of the good things to come and not the true form of these realities, it can never perfect the worshippers by the same sacrifices which are continually offered year after year. ² Otherwise, would they not have

---

9:11 Alx[**good things that have come**], Byz[good things to come (ASV, DRA, KJV, NAS, NAU, NET, NJB, NKJ)].

9:13 Alx[**goats and bulls**], Byz[bulls and goats (JNT, KJV, NKJ, TLB)].

9:14 Alx/Byz[**eternal Spirit**], Minor[Holy Spirit (DRA, ~TLB)]; Alx[**our conscience**], Byz[your conscience (ASV, KJV, NAS, NAU, NKJ, RSV)]; **dead works** *or* works that lead to death.

9:15 **covenant** *or* will *or* testament.

9:16-17 **will** *or* covenant *or* testament.

9:17 Alx/Byz[**it never takes effect**], Minor[it does not then take effect...does it?].

9:19 Alx/Byz[**and goats**], Minor[*omits* (JNT, MRD, NIV, REB)]; *compare Exodus 24:5.*

9:20 ~**Exodus 24:8**.

9:28 Alx/Byz[**so also Christ**], Minor[*omits* also (ESV, KJV, NIV, NKJ, NRS, REB, RSV)]; **bear the sins** *or* remove the sins.

10:1 Alx/Byz[**it can never perfect the worshippers by the same sacrifices which are continually offered year after year**], Major[the same sacrifices which are continually offered year after year can never perfect the worshippers (MRD, NLT, TLB)]; **the worshippers** Greek those who draw near; **perfect...continually offered** *or* continually perfect...offered.

10:2 Alx/Byz[**Otherwise would they not have ceased to be offered? If**], Minor[For then they would have ceased to be offered. Since (DRA, MRD, NLT, REB, TEV, TLB)]; Alx[**cleansed**], Byz[made clean].

ceased to be offered? If the worshippers had once been cleansed, they would no longer have any consciousness of sins. [3] But in these sacrifices there is a reminder of sins year after year. [4] For it is impossible for the blood of bulls and goats to take away sins.

[5] Therefore, when Christ came into the world, he said:

"Sacrifice and offering you did not desire,
but a body you prepared for me;

[6] *in burnt offerings and sin offerings*
you have taken no pleasure.

[7] *Then I said, 'Behold,*
I have come to do your will, O God,'
as it is written of me in the roll of the book."

[8] When he said above, *"You did not desire, nor did you take pleasure in sacrifices and offerings and burnt offerings and sin offerings"* (these are offered according to law), [9] then he said, *"Behold, I have come to do your will."* He takes away the first in order to establish the second. [10] And by that will we have been sanctified through the offering of the body of Jesus Christ once for all.

[11] And every priest stands daily at his service, offering time after time the same sacrifices, which can never take away sins. [12] But when this one had offered for all time one sacrifice for sins, he sat down at the right hand of God, [13] waiting from that time until his enemies be made a stool for his feet. [14] For by one offering he has perfected for all time those who are sanctified.

[15] And the Holy Spirit also bears witness to us; for after saying,

[16] *"This is the covenant that I will make*
with them after those days, says the Lord:
I will put my laws into their hearts,
and in their mind I will write them,"

[17] and,

"Their sins and their lawless deeds
I will remember nevermore."

[18] Where there is forgiveness of these, there is no longer any offering for sin.

[19] Therefore, brothers, since we have confidence to enter the holy place by the blood of Jesus, [20] by a new and living way which he opened for us through the veil, that is, his flesh, [21] and since we have a great priest over the house of God, [22] let us draw near with a

---

10:4 Alx/Byz[**bulls and goats**], Minor[goats and bulls].

10:5 Alx/Byz[**Sacrifice and offering**], Minor[Offering and sacrifice (~TLB)]; **Christ** *Greek he.*

10:5-7 ~**Psalms 40:6-8 LXX.**

10:8 Alx[**pleasure in sacrifices and offerings**], Byz[pleasure in sacrifice and offering (KJV, NKJ)]; Alx[**offered according to law**], Byz[offered according to the law (ASV, DRA, ESV, HCS, JNT, KJV, MRD, NAB, NAS, NAU, NET, NIV, NJB, NKJ, NLT, NRS, REB, RSV, TEV, TLB)].

10:9 Alx[**do your will**], Byz[*adds* O God (DRA, KJV, MRD, NKJ, TEV)]; *compare Psalms 39:9 LXX.*

10:10 Alx/Byz[**body of Jesus**], Minor[blood of Jesus].

10:11 Alx/Byz[**every priest**], Minor[every high priest (MRD)].

10:12 Alx[**this one**], Byz[he (ASV, ~ESV, NAS, NAU, NJB, ~NLT, ~NRS, ~REB, ~RSV, ~TEV, ~TLB)]; **offered for all time one sacrifice for sins, he sat down at the right hand of God** *or* offered one sacrifice for sins, he sat down at the right hand of God for all time.

10:15 Alx[**for after saying**], Byz[*adds* before (KJV, NKJ, ~REB, ~TEV)].

10:16 Alx[**hearts...mind**], Byz[hearts...minds (~ASV, DRA, ESV, HCS, JNT, KJV, ~MRD, NAB, ~NAS, ~NAU, NET, NIV, ~NJB, NKJ, NLT, NRS, RSV, TEV, ~TLB)].

10:16-17 ~**Jeremiah 31:33-34 LXX.**

10:17 Alx/Byz[**and, "Their sins..."** *syntax*], Minor[Then he says, "And their sins..." *clarification* (ESV, HCS, JNT, NAB, NET, NIV, NKJ, NLT, NRS, REB, RSV, TEV, TLB)].

10:22 Alx/Byz[**and our bodies washed with pure water 23**], Minor[23 and our bodies washed with pure water].

true heart in full assurance of faith, having our hearts sprinkled clean from an evil conscience and our bodies washed with pure water. 23 Let us hold fast the confession of our hope without wavering, for he who promised is faithful. 24 And let us consider how to stir up one another to love and good works, 25 not forsaking our own assembling together, as is the habit of some, but encouraging one another; and all the more, as you see the Day drawing near.

26 For if we sin deliberately after we have received the knowledge of the truth, there no longer remains a sacrifice for sins, 27 but a fearful expectation of judgment, and a fury of fire which will consume the adversaries. 28 Anyone who has rejected the law of Moses dies without mercy on the testimony of two or three witnesses. 29 How much severer punishment do you think a man will deserve who has trampled under foot the Son of God, and has regarded as an unclean thing the blood of the covenant by which he was sanctified, and has insulted the Spirit of grace? 30 For we know him who said,

"Vengeance is mine, I will repay."

And again,

"The Lord will judge his people."

31 It is a fearful thing to fall into the hands of the living God.

32 But remember the former days when, after you were enlightened, you endured a great struggle with sufferings, 33 sometimes being publicly exposed to insult and persecution; and at other times standing side by side with those who were so treated. 34 For you had compassion on the prisoners, and you joyfully accepted the plundering of your property, since you know that you yourselves have a better possession and an abiding one. 35 Therefore do not throw away your confidence, which has a great reward. 36 For you have need of endurance, so that when you have done the will of God, you may receive what was promised.

37 "For yet in a very little while,
      he who is coming will come and will not delay.

38 But my righteous one shall live by faith,
      and if he shrinks back,
         my soul has no pleasure in him."

39 But we are not of those who shrink back and are destroyed, but of those who have faith and keep their souls.

11 1 Now faith is the assurance of things hoped for, the conviction of things not seen. 2 For by it the men of old received divine approval.

3 By faith we understand that the world was created by the word of God, so that what is seen was not made out of things which are visible.

4 By faith Abel offered God a more acceptable sacrifice than Cain, through which he was commended as a righteous man, when God spoke well of his gifts. And through faith

---

10:30 Alx[**I will repay**], Byz[*adds* says the Lord (KJV, NKJ)]; ~**Deuteronomy 32:35-36**, ~Psalms 135:14.

10:34 Alx[**the prisoners**], Byz[me in my chains (KJV, NKJ)]; Alx[**you yourselves have**], Byz[you have in yourselves (KJV)], Major[you have for yourselves (ASV, NAS, NAU)], Minor[you have (DRA, JNT, MRD, NAB, ~NET, NIV, NKJ, ~NLT, REB, TEV, ~TLB)]; Alx[**an abiding one**], Byz[*adds* in heaven (KJV, MRD, NKJ, TLB)].

10:37-38 **Habakkuk 2:3-4 LXX**.

10:38 Alx[**my righteous one**], Byz[the righteous *or* the just (JNT, KJV, MRD, NKJ, TLB)].

11:1 Alx/Byz[**assurance** *or* substance], Metzger[*a single manuscript* resurrection].

11:3 Alx[**what is seen**], Byz[things which are seen (DRA, KJV, MRD, NKJ, TLB)]; **not made out of things which are visible** *or* made out of things which are not visible.

11:4 Alx/Byz[**Abel offered God**], Minor[*omits* God (JNT, REB)]; Alx/Byz[**God spoke well of his gifts**], Minor[he spoke well of his gifts to God]; Alx[**he still speaks**], Byz[he still speaks *or* he is still spoken of (~TLB)]; **more acceptable** *Greek* greater; **through faith** *Greek* through it.

he still speaks, even though he is dead. ⁵ By faith Enoch was taken up so that he should not see death. And *he was not found, because God had changed his place.* For before the change he was attested as having *pleased God.* ⁶ And without faith it is impossible to please God, for anyone who comes to him must believe that he exists and that he rewards those who earnestly seek him. ⁷ By faith Noah, being warned by God about things not yet seen, in godly fear prepared an ark for the salvation of his household, by which he condemned the world, and became an heir of the righteousness which comes by faith.

⁸ By faith Abraham obeyed when he was called to go out to a place which he was to receive as an inheritance. And he went out, not knowing where he was going. ⁹ By faith he lived in a land of promise, as in a foreign land, dwelling in tents with Isaac and Jacob, heirs with him of the same promise. ¹⁰ For he was looking forward to the city which has foundations, whose architect and builder is God. ¹¹ By faith Sarah herself, when she was barren, received power to conceive, even when she was past the age, because she considered him faithful who had promised. ¹² Therefore from one man, and him as good as dead, were born descendants as many as the stars of heaven and as the innumerable grains of sand by the seashore.

¹³ These all died in faith, not having taken hold of the promises, but having seen them and greeted them from a distance, and having acknowledged that they were strangers and exiles on the earth. ¹⁴ For people who say such things make it clear that they are seeking a country of their own. ¹⁵ And if they had been thinking of that country from which they had gone out, they would have had opportunity to return. ¹⁶ But as it is, they desire a better country, that is, a heavenly one. Therefore God is not ashamed to be called their God, for he has prepared for them a city.

¹⁷ By faith Abraham, when he was tested, offered up Isaac, and he who had received the promises was ready to offer up his only son, ¹⁸ of whom it was said, *"Through Isaac shall your descendants be called."* ¹⁹ He considered that God was able to raise men even from the dead; from which, figuratively speaking, he did receive him back. ²⁰ By faith also Isaac blessed Jacob and Esau in regard to their future. ²¹ By faith Jacob, when he was dying, blessed each of the sons of Joseph, and *worshipped as he leaned on the top of his staff.* ²² By faith Joseph, when he was at the end of his life, made mention of the exodus of the Israelites, and gave orders concerning his bones.

11:5 Alx[**before the change**], Byz[before his change (ASV, DRA, ESV, HCS, KJV, MRD, NAB, NAS, NAU, NET, NIV, NJB, NKJ, NLT, NRS, REB, RSV, TEV, ~TLB)]; Genesis 5:24 LXX.

11:8 Alx[**a place**], Byz[the place (MRD, NKJ)].

11:9 Alx/Major[**a land of promise**], Byz[the land of promise (ASV, ~DRA, ESV, HCS, JNT, KJV, MRD, NAB, NAS, NAU, NET, NIV, NJB, NKJ, NLT, NRS, REB, RSV, TEV)].

11:11 Alx[*text*], Byz[By faith Sarah herself received power to conceive, and she bore a child even when she was past the age, because she considered him faithful who had promised (ASV, ESV, KJV, NAS, NAU, NJB, NKJ, REB, RSV, TLB)], Minor[By faith he received power to generate, even though he was too old – and Sarah herself was barren – because he considered him faithful who had promised (JNT, NAB, NET, NIV, NRS, TEV)].

11:12 Alx/Byz[**as the...sand**], Minor[like...sand]; ~Genesis 22:17.

11:13 Alx/Byz[**taken hold of**], Minor[received (ASV, DRA, ESV, HCS, JNT, KJV, MRD, NAB, NAS, NAU, NET, NIV, NJB, NKJ, NLT, NRS, REB, RSV, TEV, TLB)]; Alx/Byz[**having seen them**], Minor[*adds* were assured of them (KJV, NKJ)].

11:15 Alx/Byz[**had been thinking**], Minor[are thinking (~JNT, ~MRD)]; Alx[**from which they had gone out**], Byz[from which they had come out (DRA, HCS, KJV, MRD, NAB, NJB, NKJ, NLT, ~TLB)].

11:17 Alx/Byz[**Abraham**], Minor[*omits*].

11:18 **descendants** *Greek* seed; **Genesis 21:12**.

11:20 Alx[**By faith also**], Byz[*omits* also (ASV, ESV, HCS, JNT, KJV, MRD, NAB, NAS, NAU, NIV, NJB, NKJ, NLT, NRS, REB, RSV, TEV, TLB)].

11:21 Genesis 47:31 LXX.

²³ By faith Moses, when he was born, was hidden for three months by his parents, because they saw he was a beautiful child; and they were not afraid of the king's edict. ²⁴ By faith Moses, when he was grown up, refused to be called the son of Pharaoh's daughter, ²⁵ choosing rather to share ill-treatment with the people of God than to enjoy the fleeting pleasures of sin. ²⁶ He considered abuse suffered for the Christ greater wealth than the treasures of Egypt, for he was looking ahead to his reward. ²⁷ By faith he left Egypt, not fearing the anger of the king; for he endured as seeing him who is invisible. ²⁸ By faith he kept the Passover and the sprinkling of the blood, so the destroyer of the firstborn would not touch them. ²⁹ By faith the people passed through the Red Sea as on dry land. But when the Egyptians tried to do so, they were drowned. ³⁰ By faith the walls of Jericho fell down after they had been encircled for seven days. ³¹ By faith Rahab the harlot did not perish with those who were disobedient, because she had welcomed the spies.

³² And what more shall I say? For time will fail me if I tell of Gideon, Barak, Samson, Jephthah, of David and Samuel and the prophets, ³³ who through faith conquered kingdoms, performed acts of justice, received promises, shut the mouths of lions, ³⁴ quenched the power of fire, escaped the edge of the sword, whose weakness was turned to strength, who became mighty in war, and put foreign armies to flight. ³⁵ Women received back their dead, raised to life again. Others were tortured and refused to be released, so that they might gain a better resurrection. ³⁶ And others experienced mockings and scourgings – yes, also chains and imprisonment. ³⁷ They were stoned, they were sawn in two, they were killed with the sword; they went about in skins of sheep and goats, destitute, afflicted, ill-treated – ³⁸ of whom the world was not worthy – wandering over deserts and mountains, and in caves and holes in the ground.

³⁹ And all these, though well attested by their faith, did not receive what was promised, ⁴⁰ because God had provided something better for us, that apart from us they should not be made perfect.

12 ¹ Therefore, since we are surrounded by so great a cloud of witnesses, let us also lay aside every weight, and the sin which so easily entangles us. And let us run with perseverance the race that is set before us, ² fixing our eyes on Jesus, the author and perfecter of our faith, who for the joy that was set before him endured the cross, despising the shame, and sat down at the right hand of the throne of God. ³ Consider him who endured from sinners such hostility against himself, so that you may not grow weary and lose heart.

11:²³ Alx/Byz[*text*], Minor[*adds* By faith Moses, when he was grown, destroyed the Egyptian when he observed the humiliation of his brothers].

11:²⁶ Alx/Byz[**treasures of Egypt**], Minor[treasures in Egypt (KJV, NKJ)].

11:²⁹ Alx[**as on dry land**], Byz[*omits* land].

11:³¹ **disobedient** *or* unbelieving.

11:³² Alx[**Gideon, Barak, Samson, Jephthah**], Byz[Gideon, Barak, and also Samson, and Jephthah (KJV, MRD, NKJ, TLB)].

11:³⁵ Alx/Byz[**Women received back their dead**], Minor[The dead returned to their women (MRD, NJB)].

11:³⁷ Alx[**they were sawn in two**], Byz[they were sawn in two, they were tested (ASV, DRA, KJV, NAS, NAU, NKJ, TLB)], Minor[they were tested, they were sawn in two *others* they were sawn in two, they were burned].

11:³⁸ Alx[**wandering over deserts**], Byz[wandering in deserts (ASV, DRA, HCS, KJV, MRD, NAS, NAU, NET, NIV, NJB, NKJ, NRS, REB, TEV)].

11:³⁹ Alx/Byz[**what was promised** *or* the promise], Minor[the promises].

12:¹ Alx/Byz[**entangles**], Minor[distracts].

12:² **for the joy** *or* in place of the joy.

12:³ Alx/Byz[**against himself**], Minor[against themselves (Metzger) *others omit* (MRD, NAB, NET, NIV, NJB, NLT, REB, TEV)].

⁴ In your struggle against sin, you have not yet resisted to the point of shedding your blood. ⁵ And have you forgotten the exhortation which addresses you as sons? –

"My son, do not regard lightly the discipline of the Lord,
nor lose courage when you are rebuked by him.

⁶   *For those whom the Lord loves he disciplines.*
And he scourges every son whom he receives."

⁷ It is for discipline that you endure. God is treating you as sons; for what son is there whom his father does not discipline? ⁸ If you are left without discipline, in which all have become partakers, then you are illegitimate children and not sons. ⁹ Besides this, we have had fathers of our flesh to discipline us and we respected them. Shall we not [then] submit all the more to the Father of spirits and live? ¹⁰ For they disciplined us for a short time as seemed best to them, but he disciplines us for our good, that we may share his holiness. ¹¹ For the moment all discipline seems painful rather than pleasant; but later it yields the peaceful fruit of righteousness to those who have been trained by it.

¹² Therefore lift your feeble hands and strengthen your weak knees, ¹³ and *make straight paths for your feet,* so that what is lame may not be turned aside, but rather be healed.

¹⁴ Strive for peace with all men, and for the holiness without which no one will see the Lord. ¹⁵ See to it that no one comes short of the grace of God; that no root of bitterness spring up and cause trouble, and by it many become defiled; ¹⁶ that no one be immoral or godless like Esau, who sold his own birthright for a single meal. ¹⁷ For you know that afterward, when he desired to inherit the blessing, he was rejected, for he found no place for repentance, though he sought it diligently with tears.

¹⁸ For you have not come to something that can be touched, and to a blazing fire, and to darkness and gloom and whirlwind, ¹⁹ and the blast of a trumpet, and the sound of a voice whose words made the hearers beg that no further word be spoken to them. ²⁰ For they could not endure the order that was given, *"If even a beast touches the mountain, it shall be stoned."* ²¹ The sight was so terrifying that Moses said, *"I am trembling with fear."* ²² But you have come to Mount Zion and to the city of the living God, the heavenly Jerusalem, and to myriads of angels, to a joyful assembly ²³ and church of the firstborn who are enrolled in heaven, and to God, the Judge of all, and to the spirits of righteous men made perfect, ²⁴ and

---

12:5-6 **Proverbs 3:11-12 LXX**.

12:7 Alx/Major[**It is for discipline that you endure. God**], Byz[If you endure discipline, God (KJV, NKJ)].

12:9 Alx/Byz[**respected**], Minor[respect (TLB)]; Alx[**then**], Byz[*omits* (DRA, ESV, HCS, JNT, MRD, NET, NIV, NJB, NKJ, NRS, REB, RSV, TLB)].

12:11 Alx/Byz[**For the moment**], Minor[Indeed for the moment].

12:13 ~Proverbs 4:26.

12:15 Alx[**by it**], Byz[by this (~JNT, ~NAB, NJB, NKJ)]; Alx/Byz[**many**], Minor[the many (ASV, REB, RSV)].

12:16 Alx[**his own birthright**], Byz[his birthright (DRA, ESV, HCS, JNT, KJV, MRD, NAB, NIV, NJB, NRS, REB, RSV, TEV, TLB)].

12:17 **no place for repentance** *could refer to either Esau's or his father's change of mind.*

12:18 Alx[**something**], Byz[a mountain (ASV, DRA, JNT, KJV, MRD, NAS, NAU, NIV, NKJ, NLT, ~REB)]; Alx[**gloom**], Byz[blackness (ASV, KJV, NKJ)], Minor[*omits*], *DRA reads* whirlwind and darkness and storm.

12:19 Alx/Byz[**beg that no further word**], Minor[refuse that further word].

12:20 Alx/Byz[**stoned**], Minor[*adds* or shot with an arrow (KJV, NKJ, ~TLB)]; ~**Exodus 19:12-13**.

12:21 Alx/Byz[**I am trembling with fear** *Greek* I fear and tremble], Minor[I fear and exceedingly tremble (~ASV, ~KJV, ~NKJ)]; ~**Deuteronomy 9:19**.

12:22 Alx[**angels, to a joyful assembly 23**], Byz[angels, 23 to a joyful assembly (ASV, KJV, MRD, NAS, NAU, NKJ, REB, TEV)], Minor[angels 23 in a joyful assembly, (~DRA, ~ESV, ~HCS, ~JNT, ~NAB, ~NIV, ~NLT, ~NRS, ~RSV, ~TLB)].

12:24 Alx/Byz[**speaks better**], Minor[speaks better things (HCS, JNT, KJV, NKJ, REB, TEV)].

to Jesus, the mediator of a new covenant, and to the sprinkled blood that speaks better than the blood of Abel.

²⁵ See to it that you do not refuse him who is speaking. For if they did not escape when they refused him who warned them on earth, how much less shall we escape, if we turn away from him who warns us from heaven? ²⁶ Then his voice shook the earth, but now he has promised, *"Yet once more I will shake not only the earth, but also heaven."* ²⁷ This phrase, *"Yet once more,"* indicates [the] removal of what is shaken – that is, created things – in order that what cannot be shaken may remain. ²⁸ Therefore, since we are receiving a kingdom that cannot be shaken, let us give thanks, with which we may offer to God acceptable worship with reverence and awe, ²⁹ *"for our God is a consuming fire."*

13

¹ Let brotherly love continue. ² Do not forget to show hospitality to strangers, for by so doing some people have entertained angels without knowing it. ³ Remember the prisoners, as though in prison with them, and those who are ill-treated, since you yourselves are also in the body. ⁴ Let marriage be held in honor among all, and let the marriage bed be undefiled; for God will judge the immoral and adulterous. ⁵ Keep your lives free from the love of money and be content with what you have. For God has said, *"I will never leave you, nor forsake you."* ⁶ So we say with confidence,

"The Lord is my helper.

[And] I will not be afraid.

What can man do to me?"

⁷ Remember your leaders, those who spoke to you the word of God. Consider the outcome of their life, and imitate their faith. ⁸ Jesus Christ is the same yesterday and today and forever. ⁹ Do not be carried away by shifty and strange teachings. For it is good for the heart to be strengthened by grace, not by foods, through which those who are so occupied were not benefited. ¹⁰ We have an altar from which those who serve the tabernacle have no right to eat. ¹¹ For the bodies of those animals, whose blood is brought into the holy place by the high priest as an offering for sin, are burned outside the camp. ¹² And so Jesus also suffered outside the gate to sanctify the people through his own blood. ¹³ Let us, then, go to him outside the camp, bearing the disgrace he bore. ¹⁴ For here we do not have an enduring city, but we are looking for the city which is to come. ¹⁵ Through him [then] let us continually offer up a sacrifice of praise to God, that is, the fruit of lips that acknowledge his name. ¹⁶ Do not forget to do good and to share with others, for with such sacrifices God is pleased.

12:²⁵ Alx[**on earth**], Byz[on the earth (DRA, MRD, ~NLT, ~TLB)].

12:²⁶ Alx[**I will shake**], Byz[I shake (KJV, NKJ)]; ~**Haggai 2:6 LXX**.

12:²⁷ Alx/Byz[**the removal**], Minor[*omits* the (JNT, NLT, TEV, ~TLB)].

12:²⁸ Alx/Byz[**we may offer**], Major[we offer (~DRA, ~ESV, ~NET, ~NIV, ~NJB, ~NLT, NRS, ~REB, ~RSV, ~TEV, ~TLB)]; Alx[**reverence and awe**], Byz[modesty and reverence].

12:²⁹ Deuteronomy 4:24.

13:¹ Alx/Major[**2 Do not forget to show hospitality to strangers**], Byz[Do not forget to show hospitality to strangers 2].

13:⁴ Alx[**for God will judge**], Byz[but God will judge (JNT, KJV, MRD, NKJ, ~NLT, ~TEV)].

13:⁵ Alx/Byz[**nor forsake you**], Major[nor can I forsake you]; Deuteronomy 31:6, 8; **Joshua 1:5**.

13:⁶ Alx/Byz[**and**], Minor[*omits* (ASV, DRA, ESV, HCS, JNT, MRD, NAS, NAU, NIV, NJB, NKJ, NRS, REB, RSV, TEV)]; ~Psalms 118:6 LXX.

13:⁹ Alx/Byz[**carried away**], Minor[carried about (KJV, NKJ, ~NLT, ~TLB)]; Alx[**are so occupied**], Byz[were so occupied (ASV, JNT, KJV, MRD, NAS, NAU, NET, NKJ, REB, TLB)].

13:¹⁰ Alx/Byz[**have no right to eat**], Minor[have not eaten (~TLB)].

13:¹¹ Alx/Byz[**as an offering for sin**], Minor[*omits* (~JNT, ~NJB)].

13:¹² Alx/Byz[**gate**], Alt/Peshitta[city (MRD, ~NIV, ~NLT, ~NRS, TEV, TLB)], Alt[*without textual foundation* camp (~NET)].

13:¹⁵ Alx/Byz[**then**], Minor[*omits* (MRD, NJB, REB, TLB)].

17 Obey your leaders and submit to them; for they are keeping watch over your souls, as men who will have to give account. Let them do this with joy, and not with grief, for that would be of no advantage to you.

18 Pray for us, for we are sure that we have a clear conscience, desiring to live honorably in all things. **19** I urge you all the more to do this so that I may be restored to you the sooner.

20 Now may the God of peace who brought again from the dead our Lord Jesus, that great shepherd of the sheep, through the blood of the eternal covenant, **21** equip you with every good thing to do his will, working in us that which is pleasing in his sight, through Jesus Christ, to whom be glory for ever [and ever]. Amen.

22 I urge you, brothers, bear with my word of exhortation, for I have written to you briefly. **23** You should know that our brother Timothy has been released, with whom I will see you if he comes soon.

24 Greet all your leaders and all the saints. Those who come from Italy send you greetings. **25** Grace be with you all.

13:18 Alx[**we are sure**], Byz[we trust (DRA, KJV, MRD, ~NLT, ~TLB)].

13:21 Alx[**every good thing**], Byz[every good work (KJV, MRD, NJB, NKJ)], Minor[every good work and word]; Alx[**working in us**], Byz[working in you (DRA, KJV, MRD, NAB, NKJ, NLT, RSV, TLB)], Minor[working for himself in us (~JNT, ~MRD, ~NAB, ~NIV, ~NLT, ~REB, ~TEV)]; Alx/Byz[**and ever**], Minor[omits (NET)].

13:22 Alx/Byz[**bear with my word**], Minor[that you bear with my word (DRA, MRD)].

13:23 Alx[**our brother Timothy**], Byz[brother Timothy (TLB)].

13:25 Alx[text], Byz[adds Amen (ASV, DRA, KJV, MRD, NKJ, RSV)], Minor[adds by Timothy *others* Written to the Hebrews from Italy, by Timothy (KJV) *others* Grace be with us all *others* Grace be with all the saints], Alt[*without textual foundation adds* Goodbye (~TLB)].

The Letter of James

1 ¹ James, a servant of God and of the Lord Jesus Christ, to the twelve tribes in the Dispersion: greetings.

² Consider it all joy, my brothers, when you encounter various trials, ³ for you know that the testing of your faith produces endurance. ⁴ And let endurance have its perfect result, so that you may be perfect and complete, lacking in nothing. ⁵ If any of you lacks wisdom, let him ask of God, who gives to all generously and without reproach, and it will be given to him. ⁶ But he must ask in faith, with no doubting, for he who doubts is like a wave of the sea that is driven and tossed by the wind. ⁷ For that man ought not to expect that he will receive anything from the Lord, ⁸ being a double-minded man, unstable in all his ways.

⁹ But the brother of humble circumstances is to glory in his high position. ¹⁰ And the rich man is to glory in his humiliation, because like the flower of the grass he will pass away. ¹¹ For the sun rises with its scorching heat and withers the grass. Its flower falls and its beauty is destroyed. So will the rich man fade away in the midst of his pursuits.

¹² Blessed is the man who perseveres under trial. For when he has stood the test, he will receive the crown of life that he has promised to those who love him. ¹³ Let no one say when he is tempted, "I am being tempted by God"; for God cannot be tempted by evil, and he himself does not tempt anyone. ¹⁴ But each one is tempted when he is carried away and enticed by his own desire. ¹⁵ Then when desire has conceived, it gives birth to sin. And when sin is full-grown, it brings forth death.

¹⁶ Do not be deceived, my beloved brothers. ¹⁷ Every good thing given and every perfect gift is from above, coming down from the Father of lights, with whom there is no variation or shifting shadow. ¹⁸ Of his own will he brought us forth by the word of truth, that we should be a kind of first fruits of his creatures.

¹⁹ This you know, my beloved brothers. But everyone must be quick to hear, slow to speak and slow to anger, ²⁰ for the anger of man does not perform the righteousness of God. ²¹ Therefore, putting aside all filthiness and rank growth of wickedness, in humility receive the implanted word, which is able to save your souls.

²² But prove yourselves doers of the word, and not merely hearers who deceive themselves. ²³ For if anyone is a hearer of the word and not a doer, he is like a man who looks at his natural face in a mirror. ²⁴ For he looks at himself and goes away, and

---

Title Alx/Byz[**The Letter of James**], Minor[*variations of* The General Letter of the Holy Apostle James].

1:¹ **servant** *Greek* slave.

1:³ Alx/Byz[**testing**], Minor[proving (ASV, TEV)].

1:¹² Alx[**he has promised**], Byz[the Lord has promised (ASV, KJV, NJB, NKJ, NRS)], Minor[God has promised (DRA, ESV, JNT, MRD, NAS, NAU, NET, NIV, NLT, REB, RSV, TEV, TLB)].

1:¹⁷ Alx/Byz[**no variation or shifting shadow** *or* no variation from a shifting shadow], Minor[no variation or shifting or shadow].

1:¹⁹ Alx[**This you know, my beloved brothers. But**], Byz[And so, my beloved brothers, let (JNT, KJV, ~MRD, NKJ, ~TEV, ~TLB)]; Alx[**But everyone**], Byz[*omits* But (ESV, HCS, JNT, KJV, MRD, NAB, NET, NIV, NJB, NKJ, NLT, NRS, RSV, TEV, TLB)].

1:²⁰ Alx[**perform**], Byz[produce (ESV, HCS, JNT, NAB, NAS, NAU, NET, NIV, NKJ, NLT, NRS, REB, TEV, TLB)].

1:²¹ *or* Therefore, humbly putting aside all filthiness and rank growth of wickedness, receive the implanted word, which is able to save your souls.

1:²³ **natural face** *Greek* the face of his birth.

immediately forgets what he was like. **25** But one who looks intently into the perfect law, the law of liberty, and perseveres, not being a forgetful hearer but a doer that acts, this man will be blessed in what he does.

26 If anyone thinks himself to be religious, and yet does not bridle his tongue but deceives his own heart, this man's religion is worthless. **27** Religion that is pure and undefiled in the sight of our God and Father is this: to visit orphans and widows in their distress, and to keep oneself unstained from the world.

2 **1** My brothers, show no favoritism as you hold your faith in our glorious Lord Jesus Christ. **2** For if a man comes into your synagogue with a gold ring and dressed in fine clothes, and there also comes in a poor man in shabby clothes, **3** but you pay special attention to the one who is wearing the fine clothes and say, "Have a seat here in a good place," and you say to the poor man, "You stand there," or, "Sit by my feet," **4** have you not made distinctions among yourselves, and become judges with evil thoughts?

5 Listen, my beloved brothers: has not God chosen those who are poor in the world to be rich in faith and heirs of the kingdom which he has promised to those who love him? **6** But you have dishonored the poor man. Is it not the rich who oppress you? Is it not they who drag you into court? **7** Is it not they who blaspheme the honorable name by which you have been called? **8** If you really fulfill the royal law, according to the scripture, *"You shall love your neighbor as yourself,"* you are doing well. **9** But if you show partiality, you commit sin, and are convicted by the law as transgressors. **10** For whoever keeps the whole law and yet stumbles in one point has become guilty of all of it. **11** For he who said, *"Do not commit adultery,"* said also, *"Do not murder."* If you do not commit adultery but do commit murder, you have become a transgressor of the law. **12** So speak and so act as those who are to be judged by the law of liberty. **13** For judgment will be without mercy to one who has shown no mercy. Mercy triumphs over judgment.

14 What good is it, my brothers, if a man says he has faith but has no works? Can such faith save him? **15** If a brother or sister is without clothing and in need of daily food, **16** and one of you says to them, "Go in peace, be warmed and filled," and yet you do not give them what is necessary for their body, what use is that? **17** So faith by itself, if it has no works, is dead.

1:25 Alx[**not being**], Byz[he not being (KJV, ~NIV, ~NLT, REB, TLB)].

1:26 Alx[**If anyone**], Byz[*adds* among you (KJV, NKJ)].

2:3 Alx[**but you pay special attention**], Byz[and you pay special attention (ASV, DRA, ESV, ~HCS, ~JNT, KJV, MRD, NAB, NAS, NAU, ~NET, ~NIV, NJB, NKJ, ~NLT, NRS, ~REB, RSV, ~TEV, TLB)]; Alx[**fine clothes and say**], Byz[*adds* to him (DRA, JNT, KJV, MRD, NKJ, ~NLT, REB, TEV, ~TLB)]; Alx/Byz[**"You stand there," or, "Sit"**], Minor["You stand," or, "Sit there"]; Alx[**Sit by my feet**], Byz[Sit here by my feet (HCS, KJV, MRD, NKJ, REB, TEV)]; **Have a seat here in a good place** *or* Please have a seat here; **Sit by my feet** *Greek* Sit under my footstool.

2:4 Alx[**have you not...?**], Byz[have you not then...? (ESV, JNT, KJV, ~NET)], Minor[you have then...! (TEV, TLB)].

2:5 Alx[**in the world**], Byz[of the world (JNT, MRD, ~NIV, ~REB)], Minor[of this world (~DRA, ~HCS, KJV, NAS, NAU, NKJ, ~NLT, TEV, ~TLB)].

2:8 **Leviticus 19:18**.

2:10 Alx/Byz[**keeps...stumbles**], Major[will keep...will stumble (~ASV, ~DRA, ~KJV, ~MRD, ~NKJ, ~TEV)].

2:11 Alx/Byz[**Do...Do...you do...do**], Major[You shall...You shall...you shall...shall (~DRA, ~MRD, ~NAB, ~NJB, ~NLT, ~NRS, ~REB, ~TLB)]; **Exodus 20:13, 14, Deuteronomy 5:17, 18**.

2:13 Alx/Byz[**mercy. Mercy**], Minor[mercy. And mercy (DRA, ~JNT, KJV, ~NET, ~NJB, ~NLT, ~RSV, ~TEV, ~TLB)].

2:15 Alx[**If a brother**], Byz[But if a brother (DRA, MRD)]; Alx[**and in need**], Byz[and is in need (NJB, ~NLT, ~TLB)].

18 But someone will say, "You have faith and I have works." Show me your faith without the works, and I will show you faith by my works. **19** You believe that God is one. You do well. Even the demons believe – and shudder. **20** But are you willing to know, O foolish man, that faith without works is useless? **21** Was not Abraham our father justified by works when he offered up Isaac his son on the altar? **22** You see that faith was active with his works, and faith was completed by works, **23** and the scripture was fulfilled which says, *"Abraham believed God, and it was reckoned to him as righteousness,"* and he was called the friend of God. **24** You see that a man is justified by works and not by faith alone. **25** In the same way was not Rahab the harlot also justified by works, when she received the messengers and sent them out by another way? **26** For as the body without the spirit is dead, so faith without works is dead also.

3 **1** Let not many of you become teachers, my brothers, for you know that we who teach will be judged with greater strictness. **2** For we all stumble in many ways. If anyone does not stumble in what he says, he is a perfect man, able to bridle the whole body as well. **3** If we put bits into the mouths of horses that they may obey us, we guide their whole bodies. **4** Look at the ships also; though they are so great and are driven by strong winds, they are guided by a very small rudder wherever the will of the pilot directs. **5** So also the tongue is a small part of the body, and yet it boasts of great things.

See how small a fire sets how great a forest aflame! **6** And the tongue is a fire, a world of evil among the members of the body. The tongue corrupts our whole person, sets the whole wheel of nature on fire, and is itself set on fire by hell. **7** For every species of beasts and birds, of reptiles and creatures of the sea, is tamed and has been tamed by the human race. **8** But no man can tame the tongue. It is a restless evil, full of deadly poison. **9** With it we bless the Lord and Father, and with it we curse men, who have been made in the likeness of God. **10** From the same mouth come blessing and cursing. My brothers, this ought not to be so. **11** Does a spring pour forth from the same opening both fresh and bitter water? **12** Can a fig tree, my brothers, produce olives, or a grapevine produce figs? Nor can salt water produce fresh.

2:18 Alx[**without the works**], Byz[without your works (ASV, ESV, KJV, NKJ, ~NLT, NRS, RSV, ~TLB)]; Alx[**I will show you faith**], Byz[I will show you my faith (~DRA, ESV, JNT, KJV, MRD, NAB, NAS, NAU, NIV, NJB, NKJ, NLT, NRS, REB, RSV, TEV, ~TLB)].

2:19 Alx/Byz[**God is one**], Minor[there is one God (DRA, KJV, MRD, NIV, ~NJB, NKJ, NLT, REB, TEV, ~TLB) *others* God is].

2:20 Alx[**useless**], Byz[dead (DRA, ~JNT, KJV, MRD, NKJ, ~TLB)].

2:22 Alx/Byz[**was active** *or* was working], Minor[is active *or* is working].

2:23 **Genesis 15:6**.

2:24 Alx[**You see**], Byz[You see, then (KJV, NJB, NKJ, REB, TEV, TLB)].

2:25 Alx/Byz[**messengers**], Minor[spies (MRD, NIV, TEV)].

2:26 Alx/Byz[**For**], Minor[*omits* (MRD, NIV, NJB, NLT, REB, ~TEV, TLB)].

3:3 Alx[**If we put**], Byz[Behold! We put (KJV, MRD, ~NKJ)].

3:5 Alx[**how small a fire**], Byz[a small fire (~ESV, HCS, KJV, MRD, ~NAS, ~NAU, NIV, NKJ, NRS, REB, RSV, TEV, TLB)].

3:6 Alx/Byz[**And the tongue is a fire**], Minor[*omits* And]; Alx[**a world of evil among the members of the body. The tongue corrupts** *or* a world of evil. The tongue is set among our members, corrupting our body], Byz[a world of evil. The tongue is so set among the members of the body, that it corrupts (JNT, KJV, NKJ)]; Alx/Byz[**wheel of nature** *or* course of life], Minor[wheel of our nature (DRA, JNT, MRD, NAB, NAS, NAU, NIV, ~NLT, REB, TEV, TLB)]; **hell** *Greek* Gehenna.

3:8 Alx[**a restless evil**], Byz[an uncontrollable evil (KJV, MRD, NKJ, TEV)].

3:9 Alx[**the Lord and Father**], Byz[God, even the Father (DRA, KJV, NKJ, ~TLB)].

3:12 Alx[**Nor can salt water produce fresh**], Byz[So no spring yields both salt water and fresh (~ESV, KJV, ~NET, ~NIV, NKJ, ~NLT, ~REB, ~TLB)].

¹³ Who is wise and understanding among you? By his good life let him show his deeds in the humility of wisdom. ¹⁴ But if you have bitter jealousy and selfish ambition in your heart, do not boast and be false to the truth. ¹⁵ This wisdom is not such as comes down from above, but is earthly, unspiritual, demonic. ¹⁶ For where jealousy and selfish ambition exist, there will be disorder and every evil practice. ¹⁷ But the wisdom from above is first pure, then peaceable, gentle, open to reason, full of mercy and good fruits, without uncertainty, without hypocrisy. ¹⁸ And a harvest of righteousness is sown in peace by those who make peace.

4 ¹ What causes quarrels, and what causes fights among you? Is it not your passions that are at war in your members? ² You desire and do not have; so you kill. And you covet and cannot obtain; so you fight and quarrel. You do not have, because you do not ask. ³ You ask and do not receive, because you ask with wrong motives, so that you may spend it on your pleasures. ⁴ You adulteresses, do you not know that friendship with the world is hostility toward God? Therefore whoever wishes to be a friend of the world makes himself an enemy of God. ⁵ Or do you think that the Scripture speaks without reason? He jealously desires the Spirit which he has made to dwell in us, ⁶ but he gives more grace. Therefore it says,

"God opposes the proud,
   but gives grace to the humble."

⁷ Submit yourselves therefore to God. But resist the devil and he will flee from you. ⁸ Draw near to God and he will draw near to you. Cleanse your hands, you sinners, and purify your hearts, you double-minded. ⁹ Be miserable and mourn and weep. Let your laughter be turned to mourning and your joy to gloom. ¹⁰ Humble yourselves before the Lord, and he will exalt you.

¹¹ Do not speak against one another, brothers. He who speaks against a brother or judges his brother, speaks against the law and judges the law. But if you judge the law, you are not a doer of the law but a judge of it. ¹² There is [the] one Lawgiver and Judge, the one who is able to save and destroy. But you – who are you to judge your neighbor?

3:14 Alx/Byz[**heart**], Minor[hearts (DRA, ESV, JNT, KJV, MRD, NAB, NET, NIV, NKJ, NRS, REB, RSV, ~TLB)]; Alx/Byz[**do not boast and be false to the truth**], Minor[do not boast against the truth or lie (MRD, ~NJB, ~NLT, ~TEV, ~TLB)].

3:17 Alx[**without hypocrisy**], Byz[and without hypocrisy (ESV, HCS, JNT, KJV, ~MRD, NET, NIV, NKJ, NLT, TEV, ~TLB)]; **uncertainty** or prejudice.

3:18 Alx[**a harvest** or fruit], Byz[the harvest (ASV, DRA, HCS, KJV, MRD, NAB, NAS, NAU, NET, NKJ, ~REB, RSV, TEV)].

4:1 Alx[**and what causes fights**], Byz[and fights (DRA, HCS, JNT, KJV, MRD, NAS, NAU, NIV, NJB, NKJ, NLT, NRS, REB, TEV, TLB)]; **what causes** or what is the source of.

4:2 Alx/Major[**You do not have**], Byz[And you do not have (DRA, MRD, ~TLB)], Minor[Yet you do not have (KJV, NKJ, NLT, ~TLB)].

4:4 Alx[**You adulteresses**], Byz[You adulterers and adulteresses (KJV, NKJ)], Minor[You adulterers (~ESV, DRA, MRD, NAB, ~NET, ~NIV, NJB, NLT, NRS, ~REB, ~RSV, ~TEV)].

4:5 Alx[**which he has made to dwell**], Byz[which dwells (DRA, JNT, KJV, MRD, NKJ)]; **He jealously desires the Spirit which he has made to dwell in us** or The spirit which he made to dwell in us desires jealously *compare Genesis 4:7*.

4:6 **Proverbs 3:34 LXX**.

4:7 Alx/Major[**But resist**], Byz[Resist (ESV, ~JNT, KJV, NAB, NAS, NAU, NIV, NJB, NKJ, NRS, REB, RSV, TEV, TLB)].

4:9 Alx/Byz[**mourn and weep**], Minor[mourn, weep (JNT, NAB, ~NJB, ~NLT, ~TLB) *others* mourn (MRD)]; Alx[**turned**], Byz[changed (HCS, NIV, ~NLT, TEV, ~TLB)].

4:11 Alx[**or judges his brother**], Byz[and judges his brother (KJV, NKJ, NLT, TLB)].

4:12 Alx/Byz[**the one Lawgiver and Judge**], Major[*omits* and Judge (KJV, NKJ)]; Alx/Byz[**But you**], Minor[*omits* (JNT, KJV, NJB, NKJ, ~NLT, TEV)]; Alx[**your neighbor**], Byz[another (JNT, KJV,

¹³ Come now, you who say, "Today or tomorrow we will go to such and such a city, and spend a year there and engage in business and make a profit." ¹⁴ Yet you do not know what will happen tomorrow. What is your life? For you are a mist that appears for a little while and then vanishes. ¹⁵ Instead, you ought to say, "If the Lord wills, we will live and do this or that." ¹⁶ As it is, you boast in your arrogance. All such boasting is evil. ¹⁷ Therefore, to one who knows the right thing to do and does not do it, to him it is sin.

5 ¹ Come now, you rich, weep and howl for the miseries that are coming upon you. ² Your riches have rotted and your garments are moth-eaten. ³ Your gold and silver have rusted, and their rust will be evidence against you and will eat your flesh like fire. You have laid up treasure in the last days. ⁴ Behold, the wages of the laborers who mowed your fields, which you kept back by fraud, cry out against you; and the cries of the harvesters have reached the ears of the Lord of Sabaoth. ⁵ You have lived on the earth in luxury and in pleasure; you have fattened your hearts in a day of slaughter. ⁶ You have condemned and put to death the righteous man; he does not resist you.

⁷ Therefore be patient, brothers, until the coming of the Lord. See how the farmer waits for the precious fruit of the earth, being patient over it, until it receives the early and late rain. ⁸ You too be patient; strengthen your hearts, for the coming of the Lord is near. ⁹ Do not grumble, brothers, against one another, that you may not be judged. Behold, the Judge is standing at the door. ¹⁰ As an example, brothers, of suffering and patience, take the prophets who spoke in the name of the Lord. ¹¹ Behold, we call those blessed who endured. You have heard of the endurance of Job, and you have seen the purpose of the Lord, how the Lord is full of compassion and mercy.

¹² But above all, my brothers, do not swear, either by heaven or by earth or with any other oath. But let your yes be yes and your no be no, that you may not fall under condemnation.

¹³ Is anyone among you suffering? He should pray. Is anyone cheerful? Let him sing praise. ¹⁴ Is any among you sick? Let him call for the elders of the church, and let them pray over him, anointing [him] with oil in the name of the Lord. ¹⁵ And the prayer

---

NKJ, TEV, TLB)]; *DRA divides verse 12 and 13 after* **save and destroy.**

4:¹³ Alx[**Today or tomorrow**], Byz[Today and tomorrow]; Alx/Byz[**we will go**], Major[we may go]; Alx[**a year**], Byz[one year].

4:¹⁴ Alx[**What is your life**], Byz[For what is your life (DRA, ~HCS, ~JNT, KJV, MRD, NKJ, ~TLB)]; Alx[**you are a mist**], Byz[it shall be a mist], Minor[it is a mist (DRA, KJV, MRD, NKJ, NLT, TLB)]; Alx[**and then vanishes**], Byz[and then also vanishes]; *DRA divides verse 14 and 15 after* **what will happen tomorrow.**

4:¹⁵ Alx/Byz[**we will live**], Major[we should live].

5:³ **will eat your flesh like fire. You have laid up treasure in the last days** *or* will eat your flesh, since you have stored up fire in the last days.

5:⁴ **Sabaoth** *Hebraism* armies *or* hosts.

5:⁵ Alx[**in a day of slaughter**], Byz[as in a day of slaughter (KJV, MRD, NKJ)]; **slaughter** *double entendre for a* battle *or a* feast.

5:⁷ Alx[**rain** *implied*], Byz[rain].

5:⁸ **near** *or* at hand.

5:⁹ Alx[**grumble, brothers, against one another**], Byz[grumble against one another, brothers (ESV, JNT, KJV, MRD, NET, NIV, NJB, NKJ, NLT, TEV, TLB)]; Alx/Byz[**judged**], Minor[condemned (JNT, KJV, NKJ)]; Alx/Byz[**the Judge**], Minor[a Judge].

5:¹⁰ Alx[**brothers**], Byz[my brothers (DRA, KJV, MRD, NKJ, ~REB, TEV, ~TLB)].

5:¹¹ Alx[**who endured**], Byz[who endure (KJV, NKJ, NLT)]; Alx/Byz[**and you have seen**], Major[and see (NLT, TEV, TLB)]; Alx/Byz[**how the Lord**], Major[how he (TLB)].

5:¹² Alx[**under condemnation**], Byz[into hypocrisy (~REB)].

5:¹⁴ Alx/Byz[**anointing him**], Minor[*omits* him (~NJB, ~NLT, ~NRS)]; Alx/Byz[**in the name of the Lord**], Minor[*omits* of the Lord].

offered in faith will save the sick man, and the Lord will raise him up. And if he has committed sins, he will be forgiven. **16** Therefore, confess your sins to one another, and pray for one another so that you may be healed. The prayer of a righteous man is powerful and effective. **17** Elijah was a man with a nature like ours, and he prayed earnestly that it would not rain, and it did not rain on the earth for three years and six months. **18** Then he prayed again, and the heavens gave rain and the earth produced its fruit.

19 My brothers, if anyone among you wanders from the truth and someone brings him back, **20** let him know that whoever turns a sinner from the error of his way will save his soul from death and will cover a multitude of sins.

5:16 Alx[**Therefore, confess your sins**], Byz[Confess your trespasses (KJV, MRD, NKJ, ~NLT, TLB)].

5:19 Alx[**My brothers**], Byz[Brothers (KJV, NKJ, REB, ~TLB)].

5:20 Alx/Byz[**let him know** or he must know], Minor[you must know (JNT, NIV, NLT, NRS, REB, TEV, ~TLB)]; Alx[**save his soul**], Byz[save a soul (ASV, KJV, NKJ, REB, TLB)]; Alx/Byz[**a multitude of sins**], Minor[adds Amen others add to his eternal glory. Amen].

First Peter

1 ¹ Peter, an apostle of Jesus Christ, to the chosen exiles in the Dispersion, scattered throughout Pontus, Galatia, Cappadocia, Asia and Bithynia, ² who have been chosen according to the foreknowledge of God the Father, by the sanctifying work of the Spirit, for obedience to Jesus Christ and sprinkling with his blood: may grace and peace be yours in abundance.

³ Blessed be the God and Father of our Lord Jesus Christ! In his great mercy he has caused us to be born again into a living hope through the resurrection of Jesus Christ from the dead, ⁴ to obtain an inheritance which is imperishable and undefiled and will not fade away, kept in heaven for you, ⁵ who are protected by God's power through faith for a salvation ready to be revealed in the last time. ⁶ In this you greatly rejoice, though now for a little while you may have to suffer various trials, ⁷ so that the trial of your faith, being more precious than gold which is perishable, even though tested by fire, may be found to result in praise and glory and honor at the revelation of Jesus Christ. ⁸ Though you have not seen him, you love him. And even though you do not see him now, you believe in him and rejoice with an inexpressible and glorious joy, ⁹ as you obtain the outcome of [your] faith, the salvation of your souls.

¹⁰ As to this salvation, the prophets who prophesied of the grace that would come to you inquired and searched carefully, ¹¹ seeking to know what person or time the Spirit of Christ within them was indicating when he predicted the sufferings of Christ and the glories to follow. ¹² It was revealed to them that they were not serving themselves, but you, in these things which now have been announced to you through those who preached the gospel to you [in] the Holy Spirit sent from heaven – things into which angels long to look.

¹³ Therefore, prepare your minds for action. Be sober in spirit. Set your hope fully on the grace to be given you at the revelation of Jesus Christ. ¹⁴ As obedient children, do not be conformed to the former lusts which were yours in your ignorance. ¹⁵ But as he who called you is holy, be holy yourselves in all your conduct; ¹⁶ because it is written, *"You shall be holy, for I [am] holy."*

¹⁷ If you address as Father the One who impartially judges according to each one's work, conduct yourselves in fear during the time of your exile on earth. ¹⁸ You know that you were redeemed from the futile way of life inherited from your forefathers, not with

---

Title Alx/Byz[**First Peter** *Greek* Peter A], Minor[*variations of* The First General Letter of the Apostle Peter].

1:¹ Alx/Byz[**Peter**], Alt[*without textual foundation* Cephas (~JNT)].

1:³ Alx/Byz[**caused us to be born**], Minor[caused you to be born].

1:⁴ Alx/Byz[**kept in heaven for you**], Minor[kept in heaven for us].

1:⁶ **In this you greatly rejoice** *or* Rejoice greatly in this.

1:⁷ Alx/Byz[**trial**], Minor[proof (ASV, ESV, HCS, JNT, MRD, NAB, NAS, NAU, NET, ~NIV, NJB, NKJ, NRS, RSV, TEV)]; Alx[**glory and honor**], Byz[honor and glory (KJV, NKJ)], Minor[honor (NJB)].

1:⁸ Alx[**not seen him**], Byz[not known him].

1:⁹ Alx/Byz[**your faith**], Minor[*omits* your (NLT)].

1:¹⁰ Alx[**inquired**], Byz[have inquired (DRA, KJV, NKJ, ~TLB)].

1:¹¹ **what person** *or* what circumstances *Greek* what.

1:¹² Alx/Byz[**not serving themselves, but you**], Minor[not serving themselves, but us (KJV, MRD, NKJ)]; Alx/Byz[**in the Holy Spirit**], Minor[*omits* in (Metzger)].

1:¹³ **prepare your minds for action** *Greek* gird up the loins of your mind.

1:¹⁶ Alx[**You shall be holy**], Byz[Be holy (HCS, KJV, MRD, NAB, NIV, NJB, NKJ, ~NLT, TEV, ~TLB)]; Alx/Byz[**I am holy**], Minor[*omits* am]; ~**Leviticus 19:2**.

perishable things such as silver or gold, [19] but with the precious blood of Christ, like that of a lamb without blemish or spot. [20] He was destined before the foundation of the world, but was revealed at the end of times for your sake. [21] Through him you are believers in God, who raised him from the dead and gave him glory, so that your faith and hope are in God.

[22] Since you have purified your souls by obedience to the truth for a sincere love of the brothers, love one another earnestly from a [pure] heart. [23] For you have been born again, not of perishable seed, but of imperishable, through the living and enduring word of God. [24] For,

"All flesh is like grass,
    and all its glory like the flower of grass.
The grass withers,
    and the flower falls,
[25]   but the word of the Lord stands forever."

And this is the word which was preached to you.

2 [1] Therefore, put away all malice and all deceit and hypocrisies and envies and all slanders. [2] Like newborn babes, long for the pure spiritual milk, so that by it you may grow up in your salvation, [3] for you have tasted the kindness of the Lord. [4] As you come to him, the living Stone – rejected by men but chosen and precious in the sight of God – [5] you also, like living stones, are being built into a spiritual house to be a holy priesthood, to offer spiritual sacrifices acceptable to God through Jesus Christ. [6] For it stands in scripture:

"Behold, I lay in Zion a stone,
    a cornerstone chosen and precious,
    and he who believes in him will never be put to shame."

[7] To you therefore who believe, this is precious. But for those who do not believe,

"The very stone which the builders rejected
    has become the chief cornerstone,"

[8] and,

1:20 Alx[**at the end of times**], Byz[at the ends of times (~KJV, ~NAS, ~NAU, ~NET, ~NIV, ~NKJ)], Minor[at the end of days (~NLT, ~TEV, ~TLB) *others* at the end of time (NAB, NJB, REB)].

1:21 Alx[**are believers**], Byz[believe (JNT, KJV, MRD, NAB, NET, NKJ, REB, TEV, TLB)].

1:22 Alx[**obedience to the truth**], Byz[*adds* through the Spirit (KJV, NKJ)]; Alx/Byz[**a pure heart**], Minor[the heart (ASV, DRA, ~JNT, NAS, NAU, NIV, NJB, NLT, NRS, ~REB, RSV, ~TEV, ~TLB)].

1:23 Alx[**through the living and enduring word of God** *or* through the word of the living and enduring God], Byz[through the word of God which lives and endures forever (DRA, JNT, KJV, MRD, NKJ, NLT, TEV, TLB)].

1:24 Alx[**all its glory**], Byz[all the glory of man (~JNT, KJV, ~NIV, ~NJB, NKJ, ~NLT, ~REB, ~TEV, ~TLB)]; Alx[**the flower falls**], Byz[its flower falls (DRA, KJV, NKJ, ~TLB)].

1:24-25 **Isaiah 40:6-8 LXX**.

2:1 Alx/Byz[**hypocrisies**], Minor[hypocrisy (ESV, HCS, JNT, MRD, NAB, NAS, NAU, NET, NIV, NJB, NKJ, NLT, NRS, REB, RSV, TEV, TLB)].

2:2 Alx/Byz[**in your salvation**], Major[omits (KJV, MRD, NKJ)].

2:3 Alx[**for** *or* if], Byz[if indeed (DRA, ESV, ~HCS, KJV, ~NIV, ~NJB, NKJ, ~NLT, NRS, ~REB, ~TEV, ~TLB)].

2:5 Alx[**are being built into** *or* let yourselves be built into], Byz[*omits* into (ASV, DRA, KJV, ~MRD, ~NJB, NKJ, TEV, TLB)].

2:6 Alx[**For it stands in scripture**], Byz[For it stands in the scripture (DRA, JNT, MRD, ~NLT, TEV, TLB)], Minor[For it also stands in the scripture (KJV, NKJ)]; **Isaiah 28:16 LXX**.

2:7 Alx[**those who do not believe**], Byz[those who do not obey (KJV, NKJ, ~NLT)]; Alx/Byz[**The very stone... chief cornerstone**], Minor[omits (MRD)]; **chief cornerstone** *or* capstone; Psalms 118:22.

2:8 Alx/Major[**8 and, "A stone that causes men to stumble**], Byz[and, "A stone that causes men to stumble 8]; ~Isaiah 8:14 Masoretic.

> *"A stone that causes men to stumble*
> *and a rock that makes them fall."*

They stumble because they disobey the word – as they were destined to do.

⁹ But you are *a chosen race, a royal priesthood, a holy nation, a people for God's own possession, that you may declare the praises* of him who called you out of darkness into his marvelous light.

¹⁰   Once you were not a people,
>   but now you are the people of God.
>   Once you had not received mercy,
>   but now you have received mercy.

¹¹ Beloved, I urge you as aliens and strangers to abstain from fleshly lusts which wage war against your soul. ¹² Maintain good conduct among the Gentiles, so that in case they speak against you as wrongdoers, they may, seeing your good deeds, glorify God on the day of visitation.

¹³ Submit yourselves for the Lord's sake to every human institution, whether to a king as the supreme authority, ¹⁴ or to governors as sent by him to punish those who do wrong and to praise those who do right. ¹⁵ For it is God's will that by doing right you should silence the ignorance of foolish men. ¹⁶ Live as free men, but do not use your freedom as a covering for evil; live as servants of God. ¹⁷ Honor all people, love the brotherhood, fear God, honor the king.

¹⁸ Servants, be submissive to your masters with all respect, not only to those who are good and gentle, but also to those who are overbearing. ¹⁹ For a man has grace if, mindful of God, he bears up under pain while suffering unjustly. ²⁰ For what credit is it if, when you do wrong and are beaten for it, you patiently endure? But if, when you do right and suffer for it, you patiently endure, you have favor with God. ²¹ For to this you have been called, because Christ also suffered for you, leaving you an example, that you should follow in his steps.

²²   *"He committed no sin,*
>   *and no deceit was found in his mouth."*

²³ When he was reviled, he did not revile in return. When he suffered, he uttered no threats, but he trusted himself to him who judges justly. ²⁴ He bore our sins in his own body on the tree, so that we might die to sin and live for righteousness. By his wounds you have been healed. ²⁵ For you were straying like sheep, but now you have returned to the Shepherd and Guardian of your souls.

3 ¹ You wives, in the same way be submissive to your husbands so that, even if any of them do not believe the word, they will be won over without a word by the

---

2:9 **God's** *Greek* his; Isaiah 43:20 LXX, Exodus 19:16 LXX, ~Isaiah 43:21 LXX.

2:12 Alx[**seeing your good deeds**], Byz[having seen your good deeds (~TLB)].

2:13 Alx[**Submit yourselves**], Byz[Therefore submit yourselves (NKJ)].

2:16 **servants** *Greek* slaves.

2:19 Alx/Byz[**For a man has grace**], Minor[*adds* with God (MRD, NET, ~NLT, ~TEV, ~TLB)]; Alx/Byz[**mindful of God**], Minor[mindful of goodness (MRD, NLT)].

2:21 Alx[**for you**], Byz[for us (DRA, KJV, MRD, NKJ)]; Alx/Byz[**leaving you**], Minor[leaving us (KJV, MRD, NKJ)].

2:22 Isaiah 53:9 LXX.

2:24 Alx/Byz[**our sins**], Minor[your sins]; **on the tree** *or* to the tree; **wounds** *Greek* bruises.

2:25 **Guardian** *Greek* overseer *or* bishop.

3:1 Alx/Byz[**even if any**], Minor[*omits* even (DRA, KJV, MRD, NIV, NJB, REB, RSV, TEV, TLB)]; Alx/Byz[**they will be won**], Minor[they may be won (ASV, DRA, ESV, HCS, KJV, MRD, NAB, NAS, NAU, NIV, NJB, NKJ, NRS, REB, RSV)].

behavior of their wives, ² when they see your chaste and respectful behavior. ³ Your adornment must not be merely outward – braiding the hair, and wearing gold jewelry, or putting on fine clothing. ⁴ But let it be the hidden person of the heart, with the imperishable beauty of a gentle and quiet spirit, which is precious in God's sight. ⁵ For in this way in former times the holy women also, who hoped in God, used to adorn themselves, and were submissive to their own husbands; ⁶ just as Sarah obeyed Abraham, calling him lord. And you are her children if you do what is right and are not frightened by any fear.

⁷ Husbands, in the same way be considerate as you live with your wives, and treat them with honor, as the weaker vessel, since you are joint heirs of the grace of life, so that your prayers will not be hindered.

⁸ Finally, all of you, live in harmony with one another. Be sympathetic. Love as brothers. Be compassionate and humble. ⁹ Do not return evil for evil or insult for insult, but give a blessing instead. For to this you were called, that you may inherit a blessing. ¹⁰ For,

> "He who would love life
> > and see good days
> must keep the tongue from evil
> > and the lips from speaking deceit.

¹¹ > But he must turn away from evil and do good.
> > He must seek peace and pursue it.

¹² > For the eyes of the Lord are on the righteous
> > and his ears are open to their prayer.
> But the face of the Lord is against those who do evil."

¹³ Who is there to harm you if you are zealous for what is good? ¹⁴ But even if you should suffer for the sake of righteousness, you are blessed. *Do not fear their fear, and do not be troubled,*" ¹⁵ but in your hearts reverence Christ as Lord. Always be prepared to make a defense to everyone who asks you to give an account for the hope that is in you, ¹⁶ yet do it with gentleness and respect. And keep a clear conscience, so that, when you are slandered, those who revile your good behavior in Christ may be put to shame. ¹⁷ For it is better to suffer for doing right, if that should be God's will, than for doing wrong. ¹⁸ For Christ also suffered for sins once for all, the righteous for the unrighteous, that he might bring you to

---

3:4 Alx/Byz[**gentle and quiet**], Minor[quiet and gentle (DRA, ~MRD)].

3:7 **vessel** *or* partner.

3:8 Alx[**humble**], Byz[courteous (~DRA, KJV, MRD, NKJ)].

3:9 Alx[**for to this**], Byz[knowing to this (KJV, NKJ)].

3:10 Alx[**the tongue... the lips**]; Byz[his tongue... his lips (ASV, DRA, ESV, HCS, JNT, KJV, MRD, NAS, NAU, NET, NIV, ~NJB, NKJ, ~NLT, ~NRS, REB, RSV, ~TLB)].

3:10-12 Psalms 34:12-16.

3:11 Alx[**But he**], Byz[He (DRA, ESV, JNT, KJV, MRD, NAB, NAU, NIV, NJB, NKJ, NLT, NRS, REB, RSV, TEV, TLB)].

3:13 Alx[**zealous**], Byz[imitators (KJV, NKJ)].

3:14 Alx/Byz[**and do not be troubled**], Minor[*omits* (NJB, ~TLB)]; Isaiah 8:12.

3:15 Alx[**Christ**], Byz[God (KJV, NKJ)]; Alx[**Always be prepared**], Byz[and always be prepared (HCS, KJV, MRD, NET, NJB, NKJ, NLT, TLB)].

3:16 Alx[**16 yet do it with gentleness and respect**], Byz[with gentleness and respect 16 (ASV, JNT, KJV, NAS, NAU, NIV, NKJ, REB, RSV, TLB)]; Alx[**when you are slandered** *Greek* in which you are slandered], Byz[when they slander you (DRA, KJV, ~MRD, NET, NIV, NJB, NKJ,)], Minor[if they slander you (NLT, TLB)]; Alx[**slandered**], Byz[*adds* as evildoers (KJV, MRD, NKJ, TLB)].

3:18 Alx/Byz[**suffered**], Minor[died (DRA, JNT, MRD, NAS, NAU, NIV, NJB, RSV, TEV)]; Alx/Byz[**for sins**], Minor[for our sins (DRA, MRD, NLT, REB, TLB)]; Alx/Major[**bring you to God**], Byz[bring us to God (ASV, DRA, KJV, NAS, NAU, NJB, NKJ, REB, RSV, TLB)]; **in the spirit** *or* by the Spirit.

God, being put to death in the flesh but made alive in the spirit; [19] in which also he went and preached to the spirits in prison, [20] who formerly did not obey, when the patience of God waited in the days of Noah, during the building of the ark, in which a few, that is, eight persons, were saved through water. [21] And corresponding to that, baptism now saves you – not the removal of dirt from the flesh, but an appeal to God for a good conscience – through the resurrection of Jesus Christ, [22] who has gone into heaven and is at the right hand of God, with angels and authorities and powers subject to him.

4 [1] Therefore, since Christ has suffered in the flesh, arm yourselves also with the same purpose, because he who has suffered in the flesh has ceased from sin, [2] so as to live the rest of the time in the flesh no longer for human lusts, but for the will of God. [3] For there has been enough time to do what the Gentiles like to do, living in vice, lust, drunkenness, orgies, carousing, and lawless idolatry. [4] In all this, they are surprised that you do not run with them into the same flood of dissipation, and they abuse you. [5] But they will give account to him who is ready to judge the living and the dead. [6] For this reason the gospel was preached even to those who are dead, that though they are judged in the flesh as men, they might live in the spirit according to the will of God.

[7] The end of all things is near; therefore be clear minded and sober for your prayers. [8] Above all, hold unfailing your love for one another, because love covers a multitude of sins. [9] Offer hospitality to one another without complaint. [10] As each one has received a special gift, employ it in serving one another as good stewards of God's varied grace. [11] Whoever speaks is to do so as one who is speaking the utterances of God; whoever serves is to do so as one who is serving by the strength which God supplies; so that in all things God may be glorified through Jesus Christ. To him belongs the glory and dominion for ever and ever. Amen.

[12] Beloved, do not be surprised at the fiery ordeal which comes upon you to test you, as though something strange were happening to you. [13] But rejoice that you share in the sufferings of Christ, so that you may also be overjoyed when his glory is revealed. [14] If

---

3:19 **in which also** *Greek en o kai emended to* Enoch *by Moffatt and Goodspeed.*

3:20 Alx/Byz[**when**], Minor[*adds* once (KJV, NKJ)].

3:21 Alx[**saves you**], Byz[saves us (JNT, KJV, NKJ, TLB)]; Alx/Byz[**And corresponding**], Minor[which also, corresponding (ASV, DRA, ESV, JNT, NAB, NET, NJB)]; **for a good conscience** *or* from a good conscience.

3:22 Alx/Byz[**who has gone into heaven**], Minor/Vulgate[*adds* swallowing up death, that we might be made heirs of everlasting life (DRA)].

4:1 Alx[**Christ has suffered**], Byz[*adds* for us (KJV, NKJ)], Minor[*adds* for you (MRD)]; Alx/Byz[**ceased from sin**], Minor[ceased with sin (HCS, JNT, NAB, NET, NIV, NJB, NLT, NRS, REB, TEV, ~TLB)].

4:3 Alx[**there has been enough time**], Byz[you have had lifetime enough (JNT, ~MRD, ~NAS, ~NAU, ~NET, ~NIV, NJB, ~NLT, ~NRS, ~REB, ~TEV, ~TLB)], Major[we have had lifetime enough (KJV, NKJ)]; Alx[**what the Gentiles like to do**], Byz[what the Gentiles want to do (DRA, ESV, HCS, JNT, KJV, NIV, NJB, NKJ)].

4:4 **abuse you** *or* blaspheme.

4:7 **near** *or* at hand.

4:8 Alx[**Above all**], Byz[And above all (DRA, KJV, MRD, NKJ)]; Alx[**love covers**], Byz[love will cover (KJV, NKJ)].

4:9 Alx[**complaint**], Byz[complaints (ASV, DRA, ESV, KJV, MRD, NAB, NET, NIV, NJB, NKJ, NRS, ~TLB)].

4:11 Alx/Byz[**which God supplies**], Major[that God supplies (ESV, ~HCS, JNT, MRD, NAB, NET, ~NIV, ~NJB, NLT, NRS, TEV, TLB)].

4:14 Alx/Major[**of glory**], Byz[of glory, and of power], Minor[of honor, glory, and of power (DRA)]; Alx[**rests on you**], Byz[*adds* On their part he is blasphemed, but on your part he is glorified (KJV, NKJ)].

you are insulted because of the name of Christ, you are blessed, for the Spirit of glory and of God rests on you. ¹⁵ But let none of you suffer as a murderer, or a thief, or a wrongdoer, or a troublesome meddler. ¹⁶ Yet if one suffers as a Christian, let him not be ashamed, but under that name let him glorify God. ¹⁷ For [the] time has come for judgment to begin with the household of God. And if it begins with us, what will be the outcome for those who do not obey the gospel of God? ¹⁸ And

> *"if it is hard for the righteous to be saved,*
>> *what will become of the godless man and the sinner?"*

¹⁹ Therefore, let those who suffer according to God's will do right and entrust their souls to a faithful Creator.

5 ¹ So I exhort elders among you, as a fellow elder and a witness of the sufferings of Christ and a partaker in the glory that is to be revealed, ² shepherd the flock of God that is under your care, [serving as overseers] – not under compulsion, but voluntarily, according to the will of God; and not for sordid gain, but with eagerness; ³ not as lording it over those in your charge, but being examples to the flock. ⁴ And when the Chief Shepherd appears, you will receive the unfading crown of glory.

⁵ Likewise you that are younger men be subject to elders. Clothe yourselves, all of you, with humility toward one another, for

> *"God opposes the proud,*
>> *but gives grace to the humble."*

⁶ Therefore humble yourselves under the mighty hand of God, that he may exalt you in due time. ⁷ Cast all your care on him, because he cares for you.

⁸ Be sober, be alert. Your adversary the devil prowls around like a roaring lion, seeking [someone] to devour. ⁹ But resist him, firm in your faith, knowing that the same experiences of suffering are being accomplished by your brothers throughout the world. ¹⁰ And after you have suffered a little while, the God of all grace, who has called you to his eternal glory in Christ [Jesus], will himself restore, establish, strengthen, and ground you. ¹¹ To him be the dominion forever. Amen.

4:15 Alx/Byz[**or a troublesome meddler**], Minor[*omits* (MRD)].

4:16 Alx[**under that name**], Byz[in this matter (KJV, NKJ)].

4:17 Alx/Byz[**the time has come**], Minor[it is time (ESV, NAB, NAS, NAU, NET, NIV)].

4:18 Alx/Byz[**what will become**], Minor[but what will become]; Proverbs 11:31 LXX.

4:19 Alx/Byz[**their souls**], Minor[*omits* their (~NLT, ~TLB)]; Alx[**to a faithful Creator**], Byz[as to a faithful Creator (KJV, MRD, ~NAB, ~NET, NKJ)].

5:1 Alx[**So I exhort elders**], Byz[I exhort the elders (ASV, KJV, MRD, NIV, NJB, NKJ, TEV)].

5:2 Alx/Byz[**serving as overseers**], Minor[*omits* (~MRD, REB, RSV, ~TEV, ~TLB)]; Alx[**according to the will of God**], Byz[*omits* (KJV, MRD, NKJ, RSV, TLB)].

5:5 Alx[**with humility toward one another**], Byz[with humility, to serve one another (ASV, KJV, NAS, NAU, NKJ, NLT, TEV, TLB)]; Proverbs 3:34 LXX.

5:7 Alx[**Cast**], Byz[casting (ASV, DRA, ESV, HCS, KJV, NAS, NAU, NET, NKJ)].

5:8 Alx/Byz[**be alert. Your adversary**], Minor[be alert, because your adversary (DRA, KJV, MRD, NJB, NKJ)]; Alx[**someone to devour**], Byz[whom he may devour (ASV, DRA, KJV, MRD, NKJ)], Minor[to devour].

5:10 Alx/Byz[**who has called you**], Minor[who has called us (DRA, KJV, MRD, NKJ, TLB)]; Alx/Byz[**Jesus**], Minor[*omits* (ASV, ESV, JNT, NAS, NAU, NET, NIV, NJB, NRS, REB, RSV, TEV, TLB, Metzger)]; Alx/Byz[**will himself restore**], Major[may he himself restore (KJV, MRD, NKJ)]; Alx/Byz[**restore, establish, strengthen, and ground you**], Minor[restore, establish, and strengthen you (ASV, ~DRA, ~MRD, RSV, ~TLB) *others* restore, establish, and ground you].

5:11 Alx[**the dominion**], Byz[the glory and the dominion (DRA, KJV, NKJ)], Minor[the glory, and power, and the honor (MRD)]; Alx[**forever**], Byz[for ever and ever (ASV, DRA, ESV, JNT, KJV, MRD, NAS, NAU, NIV, NJB, NKJ, NRS, REB, RSV, TLB)].

12 With the help of Silvanus, a faithful brother as I regard him, I have written to you briefly, exhorting you and testifying that this is the true grace of God. Stand fast in it. **13** She who is in Babylon, chosen together with you, sends you her greetings, and so does my son Mark. **14** Greet one another with a kiss of love. Peace to all of you who are in Christ.

5:12 Alx[**grace of God. Stand fast in it**], Byz[grace of God, in which you stand (DRA, KJV, MRD, NKJ, ~TLB)]; **Silvanus** or Silas.

5:13 Alx/Byz[**She who is in**], Minor[The church in (DRA, ~JNT, KJV, MRD, NET, NLT, NRS, REB, TEV, TLB)]; Alx/Byz[**Babylon**], Minor[Rome (TLB)].

5:14 Alx/Byz[**a kiss of love**], Minor[a holy kiss (DRA, MRD)]; Alx[**in Christ**], Byz[in Christ Jesus. Amen (DRA, KJV, ~MRD, NKJ)].

Second Peter

1 ¹ Simeon Peter, a servant and apostle of Jesus Christ, to those who have received a faith of the same kind as ours, by the righteousness of our God and Savior, Jesus Christ: ² grace and peace be multiplied to you in the knowledge of God and of Jesus our Lord.

³ His divine power has granted to us everything pertaining to life and godliness, through the true knowledge of him who called us by his own glory and excellence. ⁴ By these he has granted to us his precious and very great promises, so that through them you may escape from the corruption that is in the world because of lust, and become partakers of the divine nature. ⁵ For this very reason, make every effort to add to your faith virtue; and to virtue, knowledge, ⁶ and to knowledge, self-control, and to self-control, perseverance, and to perseverance, godliness, ⁷ and to godliness, brotherly kindness, and to brotherly kindness, love. ⁸ For if these qualities are yours and are increasing, they keep you from being ineffective or unfruitful in the knowledge of our Lord Jesus Christ. ⁹ For whoever lacks these things is blind and shortsighted, and has forgotten that he was cleansed from his old sins. ¹⁰ Therefore, brothers, be all the more eager to make your calling and election sure. For if you do these things, you will never fall; ¹¹ so there will be an entrance richly provided for you into the eternal kingdom of our Lord and Savior Jesus Christ.

¹² Therefore I will always remind you of these things, even though you know them and are firmly established in the truth you now have. ¹³ I think it right, as long as I am in this body, to stir you up by way of reminder, ¹⁴ since I know that the putting aside of my body will be soon, as our Lord Jesus Christ has made clear to me. ¹⁵ And I will see to it that after my departure you will be able at any time to call these things to mind.

¹⁶ For we did not follow cleverly devised tales when we made known to you the power and coming of our Lord Jesus Christ, but we were eyewitnesses of his majesty. ¹⁷ For he received honor and glory from God the Father when the voice came to him by the Majestic Glory, saying, "This is my Son, my Beloved, with whom I am well pleased." ¹⁸ We ourselves heard this voice coming from heaven when we were with him on the holy mountain. ¹⁹ And we have the prophetic word made more sure, and you will do well to pay attention to this as to a lamp shining in a dark place, until the day dawns and the morning star rises in your hearts. ²⁰ First of all you must understand this, that no prophecy of

---

Title Alx/Byz[**Second Peter** *Greek* Peter B], Minor[*variations of* The Second General Letter of the Holy Apostle Peter].

1:1 Alx/Byz[**Simeon**], Minor[Simon (ASV, DRA, JNT, KJV, MRD, NAS, NAU, NIV, NJB, NKJ, NLT, TEV, TLB)]; Alx/Byz[**Peter**], Alt[*without textual foundation* Cephas (~JNT)]; Alx/Byz[**our God and Savior** *or* our God, and the Savior], Minor[our God and our Savior (JNT) *others* God and our Savior (KJV) *others* our Lord and Savior (MRD)]; **servant** *Greek* slave.

1:2 Alx/Byz[**God and of Jesus**], Minor[*omits* (NJB, ~TLB) *others* our Lord Jesus Christ (MRD)].

1:3 Alx[**by his own**], Byz[through his (~KJV, NKJ, NLT)].

1:4 Alx/Byz[**precious and very great**], Minor[very great and precious (DRA, HCS, KJV, MRD, NIV, NJB, NKJ, NLT, REB, TEV)].

1:10 Alx/Byz[**all the more eager**], Minor[*adds* through good works (DRA, MRD)].

1:12 Alx[**always**], Byz[not neglect to (KJV, MRD, NKJ)].

1:13, 14 **body** *Greek* tent.

1:17 Alx[**my Son, my Beloved**], Byz[my beloved Son (ASV, DRA, ESV, HCS, KJV, MRD, NAS, NAU, NET, ~NIV, NJB, NKJ, NLT, RSV, TEV, TLB)]; Matthew 17:2, 5.

1:19 **And we have the prophetic word made more sure** *or* We also have the more sure prophetic word.

1:20 **interpretation** *or* explanation.

scripture is a matter of one's own interpretation, [21] for no prophecy was ever made by the act of human will, but men moved by the Holy Spirit spoke from God.

2 [1] But false prophets also arose among the people, just as there will also be false teachers among you, who will secretly introduce destructive heresies, even denying the Master who bought them, bringing swift destruction upon themselves. [2] And many will follow their indecency, and because of them the way of truth will be reviled. [3] And in their greed they will exploit you with false words. From long ago their condemnation has not been idle, and their destruction has not been asleep.

[4] For if God did not spare angels when they sinned, but cast them into hell and committed them to chains of darkness, to be reserved for judgment; [5] and if he did not spare the ancient world, but preserved Noah, a preacher of righteousness, with seven others, when he brought a flood upon the world of the ungodly; [6] and if he condemned the cities of Sodom and Gomorrah [to destruction] by reducing them to ashes, having made them an example of what is coming to the ungodly; [7] and if he rescued Lot, a righteous man, who was distressed by the filthy lives of lawless men [8] (for by what he saw and heard that righteous man, while living among them, felt his righteous soul tormented day after day by their lawless deeds) – [9] then the Lord knows how to rescue the godly from trial, and to keep the unrighteous under punishment for the day of judgment, [10] and especially those who indulge the flesh in its corrupt desire and despise authority.

Bold and willful, they are not afraid to revile the glorious ones, [11] whereas angels, though greater in power and might, do not bring a reviling judgment against them before the Lord. [12] But these, like irrational animals, creatures of instinct, born to be caught and killed, reviling in matters of which they are ignorant, will also be destroyed in their destruction, [13] suffering wrong for their wrongdoing. They count it a pleasure to revel in the daytime. They are blots and blemishes, reveling in their deceptions, as they carouse with you. [14] They have eyes full of an adulteress, that never cease from sin; they entice unstable souls. They have hearts trained in greed. Accursed children! [15] Forsaking the right way, they have gone astray, having followed the way of Balaam, the son of Bosor, who loved the wages of unrighteousness. [16] But he was rebuked for his own transgression by a donkey – a

---

1:21 Alx[**but men moved by the Holy Spirit spoke from God**], Byz[but holy men of God spoke, as they were moved by the Holy Spirit (DRA, KJV, MRD, NKJ, ~TLB)].

2:2 Alx/Byz[**indecency**], Minor[destructiveness (NKJ, ~TLB)].

2:3 Alx[**has not been asleep**], Byz[will not be asleep (TLB)].

2:4 Alx/Byz[**chains**], Minor[pits (ASV, JNT, NAS, NAU, NIV, NJB, NLT, REB, RSV)]; Alx/Byz[**reserved for judgment**], Minor[*adds* to be tortured (MRD)]; **hell** *Greek* Tartaros.

2:6 Alx/Byz[**to destruction**], Minor[*omits*]; Alx[**of what is coming to the ungodly**], Byz[to those who would live ungodly thereafter (ASV, DRA, HCS, JNT, KJV, MRD, NAB, NAS, NAU, NET, NJB, NKJ, RSV)].

2:8 Alx/Byz[**that righteous man**], Minor[he, being righteous (DRA, NLT, TLB)].

2:9 Alx/Byz[**from trial**], Minor[from trials (ESV, HCS, JNT, KJV, MRD, NET, NIV, NJB, NKJ, NLT, REB, TEV, TLB)]; **keep the unrighteous under punishment for** *or* hold the unrighteous for punishment in; **for the day** *or* until the day.

2:10 **glorious ones** *or* angels *Greek* glories.

2:11 Alx/Byz[**against them**], Minor[against themselves (DRA)]; Alx/Byz[**before the Lord** *or* from the Lord], Minor[*omits* (DRA, MRD)].

2:12 Alx[**will also be destroyed**], Byz[will be utterly destroyed (ASV, DRA, JNT, MRD, ~NLT, REB, TEV)].

2:13 Alx[**suffering**], Byz[receiving (DRA, JNT, KJV, MRD, NIV, NKJ, ~NLT, TLB)]; Alx/Byz[**deceptions**], Minor[love feasts (DRA, MRD, ~NET, NIV, NRS, RSV, TLB)].

2:14 Alx/Byz[**an adulteress**], Minor[adultery (ASV, DRA, ESV, HCS, KJV, MRD, NAB, NAS, NAU, NET, NIV, NJB, NKJ, NLT, NRS, RSV)].

2:15 Alx/Byz[**Bosor**], Minor[Beor (ASV, ESV, ~JNT, MRD, NAS, NAU, NIV, NKJ, NLT, RSV, TEV, TLB)].

beast without speech – who spoke with a man's voice and restrained the prophet's madness.

¹⁷ These are springs without water and mists driven by a storm. For them the blackest darkness has been reserved. ¹⁸ For speaking out arrogant words of vanity, they entice by fleshly desires, by sensuality, those who barely escape from the ones who live in error. ¹⁹ They promise them freedom, while they themselves are slaves of corruption; for whatever overcomes a man, to that he is enslaved. ²⁰ For if, after they have escaped the defilements of the world by the knowledge of [our] Lord and Savior Jesus Christ, they are again entangled in them and are overcome, the last state has become worse for them than the first. ²¹ For it would have been better for them not to have known the way of righteousness, than having known it, to turn away from the holy commandment handed on to them. ²² It has happened to them according to the true proverb,

"A dog turns back to its own vomit,"

and,

"A sow, after having washed, returns to wallowing in the mire."

3 ¹ This is now the second letter that I have written to you, beloved, and in both of them I have aroused your sincere mind by way of reminder; ² that you should remember the words spoken beforehand by the holy prophets and the commandment of the Lord and Savior spoken through your apostles. ³ First of all you must understand this, that scoffers will come in the last days, [with] scoffing, following their own lusts ⁴ and saying, "Where is the promise of his coming? For, ever since the fathers fell asleep, all things continue as they were from the beginning of creation." ⁵ They deliberately ignore this fact, that by the word of God heavens existed long ago, and the earth was formed out of water and by means of water, ⁶ through which the world at that time was destroyed, being deluged with water. ⁷ But by the same word the present heavens and earth are reserved for fire, being kept for the day of judgment and destruction of ungodly men.

⁸ But do not ignore this one fact, beloved, that with the Lord one day is like a thousand years, and a thousand years like one day. ⁹ The Lord is not slow about his promise, as some count slowness, but is patient toward you, not wishing for any to perish but for all to come to repentance. ¹⁰ But the day of the Lord will come like a thief, in which the heavens will pass away with a roar and the elements will be destroyed with fire, and the earth and the works that are in it will be laid bare. ¹¹ Since all these things are to be destroyed in this way, what sort of people ought [you] to be in lives of holiness and godliness, ¹² looking for and hastening the coming of the day of God, because of which the

---

2:17 Alx[**mists**], Byz[clouds (DRA, KJV, MRD, NKJ, TEV, TLB)]; Alx[**reserved**], Byz[*adds* forever (KJV, NKJ, TLB)].

2:18 Alx[**barely escape**], Byz[actually escape (KJV, NKJ)].

2:19 Alx[**he is enslaved**], Byz[he is also enslaved (ASV, DRA, ~KJV, NKJ)].

2:20 Alx[**our Lord**], Byz[the Lord (ASV, KJV, NAS, NAU, NKJ)].

2:21 Alx[**turn away** *or* turn back], Byz[*omits* away (JNT, KJV, NKJ)].

2:22 Alx[**It has happened**], Byz[But it has happened (~DRA, KJV, MRD, NKJ)]; ~**Proverbs 26:11**, Classical[**Heraclitus Frg. B13** "Pigs delight in the mire more than in clean water"].

3:2 Alx[**the commandment of the Lord and Savior spoken through your apostles**], Byz[the commandment of the Lord and Savior spoken through us – the apostles (KJV, ~MRD, NKJ, TLB)], Minor[your apostles of the commandments of the Lord and Savior (DRA)].

3:3 Alx[**with scoffing** *Greek* in scoffing], Byz[*omits* (~DRA, JNT, KJV, NKJ, TEV)].

3:7 Alx[**by the same word**], Byz[by his word (MRD, NAS, NAU, REB, ~TEV, TLB)].

3:9 Alx[**toward you**], Byz[toward us (KJV, NKJ, ~TLB)], Minor[because of you].

3:10 Alx[**like a thief**], Byz[*adds* in the night (KJV, NKJ)]; Alx[**be laid bare**], Byz[be burned up (ASV, DRA, JNT, KJV, NAS, NAU, NJB, NKJ, ~NLT, ~REB, RSV, TLB)], Minor[be found destroyed *others* be found dissolved *others* disappear (TEV)].

3:11 Alx[**in this way**], Byz[therefore (DRA, KJV, MRD, NKJ)]; Alx/Byz[**you**], Minor[we (NET, TLB)].

3:12 **hastening** *or* desiring.

heavens will be destroyed by fire, and the elements will melt with intense heat! [13] But according to his promise we are looking for new heavens and a new earth, in which righteousness dwells.

[14] Therefore, beloved, since you look for these things, be diligent to be found by him in peace, spotless and blameless. [15] And regard the patience of our Lord as salvation; just as also our beloved brother Paul, according to the wisdom given him, wrote to you. [16] He writes the same way in all his letters, speaking in them of these matters. His letters contain some things that are hard to understand, which ignorant and unstable people distort, as they do the other Scriptures, to their own destruction. [17] You therefore, beloved, knowing this beforehand, be on your guard so that you are not carried away by the error of lawless men and fall from your own steadfastness. [18] But grow in the grace and knowledge of our Lord and Savior Jesus Christ. To him be the glory both now and to the day of eternity. [Amen.]

3:13 Alx/Byz[**promise**], Minor[promises (DRA, NJB)].

3:15 Alx/Byz[**Paul**], Alt[*without textual foundation* Saul (~JNT)].

3:18 Alx/Byz[**Jesus Christ**], Minor[*adds* and God the Father (MRD)]; Alx/Byz[**day of eternity**], Minor[eternity of eternity (ASV, JNT, KJV, NIV, NKJ, REB, TEV, TLB)]; Alx/Byz[**Amen**], Minor[*omits* (NET, REB, ~TLB) *others add* Second Peter].

First John

1 ¹ That which was from the beginning, which we have heard, which we have seen with our eyes, which we have looked upon, and our hands have touched, concerning the Word of life – ² the life was revealed, and we have seen it, and testify to it, and proclaim to you the eternal life which was with the Father and was revealed to us – ³ that which we have seen and heard we proclaim also to you, so that you too may have fellowship with us; and our fellowship is with the Father and with his Son Jesus Christ. ⁴ And we write this that our joy may be complete.

⁵ This is the message we have heard from him and declare to you, that God is light and in him is no darkness at all. ⁶ If we say we have fellowship with him, and walk in darkness, we lie and do not practice the truth. ⁷ But if we walk in the light, as he is in the light, we have fellowship with one another, and the blood of Jesus his Son cleanses us from all sin. ⁸ If we say we have no sin, we deceive ourselves, and the truth is not in us. ⁹ If we confess our sins, he is faithful and just, and will forgive us our sins and cleanse us from all unrighteousness. ¹⁰ If we say that we have not sinned, we make him a liar, and his word is not in us.

2 ¹ My little children, I write this to you so that you may not sin. But if anyone does sin, we have an advocate with the Father, Jesus Christ the righteous. ² And he is the atoning sacrifice for our sins; and not for ours only, but also for the sins of the whole world. ³ Now by this we know that we know him: if we keep his commandments. ⁴ He who says, "I know him," but does not keep his commandments, is a liar, and the truth is not in him. ⁵ But whoever keeps his word, truly the love of God is perfected in him. By this we know that we are in him: ⁶ he who says he abides in him ought to walk [just] as he walked.

⁷ Beloved, I am writing you no new commandment, but an old commandment that you had from the beginning. The old commandment is the word that you have heard. ⁸ Yet I am writing you a new commandment, which is true in him and in you, because the darkness is passing away and the true light is already shining. ⁹ He who says he is in the light and hates his brother is in the darkness still. ¹⁰ He who loves his brother abides in the light, and there is no cause for stumbling in him. ¹¹ But he who hates his brother is in the darkness and walks in the darkness, and does not know where he is going, because the darkness has blinded his eyes.

Title Alx/Byz[**First John** Greek John A], Minor[variations of The First General Letter of the Holy Apostle John].

1:3 Alx[**proclaim also**], Byz[omits also (DRA, KJV, NKJ, NLT, TLB)].

1:4 Alx[**write this**], Byz[adds to you (DRA, KJV, MRD, NJB, NKJ, ~TLB)]; Alx/Byz[**our joy**], Minor[your joy (DRA, KJV, NKJ, ~NLT, ~TLB)].

1:5 Alx/Major[**message**], Byz[promise].

1:7 Alx[**blood of Jesus**], Byz[adds Christ (DRA, KJV, NKJ, ~TLB)]; **all sin** or every sin.

1:9 Alx/Byz[**forgive us our sins** Greek forgive us sins], Minor[forgive our sins (~JNT, NAB, NJB, REB, RSV)].

2:2 **atoning sacrifice** or bringer of mercy.

2:4 Alx/Byz[**the truth**], Minor[truth (NJB, TEV, ~TLB) others the truth of God].

2:6 Alx/Byz[**just**], Minor[omits (JNT, MRD, NIV, NJB, NLT, ~REB, TLB)].

2:7 Alx[**Beloved**], Byz[Brothers (KJV, NKJ, TLB)]; Alx[**the word that you have heard**], Byz[adds from the beginning (~JNT, KJV, NKJ, ~NLT, ~REB, ~TEV, ~TLB)].

2:10 **stumbling in him** or stumbling in it.

12   I write to you, little children,
                     because your sins are forgiven you
                             for his name's sake.
13   I write to you, fathers,
                     because you have known him
                             who is from the beginning.
            I write to you, young men,
                     because you have overcome the evil one.
14   I wrote to you, little children,
                     because you have known the Father.
            I wrote to you, fathers,
                     because you have known him
                             who is from the beginning.
            I wrote to you, young men,
                     because you are strong,
                     and the word of God abides in you,
                             and you have overcome the evil one.

¹⁵ Do not love the world or the things in the world. If anyone loves the world, the love of the Father is not in him. ¹⁶ For all that is in the world – the lust of the flesh, and the lust of the eyes, and the pride of life – is not of the Father but is of the world. ¹⁷ And the world is passing away, and the lust of it; but he who does the will of God abides forever.

¹⁸ Little children, it is the last hour; and as you have heard that Antichrist is coming, even now many antichrists have come; by this we know that it is the last hour. ¹⁹ They went out from us, but they were not of us; for if they had been of us, they would have continued with us; but they went out that it might be plain that none of them were of us. ²⁰ But you have an anointing from the Holy One, and you all know. ²¹ I write to you, not because you do not know the truth, but because you know it, and because no lie is of the truth. ²² Who is the liar but he who denies that Jesus is the Christ? This is the Antichrist, he who denies the Father and the Son. ²³ No one who denies the Son has the Father; whoever acknowledges the Son has the Father also. ²⁴ Let that abide in you which you heard from the beginning. If what you heard from the beginning abides in you, then you also will abide in the Son and in the Father. ²⁵ And this is what he has promised us – eternal life.

²⁶ These things I have written to you about those who try to deceive you. ²⁷ But the anointing which you have received from him abides in you, and you do not need that

---

2:14 Alx/Byz[**I wrote to you, fathers...14**], Major[14 I wrote to you, fathers... (ASV, ESV, KJV, NAS, NAU, NIV, NKJ, REB, RSV, TLB)]; Alx/Byz[**I wrote to you, little children**], Major[I write to you, little children (DRA, KJV, ~NIV, NKJ, ~TLB)]; Alx/Byz[**word of God**], Minor[word *others* word of God the Father].

2:17 Alx/Byz[**the lust of it**], Minor[*omits* of it (~NLT, ~TLB)]; Alx/Byz[**abides forever**], Minor[*adds* just as God abides forever].

2:18 Alx[**that Antichrist**], Byz[that the Antichrist (NAB, NET, NIV, NJB, NKJ, NLT, TEV)], Minor[the Antichrist (~TLB)].

2:19 **none of them were of us** *or* not all of them were of us *Greek* all are not of us.

2:20 Alx/Byz[**Holy One, and**], Minor[*omits* and]; Alx[**all know**], Byz[know all (ASV, DRA, JNT, KJV, NKJ, ~TLB)].

2:23 Alx[**whoever acknowledges the Son has the Father also**], Byz[*omits*].

2:24 Alx[**Let that abide in you**], Byz[Therefore let that abide in you (KJV, NKJ, NLT, REB, TEV, TLB)]; Alx/Byz[**and in the Father**], Minor[*omits* in (JNT, NLT, TEV, TLB)].

2:25 Alx/Byz[**promised us**], Minor[promised you (NJB)].

2:27 Alx/Byz[**teach you; but as**], Minor[*omits* as (HCS, NAB, ~NJB, NLT, REB, TEV, TLB)]; Alx[**his**

anyone teach you; but as his anointing teaches you about all things, and is true, and is not a lie, and just as it has taught you, you abide in him.

3 **28** And now, little children, abide in him, so that when he appears we may have confidence and not be ashamed before him at his coming. **29** If you know that he is righteous, you also know that everyone who does right is born of him. **1** See what love the Father has given us, that we should be called children of God! And so we are! The reason why the world does not know us is that it did not know him. **2** Beloved, now we are children of God; and it has not yet been revealed what we shall be. We do know that when he appears, we shall be like him, for we shall see him as he is. **3** And everyone who has this hope in him purifies himself, just as he is pure.

4 Everyone who commits sin also commits lawlessness; sin is lawlessness. **5** And you know that he appeared to take away sins, and in him there is no sin. **6** No one who abides in him sins. No one who sins has either seen him or known him. **7** Little children, let no one deceive you. He who does right is righteous, just as he is righteous. **8** He who commits sin is of the devil, for the devil has sinned from the beginning. The reason the Son of God appeared was to destroy the works of the devil. **9** No one who is of God practices sin, for God's seed remains in him; and he cannot sin, because he has been born of God. **10** By this it may be seen who are the children of God, and who are the children of the devil: whoever does not do right is not of God, nor he who does not love his brother.

11 For this is the message which you heard from the beginning, that we should love one another, **12** and not be like Cain who was of the evil one and murdered his brother. And why did he murder him? Because his own deeds were evil and his brother's righteous. **13** [So] do not marvel, brothers, if the world hates you. **14** We know that we have passed from death to life, because we love the brothers. He who does not love abides in death. **15** Anyone who hates his brother is a murderer, and you know that no murderer has eternal life abiding in him. **16** By this we know love, that he laid down his life for us. And we also ought to lay down our lives for the brothers. **17** But if anyone has the world's goods and sees his brother in need, yet closes his heart against him, how does the love of God abide in him? **18** Little children, let us not love in word or tongue but in deed and in truth.

---

anointing teaches], Byz[the same anointing teaches (KJV, ~MRD, ~NJB, NKJ, ~NLT, ~TLB)]; Alx[**abide in him** or abide in it], Byz[will abide in him (KJV, NKJ)].

2:28 Alx[**when he appears** or if he appears], Byz[whenever he appears].

2:29 Alx[**you also know**], Byz[omits also (ESV, KJV, NIV, NJB, NKJ, NRS, REB, RSV, TEV, TLB)].

3:1 Alx[**And so we are**], Byz[omits (DRA, KJV, NKJ)]; Alx/Byz[**does not know us**], Major[does not know you].

3:2 Alx[**what we shall be. We do know**], Byz[what we shall be, but we know (ESV, KJV, MRD, ~NIV, NKJ, ~NLT, REB, RSV, TEV, TLB)]; **when he appears** or when it is revealed.

3:5 Alx[**to take away sins**], Byz[to take away our sins (DRA, KJV, MRD, NIV, NKJ, NLT, TLB)].

3:10 Alx/Byz[**does not do right** or does not practice righteousness], Minor[is not righteous (DRA, ~TLB)].

3:13 Alx[**So**], Byz[omits (ASV, DRA, HCS, JNT, ESV, KJV, NAS, NAU, NIV, NJB, NKJ, NRS, REB, RSV]; Alx[**brothers**], Byz[my brothers (KJV, MRD, NIV, NKJ, TEV, ~TLB)].

3:14 Alx[**He who does not love**], Byz[adds his brother (KJV, MRD, NKJ, ~TLB) others add the brother].

3:15 Alx[**abiding in him**], Byz[abiding in himself (DRA, ~TLB) NLT, NRS, and REB make this a gender neutral plural].

3:16 Alx/Byz[**By this we know love**], Minor[By this we know the love of God (DRA, KJV)].

3:18 Alx[**Little children**], Byz[My little children (ASV, DRA, KJV, MRD, NKJ, TEV)].

¹⁹ [And] by this we shall know that we are of the truth, and shall assure our heart before him ²⁰ whenever our heart condemns us; for God is greater than our heart, and he knows everything. ²¹ Beloved, if [our] heart does not condemn, we have confidence before God; ²² and we receive from him whatever we ask, because we keep his commandments and do what pleases him. ²³ And this is his commandment: that we should believe in the name of his Son Jesus Christ, and love one another, just as he has commanded us. ²⁴ Now those who keep his commandments abide in him, and he in them. And by this we know that he abides in us, by the Spirit whom he has given us.

4 ¹ Beloved, do not believe every spirit, but test the spirits to see whether they are of God; because many false prophets have gone out into the world. ² By this you know the Spirit of God: every Spirit that confesses that Jesus Christ has come in the flesh is of God, ³ and every spirit which does not confess Jesus is not of God. This is the spirit of the Antichrist, of which you have heard that it was coming, and now it is in the world already. ⁴ You are of God, little children, and have overcome them, because he who is in you is greater than he who is in the world. ⁵ They are of the world and therefore speak as of the world, and the world listens to them. ⁶ We are of God. Whoever knows God listens to us. He who is not of God does not listen to us. By this we know the spirit of truth and the spirit of error.

⁷ Beloved, let us love one another, for love is of God; and everyone who loves is born of God and knows God. ⁸ He who does not love does not know God, for God is love. ⁹ In this the love of God was revealed among us, that God sent his only begotton Son into the world, so that we might live through him. ¹⁰ In this is love, not that we have loved God but that he loved us and sent his Son to be the atoning sacrifice for our sins. ¹¹ Beloved, if God so loved us, we also ought to love one another. ¹² No one has ever seen God; but if we love one another, God abides in us and his love is perfected in us.

¹³ By this we know that we abide in him and he in us, because he has given us of his Spirit. ¹⁴ And we have seen and testify that the Father has sent his Son as the Savior of the world. ¹⁵ If anyone confesses that Jesus is the Son of God, God abides in him, and he in God. ¹⁶ So we know and believe the love God has for us.

God is love, and he who abides in love abides in God, and God abides in him. ¹⁷ In this, love is perfected among us, that we may have confidence for the Day of Judgment;

3:19 Alx/Byz[**And by this**], Minor[*omits* And (ASV, DRA, ESV, HCS, JNT, NAS, NAU, NJB, NLT, REB, RSV, ~TEV, ~TLB)]; Alx[**we shall know**], Byz[we know (DRA, KJV, MRD, NIV, NKJ)]; Alx[**heart**], Byz[hearts (DRA, HCS, JNT, KJV, MRD, NAB, NIV, ~NJB, NKJ, ~NLT, NRS, ~REB, RSV, ~TEV, TLB)].

3:20 **whenever our heart condemns us; for God is greater than our heart** *or* that even if our heart condemns us, God is greater than our heart.

3:21 Alx/Byz[**our**], Minor[*omits*]; Alx[**does not condemn**], Byz[*adds* us (ASV, DRA, ESV, HCS, JNT, KJV, MRD, NAB, NAS, NAU, NET, NIV, NJB, NKJ, NRS, REB, RSV, TEV)].

3:23 Alx/Byz[**we should believe**], Minor[we believe (ESV, HCS, MRD, NAS, NAU, NET, ~NIV, TEV)]; Alx[**as he has commanded us**], Byz[*omits* us (~TLB)].

4:2 Alx/Byz[**By this you know the Spirit of God**], Major[By this the Spirit of God is known (DRA, MRD, NJB, ~NLT, REB, TLB)].

4:3 Alx[**does not confess Jesus**], Byz[does not confess that Jesus Christ has come in the flesh (KJV, MRD, NKJ, ~NLT, ~TLB)], Alt/Vulgate[dissolves Jesus *or* severs Jesus (DRA) *others* annuls Jesus].

4:6 **spirit of truth** *or* Spirit of truth.

4:10 Alx[**we have loved God**], Byz[we loved God (ASV, JNT, KJV, MRD, NAS, NAU, NIV, NJB, NKJ, NLT, NRS, REB, RSV, ~TLB)]; **atoning sacrifice** *or* bringer of mercy.

4:15 Alx[**If anyone**], Byz[Whoever (ASV, DRA, ESV, HCS, KJV, MRD, NAB, NAS, NAU, NJB, NKJ, NLT, NRS, RSV, TLB)]; Alx/Byz[**Jesus**], Minor[*adds* Christ].

4:16 Alx/Major[**and God abides in him**], Byz[*omits* abides (DRA, KJV, NAB, NIV, NJB, NKJ)].

because as he is, so are we in this world. [18] There is no fear in love, but perfect love casts out fear, because fear has to do with punishment. And he who fears is not made perfect in love. [19] We love because he first loved us. [20] If anyone says, "I love God," and hates his brother, he is a liar; for he who does not love his brother whom he has seen, cannot love God whom he has not seen. [21] And this commandment we have from him: that he who loves God must love his brother also.

5 [1] Everyone who believes that Jesus is the Christ is born of God, and everyone who loves the parent [also] loves the child. [2] By this we know that we love the children of God, when we love God and obey his commandments. [3] For this is the love of God, that we obey his commandments. And his commandments are not burdensome. [4] For whatever is born of God overcomes the world. And this is the victory that has overcome the world – our faith. [5] [So] who is it that overcomes the world but he who believes that Jesus is the Son of God?

[6] This is he who came by water and blood – Jesus Christ; not only by water, but by water and by blood. And it is the Spirit who bears witness, because the Spirit is the truth. [7] There are three witnesses, [8] the Spirit, the water, and the blood; and these three agree. [9] If we receive the testimony of men, the testimony of God is greater; for this is the testimony of God: that he has borne witness of his Son. [10] He who believes in the Son of God has the testimony in himself. He who does not believe God has made him a liar, because he has not believed in the testimony that God has given of his Son. [11] And this is the testimony: that God has given us eternal life, and this life is in his Son. [12] He who has the Son has life; he who does not have the Son of God does not have life.

[13] I write these things to you who believe in the name of the Son of God, so that you may know that you have eternal life. [14] And this is the confidence which we have in him, that if we ask anything according to his will he hears us. [15] And if we know that he hears us, whatever we ask, we know that we have the requests that we have asked of him.

[16] If anyone sees his brother commit a sin that does not lead to death, he will ask, and God will give him life for those whose sin is not leading to death. There is sin leading

4:19 Alx[**We love**], Byz[*adds* him (KJV, NKJ, ~NLT, TLB) *others add* God (DRA, MRD) *others add* therefore (DRA, MRD, NJB, ~TLB)].

4:20 Alx/Major[**love his brother**], Byz[love the brother (NJB)], Alt[*without textual foundation* love a brother (~NAB, ~REB) *others without textual foundation* love people (~NLT, ~NRS)]; Alx[**cannot love God**], Byz[how can he love God…? (DRA, KJV, MRD, NKJ, NLT, TLB)].

5:1 Alx/Byz[**also**], Minor[*omits* (ESV, NAS, NAU, NET, NJB, NRS, REB, RSV)].

5:2 Alx[**obey**], Byz[keep (DRA, KJV, NJB, NKJ)].

5:4 Alx/Byz[**our faith**], Minor[your faith (~TLB)].

5:5 Alx[**So**], Byz[*omits* (DRA, ESV, JNT, KJV, ~MRD, NAU, NIV, NJB, NKJ, NRS, ~REB, RSV, TEV)].

5:6 Alx[**by water and by blood**], Byz[by water and blood (DRA, ESV, JNT, KJV, MRD, NAB, NET, NIV, NJB, NKJ, NLT, NRS, RSV, ~TLB)], Minor[by water and by spirit]; Alx/Byz[**because the Spirit is the truth**], Alt/Vulgate[that Christ is the truth (DRA)].

5:7-8   Alx/Major/early-Vulgate/Peshitta/Coptic/Armenian/Ethiopic/Arabic/Slavonic[*text*], Byz/late-Vulgate[7 There are three witnesses in heaven: the Father, the Word, and the Holy Spirit; and these three are one. 8 And there are three that bear witness on earth: the Spirit, the water, and the blood; and these three agree (DRA, KJV, MRD, NKJ, ~TLB)].

5:8 **these three agree** *or* these three agree as one.

5:9 Alx[**God: that** *or* God that], Byz[God which (DRA, JNT, KJV, MRD, NIV, NJB, NKJ, ~NLT, ~REB, ~TEV)].

5:10 Alx[**testimony in himself**], Byz[testimony in him (ASV, ~JNT, NJB, ~REB, ~TEV, ~TLB)], Minor[testimony of God in himself (DRA)]; Alx/Byz[**He who does not believe God**], Minor[He who does not believe the Son (DRA, ~NLT, ~TLB)].

5:13 Alx[*text*], Byz[*adds* and that you may believe in the name of the Son of God (KJV, NKJ)].

5:16 **God** *Greek* he.

to death. I do not say that he should pray about that. [17] All wrongdoing is sin, and there is sin that does not lead to death.

[18] We know that anyone born of God does not sin; but he who was born of God keeps him, and the evil one does not touch him. [19] We know that we are of God, and the whole world is under the power of the evil one. [20] And we know that the Son of God has come and has given us understanding, that we may know him who is true; and we are in him who is true, in his Son Jesus Christ. This is the true God and eternal life. [21] Little children, keep yourselves from idols.

5:[17] Alx/Byz/Vulgate[**that does not lead to death**], Minor[*omits* not (DRA, ~TLB)].

5:[18] Alx[**keeps him**], Byz[keeps himself (ASV, KJV, MRD, ~NET, NKJ)].

5:[20] Alx/Byz[**that we may know him who is true**], Minor[to know him who is true (ASV, NAB, NET, REB, RSV, TLB)]; Alx/Byz[**him who is true**], Alt/Vulgate[the true God (DRA, ~MRD, NLT, REB, TEV, TLB)]; Alx/Byz[**eternal life**], Minor[the eternal life (MRD, ~TEV, ~TLB)]; *NJB includes verse 21 in verse 20.*

5:[21] Alx[*text*], Byz[*adds* Amen (DRA, KJV, NKJ, ~TLB)].

Second John

1 ¹ The elder to the chosen lady and her children, whom I love in the truth; and not only I, but also all who know the truth, ² because of the truth which abides in us and will be with us forever: ³ grace, mercy, and peace will be with us, from God the Father and from Jesus Christ, the Father's Son, in truth and love.

⁴ I rejoiced greatly to find some of your children walking in the truth, just as we have been commanded by the Father. ⁵ And now I ask you, lady, not as though I were writing you a new commandment, but the one we have had from the beginning, that we love one another. ⁶ And this is love, that we walk according to his commandments. This is the commandment, just as you have heard from the beginning, that you should walk in love. ⁷ For many deceivers, who do not acknowledge Jesus Christ as coming in the flesh, have gone out into the world. Any such person is the deceiver and the antichrist. ⁸ Watch yourselves, that you do not lose what we have worked for, but that you may receive a full reward. ⁹ Anyone who runs ahead and does not abide in the teaching of Christ does not have God; he who abides in the teaching has both the Father and the Son. ¹⁰ If anyone comes to you and does not bring this teaching, do not receive him into your house or give him any greeting; ¹¹ for he who greets him shares in his wicked work.

¹² Though I have much to write to you, I do not want to use paper and ink, but I hope to come to see you and talk with you face to face, so that our joy may be complete. ¹³ The children of your chosen sister greet you.

Title Alx/Byz[**Second John** *Greek* John B], Minor[*variations of* The second general letter of the holy apostle John, the theologian].

1:1 **chosen lady** *or a name* chosen Kyria *or* lady Electa *or* Electa Kyria *see MRD*.

1:3 Alx/Byz[**grace, mercy, and peace will be**], Alt[*without textual foundation* may grace, mercy, and peace be (~DRA, ~KJV, ~MRD, ~TEV, ~TLB)]; Alx/Major[**with us**], Byz[with you (DRA, KJV, MRD, NKJ)], Alx[**Jesus Christ**], Byz[the Lord Jesus Christ (KJV, MRD, NKJ)].

1:5 **lady** *or* Kyria *see MRD*.

1:7 Alx[**gone out into the world**], Byz[gone into the world (KJV)].

1:8 Alx[**you do not lose**], Byz[we do not lose (KJV, NKJ)], Alx/Byz[**we have worked**], Minor[you have worked (DRA, JNT, MRD, NIV, RSV)], Alx[**you may receive**], Byz[we may receive (KJV, NKJ)].

1:9 Alx[**runs ahead**], Byz[transgresses (DRA, ~HCS, KJV, MRD, ~NAS, ~NAU, NKJ, ~NLT, ~REB)]; Alx[**he who abides in the teaching**], Byz[*adds* of Christ (KJV, NKJ, ~NLT, TLB)].

1:11 Alx/Byz[**text**], Metzger[*Sixtine-Vulgate adds* Behold, I have forewarned you, that in the day of the Lord you may not be confounded].

1:12 Alx/Byz[**our joy**], Minor[your joy (ASV, DRA, NAS, NAU)].

1:13 Alx[**text**], Byz[*adds* Amen (KJV, NKJ)], Minor[*adds* Grace to you. Amen (MRD) *others add* The second letter of John].

Third John

1 ¹ The elder to the beloved Gaius, whom I love in truth.
² Beloved, I pray that you may be in good health and that all may go well with you, even as your soul is getting along well. ³ For I greatly rejoiced when some of the brothers arrived and testified to the truth of your life, and how you are walking in truth. ⁴ I have no greater joy than this, to hear that my children are walking in the truth.

⁵ Beloved, you are acting faithfully in whatever you accomplish for the brothers, and especially when they are strangers. ⁶ And they have testified to your love before the church. You will do well to send them on their way in a manner worthy of God. ⁷ For they went out for the sake of the Name, accepting nothing from the Gentiles. ⁸ Therefore we ought to support such men, so that we may be fellow workers in the truth.

⁹ I wrote something to the church; but Diotrephes, who loves to be first among them, does not accept what we say. ¹⁰ So if I come, I will call attention to what he is doing, gossiping against us with evil words. And not satisfied with that, he refuses to welcome the brothers himself, and also stops those who want to welcome them and puts them out of the church.

¹¹ Beloved, do not imitate what is evil, but what is good. The one who does good is of God. The one who does evil has not seen God. ¹² Demetrius has received a good testimony from everyone, and from the truth itself. And we add our testimony, and you know that our testimony is true.

¹³ I had much to write you, but I do not want to do so with pen and ink. ¹⁴ I hope to see you soon, and we will talk face to face. ¹⁵ Peace to you. The friends here send their greetings. Greet the friends there by name.

Title Alx/Byz[**Third John** *Greek* John G *gamma is the third letter in Greek*], Minor[*variations of* The Third General Letter of the Holy Apostle John to Gaius].

1:3 Alx/Byz[**For I greatly rejoiced**], Minor[*omits* For (DRA, NIV, NJB, NLT, NRS, REB, TEV, TLB)].

1:4 Alx/Byz[**joy**], Minor[grace (DRA)]; Alx[**the truth**], Byz[*omits* the (DRA, KJV, NKJ, ~TLB)].

1:5 Alx[**especially**], Byz[*omits* (HCS, JNT, KJV, NKJ, REB, TEV, ~TLB)].

1:7 Alx/Byz[**the Name**], Minor[his name (DRA, KJV, MRD, ~NEB, NKJ, ~NLT, ~NRS, ~REB, RSV, ~TEV, ~TLB)]; Alx/Byz[**Gentiles**], Major[nations], Alt[pagans (HCS, NAB, NET, NIV, ~NJB, ~NLT, ~NRS, ~REB, RSV, ~TEV, ~TLB)].

1:8 Alx[**support**], Byz[welcome (ASV, DRA, KJV, MRD, ~NIV, NJB, NKJ)].

1:9 Alx[**I wrote something**], Byz[*omits* something (KJV, NAB, NIV, ~NJB, NKJ, NLT, REB, ~TEV, ~TLB)]; Minor[I would have written (DRA, MRD)].

1:10 *DRA omits this verse.*

1:11 Alx[**God. The one**], Byz[God. But the one (KJV, MRD, NKJ, ~NLT, TLB)].

1:12 Alx[**and you know** *singular*], Byz[and you know *plural* (KJV, MRD)]; Alx/Byz[**our testimony**], Alt[*without textual foundation* my testimony (~REB, ~RSV, ~TLB)].

1:13 Alx[**to write you**], Byz[*omits* you (KJV, NKJ, TLB)].

1:14 Alx[**to see you**], Byz[*omits* you].

1:14-15 Alx[*text*], Byz[*joins both verses as verse 14* (ASV, DRA, HCS, KJV, NAS, NIV, NKJ, REB)], Minor[*adds* Amen *others add variations of* The Third General Letter of John].

Jude

1 ¹ Jude, a servant of Jesus Christ (but brother of James), to those who are called, beloved in God the Father and kept for Jesus Christ: ² may mercy, peace, and love be multiplied to you.

³ Beloved, although I was very eager to write you about our common salvation, I felt the necessity to write to you appealing that you contend for the faith which was once for all delivered to the saints. ⁴ For certain persons have crept in secretly, those who were long ago marked out for this condemnation, ungodly persons who turn the grace of our God into a license for sin and deny our only Master and Lord, Jesus Christ.

⁵ Now I desire to remind you, though you were fully informed, that [the] Lord who once saved a people out of the land of Egypt, afterward destroyed those who did not believe. ⁶ And the angels who did not keep their own domain, but abandoned their proper abode, he has kept in eternal chains under darkness for the judgment of the great day, ⁷ just as Sodom and Gomorrah and the surrounding cities, which likewise acted immorally and indulged in strange flesh, serve as an example by undergoing a punishment of eternal fire.

⁸ Yet in the same way these men in their dreamings defile the flesh, reject authority, and revile the glorious ones. ⁹ But Michael the archangel, when he disputed with the devil and argued about the body of Moses, did not dare pronounce against him a slanderous accusation, but said, "The Lord rebuke you!" ¹⁰ But these men revile whatever they do not understand. And the things that they know by instinct, like unreasoning animals do, by these things they are destroyed. ¹¹ Woe to them! For they have gone the way of Cain, and for the sake of gain they have rushed headlong into Balaam's error, and perished in Korah's rebellion. ¹² These are the ones who are blemishes in your love feasts when they feast without fear, caring for themselves; clouds without water, carried along by winds; autumn trees without fruit, twice dead, uprooted; ¹³ wild waves of the sea, casting up their own shame like foam; wandering stars, for whom the blackest darkness has been reserved into eternity.

¹⁴ It was also about these men that Enoch, in the seventh generation from Adam, prophesied, saying, "*Behold, the Lord came with ten thousands of his holy ones,* ¹⁵ *to execute*

Title Alx/Byz[**Jude**], Minor[*variations of* The General Letter of the Holy Apostle Jude, Brother of James].

1:1 Alx[**beloved**], Byz[sanctified (KJV, NKJ)]; Alx/Byz[**and kept for Jesus Christ**], Minor[*omits*]; **Jude** *Greek* Judas; **servant** *Greek* slave; **kept for** *or* kept by *or* kept in.

1:3 Alx[**our common salvation**], Byz[the common salvation (KJV)], Minor[your common salvation (DRA)].

1:4 Alx/Byz[**our only Master and Lord** *or* the only Master, and our Lord], Major[the only Lord God, and our Lord (KJV, MRD, NKJ)]; **marked out** *or* designated.

1:5 Alx/Byz[**I desire to remind you**], Minor[*adds* brothers]; Alx[**you were fully informed**], Byz[you once knew this (KJV, NKJ)], Minor[you were once fully informed (ASV, ESV, NAS, NAU, NET, NJB, RSV)]; Alx/Byz[**the Lord**], Minor[Jesus (DRA, ESV, NET, NLT) *others* God (MRD) *others* God Christ *others* he (RSV)], Alt[*without textual foundation* ADONAI *my Lord* (~JNT)]; Alx[**who once saved**], Byz[who saved (ASV, DRA, ESV, KJV, NAS, NAU, NET, NIV, NJB, NKJ, RSV, TLB)]; Alx/Major[**the land of Egypt**], Byz[Egypt (HCS, JNT, MRD, NIV, NJB, NLT, REB, TEV)].

1:8 Alx/Byz[**authority**], Minor[authorities]; **glorious ones** *or* angels *Greek* glories.

1:9 **a slanderous accusation** *or* an accusation of blasphemy.

1:12 Alx[**These are the ones who are blemishes**], Byz[These are blemishes (DRA, ESV, ~JNT, KJV, NAB, ~NET, ~NIV, NJB, NKJ, NLT, NRS, ~REB, RSV, TEV, ~TLB)]; Alx/Byz[**love feasts**], Minor[deceptions]; Alx/Byz[**when they feast**], Minor[*adds* with you (ASV, ESV, HCS, JNT, KJV, NAS, NAU, NIV, NJB, NKJ, NLT, NRS, TLB)]; Alx/Byz[**along** *or* away], Minor[about (DRA, KJV, MRD, NAB, NJB, NKJ, ~NLT, ~TLB)]; **blemishes** *or* reefs.

1:14-15 Pseudepigrapha[**1 Enoch 1:9** "Behold, he comes with ten thousands of his saints, to execute judgment upon them, and destroy the wicked, and reprove all the carnal for everything which the

*judgment on all, and to convict everyone of all their ungodly deeds which they have done in an
ungodly way, and of all the harsh things which ungodly sinners have spoken against him."* [16] These
are grumblers, finding fault, following after their own lusts; they speak arrogantly, flattering
people for their own advantage.

[17] But you must remember, beloved, the predictions of the apostles of our Lord Jesus
Christ; [18] they told you [that]: *"At the end of time there will be scoffers, following their own ungodly
lusts."* [19] These are the ones who cause divisions, worldly-minded, devoid of the Spirit. [20] But
you, beloved, build yourselves up on your most holy faith. Pray in the Holy Spirit. [21] Keep
yourselves in the love of God. Wait anxiously for the mercy of our Lord Jesus Christ to
eternal life. [22] And have mercy on some, who doubt. [23] Save others, snatching them out of fire.
And on some have mercy with fear, hating even the garment polluted by the flesh.

[24] Now to him who is able to keep you from falling and to present you without
blemish before the presence of his glory with great joy, [25] to the only God our Savior, through
Jesus Christ our Lord, be glory, majesty, dominion, and authority, before all time and now
and forever. Amen.

---

sinful and ungodly have done, and committed against him."].

1:15 Alx[**to execute judgment on all**], Byz[*adds* the ungodly among them (KJV, NKJ)], Minor[*adds* the
    ungodly (ASV, DRA, ESV, MRD, NAS, NAU, NIV, NJB, REB, RSV)]; Alx/Byz[**harsh things**],
    Minor[harsh words (JNT, KJV, MRD, NAB, NET, NIV, ~NLT, REB, TEV)].

1:16 Alx[**their own lusts**], Byz[their lusts (ASV, HCS, JNT, MRD, NAB, NET, NLT, REB, TLB)].

1:18 Alx/Byz[**that**], Minor[*omits* (ASV, ESV, HCS, JNT, KJV, NAB, NET, NIV, NJB, NRS, REB, RSV,
    TEV)]; Alx[**At the end of time**], Byz[In the last time (ASV, DRA, ESV, HCS, KJV, NAB, NAS, NAU,
    NET, NIV, NKJ, NLT, NRS, REB, RSV, TLB)]; **2 Peter 3:3**.

1:19 Alx/Byz[**cause divisions**], Minor[separate themselves (DRA, KJV, MRD)].

1:22 Alx/Byz[**have mercy on**], Minor[convince (DRA, JNT, RSV) *others omit* (MRD)]; Alx[**who doubt**],
    Byz[making a distinction (JNT, KJV, NKJ)].

1:23 Alx/Major[**snatching them out of fire**], Byz[snatching them out of the fire (ASV, DRA, ESV, HCS,
    JNT, KJV, MRD *verse 22*, NAB, NAS, NAU, NET, NIV, NJB, NKJ, NLT, NRS, REB, RSV, TEV, TLB)];
    Alx[**with fear**], Byz[*places* with fear *in the first half of the verse* (KJV, NKJ)].

1:24 Alx[**keep you from falling**], Byz[keep them from falling].

1:25 Alx[*text*], Byz[to the only wise God our Savior, be glory, and majesty, dominion, and authority, both
    now and forever. Amen (KJV, NKJ)].

The Revelation of John

1 ¹ The revelation of Jesus Christ, which God gave him to show to his servants what must soon take place. And he made it known by sending his angel to his servant John, ² who bore witness to the word of God and to the testimony of Jesus Christ – to all that he saw. ³ Blessed is he who reads the words of this prophecy, and blessed are those who hear, and who keep what is written in it; for the time is near.

⁴ John, to the seven churches which are in Asia: grace to you and peace from him who is and who was and who is to come, and from the sevenfold Spirit which is before his throne, ⁵ and from Jesus Christ, who is the faithful witness, the firstborn of the dead, and the ruler of the kings of the earth.

To him who loves us and has freed us from our sins by his blood, ⁶ and has made us a kingdom, priests to his God and Father – to him be glory and dominion for ever [and ever]. Amen.

⁷   *Behold, he is coming with the clouds.*
            And every eye will see him,
        even those who pierced him.
            And all the tribes of the earth will mourn because of him.
Even so. Amen.

⁸ "I am the Alpha and the Omega," says the Lord God, "who is, and who was, and who is to come, the Almighty."

⁹ I, John, your brother and companion in the tribulation and kingdom and patience in Jesus, was on the island called Patmos because of the word of God and the testimony of Jesus. ¹⁰ I was in the Spirit on the Lord's Day, and I heard behind me a loud voice like a trumpet, ¹¹ saying, "Write in a book what you see, and send it to the seven

---

1:Title Alx[**The Revelation of John**], Byz[Revelation], Minor[*variations of* The Revelation of Saint John the Divine and Evangelist].

1:1 **servants** *Greek* slaves; **servant** *Greek* slave.

1:2 Alx/Byz[**Christ – to all**], Minor[Christ, and to all (KJV, NET, ~TEV, TLB)].

1:3 Alx/Byz[**reads the words**], Minor[reads the word (~NAB, ~TLB)].

1:4 Alx[**peace from him**], Byz[peace from God (TEV, TLB)]; **sevenfold Spirit which is** *Greek* seven spirits which are; Isaiah 11:2 LXX.

1:5 Alx/Byz[**firstborn of the dead**], Minor[firstborn from the dead (HCS, JNT, NET, NIV, NJB, NKJ, NLT, REB, TEV, TLB)]; Alx/Byz[**loves us**], Minor[loved us (DRA, KJV, MRD, NKJ)]; Alx[**freed**], Byz[washed (DRA, KJV, NJB, NKJ)]; Alx/Byz[**from our sins**], Minor[from sins].

1:6 Alx/Byz[**a kingdom, priests**], Minor[kings and priests (DRA, KJV, ~NIV, NKJ, ~REB)]; Alx/Byz[**and ever**], Minor[*omits* (REB, TLB)].

1:7 Matthew 24:30, Mark 13:26, Luke 21:27.

1:8 Alx/Major[**the Alpha** *word* **and the Omega** *letter*], Byz[the Alpha *letter* and the Omega *letter*]; Alx/Byz[**Omega," says the Lord God**], Minor[Omega, the Beginning and the End," says the Lord (DRA, KJV, NKJ, ~NLT, ~TLB)].

1:9 Alx/Byz[**your brother and companion**], Minor[both your brother and companion (KJV, NKJ)]; Alx/Byz[**and kingdom**], Minor[and the kingdom (DRA, ESV, KJV, NAB, ~NLT, NRS, RSV, ~TLB) *others omit* (MRD)]; Alx/Byz[**patience in**], Minor[patience of (JNT, KJV, NKJ, ~NLT, ~TLB)]; Alx[**Jesus...Jesus**], Byz[Jesus Christ...Jesus Christ (KJV, MRD, NKJ, ~TLB)], Major[Christ Jesus...Jesus Christ (~DRA)]; **testimony of Jesus** *or* testimony to Jesus.

1:10 **in the Spirit** *or* in the spirit.

1:11 Alx/Byz[**saying, "Write**]; Minor[saying "I am the Alpha and the Omega, the First and the Last," and, "Write (KJV, NKJ, TLB)]; Alx/Byz[**seven churches**], Minor[*omits* seven *others add* which are in Asia (KJV, NKJ, TLB)].

churches: to Ephesus and to Smyrna and to Pergamum and to Thyatira and to Sardis and to Philadelphia and to Laodicea."

¹² Then I turned to see the voice that was speaking to me. And having turned I saw seven golden lampstands, ¹³ and in the midst of the lampstands one like a Son of Man, clothed with a robe down to the feet and girded round his chest with a golden band. ¹⁴ His head and hair were as white wool, as white as snow, and his eyes were like a flame of fire. ¹⁵ His feet were like burnished bronze, refined as in a furnace. And his voice was like the sound of many waters. ¹⁶ He held in his right hand seven stars. Out of his mouth went a sharp two-edged sword. And his face was like the sun shining in its strength.

¹⁷ And when I saw him, I fell at his feet as though dead. But he laid his right hand on me, saying, "Do not be afraid. I am the First and the Last, ¹⁸ and the Living One. I was dead, and behold, I am alive for evermore! And I have the keys of death and Hades. ¹⁹ Write, therefore, what you have seen, what is now and what will take place after this. ²⁰ The mystery of the seven stars which you saw in my right hand, and the seven golden lampstands: the seven stars are the angels of the seven churches, and the seven lampstands are the seven churches.

2 ¹ "To the angel of the church in Ephesus write:
'These are the words of him who holds the seven stars in his right hand, who walks among the seven golden lampstands. ² I know your works, toil, and your patient endurance. I know that you cannot bear evil men, but you have tested those who call themselves apostles and are not, and have found them to be false. ³ I know you have persevered and have endured for my name's sake, and you have not grown weary. ⁴ But I have this against you, that you have left your first love. ⁵ Remember then from where you have fallen, repent and do the works you did at first. If not, I will come to you and remove your lampstand from its place, unless you repent. ⁶ But this you have, that you hate the deeds of the Nicolaitans, which I also hate. ⁷ He who has an ear, let him hear what the

---

1:12 Alx[**to see**], Byz[*adds* there (~TLB)]; Alx/Byz[**was speaking**], Minor[spoke (ASV, DRA, KJV, MRD, NAB, NKJ, NRS, REB)].

1:13 Alx[**lampstands**], Byz[seven lampstands (DRA, KJV, NKJ)].

1:14 Alx/Byz[**as white wool**], Minor[white like wool (ESV, HCS, KJV, MRD, NAS, NAU, NIV, ~NJB, NKJ, NLT)].

1:15 Alx[**refined** *singular*], Byz[refined *plural* (KJV)].

1:17 Alx/Major[**his right hand** *Greek* his right], Byz[his right hand]; Alx/Byz[**saying**], Minor[*adds* to me (KJV, NKJ)].

1:18 Alx/Byz[**for evermore!** *Greek* for ever and ever], Major[*adds* Amen! (KJV, MRD, NKJ)]; Alx/Byz[**death and Hades**], Minor[Hades and death (KJV, NKJ, TLB)].

1:19 Alx/Byz[**therefore**], Minor[*omits* (KJV, NKJ, NLT, TLB)].

1:20 Alx/Byz[**the seven lampstands**], Minor[*adds* which you saw (KJV, NKJ)]; **angels** *or* messengers.

2:1 Alx/Byz[**in Ephesus**], Minor[of Ephesus (DRA, KJV, MRD, NKJ, REB, TLB)].

2:1-3:14 **angel** *or* messenger.

2:2 Alx[**toil**], Byz[your toil (ASV, DRA, ESV, HCS, JNT, KJV, MRD, NAB, NAS, NAU, NET, NIV, NJB, NKJ, NLT, NRS, REB, RSV, TEV, TLB)].

2:3 Alx/Byz[**persevered and have endured**], Minor[endured and have persevered (HCS, KJV, ~NKJ)]; Alx/Byz[**for my name's sake, and you have not grown weary**], Major[for my name's sake, and you did not grow weary (~JNT, ~NJB, ~NLT, ~TEV, ~TLB)], Minor[and for my name's sake you have labored, and have not fainted (~DRA, KJV, ~MRD, NKJ)].

2:5 Alx/Byz[**fallen**], Minor[fallen away]; Alx[**I will come to you**], Byz[*adds* quickly (KJV, MRD, NKJ)].

2:7 Alx/Byz[**Paradise**], Minor[midst of the Paradise (KJV, NKJ)]; Alx[**of God**], Byz[of my God (DRA, MRD)].

Spirit says to the churches. To him who overcomes, I will give the right to eat from the tree of life, which is in the Paradise of God.'

8 "And to the angel of the church in Smyrna write:

'These are the words of the First and the Last, who died, and came to life. 9 I know your tribulation and your poverty (but you are rich) and I know the slander of those who say that they are Jews and are not, but are a synagogue of Satan. 10 Do not fear anything you are about to suffer. Behold, the devil is about to throw some of you into prison, that you may be tested, and for ten days you will have tribulation. Be faithful even until death, and I will give you the crown of life. 11 He who has an ear, let him hear what the Spirit says to the churches. He who overcomes cannot be hurt by the second death.'

12 "And to the angel of the church in Pergamum write:

'These are the words of him who has the sharp two-edged sword. 13 I know where you dwell, where Satan's throne is. And you hold fast to my name, and did not deny my faith even in the days of Antipas my witness – my faithful! – who was killed among you, where Satan dwells. 14 But I have a few things against you, because you have some there who hold the teaching of Balaam, who taught Balak to put a stumbling block before the sons of Israel, to eat food sacrificed to idols and to practice sexual immorality. 15 So you also, likewise, have those who hold to the teaching of [the] Nicolaitans. 16 Repent therefore, or else I will soon come to you and will fight against them with the sword of my mouth. 17 He who has an ear, let him hear what the Spirit says to the churches. To him who overcomes I will give some of the hidden manna. And I will give him a white stone, with a new name written on the stone which no one knows except him who receives it.'

18 "And to the angel of the church in Thyatira write:

'These are the words of the Son of God, whose eyes are like a flame of fire, and whose feet are like burnished bronze. 19 I know your works, and love and faith, and service and your perseverance, and that your works are now more than at the first. 20

2:8 Alx/Byz[**in Smyrna**], Minor[of Smyrna (DRA, MRD, REB)].

2:9 Alx[**tribulation**], Byz[works and tribulation (KJV, MRD, NKJ)].

2:10 Alx/Byz[**anything**], Minor[what (ASV, ESV, HCS, JNT, NAS, NAU, NET, NIV, NJB, NLT, NRS, ~REB, RSV, TLB)]; Alx[**Behold**], Byz[Therefore, behold (MRD)], Minor[omits (NET, NLT, REB, TLB)]; Alx/Byz[**you will have tribulation**], Minor[you have tribulation].

2:13 Alx[**I know where you dwell**], Byz[I know your works, and where you dwell (KJV, MRD, NKJ)]; Alx/Byz[**even in the days**], Major[omits even (MRD)]; Alx[**of Antipas**], Byz[when Antipas (DRA, JNT, NJB, NLT, REB, TEV, TLB)], Major[in which Antipas (KJV, NKJ)], Minor[omits Antipas (MRD)]; Alx[**my witness – my faithful!**], Byz[my faithful witness (DRA, ESV, HCS, JNT, KJV, MRD, NAB, NET, NIV, NJB, NKJ, NLT, REB, TEV, TLB)]; **deny my faith** or deny your faith in me; **witness** Greek martyr.

2:14 Alx/Byz[**because you have**], Minor[omits because (~ESV, ~HCS, ~JNT, ~MRD, ~NAB, ~NET, ~NIV, ~NJB, ~NLT, ~NRS, ~REB, ~RSV, ~TEV, ~TLB)]; Alx/Byz[**who taught Balak**], Minor[who taught through Balak]; Alx[**to eat**], Byz[and to eat (~TLB)].

2:15 Alx/Byz[**likewise** Greek homoios], Minor[which thing I hate Greek ho miso (KJV, NKJ)]; Alx/Byz[**the Nicolaitans**], Minor[omits the (NLT, ~TLB)].

2:16 Alx/Byz[**therefore**], Minor[omits (DRA, KJV, MRD, NKJ, NLT, TLB)].

2:17 Alx/Byz[**some of the hidden manna**], Major[to eat of the hidden manna (KJV, MRD, NKJ, TLB)], Minor[to eat from the hidden manna]; Alx/Byz[**which no one knows**], Minor[which no one learns (~NET, ~NLT)].

2:18 Alx/Byz[**whose eyes are like**], Minor[who has eyes like (ESV, NAB, NAS, NAU, NET, NJB, NKJ, NRS, RSV)].

2:19 Alx/Byz[**faith...service**], Minor[service...faith (KJV, NKJ, TLB)]; Alx/Byz[**your perseverance**], Minor[omits your (ASV, ESV, HCS, JNT, NAB, NAS, NAU, NET, NIV, NRS, RSV, TLB)].

2:20 Alx/Major[**I have this against you**], Byz[I have a few things against you (DRA, KJV, NKJ)]; Alx/Byz[**tolerate**], Minor[allow (NKJ, NLT, TLB)]; Alx[**the woman Jezebel**], Byz[your woman

Nevertheless I have this against you, that you tolerate the woman Jezebel, who calls herself a prophetess and is teaching and beguiling my servants to practice sexual immorality and to eat food sacrificed to idols. 21 I gave her time to repent, but she refuses to repent of her immorality. 22 So I will cast her on a sickbed, and I will throw those who commit adultery with her into great tribulation, unless they repent of her ways. 23 And I will strike her children dead. And all the churches shall know that I am he who searches minds and hearts, and I will give to each of you according to your works. 24 But to you I say, to the rest of you in Thyatira, who do not hold this teaching, who have not learned what some call the deep things of Satan, I do not lay upon you any other burden; 25 only hold fast what you have until I come. 26 He who overcomes, and keeps my works until the end,

> to him I will give power over the nations –
>
> 27   *"He shall rule them with a rod of iron;*
> *as when potter's vessels are broken in pieces"*

28 – just as I also have received from my Father; and I will give him the morning star. 29 He who has an ear, let him hear what the Spirit says to the churches.'

3 1 "And to the angel of the church in Sardis write:
'These are the words of him who has the sevenfold Spirit of God and the seven stars. I know your works; you have a name of being alive, but you are dead. 2 Wake up, and strengthen what remains and is about to die, for I have not found your works perfect in the sight of my God. 3 Remember therefore what you have received and heard; keep it, and repent. But if you will not wake up, I will come like a thief, and you cannot know at what hour I will come upon you. 4 Yet you have a few names in Sardis, people who have not soiled their garments; and they shall walk with me in white, for they are worthy. 5 He who overcomes shall thus be clothed in white garments, and I will never

---

Jezebel (MRD)]; Alx[**calls herself**], Byz[says she is (~JNT, MRD, ~REB)]; Alx/Byz[**and is teaching and beguiling**], Minor[to teach and beguile (DRA, KJV, NKJ, TEV, TLB)]; **servants** *Greek* slaves.

2:21 Alx/Byz[*text*], Minor[I gave her time to repent of her immorality, and she did not repent (KJV, NKJ, ~TLB)].

2:22 Alx[**her ways**], Byz[their ways (DRA, KJV, MRD, NJB, NKJ, ~TEV, ~TLB)].

2:24 Alx/Byz[**to the rest**], Minor[and to the rest (~DRA, KJV, NKJ)]; Alx/Byz[**who have not learned**], Minor[and who have not learned (DRA, KJV, NAB, NIV, ~NJB, REB)]; Alx/Byz[**deep things**], Minor[depths (DRA, KJV, NKJ)]; Alx/Byz[**I do not lay upon you**], Minor[I will not lay upon you (DRA, KJV, NAB, NIV, NKJ, NLT, TEV, TLB)].

2:27 Alx[**are broken**], Byz[shall be broken (DRA, KJV, MRD, NAB, NET, NIV, NKJ, ~NLT, TEV, TLB)]; **rule** *or* shepherd; **Psalms 2:9.**

2:28 Alx[*text*], Byz[*divides verse 27 and 28 after* from my Father (ASV, ESV, HCS, KJV, MRD, NAS, NAU, NIV, NKJ, RSV, ~TEV, TLB)].

3:1 Alx/Byz[**sevenfold Spirit** *Greek* seven spirits], Minor[*omits* seven]; Alx/Byz[**you have a name**], Minor[you have the name (DRA, ESV, NAB, ~REB, RSV, TEV)].

3:2 Alx/Byz[**and is about to die**], Major[which you are about to cast away]; Alx/Byz[**I have not found your works**], Minor[I have found no works of yours (ASV, ~JNT, REB, ~TEV) *others* I have not found yours]; Alx/Byz[**my God**], Minor[*omits* my (KJV, NKJ, TLB)].

3:3 Alx[**come like a thief**], Byz[come upon you like a thief (KJV, MRD, NKJ, ~NLT)]; Alx/Major[**you cannot know**], Byz[you will not know (ASV, DRA, ESV, JNT, KJV, MRD, NAS, NAU, NIV, NKJ, ~NLT, NRS, REB, RSV, ~TEV, ~TLB)].

3:4 Alx/Byz[**Yet you have a few names in Sardis**], Minor[You have a few names even in Sardis (KJV, NKJ, ~TLB)].

3:5 Alx[**He who overcomes shall thus be clothed**], Byz[He who overcomes, the same shall be clothed (KJV, ~NKJ, ~NLT, ~TLB)].

blot out his name from the Book of Life; but I will confess his name before my Father and before his angels. 6 He who has an ear, let him hear what the Spirit says to the churches.'

7 "And to the angel of the church in Philadelphia write:

'These are the words of him who is holy, who is true,
who has the key of David,
who opens and no one shall shut,
and shuts and no one opens.

8 I know your works. See, I have set before you an open door which no one can shut. I know that you have little strength, yet you have kept my word, and have not denied my name. 9 Behold, I will make those of the synagogue of Satan who say that they are Jews and are not, but lie – look, I will make them come and bow down before your feet, and know that I have loved you. 10 Because you have kept my command to persevere, I also will keep you from the hour of trial which shall come upon the whole world, to test those who dwell on the earth. 11 I am coming soon. Hold fast to what you have, so that no one may take your crown. 12 He who overcomes, I will make him a pillar in the temple of my God, and he shall never go out of it. And I will write on him the name of my God and the name of the city of my God, the New Jerusalem, which comes down out of heaven from my God. And I will write on him my new name. 13 He who has an ear, let him hear what the Spirit says to the churches.'

14 "And to the angel of the church in Laodicea write:

'These are the words of the Amen, the faithful and true witness, the beginning of God's creation. 15 I know your works, that you are neither cold nor hot. I could wish you were cold or hot! 16 So then, because you are lukewarm, and neither hot nor cold, I will spit you out of my mouth. 17 You say that, "I am rich; I have become wealthy, and have need of nothing" – and do not know that you are wretched, miserable, poor, blind, and naked, 18 Therefore I counsel you to buy from me gold refined in the fire, that you may be rich; and white garments to clothe you, and to keep the shame of your nakedness from being seen; and salve to anoint your eyes, that you may see. 19 Those whom I love, I rebuke and chasten. So be earnest and repent. 20 Behold, I stand at the door and knock. If any one hears my voice and opens the door, I will [both] come in to him and eat with him, and he with me. 21 To him who overcomes, I will grant to sit with me on my throne, as I

3:7 Alx/Byz[**who is holy, who is true**], Minor[the true messenger]; Alx[**no one shall shut**], Byz[no one shall shut it (~TEV)], Minor[no one shuts (DRA, KJV, MRD, NKJ)]; Alx/Byz[**and shuts and no one opens**], Major[and if he is not opening, no one shall open].

3:8 Alx/Byz[**which no one can shut**], Minor[and no one can shut it (JNT, KJV, NKJ)].

3:9 Alx[**Behold, I will** *Greek* Behold, I should], Byz[Behold, I will].

3:11 Alx/Byz[**I am coming soon**], Minor[Behold, I am coming soon (DRA, KJV, NKJ, TLB)].

3:12 Alx[**which comes down** *Greek* coming down], Byz[which comes down].

3:14 Alx/Byz[**in Laodicea**], Minor[of the Laodiceans (DRA, KJV, NKJ)]; **beginning** *or* origin.

3:15 Alx[**wish you were cold or hot** *Greek* wish you were being cold or hot], Byz[wish that you are cold or hot].

3:16 Alx/Byz[**neither hot nor cold**], Major[not hot and not cold], Minor[neither cold nor hot (DRA, JNT, KJV, NKJ, NRS, ~REB, RSV, ~TLB)].

3:17 Alx/Byz[**You say that**], Major[*omits* that (ASV, DRA, ESV, HCS, JNT, KJV, MRD, NAB, NAS, NAU, NET, NIV, NJB, NKJ, NLT, NRS, REB, RSV, TEV, TLB)]; Alx[**miserable**], Byz[the miserable].

3:18 Alx[**salve to anoint your eyes**], Byz[salve so that you may anoint your eyes], Minor[anoint your eyes with salve (DRA, KJV, MRD, NKJ)].

3:19 Alx/Byz[**be earnest**], Major[be zealous (ASV, DRA, ESV, KJV, ~MRD, NAS, NAU, NKJ, RSV)].

3:20 Alx/Byz[**both**], Minor[*omits* (ASV, DRA, ESV, HCS, JNT, KJV, MRD, NAS, NAU, NET, NIV, NJB, NKJ, NLT, NRS, REB, RSV, TEV, TLB)].

also overcame and sat down with my Father on his throne. ²² He who has an ear, let him hear what the Spirit says to the churches.'"

4 ¹ After this I looked, and behold, a door standing open in heaven. And the voice which I had first heard – speaking to me like a trumpet – one saying, "Come up here, and I will show you what must take place after this." ² At once I was in the Spirit. And behold, a throne was standing in heaven, with one sitting on the throne. ³ And he who sat there was like jasper and carnelian in appearance. And round the throne was a rainbow that looked like an emerald. ⁴ And round the throne were twenty-four thrones. And seated on the thrones were twenty-four elders, clothed in white garments, and golden crowns on their heads. ⁵ From the throne come flashes of lightning, and voices and peals of thunder. And before the throne were seven lamps of fire, which is the sevenfold Spirit of God. ⁶ And before the throne there was as it were a sea of glass, like crystal.

And in the center, around the throne, are four living creatures, full of eyes in front and behind. ⁷ The first living creature was like a lion, the second creature like an ox, the third creature had the face like that of a man, and the fourth creature was like a flying eagle. ⁸ And the four living creatures, each of them with six wings, are full of eyes all around and within. And day and night they never cease to sing,

"Holy, holy, holy,
is the Lord God Almighty,
who was and is and is to come."

⁹ And whenever the living creatures shall give glory and honor and thanks to him who sits on the throne, who lives for ever and ever, ¹⁰ the twenty-four elders shall fall down before him who sits on the throne and shall worship him who lives for ever and ever; and shall cast their crowns before the throne, saying,

---

4:1 Alx/Byz[**one saying**], Minor[saying *Greek* to say (DRA, ESV, HCS, JNT, KJV, MRD, NAB, NAS, NAU, NET, NIV, NJB, NKJ, NLT, NRS, REB, RSV, TEV, TLB)].

4:2 Alx[**At once**], Byz[And at once (DRA, KJV, NLT, TLB)]; **in the Spirit** *or* in the spirit.

4:3 Alx[**And he who sat there was**], Byz[*omits* (~NAB, ~REB, ~TEV, ~TLB)]; Alx[**an emerald**], Byz[emeralds (MRD)].

4:4 Alx/Byz[**And round the throne**], Minor[*omits* And (ESV, HCS, JNT, MRD, NAB, NAU, NET, NIV, NJB, NKJ, NLT, NRS, REB, RSV, TEV, TLB)]; Alx/Byz[**twenty-four thrones**], Minor[twenty and four thrones (~ASV, ~DRA, ~KJV, MRD)]; Alx[**twenty-four elders**], Byz[the twenty-four elders], Minor[I saw twenty and four elders (~DRA, ~KJV, ~MRD, ~NAS, ~NAU, ~NKJ)]; Alx/Byz[**and golden crowns**], Minor[and they had golden crowns (~JNT, KJV, NET, NIV, NKJ, NLT, ~REB, ~TEV)].

4:5 Alx/Byz[**voices and peals of thunder**], Minor[peals of thunder and voices (KJV, NKJ)]; Alx/Byz[**the throne**], Major[his throne (MRD, TLB)]; Alx/Byz[**which is the sevenfold Spirit** *or* which are the seven spirits], Major[*omits* the].

4:6 Alx/Byz[**as it were**], Minor[*omits* (KJV, ~NJB, NKJ, NLT, TLB)].

4:7 Alx/Byz[**the face**], Major[a face (ASV, HCS, JNT, KJV, MRD, NAB, NAS, NAU, NET, NIV, NJB, NKJ, NLT, NRS, REB, TEV)]; Alx/Byz[**like that of a man**], Major[of a man (ESV, ~NJB, ~NLT, ~REB, RSV, TLB)], Minor[like a man]; Alx/Byz[**the fourth creature**], Minor[*omits* creature (NAB, NIV, NLT, REB, TEV, TLB)].

4:8 Alx/Byz[**And the four living creatures**], Minor[*omits* the (~MRD, ~NLT, ~TLB)]; Alx/Byz[**each of them**], Major[*omits* of them (HCS, JNT, NET, NIV, NJB, NKJ, NLT, REB, ~TLB, TLB)]; Alx/Byz[**Holy, holy, holy**], Minor[Holy, holy, holy, holy, holy, holy, holy, holy, holy].

4:9 Alx[**shall give glory**], Byz[should give glory], Alt[gave glory (DRA, ~TEV, TLB)].

4:10 Alx/Byz[**twenty-four**], Minor[twenty and four (~ASV, ~DRA, ~KJV, MRD)]; Alx/Byz[**shall worship**], Minor[worship (~DRA, ESV, HCS, JNT, KJV, MRD, NAB, NET, NIV, ~NJB, NKJ, NLT, NRS, REB, RSV, TEV, ~TLB)]; Alx/Byz[**and shall cast their crowns**], Minor[and cast their crowns (DRA, ESV, HCS, JNT, KJV, MRD, NAB, NET, NIV, ~NJB, NKJ, NLT, NRS, REB, RSV, TEV, TLB)].

11   "You are worthy, our Lord and God,

         to receive glory and honor and power,

     for you created all things,

         and by your will they began to exist and were created."

5 ¹ I saw in the right hand of him who sat on the throne a scroll written inside and on the back, sealed with seven seals. ² And I saw a strong angel proclaiming in a loud voice, "Who is worthy to open the scroll and break its seals?" ³ And no one in heaven or on earth or under the earth was able to open the scroll or to look into it. ⁴ And I wept greatly because no one was found worthy to open the scroll or to look into it. ⁵ Then one of the elders said to me, "Weep not. Behold, the Lion of the tribe of Judah, the Root of David, has conquered, so that he can open the scroll and its seven seals."

⁶ And between the throne and the four living creatures and among the elders, I saw a Lamb standing, as if it had been slain, with seven horns and with seven eyes, which are the [seven] spirits of God sent out into all the earth. ⁷ And he came and took it from the right hand of him who sat on the throne. ⁸ And when he had taken the scroll, the four living creatures and the twenty-four elders fell down before the Lamb, each one holding a harp and golden bowls full of incense, which are the prayers of the saints. ⁹ And they sang a new song, saying,

     "Worthy are you to take the scroll

         and to open its seals;

     for you were slain, and with your blood purchased men for God

         from every tribe and tongue and people and nation.

10   You have made them to be a kingdom and priests to our God,

         and they will reign on the earth."

¹¹ Then I looked, and I heard the voice of many angels around the throne and the living creatures and the elders, numbering myriads of myriads and thousands of thousands, ¹² saying with a loud voice,

---

4:11 Alx/Byz[**our Lord and God** *Greek* Lord and our God], Major[*adds* the Holy], Minor[O Lord (KJV, NKJ, TLB)]; Alx/Byz[**began to exist**], Minor[exist (HCS, KJV, ~MRD, ~NIV, ~NJB, NKJ, ~REB)].

5:1 Alx[**written inside and on the back**], Byz[written inside and outside (DRA, ~JNT, ~NAB, ~NET, ~NIV, NLT, ~REB, ~TEV)]; **written inside and on the back, sealed with seven seals** *or* written on the inside, and sealed on the back with seven seals.

5:2 Alx/Byz[**in a loud voice**], Minor[with a loud voice (ASV, DRA, ESV, KJV, MRD, NAS, NAU, NJB, NKJ, NLT, NRS, RSV, TLB)].

5:3 Alx/Byz[**in heaven**], Major[in heaven above (MRD)].

5:4 Alx/Byz[**to open**], Minor[*adds* and read (KJV, ~NJB, NKJ, ~NLT, ~TLB)].

5:5 Alx/Byz[**so that he can open** *Greek* to open], Major[who opens (MRD)]; Alx/Byz[**and its seven seals**], Minor[and loose its seven seals (DRA, KJV, NKJ, TLB)].

5:6 Alx/Byz[**And between**], Minor[And behold! Between (DRA, KJV, NKJ)]; Alx/Byz[**seven spirits**], Minor[*omits* seven]; **between the throne and the four living creatures and among the elders** *or* in the middle of the throne, encircled by the four living creatures and the elders.

5:7 Alx/Byz[**took it**], Minor[took the scroll (DRA, ESV, HCS, JNT, KJV, MRD, NAB, NAU, NET, NIV, NJB, NKJ, NLT, NRS, REB, RSV, TEV, TLB)].

5:8 Alx/Byz[**a harp**], Minor[harps (DRA, KJV)]; Alx/Byz[**the prayers**], Major[prayers].

5:9 Alx[**purchased men for God**], Byz[purchased us for God (DRA, KJV, MRD, NKJ)], Minor[*omits* for God]; **purchased** *or* ransomed.

5:10 Alx/Byz[**You have made them**], Minor[You have made us (DRA, KJV, NKJ)]; Alx[**a kingdom**], Byz[kings (KJV, MRD, NJB, NKJ, ~REB)]; Alx/Byz[**they will reign**], Minor[we shall reign (DRA, KJV, NKJ) *others* they reign (ASV, MRD, ~NJB)].

5:11 Alx[**I heard the voice**], Byz[I heard as it were the voice (MRD)]; Alx/Byz[**numbering myriads of myriads**], Minor[*omits* (DRA, ~NAB, ~NLT, ~TEV, ~TLB)].

"Worthy is the Lamb who was slain,
to receive the power and wealth and wisdom and might
and honor and glory and blessing!"

[13] And I heard every creature in heaven and on earth and under the earth and on the sea, and all that is in them, saying,

"To him who sits on the throne and to the Lamb
be blessing and honor and glory and power,
for ever and ever!"

[14] And the four living creatures were saying, "Amen!" And the elders fell down and worshipped.

6 [1] And I saw when the Lamb opened one of the seven seals, and I heard one of the four living creatures say, as with a voice of thunder, "Come!" [2] And I looked, and behold, a white horse, and its rider had a bow. And a crown was given to him, and he went out conquering and to conquer.

[3] When he opened the second seal, I heard the second living creature say, "Come!" [4] And out came a horse, fiery red. Its rider was permitted to take peace from the earth, and that men should slay one another. And to him was given a great sword.

[5] When he opened the third seal, I heard the third living creature say, "Come." And I looked, and behold, a black horse. And its rider had a pair of scales in his hand. [6] And I heard what sounded like a voice in the center of the four living creatures saying, "A quart of wheat for a denarius, and three quarts of barley for a denarius. And do not damage the oil and the wine!"

[7] When the Lamb opened the fourth seal, I heard the voice of the fourth living creature say, "Come!" [8] And I looked, and behold, a pale horse. And its rider's name was Death, and Hades was following with him. And they were given power over a fourth of

---

5:12 Alx[**wealth**], Byz[the wealth (TLB)], Alt/Vulgate[divinity (DRA)].

5:13 Alx/Byz[**I heard**], Minor[adds also (~NLT, ~TLB)]; Alx/Byz[**on earth**], Minor[in earth (~TLB)]; Alx/Byz[**for ever and ever**], Major[adds Amen].

5:14 Alx/Byz[**were saying**], Major[saying (ASV, DRA, ESV, HCS, JNT, KJV, MRD, NAS, NIV, NJB, NKJ, NLT, NRS, RSV, TEV)]; Alx/Byz[**Amen**], Major[the Amen]; Alx[**the elders**], Byz[the twenty-four elders (DRA, KJV, NKJ, NLT, TLB)]; Alx[**worshipped**], Byz[adds him who lives for ever and ever (DRA, KJV, NKJ, ~NLT, ~TLB)].

6:1, 3, 5, 7 **Come!** or Go!

6:1 Alx[**I saw when**], Byz[I saw that (DRA, ~HCS, ~NJB, ~NRS, ~TEV)]; Alx[**seven seals**], Byz[omits seven (KJV, NKJ, TLB)]; Alx/Byz[**Come**], Major[adds and see (DRA, KJV, MRD, NKJ)].

6:2 Alx/Byz[**And I looked, and behold**], Major[And behold (~HCS, ~JNT, ~MRD, ~NAB, ~NET, ~NIV, ~NJB, ~NRS, ~REB, ~TEV, ~TLB)].

6:3 Alx/Byz[**Come**], Minor[adds and see (DRA, KJV, NKJ)].

6:4 Alx/Byz[**And out came a horse**], Minor[And I saw, and behold, out came a horse]; Alx/Byz[**from the earth**], Minor[of the earth (~TEV, ~TLB)]; Alx/Byz[**and that men should slay**], Major[omits and (ESV, HCS, NAB, NET, NRS, REB, RSV, TEV)].

6:5 Alx/Byz[**"Come." And I looked**], Major["Come and see." And I looked (DRA, KJV, MRD, NKJ)].

6:6 Alx/Byz[**what sounded like**], Major[omits (KJV, MRD, NKJ, NLT, TLB)]; **quart** Greek choinix; a **denarius** was a day's wage for a laborer.

6:7 Alx/Byz[**the voice of**], Major[omits (MRD, NLT, REB, TEV, TLB)]; Alx/Byz[**Come**], Major[adds and see (DRA, KJV, MRD, NKJ)].

6:8 Alx/Byz[**And I looked, and behold**], Major[And behold (DRA, ~HCS, ~JNT, ~NAB, ~NET, ~NIV, ~NJB, ~NRS, ~REB, ~TEV, ~TLB)]; Alx/Byz[**Hades was following with him**], Major[omits with (DRA, ESV, NAB, NLT, RSV)]; Alx[**And they were given power**], Byz[And he was given power (DRA, MRD)].

the earth, to kill with sword and with famine and with pestilence and by wild beasts of the earth.

⁹ When he opened the fifth seal, I saw under the altar the souls of those who had been slain because of the word of God and because of the testimony they had maintained. ¹⁰ And they cried out with a loud voice, "O Sovereign Lord, holy and true, how long before you judge and avenge our blood on those who dwell on the earth?" ¹¹ Then each of them was given a white robe, and they were told to rest a little longer, until the number of their fellow servants and their brothers should be completed, who were to be killed as they had been.

¹² And I looked when he opened the sixth seal, and there was a great earthquake; and the sun became black as sackcloth made of hair, and the whole moon became like blood. ¹³ And the stars of the sky fell to the earth, as a fig tree casts its unripe figs when shaken by a great wind. ¹⁴ The sky vanished like a scroll that is rolled up, and every mountain and island was removed from its place. ¹⁵ Then the kings of the earth and the great men and the generals and the rich and the strong, and every one, slave and free, hid in the caves and among the rocks of the mountains, ¹⁶ and they said to the mountains and to the rocks, "Fall on us and hide us from the face of him who sits on the throne, and from the wrath of the Lamb. ¹⁷ For the great day of their wrath has come, and who can stand?"

7 ¹ After this I saw four angels standing at the four corners of the earth, holding back the four winds of the earth, that no wind would blow on the earth or the sea or on any tree. ² Then I saw another angel ascend from the rising of the sun, having the seal of the living God, and he called out with a loud voice to the four angels who had been given power to harm the earth and sea, ³ saying, "Harm not the earth, nor the sea, nor the trees until we have sealed the servants of our God on their foreheads." ⁴

6:9 Alx[**because of the testimony**], Byz[*adds* of the Lamb (MRD)], Minor[*omits* because of (HCS, NIV, TEV)]; **under** *or* at the foot of.

6:10 Alx/Byz[**they cried out**], Minor[they were crying out].

6:11 Alx/Byz[**was given a white robe**], Minor[were given white robes (DRA, KJV, TLB)]; Alx/Byz[**a little longer**], Major[yet longer]; Alx[**until...should be completed**], Byz[until...should complete (~ASV)], Minor[until...would be completed (HCS, ~MRD, NAB, NAU, NET, NIV, NJB, NKJ, ~NLT, NRS, ~TEV, TLB) *others* as long as...were not complete]; Alx/Byz[**who were to be killed**], Major[and those who were to be killed (~ASV, ~DRA, NAS, NAU, ~TLB)]; **servants** *or* slaves.

6:12 Alx/Byz[**and there was a great earthquake**], Minor[and behold, there was a great earthquake (DRA, ESV, KJV, NKJ, RSV)]; Alx/Byz[**the whole moon**], Minor[the moon (KJV, NJB, NKJ, NLT, TLB)].

6:13 Alx[**as a fig tree casts**], Byz[as a fig tree casting (NET, NJB, NLT, TEV)].

6:14 Alx/Byz[**The sky vanished like a scroll that is rolled up**], Minor[The sky, rolled up, vanished like a scroll (~NLT)].

6:15 Alx/Byz[**the generals and the rich**], Minor[the rich and the generals (KJV, NKJ, TLB)]; Alx/Byz[**the strong**], Minor[the powerful (ESV, HCS, JNT, KJV, ~MRD, NAB, NET, NIV, NJB, NKJ, NLT, NRS, REB, TEV, ~TLB)]; Alx/Byz[**every one, slave and free**], Minor[every slave and every free one (DRA, KJV, NIV, NKJ)].

6:17 Alx[**their wrath**], Byz[his wrath (KJV, NJB, NKJ)].

7:1 Alx[**After**], Byz[And after (KJV, MRD)]; Alx/Byz[**this**], Minor[these (DRA, KJV, MRD, ~NJB, NKJ, ~NLT, ~TLB)], Alt[*some electronic versions have the typo* his (ASV)]; Alx/Byz[**any tree**], Major[a certain tree (~TLB)].

7:2 Alx/Byz[**ascend** *Greek* ascending], Minor[having ascended (MRD)].

7:3 Alx/Byz[**nor the sea**], Minor[and the sea (~NKJ, ~TEV)]; Alx[**until we have sealed**], Byz[not until we have sealed]; **servants** *or* slaves.

7:4 Alx/Byz[**one hundred forty-four**], Major[one hundred and forty-four (ASV, KJV, MRD, NAB, NAS, NAU, NET, NJB, NKJ, REB, RSV)].

And I heard the number of those who were sealed, one hundred forty-four thousand sealed from every tribe of the sons of Israel:

5　　　From the tribe of Judah, twelve thousand were sealed,

　　　　from the tribe of Reuben twelve thousand,

　　　　from the tribe of Gad twelve thousand,

6　　　from the tribe of Asher twelve thousand,

　　　　from the tribe of Naphtali twelve thousand,

　　　　from the tribe of Manasseh twelve thousand,

7　　　from the tribe of Simeon twelve thousand,

　　　　from the tribe of Levi twelve thousand,

　　　　from the tribe of Issachar twelve thousand,

8　　　from the tribe of Zebulun twelve thousand,

　　　　from the tribe of Joseph twelve thousand,

　　　　from the tribe of Benjamin, twelve thousand were sealed.

9 After this I looked, and behold, a great multitude which no one could count, from every nation and all tribes and peoples and tongues, standing before the throne and before the Lamb, clothed in white robes, and palm branches were in their hands. 10 And they cry out with a loud voice, saying,

　　　"Salvation belongs to our God

　　　　who sits on the throne, and to the Lamb."

11 And all the angels were standing around the throne and around the elders and the four living creatures. And they fell on their faces before the throne and worshipped God, 12 saying,

　　　"Amen! Blessing and glory and wisdom

　　　and thanksgiving and honor and power and might

　　　be to our God for ever and ever!

　　　Amen."

13 Then one of the elders addressed me, saying, "Who are these, clothed in white robes, and where have they come from?" 14 And I had said to him, "My lord, you know." And he said to me, "These are they who have come out of the great tribulation. They have washed their robes and made them white in the blood of the Lamb.

15　　　Therefore, they are before the throne of God

　　　　　and serve him day and night in his temple.

　　　　And he who sits on the throne

7:5 Alx/Byz[**Reuben twelve thousand**], Minor[*adds* were sealed (DRA, KJV, NKJ)].

7:6 Alx/Byz[**twelve thousand... twelve thousand... twelve thousand**], Minor[*adds* were sealed... were sealed... were sealed (DRA, KJV, NKJ)].

7:7 Alx/Byz[**twelve thousand... twelve thousand... twelve thousand**], Minor[*adds* were sealed... were sealed... were sealed (DRA, KJV, NKJ)].

7:8 Alx/Byz[**Zebulun twelve thousand...Joseph twelve thousand**], Minor[*adds* were sealed...were sealed (DRA, KJV, NKJ)].

7:10 Alx/Byz[**cry out**], Minor[crying out (ESV, ~NET, NKJ, ~NLT, RSV, ~TLB)]; Alt[cried out (DRA, HCS, JNT, KJV, MRD, NAB, NIV, NJB *verse 9*, NRS, REB, TEV)]; Alx/Byz[**Salvation belongs to our God who sits on the throne, and to the Lamb**], Minor[Salvation belongs to him who sits on the throne of our God, even the Lamb].

7:11 Alx/Byz[**before the throne**], Minor[before his throne (MRD)].

7:12 Alx/Byz[**and ever! Amen**], Minor[*omits* Amen].

7:14 Alx/Byz[**And I had said**], Major[And I said (~ASV, DRA, ESV, HCS, ~JNT, KJV, MRD, NAB, NAS, NAU, NET, ~NIV, ~NJB, NKJ, NLT, NRS, ~REB, RSV, ~TEV, ~TLB)]; Alx/Byz[**My lord**], Minor[Lord (ESV, HCS, JNT, KJV, NIV, NJB, NKJ, NLT, NRS, RSV, TEV, TLB)]; Alx/Byz[**made them white**], Major[made white (NJB)], Minor[*adds* robes].

will spread his tent over them.

16 They will hunger no more, nor thirst anymore.
   The sun will not beat down on them,
      nor any scorching heat.
17 For the Lamb in the center of the throne will be their shepherd,
      and he will guide them to springs of living waters.
   And God will wipe away every tear from their eyes."

8 ¹ When the Lamb opened the seventh seal, there was silence in heaven for about half an hour. ² And I saw the seven angels who stand before God, and to them were given seven trumpets.

³ Another angel, who had a golden censer, came and stood over the altar. And he was given much incense to offer, with the prayers of all the saints, on the golden altar before the throne. ⁴ And the smoke of the incense, with the prayers of the saints, went up before God from the angel's hand. ⁵ Then the angel took the censer and filled it with fire from the altar and threw it on the earth. And there were peals of thunder, voices, flashes of lightning, and an earthquake.

⁶ The seven angels who had the seven trumpets prepared to sound them.

⁷ And the first sounded his trumpet. And there came hail and fire, mixed in blood. And they were thrown to the earth. And a third of the earth was burned up. And a third of the trees were burned up. And all the green grass was burned up.

⁸ The second angel sounded his trumpet. And something like a great mountain burning with fire was thrown into the sea. And a third of the sea became blood. ⁹ And a third of the living creatures which were in the sea died. And a third of the ships were destroyed.

¹⁰ The third angel sounded his trumpet. And a great star fell from heaven, blazing like a torch. And it fell on a third of the rivers and on the springs of water. ¹¹ The name of

---

7:16 Alx[**The sun will not beat down**], Byz[The sun will never beat down (~HCS, ~NJB, ~NLT, REB, ~TLB)].

7:17 Alx/Byz[**will be their shepherd, and he will guide them**], Major[is their shepherd, and he guides them]; Alx/Byz[**springs of living waters** *Greek* springs of waters of life], Minor[living springs of waters (KJV, NKJ)].

8:1 Alx[**When** *or* Whenever], Byz[When].

8:3 Alx/Byz[**over the altar**], Minor[at the altar (DRA, ESV, HCS, JNT, KJV, MRD, NAB, NAS, NAU, NET, NIV, NJB, NKJ, NLT, NRS, REB, RSV, TEV, TLB)]; Alx[**to offer** *Greek* that he would offer], Byz[that he should offer (ASV, DRA, KJV, MRD, NAS, NAU, NKJ)].

8:5 Alx/Byz[**peals of thunder, voices, flashes of lightning**], Minor[voices, peals of thunder, flashes of lightning (KJV, ~NJB, NKJ, ~NLT, ~REB, ~TEV) *others* peals of thunder, flashes of lightning, voices (MRD)].

8:6 Alx/Byz[**who had the seven**], Minor[having the seven (~JNT, NET, ~NLT, ~TEV, ~TLB)]; Alx[**prepared to sound them**], Byz[prepared themselves to sound (ASV, DRA, KJV, MRD, NAS, NAU, NKJ)].

8:7 Alx/Byz[**the first**], Minor[*adds* angel (DRA, ESV, HCS, KJV, NET, NIV, NKJ, NLT, NRS, REB, RSV, TEV, TLB)]; Alx/Byz[**mixed in blood**], Minor[mixed with blood (ASV, DRA, ESV, HCS, JNT, KJV, NAB, NAS, NAU, NET, NIV, NJB, NKJ, NLT, NRS, REB, RSV, TEV, TLB)], Alt/Peshitta[mixed in water (~MRD)]; Alx/Byz[**of the earth was burned up, and a third**], Minor[*omits* (KJV, NKJ)].

8:8 Alx/Byz[**a great mountain burning with fire**], Major[*omits* with fire (JNT, NAB, NIV, ~NLT, ~TEV, TLB)].

8:9 Alx/Byz[**which were in the sea**], Major[*omits* which were (~DRA, ESV, HCS, JNT, ~MRD, NAB, NET, NIV, NJB, NKJ, NLT, NRS, REB, RSV, TEV, ~TLB)].

8:10 Alx/Byz[**and on the springs of water**], Minor[*omits*], Alt[*without textual foundation omits* of water (REB, TLB)].

the star is Wormwood. A third of the waters became Wormwood. And many men died from the waters, because they were made bitter.

¹² The fourth angel sounded his trumpet. And a third of the sun was struck, a third of the moon, and a third of the stars, so that a third of them darkened. And a third of the day was without light, and also a third of the night.

¹³ Then I looked, and I heard an eagle flying in midheaven, saying with a loud voice, "Woe, woe, woe to those who dwell on the earth, because of the blasts of the other trumpets of the three angels who are about to sound!"

9 ¹ And the fifth angel sounded his trumpet. And I saw a star which had fallen from heaven to earth. And he was given the key of the shaft of the bottomless pit. ² He opened the bottomless pit. And smoke went up from the pit, like the smoke of a great furnace. And the sun and the air were darkened by the smoke from the pit. ³ Then out of the smoke came locusts on the earth. And they were given power like the power of scorpions of the earth. ⁴ They were told not to harm the grass of the earth or any green growth or any tree, but those of mankind who have not the seal of God on their foreheads. ⁵ And it was given them that they should not kill them, but that they would be tormented five months. And their torture was like the torture of a scorpion, when it stings a man. ⁶ And in those days men will seek death and will not be able to find it. They will long to die, and death flees from them.

⁷ In appearance the locusts were like horses prepared for battle; and on their heads, as it were, crowns like gold. And their faces were as human faces, ⁸ and they had hair as the hair of women. And their teeth were like those of lions. ⁹ They had breastplates like breastplates of iron. And the sound of their wings was like the thundering of many horses and chariots rushing into battle. ¹⁰ They have tails like scorpions, and stingers. And in their tails is their power to hurt men for five months. ¹¹ They have as king over them the angel of the abyss. His name in Hebrew is Abaddon. And in Greek he has the name Apollyon.

8:11 Alx/Byz[**A third of the waters**], Minor[*omits* of the waters]; **Wormwood** *or* Bitterness *Greek* Absinthe.

8:13 Alx/Byz[**an eagle**], Minor[an angel (KJV, NKJ)].

9:2 Alx[**great furnace**], Byz[burning furnace (MRD)].

9:4 Alx[**not to harm**], Byz[that they should not harm (ASV, DRA, KJV, MRD, NAS)]; Alx/Byz[**but those of mankind**], Minor[but only those of mankind (ASV, DRA, ESV, HCS, JNT, KJV, MRD, NAB, NAS, NAU, NET, NIV, NJB, NKJ, NLT, NRS, REB, RSV, TEV)]; Alx[**their foreheads** *Greek* the foreheads], Byz[their foreheads].

9:5 Alx[**And it was given them** *the men*], Byz[And it was given them *the locusts* (ESV, HCS, JNT, NAB, NAS, NAU, NET, NIV, NJB, NKJ, NLT, NRS, REB, RSV, TEV, TLB)]; Alx[**they would be tormented**], Byz[they should be tormented (ASV, DRA, KJV, MRD)].

9:6 Alx/Byz[**will not be able to find it**], Minor[will not find it (DRA, ESV, HCS, JNT, KJV, MRD, NAB, NAS, NAU, NIV, ~NJB, NKJ, NLT, NRS, REB, RSV, TEV)]; Alx[**death flees from them**], Byz[death will flee from them (DRA, ESV, HCS, JNT, KJV, MRD, NAB, NET, NIV, NJB, NKJ, NLT, NRS, REB, RSV, TEV, TLB)].

9:7 Alx/Byz[**crowns like gold**], Major[golden crowns (ESV, HCS, JNT, NAB, NIV, NJB, NLT, NRS, REB, RSV, TEV, TLB)].

9:10 ALX[**and stingers. And in their tails is their power to hurt**], Byz[and stingers. And in their tails they had power to hurt (HCS, MRD, NAB, NIV, ~NJB, NLT, TEV)]; Minor[and stingers were in their tails. And their power was to hurt (DRA, KJV, NKJ)]; **stingers** *Greek* stings.

9:11 Alx/Byz[**They have as king over them**], Major[Having as king over them], Minor[And they have as king over them (~KJV, ~MRD, ~NKJ)]; Alx/Byz[**the angel**], Major[an angel]; Alx[**and in Greek**], Byz[but in Greek (KJV, NKJ)]; **Abaddon** *Destruction*; **Apollyon** *Destroyer*.

¹² The first woe is past. Behold, two woes are still to come after these.

¹³ And the sixth angel sounded his trumpet. And I heard a voice from the [four] horns of the golden altar which is before God, ¹⁴ one saying to the sixth angel having the trumpet, "Release the four angels who are bound at the great river Euphrates." ¹⁵ And the four angels, who had been held ready for the hour and day and month and year, were released to kill a third of mankind. ¹⁶ And the number of the troops of horsemen was two hundred million. I heard their number. ¹⁷ And this was how I saw the horses in my vision: the riders wore breastplates the color of fire and of sapphire and of sulfur. And the heads of the horses were like the heads of lions. And out of their mouths came fire and smoke and sulfur. ¹⁸ A third of mankind was killed from these three plagues, from the fire and the smoke and sulfur that came out of their mouths. ¹⁹ For the power of the horses is in their mouth and in their tails. For their tails are like serpents and have heads, and with them they do harm.

²⁰ The rest of mankind, who were not killed by these plagues, did not repent of the works of their hands nor give up worshipping demons and idols of gold and silver and bronze and stone and wood, which can neither see nor hear nor walk; ²¹ nor did they repent of their murders, their magic potions, their sexual immorality or their thefts.

10

¹ And I saw another mighty angel coming down from heaven, wrapped in a cloud, with the rainbow over his head. And his face was like the sun, and his legs like pillars of fire. ² He had a little scroll which was open in his hand. And he set his right foot on the sea, and his left foot on the land. ³ And he cried out with a loud voice, like the roar of a lion. When he shouted, the voices of the seven thunders spoke. ⁴ And when the seven thunders spoke, I was about to write. But I heard a voice

---

9:12 Alx/Byz[**still to come after these. 13 And the sixth angel**], Minor[still to come. 13 And after these the sixth angel (~ESV, ~NAB, ~NLT, ~NRS, ~RSV, ~TEV)].

9:13 Alx/Byz[**four**], Minor[*omits* (ASV, MRD, NET, NIV, REB)].

9:14 Alx[*masculine i.e. a person* **one saying to the sixth angel**], Byz[*neuter* saying to the sixth angel], Major[*feminine i.e. a voice* saying to the sixth angel (DRA, ESV, ~HCS, JNT, KJV, NAB, NET, NIV, NJB, NKJ, NLT, NRS, REB, RSV, TEV, TLB)]; Alx/Byz[**having the trumpet**], Minor[who had the trumpet (ASV, DRA, ESV, HCS, KJV, NAB, NAS, NAU, NIV, NKJ, NLT, NRS, RSV)], Alt[*without textual foundation omits* (~TEV, ~TLB)].

9:15 Alx[**for the hour and day**], Byz[for the hour and the day (JNT, TEV)].

9:16 Alx/Byz[**the troops** *or* the army], Minor[troops *or* army (ESV, HCS, JNT, NAB, NET, TLB)]; Alx[**of horsemen** *Greek* of the horsemen], Byz[of the horse (~ESV, ~HCS, NET, ~NIV, ~NJB, ~NLT, ~TEV)], Alt[*without textual foundation omits* (~TLB)]; Alx/Byz[**two hundred million** *Greek* twenty thousands of ten thousands], Major[one hundred million *Greek* ten thousands of ten thousands], Minor[two ten thousands of ten thousands (ASV, ESV, ~KJV, MRD, NJB, RSV, REB)]; Alx/Byz[**I heard their number**], Minor[and I heard their number (DRA, KJV, MRD)].

9:17 **sapphire** *Greek* hyacinth.

9:18 Alx/Byz[**from these three plagues**], Minor[by these three (KJV, ~TLB)].

9:19 Alx/Byz[**the power of the horses**], Minor[their power (KJV, NKJ, NLT, ~TLB)]; Alx/Byz[**and in their tails**], Minor[*omits*].

9:21 Alx[**magic potions** *or* drugs *Greek* pharmakon], Byz[sorceries *Greek* pharmakeia (ASV, DRA, ESV, HCS, KJV, MRD, NAS, NAU, NET, NIV, NJB, NKJ, NLT, NRS, ~REB, RSV, TEV, TLB)].

10:1 Alx/Byz[**another mighty angel**], Major[*omits* another]; Alx/Byz[**the rainbow**], Minor[a rainbow (DRA, ESV, HCS, JNT, KJV, MRD, NAB, NET, NIV, NJB, NKJ, NLT, NRS, REB, RSV, TEV, TLB)]; Alx/Byz[**his head**], Minor[the head].

10:2 Alx[**a little scroll**], Byz[a scroll].

10:4 Alx/Byz[**seven thunders spoke**], Minor[seven thunders uttered their voices (ASV, DRA, KJV, NKJ)]; Alx/Byz[**saying**], Minor[*adds* to me (DRA, KJV, NJB, NKJ, TLB)]; Alx/Byz[**do not write them down**], Minor[do not write these down].

from heaven saying, "Seal up what the seven thunders have said, and do not write them down." [5] Then the angel, whom I saw standing on the sea and on the land,

> lifted up his right hand to heaven,

[6]   and swore in him who lives for ever and ever,

who created heaven and the things in it, the earth and the things in it, and the sea and the things in it, that there will be no more delay. [7] But in the days of the trumpet of the seventh angel, when he is about to sound, then the mystery of God is finished, as he announced to his own servants the prophets.

[8] Then the voice which I had heard from heaven spoke to me again, saying, "Go, take the scroll which is open in the hand of the angel who is standing on the sea and on the land." [9] And I went to the angel, telling him to give me the little scroll. And he said to me, "Take it and eat it. It will make your stomach bitter, but in your mouth it will be sweet as honey." [10] I took the little scroll from the angel's hand and ate it. And in my mouth it was sweet as honey. But when I had eaten it, my stomach was made bitter. [11] And they said to me, "You must again prophesy over many peoples and nations and tongues and kings."

11

[1] Then I was given a measuring rod like a staff. And one said, "Rise and measure the temple of God and the altar and those who worship there. [2] But leave out the court outside the temple and do not measure it, for it has been given over to the nations. And they will trample over the holy city for forty-two months. [3] And I will grant power to my two witnesses. And they will prophesy for twelve hundred and sixty days, clothed in sackcloth." [4] These are the two olive trees and the two lampstands that stand before the Lord of the earth. [5] And if anyone wants to harm them, fire flows out from their mouth and devours their enemies. So if anyone wants to harm them, he must be killed in this way. [6] These have the power to shut up the sky, so that rain will not fall during the days of their prophesying. And they have power over the waters to turn them into blood, and to strike the earth with every plague, as often as they desire. [7] When they have finished their testimony, the beast that comes up from the abyss will

---

10:5 Alx/Byz[**right hand**], Minor[*omits* right (DRA, KJV, NKJ)].

10:6 Alx/Byz[**swore in him**], Major[swore by him (ASV, DRA, ESV, HCS, JNT, KJV, MRD, NAB, NAS, NAU, NET, NIV, NJB, NKJ, NRS, REB, RSV, TLB)]; Alx/Byz[**and the sea and the things in it**], Minor[*omits*].

10:7 Alx/Byz[**then the mystery** *Greek* and the mystery]; Alx/Byz[**is finished**], Minor[should be finished (KJV, RSV)]; Alx[**his own servants**], Byz[his servants (ASV, DRA, ESV, HCS, JNT, KJV, MRD, NAB, NAS, NAU, NET, NIV, NJB, NKJ, NLT, NRS, REB, RSV, TEV, TLB)]; **servants** *Greek* slaves.

10:8 Alx[**the scroll**], Byz[the little scroll (KJV, MRD, NKJ)].

10:9 Alx/Byz[**telling him to give**], Minor[saying to him, "Give (KJV, NKJ)].

10:10 Alx[**the little scroll**], Byz[the scroll (DRA, ~NJB, REB, ~TLB)].

10:11 Alx/Byz[**they said to me** *Greek* they say to me], Minor[he said to me *Greek* he says to me (DRA, ~ESV, ~HCS, ~JNT, KJV, MRD, NAB, ~NIV, ~NJB, NKJ, ~NLT, ~REB, ~RSV, ~TEV, TLB)]; Alx[**nations**], Byz[over nations (~DRA, ~MRD, ~NJB, ~REB, ~TEV)]; Alx/Byz[**peoples...nations**], Alt[nations...peoples (DRA, MRD, ~NJB, ~REB, ~TEV)]; Alx/Byz[**and nations**], Major[and over nations].

11:1 Alx/Byz[**like a staff**], Minor[*adds* and the angel stood (KJV, MRD, NKJ)].

11:2 Alx/Byz[**outside the temple**], Minor[inside the temple]; Alx/Major[**forty-two** *Greek* forty and two], Byz[forty-two].

11:4 Alx/Byz[**the two lampstands**], Minor[*omits* the]; Alx/Byz[**Lord**], Minor[God (KJV, NKJ, TLB)].

11:5 Alx/Byz[**wants to harm...wants to harm**], Minor[should want to harm...should want to harm].

11:6 Alx[**the power**], Byz[*omits* the (DRA, KJV, MRD, NIV, NKJ, NLT, NRS, RSV, TEV, TLB)].

make war with them, and overcome them and kill them. [8] And their dead bodies will lie in the street of the great city which mystically is called Sodom and Egypt, where also their Lord was crucified. [9] For three days and a half men from the peoples and tribes and tongues and nations gaze at their dead body and refuse to let their dead bodies be placed in a tomb. [10] And those who dwell on the earth rejoice over them and celebrate. And they will send gifts to one another, because these two prophets tormented those who dwell on the earth. [11] But after the three and a half days a breath of life from God entered them. And they stood up on their feet, and great fear fell upon those who saw them. [12] And they heard a loud voice from heaven saying to them, "Come up here." And they went up to heaven in a cloud, while their enemies looked on. [13] And in that hour there was a great earthquake, and a tenth of the city fell. Seven thousand people were killed in the earthquake, and the rest were terrified and gave glory to the God of heaven.

[14] The second woe has passed. Behold, the third woe is coming soon.

[15] And the seventh angel sounded his trumpet. And there were loud voices in heaven, saying,

> "The kingdom of the world has become the kingdom of our Lord
> and of his Christ.
> And he will reign for ever and ever."

[16] And the twenty-four elders, who sit on their thrones before God, fell on their faces and worshipped God, [17] saying,

> "We give thanks to you, O Lord God, the Almighty,
> who is and who was,
> because you have taken your great power
> and have begun to reign.

11:8 Alx/Byz[**dead bodies** *Greek* dead body], Minor[dead bodies]; Alx/Byz[**their Lord**], Minor[our Lord (KJV, NKJ)].

11:9 Alx/Byz[**three days and a half**], Major[*omits* and]; Alx/Byz[**gaze**], Minor[will gaze (DRA, ESV, HCS, KJV, MRD, NAB, NAS, NAU, NET, NIV, NKJ, NLT, NRS, TEV, ~TLB)]; Alx/Byz[**dead body**], Minor[dead bodies (ASV, DRA, ESV, HCS, JNT, KJV, MRD, NAB, NAS, NAU, NET, NIV, NJB, NKJ, NLT, NRS, REB, RSV, TEV, TLB)]; Alx[**refuse to let**], Byz[will refuse to let (DRA, KJV, MRD, NAB, NAS, NAU, NET, ~NIV, ~NKJ, NLT, ~NRS, TEV, TLB)]; Alx/Byz[**a tomb**], Minor[tombs (DRA, KJV, ~NAB, ~NIV, ~NJB, NKJ, ~NLT, ~REB, ~TEV, ~TLB)].

11:10 Alx/Byz[**rejoice over them**], Minor[will rejoice over them (DRA, ESV, HCS, KJV, MRD, NAB, NAS, NAU, NET, NIV, NKJ, NLT, NRS, RSV, TEV, TLB)]; Alx[**celebrate**], Byz[will celebrate (~DRA, ~ESV, ~HCS, ~KJV, MRD, ~NAB, ~NAS, ~NAU, ~NET, NIV, ~NKJ, ~NLT, ~NRS, ~RSV, TEV, TLB)]; Alx/Byz[**will send gifts**], Major[will give gifts (~ESV, ~NAB, NJB, NLT, ~NRS, ~REB, ~RSV, TLB)]; Minor[send gifts (JNT)].

11:11 Alx[**entered them**], Byz[entered into them (ASV, DRA, KJV, MRD)]; Alx/Byz[**fell upon**], Major[fell on (ESV, HCS, JNT, MRD, NAB, ~NET, ~NIV, ~NJB, NKJ, ~NLT, ~NRS, ~REB, RSV, ~TEV, TLB)].

11:12 Alx[**And they heard**], Byz[And I heard (NJB, ~NLT, ~REB, ~TLB)].

11:13 Alx/Byz[**And in that**], Minor[*omits* And (HCS, JNT, NAB, NET, NIV, NJB, NKJ, NLT, NRS, REB, TEV, TLB)]; Alx[**hour**], Byz[day].

11:14 Alx/Byz[**behold**], Minor[and behold (DRA, KJV, ~NAB, ~NLT, ~REB, ~TEV, ~TLB)], Alt[*without textual foundation omits* behold (~NAB, ~NET, ~NIV, ~NJB, ~NRS, ~REB, ~TEV, ~TLB)].

11:15 Alx/Byz[**The kingdom of the world**], Minor[The kingdoms of the world (KJV, NKJ, ~NLT, ~REB, ~TEV)].

11:16 Alx/Byz[**twenty-four**], Minor[twenty and four (ASV, DRA, KJV, MRD)]; Alx/Major[**who sit** *Greek* sitting], Byz[who sit]; Alx[**before God**], Byz[before the throne of God (MRD)].

11:17 Alx/Major[**who is and who was**], Byz[*adds* and who comes (DRA, KJV, NKJ)]; Alx/Byz[**because**], Minor[and because].

18   And the nations raged.
                        And your wrath came,
                        and the time for the dead to be judged,
                   for rewarding your servants the prophets
                        and the saints and those who fear your name,
                        both small and great,
                   and for destroying those who destroy the earth."

¹⁹ And the temple of God that is in heaven was opened, and within his temple was seen the ark of his covenant. And there were flashes of lightning, and voices, and peals of thunder, and an earthquake and a great hailstorm.

12 ¹ A great sign appeared in heaven: a woman clothed with the sun, and with the moon under her feet, and on her head a crown of twelve stars. ² And she was with child. And she cried out in labor and in pain to give birth. ³ Then another sign appeared in heaven: and behold, a great red dragon with seven heads and ten horns. And on his heads were seven diadems. ⁴ And his tail swept away a third of the stars of heaven, and threw them to the earth. And the dragon stood before the woman who was about to give birth, so that he might devour her child when it was born. ⁵ And she gave birth to a son, a male child, who is to rule all the nations with a rod of iron. And her child was caught up to God and to his throne. ⁶ And the woman fled into the wilderness, where she has a place prepared from God, that there they may nourish her for one thousand two hundred and sixty days.

⁷ And there was war in heaven. Michael and his angels fought with the dragon. And the dragon and his angels fought back, ⁸ but he was not strong enough. And there was no longer a place found for them in heaven. ⁹ And the great dragon was thrown down, that ancient serpent, who is called the Devil and Satan, the deceiver of the whole world – he was thrown down to the earth. And his angels were thrown down with him. ¹⁰ Then I heard a loud voice in heaven, saying,

              "Now the salvation, and the power,
                   and the kingdom of our God
                   and the authority of his Christ have come,

---

11:18 Alx/Major[**dead to be judged**], Byz[nations to be judged]; Alx/Major[**saints and those who fear**], Byz[saints, those who fear (JNT, TEV, ~TLB)]; **servants** *Greek* slaves.

11:19 Alx/Byz[**that is in heaven**], Major[in heaven (DRA, ESV, HCS, JNT, KJV, MRD, NAB, NET, NIV, NJB, NKJ, NLT, NRS, REB, RSV, TEV, TLB)]; Alx[**his covenant**], Byz[the covenant of the Lord], Alt[*without textual foundation* the covenant (~JNT, ~NJB, ~TEV)]; Alx/Byz[**and an earthquake**], Major[*omits*].

12:2 Alx[**and she was with child, and she cried out**], Byz[and being with child she cried out (DRA, KJV, MRD, NKJ)].

12:3 Alx/Byz[**red dragon**], Minor[fiery dragon (MRD)].

12:5 Alx/Byz[**to God and to his throne**], Minor[to God and his throne (JNT, NAB, NKJ, TEV)].

12:6 Alx/Byz[**from God**], Major[by God (DRA, ESV, HCS, JNT, MRD, NAB, NAS, NAU, NET, NIV, ~NJB, NKJ, ~NLT, NRS, REB, RSV, ~TEV, ~TLB)]; Alx/Byz[**that there**], Minor[*omits* there (ESV, JNT, NET, NIV, NJB, NLT, REB, RSV, TEV, TLB)]; Alx/Byz[**they may nourish**], Minor[they nourish (ESV, HCS, NAU, NJB, NLT, ~REB, RSV, TEV, TLB)].

12:7 Alx/Byz[**fought with the dragon**], Minor[fought against the dragon (ESV, HCS, JNT, KJV, MRD, NAB, NET, NIV, ~NJB, NLT, NRS, REB, RSV, TEV, ~TLB)].

12:8 Alx/Byz[**he was not strong enough**], Minor[they were not strong enough (ASV, DRA, ~KJV, ~MRD, NAB, NAS, NAU, NJB, NKJ, NRS, RSV)]; Alx[**a place for them**], Byz[a place for him (~NET, ~NLT, ~TEV, TLB)].

12:10 Alx/Byz[**cast out**], Minor[thrown down (ASV, ESV, KJV, NAS, NAU, NET, NIV, NJB, NKJ, NLT, NRS, ~REB, RSV, TEV, TLB)].

for the accuser of our brothers has been cast out,
who accuses them before our God
day and night.

11 They overcame him by the blood of the Lamb
and by the word of their testimony,
and they loved not their lives even to death.

12 Rejoice then, O heavens
and you that dwell in them!
But woe to the earth and the sea.
For the devil has come down to you
in great wrath,
because he knows that his time is short!"

13 And when the dragon saw that he had been thrown down to the earth, he pursued the woman who had given birth to the male child. **14** But the woman was given the two wings of the great eagle, so that she might fly into the wilderness to her place, where she is nourished for a time and times and half a time, from the presence of the serpent. **15** And the serpent poured water like a river out of his mouth after the woman, to sweep her away with the flood. **16** But the earth helped the woman, and the earth opened its mouth and drank up the river which the dragon had poured out of his mouth. **17** Then the dragon was enraged with the woman, and went off to make war on the rest of her offspring, on those who keep the commandments of God and hold to the testimony of Jesus. **18** And he stood on the shore of the sea.

13

1 And I saw a beast coming out of the sea. He had ten horns and seven heads, with ten diadems on his horns. And on his heads were blasphemous name[s]. **2** The beast that I saw was like a leopard. And his feet were like those of a bear, and his mouth like the mouth of a lion. And the dragon gave him his power and his throne and great authority. **3** And one of its heads seemed to have a fatal wound. But its fatal wound was healed. And the whole earth followed the beast with wonder. **4** Men worshipped the dragon, because he gave his authority to the beast. And they worshipped the beast, saying, "Who is like the beast, and who is able to make war against him?"

12:11 **word of their testimony** *or* word of which they testified.

12:12 Alx/Byz[**woe to the earth and the sea**], Minor[woe to the inhabitants of the earth and the sea (KJV, NKJ, ~TLB)].

12:14 Alx[**where she is nourished**], Byz[that she might be nourished (~ESV, ~REB, ~RSV)].

12:17 Alx/Byz[**Jesus**], Minor[*adds* Christ (DRA, KJV, NKJ)].

12:18 Alx[**And he stood on the shore of the sea 13:1**], Byz[13:1 And I stood on the shore of the sea… (~ASV, KJV, ~MRD, ~NAS, ~NAU, ~NIV, ~NJB, NKJ, ~REB)], Alt[*places this in verse 17* (ESV, RSV, TLB)].

13:1 Alx/Byz[**ten horns and seven heads**], Minor[seven heads and ten horns (DRA, KJV, NJB, NKJ, NLT, TLB)]; Alx/Byz[**were blasphemous names**], Minor[was a blasphemous name (KJV, NET, NIV, NKJ, REB, RSV, TEV)].

13:2 Alx/Byz[**a lion**], Minor[lions (MRD)].

13:3 Alx/Byz[**And one of its heads**], Minor[And I saw one of its heads (ASV, DRA, KJV, NAB, NAS, NAU, NJB, NKJ, NLT, TLB)]; Alx/Byz[**and the whole earth followed**], Minor[and in the whole earth they followed].

13:4 Alx[**because he gave**], Byz[which had given (~ESV, ~JNT, ~MRD, ~NET, ~NIV, ~NJB, ~NRS, ~REB, ~RSV, ~TEV)], Minor[which gave (DRA, KJV, NKJ, ~NLT, ~TLB)]; Alx/Major[**and who is able**], Byz[*omits* and].

⁵ And the beast was given a mouth speaking arrogant words and blasphemies. And it was allowed to exercise authority for forty-two months. ⁶ And he opened his mouth in blasphemies against God, to blaspheme his name and his dwelling – those who dwell in heaven. ⁷ Also it was given power to make war on the saints and to conquer them. And authority was given it over every tribe and people and tongue and nation, ⁸ and all who dwell on earth will worship him, every one whose name has not been written from the foundation of the world in the book of life of the Lamb that was slain.

⁹ If anyone has an ear, let him hear.

10   If anyone is destined for captivity,
                to captivity he goes.
        If anyone is to be killed with the sword,
                he is to be killed with the sword.

Here is the endurance and faith of the saints.

¹¹ Then I saw another beast coming up out of the earth. And he had two horns like a lamb, and he spoke like a dragon. ¹² He exercises all the authority of the first beast in his presence, and makes the earth and its inhabitants worship the first beast, whose fatal wound was healed. ¹³ He performs great signs, that he should even cause fire to come down from heaven to earth in the sight of men. ¹⁴ And he deceives those who dwell on the earth because of the signs which he was given power to do in the presence of the beast. He ordered them to make an image in honor of the beast who was wounded by the sword and yet lived. ¹⁵ And it was given to him to give breath to the image of the beast so that the image of the beast could even speak, and [could] cause those who would not worship the image of the beast to be killed. ¹⁶ And he causes all, both small and great, rich and

---

13:5 Alx[**blasphemies**], Byz[blasphemy (REB, ~TEV)]; Alx[**allowed to exercise authority**], Byz[given authority to make war]; Alx[**forty-two** Greek forty and two], Byz[forty-two].

13:6 Alx[**blasphemies**], Byz[blasphemy (KJV, MRD, ~NET, NKJ, ~NLT, ~TEV, ~TLB)]; Alx/Byz[**his dwelling – those who dwell in heaven**], Minor[his dwelling and those dwelling in heaven (DRA, JNT, KJV, MRD, NAB, NIV, NJB, NKJ, TEV, TLB)].

13:7 Alx/Byz[**Also it was given power to make war on the saints and to conquer them**], Minor[omits]; Alx/Byz[**and people**], Minor[omits (KJV, NKJ, TLB)].

13:8 Alx/Byz[**worship him**], Major[worship it (ESV, JNT, NAB, ~NET, ~NIV, NJB, ~NLT, NRS, REB, RSV, TEV, ~TLB)]; Alx/Byz[**every one whose name has not**], Minor[every one whose names have not (DRA, JNT, KJV, MRD, NAB, NIV, NKJ, NLT, REB, TEV, TLB)]; Alx/Byz[**written from the foundation of the world in the book of life of the Lamb that was slain** or written in the book of life of the Lamb that was slain from the foundation of the world], Minor[omits that was (JNT, KJV, MRD, ~NJB, NKJ, REB, TLB)].

13:10 Alx/Byz[**If anyone is destined for captivity**], Major[If anyone has captives (DRA, KJV, MRD, NKJ)]; Alx[**if anyone is to be killed with the sword, he is to be killed with the sword**], Byz[if anyone kills with the sword, he must be killed with the sword (ASV, DRA, KJV, MRD, NAS, NAU, NKJ, NRS, RSV)].

13:12 Alx/Byz[**and makes the earth and its inhabitants worship the first beast**], Major[and begins to make the earth and its inhabitants worship the first beast (~NJB)], Alt[omits (MRD)].

13:13 Alx[**that he should even cause fire to come**], Byz[that fire should even come down]; Alx/Byz[**to earth**], Major[on earth (ASV, KJV, MRD, ~NJB, NKJ)], Alt[without textual foundation omits (~NET, ~TLB)].

13:14 Alx/Byz[**he deceives those**], Major[adds of mine]; Alx/Byz[**by the sword** Greek of the sword], Major[by the sword Greek from the sword].

13:15 Alx[**could cause**], Byz[omits could (ASV, HCS, ~JNT, KJV, MRD, NAS, NAU, NIV, NJB, NKJ, NLT, NRS, REB, RSV, TEV, TLB)]; Alx/Major[**to be killed**], Byz[that they should be killed]; **give breath** or give spirit.

13:16 Alx/Byz[**a mark**], Major[marks]; Alx/Major[**forehead**], Byz[foreheads (DRA, KJV, MRD, NAB, NKJ, TEV)].

poor, free and slave, to be given a mark on their right hand or their forehead, [17] and that no one can buy or sell unless he has the mark – the name of the beast or the number of his name. [18] This calls for wisdom. Let him who has understanding calculate the number of the beast. For it is the number of a man. And its number is six hundred and sixty-six.

14

[1] Then I looked, and behold, the Lamb was standing on Mount Zion, and with him a hundred and forty-four thousand who had his name and his Father's name written on their foreheads. [2] I heard a voice from heaven like the sound of many waters and like the sound of loud thunder. And the voice I heard was like the sound of harpists playing on their harps. [3] And they sing [what seemed to be] a new song before the throne and before the four living creatures and before the elders. No one could learn the song except the hundred and forty-four thousand who had been redeemed from the earth. [4] These are the ones who have not been defiled with women, for they have kept themselves chaste. These are the ones who follow the Lamb wherever he goes. They have been purchased from among men as first fruits to God and to the Lamb. [5] And no lie was found in their mouth. They are blameless.

[6] Then I saw another angel flying in mid-heaven, having an eternal gospel to proclaim to those who sit on the earth, and to every nation and tribe and tongue and people. [7] And he said with a loud voice, "Fear God, and give him glory, because the hour of his judgment has come. Worship him who made the heaven and the earth and sea and springs of water."

[8] And another angel, a second, followed, saying, "Fallen, fallen is Babylon the great, who has made all the nations drink the wine of her impure passion."

13:17 Alx/Byz[**and that**], Minor[*omits* and (ESV, HCS, JNT, MRD, NAB, NET, NIV, NRS, RSV, TEV)]; Alx/Byz[**the mark – the name**], Minor[the mark or the name (DRA, KJV, ~NAS, ~NAU, NKJ, ~REB)], Alt[the mark of the name (MRD, NAB)].

13:18 Alx[**six hundred and sixty-six**], Byz[six six six (ESV, HCS, JNT, NET, NIV, NJB, NKJ, NLT, TEV, TLB)], Major[six hundred, sixty-six (DRA, ~KJV, NRS)], Minor[six hundred and sixteen]; *Metzger notes* "the Greek form Neron Caesar written in Hebrew characters… is equivalent to 666, whereas the Latin form Nero Caesar… is equivalent to 616."

14:1 Alx/Byz[**the Lamb**], Minor[a Lamb (DRA, KJV, MRD, NKJ, TLB)]; Alx/Byz[**a hundred**], Major[a number, a hundred (MRD)]; Alx/Byz[**his name and his Father's name**], Minor[his Father's name (KJV, NKJ)].

14:2 Alx/Byz[**the voice I heard was like the sound of harpists**], Minor[I heard the voice of harpists (KJV, NKJ, TLB)].

14:3 Alx[**what seemed to be**], Byz[*omits* (ESV, HCS, JNT, MRD, NAS, NAU, NET, NIV, NJB, NLT, NRS, REB, RSV, TEV, TLB)].

14:4 Alx/Byz[**These are the ones who have not been defiled**], Minor[*omits* These are (TLB)]; Alx/Byz[**purchased**], Major[*adds* by Jesus (MRD)].

14:5 Alx/Byz[**lie**], Minor[guile (KJV, NAB, NKJ)]; Alx[**they are blameless**], Byz[for they are blameless before the throne of God (DRA, KJV, NKJ)], Minor[for they are blameless (ESV, MRD, RSV)].

14:6 Alx/Byz[**another angel**], Major[an angel (REB)]; Alx/Byz[**sit**], Minor[dwell (ASV, ESV, HCS, JNT, KJV, MRD, NAB, NAS, NAU, NET, NIV, NJB, NKJ, ~NLT, NRS, ~REB, RSV, ~TEV, ~TLB)]; **in mid-heaven** *or* at the zenith (*i.e. directly overhead*).

14:7 Alx[**Fear God**], Byz[Fear the Lord (DRA)]; Alx/Byz[**him who made** *or* the maker of], Major[him who made]; Alx[**the earth and sea**], Byz[the earth and the sea (DRA, ESV, HCS, JNT, KJV, MRD, NET, NIV, NKJ, NLT, NRS, REB, RSV, TLB)].

14:8 Alx[**And another angel, a second**], Byz[And another, a second angel (ASV, MRD)], Minor[*omits* a second (DRA, KJV, NKJ, TLB) *others omit* angel], Alt[*without textual foundation omits* another (~HCS, ~NAB, ~NET, ~NIV, ~NJB, ~NLT, ~REB, ~TEV)]; Alx/Byz[**Fallen, fallen**], Major[Fallen]; Alx/Byz[**Babylon the great**], Minor[*adds* city (KJV, NKJ, NLT, TLB)]; Alx/Byz[**who has made**], Major[*omits* who (JNT, NET, NRS, TEV)], Minor[because she has

⁹ And another angel, a third, followed them, saying with a loud voice, "If any one worships the beast and its image, and receives a mark on his forehead or on his hand, ¹⁰ he also will drink of the wine of God's wrath, which is poured in full strength into the cup of his anger. And he will be tormented with fire and sulfur in the presence of the holy angels and in the presence of the Lamb. ¹¹ And the smoke of their torment goes up for ever and ever. They have no rest day and night, those who worship the beast and his image, and whoever receives the mark of his name." ¹² Here is the endurance of the saints, those who keep the commandments of God and the faith of Jesus.

¹³ And I heard a voice from heaven, saying, "Write, 'Blessed are the dead who die in the Lord from now on!'" "Yes," says the Spirit, "that they will rest from their labors, for their deeds follow them."

¹⁴ *Then I looked, and behold, a white cloud, and seated on the cloud was one like a son of man, with a golden crown on his head,* and a sharp sickle in his hand. ¹⁵ And another angel came out of the temple, crying out with a loud voice to him who sat on the cloud, "Put in your sickle and reap, for the hour to reap has come, because the harvest of the earth is ripe." ¹⁶ So he who sat on the cloud swung his sickle over the earth, and the earth was reaped.

¹⁷ And another angel came out of the temple in heaven. And he too had a sharp sickle. ¹⁸ Then another angel [came] out from the altar, [the one who] has power over fire. And he called with a loud voice to him who had the sharp sickle, "Put in your sharp sickle. And gather the clusters of the vine of the earth, because her grapes are ripe." ¹⁹ So the angel swung his sickle on the earth and gathered the clusters from the vine of the earth, and threw them into the great wine press of the wrath of God. ²⁰ And the wine press was trodden outside the city, and blood flowed from the wine press, as high as the horses' bridles for a distance of one thousand six hundred stadia.

---

made (KJV, NKJ, NLT, TLB)]; Alx/Major[**all the nations**], Byz[all nations (DRA, ESV, HCS, KJV, MRD, ~NJB, NKJ, NRS, REB, RSV, TEV, ~TLB)].

14:⁹ Alx[**another angel, a third**], Byz[a third angel (DRA, HCS, KJV, NAB, NET, NIV, NJB, NKJ, NLT, REB, TEV, TLB)]; Alx/Major[**a mark**], Byz[the mark (~DRA, JNT, ~KJV, ~MRD, ~NAB, NET, ~NIV, ~NJB, ~NKJ, ~NLT, ~REB, TEV, ~TLB)].

14:¹⁰ Alx/Byz[**holy angels**], Minor[*omits* holy].

14:¹² Alx/Byz[**those who keep**], Minor[here are those who keep (KJV, NKJ)].

14:¹³ Alx/Byz[**a voice from heaven, saying**], Minor[*adds* to me (DRA, KJV, NJB, NKJ, ~TLB)]; Alx[**for their deeds**], Byz[and their deeds (KJV, NKJ)].

14:¹⁴ Daniel 7:13-14.

14:¹⁵ Alx/Major[**for the hour to reap has come**], Byz[for the hour of reaping has come (~NJB, NLT, ~REB, ~TEV)], Minor[for the hour has come for you to reap (KJV, NKJ, TLB)]; *some MRD databases omit everything after* **cloud**.

14:¹⁸ Alx/Byz[**came out from the altar**], Minor[*omits* came], Alt[*without textual foundation omits* came out from the altar (~TLB)]; Alx[**the one who has power** *Greek* the one having power], Byz[having power (~DRA, ~HCS, ~JNT, ~KJV, MRD, ~NAB *incorrect bracket*, ~NET, ~NIV, ~NJB, ~NKJ, ~NLT)]; Alx[**a loud voice**], Byz[a loud cry (KJV, NKJ, ~NLT, ~REB, ~TLB)]; Alx/Byz[**clusters of the vine**], Minor[clusters (~REB)]; Alx/Major[**her grapes are ripe**], Byz[the grape of the earth is ripe]; *some MRD databases omit last clause.*

14:¹⁹ Alx/Major[**the great wine press of the wrath of God** *or* the wine press of the great wrath of God (see TEV) *or* the winepress of the wrath of the great God (see MRD)], Byz[the great wine press of the wrath of God]; *in the Alx* great *is masculine and in the Byz it is feminine –* wine press *can be either masculine or feminine, while* wrath *and* God *are both masculine.*

14:²⁰ Alx/Byz[**outside the city**], Alt[*without textual foundation omits* (~MRD)]; Alx/Byz[**one thousand six hundred stadia** *about 180 miles*], Minor[1606 stadia *others* 1200 stadia *others* 1500 stadia *others omit*].

15

¹ Then I saw another sign in heaven, great and marvelous, seven angels with seven plagues, which are the last, because with them the wrath of God is finished. ² And I saw what looked like a sea of glass mixed with fire and, standing beside the sea of glass, those who had been victorious over the beast and his image and over the number of his name. They held harps of God ³ and they sang the song of Moses, the servant of God, and the song of the Lamb, saying,

"Great and marvelous are your deeds,
O Lord God the Almighty!
Just and true are your ways,
O King of the nations!

⁴ Who cannot fear, O Lord,
and glorify your name?
For you alone are righteous.
All the nations will come
and worship before you,
for your righteous acts have been revealed."

⁵ After this I looked, and the temple of the tabernacle of testimony in heaven was opened. ⁶ And the seven angels [who] had the seven plagues came out of the temple, clothed in clean bright linen, and girded around their chests with golden sashes. ⁷ Then one of the four living creatures gave to the seven angels seven golden bowls full of the wrath of God, who lives for ever and ever. ⁸ And the temple was filled with smoke from the glory of God and from his power. And no one could enter the temple until the seven plagues of the seven angels were completed.

16

¹ Then I heard a loud voice from the temple, saying to the seven angels, "Go and pour out on the earth the seven bowls of the wrath of God."

² So the first angel went and poured out his bowl to the earth. And foul and loathsome sores broke out on the people who had the mark of the beast and worshipped his image.

³ The second poured out his bowl to the sea. And it became blood like that of a dead man. And every living soul that was in the sea died.

15:2 Alx/Byz[**and his image**], Minor[*adds* and over his mark (KJV, NKJ, TLB)]; Alx/Major[**harps**], Byz[the harps (DRA, KJV, MRD, REB)].

15:3 Alx/Byz[**the servant**], Minor[a servant (HCS)]; Alx/Byz[**nations**], Minor[saints (KJV, NKJ) *others* ages (ASV, DRA, NIV, REB, RSV, TLB) *or* worlds (MRD)]; **servant** *Greek* slave.

15:4 Alx/Byz[**Who cannot fear**], Major[*adds* you (DRA, KJV, MRD, NKJ, NLT, REB, TEV)]; Alx/Byz[**righteous**], Major[holy (ASV, DRA, ESV, HCS, JNT, KJV, MRD, NAB, NAS, NAU, NET, NIV, NJB, NKJ, NLT, NRS, REB, RSV, TEV, TLB)]; Alx/Byz[**All the nations**], Minor[*omits* the nations].

15:5 Alx/Byz[**I looked**], Minor[*adds* and behold (DRA, KJV, NKJ, NLT, TLB)].

15:6 Alx/Byz[**who had**], Minor[having (DRA, ESV, HCS, JNT, KJV, NAB, NIV, NJB, NKJ, NRS, REB, RSV)]; Alx/Byz[**came out of the temple**], Minor[came out of heaven *others* came out (NJB, REB)]; Alx[**clothed**], Byz[who were clothed (JNT, NAB, NIV, NLT, REB)]; Alx/Byz[**clean bright**], Minor[clean and bright (ASV, DRA, KJV, NAS, NAU, REB)]; Alx/Byz[**linen**], Minor[stone (ASV)].

15:8 Alx/Major[**with smoke**], Byz[from the smoke (~NAB, ~NJB)].

16:1 Alx/Byz[**from the temple**], Minor[from heaven *others omit* (MRD)]; Alx/Byz[**seven bowls**], Minor[bowls (KJV, NKJ)].

16:2 Alx/Byz[**to the earth**], Minor[on the earth (DRA, ESV, HCS, JNT, KJV, MRD, NAB, NAU, NET, NIV, NJB, NKJ, NLT, NRS, REB, RSV, TEV, TLB)]; Alx/Byz[**on the people**], Minor[in the people].

16:3 Alx[**The second**], Byz[*adds* angel (DRA, ESV, KJV, MRD, NAB, NAS, NAU, NET, NIV, NJB,

⁴ The third poured out his bowl to the rivers and the springs of water. And it became blood. ⁵ And I heard the angel of the waters say,

"Righteous are you, who are and who were, O Holy One,
     because you judged these things.

⁶   For they shed the blood of saints and prophets,
               and you [have] give[n] them blood to drink.
     They deserve it."

⁷ And I heard the altar saying,

"Yes, O Lord God, the Almighty,
     true and just are your judgments."

⁸ The fourth poured out his bowl on the sun, and it was allowed to scorch men in fire. ⁹ Men were scorched by the fierce heat. And they cursed the name of God who has the power over these plagues, and they did not repent and give him glory.

¹⁰ The fifth poured out his bowl on the throne of the beast, and his kingdom was plunged into darkness. Men gnawed their tongues in agony. ¹¹ And they cursed the God of heaven because of their pains and their sores, and they did not repent of their deeds.

¹² The sixth poured out his bowl on the great river Euphrates, and its water was dried up, to prepare the way for the kings from the Rising Sun. ¹³ And I saw three unclean spirits, as frogs, coming out of the mouth of the dragon and out of the mouth of the beast and out of the mouth of the false prophet. ¹⁴ For they are spirits of demons, performing miraculous signs, which go out over the kings of the whole world to gather them for the battle on the great day of God Almighty. ¹⁵ ("Behold, I am coming like a thief! Blessed is he who stays awake and keeps his clothes with him, so that he may not go naked and be

---

NKJ, NLT, NRS, REB, RSV, TEV, TLB)]; Alx/Byz[**every living soul**], Minor[every soul (~HCS, NLT, TLB)]; Alx[**that was in the sea**], Byz[in the sea (DRA, HCS, JNT, KJV, MRD, NAB, NAS, NAU, NIV, NJB, NKJ, NLT, NRS, REB, TEV, TLB)].

16:4 Alx/Byz[**The third**], Minor[*adds* angel (ESV, KJV, MRD, NAB, NAS, NAU, NET, NIV, NJB, NKJ, NLT, NRS, REB, RSV, TEV, TLB)]; Alx[**and the springs**], Byz[and to the springs]; Alx/Byz[**it became blood**], Minor[they became blood (ESV, HCS, JNT, KJV, MRD, NAB, NAS, NAU, NET, NIV, NJB, NKJ, NLT, NRS, REB, RSV, TEV, TLB)].

16:5 Alx/Byz[**Righteous are you**], Minor[*adds* Lord (DRA, KJV, NKJ)]; Alx/Byz[**O Holy One**], Minor[holy (~MRD) *others* and the Holy One (~DRA, ~HCS, ~NET, ~NIV, ~NJB) *others* and shall be (KJV, NKJ)].

16:6 Alx/Byz[**blood**], Minor[bloods]; Alx[**have given**], Byz[gave (HCS, JNT)]; Alx/Byz[**They deserve it**], Minor[For they deserve it (DRA, KJV, MRD, NKJ)].

16:7 Alx/Byz[**I heard the altar saying**], Minor[I heard another from the altar saying (DRA, ~HCS, KJV, ~MRD, NKJ, ~NLT, ~REB, ~TEV, ~TLB)].

16:8 Alx/Byz[**The fourth**], Major[*adds* angel (DRA, KJV, NAS, NAU, NET, NIV, NJB, NKJ, NLT, NRS, REB, RSV, TEV, TLB)].

16:9 Alx[**they cursed the name**], Byz[the men cursed the name (MRD)]; Alx[**who has the power**], Byz[who has power (DRA, ESV, KJV, MRD, NAB, NET, NIV, NKJ, NLT, NRS, RSV, TEV, ~TLB)].

16:10 Alx/Byz[**The fifth**], Minor[*adds* angel (DRA, ESV, KJV, NAB, NAS, NAU, NET, NIV, NJB, NKJ, NLT, NRS, REB, RSV, TEV, TLB)].

16:12 Alx/Byz[**The sixth**], Minor[*adds* angel (DRA, ESV, KJV, NAB, NAS, NAU, NET, NIV, NJB, NKJ, NLT, NRS, REB, RSV, TEV, TLB)]; **the Rising Sun** *or* the East.

16:13 Alx/Byz[**as frogs**], Minor[like frogs (DRA, ESV, HCS, JNT, KJV, MRD, NAB, NAS, NAU, ~NET, ~NIV, ~NJB, NKJ, ~NLT, NRS, REB, RSV, ~TEV)].

16:14 Alx/Byz[**which go out**], Minor[to go out (~DRA, ~MRD, ~NAB, ~NIV, NJB, NLT, REB, ~TEV, ~TLB)]; Alx/Byz[**of the whole world**], Minor[of the earth and of the whole world (KJV, NKJ)], Alt[*without textual foundation omits* whole (~NET)]; Alx[**the great day**], Byz[that great day (KJV, NKJ, NLT, TLB)].

shamefully exposed.") **16** And they gathered them together at the place which in Hebrew is called Har-Magedon.

17 The seventh poured out his bowl to the air, and out of the temple came a loud voice from the throne, saying, "It is done!" **18** And there were flashes of lightning and voices and peals of thunder. And there was a great earthquake, such as there had not been since man came to be on the earth, so great an earthquake was it, and so mighty. **19** The great city was split into three parts, and the cities of the nations fell. Babylon the great was remembered before God, to give her the cup of the wine of the fury of his wrath. **20** And every island fled away, and the mountains were not found. **21** Huge hailstones, about a hundred pounds each, fell from heaven upon men. And men cursed God for the plague of hail, because the plague was so terrible.

17 **1** And one of the seven angels who had the seven bowls came and spoke with me, saying, "Come, I will show you the judgment of the great harlot who sits on many waters, **2** with whom the kings of the earth committed fornication, and the inhabitants of the earth were made drunk with the wine of her fornication." **3** And he carried me away in the Spirit into a wilderness, and I saw a woman sitting on a scarlet beast, and it had seven heads and ten horns which [were] full of blasphemous names. **4** The woman was wearing purple and scarlet, and adorned with gold and precious stones and pearls, having in her hand a golden cup full of abominations and of the unclean things of her immorality. **5** And on her forehead was written a name,

---

16:16 Alx/Byz[**Har-Magedon** *Hebraism* Mount Megiddo *i.e. Mount Carmel*], Minor[Ar-mageddon *Hebraism* City of Megiddo (DRA, ESV, HCS, KJV, MRD, NAB, NET, NIV, NJB, NKJ, NLT, REB, RSV, TEV, ~TLB) *others* Mageddon *Hebraism* Megiddo].

16:17 Alx/Byz[**The seventh**], Minor[*adds* angel (DRA, ESV, KJV, NAB, NAS, NAU, NET, NIV, NJB, NKJ, NLT, NRS, REB, RSV, TEV, TLB)]; Alx/Byz[**to the air**], Minor[into the air (ESV, HCS, KJV, NAB, NET, NIV, NJB, NKJ, NLT, NRS, RSV, TEV, TLB)]; Alx[**out of the temple**], Byz[*adds* of heaven (KJV, NKJ, TLB)], Minor[*adds* of God]; Alx/Byz[**a loud voice**], Minor[a voice].

16:18 Alx/Byz[**flashes of lightning and voices and peals of thunder**], Major[flashes of lightning and peals of thunder and voices (MRD)], Minor[voices and peals of thunder and flashes of lightning (KJV, NKJ)], Alt[*without textual foundation* thunder...voices...lightning (~NLT, ~TLB)]; Alx/Byz[**and there was a great earthquake**], Major[*omits* there was (ESV, NAB, NIV, NJB, NRS, REB, RSV, TEV)]; Alx[**since man came to be**], Byz[since men came to be (ASV, DRA, KJV, MRD, NKJ, NLT, NRS, RSV)].

16:19 Alx/Byz[**cities of the nations**], Alt/Peshitta[city of the nations (MRD)], Alt/Vulgate[cities of the Gentiles (DRA, NAB)], Alt[*without textual foundation* cities of the world (~NJB, ~TLB)].

16:21 **a hundred pounds** *Greek* a talent.

17:1 Alx/Byz[**spoke with me, saying**], Minor[*adds* to me (~ESV, ~JNT, KJV, ~NAB, ~NET, ~NIV, ~NJB, NKJ, ~NLT, ~NRS, ~REB, ~RSV, ~TEV)]; Alx/Byz[**many waters**], Major[the many waters (NAB, TLB)].

17:2 Alx/Major[**her fornication**], Byz[fornication (~ESV, ~NRS, ~RSV)].

17:3 Alx/Major[**a scarlet beast**], Byz[the scarlet beast]; Alx[**which were full**], Byz[which was full (ESV, HCS, NAB, NET, NIV, NJB, NKJ, NLT, NRS, REB, RSV, TEV, TLB)]; Alx/Byz[**it had seven heads**], Minor[it had the seven heads]; **in the Spirit** *or* in the spirit.

17:4 Alx/Byz[**The woman was**], Minor[*omits* was (NLT, TLB)]; Alx/Byz[**wearing purple**], Minor[clothed with purple (ASV, DRA, ESV, HCS, JNT, KJV, MRD, NAS, NAU, NET, NIV, NJB, NKJ, NRS, REB, RSV, TEV)]; Alx/Byz[**and adorned**], Major[*omits* and (HCS, ~NLT, ~TLB)]; Alx/Byz[**unclean things**], Minor[uncleanness (DRA, ESV, HCS, KJV, MRD, NJB, NKJ, NLT, NRS, REB, RSV, ~TLB)]; Alx/Major[**of her immorality**], Byz[of the immorality of the earth], Minor[of her immorality with those of the earth (MRD) *others* of her immorality with all of the earth], Alt[*without textual foundation* omits (~TLB)].

17:5 Alx/Byz[**mystery**], Minor[*omits*]; Alx/Byz[**harlots**], Alt/Vulgate[fornications (DRA)].

"MYSTERY, BABYLON THE GREAT, THE MOTHER OF HARLOTS AND OF THE ABOMINATIONS OF THE EARTH."

⁶ And I saw the woman drunk from the blood of the saints, and from the blood of the witnesses of Jesus. When I saw her, I wondered greatly. ⁷ And the angel said to me, "Why do you wonder? I will tell you the mystery of the woman and of the beast that carries her, which has the seven heads and the ten horns. ⁸ The beast that you saw was, and is not, and is about to come up out of the abyss and go to destruction. And those who dwell on the earth, whose name has not been written in the book of life from the foundation of the world, will wonder when they see the beast, because he was and is not and will come. ⁹ Here is the mind that has wisdom: The seven heads are seven mountains on which the woman sits. And they are seven kings. ¹⁰ Five have fallen, one is, the other has not yet come; and when he comes, he must remain a little while. ¹¹ The beast who was, and is not, is an eighth. He belongs to the seven and he goes to destruction. ¹² And the ten horns which you saw are ten kings, who have not yet received a kingdom. But they receive authority as kings with the beast for one hour. ¹³ These have one purpose and they give their power and authority to the beast. ¹⁴ These will make war against the Lamb. And the Lamb will overcome them, because he is Lord of lords and King of kings, and those who are with him are the called and chosen and faithful."

¹⁵ And he said to me, "The waters you saw where the harlot sits, are peoples and multitudes and nations and tongues. ¹⁶ And the ten horns you saw, they and the beast will hate the harlot. They will make her desolate and naked, and will eat her flesh and burn her up in fire. ¹⁷ For God has put it into their hearts to carry out his purpose by being of one mind and giving over their royal power to the beast, until the words of God shall be fulfilled. ¹⁸ The woman that you saw is the great city which has dominion over the kings of the earth."

17:6 Alx/Byz[**drunk from the blood**], Minor[*omits* from]; Alx/Byz[**saints, and from the blood**], Major[*omits* and (ESV, JNT, NIV, NLT, ~TLB)]; Alx/Byz[**of Jesus**], Minor[*omits*].

17:8 Alx[**go to destruction**], Byz[to go to destruction (ASV, NAS, NJB)]; Alx/Byz[**whose name has not been written**], Major[whose names have not been written (DRA, ESV, HCS, JNT, KJV, MRD, NAB, NET, NIV, NJB, NKJ, NLT, NRS, REB, RSV, TEV, TLB)]; Alx/Byz[**the beast, because he was**], Major[that the beast was (NET)], Minor[the beast, how that he was (ASV, ~NJB) *others* the beast that was (DRA, HCS, JNT, KJV, ~MRD, NKJ, ~NLT, REB, ~TEV, ~TLB)]; Alx/Byz[**and will come**], Minor[and yet is (KJV, ~NAB, ~NIV, NKJ)], Alt/Vulgate[*omits* (DRA, ~NLT, ~TLB)].

17:9 Alx/Byz[**Here is the mind**], Alt/Vulgate[And here is the mind (DRA, KJV, TLB)]; Alx[**And they are seven kings 10**], Byz[10 And they are seven kings (ASV, ESV, HCS, KJV, MRD, NAS, NAU, NIV, NJB, NKJ, REB, RSV, TLB)]; **kings** *or* emperors

17:10 Alx/Byz[**one is**], Minor[and one is (KJV, ~NLT, ~TLB)].

17:13 Alx/Byz[**they give their power**], Alt[they shall give their power (DRA, KJV, MRD, NAB, NET, NIV, NKJ, REB)].

17:16 Alx/Byz[**the ten horns that you saw, they and the beast will hate the harlot**], Minor[the ten horns that you saw on the beast, they will hate the harlot (DRA, KJV, NKJ)]; Alx/Byz[**and naked**], Major[and will make her naked (JNT, NIV, ~REB, TEV, ~TLB)]; Alx/Byz[**in fire**], Minor[with fire (ASV, DRA, ESV, HCS, JNT, KJV, MRD, NAB, NAS, NAU, NET, NIV, NKJ, NLT, NRS, ~REB, RSV, TEV, TLB)].

17:17 Alx/Byz[**the words of God**], Minor[the sayings of God]; Alx[**shall be fulfilled**], Byz[should be fulfilled (ASV, NAS)].

18

¹ After these things I saw another angel coming down from heaven, having great authority. And the earth was made bright with his splendor. ² And he called out in a mighty voice,

"Fallen, fallen is Babylon the great!

She has become a dwelling place of demons,

a prison of every unclean spirit,

a prison of every unclean bird,

[a prison of every unclean]

and hateful [beast].

³ For all nations have drunk the wine

of her impure passion.

And the kings of the earth have committed fornication with her.

And the merchants of the earth have grown rich

with the wealth of her wantonness."

⁴ Then I heard another voice from heaven, saying,

"Come out of her, my people,

so that you will not share in her sins

and receive of her plagues.

⁵ For her sins are piled up as high as heaven,

and God has remembered her iniquities.

⁶ Pay her back even as she has paid,

and redouble the double according to her deeds;

in the cup which she has mixed,

mix a double portion for her.

⁷ As she glorified herself and played the wanton,

so give her a like measure of torment and mourning.

For she says in her heart that,

'A queen I sit,

and I am not a widow,

mourning I will never see.'

18:1 Alx/Byz[**After these things**], Minor[And after these things (DRA, KJV)]; Alx/Byz[**I saw another angel**], Minor[I saw an angel].

18:2 Alx/Byz[**in a mighty voice**], Major[with a mighty voice (ASV, DRA, ESV, ~KJV, MRD, NAS, NAU, NET, NIV, NJB, ~NKJ, NLT, NRS, RSV, TLB)]; Alx/Byz[**Fallen, fallen is Babylon the great**], Major[Fallen is Babylon the great], Alt[*without textual foundation* Babylon has fallen, Babylon the great has fallen (~NJB)]; Alx[**a prison of every unclean bird, a prison of every unclean and hateful beast**], Byz[a prison of every unclean and hateful bird (ASV, DRA, JNT, KJV, NAS, NAU, NIV, NJB, NKJ, REB, RSV, TEV, ~TLB)].

18:3 Alx/Byz[**drunk**], Major[fallen by (ASV, NET)]; Alx/Byz[**the wine of her impure passion** *or* the wine of the wrath of her immorality], Minor[*omits* the wine *others omit* passion (~NIV, NJB, ~TEV)], Alt[*omits* impure (MRD)]; **passion** *or* wrath; **wealth** *or* power.

18:5 Alx/Byz[**God**], Alt[the Lord (DRA)]; Alx/Byz[**remembered her iniquities**], Minor[remembered her for her iniquities].

18:6 Alx/Byz[**6 Pay her back even as she has paid**], Minor[*adds* you (DRA, KJV, NKJ, TEV, TLB)], Alt[Pay her back even as she has paid 6 (NJB)]; Alx[**and redouble the double**], Byz[and redouble to her double (~ASV, DRA, ESV, JNT, KJV, MRD, NAB, NAS, NAU, NET, NIV, ~NJB, NKJ, NLT, NRS, REB, RSV, TEV, ~TLB)]; Alx/Byz[**the cup**], Minor[her cup (~NAB, ~NIV, TEV)].

18:7 Alx/Byz[**she says in her heart that**], Minor[*omits* that (ASV, DRA, ESV, HCS, JNT, KJV, MRD, NAB, NAS, NAU, NET, NIV, NJB, NKJ, NLT, NRS, REB, RSV, TEV, TLB)]; Alx/Major[**A queen**], Byz[As a queen (ESV, HCS, NAB, NAS, NAU, ~NET, NIV, NJB, NKJ, ~NRS)].

8   Therefore in one day her plagues will come,
                pestilence and mourning and famine,
          and she will be burned with fire;
                for mighty is the Lord God who judged her.

⁹ And the kings of the earth, who committed fornication and were wanton with her, will weep and wail over her when they see the smoke of her burning. ¹⁰ They will stand far off, in fear of her torment, and say,

          'Woe, woe, the great city,
                the mighty city, Babylon!
          In one hour has your judgment come.'

¹¹ And the merchants of the earth weep and mourn over her, because no one buys their cargoes any more – ¹² cargoes of gold, silver, precious stone and pearls; fine linen; purple, silk and scarlet cloth; every sort of citron wood, and articles of every kind made of ivory, costly wood, bronze, iron and marble; ¹³ cargoes of cinnamon and spice, of incense, myrrh and frankincense, of wine and olive oil, of fine flour and wheat; cattle and sheep; horses and chariots; and slaves and human souls.

14   The fruit you longed for
                has gone from you.
          And all your riches and splendor
                have perished.
                And they shall never find them.

¹⁵ The merchants of these things, who gained wealth from her, will stand far off, in fear of her torment, weeping and mourning, ¹⁶ saying,

          'Woe, woe, the great city,
                she who was clothed in fine linen
                      and purple and scarlet,
                and adorned [in] gold
                      and a precious stone and pearl!

17   In one hour such great wealth has been laid waste!'

18:8 Alx/Byz[**and mourning**], Minor[*omits* and (JNT, NAB, NET, NIV, REB, TEV)]; Alx/Byz[**the Lord God**], Minor[*omits* the Lord (DRA)], Alt[*without textual foundation omits* God (~TLB)]; Alx/Byz[**judged**], Minor[judges (~DRA, HCS, ~JNT, KJV, MRD, NAB, NAS, NAU, NET, NIV, NKJ, NLT, NRS, RSV, TEV, TLB)].

18:9 Alx/Major[**weep and wail over her**], Byz[weep and wail because of her (NET, NJB, NKJ, ~TEV)], Minor[bewail her and mourn over her (~KJV)], Alt[*without textual foundation omits* weep and (~NLT, ~TLB)].

18:11 Alx[**weep and mourn**], Byz[will weep and mourn (DRA, HCS, KJV, MRD, NAB, NET, NIV, NJB, NKJ, NLT, REB, TLB)].

18:12 Alx[**pearls**], Byz[pearl]; Alx/Byz[**wood**], Minor[stone (DRA)].

18:13 Alx/Byz[**and spice**], Major[*omits* (DRA, KJV, NKJ)]; Alx/Byz[**cattle and sheep**], Major[sheep and cattle]; **human souls** *or* human lives.

18:14 Alx/Major[**gone**], Byz[perished (~NJB, ~TEV)]; Alx/Major[**perished**], Byz[gone (~ESV, HCS, KJV, NAB, NAS, NET, ~NIV, ~NJB, NKJ, NLT, NRS, REB, RSV, TEV, TLB)]; Alx[**they shall never find them**], Byz[you shall never find them (KJV, ~NAB, NKJ, ~NLT, ~NRS, ~RSV, ~TEV)], Major[you can never find them].

18:15 Alx/Byz[**weeping and mourning**], Minor[both weeping and mourning (MRD)].

18:16 Alx/Byz[**saying**], Major[and saying (DRA, JNT, KJV, ~NIV, NKJ, ~NLT, TEV, ~TLB)]; Alx/Byz[**in gold**], Major[with gold (ASV, DRA, ESV, HCS, JNT, KJV, MRD, NAS, NAU, NET, NIV, ~NJB, NKJ, NLT, NRS, REB, RSV, TEV, TLB)]; Alx[**pearl**], Byz[pearls (DRA, ESV, HCS, JNT, KJV, MRD, NAB, NAS, NAU, NET, NIV, NJB, NKJ, NLT, NRS, REB, RSV, TEV, TLB)].

18:17 Alx/Major[**17 In one hour...laid waste**], Byz[In one hour...laid waste 17 (MRD)]; Alx/Byz[**all**

And every shipmaster, and all seafarers and sailors, and all who make their living by the sea, stood far off, [18] and were crying out as they saw the smoke of her burning, saying, 'What city is like the great city?' [19] And they threw dust on their heads and were crying out, weeping and mourning, saying,

'Woe, woe, the great city,
> where all who had the ships in the sea
> became rich by her wealth,
for in one hour she has been laid waste!'

[20] Rejoice over her, O heaven,
> and you saints and you apostles and you prophets,
because God has pronounced judgment for you against her!"

[21] Then a mighty angel took up a stone like a great millstone and threw it into the sea, saying,

"So will Babylon, the great city,
> be thrown down with violence,
> and will never again be found.

[22] And the sound of harpists and musicians
> and flute-players and trumpeters
> will never be heard in you again.
And no craftsman of any craft
> will ever be found in you again.
And the sound of a millstone
> will never be heard in you again.

[23] And the light of a lamp
> will never shine in you again.
And the voice of the bridegroom and bride
> will never be heard in you again.
For your merchants were the great men of the earth,
> because all the nations were deceived by your sorcery.

[24] And in her was found the blood of prophets and of saints,
> and of all who have been slain on the earth."

---

seafarers *Greek* all who sail to a place], Minor[all the company in ships (KJV, ~NIV, ~NKJ, ~TLB)].

18:18 Alx/Byz[**were crying out**], Minor[cried out (ASV, DRA, ESV, JNT, KJV, MRD, NAB, ~NIV, NKJ, ~NLT, NRS, REB, RSV, TEV)].

18:19 Alx/Byz[**were crying out**], Minor[cried out (ASV, DRA, KJV, MRD, NAB, ~NIV, NKJ, REB, TEV)], Alt[*without textual foundation omits* (~JNT, ~NJB, ~TLB)]; Alx/Byz[**saying**], Major[and saying (MRD, NJB, NKJ, TLB)], Alt[*without textual foundation omits* (~ESV, ~HCS, ~NAB, ~NET, ~NIV, ~NLT, ~NRS, ~REB, ~RSV)]; Alx/Byz[**the ships**], Minor[ships (DRA, ESV, HCS, ~JNT, KJV, MRD, NAB, NAS, NAU, NET, NIV, NJB, NKJ, ~NLT, NRS, REB, RSV, TEV)], Alt[*without textual foundation omits* (~TLB)].

18:20 Alx/Byz[**you saints and you apostles**], Minor[you holy apostles (DRA, KJV, ~NJB, NKJ, ~REB)], Alt[you angels and apostles (MRD)].

18:22 Alx/Byz[**of any craft**], Minor[*omits*].

18:23 Alx/Byz[**for your merchants**], Minor[*omits* for (NIV, NJB, REB, TEV, TLB)].

18:24 Alx[**blood** *singular*], Byz[blood *plural*].

19

¹ After these things I heard what sounded like the loud voice of a great multitude in heaven, crying,

"Hallelujah!

Salvation and glory and power belong to our God,

²   for his judgments are true and just.

He has judged the great harlot

     who corrupted the earth with her fornication,

and he has avenged

     the blood of his servants at her hand."

³ And again they said,

"Hallelujah!

The smoke from her goes up for ever and ever."

⁴ And the twenty-four elders and the four living creatures fell down and worshipped God who is seated on the throne, saying,

"Amen. Hallelujah!"

⁵ And a voice came from the throne, saying,

"Praise our God,

     all you his servants,

[and] you who fear him,

     small and great."

⁶ Then I heard what sounded like the voice of a great multitude, like the sound of many waters and like the sound of mighty peals of thunder, crying,

"Hallelujah!

For the Lord

     [our] God the Almighty reigns.

⁷ Let us rejoice and be glad

     and give him the glory!

For the marriage of the Lamb has come,

     and his bride has made herself ready.

⁸ It was given to her to clothe herself in fine linen,

     bright clean";

for the fine linen is the righteous acts of the saints.

⁹ Then the angel said to me, "Write, 'Blessed are those who are invited to the marriage supper of the Lamb.'" And he said to me, "These are true words of God." ¹⁰

19:1 Alx/Byz[**After these things**], Minor[And after these things (KJV, MRD)]; Alx/Byz[**what sounded like** or as it were], Minor[omits (KJV, MRD, NKJ, TLB)]; Alx/Byz[**glory and power**], Major[power and glory], Minor[glory and honor and power (KJV, NKJ) others power and glory and honor (MRD)], Alt[*without textual foundation* honor and power (~TLB)]; Alx/Byz[**belong to our God**], Minor[to the Lord our God (KJV, ~NKJ)].

19:2 Alx[**corrupted**], Byz[utterly corrupted]; **servants** *Greek* slaves.

19:3 Alx/Byz[**again they said**], Major[again one said or a second one said].

19:4 Alx/Major[**twenty-four**], Byz[twenty and four (~ASV, ~DRA, ~KJV)].

19:5 Alx/Byz[**from the throne**], Minor[out of the throne (~DRA, KJV, ~MRD, TLB)]; Alx/Byz[**and you who fear**], Minor[omits and (ASV, ESV, HCS, JNT, NAS, NAU, NIV, NLT, REB, RSV, TLB)]; Alx/Byz[**small and great**], Minor[both small and great (HCS, KJV, NET, NIV, NKJ, REB, ~TEV)]; **servants** *Greek* slaves.

19:6 Alx/Major[**Lord our God**], Byz[omits our (JNT, KJV, NKJ)]; Alx/Byz[**Almighty**], Minor[All Mighty (~JNT, ~NET, REB)].

19:7 Alx/Byz[**Let us...and give**], Minor[Let us...and we will give].

19:8 Alx/Byz[**bright clean**], Major[bright and clean (ASV, DRA, ESV, HCS, JNT, MRD, NAS, NAU, NIV, NRS, REB, RSV)], Minor[clean and bright (KJV, NKJ, ~TEV, TLB)].

Then I fell at his feet to worship him, but he said to me, "You must not do that! I am a fellow servant with you and your brothers who hold the testimony of Jesus. Worship God. For the testimony of Jesus is the spirit of prophecy."

11 Then I saw heaven opened, and behold, a white horse! He who sat on it is [called] Faithful and True, and in righteousness he judges and makes war. 12 His eyes are [as] a flame of fire, and on his head are many diadems. And he has a name written on him which no one knows but himself. 13 He is clothed in a robe dipped in blood, and his name has been called the Word of God. 14 The armies [which were] in heaven were following him, riding on white horses, and dressed in fine linen, shining clean. 15 From his mouth comes a sharp sword with which to strike down the nations, and he will *rule them with a rod of iron*. He treads the wine press of the fury of the wrath of God the Almighty. 16 And he has on his robe and on his thigh a name written,

KING OF KINGS AND LORD OF LORDS.

17 Then I saw one angel standing in the sun, and [in] a loud voice he cried to all the birds that fly in mid-heaven, "Come, gather for the great supper of God, 18 so that you may eat the flesh of kings, the flesh of captains, and the flesh of mighty men, the flesh of horses and their riders, and the flesh of all men, both free and slave, both small and great." 19 And I saw the beast and the kings of the earth with their armies gathered to make war against him who sits on the horse and against his army. 20 And the beast was captured, and with him the false prophet who had performed the signs in his presence, by which he deceived those who had received the mark of the beast and those who worshipped his image. These two were thrown alive into the lake of fire which burns with sulfur. 21 And the rest were killed with the sword that came from the mouth of him who sat on the horse, and all the birds were gorged with their flesh.

19:9 **the angel** *Greek* he.

19:10 **servant** *Greek* slave; **of Jesus** *or* to Jesus.

19:11 Alx/Byz[**called**], Minor[*omits*].

19:12 Alx/Byz[**as**], Major[*omits* (ASV, NAS, NAU, NJB)]; Alx[**a name written**], Byz[names written, and a name written (MRD)].

19:13 Alx/Byz[**dipped in**], Minor[sprinkled with (ASV, DRA, MRD) *others* sprinkled around with (~TEV)]; Alx/Byz[**his name has been called**], Major[his name is called (ASV, DRA, ESV, HCS, JNT, KJV, MRD, NAS, NAU, NET, ~NIV, ~NJB, NKJ, NRS, RSV, TEV)].

19:14 Alx/Byz[**which were in heaven**], Minor[in heaven (ESV, JNT, MRD, NAB, NIV, NJB, NKJ, NLT, NRS, REB, RSV, TEV, TLB)]; Alx/Byz[**shining clean**], Minor[shining and clean (ASV, DRA, ESV, JNT, KJV, MRD, NAS, NAU, NIV, NKJ, NRS, REB, RSV, TLB)].

19:15 Alx[**a sharp sword**], Byz[a sharp two edged sword (DRA, MRD)]; Alx/Byz[**fury of the wrath**], Minor[fury and the wrath (KJV, NAB, NKJ)], Alt/Peshitta[*omits* fury of (MRD)]; **rule** *or* shepherd; Psalms 2:9.

19:16 Alx/Byz[**a name written**], Minor[the name written (~NIV, ~NLT, ~REB, TEV, ~TLB)], Alt/Vulgate[written (DRA)], Alt[*without textual foundation* the words written (~MRD)].

19:17 Alx/Byz[**one angel**], Major[an angel (ASV, DRA, ESV, HCS, JNT, KJV, MRD, NAB, NAS, NAU, NIV, NJB, NKJ, NLT, NRS, REB, RSV, TEV, TLB)]; Alx/Byz[**in a loud voice**], Major[with a loud voice (ASV, DRA, ESV, KJV, MRD, NAS, NAU, ~NJB, NKJ, ~NLT, NRS, ~REB, RSV, TLB)]; Alx/Byz[**Come, gather**], Minor[Come and gather (ASV, KJV, NKJ, TEV)]; Alx/Byz[**great supper of God**], Minor[supper of the great God (KJV, NKJ, TLB)]; **in mid-heaven** *or* at the zenith (*i.e. directly overhead*).

19:18 Alx/Byz[**both free and slave**], Minor[*omits* both (DRA, JNT, MRD, NAB, NIV, NJB, NKJ, REB, TEV, TLB)]; Alx[**both small and great** *or* and small and great], Byz[and both small and great].

19:19 Alx/Byz[**their armies gathered**], Minor[his armies gathered].

19:20 Alx[**and with him the false prophet**], Byz[and the false prophet that was with him (MRD)].

20

¹ Then I saw an angel coming down from heaven, holding in his hand the key of the abyss and a great chain. ² And he seized the dragon, the ancient serpent, who is the Devil and Satan, and bound him for a thousand years. ³ And he threw him into the abyss, and shut it and sealed it over him, so that he might not deceive the nations any more, until the thousand years were ended. After these things he must be released for a short time.

⁴ Then I saw thrones, and seated on them were those to whom judgment was given. Also I saw the souls of those who had been beheaded because of their testimony of Jesus and because of the word of God, and who had not worshipped the beast or his image and had not received its mark on the forehead and on their hand. They came to life, and reigned with Christ a thousand years. ⁵ The rest of the dead did not come to life until the thousand years were ended. This is the first resurrection. ⁶ Blessed and holy is the one who has a part in the first resurrection. Over these the second death has no power, but they will be priests of God and of Christ and will reign with him for [the] thousand years.

⁷ And when the thousand years are finished, Satan will be released from his prison ⁸ and will come out to deceive the nations which are at the four corners of the earth, that is, Gog and Magog, to gather them into the war. Their number is like the sand of the seashore. ⁹ And they marched up over the broad plain of the earth and surrounded the camp of the saints and the beloved city. But fire came down from heaven and devoured them. ¹⁰ And the devil who had deceived them was thrown into the lake of fire and sulfur where both the beast and the false prophet were. And they will be tormented day and night for ever and ever.

¹¹ Then I saw a great white throne and him who sat upon it. From his presence earth and sky fled away, and no place was found for them. ¹² And I saw the dead, great and small, standing before the throne. And books were opened. Also another was opened, which is the book of life. And the dead were judged by what was written in the books,

---

20:2 Alx/Byz[**the ancient serpent**], Minor[*omits* serpent]; Alx[**the Devil and Satan**], Byz[*adds* the deceiver of the world], Major[*adds* the deceiver of the whole world (MRD)].

20:3 Alx/Byz[**shut it**], Minor[shut him (DRA, KJV, ~MRD, NKJ)]; Alx/Byz[**After these things**], Major[And after these things (DRA, KJV, ~MRD, NKJ)].

20:4 Alx/Major[**on the forehead and on their hand**], Byz[on their forehead and on their hand (ASV, DRA, ESV, HCS, JNT, KJV, NAS, NAU, NIV, NKJ, NLT, NRS, ~REB, RSV, TEV, TLB)]; Alx/Byz[**a thousand years**], Major[the thousand years].

20:5 Alx[**The rest of the dead**], Byz[And the rest of the dead], Minor[But the rest of the dead (KJV, NKJ, ~REB)]; Alx/Byz[**come to life**], Minor[come to life again (KJV, NKJ, NLT, TLB)]; Alx/Byz[**The rest of the dead did not come to life until the thousand years were ended**], Alt/Peshitta[*omits* (MRD)].

20:6 Alx[**the thousand**], Byz[a thousand (ASV, DRA, ESV, HCS, KJV, NAS, NAU, NET, NIV, NJB, NKJ, NLT, NRS, RSV, TEV, TLB)].

20:7 Alx/Byz[**And when the thousand are finished**], Minor[And after the thousand years (TEV)].

20:8 Alx/Byz[**into the war**], Minor[*omits* the (DRA, ESV, HCS, KJV, MRD, NAB, NIV, NJB, NKJ, NLT, NRS, REB, RSV, TEV, TLB)]; Alx/Byz[**their number**], Major[the number (~NJB, ~NLT, ~REB, ~TEV, ~TLB)]; *Vulgate and DRA include this verse in verse 7.*

20:9 Alx/Byz[**And they marched...beloved city, but fire**], Alt/Vulgate[8 And they marched...beloved city, 9 but fire (DRA)]; Alx[**from heaven**], Byz[out of heaven from God], Minor[from God out of heaven (DRA, KJV, MRD, NKJ, TLB)].

20:10 Alx/Byz[**10...both the beast** *or* 10...also the beast], Minor[*omits* both (ESV, HCS, JNT, KJV, NAB, NAS, NAU, NET, NIV, NJB, NKJ, ~NLT, NRS, REB, RSV, ~TEV, TLB)]; Alt/Vulgate[both the beast 10 (DRA)].

20:12 Alx/Byz[**great and small**], Minor[small and great (KJV, NKJ)]; Alx/Byz[**before the throne**], Minor[before God (KJV, NKJ, ~NLT, TLB)]; Alx/Byz[**and books were opened**], Minor[and they opened books].

according to what they had done. ¹³ The sea gave up the dead which were in it. And death and Hades gave up the dead which were in them. And all were judged according to what they had done. ¹⁴ Then death and Hades were thrown into the lake of fire. This is the second death, the lake of fire. ¹⁵ And if anyone's name was not found written in the book of life, he was thrown into the lake of fire.

21 ¹ Then I saw a new heaven and a new earth. For the first heaven and the first earth had departed, and there was no longer any sea. ² And I saw the holy city, new Jerusalem, coming down out of heaven from God, prepared as a bride adorned for her husband. ³ And I heard a loud voice out of the throne saying, "Behold, the dwelling of God is with men. And he will dwell with them, and they shall be his peoples, and God himself will be with them [as their God]. ⁴ He will wipe away every tear from their eyes, and death will be no more. Neither will there be mourning nor crying nor pain any more, [for] the former things have passed away."

⁵ And he who sits on the throne said, "Behold, I am making all things new." And he said, "Write this, for these words are trustworthy and true." ⁶ Then he said to me, "They have come to pass. I [am] the Alpha and the Omega, the beginning and the end. I will give to the one who is thirsty from the spring of the water of life without cost. ⁷ He who overcomes will inherit these things, and I will be his God and he will be my son. ⁸ But the cowardly and faithless and abominable and murderers and fornicators and sorcerers and idolaters and all the liars – their lot will be in the lake that burns with fire and sulfur, which is the second death."

20:¹³ Alx/Byz[**the dead...the dead**], Minor[dead...dead (~HCS, ~NAB, ~NLT, ~TEV, ~TLB)]; Alx/Byz[**and death and Hades**], Alt[14 and death and Hades (NJB)]; Alx/Byz[**what they had done**], Minor[what he had done (JNT, MRD, NET, NIV, NJB *verse 14*, NKJ, REB, TLB)].

20:¹⁴ Alx/Major[**This is the second death, the lake of fire**], Byz[This is the second death (DRA, KJV, NKJ)].

21:¹ Alx/Byz[**the first earth had departed**], Minor[the first earth had passed away (ASV, ESV, HCS, JNT, KJV, MRD, NAB, NAS, NAU, NET, NIV, NKJ, NRS, RSV)].

21:² Alx/Byz[**And I saw**], Minor[And I, John, saw (DRA, KJV, NKJ, TLB)].

21:³ Alx[**out of the throne**], Byz[out of heaven (KJV, MRD, NKJ)]; Alx[**his peoples**], Byz[his people (DRA, ESV, HCS, JNT, KJV, MRD, NAB, NAS, NAU, NET, NIV, NJB, NKJ, NLT, REB, RSV, TEV, TLB)]; Alx[**as their God**], Byz[omits (NAS, NAU, NET, NLT, NRS, REB, RSV, TLB)]; **dwelling** *or* tent *Greek* tabernacle; **will dwell** *Greek* will tabernacle.

21:⁴ Alx/Major[**he will wipe away**], Byz[God will wipe away (DRA, KJV, NKJ) *others add* from them]; Alx/Byz[**for**], Minor[omits (ASV, NAS, NAU, NJB, NLT, TEV, TLB)].

21:⁵ Alx[**And he said**], Byz[adds to me (DRA, KJV, NET, NKJ, NLT, TEV, TLB)], Alt[*without textual foundation* omits (~NJB)]; Alx/Byz[**for these words**], Minor[adds of God (MRD)]; Alx/Byz[**trustworthy and true**], Major[true and trustworthy (JNT, KJV, NKJ, TEV)].

21:⁶ Alx[**They have come to pass**], Byz[I have become], Minor[It has come to be (DRA, ESV, HCS, JNT, KJV, NAS, NAU, NET, NIV, NJB, NKJ, NLT, NRS, REB, RSV, TEV, TLB)], Alt[*without textual foundation* omits (~MRD)]; Alx[**I am**], Minor[I], Major[omits]; Alx/Major[the Alpha *word* and the Omega *letter*], Byz[the Alpha *letter* and the Omega *letter*]; Alx/Byz[**the beginning**], Minor[and the beginning].

21:⁷ Alx/Major[**He who overcomes will inherit**], Byz[He who overcomes will have (~JNT, ~TEV)]; Alx/Byz[**these things**], Minor[all things (KJV, ~NIV, NKJ, ~NLT, ~TLB)].

21:⁸ Alx/Byz[**faithless**], Major[adds and sinners (MRD)]; Alx[**with fire**], Byz[in fire (~NJB, ~NLT)].

⁹ And one from the seven angels, who had the seven bowls which were full of the seven last plagues, came and spoke with me, saying, "Come, I will show you the Bride, the wife of the Lamb." ¹⁰ And he carried me away in the Spirit to a great and high mountain, and showed me the holy city, Jerusalem, coming down out of heaven from God, ¹¹ having the glory of God. Its brilliance was like that of a very precious jewel, like a jasper, clear as crystal. ¹² It had a great, high wall, with twelve gates, and at the gates twelve angels. And names were written on the gates, which are [the names] of the twelve tribes of the sons of Israel. ¹³ On the east there were three gates. And on the north three gates. And on the south three gates. And on the west three gates. ¹⁴ And the wall of the city had twelve foundations, and on them twelve names, of the twelve apostles of the Lamb.

¹⁵ The one who talked with me had a measuring rod of gold to measure the city, and its gates and its walls. ¹⁶ The city is laid out as a square, and its length is [even] as great as its width. And he measured the city with the rod, twelve thousand stadia. Its length and width and height are equal. ¹⁷ He also measured its wall, a hundred and forty-four cubits by a man's measure, which is also an angel's. ¹⁸ The wall was made of jasper, and the city of pure gold, as clear as a crystal. ¹⁹ The foundations of the city wall were adorned with every kind of precious stone. The first foundation was jasper, the second sapphire, the third chalcedony, the fourth emerald, ²⁰ the fifth sardonyx, the sixth carnelian, the seventh chrysolite, the eighth beryl, the ninth topaz, the tenth chrysoprase, the eleventh jacinth, and the twelfth amethyst. ²¹ And the twelve gates were twelve pearls,

---

21:9 Alx/Major[**from the seven angels**], Byz[of the seven angels (ASV, DRA, ESV, HCS, JNT, KJV, MRD, NAB, NAS, NAU, NET, NIV, NJB, NKJ, NLT, NRS, REB, RSV, TEV, TLB)]; Alx/Byz[**which were full of the seven last plagues**], Major[full of the seven last plagues (DRA, ESV, HCS, JNT, KJV, MRD, NAB, NAS, NAU, NET, NIV, NJB, NKJ, NLT, NRS, REB, RSV, TEV, TLB)]; Alx/Byz[**came and spoke with me**], Minor[came to me and spoke with me (~JNT, KJV, NKJ, ~TEV)]; Alx/Byz[**the Bride, the wife of the Lamb**], Major[the wife, the Bride of the Lamb], Minor[the Bride of the Lamb, the wife (~KJV, ~NJB, ~NKJ, ~TLB)].

21:10 Alx/Byz[**the holy city, Jerusalem**], Major[the great city, the holy Jerusalem (KJV, NKJ)]; **in the Spirit** *or* in the spirit.

21:11 Alx/Byz[**the glory of God. Its brilliance**], Minor[the glory of God, and its brilliance (DRA, KJV, NIV, NJB, NLT, NRS, TLB)].

21:12 Alx/Byz[**It had** *Greek* having], Minor[And it had *Greek* and having (DRA, KJV, MRD, NKJ)]; Alx/Byz[**and at the gates twelve angels**], Minor[*omits* (MRD)]; Alx/Byz[**and names were written on the gates**], Minor[and their names were written on the gates]; Alx/Byz[**and names...which are the names of the twelve tribes**], Minor[and names...which are the twelve tribes (~ESV, ~JNT, NAS, ~NET, ~NIV, ~NJB, ~NLT, ~NRS, ~REB, ~RSV, ~TEV, ~TLB)].

21:13 Alx/Byz[**and on the north**], Minor[*omits* and (ESV, HCS, JNT, KJV, MRD, NAB, NET, NIV, NJB, NKJ, NLT, NRS, REB, RSV, TEV, TLB)]; Alx/Byz[**and on the south**], Minor[*omits* and (ESV, HCS, JNT, KJV, MRD, NAB, NET, NIV, NJB, NKJ, NLT, NRS, REB, RSV, TEV, TLB)]; Alx/Byz[**and on the west**], Minor[*omits* and].

21:14 Alx/Byz[**on them**], Minor[in them (DRA, KJV, ~NJB)]; Alx/Byz[**twelve names**], Minor[the twelve names (DRA, ESV, HCS, JNT, MRD, NAB, NAS, NAU, NET, NRS, RSV) *others* the names (KJV, NIV, NJB, NKJ, NLT, REB, TEV, TLB)].

21:15 Alx/Byz[**a measuring rod of gold**], Minor[*omits* measuring (KJV, NKJ)].

21:16 Alx/Byz[**even**], Major[*omits* (ASV, DRA, ESV, HCS, JNT, KJV, MRD, NAS, NAU, NET, NIV, NJB, NKJ, NLT, NRS, REB, RSV, TEV, TLB)]; Alx/Byz[**as great**], Minor[so great]; Alx/Byz[**its length and width and height are equal**], Major[its length and width and height are an equal twelve]; **twelve thousand stadia** *about 1,400 miles.*

21:17 Alx/Byz[**He also measured its wall, a hundred and forty-four**], Minor[And its wall was a hundred and forty-four (REB)]; **hundred and forty-four cubits** *about 200 feet.*

21:19 Alx/Byz[**The foundations**], Minor[And the foundations (DRA, KJV, MRD, ~TLB)].

each of the gates made of a single pearl. And the street of the city was pure gold, like a transparent crystal.

²² And I saw no temple in the city, for the Lord God Almighty and the Lamb are its temple. ²³ And the city has no need of the sun or of the moon to brighten it, for the glory of God gives it light, and its lamp is the Lamb. ²⁴ And the nations will walk by its light, and the kings of the earth will bring their glory into it. ²⁵ In the daytime (for there will be no night there) its gates will never be shut. ²⁶ They will bring into it the glory and the honor of the nations. ²⁷ Nothing unclean will ever enter it, nor any [one who] practices abomination or falsehood, but only those whose names are written in the Lamb's book of life.

22 ¹ Then he showed me a river of the water of life, clear as crystal, flowing from the throne of God and of the Lamb, ² through the middle of the street of the city; also, on either side of the river, the tree of life bearing twelve kinds of fruit, yielding its fruit each month. And the leaves of the tree were for the healing of the nations. ³ There will no longer be any curse. And the throne of God and of the Lamb will be in it, and his servants will serve him. ⁴ They will see his face, and his name will be on their foreheads. ⁵ And there will be no more night. And they will not need the light of a lamp or the light of the sun, for the Lord God will give light to them; and they will reign for ever and ever.

⁶ And he said to me, "These words are trustworthy and true. And the Lord, the God of the spirits of the prophets, has sent his angel to show his servants the things which must soon take place."

⁷ "And behold, I am coming soon. Blessed is he who keeps the words of the prophecy of this book."

⁸ And I, John, am the one who heard and saw these things. And when I heard and saw them, I fell down to worship at the feet of the angel who showed them to me. ⁹ But he

---

21:23 Alx/Byz[**to brighten it**], Minor[to shine in it (DRA, KJV, NKJ)].

21:24 Alx/Byz[**And the nations**], Minor[*adds* of those who are saved (KJV, MRD, NKJ)]; Alx/Byz[**will walk by its light**], Minor[will walk in its light (~ASV, HCS, KJV, NKJ, NLT)]; Alx[**will bring their glory**], Byz[will bring their glory and honor (DRA, KJV, NKJ)], Major[will bring him the glory and honor of the nations (~MRD)].

21:26 Alx/Byz[**glory and honor of the nations**], Minor[*adds* that they may come in].

21:27 Alx[**unclean**], Byz[defiling (KJV, NKJ, ~NLT, ~TLB)]; Alx/Byz[**one who practices**], Major[thing that causes (DRA, KJV, MRD, NKJ)].

22:1 Alx/Byz[**a river**], Major[a pure river (KJV, NKJ, ~TLB)].

22:2 Alx/Byz[**yielding its fruit each month**], Minor[yielding its fruit once each month (~MRD, NAB, NJB, REB, TEV)].

22:3 Alx/Byz[**There will no longer be any curse**], Minor[There will not be any curse there (~NJB, ~REB, ~TEV, ~TLB)]; **servants** *Greek* slaves.

22:5 Alx/Byz[**no more night**], Major[no night there (KJV, ~NJB, NKJ, NLT, TLB)], Minor[no night]; Alx/Major[**not need** *Greek* not have a need], Byz[not need]; Alx[**the light of a lamp**], Byz[a lamp (KJV, NKJ, NLT, TEV, TLB)]; Alx/Byz[**the light of the sun**], Minor[a light]; Alx[**will give light to them**], Byz[will give them light (ASV, DRA, ESV, HCS, JNT, NAB, NAS, NAU, NLT, ~NRS, REB, ~RSV, ~TEV, ~TLB)], Minor[gives them light (KJV, MRD, NKJ)].

22:6 Alx[**And he said to me**], Byz[And he says to me]; Alx/Byz[**the spirits of the prophets**], Minor[the holy prophets (KJV, NKJ, ~TLB)].

22:7 Alx/Byz[**And behold**], Minor[Behold (HCS, JNT, KJV, NAB, NET, NIV, NKJ, NLT, NRS, TEV)], Alt[*without textual foundation omits* (~NJB, ~REB, ~TLB)].

22:8 Alx/Byz[**the one who heard and saw these things**], Minor[the one who saw and heard these things (KJV, NKJ, TLB)]; Alx/Byz[**when I heard and saw them**], Minor[when I heard and when I saw them], Alt[*without textual foundation omits* (~TLB)].

22:9 Alx/Byz[**Do not do that! I am a fellow servant**], Minor[Do not do that, for I am a fellow servant

said to me, "Do not do that! I am a fellow servant with you and your brothers the prophets, and with those who keep the words of this book. Worship God." [10] And he said to me, "Do not seal up the words of the prophecy of this book, for the time is near. [11] He who does wrong, let him do wrong still. And he who is filthy, let him be made filthy still. And the righteous, let him do righteousness still. And he who is holy, let him be holy still."

[12] "Behold, I am coming soon. And my reward is with me, to render to every man according to what he is doing. [13] I am the Alpha and the Omega, the first and the last, the beginning and the end."

[14] Blessed are those who wash their robes, so that they may have the right to the tree of life, and may enter by the gates into the city. [15] Outside are the dogs and the sorcerers and the immoral persons and the murderers and the idolaters, and everyone who loves and practices falsehood.

[16] "I, Jesus, have sent my angel to give you this testimony for the churches. I am the Root and the Offspring of David, the bright Morning Star." [17] The Spirit and the Bride say, "Come." And let him who hears say, "Come." And let him who is thirsty come; let him who wishes take water of life without price.

[18] I testify to everyone who hears the words of the prophecy of this book: if anyone adds on them, God will add on him the plagues described in this book; [19] and if anyone takes away from the words of the book of this prophecy, God will take away his share from the tree of life and from the holy city, which are described in this book.

(DRA, KJV, NKJ)]; **servant** Greek slave.

22:10 Alx/Byz[**for the time is near**], Minor[because the time is near (HCS, JNT, NET, NIV, NJB, TEV)].

22:11 Alx/Byz[**let him be made filthy**], Minor[let him be filthy (DRA, ESV, KJV, MRD, NAB, NAS, NAU, NET, NIV, NJB, NKJ, NLT, NRS, REB, RSV, TEV, ~TLB)]; Alx/Byz[**let him do righteousness**], Minor[let him be righteous (DRA, ~HCS, KJV, ~NJB, NKJ, ~REB, ~TLB)].

22:12 Alx/Byz[**Behold**], Minor[And behold (KJV, NKJ)]; Alx[**according to what he is doing**], Byz[according to what he will do (KJV)], Alt[without textual foundation according to what he has done (~ESV, ~HCS, ~JNT, ~NAS, ~NAU, ~NET, ~NIV, ~REB, ~RSV, ~TEV, ~TLB)].

22:13 Alx/Major[**the Alpha** word **and the Omega** letter], Byz[the Alpha letter and the Omega letter]; Alx/Major[**the first and the last, the beginning and the end**], Byz[the first and the last, beginning and end], Minor[the beginning and the end, the first and the last (KJV, NKJ, TLB)].

22:14 Alx[**wash their robes**], Byz[do his commandments (KJV, MRD, NKJ)].

22:15 Alx/Byz[**Outside are the dogs**], Minor[But outside are the dogs (~KJV, NKJ, TEV)]; Alx/Byz[**loves and practices falsehood**], Minor[practices and loves falsehood].

22:16 Alx/Byz[**for the churches** or because of the churches], Minor[in the churches (DRA, KJV, NKJ, TEV)]; Alx/Byz[**the bright Morning Star**], Minor[the bright and morning star (DRA, KJV, NKJ)]; **you** plural.

22:17 Alx/Major[**let him who wishes**], Byz[and let him who wishes (DRA, KJV, MRD, NAB)]; Alx/Byz[**water of life**], Minor[the water of life (ASV, DRA, ESV, HCS, JNT, KJV, MRD, ~NAB, NAS, NAU, NET, NIV, NJB, NKJ, NLT, NRS, REB, RSV, TEV, TLB)].

22:18 Alx/Byz[**I testify**], Minor[For I confirm (~DRA, ~KJV, ~NKJ)]; Alx/Major[**if anyone adds on them**], Byz[if anyone adds to these things (DRA, KJV, NKJ, ~NLT, ~TLB)]; Alx/Byz[**the plagues**], Minor[the seven plagues].

22:19 Alx/Byz[**God will**], Major[may God]; Alx/Byz[**the tree of life**], Alt/Vulgate[the book of life (DRA, KJV, NKJ) Metzger notes that Erasmus had no Greek source for the last six verses of his Greek New Testament. He translated from the Latin Vulgate to provide the missing verses, and so transferred into his Greek New Testament a Latin transcription error which exists in no Greek source manuscript]; Alx/Byz[**which was described in this book**], Minor[and from the things which are described in this book (DRA, KJV, NKJ)].

20 He who testifies to these things says, "Yes, I am coming soon." Amen. Come, Lord Jesus.

21 The grace of the Lord Jesus be with all.

22:20 Alx[**Come, Lord Jesus**], Byz[Yes, come Lord Jesus (KJV, NKJ)], Minor[*adds* Christ *others add* Christ, with your saints *others add as the end of the book* with all the saints for ever and ever, Amen].

22:21 Alx/Byz[**The grace of the Lord**], Minor[The grace of our Lord (DRA, KJV, MRD, NKJ, TLB) *others omit*]; Alx[**Jesus**], Byz[Jesus Christ (DRA, KJV, MRD, NKJ, TLB)]; Alx[**be with all**], Byz[be with all the saints (HCS, MRD, NRS, RSV)], Minor[be with us all *others* be with you all (DRA, KJV, NJB, NKJ, TLB) *others* be with the saints (ASV) *others* be with your saints *others* be with all his saints (~NIV, ~NLT)]; Alx[**all…**], Byz[*adds* Amen (ASV, DRA, ESV, HCS, KJV, MRD, NAS, NAU, NIV, NJB, NKJ, NRS, RSV, TLB)].

Cross Reference Index

Cross Reference Index: Matthew

01:01 **This section also includes topical notes for: Son of David** - Genesis 5:1, 22:18; 1Chronicles 17:11; Matthew 9:27, 12:23, 15:22, 20:30-31, 21:9, 21:15, 22:42; Mark 10:47-48, 12:35; Luke 18:38-39; Pseudepigrapha[3Enoch 45:5; Psalms of Solomon 17.21; Testament of Solomon 1:7, 20:2]; Apostolic[**Papias Fragment 3:16**]; Archelaus[Disputation with Manes 34]; Clement of Alexandria[Fragments from Eusebius Ecclesiastical History Book VII.6.14; The Instructor Book I.5]; Dionysius of Alexandria[Exegetical Fragments Commentary on the Beginning of Ecclesiastes 1.1]; Irenaeus[Against Heresies Book III.1.1, 11.8, 16.2, 21.5; Demonstration of the Apostolic Preaching 29, 37; Fragments from the Lost Works 29]; Origen[Gospel of John Book I.6]; Tertullian[On the Flesh of Christ 22]

> So Matthew composed the oracles in the Hebrew language and each person interpreted them as best he could. (Papias – Fragment 3:16)

01:01-12 NT-Apocrypha[Protevangelium of James 21]

01:01-14 Pseudepigrapha[Apocalypse of Adam 7:45]

01:01-17 Luke 3:23-38; Rabbinic[Babylonian Yebamot 49b; Mishnah Yebamot 4:13]

01:01-18 Irenaeus[Fragments from the Lost Works 29]

01:02 Genesis 21:2-3, 12, 25:26, 29:35; 1Chronicles 1:34

01:03 Genesis 38:29-30; 1Chronicles 2:4-5, 9; Ruth 4:12, 18-19

01:03-05 Ruth 4:12-22

01:03-06 1Chronicles 2:9-15

01:05 Joshua 2:1

01:06 1Samuel 17:12; 2Samuel 12:24; 1Chronicles 2:13-15; Ruth 4:17, 22

01:06-11 1Chronicles 3:5, 10-16

01:09 Pseudepigrapha[Apocalypse of Zephaniah 3:4]

01:11 2Kings 24:12-16; 2Chronicles 36:10; Ezra 1:32; Jeremiah 27:20; OT-Apocrypha[1Esdras 1:32]

01:11-12 1Chronicles 3:15-17

01:12 1Chronicles 3:13, 19; Ezra 3:2

01:12-16 Irenaeus[Against Heresies Book III.21.9]

01:16 Matthew 27:17, 22; Tertullian[On the Flesh of Christ 20]; NT-Apocrypha[History of Joseph the Carpenter 16]

01:17 Clement of Alexandria[Stromata Book I.21]

01:18 Matthew 1:23-25; Luke 1:27, 35; Pseudepigrapha[2Enoch 71:2; Joseph and Aseneth 21:1]; Irenaeus[Against Heresies Book III.11.8, 16.2]; Methodius[Banquet of the Ten Virgins 11.2]; Victorinus[Apocalypse 4.7-10]

01:18-19 Rabbinic[Babylonian Sotah 3b-4a, 7a]

01:18-21 Pseudepigrapha[Martyrdom and Ascension of Isaiah 11:3-4]

01:18-24 NT-Apocrypha[Gospel of the Nativity of Mary 10]

01:18-25 Luke 1:26-27n, 2:1-7; Pseudepigrapha[Testament of Isaac 3:17; Testament of Solomon 22:20]; Rabbinic[Babylonian (Gittin 90a; Shabbat 104b; Sanhedrin 106a; Yebamot 49b); Mishnah Yebamot 4:13]

01:19 Rabbinic[Exodus Rabba on 1.15, 2.2]; NT-Apocrypha[History of Joseph the Carpenter 5]

01:19-20 NT-Apocrypha[Protoevangelium of James 14.1-2]

01:20 Pseudepigrapha[Testament of Solomon 1:7, 20:2]; Irenaeus[Against Heresies Book III.9.2, 16.2, IV.23.1]; Origen[Against Celsus Book I.66]; Tertullian[On the Flesh of Christ 20]; Epic of Gilgamesh[The Story of the Flood]

01:20-21 Cyprian[Treatise XII.Book II.7]; Gregory Thaumaturgus[Twelve Topics on the Faith 4]

01:20-24 NT-Apocrypha[History of Joseph the Carpenter 6]

01:21 Genesis 17:19; Psalms 130:8; Luke 1:31; Pseudepigrapha[Sibylline Oracles 1.325-329]; Justin[First Apology 33]; Tertullian[Five Books Against Marcion Book IV.7]; NT-Apocrypha[Protoevangelium of James 11.3]

01:23 Isaiah 7:14, 8:8, 10; Matthew 1:25; Luke 1:31, 2:21; Acts 4:12; Ephesians 4:32n; Pseudepigrapha[Testament of Solomon 6:8, 11:6, 15:12]; Rabbinic[Yalqut 766]; Cyprian[Treatise XII.Book II.6]; Irenaeus[Against Heresies Book III.9.2, 21.4; Demonstration of the Apostolic Preaching 54]; Lactantius[Epitome of the Divine Institutes 44]; Novatian[Treatise Concerning the Trinity 24]; Origen[Against Celsus Book I.34]; Tertullian[Against Praxeas 27; An Answer to the Jews 9; On the Flesh of Christ 17, 21; On the Resurrection of the Flesh 20]

01:23-25 Matthew 1:18; Rabbinic[Babylonian (Sotah 11b; Yoma 74b); Exodus Rabba on 1:15, 2:25]

01:24 NT-Apocrypha[Protoevangelium of James 14.2]

01:25 Matthew 1:21; Luke 1:31, 2:21; Pseudepigrapha[Joseph and Aseneth 21:1; Sibylline Oracles 1.325-329]

01:28 Irenaeus[Against Heresies Book III.21.4]

02:01 This section also includes topical notes for: Wise Men - Genesis 24:10; Exodus 36:1-5; Judges 19:1; Esther 1:13; Job 34:2; Psalms 49:10; Daniel 2:13; Matthew 23:34; Luke 1:5, 2:4-7, 3:1; Josephus[Antiquities 17.8.1 191; War 1.33.8 665]; Philo[Every Good Man Is Free (74); On Abraham (132); On the Confusion of Tongues (77-78, 82, 107-109) cf. {Genesis 11:24, 23:4, 47:9, Exodus 2:22}]; Rabbinic[Lamentations Rabba on 1:51]; Justin[First Apology 31, 34]; Tertullian[On Idolatry 9; On the Flesh of Christ 2]; NT-Apocrypha[Epistula Apostolorum 3; Protoevangelium of James 17.1]

02:01-02 Cyprian[Treatise XII.Book II.12, 29]; Hippolytus[Refutation of all Heresies Book VII.15]; Justin[First Apology 18]

02:01-05 NT-Apocrypha[Protoevangelium of James 21.2]

02:01-11 Irenaeus[Demonstration of the Apostolic Preaching 58]; Justin[Dialogue with Trypho 77]

02:01-12 Clement of Alexandria[Stromata Book I.15]; Irenaeus[Against Heresies Book III.16.4; Demonstration of the Apostolic Preaching 58]; Justin[Dialogue with Trypho 88, 106]; Tertullian[An Answer to the Jews 9]; NT-Apocrypha[Arabic Gospel of the Infancy of the Savior 7; Gospel of Pseudo-Matthew 16]

02:01-14 Justin[Dialogue with Trypho 102]

02:01-16 Pseudepigrapha[Sibylline Oracles 1.334-335]

02:01-18 Justin[Dialogue with Trypho 78]

02:01-19 Justin[Dialogue with Trypho 103]

02:01-23 NT-Apocrypha[Acts of Pilate IX.3; Acts of Thomas 1.32]

02:02 Numbers 24:17; Matthew 2:9; Pseudepigrapha[Aristobulus Fragment 4:5; Orphica E and T 31; Sibylline Oracles 8.476, 12.30]; Rabbinic[Deuteronomy Rabba on 1:20; Lamentations Rabba on 2:4]; Tacitus[The Histories 2.78]; Irenaeus[Against Heresies Book III.9.2]; NT-Apocrypha[Protoevangelium of James 21.2]

02:02-10 Pseudepigrapha[Ladder of Jacob 7:19-20; Testament of Judah 24.1; Testament of Levi 18.3]

02:02-11 Matthew 28:17n

02:02-16 Josephus[Antiquities 17.2.4 43-44, 17.6.5-6 174-181]

02:03-06 Tertullian[An Answer to the Jews 13]

02:04-06 Rabbinic[Bereshith Rabba 82 p. 155b cf. {Micah 5:1}]

02:05 John 7:42

02:06 2Samuel 5:2; Micah 5:1-3; 1Chronicles 11:2; Rabbinic[Jerusalem Berakhot 5a]; Irenaeus[Demonstration of the Apostolic Preaching 63]; Origen[Against Celsus Book I.51; De Principiis Book IV.1.5]

02:07-08 NT-Apocrypha[Protoevangelium of James 21.2]

02:09 Genesis 24:7; Matthew 2:2; Hippolytus[The Discourse on the Holy Theophany 3]; NT-Apocrypha[Gospel of the Nazareans Fragment 28; Protoevangelium of James 21.3]

02:10 Isaiah 39:2; Jonah 4:6

02:11 Genesis 24:26, 53; Psalms 72:10-11, 15; Isaiah 60:6; Luke 2:16; Pseudepigrapha[Sibylline Oracles 1.334; Testament of Adam 3.6; Testament of Job 32:10]; Tertullian[On the Flesh of Christ 2]

02:11-12 NT-Apocrypha[Protoevangelium of James 21.3-4]

02:11-16 Peter of Alexandria[Canonical Epistle 13]

02:12 Genesis 24:6; 1Kings 13:9; Matthew 1:20, 2:19, 22; Tacitus[The Histories 4.83-84]; Epic of Gilgamesh[The Story of the Flood]

02:13 Exodus 2:15; 1Kings 11:40; Jeremiah 26:21-23; Archelaus[Disputation with Manes 44 cf. {Exodus 2}]; Origen[Against Celsus Book I.66]; NT-Apocrypha[Papyrus Cairensis 10 735 Recto]

02:13-14 NT-Apocrypha[Arabic Gospel of the Infancy of the Savior 9]

02:13-15 Pseudepigrapha[Lives of the Prophets 2:8]

02:13-23 Rabbinic[Babylonian (Sanhedrin 107b; Shabbat 104; Sotah 47a); Jerusalem (Hagigah ii. 2; Sanhedrin vi. 9)]

02:14 Genesis 45:27; Irenaeus[Against Heresies Book III.21.3]; NT-Apocrypha[Gospel of Pseudo-Matthew 17]

02:14-15 Rabbinic[**Babylonian Sanhedrin 107b**]

When Jannai slew our Rabbis, R. Joshua b. Perahjah (and Jesus) fled to Alexandria. (Talmud -Babylonian Sanhedrin 107b, *The Babylonian Talmud a Translation and Commentary,* **Jacob Neusner; Hendrickson Publishers, Inc., 2005)**

02:15 Numbers 23:22, 24:8; Hosea 11:1; Irenaeus[Against Heresies Book III.9.2]; Justin[Dialogue with Trypho 115]; NT-Apocrypha[Arabic Gospel of the Infancy of the Savior 12; Gospel of the Nazareans Fragment 1]

02:16 Pseudepigrapha[Apocalypse of Daniel 1:10; Greek Apocalypse of Ezra 4:11; Vision of Ezra 38]; Archelaus[Disputation with Manes 44 cf. {Exodus 12}]; Irenaeus[Against Heresies Book III.16.4]; NT-Apocrypha[Apocalypse of Paul 1.26; Gospel of Pseudo-Matthew 17; Protoevangelium of James 22.1]

02:16-18 Tertullian[A Treatise on the Soul 19; On the Flesh of Christ 2]

02:18 Genesis 35:19; Jeremiah 31:15; Hippolytus[Refutation of all Heresies Book V.3]

02:19 Matthew 1:20, 2:12; Rabbinic[Babylonian Sanhedrin 107b]; Epic of Gilgamesh[The Story of the Flood]

02:20 Genesis 46:4; Exodus 4:19; Pseudepigrapha[Sibylline Oracles 1.345]; NT-Apocrypha[Extracts from the Gospel of Pseudo-Matthew 25]

02:21 Epic of Gilgamesh[The Story of the Flood]

02:22 Matthew 2:12; Mark 1:9; Luke 1:26, 2:39; John 1:45-46; Josephus[Antiquities 17.8.1 188]; Tacitus[The Histories 4.83-84]

02:23 Judges 13:5, 7, 16:17; Isaiah 11:1-2, 10, 53:2; Zechariah 3:8, 6:12; Luke 2:39; John 15:2-6n; Acts 3:18n; Pseudepigrapha[Martyrdom and Ascension of Isaiah 11.15; Testament of Judah 24.4-6]; Dead Sea Scrolls[1Q Hymns (1QHODAYOTH [1QH]) COL XIV 15-18]; Rabbinic[Babylonian Berakhot 17b; Sotah 47a]; Origen[Gospel of Matthew Book X.16]; Nag Hammadi[Gospel of Philip 62]; NT-Apocrypha[Gospel of the Nazareans Fragment 1]

03:01 NT-Apocrypha[Gospel of the Ebionites Fragment 2]

03:01-02 Tertullian[On Repentance 2]

03:01-03 Epic of Gilgamesh[The Coming of Enkidu]

03:01-06 Pseudepigrapha[Sibylline Oracles 1.336-4.165]

03:01-17 This section also includes topical notes for: John the Baptist - Mark 1:1-11; Luke 3:1-22; John 1:19-28; Acts 1:5, 22, 10:37, 11:16, 13:24-25, 18:25, 19:3-4; Pseudepigrapha[Sibylline Oracles 1.336-341]; Dead Sea Scrolls[1Q Rule of the Community (1QS) COL VIII 12-16; 4Q Tanhumin (4Q176[4QTANH]) Fragments 1-2 COL I 7-9]; Josephus[Antiquities 18.5.2.118]; Philo[Fragments Extracted From the Parallels of John of Damascus Page 367. D. cf. {2 Kings 10:18-28}; On Dreams, That they Are God-Sent (1.124-1.126) cf. {Genesis 28:11}; On the Contemplative Life Or Suppliants (37-39)]; Clement of Alexandria[Exhortation to the Heathen 1, 9]; Justin[Dialogue with Trypho 49]; Origen[Gospel of John Book II.24-27, 29-30, VI.4-25, 30-32]

03:02 Daniel 2:44; Matthew 4:17, 10:7; Mark 1:15; Constitutions of the Holy Apostles[Book II.55]; Origen[Gospel of Matthew Book X.14, XII.14]

03:03 Isaiah 40:3; Gregory Thaumaturgus[Four Homilies 4]; Irenaeus[Against Heresies Book III.9.1]; Tertullian[On Baptism 6]

03:04 Leviticus 11:21; 2Kings 1:8; Pseudepigrapha[Martyrdom and Ascension of Isaiah 2:10]; NT-Apocrypha[Gospel of the Ebionites Fragment 2]

03:05 Cyprian[Epistle LXXI.1]; NT-Apocrypha[Gospel of the Ebionites Fragment 1-2]

03:05-16 This section also includes topical notes for: Baptism - Exodus 3:1-6, 19:10-14, 30:20-21; Numbers 31:22-23; Joshua 4:14-24; 2 Kings 5:13; Psalms 51:2-6; Isaiah 1:16-18; Matthew 21:25, 28:19; Mark 1:4-5, 8-10, 11:30, 16:6; Luke 3:7-8, 12, 21, 7:29-30, 20:4; John 1:25-26, 28, 31, 33, 3:5, 22-23, 4:1-2, 10:40; Acts 1:5, 22, 2:38, 41, 8:12-13, 16, 36-38, 9:18, 10:37, 46-48, 11:16, 16:14, 15, 33, 18:8, 25, 19:4-5, 22:16; Romans 6:3-4; 1Corinthians 1:13-17, 10:1-2, 12:13, 15:29; Galatians 3:27; Ephesians 4:5, 5:26; Colossians 2:12; Hebrews 6:2; 1Peter 3:18, 21; Pseudepigrapha[4Baruch 6.25; Hellenistic Synagogal Prayers 5.5; Life of Adam and Eve Vita 6.2-3; Odes of Solomon 24.1; Testament of Judah 24.2; Testament of Levi 18.7]; Dead Sea Scrolls[1Q Rule of the Community (1QS) COL III 6-12]; Philo[On Dreams, That they Are God-Sent (2.25) cf. {Numbers 6:1-27}; On the Eternity of the World (111); On

the Life of Moses II (138-139) cf. {Exodus 30:17-21}; On the Unchangeableness of God (8-9) cf.
{Exodus 30:17-21}; Questions And Answers On Genesis II (20, 42) cf. {Genesis 7:17-18, 8:11}];
Rabbinic[Babylonian (Abodah Zarah 24a; Yoma 8b cf. {Ezekiel 36:25; Jeremiah 17:13}; Yebamot 46a,
47b, 48b); Jerusalem Pesahim 36b; Mishnah Negaim 7.1; Mishnah Pesahim 8.8 cf. {Exodus 12:43};
Numbers Rabba on 19.2]; Clement of Alexandria[Exhortation to the Heathen 11; Fragments from
Macarius Chrysocephalus Parable of the Prodigal son 6-7; Stromata Book V.6, 8; The Instructor
Book I.6]; Clement[Recognitions Book IX.7]; Irenaeus[Against Heresies Book I.3.3, 7.2, 15.3, 21.1-5,
23.5, 26.1, 30.12, 14, II.10.2, III.17.2, V.15.3; Fragments from the Lost Works 54]; Justin[Dialogue with
Trypho 12, 14, 18-19, 29, 44, 51, 88, 103, 138; First Apology 61, 65-66; On the Resurrection 8]; Liturgy
of James 32; Theodotus[Excerpts 7-8]; Nag Hammadi[A Valentinian Exposition 40-42; Apocalypse
of Adam 85; Apocryphon of John 31; Exegesis of the Soul 131-132; Gospel of Philip 57, 61, 65, 69, 73,
75, 77; Gospel of the Egyptians III 63; On the Origin of the World 122; Testimony of Truth 69;
Trimorphic Protennoia 45, 48; Tripartite Tractate 127-128; Zostrianos 5, 15]; NT-Apocrypha[Epistula
Apostolorum 42; Gospel of Judas 55; Oxyrhynchus Papyrus 840]

03:06 Tertullian[On Baptism 20]

03:07 This section also includes topical notes for: Offspring of Vipers – Matthew 12:34, 23:33-35n,
Luke 3:7, 21:23; Romans 1:18, 2:5, 5:9; Ephesians 5:6; Colossians 3:6; 1Thessalonians 1:10; Revelation
6:16-17; Pseudepigrapha[Sibylline Oracles 1.370-371, 8.1]; Dead Sea Scrolls[1Q Hymns
(1QHODAYOTH [1QH]) COL XIII 9-11; Damascus Document (CD-A) COL VIII 8-13, (CD-B) COL
XIX 14-24]; Philo[Special Laws III (103)]; Clement of Alexandria[Exhortation to the Heathen 1];
Hippolytus[Refutation of all Heresies Book IX.23-24; The Discourse on the Holy Theophany 3];
Irenaeus[Against Heresies Book III.9.1]; Origen[Gospel of John Book VI.14]; Nag
Hammadi[Authoritative Teaching 33; Book of Thomas the Contender 141]; NT-Apocrypha[Acts of
Paul in Philippi 3.38; Gospel of the Ebionites Fragment 2]

03:07-08 Archelaus[Disputation with Manes 32]; Origen[Gospel of John Book VI.13]

03:07-09 Justin[Dialogue with Trypho 44]; Tertullian[A Treatise on the Soul 21]

03:07-10 Matthew 7:16-21n; Josephus[Antiquities 18.5.2 116-119]

03:07-12 Tertullian[On Baptism 10]

03:08 Acts 3:19n; Rabbinic[Avot 5.22]; Gregory Thaumaturgus[Four Homilies 1]

03:09 John 8:33, 37, 39; Romans 4:12; Clement of Alexandria[Exhortation to the Heathen 1];
Cyprian[Epistle LXII.4]; Irenaeus[Against Heresies Book IV.7.2, 25.1, 39.3, V.34.1; Demonstration of
the Apostolic Preaching 93]; Tertullian[Against Hermogenes 12; On Modesty 20; On Monogamy 6];
Linguistics[The Hebrew word for "Stones" (אבן) is a pun for "Children" (בן)]

03:10 Matthew 7:19; Luke 13:7, 9; John 15:6; Pseudepigrapha[Apocalypse of Adam 6:2]; Clement of
Alexandria[Who is the Rich Man that shall be Saved 29]; Cyprian[Treatise XII.Book III.26; Treatises
Attributed to Cyprian On the Glory of Martyrdom 27]; Hippolytus[Refutation of all Heresies Book
V.3, 11]; Irenaeus[Against Heresies Book IV.8.3, 36.4, V.17.4; Fragments from the Lost Works 30];
Origen[Gospel of John Book VI.14]; Tertullian[On Exhortation to Chastity 6; On Repentance 4; The
Chaplet, or De Corona 13]; Nag Hammadi[Gospel of Philip 83; Gospel of Thomas 40]; NT-
Apocrypha[6Ezra 17.78; Epistula Apostolorum 28]; Epic of Gilgamesh[The Forest Journey]

03:10-12 Philo[**(On Husbandry 9-10)**]

> What can man be but the kind that is in every one of us, which is accustomed to reap the
> advantage from all that is sown or planted? But since milk is the food of infants, but
> cakes made of wheat are the food of full grown men, so also the soul must have a milk-
> like nourishment in its age of childhood, namely, the elementary instruction of
> encyclical science. But the perfect food which is fit for men consists of explanations
> dictated by prudence, and temperance, and every virtue. For these things being sown and
> implanted in the mind will bring forth most advantageous fruit, namely, good and
> praiseworthy actions. By means of this husbandry, all the trees of the passions and vices,
> which shoot forth and grow up to a height, bringing forth pernicious fruits, are rooted
> up, and cut down, and cleared away, so that not even the smallest fragment of them is
> left, from which any new shoots of evil actions can subsequently spring up. (Philo - On
> Husbandry 9-10)]

03:11 Amos 7:4; Matthew 11:3; John 1:15, 26, 31, 33; Acts 1:5, 11:16, 13:24-25, 19:4; Anonymous[Treatise
on Re-Baptism 2]; Cyprian[Treatise XII.Book I.12]; Hippolytus[The Discourse on the Holy

Theophany 3]; Irenaeus[Against Heresies Book IV.4.3]; Origen[Gospel of John Book VI.16]; Epic of Gilgamesh[The Coming of Enkidu]

03:11-12 This section also includes topical notes for: Baptism of Fire - Genesis 15:17; Exodus 19:18; Isaiah 4:2-5; Luke 3:16-17; Acts 2:3; 1Corinthians 12:13-15; Revelation 20:9-15; Pseudepigrapha[4Ezra 16.4-10; Apocalypse of Elijah 5.22-24, 5.37-38; Sibylline Oracles 1.350]; Dead Sea Scrolls[1Q Hymns (1QHODAYOTH [1QH]) COL IX 28-36, XIV 17-18; 1Q Micah Pesher (1Q14[1QPMIC]) Fragments 2-5; 1Q Zephaniah Pesher (1Q15[1QPZEPH]) 2-5; 4Q Catena(4Q177[4QCATENA]) COL III (Fragments 2+24+14+3+4+1+31) 6-7; 4Q Isaiah Pesher (4Q163[4QIS]) Fragments 4-6 COL I 14-16; 4Q Nahum Pesher (4Q169[4QPNAH]) Fragments 1 & 2 10-11]; Philo[On Dreams, That they Are God-Sent (2.212-2.214) cf. {Genesis 40:19, Revelation 19:17-21}; On Husbandry (17-20) cf. {Genesis 9:20, Deuteronomy 20:20}; On Rewards And Punishments (153-157) cf. {Leviticus 26:14-39, Revelation 20:9}; Questions And Answers On Genesis III (15) cf. {Genesis 15:9-20, 1Corinthians 3:12-15}; The Decalogue (48-49) cf. {Exodus 19:16-19}]; Rabbinic[Babylonian (Abodah Zarah 3b-4a; Sanhedrin 39b cf. {Numbers 31:23, Isaiah 66:15})]; Hippolytus[Refutation of all Heresies Book IX.22-23]; Irenaeus[Against Heresies Book I.7.1, V.18.3, 29.2]; Theodotus[Excerpts 25]; Nag Hammadi[Gospel of Philip 67; Gospel of Thomas 10]

03:12 Matthew 13:30; Pseudepigrapha[4Ezra 9.13-23]; Dead Sea Scrolls[1Q Zephaniah Pesher (1Q15[1QPZEPH]) 2-5]; Apostolic[1Clement 56:15]; Clement of Alexandria[The Instructor Book I.9]; Clement[Recognitions Book III.38]; Hippolytus[Refutation of all Heresies Book V.4]; Irenaeus[Against Heresies Book IV.33.1, 11, V.28.4, 29.1]; Tertullian[De Fuga in Persecutione 1; On Prescription Against Heretics 3; On Repentance 4; To his Wife Book I.6]; Nag Hammadi[Authoritative Teaching 25]; NT-Apocrypha[Acts of Paul in Ephesus p.1; Epistula Apostolorum 49]

03:13 Genesis 32:10; Hippolytus[The Discourse on the Holy Theophany 2]; Origen[Gospel of John Book VI.31]

03:13-14 Gregory Thaumaturgus[Four Homilies 4]; NT-Apocrypha[Gospel of the Ebionites Fragment 3; Gospel of the Nazareans Fragment 2]

03:13-17 Mark 1:9-11; Luke 3:21-22; Tertullian[Against All Heresies 5; On Baptism 9]; NT-Apocrypha[Arabic Gospel of the Infancy of the Savior 54]

03:14 Hippolytus[The Discourse on the Holy Theophany 4]

03:15 Apostolic[Ignatius - Letter to the Smyrnaeans 1:1]; Anonymous[Treatise on Re-Baptism 5]; Nag Hammadi[Gospel of Philip 72]

03:15-16 Justin[**Dialogue with Trypho 88**]

> **And then, when Jesus had gone to the river Jordan, where John was baptizing, and when he had stepped in the the water, a fire was kindled in the Jordan; and when He came out of the water, the Holy Ghost lighted on Him like a dove, [as] the apostles of this very Christ of ours wrote. (Justin Martyr - Dialogue with Trypho 88)**

03:15-17 Hippolytus[The Discourse on the Holy Theophany 5]

03:16 This section also includes topical notes for: The Dove - Genesis 8:9-12; 1Samuel 10:6, 9, 20, 23; 2Samuel 7:14; 1Chronicles 17:13; Psalms 55:6-7; 89:27; Isaiah 11:2; Ezekiel 1:1; Matthew 3:16n; Mark 1:10; Luke 3:21-22; John 1:32; Pseudepigrapha[2Baruch 22:2; 4Ezra 2.15-18; Apocalypse of Elijah 3:2; Psalms of Solomon 17.37; Sibylline Oracles 6.7]; Philo[Questions And Answers On Genesis II (42) cf. {Genesis 7:17-18, 8:11, Matthew 3:1-12, 16, Luke 3:1-18}]; Rabbinic[Babylonian Hagigah 15a]; Clement of Alexandria[Fragments from Macarius Chrysocephalus Oration VIII on Matt VIII and Book VII on Luke XIII]; Hippolytus[The Discourse on the Holy Theophany 9]; Irenaeus[Against Heresies Book I.15.1, 25.1, III.9.3, 11.3, V.1.2]; Justin[Dialogue with Trypho 8]; Tertullian[On Baptism 8; On the Flesh of Christ 3]; Nag Hammadi[Gospel of Philip 70; Testimony of Truth 39]; NT-Apocrypha[Acts of Pilate XVIII.2; Akhmim Fragment 9.36; Gospel of the Ebionites Fragment 3; Gospel of the Hebrews Fragment 2; Protoevangelium of James 9.1]

03:16-17 Pseudepigrapha[Sibylline Oracles 6.4]

03:17 Genesis 22:2; Psalms 2:7; Isaiah 42:1, 62:4; Jeremiah 31:20; Matthew 12:18n, 17:5; Mark 9:7; Luke 9:35; 2Peter 1:17; Pseudepigrapha[1Enoch 65.4-5]; Tacitus[The Histories 5.13]; Alexander of Alexandria[Epistles on Arian Heresy 1.8]; Archelaus[Disputation with Manes 49-50]; Clement[Recognitions Book I.48]; Gregory Thaumaturgus[Four Homilies 4; On the Trinity; Twelve Topics on the Faith 3]; Justin[Dialogue with Trypho 103]; Lactantius[Divine Institutes Book IV.15]; Origen[Against Celsus Book II.72; Gospel of Matthew Book X.9]; Tertullian[A Treatise on the Soul

17; Against Praxeas 19]; NT-Apocrypha[Apocalypse of Peter 1.17; Gospel of the Ebionites Fragment 3]

04:01 Hebrews 2:18; 4:15; Dionysius of Alexandria[Exegetical Fragments An Exposition of Luke 22.46; Exegetical Fragments Gospel According to Luke - An Interpretation 22.46]; NT-Apocrypha[Gospel of the Hebrews Fragment 3]

04:01-04 Tertullian[On Baptism 20]

04:01-11 Mark 1:12-13; Luke 4:1-13n; Tertullian[Five Books Against Marcion Book V.6]

04:02 Exodus 34:28; Deuteronomy 9:9; 1Kings 19:8; Pseudepigrapha[Life of Adam and Eve Vita 6:3]; Archelaus[Disputation with Manes 44 cf. {Exodus 34}]; NT-Apocrypha[Acts of Thomas 1.86, 1.156; Protoevangelium of James 2.4]

04:03 Genesis 3:1-7; Psalms 2:7; Matthew 4:6, 27:40; Archelaus[Disputation with Manes 50]; Hippolytus[The Discourse on the Holy Theophany 3]; Irenaeus[Against Heresies Book IV.6.6, V.21.2]; Tertullian[Against Praxeas 1, 26; On Fasting 8]

04:03-06 John 3:18n

04:04 This section also includes topical notes for: By Bread Alone - Deuteronomy 8:3; Luke 4:4; OT-Apocrypha[Wisdom of Solomon 16:26]; Philo[Allegorical Interpretation III (173) cf. {Exodus 16:15}; On Mating With the Preliminary Studies (170) cf. {Deuteronomy 8:3}]; Clement of Alexandria[The Instructor Book III.7]; Tertullian[On Fasting 6; On the Resurrection of the Flesh 26, 61]

04:05 Nehemiah 11:1; Isaiah 48:2, 52:1; Daniel 3:28, 9:24, 27; Matthew 27:53; Revelation 11:2, 21:2, 10, 22:19; NT-Apocrypha[Gospel of the Nazareans Fragment 3]

04:06 This section also includes topical notes for: Foot not Strike a Stone - Psalms 91:11-12; Matthew 4:3, 27:40; Luke 4:11; Dead Sea Scrolls[11Q OT-Apocryphal Psalms (11Q11[11QPSAP]) COL V 11-13]; Tertullian[Against Praxeas 1, 26]

04:07 Deuteronomy 6:16; Isaiah 7:12; 1Corinthians 10:9; Irenaeus[Against Heresies Book V.22.1]

04:08 Deuteronomy 3:27, 34:1; Pseudepigrapha[2Baruch 76:3]; NT-Apocrypha[Gospel of the Hebrews Fragment 3]; Linguistics[The Hebrew word for "Earth" (הארץ) is the same as "Land" (הארץ)]

04:09 Daniel 3:5, 10, 15; Matthew 2:11, 18:26; 1Corinthians 14:25; Revelation 4:10, 5:14, 7:11, 11:16, 19:4, 10, 22:8; Irenaeus[Against Heresies Book V.24.1, 3]; Origen[Gospel of Matthew Book XII.22, XIII.9]

04:09-10 Justin[Dialogue with Trypho 103]

04:10 Deuteronomy 6:13, 10:20, 32:43; John 2:12; Pseudepigrapha[Testament of Job 26:3]; Archelaus[Disputation with Manes 32]; Clement[Homily X.5; Recognitions Book IV.34, V.13]; Irenaeus[Against Heresies Book V.21.2, 22.2]; Justin[Dialogue with Trypho 116]; Origen[Against Celsus Book VII.64; Gospel of Matthew Book XII.22]; Peter of Alexandria[Canonical Epistle 1]; Tertullian[On Prayer 8; Scorpiace 15]

04:11 1Kings 19:5

04:11-15 Origen[Gospel of John Book X.1, 14; Gospel of Matthew Book X.12]

04:12 Matthew 14:3; Mark 6:17; Luke 3:19-20; John 4:1-3; Origen[Gospel of Matthew Book XI.16]; Tertullian[On Fasting 8]

04:12-16 Tertullian[An Answer to the Jews 6]

04:12-17 Mark 1:14-15; Luke 4:14-15, 31a

04:13 John 2:12

04:15 OT-Apocrypha[1Maccabees 5:15]; Hippolytus[Fragments - On Genesis 49.21-26]

04:15-16 Isaiah 9:1-2; Hippolytus[Fragments - On Genesis 49.12-15]

04:16 Isaiah 8:23-9:2, 58:10; Luke 1:79; Clement[First Epistle Concerning Virginity 2]; Origen[Against Celsus Book VI.66; Gospel of Matthew Book XIII.9]; NT-Apocrypha[Acts of Paul from Corinth to Italy p.8]

04:17 Daniel 2:44; Matthew 3:2, 10:7; Clement of Alexandria[Exhortation to the Heathen 9]; Hippolytus[Fragments - On Genesis 49.21-26]; Origen[Gospel of John Book X.1; Gospel of Matthew Book XII.14]

04:18 John 1:40-41; Origen[Gospel of John Book X.6]; NT-Apocrypha[Gospel of Mani Coptic Psalm book II; Gospel of the Ebionites Fragment 4]

04:18-22 Mark 1:16-20; Luke 5:1-11n; NT-Apocrypha[Acts of John 88]

04:19 2Kings 6:19; Jeremiah 16:16; Clement of Alexandria[Stromata Book VII.18]; Origen[Against Celsus Book I.62; Gospel of Matthew Book XII.21]; Teaching of Addaeus the Apostle

04:19-20 Origen[Against Celsus Book VIII.56]

04:21-22 Tertullian[On Baptism 12; On Idolatry 12]

04:23 Nag Hammadi[Gospel of Mary 8]; NT-Apocrypha[Abgar Legend]

04:23-25 This section also includes topical notes for: Healing - Matthew 8:7-16, 9:35n, 12:15, 14:14, 15:30, 19:2, 21:14; Mark 1:34, 39, 3:10, 6:5; Luke 4:40, 44, 5:15-17, 6:17-19, 9:11; Pseudepigrapha[Sibylline Oracles Prologue, 1.351-355; Testament of Adam 3.1]; Dead Sea Scrolls[4Messianic Apocalypse (4Q521) Fragment 2 COL II 7-13]; Philo[On the Migration of Abraham (124) cf. {Genesis 12:3}]; Rabbinic[Babylonian Sanhedrin 98a]; Irenaeus[Against Heresies Book I.30.13, V.12.6; Demonstration of the Apostolic Preaching 66-67]; Justin[First Apology 31-48]; Nag Hammadi[Testimony of Truth 33]; Egyptian Book of the Dead[Oration 99]

04:24 Mark 6:55-56; NT-Apocrypha[Acts of Peter p.128; Epistula Apostolorum 5]

04:25 Mark 3:7-8

05:01 Origen[Gospel of Matthew Book X.8, XI.13]

05:01-03 Origen[Gospel of Matthew Book XI.4]

05:01-12 Pseudepigrapha[Joseph and Aseneth 21:10]; Philo[On Dreams, That they Are God-Sent (1.50-1.51) cf. {Genesis 12:1-3}; On Flight And Finding (73-74) cf. {Deuteronomy 27:11-28:14}]

05:01-07:29 Clement of Alexandria[Stromata Book II.18]

05:02 Matthew 9:35n, 11:1; Mark 8:31, 9:31; Luke 11:1; OT-Apocrypha[Sirach 25:7-12]; Dead Sea Scrolls[1Q Hymns (1QHODAYOTH [1QH]) COL XV 20-25]; NT-Apocrypha[Gospel of Pseudo-Matthew 16]

05:02-11 Dead Sea Scrolls[1Q Hymns (1QHODAYOTH [1QH]) COL VI (=XIV+Fragments 15+18+22+44+9) 1-9; 4Q Psalms Pesher (4Q171[4QPPS]) COL III 9-11; 4Q Wisdom Text with Beatitudes (4Q525[4QBEAT]) Fragment 2 COL II 1-7]

05:03 Psalms 34:19; Isaiah 57:15, 61:1-2; Matthew 11:5n; Apostolic[Polycarp - Letter to the Philippians 2:3]; Archelaus[Disputation with Manes 40, 42]; Clement of Alexandria[Who is the Rich Man that shall be Saved 16-17]; Clement[Homily XV.10; Recognitions Book I.61]; Origen[Gospel of Matthew Book XIV.7; De Principiis Book II.3.7]; Tertullian[De Fuga in Persecution 12; To his Wife Book II.6]; Nag Hammadi[Gospel of Thomas 54; On the Origin of the World 110]; Indian[Dhammapada 200]

05:03-04 Pseudepigrapha[Testament of Judah 25.4]

05:03-05 Tertullian[Of Patience 11]

05:03-12 Luke 6:20-23

05:03-12 NT-Apocrypha[Epistula Apostolorum 38]

05:03-16 Methodius[Banquet of the Ten Virgins 7.3]

05:04 Isaiah 61:2-3; OT-Apocrypha[Sirach 48:24]; Cyprian[Epistle LI.23; Treatise XII.Book III.6]; Nag Hammadi[Gospel of Thomas 58]; NT-Apocrypha[Acts of Paul and Thecla 1.6; Pseudo Clementines - Kerygmata Petrou H III 26.2]

05:05 Deuteronomy 4:38; Psalms 37:11; Pseudepigrapha[1Enoch 5:7, **6:9**; Testament of Job 33:5]; Rabbinic[**Mishnah Sanhedrin 10:2**]; Apostolic[Didache 3:7]; Clement of Alexandria[Stromata Book IV.6]; Constitutions of the Holy Apostles[Book II.1, VII.7]; Cyprian[Treatise XII.Book III.5]; Irenaeus[Against Heresies Book III.22.1, V.9.4, 32.2]; Origen[De Principiis Book II.3.7]; Teaching of the Twelve Apostles 3.8; Tertullian[On Prescription Against Heretics 8]; NT-Apocrypha[Acts of Thomas 1.94; Apocalypse of Paul 1.21]

> The elect shall possess light, joy, and peace; and they shall inherit the earth.
> (Pseudepigrapha - 1Enoch 6:9)

> Who is someone who will inherit the world to come? It is one who is meek and humble.
> (Talmud - Mishnah Sanhedrin 10:2, *The Babylonian Talmud a Translation and Commentary*, Jacob Neusner; Hendrickson Publishers, Inc., 2005)

05:06 Psalms 107:5, 8; Isaiah 55:1-2; Pseudepigrapha[4Baruch 9:21]; Rabbinic[Babylonian Sanhedrin 100a cf. {Psalms 36:9}]; Clement of Alexandria[Stromata Book V.11; Who is the Rich Man that shall be Saved 17]; Cyprian[Epistle LXII.8]; Origen[De Principiis Book II.11.2]; Tertullian[On Fasting 15]; Theodotus[Excerpts 14]; Nag Hammadi[Gospel of Thomas 69]; NT-Apocrypha[Acts of Thomas 1.94; Apocalypse of Paul 1.22; Apocalypse of Peter 1.14-15]

05:06-07 Cyprian[Treatise XII.Book III.1]

05:07 Proverbs 14:21, 17:5; Matthew 18:33; James 2:13; Apostolic[1Clement 13:2]; Clement of Alexandria[Stromata Book IV.6]; Constitutions of the Holy Apostles[Book VI.23, VII.8]; NT-Apocrypha[Acts of Paul and Thecla 1.6; Acts of Thomas 1.67; Apocalypse of Paul 1.16]

05:07-09 Constitutions of the Holy Apostles[Book II.1]

05:08 Genesis 20:5; Psalms 24:3-5, 73:1; Pseudepigrapha[2Enoch 45:3; 4Ezra 7:98];
Archelaus[Disputation with Manes 42]; Clement of Alexandria[Stromata Book II.11, 20, IV.6, V.1,
VI.14, VII.3, 10]; Clement[Homily XVII.7; Recognitions Book II.22, III.27, 30]; Cyprian[Epistle XLV.2;
Treatise XII.Book III.79]; Irenaeus[Against Heresies Book IV.9.2, 20.5]; Methodius[Banquet of the
Ten Virgins 11.2]; Novatian[Treatise Concerning the Trinity 28]; Origen[Against Celsus Book VI.4,
VII.33, 45; De Principiis Book I.1.9]; Pontianus[Second Epistle]; NT-Apocrypha[Acts of Paul and
Thecla 1.5; Acts of Thomas 1.94; Martyrdom of Bartholomew]
05:09 Proverbs 10:10; Hosea 2:1; Hebrews 12:14; James 3:18; Pseudepigrapha[2Enoch 52:10]; Clement
of Alexandria[Stromata Book I.1; Who is the Rich Man that shall be Saved 24];
Clement[Recognitions Book II.27, 29]; Constitutions of the Holy Apostles[Book II.46];
Cyprian[Treatise I.24, XII.Book III.3]; Origen[Gospel of Matthew Book II.Frag]; Tertullian[Of
Patience 11; On Baptism 14; On Modesty 2, 5]; NT-Apocrypha[Acts of Paul and Thecla 1.6]
05:09-10 Clement of Alexandria[Stromata Book IV.6]
05:10 1Peter 3:14; Pseudepigrapha[2Baruch 52:6]; Apostolic[Polycarp - Letter to the Philippians 2:3];
Cyprian[Treatise XI.12, XII.Book III.16]; Tertullian[On the Resurrection of the Flesh 41; Scorpiace 9];
Zephyrinus[Second Epistle 1.1]; NT-Apocrypha[Apocalypse of Peter 1.16]
05:10-12 Pseudepigrapha[Odes of Solomon 31.6]; Cyprian[Epistle XXV.4]; Dionysius of
Alexandria[Extant Fragments Epistle to Fabius Bishop of Antioch 5]; Nag Hammadi[Apocryphon of
James 4; Gospel of Thomas 58, 68-69]
05:11 Isaiah 51:7; Matthew 10:22; 1Peter 4:14; OT-Apocrypha[2Esdras 7:14]; Tertullian[De Fuga in
Persecutione 7]; NT-Apocrypha[Acts of Thomas 1.107; Apocalypse of Paul 1.44; Epistula
Apostolorum 38, 50]
05:11-12 Constitutions of the Holy Apostles[Book II.8, V.3]; Tertullian[Of Patience 8, 11]; NT-
Apocrypha[Acts of Thomas 1.25]
05:12 Genesis 15:1; 2Chronicles 36:16; Matthew 23:30, 37; Acts 7:52; Hebrews 11:32-38; James 5:10;
Irenaeus[Against Heresies Book IV.33.9]; NT-Apocrypha[Epistula Apostolorum 40, 42; Pistis Sophia
c. 2-6]
05:13 Pseudepigrapha[Joseph and Aseneth 11:4]; Clement of Alexandria[Stromata Book I.8; The
Instructor Book III.11]; Cyprian[The Seventh Council of Carthage under Cyprian; Treatise XII.Book
III.87]; Irenaeus[Against Heresies Book IV.31.3]; Methodius[Banquet of the Ten Virgins 1.1];
Origen[Against Celsus Book VIII.70]; NT-Apocrypha[Acts of John 109]
05:13-14 Clement of Alexandria[Who is the Rich Man that shall be Saved 36]; Irenaeus[Against
Heresies Book I.6.1]
05:13-16 Mark 9:50; Luke 14:34-35
05:14 This section also includes topical notes for: Light of the World - Isaiah 2:2; John 1:9, 3:19, 8:12,
9:5, 11:9, 12:46; Philippians 2:15; Philo[On Dreams, That they Are God-Sent (1.164-1.165, 1.175-1.176)
cf. {Isaiah 6:9-10, Matthew 11:25, Luke 10:21, 18:31-34, 1Corinthians 2:7-16, 2Corinthians 4:3,
Ephesians 3:9, Colossians 1:26, 2:2-3}]; Clement[First Epistle Concerning Virginity 2, 13];
Irenaeus[Against Heresies Book IV.7.3]; Origen[Against Celsus Book V.10, VII.51; Gospel of John
Book VI.38]; Tertullian[On Idolatry 15]; Nag Hammadi[Gospel of Thomas 32]; NT-
Apocrypha[Clement Romance 67.1; Letter of Clement to James 1.3]; Indian[Dhammapada 172-173,
304, 382, 387]
05:14-15 Clement[Recognitions Book VIII.4]; Origen[Gospel of John Book I.24]; Tertullian[On the
Apparel of Women Book II.13]
05:14-16 Nag Hammadi[Gospel of Thomas 24]
05:15 This section also includes topical notes for: Lamp Under a Bushel - Matthew 6:22; Mark 4:21;
Luke 8:16; 11:33-36; John 5:35; Philo[On Abraham (161) cf. {Genesis 18:2}; On Mating With the
Preliminary Studies (8) cf. {Exodus 25:31}; That the Worse Is Wont To Attack the Better (128) cf.
{Exodus 4:14}; Special Laws I (321-323); Special Laws III (6) cf. {Exodus 34:33-35, 1 Samuel 14:27-
45}]; Clement of Alexandria[Stromata Book I.1]; Hippolytus[Refutation of all Heresies Book V.2];
Tertullian[On Prescription Against Heretics 26]; Nag Hammadi[Gospel of Thomas 33; Teachings of
Silvanus 106]
05:15-17 Rabbinic[Babylonian Shabbat 116a-b]
05:16 This section also includes topical notes for: Good Works – John 10:32; Acts 9:36; Ephesians
2:10, 5:8-9; 1Timothy 2:10, 5:10, 25, 6:18; Titus 2:7, 14, 3:8, 14; Hebrews 10:24; 1Peter 2:12;
Pseudepigrapha[4Ezra 2.15-32; Joseph and Aseneth 20:7; Odes of Solomon 11.20]; Philo[On the Birth
of Abel And the Sacrifices offered By Him And By His Brother Cain (53) cf. {Genesis 4:3,
Deuteronomy 23:21}; On the Change of Names (40, 128-129) cf. {Exodus 7:11, Deuteronomy 12:28};

On the Contemplative Life Or Suppliants (2); Special Laws IV (186) cf. {Leviticus 19:16, 19:36}]; Archelaus[Disputation with Manes 22]; Clement of Alexandria[Exhortation to the Heathen 11; Fragments from Macarius Chrysocephalus Parable of the Prodigal son 6; Fragments from the Latin Translation of Cassiodorus Comments on 1John; Stromata Book III.4, IV.26, V.1, 7, 12, 14; Who is the Rich Man that shall be Saved 1, 32]; Clement[First Epistle Concerning Virginity 2; Second Epistle Concerning Virginity 6]; Cyprian[Epistle VI.3; Treatise XII.Book III.26]; Irenaeus[Against Heresies Book I.6.2, 4, II.9.1, IV.12.5, 18.6, 36.6, 37.1, 3, 41.2, V.1.1, 8.4, 11.2]; Justin[First Apology 8, 16]; Liturgy of James 7, 21; Methodius[Banquet of the Ten Virgins 6.3]; Origen[Against Celsus Book V.10; Gospel of John Book I.24, II.11; Gospel of Matthew Book X.3]; Tertullian[On Idolatry 15; On the Apparel of Women Book II.13]; Nag Hammadi[Letter of Peter to Philip 137; Teachings of Silvanus 114; Tripartite Tractate 131]; NT-Apocrypha[Pseudo-Titus Epistle Line 319]

05:17 Matthew 3:15; Romans 3:31; Pseudepigrapha[Sibylline Oracles 1.332]; Archelaus[Disputation with Manes 40]; Clement of Alexandria[Stromata Book III.6]; Hippolytus[Fragments - On Genesis 49.12-15]; Origen[Gospel of Matthew Book X.12]; Tertullian[An Answer to the Jews 9; On Exhortation to Chastity 7; On Modesty 6; On Monogamy 7; On Prayer 11; On the Apparel of Women Book II.2; Five Books Against Marcion Book IV.7, 9, 12, 36, V.14]; NT-Apocrypha[Gospel of the Ebionites Fragment 6; Pseudo Clementines - Kerygmata Petrou H III 51.2]

05:17-18 Clement[Homily III.51]; Constitutions of the Holy Apostles[Book VI.19]; Irenaeus[Against Heresies Book IV.34.2]

05:17-7;29 Irenaeus[Demonstration of the Apostolic Preaching 95]

05:18 2Kings 19:27; Isaiah 37:18, 65:16; Jeremiah 28:6; Luke 16:17, 21:33; Pseudepigrapha[Baruch 4:1; Life of Abraham 11:5]; Rabbinic[Babylonian (Sanhedrin 111a; Shabbat 119b); Exodus Rabba on 6.2; Jerusalem Sanhedrin 20c]; Clement of Alexandria[Exhortation to the Heathen 9; Fragments from Macarius Chrysocephalus Book XIII .9]; Hippolytus[Appendix to the Works of Hippolytus - On the End of the World 2; Refutation of all Heresies Book V.19]; Irenaeus[Against Heresies Book I.3.2, II.22.4]; Nag Hammadi[Gospel of Truth 23]; NT-Apocrypha[Acts of Andrew and Matthias; Letter of Peter to James 2.5; Pseudo Clementines - Kerygmata Petrou H III 51.3]

05:19 James 2:10; Clement of Alexandria[Stromata Book II.19]; Constitutions of the Holy Apostles[Book II.5]; Cyprian[Epistle LXII.14, LXXVI.6; Treatise X.12, XII.Book III.96]; Justin[First Apology 29]; Origen[Gospel of Matthew Book XIII.15]

05:20 Matthew 6:1-6n; Clement of Alexandria[Stromata Book III.4, VI.15, 18]; Constitutions of the Holy Apostles[Book II.35]; Hippolytus[Refutation of all Heresies Book IX.23]; Justin[Dialogue with Trypho 105]; Tertullian[On Idolatry 2; On Monogamy 7]; Nag Hammadi[Gospel of Thomas 39]

05:20-22 Irenaeus[Against Heresies Book IV.13.1]

05:21 Exodus 20:13, 21:12; Leviticus 24:17; Deuteronomy 5:17; Matthew 19:18; Mark 10:19; Luke 18:20; Romans 13:9; James 2:11; Justin[First Apology 15]; NT-Apocrypha[Pseudo Clementines - Kerygmata Petrou H XI 32.1]

05:21-22 Cyprian[Treatise XII.Book III.8]; Irenaeus[Against Heresies Book II.32.1]; Tertullian[On Modesty 6; On Prayer 11]

05:21-26 Luke 12:57-59

05:22 Deuteronomy 17:8-13, 21:18, 20; Daniel 7:10; 1John 3:15; Pseudepigrapha[2Enoch 44:2; Sibylline Oracles 2.292]; Rabbinic[Babylonian (Baba Mesia 59b; Sanhedrin 58b)]; Clement of Alexandria[The Instructor Book II.6]; Constitutions of the Holy Apostles[Book II.32, 53, VI.23]; Cyprian[Epistle LIV.4; Treatise XII.Book III.13]; Fabian[Second Epistle]; Irenaeus[Against Heresies Book II.32.1, IV.16.5, 36.1]; Origen[De Principiis Book III.1.6, IV.1.19]; Tertullian[Of Patience 6; On Idolatry 2]; NT-Apocrypha[Gospel of the Nazareans Fragment 4]

05:22-23 Tertullian[On Prayer 11]

05:23-24 Constitutions of the Holy Apostles[Book II.53]; Cyprian[Epistle XXVII.1; Treatise XII.Book III.3]; Irenaeus[Against Heresies Book IV.18.1]; Teaching of the Twelve Apostles 14.2; Tertullian[Five Books in Reply to Marcion Book IV.243; Of Patience 12]; Victorinus[Apocalypse 6.9]

05:23-26 Dead Sea Scrolls[4Q Sapiential Work (4Q418[4QSAP.WORKA]) Fragment 8 3-6; (4Q417[4QSAP.WORKA]) Fragment 1 COL II 6-9; (4Q416[4QSAP.WORKA]) Fragment 2 COL II 4-7]

05:24-25 Clement of Alexandria[Stromata Book III.4]

05:25 Pseudepigrapha[Ahiqar 142]; Clement of Alexandria[Stromata Book IV.14]; Tertullian[A Treatise on the Soul 35, 38; Of Patience 12]

05:25-26 Matthew 18:34-35; Irenaeus[Against Heresies Book I.25.4]

05:26 Apostolic[Didache 1:5]; Cyprian[Treatise VIII.11, XII.Book III.57]; Origen[Gospel of Matthew Book XIV.8]; Teaching of the Twelve Apostles 1.5; Tertullian[A Treatise on the Soul 35; On the Resurrection of the Flesh 42]

05:27 Exodus 20:14; Deuteronomy 5:18; Matthew 19:18; Mark 10:19; Luke 18:20; Romans 13:9; James 2:11; Justin[First Apology 16]; NT-Apocrypha[Pseudo Clementines - Kerygmata Petrou H XI 32.1]

05:27-28 Clement of Alexandria[Stromata Book III.11]; Irenaeus[Against Heresies Book IV.13.1]; Tertullian[On Modesty 6; On Repentance 3]

05:27-32 John 8:3-11n

05:28 This section also includes topical notes for: Look at with Lust - Exodus 20:17; 2Samuel 11:2; Job 31:1; Proverbs 6:25; James 1:14-15; 2Peter 2:14; 1John 2:16; OT-Apocrypha[Sirach 9:8]; Dead Sea Scrolls[1Q Rule of the Community (1QS) COL I 5-20]; Philo[Special Laws III (9) cf. {Exodus 20:14}]; Rabbinic[**Babylonian Abodah Zarah 20a cf. {Deuteronomy 23:9}**]; Athenagoras[Plea for the Christians 32]; Clement of Alexandria[Stromata Book II.11, 14-15, III.2, 14, IV.18; The Instructor Book III.5]; Constitutions of the Holy Apostles[Book I.1]; Irenaeus[Against Heresies Book IV.16.5]; Origen[De Principiis Book III.1.6]; Tertullian[A Treatise on the Soul 15, 40, 58; On Exhortation to Chastity 9; On Idolatry 2, 23; On the Apparel of Women Book II.2; On the Resurrection of the Flesh 15]; Theophilus of Antioch[To Autolycus Book III.13]; Nag Hammadi[Authoritative Teaching 25]; NT-Apocrypha[Pseudo-Titus Epistle Line 237]

> **But is it permitted even to look? And an objection is to be raised: "You shall keep from you every evil thing" (Deuteronomy 23:9) – one should not stare at a beautiful woman, even if she is not married. (Talmud - Babylonian Abodah Zarah 20a,** *The Babylonian Talmud a Translation and Commentary,* **Jacob Neusner; Hendrickson Publishers, Inc., 2005)**

05:28-29 Clement[Recognitions Book VII.37]; Justin[First Apology 15]

05:28-30 Indian[Dhammapada 284-285]

05:29 Clement of Alexandria[The Instructor Book III.11]; Peter of Alexandria[Genuine Acts of Peter 3]

05:29-30 Matthew 18:8-9; Mark 9:43-47; Pseudepigrapha[1Enoch 27:2]; Indian[Dhammapada 360-362]

05:31 Deuteronomy 24:1-4; Matthew 19:7; Mark 10:4

05:31-32 Matthew 19:9; Mark 10:11-12; Luke 16:18

05:32 1Corinthians 7:10-11; Rabbinic[**Babylonian Sotah 90a**] Archelaus[Disputation with Manes 42]; Clement of Alexandria[Stromata Book II.23]; Origen[Gospel of Matthew Book XIV.24]; Tertullian[On Modesty 16; On Monogamy 9; Five Books Against Marcion Book IV.34]; Theophilus of Antioch[To Autolycus Book III.13]

> **The House of Shammai say, "A man should divorce his wife only because he has found grounds for it in unchastity." (Talmud - Babylonian Sotah 90a,** *The Babylonian Talmud a Translation and Commentary,* **Jacob Neusner; Hendrickson Publishers, Inc., 2005)**

05:32-33 Justin[First Apology 15]

05:33 Leviticus 19:12; Numbers 30:2-33; Deuteronomy 23:21-22; Zechariah 8:17; Apostolic[Didache 2:3]; Constitutions of the Holy Apostles[Book VI.23]; Irenaeus[Against Heresies Book IV.13.1]; Origen[Gospel of Matthew Book XIV.14]

05:33-37 This section also includes topical notes for: Oaths - James 5:12; Pseudepigrapha[Sibylline Oracles 2.68-69]; Josephus[**War 2.8.6 135**]; Philo[Special Laws II (10, 12-15, 224, 252-253) cf. {Deuteronomy 19:19}]; Rabbinic[**Babylonian Hullin 2a cf. {Deuteronomy 23:22, Ecclesiastes 5:5}**]; Clement of Alexandria[Stromata Book V.14, VII.8; The Instructor Book III.11]; Hippolytus[**Refutation of all Heresies Book IX.17**]; Irenaeus[Against Heresies Book II.32.1]

> **Whatever they [Essenes] say also is firmer than an oath; but swearing is avoided by them, and they esteem it worse than perjury for they say that he who cannot be believed without [swearing by] God is already condemned. (Josephus - War 2.8.6 135)**

But lo it is written, "But if you refrain from vowing, you will not incur guilt" (Deuteronomy 23:22). And it is written, "It is better that you should not vow than that you should vow and not fulfill it" (Ecclesiastes 5:5) and it was taught on Tannaite authority, "Better than both alternatives that he does not vow at all," the words of R. Meir. (Talmud - Babylonian Hullin 2a, *The Babylonian Talmud a Translation and Commentary*, Jacob Neusner; Hendrickson Publishers, Inc., 2005)

And no one amongst them [Esseni] is in the habit of swearing; but whatever any one says, this is regarded more binding than an oath. If, however, one will swear, he is condemned as one unworthy of credence. (Hippolytus - Refutation of all Heresies Book IX.17)

05:34 Psalms 11:4; Isaiah 66:1; Matthew 23:22; Acts 7:49; Constitutions of the Holy Apostles[Book VII.3]; Irenaeus[Against Heresies Book IV.1.5]; Justin[First Apology 16]; Origen[De Principiis Book II.1.3, IV.1.19]; Teaching of the Twelve Apostles 2.3; NT-Apocrypha[Testimony regarding the Recipients of the Epistle of Peter to James 1.2]

05:34-35 Isaiah 66:1; Pseudepigrapha[2Enoch 49:1]; Clement[Homily III.56]; Origen[Gospel of John Book VI.23; De Principiis Book II.4.1]

05:34-37 Cyprian[Treatise XII.Book III.12]; Tertullian[On Idolatry 11]

05:35 Psalms 48:2-3, 99:5; Isaiah 66:1; Lamentations 2:1; Acts 7:49; Irenaeus[Against Heresies Book IV.4.1, 36.5]; Methodius[Oration Concerning Simeon and Anna 13]; Origen[Gospel of John Book X.16]

05:36 Clement of Alexandria[Stromata Book II.5; The Instructor Book III.3]; Cyprian[Treatise II.16]; Tertullian[On the Apparel of Women Book II.6]

05:37 2Corinthians 1:17; Clement[Homily III.55, XIX.2]; Cyprian[Epistle LIV.14]; Tertullian[Against Praxeas 9; On Prescription Against Heretics 26; On the Flesh of Christ 23]

05:38 Exodus 21:24; Leviticus 24:20; Deuteronomy 19:21; Josephus[Antiquities 4.8.35 280]; Constitutions of the Holy Apostles[Book VI.23]; Origen[De Principiis Book III.1.6]; Tertullian[An Answer to the Jews 3; Of Patience 6; On Exhortation to Chastity 6]

05:38-42 Luke 6:29-30

05:39 This section also includes topical notes for: Turn the other Cheek - Proverbs 20:22, 24:29; Isaiah 50:6; Lamentations 3:30; Luke 6:29; John 18:22; Dead Sea Scrolls[Damascus Document (CD-A) COL IX 2]; Philo[On Husbandry (111-113); On the Virtues (117-120) cf. {Exodus 23:4}]; Rabbinic[Tosephta Baba Qamma ix.29]; Arnobius[Against the Heathen Book I.6]; Clement of Alexandria[Who is the Rich Man that shall be Saved 18]; Irenaeus[Against Heresies Book II.32.1, III.18.6, IV.34.4]; Origen[Against Celsus Book VII.25; De Principiis Book III.1.6]; Tertullian[Of Patience 8; On Exhortation to Chastity 6]

05:39-40 Origen[Against Celsus Book VII.61]

05:39-41 Teaching of the Twelve Apostles 1.4

05:39-42 Constitutions of the Holy Apostles[Book VII.2]

05:39-44 Indian[Dhammapada 223, 389]

05:40 1Corinthians 6:7; Clement of Alexandria[Stromata Book IV.10; The Instructor Book III.12]; Fabian[Second Epistle]; Tertullian[Of Patience 7]

05:40-41 Apostolic[Didache 1:4]

05:41 Clement of Alexandria[Who is the Rich Man that shall be Saved 31]; Irenaeus[Against Heresies Book IV.13.3]

05:42 Deuteronomy 15:7; Pseudepigrapha[Pseudo-Phocylides 1.22-23]; Clement of Alexandria[Fragments from Nicetas Bishop of Heraclea Catena on Matthew 3; Stromata Book III.6, IV.6]; Hippolytus[Refutation of all Heresies Book IX.15]; Irenaeus[Against Heresies Book II.32.1]; Tertullian[De Fuga in Persecutione 13; On Monogamy 11]

05:43 This section also includes topical notes for: Love your Neighbor - Leviticus 19:18; Deuteronomy 7:2, 23:4, 7; Matthew 19:19, 22:39; Mark 12:31-33; Luke 10:27; Romans 13:8-10; Galatians 5:14; James 2:8; Pseudepigrapha[Letter of Aristeas 1.225-226]; Dead Sea Scrolls[Damascus Document (CD-A) COL VI 15-21]; Philo[Fragments Extracted From the Parallels of John of Damascus 784 C]; Clement of Alexandria[Stromata Book II.18]; Constitutions of the Holy

Apostles[Book VI.23]; Irenaeus[Fragments from the Lost Works 4]; NT-Apocrypha[Pseudo Clementines - Kerygmata Petrou H XI 32.1]

05:43-45 Cyprian[Treatise X.15]

05:43-46 Cyprian[Treatise IX.5]

05:43-48 Luke 6:27-28, 32-36; Pseudepigrapha[Joseph and Aseneth 29:5]; Josephus[**War 2.8.6 134**]

> They [the Essenes] do nothing but according to the injunctions of their curators; only these two things are done among them at everyone's own free-will, which are to assist those that want it, and to show mercy; for they are permitted of their own accord to afford succor to such as deserve it, when they stand in need of it, and to bestow food on those that are in distress. (Josephus - War 2.8.6 134)

05:44 This section also includes topical notes for: **Pray even for Enemies** - Exodus 23:4-5; Leviticus 19:34; 2Kings 6:22; 2Chronicles 28:9-15; Psalms 7:4, 35:13-14; Proverbs 24:17-18, 25:21-22; Luke 6:27-28, 34, 35, 23:34; Acts 7:60; Romans 12:14, 20-21; 1Corinthians 4:12-13; 1Peter 3:9; Pseudepigrapha[Letter of Aristeas 1.227, 1.249; Sibylline Oracles 2.65]; Philo[Special Laws I (97, 210-211) cf. {Leviticus 9:7}]; Rabbinic[Avot 4.24 cf. {Proverbs 24:17-18}; Babylonian Berakhot 10a, 17a]; Apostolic[Polycarp - Letter to the Philippians 12:3]; Clement of Alexandria[Stromata Book VII.12; The Instructor Book I.8]; Clement[Homily III.19]; Constitutions of the Holy Apostles[Book VII.2]; Hippolytus[Refutation of all Heresies Book IX.18]; Irenaeus[Against Heresies Book II.32.1, III.18.5]; Justin[Dialogue with Trypho 85, 133; First Apology 14-15]; Lactantius[Divine Institutes Book VI.18]; Teaching of the Twelve Apostles 1.3; Tertullian[Apology 31; On Idolatry 21; On Prayer 3]; NT-Apocrypha[Acts of Peter 1.10, 1.28; Epistula Apostolorum 18; Oxyrhynchus Papyrus 1224 p.176]

05:44-45 Athenagoras[Plea for the Christians 11]; Clement of Alexandria[Stromata Book IV.14, VII.14]; Clement[Homily III.57]; Constitutions of the Holy Apostles[Book I.2]; Cyprian[Treatise XII.Book III.49]; Origen[Against Celsus Book VIII.35]; Tertullian[Of Patience 6]

05:44-46 Theophilus of Antioch[To Autolycus Book III.14]

05:44-47 Apostolic[Didache 1:3]

05:44-48 Clement of Alexandria[Stromata Book VI.12]

05:45 This section also includes topical notes for: **Sun Rise on the Evil and the Good** - Ephesians 5:1; Philo[The Cherubim Part 1 (36-38); On The Unchangeableness of God (176)]; Clement of Alexandria[Stromata Book V.3, VI.3; The Instructor Book I.8]; Clement[Recognitions Book III.38, V.13]; Constitutions of the Holy Apostles[Book II.14, 53, VII.2]; Hippolytus[Refutation of all Heresies Book V.2]; Irenaeus[Against Heresies Book II.9.1, 22.2, III.25.4, IV.13.3, 36.6, V.2.2, 27.1]; Origen[Against Celsus Book IV.28; Gospel of John Book I.11; De Principiis Book II.4.1]; Tertullian[A Treatise on the Soul 47; On the Resurrection of the Flesh 26; Five Books Against Marcion Book II.17, IV.36]; NT-Apocrypha[Apocalypse of Paul 1.16]

05:45-46 Justin[First Apology 15]

05:46 Athenagoras[Plea for the Christians 12]

05:46-47 Constitutions of the Holy Apostles[Book VII.2]; Teaching of the Twelve Apostles 1.3

05:47-48 Linguistics[The Hebrew word for "Perfect" (שלם) is written the same as "Peace offering" (שלם)]

05:48 Leviticus 19:2; Deuteronomy 18:13; Apostolic[Didache 1:4]; Clement of Alexandria[Stromata Book IV.22, VI.14, VII.13-14]; Origen[Against Celsus Book IV.29; De Principiis Book II.4.1, IV.1.37]; Tertullian[On the Apparel of Women Book II.2; Five Books Against Marcion Book I.24]; NT-Apocrypha[Epistula Apostolorum 29]

06:01 Matthew 23:5; NT-Apocrypha[Pseudo Clementines - Kerygmata Petrou H XI 29.4]

06:01-02 Origen[Gospel of Matthew Book XI.15]

06:01-04 Rabbinic[Mishna Aboth 2:13]; Tertullian[To his Wife Book II.5]; NT-Apocrypha[Acts of Thomas 1.19]

06:01-06 This section also includes topical notes for: **Pride** - Matthew 5:20, 16:6-12, 23:15-29; Mark 8:5; Luke 11:39-43, 12:1; Philo[On Dreams, That they Are God-Sent (2.140); On The Unchangeableness of God (101-103) cf. {Numbers 14:39-45, Deuteronomy 1:41-46}]; Nag Hammadi[Gospel of Thomas 14]

06:02 Pseudepigrapha[Vision of Ezra 3]; Cyprian[Treatise XII.Book III.40]; Tertullian[On the Veiling of Virgins 13]

06:02-16 This section also includes topical notes for: **Hypocrisy** - Matthew 7:5, 15:7, 22:18, 23:13-29, 24:51; Mark 7:6, 12:15; Luke 6:42, 12:1, 12:56, 13:15; Romans 12:9; 1Timothy 4:2; James 3:17; 1Peter 2:1; Philo[On the Posterity of Cain And His Exile (85-88) cf. {Deuteronomy 30:14, James 2:1-26}; **That**

the Worse Is Wont To Attack the Better (19-21) cf. {Deuteronomy 16:18-20, Isaiah 1:2-17}; On The
Unchangeableness of God (101-103) cf. {Numbers 14:39-45, Deuteronomy 1:41-46}]; Nag
Hammadi[Apocryphon of James 7]

> If, therefore, you see any one desiring meat or drink at an unseasonable time, or
> repudiating baths or ointments at the proper season, or neglecting the proper clothing
> for his body, or lying on the ground and sleeping in the open air, and by such conduct as
> this, pretending to a character for temperance and self-denial, you, pitying his self-
> deception, should show him the true path of temperance, for all the practices in which he
> has been indulging are useless and profitless labors, oppressing both his soul and body
> with hunger and all sorts of other hardships. Nor if anyone, using washings and
> purifications soils his mind, but makes his bodily appearance brilliant; nor if again out
> of his abundant wealth he builds a temple with brilliant artments of all kinds, at a vast
> expense; nor if he offers up catombs and never ceases sacrificing oxen; nor if he adorns
> temples with costly offerings, bringing timber in abundance, and skilful ornaments,
> more valuable than nay of gold or silver, still let him not be classed among pious men,
> for he also has wandered out of the way to piety, looking upon ceremonious worship as
> equivalent to sanctity, and giving gifts to the incorruptible being who will never receive
> such offerings, and flattering him who can never listen to flattery, who loves genuine
> worship (and genuine worship is that of the soul which offers the only sacrifice, plain
> truth), and rejects all spurious ministrations, and those are spurious which are only
> displays of external riches and extravagance. (Philo - That the Worse Is Wont To Attack
> the Better (19-21) cf. {Deuteronomy 16:18-20, Isaiah 1:2-17})

06:03 This section also includes topical notes for: Giving - Philo[The Cherubim: Of Cain And His
Birth Part 2 (122-123)]; Irenaeus[Against Heresies Book IV.30.3]; Theophilus of Antioch[To
Autolycus Book III.14]; Nag Hammadi[Gospel of Thomas 62]
06:03-04 Constitutions of the Holy Apostles[Book III.14]; Cyprian[Treatise XII.Book III.40]
06:03-06 Rabbinic[Jerusalem Targum Onkelos Exodus 2:23-25]
06:05 Matthew 6:16, 23:5; Luke 18:10-14; Constitutions of the Holy Apostles[Book VII.24]; Teaching of
the Twelve Apostles 8.2; NT-Apocrypha[Acts of Thomas 1.53]
06:05-06 Tertullian[On Prayer 17; 24]
06:05-15 Luke 11:2-4
06:06 2Kings 4:33; Isaiah 26:20; Archelaus[Disputation with Manes 20]; Clement of
Alexandria[Stromata Book I.6]; Clement[Homily III.55]; Nag Hammadi[Gospel of Philip 68]
06:07 Ecclesiastes 5:1; Isaiah 1:15; OT-Apocrypha[Sirach 7:14]
06:08 Matthew 6:32; Luke 12:30; Clement of Alexandria[Stromata Book VII.7]; Clement[Homily III.55];
Tertullian[On Prayer 10]; Nag Hammadi[Apocryphon of James 11]
06:09 Isaiah 29:23, 63:16, 64:7; Ezekiel 36:23, Malachi 1:6; John 1:18n; OT-Apocrypha[Sirach 23:1, 4];
Archelaus[Disputation with Manes 20]; Clement of Alexandria[Fragments from the Latin
Translation of Cassiodorus Comments on 1Peter; Stromata Book VII.12; The Instructor Book I.8];
Constitutions of the Holy Apostles[Book III.18, VII.24]; Cyprian[Treatise IV.7]; Irenaeus[Against
Heresies Book II.9.1]; Origen[De Principiis Book II.4.1]; Tertullian[Against Praxeas 23]; Nag
Hammadi[Discourse on the Eighth and Ninth 53; Gospel of Philip 52; Gospel of the Egyptians III
40]; NT-Apocrypha[Acts of Thomas 1.144]
06:09-13 1Chronicles 29:10-18; Apostolic[Didache 8:2]; Teaching of the Twelve Apostles 8.2;
Rabbinic[Babylonian Kiddushin 81a]
06:10 Matthew 26:42; Luke 22:42; OT-Apocrypha[1Maccabees 3:60]; Rabbinic[Avot 2.4];
Apostolic[Martyrdom of Polycarp 7:1]; Clement of Alexandria[Stromata Book IV.8]; Constitutions
of the Holy Apostles[Book II.56]; Cyprian[Treatise XII.Book III.19]; Nag Hammadi[Apocryphon of
James 4]; NT-Apocrypha[Acts of Thomas 1.3]
06:11 Proverbs 27:1, 30:8; Tertullian[On Fasting 15]; NT-Apocrypha[Gospel of the Nazareans
Fragment 5]
06:12 Matthew 18:32-33; OT-Apocrypha[Sirach 28:2]; Clement of Alexandria[Stromata Book VII.13];
Constitutions of the Holy Apostles[Book II.21]; Cyprian[Treatise XII.Book III.22]; Irenaeus[Against
Heresies Book V.17.1]; Nag Hammadi[Apocryphon of James 12]

06:13 1Chronicles 29:11; Psalms 18:30; Matthew 26:41; Luke 22:40; John 17:15; 2Timothy 4:18;
2Thessalonians 3:3; OT-Apocrypha[Sirach 23:1, 33:1]; Pseudepigrapha[Odes of Solomon 14:5;
Testament of Job 43:5]; Apostolic[Polycarp - Letter to the Philippians 7:2]; Clement[Homily XIX.2];
Peter of Alexandria[Canonical Epistle 9]; Tertullian[De Fuga in Persecutione 2]; Nag
Hammadi[Apocryphon of James 4]

06:14 Mark 11:25; Ephesians 4:32; Colossians 3:13; Apostolic[1Clement 13:2]; Clement of
Alexandria[Who is the Rich Man that shall be Saved 39]

06:14-15 Tertullian[On Prayer 11]

06:15 Matthew 18:35; Mark 11:25-26; NT-Apocrypha[Gospel of Mani Turfman Fragment M 801]

06:16 Isaiah 58:5; Matthew 6:5, 23:5; Justin[First Apology 16]; Teaching of the Twelve Apostles 8.1

06:16-18 Pseudepigrapha[Apocalypse of Elijah 1:13]; Philo[That the Worse Is Wont To Attack the
Better (19-21) cf. {Deuteronomy 16:20}]; Tertullian[On Fasting 8; On Prayer 18]; Nag
Hammadi[Gospel of Thomas 14]

06:16-21 Justin[Dialogue with Trypho 15]

06:17 2Samuel 12:20; Ecclesiastes 9:8

06:19 Job 24:16; Isaiah 51:8; Pseudepigrapha[Testament of Abraham 10:10]; Clement of
Alexandria[Stromata Book III.6, 12, IV.6; Who is the Rich Man that shall be Saved 13];
Irenaeus[Against Heresies Book IV.16.1]

06:19-20 James 5:2-3; Pseudepigrapha[2Baruch 14:13]; Rabbinic[Avot 2.8]; Justin[First Apology 15];
Nag Hammadi[Gospel of Thomas 76; Gospel of Truth 33]; Indian[Dhammapada 240]

06:19-21 Luke 12:33-34; Cyprian[Treatise VIII.7]; NT-Apocrypha[Acts of Thomas 1.21];
Pseudepigrapha[Joseph and Aseneth 12:15]

06:20 OT-Apocrypha[2Esdras 7:77; Sirach 29:10-11]; Pseudepigrapha[Testament of Levi 13:5];
Apostolic[Shepherd of Hermas 50:8-9]; Constitutions of the Holy Apostles[Book II.36]

06:20-21 Clement of Alexandria[Exhortation to the Heathen 10]; Cyprian[Treatise XII.Book III.1];
Origen[Gospel of Matthew Book X.14]

06:21 Luke 6:45n; Clement of Alexandria[Stromata Book VII.12]; Constitutions of the Holy
Apostles[Book III.7]; Tertullian[Ad Martyras 3]; NT-Apocrypha[Gospel of Mani Kephalaia LXXXIX;
Gospel of Mani Psalm CCLXXIV]

06:22 Matthew 5:15n; Pseudepigrapha[Testament of Issachar 4:6]; Justin[First Apology 16]

06:22-23 This section also includes topical notes for: Eye is the Lamp of the Body - Luke 11:34-36;
Philo[Special Laws III (6)]; Gregory Thaumaturgus[On the Gospel According to Matthew];
Rabbinic[Avot 5.22]; Nag Hammadi[Dialogue of the Savior 8; Teachings of Silvanus 99, 106]

06:23 Deuteronomy 15:9; Matthew 20:15; Mark 7:22; OT-Apocrypha[Sirach 14:10];
Pseudepigrapha[Joseph and Aseneth 6:6]; Origen[Against Celsus Book VII.33]

06:24 This section also includes topical notes for: God and Mammon - Luke 16:9, 13; Philo[On
Abraham (220-222) cf. {Genesis 13:5-17}]; Apostolic[2Clement 6:1]; Clement of Alexandria[Stromata
Book III.4, 12, IV.6, 22, VII.12]; Clement[Recognitions Book V.9]; Constitutions of the Holy
Apostles[Book VII.1, 6; Ecclesiastical Canons 47.81]; Cyprian[Treatise III.27]; Irenaeus[Against
Heresies Book III.8.1]; Origen[Against Celsus Book VIII.3]; Peter of Alexandria[Canonical Epistle
12]; Tertullian[A Treatise on the Soul 16; On Idolatry 12; The Chaplet, or De Corona 12; The Shows,
or De Spectaculis 26; To his Wife Book II.3]; Nag Hammadi[Gospel of Thomas 47; Testimony of
Truth 29, 68]; NT-Apocrypha[Pseudo-Titus Epistle Line 33]

06:24-32 Pseudepigrapha[Sibylline Oracles 2.56-57]

06:25 Philippians 4:6; Pseudepigrapha[Letter of Aristeas 1.140]; Clement of Alexandria[The Instructor
Book II.1, 11]; Tertullian[Of Patience 8; On Idolatry 12]; Nag Hammadi[Gospel of Thomas 36]; NT-
Apocrypha[Acts of Thomas 1.36]

06:25-26 Justin[First Apology 15]

06:25-28 Origen[Against Celsus Book VII.24]

06:25-31 Pythagoras[Golden Verses Lines 32-35]

06:25-32 Pseudepigrapha[History of the Rechabites 9.9-10]

06:25-34 Luke 12:22-34; Dead Sea Scrolls[4QSapiential Work A (4Q417[4QSap.Work A]) Fragment 1
COL I 17-27]; Tertullian[On Monogamy 16]

06:26 Job 12:7, 38:41; Song of Solomon 5:9-11; Matthew 10:31; Luke 12:7; Pseudepigrapha[Psalms of
Solomon 5:9-11]; Constitutions of the Holy Apostles[Book IV.5]; Cyprian[Treatise XII.Book III.11];
Tertullian[To his Wife Book I.4]; NT-Apocrypha[Acts of Thomas 1.28]

06:27 Tertullian[On the Apparel of Women Book II.7; The Shows, or De Spectaculis 23];
Theodotus[Excerpts]

06:28 Psalms 103:15; Philo[On Dreams, That they Are God-Sent (1.124-1.126) cf. {Genesis 28:11, 20-21};
   On Husbandry (51-53) cf. {Psalms 23:1}; Special Laws I (43-44)]; Tertullian[On Idolatry 12]

06:28-30 Tertullian[To his Wife Book I.4]

06:28-32 Nag Hammadi[Gospel of Thomas 36]

06:29 1Kings 10:1-29; 2Chronicles 9:1-31; OT-Apocrypha[1Esdras 1:4]

06:30 Psalms 90:5; Clement of Alexandria[Stromata Book IV.7]; NT-Apocrypha[Acts of Paul in
   Philippi 3.31; Acts of Thomas 1.28; Epistula Apostolorum 24]

06:31 Clement of Alexandria[Stromata Book IV.6]; Cyprian[Treatise IV.21]; Tertullian[On Idolatry 12;
   To his Wife Book I.4]

06:31-32 Constitutions of the Holy Apostles[Book IV.5]

06:31-33 Cyprian[Treatise VIII.9]

06:31-34 Cyprian[Treatise XII.Book III.11]

06:32 Matthew 6:8; Clement of Alexandria[The Instructor Book II.11]; Clement[Homily III.55]; Nag
   Hammadi[Apocryphon of James 11]

06:32-33 Clement of Alexandria[Stromata Book IV.6]; Tertullian[On Prayer 6]; Theodotus[Excerpts 12]

06:33 Psalms 37:4, 25; OT-Apocrypha[Wisdom of Solomon 7:11]; Clement of Alexandria[The Instructor
   Book II.13]; Clement[Recognitions Book II.20, 46, III.20, 37, 41]; NT-Apocrypha[Freer Logion]

06:34 Exodus 16:4, 19; Clement of Alexandria[The Instructor Book I.5, 12]; Cyprian[Treatise IV.19];
   Tertullian[On Exhortation to Chastity 12; On Prayer 6; To his Wife Book I.4]; Nag
   Hammadi[Dialogue of the Savior 53]; NT-Apocrypha[Acts of Thomas 1.28]

07:01 Romans 2:1, 14:4, 10; 1Corinthians 5:12; James 4:11; Rabbinic[Babylonian Sanhedrin 18a-19b];
   Tertullian[Of Patience 10; On Modesty 2]

> **The king does not judge, and [others] do not judge him; does not give testimony, and
> [others] do not give testimony about him. (Talmud - Babylonian Sanhedrin 18a-19b, *The
> Babylonian Talmud a Translation and Commentary*, Jacob Neusner; Hendrickson
> Publishers, Inc., 2005)**

07:01-02 Apostolic[1Clement 13:2; Polycarp - Letter to the Philippians 2:3]; Clement of
   Alexandria[Who is the Rich Man that shall be Saved 33]; Irenaeus[Against Heresies Book IV.30.3]

07:01-05 Pseudepigrapha[Sibylline Oracles 2.61-63]

07:01-06 Luke 6:37-42

07:02 Mark 4:24; Pseudepigrapha[2Enoch 44:4; Pseudo-Phocylides 11; Testament of Zebulon 8:3];
   Anonymous[Treatise Against the Heretic Novatian 13]; Clement[Homily XVIII.16]; Constitutions of
   the Holy Apostles[Book II.42, 48]; Cyprian[Treatise IV.23]; Justin[Dialogue with Trypho 115];
   Origen[Gospel of Matthew Book XIII.30]; Tertullian[On Modesty 2]

07:03-04 Hippolytus[Refutation of all Heresies Book VIII.1]

07:03-05 Rabbinic[Babylonian Arakhin 16b]; Nag Hammadi[Gospel of Thomas 26];
   Indian[Dhammapada 50, 252]

07:05 Matthew 6:2-16n; Irenaeus[Against Heresies Book IV.30.3]

07:06 **This section also includes topical notes for: Pearls before Swine** - Exodus 29:33; Leviticus
   22:10; Luke 13:32n; Pseudepigrapha[Ahiqar 1.44-45; Joseph and Aseneth 10:13]; Plato[Theaetetus
   166c-d; Republic VII 535e; Laws VIII 831d]; Apostolic[Didache 9:5]; Archelaus[Fragment of the
   Disputation with Manes 2]; Clement of Alexandria[Stromata Book I.12, II.12]; Clement[Recognitions
   Book II.1, III.1; Second Epistle Concerning Virginity 6]; Constitutions of the Holy Apostles[Book
   III.5]; Cyprian[Treatise V.1, XII.Book III.50]; Hippolytus[Refutation of all Heresies Book V.3, IX.12];
   Lactantius[Divine Institutes Book VII.26]; Methodius[Banquet of the Ten Virgins 4.4; Fragments
   Extracts from the Work on Things Created 1]; Origen[Gospel of Matthew Book X.8]; Syriac
   Martyrdom of Habib the Deacon; Teaching of the Twelve Apostles 9.5; Tertullian[On Baptism 18;
   On Prescription Against Heretics 26, 41; To his Wife Book II.5]; Nag Hammadi[Gospel of Philip 62;
   Gospel of Thomas 93; Teachings of Silvanus 97]; NT-Apocrypha[Oxyrhynchus Papyrus 840];
   Egyptian Book of the Dead[Oration 125]; Linguistics[Hebrew word for "Swine" (חזיר) is a pun for
   "Turn" (יחזר)]

07:07 Jeremiah 29:13; Mark 11:24; John 14:13-14, 15:7, 16:23-24; James 1:5; 1John 3:22, 5:14-15;
   Pseudepigrapha[Sibylline Oracles 7.90]; Clement of Alexandria[Stromata Book I.11, II.20, III.7, IV.2,
   V.1, 3, VIII.1]; Clement[Homily III.52]; Irenaeus[Against Heresies Book II.13.10, 18.3, 30.2];
   Origen[Letter to Gregory 3]; Tertullian[On Baptism 20; On Prayer 10; On Prescription Against
   Heretics 8]; Nag Hammadi[Dialogue of the Savior 10]; NT-Apocrypha[5Ezra 2.13; Acts of John 22;
   Acts of Thomas 1.53; Epistula Apostolorum 39; Gospel of the Hebrews Fragment 4b]

07:07-08 This section also includes topical notes for: Knock and It Shall be Opened – Luke 11:9-10; Pseudepigrapha[Jubilees 1.15; Odes of Solomon 33.13]; Plato[Republic VI 489b-c]; Clement of Alexandria[Stromata Book V.14; The Instructor Book III.6; Who is the Rich Man that shall be Saved 10]; Irenaeus[Against Heresies Book II.18.6]; Origen[Gospel of Matthew Book X.9, XIV.25]; Nag Hammadi[Gospel of Mary 8; Gospel of Thomas 2, 92, 94; Teachings of Silvanus 103, 106-107, 117]; NT-Apocrypha[Acts of Thomas 1.94]

07:07-12 Luke 11:9-13
07:08 Proverbs 8:17
07:09 Tertullian[On Prayer 6]
07:09-11 Clement[Homily III.56]; Cyprian[Epistle LI.23]
07:11 James 1:17; Hippolytus[Refutation of all Heresies Book V.12]
07:12 Psalms 34:14; Proverbs 25:21; Matthew 22:40; Luke 6:31; Romans 13:8-10; OT-Apocrypha[Sirach 31:15; Tobit 4:15]; Pseudepigrapha[Ahiqar 52; Life of Abraham 11:12; Letter of Aristeas 1.207]; Rabbinic[Babylonian Shabbat 31a]; Apostolic[Didache 1:2]; Archelaus[Disputation with Manes 42]; Clement[Homily XII.32]; Cyprian[Treatise IV.28]; Fabian[Second Epistle]; Teaching of the Twelve Apostles 1.3; Tertullian[Scorpiace 10]; NT-Apocrypha[Acts of Thomas 1.83; Clement Romance - Peter on his Mission Journeys H VII 4.3]

07:13 This section also includes topical notes for: Straight and Narrow Road - OT-Apocrypha[2Esdras 7:6-14]; Pseudepigrapha[2Baruch 85:13; 4Ezra 7.4-18; Testament of Abraham 11:2, 11:11, rec. B 8:16]; Philo[Every Good Man Is Free (3) cf. {Deuteronomy 30:19, Psalms 1, Jeremiah 21:8}; On Abraham (59) cf. {Deuteronomy 30:19, Psalms 1, Jeremiah 21:8}; On Husbandry (101, 104) cf. {Genesis 49:17}; On the Life of Moses II (138-139) cf. {Exodus 30:17-21}; On the Migration of Abraham (144-146) cf. {Genesis 25:27, 27:41, 29:31-30:20, 33:4, Numbers 20:17, Deuteronomy 2:27, 5:32, 17:11, 17:20, 28:14}; On The Unchangeableness of God (155-165) cf. {Numbers 20:17, Deuteronomy 2:27, 5:32, 17:11, 17:20, 28:14}]; Plato[Republic II 364d, X 619e, 621c-d]; Clement of Alexandria[Exhortation to the Heathen 10; Stromata Book IV.6, 22, V.5, VI.1]; Hippolytus[Refutation of all Heresies Book V.3]; Liturgy of James 29; Tertullian[Five Books Against Marcion Book II.13]; NT-Apocrypha[Clement Romance - Peter on his Mission Journeys H VII 7.1]; Epic of Gilgamesh[The Forest Journey]; Indian[Dhammapada 45]

07:13-14 This section also includes topical notes for: Salvation to Some and Destruction to Others - Matthew 25:29-30, 46; Luke 13:24; Romans 9:22-23; Pseudepigrapha[Life of Adam and Eve (Apocalypse of Moses) 28.4; Odes of Solomon 17.2-5, 17.14-15, 25.4, 31.13, 33.6-13, 35.1-7, 40.5-6, 42.14-20; Testament of Asher 1:3; Testament of Benjamin 3.8]; Dead Sea Scrolls[4Q 431(4QHADAYOT[4QH]) Fragment 1 5-9; 4Q Enoch (4Q201[4QENAR]) COL I 1-8; 4Q Historical Word (4Q183) 1-8; 4Q Sapiential Work (4Q418[4QSAP.WORKA]) Fragment 69 5-9; 4Q Testament of Qahat (4Q542[4QTQAHATAR]) COL II 1-8; 4Q Visions of Amram (4Q548[4QAMRAMAR]) 8-16]; Philo[On Dreams, That they Are God-Sent (1.151-1.152, 2.282) cf. {Genesis 28:12, Exodus 14:30, Leviticus 26:12}; On Flight And Finding (73-74) cf. {Deuteronomy 27:11-28:68}; On the Life of Moses I (145-146) cf. {Exodus 7:8-11:10, Matthew 25, Revelation 20:1-21:8}]; Plato[Phaedo 63c]; Clement[Homily XVIII.17]; Cyprian[Treatise XII.Book III.6]; Hippolytus[Fragments - On Susannah 18; Refutation of all Heresies Book V.3]; Irenaeus[Demonstration of the Apostolic Preaching 69]; Teaching of the Twelve Apostles 1.1; Tertullian[On Fasting 17]; Nag Hammadi[Authoritative Teaching 32-33; Gospel of Philip 66; Gospel of Thomas 49; Teachings of Silvanus 103, 106-107; Testimony of Truth 31-32]; Indian[Dhammapada 163, 244-245]

07:14 This section also includes topical notes for: Few Find It - Acts 14:22; Philo[Every Good Man Is Free (72) cf. {Deuteronomy 30:14}]; Clement of Alexandria[Stromata Book IV.2]; Origen[Against Celsus Book VI.16; Gospel of John Book X.28; Gospel of Matthew Book XII.12, XIII.30, XIV.1]; NT-Apocrypha[Epistula Apostolorum 24]

07:15 Ezekiel 22:27; Matthew 10:16, 24:11, 24; Luke 6:26, 13:32n; John 10:12; Acts 20:29; 2Peter 2:1; 1John 4:1; Revelation 16:13; Archelaus[Disputation with Manes 42]; Clement of Alexandria[Exhortation to the Heathen 1; Stromata Book I.8]; Constitutions of the Holy Apostles[Book VI.13]; Irenaeus[Against Heresies Book I.Preface.2, III.16.8]; Justin[Dialogue with Trypho 35]; Lactantius[Divine Institutes Book V.3]; Tertullian[On Prescription Against Heretics 1, 4]; NT-Apocrypha[Acts of Peter 1.8; Acts of Thomas 1.67, 1.79; Clement Romance 17.4; Epistula Apostolorum 44]

07:15-16 Justin[First Apology 16]
07:15-27 Luke 6:43-49

07:16 Isaiah 5:24; James 3:12; OT-Apocrypha[Sirach 27:6]; Archelaus[Disputation with Manes 17]; Tertullian[On Prescription Against Heretics 30]

07:16-20 Pseudepigrapha[Apocalypse of Adam 6:2]

07:16-21 This section also includes topical notes for: Trees Bearing Good Fruit – Genesis 1:12, 2:9; Judges 9:9-13; Matthew 3:7-10, 12:33, 13:33, 35; Mark 4:20; Luke 3:8-9, 6:43, 8:14-15; John 15:2-16; Romans 11:24; James 3:17; Jude 1:12; Pseudepigrapha[4Ezra 6.44, 8.6, 9.21-23, 9.32-33; Odes of Solomon 8.2, 11.1, 11.12, 11.16-16c, 11.23, 14.7; Questions of Ezra Recension A 1.37-40]; Philo[Concerning Noah's Work As A Planter (43-45, 95-99, 102-109) cf. {Genesis 2:8-9, Leviticus 19:23-25}; On Husbandry (12-20) cf. {Genesis 9:20, Deuteronomy 20:20}; On the Birth of Abel And the Sacrifices offered By Him And By His Brother Cain (124-130) cf. {Numbers 35:6-32, Joshua 20:2-3, 21:13-38}; On the Change of Names (140) cf. {Genesis 2:8-9}; On the Virtues (156-160) cf. {Leviticus 19:23-25}; The Cherubim: Of Cain And His Birth Part 2 (101-104); Special Laws I (245-246) cf. {Leviticus 6:9-11}]; Clement of Alexandria[Exhortation to the Heathen 11; Stromata Book IV.18]; Irenaeus[Against Heresies Book I.11.1, 17.3, IV.11.2-3, V.10.1-2, 12.4, 14.4; Demonstration of the Apostolic Preaching 99; Fragments from the Lost Works 55]; Liturgy of James 7, 21; Nag Hammadi[Apocalypse of Adam 76; Authoritative Teaching 31; Book of Thomas the Contender 142; Gospel of Thomas 45; Gospel of Truth 28; Trimorphic Protennoia 44; Tripartite Tractate 118]; NT-Apocrypha[Gospel of Judas 39, 43]

07:17 Tertullian[Against All Heresies 6; On the Flesh of Christ 8]

07:18 Archelaus[Disputation with Manes 5, 13]; Clement of Alexandria[The Instructor Book II.5]; Hippolytus[Refutation of all Heresies Book X.15]; Origen[De Principiis Book II.5.4]; Tertullian[Against Hermogenes 13]

07:19 Matthew 3:10; Luke 3:9, 13:6-9; John 15:6; Justin[First Apology 16]; NT-Apocrypha[6Ezra 17.78]

07:20 Matthew 7:16, 12:33

07:21 Matthew 21:31; Romans 2:13; James 1:22, 25; 1John 2:17; Apostolic[2Clement 4:2]; Clement of Alexandria[Stromata Book VII.12, 16; Who is the Rich Man that shall be Saved 29]; Cyprian[Epistle LXXII.16; Treatise XII.Book III.19]; Hippolytus[Refutation of all Heresies Book V.3]; Justin[First Apology 16]; NT-Apocrypha[Clement Romance - Peter on his Mission Journeys H VIII 7.4; Epistula Apostolorum 18; Gospel of the Nazareans Fragment 6]

07:21-23 Luke 13:25-27; Origen[Gospel of John Book X.28]

07:22 Jeremiah 14:14, 27:15; Mark 9:38; Luke 9:49; Cyprian[Treatise I.15]; Justin[Dialogue with Trypho 76]; Origen[Against Celsus Book I.6]

07:22-23 Anonymous[Treatise Against the Heretic Novatian 8]; Cyprian[Treatise XII.Book III.26]; Origen[Against Celsus Book II.49; De Principiis Book IV.1.2]

07:23 Psalms 6:8-9; Matthew 10:33, 13:41-42, 25:41; 2Timothy 2:12; Apostolic[2Clement 4:5]; Hippolytus[Appendix to the Works of Hippolytus - On the End of the World 48]; NT-Apocrypha[Gospel of the Nazareans Fragment 6]

07:24 James 1:22; Archelaus[Disputation with Manes 46]; Cyprian[Treatise I.2]; Origen[Gospel of Matthew Book XII.11; De Principiis Book III.1.6]

07:24-27 Cyprian[Treatise XII.Book III.96]

07:24-29 Luke 6:43-49n

07:25 Job 1:19; Irenaeus[Against Heresies Book II.27.3]

07:26 James 1:23; Origen[De Principiis Book III.1.6]

07:26-27 Anonymous[Treatise Against the Heretic Novatian 5]

07:27 Ezekiel 13:10-15

07:28 Matthew 11:1, 13:53, 19:1, 26:1; Luke 7:1; Pseudepigrapha[Joseph and Aseneth 15:11]; Origen[Gospel of Matthew Book XIV.14]

07:28-29 This section also includes topical notes for: Power and Authority – Psalms 62:11; Matthew 9:6, 28:18; Mark 1:22, 27, 2:10; Luke 4:32-36, 5:24; 1Corinthians 15:24; Ephesians 1:21; Philo[Every Good Man Is Free (159)]

07:29 Matthew 9:35n; Pseudepigrapha[Psalms of Solomon 17.43]

08:01-04 Mark 1:40-45; Luke 5:12-16

08:02 Numbers 12:10, 13; Matthew 28:17n; NT-Apocrypha[Epistula Apostolorum 5]

08:02-03 Origen[Gospel of John Book VI.28]

08:02-04 NT-Apocrypha[Papyrus Egerton 2 Fragment 1 Lines 22-41]

08:03 Origen[Against Celsus Book I.48]

08:04 Leviticus 13:49, 14:2-32; Matthew 9:30, 12:16; Mark 7:36; Luke 17:14; Constitutions of the Holy Apostles[Book VI.19]; Cyprian[Epistle LIV.4, LXIV.2]; Origen[Gospel of John Book II.28]

08:05 Origen[Gospel of John Book X.10]; Tertullian[On Baptism 11; On Idolatry 19]
08:05-06 Tertullian[Against the Valentinians 28]
08:05-13 Luke 7:1-10; John 4:43-54
08:07 Origen[Letter to Gregory 3]
08:07-16 Matthew 4:23-24n
08:08 Matthew 8:16n
08:09 Clement[Recognitions Book IV.33]; Irenaeus[Against Heresies Book I.7.4]
08:10 Matthew 15:28; Archelaus[Disputation with Manes 42]
08:11 Psalms 107:3; Isaiah 43:5; OT-Apocrypha[4Maccabees 13:17]; Pseudepigrapha[3Enoch 48A:10; Baruch 4:37; Testament of Levi 18:14]; Clement[Homily VIII.4; Recognitions Book IV.4]; Cyprian[Treatise IV.13]; Irenaeus[Against Heresies Book IV.8.1, V.30.4]; Justin[Dialogue with Trypho 76, 120, 140]; NT-Apocrypha[Clement Romance - Peter on his Mission Journeys H VIII 4.1]
08:11-12 Luke 13:28-29; Cyprian[Treatise XII.Book I.23]; Irenaeus[Against Heresies Book IV.36.8]; NT-Apocrypha[Narrative of Joseph 3]
08:12 This section also includes topical notes for: Weeping and Gnashing of Teeth - Psalms 112:10; Matthew 13:42, 50, 22:13, 24:51, 25:30; Luke 6:25, 13:28; Pseudepigrapha[4Ezra 7.36; Greek Apocalypse of Ezra 4:37; Sibylline Oracles 8.231, 8.86; Testament of Jacob 5:9]; Constitutions of the Holy Apostles[Book V.6]; Tertullian[On the Resurrection of the Flesh 36]; Nag Hammadi[Dialogue of the Savior 14; Gospel of Philip 68]; NT-Apocrypha[Acts of Peter 1.12; Apocalypse of Paul 1.16, 1.42; Apocalypse of Peter 1.5; Epistula Apostolorum 39; Letter of Clement to James 17.1]
08:13 Matthew 9:29, 15:28; John 4:50-51; Irenaeus[Against Heresies Book IV.37.5]
08:14 1Corinthians 9:5
08:14-22 Mark 1:29-38; Luke 4:38-43
08:15 Tertullian[A Treatise on the Soul 17]
08:16 This section also includes topical notes for: Healing with a Word - Matthew 8:8; Luke 7:7; Irenaeus[Against Heresies Book V.15.2]; Lactantius[Divine Institutes Book IV.15]; NT-Apocrypha[Epistula Apostolorum 5]
08:17 Isaiah 53:4; Irenaeus[Demonstration of the Apostolic Preaching 67]
08:18-27 Mark 4:35-41; Luke 8:22-25, 9:57-62
08:20 This section also includes topical notes for: No Where to Lay His Head - Genesis 28:11; Psalms 80:17, 84:4; Luke 9:58; 2Corinthians 8:9; Philo[On Dreams, That they Are God-Sent (1.124-1.126) cf. {Genesis 28:11, 20-21}]; Rabbinic[Jerusalem Taanit 65 cf. {Numbers 23:19}]; Clement of Alexandria[Stromata Book I.3]; Cyprian[Treatise XII.Book III.11]; Tertullian[On Idolatry 18]; Nag Hammadi[Gospel of Thomas 86]; NT-Apocrypha[Acts of Andrew (Codex Vaticanus 808) 10]
08:21 1Kings 19:20; OT-Apocrypha[Tobit 4:3]
08:21-22 Tertullian[On Monogamy 7]
08:22 Matthew 9:9; John 1:43, 21:19; Clement of Alexandria[Stromata Book III.4; The Instructor Book III.11; Who is the Rich Man that shall be Saved 23]; Cyprian[Treatise IV.10]; NT-Apocrypha[Acts of Peter 1.40]
08:23 Origen[Gospel of John Book X.14]
08:23-27 Psalms 107:23-31; Mark 4:37-41n; Luke 8:22-25; Pseudepigrapha[Testament of Adam 3.1; Testament of Naphtali 6.1-10]
08:24 This section also includes topical notes for: Asleep in the Boat - Jonah 1:4; Mark 4:38; Philo[On the Creation (87-88) cf. {Genesis 2:7-20}]; Tertullian[On Baptism 12]
08:24-26 Clement[Homily XIX.14]
08:26 Psalms 65:8, 89:10, 107:25-32; Matthew 14:31; Pseudepigrapha[2Baruch 21:6]; Archelaus[Disputation with Manes 44 cf. {Exodus 14}]; Clement of Alexandria[Stromata Book VI.14]; Irenaeus[Fragments from the Lost Works 52]; NT-Apocrypha[Epistula Apostolorum 24]
08:26-27 Egyptian Book of the Dead[Oration 57]
08:27 Psalms 107:23-30; Mark 04:37-41n; Luke 8:25
08:28 Isaiah 65:4; Origen[Gospel of John Book VI.24]; Linguistics[The Hebrew phrase "Met Him" (ויפגעו בו) in verse 8:28 is written the same as "Entreated Him" (ויפגעו בו) in verse 8:31]
08:28-34 Mark 5:1-20n; Luke 8:26-40; Justin[First Apology 18]
08:29 1Kings 17:18; Mark 1:24; Luke 4:34; Pseudepigrapha[1Enoch 16:1]; Cyprian[Treatise XII.Book II.28]; Origen[Gospel of Matthew Book XI.17]; Tertullian[Against Praxeas 26]
08:30-34 Tertullian[On Modesty 9]
08:31 Clement[Homily XIX.14]; Linguistics[The Hebrew phrase "Met Him" (ויפגעו בו) in verse 8:28 is written the same as "Entreated Him" (ויפגעו בו) in verse 8:31]

08:32 Origen[Gospel of John Book VI.24]

09:01-08 Mark 2:1-12; Luke 5:17-26

09:02 Matthew 8:6; Luke 7:48, 9:33; Anonymous[Treatise on Re-Baptism 18]; Clement of
Alexandria[The Instructor Book I.2]; Constitutions of the Holy Apostles[Book II.20]; NT-
Apocrypha[Epistula Apostolorum 5]

09:02-07 Irenaeus[Against Heresies Book V.17.2-3]

09:03 1Samuel 15:22

09:04 Zechariah 8:17; Matthew 12:25; Cyprian[Treatise IV.4]; Tertullian[A Treatise on the Soul 15; On
the Resurrection of the Flesh 15]

09:06 This section also includes topical notes for: Authority to Forgive Sins - Psalms 80:17; Matthew
7:28-29n; Mark 2:10; Luke 7:48-49; Acts 5:31n, 13:38, 26:18n; Colossians 2:13; 1John 1:9, 2:12;
Rabbinic[Babylonian Sanhedrin 38b cf. {Exodus 23:21, 24:1}]

09:06-08 Acts 9:33-35

09:08 Irenaeus[Against Heresies Book V.17.2]

09:09 Matthew 8:22; John 1:43, 21:19; Clement of Alexandria[Who is the Rich Man that shall be Saved
13]; Origen[Gospel of Matthew Book XIV.15]; Tertullian[On Baptism 12; On Idolatry 12]; Nag
Hammadi[Gospel of Philip 63]; NT-Apocrypha[Gospel of the Ebionites Fragment 4]

09:09-13 This section also includes topical notes for: Publicans and Sinners - Genesis 47:17-26; Mark
2:13-17; Luke 5:27-32; Philo[Special Laws II (92-95)]

09:10-11 Matthew 11:19n; Luke 15:1-2, 19:7

09:10-12 Tertullian[On Modesty 9]

09:10-17 Luke 7:34-50; Pseudepigrapha[Joseph and Aseneth 20:2]; Philo[On the Contemplative Life Or
Suppliants (75)]

09:11 Genesis 38:28, 42:32, 47:13-26; Luke 15:1-2

09:12 Constitutions of the Holy Apostles[Book II.14, 20, 40]; Cyprian[Epistle LI.16, LXVI.4];
Methodius[Banquet of the Ten Virgins 1.1]; Origen[Against Celsus Book III.61]

09:13 Proverbs 16:7; Hosea 6:6; Matthew 12:7; Pseudepigrapha[Apocalypse of Sedrach 15:1; Sibylline
Oracles 2.81-86, 8.334]; Apostolic[2Clement 2:4; Epistle of Barnabas 5:9]; Clement of
Alexandria[Stromata Book IV.6; Who is the Rich Man that shall be Saved 39]; Clement[Homily
III.56; Recognitions Book I.37]; Cyprian[Epistle LXXII.23]; Justin[First Apology 15]; Tertullian[On
Repentance 8; Five Books Against Marcion Book IV.27]

09:14 Isaiah 58:3; Matthew 11:18; Luke 18:12

09:14-15 Tertullian[On Fasting 2]; Nag Hammadi[Gospel of Thomas 6, 14, 104]

09:14-17 Mark 2:18-22; Luke 5:33-39

09:15 John 3:29n; Constitutions of the Holy Apostles[Book V.18]; Nag Hammadi[Gospel of Thomas 75]

09:16 Mark 2:21n; Luke 5:36

09:16-17 Archelaus[Disputation with Manes 18]; Tertullian[Five Books Against Marcion Book III.15];
Nag Hammadi[Gospel of Thomas 47]

09:17 This section also includes topical notes for: New Wine into Old Wine Skins - Job 32:19; Mark
2:22; Luke 5:37, 39; Dead Sea Scrolls[11Q TEMPLE SCROLL (11Q19[11QT]) COL XXI 4-9;
(11Q20[11QTEMPLE]) Fragment 8-9 COL I 10-11]; Philo[Fragments Preserved By Antonius Ser.
Cxxxv]; Rabbinic[Avot 4.26; Mishnah Aboth 4:20]; Irenaeus[Against Heresies Book IV.33.14]

09:18 Matthew 8:3, 28:17n; Mark 6:5, 7:32, 8:23, 25; Luke 13:13; Pseudepigrapha[Joseph and Aseneth
19:1]; Origen[Gospel of Matthew Book XI.17]

09:18-26 Mark 5:21-43; Luke 8:40-56

09:20 Leviticus 15:25; Numbers 15:38; Deuteronomy 22:12; Matthew 14:36; Mark 6:56; Dionysius of
Alexandria[Extant Fragments Epistle to Bishop Basilides 2]; Irenaeus[Against Heresies Book II.20.1,
23.1-2]; NT-Apocrypha[Epistula Apostolorum 5; Gospel of the Nazareans Fragment 29]

09:20-21 Nag Hammadi[Testimony of Truth 41]

09:20-22 Origen[Gospel of Matthew Book XI.7]

09:22 Mark 10:52; Luke 7:50, 17:19; Acts 3:16; Clement of Alexandria[Stromata Book V.1, VI.6];
Constitutions of the Holy Apostles[Book VI.28]

09:23 Tertullian[On Modesty 2]

09:24 John 11:11; Origen[Gospel of Matthew Book XII.2]

09:25 Mark 1:31, 9:27

09:27 Psalms 86:3; Matthew 1:1, 20:29-31; Pseudepigrapha[Testament of Solomon 1:7, 20:2]

09:28 Hippolytus[Fragments - On Genesis 49.12-15]

09:29 Matthew 8:13, 15:28; Clement of Alexandria[Stromata Book II.11; The Instructor Book I.6];
  Irenaeus[Against Heresies Book IV.37.5, V.17.1]
09:29-30 Matthew 20:34
09:30-31 Mark 7:36
09:32 NT-Apocrypha[Epistula Apostolorum 5]
09:32-33 Matthew 12:22; Mark 7:32, 35, 9:17, 25; Luke 11:14
09:32-34 Matthew 10:25
09:33 Mark 2:12; Lactantius[Divine Institutes Book IV.26]
09:34 Matthew 12:24; Mark 3:22; Luke 11:15; Pseudepigrapha[Testament of Solomon 2:9];
  Clement[Recognitions Book I.40]
09:35 This section also includes topical notes for: Teaching - Matthew 4:23-24n, 5:2, 7:29, 10:1, 11:1,
  13:54, 21:23, 22:16, 26:55; Mark 1:21-22, 1:34, 39, 2:13, 4:1-2, 5:2, 6:2, 6, 34, 10:1, 11:17, 12:14, 35, 14:49;
  Luke 4:15, 31, 44, 5:3, 17, 6:6, 7:21, 13:10, 22, 26, 19:47, 20:1, 21, 21:37, 23:5; John 3:2, 6:45, 59, 7:14, 28,
  35, 8:2, 20, 18:20; Dead Sea Scrolls[4Q Aramaic C (4Q536) Fragment 1 COL I 1-13]; Nag
  Hammadi[Gospel of Mary 8]
09:35-11:01 Mark 6:7-13; Luke 9:1-6
09:36 This section also includes topical notes for: Sheep with No Shepherd - Numbers 27:17; 1Kings
  22:17; 2Chronicles 18:16; Ezekiel 34:5; Zechariah 10:2; Matthew 14:14, 15:32; Mark 6:34; OT-
  Apocrypha[Judith 11:19]; Pseudepigrapha[Apocalypse of Elijah 4:1]; Philo[On the Virtues (58) cf.
  {Numbers 27:16}]; NT-Apocrypha[Apocalypse of Paul 1.48]
09:37 John 4:35; Pseudepigrapha[Joseph and Aseneth 1:2]; NT-Apocrypha[Epistula Apostolorum 41]
09:37-38 Luke 10:2; Clement of Alexandria[Stromata Book I.1]; Clement[First Epistle Concerning
  Virginity 13; Recognitions Book IV.4]; Origen[Against Celsus Book I.62]; Nag Hammadi[Gospel of
  Thomas 73]
09:38 OT-Apocrypha[1Maccabees 12:17]
10:01 Matthew 9:35; Mark 1:34, 6:7; Luke 7:21, 9:1; NT-Apocrypha[Abgar Legend]
10:01-04 Genesis 35:22-26; Mark 3:13-19; Luke 6:12-16
10:02 This section also includes topical notes for: Twelve Apostles - Luke 11:49, 22:14; John 1:40-41;
  Pseudepigrapha[4Ezra 2.18-19; Martyrdom and Ascension of Isaiah 3.13]; Dead Sea Scrolls[1Q Rule
  of the Community (1QS) COL VIII 1-9; 4Q Isaiah Pesher (4Q164[4QPIS]) Fragment I 4-6; 4Q
  Ordinances (4Q159[4QORD]) Fragments 2-4 3, 4; Damascus Document (CD-A) COL X 4-10];
  Philo[On Dreams, That they Are God-Sent (2.272-2.273) cf. {Deuteronomy 26:13}];
  Rabbinic[Babylonian Sanhedrin 2a, 43a]; Clement of Alexandria[Stromata Book VI.11];
  Clement[Recognitions Book I.40]; Constitutions of the Holy Apostles[Book VI.14]; Irenaeus[Against
  Heresies Book II.21.1, IV.8.3; Demonstration of the Apostolic Preaching 46; Fragments from the Lost
  Works 31]; Justin[Dialogue with Trypho 42]; NT-Apocrypha[Gospel of Judas 33; Gospel of the
  Ebionites Fragment 4]
10:02-04 NT-Apocrypha[Acts of Thomas 1.1; Epistula Apostolorum 2; Gospel of the Ebionites
  Fragment 4]
10:03 John 1:43; Origen[Against Celsus Book I.62]
10:04 Matthew 26:25, 27:3; Mark 14:44; John 6:64, 12:4, 13:11, 18:2, 5
10:05 Clement of Alexandria[Stromata Book III.18]; Clement[Recognitions Book I.57]; Cyprian[Epistle
  LXXV.6]; Hippolytus[Refutation of all Heresies Book V.18]; Origen[Gospel of Matthew Book XII.15];
  Tertullian[De Fuga in Persecutione 6]; NT-Apocrypha[Kerygma Petri 3b]
10:05-14 Josephus[Antiquities 18.1.5 18-22; War 2.8.2-4 119-127]
10:05-15 Mark 6:7-13; Luke 9:1-6
10:06 Jeremiah 50:6; Matthew 15:24; Irenaeus[Against Heresies Book III.13.2, IV.1.7]; NT-
  Apocrypha[Gospel of the Ebionites Fragment 4]
10:07 Matthew 3:2, 4:17; Luke 10:9, 11; Tertullian[On the Resurrection of the Flesh 33]
10:08 2Kings 5:16; Rabbinic[Babylonian Berakhot 29a]; Clement[First Epistle Concerning Virginity 12];
  Cyprian[Treatise XII.Book III.100]; Irenaeus[Against Heresies Book I.4.3, II.32.4]; Tertullian[On
  Modesty 2]; NT-Apocrypha[Clement Romance 71.3]
10:09 NT-Apocrypha[Acts of Thomas 1.20]
10:09-11 Hippolytus[Refutation of all Heresies Book IX.15]
10:10 Luke 10:4, 7; 1Corinthians 9:14; 1Timothy 5:18; Apostolic[Didache 13:2]; Archelaus[Disputation
  with Manes 42]; Irenaeus[Against Heresies Book IV.8.3]; Origen[Gospel of John Book I.26]; Teaching
  of the Twelve Apostles 13.3; Tertullian[Five Books Against Marcion Book IV.24]; Nag

Hammadi[Dialogue of the Savior 53; Gospel of Thomas 14, 42]; NT-Apocrypha[Acts of Andrew and Matthias]

10:10-11 Numbers 18:31

10:11 Clement[Recognitions Book II.1]

10:12 Constitutions of the Holy Apostles[Book II.54]; NT-Apocrypha[Clement Romance 30.3]

10:12-13 Luke 10:5-6; Constitutions of the Holy Apostles[Book III.14]

10:12-15 Clement[Recognitions Book II.30]

10:13 NT-Apocrypha[Gospel of the Nazareans Fragment 23]

10:14 Acts 13:51

10:14-15 Luke 10:10-12

10:15 Genesis 18:20-19.28; Matthew 11:24; Luke 10:4-12; 2Peter 2:6; Jude 1:7; Pseudepigrapha[4Ezra 2.9]; Irenaeus[Against Heresies Book IV.28.1]; NT-Apocrypha[Epistula Apostolorum 26]

10:16 Genesis 3:1; Luke 10:3, 13:32n; John 10:12; Acts 20:29; Romans 16:19; OT-Apocrypha[Sirach 13:17]; Pseudepigrapha[Apocalypse of Elijah 3:2]; Apostolic[2Clement 5:4; Ignatius - Letter to Polycarp 3:2]; Clement of Alexandria[Exhortation to the Heathen 10; Stromata Book VII.13; The Instructor Book I.5]; Cyprian[Treatise XII.Book III.87]; Fabian[First Epistle]; Irenaeus[Against Heresies Book V.19.1]; Tertullian[Against the Valentinians 2; On Baptism 8; Scorpiace 9]; Nag Hammadi[Gospel of Thomas 39; Teachings of Silvanus 95]; NT-Apocrypha[Acts of Andrew and Matthias; Epistula Apostolorum 44; Gospel of the Nazareans Fragment 7; Pseudo-Titus Epistle Line 479]

10:16-25 Mark 13:9-13; Luke 21:12-17

10:17 Constitutions of the Holy Apostles[Book V.3]; Tertullian[De Fuga in Persecutione 6]

10:17-18 Matthew 24:12; Irenaeus[Against Heresies Book III.18.5]; Peter of Alexandria[Canonical Epistle 9]

10:18 Deuteronomy 31:26; Cyprian[Epistle XXV.4]; Origen[Against Celsus Book II.13; Gospel of Matthew Book XII.16; De Principiis Book IV.1.2]

10:19 Exodus 4:12; Cyprian[Epistle LXXXII.1]; Tertullian[Scorpiace 11]

10:19-20 Cyprian[Epistle VIII.1, LIII.4, LV.5, LXXVI.5; Treatise XI.10, XII.Book III.16]

10:19-22 Luke 12:11-12; Clement of Alexandria[Stromata Book VII.11]

10:20 Luke 21:12-15; Pseudepigrapha[Martyrdom and Ascension of Isaiah 1:7]; Irenaeus[Against Heresies Book III.17.1]

10:21 Micah 7:6; Luke 21:16; Pseudepigrapha[3Baruch 4:17; Greek Apocalypse of Ezra 3.12-15]; Irenaeus[Against Heresies Book I.3.5]; Origen[Gospel of Matthew Book XII.16]; Tertullian[Scorpiace 10]

10:22 Daniel 12:12; Matthew 24:9, 13; Luke 21:17; OT-Apocrypha[2Esdras 6:25]; Clement of Alexandria[Who is the Rich Man that shall be Saved 32]; Constitutions of the Holy Apostles[Book V.3]; Cyprian[Epistle V.2, XXXVI.1; Treatise I.21, IX.13, XI.6]; Teaching of the Twelve Apostles 16.5; Tertullian[De Fuga in Persecutione 7; On Prescription Against Heretics 3]; Nag Hammadi[Testimony of Truth 44]; NT-Apocrypha[Acts of Thomas 1.25; Epistula Apostolorum 50]

10:23 Psalms 80:17; Matthew 16:27-28, 24:27, 30, 37, 39, 44, 25:31, 26:64; Mark 13:26, 14:62; Luke 9:26, 17:30, 18:8, 21:27; Callistus[Second Epistle 3.3]; Clement of Alexandria[Stromata Book IV.10]; Constitutions of the Holy Apostles[Book V.3, VIII.45]; Origen[Against Celsus Book I.65; Gospel of Matthew Book X.23]; Peter of Alexandria[Canonical Epistle 9]; Tertullian[De Fuga in Persecutione 6; To his Wife Book I.3]

10:24 Luke 6:40; John 13:16, 15:20; Constitutions of the Holy Apostles[Book V.12]; Fabian[Second Epistle]; Irenaeus[Against Heresies Book II.28.6]; Tertullian[A Treatise on the Soul 55; Against All Heresies 3; Five Books Against Marcion Book IV.4]

10:25 Matthew 9:34, 12:24; Mark 3:22; Luke 11:15; Pseudepigrapha[Testament of Solomon 2:9, 3:1]; Clement[Recognitions Book II.27]; Cyprian[Treatise XII.Book III.75]; Irenaeus[Against Heresies Book V.27.1]; Nag Hammadi[Dialogue of the Savior 53]

10:26 Matthew 13:11n; Mark 4:22; Luke 8:17; Pseudepigrapha[3Enoch 11:1; 4Ezra 12.37-39]; Philo[**That The Worse Is Wont To Attack The Better (128)**];Clement of Alexandria[Exhortation to the Heathen 1]; Clement[Recognitions Book III.13]; Irenaeus[Against Heresies Book I.Preface.2]; Origen[Gospel of Matthew Book XIV.9]; Tertullian[On the Veiling of Virgins 14]; Nag Hammadi[Apocryphon of John 1; Book of Thomas the Contender 138; Gospel of Philip 56, 84-85; Gospel of Thomas 5, 17, 108; Gospel of Truth 18, 24, 27, 40; On the Origin of the World 125; Treatise on the Resurrection 45; Trimorphic Protennoia 37, 41, 44, 47]; NT-Apocrypha[Gospel of Mani Kephalaia LXV]; Epic of Gilgamesh[Prologue - Gilgamesh King in Uruk]

> **This voice is itself the most manifest of all the conceptions. For, as what is laid up is hidden in darkness until light shines upon it and exhibits it, in the same manner the conceptions are stored away in an invisible place, namely, the mind, until the voice, like light, sheds its beams upon them and reveals everything. (Philo - That The Worse Is Wont To Attack The Better 128)**

10:26-27 Clement of Alexandria[Stromata Book I.12, VI.15]

10:26-31 Luke 12:2-7

10:27 Hippolytus[Fragments - On Daniel 2.2; Refutation of all Heresies Book V.2]; Origen[Gospel of Matthew Book XII.17]; Tertullian[On Prescription Against Heretics 26]; Nag Hammadi[Gospel of Thomas 33]

10:28 James 4:12; OT-Apocrypha[4Maccabees 13:14-15]; Apostolic[2Clement 5:4]; Anonymous[Treatise Against the Heretic Novatian 16]; Archelaus[Disputation with Manes 47]; Clement[Homily XVII.5]; Constitutions of the Holy Apostles[Book V.4]; Cyprian[Epistle LXXX.2, LV.7; Treatise XI.5, XII.Book III.16]; Irenaeus[Against Heresies Book III.18.5]; Justin[First Apology 19]; Novatian[Treatise Concerning the Trinity 25]; Peter of Alexandria[Genuine Acts of Peter 3]; Syriac Martyrdom of Shamuna, Guria, and Habib; Tertullian[De Fuga in Persecutione 7; On Modesty 2; On the Resurrection of the Flesh 35]; NT-Apocrypha[Acts of Paul in Ephesus p.1; Epistula Apostolorum 39]

10:29 Cyprian[Epistle LIV.5, LXVIII.1; Treatises Attributed to Cyprian On the Glory of Martyrdom 17]; Irenaeus[Against Heresies Book V.22.2]; Origen[De Principiis Book III.2.7]; Tertullian[De Fuga in Persecutione 3; On Exhortation to Chastity 1; On Monogamy 9; On the Resurrection of the Flesh 35]; Nag Hammadi[Gospel of Philip 56]

10:29-30 Clement[Homily XII.31]; Irenaeus[Against Heresies Book II.26.2, 28.9]; Novatian[Treatise Concerning the Trinity 8]; Origen[Against Celsus Book VIII.70]

10:30 1Samuel 14:45; 2Samuel 14:11; Acts 27:34; Clement of Alexandria[Stromata Book VI.17; The Instructor Book III.3]; Tertullian[On the Resurrection of the Flesh 35]; NT-Apocrypha[Acts of Andrew and Matthias]

10:31 Matthew 6:26, 12:12; Tertullian[On the Resurrection of the Flesh 35]

10:32 1Samuel 2:30; Revelation 3:5; Pseudepigrapha[4Ezra 2.47]; Apostolic[2Clement 3:2]; Anonymous[Treatise on Re-Baptism 11]; Clement of Alexandria[Stromata Book IV.9]; Constitutions of the Holy Apostles[Book V.1]; Cyprian[Epistle XXXVI.1]; Origen[Gospel of Matthew Book XII.16, 24]; NT-Apocrypha[Pseudo-Titus Epistle Line 636]

10:32-33 Luke 12:8-9; Rabbinic[Avot 4.1 cf. {1Samuel 2:30}]; Cyprian[Epistle IX.2; Treatise XI.5, XII.Book III.16]; Tertullian[Against Praxeas 26; De Fuga in Persecutione 7]

10:33 Mark 8:38; Luke 9:26; 2Timothy 2:12; Anonymous[Treatise Against the Heretic Novatian 7]; Constitutions of the Holy Apostles[Book V.4]; Cyprian[Epistle XXX.7, LIV.12]; Irenaeus[Against Heresies Book III.18.5]; Origen[Gospel of Matthew Book XII.24]; Syriac Martyrdom of Shamuna, Guria, and Habib; Tertullian[On Idolatry 13; On the Flesh of Christ 5; On the Resurrection of the Flesh 13]

10:34 Archelaus[Disputation with Manes 44 cf. {Exodus 32}; Fragment of the Disputation with Manes 1]; Clement[Homily XI.19; Recognitions Book II.26, VI.4]; Hippolytus[Refutation of all Heresies Book V.16]; Irenaeus[Against Heresies Book I.3.5]; Tertullian[Scorpiace 10; Five Books Against Marcion Book III.14]; Victorinus[Apocalypse 1.16]; Nag Hammadi[Gospel of Thomas 16]; NT-Apocrypha[Gospel of the Nazareans Fragment 23; Pseudo Clementines - Kerygmata Petrou H XI 19.1]

10:34-39 Luke 12:49, 51-53, 14:26-27, 27:49

10:35 Rabbinic[Babylonian (Sanhedrin 97a; Sotah 49b)]; NT-Apocrypha[Pseudo Clementines - Kerygmata Petrou H XI 19.3]

10:35-36 Micah 7:6; Pseudepigrapha[Sibylline Oracles 8.84]; Clement[Recognitions Book II.29]

10:37 Deuteronomy 33:9; Anonymous[Martyrdom of Justin Martyr 3]; Archelaus[Disputation with Manes 48]; Constitutions of the Holy Apostles[Book V.4]; Cyprian[Treatise VIII.16]; Tertullian[On Baptism 12; On Prayer 8; Five Books Against Marcion Book IV.19]; NT-Apocrypha[Acts of Thomas 1.61; Pistis Sophia c. 136; Two Books of Jeu c. 1-3]

10:37-38 Cyprian[Epistle XXV.4; Treatise XI.6, XII.Book III.18]; Tertullian[De Fuga in Persecutione 7]

10:38 Matthew 16:24-25n; Mark 8:34; Luke 9:23; Origen[Gospel of Matthew Book XII.22]

10:39 Matthew 16:25; Mark 8:35; Luke 9:24, 17:33; John 12:25n; Apostolic[Ignatius - Letter to the Magnesians 5:2]; Clement of Alexandria[Stromata Book IV.6]; Cyprian[Treatises Attributed to

Cyprian - On the Glory of Martyrdom 28]; Origen[Gospel of Matthew Book XII.20]; Syriac Martyrdom of Habib the Deacon; Tertullian[Scorpiace 11]

10:40 Matthew 18:5; Mark 9:37; Luke 9:48, 10:16; John 12:44, 13:20; Galatians 4:14; Archelaus[Disputation with Manes 47]; Clement of Alexandria[Who is the Rich Man that shall be Saved 31]; Constitutions of the Holy Apostles[Book VIII.46]; Teaching of the Twelve Apostles 11.4; NT-Apocrypha[Letter of Clement to James 2.5, 17.1; Two Books of Jeu c. 1-3]

10:40-11:01 Mark 9:41

10:41 1Kings 17:9-24, 18:4; 2Kings 4:8-37; Constitutions of the Holy Apostles[Book VII.28]; NT-Apocrypha[Epistula Apostolorum 42]

10:41-42 Clement of Alexandria[Stromata Book IV.6]

10:42 Pseudepigrapha[2Baruch 48:19]; Philo[Fragments Extracted From the Parallels of John of Damascus Page 349. A.-B.]; Rabbinic[Babylonian Nedarim 21a]; Cyprian[Treatise XII.Book III.1]; Origen[Gospel of Matthew Book XIV.8]; Tertullian[On Baptism 9]; NT-Apocrypha[Acts of Paul and Thecla 1.6; Arabic Gospel of the Infancy of the Savior 42; History of Joseph the Carpenter 1]

11:01 Matthew 5:2, 7:28, 9:35n, 13:53, 19:1, 26:1

11:02 Matthew 14:3; John 3:24; Constitutions of the Holy Apostles[Book V.7]

11:02-03 Origen[Gospel of Matthew Book X.20]

11:02-06 Pseudepigrapha[Sibylline Oracles 1.350]; Tertullian[On Baptism 10]

11:02-19 Luke 7:18-35

11:03 Psalms 118:26; Daniel 7:13, 9:26; Malachi 3:1; Matthew 3:11; John 1:15, 27, 6:14; Acts 19:4; Hebrews 10:37; Revelation 1:4, 8

11:03 Origen[Gospel of John Book I.7, VI.6]

11:03-06 Acts 3:18-26n; Clement of Alexandria[The Instructor Book I.10]

11:04 Malachi 3:22; Clement of Alexandria[Stromata Book VI.17]; NT-Apocrypha[Epistula Apostolorum 5]

11:04-05 Origen[Gospel of Matthew Book XII.2]

11:04-06 Egyptian Book of the Dead[Oration 99]

11:05 This section also includes topical notes for: Good News to the Poor - Isaiah 26:19, 29:18, 35:5-6, 42:7, 18, 61:1-2; Matthew 5:3; Luke 4:18, 6:20, 7:22; OT-Apocrypha[Sirach 48:5]; Pseudepigrapha[Apocalypse of Elijah 3:9; Sibylline Oracles 1.353, 6:12, 8.205]; Dead Sea Scrolls[1Q Hymns (1QHODAYOTH [1QH]) COL XXIII 14-15; **4Messianic Apocalypse (4Q521) Fragment 2 COL II 7-13**]; Tacitus[The Histories 4.81]; Apostolic[1Clement 59:4]; Clement of Alexandria[Exhortation to the Heathen 1, 12]; Constitutions of the Holy Apostles[Book VIII.1]; Irenaeus[Fragments from the Lost Works 54]; Justin[Dialogue with Trypho 12; First Apology 22]; Nag Hammadi[The Act of Peter 128]; NT-Apocrypha[Abgar Legend; Acts of Peter p.128; Epistula Apostolorum 5]

For the heavens and the earth will listen to His Messiah, *and no one* in them will turn away from the commandments of the holy ones. Strengthen yourselves, you who seek the Lord in His service! Will you not find the Lord in this, all those who hope in their heart? For the Lord will attend the pious and call the righteous by name. Over the poor His spirit will hover, and He will renew the faithful with His strength. For He will honor the pious upon the *throne of His* eternal Kingdom, freeing prisoners, restoring sight to the blind, straightening the *bent*. And in His mercy I shall *ever* cling to those who hope, and the *fruit of* good *deeds* shall not be delayed for anyone, and the Lord will perform glorious things which have never been, just as He said. For He will heal the gravely wounded, and revive the dead. He will bring good news to the poor, *and satisfy the needy*. He will lead the uprooted, and feed the hungry. (Dead Sea Scrolls - 4QMessianic Apocalypse (4Q521) Fragment 2 COL II 1-13)

11:06 Matthew 13:57; 26:31

11:07 Matthew 3:5; Pseudepigrapha[Sibylline Oracles 8.297]; Rabbinic[Babylonian Taanit 20b]; NT-Apocrypha[Acts of Thomas 1.136]

11:07-09 Indian[Dhammapada 395]

11:07-15 Tertullian[Five Books in Reply to Marcion Book II.145]

11:08 Tertullian[On Idolatry 18]; NT-Apocrypha[Acts of Thomas 1.36]; Epic of Gilgamesh[The Coming of Enkidu]

11:09 Matthew 14:5; 21:26; Luke 1:76; Irenaeus[Against Heresies Book III.10.1, 11.4]; Origen[Gospel of John Book VI.8]; Tertullian[On Monogamy 8]

11:09-11 Clement[Recognitions Book I.60]; Nag Hammadi[Gospel of Thomas 46]

11:10 Exodus 23:20; Malachi 3:1; Mark 1:2; Luke 1:76, 7:27; John 3:28; Origen[Gospel of John Book VI.10]; Tertullian[An Answer to the Jews 9]

11:11 Job 11:2, 14:1; Archelaus[Disputation with Manes 49]; Clement of Alexandria[Who is the Rich Man that shall be Saved 31]; Clement[First Epistle Concerning Virginity 6]; Irenaeus[Against Heresies Book III.10.1]; Origen[Gospel of Matthew Book X.22, XIII.15]; Tertullian[On Baptism 12]; NT-Apocrypha[Clement Romance 17.2; Pseudo Clementines - Kerygmata Petrou H II 17.2, H III 22.2, 52.1]; Epic of Gilgamesh[The Coming of Enkidu]

11:12 Ezekiel 22:26; Rabbinic[Babylonian (Baba Mesia 118a; Berakhot 32a; Qiddushin 70a; Sanhedrin 58b cf. {Job 22:8}, 105a); Genesis Rabba on 32:2 cf. {Psalms 12:6}; Mishnah Eduyoth 8.7; Pesiqta de-Rab Kahana 161a; Tosephta Berakhot 5.2 cf. {Esther 7:8}]; Clement of Alexandria[Stromata Book IV.2, V.3; Who is the Rich Man that shall be Saved 21]; Irenaeus[Against Heresies Book IV.37.7]; Origen[Gospel of John Book VI.11]; NT-Apocrypha[Gospel of the Nazareans Fragment 8]

11:12-13 Luke 16:16

11:12-15 Justin[Dialogue with Trypho 51]

11:13 Rabbinic[Babylonian Sanhedrin 11a]; Clement of Alexandria[Stromata Book V.8]; Cyprian[Treatise XII.Book I.9]; Origen[Gospel of John Book VI.14]; Tertullian[An Answer to the Jews 13; On Fasting 2; On Modesty 6]; Nag Hammadi[Apocryphon of James 6]

11:14 Malachi 4:5; Matthew 17:10-13; Mark 9:11-13; Luke 1:17; John 1:21; OT-Apocrypha[Sirach 48:10]; Pseudepigrapha[Sibylline Oracles 2.187]; Rabbinic[Seder Olam Rabba 17]; Justin[Dialogue with Trypho 49]; Origen[Gospel of John Book II.24, VI.7; Gospel of Matthew Book X.20, XII.9]; Tertullian[A Treatise on the Soul 35]

11:14-15 Hippolytus[Refutation of all Heresies Book VIII.3]; Origen[Gospel of John Book II.30]

11:15 This section also includes topical notes for: Ears to Hear - Deuteronomy 29:4; Ezekiel 3:27, 12:2; Matthew 13:9, 43; Mark 4:9, 23, 7:16; Luke 8:8, 14:35; Revelation 2:7, 13:9; Pseudepigrapha[Odes of Solomon 15.3-4]; Philo[Fragments Extracted From the Parallels of John of Damascus Page 782 cf. {Deuteronomy 29:4}; On Dreams, That they Are God-Sent (1.164-1.165) cf. {Deuteronomy 29:4}; On Flight And Finding (122-123) cf. {Deuteronomy 29:4}; On the Contemplative Life Or Suppliants (13) cf. {Genesis 12:1-4, 14:8-17, 22-24}]; Plato[Phaedo 66a-b]; Clement of Alexandria[Exhortation to the Heathen 1, 10; Stromata Book II.5, V.1, 14, VI.15]; Constitutions of the Holy Apostles[Book II.6]; Nag Hammadi[Gospel of Mary 8; Testimony of Truth 29]; NT-Apocrypha[Acts of Thomas 1.82]

11:16-17 Clement of Alexandria[The Instructor Book I.5]

11:17 Ecclesiastes 3:4; Origen[Gospel of Matthew Book X.22]; Nag Hammadi[Gospel of Thomas 43]; NT-Apocrypha[Acts of John 94]; Linguistics[Aramaic word for "Dance" is written the same as "Mourn"]

11:18 Matthew 3:4, 9:14; Luke 18:12; NT-Apocrypha[Acts of Thomas 1.82]

11:18-19 Clement of Alexandria[Stromata Book III.6]

11:19 This section also includes topical notes for: Glutton and a Drunkard - Deuteronomy 21:20; Psalms 80:17; Proverbs 23:20; Matthew 9:11; Luke 7:34, 15:1-2, 19:7; Philo[On Flight And Finding (166) cf. {Genesis 21:2}]; Clement of Alexandria[The Instructor Book II.2]; Irenaeus[Against Heresies Book IV.31.2]; Origen[Gospel of John Book II.1]; Tertullian[On Fasting 2; On Modesty 9; On Monogamy 8]

11:20 Origen[Against Celsus Book VI.16]; NT-Apocrypha[Gospel of the Nazareans Fragment 27]

11:20-24 Luke 10:1-16

11:21 Esther 4:1; Daniel 9:3; Jonah 3:5-6; Acts 3:19n; Pseudepigrapha[Joseph and Aseneth 13:2]; Tertullian[On Modesty 10]

11:21-22 Isaiah 23:1-8; Ezekiel 26:1-28:26; Joel 3:4-8; Amos 1:9-10; Zechariah 9:2-4

11:22 Isaiah 34:8; OT-Apocrypha[Judith 16:17]; Origen[Gospel of Matthew Book XIII.22]; Tertullian[On the Resurrection of the Flesh 33]; NT-Apocrypha[Epistula Apostolorum 26]

11:23 Genesis 19:24-28; Isaiah 14:11, 13-15, 29:14; Ezekiel 31:14; 2Peter 2:6; Jude 1:7; Pseudepigrapha[Psalms of Solomon 1:5]

11:23-24 Irenaeus[Against Heresies Book IV.36.3]; Tertullian[On Fasting 7]

11:24 Matthew 10:15; Luke 10:12; Pseudepigrapha[4Ezra 2.9]; Irenaeus[Against Heresies Book IV.36.4]; NT-Apocrypha[Epistula Apostolorum 26]

11:25 Psalms 136:26; 1Corinthians 1:26-29; OT-Apocrypha[Sirach 51:1; Tobit 7:17]; Rabbinic[Babylonian Baba Batra 12a]; Clement[Homily VIII.6, XVII.5, XVIII.15; Recognitions Book

IV.5]; Irenaeus[Against Heresies Book IV.1.2]; Nag Hammadi[Gospel of Thomas 62]; NT-Apocrypha[Clement Romance - Peter on his Mission Journeys H VIII 6.4; Correspondence between Seneca and Paul VII; Gospel of the Nazareans Fragment 9]

11:25-26 Cyprian[Treatise XII.Book III.22]; Tertullian[Against Praxeas 26]; Nag Hammadi[Gospel of Thomas 4]

11:25-27 Irenaeus[Against Heresies Book I.20.3]

11:25-30 Luke 10:17-24

11:27 Matthew 28:18; John 1:18, 3:35, 10:15, 13:3, 17:2; Philippians 2:9; Alexander of Alexandria[Epistles on Arian Heresy 1.5, 12]; Archelaus[Disputation with Manes 37]; Clement of Alexandria[Exhortation to the Heathen 1; Stromata Book I.28, V.13, VII.10; The Instructor Book I.5; Who is the Rich Man that shall be Saved 7]; Clement[Homily XVII.4, XVIII.4; Recognitions Book II.47]; Hippolytus[Against the Heresy of One Noetus 6]; Irenaeus[Against Heresies Book I.2.5, 15.3, II.6.1, 14.7, 30.9, IV.6.1, 3-4, 7, 7.4, 20.2]; Justin[Dialogue with Trypho 100, 136; First Apology 63]; Origen[Against Celsus Book VI.17, VII.44; Gospel of John Book I.42; De Principiis Book I.1.8, II.4.3, 6.1]; Tertullian[Against Praxeas 8, 24, 26; On Prescription Against Heretics 21; Five Books Against Marcion Book II.27]; Nag Hammadi[Dialogue of the Savior 35]; NT-Apocrypha[Gospel of the Nazareans Fragment 23]

11:28 Exodus 33:14; Jeremiah 31:25; OT-Apocrypha[Sirach 24:19, 51:23]; Clement of Alexandria[Fragments from Macarius Chrysocephalus Parable of the Prodigal son 3, 7]; Clement[Homily III.52]; Constitutions of the Holy Apostles[Book I.6]; Hippolytus[Refutation of all Heresies Book IX.17]; Irenaeus[Against Heresies Book I.20.2]; Methodius[Oration Concerning Simeon and Anna 1]; Origen[Against Celsus Book II.73, III.63]; Nag Hammadi[Authoritative Teaching 35; Gospel of Truth 33; Teachings of Silvanus 103]; NT-Apocrypha[Gospel of the Hebrews Fragment 4b]

11:28-29 Pseudepigrapha[4Ezra 2.25, 2.34]

11:28-30 Clement of Alexandria[Exhortation to the Heathen 12; Stromata Book II.5; The Instructor Book I.10]; Cyprian[Treatise XII.Book I.13, III.119]; Nag Hammadi[Gospel of Thomas 90]

11:29 Numbers 12:3; Isaiah 28:12; Jeremiah 6:16; OT-Apocrypha[Sirach 6:24, 28, 51:26]; Pseudepigrapha[2Enoch 34:1; Sibylline Oracles 8.326]; Rabbinic[Avot 3.6]; Origen[Against Celsus Book II.7]; NT-Apocrypha[Acts of Paul and Thecla 1.7; Acts of Thomas 1.67; Pseudo-Titus Epistle Line 227]

11:29-30 Pseudepigrapha[Odes of Solomon 42.7-8; Psalms of Solomon 17.30]; Apostolic[1Clement 16:17]; Clement of Alexandria[Stromata Book V.5]; Justin[Dialogue with Trypho 53]; NT-Apocrypha[Acts of Thomas 1.28]

11:30 1John 5:3; Clement[Recognitions Book X.51]; Tertullian[On Monogamy 2]

12:01 This section also includes topical notes for: Lawful to do on the Sabbath - Numbers 28:9; Deuteronomy 5:14, 23:24-26; Mark 2:23; Luke 6:1; Dead Sea Scrolls[4Q Ordinances (4Q159[4QORD]) Fragment 1 COL II 3-5]

12:01-08 Mark 2:23-28; Luke 6:1-5; Justin[Dialogue with Trypho 27]

12:02 Exodus 20:10; Deuteronomy 5:14; Hippolytus[Refutation of all Heresies Book IX.23]

12:03-04 1Samuel 21:1-7

12:03-05 Rabbinic[Babylonian Shabbat 132b]

12:04 Exodus 40:23; Leviticus 24:5-9; 1Samuel 21:1-6; OT-Apocrypha[2Maccabees 10:3]

12:05 Numbers 28:9-10; Irenaeus[Against Heresies Book V.34.3]; Origen[Gospel of Matthew Book XIV.20]; Victorinus[On the Creation of the World]

12:06 Matthew 12:41-42; Luke 11:31-32; Irenaeus[Against Heresies Book IV.9.2]

12:07 Hosea 6:6; Matthew 9:13; Pseudepigrapha[Sibylline Oracles 2.81-86]; Clement of Alexandria[Stromata Book IV.6]; Clement[Homily III.56; Recognitions Book I.37]; Cyprian[Epistle LXXII.23]; Hippolytus[Refutation of all Heresies Book IX.17]; Irenaeus[Against Heresies Book IV.17.4]; Tertullian[Five Books Against Marcion Book IV.27; On Modesty 2]

12:08 Psalms 80:17; Pseudepigrapha[Martyrdom and Ascension of Isaiah 1:4]; Archelaus[Disputation with Manes 42]; Origen[Gospel of Matthew Book XIV.20]; Tertullian[On the Flesh of Christ 15]

12:09 NT-Apocrypha[Gospel of the Nazareans Fragment 10]

12:09-14 Mark 3:1-6; Luke 6:6-11

12:10 Luke 14:3; Rabbinic[Babylonian (Shabbat 147b; Zebahim 19a)]; NT-Apocrypha[Epistula Apostolorum 5; Gospel of the Nazareans Fragment 29]

12:11 Luke 14:5; Rabbinic[Babylonian Abodah Zarah 26a; Tosephta Baba Mesia, ii.33]; Nag Hammadi[Gospel of Truth 32]

12:12 Matthew 6:26, 10:31; Luke 12:7, 24, 13:16; John 5:9, 7:23, 9:14

12:14 Matthew 27:1; Mark 11:18; Luke 19:47; John 5:16, 18

12:14-21 Mark 3:6-12; Luke 6:11

12:15 Matthew 4:23-24n; Luke 6:17-19; Origen[Gospel of Matthew Book XI.4]

12:16 Matthew 8:4, 9:30; Mark 5:43, 7:36

12:17 Origen[Gospel of John Book I.23]

12:18 This section also includes topical notes for: My Servant Whom I Have Chosen - Deuteronomy 34:5; Joshua 24:29; Isaiah 41:9, 49:5, 52:13, 53:11; Haggai 2:23; Zechariah 3:8; Luke 9:35, 23:35; Philippians 2:6-7; Dead Sea Scrolls[4Q Tanhumin (4Q176[4QTANH]) Fragments 1-2 COL I 9 - COL II 2]; Hippolytus[Treatise on Christ and Antichrist 3]; Irenaeus[Against Heresies Book III.11.6]

12:18-19 Irenaeus[Against Heresies Book I.7.2]

12:18-21 Isaiah 42:1-4

12:19 Origen[Gospel of John Book I.23]

12:19-20 Tertullian[An Answer to the Jews 9]

12:21 Isaiah 11:10; Tertullian[On the Resurrection of the Flesh 59]

12:22-23 Matthew 9:32-33

12:22-45 Mark 3:20-31; Luke 11:14-32

12:23 Matthew 1:1; Pseudepigrapha[Testament of Solomon 1:7, 20:2]

12:24 Matthew 9:34, 10:25; Pseudepigrapha[Testament of Solomon 2:9, 3:1]; Justin[Dialogue with Trypho 69]; Origen[Against Celsus Book II.9; Gospel of Matthew Book XII.2]

12:24-27 Luke 11:15-19n

12:25 Clement[Recognitions Book II.31]; Irenaeus[Against Heresies Book V.26.1]

12:26 Clement[Homily XIX.2]

12:27 Methodius[Oration on the Psalms 4]

12:28 Acts 10:38

12:29 Isaiah 49:24, 53:12; Rabbinic[Canticles Rabba on 8:19; Deuteronomy Rabba on 1:22 cf. {Psalms 149:8, Exodus 14:10, 15:1}]; Constitutions of the Holy Apostles[Book VIII.7]; Irenaeus[Against Heresies Book III.8.2, 18.6, 23.1, V.21.3, 22.1]; Methodius[Oration on the Psalms 6]; Nag Hammadi[Gospel of Thomas 34]

12:29-31 Cyprian[Treatise IV.28]

12:30 Mark 9:40; Luke 9:50; Constitutions of the Holy Apostles[Book II.56, 59]; Cyprian[The Seventh Council of Carthage under Cyprian; Treatise I.6, XII.Book III.86]; NT-Apocrypha[Clement Romance 69.4; Letter of Clement to James 18.4]

12:31 1Timothy 1:13; Apostolic[Didache 11:7]; Irenaeus[Against Heresies Book III.11.9]; NT-Apocrypha[Questions of Bartholomew V 2]

12:31-32 Teaching of the Twelve Apostles 11.7

12:32 Psalms 80:17; Luke 12:10; Rabbinic[Siphre On Numbers 15:31]; Archelaus[Disputation with Manes 31]; Constitutions of the Holy Apostles[Book VI.18]; Cyprian[Treatise XII.Book III.28]; Novatian[Treatise Concerning the Trinity 29]; Origen[Gospel of John Book II.6; De Principiis Book I.3.2]; Tertullian[On Modesty 13]

12:33 Matthew 7:16-21n; Apostolic[Ignatius - Letter to the Ephesians 14:2]; Clement[First Epistle Concerning Virginity 3]; Origen[De Principiis Book II.5.4]; Nag Hammadi[Gospel of Thomas 43]

12:33-37 Luke 6:43-45

12:34 Matthew 3:7n; 15:18; 23:33-35n; Mark 7:21; Luke 3:7, 13:32n; Clement[Homily XIX.7]

12:34-35 Clement of Alexandria[Who is the Rich Man that shall be Saved 17]; Cyprian[Epistle LIV.3]; Nag Hammadi[Gospel of Thomas 45]

12:35 Origen[De Principiis Book II.5.4]

12:36 Constitutions of the Holy Apostles[Book VII.4]; Irenaeus[Against Heresies Book II.19.2, 31.1, IV.16.5]; Origen[Gospel of Matthew Book XIV.8]; Tertullian[Of Patience 8]; NT-Apocrypha[History of Joseph the Carpenter 1]

12:36-37 Clement of Alexandria[The Instructor Book II.6]; Constitutions of the Holy Apostles[Book II.1]; Cyprian[Treatise XII.Book III.13]

12:37 Clement of Alexandria[Stromata Book I.10]; Tertullian[On Idolatry 20; Five Books Against Marcion Book II.25]

12:38 Matthew 16:1; Luke 11:16; John 6:30; 1Corinthians 1:22; Justin[Dialogue with Trypho 107]

12:38-42 Mark 8:11-12; Luke 11:29-32

12:39 Deuteronomy 32:5; Matthew 16:4; Rabbinic[**Babylonian Sanhedrin 98a**]; Irenaeus[Against Heresies Book III.20.1]; Justin[Dialogue with Trypho 108]; Linguistics[The Hebrew word for "Lusts After" (אות) is written the same as "Sign" (אות)]

> **And said R. Yohanan, "The son of David will come to a generation that is either entirely righteous or entirely wicked." (Talmud - Babylonian Sanhedrin 98a,** *The Babylonian Talmud a Translation and Commentary,* **Jacob Neusner; Hendrickson Publishers, Inc., 2005)**

12:39-40 Pseudepigrapha[Apocalypse of Elijah 3:2]; Cyprian[Treatise XII.Book II.25]

12:40 Psalms 80:17; Jonah 1:17; Pseudepigrapha[Testament of Zebulon 4:4]; Constitutions of the Holy Apostles[Book V.14]; Irenaeus[Against Heresies Book V.31.1]; Methodius[Fragments On the History of Jonah1]; Tertullian[A Treatise on the Soul 55]; NT-Apocrypha[Acts of Paul in Philippi 3.29; Gospel of the Nazareans Fragment 11]

12:41 Matthew 12:6; John 3:5, 8; Acts 3:19n; NT-Apocrypha[Pseudo Clementines - Kerygmata Petrou H XI 33.2]

12:41-42 Clement[Homily XI.33; Recognitions Book VI.14]; Irenaeus[Against Heresies Book III.21.8, IV.9.2, 33.4]; Tertullian[On the Flesh of Christ 18]

12:42 1Kings 10:1-10; 2Chronicles 9:1-12; Matthew 12:6; Pseudepigrapha[Testament of Solomon 19:3, 21:1]; Irenaeus[Against Heresies Book IV.27.1]; Origen[Gospel of Matthew Book X.17; De Principiis Book III.3.1]; NT-Apocrypha[Gospel of the Nazareans Fragment 29; Pseudo Clementines - Kerygmata Petrou H XI 33.1]

12:43 Isaiah 34:14; Pseudepigrapha[Testament of Solomon 7:7]; Irenaeus[Against Heresies Book I.16.3]

12:43-45 Luke 11:24-26

12:44 Theodotus[Excerpts]

12:45 2Peter 2:20; Pseudepigrapha[Testament of Solomon 8:2]; NT-Apocrypha[Acts of Andrew and Matthias]

12:46 Matthew 13:55; Mark 6:3; John 2:12; Acts 1:14; NT-Apocrypha[Gospel of the Nazareans Fragment 2]

12:46-50 Mark 3:31-35; Luke 8:19-21; Nag Hammadi[Gospel of Thomas 99]

12:47 Archelaus[Disputation with Manes 47]

12:47-50 NT-Apocrypha[Gospel of the Ebionites Fragment 5]

12:48 Tertullian[Five Books Against Marcion Book IV.19; On the Flesh of Christ 7]

12:50 Apostolic[2Clement 9:11]; Origen[Gospel of John Book II.6]; Theodotus[Excerpts 20]; Nag Hammadi[Gospel of Truth 33, 43; Interpretation of Knowledge 9]

13:01-02 Luke 5:1-3

13:01-09 Mark 4:1-9; Luke 8:4-8; Pseudepigrapha[Greek Apocalypse of Ezra 5:12]

13:02-03 Origen[Gospel of Matthew Book XI.4]

13:03 OT-Apocrypha[2Esdras 8:41, 9:31]; Justin[Dialogue with Trypho 125]; Tertullian[Scorpiace 11]

13:03-08 Hippolytus[Refutation of all Heresies Book VIII.2]

13:03-09 Hippolytus[Refutation of all Heresies Book V.3]

13:03-43 This section also includes topical notes for: Sower - Mark 4:3-20; Luke 8:5-15; Pseudepigrapha[4Ezra 6.43-44, 8.6, 8.41-44, 9.31-37, 16.77-78; Odes of Solomon 17.14; Questions of Ezra Recension A 1.37-40]; Philo[Questions And Answers On Genesis III (10) cf. {Genesis 15:13, Matthew 13:3-23, Mark 4:29, Luke 8:5-15}]; Rabbinic[Avot 3.22]; Plato[Phaedrus 276b-c]; Clement of Alexandria[Exhortation to the Heathen 12; Stromata Book I.1, 7]; Justin[Dialogue with Trypho 28, 136]; Nag Hammadi[Apocryphon of James 8, 12; Gospel of Thomas 9; Gospel of Truth 28; Interpretation of Knowledge 5; Tripartite Tractate 60; Apocryphon of James 7; Concept of Our Great Power 40-41; Melchizedek 1-2]; NT-Apocrypha[Gospel of Judas 44]

13:03-53 This section also includes topical notes for: Speaking in Parables - Matthew 15:15, 21:33-45, 22:1, 24:32; Mark 3:23, 4:2-34, 7:17, 12:1-12, 13:28; Luke 4:23, 5:36, 6:39, 8:4-11, 12:16, 41, 13:6, 14:7, 15:3, 18:1-9, 19:11, 20:9-19, 21:29; John 10:6; Philo[Fragments Extracted From the Parallels of John of Damascus Page 533. C., 782. A. cf. {Exodus 20:19}; On Dreams, That they Are God-Sent (1.164-1.165) cf. {Isaiah 6:9-10, Matthew 11:25, Luke 10:21, 18:31-34, 1Corinthians 2:7-16, 2Corinthians 4:3, Ephesians 3:9, Colossians 1:26, 2:2-3}; On the Contemplative Life Or Suppliants (28-29) cf. {Genesis 40:8-22, 41:12-38, Ezekiel 17:2-24, Daniel 2:1-49, 4:9-27, Galatians 4:21-31}; On the Giants (53-54) cf. {Exodus 33:7, 34:33-35, Isaiah 48:12-13, 2Corinthians 3:14-4:4, Revelation 1:17, 2:8, 22:13}; On the Posterity of Cain And His Exile (143-145) cf. {Exodus 20:19, Deuteronomy 15:8}]; Clement of Alexandria[Stromata Book VI.15]; Irenaeus[Against Heresies Book III.5.1]

13:05 OT-Apocrypha[Sirach 40:15]

13:05-06 Origen[De Principiis Book III.1.14]

13:06 Pseudepigrapha[Psalms of Solomon 18:6]

13:07 Job 31:40

13:08 Clement of Alexandria[Stromata Book VI.14, VII.12]

13:09 Matthew 11:15n, 13:43; Mark 4:23; Luke 14:35; Revelation 2:7, 13:9; Origen[Against Celsus Book VII.34]

13:10 Tertullian[On the Resurrection of the Flesh 33]

13:10-11 Origen[Gospel of Matthew Book XI.4]

13:10-17 Mark 4:10-12; Luke 8:9-10

13:11 This section also includes topical notes for: To Know the Mysteries of the Kingdom - Matthew 10:26; Luke 8:10, 12:2; John 4:25; 1Corinthians 4:1; Ephesians 3:3-4, 6:19; Colossians 2:2, 4:3; Philo[Special Laws I (63-64) cf. {Deuteronomy 18:18}]; Clement of Alexandria[Stromata Book I.2, V.12]; Origen[Gospel of Matthew Book X.4, 16]; Tertullian[On Prescription Against Heretics 22]

13:11-16 Irenaeus[Against Heresies Book IV.29.1]

13:12 Matthew 25:29; Mark 4:25; Luke 8:18, 19:26; Pseudepigrapha[4Ezra 7.25]; Origen[Gospel of Matthew Book X.19]; Tertullian[Five Books Against Marcion Book II.2]; Nag Hammadi[Gospel of Thomas 41]

13:13 Jeremiah 5:21; Archelaus[Fragment of the Disputation with Manes 2]; Clement of Alexandria[Stromata Book I.1]; Hippolytus[Refutation of all Heresies Book V.3]; Tertullian[On the Resurrection of the Flesh 33]

13:13-15 2Corinthians 3:12-18n; Pseudepigrapha[Sibylline Oracles 1.360, 1.369]

13:14 NT-Apocrypha[Abgar Legend]

13:14-15 Isaiah 6:9-10; John 12:40; Acts 28:26-27

13:15 Clement of Alexandria[Exhortation to the Heathen 10]

13:16 Isaiah 52:15; Constitutions of the Holy Apostles[Book VI.21]; Origen[Gospel of John Book X.27]; Nag Hammadi[Dialogue of the Savior 57]; NT-Apocrypha[Epistula Apostolorum 29]

13:16-17 Luke 10:23-24; Pseudepigrapha[Psalms of Solomon 17.44]; Clement of Alexandria[Who is the Rich Man that shall be Saved 29]; Methodius[Banquet of the Ten Virgins 7.7]

13:17 Pseudepigrapha[2Baruch 85:2]; Clement[Homily III.53]; Cyprian[Treatise XII.Book II.27]; Irenaeus[Against Heresies Book IV.11.1, 22.1]; Origen[Gospel of John Book VI.2]

13:18-23 Mark 4:13-20; Luke 4:11-15, 8:11-15

13:18-30 Justin[Second Apology 8]

13:19 Pseudepigrapha[Testament of Job 43:5]

13:22 Luke 12:16-21; 1Timothy 6:9-10, 17; Pseudepigrapha[Questions of Ezra 37]; Clement of Alexandria[Stromata Book VII.12; Who is the Rich Man that shall be Saved 11]

13:23 Matthew 7:16-21n; Clement[Recognitions Book IV.35]

13:23-24 Genesis 2:9

13:24-30 Philo[On Husbandry (17-20) cf. {Genesis 9:20, Deuteronomy 20:20}]

13:24-43 Pseudepigrapha[2Baruch 70.2; 4Ezra 3.20, 3.26, 4.30]; Clement of Alexandria[Stromata Book I.17, VI.8, VII.15]; Nag Hammadi[Gospel of Thomas 57; Gospel of Truth 28, 36]

13:25 Pseudepigrapha[Sibylline Oracles 1.396]; Rabbinic[Genesis Rabbah 28:8 cf. {Genesis 6:7, 12}]; Archelaus[Disputation with Manes 13]; Irenaeus[Against Heresies Book V.10.1]; Tertullian[A Treatise on the Soul 16]; NT-Apocrypha[Acts of Thomas 1.145]

13:25-30 Apostolic[Ignatius - Letter to the Ephesians 10:3]

13:27 Cyprian[Epistle V.3]

13:27-30 Victorinus[Apocalypse 7.2]

13:28 Clement of Alexandria[Stromata Book VII.15]; Irenaeus[Against Heresies Book IV.40.3]; NT-Apocrypha[Letter of Peter to James 2.3]

13:30 Matthew 3:12; Pseudepigrapha[4Ezra 9.13-23]; Dead Sea Scrolls[1Q Zephaniah Pesher (1Q15[1QPZEPH]) 2-5]; Apostolic[1Clement 56:15]; Hippolytus[Refutation of all Heresies Book IX.7]; Irenaeus[Against Heresies Book V.27.1]; Tertullian[Against Praxeas 1]; Nag Hammadi[Authoritative Teaching 25]; NT-Apocrypha[Acts of Paul in Ephesus p.1; Epistula Apostolorum 49]

13:31 Matthew 17:20; Luke 17:6; Clement of Alexandria[Stromata Book V.1; The Instructor Book I.11]; Constitutions of the Holy Apostles[Book III.5]; Nag Hammadi[Gospel of Thomas 20]

13:31-32 Clement of Alexandria[Fragments from Nicetas Bishop of Heraclea Catena on Matthew 4]; Hippolytus[Refutation of all Heresies Book V.4]; Irenaeus[Against Heresies Book I.13.2; Fragments from the Lost Works 31]; Origen[Gospel of Matthew Book XIII.5]

13:31-33 Mark 4:30-32; Luke 13:18-21

13:31-43 Tertullian[An Answer to the Jews 2]

13:32 Psalms 104:12; Ezekiel 17:23, 31:6; Daniel 4:9, 12, 18, 21; Rabbinic[Avot 3.22 cf. {Jeremiah 17:8}]

13:33 Genesis 3:17-18, 18:6; 1Corinthians 5:6; Galatians 5:9; Clement of Alexandria[Stromata Book V.12]; Nag Hammadi[Gospel of Thomas 96]

13:33-34 Hippolytus[Refutation of all Heresies Book V.3]

13:34 Irenaeus[Against Heresies Book IV.40.3]; Origen[Gospel of Matthew Book X.4]; Tertullian[On the Resurrection of the Flesh 33]; Nag Hammadi[Apocryphon of James 7; Gospel of Thomas (Prologue)]

13:34-35 Mark 4:33-34

13:35 Psalms 78:2; Archelaus[Disputation with Manes 28]; Irenaeus[Against Heresies Book II.22.1]

13:35-37 Rabbinic[Babylonian Sanhedrin 39a cf. {Genesis 2:21}]

13:36 Matthew 15:15; Mark 4:10; 7:17; Luke 8:9; Origen[Gospel of Matthew Book X.1, XI.4]

13:36-43 Pseudepigrapha[Sibylline Oracles 1.387]; Philo[On Husbandry (17-20) cf. {Genesis 9:20, Deuteronomy 20:20}]; Apostolic[Ignatius - Letter to the Ephesians 10:3]

13:37 Psalms 80:17; Origen[Gospel of Matthew Book X.2]

13:37-43 Pseudepigrapha[4Ezra 4.27-32, 4.35-36, 9.13-23; Apocalypse of Elijah 5.2-4]; Dead Sea Scrolls[4Q Enoch (4Q204[4QENAR]) COL I 16-18]; Justin[First Apology 52]; Nag Hammadi[Gospel of Thomas 21]

13:38 John 12:28; 1John 3:10; Irenaeus[Against Heresies Book IV.26.1, 41.1, 3, V.33.3]; NT-Apocrypha[Epistula Apostolorum 29]

13:39 OT-Apocrypha[2Esdras 7:113]; Pseudepigrapha[1Enoch 16:1; Testament of Job 4:6; Testament of Reuben 6:8]; Clement[Homily III.55, XIX.2]; Origen[Gospel of Matthew Book X.2]

13:40 Matthew 3:10, 7:19; John 15:6

13:40-43 Irenaeus[Against Heresies Book IV.40.2]

13:41 Psalms 80:17, 141:9; Zephaniah 1:3; Matthew 24:31; Mark 13:27

13:42 Daniel 3:6; Matthew 8:12, 13:50, 22:13, 24:51, 25:30; Luke 13:28; Pseudepigrapha[1Enoch 67.5-8; Sibylline Oracles 8.231; Vision of Ezra 59]; Justin[First Apology 16]; Origen[Gospel of Matthew Book X.2, 12]; Tertullian[On the Resurrection of the Flesh 36]; NT-Apocrypha[Acts of Paul in Corinth p.6]

13:43 Judges 5:31; 2Samuel 23:3; Daniel 12:3; Matthew 11:15n, 13:9; Mark 4:23; Luke 14:35; Revelation 2:7, 13:9; Pseudepigrapha[1Enoch 51.2-5; 2Enoch 22:10, 65:8, 65:11; 4Ezra 7:97; Apocalypse of Adam 7:52; Apocalypse of Elijah 4:19; Testament of Levi 4:2]; Hippolytus[Fragments - Scholia On Daniel 12.3; Treatise on Christ and Antichrist 65]; Irenaeus[Against Heresies Book II.32.1]; Origen[Gospel of Matthew Book X.2]; Theodotus[Excerpts 56]

13:44 Proverbs 2:4; OT-Apocrypha[Sirach 20:30]; Clement of Alexandria[Stromata Book I.1, V.4, VII.18]; Irenaeus[Against Heresies Book IV.26.1]; Origen[Gospel of Matthew Book X.4; De Principiis Book IV.1.23]; Tatian[Address to the Greeks 30]; Nag Hammadi[Acts of Peter and the Twelve Apostles 10; Gospel of Thomas 109; Teachings of Silvanus 106-107; Tripartite Tractate 127]

13:44-45 NT-Apocrypha[Acts of John 109]

13:44-46 Nag Hammadi[Gospel of Thomas 76]

13:45 Origen[Gospel of Matthew Book X.7-8]

13:45-46 Dead Sea Scrolls[4Q Aramaic LEVI (4Q214[4QTLEVIAR]) Fragment 3 COL II 1-4]; Clement of Alexandria[The Instructor Book II.13]; Cyprian[Treatise VIII.7, XII.Book III.1]; Nag Hammadi[Acts of Peter and the Twelve Apostles 2-3]

13:46 Clement of Alexandria[Fragments from Nicetas Bishop of Heraclea Catena on Matthew 5]; Clement[Recognitions Book III.62]

13:47 Habakkuk 1:14; Origen[Gospel of Matthew Book X.11-12]; NT-Apocrypha[Acts of John 109]

13:47-48 Clement of Alexandria[Stromata Book VI.11]; Nag Hammadi[Gospel of Thomas 8]

13:49 Psalms 1:5

13:49-50 Plato[Theaetetus 176e-177a]; Origen[Gospel of Matthew Book X.12]

13:50 Daniel 3:6; Matthew 8:12, 13:42, 22:13, 24:51, 25:30; Luke 13:28

13:51-52 Origen[Gospel of Matthew Book X.14]; Victorinus[Apocalypse 1.16]

13:52 Clement[Recognitions Book IV.5]; Irenaeus[Against Heresies Book IV.9.1, 26.1]; Origen[Gospel of Matthew Book X.15]

13:52-58 Tertullian[On Fasting 14]

13:53 Matthew 7:28, 11:1, 19:1, 26:1; Luke 7:1

13:53-54 Origen[Gospel of Matthew Book X.16]

13:53-58 Mark 6:1-6; Luke 4:16-30

13:54 Matthew 9:35n; John 7:15; Origen[Against Celsus Book VI.16]; Tertullian[On the Flesh of Christ 9]

13:54-56 Origen[Gospel of Matthew Book X.17]

13:55 Matthew 12:46; Luke 3:23; John 6:42; Galatians 1:19; Acts 15:5-21; Josephus[Antiquities 20. 9.1 199-203]; Justin[Dialogue with Trypho 88]; Origen[Gospel of John Book VI.7]; Tertullian[An Answer to the Jews 10]; Nag Hammadi[Gospel of Philip 73]; NT-Apocrypha[Acts of Peter 1.14]

13:57 Matthew 11:6, 26:31; John 4:44; Rabbinic[Exodus Rabba on 3:16, 4:18, 31]; Origen[Gospel of Matthew Book X.16, 18]; Nag Hammadi[Gospel of Thomas 31]

13:58 Origen[Gospel of Matthew Book X.19]

14:01 Origen[Gospel of Matthew Book X.20]

14:01-12 Mark 6:14-29; Luke 3:3, 19, 9:7-9

14:02 Origen[Gospel of John Book VI.30; Gospel of Matthew Book X.20, XII.9]

14:03 Matthew 11:2; Luke 3:19-20; John 3:24; Tertullian[Scorpiace 8]

14:03-04 Leviticus 18:16, 20:21; Origen[Gospel of Matthew Book X.21]

14:03-10 Justin[Dialogue with Trypho 49]

14:03-12 Pseudepigrapha[Sibylline Oracles 1.343]

14:04 Zadokite Fragments[Zadokite Fragments 7.1 cf. {Genesis 1:27, 7:9 Deuteronomy 17:17}]; Rabbinic[Babylonian Qiddushin 2b cf. {Deuteronomy 24:1}; Canticles Rabba on 1.4]

14:05 Matthew 11:9; 21:26, Luke 1:76, 7:26

14:12 Exodus 12:6; Pseudepigrapha[Sibylline Oracles 2.202]

14:12-13 Origen[Gospel of Matthew Book X.23]; Mark 6:29-32; Luke 9:10; John 6:1, 3

14:13-15 Origen[Gospel of Matthew Book XI.4]

14:13-21 Pseudepigrapha[Sibylline Oracles 1.357]

14:13-33 Mark 6:30-52; Luke 9:10-17; John 6:2-21

14:14 Matthew 4:23-24n, 9:36, 15:32; Origen[Gospel of Matthew Book X.24, XI.19]

14:15 Matthew 15:32; Mark 8:3; Origen[Gospel of Matthew Book X.25, XI.1, 19]

14:15-21 John 6:31-58n; NT-Apocrypha[Acts of John 93]

14:16-17 Origen[Gospel of Matthew Book XI.2]

14:16-20 2Kings 4:42-44

14:17 Matthew 15:34; Mark 8:5; Constitutions of the Holy Apostles[Book V.7]; NT-Apocrypha[Epistula Apostolorum 5]

14:17-18 1Samuel 21:3; Mark 6:38; Luke 9:13-16

14:19 Psalms 123:1; Pseudepigrapha[4Baruch 9:21; Testament of Zebulon 6.6-7]; Hippolytus[Refutation of all Heresies Book IX.16]; Irenaeus[Against Heresies Book II.24.4]; Origen[Gospel of Matthew Book XI.19]

14:19-20 Origen[Gospel of Matthew Book XI.3-4]

14:19-21 Archelaus[Disputation with Manes 44]; Clement of Alexandria[Stromata Book V.6, VI.11]

14:19-22 Matthew 15:35-39; Mark 8:6-10

14:20 2Kings 4:43-44; Irenaeus[Against Heresies Book II.22.3]

14:21 This section also includes topical notes for: Feeding the Five Thousand - 2Kings 4:42; Ruth 2:14; Mark 6:44; Luke 9:14; John 6:10; Acts 4:4; Philo[Every Good Man Is Free (75-91)]; Archelaus[Disputation with Manes 44 cf. {Exodus 16}]; Irenaeus[Against Heresies Book II.24.4]; Lactantius[Divine Institutes Book IV.15]; Origen[Gospel of Matthew Book XI.3]

14:22 Origen[Gospel of Matthew Book XI.4-5]; NT-Apocrypha[Acts of Peter 1.7]

14:22-23 Origen[Gospel of Matthew Book XI.6]; Mark 6:45-52; John 6:15-21

14:23 Luke 6:12, 9:28; NT-Apocrypha[Epistula Apostolorum 5]

14:23-25 Origen[Gospel of Matthew Book XI.5]

14:23-33 This section also includes topical notes for: Walking on the Sea - Genesis 32:10; Psalms 77:19; Pseudepigrapha[Odes of Solomon 39.11; Sibylline Oracles 1.356]; Philo[**Allegorical Interpretation III (172) cf. {Exodus 6:16, 16:14-15}**]; Lactantius[Divine Institutes Book IV.15]

There is a certain peculiarity which is attached to this word. For when it calls the soul to itself, it excites a congealing power in everything which is earthly, or corporeal, or under the influence of the external senses. On which account it is said to be "like the hoar-frost on the Earth." For when the man who beholds God, meditates a flight from the passions, "the waves are frozen," that is to say, the impetuous rush, and the increase, and the haughty pride of the waves are arrested, in order that he who might behold the living God might then pass over the Passion. (Philo - Allegorical Interpretation III (172) cf. {Exodus 6:16, 16:14-15})

14:25 Job 9:8; Psalms 77:20; Isaiah 43:16; Pseudepigrapha[Apocalypse of Elijah 2:6; Sibylline Oracles 6.13; Testament of Adam 3.1]; Archelaus[Disputation with Manes 44 cf. {Exodus 24:25}]; Tertullian[On Baptism 9]

14:25-32 Nag Hammadi[Testimony of Truth 33]

14:26 Luke 24:37; Pseudepigrapha[Sibylline Oracles 6.12]; Methodius[Oration on the Psalms 3]

14:27 Pseudepigrapha[2Enoch 1:7]; Origen[Gospel of Matthew Book XI.6]; NT-Apocrypha[Pistis Sophia c. 2-6]

14:28-29 Tertullian[On Baptism 12]

14:28-31 Philo[On Dreams That they Are God-Sent (2.11)]

14:29 John 21:7; Origen[Gospel of Matthew Book XI.5]

14:30 NT-Apocrypha[Acts of Peter 1.10]

14:30-31 Origen[Gospel of Matthew Book XI.6]

14:31 Matthew 8:26; Constitutions of the Holy Apostles[Book VII.11]; Cyprian[Treatise XII.Book III.42]; NT-Apocrypha[Epistula Apostolorum 11, 24]

14:32 Mark 4:39; Pseudepigrapha[Sibylline Oracles 8.273]

14:33 Matthew 16:16, 26:63, 27:54, 28:17n; Mark 14:61, 15:39; Luke 22:70; John 1:49, 3:18n; Origen[Gospel of Matthew Book XI.7, 17]

14:34 Origen[Gospel of Matthew Book XI.6, 16]

14:34-36 Mark 6:53-56

14:35-36 Origen[Gospel of Matthew Book XI.7-8]

14:36 Matthew 9:20-21; Mark 5:27-28; Luke 8:44; Nag Hammadi[Testimony of Truth 41]

15:01-02 Origen[Gospel of Matthew Book XI.8]

15:01-20 Mark 7:1-23

15:02 Luke 11:38

15:02-03 Irenaeus[Against Heresies Book IV.12.1, 4]

15:02-06 Rabbinic[Babylonian Sanhedrin 88b]

15:02-20 Pseudepigrapha[Letter of Aristeas 1.306-307]

15:03-04 Irenaeus[Against Heresies Book IV.9.3]

15:04 Cyprian[Epistle LXXII.19]; Origen[Gospel of Matthew Book XI.9, 10, 13]

15:04-08 This section also includes topical notes for: Honor Father and Mother - Exodus 20:12, 21:17; Leviticus 20:9; Deuteronomy 5:16; Matthew 19:19; Mark 7:10, 10:19; Luke 18:20; Ephesians 6:2; Dead Sea Scrolls[4Q Sapiential Work A(4Q416[4QSAP.WORKA]) Fragment 2 COL III 15-19; 4Q Sapiential Work (4Q418[4QSAP.WORKA]) Fragment 9 17-19]

15:05 Proverbs 28:24; Origen[Gospel of Matthew Book XI.10]

15:07 Matthew 6:2-16n; Origen[Gospel of John Book VI.12]; NT-Apocrypha[Papyrus Egerton 2 Fragment 2 Lines 43-59]

15:08 Psalms 78:36; Apostolic[1Clement 15:2; 2Clement 3:5]; Clement of Alexandria[Stromata Book II.14]

15:08-09 Isaiah 29:13

15:09 Justin[Dialogue with Trypho 48]; Origen[Gospel of Matthew Book XI.11]

15:10-11 Origen[Gospel of Matthew Book XI.12-13]; Tertullian[On Prayer 13]

15:11 Matthew 12:34; Clement of Alexandria[Stromata Book II.11; The Instructor Book II.1]; Constitutions of the Holy Apostles[Book VII.20]; Gregory Thaumaturgus[Canonical Epistle 1]; Origen[Against Celsus Book VIII.29; Gospel of Matthew Book XI.14, 16]; Tertullian[On Fasting 2]

15:11-18 Rabbinic[Babylonian Keritot 13a]

15:11-20 Romans 14:14; Nag Hammadi[Gospel of Thomas 14]

15:13 John 15:2; Pseudepigrapha[Odes of Solomon 38.17-22]; Apostolic[Ignatius - Letter to the Trallians 11:1, Letter to the Philadelphians 3:1]; Clement[Homily III.52]; Cyprian[Epistle XLVIII.4, LIV.7, LXXII.18]; Origen[Gospel of Matthew Book XI.13-14]; Tertullian[On Prescription Against Heretics 3]; Nag Hammadi[Gospel of Philip 85; Gospel of Thomas 40]

15:14 This section also includes topical notes for: The Blind Guide the Blind - Matthew 23:16-26; Luke 6:39; Romans 2:19; Philo[Allegorical Interpretation III (108-110) cf. {Deuteronomy 27:18}; On Dreams, That they Are God-Sent (1.218) cf. {Exodus 28:40-42}; On The Unchangeableness of God (127-130) cf. {Leviticus 13:11}]; Clement of Alexandria[The Instructor Book I.3]; Clement[First Epistle Concerning Virginity 11]; Cyprian[Epistle XXXIX.5; Treatise I.17]; Irenaeus[Against Heresies Book II.18.7, V.20.2]; Justin[Dialogue with Trypho 123]; Origen[Gospel of Matthew Book XI.14]; Tertullian[On Prescription Against Heretics 14]; Nag Hammadi[Apocalypse of Peter 72; Gospel of Thomas 28, 34; Testimony of Truth 33]; NT-Apocrypha[Epistula Apostolorum 43, 47; Oxyrhynchus Papyrus 840]

15:15 Matthew 13:3-53n; Mark 4:10, 7:17; Luke 8:9

15:16-17 Origen[Gospel of Matthew Book XI.14]

15:17 Pseudepigrapha[Testament of Job 38:3]; Irenaeus[Fragments from the Lost Works 16]; Novatian[On the Jewish Meats 5]

15:17-19 Origen[Against Celsus Book VIII.29]

15:17-20 Tertullian[On Prayer 13]

15:18 Matthew 12:34; Clement of Alexandria[The Instructor Book II.5]

15:18-19 Origen[Gospel of Matthew Book XI.15]

15:19 Mark 7:21-23; Romans 1:29-31; 1Corinthians 5:10-11, 6:9-10; Galatians 5:19-21; Ephesians 5:3-5; Colossians 3:5, 8; 1Timothy 1:9-10; 2Timothy 3:2-4; 1Peter 4:3; Revelation 21:8, 22:15; Clement of Alexandria[Stromata Book II.11]; Origen[Against Celsus Book VII.33]

15:21-22 Origen[Gospel of Matthew Book XI.16]

15:21-28 Mark 7:24-30

15:22 Matthew 1:1, 9:27, 20:30-31; Mark 10:47-48; Luke 18:38-39; Pseudepigrapha[Testament of Solomon 1:7, 20:2]; Origen[Gospel of Matthew Book XI.17]; NT-Apocrypha[Secret Gospel of Mark Fragment 1]

15:23 Origen[Gospel of Matthew Book XI.19]

15:24 Matthew 10:6; Luke 13:32n; Archelaus[Disputation with Manes 47]; Origen[Gospel of John Book X.26; Gospel of Matthew Book XI.17; De Principiis Book IV.1.22]; Tertullian[On Prescription Against Heretics 8; Five Books Against Marcion Book IV.7]

15:25 Matthew 28:17n; NT-Apocrypha[Secret Gospel of Mark Fragment 1]

15:25-28 Origen[Gospel of Matthew Book XI.17]

15:26 Cyprian[Treatises Attributed to Cyprian - On the Glory of Martyrdom 17]; Tertullian[On Prayer 6; On Prescription Against Heretics 8; Five Books Against Marcion Book IV.7]

15:27 Luke 16:21; Gregory Thaumaturgus[Four Homilies 2]; Nag Hammadi[Gospel of Philip 82]

15:28 Matthew 8:10, 13, 9:29; Origen[Gospel of Matthew Book XI.19]

15:28-32 Origen[Gospel of Matthew Book XI.18]

15:29 Matthew 5:1

15:29-31 Mark 7:31-37; NT-Apocrypha[Acts of Paul in Myra p.28]

15:30 Matthew 4:23-24n; Pseudepigrapha[Sibylline Oracles 8.272]; NT-Apocrypha[Epistula Apostolorum 5]

15:31 1Kings 1:48; Psalms 41:14; Justin[Dialogue with Trypho 69]

15:31-32 Origen[Gospel of Matthew Book X.19]

15:32 Matthew 9:36; Origen[Gospel of Matthew Book XII.6]

15:32-33 Matthew 14:14-15; Mark 6:34-36; Luke 9:12

15:32-39 Mark 8:1-10; NT-Apocrypha[Acts of John 93]

15:33 Mark 6:37; John 6:5

15:34-37 Matthew 14:17, 19-20; Mark 6:38-43; Luke 9:13-17; John 6:9-13

15:36 Pseudepigrapha[Testament of Zebulon 6.6-7]; Origen[Gospel of Matthew Book XI.19]

15:38 Matthew 14:21; Mark 6:44

16:01 Matthew 12:38, 19:3; Luke 11:16; John 6:30; 1Corinthians 1:22; Josephus[Antiquities 13.5.9 171-173, 18.1.2-4 11-17; War 2.8.14 162-166]; Origen[Gospel of Matthew Book XII.1]

16:01-04 Mark 8:11-13; Luke 12:54-56

16:02 NT-Apocrypha[Gospel of the Nazareans Fragment 13]

16:03 Nag Hammadi[Gospel of Thomas 91]

16:04 Jonah 1:17, 3:4-5; Matthew 12:39; Luke 11:29; Rabbinic[Babylonian Sanhedrin 98a];
   Irenaeus[Against Heresies Book III.20.1]; Justin[Dialogue with Trypho 108]; Origen[Gospel of
   Matthew Book XII.3-4]

16:05-07 Origen[Gospel of Matthew Book XII.5]

16:05-12 Mark 8:13-21

16:06 Josephus[Antiquities 13.5.9 171-173, 18.1.2-4 11-17; War 2.8.14 162-166]; Hippolytus[Refutation of
   all Heresies Book IX.23-24]; Irenaeus[Against Heresies Book IV.41.3]; Origen[Gospel of Matthew
   Book XII.6]

16:06-12 This section also includes topical notes for: Leaven - Matthew 6:1-6n; Luke 12:1;
   1Corinthians 5:6-8; Galatians 5:9; Philo**[Special Laws I (293) cf. {Leviticus 2:11}]**;
   Rabbinic[Babylonian Pesahim 5a]; Nag Hammadi[Testimony of Truth 29]

> And leaven is forbidden on account of the rising which it causes; this prohibition again having a figurative meaning, intimating that no one who comes to the altar ought at all to allow himself to be elated, being puffed up by insolence; but that such persons may keep their eyes fixed on the greatness of God, and so obtain a proper conception of the weakness of all created beings, even if they be very prosperous; and that so cherishing correct notions they may correct the arrogant loftiness of their minds, and discard all treacherous self-conceit. (Philo - Special Laws I (293) cf. {Leviticus 2:11})

16:07-08 Origen[Gospel of Matthew Book XII.7]

16:08 Origen[Gospel of Matthew Book XII.6]; NT-Apocrypha[Epistula Apostolorum 24]

16:09 Matthew 14:13-21; Mark 6:34-44; Luke 9:11-17; John 6:1-13

16:10 Matthew 15:32-38; Mark 8:1-9

16:11 Origen[Gospel of Matthew Book XII.6]

16:11-12 Pseudepigrapha[4Ezra 12.31-33]; Hippolytus[Refutation of all Heresies Book IX.23, 24]

16:12 Josephus[Antiquities 13.5.9 171-173, 18.1.2-4 11-17; War 2.8.14 162-166]

16:13 Psalms 80:17; Clement[Homily XVII.18]; Gregory Thaumaturgus[Four Homilies 4];
   Irenaeus[Against Heresies Book III.18.4]; Tertullian[Scorpiace 10]; NT-Apocrypha[Pseudo
   Clementines - Kerygmata Petrou H XVII 18.1]

16:13-14 Origen[Gospel of John Book VI.7; Gospel of Matthew Book XII.9]

16:13-16 Nag Hammadi[Gospel of Thomas 13]

16:13-19 Tertullian[On Monogamy 8]

16:13-23 1Corinthians 2:6-16n

16:13-28 Mark 8:2-9:1; Luke 9:18-27

16:14 Matthew 14:1-2; Mark 6:14-15; Luke 9:7-8; Pseudepigrapha[Lives of the Prophets 2:19; Sibylline
   Oracles 2.187]

16:15-16 Acts 3:18-26n; Origen[Gospel of Matthew Book XII.15]

16:15-18 Nag Hammadi[Acts of Peter and the Twelve Apostles 9]

16:16 Matthew 26:63; Mark 14:61; John 6:68-69; Archelaus[Disputation with Manes 47];
   Clement[Homily XVII.18]; Gregory Thaumaturgus[Four Homilies 4]; Hippolytus[The Discourse on
   the Holy Theophany 9]; Irenaeus[Against Heresies Book III.11.6, 19.2]; Origen[Gospel of Matthew
   Book XII.10-11, 40]; Tertullian[Against Praxeas 21-22]; NT-Apocrypha[Acts of Thomas 1.10; Pseudo
   Clementines - Kerygmata Petrou H XVII 18.1]

16:16-17 Novatian[Treatise Concerning the Trinity 26]; Origen[Gospel of Matthew Book XII.9, XIII.14]

16:16-18 Linguistics[Hebrew word pronounced "Peter" (פטר) means firstling, opening of the womb]

16:17 Matthew 17:5; Galatians 1:15-16; Pseudepigrapha[Joseph and Aseneth 16:8]; Clement of
   Alexandria[Stromata Book VI.15]; Dionysius of Alexandria[Extant Fragments Two Books on the
   Promises 4]; Irenaeus[Against Heresies Book III.13.2, 21.8]; Justin[Hortatory Address to the Greeks
   32]; Lactantius[Divine Institutes Book II.3]; Tertullian[Against Praxeas 21, 26; Five Books Against
   Marcion Book IV.11]; Nag Hammadi[Gospel of Philip 55]; NT-Apocrypha[Gospel of the Nazareans
   Fragment 14; Letter of Clement to James 1.2; Pseudo Clementines - Kerygmata Petrou H XVII 18.1,
   H XVII 19.6]

16:17-19 NT-Apocrypha[Acts of Peter 1.23]

16:18 Job 38:17; Psalms 9:14; Isaiah 38:10; John 1:42; Ephesians 2:20; OT-Apocrypha[Wisdom of
   Solomon 16:13]; Pseudepigrapha[Joseph and Aseneth 15:7; Odes of Solomon 22:12];
   Clement[Homily XVII.19]; Hippolytus[The Discourse on the Holy Theophany 9]; Justin[Dialogue
   with Trypho 106]; Origen[Gospel of John Book V.3, X.6; Gospel of Matthew Book XII.10, 14-15]; Nag

Hammadi[Gospel of Truth 42]; NT-Apocrypha[Acts of Thomas 1.10; Pseudo Clementines - Kerygmata Petrou H XVII 19.4]; Linguistics[Hebrew word for "Stone" (אבן) is a pun for "Will Build" (אבנה)]

16:18-19 Cyprian[Epistle XXVI.1; Treatise I.4]; Origen[Gospel of Matthew Book XII.11]; Tertullian[On Modesty 21; On Prescription Against Heretics 22]

16:19 Isaiah 22:22; Matthew 18:18; John 20:23; Pseudepigrapha[3Baruch 11:2]; Dead Sea Scrolls[Damascus Document (CD-A) COL XIII 1-22]; Josephus[War 1.5.2 111]; Cyprian[Epistle LXXIV.16]; Liturgy of James 49; Origen[Gospel of Matthew Book XII.14, XIII.31]; Nag Hammadi[Testimony of Truth 41]; NT-Apocrypha[Acts of Thomas 1.94; Clement Romance - Installation of Clement 146; Clement Romance 72.4; Letter of Clement to James 2.4]; Epic of Gilgamesh[The Forest Journey, The Death of Gilgamesh]

16:20 Matthew 17:9; Mark 9:9; Origen[Gospel of Matthew Book XII.15, 40, 43]

16:21 Hosea 6:2; Acts 2:23n; Plato[Crito 44a-b]; Gregory Thaumaturgus[Twelve Topics on the Faith 6]; Irenaeus[Against Heresies Book III.18.4]; Justin[Dialogue with Trypho 51, 100, 106]; Origen[Gospel of Matthew Book XII.17-20, XIII.8]

16:21-22 Genesis 34:30-31 LXX

16:21-23 Archelaus[Disputation with Manes 48]

16:21-28 Mark 8:31-9.1; Luke 9:22-27

16:22 OT-Apocrypha[1Maccabees 2:21]; Anonymous[Treatise on Re-Baptism 9]; NT-Apocrypha[Extracts from the Arabic Infancy Gospel 23]

16:22-23 Origen[Gospel of Matthew Book XII.21, 23]

16:23 2Samuel 19:23; 1Kings 11:14; Isaiah 8:14; Matthew 4:10; Pseudepigrapha[Testament of Job 26:3]; Origen[Gospel of Matthew Book XII.40, XIII.14]; Tertullian[Scorpiace 15]; NT-Apocrypha[Apocalypse of Peter 1.16]

16:24 Matthew 10:38; Mark 8:34; Luke 14:27; Clement[First Epistle Concerning Virginity 5]; Constitutions of the Holy Apostles[Book VI.22]; Origen[Gospel of Matthew Book XII.24-25]; Tertullian[A Treatise on the Soul 55; On Idolatry 12]; Epic of Gilgamesh[The Forest Journey]

16:24-25 This section also includes topical notes for: Take up your Cross – Genesis 31:45; Matthew 10:38; Mark 8:34; Luke 9:23; Clement of Alexandria[Exhortation to the Heathen 12]; Irenaeus[Against Heresies Book III.18.4-5, IV.5.4]; Nag Hammadi[Apocryphon of James 6; Gospel of Thomas 55]

16:25 Matthew 10:39; Luke 17:33; John 12:25; Apostolic[Ignatius - Letter to the Magnesians 5:2]; Origen[Gospel of Matthew Book XII.26-27]; NT-Apocrypha[Gospel of Mani Psalm CCLXXIII]

16:26 Psalms 49:8; Matthew 4:8-9; Pseudepigrapha[2Baruch 51:16]; Plato[**Republic IX 589d-591b**]; Apostolic[2Clement 6:2]; Clement of Alexandria[Stromata Book IV.6]; Constitutions of the Holy Apostles[Book V.4]; Justin[First Apology 15]; Origen[Gospel of Matthew Book XII.28]; Peter of Alexandria[Canonical Epistle 12]; Nag Hammadi[Interpretation of Knowledge 9]

> **How would a man profit if he received gold and silver on the condition that he was to enslave the noblest part of him to the worst? (Plato - Republic IX 591a)**

16:27 Psalms 28:4, 62:12-13, 80:17; Proverbs 24:12; Matthew 25:31; Romans 2:6; Revelation 22:12; OT-Apocrypha[Sirach 35:19, 22]; Pseudepigrapha[Apocalypse of Elijah 3:4; Sibylline Oracles 2.240]; Constitutions of the Holy Apostles[Book VII.32]; Gregory Thaumaturgus[Twelve Topics on the Faith 6]; Origen[Gospel of Matthew Book XII.29-30]; Zephyrinus[Second Epistle 1.1]; NT-Apocrypha[Acts of Peter 1.36; Acts of Thomas 1.28; Apocalypse of Peter 1.1, 1.6]

16:28 Psalms 80:17; Matthew 10:23, 20:21; Origen[Gospel of Matthew Book XII.31, 34-35]

17:01 Exodus 24:13-16; Hippolytus[Refutation of all Heresies Book V.42]; Irenaeus[Against Heresies Book II.24.4]; Origen[Gospel of Matthew Book XII.36]; NT-Apocrypha[Acts of John 90]

17:01-08 Tertullian[On Monogamy 8; On Prescription Against Heretics 22]

17:01-13 Tertullian[On Fasting 6]

17:01-21 This section also includes topical notes for: Transfiguration - Job 36:29; Psalms 27:5; 80:1-19; Isaiah 4:5; Mark 9:2-29; Luke 1:35, 9:28-43; Acts 26:13; 2Corinthians 4:4-6 cf.{Genesis 1:2-3; Revelation 1:13-17, 19:12-13}; Dead Sea Scrolls[1Q Hymns (1QHODAYOTH [1QH]) COL XV 24; 4Q Apocryphon of Moses A (4Q374[4QAPOCRMOSESA]) Fragment 2 COL II 6-10; 4Q Enoch(4Q205[4QENAR]) Fragment 2 COL II 27-30; 4Q Florilegium (4Q174[4QFLOR]) Fragments 1-3 COL II 4]; Philo[On Dreams, That they Are God-Sent (1.148, 1.218) cf. {Leviticus 26:12, Exodus 28:40-42}; On Flight And Finding (106-114) cf. {Exodus 28:32, Leviticus 10:36, 21:11, Numbers 35:2-

34}]; Rabbinic[Mekhilta On Exodus 13:20; Targum Onkelos Leviticus 23:34, 42-43; Targum Jerusalem Leviticus 23:34, 42-43]; Nag Hammadi[Gospel of Philip 58]

17:02 Genesis 1:3; Exodus 34:29; 2Peter 1:16-18; Pseudepigrapha[2Baruch 51:3; 4Ezra 7.97-98; Apocalypse of Zephaniah 5:4; Joseph and Aseneth 18:9]; Archelaus[Disputation with Manes 44 cf. {Exodus 34:35}]; Origen[Gospel of Matthew Book XII.37-38]; NT-Apocrypha[Acts of Thomas 1.8]

17:02-04 Tertullian[On the Resurrection of the Flesh 55]

17:03 Irenaeus[Against Heresies Book IV.20.9]; Origen[Gospel of Matthew Book XII.38]; Tertullian[Against Praxeas 14]

17:03-08 Tertullian[A Treatise on the Soul 17]

17:04 Origen[Gospel of Matthew Book XII.40-41]; NT-Apocrypha[Apocalypse of Peter 1.16]

17:05 Deuteronomy 18:15; Psalms 2:7; Isaiah 42:1; Matthew 3:17, 12:18; Mark 1:11; Luke 3:22; Acts 3:22; 2Peter 1:17-18; Pseudepigrapha[1Enoch 14:8; 2Baruch 22:2]; Tacitus[The Histories 5.13]; Clement of Alexandria[The Instructor Book I.11]; Clement[Homily III.53]; Cyprian[Epistle LXII.14; Treatise XII.Book I.10]; Gregory Thaumaturgus[Four Homilies 4]; Hippolytus[Against the Heresy of One Noetus 5, 18]; Origen[Gospel of Matthew Book XII.42]; Tertullian[Against Praxeas 23]; NT-Apocrypha[Apocalypse of Peter 1.17; Protoevangelium of James 19.2]; Linguistics[The Hebrew word for "Hear" (שמע) is written the same as "Obey" (שמע)]

17:06 Daniel 10:9; Habakkuk 3:2; Origen[Gospel of Matthew Book XII.43]; Tertullian[Against Praxeas 15]

17:07 Irenaeus[Against Heresies Book I.14.6]; Methodius[Oration Concerning Simeon and Anna 12]

17:08 Origen[Gospel of Matthew Book XII.43]

17:09 Psalms 80:17; Matthew 16:20; Origen[Against Celsus Book I.48; Gospel of Matthew Book XII.43]

17:10 Malachi 3:23; Pseudepigrapha[Sibylline Oracles 2.187]; Origen[Gospel of Matthew Book XIII.1]

17:10-11 Malachi 4:5-6

17:10-13 Origen[Gospel of Matthew Book XIII.2]

17:11 OT-Apocrypha[Sirach 48:10]

17:12 1Kings 19:2, 10; Psalms 80:17; Matthew 11:14; Rabbinic[Seder Olam Rabba 17]; Justin[Dialogue with Trypho 49]; Tertullian[A Treatise on the Soul 35]

17:12-13 Origen[Gospel of Matthew Book XIII.1-2]

17:13 Luke 1:17

17:14-15 Origen[Gospel of Matthew Book XIII.3]

17:14-20 Mark 9:14-29; Luke 9:37-43

17:16 2Kings 4:31

17:17 Deuteronomy 32:5, 20; Origen[Gospel of Matthew Book XIII.7]

17:18 Matthew 8:13, 9:22, 15:28; John 4:52-53; Pseudepigrapha[Life of Adam and Eve Vita 39.1-3]

17:19-20 Origen[Gospel of Matthew Book X.19]

17:20 Matthew 21:21; Mark 11:23; Luke 17:6; 1Corinthians 13:2; Plato[Laws VIII 842e-843a]; Clement of Alexandria[Stromata Book II.11, V.1, VII.12]; Clement[Homily XI.16; Recognitions Book V.2, V.34]; Cyprian[Treatise XII.Book III.42]; Origen[Gospel of Matthew Book X.19, XIII.5, 7]; Nag Hammadi[Gospel of Thomas 48, 106]; NT-Apocrypha[Acts of Peter 1.10]

17:21 Clement[First Epistle Concerning Virginity 12]; Origen[Gospel of Matthew Book XIII.7]; Tertullian[On Fasting 8]

17:22 Psalms 80:17

17:22 Origen[Gospel of Matthew Book XIII.8]

17:22-23 Mark 9:30-32; Luke 9:43-45; Origen[Gospel of Matthew Book XIII.9]

17:23 Matthew 16:21; Justin[Dialogue with Trypho 51]

17:24 Exodus 30:13, 38:26; Constitutions of the Holy Apostles[Book II.46, V.7]; Origen[Gospel of Matthew Book XIII.10, 13]; NT-Apocrypha[Epistula Apostolorum 5]

17:24-27 Dead Sea Scrolls[4Q Ordinances (4Q159[4QORD]) Fragment 1 COL II 6-7]; NT-Apocrypha[Acts of Thomas 1.143]

17:25-26 Origen[Gospel of Matthew Book XIII.11]

17:26 Philo[Every Good Man Is Free (42-43) cf. {Exodus 4:16, 7:1}]

17:27 Clement of Alexandria[The Instructor Book II.1; Who is the Rich Man that shall be Saved 21]; Irenaeus[Against Heresies Book V.24.1]; Origen[Gospel of Matthew Book XIII.11, 14]; Victorinus[Apocalypse 1.16]; NT-Apocrypha[Acts of Thomas 1.79]

18:01 Luke 22:24; Origen[Gospel of Matthew Book XIII.14-15]

18:01-04 Tertullian[On Monogamy 8]

18:01-05 Mark 9:33-37; Luke 9:46-48

18:01-06 Nag Hammadi[Gospel of Thomas 4]

18:02-03 Matthew 19:14; Mark 10:15; Luke 18:17

18:03 Apostolic[Shepherd of Hermas 27:1]; Clement of Alexandria[Stromata Book IV.25, V.1, 5]; Nag Hammadi[Gospel of Thomas 22; Gospel of Truth 19]

18:03-04 Rabbinic[Avot 4.25]; Clement of Alexandria[The Instructor Book I.5]

18:04 This section also includes topical notes for: Humility - Leviticus 26:41; Deuteronomy 8:2-16; 1Kings 21:29; 2Kings 22:19; 2Chronicles 7:14, 12:6-12, 32:26, 34:27; Job 22:29; Proverbs 15:33, 22:4; Isaiah 57:15; Daniel 10:12; Micah 6:8; Matthew 20:26, 23:12; Mark 10:43-44; Luke 14:11, 18:14, 22:26; Philippians 2:8; James 4:6, 10; 1Peter 3:8, 5:5-6; Philo[On Mating With the Preliminary Studies (107-108) cf. {Genesis 18:1-8}]; Origen[Gospel of Matthew Book XIII.18]

18:05 Matthew 10:40; Luke 10:16; John 13:20; Origen[Gospel of Matthew Book XIII.16]

18:06 Pseudepigrapha[2Baruch 48:19]; Clement of Alexandria[Stromata Book III.18]; Origen[Gospel of Matthew Book XIII.17-18, 22, 29]; NT-Apocrypha[Gospel of the Hebrews Fragment 6]

18:06-07 Constitutions of the Holy Apostles[Book II.10]

18:06-09 Luke 17:1-2

18:06-20 Mark 9:42-50

18:07 Clement[Recognitions Book III.49, 65]; Constitutions of the Holy Apostles[Book I.3]; Lactantius[Divine Institutes Book IV.30]; Origen[Gospel of Matthew Book XIII.20, 22-23]

18:08 Jude 1:6n; Tertullian[On Idolatry 7]

18:08-09 Matthew 5:29-30; Irenaeus[Against Heresies Book IV.27.4]; Origen[Gospel of Matthew Book XIII.24]

18:10 Acts 12:15; Hebrews 1:14; OT-Apocrypha[Tobit 12:15]; Pseudepigrapha[2Baruch 48:19; Prayer of Joseph Fragment A]; Clement of Alexandria[Who is the Rich Man that shall be Saved 31]; Clement[Homily XVII.7]; Constitutions of the Holy Apostles[Book II.18]; Irenaeus[Against Heresies Book I.13.3, 14.1]; Origen[Against Celsus Book VI.41, VIII.34, 36; Gospel of Matthew Book XIII.26, 28; De Principiis Book I.8.1]

18:10-14 Luke 15:3-7; Nag Hammadi[Gospel of Thomas 4]

18:11 Psalms 80:17; Luke 19:10; Tertullian[On Modesty 9]

18:11-12 Clement of Alexandria[Stromata Book III.14]

18:12 Psalms 119:176; Ezekiel 34:6, 12, 16; Constitutions of the Holy Apostles[Book II.20]; Irenaeus[Against Heresies Book I.23.2, II.24.6]

18:12-13 Methodius[Banquet of the Ten Virgins 3.5]

18:12-14 Origen[Gospel of Matthew Book XIII.29]; Nag Hammadi[Gospel of Thomas 107; Gospel of Truth 31-32]

18:14 Constitutions of the Holy Apostles[Book II.14]

18:14-17 Origen[Gospel of Matthew Book XIII.30]

18:15 Leviticus 19:17; Luke 17:3; Constitutions of the Holy Apostles[Book II.37]; NT-Apocrypha[Epistula Apostolorum 48]

18:15-17 Dead Sea Scrolls[**1QRule of the Community (1QS) Col. V 25 - Col. VI 1**]; Teaching of the Twelve Apostles 15.3

> **Each should reprove his fellow in truth, in humility, and in loving-kindness. He should not speak to him in anger or grumbling or wicked arrogance. He must not hate him in his heart. Instead, he is to rebuke him that *same* day so that he is not liable *for* sin. And let no man bring a public charge against his fellow unless he has rebuked him before witnesses. (Dead Sea Scrolls - 1QRule of the Community (1QS) Col. V 25 - Col. VI 1)**

18:15-18 Dead Sea Scrolls[Damascus Document (CD-A) COL VII 2]

18:15-20 Luke 17:3-4

18:16 Deuteronomy 17:6, 19:15; John 8:17; 2Corinthians 13:1; 1Timothy 5:19; Constitutions of the Holy Apostles[Book VIII.4]; Origen[Gospel of Matthew Book X.15]; Tertullian[On Baptism 6; On Prescription Against Heretics 15; Five Books Against Marcion Book IV.43]; Theodotus[Excerpts 13]

18:17 Constitutions of the Holy Apostles[Book II.38]; Cyprian[Epistle LIV.21, LXXV.1]

18:18 Matthew 16:19; John 20:23; Callistus[Second Epistle 5.5]; Constitutions of the Holy Apostles[Book II.11]; Liturgy of James 49; Origen[Gospel of Matthew Book XIII.31]; Urban I[Epistle 4.4]; NT-Apocrypha[Acts of Thomas 1.94; Clement Romance - Installation of Clement 146; Clement Romance 72.4]; Epic of Gilgamesh[The Forest Journey, The Death of Gilgamesh]

18:18-20 Josephus[War 1.5.2 111]

18:19 Matthew 7:7, 21:22; Mark 11:24; John 15:7, 16:23; 1John 3:22, 5:14-15; James 1:5; Cyprian[Epistle VII.2-3]; Origen[Against Celsus Book VIII.69; Gospel of Matthew Book XIV.1]; Nag Hammadi[Gospel of Thomas 48]; NT-Apocrypha[Acts of Paul and Thecla 1.25]

18:19-20 Rabbinic[Babylonian Berakhot 6a; Mishna Aboth 3:2]; Cyprian[Treatise I.12, XII.Book III.3]; Nag Hammadi[Gospel of Thomas 30]

18:20 Matthew 28:20; John 14:23; Rabbinic[Avot 3.3, 3.7]; Clement of Alexandria[Stromata Book III.10]; Origen[Against Celsus Book II.9; Gospel of Matthew Book XIII.15, XIV.1, 4]; Tertullian[On Baptism 6; On Modesty 21; On Repentance 9; To his Wife Book II.6]; Nag Hammadi[Gospel of Truth 36, 43]

18:21 Archelaus[Disputation with Manes 31]; NT-Apocrypha[Gospel of the Nazareans Fragment 15a]

18:21-22 Luke 17:3-4; Constitutions of the Holy Apostles[Book II.46]; Origen[Gospel of Matthew Book XIV.5]; Tertullian[Of Patience 12; On Prayer 7]

18:21-35 Lactantius[Divine Institutes Book VI.12]; Tertullian[On Prayer 7]

18:22 Genesis 4:24; Pseudepigrapha[Testament of Benjamin 7:4]; Dead Sea Scrolls[1Q Rule of the Community (1QS) COL V 25, COL VI 1]; Constitutions of the Holy Apostles[Book II.53]; Tertullian[On Modesty 21]; NT-Apocrypha[Gospel of the Nazareans Fragment 15b]

18:23 Origen[Gospel of Matthew Book XIV.7, 13]; NT-Apocrypha[Acts of Thomas 1.146]

18:23-24 Philo[Special Laws IV (200-202) cf. {Leviticus 19:14}]

18:24 Origen[Gospel of Matthew Book XIV.10, 12-13]

18:25-26 Origen[Gospel of Matthew Book XIV.11]

18:26 Origen[Gospel of Matthew Book XIV.13]

18:27 Luke 7:42

18:28 Origen[Gospel of Matthew Book XIV.11, 13]

18:29 Origen[Gospel of Matthew Book XIV.13]

18:31 Origen[Gospel of Matthew Book XIV.13]

18:32 Clement of Alexandria[Stromata Book I.1]; Cyprian[Epistle XXX.7; Treatise IV.22]

18:34 Matthew 5:25-26; Luke 12:58-59; Nag Hammadi[Testimony of Truth 30]

18:34-35 Origen[Gospel of Matthew Book XIV.13]

18:35 Matthew 6:15; Mark 11:25; Ephesians 4:32; Colossians 3:13; NT-Apocrypha[Gospel of Mani Turfman Fragment M 801]

19:01 Matthew 7:28, 11:1, 13:53, 26:1; Luke 9:51-55; Origen[Gospel of Matthew Book XIV.14]

19:01-02 Origen[Gospel of Matthew Book XIV.15]

19:01-12 Mark 10:1-12; Luke 16:18

19:02 Matthew 4:23-24n; Mark 10:1b; Luke 9:56-62

19:03 Matthew 16:1; Clement of Alexandria[Stromata Book III.6]

19:03-06 Origen[Gospel of Matthew Book XIV.16]

19:03-08 Tertullian[On Monogamy 9]

19:03-09 Mark 10:02-12; Dead Sea Scrolls[Damascus Document (CD-A) COL IV 20-21]; Rabbinic[Mishna Gittin 9.10]

19:03-12 Mark 10:2-12

19:04 Genesis 1:27, 5:2; Origen[De Principiis Book III.5.1]; Tertullian[Five Books Against Marcion Book IV.34]

19:04-05 Constitutions of the Holy Apostles[Book VI.14, 27]; Methodius[Discourse on the Resurrection 1.2]

19:05 Genesis 2:24; 1Corinthians 6:16; Ephesians 5:31; Cyprian[Treatises Attributed to Cyprian - On the Discipline and Advantage of Chastity 5]

19:05-06 Origen[Gospel of Matthew Book XIV.17]; Tertullian[To his Wife Book I.3, II.6]; Nag Hammadi[Apocryphon of John 23; Gospel of Philip 70, 76]

19:06 Mark 10:9; 1Corinthians 6:16; Ephesians 5:28; Zadokite Fragments[Zadokite Fragments 7.1 cf. {Genesis 1:27, 7:9 Deuteronomy 17:17}]; Rabbinic[Babylonian (Qiddushin 2b cf. {Deuteronomy 24:1}; Niddah 31b; Canticles Rabba on 1.4; Genesis Rabba on 2.24; Leviticus Rabba on 25.39 cf. {Isaiah 58:7}]; Plato[Symposium 192e]; Clement of Alexandria[Stromata Book III.6, 12]; Constitutions of the Holy Apostles[Book VI.14]; Justin[First Apology 16]; Origen[Gospel of Matthew Book XIV.16-17]; Tertullian[On Monogamy 5; Five Books Against Marcion Book IV.34]

19:07 Deuteronomy 24:1-4; Matthew 5:31

19:07-08 Irenaeus[Against Heresies Book IV.15.2]; Origen[Gospel of Matthew Book XIV.18]

19:08 Rabbinic[Babylonian Qiddushin 2b]; Clement[Gospel of Matthew Book XIV.23-24; Homily III.54]; Tertullian[Five Books Against Marcion Book IV.34]

19:09 Matthew 5:32; 1Corinthians 7:10-11; Athenagoras[Plea for the Christians 33]; Clement of Alexandria[Stromata Book II.23]

19:09-19 John 8:3-11n

19:10-11 1Corinthians 7:1-2, 7-9, 17; Origen[Gospel of Matthew Book XIV.25]

19:10-12 Clement of Alexandria[Stromata Book III.6]

19:11 Archelaus[Disputation with Manes 25]; Cyprian[Treatise II.4]

19:11-12 Clement of Alexandria[Stromata Book III.1]; Cyprian[Treatise XII.Book III.32]

19:12 This section also includes topical notes for: Eunuchs for the Kingdom - John 1:12-13; Philo[**On the Giants (60-61) cf. {Genesis 6:4}**]; Apostolic[Ignatius - Letter to the Smyrnaeans 6:1]; Athenagoras[Plea for the Christians 33]; Clement of Alexandria[Stromata Book III.7, 15]; Justin[First Apology 15, 29]; Methodius[Banquet of the Ten Virgins 2.7]; Tertullian[De Fuga in Persecutione 14; Of Patience 13; On Monogamy 3, 7, 14; On the Apparel of Women Book II.9; On the Resurrection of the Flesh 27]; Linguistics[Aramaic word for "Eunuch" is written the same as "Faithful," "Believer," or "Believing"]

Therefore he utters no fable whatever respecting the giants; but he wishes to set this fact before your eyes, that some men are born of the earth, and some are born of heaven, and some are born of God: those are born of the earth, who are hunters after the pleasures of the body, devoting themselves to the enjoyment and fruition of them, and being eager to provide themselves with all things that tend to each of them. Those again are born of heaven who are men of skill and science and devoted to learning; for the heavenly portion of us is our mind, and the mind of every one of those persons who are born of heaven studies the encyclical branches of education and every other art of every description, sharpening, and exercising, and practicing itself, and rendering itself acute in all those matters which are the objects of intellect. Lastly, those who are born of God are priests and prophets, who have not thought fit to mix themselves up in the constitutions of this world, and to become cosmopolites, but who having raised themselves above all the objects of the mere outward senses, have departed and fixed their views on that world which is perceptible only by the intellect, and have settled there, being inscribed in the state of incorruptible incorporeal ideas. (Philo - On the Giants (60-61) cf. {Genesis 6:4})

19:13 NT-Apocrypha[Secret Gospel of Mark Fragment 1]

19:13-15 Mark 10:13-16; Luke 18:15-17; Tertullian[On Monogamy 8]

19:14 Matthew 18:2-3; Clement of Alexandria[The Instructor Book I.5]; Constitutions of the Holy Apostles[Book VI.15]; Tertullian[On Baptism 18]

19:16 Matthew 19:29n; Luke 10:25; Clement of Alexandria[Stromata Book III.6]; Clement[Homily XVIII.3, 17]

19:16-21 Jude 1:21n

19:16-24 NT-Apocrypha[Gospel of the Nazareans Fragment 16]

19:16-26 Tertullian[On Monogamy 14]

19:16-30 This section also includes topical notes for: Rich Young Man - Mark 10:17-31; Luke 18:18-30; Philo[On Dreams, That they Are God-Sent (2.11) cf. {Genesis 37:5-11}]; Indian[Dhammapada 75, 97]

19:17 This section also includes topical notes for: God is Good - Leviticus 18:5; Psalms 52:1, 143:10; Mark 10:18; Luke 10:28, 18:19; Pseudepigrapha[Hellenistic Synagogal Prayers 9:5; Letter of Aristeas 1.210-211]; Philo[On Dreams, That they Are God-Sent (2.8) cf. {Genesis 37:5-11}; Special Laws IV (187) cf. {Genesis 1:1-31}]; Plato[Republic II 379c, 380b]; Clement of Alexandria[Fragments from Maximus 55; Stromata Book II.16, IV.18, V.14, VI.6, 16-17, VII.2; The Instructor Book I.8]; Clement[Homily III.57, XVII.4, XVIII.1]; Cyprian[Treatise I.2]; Hippolytus[Refutation of all Heresies Book V.2, VII.19, X.29]; Irenaeus[Against Heresies Book I.10.1, 12.2, II.5.1, 28.3, 29.2, III.25.2, IV.11.2, 14.3]; Justin[Dialogue with Trypho 63; First Apology 14, 16]; Novatian[Treatise Concerning the Trinity 30]; Origen[Against Celsus Book V.11; Gospel of John Book VI.28; De Principiis Book II.5.4]; Tatian[Address to the Greeks 7]; Tertullian[On Modesty 2]; Nag Hammadi[Asclepius 74; Gospel of Truth 42-3; Teachings of Silvanus 91; Tripartite Tractate 53]

19:17-19 Irenaeus[Against Heresies Book IV.12.5]; Egyptian Book of the Dead[Oration 125]

19:17-21 Cyprian[Treatise XII.Book III.1]; Irenaeus[Against Heresies Book IV.12.2]

19:17-22 Clement of Alexandria[Stromata Book VII.11]

19:18 Apostolic[Didache 2:3]

19:18-19 Exodus 20:12-16; Deuteronomy 5:16-20; Romans 13:9

19:19 Leviticus 19:18; Matthew 5:43n, 15:4-8n, 22:39; Luke 10:27; Tertullian[On the Apparel of Women Book II.2]

19:21 Matthew 6:20; Mark 14:5; Luke 12:33, 18:22n; John 12:5; Acts 2:45, 4:34-37; Pseudepigrapha[Sibylline Oracles 2.78-89]; Apostolic[Shepherd of Hermas 50:8-9]; Clement of Alexandria[Stromata Book IV.6, VI.12, 14; The Instructor Book II.3; Who is the Rich Man that shall be Saved 10, 14, 16, 19]; Cyprian[Treatise III.11, VIII.7]; Irenaeus[Against Heresies Book IV.13.3]; Tertullian[On Idolatry 12]; Epic of Gilgamesh[The Story of the Flood]

19:21-29 Philo[**On The Contemplative Life Or Suppliants (13)**]

> Then, because of their anxious desire for an immortal and blessed existence, thinking that their mortal life has already come to an end, they leave their possessions to their sons or daughters, or perhaps to other relations, giving them up their inheritance with willing cheerfulness; and those who know no relations give their property to their companions or friends, for it followed of necessity that those who have acquired the wealth which sees, as if ready prepared for them, should be willing to surrender that wealth which is blind to those who themselves also are still blind in their minds. (Philo - On The Contemplative Life Or Suppliants 13)

19:22 Psalms 62:10

19:23 Clement of Alexandria[Stromata Book V.5]; Origen[Against Celsus Book VII.23]; NT-Apocrypha[Acts of Thomas 1.36; Epistula Apostolorum 46]

19:23-24 Tertullian[To his Wife Book II.8]

19:24 Pseudepigrapha[4Ezra 7.4-18]; Apostolic[Shepherd of Hermas 14:6]; Clement of Alexandria[Stromata Book II.5; Who is the Rich Man that shall be Saved 2]; Origen[Against Celsus Book VI.16]; NT-Apocrypha[Acts of Peter and Andrew]; Linguistics[Aramaic word for "Camel" is written the same as "Beam"]

19:24-30 Mark 10:21-30n

19:26 This section also includes topical notes for: All Things are Possible - Genesis 18:14; Job 10:13, 42:2; Zechariah 8:6; Mark 9:23, 10:27, 14:36; Philo[Special Laws I (282) cf. {Deuteronomy 23:17-18}]; Justin[First Apology 18-19]; Tertullian[Against Praxeas 10; On Idolatry 12; On the Resurrection of the Flesh 57]; NT-Apocrypha[Epistula Apostolorum 21]

19:27 Tertullian[Five Books in Reply to Marcion Book III.10]; Nag Hammadi[Apocryphon of James 4]; NT-Apocrypha[Abgar Legend; Acts of Thomas 1.61; Pistis Sophia c. 136; Two Books of Jeu c. 1-3]

19:27-28 Victorinus[Apocalypse 4.8]

19:27-30 Tertullian[On Idolatry 12]

19:28 Psalms 80:17; Daniel 7:9-10; Zechariah 8:6; Matthew 20:21, 25:31; Mark 10:37; Luke 22:30; Revelation 3:21, 20:4; Pseudepigrapha[**1Enoch 108.12-13**; Martyrdom and Ascension of Isaiah 9.24-26, 11.40; Psalms of Solomon 17:26, 29; Sibylline Oracles 2.219, 2.242; Testament of Abraham 13:6; Testament of Job 33:1; Testament of Levi 13.9]; Rabbinic[Babylonian Sanhedrin 38b cf. {Daniel 4:17, 7:9}]; Plato[Apology 40e-41a]; Clement of Alexandria[Stromata Book VII.10]; Origen[Gospel of Matthew Book XI.3, XIV.15]; Tertullian[On Idolatry 18]; NT-Apocrypha[Acts of Thomas 1.80; Epistula Apostolorum 30; Narrative of Joseph 3; Passing of Mary; Pistis Sophia c. 96]

> I will bring them into the splendid light of those who love my holy name: and I will place each of them on a throne of glory, of glory peculiarly his own, and they shall be at rest during unnumbered periods. Righteous is the judgment of God. (Pseudepigrapha - 1Enoch 108.12-13)

19:28-30 Pseudepigrapha[Testament of Benjamin 10:7]

19:29 This section also includes topical notes for: Leave Brethren or Father or Mother – Exodus 32:27-28; Matthew 19:16; Mark 10:29-30; Luke 10:25, 18:29-30; Jude 1:21n; Pseudepigrapha[3Baruch 15:2 (Gk.); Sibylline Oracles Fragment 3.47]; Philo[On Flight and Finding (88) cf. {Exodus 32:26; Deuteronomy 33:9}; On Drunkenness (72) cf. {Deuteronomy 33:9}; On the Birth of Abel And the Sacrifices offered By Him And By His Brother Cain (124-130); Special Laws I (52)]; Rabbinic[Babylonian Sanhedrin 100a cf. {Isaiah 40:12}]; Clement of Alexandria[Stromata Book IV.4]; Constitutions of the Holy Apostles[Book VIII.10]; Irenaeus[Against Heresies Book V.33.2]; Nag Hammadi[Apocryphon of James 4; Authoritative Teaching 26-27; Testimony of Truth 41]; NT-

Apocrypha[Acts of Thomas 1.61; Pistis Sophia c. 136; Two Books of Jeu c. 1-3]; Epic of
Gilgamesh[The Story of the Flood]; Indian[Dhammapada 91, 211]

19:30 Matthew 20:16; Luke 13:30; Irenaeus[Against Heresies Book III.22.4]

19:30-20:16 Nag Hammadi[Gospel of Thomas 4]

20:01 Matthew 21:28, 33

20:01-16 Irenaeus[Against Heresies Book I.1.3, 3.1, IV.36.7]; Tertullian[On Monogamy 10]; Nag
Hammadi[Apocryphon of James 8]

20:02 OT-Apocrypha[Tobit 5:15]; Origen[Gospel of John Book I.34]

20:08 Leviticus 19:13; Deuteronomy 24:14-15

20:12 NT-Apocrypha[Acts of Thomas 1.60]

20:15 Matthew 6:23; Mark 7:22

20:16 Matthew 19:30; Mark 10:31; Luke 13:30; Clement of Alexandria[Stromata Book V.3];
Clement[Homily VIII.4]; Irenaeus[Against Heresies Book III.22.4, IV.15.2, 27.4]; Tertullian[On
Baptism 16; On Prescription Against Heretics 3]

20:17-19 Mark 10:32-34; Luke 18:31-34

20:18 Psalms 80:17; Matthew 16:21, 17:22-23; Luke 9:22; Irenaeus[Fragments from the Lost Works 55]

20:18-19 Justin[Dialogue with Trypho 106]

20:19 Matthew 16:21, 17:23, 27:19-31n; Luke 9:22, 24:7, 46; Acts 10:40; 1Corinthians 15:4;
Justin[Dialogue with Trypho 51]

20:20 Matthew 28:17n; Pseudepigrapha[Testament of Solomon 1:7, 20:2]; Irenaeus[Fragments from the
Lost Works 55]; Tertullian[On Baptism 11]

20:20-23 Tertullian[Scorpiace 12]

20:20-28 Mark 10:35-45

20:21 Matthew 19:28; Luke 22:30; Pseudepigrapha[Testament of Job 33:1]; Clement of
Alexandria[Stromata Book VII.12; The Instructor Book I.8]

20:22 Matthew 26:39; John 18:11; Clement of Alexandria[The Instructor Book I.6]

20:22-23 Nag Hammadi[First Apocalypse of James 25]

20:23 Origen[Gospel of Matthew Book XII.31]; NT-Apocrypha[Acts of Thomas 1.80; Pistis Sophia c.
96]

20:25 Psalms 10:5, 10; Constitutions of the Holy Apostles[Book II.20]; Origen[Against Celsus Book
VII.23]

20:25-26 Luke 22:25-26

20:26 Matthew 23:11; Mark 9:35; Luke 9:48

20:26-28 Constitutions of the Holy Apostles[Book III.19]

20:27 Matthew 23:11; Mark 9:35; Luke 22:26; Origen[Against Celsus Book IV.30]

20:28 Psalms 80:17; Isaiah 53:10; Luke 22:27; Philippians 2:7; 1Timothy 2:6; Callistus[Second Epistle
3.3]; Clement of Alexandria[The Instructor Book I.9]; Nag Hammadi[Teachings of Silvanus 104]

20:29-30 Matthew 9:27

20:29-34 Mark 10:46-52; Luke 18:35-43

20:30 Matthew 15:22; Origen[Gospel of Matthew Book XI.17]

20:30-31 Matthew 1:1

20:31 Pseudepigrapha[Testament of Solomon 1:7, 20:2]

20:34 Matthew 9:29-30

21:01 Zechariah 14:4; Origen[Gospel of John Book X.15]

21:01-11 Mark 11:1-11; Luke 19:28-44; John 12:12-19

21:02 Clement of Alexandria[Exhortation to the Heathen 12]

21:02-07 John 12:14-15

21:05 Isaiah 62:11; Zechariah 9:9; John 12:5; Pseudepigrapha[Sibylline Oracles 8.325];
Rabbinic[Babylonian (Berakhot 57a; Sanhedrin 98a)]; Apostolic[Epistle to Diognetus 7:3-5]; Clement
of Alexandria[Exhortation to the Heathen 12]; Irenaeus[Against Heresies Book IV.33.12;
Demonstration of the Apostolic Preaching 65]; Justin[Dialogue with Trypho 53, 88; First Apology
31, 35]; Methodius[Oration on the Psalms 2]

21:08 2Kings 9:13; Irenaeus[Against Heresies Book IV.11.3]

21:09 Job 16:19; Psalms 118:25-26, Psalms 148:1; Matthew 1:1, 21:15, 23:39; Mark 11:9; Luke 13:35;
Pseudepigrapha[Testament of Solomon 1:7, 20:2]; Rabbinic[Babylonian Sanhedrin 38b cf. {Exodus
23:21}]; Clement of Alexandria[The Instructor Book I.5]; Constitutions of the Holy Apostles[Book
VII.26, VIII.13]; Methodius[Oration on the Psalms 1]; NT-Apocrypha[Falling Asleep of Mary]

21:10 Methodius[Oration on the Psalms 3]; Origen[Gospel of John Book X.17]

21:10-13 Origen[Gospel of John Book X.15]

21:12 Zechariah 14:21; Pseudepigrapha[Psalms of Solomon 17:30]; NT-Apocrypha[Gospel of the Nazareans Fragment 25]

21:12-13 Pseudepigrapha[Psalms of Solomon 17.36]; Clement of Alexandria[The Instructor Book III.11]; Irenaeus[Against Heresies Book IV.1.6]; Nag Hammadi[Gospel of Thomas 64]

21:12-17 Mark 11:15-19; Luke 19:45-48; John 2:13-22

21:13 This section also includes topical notes for: Den of Robbers - Isaiah 56:7, 60:7; Jeremiah 7:11; Mark 11:17; Luke 19:46; Pseudepigrapha[Sibylline Oracles 2.150]; Philo[Special Laws IV (193-194) cf. {Leviticus 19:36}]; Apostolic[2Clement 14:1]; Constitutions of the Holy Apostles[Book II.17]; Cyprian[Treatise XII.Book III.100]; Justin[Dialogue with Trypho 17]

21:14 2Samuel 5:8; Matthew 4:23-24n

21:14-16 Methodius[Oration on the Psalms 7]

21:14-17 Mark 11:11

21:15 Psalms 118:25; Matthew 1:1, 21:9; Pseudepigrapha[Testament of Solomon 1:7, 20:2]; Methodius[Oration on the Psalms 3]

21:15-16 Cyprian[Epistle IX.4]; Tertullian[A Treatise on the Soul 19]

21:16 Psalms 8:3; Clement of Alexandria[The Instructor Book I.5]; Irenaeus[Against Heresies Book IV.11.3]

21:17 Psalms 8:2

21:18-22 Mark 11:13-26

21:19 Habakkuk 3:17; Mark 11:13-21; Luke 13:6; Pseudepigrapha[4Baruch 3.21-6.11]; Dead Sea Scrolls[4Q Halakhah (4Q25)[4Q HALAKAH] Fragment 3 7-8]; Philo[Concerning Noah's Work As A Planter (95-99, 112-119) cf. {Leviticus 19:23-25}; On the Virtues (156-160) cf. {Leviticus 19:23-25}]; Methodius[Banquet of the Ten Virgins 10.5]; Peter of Alexandria[Canonical Epistle 4]

21:19-20 Hippolytus[Refutation of all Heresies Book VIII.1]

21:21 Matthew 17:20; Luke 17:6; 1Corinthians 13:2; Plato[Laws VIII 842e-843a]

21:22 Matthew 7:7-11, 18:19; John 14:13-14; Clement of Alexandria[The Instructor Book III.12]; Clement[Recognitions Book IV.17]; Cyprian[Epistle XXV.4]; NT-Apocrypha[Martyrdom of Bartholomew]

21:23 Matthew 9:35n; Irenaeus[Against Heresies Book I.20.2]; Origen[Gospel of John Book VI.14]; Tertullian[On Baptism 3, 10; On Modesty 1]

21:23-27 Mark 11:27-33; Luke 20:1-8

21:25 Matthew 3:5-16n, 21:32; Luke 7:30; John 1:6, 33; Origen[Gospel of Matthew Book X.20]; Tertullian[On Baptism 10]

21:26 Matthew 14:5, 21:46

21:28 Matthew 20:1; Luke 15:11; Constitutions of the Holy Apostles[Book V.16]

21:31 Clement of Alexandria[Stromata Book II.4]; Hippolytus[Fragments - On Genesis 49.21-26; Refutation of all Heresies Book V.3]; Irenaeus[Against Heresies Book IV.20.12]

21:31-32 Tertullian[On Baptism 10]

21:32 Proverbs 8:20, 12:28, 21:21; Matthew 21:25; Luke 3:12, 7:29-30

21:33 Isaiah 5:1-2

21:33-41 This section also includes topical notes for: Parable of the Vineyard - Mark 12:1-9; Luke 20:09-16; Philo[On Flight And Finding (175) cf. {Deuteronomy 6:10}]; Tertullian[Against Praxeas 26]; Nag Hammadi[Gospel of Thomas 65]

21:33-44 Irenaeus[Against Heresies Book IV.36.1-2]

21:33-45 Matthew 13:3-53n

21:33-46 Mark 12:1-12; Luke 20:9-19

21:34 2Chronicles 24:19; Jeremiah 7:25, 25:4

21:35 Jeremiah 20:2; Matthew 22:6; Constitutions of the Holy Apostles[Book V.16]

21:36 Nehemiah 9:26; Jeremiah 26:21-23

21:39 Hebrews 13:12; Constitutions of the Holy Apostles[Book V.16]

21:42 Psalms 118:22-23; Isaiah 8:14, 28:16; Acts 4:11; 1Peter 2:7; Pseudepigrapha[Testament of Solomon 22:8, 23:4]; Origen[Gospel of John Book I.23]; Nag Hammadi[Gospel of Thomas 66]

21:42-43 Constitutions of the Holy Apostles[Book V.16]

21:42-44 Mark 12:10-11; Luke 20:17-18; Pseudepigrapha[Sibylline Oracles 1.344-346]

21:43 Origen[Against Celsus Book IV.42; Gospel of John Book X.16; Gospel of Matthew Book X.6, 23]

21:44 Daniel 2:34-35, 44-45; Origen[Gospel of John Book I.23]

21:45-46 Mark 12:12; Luke 20:19

21:46 Matthew 14:5, 16:14, 21:11, 21:26; Luke 7:16, 24:19; John 4:19, 9:17; NT-Apocrypha[Gospel of Judas 58]

22:01 Matthew 13:3-53n; NT-Apocrypha[Acts of Thomas 1.146]

22:01-14 Luke 14:15-24; Rabbinic[Ecclesiastes Rabba on 9:7 cf. {Isaiah 65:13; Malachi 3:18}]; Clement[Homily VIII.22]; Irenaeus[Against Heresies Book IV.36.5]

22:02 Pseudepigrapha[Apocryphon of Ezekiel Fragment 1 1:2, Fragment 3; Joseph and Aseneth 20:8]

22:02-14 This section also includes topical notes for: Parable of the Marriage Feast - Luke 14:16-24; Pseudepigrapha[4Ezra 2.37-41; Odes of Solomon 42.9; Testament of Isaac 6.13]; Philo[On Dreams, That they Are God-Sent (2.249) cf. {Exodus 26:11-12}; On the Birth of Abel And the Sacrifices offered By Him And By His Brother Cain (33) cf. {Genesis 33:11}; The Decalogue (41) cf. {Exodus 19:14-20:18}; Special Laws I (242) cf. {Exodus 29:26-28}]; Rabbinic[Avot 3.20, 4.21; Babylonian Hagigah 14b]; Clement[Recognitions Book IV.35]; Nag Hammadi[Authoritative Teaching 35; Gospel of Thomas 64]

22:03 Proverbs 9:3-6

22:03-14 Irenaeus[Against Heresies Book IV.39.3]; NT-Apocrypha[Acts of Thomas 1.4]

22:04 Proverbs 9:2, 5; Pseudepigrapha[Joseph and Aseneth 10:13]

22:06 Matthew 21:35

22:07 Irenaeus[Against Heresies Book IV.36.6]

22:08 NT-Apocrypha[Epistula Apostolorum 39]

22:10 Irenaeus[Against Heresies Book V.36.2]

22:11 2Kings 10:22; Pseudepigrapha[Joseph and Aseneth 20:6]

22:11-12 Tertullian[On the Resurrection of the Flesh 27]

22:11-13 Rabbinic[Babylonian Zebahim 17b]

22:11-14 Revelation 3:18n; Tertullian[On Modesty 9]

22:12 Clement of Alexandria[Fragments from Macarius Chrysocephalus Parable of the Prodigal son 2]

22:12-13 Origen[De Principiis Book II.5.2]

22:13 Matthew 8:12, 13:42, 50, 24:51, 25:30; Luke 13:28; OT-Apocrypha[Wisdom of Solomon 17:2]; Pseudepigrapha[Greek Apocalypse of Ezra 4:37; Testament of Jacob 5:9]; Clement of Alexandria[The Instructor Book I.10]; Tertullian[On the Resurrection of the Flesh 36]; Nag Hammadi[Apocryphon of John 27]; NT-Apocrypha[Apocalypse of Paul 1.16; Letter of Clement to James 17.1]

22:13-14 Irenaeus[Against Heresies Book IV.36.6]

22:14 OT-Apocrypha[2Esdras 8:3, 41]; Pseudepigrapha[4Ezra 2.17-18, 8.1-3, 9.13-23, 10.57-58; Odes of Solomon 22.8; Sibylline Oracles 1.349; Testament of Abraham 11:12]; Plato[Phaedo 69c-d]; Apostolic[Epistle of Barnabas 4:14]; Clement of Alexandria[Stromata Book I.1, 18-19, VI.7, 13, 15, VII.10]; Origen[Gospel of Matthew Book XII.12]; Tertullian[De Fuga in Persecutione 14]; Nag Hammadi[Authoritative Teaching 34; Gospel of Thomas 23; Teachings of Silvanus 115]; NT-Apocrypha[Clement Romance - Peter on his Mission Journeys H VIII 4.1]

22:15-16 Mark 3:6

22:15-18 NT-Apocrypha[Papyrus Egerton 2 Fragment 2 Lines 43-59]

22:15-22 Mark 12:13-17; Luke 20:20-26

22:16 Genesis 18:19; 1Samuel 16:7; Psalms 25:9, 51:15; Matthew 9:35n; Pseudepigrapha[Odes of Solomon 24.13, 39.13]; Tertullian[Against All Heresies 1]

22:16-21 Nag Hammadi[Gospel of Thomas 100]

22:17 Justin[First Apology 17]; Origen[Gospel of Matthew Book XIV.16]

22:18 Matthew 6:2-16n

22:19-21 Justin[First Apology 17]

22:20-21 Hippolytus[Refutation of all Heresies Book IX.21]

22:21 This section also includes topical notes for: Render Therefore to Caesar - Mark 12:17; Luke 20:25; Romans 13:7; Philo[Allegorical Interpretation III (95-99) cf. {Genesis 1:26, Exodus 31:2}; On Flight And Finding (13) cf. {Genesis 31:8-13}; The Cherubim Part 1 (14-17) cf. {Numbers 5:14-18, Deuteronomy 16:20}]; Clement of Alexandria[The Instructor Book II.1, III.12]; Constitutions of the Holy Apostles[Book II.46]; Irenaeus[Against Heresies Book III.8.1]; Tertullian[De Fuga in Persecutione 12; On Idolatry 15; On the Resurrection of the Flesh 22; Scorpiace 14; The Chaplet, or De Corona 12]

22:23 Exodus 3:15; Acts 23:8; Clement[Recognitions Book I.54]; Hippolytus[Refutation of all Heresies Book IX.24]; Justin[On the Resurrection 9]; Methodius[Discourse on the Resurrection 1.12]; Tertullian[Against All Heresies 1]

22:23-32 Acts 2:31n; Tertullian[On the Resurrection of the Flesh 36]

22:23-33 Mark 12:18-27; Luke 20:27-40; Tertullian[On Monogamy 7; To his Wife Book I.1]

22:24 Genesis 38:8; Deuteronomy 25:5; NT-Apocrypha[Epistula Apostolorum 3]

22:29 Archelaus[Disputation with Manes 28]; Clement[Homily III.50]; Irenaeus[Against Heresies Book IV.5.1-2, 33.4]; NT-Apocrypha[Pseudo Clementines - Kerygmata Petrou H III 50.1]

22:29-30 Tertullian[On Exhortation to Chastity 13]

22:29-33 Pseudepigrapha[Apocalypse of Zephaniah 5:5]

22:30 Pseudepigrapha[1Enoch 51.2-5; 2Enoch 22:10]; Rabbinic[Mishnah Ma'aseroth 4:5-6]; Clement of Alexandria[Stromata Book III.6, VI.12; The Instructor Book II.10]; Clement[Recognitions Book III.30]; Hippolytus[Fragments of Discourses or Homilies 1]; Irenaeus[Against Heresies Book II.33.5]; Methodius[Banquet of the Ten Virgins 2.7; Discourse on the Resurrection 1.1]; Origen[Against Celsus Book IV.29; Gospel of John Book II.16; De Principiis Book IV.1.29]; Tertullian[A Treatise on the Soul 37; On Monogamy 10; On the Apparel of Women Book I.2; On the Resurrection of the Flesh 62; Five Books Against Marcion Book V.10]

22:31-32 Rabbinic[Babylonian Sanhedrin 39a cf. {Deuteronomy 11:9}, 90b, 91b]; Origen[De Principiis Book II.4.1]

22:32 Exodus 3:6, 15-16; Mark 12:27n; OT-Apocrypha[4Maccabees 7:19, 16:25]; Pseudepigrapha[Hellenistic Synagogal Prayers 16:8, 16:14]; Clement[Homily III.55]; Constitutions of the Holy Apostles[Book VIII.41]; Cyprian[Epistle XXVI.1]; Irenaeus[Against Heresies Book II.30.9]; Origen[Against Celsus Book VIII.3]; Nag Hammadi[Gospel of Thomas 11]

22:33 Matthew 7:28, 13:54; Mark 11:18

22:34-40 Mark 12:28-34; Luke 10:25-28; Tertullian[An Answer to the Jews 2]

22:35 Origen[Gospel of Matthew Book XIV.16]

22:36-38 Clement of Alexandria[Who is the Rich Man that shall be Saved 27]

22:36-40 Pseudepigrapha[Testament of Benjamin 3.3-4; Testament of Naphtali 8.9; Testament of Zebulon 5.1-6.8]; Clement of Alexandria[The Instructor Book II.1]

22:37 Deuteronomy 6:5; Joshua 22:5; Anonymous[Treatise on Re-Baptism 13]; Clement of Alexandria[The Instructor Book I.7, III.12]; Irenaeus[Demonstration of the Apostolic Preaching 87]; Teaching of the Twelve Apostles 1.2; Tertullian[Scorpiace 6; Five Books Against Marcion Book II.13]

22:37-39 Pseudepigrapha[Sibylline Oracles 8.481-2]; Apostolic[Didache 1:2]

22:37-40 Philo[The Decalogue 22.108]; Rabbinic[Babylonian Berakhot 63a cf. {Proverbs 3:6}; Leviticus Rabba on 23.40; Midrash on Psalms 1.2; Numbers Rabba on 15:38; Siphra on Leviticus 19:2, 18; Siphre on Numbers 15:39]; Cyprian[Treatise XI.2]; Irenaeus[Against Heresies Book IV.12.2-3]; Justin[Dialogue with Trypho 93]; Origen[De Principiis Book II.4.2]; Tertullian[On Fasting 2; On the Resurrection of the Flesh 9]

22:39 Leviticus 19:18, 34; Matthew 5:43n, 19:19; Romans 13:9; Galatians 5:14; James 2:8; Rabbinic[Babylonian Shabbat 31a]; Athenagoras[Plea for the Christians 32]; Clement of Alexandria[Who is the Rich Man that shall be Saved 28]; Clement[Homily XII.32]; Cyprian[Epistle VI.5]; Fabian[Second Epistle]; Teaching of the Twelve Apostles 1.2; Tertullian[On the Apparel of Women Book II.2]; Nag Hammadi[Sentences of Sextus 179]

22:39-40 Clement of Alexandria[The Instructor Book III.12]

22:40 Matthew 5:43n, 7:12; Pseudepigrapha[Apocalypse of Sedrach 1:13]; Clement of Alexandria[Stromata Book V.14, VII.2]; Cyprian[Treatise IV.28]

22:41-46 Mark 12:35-37; Luke 20:41-44

22:42 Matthew 1:1; John 7:42; Archelaus[Disputation with Manes 47]

22:42-35 Apostolic[Epistle of Barnabas 12:10-11]

22:42-45 Acts 3:18-26n; Irenaeus[Fragments from the Lost Works 52]; Origen[Gospel of John Book X.23]; NT-Apocrypha[Arabic Gospel of the Infancy of the Savior 50]

22:43 2Samuel 23:2; Irenaeus[Against Heresies Book III.21.8, IV.33.4]

22:44 Psalms 110:1; Acts 2:34-35; 1Corinthians 15:25; Hebrews 1:13; Justin[Dialogue with Trypho 83]

22:45 Romans 1:3; Clement of Alexandria[Exhortation to the Heathen 1]

22:46 Mark 12:34; Luke 20:40

23:01 Luke 14:1-14

23:01-03 Pseudepigrapha[Vision of Ezra 46]; Tertullian[On Monogamy 8]

23:01-36 Luke 11:37-52

23:01-39 Mark 12:38-40; Luke 13:34-35, 20:45-47; Josephus[Antiquities 13.5.9 171-173, 17.2.4 32-45, 18.1.2-3 11-13; War 2.8.14 162-166]; Nag Hammadi[Gospel of Thomas 39]

23:02 Rabbinic[Exodus Rabbah 43:4]; NT-Apocrypha[Clement Romance 70.2; Pseudo Clementines - Kerygmata Petrou H III 51.1, H XI 29.1]

23:02-03 Clement[Homily III.19, 70]

23:02-04 Irenaeus[Against Heresies Book IV.12.4]

23:03 Malachi 2:7-8; Clement[First Epistle Concerning Virginity 11]; Constitutions of the Holy Apostles[Book II.8]

23:04 Rabbinic[Babylonian Nedarim 64a]; Clement of Alexandria[Stromata Book VI.6]; NT-Apocrypha[Pseudo Clementines - Kerygmata Petrou H XI 29.4]

23:05 Exodus 13:9; Numbers 15:38-39; Deuteronomy 6:8, 11:18; Matthew 6:1, 5; Rabbinic[Babylonian Menahot 41b]

23:06 Luke 14:7; Archelaus[Disputation with Manes 21]; Nag Hammadi[Apocalypse of Peter 79:29]

23:06-08 Cyprian[Treatise XII.Book III.5]

23:06-12 Rabbinic[Babylonian Horayot 13a-14b]

23:07 Rabbinic[Makkot 24a; Ketubot 103b]

23:07-12 Rabbinic[Mishnah Aboth 1:10]

23:08 Jeremiah 31:34; Tertullian[Five Books in Reply to Marcion Book IV.6; On Monogamy 7; On the Veiling of Virgins 1]; NT-Apocrypha[Epistula Apostolorum 41]; Indian[Dhammapada 353]

23:08-09 Origen[Gospel of John Book I.5]; Nag Hammadi[Gospel of Thomas 105]

23:08-10 Clement of Alexandria[Stromata Book VI.7]; Novatian[Treatise Concerning the Trinity 30]

23:09 Malachi 2:10; Clement of Alexandria[Stromata Book II.4, III.12; Who is the Rich Man that shall be Saved 23]; Clement[Recognitions Book VIII.8]; Cyprian[Treatise IV.9, XI.11]; Irenaeus[Against Heresies Book IV.1.2]; Tertullian[On Monogamy 6; On Prayer 2; On Repentance 8]; Theodotus[Excerpts]

23:11 Matthew 20:26-27; Mark 9:35, 10:43-44; Luke 9:48, 22:26; Pseudepigrapha[Ahiqar 150]

23:12 Job 22:29; Proverbs 29:23; Ezekiel 21:26; Matthew 18:4n; Luke 14:11, 18:14; Pseudepigrapha[Joseph and Aseneth 6:8]; Anonymous[Treatise Against the Heretic Novatian 13]; Origen[Against Celsus Book III.63]; NT-Apocrypha[Gospel of Mani Psalm CCLXXIII]

23:13 Isaiah 5:8, 11, 18; Clement[Recognitions Book II.30]; Origen[Gospel of Matthew Book X.14]; Nag Hammadi[Apocalypse of Peter 78:23-31]

23:13-15 Pseudepigrapha[4Ezra 12.31-33]; Hippolytus[Refutation of all Heresies Book IX.23]

23:13-29 Matthew 6:1-16

23:13-36 Rabbinic[Jerusalem (Berakhot 14b; Sotah 20c); Babylonian Sotah 22b]

23:14 Rabbinic[Babylonian Ketubot 100b]

23:15 Rabbinic[Babylonian Berakhot 10a]; Justin[Dialogue with Trypho 122]

23:16 Matthew 15:14, 23:24; Romans 2:19; Josephus[War 2.8.6 135]; Constitutions of the Holy Apostles[Book V.12]; NT-Apocrypha[Oxyrhynchus Papyrus 840]

23:16-26 Matthew 15:24

23:19 Exodus 29:37; NT-Apocrypha[Oxyrhynchus Papyrus 840]

23:21 1Kings 8:13; Psalms 26:8

23:22 Isaiah 66:1; Matthew 5:34; Acts 7:49

23:23 Leviticus 27:30; Deuteronomy 14:22; Isaiah 1:17; Jeremiah 22:3; Hosea 6:6; Micah 6:8; Zechariah 7:9; Rabbinic[Avot 1.16]

23:23-24 Anterus[Epistle]; Justin[Dialogue with Trypho 112]

23:23-29 Pseudepigrapha[4Ezra 12.31-33]; Hippolytus[Refutation of all Heresies Book IX.23]

23:24 Leviticus 11:4; Matthew 15:14, 23:16; Romans 2:19; Irenaeus[Against Heresies Book III.18.5, IV.33.7]; NT-Apocrypha[Epistula Apostolorum 43; Oxyrhynchus Papyrus 840]

23:25 Mark 7:4; Archelaus[Disputation with Manes 21]; NT-Apocrypha[Pseudo Clementines - Kerygmata Petrou H XI 29.2]

23:25-26 This section also includes topical notes for: Cleanse First the Inside of the Cup - Leviticus 10:10; Luke 11:39; Philo[Special Laws III (208) cf. {Leviticus 22:5}]; Plato[Sophist 227b-c]; Clement[Recognitions Book VI.11]; Tertullian[On Prayer 13]; Nag Hammadi[Gospel of Thomas 89]; Indian[Dhammapada 394]

23:25-27 Clement of Alexandria[The Instructor Book III.9]

23:25-29 Linguistics[Hebrew word for "Within Self" (קרב) is a pun for "Sepulchre" (קבר)]

23:26 John 9:40; Tertullian[On Repentance 6]

23:26-27 NT-Apocrypha[Oxyrhynchus Papyrus 840]

23:26-28 Irenaeus[Against Heresies Book IV.18.3]

23:27 Acts 23:3; Apostolic[Ignatius - Letter to the Philadelphians 6:1]; Archelaus[Disputation with Manes 42]; Hippolytus[Refutation of all Heresies Book V.3]; Justin[Dialogue with Trypho 112]; Tertullian[On the Resurrection of the Flesh 19]; Nag Hammadi[Teachings of Silvanus 106]; Indian[Dhammapada 150]

23:28 Isaiah 64:10; Jeremiah 22:5; Luke 16:15

23:29-38 Origen[Letter to Africanus 9]

23:31 Acts 7:52; Tertullian[On Prayer 14]

23:33 Luke 13:32n; Irenaeus[Against Heresies Book IV.41.3]

23:33-35 This section also includes topical notes for: The Righteous Blood Shed on the Earth - Matthew 3:7n, 12:34; Luke 3:7, 23:33-45n; Philo[Special Laws III (103)]

23:34 2Samuel 12:1; Jeremiah 7:25, 25:4; Matthew 10:23; Acts 7:52; 1Thessalonians 2:15; Pseudepigrapha[Sibylline Oracles 2.247]; Plato[Apology 30d-31b]; Irenaeus[Against Heresies Book IV.9.1]; Origen[Against Celsus Book III.46]

23:35 Genesis 4:8, 10; 2Chronicles 24:20-22; Proverbs 6:17; Zechariah 1:1; Joel 3:19; Jonah 1:4; Hebrews 11:4; Pseudepigrapha[Lives of the Prophets 15:6, 23:1]; Archelaus[Disputation with Manes 30]; Clement of Alexandria[The Instructor Book I.6]; Constitutions of the Holy Apostles[Book V.16]; Irenaeus[Against Heresies Book V.14.1]; Peter of Alexandria[Canonical Epistle 13]; Tertullian[Five Books in Reply to Marcion Book III.17]; NT-Apocrypha[Genna Marias; Gospel of the Nazareans Fragment 17; Protoevangelium of James 23.3, 24.1]

23:35-36 Pseudepigrapha[Life of Abraham 6:11]

23:35-37 Pseudepigrapha[4Ezra 1.32]

23:37 Acts 7:59; 1Thessalonians 2:15; Pseudepigrapha[4Ezra 1:30; Sibylline Oracles 2.247]; Rabbinic[Genesis Rabba on 2:4]; Clement of Alexandria[Stromata Book I.5; The Instructor Book I.5]; Clement[Homily III.19]; Irenaeus[Against Heresies Book IV.36.8, 37.1]; NT-Apocrypha[Acts of Peter 1.32]

23:37-38 Cyprian[Treatise XII.Book I.6]; Irenaeus[Against Heresies Book IV.37.5]

23:37-39 Luke 13:34-35; Clement of Alexandria[The Instructor Book I.9]

23:38 1Kings 9:7-8; Jeremiah 12:7; OT-Apocrypha[Tobit 14:4]; Constitutions of the Holy Apostles[Book VI.5]; Hippolytus[Expository Treatise Against the Jews 7]; Methodius[Oration Concerning Simeon and Anna 12]

23:39 Psalms 118:26; Rabbinic[Babylonian Sanhedrin 38b cf. {Exodus 23:21}]

24:01 Pseudepigrapha[4Ezra 5:2]

24:01-02 Mark 13:1-2; Luke 21:5-6

24:01-51 Rabbinic[Babylonian Sanhedrin 96b, 98a]

24:01-25:46 Mark 13:1-37

24:02 Jeremiah 7:14, 9:11; Luke 19:44; Rabbinic[**Babylonian Gittin 57b cf. {Psalms 137.7}**]; Clement[Homily III.15]; Cyprian[Treatise XII.Book I.15]

"And the destruction of the second Temple: 'O Lord, against the children of Edom, remember the day of Jerusalem, for they said, Destroy it, destroy it, down to the very foundations.' (Talmud - Babylonian Gittin 57b cf. {Psalms 137.7}, *The Babylonian Talmud a Translation and Commentary*, Jacob Neusner; Hendrickson Publishers, Inc., 2005)

24:02-51 Nag Hammadi[On the Origin of the World 126]

24:03 Matthew 13:39-40, 49, 24:27, 37, 39, 28:20; Rabbinic[Babylonian Sotah 49b; Canticles Rabba on 2:33 cf. {Micah 7:6; Psalms 84:52}]

24:03-05 NT-Apocrypha[Apocalypse of Peter 1.1-2]

24:03-13 Nag Hammadi[Gospel of Thomas 51]

24:03-14 Mark 13:3-13; Luke 21:7-19; Revelation 6:1-12, 13:1-8

24:03-24 Pseudepigrapha[4Ezra 4.52-5.13, 6.11-29, 7.26-44, 8.63-9.12]

24:03-51 NT-Apocrypha[Epistula Apostolorum 34; Gospel of Judas 33]

24:04 Pseudepigrapha[Apocalypse of Elijah 1:14]; Anonymous[Treatise on Re-Baptism 12]; Teaching of the Twelve Apostles 6.1; Tertullian[On Prescription Against Heretics 1]

24:04-05 Mark 13:5-6; Luke 21:8; Revelation 6:1-2, 13:1-6; Archelaus[Disputation with Manes 35]; Origen[Against Celsus Book VI.45]

24:04-31 Cyprian[Treatise XI.11]

24:05 Matthew 24:11, 23-24; John 5:43; 1John 2:18; Pseudepigrapha[Apocalypse of Elijah 3:1]; Cyprian[Epistle LXXII.16]; Nag Hammadi[Gospel of Mary 8]; NT-Apocrypha[Epistula Apostolorum 50]

24:06 Daniel 2:28-29, 45; Mark 13:32; Acts 01:07; Pseudepigrapha[2Baruch 21.8-9, 48:34, 48:37; Lives of the Prophets 2:8; Sibylline Oracles 3.636]; Rabbinic[Babylonian Sanhedrin 97a]

24:06-07 Mark 13:7-8; Luke 21:9-10; Revelation 6:3-4, 13:7

24:07 2Chronicles 15:6; Isaiah 19:2; Mark 13:8; Luke 21:11; Revelation 6:5-8; Pseudepigrapha[2Baruch 27:9; 2Enoch 70:23; 4Ezra 13:31, 15:15; Greek Apocalypse of Ezra 3.13; Sibylline Oracles 1.397, 2.23, 2.6]; NT-Apocrypha[Apocalypse of Thomas Line 7]

24:07-30 Pseudepigrapha[1Enoch 80.2-8]

24:08 Mark 13:8; 1Thessalonians 5:3; Pseudepigrapha[2Baruch 27:3]; Rabbinic[Babylonian Ketubot 111a]

24:09 Matthew 10:17, 22-23; John 15:18, 16:2

24:09-13 Mark 13:9; Luke 21:12-19; Revelation 6:9-12

24:10 Daniel 11:41

24:10-12 Teaching of the Twelve Apostles 16.4

24:10-13 Apostolic[Didache 16:4-5]

24:11 Matthew 24:5, 24; Pseudepigrapha[2Baruch 48:34; Apocalypse of Elijah 1:13; Sibylline Oracles 2.166]; Justin[Dialogue with Trypho 35, 51, 82]; Tertullian[On Prescription Against Heretics 1]; Nag Hammadi[Gospel of the Egyptians III 61]; NT-Apocrypha[Acts of Thomas 1.79]

24:12 Hippolytus[Appendix to the Works of Hippolytus - On the End of the World 8; Fragments from Commentaries - On Daniel 3.43]; Origen[Gospel of John Book VI.38; De Principiis Book II.8.3]; Tertullian[On Modesty 1]

24:12-13 Constitutions of the Holy Apostles[Book VI.13, 18]

24:13 Matthew 10:22; Tertullian[On Monogamy 15; Five Books Against Marcion Book IV.39]; Nag Hammadi[Testimony of Truth 44]

24:14 Matthew 10:18, 28:19; Mark 13:10-13; Clement[Homily XVI.21]; Justin[Dialogue with Trypho 10]; Origen[Against Celsus Book II.13]; Victorinus[Apocalypse 6.1-2]

24:15 Psalms 145:15; Ezekiel 42:13; Daniel 9:27, 11:31, 12:11; Mark 13:14; Luke 21:20; 2Thessalonians 2:3-12; 2Corinthians 3:12-18n; Revelation 13:1-6; OT-Apocrypha[1Maccabees 1:54, 6:7; 2Maccabees 8:17]; Pseudepigrapha[2Baruch 28:1; Apocalypse of Elijah 3:5]; Clement[Recognitions Book I.64]; Irenaeus[Against Heresies Book V.25.2, 5]; Victorinus[Apocalypse 13.13]

24:15-22 Hippolytus[Treatise on Christ and Antichrist 62]

24:15-28 Mark 13:14-23; Luke 21:20-24

24:16 Ezekiel 7:16; OT-Apocrypha[1Maccabees 2:28]

24:16-18 NT-Apocrypha[6Ezra 17.41-44]

24:16-20 Pseudepigrapha[Apocalypse of Elijah 4:24]

24:16-21 Mark 13:14; Luke 21:21-24; Revelation 13:7-18

24:17 Pseudepigrapha[2Baruch 53:9]

24:17-18 Luke 17:31

24:19 Pseudepigrapha[2Baruch 10:14; Apocalypse of Daniel 12:6; Sibylline Oracles 2.190]; Clement of Alexandria[Stromata Book III.6]; Tertullian[On Monogamy 16; To his Wife Book I.5]

24:21 Daniel 12:1; Joel 2:2; Revelation 7:14; Pseudepigrapha[4Ezra 2.27, 16.18-34; Testament (Assumption) of Moses 8:1]; Irenaeus[Against Heresies Book IV.33.13, V.25.2, 29.1]; Origen[De Principiis Book III.5.4]; NT-Apocrypha[Apocalypse of Thomas Line 46]

24:22 Pseudepigrapha[4Ezra 7.138-8.3, 9.13-23; Life of Abraham 19:13]; Methodius[Banquet of the Ten Virgins 2.2]; NT-Apocrypha[Epistula Apostolorum 28]

24:23-24 Matthew 24:5, 11; 1John 2:18; Anonymous[Treatise on Re-Baptism 12]

24:23-26 Archelaus[Disputation with Manes 35]

24:23-27 Origen[Against Celsus Book II.49]; Nag Hammadi[Gospel of Mary 8]

24:24 Deuteronomy 13:1-4, 6; 2Thessalonians 2:9-10; Revelation 13:13-14; Pseudepigrapha[2Baruch 48:34; Martyrdom and Ascension of Isaiah (3:13-4:22 = Testament of Hezekiah) 4:12; Sibylline Oracles 2.166]; Archelaus[Disputation with Manes 36]; Clement[Recognitions Book I.37]; Constitutions of the Holy Apostles[Book VI.13, 18]; Hippolytus[Appendix to the Works of Hippolytus - On the End of the World 23]; Irenaeus[Against Heresies Book II.32.3]; Justin[Dialogue with Trypho 51, 82]; Origen[De Principiis Book IV.1.2]; Teaching of the Twelve Apostles 16.4; Tertullian[A Treatise on the Soul 57; Five Books Against Marcion Book III.3; On Prescription Against Heretics 1]; Nag Hammadi[Gospel of the Egyptians III 61]; NT-Apocrypha[Clement Romance 17.4; Epistula Apostolorum 28]

24:25 Cyprian[Epistle LXXII.16]

24:26-27 Luke 17:23-24; NT-Apocrypha[Apocalypse of Peter 1.1]

24:27 Psalms 80:17; Matthew 24:37, 39; 1Corinthians 15:23; 1Thessalonians 2:19, 3:13, 4:15, 5:23; 2Thessalonians 2:1, 8; James 5:7-8; 2Peter 3:4, 12; 1John 2:28; Pseudepigrapha[Apocalypse of Elijah 3:4, 3:10; Sibylline Oracles 6.18]; Origen[De Principiis Book I.5.5]; Syriac Teaching of the Apostles

24:27-28 Hippolytus[Appendix to the Works of Hippolytus - On the End of the World 36; Treatise on Christ and Antichrist 64]

24:28 Job 39:30; Habakkuk 1:8; Luke 13:32n, 17:37; Irenaeus[Against Heresies Book IV.14.1]

24:29 Isaiah 13:10, 34:4; Ezekiel 32:7, 33:4; Haggai 2:6, 21; Joel 2:10, 31, 3:15; Revelation 6:12-13; Pseudepigrapha[Apocalypse of Elijah 3:6; Sibylline Oracles 2.202, 8.190]; Hippolytus[Appendix to the Works of Hippolytus - On the End of the World 37, 39]; Tertullian[A Strain of the Judgment of the Lord 180; Against Hermogenes 34]; NT-Apocrypha[Apocalypse of Thomas Line 11, 36]

24:29-31 Zechariah 12:10-14; Mark 13:24-27; Luke 21:25-28; 1Corinthians 15:51-55; 1Thessalonians 4:15-17; 2Thessalonians 2:1-2; Revelation 1:7, 6:13-15, 7:1-17, 8:1-2, 11:12, 14:1-5, 14:14-16, 16:8

24:29-36 Pseudepigrapha[4Ezra 9.1-8]

24:30 Psalms 80:17; Daniel 7:13-14; Zechariah 12:10, 12, 14; Matthew 16:27, 26:64; 1Thessalonians 4:15-17n; Revelation 1:6-7; Pseudepigrapha[1Enoch 61:9; 2Baruch 25:3; Apocalypse of Elijah 3:3, 5:36; Sibylline Oracles 2.240]; Apostolic[Didache 16:8]; Teaching of the Twelve Apostles 16.8; NT-Apocrypha[Apocalypse of Peter 1.1, 1.6; Apocalypse of Thomas Line 48]

24:30-31 Apostolic[Didache 16:6]; Constitutions of the Holy Apostles[Book VII.32]

24:31 Deuteronomy 30:4; Isaiah 27:13; Zechariah 2:6, 10; Matthew 13:41; 1Corinthians 15:52; 1Thessalonians 4:16; Pseudepigrapha[1Enoch 22:3; 4Baruch 3.2-3; Apocalypse of Abraham 31.1-2; Apocalypse of Elijah 5.2-4; Greek Apocalypse of Ezra 4:36-37; Life of Adam and Eve (Apocalypse of Moses) 22:3; Questions of Ezra RecB 13; Sibylline Oracles 8.239]; Apostolic[Didache 10:5]; Hippolytus[Treatise on Christ and Antichrist 64]; Teaching of the Twelve Apostles 10.5; NT-Apocrypha[Apocalypse of Thomas Line 24, 72; Epistula Apostolorum 28]

24:32 Matthew 13:3-53n

24:32-33 Tertullian[On the Resurrection of the Flesh 22]

24:32-35 Mark 13:28-31; Luke 21:29-33; Revelation 14:17-20

24:34 Matthew 16:28; Pseudepigrapha[2Enoch 23:4]

24:35 Isaiah 40:8; Matthew 5:18; Luke 16:17; Methodius[Discourse on the Resurrection 1.9]; Origen[Against Celsus Book V.22; Gospel of Matthew Book XIII.1; De Principiis Book III.5.1]; Tertullian[Against Hermogenes 34]; Nag Hammadi[Gospel of Thomas 11]; NT-Apocrypha[Letter of Peter to James 2.5; Pseudo Clementines - Kerygmata Petrou H III 51.3]

24:36 Zechariah 14:7; Mark 13:32; Acts 1:7; 1Thessalonians 5:1-2; Revelation 3:3; Rabbinic[Babylonian Sanhedrin 97b cf. {Habakkuk 2:3}; Exodus Rabba on 25:12 cf. {Psalms 95:7}]; Irenaeus[Against Heresies Book III.23.1]; Tertullian[Against Praxeas 26]

24:36-44 Mark 13:32-37; Luke 17:26-30, 34-36

24:37 Genesis 6:9-13; Psalms 80:17; Isaiah 54:9; Matthew 24:27, 39; 1Corinthians 15:23; 1Thessalonians 2:19, 3:13, 4:15, 5:23; 2Thessalonians 2:1, 8; James 5:7-8; 2Peter 3:4, 12; 1John 2:28; Pseudepigrapha[2Baruch 30:1; 2Enoch 70:10]; Rabbinic[Babylonian Sanhedrin 99a cf. {Isaiah 54:9}]; Clement of Alexandria[Stromata Book III.6]

24:37-39 Origen[Gospel of Matthew Book XIII.1]

24:38 NT-Apocrypha[Apocalypse of Paul 1.50]

24:38-39 Genesis 6:13-7.24; 2Peter 3:6

24:39 Psalms 80:17; Matthew 24:27, 37; 1Corinthians 15:23; 1Thessalonians 2:19, 3:13, 4:15, 5:23; 2Thessalonians 2:1, 8; James 5:7-8; 2Peter 3:4, 12; 1John 2:28

24:40 Pseudepigrapha[Apocalypse of Zephaniah 2:2]; NT-Apocrypha[6Ezra 17.19-33]

24:40-42 Nag Hammadi[Gospel of Thomas 61]

24:41 Origen[Gospel of Matthew Book XIII.17]

24:42 Matthew 25:13; Apostolic[2Clement 12:1]; Clement of Alexandria[Stromata Book V.14]; Irenaeus[Against Heresies Book IV.36.3, V.10.1]; Teaching of the Twelve Apostles 16.2

24:42-44 Luke 21:34-36; 1Thessalonians 5:2; 2Peter 3:10; Revelation 16:15; Apostolic[Didache 16:1]

24:42-51 This section also includes topical notes for: Watch - Matthew 25:13, 26:41; Mark 13:33-37, 14:38; Luke 12:37-39, 21:36; 1Thessalonians 5:4-6; Revelation 3:2-3, 16:15; Pseudepigrapha[4Ezra 2.14; Life of Adam and Eve (Apocalypse of Moses) 30.1]; Dead Sea Scrolls[4Q Sapiential Work (4Q418[4QSAP.WORKA]) Fragment 69 10-15]; Philo[Allegorical Interpretation III (188-199) cf. {Genesis 3:15, 14:21, 21:5, 27:36, 40, 32:24-31, Numbers 28:2, Deuteronomy 23:16, Matthew 24:45-51, Luke 12:35-48}; Fragments Extracted From the Parallels of John of Damascus Page 613. D.; On Dreams, That they Are God-Sent (2.170-2.176) cf. {Numbers 13:17-21, Deuteronomy 30:9, Isaiah 5:7};

Special Laws I (156) cf. {Genesis 6:16, 18:1-2, 10, 19:6, 9-11, Exodus 12:22-23, 33:8-10, 40:12, Numbers 3:25, 12:5, 2Samuel 6:10-12, Psalms 84:10, 141:3, 1Chronicles 13:13-14, 15:24-25, 2Chronicles 23:4, 34:9}]; Nag Hammadi[Book of Thomas the Contender 145; Gospel of Thomas 21, 103; Teachings of Silvanus 113-114]; Indian[Dhammapada 157]

24:43 1Thessalonians 5:2; 2Peter 3:10; Revelation 3:3, 16:15; Pseudepigrapha[Testament of Abraham 10:10]; NT-Apocrypha[Acts of Thomas 1.146]

24:43-44 Luke 12:39-40; Rabbinic[Babylonian Sanhedrin 39a cf. {Genesis 2:21}]

24:44 Psalms 80:17

24:44-46 Irenaeus[Against Heresies Book IV.26.5]

24:45 This section also includes topical notes for: Faithful and Wise Servant - Genesis 39:4; Psalms 104:27; Luke 12:42; Philo[Allegorical Interpretation III (188-199) cf. {Genesis 14:21; 21:5; 27:36, 40, Numbers 28:2, Deuteronomy 23:16}; Fragments Preserved By Antonius Ser. LVII.; On the Birth of Abel And the Sacrifices offered By Him And By His Brother Cain (124-130) cf. {Numbers 8:5-22; 35:1-34, Joshua 20:2-3, 21:13-38}]; Theonas[Epistle to Lucianus, the Chief Chamberlain 4]; NT-Apocrypha[Acts of Thomas 1.146; Clement Romance 60.2, 64.1]

24:45-47 Pseudepigrapha[Vision of Ezra 1.66]; Apostolic[Shepherd of Hermas 55:1-11]

24:45-50 Clement[Homily III.60]

24:45-51 Luke 12:41-48; Clement[First Epistle Concerning Virginity 13]

24:45-25:13 Pseudepigrapha[Sibylline Oracles 2.180]

24:46 Pseudepigrapha[Sibylline Oracles 2.179]

24:47 Matthew 25:21, 23; Theonas[Epistle to Lucianus, the Chief Chamberlain 4]

24:48 Irenaeus[Against Heresies Book IV.26.3, 37.3]; NT-Apocrypha[Clement Romance 60.2]

24:51 Matthew 6:2-16n, 8:12, 13:42, 50, 22:13, 25:30; Luke 13:28; Constitutions of the Holy Apostles[Book VII.5]; Irenaeus[Against Heresies Book IV.37.3]

25:01 Luke 12:35-36; Clement of Alexandria[Stromata Book V.3, VII.12]; Irenaeus[Against Heresies Book II.27.2]; NT-Apocrypha[Acts of Thomas 1.146; Letter of Clement to James 7.5]

25:01-10 John 3:29n

25:01-12 Pseudepigrapha[Sibylline Oracles 2.49]; Constitutions of the Holy Apostles[Book II.13]; Nag Hammadi[Gospel of Philip 82; Gospel of Thomas 75]

25:01-13 Methodius[Banquet of the Ten Virgins 6.3]; NT-Apocrypha[Epistula Apostolorum 43-44]

25:01-30 Nag Hammadi[Apocryphon of James 8]

25:02 Clement[First Epistle Concerning Virginity 3]; Irenaeus[Against Heresies Book II.24.4]

25:03 Rabbinic[Ecclesiastes Rabba on 9:7 cf. {Isaiah 65:13; Malachi 3:18}]

25:04 Origen[Against Celsus Book VI.5]

25:06 Methodius[Banquet of the Ten Virgins 6.4]

25:08 Job 18:5; Proverbs 13:9

25:08-09 Tertullian[On Modesty 22]

25:10 Revelation 19:7, 9; Pseudepigrapha[4Ezra 2.35-41]; Clement of Alexandria[Stromata Book VI.15]; NT-Apocrypha[Epistula Apostolorum 43]

25:11 Methodius[Banquet of the Ten Virgins 11.2]

25:11-12 Luke 13:25, 27

25:12 Matthew 7:23

25:13 Matthew 24:42-51n; Mark 13:35; Luke 12:40; Apostolic[2Clement 12:1]; Irenaeus[Against Heresies Book V.10.1]

25:14 Mark 13:34; Irenaeus[Against Heresies Book III.17.3]; NT-Apocrypha[Pseudo Clementines - Kerygmata Petrou H III 26.3]

25:14-30 Luke 19:11-27; Pseudepigrapha[Ahiqar 192]; Origen[Gospel of Matthew Book XIV.12]; NT-Apocrypha[Gospel of the Nazareans Fragment 18]

25:15 Origen[Gospel of Matthew Book XIV.7]

25:15-28 Clement of Alexandria[Stromata Book VII.12]

25:15-30 Pseudepigrapha[Letter of Aristeas 1.294, 1.319-321]

25:19 Matthew 18:23

25:21 Matthew 24:47, 25:23; Luke 16:10, 19:17n; Hippolytus[Refutation of all Heresies Book X.29]; Irenaeus[Against Heresies Book IV.11.2]; Justin[First Apology 44]; NT-Apocrypha[Clement Romance 64.1, 65.2]

25:21-23 Nag Hammadi[Tripartite Tractate 93]

25:23 Matthew 24:47, 25:21; Luke 16:10; Pseudepigrapha[3Baruch 15:4]; Hippolytus[Appendix to the Works of Hippolytus - On the End of the World 49; Refutation of all Heresies Book X.29]; Justin[First Apology 44]

25:24 John 4:37

25:26 NT-Apocrypha[Clement Romance 61.1]

25:26-30 Nag Hammadi[Gospel of Philip 64]

25:27 Origen[Gospel of Matthew Book XIV.8]; NT-Apocrypha[Acts of Thomas 1.146; Clement Romance 65.2]

25:27-30 Clement[Homily III.61]

25:28 Pseudepigrapha[Ahiqar 143]

25:28-29 Pseudepigrapha[4Ezra 7.25]

25:29 Matthew 13:12; Mark 4:25; Luke 8:18; Archelaus[Fragment of the Disputation with Manes 2]; Origen[De Principiis Book II.11.4]; Nag Hammadi[Apocalypse of Peter 83; Gospel of Thomas 41]

25:29-30 Matthew 7:13-14n; Pseudepigrapha[Odes of Solomon 24.9]

25:30 Matthew 8:12, 13:42, 50, 22:13, 24:51, Luke 13:28, 19:11-27; Pseudepigrapha[Greek Apocalypse of Ezra 4:37]; Clement of Alexandria[Stromata Book I.1; The Instructor Book I.10]; Tertullian[On the Resurrection of the Flesh 36]; NT-Apocrypha[Acts of Peter 1.2; Clement Romance 61.1, 65.2; Letter of Clement to James 17.1]

25:31 Deuteronomy 32:43, 33:2; Psalms 80:17; Daniel 7:13; Zechariah 14:5; Matthew 16:27, 19:28; Jude 1:14; Revelation 3:21, 20:11; Pseudepigrapha[**1Enoch 45:3**, 62:2, 69:27; Sibylline Oracles 2.240, 2.242]; NT-Apocrypha[Apocalypse of Thomas Line 48]

> **In that day shall the Elect One sit upon a throne of glory; and shall choose their conditions and countless habitations, while their spirits within them shall be strengthened, when they see Mine Elect Ones, And those who have called upon My glorious name. (Pseudepigrapha - 1Enoch 45:3)**

25:31-33 Tertullian[Five Books in Reply to Marcion Book IV.132]

25:31-34 Hippolytus[Appendix to the Works of Hippolytus - On the End of the World 41]

25:31-46 Proverbs 19:17; Isaiah 58:7; Pseudepigrapha[2Enoch 9:1; Testament of Joseph 1:5]; Josephus[**Antiquities 18.1.3 14-15**]; Clement of Alexandria[Stromata Book VII.3; Who is the Rich Man that shall be Saved 13, 30]; Cyprian[Treatise VIII.23, XII.Book II.30, III.1]; Irenaeus[Against Heresies Book IV.17.3, 18.6]; Justin[First Apology 44]; Nag Hammadi[Gospel of Philip 60; Gospel of Truth 38; Hypostasis of the Archons 95-96; Treatise on the Resurrection 45; Tripartite Tractate 135]; Egyptian Book of the Dead[**Oration 125**]

> **They [Essenes] also believe that souls have an immortal vigor in them, and that under the earth there will be rewards or punishments, according as they have lived virtuously or viciously in this life; and the latter are to be detained in an everlasting prison, but that the former shall have power to revive and live again; on account of which doctrines, they are able greatly to persuade the body of the people; and whatsoever they do about divine worship, prayers, and sacrifices, they perform them according to their direction; insomuch that the cities gave great attestations to them on account of their entire virtuous conduct, both in the actions of their lives and their discourses also. (Josephus - Antiquities 18.1.3 14-15)**

> **I have propitiated God with what he desires; I have given bread to the hungry, water to the thirsty, clothes to the naked…(Egyptian Book of the Dead - Oration 125,** *Ancient Egyptian Book of the Dead,* **Raymond O. Faulkner, trans.; Barnes and Noble Publishing, Inc., 2005 p. 139)**

25:32 Ezekiel 34:17-20; John 10:11-14n; Pseudepigrapha[Sibylline Oracles 8.417]; Irenaeus[Against Heresies Book IV.40.2]

25:32-33 Luke 13:32n; Tertullian[On Modesty 13]

25:33 Josephus[Discourse to the Greeks Concerning Hades 3-4]; Clement of Alexandria[The Instructor Book I.5, 8]; Irenaeus[Against Heresies Book V.27.1]

25:33-34 Luke 12:32

25:33-40 Clement of Alexandria[Stromata Book VII.12]

25:34 Luke 22:30; Pseudepigrapha[2Enoch 23:5; 3Enoch 42:3; 4Ezra 2:13]; Philo[Concerning Noah's Work As A Planter (43-45) cf. {Genesis 2:9, 25:27}]; Constitutions of the Holy Apostles[Book V.1]; Cyprian[Treatise IV.13, X.15]; Hippolytus[Fragments - On Genesis 49.16-20; Treatise on Christ and Antichrist 65]; Irenaeus[Against Heresies Book IV.28.2, 40.2]; Origen[Gospel of Matthew Book XI.16; De Principiis Book III.1.6]; Nag Hammadi[Gospel of Truth 21]

25:34-36 Pseudepigrapha[4Ezra 2.20-24; Testament of Jacob 2.23-25, 7.23-26; Testament of Zebulon 7.1-8.4]; Clement of Alexandria[The Instructor Book III.12]

25:34-40 Apostolic[Epistle of Barnabas 3:3-5]

25:34-46 Rabbinic[Babylonian Sanhedrin 81a; Midrash on Psalms 15:5]; Justin[Dialogue with Trypho 117]; Nag Hammadi[Gospel of Truth 33]

25:35 Job 31:32; Ezekiel 18:7, 9, 16; OT-Apocrypha[Tobit 4:17]; Pseudepigrapha[Testament of Isaac 6:21]; Clement of Alexandria[Stromata Book II.16]; Origen[Gospel of Matthew Book XIII.2]; NT-Apocrypha[Clement Romance 69.1; Letter of Clement to James 9.4]

25:35-36 Isaiah 58:7; Pseudepigrapha[Sibylline Oracles 2.83]; Clement of Alexandria[Stromata Book III.6]; Clement[Homily XII.32]; Irenaeus[Against Heresies Book IV.30.3]

25:35-37 NT-Apocrypha[Acts of Thomas 1.19]

25:36 OT-Apocrypha[Sirach 7:32-35]; Pseudepigrapha[Vision of Ezra 6]; Clement[First Epistle Concerning Virginity 12]; Cyprian[Epistle LIX.3; Treatise III.35, XII.Book III.109]; Tertullian[Scorpiace 11]

25:37 Hippolytus[Appendix to the Works of Hippolytus - On the End of the World 43]

25:38 Tertullian[On Prayer 26]

25:40 Proverbs 19:17; Matthew 10:42, 18:5; Mark 9:41; Rabbinic[Babylonian Gittin 56b, 57a cf. {Deuteronomy 23:6}]; Clement of Alexandria[Stromata Book II.16, III.6; The Instructor Book III.4, 12]; Origen[Gospel of John Book I.12]; Pontianus[Second Epistle]; Tertullian[On Prayer 26]

25:41 Mark 9:48; Jude 1:6-7n; Revelation 20:10; Pseudepigrapha[**1Enoch** 67:5-8, **69:28-29**; 2Enoch 10:4, 10:13]; Archelaus[Fragment of the Disputation with Manes 1]; Clement of Alexandria[Exhortation to the Heathen 9]; Clement[Homily XIX.2, XX.9]; Irenaeus[Against Heresies Book II.7.3, 32.1, III.23.2, IV. 27.4, 28.2, 40.1-2, 41.3, V.28.1, 35.2]; Justin[Dialogue with Trypho 76]; Origen[De Principiis Book III.1.6]; Tertullian[Against Hermogenes 11; An Answer to the Jews 10; On the Flesh of Christ 14]; Nag Hammadi[Gospel of the Egyptians III 57-58]; NT-Apocrypha[Pseudo-Titus Epistle Line 560]

> **He sat upon the throne of his glory; and the principal part of the judgment was assigned to him, the Son of man. Sinners shall disappear and perish from the face of the earth, while those who seduced them shall be bound with chains for ever. (Pseudepigrapha - 1Enoch 69:28-29)**

25:41-46 Apostolic[Ignatius - Letter to the Smyrnaeans 6:2]

25:42 Job 22:7; Origen[Gospel of Matthew Book XII.23]

25:44 Archelaus[Disputation with Manes 38]; Tertullian[A Strain of the Judgment of the Lord 344]

25:45 Tertullian[On Prayer 26]

25:46 Daniel 12:2; Matthew 7:13-14n; John 5:29; Jude 1:21n; Pseudepigrapha[2Enoch 46:3; Joseph and Aseneth 8:9; Psalms of Solomon 3.11-12, 13.11, 15.12-13; Testament of Abraham 11:11]; Archelaus[Disputation with Manes 38]; Clement of Alexandria[Exhortation to the Heathen 9; The Instructor Book III.12]; Constitutions of the Holy Apostles[Book VII.32]; Hippolytus[Appendix to the Works of Hippolytus - On the End of the World 48]; Justin[Dialogue with Trypho 5; First Apology 20-21, 45; Second Apology 8]; Tertullian[On Modesty 1]; NT-Apocrypha[Epistula Apostolorum 26, 29, 39]

26:01 Deuteronomy 31:1; Matthew 7:28, 11:1, 13:53, 19:1

26:01-05 Mark 14:1-2; Luke 22:1-6; John 11:45-53

26:02 Psalms 80:17; Matthew 20:18-19, 27:26; Mark 15:15; Luke 24:7, 20; John 19:16; Justin[Dialogue with Trypho 106]; Origen[Gospel of John Book X.14; Gospel of Matthew Book XII.4]

26:02-03 Exodus 12:1-27

26:03 NT-Apocrypha[Acts of Thomas 1.32]

26:06-13 Mark 14:3-9; John 12:1-8; Apostolic[Ignatius - Letter to the Ephesians 17:1]; Origen[Gospel of John Book I.12]

26:07 Song of Solomon 1:12; Luke 7:36-38; Clement of Alexandria[The Instructor Book II.8]

26:07-12 Tertullian[A Treatise on the Soul 17]

26:11 Deuteronomy 15:11

26:13 Pseudepigrapha[1Enoch 103:4]

26:14 Pseudepigrapha[Apocalypse of Daniel 9:7]

26:14-15 John 11:57

26:14-16 Mark 14:10-11; Luke 22:1-6; Dead Sea Scrolls[Damascus Document (CD-B) COL XX 1-12]; Philo[Special Laws IV (84, 89, 91)]; Rabbinic[Exodus Rabba on 22.26]; Justin[Dialogue with Trypho 137]; NT-Apocrypha[Acts of Thomas 1.32; Gospel of Judas 58]

26:15 Exodus 21:32; Zechariah 11:12; Pseudepigrapha[Testament of Gad 2:3]; Constitutions of the Holy Apostles[Book V.14]; Irenaeus[Demonstration of the Apostolic Preaching 80-81]; NT-Apocrypha[Acts of Thomas 1.2]; Epic of Gilgamesh[The Forest Journey]

26:17 Exodus 12:14-20; 1Corinthians 5:8; Tacitus[The Histories 5.4]; Anatolius[Paschal Canon 8]; Clement of Alexandria[Fragments found in Greek only in the Oxford Edition Last Work on the Passover]; Tertullian[An Answer to the Jews 10]; NT-Apocrypha[Gospel of the Ebionites Fragment 7]

26:17-25 Mark 14:12-21; Luke 22:7-14, 21-23; John 13:21-30

26:17-29 1Corinthians 11:23-26

26:18 Cyprian[Treatise X.5]

26:19 Zephyrinus[First Epistle]

26:20-29 This section also includes topical notes for: Last Supper - Mark 14:17-25; Luke 22:14-23; Pseudepigrapha[Jubilees 45:05]; Dead Sea Scrolls[1Q Rule of the Community (1QS) COL VI 3-7; Rule of the Congregation (1Q28a[1QSa]) COL II 11-22]; Rabbinic[Babylonian Berakhot 51b]; Clement of Alexandria[Fragments found in Greek only in the Oxford Edition Last Work on the Passover]; Constitutions of the Holy Apostles[Book VIII.12]; Hippolytus[Refutation of all Heresies Book IX.16]; Irenaeus[Against Heresies Book IV.17.5]; Justin[First Apology 66]; Liturgy of James 30; Liturgy of Mark 16; Nag Hammadi[Gospel of Philip 77]

26:21-22 Constitutions of the Holy Apostles[Book V.14]

26:23 Psalms 41:9; Clement of Alexandria[The Instructor Book II.8]; Origen[Against Celsus Book II.20]

26:24 1Samuel 22:22; Psalms 22:7-8, 16-18, 41:9, 52:1-5, 80:17; Isaiah 53:9; Mark 14:21; Luke 22:22; Pseudepigrapha[**1Enoch 38:2**; 2Baruch 10:6]; Philo[**Special Laws IV (84, 89-91) cf. {Exodus 20:17}**]; Apostolic[1Clement 46:8]; Clement of Alexandria[Stromata Book III.18]; Irenaeus[Against Heresies Book II.20.5, IV.28.1]

> When righteousness shall be manifested in the presence of the righteous themselves, who will be elected for their good works duly weighed by the Lord of spirits; and when the light of the righteous and the elect, who dwell on earth, shall be manifested; where will the habitation of sinners be? And where the place of rest for those who have rejected the Lord of spirits? It would have been better for them, had they never been born. (Pseudepigrapha - 1Enoch 38:2)

> So great and so excessive an evil is covetous desire; or rather, if I am to speak the plain truth concerning it, it is the source of all evils. For from what other source do all the thefts, and acts of rapine, and repudiation of debt, and all false accusations, and acts of insolence, and, moreover, all ravishments, and adulteries, and murders, and, in short, all mischiefs, whether private or public, or sacred or profane, take their rise?... Again, if the desire takes the direction of wishing for authority and power, it renders men's natures seditious, unequal, and tyrannical, it makes them cruel and inhuman enemies of their native countries, implacable masters unable to restrain themselves, irreconcilable forces to all who are equal to themselves in might, flatterers of those who are more powerful than themselves in order to be able to attack them treacherously ...When it affects the parts about the belly it makes men gluttonous, insatiable, intemperate, debauched, admirers of a profligate life, delighting in drunkenness, and epicurism, slaves to strong wine, and fish, and meat, pursuers of feasts and tables, wallowing like greedy dogs; owing to all which things their lives are rendered miserable and accursed, and they are reduced to an existence more grievous than any death. (Philo - Special Laws IV (84, 89, 91) cf. {Exodus 20:17})

26:26 Matthew 14:19, 15:36; Mark 6:41, 8:6; Luke 9:16; Tertullian[On Prayer 6]; NT-Apocrypha[Acts of Thomas 1.158]

26:26-28 1Corinthians 10:16-18n

26:26-29 John 6:31-58n; NT-Apocrypha[Acts of Thomas 1.4]

26:26-30 Mark 14:22-26; Luke 22:15-20; 1Corinthians 11:23-25

26:27 Irenaeus[Against Heresies Book V.33.1]; NT-Apocrypha[Epistula Apostolorum 15]

26:27-28 John 6:53-56n; Tertullian[A Treatise on the Soul 17]

26:28 Exodus 24:6-8; Isaiah 53:12; Jeremiah 31:31-34; Zechariah 9:11; Ephesians 4:32n; Hebrews 9:20; Tertullian[On Modesty 11]

26:28-29 Cyprian[Epistle LXII.9]

26:29 1Corinthians 10:16-18n; Philo[**On Dreams, That They Are God-Sent (2.249)**]; Clement of Alexandria[The Instructor Book II.2]; Origen[De Principiis Book II.11.2]; Teaching of the Twelve Apostles 9.2; NT-Apocrypha[Epistula Apostolorum 29]

> **And who can pour over the happy soul which proffers its own reason as the most sacred cup, the holy goblets of true joy, except the cup-bearer of God, the master of the feast, the Word? Not differing from the draught itself, but being itself in an unmixed state, the pure delight and sweetness, and pouring forth, and joy, and ambrosial medicine of pleasure and happiness; if we too may, for a moment, employ the language of the poets. (Philo - On Dreams, That They Are God-Sent 2.249)**

26:30 Psalms 113:1-118:29; Mark 14:26n; Luke 22:39; Philo[Special Laws II (148) cf. {Exodus 12:1-28}]; Rabbinic[Babylonian Megillah 14a; Mishnah Pesahim 5.7]; NT-Apocrypha[Acts of John 94]

26:30-31 Constitutions of the Holy Apostles[Book V.14]

26:30-35 Mark 14:26-31

26:31 Zechariah 13:7; Matthew 26:56; Luke 13:32n; John 16:32; Pseudepigrapha[Martyrdom and Ascension of Isaiah (3:13-4:22 = Testament of Hezekiah) 3:14]; Apostolic[Epistle of Barnabas 5:11]

26:31-35 Luke 22:31-34; John 13:36-38

26:32 Matthew 28:7, 16

26:33-34 Plato[Theaetetus 164c]

26:34 Matthew 26:69-75; Mark 14:66-72n; Luke 22:56-62; John 18:25-27; Philo[Every Good Man Is Free (131-136) cf. {Greek Playwright Ion}]; NT-Apocrypha[Epistula Apostolorum 11]

26:35 John 11:16; Irenaeus[Against Heresies Book V.35.2]

26:36-46 Mark 14:32-42; Luke 22:39-46; John 18:1-2

26:37 Matthew 17:1; Mark 5:37, 14:33; Luke 8:51, 9:28

26:38 Psalms 42:5-6, 11-12, 43:5; Jonah 4:9; John 12:27; OT-Apocrypha[Sirach 37:2]; Anatolius[Paschal Canon 10]; Gregory Thaumaturgus[Twelve Topics on the Faith 12]; Irenaeus[Against Heresies Book I.8.2, III.22.2]; Origen[Against Celsus Book II.9; Gospel of John Book II.21; De Principiis Book II.6.2, 8.4, IV.1.31]; Tertullian[De Fuga in Persecutione 7; On the Flesh of Christ 13; On the Resurrection of the Flesh 18]; NT-Apocrypha[Acts of Pilate XX.1]

26:39 Genesis 32:9-12; Psalms 109:25; Isaiah 51:17, 22; Hebrews 5:7-8; Pseudepigrapha[Sibylline Oracles 3.655]; Rabbinic[Avot 2.4]; Constitutions of the Holy Apostles[Book V.14]; Cyprian[Treatise IV.14, XII.Book III.19]; Irenaeus[Against Heresies Book I.8.2]; Justin[Dialogue with Trypho 99]; Origen[Against Celsus Book II.24, VII.55]; Tertullian[De Fuga in Persecutione 8]; Epic of Gilgamesh[The Forest Journey]

26:40 Mark 14:37

26:41 Matthew 6:13, 24:42-51n; Luke 11:4; Apostolic[Polycarp - Letter to the Philippians 7:2]; Clement of Alexandria[Stromata Book IV.7]; Constitutions of the Holy Apostles[Book V.6, VIII.45]; Hippolytus[Against Beron and Heli Frag 2; Fragments of Discourses or Homilies 3]; Irenaeus[Against Heresies Book V.9.2]; Origen[Gospel of Matthew Book X.2]; Peter of Alexandria[Canonical Epistle 9]; Tertullian[Ad Martyras 4; De Fuga in Persecutione 8; Of Patience 13; On Baptism 20; On Monogamy 14; On Prayer 8; On the Flesh of Christ 9; To his Wife Book I.4]

26:42 Matthew 6:10; Constitutions of the Holy Apostles[Book V.14]

26:44 2Corinthians 12:8

26:45 2Samuel 24:14; Psalms 80:17; Matthew 17:22; Mark 9:31, 10:33; Luke 9:44, 24:7; John 12:23, 13:1, 17:1

26:45-49 Irenaeus[Against Heresies Book II.20.2, 4]

26:46 John 14:31

26:47 Genesis 33:1; Constitutions of the Holy Apostles[Book V.14]; Irenaeus[Against Heresies Book I.31.1]

26:47-56 This section also includes topical notes for: Arrest - Dead Sea Scrolls[4Q Psalms Pesher (4Q171[4QPPS]) COL IV 7-8; 4Q429(4QHADAYOT[4QH]) Fragment 1 COL IV 1]; Philo[On Abraham (225) cf. {Genesis 14:13-20}, (235) cf. {Genesis 14:13-20}; On Joseph (77-79) cf. {Genesis 39:2-20}; Special Laws I (284) cf. {Exodus 12:5-7}]; Irenaeus[Fragments from the Lost Works 54]; Justin[Dialogue with Trypho 103-104]

26:47-27:56 This section also includes topical notes for: Trial - Psalms 109.2-3; Mark 14:43-15:41; Luke 22:47-23:49; John 18:3-19:37; Dead Sea Scrolls[4Q429(4QHADAYOT[4QH]) Fragment 1 COL IV 2]; Philo[Flaccus (112); On Joseph (77-79) cf. {Genesis 39:2-20}; On the Change of Names (125-129) cf. {Exodus 7:1}]; Rabbinic[Babylonian Sanhedrin 8b-9a cf. {Deuteronomy 17:6}]; Plato[Euthyphro 3b-d; Apology 18a-19d, 24b-d, 26b-c, 28a-b]; Nag Hammadi[Tripartite Tractate 121]

26:48 2Samuel 20:9; Origen[Against Celsus Book II.64]

26:48-49 Philo[**Who Is the Heir of Divine Things (44) cf. {Genesis 31:14; Exodus 18:7}**]

> **Do thou, therefore, love the virtues, and embrace them with thy soul, and then you will be not at all desirous to kiss, which is but the false money of friendship; --"For have they not yet any part or inheritance in thy house? Have they not been reckoned as aliens before thee? And has not thou sold them and devoured the money?" So that you could neither at any subsequent time recover it, after having devoured the price of their safety and their ransom. Do you pretend, therefore, to wish to kiss, or else to wage endless war against all the judges? But Aaron will not kiss Moses, though he will love him with the genuine affection of his heart. "For," says the scripture, "he loved him, and they embraced one another." (Philo - Who Is the Heir of Divine Things (44) cf. {Genesis 31:14; Exodus 18:7})**

26:49 Luke 22:47-48n

26:51 John 18:26; Epic of Gilgamesh[The Forest Journey]

26:52 Genesis 9:6; Revelation 13:10; Pseudepigrapha[Joseph and Aseneth 29:4; The Sentences of the Syriac Menander 18-19]; Tertullian[On Idolatry 19]; NT-Apocrypha[Acts of Thomas 1.86]; Indian[Dhammapada 405]; Linguistics[Hebrew word for "Destroyed" (חרב) is written the same as "Sword" (חרב)]

26:52-54 Origen[Against Celsus Book II.10]

26:53 Psalms 91:11; Pseudepigrapha[Joseph and Aseneth 25:6; Testament of Solomon 11:3]; Tertullian[Against Praxeas 26]

26:54 Daniel 2:28, 45; Plato[Crito 54d-e]

26:54-56 Josephus[War 2.8.12 159]

26:55 Matthew 9:35n; Luke 7:11, 19:21, 47, 21:37; John 18:20; Plato[Apology 33b]; Apostolic[Martyrdom of Polycarp 7:1]; Origen[Against Celsus Book II.64]; Peter of Alexandria[Canonical Epistle 9]

26:56 Zechariah 13:7; Matthew 26:31; John 16:32; Acts 3:18n; Irenaeus[Demonstration of the Apostolic Preaching 76]; Origen[Gospel of Matthew Book XIV.14]; Tertullian[An Answer to the Jews 10]

26:57-68 Mark 14:53-65; Luke 22:54-55, 63-71; John 18:13-14, 19-24

26:58 Mark 14:54; Luke 22:55; John 18:15

26:59 Psalms 27:12

26:59-60 Rabbinic[Babylonian Sanhedrin 27a]

26:59-63 Origen[Against Celsus Book I.Preface.1]

26:59-68 Mark 14:55-65; Luke 22:63-65

26:61 Matthew 27:40; John 2:19-21n; Acts 6:14; Origen[Against Celsus Book II.10; Gospel of John Book X.21]

26:63 Isaiah 53:7; Matthew 16:16-17, 27:12, 14; Luke 23:9; John 3:18n, 19:9; NT-Apocrypha[Acts of Thomas 1.2]

26:63-64 Acts 3:18-26n

26:64 Psalms 80:17; 110:1; Ezekiel 1:26; Daniel 7:13; Matthew 24:30; Mark 14:62n; 1Thessalonians 4:15-17n; 1Peter 3:22n; Pseudepigrapha[**1Enoch 62:1-15**, 69:27; 3Enoch 28:1; Testament of Job 33:3]; Rabbinic[Babylonian Sanhedrin 98a]; Clement of Alexandria[Fragments from the Latin Translation of Cassiodorus Comments on Jude]; NT-Apocrypha[Apocalypse of Peter 1.6; Epistula Apostolorum 3]

Thus the Lord commanded the kings, the princes, the exalted, and those who dwell on earth, saying, Open your eyes, and lift up your horns, if you are capable of comprehending the Elect One. The Lord of spirits sat upon the throne of his glory. And the spirit of righteousness was poured out over him. The word of his mouth shall destroy all the sinners and all the ungodly, who shall perish at his presence. In that day shall all the kings, the princes, the exalted, and those who possess the earth, stand up, behold, and perceive, that he is sitting on the throne of his glory; that before him the saints shall be judged in righteousness; And that nothing, which shall be spoken before him, shall be spoken in vain. Trouble shall come upon them, as upon a woman in travail, whose labour is severe, when her child comes to the mouth of the womb, and she finds it difficult to bring forth. One portion of them shall look upon another. They shall be astonished, and shall humble their countenance; And trouble shall seize them, when they shall behold this Son of woman sitting upon the throne of his glory. Then shall the kings, the princes, and all who possess the earth, glorify him who has dominion over all things, him who was concealed; for from the beginning the Son of man existed in secret, whom the Most High preserved in the presence of his power, and revealed to the elect. He shall sow the congregation of the saints, and of the elect; and all the elect shall stand before him in that day. All the kings, the princes, the exalted, and those who rule over all the earth, shall fall down on their faces before him, and shall worship him. They shall fix their hopes on this Son of man, shall pray to him, and petition him for mercy. Then shall the Lord of spirits hasten to expel them from his presence. Their faces shall be full of confusion, and their faces shall darkness cover. The angels shall take them to punishment, that vengeance may be inflicted on those who have oppressed his children and his elect. And they shall become an example to the saints and to his elect. Through them shall these be made joyful; for the anger of the Lord of spirits shall rest upon them. Then the sword of the Lord of spirits shall be drunk with their blood; but the saints and elect shall be safe in that day; nor the face of the sinners and the ungodly shall they thenceforwards behold. The Lord of spirits shall remain over them. (Pseudepigrapha - 1Enoch 62:1-15)

26:65 This section also includes topical notes for: Heard the Blasphemy - Leviticus 10:6, 21:10; Numbers 14:6; 2Samuel 13:19; Job 1:20, 2:12; Ezra 9:3; Jeremiah 36:24; Mark 15:37-38; Acts 14:14; Rabbinic[Babylonian (Berakhot 17b cf. {Psalms 144:14}; **Sanhedrin 60a**, 103a]; NT-Apocrypha[Acts of Thomas 1.16]

All the same are the one who actually hears [the blasphemy] and the one who hears it from the one who heard it. Both are liable to tear their garments. (Talmud - Sanhedrin 60a, *The Babylonian Talmud a Translation and Commentary*, Jacob Neusner; Hendrickson Publishers, Inc., 2005)

26:65-66 Leviticus 24:16; John 19:7
26:67 Leviticus 16:21, 24:14; Numbers 27:18, 23; Deuteronomy 34:9; Isaiah 50:6, 53:5; Micah 4:14; Mark 14:65; Pseudepigrapha[Sibylline Oracles 1.365, 8.287-289]; Rabbinic[Numbers Rabba on 27:18; Siphra On Leviticus 24:14; Tosephta Sanhedrin 1.1]; Hippolytus[The Discourse on the Holy Theophany 7]; Irenaeus[Fragments from the Lost Works 52]; Justin[First Apology 38]; Tertullian[An Answer to the Jews 14]
26:68 Jeremiah 31:31; NT-Apocrypha[Acts of Thomas 1.6]
26:69 NT-Apocrypha[Epistula Apostolorum 11]
26:69-75 Mark 14:66-72; Luke 22:56-62; John 18:15-18, 25-27
26:70 Anonymous[Treatise on Re-Baptism 9]
26:75 Isaiah 22:4; Matthew 26:34; Mark 14:30, 72; Luke 22:34; John 13:38, 18:15-18, 25-27; Philo[Every Good Man Is Free (131-136) cf. {Greek Playwright Ion}]
27:01 Matthew 12:14; Mark 3:6
27:01-02 Mark 15:1; Luke 22:66-23:2; John 18:28-32

27:02 Peter of Alexandria[Canonical Epistle 9]; NT-Apocrypha[Gospel of Mani Turfman Fragment M 132]

27:02-24 John 18:29-19:22; Philo[Special Laws IV (69-71) cf. {Deuteronomy 1:16-17}]

27:03 Matthew 26:14-15; Pseudepigrapha[Jubilees 41:23; Testament of Gad 2:3]; Irenaeus[Against Heresies Book I.31.1; Demonstration of the Apostolic Preaching 80]

27:03-04 Cyprian[Treatise XII.Book II.14]

27:03-05 Hebrews 12:17; Origen[Against Celsus Book II.11]

27:03-10 Acts 1:18-19

27:04 Deuteronomy 27:25; Matthew 27:24; Irenaeus[Against Heresies Book I.3.3]; NT-Apocrypha[Protoevangelium of James 14.1]

27:04-50 Origen[Against Celsus Book III.32]

27:05 Genesis 27:40; 2Samuel 17:33; Psalms 109.8; Rabbinic[Babylonian Sanhedrin 44b]; Plato[Phaedo 61c-62e]; Constitutions of the Holy Apostles[Book VII.2]; NT-Apocrypha[Acts of Thomas 1.84]

27:05-10 Acts 1:18-19

27:06 Deuteronomy 23:19

27:09 Irenaeus[Demonstration of the Apostolic Preaching 80-81]

27:09 Epic of Gilgamesh[The Forest Journey]

27:09-10 Jeremiah 32:6-9; Zechariah 11:12-13; Constitutions of the Holy Apostles[Book V.14]

27:10 Exodus 9:12; Jeremiah 18:2, 19:1-3; 32:6-9

27:11 Matthew 2:2; 27:29n, 37; Mark 15:9, 12, 18, 26; Luke 23:37-38; John 18:39, 19:3, 19, 21; NT-Apocrypha[Acts of Thomas 1.32]

27:11-14 Mark 15:2-5; Luke 23:3-7; John 18:33-38; Origen[Against Celsus Book I.Preface.2]; Tertullian[An Answer to the Jews 13]; NT-Apocrypha[Acts of Pilate III.2]

27:12 Isaiah 53:7; Matthew 26:63, 27:14; Luke 23:9; John 19:9

27:14 Isaiah 53:7; Matthew 26:63, 27:12; Luke 23:9; John 19:9; Pseudepigrapha[Odes of Solomon 31.10-11]; Justin[Dialogue with Trypho 102-103]

27:15-26 Mark 15:6-15; Luke 23:13-25; John 18:39-19.16

27:17-18 Origen[Against Celsus Book I.Preface.2]

27:19 Genesis 31:24, 29; Origen[Against Celsus Book II.34]; NT-Apocrypha[Acts of Pilate II.1]

27:19-26 NT-Apocrypha[Acts of Pilate IV.1-IX.5]

27:19-31 This section also includes topical notes for: Crucifixion - Genesis 21:9; 2Chronicles 36:16; Job 9:23; Proverbs 17:5; Matthew 20:19, 27:41; Mark 10:34, 15:20-33; Luke 18:32, 22:63, 23:11, 33-45n; John 19:17-27; Pseudepigrapha[Greek Apocalypse of Ezra 7.1-3; Hellenistic Synagogal Prayers 5.22; Odes of Solomon 28.9-20, 31.12; Sibylline Oracles 5.256-258, 8.290-309; Testament of Benjamin 9.3]; Philo[Flaccus (36-38)]; Apostolic[Martyrdom of Ignatius 2]; Clement of Alexandria[Fragments found in Greek only in the Oxford Edition Last Work on the Passover; Stromata Book I.21, V.14, VI.15; The Instructor Book II.8]; Irenaeus[Against Heresies Book I.24.4, 30.13, II.26.1, 32.4, IV.33.12, V.16.3, 17.4; Demonstration of the Apostolic Preaching 34, 66, 68, 74, 80, 82; Fragments from the Lost Works 54]; Justin[Dialogue with Trypho 32, 39-40, 46, 49, 63, 67, 71-73, 86, 89-91, 94, 96-101, 103-106, 111-113, 131-132, 137; First Apology 13, 21, 31, 35, 38, 41-42, 46, 48, 50, 67; Fragments from the Lost Writings of Justin 10]; Lactantius[Divine Institutes Book IV.18-19]; Tertullian[Five Books Against Marcion Book III.19]; Nag Hammadi[A Valentinian Exposition 33; Apocalypse of Peter 81-82; Gospel of Philip 63, 68, 73; Gospel of Truth 20; Interpretation of Knowledge 5; Letter of Peter to Philip 139; Second Treatise of the Great Seth 55-56]; Epic of Gilgamesh[The Forest Journey, The Search for Everlasting Life, The Return]

27:19-45 NT-Apocrypha[Questions of Bartholomew IV 62]

27:19-54 Nag Hammadi[Second Treatise of the Great Seth 58]

27:20 Josephus[Antiquities 13.10.5 288]

27:20-25 Tertullian[An Answer to the Jews 13]

27:21 Acts 3:14; Origen[Gospel of Matthew Book XIV.19]

27:22 Pseudepigrapha[Testament of Solomon 12:3]

27:22-23 Acts 3:13, 13:28

27:24 Leviticus 16:26; Deuteronomy 21:6-9; Psalms 26:6, 73:13; Matthew 27:4; Acts 18:6, 20:26; OT-Apocrypha[Susanna 1:46]; Pseudepigrapha[Testament of Levi 16:3]; Tertullian[On Baptism 9; On Prayer 13]; NT-Apocrypha[Akhmim Fragment 1.1, 11.46]

27:24-25 Constitutions of the Holy Apostles[Book V.19]; Tertullian[An Answer to the Jews 8]

27:24-26 Mark 15:15; Luke 23:24-25

27:25 2Samuel 1:16, 14:9; Jeremiah 51:35; Ezekiel 33:5; Acts 5:28; Pseudepigrapha[Life of Abraham 6:11]; Rabbinic[Babylonian Sanhedrin 43b]; Hippolytus[Fragments - On Genesis 46.5]; Origen[Gospel of Matthew Book XIV.19]; Tertullian[Five Books Against Marcion Book II.15]; NT-Apocrypha[Acts of Pilate XII.1; Passing of Mary]

27:26 Leviticus 16:7-10; Hebrews 12:6-8n; Pseudepigrapha[Life of Adam and Eve Vita 34.1-3]; NT-Apocrypha[Acts of John 101]

27:27 Clement of Alexandria[Fragments found in Greek only in the Oxford Edition Last Work on the Passover]

27:27-30 NT-Apocrypha[Gospel of Mani Turfman Fragment M 132]

27:27-31 Mark 15:16-20; John 19:2-3; Pseudepigrapha[Sibylline Oracles 1.374]; NT-Apocrypha[Gospel of the Nazareans Fragment 34]

27:28 Justin[Dialogue with Trypho 116]; Tertullian[An Answer to the Jews 14]

27:28-30 Luke 23:11; Apostolic[Epistle of Barnabas 7:9-11]

27:29 This section also includes topical notes for: Mocked - Psalms 22:1-18; Matthew 2:2, 27:11, 37; Mark 15:7, 12; Luke 18:39, 19:3, 19, 21, 23:37-38; John 19:2-5; Pseudepigrapha[Sibylline Oracles 6.24, 8.294]; Dead Sea Scrolls[4Q Non-Canonical Psalms B (4Q381) Fragment 31 7]; Clement of Alexandria[The Instructor Book II.8]; Hippolytus[Against the Heresy of One Noetus 18]; NT-Apocrypha[Acts of Thomas 1.5]

27:29-30 NT-Apocrypha[Acts of Thomas 1.158]

27:29-35 Philo[**Flaccus (74-77)**]

He [Flaccus] arrested thirty-eight members of our council of elders, which our saviour and benefactor, Augustus, elected to manage the affairs of the Jewish nation after the death of the king of our own nation, having sent written commands to that effect to Manius Maximus when he was about to take upon himself for the second time the government of Egypt and of the country, he arrested them, I say, in their own houses, and commanded them to be thrown into prison, and arranged a splendid procession to send through the middle of the market-place a body of old men prisoners, with their hands bound, some with thongs and others with iron chains, whom he led in this plight into the theatre, a most miserable spectacle, and one wholly unsuited to the times. And then he commanded them all to stand in front of their enemies, who were sitting down, to make their disgrace the more conspicuous, and ordered them all to be stripped of their clothes and scourged with stripes, in a way that only the most wicked of malefactors are usually treated, and they were flogged with such severity that some of them the moment they were carried out died of their wounds, while others were rendered so ill for a long time that their recovery was despaired of. And the enormity of this cruelty is proved by many other circumstances, and it will be further proved most evidently and undeniably by the circumstance which I am about to mention. Three of the members of this council of elders, Euodius, and Trypho, and Audro, had been stripped of all their property, being plundered of everything that was in their houses at one onset, and he was well aware that they had been exposed to this treatment, for it had been related to him when he had in the first instance sent for our rulers, under pretence of wishing to promote a reconciliation between them and the rest of the city; but nevertheless, though he well knew that they had been deprived of all their property, he scourged them in the very sight of those who had plundered them, that thus they might endure the twofold misery of poverty and personal ill treatment, and that their persecutors might reap the double pleasure of enjoying riches which did in no respect belong to them, and also of feasting their eyes to satiety on the disgrace of those whom they had plundered. (Philo - Flaccus (74-77)

27:30 Isaiah 50:6

27:31-56 Mark 15:20-41; Luke 23:26-49; John 19:17-30

27:32 Irenaeus[Against Heresies Book I.24.4]; Origen[Gospel of Matthew Book XII.24]; Tertullian[Against All Heresies 1]

27:33 Tertullian[Five Books in Reply to Marcion Book V.232]; NT-Apocrypha[Epistula Apostolorum 9]

27:33-45 NT-Apocrypha[Acts of Pilate X.1-2]

27:33-56 This section also includes topical notes for: **Passover** - Mark 15:22-41; Luke 23:33-49; John 19:17-30; Philo[Special Laws II (145, 147-148) cf. {Exodus 12:1-28}]

27:34 Psalms 69:21-22; Pseudepigrapha[Greek Apocalypse of Ezra 2:25; 7:1; Sibylline Oracles 1.368, 6.24, 8.303]; Rabbinic[Babylonian Sanhedrin 43a]; Irenaeus[Demonstration of the Apostolic Preaching 82]; Tertullian[The Chaplet, or De Corona 14]; NT-Apocrypha[Acts of Thomas 1.158; Akhmim Fragment 5.16; Apocalypse of Paul 1.44]

27:34-35 Irenaeus[Against Heresies Book IV.35.3]; Tertullian[An Answer to the Jews 10]

27:35 This section also includes topical notes for: **Naked** - Genesis 2:25; 1Samuel 19:23-24; Psalms 22:18-19; John 19:18n, 23-24n; Pseudepigrapha[Odes of Solomon 31.9]; Philo[Allegorical Interpretation II (53-58) cf. {Genesis 2:25, 3:1, Exodus 33:7, Leviticus 10:1-5}]; Archelaus[Disputation with Manes 44 cf. {Exodus 17}]

27:35-46 Psalms 109:16

27:37 Matthew 2:2, 27:11, 29; Mark 15:9, 12, 18, 26; Luke 23:37-38; John 18:39, 19:3, 19, 21

27:38 Isaiah 53:12; NT-Apocrypha[Epistula Apostolorum 9]

27:39 Psalms 22:7-8, 109:25; Lamentations 2:15; Pseudepigrapha[Testament of Job 29:4]

27:40 Matthew 4:3, 6, 26:61, 63; Mark 14:58; Luke 4:3, 9; John 2:19-21n; Rabbinic[Babylonian Yoma 39b]

27:40-43 John 3:18n

27:42 Isaiah 41:6-11; Zephaniah 3:15; John 1:49, 12:13; Pseudepigrapha[Apocalypse of Elijah 5:11]

27:43 Psalms 22:8-9; Isaiah 36:7, 20; John 5:18, 10:36, 19:7; OT-Apocrypha[Wisdom of Solomon 2:13, 18-20]

27:45 Exodus 10:21; Jeremiah 15:9; Amos 8:9; Pseudepigrapha[Sibylline Oracles 1.374]; Rabbinic[Babylonian Sanhedrin 99a cf. {Isaiah 60:2}]; Clement[Recognitions Book I.41-42]; Cyprian[Treatise XII.Book II.23]; Tertullian[An Answer to the Jews 13]; Nag Hammadi[Concept of Our Great Power 42]; NT-Apocrypha[Acts of John 97]

27:45-54 Tertullian[On Fasting 10]

27:45-56 Mark 15:33-41; Luke 23:44-49; John 19:28-30

27:46 Psalms 22:1-2; Pseudepigrapha[Testament of Solomon 6:8]; Rabbinic[Mekhilta p. 66b; Mishnah Sanhedrin iv 5; Pesiqta Rabbathi 98a cf. {Exodus 20:2}, 100 cf. {Psalms 22:1}; Siphri Deuteronomy 329, p. 139 cf. {Isaiah 44:6}; Tosephta Sanhedrin viii 7]; Constitutions of the Holy Apostles[Book V.14]; Irenaeus[Against Heresies Book I.8.2]; Tertullian[Against Praxeas 25, 26, 30]; Nag Hammadi[Gospel of Philip 68]; NT-Apocrypha[Acts of Andrew and Matthias]

27:46-50 NT-Apocrypha[Acts of Pilate XI.1]

27:48 Psalms 69:21-22; Irenaeus[Against Heresies Book IV.35.3]; NT-Apocrypha[Acts of Thomas 1.158]

27:50-52 Dead Sea Scrolls[**1QHymns (1QHodayoth [1QH]) Col. XIII 8-12**]; Tertullian[An Answer to the Jews 13]

> You made my dwelling with many fishermen, who spread *their* net on the surface of the waters and hunt the children of iniquity. You have established me there for judgment. You have strengthened the counsel of truth in my heart, and *the waters* of the covenant for those who seek it. You have closed the mouth of the young lions whose teeth are like a sword, whose fangs are like a sharpened spear *with* the venom of serpents. All their plots are to plunder – and though they lay in wait, they have not opened their mouths against me. For You, O my God, have sheltered me from the children of men, and *have* hidden Your law *within me*, until the time You reveal Your salvation through me. For in the distress of my soul You have not abandoned me; in the bitterness of my soul You heard my cry. (Dead Sea Scrolls - 1QHymns (1QHodayoth [1QH]) Col. XIII 8-12)

27:50-54 Tacitus[The Histories 5.13]

27:51 Exodus 26:31-35; Isaiah 41:6-11; Mark 15:37-38; Hebrews 10:20; Pseudepigrapha[Greek Apocalypse of Ezra 4:36; Lives of the Prophets 12:12; Sibylline Oracles 1.376, 8.305; Testament of Benjamin 9.3; Testament of Levi 10.3-4]; Clement[Homily XIX.14]; Nag Hammadi[Gospel of Philip 69, 84-85]; NT-Apocrypha[Akhmim Fragment 6.21; Gospel of the Nazareans Fragment 21, 36; Protoevangelium of James 24.3]; Egyptian Book of the Dead[Oration 98]

27:51-52 Clement[Recognitions Book I.41]; Origen[Against Celsus Book II.33]

27:51-56 Mark 15:38-41; Luke 23:45b, 47-49

27:51-60 NT-Apocrypha[Acts of Pilate XI.2-3]

27:52 Genesis 28:12; Isaiah 26:19; Daniel 12:2; Pseudepigrapha[4Ezra 2.31; Martyrdom and Ascension of Isaiah 9:17]; Clement of Alexandria[Stromata Book VI.6]; Irenaeus[Fragments from the Lost Works 28, 54]; NT-Apocrypha[Apocalypse of Thomas Line 57]

27:52-53 Ezekiel 37:12; Pseudepigrapha[Odes of Solomon 42.11-20]; Apostolic[Ignatius - Letter to the Magnesians 9:2; Papias Fragment 5:1]; Hippolytus[Refutation of all Heresies Book V.3]; Origen[Gospel of Matthew Book XII.43]; Quadratus; Nag Hammadi[Testimony of Truth 32]; NT-Apocrypha[Acts of Pilate XXVII.1; Questions of Bartholomew I 21]

27:53 Matthew 4:5; Acts 2:31n; Revelation 11:2, 21:2, 10, 22:19

27:54 John 3:18n; Pseudepigrapha[Sibylline Oracles 1.375]; Origen[Against Celsus Book II.36]; NT-Apocrypha[Akhmim Fragment 6.21]

27:55-56 Luke 8:2-3; Tertullian[On Monogamy 8]

27:56 Matthew 20:20; Nag Hammadi[Gospel of Philip 59]

27:57 NT-Apocrypha[Secret Gospel of Mark Fragment 1]

27:57-58 Deuteronomy 21:22-23

27:57-60 Justin[Dialogue with Trypho 118]

27:57-61 Mark 15:42-47; Luke 23:50-54; John 19:38-42; Pseudepigrapha[Life of Adam and Eve Vita 43.4, (Apocalypse of Moses) 40.1-2]

27:58 Genesis 50:4-6

27:59 1Kings 13:29

27:59-60 Mark 6:29; Acts 13:29; NT-Apocrypha[Acts of Thomas 1.158]

27:60 Genesis 46:4, 50:5, 13; Matthew 28:2; Mark 16:3-4; Luke 24:2; John 20:1; Rabbinic[Babylonian Sanhedrin 47a-47b]; Origen[Against Celsus Book II.69]

27:61 Matthew 27:56, 28:1; Mark 15:40, 47, 16:1; Luke 23:55-56, 24:10; John 19:25

27:62-66 Pseudepigrapha[Martyrdom and Ascension of Isaiah (3:13-4:22 = Testament of Hezekiah) 3:14]; NT-Apocrypha[Acts of Pilate XIII.1; Akhmim Fragment 8.29, 8.33]

27:63 Matthew 12:40, 16:21, 17:23, 20:19; Mark 8:31, 9:31, 10:34; Luke 9:22, 18:33, 24:7; Pseudepigrapha[Life of Abraham 11:2; Testament of Adam 3.4]; Rabbinic[Babylonian (Sanhedrin 106b cf. {Psalms 55:23}, 107b; Sotah 47a); Yalqut 766 cf. {Numbers 23:19}]; Origen[De Principiis Book III.2.4]; NT-Apocrypha[Acts of Thomas 1.48]

27:64 Matthew 12:45; Luke 11:26; 2Peter 2:20

27:66 Daniel 6:17

28:01 Matthew 27:56, 61; Mark 15:40, 47, 16:2; John 19:25; Rabbinic[Babylonian Shabbat 151a]; NT-Apocrypha[Akhmim Fragment 9.37, 12.50]

28:01-02 Origen[Against Celsus Book II.70]

28:01-04 NT-Apocrypha[Acts of Pilate XIII.1-2]

28:01-06 Dionysius of Alexandria[Extant Fragments Epistle to Bishop Basilides 1]

28:01-10 Mark 16:1-8; Luke 24:1-12; John 20:1-10

28:02 Matthew 27:51, 60; Mark 15:46; NT-Apocrypha[Secret Gospel of Mark Fragment 1]

28:02-03 Epic of Gilgamesh[The Forest Journey]

28:02-06 Nag Hammadi[Tripartite Tractate 133]

28:03 Daniel 7:9, 10:6; Matthew 17:2; Mark 9:3; Luke 9:29; Acts 1:10; Pseudepigrapha[Joseph and Aseneth 5:4, 14:9]

28:04 Pseudepigrapha[Martyrdom and Ascension of Isaiah (3:13-4:22 = Testament of Hezekiah) 3:14]

28:05-07 Mark 16:5-7; Luke 24:3

28:06 Matthew 12:40, 16:21, 17:23, 20:19; Mark 8:31, 9:31, 10:34; Luke 9:22, 18:33, 24:7

28:07 Matthew 26:32, 28:10, 16; Mark 14:28; John 21:1-23; NT-Apocrypha[Epistula Apostolorum 10]

28:08 Mark 16:8; Pseudepigrapha[Joseph and Aseneth 9:1]

28:09 Matthew 28:17n; Gregory Thaumaturgus[Four Homilies 2]; Origen[Against Celsus Book II.70]

28:10 Matthew 26:32, 28:7, 16; Mark 14:28; John 20:17, 21:1-23; NT-Apocrypha[Epistula Apostolorum 10-11]

28:11 Genesis 31:22

28:11-15 Justin[Dialogue with Trypho 108]; NT-Apocrypha[Acts of Pilate XIII.3; Akhmim Fragment 11.49]

28:13 Matthew 27:64; Clement[Recognitions Book I.42]

28:13-14 Origen[Against Celsus Book I.51]

28:16 Matthew 26:32; 28:7, 10; Mark 14:28; Nag Hammadi[Sophia of Jesus Christ III 90]

28:16-20 Mark 16:14-18; Luke 24:36-49; John 20:19-23; Acts 1:6-8

28:17 This section also includes topical notes for: Worshipped - Matthew 2:2-11, 8:2, 9:18, 14:33, 15:25, 20:20, 28:9; Mark 5:6; Luke 24:52; John 9:38; Hebrews 1:6; Revelation 4:10, 5:14; Rabbinic[Babylonian Sanhedrin 38b cf. {Exodus 23:21, 24:1}]; NT-Apocrypha[Epistula Apostolorum 11]

28:18 Daniel 7:14; Matthew 7:28-29n, 11:27; John 3:35, 13:3, 17:2; Ephesians 1:20-22; Philippians 2:9-10n; Hippolytus[Treatise on Christ and Antichrist 26]; Tertullian[Against Praxeas 16]; NT-Apocrypha[Epistula Apostolorum 19, 21; Pistis Sophia c. 2-6]

28:18-19 Cyprian[Epistle LXXII.5]

28:18-20 Pseudepigrapha[Martyrdom and Ascension of Isaiah 11:23]; Cyprian[Epistle XXIV.2, LXII.18; The Seventh Council of Carthage under Cyprian; Treatise XII.Book II.26]

28:19 This section also includes topical notes for: Trinity - Genesis 1:26, 3:22, 32:3; Matthew 3:5-16n; Mark 16:15; Acts 1:8; 1Corinthians 12:3-6; 2Corinthians 1:21-22, 13:14; 1Peter 1:2; 1John 5:6-8; Pseudepigrapha[1Enoch 60:13; 2Baruch 21.4; Greek Apocalypse of Ezra 7.16; Hellenistic Synagogal Prayers 8.2; History of the Rechabites 16.1-2; Martyrdom and Ascension of Isaiah (3:13-4:22 = Testament of Hezekiah) 3:18; Odes of Solomon 19.2, 23.22, 25.11; Sibylline Oracles Prologue; Testament of Abraham 20.15; Testament of Isaac 1.1, 2.20, 2.9; Testament of Jacob 1.1]; Philo[**Appendices A Treatise Concerning the World (1) cf. {Genesis 1:1, Deuteronomy 10:17}**; On Abraham (56) cf. {Genesis 18:3, Exodus 19:6}; **On Abraham (132) cf. {Genesis 18:3, Exodus 19:6}**; On Flight And Finding (68-71) cf. {Genesis 1:26}; On the Confusion of Tongues (146-147, 168-179) cf. {Genesis 1:26, 3:22, 11:7, 42:11, Deuteronomy 10:17, Psalms 2:7, 33:6}]; Rabbinic[Babylonian (Menahot 110a; Sanhedrin 38b cf. {Genesis 1:26-27, 11:5, 7, 35:3, 7; Deuteronomy 4:7; 2Samuel 7:23; Daniel 4:17, 7:9}); Bereshith Rabba viii p. 22d; Debarim Rabba ii. 33 p. 104c cf. {Deuteronomy 6:4; Isaiah 6:3; Zechariah 13:8}; Jerusalem Berakhot i. 8 (3c) cf. {Numbers 23:21-22}; Shemoth Rabba xxix 5, p. 51b; Siphra 4c; Siphri Numbers 143 p. 54]; Apostolic[Didache 7:1]; Anonymous[Treatise Against the Heretic Novatian 3; Treatise on Re-Baptism 1, 7]; Athenagoras[Plea for the Christians 10, 24]; Clement of Alexandria[Fragments from Macarius Chrysocephalus Parable of the Prodigal son 6-7; Stromata Book V.14, VI.16; The Instructor Book I.6, III.12; Who is the Rich Man that shall be Saved 34]; Constitutions of the Holy Apostles[Book II.26, V.7, VI.15, VII.22, 40]; Gregory Thaumaturgus[Declaration of Faith; On the Trinity; Sectional Confession of Faith 1-5, 7-10, 13-16, 18-21, 23]; Hippolytus[Against the Heresy of One Noetus 14]; Irenaeus[Against Heresies Book I.2.5-6, 4.5, 10.1, 22.1, 30.1-2, II.12.7, 16.7-8, 10, 30.9, III.17.1, IV.Preface.4, 6.7, 7.4, 20.1, 3-4, 38.3, V.1.3, 6.1, 17.1, 18.2, 28.4; Demonstration of the Apostolic Preaching 3, 5, 10; Fragments from the Lost Works 39]; Justin[Dialogue with Trypho 128-129; First Apology 6, 60-61, 65, 67]; Liturgy of James 2, 6, 10, 14-16, 20, 27, 38-39, 41, 46-49; Liturgy of Mark 5; Liturgy of the Apostles 11; Origen[Gospel of Matthew Book X.18]; Tertullian[On Baptism 13; On Modesty 21; On Prescription Against Heretics 8, 20; Five Books Against Marcion Book IV.43]; Theodotus[Excerpts 13]; Theophilus of Antioch[To Autolycus Book II.15]; Victorinus[Apocalypse 1.15]; Nag Hammadi[A Valentinian Exposition 23; Allogenes 45, 49, 52-56, 58, 61-67; Apocryphon of John 2; Gospel of Philip 59, 67; Gospel of the Egyptians III 42, 55, IV 56, 58; Gospel of Truth 38-39; Letter of Peter to Philip 137; Sophia of Jesus Christ III 104; Tripartite Tractate 127]; NT-Apocrypha[Epistula Apostolorum 5, 30]; Epic of Gilgamesh[Prologue - Gilgamesh King in Uruk]

God being one being, has two supreme powers of the greatest importance. By means of these powers the incorporeal world, appreciable only by the intellect, was put together, which is the archetypal model of this world which is visible to us, being formed in such a manner as to be perceptible to our invisible conceptions just as the other is to our eyes. (Philo - Appendices A Treatise Concerning the World (1) cf. {Genesis 1:1, Deuteronomy 10:17})

For when the wise man entreats those persons who are in the guise of three travelers to come and lodge in his house, he speaks to them not as three persons, but as one, and says, "My lord, if I have found favor with thee, do not thou pass by thy Servant." (Philo - On Abraham (132) cf. {Genesis 18:3, Exodus 19:6})

28:19-20 Clement[Homily XVII.7; Recognitions Book II.33]; Irenaeus[Demonstration of the Apostolic Preaching 86]; Justin[Dialogue with Trypho 42, 108-110; First Apology 31, 39, 45, 49-50];

Tertullian[An Answer to the Jews 5]; Nag Hammadi[Gospel of Mary 8, 19; Interpretation of Knowledge 14]

28:20 Haggai 1:13; Matthew 13:39, 49, 18:20, 24:3; John 14:23; Clement of Alexandria[Stromata Book VI.5]; Constitutions of the Holy Apostles[Book II.59]; Cyprian[Epistle LXXX.1]; Novatian[Treatise Concerning the Trinity 12]; Origen[Against Celsus Book II.9, V.12; Gospel of John Book X.7-8; Gospel of Matthew Book XII.6, 34]; Nag Hammadi[Letter of Peter to Philip 134, 140; Teachings of Silvanus 96-97]

Cross Reference Index: Mark

01:01 John 3:18n; Apostolic[**Papias Fragment 3:15, 21:1**]; Clement of Alexandria[Fragments from Eusebius Ecclesiastical History Book VI.2.15, VII.6.14; Fragments from the Latin Translation of Cassiodorus Comments on 1Peter]; Irenaeus[Against Heresies Book III.1.1, 10.5, 11.8, 16.3]

> And Mark having become the interpreter of Peter, wrote down accurately whatsoever he remembered. It was not, however, in exact order that he related the sayings or deeds of Christ. For he neither heard the Lord nor accompanied Him. But afterwards, as I said, he accompanied Peter, who accommodated his instructions to the necessities [of his hearers], but with no intention of giving a regular narrative of the Lord's sayings. Wherefore Mark made no mistake in thus writing some things as he remembered them. For of one thing he took especial care, not to omit anything he had heard, and not to put anything fictitious into the statements. (Papias – Fragment 3:15)

> But so great a light of godliness shone upon the minds of Peter's listeners that they were not satisfied with a single hearing or with the oral teaching of the divine proclamation. So, with all kinds of exhortations they begged Mark (whose Gospel is extant), since he was Peter's follower, to leave behind a written record of the teaching given to them verbally, and did not quit until they had persuaded the man, and thus they became the immediate cause of the scripture called "The Gospel According to Mark." (Papias – Fragment 21:1)

01:01-02 Origen[Against Celsus Book II.4]
01:01-03 Origen[Gospel of John Book I.14]
01:01-06 Pseudepigrapha[Sibylline Oracles 1.336]
01:01-11 Matthew 3:1-17n; Luke 3:1-18, 21-22; John 1:19-28; Pseudepigrapha[Sibylline Oracles 1.336-341]
01:02 Exodus 23:20; Malachi 3:1; Tertullian[An Answer to the Jews 9]
01:02-03 Origen[Gospel of John Book II.17]
01:03 Isaiah 40:3; Gregory Thaumaturgus[Four Homilies 4]; Victorinus[Apocalypse 4.7-10]
01:03-04 Epic of Gilgamesh[The Coming of Enkidu]
01:04 Pseudepigrapha[Sibylline Oracles 4.165]; Tertullian[On Baptism 10; On Repentance 2]; NT-Apocrypha[Extract From the Life of John according to Serapion; Gospel of the Nazareans Fragment 2]
01:04-06 NT-Apocrypha[Gospel of the Ebionites Fragment 1-2]
01:05 Josephus[Antiquities 18.5.2 116-119]
01:06 Leviticus 11:21; 2Kings 1:8; Zechariah 13:4; Pseudepigrapha[Martyrdom and Ascension of Isaiah 2:10]; Clement of Alexandria[The Instructor Book II.11]
01:06-07 Origen[Gospel of John Book VI.16]
01:07 Clement of Alexandria[Stromata Book V.8; The Instructor Book II.12]; Epic of Gilgamesh[The Coming of Enkidu]
01:09 Genesis 32:10; Origen[Gospel of John Book VI.31]; NT-Apocrypha[Gospel of the Ebionites Fragment 3; Gospel of the Nazareans Fragment 2]
01:09-11 Pseudepigrapha[Sibylline Oracles 6.4; Testament of Levi 18:7]; Tertullian[Against All Heresies 5]
01:10 Ezekiel 1:1; John 1:32; Pseudepigrapha[4Ezra 2.15-18; Joseph and Aseneth 14:2; Psalms of Solomon 17.37; Sibylline Oracles 6.7]; Clement of Alexandria[Fragments from Macarius Chrysocephalus Oration VIII on Matt VIII and Book VII on Luke XIII]; Justin[Dialogue with Trypho 8]

01:11 Genesis 22:2; Psalms 2:7; Isaiah 42:1; Matthew 12:18, 17:5; Mark 9:7; Luke 9:35; Pseudepigrapha[Martyrdom and Ascension of Isaiah 1:4; Odes of Solomon 7:15]; Tacitus[The Histories 5.13]; Gregory Thaumaturgus[Four Homilies 4]; Origen[Gospel of John Book I.32]; NT-Apocrypha[Acts of Paul and Thecla 1.37; Gospel of the Ebionites Fragment 3]

01:11-12 NT-Apocrypha[Gospel of the Hebrews Fragment 2-3]

01:12-13 Matthew 4:1-11; Luke 4:1-13n

01:13 Job 5:22; Psalms 91:11; Pseudepigrapha[Testament of Job 20:9, 40:11; Testament of Naphtali 8:4]; Clement[Homily XIX.2]; Nag Hammadi[Gospel of Thomas 27]; NT-Apocrypha[Extract From the Life of John according to Serapion; Extracts from the Gospel of Pseudo-Matthew 18.2]

01:13-14 Origen[Gospel of John Book X.1]

01:14 Luke 4:14-15; John 4:43-45

01:14-27 Origen[Gospel of John Book X.9]

01:15 Daniel 7:22; Matthew 3:2, 4:13-17; Luke 4:31a; OT-Apocrypha[Tobit 14:5]; NT-Apocrypha[Freer Logion]

01:16 Origen[Gospel of John Book X.6]; NT-Apocrypha[Gospel of the Ebionites Fragment 4]

01:16-17 Syriac Teaching of Simon Cephas in the City of Rome

01:16-20 Matthew 4:18-22; Luke 5:1-11n; NT-Apocrypha[Acts of John 88]

01:17 Jeremiah 16:16; Pseudepigrapha[Joseph and Aseneth 21:21]; Clement of Alexandria[Stromata Book VII.18]

01:19 NT-Apocrypha[Gospel of the Nazareans Fragment 33]

01:19-20 Tertullian[On Idolatry 12]

01:21 Origen[Gospel of John Book X.1]; NT-Apocrypha[Gospel of the Ebionites Fragment 4]

01:21-22 Matthew 9:35n

01:21-28 Luke 4:31b-37

01:22 Matthew 7:29; Pseudepigrapha[Psalms of Solomon 17.43]

01:23 NT-Apocrypha[Freer Logion]

01:24 Exodus 31:13-17, 34:21; Judges 16:17; 1Kings 17:18; Psalms 106:16; Pseudepigrapha[Prayer of Joseph Fragment A]; Irenaeus[Against Heresies Book IV.6.6]; Tertullian[Against Praxeas 26]

01:25 Pseudepigrapha[Life of Adam and Eve Vita 39.1-3]

01:26 NT-Apocrypha[Freer Logion]

01:27 Matthew 7:28-29n

01:29 NT-Apocrypha[Gospel of the Ebionites Fragment 4]

01:29-30 Tertullian[On Monogamy 8]

01:29-38 Matthew 8:14-17; Luke 4:38-43

01:31 NT-Apocrypha[Secret Gospel of Mark Fragment 1]

01:32 Pseudepigrapha[Joseph and Aseneth 10:16]

01:34 Matthew 4:23-24n; Pseudepigrapha[Apocalypse of Elijah 5:32]; NT-Apocrypha[Epistula Apostolorum 5]

01:39 Matthew 4:23-25, 9:35; Luke 4:44

01:40-44 NT-Apocrypha[Epistula Apostolorum 5; Papyrus Egerton 2 Fragment 1 Lines 22-41]

01:40-45 Matthew 8:1-4; Luke 5:12-16

01:41 NT-Apocrypha[Secret Gospel of Mark Fragment 1]

01:43 NT-Apocrypha[Papyrus Egerton 2 Fragment 2 Lines 43-59]

01:44 Leviticus 13:49, 14:2-32; Constitutions of the Holy Apostles[Book VI.19]

02:01-12 Matthew 9:1-8; Luke 5:17-26; NT-Apocrypha[Acts of Peter p.130]

02:03 NT-Apocrypha[Epistula Apostolorum 5]

02:07 Psalms 103:3, 130:4; Isaiah 43:25; Tertullian[On Modesty 21]

02:08 Pseudepigrapha[Joseph and Aseneth 23:8, 26:6]; Tertullian[On Baptism 10]

02:09-11 Tertullian[On Modesty 22]

02:10 Psalms 80:17; Matthew 7:28-29n, 9:6n; Acts 26:18n; Methodius[Oration Concerning Simeon and Anna 8]

02:11 Archelaus[Disputation with Manes 40]; Clement of Alexandria[The Instructor Book I.2]

02:13 Matthew 9:35n

02:13-17 Matthew 9:9-13n; Luke 5:27-32

02:14 Clement of Alexandria[Who is the Rich Man that shall be Saved 13]; Tertullian[On Idolatry 12]; NT-Apocrypha[Akhmim Fragment 14.60]

02:15 Pseudepigrapha[Joseph and Aseneth 20:8]

02:15-16 Tertullian[On Modesty 9]

02:15-22 Luke 7:36-50; Pseudepigrapha[Joseph and Aseneth 20:2]; Philo[On the Contemplative Life Or Suppliants (75)]

02:16 Genesis 38:28, 42:32, 47:13-26; Hippolytus[Refutation of all Heresies Book IX.23]

02:16-17 NT-Apocrypha[Oxyrhynchus Papyrus 1224 p.175]

02:17 Apostolic[2Clement 2:4]; Justin[On the Resurrection 8]; Nag Hammadi[Gospel of Truth 35]

02:18-20 Pseudepigrapha[Apocalypse of Elijah 1:13]; Tertullian[On Fasting 2]

02:18-22 Matthew 9:14-17n; Luke 5:33-39

02:19 Archelaus[Disputation with Manes 42]; Nag Hammadi[Gospel of Philip 82]

02:19-20 John 3:29n; Nag Hammadi[Gospel of Thomas 104]

02:20 Constitutions of the Holy Apostles[Book V.18]; NT-Apocrypha[Akhmim Fragment 7.27]

02:21 This section also includes topical notes for: New Patch on Old Garment - Matthew 9:16; Luke 5:36; Philo[Special Laws IV (203-207) cf. {Leviticus 19:19}]

02:22 Job 13:28

02:23 Deuteronomy 23:25-26

02:23-28 Matthew 12:1-8; Luke 6:1-5

02:24 Hippolytus[Refutation of all Heresies Book IX.23]

02:25 1Samuel 21:1-7

02:26 Exodus 40:23; Leviticus 24:5-9; 1Samuel 21:1-6; 2Samuel 15:35

02:27 Exodus 20:8-10, 21:12; Deuteronomy 5:12-14

02:27-28 Rabbinic[Babylonian Yoma 85b]

02:28 Psalms 80:17

03:01 Constitutions of the Holy Apostles[Book V.7]

03:01-05 Matthew 12:9-14; Luke 6:6-10

03:02 Rabbinic[Babylonian Shabbat 147b]

03:03 NT-Apocrypha[Epistula Apostolorum 5]

03:06 Exodus 31:14; Tertullian[Against All Heresies 1]

03:06-12 Matthew 12:14-21; Luke 6:11

03:08 NT-Apocrypha[Secret Gospel of Mark Fragment 1]

03:10 Matthew 4:23-24n; Mark 4:1; Luke 5:1-3

03:11 John 3:18n

03:13-19 Genesis 35:22-26; Matthew 10:1-4; Luke 6:12-16

03:14 NT-Apocrypha[Gospel of the Ebionites Fragment 4]

03:16 Pseudepigrapha[Joseph and Aseneth 15:7]

03:16-19 Nag Hammadi[Letter of Peter to Philip 133]; NT-Apocrypha[Acts of Thomas 1.1]

03:17 Origen[Gospel of Matthew Book XII.32]; NT-Apocrypha[Pseudo-Titus Epistle Line 361]

03:18 Origen[Against Celsus Book I.62]

03:20-31 Matthew 12:22-45; Luke 11:14-32

03:21 Psalms 69:9; Isaiah 28:7; Zechariah 13:3

03:22 Matthew 9:34, 10:25; Pseudepigrapha[Jubilees 10:8; Testament of Solomon 2:9-3:1]; Justin[Dialogue with Trypho 69]

03:23 Matthew 13:3-53n; Archelaus[Disputation with Manes 16]

03:27 Isaiah 49:24; Pseudepigrapha[Psalms of Solomon 5:3; Testament of Levi 18:12]; Archelaus[Disputation with Manes 16]; Irenaeus[Against Heresies Book V.21.3, 22.1]; Nag Hammadi[Gospel of Thomas 34-5]

03:28-29 Cyprian[Epistle IX.2; Treatise XII.Book III.28]; Nag Hammadi[Gospel of Thomas 44]

03:29 Luke 12:10; NT-Apocrypha[Questions of Bartholomew V 4]

03:29-30 Teaching of the Twelve Apostles 11.7

03:31-35 Matthew 12:46-50; Luke 8:19-21; Nag Hammadi[Gospel of Thomas 99]

03:35 Apostolic[2Clement 9:11]; Nag Hammadi[Interpretation of Knowledge 9]

04:01 Matthew 9:35n; Luke 5:1-3

04:01-09 Matthew 13:1-9; Luke 8:4-8

04:02 Matthew 9:35n

04:02-34 Matthew 13:3-53n

04:03 Apostolic[1Clement 24:5]

04:03-08 Hippolytus[Refutation of all Heresies Book VIII.2]; Nag Hammadi[Apocryphon of James 12]

04:03-09 Hippolytus[Refutation of all Heresies Book V.3]; Nag Hammadi[Gospel of Thomas 9]

04:05 OT-Apocrypha[Sirach 40:15]

04:09 Matthew 11:15n

04:10-12 Matthew 13:10-17; Luke 8:9-10; Nag Hammadi[Gospel of Thomas 62]

04:11 Daniel 2:27, 2:47; OT-Apocrypha[Wisdom of Solomon 2:22]; Clement of Alexandria[Stromata Book I.2, V.12]; Nag Hammadi[Tripartite Tractate 93]; NT-Apocrypha[Secret Gospel of Mark Fragment 1]

04:12 Isaiah 6:9-10; 2Corinthians 3:12-18n; Pseudepigrapha[Sibylline Oracles 1.360, 1.369]; Origen[De Principiis Book III.1.7]

04:13-20 Matthew 13:18-23; Luke 4:11-15

04:14 OT-Apocrypha[2Esdras 8:41, 9:31]

04:15 Pseudepigrapha[Joseph and Aseneth 12:9]

04:19 Indian[Dhammapada 312, 345-346]

04:19-20 Indian[Dhammapada 356-359]

04:20 Matthew 7:16-21n

04:21 Matthew 5:15n; Clement of Alexandria[Stromata Book I.1]; Tertullian[On the Apparel of Women Book II.13]; Nag Hammadi[Gospel of Thomas 33]; NT-Apocrypha[Gospel of Mani Kephalaia LXV]

04:21-25 Luke 8:16-18, 11:33-36

04:22 Matthew 10:26; Luke 12:2; Nag Hammadi[On the Origin of the World 125]

04:24 Matthew 7:2; Luke 6:38; Cyprian[Treatise XII.Book III.22]; Justin[Dialogue with Trypho 115]; Nag Hammadi[Gospel of Philip 62]

04:25 Pseudepigrapha[4Ezra 7.25; Odes of Solomon 24.9]

04:26 NT-Apocrypha[Acts of John 98, 109]

04:26-28 Nag Hammadi[Apocryphon of James 12]

04:28 Irenaeus[Against Heresies Book IV.18.4]; Tertullian[On the Veiling of Virgins 1]

04:29 Joel 3:13

04:30 Isaiah 40:18; Origen[Gospel of Matthew Book X.4]; Nag Hammadi[Dialogue of the Savior 88]

04:30-32 Matthew 13:31-32; Luke 13:18-19; Nag Hammadi[Gospel of Thomas 20]

04:31 Clement of Alexandria[Stromata Book V.1]; Irenaeus[Against Heresies Book I.13.2]

04:31-32 Hippolytus[Refutation of all Heresies Book V.4]

04:31-41 Origen[Gospel of John Book X.9]

04:32 Psalms 104:12; Ezekiel 17:23, 31:6; Daniel 4:9, 12, 18, 21; Pseudepigrapha[Joseph and Aseneth 16:23]

04:33 Nag Hammadi[Apocryphon of James 7]

04:33-34 Matthew 13:34-35

04:34 Origen[Gospel of Matthew Book XIV.12]; Tertullian[On Prescription Against Heretics 20, 22]

04:35 Psalms 107:23-31; Matthew 13:12, 25:29; Luke 19:26

04:35-41 Matthew 8:18-27; Luke 8:22-25; Pseudepigrapha[Sibylline Oracles 8.273; Testament of Adam 3.1; Testament of Naphtali 6.1-10]; NT-Apocrypha[Acts of Thomas 1.47]

04:36 Tertullian[On Baptism 9]

04:37 Jonah 1:4

04:37-41 This section also includes topical notes for: Calming the Sea - Psalms 107:23-30; Matthew 8:27; Luke 8:25; Dead Sea Scrolls[1Q Hymns (1QHODAYOTH [1QH]) COL XIII 18; 4Q429(4QHADAYOT[4QH]) Fragment 1 COL II 5]; Philo[On the Unchangeableness of God (23-26) cf. {Deuteronomy 5:31}; The Cherubim Part 1 (36-38)]; Rabbinic[Babylonian Taanit 23a]

04:38 Matthew 8:24n; Victorinus[On the Creation of the World]

04:39 Psalms 65:8, 89:10, 106:9, 107:25-32; Irenaeus[Fragments from the Lost Works 52]; Egyptian Book of the Dead[Oration 57]

04:39-41 Dead Sea Scrolls[4QAaronic Text A = Testament of Levi (4Q541[4QAhA = 4QTLevi]) Fragment 7 3]

04:41 Jonah 1:10, 16

05:01 Origen[Gospel of John Book VI.24]

05:01-15 Pseudepigrapha[Testament of Solomon 11:3]

05:01-20 This section also includes topical notes for: Demonic Possession - Matthew 8:28-34; Luke 8:26-40; NT-Apocrypha[Epistula Apostolorum 5]; Philo[Every Good Man Is Free (159); On Dreams, That they Are God-Sent (1.149) cf. {Leviticus 26:12}]

05:03 Isaiah 65:4

05:05-09 Pseudepigrapha[Testament of Solomon 1:13]

05:06 Matthew 28:17n

05:07 Genesis 14:18, 24:3; 1Kings 17:18

05:07 NT-Apocrypha[Acts of Thomas 1.45; Secret Gospel of Mark Fragment 1]

05:09 Constitutions of the Holy Apostles[Book VIII.6]
05:11 Tertullian[De Fuga in Persecutione 2]
05:11-14 Tertullian[On Modesty 9]
05:13 Pseudepigrapha[Testament of Solomon 5:12, 11:6]; Origen[Gospel of John Book VI.24]
05:18 NT-Apocrypha[Secret Gospel of Mark Fragment 1]
05:20 Ezekiel 3:18
05:21 1Kings 17:17-24; 2Kings 4:8, 17-37
05:21-43 Matthew 9:18-26; Luke 8:40-56
05:22 Irenaeus[Against Heresies Book V.13.1]; NT-Apocrypha[Infancy Story of Thomas 17.1]
05:22-43 Constitutions of the Holy Apostles[Book V.7]
05:24 NT-Apocrypha[Secret Gospel of Mark Fragment 1]
05:25 Irenaeus[Against Heresies Book II.20.1, 23.1-2]; NT-Apocrypha[Epistula Apostolorum 5]
05:27-28 Nag Hammadi[Testimony of Truth 41]
05:31 Irenaeus[Against Heresies Book I.3.3]
05:34 1Samuel 1:17, 20:42; 2Samuel 15:9; 2Kings 5:19; OT-Apocrypha[Judith 8:35]; Clement of
    Alexandria[Stromata Book IV.25, VI.14]; Constitutions of the Holy Apostles[Book II.20]; NT-
    Apocrypha[Epistula Apostolorum 51]
05:35 Pseudepigrapha[Joseph and Aseneth 19:1]; NT-Apocrypha[Epistula Apostolorum 5]
05:36 NT-Apocrypha[Acts of Thomas 1.21, 1.158]
05:38 NT-Apocrypha[Infancy Story of Thomas 17.1]
05:39 Pseudepigrapha[4Ezra 2.31]
05:40-41 NT-Apocrypha[Secret Gospel of Mark Fragment 1]
05:41 NT-Apocrypha[Infancy Story of Thomas 18.1]
05:43 NT-Apocrypha[Acts of Paul in Myra p.29; Infancy Story of Thomas 17.1]
06:01 Origen[Gospel of Matthew Book X.16]
06:01-06 Matthew 13:53-58; Luke 4:16-30
06:01-09 Tertullian[A Treatise on the Soul 25]
06:02 Matthew 9:35n; Origen[Against Celsus Book VI.16]
06:03 Pseudepigrapha[Joseph and Aseneth 4:10]; Rabbinic[Babylonian Sanhedrin 106a];
    Origen[Against Celsus Book VI.36]; Tertullian[An Answer to the Jews 10]; Nag Hammadi[Gospel of
    Philip 73]; NT-Apocrypha[Acts of Andrew and Matthias; Acts of Peter 1.23; Acts of Thomas 1.2;
    Gospel of the Nazareans Fragment 28]
06:04 John 4:44; Nag Hammadi[Gospel of Thomas 31]
06:05 Matthew 4:23-24n; Origen[Gospel of Matthew Book X.19]
06:06 Matthew 9:35n
06:07-13 Matthew 9:35-11:1; Luke 9:1-6
06:08-11 Hippolytus[(**Refutation of all Heresies Book IX.15**)]

> **And they [Esseni] traverse their native land, and on each occasion that they go on a
> journey they carry nothing except arms. And they have also in their cities a president,
> who expends the moneys collected for this purpose in procuring clothing and food for
> them. And their robe and its shape are modest. And they do not own two cloaks, or a
> double set of shoes; and when those that are in present use become antiquated, then they
> adopt others. And they neither buy nor sell anything at all; but whatever any one has he
> gives to him that has not, and that which one has not he receives. (Hippolytus -
> Refutation of all Heresies Book IX.15)**

06:09 NT-Apocrypha[Acts of Andrew and Matthias]
06:11 Matthew 10:5-14n; Luke 10:4-11; Acts 13:51; Pseudepigrapha[2Baruch 13:4]; NT-
    Apocrypha[Clement Romance 30.3]
06:13 James 5:14; Pseudepigrapha[Life of Adam and Eve Vita 36:2]; Cyprian[Epistle LXIX.2]
06:14-15 Origen[Gospel of Matthew Book X.20]
06:14-16 Matthew 14:1-2; Luke 9:7-9
06:14-29 Josephus[**Antiquities 18.5.2 116-119**]

Now some of the Jews thought that the destruction of Herod's army came from God, and
that very justly, as a punishment of what he did against John, that was called the Baptist:
for Herod slew him, who was a good man, and commanded the Jews to exercise virtue,
both as to righteousness towards one another, and piety towards God, and so to come to
baptism; for that the washing [with water] would be acceptable to him, if they made use
of it, not in order to the putting away [or the remission] of some sins [only], but for the
purification of the body; supposing still that the soul was thoroughly purified
beforehand by righteousness. Now when [many] others came in crowds about him, for
they were very greatly moved [or pleased] by hearing his words, Herod, who feared lest
the great influence John had over the people might put it into his power and inclination
to raise a rebellion, (for they seemed ready to do any thing he should advise,) thought it
best, by putting him to death, to prevent any mischief he might cause, and not bring
himself into difficulties, by sparing a man who might make him repent of it when it
would be too late. Accordingly he was sent a prisoner, out of Herod's suspicious temper,
to Macherus, the castle I before mentioned, and was there put to death. Now the Jews
had an opinion that the destruction of this army was sent as a punishment upon Herod,
and a mark of God's displeasure to him. (Josephus - Antiquities 18.5.2 116-119)

06:15 Matthew 16:14; Mark 8:28; Luke 9:19
06:16 Origen[Gospel of John Book VI.7]
06:17-18 Leviticus 18:16
06:17-27 Justin[Dialogue with Trypho 49]
06:17-29 Matthew 14:3-11; Luke 3:3, 19; Pseudepigrapha[Sibylline Oracles 1.342]
06:18 Luke 3:19-20
06:23 Esther 5:3, 6, 7:2; NT-Apocrypha[Acts of Thomas 1.23]
06:24-25 NT-Apocrypha[Apocalypse of Paul 1.51]
06:27 Tertullian[To his Wife Book II.5]
06:29-32 Matthew 14:12-13a; Luke 9:10; John 6:1, 3
06:30-51 Pseudepigrapha[Sibylline Oracles 1.356-1.357]
06:33-52 Matthew 14:13-33; Luke 9:11-17; John 6:2-21
06:34 Numbers 27:17; 1Kings 22:17; 2Chronicles 18:16; Ezekiel 34:11; Zechariah 10:2; Matthew 9:35n;
    OT-Apocrypha[Judith 11:19]; Philo[On The Virtues (58) cf. {Numbers 27:16}]; NT-Apocrypha[Acts
    of Thomas 1.47]

"Let the Lord God of spirits and of all flesh look out for himself a man to be over this
multitude, to undertake the care and superintendence of a shepherd, who shall lead
them in a blameless manner, in order that this nation may not become corrupt like a
flock which is scattered abroad, as having no Shepherd." (Philo - On The Virtues (58) cf.
{Numbers 27:16})

06:35-44 NT-Apocrypha[Acts of John 93]
06:37-44 John 6:31-58n; NT-Apocrypha[Acts of Andrew and Matthias]
06:38 Matthew 14:17-18; Pseudepigrapha[Sibylline Oracles 8.275]; Origen[Gospel of Matthew Book
    XI.2]; NT-Apocrypha[Epistula Apostolorum 5]
06:39-40 Origen[Gospel of Matthew Book XI.3, 19]
06:41 Pseudepigrapha[Testament of Zebulon 6.6-7]; Irenaeus[Against Heresies Book II.24.4];
    Origen[Gospel of Matthew Book XI.19]
06:44 Matthew 14:21n; Irenaeus[Against Heresies Book II.24.4]
06:45 Origen[Gospel of Matthew Book XI.5]; NT-Apocrypha[Acts of Thomas 1.47, 1.66]
06:45-52 Matthew 14:22-27; John 6:15-21
06:47 NT-Apocrypha[Epistula Apostolorum 5]
06:48 Job 9:8; Pseudepigrapha[Apocalypse of Elijah 3:8; Sibylline Oracles 1.356, 6.12-13; Testament of
    Adam 3.1]
06:48-52 Pseudepigrapha[Sibylline Oracles 8.273]
06:49 OT-Apocrypha[Wisdom of Solomon 17:15]
06:50 Pseudepigrapha[Joseph and Aseneth 14:11]; NT-Apocrypha[Pistis Sophia c. 2-6]

06:53-56 Matthew 14:34-36
06:55 NT-Apocrypha[Acts of Peter p.128]
06:56 Numbers 15:38; Nag Hammadi[Testimony of Truth 41]
07:01-23 Matthew 15:1-20
07:03-04 Josephus[**Antiquities 13.10.6 297**]; Hippolytus[Refutation of all Heresies Book IX.23]; Origen[Gospel of Matthew Book XI.11]

> **The Pharisees have delivered to the people a great many observances by succession from their fathers, which are not written in the laws of Moses; and for that reason it is that the Sadducees reject them, and say that we are to esteem those observances to be obligatory which are in the written word, but are not to observe what are derived from the tradition of our forefathers. And concerning these things it is that great disputes and differences have arisen among them, while the Sadducees are able to persuade none but the rich, and have not the populace obsequious to them, but the Pharisees have the multitude on their side. (Josephus - Antiquities 13.10.6 297)**

07:03-13 Rabbinic[Babylonian Sanhedrin 88b]
07:05 Irenaeus[Against Heresies Book IV.12.1, 4]
07:06 Matthew 6:2-16n; Apostolic[1Clement 15:2; 2Clement 3:5]; Clement of Alexandria[Stromata Book II.14]; NT-Apocrypha[Papyrus Egerton 2 Fragment 2 Lines 43-59]
07:06-07 Isaiah 29:13
07:07 Justin[Dialogue with Trypho 48]
07:09 Cyprian[Epistle XXXIX.5; Treatise I.19]
07:10 Exodus 20:12, 21:17; Leviticus 20:9; Deuteronomy 5:16; Matthew 15:4-8n
07:11 Josephus[War 2.9.4 175]
07:13 Cyprian[Epistle LXII.14, LXVII.2, LXXIII.3]
07:14-23 Nag Hammadi[Gospel of Thomas 14]
07:15 Pseudepigrapha[Pseudo-Phocylides 228; Sibylline Oracles 7.134]; Tertullian[Of Patience 8; On Fasting 2]
07:15-19 Rabbinic[Babylonian Keritot 13a]
07:15-23 Romans 14:14
07:16 Matthew 11:15n
07:17 Matthew 13:3-53n
07:19 Pseudepigrapha[Testament of Job 38:3]; Novatian[On the Jewish Meats 1, 5]; Origen[Gospel of Matthew Book XI.12]
07:21-23 Matthew 15:19; Galatians 5:19-21
07:22 Constitutions of the Holy Apostles[Book VII.20]
07:24 Origen[Gospel of Matthew Book XI.16]
07:24-30 Matthew 15:21-28
07:24-39 Nag Hammadi[Gospel of Philip 82]
07:27 Pseudepigrapha[Joseph and Aseneth 10:13]; Tertullian[On Prayer 6]
07:28 Nag Hammadi[Gospel of Philip 82]
07:31-37 Matthew 15:29-31
07:32 NT-Apocrypha[Epistula Apostolorum 5]
07:37 Isaiah 35:5-6; Lactantius[Divine Institutes Book IV.26]
08:01-10 Matthew 15:32-39a; Pseudepigrapha[Sibylline Oracles 1.357]; NT-Apocrypha[Acts of John 93]
08:05 Matthew 6:1-6n
08:06 Origen[Gospel of Matthew Book XI.19]
08:11 Matthew 12:38; Luke 11:16
08:11-12 Matthew 16:1-4
08:11-13 Luke 12:54-56
08:12 Matthew 12:39; Luke 11:29
08:13-21 Matthew 16:5-12n
08:15 Luke 12:1; Pseudepigrapha[4Ezra 12.31-33]; Archelaus[Disputation with Manes 44 cf. {Exodus 14}]; Hippolytus[Refutation of all Heresies Book IX.23]
08:17 NT-Apocrypha[Epistula Apostolorum 45]
08:18 Isaiah 6:9-10; Jeremiah 5:21; Ezekiel 12:2; NT-Apocrypha[Acts of Thomas 1.82]
08:19 Irenaeus[Against Heresies Book II.22.3]

08:22 NT-Apocrypha[Epistula Apostolorum 5; Secret Gospel of Mark Fragment 1]

08:23 Egyptian Book of the Dead[Oration 102]

08:27-09:01 Matthew 16:13-28; Luke 9:18-27

08:28 Mark 6:14-15; Luke 9:7-8

08:29 Pseudepigrapha[1Enoch 48:10]

08:30 Origen[Gospel of Matthew Book XII.15]

08:31 Psalms 80:17, 118:22; Matthew 5:2; Pseudepigrapha[Life of Abraham 11:2]; Irenaeus[Against Heresies Book III.16.5]; Justin[Dialogue with Trypho 106]; NT-Apocrypha[Gospel of the Hebrews Fragment 7]

08:31-35 Nag Hammadi[Apocryphon of James 6]

08:33 Pseudepigrapha[Testament of Job 26:3]

08:34 Matthew 10:38, 16:24-25n; Luke 9:23, 14:27; Tertullian[On Idolatry 12]; Nag Hammadi[Letter of Peter to Philip 138]; Epic of Gilgamesh[The Forest Journey]

08:35 Matthew 10:39; Luke 17:33; John 12:25; Apostolic[Ignatius - Letter to the Magnesians 5:2]

08:36 Apostolic[2Clement 6:2]; Clement of Alexandria[Stromata Book VI.14]; Cyprian[Treatise III.8; Epistle LXII.15]; Nag Hammadi[Interpretation of Knowledge 9]; NT-Apocrypha[Acts of Peter 1.10]

08:37 Psalms 49:8; OT-Apocrypha[Sirach 26:14]; NT-Apocrypha[Acts of Thomas 1.72]

08:38 Psalms 80:17; Pseudepigrapha[Apocalypse of Elijah 3:4; Sibylline Oracles 2.240]; Cyprian[Treatise III.28]; Tertullian[De Fuga in Persecutione 7; On Idolatry 13; On the Flesh of Christ 5]

09:01 John 21:22-23; Origen[Gospel of Matthew Book XII.31, 35]; NT-Apocrypha[Acts of Thomas 1.141-2; Secret Gospel of Mark Fragment 1]

09:01-13 Tertullian[On Fasting 6]; Nag Hammadi[Letter of Peter to Philip 134]

09:02 Exodus 24:15; Pseudepigrapha[Apocalypse of Zephaniah 5:4]; Hippolytus[Refutation of all Heresies Book V.42]; Irenaeus[Against Heresies Book I.14.6]; Origen[Gospel of Matthew Book XII.36-37]; NT-Apocrypha[Acts of John 90; Acts of Peter 1.20; Acts of Thomas 1.143; Apocalypse of Peter 1.15]

09:02-09 Tertullian[On Monogamy 8]

09:02-29 Matthew 17:1-21n; Luke 9:28-43a

09:03 Daniel 7:9; Origen[Gospel of Matthew Book XII.39]

09:04 Deuteronomy 18:15; Tertullian[Against Praxeas 14]; NT-Apocrypha[Apocalypse of Peter 1.16]

09:05-06 Origen[Gospel of Matthew Book XII.40]

09:06 Tertullian[Against Praxeas 15]

09:07 Exodus 40:34; Deuteronomy 18:15; Psalms 2:7; Matthew 3:17; Mark 1:11; Luke 3:22; 2Peter 1:17-18; Pseudepigrapha[Martyrdom and Ascension of Isaiah 1:4]; Tacitus[The Histories 5.13]

09:09 Psalms 80:17; NT-Apocrypha[Apocalypse of Peter 1.17]

09:11 Malachi 3:22; Matthew 11:14

09:11-12 Malachi 4:5-6

09:12 Psalms 22:7, 80:17; Isaiah 53:3; Malachi 3:24

09:13 1Kings 19:2, 10; Justin[Dialogue with Trypho 49]

09:14-29 Matthew 17:14-21; Luke 9:37-43

09:17 Tertullian[On Modesty 9]

09:18-20 Pseudepigrapha[Testament of Solomon 12:2]

09:23 Matthew 19:26n; Irenaeus[Against Heresies Book IV.37.5]

09:24 NT-Apocrypha[Acts of Thomas 1.65]

09:25 Pseudepigrapha[Life of Adam and Eve Vita 39.1-3]

09:26 Pseudepigrapha[Testament of Solomon 1:13]; NT-Apocrypha[Acts of Thomas 1.75]

09:27 NT-Apocrypha[Secret Gospel of Mark Fragment 1]

09:29 Pseudepigrapha[Apocalypse of Elijah 1:21]; Dead Sea Scrolls[1QGenesisApocryphon (1QapGen ar) COL XX 28-29]; Clement[First Epistle Concerning Virginity 12]; Tertullian[On Fasting 8]

09:30 Anonymous[Treatise on Re-Baptism 9]

09:30-32 Matthew 17:22-23; Luke 9:43b-45

09:31 2Samuel 24:14; Psalms 80:17; Matthew 5:2; OT-Apocrypha[Sirach 2:18]; Pseudepigrapha[Life of Abraham 11:2]; Justin[Dialogue with Trypho 106]

09:33-37 Matthew 18:1-5; Luke 9:46-48; Origen[Gospel of Matthew Book XIII.19]

09:34 Luke 22:24

09:35 Matthew 20:26-27, 23:11; Mark 10:43-44; Luke 22:26; Apostolic[Polycarp - Letter to the Philippians 5:2]

09:37 Matthew 10:40; Luke 10:16; John 13:20; Tertullian[On Prayer 26]; NT-Apocrypha[Letter of Clement to James 2.5]

09:38 Numbers 11:26-29

09:38-41 Luke 9:49-50

09:39 Pseudepigrapha[Testament of Solomon 1:13]

09:40 Matthew 12:30; Luke 11:23; Methodius[Banquet of the Ten Virgins 1.1]; NT-Apocrypha[Oxyrhynchus Papyrus 1224 p.176]

09:41 Matthew 10:42; Rabbinic[Babylonian Nedarim 21a]

09:42 NT-Apocrypha[Acts of Peter 1.6]

09:42-50 Matthew 18:6-20; Luke 17:1-2

09:43 Matthew 5:30; NT-Apocrypha[Acts of John 36; Acts of Peter 1.28]

09:44 Irenaeus[Against Heresies Book II.32.1]

09:44-48 Josephus[Discourse to the Greeks Concerning Hades 6]

09:45 Pseudepigrapha[3Enoch 44:3]

09:47 Matthew 5:29

09:48 Isaiah 66:24; OT-Apocrypha[Judith 16:17]; Pseudepigrapha[Greek Apocalypse of Ezra 4:19; Testament of Job 20:8; Vision of Ezra 34]; Apostolic[2Clement 7:4-6, 17:5]; NT-Apocrypha[Acts of Thomas 1.56; Apocalypse of Paul 1.42]

09:49 Pseudepigrapha[Testament of Levi 9:14]

09:49-50 Nag Hammadi[Gospel of Philip 59]

09:50 Matthew 5:13; Luke 14:34-35; NT-Apocrypha[Acts of John 109]

10:01 Matthew 9:35n, 19:1-2; Luke 9:51-62; NT-Apocrypha[Secret Gospel of Mark Fragment 1]

10:01-12 Luke 16:18

10:02 Clement of Alexandria[Stromata Book III.6]; Origen[Gospel of Matthew Book XIV.16]

10:02-12 Matthew 19:3-9; Dead Sea Scrolls[Damascus Document (CD-A) COL IV 20-21]

10:04 Deuteronomy 24:1-4; Matthew 5:31

10:05 Tertullian[On Monogamy 9]

10:05-06 Clement[Homily III.54]

10:06 Genesis 1:27, 5:2

10:07-08 Genesis 2:24

10:07-09 Nag Hammadi[Gospel of Philip 70, 76]

10:08 Origen[De Principiis Book II.6.3]; Tertullian[To his Wife Book II.6]

10:09 Matthew 19:6; Clement of Alexandria[Stromata Book III.6]

10:11-19 John 8:3-11n

10:12 Matthew 5:32; 1Corinthians 7:10-11; Pseudepigrapha[Life of Abraham 42:1]

10:13 2Kings 4:27

10:13-14 NT-Apocrypha[Secret Gospel of Mark Fragment 1]

10:13-15 Tertullian[On Monogamy 8]

10:13-16 Matthew 19:13-15; Luke 18:15-17

10:14 Tertullian[On Baptism 18]

10:15 Matthew 18:3; Rabbinic[Avot 4.25]; Apostolic[Shepherd of Hermas 27:1]; Nag Hammadi[Gospel of Thomas 22]

10:17 Pseudepigrapha[Sibylline Oracles Fragment 3.47]; Clement of Alexandria[Stromata Book III.6]; Irenaeus[Against Heresies Book I.20.2]

10:17-27 Tertullian[On Monogamy 14]

10:17-31 Matthew 19:16-30n; Luke 18:18-30; Clement of Alexandria[Who is the Rich Man that shall be Saved 4]; Pseudepigrapha[Joseph and Aseneth 12:15]

10:18 Matthew 19:17n; Luke 18:19; Clement[Homily III.57]; Hippolytus[Refutation of all Heresies Book V.2, VII.19]; Origen[Against Celsus Book V.11; Gospel of John Book II.7, VI.28]; Tertullian[On Modesty 2]

10:19 Exodus 20:12-16; Deuteronomy 5:16-20, 24:14; Matthew 15:4-8n; OT-Apocrypha[Sirach 4:1]

10:20 Pseudepigrapha[2Baruch 38:4]

10:21 Luke 18:22n; Pseudepigrapha[Joseph and Aseneth 10:11; Sibylline Oracles 2.78-89]; Apostolic[Shepherd of Hermas 50:8-9]; Clement of Alexandria[Who is the Rich Man that shall be Saved 14, 16, 19]; NT-Apocrypha[Secret Gospel of Mark Fragment 1]; Epic of Gilgamesh[The Story of the Flood]

10:21-30 Philo[On Dreams That they Are God-Sent (2.11)]

10:23 Clement of Alexandria[Stromata Book V.5]

10:23-24 Tertullian[To his Wife Book II.8]

10:25 Pseudepigrapha[4Ezra 7.4-18]; Apostolic[Shepherd of Hermas 14:6]; Clement of Alexandria[Who is the Rich Man that shall be Saved 26]

10:26 Clement of Alexandria[Who is the Rich Man that shall be Saved 20]

10:27 Genesis 18:14; 2Chronicles 14:10; Job 42:2; Zechariah 8:6; Justin[First Apology 18]; NT-Apocrypha[Acts of Paul in Myra p.28; Acts of Peter 1.11]

10:28 Tertullian[Five Books in Reply to Marcion Book III.10]; NT-Apocrypha[Pistis Sophia c. 136]

10:28-30 Nag Hammadi[Authoritative Teaching 26-27; Testimony of Truth 41]

10:29 Cyprian[Treatise III.12]

10:29-30 Matthew 19:29n; Luke 18:29-30; Clement of Alexandria[Who is the Rich Man that shall be Saved 22]; Tertullian[On Idolatry 12]

10:30 Jude 1:21n; Pseudepigrapha[3Baruch 15:2 (Gk.)]; Rabbinic[Babylonian Sanhedrin 100a cf. {Isaiah 40:12}]

10:31 Matthew 20:16; Luke 13:30; Clement of Alexandria[Who is the Rich Man that shall be Saved 26]

10:32-34 Matthew 20:17-19; Luke 18:31-34

10:33 Psalms 80:17

10:34 Isaiah 50:6; Matthew 27:19-31n; Pseudepigrapha[Life of Abraham 11:2; Sibylline Oracles 8.287-289]

10:35 Tertullian[On Baptism 11]

10:35-45 Matthew 20:20-28

10:38 Luke 12:50; Pseudepigrapha[Martyrdom and Ascension of Isaiah 05:14]; Anonymous[Treatise on Re-Baptism 14]; Hippolytus[Refutation of all Heresies Book V.3]; Irenaeus[Against Heresies Book I.21.2]

10:38-39 Apostolic[Papias Fragment 6:1]; Nag Hammadi[First Apocalypse of James 25]

10:40 NT-Apocrypha[Pistis Sophia c. 96]

10:43 Luke 33:25-26

10:44 Matthew 23:11; Mark 9:35; Luke 22:26; Callistus[Second Epistle 3.3]; Origen[Against Celsus Book VII.23]

10:45 Psalms 80:17; Isaiah 53:10; Clement of Alexandria[The Instructor Book I.9]; Nag Hammadi[Teachings of Silvanus 104]

10:46 NT-Apocrypha[Secret Gospel of Mark Fragment 2]

10:46-52 Matthew 20:29-34; Luke 18:35-43

10:47 Pseudepigrapha[Testament of Solomon 1:7, 20:1]; Rabbinic[Babylonian Sanhedrin 107b]

10:47-48 Matthew 1:1

10:48 Clement of Alexandria[Stromata Book VI.15]; NT-Apocrypha[Secret Gospel of Mark Fragment 1]

10:49 Melito[Fragments 9.9]

10:49-52 Nag Hammadi[Gospel of Thomas 37]

10:52 Tertullian[On Baptism 12]

11:01 Zechariah 14:4; Pseudepigrapha[Joseph and Aseneth 3:2]; Nag Hammadi[Letter of Peter to Philip 133]; NT-Apocrypha[Acts of Thomas 1.40]

11:01-10 Matthew 21:1-11; Luke 19:29-44; John 12:12-19

11:01-12 Origen[Gospel of John Book X.15]

11:02 Genesis 49:11; 1Samuel 6:7; Zechariah 9:9; Origen[Gospel of John Book X.18]

11:07-09 John 12:5

11:08 2Kings 9:13

11:09 Matthew 21:9, 23:39; Luke 13:35, 19:38; John 12:13; Rabbinic[Babylonian Pesahim 119a cf. {Psalms 118.22}; Midrash on Psalms 118:24]; Methodius[Oration on the Psalms 1]

11:09-10 Psalms 118:25-26

11:10 Job 16:19; Psalms 148:1; Constitutions of the Holy Apostles[Book VII.26]

11:11 Matthew 21:14-17

11:12-26 Matthew 21:18-22

11:13-14 Hippolytus[Refutation of all Heresies Book VIII.1]

11:13-21 Matthew 21:19; Pseudepigrapha[4Baruch 3.21-6.11]; Dead Sea Scrolls[4Q Halakhah (4Q25)[4Q HALAKAH] Fragment 3 7-8]; Philo[Concerning Noah's Work As A Planter (95-99, 112-119) cf. {Leviticus 19:23-25}; On the Virtues (156-160) cf. {Leviticus 19:23-25}]

11:15 Irenaeus[Against Heresies Book IV.1.6]; Origen[Gospel of John Book X.18]

11:15-17 Pseudepigrapha[Psalms of Solomon 17.36]

11:15-19 Matthew 21:12-13; Luke 19:45-48; John 2:13-22

11:17 Isaiah 56:7; Jeremiah 7:11; Matthew 9:35n, 21:13n; Luke 19:46; Apostolic[2Clement 14:1]; Tertullian[On Modesty 1]

11:18 Pseudepigrapha[Testament of Levi 16:3]

11:20-21 Hippolytus[Refutation of all Heresies Book VIII.1]

11:20-26 Matthew 21:19-22

11:22 Cyprian[Treatise XII.Book III.42]; NT-Apocrypha[Acts of Paul from Corinth to Italy p.79]

11:23 Matthew 17:20; Plato[Laws VIII 842e-843a]; Clement of Alexandria[Stromata Book VII.12]

11:24 Cyprian[Treatise XII.Book III.42]; Nag Hammadi[Letter of Peter to Philip 137]

11:24-25 Origen[Gospel of Matthew Book XIV.25]

11:25 Cyprian[Treatise I.13, IV.23]; Theonas[Epistle to Lucianus, the Chief Chamberlain 9]; NT-Apocrypha[Acts of Peter and Paul]

11:26 Matthew 6:14-15

11:27 NT-Apocrypha[Oxyrhynchus Papyrus 840]

11:27-33 Matthew 21:23-27; Luke 20:1-8

11:30 Matthew 3:5-16n; Tertullian[On Baptism 10]

12:01 Psalms 80:8; Isaiah 5:1-2; Pseudepigrapha[Testament of Joseph 19:12]

12:01-08 Nag Hammadi[Gospel of Thomas 65]

12:01-09 Matthew 21:33-41n; Luke 20:09-16

12:01-12 Matthew 13:3-53n, 21:33-46; Luke 20:9-19

12:03 Irenaeus[Demonstration of the Apostolic Preaching 87]

12:06 Genesis 22:2

12:07 Genesis 37:20

12:10 Pseudepigrapha[Sibylline Oracles 1.344-346; Testament of Solomon 22:7, 23.4]; NT-Apocrypha[Acts of Peter 1.24]

12:10-11 Psalms 118:22-23; Matthew 21:42-44; Luke 20:17-18

12:12 Matthew 21:45-46; Luke 20:19

12:13 Hippolytus[Refutation of all Heresies Book IX.23]; Tertullian[Against All Heresies 1]

12:13-15 NT-Apocrypha[Papyrus Egerton 2 Fragment 2 Lines 43-59]

12:13-17 Matthew 22:15-22; Luke 20:19-26; Josephus[Antiquities 18.1.1 4; War 2.8.1 118]

12:14 Matthew 9:35n; Pseudepigrapha[Odes of Solomon 24.13, 39.13]

12:15 Matthew 6:2-16n

12:17 Matthew 22:21n; Luke 20:25; Clement of Alexandria[The Instructor Book III.12]; Origen[Gospel of Matthew Book XIII.10]; Tertullian[On Idolatry 15]

12:18 Acts 23:8; Hippolytus[Refutation of all Heresies Book IX.24]; Justin[On the Resurrection 9]; Tertullian[Against All Heresies 1]

12:18-27 Matthew 22:23-33; Luke 20:27-40; Acts 2:31n; Tertullian[On Monogamy 7; On the Resurrection of the Flesh 36; To his Wife Book I.1]

12:19 Genesis 38:8; Deuteronomy 25:5

12:20 Origen[Gospel of John Book VI.2]

12:23 Clement of Alexandria[Stromata Book III.6]

12:24 Clement[Homily XVIII.20]; NT-Apocrypha[Freer Logion; Pseudo Clementines - Kerygmata Petrou H III 50.1]

12:24-25 Tertullian[On Exhortation to Chastity 13]

12:25 Pseudepigrapha[1Enoch 15:6, 51:4]; Clement of Alexandria[Stromata Book VI.12]; Irenaeus[Against Heresies Book II.33.5]; Justin[On the Resurrection 2]; Tertullian[On Monogamy 10; On the Apparel of Women Book I.2]; NT-Apocrypha[Pseudo-Titus Epistle Line 11, 323]

12:25-34 Matthew 22:34-40

12:26 Exodus 3:1-2, 6, 15-16; OT-Apocrypha[4Maccabees 7:19, 16:25]; Origen[Gospel of John Book II.10]

12:26-27 Irenaeus[Against Heresies Book II.30.9]

12:27 This section also includes topical notes for: God of the Living - Matthew 22:32; Luke 20:28; Philo[On Flight And Finding (55-58) cf. {Deuteronomy 4:4, 30:20}; Special Laws I (31) cf. {Deuteronomy 4:4}]; Rabbinic[Babylonian Taanit 5b]; Clement[Homily III.55]

12:28 Rabbinic[Makkot 23b-24a]; Origen[Gospel of Matthew Book XIV.16]

12:28-31 Clement of Alexandria[The Instructor Book II.1]

12:28-34 Tertullian[An Answer to the Jews 2]

12:29 Clement[Homily III.57]; Constitutions of the Holy Apostles[Book II.6]

12:29-30 Deuteronomy 6:4-5; Joshua 22:5; Tertullian[Five Books in Reply to Marcion Book IV.32]

12:29-31 Pseudepigrapha[Sibylline Oracles 8.481]; Cyprian[Treatise I.15, XI.2]

12:30 Apostolic[2Clement 3:4]; Justin[First Apology 16]

12:30-31 Apostolic[Didache 1:2]; Teaching of the Twelve Apostles 1.2

12:31 Leviticus 19:18; Fabian[Second Epistle]; Tertullian[On the Apparel of Women Book II.2]; Nag Hammadi[Sentences of Sextus 179]

12:31-33 Matthew 5:43n

12:32 Deuteronomy 4:35, 6:4; Isaiah 45:21; Constitutions of the Holy Apostles[Book VII.2]

12:32-34 Luke 21:2-4; Josephus[Antiquities 6.7.4 147-149]

12:33 Leviticus 19:18; Deuteronomy 6:5; Joshua 22:5; 1Samuel 15:22; Hosea 6:6; Callistus[Second Epistle 6.6]

12:34 Luke 10:25-28; Rabbinic[Mekhilta on Exodus 13:8]

12:35 Matthew 1:1, 9:35n; Pseudepigrapha[Testament of Solomon 20:1]; Clement of Alexandria[Exhortation to the Heathen 1]

12:35-37 Matthew 22:41-46; Luke 20:41-44; Acts 3:18-26n; Apostolic[Epistle of Barnabas 12:10-11]; Irenaeus[Fragments from the Lost Works 52]

12:36 2Samuel 23:2; Psalms 110:1; Pseudepigrapha[Apocalypse of Elijah 4:28]; Justin[Dialogue with Trypho 83]

12:37 Romans 1:3

12:38 Archelaus[Disputation with Manes 21]

12:38-40 Matthew 23:1-39; Luke 11:37, 13:34-35, 20:45-47

12:39 Rabbinic[Babylonian Horayot 13a-14b]; Clement of Alexandria[Stromata Book VI.13]

12:40 Exodus 22:22; Isaiah 10:2; Rabbinic[Babylonian Ketubot 100b]

12:41 2Kings 12:9; Archelaus[Disputation with Manes 42]

12:41-44 Luke 21:1-4; Josephus[Antiquities 6.7.4 147-149]; Philo[Special Laws I (275-279) cf. {Exodus 30:8-9}]; Nag Hammadi[Sentences of Sextus 379]

12:42 Commodianus[Instructions 72]; Constitutions of the Holy Apostles[Book III.7]

13:01-23 Luke 21:5-24

13:01-37 Matthew 24:1-25:46

13:02 Jeremiah 7:14, 9:11; Rabbinic[Babylonian Gittin 57b cf. {Psalms 137.7}]

13:02-37 NT-Apocrypha[Epistula Apostolorum 34]

13:03 Pseudepigrapha[Testament of Naphtali 5:2]

13:03-13 Matthew 24:3-14; Luke 21:7-19; Revelation 6:1-12, 13:1-8

13:04 Pseudepigrapha[2Baruch 25:3]

13:05 Pseudepigrapha[2Baruch 27:2; Apocalypse of Elijah 1:14]; Nag Hammadi[Gospel of Mary 8]

13:05-06 Matthew 24:4-5; Luke 21:8; Revelation 6:1-2, 13:1-6

13:06 Cyprian[Epistle LXXIV.9; Treatise I.14]

13:07 Daniel 2:28, 45; Pseudepigrapha[Apocalypse of Daniel 1:1; Apocalypse of Elijah 2:2]; Rabbinic[Babylonian Sanhedrin 97a]

13:07-08 Matthew 24:6-7; Luke 21:9-10; Revelation 6:3-4, 13:7

13:08 2Chronicles 15:6; Isaiah 8:21, 13:13, 19:2; Matthew 24:7-8; Luke 21:11; 1Thessalonians 5:3; Revelation 6:5-8; OT-Apocrypha[2Esdras 13:30-32]; Pseudepigrapha[2Baruch 27:9; 4Ezra 15:15; Sibylline Oracles 1.397, 2.23, 2.6, 3.636]

13:09 Matthew 24:9-13; Luke 21:12-19; Revelation 6:9-12; Pseudepigrapha[2Baruch 13:4]; Nag Hammadi[Letter of Peter to Philip 138-139]; NT-Apocrypha[Epistula Apostolorum 15; Pseudo-Titus Epistle Line 479]

13:09-13 Nag Hammadi[Letter of Peter to Philip 138]

13:10-13 Matthew 24:14

13:11 Matthew 10:17-20; Luke 12:11-12; Pseudepigrapha[Ahiqar 114]

13:12 Micah 7:6; Pseudepigrapha[3Baruch 4:17; Greek Apocalypse of Ezra 3.12-15; Joseph and Aseneth 11:3; Pseudo-Phocylides 47]

13:13 Daniel 12:12; Matthew 10:22; OT-Apocrypha[2Esdras 6:25]; Nag Hammadi[Testimony of Truth 44]

13:14 Ezekiel 7:12-16; Daniel 9:27, 11:31, 12:11; Matthew 24:15-21; Luke 21:20-24; 2Thessalonians 2:3-12; 2Corinthians 3:12-18n; Revelation 13:1-18; OT-Apocrypha[1Maccabees 1:54]; Pseudepigrapha[Apocalypse of Elijah 3:5]

13:14-19 Pseudepigrapha[Apocalypse of Elijah 4:24]

13:14-20 Hippolytus[Treatise on Christ and Antichrist 62]

13:16 Luke 17:31

13:17 Pseudepigrapha[Apocalypse of Daniel 12:6; Sibylline Oracles 2.190]; Clement of Alexandria[Stromata Book III.6]

13:18-20 Victorinus[Apocalypse 7.2]

13:19 Exodus 9:18; Deuteronomy 4:32; Daniel 12:1; Joel 2:2; Revelation 7:14; Pseudepigrapha[4Ezra 2.27, 16.18-34]

13:20 1Peter 2:4-9n; Pseudepigrapha[4Ezra 7.138-8.3, 9.13-23; Life of Abraham 19:13]; NT-Apocrypha[Epistula Apostolorum 28]

13:21 Nag Hammadi[Gospel of Mary 8]

13:22 Deuteronomy 13:1-3, 6; Jeremiah 6:13; Pseudepigrapha[Apocalypse of Adam 6:5; Martyrdom and Ascension of Isaiah (3:13-4:22 = Testament of Hezekiah) 4:12; Sibylline Oracles 2.166]; Apostolic[Didache 16:4]; Irenaeus[Against Heresies Book II.32.3]; Justin[Dialogue with Trypho 51, 82]; Nag Hammadi[Gospel of the Egyptians III 61]; NT-Apocrypha[Apocalypse of Peter 1.2]

13:23 Cyprian[Treatise I.17]

13:24 Joel 3:4; Pseudepigrapha[Apocalypse of Adam 5:10]; NT-Apocrypha[Apocalypse of Thomas Line 11]

13:24-25 Isaiah 13:10, 34:4; Ezekiel 32:7-8; Joel 2:10, 31, 3:15

13:24-27 Zechariah 12:10-14; Matthew 24:29-31; Luke 21:25-28; 1Corinthians 15:51-55; 1Thessalonians 4:15-17; 2Thessalonians 2:1-2; Revelation 1:7; 6:13-8:2, 11:12, 14:1-5, 14:14-16, 16:8

13:24-37 Matthew 24:29-35, 42-44; Luke 21:25-36

13:25 Isaiah 13:10, 34:4; Ezekiel 32:7; Joel 2:31; Revelation 6:12-13; Pseudepigrapha[Sibylline Oracles 2.202, 8.190]

13:26 Psalms 80:17; Daniel 7:13-14; 1Thessalonians 4:15-17n; Revelation 1:7; Pseudepigrapha[Sibylline Oracles 2.240]; NT-Apocrypha[Acts of Peter 1.24; Apocalypse of Peter 1.1; Apocalypse of Thomas Line 48]

13:27 Deuteronomy 30:4; Zechariah 2:6, 10; Apostolic[Didache 10:5]; Victorinus[Apocalypse 7.2]; NT-Apocrypha[Apocalypse of Thomas Line 72]

13:28 Matthew 13:3-53n, 24:23; Luke 21:29-33; Revelation 6:5, 11:19, 14:17-20, 16:18; NT-Apocrypha[Apocalypse of Peter 1.2]

13:29 NT-Apocrypha[Apocalypse of Thomas Line 46]

13:31 Isaiah 51:6; Origen[Against Celsus Book V.22]

13:32 Matthew 24:6, 36; Acts 01:07; Pseudepigrapha[2Baruch 21.8-9; Greek Apocalypse of Ezra 3:5]; Irenaeus[Against Heresies Book II.28.6-8, III.23.1]; Tertullian[A Treatise on the Soul 33]; NT-Apocrypha[Apocalypse of Thomas Line 5]

13:33 Irenaeus[Against Heresies Book V.10.1]

13:33-37 Matthew 24:42-51n

13:34 Luke 12:36-38

13:35 Mark 14:72; Philo[Every Good Man Is Free (131-136) cf. {Greek Playwright Ion}]; Constitutions of the Holy Apostles[Book VII.31]; NT-Apocrypha[Epistula Apostolorum 15]

13:35-37 Apostolic[Didache 16:1]

14:01 Exodus 13:1-27; 1Corinthians 5:8; Pseudepigrapha[Testament of Levi 16:3]; Tacitus[The Histories 5.4]

14:01-02 Matthew 26:1-5; Luke 22:1-2

14:01-09 Matthew 26:6-13; John 12:1-8

14:03 Mark 7:37-38

14:03-09 Matthew 26:6-13; John 12:1-8

14:06 Rabbinic[Babylonian Sanhedrin 101a]

14:07 Deuteronomy 15:11

14:08-09 Lactantius[Divine Institutes Book VI.12]

14:09 Pseudepigrapha[Joseph and Aseneth 19:8]; Rabbinic[Ecclesiastes Rabba on 1.3, 7.1; Genesis Rabba on 12.1]

14:10 Irenaeus[Against Heresies Book I.31.1]

14:10-11 Matthew 26:14-16; Luke 22:3-6; Dead Sea Scrolls[4Q429(4QHADAYOT[4QH]) Fragment 1 COL III 8-9]; Justin[Dialogue with Trypho 137]; NT-Apocrypha[Gospel of Judas 58]

14:12 Exodus 12:14-20; Deuteronomy 16:2; Tacitus[The Histories 5.4]; Anatolius[Paschal Canon 8]; Tertullian[An Answer to the Jews 8, 10]; NT-Apocrypha[Akhmim Fragment 2.5]

14:12-25 Matthew 26:17-29; Luke 22:7-23; John 13:21-30; 1Corinthians 11:23-26

14:13 Tertullian[On Baptism 19]

14:14-16 1Samuel 21:2; Matthew 26:18-19; Luke 22:11-13

14:16-26 Dead Sea Scrolls[**1QThe Rule of the Congregation (1Q28a [1QSa]) Col. II 11-21**]

> *This is the assembly* of famous men, *summoned* to the Community Council when *God* begets the Messiah among them. He shall come, the head of the entire congregation of Israel, with all the Priests of Aaron *and* the men of reputation. They shall sit *before him* by rank. Then *the Messiah* of Israel shall *come*, and the chiefs of the *clans of Israel* shall sit before him by rank, according to *commission* in their camps and marches. *Then*, all the heads of the *clans of the congregation*, with the sages, shall sit before them by rank. And *when* they gather *at the* common *table, or to drink* wine, when the common table is made ready *or* the wine for drinking, *let* no hand *reach* before the Priest for the first-fruits of bread or wine. For *he* shall *bless* the first-fruits of bread and wine and be the first *to* stretch out his hand for bread. *Afterward*, the Messiah of Israel *shall stretch out* his hand for bread. *Last,* the whole congregation shall give a blessing, *each by* rank. (1QThe Rule of the Congregation (Dead Sea Scrolls - 1Q28a [1QSa]) Col. II 11-21)

14:15 Luke 22:12; Rabbinic[Mishnah Pesahim 10.1]

14:17-25 Matthew 26:20-29n; Luke 22:14-23

14:18 1Samuel 22:22; Psalms 41:9-10; Matthew 26:21; Luke 22:21; John 13:11, 18-19; Pseudepigrapha[The Sentences of the Syriac Menander 215]

14:21 Psalms 41:9, 80:17; Matthew 26:24; Philo[Special Laws IV (84, 89-91) cf. {Exodus 20:17}]; Irenaeus[Against Heresies Book II.20.5]; Tertullian[On Prescription Against Heretics 30]; NT-Apocrypha[Apocalypse of Peter 1.3]

14:22 1Corinthians 10:16-18n; NT-Apocrypha[Gospel of the Hebrews Fragment 7]

14:22-25 John 6:31-58n

14:23 NT-Apocrypha[Epistula Apostolorum 15]

14:23-24 John 6:53-56n

14:24 Exodus 24:6-8; Isaiah 53:11; Jeremiah 31:31-34; Zechariah 9:11; Tertullian[On Modesty 11]; Nag Hammadi[Gospel of Truth 43]

14:25 1Corinthians 10:16-18n; Clement of Alexandria[The Instructor Book II.2]; Teaching of the Twelve Apostles 9.2; NT-Apocrypha[Gospel of the Hebrews Fragment 7]

14:26 Rabbinic[Mekhilta On Exodus 12.46]; NT-Apocrypha[Acts of John 94]

14:26-31 Matthew 26:30-35; Luke 22:31-34; John 13:36-38

14:27 Zechariah 13:7; Luke 13:32n; Anonymous[Treatise on Re-Baptism 6-7]

14:27-29 NT-Apocrypha[Fayyum Fragment]

14:28 Matthew 28:16-20

14:30 Mark 14:72; Philo[Every Good Man Is Free (131-136) cf. {Greek Playwright Ion}]

14:31 Pseudepigrapha[Joseph and Aseneth 24:11]; Tertullian[On Prayer 8]

14:32-42 Matthew 26:36-46; Luke 22:39-46; John 18:1-2; Pseudepigrapha[Joseph and Aseneth 14:4]

14:34 Psalms 42:5-6, 11-12, 43:5; Jonah 4:9; OT-Apocrypha[Sirach 37:2]

14:35 Pseudepigrapha[Joseph and Aseneth 11:19]; Epic of Gilgamesh[The Forest Journey]

14:35-36 Genesis 32:9-12

14:36 Matthew 19:26n; Pseudepigrapha[Apocryphon of Ezekiel Fragment 2; Martyrdom and Ascension of Isaiah 05:14]; Rabbinic[Avot 2.4]; Dionysius of Alexandria[Exegetical Fragments Gospel According to Luke - An Interpretation 22.42]

14:37 Matthew 26:40; Rabbinic[Babylonian Pesahim 109a; Mishnah Pesahim 10.8 cf. {Exodus 12:42}; Tosephta Pesahim 10.9]

14:38 Psalms 51:14; Matthew 24:42-51n; Cyprian[Treatise IV.26]

14:41 Psalms 80:17

14:43 Genesis 33:1; Irenaeus[Against Heresies Book I.31.1]

14:43-15:41 Matthew 26:47-27:56n

14:43-52 Matthew 26:47-56n; Luke 22:47-53; John 18:2-12

14:45 Luke 22:47-48n

14:47 Epic of Gilgamesh[The Forest Journey]

14:48 NT-Apocrypha[Acts of Paul in Myra p.31]

14:49 Isaiah 53:7; Matthew 9:35n; Luke 19:47, 21:37; Josephus[War 2.8.12 159]; Origen[Gospel of Matthew Book XIV.14]

14:50 Zechariah 13:7; Irenaeus[Demonstration of the Apostolic Preaching 76]; Justin[First Apology 50]

14:51 NT-Apocrypha[Secret Gospel of Mark Fragment 1]

14:51-52 Genesis 39:12-13

14:52 Amos 2:16

14:53 Matthew 26:57; Luke 22:54; John 18:13-14

14:54 Matthew 26:58; Luke 22:55-62; John 18:15-27

14:55-59 Rabbinic[Babylonian Sanhedrin 67a; Jerusalem Sanhedrin vii. 16; Tosephta Sanhedrin x. 11]

14:55-65 Matthew 26:59-68; Luke 22:63-65

14:56 Deuteronomy 17:6, 19:15

14:58 John 2:19-21n; Pseudepigrapha[2Baruch 4:2]; Cyprian[Treatise XII.Book I.15]; Origen[Gospel of John Book X.21; Gospel of Matthew Book XI.9]; Nag Hammadi[Gospel of Thomas 71]

14:60-61 Isaiah 53:7

14:61 NT-Apocrypha[Akhmim Fragment 4.10]

14:62 This section also includes topical notes for: Coming with the Clouds - Psalms 80:17, 110:1; Daniel 7:13; Matthew 26:64; Luke 22:69; 1Thessalonians 4:15-17n; 1Peter 3:22n; Pseudepigrapha[4Ezra 13.1-53; Martyrdom and Ascension of Isaiah 10.15, 11.32; Odes of Solomon 8.6, 18, 18.7, 19.5, 10, 22.7]; Rabbinic[Babylonian Sanhedrin 98a; Jerusalem Taanit 65 cf. {Numbers 23:19}; Yalqut 766 cf. {Numbers 24:23}]; Clement of Alexandria[Fragments from the Latin Translation of Cassiodorus Comments on Jude]; Irenaeus[Against Heresies Book V.30.4]; Justin[Dialogue with Trypho 14, 31; First Apology 52]; Tertullian[Five Books Against Marcion Book III.25]; Nag Hammadi[Apocryphon of James 14; On the Origin of the World 105]; NT-Apocrypha[Epistula Apostolorum 19]; Egyptian Book of the Dead[Oration 174]

14:63 Numbers 14:6; Mark 15:37-38; Rabbinic[Babylonian Sanhedrin 60a]

14:64 Leviticus 24:16; Matthew 26:65n

14:65 Matthew 26:67; Pseudepigrapha[Sibylline Oracles 8.287-289]; Irenaeus[Fragments from the Lost Works 52]; Justin[First Apology 38]; Tertullian[An Answer to the Jews 14]; NT-Apocrypha[Acts of Thomas 1.6; Akhmim Fragment 3.9]

14:66 NT-Apocrypha[Acts of Peter 1.7]

14:66-72 Matthew 26:69-75; Luke 22:55-62; John 18:15-27

14:67 Rabbinic[Babylonian Sanhedrin 107b]

14:72 Matthew 26:34, 75; Mark 13:35, 14:30; Luke 22:34, 61; John 13:38; Philo[Every Good Man Is Free (131-136) cf. {Greek Playwright Ion}]

15:01 Matthew 27:1-2; Luke 22:66-23:1; John 18:28; Nag Hammadi[Letter of Peter to Philip 139]

15:01-05 Tertullian[An Answer to the Jews 13]

15:01-15 Philo[Special Laws IV (69-71) cf. {Deuteronomy 1:16-17}]

15:02 NT-Apocrypha[Acts of Peter 1.8]

15:02-05 Matthew 27:11-14; Luke 23:3-7; John 18:33b-38; NT-Apocrypha[Acts of Pilate III.2]

15:03 Genesis 31:26-28

15:04 NT-Apocrypha[Acts of Paul and Thecla 1.16]

15:04-05 Isaiah 53:7

15:05 Pseudepigrapha[Odes of Solomon 31.10-11]; Justin[Dialogue with Trypho 102-103]; NT-Apocrypha[Akhmim Fragment 4.10]

15:06-14 Matthew 27:15-18, 20-23; Luke 23:13-23; John 18:39-40

15:07 Luke 23:18

15:07-20 Nag Hammadi[Letter of Peter to Philip 139]

15:08 Rabbinic[**Babylonian Sanhedrin 43a**]

A herald precedes him etc. This implies, only immediately before [the execution], but not previous thereto. [In contradiction to this] it was taught: On the eve of the Passover Yeshu was hanged. For forty days before the execution took place, a herald went forth and cried, He is going forth to be stoned because he has practised sorcery and enticed Israel to apostacy. Any one who can say anything in his favour, let him come forward and plead on his behalf. But since nothing was brought forward in his favour he was hanged on the eve of the Passover! Ulla retorted: Do you suppose that he was one for whom a defence could be made? Was he not a Mesith [enticer], concerning whom Scripture says, Neither shalt thou spare, neither shalt thou conceal him? With Yeshu however it was different, for he was connected with the government [or royalty, i.e., influential]. (Talmud - Babylonian Sanhedrin 43a, *The Soncino Talmud*; Judaica Press, Inc. 1973 and Soncino Press, Ltd. 1965, 1967, 1977, 1983, 1984, 1987, 1988, & 1990)

15:08-15 Tertullian[An Answer to the Jews 13]

15:10 Plato[Apology 28a-b]

15:15 Matthew 27:24-26; Luke 23:24-25; John 18:29-19:22; Hebrews 12:6-8n; Pseudepigrapha[Life of Adam and Eve Vita 34.1-3]; Justin[First Apology 38, 50]; NT-Apocrypha[Acts of John 101; Acts of Pilate IV.1-IX.5; Akhmim Fragment 2.5]

15:15-20 NT-Apocrypha[Gospel of the Nazareans Fragment 34]

15:16 Clement of Alexandria[Fragments found in Greek only in the Oxford Edition Last Work on the Passover]

15:16-19 NT-Apocrypha[Acts of Pilate X.1; Questions of Bartholomew IV 62]

15:16-20 Pseudepigrapha[Sibylline Oracles 1.374]; NT-Apocrypha[Akhmim Fragment 3.10]

15:17 Matthew 27:29n; Pseudepigrapha[Sibylline Oracles 8.294]; Clement of Alexandria[The Instructor Book II.8]; NT-Apocrypha[Apocalypse of Paul 1.44]

15:17-19 NT-Apocrypha[Gospel of Mani Turfman Fragment M 132]

15:18-23 Pseudepigrapha[Sibylline Oracles 6.24]

15:19 2Kings 2:11; NT-Apocrypha[Acts of John 97]

15:20-21 Matthew 27:31-32; Luke 23:26-32; John 19:16-17a

15:20-33 Matthew 27:19-31n; Luke 23:33-45n; John 19:17-27

15:21 Romans 16:13; Irenaeus[Against Heresies Book I.24.4]; Origen[Gospel of Matthew Book XII.24]; Tertullian[Against All Heresies 1]

15:22 Pseudepigrapha[Testament of Solomon 12:3]; NT-Apocrypha[Epistula Apostolorum 9]

15:22-33 Luke 23:33-45n; John 19:17b-27; NT-Apocrypha[Acts of Pilate X.1-2; Questions of Bartholomew IV 62]

15:22-41 Matthew 27:33-56n

15:23 Psalms 69:22; Tertullian[Five Books in Reply to Marcion Book V.232]

15:24 Psalms 22:18-19; Pseudepigrapha[Odes of Solomon 31.9]; Irenaeus[Against Heresies Book IV.35.3]; NT-Apocrypha[Akhmim Fragment 4.10-12]

15:24-25 John 19:18n, 23-24n

15:25-45 Philo[**Flaccus (83-85)**]

I have known instances before now of men who had been crucified when this festival and holiday was at hand, being taken down and given up to their relations, in order to receive the honors of sepulture, and to enjoy such observances as are due to the dead; for it used to be considered, that even the dead ought to derive some enjoyment from the natal festival of a good emperor, and also that the sacred character of the festival ought to be regarded. But this man did not order men who had already perished on crosses to be taken down, but he commanded living men to be crucified, men to whom the very time itself gave, if not entire forgiveness, still, at all events, a brief and temporary respite from punishment; and he did this after they had been beaten by scourgings in the middle of the theatre; and after he had tortured them with fire and sword; and the spectacle of their sufferings was divided; for the first part of the exhibition lasted from the morning to the third or fourth hour, in which the Jews were scourged, were hung up, were tortured on the wheel, were condemned, and were dragged to execution through the middle of the orchestra; and after this beautiful exhibition came the dancers, and the buffoons, and the flute-players, and all the other diversions of the theatrical contests. (Philo - Flaccus (83-85)

15:26 NT-Apocrypha[Acts of Paul and Thecla 1.28]

15:27 NT-Apocrypha[Epistula Apostolorum 9; Extracts from the Arabic Infancy Gospel 23]

15:27-28 Isaiah 53:12

15:29 Psalms 22:7-8, 109:25; Lamentations 2:15; Mark 14:58; John 2:19-21n; OT-Apocrypha[Wisdom of Solomon 2:17]; Rabbinic[Babylonian Yoma 39b]

15:31 Matthew 27:19-31n; Pseudepigrapha[Apocalypse of Elijah 5:11]

15:32 Isaiah 41:6-11; Zephaniah 3:15

15:33 Exodus 10:21; Amos 8:9; Pseudepigrapha[Sibylline Oracles 1.374]; Rabbinic[Babylonian Sanhedrin 99a cf. {Isaiah 60:2}]; Tertullian[An Answer to the Jews 13]; Nag Hammadi[Concept of Our Great Power 42]; NT-Apocrypha[Acts of John 97; Akhmim Fragment 5.15, 6.22]

15:33-39 Tertullian[On Fasting 10]

15:34 Psalms 22:1-2; Pseudepigrapha[Testament of Solomon 6:8]; Nag Hammadi[Gospel of Philip 68]; NT-Apocrypha[Akhmim Fragment 5.19]

15:34-37 Matthew 27:46-50; Luke 23:46; John 19:28-30; NT-Apocrypha[Acts of Pilate XI.1]

15:36 Psalms 69:22; Pseudepigrapha[Greek Apocalypse of Ezra 2:25, 7:1]; Irenaeus[Against Heresies Book IV.35.3]

15:37-38 2Kings 2:12; Matthew 27:51; Mark 14:63; Luke 23:45; Rabbinic[Babylonian Moed Qatan 25b; Mishnah Sanhedrin 7:5]; Tertullian[An Answer to the Jews 13]

15:37-39 Tacitus[The Histories 5.13]

15:38 Exodus 26:31-33; Pseudepigrapha[Lives of the Prophets 12:12; Sibylline Oracles 1.375-376, 8.305; Testament of Benjamin 9.3; Testament of Levi 10.3-4]; Nag Hammadi[Gospel of Philip 69, 84-85]; NT-Apocrypha[Akhmim Fragment 5.20; Questions of Bartholomew I 26-27]

15:38-41 Matthew 27:51-56; Luke 23:45b, 47-49

15:38-46 NT-Apocrypha[Acts of Pilate XI.2-3]

15:39 John 3:18n; Pseudepigrapha[Testament of Solomon 15:10]; NT-Apocrypha[Akhmim Fragment 11.45]

15:39-41 Plato[Phaedo 59b-c]

15:41 Luke 8:2-3; NT-Apocrypha[Secret Gospel of Mark Fragment 2]

15:42 Deuteronomy 21:22; Tertullian[On Fasting 14]; NT-Apocrypha[Acts of Peter 1.40]

15:42-46 Matthew 27:57-60; Luke 23:50-54; John 19:38-42; Justin[Dialogue with Trypho 118]

15:42-47 Pseudepigrapha[Life of Adam and Eve Vita 43.4, (Apocalypse of Moses) 40.1-2]

15:43 Genesis 50:4-5; NT-Apocrypha[Akhmim Fragment 2.3]

15:45 Genesis 50:6

15:46 Genesis 46:4, 50:5, 13; NT-Apocrypha[Akhmim Fragment 6.24, 8.33]

15:47 Matthew 27:61; Luke 23:55-56

16:01 NT-Apocrypha[Epistula Apostolorum 9; Gospel of Mani Turfman Fragment M 18; Secret Gospel of Mark Fragment 2]

16:01-02 Rabbinic[**Babylonian Shabbat 151a**]; Dionysius of Alexandria[Extant Fragments Epistle to Bishop Basilides 1]

They wait at the Sabbath limit at twilight to attend to the business of a bride, and the affairs of a corpse, to bring it a coffin and wrappings. (Talmud - Babylonian Shabbat 151a, *The Babylonian Talmud a Translation and Commentary*, Jacob Neusner; Hendrickson Publishers, Inc., 2005)

16:01-04 NT-Apocrypha[Acts of Pilate XIII.1-2]

16:01-08 NT-Apocrypha[Akhmim Fragment 13.57; Gospel of the Nazareans Fragment 26]

16:02 Matthew 28:1; Luke 24:1

16:03 NT-Apocrypha[Akhmim Fragment 10.39, 12.54]

16:03-04 Luke 24:2; John 20:1

16:04 NT-Apocrypha[Epistula Apostolorum 9]

16:05-07 Matthew 28:5-7; Luke 24:3

16:06 Rabbinic[Babylonian Sanhedrin 107b]; NT-Apocrypha[Epistula Apostolorum 10]

16:07 Matthew 26:32; Mark 14:28; NT-Apocrypha[Gospel of Mani Turfman Fragment M 18]

16:08 Matthew 28:8

16:09 John 20:11-17; Constitutions of the Holy Apostles[Book V.14]

16:09-20 NT-Apocrypha[Epistula Apostolorum 30]

16:10 NT-Apocrypha[Akhmim Fragment 7.27]

16:10-11 Luke 24:9-11; John 20:18; NT-Apocrypha[Epistula Apostolorum 9-10]

16:12-13 Luke 24:13-35

16:14 Luke 24:36-49; John 20:19-25; Constitutions of the Holy Apostles[Book V.14]; NT-Apocrypha[Epistula Apostolorum 11]

16:14-18 Matthew 28:16-20; Luke 24:36-49; John 20:19-23

16:15 Genesis 32:3; Matthew 28:19n; Acts 1:8; NT-Apocrypha[Epistula Apostolorum 30]

16:15-16 Tertullian[An Answer to the Jews 5]

16:16 Matthew 3:5-16n; Constitutions of the Holy Apostles[Book VI.15]

16:16-18 NT-Apocrypha[Acts of Pilate XIV.1]

16:17 Justin[Dialogue with Trypho 30]

16:17-18 Acts 3:6n; Constitutions of the Holy Apostles[Book VIII.1]; Cyprian[The Seventh Council of Carthage under Cyprian]; Irenaeus[Against Heresies Book II.20.3]

16:18 Pseudepigrapha[Testament of Joseph 6:2]; Apostolic[Papias Fragment 3:9, 5:1]; Nag Hammadi[A Valentinian Exposition 40]

16:19 2Kings 2:11; Psalms 110:1; Acts 1:9-14; Pseudepigrapha[Testament of Job 33:3]; Irenaeus[Against Heresies Book III.10.5]; Tertullian[Against Praxeas 30; On the Resurrection of the Flesh 51]; NT-Apocrypha[Epistula Apostolorum 3]

16:19-20 Luke 24:50-53; Nag Hammadi[Sophia of Jesus Christ III 119]

Cross Reference Index: Luke

01:01 Clement of Alexandria[Fragments from Eusebius Ecclesiastical History Book VII.6.14]; Irenaeus[Against Heresies Book III.1.1, 11.8]; Tertullian[On Prescription Against Heretics 26]; NT-Apocrypha[**Canon Muratori Line 1-8**]; Nag Hammadi[Gospel of Thomas (Prologue)]

> **At which however he [Luke] was present and so he has set it down. The third Gospel book, that according to Luke. This physician Luke after Christ's ascension (resurrection?), since Paul had taken him with him as an expert in the way (of the teaching), composed it in his own name according to (his) thinking. Yet neither did he himself see the Lord in the flesh; and therefore, as he was able to ascertain it, so he begins to tell the story from the birth of John. (NT Apochrypha - Canon Muratori Line 1-8** *New Testament Apocrypha*, Wilhelm Schneemelcher, ed.; R. McL. Wilson, trans.; Westminster John Knox Press, Volume I, 2003)**

01:02 John 1:1-18n; Irenaeus[Against Heresies Book II.22.5; Fragments from the Lost Works 2]

01:03 NT-Apocrypha[Acts of Paul in Philippi 1.1]

01:05 Exodus 6:23; 1Chronicles 24:10; Nehemiah 12:4, 17; Matthew 2:1n; Pseudepigrapha[Joseph and Aseneth 1:1]; Victorinus[Apocalypse 4.7-10]; NT-Apocrypha[Apocalypse of Paul 1.51; Extract From the Life of John according to Serapion]

01:05-18 NT-Apocrypha[Gospel of the Ebionites Fragment 1]

01:06 Deuteronomy 4:40; Ezekiel 36:37; Pseudepigrapha[2Enoch 9:1; Apocalypse of Zephaniah 3:4]; Irenaeus[Against Heresies Book III.10.1]; Origen[Gospel of Matthew Book XI.10]; Pseud-Irenaeus

01:07 Genesis 18:11, 26:5; Irenaeus[Against Heresies Book I.30.11]

01:08 Irenaeus[Against Heresies Book III.10.1]

01:09 Exodus 30:7

01:09-12 NT-Apocrypha[Genna Marias]

01:10 Daniel 9:21

01:11 Judges 6:12; Lamentations 4:20; Tertullian[On Prayer 16]

01:12 Judges 13:6

01:13 Genesis 17:19; Daniel 10:12; Origen[Gospel of John Book II.24, VI.7; Gospel of Matthew Book XIII.2]; NT-Apocrypha[Protoevangelium of James 4.1-2]

01:13-64 Irenaeus[Fragments from the Lost Works 47]

01:14 Pontianus[Second Epistle]

01:14-17 Pseudepigrapha[Testament of Job 25:1]

01:15 Leviticus 10:9; Numbers 6:2-21; Judges 13:4-5; 1Samuel 1:11; Daniel 2:18; Amos 2:11-12; Romans 12:1n; Philo[Special Laws I (247-272) cf. {Numbers 6:13-21}]; Irenaeus[Against Heresies Book III.10.1]; Origen[Gospel of John Book II.24]; Epic of Gilgamesh[The Coming of Enkidu]

01:15-17 Origen[Gospel of Matthew Book XIII.2]

01:17 Malachi 3:1, 22, 4:5-6; OT-Apocrypha[Sirach 48:10]; Rabbinic[Seder Olam Rabba 17]; Irenaeus[Against Heresies Book III.10.5, 11.4]; Justin[Dialogue with Trypho 49]; Methodius[Oration on the Psalms 2, 4]; Origen[Gospel of John Book II.24, VI.7; Gospel of Matthew Book XIII.2]; Tertullian[On Monogamy 8]

01:18 Genesis 15:8, 17:17, 18:11; Origen[Gospel of John Book VI.10]

01:19 Daniel 8:16, 9:21; OT-Apocrypha[Tobit 12:15]; Pseudepigrapha[Testament of Solomon 18:6]; NT-Apocrypha[Extract From the Life of John according to Serapion]

01:20 Hippolytus[The Discourse on the Holy Theophany 3]; Tertullian[On Idolatry 23]; NT-Apocrypha[Genna Marias]

01:20-22 NT-Apocrypha[Protoevangelium of James 10.2]

01:21 NT-Apocrypha[Protoevangelium of James 24.1]

01:22 Daniel 10:7; Tacitus[The Histories 4.81]; Tertullian[On Idolatry 23]; NT-Apocrypha[Genna Marias]

01:24 NT-Apocrypha[Protoevangelium of James 12.3]

01:25 Genesis 30:23; NT-Apocrypha[Protoevangelium of James 6.2]

01:26 Genesis 24:7; Pseudepigrapha[Sibylline Oracles 8.459]; Irenaeus[Against Heresies Book I.15.3, III.10.2, 14.2, IV.Preface.3]; NT-Apocrypha[Epistula Apostolorum 14; Extract From the Life of John according to Serapion]

01:26-27 This section also includes topical notes for: Virgin Mary - Matthew 1:18-25; Pseudepigrapha[Hellenistic Synagogal Prayers 6.2; Lives of the Prophets 2.8; Testament of Adam 3.3]; Philo[On Flight And Finding (106-114) cf. {Exodus 28:32, Leviticus 10:36, 21:11-14, Numbers 35:2-34}; On Mating With the Preliminary Studies (124-125) cf. {Genesis 38:14-26}; On the Contemplative Life Or Suppliants (68) cf. {Genesis 24:16}; On the Posterity of Cain And His Exile 133-136 cf. {Genesis 24:16}; The Cherubim: Of Cain And His Birth Part 2 (51-52) cf. {Genesis 18:11}; Special Laws I (110) cf. {Leviticus 21:13-14}; On The Unchangeableness of God (136-139) cf. {Genesis 38:11}]; Clement of Alexandria[Fragments from Nicetas Bishop of Heraclea Catena on Matthew 5; Stromata Book VI.15; The Instructor Book I.5]; Gregory Thaumaturgus[Four Homilies 2-3]; Hippolytus[Fragments - On Daniel 2.6; Refutation of all Heresies Book X.29]; Irenaeus[Against Heresies Book I.7.2, 15.3, 26.1, 27.2, 30.11-12, III.5.1, 9.2, 16.2, 18.3, 6, 19.2-3, 21.1, 4-5, 7, 10, 22.1, 4, IV.9.2, 23.2, 33.11, V.1.3, 19.1; Demonstration of the Apostolic Preaching 32-33, 35-37, 40, 53-54, 57, 59, 63; Fragments from the Lost Works 53-54]; Justin[Dialogue with Trypho 23, 43, 45, 48, 50, 57, 63, 66, 71, 76, 84-85, 87, 100-101, 105, 113, 120, 127; First Apology 33; On the Resurrection 3]; Lactantius[Divine Institutes Book IV.12]; Liturgy of James 29; Tertullian[On the Veiling of Virgins 6]; Nag Hammadi[Testimony of Truth 39-40, 45]

01:26-28 Hippolytus[Refutation of all Heresies Book V.46]; Tertullian[On the Flesh of Christ 2]; NT-Apocrypha[Gospel of the Nativity of Mary 9]

01:26-35 Rabbinic[Babylonian Sotah 4a]

01:26-38 Pseudepigrapha[Odes of Solomon 19:10; Testament of Solomon 22:20]

01:27 Genesis 24:16; Pseudepigrapha[Martyrdom and Ascension of Isaiah 11.2]; Origen[Gospel of Matthew Book X.20]; Tertullian[An Answer to the Jews 9]

01:28 Judges 6:12; Peter of Alexandria[Fragments From a Sermon]; NT-Apocrypha[Gospel of Pseudo-Matthew 9; Protoevangelium of James 11.1]

01:28-29 Gregory Thaumaturgus[Four Homilies 1]

01:29 Nag Hammadi[Gospel of Thomas 2]

01:30 Genesis 6:8; Exodus 33:16; Proverbs 12:2

01:30-31 NT-Apocrypha[Protoevangelium of James 11.2-3]

01:30-33 Cyprian[Treatise XII.Book II.11]

01:31 Genesis 16:11; Numbers 27:16-18; Judges 13:3; Isaiah 7:14; Matthew 1:21; Pseudepigrapha[Sibylline Oracles 1.325-329]; Tertullian[On the Flesh of Christ 21]; NT-Apocrypha[Protoevangelium of James 4.2]

01:31-36 Pseudepigrapha[Sibylline Oracles 8.462]

01:32 Romans 1:3; Pseudepigrapha[Testament of Job 25:1]; Irenaeus[Against Heresies Book III.10.2, 16.3]; Justin[First Apology 33]; Origen[Gospel of Matthew Book XIII.26]; NT-Apocrypha[Protoevangelium of James 11.3]

01:32-33 2Samuel 7:12-13, 16; Isaiah 9:6-8; NT-Apocrypha[Gospel of the Nativity of Mary 9]

01:33 Exodus 4:22; Numbers 24:17; Isaiah 9:7-8, 14:1, 29:23, 41:8, 44:1, 5, 21, 45:4, 49:5-6; Daniel 7:14; Micah 4:7; OT-Apocrypha[Baruch 3:35-37]; Pseudepigrapha[Hellenistic Synagogal Prayers 5.8; More Psalms of David 155.21 (5ApocSyrPs 3); Prayer of Joseph Fragment A 1-9; Testament of Benjamin 11.5]; Dead Sea Scrolls[4Q Tanhumin (4Q176[4QTANH]) Fragments 1-2 COL I 9 - COL II 2]; Philo[Concerning Noah's Work As A Planter (43-45) cf. {Genesis 2:7-9, 25:27}; On Dreams That they Are God-Sent (1.175-1.176) cf. {Genesis 28:14}, (1.255-1.256) cf. {Genesis 32:7-30}]; Hippolytus[**Fragments - On Genesis III**]; Irenaeus[Against Heresies Book III.9.2, **IV.21.3**, V.33.3; Demonstration of the Apostolic Preaching 97]; Justin[Dialogue with Trypho 36, 100, 114, 123, 125, 130, 134-135, **Dialogue with Trypho 140**]; Lactantius[Divine Institutes Book IV.13; Epitome of the Divine Institutes 44]; NT-Apocrypha[Acts of Peter and Paul; Gospel of the Hebrews Fragment 2]

She [Rebecca] says to her younger son, "Go to the flock and fetch me two kids," prefiguring the Savior's advent in the flesh to work a mighty deliverance for them who were held liable to the punishment of sin; for indeed in all the Scriptures kids are taken for emblems of sinners. His being charged to bring "two," denotes the reception of two peoples: by the "tender and good," are meant teachable and innocent souls. The robe or raiment of Esau denotes the faith and Scriptures of the Hebrews, with which the people of the Gentiles were endowed. The skins which were put upon his arms are the sins of both peoples, which Christ, when His hands were stretched forth on the cross, fastened to it along with Himself. In that Isaac asks of Jacob why he came so soon, we take him as admiring the quick faith of them that believe. That savory meats are offered, denotes an offering pleasing to God, the salvation of sinners. After the eating follows the blessing, and he delights in his smell. He announces with clear voice the perfection of the resurrection and the kingdom, and also how his brethren who believe in Israel adore him and serve him. Because iniquity is opposed to righteousness, Esau is excited to strife, and meditates death deceitfully, saying in his heart, "Let the days of the mourning for my father come on, and I will slay my brother Jacob." The devil, who previously exhibited the fratricidal Jews by anticipation in Cain, makes the most manifest disclosure of them now in Esau, showing also the time of the murder: "let the days," says he, "of the mourning for my father come on, that I may slay my brother." Wherefore Rebecca - that is, patience - told her husband of the brother's plot: who, summoning Jacob, bade him go to Mesopotamia and thence take a wife of the family of Laban the Syrian, his mother's brother. As therefore Jacob, to escape his brother's evil designs, proceeds to Mesopotamia, so Christ, too, constrained by the unbelief of the Jews, goes into Galilee, to take from thence to Himself a bride from the Gentiles, His Church. (Hippolytus - Fragments - On Genesis III)

If any one, again, will look into Jacob's actions, he shall find them not destitute of meaning, but full of import with regard to the dispensations. Thus, in the first place, at his birth, since he laid hold on his brother's heel, he was called Jacob, that is, the supplanter — one who holds, but is not held; binding the feet, but not being bound; striving and conquering; grasping in his hand his adversary's heel, that is, victory. For to this end was the Lord born, the type of whose birth he set forth beforehand, of whom also John says in the Apocalypse: "He went forth conquering, that He should conquer." In the next place, [Jacob] received the rights of the first-born, when his brother looked on them with contempt; even as also the younger nation received Him, Christ, the first-begotten, when the elder nation rejected Him, saying, "We have no king but Caesar." But in Christ every blessing [is summed up], and therefore the latter people has snatched away the blessings of the former from the Father, just as Jacob took away the blessing of this Esau. For which cause his brother suffered the plots and persecutions of a brother, just as the Church suffers this self-same thing from the Jews. In a foreign country were the twelve tribes born, the race of Israel, inasmuch as Christ was also, in a strange country, to generate the twelve-pillared foundation of the Church. Various colored sheep were allotted to this Jacob as his wages; and the wages of Christ are human beings, who from various and diverse nations come together into one cohort of faith, as the Father promised Him, saying, "Ask of Me, and I will give Thee the heathen for Thine inheritance, the uttermost parts of the earth for Thy possession." And as from the multitude of his sons the prophets of the Lord [afterwards] arose, there was every necessity that Jacob should beget sons from the two sisters, even as Christ did from the two laws of one and the same Father; and in like manner also from the handmaids, indicating that Christ should raise up sons of God, both from freemen and from slaves after the flesh, bestowing upon all, in the same manner, the gift of the Spirit, who vivifies us. But he (Jacob) did all things for the sake of the younger, she who had the handsome eyes, Rachel, who prefigured the Church, for which Christ endured patiently; who at that time, indeed, by means of His patriarchs and prophets, was prefiguring and declaring beforehand future things, fulfilling His part by anticipation in the dispensations of God, and accustoming His inheritance to obey God, and to pass through the world as in a state of pilgrimage, to follow His word, and to indicate beforehand things to come. For with God there is nothing without purpose or due signification. (Irenaeus - Against Heresies Book IV.21.3)

"Hence also Jacob, as I remarked before, being himself a type of Christ, had married the two handmaids of his two free wives, and of them begat sons, for the purpose of indicating beforehand that Christ would receive even all those who amongst Japheth's race are descendandts of Canaan, equally with the free, and would have the children fellow-heirs. (Justin Martyr - Dialogue with Trypho 140)

01:34 Genesis 24:16; NT-Apocrypha[Protoevangelium of James 13.3]

01:34-35 Gregory Thaumaturgus[Twelve Topics on the Faith 4]; Nag Hammadi[Gospel of Philip 71]

01:34-38 Pseudepigrapha[Testament of Isaac 3:17]

01:35 Genesis 1:2-3, 6:4; Exodus 4:22, 40:35; Numbers 11:25; 1Kings 8:10-11; Psalms 2:7; Isaiah 4:3; Matthew 17:1-21, 28:19n; John 1:14, 3:18n; Pseudepigrapha[2Baruch 21.6]; Philo[On The Unchangeableness of God 1.3]; Rabbinic[Targum Jerusalem Exodus 25:20, 37:9, 40:38; Psalms 17:8, 68:14, 91:1, 4, 121:5]; Cyprian[Treatise XII.Book II.10]; Hippolytus[Refutation of all Heresies Book V.30, VII.14; The Discourse on the Holy Theophany 9]; Irenaeus[Against Heresies Book III.21.4, V.1.3]; Justin[Dialogue with Trypho 100; First Apology 33]; Novatian[Treatise Concerning the Trinity 24]; Origen[Gospel of John Book VI.7; Gospel of Matthew Book X.17; De Principiis Book I.3.2, II.6.7]; Peter of Alexandria[Fragments From a Sermon; Fragments On the Godhead]; Tertullian[Against Praxeas 26-27; An Answer to the Jews 13; On the Flesh of Christ 14; The Five

Books Against Marcion Book IV.7]; NT-Apocrypha[Acts of Thomas 1.27; Gospel of the Nativity of Mary 9; Protoevangelium of James 11.3]

01:36 Gregory Thaumaturgus[Four Homilies 3]; Irenaeus[Against Heresies Book I.30.11]; NT-Apocrypha[Extract From the Life of John according to Serapion; Papyrus Cairensis 10 735 Verso; Protoevangelium of James 12.2]

01:37 Genesis 18:14; Pseudepigrapha[2Baruch 54:2]; Tertullian[On Idolatry 12]

01:38 Ruth 3:9; Pseudepigrapha[Odes of Solomon 29:11]; Irenaeus[Against Heresies Book III.22.4]; Justin[Dialogue with Trypho 100]; Tertullian[To his Wife Book II.6]; NT-Apocrypha[Protoevangelium of James 11.3]

01:39 Genesis 24:28; NT-Apocrypha[Extract From the Life of John according to Serapion]

01:39-40 NT-Apocrypha[Protevangelium of James 12.2]

01:41 Genesis 25:22; Irenaeus[Against Heresies Book III.16.4]; NT-Apocrypha[Protoevangelium of James 12.2]

01:41-42 Origen[Gospel of John Book VI.30]

01:41-43 Cyprian[Treatise XII.Book II.8]; Gregory Thaumaturgus[Four Homilies 2]; Tertullian[On the Flesh of Christ 21]

01:41-46 Tertullian[A Treatise on the Soul 26]

01:42 Genesis 24:60; Deuteronomy 28:4; Judges 5:24; OT-Apocrypha[Judith 13:18]; Pseudepigrapha[2Baruch 54:10-11]; Irenaeus[Against Heresies Book III.21.5]; Nag Hammadi[Gospel of Thomas 79]; NT-Apocrypha[Infancy Story of Thomas 19.4; Protoevangelium of James 11.1]

01:42-44 NT-Apocrypha[Protoevangelium of James 12.1-2]

01:42-55 Constitutions of the Holy Apostles[Book VIII.2]

01:43 2Samuel 24:21; Theodotus[Excerpts 50]

01:46 Psalms 34:3, 35:9; Gregory Thaumaturgus[Four Homilies 2]; Irenaeus[Against Heresies Book III.10.2, IV.7.1]; NT-Apocrypha[Protoevangelium of James 5.2]

01:46-55 OT-Apocrypha[Book of Odes 9]

01:46-56 1Samuel 2:1-10

01:47 Isaiah 17:10, 61:10; Habakkuk 3:18

01:48 Genesis 29:32, 30:13; 1Samuel 1:11, 9:16; Psalms 72:17; Malachi 3:12; Pseudepigrapha[Joseph and Aseneth 11:12]; NT-Apocrypha[Falling Asleep of Mary; Protoevangelium of James 6.2, 12.1-2]

01:49 Deuteronomy 10:21; Psalms 45:4, 6, 71:19, 111:9

01:50 Psalms 89:2, 100:5, 103:11, 13, 17

01:51 Psalms 89:11, 118:15; Proverbs 3:34; Gregory Thaumaturgus[Four Homilies 2]

01:52 Job 5:11, 12:19; Ezekiel 21:31; OT-Apocrypha[Sirach 10:14]; Pseudepigrapha[Ahiqar 150; Joseph and Aseneth 6:8; Sibylline Oracles 13.3]; Tertullian[Five Books Against Marcion Book IV.34, V.12]

01:53 1Samuel 2:5; Job 22:9; Psalms 107:9

01:54 Psalms 98:3; Isaiah 41:8; Gregory Thaumaturgus[Four Homilies 2]

01:55 Genesis 17:7, 22:17; 1Samuel 2:1-10; 2Samuel 22:51; Micah 7:20

01:56 NT-Apocrypha[Protoevangelium of James 12.3]

01:57 Nag Hammadi[Testimony of Truth 45]

01:58 Genesis 19:19

01:59 Genesis 17:12; Leviticus 12:3; Pseudepigrapha[Joseph and Aseneth 1:1]

01:59-79 Origen[Gospel of John Book II.27]

01:61 Psalms 18:1

01:62-63 Tertullian[On Idolatry 23]

01:63 Origen[Gospel of Matthew Book XIII.2]

01:64 Daniel 10:16; NT-Apocrypha[Genna Marias; Protoevangelium of James 10.2]

01:65 Origen[Gospel of John Book VI.7]

01:67 Pseud-Irenaeus

01:67-69 Cyprian[Treatise XII.Book II.7]

01:68 Exodus 4:31; Ruth 1:6; 1Kings 1:48; Psalms 41:14, 72:18, 106:48, 111:9; Pseudepigrapha[Sibylline Oracles 8.246]; Irenaeus[Against Heresies Book III.10.2]

01:68-79 1Samuel 2:1-10; OT-Apocrypha[Book of Odes 9]

01:69 2Samuel 22:3; 1Chronicles 17:4, 24; Psalms 18:3, 132:17; Ezekiel 29:21; Pseudepigrapha[2Enoch 35.2; Sibylline Oracles 8.245]; Irenaeus[Against Heresies Book III.16.3]

01:71 2Samuel 22:18; Psalms 18:18, 106:10; Irenaeus[Against Heresies Book IV.20.4]

01:72 Exodus 2:24; Psalms 106:45-46

01:72-73 Genesis 17:7; Leviticus 26:42; Psalms 105:8-9; Micah 7:20

01:73 Genesis 26:3; Jeremiah 11:5

01:73-74 Genesis 22:16-17

01:74 Psalms 97:10; Micah 4:10

01:75 Irenaeus[Against Heresies Book IV.20.4]

01:76 Isaiah 40:3; Malachi 3:1; Irenaeus[Against Heresies Book III.10.2]; Origen[Gospel of John Book VI.8]; Tertullian[On Baptism 6, 10; On Modesty 10]

01:76-77 Peter of Alexandria[Canonical Epistle 5]

01:78 Isaiah 60:1; Jeremiah 23:5; Zechariah 3:8, 6:12; Malachi 4:2; Pseudepigrapha[Testament of Job 40:3; Testament of Solomon 9:6]; Irenaeus[Against Heresies Book III.10.2, V.17.1]

01:78-79 Isaiah 9:2, 58:8, 60:1-2; Tertullian[An Answer to the Jews 6]

01:79 Psalms 107:10, 14; Isaiah 9:1-2, 42:7, 59:8; Methodius[Oration Concerning Simeon and Anna 6, 8]

01:80 Judges 13:24

02:01 Pseudepigrapha[Sibylline Oracles 3.372]; Clement of Alexandria[Stromata Book I.21]; Justin[First Apology 34]; NT-Apocrypha[Protoevangelium of James 17.1]

02:01-02 Josephus[Antiquities 17.6.5 174-181, 18.1.1 1]

02:01-06 NT-Apocrypha[Gospel of Pseudo-Matthew 13]

02:01-07 Matthew 1:18-25; Tertullian[An Answer to the Jews 9; On the Flesh of Christ 2]

02:02 Irenaeus[Against Heresies Book III.21.3]; Justin[First Apology 46]

02:04-07 Gregory Thaumaturgus[Four Homilies 1]

02:04-15 Justin[First Apology 34]

02:06 Genesis 25:24

02:07 Genesis 24:23; Pseudepigrapha[Sibylline Oracles 8.477]; Gregory Thaumaturgus[Four Homilies 2]; Irenaeus[Fragments from the Lost Works 52]; NT-Apocrypha[Epistula Apostolorum 3; Extracts from the Gospel of Pseudo-Matthew 14; Protoevangelium of James 22.2]

02:07-16 Pseudepigrapha[Lives of the Prophets 2:8]

02:08 Pseudepigrapha[Testament of Abraham 10:2]; Irenaeus[Against Heresies Book IV.7.1]; Tertullian[On the Flesh of Christ 2]

02:08-12 NT-Apocrypha[Gospel of Pseudo-Matthew 13]

02:09 NT-Apocrypha[Extracts from the Gospel of Pseudo-Matthew 21; Protoevangelium of James 4.1]

02:10 Gregory Thaumaturgus[Four Homilies 2]

02:10-11 Cyprian[Treatise XII.Book II.8]; Origen[Gospel of John Book I.13]

02:11 Pseudepigrapha[Psalms of Solomon 17:32; Testament of Solomon 17:4]; Irenaeus[Against Heresies Book III.10.3]

02:12 1Samuel 10:1; Isaiah 38:7; Pseudepigrapha[Lives of the Prophets 2.8]; Irenaeus[Fragments from the Lost Works 52]

02:13 1Kings 22:19; Daniel 7:10; Pseudepigrapha[Joseph and Aseneth 14:8]; Tertullian[On the Flesh of Christ 2]

02:14 Genesis 24:25; Psalms 51:20; Isaiah 57:19; OT-Apocrypha[Book of Odes 14]; Pseudepigrapha[2Enoch 35:1; Psalms of Solomon 18:10]; Constitutions of the Holy Apostles[Book VIII.13]; Gregory Thaumaturgus[Twelve Topics on the Faith 12]; Methodius[Oration Concerning Simeon and Anna 5]

02:15 Pseudepigrapha[Joseph and Aseneth 17:1]

02:15-18 Irenaeus[Against Heresies Book III.16.4]

02:16 Irenaeus[Fragments from the Lost Works 52]

02:19 Genesis 37:11; Daniel 7:28; Pseudepigrapha[Life of Adam and Eve (Apocalypse of Moses) 3:3]; NT-Apocrypha[Gospel of Pseudo-Matthew 33; Infancy Story of Thomas 11.2]

02:20 Irenaeus[Against Heresies Book III.10.3]; NT-Apocrypha[Protoevangelium of James 19.2]

02:21 Genesis 17:12; Leviticus 12:3; Luke 1:31; Pseudepigrapha[Sibylline Oracles 1.325-329]; Nag Hammadi[Gospel of Thomas 4]

02:21-38 NT-Apocrypha[Gospel of Pseudo-Matthew 15]

02:22 Leviticus 12:2-4, 6; Irenaeus[Against Heresies Book III.10.4]; Methodius[Oration Concerning Simeon and Anna 4]

02:22-24 Philo[Special Laws I (162) cf. {Leviticus 1:14}]

02:22-35 Tertullian[On the Flesh of Christ 2]

02:22-39 NT-Apocrypha[Acts of Pilate IX.3]

02:23 Exodus 13:2, 12, 15; Irenaeus[Against Heresies Book I.3.4]; Tertullian[On the Flesh of Christ 23]; NT-Apocrypha[Acts of Thomas 1.79; Arabic Gospel of the Infancy of the Savior 5]

02:24 Leviticus 5:11, 12:6-8; Clement of Alexandria[The Instructor Book I.5]

02:25 Isaiah 40:1, 49:13, 52:9; Jeremiah 17:7; Pseudepigrapha[2Baruch 44:8; Joseph and Aseneth 4:7];
  Hippolytus[Fragments - On Genesis 46.5]; NT-Apocrypha[Extract From the Life of John according
  to Serapion; Protoevangelium of James 24.4]

02:25-33 Tertullian[An Answer to the Jews 12]

02:25-38 NT-Apocrypha[Arabic Gospel of the Infancy of the Savior 6]

02:26 Psalms 89:49; NT-Apocrypha[Protevangelium of James 24]

02:28 Irenaeus[Against Heresies Book I.8.4]

02:28-32 Acts 3:18-26n

02:28-35 NT-Apocrypha[Acts of Pilate XVI.2]

02:29 Genesis 15:15, 46:30; OT-Apocrypha[Tobit 11:9]; Cyprian[Treatise VII.3]; Irenaeus[Against
  Heresies Book III.10.4, 16.4, IV.7.1]; Methodius[Oration on the Psalms 5]

02:29-30 Cyprian[Treatise XII.Book III.58]; Origen[Gospel of John Book X.27]

02:29-32 OT-Apocrypha[Book of Odes 13]; Methodius[Oration Concerning Simeon and Anna 8]

02:30 Job 19:27, 42:5; Psalms 67:3, 98:2; Isaiah 42:6

02:30-31 Isaiah 40:5, 52:10

02:32 Exodus 13:15; Isaiah 42:6, 46:13, 49:6, 9; Pseudepigrapha[1Enoch 48:4]; Methodius[Oration
  Concerning Simeon and Anna 12]; NT-Apocrypha[Protoevangelium of James 19.2]

02:34 Isaiah 8:14; Daniel 11:41; Hippolytus[Fragments - On Genesis 49.16-20]; Tertullian[On the Flesh
  of Christ 23]; NT-Apocrypha[Acts of Pilate XVI.7; Protoevangelium of James 17.2]

02:35 Rabbinic[Babylonian Hagigah 4b]

02:36 Constitutions of the Holy Apostles[Book III.1]; Irenaeus[Against Heresies Book I.8.4]

02:36-38 Constitutions of the Holy Apostles[Book VIII.2]; Tertullian[On Fasting 8; On the Flesh of
  Christ 2]

02:37 OT-Apocrypha[Judith 8:6]; Cyprian[Treatise IV.36]

02:38 Isaiah 52:9; Acts 3:18-26n; Irenaeus[Against Heresies Book III.10.4]; Methodius[Oration
  Concerning Simeon and Anna 11]

02:39 Matthew 2:23; Pseudepigrapha[Martyrdom and Ascension of Isaiah 11.15]

02:40 Pseudepigrapha[Joseph and Aseneth 4:7]; NT-Apocrypha[Epistula Apostolorum 3;
  Protoevangelium of James 6.1]

02:41 Exodus 12:1-27, 23:14-17; Deuteronomy 16:1-8, 16; Rabbinic[Babylonian Kallah 51a]

02:41-49 Philo[On the Migration of Abraham (139-142) cf. {Genesis 21:7}]

02:41-52 Pseudepigrapha[2Enoch 71:18]; NT-Apocrypha[Infancy Story of Thomas 19.3]

02:42 Josephus[Life 1.2 8]; Irenaeus[Against Heresies Book I.3.2]

02:42-47 NT-Apocrypha[Arabic Gospel of the Infancy of the Savior 50]

02:43 Exodus 12:15, 18

02:46 NT-Apocrypha[Acts of Thomas 1.79]

02:46-52 NT-Apocrypha[Arabic Gospel of the Infancy of the Savior 53]

02:49 Genesis 28:17; John 14:2n; Irenaeus[Against Heresies Book I.20.2]; Tertullian[Against Praxeas 26]

02:51 Pseudepigrapha[Life of Adam and Eve (Apocalypse of Moses) 3:3]; Constitutions of the Holy
  Apostles[Book VI.23]; NT-Apocrypha[Infancy Story of Thomas 11.2, 19.5]

02:52 1Samuel 2:21, 26; Proverbs 3:3-4; Pseudepigrapha[Joseph and Aseneth 4:7]; Origen[Gospel of
  Matthew Book XIII.26]; Tertullian[On Modesty 1]

03:01 Josephus[Antiquities 17.6.5-6 174-181, 17.11.4 318, 18.1.1 1, 18.2.2 35, 20.7.1 137-138; War 2.6.3 93-
  99, 2.12.8 247]; Irenaeus[Against Heresies Book I.27.2]; Tertullian[Five Books Against Marcion Book
  IV.7]

03:01-02 Clement of Alexandria[Stromata Book I.21]

03:01-06 Pseudepigrapha[Sibylline Oracles 1.336]

03:01-18 Matthew 3:1-17n; Mark 1:1-11; John 1:19-28; Acts 3:19n

03:01-22 Pseudepigrapha[Sibylline Oracles 1.336-341]

03:02 Jeremiah 1:1; Josephus[Antiquities 18.2.2 35]; Origen[Gospel of John Book VI.14]

03:02-03 NT-Apocrypha[Gospel of the Ebionites Fragment 1]

03:02-04 Epic of Gilgamesh[The Coming of Enkidu]

03:02-15 Josephus[Antiquities 18.5.2 116-119]

03:03 Mark 6:17-29; Matthew 14:1-12; Pseudepigrapha[Sibylline Oracles 4.165]; Josephus[Antiquities
  18.5.2 116-119, 18.5.4 136]; NT-Apocrypha[Gospel of the Nazareans Fragment 2]

03:04 Gregory Thaumaturgus[Four Homilies 4]; Origen[Gospel of John Book VI.10]

03:04-05 Tertullian[Five Books Against Marcion Book V.3]

03:04-06 Isaiah 40:3-5; Tertullian[On Repentance 2]

03:05 Pseudepigrapha[Psalms of Solomon 11.4]

03:06 Psalms 67:3, 98:3; Isaiah 40:3-5

03:07 Matthew 12:34, 23:33-35n; Pseudepigrapha[Sibylline Oracles 8.1]

03:07-08 Clement of Alexandria[Exhortation to the Heathen 1]

03:07-21 Matthew 3:5-16n

03:08 John 8:33; Rabbinic[Avot 5.22]; Irenaeus[Against Heresies Book V.32.2]; Tertullian[On Modesty 10, 20]; Linguistics[The Hebrew word for "Stones" (אבן) is a pun for "Children" (בן)]

03:08-09 Matthew 7:16-21n

03:09 Clement of Alexandria[Who is the Rich Man that shall be Saved 29]; Hippolytus[Refutation of all Heresies Book V.3, 11]; Origen[Gospel of John Book VI.14]; Nag Hammadi[Gospel of Thomas 40]; NT-Apocrypha[6Ezra 17.78]; Epic of Gilgamesh[The Forest Journey]

03:11 Irenaeus[Against Heresies Book IV.30.3]; Tertullian[Of Patience 7]

03:12 Luke 7:29; Tertullian[On Modesty 10]

03:12-13 Tertullian[On Idolatry 19]

03:13 Constitutions of the Holy Apostles[Book II.39]

03:14 Constitutions of the Holy Apostles[Book VIII.32]; Hippolytus[Appendix to the Works of Hippolytus - On the End of the World 38]; Origen[Gospel of John Book VI.30]; Tertullian[On Modesty 10]

03:15 Origen[Gospel of John Book VI.8]

03:16 Anonymous[Treatise on Re-Baptism 19]; Clement of Alexandria[Stromata Book V.8; The Instructor Book II.12]; Gregory Thaumaturgus[Four Homilies 4]; Origen[Gospel of John Book VI.16]; Epic of Gilgamesh[The Coming of Enkidu]

03:16-17 Matthew 3:11-12n

03:17 Apostolic[1Clement 56:15]; Clement of Alexandria[The Instructor Book I.9]; Hippolytus[Refutation of all Heresies Book V.4]; Irenaeus[Against Heresies Book I.3.5, IV.33.1]; NT-Apocrypha[Epistula Apostolorum 28, 49]

03:19 Matthew 14:1-12; Mark 6:17-29; Josephus[Antiquities 18.5.2 116-119, 18.5.4 136]

03:20 Matthew 14:3-4; Mark 6:17-18

03:21 Genesis 32:10; Ezekiel 1:1; NT-Apocrypha[Arabic Gospel of the Infancy of the Savior 54; Gospel of the Ebionites Fragment 3]

03:21-22 Matthew 3:1-17n; Mark 1:1-11; John 1:19-28; Pseudepigrapha[Sibylline Oracles 6.4]; Tertullian[Against All Heresies 5]

03:22 Genesis 22:2; Psalms 2:7; Isaiah 42:1, 44:21, 62:4; Jeremiah 31:20; Matthew 3:16n, 12:8, 17:5; Mark 9:7; Luke 9:35; John 1:32; Pseudepigrapha[4Ezra 2.15-18; Psalms of Solomon 17.37]; Tacitus[The Histories 5.13]; Clement of Alexandria[Fragments Edited by Corderius Catena on Luke; Fragments from Macarius Chrysocephalus Oration VIII on Matt VIII and Book VII on Luke XIII]; Justin[Dialogue with Trypho 8]; Tertullian[On Baptism 8]; NT-Apocrypha[Gospel of the Hebrews Fragment 2]

03:23 Genesis 41:46; Pseudepigrapha[2Enoch 67:1; 3Enoch 45:5]; Dead Sea Scrolls[Rule of the Congregation (1Q28a[1QSa]) COL I 13-18]; Clement of Alexandria[Stromata Book I.21, VI.11]; Irenaeus[Against Heresies Book I.1.3, 3.1, 25.1, II.12.1, 8, 22.1, 3-5]; Justin[Dialogue with Trypho 88]; NT-Apocrypha[Acts of Thomas 1.143; Gospel of the Ebionites Fragment 3-4]

03:23-38 Matthew 1:1-17; Irenaeus[Against Heresies Book I.27.2, III.22.4]; Justin[Dialogue with Trypho 100]

03:23-04:13 Plato[Republic VII 537d-e]

03:27 1Chronicles 3:17, 19; Ezra 3:2, 5:2

03:31 2Samuel 5:14; 1Chronicles 3:5, 14:4

03:31-32 1Samuel 16:1, 13

03:31-34 1Chronicles 2:1-15

03:32 Ruth 4:18-22

03:33 Genesis 29:35, 38:29; Ruth 4:12

03:34 Genesis 21:2-3, 25:26; 1Chronicles 1:34

03:34-36 Genesis 11:10-26; 1Chronicles 1:24-28

03:36 Pseudepigrapha[Jubilees 8:2]

03:36-38 Genesis 4:25-5:32; 1Chronicles 1:1-4

03:37 Dead Sea Scrolls[11Q Jubilees (11Q12[QJUB]) Fragment 2 1-4]

03:38 Genesis 2:7

04:01-03 Tertullian[On Fasting 8]

04:01-13 This section also includes topical notes for: Temptation on the Mountain - Matthew 4:1-11; Mark 1:12-13; Pseudepigrapha[Life of Adam and Eve Vita 6.2-3, 39.1-3]; Philo[Concerning Noah's Work As A Planter (19-22) cf. {Genesis 1:26-27}; On Rewards And Punishments (17-21) cf. {Genesis 5:24}]; Clement of Alexandria[Stromata Book II.5]; Clement[Homily VIII.21]; Constitutions of the Holy Apostles[Book VII.22]; Irenaeus[Against Heresies Book III.22.2, V.21.2; Fragments from the Lost Works 54]; Justin[Dialogue with Trypho 103, 125]; Nag Hammadi[Authoritative Teaching 29]; Epic of Gilgamesh[The Forest Journey]

04:02 NT-Apocrypha[Protoevangelium of James 2.4]

04:03 Irenaeus[Against Heresies Book IV.6.6]

04:03-09 John 3:18n

04:04 Deuteronomy 8:3; Matthew 4:4; Tertullian[On Fasting 6]

04:06 Irenaeus[Against Heresies Book V.22.2, 24.1, 3]

04:06-07 Irenaeus[Against Heresies Book V.21.2]

04:08 Deuteronomy 6:13, 10:20; Pseudepigrapha[Testament of Job 26:3]; Clement[Homily X.5; Recognitions Book IV.34]; Irenaeus[Against Heresies Book V.22.2]; Tertullian[On Prayer 8]

04:09 Ezekiel 8:3; NT-Apocrypha[Gospel of the Nazareans Fragment 3]

04:10-11 Psalms 91:11-12

04:11 Matthew 4:6n

04:11-15 Matthew 13:18-23; Mark 4:13-20

04:12 Deuteronomy 6:16; Isaiah 7:12

04:13 Pseudepigrapha[Life of Adam and Eve Vita 17:2]

04:13-16 Origen[Gospel of John Book X.1]

04:14-15 Matthew 4:12-17; Mark 1:14-15; John 4:43-45

04:14-18 Tertullian[An Answer to the Jews 12]

04:15 Matthew 9:35n

04:16 NT-Apocrypha[Infancy Story of Thomas 15.2]

04:16-30 Tertullian[Five Books Against Marcion Book IV.8]

04:16-32 Matthew 13:53-58; Mark 6:1-6

04:18 Matthew 11:5n; Clement of Alexandria[Exhortation to the Heathen 12]; Hippolytus[Fragments - On Daniel 2.17]; Irenaeus[Against Heresies Book IV.23.1]; Justin[Dialogue with Trypho 12]; Origen[Gospel of John Book I.11]; Tertullian[Against Praxeas 11]

04:18-19 Isaiah 58:6, 61:1-2; Peter of Alexandria[Canonical Epistle 2]

04:21 Josephus[War 2.8.12 159]; Origen[Gospel of John Book X.1]

04:22 Irenaeus[Against Heresies Book I.25.1]; Tertullian[An Answer to the Jews 10]; NT-Apocrypha[Infancy Story of Thomas 15.2]

04:23 Matthew 13:3-53n

04:24 Matthew 13:57; John 4:44; Constitutions of the Holy Apostles[Book II.58]; Nag Hammadi[Gospel of Thomas 31]

04:25 1Kings 17:1, 7, 18:1; Pseudepigrapha[Apocalypse of Elijah 3:1]

04:26 1Kings 17:8-16

04:27 2Kings 5:1-14; Tertullian[Five Books Against Marcion Book IV.9]

04:30 Genesis 31:7

04:31 Matthew 4:13-17, 9:35n; Mark 1:15; NT-Apocrypha[Gospel of the Ebionites Fragment 4]

04:31-34 Tertullian[Five Books Against Marcion Book IV.7]

04:31-37 Mark 1:21-28

04:32 Pseudepigrapha[Psalms of Solomon 17.43]; Tertullian[Five Books Against Marcion Book IV.13]

04:32-36 Matthew 7:28-29n

04:34 Judges 16:17; 1Kings 17:18; Archelaus[Disputation with Manes 48]; Tertullian[Five Books Against Marcion Book V.6]

04:35 Pseudepigrapha[Life of Adam and Eve Vita 39.1-3]

04:38 NT-Apocrypha[Gospel of the Ebionites Fragment 4]

04:38-43 Matthew 8:14-17; Mark 1:29-38

04:39 Pseudepigrapha[2Baruch 21:6]

04:40 Matthew 4:23-24n

04:40-41 Matthew 8:16-17; Mark 1:32-34

04:40-43 Tertullian[Five Books Against Marcion Book IV.8]

04:41 John 3:18n; Pseudepigrapha[Testament of Solomon 1:12]

04:42-44 Mark 1:35-39

04:44 Matthew 4:23-25; Mark 1:39

05:01-09 Egyptian Book of the Dead[Oration 153A-B]

05:01-11 This section also includes topical notes for: The Fishermen - Jeremiah 16:16; Ezekiel 47:10; Habbakuk 1:12-15; Matthew 4:18-22; Mark 1:16-20; Dead Sea Scrolls[1Q Hymns (1QHODAYOTH [1QH]) COL XIII 8-9; 4Q429(4QHADAYOT[4QH]) Fragment 1 COL I 1-3]

05:01-14 Tertullian[Five Books Against Marcion Book IV.9]

05:01-39 Irenaeus[Against Heresies Book III.14.3]

05:03 Matthew 9:35n, 13:1-2; Mark 3:9-10

05:03-09 This section also includes topical notes for: Let Down Your Nets - Ezekiel 47:6-10; John 21:6-8; Dead Sea Scrolls[1Q Habakkuk Pesher (1QHAB) COL I 12-14; Damascus Document (CD-A) COL IV 15-18]; Philo[On Husbandry (23-25) cf. {Genesis 4:2, 9:20}; On the Life of Moses II (250) cf. {Genesis 14:13-14}]

05:04-08 Pseudepigrapha[Testament of Zebulon 6.6-7]

05:04-09 Egyptian Book of the Dead[Oration 113]

05:05 John 21:3

05:06 John 21:6

05:08 Origen[Against Celsus Book I.63]

05:10-11 Tertullian[On Idolatry 12]

05:11 NT-Apocrypha[Abgar Legend]

05:12 NT-Apocrypha[Epistula Apostolorum 5]

05:12-14 NT-Apocrypha[Papyrus Egerton 2 Fragment 1 Lines 22-41]

05:12-16 Matthew 8:1-4; Mark 1:40-45

05:14 Leviticus 13:49, 14:2-32

05:15-17 Matthew 4:23-24n

05:16 Cyprian[Treatise IV.29]

05:16-26 Tertullian[Five Books Against Marcion Book IV.10]

05:17 Matthew 9:35n; Hippolytus[Refutation of all Heresies Book IX.23]

05:17-26 Matthew 9:1-8; Mark 2:1-12

05:20 Constitutions of the Holy Apostles[Book II.20]; Irenaeus[Against Heresies Book V.17.1]

05:21 Isaiah 43:25, 55:7; Tertullian[On Modesty 9, 21]

05:24 Psalms 80:17, Matthew 7:28-29n, 9:6n; Acts 26:18n

05:27-29 Clement of Alexandria[Who is the Rich Man that shall be Saved 13]

05:27-32 Matthew 9:9-13n; Mark 2:13-17

05:28 Genesis 31:14; NT-Apocrypha[Abgar Legend]

05:29 Tertullian[On Idolatry 12]

05:29-30 Tertullian[On Modesty 9]

05:30 Genesis 38:28, 42:32, 47:13-26; Luke 15:1-2; Hippolytus[Refutation of all Heresies Book IX.23]

05:31 Tertullian[On the Resurrection of the Flesh 9; Five Books Against Marcion Book IV.11]

05:31-32 Irenaeus[Against Heresies Book III.5.2]

05:32 Rabbinic[Babylonian Sanhedrin 99a cf. {Isaiah 57:19}]

05:33-35 Tertullian[On Fasting 2]

05:33-39 Matthew 9:14-17; Mark 2:18-22

05:34-35 John 3:29n; Tertullian[Five Books Against Marcion Book IV.11]

05:35 Constitutions of the Holy Apostles[Book V.18]

05:36 Matthew 9:16, 13:3-53n; Mark 2:21n

05:36-37 Irenaeus[Against Heresies Book IV.35.2]

05:36-39 Nag Hammadi[Gospel of Thomas 47]

05:37 Job 32:19

05:39 Matthew 9:17n

06:01 Deuteronomy 23:25-26; Matthew 12:1n; Philo[On Dreams, That they Are God-Sent (2.71-2.74) cf. {Leviticus 2:1}; Special Laws I (245-246) cf. {Leviticus 6:9-11, 9:7-14}]; Archelaus[Disputation with Manes 40]

06:01-05 Matthew 12:1-8; Mark 2:23-28

06:01-14 Tertullian[Five Books Against Marcion Book IV.12]

06:02 Hippolytus[Refutation of all Heresies Book IX.23]

06:03-04 1Samuel 21:1-7; Irenaeus[Against Heresies Book IV.8.3]

06:04 Leviticus 24:5-9

06:05 Psalms 80:17; Novatian[Treatise Concerning the Trinity 11]

06:06 Matthew 9:35n

06:06-10 Matthew 12:9-14; Mark 3:1-5

06:07 Rabbinic[Babylonian Shabbat 147b]; Hippolytus[Refutation of all Heresies Book IX.23]

06:11 Matthew 12:14-21; Mark 3:6-12

06:12 OT-Apocrypha[4Maccabees 3:13-19]; Cyprian[Epistle VII.5; Treatise IV.29]

06:12-16 Genesis 35:22-26; Matthew 10:1-4; Mark 3:13-19

06:12-19 Tertullian[Five Books Against Marcion Book IV.13]

06:13 Irenaeus[Against Heresies Book I.3.2]; NT-Apocrypha[Gospel of the Ebionites Fragment 4; Kerygma Petri 3b]

06:14-16 NT-Apocrypha[Acts of Thomas 1.1]

06:15-16 Hippolytus[**Refutation of all Heresies Book IX.21**]

> **But the adherents of another party [of Esseni], if they happen to hear any one maintaining a discussion concerning God and His laws - supposing such to be an uncircumcised person, they will closely watch him and when they meet a person of this description in any place alone, they will threaten to slay him if he refuses to undergo the rite of circumcision. Now, if the latter does not wish to comply with this request, an Essene spares not, but even slaughters. And it is from this occurrence that they have received their appellation, being denominated (by some) Zelotae, but by others Sicarii. (Hippolytus - Refutation of all Heresies Book IX.21)**

06:17-19 Matthew 4:23-24n

06:20 Isaiah 61:1; Matthew 11:5n; Apostolic[Polycarp - Letter to the Philippians 2:3]; Clement[Recognitions Book I.61]; Tertullian[To his Wife Book II.6]; Nag Hammadi[Gospel of Thomas 54]

06:20-22 Tertullian[On Idolatry 12; Five Books Against Marcion Book IV.14]

06:20-26 Deuteronomy 27:15-28:9; Matthew 5:1-12; Nag Hammadi[Book of Thomas the Contender 144-145]

06:20-38 Clement of Alexandria[Stromata Book II.18]

06:21 Psalms 126:5-6; Isaiah 61:2, 65:18; Jeremiah 31:25; Rabbinic[Babylonian Sanhedrin 100a cf. {Psalms 36:9}]

06:22 Psalms 80:17; 1Peter 4:14; Clement of Alexandria[Stromata Book IV.6]; Cyprian[Treatise III.12]

06:22-23 Constitutions of the Holy Apostles[Book V.2]; Cyprian[Epistle LV.2; Treatise XI.12, XII.Book III.16]; Tertullian[Of Patience 8]

06:22-27 NT-Apocrypha[Epistula Apostolorum 38]

06:23 2Chronicles 36:16; Acts 7:52; Origen[Gospel of Matthew Book X.18]; Tertullian[Scorpiace 9]; NT-Apocrypha[Epistula Apostolorum 42]

06:24 Pseudepigrapha[1Enoch 94:8]; Irenaeus[Against Heresies Book III.14.3]; Nag Hammadi[Gospel of Thomas 54]; NT-Apocrypha[Epistula Apostolorum 46]

06:24-26 Dead Sea Scrolls[4Q Psalms Pesher (4Q171[4QPPS]) COL III 9-11]; Tertullian[Five Books Against Marcion Book IV.15]

06:25 Isaiah 5:22, 65:13; Dionysius of Alexandria[Exegetical Fragments Commentary on the Beginning of Ecclesiastes 3.4]; Tertullian[On Fasting 15]

06:26 Jeremiah 5:31; Micah 2:11

06:27 Psalms 25:21; Apostolic[Polycarp - Letter to the Philippians 12:3]; Tertullian[A Treatise on the Soul 35]; NT-Apocrypha[Oxyrhynchus Papyrus 1224 p.176; Pseudo Clementines - Kerygmata Petrou H XI 32.1]

06:27-28 Matthew 5:44n; Athenagoras[Plea for the Christians 11]; Tertullian[Five Books Against Marcion Book IV.16]

06:27-29 Clement of Alexandria[The Instructor Book III.12]

06:27-35 Apostolic[Didache 1:3]

06:28 Constitutions of the Holy Apostles[Book I.2]; Justin[First Apology 15]; Lactantius[Divine Institutes Book VI.18]; Tertullian[Five Books Against Marcion Book IV.27]

06:29 Matthew 5:39n; Archelaus[Disputation with Manes 40]; Justin[First Apology 16]; Tertullian[Of Patience 7; Five Books Against Marcion Book IV.16]

06:29-30 Apostolic[Didache 1:4]; Constitutions of the Holy Apostles[Book VII.2]; Teaching of the Twelve Apostles 1.4

06:29-31 Irenaeus[Against Heresies Book IV.13.3]

06:30 Pseudepigrapha[Pseudo-Phocylides 1.22-23]; Apostolic[Didache 1:5]; Clement of
  Alexandria[Stromata Book III.4; Who is the Rich Man that shall be Saved 31]; Constitutions of the
  Holy Apostles[Book III.4]; Fabian[Second Epistle]; Justin[First Apology 15]; Teaching of the Twelve
  Apostles 1.5; Tertullian[On Baptism 18; On Monogamy 11; Five Books Against Marcion Book IV.16]
06:30-36 Nag Hammadi[Gospel of Thomas 95]
06:31 Matthew 7:12; Apostolic[1Clement 13:2; Didache 1:2]; Clement of Alexandria[The Instructor
  Book III.12]; Tertullian[Scorpiace 10; Five Books Against Marcion Book IV.16]; NT-
  Apocrypha[Clement Romance - Peter on his Mission Journeys H VII 4.3]
06:31-32 Teaching of the Twelve Apostles 1.3
06:32 Constitutions of the Holy Apostles[Book VII.2]; Cyprian[Treatise XII.Book III.49]
06:32-34 Athenagoras[Plea for the Christians 12]; Lactantius[Divine Institutes Book VI.11]
06:32-35 Pseudepigrapha[Pseudo-Phocylides 152]; Apostolic[2Clement 13:4]
06:33 Leviticus 25:35
06:34 Justin[First Apology 15]; Tertullian[Five Books Against Marcion Book IV.17]; NT-
  Apocrypha[Pseudo Clementines - Kerygmata Petrou H XI 32.1]
06:34-35 This section also includes topical notes for: Lending Without Usury - Matthew 5:44n;
  Philo[Special Laws II (74-78, 122) cf. {Exodus 22:25}]; Rabbinic[Babylonian Baba Mesia 60b-61a, 75b];
  Clement of Alexandria[Stromata Book II.18]
06:35 Leviticus 25:35-36; Psalms 25:8, 86:5; OT-Apocrypha[Wisdom of Solomon 15:1];
  Rabbinic[Babylonian Sanhedrin 100a cf. {Isaiah 40:12}]; Mishnah Aboth 1:11-13];
  Hippolytus[Refutation of all Heresies Book V.2]; Justin[Dialogue with Trypho 96]; Tertullian[On
  Modesty 10; Five Books Against Marcion Book IV.17]
06:35-36 Clement of Alexandria[The Instructor Book I.8]
06:36 Clement of Alexandria[Stromata Book II.19]; Clement[Recognitions Book V.13]; Cyprian[Epistle
  LI.16]; Justin[First Apology 15]; Origen[De Principiis Book IV.1.37]; Tertullian[On Modesty 2; Five
  Books Against Marcion Book IV.17]
06:36-38 Apostolic[1Clement 13:2; Polycarp - Letter to the Philippians 2:3]
06:37 Rabbinic[Babylonian Sanhedrin 18a-19b]; Constitutions of the Holy Apostles[Book II.36, 42];
  Cyprian[Treatise XII.Book III.21]; Tertullian[Of Patience 10, 12; On Modesty 2; On Prayer 7]
06:37-38 Clement of Alexandria[Who is the Rich Man that shall be Saved 33]; Constitutions of the
  Holy Apostles[Book II.21]; Tertullian[Five Books Against Marcion Book IV.17]
06:37-42 Matthew 7:1-5
06:38 Pseudepigrapha[2Enoch 44:4, 50:5; Pseudo-Phocylides 12]; Apostolic[Didache 1:3];
  Clement[Homily XVIII.16]
06:39 Matthew 13:3-53n; 15:14, 24; Tertullian[On the Resurrection of the Flesh 33; Five Books Against
  Marcion Book IV.17]; NT-Apocrypha[Epistula Apostolorum 47]
06:40 Matthew 10:24-25; John 13:16, 15:20; Constitutions of the Holy Apostles[Book V.6];
  Irenaeus[Against Heresies Book V.31.2]; Tertullian[Against All Heresies 3; On Prescription Against
  Heretics 34; Five Books Against Marcion Book IV.17]; Nag Hammadi[Dialogue of the Savior 53;
  Gospel of Thomas 108]
06:41 Pseudepigrapha[Joseph and Aseneth 11:19]; Constitutions of the Holy Apostles[Book II.17]
06:41-42 Rabbinic[**Babylonian Arakhin 16b**]; Hippolytus[Refutation of all Heresies Book VIII.1]; Nag
  Hammadi[Gospel of Thomas 26]; Indian[Dhammapada 50]

**Said R. Tarfon, "I should be surprised if there is anyone left in this generation who
accepts rebuke. If one says to someone, 'Remove the chip from your eye,' the other party
responds, 'Take the beam from your eye'!" (Talmud - Babylonian Arakhin 16b, *The
Babylonian Talmud a Translation and Commentary*, Jacob Neusner; Hendrickson
Publishers, Inc., 2005)**

06:41-46 Tertullian[Five Books Against Marcion Book IV.17]
06:42 Matthew 6:2-16n; Origen[De Principiis Book I.2.7]
06:43 Clement of Alexandria[The Instructor Book II.5]; Tertullian[Five Books Against Marcion Book
  I.2]; Nag Hammadi[Apocalypse of Peter 75]
06:43-44 Matthew 7:16-21n; Tertullian[A Treatise on the Soul 21]
06:43-49 This section also includes topical notes for: Great is the Fall - Matthew 7:24-27;
  Philo[Fragments Extracted From the Parallels of John of Damascus Page 343. D., Page 784. C. cf.
  {Genesis 28:12}]
06:44 Matthew 12:33; Nag Hammadi[Apocalypse of Peter 76]

06:45 This section also includes topical notes for: Treasures of the Heart - Matthew 6:21, 12:34-35; Luke 12:34; Romans 2:5; Philo[On Flight And Finding (79-80) cf. {Leviticus 35:16-21}]

06:46 Malachi 1:6; Clement of Alexandria[Stromata Book IV.7, VII.16, 18; Who is the Rich Man that shall be Saved 29]; Clement[Homily VIII.7; Recognitions Book IV.5]; Irenaeus[Against Heresies Book IV.37.3, V.8.4, 9.3-4, 12.3, 13.2, 5, 14.1, 4]; NT-Apocrypha[Clement Romance - Peter on his Mission Journeys H VIII 7.4; Papyrus Egerton 2 Fragment 2 Lines 43-59]

06:48-49 This section also includes topical notes for: Foundation upon the Rock - Psalms 89:14, 97:2; Proverbs 10:25; Matthew 7:24-27; Ephesians 2:20-22; Hebrews 11:10; Pseudepigrapha[Ahiqar 2.75; Joseph and Aseneth 22.13; Odes of Solomon 35.4, 38.17]; Dead Sea Scrolls[1Q Hymns (1QHODAYOTH [1QH]) COL XV 8-9]; Philo[On Dreams, That they Are God-Sent (2.8) cf. {Genesis 37:5-11}; On the Change of Names (211-212) cf. {Deuteronomy 33:6}; The Cherubim: Of Cain And His Birth Part 2 (101-104)]; Rabbinic[Avot 3.22 cf. {Jeremiah 17:8}; Babylonian Sanhedrin 26b]; Plato[Laws XII 960e]; Clement of Alexandria[Stromata Book II.2, VII.10]; Nag Hammadi[Apocryphon of James 8; Gospel of Thomas 32]; Egyptian Book of the Dead[Oration 17]; Indian[Dhammapada 7-8, 13-14, 81]

07:01 Tertullian[On Idolatry 19]

07:01-10 Matthew 8:5-13

07:01-17 Tertullian[Five Books Against Marcion Book IV.18]

07:01-50 Irenaeus[Against Heresies Book III.14.3]

07:03 Tertullian[On Baptism 11]

07:05 Pseudepigrapha[Joseph and Aseneth 10:11]

07:07 Matthew 8:16n; Tertullian[On Baptism 11]

07:08 Clement[Recognitions Book IV.33]; Irenaeus[Against Heresies Book I.7.4]

07:11 NT-Apocrypha[Acts of Peter 1.25; Infancy Story of Thomas 17.1]

07:11-15 Constitutions of the Holy Apostles[Book V.7]

07:12 Irenaeus[Against Heresies Book V.13.1]; Origen[Gospel of Matthew Book XI.17]

07:12-16 1Kings 17:9-24; 2Kings 4:32-37

07:13 NT-Apocrypha[Infancy Story of Thomas 17.1]

07:14 NT-Apocrypha[Acts of Peter 1.27; Epistula Apostolorum 5; Infancy Story of Thomas 17.1, 18.1; Secret Gospel of Mark Fragment 1]

07:15-16 NT-Apocrypha[Infancy Story of Thomas 17.1-2]

07:16 Tertullian[Five Books Against Marcion Book IV.18-19]

07:18-23 Pseudepigrapha[Sibylline Oracles 1.350]; Tertullian[On Baptism 10]

07:18-35 Matthew 11:2-19

07:19 Psalms 40:7-8, 118:26; Malachi 3:1; Clement of Alexandria[The Instructor Book I.10]

07:19-23 Matthew 11:05n; Dead Sea Scrolls**[4QMessianic Apocalypse (4Q521) Fragment 2 COL II 1-13]**

07:20-22 Tertullian[Five Books Against Marcion Book IV.18]

07:22 Isaiah 26:19, 29:18, 35:5-6, 42:7, 18, 61:1-2; Matthew 5:3, 11:5n; Luke 4:18, 6:20; OT-Apocrypha[Sirach 48:5]; Pseudepigrapha[Apocalypse of Elijah 3:9; Sibylline Oracles 1.353, 6:12, 8.205]; Dead Sea Scrolls[1Q Hymns (1QHODAYOTH [1QH]) COL XXIII 14-15]; Tacitus[The Histories 4.81]; Apostolic[1Clement 59:4]; Clement of Alexandria[Exhortation to the Heathen 1, 12]; Constitutions of the Holy Apostles[Book VIII.1]; Irenaeus[Fragments from the Lost Works 54]; Justin[Dialogue with Trypho 12; First Apology 22]; Nag Hammadi[The Act of Peter 128]; NT-Apocrypha[Abgar Legend; Acts of Peter p.128; Epistula Apostolorum 5]

07:22-23 Clement of Alexandria[The Instructor Book I.10]

07:22-28 Philo[On Dreams, That They Are God-Sent (1.124-1.126)]

07:24 1Kings 14:15; Rabbinic[Babylonian Taanit 20b]

07:24-26 Indian[Dhammapada 395]

07:24-30 Tertullian[Five Books in Reply to Marcion Book II.145]

07:25 Clement of Alexandria[The Instructor Book II.11]

07:25-26 This section also includes topical notes for: Clothed in Soft Raiment - Philo[**On Dreams, That They Are God-Sent (1.124-1.126)**]; Plato[Phaedo 64c-e]; Nag Hammadi[Gospel of Philip 57; Gospel of Thomas 78; Teachings of Silvanus 89-90]

Now no such person as this is a pupil of the sacred word, but those only are the disciples of that who are real genuine men, lovers of temperance, and orderliness, and modesty, men who have laid down continence, and frugality, and fortitude, as a kind of base and foundation for the whole of life; and safe stations for the soul, in which it may anchor without danger and without changeableness: for being superior to money, and pleasure, and glory, they look down upon meats and drinks, and everything of that sort, beyond what is necessary to ward off hunger: being thoroughly ready to undergo hunger, and thirst, and heat, and cold, and all other things, however hard they may be to be borne, for the sake of the acquisition of virtue. And being admirers of whatever is most easily provided, so as to not be ashamed of ever such cheap or shabby clothes, think rather, on the other hand, that sumptuous apparel is a reproach and great scandal to life. To these men, the soft earth is their most costly couch; their bed is bushes, and grass, and herbage, and a thick layer of leaves; and the pillows for their head are a few stones, or any little mounds which happen to rise a little above the surface of the plain. Such a life as this, is, by luxurious men, denominated a life of hardship, but by those who live for virtue, it is called most delightful; for it is well adapted, not for those who are called men, for those who really are such. Do you not see, that even now, also, the sacred historian represents the practicer of honorable pursuits, who abounds in all royal materials and appointments, as sleeping on the ground, and using a stone for his pillow; and a little further on, he speaks of himself as asking in his prayers for bread and a cloak, the necessary wealth of nature? like one who has at all times held in contempt, the man who dwells among vain opinions, and who is inclined to revile all those who are disposed to admire him; this man is the archetypal pattern of the soul which is devoted to the practice of virtue, and an enemy of every effeminate person. (Philo - On Dreams, That They Are God-Sent (1.124-1.126)

07:25-28 Tertullian[On Idolatry 18; Five Books Against Marcion Book IV.18]
07:26 Irenaeus[Against Heresies Book III.11.4]; Origen[Gospel of Matthew Book X.22]; Tertullian[On Monogamy 8]
07:27 Exodus 23:20; Malachi 3:1; Tertullian[An Answer to the Jews 9]
07:28 Clement of Alexandria[The Instructor Book I.5]; Nag Hammadi[Gospel of Thomas 46]; Epic of Gilgamesh[The Coming of Enkidu]
07:29 Pseudepigrapha[Psalms of Solomon 2:15]
07:29-30 Matthew 3:5-16n
07:30 Psalms 33:10; Matthew 21:32; Luke 3:12; Irenaeus[Against Heresies Book IV.24.1]
07:32 Origen[Gospel of Matthew Book X.22]; NT-Apocrypha[Acts of John 94]
07:34 Psalms 80:17; Matthew 11:19n; Tertullian[On Fasting 2; On Monogamy 8]
07:35 Pseudepigrapha[4Ezra 2.15-18]; Clement of Alexandria[Stromata Book VI.16]; Irenaeus[Against Heresies Book I.8.4; Fragments from the Lost Works 37]; Nag Hammadi[Teachings of Silvanus 91]; NT-Apocrypha[Epistula Apostolorum 38]
07:36 NT-Apocrypha[Acts of John 93]
07:36-48 Philo[Special Laws I (102, 282) cf. {Deuteronomy 23:17-18}]
07:36-50 Matthew 9:10-17; Mark 2:15-22; Luke 14:1-31; John 14:1-17:26; Pseudepigrapha[Joseph and Aseneth 20:2]; Philo[On the Contemplative Life Or Suppliants (75)]; Origen[Gospel of John Book I.12]; Tertullian[Five Books Against Marcion Book IV.18]
07:37-38 NT-Apocrypha[Arabic Gospel of the Infancy of the Savior 5]
07:37-50 Origen[Gospel of Matthew Book XII.4]
07:38 Matthew 26:7; Mark 14:3; John 12:3
07:38-44 John 13:5-14n
07:38-45 NT-Apocrypha[Gospel of the Nazareans Fragment 31]
07:39 Deuteronomy 18:15; Pseudepigrapha[Joseph and Aseneth 23:8]; Anonymous[Treatise Against the Heretic Novatian 11]
07:41 Hippolytus[Fragments - On The Psalms 1.3]; Origen[Gospel of Matthew Book XIV.7]
07:44 Genesis 18:4; 1Samuel 25:41; Pseudepigrapha[Joseph and Aseneth 7:1]
07:45-50 Nag Hammadi[Gospel of Philip 63]

07:46 Psalms 23:5

07:47 Clement of Alexandria[The Instructor Book II.8]; Constitutions of the Holy Apostles[Book II.24]; Cyprian[Treatise XII.Book III.116]

07:48 Anonymous[Treatise on Re-Baptism 18]

07:48-50 Matthew 9:6n; Acts 26:18n

07:50 Anonymous[Treatise on Re-Baptism 18]; Hippolytus[Appendix to the Works of Hippolytus - On the End of the World 49]; NT-Apocrypha[Acts of Thomas 1.88]

08:01-03 Tertullian[On Monogamy 8]

08:02 Pseudepigrapha[Testament of Solomon 8:2]

08:03 Matthew 27:55-56; Mark 15:40-41; Luke 23:49

08:04-11 Matthew 13:3-53n

08:04-15 Matthew 13:1-15, 18-23; Mark 4:1-20

08:05 Clement[Recognitions Book III.14]; NT-Apocrypha[Acts of John 98]

08:05-08 Hippolytus[Refutation of all Heresies Book V.3, VIII.2]

08:05-15 Matthew 13:3-43n

08:06 Jeremiah 17:8

08:08 Matthew 11:15n; Tertullian[Five Books Against Marcion Book IV.19]

08:10 Isaiah 6:9-10; 2Corinthians 3:12-18n; Pseudepigrapha[Sibylline Oracles 1.360]; Clement of Alexandria[Stromata Book I.2, V.12]; Origen[De Principiis Book III.1.7]; Nag Hammadi[Gospel of Thomas (Prologue)]

08:11 Tertullian[On the Resurrection of the Flesh 33]

08:12 Pseudepigrapha[Apocalypse of Adam 6:1]

08:14 Origen[Gospel of John Book I.12]

08:14-15 Matthew 7:16-21n

08:15 This section also includes topical notes for: Pure Heart - 1Timothy 1:5; 2Timothy 2:22; 1Peter 1:22; Dead Sea Scrolls[4Q Testament of Qahat (4Q542[4QTQAHATAR]) COL I 10]

08:16 Matthew 5:15n; Tertullian[On the Apparel of Women Book II.13; Five Books Against Marcion Book IV.19]; NT-Apocrypha[Gospel of Mani Kephalaia LXV]

08:16-18 Mark 4:21-25; Luke 11:33-36

08:17 Matthew 10:26; Luke 12:2; Clement of Alexandria[Stromata Book I.1]; Tertullian[On Repentance 6; Five Books Against Marcion Book IV.19]

08:18 Matthew 25:29; Luke 19:26; Pseudepigrapha[4Ezra 7.25; Odes of Solomon 24.9]; Clement[Homily XVIII.16]; Tertullian[De Fuga in Persecutione 11; Five Books Against Marcion Book II.2, IV.19]

08:19-21 Matthew 12:46-50; Mark 3:31-35

08:20 Tertullian[Five Books Against Marcion Book III.11]

08:20-21 Tertullian[On the Flesh of Christ 7]

08:21 Apostolic[2Clement 9:11]; Tertullian[Five Books Against Marcion Book IV.26]

08:22-25 Psalms 107:23-31; Matthew 8:18-27; Mark 4:35-41; Pseudepigrapha[Testament of Adam 3.1; Testament of Naphtali 6.1-10]

08:24 Irenaeus[Fragments from the Lost Works 52]; Egyptian Book of the Dead[Oration 57]

08:25 Psalms 107:23-30; Matthew 8:27; Mark 04:37-41n; Tertullian[Five Books Against Marcion Book IV.20]

08:26-37 Origen[Gospel of John Book VI.24]

08:26-39 NT-Apocrypha[Epistula Apostolorum 5]

08:26-40 Matthew 8:28-34; Mark 5:1-20

08:28 Genesis 14:18; 1Kings 17:18; Tertullian[Five Books Against Marcion Book IV.20]

08:29 Methodius[Oration on the Psalms 3]

08:30 Tertullian[Five Books Against Marcion Book IV.20]

08:32-33 Tertullian[On Modesty 9]

08:40-56 Matthew 9:18-26; Mark 5:21-43

08:41 Irenaeus[Against Heresies Book I.8.2]

08:41-56 Constitutions of the Holy Apostles[Book V.7]

08:43 Dionysius of Alexandria[Extant Fragments Epistle to Bishop Basilides 2]; Irenaeus[Against Heresies Book II.20.1, 23.1-2]; NT-Apocrypha[Epistula Apostolorum 5]

08:43-46 Tertullian[Five Books Against Marcion Book IV.20]

08:44 Numbers 15:38; Nag Hammadi[Testimony of Truth 41]

08:45-46 Origen[Gospel of Matthew Book X.19]

08:46 Origen[Gospel of Matthew Book XI.17]

08:48 Tertullian[Five Books Against Marcion Book IV.20]
08:49 NT-Apocrypha[Epistula Apostolorum 5]
08:51 Irenaeus[Against Heresies Book II.24.4]
08:52 Pseudepigrapha[4Ezra 2.31]
08:55 1Kings 17:22; NT-Apocrypha[Infancy Story of Thomas 17.1]
09:01-06 Matthew 9:35-11:1; Mark 6:7-13
09:01-08 Tertullian[Five Books Against Marcion Book IV.21]
09:02 NT-Apocrypha[Epistula Apostolorum 19]
09:03 Nag Hammadi[Gospel of Thomas 14]
09:03-04 Hippolytus[Refutation of all Heresies Book IX.15]
09:05 Matthew 10:5-14n; Acts 10:4-11, 13:51; Pseudepigrapha[Apocalypse of Adam 6:1];
   Hippolytus[The Discourse on the Holy Theophany 7]
09:07-08 Origen[Gospel of Matthew Book X.20]
09:07-09 Matthew 14:1-2; Mark 6:14-16
09:08 Malachi 3:23; Matthew 16:14; Mark 8:28; Luke 9:19; OT-Apocrypha[Sirach 48:10]
09:10 Matthew 14:12-13a; Mark 6:29-32; John 6:1, 3
09:10-17 Pseudepigrapha[Sibylline Oracles 1.357]; Tertullian[Five Books Against Marcion Book IV.21]
09:11 Matthew 4:23-24n
09:11-17 Matthew 14:13-33; Mark 6:33-52; John 6:2-21
09:12-17 NT-Apocrypha[Acts of John 93]
09:13 Origen[Gospel of Matthew Book XI.2]
09:13-14 Irenaeus[Against Heresies Book II.24.4]
09:13-17 John 6:31-58n
09:14 Matthew 14:21n; Origen[Gospel of Matthew Book XI.3, 19]
09:16 Pseudepigrapha[Testament of Zebulon 6.6-7]; Origen[Gospel of Matthew Book XI.19]
09:17 2Kings 4:44; Irenaeus[Against Heresies Book II.22.3]
09:18-27 Matthew 16:13-28; Mark 8:27-9:1
09:19 Matthew 4:2, 6, 14:1; Luke 9:7
09:20 John 6:68-69; Tertullian[Five Books Against Marcion Book IV.21, 34]
09:21 Origen[Gospel of Matthew Book XII.15]
09:21-22 Tertullian[Five Books Against Marcion Book IV.21]
09:22 Psalms 80:17; Hosea 6:2; Irenaeus[Against Heresies Book III.16.5]; Justin[Dialogue with Trypho
   51, 76]
09:23 Matthew 10:38, 14:27, 16:24-25n; Mark 8:34; Tertullian[On Idolatry 12]; Epic of Gilgamesh[The
   Forest Journey, The Story of the Flood]
09:23-24 Nag Hammadi[Apocryphon of James 6]
09:24 Matthew 10:39, 17:33; Apostolic[Ignatius - Letter to the Magnesians 5:2]; Cyprian[Treatise XI.12];
   Tertullian[Five Books Against Marcion Book IV.21]
09:24-27 John 12:25n
09:25 Apostolic[2Clement 6:2]; Clement of Alexandria[Stromata Book VI.14]; Cyprian[Treatise
   XII.Book III.61]; Nag Hammadi[Interpretation of Knowledge 9]
09:26 Psalms 80:17; Pseudepigrapha[Sibylline Oracles 2.240]; Constitutions of the Holy Apostles[Book
   V.4]; Tertullian[De Fuga in Persecutione 7; On Idolatry 13; On the Flesh of Christ 5; Five Books
   Against Marcion Book IV.21]; NT-Apocrypha[Apocalypse of Peter 1.1, 1.6; Apocalypse of Thomas
   Line 48]
09:27 Origen[Gospel of Matthew Book XII.35]; Nag Hammadi[Gospel of Thomas 1]
09:28 Pseudepigrapha[Apocalypse of Zephaniah 5:4; Joseph and Aseneth 11:1]; Origen[Gospel of
   Matthew Book XII.31]; Tertullian[Five Books Against Marcion Book IV.22]; NT-Apocrypha[Acts of
   John 90; Apocalypse of Peter 1.15]
09:28-29 Origen[Gospel of Matthew Book XII.39]
09:28-36 Tertullian[On Fasting 6; On Monogamy 8; Five Books Against Marcion Book IV.22]
09:28-43 Matthew 17:1-21n; Mark 9:2-29
09:30 Constitutions of the Holy Apostles[Book VI.19]; Tertullian[On Baptism 19]
09:30-31 Origen[Gospel of Matthew Book XII.38]
09:31 Origen[Against Celsus Book VI.76; Gospel of Matthew Book XII.41]
09:32-33 Origen[Gospel of Matthew Book XII.40]
09:33 Origen[Gospel of Matthew Book XII.41]; Tertullian[On Fasting 6; Five Books Against Marcion
   Book IV.22]

09:34 Exodus 24:18

09:35 Deuteronomy 18:15; Psalms 2:7; Isaiah 42:1; Matthew 3:17, 12:18n; Mark 1:11, 3:22; 2Peter 1:17-18; Pseudepigrapha[Martyrdom and Ascension of Isaiah 8:8]; Tacitus[The Histories 5.13]; Gregory Thaumaturgus[Four Homilies 4]; Tertullian[Five Books Against Marcion Book IV.22, 34]

09:41 Tertullian[Five Books Against Marcion Book IV.23]

09:42 Pseudepigrapha[2Baruch 21:6; Life of Adam and Eve Vita 39.1-3]

09:43-45 Matthew 17:22-23; Mark 9:30-32

09:44 Psalms 80:17

09:46 Luke 22:24

09:46-48 Matthew 18:1-5; Mark 9:33-37; Origen[Gospel of Matthew Book XIII.19]

09:47-48 Tertullian[Five Books Against Marcion Book IV.23]

09:48 Matthew 10:40; Luke 10:16; John 13:20; Cyprian[Epistle VI.4; Treatise X.10, XII.Book III.5]; Origen[Gospel of Matthew Book XIII.29]

09:49 Numbers 11:28

09:49-50 Mark 9:38-41

09:51 Pseudepigrapha[Psalms of Solomon 4:18]; Josephus[Antiquities 20.6.1 118]

09:51-55 Matthew 19:1; Mark 10:1a

09:51-56 Tertullian[Of Patience 3; Five Books Against Marcion Book IV.23]

09:52 Pseudepigrapha[Joseph and Aseneth 3:2]

09:53 2Samuel 17:11; NT-Apocrypha[Secret Gospel of Mark Fragment 2]

09:54 Genesis 19:24-25; 2Kings 1:9-16; Pseudepigrapha[Joseph and Aseneth 25:6]; Philo[On Dreams That They are God-Sent (1.85-86) cf. {Genesis 19:24}]

09:55 Clement of Alexandria[Fragments from Macarius Chrysocephalus Oration VIII on Matt VIII and Book VII on Luke XIII]

09:56 Cyprian[Epistle LVIII.2]; Tertullian[On the Flesh of Christ 12]

09:56-62 Matthew 19:2; Mark 10:1b

09:57-58 Irenaeus[Against Heresies Book I.8.3]; Tertullian[Five Books Against Marcion Book IV.23]

09:57-62 Matthew 8:18-22

09:58 Genesis 28:11; Psalms 80:17; Matthew 8:20n; Clement of Alexandria[Stromata Book I.3]; Tertullian[On Idolatry 18]; Nag Hammadi[Gospel of Thomas 86]

09:59-60 Archelaus[Disputation with Manes 48]; Tertullian[On Baptism 12; On Idolatry 12; On Monogamy 7; Five Books Against Marcion Book IV.23]

09:60 Clement of Alexandria[Stromata Book III.4; Who is the Rich Man that shall be Saved 23]; Irenaeus[Against Heresies Book V.9.2]

09:60-62 Irenaeus[Against Heresies Book I.8.3]

09:61 1Kings 19:20

09:62 Genesis 19:17, 26; 1Kings 19:19-21; Philo[On the Migration of Abraham (144-146) cf. {Genesis 25:27, 27:41, 29:31-30:20, 33:4, Numbers 20:17, Deuteronomy 2:27, 5:32, 17:11, 17:20, 28:14}]; Clement of Alexandria[Stromata Book VII.16]; Cyprian[Epistle VII.6; Treatise XI.7, XII.Book III.11]; Tertullian[On Idolatry 12; On Modesty 6]; NT-Apocrypha[Acts of John 109; Acts of Thomas 1.147]

10:01 Genesis 46:27; Exodus 24:1; Numbers 11:16; Pseudepigrapha[Joseph and Aseneth 2:11; Letter of Aristeas 1.46-52]; Rabbinic[Babylonian (Qiddushin 32b; Sanhedrin 2a, 16b)]; Clement of Alexandria[Stromata Book II.20]; Clement[Recognitions Book I.40]; Irenaeus[Against Heresies Book II.21.1]; Tertullian[Five Books Against Marcion Book IV.24]; NT-Apocrypha[Abgar Legend; Letter of Peter to James 2.2]

10:01-16 Matthew 11:20-24

10:02 Matthew 9:37-38; Clement of Alexandria[Stromata Book I.1]; Nag Hammadi[Gospel of Thomas 73]

10:03 Matthew 10:16; Luke 13:32n; Apostolic[2Clement 5:4]

10:04 2Kings 4:29; Clement of Alexandria[The Instructor Book III.7]; Origen[De Principiis Book IV.1.18]; Tertullian[Five Books Against Marcion Book IV.24]

10:05 1Samuel 25:5; Tertullian[On Prayer 26; Five Books Against Marcion Book IV.24]; NT-Apocrypha[Clement Romance 30.3]

10:05-06 Clement[Recognitions Book II.30]; Constitutions of the Holy Apostles[Book III.14]

10:07 Numbers 18:31; 1Corinthians 9:14; 1Timothy 5:18; Constitutions of the Holy Apostles[Book II.24]; Teaching of the Twelve Apostles 13.3; Tertullian[Five Books Against Marcion Book IV.24]; Nag Hammadi[Dialogue of the Savior 53]; NT-Apocrypha[Clement Romance 71.3]

10:08-09 Nag Hammadi[Gospel of Thomas 14]

10:09 Origen[Against Celsus Book VII.57]; Tertullian[Five Books Against Marcion Book IV.24]

10:11 Matthew 10:7-14; Mark 6:8-11; Luke 9:3-5; Acts 13:51; Tertullian[Five Books Against Marcion Book IV.24]

10:12 Genesis 19:24-28; Matthew 10:25, 11:24; Pseudepigrapha[4Ezra 2.9]; Irenaeus[Against Heresies Book IV.36.4, V.27.1]

10:12-14 Tertullian[On Fasting 7]

10:13 Esther 4:3; Isaiah 23:1-18; Daniel 9:3; Jonah 3:5; Acts 3:19n; Pseudepigrapha[Joseph and Aseneth 13:2]; Tertullian[On Modesty 10]; NT-Apocrypha[Gospel of the Nazareans Fragment 27]

10:13-14 Ezekiel 26:1-28:26; Joel 3:4-8; Amos 1:9-10; Zechariah 9:2-4

10:15 Isaiah 14:11, 13-15

10:16 Matthew 10:40; Mark 9:37; Luke 10:16; John 13:20; Clement of Alexandria[Who is the Rich Man that shall be Saved 31]; Constitutions of the Holy Apostles[Book II.20, VIII.3, 46]; Cyprian[Epistle LIV.4, LXVIII.4]; Irenaeus[Against Heresies Book III.Preface.1]; Justin[First Apology 63]; Pontianus[First Epistle]; Tertullian[Five Books Against Marcion Book IV.24]; NT-Apocrypha[Clement Romance 66.3]

10:17 OT-Apocrypha[Tobit 7:17]

10:17-19 Pseudepigrapha[Testament of Levi 18.12]

10:17-24 Matthew 11:25-30

10:18 Isaiah 14:12; Pseudepigrapha[2Enoch 29:3; Life of Adam and Eve Vita 12:1; Testament of Benjamin 3:7]; Apostolic[Papias Fragment 24:1]; Archelaus[Disputation with Manes 20, 32]; Clement[Homily XIX.2]; Constitutions of the Holy Apostles[Book VIII.7]; Irenaeus[Against Heresies Book III.17.3]; Origen[De Principiis Book I.5.5]; Tertullian[A Treatise on the Soul 17; Five Books Against Marcion Book II.10]; Nag Hammadi[Gospel of Truth 33]; NT-Apocrypha[Freer Logion]; Egyptian Book of the Dead[Oration 16]

10:19 Genesis 3:15; Psalms 91:13; Pseudepigrapha[Testament of Levi 18:12]; Rabbinic[Avot 2.15]; Apostolic[Papias Fragment 3:9, 5:1]; Anonymous[Treatise Against the Heretic Novatian 6]; Archelaus[Disputation with Manes 32]; Clement of Alexandria[Stromata Book IV.6]; Constitutions of the Holy Apostles[Book VIII.7]; Irenaeus[Against Heresies Book II.20.3, III.23.7, V.24.4]; Justin[Dialogue with Trypho 76]; Origen[Against Celsus Book VII.70; De Principiis Book IV.1.5]; Tertullian[Five Books Against Marcion Book IV.24]; Nag Hammadi[A Valentinian Exposition 40]; Egyptian Book of the Dead[Oration 19]

10:19-20 OT-Apocrypha[Sirach 11:19]

10:20 Exodus 32:32; Isaiah 4:3; Revelation 21:27n; Pseudepigrapha[Joseph and Aseneth 15:4]; Constitutions of the Holy Apostles[Book VIII.1]; Tertullian[Five Books Against Marcion Book IV.7]

10:21 Psalms 136:26; Isaiah 29:14; OT-Apocrypha[Sirach 51:1]; Clement of Alexandria[The Instructor Book I.6]; Clement[Homily VIII.6, XVIII.15]; Irenaeus[Against Heresies Book IV.1.2]; Tertullian[Against Praxeas 26; Five Books Against Marcion Book IV.25]; Nag Hammadi[Gospel of Thomas (Prologue), 62]; NT-Apocrypha[Clement Romance - Peter on his Mission Journeys H VIII 6.4]

10:22 John 3:35, 10:15; Archelaus[Disputation with Manes 37]; Clement of Alexandria[Stromata Book V.13, VII.18; The Instructor Book I.5, 8-9]; Clement[Homily XVII.4; Recognitions Book II.47]; Irenaeus[Against Heresies Book I.2.5, 15.3, II.30.9, IV.6.1, 3-4, 7, 7.4]; Justin[Dialogue with Trypho 136]; Novatian[Treatise Concerning the Trinity 26]; Origen[Against Celsus Book II.71; De Principiis Book I.3.4]; Tertullian[Against Praxeas 26]; Nag Hammadi[Dialogue of the Savior 35]

10:22-24 Tertullian[Five Books Against Marcion Book IV.25]

10:23 Nag Hammadi[Dialogue of the Savior 57]

10:23-24 Pseudepigrapha[Psalms of Solomon 17.44]

10:24 Clement[Homily III.53]; Methodius[Oration on the Psalms 2]

10:25 Tertullian[On the Flesh of Christ 7; Five Books Against Marcion Book IV.19]

10:25-28 Tertullian[An Answer to the Jews 2]

10:27 Leviticus 19:18; Deuteronomy 6:5, 10:12; Joshua 22:5; Matthew 5:43n; Pseudepigrapha[Sibylline Oracles 8.481; Testament of Issachar 5:2]; Apostolic[Didache 1:2]; Clement of Alexandria[Stromata Book II.15, IV.3]; Tertullian[On the Apparel of Women Book II.2; Five Books Against Marcion Book IV.25, V.8]

10:28 Leviticus 18:5; Nehemiah 9:29; Ezekiel 20:21; Matthew 22:35-40; Mark 12:28-34

10:29 Leviticus 19:16, 33; Pseudepigrapha[Letter of Aristeas 1.228]; Clement of Alexandria[Who is the Rich Man that shall be Saved 28]

10:30 Pseudepigrapha[Joseph and Aseneth 27:3]

10:30-35 Pseudepigrapha[Joseph and Aseneth 29:5]

10:30-37 Philo[Special Laws III (116) cf. {Exodus 22:22}]; Nag Hammadi[Gospel of Philip 78]

10:34 2Chronicles 28:15; Methodius[Oration on the Psalms 6]

10:35 Irenaeus[Against Heresies Book III.17.3]

10:36 Pseudepigrapha[Martyrdom and Ascension of Isaiah 8.15]

10:36-37 Clement of Alexandria[Who is the Rich Man that shall be Saved 28]

10:37 Pseudepigrapha[Joseph and Aseneth 23:3]

10:39 John 11:1; NT-Apocrypha[Acts of Paul and Thecla 1.18]

10:41 Pseudepigrapha[Joseph and Aseneth 14:4]; Origen[Gospel of John Book VI.24]

10:41-42 Clement of Alexandria[Who is the Rich Man that shall be Saved 10]

11:01 Matthew 5:2; NT-Apocrypha[Acts of Thomas 1.53]

11:01-04 Tertullian[Five Books Against Marcion Book IV.26]

11:01-13 Matthew 6:9-15, 7:11

11:01-54 Irenaeus[Against Heresies Book III.14.3]

11:02 Archelaus[Disputation with Manes 20]

11:03 Tertullian[On Fasting 15]; NT-Apocrypha[Gospel of the Nazareans Fragment 5]

11:04 Clement of Alexandria[Stromata Book VII.13]; Tertullian[On Modesty 2]; Nag
Hammadi[Apocryphon of James 4]

11:05 Origen[Gospel of Matthew Book XI.8]; Tertullian[On Prescription Against Heretics 11]

11:05-09 Tertullian[On Prayer 6; Five Books Against Marcion Book IV.26]

11:07 Pseudepigrapha[Joseph and Aseneth 10:2-6]

11:08 Origen[Gospel of Matthew Book XIV.25]

11:09 Clement of Alexandria[Stromata Book VIII.1]; Origen[Letter to Gregory 3]; Tertullian[On
Baptism 20; On Prayer 10; On Prescription Against Heretics 11]; Nag Hammadi[Letter of Peter to
Philip 137]; NT-Apocrypha[Acts of John 22; Epistula Apostolorum 39; Gospel of the Hebrews
Fragment 4b]

11:09-10 Acts 17:2-3; Pseudepigrapha[Jubilees 1.15; Odes of Solomon 33.13]; Clement of
Alexandria[Who is the Rich Man that shall be Saved 10]; Irenaeus[Against Heresies Book II.18.6];
Nag Hammadi[Gospel of Mary 8; Gospel of Thomas 2, 92, 94; Teachings of Silvanus 103, 106-107,
117]

11:10 Anonymous[Treatise Against the Heretic Novatian 16]; Cyprian[Epistle VII.2]

11:11 Origen[Gospel of Matthew Book XIV.25]; Tertullian[On Prayer 6]

11:11-13 Tertullian[Five Books Against Marcion Book IV.26]

11:13 Clement of Alexandria[Who is the Rich Man that shall be Saved 39]

11:14-22 Pseudepigrapha[Testament of Levi 18:12]

11:14-32 Matthew 12:22-45; Mark 3:20-33

11:15 Matthew 9:34, 10:25; Pseudepigrapha[Testament of Solomon 2:9-3:1]; Justin[Dialogue with
Trypho 69]

11:15-19 Rabbinic[Babylonian (Sanhedrin 107b; Shabbat 106; Sotah 47a); Jerusalem Shabbat 13d;
Tosephta Shabbat xi 15]; Egyptian Book of the Dead[Oration 99]

11:16 Matthew 16:1; Mark 8:11

11:18-22 Tertullian[Five Books Against Marcion Book IV.26]

11:20 Exodus 8:15, 19; Cyprian[Treatise III.26, XII.Book II.4]; Melito[Fragments 9.9]

11:21-22 Song of Solomon 5:4; Pseudepigrapha[Psalms of Solomon 5:4]; Irenaeus[Against Heresies
Book IV.33.4]

11:22 Isaiah 49:24, 53:12; Clement[Recognitions Book II.60]; NT-Apocrypha[Pseudo-Titus Epistle Line
420]

11:23 Mark 9:40; Cyprian[Epistle LXIX.3, LXXIV.14, LXXV.1]

11:23-26 NT-Apocrypha[Acts of Thomas 1.46]

11:24 Methodius[Oration Concerning Simeon and Anna 3]

11:24-26 NT-Apocrypha[Acts of Thomas 1.77]

11:25 Pseudepigrapha[2Baruch 25:3]

11:26 Pseudepigrapha[Testament of Solomon 8:2]

11:27 Pseudepigrapha[2Baruch 54:11]; Clement of Alexandria[The Instructor Book I.6]; Tertullian[Five
Books Against Marcion Book III.11]

11:27-28 Tertullian[On the Flesh of Christ 7; Five Books Against Marcion Book IV.26]; Nag
Hammadi[Gospel of Thomas 79]

11:29 Matthew 16:4; Mark 8:12; Rabbinic[Babylonian Sanhedrin 98a]; Justin[Dialogue with Trypho 108]; Tertullian[Five Books Against Marcion Book IV.27]

11:29-30 Irenaeus[Against Heresies Book III.20.1]

11:30 Psalms 80:17; Jonah 3:4

11:31 1Kings 10:1; 2Chronicles 9:1-12; Pseudepigrapha[Testament of Solomon 19:3, 21:1]; Irenaeus[Against Heresies Book IV.27.1]

11:31-32 Clement[Homily XI.33; Recognitions Book VI.14]; Irenaeus[Against Heresies Book IV.9.2]; NT-Apocrypha[Pseudo Clementines - Kerygmata Petrou H XI 33.1-2]

11:32 Jonah 3:5, 8, 10; Acts 3:19n

11:33 Tertullian[On the Apparel of Women Book II.13; Five Books Against Marcion Book IV.27]

11:33-36 Matthew 5:15n, 6:22-23; Mark 4:21-25; Luke 8:16-18

11:37 NT-Apocrypha[Acts of John 93]

11:37-52 Tertullian[Five Books Against Marcion Book IV.27]

11:37-54 Matthew 23:1-36; Mark 12:38-40; Luke 20:45-47

11:39 Matthew 23:25-26n; Pseudepigrapha[4Ezra 12.31-33]; Archelaus[Disputation with Manes 21]

11:39-40 Indian[Dhammapada 394]

11:39-41 Nag Hammadi[Gospel of Thomas 89]

11:39-43 Matthew 6:1-6n; Hippolytus[Refutation of all Heresies Book IX.23]

11:40 Clement of Alexandria[Stromata Book III.4]; Irenaeus[Against Heresies Book II.28.6]

11:40-41 Cyprian[Treatise XII.Book III.1]

11:41 Cyprian[Treatise VIII.2]; Nag Hammadi[Gospel of Thomas 3, 70]

11:42 Leviticus 27:30; Archelaus[Disputation with Manes 21]

11:42-43 Pseudepigrapha[4Ezra 12.31-33]

11:43 Rabbinic[Babylonian Horayot 13a-14b]; Clement of Alexandria[The Instructor Book III.12]

11:44 Apostolic[Ignatius - Letter to the Philadelphians 6:1]

11:46 Clement of Alexandria[Stromata Book VI.6]

11:47-51 Pseudepigrapha[4Ezra 1.32]; Justin[Dialogue with Trypho 93]

11:48 Origen[Against Celsus Book II.75]; Tertullian[On Prayer 14]

11:49 Jeremiah 7:25; Matthew 10:2n

11:49-51 Pseudepigrapha[Sibylline Oracles 2.247]

11:50 Irenaeus[Against Heresies Book V.14.1]

11:50-51 Apostolic[Polycarp - Letter to the Philippians 2:1]

11:51 Genesis 4:8, 10; 2Chronicles 24:20-21; Zechariah 1:1; NT-Apocrypha[Genna Marias]

11:52 Clement of Alexandria[Stromata Book VII.17]; Clement[Homily XVIII.16; Recognitions Book I.54, II.30, 46]; Origen[De Principiis Book IV.1.10]; Nag Hammadi[Gospel of Thomas 39, 102; Apocalypse of Peter 78:23-31]

11:53 Hippolytus[Refutation of all Heresies Book IX.23]

12:01 Matthew 6:1-6n, 2-16n, 16:6-12n; Mark 8:15; Pseudepigrapha[4Ezra 12.31-33]; Hippolytus[Refutation of all Heresies Book IX.23]

12:01-21 Tertullian[Five Books Against Marcion Book IV.28]

12:02 Matthew 13:11n; Mark 4:22; Luke 8:17; Pseudepigrapha[4Ezra 12.37-39]; Clement of Alexandria[Stromata Book I.1]; Origen[Gospel of Matthew Book XIV.9]; NT-Apocrypha[Gospel of Mani Kephalaia LXV]

12:03 Clement of Alexandria[Stromata Book VI.15]

12:04 Nag Hammadi[Letter of Peter to Philip 138]

12:04-05 Apostolic[2Clement 5:4]; Tertullian[On Modesty 2]

12:04-07 Matthew 10:26-31

12:05 Psalms 119:120

12:06 Nag Hammadi[Gospel of Philip 56]

12:06-07 Clement[Homily XII.31]; Irenaeus[Against Heresies Book II.28.9]

12:07 1Samuel 14:45; 2Samuel 14:11; Clement of Alexandria[Stromata Book VI.17]

12:08 Psalms 80:17; Pseudepigrapha[4Ezra 2.47]; Clement of Alexandria[Stromata Book IV.9]; Cyprian[Treatise III.20]; Nag Hammadi[Letter of Peter to Philip 139]

12:09 Cyprian[Epistle XXX.7]

12:10 Psalms 80:17; Matthew 12:32; Mark 3:29; Origen[De Principiis Book I.3.2]; Nag Hammadi[Gospel of Thomas 44]; NT-Apocrypha[Questions of Bartholomew V 4]

12:11 Pseudepigrapha[Ahiqar 114]; Nag Hammadi[Letter of Peter to Philip 138]

12:11-12 Clement of Alexandria[Stromata Book IV.9]

12:13-14 Nag Hammadi[Gospel of Thomas 72]

12:13-21 Pseudepigrapha[Ahiqar 137]

12:14 Exodus 2:14; NT-Apocrypha[Letter of Clement to James 5.3]

12:15 NT-Apocrypha[Epistula Apostolorum 46]

12:16 Psalms 49:17; Matthew 13:3-53n

12:16-20 Clement of Alexandria[Stromata Book III.6]; Tertullian[On Prayer 6]

12:16-21 Philo[**Allegorical Interpretation III (104-106) cf. {Deuteronomy 32:34}**); On Flight And Finding (79-80) cf. {Leviticus 35:16-21}]; Pythagoras[Golden Verses Lines 16-17]; Nag Hammadi[Gospel of Thomas 63]; Indian[Dhammapada 287]

> Since therefore we find that there are two natures which have been created and fashioned and accurately and skillfully framed by God; the one being in its own intrinsic nature pernicious and open to reproach, and accursed, and the other beneficial and praiseworthy, the one too having a spurious stamp upon it, but the other having undergone a strict test; we will utter a beautiful and suitable prayer which Moses also addressed to God, praying that God may open his treasure house, and may lay before us his sublime word pregnant with divine lights, which he calls the heaven, and may bind fast the storehouses of evil. For, just as there are storehouses of good things so are there also storehouses of evil things with God; as he says in his great song, "Behold are not these things collected with me, and sealed up in my treasure houses, against the day of vengeance when their foot shall be tripped Up?" You see then that there are several storehouses of evil things, and only one of good things. For since God is One, so also is his storehouse of good things one likewise. But there are many storehouses of evil things because the wicked are infinite in number. And in this observe the goodness of the true God, He opens the treasure house of his good things freely, but he binds fast that which contains the evil things. For it is an especial property of God to offer his good things freely and to be beforehand with men in bestowing gifts upon them, but to be slow in bringing evil on them, and Moses dwelling at length upon the munificent and gracious nature of God, says that not only have his storehouses of evil things been sealed up in all other times, but also when the soul is tripped up in the path of right reason, when it is especially fair that it should be considered worthy of punishment; for he says that, "In the day of vengeance the storehouses of evil things have been sealed up," the sacred word of scripture showing that God does not visit with his vengeance even those who sin against him, immediately, but that he gives them time for repentance, and to remedy and correct their evil conduct. (Philo - Allegorical Interpretation III (104-106) cf. {Deuteronomy 32:34})

12:17-18 Pseudepigrapha[Sibylline Oracles 1.344-346]

12:17-20 Clement[Recognitions Book X.45]

12:19 Ecclesiastes 8:15; Pseudepigrapha[1Enoch 97:8-10; Joseph and Aseneth 20:8; Testament of Abraham rec. B 5:1]

12:19-20 OT-Apocrypha[Sirach 11:19; Tobit 7:10]; Clement of Alexandria[The Instructor Book II.13]; Epic of Gilgamesh[The Search for Everlasting Life]

12:20 Jeremiah 17:11; OT-Apocrypha[Wisdom of Solomon 15:8]; Pseudepigrapha[Pseudo-Phocylides 106]; Plato[Apology 29d-30b; Phaedo 64c-e]; Clement of Alexandria[Stromata Book IV.6]; Cyprian[Treatise IV.20, VIII.13, XII.Book III.61]; Irenaeus[Against Heresies Book III.14.3]

12:21 Psalms 39:7; Romans 11:33n

12:22-23 Clement of Alexandria[Stromata Book IV.6]

12:22-24 Clement of Alexandria[The Instructor Book II.11]; Tertullian[On Idolatry 12]

12:22-28 Tertullian[Five Books Against Marcion Book IV.29]

12:22-31 Matthew 6:25-34

12:23 Cyprian[Treatise VIII.7]; Tertullian[Of Patience 8]

12:24 Job 38:41; Psalms 147:9; NT-Apocrypha[Acts of Thomas 1.28]

12:25 Theodotus[Excerpts]

12:27 1Kings 10:4-7; 2Chronicles 9:3-6; Tertullian[The Chaplet, or De Corona 4]

12:27-28 Clement of Alexandria[The Instructor Book II.11]

12:28 Tertullian[On Idolatry 12]

12:29 Tertullian[On Prayer 6]

12:30 Tertullian[Five Books Against Marcion Book IV.29]

12:30-31 Clement of Alexandria[Stromata Book IV.6]

12:31 Tertullian[Five Books Against Marcion Book III.25, IV.29]

12:32 Isaiah 41:14; Daniel 7:18, 32; Clement of Alexandria[Who is the Rich Man that shall be Saved 31]; Methodius[Oration Concerning Simeon and Anna 13]

12:32-34 Matthew 6:19-21

12:33 Apostolic[Shepherd of Hermas 50:8-9]; Clement of Alexandria[Exhortation to the Heathen 10; Stromata Book IV.6; Who is the Rich Man that shall be Saved 14]; Cyprian[Treatise XII.Book III.1]; Nag Hammadi[Gospel of Thomas 76]

12:33-34 Epic of Gilgamesh[The Story of the Flood]

12:34 Luke 6:45n; NT-Apocrypha[Gospel of Mani Kephalaia LXXXIX, Gospel of Mani Psalm CCLXXIV]

12:35 Exodus 12:11; 1Kings 18:46; 2Kings 4:29, 9:1; Job 38:3, 40:7; Proverbs 31:17; Jeremiah 1:17; Matthew 25:1-13; Apostolic[Didache 16:1]; Clement[Second Epistle Concerning Virginity 8]; Constitutions of the Holy Apostles[Book VII.31]; Cyprian[Treatise I.27]; Teaching of the Twelve Apostles 16.1; Nag Hammadi[Gospel of Thomas 103]

12:35-36 Irenaeus[Against Heresies Book IV.36.3, 37.3]; Tertullian[Five Books Against Marcion Book IV.29]

12:35-37 Clement of Alexandria[The Instructor Book II.9]; Cyprian[Treatise XI.8, XII.Book II.19, III.11]

12:35-38 Methodius[Banquet of the Ten Virgins 5.2]

12:36 Mark 13:34-36

12:37 Pseudepigrapha[Martyrdom and Ascension of Isaiah (3:13-4:22 = Testament of Hezekiah) 4:16]; Constitutions of the Holy Apostles[Book VII.31]

12:37-39 Matthew 24:42-51n

12:38 NT-Apocrypha[Acts of Thomas 1.147]

12:39 Nag Hammadi[Gospel of Thomas 103]

12:39-40 Rabbinic[Babylonian Sanhedrin 39a cf. {Genesis 2:21}]

12:39-46 Tertullian[Five Books Against Marcion Book IV.29]

12:40 Psalms 80:17; Matthew 24:43-44; Apostolic[Didache 16:1]

12:41 Matthew 13:3-53n

12:41-48 Matthew 24:45-51

12:42 Matthew 24:45n; Clement[Homily III.64]; NT-Apocrypha[Clement Romance 60.2, 64.1]

12:42-46 Pseudepigrapha[Sibylline Oracles 2.180]

12:45 Irenaeus[Against Heresies Book IV.26.3]; NT-Apocrypha[Clement Romance 60.2]

12:45-46 Origen[Letter to Africanus 7]

12:45-47 Irenaeus[Against Heresies Book IV.37.3]

12:47 Cyprian[Epistle VII.1; Treatise XII.Book III.19]

12:48 Clement of Alexandria[Stromata Book II.23]; Constitutions of the Holy Apostles[Book II.18]; Cyprian[Treatise I.21]; Irenaeus[Against Heresies Book IV.27.2]; Justin[First Apology 17]; Tertullian[On Fasting 4]

12:49 Archelaus[Fragment of the Disputation with Manes 1]; Clement[Recognitions Book VI.4]; Methodius[Banquet of the Ten Virgins 6.3; Oration Concerning Simeon and Anna 13]; Tertullian[Five Books Against Marcion Book IV.29]; Theodotus[Excerpts 26]; Nag Hammadi[Gospel of Thomas 10]; NT-Apocrypha[Pseudo Clementines - Kerygmata Petrou H XI 19.2]

12:49-53 Matthew 10:34-36; Nag Hammadi[Gospel of Thomas 16]

12:50 Mark 10:38; Anonymous[Treatise on Re-Baptism 14]; Cyprian[Epistle LXXII.22]; Origen[Gospel of John Book VI.26, 37; Gospel of Matthew Book XIV.8]; Tertullian[Of Patience 13; On Baptism 16; On Modesty 22]

12:51 Tertullian[Five Books Against Marcion Book IV.29]

12:51-53 Clement[Recognitions Book II.32]

12:53 Micah 7:6; Pseudepigrapha[Greek Apocalypse of Ezra 3.12-15; Sibylline Oracles 8.84]; Rabbinic[**Babylonian Sanhedrin 97a cf. {Micah 7:6};** Babylonian Sotah 49B]; Clement[Recognitions Book II.29]; Tertullian[Five Books Against Marcion Book IV.29]; NT-Apocrypha[Pseudo Clementines - Kerygmata Petrou H XI 19.3]

R. Nehorai says, "In the generation in which the son of David will come, children will shame elders, and elders will stand up before children. 'The daughter rises up against the mother, and the daughter-in-law against her mother-in-law' (Micah 7:6). (Talmud - Babylonian Sanhedrin 97a, *The Babylonian Talmud a Translation and Commentary*, Jacob Neusner; Hendrickson Publishers, Inc., 2005)

12:54 1Kings 18:44
12:54-56 Matthew 16:1-4; Mark 8:11-13
12:56 Matthew 6:2-16n; Nag Hammadi[Gospel of Thomas 91]
12:56-59 Tertullian[Five Books Against Marcion Book IV.29]
12:57 Constitutions of the Holy Apostles[Book II.37]
12:57-59 Matthew 5:25-26
12:58 Clement of Alexandria[Stromata Book III.4]; Irenaeus[Against Heresies Book I.25.4]
12:58-59 Origen[Gospel of Matthew Book XIV.9]
12:59 Apostolic[Didache 1:5]
13:01 Josephus[Antiquities 18.4.1 85-87]
13:01-05 Anonymous[Treatise Against the Heretic Novatian 15]
13:01-35 Irenaeus[Against Heresies Book III.14.3]
13:03 Psalms 7:12-13; Jeremiah 12:17
13:05 Psalms 7:12-13; NT-Apocrypha[Oxyrhynchus Papyrus 840]
13:06 Psalms 80:9-17; Isaiah 5:1-7; Jeremiah 24:2-6; Hosea 9:10, 16; Habakkuk 3:17; Matthew 13:3-53n; Irenaeus[Against Heresies Book IV.36.8]; NT-Apocrypha[Apocalypse of Paul 1.16; Apocalypse of Peter 1.2]
13:07 Leviticus 19:23-25
13:08 Origen[Gospel of Matthew Book X.9]
13:10 Matthew 9:35n
13:11 Origen[Against Celsus Book VIII.54]
13:12 Origen[Gospel of Matthew Book XI.19]
13:14 Exodus 20:9-10; Deuteronomy 5:13-14; Rabbinic[Babylonian Shabbat 147b]
13:14-16 Irenaeus[Against Heresies Book IV.8.2]
13:15 Matthew 6:2-16n; Tertullian[Five Books Against Marcion Book IV.30]
13:15-16 Hippolytus[Fragments - On Daniel 2.18]
13:16 Irenaeus[Against Heresies Book II.23.2]; Origen[Against Celsus Book VIII.54]
13:17 Isaiah 45:16
13:18-19 Matthew 13:31-32; Mark 4:30-32
13:19 Psalms 104:12; Ezekiel 17:23, 31:6; Daniel 4:9, 12, 18, 21; Clement of Alexandria[Stromata Book V.1; The Instructor Book I.11]; Hippolytus[Refutation of all Heresies Book V.4]; Nag Hammadi[Gospel of Thomas 20]
13:20-21 Matthew 13:33; Philo[**On Abraham (107-109) cf. {Genesis 18:1-8}**]; Tertullian[Five Books Against Marcion Book IV.30]

It has been said then that the disposition of the Egyptians is inhospitable and intemperate; and the humanity of him who has been exposed to their conduct deserves admiration, for He in the middle of the day beholding as it were three men traveling (and he did not perceive that they were in reality of a more divine nature), ran up and entreated them with great perseverance not to pass by his tent, but as was becoming to go in and receive the rites of hospitality: and they knowing the truth of the man not so much by what he said, as by his mind which they could look into, assented to his request without hesitation; and being filled as to his soul with joy, he took every possible pain to make their extemporaneous reception worthy of them; and he said to his wife, "Hasten now, and make ready quickly three measures of fine meal," and he himself went forth among the herds of oxen, and brought forth a tender and well-fed heifer, and gave it to his servant; and he having slain it, dressed it with all speed. For no one in the house of a wise man is ever slow to perform the duties of hospitality, but both women and men, and slaves and freemen, are most eager in the performance of all those duties towards strangers. (Philo - On Abraham (107-109) cf. {Genesis 18:1-8})

13:21 Philo[On Mating With the Preliminary Studies (100-101) cf. {Exodus 16:36}; On the Birth of Abel And the Sacrifices offered By Him And By His Brother Cain (60) cf. {Genesis 18:6}]; Nag Hammadi[Gospel of Thomas 96]

13:22 Matthew 9:35n

13:22-30 Matthew 7:13-14, 21-23

13:23 Pseudepigrapha[4Ezra 8.3]

13:24 Origen[Gospel of Matthew Book XII.12]; Tertullian[On Fasting 17]; NT-Apocrypha[Epistula Apostolorum 24]

13:25 Rabbinic[Babylonian Abodah Zarah 3b]; Melito[Fragments 9.9]

13:25-28 Tertullian[Five Books Against Marcion Book IV.30]

13:26 Matthew 9:35n; Justin[First Apology 16]

13:26-27 Origen[Against Celsus Book II.49]

13:27 Psalms 6:8-9; OT-Apocrypha[1Maccabees 3:6]; Archelaus[Disputation with Manes 38]

13:28 Matthew 22:13, 25:30; Pseudepigrapha[Sibylline Oracles 8.231, 8.86]; Irenaeus[Against Heresies Book IV.8.1]

13:28-29 Pseudepigrapha[2Enoch 42:5]

13:29 Psalms 107:3; Isaiah 43:5, 49:12, 59:19; Malachi 1:11; Matthew 8:11-12; Pseudepigrapha[Baruch 4:37; Psalms of Solomon 11.1-3, 17.31]; Clement[Homily VIII.4; Recognitions Book IV.4]; NT-Apocrypha[Clement Romance - Peter on his Mission Journeys H VIII 4.1; Epistula Apostolorum 30]

13:30 Matthew 19:30, 20:16; Mark 10:31

13:32 This section also includes topical notes for: Naming the Animals - Genesis 2:19-20; Matthew 7:6, 15, 10:16, 12:34, 15:24, 23:33, 24:28, 25:32-33, 26:31; Mark 14:27; Luke 10:3, 17:37; John 10:7-27, 21:16-17; Philo[Fragments Extracted From the Parallels of John of Damascus Page 748. B. cf. {Genesis 3:19-20}]; Rabbinic[Genesis Rabba on 25.20]; Clement of Alexandria[Stromata Book IV.6]; Irenaeus[Against Heresies Book I.31.4, IV.41.3]; Nag Hammadi[Acts of Peter and the Twelve Apostles 4, 7-8; Book of Thomas the Contender 141; Gospel of Philip 60, 64, 71, 78; Teachings of Silvanus 86, 94, 105, 107]; Plato[Republic X 620d]

13:33 Origen[Gospel of Matthew Book XII.20]

13:34 Deuteronomy 32:11; Psalms 91:4; Isaiah 31:5; Pseudepigrapha[4Ezra 1:30]; Clement of Alexandria[Stromata Book I.5]; Clement[Homily III.19]; Irenaeus[Against Heresies Book IV.36.8]

13:34-35 Matthew 23:1-39; Mark 12:38-40; Luke 20:45-47

13:35 1Kings 9:7; Psalms 69:26, 118:26; Jeremiah 12:7, 22:5; OT-Apocrypha[Tobit 14:4]; Rabbinic[Babylonian Sanhedrin 38b cf. {Exodus 23:21}]

14:01 NT-Apocrypha[Acts of John 93]

14:01-14 Matthew 23:1

14:01-31 Pseudepigrapha[Joseph and Aseneth 20:2]; Philo[On the Contemplative Life Or Suppliants (75)]

14:01-16:31 Luke 7:36-50

14:03 Rabbinic[Babylonian (Shabbat 147b; Zebahim 19a)]; Irenaeus[Against Heresies Book IV.8.2]

14:05 Deuteronomy 22:4; Matthew 12:11

14:07 Matthew 13:3-53n

14:07-24 Philo[On Husbandry (152-155, 157-158, 165-166) cf. {Deuteronomy 20:5, 28:30}]

14:08 Clement of Alexandria[The Instructor Book II.1]

14:08-11 Proverbs 25:6-7

14:10 Clement of Alexandria[The Instructor Book II.1]

14:11 Ezekiel 17:24, 21:31; Matthew 18:4n, 23:12; Luke 18:14; Pseudepigrapha[Ahiqar 150]; Clement of Alexandria[Stromata Book II.22; The Instructor Book III.12]; Constitutions of the Holy Apostles[Book II.2]; Cyprian[Epistle V.3; Treatise XII.Book III.5]; Lactantius[Divine Institutes Book V.16]; Origen[De Principiis Book III.1.12]

14:12 Nag Hammadi[Acts of Peter and the Twelve Apostles 11-12]

14:12-13 Clement of Alexandria[The Instructor Book II.1]; Irenaeus[Against Heresies Book V.33.2]

14:12-14 Rabbinic[Avot 2.3]; Cyprian[Treatise XII.Book III.1]; Tertullian[Five Books Against Marcion Book IV.31]

14:13 Deuteronomy 14:29; OT-Apocrypha[Tobit 2:2]; Constitutions of the Holy Apostles[Book II.28]

14:14 Acts 2:31n; Pseudepigrapha[2Enoch 50:5]; Irenaeus[Against Heresies Book V.36.3]; Tertullian[On the Resurrection of the Flesh 33]

14:15 NT-Apocrypha[5Ezra 2.38]

14:15-16 Clement of Alexandria[The Instructor Book II.1]

14:16 Pseudepigrapha[2Enoch 42:5; Apocryphon of Ezekiel Fragment 1 1:2, Fragment 3];
   Tertullian[Five Books Against Marcion Book IV.31]; NT-Apocrypha[Acts of Thomas 1.146]
14:16-23 Nag Hammadi[Gospel of Thomas 64]
14:16-24 Matthew 22:2-14n; Rabbinic[Ecclesiastes Rabba on 9:7 cf. {Isaiah 65:13; Malachi 3:18}]
14:18-21 Tertullian[Five Books Against Marcion Book IV.31]
14:20 Deuteronomy 24:5; Clement of Alexandria[Stromata Book III.12]
14:23 Tertullian[Five Books Against Marcion Book IV.31]
14:24 NT-Apocrypha[Epistula Apostolorum 39]
14:26 Exodus 32:29; Deuteronomy 33:9; Matthew 10:37; Dead Sea Scrolls[4Q Testimonia
   (4Q175[4QTEST]) 14-17]; Philo[**On Drunkenness (72-76) cf. {Deuteronomy 33:9}; On Flight And
   Finding (88-92) cf. {Exodus 32:26, Deuteronomy 33:9}**; On the Birth of Abel And the Sacrifices
   offered By Him And By His Brother Cain (124-130) cf. {Numbers 8:5-22, 35:6-32, Joshua 20:2-3,
   21:13-38}; Special Laws I (52) cf. {Leviticus 19:34}]; Plato[Laws VI 776a-b]; Clement of
   Alexandria[Stromata Book III.15; Who is the Rich Man that shall be Saved 22]; Irenaeus[Against
   Heresies Book IV.8.3]; Origen[Gospel of Matthew Book XIII.25]; Tertullian[On Idolatry 12; On
   Prayer 8; Scorpiace 11]; Nag Hammadi[Exegesis of the Soul 135; Gospel of Thomas 101, 105; On the
   Origin of the World 104]; NT-Apocrypha[Acts of Thomas 1.61; Pistis Sophia c. 136; Two Books of
   Jeu c. 1-3]

> This is he "who says to his father and to his mother," his mortal parents, "I have not seen
> you," ever since I have beheld the things of God, who "does not recognize his sons," ever
> since he has become an acquaintance of wisdom, who "disowns his Brethren," ever since
> he has ceased to be disowned by God, and has been thought worthy of perfect salvation.
> (Philo - On Drunkenness (72-76) cf. {Deuteronomy 33:9})

> We must, therefore, say what is suitable on each of these heads, beginning with the first
> order. It is with exceeding propriety that the command is given to flee only to those cities
> which have been assigned to the tribe of Levi; for the Levites themselves are in a manner
> fugitives, inasmuch as they, for the sake of pleasing God, have left parents, and children,
> and brethren, and all their mortal relations. Therefore the original leader of the company
> is represented as saying to his father and mother, "I have not seen you, and my brethren I
> do not know, and my sons I Disown," in order to be able to serve the living God without
> allowing any opposite attraction to draw him away. (Philo - On Flight And Finding (88-
> 92) cf. {Exodus 32:26, Deuteronomy 33:9})

14:26-27 Clement of Alexandria[Stromata Book VII.12]; Nag Hammadi[Gospel of Thomas 55]
14:27 Matthew 10:38, 16:24; Mark 8:34; Luke 9:23; Irenaeus[Against Heresies Book I.3.5]
14:27-30 Tertullian[On Idolatry 12]
14:28 Genesis 11:3; Origen[Gospel of John Book VI.1]; NT-Apocrypha[Pseudo-Titus Epistle Line 169]
14:29 Pseudepigrapha[The Sentences of the Syriac Menander 344]
14:31 Pseudepigrapha[The Sentences of the Syriac Menander 340]
14:31-32 Nag Hammadi[Gospel of Thomas 98]
14:31-35 Linguistics[Aramaic words for "Salt" and "King" are homonyms]
14:32 2Samuel 8:10, 11:7; Psalms 122:6
14:33 Archelaus[Disputation with Manes 40, 42]; Cyprian[Treatise IV.19, XI.7, XII.Book III.11]
14:34 NT-Apocrypha[Acts of John 109]
14:34-35 Matthew 5:13; Mark 9:50; Origen[Against Celsus Book VIII.70]
14:34-36 Nag Hammadi[Gospel of Thomas 114]
14:35 Matthew 11:15n
15:01 Pseudepigrapha[Joseph and Aseneth 9:2]
15:01-02 Tertullian[On Modesty 9]
15:01-07 Matthew 18:10-14
15:01-10 Tertullian[Five Books Against Marcion Book IV.32]
15:02 Luke 5:29-30; Hippolytus[Refutation of all Heresies Book IX.23]
15:03 Matthew 13:3-53n
15:03-07 Nag Hammadi[Gospel of Thomas 107]
15:03-10 Tertullian[On Modesty 7; On Repentance 8]

15:04 Ezekiel 34:11, 16; Irenaeus[Against Heresies Book I.8.4, 16.1, II.24.6, III.23.8]

15:04-06 Constitutions of the Holy Apostles[Book II.20]; Methodius[Banquet of the Ten Virgins 3.5]

15:04-07 Nag Hammadi[Gospel of Truth 31-32]

15:04-10 Hippolytus[Refutation of all Heresies Book V.47]

15:05 Isaiah 49:22

15:06 Anatolius[Paschal Canon 10]; Canticle of Mar Jacob the Teacher on Edessa

15:06-10 Anonymous[Treatise Against the Heretic Novatian 15]

15:07 Rabbinic[Babylonian Sanhedrin 99a cf. {Isaiah 57:19}]; Clement of Alexandria[Stromata Book II.15]; Constitutions of the Holy Apostles[Book II.13, VIII.8; Ecclesiastical Canons 47.52]; Cyprian[Epistle XLVI.2, LI.22]; Tertullian[On Repentance 8]

15:07-10 Pseudepigrapha[Joseph and Aseneth 15:8]

15:08 Irenaeus[Against Heresies Book I.8.4, 16.1]; Methodius[Banquet of the Ten Virgins 9.4]; Tertullian[On Prescription Against Heretics 11]

15:10 Clement of Alexandria[Stromata Book II.15; Who is the Rich Man that shall be Saved 39]; Tertullian[On Repentance 8]

15:11 Genesis 38:28, 42:32, 47:13-26; Irenaeus[Against Heresies Book IV.36.7]

15:11-24 Pseudepigrapha[Apocalypse of Sedrach 6:4]

15:11-32 Philo[Special Laws II (18-19)]; Clement of Alexandria[Fragments from Macarius Chrysocephalus Parable of the Prodigal son 1]; Tertullian[Of Patience 12; On Repentance 8]

15:12 OT-Apocrypha[1Maccabees 10:29-30; Tobit 3:17]

15:13 Proverbs 29:3; Pseudepigrapha[Hellenistic Synagogal Prayers 11:9]; Pythagoras[Golden Verses Line 37]; Constitutions of the Holy Apostles[Book VIII.9]

15:15 Pseudepigrapha[Joseph and Aseneth 3:5]

15:17 Clement of Alexandria[Stromata Book IV.6]

15:18 Exodus 10:16; Psalms 51:6

15:18-21 Pseudepigrapha[Joseph and Aseneth 7:4]

15:19 Pseudepigrapha[Joseph and Aseneth 6:8]

15:19-21 Pseudepigrapha[Joseph and Aseneth 11:5, 12:5]

15:20 OT-Apocrypha[Tobit 11:9]; Pseudepigrapha[Hellenistic Synagogal Prayers 11:9]

15:21 Constitutions of the Holy Apostles[Book II.40]

15:22 Genesis 41:42; Pseudepigrapha[Joseph and Aseneth 15:10]

15:22-23 Irenaeus[Against Heresies Book IV.14.2]

15:23 Pseudepigrapha[Joseph and Aseneth 20:8]; Methodius[Banquet of the Ten Virgins 7.4]; Tertullian[On Modesty 9]

15:24 Pseudepigrapha[Joseph and Aseneth 8:9, 11:5, 19:10]

15:25 Daniel 3:5, 10, 15; Origen[Gospel of Matthew Book XIV.1]

15:29-32 Tertullian[On Repentance 8]

15:31 NT-Apocrypha[Gospel of the Hebrews Fragment 5]

15:32 Pseudepigrapha[Joseph and Aseneth 8:9, 11:5]

16:01 Pseudepigrapha[Joseph and Aseneth 3:5]

16:01-09 Pseudepigrapha[Letter of Aristeas 1.187-189]

16:01-31 Irenaeus[Against Heresies Book III.14.3]

16:03 Isaiah 22:19; Pseudepigrapha[Pseudo-Phocylides 152]

16:04-09 Pseudepigrapha[4Ezra 7.80, 7.85]

16:05-07 Origen[Gospel of Matthew Book XIV.8]

16:07 NT-Apocrypha[Infancy Story of Thomas 12.2]

16:08 1Thessalonians 5:5n; Cyprian[Epistle LXXII.19]; Nag Hammadi[Gospel of Thomas 50]; NT-Apocrypha[Epistula Apostolorum 39]

16:09 Pseudepigrapha[1Enoch 39:4, 63:10; 4Ezra 2:11]; Clement of Alexandria[Who is the Rich Man that shall be Saved 13, 31]; Irenaeus[Against Heresies Book IV.30.3]; Methodius[Apostolic Words from the Discourse on the Resurrection 5]; Tertullian[De Fuga in Persecutione 13; Of Patience 7]; NT-Apocrypha[5Ezra 2.11]

16:10-11 Pseudepigrapha[4Ezra 7.18]

16:10-12 Apostolic[2Clement 8:5]; Hippolytus[Refutation of all Heresies Book X.29]

16:11 Irenaeus[Against Heresies Book II.34.3]

16:11-12 Cyprian[Treatise VIII.8]; Tertullian[Five Books Against Marcion Book IV.33]

16:13 Matthew 6:24n; Apostolic[2Clement 6:1]; Clement of Alexandria[Stromata Book III.4, VII.12]; Tertullian[On Idolatry 12; Five Books Against Marcion Book IV.33; To his Wife Book II.3]; Nag Hammadi[Gospel of Thomas 47]

16:14 Cyprian[Treatise VIII.12]; Hippolytus[Refutation of all Heresies Book IX.23]; Origen[Gospel of Matthew Book XI.9]

16:15 1Kings 8:39; 1Chronicles 28:9; Proverbs 24:12; Constitutions of the Holy Apostles[Book VII.8]; Cyprian[Epistle LXVI.4]; Tertullian[On the Apparel of Women Book II.13; Five Books Against Marcion Book IV.33]; NT-Apocrypha[6Ezra 17.55-64]

16:16 Matthew 11:12-13; Rabbinic[Babylonian Sanhedrin 11a]; Archelaus[Disputation with Manes 13, 40]; Clement of Alexandria[Stromata Book V.8]; Irenaeus[Against Heresies Book IV.4.2]; Origen[Gospel of John Book VI.8; Gospel of Matthew Book X.21, XI.1]; Tertullian[An Answer to the Jews 13; On Fasting 2; On Modesty 6; Five Books Against Marcion Book IV.33, V.2, 8]; Nag Hammadi[Apocryphon of James 6]

16:17 Matthew 5:18; Clement of Alexandria[Fragments Edited by Corderius Catena on Luke]; Tertullian[Five Books Against Marcion Book IV.33]

16:18 Matthew 5:32, 19:1-12; Mark 10:1-12; John 8:3-11n; 1Corinthians 7:10-11; Tertullian[Five Books Against Marcion Book IV.34]

16:19 Proverbs 31:22; Archelaus[Disputation with Manes 41]

16:19-31 Dead Sea Scrolls[4Q Enoch (4Q206[4QENAR]) Fragment I 1-7]; Philo[On Rewards And Punishments (152)]; Irenaeus[Against Heresies Book II.34.1, IV.1.4]; Tertullian[Five Books in Reply to Marcion Book IV.139; On Fasting 16; On Idolatry 13; Five Books Against Marcion Book IV.34]

16:21 Pseudepigrapha[Joseph and Aseneth 10:13]; Nag Hammadi[Gospel of Philip 82]

16:22 Pseudepigrapha[Apocalypse of Sedrach 14:6]

16:22-25 Pseudepigrapha[Testament of Abraham 20.14-15]

16:22-28 Pseudepigrapha[**1Enoch 22:3-14**]; Dead Sea Scrolls[4Q Enoch (4Q206[4QENAR]) Fragment 1 1-7]; Josephus[Discourse to the Greeks Concerning Hades 1-4]

Then Raphael, one of the holy angels who were with me, answered and said, These are the delightful places where the spirits, the souls of the dead, will be collected; for them were they formed; and here will be collected all the souls of the sons of men. These places, in which they dwell, shall they occupy until the day of judgment, and until their appointed period. Their appointed period will be long, even until the great judgment. And I saw the spirits of the sons of men who were dead; and their voices reached to heaven, while accusing. Then I inquired of Raphael, an angel who was with me, and said, Whose spirit is that, the voice of which reaches to heaven, and accuses? He answered, saying, This is the spirit of Abel who was slain by Cain his brother; and who will accuse that brother, until his seed be destroyed from the face of the earth; Until his seed perish from the seed of the human race. At that time therefore I inquired respecting him, and respecting the general judgment, saying, Why is one separated from another? He answered, Three separations have been made between the spirits of the dead, and thus have the spirits of the righteous been separated. Namely, by a chasm, by water, and by light above it. And in the same way likewise are sinners separated when they die, and are buried in the earth; judgment not overtaking them in their lifetime. Here their souls are separated. Moreover, abundant is their suffering until the time of the great judgment, the castigation, and the torment of those who eternally execrate, whose souls are punished and bound there for ever. And thus has it been from the beginning of the world. Thus has there existed a separation between the souls of those who utter complaints, and of those who watch for their destruction, to slaughter them in the day of sinners. Such has been made for the spirits of men who were not righteous but sinners, who were complete in transgression, and of the transgressors they shall be companions: but their spirits shall not be slain in the day of judgment nor shall they be raised from thence.' (Pseudepigrapha - 1Enoch 22:3-14)

16:22-31 Archelaus[Disputation with Manes 41]

16:23 OT-Apocrypha[4Maccabees 13:15]; Pseudepigrapha[4Ezra 7:36; Hellenistic Synagogal Prayers 16:4]; Tertullian[Five Books Against Marcion Book IV.34]; NT-Apocrypha[Epistula Apostolorum 27]

16:23-24 Tertullian[A Treatise on the Soul 7, 9]

16:23-26 Pseudepigrapha[Apocalypse of Elijah 5:27]

16:24 Pseudepigrapha[2Enoch 63:4]

16:25 Cyprian[Treatise XII.Book III.61]

16:26 OT-Apocrypha[2Esdras 7:36]; Pseudepigrapha[1Enoch 22:9; Prayer of Jacob 1:11]; Tertullian[A Treatise on the Soul 57; The Martyrdom of Perpetua and Felicitas 2]; NT-Apocrypha[Acts of Thomas 1.55]

16:28 Irenaeus[Against Heresies Book II.24.4]; Methodius[Apostolic Words from the Discourse on the Resurrection 19]

16:29 Tertullian[On Prescription Against Heretics 8; Five Books Against Marcion Book IV.34]

16:29-31 Pseudepigrapha[4Ezra 7.130-131]

16:31 Acts 3:18n; Irenaeus[Against Heresies Book IV.1.3]

17:01 Clement[Recognitions Book III.65]; Lactantius[Divine Institutes Book IV.30]; NT-Apocrypha[Epistula Apostolorum 29]

17:01-02 Apostolic[1Clement 46:8]

17:01-04 Matthew 18:21-22, 67; Mark 9:42; Tertullian[Five Books Against Marcion Book IV.35]

17:01-37 Irenaeus[Against Heresies Book III.14.3]

17:03 Leviticus 19:17; NT-Apocrypha[Gospel of Mani Psalm CCXXXIX]

17:03-04 Matthew 18:15-18n; Clement of Alexandria[The Instructor Book III.12]

17:04 Psalms 119:164; Hippolytus[Refutation of all Heresies Book V.2]; NT-Apocrypha[Gospel of the Nazareans Fragment 15a]

17:05-06 Clement of Alexandria[Stromata Book V.1]

17:06 Clement[Recognitions Book V.34]

17:07-10 Cyprian[Treatise XII.Book III.51]

17:10 2Samuel 6:22; Cyprian[Epistle XXVI.2]

17:11-21 Tertullian[Five Books Against Marcion Book IV.35]

17:12 Leviticus 13:45-46

17:14 Leviticus 13:49, 14:1-32; Constitutions of the Holy Apostles[Book VI.19]

17:15 2Kings 5:15

17:16 Nag Hammadi[Gospel of Thomas 14]

17:20 NT-Apocrypha[Apocalypse of Peter 1.1]

17:20-21 Pseudepigrapha[4Ezra 2.37-38]; Dead Sea Scrolls[4Q Songs of the Sabbath Sacrifice (4Q401[4QSHIRSHABB]) Fragment 14 COL I 5-6]; Philo[Every Good Man Is Free (68) cf. {Deuteronomy 30:14}]; Clement of Alexandria[Exhortation to the Heathen 9, 11; Who is the Rich Man that shall be Saved 17]; Irenaeus[Against Heresies Book III.21.4, IV.8.1]; Justin[Dialogue with Trypho 51]; Origen[De Principiis Book I.3.6]; Nag Hammadi[Gospel of Thomas 3, 82, 113; Teachings of Silvanus 107; Trimorphic Protennoia 50]

17:20-37 Matthew 24:23-28, 36-41

17:21 Cyprian[Treatise XII.Book III.52]; Hippolytus[Refutation of all Heresies Book V.2-3]; Origen[Gospel of Matthew Book X.14, XII.14, 35]; Peter of Alexandria[Canonical Epistle 5]

17:21-23 Nag Hammadi[Gospel of Mary 8]

17:22 Psalms 80:17; Nag Hammadi[Gospel of Thomas 38]

17:23 NT-Apocrypha[Apocalypse of Peter 1.1]

17:24 Psalms 80:17; Pseudepigrapha[Apocalypse of Elijah 3:4; Sibylline Oracles 6.18]

17:25-30 Tertullian[Five Books Against Marcion Book IV.35]

17:26 Genesis 6:5-12; Psalms 80:17; Pseudepigrapha[2Enoch 70:10]; Rabbinic[Babylonian Sanhedrin 99a cf. {Isaiah 54:9}]; NT-Apocrypha[Apocalypse of Paul 1.15]

17:26-30 Irenaeus[Against Heresies Book IV.36.3]

17:27 Genesis 6:11-13, 7:6-24

17:28 Genesis 18:20-19:25; Clement of Alexandria[Stromata Book III.6]

17:28-29 Tertullian[To his Wife Book I.5]

17:29 Genesis 19:15-29

17:30 Psalms 80:17

17:31 Matthew 24:17-18; Mark 13:15-16

17:31-32 Genesis 19:17, 26; Cyprian[Treatise XI.7]

17:31-33 Pseudepigrapha[Apocalypse of Elijah 4:24]

17:32 Tertullian[Five Books Against Marcion Book IV.35]

17:33 Matthew 10:39, 16:25; Mark 8:35; Luke 9:24; John 12:25n; Apostolic[Ignatius - Letter to the Magnesians 5:2]

17:34 Pseudepigrapha[Apocalypse of Zephaniah 2:2]; Irenaeus[Against Heresies Book V.27.1]; Nag Hammadi[Gospel of Thomas 61]

17:37 Job 39:30; Matthew 24:28; Luke 13:32n; Dead Sea Scrolls[4Q Word of the Luminaries (4Q504[4QDIBHAM]) Fragment 6 6-9]

18:01 Origen[Gospel of Matthew Book XIII.23]; Tertullian[On Fasting 10; On the Resurrection of the Flesh 33]; Nag Hammadi[Gospel of Thomas 14]

18:01-02 Origen[Gospel of Matthew Book XIV.25]

18:01-08 Tertullian[Five Books Against Marcion Book IV.36]

18:01-09 Matthew 13:3-53n

18:01-43 Irenaeus[Against Heresies Book III.14.3]

18:02 Pseudepigrapha[Joseph and Aseneth 28:7]

18:02-03 Tertullian[On Prescription Against Heretics 11]

18:02-05 Hippolytus[Treatise on Christ and Antichrist 56]

18:03 Exodus 22:22; Cyprian[Epistle VII.2]

18:06-08 Clement[Homily XVII.5]

18:07 Judges 11:36; Psalms 22:3; OT-Apocrypha[Sirach 35:22]; Tertullian[Scorpiace 11]

18:07-08 Irenaeus[Against Heresies Book IV.27.4]

18:08 Psalms 80:17; Rabbinic[Babylonian Sanhedrin 96b]; Clement of Alexandria[Stromata Book III.6]; Constitutions of the Holy Apostles[Book VI.18]; Cyprian[Epistle LXXIII.9; Treatise I.26]; Irenaeus[Against Heresies Book IV.33.11]; Origen[Gospel of John Book VI.38; Gospel of Matthew Book XIII.1]

18:09 Ezekiel 33:13

18:09-14 Tertullian[On Prayer 17]

18:10 Irenaeus[Against Heresies Book IV.36.8]

18:10-11 Origen[Gospel of John Book VI.13]

18:10-14 Clement of Alexandria[Fragments from Macarius Chrysocephalus Parable of the Prodigal son 4]; Cyprian[Treatise IV.6]; Tertullian[Five Books Against Marcion Book IV.36]

18:11 Pseudepigrapha[Joseph and Aseneth 11:19]; Hippolytus[Refutation of all Heresies Book IX.23]; Origen[Against Celsus Book III.64]

18:12 Genesis 14:20; Pseudepigrapha[Apocalypse of Elijah 1:13]

18:13 2Kings 5:18; Psalms 25:11, 51:1, 79:9; Daniel 9:19; Pseudepigrapha[Joseph and Aseneth 10:15, 11:19]

18:13-14 Origen[Against Celsus Book III.64]

18:14 Matthew 18:4n, 23:12; Luke 14:11; Pseudepigrapha[Ahiqar 150]; Clement of Alexandria[The Instructor Book III.12]; Constitutions of the Holy Apostles[Book VII.8]; Cyprian[Treatise I.21]; Origen[De Principiis Book III.1.12]; NT-Apocrypha[Protoevangelium of James 5.1, 20.3]

18:15-17 Matthew 19:13-15; Mark 10:13-16

18:16 Tertullian[On Baptism 18]

18:17 Rabbinic[Avot 4.25]; Apostolic[Shepherd of Hermas 27:1]; Origen[Gospel of Matthew Book XIII.19]; Nag Hammadi[Gospel of Thomas 22]

18:18 Deuteronomy 14:22; Jude 1:21n; Pseudepigrapha[Sibylline Oracles Fragment 3.47]; Clement of Alexandria[Stromata Book III.6, VII.12]; Clement[Homily XVIII.3, 17]; Irenaeus[Against Heresies Book I.20.2]; Justin[Dialogue with Trypho 101]

18:18-22 Tertullian[Five Books Against Marcion Book IV.36]

18:18-27 Tertullian[On Monogamy 14]

18:18-30 Matthew 19:16-30n; Mark 10:17-31

18:19 Matthew 19:17n; Mark 10:18; Clement[Homily III.57]; Hippolytus[Refutation of all Heresies Book V.2, VII.19]; Origen[Gospel of John Book VI.28; De Principiis Book I.2.13]; Tertullian[On Modesty 2; Five Books Against Marcion Book IV.36]

18:20 Exodus 20:12-16; Deuteronomy 5:16-20; Matthew 15:4-8n; John 8:3-11n; Pseudepigrapha[Life of Abraham 11:10]

18:21 Pseudepigrapha[2Baruch 38:4]

18:22 This section also includes topical notes for: Give to the Poor - Matthew 19:21; Mark 10:21; OT-Apocrypha[Sirach 29:11]; Philo[On the Contemplative Life Or Suppliants (13)]; Apostolic[Shepherd of Hermas 50:8-9]; Clement of Alexandria[Who is the Rich Man that shall be Saved 16, 19]; Tertullian[On Idolatry 12]; NT-Apocrypha[Acts of Thomas 1.21]; Epic of Gilgamesh[The Story of the Flood]

18:22-30 Mark 10:21-32n

18:23 NT-Apocrypha[Secret Gospel of Mark Fragment 1]

18:24 Clement of Alexandria[Stromata Book V.5]; NT-Apocrypha[Epistula Apostolorum 46]

18:24-25 Tertullian[To his Wife Book II.8]

18:25 Pseudepigrapha[4Ezra 7.4-18]; Apostolic[Shepherd of Hermas 14:6]

18:26 Clement of Alexandria[Who is the Rich Man that shall be Saved 20]

18:27 Constitutions of the Holy Apostles[Book V.7]; Irenaeus[Against Heresies Book II.10.4, IV.20.5, V.5.2, 25.4; Demonstration of the Apostolic Preaching 97]; Justin[First Apology 18]; Tertullian[Against Praxeas 10; On Baptism 2; On Idolatry 12]; Theophilus of Antioch[To Autolycus Book II.13]

18:28 Tertullian[Five Books in Reply to Marcion Book III.10]; NT-Apocrypha[Pistis Sophia c. 136]

18:28-30 NT-Apocrypha[Two Books of Jeu c. 1-3]

18:29 Indian[Dhammapada 43]

18:29-30 Matthew 19:29n; Mark 10:29-30; Cyprian[Epistle LV.2; Treatise XI.12, XII.Book III.16]; Irenaeus[Against Heresies Book V.33.2]; Epic of Gilgamesh[The Story of the Flood]

18:30 Jude 1:21n

18:31 Psalms 80:17; Acts 3:18n

18:31-33 Justin[Dialogue with Trypho 106]

18:31-34 Matthew 20:17-19; Mark 10:32-34

18:32 Matthew 27:19-31n; Pseudepigrapha[Sibylline Oracles 8.287-289]

18:33 Justin[Dialogue with Trypho 51]

18:35-43 Matthew 20:29-34; Mark 10:46-52

18:38 Tertullian[Five Books Against Marcion Book IV.38]

18:38-39 Matthew 1:1

18:38-40 Tertullian[Five Books Against Marcion Book IV.36]

18:42 Tertullian[On Baptism 12; On Prescription Against Heretics 14; Five Books Against Marcion Book IV.36]

19:01-48 Irenaeus[Against Heresies Book III.14.3]

19:02-09 Clement of Alexandria[Who is the Rich Man that shall be Saved 13]

19:05 Pseudepigrapha[Joseph and Aseneth 3:2]; Clement[Homily III.63]; Irenaeus[Against Heresies Book I.8.3]; NT-Apocrypha[Clement Romance 63.1]

19:08 Exodus 21:37, 22:1; Numbers 5:6; Pseudepigrapha[Joseph and Aseneth 10:11]; Irenaeus[Against Heresies Book IV.12.5]

19:08-09 Cyprian[Treatise VIII.8, XII.Book III.1]; Tertullian[Five Books Against Marcion Book IV.37]

19:08-10 Clement of Alexandria[Stromata Book IV.6]

19:09 Cyprian[Epistle LXII.4]; NT-Apocrypha[Clement Romance 63.1]

19:10 Psalms 80:17; Ezekiel 34:16; Matthew 18:11; Constitutions of the Holy Apostles[Book II.20]; Tertullian[On the Resurrection of the Flesh 9, 34; Five Books Against Marcion Book IV.37]

19:11 Matthew 13:3-53n

19:12 Origen[Gospel of Matthew Book XIV.13]

19:12-13 Tertullian[Five Books Against Marcion Book IV.39]

19:12-27 Pseudepigrapha[Ahiqar 193]; Origen[Gospel of Matthew Book XIV.12]

19:13 Origen[Gospel of Matthew Book XIV.7]; NT-Apocrypha[Acts of Thomas 1.146]

19:14 Origen[De Principiis Book II.4.4]

19:15 Tertullian[On Exhortation to Chastity 10]

19:17 This section also includes topical notes for: Faithfulness - Matthew 25:21; Philo[Concerning Noah's Work As A Planter (102-109) cf. {Leviticus 19:23}; Special Laws IV (218) cf. {Exodus 23:11}]; Justin[First Apology 44]; Origen[Against Celsus Book VIII.74; Gospel of Matthew Book XIV.9; De Principiis Book II.11.2]

19:19 Origen[Gospel of Matthew Book XIV.9; De Principiis Book II.11.2]

19:20-24 Tertullian[On Prescription Against Heretics 26]

19:22 Clement of Alexandria[Stromata Book I.1]; Tertullian[Five Books Against Marcion Book IV.37]

19:22-26 Nag Hammadi[Gospel of Philip 64]

19:23 NT-Apocrypha[Clement Romance 61.1]

19:24-26 Pseudepigrapha[Ahiqar 143]

19:26 Matthew 13:12; Mark 4:25; Luke 8:18; Pseudepigrapha[4Ezra 7.25; Odes of Solomon 24.9]; Clement of Alexandria[Stromata Book VII.10]; Irenaeus[Against Heresies Book I.6.4]; Origen[De Principiis Book II.11.4]

19:27 1Samuel 15:33; Matthew 25:14-30; Methodius[Oration on the Psalms 1]; Origen[Gospel of Matthew Book XIV.13]

19:29 Origen[Gospel of John Book X.15]

19:29-44 Matthew 21:1-11; Mark 11:1-10; John 12:12-19

19:30 1Samuel 6:7

19:30-35 John 12:14-15

19:35 John 12:5

19:36 2Kings 9:13

19:37-38 Methodius[Oration on the Psalms 3]

19:38 Psalms 118:26; Mark 11:9; Rabbinic[Babylonian Sanhedrin 38b cf. {Exodus 23:21}]; Methodius[Oration on the Psalms 1]; NT-Apocrypha[Falling Asleep of Mary]

19:40 Habakkuk 2:11; Pseudepigrapha[4Ezra 5:5]; Cyprian[Epistle IX.4]; Origen[Gospel of John Book X.17]; NT-Apocrypha[Acts of Andrew (Codex Vaticanus 808) 16]

19:41 2Kings 8:11

19:41-42 Origen[Gospel of John Book X.15, 18]

19:41-44 Tertullian[An Answer to the Jews 13]

19:42 Deuteronomy 32:28-29; Isaiah 6:9-10; Irenaeus[Against Heresies Book I.20.2]

19:42-44 Lactantius[Divine Institutes Book IV.20]

19:43-44 Josephus[War 6.1.1-6.10.1 1-435]; Clement[Homily III.15]

19:44 2Samuel 17:13; Job 10:12; Psalms 137:9; Isaiah 29:3; Jeremiah 6:15; Hosea 10:14, 14:1; Nahum 3:10; OT-Apocrypha[Wisdom of Solomon 3:7]; Dead Sea Scrolls[4Q Isaiah Pesher (4Q161[4QPIS]) Fragment 1 COL II 2]; Rabbinic[Babylonian Gittin 57b cf. {Psalms 137.7}]; Clement[Recognitions Book I.37]; Constitutions of the Holy Apostles[Book V.15]

19:45-46 Pseudepigrapha[Psalms of Solomon 17.36]; Clement of Alexandria[The Instructor Book III.11]

19:45-48 Matthew 21:12-17; Mark 11:15-19; John 2:13-22

19:46 Isaiah 56:7; Jeremiah 7:11; Matthew 21:13n; Apostolic[2Clement 14:1]; Tertullian[On Modesty 1]

19:47 Matthew 9:35n; Luke 21:37

20:01 Matthew 9:35n

20:01-08 Matthew 21:23-27; Mark 11:27-33

20:04 Matthew 3:5-16n; Tertullian[On Baptism 10]

20:04-06 Tertullian[Five Books Against Marcion Book IV.38]

20:08 Tertullian[Five Books Against Marcion Book IV.38]

20:09 Isaiah 5:1-2

20:09-16 Mark 12:1-9

20:09-19 Matthew 13:3-53n; Matthew 21:33-41n

20:10-12 2Chronicles 36:15-16

20:15 Pseudepigrapha[Apocryphon of Ezekiel Fragment 1 2:6]

20:17 Psalms 118:22; Isaiah 28:16; Matthew 21:42; Pseudepigrapha[Testament of Solomon 22:8, 23:4]

20:17-19 Matthew 21:42-46; Mark 12:10-12

20:18 Isaiah 8:14; Daniel 2:34, 44

20:19 NT-Apocrypha[Acts of Thomas 1.164]

20:19-26 Matthew 21:45, 22:45

20:20 Tertullian[Five Books Against Marcion Book IV.19]

20:20-26 Matthew 22:15-22; Mark 12:13-17

20:21 Matthew 9:35n; Pseudepigrapha[Odes of Solomon 24.13, 39.13]; NT-Apocrypha[Epistula Apostolorum 24]

20:25 Matthew 22:21n; Mark 12:17; Clement of Alexandria[The Instructor Book III.12]; Origen[Gospel of Matthew Book XIII.10]; Tertullian[On Idolatry 15; Five Books Against Marcion Book IV.38]

20:26-38 Tertullian[On Monogamy 7]

20:27 Acts 5:17, 23:8; Josephus[Antiquities 18.1.4 16-17; War 2.8.14 162-166]; Hippolytus[Refutation of all Heresies Book IX.24]; Justin[On the Resurrection 9]; Tertullian[Against All Heresies 1]

20:27-33 Tertullian[Five Books Against Marcion Book IV.38; On the Resurrection of the Flesh 36]

20:27-38 Acts 2:31n

20:27-40 Matthew 22:23-33; Mark 12:18-27; Tertullian[To his Wife Book I.1]

20:28 Genesis 38:8; Deuteronomy 25:5; Mark 12:27n

20:33-34 Tertullian[Five Books Against Marcion Book IV.38]

20:34 Clement of Alexandria[The Instructor Book I.4]

20:34-35 Clement of Alexandria[Stromata Book III.12]; Justin[On the Resurrection 3]

20:34-36 Tertullian[On Exhortation to Chastity 13]; Nag Hammadi[Tripartite Tractate 132]

20:34-38 Cyprian[Treatise XII.Book III.32]

20:35 Clement of Alexandria[Stromata Book III.6, VI.12, 16]; Cyprian[Epistle LXXX.1];
   Irenaeus[Against Heresies Book II.33.5]; Justin[Dialogue with Trypho 81]; Pontius the Deacon[The
   Life and Passion of Cyprian 1]

20:35-36 Cyprian[Treatise II.22]; Tertullian[On Monogamy 10; On the Apparel of Women Book I.2;
   Five Books Against Marcion Book IV.38-39]; Nag Hammadi[Gospel of Truth 43]

20:36 Genesis 6:2; Jude 1:21n; Pseudepigrapha[2Baruch 51:9]; Clement of Alexandria[Stromata Book
   VI.13, VII.10]; Origen[Against Celsus Book IV.29; Gospel of Matthew Book XI.14; De Principiis Book
   IV.1.29]; Tertullian[On the Resurrection of the Flesh 62; Five Books Against Marcion Book III.9,
   V.10; To his Wife Book I.1]

20:37 Exodus 3:2, 6, 15; OT-Apocrypha[4Maccabees 7:19, 16:25]

20:38 Pseudepigrapha[Hellenistic Synagogal Prayers 16:8-14]; Clement[Homily III.55]; Constitutions
   of the Holy Apostles[Book VI.30]; Novatian[Treatise Concerning the Trinity 25]; Nag
   Hammadi[Gospel of Thomas 18]

20:39-44 Tertullian[Five Books Against Marcion Book IV.38]

20:41-44 Matthew 22:41-46; Mark 12:35-37; Acts 3:18-26n; Apostolic[Epistle of Barnabas 12:10-11];
   Clement of Alexandria[Exhortation to the Heathen 1]; Irenaeus[Fragments from the Lost Works 52]

20:42-43 Psalms 110:1

20:44 Romans 1:3

20:45-47 Matthew 23:1-39; Mark 12:38-40; Luke 11:37-54

20:46 Rabbinic[Babylonian Horayot 13a-14b]; Archelaus[Disputation with Manes 21]; Clement of
   Alexandria[Stromata Book VI.13]

20:47 Rabbinic[Babylonian Ketubot 100b]

21:01-04 Mark 12:32-34, 41-44; Philo[Special Laws I (275-279) cf. {Exodus 30:8-9}]; Nag
   Hammadi[Sentences of Sextus 379]; Indian[Dhammapada 224]

21:02 Commodianus[Instructions 72]; Gregory Thaumaturgus[Oration and Panegyric Addressed to
   Origen 3]

21:03-04 Constitutions of the Holy Apostles[Book III.7]; Cyprian[Treatise VIII.15]

21:04 Irenaeus[Against Heresies Book IV.18.2]

21:05-36 Matthew 24:1-25:46; Mark 13:1-37

21:06 Rabbinic[Babylonian Gittin 57b cf. {Psalms 137.7}]

21:06-36 NT-Apocrypha[Epistula Apostolorum 34]

21:07 Pseudepigrapha[2Baruch 25:3; 4Ezra 4.33]; Tertullian[Five Books Against Marcion Book IV.39]

21:07-19 Matthew 24:3-14; Mark 13:03-13; Revelation 6:1-12, 13:1-8

21:08 Daniel 7:22; Matthew 24:4-5; Mark 13:5-6; Revelation 6:1-2, 13:1-6; Alexander of
   Alexandria[Epistles on Arian Heresy 2.5]; Tertullian[Five Books Against Marcion Book IV.39, V.1]

21:08-09 Hippolytus[Appendix to the Works of Hippolytus - On the End of the World 8, 10]

21:09 Daniel 2:28, 45

21:09-10 Matthew 24:6-7; Mark 13:7-8; Revelation 6:3-4, 13:7

21:09-14 Tertullian[Five Books Against Marcion Book IV.39]

21:10 2Chronicles 15:6; Isaiah 19:2; Pseudepigrapha[4Ezra 15:15; Apocalypse of Daniel 1:1; Sibylline
   Oracles 1.397, 2.23, 2.6, 3.636]; NT-Apocrypha[Epistula Apostolorum 37]

21:10-11 Victorinus[Apocalypse 6.3-4]

21:11 Isaiah 19:17; Ezekiel 38:19, 22; Matthew 24:7; Mark 13:8; 1Thessalonians 5:3; Revelation 6:5-8;
   Pseudepigrapha[2Baruch 27:9]; NT-Apocrypha[Apocalypse of Thomas Line 7, 11]

21:12 Nag Hammadi[Apocryphon of James 5; Letter of Peter to Philip 138-139]; NT-
   Apocrypha[Epistula Apostolorum 15]

21:12-19 Matthew 24:9-13; Mark 13:9; Revelation 6:9-12

21:14-15 Cyprian[Epistle LXXVI.5; Treatise XI.10]

21:15 Luke 12:11-12

21:16-17 Tertullian[Five Books Against Marcion Book IV.39]

21:17 Cyprian[Treatise XII.Book III.29]

21:18 1Samuel 14:45; Hippolytus[Treatise on Christ and Antichrist 64]

21:18-19 Constitutions of the Holy Apostles[Book V.7]

21:19 Pseudepigrapha[2Enoch 50:2]

21:19-20 Tertullian[Five Books Against Marcion Book IV.39]

21:20 Matthew 24:15; Mark 13:14; 2Thessalonians 2:3-12; Revelation 13:1-6; Origen[Against Celsus Book II.13; Gospel of Matthew Book XIV.19]

21:20-23 Hippolytus[Treatise on Christ and Antichrist 62]

21:21 Victorinus[Apocalypse 12.6]

21:21-24 Matthew 24:16-21; Mark 13:14; Revelation 13:7-18

21:22 Deuteronomy 32:35; Jeremiah 46:10; Hosea 9:7; Tertullian[Five Books Against Marcion Book IV.39]

21:23 Pseudepigrapha[Apocalypse of Daniel 12:6; Sibylline Oracles 2.190]; Clement of Alexandria[Stromata Book III.6]; Tertullian[On Monogamy 16; Five Books Against Marcion Book IV.33; To his Wife Book I.5]

21:24 Genesis 34:26; Deuteronomy 28:64; Ezra 9:7; Psalms 79:1; Isaiah 63:18; Jeremiah 21:7; Ezekiel 32:9; Daniel 9:26, 12:7; Zechariah 12:3; OT-Apocrypha[1Maccabees 3:45, 51; Sirach 28:18; Tobit 14:5]; Pseudepigrapha[Joseph and Aseneth 26:5; Psalms of Solomon 17:25]; NT-Apocrypha[Apocalypse of Thomas Line 8]

21:24-31 Tertullian[On the Resurrection of the Flesh 22]

21:25 Psalms 46:2-4, 65:8, 89:10; Isaiah 13:10, 24:19; Ezekiel 32:7; Joel 2:30-31, 3:3; Jonah 1:15; Revelation 6:12-13; OT-Apocrypha[Wisdom of Solomon 5:22]; NT-Apocrypha[Apocalypse of Thomas Line 24]

21:25-26 Pseudepigrapha[2Baruch 25:4]

21:25-28 Zechariah 12:10-14; Matthew 24:29-31; Mark 13:24-27; 1Corinthians 15:51-55; 1Thessalonians 4:15-17; 2Thessalonians 2:1-2; Revelation 1:7, 6:13-8:2, 11:12, 14:1-5, 14:14-16, 16:8

21:25-38 Matthew 24:29-35, 42-44; Mark 13:24-37; Tertullian[Five Books Against Marcion Book IV.39]

21:26 Isaiah 34:4; Joel 2:10; Haggai 2:6, 21; Pseudepigrapha[4Ezra 15:18]; Tertullian[A Strain of the Judgment of the Lord 180]; NT-Apocrypha[Apocalypse of Thomas Line 11, 21]

21:27 Psalms 80:17; Daniel 7:13; Revelation 1:7; NT-Apocrypha[Apocalypse of Thomas Line 48]

21:28 Pseudepigrapha[1Enoch 51:2; 2Baruch 23:7; 3Enoch 48A:5]; Hippolytus[Treatise on Christ and Antichrist 64]

21:29 Matthew 13:3-53n

21:29-33 Matthew 24:32; Mark 13:28; Revelation 8:5, 11:19, 14:17-20, 16:18

21:31 Cyprian[Treatise VII.2]

21:33 Psalms 119:89; Isaiah 40:8; Nag Hammadi[Gospel of Thomas 111]

21:34 Isaiah 5:11-13; Irenaeus[Against Heresies Book IV.37.3]; Methodius[Banquet of the Ten Virgins 5.5]; NT-Apocrypha[Acts of Thomas 1.36]; Indian[Dhammapada 315]

21:34-35 Irenaeus[Against Heresies Book IV.36.3]

21:34-36 Matthew 24:42-44; 1Thessalonians 5:2; 2Peter 3:10; Revelation 16:15

21:35 Isaiah 24:17; Jeremiah 25:29

21:36 Psalms 80:17; Matthew 24:42-51n; Cyprian[Epistle LXXX.1]; Tertullian[On the Resurrection of the Flesh 22]

21:37 Matthew 9:35n; Luke 19:47; Tertullian[Against Praxeas 31]; Nag Hammadi[Letter of Peter to Philip 133]

22:01 Exodus 12:1-27; 1Corinthians 5:8; Tacitus[The Histories 5.4]; Tertullian[Five Books Against Marcion Book IV.40]

22:01-06 Matthew 26:1-5, 26:14-16n, Mark 14:10-11; John 11:45-53; Dead Sea Scrolls[4Q429(4QHADAYOT[4QH]) Fragment 1 COL III 8-9]

22:02 NT-Apocrypha[Acts of Thomas 1.164]

22:03 Tertullian[Five Books Against Marcion Book V.6]; Nag Hammadi[Concept of Our Great Power 41]

22:03-04 John 13:30; Rabbinic[Exodus Rabba on 32:7; Genesis Rabba on 38:1]

22:03-06 Justin[Dialogue with Trypho 137]; NT-Apocrypha[Gospel of Judas 58]

22:04-06 1Samuel 21:7

22:07 Exodus 12:6, 14-15, 18-20; Tacitus[The Histories 5.4]; Anatolius[Paschal Canon 8]; Tertullian[An Answer to the Jews 8, 10]

22:07-23 Matthew 26:17-29; Mark 14:12-25; John 13:21-30; 1Corinthians 11:23-26

22:08 Exodus 12:8-11; Cyprian[Treatises Attributed to Cyprian - On the Glory of Martyrdom 11]

22:10 1Samuel 10:2-7; Tertullian[On Baptism 19]

22:11-13 Mark 14:14-16

22:14 Matthew 10:2n

22:14-23 Matthew 26:20-29n; Mark 14:17-25

22:15 Cyprian[Epistle LIII.2]; Tertullian[A Treatise on the Soul 16; Five Books Against Marcion Book IV.40]; NT-Apocrypha[Gospel of the Ebionites Fragment 7]

22:15-20 Tertullian[Five Books Against Marcion Book V.8]

22:16 Hippolytus[Fragments - Writings of Hippolytus 2]

22:19 Exodus 12:14; Deuteronomy 16:3; 1Corinthians 10:16-18n; Constitutions of the Holy Apostles[Book V.19]; NT-Apocrypha[Epistula Apostolorum 15]

22:19-20 John 6:31-58n; Tertullian[A Treatise on the Soul 17; Five Books Against Marcion Book IV.40]

22:20 Exodus 24:6-8; Jeremiah 31:31-34, 32:40; Zechariah 9:11; Tertullian[On Fasting 14]

22:20-23 NT-Apocrypha[Papyrus Egerton 2 Fragment 2 Lines 43-59]

22:21 Psalms 41:9; Mark 14:18; Tertullian[On Modesty 11]

22:22 Psalms 80:17; Matthew 26:24; Tertullian[Five Books Against Marcion Book IV.41]

22:24 Matthew 18:1; Mark 9:34; Luke 9:46

22:25 Pseudepigrapha[Joseph and Aseneth 21:8]; Origen[Against Celsus Book VII.23]

22:25-30 Nag Hammadi[Gospel of Thomas 2]

22:26 Matthew 20:25-27, 23:11; Mark 9:35, 10:42-44

22:27 John 13:12-15; Pseudepigrapha[Testament of Joseph 17:8]; Origen[Against Celsus Book II.7]

22:28 Origen[Gospel of John Book I.31]; Tertullian[On Idolatry 18]

22:29 Tertullian[Against Praxeas 26]

22:30 Matthew 19:28; Pseudepigrapha[3Enoch 48:1:10; Martyrdom and Ascension of Isaiah 9.24-26, 11.40; Testament of Job 33:1; Testament of Levi 13.9]; Clement of Alexandria[Stromata Book VII.10]; NT-Apocrypha[Epistula Apostolorum 30; Pistis Sophia c. 96]

22:31 Job 1:6; Amos 9:9; Cyprian[Treatise IV.30]

22:31-32 Clement of Alexandria[Stromata Book IV.9]; Constitutions of the Holy Apostles[Book VI.5]; Cyprian[Epistle VII.5]; Tertullian[De Fuga in Persecutione 2]

22:31-34 Matthew 26:31-35; Mark 14:27-31; John 13:36-38

22:32 Psalms 51:15; Cyprian[Epistle II.1]

22:34 Mark 14:72; Philo[Every Good Man Is Free (131-136) cf. {Greek Playwright Ion}]; Constitutions of the Holy Apostles[Book V.14]; Tertullian[Five Books Against Marcion Book IV.41]

22:35 Matthew 10:9-10; Mark 6:8-9; Luke 9:3, 10:4

22:36-38 1Samuel 21:8-9

22:37 Isaiah 53:12; Pseudepigrapha[Psalms of Solomon 16:5]

22:38 Deuteronomy 3:26

22:39-46 Matthew 26:36-46; Mark 14:32-42; John 18:1-2

22:40 Tertullian[On Prayer 8]

22:40-46 Galatians 5:24

22:41-42 Genesis 32:9-12

22:41-43 Epic of Gilgamesh[The Forest Journey]

22:42 Rabbinic[Avot 2.4]; Constitutions of the Holy Apostles[Book V.14]; Cyprian[Epistle LIII.2]; Hippolytus[Fragments of Discourses or Homilies 3]; Tertullian[On Prayer 4]; NT-Apocrypha[Acts of Thomas 1.3]

22:42-44 Justin[Dialogue with Trypho 103]

22:43 NT-Apocrypha[Gospel of the Nazareans Fragment 32]

22:44 Pseudepigrapha[Joseph and Aseneth 4:9]; Irenaeus[Against Heresies Book III.22.2, IV.35.3]

22:47 Genesis 33:1; Constitutions of the Holy Apostles[Book V.14]

22:47-23:49 Matthew 26:47-27:56n

22:47-48 This section also includes topical notes for: **Kiss of Betrayal** - Genesis 31:28, 33:4; Matthew 26:48-50; Mark 14:44-46; Philo[Who Is the Heir of Divine Things (44) cf. {Genesis 31:28, 33:4}]; Rabbinic[Canticles Rabba 1.2; Jerusalem Targum Deuteronomy 34:5]; Irenaeus[Against Heresies Book I.31.1, II.20.2, 4]

22:47-49 Tertullian[Five Books Against Marcion Book IV.41]

22:47-53 Matthew 26:47-56n; Mark 14:43-52; John 18:3-12

22:48 Psalms 80:17; Peter of Alexandria[Fragments On the Advent of our Savior]

22:50 Epic of Gilgamesh[The Forest Journey]

22:53 Luke 19:47, 21:37

22:54 Matthew 26:57; Mark 14:53; John 18:13-14; NT-Apocrypha[Acts of John 94]

22:54-62 Tertullian[Five Books Against Marcion Book IV.41]

22:55-62 Matthew 26:58, 69-75; Mark 14:54, 66-72; John 18:15-27

22:61 Philo[Every Good Man Is Free (131-136) cf. {Greek Playwright Ion}]; Tertullian[On Repentance 3]; NT-Apocrypha[Acts of Peter 1.7]
22:62 Isaiah 22:4
22:63 Matthew 27:19-31n, 29n
22:63-65 Matthew 26:59-68; Mark 14:55-65
22:63-71 Philo[On Joseph (77-79) cf. {Genesis 39:2-20}]

> I would rather choose to die than to speak merely with the object of gratifying the ear, and to conceal the truth, disregarding all thought of what is really advantageous. "Now then," as the tragedian says: "Now then let fire, let biting steel come on; Burn, scorch my flesh, and glut your appetite, Drinking my dark, warm blood; for here I swear, Sooner shall those bright stars which deck the heaven Descend beneath the earth, the earth itself Soar upwards to the sky, than servile words of flattery creep from out my mouth to thee." But the people, when it is the master, cannot endure a statesman of so masculine a spirit, and one who keeps so completely aloof from the passions, from pleasure, from fear, from grief, from desire; but it arrests its well-wisher and friend and punishes him as an enemy, in doing which it first of all inflicts upon itself the most grievous of all punishments, namely, ignorance; in consequence of which state it does not itself learn that lesson which is the most beautiful and profitable of all, namely, obedience to its governor, from which the knowledge how to govern subsequently springs. (Philo - On Joseph (77-79) cf. {Genesis 39:2-20})

22:66-67 Tertullian[Five Books Against Marcion Book IV.41]
22:66-71 John 18:19-24
22:66-23:01 Matthew 27:1-2; Mark 15:1; John 18:28
22:67 Jeremiah 38:15
22:68 Daniel 7:13
22:69 Psalms 80:17, 110:1; Mark 14:62n; 1Peter 3:22n; Pseudepigrapha[Testament of Job 33:3]
22:69-71 Tertullian[Five Books Against Marcion Book IV.41]
22:70 John 3:18n
23:01-05 Matthew 27:11-14; Mark 15:1-5; John 18:28-38
23:01-24 John 18:29-19:22; Philo[Special Laws IV (69-71) cf. {Deuteronomy 1:16-17}]
23:02 1Kings 18:17; John 18:29-33a; Constitutions of the Holy Apostles[Book V.14]; NT-Apocrypha[Acts of Pilate I.1-III.1]
23:03 Tertullian[Five Books Against Marcion Book IV.42]
23:03-07 Matthew 27:11-14; Mark 15:2-5; John 18:33b-38; NT-Apocrypha[Acts of Pilate III.2]
23:04 Pseudepigrapha[Odes of Solomon 31.8]
23:05 Matthew 9:35n
23:06-16 NT-Apocrypha[Acts of Thomas 1.32; Gospel of Mani Turfman Fragment M 132]
23:07 Tertullian[Five Books Against Marcion Book IV.42]
23:09 NT-Apocrypha[Acts of Thomas 1.106]
23:10 Genesis 31:26-28
23:11 Matthew 27:19-31n, 29n
23:12 Origen[Gospel of Matthew Book XII.1]
23:13-23 Matthew 27:15-18, 20-23; Mark 15:6-14; John 18:39-40
23:13-25 Tertullian[An Answer to the Jews 13]
23:14 Genesis 31:35; Pseudepigrapha[Odes of Solomon 31.8]; Constitutions of the Holy Apostles[Book V.14]
23:15 Lactantius[Divine Institutes Book IV.18]
23:18 Mark 15:7; Josephus[Antiquities 18.3.2 60-62; War 2.9.4 175-177, 2.12.3-4 232-235]; Origen[Gospel of Matthew Book XIV.17]; NT-Apocrypha[Acts of Paul and Thecla 1.20]
23:21 Constitutions of the Holy Apostles[Book V.14]; Origen[Against Celsus Book VIII.42; Gospel of Matthew Book XII.1]
23:22 Pseudepigrapha[Odes of Solomon 31.8]
23:24-25 Matthew 27:24-26; Mark 15:15; NT-Apocrypha[Acts of Pilate IV.1-IX.5]
23:25 Leviticus 16:7-10; Tertullian[Five Books Against Marcion Book IV.42]; Josephus[**Antiquities 18.3.2-3 60-64**]

But Pilate undertook to bring a current of water to Jerusalem, and did it with the sacred money, and derived the origin of the stream from the distance of two hundred furlongs. However, the Jews were not pleased with what had been done about this water; and many ten thousands of the people got together, and made a clamor against him, and insisted that he should leave off that design. Some of them also used reproaches, and abused the man, as crowds of such people usually do. So he habited a great number of his soldiers in their habit, who carried daggers under their garments, and sent them to a place where they might surround them. So he bid the Jews himself go away; but they boldly casting reproaches upon him, he gave the soldiers that signal which had been beforehand agreed on; who laid upon them much greater blows than Pilate had commanded them, and equally punished those that were tumultuous, and those that were not; nor did they spare them in the least: and since the people were unarmed, and were caught by men prepared for what they were about, there were a great number of them slain by this means, and others of them ran away wounded. And thus an end was put to this sedition. Now there was about this time Jesus, a wise man, if it be lawful to call him a man; for he was a doer of wonderful works, a teacher of such men as receive the truth with pleasure. He drew over to him both many of the Jews and many of the Gentiles. He was [the] Christ. And when Pilate, at the suggestion of the principal men amongst us, had condemned him to the cross, those that loved him at the first did not forsake him; for he appeared to them alive again the third day; as the divine prophets had foretold these and ten thousand other wonderful things concerning him. And the tribe of Christians, so named from him, are not extinct at this day. (Josephus - Antiquities (18.3.2-3 60-64) - The Testimonium Flavianum)

23:26 Irenaeus[Against Heresies Book I.24.4]; Origen[Gospel of Matthew Book XII.24]; Tertullian[Against All Heresies 1]

23:26-32 Matthew 27:31-32; Mark 15:20-21; John 19:16-17a

23:27 Zechariah 12:10-14

23:28 Jeremiah 9:19

23:28-30 Plato[Apology 39c-d]

23:29 Isaiah 54:1; Pseudepigrapha[2Baruch 10:14]; Nag Hammadi[Gospel of Thomas 79]

23:29-30 Pseudepigrapha[Apocalypse of Elijah 2:34-38]

23:30 Hosea 10:8

23:31 Proverbs 11:31; Tertullian[On Repentance 4]

23:33 John 19:17-18n; Tertullian[Five Books Against Marcion Book IV.42]; NT-Apocrypha[Epistula Apostolorum 9]

23:33-34 Isaiah 53:12

23:33-45 This section also includes topical notes for: Crucifixion - Genesis 31:44, 47, 54A, 33:5, 35:4, 40:12-22; Exodus 39:23; Numbers 13:23; Isaiah 41:6-11, 53:12; Deuteronomy 18:18; Psalms 22:1-31; Matthew 20:19, 27:19-31n, 41; Mark 15:20-33; John 19:17b-27; Pseudepigrapha[Greek Apocalypse of Ezra 7.1-3; Hellenistic Synagogal Prayers 5.22; Odes of Solomon 28.9-20, 31.12; Sibylline Oracles 5.256-258, 8.290-309; Testament of Benjamin 9.3]; Dead Sea Scrolls[1Q Hymns (1QHODAYOTH [1QH]) COL XII 8-15, COL XIII 27-39, COL XVII 24-29; 4Q Nahum Pesher (4Q169[4QPNAH]) Fragments 3 & 4 COL I 6-7; 4Q429(4QHADAYOT[4QH]) Fragment 1 COL IV 3-12]; Philo[Every Good Man Is Free (25) cf. {Fragment of Euripedes From the Syleus. Fr. 2}; Flaccus (74-77, 83-85, 159); On Dreams, That they Are God-Sent (2.213) cf. {Genesis 40:18-22}; On Joseph (77-79) cf. {Genesis 39:2-20}; On the Change of Names (140) cf. {Hosea 14:8-9}; On the Confusion of Tongues (185-186, 193) cf. {Genesis 11:7}; On the Life of Moses I (123) cf. {Exodus 10:21-23}; On the Migration of Abraham (139-142) cf. {Genesis 22:2-14, Exodus 1:19}; On the Posterity of Cain And His Exile (26) cf. {Deuteronomy 21:23, Gal 3:13}; Special Laws III (151-152) cf. {Deuteronomy 21:23}]; Rabbinic[Babylonian Sanhedrin 43a, 67a, 99a cf. {Isaiah 60:2}; Esther Rabba on 9:2; Tosephta Sanhedrin 9.7]; Apostolic[Martyrdom of Ignatius 2]; Clement of Alexandria[Fragments found in Greek only in the Oxford Edition Last Work on the Passover; Stromata Book I.21, V.14, VI.15; The Instructor Book II.8]; Irenaeus[Against Heresies Book I.24.4, 30.13, II.26.1, 32.4, IV.33.12, V.16.3, 17.4; Demonstration of the Apostolic Preaching 34, 66, 68, 74, 80, 82; Fragments from the Lost Works 54]; Justin[Dialogue with Trypho 39-40, 46, 49, 63, 67, 71-73, 86, 89-91, 94, 96-101, 103-106, 111-113, 131-

132, 137; First Apology 13, 21, 31, 35, 38, 41-42, 46, 48, 50, 67; Fragments from the Lost Writings of
Justin 10]; Lactantius[Divine Institutes Book IV.18-19]; Tertullian[Five Books Against Marcion Book
III.19]; Nag Hammadi[Gospel of Philip 56]; NT-Apocrypha[Acts of Pilate X.1-2; Questions of
Bartholomew IV 62]; Epic of Gilgamesh[The Forest Journey, The Search for Everlasting Life, The
Return]

23:33-49 Matthew 27:33-56n

23:34 Psalms 22:18-19; Matthew 5:44n; John 19:23; Pseudepigrapha[Odes of Solomon 31.9]; Philo[**On
Dreams, That They Are God-Sent (2.213)**; **On The Change Of Names (140)**];
Archelaus[Disputation with Manes 44 cf. {Exodus 8}]; Clement[Homily III.19, XI.20; Recognitions
Book VI.5]; Constitutions of the Holy Apostles[Book II.16, V.14]; Irenaeus[Against Heresies Book
III.16.9, 18.5, IV.35.3]; NT-Apocrypha[Gospel of the Nazareans Fragment 24, 35];
Indian[Dhammapada 399]

> Like those who are fixed to a cross, nailed as it were to the tree of hopeless and helpless
> ignorance. (Philo - On Dreams, That They Are God-Sent 2.213)

> For if there be any good thing among existing things, that, or I should rather say the
> whole heaven and the whole world, if one must tell the truth, is the fruit of God; being
> preserved upon his eternal and everflourishing nature as upon a tree. But it belongs to
> wise and understanding men to understand and to confess such things as these, and not
> to the ignorant. (Philo - On The Change Of Names 140)

23:35 Isaiah 41:6-11, 42:1; Matthew 12:18n; Pseudepigrapha[Martyrdom and Ascension of Isaiah 8:8]
23:35-36 Psalms 22:7-8
23:36 Psalms 69:22; Matthew 27:19-31n, 29n; Pseudepigrapha[Greek Apocalypse of Ezra 2:25, 7:1;
Sibylline Oracles 6.24]; Irenaeus[Against Heresies Book IV.35.3]
23:37 Pseudepigrapha[Apocalypse of Elijah 5:11]
23:39 Pseudepigrapha[2Enoch 7:1]; Constitutions of the Holy Apostles[Book V.14]; NT-
Apocrypha[Akhmim Fragment 4.13]
23:39-43 Tertullian[On Modesty 22]; NT-Apocrypha[Acts of Thomas 1.6]
23:42 Genesis 40:2, 14
23:43 Pseudepigrapha[Apocalypse of Sedrach 15:2; Life of Adam and Eve Vita 25:3];
Rabbinic[Babylonian Sanhedrin 43b]; Origen[Gospel of John Book X.21]; NT-Apocrypha[Acts of
Pilate XXVI.1; Narrative of Joseph 3]
23:44 Exodus 10:21; Rabbinic[Babylonian Sanhedrin 99a cf. {Isaiah 60:2}]; Nag Hammadi[Concept of
Our Great Power 42]; NT-Apocrypha[Acts of John 97]
23:44-45 Amos 8:9; Pseudepigrapha[Sibylline Oracles 1.374-1.376]; Origen[Against Celsus Book II.33];
Tertullian[An Answer to the Jews 13]
23:44-47 Tacitus[The Histories 5.13]; Tertullian[On Fasting 10]
23:45 Exodus 26:31-33, 36:35; Amos 8:3; Pseudepigrapha[Lives of the Prophets 12:12; Sibylline Oracles
8.305; Testament of Benjamin 9.3; Testament of Levi 10.3-4]; Julius Africanus[**Fragments of the Five
Books of Chronography XVIII.1**]Tertullian[**Apology 21**]; Nag Hammadi[Gospel of Philip 69, 84-5]

> And yet, nailed upon the cross, He exhibited many notable signs, by which His death
> was distinguished from all others. At His own free-will, He with a word dismissed from
> Him His spirit, anticipating the executioner's work. In the same hour, too, the light of
> day was withdrawn, when the sun at the very time was in his meridian blaze. Those who
> were not aware that this had been predicted about Christ, no doubt thought it an eclipse.
> You yourselves have the account of the world-portent still in your archives. (Tertullian -
> Apology 21)

On the whole world there pressed a most fearful darkness; and the rocks were rent by an earthquake, and many places in Judea and other districts were thrown down. This darkness Thallus, in the third book of his History, calls, as appears to me without reason, an eclipse of the sun. For the Hebrews celebrate the passover on the 14th day according to the moon, and the passion of our Savior falls on the day before the passover; but an eclipse of the sun takes place only when the moon comes under the sun. And it cannot happen at any other time but in the interval between the first day of the new moon and the last of the old, that is, at their junction: how then should an eclipse be supposed to happen when the moon is almost diametrically opposite the sun? (Julius Africanus – (Fragments of the Five Books of Chronography XVIII.1)

23:45-49 Matthew 27:51-56; Mark 15:38-41

23:45-54 NT-Apocrypha[Acts of Pilate XI.2-3]

23:45-55 Tertullian[Five Books Against Marcion Book IV.42]

23:46 Genesis 49:33; Psalms 31:5-6; Matthew 27:46-50; John 19:28-30; Pseudepigrapha[Life of Adam and Eve (Apocalypse of Moses) 42:8]; Constitutions of the Holy Apostles[Book V.6, 14]; Justin[Dialogue with Trypho 105]; Tertullian[Against Praxeas 25-26, 30]; NT-Apocrypha[Acts of Pilate XI.1; Protoevangelium of James 23.3]

23:47 NT-Apocrypha[Akhmim Fragment 8.28]

23:48 Plato[Phaedo 60a-c]; NT-Apocrypha[Akhmim Fragment 7.25; Gospel of the Nazareans Fragment 24]

23:49 Psalms 38:12, 88:8-9; Luke 8:2-3

23:50-52 Genesis 50:4-5

23:50-54 Matthew 27:57-60; Mark 15:42-46; John 19:38-42; Justin[Dialogue with Trypho 118]

23:50-56 Pseudepigrapha[Life of Adam and Eve Vita 43.4, (Apocalypse of Moses) 40.1-2]

23:53 Genesis 46:4, 50:5, 13; Deuteronomy 21:22; Rabbinic[Babylonian Sanhedrin 47a-47b]; Origen[Against Celsus Book II.69]

23:54 NT-Apocrypha[Akhmim Fragment 2.5]

23:55-56 Matthew 27:61; Mark 15:47

23:56 Exodus 12:16, 20:10; Leviticus 23:8; Deuteronomy 5:14; Dionysius of Alexandria[Extant Fragments Epistle to Bishop Basilides 1]

24:01 Matthew 28:1; Mark 16:2; Rabbinic[Babylonian Shabbat 151a]; Tertullian[Five Books Against Marcion Book IV.43]

24:01-02 Dionysius of Alexandria[Extant Fragments Epistle to Bishop Basilides 1]; NT-Apocrypha[Acts of Pilate XIII.1-2]

24:01-03 NT-Apocrypha[Epistula Apostolorum 9]

24:01-12 Matthew 28:1-10; Mark 16:1-8; John 20:1-10

24:01-53 Irenaeus[Against Heresies Book III.14.3]

24:03 Tertullian[Five Books Against Marcion Book IV.43]

24:04 OT-Apocrypha[2Maccabees 3:26]; Pseudepigrapha[2Enoch 1:4-7; Martyrdom and Ascension of Isaiah (3:13-4:22 = Testament of Hezekiah) 3:17]

24:05-06 NT-Apocrypha[Gospel of Mani Turfman Fragment M 18]

24:06 NT-Apocrypha[Acts of Thomas 1.169]

24:06-07 Tertullian[Five Books Against Marcion Book IV.43]

24:07 Psalms 80:17; Matthew 16:21, 17:22-23, 20:18-19; Mark 8:21, 9:31, 10:33-34; Luke 9:22, 18:31-33; Pseudepigrapha[Life of Abraham 11:2]

24:09-11 Mark 16:10-11; John 20:18

24:10 NT-Apocrypha[History of Joseph the Carpenter 4]

24:11 Genesis 45:26

24:11-41 NT-Apocrypha[Epistula Apostolorum 10]

24:12 1Corinthians 15:5a

24:13 Clement of Alexandria[Stromata Book VI.15]

24:13-19 Tertullian[Five Books Against Marcion Book IV.43]

24:13-35 Mark 16:12-13a

24:15 Origen[Against Celsus Book II.62]

24:18 Constitutions of the Holy Apostles[Book V.14]

24:18-21 Origen[Gospel of John Book I.7]

24:19 Judges 6:8; Rabbinic[Babylonian Sanhedrin 107b]

24:19-27 Josephus[Antiquities 18.3.3 63-64]

24:20-21 Anonymous[Treatise on Re-Baptism 9]

24:21 Isaiah 41:14, 43:14, 44:24; Irenaeus[Against Heresies Book V.31.1-2; Fragments from the Lost Works 31]; Tertullian[Five Books Against Marcion Book IV.43]

24:25 Deuteronomy 18:15; Psalms 22:1-31; Irenaeus[Against Heresies Book III.16.5]; Tertullian[Five Books Against Marcion Book IV.43]; NT-Apocrypha[Epistula Apostolorum 35]

24:25-27 Isaiah 53:1-12; Acts 2:23n, 3:18-26 n, 9:22; 1Corinthians 2:6-16n

24:26 Irenaeus[Against Heresies Book IV.26.1]; Justin[Dialogue with Trypho 106]

24:27 Deuteronomy 18:15; Psalms 22:1-18; 2Corinthians 3:12-18n; Josephus[War 2.8.12 159]; Apostolic[Ignatius - Letter to the Philadelphians 5:2, 9:2; Polycarp - Letter to the Philippians 6:3; Epistle of Barnabas 1:7, 3:6]; Irenaeus[Against Heresies Book II.32.4, 35.4, III.Preface.1, IV.10.1]; Tertullian[On Prescription Against Heretics 22]; NT-Apocrypha[Acts of Thomas 1.59]

24:27-49 Nag Hammadi[Letter of Peter to Philip 133]

24:29 Judges 19:9

24:30-31 Origen[Against Celsus Book II.68]

24:31 2Kings 6:17; OT-Apocrypha[2Maccabees 3:34]; Origen[Against Celsus Book II.62]

24:31-32 Acts 17:2-3

24:32 Psalms 39:4; Origen[Gospel of John Book I.10, X.13]

24:32-42 Justin[On the Resurrection 9]

24:34 1Corinthians 15:5a; Theodotus[Excerpts 42]

24:36 Nag Hammadi[Gospel of Mary 8; Gospel of Truth 36; Sophia of Jesus Christ III 91]

24:36-49 Matthew 28:16-20; Mark 16:14-18; John 20:19-25

24:37 NT-Apocrypha[Epistula Apostolorum 11]

24:37-39 Tertullian[Five Books Against Marcion Book IV.43]

24:38 Pseudepigrapha[Joseph and Aseneth 10:5]

24:39 Genesis 27:21; Apostolic[Ignatius - Letter to the Smyrnaeans 3:1]; Hippolytus[Fragments - Writings of Hippolytus 3]; Irenaeus[Against Heresies Book V.2.3]; Tertullian[On the Flesh of Christ 5, To his Wife Book I.4]; Nag Hammadi[Trimorphic Protennoia 47]; NT-Apocrypha[Epistula Apostolorum 11-12]

24:41 Tertullian[Five Books Against Marcion Book IV.43]

24:41-44 Clement of Alexandria[The Instructor Book II.1]

24:42 Justin[Fragments from the Lost Works of Justin, On the Resurrection 9]; Tertullian[The Chaplet, or De Corona 14]

24:42-43 Origen[Gospel of Matthew Book XI.2]

24:44 Josephus[War 2.8.12 159]; Irenaeus[Against Heresies Book IV.1.6, 10.1]; Tertullian[An Answer to the Jews 8]; NT-Apocrypha[Epistula Apostolorum 19]

24:44-46 This section also includes topical notes for: Opening the Mind - 2Corinthians 3:12-18n; Acts 3:18n, 9:22; Pseudepigrapha[4Ezra 14.22-26, 14.39-48]; Philo[Special Laws III (6)]; Plato[Theaetetus 152c-d]; Clement of Alexandria[Exhortation to the Heathen 1; Fragments from Eusebius Ecclesiastical History Book VII.2.1; Stromata Book I.2, 12, V.4, VI.7, 9, 11]; Irenaeus[Against Heresies Book I.25.5, 30.14, II.27.3, 32.4, 35.4, III.Preface.1, 1.1, 12.3, 16.5, IV.26.1; Demonstration of the Apostolic Preaching 40-42, 52, 86]; Justin[Dialogue with Trypho 39, 56-58, 77, 92-93, 106, 123; First Apology 30-31, 50]; Lactantius[Divine Institutes Book IV.20]; Nag Hammadi[Authoritative Teaching 27-28; Gospel of Truth 27, 30-31; Trimorphic Protennoia 36, 50; Tripartite Tractate 127]; NT-Apocrypha[Epistula Apostolorum 11, 19, 31]

24:44-47 1Corinthians 2:6-16n; Apostolic[Ignatius - Letter to the Philadelphians 5:2, 9:2; Polycarp - Letter to the Philippians 6:3; Epistle of Barnabas 1:7, 3:6]; Cyprian[Treatise XII.Book I.4]

24:44-48 Acts 2:23n

24:45 Acts 17:2-3

24:45-48 Tertullian[An Answer to the Jews 5]

24:46 Isaiah 53:1-12; Hosea 6:2; NT-Apocrypha[Pistis Sophia c. 136]

24:47 Tertullian[Five Books Against Marcion Book IV.43]; NT-Apocrypha[History of Joseph the Carpenter 1; Kerygma Petri 3a]

24:48 Tacitus[The Histories 4.81]

24:48-49 Tertullian[Five Books in Reply to Marcion Book IV.104]

24:49 Acts 1:4; Tertullian[Against Praxeas 26]; NT-Apocrypha[Acts of Thomas 1.27; History of Joseph
   the Carpenter 1]
24:50 Genesis 31:55; OT-Apocrypha[Sirach 50:20]
24:50-51 Acts 1:4-11n, 1:9-11
24:50-53 Mark 16:19-20
24:51 2Kings 2:11; Acts 1:9-11; Justin[Fragments from the Lost Works of Justin, On the Resurrection 9]
24:52 Matthew 28:17n; Mark 16:19; Acts 1:12-14; NT-Apocrypha[Apocalypse of Peter 1.17]
24:53 OT-Apocrypha[Sirach 50:22]

Cross Reference Index: John

01:01 Genesis 1:1; Pseudepigrapha[2 Enoch 33:4; Hellenistic Synagogal Prayers 5:20, 12:10, 16:5, 14; Odes of Solomon 41:14]; Plato[Timaeus 37c-38b]; Apostolic[Papias Fragment 6:1, 19:1, 20:1]; Alexander of Alexandria[Epistles on Arian Heresy 2.3]; Clement of Alexandria[Exhortation to the Heathen 1; Fragments from Eusebius Ecclesiastical History Book VII.6.14]; The Instructor Book I.8]; Cyprian[Treatise XII.Book II.6]; Dionysius of Alexandria[Extant Fragments Epistle to Dionysius Bishop of Rome - Book II.12]; Gregory Thaumaturgus[Four Homilies 4; Sectional Confession of Faith 7, 15]; Irenaeus[Against Heresies Book III.1.1, 11.8; Demonstration of the Apostolic Preaching 43]; Methodius[Banquet of the Ten Virgins 3.6]; Novatian[Treatise Concerning the Trinity 13, 15]; Origen[Against Celsus Book V.24, VI.65, VIII.6; Gospel of John Book I.16]; Tertullian[Against Hermogenes 18, 20; Against Praxeas 7-8, 12-13, 16, 19; On Prescription Against Heretics 3]; Theophilus of Antioch[To Autolycus Book II.22]; Victorinus[Apocalypse 4.7-10]; NT-Apocrypha[Acts of John 98, 109; Canon Muratori Line 9-16; Epistula Apostolorum 17]

> Here begins the summary of the Gospel According to John: The Gospel of John was made known and given to the churches by John while he was still in the flesh, as a man of Hierapolis by the name of Papias, a beloved disciple of John, has related in the exoteric – that is, the last – part of his five books. Indeed, he wrote down the Gospel correctly as John dictated (Papias – Fragment (19:1) from Codex Vaticanus Alexandrinus)

01:01-02 Apostolic[Ignatius - Letter to the Magnesians 8:2]; Methodius[Fragments Extracts from the Work on Things Created 8]; Novatian[Treatise Concerning the Trinity 30]; Origen[Gospel of Matthew Book X.14; De Principiis Book II.9.4]; Nag Hammadi[Gospel of Thomas 18]

01:01-03 Pseudepigrapha[Odes of Solomon 16:7]; Alexander of Alexandria[Epistles on Arian Heresy 1.4]; Clement[Recognitions Book VIII.34]; Hippolytus[Against the Heresy of One Noetus 12]; Lactantius[Divine Institutes Book IV.8]; Origen[De Principiis Book I.7.1]; Tertullian[Against Hermogenes 21; Against Praxeas 21]; Victorinus[On the Creation of the World]

01:01-04 Pseudepigrapha[Ahiqar 95]; Hippolytus[Refutation of all Heresies Book V.11]; Origen[Gospel of John Book I.42, II.1-6, 13]

01:01-05 Cyprian[Treatise XII.Book II.3]

01:01-08 Pseudepigrapha[Odes of Solomon 12.3]

01:01-14 This section also includes topical notes for: The Word - Genesis 1:3, 15:1, 4, 19:24; Exodus 9:20-21; Deuteronomy 5:5; 2Samuel 7:4, 24:11; 1Kings 6:11, 13:20, 16:1, 17:2, 8, 18:1, 31, 19:9, 21:17, 28; 2Kings 20:4; 1Chronicles 22:8; 2Chronicles 11:2, 12:7; Psalms 2:7, 18:30, 33:4-15, 107:20, 119:50, 89, 105, 123, 140, 160; 138:2; Proverbs 8:22-31; Isaiah 9:8; 40:8, 55:11; Jeremiah 1:2, 4, 11, 13, 2:1, 13:3, 8, 16:1, 18:5, 24:4, 28:12, 32:6, 33:1, 19, 23, 34:12, 36:27, 39:15, 42:7; Ezekiel 1:3, 3:16, 6:1, 7:1, 11:14, 12:17, 21, 26, 13:1, 14:2, 12, 15:1, 16:1, 17:1, 11, 18:1, 20:2, 20:45, 21:1, 18, 22:1, 17, 23, 23:1, 24:1, 15, 20, 25:1, 26:1, 27:1, 28:1, 11, 20, 29:1, 30:1, 20, 31:1, 32:1 32:17, 33:1, 23, 34:1, 35:1, 36:16, 37:15, 38:1; Daniel 9:2; Jonah 1:1, 3:1; Haggai 2:20; Zechariah 4:8, 6:9, 7:1, 8; Luke 1:2; Hebrews 11:3; 1John 1:1; Revelation 19:13; Pseudepigrapha[2Baruch 21.4-5; 2Enoch 71:33-35; 4Ezra 6.38-39, 6.43, 16.56; Ezekiel the Tragedian 1.99; Hellenistic Synagogal Prayers 5.20; Odes of Solomon 29.9-10, 37.3, 39.9, 41.11, 41.14; Orphica (E and T) 1.6-45; Pseudo-Philo 60.2; Sibylline Oracles 8.439-455]; Josephus[Discourse to the Greeks Concerning Hades 6]; Philo[Allegorical Interpretation III (95); On Dreams, That they Are God-Sent (1.85-86, 1.215, 1.237-1.239, 2.249) cf. {Genesis 1:1, 19:24, 31:13, 32:24-32, Exodus 26:11-12, Leviticus 16:17, Deuteronomy 1:31, 10:10, Psalms 2.7, 33:6, 119:1-176}; On Flight And Finding (13, 75-76, 95-112, 117-118) cf. {Genesis 31:8-13, Exodus 25:22, 28:32, Leviticus 10:6, 36, 21:11, Numbers 23:19, 35:1-34, Deuteronomy 1:31, Psalms 119:160}; On the Change of Names (87) cf. {Genesis 32:24-30}; On the Confusion of Tongues (146-147, 168-179) cf. {Genesis 1:26, 3:22, 11:7, 42:11, Deuteronomy 10:17, Psalms 2:7, 33:6}; On the Migration of Abraham (6) cf. {Psalms 2:7, 33:6}; Questions And Answers On Genesis I (4, 8) cf. {Genesis 1:26, 2:7, 15, Matthew 22:15-22, Mark 12:13-17, John 20:20-26}; Questions And Answers On Genesis II (62) cf. {Genesis 1:26, 9:6, Luke 1:26-38, John 1:1-18, Colossians 1:15-18, Philippians 2:6-11}; Special Laws I (81) cf. {Psalms 33:6}; Who Is the Heir of Divine Things (215-220) cf. {Genesis 1:1, Exodus 25:31-40}]; Rabbinic[Babylonian Sanhedrin 38b cf. {Genesis 19:24}, 99a cf. {Numbers 15:3}]; Apostolic[Epistle to Diognetus 11:2-5]; Athenagoras[Plea for the Christians 10, 24]; Clement of Alexandria[Exhortation to the Heathen 1, 9-12; Fragments

from Nicetas Bishop of Heraclea Catena on Matthew 5; Fragments from the Latin Translation of Cassiodorus Comments on 1John; Stromata Book II.6, V.6, 11, 14, VI.3, 5, 11, 16, VII.3, 9-10; The Instructor Book I.1-3, 5-12, II.2, 8, 13, III.1, 12]; Hippolytus[Against the Heresy of One Noetus 14; Refutation of all Heresies Book X.29]; Irenaeus[Against Heresies Book I.1.1-2, 4.1, 8.5, 9.2-3, 10.3, 12.3-4, 14.1, 3, 8, 15.2, 5, II.2.4-5, 11.1, 12.5-6, 13.2, 6-7, 14.1, 8, 16.6-11, 18.4, 19.9, 25.3, 27.2, 28.2, 4-6, 30.9; III.8.2-3, 9.3, 11.1-4, 8, 16.6-9, 17.4, 18.1-2, 6, 19.1-3, 20.1-2, 22.1, 3, 25.5, IV.Preface.3, 1.1, 5.3-5, 6.1-3, 5-6, 7.4, 12.4, 20.1-4, 7, 11, 24.1-2, 28.2, 31.2, 32.1, 33.11, 15, 33.3, 34.4, 35.4, 36.8, V.1.1, 3, 2.2-3, 8.4, 9.3; 12.6, 14.1-2, 15.2-4, 16.2-3, 17.1, 3, 18.1-3, 19.2, 21.3, 22.1, 24.4, 36.3; Demonstration of the Apostolic Preaching 24, 29, 37-38, 43, 53, 94; Fragments from the Lost Works 8, 19, 47, 52-54]; Justin[Dialogue with Trypho 61-62, 102, 105; Discourse to the Greeks 5; First Apology 5, 12, 14, 21-23, 36, 63, 66; Fragments from the Lost Writings of Justin 10-11; Hortatory Address to the Greeks 16, 38; On the Resurrection 1; Second Apology 6, 8, 10, 13]; Tatian[Address to the Greeks 5, 7]; Tertullian[On Monogamy 5]; Theophilus of Antioch[To Autolycus Book II.10, 18, 22]; NT-Apocrypha[Epistula Apostolorum 3]

01:01-18 This section also includes topical notes for: Incarnation - Pseudepigrapha[Hellenistic Synagogal Prayers 1.8, 5.4, 5.6, 5.20, 6.2, 7.15; Martyrdom and Ascension of Isaiah 3.13; Odes of Solomon 12:3, 16:10, 19.6-11, 32:2, 41.9; Sibylline Oracles Prologue, 1.324-325; Testament of Adam 3.1; Testament of Asher 7.3-6; Testament of Naphtali 8.3; Testament of Zebulon 9.8]; Dead Sea Scrolls[1Q Genesis Apocryophon(1QAPGENAR) COL II 1-26]; Philo[On the Migration of Abraham (139-142) cf. {Genesis 22:2-14, Exodus 1:19}; On the Posterity of Cain And His Exile (30-31) cf. {Genesis 17:1-22, 18:1-21}; On the Prayers And Curses Uttered By Noah When He Became Sober (24) cf. {Deuteronomy 21:15-17}; Questions And Answers On Genesis III (10) cf. {Genesis 15:13, Luke 1:26-38, John 1:1-18, Colossians 1:15-18, Philippians 2:6-11}]; Clement of Alexandria[Exhortation to the Heathen 10-11; Fragments from Nicetas Bishop of Heraclea Catena on Matthew 5; Stromata Book VI.15; The Instructor Book I.2, 8]; Hippolytus[Refutation of all Heresies Book X.23]; Irenaeus[Against Heresies Book I.9.1, III.4.2, 9.1, 11.3, 17.4, 18.2, V.1.1-3, 17.1, 18.1, 3, 19.2, 20.1, 25.5; Demonstration of the Apostolic Preaching 3, 99-100; Fragments from the Lost Works 52, 54]; Justin[Dialogue with Trypho 45, 48, 67, 78, 126; First Apology 31, 46; Fragments from the Lost Writings of Justin 10; Hortatory Address to the Greeks 38; On the Resurrection 1]; Nag Hammadi[A Valentinian Exposition 29, 32; Apocryphon of John 6; Concept of Our Great Power 42, 44; Gospel of Philip 55; Gospel of the Egyptians III 49-50, 53-54, 64; Gospel of Truth 16, 23-24, 37, 40; Hypostasis of the Archons 96; Teachings of Silvanus 106, 111-113, 115; Testimony of Truth 39-40; Treatise on the Resurrection 44; Trimorphic Protennoia 46; Tripartite Tractate 51, 54, 57, 62, 66, 93, 95-96, 98, 113-115, 125, 130]; NT-Apocrypha[Canon Muratori Line 20; Questions of Bartholomew IV 60]

01:02 Proverbs 8:22; Origen[Gospel of Matthew Book X.2]; Tertullian[Against Praxeas 15]

01:03 Psalms 33:6; OT-Apocrypha[Wisdom of Solomon 9:1]; Pseudepigrapha[Hellenistic Synagogal Prayers 3:1, 12:12-15, 28, 14:1]; Alexander of Alexandria[Epistles on Arian Heresy 2.3]; Clement of Alexandria[Stromata Book I.9, VI.7, 11, 15-17, VII.3; The Instructor Book I.7, 11, III.5]; Irenaeus[Against Heresies Book I.22.1, II.2.5, III.21.10, IV.32.1]; Novatian[Treatise Concerning the Trinity 13, 15, 17, 21]; Origen[De Principiis Preface.2, 4, I.2.10, IV.1.30]; Tatian[Address to the Greeks 19]; Tertullian[Against Hermogenes 22, 45; Against Praxeas 7, 12, 15, 19; On the Resurrection of the Flesh 5; Five Books Against Marcion Book V.19]

01:03-04 Pseudepigrapha[Joseph and Aseneth 12:2]; Clement of Alexandria[Fragments from the Latin Translation of Cassiodorus Comments on 1John; The Instructor Book II.9]; Hippolytus[Refutation of all Heresies Book V.3-4]; Origen[Against Celsus Book VI.5; Gospel of John Book I.22]

01:03-05 Origen[Gospel of John Book I.24]

01:04 Pseudepigrapha[Odes of Solomon 3:9]; Clement of Alexandria[Stromata Book IV.7; The Instructor Book I.6]; Origen[Gospel of John Book Book II.9]; Nag Hammadi[Letter of Peter to Philip 134]; NT-Apocrypha[Epistula Apostolorum 39]

01:04-09 Pseudepigrapha[Sibylline Oracles Fragment 1.27]

01:05 Isaiah 9:1; Pseudepigrapha[Odes of Solomon 18:6]; Archelaus[Disputation with Manes 13, 24]; Clement of Alexandria[The Instructor Book II.9-10]; Methodius[Oration on the Psalms 3]; Origen[Against Celsus Book VII.51; Gospel of John Book Book II.22]; Tatian[Address to the Greeks 13]; Nag Hammadi[Letter of Peter to Philip 133]

01:06 Matthew 3:1; Mark 1:4; Luke 3:1-2; Origen[Gospel of John Book II.24]

01:06-36 Tertullian[On Baptism 10]

01:07 Origen[Gospel of John Book II.29]

01:08 Isaiah 9:1; Pseudepigrapha[2 Enoch 46:3]

01:09 Pseudepigrapha[2Baruch 18:2; 4Baruch 9:4, 20]; Clement of Alexandria[Stromata Book II.5]; Constitutions of the Holy Apostles[Book V.16]; Gregory Thaumaturgus[Four Homilies 4]; Hippolytus[Refutation of all Heresies Book V.4, VII.10]; Lactantius[Divine Institutes Book III.26]; Origen[Against Celsus Book VI.59; Gospel of John Book I.24]; Tertullian[Against Praxeas 12]

01:09-10 Cyprian[Treatise XII.Book I.7]

01:10 Pseudepigrapha[Joseph and Aseneth 12:2]; Origen[Gospel of Matthew Book XIII.20]

01:10-11 Hippolytus[Against the Heresy of One Noetus 12]; Novatian[Treatise Concerning the Trinity 13]

01:11 Pseudepigrapha[Odes of Solomon 7:12]; Clement of Alexandria[Stromata Book VII.13]; Cyprian[Treatise IV.9]; Justin[First Apology 31]; Methodius[Oration Concerning Simeon and Anna 1]; Tertullian[Five Books in Reply to Marcion Book V.43]; Nag Hammadi[Apocryphon of James 9; Dialogue of the Savior 33]

01:11-12 Cyprian[Treatise XII.Book I.3]

01:12 Isaiah 9:1; Archelaus[Disputation with Manes 28]; Clement of Alexandria[Stromata Book IV.6]; Tertullian[On Prayer 2]

01:12-13 Matthew 19:12n; Philo[On the Giants (60-61) cf. {Genesis 6:4}]; NT-Apocrypha[Acts of Thomas 1.45, 1.48]

01:13 Pseudepigrapha[Joseph and Aseneth 28:11]; Clement of Alexandria[Stromata Book II.13]; Irenaeus[Against Heresies Book V.1.3, 18.3]; Tertullian[On the Flesh of Christ 13, 24]; NT-Apocrypha[Epistula Apostolorum 3]

01:13-14 Irenaeus[Against Heresies Book III.16.2]

01:14 Exodus 4:22; Psalms 2:7, 119:160; Song of Solomon 7:5-6; Isaiah 60:1-2; Ezekiel 37:27; Luke 1:35; 1Timothy 3:16n; Pseudepigrapha[Hellenistic Synagogal Prayers 1:2, 12:9; Odes of Solomon 12:12; Prayer of Joseph Fragment A; Psalms of Solomon 7:6; Sibylline Oracles 12.232, 12.33, 8.470]; Apostolic[Ignatius - Letter to the Ephesians 7:2, 19:3]; Clement of Alexandria[Stromata Book V.3; The Instructor Book I.3]; Dionysius of Alexandria[Extant Fragments Two Books on the Promises 6]; Gregory Thaumaturgus[Four Homilies 2]; Hippolytus[Fragments - On Proverbs 9.1]; Irenaeus[Demonstration of the Apostolic Preaching 31, 94]; Novatian[Treatise Concerning the Trinity 10, 13, 17, 24, 30]; Origen[Against Celsus Book VI.68; Gospel of Matthew Book XI.14, XII.30, XIII.2, XIV.17]; Peter of Alexandria[Fragments From a Sermon; Fragments On the Godhead]; Tertullian[Against Praxeas 15, 21, 26; On Modesty 6, 16; On the Flesh of Christ 18, 20; On the Resurrection of the Flesh 37]; Nag Hammadi[Dialogue of the Savior 33; Gospel of Thomas 28, 78]; NT-Apocrypha[Acts of John 98; Acts of Thomas 1.60, 1.22; Epistula Apostolorum 3, 14, 39]

01:14-16 Irenaeus[Against Heresies Book III.10.2]

01:15 Irenaeus[Fragments from the Lost Works 27]; Novatian[Treatise Concerning the Trinity 14]

01:15-18 Origen[Gospel of John Book II.29, VI.10]

01:16 Clement of Alexandria[Stromata Book I.17]; Hippolytus[Fragments - On Genesis 49.21-26]

01:16-17 Tertullian[On Baptism 5]

01:17 Exodus 31:18, 34:6, 28; Psalms 25:10, 40:11, 85:11; 1Peter 1:10-13n; Clement of Alexandria[The Instructor Book I.7; Who is the Rich Man that shall be Saved 8]; Gregory Thaumaturgus[Four Homilies 2]; Origen[Gospel of John Book VI.3]; Peter of Alexandria[Fragments On the Godhead]; Tertullian[An Answer to the Jews 2; Of Patience 6]; NT-Apocrypha[Acts of John 98]

01:18 This section also includes topical notes for: God the Father - Genesis 32:30; Exodus 33:20; 1Chronicles 29:10; Psalms 89:26; Isaiah 9:6; Matthew 6:9; Romans 1:7; 1Corinthians 1:3, 8:6; 2Corinthians 1:2; Galatians 1:3-4; Ephesians 1:2; Philippians 1:2; Colossians 1:2; 1Thessalonians 1:1; 2Thessalonians 1:1-2; Titus 1:4; Philemon 1:3; Pseudepigrapha[Hellenistic Synagogal Prayers 12:9-10; Jubilees 1.25; Odes of Solomon 9.5; Prayer of Jacob 1.1-10]; Josephus[Discourse to the Greeks Concerning Hades 6]; Philo[On Rewards And Punishments (163-167) cf. {Deuteronomy 30:3-4}; Special Laws I (332) cf. {Deuteronomy 14:1}; Special Laws II (165)]; Alexander of Alexandria[Epistles on Arian Heresy 1.4, 2.3]; Archelaus[Disputation with Manes 5, 32, 47]; Athenagoras[Plea for the Christians 10, 24]; Clement of Alexandria[Fragments from the Latin Translation of Cassiodorus Comments on 1John, 1Peter, 2John; Stromata Book V.1, 11-12, 14; VI.16-17; VII.1-2, 10; The Instructor Book I.1, 5, 8; Who is the Rich Man that shall be Saved 37]; Gregory Thaumaturgus[On the Trinity]; Hippolytus[Against the Heresy of One Noetus 5]; Irenaeus[Against Heresies Book I.2.1, II.1.1, 13.4, 6-8, 16.6-11, 18.6-7, 19.4, 25.4, 28.1, 3-6, 8-9, 30.9, 31.1, 34.3, 35.3-4, III.1.2, 3.3, 5.1, 6.1, 11.6-7, 12.5, IV.Preface.4, 5.5, 6.2-6, 9.3, 11.1-3, 13.1, 16.5, 17.6, 19.1, 3, 20.1-8, 11, 27.4, 28.1-2, 31.1-2, 33.3, 7, 34.3, 5, 35.1, 4, 36.1, 5-6, 8, 38.2-3, 40.1-2, 41.4, V.1.1, 3, 2.1, 4.1-2, 6.1, 14.2, 15.1-2, 4, 16.1-3, 17.1-2, 18.1-2, 19.2, 20.1, 21.2-3, 22.1-2, 25.5, 26.2, 36.2-3; Demonstration of the

Apostolic Preaching 8, 47, 52-53, 99, 100; Fragments from the Lost Works 39]; Justin[Dialogue with Trypho 118, 127; First Apology 8, 22; Hortatory Address to the Greeks 19; On the Resurrection 1]; Methodius[Apostolic Words from the Discourse on the Resurrection 19; Concerning Free Will 11.2]; Origen[Against Celsus Book II.71, VII.27; De Principiis Book I.1.8, II.4.3]; Tertullian[Against Praxeas 8, 15, 21; An Answer to the Jews 9; On Prescription Against Heretics 3]; Theophilus of Antioch[To Autolycus Book I.4]; Nag Hammadi[A Valentinian Exposition 22; Authoritative Teaching 33; Eugnostos the Blessed III 73-75; Gospel of Truth 38-40; Interpretation of Knowledge 9; Prayer of Thanksgiving 64; Sophia of Jesus Christ III 95, 98-99; Teachings of Silvanus 91, 98]; NT-Apocrypha[Acts of Peter 1.7; Acts of Thomas 1.48]

01:19 1Samuel 9:15; Origen[Gospel of John Book VI.2]

01:19-20 Origen[Gospel of John Book VI.6]

01:19-21 Origen[Gospel of John Book VI.4]

01:19-28 Matthew 3:1-17n; Mark 1:1-11; Luke 3:1-18, 21-22; Pseudepigrapha[Sibylline Oracles 1.336-341]

01:20 Hippolytus[The Discourse on the Holy Theophany 3]; Origen[Gospel of John Book V.3, VI.30]

01:21 Deuteronomy 18:15, 18; Malachi 4:5; Origen[Gospel of John Book VI.7-8]; Tertullian[A Treatise on the Soul 35]

01:23 Isaiah 40:3; Pseudepigrapha[Sibylline Oracles 1.336]; Clement of Alexandria[Exhortation to the Heathen 1]; Gregory Thaumaturgus[Four Homilies 4]; Tertullian[An Answer to the Jews 9]; Epic of Gilgamesh[The Coming of Enkidu]

01:24 Hippolytus[Refutation of all Heresies Book IX.23]

01:24-25 Origen[Gospel of John Book VI.13-14]

01:25 Origen[Gospel of John Book V.3, VI.4-5]

01:25-33 Matthew 3:5-16n

01:26 Pseudepigrapha[Odes of Solomon 30:6]; Origen[Gospel of John Book II.29, VI.15]

01:26-27 Cyprian[Treatise XII.Book II.19]; Origen[Against Celsus Book II.9, V.12; De Principiis Book IV.1.30]

01:27 Pseudepigrapha[Joseph and Aseneth 12:5]; Clement of Alexandria[Stromata Book V.8]; Gregory Thaumaturgus[Four Homilies 4]; Hippolytus[The Discourse on the Holy Theophany 3]; Epic of Gilgamesh[The Coming of Enkidu]

01:28 Origen[Gospel of John Book VI.24; Gospel of Matthew Book XIV.15]

01:28-29 Genesis 32:10

01:29 1Samuel 9:17; Isaiah 53:6-7; Jeremiah 11:19; Pseudepigrapha[2Enoch 64:5; Testament of Benjamin 3:7-8; Testament of Joseph 19.8]; Clement of Alexandria[Fragments found in Greek only in the Oxford Edition Last Work on the Passover; Fragments from Macarius Chrysocephalus Parable of the Prodigal son 2; The Instructor Book I.5]; Cyprian[Treatise XII.Book II.15]; Gregory Thaumaturgus[Four Homilies 4]; Hippolytus[Fragments - On Daniel 2.15; Treatise on Christ and Antichrist 6, 45]; Irenaeus[Against Heresies Book III.10.2]; Justin[Dialogue with Trypho 40]; Liturgy of James 41; Origen[Gospel of John Book I.5-6, 37, VI.32; Gospel of Matthew Book XIII.8]; Tertullian[Against Praxeas 21; An Answer to the Jews 9]; NT-Apocrypha[Acts of Pilate XVIII.2]

01:29-31 Origen[Gospel of John Book I.23, II.29]

01:29-34 Tertullian[Against All Heresies 5]

01:30 Pseudepigrapha[Odes of Solomon 28:19]

01:31 Pseudepigrapha[2Baruch 29:3]

01:31-32 Pseudepigrapha[Sibylline Oracles 6.4]

01:32 1Samuel 10:6, 9, 20, 23; 2Samuel 7:14; 1Chronicles 17:13; Psalms 89:27; Isaiah 11:2; Matthew 3:16n; Mark 1:10; Luke 3:21-22; Pseudepigrapha[Psalms of Solomon 17.37]; Justin[Dialogue with Trypho 8]; Origen[Gospel of John Book II.6]

01:32-34 Origen[Against Celsus Book I.48]

01:32-38 Origen[Gospel of John Book II.29]

01:33 Acts 11:16n; Origen[Gospel of John Book II.24]

01:34 John 3:18n

01:35 Origen[Gospel of Matthew Book X.1]

01:36 Pseudepigrapha[Testament of Benjamin 3.8; Testament of Joseph 19.8]; Clement of Alexandria[Fragments found in Greek only in the Oxford Edition Last Work on the Passover; The Instructor Book I.5]; Justin[Dialogue with Trypho 40]; Tertullian[An Answer to the Jews 9]

01:36-37 Cyprian[Treatise XII.Book II.29]

01:38 Origen[Gospel of Matthew Book XII.22]

01:39 NT-Apocrypha[Secret Gospel of Mark Fragment 1]

01:40 Origen[Gospel of Matthew Book X.1]

01:41 1Samuel 2:10; Psalms 2:2; Acts 3:18-26n; Origen[Gospel of John Book X.6]

01:42 Origen[Gospel of John Book I.7]; NT-Apocrypha[Gospel of the Nazareans Fragment 14]

01:43 1Kings 19:19

01:43-48 Nag Hammadi[Letter of Peter to Philip 133]

01:45 Deuteronomy 18:18; Isaiah 7:14, 9:6; Ezekiel 34:23; Acts 2:23n, 3:18-26n; Pseudepigrapha[3Enoch 45:5]; Irenaeus[Against Heresies Book IV.10.1]; Justin[Dialogue with Trypho 137]

01:46 2Kings 6:13, 10:16; Origen[Gospel of John Book I.7]

01:47 Psalms 32:2; Zephaniah 3:13; Clement of Alexandria[Stromata Book VI.14]; Irenaeus[Against Heresies Book III.11.6]

01:49 Genesis 27:29; Exodus 4:22; 2Samuel 7:14; Psalms 2:7; Zephaniah 3:15; John 3:18n; Dead Sea Scrolls[4Q Isaiah Pesher (4Q163[4QIS]) Fragments 18-19 1-6]; Irenaeus[Against Heresies Book III.11.6]; Justin[Dialogue with Trypho 135]; Tertullian[Against Praxeas 21, 23]

01:50 Irenaeus[Against Heresies Book IV.9.2]; Tertullian[Against Praxeas 21]

01:51 Genesis 28:12; Psalms 80:17; Pseudepigrapha[Apocalypse of Elijah 5:39]; Philo[On Dreams, That they Are God-Sent (1.151-1.152) cf. {Genesis 28:12}; Special Laws I (85-87) cf. {Exodus 28:2-40}]; Origen[Against Celsus Book I.48]

02:01 NT-Apocrypha[Epistula Apostolorum 5]

02:01-10 Tertullian[A Treatise on the Soul 17]

02:01-11 Hippolytus[Refutation of all Heresies Book V.3]; Tertullian[On Baptism 9; On Monogamy 8]

02:01-12 Philo[Allegorical Interpretation, III (82) cf. {Genesis 14:18-20, Deuteronomy 4:39}]; Irenaeus[Against Heresies Book II.22.3]; Origen[Gospel of John Book X.7]

02:03 Constitutions of the Holy Apostles[Book V.7]; Irenaeus[Against Heresies Book III.11.5]

02:04 Hippolytus[Refutation of all Heresies Book VII.15]; Irenaeus[Against Heresies Book III.16.7]; Nag Hammadi[Gospel of Thomas 101]

02:04-05 Genesis 27:13

02:05 Genesis 41:55; Tertullian[On Baptism 13]

02:07 Methodius[Oration on the Psalms 3]

02:07-11 Philo[On Dreams, That They Are God-Sent (2.249)]

02:09 Genesis 27:17, 25

02:11 Isaiah 8:23, 9:1; Pseudepigrapha[Apocalypse of Elijah 3:12; Lives of the Prophets 1:2]; Irenaeus[Against Heresies Book V.5.2]; NT-Apocrypha[Acts of Thomas 1.29]

02:12 Matthew 4:13; NT-Apocrypha[Epistula Apostolorum 5]

02:12-25 Origen[Gospel of John Book X.1]

02:13 Exodus 12:1-27; Origen[Gospel of John Book X.11, 16, 28]

02:13-17 Clement of Alexandria[The Instructor Book III.11]; Origen[Gospel of John Book X.15]

02:13-22 Matthew 21:12-13; Mark 11:15-18; Luke 19:45-46

02:14-15 Irenaeus[Against Heresies Book IV.1.6]

02:14-16 Pseudepigrapha[Psalms of Solomon 17.36]; Origen[Book X.19]

02:16 Zechariah 14:21; John 14:2n; Origen[De Principiis Book II.4.1]; Tertullian[Against Praxeas 21]

02:16-18 Irenaeus[Against Heresies Book IV.1.7]

02:17 Psalms 69:9-10

02:18-19 Origen[Gospel of John Book X.20]

02:19 Rabbinic[Babylonian Yoma 39b]; Cyprian[Treatise XII.Book I.15]; Hippolytus[Treatise on Christ and Antichrist 6]; Novatian[Treatise Concerning the Trinity 21]; Origen[Against Celsus Book III.32, VIII.19]; Tertullian[On Modesty 16; On the Resurrection of the Flesh 18]

02:19-20 Lactantius[Divine Institutes Book IV.18]

02:19-21 This section also includes topical notes for: Temple of Body - Zechariah 6:12; Matthew 26:61, 27:40; Mark 14:58, 15:29; 1Corinthians 3:16, 6:19; Ephesians 2:20-22; Revelation 3:12; Dead Sea Scrolls[4Q Florilegium (4Q174[4QFLOR]) Fragments 1-3 COL I 6-13]; Philo[On Dreams, That they Are God-Sent (1.149) cf. {Leviticus 26:12}, (1.215, 2.272-2.273) cf. {Leviticus 16:17, Deuteronomy 26:13}; On Rewards And Punishments (123-125) cf. {Leviticus 26:11-12}]; Clement of Alexandria[Fragments from the Unpublished Disputation against Iconoclasts - of Nicephorus of Contantinople]; Irenaeus[Against Heresies Book V.6.2; Fragments from the Lost Works 40]; Justin[Fragments from the Lost Writings of Justin 10]; Victorinus[Apocalypse 11.19]; Nag Hammadi[Gospel of Thomas 71]

02:19-22 Tertullian[Five Books in Reply to Marcion Book IV.98]

02:20 Origen[Gospel of John Book X.22]

02:20-21 Gregory Thaumaturgus[Twelve Topics on the Faith 9]

02:21 Origen[Against Celsus Book VIII.19; Gospel of John Book X.23]; Tertullian[On the Resurrection of the Flesh 18]

02:22 Origen[Gospel of John Book X.27]

02:23 Pseudepigrapha[Apocalypse of Elijah 3:12; Sibylline Oracles 1.340]; Irenaeus[Against Heresies Book II.22.3]

02:23-25 Origen[Gospel of John Book X.28]

02:25 Pseudepigrapha[Joseph and Aseneth 23:8]; Irenaeus[Against Heresies Book III.9.3]; Origen[Gospel of Matthew Book X.14]

03:01 Rabbinic[Babylonian (Sanhedrin 43a; Taanit 19b-20a)]; Hippolytus[Refutation of all Heresies Book IX.23]

03:01-02 Pseudepigrapha[Sibylline Oracles 8.316]

03:02 Matthew 9:35n; Tacitus[The Histories 4.81]; NT-Apocrypha[Papyrus Egerton 2 Fragment 2 Lines 43-59; Secret Gospel of Mark Fragment 1]

03:03 Pseudepigrapha[Apocalypse of Elijah 1:6; Testament of Job 38:2]; Anonymous[Treatise on Re-Baptism 3]; Clement of Alexandria[Stromata Book III.5]

03:03-07 This section also includes topical notes for: Born Again - 1Peter 1:23; Philo[On Dreams, That they Are God-Sent (2.25) cf. {Numbers 6:2}]; Plato[Phaedo 77d-e]; Clement of Alexandria[Exhortation to the Heathen 9]; Cyprian[Epistle I.3]; Irenaeus[Against Heresies Book II.22.4; Demonstration of the Apostolic Preaching 3; Fragments from the Lost Works 34]; Nag Hammadi[Dialogue of the Savior 59; Gospel of Philip 67, 69; Gospel of the Egyptians III 63]

03:04 NT-Apocrypha[Acts of Thomas 1.132]

03:05 Ezekiel 36:25-27; Pseudepigrapha[Joseph and Aseneth 8:9]; Anonymous[Treatise on Re-Baptism 3, 15]; Clement[Homily XI.26; Recognitions Book VI.9]; Constitutions of the Holy Apostles[Book VI.15]; Cyprian[Epistle LXXI.1, LXXII.21]; Irenaeus[Against Heresies Book III.17.2]; Justin[First Apology 61]; Tertullian[A Treatise on the Soul 39; On Baptism 12]; NT-Apocrypha[Acts of Thomas 1.45; Pseudo Clementines - Kerygmata Petrou H XI 26.2]

03:05-06 Cyprian[The Seventh Council of Carthage under Cyprian; Treatise XII.Book I.12, XII.Book III.25]; Hippolytus[Refutation of all Heresies Book VIII.3]

03:05-23 Matthew 3:5-16n

03:06 Clement of Alexandria[Stromata Book III.12]; Clement[First Epistle Concerning Virginity 8]; Hippolytus[Against the Heresy of One Noetus 16; Refutation of all Heresies Book V.2]; Tertullian[Against Praxeas 27; Five Books in Reply to Marcion Book II.337; On the Flesh of Christ 18]

03:07 Pseudepigrapha[2Baruch 18:2]

03:08 Ecclesiastes 11:5; OT-Apocrypha[Sirach 16:21]; Apostolic[Ignatius - Letter to the Philadelphians 7:1]; Anonymous[Treatise on Re-Baptism 18]; Origen[De Principiis Book I.3.4]

03:08-13 Pseudepigrapha[4Ezra 4.1-12]

03:11 Hippolytus[Against the Heresy of One Noetus 5]

03:11-13 Pseudepigrapha[4Ezra 4.21]

03:12 OT-Apocrypha[Wisdom of Solomon 9:16; 18:15]; Pseudepigrapha[2Enoch 46:3]; Nag Hammadi[Book of Thomas the Contender 138]

03:12-18 Pseudepigrapha[1Enoch 46:1-3; 48:2-7]

03:13 This section also includes topical notes for: Son of Man - Deuteronomy 30:12; Proverbs 30:4; Daniel 7:13; OT-Apocrypha[2Esdras 4:8]; Pseudepigrapha[**1Enoch 46:1-4, 48:2-7, 69:26-29;** Baruch 3:29; Odes of Solomon 22.1, 36.3]; Archelaus[Disputation with Manes 47]; Hippolytus[Against the Heresy of One Noetus 4-5]; Irenaeus[Against Heresies Book I.12.4, 15.3, III.16.7, 18.4, 6, 19.1-3, 20.2, 22.1, IV.20.11, 33.2, 11, 40.2, V.17.3, 21.1-3; Demonstration of the Apostolic Preaching 36, 92; Fragments from the Lost Works 52]; Justin[Dialogue with Trypho 96, 100]; Novatian[Treatise Concerning the Trinity 13]; Tertullian[Against Praxeas 30]; Nag Hammadi[Apocryphon of James 3, 14; Prayer of the Apostle Paul A.I; Testimony of Truth 30-32, 40-41; Treatise on the Resurrection 44]

There I beheld the Ancient of days, whose head was like white wool, and with him another, whose countenance resembled that of man. His countenance was full of grace, like that of one of the holy angels. Then I inquired of one of the angels, who went with me, and who showed me every secret thing, concerning this Son of man; who he was; whence he was and why he accompanied the Ancient of days. He answered and said to me, This is the Son of man, to whom righteousness belongs; with whom righteousness has dwelt; and who will reveal all the treasures of that which is concealed: for the Lord of spirits has chosen him; and his portion has surpassed all before the Lord of spirits in everlasting uprightness. (Pseudepigrapha - 1Enoch 46:1-4)

In that hour was this Son of man invoked before the Lord of spirits, and his name in the presence of the Ancient of days. Before the sun and the signs were created, before the stars of heaven were formed, his name was invoked in the presence of the Lord of spirits. A support shall he be for the righteous and the holy to lean upon, without falling; and he shall be the light of nations. He shall be the hope of those whose hearts are troubled. All, who dwell on earth, shall fall down and worship before him; shall bless and glorify him, and sing praises to the name of the Lord of spirits. Therefore the Elect and the Concealed One existed in his presence, before the world was created, and for ever. In his presence he existed, and has revealed to the saints and to the righteous the wisdom of the Lord of spirits; for he has preserved the lot of the righteous, because they have hated and rejected this world of iniquity, and have detested all its works and ways, in the name of the Lord of spirits. For in his name shall they be preserved; and his will shall be their life. In those days shall the kings of the earth and the mighty men, who have gained the world by their achievements, become humble in countenance. (Pseudepigrapha - 1Enoch 48:2-7)

There was great joy among them and they blessed and glorified and extolled because the name of that Son of Man had been revealed to them. He sat on the throne of his glory and the sum of judgment was given to the Son of Man and he caused the sinners to pass away and be destroyed from off the face of the earth and those who have led the world astray. With chains shall they be bound and in their assemblage-place of destruction shall they be imprisoned and all their works vanish from the face of the earth. From henceforth there shall be nothing corruptible; for that Son of Man has appeared and has seated himself on the throne of his glory and all evil shall pass away before his face and the word of that Son of Man shall go forth and be strong before the Lord of Spirits. (Pseudepigrapha - 1Enoch 69:26-29)

03:13-14 Psalms 80:17
03:14 Numbers 21:8-9; Isaiah 52:13; Irenaeus[Against Heresies Book IV.1.7]; Justin[Dialogue with Trypho 91, 94, 112]; Tertullian[Five Books Against Marcion Book II.22]
03:14-15 Apostolic[Epistle of Barnabas 12:7]; Cyprian[Treatise XII.Book II.20]; Hippolytus[Refutation of all Heresies Book V.11]
03:14-16 Jude 1:21n
03:14-18 Nag Hammadi[Testimony of Truth 49]
03:15-16 Clement of Alexandria[Stromata Book V.13]
03:16 Exodus 4:22; Psalms 2:7; Ephesians 4:32n; 1John 4:9; Pseudepigrapha[4Ezra 8.59-60, 9.10-11; Greek Apocalypse of Ezra 6.16; Jubilees 2.20; Odes of Solomon 9:7]; Dead Sea Scrolls[4Q Jubilees (4Q216[4QJUB[) Fragment 1 COL VII 11-12]; Apostolic[Martyrdom of Ignatius 2]; Anonymous[Treatise on Re-Baptism 13]; Irenaeus[Against Heresies Book IV.29.1-2, 33.15, 41.2]; Nag Hammadi[Exegesis of the Soul 132; Gospel of Philip 73; Gospel of Truth 38-40; Treatise on the Resurrection 46; Tripartite Tractate 86-87]; NT-Apocrypha[Epistula Apostolorum 26]
03:16-18 Exodus 4:22; Psalms 2:7; Luke 1:35; John 1:18; Acts 13:33; Hebrews 1:5, 5:5, 11:17; 1John 4:9; Pseudepigrapha[Hellenistic Synagogal Prayers 8.1, 10.17; Odes of Solomon 29.6, 36.3, 41.10, 41.13;

Prayer of Joseph Fragment A 1-9]; Anonymous[Martyrdom of Justin Martyr 1]; Clement of
Alexandria[Exhortation to the Heathen 10; Fragments from the Latin Translation of Cassiodorus
Comments on 1John, 2John; Stromata Book IV.21, V.1, VI.5, 7, 12, 14-17, VII.1-3; The Instructor Book
I.3, 7, 9; Who is the Rich Man that shall be Saved 8, 12, 37]; Irenaeus[Against Heresies Book I.5.1, 7.2,
9.2-3, 10.3, 14.1, 24.4, II.7.2, 10.2, 26.1, 28.6, 8, 30.9, 32.4, III.1.2, 6.1, 6.4, 11.8, 12.7, 16.6-8, 17.4, 18.1, 6,
19.1, 3, 20.2, 22.1, 3, IV.Preface.3, 1.4, 5.4, 6.2, 6, 9.2, 13.1, 20.3, 5, 7-8, 11, 24.2, 26.1, 27.1-2, 33.3-4, 7,
11, 34.3, 36.2, 5, 7, 38.3, V.5.2, 6.1, 14.4, 17.2, 20.1, 21.2, 25.5, 26.2, 28.4, 36.3; Demonstration of the
Apostolic Preaching 34, 36-37, 43-45, 47, 49, 52, 56, 61-62, 64, 66-67, 72, 92, 95, 99-100; Fragments
from the Lost Works 39, 52-54]; Justin[Dialogue with Trypho 43, 85, 100, 102-103, 105, 108, 111, 115,
117-118, 122, 129, 132, 137; First Apology 12, 21-23, 30, 33 cf. {Exodus 4:22, 46, 53, 63}; Fragments
from the Lost Writings of Justin 2]; Tertullian[Against Praxeas 21]

03:16-19 Clement of Alexandria[Stromata Book VII.2]; Nag Hammadi[Teachings of Silvanus 112-113]
03:17 Pseudepigrapha[Sibylline Oracles 8.254]; NT-Apocrypha[Acts of Peter 1.7; Extracts from the
Arabic Infancy Gospel 40]

03:18 This section also includes topical notes for: Son of God - Matthew 4:3-6, 14:33, 26:63, 27:40-43,
27:54; Mark 1:1, 3:11, 15:39; Luke 1:35, 4:3-9, 41, 22:70; John 1:34, 49, 3:18, 5:25, 9:35, 10:36, 11:4, 27,
19:7, 20:31; Acts 8:37, 9:20; Romans 1:4; 2Corinthians 1:19; Galatians 2:20; Ephesians 4:13; Hebrews
4:14, 6:6, 7:3, 10:29; 1John 3:8, 4:15, 5:5, 10-13, 20; Revelation 2:18; Pseudepigrapha[4Ezra 2.47, 7.28-
29; History of the Rechabites 16.2; Sibylline Oracles 1.331]; Dead Sea Scrolls[**4Q Aramaic
Apocalypse (4Q246) Col II 1-8**]; Philo[On Husbandry (51-53) cf. {Exodus 20:20-21, Psalms 23:1}; On
the Confusion of Tongues (62-63) cf. {Zechariah 6:12}, (146-147, 168-179) cf. {Genesis 1:26, 3:22, 11:7,
42:11, Deuteronomy 10:17, Psalms 2:7, 33:6}]; Rabbinic[Jerusalem Shabbat 8d]; Clement of
Alexandria[Stromata Book II.15, IV.26]; Origen[Gospel of John Book X.28]; Nag Hammadi[A
Valentinian Exposition 22; Tripartite Tractate 133]; NT-Apocrypha[Gospel of Judas 34]

**He will be called the Son of God, and they will call him the son of the Most High…
Their kingdom will be an eternal kingdom, and all their paths will be in truth. They will
judge the earth in truth, and all will make peace. The sword will cease from the earth,
and all the provinces will pay them homage. (Dead Sea Scrolls - 4Q Aramaic Apocalypse
(4Q246) Col II 1-8)**

03:18-19 Cyprian[Treatise XII.Book I.7, III.31]
03:18-21 Irenaeus[Against Heresies Book V.27.2]
03:19 This section also includes topical notes for: The Light - Isaiah 9:8; John 12:25;
Pseudepigrapha[4Ezra 6.38-40; Odes of Solomon 10.1, 11.11, 12.7, 22.12, 25.7, 29.7, 32.1, 36.3, 41.14;
Sibylline Oracles 8.271]; Dead Sea Scrolls[1QRule of the Community (1QS) COL III 3];
Philo[Fragments Extracted From the Parallels of John of Damascus Page 370. B. cf. {Genesis 1:4}; On
Dreams, That they Are God-Sent (1.218) cf. {Exodus 28:40-42}; On the Creation (31)]; Clement of
Alexandria[Exhortation to the Heathen 1, 9-11]; Dionysius of Alexandria[Exegetical Fragments
Commentary on the Beginning of Ecclesiastes 2.13]; Irenaeus[Against Heresies Book I.4.1, 5, 8.5, 9.2-
3, 29.1-2, 30.1, 30.12, II.16.4, 18.5, 30.9, III.11.4; Fragments from the Lost Works 47, 53];
Justin[Dialogue with Trypho 17, 24, 121-122, 135]; Nag Hammadi[Gospel of Philip 58, 78; Gospel of
Thomas 77; Letter of Peter to Philip 133; On the Origin of the World 108; Teachings of Silvanus 98-
99, 101-103; Trimorphic Protennoia 47]; NT-Apocrypha[Epistula Apostolorum 19; Extract from the
Latin Infancy Gospel in the Arundel Manuscript 73-74]; Egyptian Book of the Dead[Oration 21];
Epic of Gilgamesh[The Forest Journey]
03:19-21 Pseudepigrapha[Apocalypse of Adam 6:5]
03:20 Job 24:13-17
03:21 OT-Apocrypha[Tobit 4:6]; Tertullian[On the Apparel of Women Book II.13]; Nag
Hammadi[Book of Thomas the Contender 138]
03:21-22 Novatian[Treatise Concerning the Trinity 21]
03:22 NT-Apocrypha[Secret Gospel of Mark Fragment 1]
03:23-24 Josephus[Antiquities 18.5.2 116-119]
03:23-26 Origen[Gospel of John Book X.2]
03:24 Matthew 14:3; Mark 6:17; John 9:20
03:26 NT-Apocrypha[Secret Gospel of Mark Fragment 1]
03:27 Pseudepigrapha[Psalms of Solomon 5:3]; Cyprian[The Seventh Council of Carthage under
Cyprian; Treatise XII.Book III.4]
03:28 Malachi 3:1; John 1:20

03:28-29 Cyprian[Treatise XII.Book II.19]

03:29 This section also includes topical notes for: Bride and Bridegroom - Genesis 29:20-28; Isaiah 62:5; Matthew 9:15, 25:1-10; Mark 2:29-20; Luke 5:34-35; OT-Apocrypha[1Maccabees 9:39]; Pseudepigrapha[History of the Rechabites 14.3; Odes of Solomon 38.11, 42.8-9]; Philo[Special Laws I (110) cf. {Leviticus 21:14}]; Clement of Alexandria[Fragments from Macarius Chrysocephalus Parable of the Prodigal son 2; Stromata Book II.6]; Irenaeus[Against Heresies Book I.7.1, 5, 13.3, 30.2, II.27.2, V.9.4, 35.2]; Nag Hammadi[Authoritative Teaching 22; Exegesis of the Soul 132; Gospel of Philip 65, 82; Tripartite Tractate 93, 122]; Epic of Gilgamesh[The Coming of Enkidu, Ishtar and Gilgamesh]

03:30 Clement of Alexandria[Stromata Book VI.11]; Tertullian[On Prayer 1]

03:30-31 Tertullian[On Baptism 10]

03:31 Pseudepigrapha[Odes of Solomon 41.8]; Clement[First Epistle Concerning Virginity 8]; Hippolytus[Fragments - On The Psalms 1.6]; Novatian[Treatise Concerning the Trinity 14]

03:31-32 Tertullian[On Prayer 1]

03:31-33 Clement of Alexandria[Exhortation to the Heathen 4]

03:33 Clement of Alexandria[Fragments from Macarius Chrysocephalus Parable of the Prodigal son 1, 6]

03:34 Tertullian[On Fasting 17]

03:34-35 Novatian[Treatise Concerning the Trinity 20]; Victorinus[Apocalypse 1.16]

03:35 Daniel 1:2; Matthew 11:27; Luke 10:22; Tertullian[Against Praxeas 16]

03:35-36 Tertullian[Against Praxeas 21]

03:36 This section also includes topical notes for: Obey not the Son and Don't See Life - Romans 13:4; Revelation 6:16-17, 19:15; Pseudepigrapha[Apocalypse of Elijah 5:1; Sibylline Oracles 8.255]; Rabbinic[Babylonian Sanhedrin 38b cf. {Exodus 23:21, 24:1}]; Clement of Alexandria[Stromata Book V.13; The Instructor Book I.6]; Constitutions of the Holy Apostles[Book V.20]; Cyprian[Treatise XII.Book II.27]; Irenaeus[Against Heresies Book IV.37.5]; Justin[Dialogue with Trypho 138]; NT-Apocrypha[Gospel of the Ebionites Fragment 6]

04:01 Pseudepigrapha[3Baruch 5:3 (Gk.)]; Clement of Alexandria[Stromata Book I.21]

04:01-02 Matthew 3:5-16n

04:01-03 Matthew 4:12

04:01-25 Tertullian[On Modesty 11]

04:02 Tertullian[On Baptism 11]

04:04 Cyprian[Epistle VIII.1]

04:04-42 Philo[Concerning Noah's Work As A Planter (77-79) cf. {Numbers 20:5-13}; On Flight And Finding (95-105, 197-210) cf. {Jeremiah 2:13}; On the Posterity of Cain And His Exile (128-129, 138-139) cf. {Genesis 2:10, 24:15-21}; On The Unchangeableness of God (155-163) cf. {Genesis 18:27, 48:15, Deuteronomy 28:12, Jeremiah 2:13}]; Irenaeus[Against Heresies Book III.17.2]

04:05 Genesis 33:19, 48:22; Joshua 24:32

04:06 Clement of Alexandria[The Instructor Book I.9]; Irenaeus[Against Heresies Book III.22.2]; Tertullian[On Baptism 9]; NT-Apocrypha[Acts of Thomas 1.47]

04:07 Rabbinic[Babylonian Shabbat 16b; Mishnah Niddah 4.1]

04:07-14 Hippolytus[Refutation of all Heresies Book V.14]

04:07-15 Nag Hammadi[Gospel of Thomas 108]

04:09 Ezra 4:1-5, 9:1-10:44; Nehemiah 4:1-2; OT-Apocrypha[Sirach 50:25]; Methodius[Oration Concerning Simeon and Anna 8]

04:10 Genesis 26:19; Jeremiah 2:13; Zechariah 14:8; Pseudepigrapha[Odes of Solomon 11:7]; Hippolytus[Refutation of all Heresies Book V.4]

04:10-11 This section also includes topical notes for: Living Water - Song of Solomon 4:12-15; Jeremiah 2:13, 17:13; Zechariah 14:8; John 7:38; OT-Apocrypha[Sirach 24:30-34]; Pseudepigrapha[Odes of Solomon 6.13, 11.7, 26.11-13, 30.1-7]; Dead Sea Scrolls[11Q New Jerusalem (11Qi8[11QNJAR]) Fragment 24 1-5; 1Q Hymns (1QHODAYOTH [1QH]) COL XVI 6-16]; Josephus[Against Apion 1.22 164]; Philo[Special Laws IV (140-141) cf. {Deuteronomy 6:7}]; Rabbinic[Avot 1.4, 6.1; Targum Neofiti Deuteronomy 2:6]; Clement of Alexandria[Stromata Book II.2]; Irenaeus[Against Heresies Book V.18.2; Fragments from the Lost Works 52]; Justin[Dialogue with Trypho 14, 19, 114, 140]; Nag Hammadi[Apocryphon of John 4; Gospel of Philip 75; Gospel of Thomas 13; Trimorphic Protennoia 37, 46, 48; Tripartite Tractate 66, 76-77, 80, 85, 90]; NT-Apocrypha[Oxyrhynchus Papyrus 840]

04:10-14 Apostolic[Ignatius - Letter to the Romans 7:2]

04:10-15 John 6:31-58n; Pseudepigrapha[Odes of Solomon 6:18]
04:11 Genesis 21:19
04:12 Tertullian[Five Books Against Marcion Book IV.35]
04:13-14 Clement of Alexandria[The Instructor Book I.9]; Cyprian[Epistle LXII.8]
04:14 Isaiah 58:11; Jude 1:21n; Pseudepigrapha[1Enoch 48:1; Odes of Solomon 10:2]; Apostolic[Didache 10:3]; Hippolytus[Refutation of all Heresies Book V.22; The Discourse on the Holy Theophany 2]; Irenaeus[Against Heresies Book IV.36.4; Fragments from the Lost Works 52]; NT-Apocrypha[Oxyrhynchus Papyrus 840]
04:16-18 Tertullian[On Monogamy 8]
04:20 Deuteronomy 11:29, 12:5-14, 27:12; Joshua 8:33; Psalms 122:1-5; Origen[De Principiis Book I.1.4]; Tertullian[Five Books Against Marcion Book IV.35]
04:21 1Kings 8:27; Isaiah 66:1; Malachi 1:11; Hippolytus[Refutation of all Heresies Book V.4]; Novatian[Treatise Concerning the Trinity 6]; Origen[Against Celsus Book VI.70]
04:22 Isaiah 2:3; Tertullian[Five Books Against Marcion Book IV.35]; Nag Hammadi[Gospel of Thomas 43]
04:23 Clement of Alexandria[Stromata Book I.6, V.11]; Cyprian[Treatise IV.2]; Nag Hammadi[Gospel of Philip 69]
04:23-24 Origen[De Principiis Book I.1.4]; Tertullian[On Prayer 28]
04:24 Dionysius of Alexandria[Extant Fragments Epistle to Dionysius Bishop of Rome - Book I.4]; Gregory Thaumaturgus[Sectional Confession of Faith 10, 14]; Irenaeus[Fragments from the Lost Works 37]; Novatian[Treatise Concerning the Trinity 6]; Origen[Against Celsus Book II.71, VI.70; De Principiis Book I.1.1]; Tatian[Address to the Greeks 4]; Tertullian[Against Hermogenes 32; Against Praxeas 7; On the Resurrection of the Flesh 7]
04:25 Matthew 13:11n; Origen[Gospel of John Book I.7]; Tertullian[Against Praxeas 21]
04:25-42 Acts 3:18-26n
04:27 Clement[Second Epistle Concerning Virginity 15]
04:31-34 Tertullian[On Fasting 15]
04:32 Apostolic[Didache 10:3]; Cyprian[Treatise XII.Book III.60]
04:32-34 Clement of Alexandria[The Instructor Book I.6]
04:34 Cyprian[Treatise XII.Book III.60]; Novatian[On the Jewish Meats 5]; Tertullian[Against Praxeas 21]; NT-Apocrypha[Acts of Thomas 1.5; Protoevangelium of James 2.4]
04:35 Irenaeus[Against Heresies Book IV.23.1]; NT-Apocrypha[Acts of Thomas 1.147]
04:36 Isaiah 9:2
04:37 Job 31:8; Micah 6:15; Irenaeus[Against Heresies Book IV.25.3]
04:38 Novatian[Treatise Concerning the Trinity 21]
04:41 Irenaeus[Against Heresies Book IV.1.7]
04:43-45 Mark 1:14; Luke 4:14-15
04:44 Matthew 13:57; Mark 6:4; Luke 4:24; Constitutions of the Holy Apostles[Book II.58]; Nag Hammadi[Gospel of Thomas 31]
04:46 John 2:1-11; Origen[Gospel of Matthew Book XI.17]
04:48 Daniel 4:2, 37; OT-Apocrypha[Wisdom of Solomon 8:8]; Pseudepigrapha[Apocalypse of Adam 6:5; Apocalypse of Elijah 5:25]; Origen[Gospel of Matthew Book XI.17]
04:50 1Kings 17:23; Irenaeus[Against Heresies Book II.22.3]
05:01-05 Irenaeus[Against Heresies Book II.22.3]
05:01-09 Tertullian[An Answer to the Jews 13; On Baptism 5]
05:02 Nehemiah 3:1, 3:32, 12:39
05:05 Deuteronomy 2:14; Irenaeus[Against Heresies Book II.23.2, 24.4]
05:10 Nehemiah 13:19; Jeremiah 17:21
05:14 Cyprian[Epistle VI.2, LI.26; Treatise II.2, XII.Book III.27]; Irenaeus[Against Heresiies Book IV.36.6, V.15.2]; NT-Apocrypha[Freer Logion; Papyrus Egerton 2 Fragment 2 Lines 43-59]
05:16-18 Genesis 31:38-41
05:17 Pseudepigrapha[Letter of Aristeas 1.210]; Philo[Allegorical Interpretation I 3]; Rabbinic[Shemoth Rabba xxx. 9 p. 53c, d]; Clement of Alexandria[Stromata Book I.1]; Methodius[Banquet of the Ten Virgins 2.1; Discourse on the Resurrection 1.15]; Novatian[Treatise Concerning the Trinity 28]; Tertullian[Against Praxeas 21]
05:17-18 Tertullian[An Answer to the Jews 9]
05:17-26 Pseudepigrapha[Artapanus Fragment 3 (PrEv 9.27.23)]
05:18 John 1:18n; OT-Apocrypha[Wisdom of Solomon 2:16]

05:19 John 14:10-17n; Clement of Alexandria[Stromata Book I.1]; Novatian[Treatise Concerning the Trinity 14, 21]; Origen[Gospel of John Book X.21; De Principiis Book I.2.12]; Tertullian[Against Praxeas 15]; Nag Hammadi[Gospel of Thomas 27, 84]

05:19-27 Tertullian[Against Praxeas 21]

05:19-30 Philo[**Special Laws I (65)**]

> **...Some other prophet will appear to them on a sudden, inspired like himself [Moses], who will preach and prophesy among them, saying nothing of his own... (Philo - Special Laws I 65)**

05:20 Pseudepigrapha[Apocalypse of Elijah 5:25]

05:21 Deuteronomy 32:39; 1Samuel 2:6; 2Kings 5:7; Hosea 6:2; Pseudepigrapha[Joseph and Aseneth 20:7]; Tertullian[Against Praxeas 24]; NT-Apocrypha[Epistula Apostolorum 21]

05:22 Daniel 7:10, 13; Pseudepigrapha[1Enoch 69:27; Apocalypse of Elijah 5:25]; Josephus[Discourse to the Greeks Concerning Hades 6]; Tertullian[Against Praxeas 16]

05:22-23 Cyprian[Treatise XII.Book II.28, III.33]

05:23 Clement[Recognitions Book II.48]; Hippolytus[Against the Heresy of One Noetus 7]; Lactantius[Epitome of the Divine Institutes 49]; Origen[Against Celsus Book VIII.9]; NT-Apocrypha[Letter of Clement to James 17.1]

05:24 Pseudepigrapha[Joseph and Aseneth 8:9]; Clement of Alexandria[Stromata Book V.13; The Instructor Book I.6]; Justin[Dialogue with Trypho 136]; Nag Hammadi[Gospel of Thomas 1]; NT-Apocrypha[Epistula Apostolorum 21]

05:24-25 Tertullian[On the Resurrection of the Flesh 37]; NT-Apocrypha[Epistula Apostolorum 28-29]

05:24-29 Jude 1:21n

05:25 John 3:18n; Constitutions of the Holy Apostles[Book V.7]; Hippolytus[Appendix to the Works of Hippolytus - On the End of the World 36; Treatise on Christ and Antichrist 65]

05:26 Pseudepigrapha[Odes of Solomon 3:9]; Novatian[Treatise Concerning the Trinity 14]

05:27 Psalms 80:17; John 3:13n; Pseudepigrapha[1Enoch 69:26-29]; Origen[Gospel of John Book I.40]

05:27-30 Pseudepigrapha[Apocalypse of Elijah 5:24-25]

05:28 Isaiah 26:19; Ezekiel 37:12; Irenaeus[Against Heresies Book V.13.1]; NT-Apocrypha[Epistula Apostolorum 29]

05:28-29 Tertullian[On the Resurrection of the Flesh 37]

05:29 Daniel 12:2; Acts 2:31n; Lactantius[Divine Institutes Book II.13]; Tertullian[On the Resurrection of the Flesh 50]

05:30 Numbers 16:28

05:31 Origen[Against Celsus Book I.48]; Tertullian[On Prescription Against Heretics 23]

05:31-32 Cyprian[Epistle LXVIII.2]

05:33 John 1:19-27; 3:27-30

05:33-35 Tertullian[Five Books in Reply to Marcion Book II.145]

05:33-39 Acts 3:18-26n

05:34 Tertullian[On the Apparel of Women Book II.13]

05:35 Psalms 132:16; Matthew 5:15n; Pseudepigrapha[2Baruch 18:2; 2Enoch 46:3]; Irenaeus[Fragments from the Lost Works 47]; Tertullian[An Answer to the Jews 9]

05:36-37 Tertullian[Against Praxeas 21]

05:37 Deuteronomy 4:12; Matthew 3:17; Mark 1:11; Luke 3:22; Hippolytus[Refutation of all Heresies Book V.3]

05:39 Jude 1:21n; Constitutions of the Holy Apostles[Book II.5]; Gregory Thaumaturgus[Four Homilies 2]; Methodius[Banquet of the Ten Virgins 8.4; Oration on the Psalms 4]; Origen[Against Celsus Book V.16; Gospel of John Book V.4, VI.12; De Principiis Book IV.1.19]; Tertullian[On Prescription Against Heretics 8]; NT-Apocrypha[Papyrus Egerton 2 Fragment 1 Lines 1-20]

05:39-40 Cyprian[Treatise XII.Book I.18]; Irenaeus[Against Heresies Book IV.10.1]

05:39-46 2Corinthians 3:12-18n

05:40 Pseudepigrapha[Odes of Solomon 3:9]

05:43 Philippians 2:9; Cyprian[Treatise XII.Book II.5]; Irenaeus[Against Heresies Book V.25.4; Against Praxeas 16, 21, 23; An Answer to the Jews 13; On Prayer 3]; Nag Hammadi[Gospel of Truth 38]

05:44 2Kings 19:15, 19; Isaiah 37:20; Daniel 3:45; Tertullian[On the Veiling of Virgins 2]

05:45 Deuteronomy 31:26-27

05:45-46 Acts 2:23n; NT-Apocrypha[Papyrus Egerton 2 Fragment 1 Lines 1-20]

05:45-47 Archelaus[Disputation with Manes 45]; Cyprian[Treatise XII.Book I.18]

05:46 Deuteronomy 18:15; Acts 3:18-26n; Apostolic[Ignatius - Letter to the Philadelphians 5:2, 9:2; Polycarp - Letter to the Philippians 6:3; Epistle of Barnabas 1:7, 3:6]; Archelaus[Disputation with Manes 41]; Constitutions of the Holy Apostles[Book II.5]; Irenaeus[Against Heresies Book IV.10.1]; Justin[Dialogue with Trypho 136]; Origen[Gospel of John Book VI.12; Gospel of Matthew Book X.18, 22]

05:46-47 Irenaeus[Against Heresies Book IV.1.3]; Origen[Against Celsus Book II.4]

06:01 Matthew 14:12-13a; Mark 6:29-32; Luke 9:10; Pseudepigrapha[Joseph and Aseneth 8:5; Testament of Jacob 7:23]; Irenaeus[Against Heresies Book II.22.3]

06:01-13 Pseudepigrapha[Sibylline Oracles 1.357]

06:01-14 Tertullian[An Answer to the Jews 10]

06:01-15 Matthew 14:13-21; Mark 6:30-44; Luke 9:10-17

06:02 Matthew 14:13-33; Mark 6:33-52

06:02-21 Dead Sea Scrolls[Damascus Document (CD-A) COL XIII 1; Rule of the Congregation (1Q28a[1QSa]) COL I 13-16]

06:04-21 Matthew 14:13-33; Mark 6:33-52; Luke 9:11-17

06:05-13 NT-Apocrypha[Acts of John 93]

06:07-14 John 6:31-58n

06:09 2Kings 4:42-44; Origen[Gospel of Matthew Book XI.2]; NT-Apocrypha[Epistula Apostolorum 5]

06:09-11 Irenaeus[Against Heresies Book II.24.4]

06:10 Matthew 14:21n; Origen[Gospel of Matthew Book XI.19]

06:11 Pseudepigrapha[Testament of Zebulon 6.6-7]; Irenaeus[Against Heresies Book III.11.5]; Methodius[Oration on the Psalms 3]

06:12 Rabbinic[Jerusalem Sanhedrin 23C]

06:13 Irenaeus[Against Heresies Book II.22.3]; Origen[Gospel of Matthew Book XI.19]

06:15 1Samuel 10:21; Josephus[Antiquities 6.4.5 62]; Tertullian[On Idolatry 18]

06:16-21 Matthew 14:22-27; Mark 6:45-52

06:18-21 Pseudepigrapha[Sibylline Oracles 8.273]

06:19 Job 9:8; Pseudepigrapha[Sibylline Oracles 6.12-13; Testament of Adam 3.1]

06:21 Psalms 107:30

06:26-27 John 6:31-58n; Novatian[On the Jewish Meats 5]

06:27 Numbers 8:11; Ruth 2:12; Psalms 80:17; Acts 3:18-26n; Jude 1:21n; Rabbinic[Ruth Rabba on 2:12]; Apostolic[Didache 10:3]; Clement of Alexandria[Stromata Book I.1, III.12, VI.1]; Clement[First Epistle Concerning Virginity 13]; Constitutions of the Holy Apostles[Book II.61]; Methodius[Oration on the Psalms 1]; Tertullian[On Fasting 15]

06:29 Constitutions of the Holy Apostles[Book II.61]; Hippolytus[Against the Heresy of One Noetus 7]

06:29-30 Tertullian[Against Praxeas 21]

06:31 Exodus 16:4; Numbers 11:7-9; Psalms 78:24-25, 105:40; Nehemiah 9:15; Origen[Gospel of Matthew Book XII.33]; Tertullian[On the Resurrection of the Flesh 37]

06:31-32 Exodus 16:15; Tertullian[An Answer to the Jews 3]

06:31-33 Pseudepigrapha[Sibylline Oracles Fragment 3.49]

06:31-58 This section also includes topical notes for: Spiritual Food - Deuteronomy 8:3; Nehemiah 9:20; Psalms 78:24; Matthew 14:15:26, 26:26-29; Mark 6:37-44, 14:22-25; Luke 9:13-17, 22:19-20; John 4:10-15, 6:7-14, 6:26-27; Acts 14:17; Hebrews 5:11-14; 1Corinthians 10:3-4, 11:23-29; Philo[Concerning Noah's Work As A Planter (77-79) cf. {Genesis 26:32}; On the Change of Names (174) cf. {Genesis 45:18}]; Rabbinic[Babylonian Sukkah 52a]; Plato[Republic IX 585b-d]; Clement of Alexandria[The Instructor Book I.6, II.1-2]; Irenaeus[Against Heresies Book IV.38.2, V.22.2; Fragments from the Lost Works 31]; Theodotus[Excerpts 14]; Nag Hammadi[A Valentinian Exposition 44; Authoritative Teaching 31-32, 35; Gospel of Philip 55, 57, 73, 80]

06:32 Exodus 16:4; Tertullian[Against Praxeas 21]

06:32-35 Philo[Allegorical Interpretation II (86)]

06:32-40 Liturgy of the Apostles 14

06:33 Apostolic[Ignatius - Letter to the Ephesians 5:2]; Origen[Gospel of John Book I.23; Gospel of Matthew Book XII.5]; Tertullian[On Prayer 6]; NT-Apocrypha[Acts of John 98]

06:33-37 Pseudepigrapha[Odes of Solomon 41:11]

06:35 OT-Apocrypha[Sirach 24:21]; Pseudepigrapha[Joseph and Aseneth 8:5]; Cyprian[Treatise XII.Book I.22]; Hippolytus[Fragments - On Genesis 49.16-20]; Irenaeus[Against Heresies Book II.11.1]; Origen[Gospel of John Book I.23]; Tertullian[On Prayer 6]; NT-Apocrypha[Acts of John 98]

06:36 Nag Hammadi[Apocryphon of James 13]

06:37 NT-Apocrypha[Gospel of the Nazareans Fragment 23]

06:37-38 Cyprian[Epistle LXXII.11]

06:37-46 Tertullian[Against Praxeas 21]

06:38 Exodus 19:18, 33:9; Pseudepigrapha[Prayer of Joseph Fragment A; Sibylline Oracles 3.655];
Philo[On the Posterity of Cain And His Exile (30-31) cf. {Genesis 17:1-22, 18:1-21}];
Archelaus[Disputation with Manes 47]; Cyprian[Treatise II.7, IV.14, XII.Book III.19];
Novatian[Treatise Concerning the Trinity 26]; Tertullian[Against Praxeas 8; On Prayer 4]

06:38-40 Tertullian[On the Resurrection of the Flesh 34]

06:39 Tertullian[On the Resurrection of the Flesh 36]; NT-Apocrypha[Gospel of the Nazareans
Fragment 23]

06:39-54 Nag Hammadi[Testimony of Truth 34-35]

06:40 Jude 1:21n; Clement of Alexandria[The Instructor Book I.6]

06:41 Origen[Gospel of John Book I.23]; NT-Apocrypha[Abgar Legend]

06:42 Pseudepigrapha[3Enoch 45:5]; Irenaeus[Against Heresies Book I.25.1]

06:44 Hippolytus[Refutation of all Heresies Book V.3]; Origen[Gospel of Matthew Book XIV.14];
Tertullian[A Treatise on the Soul 16; Against Praxeas 24]; Nag Hammadi[Exegesis of the Soul 134-
135]

06:45 Isaiah 54:13; Jeremiah 31:33; Matthew 9:35n; Acts 3:18n; Constitutions of the Holy Apostles[Book
VIII.32]

06:46 Genesis 32:30; Novatian[Treatise Concerning the Trinity 14]; NT-Apocrypha[Acts of Peter 1.7]

06:47 Jude 1:21n

06:48 Pseudepigrapha[Joseph and Aseneth 8:5]; Irenaeus[Against Heresies Book II.11.1]; NT-
Apocrypha[Acts of John 98]

06:48-50 Origen[Gospel of John Book X.13]

06:48-51 Philo[Allegorical Interpretation II (86)]

06:49 Numbers 14:23; Deuteronomy 1:35; Tertullian[On the Resurrection of the Flesh 37]

06:50-58 Jude 1:21n

06:51 Novatian[Treatise Concerning the Trinity 14]; Origen[Gospel of Matthew Book XI.14, XII.5, 33];
Tertullian[On the Flesh of Christ 13; On the Resurrection of the Flesh 37]

06:53 Leviticus 17:10-14; Psalms 80:17; Cyprian[Treatise IV.18; XII.Book I.22, III.25];
Hippolytus[Appendix to the Works of Hippolytus - On the Seventy Apostles 15; Refutation of all
Heresies Book V.3]; Origen[Gospel of John Book VI.26, X.13]; Tertullian[On Baptism 16]; Nag
Hammadi[Gospel of Philip 57]

06:53-55 Clement of Alexandria[The Instructor Book I.6]

06:53-56 This section also includes topical notes for: The Flesh and Blood - Ezekiel 39:17-19;
Matthew 26:27-28; Mark 14:23-24; Luke 22:20; 1Corinthians 10:16-21, 11:25-27; Dead Sea Scrolls[1Q
Hymns (1QHODAYOTH [1QH]) COL XIII 7]; Philo[Every Good Man Is Free (25) cf. {Fragment of
Euripedes From the Syleus. Fr. 2}; On Dreams, That they Are God-Sent (2.246-2.249) cf. {Exodus
26:11-12, Leviticus 26:12, Psalms 45:5}; On Joseph (77-79) cf. {Genesis 39:2-20}]; Clement of
Alexandria[The Instructor Book II.2]; Gregory Thaumaturgus[Twelve Topics on the Faith 10]

06:56 Romans 8:9-11n

06:58 Cyprian[Treatise IV.18]; Tertullian[On the Resurrection of the Flesh 37]

06:59 Matthew 9:35n

06:62 Psalms 80:17; Novatian[Treatise Concerning the Trinity 14]

06:63 Tertullian[On the Resurrection of the Flesh 37, 50]

06:64 Anonymous[Treatise Against the Heretic Novatian 14]

06:65 Cyprian[Epistle LXXII.18]

06:66 Hippolytus[Appendix to the Works of Hippolytus - On the Seventy Apostles 15]

06:66-68 Tertullian[Against Praxeas 21; On Prescription Against Heretics 3]

06:67 Anonymous[Treatise Against the Heretic Novatian 8]; Constitutions of the Holy Apostles[Book
VI.22]; Cyprian[Epistle LIV.7]

06:67-69 Cyprian[Epistle LXVIII.8]

06:68 Jude 1:21n; Origen[Gospel of Matthew Book XII.17]

06:69 Matthew 16:16; Mark 8:29; Luke 9:20; Irenaeus[Against Heresies Book III.11.6]

06:70 Tertullian[An Answer to the Jews 14]; NT-Apocrypha[Kerygma Petri 3b]

06:71 Irenaeus[Against Heresies Book I.31.1]

07:01-53 Tertullian[Against Praxeas 22]

07:02 Leviticus 23:34; Deuteronomy 16:13, 16

07:05 Tertullian[On the Flesh of Christ 7]

07:12 Rabbinic[Babylonian (Sanhedrin 106b cf. {Psalms 55:23}, 107b; Sotah 47a); Yalqut 766 cf. {Numbers 23:19}]

07:14 Matthew 9:35n; Pseudepigrapha[Ezekiel the Tragedian 2]

07:15 Dead Sea Scrolls[4Q Elect of God (4Q534[4QMESSAR]) COL 1 7-11]; Origen[Against Celsus Book VI.16; Gospel of Matthew Book X.17]

07:16 Clement of Alexandria[Stromata Book I.17]

07:17 Numbers 16:28; Clement of Alexandria[Stromata Book I.7]

07:18 Psalms 92:16; Clement of Alexandria[Stromata Book I.17, 20]; Origen[Gospel of John Book I.40]; NT-Apocrypha[Epistula Apostolorum 50]

07:19 Pseudepigrapha[Ezekiel the Tragedian 12]

07:20 Clement[Recognitions Book I.40]

07:22 Genesis 17:10-13; Leviticus 12:3; Victorinus[On the Creation of the World]

07:22-23 Rabbinic[Babylonian Yoma 85b]

07:23 John 5:9

07:24 Isaiah 11:3-4; Pseudepigrapha[Pseudo-Phocylides 9; Vision of Ezra 39]; Constitutions of the Holy Apostles[Book II.37]

07:27 1Samuel 16:7

07:28 Matthew 9:35n

07:30 Irenaeus[Against Heresies Book III.16.7]; NT-Apocrypha[Papyrus Egerton 2 Fragment 1 Lines 22-41]

07:32 Pseudepigrapha[Ezekiel the Tragedian 104]; Hippolytus[Refutation of all Heresies Book IX.23]

07:33 Nag Hammadi[Apocryphon of James 2]

07:34 Proverbs 1:28; Nag Hammadi[Gospel of Thomas 38]

07:34-36 Nag Hammadi[Gospel of Thomas 59]

07:35 Matthew 9:35n

07:37 Leviticus 23:36; Isaiah 12:3, 49:10, 55:1; Pseudepigrapha[Odes of Solomon 11:7, 30.1-7]; Origen[Gospel of John Book VI.10, 22]; Nag Hammadi[Gospel of Thomas 28, 108]

07:37-38 Pseudepigrapha[Odes of Solomon 6:18]; Cyprian[Treatise XII.Book I.22]; Tertullian[On Baptism 9]

07:37-39 Cyprian[Epistle LXII.8]; Tertullian[Five Books in Reply to Marcion Book III.6]

07:38 Proverbs 18:4; Song of Solomon 4:15; Isaiah 43:19, 58:11; Ezekiel 47:1-12; Joel 3:18; Zechariah 14:8; John 4:10-11n; OT-Apocrypha[Sirach 24:30-34]; Hippolytus[The Discourse on the Holy Theophany 2]

07:38-39 Anonymous[Treatise on Re-Baptism 14]

07:39 Irenaeus[Against Heresies Book V.18.2]; Origen[Gospel of Matthew Book XII.40]

07:40 Deuteronomy 18:15

07:42 2Samuel 7:12; Psalms 89:3-4; Jeremiah 23:5; Micah 5:1-2; Pseudepigrapha[Psalms of Solomon 17:21]; Josephus[War 2.8.12 159]; Justin[First Apology 34]; Origen[Against Celsus Book I.51]

07:45-48 Hippolytus[Refutation of all Heresies Book IX.23]

07:47 Rabbinic[Babylonian (Sanhedrin 106b cf. {Psalms 55:23}, 107b; Sotah 47a); Yalqut 766 cf. {Numbers 23:19}]

07:48 Pseudepigrapha[Fragments of Pseudo-Greek Poets 8]

07:49 Deuteronomy 27:26

07:50 John 3:1-2

07:51 Deuteronomy 19:18

07:52 2Kings 14:25

07:53-08:11 Apostolic[Papias Fragment 3:17, 23:1, 26:1]

08:02 Matthew 9:35n

08:03 Numbers 5:12; Hippolytus[Refutation of all Heresies Book IX.23]

08:03-11 This section also includes topical notes for: Adultery - Matthew 5:27-32, 19:9-19; Mark 10:11-19; Luke 16:18, 18:20; Romans 2:22, 13:9; Galatians 5:19; James 2:11; 2Peter 2:14; Revelation 2:22; Josephus[Antiquities 15.7.10 259]; Philo**The Cherubim Part (14-17) cf. {Numbers 5:14-18, Deuteronomy 16:20}**; Special Laws III (52-54, 58-63) cf. {Deuteronomy 22:13}]; Rabbinic[Aboth de Rabbi Nathan 2.5a cf. {Job 31:1}; Mishnah Gittin 9:3]; Irenaeus[Against Heresies Book II.32.1]

Now of the kind of opposition of place which is connected with standing in front of a judge for judgment, we have an example in the case of the woman who has been suspected of having committed adultery. For, says Moses, "the priest shall cause the woman to stand in front of her lord, and she shall uncover her Head." ...And therefore it is enjoined to the priest and prophet, that is to say to reason, "to place the soul in front of God, with the head uncovered," that is to say the soul must be laid bare as to its principal design, and the sentiments which it nourished must be revealed, in order that being brought before the judgment seat of the most accurate vision of the incorruptible God, it may be thoroughly examined as to all its concealed disguises, like a base coin, or, on the other hand, if it be found to be free from all participation in any kind of wickedness, it may wash away all the calumnies that have been uttered against its bringing him for a testimony to its purity, who is alone able to behold the soul naked. (Philo - The Cherubim Part (14-17) cf. {Numbers 5:14-18, Deuteronomy 16:20})

08:04 Pseudepigrapha[Joseph and Aseneth 4:10]
08:05 Leviticus 20:10; Deuteronomy 21:22, 22:22-24
08:07 Deuteronomy 17:6-7
08:10 Pseudepigrapha[Odes of Solomon 19:10]
08:11 Callistus[Second Epistle 6.6]; Constitutions of the Holy Apostles[Book II.24]; NT-Apocrypha[Freer Logion; Protoevangelium of James 16.2]
08:12 Isaiah 42:8, 49:6, 60:1, 3; Matthew 5:14n; John 9:5; Pseudepigrapha[2Enoch 46:3; Apocalypse of Daniel 14:16; Odes of Solomon 12:3, 18:14; Sibylline Oracles Fragment 1.27]; Dead Sea Scrolls[4QAaronic Text A = Testament of Levi (4Q541[4QAhA = 4QTLevi]) Fragment 24 COL II 6]; Clement of Alexandria[Stromata Book I.13]; Cyprian[Epistle LXII.18; Treatise X.11, XII.Book II.7]; Nag Hammadi[Letter of Peter to Philip 133]
08:14 Acts 3:18-26n
08:14-15 Novatian[Treatise Concerning the Trinity 15]
08:15 1Samuel 16:7
08:16 Hippolytus[Against the Heresy of One Noetus 7]
08:16-19 Tertullian[Against Praxeas 22]
08:17 Deuteronomy 19:15
08:17-18 Acts 3:18-26n; Novatian[Treatise Concerning the Trinity 26]
08:18 Hippolytus[Against the Heresy of One Noetus 7]
08:19 Nag Hammadi[Dialogue of the Savior 35]
08:20 Matthew 9:35n
08:21 Deuteronomy 24:16
08:23 Pseudepigrapha[Odes of Solomon 41.8]; Novatian[Treatise Concerning the Trinity 15]
08:24 Clement of Alexandria[Stromata Book V.13]; Cyprian[Treatise XII.Book I.5]
08:24-28 Apostolic[2Clement 17:5]
08:25 Deuteronomy 15:12; Acts 3:18-26n
08:26 Tertullian[Against Praxeas 8]
08:26-29 Tertullian[Against Praxeas 22]
08:28 Psalms 80:17; Isaiah 43:10; Acts 3:18-26n; Dead Sea Scrolls[4Q Elect of God (4Q534[4QMESSAR]) COL 1 7-11]
08:31-32 Cyprian[Treatise IX.13, XI.8]; Origen[Gospel of Matthew Book XII.15]
08:32 1Peter 2:13; Pseudepigrapha[Ezekiel the Tragedian 104]; Nag Hammadi[Gospel of Philip 84-85]
08:32-34 Nag Hammadi[Gospel of Philip 77]
08:32-36 Clement of Alexandria[Stromata Book II.5]
08:33 Nehemiah 9:36; Matthew 3:9; Luke 3:8; NT-Apocrypha[Apocalypse of Paul 1.3]
08:34 Genesis 4:7; Clement[Recognitions Book V.12]; Cyprian[Treatise IV.6]; Irenaeus[Against Heresies Book III.8.1]; Origen[Gospel of Matthew Book XIII.11]
08:35 Exodus 21:2
08:36 Irenaeus[Against Heresies Book III.19.1]
08:38 Tertullian[Against Praxeas 22]
08:39 Origen[Gospel of John Book VI.2]; Tertullian[On Monogamy 6]
08:40 Psalms 15:2; Gregory Thaumaturgus[Twelve Topics on the Faith 8]; Origen[Against Celsus Book I.66, II.25, VII.16]; Tertullian[Against Praxeas 22; On the Flesh of Christ 15]

08:41 Genesis 38:24; Deuteronomy 32:6; Isaiah 63:16, 64:8; Malachi 2:10; Nag Hammadi[Gospel of Thomas 105]

08:42 Novatian[Treatise Concerning the Trinity 15]; Tertullian[Against Praxeas 22]

08:44 Genesis 3:4; OT-Apocrypha[Wisdom of Solomon 2:24]; Pseudepigrapha[Joseph and Aseneth 12:9]; Anterus[Epistle]; Archelaus[Disputation with Manes 13, 29, 32-33]; Clement of Alexandria[Stromata Book I.17]; Constitutions of the Holy Apostles[Book II.21]; Hippolytus[Refutation of all Heresies Book V.12]; Irenaeus[Against Heresies Book V.22.2, 23.2]; Origen[Gospel of Matthew Book XII.40]; Tertullian[Against Praxeas 1]; Nag Hammadi[Gospel of Philip 60-61]; NT-Apocrypha[Acts of Peter 1.16; Acts of Thomas 1.143; Pseudo Clementines - Kerygmata Petrou H III 25.2]

08:46 Origen[De Principiis Book II.6.4]

08:49 Malachi 1:6; Tertullian[Against Praxeas 22]

08:51 Gregory Thaumaturgus[Twelve Topics on the Faith 7]; Novatian[Treatise Concerning the Trinity 15]

08:52 Zechariah 1:5

08:53 OT-Apocrypha[Sirach 44:19]

08:54-56 Tertullian[Against Praxeas 22]

08:56 Acts 3:18-26n; Pseudepigrapha[Sibylline Oracles 6.19; Testament of Levi 18:14]; Irenaeus[Against Heresies Book IV.5.3, 5]; Origen[Gospel of John Book II.28]; Nag Hammadi[Gospel of Philip 82]

08:56-57 Irenaeus[Against Heresies Book II.22.6]

08:56-58 NT-Apocrypha[Gospel of Pseudo-Matthew 30]

08:57-59 Pseudepigrapha[Odes of Solomon 28:19]

08:58 This section also includes topical notes for: Pre-incarnate - Genesis 19:24, 27:24; Isaiah 43:10, 13; Pseudepigrapha[Prayer of Joseph Fragment A]; Philo[On Abraham (132) cf. {Genesis 18:3}; On Flight and Finding (68-70) cf. {Genesis 1:26}]; Clement of Alexandria[The Instructor Book I.7]; Gregory Thaumaturgus[Twelve Topics on the Faith 5]; Irenaeus[Against Heresies Book IV.13.4; Demonstration of the Apostolic Preaching 29, 43-46, 51-52; Fragments from the Lost Works 52-54]; Justin[Dialogue with Trypho 56-61, 87, 113, 126-130]; Novatian[Treatise Concerning the Trinity 15]; Origen[Against Celsus Book VIII.12]

08:59 Irenaeus[Fragments from the Lost Works 52]; NT-Apocrypha[Acts of Peter 1.32]

09:01 Constitutions of the Holy Apostles[Book V.7]; Hippolytus[Refutation of all Heresies Book V.4]; Irenaeus[Against Heresies Book II.16.9]; Origen[Gospel of John Book I.5]; NT-Apocrypha[Epistula Apostolorum 5]

09:01-38 Irenaeus[Against Heresies Book V.15.2-3]

09:01-41 Methodius[Oration on the Psalms 3]

09:02 Exodus 20:5; Ezekiel 18:20; Pseudepigrapha[Odes of Solomon 11:3; Testament of Job 23:6]

09:02-03 Clement[Homily XIX.22]

09:04 Jeremiah 13:16; Tertullian[Against Praxeas 22]

09:04-05 Origen[Gospel of John Book I.24]

09:05 Isaiah 49:6; Matthew 5:14n; John 8:12

09:06 Egyptian Book of the Dead[Oration 102]

09:07 2Kings 5:10; Isaiah 8:6; Pseudepigrapha[Lives of the Prophets 1:2]

09:16 Hippolytus[Refutation of all Heresies Book IX.23]

09:24 Joshua 7:19; Psalms 68:35

09:29 Numbers 12:2, 8; NT-Apocrypha[Papyrus Egerton 2 Fragment 1 Lines 1-20]

09:30 Irenaeus[Against Heresies Book V.13.1, 15.2]

09:31 Psalms 34:15, 66:18, 145:19; Proverbs 15:8, 29; Isaiah 1:15; Pseudepigrapha[Joseph and Aseneth 4:7]; Cyprian[Epistle LXIII.2, LXVII.2, LXIX.2; The Seventh Council of Carthage under Cyprian]

09:34 Psalms 51:5, 7

09:35 John 3:18n; NT-Apocrypha[Epistula Apostolorum 30]

09:35-38 Tertullian[Against Praxeas 22]

09:38 Matthew 28:17n

09:39 Origen[Against Celsus Book VII.39]

10:01 Anonymous[Treatise Against the Heretic Novatian 2]; NT-Apocrypha[Epistula Apostolorum 44]

10:01-03 Clement of Alexandria[Stromata Book V.13]

10:01-09 Apostolic[Ignatius - Letter to the Philadelphians 9:1; Shepherd of Hermas 89:1-8]; Clement of Alexandria[Stromata Book VI.8]

10:01-16 Nag Hammadi[Apocryphon of James 8]

10:01-18 NT-Apocrypha[Acts of Thomas 1.26]

10:03 Psalms 95:7; Clement[Homily III.52]; Origen[Letter to Gregory 3]

10:04 Psalms 80:2

10:06 Matthew 13:3-53n

10:07 Clement of Alexandria[Stromata Book V.13]; Hippolytus[Refutation of all Heresies Book V.12]

10:07-09 Pseudepigrapha[Odes of Solomon 12:3]

10:07-10 Pseudepigrapha[Odes of Solomon 17:9-11; 42:17]

10:07-14 Nag Hammadi[Authoritative Teaching 32-33; Teachings of Silvanus 106-107, 117]

10:07-27 Luke 13:32n

10:08 Jeremiah 23:1-2; Ezekiel 34:2-3; Anonymous[Treatise Against the Heretic Novatian 2]; Clement
of Alexandria[Stromata Book I.17]; Hippolytus[Refutation of all Heresies Book V.30];
Irenaeus[Against Heresies Book III.4.1]; Origen[Gospel of John Book I.42; Gospel of Matthew Book
X.14]

10:08-10 Origen[Against Celsus Book VII.70]

10:09 Numbers 27:17; Psalms 118:20; Clement of Alexandria[Exhortation to the Heathen 1];
Clement[Homily III.52]; Cyprian[Treatise XII.Book II.27, III.24]; Hippolytus[Refutation of all
Heresies Book V.3]; Origen[Gospel of John Book I.11; Gospel of Matthew Book XII.12]; NT-
Apocrypha[Acts of John 94, 98, 109]

10:10 Jude 1:21n; Pseudepigrapha[Odes of Solomon 3:9]; Gregory Thaumaturgus[Twelve Topics on
the Faith 7]

10:11 Isaiah 40:11; Ezekiel 34:11-16, 23, 37:24; Rabbinic[Babylonian Yoma 66b]; Clement of
Alexandria[Stromata Book I.26; The Instructor Book I.7, 11]; Peter of Alexandria[Genuine Acts of
Peter 3]; Tertullian[On Modesty 7]; NT-Apocrypha[Acts of Peter 1.10; Acts of Thomas 1.39; Extracts
from the Arabic Infancy Gospel 40]

10:11-12 Constitutions of the Holy Apostles[Book II.20]; Cyprian[Epistle II.1]

10:11-14 This section also includes topical notes for: Good Shepherd - Psalms 23:1; 80:1; Matthew
25:32; Hebrews 13:20; 1Peter 5:4; Pseudepigrapha[4Ezra 2.34; Psalms of Solomon 17.40]; Dead Sea
Scrolls[4Q Genesis Pesher (4Q254) Fragment 6 1-4]; Philo[On Dreams, That they Are God-Sent
(1.255-1.256) cf. {Genesis 32:24-32}; On Husbandry (41-42) cf. {Genesis 30:36, 46:31-47:6; Exodus
23:20}, **(51-53) cf. {Genesis 30:36, 46:31-47:6; Exodus 23:20}**, (64-66) cf. {Genesis 30:36, 46:31-47:6;
Exodus 23:20}; On the Virtues (58) cf. {Numbers 27:16}]; Clement of Alexandria[Exhortation to the
Heathen 11; The Instructor Book I.4, 6, 9]

> ...For God, like a shepherd and a king, governs (as if they were a flock of sheep) the
> earth, and the water, and the air, and the fire, and all the plants, and living creatures that
> are in them, whether mortal or divine; and he regulates the nature of the heaven, and the
> periodical revolutions of the sun and moon, and the variations and harmonious
> movements of the other stars, ruling them according to law and justice; appointing, as
> their immediate superintendent, his own right reason, his first-born son, who is to
> receive the charge of this sacred company, as the lieutenant of the great king; for it is
> said somewhere, "Behold, I am he! I will send my messenger before thy face, who shall
> keep thee in the Road." Let therefore all the world, the greatest and most perfect flock of
> the living God, say "The Lord is my shepherd, and he shall cause me to lack nothing,"
> and let every separate individual say the same thing; not with the voice which proceeds
> from his tongue and his mouth, extending only through a scanty portion of the air, but
> with the wide spreading voice of the mind, which reaches to the very extremities of this
> universe; for it is impossible that there should be a deficiency of anything that is
> necessary, where God presides, who is in the habit of bestowing good things in all
> fullness and completeness in all living beings. (Philo - On Husbandry (51-53) cf.
> {Genesis 30:36, 46:31-47:6; Exodus 23:20})

10:12 Tertullian[De Fuga in Persecutione 11]; NT-Apocrypha[Acts of Peter 1.8; Acts of Thomas 1.25;
Epistula Apostolorum 44]

10:12-13 Clement[First Epistle Concerning Virginity 13]

10:14 Pseudepigrapha[Odes of Solomon 8:12]; NT-Apocrypha[Acts of Thomas 1.25]

10:15 Matthew 11:27; Luke 10:22; Alexander of Alexandria[Epistles on Arian Heresy 2.4];
Tertullian[Against Praxeas 22]

10:16 Isaiah 56:8; Ezekiel 34:23, 37:24; Clement of Alexandria[Stromata Book VI.14; The Instructor Book I.7]; Cyprian[Epistle LXXV.5; Treatise I.8]; NT-Apocrypha[Acts of John 100]

10:17 Pseudepigrapha[Joseph and Aseneth 15:8]; Gregory Thaumaturgus[Twelve Topics on the Faith 10]

10:17-18 Rabbinic[Jerusalem Berakhot i. 8. (3c) cf. {Numbers 23:24}]; Hippolytus[Refutation of all Heresies Book X.23]; Tertullian[Against Praxeas 22]

10:18 Cyprian[Treatise VI.14, XII.Book II.24]; Dionysius of Alexandria[Exegetical Fragments Gospel According to Luke - An Interpretation 22.44]; Hippolytus[Against the Heresy of One Noetus 18]; Novatian[Treatise Concerning the Trinity 21]; Origen[Against Celsus Book II.16; Gospel of John Book VI.35; De Principiis Book II.6.3, 8.4, IV.1.31]

10:20 OT-Apocrypha[Wisdom of Solomon 5:4]

10:22 OT-Apocrypha[1Maccabees 4:59]; NT-Apocrypha[Gospel of the Nativity of Mary 2]

10:24 Origen[Against Celsus Book I.48]

10:24-30 Tertullian[Against Praxeas 22]

10:25 Tertullian[Five Books Against Marcion Book II.5]; NT-Apocrypha[Papyrus Egerton 2 Fragment 2 Lines 43-59]

10:27 Archelaus[Disputation with Manes 25]; Clement of Alexandria[Stromata Book VI.14]; Tertullian[On Modesty 7]

10:27-28 Jude 1:21n; Novatian[Treatise Concerning the Trinity 15]

10:28 Pseudepigrapha[Joseph and Aseneth 12:11; Odes of Solomon 3:9]; NT-Apocrypha[5Ezra 2.25; Epistula Apostolorum 28]

10:29 Constitutions of the Holy Apostles[Book VIII.11]

10:30 Alexander of Alexandria[Epistles on Arian Heresy 1.9, 2.3]; Cyprian[Epistle LXXV.5; Treatise I.6]; Dionysius of Rome[Against the Sabellians 3]; Gregory Thaumaturgus[Four Homilies 4]; Hippolytus[Against the Heresy of One Noetus 7]; Novatian[Treatise Concerning the Trinity 13, 15, 27]; Origen[Against Celsus Book VIII.12]; Tertullian[Against Hermogenes 18; Against Praxeas 8, 20, 24-25; On Prayer 2]

10:31 NT-Apocrypha[Papyrus Egerton 2 Fragment 1 Lines 22-41]

10:31-33 Tertullian[An Answer to the Jews 9]

10:32 Tertullian[Against Praxeas 22]

10:33 Leviticus 24:16; Methodius[Oration on the Psalms 7]; Novatian[Treatise Concerning the Trinity 27]

10:34 Exodus 7:1, 22:27; Psalms 82:6; Hippolytus[Refutation of all Heresies Book V.2, X.30]

10:34-38 Cyprian[Treatise XII.Book II.6]; Tertullian[Against Praxeas 22]

10:35-36 Novatian[Treatise Concerning the Trinity 15]

10:36 Jeremiah 1:5; John 3:18n; Pseudepigrapha[Apocalypse of Elijah 1:6]; Novatian[Treatise Concerning the Trinity 27]; Origen[Gospel of John Book I.23]; NT-Apocrypha[Epistula Apostolorum 39]

10:37-38 Tertullian[An Answer to the Jews 13]

10:38 NT-Apocrypha[Acts of John 100; Acts of Peter 1.20; Epistula Apostolorum 17, 31, 39]

10:39 NT-Apocrypha[Papyrus Egerton 2 Fragment 1 Lines 22-41]

10:40 Matthew 3:5-16n; John 1:28; NT-Apocrypha[Secret Gospel of Mark Fragment 1]

10:41 Origen[Gospel of Matthew Book X.20]

11:01 Luke 10:38-39

11:01-18 Origen[Gospel of John Book VI.24]

11:02 John 12:3; NT-Apocrypha[Secret Gospel of Mark Fragment 1]

11:04 John 3:18n

11:05 NT-Apocrypha[Secret Gospel of Mark Fragment 2]

11:06 Pseudepigrapha[Testament of Abraham 20:11]

11:09 Jeremiah 13:16

11:10 Pseudepigrapha[Joseph and Aseneth 6:6]; NT-Apocrypha[Akhmim Fragment 5.18]

11:11-14 Pseudepigrapha[4Ezra 2.31]

11:12 Novatian[Treatise Concerning the Trinity 26]

11:16 Plato[Phaedo 61c-d]

11:24 Daniel 12:2

11:24-25 Acts 2:31n

11:25 Pseudepigrapha[Odes of Solomon 3:9]; Constitutions of the Holy Apostles[Book V.7]; Cyprian[Treatise VII.21]; Gregory Thaumaturgus[Twelve Topics on the Faith 7]; Irenaeus[Against

Heresies Book IV.5.2; Fragments from the Lost Works 52]; Origen[Gospel of John Book I.10-11]; Nag Hammadi[Letter of Peter to Philip 134]; NT-Apocrypha[Acts of John 98, 109; Martyrdom of the Holy Apostle Paul 1.4]

11:25-26 Nag Hammadi[Gospel of Thomas 11]

11:26 Novatian[Treatise Concerning the Trinity 16]

11:27 John 3:18n; Tertullian[Against Praxeas 22]

11:32-33 NT-Apocrypha[Secret Gospel of Mark Fragment 1]

11:33 Gregory Thaumaturgus[Twelve Topics on the Faith 12]

11:34 Genesis 29:6

11:35 Genesis 29:11

11:39 Genesis 29:7-10; Pseudepigrapha[Testament of Abraham 20:11]; Origen[Gospel of John Book I.5; Gospel of Matthew Book XII.2]; NT-Apocrypha[Epistula Apostolorum 5]

11:39-44 Constitutions of the Holy Apostles[Book V.7]

11:41 Tertullian[Against Praxeas 26]

11:41-42 Tertullian[Against Praxeas 23; On Repentance 9]

11:43 Clement of Alexandria[The Instructor Book I.2]; NT-Apocrypha[Secret Gospel of Mark Fragment 1]

11:43-44 Irenaeus[Against Heresies Book II.22.3]

11:45-57 Matthew 26:1-5; Mark 14:1-2; Luke 22:1-2

11:48 Constitutions of the Holy Apostles[Book VI.25]

11:49-52 Pseudepigrapha[Odes of Solomon 31.12]

11:50 Jonah 1:12-15; NT-Apocrypha[Akhmim Fragment 11.48]

11:51 Exodus 28:30; Numbers 27:21; Constitutions of the Holy Apostles[Book VIII.2]

11:52 Pseudepigrapha[Odes of Solomon 10:5]; Hippolytus[Treatise on Christ and Antichrist 6]

11:54 2Samuel 13:25; Irenaeus[Against Heresies Book II.22.3]

11:55 2Chronicles 30:17

12:01 Irenaeus[Against Heresies Book II.22.3; Fragments from the Lost Works 54]; NT-Apocrypha[Secret Gospel of Mark Fragment 1]

12:01-08 Matthew 26:6-13; Mark 14:3-9

12:03 Luke 7:37-38; Pseudepigrapha[Joseph and Aseneth 17:4]

12:04-06 Pseudepigrapha[Letter of Aristeas 1.270]

12:05 1Kings 1:38, 44; Zechariah 9:9; Matthew 21:5; Mark 11:7-9; Luke 19:35; NT-Apocrypha[Arabic Gospel of the Infancy of the Savior 5]

12:05-06 Origen[Gospel of Matthew Book XI.9]

12:06 Pseudepigrapha[3Enoch 27:2]; Constitutions of the Holy Apostles[Book V.14, VII.2]; NT-Apocrypha[Acts of Thomas 1.84]

12:08 Deuteronomy 15:11

12:12-14 Origen[Gospel of John Book X.18]

12:12-15 Origen[Gospel of John Book X.15]

12:12-19 Matthew 21:1-11; Mark 11:1-10; Luke 19:28-44

12:13 Leviticus 23:40; Psalms 118:25-26; Zephaniah 3:15; Rabbinic[Babylonian Sanhedrin 38b cf. {Exodus 23:21}]; Constitutions of the Holy Apostles[Book VII.26]; Methodius[Oration on the Psalms 1]

12:14-15 Rabbinic[Babylonian Sanhedrin 98a]

12:15 Isaiah 35:4, 40:9; Zephaniah 3:14; Zechariah 9:9; Pseudepigrapha[Sibylline Oracles 8.325]; Justin[First Apology 31, 35]

12:20 Novatian[Treatise Concerning the Trinity 26]

12:23 Psalms 80:17

12:24 Origen[Against Celsus Book VIII.43]; NT-Apocrypha[Papyrus Egerton 2 Fragment 2 Lines 60-75]

12:25 This section also includes topical notes for: He that Hates his Life in this World Shall Keep It - Matthew 10:39, 16:25; Mark 8:35; Luke 9:24, 17:33; John 3:19; Jude 1:21n; Philo[Fragments Extracted From the Parallels of John of Damascus Page 370. B. cf. {Genesis 1:4}; On Dreams, That they Are God-Sent (1.218) cf. {Exodus 28:40-43}]; Rabbinic[Babylonian Taanit 31a]; Apostolic[Ignatius - Letter to the Magnesians 5:2]; Clement of Alexandria[Stromata Book IV.6]; Cyprian[Epistle LV.7, LXXX.2; Treatise XI.5, XII.Book III.16]; Nag Hammadi[Gospel of Thomas 56, 110; Testimony of Truth 41]; Indian[Dhammapada 83-84, 95, 99, 167, 254, 345-347]

12:26 OT-Apocrypha[4Maccabees 17:20]; Origen[Gospel of John Book I.24]; NT-Apocrypha[Epistula Apostolorum 41]; Epic of Gilgamesh[The Forest Journey]

12:27 Psalms 6:3-4; 31:10, 42:5-6, 11-12; Gregory Thaumaturgus[Twelve Topics on the Faith 12]; Irenaeus[Against Heresies Book I.8.2]; Origen[De Principiis Book II.8.4, IV.1.31]

12:27-28 Tertullian[Against Praxeas 23]

12:28 Rabbinic[Tosefta Sotah 13:2]; Tertullian[On Prayer 3]

12:28-30 Tacitus[The Histories 5.13]

12:29 Genesis 21:17; Job 37:5

12:30 Tertullian[Against Praxeas 23]

12:31 Pseudepigrapha[Life of Adam and Eve Vita 12:1; Martyrdom and Ascension of Isaiah 2:4; Testament of Solomon 2:9]; Apostolic[Epistle of Barnabas 18:1-2; Papias Fragment 24:1]; Origen[Against Celsus Book VII.17]; NT-Apocrypha[Freer Logion; Papyrus Egerton 2 Fragment 1 Lines 1-20; Two Books of Jeu c. 1-3]

12:31-32 Origen[Gospel of Matthew Book XII.18]

12:32 Irenaeus[Against Heresies Book IV.1.7]; NT-Apocrypha[Epistula Apostolorum 12]

12:34 Psalms 80:17, 89:4, 27, 36, 110:4; Daniel 7:14; Isaiah 9:7; Ezekiel 37:25; Anonymous[Treatise on Re-Baptism 9]; Clement[Recognitions Book I.43]

12:35 Pseudepigrapha[Odes of Solomon 18:14]; Cyprian[Treatises Attributed to Cyprian - On the Glory of Martyrdom 27]; Nag Hammadi[Letter of Peter to Philip 133; Teachings of Silvanus 102-103]

12:36 1Thessalonians 5:5n; Nag Hammadi[Gospel of Thomas 50]; NT-Apocrypha[Epistula Apostolorum 39]

12:37 NT-Apocrypha[Epistula Apostolorum 30]

12:38 Isaiah 53:1; NT-Apocrypha[Epistula Apostolorum 33]

12:39 NT-Apocrypha[Abgar Legend]

12:40 Isaiah 6:10; 2Corinthians 3:12-18n; Pseudepigrapha[Sibylline Oracles 1.360, 1.369]; Pythagoras[Golden Verses Lines 55-61]; Tertullian[On Fasting 6]

12:41 Isaiah 6:1

12:43 Constitutions of the Holy Apostles[Book V.6]; Tertullian[On the Veiling of Virgins 2]

12:44 Justin[Dialogue with Trypho 136]; NT-Apocrypha[Epistula Apostolorum 28]

12:44-45 Tertullian[Against Praxeas 23]

12:48 Origen[Gospel of John Book II.9]; Victorinus[Apocalypse 1.16]

12:49-50 John 14:10-17n; Tertullian[Against Praxeas 23]

12:50 Jude 1:21n; Pseudepigrapha[Joseph and Aseneth 12:2]

13:01 Hippolytus[Against the Heresy of One Noetus 8]; Tertullian[Against Praxeas 23]

13:01-05 Tertullian[The Chaplet, or De Corona 8]

13:01-07 Pseudepigrapha[Joseph and Aseneth 7:1; 20:2]

13:01-12 Tertullian[On Baptism 9]

13:01-17 Tertullian[On Idolatry 18]

13:01-35 Hippolytus[**Refutation of All Heresies Book IX.16-17**]

Then again they [Esseni] come together into one place, and encircle themselves with linen girdles, for the purpose of concealing their private parts. And in this manner they perform ablutions in cold water; and after being thus cleansed, they repair together into one apartment, - now no one who entertains a different opinion from themselves assembles in the house, - and they proceed to partake of breakfast. And when they have taken their seats in silence, they set down loaves in order, and next some one sort of food to eat along with the bread, and each receives from these a sufficient portion. No one, however, tastes these before the priest utters a blessing, and prays over the food. And after breakfast, when he has a second time offered up supplication, as at the beginning, so at the conclusion of their meal they praise God in hymns. Next, after they have laid aside as sacred the garments in which they have been clothed while together taking their repast within the house - (now these garments are linen) - and having resumed the clothes which they had left in the vestibule, they hasten to agreeable occupations until evening. And they partake of supper, doing all things in like manner to those already mentioned. And no one will at any time cry aloud, nor will any other tumultuous voice be heard. But they each converse quietly, and with decorum one concedes the conversation to the other, so that the stillness of those within the house appears a sort of mystery to those outside. And they are invariably sober, eating and drinking all things by measure. All then pay attention to the president; and whatever injunctions he will issue, they obey as law. (Hippolytus - Refutation of All Heresies Book IX.16-17)

13:01-38 Gregory Thaumaturgus[Twelve Topics on the Faith 5]

13:02 Irenaeus[Against Heresies Book I.31.1]; Origen[De Principiis Book III.2.4]; Tertullian[An Answer to the Jews 14]

13:02-27 Origen[Gospel of John Book X.30]

13:03 Tertullian[Against Praxeas 23]

13:04-05 Constitutions of the Holy Apostles[Book III.19]

13:04-17 Nag Hammadi[Gospel of Philip 72]

13:04-23 Hippolytus[Refutation of all Heresies Book IX.16]

13:05 Clement of Alexandria[The Instructor Book II.8]; Irenaeus[Against Heresies Book IV.22.1]; NT-Apocrypha[Gospel of the Nazareans Fragment 31]

13:05-14 This section also includes topical notes for: Washing the Disciples' Feet - Exodus 30:19-21; Luke 07:38-44; Philo[On Dreams, That they Are God-Sent (1.148) cf. {Leviticus 26:12}; On the Life of Moses II (138-139) cf. {Exodus 30:17-21}; Philo[Special Laws I (207) cf. {Exodus 29:17}]; Rabbinic[Babylonian Zebahim 17b, 19b]; Clement of Alexandria[Fragments found in Greek only in the Oxford Edition Last Work on the Passover; Fragments from Macarius Chrysocephalus Parable of the Prodigal son 1]

13:08 Origen[Against Celsus Book II.7]

13:09-10 Tertullian[On Baptism 12]

13:10 Tertullian[On Baptism 15; On Repentance 6]; NT-Apocrypha[Oxyrhynchus Papyrus 840]

13:11 Mark 14:18

13:13 Pseudepigrapha[The Sentences of the Syriac Menander 366]; Origen[Gospel of John Book I.23, 31]

13:14-15 Cyprian[Epistle V.2; Treatise XII.Book III.39]

13:15 Luke 22:27; NT-Apocrypha[Epistula Apostolorum 42]

13:16 Matthew 10:24; Luke 6:40; John 15:20; Cyprian[Epistle VI.4]; Tertullian[Against All Heresies 3]; Nag Hammadi[Dialogue of the Savior 53]

13:16-17 Cyprian[Treatise XII.Book III.5]

13:17 Constitutions of the Holy Apostles[Book VI.23]

13:18 Genesis 25:26; Psalms 41:9-10; Pseudepigrapha[Ahiqar 139; The Sentences of the Syriac Menander 215]; Dead Sea Scrolls[1Q Hymns (1QHODAYOTH [1QH]) COL XIII 22-24]; Josephus[War 2.8.12 159]; Rabbinic[Babylonian Sanhedrin 106b-107a]; NT-Apocrypha[Gospel of the Nazareans Fragment 23]

13:18-19 Mark 14:18

13:19 Isaiah 43:10, 46:10; Acts 3:18-26n; Apostolic[2Clement 17:5]

13:20 Matthew 10:40; Mark 9:37; Luke 9:48, 10:16; Constitutions of the Holy Apostles[Book VIII.46]; NT-Apocrypha[Letter of Clement to James 2.5, 17.1]

13:21 Constitutions of the Holy Apostles[Book V.14]; Gregory Thaumaturgus[Twelve Topics on the Faith 12]

13:21-30 Matthew 26:20-25; Mark 14:17-21; Luke 22:21-23

13:23 Pseudepigrapha[Joseph and Aseneth 10:4]; NT-Apocrypha[Acts of John 89; Secret Gospel of Mark Fragment 2]

13:23-25 Apostolic[Papias Fragment 12:1]

13:25 Tertullian[On Prescription Against Heretics 22]; NT-Apocrypha[Acts of John 89]

13:26 Irenaeus[Against Heresies Book I.31.1]

13:26-27 Genesis 33:10-16

13:26-31 NT-Apocrypha[Gospel of Judas 56]

13:27 1Samuel 21:7, 22:22; Archelaus[Disputation with Manes 33]; Cyprian[Treatise XII.Book III.80]; Origen[Gospel of Matthew Book XIII.8; De Principiis Book III.2.1]; Nag Hammadi[Concept of Our Great Power 41]

13:29 Pseudepigrapha[3Enoch 27:2]

13:30 Luke 22:3-4

13:31 Psalms 80:17; NT-Apocrypha[Epistula Apostolorum 19, 36]

13:31-32 Tertullian[Against Praxeas 23]

13:33 John 7:34; Clement of Alexandria[Stromata Book III.15, VI.12; The Instructor Book I.5]; Nag Hammadi[Gospel of Truth 19]

13:34 John 3:23, 15:12, 17; 2John 5:1; Constitutions of the Holy Apostles[Book VI.23]; NT-Apocrypha[Epistula Apostolorum 18]

13:34-35 Nag Hammadi[Gospel of Thomas 25]

13:35 Constitutions of the Holy Apostles[Book II.3]; Fabian[Second Epistle]; Zephyrinus[Second Epistle 1.1]

13:36 Nag Hammadi[Gospel of Thomas 24]; NT-Apocrypha[Acts of Peter 1.35]

13:36-38 Matthew 26:31-35; Mark 14:27-31; Luke 22:31-34

13:38 Mark 14:72; Philo[Every Good Man Is Free (131-136) cf. {Greek Playwright Ion}]

14:01 Exodus 14:21

14:01-16:33 Pseudepigrapha[Hellenistic Synagogal Prayers 7:15; 9:9]

14:01-17:26 Luke 7:36-50; Pseudepigrapha[Joseph and Aseneth 20:2]; Philo[On the Contemplative Life Or Suppliants (75)]

14:02 This section also includes topical notes for: My Father's House - 1Kings 5:5; Luke 2:49; John 2:16; Hebrews 11:10-16; Pseudepigrapha[1Enoch 45:3; 2Baruch 48:6; 2Enoch 61:2; 4Ezra 7.95, 10.55-56; Hellenistic Synagogal Prayers 2.11, 14.3; History of the Rechabites 16.7; Joseph and Aseneth 15:7; Odes of Solomon 11:23; Testament of Abraham 20:14-15]; Dead Sea Scrolls[11Q Hymns (11Q15) 1-6; 4Q Enoch (4Q204[4QENAR]) COL VI 20-30]; Philo[Concerning Noah's Work As A Planter (43-45) cf. {Genesis 25:27}; On Dreams, That they Are God-Sent (1.255-1.256) cf. {Genesis 31:18}]; Rabbinic[Babylonian Baba Batra 75b; Mishnah Sanhedrin 4:5]; Clement of Alexandria[Stromata Book IV.6, 26, VI.13-14; Who is the Rich Man that shall be Saved 32]; Irenaeus[Against Heresies Book III.19.3, V.36.1-2]; Justin[First Apology 8]; Tertullian[On Monogamy 10; On the Resurrection of the Flesh 41]; Nag Hammadi[Eugnostos the Blessed III. 84-85; Gospel of Truth 25; On the Origin of the World 104; Trimorphic Protennoia 50; Tripartite Tractate 136]; NT-Apocrypha[Gospel of Judas 45]; Egyptian Book of the Dead[Oration 17, 127]

14:02-03 Pseudepigrapha[Odes of Solomon 3:5]

14:03 Origen[Against Celsus Book VI.20]

14:05 Nag Hammadi[Dialogue of the Savior 73]

14:05-11 Tertullian[Against Praxeas 24]

14:06 Pseudepigrapha[Odes of Solomon 3:9, 11:3]; Clement of Alexandria[Stromata Book I.5, V.3]; Cyprian[Epistle LXXII.17, LXXIII.9; The Seventh Council of Carthage under Cyprian; Treatise XII.Book II.27, III.24]; Dionysius of Alexandria[Exegetical Fragments Commentary on the Beginning of Ecclesiastes 2.14]; Gregory Thaumaturgus[Twelve Topics on the Faith 7]; Hippolytus[Expository Treatise Against the Jews 6]; Irenaeus[Against Heresies Book III.5.1]; Lactantius[Epitome of the Divine Institutes 49]; Origen[Against Celsus Book I.66, VI.66, VIII.12; Gospel of John Book I.11, 22, VI.3; Gospel of Matthew Book XII.33, 40, XIII 9; De Principiis Preface 1]; Tertullian[Against Praxeas 24; On Repentance 4; On the Veiling of Virgins 1]; Nag Hammadi[Letter of Peter to Philip 134]; NT-Apocrypha[Acts of John 94, 98, 109]

14:06-07 Irenaeus[Against Heresies Book IV.7.3]

14:06-09 Novatian[Treatise Concerning the Trinity 28]

14:07 Colossians 1:15n; Irenaeus[Against Heresies Book III.13.2]

14:07-09 Nag Hammadi[Dialogue of the Savior 35]

14:08-09 Alexander of Alexandria[Epistles on Arian Heresy 1.9]; Hippolytus[Against the Heresy of One Noetus 7]

14:09 Alexander of Alexandria[Epistles on Arian Heresy 2.3]; Gregory Thaumaturgus[Four Homilies 4]; Origen[Against Celsus Book VII.43; De Principiis Book I.2.6, II.4.3]; Tertullian[An Answer to the Jews 9]

14:09-10 Irenaeus[Against Heresies Book III.13.2]; Tertullian[Against Praxeas 20]

14:10 Alexander of Alexandria[Epistles on Arian Heresy 2.3]; Dionysius of Rome[Against the Sabellians 3]; NT-Apocrypha[Acts of John 100; Epistula Apostolorum 25]

14:10-11 NT-Apocrypha[Epistula Apostolorum 39]

14:10-17 This section also includes topical notes for: I Speak Not from Myself - John 5:9, 12:49-50; Romans 8:9-11n; Philo[Special Laws I (65) cf. {Deuteronomy 18:18}]; Clement of Alexandria[The Instructor Book I.5, 7]; Nag Hammadi[Gospel of Philip 74; Gospel of Truth 37; Teachings of Silvanus 100; Trimorphic Protennoia 48]

14:10-20 NT-Apocrypha[Epistula Apostolorum 17]

14:11 Hippolytus[Refutation of all Heresies Book IX.7]; Irenaeus[Against Heresies Book V.18.1]; Origen[Against Celsus Book VIII.12]

14:12 Hippolytus[Against the Heresy of One Noetus 8]; Novatian[Treatise Concerning the Trinity 28]; NT-Apocrypha[Epistula Apostolorum 13; Pseudo-Titus Epistle Line 275]

14:13 Lactantius[Epitome of the Divine Institutes 49]; Nag Hammadi[Apocryphon of James 11]; NT-Apocrypha[Epistula Apostolorum 36]

14:13-14 Origen[Gospel of Matthew Book XII.8]

14:15 OT-Apocrypha[Wisdom of Solomon 6:18]; Cyprian[Treatise I.2]; NT-Apocrypha[Epistula Apostolorum 24, 36, 39]

14:15-16 Archelaus[Disputation with Manes 34]; Novatian[Treatise Concerning the Trinity 28]

14:16 Pseudepigrapha[Hellenistic Synagogal Prayers 7.15]; Rabbinic[Sanhedrin 98b]; Irenaeus[Against Heresies Book I.4.5, III.11.9]; Methodius[Banquet of the Ten Virgins 9.2]; Tertullian[Against Praxeas 9, 25]; NT-Apocrypha[Two Books of Jeu c. 1-3]

14:16-18 Novatian[Treatise Concerning the Trinity 29]

14:16-26 Matthew 28:19n

14:17 Pseudepigrapha[Jubilees 25:14]; Irenaeus[Demonstration of the Apostolic Preaching 100]

14:17-19 Pseudepigrapha[Odes of Solomon 3:8-10]

14:18 Archelaus[Disputation with Manes 27]

14:19 Origen[Gospel of John Book VI.2]

14:20 NT-Apocrypha[Epistula Apostolorum 19, 31, 39]

14:21 NT-Apocrypha[Epistula Apostolorum 24]

14:23 Proverbs 8:17; Ezekiel 37:27; Pseudepigrapha[1Enoch 45:3]; Novatian[Treatise Concerning the Trinity 28]; Origen[Against Celsus Book VIII.18; De Principiis Book I.1.2]; NT-Apocrypha[Epistula Apostolorum 36]

14:26 This section also includes topical notes for: Holy Spirit - Pseudepigrapha[Odes of Solomon 3:10]; Dead Sea Scrolls[1Q Rule of the Community (1QS) COL VIII 15-16]; Athenagoras[Plea for the Christians 10, 24]; Clement of Alexandria[Exhortation to the Heathen 9, 12; Fragments from the Latin Translation of Cassiodorus Comments on 1Peter; Stromata Book VI.15, VII.2]; Irenaeus[Against Heresies Book I.4.5, 11.1, II.16.6-8, 19.9, 28.2, III.17.3, IV.20.1, 3, 8, 36.6, 38.2-3, V.1.1, 3, 6.1, 18.2, 28.4; Fragments from the Lost Works 8, 26, 39]; Novatian[Treatise Concerning the Trinity 28]; Origen[De Principiis Book I.3.4; Gospel of John Book II.6]; Tertullian[On Fasting 10; On Prescription Against Heretics 27; On the Veiling of Virgins 1]; NT-Apocrypha[Two Books of Jeu c. 1-3]

14:27 Haggai 2:9; Cyprian[Treatise I.24, XII.Book III.3]; Origen[Gospel of John Book VI.1]; Tertullian[To his Wife Book II.6]; Nag Hammadi[Gospel of Mary 8]; NT-Apocrypha[Acts of Thomas 1.69; Epistula Apostolorum 30]

14:27-28 Origen[Against Celsus Book VIII.14]

14:28 Alexander of Alexandria[Epistles on Arian Heresy 1.12]; Cyprian[Treatise XII.Book III.58]; Gregory Thaumaturgus[Four Homilies 4]; Irenaeus[Against Heresies Book II.28.8];

Methodius[Banquet of the Ten Virgins 7.1]; Novatian[Treatise Concerning the Trinity 26, 28]; Tertullian[Against Praxeas 9, 14]; NT-Apocrypha[Epistula Apostolorum 13]

14:30 Pseudepigrapha[Martyrdom and Ascension of Isaiah 2:4; Testament of Solomon 2:9]; Apostolic[Epistle of Barnabas 18:1-2]; Hippolytus[Fragments - On Proverbs 30.19]; Origen[Against Celsus Book VIII.36; De Principiis Book II.6.4]; Tertullian[Five Books in Reply to Marcion Book II.220]; NT-Apocrypha[Freer Logion]

14:31 Origen[Gospel of Matthew Book XIII.10]; NT-Apocrypha[Two Books of Jeu c. 1-3]

15:01 Numbers 13:23; Psalms 80:9-17; Jeremiah 2:21; Pseudepigrapha[2Baruch 39:7; 2Enoch 50:2; Odes of Solomon 17:16]; Clement of Alexandria[Stromata Book I.9]; Cyprian[Epistle LXII.2]; Hippolytus[Treatise on Christ and Antichrist 8]; Methodius[Banquet of the Ten Virgins 5.5, 10.5]; Novatian[Treatise Concerning the Trinity 28]; Origen[Gospel of John Book I.23; Gospel of Matthew Book XI.13]; Teaching of the Twelve Apostles 9.2; Tertullian[Against Praxeas 25]; Nag Hammadi[Tripartite Tractate 51, 62]; NT-Apocrypha[Acts of Thomas 1.36]

15:01-02 Clement of Alexandria[The Instructor Book I.8, II.2]

15:01-06 Nag Hammadi[Book of Thomas the Contender 144; Teachings of Silvanus 107-108]

15:02 Pseudepigrapha[Odes of Solomon 24.9]; Tertullian[Five Books in Reply to Marcion Book II.19]

15:02-06 This section also includes topical notes for: The Branch - Genesis 40:9-14; Exodus 25:32; Numbers 13:23; Psalms 80:15; Isaiah 4:2-5, 11:1; Jeremiah 23:5, 33:15; Zechariah 3:8-9, 6:12; Matthew 2:23, 7:16-21n; Pseudepigrapha[Odes of Solomon 39.10]; Dead Sea Scrolls[4Q Genesis Pesher (4Q252[4QPGEN) COL V 1-6]; Philo[On Dreams, That they Are God-Sent (2.170-2.176) cf. {Numbers 13:17-21, Deuteronomy 30:9, Isaiah 5:7}; On the Change of Names (224) cf. {Numbers 13:17-27}]; Apostolic[Shepherd of Hermas 53:1-8]; Nag Hammadi[Authoritative Teaching 22; Trimorphic Protennoia 45]

15:03 Origen[Gospel of John Book X.21]

15:04 Nag Hammadi[Apocryphon of James 9; Trimorphic Protennoia 50]; NT-Apocrypha[Epistula Apostolorum 19]

15:04-06 Tertullian[Five Books in Reply to Marcion Book II.19]

15:04-08 Justin[Dialogue with Trypho 110]

15:05 Methodius[Banquet of the Ten Virgins 5.5]; Origen[Gospel of John Book I.23]

15:06 Ezekiel 15:1-8; NT-Apocrypha[6Ezra 17.78]

15:09 OT-Apocrypha[Wisdom of Solomon 3:9]; Pseudepigrapha[Odes of Solomon 8:19-21]; Irenaeus[Against Heresies Book III.20.2]

15:09-10 Novatian[Treatise Concerning the Trinity 28]

15:10 NT-Apocrypha[Epistula Apostolorum 24, 36]

15:11-12 Clement of Alexandria[Stromata Book II.15]

15:12 John 13:34, 15:17; 1John 3:23; 2John 5:1; Cyprian[Epistle VII.3; Treatise I.14]

15:12-13 Cyprian[Treatise XII.Book III.3]

15:13 Pseudepigrapha[Apocalypse of Sedrach 1:25]; Plato[Phaedo 67e-68b]; Constitutions of the Holy Apostles[Book III.19]; Nag Hammadi[Gospel of Philip 53]

15:14-15 Cyprian[Epistle LXII.14]

15:15 Exodus 33:11; Plato[Apology 39e-40a]; Constitutions of the Holy Apostles[Book VI.21]; Irenaeus[Against Heresies Book IV.13.4]; Novatian[Treatise Concerning the Trinity 28]; Origen[Gospel of John Book I.31]

15:16 Irenaeus[Against Heresies Book IV.14.1]; NT-Apocrypha[Gospel of the Nazareans Fragment 23]

15:18 NT-Apocrypha[Epistula Apostolorum 38]

15:18-20 Cyprian[Epistle LV.6; Treatise XI.11, XII.Book III.29]

15:19 NT-Apocrypha[Gospel of the Nazareans Fragment 23]

15:20 Matthew 10:24; Luke 6:40; John 13:16; Constitutions of the Holy Apostles[Book V.3]; Novatian[Treatise Concerning the Trinity 29]

15:21 Novatian[Treatise Concerning the Trinity 28]; Peter of Alexandria[Fragments Up to the Time of the Destruction of Jerusalem 2]; NT-Apocrypha[Epistula Apostolorum 15]

15:22 Origen[Gospel of John Book I.42, II.9; De Principiis Book I.3.6]

15:23 Methodius[Oration on the Psalms 7]

15:25 Psalms 35:19, 69:4-5; Pseudepigrapha[Psalms of Solomon 7:1]; Rabbinic[Yoma 9b]

15:26 Matthew 28:19n; Pseudepigrapha[Joseph and Aseneth 19:11; Odes of Solomon 3:10]; Irenaeus[Against Heresies Book I.4.5]; Tertullian[On Modesty 21; On Prescription Against Heretics 27]; NT-Apocrypha[Two Books of Jeu c. 1-3]

16:01-04 Nag Hammadi[Letter of Peter to Philip 138]

16:01-33 Gregory Thaumaturgus[Twelve Topics on the Faith 5]

16:02 Pseud-Irenaeus

16:02-03 Cyprian[Treatise XII.Book III.16]

16:02-04 Cyprian[Epistle LV.2; Treatise XI.11]

16:05-15 NT-Apocrypha[Abgar Legend]

16:06 Irenaeus[Against Heresies Book I.15.2]

16:06-07 Tertullian[On Baptism 10]

16:07 Pseudepigrapha[Hellenistic Synagogal Prayers 7.15]; Clement of Alexandria[Fragments from the Latin Translation of Cassiodorus Comments on 1Peter]; Irenaeus[Against Heresies Book I.4.5, III.17.2]; Novatian[Treatise Concerning the Trinity 29]; NT-Apocrypha[Two Books of Jeu c. 1-3]

16:07-13 Pseudepigrapha[Testament of Judah 20:5]

16:07-15 Matthew 28:19n

16:08 Archelaus[Disputation with Manes 13, 27]; NT-Apocrypha[Freer Logion]

16:10 NT-Apocrypha[Epistula Apostolorum 29]

16:11 Pseudepigrapha[Martyrdom and Ascension of Isaiah 2:4; Testament of Solomon 2:9]; Apostolic[Epistle of Barnabas 18:1-2; Papias Fragment 24:1]; Origen[Against Celsus Book VII.17; Gospel of Matthew Book XI.14, XII.18]; NT-Apocrypha[Freer Logion]

16:12-13 Origen[Against Celsus Book II.2; De Principiis Book I.3.4]; Tertullian[On Monogamy 2; On Prescription Against Heretics 22; On the Veiling of Virgins 1]; Theognostus[Seven Books of Hypotyposes or Outlines 2]

16:13 Psalms 25:5; Novatian[Treatise Concerning the Trinity 29]; Tertullian[Against Praxeas 31; On Fasting 10; On Prescription Against Heretics 8; On the Veiling of Virgins 1]

16:14 Archelaus[Disputation with Manes 34]; Novatian[Treatise Concerning the Trinity 16]; Tertullian[On Monogamy 2]

16:14-15 Origen[Gospel of John Book II.12]

16:15 Tertullian[Against Praxeas 17]

16:17 NT-Apocrypha[Epistula Apostolorum 29]

16:20 Pseudepigrapha[Joseph and Aseneth 11:6]; Cyprian[Treatise VII.5, XI.11]; Dionysius of Alexandria[Exegetical Fragments Commentary on the Beginning of Ecclesiastes 3.4]; Tertullian[On Idolatry 13; The Chaplet, or De Corona 13; The Shows, or De Spectaculis 28]

16:21 Isaiah 13:8, 21:3, 26:17; Micah 4:9; Pseudepigrapha[4Ezra 16.35-39]

16:22 Isaiah 66:14; Cyprian[Treatise VII.5]; Gregory Thaumaturgus[Four Homilies 1, 2]

16:23 Cyprian[Treatise IV.3]; Nag Hammadi[Letter of Peter to Philip 137]

16:24 Tertullian[The Martyrdom of Perpetua and Felicitas 6]

16:25 Origen[Against Celsus Book IV.87]; Nag Hammadi[Apocryphon of James 7]; NT-Apocrypha[Epistula Apostolorum 29; Pistis Sophia c. 2-6]

16:26 Hippolytus[The Discourse on the Holy Theophany 9]

16:27 Clement of Alexandria[The Instructor Book I.3]

16:27-28 Pseudepigrapha[Odes of Solomon 41.8]

16:28 Cyprian[Treatise VII.7]; Hippolytus[Against the Heresy of One Noetus 16]; Methodius[Oration on the Psalms 7]; Tertullian[Against Praxeas 24]; Nag Hammadi[Gospel of Thomas 49]

16:29 Nag Hammadi[Apocryphon of James 7]

16:30 Pseudepigrapha[Joseph and Aseneth 13:11]; Tertullian[On Prescription Against Heretics 3]

16:32 Zechariah 13:7; Constitutions of the Holy Apostles[Book V.14]; NT-Apocrypha[Epistula Apostolorum 29]

16:33 Alexander of Alexandria[Epistles on Arian Heresy 1.12]; Constitutions of the Holy Apostles[Book V.3]; Cyprian[Treatise IX.12, XI.11, XII.Book III.6]; Dionysius of Alexandria[Exegetical Fragments An Exposition of Luke 22.46]; Gregory Thaumaturgus[Twelve Topics on the Faith 12]; Origen[Against Celsus Book VI.59; VIII.70; De Principiis Book III.2.5]

17:01 Origen[Gospel of John Book I.23]; Tertullian[Against Praxeas 25]

17:01-09 Pseudepigrapha[Odes of Solomon 31:4]

17:01-26 Nag Hammadi[Gospel of Truth 38-40]

17:02 Gregory Thaumaturgus[Four Homilies 2]; NT-Apocrypha[Epistula Apostolorum 28; Gospel of the Nazareans Fragment 23]

17:02-03 Jude 1:21n

17:03 OT-Apocrypha[Wisdom of Solomon 15:3]; Constitutions of the Holy Apostles[Book V.16, VI.23]; Cyprian[Epistle LXXII.17; Treatise IV.28, V.23, XI.2]; Irenaeus[Against Heresies Book IV.1.2]; Novatian[Treatise Concerning the Trinity 16]; Origen[Gospel of John Book II.2]

17:03-04 Novatian[Treatise Concerning the Trinity 26]

17:03-05 Cyprian[Treatise XII.Book II.1]

17:04 Constitutions of the Holy Apostles[Book VIII.1, 12]

17:05 Hippolytus[Fragments - On Genesis 49.21-26]; Irenaeus[Against Heresies Book IV.14.1];
   Novatian[Treatise Concerning the Trinity 13, 16, 26]; Origen[Gospel of Matthew Book XIII.20]

17:06 Constitutions of the Holy Apostles[Book VIII.1, 12]; Gregory Thaumaturgus[On the Trinity];
   Tertullian[Against Praxeas 17; On Prayer 3]; NT-Apocrypha[Gospel of the Nazareans Fragment 23]

17:07 Pseudepigrapha[Joseph and Aseneth 13:11]

17:09 NT-Apocrypha[Gospel of the Nazareans Fragment 23]

17:10 Origen[De Principiis Book I.2.10]

17:11 Pseudepigrapha[Odes of Solomon 8:19-21]; Constitutions of the Holy Apostles[Book VIII.1];
   Origen[Gospel of Matthew Book XIII.20]; Tertullian[Against Praxeas 25]; NT-Apocrypha[Acts of
   Peter 1.27]

17:11-12 Pseudepigrapha[Odes of Solomon 33.13]

17:12 Psalms 41:9, 109:4-8; Proverbs 24:22; Isaiah 57:4; Pseudepigrapha[Apocalypse of Elijah 2:40];
   Josephus[War 2.8.12 159]; Irenaeus[Against Heresies Book II.20.5]; Nag Hammadi[Teachings of
   Silvanus 114]; NT-Apocrypha[5Ezra 2.25; Acts of Peter 1.7; Apocalypse of Peter 1.14-15]

17:13-14 Origen[Gospel of Matthew Book XIII.20]

17:14 Tertullian[On Prayer 12]

17:14-18 NT-Apocrypha[Acts of Thomas 1.25]

17:16 Irenaeus[Against Heresies Book I.6.4]; Origen[Gospel of Matthew Book XIII.21; De Principiis
   Book II.3.6]

17:17 Psalms 119:142, 160; Clement of Alexandria[The Instructor Book III.2]; Constitutions of the Holy
   Apostles[Book VIII.11]

17:20 Cyprian[Treatise IV.30]; NT-Apocrypha[Epistula Apostolorum 34]

17:20-23 Origen[De Principiis Book I.6.2]

17:21 Cyprian[Epistle LXXIV.3]; Origen[Against Celsus Book VIII.12; Gospel of John Book I.24; Gospel
   of Matthew Book XIII.20; De Principiis Book III.6.1]

17:21-22 Origen[De Principiis Book II.3.5]

17:21-23 NT-Apocrypha[Epistula Apostolorum 17, 39]

17:21-26 Clement of Alexandria[The Instructor Book I.8]

17:22 Pseudepigrapha[Testament of Judah 25:3]; Origen[Against Celsus Book VIII.12]

17:22-23 Hippolytus[Refutation of all Heresies Book X.30]

17:23 Clement of Alexandria[The Instructor Book I.3]; Origen[Gospel of Matthew Book XIII.20]

17:24 Pseudepigrapha[Odes of Solomon 3:5, 41:15]; Cyprian[Treatise VII.22; XII.Book III.58];
   Irenaeus[Against Heresies Book IV.14.1]; Origen[De Principiis Book II.3.5, 11.6, III.6.1]; Nag
   Hammadi[Treatise on the Resurrection 44]

17:25 Constitutions of the Holy Apostles[Book VIII.1]; Origen[De Principiis Book II.5.4]

18:01 Constitutions of the Holy Apostles[Book V.14]

18:01-02 Matthew 26:36-46; Mark 14:32-42; Luke 22:39-46

18:01-11 Matthew 26:47-56n; Mark 14:43-50; Luke 22:47-53

18:02-05 Irenaeus[Against Heresies Book I.31.1]

18:03 Genesis 33:1

18:03-12 Mark 14:43-52; Luke 22:47-53

18:03-19:37 Matthew 26:47-27:56n

18:04 Origen[Against Celsus Book II.10]; NT-Apocrypha[Epistula Apostolorum 10]

18:06 NT-Apocrypha[Acts of Thomas 1.157]

18:09 John 6:39

18:10 Genesis 34:25; Epic of Gilgamesh[The Forest Journey]

18:11 Genesis 34:30; Matthew 26:39; Mark 14:36; Luke 22:42; Pseudepigrapha[Joseph and Aseneth
   29:4]; Dionysius of Alexandria[Exegetical Fragments Gospel According to Luke - An Interpretation
   22.42]

18:12 NT-Apocrypha[Acts of John 94]

18:13 Josephus[Antiquities 18.2.2 35]

18:13-14 Matthew 26:57; Mark 14:53; Luke 22:54

18:14 John 11:49-50; Pseudepigrapha[Odes of Solomon 31.12]

18:15 NT-Apocrypha[Gospel of the Nazareans Fragment 33]

18:15-27 Matthew 26:58, 69-75; Mark 14:54, 66-72; Luke 22:55-62

18:16 Pseudepigrapha[Joseph and Aseneth 10:2]

18:17 NT-Apocrypha[Passing of Mary]

18:19-24 Matthew 26:59-66; Mark 14:55-64; Luke 22:66-71

18:20 Isaiah 45:19; Matthew 9:35n; Tertullian[On Prescription Against Heretics 26]

18:22 Genesis 31:36; Exodus 22:27; NT-Apocrypha[Acts of Thomas 1.6]

18:22-23 Cyprian[Epistle LIV.4]

18:23 Cyprian[Epistle LXIV.2, LXVIII.3]

18:24 Josephus[Antiquities 18.2.2 35]

18:25-27 Matthew 26:71-75; Mark 14:69-72; Luke 22:58-62

18:28 Genesis 31:35; Matthew 27:1-2; Mark 15:1; Luke 22:66-23:1; Clement of Alexandria[Fragments found in Greek only in the Oxford Edition Last Work on the Passover]; Peter of Alexandria[Fragments Up to the Time of the Destruction of Jerusalem 7]; Tertullian[An Answer to the Jews 10]; NT-Apocrypha[Acts of Thomas 1.32]

18:28-38 Matthew 27:11-14; Mark 15:1-5; Luke 23:1-5

18:29-33 NT-Apocrypha[Acts of Pilate I.1-III.1]

18:29-19:22 Matthew 27:2-24; Mark 15:1-15; Luke 23:1-24; Philo[Special Laws IV (69-71) cf. {Deuteronomy 1:16-17}]

18:33 Clement of Alexandria[Fragments found in Greek only in the Oxford Edition Last Work on the Passover]; Origen[Gospel of John Book I.23]

18:33-38 NT-Apocrypha[Acts of Pilate III.2-IV.1]

18:35 Genesis 31:26

18:36 Origen[Against Celsus Book I.61; Gospel of John Book I.23; Gospel of Matthew Book XIII.9]; Tertullian[On Idolatry 18-19]; NT-Apocrypha[Acts of John 94; History of Joseph the Carpenter 8; Gospel of Mani Turfman Fragment M 132; Martyrdom of the Holy Apostle Paul 1.4]

18:37 Hippolytus[Treatise on Christ and Antichrist 6]

18:37-38 Nag Hammadi[Gospel of Philip 62]

18:38 Genesis 31:35; Pseudepigrapha[Odes of Solomon 31.8]; Constitutions of the Holy Apostles[Book V.14]

18:39-40 Matthew 27:15-18, 20-23; Mark 15:6-14; Luke 23:13-23

19:01 Hebrews 12:6-8n; Apostolic[Martyrdom of Polycarp 8:1]; Justin[First Apology 38, 50]; NT-Apocrypha[Acts of John 101]

19:01-03 Pseudepigrapha[Sibylline Oracles 1.374]; NT-Apocrypha[Gospel of the Nazareans Fragment 34]

19:02 Clement of Alexandria[The Instructor Book II.8]; Origen[De Principiis Book III.3.4]; Nag Hammadi[Letter of Peter to Philip 139]

19:02-05 Matthew 27:27-30n; Pseudepigrapha[Sibylline Oracles 8.294]

19:02-16 NT-Apocrypha[Gospel of Mani Turfman Fragment M 132]

19:03 Genesis 33:5; NT-Apocrypha[Acts of Thomas 1.6]

19:04 Pseudepigrapha[Odes of Solomon 31.8]

19:04-15 NT-Apocrypha[Acts of Pilate IV.1-IX.5]

19:05 Clement of Alexandria[The Instructor Book II.8]; Nag Hammadi[Letter of Peter to Philip 139]

19:06 Constitutions of the Holy Apostles[Book V.19]; Origen[Gospel of John Book I.12; Gospel of Matthew Book XIV.17]

19:07 Leviticus 24:16; John 3:18n

19:08-16 Tertullian[An Answer to the Jews 13]

19:09 Pseudepigrapha[Odes of Solomon 31.10-11]; Clement of Alexandria[Fragments found in Greek only in the Oxford Edition Last Work on the Passover]; Justin[Dialogue with Trypho 102-103]

19:10 Genesis 31:29

19:11 Cyprian[Treatise IV.26; XII.Book III.80]; Irenaeus[Against Heresies Book IV.18.3]; Origen[De Principiis Book III.2.6]; NT-Apocrypha[Acts of Thomas 1.140]

19:12 Constitutions of the Holy Apostles[Book V.19]; Tertullian[An Answer to the Jews 8]

19:13 NT-Apocrypha[Akhmim Fragment 3.7]

19:13-14 Peter of Alexandria[Fragments Up to the Time of the Destruction of Jerusalem]

19:14 Hippolytus[Fragments - On Daniel 2.6]; NT-Apocrypha[Acts of John 97]

19:15 Constitutions of the Holy Apostles[Book V.19, VI.25]; Irenaeus[Against Heresies Book IV.21.3]; Origen[Gospel of John Book I.12; Gospel of Matthew Book XIV.17, 19]

19:16-17 Matthew 27:31-32; Mark 15:20-21; Luke 23:26-32

19:17 Leviticus 16:7-10; Galatians 3:13n; Pseudepigrapha[Testament of Solomon 12:3];
Rabbinic[Pesikta Rabbati 36:2 cf. {Psalms 22:15-16}]; Tertullian[An Answer to the Jews 10; Five
Books in Reply to Marcion Book IV.94]; NT-Apocrypha[Epistula Apostolorum 9]

19:17-18 Philo[On Dreams That they Are God-Sent (1.175-1.176) cf. {Genesis 28:14}]; Origen[Gospel of
Matthew Book XII.24]

19:17-27 Matthew 27:19-31n; Mark 15:20-33; Luke 23:33-45n; NT-Apocrypha[Acts of Pilate X.1-2]

19:17-30 Matthew 27:33-56n

19:17-37 NT-Apocrypha[Questions of Bartholomew IV 62]

19:18 This section also includes topical notes for: The Word and the Tree - Matthew 27:35n; Mark
15:24-25; Philo[Concerning Noah's Work As A Planter (43-45) cf. {Genesis 2:9, 25:27}; On Dreams,
That they Are God-Sent (1.175-1.176) cf. {Genesis 28:14}]; NT-Apocrypha[Epistula Apostolorum 9]

19:19-20 Tertullian[Five Books in Reply to Marcion Book IV.113]

19:20 Pseudepigrapha[Testament of Job 20:7]

19:23 Philo[Allegorical Interpretation II (56-58) cf. {Leviticus 10:1, 16:1}]; Irenaeus[Demonstration of
the Apostolic Preaching 80]

19:23-24 Philo[On Flight And Finding (106-114) cf. {Exodus 28:32, Leviticus 10:36, 21:11, Numbers
35:2-34}]; Cyprian[Treatise I.7]; Tertullian[An Answer to the Jews 10]

19:24 Exodus 39:23; Psalms 22:18-19; Pseudepigrapha[Odes of Solomon 31.9]; Irenaeus[Against
Heresies Book IV.35.3]

19:26 Pseudepigrapha[Sibylline Oracles 8.291]; Hippolytus[Refutation of all Heresies Book V.21];
Origen[Gospel of John Book I.6]; Tertullian[On Prescription Against Heretics 22]; NT-
Apocrypha[Secret Gospel of Mark Fragment 2]

19:26-27 NT-Apocrypha[Falling Asleep of Mary]

19:28 Psalms 22:15, 63:2; Josephus[War 2.8.12 159]; Tertullian[An Answer to the Jews 10]; NT-
Apocrypha[Akhmim Fragment 5.17]

19:28-29 Psalms 69:21-22

19:28-30 NT-Apocrypha[Acts of Pilate XI.1]

19:29 Irenaeus[Demonstration of the Apostolic Preaching 82]

19:29-30 Ruth 2:14; Matthew 27:46-50; Mark 15:34-37; Luke 23:46; Rabbinic[Ruth Rabba on 2:14];
Irenaeus[Against Heresies Book IV.35.3]

19:30 Job 19:26-27; Pseudepigrapha[Life of Adam and Eve Vita 45:3]; Apostolic[Epistle of Barnabas
7:3]; NT-Apocrypha[Akhmim Fragment 5.17]

19:31 Deuteronomy 21:22-23; Pseudepigrapha[Martyrdom and Ascension of Isaiah (3:13-4:22 =
Testament of Hezekiah) 3:13]; Peter of Alexandria[Fragments Up to the Time of the Destruction of
Jerusalem]; Tertullian[Five Books Against Marcion Book V.4]; NT-Apocrypha[Akhmim Fragment
2.5, 4.14, 5.15]

19:32 Origen[Gospel of John Book X.13]

19:32-33 Origen[Against Celsus Book II.16]

19:32-37 Tertullian[An Answer to the Jews 10]

19:33-34 Tertullian[On Modesty 22]

19:34 Genesis 2:21; Pseudepigrapha[Ladder of Jacob 7.30-34; Sibylline Oracles 8.296]; Dead Sea
Scrolls[1Q Hymns (1QHODAYOTH [1QH]) COL X 10-35]; Irenaeus[Against Heresies Book IV.33.2,
35.3]; Tertullian[On Baptism 9, 16]; Nag Hammadi[Interpretation of Knowledge 10]; NT-
Apocrypha[Acts of John 97, 101; Acts of Thomas 1.165; Apocalypse of Paul 1.44; Arabic Gospel of
the Infancy of the Savior 35]

19:34-45 Origen[Against Celsus Book II.36]

19:36 Exodus 12:10, 46; Numbers 9:12; Psalms 34:20-21; Origen[Gospel of Matthew Book X.22]

19:37 Zechariah 12:10; Revelation 1:7; Archelaus[Disputation with Manes 50]; Constitutions of the
Holy Apostles[Book V.19]; Hippolytus[Appendix to the Works of Hippolytus - On the End of the
World 40]; Tertullian[On the Resurrection of the Flesh 22, 51]

19:38 Genesis 50:4-6; 1Kings 13:29

19:38-42 Matthew 27:57-60; Mark 15:42-46; Luke 23:50-54; Pseudepigrapha[Life of Adam and Eve Vita
43.4, (Apocalypse of Moses) 40.1-2]; Justin[Dialogue with Trypho 118]; NT-Apocrypha[Acts of
Pilate XI.3]

19:39 John 3:1-2; Apostolic[Papias Fragment 25:1]

19:39-40 Rabbinic[Mishnah Shabbat 23.5]

19:40 Rabbinic[Babylonian Sanhedrin 47a-47b]

19:41 Origen[Against Celsus Book II.69]; NT-Apocrypha[Akhmim Fragment 6.24; Secret Gospel of Mark Fragment 1]

19:41-42 Genesis 46:4, 50:5, 13

20:01 Mark 16:3-4; Rabbinic[Babylonian Shabbat 151a]; Dionysius of Alexandria[Extant Fragments Epistle to Bishop Basilides 1]; NT-Apocrypha[Acts of Pilate XIII.1-2]

20:01-10 Matthew 28:1-10; Mark 16:1-8; Luke 24:1-12

20:02 NT-Apocrypha[Acts of John 90]

20:07 Pseudepigrapha[Apocalypse of Abraham 11:3]

20:09 Psalms 16:9; Josephus[War 2.8.12 159]

20:11 Constitutions of the Holy Apostles[Book V.14]; NT-Apocrypha[Epistula Apostolorum 9]

20:11-18 Mark 16:9-11

20:12 Exodus 25:18-22, 37:8-9; Numbers 7:89; 2Samuel 6:2; 1Kings 6:27, 8:6-7; 2Kings 19:15; 2Chronicles 3:12-13, 5:7-8; Psalms 99:1; Pseudepigrapha[Martyrdom and Ascension of Isaiah (3:13-4:22 = Testament of Hezekiah) 3:17]

20:14-15 NT-Apocrypha[Epistula Apostolorum 10]

20:15-17 NT-Apocrypha[Gospel of Mani Coptic Psalm book II]

20:17 Psalms 22:23; John 1:18n; Clement[Second Epistle Concerning Virginity 15]; Hippolytus[Against the Heresy of One Noetus 6]; Irenaeus[Against Heresies Book V.31.1]; Novatian[Treatise Concerning the Trinity 26]; Origen[Gospel of John Book VI.37, X.21]; Tertullian[Against Praxeas 25, 28; To his Wife Book I.4]; NT-Apocrypha[Acts of Peter 1.31; Acts of Thomas 1.8; Epistula Apostolorum 10]

20:18 Mark 16:10-11; Luke 24:9-11

20:19 NT-Apocrypha[Acts of John 115; Acts of Peter 1.5; Acts of Thomas 1.27; Akhmim Fragment 12.50; Passing of Mary]

20:19-20 NT-Apocrypha[Epistula Apostolorum 11]

20:19-23 Matthew 28:16-20; Mark 16:14-18; Luke 24:36-49; Nag Hammadi[Letter of Peter to Philip 140]

20:19-25 Mark 16:14; Luke 24:36-49

20:19-26 Nag Hammadi[Gospel of Mary 8]

20:20 Irenaeus[Against Heresies Book V.7.1, 31.2]

20:21 Cyprian[Treatise I.4]; NT-Apocrypha[Acts of Peter 1.5; Acts of Thomas 1.27]

20:21-22 NT-Apocrypha[Epistula Apostolorum 30]

20:21-23 Cyprian[Epistle LXXII.7, LXXV.11]

20:22 Genesis 2:7; Ezekiel 37:9; OT-Apocrypha[Wisdom of Solomon 15:11]; Pseudepigrapha[4Ezra 14.22-26, 14.39-48; Joseph and Aseneth 19:11; Odes of Solomon 18.15]; Rabbinic[Targum Pseudo-Jonathan on Exodus 20:18]; Anonymous[Treatise on Re-Baptism 3]; Irenaeus[Against Heresies Book III.1.1; Fragments from the Lost Works 52]; Origen[Against Celsus Book VII.51; Gospel of Matthew Book XII.11; De Principiis Book I.3.2, 7]; Tertullian[Five Books in Reply to Marcion Book IV.104]; Nag Hammadi[Gospel of Philip 63; Trimorphic Protennoia 36-45]; NT-Apocrypha[Acts of Thomas 1.81]

20:22-23 Cyprian[Epistle LXXIV.16]; Novatian[Treatise Concerning the Trinity 29]; Urban I[Epistle 4.4]

20:23 Matthew 16:19, 18:18; Cyprian[The Seventh Council of Carthage under Cyprian]; Tertullian[On Modesty 2, 21]; NT-Apocrypha[Acts of Thomas 1.94; Letter of Clement to James 2.4]

20:24 Irenaeus[Against Heresies Book I.18.3]

20:25 Constitutions of the Holy Apostles[Book V.19]; Irenaeus[Against Heresies Book V.7.1]; NT-Apocrypha[Akhmim Fragment 6.21; Protoevangelium of James 19.3]

20:26 Irenaeus[Fragments from the Lost Works 52]; Nag Hammadi[Sophia of Jesus Christ III 91]; NT-Apocrypha[Acts of Peter 1.5; Acts of Thomas 1.27]

20:26-27 Origen[Against Celsus Book II.62-63]; NT-Apocrypha[Epistula Apostolorum 11]

20:26-29 Cyprian[Treatise I.12]

20:27 Genesis 27:21; Pseudepigrapha[Sibylline Oracles 8.320]; Hippolytus[Fragments - Writings of Hippolytus 3]; Irenaeus[Against Heresies Book V.7.1, 31.2]; Origen[Against Celsus Book II.61]; Tertullian[A Treatise on the Soul 17]; NT-Apocrypha[Acts of John 90; Akhmim Fragment 6.21; Epistula Apostolorum 2]

20:27-29 Cyprian[Treatise XII.Book II.6]

20:28 Psalms 35:23; Pseudepigrapha[Joseph and Aseneth 22:3]; Novatian[Treatise Concerning the Trinity 13, 30]; Tertullian[An Answer to the Jews 7]; Nag Hammadi[Letter of Peter to Philip 133]; NT-Apocrypha[Acts of Thomas 1.10, 1.144, 1.166]

20:29 Pseudepigrapha[4Ezra 1:37]; Clement of Alexandria[Stromata Book II.2]; Origen[Gospel of John Book X.27]; Tertullian[On the Resurrection of the Flesh 34]; Nag Hammadi[Apocryphon of James 12-13]; NT-Apocrypha[Abgar Legend; Epistula Apostolorum 29]

20:30 Pseudepigrapha[Lives of the Prophets 1:2]

20:31 John 3:18n; Irenaeus[Against Heresies Book III.16.5]; Tertullian[Against Praxeas 21, 25]

21:01 NT-Apocrypha[Akhmim Fragment 14.60]

21:01-08 Luke 5:1-11n

21:02-08 NT-Apocrypha[Gospel of Mani Coptic Psalm book II]

21:04-05 Clement of Alexandria[The Instructor Book I.5]

21:06 NT-Apocrypha[Acts of Thomas 1.47]

21:06-07 Clement of Alexandria[The Instructor Book II.1]

21:06-08 Pseudepigrapha[Testament of Zebulon 6.6-7]

21:07 NT-Apocrypha[Secret Gospel of Mark Fragment 2]

21:11 Greek[Archimedes, On the Measurement of the Cycle]

21:15 Cyprian[Treatise I.4]; NT-Apocrypha[Gospel of the Nazareans Fragment 14]

21:15-17 Genesis 50:21; Dead Sea Scrolls[Damascus Document (CD-A) COL XIV 7-12]

21:15-18 Pseudepigrapha[Joseph and Aseneth 4:3, 14:4]

21:16 2Samuel 5:2; Psalms 78:71

21:16-17 Luke 13:32n

21:17 Cyprian[Epistle II.1]; Nag Hammadi[Gospel of Philip 81]

21:18 Tertullian[Scorpiace 15]; NT-Apocrypha[Letter of Clement to James 2.1]

21:18-19 Origen[Against Celsus Book II.45]

21:20 John 13:25; Apostolic[Papias Fragment 12:1]; Clement[First Epistle Concerning Virginity 6]; Tertullian[On Prescription Against Heretics 22]; NT-Apocrypha[Secret Gospel of Mark Fragment 2]

21:22 Hippolytus[Appendix to the Works of Hippolytus - On the End of the World 21]

21:22-23 Deuteronomy 33:6; Mark 9:1

21:23 Tertullian[A Treatise on the Soul 50]

21:25 Philo[Special Laws IV (237-238)]; Origen[Gospel of John Book I.11; Gospel of Matthew Book XIV.12; De Principiis Book II.6.1]; Nag Hammadi[Gospel of Thomas (Prologue)]

Cross Reference Index: Acts

01:01 Luke 1:1-4; Clement of Alexandria[Fragments from Eusebius Ecclesiastical History Book VI.6.14; Fragments from the Latin Translation of Cassiodorus Comments on 1Peter]; Constitutions of the Holy Apostles[Book II.5]; NT-Apocrypha[Acts of Paul in Philippi 1.1; **Canon Muratori Line 34-39**]

But the acts of all apostles are written in one book. For the 'most excellent Theophilus' Luke summarises the several things that in his own presence have come to pass, as also by the omission of the passion of Peter he makes quite clear, and equally by (the omission) of the journey of Paul, who from the city (of Rome) proceeded to Spain. The epistles, however, of Paul themselves make clear to those who wish to know it which there are (i.e. from Paul), from what place and for what cause they were written. (NT Apochrypha - Canon Muratori Line 34-39 *New Testament Apocrypha*, **Wilhelm Schneemelcher, ed.; R. McL. Wilson, trans.; Westminster John Knox Press, Volume I, 2003)**

01:02 2Kings 2:11; Pseudepigrapha[Martyrdom and Ascension of Isaiah 9.33-35]; NT-Apocrypha[Acts of Thomas 1.8]

01:03 This section also includes topical notes for: The Passion - Genesis 50:3; Galatians 5:24; Pseudepigrapha[Sibylline Oracles Prologue]; Philo[Allegorical Interpretation III (188-199) cf. {Genesis 27:6, 32:24-31}; On Dreams, That they Are God-Sent (1.255-1.256) cf. {Genesis 32:24-32}; On the Contemplative Life Or Suppliants (88-90) cf. {Exodus 14:3-14}; Special Laws II (147) cf. {Exodus 12:1-28}]; Clement of Alexandria[Stromata Book I.21; The Instructor Book I.10, II.8]; Constitutions of the Holy Apostles[Book V.7]; Hippolytus[Refutation of all Heresies Book IX.17]; Irenaeus[Against Heresies Book I.3.3, 8.2, 25.1, II.20.2-4, V.16.3; Fragments from the Lost Works 55]; Justin[Dialogue with Trypho 106, 125; First Apology 31; Fragments from the Lost Writings of Justin 10]; Origen[Against Celsus Book II.63]; NT-Apocrypha[Canon Muratori Line 21]; Indian[Dhammapada 422]

01:04 Pseudepigrapha[Martyrdom and Ascension of Isaiah 8:24]; Tertullian[Five Books in Reply to Marcion Book II.328]

01:04-05 Anonymous[Treatise on Re-Baptism 2]

01:04-08 Nag Hammadi[Letter of Peter to Philip 133]

01:04-11 This section also includes topical notes for: Ascension - Luke 24:49-51; Philo[On Dreams, That they Are God-Sent (1.137-1.139, 1.151-1.152, 1.218) cf. {Genesis 28:12, Exodus 28:40-42}]; Irenaeus[Against Heresies Book I.24.4, 25.1, 30.14, II.32.3, III.19.3, V.31.2; Demonstration of the Apostolic Preaching 83; Fragments from the Lost Works 53-54]; Justin[Dialogue with Trypho 17, 36, 39, 108, 126, 132; First Apology 45-46, 50]

01:05 Matthew 3:11; Mark 1:8; Luke 3:16; John 1:33; Anonymous[Treatise on Re-Baptism 19]; Origen[Against Celsus Book VII.51]; NT-Apocrypha[Martyrdom of the Holy Apostle Paul 1.6]

01:05-22 Matthew 3:5-16n

01:06 Malachi 3:22

01:06-08 Tertullian[Five Books in Reply to Marcion Book IV.104]

01:07 Matthew 24:6, 36; Mark 13:32; Pseudepigrapha[2Baruch 21.8-9]; Clement of Alexandria[Stromata Book III.6]; Cyprian[Treatise XII.Book III.89]; Gregory Thaumaturgus[Twelve Topics on the Faith 12]; Irenaeus[Against Heresies Book III.23.1]

01:08 Genesis 32:3; Isaiah 32:15, 49:6; Matthew 28:19n; Mark 16:15; Luke 24:47-48; Pseudepigrapha[Martyrdom and Ascension of Isaiah 11:23; Psalms of Solomon 8:15]; Tacitus[The Histories 4.81]; Origen[Gospel of John Book II.28; Gospel of Matthew Book X.18; De Principiis Book I.3.7]; Nag Hammadi[Letter of Peter to Philip 137]; NT-Apocrypha[Epistula Apostolorum 30]

01:09 Mark 16:19; Pseudepigrapha[2Enoch 3:1, 67:3; Sibylline Oracles 1.381]; Josephus[Antiquities 4.8.48 326]; Constitutions of the Holy Apostles[Book V.7]; Justin[On the Resurrection 9]; Lactantius[Divine Institutes Book IV.12]; NT-Apocrypha[Apocalypse of Peter 1.17; Epistula Apostolorum 51]

01:09-10 Tertullian[On the Resurrection of the Flesh 51]

01:09-11 Luke 24.50-51

01:10 Genesis 32:1; OT-Apocrypha[2Maccabees 3:26]; Pseudepigrapha[2Enoch 1:4; Life of Adam and Eve (Apocalypse of Moses) 33:1]

01:10-11 Tertullian[On Baptism 19]

01:11 Pseudepigrapha[4Baruch 9:20; Testament of Job 39:12]; Tertullian[Against Praxeas 31; On the Flesh of Christ 24; On the Resurrection of the Flesh 22]

01:12 Syriac Teaching of the Apostles; Nag Hammadi[Letter of Peter to Philip 139]

01:12-13 Nag Hammadi[Letter of Peter to Philip 133]

01:12-14 Mark 16:19; Luke 24:52

01:13 Matthew 10:2-4; Mark 3:16-19; Luke 6:14-16; Rabbinic[Babylonian Sotah 48b]; NT-Apocrypha[Acts of Thomas 1.1]

01:14 Cyprian[Treatise I.25, IV.8]; Nag Hammadi[Gospel of Thomas 12]

01:15 Cyprian[Epistle LXVII.4]

01:15-20 Tertullian[On Prescription Against Heretics 20]

01:16 Psalms 41:9-10; Josephus[War 2.8.12 159]; Irenaeus[Against Heresies Book I.31.1, III.12.1]

01:16-26 Psalms 109:8

01:18 Genesis 27:40; Matthew 27:3-10; OT-Apocrypha[Wisdom of Solomon 4:19]; Apostolic[Papias Fragment 18:1]; Constitutions of the Holy Apostles[Book VII.2]; NT-Apocrypha[Acts of Thomas 1.84]

01:19 Matthew 27:3-8

01:19-26 Apostolic[Papias Fragment 3:9-10, 5:1]

01:20 Psalms 69:25-26, 109:8; Constitutions of the Holy Apostles[Book VI.12]; Irenaeus[Against Heresies Book II.20.2, III.12.1]

01:20-26 NT-Apocrypha[Gospel of Judas 36]

01:21 NT-Apocrypha[Acts of Paul in Philippi 3.4]

01:22 Matthew 3:16; Mark 1:9, 16:19; Luke 3:21, 24:51; Acts 2:31n

01:24 NT-Apocrypha[Acts of Paul and Thecla 1.24; Acts of Peter 1.2]

01:25 Deuteronomy 9:16, 17:20

01:26 Proverbs 16:33; Irenaeus[Against Heresies Book II.20.5]

02:01 Leviticus 23:15-21; Deuteronomy 16:9-11

02:01-04 Rabbinic[Babylonian Sotah 48b]; Liturgy of James 32; Tertullian[On Fasting 10; On Prayer 25]

02:01-21 Philo[Special Laws II (176-177, 179-180) cf. {Leviticus 23:15-17}]; Irenaeus[Against Heresies Book III.12.1]

02:01-47 Justin[First Apology 39]

02:02 Proverbs 1:23

02:02-04 Acts 11:16n; Dead Sea Scrolls[4Q Liturgy of the Three Tongues of Fire (4Q376) COL II 1-3]; Rabbinic[Targum Pseudo-Jonathan on Exodus 20:18]; Cyprian[Treatise XII.Book III.101]

02:03 Numbers 11:25; Matthew 3:11-12n; Hippolytus[The Discourse on the Holy Theophany 9]; Nag Hammadi[Gospel of Truth 27]

02:03-04 Pseudepigrapha[4Ezra 14.39-48]

02:03-13 Pseudepigrapha[Testament of Benjamin 9.3]

02:04 OT-Apocrypha[Sirach 48:12]; Constitutions of the Holy Apostles[Book V.20]

02:05 Deuteronomy 2:25

02:06 Archelaus[Disputation with Manes 36]

02:09-10 Tertullian[An Answer to the Jews 7]

02:11 OT-Apocrypha[Sirach 36:7]; Pseudepigrapha[2Enoch 54:1; Testament of Job 38:1]; NT-Apocrypha[Acts of Paul and Thecla 1.1, 1.18; Acts of Peter 1.5, 1.17]

02:13 Job 32:18; Tertullian[On Fasting 10]

02:14 Job 32:11

02:14-15 Tertullian[On Prayer 25]

02:15 Pseudepigrapha[2Enoch 51:1]; Tertullian[On Fasting 10]

02:17 Isaiah 2:2; Novatian[Treatise Concerning the Trinity 29]; NT-Apocrypha[Epistula Apostolorum 30]

02:17-18 Anonymous[Treatise on Re-Baptism 15]; Tertullian[On the Resurrection of the Flesh 63; Five Books Against Marcion Book V.8]

02:17-21 Joel 2:28-32

02:18 Numbers 11:29

02:19-22 Pseudepigrapha[Apocalypse of Elijah 5:1]

02:20 Hippolytus[Appendix to the Works of Hippolytus - On the End of the World 37]

02:22 Tertullian[Against Praxeas 17; On Modesty 21; On the Flesh of Christ 15]; NT-
Apocrypha[Epistula Apostolorum 30]

02:22-24 Nag Hammadi[Letter of Peter to Philip 139]

02:22-27 Irenaeus[Against Heresies Book III.12.2]

02:23 This section also includes topical notes for: Foreknowledge of God – Isaiah 46:10; Matthew
16:21, 27:35; Mark 15:24; Luke 24:25-27, 33, 44-48; John 1:45, 5:45-46, 19:18; Acts 3:18n, 18:28, 26:22-
23; 1Corinthians 2:7-8; 2Corinthians 3:14-18, 4:3; 1Peter 1:2; Pseudepigrapha[2Baruch 23.3-4; 4Ezra
6.1-6, 7.74; Hellenistic Synagogal Prayers 8.5, 9.5; Jubilees 1.4-5, 1.26, 32.21-26; Odes of Solomon 7.9-
10, 8.13]; Dead Sea Scrolls[1Q Hymns (1QHODAYOTH [1QH]) COL VII (=XV+Fragments
10+32+34+42) 18-26, COL IX 7; 1Q Rule of the Community (1QS) COL III 13-20, COL IV 1; 4Q Ages
of Creation (4Q180[4QAGESCREAT]) Fragment 2-4 COL II 9-10; 4Q Songs of the Sabbath Sacrifice
(4QSHIRSHABB]) Fragment 4 12-15; Damascus Document (CD-A) COL II 5-10]; Philo[On the
Creation (45-48) cf. {Genesis 1:14, Acts 2:23}; On The Unchangeableness of God (23-32) cf.
{Deuteronomy 5:31, 2Peter 3}]; Apostolic[Ignatius - Letter to the Ephesians 18:2, 20:1]; Clement of
Alexandria[Fragments from the Latin Translation of Cassiodorus Comments on 1Peter; Stromata
Book II.8, 13, VI.14, 17, VII.7; The Instructor Book I.7]; Hippolytus[Refutation of all Heresies Book
X.28]; Irenaeus[Against Heresies Book II.16.11, 28.7, 33.5, III.1.1, 16.7, 21.8, IV.11.1, 14.2, 29.2, 32.2,
39.4, V.1.1, 31.1, 36.1]; Justin[Dialogue with Trypho 16, 42, 70, 92, 96, 103, 118, 134, 136, 140-141; First
Apology 28, 44-45; On the Resurrection 10]; Nag Hammadi[Apocryphon of John 5, 8; Eugnostos the
Blessed III 73; Gospel of Philip 55; Gospel of Truth 21, 28, 38, 41; Sentences of Sextus 311-2; Sophia
of Jesus Christ III. 91-92, 95; Teachings of Silvanus 116; Tripartite Tractate 125]

02:23-41 Apostolic[Epistle to Diognetus 8:9-9:6]

02:24 2Samuel 22:6; Psalms 17:6, 18:4, 116:3; Matthew 28:5-6; Mark 16:6; Luke 24:5; Apostolic[Polycarp
- Letter to the Philippians 1:2]; Hippolytus[Refutation of all Heresies Book V.14];
Irenaeus[Fragments from the Lost Works 54]

02:25-28 Psalms 16:8-11

02:25-36 Pseudepigrapha[Apocalypse of Zephaniah 5:5]

02:26-28 Clement of Alexandria[Stromata Book VI.6]

02:27 Irenaeus[Against Heresies Book III.19.3]; Origen[Gospel of John Book I.34]

02:29 Exodus 2:15; 1Kings 2:10; Josephus[Antiquities 13.8.4 249, 16.7.1 179-183]; Nag Hammadi[Letter
of Peter to Philip 134-5]

02:30 2Samuel 7:12-13; Psalms 89:3-4, 132:11; Pseudepigrapha[Martyrdom and Ascension of Isaiah
11:23]; Tertullian[On the Flesh of Christ 21]; NT-Apocrypha[Acts of Paul from Corinth to Italy p.8]

02:30-38 Irenaeus[Against Heresies Book III.12.2]

02:31 This section also includes topical notes for: Resurrection - Psalms 16:10; Matthew 22:23-32,
27:53; Mark 12:18-27; Luke 14:14, 20:27-38; John 5:29, 11:24-25; Acts 1:22, 2:31, 4:2, 33, 17:18, 32, 23:6-
8, 24:15, 21, 26:23; Romans 1:4, 6:5; 1Corinthians 15:12-56; Philippians 3:10-11; 2Timothy 2:18;
Hebrews 6:2, 11:35; 1Peter 1:3, 3:21; Revelation 20:5-6; Pseudepigrapha[Hellenistic Synagogal
Prayers 5.6, 5.22, 12.49-50; History of the Rechabites 13.5; Martyrdom and Ascension of Isaiah 11.20-
21; Odes of Solomon 17.13; Sibylline Oracles Prologue; Testament of Adam 3.3-4; Testament of
Benjamin 9.3]; Dead Sea Scrolls[1Q Hymns (1QHODAYOTH [1QH]) COL XII 22-28];
Philo[Concerning Noah's Work As A Planter (177); On Dreams, That they Are God-Sent (1.218) cf.
{Exodus 28:40-42}; On Flight And Finding (55-58) cf. {Deuteronomy 4:4, 30:20}; On Rewards And
Punishments (172) cf. {Isaiah 54:1}; Special Laws IV (169) cf. {Deuteronomy 17:18-29}];
Rabbinic[Babylonian Sanhedrin 106a cf. {Numbers 24:23}; Yalqut 766]; Clement of
Alexandria[Fragments found in Greek only in the Oxford Edition Last Work on the Passover;
Fragments from the Latin Translation of Cassiodorus Comments on 1Peter; Stromata Book VI.15;
The Instructor Book I.5, 10]; Gregory Thaumaturgus[Twelve Topics on the Faith 9];
Irenaeus[Against Heresies Book I.26.1, 27.3, 30.13-14, II.32.3, III.1.1, 12.2, 19.3, IV.33.13, V.31.2;
Demonstration of the Apostolic Preaching 72-73]; Justin[Dialogue with Trypho 36, 45-46, 72, 97, 99-
100, 108, 118, 132; First Apology 21, 38]; Lactantius[Divine Institutes Book IV.19]; Origen[Gospel of
John Book I.34]; NT-Apocrypha[Acts of Pilate XVII.1-XXVI.1; Canon Muratori Line 21; Questions of
Bartholomew I 10-20]; Egyptian Book of the Dead[Oration 8]

02:32 Tacitus[The Histories 4.81]

02:33 Acts 11:16n; Matthew 28:19n; Pseudepigrapha[Testament of Job 33:3]; Dead Sea Scrolls[4Q
Liturgy of the Three Tongues of Fire (4Q376) COL II 1-3]; Anonymous[Treatise Against the Heretic
Novatian 3]; Victorinus[Apocalypse 1.16]; NT-Apocrypha[Epistula Apostolorum 3]

02:33-34 1Peter 3:22n

02:34 Justin[Dialogue with Trypho 83]

02:34-35 Psalms 110:1

02:36 Psalms 20:7; Justin[Dialogue with Trypho 133, 136; On the Resurrection 10]; Tertullian[Against
      Praxeas 28]

02:37 Psalms 109:16

02:38 Acts 3:19n, 11:16n; Ephesians 4:32n; Dead Sea Scrolls[4Q Liturgy of the Three Tongues of Fire
      (4Q376) COL II 1-3]; Justin[Dialogue with Trypho 95]; NT-Apocrypha[Acts of Thomas 1.132]

02:38-39 Cyprian[Epistle LXXII.17]

02:38-41 Genesis 50:17; Matthew 3:5-16n

02:39 Isaiah 57:19; Joel 2:32, 3:5; OT-Apocrypha[Sirach 24:32]

02:40 Deuteronomy 32:5; Psalms 78:8; Rabbinic[Babylonian Sanhedrin 98a]

02:41 Clement of Alexandria[Stromata Book I.18]; Irenaeus[Against Heresies Book IV.23.2]; NT-
      Apocrypha[Gospel of the Nazareans Fragment 35; Martyrdom of the Holy Apostle Paul 1.1]

02:42 Irenaeus[Fragments from the Lost Works 36]; Nag Hammadi[Apocryphon of James 8]

02:42-47 1Corinthians 10:16-18n; Pseudepigrapha[Martyrdom and Ascension of Isaiah 3.13]; Dead Sea
      Scrolls[1Q Rule of the Community (1QS) COL V 1-23]; Josephus[**War 2.8.4 119-127**]; Philo[**Every
      Good Man Is Free (85-87)**]; Plato[Republic III 416d-417b, IV 423e-424b, V 449c-450c, 457c-d, VIII
      543a]; Hippolytus[**Refutation of all Heresies Book IX.14-15**]; Irenaeus[Against Heresies Book
      II.31.3; Demonstration of the Apostolic Preaching 1-111]; Justin[First Apology 14, 67]

> They [Essenes] have no one certain city, but many of them dwell in every city; and if any
> of their sect come from other places, what they have lies open for them, just as if it were
> their own; and they go in to such as they never knew before, as if they had been ever so
> long acquainted with them. For which reason they carry nothing at all with them when
> they travel into remote parts, though still they take their weapons with them, for fear of
> thieves. Accordingly, there is, in every city where they live, one appointed particularly to
> take care of strangers, and to provide garments and other necessaries for them. But the
> habit and management of their bodies is such as children who are in fear of their
> masters. Nor do they allow the change of shoes until [the shoes] be first torn to pieces, or
> worn out by time. Nor do they either buy or sell any thing to one another; but every one
> of them gives what he has to him that wants it, and receives from him again in lieu of it
> what may be convenient for himself; and although there be no requital made, they are
> fully allowed to take what they want of whomsoever they please. (Josephus - War 2.8.4
> 119-127)

> In the first place, then, there is no one [Essene] who has a house so absolutely his own
> private property, that it does not in some sense also belong to every one: for besides that
> they all dwell together in companies, the house is open to all those of the same notions,
> who come to them from other quarters; then there is one magazine among them all; their
> expenses are all in common; their garments belong to them all in common; their food is
> common, since they all eat in messes; for there is no other people among which you can
> find a common use of the same house, a common adoption of one mode of living, and a
> common use of the same table more thoroughly established in fact than among this tribe:
> and is not this very natural? For whatever they, after having been working during the
> day, receive for their wages, that they do not retain as their own, but bring it into the
> common stock, and give any advantage that is to be derived from it to all who desire to
> avail themselves of it; and those who are sick are not neglected because they are unable
> to contribute to the common stock, inasmuch as the tribe have in their public stock a
> means of supplying their necessities and aiding their weakness, so that from their ample
> means they support them liberally and abundantly; and they cherish respect for their
> elders, and honor them and care for them, just as parents are honored and cared for by
> their lawful children: being supported by them in all abundance both by their personal
> exertions, and by innumerable contrivances. (Philo - Every Good Man Is Free 85-87)

The tenets of the Esseni - And they despise wealth, and do not turn away from sharing their goods with those that are destitute. No one among them, however, enjoys a greater amount of riches than another. For a regulation with them is, that an individual coming forward to join the sect must sell his possessions, and present the price of them to the community. And on receiving the money, the head of the order distributes it to all according to their necessities. Thus there is no one among them in distress. And they do not use oil, regarding it as a defilement to be anointed. And there are appointed overseers, who take care of all things that belong to them in common, and they all appear always in white clothing. (Hippolytus - Refutation of all Heresies Book IX.14-15)

02:43 Pseudepigrapha[Apocalypse of Elijah 5:1]

02:44 Acts 4:32-35; Apostolic[Epistle of Barnabas 4:10]

02:45 Matthew 19:21; Mark 10:21; Luke 12:33, 18:22; Epic of Gilgamesh[The Story of the Flood]

02:46 Ecclesiastes 9:7; NT-Apocrypha[Acts of Peter 1.41]

02:47 NT-Apocrypha[Acts of Peter 1.9, 1.31, 1.33]

03:01 Daniel 9:21; Pseudepigrapha[2Enoch 51:5]; Tertullian[On Prayer 25]

03:01-11 Tertullian[On Modesty 21]

03:02-10 Philo[On the Posterity of Cain And His Exile (147) cf. {Genesis 24:17-20}]; Irenaeus[Against Heresies Book II.32.4, III.12.3]; Nag Hammadi[Acts of Peter and the Twelve Apostles 11]

03:02-26 Nag Hammadi[Letter of Peter to Philip 139]

03:05 Tertullian[On Prescription Against Heretics 7]

03:06 This section also includes topical notes for: Healing in the Name of Jesus - Mark 16:17-18; Acts 9:34; Rabbinic[Jerusalem (Abodah Zarah 40d; Shabbat 14d cf. {Leviticus 18:5, Ecclesiastes 10:5}); Tosephta Hullin, ii. 22-23 cf. {Ecclesiastes 10:8}]; Cyprian[Treatise XII.Book III.61]; NT-Apocrypha[Acts of Paul in Myra p.29]

03:08 Isaiah 35:6

03:10 Pseudepigrapha[3Baruch]

03:12 Pseudepigrapha[Apocalypse of Elijah 5:4]; Irenaeus[Against Heresies Book III.12.3]; NT-Apocrypha[Acts of Peter 1.28]

03:13 Exodus 3:6, 15; Isaiah 52:13, 53:11; Pseudepigrapha[2Baruch 70:10; Hellenistic Synagogal Prayers 15:3; Odes of Solomon 31.8; Prayer of Manasseh 1; Rabbinic[Babylonian Sanhedrin 43a]; Tertullian[An Answer to the Jews 8]; Nag Hammadi[Letter of Peter to Philip 133]

03:14 Matthew 27:15-23; Mark 15:6-14; Luke 23:13-23; John 19:12-15; Clement of Alexandria[The Instructor Book III.11]; Hippolytus[Expository Treatise Against the Jews 9]

03:15 Apostolic[Epistle of Barnabas 18:1-2]; Irenaeus[Against Heresies Book II.22.4]; Justin[Dialogue with Trypho 93]

03:17 Pseudepigrapha[Joseph and Aseneth 6:7]; Clement of Alexandria[Stromata Book VI.6]; NT-Apocrypha[Kerygma Petri 3c]

03:17-30 NT-Apocrypha[Acts of Peter 1.2]

03:18 This section also includes topical notes for: Foretold by the Prophets - Matthew 2:23, 26:56; Luke 16:31, 18:31, 24:44-46; John 1:45, 6:45; Acts 2:23n, 13:27, 24:24, 26:22, 28:23; Romans 1:2, 3:21, 16:26; Hebrews 1:1; Revelation 10:7; Josephus[War 2.8.12 159]; Rabbinic[Babylonian Sanhedrin 99a]; Anonymous[Martyrdom of Justin Martyr 1]; Irenaeus[Against Heresies Book I.7.2]; Justin[Dialogue with Trypho 126, 136]

03:18-24 Nag Hammadi[Tripartite Tractate 113]

03:18-26 This section also includes topical notes for: Christ - Psalms 2:2; Daniel 9:25-26; Matthew 11:3-6; 16:15-16, 22:42-45, 26:63-64; Mark 12:35-37; Luke 2:28-32, 38, 20:41-44, 24:25-27; John 1:41, 45, 4:25-26, 29, 42, 5:33, 36-37, 39, 46, 6:27, 8:14, 17-18, 25, 28, 56, 13:19; Acts 3:18n, 20, 24, 4:26-27, 9:22, 13:27, 17:2-3, 26:6-7, 22-23, 28:23; Romans 1:1-3; 1Corinthians 15:3; 1Peter 1:10-11; 2 Peter 1:16-18; 1John 5:6-9; Pseudepigrapha[Hellenistic Synagogal Prayers 2.19; Odes of Solomon 9.3, 10.4, 17.6-17, 41.3, 41.15; Psalms of Solomon 17.32; Sibylline Oracles 2.45, 8.217-250; Testament of Benjamin 11.2-5]; Dead Sea Scrolls[1Q Hymns (1QHODAYOTH [1QH]) COL XIII 12-17, XV 10-15; 4Q Aramaic Apocalypse (4Q246) COL I 7, COL II 8; 4Q Aramaic TextA=Testament of Levi(?) (4Q541[4QAHA=4QTLEVIS?]) Fragment 9 COLI 1-7; 4Q Bless Oh My Soul (4Q434[4QBARKINAPSHI]) Fragment 1 COL I 1-9]; Josephus[Antiquities 18.3.2-3 60-64; Discourse to the Greeks Concerning Hades 6]; Philo[Concerning Noah's Work As A Planter (177); Every Good Man Is Free (20, 42-43) cf. {Exodus 4:16, 7:1}; On Dreams, That they Are God-Sent (1.175-1.176,

1.255-1.256, 2.229-2.231) cf. {Genesis 28:14, 32:24-31, Leviticus 16:17, Deuteronomy 10:10}; On Flight
And Finding (106-114) cf. {Exodus 28:32, Leviticus 10:36, 21:10-14, Numbers 35:2-34}; On the Change
of Names (128-129) cf. {Genesis 17:16, Exodus 4:16, 7:1, Deuteronomy 33:1}]; Rabbinic[Babylonian
(Sanhedrin 93b, 98b-99a; Sukkah 52a cf. {Psalms 2:7-8})]; Clement of Alexandria[Exhortation to the
Heathen 1; Stromata Book V.11, VI.5, 7, 15; The Instructor Book I.5]; Hippolytus[Refutation of all
Heresies Book IX.25]; Irenaeus[Against Heresies Book I.2.5, 3.1, 4.1, 4.5, 7.2, 8.4, 10.3, 11.1, 12.4, 15.3,
19.1, 21.2-3, 24.2, 24.4, 26.1, 29.1-2, 30.1-2, 30.11-14, II.16.10-11, 19.9, III.1.2, 5.3, 9.3, 11.6-7, 12.2-3,
12.5, 16.1, 17.1, 18.3-4, 19.2, 21.5, IV.Preface.3, 1.4, 1.6, 6.2, 6.6, 9.2, 11.3, 26.1, 27.1-2, 33.3-5, 35.4,
V.21.3, 22.1, 25.5, 26.2; Demonstration of the Apostolic Preaching 36, 49, 58, 61-64, 66, 71, 73-74, 77,
91; Fragments from the Lost Works 39, 52-54]; Justin[Dialogue with Trypho 8, 10, 34, 39, 43, 45-49,
67, 76, 85, 89, 96, 108, 110, 113-116, 118, 120-121, 128, 132, 134, 136, 138-139, 142; Second Apology 6];
Nag Hammadi[Gospel of Philip 53, 74; Gospel of Truth 16; Teachings of Silvanus 98-99, 101-104,
106, 109-110; Trimorphic Protennoia 38]

03:19 This section also includes topical notes for: Repent - Matthew 3:8, 11:21, 12:41; Luke 10:13,
11:32; Acts 2:38, 26:20; Pseudepigrapha[4Ezra 7.138-140]; Dead Sea Scrolls[1Q Rule of the
Community (1QS) COL III 6-12]; Philo[On Rewards And Punishments (163-170) cf. {Leviticus 26:1-
45, Isaiah 54:1-13, Ezekiel 20:33-38}; On the Unchangeableness of God (8-9) cf. {Exodus 30:17-21}; On
the Virtues (179-184) cf. {Leviticus 26:1-12, Deuteronomy 30:11, Galatians 5:16-26}; Questions And
Answers On Genesis II (42) cf. {Genesis 7:17-18, 8:11, Matthew 3:1-12, 16, Luke 3:1-18}; The
Cherubim Part 1 (14-17) cf. {Numbers 5:14-18, Deuteronomy 16:20}; Special Laws I (235-237) cf.
{Leviticus 6:1-7}]; Clement of Alexandria[Exhortation to the Heathen 12; Fragments from Antonius
Melissa Book I.17; Stromata Book VI.6, 12, 14; The Instructor Book I.2]; Irenaeus[Against Heresies
Book I.10.1]; Justin[Dialogue with Trypho 26, 100, 107, 138, 141]; Theophilus of Antioch[To
Autolycus Book III.11]; Nag Hammadi[Gospel of Truth 35]

03:19-21 Tertullian[On the Resurrection of the Flesh 23]

03:20 NT-Apocrypha[Acts of John 22]

03:22-23 Deuteronomy 18:15-20; Clement[Homily III.53; Recognitions Book I.36]

03:23 Leviticus 23:29; Deuteronomy 18:19

03:24 Rabbinic[Babylonian Sanhedrin 99a]

03:25 Genesis 12:3, 18:18, 22:18, 26:4, 28:14

03:26 Pseudepigrapha[2Baruch 70:10]; Nag Hammadi[Letter of Peter to Philip 133]

04:01 Josephus[Antiquities 18.1.4 16-17; War 2.8.14 162-166]

04:02 Acts 2:31n; Cyprian[Epistle LXVII.4]; Irenaeus[Against Heresies Book III.12.3]

04:04 Matthew 14:21n; Irenaeus[Against Heresies Book IV.23.2]; NT-Apocrypha[Gospel of the
Nazareans Fragment 35]

04:06 Josephus[Antiquities 18.2.2 35, 18.8.1 259]

04:07 NT-Apocrypha[Acts of Thomas 1.106, 1.140]

04:07-12 Egyptian Book of the Dead[Oration 63A]

04:08 Irenaeus[Against Heresies Book III.12.4]; NT-Apocrypha[Martyrdom of the Holy Apostle Paul
1.3]

04:08-12 Cyprian[Treatise XII.Book II.16]

04:11 Psalms 118:22; Matthew 21:42; Pseudepigrapha[Testament of Solomon 22:8, 23:4]; Origen[Gospel
of John Book I.23]

04:12 Revelation 12:10n; Anonymous[Treatise on Re-Baptism 6]; Irenaeus[Demonstration of the
Apostolic Preaching 95-96]; Nag Hammadi[Gospel of Truth 16-17]; NT-Apocrypha[Acts of Paul in
Ephesus p.2]

04:13 Origen[Gospel of Matthew Book X.14]; Nag Hammadi[Letter of Peter to Philip 134-135]

04:18 Nag Hammadi[Letter of Peter to Philip 139]

04:19 Hippolytus[Against the Heresy of One Noetus 6]

04:22 Irenaeus[Against Heresies Book III.12.5]

04:24 Exodus 20:11; 2Kings 19:15; Nehemiah 9:6; Psalms 146:6; Isaiah 37:16; OT-Apocrypha[Judith
9:12]; Pseudepigrapha[Joseph and Aseneth 8:9; Testament of Job 2:4]; Irenaeus[Against Heresies
Book III.12.5]; NT-Apocrypha[Acts of Paul and Thecla 1.24]

04:25 Irenaeus[Demonstration of the Apostolic Preaching 74]

04:25-26 Psalms 2:1-2

04:26-27 Acts 3:18-26n

04:27 Isaiah 61:1; Matthew 27:1-2; Mark 15:1-5; Luke 23:7-11; John 18:28-29; Pseudepigrapha[2Baruch
70:10]; Tertullian[Against Praxeas 28; On Baptism 7]; Nag Hammadi[Letter of Peter to Philip 133]

04:29 Nag Hammadi[Letter of Peter to Philip 134-135]; NT-Apocrypha[Acts of Paul in Sidon p.37]

04:30 Pseudepigrapha[Apocalypse of Elijah 5:1]; Nag Hammadi[Letter of Peter to Philip 133]

04:31 Irenaeus[Against Heresies Book III.12.5]; Nag Hammadi[Letter of Peter to Philip 134-135]

04:32 Acts 2:44-45; Apostolic[Didache 4:8; Epistle of Barnabas 4:10]; Cyprian[Epistle VII.3; Treatise VIII.25, XII.Book III.3]; Origen[Against Celsus Book VIII.12; Gospel of Matthew Book XIV.1]; Teaching of the Twelve Apostles 4.8; Epic of Gilgamesh[The Story of the Flood]

04:32-37 Fabian[Second Epistle]; Urban I[Epistle 1.1]

04:33 Acts 2:31n; 1Peter 1:10-13n; Irenaeus[Against Heresies Book III.12.5]

04:34 Deuteronomy 15:4

04:34-35 Tertullian[De Fuga in Persecutione 12]

04:34-05:11 Josephus[Antiquities 18.1.5 22]

04:35 Matthew 19:21; Mark 10:21; Luke 12:33, 18:22

05:01 Clement of Alexandria[Stromata Book I.23]

05:01-06 Tertullian[On Modesty 21]

05:01-11 Dead Sea Scrolls[1Q Rule of the Community (1QS) COL VII 19-20; Damascus Document (CD-A) COL XIII 13-16]; Constitutions of the Holy Apostles[Book VII.2]; Urban I[Epistle 2.2]; NT-Apocrypha[Acts of Peter p.139]

05:02 Joshua 7:1; OT-Apocrypha[2Maccabees 4:32]

05:03-04 Cyprian[Treatise XII.Book III.30]

05:04 Deuteronomy 23:21

05:05 Pseudepigrapha[2Enoch 71:9]

05:06 Leviticus 10:4

05:07 OT-Apocrypha[3Maccabees 4:17]

05:10 Leviticus 10:4; Pseudepigrapha[2Enoch 71:9]; Archelaus[Fragment of the Disputation with Manes 1]

05:13-16 Tertullian[On Modesty 21]

05:15 Irenaeus[Demonstration of the Apostolic Preaching 71]

05:16 NT-Apocrypha[Acts of Peter p.128]

05:17 Luke 20:27; Josephus[Antiquities 18.1.4 16-17; War 2.8.14 162-166]

05:17-26 Pseudepigrapha[Artapanus Fragment 3 (PrEv 9.27.23)]

05:20 Origen[Gospel of John Book X.19]

05:21 Exodus 12:21; OT-Apocrypha[1Maccabees 12:6; 2Maccabees 1:10]

05:26 Nag Hammadi[Letter of Peter to Philip 139]; NT-Apocrypha[Acts of Thomas 1.164]

05:28 Matthew 27:25; Pseudepigrapha[Life of Abraham 6:11]

05:29 Hippolytus[Against the Heresy of One Noetus 6]; Polycrates of Ephesus[Epistle]

05:29-30 Origen[Gospel of John Book X.19]

05:30 Exodus 3:15; Deuteronomy 21:22; Daniel 3:26, 3:52; Acts 10:39; Galatians 3:13n; Pseudepigrapha[2Enoch 7:1]; Dead Sea Scrolls[11Q TEMPLE SCROLL (11Q19[11QT]) COL LXIV 7-12]; Irenaeus[Against Heresies Book III.12.5]

05:30-31 Nag Hammadi[Letter of Peter to Philip 139]

05:31 This section also includes topical notes for: Remission of Sin - Psalms 118:16; Matthew 9:6n; Acts 26:18n; Apostolic[Epistle of Barnabas 18:1-2]; Justin[Dialogue with Trypho 116]; NT-Apocrypha[Kerygma Petri 3a]

05:32 Justin[Dialogue with Trypho 138]

05:33-39 Josephus[**Antiquities 20.5.1 97-99, 20.5.2 102**]

Now it came to pass, while Fadus was procurator of Judea, that a certain magician, whose name was Theudas, persuaded a great part of the people to take their effects with them, and follow him to the river Jordan; for he told them he was a prophet, and that he would, by his own command, divide the river, and afford them an easy passage over it; and many were deluded by his words. However, Fadus did not permit them to make any advantage of his wild attempt, but sent a troop of horsemen out against them; who, falling upon them unexpectedly, slew many of them, and took many of them alive. They also took Theudas alive, and cut off his head, and carried it to Jerusalem. This was what befell the Jews in the time of Cuspius Fadus's government. (Josephus - Antiquities 20.5.1 97-99)

> The sons of Judas of Galilee were now slain; I mean of that Judas who caused the people to revolt, when Cyrenius came to take an account of the estates of the Jews, as we have showed in a foregoing book. The names of those sons were James and Simon, whom Alexander commanded to be crucified. (Josephus - Antiquities 20.5.2 102)

05:35-39 Clement[Recognitions Book I.65]
05:36 Josephus[Antiquities 17.10.5 271-272, 17.10.8 285]
05:36-37 Origen[Against Celsus Book VI.11; Gospel of John Book VI.6]
05:38-39 Origen[Against Celsus Book I.57]
05:39 OT-Apocrypha[2Maccabees 7:19; Wisdom of Solomon 12:13-14]
05:40 Rabbinic[Bammidbar Rabba xix. 3; Bereshith Rabba vii. 2; Jerusalem (Qiddushin 64d; Yebamot 4a); Pesiqta de-Rab Kahana 35b, 36a; Tanhuma 56b, 57a]
05:40-41 Constitutions of the Holy Apostles[Book V.2]
05:41 Pseudepigrapha[2Baruch 52:6]; Origen[Against Celsus Book II.45]; Nag Hammadi[Letter of Peter to Philip 138]
05:42 Irenaeus[Against Heresies Book III.12.5]
06:01 Pseudepigrapha[Testament of Job 10:2]
06:01-06 Dead Sea Scrolls[Damascus Document (CD-A) COL XIV 12-17]; Apostolic[Ignatius - Letter to the Trallians 2:3]; Tertullian[Against All Heresies 1]
06:02 Exodus 18:17-23; Clement of Alexandria[The Instructor Book II.7]
06:03 Exodus 31:3, 35:31; Numbers 27:16; Victorinus[On the Creation of the World]
06:03-07 Irenaeus[Against Heresies Book IV.15.1]
06:05 Hippolytus[Refutation of all Heresies Book VII.24]; Irenaeus[Against Heresies Book I.26.3]; Nag Hammadi[Letter of Peter to Philip 133]
06:05-08 Pseudepigrapha[Joseph and Aseneth 4:7]
06:06 Numbers 27:18, 23; Deuteronomy 34:9; Constitutions of the Holy Apostles[Book V.2]
06:08 1Peter 1:10-13n
06:08-07:60 Constitutions of the Holy Apostles[Book II.49, VIII.46]
06:13 Exodus 20:16; Proverbs 14:5, 24:28; Jeremiah 26:11
06:13-14 Rabbinic[Genesis Rabbah 98:9 cf. {Genesis 49:11}; Leviticus Rabbah 9:7 cf. {Leviticus 7:11-12}]
06:14 Rabbinic[**Babylonian Yoma 39b cf. {Zechariah 11:1}**]

> Forty years before the destruction of the Temple the lot [For the Lord] did not come up in the right hand; nor did the crimson-coloured strap become white; nor did the westernmost light shine; and the doors of the Hekal [courtyard] would open by themselves, until R. Johanan b. Zakkai rebuked them, saying: Hekal, Hekal, why wilt thou be the alarmer thyself? I know about thee that thou wilt be destroyed, for Zechariah ben Ido has already prophesied concerning thee: Open thy doors, O Lebanon, that the fire may devour thy cedars. (Talmud - Babylonian Yoma 39b, *The Soncino Talmud*; Judaica Press, Inc. 1973 and Soncino Press, Ltd. 1965, 1967, 1977, 1983, 1984, 1987, 1988, & 1990)

06:15 Pseudepigrapha[Joseph and Aseneth 18:9]; Tertullian[On the Resurrection of the Flesh 55]; NT-Apocrypha[Acts of Paul and Thecla 1.3]
07:01-60 Origen[De Principiis Book II.4.2]
07:02 Genesis 11:31-12:1, 15:7; Psalms 29:3; Pseudepigrapha[Apocalypse of Elijah 1:5]
07:02-04 Tertullian[On the Pallium 2]
07:02-08 Irenaeus[Against Heresies Book III.12.10]
07:03 Genesis 12:1; Pseudepigrapha[Apocalypse of Elijah 5:4]; Irenaeus[Demonstration of the Apostolic Preaching 24]
07:04 Genesis 11:31-12:1, 4-5
07:05 Genesis 12:7, 13:15, 15:18, 16:1, 17:8, 24:7, 48:4; Deuteronomy 2:5; Irenaeus[Against Heresies Book V.32.2]
07:06 Exodus 2:22; Tertullian[An Answer to the Jews 2]
07:06-07 Genesis 15:13-14
07:07 Exodus 3:12
07:08 Genesis 17:10-14, 21:2-4, 25:26, 29:31-30:24, 35:16-18; 1Chronicles 1:34
07:08-14 Pseudepigrapha[Hellenistic Synagogal Prayers 12.64]

07:09 Genesis 37:11, 28, 39:2-3, 23, 45:4
07:09-10 Genesis 39:21
07:10 Genesis 41:37-44, 45:8; Psalms 105:21
07:11 Genesis 41:54-57, 42:5
07:12-13 Genesis 42:1-2
07:13 Genesis 42:16, 45:1, 3-4, 16
07:14 Genesis 45:9-11, 18-19, 23, 46:27; Exodus 1:5; Deuteronomy 10:22; Philo[On the Migration of Abraham (199-201) cf. {Genesis 46:27, Deuteronomy 10:22}]; Irenaeus[Demonstration of the Apostolic Preaching 25]
07:15 Genesis 46:1-7, 49:33; Exodus 1:6; Deuteronomy 26:5; Pseudepigrapha[Jubilees 46:10]; Tertullian[On the Pallium 2]
07:16 Genesis 23:2-20, 33:19, 49:29-30, 50:7-13; Joshua 24:32
07:17 Genesis 47:27; Exodus 1:20; Psalms 105:24
07:17-19 Exodus 1:7-11
07:19 Exodus 1:17, 22
07:20 Exodus 2:2; Josephus[Antiquities 2.9.6-7 230-232]
07:21 Exodus 2:3-10
07:22 1Kings 5:10; Josephus[Antiquities 2.10.1-11.1 241-255]; Clement of Alexandria[Stromata Book I.23]; Origen[Against Celsus Book III.46]
07:23 Pseudepigrapha[Jubilees 47:10]
07:23-24 Exodus 2:11-12
07:26 Exodus 2:13
07:27-28 Exodus 2:14
07:29 Exodus 2:11-15, 21-22, 18:3-4
07:30 Exodus 3:2; Pseudepigrapha[Jubilees 48:2]
07:31 Exodus 3:3-4
07:32 Exodus 3:6, 15
07:33-34 Exodus 3:5-10
07:34 Exodus 3:1-10
07:35 Exodus 2:14, 3:2; Deuteronomy 33:16; Psalms 19:15, 78:35
07:36 Exodus 7:3, 14:21, 33, 15:4; Numbers 14:33; Psalms 105:27; Pseudepigrapha[Testament of Solomon 25:4]
07:36-41 Pseudepigrapha[Testament (Assumption) of Moses 3:11]
07:37 Deuteronomy 18:15, 18; Pseudepigrapha[Testament of Benjamin 9:2]; Clement[Homily III.53]
07:38 Exodus 19:1-6, 20:1-17, 31:18; Deuteronomy 4:10, 5:1-33, 9:10, 18:15, 32:47, 33:3; Irenaeus[Against Heresies Book IV.15.1]
07:38-41 Tertullian[An Answer to the Jews 1]
07:39 Numbers 14:3
07:39-40 Tertullian[Of Patience 5]
07:40 Exodus 32:1, 23
07:41 Exodus 32:2-6, 8; Deuteronomy 4:28; Psalms 115:4; Jeremiah 1:16
07:42 Jeremiah 7:18, 8:21, 9:13
07:42-43 Amos 5:25-27; Origen[Against Celsus Book V.8]
07:43 Pseudepigrapha[Testament of Solomon 26:1]
07:44 Exodus 25:9, 25:40, 27:21; Numbers 1:5; Pseudepigrapha[Sibylline Oracles 4.10]
07:45 Genesis 17:8, 48:4; Deuteronomy 32:49; Joshua 3:14-17, 18:1, 23:9, 24:18; Tertullian[On the Pallium 2]
07:45-46 2Samuel 7:1-16; 1Chronicles 17:1-14; 2Chronicles 6:7-8; Psalms 132:1-5
07:45-47 1Kings 8:17-20
07:47 1Kings 6:1-38; 2Chronicles 3:1-17, 5:1, 6:2, 10, 18, 22:6
07:48 Isaiah 16:12; Pseudepigrapha[Sibylline Oracles 4.8]
07:49 Irenaeus[Demonstration of the Apostolic Preaching 45]
07:49-50 Isaiah 66:1-2
07:51 This section also includes topical notes for: Circumcision - Exodus 32:9, 33:3, 5; Leviticus 26:41; Numbers 27:14; Deuteronomy 10:16, 30:6; Isaiah 63:10; Jeremiah 4:4, 6:10, 9:26; Ezekiel 44:7-9; Romans 2:29; Colossians 2:11; Pseudepigrapha[4Ezra 1.32; Jubilees 1.23; Odes of Solomon 11.2]; Dead Sea Scrolls[1Q Habakkuk Pesher (1QHAB) COL XI 12-13; 4Q Bless Oh My Soul (4Q434[4QBARKINAPSHI]) Fragment 1 COL I 4; 4Q Catena(4Q177[4QCATENA]) COL II

(Fragments 11+10+26+9+20+7) 16; 4Q Word of the Luminaries (4Q504[4QDIBHAM]) Fragment 4 11]; Philo[Special Laws I (6)]; Rabbinic[Babylonian Keritot 9a]; Clement of Alexandria[Stromata Book IV.25, V.8]; Hippolytus[Refutation of all Heresies Book IX.21]; Irenaeus[Against Heresies Book IV.16.1-2, 22.2, IV.25.1; Demonstration of the Apostolic Preaching 24]; Justin[Dialogue with Trypho 12, 15-16, 18-19, 24, 27-29, 41, 43, 47, 92, 113-114, 123, 137]; Tertullian[An Answer to the Jews 3]; Nag Hammadi[Gospel of Philip 82; Gospel of Thomas 53]

07:51-52 Tertullian[An Answer to the Jews 13]

07:52 1Kings 19:10, 14; 2Chronicles 36:16; Nehemiah 9:26; Apostolic[Ignatius - Letter to the Philadelphians 5:2, 9:2; Polycarp - Letter to the Philippians 6:3; Epistle of Barnabas 1:7, 3:6]; Hippolytus[Expository Treatise Against the Jews 9]; Justin[Dialogue with Trypho 93]; Origen[Gospel of Matthew Book X.18; Letter to Africanus 9]

07:53 Deuteronomy 33:2; Pseudepigrapha[2Enoch 15:1; Jubilees 1:28]; Rabbinic[Exodus Rabbah 29:2 cf. {Psalms 68:17-18}]

07:54 Job 16:9; Psalms 35:16, 36, 37:12, 112:10

07:55 Isaiah 6:1, 63:3; Pseudepigrapha[Life of Adam and Eve (Apocalypse of Moses) 33:1]; Tertullian[Against Praxeas 30]

07:55-56 1Peter 3:22n

07:56 Pseudepigrapha[Sibylline Oracles 2.245]; Constitutions of the Holy Apostles[Book VI.30]; Irenaeus[Against Heresies Book III.12.13]

07:57 Job 16:10; Pseudepigrapha[2Baruch 22:1]

07:58 Leviticus 24:14; Numbers 15:35; Deuteronomy 17:7

07:59 Psalms 31:5; Peter of Alexandria[Canonical Epistle 9]; Tertullian[Scorpiace 15]; NT-Apocrypha[Protoevangelium of James 23.3]

07:59-60 Tertullian[Of Patience 14; On the Resurrection of the Flesh 55]

07:60 Matthew 5:44n; Clement[Recognitions Book VI.5]; Cyprian[Treatise IX.16]; Pseud-Irenaeus

08:01 Irenaeus[Against Heresies Book V.12.5]; Nag Hammadi[Letter of Peter to Philip 133]

08:03 Acts 22:4-5, 26:9-11; Irenaeus[Against Heresies Book V.12.5]

08:05-40 Nag Hammadi[Letter of Peter to Philip 133]

08:09 Irenaeus[Against Heresies Book II.32.4]; Tertullian[A Treatise on the Soul 57]

08:09-11 Josephus[Antiquities 20.7.2 142]; Clement[Homily IV.4]

08:09-24 Hippolytus[Refutation of all Heresies Book V.2]; Tertullian[Against All Heresies 1; On Idolatry 9]

08:10 Pseudepigrapha[Testament of Solomon 2:4]; Origen[Against Celsus Book VI.11]; NT-Apocrypha[Acts of Peter 1.4]

08:12-38 Matthew 3:5-16n

08:13 Clement[Recognitions Book III.49]

08:13-24 Clement of Alexandria[Fragments from Eusebius Ecclesiastical History Book VI.2.15; Stromata Book II.11]; Constitutions of the Holy Apostles[Book IV.7, VI.7]; Irenaeus[Against Heresies Book I.23.1-5, 27.1, 27.4, II.Preface.1, 9.2, 31.1-2, 32.4, III.Preface.1, 4.3, 12.12, IV.33.3]; Justin[Dialogue with Trypho 120; First Apology 23, 56; Second Apology 15]; Nag Hammadi[Gospel of Philip 64]

08:17 Cyprian[Epistle LXXI.1]

08:18 This section also includes topical notes for: Laying on of Hands - Numbers 8:10, 27:18, 23; Deuteronomy 34:9; 1Timothy 4:14; Hebrews 6:2; Philo[Special Laws I (201-204) cf. {Leviticus 1:4}]; Rabbinic[Jerusalem Bikkurim 65c; Siphre on Numbers 27:18; Targum Jerusalem Ruth 2:12 cf. {Deuteronomy 23:16, 1Chronicles 2:55}]; Hippolytus[Refutation of all Heresies Book X.8]; Origen[De Principiis Book I.3.2]; NT-Apocrypha[Acts of Peter 1.23]

08:18-21 Tertullian[A Treatise on the Soul 34]

08:20 Daniel 2:5, 3:29; Cyprian[Treatise XII.Book III.100; Treatises Attributed to Cyprian Exhortation to Repentance]; Tertullian[De Fuga in Persecutione 12]

08:20-21 Anonymous[Treatise on Re-Baptism 16]

08:21 Deuteronomy 12:12, 14:27, 29; Psalms 78:37; Tertullian[On Idolatry 9]

08:22 Pseudepigrapha[Joseph and Aseneth 9:2]

08:23 Deuteronomy 29:17; Isaiah 58:6; Lamentations 3:15

08:24 Exodus 8:4, 24, 9:28, 10:17

08:25 Rabbinic[Babylonian Shabbat 116a]

08:26 Daniel 8:4, 9; Origen[Gospel of John Book I.15]

08:26-27 Linguistics[Aramaic words for "Treasury" and "Gaza" are homonyms]

08:26-40 Tertullian[On Baptism 4, 18]

08:27 Deuteronomy 23:1; 1Kings 8:41; Psalms 68:32; Isaiah 56:3-7; Jeremiah 34:19; Zephaniah 3:10; Linguistics[Aramaic word for "Eunuch" is written the same as "Faithful," "Believer," or "Believing"]

08:27-39 Irenaeus[Against Heresies Book IV.23.2]

08:28 Pseudepigrapha[Joseph and Aseneth 5:4]

08:30 Clement of Alexandria[Stromata Book I.10]

08:32 Irenaeus[Against Heresies Book III.12.8]

08:32-33 Isaiah 53:7-8

08:32-35 Acts 17:2-3

08:36-37 Cyprian[Treatise XII.Book III.43]

08:37 John 3:18n; Irenaeus[Against Heresies Book III.12.8]; Pontius the Deacon[The Life and Passion of Cyprian 2]

08:38 Pseudepigrapha[2Baruch 6:4]

08:39 1Kings 18:12; 2Kings 2:16; Ezekiel 11:24; NT-Apocrypha[Passing of Mary]

09:01 Pseudepigrapha[Joseph and Aseneth 7:4]; Irenaeus[Against Heresies Book V.12.5]

09:01-02 Justin[Dialogue with Trypho 134]

09:01-12 Pseudepigrapha[Joseph and Aseneth 14:1-9]

09:01-19 Acts 6:12-18, 22:6-16

09:01-29 OT-Apocrypha[2Maccabees 3:24-40; 4Maccabees 4:1-14]

09:01-31 Tertullian[On Baptism 13]

09:02 OT-Apocrypha[1Maccabees 15:21]; Pseudepigrapha[Odes of Solomon 24.13, 39.13]; Tertullian[On Prayer 11]; Nag Hammadi[Gospel of Truth 18; Teachings of Silvanus 103]; NT-Apocrypha[Epistula Apostolorum 33]

09:03 Nag Hammadi[Letter of Peter to Philip 134]; NT-Apocrypha[Pseudo Clementines - Kerygmata Petrou H XVII 19.4]

09:03-05 Nag Hammadi[Apocalypse of Paul 18]

09:03-07 NT-Apocrypha[Abgar Legend]

09:03-08 Tertullian[Five Books Against Marcion Book V.1]

09:03-09 Pseudepigrapha[Joseph and Aseneth 6:1]

09:03-19 Philo[On the Virtues (179-182) cf. {Deuteronomy 30:11-14}]

09:04 Genesis 46:2; Exodus 2:4; 1Samuel 3:4; NT-Apocrypha[Epistula Apostolorum 33]

09:04-05 Origen[Gospel of John Book I.12]

09:04-08 NT-Apocrypha[Epistula Apostolorum 31]

09:05 Constitutions of the Holy Apostles[Book VIII.46]; Cyprian[Treatises Attributed to Cyprian - On the Glory of Martyrdom 4]

09:06 Ezekiel 3:22

09:07 Deuteronomy 4:12; Daniel 10:7; OT-Apocrypha[Wisdom of Solomon 18:1]

09:09 Pseudepigrapha[Joseph and Aseneth 10:17]

09:10-17 Pseudepigrapha[Joseph and Aseneth 19:1]

09:11 Tertullian[On Baptism 18]; NT-Apocrypha[Gospel of Pseudo-Matthew 3]

09:15 Jeremiah 50:25; Origen[De Principiis Book III.2.5]; Tertullian[On Modesty 14]; NT-Apocrypha[Apocalypse of Paul 1.45; Epistula Apostolorum 31]

09:15-16 Irenaeus[Against Heresies Book III.15.1]

09:16 Nag Hammadi[Letter of Peter to Philip 138]

09:18 Matthew 3:5-16n; NT-Apocrypha[Epistula Apostolorum 31]

09:20 John 3:18n; Irenaeus[Against Heresies Book III.12.9]

09:22 This section also includes topical notes for: Proving the Christ - Luke 24:25-27, 44-46; Acts 3:18-26n, 8:27-39; 17:3, 28:23; Rabbinic[Babylonian Sotah 47a]; Clement of Alexandria[Stromata Book VI.15]; Irenaeus[Against Heresies Book II.32.4, 35.4, III.Preface.1, IV.23.2, 24.1, V.14.4]; Justin[Dialogue with Trypho 39, 56-58, 77, 92-93, 123]

09:25 Joshua 2:15; 2Corinthians 11:32-33; NT-Apocrypha[Pseudo-Titus Epistle Line 298]

09:34 Acts 3:6n

09:36 Pseudepigrapha[Vision of Ezra 3]; NT-Apocrypha[History of Joseph the Carpenter 32]

09:36-43 Tertullian[On Modesty 21]

09:37 1Kings 17:19

09:38 Numbers 22:16

09:40 2Kings 4:35; Pseudepigrapha[Joseph and Aseneth 11:19]; Archelaus[Fragment of the Disputation with Manes 1]; Cyprian[Treatise VIII.6]

09:43 Tertullian[On Baptism 18]

10:01 Pseudepigrapha[Joseph and Aseneth 1:3]

10:01-04 Tertullian[On Fasting 8]

10:01-05 Irenaeus[Against Heresies Book III.12.7]

10:01-48 Constitutions of the Holy Apostles[Book VI.12]

10:01-11:30 Pseudepigrapha[Joseph and Aseneth 7:1]

10:02 OT-Apocrypha[Tobit 12:8]; Pseudepigrapha[Joseph and Aseneth 10:11; Vision of Ezra 3]; Cyprian[Treatise IV.32]; Nag Hammadi[Teachings of Silvanus 108-109, 114]

10:03-16 Pseudepigrapha[Joseph and Aseneth 14:1-6]

10:04 Cyprian[Treatise IV.32]; NT-Apocrypha[Gospel of the Nativity of Mary 3]

10:09 Pseudepigrapha[2Enoch 51:5]; Tertullian[On Fasting 10; On Prayer 25]

10:09-15 Origen[Against Celsus Book II.1]

10:10 Genesis 15:12

10:10-15 Clement of Alexandria[The Instructor Book II.1]

10:10-16 Rabbinic[Babylonian Horayot 11a]

10:12 Genesis 1:24

10:14 Leviticus 11:1-47; Ezekiel 4:14, 21:5; Origen[Against Celsus Book V.49]

10:14-15 Tertullian[Of Patience 8]

10:15 Irenaeus[Against Heresies Book III.12.7]; Novatian[On the Jewish Meats 2]

10:22 OT-Apocrypha[1Maccabees 10:25, 11:30, 33]; Nag Hammadi[Teachings of Silvanus 108-109, 114]; NT-Apocrypha[Acts of Peter 1.4]

10:24 Pseudepigrapha[Joseph and Aseneth 5:3]

10:26 OT-Apocrypha[Wisdom of Solomon 7:1]; Cyprian[Treatise IX.24]

10:28 Pseudepigrapha[Joseph and Aseneth 8:5]; Cyprian[Epistle LVIII.5]; Tertullian[On Modesty 9]

10:28-29 Irenaeus[Against Heresies Book III.12.15]

10:30 OT-Apocrypha[2Maccabees 11:8]; Tertullian[On Fasting 8]

10:34 Deuteronomy 10:17; 2Chronicles 19:7; Daniel 2:8; Romans 2:11; OT-Apocrypha[Sirach 35:12]; Pseudepigrapha[1Enoch 63:8-9; Joseph and Aseneth 7:7]; NT-Apocrypha[Apocalypse of Paul 1.16]

10:34-35 Clement of Alexandria[Stromata Book VI.8]; Irenaeus[Against Heresies Book III.12.7]; Acts 17:2-3

10:35 Psalms 15:2

10:36 Psalms 107:20, 147:18; Isaiah 52:7; Nahum 1:15, 2:1; OT-Apocrypha[Wisdom of Solomon 6:7; 8:3]; Hippolytus[Against the Heresy of One Noetus 13]

10:36-38 Matthew 28:19n

10:37 Matthew 3:5-16n

10:37-44 Irenaeus[Against Heresies Book III.12.7, 13]

10:38 1Samuel 16:13; Isaiah 58:11, 61:1; Pseudepigrapha[2Baruch 70.10; Psalms of Solomon 17.37]; Dead Sea Scrolls[**4QBless, Oh My Soul (4Q434 [4QBarki Napshi])** Fragment 1 COL I 1-7]; Origen[Against Celsus Book VIII.64]

> **Bless, my soul, the Lord for all His marvels forever, and blessed be His name. For He has saved the soul of the poor, and has not despised the humble, and He has not forgotten the oppression of the needy. He has opened His eyes on the oppressed, and has heard the cry of the orphans, and has turned His ears to their cry. In the abundance of His mercy He has shown favor to the meek, and has opened their eyes to see His ways, and *their ears* to hear His teaching. He has circumcised the foreskin of their heart, and has delivered them in His kindness, and has set their feet firmly on the path. He has not forsaken them in their many sorrows, and has not given them into the hands of the violent, nor judged them with the wicked, nor *turned* His anger against them, nor destroyed them in His wrath. *Though* the fury *of* His wrath does not grow weary, He has not judged them in the fire of His zeal, *but* in the greatness of His mercy. (Dead Sea Scrolls - 4QBless, Oh My Soul (4Q434 [4QBarki Napshi]) Fragment 1 COL I 1-7)**

10:38-41 Tacitus[The Histories 4.81]

10:39 Deuteronomy 21:22; Acts 5:30; Galatians 3:13n; Pseudepigrapha[2Enoch 7:1]; Nag Hammadi[Letter of Peter to Philip 139]

10:40 Hosea 6:2; Pseudepigrapha[Life of Abraham 11:2]; NT-Apocrypha[Pistis Sophia c. 136]

10:41 Nag Hammadi[Treatise on the Resurrection 46]

10:42 Apostolic[2Clement 1:1; Polycarp - Letter to the Philippians 2:1]; Constitutions of the Holy Apostles[Book V.20]; Irenaeus[Against Heresies Book IV.20.2]; NT-Apocrypha[Acts of Thomas 1.28, 1.30; Epistula Apostolorum 16]

10:43 Isaiah 33:24, 53:5-6; Jeremiah 31:34; Daniel 9:24; Rabbinic[Babylonian Sanhedrin 99a]; NT-Apocrypha[Kerygma Petri 3a]

10:44-46 Tertullian[On Fasting 8]

10:44-48 Anonymous[Treatise on Re-Baptism 5]

10:46-48 Matthew 3:5-16n

10:47 Cyprian[Epistle LXXI.1]; Irenaeus[Against Heresies Book III.12.15]

11:02 Justin[Dialogue with Trypho 8. 10]

11:03 Tertullian[On Modesty 9]

11:05-10 Rabbinic[Babylonian Horayot 11a]

11:06 Genesis 1:24, 30

11:15 Constitutions of the Holy Apostles[Book VI.12]

11:15-17 Anonymous[Treatise on Re-Baptism 2]

11:16 This section also includes topical notes for: Receiving the Holy Spirit - Matthew 3:5-16n; John 1:33; Acts 1:5, 2:2-4, 33, 38; Dead Sea Scrolls[4Q Word of the Luminaries (4Q504[4QDIBHAM]) COL V 15-16]

11:18 OT-Apocrypha[Wisdom of Solomon 12:19]

11:19 Acts 8:1-4

11:21 2Samuel 03:12

11:22 Isaiah 5:9

11:23 Psalms 10:17

11:26 Tacitus[The Annals 15.44]; Theophilus of Antioch[To Autolycus Book I.1]; Nag Hammadi[Gospel of Philip 62]

11:27-28 Josephus[**Antiquities 20.2.5 49-53**, 20.5.2 101]

Now her [Helena's] coming was of very great advantage to the people of Jerusalem; for a famine did oppress them at that time, and many people died for want of what was necessary to procure food. Queen Helena sent some of her servants to Alexandria with money to buy a great quantity of corn, and others of them to Cyprus, to bring a cargo of dried figs. And as soon as they came back, and had brought those provisions, which was done very quickly, she distributed food to those that were in want of it, and left a most excellent memorial behind her of this benefaction, which she bestowed on our whole nation. And when her son Izates was informed of this famine, he sent great sums of money to the principal men in Jerusalem. However, what favors this queen and king conferred upon our city Jerusalem shall be further related hereafter. (Josephus - Antiquities 20.2.5 49-53)

11:28 Acts 21:10; Constitutions of the Holy Apostles[Book VIII.2]

11:30 Acts 15:2-6n

12:02 Rabbinic[Babylonian Sanhedrin 43a]; Clement of Alexandria[Fragments from Eusebius Ecclesiastical History Book VII.2.2]

12:02-17 Clement of Alexandria[Fragments from Eusebius Ecclesiastical History Book VI.2.15]

12:03 Tacitus[The Histories 5.4]; NT-Apocrypha[Epistula Apostolorum 15]

12:03-05 Pseudepigrapha[Joseph and Aseneth 10:2]

12:04 Peter of Alexandria[Canonical Epistle 13]

12:05 OT-Apocrypha[Judith 4:9]

12:06-17 Pseudepigrapha[ArtapanusFragment 3 (PrEv 9.27.23)]

12:07 1Kings 19:5; NT-Apocrypha[Protoevangelium of James 4.1]

12:10 OT-Apocrypha[Sirach 19:26]

12:11 Exodus 18:4; Daniel 3:28, 6:23; Pseudepigrapha[Joseph and Aseneth 13:11]

12:13-15 Origen[Gospel of Matthew Book XIII.28]

12:15 Pseudepigrapha[Testament of Job 23:2]

12:17 Nag Hammadi[Gospel of Thomas 12]

12:18-19 Peter of Alexandria[Canonical Epistle 13]

12:20 1Kings 5:11, 25; Ezekiel 27:17
12:20-23 Josephus[**Antiquities 19.8.2 343-352**]

Now when Agrippa had reigned three years over all Judea, he came to the city Cesarea, which was formerly called Strato's Tower; and there he exhibited shows in honor of Caesar, upon his being informed that there was a certain festival celebrated to make vows for his safety. At this festival, a great multitude came together of the principal persons, and such as were of dignity through his province. On the second day of shows he put on a garment made wholly of silver, and of a contexture truly wonderful, and came into the theater early in the morning; at which time the silver of his garment being illuminated by the fresh reflection of the sun's rays upon it, shone out after a surprising manner, and was so resplendent as to spread a horror over those that looked intently upon him; and presently his flatterers cried out, one from one place, and another from another, (though not for his good,) that he was a god; and they added, "Be thou merciful to us; for although we have hitherto reverenced thee only as a man, yet shall we henceforth own thee as superior to mortal nature." Upon this the king did neither rebuke them, nor reject their impious flattery. But as he presently afterward looked up, he saw an owl sitting on a certain rope over his head, and immediately understood that this bird was the messenger of ill tidings, as it had once been the messenger of good tidings to him; and fell into the deepest sorrow. A severe pain also arose in his belly, and began in a most violent manner. He therefore looked upon his friends, and said, "I, whom you call a god, am commanded presently to depart this life; while Providence thus reproves the lying words you just now said to me; and I, who was by you called immortal, am immediately to be hurried away by death. But I am bound to accept what Providence allots, as it pleases God; for we have by no means lived ill, but in a splendid and happy manner." When he said this, his pain became violent. Accordingly he was carried into the palace, and the rumor went abroad every where, that he would certainly die in a little time. But the multitude presently sat in sackcloth, with their wives and children, after the law of their country, and besought God for the king's recovery. All places were also full of mourning and lamentation. Now the king rested in a high chamber, and as he saw them below lying prostrate on the ground, he could not himself forbear weeping. And when he had been quite worn out by the pain in his belly for five days, he departed this life, being in the fifty-fourth year of his age, and in the seventh year of his reign; for he reigned four years under Caius Caesar, three of them were over Philip's tetrarchy only, and on the fourth he had that of Herod added to it; and he reigned, besides those, three years under the reign of Claudius Caesar; in which time he reigned over the forementioned countries, and also had Judea added to them, as well as Samaria and Cesarea. The revenues that he received out of them were very great, no less than twelve millions of drachme. Yet did he borrow great sums from others; for he was so very liberal that his expenses exceeded his incomes, and his generosity was boundless. (Josephus - Antiquities 19.8.2 343-352)

12:22 Ezekiel 28:2, 6, 9
12:23 2Kings 19:35; Daniel 5:20; OT-Apocrypha[1Maccabees 7:41; 2Maccabees 9:9; Judith 16:17; Sirach 48:21]; Pseudepigrapha[Life of Abraham 44:9; Testament of Job 20:8]; Lactantius[Of the Manner in which the Persecutors Died 33]
13:01 Numbers 8:10; Josephus[Antiquities 15.10.5 373-379]; NT-Apocrypha[Acts of Barnabas]
13:02-03 Gregory Thaumaturgus[Sectional Confession of Faith 11]
13:05 Dionysius of Alexandria[Extant Fragments Two Books on the Promises 5]
13:06-11 Tertullian[On Idolatry 9]
13:06-12 Tertullian[On Modesty 21]
13:08 Tertullian[A Treatise on the Soul 57]
13:09 NT-Apocrypha[Epistula Apostolorum 31]
13:10 Proverbs 10:9; Jeremiah 5:27; Hosea 14:10; OT-Apocrypha[Sirach 1:30]; Origen[Gospel of John Book VI.10]; NT-Apocrypha[Epistula Apostolorum 35]
13:11 Judges 2:15; 1Samuel 12:15

13:13 Dionysius of Alexandria[Extant Fragments Two Books on the Promises 5]; NT-Apocrypha[Acts of Paul in Sidon p.35]

13:16 Nag Hammadi[Teachings of Silvanus 108-109, 114]

13:17 Exodus 1:7, 6:1, 6, 12:42, 51; Deuteronomy 4:34, 37, 5:15, 9:26, 29, 10:15; Isaiah 1:2; OT-Apocrypha[Wisdom of Solomon 19:10]; Tertullian[An Answer to the Jews 3]

13:17-19 Tertullian[On the Pallium 2]

13:18 Exodus 16:35; Numbers 14:34; Deuteronomy 1:31; Pseudepigrapha[Hellenistic Synagogal Prayers 5:12]

13:19 Deuteronomy 7:1; Joshua 14:1; Jeremiah 3:18

13:20 Judges 2:16; 1Samuel 3:20; 1Kings 6:1

13:21 1Samuel 8:5, 10, 19, 10:20-21, 24, 11:15

13:22 1Samuel 13:14, 15:23, 16:1, 12-13; Psalms 89:20-21; Isaiah 44:28; Apostolic[1Clement 18:1]; Constitutions of the Holy Apostles[Book VI.2]

13:23 2Samuel 7:12; Isaiah 11:1; Pseudepigrapha[Testament of Solomon 17:4]

13:24 Mark 1:4; Luke 3:3

13:25 Matthew 3:11; Mark 1:7; Luke 3:16; John 1:20, 27; Pseudepigrapha[Joseph and Aseneth 12:5]

13:26 Psalms 107:20, 147:18; Nag Hammadi[Teachings of Silvanus 108-109, 114]

13:27 Acts 3:18-26n; 2Corinthians 3:12-18n; Pseudepigrapha[Joseph and Aseneth 6:7]

13:28 Matthew 27:22-23; Mark 15:13-14; Luke 23:21-23; John 19:15; Pseudepigrapha[Odes of Solomon 31.8]

13:29 Matthew 27:57-61; Mark 15:42-47; Luke 23:50-56; John 19:38-42

13:31 Acts 1:3; Tacitus[The Histories 4.81]

13:33 Psalms 2:7

13:34 Isaiah 55:3

13:35 Psalms 16:10

13:36 Judges 2:10; 1Kings 2:10

13:38 Matthew 9:6n; Acts 26:18n

13:41 Habakkuk 1:5

13:46 Jude 1:21n; Tertullian[De Fuga in Persecutione 6]

13:46-47 Cyprian[Treatise XII.Book I.21]

13:47 Isaiah 42:6; 49:6; NT-Apocrypha[Epistula Apostolorum 31]

13:48 Jude 1:21n; Clement[Recognitions Book I.42]

13:50 NT-Apocrypha[Acts of Paul and Thecla 1.21; Acts of Paul in Antioch 1:1]

13:51 Matthew 10:14; Mark 6:11; Luke 9:5, 10:11

14:04 Teaching of the Twelve Apostles 11.4

14:07 Exodus 20:11

14:10 Ezekiel 2:1

14:14 OT-Apocrypha[Judith 14:16]; Teaching of the Twelve Apostles 11.4

14:14-15 Cyprian[Treatise IX.24]

14:15 Exodus 20:11; Psalms 146:6; Jeremiah 2:5; Galatians 5:24; OT-Apocrypha[4Maccabees 12:13; Wisdom of Solomon 7:3]; Pseudepigrapha[Testament of Job 2:4]; NT-Apocrypha[Acts of Paul and Thecla 1.17, 1.24; Acts of Paul in Ephesus p.2; Acts of Paul in Myra p.29]

14:15-17 Tertullian[On Repentance 5]

14:17 Leviticus 26:4; Psalms 145:16, 147:8; Jeremiah 5:24; John 6:31-58n

14:19 NT-Apocrypha[Acts of Paul and Thecla 1.21; Acts of Paul in Antioch 1:1; Acts of Peter 1.32]

14:22 Apostolic[Epistle of Barnabas 7:11]; Peter of Alexandria[Canonical Epistle 9]; Nag Hammadi[Letter of Peter to Philip 138]

14:23 Acts 15:2-6n; Pseudepigrapha[Joseph and Aseneth 13:15]; Archelaus[Disputation with Manes 51]; Clement of Alexandria[Stromata Book VI.13]

14:27 Dionysius of Alexandria[Extant Fragments Epistle Against Bishop Germanus 6]

15:01 Leviticus 12:3

15:01-20 Josephus[Antiquities 20.2.3-4 34-48]

15:01-31 Tertullian[On Idolatry 24]

15:01-41 Constitutions of the Holy Apostles[Book VI.12]

15:02-06 This section also includes topical notes for: Elders – Exodus 24:1-11; Numbers 11:24-25; Acts 11:30, 14:23, 15:22-23, 16:4, 20:17, 21:18; 1Timothy 5:17; Titus 1:5; James 5:14; 1Peter 5:1; Revelation 4:4, 10, 5:5-14, 7:11-13, 11:16, 14:3, 19:4; Pseudepigrapha[Letter of Aristeas 1.46-52]; Philo[On the Contemplative Life Or Suppliants (67)]; Rabbinic[Babylonian Qiddushin 32b]; Clement of

Alexandria[Stromata Book VI.13, VII.1]; Irenaeus[Against Heresies Book III.2.1, IV.26.2-3, 5, V.33.3];
Justin[Dialogue with Trypho 78]; Indian[Dhammapada 260-261]

15:04 OT-Apocrypha[Judith 8:26]

15:05 Hippolytus[Refutation of all Heresies Book IX.23]; Irenaeus[Against Heresies Book I.26.2];
Justin[Dialogue with Trypho 92]

15:05-21 Matthew 13:55

15:05-29 Tertullian[Five Books Against Marcion Book V.2]

15:05-31 Rabbinic[Echah Rabba on i. 1 p. 10a]

15:07 NT-Apocrypha[Epistula Apostolorum 1]

15:07-08 Acts 10:1-44; Anonymous[Treatise on Re-Baptism 2]

15:07-11 Tertullian[On Modesty 21]

15:08 Acts 2:4; NT-Apocrypha[Acts of Paul and Thecla 1.24; Acts of Peter 1.2]

15:09 Anonymous[Treatise on Re-Baptism 5]

15:10 Exodus 17:2; Rabbinic[Babylonian Berakhot 13a, 14b]; Tertullian[On Modesty 6; On Monogamy
7]

15:11 1Peter 1:10-13n

15:13-17 Anonymous[Treatise on Re-Baptism 12]

15:14 Deuteronomy 14:2; Irenaeus[Against Heresies Book IV.20.12]

15:14-15 Irenaeus[Against Heresies Book III.12.14]

15:16 Jeremiah 12:15

15:16-18 Amos 9:11-12

15:18 Isaiah 45:21

15:20 Genesis 9:4; Exodus 34:15; Leviticus 3:17, 17:10-16, 18:6-23, 26; Pseudepigrapha[1Enoch 7:5;
Joseph and Aseneth 21:10; Pseudo-Phocylides 1.31; Sibylline Oracles 2.96]; Rabbinic[Babylonian
Sanhedrin 56a, 74a]; Origen[Gospel of Matthew Book XI.12]; Teaching of the Twelve Apostles 6.3;
Nag Hammadi[The Exegesis of the Soul 127-130]; NT-Apocrypha[Clement Romance - Peter on his
Mission Journeys H VII 4.2; Epistula Apostolorum 18]

15:22-23 Acts 15:2-6n

15:23 Clement of Alexandria[The Instructor Book II.7]

15:24 Clement of Alexandria[Stromata Book IV.15]

15:28-29 Clement of Alexandria[The Instructor Book II.7]; Cyprian[Treatise XII.Book III.119];
Origen[Against Celsus Book VIII.29]

15:28-30 Tertullian[On Modesty 12]

15:29 Genesis 9:4; Leviticus 3:17, 17:10-14; OT-Apocrypha[4Maccabees 5:2]; Pseudepigrapha[Pseudo-
Phocylides 31]; Sibylline Oracles 2.96]; Teaching of the Twelve Apostles 6.3; Nag
Hammadi[Exegesis of the Soul 127-130]; NT-Apocrypha[Clement Romance - Peter on his Mission
Journeys H VII 4.2; Epistula Apostolorum 18]

15:32 Constitutions of the Holy Apostles[Book VIII.2]

15:38 Acts 13:13

15:39 NT-Apocrypha[Acts of Barnabas]

16:01-03 Clement of Alexandria[Stromata Book VI.15]; Tertullian[On Modesty 17]

16:03 Origen[Gospel of John Book X.5]; Tertullian[On Monogamy 14; Five Books Against Marcion
Book V.3]

16:04 Acts 15:2-6n; Syriac Teaching of the Apostles; Tertullian[On Modesty 12]

16:08 Irenaeus[Against Heresies Book III.14.1]

16:09 Joshua 10:6

16:13 Irenaeus[Against Heresies Book III.14.1]

16:14 OT-Apocrypha[2Maccabees 1:4]

16:14-33 Matthew 3:5-16n

16:15 NT-Apocrypha[Acts of Peter 1.29]

16:16 Cyprian[Epistle LXXV.15]; Irenaeus[Against Heresies Book I.13.3]; Tertullian[The Shows, or De
Spectaculis 26]

16:17 Revelation 12:10n; Pseudepigrapha[Joseph and Aseneth 8:2]

16:18 Lactantius[Divine Institutes Book II.16]

16:20 1Kings 18:17; Amos 7:10

16:23-30 Pseudepigrapha[Artapanus Fragment 3 (PrEv 9.27.23)]

16:23-34 Pseudepigrapha[Testament of Joseph 8:5]

16:25 Cyprian[Treatise XII.Book III.14]; Tertullian[On Prayer 24]

16:28 Pseudepigrapha[Joseph and Aseneth 8:9]

16:34 Pseudepigrapha[Joseph and Aseneth 7:1, 20:8]

16:36 Judges 18:6; Pseudepigrapha[Joseph and Aseneth 20:10]; NT-Apocrypha[Epistula Apostolorum 51]

17:02-03 This section also includes topical notes for: Opening Scripture - Genesis 3:5; Genesis 21:19; Numbers 22:31, 24:4, 16; 2Kings 6:17, 20; Job 33:15-16, 36:10-12; Psalms 40:6, 119:18, 130, 146:8; Proverbs 20:13; Isaiah 22:22, 48:8, 50:5; Matthew 7:7-8; Luke 11:9-10, 24:31-32, 45; Acts 3:18-26n, 8:32-35, 10:34-45, 26:18; 2Corinthians 3:12-18n; Ephesians 6:19; Revelation 3:7, 5:2-9; Philo[Special Laws III (6)]; Irenaeus[Against Heresies Book II.32.4, 35.4; III.Preface.1]

17:03 Acts 9:22; Justin[Dialogue with Trypho 39, 56-58, 77, 92-93, 123]

17:09-10 Peter of Alexandria[Canonical Epistle 12]

17:11 2Corinthians 3:12-18n

17:15-34 Clement of Alexandria[Stromata Book VI.18]

17:18 Acts 2:31n; Clement of Alexandria[Stromata Book I.11]

17:21 Tertullian[A Treatise on the Soul 3]

17:22-23 Clement of Alexandria[Stromata Book V.12]

17:22-28 Clement of Alexandria[Stromata Book I.19]

17:23 OT-Apocrypha[Wisdom of Solomon 14:20; 15:17]; Pseudepigrapha[2Enoch 67:3]; Hippolytus[Refutation of all Heresies Book VII.21]; Origen[Gospel of John Book X.5]

17:24 Exodus 20:11; 1Kings 8:27; Psalms 146:5; OT-Apocrypha[Tobit 7:17; Wisdom of Solomon 9:9]; Irenaeus[Against Heresies Book III.12.9]; Tertullian[Against Praxeas 16]

17:24-25 Isaiah 42:5; OT-Apocrypha[Wisdom of Solomon 9:1]; Clement of Alexandria[Stromata Book V.11]

17:25 Psalms 50:12; Isaiah 57:15; Pseudepigrapha[Joseph and Aseneth 12:1]

17:26 Genesis 1:14, 28, 10:1-32; Deuteronomy 32:8; Psalms 74:17; OT-Apocrypha[Wisdom of Solomon 7:18]

17:27 Deuteronomy 4:29; Psalms 145:18; Isaiah 55:6; Jeremiah 23:23; OT-Apocrypha[Wisdom of Solomon 13:6]

17:28 Pseudepigrapha[Aristobulus Frag 4:6]; Greek[Epimenides, de Oraculis; Aratus, Phaenomena 5 Line 5; Cleanthes]; Origen[Against Celsus Book IV.5; De Principiis Book II.1.3]; Socrates Scholasticus Book 3.16

17:29 Genesis 1:27; Deuteronomy 4:28; Isaiah 40:18-20, 44:9-20; OT-Apocrypha[Wisdom of Solomon 13:10]; Pseudepigrapha[Joseph and Aseneth 2:3]

17:30 OT-Apocrypha[Sirach 28:7]; Pseudepigrapha[Joseph and Aseneth 6:7]; Clement of Alexandria[Stromata Book VI.6]; NT-Apocrypha[Kerygma Petri 3c]

17:31 Psalms 9:9, 96:13, 98:9; NT-Apocrypha[Martyrdom of the Holy Apostle Paul 1.4]

17:32 Acts 2:31n; Pseudepigrapha[Pseudo-Phocylides 104]; Tertullian[On the Resurrection of the Flesh 39]

18:01-02 Josephus[**Antiquities 18.3.5 81-84**]

> There was a man who was a Jew, but had been driven away from his own country by an accusation laid against him for transgressing their laws, and by the fear he was under of punishment for the same; but in all respects a wicked man. He, then living at Rome, professed to instruct men in the wisdom of the laws of Moses. He procured also three other men, entirely of the same character with himself, to be his partners. These men persuaded Fulvia, a woman of great dignity, and one that had embraced the Jewish religion, to send purple and gold to the temple at Jerusalem; and when they had gotten them, they employed them for their own uses, and spent the money themselves, on which account it was that they at first required it of her. Whereupon Tiberius, who had been informed of the thing by Saturninus, the husband of Fulvia, who desired inquiry might be made about it, ordered all the Jews to be banished out of Rome; at which time the consuls listed four thousand men out of them, and sent them to the island Sardinia; but punished a greater number of them, who were unwilling to become soldiers, on account of keeping the laws of their forefathers. Thus were these Jews banished out of the city by the wickedness of four men. (Josephus - Antiquities 18.3.5 81-84)

18:05 Matthew 3:5-16n
18:06 Pseudepigrapha[Life of Abraham 6:11]
18:09 Joshua 1:9; Jeremiah 1:19; NT-Apocrypha[Acts of Paul in Myra p.31; Acts of Thomas 1.1]
18:09-10 Isaiah 41:10, 43:5; Jeremiah 1:8
18:18 Numbers 6:2, 9, 18; Origen[Gospel of Matthew Book XI.8]
18:25 Matthew 3:5-16n
18:27 1Peter 1:10-13n
18:28 Acts 2:23n; 2Corinthians 3:12-18n; Methodius[Oration Concerning Simeon and Anna 6]
19:01 Pseudepigrapha[Testament of Solomon 8:11]
19:01-07 Tertullian[On Baptism 10]
19:02 Origen[Gospel of John Book VI.17]
19:03-05 Matthew 3:5-16n
19:04 Mark 1:4, 8; Luke 3:4, 16; John 1:26-27
19:09 Tertullian[On Prayer 11]; NT-Apocrypha[Acts of Thomas 1.131]
19:11-17 Justin[Second Apology 6]
19:13 Josephus[Antiquities 8.2.5 45-48]
19:14 Constitutions of the Holy Apostles[Book VIII.2]
19:15 Cyprian[Epistle LXXV.15]
19:15-16 Lactantius[Divine Institutes Book II.16]
19:18 Pseudepigrapha[Joseph and Aseneth 10:12]
19:19 Deuteronomy 18:10-14; Pseudepigrapha[Pseudo-Phocylides 149]
19:23 Tertullian[On Prayer 11]
19:24 NT-Apocrypha[Acts of Paul in Ephesus p.1]
19:24-27 Pseudepigrapha[Testament of Solomon 7:5, 8:11]
19:26-30 Peter of Alexandria[Canonical Epistle 13]
19:27 Isaiah 40:17; OT-Apocrypha[Wisdom of Solomon 3:17]
19:28 OT-Apocrypha[Bel and the Dragon 18:41]; Pseudepigrapha[Sibylline Oracles 5.293]
19:34 Pseudepigrapha[Testament of Solomon 7:5, 8:11]
20:05-06 Irenaeus[Against Heresies Book III.14.1]
20:06 Tacitus[The Histories 5.4]
20:07 1Corinthians 10:16-18n
20:07-09 Origen[Gospel of John Book V.4]
20:08 Pseudepigrapha[Joseph and Aseneth 14:9]
20:09 NT-Apocrypha[Martyrdom of the Holy Apostle Paul 1.1]
20:09-12 Tertullian[On Modesty 21]
20:10 1Kings 17:21
20:17 Acts 15:2-6n
20:24 2Timothy 4:7; 1Peter 1:10-13n; Hippolytus[Refutation of all Heresies Book IX.18]
20:25 Pseudepigrapha[Joseph and Aseneth 13:11]; Irenaeus[Against Heresies Book III.14.2]; NT-Apocrypha[Acts of Peter 1.1]

20:26 OT-Apocrypha[Susanna 1:46]; Pseudepigrapha[Life of Abraham 6:11]

20:28 Psalms 74:2; Apostolic[1Clement 7:4]; Constitutions of the Holy Apostles[Book II.57]; Irenaeus[Against Heresies Book III.14.2]; Tertullian[On Modesty 7]

20:28-31 Hippolytus[Refutation of all Heresies Book IX.1]

20:29 NT-Apocrypha[Acts of Peter 1.8; Epistula Apostolorum 44]

20:29-11 Cyprian[Epistle V.3]

20:32 This section also includes topical notes for: Inheritance - Deuteronomy 10:9, 12:9, 18:2, 33:3-4; Joshua 13:33; Psalms 2:7-8; Acts 26:18; Galatians 3:18; Ephesians 1:14-18, 5:5; Colossians 1:12, 3:24; Hebrews 9:15, 11:8; 1Peter 1:4, 10-13n; OT-Apocrypha[Wisdom of Solomon 5:5]; Pseudepigrapha[2Baruch 44.13-15; 4Ezra 7.6-9, 7.96-97; Hellenistic Synagogal Prayers 2.11; Joseph and Aseneth 13:15; Odes of Solomon 11.16-18, 23.19]; Philo[Every Good Man Is Free (42-43) cf. {Exodus 4:16, 7:1}; On Flight And Finding (55-58) cf. {Deuteronomy 4:4, 30:20}; Special Laws II (124-128) cf. {Numbers 36:1-12}]; Rabbinic[Babylonian (Sanhedrin 91b, 100a cf. {Proverbs 8:21}; Zebahim 119a)]; Plato[Phaedo 83d-e, 108b-c]; Clement of Alexandria[Exhortation to the Heathen 9-10, 12; Fragments from Macarius Chrysocephalus Parable of the Prodigal son 1-2; Fragments from the Latin Translation of Cassiodorus Comments on Jude; Stromata Book VI.12, 14, VII.2, 10; Who is the Rich Man that shall be Saved 3]; Irenaeus[Against Heresies Book III.5.3, IV.8.1-3, 9.1, 24.2, 26.1, 30.4, 41.3, V.1.3, 9.4, 30.4, 32.1-2, 33.1, 36.3; Demonstration of the Apostolic Preaching 46; Fragments from the Lost Works 19, 36]; Justin[Dialogue with Trypho 25-26, 113, 116, 120, 130, 135, 139-140; Fragments from the Lost Writings of Justin 5]; Lactantius[Divine Institutes Book IV.20]; Nag Hammadi[Apocryphon of John 25-26; Gospel of Philip 52, 59; Gospel of Thomas 3; Gospel of Truth 20, 42; Tripartite Tractate 131]

20:33 1Samuel 12:3; Pseudepigrapha[Joseph and Aseneth 2:4]

20:35 Matthew 10:8; OT-Apocrypha[Sirach 4:31]; Apostolic[1Clement 2:1]; Constitutions of the Holy Apostles[Book IV.3, VI.23]

20:37 Genesis 33:4, 45:14

20:38 Peter of Alexandria[Genuine Acts of Peter 3]; NT-Apocrypha[Acts of Peter 1.1]

21:08 Acts 6:5, 8:5

21:09 Joel 2:28

21:09-10 Constitutions of the Holy Apostles[Book VIII.2]

21:10 Acts 11:28

21:11 Tertullian[Scorpiace 15]

21:13 Tertullian[De Fuga in Persecutione 6]

21:14 Apostolic[Martyrdom of Polycarp 7:1]

21:18 Acts 15:2-6n; Clement of Alexandria[Fragments from Eusebius Ecclesiastical History Book VI.2.1]; Nag Hammadi[Gospel of Thomas 12]

21:20-26 Tertullian[On Monogamy 14]

21:23-24 Numbers 6:5, 13-21

21:23-26 Tertullian[Five Books Against Marcion Book V.3]

21:24 Numbers 6:9; Origen[Gospel of John Book X.5]

21:25 Acts 15:29; Pseudepigrapha[Sibylline Oracles 2.96]; Nag Hammadi[Exegesis of the Soul 127-130]; NT-Apocrypha[Clement Romance - Peter on his Mission Journeys H VII 4.2]

21:26 Numbers 6:1-21; OT-Apocrypha[1Maccabees 3:49]; Josephus[Antiquities 15.11.5 417; War 5.5.2 193-4, 6.2.4 124-126]; Origen[Against Celsus Book II.1; Gospel of John Book X.5; Gospel of Matthew Book XI.8]

21:28 Ezekiel 44:7

21:29 Acts 20:4

21:37-38 Josephus[**Antiquities 20.8.6 169-172**; War 2.13.5 261]

These works, that were done by the robbers, filled the city with all sorts of impiety. And now these impostors and deceivers persuaded the multitude to follow them into the wilderness, and pretended that they would exhibit manifest wonders and signs, that should be performed by the providence of God. And many that were prevailed on by them suffered the punishments of their folly; for Felix brought them back, and then punished them. Moreover, there came out of Egypt about this time to Jerusalem one that said he was a prophet, and advised the multitude of the common people to go along with him to the Mount of Olives, as it was called, which lay over against the city, and at the distance of five furlongs. He said further, that he would show them from hence how, at his command, the walls of Jerusalem would fall down; and he promised them that he would procure them an entrance into the city through those walls, when they were fallen down. Now when Felix was informed of these things, he ordered his soldiers to take their weapons, and came against them with a great number of horsemen and footmen from Jerusalem, and attacked the Egyptian and the people that were with him. He also slew four hundred of them, and took two hundred alive. But the Egyptian himself escaped out of the fight, but did not appear any more. And again the robbers stirred up the people to make war with the Romans, and said they ought not to obey them at all; and when any persons would not comply with them, they set fire to their villages, and plundered them. (Josephus - Antiquities 20.8.6 169-172)

21:39 NT-Apocrypha[Epistula Apostolorum 31, 33]
22:03 Acts 5:34; Pseudepigrapha[Joseph and Aseneth 4:7]; NT-Apocrypha[Epistula Apostolorum 31, 33]
22:05 Acts 8:3, 26:9-11; Clement[Recognitions Book I.71]
22:05-06 NT-Apocrypha[Epistula Apostolorum 33]
22:06-16 Acts 6:12-18; 9:1-19
22:07 NT-Apocrypha[Epistula Apostolorum 31]
22:08 Irenaeus[Against Heresies Book III.15.1]
22:09 OT-Apocrypha[Wisdom of Solomon 18:1]
22:10 Pseudepigrapha[Joseph and Aseneth 14:8]
22:11 Deuteronomy 28:28; Tertullian[Against Praxeas 15]; NT-Apocrypha[Epistula Apostolorum 31]
22:14 Exodus 3:15
22:16 Joel 2:32; Matthew 3:5-16n; Cyprian[The Seventh Council of Carthage under Cyprian]
22:23 Pseudepigrapha[Joseph and Aseneth 10:14; Testament of Job 28:3]
22:28 Tertullian[On Modesty 22]
23:01 Hippolytus[Refutation of all Heresies Book IX.21]; NT-Apocrypha[Epistula Apostolorum 38]
23:02 Acts 24:1; Josephus[Antiquities 20.5.2 103, 20.6.2 131, 20.9.2 205; War 2.12.6 243]; Tertullian[On Modesty 14]; NT-Apocrypha[Acts of Andrew and Matthias]
23:03 Leviticus 19:15; Deuteronomy 28:22; Ezekiel 13:10-15
23:04-05 Cyprian[Epistle LIV.4, LXIV.2, LXVIII.3]
23:05 Exodus 22:27-28
23:06 Acts 26:5; Philippians 3:5; Tertullian[On the Resurrection of the Flesh 39]
23:06-08 Acts 2:31n
23:06-09 Josephus[Antiquities 13.5.9 171-173, **18.1.2-4 11-17**; War 2.8.14 162-166]; Hippolytus[Refutation of all Heresies Book IX.23-24]

Now, for the Pharisees, they live meanly, and despise delicacies in diet; and they follow the conduct of reason; and what that prescribes to them as good for them they do; and they think they ought earnestly to strive to observe reason's dictates for practice. They also pay a respect to such as are in years; nor are they so bold as to contradict them in any thing which they have introduced; and when they determine that all things are done by fate, they do not take away the freedom from men of acting as they think fit; since their notion is, that it hath pleased God to make a temperament, whereby what he wills is done, but so that the will of man can act virtuously or viciously. They also believe that souls have an immortal rigor in them, and that under the earth there will be rewards or punishments, according as they have lived virtuously or viciously in this life; and the latter are to be detained in an everlasting prison, but that the former shall have power to revive and live again; on account of which doctrines they are able greatly to persuade the body of the people; and whatsoever they do about Divine worship, prayers, and sacrifices, they perform them according to their direction; insomuch that the cities give great attestations to them on account of their entire virtuous conduct, both in the actions of their lives and their discourses also. But the doctrine of the Sadducees is this: That souls die with the bodies; nor do they regard the observation of any thing besides what the law enjoins them; for they think it an instance of virtue to dispute with those teachers of philosophy whom they frequent: but this doctrine is received but by a few, yet by those still of the greatest dignity. But they are able to do almost nothing of themselves; for when they become magistrates, as they are unwillingly and by force sometimes obliged to be, they addict themselves to the notions of the Pharisees, because the multitude would not otherwise bear them. (Josephus - Antiquities 18.1.2-4 11-17)

23:08 Matthew 22:23; Mark 12:18; Luke 20:27; Josephus[Antiquities 18.1.4 16-17; War 2.8.14 162-166]; Rabbinic[Babylonian Sanhedrin 90a]; Justin[On the Resurrection 9]; Tertullian[Against All Heresies 1]

23:11 Pseudepigrapha[2Enoch 1:7]; NT-Apocrypha[Acts of Thomas 1.1]

23:34 NT-Apocrypha[Epistula Apostolorum 33]

24:01 Acts 23:2; Josephus[Antiquities 20.5.2 103, 20.6.2 131, 20.9.2 205; War 2.12.6 243]

24:02 OT-Apocrypha[2Maccabees 4:6]

24:03 Apostolic[Didache 9:1]

24:05 1Samuel 25:25; Psalms 1:1; Proverbs 22:10, 29:8; Rabbinic[Babylonian Shabbat 116a]

24:10 Josephus[War 2.12.8 247]

24:14 Acts 3:18n; OT-Apocrypha[4Maccabees 12:17]; Pseudepigrapha[Odes of Solomon 11:3]

24:15 Daniel 12:2; Acts 2:31n; Lactantius[Divine Institutes Book II.13]; NT-Apocrypha[Epistula Apostolorum 39]

24:16 Proverbs 3:4; Romans 2:15n; Hippolytus[Refutation of all Heresies Book IX.21]

24:17 Pseudepigrapha[Vision of Ezra 3]

24:18 Acts 21:17-28

24:21 Acts 2:31n, 23:6

24:22 Pseudepigrapha[Odes of Solomon 11:3]

24:24-25 Josephus[**Antiquities 20.7.1-2 137-144**]; Tacitus[The Histories 5.10]

When Agrippa had received these countries as the gift of Caesar, he gave his sister Drusilla in marriage to Azizus, king of Emesa, upon his consent to be circumcised; for Epiphanes, the son of king Antiochus, had refused to marry her, because, after he had promised her father formerly to come over to the Jewish religion, he would not now perform that promise. He also gave Mariamne in marriage to Archelaus, the son of Helcias, to whom she had formerly been betrothed by Agrippa her father; from which marriage was derived a daughter, whose name was Bernice. But for the marriage of Drusilla with Azizus, it was in no long time afterward dissolved upon the following occasion: While Felix was procurator of Judea, he saw this Drusilla, and fell in love with her; for she did indeed exceed all other women in beauty; and he sent to her a person whose name was Simon - one of his friends; a Jew he was, and by birth a Cypriot, and one who pretended to be a magician, and endeavored to persuade her to forsake her present husband, and marry him; and promised, that if she would not refuse him, he would make her a happy woman. Accordingly she acted ill, and because she was desirous to avoid her sister Bernice's envy, for she was very ill treated by her on account of her beauty, was prevailed upon to transgress the laws of her forefathers, and to marry Felix; and when he had had a son by her, he named him Agrippa. But after what manner that young man, with his wife, perished at the conflagration of the mountain Vesuvius, in the days of Titus Caesar, shall be related hereafter. (Josephus - Antiquities 20.7.1-2 137-144)

24:25 NT-Apocrypha[Acts of Paul and Thecla 1.17]
24:26 Tertullian[De Fuga in Persecutione 12]
24:27-25:02 Josephus[Antiquities 20.8.9-10 182-186]
25:13 Acts 26:27-28; Josephus[Antiquities 20.7.3 145]
26:04-05 Josephus[Life 1.2 12]
26:05 Acts 23:6; Philippians 3:5
26:06 NT-Apocrypha[Epistula Apostolorum 32]
26:07 NT-Apocrypha[Epistula Apostolorum 30]
26:09 Rabbinic[Babylonian Abodah Zarah 17a]
26:11 Acts 8:3; 22:4-5
26:12 NT-Apocrypha[Epistula Apostolorum 33]
26:12-18 Acts 2:6-16, 9:1-19
26:13 Matthew 17:1-21n
26:14 Greek[Euripedes, Bacchae 794s]; NT-Apocrypha[Epistula Apostolorum 31, 33]
26:15 Irenaeus[Against Heresies Book III.15.1]
26:16 Ezekiel 2:1; Pseudepigrapha[4Ezra 2.38; Joseph and Aseneth 14:8]
26:16-18 Ephesians 4:32n
26:17 1Chronicles 16:35; Jeremiah 1:7-8, 19
26:17-18 Clement of Alexandria[Stromata Book I.19]; NT-Apocrypha[Epistula Apostolorum 31]
26:18 This section also includes topical notes for: Forgiveness-Pardoning of Sin-Turning to God –
Exodus 3:3-6; Deuteronomy 30:10, 33:3-4; Psalms 7:11-13, 22:27, 80:3-19, 85:4, 119:58-60; Proverbs 1:23; Isaiah 6:10, 31:6, 35:5, 42:7, 16, 59:20, 61:1; Jeremiah 18:8, 23:22, 26:3, 31:18-19, 34:15, 44:5; Ezekiel 14:6, 18:21, 27-32, 33:9-14, 19; Daniel 9:13, 12:3; Hosea 12:6; Joel 2:12-13, Jonah 3:8-10, Malachi 2:6, 4:6; Matthew 9:6n; Mark 2:10; Luke 5:24, 7:48-50; Acts 5:31n, 13:38, 17:2-3, 20:32n, Ephesians 1:17; Colossians 1:14, 2:13; James 5:15; 1John 1:9, 2:12; OT-Apocrypha[Wisdom of Solomon 5:5]; Pseudepigrapha[4Ezra 7.133; Hellenistic Synagogal Prayers 11.6; Joseph and Aseneth 8:9; Jubilees 1.15; Letter of Aristeas 1.2; Odes of Solomon 11.9-21, 21.3; Testament of Asher 1.1-2.10; Testament of Dan 5.9-11; Testament of Joseph 20.2-3; Testament of Levi 19.2; Testament of Zebulon 9.7-8]; Philo[Fragments Preserved By Antonius Ser. Viii.]; Rabbinic[Babylonian (Baba Batra 25a; Sanhedrin 38b cf. {Exodus 23:21, 24:1})]; Plato[Apology 31c-d; Republic VII 514a-517a, **VII 518a-c**, VII 520c, 532b-c, 533d-e]; Apostolic[1Clement 59:2]; Clement of Alexandria[Exhortation to the Heathen 1, 8, 11; Fragments from Macarius Chrysocephalus Parable of the Prodigal son 2; Fragments from the Latin Translation of Cassiodorus Comments on Jude; Stromata Book II.23, IV.6, VI.6, VII.7; The Instructor Book I.1, 6; Who is the Rich Man that shall be Saved 39];

Hippolytus[Refutation of all Heresies Book IX.18]; Irenaeus[Against Heresies Book II.32.2, III.25.7, IV.Preface.1, 29.2, 39.4, 40.1, 41.3, V.24.4; Demonstration of the Apostolic Preaching 41]; Justin[Dialogue with Trypho 16, 107]; Origen[Gospel of John Book II.14]; Tertullian[An Answer to the Jews 13]; Theophilus of Antioch[To Autolycus Book III.11]; Nag Hammadi[Apocryphon of John 1; Exegesis of the Soul 131-132; Gospel of Truth 21-22, 30, 35; Teachings of Silvanus 93-94, 103; Testimony of Truth 30, 40-41; Trimorphic Protennoia 49; Tripartite Tractate 130]; NT-Apocrypha[Epistula Apostolorum 5, 21, 33, 38-39, 42]; Indian[Dhammapada 87-88, 146]

> Any one who has common sense will remember that the bewilderments of the eyes are of two kinds, and arise from two causes, either from coming out of the light or from going into the light, which is true of the mind's eye, quite as much as of the bodily eye; and he who remembers this when he sees any one whose vision is perplexed and weak, will not be too ready to laugh; he will first ask whether that soul of man has come out of the brighter light, and is unable to see because unaccustomed to the dark, or having turned from darkness to the day is dazzled by excess of light. And he will count the one happy in his condition and state of being, and he will pity the other; ...But then, if I am right, certain professors of education must be wrong when they say that they can put a knowledge into the soul which was not there before, like sight into blind eyes...Whereas, our argument shows that the power and capacity of learning exists in the soul already; and that just as the eye was unable to turn from darkness to light without the whole body, so too the instrument of knowledge can only by the movement of the whole soul be turned from the world of becoming into that of being, and learn by degrees to endure the sight of being, and of the brightest and best of being, or in other words, of the good...And must there not be some art which will effect conversion in the easiest and quickest manner; not implanting the faculty of sight, for that exists already, but has been turned in the wrong direction, and is looking away from the truth? (Plato - Republic VII 518a-c)

26:20 Acts 3:19n, 9:20, 28-29
26:22 Rabbinic[Babylonian Sanhedrin 99a]; Clement of Alexandria[Stromata Book VI.15]; Irenaeus[Against Heresies Book IV.10.1]; Tertullian[On the Resurrection of the Flesh 39]
26:22-23 Acts 2:23n, 3:18-26n
26:22-27 1Corinthians 2:6-16n
26:23 Isaiah 42:6, 49:6; Acts 2:31n; Irenaeus[Against Heresies Book III.19.3]
26:25 OT-Apocrypha[Judith 10:13]
26:26 Tertullian[Fragment Concerning the Execreable god of the Heathen 1]
26:27-28 Acts 25:13n
26:28 1Kings 21:7
27:01-44 Irenaeus[Against Heresies Book III.14.1]
27:09 Leviticus 16:29
27:19 Jonah 1:5
27:34 1Samuel 14:45; 2Samuel 14:11
27:35 Tertullian[On Prayer 24]
27:40 NT-Apocrypha[Acts of Paul from Corinth to Italy p.7]
27:41 NT-Apocrypha[Letter of Clement to James 14.4]
28:01-06 Pseudepigrapha[Testament of Joseph 6:2]
28:02 Tertullian[On Idolatry 20]
28:03 Tertullian[Scorpiace 1]
28:11 Irenaeus[Against Heresies Book III.14.1]
28:17-29 Tertullian[Five Books in Reply to Marcion Book II.42]
28:19 Acts 25:11
28:23 Acts 3:18-26n, 9:22; Irenaeus[Against Heresies Book IV.10.1]
28:25 Hippolytus[The Discourse on the Holy Theophany 8]; NT-Apocrypha[Abgar Legend]
28:26 Pseudepigrapha[Sibylline Oracles 1.360, 1.369]; Methodius[Oration Concerning Simeon and Anna 11]
28:26-27 Isaiah 6:9-10; Tertullian[On Fasting 6]
28:27 Clement of Alexandria[Exhortation to the Heathen 10]

28:28 Psalms 67:2-3, 98:3; Isaiah 40:5; NT-Apocrypha[Epistula Apostolorum 31]
28:31 Nag Hammadi[Letter of Peter to Philip 134-5]

Cross Reference Index: Romans

01:01 Psalms 78:70, 105:26; Tertullian[On Modesty 14]

01:01-03 Acts 3:18-26n

01:01-04 Irenaeus[Against Heresies Book III.16.3]; Origen[De Principiis Book II.4.2]

01:01-05 Origen[Gospel of John Book II.6]

01:02 2Corinthians 3:12-18n; Rabbinic[**Babylonian Berakhot 34b**; Babylonian Sanhedrin 99a]; Apostolic[Ignatius - Letter to the Magnesians 9:2, Letter to the Philadelphians 5:2, 9:2; Polycarp - Letter to the Philippians 6:3; Epistle of Barnabas 1:7, 3:6]

R. Hiyya bar Abba said R. Yohanan said, " All of the prophets prophesied only concerning the days of the Messiah, but as to the world that will come [thereafter], 'Eye has not seen, God, beside you.'" (Talmud - Babylonian Berakhot 34b, *The Babylonian Talmud a Translation and Commentary*, Jacob Neusner; Hendrickson Publishers, Inc., 2005)

01:03 2Samuel 7:12-14a; 1Kings 5:5; Matthew 22:45; Mark 12:37; Luke 1:32, 20:44; Pseudepigrapha[Hellenistic Synagogal Prayers 6:2]; Origen[Gospel of John Book X.4; Gospel of Matthew Book XI.17]; Tertullian[On the Flesh of Christ 22]; NT-Apocrypha[Acts of Paul in Philippi 3.5]

01:03-04 Matthew 28:19n; Irenaeus[Against Heresies Book III.22.1]; Tertullian[Against Praxeas 27]

01:04 Exodus 3:14; John 3:18n; Acts 2:31n; Pseudepigrapha[Testament of Levi 18:7]; Origen[Gospel of Matthew Book XI.17]

01:05 1Peter 1:10-13n; Pseudepigrapha[Hellenistic Synagogal Prayers 11:3]

01:07 Numbers 6:25-26; John 1:18n; Pseudepigrapha[2Baruch 78:3]; Tertullian[Against Praxeas 13]

01:08 Exodus 3:14; Anonymous[Treatise on Re-Baptism 9]; Cyprian[Epistle XXX.2]; Origen[Gospel of Matthew Book XIII.20]; Tertullian[Against Praxeas 28]

01:09 Deuteronomy 11:13; 1Samuel 12:5; Pseudepigrapha[2Baruch 86:1]

01:11-12 Clement of Alexandria[Stromata Book V.1, 4]

01:13 Acts 19:21

01:14 Rabbinic[Mishnah Aboth 4:1]; Origen[Against Celsus Book III.54; Gospel of John Book IV.2]

01:16 Psalms 119:46; Revelation 12:10n; Irenaeus[Against Heresies Book III.5.3]

01:16-18 Tertullian[Five Books Against Marcion Book V.13]

01:17 Psalms 98:2; Isaiah 51:5, 8; Habakkuk 2:4; Pseudepigrapha[2Baruch 54:17]; Rabbinic[Babylonian Makkot 23b cf. {Habbukkuk 2:4}]; Clement of Alexandria[Stromata Book II.6, V.1]; Hippolytus[Treatise on Christ and Antichrist 64]; Irenaeus[Against Heresies Book IV.34.2]; Tertullian[On Exhortation to Chastity 7]

01:18 Psalms 73:6; Proverbs 11:5; Pseudepigrapha[1Enoch 91:7]; Irenaeus[Against Heresies Book IV.27.4]

01:18-23 Origen[Against Celsus Book VI.3]

01:18-32 Philo[On the Contemplative Life Or Suppliants (59-62)]

01:19 Pseudepigrapha[2Baruch 54:17]; Origen[Against Celsus Book IV.30]

01:19-21 Lactantius[Divine Institutes Book II.3]

01:19-22 Origen[Against Celsus Book III.47]

01:19-32 OT-Apocrypha[Wisdom of Solomon 13:1-15:19]

01:20 Job 12:7-9; Psalms 8:4, 19:2; Isaiah 40:26, 28; Clement[Recognitions Book II.21]; Novatian[Treatise Concerning the Trinity 3]; Origen[Against Celsus Book VI.59, VII.37; Gospel of Matthew Book XI.18]; Tatian[Address to the Greeks 4]; Tertullian[A Treatise on the Soul 18; Five Books Against Marcion Book V.16]; Nag Hammadi[Tripartite Tractate 54, 56-7]

01:20-21 Pseudepigrapha[2Baruch 54:18]

01:20-23 Tertullian[Five Books Against Marcion Book IV.25]

01:20-27 Hippolytus[Refutation of all Heresies Book V.2]

01:21 2Kings 17:15; Psalms 76:6, 94:11; Jeremiah 2:5; OT-Apocrypha[2Esdras 8:60; Wisdom of Solomon 13:1]; Pseudepigrapha[1Enoch 99:8]; Irenaeus[Against Heresies Book IV.33.1]; Methodius[Banquet of the Ten Virgins 8.13]; Origen[Against Celsus Book III.47, VII.47]

01:21-23 Lactantius[Divine Institutes Book IV.1]; Origen[Against Celsus Book IV.30]

01:21-25 Pseudepigrapha[Hellenistic Synagogal Prayers 12:68]; Clement of Alexandria[Exhortation to the Heathen 8]

01:22 Jeremiah 10:14; Clement of Alexandria[Stromata Book I.27]; Lactantius[Divine Institutes Book VI.6]; Nag Hammadi[Teachings of Silvanus 111-112]

01:22-23 Origen[Against Celsus Book III.73]

01:23 Deuteronomy 4:15-19; Psalms 106:20; Jeremiah 2:11; OT-Apocrypha[Wisdom of Solomon 11:15, 12:24]; Nag Hammadi[Letter of Peter to Philip 133]

01:23-25 Origen[Against Celsus Book VII.47]

01:24 Origen[Against Celsus Book V.32]

01:25 Jeremiah 13:25, 16:19; Pseudepigrapha[Assumption of Moses 5:4; Hellenistic Synagogal Prayers 12:85]; Apology of Aristides 3; Constitutions of the Holy Apostles[Book V.12]; Irenaeus[Against Heresies Book II.9.2]; Origen[Against Celsus Book VI.4]; Tertullian[On the Resurrection of the Flesh 26]

01:25-26 Cyprian[Treatise XII.Book III.10]

01:26 Pseudepigrapha[Pseudo-Phocylides 192; Sibylline Oracles 3.185; Testament of Joseph 7:8]; Plato[Laws VIII 836c-e, 840d-e]; Origen[Against Celsus Book V.32]; Tertullian[The Chaplet, or De Corona 6]

01:26-27 Clement of Alexandria[The Instructor Book II.10]; Cyprian[Epistle I.9]

01:27 Leviticus 18:22, 20:13; Pseudepigrapha[Apocalypse of Elijah 1:16; Pseudo-Phocylides 190]; Origen[Against Celsus Book VII.49]

01:28 OT-Apocrypha[2Maccabees 6:4; 3Maccabees 4:16]; Constitutions of the Holy Apostles[Book V.12]; Irenaeus[Against Heresies Book IV.29.1]; Origen[Against Celsus Book V.32, VII.48]; Tatian[Address to the Greeks 40]; Tertullian[Five Books in Reply to Marcion Book II.48]

01:29 Pseudepigrapha[Pseudo-Phocylides 71]

01:29-31 OT-Apocrypha[4Maccabees 1:26, 2:15]; Pseudepigrapha[Sibylline Oracles 1.175]

01:30 Pseudepigrapha[Vision of Ezra 50]

01:30-32 Cyprian[Epistle LXVII.9]

01:32 Pseudepigrapha[2Enoch 10:4]; Apostolic[1Clement 35]; Fabian[First Epistle]

02:01 Matthew 7:1; Luke 6:37

02:01-03 Cyprian[Treatise XII.Book III.21]

02:02 Tertullian[Five Books Against Marcion Book V.13]

02:03 Pseudepigrapha[Psalms of Solomon 15:8]

02:04 OT-Apocrypha[Wisdom of Solomon 11:23]; Pseudepigrapha[Hellenistic Synagogal Prayers 11:4; Testament of Abraham 10:14]; Irenaeus[Demonstration of the Apostolic Preaching 8]; NT-Apocrypha[Apocalypse of Sedrach 14]

02:04-05 Origen[De Principiis Book III.1.11]

02:04-06 Cyprian[Treatise IX.4, XII.Book III.35]

02:04-07 Irenaeus[Against Heresies Book IV.37.1]

02:04-10 Origen[De Principiis Book III.1.6]

02:05 Deuteronomy 9:27; Psalms 110:5; Zephaniah 1:14; Luke 6:45n; Pseudepigrapha[Apocalypse of Elijah 1:19, 5:24; Psalms of Solomon 9:5; Testament of Levi 3:2]; Irenaeus[Against Heresies Book IV.33.15]

02:05-11 Apostolic[Epistle of Barnabas 4:12]

02:06 Psalms 62:12-13; Proverbs 24:12; OT-Apocrypha[Sirach 16:14]; Pseudepigrapha[Joseph and Aseneth 28:3]; Clement of Alexandria[Stromata Book IV.22]; Tertullian[An Answer to the Jews 9]; NT-Apocrypha[Epistula Apostolorum 29]

02:07 Jude 1:21n; Pythagoras[Golden Verses Line 71]

02:07-09 Theophilus of Antioch[To Autolycus Book I.14]

02:09 Deuteronomy 28:53; Isaiah 28:22]

02:11 Deuteronomy 10:17; 2Chronicles 19:7; Acts 10:34; OT-Apocrypha[Sirach 35:12]; Pseudepigrapha[1Enoch 63:8-9]; Anonymous[Treatise Against the Heretic Novatian 16]; Origen[De Principiis Book I.7.5, 8.4]; Peter of Alexandria[Canonical Epistle 7]; NT-Apocrypha[Acts of Peter and Paul; Epistula Apostolorum 24]

In his judgments he pays no respect to persons; and we must depart from his presence, on account of our evil deeds. (Pseudepigrapha - 1Enoch 63:8-9)

02:12 Cyprian[Treatise XII.Book III.99]

02:12-16 Tertullian[Five Books Against Marcion Book V.13]

02:13 Cyprian[Treatise XII.Book III.96]; Dionysius of Alexandria[Extant Fragments Epistle to Dionysius Bishop of Rome - Book II.10]; Tertullian[On Exhortation to Chastity 7]

02:14 Pseudepigrapha[Apocalypse of Sedrach 15:4; Hellenistic Synagogal Prayers 11:3, 12:43]; Plato[Laws VIII 836c-e, 840d-e]; Clement of Alexandria[Stromata Book II.9]; Tertullian[The Chaplet, or De Corona 6]

02:14-15 Pseudepigrapha[2Baruch 48:40, 57.2-3]; Archelaus[Disputation with Manes 28]; Clement of Alexandria[Stromata Book I.19]; Justin[Dialogue with Trypho 93]

02:14-16 Philo[On Husbandry (179) cf. {Numbers 6:9}]

02:15 This section also includes topical notes for: Conscience - Isaiah 51:7; Jeremiah 31:33; Acts 24:16; 1Peter 3:21; OT-Apocrypha[Wisdom of Solomon 17:11]; Pseudepigrapha[2Baruch 57:2; Testament of Reuben 4:3]; Philo[Fragments Extracted From the Parallels of John of Damascus Page 349. A-B.; On The Unchangeableness of God (134-135) cf. {Leviticus 14:35}]; Rabbinic[Siphri Numbers 115 P.35]; Clement of Alexandria[Exhortation to the Heathen 10]; Hippolytus[Refutation of all Heresies Book IX.21]; Irenaeus[Against Heresies Book III.4.2]; Justin[Dialogue with Trypho 141]; Origen[Gospel of Matthew Book XI.15]

02:15-16 Pseudepigrapha[3Enoch 11:1; 4Ezra 16.54-55, 16.63; Hellenistic Synagogal Prayers 2.4, 2.11; Odes of Solomon 16.8; Psalms of Solomon 14.6, 17.25; Sibylline Oracles 8.282-285]; Clement of Alexandria[Stromata Book II.13, V.14; The Instructor Book I.3]; Irenaeus[Against Heresies Book IV.18.3, 19.2]; Origen[De Principiis Book II.10.4]

02:16 Origen[Gospel of John Book I.6, 14, V.4]; Nag Hammadi[Teachings of Silvanus 116]

02:17 Micah 3:11; Pseudepigrapha[2Baruch 48:22; Psalms of Solomon 17:1]

02:17-20 Clement of Alexandria[Stromata Book I.27]

02:21 Psalms 50:16-21; Tertullian[Five Books Against Marcion Book V.13]

02:22 John 8:3-11n; Pseudepigrapha[Joseph and Aseneth 10:12; Testament of Levi 14:4]

02:23 Origen[Against Celsus Book VIII.10]

02:24 Isaiah 52:5; Ezekiel 36:20-22; Clement of Alexandria[Stromata Book III.18]; Cyprian[Epistle VI.3]; Tertullian[An Answer to the Jews 13; On Idolatry 14; Five Books Against Marcion Book V.13]

02:25 Clement of Alexandria[Stromata Book VII.9]

02:25-26 Origen[Gospel of Matthew Book XI.12]

02:25-29 Jeremiah 4:4, 9:25

02:26 Leviticus 18:5; Deuteronomy 30:16

02:27 Plato[Laws VIII 836c-e, 840d-e]

02:28 Archelaus[Disputation with Manes 40]; Clement[Recognitions Book V.34]

02:28-29 Origen[De Principiis Book IV.1.21]; Tertullian[Five Books Against Marcion Book V.13; On the Resurrection of the Flesh 26; To his Wife Book I.2]

02:29 Deuteronomy 30:6; Acts 7:51n; Pseudepigrapha[Jubilees 1:23]; Archelaus[Disputation with Manes 42]; Clement of Alexandria[Stromata Book VII.12]; Origen[Against Celsus Book VII.21; Gospel of John Book I.2, 40]

03:01 Pseudepigrapha[2Baruch 14:4]

03:01-02 Deuteronomy 4:7-8; Psalms 103:7, 147:19-20

03:02 Origen[Gospel of Matthew Book X.6]

03:03 Pseudepigrapha[Psalms of Solomon 8:28]; Apostolic[Ignatius - Letter to the Ephesians 14:2]; Cyprian[Treatise I.22]

03:03-04 Cyprian[Epistle LIV.7, LXVII.8, LXVIII.8; The Seventh Council of Carthage under Cyprian]

03:03-10 Callistus[Second Epistle 6.6]

03:04 Psalms 51:4-6, 116:11; Pseudepigrapha[Joseph and Aseneth 25:8]

03:05-06 Clement of Alexandria[The Instructor Book I.8]

03:08 Clement of Alexandria[Stromata Book III.4]; Cyprian[Treatise XII.Book III.98]; Irenaeus[Against Heresies Book I.25.3]

03:10-12 Psalms 14:1-3, 53:1-4; Ecclesiastes 7:20

03:11 Irenaeus[Against Heresies Book I.19.1]

03:13 Psalms 5:9-10, 140:3-4; Tertullian[Of Patience 6]

03:13-18 Cyprian[Treatise X.8]

03:14 Psalms 10:7

03:15 Constitutions of the Holy Apostles[Book II.21]

03:15-17 Proverbs 1:16; Isaiah 59:7-8

03:16-18 Clement of Alexandria[Stromata Book I.27]

03:18 Psalms 36:1-2

03:19 Tertullian[Five Books Against Marcion Book V.13]

03:20 Genesis 6:12; Psalms 143:2; Ecclesiastes 7:20; Galatians 2:16; Archelaus[Disputation with Manes 40]; Clement of Alexandria[Stromata Book II.7, IV.3]; Irenaeus[Against Heresies Book V.22.1]

03:21 Psalms 71:2, 15, 18, 24; Isaiah 51:5, 8; Daniel 9:16; Acts 3:18n; Irenaeus[Against Heresies Book IV.34.2]

03:21-22 Clement of Alexandria[The Instructor Book I.8]; Tertullian[Five Books Against Marcion Book V.13]

03:22 Galatians 2:16

03:23 Pseudepigrapha[4Ezra 7.46-47; Questions of Ezra Recension A 1.4-5]; Irenaeus[Against Heresies Book IV.27.2]

03:23-24 Cyprian[Treatise XII.Book II.27]

03:23-26 Callistus[Second Epistle 6.6]

03:24 Psalms 130:7

03:25 Leviticus 16:13-15; Pseudepigrapha[Testament of Abraham 10:14]; Hippolytus[Against the Heresy of One Noetus 7]; Origen[Gospel of John Book I.22; Gospel of Matthew Book XII.21]

03:25-26 Origen[Gospel of John Book I.23]

03:26 Clement of Alexandria[The Instructor Book I.8]; Tertullian[On Modesty 2]

03:28 Apostolic[Ignatius - Letter to the Magnesians 8:1]

03:29 Clement of Alexandria[Stromata Book VI.6]; Origen[Gospel of Matthew Book XI.18]; Tertullian[On Modesty 7]

03:29-30 Clement of Alexandria[Stromata Book V.3]

03:30 Deuteronomy 6:4; Irenaeus[Against Heresies Book III.10.2, IV.22.2]

03:31 Tertullian[On Modesty 6]

04:01-02 Archelaus[Disputation with Manes 40]

04:01-05 Clement of Alexandria[Stromata Book I.7]

04:01-25 Tertullian[An Answer to the Jews 3; On Monogamy 6]

04:03 Genesis 15:6; Galatians 3:6; Apostolic[1Clement 10]; Clement of Alexandria[Stromata Book V.1]; Irenaeus[Against Heresies Book IV.5.3, 8.1; Demonstration of the Apostolic Preaching 24, 35]; Tertullian[Of Patience 6]

04:05 Clement of Alexandria[Stromata Book V.1]

04:07 Tertullian[Scorpiace 6]

04:07-08 Psalms 32:1-2; Ephesians 4:32n; Clement of Alexandria[Stromata Book II.15]

04:07-09 Apostolic[1Clement 50:6]

04:08 Exodus 3:14

04:09 Genesis 15:6; Clement of Alexandria[Stromata Book V.1]; Tertullian[Of Patience 6]

04:10-11 Genesis 17:10-11

04:11 Apostolic[Epistle of Barnabas 13:7]; Gregory Thaumaturgus[Four Homilies 2]; Irenaeus[Demonstration of the Apostolic Preaching 24]; Origen[Gospel of John Book VI.2]; Tertullian[On the Apparel of Women Book II.2; Five Books Against Marcion Book V.3]

04:11-12 Tertullian[On Monogamy 6]

04:12 Irenaeus[Against Heresies Book IV.7.2]

04:13 Genesis 17:4-6, 18:18, 22:17-18; OT-Apocrypha[Sirach 44:21]; Pseudepigrapha[2Baruch 14:13, 51:3; Hellenistic Synagogal Prayers 12:62; Jubilees 19:21]; Irenaeus[Demonstration of the Apostolic Preaching 35]

04:14 Galatians 3:18

04:15 Pseudepigrapha[2Baruch 15:2; Jubilees 33:16]

04:16 Galatians 3:7; Rabbinic[Tanna De-Be Eliyyahu 9]; Tertullian[On the Apparel of Women Book II.2]

04:17 Isaiah 48:13; OT-Apocrypha[Sirach 44:19]; Pseudepigrapha[2Baruch 21:5, 48:8; Joseph and Aseneth 12:2, 20:7]; Apostolic[Epistle of Barnabas 13:7]; Origen[Gospel of John Book II.7]

04:17-18 Genesis 17:5

04:18 Genesis 15:5

04:19 Genesis 17:17

04:22 Genesis 15:6; Clement of Alexandria[Stromata Book V.1]; Tertullian[Of Patience 6]
04:24 Isaiah 53:12
04:25 Isaiah 53:4-5; Tertullian[Scorpiace 7]; NT-Apocrypha[Gospel of the Nazareans Fragment 26]
05:01 Isaiah 32:17, 53:5; Tertullian[Five Books Against Marcion Book V.13]
05:02 Pseudepigrapha[Odes of Solomon 7:3]
05:02-05 Cyprian[Treatise XI.9, XII.Book III.6]
05:03 Pseudepigrapha[Testament of Joseph 10:1]; Tertullian[Scorpiace 13]
05:03-05 Clement of Alexandria[Stromata Book IV.22]; Origen[Gospel of John Book I.24]
05:04 Syriac Acts of Sharbil
05:04-05 Clement of Alexandria[Stromata Book II.22]
05:05 Psalms 22:5-6, 25:20; OT-Apocrypha[Sirach 18:11]
05:06-10 Irenaeus[Against Heresies Book III.16.9]
05:07-08 Origen[Against Celsus Book IV.28]
05:08 Clement of Alexandria[The Instructor Book I.9]
05:08-09 Cyprian[Epistle LI.18]
05:12 Genesis 2:17, 3:6, 19; OT-Apocrypha[2Esdras 3:21, 26; Wisdom of Solomon 2:24];
　　Pseudepigrapha[2Baruch 17:3, 23:4, 54:15]; Gregory Thaumaturgus[Twelve Topics on the Faith 12];
　　Nag Hammadi[Tripartite Tractate 108]
05:12-14 Clement of Alexandria[Stromata Book III.9]; Nag Hammadi[Gospel of Philip 74]
05:12-21 Pseudepigrapha[2Baruch 54:14-15, 19; Life of Adam and Eve (Apocalypse of Moses) 14:2];
　　OT-Apocrypha[Sirach 15:11-20]
05:12-22 Pseudepigrapha[4Ezra 3.19-22, 26, 4.30-32, 7:46-48, 116-119]
05:13 Clement of Alexandria[Stromata Book IV.3]; Origen[Gospel of John Book II.9]
05:14 Pseudepigrapha[Sibylline Oracles 1.333]; Archelaus[Disputation with Manes 29]; Gregory
　　Thaumaturgus[Four Homilies 2]; Hippolytus[Refutation of all Heresies Book VII.13];
　　Irenaeus[Against Heresies Book III.18.7, 22.3]; Justin[Dialogue with Trypho 40]; Methodius[Banquet
　　of the Ten Virgins 4.2]; Origen[Against Celsus Book IV.40]
05:15 Isaiah 53:11; 1Peter 1:10-13n; Pseudepigrapha[Sibylline Oracles 8.259]
05:16 OT-Apocrypha[2Esdras 7:118]; Nag Hammadi[Interpretation of Knowledge 14]
05:17 Pseudepigrapha[Life of Adam and Eve (Apocalypse of Moses) 14:2]; Irenaeus[Against Heresies
　　Book III.16.9]
05:19 Isaiah 53:11; Irenaeus[Against Heresies Book III.18.7, 21.10]
05:20 Pseudepigrapha[Life of Abraham 39:6]; Irenaeus[Against Heresies Book III.23.8]; Tertullian[On
　　the Resurrection of the Flesh 34]
05:20-21 Tertullian[On the Resurrection of the Flesh 47; Five Books Against Marcion Book V.13]
05:21 Jude 1:21n; Pseudepigrapha[Joseph and Aseneth 8:9]
06:01-12 Tertullian[On Modesty 17]
06:02 Clement of Alexandria[Stromata Book III.11]
06:03 Constitutions of the Holy Apostles[Book V.16]; Tertullian[On Monogamy 17]
06:03-04 Matthew 3:5-16n; Irenaeus[Against Heresies Book III.16.9]; Tertullian[On Repentance 6]
06:03-06 Tertullian[On the Resurrection of the Flesh 47]
06:04 Colossians 2:12; Methodius[Discourse on the Resurrection 1.13]; Origen[Against Celsus Book
　　II.69; Gospel of John Book I.25, X.20; Gospel of Matthew Book XIII.9]; Tertullian[A Treatise on the
　　Soul 40]; NT-Apocrypha[Acts of Paul in Philippi 3.31]
06:05 Acts 2:31n; Clement of Alexandria[Stromata Book VII.12]; Constitutions of the Holy
　　Apostles[Book VII.39]
06:06 Pseudepigrapha[Odes of Solomon 17.4, 17.12, 21.2]; Clement of Alexandria[Stromata Book III.11,
　　IV.7]; NT-Apocrypha[Acts of Thomas 1.48]
06:06-07 Clement of Alexandria[Stromata Book VII.3]
06:07 Irenaeus[Against Heresies Book III.23.6]
06:08 Tertullian[On Repentance 6; On the Resurrection of the Flesh 47]
06:09 Irenaeus[Against Heresies Book III.16.9]; Origen[Against Celsus Book II.16; Gospel of Matthew
　　Book XII.4]; Victorinus[Apocalypse 1.5]
06:10 OT-Apocrypha[4Maccabees 7:19]; Origen[Against Celsus Book II.69; Gospel of John Book I.11]
06:11-13 Tertullian[On the Resurrection of the Flesh 47]
06:12 Genesis 4:7; Irenaeus[Against Heresies Book V.14.4]; Origen[Gospel of Matthew Book XII.35,
　　XIV.3, 7]
06:12-19 Callistus[Second Epistle 6.6]

06:13 Apostolic[Polycarp - Letter to the Philippians 4:1]; Clement of Alexandria[Stromata Book III.11]

06:14-15 Clement of Alexandria[Stromata Book III.8]; Tertullian[Of Patience 6]

06:16 1Peter 2:13; Clement of Alexandria[Stromata Book III.4]

06:19-23 Tertullian[On the Resurrection of the Flesh 47]

06:20-23 Clement of Alexandria[Stromata Book IV.3]

06:21 Ezekiel 16:61, 63

06:22 Clement of Alexandria[Stromata Book II.22]

06:22-23 Jude 1:21n

06:23 Pseudepigrapha[2Enoch 30:16]; Irenaeus[Against Heresies Book III.19.1]

07:01 Tertullian[To his Wife Book II.2]

07:01-03 Origen[Gospel of Matthew Book XII.4]; Tertullian[On Monogamy 9]

07:01-06 Pseudepigrapha[Sibylline Oracles 8.300]

07:02 Callistus[Second Epistle 3.3]; Clement of Alexandria[Stromata Book III.12]

07:02-03 Tertullian[On Monogamy 13]

07:03 Origen[Gospel of Matthew Book XIV.23-24]

07:04 Clement of Alexandria[Stromata Book III.12]

07:04-08 Tertullian[Five Books Against Marcion Book V.13]

07:05 Pseudepigrapha[Joseph and Aseneth 12:5]

07:05-08:13 Nag Hammadi[Authoritative Teaching 23]

07:05-25 Plato[Phaedo 66e-67e]

07:06 Pseudepigrapha[Joseph and Aseneth 8:9]; Clement of Alexandria[Stromata Book IV.3];
  Irenaeus[Demonstration of the Apostolic Preaching 90]

07:07 Exodus 20:17; Deuteronomy 5:21; OT-Apocrypha[4Maccabees 2:5; Life of Adam and Eve
  (Apocalypse of Moses) 19:3]; Clement of Alexandria[Stromata Book III.11]

07:07-10 Methodius[Apostolic Words from the Discourse on the Resurrection 1]

07:08-09 Origen[Gospel of John Book II.9]

07:09 Pseudepigrapha[Joseph and Aseneth 19:10]; Clement[First Epistle Concerning Virginity 8];
  Origen[Against Celsus Book III.62]

07:10 Genesis 2:17; Leviticus 18:5; Pseudepigrapha[Psalms of Solomon 14:1]; Rabbinic[Babylonian
  Yoma 72b]

07:11 Genesis 3:13; Rabbinic[Babylonian Hagigah 16a]

07:12 OT-Apocrypha[2Esdras 9:37]; Clement of Alexandria[Stromata Book III.12, IV.3; The Instructor
  Book I.8; Who is the Rich Man that shall be Saved 9]; Origen[Against Celsus Book VII.20; Gospel of
  Matthew Book XI.14]; Tertullian[On Modesty 6]

07:12-13 Origen[De Principiis Book II.5.4]

07:12-15 Methodius[Apostolic Words from the Discourse on the Resurrection 1]

07:13-14 Tertullian[Five Books Against Marcion Book V.13]

07:14 Psalms 51:5, 7; Clement of Alexandria[Stromata Book IV.3]; Novatian[On the Jewish Meats 2];
  Origen[Against Celsus Book VII.20; Gospel of John Book X.5; Gospel of Matthew Book XI.14]

07:15 Galatians 5:17; Lactantius[Divine Institutes Book IV.24]; Methodius[Discourse on the
  Resurrection 3.1]

07:15-18 Methodius[Apostolic Words from the Discourse on the Resurrection 2]

07:17 Tertullian[On the Resurrection of the Flesh 46]

07:17-18 Clement of Alexandria[Stromata Book III.11]

07:18 Genesis 6:5, 8:21; Clement[First Epistle Concerning Virginity 8]; Irenaeus[Against Heresies Book
  III.20.3, IV.36.8]; Tertullian[On Modesty 17]

07:19 Methodius[Apostolic Words from the Discourse on the Resurrection 1-2]; Nag Hammadi[Gospel
  of Philip 83]

07:20 Clement of Alexandria[Stromata Book III.11]; Tertullian[On the Resurrection of the Flesh 46]

07:22 Nag Hammadi[Letter of Peter to Philip 137]

07:22-25 Methodius[Apostolic Words from the Discourse on the Resurrection 3]

07:23 OT-Apocrypha[2Esdras 7:72]; Origen[Gospel of Matthew Book XII.4; De Principiis Book III.4.2,
  4]; Tertullian[On the Resurrection of the Flesh 46, 51; Five Books Against Marcion Book V.14]

07:23-24 Clement of Alexandria[Stromata Book III.11]

07:24 Pseudepigrapha[Joseph and Aseneth 27:10]; Clement of Alexandria[Stromata Book III.3];
  Irenaeus[Against Heresies Book III.20.3]; Origen[Against Celsus Book VII.50, VIII.54]

08:02 Galatians 5:18-23n; Origen[De Principiis Book III.4.4]; Tertullian[On the Resurrection of the Flesh
  46]

08:02-03 Tertullian[Five Books Against Marcion Book V.13]

08:02-04 Clement of Alexandria[Stromata Book III.11]; Methodius[Apostolic Words from the Discourse on the Resurrection 3]

08:02-08 Tertullian[On Modesty 17]

08:03 Leviticus 16:1-34; 1Timothy 3:16n; Gregory Thaumaturgus[Twelve Topics on the Faith 12]; Irenaeus[Against Heresies Book III.20.2]; Origen[Gospel of John Book II.21; Gospel of Matthew Book XIV.7]; Tertullian[On the Resurrection of the Flesh 16, 46; Five Books Against Marcion Book V.14]

08:04-15 Nag Hammadi[Apocryphon of James 11-12]

08:05 Tertullian[A Treatise on the Soul 40]

08:05-06 Tertullian[On Exhortation to Chastity 10]

08:05-13 Tertullian[Five Books Against Marcion Book V.14]

08:05-16 Clement of Alexandria[Stromata Book III.11]

08:06 Ephesians 2:1; Colossians 2:11; Rabbinic[Ecclesiastes Rabba on 1:8]; Irenaeus[Against Heresies Book I.6.2]; Origen[Gospel of Matthew Book XI.3]

08:06-07 Clement[First Epistle Concerning Virginity 8]

08:06-13 Tertullian[On the Resurrection of the Flesh 46]

08:07 Novatian[Treatise Concerning the Trinity 29]; Origen[De Principiis Book III.4.5]

08:07-08 Clement of Alexandria[Stromata Book IV.7]

08:08 Origen[Against Celsus Book VII.38]; Tertullian[On Fasting 17; On the Resurrection of the Flesh 10; Five Books Against Marcion Book V.10]

08:08-09 Origen[Gospel of Matthew Book XIII.2]

08:08-13 Irenaeus[Against Heresies Book V.10.2]

08:09 OT-Apocrypha[2Esdras 7:11]; Clement of Alexandria[Stromata Book II.20; The Instructor Book I.6]; Clement[First Epistle Concerning Virginity 8]; Gregory Thaumaturgus[Sectional Confession of Faith 10]; Irenaeus[Against Heresies Book V.8.1]; Novatian[Treatise Concerning the Trinity 29]; Origen[Against Celsus Book VII.45; De Principiis Book III.4.2]; Tertullian[On the Resurrection of the Flesh 49]

08:09-11 This section also includes topical notes for: Spirit of God Dwells in You - John 6:38, 14:10-17; 1Corinthians 3:16; 2Corinthians 6:16; Ephesians 3:17; 2Timothy 1:14; James 4:5; 1John 3:24, 4:12-16; 2John 1:9; Philo[On the Prayers And Curses Uttered By Noah When He Became Sober (64) cf. {Genesis 9:27}]; Apostolic[Ignatius - Letter to the Ephesians 15:3, Letter to the Philadelphians 7:2; Epistle of Barnabas 4:11, 6:14-15; Martyrdom of Ignatius 2]; Clement of Alexandria[Stromata Book II.20; Who is the Rich Man that shall be Saved 33]; Irenaeus[Against Heresies Book III.21.4, V.6.2, 20.2; Fragments from the Lost Works 26]; Justin[Dialogue with Trypho 115; Hortatory Address to the Greeks 8, 32, 35]; Tatian[Address to the Greeks 15]; Nag Hammadi[Gospel of Philip 61; Gospel of Truth 42; Teachings of Silvanus 87]

08:09-27 Matthew 28:19n

08:10 Clement of Alexandria[Stromata Book IV.7]

08:11 Gregory Thaumaturgus[Sectional Confession of Faith 10]; Hippolytus[Against the Heresy of One Noetus 4]; Irenaeus[Against Heresies Book III.16.9, V.7.1]; Methodius[Apostolic Words from the Discourse on the Resurrection 3]; Origen[Gospel of Matthew Book XIV.3]; Tertullian[Against Praxeas 28; Five Books Against Marcion Book V.14]

08:11-12 Hippolytus[Refutation of all Heresies Book V.30]

08:12 Tertullian[On Modesty 17]

08:12-14 Cyprian[Treatise X.14]

08:13 Clement of Alexandria[Stromata Book IV.7]; Origen[Against Celsus Book V.49, VII.38, 52]; Nag Hammadi[Interpretation of Knowledge 20]

08:14 Deuteronomy 14:1; Origen[Against Celsus Book IV.95, VI.70]

08:14-15 Gregory Thaumaturgus[Sectional Confession of Faith 10]

08:14-19 Pseudepigrapha[Jubilees 1.25]; Clement of Alexandria[Stromata Book VI.14, VII.11]; Irenaeus[Against Heresies Book IV.16.5, 41.2-3; Fragments from the Lost Works 36]; Justin[Dialogue with Trypho 23, 45, 123-124]; Nag Hammadi[Apocryphon of James 16; Gospel of Philip 62, 67, 75, 85; Gospel of Thomas 3, 50; Gospel of Truth 27; Sentences of Sextus 376a]

08:15 Pseudepigrapha[Apocryphon of Ezekiel Fragment 2]; Clement of Alexandria[Stromata Book IV.7]; Irenaeus[Against Heresies Book III.6.1, 20.2, IV.9.2, V.8.1]; Origen[Against Celsus Book I.57; Gospel of John Book I.31; Gospel of Matthew Book XIII.26]; Theodotus[Excerpts 19]; NT-Apocrypha[Acts of Paul in Ephesus p.2; Acts of Paul in Philippi 3.8]

08:15-16 Clement of Alexandria[Exhortation to the Heathen 9]
08:16 Origen[Gospel of Matthew Book XIII.2]
08:16-17 Cyprian[Epistle LV.1, LXXX.2; Treatise XI.8, XII.Book III.16]
08:16-21 Apostolic[Papias Fragment 15:1]
08:17 Galatians 4:5-7; Pseudepigrapha[Joseph and Aseneth 24:14]; Clement of Alexandria[Exhortation
    to the Heathen 11]; Hippolytus[The Discourse on the Holy Theophany 8]; Tertullian[Scorpiace 13];
    NT-Apocrypha[Acts of Paul and Thecla 1.5; Epistula Apostolorum 19]
08:17-18 Clement of Alexandria[Stromata Book IV.7]; Tertullian[On the Resurrection of the Flesh 40]
08:18 Pseudepigrapha[2Baruch 15:8, 32:6]; Cyprian[Epistle LV.10, LXXVI.7, LXXX.2; Treatise XI.13,
    XII.Book III.17; Treatises Attributed to Cyprian On the Glory of Martyrdom 18]; Pseud-Irenaeus;
    Syriac Martyrdom of Habib the Deacon; Syriac Martyrdom of Shamuna, Guria, and Habib;
    Tertullian[On the Resurrection of the Flesh 10]; NT-Apocrypha[Apocalypse of Paul 1.49]
08:19 OT-Apocrypha[2Esdras 7:75]; Hippolytus[Refutation of all Heresies Book VII.13];
    Irenaeus[Against Heresies Book V.32.1]; Origen[Gospel of John Book I.24; De Principiis Book I.7.5]
08:19-20 Origen[Against Celsus Book VIII.5]
08:19-21 Origen[Against Celsus Book V.13, VII.65]; Tertullian[Against Hermogenes 11]
08:19-22 Hippolytus[Refutation of all Heresies Book VII.15]
08:20 Genesis 3:17-19, 5:29; Ecclesiastes 1:2; Origen[Against Celsus Book VII.50; Gospel of John Book
    I.17, 24]
08:20-21 Origen[De Principiis Book II.9.7, III.5.1, 4]
08:20-23 Origen[De Principiis Book I.7.5]
08:21 Irenaeus[Against Heresies Book V.36.3]
08:21-22 Archelaus[Disputation with Manes 37]
08:22 OT-Apocrypha[2Esdras 10:9]; Hippolytus[Refutation of all Heresies Book VII.13]; Origen[Gospel
    of John Book I.17]; Theophilus of Antioch[To Autolycus Book II.17]
08:23 Irenaeus[Against Heresies Book IV.8.1]; Tertullian[Five Books in Reply to Marcion Book II.328];
    NT-Apocrypha[Acts of Paul in Ephesus p.2; Acts of Paul in Philippi 3.8]
08:24 Origen[Gospel of John Book I.24]
08:24-25 Clement of Alexandria[Stromata Book IV.7]; Cyprian[Treatise IX.13, XII.Book III.45]
08:26 Isaiah 28:11; Clement of Alexandria[Stromata Book VII.8]; Tertullian[On Monogamy 3]
08:27 Psalms 139:1; Nag Hammadi[Gospel of Truth 20]
08:28 Pseudepigrapha[Psalms of Solomon 4:25]
08:28-29 Clement of Alexandria[The Instructor Book III.3]
08:28-30 Clement of Alexandria[Stromata Book IV.7]
08:29 Genesis 1:27; Irenaeus[Against Heresies Book III.20.2]; Justin[First Apology 14]; Origen[Gospel
    of Matthew Book XII.29, XIII.27]; NT-Apocrypha[Acts of Thomas 1.48, 1.60]
08:29-30 Nag Hammadi[Gospel of Truth 41]
08:31 Psalms 118:6; Origen[Gospel of John Book II.22]
08:32 Genesis 22:16; Alexander of Alexandria[Epistles on Arian Heresy 1.8]; Origen[Against Celsus
    Book VIII.43; Gospel of Matthew Book XIII.8-9; Letter to Africanus 5]; Tertullian[Against Praxeas 30;
    De Fuga in Persecutione 12; Scorpiace 7]
08:33 Isaiah 50:8; 1Peter 2:4-9n
08:34 Job 34:29; Psalms 110:1; 1Peter 3:22n; Irenaeus[Against Heresies Book III.16.9]
08:35 Pseudepigrapha[2Enoch 66:6; Odes of Solomon 28:5]; Clement of Alexandria[Fragments from
    Macarius Chrysocephalus Parable of the Prodigal son 7]; Cyprian[Epistle VII.5, XXV.4];
    Origen[Gospel of Matthew Book XIII.29, XIV.17; De Principiis Book III.1.12]; Tertullian[Scorpiace
    13]
08:35-37 Cyprian[Treatise XI.6, XII.Book III.18]
08:35-39 Origen[Against Celsus Book I.Preface.3]
08:36 Psalms 44:22-23; Zechariah 11:4; Irenaeus[Against Heresies Book II.22.2, IV.16.1]
08:36-37 Clement of Alexandria[Stromata Book IV.7]
08:37 Origen[Against Celsus Book I.Preface.4]
08:38 Pseudepigrapha[Life of Adam and Eve Vita 21:1, 28:2; Testament of Job 47:9; Testament of
    Solomon 20:15-16]; Apostolic[Ignatius - Letter to the Trallians 5:2; Martyrdom of Polycarp 14:1]
08:38-39 Clement of Alexandria[Stromata Book IV.14]; Origen[De Principiis Book III.2.5]
09:01 Archelaus[Disputation with Manes 34]; Gregory Thaumaturgus[Sectional Confession of Faith
    10]
09:03 Exodus 32:32

09:03-05 Cyprian[Treatise XII.Book II.6]

09:04 Exodus 4:22, 16:10; Deuteronomy 7:6, 14:1-2; Hosea 11:1; OT-Apocrypha[2Maccabees 6:23; Sirach 44:12, 18]; Tertullian[On Modesty 8]; NT-Apocrypha[Acts of Paul in Ephesus p.2; Acts of Paul in Philippi 3.8]

09:05 Exodus 13:5; Psalms 41:14; Hippolytus[Against the Heresy of One Noetus 6-7]; Irenaeus[Against Heresies Book III.16.3]; Methodius[Oration Concerning Simeon and Anna 1]; Novatian[Treatise Concerning the Trinity 13, 30]; Tertullian[Against Praxeas 13, 15; An Answer to the Jews 10]

09:06 Numbers 23:19; Rabbinic[Babylonian Qiddushin 36a]; Origen[De Principiis Book IV.1.21, 23]

09:07 Genesis 21:12

09:07-08 Justin[Dialogue with Trypho 44]

09:08 Exodus 14:4; Origen[De Principiis Book IV.1.21-22]

09:09 Genesis 18:10, 14

09:10 Genesis 25:21

09:10-13 Irenaeus[Against Heresies Book IV.21.2]; Tertullian[On Modesty 8]

09:11 1Peter 2:4-9n

09:11-12 Origen[De Principiis Book II.9.7]

09:11-14 Origen[Gospel of John Book II.25]

09:12 Genesis 25:23

09:13 Malachi 1:2-3

09:14 Deuteronomy 32:4; Clement of Alexandria[Stromata Book IV.26]; Origen[De Principiis Book I.7.4]

09:15 Exodus 33:19; Clement of Alexandria[Stromata Book IV.6]

09:16 Isaiah 49:10; Pseudepigrapha[Assumption of Moses 12:7]; Origen[De Principiis Book III.1.7, 18]

09:17 Exodus 9:16

09:17-18 Rabbinic[Shemoth Rabba xiii. 3, p. 24b cf. {Exodus 9:16, 10:1}]

09:18 Exodus 4:21, 7:3, 9:12; Origen[De Principiis Book III.1.7-8, 14]

09:18-21 Origen[De Principiis Book III.1.20]

09:19 Pseudepigrapha[2Baruch 3:7]

09:19-20 OT-Apocrypha[Wisdom of Solomon 12:12]

09:19-21 Methodius[Discourse on the Resurrection 1.8]

09:20 Job 9:12; Isaiah 29:16, 45:9; Tertullian[On the Resurrection of the Flesh 7]

09:20-21 Origen[De Principiis Book III.1.7]

09:21 Jeremiah 18:6; OT-Apocrypha[Wisdom of Solomon 15:7]

09:22 Isaiah 13:5, 54:16; Jeremiah 50:25; Pseudepigrapha[2Baruch 24:2, 59:6]

09:22-23 Matthew 7:13-14n; Nag Hammadi[Gospel of Truth 25]

09:23 Isaiah 45:9; Pseudepigrapha[Joseph and Aseneth 21:16; Sibylline Oracles 2.81-86]

09:24 Pseudepigrapha[Jubilees 02:19]

09:25 Hosea 2:23-25; Irenaeus[Against Heresies Book I.10.3, III.9.1; Demonstration of the Apostolic Preaching 93]

09:25-26 Irenaeus[Against Heresies Book IV.20.12]

09:26-27 Hosea 2:1

09:26-28 Hosea 1:10; Isaiah 10:22-23

09:28 Isaiah 28:22; Daniel 5:28; Irenaeus[Demonstration of the Apostolic Preaching 87]

09:29 Isaiah 1:9

09:31 Deuteronomy 16:20; Proverbs 15:9; Isaiah 51:1; OT-Apocrypha[Sirach 27:8; Wisdom of Solomon 2:11]

09:32-33 Isaiah 8:14; Clement of Alexandria[Stromata Book VI.15]; Tertullian[An Answer to the Jews 10, 14]

09:33 Isaiah 28:16; Pseudepigrapha[Sibylline Oracles 1.345, 8.246]; Tertullian[Five Books Against Marcion Book IV.13]

10:01-03 Pseudepigrapha[Sibylline Oracles 1.369-370]

10:02-04 Clement of Alexandria[Stromata Book II.9]; Tertullian[Five Books Against Marcion Book V.14]

10:03-04 Irenaeus[Against Heresies Book IV.12.4]

10:04 Clement of Alexandria[Stromata Book IV.21]; Hippolytus[The Discourse on the Holy Theophany 5]

10:05 Leviticus 18:5; Pseudepigrapha[2Baruch 67:6]; NT-Apocrypha[Epistula Apostolorum 39]

10:06 Deuteronomy 9:4; OT-Apocrypha[2Esdras 4:8]; Pseudepigrapha[Baruch 3:29]

10:06-07 Proverbs 30:4; Irenaeus[Against Heresies Book III.18.2]; Nag Hammadi[Dialogue of the Savior 36]

10:06-08 Deuteronomy 30:12-14; Origen[Gospel of John Book I.42, II.9; De Principiis Book I.3.6]

10:07 Psalms 71:20, 107:26; OT-Apocrypha[Wisdom of Solomon 16:13]

10:08 Irenaeus[Fragments from the Lost Works 36]

10:08-10 Peter of Alexandria[Canonical Epistle 5]

10:08-11 Clement of Alexandria[Stromata Book IV.16]

10:09 Rabbinic[Babylonian Yoma 36b]; Irenaeus[Against Heresies Book III.18.2]

10:09-10 Pseudepigrapha[4Ezra 2.47]

10:09-13 Revelation 12:10n

10:10 Origen[Gospel of Matthew Book XII.24, XIV.3]; Tertullian[A Treatise on the Soul 15; On Fasting 2]

10:10-11 Clement of Alexandria[Stromata Book IV.7, IV.9]

10:11 Isaiah 28:16

10:12 Clement of Alexandria[Stromata Book VI.6]

10:13 Joel 2:32, 3:5

10:14 NT-Apocrypha[Kerygma Petri 3b]

10:14-17 Clement of Alexandria[Stromata Book II.6]; Tertullian[An Answer to the Jews 3]

10:15 Isaiah 52:7; Nahum 1:15, 2:1; Irenaeus[Against Heresies Book III.13.1; Demonstration of the Apostolic Preaching 86]; Origen[Gospel of John Book I.10]

10:16 Isaiah 53:1

10:18 Psalms 19:4-5; Clement of Alexandria[The Instructor Book II.8]; Hippolytus[Refutation of all Heresies Book V.2]; Tertullian[An Answer to the Jews 5, 7]

10:19 Deuteronomy 32:21; Pseudepigrapha[3Baruch 16:3]; Irenaeus[Demonstration of the Apostolic Preaching 95]

10:19-21 Clement of Alexandria[Stromata Book II.9]

10:20-21 Isaiah 65:1-2

10:21 Justin[Dialogue with Trypho 97]; Tertullian[An Answer to the Jews 13]

11:01-02 Psalms 94:14

11:02 1Samuel 12:22; Jeremiah 31:37

11:03 1Kings 19:10, 14

11:04 1Kings 19:18; OT-Apocrypha[2Maccabees 2:4]; Constitutions of the Holy Apostles[Book VIII.1]; Origen[De Principiis Book IV.1.13]

11:05 Origen[Gospel of Matthew Book XI.17]

11:07 Peter of Alexandria[Fragments Up to the Time of the Destruction of Jerusalem 1]

11:08 Deuteronomy 29:3-4; Isaiah 6:9, 29:10

11:09 Clement of Alexandria[Stromata Book VI.15]

11:09-10 Psalms 35:8, 69:22-23

11:11 Deuteronomy 32:21; Clement of Alexandria[Stromata Book II.9]

11:11-12 Origen[Against Celsus Book VI.80]

11:11-36 Tertullian[On Modesty 8]

11:15 OT-Apocrypha[Sirach 10:20]

11:16 Numbers 15:17-21; Nehemiah 10:37; Ezekiel 44:30; Irenaeus[Against Heresies Book I.8.3]; Nag Hammadi[Interpretation of Knowledge 19]

11:16-28 Philo[Fragments Extracted From the Parallels of John of Damascus Page 748. B cf. {Genesis 3:19-20}; On Dreams, That they Are God-Sent (2.170-2.176) cf. {Numbers 13:17-21, Deuteronomy 30:9, Isaiah 5:7}]

11:17 Exodus 3:14; Judges 9:9; Clement of Alexandria[Stromata Book VI.15]; Irenaeus[Against Heresies Book IV.27.3, V.10.1]

11:17-20 Tertullian[Five Books in Reply to Marcion Book II.19]

11:20-21 Anonymous[Treatise on Re-Baptism 9]; Cyprian[Epistle VI.4; Treatise XII.Book III.5]

11:21 Pseudepigrapha[2Baruch 13:10]; Irenaeus[Against Heresies Book IV.27.3]

11:22 Clement of Alexandria[The Instructor Book I.8]; Tertullian[On Modesty 2]

11:25 OT-Apocrypha[2Esdras 4:35]; Pseudepigrapha[2Baruch 23:5; Sibylline Oracles 1.369-370]

11:25-26 Origen[Gospel of Matthew Book XIV.20]

11:26 Pseudepigrapha[Testament of Benjamin 10:11]; Irenaeus[Against Heresies Book IV.1.7]

11:26-27 Psalms 14:7; Isaiah 59:20-21

11:27 Isaiah 27:9; Jeremiah 31:33-34

11:29 Psalms 110:4

11:30 Pseudepigrapha[Joseph and Aseneth 12:5]

11:32 Irenaeus[Against Heresies Book I.10.3, III.20.2]

11:33 This section also includes topical notes for: Depth of the Riches - Job 5:9, 9:10; Psalms 77:20; Isaiah 45:15, 55:8; Luke 12:21; 2Corinthians 6:10; Ephesians 3:8; Colossians 1:27; Hebrews 11:26; OT-Apocrypha[Wisdom of Solomon 17:1]; Pseudepigrapha[2Baruch 14:8; Hellenistic Synagogal Prayers 4:30]; Philo[Concerning Noah's Work As A Planter (65-69) cf. {Numbers 18:20, Deuteronomy 10:9}]; Clement of Alexandria[Stromata Book V.12; The Instructor Book III.12]; Irenaeus[Against Heresies Book I.10.3]; Methodius[Oration Concerning Simeon and Anna 3]; Novatian[Treatise Concerning the Trinity 3, 8]; Origen[Gospel of John Book II.1; De Principiis Book IV.1.26]; Tertullian[Five Books Against Marcion Book II.2, V.14]; Nag Hammadi[Gospel of Truth 37]

11:33-36 Cyprian[Treatise XII.Book III.53]

11:34 Job 15:18; Isaiah 40:13; Jeremiah 23:18; Pseudepigrapha[2Enoch 33:4]; Clement[Recognitions Book V.25]; Irenaeus[Against Heresies Book V.1.1]; Tertullian[Against Hermogenes 45; Against Praxeas 19; Scorpiace 7; Five Books Against Marcion Book II.2]

11:34-35 Tertullian[Against Hermogenes 17; Five Books Against Marcion Book V.14]

11:35 Job 41:3, 11

11:36 Irenaeus[Against Heresies Book I.3.4]; Origen[Against Celsus Book VI.65]

12:01 This section also includes topical notes for: Living Sacrifice - Leviticus 10:9; Numbers 6:2-21; Judges 13:4-5; 1Samuel 1:11; Daniel 2:18; Amos 2:11-12; Luke 1:15; Pseudepigrapha[Sibylline Oracles 8.408; Testament of Levi 3:6]; Philo[Special Laws I (166-167) cf. {Exodus 12:5, 29:1, Leviticus 1:3-10, 3:1-6, 4:3-32, 5:15-18, 6:6, 9:2-3, 14:10, 22:19, 23:12-18, Numbers 6:16, 28:19, 29:2, 8, 13-36}; Special Laws II (162) cf. {Leviticus 23:4-14}]; Athenagoras[Plea for the Christians 13]; Teaching of the Twelve Apostles 14.2; Tertullian[On Prayer 15; On the Resurrection of the Flesh 47]; Nag Hammadi[Teachings of Silvanus 104]; NT-Apocrypha[Acts of Peter 1.29]

12:01-02 Cyprian[Epistle LXXVI.3; Treatise XI.8]

12:02 Clement of Alexandria[Stromata Book II.9]; Constitutions of the Holy Apostles[Book II.55]; Hippolytus[Refutation of all Heresies Book IX.22]

12:03 Archelaus[Disputation with Manes 42]; Irenaeus[Against Heresies Book V.20.2]

12:04 Pseudepigrapha[Odes of Solomon 17:16]

12:04-05 Justin[Dialogue with Trypho 42]

12:04-08 Nag Hammadi[Interpretation of Knowledge 15-19; Trimorphic Protennoia 49]

12:05 1Corinthians 12:12; Clement of Alexandria[The Instructor Book I.5]

12:06 Justin[Dialogue with Trypho 88]; Tertullian[On Modesty 8]

12:08 1Corinthians 12:4-11

12:08-13 Clement of Alexandria[The Instructor Book III.12]

12:09 Psalms 97:10; Amos 5:15; Matthew 6:2-16n; Clement of Alexandria[Stromata Book IV.7; The Instructor Book II.6]; Tertullian[Of Patience 10]

12:09-10 Clement of Alexandria[Stromata Book II.9]; Tertullian[Five Books Against Marcion Book V.14]

12:10 Apostolic[Polycarp - Letter to the Philippians 10:1]; NT-Apocrypha[Acts of Peter and Paul]

12:11 Origen[De Principiis Book II.8.3]

12:12 Tertullian[Five Books Against Marcion Book V.14]

12:13 Cyprian[Epistle LIX.3]

12:14 Matthew 5:44n; Luke 6:28; Clement of Alexandria[Stromata Book IV.16]; Cyprian[Treatise XII.Book III.13]; Lactantius[Divine Institutes Book VI.18]; Origen[Against Celsus Book VIII.38]

12:15 Psalms 35:13; OT-Apocrypha[Sirach 7:34]; Tertullian[On Fasting 13; On Idolatry 13]

12:15-16 1Corinthians 9:20n

12:16 Genesis 18:8; Proverbs 3:7; Isaiah 5:21; Pseudepigrapha[Letter of Aristeas 1.257, 1.266]; Rabbinic[Exodus Rabba on 33:12; Leviticus Rabba on 1.1; Mekhilta On Exodus 18:12]; Irenaeus[Against Heresies Book V.22.2]; Peter of Alexandria[Canonical Epistle 11]

12:16-19 Tertullian[Five Books Against Marcion Book V.14]

12:17 Proverbs 3:4; 1Peter 2:12n; Pseudepigrapha[Apocalypse of Sedrach 7:9; Joseph and Aseneth 23:9]; Apostolic[Polycarp - Letter to the Philippians 6]; Clement[First Epistle Concerning Virginity 13]; Cyprian[Treatise XII.Book III.23]; Tertullian[Of Patience 10; On Exhortation to Chastity 6; On the Apparel of Women Book II.13]; NT-Apocrypha[Acts of John 81; Acts of Paul in Antioch 1:1; Acts of Peter 1.28]

12:18 Clement of Alexandria[Stromata Book II.9]

12:19 Leviticus 19:18; Deuteronomy 32:35; Pseudepigrapha[2Enoch 50:4; Joseph and Aseneth 28:14; Testament of Gad 6:7]; Cyprian[Treatise V.17]; Lactantius[Divine Institutes Book VI.18]; Tertullian[Of Patience 10; Five Books Against Marcion Book II.18, IV.16]; Zephyrinus[Second Epistle 1.1]; NT-Apocrypha[Acts of Pilate XII.1]

12:20 2Kings 6:22; Proverbs 25:21-22; Rabbinic[Babylonian Sukkah 52a]

12:20-21 Matthew 5:44n

12:21 Pseudepigrapha[Testament of Benjamin 4:3]; Clement of Alexandria[Stromata Book II.9]; Cyprian[Treatise XII.Book III.23]

13:01 Proverbs 8:15; OT-Apocrypha[Sirach 4:27; Wisdom of Solomon 6:3]; Pseudepigrapha[Prayer of Jacob 1.1-7; Prayer of Joseph Fragment A 1-9]; Apostolic[Martyrdom of Polycarp 14:1]; Constitutions of the Holy Apostles[Book IV.13]; Irenaeus[Against Heresies Book V.24.1]; Tertullian[On Idolatry 15; Scorpiace 14]

13:01-02 Origen[Against Celsus Book VIII.65]

13:01-03 Josephus[War 2.8.7 140]; Plato[Laws XI 917a]

13:01-04 Theophilus of Antioch[To Autolycus Book I.11]

13:01-07 Irenaeus[Against Heresies Book IV.36.6]

13:02 Fabian[Second Epistle]

13:02-04 Hippolytus[Refutation of all Heresies Book IX.18]

13:03 Pseudepigrapha[Letter of Aristeas 1.240-241]; Cyprian[Treatise XII.Book III.38]

13:03-04 Rabbinic[Avot 3.2]; Clement of Alexandria[The Instructor Book I.9]

13:04 John 3:36n; Constitutions of the Holy Apostles[Book IV.13]; Dionysius of Alexandria[Extant Fragments Epistle to Hermammon 6]; Irenaeus[Against Heresies Book V.24.1-2]; Tertullian[A Treatise on the Soul 33]

13:06 Dionysius of Alexandria[Extant Fragments Epistle to Hermammon 6]; Irenaeus[Against Heresies Book V.24.1]; Tertullian[Scorpiace 14]

13:07 Matthew 22:21n; Mark 12:17; Luke 20:25; Passion of the Scillitan Martyrs

13:07-08 Constitutions of the Holy Apostles[Book IV.13]; Cyprian[Treatise XII.Book III.5]; Theophilus of Antioch[To Autolycus Book III.14]

13:08 Clement of Alexandria[Stromata Book IV.7]

13:08-10 Matthew 5:43n; Clement of Alexandria[Stromata Book IV.3]

13:09 Exodus 20:13-17; Leviticus 19:18; Deuteronomy 5:17-19:21; John 8:3-11n; OT-Apocrypha[4Maccabees 2:6]; Pseudepigrapha[Life of Abraham 11:10]; Clement of Alexandria[Stromata Book VII.16]; Tertullian[An Answer to the Jews 2; On the Apparel of Women Book II.2; Five Books Against Marcion Book V.14]; Nag Hammadi[Sentences of Sextus 179]

13:09-10 Rabbinic[**Babylonian Shabbat 31a**]; Irenaeus[Against Heresies Book IV.12.2]

There was another case of a gentile who came before Shammai. He said to him, "Convert me on the stipulation that you teach me the entire Torah while I am standing on one foot." He drove him off with the building cubit that he had in his hand. He came before Hillel: "Convert me." He said to him, "'What is hateful to you, to your fellow don't do.' That's the entirety of the Torah; everything else is elaboration. So go, study." (Talmud - Babylonian Shabbat 31a, *The Babylonian Talmud a Translation and Commentary*, Jacob Neusner; Hendrickson Publishers, Inc., 2005)

13:10 OT-Apocrypha[Wisdom of Solomon 6:18]; Pseudepigrapha[Apocalypse of Sedrach 1:14]; Clement of Alexandria[Stromata Book IV.18]; Fabian[Second Epistle]; Irenaeus[Demonstration of the Apostolic Preaching 87, 95]

13:11-12 Clement of Alexandria[Stromata Book IV.22]

13:12 Origen[Gospel of Matthew Book XI.6, XII.37]; NT-Apocrypha[Epistula Apostolorum 39]

13:12-13 Clement of Alexandria[The Instructor Book II.4]; Cyprian[Treatise X.10]; Tertullian[On Modesty 7]

13:12-14 Clement of Alexandria[Stromata Book III.7]

13:13 Pseudepigrapha[Pseudo-Phocylides 69; Sibylline Oracles 1.175]; Clement of Alexandria[Stromata Book IV.26]; Origen[Gospel of Matthew Book XII.37]; Tertullian[On Fasting 9, 17]; NT-Apocrypha[Acts of Paul in Ephesus p.1]

13:14 Clement of Alexandria[The Instructor Book III.11]; Clement[First Epistle Concerning Virginity 7]; Origen[De Principiis Book II.3.2]; Tertullian[On Monogamy 17]

14:01 Cyprian[Epistle LXXIII.6]

14:01-23 Rabbinic[Babylonian (Nedarim 81b; Shabbat 94b)]

14:02 Genesis 1:29, 9:3; Clement of Alexandria[Stromata Book VI.1]

14:03 Clement of Alexandria[Stromata Book III.6; The Instructor Book II.1]

14:04 Anonymous[Treatise Against the Heretic Novatian 12]; Cyprian[Epistle LI.18]; Hippolytus[Refutation of all Heresies Book IX.7]; Tertullian[On Modesty 2]

14:06 Colossians 2:16; Clement of Alexandria[The Instructor Book II.1]

14:08 OT-Apocrypha[4Maccabees 7:19]; NT-Apocrypha[Martyrdom of the Holy Apostle Paul 1.4]

14:09 Irenaeus[Against Heresies Book III.18.2]; Methodius[Apostolic Words from the Discourse on the Resurrection 20]; Origen[Against Celsus Book II.65; Gospel of John Book VI.18]; NT-Apocrypha[Acts of Thomas 1.30]

14:10 2Corinthians 5:10; Apostolic[Polycarp - Letter to the Philippians 6:2]

14:11 Isaiah 45:23, 49:18; Jeremiah 22:24; Ezekiel 5:11; Pseudepigrapha[Martyrdom and Ascension of Isaiah 9.27-32]

14:12 Rabbinic[Mishna Aboth 4:22]

14:12-13 Cyprian[Epistle LXXV.17]

14:13 Tertullian[To his Wife Book II.1]

14:15 Irenaeus[Against Heresies Book III.18.3]; Origen[Against Celsus Book I.Preface.6, VIII.28, Letter to Africanus 5]

14:16-17 Clement of Alexandria[The Instructor Book II.1]

14:17 Clement of Alexandria[Stromata Book III.6]; Cyprian[Treatise XII.Book III.60]; Novatian[On the Jewish Meats 5]; Tertullian[On Fasting 15; On Prayer 12]

14:19 Clement of Alexandria[Stromata Book III.12]

14:20 Teaching of the Twelve Apostles 6.3

14:20-21 Clement of Alexandria[The Instructor Book II.1]; Tertullian[On Fasting 15]

14:21 Clement of Alexandria[Stromata Book III.12]; Origen[Against Celsus Book VIII.28]

14:23 Dionysius of Alexandria[Extant Fragments Epistle to Bishop Basilides 4]; Origen[Gospel of Matthew Book XI.12, 14, XII.21]

15:03 Psalms 69:9-10

15:04 OT-Apocrypha[1Maccabees 12:9]; Clement of Alexandria[Stromata Book IV.5]; Fabian[First Epistle]

15:05 Tertullian[On Modesty 2]

15:06 Pseudepigrapha[4Baruch 9:14]

15:08 Psalms 89:3; Micah 7:20; OT-Apocrypha[Sirach 36:20]; Pseudepigrapha[Odes of Solomon 31:13]

15:09 2Samuel 22:50; Psalms 18:49-50

15:10 Deuteronomy 32:43

15:11 Psalms 117:1

15:12 Isaiah 11:10; Tertullian[On the Resurrection of the Flesh 59]

15:13 Gregory Thaumaturgus[Sectional Confession of Faith 10]

15:13-14 Clement of Alexandria[Stromata Book IV.7]

15:14 NT-Apocrypha[Fragments of a Dialogue between John and Jesus]

15:15-16 Archelaus[Disputation with Manes 34]

15:15-17 Justin[Dialogue with Trypho 116]

15:15-20 Gregory Thaumaturgus[Sectional Confession of Faith 11]

15:16 Isaiah 66:20; OT-Apocrypha[4Maccabees 7:8]; Cyprian[Epistle IX.4]

15:18 Archelaus[Disputation with Manes 34]

15:19 Origen[Against Celsus Book VII.21; Gospel of John Book V.3]; NT-Apocrypha[Acts of Peter and Paul]

15:21 Isaiah 52:15

15:26 1Corinthians 16:1-4

15:27 1Corinthians 9:11; Teaching of the Twelve Apostles 4.8

15:29 Clement of Alexandria[Stromata Book V.10]

15:33 Pseudepigrapha[Testament of Dan 5:2]

16:02 Acts 18:2

16:05 Exodus 3:14

16:07 Teaching of the Twelve Apostles 11.4

16:11 NT-Apocrypha[Acts of Peter 1.6]

16:13 Mark 15:21

16:14 Hippolytus[Appendix to the Works of Hippolytus - On the Seventy Apostles 37]

16:15 Pseudepigrapha[Testament of Job 51:2]
16:16 Clement of Alexandria[The Instructor Book III.11]; Tertullian[On Prayer 18]; Nag
    Hammadi[Gospel of Philip 58; Letter of Peter to Philip 140]
16:17 Irenaeus[Against Heresies Book I.31.4, II.14.2]
16:17-18 NT-Apocrypha[Epistula Apostolorum 50]
16:17-19 Clement[First Epistle Concerning Virginity 11]
16:18 Clement[First Epistle Concerning Virginity 13]
16:19 Clement of Alexandria[The Instructor Book I.5]
16:20 Genesis 3:15; Constitutions of the Holy Apostles[Book VIII.8]; Theonas[Epistle to Lucianus, the
    Chief Chamberlain 9]; NT-Apocrypha[Acts of Peter 1.6]
16:21 Acts 16:1; Constitutions of the Holy Apostles[Book VI.18]; NT-Apocrypha[Acts of Barnabas]
16:22 Pseudepigrapha[Testament of Job 51:4]
16:23 Acts 19:29; 1Corinthians 1:14; 2Timothy 4:20; NT-Apocrypha[Acts of Peter 1.1]
16:25 Origen[Gospel of John Book VI.2]
16:25-26 Origen[Against Celsus Book II.4, III.61]
16:26 Acts 3:18n; Rabbinic[Babylonian Sanhedrin 99a]
16:26-27 Clement of Alexandria[Stromata Book IV.3]
16:27 OT-Apocrypha[4Maccabees 18:24]; Pseudepigrapha[Pseudo-Phocylides 54]

Cross Reference Index: First Corinthians

01:01 Origen[Gospel of Matthew Book XIV.1]

01:02 Psalms 99:6; Joel 3:5; Acts 18.1

01:03 John 1:18n; Pseudepigrapha[2Baruch 78:3]; Tertullian[Five Books Against Marcion Book V.5]

01:05 Origen[Gospel of John Book VI.1]

01:07 Pseudepigrapha[Martyrdom and Ascension of Isaiah (3:13-4:22 = Testament of Hezekiah) 4:13]; Rabbinic[Babylonian Sanhedrin 97b]

01:09 Deuteronomy 7:9; Clement of Alexandria[Stromata Book II.6, V.1]

01:10 Anonymous[Treatise on Re-Baptism 2]; Constitutions of the Holy Apostles[Book II.44]; Cyprian[Treatise I.8, XII.Book III.86]; Origen[Gospel of Matthew Book XIV.1; De Principiis Book I.6.2]; Tertullian[On Prescription Against Heretics 5, 26]

01:10-13 Apostolic[1Clement 46:5-9]

01:11-12 Tertullian[On Baptism 14]

01:12 Acts 18:24; Origen[Gospel of Matthew Book XIV.1]

01:13-17 Matthew 3:5-16n

01:14 Acts 18:8, 19.29; Romans 16:23; Clement of Alexandria[Fragments from the Books of the Hypotyposes Book V]; Tertullian[On Baptism 14]

01:14-15 Tertullian[On Modesty 14]

01:16 1Corinthians 16:15; NT-Apocrypha[Acts of Paul in Philippi 1.1]

01:16-17 Tertullian[On Baptism 14]

01:17-18 Colossians 1:20

01:17-24 Cyprian[Treatise XII.Book III.69]

01:17-25 Pseudepigrapha[Sibylline Oracles 8.246]

01:18 Pseudepigrapha[Martyrdom and Ascension of Isaiah 9.26]; Irenaeus[Against Heresies Book I.3.5]; Justin[Dialogue with Trypho 138]; Origen[Against Celsus Book III.47]; Theodotus[Excerpts 27]; Nag Hammadi[Apocryphon of James 5-6]

01:18-19 Tertullian[Five Books Against Marcion Book V.5]

01:19 Psalms 33:10; Isaiah 29:14; Clement of Alexandria[Stromata Book I.3]; Tertullian[Five Books Against Marcion Book V.19]

01:19-20 Clement of Alexandria[Stromata Book V.1]

01:19-24 Clement of Alexandria[Stromata Book I.18]

01:20 Job 12:17; Isaiah 19:11, 33:18, 44:25; Apostolic[Ignatius - Letter to the Ephesians 18:1]; Tertullian[On Idolatry 9; On the Resurrection of the Flesh 3; Five Books Against Marcion Book V.5]; Nag Hammadi[Teachings of Silvanus 111-112]

01:20-22 Lactantius[Divine Institutes Book IV.2]

01:21 Methodius[Oration on the Psalms 6]; Origen[Against Celsus Book V.16; Gospel of Matthew Book XI.17, XII.30]; Tertullian[On Modesty 9; Five Books Against Marcion Book II.2, V.5]

01:22 Clement of Alexandria[Stromata Book I.2]; Tertullian[Five Books Against Marcion Book V.5]

01:22-24 Cyprian[Treatise XII.Book II.1]

01:23 Clement of Alexandria[Stromata Book VI.15]; Irenaeus[Against Heresies Book III.18.2]; Origen[Gospel of Matthew Book X.16]; Tertullian[An Answer to the Jews 10; Five Books Against Marcion Book V.5]

01:23-24 Origen[Against Celsus Book I.13]

01:24 Deuteronomy 4:37, 9:29; Job 12:13; Psalms 106:8; Jeremiah 10:12, 27:5, 32:17, 51:15; Habakkuk 3:19; OT-Apocrypha[Wisdom of Solomon 7:24]; Pseudepigrapha[2Baruch 21.6; Prayer of Jacob 1.1-7; Prayer of Joseph Fragment A 1-9]; Clement of Alexandria[Stromata Book I.20, 26, VI.6, VII.2]; Justin[Dialogue with Trypho 105, 128; First Apology 23; Second Apology 10]; Melito[Fragments 9.9]; Origen[Gospel of John Book I.23; Gospel of Matthew Book XIV.1; De Principiis Book I.2.1, 9]; Tertullian[Against Praxeas 19]

01:25 Tertullian[Five Books Against Marcion Book II.2, V.5]

01:26 Irenaeus[Against Heresies Book II.19.7]; Origen[Against Celsus Book VI.14; De Principiis Book III.4.2]; Nag Hammadi[Gospel of Truth 21-22]

01:26-27 Origen[Gospel of John Book IV.2]; Tertullian[To his Wife Book II.6]

01:26-28 Origen[Against Celsus Book III.48]

01:26-29 Origen[De Principiis Book IV.1.4]; NT-Apocrypha[Correspondence between Seneca and Paul VII]

01:27 Origen[Against Celsus Book III.73, VII.44]; Tertullian[Against Praxeas 10; On Baptism 2; On the Flesh of Christ 4; On the Resurrection of the Flesh 57; Five Books Against Marcion Book V.5, 19]

01:27-28 Tertullian[De Fuga in Persecutione 2]; Origen[Against Celsus Book VI.4]

01:28 Irenaeus[Against Heresies Book II.19.7]; Origen[Gospel of Matthew Book XI.17]

01:29 Irenaeus[Against Heresies Book III.20.1]; Origen[De Principiis Book III.1.12]; Tertullian[Five Books Against Marcion Book V.5]

01:30 Jeremiah 23:5-6; Origen[Against Celsus Book V.39, VI.44; Gospel of John Book I.11, 23, XII.11, 25]

01:31 Jeremiah 9:22-24; Apostolic[1Clement 13]; Clement of Alexandria[The Instructor Book I.6]; Tertullian[Five Books Against Marcion Book V.5]; NT-Apocrypha[History of Joseph the Carpenter 2]

02:02 Origen[Against Celsus Book II.66, IV.30; Gospel of Matthew Book XII.18; De Principiis Book IV.1.31]; Tertullian[On Modesty 14; On the Flesh of Christ 5]

02:03 Pseudepigrapha[Joseph and Aseneth 9:1, 15:5]

02:04 Origen[Gospel of John Book I.10; Gospel of Matthew Book XIV.14; De Principiis Book IV.1.7]

02:04-05 Gregory Thaumaturgus[Sectional Confession of Faith 12]; Origen[Against Celsus Book I.62, VI.2]

02:05 Clement of Alexandria[Stromata Book I.11, V.1]

02:06 Pseudepigrapha[Sibylline Oracles 2.219]; Irenaeus[Against Heresies Book I.8.4, III.2.1, V.6.1]; Origen[Against Celsus Book II.24, III.59; Gospel of John Book VI.32; De Principiis Book III.2.1, IV.1.7]; Nag Hammadi[Gospel of Philip 81]; NT-Apocrypha[Epistula Apostolorum 28]

02:06-07 Clement of Alexandria[Stromata Book V.10, 12]; Origen[De Principiis Book IV.1.11]; Tertullian[On Modesty 8; On the Pallium 4; Five Books Against Marcion Book V.5]

02:06-08 Pseudepigrapha[Apocalypse of Adam 6:8]; Origen[Against Celsus Book III.19; De Principiis Book III.3.1-2, IV.1.13]

02:06-16 This section also includes topical notes for: God`s Wisdom in a Mystery - Exodus 4:22; Isaiah 9:1-8, 42:1-4, 49:1-7, 52:13-53:12; Matthew 16:13-23; Luke 24:25-27, 24:44-47; Acts 26:22-27; 2Corinthians 3:12-18, 4:3-6; Ephesians 3:3-9; Pseudepigrapha[4Ezra 4.1-12; Hellenistic Synagogal Prayers 10.12-13; Joseph and Aseneth 22.13; Odes of Solomon 8.8-12, 18.14]; Dead Sea Scrolls[1Q Habakkuk Pesher (1QHAB) COL VII 4-14; 1Q Hymns (1QHODAYOTH [1QH]) COL XIII 25-26]; Plato[Timaeus 51e]; Tacitus[The Histories 1.22]; Clement of Alexandria[Exhortation to the Heathen 11-12; Stromata Book I.12, V.4,10, 12, 14, VI.9, 11, 15; The Instructor Book I.6, III.1]; Irenaeus[Against Heresies Book I.Preface.2, 3.1, 3, 6.1, 12.4, 15.2, 21.4, 29.3, 30.14, 31.1, 3-4, II.13.10, 14.1, 7, 16.0-11, 18.1, 22.3, 24.1, 25.4, 28.1-2, 4, 6, 30.7, 9, III.1.1, 2.1, 3.1, 5.1, 7.1, IV.18.4, 29.1, 33.3, 15, V.6.1, 8.2, 4, 9.1-4, 10.1-2, 11.1, 12.2-3; Fragments from the Lost Works 26, 36]; Justin[Dialogue with Trypho 4, 7, 38, 55, 91, 94, 106, 111, 114-115, 125, 131, 134, 138, 141; Hortatory Address to the Greeks 8, 35]; Origen[De Principiis Book IV.1.10]; Tatian[Address to the Greeks 15]; Nag Hammadi[A Valentinian Exposition 22, 25; Apocryphon of John 6-8; Gospel of the Egyptians IV. 57-8; Gospel of Truth 18, 37; Prayer of the Apostle Paul A.I; Teachings of Silvanus 107, 116; Testimony of Truth 41; Trimorphic Protennoia 41; Tripartite Tractate 66, 126]

02:07 Lactantius[Divine Institutes Book II.3]; Origen[Against Celsus Book III.61; Gospel of Matthew Book XII.38, XIII.3]

02:07-08 Acts 2:23n; Pseudepigrapha[Martyrdom and Ascension of Isaiah 11.15]; Justin[Dialogue with Trypho 95]; Origen[Gospel of Matthew Book XIII.8]

02:08 Pseudepigrapha[Martyrdom and Ascension of Isaiah 10:11; Sibylline Oracles 1.369-370]; Hippolytus[The Discourse on the Holy Theophany 4]; Justin[First Apology 36, 49]; Tertullian[On Modesty 9; Five Books Against Marcion Book V.6]; NT-Apocrypha[Epistula Apostolorum 28]

02:09 This section also includes topical notes for: Eye Saw Not - Isaiah 52:15, 64:3-4, 65:16; Jeremiah 3:16; OT-Apocrypha[Sirach 1:10]; Pseudepigrapha[4Ezra 7:15]; Josephus[Discourse to the Greeks Concerning Hades 7]; Rabbinic[Babylonian (Berakhot 34b; Sanhedrin 99a cf. {Isaiah 64:3})]; Plato[Phaedo 114b-c]; Apostolic[1Clement 34:8; 2Clement 11:7, 14:5; Martyrdom of Polycarp 2:4]; Alexander of Alexandria[Epistles on Arian Heresy 1.5]; Clement of Alexandria[Exhortation to the Heathen 10, 12; Stromata Book II.4, IV.18, V.4, 6, VI.8; The Instructor Book I.6, II.13, III.12; Who is

the Rich Man that shall be Saved 23]; Clement[First Epistle Concerning Virginity 9]; Constitutions of the Holy Apostles[Book VII.32]; Hippolytus[Against Plato on the cause of the Universe 3; Appendix to the Works of Hippolytus - On the End of the World 44; Refutation of all Heresies Book V.19, 21-22]; Irenaeus[Against Heresies Book V.36.3]; Lactantius[Divine Institutes Book IV.1]; Liturgy of James 31; Novatian[Treatise Concerning the Trinity 7]; Origen[De Principiis Book III.6.4]; Tertullian[Five Books in Reply to Marcion Book II.24; On the Resurrection of the Flesh 26]; Theophilus of Antioch[To Autolycus Book I.14]; Nag Hammadi[Dialogue of the Savior 57; Gospel of Philip 76; Gospel of the Egyptians III.68; Gospel of Thomas 17; Prayer of the Apostle Paul A.I]; NT-Apocrypha[Acts of Peter 1.39; Acts of Thomas 1.36; Gospel of Judas 47; Gospel of Mani Turfman Fragment M 789; Pseudo-Titus Epistle Line 5]; Epic of Gilgamesh[The Search for Everlasting Life]

02:09-11 Gregory Thaumaturgus[Sectional Confession of Faith 12]

02:10 Job 11:7; Daniel 2:22; Pseudepigrapha[Testament of Job 37:6]; Clement of Alexandria[Stromata Book II.2, VI.18]; Irenaeus[Against Heresies Book II.28.7]; Origen[Gospel of Matthew Book XIV.11; De Principiis Book I.3.4]; Nag Hammadi[Trimorphic Protennoia 50]

02:10-11 Proverbs 20:27; Matthew 28:19n

02:11 Zechariah 12:1; Origen[Gospel of Matthew Book XIII.2, XIV.6]; Tertullian[Against Hermogenes 18; Against Praxeas 8, 19; Five Books Against Marcion Book II.2]

02:12 Novatian[Treatise Concerning the Trinity 29]; Origen[Gospel of John Book I.6]

02:13 Clement of Alexandria[Stromata Book I.17, V.4]; Hippolytus[Refutation of all Heresies Book VII.14]; Origen[Gospel of Matthew Book XIV.14]

02:13-14 Clement[First Epistle Concerning Virginity 11]; Hippolytus[Refutation of all Heresies Book V.3]

02:14 Clement of Alexandria[Stromata Book I.12, VI.18]; Gregory Thaumaturgus[Sectional Confession of Faith 12]; Hippolytus[Refutation of all Heresies Book V.29]; Irenaeus[Against Heresies Book V.8.4; Demonstration of the Apostolic Preaching 100; Fragments from the Lost Works 36]; Lactantius[Divine Institutes Book II.3]; Origen[Against Celsus Book VI.71; Gospel of John Book I.3]; Tertullian[On Fasting 3; Five Books Against Marcion Book II.2]; Urban I[Epistle 7.7]

02:14-15 Pseudepigrapha[Letter of Aristeas 1.127]; Irenaeus[Against Heresies Book I.8.3]; Origen[Gospel of John Book II.15]

02:15 Clement of Alexandria[Stromata Book I.11]; Irenaeus[Against Heresies Book IV.33.1, 15]

02:16 Isaiah 40:13; Jeremiah 23:18; OT-Apocrypha[Wisdom of Solomon 9:13]; Apostolic[Ignatius - Letter to the Ephesians 3:2]; Origen[Gospel of John Book I.6, X.18; Gospel of Matthew Book XI.3]; NT-Apocrypha[Epistle to the Laodiceans 1:14]

03:01 Tertullian[On Prescription Against Heretics 27]

03:01-02 Pseudepigrapha[Odes of Solomon 8:14]

03:01-03 Clement of Alexandria[Stromata Book V.10; The Instructor Book I.6]; Cyprian[Treatise XII.Book III.3]; Irenaeus[Against Heresies Book V.8.4]

03:02 Hebrews 5:12-13; Archelaus[Disputation with Manes 41]; Irenaeus[Against Heresies Book IV.38.1]; Origen[Gospel of Matthew Book XII.31]; Tertullian[On Monogamy 11]

03:02-03 Origen[Against Celsus Book II.66]

03:03 Anonymous[Treatise Against the Heretic Novatian 14]; Irenaeus[Against Heresies Book IV.38.2]

03:03-04 Tertullian[On Baptism 14]

03:04 1Corinthians 1:12

03:06 Acts 18:4-11, 24-28; Pseudepigrapha[Sibylline Oracles 5.262]; Gregory Thaumaturgus[Sectional Confession of Faith 7]; Irenaeus[Against Heresies Book V.6.2]

03:06-07 Origen[De Principiis Book III.1.18]

03:06-08 Novatian[Treatise Concerning the Trinity 27]

03:06-09 Tertullian[An Answer to the Jews 3]

03:06-10 Pseudepigrapha[Odes of Solomon 38:17]

03:07 Archelaus[Disputation with Manes 13]; Irenaeus[Against Heresies Book IV.25.3]; Methodius[Discourse on the Resurrection 1.15]

03:08 Tertullian[On Monogamy 10]

03:08-09 Clement of Alexandria[Stromata Book I.1]

03:09 Dionysius of Alexandria[Exegetical Fragments Commentary on the Beginning of Ecclesiastes 1.18]; Origen[Against Celsus Book IV.1]; NT-Apocrypha[Acts of Thomas 1.39; Pseudo Clementines - Kerygmata Petrou H XVII 19.7]

03:10 Isaiah 3:3; Archelaus[Disputation with Manes 51]; Tertullian[An Answer to the Jews 13; Five Books Against Marcion Book V.6]

03:10-15 Clement of Alexandria[Stromata Book V.4]; Irenaeus[Against Heresies Book V.29.1]; Justin[First Apology 17]

03:11 Isaiah 28:16; Archelaus[Disputation with Manes 48]; Tertullian[Five Books Against Marcion Book V.6]

03:11-15 Lactantius[Divine Institutes Book VI.9]

03:12 Anonymous[Treatise Against the Heretic Novatian 7]; Clement of Alexandria[Stromata Book VI.17]; Origen[Against Celsus Book V.15, VI.70; De Principiis Book II.10.4]

03:12-15 This section also includes topical notes for: Prove Each Man`s Work - Numbers 31:22-23; 1Kings 7:51; 2Chronicles 15:8; Proverbs 19:17; 1Peter 1:7n; Revelation 3:18n; Pseudepigrapha[4Ezra 7.52-61]; Rabbinic[Babylonian Sotah 49a; Yalqut on Psalms 60:9 cf. {Daniel 1:6}]; Plato[Republic III 415a-c, **VI 502e-503a**, VIII 546e]; Apostolic[Martyrdom of Polycarp 15:2]; Origen[Against Celsus Book IV.13]; NT-Apocrypha[Epistula Apostolorum 39]

> We were saying, as you will remember, that they were to be lovers of their country, tried by the test of pleasures and pains, and neither in hardships, nor in dangers, nor at any other critical moment were to lose their patriotism--he was to be rejected who failed, but he who always came forth pure, like gold tried in the refiner's fire, was to be made a ruler, and to receive honors and rewards in life and after death. (Plato - Republic VI 502e-503a)

03:13 Malachi 3:19; Pseudepigrapha[Testament of Abraham 13:13]; Apostolic[1Clement 47]; Cyprian[Epistle LI.20]; NT-Apocrypha[Acts of Paul in Ephesus p.2]

03:13-15 Pseudepigrapha[Testament of Abraham 12:10-14]; Justin[Dialogue with Trypho 116]

03:14 Pseudepigrapha[4Ezra 7:99]; NT-Apocrypha[Acts of Paul in Philippi 3.36]

03:15 Amos 4:11; Apostolic[2Clement 7:4-6]; Nag Hammadi[Gospel of Truth 42]; Egyptian Book of the Dead[Oration 19, 22, 24, 63B]

03:16 John 2:19-21n; Romans 8:9-11n; 1Corinthians 6:19; 2Corinthians 6:16; Apostolic[Ignatius - Letter to the Ephesians 15:3, Letter to the Philadelphians 7:2; Epistle of Barnabas 4:11, 6:14-15]; Clement of Alexandria[Exhortation to the Heathen 11; Stromata Book VII.13]; Cyprian[Epistle LIX.2]; Tertullian[A Treatise on the Soul 53; On Modesty 6; On the Resurrection of the Flesh 10; Five Books Against Marcion Book V.6; To his Wife Book II.3]

03:16-17 Cyprian[Treatise XII.Book III.27]; Gregory Thaumaturgus[Sectional Confession of Faith 21]; Irenaeus[Fragments from the Lost Works 40]; Tertullian[On the Apparel of Women Book II.1]

03:16-18 Tertullian[On Modesty 16]

03:17 Psalms 66:5, 79:1; Archelaus[Disputation with Manes 19]; Irenaeus[Against Heresies Book IV.8.3, V.6.2]; Tertullian[Five Books Against Marcion Book V.6]

03:18 Tertullian[On Prescription Against Heretics 7; Five Books Against Marcion Book V.6]

03:18-19 Origen[Against Celsus Book I.13]

03:18-20 Cyprian[Treatise IX.2, XII.Book III.69]

03:19 Job 5:12-13; Clement of Alexandria[Exhortation to the Heathen 11]; Origen[Against Celsus Book VI.12, VII.23; Gospel of John Book II.4]; Tertullian[On the Resurrection of the Flesh 3; Five Books Against Marcion Book V.6]; Urban I[Epistle 6.6]; Nag Hammadi[Teachings of Silvanus 111-112]

03:19-20 Clement of Alexandria[Stromata Book I.3, 11]

03:20 Psalms 94:11; Tertullian[Five Books Against Marcion Book V.6]

03:21 Tertullian[On the Apparel of Women Book II.3; Five Books Against Marcion Book V.6]

03:21-23 Tertullian[Five Books Against Marcion Book V.7]

03:22 Tertullian[On the Resurrection of the Flesh 59]

04:01 Apostolic[Ignatius - Letter to the Trallians 2:3]

04:03 Tertullian[On the Apparel of Women Book II.13]

04:04 Job 27:6; Psalms 143:2; Apostolic[Ignatius - Letter to the Romans 5:1]; Irenaeus[Against Heresies Book IV.9.2]

04:05 Pseudepigrapha[2Baruch 83:3; 4Ezra 12.37-39]; Origen[Gospel of Matthew Book XI.15, XIII.30]; Tertullian[Five Books Against Marcion Book V.7]; Nag Hammadi[Gospel of Thomas 5-6]; NT-Apocrypha[Canon Muratori Line 23]

04:07 Cyprian[Treatise XII.Book III.4]; Tertullian[On Modesty 14; On Prayer 22; On the Veiling of Virgins 13]

04:08 Tertullian[On Fasting 12; On Modesty 14]; Nag Hammadi[Apocryphon of James 4]

04:09 OT-Apocrypha[4Maccabees 17:14; Joseph and Aseneth 15:5]; Origen[Gospel of John Book I.24]; Tertullian[Five Books Against Marcion Book V.7]

04:09-12 Clement of Alexandria[Stromata Book IV.7]

04:10 Proverbs 3:7

04:12 Psalms 109:28; Acts 18:3

04:12-13 Matthew 5:44n; Origen[Against Celsus Book V.63, VII.46]

04:13 Proverbs 21:18; Lamentations 3:45; OT-Apocrypha[Tobit 5:19]; Origen[Gospel of John Book VI.37]

04:14 OT-Apocrypha[Wisdom of Solomon 11:10]; Apostolic[Papias Fragment 15:1]

04:15 Clement of Alexandria[Stromata Book III.15, V.2]; Methodius[Banquet of the Ten Virgins 3.9]; Tertullian[On Monogamy 6; Five Books Against Marcion Book V.8]; NT-Apocrypha[Epistula Apostolorum 41]

04:16 1Corinthians 11:1; Philippians 3:17

04:17 Pseudepigrapha[1Enoch 104:13]

04:19 Clement of Alexandria[Stromata Book VII.16]; Tertullian[A Treatise on the Soul 53]

04:19-20 Clement of Alexandria[Stromata Book I.11]; Origen[Gospel of John Book I.10]

04:20 Cyprian[Treatise XII.Book III.96]

04:21 Clement of Alexandria[The Instructor Book I.7]

05:01 Leviticus 18:7-88; Deuteronomy 22:30, 27:20; Pseudepigrapha[Pseudo-Phocylides 179]; Rabbinic[Babylonian (Qiddushin 77a; Sanhedrin 58a-b; Yebamot 22a)]; Tertullian[On Modesty 2; Five Books Against Marcion Book V.7]; NT-Apocrypha[Pseudo-Titus Epistle Line 200]

05:02 Tertullian[On Modesty 13]

05:03 Tertullian[On Fasting 13; On Modesty 14]

05:04 Cyprian[Epistle XI.1]; Origen[Gospel of Matthew Book XIV.1]

05:05 Clement of Alexandria[Fragments from the Latin Translation of Cassiodorus Comments on 1Peter]; Hippolytus[Refutation of all Heresies Book IX.18]; Tertullian[On Modesty 2, 13; Five Books Against Marcion Book V.7]; Urban I[Epistle 2.2]

05:06 Galatians 5:9; Irenaeus[Against Heresies Book IV.27.4]; Tertullian[On Modesty 13, 18; On the Apparel of Women Book II.3]

05:06-08 Matthew 16:6-12n; Rabbinic[Babylonian Berakhot 17a]

05:06-09 Tertullian[Five Books in Reply to Marcion Book II.89]

05:07 Exodus 12:5, 19, 21; Isaiah 53:7; Archelaus[Disputation with Manes 49]; Clement of Alexandria[Stromata Book III.18, V.10]; Cyprian[Treatise II.16]; Hippolytus[Fragments of Discourses or Homilies 5; Refutation of all Heresies Book X.29]; Origen[Gospel of John Book X.11]; Peter of Alexandria[Fragments Up to the Time of the Destruction of Jerusalem]; Tertullian[An Answer to the Jews 11; Five Books Against Marcion Book V.7]

05:07-08 Exodus 13:7; Apostolic[Ignatius - Letter to the Magnesians 10:2]; Cyprian[Treatise XII.Book III.11]; Hippolytus[Refutation of all Heresies Book VIII.7, 11]

05:08 Exodus 12:3-20, 13:7, 23:15, 34:18; Leviticus 23:6; Deuteronomy 16:3; Ezekiel 45:21; Matthew 26:17; Mark 14:1; Luke 22:1; Philo[Special Laws II (155, 161) cf. {Leviticus 23:6}]; Origen[Gospel of John Book X.13; Gospel of Matthew Book XII.5]

05:09-10 Nag Hammadi[Exegesis of the Soul 131]

05:09-11 Tertullian[On Modesty 18]

05:10 Pseudepigrapha[Sibylline Oracles 1.175]; Tertullian[A Treatise on the Soul 35; On Idolatry 14, 24]

05:11 Pseudepigrapha[Pseudo-Phocylides 69]; Clement of Alexandria[Stromata Book III.18; The Instructor Book II.1]; Fabian[First Epistle; Second Epistle]; Irenaeus[Against Heresies Book IV.27.4]; Origen[Gospel of Matthew Book XIII.30]; Tertullian[Five Books Against Marcion Book IV.9; To his Wife Book II.3]

05:12 Tertullian[On Modesty 2, 19]

05:13 Deuteronomy 17:7, 19:19, 21:21, 22:24, 24:7; Joshua 7:13; Tertullian[Against Hermogenes 11; Five Books Against Marcion Book V.7, 18]

06:01 Rabbinic[Babylonian Gittin 88b]; Constitutions of the Holy Apostles[Book II.45]; NT-Apocrypha[Letter of Clement to James 5.2]

06:01-02 Cyprian[Treatise XII.Book III.44]

06:01-03 Clement of Alexandria[Stromata Book VII.14]; Tertullian[To his Wife Book II.6]

06:01-06 Tertullian[On Modesty 2]

06:02 Daniel 7:22; OT-Apocrypha[Wisdom of Solomon 3:8]; Apostolic[Polycarp - Letter to the Philippians 11:2]

06:02-03 Tertullian[On Idolatry 18]

06:03 Pseudepigrapha[1Enoch 13:10, 14:3]; Dead Sea Scrolls[4Q Enoch (4Q202[4QENAR]) COL VI 5-10, (4Q204[4QENAR]) COL VI 5-17]; Origen[Gospel of Matthew Book X.13]; Tertullian[On Modesty 14; On Repentance 7; On the Apparel of Women Book I.2; Five Books Against Marcion Book II.9]; NT-Apocrypha[Acts of Paul and Thecla 1.6; Letter of Clement to James 5.2]

06:04 Cyprian[Treatises Attributed to Cyprian - On the Glory of Martyrdom 28]

06:07 Apostolic[Ignatius - Letter to the Ephesians 10:3]; Fabian[Second Epistle]

06:07-09 Clement of Alexandria[Stromata Book VII.14]; Cyprian[Treatise XII.Book III.44]

06:09 Pseudepigrapha[Sibylline Oracles 1.175, 3.185; Testament of Jacob 7:19]; Apostolic[Ignatius - Letter to the Philadelphians 3:3; Polycarp - Letter to the Philippians 5:3]; Cyprian[Treatise IV.12]

06:09-10 Apostolic[Ignatius - Letter to the Ephesians 16:1]; Clement of Alexandria[The Instructor Book III.11]; Irenaeus[Against Heresies Book IV.27.4]

06:09-11 Pseudepigrapha[Joseph and Aseneth 12:5; Testament of Job 25:1]; Clement of Alexandria[Stromata Book III.18]; Cyprian[Treatise XII.Book III.65]; Irenaeus[Against Heresies Book V.11.1]; Tertullian[On Modesty 16]

06:10 Pseudepigrapha[Pseudo-Phocylides 69]; Anonymous[Treatise on Re-Baptism 13]; Cyprian[Epistle LIV.4]; Origen[Against Celsus Book VIII.38, 41]

06:11 Gregory Thaumaturgus[Sectional Confession of Faith 21]; Tertullian[A Treatise on the Soul 21]

06:11-12 Irenaeus[Against Heresies Book IV.37.4]

06:11-13 Clement of Alexandria[Stromata Book VII.14]

06:12 1Corinthians 10:23; OT-Apocrypha[Sirach 37:28]

06:13 OT-Apocrypha[Sirach 36:18]; Clement of Alexandria[Stromata Book III.5-6, 18; The Instructor Book I.6, II.1]; Gregory Thaumaturgus[Canonical Epistle 1]; Novatian[On the Jewish Meats 1, 5]

06:13-14 Irenaeus[Against Heresies Book V.6.2]; Tertullian[On Modesty 16; Five Books Against Marcion Book V.7]

06:14 Archelaus[Disputation with Manes 49]; Irenaeus[Against Heresies Book V.7.1]; NT-Apocrypha[Freer Logion]

06:15 Clement of Alexandria[The Instructor Book II.10]; Cyprian[Treatises Attributed to Cyprian - On the Discipline and Advantage of Chastity 6]; Tertullian[On the Resurrection of the Flesh 10; Five Books Against Marcion Book IV.34, V.7; To his Wife Book II.3]

06:15-17 Cyprian[Treatise XII.Book III.62]

06:15-18 Tertullian[On Modesty 16]

06:16 Genesis 2:24; Matthew 19:6; Clement of Alexandria[Stromata Book III.18]

06:17 Deuteronomy 10:20; Psalms 73:28; Pseudepigrapha[Odes of Solomon 3:8]; Origen[Against Celsus Book II.9, VI.47; Gospel of Matthew Book XIV.7, 16; De Principiis Book II.6.3]

06:18 OT-Apocrypha[Sirach 23:17]; Pseudepigrapha[Testament of Reuben 5:5]; Clement of Alexandria[Stromata Book III.12]; Cyprian[Epistle LI.26]; Origen[Gospel of John Book I.5]; Nag Hammadi[Exegesis of the Soul 127-130]; NT-Apocrypha[Acts of Thomas 1.86]

06:18-20 Cyprian[Treatise XII.Book III.63]

06:19 John 2:19-21n; 1Corinthians 3:16; 2Corinthians 6:16; Matthew 28:19n; Clement of Alexandria[Stromata Book VII.11]; Cyprian[Treatise II.2]; Gregory Thaumaturgus[Sectional Confession of Faith 21]; NT-Apocrypha[Acts of Thomas 1.12, 1.87, 1.156]

06:19-20 Clement[First Epistle Concerning Virginity 12]; Constitutions of the Holy Apostles[Book V.16]; Cyprian[Treatise XII.Book III.11]; Tertullian[On Modesty 6, 16; On the Apparel of Women Book II.1, 3]

06:20 Cyprian[Treatise IV.11, XI.6]; Irenaeus[Against Heresies Book V.13.3]; Origen[Gospel of Matthew Book XII.28; Letter to Africanus 5]; Tertullian[On Modesty 6; On the Resurrection of the Flesh 16; Five Books Against Marcion Book V.7]; NT-Apocrypha[Acts of Thomas 1.2, 1.72]

07:01 Pseudepigrapha[2Enoch 59:1; Testament of Solomon 2:3]; Tertullian[On Monogamy 3]

07:01-02 Tertullian[On Monogamy 11]

07:01-03 Clement of Alexandria[Stromata Book III.15]; Tertullian[On Modesty 16]

07:01-06 Methodius[Banquet of the Ten Virgins 3.12]

07:01-07 Cyprian[Treatise XII.Book III.32]

07:01-40 Tertullian[On Exhortation to Chastity 3; On the Veiling of Virgins 4; To his Wife Book I.3]

07:02 Origen[Gospel of Matthew Book XIV.23]

07:03 Clement of Alexandria[Stromata Book III.18]; Tertullian[Of Patience 5]

07:05 Clement of Alexandria[Stromata Book III.6, 12, 15, 18]; Origen[Gospel of Matthew Book XIV.1-2]; Tertullian[On Exhortation to Chastity 1, 10; On the Veiling of Virgins 10]

07:05-06 Irenaeus[Against Heresies Book IV.15.2]

07:35 Archelaus[Disputation with Manes 5]; Clement of Alexandria[Stromata Book IV.5, 23]; Tertullian[To his Wife Book I.3-4]

07:36-37 Methodius[Banquet of the Ten Virgins 3.14]

07:37 Tertullian[On Monogamy 3]

07:38 Clement of Alexandria[Stromata Book IV.23]; Methodius[Banquet of the Ten Virgins 2.7]

07:38-40 Tertullian[On Modesty 16]

07:39 Tertullian[On Monogamy 7, 11; The Chaplet, or De Corona 13; Five Books Against Marcion Book V.7; To his Wife Book II.1-2]

07:39-40 Clement of Alexandria[Stromata Book III.12]; Cyprian[Treatise XII.Book III.62]; Origen[Gospel of Matthew Book XIV.18, 23]; Tertullian[Of Patience 13]

07:40 Gregory Thaumaturgus[Sectional Confession of Faith 21]; Novatian[Treatise Concerning the Trinity 29]; Tertullian[On Monogamy 3]

08:01 Apostolic[Epistle to Diognetus 12:5]; Clement of Alexandria[Stromata Book II.11, IV.15]; Irenaeus[Against Heresies Book II.26.1]; Nag Hammadi[Gospel of Philip 77]

08:01-03 Clement of Alexandria[Stromata Book I.11]

08:01-13 Tertullian[On Idolatry 16]

08:02 Cyprian[Treatise XII.Book III.21]; Tertullian[On Modesty 14; On Prescription Against Heretics 27]

08:03 Origen[Gospel of Matthew Book XIV.23]

08:04 Deuteronomy 4:35, 39, 6:4; Clement of Alexandria[Stromata Book VI.18]; Irenaeus[Against Heresies Book III.6.5]; Novatian[On the Jewish Meats 7]; Origen[Against Celsus Book VIII.24]; Teaching of the Twelve Apostles 6.3; Tertullian[Five Books Against Marcion Book V.7; The Shows, or De Spectaculis 13]; NT-Apocrypha[Acts of Paul in Ephesus p.1]

08:04-13 Hippolytus[Refutation of all Heresies Book IX.21]

08:05 Psalms 136:2; Pseudepigrapha[Apocalypse of Zephaniah A]; Origen[Against Celsus Book VIII.4; Gospel of John Book I.34]; Tertullian[Against Hermogenes 4; Five Books Against Marcion Book III.15, V.7, 11]

08:05-06 Origen[Against Celsus Book IV.29]; Tertullian[Five Books in Reply to Marcion Book IV.40]

08:06 Malachi 2:10; John 1:18n; Matthew 28:19n; Pseudepigrapha[Hellenistic Synagogal Prayers 12:12, 68]; Clement of Alexandria[The Instructor Book II.1]; Hippolytus[Against the Heresy of One Noetus 3]; Tertullian[Five Books Against Marcion Book V.7]

08:07 Clement of Alexandria[Stromata Book IV.15, V.3]; Tertullian[On Modesty 14]

08:07-08 Clement of Alexandria[Stromata Book II.15; The Instructor Book II.1]

08:08 Clement of Alexandria[Stromata Book IV.23]; Cyprian[Treatise XII.Book III.60]; Origen[Against Celsus Book VIII.29; Gospel of Matthew Book XI.12, 14]; Tertullian[On Fasting 2]

08:09 Clement of Alexandria[Stromata Book IV.15]

08:10 Pseudepigrapha[Sibylline Oracles 2.96]; Tertullian[On Idolatry 10; The Chaplet, or De Corona 11]

08:11 Clement of Alexandria[Stromata Book IV.15]; Irenaeus[Against Heresies Book III.18.3]

08:11-12 Origen[Gospel of Matthew Book XIII.22]

08:11-13 Clement of Alexandria[The Instructor Book II.1]

08:12 Tertullian[On Modesty 14]

08:12-13 Clement[Second Epistle Concerning Virginity 5]

08:13 Cyprian[Epistle LXI.2]; Origen[Against Celsus Book VIII.28]

09:01 Tertullian[Against Praxeas 15; On Modesty 14]

09:01-05 Tertullian[On Monogamy 8]

09:04-05 Tertullian[On Exhortation to Chastity 8]

09:05 Clement of Alexandria[Stromata Book III.6]

09:06 Tertullian[On Modesty 19]

09:07 Deuteronomy 20:6; Tertullian[Five Books Against Marcion Book V.7]

09:08-10 Origen[Against Celsus Book II.3]

09:09 Deuteronomy 25:4; Archelaus[Disputation with Manes 21]; Tertullian[Five Books Against Marcion Book III.5, V.7]

09:09-10 Origen[Against Celsus Book IV.49; De Principiis Book II.4.2, IV.1.12]; Tertullian[An Answer to the Jews 3]

09:09-18 Tertullian[On Exhortation to Chastity 8]

09:10 OT-Apocrypha[Sirach 6:19]; Origen[Gospel of Matthew Book XII.4]

09:11 Romans 15:27

09:13 Leviticus 6:16, 26; Numbers 18:8, 31; Deuteronomy 18:1-3

09:13-14 Tertullian[Five Books Against Marcion Book V.7]

09:14 Matthew 10:10; Luke 10:7; Clement of Alexandria[The Instructor Book II.1]

09:15 Tertullian[On Modesty 14; Five Books Against Marcion Book V.7]

09:16 Jeremiah 20:9; Tertullian[An Answer to the Jews 6]

09:17 NT-Apocrypha[Acts of John 113]

09:18 Rabbinic[Mishnah Aboth 1.11-13, 4.15]

09:19 1Peter 3:1; Clement of Alexandria[Stromata Book VI.15, VII.9]; Origen[Gospel of Matthew Book XII.41]; Tertullian[On Fasting 13; On Idolatry 18]

09:19-22 Philo[On Dreams, That they Are God-Sent (1.149) cf. {Leviticus 26:12}]

09:19-25 Clement of Alexandria[Stromata Book IV.15]

09:20 Ecclesiastes 3:4; Romans 12:15; Pseudepigrapha[Letter of Aristeas 1.257]; Rabbinic[Aboth De Rabbi Nathan 15; Babylonian Shabbat 31a; Derekh Eretz Rabba 8.4; Derekh Eretz Zuta 5.5; Exodus Rabba on 34.28; Genesis Rabba on 18.8; Mishnah Aboth 1.12, 2.5; Tosephta Berakhot 2.24]

09:20-21 Clement of Alexandria[Stromata Book I.1]

09:20-22 Origen[Gospel of John Book X.5; Gospel of Matthew Book XI.8]; Tertullian[On Prescription Against Heretics 24; Five Books Against Marcion Book V.3]

09:22 Clement of Alexandria[Stromata Book V.3]; Cyprian[Epistle LI.15]; Tertullian[On Idolatry 14; On Monogamy 14]; NT-Apocrypha[Correspondence between Seneca and Paul X]

09:24 Pseudepigrapha[3Baruch 12:6 (Gk.); Hellenistic Synagogal Prayers 2:8; Sibylline Oracles 2.39]; Apostolic[Ignatius - Letter to Polycarp 1:2-3, 2:3]; Cyprian[Treatises Attributed to Cyprian - On the Glory of Martyrdom 28]

09:24-25 Cyprian[Epistle VIII.1; Treatise XI.8, XII.Book III.26]

09:25 Pseudepigrapha[2Baruch 15:8; Greek Apocalypse of Ezra 6:17; Testament of Benjamin 4:1]

09:24-27 This section also includes topical notes for: Win the Crown - 2Timothy 2:5, 4:7-8; James 1:12; 1Peter 5:2-4; Revelation 2:10; Pseudepigrapha[4Ezra 2.43-47, 7.127-129; Greek Apocalypse of Ezra 6.17; Hellenistic Synagogal Prayers 2.8; Letter of Aristeas 1.58, 1.280-281, 1.320; Martyrdom and Ascension of Isaiah 9.12, 9.24-26, 11.40; Odes of Solomon 1.1-3, 5.12, 9.8-11, 11.16a, 17.1, 20.7; Questions of Ezra Recension A 1.6; Sibylline Oracles 2.35-55; Testament of Benjamin 4.1-2]; Dead Sea Scrolls[11Q New Jerusalem (11Qi8[11QNJAR]) Fragment 14 1-5]; Philo[**Allegorical Interpretation II (108) cf. {Leviticus 11:29-44}; On the Migration of Abraham (132-133) cf. {Genesis 18:23, Deuteronomy 10:20}**]; Rabbinic[Avot 6.7 cf. {Proverbs 4:9}; Bablyonian Berakhot 17a; Ecclesiastes Rabba on 7:2]; Plato[Phaedo 60e-61a; Republic X 612d-e, 613b-c, 621c-d]; Apostolic[Martyrdom of Ignatius 5]; Clement of Alexandria[Exhortation to the Heathen 1, 10; Fragments from Maximus 55; Stromata Book VII.3, 11; The Instructor Book I.2, III.8; Who is the Rich Man that shall be Saved 3]; Irenaeus[Against Heresies Book IV.37.6-7, V.29.1]; Tertullian[The Shows, or De Spectaculis 29]; Nag Hammadi[Authoritative Teaching 26; Interpretation of Knowledge 21; Teachings of Silvanus 87, 89, 112, 114; Testimony of Truth 45]; NT-Apocrypha[Epistula Apostolorum 38]; Epic of Gilgamesh[Ishtar and Gilgamesh]

Therefore do thou array against it the wisdom which contends with serpents; and struggle in this most glorious struggle, and labour to win the crown in the contest against pleasure, which subdues every one else; winning a noble and glorious crown, such as no assembly of men can confer. (Philo - Allegorical Interpretation II (108) cf. {Leviticus 11:29-44})

And he also, with a wish further to excite an irresistible desire of what is good, enjoins one to cleave to it; for he says, "Thou shalt fear the Lord thy God, and him only shalt thou serve; and thou shalt cleave to Him." What, then, is this cleaving? What? Surely it is piety and faith; for these virtues adapt and invite the mind to incorruptible nature. For Abraham also, when he believed, is said to have "come near to God." If, therefore, while you are walking you are neither fatigued, so as to give way and stumble, nor are so careless as to turn to either the right hand or to the left hand, and so to stray and miss the direct road which lies between the two; but if, imitating good runners, you finish the course of life without stumbling or error, you will deservedly obtain the crown and worthy prize of victory when you have arrived at your desired end. (Philo - On the Migration of Abraham (132-133) cf. {Genesis 18:23, Deuteronomy 10:20})

09:25 OT-Apocrypha[Wisdom of Solomon 4:2]; Apostolic[2Clement 7:1-3, 20:1-4; Martyrdom of Polycarp 17:1]; Clement of Alexandria[Stromata Book III.16]; Tertullian[Ad Martyras 3]; Theonas[Epistle to Lucianus, the Chief Chamberlain 2]; NT-Apocrypha[Pseudo-Titus Epistle Line 257]

09:26 Origen[Against Celsus Book VII.52]

09:27 Apostolic[Ignatius - Letter to the Trallians 12:3]; Clement of Alexandria[Stromata Book III.16]; Clement[First Epistle Concerning Virginity 9]; Origen[Against Celsus Book V.49]; Tertullian[On Fasting 8]

10:01 Exodus 13:21-22, 14:22-29; Psalms 105:39; OT-Apocrypha[Wisdom of Solomon 19:7]; Pseudepigrapha[Joseph and Aseneth 8:5]; Clement of Alexandria[Stromata Book VII.16]; Cyprian[Treatise XII.Book I.4]

10:01-02 Matthew 3:5-16n; Cyprian[Epistle LXXV.15]

10:01-04 Origen[Against Celsus Book IV.49]

10:01-08 Irenaeus[Against Heresies Book IV.27.3]

10:03 Exodus 16:4, 35; Deuteronomy 8:3; Psalms 78:24-29; Apostolic[Didache 10:3]

10:03-04 John 6:31-58n; Clement of Alexandria[Stromata Book VII.16]

10:04 Exodus 17:6; Numbers 20:7-11; Psalms 78:15; Clement[Recognitions Book I.35]; Gregory Thaumaturgus[Sectional Confession of Faith 22]; Irenaeus[Demonstration of the Apostolic Preaching 46; Fragments from the Lost Works 52]; Justin[Dialogue with Trypho 12, 113-114]; Origen[Gospel of Matthew Book XII.10-11; De Principiis Book IV.1.13]; Tertullian[An Answer to the Jews 9; Of Patience 5; Five Books Against Marcion Book III.5, IV.35, V.7]

10:05 Numbers 14:16, 23, 29-30; Psalms 78:31; Irenaeus[Against Heresies Book IV.36.6]

10:06 Numbers 11:4, 34; Psalms 106:14; Cyprian[Epistle LXXV.15]; Tertullian[On Idolatry 5; On the Resurrection of the Flesh 59; Five Books Against Marcion Book V.7]

10:07 Exodus 32:6; Clement of Alexandria[The Instructor Book I.11]; Tertullian[An Answer to the Jews 1; On Fasting 6; On Idolatry 3]

10:07-10 Tertullian[Five Books Against Marcion Book V.7]

10:08 Numbers 25:1-18, 26:62; Clement of Alexandria[The Instructor Book II.10]; Tertullian[On Modesty 6]

10:09 Numbers 21:5-6; Psalms 78:18

10:10 Exodus 16:2; Numbers 14:2, 36, 16:11-35, 41-49; Psalms 106:25-27

10:11 Pseudepigrapha[4Ezra 2.34-35]; Hippolytus[Fragments - On Susannah 17; Refutation of all Heresies Book V.3]; Irenaeus[Against Heresies Book IV.14.3]; Origen[Against Celsus Book IV.43; Gospel of John Book I.8; De Principiis Book IV.1.13]; Tertullian[Against Praxeas 16; On Idolatry 5; On the Apparel of Women Book II.9; Five Books Against Marcion Book V.7; To his Wife Book I.2, 5]

10:12 Clement of Alexandria[Stromata Book III.1]; Clement[Second Epistle Concerning Virginity 13]; Cyprian[Epistle LI.18; Treatise XII.Book III.21]

10:13 Deuteronomy 7:9; Psalms 145:13; Clement of Alexandria[Stromata Book II.6, V.1]; Cyprian[Treatise XII.Book III.91]; Origen[Gospel of Matthew Book XI.6; De Principiis Book III.2.3]; NT-Apocrypha[Pseudo-Titus Epistle Line 247]

10:14 Tertullian[The Chaplet, or De Corona 10]

10:14-22 Pseudepigrapha[Joseph and Aseneth 8:5]

10:16 Matthew 26:26-29; Mark 14.22-25; Luke 22:19-20; Rabbinic[Babylonian Berakhot 51a; Mishnah Pesahim 10.7]; Irenaeus[Against Heresies Book III.18.2, V.2.2]; Nag Hammadi[Gospel of Philip 75]; NT-Apocrypha[Acts of Thomas 1.121]

10:16-18 This section also includes topical notes for: Eucharist - 1Samuel 21:6; Matthew 26:26-29; Mark 14:22-23; Luke 22:19-20; 1Corinthians 11:23-24; Pseudepigrapha[Jubilees 45:05]; Philo[On Dreams, That They Are God-Sent (2.249)]; Clement of Alexandria[Stromata Book IV.25; The Instructor Book I.6, II.2]; Hippolytus[Refutation of all Heresies Book IX.16]; Irenaeus[Against Heresies Book I.13.2, IV.18.4-5, V.1.3, 2.2-3; Fragments from the Lost Works 13, 37]; Justin[Dialogue with Trypho 41, 70, 117; First Apology 65, 67]; Nag Hammadi[A Valentinian Exposition 43-44; The Acts of Peter 128]; Epic of Gilgamesh[Ishtar and Gilgamesh, The Death of Gilgamesh]

10:16-21 John 6:53-56n

10:18 Leviticus 7:6, 15; Origen[De Principiis Book IV.1.21]; Teaching of the Twelve Apostles 6.3

10:19 Tertullian[A Treatise on the Soul 3]

10:20 Leviticus 17:7; Deuteronomy 32:17; Psalms 106:37; Pseudepigrapha[1Enoch 19.1; Baruch 4:7]; Clement of Alexandria[The Instructor Book II.1]; Clement[Recognitions Book II.71]; Constitutions of the Holy Apostles[Book VII.21]

10:21 Isaiah 65:11; Malachi 1:7, 12; Cyprian[Epistle IX.2, XXX.3; Treatise III.15]; Tertullian[The Shows, or De Spectaculis 13]; NT-Apocrypha[Clement Romance - Peter on his Mission Journeys H VII 4.2]

10:22 Deuteronomy 32:21

10:23 1Corinthians 6:12; OT-Apocrypha[Sirach 37:28]; Clement of Alexandria[The Instructor Book II.1, 13; Stromata Book III.5]; Cyprian[Treatise II.9, XII.Book III.92]; Origen[De Principiis Book II.7.4]; Tertullian[On Baptism 17; On the Apparel of Women Book II.10; To his Wife Book II.6; On Exhortation to Chastity 8]

10:23-31 Clement of Alexandria[Stromata Book IV.7]

10:24 Tertullian[On the Apparel of Women Book II.2]

10:25 Clement of Alexandria[The Instructor Book II.1; Stromata Book IV.15]; Novatian[On the Jewish Meats 5]; Tertullian[On Fasting 2]

10:25-27 Tertullian[Five Books Against Marcion Book V.7]

10:25-31 Hippolytus[Refutation of all Heresies Book IX.21]

10:26 Psalms 50:12, 89:12; Apostolic[1Clement 54]; Clement of Alexandria[Stromata Book IV.15, VI.11, 17]

10:26-28 Psalms 24:1; Clement of Alexandria[Exhortation to the Heathen 10]

10:27 Clement of Alexandria[The Instructor Book II.1]

10:27-29 Tertullian[On Idolatry 16]

10:28 Apostolic[1Clement 54]; Tertullian[The Chaplet, or De Corona 10]

10:28-31 Clement of Alexandria[Stromata Book IV.15]

10:31 Clement of Alexandria[The Instructor Book II.1]; Clement[Second Epistle Concerning Virginity 6]; Origen[Against Celsus Book VIII.32; Gospel of Matthew Book XI.12]

10:32-33 Clement[Second Epistle Concerning Virginity 5]; Tertullian[On Idolatry 14]

10:33 Cyprian[Epistle LI.15]; NT-Apocrypha[Correspondence between Seneca and Paul X]

11:01 1Corinthians 4:16; Philippians 3:17; Clement of Alexandria[Stromata Book II.22]; Clement[First Epistle Concerning Virginity 6]; Cyprian[Epistle LI.15]; Origen[Gospel of Matthew Book X.15]; Nag Hammadi[Exegesis of the Soul 133]

11:01-16 Tertullian[On Prayer 20]

11:01-34 Tertullian[On the Veiling of Virgins 16]

11:02 Cyprian[Epistle LXII.2]; NT-Apocrypha[Acts of Paul in Philippi 1.5]

11:02-03 Ephesians 5:22-33n

11:02-16 Pseudepigrapha[Joseph and Aseneth 15:1]; Tertullian[On Monogamy 2; On the Apparel of Women Book II.7]

11:03 Genesis 3:16; Clement of Alexandria[Stromata Book IV.8, V.6; The Instructor Book III.11]; Constitutions of the Holy Apostles[Book I.8, III.6, 9]; Origen[De Principiis Book II.6.1]; Tertullian[Against Praxeas 14; On the Veiling of Virgins 6-7; Five Books Against Marcion Book V.8]; Victorinus[Apocalypse 1.14]

11:03-16 Tertullian[On Prayer 15]

11:04 Cyprian[Treatise III.2]

11:04-05 Irenaeus[Against Heresies Book III.11.9]; Tertullian[On Prayer 22]

11:05 Clement of Alexandria[The Instructor Book III.11]; Tertullian[On Prayer 21]; Victorinus[Apocalypse 10.3]

11:05-06 Rabbinic[Babylonian (Sotah 8b cf. {Numbers 5:18}; Yebamot 48a); Jerusalem Moed Qatan 81c; Numbers Rabba on 16.6; Siphre on Deuteronomy 21:12]; Tertullian[Five Books Against Marcion Book V.8]

11:06 Pseudepigrapha[Testament of Job 23:7]; Tertullian[On the Veiling of Virgins 17]

11:07 Genesis 1:26-27, 5:1, 9:6; OT-Apocrypha[Sirach 17:3; Wisdom of Solomon 2:23]; Pseudepigrapha[Testament of Naphtali 2:5]; Clement of Alexandria[Stromata Book IV.8]; Methodius[Apostolic Words from the Discourse on the Resurrection 11]; Tertullian[On Exhortation to Chastity 1; On Idolatry 15; Five Books Against Marcion Book V.8]

11:08 Genesis 2:21-23; Clement of Alexandria[Stromata Book IV.8]

11:09 Genesis 2:18-23; Tertullian[Five Books Against Marcion Book V.8]

11:10 Genesis 6:2, 24:65; Psalms 138:1; Dead Sea Scrolls[Damascus Document (CD-A) COL XV 17]; Clement of Alexandria[Fragments from the Books of the Hypotyposes Book III.]; Irenaeus[Against Heresies Book I.8.2]; Tertullian[On Prayer 22; On the Veiling of Virgins 7; The Chaplet, or De Corona 14; Five Books Against Marcion Book V.7-8]

11:11 Clement of Alexandria[Stromata Book IV.8]

11:14 Pseudepigrapha[Pseudo-Phocylides 212]; Tertullian[On Prayer 22; On the Veiling of Virgins 16; The Chaplet, or De Corona 6]

11:14-15 Tertullian[On the Veiling of Virgins 7]

11:15 Zechariah 9:11

11:16 Cyprian[Epistle LXXII.13, 26]; Tertullian[On the Veiling of Virgins 8]

11:17 Anonymous[Treatise Against the Heretic Novatian 14]

11:17-34 Apostolic[Ignatius - Letter to the Smyrnaeans 8:2]

11:18 Tertullian[On Prescription Against Heretics 5, 39]

11:18-19 Tertullian[Five Books Against Marcion Book V.8]

11:19 Deuteronomy 13:3; Archelaus[Disputation with Manes 39]; Clement of Alexandria[Stromata Book VII.15]; Cyprian[Treatise I.10, XII.Book III.93]; Hippolytus[Refutation of all Heresies Book IX.1]; Justin[Dialogue with Trypho 35]; Lactantius[Divine Institutes Book IV.30]; Methodius[Apostolic Words from the Discourse on the Resurrection 2]; Origen[Against Celsus Book III.13]; Tertullian[Against the Valentinians 5; On Prescription Against Heretics 1, 4-5, 30, 39; On the Resurrection of the Flesh 40, 63]; NT-Apocrypha[Epistula Apostolorum 29]

11:20 Clement of Alexandria[The Instructor Book II.2]

11:20-34 1Corinthians 10:16-18n

11:21-22 Clement of Alexandria[The Instructor Book II.1]

11:22 Clement of Alexandria[The Instructor Book III.11]

11:23 Constitutions of the Holy Apostles[Book VIII.12]; NT-Apocrypha[Gospel of the Hebrews Fragment 7]

11:23-26 Matthew 26:26-29; Mark 14:22-25; Luke 22:14-20; Cyprian[Epistle LXII.10]

11:23-29 John 6:31-58n; Tertullian[Five Books Against Marcion Book V.8]

11:24 Leviticus 24:7; Psalms 38:1, 70:1; OT-Apocrypha[Wisdom of Solomon 16:6]

11:24-25 Matthew 26:26-28; Mark 14:22-24; Luke 22:19-20

11:24-26 NT-Apocrypha[Epistula Apostolorum 15]

11:25 Exodus 24:6-8; Jeremiah 31:31-34, 32:40; Tertullian[A Treatise on the Soul 17]

11:26 Constitutions of the Holy Apostles[Book VII.25]; Cyprian[Epistle XI.1, LXII.17]

11:27 Cyprian[Epistle IX.2, X.1, LXXIV.21; Treatise III.15, XII.Book III.94]

11:27-28 Clement of Alexandria[Stromata Book I.1]

11:27-30 NT-Apocrypha[Acts of Thomas 1.51]

11:28 Origen[Gospel of Matthew Book X.25]

11:29 Constitutions of the Holy Apostles[Book VII.25]

11:30 Pseudepigrapha[4Ezra 2.31]; Origen[Gospel of Matthew Book X.24, XI.14]

11:31-32 Clement of Alexandria[Stromata Book I.1]

11:32 Clement of Alexandria[Stromata Book I.27]; Hippolytus[Refutation of all Heresies Book V.9]

11:33 Cyprian[Treatise XII.Book III.60]

11:33-34 Clement of Alexandria[The Instructor Book II.1]

12:01 Tertullian[Five Books Against Marcion Book V.8]

12:01-11 Justin[Dialogue with Trypho 39]; Tertullian[A Treatise on the Soul 9]

12:02 Psalms 115:5; Habakkuk 2:18-19; OT-Apocrypha[3Maccabees 4:16]

12:02-04 Clement of Alexandria[The Instructor Book I.6]

12:03 Numbers 21:3; Novatian[Treatise Concerning the Trinity 29]; Origen[De Principiis Book I.3.2, 7]; Teaching of the Twelve Apostles 11.7; Nag Hammadi[Apocryphon of James 3]

12:03-06 Matthew 28:19n

12:03-13 Gregory Thaumaturgus[Sectional Confession of Faith 22]

12:04-06 Irenaeus[Against Heresies Book II.28.7]; Origen[Gospel of John Book II.6]

12:04-07 Irenaeus[Against Heresies Book IV.20.6]; Origen[De Principiis Book I.3.7]

12:04-09 Justin[Dialogue with Trypho 88]

12:04-10 Irenaeus[Against Heresies Book II.30.8, 32.4, III 1.1, V.20.1, 22.2]

12:04-12 Tertullian[On Baptism 20]

12:04-31 Tertullian[Five Books Against Marcion Book V.8]

12:06 Origen[De Principiis Book I.3.8]

12:07-11 Clement of Alexandria[Stromata Book IV.21]

12:08 Constitutions of the Holy Apostles[Book VIII.1]; Origen[Against Celsus Book III.46; Gospel of Matthew Book XIV.6]; Tertullian[On Prescription Against Heretics 14]

12:08-09 Origen[Against Celsus Book VI.13]

12:08-10 Clement[First Epistle Concerning Virginity 11]

12:08-31 Nag Hammadi[Interpretation of Knowledge 15-19; Trimorphic Protennoia 49]

12:10 Hippolytus[Refutation of all Heresies Book IX.22]

12:11 Romans 12:6-8; Origen[De Principiis Book I.3.7]

12:12 Romans 12:4-5; Apostolic[1Clement 37]; Origen[Gospel of John Book X.20]

12:13 Matthew 3:5-16n; Clement of Alexandria[Stromata Book V.5, 6; The Instructor Book I.6]; NT-Apocrypha[Acts of Peter p.137]

12:13-15 Matthew 3:11-12n

12:18 Archelaus[Disputation with Manes 18]

12:21 Origen[Gospel of Matthew Book XIII.24]

12:23 Tertullian[On the Resurrection of the Flesh 9]

12:25-26 Origen[Gospel of Matthew Book XIV.1]

12:26 Cyprian[Epistle LI.15, LIX.1]; Tertullian[On Repentance 9]

12:27 Origen[Gospel of John Book X.20, 23; Gospel of Matthew Book XIV.17]; Tertullian[On Modesty 6]

12:28 Ephesians 4:11; Irenaeus[Against Heresies Book III.11.4, 24.1]; Origen[Gospel of Matthew Book XI.15, XIV.1]; Victorinus[Apocalypse 10.3]

12:31 Origen[Gospel of Matthew Book XIV.23]

13:01 Psalms 150:5; Clement of Alexandria[Stromata Book IV.18]; Origen[Gospel of John Book VI.12]; Tertullian[Five Books Against Marcion Book V.8]; NT-Apocrypha[Gospel of Pseudo-Matthew 31]

13:01-04 Cyprian[Treatise X.13]

13:01 Pseudepigrapha[Testament of Job 38:1, 48:2]

13:01-03 Pseudepigrapha[Apocalypse of Sedrach 1:2]

13:01-13 Plato[Symposium 188c-e, 196b-197e]; Apostolic[1Clement 49:1-50:3]; Irenaeus[Against Heresies Book I.10.1, II.26.1, IV.33.8]; Nag Hammadi[Gospel of Philip 62, 77, 79]

13:02 Matthew 17:20, 21:21; Mark 11:23; Plato[Laws VIII 842e-843a]; Clement of Alexandria[Stromata Book V.1, VII.12]; Irenaeus[Against Heresies Book IV.12.2]; Origen[Gospel of Matthew Book XIII.5, 7]; NT-Apocrypha[Fragments of a Dialogue between John and Jesus]

13:02-03 Methodius[Banquet of the Ten Virgins 9.4]

13:02-05 Cyprian[Treatise I.14]

13:02-08 Cyprian[Treatise XII.Book III.3]

13:03 Daniel 3:19; Anonymous[Treatise on Re-Baptism 13]; Archelaus[Disputation with Manes 42]; Clement of Alexandria[Stromata Book IV.18, VII.10]; Cyprian[Epistle LXXII.21]; Tertullian[Against Praxeas 1]

13:04 Clement of Alexandria[The Instructor Book III.1]; Peter of Alexandria[Canonical Epistle 10]

13:04-07 Cyprian[Treatise IX.15]

13:04-08 Clement of Alexandria[Who is the Rich Man that shall be Saved 38]

13:05 Zechariah 8:17; Origen[Gospel of Matthew Book XII.41]; Tertullian[On the Apparel of Women Book II.2]

13:07 Proverbs 10:12; Clement of Alexandria[Stromata Book IV.7, 18, VII.12]

13:07-08 Clement of Alexandria[The Instructor Book II.1]; Cyprian[Treatise I.14]; Origen[Gospel of Matthew Book XII.23]

13:08-10 Archelaus[Disputation with Manes 37]

13:09 Archelaus[Disputation with Manes 13]; Irenaeus[Against Heresies Book II.28.7, 9, V.7.2]

13:09-10 Archelaus[Disputation with Manes 36]; Irenaeus[Against Heresies Book IV.9.2];
  Origen[Gospel of Matthew Book X.9]

13:10 Methodius[Banquet of the Ten Virgins 9.2]; Origen[Against Celsus Book VI.20; Gospel of
  Matthew Book XII.6]

13:11 Clement of Alexandria[The Instructor Book I.6]; Origen[Gospel of Matthew Book XI.2-3, XIII.26];
  Tertullian[On Modesty 1]

13:12 Genesis 32:31; Numbers 12:8; 2Corinthians 3:14-18n; Pseudepigrapha[Testament of Job 33:8];
  Archelaus[Disputation with Manes 41]; Clement of Alexandria[Stromata Book I.19, V.1; The
  Instructor Book I.6]; Cyprian[Treatise XII.Book III.53]; Irenaeus[Against Heresies Book V.7.2];
  Methodius[Banquet of the Ten Virgins 5.7, 9.2]; Origen[Against Celsus Book VI.20, VII.38, 50;
  Gospel of John Book X.27]; Tertullian[Against Praxeas 14; Five Books in Reply to Marcion Book
  IV.82]

13:13 Apostolic[Epistle of Barnabas 1:6]; Clement of Alexandria[Stromata Book IV.7, V.1; Who is the
  Rich Man that shall be Saved 38]; Irenaeus[Against Heresies Book II.28.3, IV.12.2]; Tertullian[Five
  Books Against Marcion Book V.8]; Nag Hammadi[Apocryphon of James 8]; NT-Apocrypha[Gospel
  of Mani Turfman Fragment M 801]

14:05 Numbers 11:29

14:06 Clement of Alexandria[Stromata Book VII.10]; Irenaeus[Against Heresies Book I.14.1]

14:07 NT-Apocrypha[Gospel of Pseudo-Matthew 31]

14:08 Origen[Gospel of John Book VI.12]

14:09-13 Clement of Alexandria[Stromata Book I.16]

14:12 Rabbinic[Babylonian Sanhedrin 97b]

14:15 Pseudepigrapha[Testament of Job 43:2]; Origen[Gospel of Matthew Book XIV.25; De Principiis
  Book II.8.2]; Tertullian[On Prayer 28]

14:16 1Chronicles 16:36

14:20 Jeremiah 4:22; Clement of Alexandria[The Instructor Book I.6]; Irenaeus[Against Heresies Book
  IV.28.3; Demonstration of the Apostolic Preaching 46, 96]; Tertullian[Against the Valentinians 2]

14:21 Isaiah 28:11-12; Constitutions of the Holy Apostles[Book VIII.1]; Tertullian[Five Books Against
  Marcion Book V.8]

14:22-24 Hippolytus[Refutation of all Heresies Book IX.22]

14:25 1Kings 18:39; Daniel 2:47; Isaiah 45:14; Zechariah 8:23; Pseudepigrapha[2Baruch 83:3];
  Apostolic[Polycarp - Letter to the Philippians 4:3]; NT-Apocrypha[6Ezra 17.55-64]

14:25-26 Tertullian[Five Books Against Marcion Book V.8]

14:26 Pseudepigrapha[Testament of Job 47:9]

14:29 Teaching of the Twelve Apostles 10.7, 11.7; Victorinus[Apocalypse 10.3]

14:29-30 Cyprian[Epistle LXX.3]

14:30 Cyprian[Epistle LXXIII.10]

14:31 Hippolytus[Refutation of all Heresies Book IX.22]; Teaching of the Twelve Apostles 10.7

14:32 Novatian[Treatise Concerning the Trinity 29]; Origen[Gospel of John Book VI.7; Gospel of
  Matthew Book XIII.2]; Tertullian[Five Books Against Marcion Book IV.4]

14:33 Constitutions of the Holy Apostles[Book VIII.46]

14:34 Genesis 3:16; Constitutions of the Holy Apostles[Book III.6]; Tertullian[Five Books Against
  Marcion Book V.8]

14:34-35 Cyprian[Treatise XII.Book III.46]; Tertullian[On Baptism 17; On the Veiling of Virgins 9; Five
  Books Against Marcion Book V.8]

14:35 Tertullian[On the Veiling of Virgins 3]

14:39 Hippolytus[Refutation of all Heresies Book IX.22]

14:40 Clement[First Epistle Concerning Virginity 2]

15:02 Origen[Against Celsus Book VI.10]; Tertullian[Five Books Against Marcion Book I.20]

15:03 Isaiah 53:5-12; Acts 3:18-26n; Tertullian[Against Praxeas 15, 29]; NT-Apocrypha[Acts of Paul in
  Philippi 3.4]

15:03-04 Irenaeus[Against Heresies Book III.18.3]; Tertullian[A Treatise on the Soul 55; Against
  Praxeas 30; On the Resurrection of the Flesh 48; Five Books Against Marcion Book III.8]

15:03-08 Origen[Against Celsus Book II.63]

15:03-11 Archelaus[Disputation with Manes 34]

15:04 Psalms 16:8-10; Hosea 6:2; Jonah 1:17; Pseudepigrapha[Life of Abraham 11:2]; NT-
  Apocrypha[Pistis Sophia c. 136]

15:05 Matthew 28:16-17; Mark 16:14; Luke 24:12, 34, 36; John 20:19; Teaching of the Twelve Apostles 11.4; NT-Apocrypha[Letter of Clement to James 1.3]

15:06 Pseudepigrapha[4Ezra 2.31]

15:06-07 NT-Apocrypha[Acts of Pilate XIV.1, XVI.5]

15:07 Teaching of the Twelve Apostles 11.4; Nag Hammadi[First Apocalypse of James 31]; NT-Apocrypha[Gospel of the Hebrews Fragment 7]

15:08 Acts 9:3-6; Apostolic[Ignatius - Letter to the Romans 9:2]; Irenaeus[Against Heresies Book I.8.2]; Tertullian[Against Praxeas 15]; NT-Apocrypha[Pseudo Clementines - Kerygmata Petrou H XVII 19.4]

15:08-09 NT-Apocrypha[Epistula Apostolorum 31]

15:09 Acts 8:3; Origen[De Principiis Book I.8.2]

15:10 Irenaeus[Against Heresies Book IV.24.1]; Origen[De Principiis Book III.2.5]

15:11 Irenaeus[Against Heresies Book III.13.1]; Tertullian[On Modesty 19; Five Books Against Marcion Book IV.4]

15:12 Josephus[Antiquities 18.1.4 16-17; War 2.8.14 162-166]; Irenaeus[Against Heresies Book III.18.3]; Julius Africanus[Epistle to Aristides 1]; Origen[Against Celsus Book III.11]; Tertullian[On Prescription Against Heretics 33; Five Books Against Marcion Book V.9]; NT-Apocrypha[Apocalypse of Paul 1.42]

15:12-13 Justin[On the Resurrection 2]

15:12-18 Tertullian[On the Resurrection of the Flesh 48]

15:12-20 Archelaus[Disputation with Manes 49]

15:12-56 Acts 2:31n; Apostolic[1Clement 24:1-5]

15:13 Irenaeus[Against Heresies Book V.13.4]

15:13-18 Tertullian[Five Books Against Marcion Book III.8]

15:15 Origen[Gospel of John Book X.21]

15:18 Pseudepigrapha[4Ezra 2.31]

15:19 Pseudepigrapha[2Baruch 21:13]; Lactantius[Divine Institutes Book VI.9]; Tertullian[On the Resurrection of the Flesh 24]

15:20 Pseudepigrapha[4Ezra 2.31; Sibylline Oracles 8.314]; Hippolytus[Fragments - Writings of Hippolytus 3]; Origen[Gospel of Matthew Book XII.20]

15:20-22 Irenaeus[Against Heresies Book III.23.1]

15:21 Genesis 3:17-19; Pseudepigrapha[2Baruch 17:3]; Archelaus[Disputation with Manes 43]; Tertullian[On the Resurrection of the Flesh 48; Five Books Against Marcion Book V.9]

15:22 Irenaeus[Against Heresies Book III.18.1, 23.8, V.1.3]; Methodius[Banquet of the Ten Virgins 3.6-7; Discourse on the Resurrection 1.13]; Origen[Against Celsus Book IV.40, VI.36; Gospel of Matthew Book XIII.8]; Tertullian[Five Books in Reply to Marcion Book II.245; On Monogamy 17]

15:22-23 Tertullian[On the Resurrection of the Flesh 48]

15:22-24 Origen[Gospel of John Book X.21]

15:23 Pseudepigrapha[2Baruch 14:1a]; Apostolic[1Clement 37:3]; Cyprian[Treatise I.17]

15:23-28 Hippolytus[Against the Heresy of One Noetus 6]

15:24 Daniel 2:44; Matthew 7:28-29n

15:24-25 Pseudepigrapha[2Baruch 73:1]; Tertullian[Against Praxeas 4]

15:25 Psalms 110:1; Irenaeus[Against Heresies Book V.36.1-2]; Origen[De Principiis Book I.6.1]; Tertullian[Five Books Against Marcion Book V.9]

15:25-26 Origen[Against Celsus Book VI.35; Gospel of John Book I.16, X.23]

15:25-28 Irenaeus[Against Heresies Book V.36.2]

15:26 Irenaeus[Against Heresies Book III.23.7]; Origen[Gospel of John Book VI.37; Gospel of Matthew Book XII.33]; Tertullian[On the Resurrection of the Flesh 51]

15:27 Psalms 8:6-7; Tertullian[Five Books Against Marcion Book V.9]

15:27-28 Tertullian[Against Praxeas 4]

15:28 Apostolic[Polycarp - Letter to the Philippians 2:1]; Origen[Gospel of John Book I.37; De Principiis Book III.5.7, 6.6]

15:29 Matthew 3:5-16n; OT-Apocrypha[2Maccabees 12:43]; Pseudepigrapha[Questions of Ezra 32]; Tertullian[Five Books Against Marcion Book V.10]

15:29-32 Tertullian[On the Resurrection of the Flesh 48]

15:31 Cyprian[Treatise XI.13]

15:32 Isaiah 22:13, 56:12; OT-Apocrypha[Wisdom of Solomon 2:5]; Anterus[Epistle]; Archelaus[Disputation with Manes 49]; Constitutions of the Holy Apostles[Book III.7];

Tertullian[On Fasting 17; On Modesty 22; On Monogamy 16; On the Resurrection of the Flesh 49];
NT-Apocrypha[Apocalypse of Paul 1.15]; Epic of Gilgamesh[The Search for Everlasting Life]

15:32-33 Clement of Alexandria[Stromata Book I.14]

15:33 Greek[Menander, Thais Fragment 218 Kock (1024 Nauck)]; Cyprian[Epistle LIV.21; Treatise
XII.Book III.95]; Fabian[First Epistle]; Socrates Scholasticus Book 3.16; Tertullian[To his Wife Book
I.8]

15:34 OT-Apocrypha[Wisdom of Solomon 13:1]; Clement of Alexandria[Stromata Book III.16]

15:35 Origen[Against Celsus Book VIII.30]; Tertullian[On the Resurrection of the Flesh 48; Five Books
Against Marcion Book V.10]

15:35-38 Origen[Against Celsus Book V.18]

15:35-53 Nag Hammadi[Treatise on the Resurrection 47-48]

15:36 Cyprian[Treatise XII.Book III.58]; Irenaeus[Against Heresies Book V.7.1]; Minucius Felix[The
Octavius 34]; NT-Apocrypha[Apocalypse of Peter 1.4]

15:36-39 Tertullian[On the Resurrection of the Flesh 52]

15:36-44 This section also includes topical notes for: Raised Imperishable - Pseudepigrapha[4Ezra
2.44-45, 5.45, 6.26, 7.32, 7.97-98, 7.113-114; Life of Adam and Eve (Apocalypse of Moses) 28.4; Odes
of Solomon 8.3-5, 17.13, 22.10, 33.12, 40.6; Sibylline Oracles 4.179-192]; Dead Sea
Scrolls[4QMessianic Apocalypse (4Q521) Fragment 5 COL II 6-15]; Josephus[Discourse to the
Greeks Concerning Hades 5-6]; Philo[On Flight And Finding (55-58) cf. {Deuteronomy 4:4, 30:20}];
Rabbinic[**Babylonian Sanhedrin 90b**, 91b-92a]; Athenagoras[Plea for the Christians 36; The Treatise
2, 3, 7, 11, 13-25]; Clement of Alexandria[Exhortation to the Heathen 10; The Instructor Book I.5-6];
Hippolytus[Refutation of all Heresies Book IX.22-23]; Irenaeus[Against Heresies Book I.22.1, 23.5,
27.3, II.14.4, 29.1-3, 33.5, III.19.2, IV.24.2, 38.4, V.2.3, 3.2-3, 4.1, 15.1, 31.1-2, 32.1-2, 33.1-2, 34.1-2, 35.1-
2, 36.1; Fragments from the Lost Works 12, 50]; Justin[Dialogue with Trypho 69, 80, 113; First
Apology 18, 52; On the Resurrection 2-10]; Tatian[Address to the Greeks 6]; Tertullian[Five Books
Against Marcion Book III.25]; Nag Hammadi[Dialogue of the Savior 84-85; Gospel of Truth 20]

"Now if a grain of wheat, which is buried naked, comes forth in many garments, the
righteous, who are buried in their garments, all the more so [will rise in many
garments]!" (Talmud - Babylonian Sanhedrin 90b, *The Babylonian Talmud a Translation
and Commentary,* Jacob Neusner; Hendrickson Publishers, Inc., 2005)

15:37 NT-Apocrypha[Acts of Paul in Philippi 3.26]

15:37-44 Tertullian[Five Books Against Marcion Book V.10]

15:38 Genesis 1:11

15:38-50 Nag Hammadi[Gospel of Philip 66]

15:39 Genesis 1:20, 24, 8:17; Pseudepigrapha[Apocalypse of Zephaniah 10:14]

15:39-42 Origen[De Principiis Book II.10.2]

15:40-41 Tertullian[On the Resurrection of the Flesh 49]

15:40-42 Origen[Against Celsus Book V.10]

15:41 Pseudepigrapha[2Baruch 51:1]; Clement of Alexandria[Stromata Book VI.13-14]; Dionysius of
Alexandria[Extant Fragments Refutation on the Ground of the Constitution of the Universe];
Irenaeus[Against Heresies Book II.16.5]; Origen[Against Celsus Book IV.57; De Principiis Book
II.9.3]; Tertullian[Scorpiace 6; Five Books Against Marcion Book V.20]

15:41-42 Methodius[Banquet of the Ten Virgins 7.3]; Origen[Against Celsus Book IV.30; Gospel of
Matthew Book X.3]

15:41-44 Cyprian[Treatise XII.Book III.58]

15:41-45 Tertullian[On the Resurrection of the Flesh 52]

15:42 Irenaeus[Against Heresies Book V.7.1]; Methodius[Apostolic Words from the Discourse on the
Resurrection 5; Discourse on the Resurrection 1.13]; NT-Apocrypha[Correspondence between
Seneca and Paul XIV]

15:42-43 Origen[De Principiis Preface.5]

15:42-44 Origen[Against Celsus Book V.19]

15:42-47 Tertullian[On the Resurrection of the Flesh 53]

15:43-44 Irenaeus[Against Heresies Book V.7.2]

15:44 Pseudepigrapha[Apocalypse of Elijah 5:32]; Athenagoras[Plea for the Christians 31];
Clement[First Epistle Concerning Virginity 11]; Irenaeus[Against Heresies Book II.19.6];
Origen[Against Celsus Book IV.57; De Principiis Book II.10.1]

15:45 Genesis 2:7; Pseudepigrapha[2Enoch 42:5; Sibylline Oracles 8.259]; Gregory Thaumaturgus[Twelve Topics on the Faith 3]; Irenaeus[Against Heresies Book V.16.3]; Origen[Gospel of John Book I.20]; Tertullian[Five Books in Reply to Marcion Book II.245; On the Resurrection of the Flesh 49, 51; Five Books Against Marcion Book V.10]

15:45-46 Irenaeus[Against Heresies Book V.12.2]

15:45-47 Victorinus[On the Creation of the World]; Nag Hammadi[Apocryphon of John 14]

15:46 Tertullian[A Treatise on the Soul 11; On Baptism 5; On Monogamy 5; Five Books Against Marcion Book V.10]

15:46-50 Archelaus[Disputation with Manes 40]

15:47 Genesis 2:7; Pseudepigrapha[Sibylline Oracles 8.445]; Cyprian[Treatise II.23]; Gregory Thaumaturgus[Twelve Topics on the Faith 3]; Hippolytus[Fragments - On Genesis 49.21-26]; Tertullian[Five Books in Reply to Marcion Book II.245; On the Flesh of Christ 8; Five Books Against Marcion Book V.10]

15:47-49 Cyprian[Treatise X.14, XII.Book II.10, III.11]; Tertullian[On the Resurrection of the Flesh 49]

15:48 Irenaeus[Against Heresies Book I.8.3]

15:48-49 Irenaeus[Against Heresies Book V.9.3]

15:48-51 Origen[Against Celsus Book V.19]

15:49 Genesis 5:3; Irenaeus[Against Heresies Book III.20.2, V.11.2]; Methodius[Discourse on the Resurrection 1.13]; Tertullian[Five Books Against Marcion Book V.10]; Theodotus[Excerpts 24]; NT-Apocrypha[Apocalypse of Thomas Line 59]

15:49-50 Methodius[Apostolic Words from the Discourse on the Resurrection 5]

15:50 Clement of Alexandria[Stromata Book II.20, III.17]; Irenaeus[Against Heresies Book I.30.13, V.9.1, 10.1-2]; Methodius[Apostolic Words from the Discourse on the Resurrection 6; Discourse on the Resurrection 1.13]; Novatian[Treatise Concerning the Trinity 10]; Tertullian[On the Apparel of Women Book II.7; On the Resurrection of the Flesh 48-51; Five Books Against Marcion Book V.10, 12, 14]; Nag Hammadi[Gospel of Philip 56]; NT-Apocrypha[Pseudo-Titus Epistle Line 74]

15:50-53 Pseudepigrapha[Martyrdom and Ascension of Isaiah (3:13-4:22 = Testament of Hezekiah) 4:18]

15:51 Pseudepigrapha[2Baruch 49:3, 51:1; 4Ezra 2.31; Testament of Benjamin 10:8; Questions of Ezra RecB 13]

15:51-52 Pseudepigrapha[**1Enoch 50:1**]; Origen[Against Celsus Book V.17]; Tertullian[Five Books Against Marcion Book V.20]

> **In those days the saints and the chosen shall undergo a change. The light of day shall rest upon them; and the splendor and glory of the saints shall be changed. (Pseudepigrapha - 1Enoch 50:1)**

15:51-53 Tertullian[On the Resurrection of the Flesh 42]

15:51-55 Zechariah 12:10-14; Matthew 24:29-31; Mark 13:24-27; Luke 21:25-28; 1Thessalonians 4:15-17n; 2Thessalonians 2:1-2; Revelation 1:7, 6:13-8:2, 8:5, 11:12, 11:19, 14:1-5, 14:14-16, 16:8, 16:18

15:52 1Thessalonians 4:15-17; Pseudepigrapha[2Baruch 30:2; 4Baruch 3.2-3; 4Ezra 6:20, 23-26; Apocalypse of Abraham 31.1-2; Greek Apocalypse of Ezra 4:36-37; Life of Adam and Eve (Apocalypse of Moses) 22:3; Sibylline Oracles 8.239]; Apostolic[Didache 16:6]; Clement of Alexandria[Who is the Rich Man that shall be Saved 3]; Hippolytus[Appendix to the Works of Hippolytus - On the End of the World 37]; Irenaeus[Against Heresies Book V.13.1]; Origen[Against Celsus Book II.65; Gospel of Matthew Book XIV.9]; Tertullian[A Treatise on the Soul 55; On Prayer 29; On the Resurrection of the Flesh 57; Five Books Against Marcion Book V.10, 12]; Nag Hammadi[Treatise on the Resurrection 46]

15:52-54 Pythagoras[Golden Verses Line 71]; Nag Hammadi[Tripartite Tractate 114]

15:52-56 Tertullian[On the Resurrection of the Flesh 51]

15:53 Pseudepigrapha[2Enoch 8:5]; Irenaeus[Against Heresies Book V.2.3, 10.2, 13.3, 13.5]; Methodius[Apostolic Words from the Discourse on the Resurrection 5; Discourse on the Resurrection 1.13]; Origen[Against Celsus Book VII.32]; Tertullian[On the Apparel of Women Book II.6; On the Resurrection of the Flesh 50, 57, 60; Five Books Against Marcion Book V.10, 12; To his Wife Book I.7]; Victorinus[Apocalypse 1.16]

15:53-54 Jude 1:21n

15:53-55 Cyprian[Treatise XII.Book III.58]; Tertullian[On the Resurrection of the Flesh 54]

15:53-56 Origen[De Principiis Book II.3.2]

15:54 Isaiah 25:8; Pseudepigrapha[1Enoch 62:18; Odes of Solomon 15:8]; Archelaus[Disputation with Manes 29]; Athenagoras[The Treatise 18]; Irenaeus[Against Heresies Book I.10.3]; Methodius[Discourse on the Resurrection 1.13]; Origen[Against Celsus Book VI.36]; Tertullian[Five Books in Reply to Marcion Book II.354]; Nag Hammadi[Treatise on the Resurrection 45]

15:54-55 Archelaus[Disputation with Manes 30]; Irenaeus[Against Heresies Book III.23.7]

15:55 Hosea 13:14; Pseudepigrapha[Hellenistic Synagogal Prayers 5:7; Sibylline Oracles 8.415]; Clement of Alexandria[The Instructor Book II.8]; Gregory Thaumaturgus[On All the Saints]; Tertullian[On the Resurrection of the Flesh 47; Five Books Against Marcion Book V.10]; NT-Apocrypha[Acts of Pilate XXI.2]

15:56 Archelaus[Disputation with Manes 28]

15:58 2Chronicles 15:7; Isaiah 65:23; Apostolic[Polycarp - Letter to the Philippians 10:1]; Fabian[First Epistle]; Tertullian[De Fuga in Persecutione 9]; NT-Apocrypha[Epistle to the Laodiceans 1:14]

16:01 Romans 15:25-26

16:05 Acts 19:21

16:08 Leviticus 23:15-21; Deuteronomy 16:9-11

16:09 Acts 19:8-10

16:10 1Corinthians 4:17

16:13 Psalms 31:25; NT-Apocrypha[Acts of Peter 1.6]

16:13-14 Fabian[First Epistle]

16:15 1Corinthians 1:16

16:15-17 NT-Apocrypha[Acts of Paul in Philippi 1.1]

16:19 Acts 18:2

16:20 Pseudepigrapha[Joseph and Aseneth 19:11]; Tertullian[On Prayer 18]

16:22 Apostolic[Didache 10:6]; Constitutions of the Holy Apostles[Book VII.26]; Teaching of the Twelve Apostles 10.6

16:23 NT-Apocrypha[Acts of Thomas 1.13]

Cross Reference Index: Second Corinthians

01:01 Acts 18:1; Origen[Gospel of Matthew Book XIV.1]

01:02 John 1:18n; Pseudepigrapha[2Baruch 78:3]

01:03 Pseudepigrapha[Hellenistic Synagogal Prayers 9:8]; Constitutions of the Holy Apostles[Book VIII.5]; Tertullian[Five Books Against Marcion Book V.11]

01:05 Psalms 34:19-20, 94:19; Justin[Dialogue with Trypho 117]

01:08 1Corinthians 15:32; Tertullian[On the Resurrection of the Flesh 48]

01:09-10 Clement of Alexandria[Stromata Book I.11]

01:12 1Peter 1:10-13n; Clement of Alexandria[Stromata Book IV.16]; Hippolytus[Refutation of all Heresies Book IX.21]

01:16 Acts 19:21

01:18 Deuteronomy 7:9

01:19 John 3:18n; Acts 18:5

01:21 Clement of Alexandria[Stromata Book VI.14]

01:21-22 Matthew 28:19n; Gregory Thaumaturgus[Sectional Confession of Faith 20]; Tertullian[On Baptism 10]

01:22 Pseudepigrapha[4Ezra 2.39]; Tertullian[Five Books in Reply to Marcion Book II.328; On the Resurrection of the Flesh 53]

01:22-23 Nag Hammadi[Gospel of Truth 36]

01:24 Dionysius of Alexandria[Extant Fragments Epistle to Bishop Basilides 4]

02:04 NT-Apocrypha[Acts of Paul in Philippi 2.5, 3.2]

02:05-11 Tertullian[On Modesty 13]

02:09 Pseudepigrapha[Testament of Job 12:1]

02:10 Cyprian[Epistle LIV.16; Treatises Attributed to Cyprian Exhortation to Repentance]

02:11 Pseudepigrapha[Testament of Job 6:4]

02:13 Acts 20:1

02:14-16 Clement of Alexandria[The Instructor Book II.8]

02:15 Pseudepigrapha[Testament of Levi 2]; Origen[Against Celsus Book I.48]; Pseud-Irenaeus

02:15-16 Irenaeus[Against Heresies Book IV.28.3]

02:17 Irenaeus[Against Heresies Book IV.26.4]

03:02 Apostolic[Polycarp - Letter to the Philippians 11:3]

03:02-03 Irenaeus[Against Heresies Book III.4.2]

03:03 Exodus 24:12, 31:18, 32:15, 34:1; Deuteronomy 9:10-11; Proverbs 3:3, 7:3; Jeremiah 31:33; Ezekiel 11:19, 36:26; Irenaeus[Against Heresies Book V.13.4]; Justin[Dialogue with Trypho 114]; Origen[Gospel of Matthew Book XII.20]

03:05-06 Origen[Against Celsus Book VI.70]

03:06 Exodus 24:8; Jeremiah 31:31-34, 32:40; Pseudepigrapha[Joseph and Aseneth 8:9]; Rabbinic[Exodus Rabbah 5:9; Yoma 72b]; Justin[Dialogue with Trypho 24]; Methodius[Oration Concerning Simeon and Anna 8]; Origen[Gospel of John Book IV.2; De Principiis Book I.1.2]; Tertullian[On Modesty 17; Five Books Against Marcion Book V.11]

03:06-07 Archelaus[Disputation with Manes 28]

03:06-08 Origen[Against Celsus Book VII.20]

03:06-11 Archelaus[Disputation with Manes 40]

03:07 Exodus 34:29-30; Archelaus[Disputation with Manes 28, 43]; Origen[Gospel of Matthew Book X.15, XI.14]

03:07-08 Tertullian[Five Books Against Marcion Book V.11]

03:07-18 NT-Apocrypha[Acts of Thomas 1.13]

03:09 Deuteronomy 27:26

03:10 Exodus 34:29-30, 35; Origen[Gospel of Matthew Book X.9]

03:12-18 **This section also includes topical notes for: The Veil is Taken Away** – Exodus 34:33-35; Deuteronomy 32:29; Job 34:16; Psalms 107:43; Proverbs 8:9; Nehemiah 8:8, 13; Jeremiah 9:11; Isaiah

6:9, 40:21, 43:10, 44:18; Hosea 14:10; Amos 5:13; Daniel 5:7-8, 15-17, 12:9; Matthew 13:13-15; 24:15; Mark 4:12, 13:14; Luke 8:10, 24:27, 44-46; John 5:39-46, 12:40; Acts 13:27, 17:2-3, 11, 18:28; Romans 1:2; 1Corinthians 2:6-16n; Hebrews 6:20, 8:5n; Pseudepigrapha[4Ezra 14.3-6, 14.22-26; Odes of Solomon 8.8-12, 11.14; Testament of Judah 16.4]; Dead Sea Scrolls[4Q Mysteries (4Q300[4QMYST]) Fragment COL II 2-5]; Philo[On Dreams That They are God Sent (1.164-165); On Mating With the Preliminary Studies (124-125) cf. {Genesis 38:14-16}; On the Giants (53-54) cf. {Exodus 33:7, 34:33-35}]; Rabbinic[Aboth de Rabbi Nathan 12; **Babylonian Yoma 72b cf. {Deuteronomy 4:44}**; Mekhilta on Exodus 12:1; Mishnah Aboth 5.22; Siphra on Leviticus 13:49]; Plato[Republic VII 514a-517a, 532b-c]; Apostolic[Epistle of Barnabas 10:11-12]; Archelaus[Disputation with Manes 31, 41, 43-44; Fragment of the Disputation with Manes 2, 3]; Clement of Alexandria[Exhortation to the Heathen 1; Stromata Book I.1, 12, IV.18, V.4, 6, 8-10, VI.9, 11, 15]; Clement[Recognitions Book I.40]; Cyprian[Treatise XII.Book I.4]; Irenaeus[Against Heresies Book I.6.1-2, 29.3, IV.26.1, 29.1]; Justin[Dialogue with Trypho 7, 55, 68, 90, 114-115, 123, 126; First Apology 31, 36; Hortatory Address to the Greeks 29]; Lactantius[Divine Institutes Book IV.20]; Liturgy of James 27; Methodius[Banquet of the Ten Virgins 5.7]; Origen[Against Celsus Book V.60; De Principiis Book I.1.2; Gospel of John Book I.8, X.24; Gospel of Matthew Book XII.9-11]; Tertullian[Five Books Against Marcion Book V.11]; Nag Hammadi[A Valentinian Exposition 25; Gospel of Philip 84; Hypostasis of the Archons 94; Trimorphic Protennoia 50; Tripartite Tractate 123]; NT-Apocrypha[Epistula Apostolorum 11; Kerygma Petri 4a]

R. Joshua b. Levi said: What is the meaning of the Scriptural verse: And this is the law which Moses set [before the children of Israel]? If he is meritorious it becomes for him a medicine of life, if not, a deadly poison. That is what Raba [meant when he] said: If he uses it the right way it is a medicine of life unto him; he who does not use it the right way, it is a deadly poison. (Talmud - Babylonian Yoma 72b, *The Soncino Talmud*; Judaica Press, Inc. 1973 and Soncino Press, Ltd. 1965, 1967, 1977, 1983, 1984, 1987, 1988, & 1990)

03:13 Exodus 34:33, 35, 36:35
03:14 Clement of Alexandria[Stromata Book IV.16]; Origen[Gospel of John Book X.18]
03:14-18 This section also includes topical notes for: Looking as in a Mirror - Acts 2:23n;
   1Corinthians 13:12; Pseudepigrapha[Odes of Solomon 13.1]; Philo[On the Contemplative Life Or Suppliants (78)]; Irenaeus[Against Heresies Book IV.9.2]; Origen[Gospel of John Book I.16, X.27]
03:15-18 Gregory Thaumaturgus[Sectional Confession of Faith 20];
03:16 Exodus 34:34
03:16-17 Origen[Gospel of Matthew Book X.14, XI.14]
03:17 Novatian[Treatise Concerning the Trinity 29]; Origen[Against Celsus Book VI.70]
03:18 Exodus 16:7, 10, 24:17; Pseudepigrapha[Apocalypse of Zephaniah 5:4; Joseph and Aseneth 18:9; Odes of Solomon 13:1]; Apostolic[1Clement 36:2]; Methodius[Oration Concerning Simeon and Anna 1]; Origen[Gospel of Matthew Book XII.11]; NT-Apocrypha[Apocalypse of Thomas Line 59]
04:01-02 Tertullian[On Modesty 15]
04:03 Acts 2:23n; Pseudepigrapha[Hellenistic Synagogal Prayers 10.4]; Nag Hammadi[Gospel of Truth 18]
04:03-06 1Corinthians 2:6-16n; Dead Sea Scrolls[1Q Mysteries (1Q27[1QMYST]) Fragment 1 COL I 3-4]
04:04 Colossians 1:15n; Pseudepigrapha[Martyrdom and Ascension of Isaiah 2:4];
   Archelaus[Disputation with Manes 13; Fragment of the Disputation with Manes 2];
   Irenaeus[Against Heresies Book III.7.1, IV.29.1, V.3.3; Fragments from the Lost Works 46];
   Lactantius[Divine Institutes Book II.15]; Origen[Gospel of Matthew Book XI.14; De Principiis Book IV.1.37]; Tertullian[On Modesty 9; Five Books Against Marcion Book V.11]; NT-Apocrypha[Freer Logion]
04:04-06 Matthew 17:1-21n
04:05-06 Tertullian[Five Books Against Marcion Book V.12]
04:06 Genesis 1:3; Job 37:15; Psalms 112:4; Isaiah 9:1-2; Pseudepigrapha[2Enoch 26:1; Joseph and Aseneth 14:1]; Lactantius[Divine Institutes Book II.11]; Origen[Against Celsus Book VI.5]; Tertullian[Five Books Against Marcion Book V.11]
04:06-07 Tertullian[On the Resurrection of the Flesh 44]
04:07 Lamentations 4:2; Clement of Alexandria[Who is the Rich Man that shall be Saved 34]; Origen[Gospel of John Book IV.2; De Principiis Book IV.1.7]; Tertullian[Of Patience 10; Five Books Against Marcion Book V.11]

04:08 Tertullian[Scorpiace 13; Five Books Against Marcion Book V.12]; NT-Apocrypha[Pseudo-Titus Epistle Line 48]

04:08-09 Clement of Alexandria[Stromata Book IV.21]

04:08-12 Tertullian[Five Books Against Marcion Book V.11]

04:10 Irenaeus[Against Heresies Book V.13.4]; Origen[Against Celsus Book VII.38; Gospel of John Book I.25, 35; Gospel of Matthew Book XIII.16]

04:10-11 Tertullian[On the Resurrection of the Flesh 44; Five Books Against Marcion Book V.11]

04:11 Irenaeus[Against Heresies Book V.13.5]

04:13 Psalms 116:10; Novatian[Treatise Concerning the Trinity 29]

04:14 Apostolic[Polycarp - Letter to the Philippians 2:2]; Tertullian[On the Resurrection of the Flesh 44; Five Books Against Marcion Book V.11; The Shows, or De Spectaculis 26]

04:16 Origen[Gospel of Matthew Book X.15]; Syriac Martyrdom of Shamuna, Guria, and Habib; Tertullian[On the Resurrection of the Flesh 16, 40]; Nag Hammadi[Letter of Peter to Philip 137]

04:16-18 Tertullian[Five Books Against Marcion Book V.11]

04:17 Pseudepigrapha[2Baruch 15:8, 48:50]

04:17-18 Origen[Against Celsus Book VI.19]; Tertullian[On the Resurrection of the Flesh 40]

04:18 Pseudepigrapha[Joseph and Aseneth 12:15]; Clement of Alexandria[The Instructor Book III.2; Who is the Rich Man that shall be Saved 25]; Origen[Against Celsus Book VI.59; Gospel of Matthew Book XII.23, XIII.1, 20; De Principiis Book III.6.4]; Theodotus[Excerpts 11]

04:18-05:01 Origen[De Principiis Book II.3.6]

05:01 Job 4:19; Jude 1:21n; OT-Apocrypha[Wisdom of Solomon 9:15]; Origen[Against Celsus Book VII.32; De Principiis Book III.6.4]; Syriac Martyrdom of Shamuna, Guria, and Habib; Tertullian[Five Books in Reply to Marcion Book II.340; On the Apparel of Women Book II.6; On the Resurrection of the Flesh 41; Five Books Against Marcion Book V.12]

05:01-02 Pseudepigrapha[2Baruch 48:6]

05:01-03 Clement of Alexandria[Stromata Book IV.26]

05:01-04 Pseudepigrapha[Martyrdom and Ascension of Isaiah (3:13-4:22 = Testament of Hezekiah) 4:18]; Methodius[Apostolic Words from the Discourse on the Resurrection 5]

05:01-05 Pseudepigrapha[3Enoch 18:22; Life of Adam and Eve (Apocalypse of Moses) 31:1]

05:02 Tertullian[Five Books Against Marcion Book V.12]

05:02-03 Tertullian[On the Resurrection of the Flesh 41]

05:03 Rabbinic[Babylonian Sanhedrin 90b]; Nag Hammadi[Gospel of Philip 56]

05:03-04 Pseudepigrapha[2Enoch 22:8]; Tertullian[On the Resurrection of the Flesh 42; Five Books Against Marcion Book V.12]

05:04 OT-Apocrypha[Wisdom of Solomon 9:15]; Pseudepigrapha[4Ezra 14:15]; Irenaeus[Against Heresies Book II.19.6, IV.36.6, V.8.1]; Origen[Against Celsus Book VII.32; Gospel of Matthew Book XIII.21]; Tertullian[On the Resurrection of the Flesh 54; To his Wife Book I.7]

05:04-05 Gregory Thaumaturgus[Sectional Confession of Faith 21]

05:05 Tertullian[Five Books in Reply to Marcion Book II.328; On Baptism 10; On the Resurrection of the Flesh 51, 53]

05:06 Origen[Against Celsus Book VII.50; Gospel of Matthew Book XIV.12]

05:06-08 Nag Hammadi[Gospel of Mary 8]

05:06-10 Tertullian[On the Resurrection of the Flesh 43]

05:07 Clement of Alexandria[Stromata Book IV.26, V.6; The Instructor Book III.2]; Methodius[Apostolic Words from the Discourse on the Resurrection 5]

05:08 Origen[Against Celsus Book VII.50]

05:09 Clement of Alexandria[Stromata Book IV.26]

05:10 Ecclesiastes 12:14; Romans 14:10; Apostolic[Polycarp - Letter to the Philippians 6:2; Epistle of Barnabas 4:12]; Clement of Alexandria[Stromata Book III.8]; Cyprian[Treatise XII.Book II.28, III.56]; Origen[Gospel of Matthew Book XII.30, XIII.30, XIV.8; De Principiis Book III.1.20]; Tertullian[On Prescription Against Heretics 44; On the Resurrection of the Flesh 60; Five Books Against Marcion Book V.12]; NT-Apocrypha[Epistula Apostolorum 26; History of Joseph the Carpenter 1]

05:11 Clement[Second Epistle Concerning Virginity 3]

05:12 1Samuel 16:7

05:14 Pseudepigrapha[Sibylline Oracles 1.371]

05:14-17 Clement of Alexandria[Stromata Book III.8]

05:15 Cyprian[Treatise XI.6]

05:16 Clement of Alexandria[Fragments from the Books of the Hypotyposes Book IV.]; Origen[Against Celsus Book VI.68, VII.39; Gospel of Matthew Book XI.17; De Principiis Book II.6.7]

05:17 Isaiah 43:18; Pseudepigrapha[4Ezra 7.138-140]; Constitutions of the Holy Apostles[Book VI.18]; Hippolytus[Refutation of all Heresies Book X.29]; Tertullian[On Fasting 14; On Modesty 6; Five Books Against Marcion Book IV.11, V.2, 12, 19]

05:19 Pseudepigrapha[Joseph and Aseneth 11:10]; Methodius[Oration Concerning Simeon and Anna 2]; Origen[Gospel of John Book I.6]

05:19-20 Liturgy of the Apostles 8

05:20 Isaiah 52:7; Origen[Against Celsus Book VIII.1; De Principiis Book III.1.20]

05:21 Pseudepigrapha[Psalms of Solomon 17.36; Testament of Benjamin 3.8; Testament of Judah 24.2]; Archelaus[Disputation with Manes 50]; Clement of Alexandria[The Instructor Book III.12]; Justin[Dialogue with Trypho 102]; Origen[Against Celsus Book I.69, IV.15; Gospel of John Book II.21; Gospel of Matthew Book XIV.7, 20]

06:02 Isaiah 49:8

06:03 Clement[Second Epistle Concerning Virginity 3]

06:03-07 Clement of Alexandria[Stromata Book IV.21]

06:04 Clement of Alexandria[Stromata Book I.1]; Gregory Thaumaturgus[Sectional Confession of Faith 21]

06:05 Acts 16:23

06:05-06 Tertullian[On Modesty 15]

06:06-07 Gregory Thaumaturgus[Sectional Confession of Faith 21]

06:07 Apostolic[Polycarp - Letter to the Philippians 4:1]; Clement of Alexandria[Stromata Book VI.12]; Tertullian[On the Resurrection of the Flesh 7]; NT-Apocrypha[Acts of Paul from Corinth to Italy p.8]

06:09 Psalms 118:17

06:10 Romans 11:33n

06:10-11 Clement of Alexandria[Stromata Book I.1]

06:11 Psalms 119:32; Clement of Alexandria[Fragments from the Books of the Hypotyposes Book IV]

06:13 Apostolic[Papias Fragment 15:1]

06:14 Deuteronomy 32:10; Alexander of Alexandria[Epistles on Arian Heresy 2.3]; Clement of Alexandria[The Instructor Book I.4]; Constitutions of the Holy Apostles[Book VIII.34]; Cyprian[Epistle LXXII.15; Treatise XII.Book III.62]; Tertullian[On Idolatry 13; Five Books Against Marcion Book III.8]

06:14-15 Alexander of Alexandria[Epistles on Arian Heresy 1.7]; Callistus[Second Epistle 2.2]; Clement of Alexandria[Stromata Book V.9]

06:14-16 Tertullian[On the Apparel of Women Book I.2]

06:14-07:01 Pseudepigrapha[2Enoch 34:1]

06:15 1Kings 18:21; Pseudepigrapha[Lives of the Prophets 4:6; Sibylline Oracles 2.166; Testament of Reuben 4:7]

06:16 Leviticus 26:11-12; Jeremiah 32:28; Ezekiel 37:27; Romans 8:9-11n; 1Corinthians 3:16, 6:19; Pseudepigrapha[Hellenistic Synagogal Prayers 10:10]; Apostolic[Ignatius - Letter to the Ephesians 15:3, Letter to the Philadelphians 7:2; Epistle of Barnabas 4:11, 6:14-15; Martyrdom of Ignatius 2]; Archelaus[Disputation with Manes 19]; Clement of Alexandria[Exhortation to the Heathen 11; Stromata Book VII.11]; Constitutions of the Holy Apostles[Book VIII.6]; Origen[Against Celsus Book VIII.18]; Tertullian[A Treatise on the Soul 53]; NT-Apocrypha[Acts of Paul and Thecla 1.5]

06:16-18 Clement of Alexandria[Stromata Book III.11, IV.21]; Tertullian[On Modesty 15]

06:17 Isaiah 52:4, 11; Ezekiel 20:34, 41; Constitutions of the Holy Apostles[Book VI.4]; Tertullian[On Modesty 18; Five Books Against Marcion Book V.18]

06:17-18 Clement of Alexandria[Stromata Book V.9]

06:18 2Samuel 7:8, 14; Isaiah 43:6; 1Chronicles 17:13; Jeremiah 31:9; Pseudepigrapha[Apocalypse of Zephaniah 2:9]

07:01 Pseudepigrapha[Hellenistic Synagogal Prayers 10:10]; Clement of Alexandria[Stromata Book III.8, 11]; Constitutions of the Holy Apostles[Book VII.39; VIII.6, 8, 13]; Tertullian[On Modesty 15; Five Books Against Marcion Book V.12]; Nag Hammadi[Exegesis of the Soul 127-130; Teachings of Silvanus 108-109, 114]

07:01-11 Clement of Alexandria[Stromata Book IV.21]

07:02 Irenaeus[Against Heresies Book IV.26.4]

07:04 Methodius[Oration Concerning Simeon and Anna 6]; NT-Apocrypha[Acts of John 33]

07:05 2Corinthians 2:13; Tertullian[On the Resurrection of the Flesh 40]

07:06 Isaiah 49:13

07:09 Tertullian[Five Books Against Marcion Book I.29]

07:10 Revelation 12:10n; OT-Apocrypha[Sirach 38:18]; Cyprian[Treatises Attributed to Cyprian - Exhortation to Repentance]

07:15 Psalms 2:11; Pseudepigrapha[Joseph and Aseneth 9:1]

08:01 Irenaeus[Against Heresies Book IV.33.8]

08:04 Romans 15:26

08:09 1Peter 1:10-13n; Gregory Thaumaturgus[Four Homilies 1]; Peter of Alexandria[Fragments On the Godhead]

08:12 Proverbs 3:27-28; Clement of Alexandria[Stromata Book IV.6]

08:12-13 Cyprian[Treatise XII.Book III.2]

08:12-14 Clement of Alexandria[Stromata Book II.19]

08:14-15 Cyprian[Treatise XII.Book III.1]

08:15 Exodus 16:18

08:16 Origen[De Principiis Book III.2.4]

08:20-21 Clement of Alexandria[The Instructor Book III.11]

08:21 Proverbs 3:4; Tertullian[On the Apparel of Women Book II.13]

09:06 Proverbs 11:24, 22:9; Galatians 6:7-9n

09:06-07 Cyprian[Treatise XII.Book III.1]

09:07 Deuteronomy 15:10; Proverbs 22:8; Pseudepigrapha[2Enoch 61:15]; Clement of Alexandria[Who is the Rich Man that shall be Saved 31]

09:09 Psalms 112:9

09:09-12 Cyprian[Treatise XII.Book III.1]

09:10 Isaiah 55:10; Hosea 10:12; Cyprian[Treatise VIII.9]

09:12 Cyprian[Treatise VIII.9]

09:13 Clement of Alexandria[Stromata Book III.1]

09:14-15 Archelaus[Disputation with Manes 35]

09:15 Clement of Alexandria[Stromata Book III.1]

10:01 Apostolic[Polycarp - Letter to the Philippians 10:1; Epistle to Diognetus 7:3-5]

10:03 Clement of Alexandria[Stromata Book II.20]

10:03-04 Origen[Against Celsus Book VII.46]

10:03-05 Clement of Alexandria[Stromata Book IV.7]; Origen[Against Celsus Book V.64]

10:04 Proverbs 21:22; Tertullian[On Idolatry 19]

10:05 Clement of Alexandria[Stromata Book VII.3]; Methodius[Apostolic Words from the Discourse on the Resurrection 1-2]; Origen[Against Celsus Book IV.1, V.1; De Principiis Book III.2.4]

10:08 Jeremiah 24:6

10:09 Tertullian[On Modesty 14]

10:13 Tertullian[On Prayer 22]

10:13-14 Cyprian[Treatise XII.Book III.37]

10:13-16 Gregory Thaumaturgus[Sectional Confession of Faith 11]

10:15-16 Clement of Alexandria[Stromata Book VI.18]

10:17 Jeremiah 9:22-24; Apostolic[1Clement 13]; Clement of Alexandria[The Instructor Book I.6]; NT-Apocrypha[History of Joseph the Carpenter 2]

11:02 Clement of Alexandria[The Instructor Book I.5]; Cyprian[Epistle LXXIV.14]; Methodius[Banquet of the Ten Virgins Introduction, 4.5]; Tertullian[Five Books in Reply to Marcion Book IV.51; On Modesty 20; Five Books Against Marcion Book V.12]

11:02-03 Clement of Alexandria[Stromata Book III.11]

11:03 Genesis 3:13; Pseudepigrapha[2Enoch 31:6; Life of Adam and Eve (Apocalypse of Moses) 14:2]; Clement of Alexandria[Exhortation to the Heathen 1; Stromata Book III.12, 14]; Clement[First Epistle Concerning Virginity 5]; Tertullian[An Answer to the Jews 10]; NT-Apocrypha[Protoevangelium of James 13.1; Pseudo-Titus Epistle Line 417]

11:04 Hippolytus[Refutation of all Heresies Book IX.18]; Irenaeus[Against Heresies Book I.8.1]

11:05 Tertullian[Five Books Against Marcion Book I.14]

11:06 Clement of Alexandria[Stromata Book VI.18]; Origen[Gospel of John Book IV.2]

11:09 Philippians 4:15-18

11:12 Methodius[Banquet of the Ten Virgins 3.8]

11:13 Clement[First Epistle Concerning Virginity 13]; Constitutions of the Holy Apostles[Book VI.9];
    Justin[On the Resurrection 10]; Tertullian[Five Books Against Marcion Book V.12]; NT-
    Apocrypha[Acts of Thomas 1.79; Epistula Apostolorum 1, 7]

11:13-15 Pseudepigrapha[Testament of Job 6:4]

11:14 Pseudepigrapha[Life of Adam and Eve (Apocalypse of Moses) 17:1; Life of Adam and Eve Vita
    9:1, 9.3, 12.1, 17.1]; Clement of Alexandria[Stromata Book VI.8]; Clement[Recognitions Book II.18];
    Methodius[Banquet of the Ten Virgins 10.5]; Origen[Against Celsus Book VIII.4]; Tertullian[A
    Treatise on the Soul 57; On Prescription Against Heretics 6; On the Resurrection of the Flesh 55; Five
    Books Against Marcion Book V.12]

11:14-15 Tertullian[An Answer to the Jews 10]

11:15 Pseudepigrapha[Joseph and Aseneth 28:3]; NT-Apocrypha[Acts of Thomas 1.79]

11:18 Tertullian[On the Apparel of Women Book II.3]

11:19 Theonas[Epistle to Lucianus, the Chief Chamberlain 9]

11:20 Psalms 53:5; Tertullian[On Modesty 14]

11:22 Origen[De Principiis Book II.4.2]

11:23 Acts 16:23; Archelaus[Disputation with Manes 35]; Clement of Alexandria[Stromata Book IV.20];
    Tertullian[Scorpiace 13]; NT-Apocrypha[Pseudo-Titus Epistle Line 61]

11:24 Deuteronomy 25:3

11:25 Acts 14:19, 16:22; Apostolic[1Clement 5:6]

11:26 Acts 9:23, 14:5

11:27 Pseudepigrapha[2Enoch 66:6]; Tertullian[On Fasting 8]

11:29 Clement[First Epistle Concerning Virginity 12]; Cyprian[Epistle XI.1, LIX.1]; Origen[Gospel of
    John Book X.5; Gospel of Matthew Book XI.3, XII.23]

11:31 Clement of Alexandria[Stromata Book V.6]

11:32-33 Peter of Alexandria[Canonical Epistle 9]

11:33 Acts 9:23-25

12:01 Tertullian[Five Books in Reply to Marcion Book III.303]

12:01-03 Pseudepigrapha[2Enoch 42:3]

12:01-04 Pseudepigrapha[Apocalypse of Zephaniah 5:6]

12:02 Pseudepigrapha[2Enoch 8:1, 42:3; Life of Adam and Eve (Apocalypse of Moses) 37:5; Testament
    of Job 39:12, 48:2; Testament of Levi 2:7]; Hippolytus[Refutation of all Heresies Book V.3];
    Origen[Against Celsus Book I.48, VI.21]; Nag Hammadi[Apocalypse of Paul 19]; NT-
    Apocrypha[Apocalypse of Paul 1.11, 1.19]

12:02-03 Methodius[Discourse on the Resurrection 3.9]

12:02-04 Pseudepigrapha[Life of Adam and Eve Vita 25:3]; Irenaeus[Against Heresies Book II.30.7];
    Tertullian[A Treatise on the Soul 9]

12:03 Pseudepigrapha[1Enoch 39:3]; Irenaeus[Against Heresies Book V.2.3]

> **A cloud then snatched me up, and the wind raised me above the surface of the earth, placing me at the extremity of the heavens. (Pseudepigrapha - 1Enoch 39:3)**

12:03-05 Origen[Gospel of John Book X.5]

12:04 Pseudepigrapha[2 Baruch 4:7; 2 Enoch 8:1]; Hippolytus[Refutation of all Heresies Book VII.14];
    Irenaeus[Against Heresies Book V.5.1]; Origen[Against Celsus Book VI.6, VII.43; Gospel of John
    Book VI.2; De Principiis Book II.7.4]; Tertullian[On Prescription Against Heretics 24]; NT-
    Apocrypha[Apocalypse of Paul 1.19, 1.21]

12:07 Numbers 33:55; Job 2:6; Ezekiel 28:24; Tertullian[De Fuga in Persecutione 2]; NT-
    Apocrypha[Acts of Peter 1.17, 1.32]

12:07-08 Tertullian[Five Books Against Marcion Book V.12]

12:07-09 Cyprian[Treatise VII.13, XII.Book III.6]; Irenaeus[Against Heresies Book V.3.1]

12:07-10 Tertullian[On Modesty 13]

12:08-09 Archelaus[Disputation with Manes 34]

12:09 Irenaeus[Against Heresies Book III.20.1]; Tertullian[De Fuga in Persecutione 2; On Modesty 13;
    On the Resurrection of the Flesh 9, 47; Five Books Against Marcion Book V.12]

12:10 Tertullian[On the Apparel of Women Book II.3; Scorpiace 13]

12:12 OT-Apocrypha[Wisdom of Solomon 10:16]; Tertullian[To his Wife Book II.6]; NT-
    Apocrypha[Epistula Apostolorum 30]

12:21 Cyprian[Epistle LI.26; Treatises Attributed to Cyprian Exhortation to Repentance]; Tertullian[On
    Modesty 15]

13:01 Deuteronomy 17:6, 19:15; Tertullian[On Baptism 6; On Prescription Against Heretics 22; Five Books Against Marcion Book IV.43, V.12]; Theodotus[Excerpts 13]

13:02 Cyprian[Treatises Attributed to Cyprian - Exhortation to Repentance]; Tertullian[Five Books Against Marcion Book V.12]

13:03 Archelaus[Disputation with Manes 26, 34]; Origen[Gospel of John Book VI.3, X.8; De Principiis Preface.1, II.6.7, IV.1.29]

13:04 Hippolytus[Fragments - On Genesis 49.16-20]; Irenaeus[Fragments from the Lost Works 52]; Origen[Gospel of Matthew Book X.22; De Principiis Book IV.1.31]

13:05 Clement of Alexandria[The Instructor Book III.3]

13:10 Tertullian[Five Books Against Marcion Book V.12]

13:12 Tertullian[On Prayer 18]

13:13 Gregory Thaumaturgus[Sectional Confession of Faith 20]; NT-Apocrypha[Acts of Pilate XXVII.1]

13:14 Matthew 28:19n

Cross Reference Index: Galatians

01:01 Apostolic[Polycarp - Letter to the Philippians 12:2]; Hippolytus[Treatise on Christ and Antichrist 8]; Irenaeus[Against Heresies Book III.13.2]; Novatian[Treatise Concerning the Trinity 13]; Tertullian[Against Praxeas 28; Five Books Against Marcion Book V.1]; NT-Apocrypha[Acts of Peter and Paul; Epistle to the Laodiceans 1:1]

01:03 NT-Apocrypha[Epistle to the Laodiceans 1:2]

01:03-04 John 1:18n

01:04 Origen[Against Celsus Book VI.54]; NT-Apocrypha[Freer Logion; Letter of Clement to James 1.5]

01:05 OT-Apocrypha[4Maccabees 18:24]

01:06 Tertullian[On Prescription Against Heretics 27]; NT-Apocrypha[Acts of Paul in Philippi 3.2]

01:06-07 Tertullian[Five Books Against Marcion Book I.20, V.2]

01:06-08 Archelaus[Disputation with Manes 35]

01:06-09 Clement of Alexandria[Stromata Book VII.16]; Cyprian[Epistle XXII.3, LXII.10]; Tertullian[Five Books Against Marcion Book V.12]

01:08 Archelaus[Disputation with Manes 40]; Irenaeus[Against Heresies Book I.31.2]; Tertullian[On Prescription Against Heretics 6, 29; On the Flesh of Christ 6, 24; Five Books Against Marcion Book IV.4, V.2]; Nag Hammadi[Testimony of Truth 73]

01:08-09 Alexander of Alexandria[Epistles on Arian Heresy 1.13]; Clement of Alexandria[Stromata Book I.10]; Tertullian[On Prescription Against Heretics 4]

01:09 Hippolytus[Refutation of all Heresies Book IX.18]

01:10 Cyprian[Epistle LIV.8, LXI.5, LXII.15; Treatise II.5, XII.Book III.55]; Tertullian[On Idolatry 14]

01:11 NT-Apocrypha[Epistle to the Laodiceans 1:4]

01:11-24 Tertullian[Five Books Against Marcion Book V.2]

01:12 Novatian[Treatise Concerning the Trinity 13]

01:13 Acts 8:3, 22:4-5, 26:9-11; Tertullian[On Prescription Against Heretics 23]; NT-Apocrypha[Epistula Apostolorum 31, 33]

01:14 Acts 22:3; Josephus[Antiquities 13.10.6 297]; Rabbinic[Babylonian Sanhedrin 88b]; Irenaeus[Against Heresies Book IV.12.1, 4]; Tertullian[On Modesty 1]

01:15 Isaiah 49:1; Jeremiah 1:5; Origen[Gospel of Matthew Book XIII.27]; Nag Hammadi[Apocalypse of Paul 18]

01:15-16 Irenaeus[Against Heresies Book V.12.5, 15.3]

01:16 Acts 9:3-6, 22:6-10, 26:13-18; Justin[Hortatory Address to the Greeks 32]; NT-Apocrypha[Epistula Apostolorum 31]

01:17 NT-Apocrypha[Acts of Paul in Philippi 3.4]

01:18 Acts 9:26-30; Tertullian[On Prescription Against Heretics 23]

01:19 Matthew 13:55; Origen[Against Celsus Book I.47; Gospel of Matthew Book X.17]; Teaching of the Twelve Apostles 11.4

01:23 NT-Apocrypha[Epistula Apostolorum 33]

01:24 Tertullian[On Prescription Against Heretics 23]

02:01 Acts 11:30, 15:2

02:01-02 Irenaeus[Against Heresies Book III.13.3]

02:01-05 Tertullian[Five Books Against Marcion Book V.3]

02:02 Tertullian[Five Books Against Marcion Book IV.2]; NT-Apocrypha[Epistula Apostolorum 27]

02:04 Hippolytus[Fragments - On Susannah 12]; Origen[Gospel of Matthew Book XIV.9]; Tertullian[On Modesty 6; Five Books Against Marcion Book I.20]

02:05 Origen[Against Celsus Book VII.21]

02:06 Deuteronomy 10:17; OT-Apocrypha[Sirach 35:13]

02:08 Irenaeus[Against Heresies Book III.13.1]; NT-Apocrypha[Epistula Apostolorum 31]

02:08-09 Gregory Thaumaturgus[Sectional Confession of Faith 11]

02:09 1Peter 1:10-13n; Pseudepigrapha[Joseph and Aseneth 17:6]; Apostolic[1Clement 5:2]; Clement of Alexandria[Stromata Book VI.18]; Cyprian[Treatise XII.Book III.37]; Methodius[Oration on the Psalms 2]; Tertullian[On Prescription Against Heretics 23]

02:09-10 Tertullian[Five Books Against Marcion Book V.3]

02:10 Pseudepigrapha[Sibylline Oracles 2.78-89]

02:11 NT-Apocrypha[Pseudo Clementines - Kerygmata Petrou H XVII 19.4-6]

02:11-14 Pseudepigrapha[Joseph and Aseneth 7:1]; NT-Apocrypha[Letter of Peter to James 2.4]

02:12 Origen[Against Celsus Book II.1]; Tertullian[Five Books Against Marcion Book V.3]

02:12-13 Irenaeus[Against Heresies Book III.12.15]; Tertullian[On Prescription Against Heretics 23]

02:13-14 Tertullian[Five Books Against Marcion Book IV.3]

02:15 Pseudepigrapha[Jubilees 23:24]

02:16 Genesis 6:12; Psalms 143:2; Romans 3:20, 22; Apostolic[Ignatius - Letter to the Magnesians 8:1]; Tertullian[Five Books Against Marcion Book V.3]

02:17 NT-Apocrypha[Letter of Peter to James 2.4]

02:18 Archelaus[Disputation with Manes 40]; Tertullian[On Modesty 14; Five Books Against Marcion Book V.3]

02:19 OT-Apocrypha[4Maccabees 7:19]; Tertullian[Five Books Against Marcion Book V.13]

02:19-20 Clement of Alexandria[Stromata Book III.18]

02:20 John 3:18n; Origen[Gospel of John Book I.6, X.8; Gospel of Matthew Book XII.25; De Principiis Book IV.1.29]

02:21 Apostolic[Ignatius - Letter to the Magnesians 8:1]

03:01 Archelaus[Disputation with Manes 49]; Tertullian[On Prescription Against Heretics 27]

03:01-4:31 Tertullian[On Monogamy 6, 14]

03:03 Clement of Alexandria[Stromata Book III.17, VI.14; Commentary on the Gospel of Matthew Book XI.8, XII.5; De Principiis Book I.3.4]

03:05-09 Irenaeus[Against Heresies Book IV.21.1]

03:06 Genesis 15:6; Romans 4:3; Irenaeus[Against Heresies Book V.32.2]; Tertullian[Five Books Against Marcion Book V.3; Of Patience 6]

03:06-09 Cyprian[Epistle LXII.4; Treatise XII.Book I.5]

03:07 Romans 4:16; Tertullian[On Monogamy 6; Five Books Against Marcion Book V.3]

03:08 Genesis 12:3, 18:18, 22:18, 26:4, 28:14; OT-Apocrypha[Sirach 44:21]; Tertullian[On the Flesh of Christ 22]

03:09 Tertullian[Five Books Against Marcion Book V.3]

03:10 Deuteronomy 27:26, 28:58, 30:10; OT-Apocrypha[4Maccabees 5:20]; Constitutions of the Holy Apostles[Book VI.25]; Lactantius[Divine Institutes Book IV.25]

03:11 Habakkuk 2:4; Irenaeus[Demonstration of the Apostolic Preaching 35]; Tertullian[On Exhortation to Chastity 7; Five Books Against Marcion Book V.3]

03:12 Leviticus 18:5; Archelaus[Disputation with Manes 28]; Clement of Alexandria[Stromata Book II.10]; NT-Apocrypha[Epistula Apostolorum 39]

03:13 This section also includes topical notes for: Hang on Cross - Genesis 31:44-49; Exodus 32:32; Deuteronomy 21:23, 27:26, 28:66; Acts 5:30, 10:39; John 19:17; Pseudepigrapha[2Enoch 7:1; Martyrdom and Ascension of Isaiah 11.21; Odes of Solomon 27.1-3; Sibylline Oracles 5.256-258]; Dead Sea Scrolls[11Q TEMPLE SCROLL (11Q19[11QT]) COL LXIV 7-12]; Philo[Concerning Noah's Work As A Planter (43-45) cf. {Genesis 2:9, 25:27}; On the Change of Names (140) cf. {Hosea 14:8-9}; On the Posterity of Cain And His Exile (26) cf. {Deuteronomy 21:23, Galatians 3:13}]; Rabbinic[Exodus Rabba on 34.1; Babylonian Sanhedrin 45b-46b]; Apostolic[Didache 16:5]; Archelaus[Disputation with Manes 28, 31]; Clement of Alexandria[Stromata Book V.11; The Instructor Book I.5]; Irenaeus[Against Heresies Book III.18.3, IV.10.2, V.18.1, 3, 19.1; Demonstration of the Apostolic Preaching 34; Fragments from the Lost Works 53]; Justin[Dialogue with Trypho 86, 89-90, 93-97, 111; First Apology 41]; Origen[Gospel of Matthew Book XI.8]; Tertullian[Against Praxeas 29; An Answer to the Jews 10-11; De Fuga in Persecutione 12; Of Patience 8; Five Books Against Marcion Book III.18, V.3]; Nag Hammadi[Apocryphon of James 13; Gospel of Truth 18, 20; Interpretation of Knowledge 4; Teachings of Silvanus 106; Trimorphic Protennoia 50]; NT-Apocrypha[Gospel of the Nazareans Fragment 32]

03:15 Tertullian[Five Books Against Marcion Book V.4]

03:16 Genesis 12:7, 13:15, 17:7-8, 24:7; Irenaeus[Against Heresies Book V.32.2]; Tertullian[An Answer to the Jews 1; Of Patience 6; On the Flesh of Christ 22; Five Books Against Marcion Book V.4]

03:17 Exodus 12:40; Novatian[On the Jewish Meats 2]

03:18 Acts 20:32n; Romans 4:14

03:19 Leviticus 26:46; Deuteronomy 5:4; Pseudepigrapha[Jubilees 1:28; Testament of Dan 6:2]; Rabbinic[Exodus Rabbah 29:2 cf. {Psalms 68:17-18}; Pesikta Rabbati 21:5]; Clement of Alexandria[Stromata Book I.26]; Hippolytus[Refutation of all Heresies Book VII.19]; Irenaeus[Against Heresies Book V.21.1]

03:20 Hippolytus[Fragments - On Numbers]; Novatian[Treatise Concerning the Trinity 30]; Tertullian[Five Books in Reply to Marcion Book IV.51]

03:22 Tertullian[Five Books Against Marcion Book V.13]

03:23-24 Clement of Alexandria[Stromata Book I.26]

03:23-28 Clement of Alexandria[The Instructor Book I.6]

03:24 Clement of Alexandria[Stromata Book I.5, II.7; The Instructor Book I.11; Who is the Rich Man that shall be Saved 9]; Irenaeus[Against Heresies Book IV.1.7]

03:26 Tertullian[Five Books Against Marcion Book V.3]

03:27 Matthew 3:5-16n; Cyprian[Epistle LIX.2, LXXIII.5, LXXIV.12]; Tertullian[On Baptism 12; On Modesty 6; On Monogamy 7, 17; Five Books Against Marcion Book III.12]; NT-Apocrypha[Pseudo-Titus Epistle Line 358]

03:28 Clement of Alexandria[Exhortation to the Heathen 11; Stromata Book V.5]; Tertullian[On the Apparel of Women Book I.2]; NT-Apocrypha[Acts of Thomas 1.4, 1.83]

03:29 Romans 4:13; Tertullian[Five Books Against Marcion Book V.3]

04:01 Origen[Gospel of Matthew Book XIII.26]

04:01-02 Origen[Gospel of Matthew Book X.9]

04:01-03 Clement of Alexandria[Stromata Book I.11]

04:01-04 Nag Hammadi[Gospel of Philip 60]

04:01-05 Clement of Alexandria[The Instructor Book I.6]

04:03 Pseudepigrapha[Testament of Solomon 8:2, 18:2]; Archelaus[Disputation with Manes 13]; Tertullian[Five Books Against Marcion Book V.4]

04:04 OT-Apocrypha[Tobit 14:5]; Pseudepigrapha[2Baruch 29:8, 40:4]; Archelaus[Disputation with Manes 49]; Cyprian[Treatise XII.Book II.8]; Irenaeus[Against Heresies Book III.16.7, 22.1, V.21.1]; Novatian[Treatise Concerning the Trinity 11]; Origen[Gospel of Matthew Book XIII.26]; Tertullian[On the Flesh of Christ 20; On the Veiling of Virgins 6; Five Books Against Marcion Book V.4, 8]

04:04-05 Irenaeus[Against Heresies Book III.16.3]; Methodius[Oration Concerning Simeon and Anna 4]

04:05 Irenaeus[Against Heresies Book III.20.2, IV.8.1, V.18.2]; NT-Apocrypha[Acts of Paul in Ephesus p.2; Acts of Paul in Philippi 3.8]

04:05-06 Tertullian[Five Books Against Marcion Book V.4]

04:06 Pseudepigrapha[Apocryphon of Ezekiel Fragment 2]; Irenaeus[Demonstration of the Apostolic Preaching 5]; Theodotus[Excerpts]

04:06-07 Clement of Alexandria[Exhortation to the Heathen 9]

04:07 Romans 8:15-17; Clement of Alexandria[The Instructor Book I.6]

04:08 2Chronicles 13:9; Isaiah 37:19; Jeremiah 2:11; Irenaeus[Against Heresies Book II.9.2]; Tertullian[Five Books Against Marcion Book V.4]; Nag Hammadi[Gospel of Philip 54]

04:08-09 Irenaeus[Against Heresies Book III.6.5]; Tertullian[An Answer to the Jews 4]

04:09 Pseudepigrapha[Testament of Solomon 8:2; 18:2]; Clement of Alexandria[Exhortation to the Heathen 5]; Constitutions of the Holy Apostles[Book V.16]; Tertullian[On Prescription Against Heretics 33; Five Books Against Marcion Book V.4]

04:10 Pseudepigrapha[1Enoch 72:1-82:20]; Tertullian[On Fasting 2, 14; Five Books Against Marcion Book V.4]; NT-Apocrypha[Kerygma Petri 2c]

04:10-11 Origen[Against Celsus Book VIII.21]

04:12 NT-Apocrypha[Correspondence between Seneca and Paul XII]

04:16 Amos 5:10; Clement of Alexandria[The Instructor Book I.9]; Cyprian[Epistle LXI.5]

04:19 Pseudepigrapha[Odes of Solomon 14:10]; Apostolic[Papias Fragment 15:1]; Clement of Alexandria[Stromata Book III.15]; Methodius[Banquet of the Ten Virgins 3.9, 8.8]; Tertullian[Five Books Against Marcion Book V.8; On Monogamy 14]

04:19-31 Tertullian[Five Books in Reply to Marcion Book III.3]

04:21-24 Origen[Against Celsus Book II.3, IV.44; De Principiis Book IV.1.13]

04:21-26 Tertullian[Five Books Against Marcion Book V.4]

04:21-31 Tertullian[On Monogamy 6]

04:22 Genesis 16:15, 21:2, 9; Tertullian[Five Books Against Marcion Book III.5]

04:22-24 This section also includes topical notes for: Allegory – Proverbs 1:6; Pseudepigrapha[Letter of Aristeas 1.141-171]; Philo[On Husbandry (131-135), (142-145), cf. {Leviticus 11:1-47}; Special Laws I (166-167); Special Laws IV (106-113) cf. {{Leviticus 11:1-47; Deuteronomy 14:10}; Who is the Heir of Divine Things (239) cf. {Leviticus 11:21}]; Apostolic[Epistle of Barnabas 10.12]; Clement of Alexandria[Stromata Book I.5, II.5, 15, V.6, 8, 9, 11, VI.6, VII.18; The Instructor Book II.1]; Irenaeus[Against Heresies Book II.20.4-5, 21.1-2, 23.1-2, 24.3-5, 25.1, IV.14.3, 20.1, 12, 25.3, 26.1, 30.3-4, 31.1, 32.2, 33.9-10, 35.3, V.8.4, 20.2, 26.2; Demonstration of the Apostolic Preaching 24, 26; Fragments from the Lost Works 8, 17, 19, 27-28, 41-48]; Justin[Dialogue with Trypho 20-21, 40, 42, 44, 53-54, 68, 90-91, 111, 120, 131, 134, 140; Fragments from the Lost Writings of Justin 10]; Theophilus of Antioch[To Autolycus Book II.15-17]

04:23 Genesis 17:16

04:24 Origen[Gospel of Matthew Book X.14]; Tertullian[Five Books Against Marcion Book III.5]

04:26 Psalms 87:5; Pseudepigrapha[3Enoch 48A:3; 4Baruch 5:35; 4Ezra 10:7]; Apostolic[Polycarp - Letter to the Philippians 3:3]; Clement[First Epistle Concerning Virginity 5]; Hippolytus[Refutation of all Heresies Book V.2]; Irenaeus[Against Heresies Book V.35.2]; Origen[Gospel of Matthew Book XI.17, XIV.13]; Tertullian[Five Books Against Marcion Book III.25, V.15]

04:26-27 NT-Apocrypha[Epistula Apostolorum 33]

04:27 Isaiah 54:1; Apostolic[2Clement 2:1]; Hippolytus[Refutation of all Heresies Book V.3]; Irenaeus[Against Heresies Book I.10.3; Demonstration of the Apostolic Preaching 94]; Origen[Gospel of Matthew Book X.23]; Tertullian[Five Books in Reply to Marcion Book III.2]

04:28 Irenaeus[Against Heresies Book IV.7.2, V.32.2]; Tertullian[On Monogamy 6]

04:29-30 Genesis 21:9-10

04:30 Clement of Alexandria[Stromata Book I.11]

04:31 Apostolic[Papias Fragment 15:1]; Tertullian[On Monogamy 6; On the Apparel of Women Book II.7; Five Books Against Marcion Book V.4]

05:01 Tertullian[An Answer to the Jews 4; On Fasting 2; On Modesty 6; Five Books Against Marcion Book V.4]

05:02 Origen[Against Celsus Book V.48]

05:02-06 Tertullian[On Modesty 17]

05:03 Hippolytus[Refutation of all Heresies Book VIII.11]

05:04 Apostolic[Ignatius - Letter to the Magnesians 8:1]

05:05 Tertullian[On the Resurrection of the Flesh 23]

05:05-06 Clement of Alexandria[Stromata Book II.22]

05:06 Tertullian[Five Books Against Marcion Book V.4]

05:07 Pseudepigrapha[Sibylline Oracles 2.39]; Tertullian[On Prescription Against Heretics 27]

05:08 Origen[Against Celsus Book VI.57; De Principiis Book III.1.7]

05:09 Matthew 16:6-12n; 1Corinthians 5:6; Constitutions of the Holy Apostles[Book II.17]

05:10 Tertullian[Five Books Against Marcion Book V.4]

05:11 Tertullian[An Answer to the Jews 10]

05:12 Deuteronomy 23:2; Tertullian[A Treatise on the Soul 16; On Modesty 1]

05:13 Clement of Alexandria[Stromata Book III.5]; Tertullian[On Modesty 6; On the Apparel of Women Book II.7]; NT-Apocrypha[Pseudo-Titus Epistle Line 137]

05:14 Leviticus 19:18; Matthew 5:43n; Rabbinic[Makkot 23b-24a]; Irenaeus[Demonstration of the Apostolic Preaching 86]; Tertullian[On the Apparel of Women Book II.2; Five Books Against Marcion Book V.4]

05:14-15 Cyprian[Treatise XII.Book III.3]

05:15 Cyprian[Epistle VI.5]; Origen[Gospel of Matthew Book XIV.1]

05:16 NT-Apocrypha[Pseudo-Titus Epistle Line 140]

05:16-17 Tertullian[A Treatise on the Soul 40]

05:16-23 Pseudepigrapha[3Baruch 13:3-4; Sibylline Oracles 2.68-78; Testament of Levi 17.11]; Dead Sea Scrolls[1Q Rule of the Community (1QS) COL I 5-20; IV 2-15]; Philo[On the Virtues (179-182) cf. {Deuteronomy 30:11-14}]; Plato[Phaedo 80e-81e, 83d-e; Republic III 395e-396d]; Clement of Alexandria[Stromata Book IV.8]; Irenaeus[Against Heresies Book II.31.3, 32.1-2, V.11.1]; Justin[Dialogue with Trypho 110; Discourse to the Greeks 5; First Apology 10, 12]; Nag Hammadi[On the Origin of the World 106]; NT-Apocrypha[Epistula Apostolorum 43]; Egyptian Book of the Dead[Oration 125]

05:16-26 Acts 3:19n

05:17 Romans 7:15-23; Clement of Alexandria[Stromata Book VI.16, VII.12]; Hippolytus[Refutation of all Heresies Book V.21]; Methodius[Banquet of the Ten Virgins 8.17]; Novatian[Treatise Concerning the Trinity 29]; Origen[Against Celsus Book VIII.23; Gospel of Matthew Book XIV.3; De Principiis Book III.2.3, 4.2]; Tertullian[On Monogamy 1; On the Resurrection of the Flesh 10]

05:17-22 Cyprian[Treatise IV.16]

05:17-24 Cyprian[Treatise XII.Book III.64]

05:18-21 Pythagoras[Golden Verses Lines 9-11]

05:18-23 This section also includes topical notes for: Led by the Spirit You Are Not Under the Law - Romans 8:22; Philo[On the Birth of Abel And the Sacrifices offered By Him And By His Brother Cain (124-130) cf. {Leviticus 25:38-39}]; Nag Hammadi[Gospel of Philip 65]

05:19 John 8:3-11n; Tertullian[On the Resurrection of the Flesh 45]

05:19-21 Matthew 15:19; Mark 7:21-23; Pseudepigrapha[Pseudo-Phocylides 71]; Apostolic[Didache 5:1; Epistle of Barnabas 20:1-2]; Cyprian[The Seventh Council of Carthage under Cyprian]; Origen[De Principiis Book III.4.2]; Tertullian[On Modesty 17; Five Books Against Marcion Book V.10]; NT-Apocrypha[Questions of Bartholomew IV 38, 44]

05:19-22 Apostolic[1Clement 30:1, 35:5]

05:19-23 Apostolic[Shepherd of Hermas 92:1-3]

05:20 Clement of Alexandria[Stromata Book VI.16]; Tertullian[On Prescription Against Heretics 6, 33]; NT-Apocrypha[Acts of Paul in Ephesus p.1]

05:21 Fabian[Second Epistle]; Irenaeus[Against Heresies Book I.6.3]; Tertullian[On the Resurrection of the Flesh 49]

05:22 Clement[First Epistle Concerning Virginity 9]; Hippolytus[Fragments - On Psalms 77.1-78.72]; Origen[De Principiis Book I.3.4]

05:22-23 Clement of Alexandria[Who is the Rich Man that shall be Saved 3]; Methodius[Banquet of the Ten Virgins 10.5]

05:24 Luke 22:40-46; Acts 1:3, 14:15; Philo[On Dreams That they Are God-Sent (1.255-1.256) cf. {Genesis 32:7-30}]; Clement of Alexandria[Fragments from the Books of the Hypotyposes Book V]; Clement[First Epistle Concerning Virginity 7]; Cyprian[Treatise II.6]

05:24-25 Clement of Alexandria[Stromata Book IV.7]

05:25 Clement of Alexandria[Stromata Book V.6]; Origen[Against Celsus Book VII.52]; Nag Hammadi[Interpretation of Knowledge 20]

05:25-26 Clement of Alexandria[The Instructor Book III.12]

05:26 Clement of Alexandria[Stromata Book I.8]; Tertullian[Of Patience 10]

06:01 OT-Apocrypha[Wisdom of Solomon 17:17]; Callistus[Second Epistle 5.5]

06:01-02 Cyprian[Epistle LI.18; Treatise XII.Book III.9]

06:02 Clement of Alexandria[Stromata Book III.1; The Instructor Book III.12]; Origen[Gospel of Matthew Book XIV.16]; Tertullian[Five Books Against Marcion Book V.4]

06:03-04 Clement[First Epistle Concerning Virginity 3]

06:04 Callistus[Second Epistle 5.5]

06:07 Job 4:8; Proverbs 22:8; Pseudepigrapha[2Enoch 42:11; Testament of Levi 13:6]; Dead Sea Scrolls[4Q Aramaic Levi (4Q213[4QTLEVIAR]) Fragment 5 COL I 7-18]; Apostolic[Polycarp - Letter to the Philippians 5:1]; Clement of Alexandria[The Instructor Book III.12; Who is the Rich Man that shall be Saved 41]; Cyprian[Epistle LXVII.5; Treatise III.28]; Tertullian[On Modesty 2; Five Books Against Marcion Book V.4]

06:07-09 2Corinthians 9:6; Justin[Fragments from the Lost Writings of Justin 12]; Nag Hammadi[Gospel of Philip 52]

06:08 Jude 1:21n; Clement of Alexandria[Stromata Book IV.7]

06:08-10 Clement of Alexandria[Stromata Book I.1]

06:09 Clement of Alexandria[The Instructor Book III.12]; Tertullian[On the Resurrection of the Flesh 23; Five Books Against Marcion Book V.4]

06:09-10 Cyprian[Treatise VIII.24, IX.13]

06:10 Constitutions of the Holy Apostles[Book VII.2]; Tertullian[Five Books Against Marcion Book V.4]

06:13 Tertullian[On the Apparel of Women Book II.3]

06:14 Colossians 1:20; Pseudepigrapha[Lives of the Prophets 2.14]; Apostolic[Ignatius - Letter to the Romans 7:2]; Clement of Alexandria[Stromata Book II.20, IV.3]; Cyprian[Treatise II.6, XII.Book III.11; Treatises Attributed to Cyprian On the Glory of Martyrdom 28]; Irenaeus[Against Heresies Book I.3.5]; Origen[Against Celsus Book II.69; Gospel of John Book X.20; Gospel of Matthew Book

XII.18, 25, 27, XIII.21]; Tertullian[Five Books Against Marcion Book V.4]; NT-Apocrypha[Pseudo-Titus Epistle Line 24; Two Books of Jeu c. 1-3]

06:15 Clement of Alexandria[Exhortation to the Heathen 11]; Hippolytus[Refutation of all Heresies Book X.29]

06:16 Psalms 125:5, 128:6; NT-Apocrypha[Acts of Paul in Philippi 3.36]

06:17 OT-Apocrypha[3Maccabees 2:29]; Cyprian[Epistle XXXIII.2]; Peter of Alexandria[Canonical Epistle 1]; Tertullian[On the Resurrection of the Flesh 10]; NT-Apocrypha[Acts of Paul in Philippi 3.34-35]

06:18 NT-Apocrypha[Epistle to the Laodiceans 1:19]

Cross Reference Index:
Ephesians

01:01 Acts 18:19-21, 19:1

01:02 John 1:18n

01:04 This section also includes topical notes for: Predestination - Pseudepigrapha[Joseph and Aseneth 8:9]; Dead Sea Scrolls[1Q Rule of the Community (1QS) COL III 15-16]; Apostolic[Ignatius - Letter to the Ephesians (Prologue)]; Clement of Alexandria[Stromata Book VII.2, 5, 17; The Instructor Book I.7]; Irenaeus[Against Heresies Book II.2.4, III.22.3, V.1.1]; Origen[De Principiis Book III.5.4]; Tertullian[On the Apparel of Women Book II.9]; Nag Hammadi[Treatise on the Resurrection 46]

01:04-05 Clement of Alexandria[Stromata Book VI.9]

01:05 Clement of Alexandria[Stromata Book II.16, 19; The Instructor Book I.5]; Irenaeus[Against Heresies Book III.20.2, IV.8.1, V.18.2]; NT-Apocrypha[Acts of Paul in Ephesus p.2; Acts of Paul in Philippi 3.8]

01:06 Deuteronomy 32:15, 33:5, 26; Isaiah 44:2; Daniel 3:35; OT-Apocrypha[Sirach 45:1, 46:13]; Pseudepigrapha[Martyrdom and Ascension of Isaiah 1:4]

01:07 Acts 26:18n; Colossians 1:14; 1Peter 1:10-13n; Apostolic[1Clement 7:4]; Irenaeus[Against Heresies Book V.1.1, 2.1-2, 14.3]

01:09-10 Lactantius[Divine Institutes Book IV.2]; Tertullian[On Monogamy 5; Five Books Against Marcion Book V.17]

01:10 Hippolytus[Against Beron and Heli Frag 2]; Irenaeus[Against Heresies Book I.3.4, 10.1, 16.6, 20.2; Demonstration of the Apostolic Preaching 30]; Tertullian[An Answer to the Jews 14]; NT-Apocrypha[Epistula Apostolorum 13]

01:12 Tertullian[Five Books Against Marcion Book V.17]

01:13 Revelation 12:10n; Pseudepigrapha[4Ezra 2.39]; Clement of Alexandria[Fragments from Macarius Chrysocephalus Parable of the Prodigal son 1, 6]

01:13-14 Irenaeus[Against Heresies Book V.8.1]; Tertullian[Five Books in Reply to Marcion Book II.328]

01:14 Malachi 3:17; Tertullian[On the Resurrection of the Flesh 53]

01:14-18 Acts 20:32n

01:17 Isaiah 11:2; Acts 26:18n; OT-Apocrypha[Wisdom of Solomon 7:7]; Pseudepigrapha[Testament of Job 33:3]; Origen[Gospel of Matthew Book XII.10]; Tertullian[Against Praxeas 28; Five Books Against Marcion Book V.17]

01:17-18 Pseudepigrapha[Hellenistic Synagogal Prayers 8.1]

01:18 Pseudepigrapha[Joseph and Aseneth 6:6; 21:16]; Teaching of Addaeus the Apostle; Egyptian Book of the Dead[Oration 98]

01:18-22 Tertullian[Five Books Against Marcion Book V.17]

01:19 Isaiah 40:26; Daniel 4:27; NT-Apocrypha[Freer Logion]

01:20 Psalms 110:1; Pseudepigrapha[Testament of Job 33:3]; Irenaeus[Against Heresies Book IV.25.1]

01:21 Matthew 7:28-29n; Pseudepigrapha[Prayer of Joseph Fragment A; Psalms of Solomon 2:19; Testament of Adam 4:1]; Hippolytus[Refutation of all Heresies Book VII.13]; Irenaeus[Against Heresies Book IV.19.2, 24.2]; Methodius[Banquet of the Ten Virgins 3.6]; Origen[Gospel of John Book I.15, 34; De Principiis Book I.5.1]; Nag Hammadi[Gospel of Philip 54; Prayer of the Apostle Paul A.I]; NT-Apocrypha[Acts of Thomas 1.119; Epistula Apostolorum 3]

01:22 Psalms 8:6-7

01:23 Jeremiah 23:24; Colossians 1:18; Tertullian[On Monogamy 13; Five Books Against Marcion Book V.17]

02:01 Romans 8:6

02:01-02 Tertullian[Five Books Against Marcion Book V.17]

02:02 Pseudepigrapha[2Enoch 3:1; 29:4; 4Baruch 9:17; Martyrdom and Ascension of Isaiah 2:4, 10.31; Testament of Job 42:4]; Apostolic[Epistle of Barnabas 18:1-2]; Archelaus[Disputation with Manes 44]; Clement[First Epistle Concerning Virginity 11]; Irenaeus[Against Heresies Book V.24.4];

Origen[Against Celsus Book VII.52; Gospel of Matthew Book XIII.8; De Principiis Book II.11.5]; Tertullian[A Strain of the Judgment of the Lord 180]; NT-Apocrypha[Acts of Paul in Philippi 3.22; Freer Logion]

02:03 Pseudepigrapha[Life of Adam and Eve (Apocalypse of Moses) 3:2]; Clement of Alexandria[Stromata Book III.18]; Origen[Against Celsus Book IV.72]; Tertullian[A Treatise on the Soul 16, 21; On Modesty 17; Five Books Against Marcion Book V.17]; NT-Apocrypha[Acts of Paul in Philippi 3.19]

02:03-05 Clement of Alexandria[Exhortation to the Heathen 2]

02:05 Colossians 2:13; Pseudepigrapha[Joseph and Aseneth 15:5]; Clement of Alexandria[Stromata Book II.10, III.9]

02:05-08 1Peter 1:10-13n

02:05-09 Apostolic[Polycarp - Letter to the Philippians 1:3]

02:06 Origen[Gospel of Matthew Book X.14]

02:07 Irenaeus[Against Heresies Book IV.5.1]; Origen[De Principiis Book II.3.5]

02:08-09 Peter of Alexandria[Fragments On the Godhead]

02:10 Matthew 5:16n; Tertullian[On Baptism 8]

02:10-20 Tertullian[Five Books Against Marcion Book V.17]

02:11 Clement of Alexandria[Stromata Book VII.9]

02:12 Pseudepigrapha[Apocalypse of Elijah 1:14]; Clement of Alexandria[Exhortation to the Heathen 2]; Origen[Gospel of John Book X.18; Gospel of Matthew Book X.16]; Tertullian[Five Books Against Marcion Book V.11; To his Wife Book II.2]

02:13 Isaiah 57:19; Pseudepigrapha[2Baruch 42:3]; Clement of Alexandria[Stromata Book II.10]; Irenaeus[Against Heresies Book III.18.3, V.14.3]

02:14 Isaiah 9:5-6; Micah 5:4; Pseudepigrapha[2Baruch 54:5]; Gregory Thaumaturgus[Four Homilies 3]; Hippolytus[Fragments - On Daniel 2.15]; Origen[Gospel of John Book I.30; Gospel of Matthew Book XII.25]; Teaching of Addaeus the Apostle

02:14-16 Clement of Alexandria[Stromata Book VI.13]

02:15 Daniel 12:3; Colossians 2:14; Irenaeus[Against Heresies Book V.14.3]

02:16 Colossians 1:20

02:17 Isaiah 52:7, 57:19; Zechariah 9:10; Pseudepigrapha[2Baruch 42:3]; Constitutions of the Holy Apostles[Book II.54]; Hippolytus[Refutation of all Heresies Book V.3]; Irenaeus[Against Heresies Book III.5.3]

02:17-18 Cyprian[Treatise XII.Book II.27]

02:18 Pseudepigrapha[Odes of Solomon 7:3]

02:19 Pseudepigrapha[Odes of Solomon 3:6; Testament of Job 18:4]; Tertullian[To his Wife Book II.2]

02:19-22 Apostolic[Ignatius - Letter to the Ephesians 15:3, Letter to the Philadelphians 7:2; Epistle of Barnabas 4:11, 6:14-15]; Justin[Dialogue with Trypho 114]

02:20 Isaiah 28:16; Matthew 21:42; Cyprian[Epistle LXVIII.8]; Irenaeus[Against Heresies Book III.5.3]; Origen[Against Celsus Book VIII.19; Gospel of John Book X.20]; Tertullian[Five Books Against Marcion Book IV.39, V.17]; NT-Apocrypha[Acts of Andrew (Codex Vaticanus 808) 16]

02:20-21 Clement of Alexandria[Stromata Book VI.11]; Tertullian[An Answer to the Jews 13]

02:20-22 Luke 6:48-49n; John 2:19-21n; Dead Sea Scrolls[1QRule of the Community (1QS) COL VIII 5-9]

03:01 NT-Apocrypha[Acts of Paul in Philippi 3.1]

03:03-04 Clement of Alexandria[Stromata Book I.28]

03:03-05 Clement of Alexandria[Stromata Book V.10]; Hippolytus[Refutation of all Heresies Book VII.14]; Nag Hammadi[Trimorphic Protennoia 50]

03:03-09 1Corinthians 2:6-16n

03:05 Clement of Alexandria[Stromata Book V.13]; Origen[Gospel of John Book VI.2]

03:06 Colossians 1:26-27; Pseudepigrapha[Joseph and Aseneth 15:5; 24:14]; NT-Apocrypha[Epistula Apostolorum 32]

03:07-08 1Peter 1:10-13n

03:08 Romans 11:33n; Archelaus[Disputation with Manes 34-35]; Origen[Gospel of Matthew Book XIII.29]

03:08-09 Gregory Thaumaturgus[Oration and Panegyric Addressed to Origen 15]; Tertullian[Five Books Against Marcion Book V.18]

03:09 OT-Apocrypha[3Maccabees 2:3]; Nag Hammadi[Teachings of Silvanus 115]

03:10 Pseudepigrapha[Testament of Solomon 20:15-16]; Apostolic[Ignatius - Letter to the Trallians 5:2; Martyrdom of Polycarp 14:1]; Clement of Alexandria[Stromata Book I.4]; Methodius[Banquet of the Ten Virgins 3.6]; Tertullian[Five Books Against Marcion Book V.18]

03:10-11 Clement of Alexandria[Stromata Book I.17]

03:14-15 Clement of Alexandria[Stromata Book VI.7]; Tertullian[Five Books in Reply to Marcion Book IV.42; On Repentance 8]

03:14-17 Methodius[Banquet of the Ten Virgins 8.8]

03:14-18 Hippolytus[Refutation of all Heresies Book V.29]

03:15 Psalms 147:4; Pseudepigrapha[Hellenistic Synagogal Prayers 12:2]; Constitutions of the Holy Apostles[Book VIII.12]; Hippolytus[Against the Heresy of One Noetus 3; Refutation of all Heresies Book V.2]; Theodotus[Excerpts]

03:16 Pseudepigrapha[Joseph and Aseneth 21:16]

03:17 Romans 8:9-11n; Apostolic[Ignatius - Letter to the Ephesians 15:3, Letter to the Philadelphians 7:2; Epistle of Barnabas 4:11, 6:14-15]; Tertullian[On the Resurrection of the Flesh 40]

03:19 Nag Hammadi[Apocryphon of James 2]

03:21 Pseudepigrapha[4Maccabees 18.24]

04:01 Cyprian[Epistle LXXIV.24]; Tertullian[On Exhortation to Chastity 10]

04:01-06 Tertullian[On the Veiling of Virgins 2]

04:02 Colossians 3:12-13

04:02-03 Cyprian[Epistle LI.24; Treatise IX.15]

04:03 Cyprian[Treatise I.8]

04:03-06 Cyprian[The Seventh Council of Carthage under Cyprian]

04:04 Pseudepigrapha[Testament of Judah 25:3]; Constitutions of the Holy Apostles[Book II.44]; Cyprian[Treatise I.4]

04:04-06 Pseudepigrapha[2Baruch 48:24]; Tertullian[Five Books in Reply to Marcion Book IV.40; On Baptism 15]

04:05 Matthew 3:5-16n; Anonymous[Treatise on Re-Baptism 10]; Tertullian[On Baptism 12; Five Books Against Marcion Book V.10]

04:05-06 Cyprian[Epistle LXXIV.26]; Irenaeus[Against Heresies Book IV.32.1]; Tertullian[On Exhortation to Chastity 7]; NT-Apocrypha[Acts of Paul in Ephesus p.1]

04:06 Cyprian[Epistle LXXIV.24]; Hippolytus[Against the Heresy of One Noetus 14]; Irenaeus[Against Heresies Book II.2.5, IV.20.2, V.18.2; Demonstration of the Apostolic Preaching 5]

04:07 1Peter 1:10-13n

04:07-08 Justin[Dialogue with Trypho 88]

04:08 Psalms 68:18-19; Pseudepigrapha[Apocalypse of Elijah 1:4; Greek Apocalypse of Ezra 7:2-3]; Apostolic[Ignatius - Letter to the Magnesians 9:2]; Justin[Dialogue with Trypho 39]; Tertullian[Five Books Against Marcion Book V.8, 18]

04:08-10 Pseudepigrapha[Odes of Solomon 22.1, 29.4, 42.11-20]; Irenaeus[Demonstration of the Apostolic Preaching 83]; Nag Hammadi[Apocalypse of Paul 23:14-17]

04:09 This section also includes topical notes for: Descended into the Lower Parts of the Earth - Psalms 63:10; Pseudepigrapha[Prayer of Joseph Fragment A; Sibylline Oracles 1.378]; Clement of Alexandria[Stromata Book VI.6]; Irenaeus[Against Heresies Book IV.22.1, V.31.1-2; Demonstration of the Apostolic Preaching 78]; Tertullian[Against Praxeas 30]; Nag Hammadi[Testimony of Truth 32]

04:09-10 Irenaeus[Fragments from the Lost Works 52]

04:10 Irenaeus[Against Heresies Book III.21.6]; Novatian[Treatise Concerning the Trinity 17]; Origen[Against Celsus Book I.35]

04:11 Origen[Gospel of John Book I.5]

04:11-12 Clement of Alexandria[Stromata Book I.1]

04:11-13 Clement of Alexandria[Stromata Book IV.21]

04:12 Apostolic[Ignatius - Letter to the Romans 3:3]; Clement of Alexandria[Stromata Book VI.14]

04:13 John 3:18n; Clement of Alexandria[Stromata Book VI.11, 13, VII.2, 11, 14]; Hippolytus[Treatise on Christ and Antichrist 3]; Origen[Gospel of John Book X.20; Gospel of Matthew Book X.3, XIII.26; De Principiis Book I.6.2]

04:13-15 Clement of Alexandria[The Instructor Book I.5]

04:14 Isaiah 57:20; OT-Apocrypha[Sirach 5:9]; Clement of Alexandria[Stromata Book I.8]; Irenaeus[Against Heresies Book I.31.4, II.14.2]; Origen[Against Celsus Book V.18]

04:16 Colossians 2:19; Irenaeus[Against Heresies Book III.19.3, IV.32.1]; Tertullian[Five Books Against Marcion Book V.8]

04:17-19 Clement of Alexandria[Exhortation to the Heathen 9]

04:17-20 Tertullian[On Modesty 17]

04:18 This section also includes topical notes for: Ignorance - Pseudepigrapha[Apocalypse of Elijah 1:13; Odes of Solomon 23.4]; Philo[On Joseph (77-79) cf. {Genesis 39:2-20}; On the Virtues (179-184) cf. {Leviticus 26:1-12, Deuteronomy 30:11, Galatians 5:16-26}]; Rabbinic[Avot 2.8; **Babylonian Sanhedrin 92a cf. {Isaiah 5:13}**]; Apostolic[2Clement 19:2]; Clement of Alexandria[Stromata Book VII.10; The Instructor Book I.1]; Irenaeus[Against Heresies Book II.20.3, IV.36.7, V.12.4]; Nag Hammadi[Apocryphon of James 8; Gospel of Truth 21-22, 25-26, 28-30, 32, 38]

> Said R. Eleazar, "Any man who has no knowledge in the end will go into exile, as it is said, 'Therefore my people have gone into exile, because they have no knowledge' (Isaiah 5:13)." (Talmud - Babylonian Sanhedrin 92a, *The Babylonian Talmud a Translation and Commentary*, Jacob Neusner; Hendrickson Publishers, Inc., 2005)

04:19 Pseudepigrapha[Pseudo-Phocylides 6]

04:20-24 Clement of Alexandria[Stromata Book III.4; The Instructor Book III.3]

04:21-24 Pseudepigrapha[4Ezra 7.138-140]

04:22 Colossians 3:9; Tertullian[On the Resurrection of the Flesh 49]

04:22-23 Tertullian[On Fasting 8]

04:22-24 Clement of Alexandria[Stromata Book VII.3]; Cyprian[Treatise XII.Book III.11]; Nag Hammadi[Letter of Peter to Philip 137]; NT-Apocrypha[Acts of Thomas 1.48]

04:22-32 Tertullian[On the Resurrection of the Flesh 45]

04:24 Genesis 1:26; Colossians 3:10; OT-Apocrypha[Wisdom of Solomon 9:3]; Pseudepigrapha[Odes of Solomon 17.4]; Clement of Alexandria[Stromata Book III.14]; Lactantius[Divine Institutes Book II.11]

04:24-29 Clement of Alexandria[Stromata Book I.18]

04:25 Zechariah 8:16; Pseudepigrapha[2Enoch 42:12; Pseudo-Phocylides 6]; Irenaeus[Against Heresies Book IV.37.4]; Tertullian[Five Books Against Marcion Book V.18]

04:25-29 Clement of Alexandria[The Instructor Book III.12]

04:26 Deuteronomy 24:15; Psalms 4:4-5; Apostolic[Polycarp - Letter to the Philippians 12:1]; Clement of Alexandria[Stromata Book V.5]; Constitutions of the Holy Apostles[Book II.53]; Cyprian[Treatise XII.Book III.8]; Hippolytus[Appendix to the Works of Hippolytus - On the End of the World 23]; Lactantius[Divine Institutes Book VI.18; Treatise on the Anger of God 21]; Tertullian[Of Patience 12; On Modesty 19; On Prayer 11; Five Books Against Marcion Book V.18]

04:27 Clement[Homily XIX.2]; Cyprian[Epistle LXI.2]; Origen[De Principiis Book III.2.4]; Tertullian[De Fuga in Persecutione 9; On Prayer 22]

04:28 Hippolytus[Refutation of all Heresies Book IX.15]; NT-Apocrypha[Acts of Thomas 1.58]

04:28-29 Tertullian[On Modesty 17]

04:29 Clement of Alexandria[The Instructor Book II.6]; Cyprian[Epistle XLI.2; Treatise XII.Book III.13]; Irenaeus[Against Heresies Book IV.37.4]

04:29-32 Anterus[Epistle]

04:30 Isaiah 63:10; Pseudepigrapha[4Ezra 2.39]; Clement of Alexandria[Fragments from Macarius Chrysocephalus Parable of the Prodigal son 1, 6]; Tertullian[Ad Martyras 1; On Prayer 11]

04:30-31 Cyprian[Treatise IX.16, XII.Book III.7]

04:31 Pseudepigrapha[Pseudo-Phocylides 64]; Tertullian[On Prayer 11]

04:32 This section also includes topical notes for: God for Christ's Sake Forgave You - Matthew 1:21, 26:28; John 3:16; Acts 2:38, 26:16-18; Romans 4:7-8; Colossians 3:13; James 5:15-20; 1John 1:7-9, 2:1-2, 12; Dead Sea Scrolls[1Q Habakkuk Pesher (1QHAB) COL VIII 1-3]; Tertullian[On Modesty 2]

05:01 Apostolic[Epistle to Diognetus 10:4-6; Papias Fragment 15:1; Polycarp - Letter to the Philippians 10:2]; Origen[Against Celsus Book VI.63]

05:01-02 Clement of Alexandria[The Instructor Book III.12]

05:01-11 Clement of Alexandria[Stromata Book III.4]

05:01-21 Anterus[Epistle]

05:02 Exodus 29:18; Psalms 40:7; Ezekiel 20:41; Pseudepigrapha[4Ezra 6.44; Martyrdom and Ascension of Isaiah 6.17; Odes of Solomon 11.15, 11.21]; Rabbinic[Babylonian Sanhedrin 93b]; Irenaeus[Against Heresies Book I.4.1, 21.3]; Liturgy of James 5; Origen[De Principiis Book II.6.6]; Nag

Hammadi[Dialogue of the Savior 2; Gospel of Philip 78; Gospel of Truth 34]; Indian[Dhammapada 54-56]

05:03 Tertullian[On Modesty 17]

05:03-04 Clement of Alexandria[The Instructor Book II.6, 10]

05:03-05 Pseudepigrapha[Pseudo-Phocylides 6]

05:04 Clement of Alexandria[The Instructor Book II.7]; Cyprian[Treatise XII.Book III.41]; Irenaeus[Against Heresies Book IV.28.2]

05:04-05 Theonas[Epistle to Lucianus, the Chief Chamberlain 2]

05:05 Acts 20:32n; Pseudepigrapha[Testament of Judah 19:1]; Clement of Alexandria[The Instructor Book III.4]; Cyprian[Epistle LI.27]; Tertullian[On Idolatry 11]

05:05-06 Tertullian[On Modesty 17]

05:05-13 Gregory Thaumaturgus[Canonical Epistle 2]

05:06 Clement[First Epistle Concerning Virginity 3]; Cyprian[Treatise I.23]; NT-Apocrypha[Acts of Paul in Philippi 3.22]

05:06-07 Anonymous[Treatise Against the Heretic Novatian 17]; Cyprian[Epistle XXXIX.6, LXIII.5]; Irenaeus[Against Heresies Book IV.27.4]

05:07-08 Tertullian[On Modesty 18]

05:08 Apostolic[Papias Fragment 15:1]; Clement of Alexandria[The Instructor Book I.6]; Origen[Gospel of John Book II.14]; Tertullian[A Treatise on the Soul 21]; NT-Apocrypha[Epistula Apostolorum 39]

05:11 Tertullian[Five Books Against Marcion Book V.18; On Modesty 21]; NT-Apocrypha[Epistula Apostolorum 39]

05:11-12 Tertullian[On Idolatry 9; On Modesty 18]

05:12 Pseudepigrapha[2Enoch 34:1]; Tertullian[On Modesty 17]

05:13 Irenaeus[Against Heresies Book I.8.5]

05:14 Isaiah 26:19, 51:17, 52:1, 60:1; Pseudepigrapha[4Ezra 2.31; Odes of Solomon 15:2; Sibylline Oracles 1.371]; Archelaus[Disputation with Manes 43]; Clement of Alexandria[Exhortation to the Heathen 11]; Hippolytus[Refutation of all Heresies Book V.2; Treatise on Christ and Antichrist 65]; Nag Hammadi[Gospel of Truth 33]

05:15 Clement[Second Epistle Concerning Virginity 6]

05:15-16 Hippolytus[Appendix to the Works of Hippolytus - On the End of the World 11]

05:16 Daniel 2:8; Amos 5:13; Origen[Against Celsus Book VI.54]; Tertullian[De Fuga in Persecutione 9]

05:18 Proverbs 23:31; Pseudepigrapha[Sibylline Oracles 2.95; Testament of Job 43:2; Testament of Judah 14:1]; Clement of Alexandria[The Instructor Book II.2]; Tertullian[On Modesty 17; Five Books Against Marcion Book V.18]

05:19 Psalms 33:2-3; Pseudepigrapha[Sibylline Oracles 8.497]; Clement of Alexandria[The Instructor Book II.4]; Tertullian[Five Books Against Marcion Book V.18; To his Wife Book II.6]

05:20 Colossians 3:16-17

05:21 Apostolic[1Clement 2]

05:21-29 Clement of Alexandria[Stromata Book IV.8]

05:22 Genesis 3:16; Colossians 3:18; Clement of Alexandria[The Instructor Book III.12]

05:22-24 Apostolic[1Clement 1:3]

05:22-25 Tertullian[Five Books Against Marcion Book V.18]

05:22-33 This section also includes topical notes for: Wives Submit to Husbands - 1Corinthians 11:2-3; 1Peter 3:1-7n; Philo[Questions And Answers On Genesis I (27) cf. {Genesis 2:21, John 19:34, Ephesians 5:21-33, Colossians 1:18-19}]; Plato[Meno 71e]; Nag Hammadi[Interpretation of Knowledge 16-17, 21]

05:22-06:09 Pseudepigrapha[Pseudo-Phocylides 175]

05:23 Philo[On Rewards And Punishments (114, 123-125) cf. {Deuteronomy 28:6-13, 33:12}]; Clement of Alexandria[Stromata Book V.6; The Instructor Book I.5]; Dionysius of Alexandria[Exegetical Fragments Commentary on the Beginning of Ecclesiastes 2.14]; Irenaeus[Against Heresies Book III.16.6, 19.3, IV.33.10, V.18.2, 20.2]; Nag Hammadi[Exegesis of the Soul 133; Gospel of Truth 41]; NT-Apocrypha[Questions of Bartholomew II 7]

05:23-25 Nag Hammadi[Tripartite Tractate 59]

05:25 Colossians 3:19; Clement of Alexandria[The Instructor Book III.12]; Justin[Dialogue with Trypho 134]; Origen[Gospel of Matthew Book XIV.16]

05:25-26 Cyprian[Epistle LXXIII.6, LXXV.2]; Methodius[Banquet of the Ten Virgins 3.1, 3.8]

05:25-29 Apostolic[Ignatius - Letter to Polycarp 5:1]

05:26 Ezekiel 16:9; Matthew 3:5-16n; NT-Apocrypha[Acts of Thomas 1.25]

05:26-27 Tertullian[On Modesty 18]

05:27 Constitutions of the Holy Apostles[Book II.61]; Origen[Gospel of Matthew Book XII.12]

05:28 Matthew 19:6

05:28-29 Cyprian[Treatises Attributed to Cyprian - On the Discipline and Advantage of Chastity 5]; Tertullian[Five Books Against Marcion Book V.18]

05:28-32 Methodius[Banquet of the Ten Virgins 3.1]

05:29-33 Nag Hammadi[Interpretation of Knowledge 15]

05:30 Irenaeus[Against Heresies Book V.2.3]

05:31 Genesis 2:24; Methodius[Banquet of the Ten Virgins 3.8]; Tertullian[On Exhortation to Chastity 5; Five Books Against Marcion Book V.18; To his Wife Book II.6]

05:31-32 Cyprian[Epistle XLVIII.1]; Origen[Against Celsus Book IV.49; Gospel of Matthew Book XIV.17]; Tertullian[A Treatise on the Soul 11; Five Books Against Marcion Book III.5]; Nag Hammadi[Gospel of Philip 64]

05:32 Irenaeus[Against Heresies Book I.8.4]; Tertullian[A Treatise on the Soul 21; On Fasting 3; Five Books Against Marcion Book V.18]

06:01 Colossians 3:20; Plato[Republic IV 425b]; Clement of Alexandria[The Instructor Book III.12]

06:01-02 Tertullian[Five Books Against Marcion Book V.18]

06:01-03 Cyprian[Treatise XII.Book III.70]

06:02 Matthew 15:4-8n

06:02-03 Exodus 20:12; Deuteronomy 5:16, 15:16; Origen[De Principiis Book II.4.2, IV.1.19]

06:04 Deuteronomy 6:7, 20-25; Psalms 78:4; Proverbs 2:2, 3:11, 19:18, 22:6; Isaiah 11:5; Colossians 3:21; Pseudepigrapha[Pseudo-Phocylides 207]; Constitutions of the Holy Apostles[Book II.2]; Cyprian[Treatise XII.Book III.71]; Teaching of the Twelve Apostles 4.9; Tertullian[Five Books Against Marcion Book V.18]

06:04-09 Clement of Alexandria[The Instructor Book III.12]

06:05 1Peter 2:18; Pseudepigrapha[2Enoch 66:2; Joseph and Aseneth 9:1; Testament of Reuben 4:1]; Constitutions of the Holy Apostles[Book IV.11, VII.13]; Teaching of the Twelve Apostles 4.11

06:05-06 Cyprian[Treatise XII.Book III.72]

06:05-09 Apostolic[Ignatius - Letter to Polycarp 4:1-3]

06:06 Constitutions of the Holy Apostles[Book IV.12]

06:07 2Chronicles 19:6; Constitutions of the Holy Apostles[Book VII.13]

06:08 Colossians 3:22-25; Peter of Alexandria[Canonical Epistle 6]

06:09 Leviticus 25:43; Deuteronomy 10:17; 2Chronicles 19:17; Colossians 3:25, 4:1; Cyprian[Treatise XII.Book III.73]; Peter of Alexandria[Canonical Epistle 7]; Teaching of the Twelve Apostles 4.1; Tertullian[On Exhortation to Chastity 7]; NT-Apocrypha[Acts of Peter and Paul; Epistula Apostolorum 24]

06:10 Isaiah 40:26; Pseudepigrapha[Apocalypse of Elijah 4:16]

06:10-17 Fabian[Third Epistle]

06:10-20 Pseudepigrapha[Life of Adam and Eve (Apocalypse of Moses) 20:2]

06:11 Clement of Alexandria[Stromata Book II.20, VII.11]; Origen[Against Celsus Book VIII.55, 73]; Tertullian[Five Books Against Marcion Book V.18]

06:11-12 Justin[Dialogue with Trypho 116]; Origen[Against Celsus Book VIII.34]

06:11-17 1Thessalonians 05:06-08; Nag Hammadi[Dialogue of the Savior 2; Letter of Peter to Philip 137; Teachings of Silvanus 84]

06:12 Pseudepigrapha[Life of Adam and Eve Vita 21:1, 28:2; Martyrdom and Ascension of Isaiah 1:4; Testament of Levi 3:10; Testament of Solomon 8:3, 18:2, 20:15-16]; Apostolic[Ignatius - Letter to the Trallians 5:2]; Archelaus[Disputation with Manes 13]; Clement of Alexandria[Stromata Book III.16, IV.7, V.14]; Irenaeus[Against Heresies Book I.5.4, 10.1, 21.5, 23.3, 24.4, II.28.6, 30.3-4, 6]; Justin[Dialogue with Trypho 41, 49, 105, 131]; Novatian[On the Jewish Meats 1]; Origen[Gospel of John Book X.18; Gospel of Matthew Book X.14, XII.13, XIII.4; De Principiis Book III.2.4]; Tertullian[On Fasting 17; On Prescription Against Heretics 39; Five Books Against Marcion Book V.18]; Nag Hammadi[Apocalypse of Paul 19, 23; Authoritative Teaching 25; Dialogue of the Savior 20; Eugnostos the Blessed III. 87; Exegesis of the Soul 131; Gospel of the Egyptians III. 43, 53, IV. 57; Hypostasis of the Archons 86; Letter of Peter to Philip 135-136; On the Origin of the World 102; Sophia of Jesus Christ III. 109, 111; Teachings of Silvanus 91, 105-106, 114, 117; Testimony of Truth 32, 42; Trimorphic Protennoia 49]; NT-Apocrypha[Epistula Apostolorum 28]

06:12-13 Origen[De Principiis Book III.2.1]

06:12-17 Cyprian[Epistle LV.8; Treatise XII.Book III.117]; Methodius[Apostolic Words from the
   Discourse on the Resurrection 2]
06:12-18 Pseudepigrapha[Apocalypse of Elijah 1.23-27]
06:13 Clement of Alexandria[Stromata Book VII.11]
06:13-14 Tatian[Address to the Greeks 16]
06:13-16 OT-Apocrypha[Wisdom of Solomon 5:17-21]
06:13-17 Pseudepigrapha[Testament of Levi 8:2]
06:14 Isaiah 11:5, 59:17; Pseudepigrapha[Apocalypse of Elijah 4:31]
06:14-15 NT-Apocrypha[Acts of Thomas 1.147]
06:14-17 Clement of Alexandria[Exhortation to the Heathen 11]; Tertullian[Five Books Against
   Marcion Book III.14]
06:15 Isaiah 52:7; Nahum 1:15, 2:1; Clement of Alexandria[Fragments from Macarius Chrysocephalus
   Parable of the Prodigal son 6; The Instructor Book II.13]
06:16 Psalms 7:13; Methodius[Oration Concerning Simeon and Anna 10]; Origen[Gospel of Matthew
   Book XI.9]; Tertullian[De Fuga in Persecutione 9]
06:17 Isaiah 11:4, 49:2, 59:17; Hosea 6:5; Apostolic[Ignatius - Letter to Polycarp 6:2];
   Methodius[Banquet of the Ten Virgins 8.12]; Tatian[Address to the Greeks 16]; Tertullian[An
   Answer to the Jews 9]; Indian[Dhammapada 40]
06:18 Apostolic[Polycarp - Letter to the Philippians 12:3]; Tertullian[On Fasting 10; On Prayer 23, 28]
06:19 Acts 17:2-3
06:19-20 Tertullian[Five Books Against Marcion Book V.18]
06:21 Acts 20:4; 2Timothy 4:12
06:22 Colossians 4:7-8
06:24 Pseudepigrapha[Psalms of Solomon 4:25]

Cross Reference Index: Philippians

01:01 Acts 16:12
01:02 John 1:18n; NT-Apocrypha[Epistle to the Laodiceans 1:2]
01:03 NT-Apocrypha[Epistle to the Laodiceans 1:3]
01:05 Apostolic[Polycarp - Letter to the Philippians 1]
01:07 1Peter 1:10-13n; Clement of Alexandria[Stromata Book IV.13]
01:09-10 Clement of Alexandria[Stromata Book I.11]
01:11 Proverbs 3:9, 11:30; Amos 6:13
01:12 NT-Apocrypha[Epistle to the Laodiceans 1:5]
01:13 Acts 28:30; NT-Apocrypha[Epistle to the Laodiceans 1:6]
01:13-14 Clement of Alexandria[Stromata Book IV.5]
01:14-18 Tertullian[Five Books Against Marcion Book V.20]
01:18 Cyprian[Epistle LXXII.14, LXXIV.20]; NT-Apocrypha[Epistle to the Laodiceans 1:6]
01:19 Job 13:16; NT-Apocrypha[Epistle to the Laodiceans 1:7]
01:20 Tertullian[On the Apparel of Women Book II.11]
01:20-24 Clement of Alexandria[Stromata Book III.9]
01:21 Cyprian[Treatise VII.7; Treatises Attributed to Cyprian On the Glory of Martyrdom 14]; NT-Apocrypha[Epistle to the Laodiceans 1:8]
01:22 Psalms 104:13; Irenaeus[Against Heresies Book V.12.4]
01:22-24 NT-Apocrypha[Acts of Paul in Philippi 2.3]
01:23 Pseudepigrapha[2Baruch 3:7]; Origen[Gospel of John Book I.17; De Principiis Book I.7.5, II.11.5]; Tertullian[Of Patience 9; On Exhortation to Chastity 12; The Shows, or De Spectaculis 28; To his Wife Book I.5]
01:23-24 Peter of Alexandria[Canonical Epistle 10]
01:24 NT-Apocrypha[Acts of Paul in Philippi 1.6]
01:27 Apostolic[Polycarp - Letter to the Philippians 5:2]; NT-Apocrypha[Epistula Apostolorum 38]
01:29-30 Clement of Alexandria[Stromata Book IV.13]; Tertullian[Scorpiace 13]
01:30 Acts 16:19-40
02:01-02 Clement of Alexandria[Stromata Book IV.13]
02:02 NT-Apocrypha[Epistle to the Laodiceans 1:9]
02:03 Tertullian[Of Patience 10]
02:04 Apostolic[Martyrdom of Polycarp 1:2]; Tertullian[On the Apparel of Women Book II.2]
02:05-07 Clement of Alexandria[Exhortation to the Heathen 1, 10]
02:05-09 Origen[Against Celsus Book IV.18]
02:06 Origen[Against Celsus Book VI.15; Gospel of John Book I.37; Gospel of Matthew Book XIV.17]; Pseud-Irenaeus; Tertullian[Against Praxeas 7; On the Resurrection of the Flesh 6]
02:06-07 Matthew 12:18n; Hippolytus[Refutation of all Heresies Book X.7]; Origen[Against Celsus Book IV.15; De Principiis Book IV.1.32]; Tertullian[Five Books Against Marcion Book V.20]
02:06-08 Pseudepigrapha[Apocalypse of Elijah 1:6]; Phileas[Epistle to the People of Thmuis 1]; NT-Apocrypha[Acts of Thomas 1.15]
02:06-09 Pseudepigrapha[Odes of Solomon 41:12]; Origen[Gospel of John Book X.8]; Nag Hammadi[Apocryphon of James 14]
02:06-11 Cyprian[Treatise XII.Book II.13, III.39]; Novatian[Treatise Concerning the Trinity 22]
02:07 Isaiah 53:3, 11; Archelaus[Disputation with Manes 50]; Clement of Alexandria[The Instructor Book III.1]; Hippolytus[Expository Treatise Against the Jews 4; Refutation of all Heresies Book V.14; The Discourse on the Holy Theophany 2]; Origen[Gospel of Matthew Book XI.17, XII.29, XIII.10]; Peter of Alexandria[Fragments On the Godhead]
02:07-08 NT-Apocrypha[Acts of Thomas 1.72]
02:07-09 Hippolytus[Fragments - On Genesis 49.21-26]
02:08 Matthew 18:4n; Irenaeus[Against Heresies Book III.12.9, IV.24.2, V.16.3; Demonstration of the Apostolic Preaching 34]; Origen[Against Celsus Book VI.15; Gospel of John Book I.37, X.4];

Tertullian[On the Flesh of Christ 4; Five Books Against Marcion Book V.20]; Nag Hammadi[Teachings of Silvanus 110-111]

02:09 John 5:43; Pseudepigrapha[3Enoch 12:5; Martyrdom and Ascension of Isaiah 10.7-8; Prayer of Joseph Fragment A]; Archelaus[Disputation with Manes 48]; Nag Hammadi[Apocryphon of John 7; Gospel of Philip 54; Prayer of the Apostle Paul A.I]; NT-Apocrypha[Acts of Thomas 1.27]

02:09-10 Clement of Alexandria[Stromata Book VI.10; The Instructor Book I.7]; Cyprian[Treatise IX.24]; Irenaeus[Against Heresies Book I.15.1-3, II.24.1-2, IV.17.6]; Justin[Dialogue with Trypho 75, 89-91, 113, 115, 131-132; First Apology 33, 46]

02:09-11 Origen[Gospel of John Book VI.26]

02:10 Pseudepigrapha[Martyrdom and Ascension of Isaiah 9.27-32, 10:16]; Apostolic[Polycarp - Letter to the Philippians 2:1]; Clement of Alexandria[Fragments from the Latin Translation of Cassiodorus Comments on 1John]; Hippolytus[Treatise on Christ and Antichrist 26]; Liturgy of Mark 19; Methodius[Oration on the Psalms 7]; Tertullian[Five Books in Reply to Marcion Book IV.41]

02:10-11 Isaiah 45:23; Clement of Alexandria[Stromata Book I.24]; Irenaeus[Against Heresies Book I.10.1]; Origen[Against Celsus Book VIII.59; De Principiis Book I.2.10]

02:11 Hippolytus[Appendix to the Works of Hippolytus - On the End of the World 39]

02:12 Psalms 2:12; Revelation 12:10n; Pseudepigrapha[2Enoch 66:2; Joseph and Aseneth 9:1]; Anonymous[Treatise on Re-Baptism 13]; NT-Apocrypha[Epistle to the Laodiceans 1:10]

02:13 Archelaus[Disputation with Manes 38]; Origen[De Principiis Book III.1.7, 19]; NT-Apocrypha[Epistle to the Laodiceans 1:11]

02:14 NT-Apocrypha[Epistle to the Laodiceans 1:12]

02:14-15 Cyprian[Treatise XII.Book III.14]

02:15 Deuteronomy 32:5; Daniel 12:3; Pseudepigrapha[Apocalypse of Adam 7:52]; Rabbinic[Babylonian Sanhedrin 98a]; Apostolic[Papias Fragment 15:1]; Clement of Alexandria[The Instructor Book III.12]; Cyprian[Epistle VI.3; Treatise XII.Book III.26]; Irenaeus[Against Heresies Book IV.5.3; Demonstration of the Apostolic Preaching 35]; Tertullian[On Idolatry 15]; Nag Hammadi[Letter of Peter to Philip 137]

02:15-16 Clement[First Epistle Concerning Virginity 9; Second Epistle Concerning Virginity 6]

02:16 Isaiah 49:4, 65:23; Pseudepigrapha[Sibylline Oracles 2.39]; Apostolic[Polycarp - Letter to the Philippians 9:2]; Nag Hammadi[Gospel of Philip 63]; NT-Apocrypha[Epistula Apostolorum 27]

02:17 Clement of Alexandria[Stromata Book IV.13]; Teaching of the Twelve Apostles 14.2; Tertullian[Scorpiace 13]

02:19 NT-Apocrypha[Acts of Peter 1.4]

02:20-21 Clement of Alexandria[Stromata Book IV.13]

02:21 Cyprian[Treatise XII.Book III.11]

02:27 NT-Apocrypha[Acts of Paul in Philippi 2.3-4]

03:01 NT-Apocrypha[Epistle to the Laodiceans 1:13]

03:01-02 Tertullian[An Answer to the Jews 3]

03:02 Psalms 22:16, 20; Anonymous[Treatise Against the Heretic Novatian 1]; Cyprian[Epistle LIV.19]; Hippolytus[Appendix to the Works of Hippolytus - On the End of the World 11]; Nag Hammadi[Apocalypse of Peter 78:23-31]

03:03 Origen[Gospel of Matthew Book XII.3]; Tertullian[On the Apparel of Women Book II.9; To his Wife Book I.2]

03:03-04 Tertullian[On the Apparel of Women Book II.3]

03:04-07 Tertullian[Five Books Against Marcion Book V.20]

03:05 Acts 23:6, 26:5; Romans 11:1; Hippolytus[Refutation of all Heresies Book IX.23]; Tertullian[An Answer to the Jews 1]; NT-Apocrypha[Epistula Apostolorum 31]

03:06 Acts 8:3, 22:4-5, 26:9-11; Pseudepigrapha[2Baruch 67:6]

03:08 Origen[Gospel of Matthew Book X.9]; Tertullian[Of Patience 13; Five Books Against Marcion Book V.20; To his Wife Book II.2]; NT-Apocrypha[Acts of Paul in Philippi 3.35]

03:09 Tertullian[Five Books Against Marcion Book V.20]

03:10 Irenaeus[Fragments from the Lost Works 36]; Origen[Against Celsus Book II.69]

03:10-11 Acts 2:31n

03:11 Irenaeus[Against Heresies Book V.13.4]; NT-Apocrypha[Acts of Paul in Philippi 3.35]

03:11-12 Lactantius[Divine Institutes Book VII.24]

03:11-14 Tertullian[On the Resurrection of the Flesh 23]

03:12 Irenaeus[Against Heresies Book IV.9.2]; Tertullian[To his Wife Book II.2, 6]

03:12-15 Clement of Alexandria[The Instructor Book I.6]

03:13 Archelaus[Disputation with Manes 48]; Tertullian[On Modesty 6]

03:13-14 Tertullian[To his Wife Book I.3]

03:14 Pseudepigrapha[3Baruch 12:6 (Gk.)]; Apostolic[1Clement 5:5]; Clement[First Epistle Concerning Virginity 5]; Novatian[On the Jewish Meats 1]; Peter of Alexandria[Canonical Epistle 8, 11]

03:15 Apostolic[Ignatius - Letter to the Smyrnaeans 11:3]; Clement of Alexandria[Stromata Book VI.14]; Hippolytus[Fragments - On Genesis 49.21-26]; Tertullian[On Fasting 10; The Chaplet, or De Corona 4]

03:17 1Corinthians 4:16, 11:1

03:18 Apostolic[Polycarp - Letter to the Philippians 12:3]

03:18-19 NT-Apocrypha[Epistula Apostolorum 7]

03:19 Hosea 4:7; Pseudepigrapha[Apocalypse of Elijah 1:13; Pseudo-Phocylides 69]; Archelaus[Disputation with Manes 38]; Clement of Alexandria[The Instructor Book II.1]; Clement[First Epistle Concerning Virginity 13]; Origen[Gospel of Matthew Book XI.14]; Tertullian[Of Patience 16; On the Veiling of Virgins 14; To his Wife Book I.8]; NT-Apocrypha[Acts of Thomas 1.12; Epistula Apostolorum 38, 47]

03:19-21 Cyprian[Treatise XII.Book III.11]

03:20 Pseudepigrapha[Apocalypse of Elijah 1:10; Martyrdom and Ascension of Isaiah (3:13-4:22 = Testament of Hezekiah) 4:13; Testament of Solomon 17:4]; Rabbinic[Babylonian Sanhedrin 97b]; Clement of Alexandria[Stromata Book III.15, IV.3]; Origen[Gospel of John Book II.4; Gospel of Matthew Book X.14, XII.10]; Tertullian[The Chaplet, or De Corona 13; Five Books Against Marcion Book III.25, V.20]

03:20-21 Irenaeus[Against Heresies Book V.13.3]; Tertullian[On the Resurrection of the Flesh 47]

03:21 Pseudepigrapha[2Baruch 51:3; Martyrdom and Ascension of Isaiah (3:13-4:22 = Testament of Hezekiah) 4:18]; Apostolic[Polycarp - Letter to the Philippians 2:1]; Cyprian[Epistle LXXVI.2; Treatise VII.22]; Methodius[Apostolic Words from the Discourse on the Resurrection 12]; Origen[Against Celsus Book VII.50; Gospel of Matthew Book XII.29, XIII.21]; Tertullian[On the Resurrection of the Flesh 55; Five Books Against Marcion Book V.20]

04:01 Clement[Second Epistle Concerning Virginity 6]

04:03 Exodus 32:32-33; Psalms 69:28-29; Daniel 12:1; Revelation 21:27n; Pseudepigrapha[Apocalypse of Zephaniah 3:8]; Clement[First Epistle Concerning Virginity 6]; Constitutions of the Holy Apostles[Book VIII.8]; Origen[Gospel of John Book VI.36]; Tertullian[The Chaplet, or De Corona 13; To his Wife Book I.4]

04:05 Psalms 145:18; OT-Apocrypha[Wisdom of Solomon 2:19]; Clement of Alexandria[Exhortation to the Heathen 9]; Tertullian[On the Apparel of Women Book II.13]

04:06 Apostolic[Didache 9:1]; Clement[Second Epistle Concerning Virginity 1]; Nag Hammadi[Letter of Peter to Philip 137]; NT-Apocrypha[Epistle to the Laodiceans 1:14]

04:06-07 Tertullian[On Prayer 11]

04:07 Isaiah 26:3; Theonas[Epistle to Lucianus, the Chief Chamberlain 9]

04:08 Tertullian[On the Apparel of Women Book II.13]; NT-Apocrypha[Epistle to the Laodiceans 1:15]

04:08-09 Clement of Alexandria[Stromata Book III.18]; Origen[De Principiis Book II.5.3]

04:09 NT-Apocrypha[Epistle to the Laodiceans 1:16]

04:11-13 Clement of Alexandria[Stromata Book IV.16]

04:13 OT-Apocrypha[Wisdom of Solomon 7:23]; Origen[Against Celsus Book VIII.70; Gospel of John Book I.38, X.28; Gospel of Matthew Book XII.12; De Principiis Book III.2.5]

04:15 Apostolic[1Clement 47:2; Polycarp - Letter to the Philippians 11:3]

04:16 Acts 17:1; 2Corinthians 11:9

04:17 Irenaeus[Against Heresies Book IV.8.3]

04:18 Genesis 8:21; Exodus 29:18; Isaiah 56:7; Ezekiel 20:41; OT-Apocrypha[Sirach 35:6]; Clement of Alexandria[Stromata Book VII.3]; Cyprian[Treatise IV.33]; Irenaeus[Against Heresies Book IV.18.4]; Nag Hammadi[Teachings of Silvanus 104]

04:19 Pseudepigrapha[Joseph and Aseneth 21:16]; Tertullian[To his Wife Book I.4]

04:20 Pseudepigrapha[4Maccabees 18.24]

04:22 NT-Apocrypha[Acts of Peter 1.3; Epistle to the Laodiceans 1:18; Martyrdom of the Holy Apostle Paul 1.1]

04:23 NT-Apocrypha[Epistle to the Laodiceans 1:19]

Cross Reference Index: Colossians

01:02 John 1:18n; Cyprian[Treatise IV.31]

01:05 Clement[First Epistle Concerning Virginity 4]; Origen[Against Celsus Book VI.64]

01:05-06 Tertullian[Five Books Against Marcion Book V.19]

01:06 1Peter 1:10-13n

01:07 Colossians 4:12; Philemon 1:23

01:09-11 Clement of Alexandria[Stromata Book V.10]

01:10 Apostolic[Shepherd of Hermas 53:1-8]; Tertullian[On Exhortation to Chastity 10]

01:12 Acts 20:32n

01:13 Pseudepigrapha[Joseph and Aseneth 15:12]; Nag Hammadi[Dialogue of the Savior 3; Hypostasis of the Archons 86]

01:14 Acts 26:18n; Ephesians 1:7; Irenaeus[Against Heresies Book V.2.2]

01:14-15 Irenaeus[Against Heresies Book III.16.3]

01:14-22 Nag Hammadi[Interpretation of Knowledge 12, 14]

01:15 This section also includes topical notes for: Image of God - Genesis 1:26-27, 9:6; John 14:7; 2Corinthians 4:4; Pseudepigrapha[Hellenistic Synagogal Prayers 5:20; 12:10; Prayer of Joseph Fragment A]; Philo[Concerning Noah's Work As A Planter (43-45) cf. {Genesis 2:9, 25:27}; On the Confusion of Tongues (146-147, 168-179) cf. {Genesis 1:26, 3:22, 11:7, 42:11, Deuteronomy 10:17}; On the Creation (69-70, 79-80) cf. {Genesis 1:26, John 14:9}]; Constitutions of the Holy Apostles[Book VIII.12]; Cyprian[Treatise XII.Book II.1]; Dionysius of Rome[Against the Sabellians 2]; Justin[Dialogue with Trypho 138]; Methodius[Banquet of the Ten Virgins 3.3]; Novatian[Treatise Concerning the Trinity 21]; Origen[Against Celsus Book VII.27; Gospel of John Book I.7, 20, VI.2, X.25; Gospel of Matthew Book XIII.10, XIV.7; De Principiis Book I.1.8, 2.1, 2.5, II.4.3, IV.1.37]; Tertullian[Against Praxeas 7; An Answer to the Jews 9; Five Books Against Marcion Book V.19-20]; Nag Hammadi[Apocryphon of John 14; Eugnostos the Blessed III.76; First Apocalypse of James 25; Gospel of Truth 38; Sophia of Jesus Christ III. 101; Teachings of Silvanus 100, 115; Tripartite Tractate 116]; NT-Apocrypha[Acts of Peter 1.2; Gospel of the Hebrews Fragment 2]

01:15-16 Origen[Gospel of John Book II.8]

01:15-17 This section also includes topical notes for: Creation – Genesis 1:1-2:3; Pseudepigrapha[Hellenistic Synagogal Prayers 3.1, 4.21, 5.1, 9.7, 14.1, 15.1; Jubilees 2.2; Sibylline Oracles 3.35]; Philo[Allegorical Interpretation III (95)]; On the Creation (16-19)]; Apostolic[Ignatius - Letter to the Magnesians 6:1]; Clement of Alexandria[Exhortation to the Heathen 1; Stromata Book II.4, VI.16, The Instructor Book I.3, III.12]; Hippolytus[Refutation of all Heresies Book X.29]; Irenaeus[Against Heresies Book I.17.1, 24.1, 25.1, 26.1-2, 27.2, 29.1, II.2.4-5, 3.2, 4.1, 7.5, 9.1, II.10.4, 11.1, 14.1, 4, 15.1-3, 16.1-3, 28.1, 3, 30.3-9, 31.1, 34.2, III.1.2, 11.1-2, 12.9, 11, IV.20.4, 24.1, 32.1, 36.1, 38.3, V.18.1-2; Demonstration of the Apostolic Preaching 3; Fragments from the Lost Works 6]; Origen[De Principiis Book II.6.1]; Tatian[Address to the Greeks 5]; Theophilus of Antioch[To Autolycus Book II.10]

01:15-20 Pseudepigrapha[Odes of Solomon 17:16]

01:16 Pseudepigrapha[2Enoch 20:1; Apocalypse of Elijah 1:8-10, 4:10; Apocalypse of Zephaniah A; Hellenistic Synagogal Prayers 3:1; 4:11, 12:14, 12:81; Psalms of Solomon 2:19; Testament of Adam 4:1; Testament of Levi 3:8; Testament of Solomon 20:15-16]; Apostolic[Ignatius - Letter to the Trallians 5:2; Martyrdom of Polycarp 14:1]; Hippolytus[Appendix to the Works of Hippolytus - On the End of the World 39, 43]; Irenaeus[Against Heresies Book I.4.5]; Justin[Second Apology 6]; Novatian[Treatise Concerning the Trinity 13]; Origen[De Principiis Book II.9.4]; Tertullian[Against the Valentinians 16; Five Books Against Marcion Book I.16]; Nag Hammadi[Teachings of Silvanus 115]; NT-Apocrypha[Acts of Andrew (Codex Vaticanus 808) 6]

01:16-17 Alexander of Alexandria[Epistles on Arian Heresy 1.6]

01:16-18 Origen[De Principiis Book I.7.1, IV.1.20]

01:17 Proverbs 8:23-27; Pseudepigrapha[Hellenistic Synagogal Prayers 12:11; Prayer of Joseph Fragment A]

01:18 Ephesians 1:22-23; Cyprian[Treatise XII.Book II.1]; Hippolytus[Fragments - Writings of Hippolytus 3]; Irenaeus[Against Heresies Book II.22.4, III.19.3, IV.20.2]; Irenaeus[Demonstration of the Apostolic Preaching 40]

01:19 Hippolytus[Refutation of all Heresies Book V.7, VIII.6]; Origen[Gospel of John Book I.11]

01:19-24 Tertullian[Five Books Against Marcion Book V.19]

01:20 1Corinthians 1:17-18; Galatians 6:14; Ephesians 2:16; Philo[Concerning Noah's Work As A Planter (43-45) cf. {Genesis 2:7-9, 25:27}]; Apostolic[1Clement 7:4]

01:21 Pseudepigrapha[Joseph and Aseneth 12:5]; Irenaeus[Against Heresies Book V.14.2]; Tertullian[On the Resurrection of the Flesh 23]

01:22 Pseudepigrapha[1Enoch 102:5]

01:23 Apostolic[Ignatius - Letter to the Ephesians 10:2]

01:23-24 Archelaus[Disputation with Manes 35]

01:25 NT-Apocrypha[Epistula Apostolorum 13]

01:25-27 Clement of Alexandria[Stromata Book V.10]

01:26 Hippolytus[Refutation of all Heresies Book V.30]

01:26-27 Clement of Alexandria[Stromata Book I.2]; Lactantius[Divine Institutes Book IV.2]

01:27 Romans 11:33n; Pseudepigrapha[Joseph and Aseneth 21:16]; Clement of Alexandria[Stromata Book V.10]

01:28 Clement of Alexandria[Stromata Book I.1, VI.14]

02:02-03 This section also includes topical notes for: Treasures of Wisdom - 2Timothy 1:14; Pseudepigrapha[1Enoch 46:3-4; 4Ezra 7.77; Odes of Solomon 11.16-18; Sibylline Oracles 2.45-55]; Rabbinic[Babylonian Sanhedrin 100a cf. {Proverbs 8:21}]; Clement of Alexandria[Exhortation to the Heathen 11-12; Stromata Book I.12, V.4, 10, 12, 14, VI.9, 11, 15; The Instructor Book I.6, III.1]; Irenaeus[Against Heresies Book I.Preface.2, 3.3, 12.4, 30.14, 31.1, 3-4, II.13.10, 14.1, 7, 16.9, 22.3, 24.1, 28.1-2, 28.6, 30.7, III.1.1, 2.1, 3.1, 5.1, 7.1, IV.26.1, V.6.1]; Justin[Dialogue with Trypho 91, 94, 106, 111, 125, 131, 134, 138, 141]; Tatian[Address to the Greeks 30]; Nag Hammadi[A Valentinian Exposition 26; Acts of Peter and the Twelve Apostles 10; Gospel of the Egyptians IV. 57-58; Gospel of Truth 18; Teachings of Silvanus 88, 106-107, 116; Trimorphic Protennoia 41]

02:03 Proverbs 2:3-4; Isaiah 45:3; OT-Apocrypha[Sirach 1:24]; Pseudepigrapha[3Enoch 8:1]; Origen[Gospel of Matthew Book X.5]

02:04 Athenagoras[Plea for the Christians 10]; Clement of Alexandria[Stromata Book I.11]; Methodius[Oration Concerning Simeon and Anna 8]; NT-Apocrypha[Epistle to the Laodiceans 1:4]

02:05 Tertullian[On Fasting 13]

02:06-08 Clement of Alexandria[Stromata Book I.11]

02:06-09 Archelaus[Disputation with Manes 35]

02:08 Pseudepigrapha[Testament of Solomon 8:3; 18:2]; Josephus[War 2.8.7 141-142]; Apology of Aristides 3; Clement of Alexandria[Stromata Book VI.15]; Clement[First Epistle Concerning Virginity 11]; Cyprian[Epistle LI.16; Treatise IX.2]; Hippolytus[Appendix to the Works of Hippolytus - On the End of the World 11]; Origen[Against Celsus Book I.Preface.5]; Tertullian[A Treatise on the Soul 3; On Prescription Against Heretics 7; Five Books Against Marcion Book V.19]; NT-Apocrypha[Acts of Peter 1.1]

02:09 Hippolytus[Refutation of all Heresies Book V.7, X.6]; Irenaeus[Against Heresies Book I.3.4]; Origen[Gospel of John Book I.11; De Principiis Book II.6.4]; Tertullian[Five Books in Reply to Marcion Book IV.98; Five Books Against Marcion Book III.6]

02:10 Cyprian[Treatise IX.2]; NT-Apocrypha[Acts of Thomas 1.119]

02:10-15 Apostolic[Ignatius - Letter to the Trallians 5:2]

02:11 Acts 7:51n; Romans 8:6; Clement of Alexandria[Stromata Book III.5]; Cyprian[Treatise XII.Book I.8]; Hippolytus[Refutation of all Heresies Book VIII.3]; Irenaeus[Against Heresies Book IV.16.1]; Tertullian[On the Resurrection of the Flesh 7; To his Wife Book I.2]

02:12 Matthew 3:5-16n; Romans 6:4; Tertullian[On Repentance 6]

02:12-13 Tertullian[On the Resurrection of the Flesh 23]

02:13 Matthew 9:6n; Acts 26:18n; Ephesians 2:1-5, 4:32n; Tertullian[Five Books Against Marcion Book V.19]

02:13-14 Constitutions of the Holy Apostles[Book VIII.8]; Tertullian[On Modesty 19]

02:14 Genesis 35:4; Ephesians 2:15; Hippolytus[Fragments - On Daniel 2.15]; Irenaeus[Against Heresies Book V.17.3; Fragments from the Lost Works 37]; Origen[Against Celsus Book I.55; Gospel of Matthew Book XIV.19]

02:14-15 Hippolytus[Refutation of all Heresies Book VIII.3]; Origen[Gospel of John Book VI.37]; Tertullian[An Answer to the Jews 10]

02:15 Pseudepigrapha[Testament of Solomon 20:15-16]; Novatian[Treatise Concerning the Trinity 21]; Origen[Gospel of Matthew Book XII.18, 25, 40]

02:16 Romans 14:1-6; Irenaeus[Fragments from the Lost Works 38]; Origen[Against Celsus Book VIII.23; Gospel of John Book X.11; Gospel of Matthew Book XI.12; De Principiis Book IV.1.13]; NT-Apocrypha[Acts of Peter 1.1]

02:16-17 Hebrews 8:5; Tertullian[Five Books Against Marcion Book V.19]

02:16-18 NT-Apocrypha[Kerygma Petri 2c]

02:17 Irenaeus[Against Heresies Book IV.11.4]; Origen[Gospel of Matthew Book XII.5]

02:18 Pseudepigrapha[Martyrdom and Ascension of Isaiah 7:21]; Athenagoras[Plea for the Christians 10]; Clement of Alexandria[Stromata Book III.6]; Clement[First Epistle Concerning Virginity 11]; Cyprian[Treatise IX.24]; Irenaeus[Fragments from the Lost Works 36]; Tertullian[On Prescription Against Heretics 33; Five Books Against Marcion Book V.19]

02:18-19 Novatian[On the Jewish Meats 5]; Origen[Against Celsus Book V.8]

02:19 Ephesians 4:16; Irenaeus[Against Heresies Book IV.32.1, V.14.4]; Tertullian[Five Books Against Marcion Book V.19]

02:20 Pseudepigrapha[Testament of Solomon 8:3, 18:2]; Cyprian[Treatise XII.Book III.11; Treatises Attributed to Cyprian On the Glory of Martyrdom 28]; Tertullian[On Repentance 6; On the Resurrection of the Flesh 23, 46]

02:21 Novatian[On the Jewish Meats 5]

02:21-22 Origen[Gospel of Matthew Book XI.13]; Tertullian[Five Books Against Marcion Book V.19]

02:22 Isaiah 29:13; Pseudepigrapha[Testament of Reuben 4:1]; Justin[Dialogue with Trypho 48]; NT-Apocrypha[Acts of Peter 1.1]

02:23 Clement of Alexandria[Stromata Book III.6]; Novatian[On the Jewish Meats 5]

03:01 Psalms 110:1; 1Peter 3:22n; Pseudepigrapha[Testament of Job 36:3]; Victorinus[Apocalypse 20.4-5]

03:01-03 Tertullian[On the Resurrection of the Flesh 23]

03:01-04 Cyprian[Treatise X.14; Treatise XII.Book III.11]

03:02 Lactantius[Divine Institutes Book III.27]; Origen[Gospel of Matthew Book XI.13]; Urban I[Epistle 6.6]

03:03 Origen[De Principiis Book II.6.7]

03:03-04 Origen[Gospel of John Book II.30; Gospel of Matthew Book XII.33; De Principiis Book IV.1.31]

03:04 Clement of Alexandria[Stromata Book III.5]; Origen[Gospel of John Book VI.3]

03:05 Pseudepigrapha[Testament of Judah 19:1]; Clement of Alexandria[Stromata Book VI.16]; Clement[First Epistle Concerning Virginity 8]; Irenaeus[Against Heresies Book V.12.3]; Origen[Against Celsus Book V.49, VII.38]; Tertullian[On Idolatry 11; On Modesty 17]

03:05-06 Clement of Alexandria[The Instructor Book III.11]; Cyprian[Epistle LI.27]

03:08 Origen[Against Celsus Book IV.72]; Tertullian[On Modesty 17]

03:08-09 Clement of Alexandria[Stromata Book VII.3]

03:08-10 Nag Hammadi[Letter of Peter to Philip 137]

03:09 Irenaeus[Against Heresies Book V.12.3]; NT-Apocrypha[Acts of Thomas 1.48; 1.58]

03:10 Genesis 1:26; Ephesians 4:24; Pseudepigrapha[Odes of Solomon 17.4]; Clement of Alexandria[Stromata Book III.5]; Irenaeus[Against Heresies Book V.12.4]; Lactantius[Divine Institutes Book II.11]; Nag Hammadi[Teachings of Silvanus 114]

03:11 Clement of Alexandria[Stromata Book IV.8, V.5]; Irenaeus[Against Heresies Book I.3.4]; Peter of Alexandria[Canonical Epistle 7]

03:12-15 Clement of Alexandria[Stromata Book IV.7-8]

03:13 Ephesians 4:2, 32

03:16 Pseudepigrapha[Sibylline Oracles 8.497]; Clement of Alexandria[The Instructor Book II.4]; Tertullian[To his Wife Book II.6]; NT-Apocrypha[Acts of Thomas 1.88]

03:17 Ephesians 5:19-20; Origen[Against Celsus Book VIII.32]

03:18 Genesis 3:16; Ephesians 5:22; 1Peter 3:1; Apostolic[1Clement 1:3]; Origen[Against Celsus Book V.5]

03:18-22 NT-Apocrypha[Acts of Peter and Paul]

03:18-25 Clement of Alexandria[Stromata Book IV.8]

03:18-04:01 Pseudepigrapha[Pseudo-Phocylides 175]

03:19 Ephesians 5:25; 1Peter 3:7; Pseudepigrapha[The Sentences of the Syriac Menander 47];
    Irenaeus[Against Heresies Book III.7.2]
03:20 Ephesians 6:1; 1Peter 5:5; Plato[Republic IV 425b]
03:21 Ephesians 6:4; Pseudepigrapha[Pseudo-Phocylides 207]
03:22 1Peter 2:18; Apostolic[Ignatius - Letter to Polycarp 4:1-3]; Constitutions of the Holy
    Apostles[Book IV.12]; Teaching of the Twelve Apostles 4.11
03:24 Acts 20:32n; Constitutions of the Holy Apostles[Book IV.12]
03:25 Deuteronomy 10:17; 2Chronicles 19:17; Ephesians 6:5-9; Apostolic[Epistle of Barnabas 4:12];
    Tertullian[On Exhortation to Chastity 7]; NT-Apocrypha[Acts of Peter and Paul; Epistula
    Apostolorum 24]
04:01 Leviticus 25:43, 53; Ecclesiastes 5:7; Ephesians 6:9; Apostolic[Ignatius - Letter to Polycarp 4:1-3];
    Clement of Alexandria[Stromata Book IV.8]; Constitutions of the Holy Apostles[Book IV.12];
    Teaching of the Twelve Apostles 4.1
04:02 Clement of Alexandria[The Instructor Book III.12]; Cyprian[Epistle VII.5; Treatise XII.Book
    III.120]; Tertullian[On Fasting 10]
04:02-04 Clement of Alexandria[Stromata Book V.10]
04:03 Apostolic[Ignatius - Letter to the Philadelphians 9:1]
04:05 Ephesians 5:16; Clement of Alexandria[The Instructor Book III.12]
04:06 Clement of Alexandria[Stromata Book II.1]; Clement[First Epistle Concerning Virginity 11];
    Origen[Against Celsus Book III.33]; Theonas[Epistle to Lucianus, the Chief Chamberlain 8]
04:07 Acts 20:4; 2Timothy 4:12
04:08 Ephesians 6:21-22
04:09 Philemon 1:10; Clement of Alexandria[The Instructor Book III.12]
04:10 Acts 12:12, 25, 13:13, 15:27-39, 19:29, 27:2; Philemon 1:24
04:11 NT-Apocrypha[Acts of Thomas 1.39]
04:12 Colossians 1:7; Philemon 1:23; Clement of Alexandria[Stromata Book VI.14]
04:14 2Timothy 4:10-11; Philemon 1:24; Irenaeus[Against Heresies Book III.14.1]; NT-
    Apocrypha[Canon Muratori Line 3]
04:16 Pseudepigrapha[2Baruch 86:1]; NT-Apocrypha[Epistle to the Laodiceans 1:20]
04:17 Philemon 1:2

Cross Reference Index: First Thessalonians

01:01 John 1:18n; Acts 17:1; Origen[Gospel of Matthew Book XIV.1]
01:03 OT-Apocrypha[4Maccabees 17:4]; Apostolic[Epistle of Barnabas 1:6]
01:04 1Peter 2:4-9n; NT-Apocrypha[Epistula Apostolorum 26]
01:06 Acts 17:5-9
01:08 OT-Apocrypha[4Maccabees 16:12]
01:09 Pseudepigrapha[Joseph and Aseneth 11:10]; Justin[Dialogue with Trypho 134]; NT-
    Apocrypha[Acts of Paul in Myra p.29]
01:09-10 Tertullian[An Answer to the Jews 1; On the Resurrection of the Flesh 24]
01:10 Pseudepigrapha[Martyrdom and Ascension of Isaiah (3:13-4:22 = Testament of Hezekiah) 4:13;
    Sibylline Oracles 8.1]
02:02 Acts 16:19-24, 17:1-9
02:03 Tertullian[On Modesty 17]
02:04 Jeremiah 11:20; Clement of Alexandria[Stromata Book VII.12]
02:05-07 Clement of Alexandria[Stromata Book I.1]
02:06 Teaching of the Twelve Apostles 11.4
02:06-07 Clement of Alexandria[The Instructor Book I.5]
02:07 Origen[Gospel of Matthew Book XIII.29]
02:12 Cyprian[Epistle LXXX.1]; Tertullian[On Exhortation to Chastity 10]; NT-Apocrypha[5Ezra 2.37]
02:14 Acts 17:5
02:14-15 Origen[Gospel of Matthew Book X.18; Letter to Africanus 9]
02:15 Acts 4:5, 19, 7:13, 9:23, 13:45, 14:2, 17:5, 18:12; Tertullian[Five Books Against Marcion Book V.15]
02:16 Genesis 15:16; Pseudepigrapha[Psalms of Solomon 1:1; Testament of Levi 6:11]
02:17 Clement of Alexandria[The Instructor Book III.2]
02:18 Pseudepigrapha[Psalms of Solomon 2:8]
02:19 Tertullian[On the Resurrection of the Flesh 24]
03:01 Acts 17:15
03:03 Rabbinic[Ecclesiastes Rabba on 4:14; Midrash on Psalms 9:2]
03:06 Acts 18:5
03:09 Apostolic[Didache 9:1]
03:11 OT-Apocrypha[Judith 12:8]
03:13 Zechariah 14:5; Pseudepigrapha[Martyrdom and Ascension of Isaiah (3:13-4:22 = Testament of
    Hezekiah) 4:14-16]; Apostolic[Didache 16:7]; Tertullian[On the Resurrection of the Flesh 24]; NT-
    Apocrypha[Apocalypse of Thomas Line 48]; Egyptian Book of the Dead[Oration 27]
04:03 Cyprian[Treatises Attributed to Cyprian - On the Discipline and Advantage of Chastity 6];
    Tertullian[On Exhortation to Chastity 1]; Nag Hammadi[Exegesis of the Soul 127-130]
04:03-05 Tertullian[Five Books Against Marcion Book V.15; On Modesty 17]
04:03-08 Clement of Alexandria[Stromata Book IV.12]
04:04 Tertullian[On the Resurrection of the Flesh 16]; NT-Apocrypha[Apocalypse of Thomas Line 56]
04:05 Psalms 79:6; Jeremiah 10:25
04:06 Psalms 94:2; OT-Apocrypha[Sirach 5:3]; Pseudepigrapha[2Enoch 60:1]; Cyprian[Treatise
    XII.Book III.88]
04:08 Ezekiel 36:27, 37:14; Tertullian[On Baptism 10]
04:09 Jeremiah 31:33-34; Clement of Alexandria[The Instructor Book I.6]
04:11 Tertullian[On Idolatry 5]
04:12 Apostolic[Didache 16:6]; Hippolytus[Treatise on Christ and Antichrist 66]
04:13 OT-Apocrypha[Wisdom of Solomon 3:18]; Cyprian[Treatise VII.21]; Tertullian[Of Patience 9]
04:13-14 Cyprian[Treatise XII.Book III.58]
04:13-15 Pseudepigrapha[4Ezra 2.31]
04:13-16 Origen[Against Celsus Book II.65]
04:13-17 Tertullian[On the Apparel of Women Book II.7; On the Resurrection of the Flesh 24, 57]

04:14 Pseudepigrapha[Martyrdom and Ascension of Isaiah (3:13-4:22 = Testament of Hezekiah) 4:16]

04:15 Pseudepigrapha[Testament of Abraham 13:4]; Hegesippus 1.1

04:15-17 This section also includes topical notes for: Rapture - Zechariah 12:10-14; Matthew 24:29-31, 26:64; Mark 13:24-27, 14:62n; Luke 21:25-28; 1Corinthians 15:51-55; 2Thessalonians 2:1-2; Revelation 1:6-7, 6:13-8:2, 8:5, 11:12, 11:19, 14:1-5, 14:14-20, 16:8, 16:18; Pseudepigrapha[4Ezra 6.26; Apocalypse of Abraham 31.1-2; Apocalypse of Elijah 5.2-4; Greek Apocalypse of Ezra 4.36-37]; Dead Sea Scrolls[4Q 431(4QHADAYOT[4QH]) Fragment 1 7-8]; Philo[On Dreams, That they Are God-Sent (1.137-1.139, 1.151-1.152) cf. {Genesis 28:12}; On Rewards And Punishments (117, 163-170) cf. {Deuteronomy 30:1-9}; On the Confusion of Tongues (197) cf. {Deuteronomy 30:1-9}; **Special Laws I (207)]**; Rabbinic[**Babylonian Baba Batra 75b cf. {Isaiah 60:8}**; Sanhedrin 92b); Mekhilta On Exodus 14:21, 24]; Plato[Timaeus 90a]; Clement of Alexandria[Who is the Rich Man that shall be Saved 3]; Methodius[Banquet of the Ten Virgins 6.4]; Origen[Against Celsus Book V.17]; Tertullian[On the Resurrection of the Flesh 41; Five Books Against Marcion Book III.25, V.15, V.20]; Nag Hammadi[Dialogue of the Savior 38; Interpretation of Knowledge 10; Tripartite Tractate 138]

By the command that the feet of the victim should be washed, it is figuratively shown that we must no longer walk upon the earth, but soar aloft and traverse the air. For the soul of the man who is devoted to God, being eager for truth, springs upward and mounts from earth to heaven; and, being borne on wings, traverses the expanse of the air, being eager to be classed with and to move in concert with the sun, and moon, and all the rest of the most sacred and most harmonious company of the stars, under the immediate command and government of God, who has a kingly authority without any rival, and of which he can never be deprived, in accordance with which he justly governs the universe. (Philo - Special Laws I 207)

And lest you suppose that there will be pain in the ascension, scripture states, "Who are these that fly as a cloud and as the doves to their cotes." (Isaiah 60:8) (Talmud - Babylonian Baba Batra 75b, *The Babylonian Talmud a Translation and Commentary*, Jacob Neusner; Hendrickson Publishers, Inc., 2005)

04:16 Pseudepigrapha[4Ezra 6:23; Apocalypse of Elijah 5:36; Greek Apocalypse of Ezra 4:36; Joseph and Aseneth 4:1; Life of Adam and Eve (Apocalypse of Moses) 22:3; Questions of Ezra RecB 13; Sibylline Oracles 8.239]; Constitutions of the Holy Apostles[Book VII.32]; Hippolytus[Appendix to the Works of Hippolytus - On the End of the World 37]; Tertullian[A Treatise on the Soul 55; On Prayer 29]

04:17 Clement of Alexandria[Stromata Book VI.13]; Origen[De Principiis Book II.11.5]; Tertullian[A Treatise on the Soul 55]; NT-Apocrypha[Apocalypse of Thomas Line 65; Epistula Apostolorum 38]

05:01 OT-Apocrypha[Wisdom of Solomon 8:8]

05:01-02 Archelaus[Disputation with Manes 38]

05:01-03 Tertullian[On the Resurrection of the Flesh 24]

05:02 Matthew 24:42-44; Luke 12:39, 21:34-36; 2Peter 3:10; Revelation 16:15; OT-Apocrypha[Wisdom of Solomon 18:14]; Pseudepigrapha[Apocalypse of Elijah 2:40]; Rabbinic[Babylonian Sanhedrin 39a cf. {Genesis 2:21}]

05:02-03 Cyprian[Treatise XII.Book III.89]; NT-Apocrypha[6Ezra 17.36-40]

05:03 Isaiah 13:8; Jeremiah 6:14, 8:11; Ezekiel 13:10; Matthew 24:8; Mark 13:8; OT-Apocrypha[Wisdom of Solomon 17:14]; Pseudepigrapha[**1Enoch 62:4**; Testament of Job 18:4]; Irenaeus[Against Heresies Book V.30.2]

For when they shall say, peace and safety; then sudden destruction comes upon them, as travail upon a woman with child; and they shall not escape. (Pseudepigrapha - 1Enoch 62:4)

05:04-05 Tertullian[On Modesty 7]

05:04-06 Matthew 24:42-51n

05:05 This section also includes topical notes for: Sons of Light - Luke 16:8; John 12:36; Dead Sea Scrolls[1Q Rule of the Community (1QS) COL III 13-26; 1Q War Scroll (1QM[+1Q33]) Col I 1-16; 4Q Catena (4Q177[4QCATENA]) COL IV (Fragments 19+12+13I+15) 12-16; 4Q Visions of Amram (4Q548[4QAMRAMAR]) 8-16]; Clement of Alexandria[Exhortation to the Heathen 10];

Irenaeus[Against Heresies Book I.14.6]; Origen[Gospel of Matthew Book XII.37]; Tertullian[De Fuga in Persecutione 9]; Nag Hammadi[First Apocalypse of James 25; Sophia of Jesus Christ III 119; Trimorphic Protennoia 37, 41-42, 45, 49]; NT-Apocrypha[Epistula Apostolorum 28, 39]

05:05-08 Clement of Alexandria[The Instructor Book II.9]

05:06-08 Ephesians 6:11-17; Clement of Alexandria[Stromata Book IV.22]; Nag Hammadi[Teachings of Silvanus 84]

05:08 Job 2:9, Isaiah 59:17; OT-Apocrypha[Wisdom of Solomon 5:18]; Pseudepigrapha[Apocalypse of Elijah 4:31]; Apostolic[Ignatius - Letter to Polycarp 6:2; Epistle of Barnabas 1:6]; Nag Hammadi[Letter of Peter to Philip 137]

05:09 Revelation 12:10n

05:10 Clement of Alexandria[The Instructor Book I.9]

05:12-13 Apostolic[1Clement 21]

05:13-15 Clement of Alexandria[The Instructor Book III.12]

05:14 Proverbs 14:29; Isaiah 57:15; Origen[De Principiis Book IV.1.19]; Tertullian[De Fuga in Persecutione 9]

05:15 Proverbs 20:22; Pseudepigrapha[Apocalypse of Sedrach 7:9; Joseph and Aseneth 23:9]; NT-Apocrypha[Acts of John 81; Acts of Peter 1.28]

05:16 Tertullian[On Exhortation to Chastity 6]

05:16-18 Gregory Thaumaturgus[Four Homilies 2]

05:17 Origen[Gospel of Matthew Book XIV.25]; Tertullian[On Fasting 10; On Prayer 23]

05:19 Numbers 11:26-29

05:19-20 Tertullian[Five Books Against Marcion Book V.15]

05:19-22 Clement of Alexandria[The Instructor Book III.12]

05:21 Clement of Alexandria[Stromata Book I.11]; Dionysius of Alexandria[Extant Fragments Epistle to Philemon, A Presbyter]; Tertullian[On Prescription Against Heretics 4; On the Veiling of Virgins 16]

05:22 Job 1:1, 8, 2:3; Apostolic[Polycarp - Letter to the Philippians 11:1]

05:23 Pseudepigrapha[Testament of Dan 5:2]; Josephus[Antiquities 1.1.2 34]; Irenaeus[Against Heresies Book V.6.1]; Origen[Gospel of Matthew Book XIII.2, XIV.3]; Tertullian[On the Apparel of Women Book II.7; On the Resurrection of the Flesh 47, 57; Five Books Against Marcion Book V.15]; Nag Hammadi[Prayer of the Apostle Paul A.I]; NT-Apocrypha[Epistula Apostolorum 22]

05:26 Tertullian[On Prayer 18]; NT-Apocrypha[Epistle to the Laodiceans 1:17]

Cross Reference Index: Second Thessalonians

01:01 Acts 17:1
01:01-02 John 1:18n
01:02 NT-Apocrypha[Acts of Paul and Thecla 1.37]
01:04 Tertullian[Scorpiace 13]
01:06-09 Tertullian[Five Books Against Marcion Book V.16]
01:06-10 Irenaeus[Against Heresies Book IV.27.4, 33.11]
01:07 Zechariah 14:5; Pseudepigrapha[1Enoch 61:10; 2Baruch 29:3; 3Baruch 1:8 (Gk.); Apocalypse of Elijah 3:3]
01:07-08 Pseudepigrapha[Martyrdom and Ascension of Isaiah (3:13-4:22 = Testament of Hezekiah) 4:14-18]
01:08 Psalms 79:6; Isaiah 66:4, 15; Jeremiah 10:25
01:09 Isaiah 2:10, 19, 21; Pseudepigrapha[1Enoch 62:2]
01:10 Psalms 67:36, 68:36, 89:8; Isaiah 2:11, 17, 49:3; NT-Apocrypha[Apocalypse of Paul 1.21]
01:12 Isaiah 24:15, 66:5; Malachi 1:11
02:01-02 Zechariah 12:10-14; Matthew 24:29-32; Mark 13:24-28; Luke 21:25-33; 1Corinthians 15:51-55; 1Thessalonians 4:15-17; Revelation 1:7, 6:13-8:2, 8:5, 11:12, 11:19, 14:1-5, 14:14-20, 16:8, 16:18; OT-Apocrypha[2Maccabees 2:7]
02:01-10 Tertullian[On the Resurrection of the Flesh 24]
02:01-11 Hippolytus[Treatise on Christ and Antichrist 63]
02:01-12 Origen[Against Celsus Book VI.46]
02:01-17 Lactantius[Divine Institutes Book VII.17]
02:02 Origen[Against Celsus Book III.11]
02:03 Psalms 89:23; Isaiah 57:3; Pseudepigrapha[Apocalypse of Daniel 9:9; Apocalypse of Elijah 1:10, 2:40; Greek Apocalypse of Ezra 4:21; Jubilees 10:3; Psalms of Solomon 2:1; Sibylline Oracles 3.570]; Justin[Dialogue with Trypho 110]; Origen[Gospel of Matthew Book XIV.11]; NT-Apocrypha[Acts of Peter 1.7; Apocalypse of Peter 1.14-15]
02:03-04 Pseudepigrapha[Apocalypse of Elijah 1:2]; Irenaeus[Against Heresies Book III.6.5, 7.2, V.25.1, 29.2, 30.2-4, 35.1]; Origen[Against Celsus Book II.49, VI.45; Gospel of Matthew Book XIV.10]; Teaching of the Twelve Apostles 16.4; Tertullian[Five Books Against Marcion Book V.16]; Victorinus[Apocalypse 12.7-9]
02:03-08 Hippolytus[Appendix to the Works of Hippolytus - On the End of the World 22]
02:03-12 Matthew 24:15; Marl 13:14; Luke 21:20; Revelation 13:1-18
02:04 Daniel 11:36; Ezekiel 28:2; Pseudepigrapha[Apocalypse of Elijah 3:5; Martyrdom and Ascension of Isaiah (3:13-4:22 = Testament of Hezekiah) 4:7]; Origen[Gospel of Matthew Book XI.6]; Tertullian[A Treatise on the Soul 57]; NT-Apocrypha[Acts of Paul in Philippi 3.11]
02:06 1Peter 1:10-13n; Pseudepigrapha[Life of Abraham 51:5]
02:06-07 Pseudepigrapha[Greek Apocalypse of Ezra 4:25]
02:06-12 Origen[Against Celsus Book II.49]
02:07-11 Constitutions of the Holy Apostles[Book VII.32]; Victorinus[Apocalypse 11.7]
02:08 Job 4:9; Psalms 33:6; Isaiah 11:4; Ezekiel 21:24; Pseudepigrapha[1Enoch 62:2; 4Ezra 13.10; Apocalypse of Elijah 2:41; Martyrdom and Ascension of Isaiah (3:13-4:22 = Testament of Hezekiah) 4:18]; Irenaeus[Against Heresies Book III.7.2, V.25.3]; Origen[Gospel of John Book II.4]; Teaching of the Twelve Apostles 16.4; Victorinus[Apocalypse 1.16]
02:08-10 Irenaeus[Against Heresies Book III.16.8]; Justin[Dialogue with Trypho 110]
02:09 Matthew 24:24; Pseudepigrapha[Apocalypse of Elijah 3:6; Martyrdom and Ascension of Isaiah (3:13-4:22 = Testament of Hezekiah) 4:9]; Origen[Against Celsus Book VI.45]; NT-Apocrypha[Epistula Apostolorum 30]
02:09-10 Origen[Gospel of Matthew Book XII.2]
02:09-12 Tertullian[Five Books Against Marcion Book V.16]

02:10 Plato[Republic VI 492e]; Cyprian[Treatise III.33]; Tertullian[On Prescription Against Heretics 9];
    Nag Hammadi[Gospel of Philip 52; Gospel of Truth 26]
02:10-12 Cyprian[Epistle LIV.13]; Irenaeus[Against Heresies Book V.28.2]
02:11 Cyprian[Epistle LXIII.2]; Irenaeus[Against Heresies Book IV.29.1]
02:11-12 Origen[Gospel of John Book II.24]
02:12 Origen[Gospel of Matthew Book XI.14]; Nag Hammadi[Dialogue of the Savior 1]
02:13 Deuteronomy 33:12; Clement[First Epistle Concerning Virginity 4]; Tertullian[On Prescription
    Against Heretics 9]
02:15 Tertullian[On Modesty 1; On Monogamy 2]
02:15-17 Anterus[Epistle]
03:01 Psalms 147:15
03:01-02 Clement of Alexandria[Stromata Book V.3]
03:01-03 Anterus[Epistle]
03:02 Isaiah 25:4; Hippolytus[Treatise on Christ and Antichrist 1]
03:04 Anterus[Epistle]
03:05 1Chronicles 29:18
03:06 Cyprian[Epistle LIV.21; Treatise I.23, XII.Book III.68]; Tertullian[On Modesty 14, 18; On
    Monogamy 2]
03:06-12 Tertullian[On Idolatry 5]
03:08 Jeremiah 20:18; Cyprian[Epistle V.2]
03:10 Pseudepigrapha[Pseudo-Phocylides 153]; Constitutions of the Holy Apostles[Book II.63];
    Teaching of the Twelve Apostles 12.3; Tertullian[Five Books Against Marcion Book V.16]
03:11 Tertullian[On Modesty 14]
03:14-15 Cyprian[Treatise XII.Book III.68]; Tertullian[On Modesty 13]
03:15 Apostolic[Polycarp - Letter to the Philippians 11:4]

Cross Reference Index:
First Timothy

01:01 Psalms 24:5; Pseudepigrapha[Hellenistic Synagogal Prayers 3:27]; Apostolic[Ignatius - Letter to the Philadelphians 5:2]; Tertullian[On Prayer 3]

01:02 John 1:18n; Acts 16:1

01:03 Cyprian[Treatise IX.8]; Irenaeus[Against Heresies Book I.31.4, II.14.2]

01:04 Irenaeus[Fragments from the Lost Works 36]; Tertullian[A Treatise on the Soul 2; On Prescription Against Heretics 7, 33]

01:05 Luke 8:15n; Pseudepigrapha[Letter of Aristeas 1.234]; Clement of Alexandria[Stromata Book I.27, IV.17, VI.12, VII.3, 10]; Hippolytus[Refutation of all Heresies Book IX.21]

01:07 Origen[Gospel of Matthew Book XII.41]

01:07-08 Clement of Alexandria[Stromata Book I.27]

01:09 Archelaus[Disputation with Manes 31]; Clement of Alexandria[Stromata Book IV.3, VII.2]; Irenaeus[Against Heresies Book IV.16.3; Demonstration of the Apostolic Preaching 35]

01:10 Irenaeus[Fragments from the Lost Works 51]

01:13 Pseudepigrapha[Joseph and Aseneth 6:7]; Cyprian[Epistle LXXII.13]; Tertullian[On Modesty 18]; NT-Apocrypha[Acts of Peter 1.2]

01:15 Origen[Against Celsus Book I.63]; Tertullian[On Modesty 18]; NT-Apocrypha[Acts of Paul in Philippi 3.6]

01:16 Jude 1:21n; Tertullian[On Modesty 18; On Repentance 4]

01:17 OT-Apocrypha[Tobit 13:7, 11]; Pseudepigrapha[4Maccabees 18.24; Hellenistic Synagogal Prayers 3:1, 4:29, 9:4]; Apostolic[1Clement 61:2; 2Clement 20:5]; Methodius[Oration Concerning Simeon and Anna 6, 10]; Novatian[Treatise Concerning the Trinity 3]; Tertullian[Against Praxeas 15]; Nag Hammadi[Letter of Peter to Philip 133; Tripartite Tractate 115]; NT-Apocrypha[Martyrdom of the Holy Apostle Paul 1.7]

01:17-18 NT-Apocrypha[Martyrdom of the Holy Apostle Paul 1.2]

01:18 Tertullian[On Prescription Against Heretics 25]

01:18-19 Clement of Alexandria[Stromata Book II.6]

01:19 Hippolytus[Refutation of all Heresies Book IX.21]; Tertullian[On Idolatry 11; On Modesty 13]

01:20 Archelaus[Disputation with Manes 13]; Hippolytus[Refutation of all Heresies Book IX.18]; Tertullian[De Fuga in Persecutione 2; On Modesty 13; On Prescription Against Heretics 3]

02:01-02 Athenagoras[Plea for the Christians 37]; Origen[Against Celsus Book VIII.73]

02:01-04 Rabbinic[Mishna Aboth 3:2]

02:02 Ezra 6:10; Jeremiah 29:7; OT-Apocrypha[2Maccabees 3:11]; Pseudepigrapha[Baruch 1:11]; Constitutions of the Holy Apostles[Book VIII.12-13]; Tertullian[Apology 31; To his Wife Book I.7]; Theophilus of Antioch[To Autolycus Book III.14]

02:04 Ezekiel 18:23; Pseudepigrapha[Hellenistic Synagogal Prayers 8:5, 11:8]; Constitutions of the Holy Apostles[Book VIII.9]; Fabian[First Epistle]; Methodius[Banquet of the Ten Virgins 2.7]

02:05 Genesis 3:24; Exodus 13:21; 14:19; Psalms 121:4; 1Timothy 3:16n; Hebrews 7:26-28n; 1John 2:1-2; Pseudepigrapha[Hellenistic Synagogal Prayers 4.22, 6.13]; Philo[On Dreams That they Are God-Sent (2.229-2.231) cf. {Leviticus 16:17; Deuteronomy 10:10}]; Clement of Alexandria[The Instructor Book III.1]; Hippolytus[Fragments - On Numbers]; Irenaeus[Against Heresies Book III.18.6]; Lactantius[Divine Institutes Book IV.25]; Novatian[Treatise Concerning the Trinity 21]; Tertullian[Against Praxeas 27; On the Flesh of Christ 15; On the Resurrection of the Flesh 51, 63]; NT-Apocrypha[Acts of Paul in Ephesus p.1]

02:06 Psalms 49:8; Clement of Alexandria[Fragments from Eusebius Ecclesiastical History Book VII.]

02:07 2Timothy 1:11; Apostolic[1Clement 60:4]; Tertullian[On Modesty 14]; NT-Apocrypha[Acts of Paul from Corinth to Italy p.7; Epistula Apostolorum 38]

02:07-12 Pseudepigrapha[3Enoch 48A:5]

02:08 Psalms 141:2; Pseudepigrapha[Testament of Solomon 1:00]; Irenaeus[Against Heresies Book V.17.1]; Tertullian[On Baptism 8; On Prayer 13, 23]; NT-Apocrypha[Acts of Peter and Paul]

02:09 1Peter 3:3; Clement of Alexandria[The Instructor Book III.11]; Tertullian[The Chaplet, or De Corona 14]

02:09-10 Clement of Alexandria[The Instructor Book II.13]; Cyprian[Treatise II.8, XII.Book III.36]; Tertullian[On Prayer 20]

02:11-12 Tertullian[On Baptism 1; On the Veiling of Virgins 9]

02:11-14 Cyprian[Treatise XII.Book III.46]

02:12 Genesis 3:16

02:13 Genesis 1:27, 2:7, 21-22

02:14 Genesis 3:1-6, 13; Pseudepigrapha[2Enoch 30:17; Life of Adam and Eve (Apocalypse of Moses) 14:2; Sibylline Oracles 1.42]; Tertullian[Five Books in Reply to Marcion Book II.188]; NT-Apocrypha[Protoevangelium of James 13.1]

02:15 Clement of Alexandria[Stromata Book III.12]

03:01 Archelaus[Disputation with Manes 51]; Tertullian[A Treatise on the Soul 16]; NT-Apocrypha[Letter of Clement to James 3.2]

03:01-02 Apostolic[1Clement 42:4-5]; Origen[Gospel of Matthew Book XIV.22]; Tertullian[On Exhortation to Chastity 7]

03:01-07 Tertullian[On Monogamy 12]

03:02 Athenagoras[Plea for the Christians 33]; Clement of Alexandria[Stromata Book III.18]; Constitutions of the Holy Apostles[Book II.2, VI.17]; Irenaeus[Against Heresies Book III.3.1-4]

03:02-07 Titus 1:6-9; Rabbinic[Exodus Rabba on 2:14; Mishnah Sanhedrin 4:4; Siphre On Numbers 11:16]

03:03 Clement[First Epistle Concerning Virginity 13]

03:04 Clement of Alexandria[Stromata Book III.18]; Constitutions of the Holy Apostles[Book II.2]; Teaching of the Twelve Apostles 15.1

03:05 Apostolic[Polycarp - Letter to the Philippians 11:2]

03:06 Constitutions of the Holy Apostles[Book II.2]; Origen[Against Celsus Book III.31]; Pontius the Deacon[The Life and Passion of Cyprian 2]; Nag Hammadi[Apocryphon of James 7]

03:08-13 Apostolic[Polycarp - Letter to the Philippians 5:2]

03:09 Pseudepigrapha[4Baruch 7:2]; Hippolytus[Refutation of all Heresies Book IX.21]

03:10 Origen[Gospel of Matthew Book XII.14]

03:12 Constitutions of the Holy Apostles[Book VI.17]; Origen[Gospel of Matthew Book XIV.22]

03:15 Pseudepigrapha[Joseph and Aseneth 14:8]; Constitutions of the Holy Apostles[Book III.15]; Irenaeus[Against Heresies Book III.1.1, 11.8]; Origen[Against Celsus Book V.33; Gospel of John Book X.16; Gospel of Matthew Book XI.15]; Pseud-Irenaeus; Victorinus[Apocalypse 1.16]

03:16 This section also includes topical notes for: God Incarnate - Genesis 18:1-33; John 1:14; Romans 8:3; 1Timothy 2:5; OT-Apocrypha[4Maccabees 6:31, 7:16, 16:1]; Dead Sea Scrolls[4Q Visions of Amram (4Q543[4QAMRAMAR]) Fragment 3 1-3]; Philo[On Dreams, That they Are God-Sent (1.237-1.239) cf. {Genesis 31:13, Deuteronomy 1:31}, (2.229-2.231) cf. {Leviticus 16:17, Deuteronomy 10:10}]; Clement of Alexandria[Fragments from Eusebius Ecclesiastical History Book VII.]; Nag Hammadi[Treatise on the Resurrection 44; Tripartite Tractate 133]; NT-Apocrypha[Freer Logion]

04:01 Isaiah 19:14; Pseudepigrapha[4Baruch 7:2]; Alexander of Alexandria[Epistles on Arian Heresy 2.5]; Clement of Alexandria[Stromata Book III.6]; Irenaeus[Against Heresies Book I.31.4, II.14.2]; Novatian[Treatise Concerning the Trinity 29]; Peter of Alexandria[Genuine Acts of Peter 3]

04:01-02 Tertullian[On Fasting 12]

04:01-03 Justin[Dialogue with Trypho 82]; Origen[Against Celsus Book V.64; Gospel of Matthew Book XIV.16; De Principiis Book II.7.3]; Tertullian[On Fasting 2; On Monogamy 15; On Prescription Against Heretics 1, 7]

04:01-04 Archelaus[Disputation with Manes 35]

04:01-05 Pseudepigrapha[Apocalypse of Elijah 1:13]; Clement of Alexandria[Stromata Book III.12]; Novatian[On the Jewish Meats 5]

04:01-15 Hippolytus[Refutation of all Heresies Book VIII.13]

04:02 Matthew 6:2-16n; Constitutions of the Holy Apostles[Ecclesiastical Canons 47.53]; Hippolytus[Refutation of all Heresies Book IX.21]

04:03 Genesis 9:3; Clement of Alexandria[Stromata Book III.6]; Hippolytus[Refutation of all Heresies Book VII.18]; Irenaeus[Against Heresies Book I.24.2, 28.1]; Tertullian[On Prescription Against Heretics 33]

04:03-05 Hippolytus[Refutation of all Heresies Book IX.16]

04:04 Genesis 1:31

04:04-05 Origen[Against Celsus Book VIII.32]; Tertullian[On the Apparel of Women Book II.9]

04:05 Origen[Gospel of Matthew Book XI.14]

04:06-08 Clement of Alexandria[The Instructor Book III.12]

04:07 Irenaeus[Against Heresies Book I.8.1]; Minucius Felix[The Octavius 11]; Origen[Against Celsus Book VII.52]

04:08 Jude 1:21n; Clement of Alexandria[Exhortation to the Heathen 11]; Dionysius of Alexandria[Extant Fragments Epistle to Bishop Basilides 1]

04:10 Plato[Timaeus 48d]; Clement of Alexandria[Exhortation to the Heathen 9; Stromata Book VI.17]; Constitutions of the Holy Apostles[Book VII.1]; Origen[Against Celsus Book IV.28; Gospel of John Book VI.37-38]; Tertullian[On Modesty 2]

04:12 Pseudepigrapha[1Enoch 104:10-11; Martyrdom and Ascension of Isaiah (3:13-4:22 = Testament of Hezekiah) 3:22]; Clement of Alexandria[Stromata Book IV.16]; Cyprian[Epistle LXIV.3]

04:13 Origen[Gospel of Matthew Book X.4, 15]

04:14 Acts 8:18n; Rabbinic[Babylonian Sanhedrin 13b]; Hippolytus[Refutation of all Heresies Book IX.22]

04:15 Tertullian[On Exhortation to Chastity 10]

04:16 Origen[Gospel of John Book II.11]

05:01 Leviticus 19:32

05:02 NT-Apocrypha[Acts of Peter p.137]

05:03 Cyprian[Treatise XII.Book III.74]; Tertullian[Of Patience 13]

05:05 Jeremiah 49:11; Pseudepigrapha[Joseph and Aseneth 13:2]

05:06 Cyprian[Treatise XII.Book III.74]; Urban I[Epistle 6.6]

05:08 Cyprian[Treatise XII.Book III.75]

05:09 Athenagoras[Plea for the Christians 33]; Constitutions of the Holy Apostles[Book III.1, VI.17]; Origen[Gospel of Matthew Book XIV.22]; Tertullian[On the Veiling of Virgins 9]

05:09-10 Tertullian[Of Patience 13; To his Wife Book I.7]

05:09-16 Pseudepigrapha[Testament of Job 10:2]

05:10 Clement of Alexandria[Fragments from Eusebius Ecclesiastical History Book VII]; Tertullian[To his Wife Book II.4]

05:11 Constitutions of the Holy Apostles[Book III.1]

05:11-12 Cyprian[Treatise XII.Book III.74]

05:13 Pseudepigrapha[Sibylline Oracles 3.43]; Clement[First Epistle Concerning Virginity 11]; Tertullian[To his Wife Book I.8]

05:14 Tertullian[On Monogamy 13]

05:14-15 Clement of Alexandria[Stromata Book III.12]

05:15 Irenaeus[Against Heresies Book III.16.1]

05:17 Acts 15:2-6n; Pseudepigrapha[Hellenistic Synagogal Prayers 14:6]; Tertullian[On Fasting 17; The Martyrdom of Perpetua and Felicitas 4]

05:18 Numbers 18:31; Deuteronomy 25:4; 2Chronicles 15:7; Matthew 10:10; Luke 10:7; Clement of Alexandria[Fragments from Eusebius Ecclesiastical History Book VII; Stromata Book II.18]]

05:19 Deuteronomy 17:6, 19:15

05:19-20 Cyprian[Treatise XII.Book III.76-77]

05:20 Hippolytus[Fragments - On Proverbs 27.22]

05:21 Pseudepigrapha[Joseph and Aseneth 16:14]; Clement of Alexandria[Fragments from Eusebius Ecclesiastical History Book VII; Stromata Book I.1]; Tertullian[On Prescription Against Heretics 37]

05:22 Cyprian[Epistle VI.4]; Tertullian[On Baptism 18; On Modesty 18]

05:23 Clement of Alexandria[The Instructor Book II.2]; Tertullian[On Fasting 9; The Chaplet, or De Corona 8]

06:01 Isaiah 52:5; Apostolic[1Clement 16:17]

06:02 Clement of Alexandria[The Instructor Book III.12]; Constitutions of the Holy Apostles[Book IV.12]

06:03 Irenaeus[Against Heresies Book I.31.4, II.14.2]

06:03-04 Alexander of Alexandria[Epistles on Arian Heresy 1.13]; Tertullian[On Prescription Against Heretics 15]

06:03-05 Apostolic[Ignatius - Letter to the Ephesians 16:1-2]; Clement of Alexandria[Stromata Book I.8]; Cyprian[Epistle XXXIX.6, LXXIII.3]

06:04 Irenaeus[Against Heresies Book III.12.11]

06:04-05 Irenaeus[Fragments from the Lost Works 36]

06:05 Malchion[Epistle Against Paul of Samosata 2]; Origen[Gospel of Matthew Book XI.9]

06:06 Clement of Alexandria[Exhortation to the Heathen 11]; Cyprian[Treatise VII.8]

06:07 Job 1:21; Psalms 49:17; Ecclesiates 5:14-15; Pseudepigrapha[Pseudo-Phocylides 110]; Philo[Special Laws I (295) cf. {Leviticus 2:11}]; Apostolic[Polycarp - Letter to the Philippians 4:1]; Cyprian[Treatise IV.19]; Gregory Thaumaturgus[Metaphrase of the Book of Ecclesiastes 5]

06:07-10 Cyprian[Treatise VIII.10, XII.Book III.61]

06:08 Genesis 28:20; Proverbs 30:8; Novatian[On the Jewish Meats 6]; Tertullian[To his Wife Book I.4]

06:08-10 Lactantius[Divine Institutes Book VI.12]

06:09 Proverbs 23:4, 28:22; Philo[Fragments Extracted From the Parallels of John of Damascus Page 774. B.]; Cyprian[Treatise III.12]

06:10 Pseudepigrapha[Ahiqar 137; Pseudo-Phocylides 1.42-44; Sibylline Oracles 2.111, 8.17]; Apostolic[Polycarp - Letter to the Philippians 4:1]; Clement of Alexandria[The Instructor Book II.3]; Clement[First Epistle Concerning Virginity 8]; Novatian[On the Jewish Meats 6]; Origen[Gospel of Matthew Book XI.9]; Tertullian[Of Patience 7; On Idolatry 11]; Urban I[Epistle 6.6]; Indian[Dhammapada 355]

06:11 1Samuel 2:27; 1Kings 13:1; Clement[First Epistle Concerning Virginity 9]

06:11-12 Peter of Alexandria[Canonical Epistle 14]

06:12 Jude 1:21n; Pseudepigrapha[4Ezra 2.47]

06:13 John 18:37; Pseudepigrapha[Joseph and Aseneth 8:9]; Clement of Alexandria[Fragments from Eusebius Ecclesiastical History Book VII.]; Tertullian[On Prescription Against Heretics 25, 37]

06:14-15 Tertullian[On the Resurrection of the Flesh 23]

06:15 Deuteronomy 10:17; Revelation 19:16; OT-Apocrypha[2Maccabees 12:15, 13:4; 3Maccabees 5:35; Sirach 46:5]; Philo[Every Good Man Is Free (42-43) cf. {Exodus 4:16, 7:1}]; Nag Hammadi[Eugnostos the Blessed III 78; Sophia of Jesus Christ III 102]; NT-Apocrypha[Epistula Apostolorum 3]

06:16 Exodus 33:20; Psalms 104:2; Pseudepigrapha[Hellenistic Synagogal Prayers 4:33, 13:5]; Clement of Alexandria[Fragments from the Latin Translation of Cassiodorus Comments on 1John; Stromata Book VI.3, 9]; Constitutions of the Holy Apostles[Book VIII.15]; Hippolytus[The Discourse on the Holy Theophany 7]; Methodius[Banquet of the Ten Virgins 6.1]; Novatian[Treatise Concerning the Trinity 18, 30]; Passion of the Scillitan Martyrs; Tertullian[Against Praxeas 15-16]; Nag Hammadi[Letter of Peter to Philip 134]; NT-Apocrypha[Acts of Peter 1.20]

06:17 Psalms 62:10-11; Pseudepigrapha[Pseudo-Phocylides 62]; Novatian[On the Jewish Meats 5]; NT-Apocrypha[Acts of Peter and Paul]

06:17-18 Origen[Against Celsus Book VII.21]

06:19 Jude 1:21n

06:20 Pseudepigrapha[Greek Apocalypse of Ezra 6:3]; Clement of Alexandria[Stromata Book VII.7, 17]; Irenaeus[Against Heresies Book I.Preface.1, 11.1, 13.1, 15.4, 23.4, II.Preface.1, 13.10, 31.1, 35.2, III 4.3, 10.3, 11.1-2, 12.12, 15.2, IV.6.4, 35.1, 41.4, V.Preface.1, V.26.2; Demonstration of the Apostolic Preaching 99]; Origen[Against Celsus Book III.11; Gospel of Matthew Book XII.12]; Tertullian[On Prescription Against Heretics 25; On the Resurrection of the Flesh 23]

06:20-21 Clement of Alexandria[Stromata Book II.11]; Hippolytus[Treatise on Christ and Antichrist 1]; Nag Hammadi[Teachings of Silvanus 94-5]

Cross Reference Index: Second Timothy

01:02 John 1:18n; Acts 16:1

01:03 Hippolytus[Refutation of all Heresies Book IX.21]; Origen[Against Celsus Book V.61; De Principiis Book II.4.2]

01:05 Acts 16:1

01:07-08 Clement of Alexandria[Stromata Book IV.7]; Tertullian[Scorpiace 13]

01:09 1Peter 1:10-13n

01:10 Pseudepigrapha[Hellenistic Synagogal Prayers 5:7]; Origen[Against Celsus Book III.61]

01:11 1Timothy 2:7; NT-Apocrypha[Acts of Paul from Corinth to Italy p.7]

01:12-14 Pseudepigrapha[Greek Apocalypse of Ezra 6:3]

01:14 Romans 8:9-11n; Colossians 02:02-03n; Apostolic[Ignatius - Letter to the Ephesians 15:3, Letter to the Philadelphians 7:2; Epistle of Barnabas 4:11, 6:14-15]; Tertullian[On Prescription Against Heretics 25]

01:15 Plato[Cratylus 384c]; Hippolytus[Appendix to the Works of Hippolytus - On the Seventy Apostles 25-26; Refutation of all Heresies Book X.24]; Tertullian[Against Hermogenes 1; De Fuga in Persecutione 2; On Prescription Against Heretics 3; On the Resurrection of the Flesh 24]; NT-Apocrypha[Acts of Paul and Thecla 1.1]

01:16 NT-Apocrypha[Acts of Paul and Thecla 1.2]

01:16-18 Origen[De Principiis Book III.1.20]

01:18 Tertullian[On the Resurrection of the Flesh 23]

02:01 Tertullian[On Prayer 19]

02:01-02 Clement of Alexandria[Stromata Book I.1]; Hippolytus[Treatise on Christ and Antichrist 1]

02:02 Clement of Alexandria[Fragments from Eusebius Ecclesiastical History Book VII.]; Tertullian[On Prescription Against Heretics 25]

02:03 Tertullian[On Prescription Against Heretics 33]; NT-Apocrypha[Acts of Paul from Corinth to Italy p.8; Martyrdom of the Holy Apostle Paul 1.2]

02:03-04 Tertullian[On Exhortation to Chastity 12]

02:04 Cyprian[Epistle LXV.1]; NT-Apocrypha[Acts of Peter 1.36; Martyrdom of the Holy Apostle Paul 1.2]

02:04-05 Cyprian[Treatise XI.8, XII.Book III.11]

02:05 1Corinthians 9:24-27n; Clement[First Epistle Concerning Virginity 5]; Constitutions of the Holy Apostles[Book II.14]; Origen[Against Celsus Book VI.44, VIII.56]

02:07 Proverbs 2:6

02:08 Tertullian[On the Flesh of Christ 22]

02:10 Revelation 12:10n

02:11 Origen[Against Celsus Book II.69]; Tertullian[Scorpiace 13]

02:11-12 Cyprian[Treatise XI.5]

02:12 Matthew 10:33; Luke 12:9; Apostolic[Polycarp - Letter to the Philippians 5:2]; Irenaeus[Against Heresies Book III.18.5]; Tertullian[On Idolatry 13]; Nag Hammadi[Testimony of Truth 44]

02:13 Numbers 23:19

02:14 Clement of Alexandria[Stromata Book I.10]; Tertullian[On Prescription Against Heretics 37]

02:15 Clement[First Epistle Concerning Virginity 13]; Constitutions of the Holy Apostles[Book VII.31]; Origen[Against Celsus Book V.1]; NT-Apocrypha[Acts of Paul from Corinth to Italy p.8]

02:16 Cyprian[Treatises Attributed to Cyprian - Exhortation to Repentance]

02:16-17 Clement of Alexandria[Stromata Book I.10]

02:17 Alexander of Alexandria[Epistles on Arian Heresy 2.5]; Cyprian[Epistle LXXII.15; Treatise III.34, XII.Book III.78]; Tertullian[On Prescription Against Heretics 3, 7]

02:17-18 Josephus[Antiquities 18.1.4 16-17; War 2.8.14 162-166]; Irenaeus[Against Heresies Book II.31.2]

02:18 Acts 2:31n; Nag Hammadi[Gospel of Philip 73; Gospel of Thomas 51; Treatise on the Resurrection 49]; NT-Apocrypha[Acts of Paul and Thecla 1.14; Acts of Paul in Philippi 1.2]

02:19 Leviticus 24:16; Numbers 16:5; Job 36:10; Isaiah 26:13, 28:16; OT-Apocrypha[Sirach 17:26, 23:10, 35:3]; Constitutions of the Holy Apostles[Book II.54]; Tertullian[On Prescription Against Heretics 3; To his Wife Book I.4]

02:20 Cyprian[Epistle L.3, LI.25]

02:20-21 Origen[Against Celsus Book IV.70; De Principiis Book II.9.8, III.1.20]

02:22 Luke 8:15n; Pseudepigrapha[Letter of Aristeas 1.234]; Clement of Alexandria[Stromata Book IV.17, VI.12, VII.3, 10]

02:23 Clement of Alexandria[Stromata Book V.1]; Irenaeus[Against Heresies Book IV.Preface.3]

02:23-24 Cyprian[Treatise XII.Book III.53]

02:24 Cyprian[Epistle LXXIII.10]; Zephyrinus[First Epistle; Second Epistle 1.1]

02:26 NT-Apocrypha[Narrative of Joseph 3]

03:01 Tertullian[On Fasting 12]

03:01-03 Hippolytus[Treatise on Christ and Antichrist 27]

03:01-05 Pseudepigrapha[Testament of Dan 5:4]; Tertullian[On Modesty 1]

03:01-09 Cyprian[Treatise I.16]

03:02 Clement of Alexandria[Stromata Book I.17]

03:03-04 Constitutions of the Holy Apostles[Book II.43]

03:04 Alexander of Alexandria[Epistles on Arian Heresy 1.13]

03:05 Anterus[Epistle]; Clement[First Epistle Concerning Virginity 3]

03:05-06 Apostolic[Polycarp - Letter to the Philippians 6:3]

03:06 Archelaus[Disputation with Manes 38]; Irenaeus[Against Heresies Book I.13.3]

03:06-07 Origen[Against Celsus Book VI.24]

03:07 Exodus 7:11; Irenaeus[Against Heresies Book IV.9.3, V.20.2]

03:08 Exodus 7:11, 22; Pseudepigrapha[Life of Abraham 47:1; Testament of Solomon 25:4]; Dead Sea Scrolls[Damascus Document (CD-A) COL V 18-21]; Philo[**On the Migration of Abraham (83) cf. {Exodus 7:11-12}**]; Rabbinic[Targum Jonathan cf. {Exodus 7:11-8:19}]; Apostolic[Ignatius - Letter to the Ephesians 16:1-2]; Anterus[Epistle]; Constitutions of the Holy Apostles[Book VIII.1]; Origen[Against Celsus Book IV.51]; Tertullian[On Idolatry 9]

> **Do you not see that conjurors and enchanters, who attempting to contend against the divine word with their sophistries, and who daring to endeavor to do other things of a similar kind, labor not so much to display their own knowledge, as to tear to pieces and turn into ridicule what was Done? For they even transform their rods into the nature of serpents, and change water into the complexion of blood, and by their incantations they attract the remainder of the frogs to the land, and, like miserable men as they are, they increase everything for their own destruction, and while thinking to deceive others they are deceived themselves. (Philo - On the Migration of Abraham (83) cf. {Exodus 7:11-12})**

03:08-09 Archelaus[Disputation with Manes 36, 45]

03:11 Psalms 34:19-20; Acts 13:14-14:20; Pseudepigrapha[Psalms of Solomon 4:23]; Origen[Gospel of John Book I.5]; NT-Apocrypha[Acts of Paul in Ephesus p.3]

03:12 Cyprian[Treatise VII.8]; Justin[Dialogue with Trypho 110]; Origen[Gospel of Matthew Book X.18]

03:13 Cyprian[Treatise VI.7]

03:15 Psalms 119:98; Revelation 12:10n

03:15-17 Clement of Alexandria[Exhortation to the Heathen 9]

03:16 Philo[On the Migration of Abraham (35)]; Apostolic[1Clement 45:2]; Origen[Gospel of John Book I.5]; Tertullian[On the Apparel of Women Book I.3]; NT-Apocrypha[Canon Muratori Line 18-20]

04:01 Irenaeus[Against Heresies Book IV.20.2]; Justin[Dialogue with Trypho 118]; NT-Apocrypha[Apocalypse of Peter 1.1; Epistula Apostolorum 16]

04:01-04 Tertullian[On Prescription Against Heretics 37]

04:03 Irenaeus[Against Heresies Book II.21.2]

04:03-04 Cyprian[Treatise XII.Book III.67]; Origen[Gospel of John Book X.13]

04:04-05 Pseudepigrapha[Apocalypse of Elijah 1:13]

04:05 Pseudepigrapha[2Enoch 50:3]

04:06 Tertullian[Scorpiace 13]

04:06-08 Cyprian[Epistle VIII.1; Treatise XII.Book III.16]

04:07 Pseudepigrapha[Sibylline Oracles 2.39]; Constitutions of the Holy Apostles[Book VIII.41]

04:07-08 1Corinthians 9:24-27n; Archelaus[Disputation with Manes 35]

04:08 OT-Apocrypha[Wisdom of Solomon 5:16]; Pseudepigrapha[2Baruch 15:8; Apocryphon of Ezekiel Fragment 1 2:6; Greek Apocalypse of Ezra 6:17; Testament of Benjamin 4:1]; Apostolic[2Clement 7:1-3, 20:1-4; Martyrdom of Polycarp 17:1]; Hippolytus[Treatise on Christ and Antichrist 31]; Tertullian[Of Patience 14; The Chaplet, or De Corona 15]; NT-Apocrypha[Freer Logion]

04:09 NT-Apocrypha[Acts of Paul in Philippi 1.16]

04:10 2Corinthians 8:23; Galatians 2:3; Colossians 4:14; Philemon 1:24; Titus 1:4; Apostolic[Polycarp - Letter to the Philippians 9:2]; NT-Apocrypha[Acts of Paul and Thecla 1.1; Martyrdom of the Holy Apostle Paul 1.1]

04:10-11 Irenaeus[Against Heresies Book III.14.1]

04:11 Acts 12:12, 25, 13:13, 15:37-39; Colossians 4:10, 14; Philemon 1:24

04:12 Acts 20:4; Ephesians 6:21-22; Colossians 4:7-8

04:13 Acts 20:6; Tertullian[On Prayer 15; The Chaplet, or De Corona 8]

04:14 2Samuel 03:39; 1Timothy 1:20; NT-Apocrypha[Acts of Paul and Thecla 1.1]

04:14-15 Psalms 62:12-13; Proverbs 24:12

04:15 Psalms 28:4

04:17 Psalms 22:22; Daniel 6:21, 28; OT-Apocrypha[1Maccabees 2:60]; Pseudepigrapha[Joseph and Aseneth 12:11]

04:18 Pseudepigrapha[4Maccabees 18.24]

04:19 Acts 18:2; 2Timothy 1:16-17; NT-Apocrypha[Acts of Paul and Thecla 1.2]

04:20 Acts 19:22, 20:4, 21:29; Romans 16:23

04:21 Irenaeus[Against Heresies Book III.3.3]; NT-Apocrypha[Acts of Paul in Philippi 1.1]

Cross Reference Index: Titus

01:02 Jude 1:21n; Pseudepigrapha[Odes of Solomon 3:10]; Irenaeus[Against Heresies Book II.16.4]

01:04 John 1:18n; 2Corinthians 8:23; Galatians 2:3; 2Timothy 4:10

01:05 Acts 15:2-6n

01:05-06 Origen[Gospel of Matthew Book XIV.22]; Tertullian[On Exhortation to Chastity 7]

01:06 Clement of Alexandria[Stromata Book III.18]; Constitutions of the Holy Apostles[Book VI.17]; Tertullian[To his Wife Book I.7]

01:06-09 1Timothy 3:2-7; Tertullian[On Monogamy 12]

01:07 Apostolic[1Clement 42:4-5]; Clement[First Epistle Concerning Virginity 13]; Cyprian[Epistle LXVII.5]

01:09-10 Origen[Against Celsus Book III.48]

01:10 Clement of Alexandria[Stromata Book I.8]

01:12 Greek[Epimenides, de Oraculis]; Plato[Laws VIII 831d]; Origen[Against Celsus Book III.43]; Socrates Scholasticus Book 3.16; Tatian[Address to the Greeks 27]; Tertullian[A Treatise on the Soul 20]

01:12-13 Clement of Alexandria[Stromata Book I.14]

01:15 Clement of Alexandria[Stromata Book III.18]; Cyprian[Epistle LVIII.4]; Hippolytus[Refutation of all Heresies Book IX.21]; Novatian[On the Jewish Meats 5]; Origen[Gospel of Matthew Book XI.12]; Tertullian[The Chaplet, or De Corona 10]

01:15-16 Tertullian[Five Books in Reply to Marcion Book II.48]

01:16 Psalms 14:1; Clement of Alexandria[Stromata Book IV.9]; NT-Apocrypha[Epistula Apostolorum 39]

02:03-05 Clement of Alexandria[Stromata Book IV.20]

02:05 Pseudepigrapha[Testament of Dan 6:2]

02:07 Peter of Alexandria[Canonical Epistle 10]

02:11 Genesis 35:7; 1Peter 1:10-13n; Revelation 12:10n; OT-Apocrypha[2Maccabees 3:30; 3Maccabees 6:9]

02:11-13 Clement of Alexandria[Exhortation to the Heathen 1]

02:12 Pseudepigrapha[Apocalypse of Elijah 1:15; Aristobulus Fragment 4:8]; Socrates Scholasticus Book 3.16

02:13 Hippolytus[Treatise on Christ and Antichrist 66]

02:14 Exodus 19:5; Deuteronomy 4:20, 7:6, 14:2, 26:18; Psalms 130:8; Ezekiel 37:23; 1Peter 2:9; Apostolic[1Clement 33:1; Polycarp - Letter to the Philippians 6:3]; Clement of Alexandria[Stromata Book I.18]

03:01 Apostolic[1Clement 2:7]; Constitutions of the Holy Apostles[Book IV.13]; Tertullian[On Idolatry 15]

03:02 Cyprian[Treatise XII.Book III.107]

03:03-05 Clement of Alexandria[Exhortation to the Heathen 1]

03:03-06 Origen[Against Celsus Book I.64]

03:03-07 Pseudepigrapha[Testament of Job 25:1]

03:04 Psalms 31:20; OT-Apocrypha[Wisdom of Solomon 1:6]

03:05 Deuteronomy 9:5; Pseudepigrapha[Hellenistic Synagogal Prayers 10:8; Joseph and Aseneth 8:9]; Cyprian[Epistle LXXIII.6]; Methodius[Banquet of the Ten Virgins 3.1, 3.8; Oration Concerning Simeon and Anna 8]; Origen[Gospel of Matthew Book XIII.27-28]; Tertullian[On Modesty 1]

03:06 Joel 2:28, 3:1

03:07 Jude 1:21n

03:08 Matthew 5:16n

03:09 Archelaus[Fragment of the Disputation with Manes 3]; Tertullian[On Prescription Against Heretics 7]

03:10 Dionysius of Alexandria[Exegetical Fragments Commentary on the Beginning of Ecclesiastes 3.7]; Irenaeus[Against Heresies Book I.16.3, III.3.4]

03:10-11 Cyprian[Epistle LIV.21; Treatise XII.Book III.78]; Origen[Against Celsus Book V.63]; Tertullian[On Prescription Against Heretics 6, 15]
03:11 Cyprian[Epistle LXXIII.2]
03:12 Acts 20:4; Ephesians 6:21-22; Colossians 4:7-8; 2Timothy 4:12
03:13 Acts 18:24; 1Corinthians 16:12

Cross Reference Index: Philemon

01:02 Colossians 4:17
01:03 John 1:18n
01:09 NT-Apocrypha[Acts of Paul in Philippi 3.1]
01:10 Colossians 4:9
01:23 Colossians 1:7, 4:12
01:24 Acts 12:12, 25, 13:13, 15:37-39, 19:29, 27:2; Colossians 4:10, 14; 2Timothy 4:10-11

Cross Reference Index: Hebrews

01:01 Hosea 12:10; Acts 3:18n; Rabbinic[Jerusalem Berakhot 12d, 13a]; Clement of Alexandria[Fragments from Eusebius Ecclesiastical History Book VI.6.14, VII.6.14; Fragments from the Latin Translation of Cassiodorus Comments on 1Peter; Stromata Book I.4, V.6, VI.7, 10, VII.16]; Methodius[Banquet of the Ten Virgins 4.1, 5.7]; Origen[Letter to Africanus 10]; NT-Apocrypha[Epistula Apostolorum 3, 19]

01:01-02 Origen[Gospel of John Book II.6]

01:02 Psalms 2:8; Jeremiah 23:20; Lactantius[Divine Institutes Book IV.2]

01:03 Job 7:21; Psalms 110:1, 113:5; 1Peter 3:22n; OT-Apocrypha[Wisdom of Solomon 7:25]; Pseudepigrapha[Life of Adam and Eve Vita 39.1-3; Odes of Solomon 36:4; Testament of Job 33:3]; Alexander of Alexandria[Epistles on Arian Heresy 1.12, 2.3]; Clement of Alexandria[Stromata Book VII.3, 10]; Gregory Thaumaturgus[Four Homilies 4]; Hippolytus[Refutation of all Heresies Book X.29; The Discourse on the Holy Theophany 7]; Irenaeus[Against Heresies Book I.2.6, 5.1, II.16.4, 6-7, 30.9]; Lactantius[Divine Institutes Book IV.29]; Methodius[Oration Concerning Simeon and Anna 10]; Origen[Against Celsus Book VIII.12; De Principiis Book I.2.5, 7-8, IV.1.28]; Tertullian[An Answer to the Jews 9; Five Books in Reply to Marcion Book V.269]; NT-Apocrypha[Epistula Apostolorum 3; Kerygma Petri 2a]

01:03-04 Apostolic[1Clement 36:2]

01:03-06 Nag Hammadi[Teachings of Silvanus 112-113]

01:03-08 Tatian[Address to the Greeks 7]

01:04 Pseudepigrapha[Prayer of Joseph Fragment A]

01:04-06 NT-Apocrypha[Gospel of Judas 48]

01:04-14 Pseudepigrapha[Sibylline Oracles 7.33]

01:05 2Samuel 7:14; 1Chronicles 17:13; Psalms 2:7; Apostolic[1Clement 36:4]; Origen[Gospel of John Book I.32]

01:05-06 Nag Hammadi[Gospel of Truth 37; Prayer of the Apostle Paul A.I; Tripartite Tractate 125]

01:06 Deuteronomy 32:43; Psalms 89:28, 97:7; Matthew 28:17n; Pseudepigrapha[Life of Adam and Eve Vita 14:1]; Dead Sea Scrolls[4Q369(4QPEnosh) 4QPrayer of Enosh COL II 6-8]; Justin[Dialogue with Trypho 138]; NT-Apocrypha[Gospel of the Hebrews Fragment 2]

01:07 Psalms 104:4; Pseudepigrapha[2Enoch 29:1, 39:5; 4Ezra 8:20-22]; Apostolic[1Clement 36:3]; Origen[De Principiis Book II.8.3]

01:08 Irenaeus[Demonstration of the Apostolic Preaching 47]

01:08-09 Psalms 45:6-7

01:09 Nag Hammadi[Gospel of Philip 74]

01:10-12 Psalms 102:25-28

01:11 Isaiah 50:9, 51:6; Origen[Gospel of John Book X.18]

01:12 Isaiah 34:4

01:13 Psalms 110:1; Apostolic[1Clement 36:5]

01:14 Psalms 34:8-9, 91:11; Daniel 7:10; Revelation 12:10n; Pseudepigrapha[Life of Adam and Eve Vita 14:1]; Athenagoras[Plea for the Christians 10]; Origen[Against Celsus Book V.3, VIII.34; Gospel of Matthew Book XII.13; De Principiis Book I.5.1, III.3.5]; Tertullian[A Strain of Sodom 38; Five Books Against Marcion Book II.9]; NT-Apocrypha[Apocalypse of Paul 1.10]

02:01 Origen[De Principiis Book III.2.4]

02:02 Tertullian[Five Books Against Marcion Book IV.34]

02:04 NT-Apocrypha[Epistula Apostolorum 30]

02:05 Deuteronomy 32:8; OT-Apocrypha[Sirach 17:17]; Cyprian[Epistle LXVI.4]

02:05-09 Tertullian[An Answer to the Jews 14]

02:06-08 Psalms 8:4-7

02:09 1Peter 1:10-13n; Rabbinic[Babylonian Sanhedrin 43b]; Origen[Gospel of John Book I.40, II.6]

02:09-11 Dead Sea Scrolls[1Q Rule of the Community (1QS) COL III 6-12]; Philo[Special Laws I (201-204) cf. {Leviticus 1:4}]; Irenaeus[Against Heresies Book V.6.1]; Nag Hammadi[Gospel of Truth 21]

02:10 Revelation 12:10n; Tertullian[On Exhortation to Chastity 12]
02:11 Exodus 31:13; Clement of Alexandria[Exhortation to the Heathen 11]; Origen[Gospel of John Book I.39]
02:12 Psalms 22:22-23
02:13 2Samuel 22:3; Isaiah 8:17-18, 12:2
02:14 Apostolic[Papias Fragment 24:1]
02:14-15 Origen[Gospel of Matthew Book XIII.8-9]
02:16 Isaiah 41:8-9; Methodius[Oration Concerning Simeon and Anna 13]
02:17 Exodus 4:16; 1Samuel 2:35; Hebrews 7:26-28n; Justin[Dialogue with Trypho 96, 115-116]
03:01 Hebrews 7:26-28n; Justin[Dialogue with Trypho 96, 115-116]
03:02 Numbers 12:7; 1Chronicles 17:14; Psalms 149:2; Isaiah 17:7; Apostolic[1Clement 17:5]; Clement of Alexandria[Stromata Book IV.17]
03:02-06 Nag Hammadi[Prayer of the Apostle Paul B.I]
03:04 Isaiah 40:28
03:05 Numbers 12:7; Joshua 1:2; Apostolic[1Clement 43:1]; Clement of Alexandria[Stromata Book IV.17]; Irenaeus[Against Heresies Book III.6.5]
03:05-06 Archelaus[Disputation with Manes 41]
03:07-04:13 Pseudepigrapha[Joseph and Aseneth 8:9; Odes of Solomon 11:12]
03:07-11 Psalms 95:7-11; Gregory Thaumaturgus[Sectional Confession of Faith 23]
03:08 Exodus 15:23, 17:7; Numbers 20:2-5
03:09 Deuteronomy 6:16
03:11 Numbers 14:21-23
03:11-18 Pseudepigrapha[Apocalypse of Elijah 2:53]
03:12 Jeremiah 16:12, 18:12
03:14 Origen[Letter to Gregory 3]
03:15 Psalms 95:7-8
03:16 Exodus 17:1
03:16-18 Numbers 14:1-35
03:18 Psalms 95:11
04:01 Pseudepigrapha[Odes of Solomon 25:12]
04:01-11 Pseudepigrapha[Apocalypse of Elijah 2:53]
04:03 Psalms 95:11; Pseudepigrapha[2Baruch 73:1; 2Enoch 53:3]
04:04 Genesis 2:2
04:05 Psalms 95:11
04:07 Psalms 95:7-8
04:08 Deuteronomy 31:7; Joshua 22:4
04:08-09 Clement of Alexandria[Stromata Book II.22]
04:09 NT-Apocrypha[5Ezra 2.24]
04:10 Genesis 2:2
04:10-11 Nag Hammadi[Dialogue of the Savior 1]
04:12 Isaiah 49:2; OT-Apocrypha[Wisdom of Solomon 7:22-30, 18:15]; Pseudepigrapha[2Baruch 83:3; Ahiqar 2.18; Odes of Solomon 12:5; Pseudo-Phocylides 124]; Justin[Dialogue with Trypho 91]; Origen[Gospel of John Book I.36]; Nag Hammadi[Gospel of Truth 26]
04:12-13 Tertullian[An Answer to the Jews 9]
04:13 Pseudepigrapha[1Enoch 9:5]; Melito[Fragments 9.9]
04:14 John 3:18n; Methodius[Banquet of the Ten Virgins 9.4]; Origen[Against Celsus Book VIII.34; Gospel of John Book I.3, 23]
04:14-15 Hebrews 7:26-28n; Justin[Dialogue with Trypho 96, 115-116]
04:14-05:10 Apostolic[Ignatius - Letter to the Philadelphians 9:1]
04:15 Pseudepigrapha[Psalms of Solomon 17:36]; Archelaus[Disputation with Manes 42]; Origen[De Principiis Book II.6.4]; Tertullian[On Prescription Against Heretics 3]; Nag Hammadi[Tripartite Tractate 115]; NT-Apocrypha[Extract From the Life of John according to Serapion]
04:16 1Peter 1:10-13n
05:01 Exodus 18:19; Hebrews 7:26-28n
05:01-03 Liturgy of James 27
05:01-10 Dead Sea Scrolls[11Q Melchizedek (11Q13[11QMELCH]) COL II 7-14]
05:03 Leviticus 9:7, 16:6, 15
05:04 Exodus 28:1; Constitutions of the Holy Apostles[Book III.10]

05:05 Psalms 2:7; Hebrews 7:26-28n; Constitutions of the Holy Apostles[Book II.27]

05:05-10 Justin[Dialogue with Trypho 33, 96, 115-116]; Tertullian[An Answer to the Jews 14]

05:06 Psalms 110:4; OT-Apocrypha[1Maccabees 14:41]; Irenaeus[Demonstration of the Apostolic Preaching 48]; Justin[Dialogue with Trypho 113]; Lactantius[Divine Institutes Book IV.14]; Origen[Gospel of John Book I.3]

05:06-10 Pseudepigrapha[2Enoch 71:33-35]

05:07 Psalms 22:25; Matthew 26:36-46; Mark 14:32-42; Luke 22:39-46; Novatian[Treatise Concerning the Trinity 31]; Tertullian[On Repentance 9]; Nag Hammadi[Teachings of Silvanus 108-109, 114]

05:09 Isaiah 45:17; Revelation 12:10n

05:09-14 Pseudepigrapha[Testament of Solomon 3:5]

05:10 Psalms 110:4; Hebrews 7:26-28n; Justin[Dialogue with Trypho 113]; Tertullian[An Answer to the Jews 2]

05:11 Clement of Alexandria[Exhortation to the Heathen 10]

05:11-13 Philo[**Every Good Man Is Free (160)**]

> And all the souls which are not as yet partakers of either of these two classes, neither of that which is enslaved, nor of that by which prudence is confirmed, but which are still naked like those of completely infant children; those we must nurse and cherish carefully, prescribing for them at first tender food instead of milk, namely, instruction in the encyclical sciences, and after that stronger food, such as is prepared by philosophy, by which they will be strengthened so as to become manly, and in good condition, and conducted on to a favourable end, not more that are recommended by you than enjoined by the oracle, "To live in conformity to nature." (Philo - Every Good Man Is Free 160)

05:11-14 John 6:31-58n; Tertullian[On Monogamy 11]

05:12 Pseudepigrapha[1Enoch 61:7]; Origen[Gospel of John Book I.20]

05:12-14 1Peter 2:2; Apostolic[Shepherd of Hermas 27:1]; Clement of Alexandria[Stromata Book V.10, VI.8]; Origen[Against Celsus Book III.53]; Nag Hammadi[Gospel of Philip 81]

05:13 1Corinthians 3:2; Philo[On Husbandry (9-11) cf. {Genesis 9:20}]; Apostolic[Polycarp - Letter to the Philippians 9:1]

05:13-14 Clement of Alexandria[Stromata Book I.11]

05:14 Genesis 2:17, 3:5; Clement of Alexandria[Stromata Book I.6, VII.1]; Lactantius[Divine Institutes Book VII.26]; Origen[Against Celsus Book VI.13]

06:01 Pseudepigrapha[Joseph and Aseneth 9:2]; Clement of Alexandria[Stromata Book V.10, VI.14]; Tertullian[On Modesty 19]

06:02 Matthew 3:5-16n; Acts 2:31n, 8:18n; Cyprian[Epistle LXXII.24]

06:04 Theognostus[Seven Books of Hypotyposes or Outlines 3]

06:04-06 Justin[Fragments from the Lost Writings of Justin 3-4]

06:04-08 Tertullian[On Modesty 19]

06:05 Joshua 21:45, 23:15

06:06 Ezekiel 18:24; John 3:18n; Rabbinic[Shemoth Rabba xiii. 3, p. 24b cf. {Exodus 9:16, 10:1}]; Tertullian[On Modesty 9]

06:07 Genesis 1:11; Deuteronomy 11:11

06:08 Genesis 3:17-18; 1Samuel 15:29; Archelaus[Disputation with Manes 5]

06:09 Revelation 12:10n

06:11-20 Clement of Alexandria[Stromata Book II.22]

06:12 Pseudepigrapha[Psalms of Solomon 12:6]

06:13 Philo[**Allegorical Interpretation III (204-205) cf. {Genesis 22:16-17; Numbers 12:7}**]

But some men have said that it is inconsistent with the character of God to swear at all; for that an oath is received for the sake of the confirmation which it supplies; but God is the only faithful being, and if any one else who is dear to God; as Moses is said to have been faithful in all his House. And besides, the mere words of God are the most sacred and holy of oaths, and laws, and institutions. And it is a proof of his exceeding power, that whatever he says is sure to take place; and this is the most especial characteristic of an oath. So that it would be quite natural to say that all the words of God are oaths confirmed by the accomplishment of the acts to which they relate. They say, indeed, that an oath is a testimony borne by God concerning a matter which is the subject of doubt. But if God swears he is bearing testimony to himself, which is an absurdity. For the person who bears the testimony, and he on whose behalf it is borne, ought to be two different persons. What, then, are we to say? In the first place, that it is not a matter of blame for God to bear testimony to himself. For what other being could be competent to bear testimony to him? In the second place, He himself is to himself every thing that is most honorable--relative, kinsman, friend, virtue, prosperity, happiness, knowledge, understanding, beginning, end, entirety, universality, judge, opinion, intention, law, action, supremacy. (Philo - Allegorical Interpretation III (204-205) cf. {Genesis 22:16-17; Numbers 12:7})

06:13-14 Genesis 22:16-17
06:13-18 Pseudepigrapha[Testament (Assumption) of Moses 3:9]
06:14 OT-Apocrypha[Sirach 44:21]
06:16 Exodus 22:10-11
06:18 Numbers 23:19
06:18-19 2Corinthians 3:12-18n
06:19 Leviticus 16:2-3, 12
06:20 Psalms 110:4; 2Corinthians 3:12-18; Hebrews 7:26-28n
06:20-07:17 Pseudepigrapha[2Enoch 71:33-35]
06:20-07:28 Justin[Dialogue with Trypho 33]
06:20-08:04 Justin[Dialogue with Trypho 96, 113, 115-116]
07:01 Pseudepigrapha[Hellenistic Synagogal Prayers 12:10]; Clement of Alexandria[Stromata Book
    IV.25]; Justin[Dialogue with Trypho 113]
07:01-02 Genesis 14:17-20
07:01-03 Tertullian[Against All Heresies 8; An Answer to the Jews 2]
07:01-21 Rabbinic[Babylonian Nedarim 32b cf. {Genesis 14:18-19; Psalms 110:1-4}]
07:02 Clement of Alexandria[Stromata Book II.5]
07:03 Psalms 110:4; John 3:18n; Pseudepigrapha[Apocalypse of Abraham 17:10; Testament of Job 33:7];
    Lactantius[Divine Institutes Book IV.13]; NT-Apocrypha[Fragments of a Dialogue between John
    and Jesus]
07:04 Genesis 14:20
07:05 Genesis 35:11; Numbers 18:21
07:07-08 Origen[De Principiis Book III.1.10]
07:10 Genesis 14:17; Tertullian[An Answer to the Jews 2]
07:10-28 Dead Sea Scrolls[11Q Melchizedek (11Q13[11QMELCH]) COL II 7-14]
07:11 Psalms 110:4; Justin[Dialogue with Trypho 113]; Origen[Gospel of John Book I.3]
07:14 Genesis 49:10; Isaiah 11:1; Julius Africanus[Epistle to Aristides 1]
07:15 Psalms 110:4; Tertullian[An Answer to the Jews 2]
07:15-17 Justin[Dialogue with Trypho 113]
07:17 Psalms 110:4; Tertullian[An Answer to the Jews 2]
07:19 Tertullian[Five Books in Reply to Marcion Book IV.208]
07:21 Psalms 110:4; Hippolytus[Refutation of all Heresies Book V.19, 22]
07:22 OT-Apocrypha[Sirach 29:14]
07:25 Pseudepigrapha[Hellenistic Synagogal Prayers 4.22, 6.13]
07:26-28 This section also includes topical notes for: High Priest Forever - 1Timothy 2:5; Hebrews
    2:17, 3:1, 4:14-15, 5:1, 5, 10, 6:20, 8:1-3, 9:11, 24-26; Pseudepigrapha[Hellenistic Synagogal Prayers
    7:4; Testament of Levi 8.14]; Philo[On Dreams, That they Are God-Sent (1.215, 2.229-2.231) cf.

{Genesis 1:1, 32:24-32, Leviticus 16:17, Deuteronomy 10:10, Psalms 2.7, 33:6, 119:1-176}; On Flight
And Finding (106-112, 117-118) cf. {Exodus 28:32, Leviticus 10:6, 36, 21:11, Numbers 35:2-34, Psalms
119:160}; Special Laws I (81, 85-87, 97, 244) cf. {Exodus 28:4-42, Leviticus 9:7-14, Psalms 33:6}];
Clement of Alexandria[Exhortation to the Heathen 12; Stromata Book II.5, VII.2-3; The Instructor
Book II.8]; Nag Hammadi[A Valentinian Exposition 25]

07:26-08:01 Tertullian[On Modesty 22]

07:27 Exodus 29:38; Leviticus 9:7, 16:6, 11, 15; Numbers 28:3; Pseudepigrapha[Pseudo-Philo 32.2-4]

08:01 Psalms 110:1; 1Peter 3:22n; Pseudepigrapha[Testament of Job 33:3]; NT-Apocrypha[Epistula
Apostolorum 3, 51]

08:01-03 Hebrews 7:26-28n

08:01-05 Pseudepigrapha[Sibylline Oracles 4.10]

08:02 Numbers 24:6; Pseudepigrapha[2Baruch 4:3]; Lactantius[Divine Institutes Book IV.25]

08:05 This section also includes topical notes for: Pattern that was Showed to Moses - Exodus 25:39-
40; Colossians 02:16-17; Hebrews 10:01; Pseudepigrapha[2Baruch 59:3; 4Ezra 2.39-40; Jubilees 1.4-5,
1.26; Odes of Solomon 11.4-12; Sibylline Oracles 1.333; Testament of Job 48:2]; Philo[Appendices A
Treatise Concerning the World (1); Concerning Noah's Work as a Planter (27)]; Plato[Sophist 266b-c;
Republic VII 514a-517a, 532b-c]; Archelaus[Disputation with Manes 30]; Clement of
Alexandria[Stromata Book I.26, VI.9, 11; The Instructor Book I.7]; Clement[Recognitions Book I.40];
Irenaeus[Against Heresies Book II.14.3, 16.1, 3, 23.1, 30.9, IV.11.4, 14.3, 20.1, 32.2, V.35.2;
Demonstration of the Apostolic Preaching 9, 40]; Justin[Hortatory Address to the Greeks 29];
Methodius[Banquet of the Ten Virgins 5.7]; Origen[Gospel of John Book VI.32, X.27; De Principiis
Book II.6.7, III.6.8, IV.1.13, 24]; Tertullian[Five Books Against Marcion Book V.11]; Nag Hammadi[A
Valentinian Exposition 35-36; Allogenes 60; Gospel of Philip 67, 84-85; Hypostasis of the Archons
87, 96; Teachings of Silvanus 99; Trimorphic Protennoia 42]

08:08 Irenaeus[Demonstration of the Apostolic Preaching 90]

08:08-09 NT-Apocrypha[Kerygma Petri 2d]

08:08-10 Clement of Alexandria[Stromata Book VI.5]

08:08-12 Jeremiah 31:31-34

08:09 Exodus 19:5

08:10 Pseudepigrapha[4Ezra 1:29]

08:10-12 Clement of Alexandria[Exhortation to the Heathen 11]

08:11 Tertullian[On Repentance 6]

08:13 Archelaus[Disputation with Manes 13]; Lactantius[Divine Institutes Book IV.20]

09:01 Pseudepigrapha[Testament of Job 48:2]

09:02 Exodus 25:23-40, 26:1-30; 2Chronicles 13:11

09:03 Exodus 26:31-33; Tertullian[Five Books in Reply to Marcion Book IV.148]

09:03-04 Tertullian[Five Books in Reply to Marcion Book IV.149]

09:04 Exodus 16:33, 25:10-16, 21, 30:1-6; Numbers 17:8-10, 25; Deuteronomy 9:9, 10:3-5;
Methodius[Oration Concerning Simeon and Anna 9]

09:05 Exodus 25:18-22

09:06 Numbers 18:2-6

09:07 Exodus 30:10; Leviticus 16:2-34; Tertullian[Five Books in Reply to Marcion Book IV.177]

09:09 Hippolytus[Refutation of all Heresies Book IX.21]

09:10 Leviticus 11:2, 25, 15:18, 19:13; Numbers 19:13; Origen[Gospel of Matthew Book XIV.20]

09:11 Hebrews 7:26-28n; Pseudepigrapha[Sibylline Oracles 4.10]; Justin[Dialogue with Trypho 96, 115-
116]

09:11-12 Tertullian[Five Books in Reply to Marcion Book IV.208]

09:11-20 Tertullian[On Modesty 11]

09:12 Daniel 9:24

09:13 Leviticus 16:3, 14-16, 17:11; Numbers 19:9, 17-19; Tertullian[Five Books in Reply to Marcion Book
IV.91]

09:14 Matthew 28:19n; Clement of Alexandria[Stromata Book III.7]; Hippolytus[Refutation of all
Heresies Book IX.21]; Origen[Gospel of John Book VI.32]

09:14-20 Apostolic[1Clement 7:4]

09:15 Jeremiah 31:31; Acts 20:32n; Pseudepigrapha[Testament of Dan 6:2]; Rabbinic[Babylonian
Sanhedrin 43b]; Clement of Alexandria[The Instructor Book I.5, III.1]; Irenaeus[Fragments from the
Lost Works 27]; Justin[Dialogue with Trypho 34, 67, 118, 122]

09:19 Leviticus 14:4; Numbers 19:6; Tertullian[Five Books in Reply to Marcion Book IV.103]

09:19-20 Exodus 24:3-8
09:19-22 Tertullian[Five Books in Reply to Marcion Book IV.87]
09:21 Exodus 40:9; Leviticus 8:15, 19, 17:11
09:22 Leviticus 17:11
09:24-26 Hebrews 7:26-28n
09:26 Pseudepigrapha[4Ezra 2.34-35; Testament of Job 4:6; Testament of Levi 18:9; Testament of
   Reuben 6:8]; Justin[Dialogue with Trypho 117]; Origen[De Principiis Book II.3.5]; Tertullian[To his
   Wife Book I.2]
09:27 Genesis 3:19; Pythagoras[Golden Verses Line 15]; Indian[Dhammapada 128]
09:28 Isaiah 53:12; Pseudepigrapha[Martyrdom and Ascension of Isaiah (3:13-4:22 = Testament of
   Hezekiah) 4:13; Testament of Job 48:2]; Rabbinic[Babylonian Sanhedrin 97b]; Irenaeus[Against
   Heresies Book IV.33.1]; Justin[Dialogue with Trypho 40, 52, 110-111, 120; First Apology 52]
10:01 Hebrews 08:05; Philo[On Husbandry (131-135, 142-145) cf. {Leviticus 11:4}; Special Laws I (166-
   167) cf. {Exodus 12:5, 29:1, Leviticus 1:3-10, 3:1-6, 4:3-32, 5:15-18, 6:6, 9:2-3, 14:10, 22:19, 23:12-18,
   Numbers 6:16, 28:19, 29:2, 8, 13-36}; Special Laws IV (106-113) cf. {Leviticus 11:3, Deuteronomy
   14:10}; Who Is the Heir of Divine Things (239) cf. {Leviticus 11:21}]; Apostolic[Epistle of Barnabas
   10:1-12]; Irenaeus[Against Heresies Book IV.11.4]; Origen[Gospel of Matthew Book X.15, XI.12,
   XII.5]; Tertullian[Five Books in Reply to Marcion Book IV.82, 207-208]
10:01-09 Nag Hammadi[Gospel of Philip 54]
10:01-14 Pseudepigrapha[Testament of Job 33:7]
10:03 Leviticus 16:34; Numbers 5:15
10:04 Leviticus 16:15, 21; Isaiah 1:11
10:05-09 Psalms 40:6-9
10:06 Leviticus 4:14
10:10 Nag Hammadi[Dialogue of the Savior 2]
10:11 Exodus 29:38; Deuteronomy 10:8, 18:7
10:11-12 NT-Apocrypha[Epistula Apostolorum 51]
10:12-13 Psalms 110:1
10:14 Nag Hammadi[Dialogue of the Savior 2]
10:16-17 Jeremiah 31:33-34
10:20 Liturgy of James 27; Nag Hammadi[Trimorphic Protennoia 47]
10:21 Zechariah 6:11; Justin[Dialogue with Trypho 96, 115-116]
10:22 Exodus 29:4; Leviticus 8:6, 30, 16:4; Isaiah 38:3; Ezekiel 36:25; Hippolytus[Refutation of all
   Heresies Book IX.21]; Tertullian[Apology 30]
10:23 Apostolic[2Clement 11:6]
10:25 Ezekiel 7:4
10:26 NT-Apocrypha[Epistula Apostolorum 50]
10:26-27 Clement of Alexandria[Stromata Book II.13]
10:26-29 Tertullian[On Baptism 8]
10:26-31 Philo[**Fragments Extracted From The Parallels Of John Of Damascus Page 343. D.**]

> **When a man rightly establishes himself in a virtuous life, with meditation, and practice,
> and good government, and when having been known by all men as a pious man and one
> who fears God, he falls into sin, that is a great fall, for he has ascended up to the height
> of heaven, and fallen down into the abyss of hell. (Philo - Fragments Extracted From The
> Parallels Of John Of Damascus Page 343. D.)**

10:27 Isaiah 26:11; Zephaniah 1:18
10:28 Numbers 35:30; Deuteronomy 17:6, 19:15; Psalms 109:12; Theodotus[Excerpts 13]
10:29 Exodus 24:8; Zechariah 12:40; John 3:18n; 1Peter 1:10-13n; Apostolic[1Clement 7:4];
   Origen[Against Celsus Book VIII.10]
10:30 Deuteronomy 32:35-36; Psalms 135:14; Anonymous[Treatise Against the Heretic Novatian 7];
   Dionysius of Alexandria[Extant Fragments Epistle to Fabius Bishop of Antioch 2]; Lactantius[Divine
   Institutes Book VI.18]; Tertullian[Of Patience 10; Five Books Against Marcion Book IV.16]
10:30-32 Pseudepigrapha[2Enoch 50:3-4]
10:32 Methodius[Banquet of the Ten Virgins 3.8]
10:32-39 Clement of Alexandria[Stromata Book IV.16]
10:33-34 Syriac Teaching of the Apostles
10:34 Pseudepigrapha[Joseph and Aseneth 12:15]

10:37 Isaiah 26:20; Apostolic[1Clement 23]

10:37-38 Habakkuk 2:3-4

10:38 Tertullian[On Exhortation to Chastity 7]

11:01-02 Clement of Alexandria[Stromata Book II.2]

11:01-40 Clement of Alexandria[Stromata Book IV.17]

11:03 Genesis 1:1-31; Psalms 33:6-9; John 1:1-18n; Pseudepigrapha[2Baruch 14:17; 54:17; 2Enoch 24:2, 25:1; 48:5; Joseph and Aseneth 12:2]

11:03-04 Clement of Alexandria[Stromata Book II.4]

11:04 Genesis 4:3-10; Tertullian[An Answer to the Jews 2]

11:05 Genesis 5:21-24; OT-Apocrypha[Sirach 44:16; Wisdom of Solomon 4:10]; Pseudepigrapha[1Enoch 70:1-4; 2Enoch 1:1]; Apostolic[1Clement 10]; Tertullian[A Treatise on the Soul 50; An Answer to the Jews 2]

11:06 Exodus 3:14; OT-Apocrypha[Wisdom of Solomon 10:17]; Clement of Alexandria[Stromata Book II.2]

11:07 Genesis 6:8, 13-7:1; Psalms 37:29; Ezekiel 14:14, 20; Tertullian[An Answer to the Jews 2]; Nag Hammadi[Teachings of Silvanus 108-109, 114]

11:08 Genesis 12:1-5, 15:7; Acts 20:32n

11:08-16 Pseudepigrapha[Testament of Job 18:4]

11:08-17 Justin[Dialogue with Trypho 92]

11:09 Genesis 12:8, 13:12, 23:4, 26:3, 35:12, 27; Pseudepigrapha[Joseph and Aseneth 24:14; Testament of Abraham rec.A 8:6]; Tertullian[An Answer to the Jews 1]

11:10 Luke 6:48-49n; OT-Apocrypha[2Maccabees 4:1; Wisdom of Solomon 13:1]; Pseudepigrapha[4Ezra 10:27; Testament of Job 39:12]; Alexander of Alexandria[Epistles on Arian Heresy 2.3]; Methodius[Banquet of the Ten Virgins 5.7]

11:10-16 John 14:2; Pseudepigrapha[4Ezra 7.4-18]; Dead Sea Scrolls[1Q Rule of the Community (1QS) COL II 21-25]; Philo[On Abraham (62-63) cf. {Genesis 12:1-4}; On Dreams, That they Are God-Sent (1.255-1.256) cf. {Genesis 32:24-32}; On Flight And Finding (75-76, 175) cf. {Numbers 35:6, 9-32, Deuteronomy 6:10-11, 33:27}; On Husbandry (64-66) cf. {Genesis 46:31-47:4}; On the Birth of Abel And the Sacrifices offered By Him And By His Brother Cain (124-130) cf. {Numbers 35:6-32, Joshua 20:2-3, 21:13-38}; On the Confusion of Tongues (77-78, 82, 107-109) cf. {Genesis 11:4, 23:4, 47:9, Exodus 2:22}; Philo[**On the Giants (61)**; Special Laws II (44-48) cf. {Leviticus 23:2}]; Plato[**Republic IX 592a-b**]; Clement of Alexandria[Exhortation to the Heathen 10]; Justin[Dialogue with Trypho 119]; Nag Hammadi[Gospel of Thomas 49]; Indian[Dhammapada 415]

> **...those who are born of God are priests and prophets, who have not thought fit to mix themselves up in the constitutions of this world, and to become cosmopolites, but who having raised themselves above all the objects of the mere outward senses, have departed and fixed their views on that world which is perceptible only by the intellect, and have settled there, being inscribed in the state of incorruptible incorporeal ideas. (Philo - On the Giants 61)**

> **You mean that he will be a ruler in the city of which we are the founders, and which exists in idea only; for I do not believe that there is such an one anywhere on earth? In heaven, I replied, there is laid up a pattern of it, I think, which he who desires may behold, and beholding, may set his own house in order. But whether such an one exists, or ever will exist in fact, is no matter; for he will live after the manner of that city, having nothing to do with any other. (Plato - Republic IX 592a-b)**

11:11 Genesis 17:19, 18:11-14, 21:2

11:12 Genesis 15:5-6, 22:17, 32:12-13; Exodus 32:13; Deuteronomy 1:10, 10:22; Isaiah 51:2; OT-Apocrypha[Sirach 44:21]; Pseudepigrapha[Greek Apocalypse of Ezra 2:32]

11:13 Genesis 23:4, 24:37, 47:9; 1Chronicles 29:15; Psalms 39:13; Irenaeus[Against Heresies Book V.32.2]; Tertullian[On Exhortation to Chastity 12]

11:13-16 Pseudepigrapha[Apocalypse of Elijah 1:10-13]

11:14-16 Apostolic[Shepherd of Hermas 50:1-3; Epistle to Diognetus 5:5-16]

11:16 Exodus 3:6, 15, 4:5; Origen[Gospel of John Book II.11]

11:17 Genesis 22:1-24; OT-Apocrypha[1Maccabees 2:52; Sirach 44:20]; Apostolic[1Clement 10]

11:18 Genesis 21:12

11:20 Genesis 27:27-29, 38-40

11:21 Genesis 47:31-48:20; Linguistics[Hebrew phrase for "Top of the Staff" (מטהף) is written the same as "Head of the Bed" (מטהף) found in Genesis 47:31]

11:22 Genesis 50:24-25; Exodus 13:19

11:23 Exodus 1:22, 2:2; Methodius[Banquet of the Ten Virgins 7.5]

11:24 Exodus 2:10-12; Pseudepigrapha[Ezekiel the Tragedian 41]

11:24-26 Origen[De Principiis Preface 1]

11:25 OT-Apocrypha[4Maccabees 15:2, 8]; Clement of Alexandria[Stromata Book II.4]

11:26 Psalms 69:10, 89:51; Romans 11:33n

11:27 Exodus 2:15, 12:51; Numbers 12:8; OT-Apocrypha[Sirach 2:2]

11:28 Exodus 12:21-30, 48; 2Kings 23:21; OT-Apocrypha[Wisdom of Solomon 18:25]

11:29 Exodus 14:21-31

11:30 Joshua 6:12-21

11:31 Joshua 2:1-21, 6:17, 21-25; Apostolic[1Clement 12]

11:32 Judges 4:6, 6:11, 12:7, 13:24, 15:20; 1Samuel 3:20, 7:15, 16:10; Clement of Alexandria[Stromata Book II.4]; Peter of Alexandria[Canonical Epistle 9]

11:32-38 Tertullian[An Answer to the Jews 13]

11:33 Judges 4:15, 7:22, 11:33, 14:6-7; 1Samuel 17:34-36; 2Samuel 8:15; Psalms 15:2; Daniel 6:1-27

11:34 Judges 16:28; 1Samuel 17:49, 52; 1Kings 19:10; Psalms 46:7; Daniel 3:23-25

11:35 1Kings 17:17-24; 2Kings 4:25-37; Acts 2:31n; OT-Apocrypha[2Maccabees 6:18-7:42]

11:36 1Kings 22:26-27; 2Chronicles 18:25-26, 36:16; Jeremiah 20:1-18, 37:1-38:28

11:36-37 Cyprian[Epistle VIII.1]

11:36-40 Clement of Alexandria[Stromata Book IV.16]

11:37 1Kings 19:10, 13, 19, 2:26; 2Kings 2:8, 13; 2Chronicles 24:21; Jeremiah 26:23; Pseudepigrapha[Ascension of Isaiah 5:11-14; Lives of the Prophets 1:1; Martyrdom and Ascension of Isaiah 5:11-14]; Apostolic[1Clement 17:1]; Constitutions of the Holy Apostles[Book V.16]; Origen[Gospel of Matthew Book X.18; Letter to Africanus 9]; NT-Apocrypha[Apocalypse of Paul 1.49]

11:37-38 Origen[Against Celsus Book VII.7, 18]

11:38 Judges 6:2; 1Samuel 13:6; 1Kings 18:4, 19:4; Pseudepigrapha[Apocalypse of Daniel 14:9]

11:39-40 Pseudepigrapha[Apocalypse of Elijah 1:13]

11:40 Psalms 37:13; Tertullian[On the Veiling of Virgins 1]

12:01 OT-Apocrypha[4Maccabees 16:16, 17:10-15]; Pseudepigrapha[Sibylline Oracles 2.39]; Apostolic[Ignatius - Letter to Polycarp 1:2-3]

12:01-02 Clement of Alexandria[Stromata Book IV.16]

12:02 Psalms 110:1; 1Peter 3:22n; Tertullian[Five Books in Reply to Marcion Book II.216]; NT-Apocrypha[Epistula Apostolorum 3]

12:03 Numbers 17:3; Deuteronomy 20:3

12:04 OT-Apocrypha[2Maccabees 13:14]

12:04-11 Pseudepigrapha[2Baruch 13:10]

12:05 Deuteronomy 8:5

12:05-06 Proverbs 3:11-12; Clement of Alexandria[Stromata Book I.5]; Tertullian[Of Patience 11]

12:06 Job 5:17; Apostolic[1Clement 56:4]; Clement of Alexandria[The Instructor Book I.9]; Cyprian[Epistle VII.5]; Origen[De Principiis Book III.1.12]

12:06-08 This section also includes topical notes for: Chastisement from God - 2Samuel 7:14; Matthew 27:26; Mark 15:15; John 19:1; Revelation 3:19; Pseudepigrapha[Life of Adam and Eve Vita 34.1-3]; Philo[**On Mating With the Preliminary Studies (177) cf. {Proverbs 3:11-12}**]

It is from this consideration, as it appears to me that one of the disciples of Moses, by name the peaceful, who in his native language is called Solomon, says, "My son, neglect not the instruction of God, and be not grieved when thou art reproved by him; for whom the Lord loves he chastens; and scourges every son whom he received." Thus, then, scourging and reproof are looked upon as good, so that by means of it agreement and relationship with God arise. For what can be more nearly related than a son is to his father, and a father to his son? (Philo - On Mating With the Preliminary Studies (177) cf. {Proverbs 3:11-12})

12:07 Pseudepigrapha[Psalms of Solomon 10:2, 14:1]
12:08 Constitutions of the Holy Apostles[Book II.8]
12:09 Numbers 16:22, 27:16; OT-Apocrypha[2Maccabees 3:24]
12:12 Job 4:3; Isaiah 35:3; OT-Apocrypha[Sirach 25:23]
12:13 Proverbs 4:26
12:14 Psalms 34:15
12:15 Deuteronomy 29:17-18; 1Peter 1:10-13n; Methodius[Discourse on the Resurrection 1.5]
12:16 Genesis 25:29-34
12:17 Genesis 27:30-40; Matthew 27:3-5; OT-Apocrypha[Wisdom of Solomon 12:10]
12:18 Exodus 19:12
12:18-19 Exodus 19:16-22, 20:18-21; Deuteronomy 4:11-12, 5:22-27
12:20 Exodus 19:12-13
12:21 Deuteronomy 9:19; OT-Apocrypha[1Maccabees 13:2]; Clement of Alexandria[Exhortation to the Heathen 9]
12:22 Psalms 74:2; Pseudepigrapha[4Baruch 5:35; Martyrdom and Ascension of Isaiah (3:13-4:22 = Testament of Hezekiah) 3:15]; Origen[Against Celsus Book VII.29]; NT-Apocrypha[Epistula Apostolorum 33]
12:22-23 Origen[Against Celsus Book VIII.5; Gospel of John Book X.11; Gospel of Matthew Book XII.20; De Principiis Book IV.1.22]
12:22-24 Pseudepigrapha[Testament of Dan 6:2; Testament of Job 48:2]
12:23 Genesis 18:25; Psalms 50:6; Pseudepigrapha[1Enoch 22:9]; Clement of Alexandria[Stromata Book VI.14]; Constitutions of the Holy Apostles[Book II.25]
12:24 Genesis 4:10; Tertullian[On the Veiling of Virgins 1]
12:25 Exodus 20:19
12:26 Exodus 19:18; Judges 5:4; Psalms 68:9, 77:19, 114:7; Haggai 2:6, 21
12:26-27 Tertullian[On Monogamy 16]
12:27 Isaiah 66:22
12:28 Daniel 7:14, 18; Pseudepigrapha[2Enoch la:4]
12:29 Deuteronomy 4:24, 9:3; Isaiah 33:14; Philo[The Decalogue (48-49) cf. {Exodus 19:16-19}]; Hippolytus[Refutation of all Heresies Book V.27]; Origen[Against Celsus Book VI.70]; Nag Hammadi[Gospel of Truth 25]

It is, therefore, with great beauty, and also with a proper sense of what is consistent with the dignity of God, that the voice is said to have come forth out of the fire; for the oracles of God are accurately understood and tested like gold by the fire. And God also intimates to us something of this kind by a figure. Since the property of fire is partly to give light, and partly to burn, those who think fit to show themselves obedient to the sacred commands shall live for ever and ever as in a light which is never darkened, having his laws themselves as stars giving light in their soul. But all those who are stubborn and disobedient are for ever inflamed, and burnt, and consumed by their internal appetites, which, like flame, will destroy all the life of those who possess them. (Philo - The Decalogue (48-49) cf. {Exodus 19:16-19})

13:02 Genesis 18:1-8, 19:1-3; Judges 6:11, 13:3; Pseudepigrapha[Pseudo-Phocylides 24-25; Testament of Abraham 2:2; Testament of Job 23:2]; Plato[Republic II 381d]; Tertullian[On Prayer 26]
13:04 Pseudepigrapha[Pseudo-Phocylides 1.177-178]; Clement of Alexandria[Stromata Book IV.20]; Clement[First Epistle Concerning Virginity 4]; Constitutions of the Holy Apostles[Book VI.28]

13:05 Genesis 28:15; Deuteronomy 31:6, 8; Joshua 1:5; Pseudepigrapha[Pseudo-Phocylides 6]; Clement of Alexandria[Stromata Book II.20]

13:06 Psalms 118:6-7; Pseudepigrapha[Odes of Solomon 7:3]

13:07 OT-Apocrypha[Sirach 33:19; Wisdom of Solomon 2:17]; Apostolic[Didache 4:1]; Clement[First Epistle Concerning Virginity 6]; Teaching of the Twelve Apostles 4.1

13:08 Psalms 102:28; Plato[Republic II 383a]; Alexander of Alexandria[Epistles on Arian Heresy 2.3]; Irenaeus[Against Heresies Book II.34.2, IV.11.2]

13:08-09 1Peter 1:10-13n

13:09 Apostolic[Ignatius - Letter to the Magnesians 8:1]

13:09-14 Pseudepigrapha[Testament of Job 20:7]

13:10-13 Tertullian[An Answer to the Jews 14]

13:11 Leviticus 6:23, 16:27

13:12 Apostolic[1Clement 7:4]

13:12-13 Tertullian[Five Books in Reply to Marcion Book IV.113]

13:13 Exodus 33:7; Leviticus 24:14; Numbers 15:35

13:14-16 Clement of Alexandria[Stromata Book IV.20]

13:15 Leviticus 7:12; 2Chronicles 29:31; Psalms 34:2, 50:14, 23; Isaiah 57:19; Hosea 14:2, 13; Pseudepigrapha[4Ezra 2.47; Odes of Solomon 8:2; Psalms of Solomon 15:2-3]; Irenaeus[Fragments from the Lost Works 37]; Teaching of the Twelve Apostles 14.2

13:17 Isaiah 62:6; Ezekiel 3:17; Apostolic[1Clement 21]

13:18 Hippolytus[Refutation of all Heresies Book IX.21]

13:20 Exodus 24:8; Isaiah 55:3, 61:8, 63:11; Jeremiah 32:40, 50:5; Ezekiel 16:60, 37:26; Zechariah 9:11; John 10:11-14n; Pseudepigrapha[Testament of Dan 5:2]; Epic of Gilgamesh[The Coming of Enkidu]

13:21 Pseudepigrapha[4Maccabees 18.24]; Clement of Alexandria[Stromata Book VI.14, VII.7-10]

13:22 Pseudepigrapha[2Baruch 81:1]

Cross Reference Index: James

01:01 Jeremiah 15:7; Matthew 13:55; Mark 6:3; Acts 15:13; Galatians 1:19; OT-Apocrypha[2Maccabees 1:27]; Nag Hammadi[Gospel of Thomas 12]; NT-Apocrypha[Epistula Apostolorum 30]

01:02 OT-Apocrypha[Sirach 2:1; Wisdom of Solomon 3:4]; Pseudepigrapha[2Baruch 52:6]

01:03 Proverbs 27:21; OT-Apocrypha[4Maccabees 1:11]; Pseudepigrapha[Testament of Joseph 10:1]; NT-Apocrypha[Epistula Apostolorum 36]

01:04 OT-Apocrypha[4Maccabees 15:7]; Clement of Alexandria[Stromata Book VI.14]

01:05 Proverbs 2:3-6; Clement[First Epistle Concerning Virginity 11]

01:08 Pseudepigrapha[Apocalypse of Elijah 1.26-27]

01:09-10 Lactantius[Divine Institutes Book V.16]

01:10 NT-Apocrypha[Epistula Apostolorum 46]

01:10-11 Psalms 102:4, 11; Isaiah 40:6-7

01:11 Job 14:2

01:12 1Corinthians 9:24-27n; Daniel 12:12; Pseudepigrapha[2Baruch 15:8; 2Enoch 50:3; Apocalypse of Elijah 1:8, 14; Greek Apocalypse of Ezra 6:17; Testament of Benjamin 4:1]; Apostolic[2Clement 7:1-3, 20:1-4; Martyrdom of Polycarp 17:1]; Constitutions of the Holy Apostles[Book II.8]; Tertullian[The Chaplet, or De Corona 15]; Nag Hammadi[Gospel of Thomas 58; Testimony of Truth 44]

01:13 OT-Apocrypha[Sirach 15:11-20]; Dionysius of Alexandria[Exegetical Fragments An Exposition of Luke 22.46; Exegetical Fragments Gospel According to Luke - An Interpretation 22.46]; Tertullian[On Prayer 8]

01:14 Pseudepigrapha[1Enoch 98:4]

01:15 Pseudepigrapha[Life of Adam and Eve (Apocalypse of Moses) 19:3]

01:17 Psalms 136:7; Pseudepigrapha[2Enoch 33:4; Joseph and Aseneth 12:15; Life of Adam and Eve (Apocalypse of Moses) 36:3]; Nag Hammadi[Gospel of Truth 35; Letter of Peter to Philip 133]

01:18 Psalms 119:43; Methodius[Oration on the Psalms 7]

01:19 Proverbs 15:1; Ecclesiastes 5:1, 7:9; OT-Apocrypha[Sirach 5:11]; Pseudepigrapha[Pseudo-Phocylides 57]

01:19-20 Fabian[Third Epistle]

01:21 OT-Apocrypha[Sirach 3:17]; Pseudepigrapha[Hellenistic Synagogal Prayers 11:3]; Irenaeus[Against Heresies Book V.10.1]; Nag Hammadi[Dialogue of the Savior 2]

01:22 Pseudepigrapha[Apocalypse of Zephaniah 10:8]

01:23 Ezekiel 33:32; Pseudepigrapha[Odes of Solomon 13:1; Testament of Job 33:8]

01:25 Psalms 19:8; Pseudepigrapha[Hellenistic Synagogal Prayers 11:3]; Irenaeus[Against Heresies Book III.5.3, IV.13.2-3, 16.5]

01:26 Psalms 34:14, 39:1, 141:3

01:27 Psalms 10:14, 18; Zechariah 7:9-10; Pseudepigrapha[4Ezra 2.20-24; Apocalypse of Elijah 1:2; Sibylline Oracles 2.76]; Clement of Alexandria[Stromata Book VI.9; Who is the Rich Man that shall be Saved 34]; Clement[First Epistle Concerning Virginity 12]; Irenaeus[Against Heresies Book IV.17.3]; Nag Hammadi[Sentences of Sextus 340]; NT-Apocrypha[5Ezra 2.21]; Egyptian Book of the Dead[Oration 125]

02:01 Job 34:19; NT-Apocrypha[Acts of Peter and Paul; Epistula Apostolorum 24, 46]

02:01-06 Pseudepigrapha[Sibylline Oracles 2.90-94]

02:01-08 Lactantius[Divine Institutes Book V.16]

02:01-26 1John 3:17-18; Philo[On Dreams, That they Are God-Sent (2.302) cf. {Exodus 7:15, Deuteronomy 30:14}; On the Posterity of Cain And His Exile (85-88) cf. {Deuteronomy 30:14}]

02:02-09 Nag Hammadi[Acts of Peter and the Twelve Apostles 11-12]

02:05 Pseudepigrapha[Apocalypse of Elijah 1:14]

02:05-07 Nag Hammadi[Gospel of Thomas 54]

02:06 Proverbs 14:21

02:07 Deuteronomy 28:10; Jeremiah 14:9; Pseudepigrapha[Apocalypse of Adam 3:18]

02:08 Leviticus 19:18; Matthew 5:43n; Clement of Alexandria[Stromata Book VI.18]; Tertullian[On the Apparel of Women Book II.2]; Nag Hammadi[Sentences of Sextus 179]

02:09 Leviticus 19:15; Deuteronomy 1:17

02:10 OT-Apocrypha[4Maccabees 5:20]

02:10-12 Apostolic[Ignatius - Letter to the Magnesians 8:1]

02:11 Exodus 20:13-14; Deuteronomy 5:17-18; John 8:3-11n; Pseudepigrapha[Life of Abraham 11:10]

02:12 Irenaeus[Against Heresies Book III.5.3, IV.13.2-3, 16.5]

02:13 OT-Apocrypha[Tobit 4:10]; Cyprian[Epistle LXXII.23]; Hippolytus[Appendix to the Works of Hippolytus - On the End of the World 47]

02:14 Urban I[Epistle Introduction]

02:15 Pseudepigrapha[Vision of Ezra 6]

02:16 Judges 18:6; NT-Apocrypha[Epistula Apostolorum 51]

02:19 Deuteronomy 6:4; NT-Apocrypha[Acts of John 78; Acts of Paul in Ephesus p.1]

02:21 Genesis 22:1-14

02:22 Clement of Alexandria[Stromata Book VI.14]

02:23 Genesis 15:6; 2Chronicles 20:7; Isaiah 41:8; OT-Apocrypha[Wisdom of Solomon 7:27]; Pseudepigrapha[Apocalypse of Abraham 9:7; Apocalypse of Zephaniah 9:5; Jubilees 19:9; Testament of Abraham 1:6]; Apostolic[1Clement 10]; Clement of Alexandria[Stromata Book II.5]; Irenaeus[Against Heresies Book IV.13.4, 16.2]; Tertullian[An Answer to the Jews 2; Of Patience 6]

02:25 Joshua 2:1-21, 15, 6:17

03:01 Tertullian[Five Books in Reply to Marcion Book IV.6; The Martyrdom of Perpetua and Felicitas 4]

03:01-02 Urban I[Epistle Introduction]

03:01-12 Dead Sea Scrolls[1QRule of the Community (1QS) COL X 21 - XI 2]

03:02 OT-Apocrypha[Sirach 14:1]; Clement of Alexandria[Stromata Book VI.14]; Clement[First Epistle Concerning Virginity 11]; Lactantius[Divine Institutes Book VI.13]; Peter of Alexandria[Genuine Acts of Peter 3]; NT-Apocrypha[Gospel of the Nazareans Fragment 15a]

03:03 Psalms 32:9

03:05 Pseudepigrapha[Pseudo-Phocylides 144]

03:06 Proverbs 16:27; OT-Apocrypha[Sirach 5:13]; Pseudepigrapha[1Enoch 48:7; The Sentences of the Syriac Menander 424]

03:07 Genesis 9:2; Pseudepigrapha[Testament of Job 3:3]

03:08 Psalms 140:4; Tertullian[Of Patience 6]

03:09 Genesis 1:26; 1Chronicles 29:10; Isaiah 63:16; OT-Apocrypha[Sirach 23:1, 4]; Pseudepigrapha[2Enoch 44:1]

03:10 OT-Apocrypha[Sirach 5:13, 28:12]

03:11 Pseudepigrapha[Joseph and Aseneth 16:16]

03:13 OT-Apocrypha[Sirach 3:17]; Urban I[Epistle Introduction]

03:15 Clement[First Epistle Concerning Virginity 11]

03:17 Matthew 6:2-16n, 7:16-21n

03:18 Isaiah 32:17; NT-Apocrypha[Protoevangelium of James 6.2]

04:01 Pseudepigrapha[Apocalypse of Elijah 1:16]

04:02 OT-Apocrypha[1Maccabees 8:16]; Pseudepigrapha[Greek Apocalypse of Ezra 1:14]

04:03 Clement of Alexandria[Stromata Book VII.7]

04:04 Isaiah 57:3; Pseudepigrapha[Apocalypse of Elijah 1:2]

04:05 Genesis 6:3; Exodus 20:5; Romans 8:9-11n; Apostolic[Ignatius - Letter to the Ephesians 15:3, Letter to the Philadelphians 7:2; Epistle of Barnabas 4:11, 6:14-15]

04:06 Job 22:29; Proverbs 3:34; Matthew 18:4n; 1Peter 1:10-13n; Pseudepigrapha[Letter of Aristeas 1.257; Joseph and Aseneth 6:8]; Apostolic[1Clement 30:1]; Anonymous[Treatise Against the Heretic Novatian 13]; Clement of Alexandria[Stromata Book III.6, IV.17]; Clement[First Epistle Concerning Virginity 8]

04:07 Pseudepigrapha[Testament of Naphtali 8:4]; Justin[Dialogue with Trypho 116]

04:08 Psalms 18:21, 25; Isaiah 1:16; Hosea 12:7; Zechariah 1:3; Malachi 3:7; Pseudepigrapha[Apocalypse of Elijah 1:26-27; Testament of Dan 6:2]

04:10 Job 5:11; Matthew 18:4n; Pseudepigrapha[Letter of Aristeas 1.263-264]

04:11 Psalms 101:5; OT-Apocrypha[Wisdom of Solomon 1:11]

04:12 Dionysius of Alexandria[Extant Fragments Epistle to Dionysius Bishop of Rome - Book II.10]

04:13 Pseudepigrapha[1Enoch 97:8-10]

04:13-14 Proverbs 27:1

04:13-15 Tertullian[On Exhortation to Chastity 12]

04:14 Psalms 39:6, 12; Hosea 13:3; Pseudepigrapha[2Baruch 14:10; 4Ezra 7.61; Hellenistic Synagogal Prayers 2:10; Pseudo-Phocylides 117]; Nag Hammadi[Gospel of Truth 21, 25]

04:17 Deuteronomy 23:22, 24:15; Origen[De Principiis Book I.3.6]

05:01-03 Pseudepigrapha[**1Enoch 94:7-8**]; Apostolic[2Clement 7:4-6]

> **Woe to those who build up their houses with crime; for from their very foundations shall their houses be demolished, and by the sword shall they themselves fall. Those, too, who acquire gold and silver, shall justly and suddenly perish. Woe to you who are rich, for in your riches have you trusted; but from your riches you shall be removed; because you have not remembered the Most High in the days of your prosperity. (Pseudepigrapha - 1Enoch 94:7-8)**

05:02 Job 13:28; Isaiah 51:8; Revelation 16:15; Pseudepigrapha[Joseph and Aseneth 2:4]

05:02-03 Matthew 6:19-20

05:03 Psalms 21:10; OT-Apocrypha[Judith 16:17; Sirach 29:10]; Pseudepigrapha[2Baruch 23:7]

05:04 Genesis 4:10; Leviticus 19:13; Deuteronomy 24:14-15; Psalms 18:7; Isaiah 5:9; Malachi 3:5; OT-Apocrypha[Tobit 4:14]; Pseudepigrapha[Pseudo-Phocylides 19-21; Testament of Job 12:4]

05:05 Jeremiah 12:3, 25:34

05:06 Hosea 1:6; OT-Apocrypha[Wisdom of Solomon 2:10, 12, 19]

05:07 Deuteronomy 11:14; Jeremiah 5:24; Hosea 6:3; Joel 2:23; Pseudepigrapha[Testament of Abraham 13:4]

05:10 Daniel 9:6; OT-Apocrypha[4Maccabees 9:8]

05:11 Exodus 34:6; Job 1:21-22, 2:10, 42:11; Psalms 103:8, 111:4; Daniel 12:12; Pseudepigrapha[Testament of Job 1:5; 37:1]

05:12 Matthew 5:33-37n; Pseudepigrapha[2Enoch 49:1]; Josephus[War 2.8.6 135]; Clement of Alexandria[Stromata Book VII.11]; Clement[Homily XIX.2]; Tertullian[On Idolatry 11]; NT-Apocrypha[Testimony regarding the Recipients of the Epistle of Peter to James 1.2]

05:13 Pseudepigrapha[Psalms of Solomon 3:2]

05:14 Mark 6:13; Acts 15:2-6n; Pseudepigrapha[Life of Adam and Eve Vita 36:2; Testament of Adam 1:7]; Constitutions of the Holy Apostles[Book III.15]; Cyprian[Epistle LXIX.2]

05:15 Acts 26:18n; Plato[Republic II 364e]

05:15-20 Ephesians 4:32n

05:16 Teaching of the Twelve Apostles 4.14; NT-Apocrypha[Epistula Apostolorum 40]

05:17 1Kings 17:1; Tertullian[On Fasting 6]

05:17-18 Rabbinic[Babylonian Sanhedrin 113a]; Clement[Recognitions Book V.29]; Tertullian[On Prayer 29]

05:18 1Kings 18:42-45

05:19 NT-Apocrypha[Epistula Apostolorum 47]

05:20 Psalms 32:1, 51:15, 85:3; Proverbs 10:12; Apostolic[1Clement 49]; Clement of Alexandria[Stromata Book IV.18]

Cross Reference Index: First Peter

01:02 Exodus 24:7; Daniel 3:31, 6:26; Matthew 28:19n

01:03 Acts 2:31n; OT-Apocrypha[Sirach 16:12]; Clement of Alexandria[Fragments from the Latin Translation of Cassiodorus Comments on 1Peter]

01:04 Acts 20:32n; Pseudepigrapha[Joseph and Aseneth 12:15]; NT-Apocrypha[Freer Logion]

01:05 Revelation 12:10n

01:06 Clement of Alexandria[Fragments from the Latin Translation of Cassiodorus Comments on 1Peter]

01:06-09 Clement of Alexandria[Stromata Book IV.20]

01:07 This section also includes topical notes for: Tested Like Gold - Job 23:10; Psalms 66:10; Proverbs 17:3; Isaiah 48:10; Zechariah 13:9; Malachi 3:3; 1Corinthians 3:12-15; Revelation 3:18n; OT-Apocrypha[Sirach 2:5]; Pseudepigrapha[4Ezra 16:73]; Philo[Questions And Answers On Genesis III (15) cf. {Genesis 15:9-20}; The Decalogue (48-49) cf. {Exodus 19:16-19}]; Plato[Republic VI 502e-503a]; Clement of Alexandria[Stromata Book II.18, IV.16]; Irenaeus[Against Heresies Book V.29.1]; Justin[Dialogue with Trypho 116]; NT-Apocrypha[Epistula Apostolorum 36]; Indian[Dhammapada 230]

01:08 Apostolic[Polycarp - Letter to the Philippians 1:3]; Irenaeus[Against Heresies Book IV.9.2, V.7.2]

01:09 Origen[De Principiis Book II.8.3]; Nag Hammadi[Dialogue of the Savior 2]

01:09-10 Revelation 12:10n

01:10 Clement of Alexandria[Fragments from the Latin Translation of Cassiodorus Comments on 1Peter]; NT-Apocrypha[Epistula Apostolorum 19]

01:10-11 Acts 3:18-26n; Apostolic[Ignatius - Letter to the Magnesians 9:2, Letter to the Philadelphians 5:2, 9:2; Polycarp - Letter to the Philippians 6:3; Epistle of Barnabas 1:7, 3:6]

01:10-12 Dead Sea Scrolls[4Q Enoch (4Q201[4QENAR]) COL I 2-4]; NT-Apocrypha[Kerygma Petri 4a]

01:10-13 This section also includes topical notes for: Grace - Psalms 84:11; Proverbs 3:34; Zechariah 12:10; John 1:17; Acts 4:33, 6:8, 15:11, 18:27, 20:24, 32; Romans 1:5, 5:15; 2Corinthians 1:12, 8:9; Galatians 2:9; Ephesians 1:7, 2:5-8, 3:7-8, 4:7; Philippians 1:7; Colossians 1:6; 2Thessalonians 2:6; 2Timothy 1:9; Titus 2:11; Hebrews 2:9, 4:16, 10:29, 12:15, 13:8-9; James 4:6; 1Peter 4:10-11, 5:4-5; 2Peter 3:15-18; Pseudepigrapha[4Ezra 2.32, 7.133; Odes of Solomon 4.4, 5.3, 6.6, 7.10, 9.5, 11.1, 20.7, 9, 21.2, 23.2, 4, 24.13, 25.4, 29.2, 5, 31.3, 7, 33.1, 10, 34.6, 37.4, 41.3]; Philo[On The Unchangeableness of God (106-108) cf. {Genesis 6:8}]; Rabbinic[Babylonian Yoma 72b]; Anonymous[Martyrdom of Justin Martyr 3]; Clement of Alexandria[Exhortation to the Heathen 1, 9, 11; Fragments from Macarius Chrysocephalus Oration VIII on Matt VIII and Book VII on Luke XIII; Fragments from the Latin Translation of Cassiodorus Comments on 1Peter; Stromata Book V.11, 13, VI.18, VII.10; The Instructor Book I.6-8; Who is the Rich Man that shall be Saved 16, 21]; Cyprian[Epistle LXXV.14]; Irenaeus[Against Heresies Book I.6.4, 10.1, 23.3, 25.3, 28.3, 7, 32.4, 34.3, IV.11.3, 13.3, 20.7, 36.4, V.2.1, 22.2; Demonstration of the Apostolic Preaching 99; Fragments from the Lost Works 7]; Justin[Dialogue with Trypho 92, 100, 116, 119; Second Apology 13]; Nag Hammadi[Authoritative Teaching 32; Gospel of Mary 9; Gospel of Philip 58; Gospel of the Egyptians III. 61; Gospel of Truth 16, 34, 36; Interpretation of Knowledge 12, 15]; NT-Apocrypha[Epistula Apostolorum 6]

01:11 Psalms 22:1-31; Isaiah 53:1-12; Tertullian[On Baptism 11]; NT-Apocrypha[Kerygma Petri 4a]

01:12 Pseudepigrapha[1Enoch 1:2, 16:3; 2Enoch 24:3]; Clement of Alexandria[Fragments from the Latin Translation of Cassiodorus Comments on 1Peter; Who is the Rich Man that shall be Saved 23]; Irenaeus[Against Heresies Book II.16.9, IV.34.1, V.36.3]; Origen[Gospel of Matthew Book X.13]; NT-Apocrypha[Epistula Apostolorum 19]

01:13 Proverbs 31:17; Apostolic[Polycarp - Letter to the Philippians 2:1]; Clement of Alexandria[Fragments from the Latin Translation of Cassiodorus Comments on 1Peter]; Nag Hammadi[Letter of Peter to Philip 137]

01:14 Pseudepigrapha[Hellenistic Synagogal Prayers 7.14; Odes of Solomon 11.10]; Apostolic[Papias Fragment 15:1]; Clement of Alexandria[Exhortation to the Heathen 12; The Instructor Book I.2]; Nag Hammadi[Gospel of Philip 84; Gospel of Truth 17]

01:14-16 Clement of Alexandria[Stromata Book III.18]

01:15 Clement of Alexandria[Fragments from the Latin Translation of Cassiodorus Comments on 1Peter]; Clement[First Epistle Concerning Virginity 7]; Tertullian[On Monogamy 3]

01:16 Leviticus 11:44-45, 19:2, 20:7, 26; Tertullian[On Exhortation to Chastity 1]

01:17 2Chronicles 19:7; Psalms 28:4, 62:12, 89:27; Proverbs 24:12; Isaiah 59:18, 64:8; Jeremiah 3:19, 17:10; OT-Apocrypha[Sirach 23:4; Wisdom of Solomon 14:3]; Anonymous[Treatise on Re-Baptism 13]; Tertullian[On Exhortation to Chastity 7]

01:17-19 Clement of Alexandria[The Instructor Book III.12]

01:17-23 Clement of Alexandria[Fragments from the Latin Translation of Cassiodorus Comments on 1Peter]

01:18 Isaiah 52:3

01:18-19 Irenaeus[Against Heresies Book III.5.3]; Origen[Gospel of Matthew Book XII.28]

01:19 Apostolic[1Clement 7:4]; Constitutions of the Holy Apostles[Book II.57]; Justin[Dialogue with Trypho 40]; Tertullian[On Modesty 16]

01:20 Apostolic[Ignatius - Letter to the Ephesians (Prologue)]; Tertullian[On the Apparel of Women Book II.9]; NT-Apocrypha[Protoevangelium of James 7.2]

01:21 Apostolic[Polycarp - Letter to the Philippians 2:1]

01:21-22 Clement of Alexandria[Stromata Book III.18]

01:22 Luke 8:15n

01:23 Daniel 6:27; John 3:3-7n; Josephus[Discourse to the Greeks Concerning Hades 5-6]; Pythagoras[Golden Verses Lines 69-71]; Justin[Dialogue with Trypho 135]

01:23-25 NT-Apocrypha[Correspondence between Seneca and Paul XIV]

01:24 Hippolytus[Refutation of all Heresies Book V.5]

01:24-25 Isaiah 40:6-9

01:25 Clement of Alexandria[Fragments from the Latin Translation of Cassiodorus Comments on 1Peter]

02:01 Matthew 6:2-16n

02:01-03 Clement of Alexandria[The Instructor Book I.6]

02:02 Hebrews 5:12-14; Revelation 12:10n; Apostolic[Shepherd of Hermas 27:1]; Archelaus[Disputation with Manes 41]; Clement of Alexandria[The Instructor Book I.7]; Constitutions of the Holy Apostles[Book V.16]; Origen[Gospel of Matthew Book XII.31, XIII.26-28]; Nag Hammadi[Gospel of Philip 81]

02:03 Psalms 34:8-9; Pseudepigrapha[Odes of Solomon 19:1]; Irenaeus[Fragments from the Lost Works 36]

02:04 Psalms 118:22; Isaiah 28:16; Pseudepigrapha[Sibylline Oracles 1.345-6; Testament of Solomon 23:4]; Origen[Against Celsus Book VIII.19]

02:04-08 Tertullian[An Answer to the Jews 13-14]

02:04-09 This section also includes topical notes for: Elect – Mark 13:20; Romans 8:33, 9:11; 1Thessalonians 1:4; Pseudepigrapha[2Baruch 23.3-5, 48.20; 4Ezra 7.74, 9.13-23; Odes of Solomon 8.13, 18, 23.3, 33.13; Vision of Ezra 1.64-66]; Clement of Alexandria[Fragments from the Latin Translation of Cassiodorus Comments on 1John, 2John; Stromata Book IV.26, V.1, 6, 12-13, VI.7, 13, 15, VII.2, 5, 7, 10, 12; Who is the Rich Man that shall be Saved 36]; Irenaeus[Against Heresies Book I.6.4, IV.33.14]; Justin[Dialogue with Trypho 69; First Apology 45]; Nag Hammadi[A Valentinian Exposition 35-36; Gospel of Thomas 49-50; Gospel of Truth 21, 38; Treatise on the Resurrection 45; Tripartite Tractate 129-130]; NT-Apocrypha[Epistula Apostolorum 36-37]

02:05 Exodus 19:6; Isaiah 61:6; Apostolic[Ignatius - Letter to the Ephesians 9:1, 15:3]; Clement of Alexandria[Fragments from the Latin Translation of Cassiodorus Comments on 1Peter; Fragments from the Unpublished Disputation against Iconoclasts, of Nicephorus of Contantinople]; Irenaeus[Against Heresies Book V.34.3]; Lactantius[Divine Institutes Book IV.13]; Origen[Gospel of John Book X.20, 23]; Teaching of the Twelve Apostles 14.2; Tertullian[On Prayer 28]; Nag Hammadi[Teachings of Silvanus 104, 106, 109; Apocalypse of Peter 70:26-27]

02:05-10 Josephus[War 2.8.12 159]

02:06 Isaiah 28:16; Pseudepigrapha[Sibylline Oracles 8.254]; Irenaeus[Against Heresies Book III.5.3]; Methodius[Oration Concerning Simeon and Anna 6]

02:06-07 Matthew 21:42; Irenaeus[Against Heresies Book III.21.7]

02:06-08 Pseudepigrapha[Sibylline Oracles 8.246; Testament of Solomon 22:8]

02:07 Psalms 118:22; Pseudepigrapha[Testament of Solomon 23:4]; Apostolic[Epistle of Barnabas 6:4]

02:07-08 Clement of Alexandria[Stromata Book VI.15]

02:08 Isaiah 8:14-15; Tertullian[Five Books Against Marcion Book IV.13]

02:09 This section also includes topical notes for: Priests and Kings - Exodus 19:5-6, 23:22;
Deuteronomy 4:20, 7:6, 10:15, 14:2, 26:18; Isaiah 9:2, 42:12, 43:20-21, 61:6; Malachi 3:17; Titus 2:14;
Revelation 1:6; Pseudepigrapha[Joseph and Aseneth 8:9; Jubilees 16:19; Odes of Solomon 11.19];
Philo[On Abraham (56, 132) cf. {Genesis 18:3, Exodus 19:6}; On Flight And Finding (106-114) cf.
{Exodus 28:32, Leviticus 10:36, 21:11-14, Numbers 35:2-34}; On the Life of Moses II (274) cf. {Exodus
32:26}; Special Laws I (141-142) cf. {Leviticus 27:30-33, Numbers 35:2-8}; Special Laws II (164) cf.
{Leviticus 23:10-12}]; Clement of Alexandria[Exhortation to the Heathen 4; Fragments from the
Latin Translation of Cassiodorus Comments on 1Peter]; Clement[First Epistle Concerning Virginity
9]; Constitutions of the Holy Apostles[Book II.25, 57, III.15, VIII.12]; Irenaeus[Against Heresies Book
V.34.3]; Justin[Dialogue with Trypho 116]; Methodius[Oration Concerning Simeon and Anna 13];
Origen[Against Celsus Book V.10]; Teaching of the Twelve Apostles 13.3; Victorinus[Apocalypse
1.6]; Nag Hammadi[Teachings of Silvanus 109]; NT-Apocrypha[Epistula Apostolorum 21]

02:10 Hosea 1:6, 9, 2:1, 23, 25; Methodius[Banquet of the Ten Virgins 4.4]; Tertullian[An Answer to the
Jews 3]

02:11 Genesis 23:4; Psalms 39:13; Pseudepigrapha[Apocalypse of Elijah 1:17]; Apostolic[Didache 1:4;
Polycarp - Letter to the Philippians 5:3]; Constitutions of the Holy Apostles[Book VII.2]; Teaching of
the Twelve Apostles 1.4

02:11-12 Clement of Alexandria[Stromata Book III.11]; Cyprian[Epistle VI.3]

02:12 Isaiah 10:3; Matthew 5:16n; Romans 12:17; Pseudepigrapha[Joseph and Aseneth 20:7]; Dead Sea
Scrolls[4Q Isaiah Pesher (4Q161[4QPIS)) Fragment 1 COL II 2]; Rabbinic[Jerusalem Baba Mesia 8c];
Apostolic[Polycarp - Letter to the Philippians 10:2]; Clement of Alexandria[The Instructor Book
III.11]; Clement[First Epistle Concerning Virginity 2]

02:13 John 8:32; Romans 6:16; 1Corinthians 7:20; Rabbinic[Mekhilta On Exodus 20:2]; Constitutions of
the Holy Apostles[Book IV.13]; Tertullian[Scorpiace 14]

02:13-14 Pseudepigrapha[Letter of Aristeas 1.240-241]; Tertullian[On Idolatry 15]

02:15-16 Clement of Alexandria[Stromata Book III.11]

02:16 Irenaeus[Against Heresies Book IV.16.5, 37.4]

02:17 Proverbs 24:21; Pseudepigrapha[The Sentences of the Syriac Menander 9]; Apostolic[1Clement 2;
Polycarp - Letter to the Philippians 10:1]; Clement of Alexandria[Exhortation to the Heathen 10];
Tatian[Address to the Greeks 4]; Nag Hammadi[Teachings of Silvanus 108-109, 114]

02:18 Ephesians 6:5; Colosians 3:22; Clement of Alexandria[The Instructor Book III.11]; Constitutions
of the Holy Apostles[Book IV.11]

02:19 Pseudepigrapha[2Enoch 50:3, 51:3]; Hippolytus[Refutation of all Heresies Book IX.21]

02:20 Tertullian[Scorpiace 12]; Apostolic[Polycarp - Letter to the Philippians 8:2]; Cyprian[Treatise
X.11]

02:21-22 Justin[Dialogue with Trypho 67]

02:21-23 Cyprian[Treatise IX.9, XII.Book III.39]

02:22 Isaiah 53:9; Pseudepigrapha[Psalms of Solomon 17.36; Testament of Benjamin 3.8; Testament of
Judah 24.2]; Clement of Alexandria[The Instructor Book I.1, III.12]; Justin[Dialogue with Trypho
102]; Origen[Against Celsus Book I.69, IV.15]; Tertullian[An Answer to the Jews 10]

02:22-24 Apostolic[Polycarp - Letter to the Philippians 8:1]

02:23 Isaiah 53:7; Jeremiah 11:20; Constitutions of the Holy Apostles[Ecclesiastical Canons 47.28];
Irenaeus[Against Heresies Book III.16.9, IV.20.2]

02:24 Isaiah 53:5-12; Clement of Alexandria[Stromata Book II.15]; Justin[Dialogue with Trypho 17, 95,
137]

02:25 Job 10:12; Isaiah 53:6; Ezekiel 34:5-6, 16; OT-Apocrypha[Wisdom of Solomon 1:6];
Pseudepigrapha[Joseph and Aseneth 12:5]; Irenaeus[Fragments from the Lost Works 54]

03:01 1Corinthians 9:19; Colossians 3:18; Pseudepigrapha[Letter of Aristeas 1.227, 1.266];
Josephus[Antiquities 20.2.3 35]; Apostolic[1Clement 1:3]; Tertullian[To his Wife Book II.6]

03:01-04 Clement of Alexandria[The Instructor Book III.11]

03:01-06 Tertullian[On Prayer 20]

03:01-07 Ephesians 5:22-33n

03:03 1Timothy 2:9; Tertullian[The Chaplet, or De Corona 14]; NT-Apocrypha[Apocalypse of Peter 1.7]

03:03-04 Cyprian[Treatise II.8]

03:04 Cyprian[Treatise XII.Book III.36]

03:06 Genesis 18:12; Proverbs 3:25; Constitutions of the Holy Apostles[Book VI.29]

03:07 Ephesians 5:25; Colossians 3:19; Pseudepigrapha[Joseph and Aseneth 24:14]; Origen[Gospel of Matthew Book XIV.16]; Tertullian[Of Patience 5]

03:08 Matthew 18:4n; Clement of Alexandria[The Instructor Book III.11]; Justin[Dialogue with Trypho 81]

03:09 Matthew 5:44n; Pseudepigrapha[Apocalypse of Sedrach 7:9; Joseph and Aseneth 23:9]; Apostolic[Polycarp - Letter to the Philippians 2:2]; Tertullian[On Idolatry 21; On Prayer 11]; NT-Apocrypha[Acts of John 81; Acts of Thomas 1.58]

03:10 Clement of Alexandria[Fragments from the Latin Translation of Cassiodorus Comments on 1Peter]

03:10-12 Psalms 34:12-17

03:11 Tertullian[On Monogamy 6]

03:13 Isaiah 50:9; Apostolic[Polycarp - Letter to the Philippians 6:3]; Clement of Alexandria[The Instructor Book III.12]; Teaching of the Twelve Apostles 1.3

03:14 Matthew 5:10; Pseudepigrapha[2Enoch 51:3]; Nag Hammadi[Gospel of Thomas 58]

03:14-15 Isaiah 8:12-13

03:15 Origen[Against Celsus Book III.33, VII.12]

03:16 Hippolytus[Refutation of all Heresies Book IX.21]

03:18 Matthew 28:19n; Cyprian[Treatise XII.Book II.27]; Tertullian[On Modesty 22]

03:18-20 Pseudepigrapha[Martyrdom and Ascension of Isaiah 9:17]; Origen[Gospel of John Book VI.18]

03:18-21 Matthew 3:5-16n; Origen[De Principiis Book II.5.3]

03:19 Pseudepigrapha[1Enoch 9:10, 10:11-15; Life of Abraham 32:13; Sibylline Oracles 1.378, 8.310]; Hippolytus[Treatise on Christ and Antichrist 26]; Tertullian[A Treatise on the Soul 55]; NT-Apocrypha[Akhmim Fragment 10.41; Epistula Apostolorum 27]

03:19-20 Clement of Alexandria[Stromata Book VI.6]; Irenaeus[Against Heresies Book IV.27.2]

03:20 Genesis 6:1-7:24; Pseudepigrapha[Hellenistic Synagogal Prayers 12:59; Sibylline Oracles 1.205]; Apostolic[1Clement 7]; Constitutions of the Holy Apostles[Book VIII.12]; Irenaeus[Against Heresies Book I.18.3, IV.36.4]; Tertullian[Against All Heresies 2; On Monogamy 4]

03:20-21 Cyprian[Epistle LXXIII.11, LXXV.2]

03:21 Acts 2:31n; Romans 2:15n; Cyprian[Epistle LXXIV.15]; Hippolytus[Refutation of all Heresies Book IX.21]; Tertullian[On Modesty 9]

03:22 This section also includes topical notes for: Right Hand of God - Matthew 26:64; Mark 14:62n; Luke 22:69; Acts 2:33-34, 7:55-56; Romans 8:34; Colossians 3:1; Hebrews 1:3, 8:1, 12:2; Pseudepigrapha[Martyrdom and Ascension of Isaiah 1:4]; Apostolic[Martyrdom of Polycarp 14:1]; Gregory Thaumaturgus[Twelve Topics on the Faith 6]; Irenaeus[Against Heresies Book I.30.14, III.5.3; Demonstration of the Apostolic Preaching 38, 85; Fragments from the Lost Works 54]; Justin[Dialogue with Trypho 32, 36]

04:02 Pseudepigrapha[Testament of Abraham 12:14]

04:03 Clement of Alexandria[Stromata Book VI.16; The Instructor Book III.12]

04:05 Apostolic[2Clement 1:1]; Clement of Alexandria[Fragments from the Latin Translation of Cassiodorus Comments on 1Peter]; Irenaeus[Against Heresies Book IV.20.2]; NT-Apocrypha[Apocalypse of Peter 1.1; Epistula Apostolorum 16]

04:06 Pseudepigrapha[Life of Abraham 32:13; Sibylline Oracles 8.310]; Cyprian[Treatise XII.Book II.27]; Nag Hammadi[Interpretation of Knowledge 20]

04:07 Pseudepigrapha[2Baruch 23:7]; Apostolic[Polycarp - Letter to the Philippians 7:2]

04:08 Psalms 32:1; Proverbs 10:12; Pseudepigrapha[Apocalypse of Sedrach 1:2]; Apostolic[1Clement 49:5; 2Clement 16:4]; Clement of Alexandria[Fragments from the Latin Translation of Cassiodorus Comments on 1John, 2John; Stromata Book I.27, II.15, IV.18; The Instructor Book III.12; Who is the Rich Man that shall be Saved 38]; Tertullian[Scorpiace 6]; Nag Hammadi[Gospel of Philip 78]

04:08-09 Pseudepigrapha[Sibylline Oracles 2.78-89]

04:10 Justin[Dialogue with Trypho 88]

04:10-11 1Peter 1:10-13n

04:11 Clement[First Epistle Concerning Virginity 11]; Theonas[Epistle to Lucianus, the Chief Chamberlain 2]

04:12 Pseudepigrapha[Testament of Joseph 2.6]; Cyprian[Treatise XI.13]; Teaching of the Twelve Apostles 16.5; Tertullian[Scorpiace 12]

04:12-14 Clement of Alexandria[Stromata Book IV.7]; Cyprian[Epistle LV.2; Treatise XI.9]

04:14 Psalms 89:50-51; Isaiah 11:2; Irenaeus[Against Heresies Book IV.33.9]

04:15 Cyprian[Epistle VI.4]

04:15-16 Cyprian[Treatise XII.Book III.37]

04:17 Jeremiah 25:29; Ezekiel 9:6; Justin[Dialogue with Trypho 138]

04:18 Proverbs 11:31

04:19 Psalms 31:5; OT-Apocrypha[2Maccabees 1:24]; Pseudepigrapha[Joseph and Aseneth 13:15]

05:01 Acts 15:2-6n; Tacitus[The Histories 4.81]

05:01-04 Tertullian[On Modesty 21]

05:02 John 21:15-17

05:02-03 Tertullian[Five Books in Reply to Marcion Book IV.6]

05:02-04 1Corinthians 9:24-27n

05:04 John 10:11-14n; Pseudepigrapha[2Baruch 15:8; Greek Apocalypse of Ezra 6:17; Testament of
    Benjamin 4:1]; Apostolic[2Clement 7:1-3, 20:1-4; Martyrdom of Polycarp 17:1]; Irenaeus[Fragments
    from the Lost Works 54]; Methodius[Oration on the Psalms 6]

05:04-05 1Peter 1:10-13n

05:05 Proverbs 3:34; Colossians 3:20; Pseudepigrapha[Ahiqar 150; Joseph and Aseneth 6:8; Letter of
    Aristeas 1.257, 1.263-264]; Apostolic[1Clement 2, 30:1]; Polycarp - Letter to the Philippians 10:2];
    Clement of Alexandria[Stromata Book III.6, IV.17]; Clement[First Epistle Concerning Virginity 8];
    Constitutions of the Holy Apostles[Book VII.5, VIII.2]; Cyprian[Epistle XIV.3, XIX.1]

05:05-06 Matthew 18:4n

05:06 Job 22:29; Matthew 23:12; Luke 14:11, 18:14; Origen[Against Celsus Book III.63; Gospel of
    Matthew Book XII.43]; Pseud-Irenaeus; NT-Apocrypha[Protoevangelium of James 15.2]

05:07 Psalms 55:23; OT-Apocrypha[Wisdom of Solomon 12:13]; Pseudepigrapha[Apocalypse of Elijah
    3:1]

05:08 Job 1:7; Psalms 22:14; Ezekiel 22:25; Pseudepigrapha[Apocalypse of Elijah 1:4, 2.7; Joseph and
    Aseneth 12:9; Testament of Solomon 2:3]; Plato[**Theaetetus 176a-c**]; Clement[First Epistle
    Concerning Virginity 5]; Cyprian[Treatise X.1]; Fabian[First Epistle]; Justin[Dialogue with Trypho
    116]; Origen[De Principiis Book III.3.5]; Nag Hammadi[Teachings of Silvanus 95, 108]; Epic of
    Gilgamesh[The Forest Journey]

> **...for there must always be something opposed to the good; nor is it possible that it
> should have its seat in heaven. But it must inevitably haunt human life, and prowl about
> this earth. (Plato - Theaetetus 176a-c, *Plato Complete Works*, John M. Cooper, ed.;
> Hackett Publishing Company, 1997, p. 195)**

05:10 Clement of Alexandria[Fragments from the Latin Translation of Cassiodorus Comments on
    1Peter; Stromata Book VI.14]

05:12 Acts 15:22, 40

05:13 Acts 12:12, 25, 13:13, 15:37-39; Colossians 4:10; Philemon 1:24; Apostolic[Papias Fragment 3:15,
    21:1]

> **Peter mentions Mark in his first epistle which, they say, he composed in Rome itself, as
> he himself indicates, referring to the city metaphorically as Babylon in these words: "She
> who is in Babylon, who is likewise chosen, sends you greetings, as does Mark, my son."
> (Papias – Fragment 21:1)**

05:14 Tertullian[On Prayer 18]; Nag Hammadi[Gospel of Mary 8; Letter of Peter to Philip 140]

Cross Reference Index:
Second Peter

01:02 Jude 1:2

01:02-04 Pseudepigrapha[Apocalypse of Elijah 1:13]

01:03 1Peter 2:9

01:04 Clement of Alexandria[Stromata Book VII.16]; Hippolytus[Refutation of all Heresies Book X.29]; Novatian[Treatise Concerning the Trinity 20]

01:06-07 Galatians 5:22-23; OT-Apocrypha[Wisdom of Solomon 6:17-20]

01:09 Deuteronomy 28:28; Tertullian[On Baptism 8]

01:10 NT-Apocrypha[Epistula Apostolorum 26]

01:11 Pseudepigrapha[Joseph and Aseneth 14:1]; Clement of Alexandria[Stromata Book VI.14]

01:12 Jude 1:5

01:14 John 21:18-19; 2Corinthians 5:1

01:16 Irenaeus[Against Heresies Book II.22.5; Fragments from the Lost Works 2]

01:16-18 Acts 3:18-26n

01:17 Tertullian[Five Books in Reply to Marcion Book II.350]

01:17-18 Matthew 17:1-5; Mark 9:2-7; Luke 9:28-35; NT-Apocrypha[Acts of Peter 1.20; Apocalypse of Peter 1.15]

01:19 Revelation 2:28, 22:16; OT-Apocrypha[2Esdras 12:42]; Pseudepigrapha[4Ezra 12:43]; NT-Apocrypha[Acts of Paul from Corinth to Italy p.8]

01:19-21 Josephus[War 2.8.12 159]

01:20 Plato[Timaeus 72a-b]; Irenaeus[Against Heresies Book I.Preface.1, 3.6, II.27.2, III.21.3]; Justin[Dialogue with Trypho 114]; Tertullian[On the Apparel of Women Book II.2]; Nag Hammadi[Testimony of Truth 37; Tripartite Tractate 112]

01:21 2Timothy 3:16; 1Peter 1:11; Hippolytus[Refutation of all Heresies Book IX.22; Treatise on Christ and Antichrist 2]; NT-Apocrypha[Acts of Paul in Ephesus p.5]

02:01 Matthew 24:11; Jude 1:4; Hippolytus[Appendix to the Works of Hippolytus - On the End of the World 10]; Irenaeus[Against Heresies Book III.18.5]; Justin[Dialogue with Trypho 82; On the Resurrection 10]; Lactantius[Divine Institutes Book IV.30]; Tertullian[On Prescription Against Heretics 1]; Nag Hammadi[Gospel of the Egyptians III.61]; NT-Apocrypha[Acts of Thomas 1.79; Apocalypse of Peter 1.14-15; Epistula Apostolorum 1, 7]

02:01-03 Pseudepigrapha[Martyrdom and Ascension of Isaiah 3.21-31]; Apostolic[Shepherd of Hermas 43:11]

02:01-22 Jude 1:4-13; Apostolic[Ignatius - Letter to the Ephesians 16:1-2]

02:02 Psalms 119:30; Isaiah 52:5; OT-Apocrypha[Wisdom of Solomon 5:6]

02:03 Romans 16:18; 1Thessalonians 2:5

02:04 This section also includes topical notes for: Fallen Angels - Genesis 6:1-4; Job 41:23; Jude 1:6; Pseudepigrapha[1Enoch 10:4-6, 11-14, 12:4-13:1, 91:15; 2Baruch 56.11-16; 2Enoch 7:1; Life of Adam and Eve Vita 12:1-2; Sibylline Oracles 1.98; Testament of Levi 3:2; Vision of Ezra 8]; Dead Sea Scrolls[1Q The Book of Giants (1Q23[1QENGIANTSAR]) Fragment 8 3-15; 4Q Ages of Creation (4Q180[4QAGESCREAT]) Fragment 1 7-10, Fragment 2 2-4; 4Q Enoch (4Q201[4QENAR]) COL V 5, (4Q202[4QENAR]) COL II 1-28, COL III 1-6, COL IV 9-11, COL VI 5-7, (4Q204[4QENAR]) COL V 1, COL VI 15, Fragment 5 COL II 18-19, (4Q206[4QENAR]) Fragment 4 COL 1 10-13]; Archelaus[Disputation with Manes 32-33]; Athenagoras[Plea for the Christians 24]; Clement of Alexandria[Fragments from the Latin Translation of Cassiodorus Comments on Jude; Stromata Book V.1, VII.14; The Instructor Book III.2]; Hippolytus[Refutation of all Heresies Book X.30]; Irenaeus[Against Heresies Book I.10.1, 3, 15.6, IV.16.2, 36.4, 40.3, 41.1, V.29.2; Demonstration of the Apostolic Preaching 18]; Justin[Second Apology 5]; Lactantius[Divine Institutes Book II.16]; Tertullian[On the Apparel of Women Book I.2, II.10]; Nag Hammadi[A Valentinian Exposition 38-39; Apocryphon of John 29]; NT-Apocrypha[Gospel of Judas 46, 55]

02:05 Genesis 6:1-7:24, 8:18; 2Peter 3:6; Pseudepigrapha[Hellenistic Synagogal Prayers 12:58; Jubilees 7:34-35; Sibylline Oracles 1.149]; Apostolic[1Clement 7]

02:05-09 Tertullian[An Answer to the Jews 2]

02:06 Genesis 19:24; Jude 1:7

02:07 Genesis 19:1-16, 29; OT-Apocrypha[3Maccabees 2:13; Wisdom of Solomon 10:6]; Pseudepigrapha[Hellenistic Synagogal Prayers 12:62]

02:09 1Corinthians 10:13; Jude 1:6; NT-Apocrypha[Epistula Apostolorum 26]

02:10 Jude 1:7-8; Apostolic[1Clement 30:1]

02:11 Jude 1:9

02:11-12 Cyprian[Treatise XII.Book III.11]

02:12 Jude 1:10

02:13-15 Cyprian[Epistle VII.1]; Indian[Dhammapada 308]

02:14 John 8:3-11n

02:14-18 Pseudepigrapha[Joseph and Aseneth 21:21]

02:15 Numbers 22:7, 31:16; Deuteronomy 23:5; Nehemiah 13:2; Jude 1:11; Revelation 2:14

02:16 Numbers 22:4-35; Cyprian[Treatise XI.10]; NT-Apocrypha[Acts of Peter 1.12]

02:17 Jude 1:13; Pseudepigrapha[**1Enoch 15:9**]; Nag Hammadi[Apocalypse of Peter 79:30-31]

> **The spirits of the giants shall be like clouds, which shall oppress, corrupt, fall, contend, and bruise the earth. (Pseudepigrapha - 1Enoch 15:9)**

02:19 John 8:34; Pseudepigrapha[4Ezra 12.42]; Irenaeus[Against Heresies Book IV.Preface.4]

02:20 Matthew 12:45

02:21 Proverbs 21:16; Luke 12:47-48

02:22 Proverbs 26:11; Greek[Heraclitus Frg. B13]; Hippolytus[Refutation of all Heresies Book IX.1]; Lactantius[Divine Institutes Book III.8]; Nag Hammadi[Gospel of Philip 79; Gospel of Truth 33]; Indian[Dhammapada 344]

03:02 Jude 1:17

03:03 Jude 1:18; Pseudepigrapha[1Enoch 72:2; Testament of Dan 5:4]; Apostolic[Didache 16:3]; Hippolytus[Appendix to the Works of Hippolytus - On the End of the World 10]; Origen[Gospel of John Book X.20]

03:04 Jeremiah 17:15; Ezekiel 12:22; Pseudepigrapha[4Ezra 2.31]

03:05 Genesis 1:2, 6-9; Pseudepigrapha[2Enoch 33:4; 47:4; Joseph and Aseneth 12:2]

03:05-14 Tertullian[A Strain of Jonah the Prophet 151]

03:06 Genesis 7:11-21; 2Peter 2:5; Pseudepigrapha[1Enoch 83:3-5; Artapanus Fragment 3 (PrEv 9.27.37)]

03:07 Pseudepigrapha[Fragments of Pseudo-Greek Poets 6]; NT-Apocrypha[Acts of Paul in Ephesus p.2; Apocalypse of Thomas Line 50; Epistula Apostolorum 26]

03:08 Psalms 90:4; Pseudepigrapha[2Baruch 48.13; Apocalypse of Elijah 5:37; Jubilees 4:30]; Dead Sea Scrolls[11Q Jubilees (11Q12[QJUB]) Fragment 4 1-4]; Rabbinic[Sanhedrin 97a-97b]; Apostolic[Epistle of Barnabas 15:4]; Irenaeus[Against Heresies Book V.23.2, 28.3]

03:09 Habakkuk 2:3; 1Timothy 2:4; OT-Apocrypha[Sirach 35:19]; Pseudepigrapha[2Baruch 21:21, 48:40]; Archelaus[Disputation with Manes 27]

03:10 Matthew 24:42-44; Luke 12:34-40; 1Thessalonians 5:2-4; Revelation 3:3, 16:15; Pseudepigrapha[1Enoch 1:6, 52:6-9; 4 Ezra 13:10-11; Apocalypse of Elijah 1:4; Greek Apocalypse of Ezra 4:38; Testament of Solomon 8:2]; Rabbinic[Babylonian Sanhedrin 39a cf. {Genesis 2:21}]; Origen[Gospel of John Book X.20]; Tertullian[Against Hermogenes 34]; NT-Apocrypha[Apocalypse of Peter 1.5]

03:10-13 Pseudepigrapha[Apocalypse of Elijah 5:38]

03:12 Pseudepigrapha[Sibylline Oracles 2.199; Testament of Abraham 13:4]; Rabbinic[Sanhedrin 97b]; Hippolytus[Appendix to the Works of Hippolytus - On the End of the World 37]

03:13 Isaiah 60:21, 65:17, 66:22; 1Corinthians 6:9-10; Revelation 21:1n, 21:27, 22:15; Pseudepigrapha[1Enoch 45:4, 72:2; Jubilees 1:29]; Origen[Gospel of John Book X.20]

03:15 Romans 2:4; 2Peter 3:9; Revelation 12:10n

03:15-16 Apostolic[Polycarp - Letter to the Philippians 7:1]; Irenaeus[Against Heresies Book IV.41.4]

03:15-17 Nag Hammadi[Gospel of Thomas 57]

03:15-18 1Peter 1:10-13n

03:16 Clement of Alexandria[Stromata Book VII.16]; Irenaeus[Against Heresies Book I.27.2]; Lactantius[Divine Institutes Book II.3]; Tertullian[On Fasting 11; On Prescription Against Heretics 39]
03:17 Mark 13:5, 1Corinthians 10:12
03:18 OT-Apocrypha[Sirach 18:10]

Cross Reference Index:
First John

01:01 Isaiah 43:13; John 1:1-18n; Pseudepigrapha[Joseph and Aseneth 12:2]; Dionysius of Alexandria[Extant Fragments Two Books on the Promises 4]; Origen[Against Celsus Book I.48, VII.34]; Tertullian[A Treatise on the Soul 17; Against Praxeas 15; Of Patience 3; To his Wife Book I.4]; Nag Hammadi[Gospel of Truth 30]; NT-Apocrypha[Acts of Thomas 1.143; Epistula Apostolorum 1, 2, 12, 31]

01:01-02 Tertullian[On the Flesh of Christ 12; Five Books in Reply to Marcion Book III.299]

01:01-03 Dionysius of Alexandria[Extant Fragments Two Books on the Promises 6]; Nag Hammadi[Apocryphon of James 3, 9]; NT-Apocrypha[Canon Muratori Line 27-34]

01:02 John 1:14; Tacitus[The Histories 4.81]; Clement of Alexandria[Fragments from the Latin Translation of Cassiodorus Comments on 1John]

01:03 Pseudepigrapha[**1Enoch 105:1-2**]; Tertullian[Against Praxeas 28]

> In those days, saith the Lord, they shall call to the children of the earth, and make them listen to their wisdom. Show them that you are their leaders; And that remuneration shall take place over the whole earth; for I and my Son will for ever hold communion with them in the paths of uprightness, while they are still alive. Peace shall be yours. Rejoice, children of integrity, in the truth. (Pseudepigrapha - 1Enoch 105:1-2)

01:05 Pseudepigrapha[Sibylline Oracles Fragment 3.34]; Clement of Alexandria[Fragments from the Latin Translation of Cassiodorus Comments on 1John]; Irenaeus[Against Heresies Book I.12.2, II.18.4, 28.4]; Origen[Against Celsus Book II.71, V.11; Gospel of John Book II.20; De Principiis Book I.1.1, IV.1.28]; Tertullian[On Repentance 6]; NT-Apocrypha[Acts of John 94; Epistula Apostolorum 39]

01:05-07 Tertullian[On Modesty 7]

01:06 Origen[Gospel of John Book II.20]; Nag Hammadi[Book of Thomas the Contender 138]

01:06-07 Pseudepigrapha[Sibylline Oracles Fragment 1.27]; Clement of Alexandria[Stromata Book III.4]

01:06-10 Indian[Dhammapada 262-268]

01:07 Proverbs 20:9; Isaiah 2:5; Apostolic[1Clement 7:4]; Clement of Alexandria[Fragments from the Latin Translation of Cassiodorus Comments on 1John]

01:07-09 Ephesians 4:32n

01:07-02:02 Tertullian[On Modesty 19]

01:08 Pseudepigrapha[4Ezra 16.53-54]; Cyprian[Treatise IV.22, XII.Book III.54]; Gregory Thaumaturgus[Metaphrase of the Book of Ecclesiastes 7]; Peter of Alexandria[Genuine Acts of Peter 3]

01:08-09 Cyprian[Treatise VIII.3]

01:09 Deuteronomy 32:4; Psalms 32:5; Proverbs 28:13; Matthew 9:6n; Acts 26:18n; NT-Apocrypha[Acts of Peter 1.2]

01:10 Clement of Alexandria[Fragments from the Latin Translation of Cassiodorus Comments on 1John]

02:01 Pseudepigrapha[Hellenistic Synagogal Prayers 4.22, 6.13]; Apostolic[Papias Fragment 15:1]; Clement of Alexandria[Fragments from the Latin Translation of Cassiodorus Comments on 1John; Stromata Book VI.14]; Irenaeus[Against Heresies Book III.17.3]; Origen[Gospel of John Book I.23]; Peter of Alexandria[Canonical Epistle 11]

02:01-02 Ephesians 4:32n; Cyprian[Epistle LI.18]; Origen[Gospel of John Book I.38, VI.37; De Principiis Book II.7.4]

02:02 Origen[Against Celsus Book III.49, IV.28, VIII.13]

02:02-03 Clement of Alexandria[Fragments from the Latin Translation of Cassiodorus Comments on 1John]

02:02-06 Clement of Alexandria[The Instructor Book III.12]

02:03-04 Cyprian[Epistle XXIV.2]

02:04 Clement of Alexandria[Stromata Book III.5]; NT-Apocrypha[Epistula Apostolorum 27, 36]

02:05 Clement of Alexandria[Fragments from the Latin Translation of Cassiodorus Comments on 1John]

02:06 Cyprian[Epistle LV.1; Treatise II.7, IX.9, XII.Book.III.11]; Origen[De Principiis Book IV.1.31]; Tertullian[On Monogamy 3]

02:07-10 Clement of Alexandria[Fragments from the Latin Translation of Cassiodorus Comments on 1John]

02:08 John 13:34; Tertullian[On Modesty 7]

02:09 Cyprian[Treatise XII.Book III.3]

02:09-11 Cyprian[Treatise X.11]

02:10 Psalms 119:165

02:11 Anonymous[Treatise Against the Heretic Novatian 13]; Nag Hammadi[Gospel of Philip 64]

02:12 Psalms 25:11; Matthew 9:6n; Acts 26:18n; Ephesians 4:32n

02:12-13 Apostolic[Papias Fragment 15:1]

02:12-17 Clement of Alexandria[Fragments from the Latin Translation of Cassiodorus Comments on 1John]

02:15 Pseudepigrapha[1Enoch 48:6-7; Apocalypse of Elijah 1:2]; Cyprian[Treatise VII.24]; Origen[Gospel of Matthew XII.36]

02:15-16 Philo[**Fragments Extracted From The Parallels Of John Of Damascus Page 370. B.**]

It is as impossible that the love of the world can co-exist with the love of God, as for light and darkness to co-exist at the same time with one another. (Philo - Fragments Extracted From The Parallels Of John Of Damascus Page 370. B.)

02:15-17 Cyprian[Treatise II.7, IV.14, XII.Book III.11]

02:16 Proverbs 27:20; Matthew 5:28n; Tertullian[On Modesty 6]

02:17 OT-Apocrypha[Wisdom of Solomon 5:15]; Pseudepigrapha[Testament of Job 33:4]; Cyprian[Treatise XII.Book III.19]

02:18 Pseudepigrapha[Greek Apocalypse of Ezra 4.25-37; Martyrdom and Ascension of Isaiah 4.2-13; Psalms of Solomon 2:1]; Apostolic[Papias Fragment 15:1]; Hippolytus[Appendix to the Works of Hippolytus - On the End of the World 10]; Irenaeus[Against Heresies Book I.13.1, III.16.5, 8, IV.Preface.3]; Justin[Dialogue with Trypho 82, 110]; Origen[Gospel of Matthew Book XI.1]; Tertullian[On Fasting 11]

02:18-19 Clement of Alexandria[Stromata Book III.6]; Cyprian[Epistle LXIX.3, LXXV.1]

02:19 Apostolic[Ignatius - Letter to the Ephesians 4:2-5:2]; Clement of Alexandria[Fragments from the Latin Translation of Cassiodorus Comments on 1John]; Cyprian[Epistle LIV.7; Treatise I.9, XII.Book III.78]; Tertullian[On Prescription Against Heretics 3]; NT-Apocrypha[Epistula Apostolorum 29]

02:20 Pseudepigrapha[Testament of Solomon 4:12]; Clement of Alexandria[Stromata Book VI.14]; Nag Hammadi[Gospel of Philip 69; Gospel of Truth 22]

02:21-22 Cyprian[Treatise XII.Book III.79]

02:22 Pseudepigrapha[Greek Apocalypse of Ezra 4.25-37]; Irenaeus[Against Heresies Book I.13.1]; Justin[Dialogue with Trypho 110]; Tertullian[Against Praxeas 28]

02:22-23 Clement of Alexandria[Fragments from the Latin Translation of Cassiodorus Comments on 1John]

02:23 Pseudepigrapha[4Ezra 2.47]; Cyprian[Treatise XI.5, XII.Book II.27]; Origen[Gospel of John Book II.28]

02:25 Jude 1:21n

02:26 Justin[Dialogue with Trypho 82]

02:27 Jeremiah 31:34; Clement of Alexandria[Stromata Book VI.14]; Nag Hammadi[Gospel of Philip 69]

02:28 Pseudepigrapha[Testament of Abraham 13:4]; Apostolic[Papias Fragment 15:1]

02:29 Clement of Alexandria[Fragments from the Latin Translation of Cassiodorus Comments on 1John]; Justin[Dialogue with Trypho 135]; Tertullian[On Fasting 11]

03:01 John 1:12; Nag Hammadi[Gospel of Truth 43]

03:01-02 Apostolic[Papias Fragment 15:1]; Clement of Alexandria[Fragments from the Latin Translation of Cassiodorus Comments on 1John]; Tertullian[On Modesty 2]

03:02 Origen[Against Celsus Book IV.29; De Principiis Book III.6.1]; Tertullian[On the Resurrection of the Flesh 23]

03:03 Tertullian[On Monogamy 3]

03:03-10 Tertullian[On Modesty 19]

03:04-10 Apostolic[Ignatius - Letter to the Ephesians 8:2, 14:2]

03:05 Isaiah 53:4, 9, 11; John 1:29; Pseudepigrapha[Testament of Benjamin 3.8; Testament of Judah 24.2; Psalms of Solomon 17.36; Clement of Alexandria[The Instructor Book I.1, III.12]; Justin[Dialogue with Trypho 67, 102]; Tertullian[On Modesty 22]

03:06 Justin[Dialogue with Trypho 111]

03:07 Apostolic[Papias Fragment 15:1]

03:08 John 3:18n; Pseudepigrapha[Joseph and Aseneth 12:9]; Apostolic[Papias Fragment 24:1; Polycarp - Letter to the Philippians 7:1]

03:08-10 Clement of Alexandria[Fragments from the Latin Translation of Cassiodorus Comments on 1John]

03:09 Justin[Dialogue with Trypho 67, 102, 135]

03:10 Hippolytus[Appendix to the Works of Hippolytus - On the End of the World 10]

03:10-15 Cyprian[Treatise XII.Book III.3]

03:11 John 13:34

03:12 Genesis 4:8; NT-Apocrypha[Acts of Andrew (Codex Vaticanus 808) 8]

03:13 NT-Apocrypha[Epistula Apostolorum 38]

03:14 John 5:24; Pseudepigrapha[Joseph and Aseneth 8:9]

03:14-15 Clement of Alexandria[Who is the Rich Man that shall be Saved 37]

03:15 Jude 1:21n; Pseudepigrapha[Testament of Benjamin 7.5]; Cyprian[Treatise IV.24, X.11]; Tertullian[On Idolatry 2]

03:15-16 Clement of Alexandria[Fragments from the Latin Translation of Cassiodorus Comments on 1John]

03:16 Tertullian[De Fuga in Persecutione 9; Scorpiace 12]

03:17 Deuteronomy 15:7-8; Cyprian[Treatise VIII.16, XII.Book III.1]; Nag Hammadi[Sentences of Sextus 370-371]

03:17-18 James 2:1-26n

03:18 Apostolic[Papias Fragment 15:1]

03:18-19 Clement of Alexandria[Stromata Book IV.16]

03:20 Tertullian[A Treatise on the Soul 15]; Nag Hammadi[Gospel of Truth 42]

03:20-21 Clement of Alexandria[Fragments from the Latin Translation of Cassiodorus Comments on 1John]

03:23 John 13:34, 15:12, 17

03:24 Romans 8:9-11n; Clement of Alexandria[Fragments from the Latin Translation of Cassiodorus Comments on 1John]

04:01 Hippolytus[Appendix to the Works of Hippolytus - On the End of the World 10]; Justin[Dialogue with Trypho 82]; Nag Hammadi[Gospel of the Egyptians III 61]

04:01-02 Irenaeus[Against Heresies Book III.16.8]

04:01-03 Tertullian[Five Books Against Marcion Book V.16]

04:02-03 Apostolic[Polycarp - Letter to the Philippians 7:1]; Cyprian[Treatise XII.Book II.8]; Tertullian[Against Praxeas 28]

04:03 Cyprian[Epistle LXXII.15]; Justin[Dialogue with Trypho 110]; Tertullian[On Prescription Against Heretics 33; On the Flesh of Christ 14; On the Resurrection of the Flesh 22]; NT-Apocrypha[Apocalypse of Paul 1.41]

04:04 Apostolic[Papias Fragment 15:1]; Cyprian[Treatise XI.10, XII.Book III.10]

04:06 Pseudepigrapha[Psalms of Solomon 8:14]

04:07 Philo[Fragments Extracted From the Parallels of John of Damascus 784 C]; Justin[Dialogue with Trypho 135]

04:07-08 Anonymous[Treatise on Re-Baptism 13]

04:08 Clement of Alexandria[Stromata Book IV.18; Who is the Rich Man that shall be Saved 37]; Lactantius[Divine Institutes Book I.7]

04:09 John 3:16

04:12 John 1:18; Pseudepigrapha[Sibylline Oracles Fragment 1.10, 3.17]; Novatian[Treatise Concerning the Trinity 18]; Tertullian[Against Praxeas 15]

04:12-16 Romans 8:9-11n

04:15 John 3:18n; Pseudepigrapha[4Ezra 2.47]; Lactantius[Epitome of the Divine Institutes 49]; Tertullian[Against Praxeas 31]

04:16 Clement of Alexandria[Fragments from the Latin Translation of Cassiodorus Comments on 1John; Stromata Book IV.16, 18, V.1; Who is the Rich Man that shall be Saved 37]; Cyprian[Treatise I.14, XII.Book III.3]

04:17 NT-Apocrypha[Epistula Apostolorum 26]

04:18 Clement of Alexandria[Fragments from the Latin Translation of Cassiodorus Comments on 1John; Stromata Book IV.16; Who is the Rich Man that shall be Saved 38]; Origen[Gospel of Matthew Book XIII.26]; Phileas[Epistle to the People of Thmuis 1]; Tertullian[De Fuga in Persecutione 9, 14; Scorpiace 12]

04:19 Pseudepigrapha[Odes of Solomon 3:3]

04:20 Pseudepigrapha[Apocalypse of Sedrach 1:10]; Cyprian[Treatise XII.Book III.3]

04:21 Pseudepigrapha[Apocalypse of Sedrach 1:12]; Nag Hammadi[Sentences of Sextus 370-371]

05:01 Alexander of Alexandria[Epistles on Arian Heresy 1.11]; Irenaeus[Against Heresies Book III.16.8]; Justin[Dialogue with Trypho 135]; Tertullian[Against Praxeas 28]

05:03 Deuteronomy 30:11; John 14:15; Clement of Alexandria[Stromata Book IV.16; The Instructor Book III.11]

05:04 Justin[Dialogue with Trypho 135]

05:05 John 3:18n

05:06 Anonymous[Treatise on Re-Baptism 15]; Clement of Alexandria[Fragments from the Latin Translation of Cassiodorus Comments on 1John]; Tertullian[On Baptism 16]

05:06-07 Justin[Fragments from the Lost Writings of Justin 10]

05:06-08 Genesis 1:26, 3:22; Matthew 28:19n; Luke 1:35; John 14:16-26, 15:26, 16:7-15; Acts 2:33, 10:36-38; Romans 1:3-4, 8:9-27; 1Corinthians 2:10-11, 6:19, 8:6, 12:3-6; 2Corinthians 1:21-22, 13:14; Hebrews 9:14; 1Peter 1:2, 3:18; Nag Hammadi[Trimorphic Protennoia 37]

05:06-09 Acts 3:18-26n

05:07 Cyprian[Treatise I.6]

05:08 Anonymous[Treatise on Re-Baptism 19]; Clement of Alexandria[Fragments from the Latin Translation of Cassiodorus Comments on 1John]; Origen[Gospel of John Book VI.26]

05:10-13 John 3:18n

05:11 John 3:36

05:11-13 Jude 1:21n

05:12 Tertullian[Against Praxeas 31]

05:14 Clement of Alexandria[Fragments from the Latin Translation of Cassiodorus Comments on 1John]

05:16 Pseudepigrapha[Jubilees 21:22; Testament of Issachar 7:1]; Hippolytus[Refutation of all Heresies Book IX.7]; Origen[Gospel of Matthew Book XIII.30]; Tertullian[On Modesty 2, 19]

05:16-17 Clement of Alexandria[Stromata Book II.15]

05:16-18 Tertullian[On Modesty 19]

05:18 Justin[Dialogue with Trypho 135]

05:19 Archelaus[Disputation with Manes 14]; Dionysius of Alexandria[Exegetical Fragments An Exposition of Luke 22.46; Exegetical Fragments Gospel According to Luke - An Interpretation 22.46]; Methodius[Apostolic Words from the Discourse on the Resurrection 5]; Origen[De Principiis Book I.5.5, II.3.6]

05:19-20 Clement of Alexandria[Fragments from the Latin Translation of Cassiodorus Comments on 1John]

05:20 Jeremiah 24:7; John 3:18n; Jude 1:21n; Nag Hammadi[Letter of Peter to Philip 133]

05:21 Pseudepigrapha[Epistle of Jeremiah 1:72]; Apostolic[Papias Fragment 15:1]; Tertullian[The Chaplet, or De Corona 10]

Cross Reference Index: Second John

01:01 Apostolic[Papias Fragment 3:4-7, Fragment 5:1, Fragment 7:1]; Clement of
  Alexandria[Fragments from the Latin Translation of Cassiodorus Comments on 2John]
01:04 2Kings 20:3; NT-Apocrypha[Epistula Apostolorum 38]
01:05 John 13:34, 15:12, 17
01:07 Pseudepigrapha[Martyrdom and Ascension of Isaiah 4.2-13]; Irenaeus[Against Heresies Book
  I.13.1]; Justin[Dialogue with Trypho 110]; NT-Apocrypha[Apocalypse of Peter 1.2]
01:07-08 Irenaeus[Against Heresies Book III.16.8]
01:07-10 Tertullian[On Fasting 11]
01:08 Ruth 2:12
01:09 Romans 8:9-11n
01:10 Alexander of Alexandria[Epistles on Arian Heresy 2.6]; Clement of Alexandria[Fragments from
  the Latin Translation of Cassiodorus Comments on 2John]
01:10-11 Cyprian[The Seventh Council of Carthage under Cyprian]; Irenaeus[Against Heresies Book
  I.16.3]
01:12 Numbers 12:8; NT-Apocrypha[Correspondence between Seneca and Paul VI]
01:13 Apostolic[Papias Fragment 15:1]

Cross Reference Index: Third John

01:01 Acts 19:29; Romans 16:23; 1Corinthians 1:14; Apostolic[Papias Fragment 3:4-7, Fragment 5:1,
  Fragment 7:1]
01:04 Apostolic[Papias Fragment 15:1]; NT-Apocrypha[Epistula Apostolorum 38]
01:11 Pseudepigrapha[Pseudo-Phocylides 77]; Tertullian[On Monogamy 6]
01:13 NT-Apocrypha[Correspondence between Seneca and Paul VI]
01:14 Numbers 12:8

Cross Reference Index: Jude

01:01 Matthew 13:55; Mark 6:3; Clement of Alexandria[Fragments from the Latin Translation of Cassiodorus Comments on Jude]; Origen[Gospel of Matthew Book X.17, XIII.27]

01:02 2Peter 1:2

01:03 Clement of Alexandria[Stromata Book VII.16]; Irenaeus[Fragments from the Lost Works 36]

01:03-16 2Peter 2:1-17

01:04 2Peter 2:1; Pseudepigrapha[1Enoch 48:10]; Irenaeus[Against Heresies Book III.18.5]

01:04-14 Clement of Alexandria[Fragments from the Latin Translation of Cassiodorus Comments on Jude]

01:05 Exodus 12:51; Numbers 14:29-37; 2Peter 1:12; Pseudepigrapha[1Enoch 10:4]

01:05-06 Clement of Alexandria[The Instructor Book III.8]

01:06 This section also includes topical notes for: Everlasting Darkness - Genesis 6:1-4; Matthew 18:8, 25:41; 2Peter 2:4n, 9; Pseudepigrapha[1Enoch 10:6, 12, 12:4, 22:11; 2Baruch 48:9; 2Enoch 7:1; 4Ezra 7.36; Sibylline Oracles 1.98, 1.350]; Dead Sea Scrolls[4Q Enoch (4Q202[4QENAR]) COL II 1-28, (4Q202[4QENAR]) COL III 1-6, (4Q202[4QENAR]) COL IV 9-11, (4Q202[4QENAR]) COL VI 5-7, (4Q204[4QENAR]) COL VI 15]; Philo[On Dreams, That they Are God-Sent (1.114) cf. {Exodus 10:21}]; Apostolic[Ignatius - Letter to the Trallians 5:2]; Hippolytus[Refutation of all Heresies Book IX.22-23]; Irenaeus[Against Heresies Book I.10.1, IV.6.5]; Justin[First Apology 8]; NT-Apocrypha[Epistula Apostolorum 26]

01:06-07 Pseudepigrapha[Testament of Solomon 1:13]

01:07 Genesis 19:1-25; 2Peter 2:6; Pseudepigrapha[4Ezra 2.9; Testament of Naphtali 3:4]; Irenaeus[Against Heresies Book IV.36.4]; Tertullian[To his Wife Book II.2]

01:07-08 2Peter 2:10

01:08 Origen[Gospel of Matthew Book X.24]

01:08-17 Clement of Alexandria[Stromata Book III.2]

01:09 Deuteronomy 34:6; Daniel 10:13, 21, 12:1; Zechariah 3:2; Revelation 12:7; Pseudepigrapha[Assumption of Moses All:All; Life of Adam and Eve Vita 15:3, 39.1-3; Testament of Solomon 1:7]

01:10 2Peter 2:12

01:11 Genesis 4:3-8; Numbers 16:1-50, 21:7, 22:1-35, 31:16; 2Peter 2:11, 15; Cyprian[Epistle LXXV.8]; Irenaeus[Against Heresies Book IV.26.3]

01:12 Proverbs 25:14; Ezekiel 34:8; Matthew 7:16-21n; Apostolic[Ignatius - Letter to the Smyrnaeans 8:2]

01:12-13 Indian[Dhammapada 308]

01:13 Isaiah 57:20; 2Peter 2:17; OT-Apocrypha[Wisdom of Solomon 14:1]; Pseudepigrapha[1Enoch 18:15, 21:5; 2Enoch 11:2; 40:13; Apocalypse of Elijah 4:11; Testament of Levi 3:2; Testament of Solomon 16:2]; Irenaeus[Against Heresies Book I.6.3]; Theophilus of Antioch[To Autolycus Book II.15]

01:14 Genesis 5:21-24; Deuteronomy 33:2; Zechariah 14:5; Pseudepigrapha[1Enoch 60:8, 93:3; 2Enoch 71:32; Jubilees 7:39; Martyrdom and Ascension of Isaiah (3:13-4:22 = Testament of Hezekiah) 4:14]

01:14-15 Pseudepigrapha[**1Enoch 1:9**]; Dead Sea Scrolls[4Q Enoch (4Q204[4QENAR]) COL I 16-18]; Anonymous[Treatise Against the Heretic Novatian 16]; Tertullian[**On the Apparel of Women Book I.3**]

Behold, he comes with ten thousands of his saints, to execute judgment upon them, and destroy the wicked, and reprove all the carnal for everything which the sinful and ungodly have done, and committed against him. (Pseudepigrapha - 1Enoch 1:9)

I am aware that the Scripture of Enoch, which has assigned this order (of action) to angels, is not received by some, because it is not admitted into the Jewish canon either. I suppose they did not think that, having been published before the deluge, it could have safely survived that world-wide calamity, the abolisher of all things. If that is the reason (for rejecting it), let them recall to their memory that Noah, the survivor of the deluge, was the great-grandson of Enoch himself; and he, of course, had heard and remembered, from domestic renown and hereditary tradition, concerning his own great-grandfather's "grace in the sight of God," and concerning all his preachings; since Enoch had given no other charge to Methuselah than that he should hand on the knowledge of them to his posterity. Noah therefore, no doubt, might have succeeded in the trusteeship of (his) preaching; or, had the case been otherwise, he would not have been silent alike concerning the disposition (of things) made by God, his Preserver, and concerning the particular glory of his own house. If (Noah) had not had this (conservative power) by so short a route, there would (still) be this (consideration) to warrant our assertion of (the genuineness of) this Scripture: he could equally have renewed it, under the Spirit's inspiration, after it had been destroyed by the violence of the deluge, as, after the destruction of Jerusalem by the Babylonian storming of it, every document of the Jewish literature is generally agreed to have been restored through Ezra. But since Enoch in the same Scripture has preached likewise concerning the Lord, nothing at all must be rejected by us which pertains to us; and we read that "every Scripture suitable for edification is divinely inspired." By the Jews it may now seem to have been rejected for that (very) reason, just like all the other (portions) nearly which tell of Christ. Nor, of course, is this fact wonderful, that they did not receive some Scriptures which spake of Him whom even in person, speaking in their presence, they were not to receive. To these considerations is added the fact that Enoch possesses a testimony in the Apostle Jude. (Tertullian - On the Apparel of Women Book I.3)]

01:14-16 Pseudepigrapha[Life of Adam and Eve Vita 51:9]
01:15 Malachi 3:13; Pseudepigrapha[Joseph and Aseneth 23:7]
01:16 Leviticus 19:15; Daniel 11:36; Pseudepigrapha[1Enoch 5:4]; Dead Sea Scrolls[4Q Enoch (4Q201[4QENAR]) COL II 12-17]
01:17 2Peter 3:2
01:18 Isaiah 3:4; 2Peter 3:3
01:18-19 Hippolytus[Appendix to the Works of Hippolytus - On the End of the World 10]
01:19 Novatian[Treatise Concerning the Trinity 29]
01:20 Clement of Alexandria[Fragments from the Latin Translation of Cassiodorus Comments on Jude]
01:21 This section also includes topical notes for: Everlasting Life - Psalms 21:4, 121:8, 133:3; Isaiah 25:8; Daniel 12:2; Matthew 19:16-21, 29, 25:46; Mark 10:30; Luke 18:18, 30, 20:36; John 3:14-16, 4:14, 5:24-25, 29, 39, 6:27, 40, 47, 50-58, 68, 10:10, 27, 28, 12:25, 50, 17:2-3; Acts 13:46, 48; Romans 2:7, 5:21, 6:22-23; 1Corinthians 15:53-54; 2Corinthians 5:1; Galatians 6:8; 1Timothy 1:16, 4:8, 6:12, 19; 2Timothy 1:10; Titus 1:2, 3:7; 1John 2:25, 3:15, 5:11-13, 20; Jude 1:21; Revelation 1:18; Pseudepigrapha[Odes of Solomon 15.10, 17.14-15, 31.7, 38.3, 40.6; Sibylline Oracles 1.349]; Dead Sea Scrolls[4Q Ages of Creation (4Q181[4QAGESCREAT]) Fragment 1 3-6]; Philo[Special Laws I (345) cf. {Deuteronomy 4:4}]; Clement of Alexandria[Exhortation to the Heathen 12; Stromata Book VII.2; The Instructor Book I.10; Who is the Rich Man that shall be Saved 1, 10-11, 20, 42]; Hippolytus[Refutation of all Heresies Book IX.22-23]; Irenaeus[Against Heresies Book I.10.1, II.28.7, IV.6.5, V.3.3, 5.2; Fragments from the Lost Works 37]; Justin[First Apology 8; On the Resurrection 1]; Nag Hammadi[Testimony of Truth 38; Tripartite Tractate 128]

01:22 Cyprian[Epistle LI.14]

01:22-23 Pseudepigrapha[Testament of Naphtali 3:3]; Clement of Alexandria[Stromata Book VI.8]

01:22-24 Clement of Alexandria[Fragments from the Latin Translation of Cassiodorus Comments on Jude]

01:23 Amos 4:11; Zechariah 3:2, 4; Clement of Alexandria[Stromata Book V.5]; Tertullian[On Modesty 18]

Cross Reference Index: Revelation

01:01 Daniel 2:28-29, 45; Amos 3:7; Pseudepigrapha[2Baruch 10:3; Testament of Job 1:4, 47:9];
Apostolic[Papias Fragment 3:4-7, Fragment 5:1, Fragment 7:1, Fragment 10:1]; Justin[Dialogue with
Trypho 81]

01:01-02 Dionysius of Alexandria[Extant Fragments Two Books on the Promises 4]

01:03 Victorinus[Apocalypse 10.3]

01:04 Exodus 3:14; Isaiah 11:2, 41:4; Revelation 4:5

01:05 Psalms 89:28, 38, 130:8; Isaiah 40:2, 55:4; Jeremiah 42:5; Apostolic[1Clement 7:4];
Irenaeus[Against Heresies Book III.19.3, 22.4; Demonstration of the Apostolic Preaching 38];
Methodius[Apostolic Words from the Discourse on the Resurrection 13]; Pseud-Irenaeus

01:06 Exodus 19:6, 23:22; Isaiah 61:6; 1Peter 2:9n; Revelation 5:10; Tertullian[On Exhortation to
Chastity 7; On Monogamy 7]; Nag Hammadi[Gospel of Thomas 2]

01:06-07 1Thessalonians 4:15-17n

01:07 Genesis 12:3, 28:14; Daniel 7:13; Zechariah 12:10-14; Matthew 24:29-31; Mark 13:24-27; Luke
21:25-28; John 19:24, 37; 1Corinthians 15:51-55; 1Thessalonians 4:15-17; 2Thessalonians 2:1-2;
Revelation 6:13-8:2, 8:5, 11:12, 11:19, 14:1-5, 14:14-16, 16:8, 16:18; Rabbinic[Sukkah 52a cf. {Zechariah
12:10-12}]; Tertullian[Against All Heresies 5; An Answer to the Jews 14; On the Resurrection of the
Flesh 51]

01:08 Exodus 3:14; Isaiah 41:4; Amos 4:13; Revelation 22:13n; Pseudepigrapha[2Baruch 21:9;
Aristobulus Fragment 4:5; Orphica E and T 39; Testament of Isaac 6:34]; Clement of Alexandria[The
Instructor Book I.6]; Origen[De Principiis Book I.2.10]; Tertullian[Against Praxeas 17]

01:09 Daniel 8:1; Apostolic[Papias Fragment 6:1]; Clement of Alexandria[Who is the Rich Man that
shall be Saved 42]; Dionysius of Alexandria[Extant Fragments Two Books on the Promises 4]

01:09-19 Pseudepigrapha[Testament of Job 2:1]

01:10 Exodus 19:16; Pseudepigrapha[2Enoch 33:2]; Teaching of the Twelve Apostles 14.1; Tertullian[A
Treatise on the Soul 8]

01:10-12 Pseudepigrapha[History of the Rechabites 1:3]

01:11 Isaiah 30:8

01:11-13 Irenaeus[Against Heresies Book V.20.1]

01:12 Exodus 25:31, 37; Zechariah 4:2; Pseudepigrapha[Apocalypse of Sedrach 2:1]; Irenaeus[Against
Heresies Book IV.20.11]

01:12-18 Cyprian[Treatise XII.Book II.26]

01:13 Ezekiel 1:26, 9:2, 11; Daniel 7:13, 10:5; Pseudepigrapha[Joseph and Aseneth 14:14]; Tertullian[An
Answer to the Jews 11, 14]; Victorinus[On the Creation of the World]

01:13-15 Pseudepigrapha[Apocalypse of Zephaniah 6:12]

01:13-16 Pseudepigrapha[Joseph and Aseneth 14:9]

01:13-17 Matthew 17:1-21n

01:13-18 Nag Hammadi[Apocalypse of Paul 22]

01:13-21 Cyprian[Treatise XII.Book III.59]

01:14 Daniel 7:9; Pseudepigrapha[**1Enoch 71:10**; 2Enoch 1:5; Apocalypse of Abraham 11:3; Joseph and
Aseneth 5:4; Sibylline Oracles 6.28]; Cyprian[Treatise II.16]

> **With them was the Ancient of days, whose head was white as wool, and pure, and his
> robe was indescribable. (Pseudepigrapha - 1Enoch 71:10)**

01:14-15 Daniel 10:6

01:15 Ezekiel 1:24, 43:2; Irenaeus[Against Heresies Book IV.14.2]

01:16 Isaiah 49:2; Pseudepigrapha[2Enoch 1:5; Joseph and Aseneth 18:9; Testament of Solomon 8:2];
Tertullian[An Answer to the Jews 9; Five Books Against Marcion Book III.14]; Nag
Hammadi[Gospel of Thomas 98]

01:17 Isaiah 44:2, 6, 48:12; Ezekiel 1:28; Daniel 8:18; Revelation 2:8, 22:13; Pseudepigrapha[3Enoch 1:7; 4Ezra 10:30]; Irenaeus[Against Heresies Book IV.20.11]; Nag Hammadi[Gospel of Thomas (Prologue)]

01:17-18 Origen[Gospel of John Book I.35]

01:18 Deuteronomy 32:40; Job 38:17; Jude 1:21n; OT-Apocrypha[Sirach 18:1]; Pseudepigrapha[Odes of Solomon 15:9]; Rabbinic[Taanit 2a-2b cf. {Ezekiel 37:13}; Sanhedrin 113a cf. {1Kings 17:1, 17-23}]; Origen[Gospel of John Book I.23]

01:19 Isaiah 48:6; Daniel 2:28-29, 45; Pseudepigrapha[2Enoch 39:2]

01:20 Ezekiel 3:12; Pseudepigrapha[Testament of Solomon 8:2]

01:20-02:01 Tertullian[On Modesty 14]

02:01 Amos 1:6; Pseudepigrapha[Martyrdom and Ascension of Isaiah (3:13-4:22 = Testament of Hezekiah) 3:15; Testament of Job 51:4; Testament of Solomon 8:2]

02:02 Justin[On the Resurrection 10]

02:03 NT-Apocrypha[Epistula Apostolorum 15]

02:04 Tertullian[On Repentance 8]

02:05 Anonymous[Treatise Against the Heretic Novatian 13]; Cyprian[Epistle XII.1, XXVII.1; Treatise III.16; Treatises Attributed to Cyprian-Exhortation to Repentance]; Tertullian[On the Apparel of Women Book I.2]

02:06 Psalms 139:21; Hippolytus[Refutation of all Heresies Book VII.24]; Irenaeus[Against Heresies Book I.26.2-3]; Tertullian[Against All Heresies 2]

02:07 Genesis 2:8-9, 3:3, 22, 24; Ezekiel 28:13, 31:8-9; Revelation 22:2; Pseudepigrapha[1Enoch 25:5; 2Baruch 4:7; 2Enoch 8:3; 4Ezra 2:11, 8:52; Greek Apocalypse of Ezra 5.20-23; Life of Adam and Eve Vita 25:3; Odes of Solomon 20:7]; Cyprian[Treatise XII.Book III.16]; Methodius[Banquet of the Ten Virgins 3.3]; Tertullian[On Repentance 8]; NT-Apocrypha[Pseudo-Titus Epistle Line 619]

02:08 Psalms 109:21; Isaiah 44:6, 48:12; Revelation 1:17, 22:13; Pseudepigrapha[Martyrdom and Ascension of Isaiah (3:13-4:22 = Testament of Hezekiah) 3:15]; Tertullian[On Modesty 14]

02:09 Pseudepigrapha[Sibylline Oracles 7.135; Testament of Job 3:6]; Clement[Recognitions Book V.34]

02:10 Daniel 1:12, 14; Zechariah 6:14; 1Corinthians 9:24-27n; OT-Apocrypha[2Maccabees 13:14]; Pseudepigrapha[2Baruch 15:8; Apocalypse of Elijah 1:8; Greek Apocalypse of Ezra 6:17; Testament of Benjamin 4:1]; Apostolic[2Clement 7:1-3, 20:1-4; Martyrdom of Polycarp 17:1]; Cyprian[Epistle XXXVI.1; Treatise XI.10, XII.Book III.16]; Tertullian[Scorpiace 12; The Chaplet, or De Corona 15]

02:11 Revelation 20:14, 21:8; Rabbinic[Palestinian Targum Deuteronomy 33:6]; Tertullian[On Repentance 8]

02:12 Isaiah 49:2; OT-Apocrypha[Wisdom of Solomon 18:15-16]; Tertullian[An Answer to the Jews 9; On Modesty 14]

02:13 Ezekiel 12:2; Pseudepigrapha[Testament of Job 3:6]; Tertullian[Scorpiace 12]

02:14 Numbers 25:1-2, 31:16; Irenaeus[Against Heresies Book I.28.2, II.14.5; Fragments from the Lost Works 45]; Tertullian[On Prescription Against Heretics 33; On Repentance 8]

02:14-15 Plato[Republic III 416d-417b, IV 423e-424b, V 449c-450c, 457c-d, VIII 543a]; Irenaeus[Against Heresies Book I.26.3]

02:15 Tertullian[On Repentance 8]

02:16 Isaiah 49:2; Jeremiah 21:5

02:17 Exodus 16:14-15, 32; Psalms 78:24; Isaiah 62:2, 65:15; OT-Apocrypha[2Maccabees 2:4-8]; Pseudepigrapha[2Baruch 29:8]; Irenaeus[Against Heresies Book V.10.2]; Tertullian[On Repentance 8]; Nag Hammadi[Gospel of Truth 27]

02:18 Daniel 10:6; John 3:18n; Pseudepigrapha[Apocalypse of Zephaniah 6:13; Joseph and Aseneth 22.7-8]; Tertullian[On Modesty 14, 19]

02:20 Numbers 25:1-2; 1Kings 16:31; 2Kings 9:22, 30; Tertullian[On Repentance 8]

02:20-22 Tertullian[On Modesty 19]

02:22 John 8:3-11n

02:23 Psalms 7:9-10, 62:12-13; Proverbs 24:12; Jeremiah 11:20, 17:10; Ezekiel 33:27; Cyprian[Epistle VIII.1; Treatise III.27, IV.4, VII.17, XII.Book.III.56]; Egyptian Book of the Dead[Oration 27, 30A]

02:24 Tertullian[On Idolatry 2]

02:26 Pseudepigrapha[Joseph and Aseneth 12:2]

02:26-27 Psalms 2:8-9; Pseudepigrapha[Psalms of Solomon 17:23-24]; Tertullian[On Idolatry 18]

02:26-28 NT-Apocrypha[Pseudo-Titus Epistle Line 634]

02:27 Pseudepigrapha[Sibylline Oracles 8.248]; Tertullian[On Repentance 4]

02:28 Pseudepigrapha[Joseph and Aseneth 14:1]

02:29 Tertullian[On Repentance 8]

03:01 Tertullian[On Modesty 14]

03:02 Ezekiel 34:4

03:02-03 Matthew 24:42-51n

03:03 Matthew 24:36; Pseudepigrapha[Life of Adam and Eve (Apocalypse of Moses) 19:3]; Rabbinic[Babylonian Sanhedrin 39a cf. {Genesis 2:21}]

03:04 Revelation 16:15; Pseudepigrapha[4Ezra 2:40]

03:04-05 Pseudepigrapha[2Enoch 22:9]; Tertullian[On the Resurrection of the Flesh 27]

03:05 Exodus 32:32-33; Psalms 69:28-29; Daniel 12:1; Malachi 3:16; Matthew 10:32; Luke 12:8; Revelation 3:18n, 20:12, 21:27n; Pseudepigrapha[3Enoch 18:24; Apocalypse of Zephaniah 3:8; Odes of Solomon 23.20]

03:06 Exodus 19:6; Tertullian[On Repentance 8]

03:07 Job 12:14; Isaiah 22:22; Hosea 12:9; Acts 17:2-3; Pseudepigrapha[Odes of Solomon 17:9-11, 42:17]; Gregory Thaumaturgus[Oration and Panegyric Addressed to Origen 15]; Irenaeus[Against Heresies Book IV.20.2]; Origen[Gospel of John Book V.4]; Tertullian[On Modesty 14]

03:08 Dionysius of Alexandria[Extant Fragments Epistle Against Bishop Germanus 6]

03:09 Psalms 86:9; Isaiah 43:4, 45:14, 49:23, 60:14; Pseudepigrapha[Sibylline Oracles 7.135; Testament of Job 3:6]

03:10 Tertullian[Scorpiace 12]

03:11 Zechariah 2:14; Pseudepigrapha[Greek Apocalypse of Ezra 6:17]; Apostolic[2Clement 7:1-3, 20:1-4; Martyrdom of Polycarp 17:1]; Cyprian[Treatise I.20, IX.13, XI.8]

03:12 Isaiah 62:2-3, 65:15; Ezekiel 48:35; John 2:19-21n; Revelation 21:2; Pseudepigrapha[2Baruch 44.9-15; Apocalypse of Elijah 1:9; Joseph and Aseneth 17:6; Martyrdom and Ascension of Isaiah (3:13-4:22 = Testament of Hezekiah) 3:16]; Rabbinic[Babylonian (Baba Batra 75b; Ketubot 111b)]; Clement of Alexandria[Stromata Book IV.26; The Instructor Book II.13]; Irenaeus[Against Heresies Book V.36.1-2]; Origen[Gospel of John Book X.26]; Nag Hammadi[Apocryphon of James 13]; NT-Apocrypha[Clement Romance 62.4; Epistula Apostolorum 33]

03:13 Tertullian[On Repentance 8]

03:14 Proverbs 8:22; Isaiah 65:16; Commodianus[Instructions 43]; Hippolytus[Refutation of all Heresies Book V.21, 37]; Pseud-Irenaeus; Tertullian[On Modesty 14]

03:16 NT-Apocrypha[Apocalypse of Paul 1.31]

03:17 Hosea 12:8; Zechariah 11:5; Anonymous[Treatise Against the Heretic Novatian 2]; Tertullian[On Repentance 8]

03:17-18 Cyprian[Treatise VIII.14]

03:18 This section also includes topical notes for: Garments - 1Kings 7:51; 2Chronicles 15:8; Proverbs 19:17; Isaiah 55:1; Matthew 22:11-14; 1Corinthians 3:12-15; 1Peter 1:7n; Revelation 3:5; Pseudepigrapha[**1Enoch 62:15-16**; 2Enoch 22:9; 4Ezra 2.39-40; Hellenistic Synagogal Prayers 10.8; History of the Rechabites 5.3-4; Martyrdom and Ascension of Isaiah 1.5, 3.25, 7.16, 8.14, 8.26, 9.2, 9.8-11, 9.24-26, 11.40; Odes of Solomon 8.9, 11.10-11, 21.3, 25.8; Psalms of Solomon 17:43; Testament of Abraham 12:14]; Rabbinic[Babylonian Sanhedrin 90b]; Clement of Alexandria[Fragments from Macarius Chrysocephalus Parable of the Prodigal son 1, 6; The Instructor Book I.6]; Irenaeus[Against Heresies Book II.14.2, IV.36.6]; Justin[Dialogue with Trypho 15, 116-117]; Nag Hammadi[Authoritative Teaching 32; Concept of Our Great Power 46; Sentences of Sextus 346; Teachings of Silvanus 87, 89, 105, 107, 112; Trimorphic Protennoia 45, 49]; NT-Apocrypha[Epistula Apostolorum 19, 21]; Egyptian Book of the Dead[Oration 125, 171]; Epic of Gilgamesh[Ishtar and Gilgamesh]

> The saints and the elect have arisen from the earth, have left off to depress their countenances, and have been clothed with the garment of life. That garment of life is with the Lord of spirits, in whose presence your garment shall not wax old, nor shall your glory diminish. (Pseudepigrapha - 1Enoch 62:15-16)

03:19 Proverbs 3:12; Hebrews 12:6-8n; Cyprian[Treatise III.14]; Tertullian[Of Patience 11]; NT-Apocrypha[Pseudo-Titus Epistle Line 63]

03:20 Song of Solomon 5:2

03:21 Cyprian[Epistle XXV.4]; Hippolytus[Refutation of all Heresies Book X.30]; Tertullian[Against Praxeas 30; On Idolatry 18; On Repentance 8]; Nag Hammadi[Gospel of Thomas 2]; NT-Apocrypha[Pseudo-Titus Epistle Line 640]

04:01 Exodus 19:24; Psalms 78:23; Daniel 2:28-29, 45; Pseudepigrapha[2Baruch 10:3, 22:2, 23:7; 2Enoch 20:1; Joseph and Aseneth 10:16]

04:01-11 Pseudepigrapha[Testament of Levi 3:9]

04:02 1Kings 22:19; 2Chronicles 18:18; Psalms 11:4, 47:8, 103:19; Isaiah 6:1; OT-Apocrypha[Sirach 1:8]; Pseudepigrapha[2Enoch 20:3]

04:02-03 Ezekiel 1:26-28; Pseudepigrapha[1Enoch 14:18]

04:03 Ezekiel 10:1; Tertullian[On the Apparel of Women Book I.7]

04:04 Isaiah 24:23; Zechariah 6:11; Acts 15:2-6n; Pseudepigrapha[2Enoch 4:1, 22:9; 3Enoch 18:1; Apocalypse of Elijah 4:10; Apocalypse of Zephaniah a; Martyrdom and Ascension of Isaiah 7:23; Testament of Job 33:1]; Rabbinic[Berakhot 17a]; Clement of Alexandria[Stromata Book VI.13]; Tertullian[The Chaplet, or De Corona 14]; Nag Hammadi[Gospel of Thomas 52 cf. {Genesis 15:1, 4; 2Samuel 7:4, 24:11; 1Kings 6:11, 13:20, 16:1, 17:2, 8, 18:1, 31, 19:9, 21:17, 28; 2Kings 20:4; 1Chronicles 22:8; 2Chronicles 11:2, 12:7; Jeremiah 1:2, 4, 11, 13, 2:1, 13:3, 8, 16:1, Jer 18:5, 24:4, 28:12, 32:6, 33:1, 19, 23, 34:12, 36:27, 39:15, 42:7; Ezekiel 1:3, 3:16, 6:1, 7:1, 11:14, 12:17, 21, 26, 13:1, 14:2, 12, 15:1, 16:1, 17:1, 11, 18:1, 20:2, 45, 21:1, 18, 22:1, 17, 23, 23:1, 24:1, 15, 20, 25:1, 26:1, 27:1, 28:1, 11, 20, 29:1, 30:1, 20, 31:1, 32:1-17, 33:1, 23, 34:1, 35:1, 36:16, 37:15, 38:1; Daniel 9:2; Jonah 1:1; 3:1; Haggai 2:20; Zechariah 4:8, 6:9, 7:1, 8}]

04:04-06 Victorinus[On the Creation of the World]

04:05 Exodus 19:16; Esther 1:1; Ezekiel 1:13; Zechariah 4:2; Revelation 1:4, 8:5, 11:19, 16:18; Pseudepigrapha[2Baruch 59.11]; NT-Apocrypha[Apocalypse of Thomas Line 49]

04:06 Ezekiel 1:18, 22, 10:12; Pseudepigrapha[2Enoch 1a:4, 3:3, 27:2; Life of Adam and Eve Vita 29:2]

04:06-07 Ezekiel 1:5-10, 10:14

04:07 Pseudepigrapha[Apocalypse of Abraham 18:5; Testament of Naphtali 5:6]; Irenaeus[Against Heresies Book III.11.8]; Novatian[Treatise Concerning the Trinity 8]

04:08 Exodus 3:14; Isaiah 6:2-3, 41:4; Ezekiel 1:18, 10:12; Amos 4:13; Pseudepigrapha[2Enoch 22:10; Apocalypse of Elijah 5:2]; Tertullian[On Prayer 3]

04:09 Daniel 4:31, 34, 6:27, 12:7; NT-Apocrypha[Apocalypse of Paul 1.44]

04:09-10 1Kings 22:19; 2Chronicles 18:18; Psalms 47:8; Ezekiel 1:26-27; OT-Apocrypha[Sirach 1:8]

04:10 Isaiah 6:1; Matthew 28:17n; Acts 15:2-6n; Revelation 04:04n; Pseudepigrapha[3Enoch 18:1]; NT-Apocrypha[Apocalypse of Paul 1.14]

04:11 1Chronicles 29:11; Pseudepigrapha[1Enoch 9:4-5]; OT-Apocrypha[3Maccabees 2:3; Sirach 18:1; Wisdom of Solomon 1:14]; Nag Hammadi[Gospel of Truth 37]

05:01 1Kings 22:19; 2Chronicles 18:18; Psalms 47:8; Isaiah 6:1, 29:11; Jeremiah 32:10; Ezekiel 1:26-27, 2:9-10; Daniel 12:4, 9; OT-Apocrypha[Sirach 1:8]; Pseudepigrapha[2Enoch 20:3; 4Baruch 3:10]; NT-Apocrypha[Apocalypse of Paul 1.41]

05:01-05 Pseudepigrapha[Odes of Solomon 23.5-10]; Clement of Alexandria[Exhortation to the Heathen 1]; Cyprian[Treatise XII.Book II.11]; Origen[Gospel of John Book V.4]; Nag Hammadi[Apocryphon of John 31; Gospel of the Egyptians III. 43, IV. 57-58; Gospel of Truth 19-20, 23; Trimorphic Protennoia 49-50]

05:01-06 Rabbinic[Shabbat 116a]

05:01-09 Dead Sea Scrolls[14 Aramaic Proto-Esther 4Q550 4Q Proto Esther (4QPERESTHER) 4-7; 4Q Isaiah Pesher (4Q163[4QIS]) Fragments 15-16 1-4]

05:02-09 Acts 17:2-3

05:03 Exodus 20:4; Deuteronomy 5:8

05:04 Pseudepigrapha[2Enoch 1:3]

05:05 Genesis 49:9-10; Isaiah 11:1, 10; Pseudepigrapha[Testament of Benjamin 11.2; Testament of Dan 5.10; Testament of Gad 8.1-2; Testament of Levi 2.11]; Hippolytus[Treatise on Christ and Antichrist 6]; Tertullian[Five Books in Reply to Marcion Book II.236]

05:05-06 Pseudepigrapha[Testament of Benjamin 3.8; Testament of Joseph 19.8]

05:05-14 Acts 15:2-6n

05:06 Isaiah 53:7; Jeremiah 11:19; Zechariah 4:10; Clement of Alexandria[Stromata Book V.6]; Irenaeus[Against Heresies Book IV.20.11]; Origen[Gospel of John Book VI.35]; Victorinus[On the Creation of the World]

05:06-10 Cyprian[Treatise XII.Book II.15]

05:06-06:01 Revelation 6:16, 7:9-17, 12:11, 13:8-11, 14:1-10, 15:3, 17:4, 19:7-9, 21:9-27; Dead Sea Scrolls[4Q Enoch (4Q204[4QENAR]) Fragment 4]

05:07 1Kings 22:19; 2Chronicles 18:18; Psalms 47:8-9; Isaiah 6:1; Ezekiel 1:26-27; OT-Apocrypha[Sirach 1:8]

05:08 Psalms 141:2; Revelation 04:04n; Pseudepigrapha[3Baruch 11:8 (GK.)]; Irenaeus[Against Heresies Book IV.17.6; Fragments from the Lost Works 37]; Methodius[Banquet of the Ten Virgins 5.7]; Origen[Against Celsus Book VIII.17]; NT-Apocrypha[Apocalypse of Paul 1.14]

05:09 Psalms 33:3, 40:3-4, 96:1, 98:1, 144:9, 149:1; Isaiah 42:10, 53:7; Apostolic[1Clement 7:4]; Tertullian[On the Resurrection of the Flesh 56]; NT-Apocrypha[Acts of Thomas 1.72]

05:10 Exodus 19:6; Isaiah 61:1, 6; Hippolytus[Refutation of all Heresies Book X.30]

05:11 1Kings 22:19; Daniel 7:10; Pseudepigrapha[1Enoch 14:22, **40:1**; Apocalypse of Zephaniah 4:1; Joseph and Aseneth 16:17]

After this I beheld thousands of thousands, and myriads of myriads, and an infinite number of people, standing before the Lord of spirits. (Pseudepigrapha - 1Enoch 40:1)

05:12 1Chronicles 29:11; Isaiah 53:7

05:13 1Kings 22:19; 2Chronicles 18:18; Psalms 47:8, 146:6; Isaiah 6:1; Ezekiel 1:26-27; OT-Apocrypha[Sirach 1:8]

05:14 Matthew 28:17n; NT-Apocrypha[Apocalypse of Paul 1.14; Extract from the Latin Infancy Gospel in the Arundel Manuscript 73]

06:01 Pseudepigrapha[Sibylline Oracles 8.244]

06:01-02 Matthew 24:4-5; Mark 13:5-6; Luke 21:8; Revelation 13:1-6

06:01-12 Matthew 24:3-14 Mark 13:3-13; Luke 21:7-19; Revelation 13:1-8

06:02 Irenaeus[Against Heresies Book IV.21.3]; Tertullian[The Chaplet, or De Corona 15]

06:02-05 Zechariah 1:8, 6:1-3, 6

06:03-04 Matthew 24:6-7; Mark 13:7-8; Luke 21:9-10; Revelation 13:7

06:04 Pseudepigrapha[2Baruch 51.11]; Tertullian[On Modesty 20]

06:05-08 Matthew 24:7; Mark 13:8; Luke 21:11

06:06 2Kings 7:1; Pseudepigrapha[Joseph and Aseneth 8:5]

06:08 Jeremiah 14:12, 15:2-3, 21:7; Ezekiel 5:12, 17, 14:21, 29:5, 33:27; Hosea 13:14; Pseudepigrapha[Odes of Solomon 15:9]; Tertullian[On Modesty 20]

06:09 Clement of Alexandria[The Instructor Book II.11]; Cyprian[Treatises Attributed to Cyprian - On the Glory of Martyrdom 30]; Tertullian[A Treatise on the Soul 8, 55; Scorpiace 12]; NT-Apocrypha[Epistula Apostolorum 15]

06:09-10 Tertullian[Five Books in Reply to Marcion Book IV.186; On the Resurrection of the Flesh 25]

06:09-12 Matthew 24:8-9; Mark 13:8-9; Luke 21:12-19; 1Thessalonians 5:3; Cyprian[Treatise IX.21, XII.Book III.16]; Tertullian[On the Resurrection of the Flesh 38]

06:10 Deuteronomy 32:43; 2Kings 9:7; Psalms 79:5, 10; Zechariah 1:12; Pseudepigrapha[Sibylline Oracles 3.313]; Cyprian[Treatise III.18]; Origen[Gospel of Matthew Book XII.35]; Tertullian[On Prayer 5]

06:11 Pseudepigrapha[2Baruch 23:5; 2Enoch 22:8-9; 4Ezra 2:40-41]; Clement of Alexandria[The Instructor Book II.11]; NT-Apocrypha[5Ezra 2.39-40]; Egyptian Book of the Dead[Oration 125, 171]

06:12 Isaiah 50:3; Jeremiah 10:22; Ezekiel 38:19; Joel 2:31, 3:4, 15; Revelation 11:13, 16:18; Pseudepigrapha[Apocalypse of Elijah 3:8; Apocryphon of Ezekiel Fragment 2; Sibylline Oracles 2.205]; NT-Apocrypha[Apocalypse of Thomas Line 13, 17, 36]

06:12-13 Isaiah 13:10; Ezekiel 32:7-8; Joel 2:10, 31, 3:15

06:12-14 Pseudepigrapha[Sibylline Oracles 8.233]

06:12-17 Anonymous[Treatise Against the Heretic Novatian 17]

06:13 Matthew 24:29; Mark 13:24-25; Luke 21:25; Pseudepigrapha[Sibylline Oracles 8.190]; NT-Apocrypha[Epistula Apostolorum 34]

06:13-14 Isaiah 34:4; Tertullian[Against Hermogenes 34]

06:13-08:02 Zechariah 12:10-14; Matthew 24:29-31; Mark 13:24-27; Luke 21:25-28; 1Corinthians 15:51-55; 1Thessalonians 4:15-17; 2Thessalonians 2:1-2; Revelation 8:5, 11:12, 11:19, 14:1-5, 14:14-20, 16:8, 16:18

06:14 Ezekiel 26:15; Revelation 16:20; Pseudepigrapha[Sibylline Oracles 3:82, 8.413]; Hippolytus[Appendix to the Works of Hippolytus - On the End of the World 37]; Nag Hammadi[Gospel of Thomas 111]

06:15 Isaiah 2:10, 19, 21, 24:21, 34:12; Jeremiah 4:29; Pseudepigrapha[3Enoch 32:2; Apocalypse of Daniel 2:15]; NT-Apocrypha[Apocalypse of Thomas Line 44]

06:16 1Kings 22:19; 2Chronicles 18:18; Psalms 47:8; Isaiah 6:1; Ezekiel 1:26-27; Hosea 10:8; Luke 23:30; Revelation 5:6-6:1; OT-Apocrypha[Sirach 1:8]; Pseudepigrapha[Apocalypse of Elijah 2:34]

06:16-17 John 3:36n

06:17 Joel 2:11, 3:4; Nahum 1:6; Zephaniah 1:14; Malachi 3:2; Pseudepigrapha[Apocalypse of Zephaniah 12:6]

07:01 Jeremiah 49:36; Ezekiel 7:2, 37:9; Daniel 7:2; Zechariah 2:10, 6:5; Pseudepigrapha[4Ezra 2:40]; NT-Apocrypha[Apocalypse of Thomas Line 24, 70]

07:02 Job 31:35; 1Samuel 21:14; 1Kings 20:38, 41; Isaiah 41:25; Ezekiel 9:2; Rabbinic[Babylonian Horayot 12a]

07:02-05 Origen[Gospel of John Book I.2]

07:03 Ezekiel 9:4, 6; Pseudepigrapha[Apocalypse of Elijah 1:9; Psalms of Solomon 15:6]; Clement of Alexandria[Fragments from Macarius Chrysocephalus Parable of the Prodigal son 1, 6]; Cyprian[Treatise V.22]; Tertullian[A Strain of the Judgment of the Lord 237]; NT-Apocrypha[Apocalypse of Thomas Line 72]

07:03-08 Pseudepigrapha[4Baruch 6.25; 4Ezra 2.39]

07:03-09 Josephus[War 2.8.2-5 119-131]

07:04 Isaiah 49:6; Irenaeus[Against Heresies Book IV.29.2]; Methodius[Banquet of the Ten Virgins 6.5]; NT-Apocrypha[5Ezra 2.38]

07:04-08 Pseudepigrapha[Apocalypse of Elijah 5.4]

07:05-07 Irenaeus[Against Heresies Book V.30.2]

07:05-08 Genesis 35:22-26; Pseudepigrapha[Apocalypse of Daniel 8:2; Testament of Dan 5:4-7]; Rabbinic[Numbers Rabbah 2:10]

07:06 Genesis 48:1; Judges 17:1-13; Hosea 5:3

07:09 Leviticus 23:40, 43; OT-Apocrypha[2Maccabees 10:7]; Pseudepigrapha[4Ezra 2:42, 13.32-39]; Methodius[Banquet of the Ten Virgins 1.5]; NT-Apocrypha[5Ezra 2.39-40, 2.46; Apocalypse of Paul 1.12]

07:09-14 Pseudepigrapha[2Enoch 22:8-9]; Egyptian Book of the Dead[Oration 125, 171]

07:09-15 Cyprian[Treatise XI.11]

07:09-17 Revelation 5:6-6:1; Cyprian[Treatise XII.Book III.16]

07:10 1Kings 22:19; 2Chronicles 18:18; Psalms 47:8; Isaiah 6:1; Ezekiel 1:26-27; Revelation 12:10n; OT-Apocrypha[Sirach 1:8]

07:11 Psalms 97:7; Pseudepigrapha[2Baruch 51:11]

07:11-13 Acts 15:2-6n

07:13 Pseudepigrapha[Apocalypse of Elijah 5:6]; NT-Apocrypha[5Ezra 2.45]

07:14 Genesis 49:11; Exodus 19:10, 14; Ezekiel 37:3; Daniel 12:1; Matthew 24:21; Mark 13:19; Pseudepigrapha[4Ezra 2.27; Sibylline Oracles 14.302]; Cyprian[Treatise XI.Preface.3]; Irenaeus[Against Heresies Book V.28.4]; Tertullian[Scorpiace 12]

07:15 1Kings 22:19; 2Chronicles 18:18; Psalms 47:8; Isaiah 6:1; Ezekiel 1:26-27, 37:27; Pseudepigrapha[1Enoch 45.4]; OT-Apocrypha[Sirach 1:8]

07:16 Pseudepigrapha[Apocalypse of Elijah 1:9, 5:6]

07:16-17 Isaiah 49:10

07:17 Psalms 23:1-2; Isaiah 25:8, 49:10; Jeremiah 2:13, 31:16; Ezekiel 34:23; Pseudepigrapha[Odes of Solomon 6:18, 11:6; Testament of Benjamin 3.8; Testament of Joseph 19.8]; Tertullian[On the Resurrection of the Flesh 58]; Nag Hammadi[Tripartite Tractate 60]

08:01 Habakkuk 2:20; Zephaniah 1:7; OT-Apocrypha[Wisdom of Solomon 18:14]

08:01-13 Victorinus[On the Creation of the World]

08:01-09:21 Philo[On Rewards And Punishments (131-136, 139-151, 168-170) cf. {Leviticus 26:14-39, Deuteronomy 28:23, 30:3-10, Revelation 8:1-9:21, 11:1-6, 13:16-17, 16:1-21}]

08:02 Joshua 6:4, 6; OT-Apocrypha[Tobit 12:15]; Pseudepigrapha[Life of Adam and Eve (Apocalypse of Moses) 22:3]

08:02-06 Pseudepigrapha[4Baruch 3.2-3]

08:03 Exodus 30:1-3, 7; Amos 9:1; OT-Apocrypha[Tobit 12:12]; Pseudepigrapha[3Baruch 11:8 (Gk.)]; NT-Apocrypha[Epistula Apostolorum 13]

08:03-04 Psalms 141:2; Tertullian[Five Books in Reply to Marcion Book IV.246; On Prayer 16]

08:05 Exodus 19:16-19; Leviticus 16:12; Esther 1:1; Isaiah 29:6; Ezekiel 10:2; Revelation 11:19; Revelation 16:18; NT-Apocrypha[Epistula Apostolorum 34]

08:07 Exodus 9:23-25; Ezekiel 5:2, 12, 38:22; Joel 3:3; Zechariah 13:9; OT-Apocrypha[Sirach 39:29; Wisdom of Solomon 16:22]; NT-Apocrypha[Epistula Apostolorum 34]

08:07-12 Pseudepigrapha[Life of Abraham 4:3]; Rabbinic[Exodus Rabbah 12:2]

08:08 Exodus 7:20-21; Jeremiah 51:25; Pseudepigrapha[1Enoch 18:13, 21:3]

08:10 Isaiah 14:12; Daniel 8:10; Pseudepigrapha[1Enoch 86:1; Sibylline Oracles 5.155]; NT-Apocrypha[Epistula Apostolorum 34]

08:11 Exodus 15:23; Jeremiah 9:14, 23:15

08:12 Exodus 10:21; Isaiah 13:10; Ezekiel 32:7-8; Joel 2:10, 3:15; Amos 8:9; Pseudepigrapha[Life of Adam and Eve (Apocalypse of Moses) 36:3]

08:13 Isaiah 24:17, 26:21; Hosea 4:1

09:01 Pseudepigrapha[1Enoch 86:1; 2Enoch 42:1; Sibylline Oracles 5.155]; Cyprian[Treatise XII.Book III.59]; NT-Apocrypha[Epistula Apostolorum 34]

09:01-02 Revelation 9:11, 11:7, 17:8, 20:1-3; Dead Sea Scrolls[4Q Enoch (4Q204[4QENAR]) COL VIII 28-30]

09:02 Genesis 19:28; Exodus 19:18; Joel 2:10; Pseudepigrapha[4Ezra 7:36]; NT-Apocrypha[Apocalypse of Thomas Line 18]

09:03 Exodus 10:12-15; OT-Apocrypha[Wisdom of Solomon 16:9]

09:04 Ezekiel 9:4, 6; Pseudepigrapha[Psalms of Solomon 15:6]; Cyprian[Treatise V.22]

09:06 Job 3:21; Jeremiah 8:3; Hosea 10:8; Pseudepigrapha[Apocalypse of Daniel 12:3; Apocalypse of Elijah 2:5, 2:32; Sibylline Oracles 2.307, 8.353]

09:07 Job 39:19; Joel 2:4-5

09:07-10 Pseudepigrapha[Joseph and Aseneth 16:18]

09:08 Joel 1:6; Pseudepigrapha[Apocalypse of Zephaniah 6:8]

09:09 Joel 2:5

09:10 Clement of Alexandria[Stromata Book III.18]

09:11 Job 26:6, 28:22; Psalms 88:12; Proverbs 15:11; Revelation 9:1-2; Pseudepigrapha[Odes of Solomon 33:1, 38:9]; Dead Sea Scrolls[4Q Enoch (4Q204[4QENAR]) COL VIII 28-30]; NT-Apocrypha[Acts of Thomas 1.32]

09:13 Exodus 27:2, 30:1-3, 40:5; Dead Sea Scrolls[4QSongs of the Sabbath Sacrifice (4Q403 [4QShirShabb]) COL I 41-43]

09:13-18 Pseudepigrapha[Sibylline Oracles 5.93]

09:14 Genesis 15:18; Deuteronomy 1:7; Joshua 1:4; Pseudepigrapha[Testament of Solomon 17:4]

09:15 Pseudepigrapha[Life of Abraham 4:3; Sibylline Oracles 3.544, 5.103]

09:17 Job 41:10-12; Pseudepigrapha[2Enoch 1:5]; NT-Apocrypha[Apocalypse of Thomas Line 26]

09:18 Pseudepigrapha[Life of Abraham 4:3; Sibylline Oracles 3.544, 5.103]

09:20 Deuteronomy 32:17; Psalms 96:5, 115:4-7, 135:15-17; Isaiah 2:8, 20, 17:8; Daniel 5:4, 23; Micah 5:12; Pseudepigrapha[Joseph and Aseneth 2:3, 9:2]

09:21 Exodus 20:13-15; 2Kings 9:22; Nahum 3:4

10:01 Exodus 13:21; Pseudepigrapha[Joseph and Aseneth 14:9, 18:9]; Tertullian[The Chaplet, or De Corona 15]

10:02 Ezekiel 2:9

10:03 1Samuel 7:10; Psalms 29:3; Jeremiah 25:30; Amos 1:2, 3:8; Hosea 11:10

10:03-04 Pseudepigrapha[2Baruch 59.11]

10:04 Daniel 8:26, 12:4, 9; Origen[Against Celsus Book VI.6; Gospel of John Book V.3]

10:05-06 Deuteronomy 32:40; Daniel 12:7

10:06 Genesis 14:19, 22; Exodus 20:11; Nehemiah 9:6; Psalms 146:6; Pseudepigrapha[Testament of Job 2:4]

10:07 Jeremiah 7:25, 25:4; Daniel 9:6, 10, 12:7; Amos 3:7; Zechariah 1:6; Acts 3:18n

10:09 Psalms 119:103; Jeremiah 33:9; Origen[Against Celsus Book VI.6]

10:09-10 Ezekiel 2:8, 3:1-3; Origen[Gospel of John Book V.4]

10:11 Jeremiah 1:10, 25:30; Ezekiel 25:2; Daniel 3:4, 7:14

11:01 Ezekiel 40:3; Zechariah 2:1-2; Pseudepigrapha[Apocalypse of Elijah 4:7]

11:01-06 Philo[On Rewards And Punishments (131-136, 139-151, 168-170) cf. {Leviticus 26:14-39, Deuteronomy 28:23, 30:3-10, Revelation 8:1-9:21, 11:1-6, 13:16-17, 16:1-21}]

11:02 Psalms 79:1; Isaiah 63:18; Zechariah 12:3; Luke 21:24

11:03 2Kings 19:2; Isaiah 37:2; Pseudepigrapha[Apocalypse of Elijah 3:1, 4.7, 5.32]; Hippolytus[Appendix to the Works of Hippolytus - On the End of the World 21; Treatise on Christ and Antichrist 47, 61]; Tertullian[A Treatise on the Soul 50]

11:03-12 NT-Apocrypha[Acts of Pilate XXV 1; Gospel of Bartholomew H:16-17; History of Joseph the Carpenter 31]

11:03-13 Pseudepigrapha[Apocalypse of Daniel 14:1-11]

11:04 Zechariah 4:3, 10-14

11:04-06 Hippolytus[Treatise on Christ and Antichrist 47]

11:05 2Samuel 22:9; 2Kings 1:10; Psalms 97:3; Jeremiah 5:14

11:06 Exodus 7:17-20; 1Samuel 4:8; 1Kings 17:1; Hippolytus[Appendix to the Works of Hippolytus - On the End of the World 21]

11:07 Daniel 7:3, 7, 21; Revelation 9:1-2, 13:5-7, 17:8; Dead Sea Scrolls[4Q Enoch (4Q204[4QENAR]) COL VIII 28-30]; Nag Hammadi[On the Origin of the World 118-119]

11:07-11 Pseudepigrapha[Apocalypse of Elijah 4:13]

11:08 Isaiah 1:9-10; Jeremiah 22:8; Ezekiel 11:6, 16:46, 49; Joel 3:19; Pseudepigrapha[Sibylline Oracles 6.21]

11:09 Psalms 79:2

11:10 Pseudepigrapha[Joseph and Aseneth 11:6]

11:10-11 Psalms 105:38

11:11 Genesis 15:12; Exodus 15:16; Ezekiel 37:10

11:11-12 Josephus[Antiquities 4.8.48 326]

11:12 2Kings 2:11; Zechariah 12:10-14; Matthew 24:29-31; Mark 13:24-27; Luke 21:25-28; 1Corinthians 15:51-55; 1Thessalonians 4:15-16; 2Thessalonians 2:1-2; Revelation 1:7, 6:13-8:2, 8:5, 11:19, 14:1-5, 14:14-16, 16:8, 16:18; Pseudepigrapha[Apocalypse of Elijah 4:19]

11:13 Ezra 1:2; Ezekiel 38:19-20; Daniel 2:18; Jonah 1:9; Revelation 6:12, 16:18; NT-Apocrypha[Epistula Apostolorum 34]

11:15 Exodus 15:18; Psalms 2:2, 10:16, 22:28-29; Daniel 2:44, 7:14, 27; Obadiah 1:21; Zechariah 14:9; Pseudepigrapha[2Enoch 1:5; Joseph and Aseneth 19:5; Sibylline Oracles 4.174-175]; Novatian[Treatise Concerning the Trinity 20]

11:16 Acts 15:2-6n; Revelation 04:04n; Pseudepigrapha[Testament of Job 33:1]; Clement of Alexandria[Stromata Book VI.13]; NT-Apocrypha[Apocalypse of Paul 1.14]

11:16-17 Cyprian[Treatise XII.Book III.20]

11:17 2Samuel 7:8; Amos 4:13

11:18 Exodus 15:14; Psalms 2:1, 46:7, 61:6, 99:1, 115:13; Jeremiah 30:23, 51:25; Daniel 9:6, 10; Amos 3:7; Micah 6:9; Zechariah 1:6; Pseudepigrapha[Apocalypse of Elijah 5:4]

11:19 Exodus 9:24, 19:16; 1Kings 8:1, 6; 2Chronicles 5:7; Esther 1:1; Isaiah 29:6; Ezekiel 1:13; Revelation 8:5, 16:18, 21; OT-Apocrypha[2Maccabees 2:4-8]; Pseudepigrapha[2Baruch 59.11]; Irenaeus[Against Heresies Book IV.18.6]; NT-Apocrypha[Epistula Apostolorum 34]

12:01 Genesis 37:9; Psalms 104:2; Isaiah 7:14; Pseudepigrapha[Joseph and Aseneth 5:5; Testament of Naphtali 5:1]; Nag Hammadi[On the Origin of the World 126]

12:01-03 Pseudepigrapha[2Baruch 25:4]

12:01-06 Pseudepigrapha[2Enoch 72:3]; Hippolytus[Treatise on Christ and Antichrist 60]; Methodius[Banquet of the Ten Virgins 8.4]

12:01-17 Pseudepigrapha[Testament of Asher 7:3; Testament of Solomon 12:1]

12:01-13:18 Pseudepigrapha[Sibylline Oracles 8.88]

12:02 Isaiah 26:17, 66:7; Micah 4:10; Pseudepigrapha[4Ezra 4.40-43]; Rabbinic[Babylonian Ketubot 111a]; NT-Apocrypha[6Ezra 17.36-40]

12:03 Isaiah 14:29, 27:1; Ezekiel 29:3; Daniel 7:7, 24; Pseudepigrapha[Odes of Solomon 22:5; Sibylline Oracles 8.88]

12:03-07 NT-Apocrypha[6Ezra 15.29]

12:04 Daniel 8:10; Pseudepigrapha[Sibylline Oracles 1.314]

12:05 Psalms 2:9; Isaiah 7:14, 66:7; Pseudepigrapha[Sibylline Oracles 8.196, 8.248]; Anonymous[Treatise Against the Heretic Novatian 14]; NT-Apocrypha[History of Joseph the Carpenter 6]

12:06 1Kings 17:1-7; Hosea 2:16; Pseudepigrapha[Apocalypse of Adam 7:9]

12:07 Daniel 10:13, 21, 12:1; Jude 1:9; Pseudepigrapha[Sibylline Oracles 5.514; Testament of Abraham 1:4; Testament of Levi 5:6; Testament of Solomon 1:7]; Rabbinic[Exodus Rabbah 18:5; Ruth Rabba on 1]; Clement[First Epistle Concerning Virginity 5]; NT-Apocrypha[Apocalypse of Paul 1.14; Apocalypse of Thomas Line 71]

12:07-09 Apostolic[Papias Fragment 24:1]

12:07-12 Pseudepigrapha[Life of Adam and Eve Vita 14:1]

12:08 Daniel 2:35

12:09 Genesis 3:1, 14; Job 2:1; Isaiah 14:12; Luke 10:18; Pseudepigrapha[Joseph and Aseneth 12:9; Life of Adam and Eve Vita 12:1; Lives of the Prophets 12:13; Testament of Benjamin 3:7]; Rabbinic[Babylonian Sanhedrin 97b]; Apostolic[Papias Fragment 11:1]; Clement of

Alexandria[Exhortation to the Heathen 1; The Instructor Book III.2]; Irenaeus[Against Heresies
Book I.27.4, IV.Preface.4]; Teaching of the Twelve Apostles 16.4; Tertullian[An Answer to the Jews
10; To his Wife Book I.6]; Nag Hammadi[Apocryphon of John 10]; NT-Apocrypha[Acts of Peter 1.6;
Apocalypse of Peter 1.2]

12:09-10 Zechariah 3:1

12:10 This section also includes topical notes for: Salvation - Job 1:9-11, 2:4; Acts 4:12, 16:17; Romans
1:16, 10:9-13; 2Corinthians 7:10; Ephesians 1:13; Philippians 2:12; 1Thessalonians 5:9; 2Timothy 2:10,
3:15; Titus 2:11; Hebrews 1:14, 2:10, 5:9, 6:9; 1Peter 1:5, 9-10, 2:2; 2Peter 3:15; Revelation 7:10, 19:1;
Rabbinic[Babylonian Sanhedrin 98b]; Anonymous[Martyrdom of Justin Martyr 5]; Clement of
Alexandria[Exhortation to the Heathen 1, 9-12; Fragments from the Latin Translation of
Cassiodorus Comments on 1John, 1Peter; Stromata Book II.16, V.13, VI.6, 12-15, VII.2, 7, 12; The
Instructor Book I.1-2, 6, 8, 10; Who is the Rich Man that shall be Saved 1-2, 18, 20, 29];
Irenaeus[Against Heresies Book I.6.2, 10.3, 22.1, 23.2, 5, 24.5, 27.3, 28.1, 31.3, II.20.3, 29.1, 34.3, III.1.1,
4.2, 5.2, 12.5, 18.1-2, 6, IV.8.1, 14.1-2, 15.1-2, 16.2, 28.3, 33.1, 4, 15, 41.4, V.2.2, 5.2, 11.1-2, 12.4, 14.1-2,
19.2, 20.1, 21.3; Demonstration of the Apostolic Preaching 88; Fragments from the Lost Works 10];
Justin[Dialogue with Trypho 8, 24, 35, 45-47, 74, 91-92, 94, 100, 102, 105, 111, 121, 138, 141; First
Apology 14, 16; Fragments from the Lost Writings of Justin 10; On the Resurrection 8, 10];
Tertullian[A Treatise on the Soul 35]; Epic of Gilgamesh[The Story of the Flood]

12:11 Revelation 5:6-6:1; Pseudepigrapha[Testament of Judah 25:4]

12:12 Deuteronomy 32:43; Psalms 96:11; Isaiah 44:23, 49:13

12:14 Exodus 19:4; Isaiah 40:31; Ezekiel 17:3, 7; Daniel 7:25, 12:7; Pseudepigrapha[Apocalypse of Elijah
3:1; Testament of Naphtali 5:6]; Irenaeus[Against Heresies Book II.31.3]

12:15 Pseudepigrapha[Apocalypse of Elijah 1:4]; Rabbinic[Exodus Rabba on 9:4]

12:16 Numbers 16:30, 32; Deuteronomy 11:6

12:17 Genesis 3:15; Daniel 7:7, 21; Pseudepigrapha[Lives of the Prophets 12:13]

13:01 Isaiah 27:1; Daniel 7:3, 7, 24; Revelation 17:3; Pseudepigrapha[4Ezra 11:1]

13:01-04 Clement of Alexandria[The Instructor Book II.1]; Irenaeus[Against Heresies Book V.29.2]

13:01-06 Matthew 24:4-5, 24:15; Mark 13:5-6, 13:14; Luke 21:8, 21:20; 2Thessalonians 2:3-12; Revelation
6:1-2

13:01-17 Pseudepigrapha[Sibylline Oracles 3.63-74]

13:01-08 Matthew 24:3-14; Mark 13:3-13; Luke 21:7-19; Revelation 6:1-12

13:01-18 Irenaeus[Against Heresies Book V.30.4]; Lactantius[Divine Institutes Book VII.17]

13:02 Daniel 7:4-6; Hosea 13:7; Irenaeus[Against Heresies Book V.28.2]

13:04 Exodus 15:11; Psalms 89:7; Pseudepigrapha[Martyrdom and Ascension of Isaiah (3:13-4:22 =
Testament of Hezekiah) 4:8]

13:05 Daniel 7:8, 11, 20; Pseudepigrapha[Apocalypse of Elijah 3:1]

13:05-06 Daniel 11:36

13:05-07 Daniel 7:25

13:07 Daniel 7:7-8, 21; Matthew 24:6-7; Mark 13:7-8; Luke 21:9-10; Revelation 6:3-4

13:07-18 Matthew 24:16-21; Mark 13:14; Luke 21:21-24

13:08 Exodus 32:32-33; Psalms 69:28; Isaiah 53:7; Daniel 12:1; Pseudepigrapha[Apocalypse of
Zephaniah 3:8]; Apostolic[Ignatius - Letter to the Ephesians (Prologue)]; Nag Hammadi[Gospel of
Truth 20]

13:08-11 Revelation 5:6-6:1

13:08-14 Pseudepigrapha[Martyrdom and Ascension of Isaiah (3:13-4:22 = Testament of Hezekiah) 4:8-
12]

13:09-10 Jeremiah 15:2, 43:11

13:10 Pseudepigrapha[The Sentences of the Syriac Menander 18-19]; Rabbinic[Babylonian Baba Batra
8b]

13:11 Daniel 8:3; Irenaeus[Against Heresies Book V.28.2]

13:11-18 Hippolytus[Treatise on Christ and Antichrist 48]; Nag Hammadi[Concept of Our Great
Power 44]

13:13 1Kings 18:24-39; Pseudepigrapha[Apocalypse of Elijah 3:6]

13:14 Deuteronomy 13:2-4; Pseudepigrapha[1Enoch 54:6]; Irenaeus[Against Heresies Book V.28.2]

13:15 Daniel 3:5-6

13:16 Exodus 28:36; Isaiah 44:5; Pseudepigrapha[Psalms of Solomon 15.9]

13:16-17 This section also includes topical notes for: Mark of the Beast - Revelation 14:9-11, 15:2,
16:2, 19:20, 20:4; Pseudepigrapha[Testament of Solomon 17:4]; Dead Sea Scrolls[Damascus

Document (CD-B) COL XIX 12]; Philo[On Rewards And Punishments (131-136, 139-151, 168-170) cf. {Leviticus 26:14-39, Deuteronomy 28:23, 30:3-10, Revelation 8:1-9:21, 11:1-6, 13:16-17, 16:1-21}]

13:17 Pseudepigrapha[3Maccabees 2.29]

13:18 Ezra 2:13; Pseudepigrapha[Apocalypse of Daniel 9:25; Sibylline Oracles 1.141]; Hippolytus[Appendix to the Works of Hippolytus - On the End of the World 28]; Irenaeus[Against Heresies Book V.28.2, 29.2, 30.1-3]; Nag Hammadi[Gospel of Thomas 100]

14:01 Isaiah 4:5; Ezekiel 9:4; Joel 3:5; Revelation 7:3; Pseudepigrapha[4Ezra 13.32-39; Apocalypse of Elijah 1:9; Testament of Solomon 17:4]; Cyprian[Treatise XII.Book II.22]

14:01-05 Matthew 24:29-31; Mark 13:24-27; Luke 21:25-28; 1Corinthians 15:51-55; 1Thessalonians 4:15-17; 2Thessalonians 2:1-2; Revelation 6:6:13-8:2, 8:5, 11:12, 11:19, 14:14-16, 16:8, 16:18; Methodius[Banquet of the Ten Virgins 1.5]; Origen[Gospel of John Book I.2]

14:01-10 Revelation 5:6-6:1

14:02 Ezekiel 1:24, 43:2

14:03 Psalms 33:3, 40:3-4, 96:1, 98:1, 144:9, 149:1; Isaiah 42:10; Acts 15:2-6n; Josephus[**War 2.8.2-3 119-123**]; Tertullian[On the Resurrection of the Flesh 56]

> These Essenes reject pleasures as an evil, but esteem continence, and the conquest over our passions, to be virtue. They neglect wedlock, but choose out other persons children, while they are pliable, and fit for learning, and esteem them to be of their kindred, and form them according to their own manners. They do not absolutely deny the fitness of marriage, and the succession of mankind thereby continued...They think that oil is a defilement; and if any one of them be anointed without his own approbation, it is wiped off his body; for they think to be sweaty is a good thing, as they do also to be clothed in white garments. (Josephus - War 2.8.2-3 119-123)

14:04 Pseudepigrapha[Joseph and Aseneth 4:7; Vision of Ezra 10]; Cyprian[Treatise II.4, XII.Book III.21, 32]; Methodius[Banquet of the Ten Virgins 6.5]; Pseud-Irenaeus; Tertullian[On the Resurrection of the Flesh 27]; NT-Apocrypha[Acts of Paul and Thecla 1.12; Pseudo-Titus Epistle Line 12]

14:05 Psalms 32:2; Isaiah 53:9; Zephaniah 3:13; Revelation 3:13

14:06 Origen[De Principiis Book IV.1.25]

14:06-07 Cyprian[Treatise XI.Preface.3, 2]

14:07 Jeremiah 13:16; Pseudepigrapha[Testament of Job 2:4]; Nag Hammadi[Teachings of Silvanus 108-109, 114]

14:08 Isaiah 21:9; Jeremiah 25:15-31, 51:7-8; Daniel 4:27; Revelation 18:2; Pseudepigrapha[4Ezra 15:47; Sibylline Oracles Fragment 3.39, 5.143]; Rabbinic[Leviticus Rabba on 13:5]

14:08-09 Plato[Laws VIII 831d]

14:09 Pseudepigrapha[Psalms of Solomon 15.9]

14:09-11 Revelation 13:16-17n; Pseudepigrapha[3Maccabees 2.29]; Cyprian[Treatise XI.3]

14:10 Genesis 19:24; Psalms 11:4, 6, 75:8-9; Isaiah 51:17, 22; Jeremiah 25:15; Ezekiel 38:22; OT-Apocrypha[3Maccabees 2:5]; Rabbinic[Numbers Rabba on 11:1]; NT-Apocrypha[Epistula Apostolorum 44]

14:10-11 Pseudepigrapha[1Enoch 27:1-3]

14:11 Isaiah 34:10; Pseudepigrapha[Martyrdom and Ascension of Isaiah (3:13-4:22 = Testament of Hezekiah) 4:12]

14:12 Deuteronomy 28:1-2

14:13 Rabbinic[Mishna Aboth 6:9; Lamentations Rabba on 1:50]

14:14 2Samuel 12:30; 1Chronicles 20:2; Daniel 7:13

14:14-16 Zechariah 12:10-14; Matthew 24:29-31; Mark 13:24-27; Luke 21:25-28; 1Corinthians 15:51-55; 1Thessalonians 4:15-17; 2Thessalonians 2:1-2; Revelation 1:7, 6:13-8:2, 8:5, 11:12, 11:19, 14:1-5, 16:8, 16:18

14:15 Jeremiah 51:33; Joel 3:13; Pseudepigrapha[Sibylline Oracles 1.387]

14:16 Zechariah 5:2

14:16-17 Cyprian[Treatise XII.Book III.20]

14:17-20 Matthew 24:32; Mark 13:28; Luke 21:29-33

14:18 Jeremiah 25:30; Joel 3:13; Pseudepigrapha[Joseph and Aseneth 25:2]

14:19-20 Lamentations 1:15; Isaiah 63:2-3

14:20 Revelation 19:15; Pseudepigrapha[4Ezra 15:36; Apocalypse of Daniel 4:8]

15:01 Leviticus 26:21; Revelation 15:7-17:1n; Pseudepigrapha[2Baruch 27:4; 3Baruch 4:1 (Gk.)]

15:02 Revelation 13:16-17n; Pseudepigrapha[2Enoch 3:3; Joseph and Aseneth 4:1; Life of Adam and Eve Vita 29:2]

15:02-04 Cyprian[Treatise XII.Book III.20]

15:03 Exodus 15:1, 11, 34:10; Numbers 12:7; Deuteronomy 34:5; Joshua 1:2, 7, 14:7; Psalms 92:5, 111:2, 139:14, 145:17; Jeremiah 10:10; Amos 4:13; Revelation 5:6-6:1; OT-Apocrypha[Tobit 13:7, 11]; Pseudepigrapha[1Enoch 9:4; 3Baruch 4:1 (Gk.)]

15:03-04 Deuteronomy 32:4; Jeremiah 10:6-7

15:04 Psalms 86:9, 98:2; Isaiah 2:2; Jeremiah 11:20, 16:19; Malachi 1:11; Dead Sea Scrolls[1Q Micah Pesher (1Q14[1QPMIC]) Fragments 22-23 4-5]

15:05 Exodus 38:21, 40:34; Daniel 10:5

15:06 Leviticus 26:21; Pseudepigrapha[Joseph and Aseneth 14:14]

15:07 Psalms 75:8; Jeremiah 25:15

15:07-17:01 This section also includes topical notes for: Apocalypse - Revelation 15:1, 21:9; Dead Sea Scrolls[11Q New Jerusalem (11Q18[11QNJAR]) Fragment 17 1-2]; Philo[Concerning Noah's Work As A Planter (77-79) cf. {Numbers 20:5-13}; On Dreams, That they Are God-Sent (2.212-2.214) cf. {Genesis 40:19, Revelation 19:17-21}; On Rewards And Punishments (131-136, 139-151, 153-157, 168-170) cf. {Leviticus 26:14-39, Deuteronomy 28:23, 30:3-10, Revelation 8:1-9:21, 11:1-6, 13:16-17, 16:1-21, 20:9}; On the Confusion of Tongues (197) cf. {Deuteronomy 30:4, Revelation 20:4, 21:24}]; Irenaeus[Against Heresies Book IV.30.4]

15:08 Exodus 40:34-35; 1Kings 8:10-11; 2Chronicles 5:13-14; Isaiah 6:1, 4; Ezekiel 44:4

16:01 Psalms 69:25; Isaiah 66:6; Ezekiel 14:19, 23:31; Zephaniah 3:8

16:01-02 Jeremiah 10:25

16:01-21 Philo[On Rewards And Punishments (131-136, 139-151, 168-170) cf. {Leviticus 26:14-39, Deuteronomy 28:23, 30:3-10, Revelation 8:1-9:21, 11:1-6, 13:16-17, 16:1-21}]; Tertullian[On the Resurrection of the Flesh 25]

16:02 Exodus 9:10; Deuteronomy 28:35; Revelation 13:16-17n; Pseudepigrapha[3Maccabees 2.29]

16:03-04 Exodus 7:17-24

16:04 Psalms 78:44

16:05 Deuteronomy 32:4; Psalms 119:137, 145:17; Pseudepigrapha[1Enoch 66:2; 2Enoch 19:4; Sibylline Oracles 7.35]; Origen[Gospel of John Book I.40]

16:06 Psalms 79:3; Isaiah 49:26

16:07 Psalms 19:9-10, 119:137; Daniel 3:27; Amos 4:13; Pseudepigrapha[Apocalypse of Elijah 5:24]; Origen[Gospel of John Book I.40]; NT-Apocrypha[Apocalypse of Paul 1.16; Apocalypse of Peter 1.7]

16:08 Matthew 24:29-31; Mark 13:24-27; Luke 21:25-28; 1Corinthians 15:51-55; 1Thessalonians 4:15-17; 2Thessalonians 2:1-2; Revelation 1:7, 6:13-8:2, 11:12, 14:1-5, 14:14-16

16:09 Isaiah 52:5

16:10 Exodus 10:21-22; Isaiah 8:22

16:11 Daniel 2:18

16:12 Psalms 106:9; Isaiah 11:15-16, 41:2, 25, 44:27, 46:11, 51:10; Jeremiah 50:38, 51:36

16:13 Exodus 8:3; 1Kings 22:21-23; Psalms 78:45, 105:30

16:14 Amos 4:13

16:15 Genesis 35:2; Isaiah 14:13, 52:1, 59:6, 61:10; Ezekiel 42:14; Zechariah 3:4; Matthew 24:42-51n; Luke 12:34-40; 1Thessalonians 5:2; James 5:2; 2Peter 3:10; Revelation 3:3-4; Rabbinic[Babylonian Sanhedrin 39a cf. {Genesis 2:21}]; Cyprian[Treatise XII.Book III.16]; Nag Hammadi[Gospel of Philip 56]

16:16 Judges 5:19; 2Kings 9:27, 23:29; 2Chronicles 35:22; Zechariah 12:11; Pseudepigrapha[4Ezra 13:34]

16:17 Isaiah 66:6; Pseudepigrapha[Apocalypse of Daniel 3:7]

16:18 Exodus 19:16-19, 24; Esther 1:1; Daniel 12:1; Revelation 8:5, 11:9, 13; Pseudepigrapha[2Baruch 59.11]; NT-Apocrypha[Apocalypse of Thomas Line 46]

16:18-19 NT-Apocrypha[Epistula Apostolorum 34]

16:19 Psalms 75:8; Isaiah 51:17, 22; Jeremiah 25:15; Pseudepigrapha[Sibylline Oracles 5.143]

16:20 Revelation 6:14

16:21 Exodus 9:23-24; Numbers 11:33; Revelation 11:19; NT-Apocrypha[Epistula Apostolorum 34]

17:01 Jeremiah 51:13; Pseudepigrapha[4Ezra 16.47-50; Sibylline Oracles 2.18, 8.194]; Cyprian[Treatise II.12]

17:01-04 Cyprian[Treatise XII.Book III.36]

17:01-18 Tertullian[An Answer to the Jews 9; On the Apparel of Women Book II.12]

17:02 Isaiah 23:17; Jeremiah 25:15, 51:7; Nahum 3:4

17:03 Isaiah 21:1; Revelation 13:1

17:04 Jeremiah 51:7; Ezekiel 28:13; Pseudepigrapha[4Ezra 15:47; Joseph and Aseneth 2:3]

17:05 Pseudepigrapha[4Ezra 16.47-50]

17:06 Isaiah 34:7; Tertullian[Scorpiace 12]

17:08 Exodus 32:32-33; Psalms 69:28; Daniel 7:3, 12:1; Revelation 9:1-2, 11:7, 21:27n; Dead Sea
    Scrolls[4Q Enoch (4Q204[4QENAR]) COL VIII 28-30]; Apostolic[Ignatius - Letter to the Ephesians
    (Prologue)]; Irenaeus[Against Heresies Book V.30.4]; Nag Hammadi[Gospel of Truth 20]; NT-
    Apocrypha[Apocalypse of Peter 1.17]

17:09 Pseudepigrapha[1Enoch 21:3; Apocalypse of Daniel 7:5; Sibylline Oracles 11.113, 13;45];
    Hippolytus[Treatise on Christ and Antichrist 29]

17:11 Pseudepigrapha[Sibylline Oracles 4.138]

17:12 Daniel 7:20, 24; Irenaeus[Against Heresies Book V.26.1]

17:14 Deuteronomy 10:17; Psalms 136:3; Daniel 2:47; 1Timothy 6:15; Revelation 5:6-6:1, 19:16n; OT-
    Apocrypha[2Maccabees 13:4; 3Maccabees 5:35]; Pseudepigrapha[1Enoch 9:4]; Tertullian[On
    Baptism 16]; NT-Apocrypha[Epistula Apostolorum 3, 39]

17:15 Jeremiah 51:13; Pseudepigrapha[4Ezra 16.47-50]; Anonymous[Treatise Against the Heretic
    Novatian 5]

17:16 Leviticus 21:9; Psalms 27:2; Jeremiah 34:22; Ezekiel 16:39, 23:29, 26:19; Hosea 2:5; Micah 3:3;
    Pseudepigrapha[Sibylline Oracles 8.142, 8.96]

17:17 Egyptian Book of the Dead[Oration 27]

17:18 Psalms 2:2, 89:28; Isaiah 24:21; Pseudepigrapha[Apocalypse of Daniel 7:5]

18:01 Ezekiel 43:2; Pseudepigrapha[Sibylline Oracles 3.302, 5.162, 14.208; Testament of Job 25:1]

18:01-24 Tertullian[On the Resurrection of the Flesh 25]

18:02 Isaiah 13:21, 21:9, 34:11, 14; Jeremiah 9:10, 50:39, 51:7-8; Pseudepigrapha[Baruch 4:35; Sibylline
    Oracles 5.143]; Tertullian[On the Resurrection of the Flesh 22]

18:03 Isaiah 23:8, 17; Jeremiah 25:15, 51:7; Ezekiel 27:12, 18, 33

18:04 Isaiah 48:20, 52:11; Jeremiah 50:8, 51:6, 45; Cyprian[Treatise III.10]; Tertullian[The Chaplet, or De
    Corona 13]

18:04-05 Jeremiah 51:9

18:04-09 Cyprian[Treatise XII.Book III.34]

18:05 Genesis 18:20-21

18:06 Psalms 137:8; Isaiah 40:2; Jeremiah 16:18, 50:15, 29

18:07 Pseudepigrapha[4Ezra 15:49; Apocalypse of Daniel 7:10; Sibylline Oracles 5.169, 5.173, 11.290]

18:07-08 Isaiah 47:7-9; Pseudepigrapha[Sibylline Oracles 3.77]

18:08 Leviticus 21:9; Isaiah 47:14; Jeremiah 50:31, 34

18:09 Ezekiel 27:30-35

18:09-10 Ezekiel 26:16-17

18:10 Daniel 4:30; Pseudepigrapha[Apocalypse of Daniel 7:2]

18:11 Ezekiel 27:36; Pseudepigrapha[Apocalypse of Elijah 2:31]

18:11-20 Nag Hammadi[Gospel of Thomas 64]

18:12 Ezekiel 27:12-22

18:13 Genesis 36:6; Ezekiel 27:12-13, 22; Pseudepigrapha[Testament of Job 32:10]

18:15 Ezekiel 27:31, 36

18:16 Ezekiel 28:13; Pseudepigrapha[Apocalypse of Daniel 7:2, 7:10]

18:17 Ezekiel 27:27-29

18:17-19 Pseudepigrapha[Apocalypse of Daniel 7:13]

18:18 Isaiah 34:10; Jeremiah 22:8; Ezekiel 27:32

18:19 Ezekiel 26:19, 27:25-36; Pseudepigrapha[Apocalypse of Daniel 7:2; Joseph and Aseneth 10:14;
    Testament of Job 28:3]

18:20 Deuteronomy 32:43; Psalms 96:11; Isaiah 44:23, 49:13; Jeremiah 51:48

18:21 Jeremiah 51:63-64; Ezekiel 26:12, 21

18:21-22 Pseudepigrapha[Sibylline Oracles 5.143]

18:22 Isaiah 24:8; Jeremiah 25:10; Ezekiel 26:13; Pseudepigrapha[Sibylline Oracles 8.115]

18:23 Isaiah 23:8, 34:12, 47:9; Jeremiah 7:34, 16:9, 25:10; Nahum 3:4

18:24 Jeremiah 51:49; Ezekiel 24:7, 36:18

19:01 Psalms 104:35; Daniel 10:6; Revelation 12:10n; OT-Apocrypha[Tobit 13:18];
    Pseudepigrapha[1Enoch 39:7; Psalms of Solomon 8:2]

> **All the holy and the elect sung before him, in appearance like a blaze of fire; their mouths being full of blessings, and their lips glorifying the name of the Lord of spirits. And righteousness incessantly dwelt before him. (Pseudepigrapha - 1Enoch 39:7)**

19:02 Deuteronomy 32:43; 2Kings 9:7; Psalms 19:9-10, 79:10, 119:137; Jeremiah 51:25; Pseudepigrapha[4Ezra 16.47-50; Apocalypse of Elijah 5:24]; NT-Apocrypha[Apocalypse of Paul 1.16, 1.18; Apocalypse of Peter 1.7]

19:03 Psalms 104:35; Isaiah 34:10

19:04 1Kings 22:19; 2Chronicles 18:18; Psalms 47:8, 106:48; Isaiah 6:1; Ezekiel 1:26-27; Acts 15:2-6n; Revelation 4:4n; OT-Apocrypha[Sirach 1:8]; Pseudepigrapha[2Enoch 20:3]; Tertullian[Scorpiace 2]; NT-Apocrypha[Apocalypse of Paul 1.14]

19:05 Psalms 22:24, 115:13, 134:1, 135:1, 20

19:06 Exodus 15:18; 1Chronicles 16:31; Psalms 22:28-29, 93:1, 97:1, 99:1, 104:35; Ezekiel 1:24, 43:2; Daniel 7:14; Amos 4:13; Zechariah 14:9; Pseudepigrapha[2Baruch 59.11]

19:06-07 Cyprian[Treatise XII.Book II.19]

19:07 1Chronicles 16:28; Psalms 118:24

19:07-09 Revelation 5:6-6:1

19:08 Isaiah 61:10

19:09 Matthew 22:2-3; Pseudepigrapha[3Enoch 48A:10; Testament of Benjamin 3.8; Testament of Job 23:2; Testament of Joseph 19.8]

19:10 Pseudepigrapha[2Enoch 1:7; Apocalypse of Zephaniah 6:15; Martyrdom and Ascension of Isaiah 7:21, 8:6]; Cyprian[Treatise IX.24]; NT-Apocrypha[Gospel of Pseudo-Matthew 3]

19:11 Psalms 9:9, 72:2, 96:13, 98:9; Isaiah 11:4; Ezekiel 1:1; Zechariah 1:8, 6:3, 6; OT-Apocrypha[2Maccabees 3:25; 11:8]; Origen[Gospel of John Book I.42]

19:11-13 Cyprian[Treatise XII.Book II.3]

19:11-14 Origen[Gospel of John Book II.4]

19:11-16 Cyprian[Treatise XII.Book II.30]; Origen[Gospel of John Book II.4]

19:11-17 Irenaeus[Against Heresies Book IV.20.11]

19:11-21 Pseudepigrapha[4Ezra 13.1-53]

19:12 Isaiah 62:2-3; Daniel 10:6; Pseudepigrapha[2Enoch 1:5; Apocalypse of Zephaniah A; Sibylline Oracles 6.28]; Lactantius[Epitome of the Divine Institutes 42]

19:12-13 Matthew 17:1-21n

19:13 Isaiah 63:1-3; John 1:1-18n; Novatian[Treatise Concerning the Trinity 13]

19:15 Psalms 2:9; Isaiah 11:4, 49:2, 63:1-6; Lamentations 1:15; Joel 3:13; Amos 4:13; John 3:36n; Revelation 14:20; Pseudepigrapha[3Enoch 32:1; Psalms of Solomon 17.24; Sibylline Oracles 8.248]; Dead Sea Scrolls[4Q Isaiah Pesher (4Q161[4QPIS]) Fragment 8-10 COL III 15-17; 4Q Bless Oh My Soul (4Q436[4QBARKINAPSHI]) Fragment 1 7]; Tertullian[An Answer to the Jews 9]; NT-Apocrypha[History of Joseph the Carpenter 6]

19:16 Deuteronomy 10:17; Daniel 2:47; 1Timothy 6:15; Revelation 17:14; OT-Apocrypha[2Maccabees 13:4; 3Maccabees 5:35]; Pseudepigrapha[1Enoch 9:4]; Dead Sea Scrolls[4Q Enoch (4Q202[4QENAR]) COL III 14]; NT-Apocrypha[Epistula Apostolorum 3; Gospel of the Nativity of Mary 9]

19:16-18 Ezekiel 39:17-20

19:17 Ezekiel 39:4; Pseudepigrapha[4Ezra 2.38]

19:17-21 Matthew 3:11-12n; Dead Sea Scrolls[4Q Nahum Pesher (4Q169[4QPNAH]) Fragments 3 & 4 COL II 4-6]; Philo[On Dreams, That they Are God-Sent (2.212-2.214) cf. {Genesis 40:19, Revelation 19:17-21}]

19:19 Psalms 2:2; Pseudepigrapha[4Ezra 13:34]

19:19-20:10 Dead Sea Scrolls[1Q Hymns (1QHODAYOTH [1QH]) COL XIV 29-33; 1Q War Scroll (1QM[+1Q33]) COL 1-17]

19:20 Numbers 16:33; Psalms 55:16; Isaiah 30:33; Daniel 7:11; Revelation 13:16-17n; Pseudepigrapha[1Enoch 10:6; 2Enoch 10:2; 3Maccabees 2.29; Apocalypse of Zephaniah 6:2; Joseph and Aseneth 12:11; Martyrdom and Ascension of Isaiah (3:13-4:22 = Testament of Hezekiah) 4:9, 4:15; Sibylline Oracles 2.292, 8.102]; Josephus[Discourse to the Greeks Concerning Hades 2]; Irenaeus[Against Heresies Book V.28.2]; NT-Apocrypha[6Ezra 17.78]

19:20-20:15 Pseudepigrapha[Sibylline Oracles 3.63-74, 4.176-178]

19:21 Isaiah 11:4; Ezekiel 39:17, 21; Dead Sea Scrolls[4Q Bless Oh My Soul (4Q436[4QBARKINAPSHI]) Fragment 1 7]; Tertullian[An Answer to the Jews 9]

20:01 Pseudepigrapha[2Enoch 42:1]

20:01-03 Revelation 9:1-2; Dead Sea Scrolls[4Q Enoch (4Q204[4QENAR]) COL VIII 28-30]; Pseudepigrapha[1Enoch 21:1-10]

20:01-10 Dead Sea Scrolls[1Q War Scroll (1QM[+1Q33]) COL III 11; 4Q Blessings (4Q286[4QBREAKOT]) Fragment 7 COL II 1-10; 4Q Catena(4Q177[4QCATENA]) COL IV (Fragments 19+12+13I+15) 9-16; 4Q Enoch (4Q202[4QENAR]) COL IV 9-11]

20:02 Genesis 3:1; Pseudepigrapha[Joseph and Aseneth 12:9; Testament of Asher 7:3; Testament of Benjamin 3:7; Testament of Judah 25:3]; Rabbinic[Babylonian Sanhedrin 97b]; Apostolic[Papias Fragment 24:1]; Clement of Alexandria[Exhortation to the Heathen 1; The Instructor Book III.2]; Irenaeus[Against Heresies Book III.23.7]; Tertullian[On the Resurrection of the Flesh 25]; Nag Hammadi[Apocryphon of John 10]; NT-Apocrypha[Acts of Pilate XXII 1; Apocalypse of Paul 1.21]; Epic of Gilgamesh[The Forest Journey]

20:02-03 Pseudepigrapha[Sibylline Oracles 8.197]

20:02-04 Pseudepigrapha[4Ezra 7.28, 11:44-46, 12:32-34; Apocalypse of Elijah 5.37-39]; Rabbinic[Babylonian (Ketubot 111b; Sanhedrin 97a)]; Plato[Republic X 614b-616b]; Irenaeus[Against Heresies Book V.32.1, 33.3, 4, 34.2, 35.1, 36.3]; Justin[Dialogue with Trypho 80-81]; Theodotus[Excerpts 57]

20:02-07 Pseudepigrapha[4Ezra 7:25-44]; Apostolic[Papias Fragment 3:12-13, 5:1, 7:1, 14:1, 16:1, 17:1; Irenaeus - Against Heresies 5.33.3]

20:03 Isaiah 24:21; Pseudepigrapha[1Enoch 18:16, 21:6; Apocalypse of Elijah 5:35]; Lactantius[Divine Institutes Book VII.26]; Tertullian[Against Hermogenes 11]

20:03-04 Tertullian[A Strain of the Judgment of the Lord 237]

20:03-08 Rabbinic[Canticles Rabba on 8:19]

20:04 Ezekiel 37:10; Daniel 7:9, 22, 27; Matthew 19:28; Revelation 13:16-17n; Pseudepigrapha[4Ezra 2.16-17, 2.24; Apocalypse of Elijah 1:9, 5:39; Martyrdom and Ascension of Isaiah (3:13-4:22 = Testament of Hezekiah) 4:16 9.24-26, 11.40; Psalms of Solomon 15.9; Testament of Job 33:1; Testament of Judah 25:4]; Philo[On the Confusion of Tongues (197) cf. {Deuteronomy 30:4, Revelation 20:4, 21:24}]; Nag Hammadi[Gospel of Thomas 2]; NT-Apocrypha[Epistula Apostolorum 15]

20:04-05 Cyprian[Treatise XI.12]; Justin[Dialogue with Trypho 81]

20:04-06 Tertullian[On the Resurrection of the Flesh 25]

20:04-09 Rabbinic[Babylonian Sanhedrin 39a cf. {Numbers 23:9}]

20:05 Irenaeus[Against Heresies Book V.36.3]

20:05-06 Acts 2:31n

20:06 Isaiah 61:6; Pseudepigrapha[Apocalypse of Elijah 5:37]; Rabbinic[Palestinian Targum Deuteronomy 33:6]; Hippolytus[Treatise on Christ and Antichrist 65]; Methodius[Banquet of the Ten Virgins 9.3]

20:07 Lactantius[Divine Institutes Book VII.26]

20:07-10 Pseudepigrapha[Sibylline Oracles 3.319]

20:08 Joshua 11:4; Judges 7:12; 1Samuel 13:5; Ezekiel 7:2, 38:1-39:16; Pseudepigrapha[3Enoch 45:5]; Rabbinic[Babylonian (Abodah Zarah 3b; Berakhot 10a; Shabbat 118a; Sanhedrin 94a, 97b); Canticles Rabba on 4:20; Leviticus Rabba on 30:5; Seder Olam Rabba 17]

20:09 2Kings 1:10, 12, 6:14; Psalms 78:18, 87:2; Jeremiah 11:15, 12:7; Ezekiel 38:22, 39:6; Habakkuk 1:6; Philo[On Rewards And Punishments (153-157) cf. {Leviticus 26:14-39, Revelation 20:9}]

20:09-15 Matthew 3:11-12n

20:10 Genesis 19:24; Psalms 11:4; Isaiah 30:33; OT-Apocrypha[3Maccabees 2:5]; Pseudepigrapha[1Enoch 10:13, 67:7; Sibylline Oracles 8.102]; Dead Sea Scrolls[4Q Enoch (4Q204[4QENAR]) COL V 1-3]; Tertullian[On the Resurrection of the Flesh 58]

> **Through that valley also rivers of fire were flowing, to which those angels shall be condemned, who seduced the inhabitants of the earth. (Pseudepigrapha - 1Enoch 67:7)**

20:10-15 Pseudepigrapha[2Baruch 44.15; 2Enoch 10:2; 4Ezra 7.35-44, 7.70, 7.73-74, 7.112-115, 9.1-8, 12.34; Apocalypse of Abraham 31.2-8; Apocalypse of Elijah 5.22-35; Greek Apocalypse of Ezra 7.13; Life of Adam and Eve (Apocalypse of Moses) 22.4]; Josephus[Discourse to the Greeks Concerning Hades 2,6]; Rabbinic[Avot 2.1, 3.3, 4.29; Babylonian (Shabbat 118a; Babylonian Taanit 5a cf. {Jeremiah 10:15}]; Plato[Phaedo 113e-114b; Republic III 386c-387a, X 614b-616b]; Anonymous[Martyrdom of Justin Martyr 5]; Clement of Alexandria[Stromata Book V.14; Who is the Rich Man that shall be Saved 33, 37]; Hippolytus[Refutation of all Heresies Book IX.22-23, 25]; Irenaeus[Against Heresies Book I.10.1, 22.1, II.29.1-2, 33.5, III.3.3, IV.20.8, 22.2, 36.3, 40.1, V.18.3,

26.2, 30.4, 35.2; Demonstration of the Apostolic Preaching 56, 85; Fragments from the Lost Works 35,
50]; Justin[Dialogue with Trypho 45, 64, 117-119, 130, 135, 140-141; First Apology 19-20, 28, 52;
Fragments from the Lost Writings of Justin 3-4; Hortatory Address to the Greeks 27];
Lactantius[Divine Institutes Book VII.23-24]; Nag Hammadi[Apocryphon of John 27, 31; Book of
Thomas the Contender 142-143; Gospel of Truth 26; Hypostasis of the Archons 95; On the Origin of
the World 102, 126; Teachings of Silvanus 104-105, 110, 114]; Egyptian Book of the Dead[Oration 17,
39, 63B, 98, 108]; Epic of Gilgamesh[The Search for Everlasting Life]

> He [R. Isaac] said to him [R. Nahman], "This is what R. Yohanan said, 'There is one thing
> that brings a burning to the wicked in Gehenna, and what is that? It is idolatry. Here it is
> written, "the vanities by which they are instructed are nothing but a piece of wood." and
> elsewhere: they are a vanity, a work of delusion" (Jeremiah 10:15).'" (Talmud -
> Babylonian Taanit 5a, *The Babylonian Talmud a Translation and Commentary*, Jacob
> Neusner; Hendrickson Publishers, Inc., 2005)

> Those who appear to be incurable by reason of the greatness of their crimes - who have
> committed many and terrible deeds of sacrilege, murders foul and violent, or the like -
> such are hurled into Tartarus, which is their suitable destiny, and they never come
> out...(Plato - Phaedo 113e-114b)

20:10-21:04 Nag Hammadi[Concept of Our Great Power 45-47]
20:11 1Kings 10:18; Psalms 114:3-7; Daniel 2:35; Pseudepigrapha[3Enoch 28:8]; Hippolytus[Appendix
  to the Works of Hippolytus - On the End of the World 43]; Tertullian[Against Hermogenes 34]; NT-
  Apocrypha[Gospel of the Nazareans Fragment 26]
20:11-12 Daniel 7:9-10
20:11-13 Anonymous[Treatise Against the Heretic Novatian 17]
20:11-15 Pseudepigrapha[**1Enoch 47:3**; 4Ezra 6.1-6; Martyrdom and Ascension of Isaiah (3:13-4:22 =
  Testament of Hezekiah) 4:18; Sibylline Oracles 2.214-338]; Dead Sea Scrolls[1Q Hymns
  (1QHODAYOTH [1QH]) COL XII 20, XV 12; 1Q Mysteries (1Q27[1QMYST]) Fragment COL I 5-7;
  1Q Rule of the Community (1QS) COL IV 16-23; 4Q Enoch (4Q204[4QENAR]) COL V 1-9,
  (4Q212[4QENAR]) COL IV 19-26; 4Q Mysteries (4Q300[4QMYST]) Fragment 3 3-6; 4Q Sapiential
  Work (4Q418[4QSAP.WORKA]) Fragment 2 1-7, 69 5-9]; Damascus Document (CD-A) COL II 5-10];
  Philo[On Flight And Finding (117-118) cf. {Leviticus 35:25}; On the Unchangeableness of God (8-9)
  cf. {Exodus 30:17-21}, (127-130) cf. {Leviticus 13:11}; The Cherubim Part 1 (14-17) cf. {Numbers 5:14-
  18, Deuteronomy 16:20}]; Rabbinic[Mishna Aboth 2:1]; Irenaeus[Against Heresies Book V.35.2]

> At that time I beheld the Ancient of days, while he sat upon the throne of his glory,
> while the book of the living was opened in his presence, and while all the powers which
> were above the heavens stood around and before him. (Pseudepigrapha - 1Enoch 47:3)

20:12 Exodus 32:32-33; Psalms 69:28; Isaiah 4:3; Daniel 12:1; Revelation 21:27n; OT-Apocrypha[Sirach
  16:12]; Pseudepigrapha[2Baruch 24:1; 3Enoch 18:24; 4Ezra 6:20; Joseph and Aseneth 15:4;
  Martyrdom and Ascension of Isaiah 9:22]
20:12-13 Psalms 28:4, 62:12; Proverbs 24:12; Isaiah 59:18; Jeremiah 17:10; Apostolic[Epistle of Barnabas
  4:12]
20:12-14 Tertullian[On the Resurrection of the Flesh 25]
20:13 Pseudepigrapha[1Enoch 51:1, 61:5; Odes of Solomon 15:9, 42:11]; Methodius[Apostolic Words
  from the Discourse on the Resurrection 9]; NT-Apocrypha[Apocalypse of Peter 1.4]
20:13-15 Tertullian[On the Resurrection of the Flesh 58]
20:14 Isaiah 25:8; Pseudepigrapha[Apocalypse of Elijah 5:38; Sibylline Oracles 2.292; Testament of
  Judah 25:3]; Rabbinic[Palestinian Targum Deuteronomy 33:6]
20:14-15 Pseudepigrapha[1Enoch 10:13]; Dead Sea Scrolls[4Q Enoch (4Q204[4QENAR]) COL V 1-3];
  NT-Apocrypha[6Ezra 17.78]
20:15 Exodus 32:32-33; Psalms 69:28; Isaiah 30:33; Daniel 12:1; Revelation 21:27n;
  Pseudepigrapha[Joseph and Aseneth 15:4]
21:01 This section also includes topical notes for: New Heaven and Earth - Isaiah 65:17, 66:22; 2Peter
  3:13; Pseudepigrapha[1Enoch 72:3; 2Baruch 44.12; Apocalypse of Elijah 5:38; Odes of Solomon 6:18;
  Pseudo-Philo 3.10; Sibylline Oracles 5.157, 5.447; Testament of Adam 3.3]; Rabbinic[Babylonian
  Sanhedrin 97b]; Plato[Phaedo 109e-110b]; Hippolytus[Appendix to the Works of Hippolytus - On

the End of the World 37]; Irenaeus[Against Heresies Book V.33.3-4, 34.2, 35.2, 36.1]; Justin[Dialogue
with Trypho 113]; Tertullian[Against Hermogenes 34]; Nag Hammadi[Gospel of Thomas 11, 111]

21:01-06 Irenaeus[Against Heresies Book V.36.1-2]

21:01-21 Dead Sea Scrolls[**4Q Enoch (4Q212[4QENAR]) COL IV 19-26**; 4Q New Jerusalem
(4Q554[4QNJar]) Fragment 1 COL I 9-22, COL II 7-22, COL III 13-22, Fragment 2 COL II 13-15];
Rabbinic[Babylonian Taanit 5a]

> And *afterward, in* the ninth week, justice will be revealed to all the sons of the earth: all
> *their evil deeds shall vanish* from the entire earth, and they will be thrown into the *Pit*.
> All *of them will see* the way of eternal truth. And *afterward will come* the time of the
> great eternal judgment. The former heavens will pass away, and *new* heavens will rise
> *for* endless shining weeks *of righteousness.* (Dead Sea Scrolls - 4Q Enoch
> (4Q212[4QENAR]) COL IV 19-26)

21:02 Nehemiah 11:1, 18; Isaiah 52:1, 61:10; Revelation 3:12; Pseudepigrapha[2Baruch 44.9-15; 3Enoch
48A:3; Martyrdom and Ascension of Isaiah (3:13-4:22 = Testament of Hezekiah) 3:16; Testament of
Job 18:4]; Rabbinic[Babylonian (Baba Batra 75b; Ketubot 111b)]; Clement of Alexandria[Stromata
Book IV.26; The Instructor Book II.13]; Irenaeus[Against Heresies Book V.35.1-2]; Lactantius[Divine
Institutes Book VII.24]; Origen[Gospel of Matthew Book XIV.13]; Tertullian[Five Books Against
Marcion Book III.25; The Shows, or De Spectaculis 30]

21:02-04 Irenaeus[Fragments from the Lost Works 50]

21:02-10 NT-Apocrypha[Epistula Apostolorum 33]

21:03 Leviticus 26:11-12; 1Kings 8:27; Psalms 95:7; Isaiah 8:8; Jeremiah 31:1; Ezekiel 37:27; Zechariah
2:10, 14; Pseudepigrapha[2Enoch 20:3; Prayer of Joseph Fragment A]; Apostolic[Ignatius - Letter to
the Ephesians 15:3, Letter to the Philadelphians 7:2; Epistle of Barnabas 4:11, 6:14-15]

21:04 Isaiah 25:8, 35:10, 43:18, 51:11, 65:17, 65:19; Jeremiah 31:16; Pseudepigrapha[2Baruch 73:2-3;
2Enoch 65:9; Apocalypse of Elijah 5:38]; Josephus[Discourse to the Greeks Concerning Hades 6];
Tertullian[On Modesty 6; On the Resurrection of the Flesh 58]

21:04-07 Nag Hammadi[Apocryphon of James 14]

21:05 1Kings 22:19; 2Chronicles 18:18; Psalms 47:8; Isaiah 6:1, 43:19; Ezekiel 1:26-27; OT-
Apocrypha[Sirach 1:8]; Pseudepigrapha[2Baruch 73:1]

21:05-22:05 Pseudepigrapha[Testament of Levi 5:1]

21:06 Psalms 36:9; Isaiah 44:6, 48:12, 55:1; Jeremiah 2:13; Zechariah 14:8; Revelation 22:13n;
Pseudepigrapha[**1Enoch 48:1**; Odes of Solomon 3:1, 6:18, 30.1-7]; Philo[Concerning Noah's Work As
A Planter (77-79) cf. {Numbers 20:5-13}]; Clement of Alexandria[Stromata Book VI.16];
Cyprian[Treatise XII.Book II.1]; Tertullian[Against All Heresies 5]

> In that place I beheld a fountain of righteousness, which never failed, encircled by many
> springs of wisdom. Of these all the thirsty drank, and were filled with wisdom, having
> their habitation with the righteous, the elect, and the holy. (Pseudepigrapha - 1Enoch
> 48:1)

21:06-07 Cyprian[Treatise XII.Book II.6, III.100]

21:07 Leviticus 26:12; 2Samuel 7:14; 1Chronicles 17:13; Ezekiel 11:20; Zechariah 8:8

21:08 Genesis 19:24; Psalms 11:4; Isaiah 30:33; Ezekiel 38:22; OT-Apocrypha[3Maccabees 2:5];
Pseudepigrapha[2Enoch 10:2, 5; Sibylline Oracles 2.255, 8.102]; Josephus[Discourse to the Greeks
Concerning Hades 2]; Rabbinic[Palestinian Targum Deuteronomy 33:6]; Tertullian[De Fuga in
Persecutione 7; On Modesty 19; Scorpiace 12]; NT-Apocrypha[Acts of Thomas 1.56]

21:09 Revelation 15:7-17:1n

21:09-11 Cyprian[Treatise XII.Book II.19]

21:09-21 Pseudepigrapha[4Ezra 10:27]

21:09-27 Revelation 5:6-6:1

21:10 Ezekiel 40:1-2; Pseudepigrapha[Testament of Naphtali 5:2]; NT-Apocrypha[Apocalypse of Paul
1.23; Clement Romance 62.4]

21:10-11 Justin[Dialogue with Trypho 113]; Epic of Gilgamesh[The Search for Everlasting Life]

21:10-21 Dead Sea Scrolls[11Q New Jerusalem (11Qi8[11QNJAR]) Fragment 24 1-5; 4Q Isaiah Pesher
(4Q164[4QPIS]) Fragment 1 1-6]

21:10-23 Tertullian[Five Books Against Marcion Book III.25]

21:11 Isaiah 58:8, 60:1-2, 19; Ezekiel 43:2

21:12 Exodus 39:14, 40:5; Isaiah 62:6; NT-Apocrypha[Epistula Apostolorum 30]

21:12-13 Exodus 28:21; Ezekiel 48:30-35

21:14 Cyprian[Epistle LXVIII.8]

21:15 Ezekiel 40:3, 5

21:16 Ezekiel 43:16; Zechariah 2:6

21:16-17 Ezekiel 48:16-17

21:17 Deuteronomy 3:11; Pseudepigrapha[Odes of Solomon 6:18]; Nag Hammadi[Gospel of Thomas 88]

21:18 Pseudepigrapha[Vision of Ezra 57]

21:18-21 Irenaeus[Against Heresies Book V.34.4]; Epic of Gilgamesh[The Search for Everlasting Life]

21:19 Exodus 28:17-20; Isaiah 54:11-12; Ezekiel 28:13; OT-Apocrypha[Tobit 13:17]; Pseudepigrapha[Life of Abraham 26:10]

21:19-21 Rabbinic[Babylonian (Baba Batra 75b; Sanhedrin 100a cf. {Isaiah 54:12})]; Plato[Republic X 616b-c]

21:20 Pseudepigrapha[Joseph and Aseneth 18:6]

21:21 Isaiah 54:11-12

21:22 Amos 4:13; Pseudepigrapha[Sibylline Oracles 5.423]

21:22-23 Pseudepigrapha[Testament of Benjamin 3.8; Testament of Joseph 19.8]

21:23 Isaiah 24:23, 60:1, 19-20; Pseudepigrapha[4Ezra 2:35]

21:23-24 Justin[Dialogue with Trypho 113]

21:24 Psalms 68:30; Isaiah 60:3, 5; Pseudepigrapha[Psalms of Solomon 17:34 (31)]; Philo[On the Confusion of Tongues (197) cf. {Deuteronomy 30:4, Revelation 20:4, 21:24}]

21:25 Zechariah 14:7

21:25-26 Isaiah 60:11

21:26 Psalms 72:10-11; Pseudepigrapha[Psalms of Solomon 17:34 (31)]

21:27 This section also includes topical notes for: Book of Life - Exodus 32:32-33; Psalms 56:8, 69:28, 87:6, 139:16; Isaiah 4:3, 35:8, 52:1; Ezekiel 33:29; Daniel 12:1; Malachi 3:16; Luke 10:20; Philippians 4:3; Revelation 3:5, 17:8, 20:12, 15, 22:19; Pseudepigrapha[Apocaplypse of Zephaniah 7.1-11, 9.1-3; Odes of Solomon 9.11-12]; Dead Sea Scrolls[4Q Sapiential Work (4Q418[4QSAP.WORKA]) Fragment 43 11-12; 4Q Sapiential WorkA (4Q417[4QSAP.WORKA]) Fragment 2 COL I 15-16; 4Q Word of the Luminaries (4Q504[4QDIBHAM]) COL VI 14; Damascus Document (CD-B) COL XX 19-22]; Apostolic[Shepherd of Hermas 3:2]; Tertullian[On the Resurrection of the Flesh 25]; Nag Hammadi[Gospel of Truth 19, 21, 23]; Epic of Gilgamesh[The Death of Enkidu]

22:01 Psalms 46:5; Ezekiel 47:1; Joel 3:18; Zechariah 14:8; Pseudepigrapha[1Enoch 14:19; Odes of Solomon 6:8]

22:01-02 Genesis 2:9-10; Pseudepigrapha[Odes of Solomon 11.16a-16c]; Apostolic[Epistle of Barnabas 11:10]

22:01-05 Pseudepigrapha[Sibylline Oracles 2.313-338, 4.179-192]

22:02 Genesis 3:22; Jeremiah 3:17; Ezekiel 47:12; Joel 1:14; Pseudepigrapha[1Enoch 25:5; 2Enoch 8:2; 4Ezra 2:11, 2:19, 8:52; Life of Adam and Eve (Apocalypse of Moses) 9:3; Psalms of Solomon 14:3; Testament of Levi 9:12, 18:11]; Rabbinic[Avot 6.7 cf. {Proverbs 3:18}; Babylonian Ketubot 111b]; NT-Apocrypha[5Ezra 2.12; Apocalypse of Peter 1.16]; Egyptian Book of the Dead[Oration 98]

22:02-03 NT-Apocrypha[Pseudo-Titus Epistle Line 624]

22:03 Zechariah 14:11

22:04 Psalms 17:15, 42:3; Pseudepigrapha[4Ezra 7:98; Testament of Levi 18:11]; NT-Apocrypha[Acts of Thomas 1.94; Apocalypse of Paul 1.12]

22:05 Isaiah 60:19-20; Daniel 7:18, 27; Zechariah 14:7; Pseudepigrapha[4Ezra 2:35]; Nag Hammadi[Gospel of Thomas 2]

22:06 Numbers 27:16; Daniel 2:28-29, 45; Pseudepigrapha[Testament of Job 1:4]

22:07 Isaiah 40:10

22:07-08 Dionysius of Alexandria[Extant Fragments Two Books on the Promises 4]

22:08 Pseudepigrapha[Apocalypse of Zephaniah 6:15, B; Martyrdom and Ascension of Isaiah 7:21, 8:6]

22:09 Cyprian[Treatise IX.24]

22:10 Daniel 12:4; Victorinus[Apocalypse 10.3]

22:10-12 Cyprian[Treatise IX.21, XII.Book III.23]

22:11 Isaiah 56:1; Ezekiel 3:27; Daniel 12:10; Pseud-Irenaeus

22:12 Psalms 28:4, 62:12; Proverbs 24:12; Isaiah 40:10, 59:18, 62:11; Jeremiah 17:10;
Pseudepigrapha[4Ezra 7:99]; Apostolic[1Clement 34:3; Epistle of Barnabas 21:3]; Clement of
Alexandria[Stromata Book IV.22]

22:13 This section also includes topical notes for: Alpha and Omega - Isaiah 41:1-4, 44:6, 48:12;
Revelation 1:8, 21:6; Rabbinic[Shemoth Rabba xxix. 5, p. 51b; Siphri Deuteronomy 329 p. 139 cf.
{Isaiah 44:6}]; Clement of Alexandria[Stromata Book IV.25, VI.16]; Irenaeus[Against Heresies Book
I.14.3, 15.1-2, II.34.2, IV.20.4, 25.1]; Justin[Hortatory Address to the Greeks 25]; Origen[Gospel of
John Book I.22-23]; Tertullian[Against All Heresies 5; Five Books Against Marcion Book II.5, III.25];
Nag Hammadi[Teachings of Silvanus 113; The Thunder: Perfect Mind 13; Tripartite Tractate 52, 57]

22:13-14 Cyprian[Treatise XII.Book II.22]

22:14 Genesis 2:9, 3:22; Psalms 118:19; Ezekiel 47:12; Pseudepigrapha[1Enoch 25:5; 4Ezra 2:11; Greek
Apocalypse of Ezra 5.20-23; Odes of Solomon 11.18]

22:14-15 Tertullian[On Modesty 19]

22:15 Hippolytus[Treatise on Christ and Antichrist 65]; NT-Apocrypha[Oxyrhynchus Papyrus 840]

22:16 Numbers 24:17; Isaiah 11:1, 10; Malachi 3:1

22:17 Isaiah 55:1; Pseudepigrapha[Odes of Solomon 30:1-7]; Irenaeus[Against Heresies Book III.4.1]

22:18 Deuteronomy 13:1, 29:19; Pseudepigrapha[3Baruch 1:7 (Slav.)]; NT-Apocrypha[Apocalypse of
Paul 1.51]

22:18-19 Deuteronomy 4:2, 12:32; Pseudepigrapha[2Enoch 48:7; Letter of Aristeas 1.311];
Tertullian[Against Hermogenes 22]; NT-Apocrypha[History of Joseph the Carpenter 30]

22:19 Genesis 2:9, 3:22; Ezekiel 47:12; Revelation 21:27n; Pseudepigrapha[Testament of Levi 18:11];
Irenaeus[Against Heresies Book V.30.1]

22:20 Teaching of the Twelve Apostles 10.6

Cross Reference Index: Sayings (Agrapha) of the Lord

Of Unknown Origin cited by the Patristic Fathers

Papias[As the elders who saw John the disciple of the Lord remembered that they had heard from him how the Lord taught in regard to those times, and said: "The days will come in which vines shall grow, having each ten thousand branches, and in each branch ten thousand twigs, and in each true twig ten thousand shoots, and in every one of the shoots ten thousand clusters, and on every one of the clusters ten thousand grapes, and every grape when pressed will give five-and-twenty metretes of wine. And when any one of the saints shall lay hold of a cluster, another shall cry out, 'I am a better cluster, take me; bless the Lord through me.' In like manner, [He said] that a grain of wheat would produce ten thousand ears, and that every ear would have ten thousand grains, and every grain would yield ten pounds of clear, pure, fine flour; and that apples, and seeds, and grass would produce in similar proportions; and that all animals, feeding then only on the productions of the earth, would become peaceable and harmonious, and be in perfect subjection to man." [Testimony is borne to these things in writing by Papias, an ancient man, who was a hearer of John and a friend of Polycarp, in the fourth of his books; for five books were composed by him. And he added, saying, "Now these things are credible to believers. And Judas the traitor," says he, "not believing, and asking, 'How shall such growths be accomplished by the Lord?' the Lord said, 'They shall see who shall come to them.' These, then, are the times mentioned by the prophet Isaiah: 'And the wolf shall lie, down with the lamb,' etc." (Fragment IV)]

Justin[Wherefore also our Lord Jesus Christ said, 'In whatsoever things I shall take you, in these I shall judge you.' (Dialogue with Trypho 47)]; Josephus[In whatsoever ways I shall find you in them shall I judge you entirely. (Discourse to the Greeks Concerning Hades 8)]; MS Pepys 2498[And he will judge everyone just as he finds them, and to each he will apportion reward just as they have deserved. (Chapter 7:20 cf. {Luke 3:18}) - *The Magdalene Gospel A Journey Behind the New Testament*, Yuri Kuchinsky; Roots Publishing, 2002 p. 375)]

Apostolic[Ignatius-Letter to the Magnesians 5]; Clement of Alexandria[Rightly, therefore, the Scripture, in its desire to make us such dialecticians, exhorts us: "Be ye skillful money-changers" rejecting some things, but retaining what is good. (Stromata Book I.28), For there is genuine coin, and other that is spurious; which no less deceives unprofessionals, that it does not the money-changers; who know through having learned how to separate and distinguish what has a false stamp from what is genuine. So the money-changer only says to the unprofessional man that the coin is counterfeit. But the reason why, only the banker's apprentice, and he that is trained to this department, learns. (Stromata Book II.4), So that, if one confesses that he has not a heart that has been made right, he has not the table of the money-changers or the test of words. And how can he be any longer a money-changer, who is not able to prove and distinguish spurious coin, even offhand? (Stromata VI.10), [The apostle] calls "approved," either those who in reaching faith apply to the teaching of the Lord with some discrimination (as those are called skillful money-changers, who distinguish the spurious coin from the genuine by the false stamp), or those who have already become approved both in life and knowledge. (Stromata VII.15)]; Constitutions of the Holy Apostles [And in doing this, do not judge thy bishop, or any of thy neighbors among the laity; for if thou judge thy brother, thou becomest a judge, without being constituted such by anybody, for the priests are only entrusted with the power of judging. For to them it is said, "Judge righteous judgment;" and again "Approve

yourselves to be exact money-changers… But it is the duty of the bishop to judge rightly, as it is written, "Judge righteous judgment;" and elsewhere, "Why do ye not even of yourselves judge what is right?" Be ye therefore as skillful dealers in money…" (Book 2.4-5)]; Dionysius[I received this vision as being what was in accordance with the apostolic word, which thus urges all who are endowed with greater virtue, "Be ye skillful money-changers." (Epistle VII)]; Socrates Scholasticus[Moreover, both Christ and his Apostle enjoin us 'to become discriminating money-changers,' so that we might 'prove all things, and hold fast that which is good': directing us also to 'beware lest any one should spoil us through philosophy and vain deceit.' (Book 3.16)]; Athanasius[And he that writes of the human attributes of the Word knows also what concerns His Godhead: and he who expounds concerning His Godhead is not ignorant of what belongs to His coming in the flesh: but discerning each as a skilled and 'approved money-changer…' (De Sententia Dionysii 9); But like good money-changers be satisfied with the reading…(Personal Letters 52)]; NT-Apocrypha[Then Peter said: "If, therefore, some of the Scriptures are true and some false, with good reason said our Master, 'Be ye good money-changers,' inasmuch as in the Scriptures there are some true sayings and some spurious. (Clementine Homilies Homily 2.51), Then Peter: "As to the mixture of truth with falsehood, I remember that on one occasion He, finding fault with the Sadducees, said, 'Wherefore ye do err, not knowing the true things of the Scriptures; and on this account ye are ignorant of the power of God.' But if He cast up to their that they knew not the true things of the Scriptures, it is manifest that there are false things in them. And also, inasmuch as He said, 'Be ye prudent money-changers,' it is because there are genuine and spurious words. And whereas He said, 'Wherefore do ye not perceive that which is reasonable in the Scriptures?' He makes the understanding of him stronger who voluntarily judges soundly. (Clementine Homilies Homily 3.50), "But if any one of those present, being able to instruct the ignorance of men, shrink from it, thinking only of his own ease, let him expect to hear this sentence: 'O wicked and slothful servant, thou oughtest to have given my money to the exchangers, and I at my coming should have got my own. Cast out the unprofitable servant into the outer darkness.' And with good reason; 'for,' says He, 'it is thine, O man, to prove my words, as silver and money are proved among the exchangers.' (Clementine Homilies Homily 3.61)]

Clement of Alexandria[For it is not in the way of envy that the Lord announced in a Gospel, "My mystery is to me and the sons of my house." (Stromata Book V.10)]

Origen["But the Saviour himself saith: He who is near me is near the fire; he who is far from me, is far from the kingdom." (Homily in Jeremiah XX.3)]

Topical Notes Index

Matthew 27:19-31	Crucifixion
Matthew 27:29	Mocked
Matthew 27:33-56	Passover
Matthew 27:35	Naked
Matthew 28:17	Worshipped
Matthew 28:19	Trinity
Mark 02:21	New Patch on Old Garment
Mark 04:37-41	Calming the Sea
Mark 05:01-20	Demonic Possession
Mark 12:27	God of the Living
Mark 14:62	Coming with the Clouds
Luke 01:26-27	Virgin Mary
Luke 04:01-13	Temptation on the Mountain
Luke 05:01-11	The Fishermen
Luke 05:03-09	Let Down Your Nets
Luke 06:34-35	Lending Without Usury
Luke 06:43-49	Great is the Fall
Luke 06:45	Treasures of the Heart
Luke 06:48-49	Foundation upon the Rock
Luke 07:25-26	Clothed in Soft Raiment
Luke 08:15	Pure Heart
Luke 13:32	Naming the Animals
Luke 18:22	Give to the Poor
Luke 19:17	Faithfulness
Luke 22:47-48	Kiss of Betrayal
Luke 23:33-45	Crucifixion
Luke 24:44-46	Opening the Mind
John 01:01-14	The Word
John 01:01-18	Incarnation
John 01:18	God the Father
John 02:19-21	Temple of Body
John 03:03-07	Born Again
John 03:13	Son of Man
John 03:18	Son of God
John 03:19	The Light
John 03:29	Bride and Bridegroom
John 03:36	Obey not the Son and Don't See Life
John 04:10-11	Living Water
John 06:31-58	Spiritual Food

Bibliography

The American Standard Version, Thomas Nelson & Sons, 1901

Ancient Egyptian Book of the Dead, Raymond O. Faulkner, trans.; Barnes and Noble Publishing, Inc., 2005

The Apocrypha and Pseudepigrapha of the Old Testament, R.H. Charles; Clarendon Press, 1913

The Apostolic Fathers, Michael W. Holmes, ed.; J. B. Lightfoot and J. R. Harmer, trans.; Baker Book House, Second Edition, 1989

The Apostolic Fathers with Justin Martyr and Irenaeus, Phillip Schaff; Public Domain - http://www.ccel.org/ccel/schaff/anf01.txt

The Babylonian Talmud a Translation and Commentary, Jacob Neusner; Hendrickson Publishers, Inc., 2005

BibleWorks 7 for Windows; BibleWorks 2007

Biblia Sacra Luxta Vulgatam Versionem, R. Weber, B. Fischer, J. Gribomont, H. F. D. Sparks, and W. Thiele; Deutsche Bibelgesellschaft, Stuttgart, 1969, 1975, 1983

The Book of Enoch the Prophet, Richard Laurence, trans.; Wizards Bookshelf, 1983

Christianity in Talmud and Midrash, R. Travers Herford; Wipf and Stock Publishers, 2003

The Demonstration of the Apostolic Preaching, Armitage Robinson, trans.; The Macmillan Co., 1920

The Dead Sea Scrolls Translated; the Qumran Texts in English, Florentino Garcia Martinez, ed.; Wilfred g. E. Watson, trans.; E. J. Brill and William B. Eerdmans, Second Edition, 1996

Dhammapada: The Buddha's Path of Wisdom, Acharya Buddharakkhita trans.; Buddhist Publication Society, 1985

Die Schriften des Neuen Testaments in ihrer altesten erreichbaren Textgestalt, 4 volumes, Soden, Hermann von 1902-1910

The Douay-Rheims American Edition; 1899

The Early Church Fathers Volumes 1-38, Philip Schaff & Alexander Roberts; Hendrickson Publishers, Inc., 1994

The Eclogues of Virgil, Eclogue IV, J. W. MacKail trans., 1934

The English Standard Version, Crossway Bibles, 2001, 2007

The Englishman's Hebrew and Chaldee Concordance of the Old Testament, George V. Wigram ed.; Baker Book House, 1980

The Epic of Gilgamesh, N. K. Sandars; Penguin Books, 1972

Fathers of the Second Century: Hermas, Tatian, Athenagoras, Theophilus, and Clement of Alexandria (Entire), Phillip Schaff; Public Domain - http://www.ccel.org/ccel/schaff/anf02.txt

Fathers of the Third Century: Tertullian, Part Fourth; Minucius Felix; Commodian; Origen, Parts First and Second, Phillip Schaff; Public Domain - http://www.ccel.org/ccel/schaff/anf04.txt

Fathers of the Third Century: Hippolytus, Cyprian, Caius, Novatian, Appendix, Phillip Schaff; Public Domain - http://www.ccel.org/ccel/schaff/anf05.txt

A Greek-English Lexicon of the New Testament and other Early Christian Literature, 3rd Edition, Walter Bauer, Frederick William Danker; the University of Chicago Press, 1957, 1979, 2000

The Greek New Testament, Barbara Aland, Kurt Aland, Johannes Karavidopoulos, Carlo M. Martini, and Bruce M. Metzger, ed.; United Bible Societies, Fourth Revised Edition, 1983

The Greek New Testament, Stephanus (Robert Estienne) 1550; Online Bible Foundation and Woodside Fellowship of Ontario, Canada, 1994

The Greek New Testament, Lobegott Friedrich Konstantin von Tischendorf; Eighth Edition 1869-1872

The Greek New Testament Text of the Greek Orthodox Church, Orthodox Skite St. Spyridon, 1904

The Golden Verses Of Pythagoras And Other Pythagorean Fragments, Florence M. Firth; Theosophical Publishing House, 1904

Hebrew Gospel of Matthew, George Howard; Mercer University Press, Second Edition, 1995

Holman Christian Standard Bible; Holman Bible Publishers, 1999, 2000, 2002, 2003

The Holy Bible, American Standard Version; Thomas Nelson and Sons, 1901

The Holy Bible, Authorized (King James) Version; 1611, Blayney Revision 1769

The Holy Bible, English Standard Version; Crossway Bibles, 2001, 2007

The Holy Bible, New International Version; International Bible Society, 1973, 1978, 1984

The Holy Bible, New Living Translation, second edition; Tyndale House Publishers, Inc., 2004

Jewish New Testament, David H. Stern; Jewish New Testament Publications, Inc., 1989

Jewish New Testament Commentary, David H. Stern; Jewish New Testament Publications, Inc., 1992

Josephus and the New Testament, Steve Mason; Hendrickson Publishers, Second Edition, 2003

The King James Version; Blayney Edition, 1611, 1769

The Living Bible, Paraphrased; Tyndale House Publishers, 1971

The Magdalene Gospel A Journey Behind the New Testament, Yuri Kuchinsky; Roots Publishing, 2002

Murdock Translation of the NT Peshitta, James Murdock, 1851

The Nag Hammadi Library in English, James M. Robinson, ed.; Members of the Coptic Gnostic Library Project of the Institute for Antiquity and Christianity, Claremont, California, trans.; Harper San Francisco, Third Edition, 1990

New American Bible with Revised New Testament; Confraternity of Christian Doctrine, 1970, 1986, 1991

New American Standard Bible; Lockman Foundation, 1960, 1962, 1963, 1968, 1971, 1972, 1973, 1975, 1977

New American Standard Bible (1995 Update); Lockman Foundation, 1988, 1995

New English Translation; Biblical Studies Foundation, 2004, 2005

New International Version; International Bible Society, Zondervan Publishing House, 1973, 1978, 1984

New Jerusalem Bible; Darton, Longman & Todd Limited and Doubleday, 1985

New King James Version; Thomas Nelson, Inc., 1982

New Living Translation, Second Edition; Tyndale House Publishers, Inc., 2004

New Revised Standard Version; Division of Christian Education of the National Council of the Churches of Christ in the United States of America, 1989

New Testament Apocrypha, Wilhelm Schneemelcher, ed.; R. McL. Wilson, trans.; Westminster John Knox Press, Volumes I and II, 2003

The New Testament and Rabbinic Judaism, David Daube; Ayer Company, Publishers, Inc., Reprint Edition, 1992

The New Testament in the Original Greek, Maurice A. Robinson and William G. Pierpont; Chilton Book Publishing, First Edition, 2005

The New Testament in the Original Greek, Brooke Foss Westcott and Fenton John Anthony Hort; London: Macmillan, 1881

Novum Testamentum Graece, Erwin Nestle, Barbara Aland, Kurt Aland, Johannes Karavidopoulos, Carlo M. Martini, and Bruce M. Metzger, ed.; Deutsche Bibelgesellschaft, 27th Edition, 1993

The Old Testament Pseudepigrapha Volume 1 and 2, James H. Charlesworth; Doubleday, 1985

The Pepysian Gospel Harmony, Margery Goates, ed.; Early English Texts Society / Oxford University Press Edition, volume 157, 1922

Phaedo by Plato 360 BC, Benjamin Jowett, trans.; C. Scribner's sons, 1871

Plato Complete Works, John M. Cooper, ed.; Hackett Publishing Company, 1997

Reclaiming the Dead Sea Scrolls, Lawrence H. Schiffman; The Jewish Publication Society, 1994

The Republic by Plato 360 BC, Benjamin Jowett, trans.; C. Scribner's sons, 1871

Revised English Bible; Oxford University Press, Cambridge University Press, 1989

Revised Standard Version; Division of Christian Education of the National Council of Churches of Christ in the United States of America, 1952 (2nd Edition New Testament 1971)

The Soncino Talmud; Judaica Press, Inc. 1973 and Soncino Press, Ltd. 1965, 1967, 1977, 1983, 1984, 1987, 1988, & 1990

The Syriac New Testament and Psalms; United Bible Societies, 1905

Tacitus – The Histories, Kenneth Wellesley, tr.; Penguin Books, 1991

A Textual Commentary on the Greek New Testament, Bruce M. Metzger; Deutsche Bibelgesellschaft, D-Stuttgart, second edition, 2002

Textus Receptus, F. H. A. Scrivner 1894 – Theodore Beza 1598; Online Bible Foundation and Woodside Fellowship of Ontario, Canada, 1994

Theatetus by Plato 360 BC, Benjamin Jowett, trans.; C. Scribner's sons, 1871

Today's English Version (Good News Bible); Thomas Nelson, Inc., 1966, 1971, 1976

The Works of Flavius Josephus, William Whiston, trans. 1737

The Works of Philo, C. D. Yonge, trans.; Hendrickson Publishers, 1993

The Works of Philo Judaeus - The contemporary of Josephus, Charles Duke Yonge, trans.; H. G. Bohn, 1854-1890.

for links to many of the ancient
documents cross referenced in this book,

please visit

www.cornerstonepublications.org

for links to many of the ancient
documents cross referenced in this book,

please visit